# Association For Consumer Research

# Think BIG:
# Big Ideas, Big Findings

## 2010

## Volume XXXVIII
## PROCEEDINGS

**Editors**
Darren W. Dahl
Gita V. Johar
Stijn M.J. van Osselaer

**Advances in Consumer Research, Volume 38**

Darren W. Dahl, Gita V. Johar, Stijn M.J. van Osselaer, Editors

2012 Copyright © ASSOCIATION FOR CONSUMER RESEARCH

International Standard Book Number (ISBN): 978-0-915552-67-2

**Association for Consumer Research**
Labovitz School of Business & Economics
University of Minnesota Duluth
11 East Superior Street, Suite 210
Duluth, MN 55802

www.acrwebsite.org

# Preface

The 41st annual conference of the Association for Consumer Research (ACR) was held in sunny Jacksonville, Florida, October 6 to October 9, 2010. This volume summarizes the research presented during the conference.

The theme of ACR 2010 was: "Think BIG. Big Ideas. Big Findings." The conference showcased lots of "big picture" theories and "big" phenomena that are of real importance to consumers' lives. In the grand scheme of things, the 2010 conference was pretty much like any other ACR Conference. That is probably a good thing. Lots of interesting talks, catching up with far-flung colleagues and friends, and meeting new ones are the constants that make ACR a central event in a consumer researcher's year.

We did make some changes to the conference to promote big picture communication: (a) Every session had four, shorter talks (which necessitated doing away with the traditional role of discussant in Special Sessions), (b) We asked session chairs to kick-start discussion about big picture implications at the end of special and competitive paper sessions. (c) Abstracts in the program were shorter, encouraging authors to clearly communicate their big picture ideas.

We also made some other changes to encourage communication between junior and senior researchers, to green the conference, and to make the conference even more fun: (a) ACR newcomers could sign up on the registration form to meet ACR regulars for research chats during coffee breaks, (b) posters featuring working papers were kept up throughout the conference, (c) the conference was greened by using shorter program booklets, a build-your-own-program internet tool, and by offering participants the option of buying carbon offsets for travel to the conference, and (d) DJoy Srivastava rocked the beach at the Saturday night closing party. We have never seen so many of our peers have such a good time on the dance floor.

We are immensely grateful to the ACR community for presenting their work, asking constructive questions during talks, and doing a lot of reviewing. We would especially like to thank the Associate Editors and the members of the Program Committee for assessing many Competitive Papers and Special Session proposals. Many thanks go out to the Roundtables Chairs, Raj Ragunathan and Eduardo Andrade, to the Film Festival Chairs, Russ Belk and Rob Kozinets, to the Doctoral Consortium Chairs, Priya Raghubir and Patti Williams, and to the Working Paper Chairs, Jen Argo and Kristin Diehl. We thank Geeta Menon, the ACR President, for totally entrusting us with the whole enterprise. Finally, we thank the wonderful team of people who really did most of the work: Annette Bartels, Aleksey Cherfas, Phil Hamlin, Paula Rigling, Rajiv Vaidyanathan, the Phd student volunteers, and the folks at Omnipress.

You rock!

Darren Dahl, University of British Columbia
Gita Johar, Columbia University
Stijn van Osselaer, Erasmus University
*2010 ACR Conference Co-Chairs and Proceedings Editors*

# Table of Contents

## ACR Presidential Address 2010

## Invited ACR 2010 Presidential Session

## ACR Fellows Addresses

# Special Session Summaries

## Competitive Papers—Full

# Competitive Papers—Extended Abstracts

# Film Festival

# Roundtable Summaries

*Raj Raghunathan*
*Darren Dahl, University of British Columbia, Canada*
*Kelly Haws, Texas A&M University, USA*
*Gita Johar, Columbia University, USA*
*Aparna Labroo, University of Chicago, USA*
*Rhiannon MacDonnell, University of Calgary, Canada*
*Himanshu Mishra, University of Utah, USA*
*Vicki Morwitz, New York University, USA*
*Joseph Nunes, University of Southern California, USA*
*Stijn van Osselaer, Erasmus University Rotterdam, The Netherlands*
*Deborah Small, University of Pennsylvania, USA*

*Andrew Gershoff, University of Texas at Austin, USA*
*Susan Dobscha, Bentley College, USA*
*Amitav Chakravarti, New York University, USA*
*Julie Irwin, University of Texas at Austin, USA*
*Karen Page Winterich, Pennsylvania State University, USA*
*Michael Luchs, William and Mary, USA*
*Bram Van den Bergh, Erasmus University Rotterdam, The Netherlands*
*Rebecca Walker Naylor, Ohio State University, USA*
*Kelly Haws, Texas A&M University, USA*
*Vladas Griskevicius, University of Minnesota, USA*

*Eduardo B. Andrade, University of California, Berkeley, USA*
*Clayton Critcher, Cornell University, USA*
*Jeff Galak, Carnegie Mellon University, USA*
*Chris Janiszewski, University of Florida, USA*
*Peter McGraw, University of Colorado, USA*
*Tom Meyvis, New York University, USA*
*Leif D. Nelson, University of California, Berkeley, USA*
*Joseph P. Simmons, Yale University, USA*
*Stacy Wood, University of South Carolina, USA*

*Michal Strahilevitz , Golden Gate University, USA*
*David Mick, University of Virginia, USA*
*Deborah Small, Wharton School of Business, USA*
*Carlos J. Torelli, University of Minnesota, USA*
*Andrew M. Kaikati, Terry College of Business, University of Georgia, USA*
*Kelly Goldsmith, Kellogg School, Northwestern University, USA*
*Michael Norton, Harvard School of Business, USA*
*Nicole Verrochi, University of Pittsburg, USA*
*Sankar Sen, Zicklin School of Business, Baruch Colege/CUNY, USA*
*Sergio Carvalho, University of Manitboa, Canada*
*Karen Page Winterich, Pennsylvania State University, USA*
*Christopher Olivola, Cognitive, Perceptual and Brain Sciences, University College London, UK*
*Ekant Veer, University of Canterbury, New Zealand*
*Susan Dobscha, Bentley University, USA*
*Uri Simonsohn, Wharton School of Business, USA*
*Wendy Liu, U.C. San Diego, USA*
*Stacy Wood, University of South Carolina, USA*
*Aronte Bennett, Villanova University, USA*
*Andrea Scott, Pepperdine University, USA*
*Jing (Alice) Wang, University of Iowa, USA*
*Lalin Anik, Harvard School of Business, USA*
*Shuili Du, Simmons College School of Management, USA*
*Stefanie Rosen, University of South Carolina, USA*
*Zoe Chance, Harvard School of Business, USA*
*Aditi Grover, Plymouth State University, USA*
*Susan Harmon, Pacific Lutheran University, USA*
*Diane Martin, University of Portland, USA*

# Working Papers

# Author Index

# ACR Presidential Address 2010

## Navigating The PhD Waters: The Role of Advisors

Geeta Menon, Abraham Krasnoff Professor of Global Business Stern School of Business, NYU, USA
(This is a slightly expanded version of the talk.)

When I thought of today's talk over a year ago, it was crystal clear to me what the topic should be – PhD education. It is one part of our profession that gives me tremendous joy, and so it seemed like a perfect topic to focus on with a captive audience. However, having decided on the topic, the nuances of creating an impact by speaking about the less obvious was a challenge. After all there are several doctoral consortia, and many focus on the path to success for PhD students. So what could I speak about that was different, but still relevant? A topic discussed far less in these public forums is the nature of the Advisor-Student relationship itself: doctoral student training, our relationships with our students, and our presence in their lives for their continued success. So I will focus today on the role of Advisors in PhD education.

I joined the PhD program in Business Administration at the University of Illinois, Urbana-Champaign in 1986, or the time long before Google Scholar. Yes, o young ones, there was that time where the first name of an author could only be found after a visit to the stacks or on microfiche. I had applied to a PhD program, was admitted, and was now venturing forth, bravely and coldly, to the Midwest. And I got hooked on soap operas and used them to educate myself on American culture. I had no idea what I wanted to do or what I wanted to accomplish, but somehow I stumbled along, each year to something better. Now I realize that I wasn't really stumbling, but that my education was a process – a process shaped by my relationship with my Advisor, Seymour Sudman, and the other members of my committee (Carolyn Simmons, Thom Srull and Bob Wyer). As well as by my relationship with my peers in the PhD program – we supported each other, looked out for each other, and saw each through fairly hard times. It's a time when deep bonds are formed and one's world view is affected for life.

From a Student's perspective, PhD education is about learning new things, apprenticing with experts in the field, and eventually striving for independence and excellence in the profession. From an Advisor's perspective the education process is about creating a new generation of scholars who push the boundaries of knowledge, getting satisfaction from the process, and if some glory is reflected back on them, great! Additionally, there could also be a research synergy that is created for an Advisor across Students.

For students graduating with a behavioral focus in Marketing from a Business school, which tends to be true for most ACR attendees, the Marketing PhD is somewhat different in structure from a PhD in Psychology. For example, the Psychology PhD program typically consists of the "lab-model" where a group of students work with a faculty advisor who is the primary researcher. While the Advisor is a key player in this model, there also is an in-built mentorship or support system (or competition) from other students in the lab. This "lab" of students lives within a bigger doctoral student pool. On the other hand, when a student is working towards a PhD in Marketing in a Business School, s/he is typically working with a faculty advisor one-on-one. And the PhD student pools in a marketing PhD program are typically smaller than those in Psychology departments. Therefore, the Advisor-Student relationship is very central to the education process. Understanding what each group looks for in the other is important.

So my goals today are to help us:
- Understand the PhD landscape,
- Understand the critical Advisor-Student relationship better in terms of what we are doing right, what we are doing less well, and how we can improve.

So like any curious researcher, I collected data.

## WHAT DO WE KNOW ABOUT THE PHD LANDSCAPE?

The first question that I asked myself was what is the size of the total Marketing PhD Student pool compared to the Marketing Faculty Advisor pool. Was there a dearth of one group versus the other?

I included a question in the most recent Marketing Academia Labor Market Survey regarding how many faculty members work with doctoral students in each of the schools surveyed.

- This survey was conducted using Qualtrics from mid-April to mid-May 2010 among 141 schools, out of which 117 responded.[1]
- 16 schools responded that they do not have a PhD program, and of the remaining 101 schools, the average size of a department is 12.5 faculty members, and the average size of the PhD program in marketing is 6.6.
- Additionally, respondents reported that on average, 50% of their faculty work with doctoral students in some capacity, either supervising them on their thesis or working with them on projects with the intention of publishing papers.
- Simple math indicates that the student-faculty ratio is about 1:1, enough for a student to get plenty of attention from a faculty member! It's like pre-school or even better!

Thus, there is an ample supply of faculty members who could serve as potential Advisors to the market of PhD students who are ready to go forth and conquer. Of course, in reality we know that some faculty Advisors have clusters of students and therefore this simple math can only go so far, but at least it gives us an indication of the basic numbers.

The next step was to zoom in on the Advisor-Student relationship.

## UNDERSTANDING THE ADVISOR-STUDENT RELATIONSHIP

In order to understand the Advisor-Student relationship, I surveyed both advisors and students. Additionally, I wanted to know whether the perspective of students changes once they become faculty members, so I also included a group that graduated a few years ago. Here's what I did:

After the AMA doctoral consortium in Texas Christian University this past June, I sent a survey to three groups of respondents:

---

[1]     The list of schools across Asia, Europe, North America, and Oceania was compiled using combinations of the UT-Dallas lists of the 100 most productive schools in the U.S. and the 100 most productive schools in the world, together with Chris Janiszewski's and my personal knowledge of schools that regularly interview at the AMA Summer Educators' Conference. Respondents were department chairs and area heads in Marketing.

- Faculty who were invited to the 2010 AMA Doctoral, and a handful of other faculty members; Of the 135 contacted, 82 responded, a response rate of 61%.
- PhD students who were Fellows at the 2010 Doctoral Consortium; Of the 97 contacted, 58 responded, a response rate of 60%; and,
- PhD students who were Fellows at the 2005 Doctoral Consortium at the University of Connecticut; Of the 81 contacted, 45 responded, a response rate of 56%.

The responses rates were much higher for behavioral (versus non-behavioral) faculty and students, and so I'm going to treat this sample as fairly indicative of the ACR audience.

I asked all three groups of respondents to evaluate the importance of 32 traits in Advisors and Students. Since all traits were positively framed, respondents were given specific instructions:

*"Of course, you may be tempted to choose "7" on most of these options, but let's try to aim for a (normal or bi-modal, etc.) non-skewed distribution of your responses across these traits. In other words, skim through the traits first, and then use the scale discerningly."*

Well, while the two Student groups used the scales more discerningly, faculty respondents just chose to disregard these instructions, and all 32 traits loaded onto one factor!

Despite such hiccups, the analyses revealed some interesting information that I have categorized into the following sections:
A. "Seven Deadly Sins of an Advisor,"
B. "Seven Deadly Sins of a Student,"
C. "Are We All on the Same Page Regarding the Advisor's Role?" and
D. "Guiding Light from Advisors Over the Years."

A general point of clarification – there wasn't much difference in the themes of the qualitative data obtained from Advisors and Students in the Seven Deadly Sins. However, when I present the Seven Deadly Sins of an Advisor, the verbatim I report are from Students, and vice versa.

## A. SEVEN DEADLY SINS OF AN ADVISOR

I asked the 2010 Consortium faculty and student attendees what, in their opinion, were the top three traits an Advisor should and should not possess in an open-ended format. I did a content-analysis of these top-threes.

### Positives

On the positive side, the most-mentioned traits were the Advisor's:
- Passion for research
- Productivity
- Ability to be a research role-model

All of these oft-mentioned positives have to do with the Advisor's research acumen. [At least that's what I called it till a colleague asked me why Indians speak in 18th century English, and so I changed this to "research talent and expertise."]

### Negatives

On the negative side, the most mentioned traits are listed below. The main point is a numbered, paraphrased title, and the bullets within are reproduced verbatim from the responses as examples.

*#1 Rigidity: My way or the highway*
- "Controlling"
- "Dogmatic/strong ideas"
- "Stifling student creativity"

*#2 Attitude$_{Student}$: I need therapy, but instead I choose to be…*
- "Mean-spirited"
- "Verbally abusive"
- "Disrespectful"
- "Bossy"
- "Gossiping"

*#3 Selfishness: How is this going to help me?*
- "Focus on own productivity"
- "Believes in hierarchy and that students are minions"
- "Indifferent to student performance"

*#4 Egotism: I reign supreme*
- "God complex"
- "Infallible"
- "Dictates research agenda"

*#5 Inaccessibility: "I am out of the office" auto-reply*
- "MIA"/"Out of contact"
- "Non-responsive to phone calls and e-mails"
- "Overcommitted"/"tired"
- "Takes too long to give feedback"

And you can't have Accessibility without Diagnosticity!

*#6 Non-diagnosticity: Feedback with little guidance*
- "Shooting down ideas"
- "Too critical"
- "On the flip side, too much sugar-coating of comments"

*#7 Unfortunately Unaware: La la la…*
- "Not pushing student enough"
- "Not being wind beneath sails"

While the positives had to do with the Advisor's research talent, the negative traits had to do with the Advisor:
a. Doing "bad" stuff (#1 and 2),
b. Having personality issues (#3 and 4), or
c. Doing nothing (#5, 6 and 7).

### Bottom line

The good news is that as Advisors we at least know what we want to accomplish intellectually! But we can be in a better place by improving social dynamics with Students. Two recommendations emerge:
a. To Advisors: Don't do bad stuff, self-regulate in interactions with Students when necessary, and try to do good stuff and advise;
b. To Students: Either
   i. Lower your expectations and accept that Advisors may sometimes be nasty/mean or lazy/aloof/absent (I know, this stinks),
   or
   ii. Pick Advisors not just based on research talent but also based on personality and availability. Talk to other senior students. I think that it often comes down to a forecasting/selection problem from the point of view of the Student: they think that all that will matter is research talent so they pick the research star of the department (who happens to be nasty and absent… Just speculating – I do after all have Presidential license! ☺ )

## B. SEVEN DEADLY SINS OF A STUDENT

I also asked each respondent to list the top three traits that a Student should and should not possess in an open-ended question.

### Positives

The three most-mentioned positives were:
- Intellectual curiosity
- Creativity
- Perseverance (hard-working, diligence, motivated)

### Negatives

These same positive traits were also mentioned in the opposite valence as negatives, along with several others:

#### #1 *Lack of intellectual curiosity*
- "Not inquisitive"
- "Not passionate"
- "Not committed"

#### #2 *Close-minded*
- "Stubborn refusal to give up an idea"
- "Too narrow"
- "Inability to listen"

#### #3 *Lazy or Passive*
- "Procrastination"
- "Looking for the easy way"
- "Need for rapid closure"

#### #4 *Perfectionist*
- "Too detail-oriented"

#### #5 *Thin-skinned*
- "Emotionally fragile"
- "Can't take criticism"

#### #6 *Over-confidence*
- "Sense of entitlement"
- "Arrogance"
- "Cocky"

#### #7 *I not We*
- "Not a good team player"
- "Overly competitive with other students in the program"
- "Doesn't work well with others"

### Bottom line

These overall results are not surprising: We want intellectually curious, open-minded, hardworking, thorough but not OCD, sensitive, humble, cooperative students!

But maybe not…

Interestingly, while there seemed to be an "ideal" Advisor (i.e., a good researcher, available, helpful, and nice), the data are more ambiguous regarding the "ideal" Student. For example, there is a conflict between #3 and #4 (do you want someone who works fast or is a perfectionist?) and between #5 and #6 (do you want someone humble or confident?). The data indicate greater heterogeneity of preferences when it comes to an ideal Student compared to an ideal Advisor. And one size does not fit all.

## C. ARE WE ALL ON THE SAME PAGE REGARDING THE ADVISOR'S ROLE?

So far I have been focusing on the synergies of responses across groups of Advisors and Students. I would like to now focus on some interesting points of differences in perceptions between the groups in terms of the evolving role of Advisors during a Student's professional journey:
- a. As a student
- b. While on the job market, and
- c. Post-PhD

As an aside, I will be presenting some charts – All scales are 7-point scales, unless otherwise specified, and a higher number indicates more of whatever is being measured.

### (a) While the Student is a Student

The time as a PhD student is a critical one in terms of both intellectual training, as well as in terms of developing and refining good "research habits." But what Students think they want and what Advisors think they need to deliver maybe disjointed, and so I asked a few questions pertaining to Advising goals and the level of involvement.

*(i) What could Advisors use more of?*

Advisors say they wish they had more Time, Students say they wish Advisors had more Personality.

Faculty reported that the biggest problem they perceive in the advising environment is lack of time to advice. However, while Students did mention that Advisors are overcommitted, they reported the bigger issues are personality-related: rigid, selfish and egotistical. Students do believe that Advisors have the intellectual component (thank goodness!), but they would also like to receive respectful guidance.

However, Advisors don't seem to realize this. They rated the importance of being Socially Aware (a measure that I am using as a surrogate for treating people with respect) as much less important a trait in an Advisor (3.8) compared to both groups of Students (4.8 and 5.6). Similarly, having a "Charming personality" was rated much lower by faculty (2.6) than the two groups of Students (4.0 and 4.2). While these traits are not the most important (given the overall middle-of-the range ratings on 7-point scales), we, as Advisors, should pay more attention to personality-related traits since there is a disparity in ratings between groups. Sensitivity to the way we interact with doctoral students is an important issue that we should keep in mind.

*(ii) What specific activities should Advisors participate in to facilitate the PhD education process?*

When asked this question, many faculty members mentioned:
1. Provide the big picture
2. Help with methodology and analyses
3. Keep abreast of the literature so that Students don't go astray. These can be classified as the "intellectual" components of advising.

However, it turns out that Students don't mention anything so sophisticated or highbrow in their responses. In fact, when asked to rate the traits of "Well read in the field" and "Has intellectual breadth" on importance in an Advisors, faculty rated these traits at 6.2 and 6.3. Students, both the 2005 and the 2010 samples, rated these traits between 5.1 and 5.3.

So what do Students want Advisors to do more of? They universally identified three sets of activities that they would like their Advisors to do more of:
1. Have regular meetings/provide constant feedback;
2. Make a schedule/check up on Student's progress; and
3. Interact personally/have lunch together occasionally/and drinks!

All three have to do with "logistical details." AKA, some form of hand-holding.

Thankfully, given the specific nature of the feedback from Students, these action items are simple to implement, if not already in place. However, Advisors, if you're not planning to check up on your students, you should make sure that students realize it is their task to chase you and harass you.

### (iii) How directive should an Advisor be?

One of the scaled questions asked, "How directive do you think an Advisor should be as far as a Student's research is concerned?" Faculty expressed that they should be less directive (4.2) than recent graduates (5.6) and current students (5.1) desire.

What is the issue here? I have been involved in reviews of PhD programs and have given quite a lot of thought to different forms of advising that I have seen over the years. In general, at the two ends of a spectrum of advising, there is the "Apprenticeship" approach and the "Sink or Swim" approach. In general, I have been a fan of the Apprenticeship approach. A discussion with a colleague recently, though, made me rethink my stand. He pointed out that too much of an Apprenticeship approach may hinder the independence of the PhD student, making them less likely to succeed in a world where they need to struggle as Assistant Professors and get tenure. [Besides, we have scientific evidence that the Apprenticeship model may convert an Anakin Skywalker into a Darth Vader!]

I still do believe that Apprenticeship is important, and maybe there is a happy medium between this and the "Sink or Swim" approach in the role an Advisor plays in the Student's life.

## (b) While the Student is on the Job Market

When on the job market, the set of demands on an Advisor is very different. The job market generally lasts for only a few months, but it has a lasting impact. So I wanted to gauge the levels of satisfaction with the role of the Advisor during this phase.

I asked respondents a hard-to-answer, ambiguous and complex question: "In your opinion, what percentage of PhD students in marketing are satisfied with the role that their advisor plays in their (a) overall PhD education; and (b) job placement?" In answering this question, respondents were asked to think about Students and Advisors around them to make the question slightly more tangible.

Regardless of the craziness of the question (and my Advisor's voice in my head saying, "I wrote Asking Questions! Did you not read it?"), the responses were indeed interesting. Faculty perceptions of themselves as Advisors are worse than student perceptions. Faculty reported on average that about 40% of students were satisfied with the role of their advisors in their overall PhD education. But the Student samples reported 60%. A similar pattern holds for job placement (40%, 54%, and 59% respectively).

Bottom line – Advisors, forgive yourselves! We are doing a lot better in the eyes of our Students than we give ourselves credit for. Yes, there is room for improvement (after all the satisfaction percentages are only a little over the half-way mark), but let's not try too hard to fix something that is only a little broken!

## (c) After the Student gets a PhD

Once Students are gainfully employed, the question arises regarding the continuing role of Advisors. Anecdotally, I know several colleagues of mine who say that they wash their hands off their Students once that time comes, and yet others who continue to hover like helicopter parents. So I investigated this issue empirically.

### (i) Mentoring after graduation

Respondents were asked: "How much (a) SHOULD, and (b) WILL an advisor continue to mentor their student after s/he graduates?"

- All three groups are equivalent in their beliefs regarding how much faculty members SHOULD mentor after graduation (Faculty = 5.7, Recent graduates = 5.5 and Current students = 5.8).
- However, Advisors believe they mentor Students after they graduate as much as they think they should (5.6); I call this group Idealists.
- Recent graduates (i.e., 2005 Doctoral Consortium students) do not believe that Advisors have continued involvement in mentoring after graduation (3.8); I call this group the Disappointed.
- Those that haven't yet graduated (i.e., 2010 Doctoral Consortium students) believe that their Advisors should continue to be involved, though they are not sure that they actually will be (4.6); I call this group the Pessimists, albeit not sufficiently so.

All three groups believe that Advisors should continue to be involved in their career, and yet according to the 2005 Students (who are probably the most recent beneficiaries of their Advisors' goodwill), Advisors are not as involved.

From an Advisor's viewpoint, however, consider issues of Promotion and Tenure down the road for our students. As good Advisors, we hopefully have internal compasses that tell us to what extent we should be involved (that is, till the student is flying on their own), and when to let go (that is, when students should establish an area of research of their own, and gain an independent reputation). Therefore, it is likely that Advisors are involved to the extent they believe that they should be involved, and that is just not the same amount as what Students expect. So again, it is up to us to either step it up or at least manage expectations.

### (ii) How important is the Advisor-Student relationship to future success of the Student?

Both groups of "Students," the 2005 and the 2010 doctoral consortia attendees, rated this relationship as extremely important to their future success (6.5 and 6.6 out of 7). Faculty members, however, rated this relationship as less critical to success, albeit on the positive side of the 7-point scale (5.0). Since the Students that graduated a few years ago still think that the Advisor is critical to their success, Advisors need to acknowledge this more and need to: (a) either manage these expectations, or (b) work harder towards getting students to be more self-sufficient.

## Bottom line

- Advisors need to be more attentive to personality issues when it comes to dealing with Students (maybe); and
- We need to revisit and manage the expectations of Students better in terms of:
  - Our role in their current PhD life (e.g., Schedule-keeper? Or idea-bouncer?)
  - Our role in their future academic life as young professors. Are we really that central to a Student's future success? I hope the answer is No.

An intriguing question is that given that all Advisors were Students at some point, why do these differences exist? I see four possibilities:

1. Advisors have moved on, forgotten, and now have a different perspective;
2. Times are different. Personality may have been considered irrelevant before (heck, it may even have been cool to be the crazy professor), but now Students want you to be nice;

3. There is a survival bias and the most successful academics are those that did not care whether their Advisor was charming; or
4. Students are now a coddled bunch and expect to have a lot of hand-holding.

You pick the poison(s)!

## D. GUIDING LIGHT FROM ADVISORS OVER THE YEARS

Finally, I asked all respondents who have been in academia for as many as 40 years to as few as 2 years what was the best piece of advice they received from their Advisor. Here are the ones that resonated most with me and they are a reminder, in my opinion, of what we need to reinforce in our roles as Advisors:

### (a) "It's a marathon, not a sprint."

It is important to think of the PhD education process as the antecedent to a life-long research adventure full of discoveries, akin to a life-long marathon. If these discoveries are packaged into synergistic research areas, a body of knowledge is generated. However, if we think of research as a bunch of publications, then the journey becomes more like a number of sprints strung together, rather than a marathon.

The kind of student that enters the PhD program is somewhat different today than 20 years ago, and some even join the PhD program with publications. Yet, doctoral programs now last 5 or 6 years instead of 3 or 4 because we hire junior faculty members for their record+potential, as opposed to the old days when we hired based on potential. All that is well and good, but I also fear that this change in our education system will slowly decompose the contributions of the next generation into a series of sprints if our focus shifts to publishing, rather than create an impact with a marathon.

So what can we do to encourage a marathon approach among Students? It is important to focus students on some of the basic characteristics that will maintain the excitement of research through the years ahead. Here's what some Advisors had to say:

*Study something that excites you, not something that is "in".*

Chris Janiszewski spoke about this last year in his Presidential address. Other Advisors have said:

*"Follow your inspiration."*

*"Study what you are passionate about
and academia ceases to be work."*

*"Don't follow the herd."*

*"Risky research is not all that risky – this is the work that garners
the most attention and changes the way people think."*

*Try to explore the topic in various ways (width)
and as well as you can (depth):*

*"Build a program of research."*

*"Work on multiple projects at once
but don't spread yourself too thin."*

*"Publish in top journals."*

### (b) "When the going gets tough, the tough get going."

An aspect of research life is rejection, criticism and very often having to rework a project that you have already invested a year or two into (the Reject/Resubmit or the "new manuscript" syndrome). The key is perseverance! As many Advisors have noted, the correlation between smartness and perseverance is not perfect. Brilliant ideas are a dime a dozen, but brilliant ideas, done, redone and then disseminated are fewer and far between. One Advisor said:

*"It's not the smartest people who succeed in our field, but it's the
people who keep working and don't give up."*

### (c) "Take yourself seriously, but not too seriously."

I believe very strongly that everyone needs work-life balance, whatever that "life" component may be. So for those of us that need something beyond work, let's take our work seriously, but let's also try to find ways to incorporate other things that inject joy into our lives; who knows they may trigger a lot of creative thinking and produce impactful research as a side benefit!

I encourage my PhD students to enjoy whatever it is that rocks their boat: their kids, travel, cooking, gardening, drinking, bartending, karaoke, reading, working at the zoo, sky-diving, cross-dressing… you name it.

### (d) "Personal issues come and go but you will always have your dissertation."

I have had several students over the years that joined the PhD program with families, or had a baby or two during the program. They balk at the age-old wisdom that the dissertation is like a baby. And while surfing the web and talking to colleagues, I found these compelling arguments about why a dissertation is harder than having a baby:

1. Unlike advisors, you can switch doctors without having to start over.
2. Conceiving a baby is WAY more fun than conceiving a topic.
3. Friends and relatives don't question the worth of a baby.
4. No one will complain if your baby is too similar to another one.
5. If you produce 8 dissertations, nobody will give you your own TV show.

So let's stop calling the dissertation a baby, and call it what it is – a big (though sometimes fulfilling) pain, which if doesn't kill you, makes you stronger.

### (e) "Pass the torch."

As Advisors, we are role models setting an example for our Students, and much like our children, they pick up behaviors and attitudes that are both communicated deliberately as well as non-consciously. Have you ever noticed a child may end up a Phillies fan because one of the parents is a Phillies fan? PhD students tend to do the same thing. No, they may not become Phillies fans, but they mimic behaviors and attitudes. It is important to behave in a way that one is proud of when emulated. And as one Advisor said, "Whatever you get from me, pass it forward." We are, after all, creating the next generation of researchers.

## ACKNOWLEDGEMENTS

I would now like to say a few words of thanks to ACR.

a. In order to recognize the "marathon, not a sprint" thinking, ACR has instituted the annual Early Career Award for contributions to consumer research. This award will be presented for the first time at tomorrow's luncheon.

b. In today's talk, I have focused on Advisor-Student relationships, but of course Advisors can spawn off a whole line of research with Students, and more interestingly (and very true in my case), can be influenced by their Students' research. This is an extremely important aspect of an Advisor's role in PhD education that I did not have the time to talk about.

As an illustration, there is a special session chaired by Nidhi Agrawal and Ellie Kyung that was invited by the three ACR co-chairs immediately following this luncheon. This session highlights synergy in research on Consumer Well-Being across several students I have been lucky enough to interact with during my twenty years as a faculty member. I have been influenced by their very intellectual minds in my own work.

c. Finally, ACR is a forum that fosters mentorship both intellectually with cutting-edge research, and socially by bringing together different generations of scholar.

A few other acknowledgements…

Thanks to *The Bold and the Beautiful*: Darren Dahl, Gita V. Johar and Stijn van Ossalaer for an amazing conference and Priya Raghubir and Patti Williams for a thought-provoking doctoral symposium.

To *All My Children* who have enriched my life professionally and personally: Eric Yorkston, Suresh Ramanathan, Nidhi Agrawal, Manoj Thomas, Ellie Kyung, Amit Bhattacharjee and Rohaan Menon. (The last one is my biological child and my rock.) And to other students who I have had the pleasure of learning from over the years: Gita V. Johar, Priya Raghubir, Raj Raghunathan, Suchi Chandran and Cenk Bülbül.

To *The Young and the Restless*, each of who contributed in unique ways along the way and I am so grateful: Amitav Chakravarti, Rohit Deo, Ellie Kyung, Gavan Fitzsimons, Tom Meyvis, Vicki Morwitz, Priya Nair, Priya Raghubir, Akshay Rao, Sankar Sen and Nicole Verrochi.

## DEDICATIONS

**To Seymour Sudman,**
Who set very high standards as an Advisor and ignited my enthusiasm for PhD Education.

**To my parents**
Who channeled my thirst for knowledge and taught me that the education process never ends.

## THANK YOU!

# Invited ACR 2010 Presidential Session

## All My Children: Fostering Diverse Approaches to Consumer Well-Being Research

Co-chairs:
Nidhi Agrawal, Northwestern University, USA
Ellie Kyung, Dartmouth College, USA

In conjunction with her address which underscored the importance of doctoral education, ACR President Geeta Menon hosted an ACR session on an issue that has significantly influenced her work: consumer well-being. To that end, her past and present student collaborators presented on a broad range of topics related to improving consumer decision-making processes and their public policy implications.

### GOAL

The goals of this session were two-fold. First, to showcase examples of theoretically grounded work in the realm of consumer well-being. And second, to promote further research in the realm of consumer well-being, while illustrating the importance of developing new scholars in our field through supporting doctoral education.

### SESSION SUMMARY

With the proliferation of channels, firms, products, and services over time, the consumer world has become increasingly complex. Consumers are often faced with competing goals or objectives that can materially affect their well-being. Thus, there is a need to understand how to empower consumers through designing better messages, decision-making contexts, choice settings and behavioral motivations and aid them in achieving their well-being goals. Much attention has been drawn to this important, growing area of research in recent years, and this session showcased varied approaches to studying consumer well-being. **Geeta Menon** opened the session by discussing her interest in consumer health and well-being research and her work with doctoral students.

The first group of papers addressed novel issues related to impulsive behavior. **Suresh Ramanathan** presented his work suggesting that indulgence maybe viewed as sticky and recurrent desires rather than weak self-control. This implies a more 'active' and goal-directed view of self-control problems in domains of impulsive behavior. Following this, **Nidhi Agrawal** discussed when and why health messages designed with the good intention of promoting healthy behaviors might backfire on consumers' subsequent self-

control in unrelated domains. **Manoj Thomas** talked about how forms of payment used can influence impulsivity and the purchase of unhealthy food products.

The second group of papers examined the role that ethics can play in consumer choices. **Suchi Chandran** moved the discussion to a new domain of ethical consumption by asking how mood, self-esteem and consumption visibility influence attitudes towards ethical products. Then **Amit Bhattacharjee** took a different view of the evaluation of products from a social value perspective by discussing consumer perceptions of the relationship between firm profit generation and social value creation.

The final group of papers examined ways in which consumers can take control over their environment and decision making to improve their well-being. **Eric Yorkston** examined how consumers can use today's technologies to the counter background sounds – typically under the control of external agents – that might otherwise negatively affect their behavior. **Ellie Kyung** discussed why consumers treat their private information so lightly in the digital age and identify methods to encourage them to value and protect their personal information. Building on this question of how to encourage consumers to actually behave in ways that maximize their well-being, **Raj Raghunathan** examined the pursuit of happiness. His studies examined why consumers believe they should make choices to maximize happiness, but do not make choices consistent with this goal. Finally, **Priya Raghubir** discussed how consumers' subjective value of money can depend upon different payments forms, currencies and denomination, affecting critical saving and spending decisions. She discussed methods to improve financial decision-making.

Together, these papers presented a variety of perspectives to studying consumer well-being. Each showcased ideas that contribute to the understanding of consumer well-being while advancing existing theory. **Gita Johar** concluded the session by discussing the key points across these presentations and highlighting the commonalities across these papers. She presented an integrative view of the various papers and emphasized the importance of studying consumer well-being.

## Short Abstracts
*(Presenting authors in italics.)*

### On Indulgence as Sticky and Recurrent Desires Rather Than Weak Self-Control
*Suresh Ramanathan*, University of Chicago

Indulgence has often been ascribed to weakness in the ability to avoid temptations. Using a new Dynamical Systems approach, we will argue that indulgence is driven by desires that strengthen over time and recur more frequently for people who are impulsive. Further, such people get "stuck" in these states of desire for longer periods of time. Contrary to the prevailing view of indulgence, we find no diminution in avoidance reactions over time, suggesting that casting indulgence as a failure of self-control may not be always an accurate view of the phenomenon.

### Preventing One Disease, Promoting Another? Carry-Over Effects of Health Messages on Subsequent Self-Control
*Nidhi Agrawal*, Northwestern University
Echo Wen Wan, University of Hong Kong

We examine the deleterious effects of health messages that communicate high risk of disease on consumers' subsequent self-control in other domains. Processing high- versus low-risk health messages impairs subsequent self-control via both motivational (e.g., depletion from trade-offs) and emotional (e..g, anxiety from risk perception) processes.

*Advances in Consumer Research*
*Volume 38, ©2012*

## Credit Cards and Purchase of Unhealthy Food Products: The Roles of Impulsivity, Deprivation and Intrusive Desires
*Manoj Thomas*, Cornell University
Kalpesh Desai, SUNY Buffalo
Satheeshkumar Seenivasan, SUNY Buffalo

Some food items that are commonly considered unhealthy also tend to elicit intrusive desires. Mode of payment can influence consumers' ability to control these intrusive desires. Paying by credit cards makes consumers more likely to buy such food items, and this effect is stronger when consumers are chronically impulsive or have been suppressing their desires.

## Loving, Feeling and Helping: The Impact of Mood, Self Esteem and Visibility of Consumption on Attitudes towards Ethical Products
*Sucharita Chandran* , Boston University
Shuili Du, Simmons College

Research suggests that buying ethical products makes consumers feel good and that providing an 'ethical guarantee' can be impactful. Here, we investigate the role of self esteem, mood and visibility of consumption (private or public) on attitudes, intentions to buy and willingness to pay for ethical products.

## Is Profit Evil? Incentive Neglect and the Association of Profit with Social Harm
*Amit Bhattacharjee*, University of Pennsylvania
Jason Dana, University of Pennsylvania
Jonathan Baron, University of Pennsylvania

Multiple studies find a strong negative correlation between perceived profit and social value across both industries and specific firms, moderated only by perceived firm motives. Similarly, we find that hypothetical organizations are viewed as creating less social value when described as for-profit rather than non-profit. People report little faith in the power of markets to create and reward value, neglecting the incentive properties of profit and focusing instead on the perceived intentions of firms.

## Success through Supplanting Sounds
*Eric Yorkston*, Texas Christian University
Leonardo Nicolao, Texas Christian University

Ancillary sounds, such as background music, can strongly effect consumers' behavior. These sounds are often determined by external agents and outside the control of individual consumers. We suggest that utilizing current technologies, consumers can take active control over environmental sounds and the behavioral consequences they have on their consumer welfare.

## Examining the "Privacy Paradox": The Role of Perceived Constraints
*Ellie Kyung*, Dartmouth College

In this digital age, it has become increasingly easy to solicit, collect, and disseminate personal information from consumers. Although consumers largely agree that privacy is important and that their information is valuable, they regularly share information in relatively unprotected forums in exchange for very little, if anything at all. We discuss reasons why consumers behave in this paradoxical manner and how to encourage them to protect their personal information.

## People Say Happiness is the Ultimate Goal, But Do They Act Like They Mean This?
*Raj Raghunathan*, University of Texas, Austin
Sunaina Chugani, University of Texas, Austin
Ashesh Mukherjee, McGill University

Although lay-people agree that life's ultimate goal is happiness maximization, our findings show they do not behave in a manner that is consistent with this goal. Our findings seem to suggest that, while people realize that they "should" select the intrinsically-motivating job, they can't help but select the extrinsically-motivating one.

## Subjective Value of Money
*Priya Raghubir*, New York University
Joydeep Srivastava, University of Maryland

In our published and ongoing work we have shown that money is subjectively valued and is not fungible across forms, denominations, and currencies. People spend and save differently as a function of whether they are paying using legal tender versus credit cards, debit cards, and gift certificates. Further, the maximum price they are willing to pay for a product differs depending on whether it is in local or foreign currency, with the amount further contingent on whether the face value of the foreign currency is a multiple or fraction of the home currency. Finally, even when consumers are paying using legal tender in their home currency, the denomination of the bills they carry affects their likelihood of purchase.

# ACR Fellows Addresses

## Fellow's Address: In Defense of Bumbling

Joseph W. Alba, University of Florida, USA

As my comments may elicit little sympathy, I will begin on a note of widespread agreement: This honor is undeserved. It is undeserved for many reasons, but the foremost is that ACR has chosen to bestow it on someone who has experienced a continued inability to adapt to the culture of consumer research.

I began my career as an outsider to consumer research, ignorant of its substance and traditions. To acclimate, I delved into the leading consumer and marketing journals—an experience that was simultaneously stimulating and perplexing. I quickly apprehended many of the themes of the discipline but was bemused by some of its methods and philosophical leanings. For example, I was surprised to encounter in one of my first readings a section labeled "manipulation checks." True to its title, the authors proceeded to report that they had successfully manipulated their independent variables. I was not particularly heartened by this outcome because my experience with experimental manipulations was that they required little confirmation. If a memory experiment varied the interval between stimulus presentation and recall, for instance, the manipulation could be checked with a watch or calendar, and there was little need to apprise the reader of its success. As I read further, it became clear why consumer articles contained manipulation checks. They were engaged in an alien practice that involved the manipulation and measurement of "constructs," which I was further chagrined to learn were hypothetical.

To understand how a construct could be unfamiliar to someone who by this time had read deeply (but obviously not broadly) about human behavior, one must appreciate the roots of cognitive psychology. As reflected in the verbal-learning paradigm, its associationistic accounts, and its functionalist orientation, much early work on memory occurred under the umbrella of behaviorism. Memory was taken to be a function of the learning environment and the individual's history (Watkins 1990), and in almost no instance did manipulation of these variables require verification.

It is no secret that consumer research has rarely aligned itself with the functionalist perspective. My personal affection for functionalism notwithstanding, I am disinclined to proselytize—a futile endeavor in any event. However, I would contend that functionalism is not a cult and that its current lack of popularity should be viewed as a matter of taste rather than scientific legitimacy.

Nonetheless, life in this non-functionalist world has been edifying, and the many issues we investigate, mostly with the aid of constructs, are interesting and important. If finding a comfort zone within consumer research required only that I relax my philosophical proclivities, I would have acclimated long ago. However, there is an additional word that has proven vexatious. It is a weighty word, but one that previously had failed to evoke a valenced response from me. That word is *theory*—a word that becomes even more ominous when used accusatorily in the sentence: "Where's your theory?" After nearly 30 years, I should accept the possibility that I may never comes to terms with this question. However, if I am to maintain even a flicker of hope, I must first understand its intent.

### WHAT IS THEORY?

I suspect that when people express a preference for theory, they are at various times using the term in at least one of three ways. The first is as a formalization, a view of theory that conforms most closely to a textbook definition, as in "a statement of relations among concepts within a set of boundary assumptions and constraints" (Bacharach 1989, p. 498). One may quibble about the particulars, but such a definition is unlikely to generate much controversy. A second use of the term is as a synonym for process. That is, when asked to supply a theory, the researcher is really being asked to describe the cognitive (or affective) processes that underlie some reported effect. It is difficult to argue with this sense of theory, as well, insofar as it reflects intellectual curiosity. We wish to understand a phenomenon as well as it can be understood. Finally, request for theory can reflect a philosophical disposition that we commonly refer to as the hypothetico-deductive approach. The popularity of the approach is plainly evident in our literature in the form of explicit and extensively reasoned a priori hypotheses, which too suggests a lack of controversy.

Given the apparent reasonableness and general acceptance of each connotation of the word, there seems to be little reason to fear theory. However, one can acknowledge the validity of each view while also questioning the need to conform to any of them. I will try to make my case on substantive grounds, but I must also confess that the issue is personal. The simple fact is that I violate the prescription for theory in all of its senses. My empirical efforts typically focus on only one or two independent and dependent variables, thereby affording little opportunity to build a theory in the classic sense. I have an appreciation for process, and there are instances in which I seek to understand the process underlying an effect, but process rarely serves as my initial motivation. Finally, my favorite form of hypothesis barely qualifies as a hypothesis at all. I am drawn primarily to research questions that are two-tailed, which itself may be an overstatement. My favorite research questions begin with the words "I wonder … ." Formal hypotheses that have appeared in my published research have been inserted under protest.

Having failed at theory, I am sensitive to my outlier status. My self-esteem is further damaged by the realization that I fall into the category of investigators described by Wegner (1992) as "bumblers," that is, people who go through life simply trying things. Worse yet, if I have accurately captured the multiple meanings of theory as used in our field, I am unlikely to ever escape bumbler status. The most obvious reason is that I lack the ability to do anything else. The other reason, however, is that my functionalist instincts prevent me from adhering to the theory orthodoxy. Fortunately, I am not alone, and I can take great comfort in the accomplishments of other bumblers. It is not my original observation that some of the greatest achievements in the natural sciences were realized through induction and observation (see, e.g., Barwise 1995; Ehrenberg 1995; Peter 1991; Rozin 2001; Watkins 1990). Closer to home, it is Greenwald (2004, p.275) who has

> "... long questioned the wisdom of a principle of proper method in psychology that is now widely advocated—the belief that empirical research is valuable only to the extent that it advances theory.
> ... Among the important works that have managed to achieve publication without advancing theory are some of the major works by Asch (conformity), Sherif (norm formation), Milgram (obedience), and Zajonc (mere exposure)."

## WHY THE OBSESSION?

In trying to understand the emphasis on theory in consumer research, at least three explanations come to mind. Each has its own merits, but it is unclear that any one is completely valid.

### Good Intentions

It is widely acknowledged that research in the fields of business, including marketing, was not highly developed 40 years ago. The stinging criticisms leveled by prestigious organizations prompted colleges of business to shift from a vocational to a scientific mode which, from a research perspective, translated into a shift from a descriptive to a theoretical orientation (see MacInnis and Folkes 2010 for a discussion).

Given the status quo, it is difficult to find fault with this shift, but there is much irony in the zeal—and narrowness—with which the theoretical approach has been promoted in our discipline. As a point of fact, theory testing is relatively rare in the so-called "hard" sciences that consumer research wishes to emulate. Emphasis on experimentation vies with an emphasis on description, and research is often motivated by a simple desire to probe the existence of a relationship between two variables (Rozin 2001, 2006). Graphs, which exhibit a strong relationship to the perceived hardness of a science, tend to be used toward descriptive rather than theoretical ends (Smith et al. 2002). These natural sciences recognize the evolutionary nature of science, embrace its multiple objectives, and are unembarrassed that a scientific paper can serve simply to report a set of empirical observations (Thomson 1994).

So, how is it that we have deviated from the practices of science while believing that we were conforming to them. Although our original intentions were laudable, we may have committed two errors in our execution. First, we may have over-interpreted the call for theory. Business research in previous generations was at its worst when its descriptions lacked generalizability and broad insight. However, neither generalizability nor profundity is isomorphic with theory. Phenomena, as I note later, are generalizable by their nature, and important phenomena spark the imagination.

Second, the consistent emphasis on theory in the ensuing years converted a notion into a rule, which is accompanied by the danger of mindless application (cf. Baron 1994; Langer 1989). Reflexive obedience to theory can be self-defeating and, in some contexts, immoral. We would question the values of a discipline that withheld publication of a welfare-enhancing discovery. We should care little about whether a discovery stems from the predictions of a formal theory, the meeting of a serendipitous outcome and a prepared mind, or simple luck. A cure is a cure, even when the mechanisms of the cure are not fully understood—and there has been no shortage of discoveries in the natural sciences that owe their existence to good fortune (Myers 2008).

Mature sciences exploit the multiple avenues to discovery. Consider Mukherjee's (2010, p. 45) characterization of cancer drug identification:

> *"Traditionally, three strategies have produced anticancer drugs. The first relies on serendipity: someone hears of a chemical that works on some cell, it is tested on cancer and—lo!—it is found to kill cancer cells while sparing normal stem cells. The second approach involves discovering a protein present or especially active in cancer cells—and relatively inactive in normal cells—and targeting that protein with a drug. ... The final strategy involves identifying some behavior of a cancer cell that renders it uniquely sensitive to a particular chemical."*

These "strategies" appear to map onto luck, deduction, and induction, respectively. Is consumer research more rigid simply because its discoveries lack import?

### Confidence

Inexplicable empirical effects prompt skepticism, and therefore requests for a process explanation are not unreasonable. Confidence in the reliability and validity of a relationship between two variables can be enhanced by a plausible causal explanation (Alba and Hutchinson 2000). Again, however, our faith in the ability of theory to achieve our objective may be misplaced. In the social sciences we are fond of noting that no theory is likely to be correct and that a theory lasts until it is displaced by a superior theory. Hence, just as production of reasons for an outcome can lead to overconfidence in its likelihood, we should acknowledge that theory can provide a fall sense of security—if not mortification. As Steven Weinberg, Nobel prize winner, ruefully noted after devising a theory to explain the reported discovery of (nonexistent) trimuons, "I've always been embarrassed that we managed to come up with a theory" (Overbye 2007).

We might dismiss embarrassment as infrequent, but the same is not true of frustration, which can arise particularly when theories are abundant. Watkins (1990) identified a period in the history of memory research that he dubbed "an era of cheap theories," an era that accompanied the ebb of functionalism and a growth in the popularity of memory constructs. Each of these theories was sophisticated, but clearly not all (or any) were correct. Those of us who were compelled to learn these theories are particularly sensitive to the havoc that can be wreaked by intelligent people armed with a large toolbox of constructs.

A final irony of the confidence-driven call for theory involves research from within our own field regarding the time at which a process explanation is offered. When process is articulated a priori, it conforms to our hypothetico-deductive instincts. When offered after the fact, the temptation is to view it as "mere" speculation. My fellow Fellows (Brinberg, Lynch, and Sawyer 1992; Sternthal, Tybout, and Calder 1987) have spoken eloquently about this misconception but with an apparent lack of persuasiveness. The implications are as significant pragmatically as they are conceptually. Researchers who speculate are frequently asked to go to great lengths to confirm their speculations within the same research report, a demand that I later suggest can be suffocating. Further, anticipating that the review process will demand a test of speculation, authors are understandably tempted to reframe their speculation as expectation—a weak form of fraud that is easy to rationalize.

In short, confidence has its costs. These costs are regrettable because they are avoidable. Those who earnestly seek confidence should explain their desire for process. If confidence is the goal, it can be achieved in the absence of theory via tests of robustness.

### Direction

A third source of affection for theory is very pragmatic and is captured famously by Lewin's (1951, p. 169) assertion that "there is nothing so practical as a good theory." When compared to random experimentation, theory does indeed convey advantage. However, for two obvious reasons, theory fails as a compelling directive if its benefit derives from practicality. First, pragmatics cannot be dictated. An important but inefficiently obtained discovery is a discovery nonetheless. With the possible exception of consumer researchers, it would be a rare patient who refused a remedy based on how it was discovered.

Second, it is not the case that scientists are faced with a binary choice between theory-based inspiration and random exploration. Bumblers in particular are familiar with the process of abduction—or "informed curiosity" (Rozin 2001). There is no reason to believe that research inspired by a hunch and then rigorously pursued is any less likely to shed light on consumer behavior than is research derived from a structured theory. In fact, as argued below, a reverse argument can plausibly be made.

Third, for those who rely on theory to confer scientific legitimacy on their efforts, abduction should not be viewed as having less serious philosophical underpinnings than the hypothetico-deductive approach or being any more detached from our ultimate scientific objectives (Haig 2005; *Stanford Encyclopedia of Philosophy* 2010).

## NO FREE LUNCH

The theory imperative is more than a matter of philosophy. By uncritically accepting the advantages of theory, we ignore some very consequential tradeoffs. I will describe four.

### Why Versus What

It has been argued that "The primary goal of a theory is to answer questions of *how*, *when*, and *why*, unlike the goal of description, which is to answer the question of *what*" (Bacharach 1989, p. 498). True enough, but it is bumblers who have a special appreciation for the fact that *what* precedes all other questions, and it amazes bumblers and functionalists (and this bumbling functionalist) that such an assertion could be controversial.

It is notable that our colleagues on the non-behavioral side of marketing have debated the merits of an extreme form of *what*. We are reminded of this controversy by the recent passing of Andrew Ehrenberg, who advocated the Empirical-then-Theoretical (EtT) approach (Ehrenberg 1993), wherein one first establishes an empirical generalization and then develops a model to explain it. Although behavioral bumblers can relate to the spirit of this recommendation, we are less ambitious and less contentious. We believe neither that *what* needs to rise to the level of an empirical generalization or that a theory needs to be preceded by a well-establish empirical generalization. We do agree with the general sentiment that data serve as the building blocks for theory and that some respect should be accorded an inductive (or abductive) approach to theory construction. To reprise an earlier irony, the hard sciences readily acknowledge this reality, such as when epidemiology provides a starting point for the investigation of an ultimately microbiological phenomenon.

If pursuit of *why* versus *what* reflected nothing more than idiosyncratic preferences, the issue would not preoccupy us. However, some have argued that theory can inhibit discovery—if for no other reason that resources are finite and effort devoted to hypothesis testing might come at the expense of hypothesis generation (McGuire 1989). A more extreme position contends that the theory orientation may actively stifle discovery:

> *"... theory is likely to obstruct research progress when the researcher's primary goal is to test the theory. In testing a theory, the theory can dominate research in a way that blinds the researcher to potentially informative observations" (Greenwald et al. 1986, p. 217; see also Rozin 2001).*

Mortensen and Cialdini (2010) make this point in a folksier manner by referring to the story of the drunk who searches for his car keys under the lamppost, not because the keys were lost under the lamppost but because the light is better there. As with EtT, it is curious that Mortensen and Cialdini would feel a need to promote a cyclical approach involving observation, theory, and experimenta-

tion. Given the rigors of the journal review process, it is less surprising that Cronbach (1986) felt the need to remind us that hypothesis testing follows a great deal of preparatory work and to urge tolerance of—and much patience with—the exploratory phase of the cycle, else good ideas be discarded prematurely. Indeed, Cronbach attributed dissatisfaction in the social sciences to "idolization of formal theory" and over-valuation of "theory-choice."

Finally, it is important not to misconstrue abduction as a lowering of standards or a trading off against rigor. When an effect lacks a causal explanation, there is all the more reason to demonstrate its robustness and probe its boundaries. There is simply less of a need to provide an empirically grounded process explanation in the short term.

## INCREMENTAL VERSUS ORIGINAL

With regard to the broader field of marketing, Rust (2006) has mused about outright hostility to original theory. I have not detected any such hostility, per se, in consumer research, but I join others in questioning the extent to which consumer research generates much original theory (MacInnis and Folkes 2010). Regardless of how one answers this question, it is undeniable that we have been unabashed borrowers of ideas developed elsewhere. The value of this strategy is a matter of opinion, but insofar as abduction is absent from our research, the risk of incrementalism lurks. Some go so far as to characterize abduction as a necessary condition for innovation (Martin 2010). Incrementalism has unfortunate negative connotations in that truth-finding can often be likened to a slow construction process. Insofar as the foundation for consumer research is provided by external disciplines, the larger question concerns the magnitude of our contribution. No metric exists, but my subjective impression is that consumer research frequently runs the risk of examining near-tautologies (Wallach and Wallach 1994), wherein the predicted outcome is a necessary consequence of the established premises. Near-tautologies appear in the literature, in part because they can add nuance to an outcome, including a demonstration of practical significance—and what could be more practical than consumption?

There are two additional dangers that accompany incrementalism. The first speaks to the legitimacy of our enterprise. Popper notwithstanding, it has been argued that psychological research is more apt to engage in confirmation than falsification of theory, and that such mis-testing of theories can forestall true understanding a phenomenon (Greenwald et al. 1986). Whatever the extent of this problem in the basic sciences, it is exacerbated in consumer research because we borrow theories for the express purpose of illustrating their relevance to consumer behavior. We have little scientific or personal incentive to borrow a theory in order to demonstrate its lack of relevance (for what journal would publish a paper about the irrelevance of a theory from another field). Worse yet, intolerance of messiness in the testing of a borrowed theory leads to sanitized confirmation of the theory (McGuire 1989).

The second danger is that dogged pursuit of any theory runs the risk of producing evanescent minutia. Research findings are produced at a prodigious rate. When the findings are produced in service to a theory, their practical contribution may evaporate with the nearly inevitable disconfirmation of the theory. In the present context, this problem may be understood via the distinction between data and phenomena. Haig (2005, p. 374) argues:

> *"Unlike phenomena, data are idiosyncratic to particular investigative contexts. Because data result from the interaction of a large number of causal factors, they are not as stable and general as phenomena, which are produced by a relatively small*

*number of causal factors. Data are ephemeral and pliable, whereas phenomena are robust and stubborn."*

Similarly, in criticizing the proliferation of memory theories, Watkins (1990, p. 332) argued:

*"... research designed to address some person's individual theory is unlikely to be of any use once that person allows the theory to wither and die. ... Were we to shed mediationism, theorizing would in all likelihood become less labyrinthian, and research questions more straightforward. ... (T)he essential findings would be simpler. And simple findings, like simple items of furniture, can be used and reused. They would form a cumulative body of knowledge, and so would free future generations of researchers from the need to start anew."*

As a practical matter, we should also recognize the problem that esoterica poses for our community. As research questions become narrower, a field can become so balkanized that its members find topics outside their own area of interest to be arcane or incomprehensible (Reis and Stiller 1992). As a matter of science it is awkward to argue against deep understanding, but as a matter of influence it is less so. If we wish to understand consumers for the sake of understanding consumers, the deeper we will plunge. If we wish to speak to potential users of our findings, higher-order interactions will be a deterrent. Large main effects, whether accompanied by theory or not, are more likely to serve as an impetus for action—and appropriately so. Our friends in marketing science know this well, perhaps because they have a salient external constituency. Their ability to produce empirical generalizations about fundamental marketing phenomena has advanced understanding and practice, irrespective of underlying theory (Hanssens 2009). We, on the other hand, have historically shied away from managerial prescriptions, but policy makers constitute an appealing constituency that could benefit from fundamental and enduring truths we might offer (e.g., Johnson and Goldstein 2003; Thaler and Sunstein 2008).

**Impossible Versus Possible**

Intellectual curiosity is admirable, but it is fair to ask whether we place undue stress on scientists by raising the bar for an acceptable contribution to an unreasonable height (Sutton and Staw 1995). Consider the following observation that captures very well the view of our leading consumer journal:

*"This focus on the underlying process is critical and something that tends to distinguish BDT articles that appear in JCR from BDT articles that appear in other journals. BDT researchers who submit to JCR are encouraged not only to illustrate the phenomenon but also to develop theory that specifies why phenomena occur, how they occur, and under what conditions" (Kahn, Luce, and Nowlis 2006, p. 131)*

Such a policy is disturbing on multiple levels. First, some phenomena are not easily understood, and the importance of a phenomenon is not diminished by its mystery. For some widely appreciated phenomena, the record shows that a satisfactory understanding might await decades of effort rather than a manuscript's worth. Indeed, by one measure the most influential article ever published in *JCR* (Huber, Payne, and Puto 1982) continues to this day to inspire a search for understanding (Tsetsos, Usher, and Chater 2010). Second, some phenomena are not reducible, at least within the confines of our current state of knowledge and the collective intelligence of the community. Gravity was not reduced to a "process" until Einstein

tackled it. Looking forward, some decision phenomena (e.g., loss aversion) and some psychophysical phenomena (e.g., visual dominance) may ultimately find process explanations, but the work that uncovers the processes may vie for a Nobel Prize. Looking back, it is clear that a bar set at this level would have disqualified luminaries of decision research (including previous Nobel Prize winners) from publishing in consumer journals. We do not know how many consumer phenomena have gone undocumented as a consequence of our restrictive policy, but we can be grateful that the policy has not been monolithic. One might argue that Huber et al. were able to evade the theory police by demonstrating a violation of classic choice theory. If so, theirs is an exception that proves the rule. If an intriguing but mysterious phenomenon merits publication only if it addresses existing theory, we need to reassess.

Finally, we should not minimize the dispiriting effect our policy has on our research efforts more generally. It is all the more lamentable when considered in light of the tolerance other scientific fields exhibit with regard to the question of the possible:

*"One reason researchers believe that heart disease and many cancers can be prevented is because of observational evidence that the incidence of these diseases differ greatly in different populations and in the same population over time. Breast cancer is not the scourge among Japanese women that it is among American women, but it takes only two generations in the United States before Japanese-Americans have the same breast cancer rates as any other ethnic group. This tells us that something about the American lifestyle or diet is a cause of breast cancer. Over the last 20 years, some two dozen large studies ... have so far failed to identify what that factor is. They may be inherently incapable of doing so. Nonetheless, we know that such a carcinogenic factor of diet or lifestyle exists, waiting to be found." (Taubes 2007)*

**Yours Versus Mine**

The preceding quote illustrates yet another disturbing aspect of an uncompromising stance on theory—one that is especially bothersome to researchers who take a cognitive perspective. Causality can be described at a variety of levels. The epidemiological finding regarding breast cancer is causal but devoid of process. The cause that is tractable at this juncture exists at the level of nature versus nurture. To identify the cause as one or the other is nontrivial, and this level of explanation may suffice depending on one's taste and objectives. Cognitive researchers, on the other hand, are held to cognitive explanations. The wisdom of this requirement grows more questionable by the day as research increasingly shows how physical cause competes with psychological cause to explain behavior (e.g., Iacoboni 2008). We would do well to abandon the conceit that we can identify true cause at this stage of development.

A more catholic view of theory is not novel within the philosophy of science. Cook and Campbell's (1979) primer on theory reminds us that different scientists may legitimately use theory in different ways. Not everyone is—or should be required to be—an essentialist. Positivists who appeal to theory as a convenience rather than a reflection of truth use a theory only insofar as it aids prediction. In other words, one's view of theory is a matter of taste and, to repeat myself, taste should not be dictated.

Finally, a recognition that different scholars might view theory differently would be a triumph of pluralism over orthodoxy, which in turn would eliminate the contradictions we conveniently ignore. As noted, our peers in marketing science enjoy greater freedom to approach market behavior from an engineering perspective (Moorthy 1993). Within consumer research, classic ethnography may be favorably viewed as dustbowl empiricism in the sense of a being an exercise in uncontaminated induction. Insofar as cognitively oriented consumer researchers must account for process, our field should be held accountable for its double standard.

## CONCLUSION

Theory has many virtues, but we should not regard theory as a defining feature of scholarship. Likewise, a request for pluralism should not be taken as radical (Simonson et al. 2001). The hypothetico-deductive approach is an esteemed mode of scientific practice, cause-effect relationships are desirable, and process explanations enrich our understanding. However, it is not illegitimate to engage in abduction, to pursue the truth via an effect-cause sequence (with a significant delay between effect and cause), or simply to acknowledge that an if-then statement can be valuable even if the intervening causal link has not or cannot be identified (Rozin 2009). When serendipity strikes, we should celebrate it rather than banish the discoverer to a hellish investigative journey. We should routinely strive for interestingness, robustness, and generalizability—but we can do so both within and beyond the confines of theory.

I noted the irony of using the theory-oriented approach to boost our self-image through emulation of real science. With the benefit of 40 years of hindsight, we can also ask whether theory has served its purpose (Hubbard and Lindsay 2002). The results from a very informal mental meta-analysis of addresses given by leading consumer researchers are not consistent with a self-confident field that can point with pride to its many important and novel discoveries. One is struck instead by the frequency with which we question the parameters and contribution of our field. I cannot prove that our obsession with theory is responsible for this state of affairs, but it seems that discovery might be more frequent if we relaxed the constraints a bit. To reference one more Nobel Prize winner, the words of E.O. Wilson (1998, p. 6-7) are sobering:

*"Original discovery is everything." ... "The true and final test of a scientific career is how well the following declarative sentence can be completed: He (or she) discovered that ..."*

I suspect that Wilson would not be satisfied with a career in which the scientist "discovered" how a finding in a different discipline could be applied to one's own. Wilson's stringent criterion for a successful career is accompanied, however, by a less stringent road to success:

*"Advice to the novice scientist: There is no fixed way to make and establish a scientific discovery. Throw everything you can at the subject, so long as the procedures can be duplicated by others."*

## APPRECIATION

This recognition, undeserved as it is, would not have been possible without the support and understanding of many. My wife, Pat, and my daughters, Elli and Billie, have provided much needed affection and have exhibited a saintly degree of patience. My academic advisors guided the baby steps of my career as a parent guides a child. Lynn Hasher watched over me while simultaneously treating me as a colleague. Bob Weisberg was brilliant but approachable. In subsequent years I benefited from a stupendously talented group of graduate students who inspired many research projects and will always be a source of pride. Many colleagues provided support when it was most needed. Jim Bettman and Brian Sternthal, in particular, helped pave the path to this day. They did so at a time when neither had a personal connection to me. I have also benefited enormously

from the everyday assistance of my local colleagues. In particular, John Lynch and Wes Hutchinson have been an inspiration. They are paragons not only of scholarliness but also of virtue.

## REFERENCES

Alba, Joseph W. and J. Wesley Hutchinson (2000), "Knowledge Calibration: What Consumers Know and What They Think They Know," *Journal of Consumer Research*, 27 (September), 123-156.

Bacharach, Samuel B. (1989), "Organizational Theories: Some Criteria for Evaluation," *Academy of Management Review*, 14 (October), 496-515.

Baron, Jonathan (1994), "Nonconsequentialist Decisions," *Behavioral and Brain Sciences,* 17(March), 1-10.

Barwise, Patrick (1995), "Good Empirical Generalizations," *Marketing Science*, 14 (Summer), G29-G35.

Bass, Frank M. (1995), "Empirical Generalizations and Marketing Science: A Personal View," *Marketing Science*, 14 (Summer), G6-G19.

Brinberg, David, John G. Lynch, Jr., and Alan G. Sawyer (1992), "Hypothesized and Confounded Explanations in Theory Tests: A Bayesian Analysis," *Journal of Consumer Research*, 19 (September), 139-154.

Cook, Thomas D. and Donald T. Campbell (1979), *Quasi-Experimentation: Design & Analysis Issues for Field Settings*, Chicago: Rand McNally.

Cronbach, Lee J. (1986), "Social Inquiry by and for Earthlings," in *Metatheory in Social Science*, eds. D.W. Fisk and R.A. Shweder, Chicago: University of Chicago Press, 83-107.

Ehrenberg, A.S.C. (1993), "Theory or Well-Based Results: Which Comes First?," in *Research Traditions in Marketing*, eds. G. Laurent, G. Lilien, and B. Pras, Boston: Kluwer, 79-131.

_____ (1995), "Empirical Generalisations, Theory, and Method," *Marketing Science*, 14 (Summer), G20-G28.

Greenwald, Anthony G., (2004), "The Resting Parrot, the Dessert Stomach, and Other Perfectly Defensible Theories," in *Perspectivism in Social Psychology: The Yin and Yang of Scientific Progress*, eds. J.T. Jost, M..R. Banaji, and D.A. Prentice, Washington, DC: American Psychological Association, 275-285.

_____ Anthony R. Pratkanis, Michael R. Leippe, and Michael H. Baumgardner (1986), "Under What Conditions Does Theory Obstruct Research Progress?," *Psychological Review*, 93 (April), 216-229.

Haig, Brian D. (2005), "An Abductive Theory of Scientific Method," *Psychological Methods*, 10 (December), 371-388.

Hanssens, Dominique M. (2009), *Empirical Generalizations about Marketing Impact*, Cambridge, MA: Marketing Science Institute.

Hubbard, Raymond and R. Murray Lindsay (2002), "How the Emphasis on 'Original' Empirical Marketing Research Impedes Knowledge Development," *Marketing Theory*, 2 (December), 381-402.

Huber, Joel, John W. Payne, and Christopher Puto (1982), "Adding Asymmetrically Dominated Alternatives: Violations of Regularity and the Similarity Hypothesis," *Journal of Consumer Research*, 9 (June), 90-98.

Iacoboni, Marco (2008), *Mirroring People*, New York: Farrar, Straus, and Giroux.

Johnson, Eric J. and Daniel Goldstein (2003), "Do Defaults Save Lives? *Science*, 302 (November 21), 1338-1339.

Kahn, Barbara E., Mary Frances Luce, and Stephen M. Nowlis (2006), "Debiasing Insights from Process Tests," *Journal of Consumer Research*, 33 (June), 131-138.

Langer, Ellen J. (1989), *Mindfulness*, Cambridge, MA: Da Capo Press.

Lewin, Kurt (1951), *Field Theory in Social Science: Selected Theoretical Papers*, ed. D. Cartwright, New York: Harper & Row.

MacInnis, Deborah J. and Valerie S. Folkes (2010), "The Disciplinary Status of Consumer Behavior: A Sociology of Science Perspective on Key Controversies," *Journal of Consumer Research*, 36 (April), 899-914.

Martin, Roger L. (2010), "Innovation's Accidental Enemies," *Bloomberg BusinessWeek*, January 14.

McGuire, William J. (1989), "A Perspectivist Approach to the Strategic Planning of Programmatic Scientific Research," in *Psychology of Science: Contributions to Metascience*, eds. B. Gholson, W.R. Shadish, Jr., R.A. Neimeyer, and A.C. Houts, New York: Cambridge, 214-245.

Moorthy, K. Sridhar (1993), "Theoretical Modeling in Marketing," *Journal of Marketing*, 57 (April), 92-106.

Mortensen, Chad R. and Robert B. Cialdini (2009), "Full-Cycle Social Psychology for Theory and Application," *Social and Personality Psychology Compass*, 4 (February), 53-63.

Mukherjee, Siddhartha (2010), "The Cancer Sleeper Cell," *New York Times Magazine*, October 31, 40-45.

Myers, Morton A. (2008), *Happy Accidents: Serendipity in Modern Medical Breakthroughs*, New York: Arcade Publishing.

Overbye, Dennis (2007), "At the Fermilab, the Race Is on for the 'God Particle,'" *New York Times*, July 24.

Peter, J. Paul (1991), "Philosophical Tensions in Consumer Inquiry," in *Handbook of Consumer Behavior*, eds. T.S. Robertson and H.H. Kassarjian, Englewood Cliffs, NJ: Prentice-Hall, 533-547.

Reis, Harry T. and Jerome Stiller (1992), "Publication Trends in *JPSP*: A Three-Decade Review," *Personality and Social Psychology Bulletin*, 4 (August), 465-472.

Rozin, Paul (2001), "Social Psychology and Science: Some Lessons from Solomon Asch," *Personality and Social Psychology Review*, 5 (February), 2-14.

_____ (2006), "Domain Denigration and Process Preference in Academic Psychology," *Perspectives on Psychological Science*, 1 (4), 365-376.

_____ (2009), "What Kind of Empirical Research Should We Publish, Fund, and Reward?," *Perspectives on Psychological Science*, 4 (4), 435-439.

Rust, Roland T. (2006), "From the Editor: The Maturation of Marketing as an Academic Discipline," *Journal of Marketing*, 70 (July), 1-2.

Simonson, Itamar, Ziv Carmon, Ravi Dhar, Aimee Drolet, and Stephen M. Nowlis (2001), "Consumer Research: In Search of Identity," *Annual Review of Psychology*, 52, 249-275.

Smith, Laurence D., Lisa A. Best, D. Alan Stubbs, Andrea Bastiani Archibald, and Roxann Roberson-Nay (2002), "Constructing Knowledge: The Role of Graphs and Tables in Hard and Soft Psychology," *American Psychologist*, 57 (October), 749-761.

*Stanford Encyclopedia of Philosophy* (2010), "Charles Sanders Peirce," http://plato.stanford.edu/entries/peirce/

Sternthal, Brian, Alice M. Tybout, and Bobby J. Calder (1987), "Confirmatory Versus Comparative Approaches to Judging Theory Tests," *Journal of Consumer Research*, 14 (June), 114-125.

Sutton, Robert I. and Barry M. Staw (1995), "What Theory Is Not," *Administrative Science Quarterly*, 40 (September), 371-384.

Taubes, Gary (2007), "Do We Really Know What Makes Us Healthy?" *New York Times*, September 16.

Thaler, Richard H. and Cass R. Sunstein (2008), *Nudge: Improving Decisions About Health, Wealth, and Happiness*, New Haven, CT: Yale University Press.

Thomson, Keith Stewart (1994), "Scientific Publishing: An Embarrassment of Riches," *American Scientist*, 82 (November-December), 508-511.

Tsetsos, Konstantinos, Marius Usher, and Nick Chater (2010), "Preference Reversal in Multiattribute Choice," *Psychological Review*, 117 (October), 1275-1293.

Wallach, Lise and Michael A. Wallach (1994), "Gergen Versus the Mainstream: Are Hypotheses in Social Psychology Subject to Empirical Test?," *Journal of Personality and Social Psychology*, 67 (August), 233-242.

Watkins, Michael J. (1990), "Mediationism and the Obfuscation of Memory," *American Psychologist*, 45 (March), 328-335.

Wegner, Daniel T. (1992), "The Premature Demise of the Solo Experiment," *Personality and Social Psychology Bulletin*, 4 (August), 504-508.

Wilson, Edward O. (1998), "Scientists, Scholars, Knaves and Fools," *American Scientist*, 86 (January-February), 6-7.

# Fellow's Address: Substantive Consumer Research

John G. Lynch, Jr., University of Colorado-Boulder, USA

I'm humbled and honored to be added to the ranks of the Fellows of the Association for Consumer Research. It's a particular honor and delight to be recognized along with Brian Sternthal and Joe Alba, two of the people I most admire in our profession.

Joe and I were part of Brian's AE team when Brian was Editor of *JCR*, and I would say Brian was my favorite boss ever. We share a deep interest in philosophy of science and methodology, and it was a pure pleasure to exchange ideas with Brian about issues raised by manuscripts I handled for him. And I don't think he ever reversed one of my recommendations -- showing great insight and discernment on his part. Joe was my colleague at University of Florida, lifetime friend, and coauthor on two of my favorite papers on my vita. Joe declining my repeated lunch invitations extended over 15 years as colleagues. So he also showed impeccable discernment and wisdom, and batted 1.000 in his own way. All kidding aside, Joe is the scholar I most often tell my doctoral students to emulate. His simple experiments build on each other to create great insight, and his writing is a model of clarity.

## KVETCHING

I want to go negative and talk with you today about what I see as a two unhealthy trends in our field. The first trend is the tendency for our best young scholars and reviewers to think that the goal of every paper must be primarily to make a theoretical contribution – preferably with a mediation analysis. The second is our collective acceptance that our field is made up of multidisciplinary silos. Debbie MacInnis and Valerie Folkes (2010) make a compelling case that the original vision of *JCR* and ACR as homes for truly interdisciplinary work has long given way to a reality that we are a multi-disciplinary rather than an inter-disciplinary field. We nestle together in the pages of *JCR*, but we aren't really informing each other's work as much as we wish, and it is quite unusual for a given paper to draw strongly from ideas in two or more different disciplines –say psychology and economics.

Some people don't see either of these as problems, but I do. My thesis is that if we would more often look to the substantive domain as inspiration for our research, three good things would happen. Our work will be of interest to a wider public, we will have more vibrant mutual influence with adjacent social science disciplines, and in our dialogue within our field, consumer researchers of different primary disciplinary orientations will benefit more richly from each other's work.

## BRINBERG AND MCGRATH'S VALIDITY NETWORK SCHEMA

Brinberg and McGrath developed their "Validity Network Schema" in a book and several articles in the 80s, and what I'm going to say in the rest of my remarks uses their foundation. The Figure below is from McGrath and Brinberg (1985). They pointed out that all research requires combining elements and relations from three domains: the conceptual domain, the methodological domain, and the substantive domain. Examples of concepts might be accessibility, diagnosticity, construal level, resource slack, or consideration set. Methods might be ethnography, meta-analysis, structural equation model of survey responses, mediation analysis, or 2 x 2 factorial design. Substantive phenomena might be price sensitivity

on the Internet, household budgeting, or "Yes…Damn" agreeing to future activities that one later regrets. Scholars have different priorities on these three domains that produce conflicts in judgments of what constitutes "good" research.

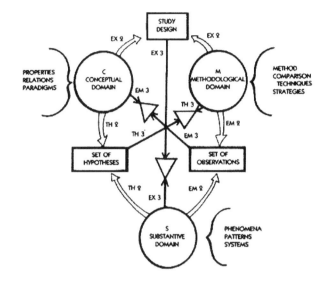

EXPERIMENTAL PATH: Building a design, and implementing it by using it on a set of substantive events.

THEORETICAL PATH: Building a set of hypotheses, and testing them by evaluating them with an appropriate set of methods.

EMPIRICAL PATH: Building a set of observations, and explaining them by construing them in terms of a set of meaningful concepts.

**Figure: Validity Network Schema, from Brinberg and McGrath (1985, p. 22)**

Brinberg and McGrath noted that researchers typically start with an interest in one domain, tie it to a second, and then choose elements from the remaining domain as a matter of convenience.

- In the "theoretical path", one builds a "set of hypotheses" by first combining elements and relations from the conceptual and substantive domains and then finding some convenient methodology to test them.
- In the "empirical path", one builds a "set of observations" by combining elements and relations from the substantive and methodological domains and then picks some convenient concepts to explain them.
- In the "experimental path"[1], one creates a "study design" by first combining elements and relations from the conceptual and methodological domains and then picks some convenient substantive context as a way to operationalize the test of interest.

Brinberg and McGrath take pains to say that each of these paths is equally legitimate. But I was trained as an experimental social psychologist, and I made my reputation in this field in my first 15 years as a rigorous practitioner of the "experimental" path. I didn't place much value on "applied" research, and I got my ideas for my papers from the pages of journals, as in my work on the accessibility diagnosticity (e.g., Lynch, Marmorstein, and Weigold 1988; Simmons, Bickart, and Lynch 1993), or research explaining contrast effects

---

1. "Experimental" path may be a misleading term. It is not necessary for the concepts to be tied to *experimental* methods to be "experimental path" – just that the substantive context for the research remains as a tertiary focus.

**15**

*Advances in Consumer Research*
*Volume 38, ©2012*

(e.g., Lynch, Chakravarti, and Mitra 1991). I see a lot of people with similar attitudes rising to positions of influence in our field.

But at my current stage of career, I think the "theoretical" path and the "empirical" path have gotten a bum rap. My beef is that the experimental path has become almost monolithic in the pages of *JCR* and *JCP*. The young scholars who I most respect seem to undervalue empirical path papers and to have an overly narrow view of what constitutes a good theoretical path project. Let me elaborate.

## The Empirical Path

The "empirical path" is alive and well among our marketing science brethren, but not in consumer research. If one looks at the last 10 O'Dell Award winners, I'd classify half as "empirical path" marketing science -- e.g., Mela, Gupta, and Lehmann (1998) work showing how advertising makes people become less price sensitive in the long run and price promotion makes them more price sensitive. And there's a rich tradition of "empirical generalizations" papers that carefully show some facts about the marketplace.

In consumer research, reviewers make it tough to publish this kind of "atheoretical" empirical path research. That's a shame. I've found such papers to be particularly useful in my own work. They tell us what neglected topics in consumer research might prove to be truly important.

In the early 80s, I was slaving away with many others on models of multi-attribute combination rules. It was edifying to read primarily descriptive papers like Hoyer (1984). Hoyer showed that consumers engage in *very* low in-aisle search, and only 9% could give more than one reason for why they bought the brand of detergent they purchased. So much for multi-attribute combination rules. Papers like Wayne's made me conclude that I should shift my focus to *very* low-level consumer information processing, including processing below the level of conscious awareness (e.g., Lynch and Srull 1982; Feldman and Lynch 1988; Lynch Marmorstein and Weigold 1988; Alba, Hutchinson, and Lynch 1991).

Similarly, it was an eye-opener to read Hauser (1978) document that 78% of the explainable uncertainty in consumer choice outcomes is driven by what brands are considered at all, with only 22% of the explainable uncertainty tied to attribute-based preferences among considered brands. That led me and my colleagues and students to conclude that we should try to understand the workings of consideration sets (e.g., Lynch and Srull 1982; Alba and Chattopadhyay 1985; Nedungadi 1990; Alba et al. 1991; Hutchinson, Raman, and Mantrala 1994; Mitra and Lynch 1995; Alba et al. 1997; Diehl, Kornish, and Lynch 2003).

## The Theoretical Path

A lot of people code research motivated by a problem in the world as "applied" and they think the task of a theorist is to identify construct-to-construct relations in some nomological net. Brinberg and McGrath remind us that the "theoretical path" is not just about construct-to-construct relations. It is also about relations between concepts and substantive phenomena. One can make important theoretical contributions either by starting with concepts and then linking to substantive phenomena or by starting with substantive phenomena then searching for concepts to explain the phenomena.

For readers who want to contribute to theory, I want to recommend this latter path to you – start with the consumer phenomenon and then try to explain it rather than always starting with concepts in the literature and then thinking of where they might apply. Gal Zauberman and I were amused and frustrated by our own foibles – apparently shared by others. We committed the "Yes…Damn!" effect, saying yes to attractive activities in a month that we would

say no to tomorrow because we believed we'd have more spare time in a month. At the same time, we persistently fooled ourselves into believing that next week would be the week that we would stop procrastinating on some important but not urgent task. These substantive facts led us to conceptualize those phenomena in terms of our resource slack theory of discounting (Zauberman and Lynch 2005).

Sometimes the theorist's task is not to conceptualize some individual behavior, but also some more macro consumption system. If the substantive phenomena are themselves really important, it is a real theoretical contribution to put structure on those phenomena. This almost always required combination of concepts from several disciplines. That is what we tried to do in our work on online shopping, first in the Alba et al. (1997) *Journal of Marketing* paper on interactive home shopping with our Florida colleagues, then with Dan Ariely in our (2000) wine online work, and then in Diehl, Kornish, and Lynch (2003) and Ariely, Lynch, and Aparicio (2004) about the role of screening agents. In all those cases, one of the major substantive questions was whether online shopping would lead to increased price sensitivity and ruinous price competition. My colleagues and I reasoned that retailers provide information similar to information provided by advertising. We used concepts from other literatures on the economic effects of advertising (Mitra and Lynch 1995, 1996) to make novel statements about when online shopping would or would not lead to increased price sensitivity and price competition.

## THE SUBSTANTIVE DOMAIN AS A PLATFORM FOR CONVERSATION

### What's Interesting?

Abelson (1995) said that research is "interesting" if it shifts one's beliefs about something that one cared about already. If I write about some topic that most people don't have any beliefs about, or if there's not a reason they'd care about their prior beliefs, it is harder for me to convince those people that my work is interesting. I liked my "experimental path" papers and early in my career, I considered it a badge of honor if only "in the know" could appreciate my papers. But later I came to realize that there were costs of being so specialized in my approach, and that I limited my audience in doing so. When I came into the field doing mathematical models of information integration, I found that behavioral people who understood the psychological issues couldn't follow the methods, and the people who understood the mathematical methods didn't understand the psychological literatures. So I switched what I studied.

If one's goal is to attract the interest of a broad rather than a narrow subset of colleagues, one can raise one's chances of success by choosing problems motivated by questions about the substantive domain. Think about how AMA interviewers perk up more when interviewees motivate their research with some real world behavior that the interviewers understand rather than leading with a literature-based motivation. When we lead with substantive phenomena, more in the audience have prior beliefs, and the topics are things they more readily care about. When we follow the "experimental" path, in contrast, it is common that a smaller set of people understands both the concepts and the methods.

I contend that substantively motivated research can a) attract broader interest among to lay people (as reflected in popular press coverage); b) stimulate greater interest and citations from scholars in adjacent social sciences; and c) inspire more vibrant within-field conversations among scholars with very different disciplinary orientations.

## Influence on the Outside World

I would argue that substantive papers are especially likely to get significant press. People are interested in our work that illuminates some real world substantive phenomenon that people can see in themselves – more so than our papers that are primarily about constructs or methods.

## Influence on Scholars in Adjacent Social Sciences

A more important measure of the success of our field is the degree to which scholars in other fields use our ideas and findings. Just individual scholars are judged less successful if they are the only ones citing their own work, we cannot judge ourselves to be successful as a field if our work is used only by others in our same field. Many have noted that we consumer researchers seem to import from other social sciences more than we export.

I contend that our prospects for export are greater for work that aims to make a contribution to the substantive domain. Substantive topics are inherently interdisciplinary, and that means I perceive that I learn a lot from work on the same topic from a scholar in another field and he or she might have the same perception.

Lately I've gotten into the field of consumer financial decision-making. This is a field where we consumer researchers can make important contributions to science and society. It's also a field that lends itself to learning from our colleagues in allied social sciences. Last year we at CU hosted the First Annual Boulder Summer Conference on Consumer Financial Decision Making. It was a remarkable conference because of the set of people in the room. We had scholars from Finance, Economics, Decision Sciences, Consumer Sciences, Marketing, Neuroscience, Psychology, and Behavioral Economics, learning from each other and from regulators, and consumer advocates in a common conversation. Candidly, I felt that I learned more from the average talk at this financial decision making conference than from the average talk I attend at ACR, where I feel there is more overlap between what I know and what the other attendees know. The benefit of interdisciplinary interchange is also what motivated Shlomo Benartzi, Stefano Della Vigna, George Loewenstein and me to propose and co-edit the *JMR* Special Interdisciplinary Issue on Consumer Financial Decision Making. We were very pleased with the 85 submissions we got from leading figures across those fields, and our hope is that this special issue will generate significant cross-field citation.

My conjecture is that interdisciplinary export and import is stronger for work that has a substantive focus than for most of what we do that starts in the conceptual or methodological domains. It's not just consumer financial decision-making, but other core topics we study. I was pleased to see Pierre Chandon and Brian Wansink (2007) win this year's *JCR* Award for their paper on health halos. Brian and then Pierre were pioneers in choosing a substantive topic of food consumption that was not "mainstream" consumer research when they started, though it has become mainstream due to their scholarly leadership. Their paper is the third most cited paper published in the 2007 issue of *JCR*, and almost 40% of those citations come from outside of consumer research and marketing. That's no accident; their own references came almost half from outside of consumer research and marketing, drawing from journals in economics, psychology, sociology, dietary science, medicine, judgment and decision-making, and nutrition.

## Influence on Consumer Researchers with Different Disciplinary Orientations

If substantively motivated research gives stronger motivation for exchange with adjacent disciplines, it also gives us a stronger rea-son to talk with each other and learn from fellow consumer researchers despite our different disciplinary orientations. I mentioned earlier the MacInnis and Folkes (2010) paper on the sociology of science of consumer research. It did a great job of documenting that the original vision of our field as an interdisciplinary social science had long given way to a multidisciplinary reality. Scholars (almost all housed in marketing departments) come from different disciplinary orientations that are rarely combined in a single paper.

This is an excellent and compelling paper, but I found it depressing. I know that there is truth to what Debbie and Valerie say because I see it in my role as ACR's representative to the *JCR* Policy Board. Two years ago the American Economic Association decided to drop its sponsorship of *JCR*, and we regularly have to provide help to the presidents of other sponsoring associations to identify appropriate representatives to that board. We have ceased to be relevant to them.

For my part, I think the original vision of the founders of *JCR* and ACR was inspiring. I don't want to let it go. I submit that we can find our way back to that interdisciplinary path with more substantively motivated consumer research. In the process, we can be a more influential field.

## CONCLUSION

There is more than one path to contribute to consumer research. We do not always have to follow the "experimental" path of reading the journals to get ideas about construct-to-construct relations, then designing a study to test the ideas in some convenient substantive context. We can also follow Brinberg and McGrath's (1986) "theoretical" & "empirical" paths that prioritize understanding something new about the substantive domain.

A larger role for substantively motivated research can help our field in three ways. Substantively motivated consumer research can remove our paradigmatic blinders to help us see new topics for research that later scholars will recognize as truly central topics for consumer research. It can increase our influence in the public domain and among other social sciences. And it can increase our ability to learn from each other as an interdisciplinary field.

## THANKS

Nobody receives such an honor as we received today without a lot of help. My wife Pat and my parents John and Bobby Gay are in my heart today. I'm the product of great colleagues and doctoral students at Florida, at Duke, and now at Colorado. But I particularly want to thank three people to whom I owe a deep debt of gratitude.

In my PhD program in social psychology at the University of Illinois, Bob Wyer taught me to get in the habit of generating testable research hypotheses. Thanks to Bob, I can't read a journal article without scribbling ideas in the margins. Bob remains my model for how I aspire to treat my students. I'm always telling them things Bob said to me that have some analogy to their situation – e.g., "word salad" to point out some particularly tortured prose, or Bob's famous line on the 6th draft of my thesis, "The need for excellence is beginning to be exceeded by the need for closure." Bob managed to be critical and so enthusiastic at the same time. That's a winning combination. His attitude about the excitement of research gave me the value system that has carried me through my career. I'll always be grateful that the Editor of *JESP*, one of the most productive authors in the history of social psychology and the most hotly sought advisor at the University of Illinois made time for a screw-up of a PhD student whenever I came knocking on his door.

Based on Bob's recommendation, Joel Cohen hired me at University of Florida when I knew nothing about consumer behavior and marketing. Joel has been a lifetime mentor and friend. I wish I were as good a senior colleague to assistant professors at Florida, Duke, and CU as Joel was to me. When I didn't know anyone in the field, Joel introduced me around at ACR to big names like Jim Bettman, Carol Scott, Alice Tybout, and Peter Wright, and encouraged them to take me seriously. Joel stimulated my thinking. When I first arrived doing work on information integration, Joel needled me about its relevance to consumer decision making when inputs came from memory. I harrumphed, but eventually concluded that Joel's "irritating" question was a good one, leading me to collaborate with Thom Srull to develop distinctions among stimulus-based, memory-based, and mixed choice. Joel and Bill Wilkie hired five people in my assistant professor cohort went on to become ACR or SCP Presidents, making my early years assistant professor nirvana. I'm proud that along with those guys and others hired later, I was a part of the "Florida School" that produced a large body of research highlighting the role of memory, attention, and basic information processes in consumer decision-making.

When I moved to Duke, I was fortunate to have another set of outstanding colleagues and students whom I truly love. But I want to single out Jim Bettman. Jim has been like a brother to me – a smarter older brother who still has all his hair and great taste in music. Jim is a glue guy who created an exciting and collaborative culture at Duke. He is generous to a fault, and more *JCR* and *JCP* authors have thanked him than any other person in the field. He and I had the pleasure of co-chairing doctoral dissertations by many brilliant Duke students over the years, whose reflected glory I'm sure played a role in my receiving this honor today.

## REFERENCES

Abelson, Robert P. (1995), *Statistics as Principled Argument*, Hillsdale, NJ: Lawrence Erlbaum Associates.

Alba, Joseph W. and Amitava Chattopadhyay (1985), "Effects of Context and Part-Category Cues on Recall of Competing Brands," *Journal of Marketing Research*, 22 (August), 340-349.

Alba, Joseph W., J. Wesley Hutchinson, and John G. Lynch, Jr., (1991) "Memory and Decision Making," in H. Kassarjian and T. Robertson (Eds.) *Handbook of Consumer Behavior*. Englewood Cliffs, NJ: Prentice Hall, 1-49.

Alba, Joseph, John Lynch, Barton Weitz, Chris Janiszewski, Richard Lutz, Alan Sawyer, Stacy Wood (1997), "Interactive Home Shopping: Consumer, Retailer, and Manufacturer Incentives to Participate in Electronic Marketplaces," *Journal of Marketing*, 61 (July), 38-53.

Ariely, Dan and Jonathan Levav (2000). Sequential Variety-Seeking in Group Settings: Taking the Road Less Traveled and Less Enjoyed. *Journal of Consumer Research*, 27(3), 279-290.

Ariely, Dan, John G. Lynch, Jr., and Manuel Aparicio (2004) "Learning by Collaborative and Individual-Based Recommendation Agents," *Journal of Consumer Psychology*, 14 (1&2), 81-95.

Brinberg, D., and McGrath, J.E. (1985). *Validity and the Research Process*: Beverly Hills, Ca., Sage Publications.

Chandon, Pierre, and Brian Wansink (2007), "The Biasing Health Halos of Fast-Food Restaurant Health Claims: Lower Calorie Estimates and Higher Side-Dish Consumption Intentions," *Journal of Consumer Research*, 54 (October), 301-314.

Diehl, Kristin, Laura J. Kornish, and John G. Lynch, Jr. (2003) "Smart Agents: When Lower Search Costs for Quality Information Increase Price Sensitivity," *Journal of Consumer Research*, 30 (June), 56-71.

Hutchinson, J. Wesley, Kalyan Raman and Murali Mantrala (1994), "Finding Choice Alternatives in Memory: Probability Models of Brand Name Recall," *Journal of Marketing Research*, 31 (November), 441-461.

Lynch, John G., Jr. and Dan Ariely (2000), "Wine Online: Search Costs and Competition on Price, Quality, and Distribution," *Marketing Science*, 19 (1), 83-103.

Lynch, John G., Jr., Dipankar Chakravarti, and Anusree Mitra (1991), "Contrast Effects in Consumer Judgments: Changes in Mental Representations or in the Anchoring of Rating Scales?" *Journal of Consumer Research*, 18 (December), 284-297.

Lynch, John G., Jr., Howard Marmorstein, and Michael F. Weigold (1988), "Choices from Sets Including Remembered Brands: Use of Recalled Attributes and Prior Overall Evaluations," *Journal of Consumer Research*, 15 (September), 169-184.

Lynch, John G., Jr. and Thomas K. Srull (1982), "Memory and Attentional Factors in Consumer Choice," *Journal of Consumer Research*, 9 (June), 18-37.

MacInnis Deborah J. and Valerie S. Folkes (2010), "The Disciplinary Status of Consumer Behavior: A Sociology of Science Perspective on Key Controversies," *Journal of Consumer Research*, 36 (6) 899-914.

Mela, Carl F., Sunil Gupta, and Donald R. Lehmann (1997), "The Long-Term Impact of Promotion and Advertising on Consumer Brand Choice," *Journal of Marketing Research*, 34, 2 (May), 248-261.

Mitra, Anusree, and John G. Lynch, Jr. (1996), "Advertising Effects on Prices Paid and Liking for Brands Selected," *Marketing Letters*, 7 (1), 19-29.

Mitra, Anusree, and John G. Lynch, Jr. (1995), "Toward a Reconciliation of Market Power and Information Theories of Advertising Effects on Price Elasticity," *Journal of Consumer Research*, 21 (March), 644-659.

Nedungadi, Prakash (1990), "Recall and Consumer Consideration Sets - Influencing Choice without Altering Brand Evaluations," *Journal of Consumer Research*, 17 (3), 263-76.

Zauberman, Gal and John G. Lynch, Jr. (2005) "Resource Slack and Discounting of Future Time versus Money," *Journal of Experimental Psychology: General*, 134 (1), 23-37.

# Fellow's Address: Three Silos and a Theory:
## Developing Nomological Networks to Explain Consumer Behavior

Brian Sternthal, Kellogg School of Management, Northwestern University, USA

Preparing for this talk prompted me to reflect on the evolution and direction of consumer research during the 40 years I have been in the field. When I started my career, there was an emphasis of developing a discipline base for studying consumer research, whether that discipline was economics, psychology, sociology, anthropology or home economics. There was also an emphasis on a multi-disciplinary approach to investigating consumer behavior. The first issue of *JCR*, published in June 1974, contained articles dealing with consumer economics, family decision making, statistical decision models and persuasive message effects. The *JCR* editorial board was represented by people from industry, as well as by academics trained in economics, home economics, human ecology, psychology and marketing.

Today, the multi-disciplinary focus remains and knowledge in the various domains has expanded dramatically. *JCR* annually publishes about twice as many articles as were published in 1974, and there are almost as many *JCR* Associate Editors as there were editorial board members when *JCR* was launched. The rapid accretion of knowledge in consumer research provides an opportunity that would not be possible without this development. It is to integrate knowledge that has been accumulated in disparate areas as a basis for developing a more general understanding of consumer behavior. Investigators in consumer research have an advantage in pursuing this analysis because the field is sufficiently small that integrating disparate theoretical views does not undermine a researchers' visibility, which often motivates a narrow focus by investigators in basic disciplines.

The opportunity to develop a more general understanding of consumer behavior emerges regardless of the domain in which this is done. For example, consumer culture research has provided rich descriptions of star trek fans (Kozinets 2001), mountain men (Belk and Costa 1998), Harley owners (Schouten and McAlexander 1995), and Burning Man (Kozinets, 2002). A more general understanding of these behaviors might be achieved by examining the factors that are common to these behavioral domains and that distinguish one from another. At issue is what explains the adoption of these unique behaviors and what prompts the choice of a specific alternative? Along the same lines, the demonstration of a variety of intriguing effects related to judgment and choice (e.g., attraction, compromise, compatibility, conjunction, contagion; cf., Gilovich, Griffin and Kahneman 2002) presents the opportunity to develop a more general understanding of consumer motivations by assessing when each of these decision strategies is likely to be invoked. Finally, investigations conducted under the rubric of information processing have reported the effects of a variety of factors related to resource allocation including repetition, involvement, and regulatory depletion. Each of these domains offers insight about how people make decisions. However, these insights have not been elevated to a level that informs understanding of how consumers make judgments beyond the variables investigated.

In this talk, I shall illustrate the development of a more general theory by examining how integrating disparate lines of inquiry pertaining to consumers' resource allocation accelerates the development of knowledge about consumer self-regulation in decision making. Three distinct areas of research will be examined as a basis for developing the more general theory: repetition, involvement, and regulatory depletion effects. The goal of this analysis is to develop converging inferences that offer a more general understanding of consumers regulate their resource allocation in rendering judgments than would be possible with a less encompassing analysis.

## REPETITION EFFECTS

Investigations of repetition effects typically involve varying the number of exposures to a persuasive message and examining recipients' evaluation of the advocacy. A repeated finding is that repetition of a persuasive message is nonmonotonically related to persuasion (Anand and Sternthal 1991; Cacioppo and Petty 1979). In response to successive exposures to a persuasive message, recipients first process the message content. Once this information is learned, they either process their own message-relevant thoughts, other idiosyncratic thoughts, or simply stop thinking about the message (Greenwald 1968). Because the message is designed with the intent to influence judgment, thoughts that represent this content are more likely to be persuasive than the idiosyncratic ones generated by the message recipient. Thus, it is the rehearsal of message information that enhances persuasion, and the rehearsal of message recipients' idiosyncratic thoughts or the absence of thought generation that cause it to decline, a phenomenon that is referred to as wearout. At some point, additional exposures beyond those needed to produce wearout reverse this decline and enhance message persuasion. This outcome is thought to occur because the rehearsal of one's own thoughts makes message information less accessible and thus again informative to the message recipient (Anand and Sternthal 1991).

This account for repetition effects suggests that individuals regulate their resource allocation to the message content so as to help them make judicious decisions. As message exposures mount, the allocation is initially to the message, then to other thoughts and then to the message once again. This theorizing is supported by the demonstration that an increase in the number of exposures is accompanied by an initial increase and then a decrease and an increase once again in the number of arguments supporting the message, and the reverse for arguments that are counter the advocacy (counterarguments).

Although this account has survived 20 years of scrutiny, it is incomplete. It presents the notion that consumers self-regulate by changing the focus of their processing; but it does not indicate what prompts this shift beyond the fact that it occurs after a number of exposures to the same message. Some insight about what triggers the shift between processing the message and one's own thoughts is offered in a repetition study conducted by Smith and Dorfman (1975). Their stimuli were complex and abstract patterns composed of black and white rectangles rather than persuasive message content. Yet, the same pattern of responses was observed as those found when the stimulus was a persuasive message: Judgments became increasingly favorable on initial exposures, declined as exposures continued to mount, and then become more favorable again. Because of the abstract nature of the stimulus, these outcomes are not readily explained in terms of individuals' message and own thoughts, but they can be accounted for in terms of Berlyne's (1970) notion of positive habituation and tedium. According to this view, in response to initial exposures individuals experience habituation to the stimulus accompanied by a feeling of increased confidence about what the nature of the stimulus, which is reflected in enhanced persuasion. Further exposures to the stimulus prompt the onset of tedium, a feeling that results in less favorable assessments of the stimulus.

Applying Smith and Dorfman's findings to the repetition effects observed when the stimulus is a persuasive message suggests that a metacognitive process is responsible for the effects of repeating a persuasive message. Specifically, initial exposures to a persuasive message enhance the feeling of confidence about the knowledge that has been acquired. At some point, however, message content is known and confidence asymptotes. It is supplanted by a feeling of tedium, which prompts either a scrutiny of the message by activating extra-communication thoughts such as counterarguments, or a cessation of thinking about the message. In either event, evaluation of the message advocacy declines. Continued repetition of the message activates the processing of its content anew because message recipients processing of their own thoughts reduces the tedium attendant to processing the message and lowers confidence that they have internalized message content.

Thus, the emerging view is that the effects of message repetition are guided by metacognitions in the form of confidence and tedium that serve an executive function in directing the amount and type of thought generation. As plausible as this account might be in explaining the effects of repetition on the activation of support and counterarguments and the attendant persuasive effects, the evidence favoring this view is incomplete. It would be bolstered by the evidence to document that the metacognitive processes hypothesized are operative in the context of persuasive message repetitions. It can also be bolstered by examining other contexts in which resource allocation is likely to be influenced by metacognitive processes similar those thought to be activated to regulate the processing of message repetitions.

## MESSAGE INVOLVEMENT

Additional insight about the resource allocation process is provided by work on involvement. A seminal finding is that when experiencing a resource limitation, consumers use cues that accommodate this limitation to make a judgment. Along these lines is the observation that individuals who have low involvement in a message issue use the credibility of a message source, or the number of arguments made in favor of an advocacy, or some other so-called peripheral cue rather than message content as a basis for making a judgment (Cacioppo, Petty, and Schumann 1983). In contrast, those who are highly involved are more likely to rely on a central cue such as the message content in rendering their judgments. This suggests that decision makers select the cues that enable them to accommodate the resources they are willing to devote to a processing task to render a judgment about an object. However, it has also been demonstrated that highly involved individuals are willing to process source and message cues in circumstances when both inform their judgments (Petty and Cacioppo 1979). Apparently, what distinguishes which cues are central and peripheral depends on their perceived value in evaluating an object. Thus, highly involved individuals exhibit discretion in their resource allocation by processing source cues in instances when they are deemed useful and considering them peripheral to judgment when they are not.

Finally, there are demonstrations that the level of involvement can prompt regulation of how a particular cue is processed. When individuals are highly involved in a message issue, the color of an object presented in an ad serves as a cue to elaborate on the benefits of the advertised brand. However, when they allocate relatively few resources, this same color cue is processed heuristically as a basis for judgment (Meyers-Levy and Peracchio 1995).

Research on involvement thus suggests that individuals are judicious in their resource allocation. When they have interest in an issue, they allocate substantial resources to the processing of message information, whereas when the issue is peripheral to their interests they rely on cues that accommodate this resource allocation in making a judgment. In some cases, high involvement entails elaboration of a single cue such the message source, the color of an object

presented an ad, or message content, and in others it give rise to the processing of multiple cues such as the message and source. Under low involvement, individuals process cues that are less resource demanding or they process cues in a less elaborate manner.

These observations raise the question of how do those varying in involvement decide which cues to process as a basis for their judgments. As suggested for repetition effects, one possibility is that individuals select cues on the basis of metacognitions prompted by stimulus processing. Along these lines, individuals' level of issue involvement prompts the activation of a threshold for the onset of tedium, which guides both the selection of the cues that will serve as a basis for judgment and the depth at which cues are processed. As was the case for repetition effects, evidence documenting this process has not been reported. However, there is emerging evidence that implicates the coordination of cognitive and metacognitive processes in resource allocation. This research pertains to the effects of depletion on subsequent task resource expenditure.

## RESOURCE ALLOCATION
## AND THE DEPLETION EFFECT

The depletion effect refers to the phenomenon where the resources allocated to the initial task affect those allocated to subsequent task: the greater the allocation to the initial task the fewer the resources devoted to a subsequent task. In most demonstrations of this phenomenon, the two tasks are not related. For example, as part of a food tasting study participants in the high depletion condition were asked to refrain from eating cookies, whereas this requirement was not imposed on those in the low depletion condition (Baumeister et al., 1998). All participants then performed a second task, which involved an attempt to complete an unsolvable puzzle. Those who refrained from eating cookies spent less time on the puzzle than those who did not have to engage in such initial self-regulation, thus providing evidence for the depletion effect. In everyday situations, the depletion effect is observed when regulation of some activity such as smoking or drinking results in the lack of regulation of a subsequent activity such as eating or shopping.

The initial explanation offered for the depletion effect was cast in terms of a resource limitation (Baumeister et al., 1998). To the extent that people allocate resources to an initial task, they have fewer resources to allocate to a subsequent task. This is based on the notion that there is a single pool of resources that can be consumed or significantly reduced by the performance of an arduous self-regulatory activity. Replenishment requires rest, consumption of food that provides energy (Gailliot et al., 2007), or practicing task performance (Muraven, Baumeister and Tice, 1999).

A substantial number of studies document that the depletion effect is unlikely to be attributable to a resource limitation. In these studies, individuals exhibit the same level of performance whether they are highly or less depleted when provided with the motivation to do so. This is achieved by paying depleted individuals for their performance on a persistence task (Baumeister et al., 2005), suggesting that persistence is warranted because the issue is important (Muraven and Slessareva, 2003), and informing participants of the time they have spent in performing a persistence task (Wan and Sternthal, 2008). In addition, there is growing evidence that the depletion effect can be reversed so that highly depleted individuals exhibit better performance on a subsequent task than those who are less depleted. This reversal has been documented by presenting two initial tasks prior to the critical task rather than a single initial task (Converse and DeShon, 2009), using two tasks that involve similar activities rather than the unrelated tasks typically employed in depletion research

(Dewitte, Bruyneel, and Geyskens, 2009), and by prompting participants to adopt a high level of construal (Agrawal and Wan, 2009).

These observations suggest that the depletion effect is better explained in terms of individuals' motivation to allocate resources they have rather than a resource limitation. A monitoring view offers such an explanation (Agrawal and Wan 2009; Baumeister et al. 2005; Baumeister 2002; Baumeister and Vohs 2007). According to this view, people set a goal and a standard that is necessary to achieve this goal, and continually adjust the allocation of resources needed to achieve this standard. For example, a consumer might consider $200 an appropriate amount to spend on a pair of shoes and continue to search until an appropriate pair that is within this budget is found. However, when people are depleted, they abandon such goals and standards and focus on their fatigue as a basis for resource allocation: the more tired they feel, the less the effort allocated to the task. Because all participants in the typical two task procedure used to demonstrate the depletion effect typically experience some level of fatigue, their performance of a focal task would depend on the amount of fatigue experienced. In contrast, if a standard of performance were made salient, it would serve as a basis for resource allocation to the second task. And if the initial task served as a standard for performance of a subsequent task, those who set a high standard by engaging in an initially highly depleting task would exhibit better performance on the subsequent task than those who engaged in a less depleting initial task.

A critical assumption underlying these predictions is that the same cue can serve both as a means of interpreting a behavior (fatigue implies less performance) and as a standard for a behavior (fatigue implies a high standard for subsequent performance). Support for this assumption is found in research on context effects (Nam and Sternthal 2008). Experts and novices with regard to musical instruments were presented a persuasive message advocating the purchase of a musical system. The qualities of this product were ambiguous. This ad was presented in the context of an ad for a BMW, toward which message recipients were favorable, or Hyundai toward which they were unfavorable. Experts used this contextual information to interpret the target musical system and thus exhibited assimilation: they were more favorable when the context was BMW than when it was Hyundai. In contrast, novices used the contextual information as a standard and thus exhibited comparison contrast: they were more favorable when the context was Hyundai than when it was BMW.

Several studies identified earlier offer support for the monitoring prediction that more depleted individuals will exhibit superior second task performance than less depleted ones and that this outcome is likely when the resources allocated to the first task are viewed as a standard for subsequent task performance. For example, having people perform multiple initial tasks makes the initial task salient as a standard for performance (Converse and DeShon 2009), which leads more depleted people to set a higher standard. Along the same lines, when the initial and subsequent tasks are similar, the relationship between the tasks makes the initial task salient as a standard for subsequent performance. And prompting people to adopt a high level of construal enhances the connection between the unrelated initial and second tasks in a depletion procedure, which makes the initial task accessible as a standard. In contrast, a low level construal makes salient the fatigue produced by an initial task as the basis for subsequent performance, and thus the more resources allocated to the initial task, the fewer allocated to the subsequent task (Agrawal and Wan 2009).

Recent research that I have conducted with Echo Wen Wan and Alice Isen examining the moderating role of positive affect on deple-

tion offers additional evidence favoring the monitoring account. In these studies, participants were presented information that stimulates either positive or neutral affect immediately after being highly or less depleted by an initial task. Neutral affect was stimulated by having people consider an event with a neutral outcome, whereas positive affect involved having people think about an event that had a favorable outcome. Performance on the subsequent task by those in neutral affect provided evidence for a depletion effect: highly depleted individuals exhibited poorer performance on the subsequent task than those who were less depleted. In contrast, those experiencing positive affect performed better when the initial task had been highly depleting rather than less depleting. Apparently, positive affect activated between the two tasks stimulated the use of the effort induced by the initial task as a standard for the performance of the subsequent task. Moreover, the depletion effect found in the neutral affect condition was mediated by participants' feeling of fatigue, whereas for those experiencing positive affect, performance of the second task was mediated by the perception of effort required to perform this task. These findings thus support the view that those in the neutral affect condition used the fatigue induced by the initial task as a basis for subsequent performance, and those experiencing positive affect used the first task as a standard for performance of the second task.

The monitoring model not only suggests that prompting people to focus on their goal rather than their fatigue enhances performance on a subsequent task, but also predicts that the depletion effect should be moderated by the framing of the initial task. Given the premise that depletion effects occur because a feeling of fatigue serves as the basis for reducing the resource allocation to a subsequent task, altering how this feeling is experienced might be used to enhance the allocation of resources to a subsequent task and overcome the depletion effect. If the initial and subsequent tasks are framed as a single task, individuals should not have the opportunity to reflect on the experienced in performing the initial task when determining their allocation to the subsequent task, and this should eliminate the depletion effect. Alternatively, the depletion effect should be eliminated if the initial task is framed as one that facilitates the second task, or at least draws attention away from the fatigue resulting from first task performance.

These predictions are confirmed in several studies. In research conducted with Echo Wen Wan, participants were presented a two-task depletion procedure where the second task involved customizing products such as a suit or other clothing and accessories. When the two tasks were represented as a single task, the depletion effect found when the procedures were represented as two separate tasks was eliminated. This outcome occurred because the feeling of fatigue that mediated the depletion effect was not observed in the one task condition. Indeed, participants in the one task condition did not differ in their perception of fatigue whether the initial task was highly resource demanding or not.

There is also evidence that framing the initial task as enhancing subsequent performance eliminates the depletion effect. Martijn and colleagues (2002) found that individuals who were informed that working hard on a task enhances subsequent performance exhibited better performance on this latter task than either those who were highly depleted, but not informed about the effect of prior effort exertion, or those who were not initially depleted. Along similar lines, Clarkson et al. (2010) observed that those highly depleted by an initial task worked harder on a subsequent task when they were told that a feature of the initial task (i.e., the color of the paper on which the task was completed) was known to be exhausting than when this feature was described as replenishing. Apparently, the attribution of the fatigue to a feature in the initial task that was not present in the subsequent task led to the inference that substantial resources were available for performing the latter task. However, when people felt that they were tired despite the presence of a replenishing feature, they inferred that fatigue induced by the initial task was indeed substantial, focused on this feeling of fatigue in determining resource allocation, and limited their allocation to the subsequent task.

The view emerging from depletion research is that the effect of initial task performance on the resources allocated to a subsequent task is guided by two factors. One is cognitive; the standard that the individual sets for task performance determines the resources allocated to it. The other factor is metacognitive; the feelings prompted by the performance of an initial task guide the subsequent resource allocation. The depletion occurs because the greater the resource allocation to an initial task, the greater the feeling of fatigue, and thus the fewer the resources allocated to a subsequent task. Stated another way, the metacognitive experience attendant to an initial task guides the resource allocation to a subsequent task. In accord with this interpretation, the depletion effect can be overcome by making salient cognitions related to the standard for performance of the second task, ignoring the metacognitive experience of fatigue attributable to the previous resource allocation, or by interpreting this experience in terms other than fatigue that stimulates substantial allocation to a subsequent task.

## AN INTEGRATED VIEW

The repetition, involvement and depletion literatures reviewed not only offers insight about the processes that explain the effects of these variables, each of these literatures offers insight about some facet of the regulatory process. And collectively they suggest that the cognitive operations individuals engage in when performing an information processing task are dependent on the metacognitions they activate. Some metacognitions promote the allocation of resources to a task, whereas other metacognitions limit such an allocation.

The analysis of repetition effects described earlier suggests that individuals' willingness to sustain the processing of a repeated message depends on metacognitions related to confidence and tedium. Actions taken are influenced by whether a subjective feeling of confidence is evoked in responding to a stimulus, which promotes resource allocation, or a subjective experience of tedium is activated, which limits resource allocation.

Depletion effects can be explained using these same concepts, though the focus of these investigations is on metacognitions that limit resource allocation. Depletion research suggests that tedium or fatigue might prompt a reduction in resource allocation. Repetition research is informative about the mechanism underlying depletion effects; it suggests that metacognitions related to the feelings of confidence that emerge upon learning and mastering tasks are likely to propel the resource allocation observed under low depletion. This account explains the observation that when individuals are highly depleted, presenting an initial task as enhancing the performance of a subsequent task prompts a resource allocation that eliminates the depletion effect found in the absence of this motivation.

Depletion research also informs an understanding of repetition effects. Investigations of the depletion effect document that the feeling of fatigue can be managed by having people interpret the subjective experience of tedium in terms of goal attainment or to limit access to this feeling. These findings offer a starting point for managing wearout effects of repeated message exposures.

Investigations of involvement effects suggest that those under high involvement exhibit discretion in the allocation of their substantial resources. They engage in the processing of so-called peripheral

cues such as the message source based on an assessment of whether this information contributes to the judgment of a message advocacy. This observation suggests that regardless of involvement, there is a point at which the enhancement of confidence resulting from a resource allocation is offset by the tedium involved in processing additional information. The point at which this occurs differs between those who are highly and less involved. Applying this observation to depletion effects raises the possibility that non-depleted individuals will exhibit similar discretion and limit their resource allocation when this allocation is perceived to contribute more to fatigue than to confidence. Some evidence supporting this view is found in the demonstration that making salient an initial task as a standard for second task performance reduces the resource allocation that would otherwise occur. Demonstrations of naturally occurring social conditions when this outcome obtains awaits empirical demonstration.

## ACKNOWLEDGEMENTS

The honor of being named an ACR Fellow is the result of a collaboration with mentors, colleagues and students. I am grateful to Jim Engel, whose passion for consumer research stimulated my interest in the area, to Tony Greenwald who taught me the how to think theoretically, to Roger Blackwell, who showed me how to advance research from ideas to outcomes, to Sid Levy who encouraged me to think abstractly, to Sam Craig who taught me how to make collaboration enjoyable, and to Alice Tybout whose wisdom about how to relate to people and ideas guided my personal and professional development.

I have benefitted from having intellectually stimulating colleagues. Collaborations with Bobby Calder enhanced my ability to situate research in a body of thought, and research conducted with Angela Lee has enhanced my experimental skills and provided insight about how to sustain research programs. I have learned from an affiliation and collaboration with doctoral students: Ruby Dholakia, Sue Jung Grant, Chris Janiszewski, Punam Keller, Durairaj Maheswaran, Joan Meyers-Levy, Prashant Malaviya, Michelle Roehm, Debbie Roedder John, Carol Scott, Echo Wen Wan and Richard Yalch. What is most gratifying is that these individuals exerted the effort to educate the next generation of scholars.

Finally, I want to acknowledge Joe Alba and John Lynch with whom I am sharing the honor of being inducted as an ACR Fellow and who served with me as editors of the *Journal of Consumer Research*. I benefited greatly from their skills, wisdom and passion for excellence.

## REFERENCES

Agrawal, Nidhi, and Echo Wen Wan (2009), "Regulating Risk or Risking Regulation? Construal Levels and Depletion Effects in the Processing of Health Messages," *Journal of Consumer Research*, 36 (October), 448–62.

Anand, Punam and Brian Sternthal (1990), "Ease of Message Processing as a Moderator of Repetition Effects in Advertising," *Journal of Advertising Research*, 27 (August), 345-353.

Baumeister, Roy F. (2002), "Yielding to Temptation: Self-Control Failure, Impulsive Purchasing and Consumer Behavior," *Journal of Consumer Research*, 28 (March), 670–76.

Baumeister, Roy. F., Ellen Bratslavsky, Mark Muraven, and Dianne M. Tice (1998), "Ego Depletion: Is the Active Self a Limited Resource?" *Journal of Personality and Social Psychology*, 74, 1252-1265.

Baumeister, Roy. F., C. Nathan DeWall, Natalie J. Ciarocco, and Jean M. Twenge, (2005), "Social Exclusion Impairs Self-regulation," *Journal of Personality and Social Psychology*, 88, 589-604.

Baumeister, Roy. F., and Kathleen D. Vohs (2007), "Self-Regulation, Ego Depletion, and Motivation," *Social and Personality Psychology Compass*, 1, 1-14.

Berlyne, Donald, E. (1970), "Novelty, Complexity and Hedonic Value," *Perception and Psychophysics*, 8, 279-286.

Belk, Russell W. and Janeen Arnold Costa (1998), "The Mountain Man Myth: A Contemporary Consuming Fantasy," *Journal of Consumer Research*, 25 (December), 218-240.

Cacioppo, John T. and Richard E. Petty (1979), "Effects of Message Repetition and Position on Cognitive Response, Recall, and Persuasion," *Journal of Personality and Social Psychology*, 37, 97-109.

Cacioppo, John T. Richard E. Petty and David Schumann (1983), "Central and Peripheral Routes to Advertising Effectiveness: The Moderating Role of Involvement," *Journal of Consumer Research*, 10 (September), 135-146.

Clarkson, Joshua J., Edward R. Hirt, Lile Jia, and Marla B. Alexander, (2010), "When Perception is More than Reality: The Effects of Perceived versus Actual Resource Depletion on Self-regulatory Behavior," *Journal of Personality and Social Psychology,* 98, 29-46.

Converse, Patrick D., and Richard P. DeShon (2009), "A Tale of Two Tasks: Reversing the Self-regulatory Resource Depletion Effect," *Journal of Applied Psychology,* 94, 1318-1324.

Dewitte, Siegfried, Sabrina Bruyneel, and Kelly Geyskens (2009), "Self-regulating Enhances Self-regulation in Subsequent Consumer Behavior Decisions Involving Similar Response Conflicts," *Journal of Consumer Research,* 36, 394-405.

Gailliot, Matthew.T. Roy F. Baumeister, C. Nathan DeWall, Jon K. Maner, E. Ashby Plant, Dianne M. Tice, Lauren E. Brewer, and Brandon J. Schmeichel (2007), "Self-control Relies on Glucose as a Limited Energy Source: Willpower is More than a Metaphor," *Journal of Personality and Social Psychology,* 92, 325-336.

Gilovich, Thomas, Dale Griffin and Daniel Kahneman (2002), *Heuristics and Biases: The Psychology of Intuitive Judgment,* Cambridge University Press, New York, USA.

Greenwald, Anthony G. (1968), "Cognitive Learning, Cognitive Response to Persuasion, and Attitude Change," in *Psychological Foundations of Attitudes*, eds. A. G. Greenwald, T. C. Brock, and T. M. Ostrom, New York: Academic Press, 147-170).

Kozinets Robert V. (2001), "Utopian Enterprise: Articulating the Meanings of Star Trek's Culture of Consumption," *Journal of Consumer Research*, 28 (June), 67-88.

Kozinets, Robert V. (2002), "Can Consumers Escape the Market? Emancipatory Illuminations from Burning Man," *Journal of Consumer Research*, 29 (June), 20-38.

Martijn, Carolien, Petra Tenbült, Harald Merckelbach, Ellen Dreezens and Nanne K. De Vriesgetting (2002), "A Grip On Ourselves: Challenging Expectancies About Loss Of Energy After Self–Control," *Social Cognition*, 20 (6), 441–60.

Meyers-Levy, Joan and Laura A. Peracchio (1995), "Understanding the Effects of Color: How the Correspondence between Available and Required Resources Affects Attitudes," *Journal of Consumer Research*, 22 (September), 121-138.

Muraven, Mark, Roy F. Baumeister, and Dianne M. Tice (1999), "Longitudinal Improvement of Self-Regulation through Practice: Building Self-Control Strength through Repeated Exercise," *Journal of Social Psychology*, 139 (4), 446–57.

Muraven, Mark, and Elisaveta Slessareva (2003), "Mechanisms of Self-control Failure: Motivation and Limited Resources," *Personality and Social Psychology Bulletin*, 29, 894-906.

Nam Myungwoo, and Brian Sternthal (2008), "The Effects of a Different Category Context on Target Brand Evaluations," *Journal of Consumer Research*, 35 (December), 668-679.

Petty, Richard E. and John T. Cacioppo (1979). "Issue Involvement Can Increase or Decrease Persuasion by Enhancing Message-Relevant Cognitive Responses," *Journal of Personality and Social Psychology*, 37 (October), 1915-1926.

Schouten, John W. and James H. McAlexander (1995), "Subcultures of Consumption: An Ethnography of the New Bikers," *Journal of Consumer Research*, 22 (1), 43-61.

Smith, Gene F. and Donald D. Dorfman (1975), "The Effect of Stimulus Uncertainty on the Relationship Between Frequency of Exposure and Liking," *Journal of Personality and Social Psychology,* 31 (1), 150-155

Wan, Echo Wen and Brian Sternthal (2008), "Regulating the Effects of Depletion Through Monitoring," *Personality and Social Psychology Bulletin*, 34 (1), 47–60.

# Special Session Summaries

SPECIAL SESSION

## Services as Social Structures: Consumer Collectives and Transformative Services Research

Laurel Anderson, Arizona State University, USA
Amy Ostrom, Arizona State University, USA

### EXTENDED ABSTRACTS

**"Conceptualizing Transformative Service Research"**
*Laurel Anderson, Arizona State University, USA*
*Amy Ostrom, Arizona State University, USA*

In our presentation we seek to offer an alternate paradigm within which to consider the role of services and the service consumer within society. We pull especially from theories of social structure and ecosocial environments to frame our most dominant premises:

1. Services are so ubiquitous that they, to a large degree, structure the world within which consumers live, the ecosocial environment.
2. Reciprocally, other components of the ecosocial environment influence services and the success of services.
3. At times, there is a tension between these service social structures and the agency of individuals or groups of consumers.
4. In some sense, given services contribution to the social structure and ecosocial environment within which consumers live and their impact on consumer well-being, many services approach the level of a public good.
5. Services can be intentional, unconscious, or unintentional of their transformational impacts.

We utilize this paradigm to frame the area of transformative services research (TSR). In this conceptualization and theory building we both build on and add to the transformative consumer research stream. We define TSR as service research that strives to create uplifting changes and improvements in the well-being of both individuals and communities (Anderson, Ostrom, and Bitner 2010).

This transformative view is especially apt for looking at services because service consumers are often vulnerable (Baker, Gentry and Rittenburg 2005) in that they often lack a degree of control and agency, service consumers are often disadvantaged, most especially with regard to expertise and decreased knowledge in comparison to the service provider, and services are consumer-centric, experiential and co-created, thus more intimate than physical goods.

From this macro level view of services, it is apparent that services have the ability to uplift and transform individual consumers and communities. Conversely, "they also, often unwittingly, have the ability to marginalize, judge, and stigmatize citizens and communities and to compromise sustainability" (Anderson et al. 2010). If services create socio-cultural structures, they can be considered envirogenic (Jamner and Stokol 2000) and can act as stressors, as enablers of well-being or ill-being, as providers of resources and/or as sources of safety or danger. Furthermore, even though we are focused on the collective consumer, well-being is influenced not only by the environment, but also by personal attributes. There is a dynamic interplay between structure and person. The level of congruence

between the individual and the environment (structure) is connected to well-being. We will use research examples focused on consumer collectives to illustrate our above premises.

### REFERENCES

Anderson, Laurel, Amy Ostrom and Mary Jo Bitner (2010), "Services as Social Structures: Consumer Collectives and Transformative Services Research," Working paper.

Baker, Stacey Menzel, James W. Gentry, and Terri L. Rittenburg (2005), "Building Understanding of the Domain of Consumer Vulnerability," *Journal of Macromarketing*, 25 (2): 128-139.

Mick, David Glen (2006), "Meaning and Mattering through Transformative Consumer Research," Presidential Address to the Association for Consumer Research, in *Advances in Consumer Research*, Vol. 33, ed. Cornelia Pechmann and Linda L. Price, Provo, UT: Association for Consumer Research, 1-4.

Jamner, Margaret Schneider, and Daniel Stokols, editors (2000), "Promoting Human Wellness: New Frontiers for Research, Practice, and Policy," Berkeley: University of California Press.

**"There's No Place Like Home...Or Is There?"**
*Stacey Menzel Baker, University of Wyoming, USA*
*Jose Antonio Rosa, University of Wyoming, USA*

When Dorothy's home is destroyed by a tornado in *The Wizard of* Oz, she sweetly declares, "There's no place like home." Her words resonate with viewers who have formed their own place attachments, which occur when individuals bond with particular physical spaces (Milligan 1998). Attachment to home or place develops over time and is formed through decommodification and singularization processes (e.g., acquisition, decoration, ritual performance) that facilitate home becoming "me" or "mine" (Kleine and Baker 2004). Disruption of strong place attachments, such as those wrought by natural hazard events, leads to a profound sense of loss and necessitates renegotiation of self (Brown and Perkins 1992). In addition, when multiple displacements occur simultaneously, as they do in disaster, there is a loss of sense of *community*, and a desire to sustain community by keeping people *in* community. Such severe injuries create dependence and require the infusion of outside resources and services (shelter, food, clothing, financial assistance) into individuals' lives and community for them to recover. Business, government, and non-profit services provide the resources which assist consumers in reconstituting the world in which they live.

The present research explores the tensions between community and individual identity reconstitution processes as housing (collective) versus home-creation (individual) needs are negotiated in disaster recovery. Qualitative, longitudinal data collected in a rural community in the Western United States impacted by a tornado inform our purpose. The tornado caused two deaths, rendered 100 homes uninhabitable, and left one-quarter of the community's residents homeless. To understand how housing/home needs were negotiated, members of multiple constituent groups were questioned about how recovery resources were garnered and distributed, as well as how resources were received and used.

Tensions between collective and individual identity reconstitution processes arose immediately after the tornado touched down, and continued throughout the entire data collection process (multiple site visits over the course of a year). Narratives reveal that the social and economic structure imposed by service providers supplying resources were at odds with survivors' familiar processes of home creation and the development of place attachment. We know that place attachments facilitate adaptation (Milligan 1998); yet our data show numerous impediments to reconstructing home: (1) recipients of burdens of costs versus the gift of benefits, (2) shared versus personal responsibility, (3) equality versus individuation motivations, and (4) personal privacy versus public transparency. Each constraint will be explored in the presentation.

Consider federal funds made possible the allocation of 60 identical trailers for displaced survivors. All were white on the exterior, all had the same floor plan, all had the same color of paint on the walls, and so forth. In other words, the behaviors, cognitions, and affect that typically lead to place attachment (e.g., freedom of choice over which home to inhabit and how to decorate it once occupied) were constrained by the commoditized state of the housing. The standardization of the trailers as well as rules against decorating trailers served to hinder positive adaptation by survivors. Though residents were displaced, they did not also want to feel misplaced. Survivors fought back and resisted the homogenizing forces of living in a commoditized home. Some broke the "rules" and hung things on the walls, while others viewed the housing as temporary and got out as quickly as possible, and still others had little choice and were forced to make the standardized housing their homes.

The presentation concludes with a discussion on (1) how transformative service research may play a role in community development or reconstitution and (2) the types of home-rebuilding services in disaster recovery that contribute to individual and community transformation. The data collection and analysis of this research is complete.

## REFERENCES

Brown, B.B., & Perkins, D.D. (1992), Disruptions in place attachment. In I. Altman & S. Low (Eds.), Place attachment (pp. 279-304). New York: Plenum.

Kleine, Susan Schultz and Stacey Menzel Baker (2004), "An Integrative Review of Material Possession Attachment." Academy of Marketing Science Review, 2004 no. 1

Milligan, M. J. (1998), "Interactional Past and Potential: The Social Construction of Place Attachment", *Symbolic Interaction,* Vol 21, pp 1-33.

### "When Consumer Well-Being Meets Small Business Ownership: Transforming Financial Service Systems to Eradicate Disparate Treatment and Discrimination"

*Sterling A. Bone, Brigham Young University, USA*
*Glenn L. Christensen, Brigham Young University, USA*
*Jerome D. Williams, University of Texas at Austin, USA*

Service systems are inherently complex because of the number and intricacy of the steps that construct them. This complexity creates a critical tension among service agents' abilities to follow formal procedures and structure to deliver desired service outcomes (Shostack 1987). The discretionary nature of many service systems requires employees to diverge from the normative to meet dueling demands of the firm and of their customers (Bone and Mowen 2010). Bone and Mowen conclude that service agents in roles that require decision latitude may exert personal biases that result in disparate or discriminatory actions taken toward customers.

Complexity and divergence in service systems increases the risk that disparate, and even discriminatory actions will be taken by firms and their agents to achieve desired firm and employee outcomes. Prior research has argued that disparate or discriminatory actions are a threat to consumers that are in transitory states of vulnerability (Baker, Gentry, and Rittenburg 2005).

Particularly among immigrants, individuals, at an increasing rate, are starting small businesses in pursuit of their dreams in order to avoid barriers that come with traditional jobs (Kelleher 2008). Yet only two out of 10 small businesses succeed in the first year (Fairlie 2009). Stimulating growth and survival of small business is a pressing concern for federal, state, and economic stakeholders. Recent U.S. Senate hearings held on minority entrepreneurship call for transformative efforts to help minority-owned enterprises as service consumers overcome the "tremendous hurdles" that they "must face each day to gain fair and adequate access to venture capital, credit, and business and technical training" (Kerry 2008).

Census and economic research has reported that minority entrepreneurs are the most vulnerable to marketplace discrimination among consumer groups (Wainwright 2007). Where is discrimination among small business owners most likely to manifest its ugly head? A report from the U.S. Chamber of Commerce (2005) concludes that lack of access to capital and credit is the most common obstacle for African American and Hispanic business owners. Moreover, Wainwright (2007) reported finding quantitative evidence that minority-owned businesses are substantially and significantly more likely to be denied credit than are white-owned businesses. These consumers must maneuver complex service systems to garner the required resources.

In this paper we seek to disentangle the socio-cultural barriers in the small business bank lending service system. We argue that transformative service research can stimulate dialogue and intervention strategies to provide greater access to capital financing for racial/ethnic minority consumers, who out of necessity, start their own businesses. We employ an in-depth interview method to investigate the pilgrimage of consumers seeking to improve their quality of life through small business start-ups. The method chosen was the Zaltman Metaphor Elicitation Technique (ZMET) (Zaltman 1997), an in-depth interview format that focuses on uncovering the informants' emotions, beliefs, and values. We purposefully sampled small business owner informants to represent three racial/ethnic groups of small business owners: White/Caucasian, Hispanic, and African-American. Thirty-nine informants who owned a small U.S. business were recruited for this study. Sixteen were White, 13 were Hispanic, and 10 were African American. Informants were asked to prepare for their 90-minute interview by writing down at least five thoughts and feelings about seeking financing for their businesses. Informants were also asked to find a picture that represented each of their thoughts or feelings. The combination of the approaches elicited rich and descriptive insights into the informants' perceived vulnerability. Interviewers were matched to the informant based on their race and language of origin. This step was taken to enhance conversational flow and to ensure cultural sensitivity.

We contrast interviews conducted with the "White" majority to those conducted with minority consumers (African-American and Hispanic). Interpretive analyses use historical, political and sociological ideology perspectives to inform this comparison of consumer experiences. We identify compelling differences in the barriers and conditions encountered in capital-seeking marketplace exchanges, factors that increase the likelihood of vulnerability in this service system, and in the coping mechanisms employed to protect from disparate treatment.

Our findings suggest that minorities perceive heightened restrictions of access to financial resources. Both minority and majority consumers describe their interactions with banks as a "financial pipeline." Akin to water as an essential resource for survival, majority White informants describe their experiences seeking financial resources as embodied in the deep-metaphor of movement, where financial resources "flow" or "run" at their request. Minority consumers, however, describe the availability of resources as a "slow drip" a "dribble," or a faucet or spicket that is "locked" or unavailable to them.

We also contrast the relationships that minority and majority consumers describe having with actors in the lending service system (e.g., loan officers, loan sharks). Drawing upon historical ideologies minority consumers describe their relationships as fettered, shackled, and oppressed (Crockett and Wallendorf 2004). Majority consumers, however, describe their relationships as emancipated, free and balanced.

We draw conclusions from these and other themes and suggest that consumer researchers and public policy stakeholders consider transformative efforts to protect minority consumers from disparate treatment. We propose an agenda for future transformative service research by outlining specific intervention strategies to reduce discriminatory and disparate treatment in service systems.

## REFERENCES

Baker, Stacy Menzel, James W. Gentry, and Terr L. Rittenburg (2005), "Building Understanding of the Domain of Consumer Vulnerability," *Journal of Macromarketing*, 5(2), 128-139.

Bone, Sterling A. and John C. Mowen (2010), "By-The-Book Decision-Making: How Service Employee Desire For Decision Latitude Influences Customer Selection Decisions," *Journal of Service Research*.

Crockett, David and Melanie Wallendorf (2004), "The Role of Normative Political Ideology in Consumer Behavior," *Journal of Consumer Research*, 31 (December), 511-528.

Fairlie, Robert W. (2009), *Kauffman Index of Entrepreneurial Activity: 1996-2008,* Ewing Marion Kauffman Foundation.

Kelleher, Elizabeth (2008), "Immigrants Fuel Small Business Growth in the United States," *America.Gov,* (http://www.america.gov/st/econ-english/2008/March/20070302160834berehellek0.7271845.html), March 7, 2008.

Kerry, John F. (2008), "Statement of Senator John F. Kerry on Business Start-up Hurdles in Underserved Communities: Access to Venture Capital and Entrepreneurship Training, "*Small Business Committee Hearing: September 11, 2008,* United States Senate.

Shostack, G. Lynn (1987), "Service Positioning Through Structural Change," *Journal of Marketing,* 51 (January), 34-43.

U.S. Chamber of Commerce (2005), "Access to capital, what funding sources work for you?, U.S. Chamber of Commerce, Washington DC, 55.

Wainwright, Jon S. (2007), "Testimony Concerning the Current State of Minority-Owned and Women-Owned Business Enterprises in the United States," *United States Senate Committee Hearings on Small Business and Entrepreneurship,* May 22, 2007.

Zaltman, Gerald (1997), "Rethinking Market Research: Putting People Back In," *Journal of Marketing Research*, 34 (November), 424-437.

## "From Patient to Agent: Collective Practices and Identity Work in an Emotional Community"

*Susan Dunnett, University of Edinburgh, UK*
*Douglas Brownlie, University of Stirling, UK*
*Paul Hewer, University of Strathclyde, UK*

This study unpacks the technology–in short, the practices–through which consumers transform themselves in a market context. It focuses on a site where selfhood has fallen under intense pressure-a community framed by the condition of serious illness. In a service setting, that of healthcare, which has undergone (and is still undergoing) a significant process of "marketisation" (Lupton 1997) it investigates an under-researched aspect of communal consumption–the sharing of social support resources in order to realise agency in service interactions.

Lupton has noted (1997) that where the patient as consumer is examined, the privileged representation is that of 'dispassionate, thinking, calculating subject'. She argues that this depiction draws heavily on models of consumer behaviour where consumers are seen as rational economic decision-makers who benefit from sovereignty of choice. The conceptualisation of the patient as consumer of a healthcare system remains contentious. It has met with resistance from researchers and medical professionals alike, largely due to its perceived role in eroding the traditional power balance of the service encounter and thus creating the often undesired burden of consumer choice (Henwood et al 2003; Shankar et al 2006). The archetypal counterpart to the consumerist patient is the passive or dependent patient, a model of unquestioning compliance (Lupton 1997). The study at hand would suggest that beyond both of these simple conceptualisations, substantial emotional and social turmoil conditions a complex disempowerment in the diagnosed.

Taking its cue from previous consumer research into at-risk groups living with serious illnesses (eg. Kates, 2002; Wong and King, 2007), this study explores the lived experience of people suffering from multiple myeloma. Its context is a support group community, presented here as a form of Maffesoli's emotional community (1996). Through a phenomenological approach (Thompson et al 1989), attention is drawn to an under-explored phenomenon, that of collective enablement of self-identity. The personal movement revealed is from a position of passivity, fear and objectification to one of *perceived* control, understanding and skilled navigation of healthcare services.

Further, it seeks to assert that community can be a technology which enables the consumer to make most effective use of the marketplace. The support groups under study are discursively positioned as receptacles of first-hand market information, with much of the narrative exchange within the group being concerned with navigating the healthcare, pharmaceutical and health insurance industries. Crucially this culture of information-exchange fosters a sense of belonging. The group provides a safe space for members to 'forge new meanings and incorporate these meanings into changing self-conceptions' (Kates 2002: 636). Carrying out this arduous business of *identity work*, informants make a journey from patient to agent that empowers them with a sense of self-confidence and a newly-found ability to negotiate and manipulate health care services.

The notion of patient as agent draws attention to the necessity of mediation of the marketplace. As the literature tells us, the consumption of goods and services is a transaction that offers substantial opportunities for creative self-realisation (Arnould and Thompson 2005). However, to make the most effective use of marketplace services-as this study shows-requires much of the consumer: initiative, knowledge-gathering, energy and stamina, entrepreneurship and wise judgment are among the qualities that enable exploitation of its opportunities, as informant Marie's agentic narrative highlights:

Marie: So I met my oncologist, and he's trying to give me this drug, and I says, well how many milligrams you gonna give me? He says, two hundred. I says well that's too high. I said, I'm no way gonna take two hundred milligrams. So he dropped it down to a hundred.

The resources made available through support groups offer informants *access* to a new self-and in transforming into a skilled consumer, they are transforming the nature of the market itself. As such consumption communities can be conceptualised as a consumer-led solution to the dark side of empowerment–the burden of personal responsibility (eg. Lupton 1997; Shankar et al 2006). The extant literature has been slow to identify and explore helping behaviour in consumption communities. However, we answer Kozinets' (2002) call for consumption communities to be characterised as an 'ameliorative' to the effects of the marketplace (ibid: 34) by highlighting the emotional texture of exchange within such groups. In addition, conclusions are drawn about the incremental, complex nature of identity work, and the collective practices that empower it. Transformation is manifested in the newly-diagnosed patient's journey from dislocation and passivity to the empowered status of 'skilled consumer'.

Perhaps, too, we may draw on Price & Arnould's assertion (1999: 40) that 'buyer-seller or service provider-client relationships often pit the goals of one against those of the other' to conclude that the structural imperative of institutional medicine to make a profit (in the U.S.A. at least) inherently limits its ability to deliver the type of care desired by consumers. Nevertheless, this is still a market where the well-being of the consumer is the proclaimed mission of the service provider. Thus we can point to potential for improvement in the development of goods and services to fit better with the needs of the consumer. On this latter note, the study's findings have implications for patient information services, doctor/patient relations and the wider culture of institutional medicine. The planning of effective healthcare services would take account of the current deficit in acknowledgement of the consumer's involuntary renegotiation of self. As put by Frank (1995): 'The scope of modernist medi-cine–defined in practices ranging from medical school curricula to billing categories–does not include helping patients learn to think differently about their post-illness worlds and construct new relationships to those worlds.' (ibid: 6). In practical terms, a deeper understanding of the processes of patienthood would seem to involve an acceptance that self-empowerment through narrative is key to the journey from passive suffering to agency. Data collection and analysis are complete.

## REFERENCES

Arnould, E.J. and Thompson, C.J. (2005) Consumer Culture Theory (CCT): Twenty Years of Research, *Journal of Consumer Research*, Vol. 31, March, pp. 1-49.

Frank, A.W. (1995), *The Wounded Storyteller: Body, Illness and Ethics*, Chicago, The University of Chicago Press.

Henwood, F., Wyatt, S., Hart, A. and Smith, J. (2003) 'Ignorance is bliss sometimes': constraints in the emergence of the 'informed patient' in the changing landscapes of health information, *Sociology of Health and Illness*, Vol. 25 No. 6, pp. 589-607.

Kates, S.M. (2002), AIDS and community-based organizations: the marketing of therapeutic discourse, *European Journal of Marketing*, Vol. 36, No. 5/6, pp. 621-641.

Kozinets, R.V. (2002), Can Consumer Escape the Market? Emancipatory Illuminations from Burning Man, *Journal of Consumer Research*, Vol. 29 June, pp. 20-38.

Lupton, D. (1997), Consumerism, Reflexivity and the Medical Encounter, *Social Science and Medicine*, Vol. 45, No.3, pp. 373-381.

Maffesoli, M. (1996), *The Time of the Tribes*, London, Sage Publications.

Price, L.L. and Arnould, E.J. (1999), Commercial Friendships: Service Provider Client Relationships in Context, *Journal of Marketing*, Vol. 63, October, pp. 38-56.

Shankar, A., Cherrier, H., and Canniford, R. (2006), Consumer Empowerment: A Foucauldian Interpretation, *European Journal of Marketing*, Vol. 40, No. 9/10, pp. 1013-1030.

Thompson, C.J., Locander, W.B., Pollio, H.R. (1989), Putting Consumer Experience Back into Consumer Research: The Philosophy and Method of Existential-Phenomenology, *Journal of Consumer Research*, Vol. 16, September, pp. 133-146.

Wong, N. and King, T. (2008), The Cultural Construction of Risk Understandings Through Illness Narratives, *Journal of Consumer Research*, Vol. 34, February, pp. 579-594.

# The Effects of Incidental Cues on Goals and Motivation
Leonard Lee, Columbia University, USA

## EXTENDED ABSTRACT

### "From Physical Strength to Mental Resolve: Why Flexing Muscles Increases Willpower"
*Iris W. Hung, National University of Singapore, Singapore*
*Aparna A. Labroo, University of Chicago, USA*

"The mind commands the body and it obeys," ~ St Augustine

To withstand physical pain and build resistance, to overcome tempting food when one is on a diet, to consume unpleasant medicine to become healthier, or to attend to disturbing but essential information are all activities that are immediately unpleasant but result in long term benefits and involve self-control dilemmas. Exerting self control during such dilemmas requires willpower—and people have to try to strengthen their resolve by employing thoughts that facilitate long term actions and suppress thoughts of succumbing to the temptation of avoiding pain or medicine or eating indulgent food. As a result of facing a self control dilemma, people sometimes clench their fists or jaws and stiffen their muscles as their mind commands their body to resist the temptation. But willpower is a limited resource and exerting willpower is difficult, it is likened metaphorically to a muscle that is easily depleted, resulting in people giving in to the temptation. The fact that the mind tries to and ultimately learns to control the body and it obeys has never been in question, but the current research examines the reverse—a role our bodies might play in strengthening our resolve or will power. If willpower is like a muscle, could simply flexing one's muscles facilitate self control?

Recent findings in psychology are starting to establish that the relationship between the mind and the body is more complex than previously presumed. In particular, research is increasingly beginning to show that merely simulating many of the bodily actions that usually result from or accompany thought might also facilitate accessibility to those very thoughts, and in this manner our bodies might exert a powerful effect on our minds. For instance, standing upright rather than slouching not only results from feeling powerful or powerless, but also can result in people feeling powerful or powerless, respectively, and merely simulating the posture in an easy chair can evoke feelings of comfort and relaxation. Simulating motor approach toward a product that is being evaluated and results in increased preference because people usually associate positive feelings with approach, and writing with the dominant hand rather than the non dominant one can help validate ones thoughts. Adding to those findings, we propose that our bodies are instrumental in the recruitment of long range thoughts and in the suppression of immediate temptation thoughts and can therefore increase willpower and facilitate self control. Following the logic of other studies in embodied cognition, we argue that simulating the very actions that accompany or result when one is engaged in recruiting willpower—mentally pulling in long range thoughts and mentally banishing temptations—actions such as clenched fists and stiffened muscles, will also increase resolve and perceived willpower by helping recruit long range thoughts, banish temptation thoughts, and engage effectively in self control.

Across five experiments, we demonstrate that when participants contract their muscles, they feel more willpower and this enhanced perception of willpower mediates increased self control. Experiment

1 demonstrated that respondents have more long range healthfulness thoughts and are able to submerge their hand in an ice bucket (that presumably improves blood circulation but is painful to do) longer when they simultaneously contract finger muscles (vs. expanded it or do not do any muscle exercise). Experiment 2 demonstrated that contracting (vs. expanding) leg muscles also elicits willpower that enabled respondents to consume more of a bitter health drink (a vinegar concoction), but only among participants with health goals. When an irrelevant goal was primed, muscle contraction had no effect. Experiment 3 showed that participants are better able to resist tempting vice foods *while* they are contracting (vs. expanding) their biceps, rather than if they make the choice <u>after</u> they contract their muscles which results in depletion. Experiments 4a and 4b further examine the effect of muscle contraction in a field study to investigate whether participants are more willing to look at unpleasant charity materials (Experiment 4a) or purchase healthy food in a cafeteria (Experiment 4b) when contracting muscles.

Thus, our results demonstrate that muscle contraction elicits willpower and helps recruit thoughts that benefit long range actions. It is truly remarkable that small bodily actions can have big consequences. Of course, simply engaging in such actions is not a cure for all self control problems, but to the extent that these actions build the willpower muscle that is otherwise easily depleted from engaging in self control, a problem faced by most of us much of the time, has important consequences.

### "Kindling the Motivational System: Impact of Incidental Hedonic Cues on Goal Pursuit"
*Monica Wadhwa , INSEAD, France*
*Baba Shiv, Stanford University, USA*

Our consumption environment is abundant in cues that are high in hedonic value (i.e., cues that are desirable). A whiff of a fragrance, a sample of a refreshing drink or an advertisement picturing romantic images are some such cues that we commonly experience in our everyday lives. While recent research on consumption motivation suggests that experiencing such high hedonic value consumption cues can lead to general reward-seeking behaviors (e.g., Wadhwa, Shiv and Nowlis 2008; Van den Bergh, Dewitte and Warlop 2008), relatively little is understood about whether and how experiencing such cues impact consumer's subsequent goal related behaviors. Since most of consumer choices and behaviors are goal driven (Bettman, Luce and Payne 1998), investigating how such experiences with hedonic cues impact subsequent goal related behaviors is consequential both from the marketers' and consumers' perspectives. Drawing upon the synthesis of research on consumption motivation and recent evidence in neuroscience (Berridge 2007; Salamone 2007), in the present research, we propose that the motivational drive activated by brief experiences with hedonic cues can enhance pursuit of a subsequently adopted goal associated with a desirable outcome.

We test the aforementioned hypotheses, in a series of studies, across different consumer goals and different dependent variables. In study 1, we sought to examine the basic research question—whether or not a brief experience with a hedonic cue can enhance pursuit of a subsequently adopted goal. In line with the general-motivational drive hypothesis, our findings demonstrate that participants who had experienced a hedonic cue (romantic images) were more likely to persist on a subsequent goal involving unscrambling unsolvable anagrams as compared to those who were exposed to a neutral cue (nature images).

In study 2, we sought to provide further support for the general motivational drive proposition. Specifically, we argue that when the motivational drive activated in response to experience with hedonic cues is satiated, impact of hedonic cues on subsequent goal pursuit behaviors should get attenuated. In this study, we carried out the motivational-drive manipulation by employing a sampling paradigm, whereby participants sampled either Hawaiian Punch (motivational drive-induced) or water (motivational drive-not induced). Subsequently, we carried out the motivational drive- satiation manipulation, which was adapted from Wadhwa et al. (2008). Specifically, participants who had experienced the hedonic cue either received a surprise reward (candy bar) after the hedonic cue experience but before the goal adoption (motivational drive-satiated), or they received the candy bar at the end of the study (motivational drive-induced). As in study-1, participants then worked on an intellectual goal that involved unscrambling unsolvable anagrams. Mirroring the results of study-1, study 2 results show that those who had experienced the hedonic cue persisted longer on the anagrams than those who had not experienced the hedonic cue. Further, in line with general motivational hypothesis, when the induced motivational drive was satiated, the impact of experiencing hedonic cue on subsequent goal persistence was attenuated. Study 3 examines the role of individual differences related to behavioral activation system (BAS) in moderating the impact of brief exposure to hedonic cues on subsequent goal pursuit. The BAS system has been linked to appetitive motives and behaviors such that in the presence of rewarding cues, individuals with a high rather than low BAS sensitivity tend to exhibit an increased tendency to act on the rewarding impact of such hedonic cues (Carver and White 1994). Drawing upon this research, we argue that a brief experience with a hedonic cue will enhance subsequent goal pursuit for those who have a high sensitivity to BAS as compared to those who have low sensitivity to BAS. As in study, participants were either exposed to romantic images (motivational drive-induced) or nature images (motivational drive-not induced). Subsequently, participants worked on a persistence goal that required squeezing a hand dynamometer (a gauge that records force). As predicted, our results show that those high than those low on BAS sensitivity showed enhanced goal pursuit (as measured by persistence on the hand-dynamometer task) subsequent to a brief experience with the hedonic cue. These participants also persisted longer on the hand-dynamometer task as compared to those in the motivational drive-not induced condition.

The general-motivational drive conceptualization suggests that a brief exposure to a hedonic cue is likely to enhance pursuit of goals associated with a desirable outcome. In study-4, we explicitly test the role of goal desirability in moderating the general-motivational effects. Drawing upon research on goal systems, we manipulated goal desirability by making either the desirable or undesirable outcome contingency associated with the goal salient (adapted from Roney, Higgins and Shah 1995). Specifically, subsequent to the motivational drive manipulation, participants were told that they would be participating in another study on persistence, which comprises of two tasks. Participants were further informed that their performance on the initial persistence task would decide the persistence task they would subsequently work on. One of the alternatives for the second persistence task was a desirable outcome, while the other one was an undesirable outcome. All the participants were informed about both the alternatives for the second persistence task. However, for half of the participants, the desirable outcome contingency was emphasized, while for the other half, the undesirable outcome contingency was emphasized. In the first persistence task, participants'

goal was to squeeze the hand dynamometer for as long as they could at the level of force that was individually identified for them at the beginning of the experiment. Our results show that when the goal was framed such that the focus was on the desirable outcome, a brief experience with the hedonic cue enhanced persistence on the subsequent handgrip persistence task. However, when the goal was framed, such that emphasis was on the undesirable outcome, the impact of experiencing the hedonic cue on subsequent hand dynamometer persistence task was attenuated.

In sum, our findings suggest that a brief experience with a hedonic cue can enhance pursuit of a subsequently adopted goal that is unrelated to the experienced hedonic cue. Implications for marketers and policy makers are discussed.

### "Climbing the Goal Ladder: How Upcoming Actions Increase Level of Aspiration"
*Minjung Koo, Sungkyunkwan University, Korea*
*Ayelet Fishbach, University of Chicago, USA*

People's goals often follow a "goal ladder" in which each goal is a step toward another, more challenging goal. For example, career paths often follow a goal ladder in which an entry-level position is a step toward a more advanced position in the organization. Even more mundane goals, such as playing a computer game, often include different levels in which a person can move up, for example, by advancing from "level 3" to "level 4." Regardless of the specific features of the goal ladder, individuals face a dilemma between moving up to a more advanced level versus repeating the current level for their next pursuit. As such, we explore whether the way individuals monitor their current goal—either in terms of remaining or completed actions—influences their aspiration level for their next goal.

We position our theory in previous goal research, which explores the impact of discrepancies (i.e., remaining actions; Carver and Scheier 1998; Hull 1932), as well as successful past pursuits (Bandura 1991) on motivation to pursue a focal goal. In departure from previous research, we compare these foci against each other and explore their relative impact on the choice of what to do once the focal goal is achieved. Building on research by Fishbach and colleagues (Fishbach et al 2006; Koo and Fishbach 2008), we predict that an emphasis on remaining actions focuses individuals on making progress, leading to a desire to move up, whereas an emphasis on completed actions focuses individuals on their commitment to the current goal, leading to a desire to repeat the present goal level. That is, when the focus is on remaining actions, people consider their progress and wish to decrease the discrepancy between their current position and the state of goal completion; that is, people wish to move forward (Carver and Scheier 1998). In a goal ladder, a desire to move forward translates into not only greater motivation to complete the present goal level but into a greater level of aspiration, such that a person wishes to move up to the next level. In contrast, when the focus is on completed actions, the actions increase the sense of personal commitment to the goal. Because the goal appears more valuable and feasible (Atkinson 1957; Feather 1982), people wish to adhere to this goal at the next opportunity (Aronson 1997; Bem 1972).

Our results across five studies support these predictions. In Study 1 we asked undergraduate students to elaborate on their remaining versus completed academic tasks. As expected, we found that elaborating on remaining (vs. completed) academic tasks increased undergraduate participants' eagerness to begin their careers but decreased their satisfaction with their present college academic life. Furthermore, the satisfaction measure was negatively correlated with the desire to begin their career, implying a trade-off exists between pursuing the goal for the sake of engagement and for the sake of moving up.

Study 2 extended these findings by separating the effect of time frame (past vs. future) from the focus on completed versus remaining actions. We asked students in beginner-level foreign language course to first consider what materials they had covered (in the past) versus would cover (in the future) in their current class. We then asked those in the remaining-actions conditions to consider either the topics they did not or would not cover in this class. Those in the completed-actions conditions considered either the topics they had covered or would cover in this class. As expected, regardless of the past and future frame, participants who focused on remaining actions aimed for a higher level as their ultimate goal in their language (among five levels) than those who focused on completed actions. This study also demonstrated more clearly that a focus on remaining (vs. completed) actions increase not only the desire to move to something else but the desire to move up to a more advanced goal as we assessed the ultimate level of mastery.

Study 3 built on the previous studies by testing the underlying inferences for these effects and including a control condition. Participants evaluated several unfamiliar musical pieces and their evaluation of each piece was followed by information on the portion they had completed, the portion of the task that remained, or the number of the next piece to be evaluated (control). After completing the initial task, participants indicated their enjoyment of the task and could choose a lower, a higher, or a similar task level for their next task. As expected, monitoring remaining (vs. completed) actions decreased participants' enjoyment of the initial task but increased their level of aspiration, as reflected in their choice of a higher-level review task. Those in the control condition fell in the middle on these measures, demonstrating unique effects for completed and remaining actions. In addition, as direct evidence for underlying inferences, we found they more likely inferred task value when they monitored completed (vs. remaining) actions, whereas they inferred higher need for progress when they monitored remaining (vs. completed) actions.

Study 4 was a field experiment involving employees at an advertising company. We found that when employees considered what they had yet to achieve (vs. what they had already achieved), they were motivated to move on to new, more challenging roles but experienced decreased satisfaction from their current roles. Finally, participants in Study 5 strategically sought information on the remaining (vs. completed) portion of the task when they expected to move to a more advanced level. Individuals appear to attend to information that matches their level of aspiration and that can best help them maintain their motivation to progress or not on a goal ladder.

Taken together, the current research sheds new light on the classic problem of what determines people's levels of aspiration (Dembo 1931) by showing that the focus on remaining actions and goal progress increase people's levels of aspiration beyond their present goal. In addition, it explores the motivational cost of the focus on making progress on a goal: It lowers the intrinsic value from engaging in a present goal.

### "Crossing the Virtual Boundary: The Effect of Incidental Cues on Task Accomplishment"

*Min Zhao, University of Toronto, Canada*
*Leonard Lee, Columbia University, USA*
*Dilip Soman, University of Toronto, Canada*

Consumers' lifespans are filled with a large set of experiences that are task-oriented such as sending a package in the post office or getting a transaction done at a bank. Often times there are physi-cal or temporal gaps between the point where the individual starts to engage in the activity and the actual activity itself, and these gaps may have multiple effects on individuals' queuing decision or their satisfaction.

Our research shows that in situations like these, an individual's approach towards the final activity might not be continuous, but rather is marked with a discontinuity. In particular, the incidental physical and informational cues in the context surrounding such tasks create discontinuities by serving as a virtual boundary which defines the starting point of the task system. These cues could be embedded within the physical context of the waiting environment such as whether people are inside a designated waiting area, an informational intervention such as an irrelevant sign-in form, or even appropriate semantic cues such as whether the term "wait inside" or "wait outside" is used to refer to the same waiting area. We argue that prior to this boundary, people are outside the system. However, once they pass this virtual boundary, they are inside the system and adopt an implemental *in-system* mindset which can increase their commitment to the task at hand (Gollwitzer 1999). Further, we propose that this increase in commitment is also characterized by a general increase in optimism and action orientation.

We conducted five experiments using a variety of incidental cues in different waiting environments to test our hypotheses.

In experiment 1, participants were asked to assume that they were waiting in the post office to send a small package. We manipulated an incidental physical cue (the presence and length of a queue-guide next to the queue) at three levels: no guide, short guide which excluded the participant, and long guide which included the participant; participants in all three conditions always stood in the same position of the queue. We found that participants in the long-guide condition (and had thus crossed the virtual boundary) were more likely to stay in the line rather than pay for immediate service, showing increased commitment to the task at hand.

In experiment 2, we investigated the interaction between two different informational cues in a visa-application scenario with a 2 (Waiting Time: Integrated vs. Segregated) x 2 (Immediate Start: Yes vs. No) between-subjects design, while holding the total waiting time for the visa application constant. The result showed that participants indicated a stronger commitment to the visa-application process when the waiting was segregated into three small waits which helped them cross the virtual boundary earlier, compared with a long integrated waiting. However, when an initial registration upon arrival was added to the beginning of the waiting such that participants perceived themselves to start immediately and thus increased their overall commitment, the difference between integrated and segregated waiting was attenuated.

In experiments 3–5, we employed real-waiting scenarios and tested the underlying mechanism through measuring participants' optimism and action orientation. In all three studies, participants were told that the experimental session was divided into two parts and they had to wait after the first part for the experimenter to set up the second part.

Experiment3 used a 2 (Waiting Location: Old Room vs. New Room) x 2 (Timing of Consent for the Second Session: First vs. Last) between-subjects design, and the second part of the session was supposed to be in the new room in all conditions. We found that for participants who waited in the old room, signing the consent form first led to a more optimistic estimation of the time needed to complete the second part of the session, compared with signing the consent form after answering the time-prediction question. However, this effect was attenuated for participants who were already waiting in the new room and thus already had increased commitment.

In experiment 4, we adopted a 2 (Semantic Frame: Waiting vs. No Waiting) x 2 (Membership Badge: Yes vs. No) between-subjects design. The results showed that when we framed the time spent on the filler task before the focal study as waiting, wearing a member badge led to significantly more optimistic estimation for the time needed to complete the focal study compared with not wearing such a badge. However, if the time on the filler task was not framed as waiting, this effect was attenuated. Further, we observed the same result pattern for participants' CRT scores (Frederick 2005), showing that increased commitment was also characterized by increased cognitive effort and action orientation.

In experiment 5, we asked all participants to wait in the same waiting area for the second part of the study session to be ready, but framed it as "waiting *inside* the waiting area", or "waiting *outside* in the waiting area" (relative to the study room). The results showed that people who perceived themselves to be waiting "inside" (vs. "outside") were more optimistic in two unrelated tasks—they predicted a higher chance of hitting a golf ball into a hole, and preferred riskier gamble options. Further, people with an "inside" mindset were more likely to choose a computer from a given set compared to people with an "outside" mindset who were more likely to defer their choice. These results showed that people who crossed the virtual boundary adopt an in-system mindset, leading to greater action orientation and optimism in general, even in unrelated task domains.

Overall, the results in this work provided convergent evidence for the effect of incidental cues in the waiting environment on task commitment, optimism, and action orientation. These findings add to literature on the effect of incidental cues on judgment and behavior, the goal literature, as well as the queuing literature.

SPECIAL SESSION
# Do Consumers Get the Message? An Examination of How Consumers Respond to Health Information

Maura L. Scott, University of Kentucky, USA
Katherine E. Loveland, Arizona State University, USA

## EXTENDED ABSTRACTS

### "Effects of Decisional Status and Construal Level on the Persuasiveness of Health-Related Messages and Products"

Gergana Y. Nenkov, Boston College, USA
J. Jeffrey Inman, University of Pittsburgh, USA

Many products and messages in the marketplace emphasize important health-related goals that consumers might achieve by consuming them–e.g., nutrition, fitness, weight loss. Some products and messages, however, are described using high levels of construal, whereas others are described using low-levels. For instance, Kellogg's *Smart Start®* line of cereals are all positioned as nutritional, but some are called *Healthy Heart*, emphasizing the reason for getting nutrition (high-level construal), while others are called *Antioxidants*, emphasizing the means of getting nutrition (low-level construal). An important question arises regarding which construal level will be more effective in persuading consumers to choose a particular product or perform a particular behavior (Lee, Keller, and Sternthal 2009). Building on construal level theory (e.g., Trope, Liberman, and Wakslak 2007), behavior identification theory (Vallacher and Wegner 1987), and the mindset theory of action phases (e.g., Gollwitzer 1990) we argue that the differential cognitive tuning created by pre- vs. post-decisional mindsets make consumers in the pre- vs. post-decisional action phase differentially receptive to messages framed using different construals.

Four studies examine the interactive effects of pre- and post-decisional status and construal level on the persuasiveness of health-related messages and products. We find that consumers in the pre-decisional action phase are more persuaded by health-related messages described using high-level construal, whereas consumers in the post-decisional phase are more persuaded by messages described using low-level construal. We test our thesis by manipulating construal level directly and indirectly, employing different targets, and examining several aspects of persuasion-choice (study 1), anticipated effortful goal pursuit (study 2), behavioral intentions (study 3), and actual behavior (study 4). We provide process evidence and show that consumers at the pre- vs. post-decisional action phase identify their goals and behaviors at different construal levels.

In study 1 (n=150) participants choose between two products promoting the same goal (i.e., nutrition), with one product stressing the abstract aspects of the goal–why one should obtain nutrition (i.e., "HEALTHY HEART: For a long and healthy life"), and the other stressing its concrete aspects–how one can obtain it (i.e., "ANTI-OXIDANTS: with Antioxidants A, C, and E, and Beta Carotene"). Participants in a deliberative (i.e., predecisional) mindset were more likely to choose the product positioned in terms of abstract construals; those in an implemental (i.e., post-decisional) mindset exhibited preference for the product positioned in concrete construals.

In study 2 (n=175) we extend previous findings by examining a different aspect of persuasion, a different construal manipulation, and a new dependent variable –anticipated effortful goal pursuit. Participants saw a brochure featuring a persuasive argument about weight control emphasizing either why one should control their weight or how one can control it. Results revealed that deliberative (implemental) mindset participants are more persuaded to pursue

the goal and anticipate more effortful goal pursuit in the high-level (low-level) construal condition.

In study 3 (n=103) we explore the effects of social distance construal framing on behavioral intentions, and test our proportion that consumers in the pre- vs. post-decisional action phases construe their goals and behaviors at different levels of construal. Participants evaluated one of two ads for a healthy product (orange juice), targeted at either a close (i.e., your family, low-level) or distant (i.e., families nationwide, high-level) construal. Participants in a predecision mindset were more persuaded to buy the product by the high-level construal ad, whereas those in the postdecision mindset were more persuaded by the low-level construal ad. Consumers in a predecisional, deliberative mindset are more likely to construe behaviors in abstract, high levels.

In study 4 (n=47) we employ temporal construal and examine whether its differential effect for people in a deliberative vs. implemental mindset would affect their behavior. Individuals participated in a study that purportedly examined decision making processes, whose purpose was to prime deliberative and implemental mindsets; in exchange, $5 would be donated to a foundation in their name. One foundation was described using high-level (i.e., future) construals, and the other was described using low-level (i.e., present) construals. Participants in a deliberative (implemental) mindset allocated significantly more money to the foundation described using future (present) construal framing, providing convergent support for our predictions.

This paper contributes to two emerging streams in consumer research–one examining the effectiveness of messages and information represented at low- vs. high-levels of construal (Kim, Rao, and Lee 2009; Lee, Keller, and Sternthal 2009) and another studying the effects of action phase mindsets on consumer behavior (Chandran and Morwitz 2005; Cheema and Patrick 2008; Dhar, Huber, and Khan 2007). It also makes important contributions to the literature on action phase mindsets (see e.g., Gollwitzer 1990) by empirically demonstrating that predecisional consumers construe information at high level, whereas postdecisional ones construe information at low-levels. Finally, findings from the current set of studies offer important implications for the design and presentation of health-related products and persuasive messages, suggesting that products and messages should be framed at a different level of construal when targeting consumers at the different stages of their decision-making process.

### "When 1-in-3 is Greater than 4-in-10: Why Lower Probability Events Can Be More Persuasive in Public Service Announcements"

Ann Schlosser, University of Washington, USA

Using ratios in public service announcements (PSAs) is a common tactic to persuade individuals of the seriousness of an issue and motivate them to act. I argue that the numbers used to represent a probability can influence consumers' beliefs about the seriousness of a problem and their willingness to act. Specifically, I propose that when events are represented in ratios using very small numbers (denominators<5), consumers perceive a problem to be more serious and are more willing to act than when ratios use large numbers (denominators ≥ 10). This is because ratios using small numbers (e.g., 1-in-4) are easier to visualize than larger ratios (e.g., 25-in-100).

People can process information using images or analytically (Epstein 1991; Green and Brock 2000). Imagery processing involves encoding information in the form of concrete, imagistic, and sensory representations, whereas discursive processing involves encoding information as abstract symbols, words, and numbers (MacInnis and Price 1987). Because of their different foci, they can lead to different outcomes (Schlosser 2003). People tend to perceive greater risk when ratios are in larger than smaller ratios (Pinto-Pradas et al. 2006; Yamagashi 1997). Although this may appear to contradict the predictions given here, the "small"-numbered ratios used previously had denominators of 10 or more. I propose that it is difficult to vividly imagine 10 or more people, hence people use discursive rather than imagery processing (i.e., focus on numbers). In the present studies, small-numbered ratios have denominators less than five.

In study 1, participants imagined a serious virus (worse than H1N1) that the Health Department wants to inform the public about. They were given three different pairs of ratios (in randomized order) and indicated which of the two made the incidence seem worse to them. The pairs were (1) 1-in-3 vs. 4-in-10 (or 6-in-15), (2) 1-in-3 vs. 35-in-100, and (3) 35-in-100 vs. 4-in-10 (or 6-in-15). If the paired comparison includes 1-in 3, which is easier to visualize and thus should seem more serious than large-numbered ratios, then more participants would select the 1-in-3 ratio as worse than 4-in-10, 6-in-15 and 35-in-100, although it represents a lower probability (i.e., 33% vs. 40% and 35%). For the third pair involving comparing two relatively large numbers, I expected that individuals would rely on discursive processing and thus more individuals would perceive the 35-in-100 ratio to be worse (because 35>4 and 6). All participants were given three pairs of ratios and were randomly assigned to (1) the order of presentation for the three pairs of ratios, and (2) whether 40% was 4-in-10 or 6-in-15. The ratio for 40% was varied to examine whether the ease in comparing the ratios numerically would alter the results. It did not. As predicted, over 59% of participants found the 1-in-3 probability of illness to be worse than a 4-in-10, 6-in-15, and 35-in-100 chance of contracting the illness. In contrast, over 80% of participants chose the 4-in-10 and 6-in-15 options over the 35-in-100 option. It may be that processing large-numbered ratios discursively caused participants to correctly identify the higher-probability ratio.

In studies 2 and 3, participants received a single ratio in a PSA and then indicated how serious the problem seemed and their willingness to act. In study 2, participants were randomly assigned to one of four PSAs titled "Skin cancer affects X in Y Americans" where "X in Y" was a smaller- or larger- ratio reflecting 25% (1-in-4, 25-in-100) or 30% (3-in-10, 30-in-100). All other information was the same. I expected that by encouraging discursive processing and thus a focus upon the first number in the ratio, participants would perceive melanoma to be more serious and be more willing to take preventative actions in the 30-in-100 than 3-in-10 condition. In contrast, by encouraging imagery processing and thus a focus upon the few people *un*affected, the 1-in-4 ad should persuade individuals of the seriousness of the problem and motivate them to act. Participants' perceptions of the problem and willingness to act should be as high if not higher in the 1-in-4 than 25-in-100 and 3-in-10 conditions. The results support these predictions.

Study 3 extends the findings of the first two by testing the role of imagery processing in explaining the effects. Specifically, participants were presented with a drunk-driving PSA and told that either 3-in-10 or 30-in-100 cars will be involved in a drunk-driving accident. In addition they were either encouraged to visualize being in one of the 10 (vs. 100) cars or not. Replicating the results of

study 2, when imagery processing was *not* encouraged, perceptions of the problem and willingness to act were higher when the ratio was 30-in-100 than 3-in-10. In contrast, when imagery processing was encouraged, perceptions of the problem and willingness to act were higher when the ratio was 3-in-10 than 30-in-100.

Collectively, the results suggest that when designing PSAs with ratios, the numbers used have important implications for consumers' beliefs about the seriousness of an issue and their willingness to act. The results also suggest that imagery processing plays an important role in whether smaller-numbered ratios will be more or less persuasive than larger-numbered ratios.

## "The Effect of Model Size and Self-Awareness on Health Message Compliance"

*Katherine E. Loveland, Arizona State University, USA*
*Elizabeth Gelfand Miller, Boston College, USA*
*Naomi Mandel, Arizona State University, USA*

In recent years, obesity incidence has risen in the United States (cdc.gov). One way that the government has tried to address this issue is through the use of public service announcements (PSA) promoting a healthier lifestyle. We examine how external cues, such as these PSAs, interact with consumer characteristics to influence healthy food choices. We predict two factors are most likely to impact the effectiveness of a health message: the visual cue provided by the body type of the model that is paired with the message and the consumer's level of self-awareness (SA) at the time of message exposure. Previous work is inconclusive regarding the impact of heavy vs. thin others on consumption. Campbell and Mohr (2009) demonstrated that exposure to an overweight prime, as compared to a normal weight prime, leads to increased consumption, suggesting that the use of a heavy model will lead to less healthful choices. Other work has demonstrated that exposure to thin primes, compared to neutral primes, can lead to increased consumption (e.g. Mills et al. 2002; Seddon and Berry 1996; Strauss et al. 1994). This suggests that the use of a thin model will lead to less healthful choices. We propose that one reason for these earlier contradictory findings is that the effect of model size on consumption decisions should vary based on SA level.

While previous work in the area of SA has demonstrated that compliance is generally higher when SA is high, as compared to low (c.f. Carver 2003), we predict that SA is likely to interact with model size, due to the automatic social comparison that occurs when individuals are exposed to a comparison standard. Additionally, since higher levels of SA lead to more accurate assessments of the self (Pryor et al. 1977), the social comparison information provided by a thin (or heavy) model will be interpreted differently depending on the level SA. Specifically, because college-aged females are often relatively thin, when SA is high, exposure to a thin (vs. heavy) model should allow participants to make a realistic assessment of how they are similar to the thin model, leading to higher body-esteem and consequently higher message compliance. On the other hand, because most young women feel constant pressure to be thinner, regardless of how thin they actually are, when SA is low, exposure to a thin (vs. heavy) model should lead consumers to judge themselves overly harshly by focusing on how they are different from the thin model, leading to lower body self-esteem and subsequently lower message compliance.

In study 1, 178 students participated for partial course credit. Participants were randomly assigned in a 2 (level of SA: high vs. low) x 4 (model size: thin, moderately heavy, obese, or no model) design. All participants viewed an ad with the same written content, emphasizing the importance of eating a healthful diet and giving specific tips on how to make healthful food decisions; the size of the model paired with the message varied by condition. Next, participants selected snacks that they would like for the coming week from 10 pretested options, in which 5 were healthful (e.g. trail mix) and 5 were not (e.g. potato chips). In the low SA condition, participants selected the most healthful snacks when an obese model was depicted. In the high SA condition, participants selected the most healthful snacks when a thin model was depicted.

In study 2, 203 female students participated. The design was similar to study 1; however, SA was manipulated using mirrors and included an "escape" condition. We found a significant main effect for SA ($F(2, 191)=4.02$, $p<.05$), as well as a significant interaction between model size and level of SA ($F(6, 191)=2.54$, $p<.05$) on message compliance (as measured by plans to consume a healthful diet in the coming week). Planned comparison revealed several interesting findings. Self-awareness only affected responses when a thin model was present, suggesting that SA only plays a role in message compliance when there is a relevant social comparison standard present. When SA was high and a thin model was pictured, participants were significantly more likely to comply with the message compared to when SA was low and a thin model was pictured. These findings were fully mediated by Body Self-Esteem (BSE, Franzoi and Shields 1984).

Our results suggest that the way in which social comparison information is processed, and its subsequent impact on message compliance for PSAs, varies based on level of SA. When SA is high, using a thin model leads to assimilative processing, leading to higher BSE and subsequently higher message compliance in the form of more healthful food choices. When SA is low, using a thin model leads to contrastive processing, leading to lower BSE, and subsequently lower compliance. As the results from studies 1 and 2 show some discrepancies, we are collecting data in a third study in which BMI and weight locus of control are measured as possible moderators.

### "The Effects of Vanity Sizing on Self-esteem and Shopping Behavior"

*Darren Dahl, University of British Columbia, Canada*
*JoAndrea Hoegg, University of British Columbia, Canada*
*Andrea Morales, Arizona State University, USA*
*Maura L. Scott, University of Kentucky, USA*

Consumers experience pressure to look thin from a variety of sources (Abramowitz 2007) and this can affect self-esteem (Smeesters and Mandel 2006). In a recent study, 89% of girls 13–17 indicated that the *fashion industry* placed "a lot of pressure on girls to be thin" and 75% stated fashion is very important to them (Salamond 2010). Consumers are also getting larger; 67% of Americans are overweight or obese (CDC 2008). In response, many retailers adapt clothing sizes (Kinley 2003). Vanity sizing refers to companies adjusting "the measurement specifications for each size [of a garment] to enable consumers to fit into smaller sizes" (Alexander et al. 2005).

"Fashion can be viewed as how one would like to be (the ideal self) vs. how one really is (the actual self)" (Kinley 2003); hence vanity sizing can be compared to the notion of an "ego size." Consumers use the ego size as a reference point, which can be inconsistent from retailer to retailer, and deviations from this reference point can influence consumers differently depending on their self-esteem. Consumers with low body image self-esteem may be more aware of food/nutrition information, their own weight and size, and reflect a magnified response to the effects of clothing size variation. Awareness of their own size leads to a strong reference point from which to compare oneself and leads to expectancy disconfirmation (positive or negative) in the face of vanity sizing or inflated sizing

(e.g., clothing that is perceived to 'run small'). In some cases, this heightens the consumer's resolve to purchase something, namely a non-sized product. Individuals with high body image self-esteem have confidence in their appearance and are likely to be less tied to "numbers;" hence, they are not upset when sizes change.

Our research examines the benefits and drawbacks of varying clothing sizes. We examine the moderating effect of different types of self-esteem on consumers' responses to clothing sizes. Four experiments demonstrate that consumers' attitude toward the retailer, purchase intentions, and loyalty vary depending on clothing size variations and body-esteem. Study 1 establishes the basic effect that consumers are affected both positively and negatively by clothing size. Studies 2 and 3 demonstrate the moderating effects of different types of self-esteem on a consumer's response to size variations. Study 4 demonstrates that vanity sizing may not be effective if people are suspicious of marketing tactics. Our findings both highlight the importance of using vanity sizing strategically as well as show the negative impact of "inflated" sizes.

Study 1 was a one-way (size: smaller, larger) between subjects experiment. Participants recorded six body measurements using a tape-measure and a mirror, and provided the measurements to the administrator. The administrator cross-checked each measurement with a fictitious size chart, then gave participants either a smaller or larger suit size. Participants in larger suit size conditions had a significantly less favorable impression of the retailer and lower purchase intention, relative to those in the smaller size condition. We demonstrate that the numeric clothing size label is important to consumers, beyond whether or not the clothing fits.

Study 2 was a 2(size: smaller, larger) x (body image–continuous) design. We found a significant interaction between body esteem and clothing size on impression of the retailer and the suit. In the larger size conditions, people with lower body esteem exhibited more negative attitudes toward the clothing and the retailer. We demonstrate the impact of clothing sizes on preferences, and show the moderating effect of body-esteem. Study 3 tests whether specifically body-esteem or any self-esteem boost would mitigate the effects of vanity sizing. Study 3 was a 2(size: smaller, larger) x 2(esteem: body, intelligence), between subjects experiment. We created a physical store with various products available. Participants tried on jeans labeled in their typical size (labels were adjusted, so the jeans would be larger or smaller) and other sizes. We find that only body-esteem, rather than any type of self esteem, can counter the effects of vanity sizing. Individuals primed with high body image self esteem were not affected by vanity sizing.

Study 4 was a 2(size: smaller, larger) x 2(suspicion: yes, no) between subjects experiment. To manipulate suspicion, participants either read a neutral article or one suggesting that marketers manipulate information to sell products. We find that suspicion reduces the influence of vanity sizing; suspicious participants were less affected by vanity- or inflated-sizing relative to their unsuspicious counterparts.

Our research contributes to the body-esteem and consumption behavior literature. Extant literature has examined dis-/confirmation from reference points such as the media (Smeesters et al. 2010) or others consumers (McFerran et al. 2009); we provide new knowledge on how consumers behave when the reference point is one's own clothing

# Standards and Construction of Hedonic Value

Meng Zhu, Carnegie Mellon University, USA
Carey Morewedge, Carnegie Mellon University, USA

## EXTENDED ABSTRACT

### "The AB Identification Survey: Identifying Absolute versus Relative Determinants of Happiness"

*Christopher K. Hsee, University of Chicago, USA*
*Adelle X. Yang, University of Chicago, USA*

Some variables are inherently evaluable and others are inherently inevaluable. To say that a variable is inherently evaluable (for simplicity, call it a type A variable), we mean that human beings have an innate, shared and stable scale to assess which level of the variable is desirable and which is not (ambient temperature, amount of sleep, etc); to say that a variable is inherently inevaluable (type B), we mean that human beings have no innate scale to gauge its desirability and in order to evaluate its desirability one must rely on external reference information, such as social comparison (the size of a diamond, the horsepower of a car, etc).

The distinction between type A and type B variables carries important social implications. For instance, improving the value of a type A variable for all the members in a society will absolutely raise the happiness of all, whereas improving the value of a type B variable for all the members in a society is merely a zero sum game and will not raise the happiness of all. Therefore from a congregate point of view, policymakers should direct the resources to improving type A variables in order to increase happiness across time.

In this paper we propose the AB Identification Survey (ABIS), a simple and practical method to identify whether a given a variable is type A or type B. The procedure of the ABIS is as follows. Suppose that we wish to identify whether a given variable X, say men's height, is type A or type B, assuming that greater X is more desirable and that the average X value in the given population is $x_m$, for example, the average height of men is 5'9". ABIS consists of two versions, the JE version and the simulated-SE version. Each version is simple and contains only two questions. The JE version reads as follows:

1. How tall are you? ____
2. As you may know, some men are tall and others are short, and men's average height is about 5'9". Given that, how do you feel about your height? Give a number between 1 (very unhappy) and 7 (very happy): _____

The simulated-SE version reads as follows:

1. How tall are you? ____
2. Suppose that you were living in a society where *every man were of your height*. Given that, how would you feel about your height? Give a number between 1 (very unhappy) and 7 (very happy): _____

Recruit a sample of men (whose height distribution should be representative of that of the target population) and ask half the sample to answer the JE version of ABIS and the other half the simulated-SE version.

After data are collected, run two regressions. One regresses the happiness ratings from the JE version of ABIS on the target variable X (e.g., height) and control variables, if any. The other regresses the happiness ratings from the Simulated-SE version of ABIS on X and control variables, if any. Let $\beta_{JE}$ and $\beta_{Simulated-SE}$ denote the estimated regression coefficients of X from the two models, respectively. Then we can simply use the following formula to identify whether X is type A or type B: AB coefficient=$\beta_{Simulated-SE}/\beta_{JE}$.

$\beta_{Simulated-SE}$ reflects the non-comparative effect of X, and $\beta_{JE}$ reflects the total effect of X. Generally speaking, The AB coefficient reflects the size of the non-comparative effect relative to the total effect. The greater the AB coefficient, the more X is a type A variable; the smaller the AB coefficient, the more X is a type B variable.

We report three studies. The first study is a validation study. It compares the results of the ABIS with the results of a cleaner but less practical experimental method and shows that the two studies produce very similar results. In addition, we report two studies to show how to apply this method to identifying a series of naturally occurring variables as type A or type B. The first survey was conducted among 453 undergraduate students, the second among 352 business students with work experiences. Our surveys have revealed interesting findings. For undergraduate students, the two top type A variables are vacation time and winter dorm temperature; the two top type B variables are home size and height (meter). For business students, top type A variables were insomnia and vacation time, and top type B variables are income and car price.

The ABIS can be used to inform policymakers where to invest resources. From the perspective of an individual, improving either type A variables or type B variables will increase happiness: "I will be happier than you if I can afford more comfortable temperature or I can afford more expensive jewelry." For that individual, pursuing both type A and type B variables is rational. But from the perspective of a society, improving type B variables is a zero-sum game and only improving type A variables can improve the happiness of all. Since this distinction applies only at the societal level but not at the individual level, policymakers, rather than individuals, are better suited to distinguish type A and type B variables. ABIS is an instrument they can use in this endeavor.

### "Social Standards and the Construction of Hedonic Value"

*Meng Zhu, Carnegie Mellon University, USA*
*Carey Morewedge, Carnegie Mellon University, USA*
*Daniel Gilbert, Harvard University, USA*
*Kristian Myrseth, ESMT, Germany*
*Karim Kassam, Carnegie Mellon University, USA*
*Timothy Wilson, University of Virginia, USA*

A contrast effect occurs when a standard of comparison influences judgment of a target stimulus, such that the target is considered less like the standard when in its presence than when judged in the absence of that standard. Contrast effects are prevalent in noetic (information based judgments) and psychophysics, yet the evidence for hedonic contrast effects has been mixed (Novemsky & Ratner 2003). We develop an attentional model to explain when and why comparative value influences hedonic value. Specifically, we propose that hedonic contrast effects are particularly elusive in experience because forecasters fail to account for (1) attentional requirements of comparison, as noticing the difference between a standard and a target requires considerable cognitive resources; (2) different attentional requirement of forecasting vs. experience—forecasters' mental representations of experiences consume fewer resources than having the forecasted experience. Thus, we predict that comparative value will influence hedonic experiences when experiences are unengaging or when comparisons are easy to make. We report four experiments that tested our theory by examining how social comparison, which is automatic, well-practiced and often occurs without conscious awareness, influences hedonic value and decision making. We predict that social standards will evoke hedonic contrast effects in situations where nonsocial standard don't.

Study 1 tested whether social standards produce a greater influence on hedonic value and whether forecasters can correctly predict this difference. Participants were presented two food items, Lay's Potato Chips (target food) and another item (standard food), either Godiva Raspberry Chocolate (better standard) or King Oscar canned sardines (worse standard). We manipulated social comparison by telling half of the participants that they will be paired with another participant in the same experiment session and each of them will be randomly assigned to sample different food item (partner condition). The other half of the participants were simply assigned to evaluate one of the two food items (no-partner condition). All participants were then assigned by computer to evaluate the target food (potato chips). Experiencers reported how much they enjoyed eating chips and forecasted predicted how much they would enjoy eating chips. As predicted, experiencers in the partner condition rated chips more enjoyable when their partner was assigned to sardines as compared to chocolate, whereas in the no-partner condition, experiencers enjoyed chips the same no matter what the alternative food was. However, forecasters predicted that hedonic contrasts would occur in both the partner and no-partner conditions.

To test whether social standards are more influential because comparing to social standards requires fewer attentional resources, Study 2 employed a 2(cognitive load: low vs. high) x 2(standard food: chocolate vs. sardines) design. All participants were paired with another participant and assigned to evaluate chips. To manipulate cognitive load, participants were asked to remember a series of number and letter, either B4 (low load condition) or 8K3YW17L (high load condition) while performing the food evaluation task. In the low load condition, participants enjoyed chips more when their partner was assigned to sardines than chocolate. However, in the high load condition, enjoyment of chips was the same regardless of the standard. These results are consistent with our attention based explanation showing that hedonic contrasts are attenuated when experiencers don't have enough cognitive resource to pay attention to other people and compare their experiences. Study 3 examined whether hedonic contrast occurs because people compare their experience to the alternative enjoyed by another person or because they compare their imagined happiness to another person. In doing so, we manipulated the modality of standards. We predict that social standards of a different modality will have a weaker effect on the target experience, as it is more difficult to compare to standards of a different modality rather than standards of the same modality. All participants were assigned to eat potato chips and their partners were assigned to experience a superior or inferior alternative. Half of the participants were told that their partners were experiencing either chocolate or sardines (same modality condition); whereas others were told that their partners were listening to a sound clip of either jungle waterfall or vacuum cleaner (different modality condition), which was rated in a pre-test as being as pleasant as chocolate or sardines. We found that hedonic contrast occurred only when partners were experiencing easy-to compare same-modality alternatives, thus supporting our theorization that social standards produce a greater influence on hedonic value because social comparisons are easier not because they are fundamentally different.

Study 4 directly tested whether social comparison can lead to suboptimal decisions. We predict that a superior social standard

can lead people to choose a lower –value, difficult-to-compare option than a higher-value, easy-to-compare option. Upon arrival, participants were paired with another participant and completed an animal trivial. Participants were then asked to choose a prize from a set of four prizes—two from a superior category (chocolates: Godiva & Hershey's) and two from an inferior category (snack bars: Granola Bar & Power Bar). Results from a separate pretest indicated that Godiva was ranked as the best prize, Hershey's was ranked as the 2nd best, Granola Bar was ranked as the 3rd best, and Power Bar was ranked as the worst prize to get for participating in a psychology experiment. In the social comparison condition, participants were told that their partner was randomly assigned to choose first and Godiva was no longer available after being chosen by the partner. In the control, participants was simply asked to choose a prize and told that Godiva was out of stock. Consistent with our prediction, we found that participants in the social condition were more likely to choose the inferior Granola Bar instead of Hershey's than the control.

## "Absolute and Relative Choices of Maximizers and Satisficers"

*Kimberlee Weaver, Virginia Tech, USA*
*Norbert Schwarz, University of Michigan, USA*
*Kim Daniloski, Virginia Tech, USA*
*Keenan Cottone, University of Michigan USA*

According to the theory of bounded rationality, cognitive and situational limitations can prevent individuals from optimizing or "maximizing" the outcome of many decisions (Simon 1955). Recently, Schwartz et al. (2002) extended these theoretical insights into an individual differences scale. "Maximizers" are consumers who exhaustively examine every possibility before deciding which choice is best, while "satisficers" are more likely to choose the first available option that meets a threshold of acceptability. In the current paper, we investigate a new question that past work has not considered: whether maximizers and satisficers not only differ in the amount of effort they put forth in trying to achieve their standards, but whether they also differ in the *type* of standard they choose to pursue in consumer choice situations. Past work has remained agnostic about which type of standard maximizers and satisficers emphasize when making decisions (Schwartz et al. 2002; Simon 1955). However, there has been an implicit assumption that maximizers and satisficers are aspiring toward the *same* standard, and that the major difference between the two types of decision makers is in the amount of effort they expend in trying to achieve it, with maximizers expending more effort and satisficers truncating the search process at an earlier point. In contrast to this implicit assumption, our major hypothesis in the current paper is that maximizers and satisficers may actually aspire toward different standards; with maximizers being more interested in pursuing the relative best, and satisficers more interested in pursuing the absolute best.

Generally speaking, there are two types of standards that consumers can use when judging what is "best": *absolute* standards and *relative* standards. To illustrate this distinction, imagine that a consumer can choose to live in one of two possible worlds. In World A, she will drive a car that is a medium quality brand rated 7/10 in parts and performance by Automotive Weekly. Nearly all of her acquaintances will drive cars that are luxury models rated 9/10. In World B, she will drive a car that is a fair quality brand, rated 6/10 in parts and performance by Automotive Weekly. Nearly all of her acquaintances will drive cars that are low quality models rated 4/10. Consumers who aspire toward an *absolute* standard search for the objectively best outcome and would likely choose to live in World

A, since the car the consumer will have is rated more highly than the car they will have in World B (i.e., 7/10 in parts and performance versus 6/10). On the other hand, consumers who aspire toward a *relative* standard search for an outcome that is best in the relative sense that it exceeds what others have. They would thus prefer to live in World B since the car the consumer will have is better than the cars driven by others (i.e., 6/10 on parts and performance versus 4/10) (Solnick and Hemenway 2005).

Results from three studies confirmed hypotheses by showing that maximizers pursue relative standards more than satisficers. Specifically, study 1 showed that maximizers were more willing than satisficers to accept *objectively worse* products or outcomes when they were paired with superior social position (e.g., Option B above). Studies 2 and 3 sought to establish the psychological mechanism driving the effect by manipulating the public visibility of the decision outcome. If maximizers' emphasis on social comparison reflects a concern for information *about* the absolute standards as proposed by past work (Iyengar et al. 2006; Schwartz et al. 2002), then they should choose the same option regardless of whether the outcome of their decision will be publicly visible or not. In contrast, if maximizers are motivated by social rivalry, then the standards they use may shift from public to private contexts. Both studies showed interactions between the maximizer/satisficer variable and the public visibility variable, supporting the social rivalry explanation. Maximizers accepted objectively inferior products that were paired with superior social position more than satisficers in public (e.g., house, car). However, the two groups of decision makers were equally likely to maximize absolute quality when then outcome was private and known only to the decision maker (e.g., pajamas, brand of mattress). The final study also indicated that maximizers prefer counterfeit products –those that have low internal quality, but have the outside appearance of high quality items—more than satisficers.

In conclusion, the current results examine a new theoretical question that past work has not considered and show that maximizers and satisficers not only differ in the amount of effort they put forth in trying to achieve their standards, but also differ in the *type* of standard they choose to pursue in consumer choice situations, with maximizers emphasizing relative standards and satisficers emphasizing absolute standards. In examining this question we bridge two literatures, the first on maximizing and satisficing in decision making and the other on relative and absolute choices, which has been studied in the decision making, psychology and consumer behavior literatures (e.g., Easterlin, 1974; Huguet, 2009; Zhou & Soman 2003).

### "Integrate or Separate Future Pain? The Impact of Current Pain"

*Eduardo B. Andrade, University of California, Berkeley, USA*
*Marco Aurelio Bianchini, Universidade Federal de Santa Catarina, Brazil*
*Newton Lucchiari, Universidade Federal de Santa Catarina, Brazil*

It is often the case that health-related treatments can take place either in one single, or in two or more, periods (e.g., extract two wisdom teeth). When no clinically dominant option is available, the doctor allows the patient to decide whether to undergo the unpleasant experience all at once or to separate it into multiple events. Although several considerations are at stake, the decision is in part a matter of one's ability to project and willingness to deal with the future painful experience. Interestingly, patients are often not experiencing any level of pain at the time of the decision (e.g., a teenager who, comfortably seated at the plastic surgeon's office, decides to undergo breast and nose surgeries all at once). Two

questions emerge from this type of scenario: (a) do patients prefer to integrate or to separate future painful treatments? And (b) does the current level of pain influence their preference?

In line with previous theoretical suggestions (Kahneman and Tversky 1979; Thaler *1985)*, we hypothesize that patients are more likely to integrate future pain. However, this preference, we argue, is partially due to the fact that they are often not experiencing any pain at the time of the decision. When pain is experienced at the time of the decision, patients might question their capacity to endure the future unpleasantness all at once (Linville and Fischer 1991). Thus, the preference for integration of pain could be reduced when a "sample" of pain is provided directly before patients make their choice.

We tested this possibility in a field experiment in a public dental clinic. Sixty-two patients with periodontal disease in both sides of the mouth (50% male) underwent a sequence of two standard and required dental examinations: one painless (i.e., general clinical exam) and one painful (i.e., pocketing and bleeding on probing exam). Our manipulation simply consisted of randomizing the order of examinations. Half of the patients were randomized to a painless-painful order whereas the order was reversed for the other half. After *each* dental examination, the patients were asked whether they preferred to have the future periodontal therapy (i.e., scaling and root planing in both sides of the mouth) in either one single intervention or in two interventions performed one week apart from one another. The results show that, in general, patients were more likely to integrate than to separate the future painful experience. However, the preference for integration diminished significantly when they experienced mild levels of pain at the time of the decision. Whereas patients, on average, preferred to integrate future pain after a painless examination, preference for integration did not differ from chance when the decision was made after a painful examination. The effect emerged when comparisons were made within and between subjects.

Given that patients' currently experienced pain can so easily influence their choice, health professionals should be aware of such effects when delegating the choice of future painful experiences to patients. Finally, it is an open question whether visceral information about pain at the time of decision can help patients make choices about integration versus separation with which they will, in retrospect, be more satisfied.

### REFERENCES

Easterlin, R. A. (1974), "Does Economic Growth Improve the Human Lot? Some Empirical Evidence," in *Nations and Households in Economic Growth,* P.A. David and M.W. Reder, eds. New York and London: Academic Press.

Huguet P, Dumas F, Marsh H, Wheeler L, Seaton M, Nezlek J, Suls J, & Régner I. (2009), "Clarifying the Role of Social Comparison in the Big-Fish-Little-Pond Effect (BFLPE): An Integrative Study," *Journal of Personality and Social Psychology,* 97 (July), 156-170.

Iyengar, S. S. Wells, R. E., & Schwartz, B. (2006). Doing Better But Feeling Worse: Looking for the "Best" Job Undermines Satisfaction. *Psychological Science,* 17 (February), 143-150.

Linville, P., & Fischer, G. *(1991).* Preferences for separating or combining events. *Journal of Personality and Social Psychology,* 60, 5–23

Loewenstein, G., O'Donoghue, T. and Rabin, M. (2003). Projection bias in predicting future utility. Quarterly Journal of Economics, 118, 1209-1248.

Gilbert, D. T., & Wilson, T. D. (2007). Prospection: Experiencing the future. *Science, 317,* 1351-1354.

Hsee, C. K. & Zhang, J. (2004). Distinction bias: Misprediction and mischoice due to joint evaluation. *Journal of Personality and Social Psychology, 86,* 680-695.

Kahneman, D., & Miller, D. T. (1986). Norm theory: Comparing reality to its alternatives. *Psychological Review, 93,* 136–153.

Kahneman, D., & Tversky, A. *(1979).* Prospect theory: An analysis of decision. Econometrica, 47(2), 263-291.

Medvec, V. H., Madey, S. F., & Gilovich, T. (1995). When less is more: Counterfactual thinking and satisfaction among Olympic medalists. *Journal of Personality and Social Psychology, 69,* 603-610.

Novemsky, N., & Ratner, R. K. (2003). The time course and impact of consumers' erroneous beliefs about hedonic contrast effects. *Journal of Consumer Research, 29,* 507-516.

Parducci, A. (1995). *Happiness, pleasure, and judgment: The contextual theory and its applications.* Mahwah, NJ: Lawrence Erlbaum Associates.

Schwartz, B. Ward, A. Monterosso, J. Lyubomirsky, S. White, K., Lehman, D. R. (2002). Maximizing versus satisficing: Happiness is a matter of choice. *Journal of Personality and Social Psychology,* 83 (November), 1178-1197.

Simon, H. A. (1955), "A behavioral model of rational choice," *Quarterly Journal of Economics,* 59, 99-118.

Solnick, S. J., & Hemenway, D. (2005), "Are positional concerns stronger in some domains than in others?" *American Economic Review, 95, 147-151.*

Thaler, R. H. (1985), Mental accounting and consumer choice, *Marketing Science,* 4 199-214.

Zellner, D. A., Rohm, E. A., Bassetti, T. L., and Parker, S. (2003). Compared to what? Effects of categorization on hedonic contrast. *Psychonomic Bulletin & Review, 10,* 468-473.

Zhou, R. & Soman D. (2003), "Looking Back: Exploring the Psychology of Queuing and the Effect of the Number of People Behind," *Journal of Consumer Research,* 29 (March), 517-530.

# Constraining the Consumption Environment to Enhance Consumer Creativity

Anne-Laure Sellier, New York University, USA

## EXTENDED ABSTRACTS

### "The Influence of Ambient Noise on Creative Cognition and Behavior"

*Ravi Mehta, University of British Columbia, Canada*
*Rui (Juliet) Zhu, University of British Columbia, Canada*
*Amar Cheema, University of Virginia, USA*

Recent years have seen a rapid shift in consumer markets from being product- and firm- centric to one encouraging consumer involvement in mutual value creation by leveraging consumer creativity (Prahalad and Ramaswamy 2004). In parallel, there has been a surge in research studying various aspects of consumer creativity, such as consumer created content (e.g., Moreau and Herd 2010) and the effects of constraints on consumer creativity (Moreau and Dahl 2009). Our research builds on this research by exploring the effects of an important environmental variable on consumers' creative performance. It is well accepted that consumers' physical surroundings can significantly affect their decisions, whether it is color, aesthetics or ambient scents. We focus on one aspect of physical surroundings that has received less attention –ambient noise.

Although ambient noise is always present in consumption contexts, its effects on cognition and behavior are not well-understood. Our research contributes to this literature by exploring the underlying process through which noise may affect creative cognition. Specifically, we examine how different levels of background noise may affect consumer creativity and behavior.

We propose that moderate compared to low levels of noise can actually enhance creativity. Based on prior research (e.g., Nagar and Pandey 1987), we theorize that a higher noise level distracts individuals and increases processing difficulty, which causes individuals to process more abstractly (Alter and Oppenheimer 2008). Because empirical work on construal level has shown that abstract construal enhances creative performance (e.g., Smith 1995), we hypothesize that a moderate level of ambient noise may increase processing difficulty, activate an abstract construal level, which subsequently may enhance creativity. Our experiments provide systematic support to our theorizing.

In our research, we only use moderate (70 dB) and low (50 dB) levels of noise intensity. Although prior research has also used high noise levels (e.g., 95 dB, Nagar and Pandey 1987), such high intensity is (1) unlikely to be sustainable in a consumer environment and (2) has constantly shown negative effects across various studies and variety of tasks (e.g., Nagar and Pandey 1987). Consequently, high noise levels were excluded from our study. In addition to intensity, different types of noises have been used in past research, such as white noise, pink noise, jet engine noises, and incessant ringing of alarm clocks. In the present research, we blend a combination of different types of ambient noises to create a soundtrack of constantly varying background noise.

In Study 1, we test our main hypothesis that a moderate (vs. low) level of noise can enhance performance on a creative task. We used Remote Associates Tests as our focal task to measure creativity. Results showed that respondents in the moderate noise condition performed significantly better on Remote Associate Tests compared to respondents in the low noise condition. Study 2 tests our central thesis in a more consumer relevant context. It examines whether a moderate (vs. low) level of noise enhances persuasion when a persuasive message requires creative cognition to comprehend. Results again support our theorizing.

In Study 3 we test our proposition that alternative levels of noise affect the two key dimensions of creativity identified in prior research–novelty and appropriateness-such that a moderate level of noise would enhance both dimensions. In this study, we presented our participants with a dilemma problem and asked them to generate as many solutions as they could think of. In addition, to test the underlying process proposed earlier, we measured processing difficulty and construal level as participants completed the survey. All generated ideas were rated along the novelty and appropriateness dimensions by a separate set of 14 judges each. As hypothesized, ideas generated by those in the moderate (vs. low) noise condition were judged to be significantly higher on both the novelty and appropriateness dimensions. The multiple mediation analysis provided support to our theorizing by demonstrating that a moderate level of noise enhanced processing difficulty which in turn induced a higher construal level, consequently leading to higher ratings on both novelty and appropriateness.

In Study 4, we examine how noise affects individuals' acceptance of creative, innovative products. In our first three studies, we manipulated noise at two levels. However, in real life, consumers come across a wide range of noise intensities. Thus, we conducted this study in a student lounge area and measured ambient noise level when the study sessions were run. Regression analysis revealed that as noise level increased, respondents reported a higher willingness-to-buy for innovative products, that is, they were more likely to accept these products.

### "Restricting Choice of Inputs Increases Creativity for Experienced Consumers"

*Anne-Laure Sellier, New York University, USA*
*Darren Dahl, University of British Columbia, Canada*

Our research explores the influence of input choice set on both consumers' self-perceptions and actual realization of creative output. It questions whether increasing choice of creative inputs (e.g., offering more choice of ingredients for a cook) leads to more creative outcomes.

Theoretically, because increasing choice of inputs offers increasing solution spaces, more choice should increase the likelihood that a more creative solution is produced. Previous investigations support this notion, finding that sufficient input choice plays a positive role in achieving creative outcomes (e.g., Amabile and Gitomer 1984). Consistent with such findings, suppliers of creative inputs (e.g., art stores) display choice options on entire walls; the implicit assumption being that more choice helps when people are selecting inputs for a creative task. Most consumers also believe that more choice is better (Schwartz 2004). It follows that consumers being provided with extensive rather than limited choice of creative inputs should feel more creative (H1).

Focusing on actual creativity, however, we challenge this lay belief to propose that increasing choice hurts creativity. In particular, we test the critical role of input choice in shaping creativity for consumers who are experienced in a creative task. In doing so, we primarily draw on the choice overload literature (e.g., Iyengar and Lepper 2000; Schwartz 2004) to test the prediction that input choice has a dehabilitating effect on experienced consumers' actual creativity, when compared to consumers with limited experience in the creative task (H2). The more choice a consumer has, the less constrained s/he is, and the more likely it is that s/he will retrieve an existing solution to the problem under study (e.g., Park and Smith 1989), thereby sticking to the top-down process described as the "path-of-least-resistance" (POLR, Ward 1994), which leads consumers to adopt a less rather than more creative solution. This adverse effect of choice should only apply to experienced consumers, since they have the domain-relevant skills allowing them to identify the vast number of possible creative solutions in the choice space (Amabile 1983). In contrast, inexperienced consumers are unlikely to be sensitive to a change in the input choice set, and should merely display a general tendency to stick to the POLR. In sum, restricting choice should positively affect creativity for experienced consumers, and have no impact on inexperienced consumers.

Further, we identify that a decrease in enjoyment with the creative process causes the dehabilitating effect of choice (H3). Too much choice has been linked to decision-making paralysis, and generally found to be detrimental to consumers' emotional well-being, particularly when consumers do not know a priori exactly what they want (Schwartz 2004), as is the case with creative outcomes. Restricting choice in creative consumption contexts should be conducive to a more enjoyable and playful creative experience, which in turn should transcend into the creative outcome (e.g., Isen 1999). Again, this positive experience should only affect experienced consumers, for only they are affected by the daunting vastness of creative possibilities.

We tested our predictions in a field study, in which 76 experienced and inexperienced knitters (mean age=29.82 years) created a scarf over a week, after choosing yarn from a limited (6 colors) versus a relatively extensive (12 colors) choice set. At the end of the week, participants returned their completed scarf, reported how creative they thought their scarf was and assessed how pleasant the creative process had been. After all scarves were collected, two experts in creative knitting evaluated the creativity of the scarves (randomized order) through handling and inspection.

Our key findings are that, focusing on the knitters' self-reported measure of creativity, knitters rated their own scarf as less creative under limited rather than extensive choice, in support of H1. In contrast, the averaged knitting experts' creativity ratings (Pearson-$r$=.66, $p$<.01) revealed a very different pattern when it was subjected to a Choice x Knitting level ANOVA. As predicted, we found a significant Choice x Knitting level interaction, $F(1, 72)$=7.75, $p$<.007, $r^2$=10. In support of H2, the analysis of simple effects further revealed that scarves knit by experienced knitters under limited rather than extensive choice were significantly more creative. Scarves knit by inexperienced knitters were equally creative under limited and extensive choice, $t$<1. Finally, in support of H3, we found that the averaged measures of knitters' enjoyment mediated the knitting experts' creativity ratings. Of particular interest, a limited choice made the task more enjoyable for experienced knitters, and that enjoyment led to more objectively rated creativity. We discuss these key findings, as well as other measures further supporting our conceptualization.

### "Designing Memories"
*Kelly B. Herd, University of Colorado, USA*
*C. Page Moreau, University of Colorado, USA*

While constraints can be beneficial, they also have the potential to diminish perceived autonomy during a creative activity. Finding the right balance between structure and freedom in any given creative activity is, therefore, challenging. This research examines an important factor likely to influence where that optimal balance lies. Specifically, we investigate how the purpose for which the creative task is performed influences consumers' creative experiences and evaluations of the creative product. In two studies, we engage participants in creative tasks (customizing a storage box, creating a scrapbook page) during which we either manipulate (Study 1) or

measure (Study 2) the extent to which the created product is intended to hold/capture something special. Both studies demonstrate that constraints have a positive influence on participants' experiences and product evaluations when the purpose of the product is less special. When the purpose is special, however, constraints do not have a positive influence on either measure.

In Study 1, 100 female participants were told that they would be choosing design options for a box, which would then be assembled to their specifications. Two factors were manipulated between-participants: (1) the purpose of the box (functional: "storage box" vs. special: "memory box") and (2) the constraints operating (low vs. high). Upon arriving, participants in the "functional" condition were asked to think about and describe the items they would place in the storage box. Participants in the "special' condition did the same for the memory box.

All participants were given an order form showing a drawing of a plain box indicating all the choices they could make in the customization task. They were then given a packet containing the second manipulation. Participants made 7 design choices. In the "low constraint" condition, the options were arranged in the packet according to the choices they would have to make. (e.g., the wide ribbon on the lid was Option A, and this condition showed all the "A" options on one page). In the "high constraint" condition, the options were presented in eight coordinated arrangements in which all seven customization decisions had already been made. Participants were told that these were merely suggestions, but creating an entirely unique design in this condition required more effort as participants had to search across pages to see all of their options.

Results showed that participants designing storage boxes had a more positive experience than those designing memory boxes. We also found an interaction, such that under high constraints, participants designing storage boxes reported more positive experiences than those designing memory boxes. When low constraints were in place, participants' experiences did not depend on the box's purpose. There was also a main effect of the box's purpose on expectations, such that participants designing storage boxes reported higher expectations than those designing memory boxes. An interaction also emerged: High constraints produced higher expectations for storage boxes than for memory boxes. Under low constraints, expectations did not depend on the box type.

Study 2 was a 2-part study, with 73 female participants. In the first session, participants were given a packet in which they were asked to either (1) think back 4 weeks ("past") or (2) think forward 4 weeks ("future") and to describe (on paper) an experience/event that was (or was expected to be) particularly meaningful, fun, or positive. Participants then indicated how special that event was (or was expected to be). Next, they were they asked to create a scrapbook page capturing that event. All scrapbooking materials were held constant. Participants evaluated their scrapbook pages and left them with us until the second session, 4 weeks later. At that time, participants in both conditions described and evaluated the event their scrapbook page again.

Participants scrapbooking an event that had already occurred were more constrained because the details of the event were fixed (e.g., pictures were or were not taken). Participants scrapbooking a future event could control, to some degree, the details of the event to come. Regression was used to assess the effects of the time manipulation and the measured specialness of the event on evaluations of the scrapbook page. An interaction emerged (F(1, 73)=5.02, p<.05), and a spotlight analysis was used to interpret the results. Those scrapbooking a past event (high constraints) reported higher evaluations of their pages when the event was less special. For those scrapbooking a future event (low constraints), the pattern was reversed. These findings are similar to those observed in Study 1, demonstrating that the specialness of the purpose of a creative activity moderates the effectiveness of constraints.

### "The Blank Page: How Constraining the Creative Task Influences Creative Processes and Outcomes"
*Caneel K. Joyce, London School of Economics, UK*

Freedom and choice are often associated with creativity. Findings from creativity research can be seen as supporting this association, showing that constraints on freedom such as surveillance and a lack of choice can decrease the intrinsic motivation to create (Amabile & Gitomer, 1984; Amabile, 1983). In seeming opposition, decision making research has revealed a "Paradox of Choice" (Schwartz, 2004) in that too much choice can be paralyzing and tends to undermine good judgment and intrinsic motivation (Iyengar & Lepper, 2000). Given that judgment and choice are important, but often-overlooked aspects of creativity, the extent of choice available to a creator regarding which problems to solve and which solutions to consider may have a major impact on the creative process and subsequent outcomes.

This research uses a multi-method approach to examine how constraining a creative task affects creative processes and outcomes. Creative tasks are characterized as more or less constrained, depending the size of the search space the creator is permitted or opts to explore. A search space is bound by constraints that limit the range of options available, and that direct the creator towards certain options over others. In practical terms, such constraints limit the range of problems that may be solved, as well as the range of solutions considered.

Three studies examined the effects of constraint on the creative task where constraint is conceptualized as a continuum. Study 1 was a laboratory experiment centered around a written product design task. First, participants were given a prompt instructing them to do internet research and then use their research to design a product to address some health-related problem. Constraint was manipulated by varying the degree of choice the participant had in defining that problem: The low constraint group could address any health-related issue; the low-moderate constraint group could address any one of five specific health-related issues, the high-moderate, one of three; and the high constraint group was given one specific issue to address. All four groups were given access to the same database of articles for their research, and their search behavior was tracked unobtrusively. All groups had 40 minutes to allocate as they wished between research and writing the product proposal. Proposal creativity was rated using the consensual assessment technique (Amabile, 1983).

Results showed a curvilinear effect of constraint on creativity, such that both the low-moderate and high-moderate constraint groups' product proposals were rated as more creative than either the low or high constraint groups. These effects were not accounted for by alternative explanations such as time allocation during the task, or decreased intrinsic motivation. Analysis of the internet research data found differences in search behavior across groups in search behavior. Specifically, the two moderate constraint groups ran fewer unique searches in the database, spending more time with each search result than either the high or low constraint groups. This suggests that moderate constraint leads to a deeper engagement with new information, and greater certainty about the appropriateness of creative search strategies.

Studies 2 and 3 were field studies that examined the role of constraint in 43 new product development teams. In Study 2, constraint was measured rather than operationalized. Raters scored the limiting aspect of constraint by responding to the question, "What percentage of possible ideas have been eliminated in solving the problem, or the types of solutions that address the problem" on a scale of 1-100%. Higher scores meant the project was more constrained (a greater percentage of all possible ideas being eliminated ex-ante) by virtue of the mission statement sentence. Inter-rater reliability was high (ICC=.80). Raters scored the directing aspect of constraint by responding to the question, "How constrained is the solution the team is trying to make" (ICC=.75). Each team submitted a mission statement for their new product, and two trained raters coded the content from these statements. Through quantitative analysis, Study 2 found that the degree of constraint that new product development teams voluntarily imposed on their projects at the beginning of the semester predicted the creativity of their product proposals more than ten weeks later. The results held up even when controlling for task conflict.

For Study 3, all 43 teams were ranked according to their constraint score as in Study 2 and sorted into high, moderate, and low constraint groups. One team was selected from each group based on the information richness of the data available, and was subjected to case study analysis using interview, observation, and archival data. We examined the data for these three teams. The result was a novel framework conceptualizing creativity as a hypothesis-testing activity.

These three studies suggest that while some amount of choice is important for encouraging creativity, too much can be counterproductive.

## REFERENCES

Alter, A. L., and D. M. Oppenheimer (2008), "Effects of Fluency on Psychological Distance and Mental Construal (or Why New York is a Large City, but New York is a Civilized Jungle)," *Psych. Sci.*, 19, 161-167.

Amabile, T. M. (1983), "The Social Psychology of Creativity: A Componential Conceptualization," *J. of Pers. and Soc. Psych.*, 45(2), 357-76.

Amabile, T. M. and J. Gitomer (1984), "Children's Artistic Creativity: Effects of Choice in Task Materials," *Pers. and Soc. Psych. Bull.*, 10(June), 209-15.

Burroughs, J. E. and D. G. Mick (2004), "Exploring Antecedents and Consequences of Consumer Creativity in a Problem-Solving Context," *J. of Cons. Res.*, 31(2), 402-11.

Dahl, D. W., and C. P. Moreau (2007), "Thinking Inside the Box: Why Consumers Enjoy Constrained Creative Experiences," *J. of Mark. Res.*, 44(August), 357-69.

Isen, A. (1999), "On the Relationship Between Affect and Creative Problem Solving," in S. W. Russ (Ed.), *Affect, Creative Experience and Psychological Adjustment*, Philadelphia: Brunne/Mazel, 3-18.

Iyengar, S. S. and M. R. Lepper (2000), "When Choice is Demotivating : Can One Desire Too Much of a Good Thing?," *J. of Pers. and Soc. Psych.*, 79(6), 995-1006.

Moreau, C. P. and D. W. Dahl, (2009), "Constraints and Consumer Creativity," in A. B. Markman, and Kristin L. Wood (Eds.), *Tools for Innovation: The Science Behind the Practical Methods that Drive New Ideas*, New York: Oxford University Press, 104-27.

Moreau, C. P. and K. B. Herd (2010), "To Each His Own? How Comparisons With Others Influence Consumers' Evaluations of Their Self-Designed Products", *J. of Cons. Res.*, 36 (February), 806-819.

Nagar, D. and J. Pandey (1987), "Affect and Performance on Cognitive Task as a Function of Crowding and Noise," *J. of App. Soc. Psych.*, 17 (2), 147-57.

Park, C. W. and D. Smith (1989), "Product-Level Choice: A Top-Down or Bottom-Up Process?," *J. of Cons. Res.*, 16(December), 289-99.

Prahalad, C.K. and V. Ramaswamy (2004), "Co-Creating Unique Value with Customers," *Strat. & Leadership*, 32 (3), 4-9.

Schwartz, B. (2004), *The Paradox of Choice*, New York: Harper Collins Publishers.

Smith, S. M. (1995), "Fixation, Incubation, and Insight in Memory and Creative Thinking," *The Creative Cognition Approach*, S. M. Smith, T. B. Ward, and R. A. Finke (ed.), Cambridge, MA: MIT Press. pp. 135-156.

Ward, T. B. (1994), "Structured Imagination: The Role of Category Structure in Exemplar Generation," *Cog. Psych.*, 27(1), 1-40.

# Effects of Choice Architecture and Menu Labeling on Food and Beverage Consumption

Jason Riis, Harvard Business School, USA
Janet Schwartz, Duke University, USA

## EXTENDED ABSTRACTS

### "Would You Like to Downsize that Meal? Prompting Self-control Is More Effective than Calorie Labeling in Reducing Calorie Consumption in Fast Food Meals"

*Janet Schwartz, Duke University, USA*
*Jason Riis, Harvard Business School, USA*
*Brian Elbel, New York University, USA*
*Dan Ariely, Duke University, USA*

Concern about rising obesity rates has led several jurisdictions to mandate calorie labeling of all items sold in fast food restaurant chains. Thus far however, such interventions have shown little evidence of influencing consumer choice. Much behavioral research suggests that self-control, and not lack of information, may be a more important contributor to problematic health behaviors such as overeating (Volpp, 2010; Thaler & Shefrin, 1981). This view is supported by recent Pew and Gallup surveys which show that most American consumers are 1) aware that they are overweight, 2) wish to lose weight, and 3) are aware that they should be eating less. In light of this, we tested an intervention that made a self control opportunity salient to customers at the point of purchase. In two field experiments conducted at a national fast food restaurant, this intervention proved effective in reducing average calories purchased per meal. In our second study, this intervention was compared a calorie labeling intervention–the portion control intervention was significantly more effective.

Both experiments were conducted at an Asian-style fast-food restaurant. Meal ordering during the studies worked using the restaurant's standard procedure, whereby customers first ordered a side dish (e.g., fried rice), and then ordered entrees (e.g., stir fried chicken). In Study 1 customers (N=238) were asked by restaurant staff if they wanted to "cut over 200 calories from their meal" by taking a half-portion of their side dish (which ranged in calories from 440-570). In one condition, on two consecutive days, restaurant customers were invited to take the half portion for no discount. In a second condition, on two different days, a nominal (25 cent) discount was offered for taking the half portion. Baseline data were collected on two consecutive days preceding each intervention. On these baseline days, the half portion offer was not made to customers. In all conditions, customers were unaware that a study was taking place and all data were recorded through individual cash register receipts.

While customers almost never spontaneously asked for a half portion side dish on the baseline days, 36% took the half portion when it was offered without a discount. Similarly, 30% took the half portion when offered with the nominal discount. These acceptance rates were not significantly different, suggesting that customers took the half portion because they wanted less food, not because they wanted to save money. Across the intervention conditions, store customers purchased an average of 71 fewer calories than customers on baseline days (p<.05). Furthermore, there was no evidence of compensation, that is, customers who opted for the half portion of their side dish did not go on to purchase higher calorie entrees.

In Study 2 we repeated the half portion intervention (with a younger, predominantly college, population; N=994). In this study, the offer always included the nominal 25 cent discount. (Although offer acceptance was just as high without the discount in Study 1, inclusion of the discount is more consistent with retail norms, and is

hence easier for employees who repeatedly make the verbal offer.) Calorie labeling was also introduced in this study to directly assess its relative impact compared to that of the half portion offer. The study was conducted in 2 three-week blocks. Calorie labels were added to menu items for the second block. During block 1 (pre-label), data were collected for a 3 day baseline period, then for a 4 day intervention, and then for another 3 day baseline period. The sequence during block 2 (post-label) was identical.

Seventeen percent of customers accepted the half portion offer (across labeling conditions), thus reducing the overall number of calories per meal served by 34 (p<.05). As in Study 1, customers did not compensate for these saved calories by ordering higher calorie entrees. While the half portion intervention did significantly reduce the average number of calories per meal, the labeling intervention did not. In fact, calories per meal went up slightly after labeling was introduced in the stores. The half portion intervention led to calorie savings both before and after labeling was introduced, but the savings were marginally smaller during the labeling period.

In sum, calorie labeling alone did not reduce the number of calories purchased per meal. However, a simple prompt to take a smaller portion (and thus fewer calories) significantly reduced calories purchased per meal.

We conclude that retailers who wish to help their customers eat less, can do so effectively by providing self control opportunities, such as smaller portion options. Such self control opportunities are more effective than simple calorie labels, and they may be cost-effective since many customers are eager to take smaller portions for no discount, or for a nominal discount.

### "Simple Strategies for Communicating Health Information"

*Julie S. Downs, Carnegie Mellon University, USA*
*Jessica Wisdom, Carnegie Mellon University, USA*
*George Loewenstein, Carnegie Mellon University, USA*

This paper explores whether innovative strategies for providing nutrition information might work better than traditional, typically numerical approaches such as simple calorie labeling.

Participants were 735 passers by, recruited in public locations to complete a short survey in exchange for a free snack of their choosing. The sample was diverse on many dimensions: aged 18 to 87 (mean=31), 44% female, 68% white, 7% African American, 9% Asian, and 16% other or mixed ethnic heritage, reflecting the population in the neighborhoods where recruitment occurred.

Before completing the survey, participants were asked to choose their snack from a list of seven available options, which ranged from relatively healthful (a 40-calorie package of freeze-dried apple slices) to decadent (a 470-calorie, deep-fried, frosted apple pie). The manner in which these snacks were presented was manipulated to test different techniques for communicating health information, compared to a control condition (over-represented in randomization in order to power collapsed comparisons), which presented the seven snacks with no nutritional information, in an arbitrary (constant) order. The first category of information was numeric, based on calorie content (including a simple presentation of the number of calories in each option, and other alternatives providing guidance for caloric consumption or other aids to interpret the information). The second category did not provide explicit information about calorie content, but rather presented heuristic cues suggesting how healthful each option was (including letter grades and simple images). The third category did not provide additional information, but rather ranked the items from least- to most-caloric, allowing satisficing behavior (finding an attractive option and then discontinuing the search) to default to a more healthful choice. This ascending order was also combined in one condition with simple calorie information, in order to look for possible interactions. Participants then completed the short survey, which included a short list of demographic questions.

Participants in the control condition selected snacks with the highest average number of calories compared to all other conditions, suggesting that any technique for communicating health information might have some benefit. An analysis of variance comparing controls to numeric information and heuristic cues found a statistically significant main effect between these three categories of communication, $F(2,591)=3.46$, $p=.03$; post-hoc tests found that the menus using heuristic cues led to significantly lower-calorie choices (M=186) compared to controls (M=222, p=.03), with numeric information falling in between (M=200), not statistically different from either of the other two groups. Interestingly, this pattern appears to be driven by overweight participants, with the difference between controls and those receiving heuristic cues being much larger among participants with a BMI of greater than 25 (237 vs. 165, p<.01) compared to those with a BMI in the normal-weight range (212 vs. 196, p=.53). Our comparison of ascending vs. arbitrary ordering of snacks found a marginally significant beneficial effect of presenting snacks in an ascending order, $F(1,302)=3.67$, $p=.056$, but no main effect of calorie information and no significant interaction between order and information.

This study includes several limitations, including an unrealistic setting, and that our participants may not have been seeking out a snack at that moment but may have merely taken the opportunity because it was free. Furthermore, we do not know whether they ate their snack at that time, or if the high- versus low-calorie snacks had differential effects on their consumption later in the day. Nonetheless, these preliminary results show promise for more intuitive approaches to presenting nutrition information, and suggest that eating behaviors may be malleable through information-only approaches. Further research is needed to assess whether these effects can carry over to more complex food choices in naturalistic settings, and whether aggregation problems in assessing calorie information can be attenuated by using simpler cues.

**"Effectiveness of Menu Labeling and Choice Architecture on Food and Beverage Purchases at a Large Hospital Cafeteria"**
*Jason Riis, Harvard Business School, USA*
*Susan Barraclough, Massachusetts General Hospital, USA*
*Doug Levy, Massachusetts General Hospital, USA*
*Lillian Sonnenberg, Massachusetts General Hospital, USA*
*Anne Thorndike, Massachusetts General Hospital, USA*

Although many public health and physician organizations agree that environmental interventions are needed to reverse the current trend of obesity, there are few studies of these types of interventions. The current study incorporates a two-phase environmental intervention in a large hospital cafeteria. In the first phase, a simplified menu labeling system was applied throughout the cafeteria. Since calorie labeling interventions have shown limited success in changing customer purchase behavior, this study implements a simpler and more meaningful labeling scheme whereby all foods in the cafeteria were labeled as red, yellow, or green (with green being the healthiest). The second phase of the study alters the choice architecture of the food and beverages in the cafeteria, making it easier for customers to make healthy choices. We will compare the purchase patterns made during these two 2-month intervention phases with purchase patterns during a 4-month baseline period.

The setting for the study is the main cafeteria at large hospital in Massachusetts. More than 5000 individuals visit the cafeteria during a typical weekday and daily revenues exceed $20,000. Just over a quarter of the revenues come from employees who use a "meal card" which allows purchases to be directly deducted from their paychecks. The purchases of these individuals can hence be tracked over time.

The first phase of the intervention will be a point-of-purchase labeling intervention designed to educate the employees, patients, and visitors about the nutritional content of the foods and beverages of the cafeteria. All foods and beverages in the cafeteria will be labeled as red, yellow, or green to reflect the nutritional content based on the United States Department of Agriculture's My Pyramid healthy eating recommendations. Displays around the cafeteria will inform customers that Red items should be consumed rarely, as they are high in calories or unhealthy fat while Green items, which feature fresh fruits and vegetables, whole grains, and healthy proteins, should be consumed often. Yellow items are intermediate. The red-yellow-green categories were developed by a team of nutritionists at the hospital.

Following the two months of Phase 1, the second phase of the cafeteria intervention will begin. The labeling scheme will not change from Phase 1; food and beverages will continue to be labeled red, yellow, and green; but choice architecture changes will be made.

The intervention at Phase 2 will involve a series of changes to the layout of the cafeteria and the standard servings of some items. These changes are designed to increase the purchase rates of green items by making them more convenient to select, and by making them the default choice whenever possible. Two such interventions involve beverages and side salads. Water and diet soda (both green items) will appear at many more locations around the cafeteria, including several prominent, easy-access baskets near each food service station. Side salads will become be the default side dish. Currently, customers who want a side salad must make a separate trip to the salad bar. Now, customers will be offered a side salad with every entrée (including pizza, burgers, and sandwiches).

Cash registers have been programmed to record individual food items and their associated red-yellow-green label. Baseline data have been collected since November of 2009. Phase 1 began on March 1, 2010 when green-yellow-red labels were placed on all menu boards in the cafeteria. The convenience and default interventions of Phase 2 will begin on May 1, 2010. Data analysis will begin in early July and results will be ready for reporting by the beginning of August.

In addition to analyzing cafeteria-wide purchase trends, we are following a cohort of several hundred meal card users. For each user in the cohort, we will be able to determine their age, sex, race/ethnicity, and job type. We will collect data on all of their purchases at baseline and during the intervention phases, allowing us to assess how the interventions affect individual-level behavioral changes and to identify the characteristics of purchasers most likely to change their behavior in response to the intervention.

Our principal outcomes are total daily and weekly cafeteria revenues for green or red labeled foods, as well as the proportion of daily revenues that are from green or red labeled foods. Analyses of meal card user purchases will be based on similar measures of spending, using time series analysis.

# "Does Calorie Labeling at Restaurants Affect Consumers' Decisions of Where to Dine?"

*Brian Elbel, New York University, USA*
*Courtney Abrams, New York University, USA*

Previous investigations of the effectiveness of calorie labeling interventions have relied on analyses of point-of-purchase surveys and receipts. However, customers may alter their behavior in ways that would not be evidenced in point-of-purchase studies. After seeing the calorie content of the generally energy-dense offerings at fast food restaurants, customers may stop going to fast food restaurants, may limit the frequency of their fast food restaurant visits, and may substitute other types of (non-labeling) restaurants. On the other hand, health-conscious diners may welcome the transparency of information and increase the frequency with which they eat at chain fast food restaurants, versus non-labeling restaurants. In this study we examine whether mandatory, city-wide calorie labeling policies influenced the restaurant choices of adults; establish why mandatory, city-wide calorie labeling do or do not influence restaurant choices; and determine to what extent individual- and community-level factors interact with the influence of calorie labeling on restaurant choice.

In order to include individuals who may have stopped going to restaurants, reduced frequency, or substituted other types of restaurants as a result of calorie labeling, we conducted a random digit dial telephone survey. We employ a difference-in-difference design, examining changes in the data from pre- to post in a large northeastern city where mandatory menu labeling was enacted in January 2010, and compare with changes from pre- to post in a control (non-labeling) city. The difference-in-difference design allows us to isolate the impact of the policy change and net out any possible non-treatment related trends that may influence food choice, such as food pricing, the growth or change in the fast food industry, or health information diffusions. The telephone survey was fielded simultaneously in both cities.

Pre-labeling data was collected in both cities December 7th-24th, 2009. A total of 1,542 telephone surveys were conducted; 755 from the labeling city and 787 from the non-labeling city. All data has been coded and entered into SAS, cleaned, and weighted. Labeling laws in the city of interest went into effect January 1, 2010 and were fully implemented by February 1, 2010. Post-labeling phone surveying will begin in both cities May 3rd, 2010. Approximately 1,500 post-labeling surveys will be conducted. All data will be coded, entered, cleaned, weighted, and analyzed by August, 2010.

We examine changes in frequency of eating at (or getting take-out from) restaurants affected by the labeling law. Individuals reported the number of times they ate breakfast, lunch, dinner, and snacks from a big chain fast food restaurant in the past week. They also reported the number of times they ate breakfast, lunch, dinner, and snacks from a big chain casual dining restaurant in the past week.

Individuals were also asked whether they had changed the frequency of eating fast food in the past three months (and whether it increased or decreased). Those who did make changes provided the reason(s), including: nearby restaurants opening or closing, seeing calorie or nutrition information in a fast food restaurant, seeing calorie or nutrition information in another type of restaurant, wanting to eat healthier food, changes in financial situation or food budget, wanting to eat or cook more at home, or other.

Respondents were also asked whether they had noticed calorie or nutrition information at a restaurant. All consumers who noticed calorie or nutrition information on a menu at any type of restaurant were asked to describe its impact on their restaurant-going behavior. Specifically, they were asked to recall in what type(s) of restaurant they saw the information, whether seeing the information changed their eating, and if so, how. The answers pertaining to restaurant-related behavior included eating fast food less often, stopping eating fast food, eating at non-fast food restaurants more often, and eating at non-fast food restaurants less often.

Factors including gender, age, race/ethnicity and income are all related to food choice. Income is expected to be highly relevant to calorie labeling and restaurant choice. Because fast foods are generally cheaper than most other foods (Darmon et al. 2004; Drewnowski 2004; Monsivais and Drewnowski 2007), consumers with lower income may be less likely to be able to substitute away from fast food in response to calorie labeling. Moreover, controlling for income, those who even perceive price to be a barrier to purchasing foods have been shown to have a less healthy diet (Beydoun and Wang 2008; Beydoun et al. 2008). We will examine differences across gender, age, race/ethnicity, educational achievement, employment status, household income, health status and weight status.

Results from this study will substantially increase our knowledge of how consumers are responding to mandatory calorie labeling. Additionally, the rich data we have collected will provide insight as to why consumers are responding as they do, and how we might make labeling and other policies more effective. Given the rate at which labeling policies are increasingly being adopted, and the need for more effective obesity policies, these insights will substantially inform this debate.

# Influence of Social Norms on Consumption: Psychology, Biology, and Behavior

Vladas Griskevicius, University of Minnesota Carlson School of Management, USA
Noah J. Goldstein, UCLA Anderson School of Management, USA

## EXTENDED ABSTRACT

### "Reciprocity by Proxy: Expanding the Boundaries of the Norm of Reciprocity to Induce Environmental Action"

*Noah J. Goldstein, UCLA, USA*
*Vladas Griskevicius, University of Minnesota, USA*
*Robert B. Cialdini, Arizona State University, USA*

The central goals of the current investigation were to challenge the wisdom of a motivational strategy commonly used in cause-related marketing campaigns (Varadarajan, Rajan, and Menon 1988), and to explore whether a seemingly small—but theoretically crucial—change to that strategy would prove more psychologically powerful and behaviorally compelling. We suggested that rather than offering to perform a favor for causes, organizations, and people that the target individuals value on the condition that the targets takes the first step (which we call an *Incentive-by-Proxy* approach), a more effective strategy—one that harnessed the obligating force of the norm of reciprocity (Gouldner 1960) to the fullest extent—would be to deliver the favor first on their behalf and then ask those individuals to repay the already completed favor via the desired behavior (which we call a *Reciprocity-by-Proxy* approach).

We argue that the effectiveness of the Reciprocity-by-Proxy normative approach lies in its ability to produce a strong sense of obligation toward the favor-doing proxy. Although the focus of his work was on gifts and favors that were mostly direct in nature, the anthropologist Marcel Mauss (1954) argued that three different normative obligations influence gift-giving and favor-doing processes in all human cultures: an obligation to give, an obligation to receive, and an obligation to repay. We contend that the Reciprocity-by-Proxy strategy should be an especially effective motivational tool because it is the only reciprocation-based influence strategy that we know that utilizes all three obligations simultaneously. That is, in a sense, targets have received in the process of giving to the valued cause (via the favor-doing proxy), and as a consequence, they are obligated to repay the favor-doer. Consequently, the individual should feel a sense of indebtedness toward the favor-doer, which will lead them to reciprocate the gesture by complying with the request.

A large field experiment in a hotel produced two findings. First, in-room signs explaining that if guests reused their towels, the hotel would donate money to a pro-environmental organization (the Incentive-by-Proxy sign) were not any more successful than a standard environmental control sign at motivating the desired behavior. Second, the Reciprocity-by-Proxy sign indicating that the hotel had already made the donation and asking guests to pitch in for that donation—a message we have never seen employed in any hotel—was the most effective.

These findings are noteworthy in that the Incentive-by-Proxy and Reciprocity-by-Proxy appeals carried similar content (in the form of monetary donations to a worthy cause) but differentially activated a crucial psychological motivation. The results of the field experiment and a follow-up pilot study strongly suggest that the superior level of prosocial conduct observed in the Reciprocity-by-Proxy condition was due to participants' greater sense of obligation to the hotel and not to potential alternative motivations. Specifically, participants who viewed the Reciprocity-by-Proxy messages were more likely to feel they would owe it to the hotel management to reuse their towels than were all other participants. Moreover, *only*

for Reciprocity-by-Proxy participants did we find a significant positive correlation between their personal endorsement of the reciprocation norm and the extent to which they felt they owed it to the hotel management to reuse their towels.

We conducted three additional experiments to replicate the findings, rule out any remaining potential alternative explanations, reveal in greater detail the psychological mechanism driving the phenomenon, and explore possible boundary conditions for the effect. Specifically, Experiment 2 replicated the field experiment in a different context and with a different behavior (i.e. volunteering time and effort to complete a task), and showed that Reciprocity-by-Proxy approaches need not explicitly portray a target's compliance with the request as helping to recover the costs of their actions. In Experiment 3, we examined the effectiveness of these approaches in yet a different context and with yet a different behavior—gift-giving. In conjunction with the findings of the survey study that was paired with the field experiment, the results of Experiment 3 yielded strong support for our contention that the Reciprocity-by-Proxy approach's effectiveness is mediated by the perception of indebtedness and obligation that the norm of reciprocation elicits in the target individual. Finally, Experiment 4 provided further support for our reciprocation-based account and revealed an important boundary condition for the effect by demonstrating that the approach is only effective when the favor to the third party has been performed on behalf of the target individuals—an approach that makes clear to the targets that the favor-doer was attempting to support his or her interests and goals when performing the favor.

## REFERENCES

Gouldner, Alvin W. (1960), "The Norm of Reciprocity: A Preliminary Statement," *American Sociological Review, 25,* 161-78.

Mauss, Marcel. (1954), *The Gift: Forms and Functions of Exchange in Archaic Societies.* Glencoe, IL: Free Press.

Varadarajan, P. Rajan and Anil Menon (1988), "Cause-related Marketing: A Coalignment of Marketing Strategy and Corporate Philanthropy," *Journal of Marketing*, 52 (July), 58-74.

### "Using Space as a Weapon: The Effects on Social Norm Violations on Consumer Territorial Defense"

*Lily Lin, University of British Columbia, Canada*
*Darren W. Dahl, University of British Columbia, Canada*
*Jennifer J. Argo, University of Alberta, Canada*

There are numerous examples in the consumer context of social scripts and norms people are expected to follow. In a restaurant setting, for example, people are expected to arrive on time for their reservations so they would not hold up other people's tables. Additionally, there is an implicit norm among many societies that people's personal space should be respected. Therefore, hovering over someone's space while they enjoyed their meal or browsed for books at the bookstore is often seen as inappropriate. While prior research in the social norms domain had focused mainly on identifying what norms are and how one could change behavior through the promotion of norms (e.g., Goldstein, Cialdini and Griskevicius 2008; Joly, Stapel and Lindenberg 2008), no research in the consumer context has examined consumers' reactions toward those who are the violators of these well-established norms. Hence, the purpose of the current research is to examine whether and how individuals would punish another consumer who had violated a social norm. Importantly, the aim of the research is to explore the conditions under which people would be willing to engage in punishing another at a cost to oneself.

According to the research on altruistic punishment and human cooperation, individuals often punish violators of social norms as a way to restore order in society. Importantly, punishment will often take place even when it is not in the best interest for the punisher. For example, when norm violators are detected in the form of selfish behaviors in economic games, other players in the game were willing to punish these defectors even if it was costly and did not lead to any material gains (Fehr and Fischbacher 2004).

The present research extended the research in altruistic punishment by testing actions taken against norm violators in two contexts. In our studies, the degree of punishment was operationalized through the level of territorial defense shown. Territorial defense, or the tendency to occupy one's territory or space for a prolonged period of time, is an interesting phenomenon that has been demonstrated in real-life contexts such as parking lots and public pay phones (e.g., Ruback and Juieng 1997). Specifically, the researchers observed that individuals were especially likely to protect and spend more time at their space when they recognized that others were waiting to occupy the same space. By employing territorial defense as the measure of punishment, our research was not only able to demonstrate altruistic punishment in a subtle, but interesting way, but we were also able to gain a better understanding of the thought processes and consumption experiences of those who chose to punish the norm violators.

Study 1 examined consumers' actions against another individual who had violated a norm against the self (i.e., invasion of personal space) in a 2 (norm violation: hovering vs. no hovering) by 2 (wait time: short vs. long) between-subjects design. To manipulate norm violation, a confederate either hovered over the participant or waited in a designated waiting area as the participant completed a food sampling task. To manipulate wait time, the participant had to wait for either a short or long amount of time before s/he could begin the task. The purpose of this manipulation was to ensure that the amount of time spent by the participant at their space was not simply driven by the anchor and adjustment effect. Results showed that those who did not have to wait for a long time themselves demonstrated more territorial defense when the confederate was a norm violator. Additionally, the results from the level of enjoyment felt during the task revealed that participants chose to spend more time on the task even though it did not provide them with a more positive consumption experience.

In Study 2, a 2 (norm violation: late vs. on time) by 2 (wait time: short vs. long) between-subjects design was utilized to examine consumers' actions toward another consumer who had violated a norm against the system (i.e., being late for an appointment). Replicating the patterns of results from the previous study, participants in the norm violation condition demonstrated more territorial defense than those in the no violation condition. Importantly, participants who spent more time at their space were not more involved with the task, and did not enjoy the task more than those who spent less time at their space. Overall, participants in the study engaged in altruistic punishment through the protection of their territory.

## REFERENCES

Fehr, Ernst and Urs Fischbacher (2004), "Third-Party Punishment and Social Norms," *Evolution and Human Behavior*, 25 (2), 63-87.

Goldstein, Noah J., Robert B. Cialdini and Vladas Griskevicius (2008), "A Room With a Viewpoint: Using Social Norms to Motivate Environmental Conservation in Hotels," *Journal of Consumer Research*, 35 (3), 472-82.

Joly, Janneke F., Diederik A. Stapel, and Siegwart M. Lindenberg (2008), "Silence and Table Manners: When Environment Activate Norms," *Personality and Social Psychology Bulletin*, 34 (8), 1047-56.

Ruback, R. Barry and Daniel Juieng (1997), "Territorial Defense in Parking Lots: Retaliation Against Waiting Drivers," *Journal of Applied Social Psychology*, 27 (9), 821-34.

### "Neural Mechanisms of Social Normative Influence"

*Michael I. Norton, Harvard Business School, USA*
*Malia F. Mason, Columbia Business School, USA*
*Rebecca Dyer, Yale University, USA*

The iconic Lacoste green crocodile logo–initially created in honor of the 1920's French tennis star Rene Lacoste–has waxed and waned in popularity over the years, enjoying enormous popularity in the United States in the late 1970's and early 1980's while nearly disappearing from sight in the 1990's, only to reemerge in this decade as a desired status symbol. One reason to buy clothing featuring this crocodile might be to emulate Lacoste himself, of course, but we would be surprised if American teenagers have any awareness of the origins of the logo. Instead, such trends are often driven by the adoption–and rejection–of products by others: The value of little green crocodiles depends critically on the value that others attach to that symbol (Berger & Heath, 2007; Cialdini & Goldstein, 2004).

In this paper, we model the process by which social norms impact preferences in a one-hour experimental session, using a paradigm in which we train participants to see symbols as socially valued or not by providing them with feedback about the preferences of others. We then examine the impact of this social feedback on the brain activity that participants exhibit while viewing objects that have been endorsed or rejected by their peers, exploring the neural processes underlying changes in valuation due to social normative influence.

We first exposed participants to information about others' preferences for abstract symbols in a "social norms" phase. During this phase, participants learned that some abstract symbols were "popular" (preferred by others on 90% of trials) while others were "unpopular" (preferred on just 10% of trials). To confirm that our social tagging manipulation impacted liking for the stimuli, we conducted a behavioral version of this social influence phase, in which participants ($N=32$) rated all symbols on a 5-point scale both before and after the social influence task. As expected, popular symbols were rated significantly higher after the social norms phase than before, while attitudes towards unpopular symbols showed a marginally significant decrease.

In the fMRI experiment, we assessed brain activity when participants ($N=12$) were exposed to these socially tagged (popular and unpopular) symbols, as well as new symbols about which they had not been provided normative information. As expected, mPFC, a brain region involved in thinking about the attitudes and preferences of others (Amodio and Frith 2006), was more active when participants viewed symbols that had been socially tagged than symbols for which they had no prior social information, suggesting a possible index of normative influence at the level of the brain. Also as predicted, we found that a region involved in the experience of reward–the caudate, part of the striatum–exhibited greater activity in response to popular symbols, providing a possible neural index of informational influence.

These results suggest that predicting whether a symbol is socially valued may require integrating data from both the mPFC and the caudate. Looking solely at the mPFC reveals only whether a symbol is socially tagged or not, while looking solely at the caudate reveals only whether a symbol is liked or disliked; only by looking at both regions together can we identify those symbols that have become valued as a result of social normative influence.

## REFERENCES

Amodio, D. M. & Frith, C. D. (2006). Meeting of minds: The medial frontal cortex and social cognition. *Nature Reviews Neuroscience*, 7, 268–277.

Berger, J. & Heath, C. (2007). Where consumers diverge from others: Identity-signaling and product domains. *Journal of Consumer Research*, 34, 121-134.

Cialdini, R. B. & Goldstein, N. J. (2004). Social influence: Compliance and conformity. *Annual Review of Psychology*, 55, 591-621.

### "Going Against the Grain: The Evolutionary Roots of Normative Influence"

*Vladas Griskevicius, University of Minnesota, USA*
*Noah J. Goldstein, UCLA , USA*
*Joseph Redden, University of Minnesota, USA*

Much research shows that people are strongly influenced by social norms. Consumers, for example, are more likely to purchase a product upon learning that many others have bought it, and hotel guests are more likely to reuse a towel when informed that many other guests reuse their towels (e.g., Goldstein, Cialdini, and Griskevicius 2008). Social norms often influence behavior in a heuristic manner, whereby people are often unaware that their actions are being influenced by the norms in the situation. The automaticity of normative influence is consistent with the evolutionary underpinning of heuristic attunement to norms. Across social species, for example, individuals who follow the crowd gain an adaptive survival advantage because following the herd decreases the likelihood that a given individual will be eaten by prey.

Although people are heuristically influenced by social norms, an evolutionary perspective suggests that organisms generally do not evolve domain-general heuristics. Instead, organisms manifest different biases in different evolutionary recurring domains (e.g., survival, reproduction, etc.) (Sundie et al. 2006). We suggest that whereas following social norms is adaptive in the evolutionary critical domain of survival, blindly following the herd is unlikely to be adaptive in the domain of mating. Thus, whereas susceptibility to social norms should be exacerbated when survival-related motives are active, people might not follow norms when mating motives are activated (Griskevicius et al. 2009).

In Study 1, we activated either self-protection, mating, or control motives by having participants read a short pre-tested story. Then, participants entered a multi-person chat room in which they were asked to indicate their preferences for various works of art. Before participants could indicate their like or dislike for the artworks, they were able to see the preferences of their peers in the chat room, which were designed to either create a social norm for liking *or* a norm against liking a given piece of art.

In the control motive condition, participants were moderately influenced by the norm, whereby preferences for liking or disliking the art were swayed in the direction of the norm. Consistent with predictions, when self-protection motives were active, people were significantly more influenced by the norm, being especially susceptible to following the herd when self-protection motives were active. However, when mating motives were active, participants responded in a drastically different manner: People, especially men, went against the norm. Mating motives led people to flout norms, doing the opposite of what everyone else was doing.

Study 2 examined an important boundary condition for when mating motives influenced susceptibility to social norms: whether the topic was *subjective* (e.g., preference for a product in a category in which there are multiple products of relatively equal quality) versus *objective* (e.g., preference for a product within a category in which one of the products is verifiably superior). After eliciting a mating or a neutral motive, participants responded to a survey in which they could see the responses of previous individuals. Half of the survey questions were relatively subjective (e.g., do you prefer a Mercedes-Benz or a BMW), and half were objective (e.g., do you think it's more expensive to live in New York or San Francisco). As in Study 1, findings showed that when choices were subjective, mating motives led people, especially men, to go against the group. However, mating motives did not influence choices for objective items.

Because mating motives likely motivate individuals to want to stand out from the crowd in a new way, Study 3 examined whether mating motives would lead people to desire products that were "new" and, thus, uncommon. Control or mating motives were activated. Then, participants chose among products that were labeled "new", "classic", or had no label. Findings showed that mating motives led people to choose a product significantly more when it was labeled as "new" compared to having no label or being labeled as "classic." Overall, consistent with evolutionary considerations of the adaptive functions of following social norms, we found that mating motives can consistently lead people to go against the prevailing social norm.

## REFERENCES

Goldstein, N. J., Cialdini, R. B., & Griskevicius, V. (2008). A room with a viewpoint: Using social norms to motivate environmental conservation in hotels. *Journal of Consumer Research, 35*, 472-482.

Griskevicius, V., Goldstein, N. J., Mortensen, C. R., Sundie, J. M., Cialdini, R. B., & Kenrick, D. T. (2009). Fear and loving in Las Vegas: Evolution, emotion, and persuasion. *Journal of Marketing Research, 46*, 385-395.

Sundie, J. M., Cialdini, R. B., Griskevicius, V., & Kenrick, D. T. (2006). Evolutionary social influence. In *Evolution and Social Psychology*, ed. Mark Schaller, Jeffry A. Simpson and Douglas T. Kenrick, New York, NY: Psychology Press, 287-316.

# Consumer Motivation: When Initial Consumption Influences Subsequent Actions

Stacey Finkelstein, University of Chicago, USA
Ying Zhang, University of Texas at Austin, USA

## EXTENDED ABSTRACTS

### "Motivational Consequences of Perceived Velocity in Goal Pursuit"

*Szu-Chi Huang, University of Texas at Austin, USA*
*Ying Zhang, University of Texas at Austin, USA*

A large body of research has documented that as people make progress and move closer to the end point, their motivation increases and they exert more effort in the pursuit (Hull 1932; Kivetz, Urminsky, and Zheng 2006). However, because movement toward goal attainment is a dynamic process, trying to understand the motivational consequences of progress by focusing on the level of progress alone would neglect the temporal aspect of movement and miss out on the rate of progress, a psychological equivalent of velocity (Carver and Scheier 1998). For companies that try to encourage repeat purchases, should they design a loyalty program that allows consumers to experience a fast or slow rate of progress? Should companies use the same point structure to motivate customers who just joined a loyalty program as the one used to motivate those who are getting close to redemption?

In order to address these questions, we build on the research on the dynamics of self-regulation (Fishbach and Dhar 2005), and posit that people are concerned about different questions as they move from earlier stages to later stages of goal pursuit, and the velocity in goal pursuit allows them to make different inferences. Specifically, when people start pursuing a goal and the progress level is low, the perceived attainability of the goal is relatively low and people's commitment to goal is ambiguous. In this situation, individuals' motivation in further pursuit is determined by whether the goal is perceived to be attainable.

Consumers are less likely to commit to goals that are beyond their reach (Bandura 1997). Thus, high (vs. low) perceived velocity suggests that one is moving toward the ideal state at a faster rate, and signals higher attainability of the goal, thus motivating the person to persist in the pursuit. On the other hand, when the progress level on the goal is relatively high, people feel more confident about achieving the goal (Wood and Bandura 1989). Thus, low (vs. high) velocity of goal pursuit suggests that more effort will be needed and thus increases one's motivation in the pursuit.

Four studies tested present predictions. The first study tested the hypothesis in the context of public goal pursuit through conducting a field study. We launched a campus campaign with the Relief Nursery of Central Texas, a social-profit organization dedicated to the cause of preventing child abuse, and created different flyers to solicit volunteer hours for the organization. The results showed that when the progress on volunteer recruitment was low, information of high (vs. low) velocity was more motivating and led to higher percentage of people willing to volunteer as well as more hours people were willing to volunteer for; in contrast, information of low (vs. high) velocity was more motivating when the progress on recruitment was high.

In Study 2 and Study 3, participants took computer-based tasks and were offered the chance to accumulate 700 points to win cash rewards. We manipulated participants' progress and perceived velocity by offering them feedback on their performances. In Study 2, we gave them three extremely difficult questions and measured the amount of time participants spent on these questions as the indicator of their motivation for the reward. We found that when the progress level was low, the participants who thought they were gaining points fast (vs. slow) persisted longer in the task, while the reverse was true when the progress level on the goal was high.

In Study 3 we asked participants about their perceived attainability of the goal and their concern about reducing the discrepancy, in addition to their persistence in trying to reach the goal. We found that low (vs. high) speed led to lower perceived attainability of the goal when the progress was low, but not when the progress was high. Also, we found that low (vs. high) speed led to higher concern about closing the gap when the progress was high, but not when the progress was low. In addition, when the progress on the goal was low, perceived attainability of the goal significantly predicted one's persistence, but when the progress was high, the concern for reducing the gap predicted their motivation for the pursuit.

In Study 4, we collaborated with a local coffee shop and distributed two versions of loyalty cards to their customers: the "uniform velocity" card that allowed customers to get a fixed number of points for purchases made at all stages of the program, and the "variable velocity" card that allowed customers to accumulate points at a faster rate at the initial stage of the program and at a slower rate when they approached the redemption point. We found that, compared with the uniform velocity program, the variable velocity program effectively enhanced customers' motivation for redemption and increased their purchase frequency at the shop.

### "Exposure to Healthy Food Increases the Appetite"

*Stacey Finkelstein, University of Chicago, USA*
*Ayelet Fishbach, University of Chicago, USA*

Consumers often experience a conflict between the health goal and the motive to satisfy their appetite (Geyskens et al. 2008; Herman & Polivy 1975; Scott et al. 2008; Vohs & Faber, 2008). Further, consumers generally believe that healthy food is less fulfilling than unhealthy alternatives, further increasing this conflict (Chandon & Wansink, 2007; Raghunathan, Naylor, and Hoyer, 2006).

To explore this conflict, we use a goal analysis (Kruglanski et al. 2002). In particular, we draw on research on the Dynamics of Self-Regulation (Fishbach and Dhar, 2005), which suggests that whether consumers infer commitment to their goals (versus progress towards their goal) influences the course of self-regulation over time. While an experience of commitment encourages goal-congruent actions due to an increased sense that the goal is valuable and attainable, an experience of progress on one goal will result in relaxing one's effort and moving away to another, competing motivation, which is presumably somewhat neglected.

In 3 studies, we test whether exposure to healthy food cues increases the strength of the motive to satisfy one's appetite as manifested by a stronger hunger experience and increased food consumption. This effect is driven by a perception of progress towards a person's goal of being a healthy individual as a result of exposure to healthy food cues. Consequently, consumers feels that the competing motivation of satisfying their hunger was neglected and increase food consumption. Further, we propose that this effect is stronger for less committed individuals who are more likely to infer progress on the health goal without an increase in commitment to the health goal.

Three studies manipulate exposure to healthy products and product labels (versus tasty products or regular product labels) and show a boost in experienced hunger, perceived progress towards the health goal, and actual food consumption as well as moderation by importance of watching one's weight. In study 1, we measured participants' experience of hunger over time. First, participants rated their hunger at the present moment. After, they tasted a sample of a protein bar that was either described as healthy or tasty or they did not taste a sample (control condition). After sampling and completing a distracter task (sampling conditions) or just completing the distracter task (control condition), participants rated their hunger a second time. In support of our hypothesis, those who sampled the item framed as healthy grew hungrier over time while those who did not taste a sample showed no difference in hunger and those who tasted the item framed as tasty were less hungry after sampling.

In study 2, we explored whether merely viewing low-fat food (e.g., fat-free cheese) versus regular (e.g., regular cheese) labels would lead participants to infer they have made progress towards their health goal. Consequently, after viewing low-fat labels, people should consume more of a neutral snack to satisfy their hunger. As predicted, participants who viewed low-fat labels reported having made more progress towards their health goal, thus activating the conflicting measure to satisfy their appetite as measured by an increase in consumption.

Clearly, there are individual differences in importance of weight-watching. For consumers who are less concerned with watching their weight, viewing low-fat labels leads to (often illusionary) progress towards one's health goal. However, for those whom weight-watching is a high priority, viewing low-fat labels and seeing that these items are pervasive in one's environment reflects that the items are common as well as that one searches for these items. Study 3 tests these predictions. Participants were exposed to either low-fat or regular labels and given a chance to consume a snack that was unrelated to the initial exposure during a presumably unrelated task. After completing this task, participants also rated how important it was for them to watch their weight using items from the restrained eater's scale (Polivy & Herman, 1975). We find that those who are less concerned with watching their weight consume more of a neutral snack when they view low-fat versus regular labels. However, those who were highly concerned with watching their weight, viewing low-fat labels did not increase consumption compared to those who viewed regular labels.

These findings have implications for marketers who use sampling to promote their product, especially in the food categories (e.g., Wadhwa, Shiv, and Nowlis, 2008). The drawback in giving away samples is that these samples can potentially make consumers feel less hungry and therefore reduce subsequent purchases and consumption. For example, grocery shoppers might satisfy their hunger with food samples and subsequently buy less food in the store. As the above findings suggest, one factor that influences the direction of impact is the perceived healthfulness of the sample.

### "Too Much of A Different Thing? The (De)motivating effects of Variety on Goal Pursuit."

*Jordan Etkin, University of Maryland, USA*
*Rebecca Ratner, University of Maryland, USA*

In the course of goal pursuit, consumers must make a series of choices about the products they use to help them maximize their likelihood of goal attainment. These chosen products, or means of goal attainment, will likely vary in many ways. How might the variety among chosen means affect subsequent motivation to pursue the goal?

The tendency for consumers to seek variety and change in choice over time has been construed as a goal-directed phenomenon (Ariely and Levav 2000; Kahn and Ratner 2005; Ratner, Kahn, and Kahneman 1999). Indeed, previous research has explored some of the inferences consumers make based on the perceived variety among products (Berger et al. 2007). Interpreting this finding from a goal systems perspective, if consumers make inferences about the "focus" of the means to their goal based on the relative similarity of the products that they choose, then this inference of "focus" may transfer from the products themselves to their associated goal. As a result, consumers may perceive themselves as more focused on a particular goal when they choose similar (vs. dissimilar) means of goal attainment, consequently affecting their motivation to pursue that goal.

We propose that the similarity of means chosen in the course of goal pursuit will affect subsequent motivation to pursue the goal, due to the inferences of focus on goal pursuit that consumers draw from the focus of the means set. Further, we propose that the amount of progress consumers feel that they have made towards attaining their goal will moderate the effect of means similarity on motivation, such that similar (vs. dissimilar) means will increase motivation when people feel that they have made high progress toward their goal.

Three studies were conducted to test these predictions. Each study used fitness goals as the target goal and followed the same basic procedure. All participants were shown a series of protein supplements and were asked to choose the three that they would most like to try after their next three workouts. Perceived goal progress was either measured or manipulated, followed by the key dependent measures of interest (motivation, perceived focus, etc.). In study 1, means similarity was manipulated by varying the set of protein supplements between participants, such that half of participants saw a set of six PowerBar protein bars (similar set) and half saw a set of six assorted protein supplements, such as a protein powder, a protein bar, etc. (dissimilar set). Participants were either surveyed before beginning a workout (low progress) or after finishing a workout (high progress). In study 2, all participants saw the same set of PowerBar protein supplements and means similarity was manipulated in a separate priming task, holding actual similarity constant; perceived progress was measured across participants and treated as a continuous variable in subsequent analyses. In study 3, means similarity was manipulated as in study 1 and perceived goal progress was manipulated in a separate priming task, holding actual progress constant.

Across all studies we found consistent support for our predictions: means similarity had a systematic affect on motivation to pursue the associated goal. Specifically, choosing from a set of similar (vs. dissimilar) means to a goal increased motivation, but only when consumers inferred that they had made high progress toward their goal. Further, in all three studies the effect of means similarity on motivation was mediated by perceived focus on goal pursuit in the high progress condition. These results persisted regardless of how means similarity was manipulated and whether perceived goal progress was measured or manipulated separately.

This research demonstrates that in addition to motivation affecting the amount variety chosen among means, the variety among means themselves may also affect subsequent motivation. In particular, the relative focus of a set of means chosen in the course of goal pursuit (similarity vs. dissimilarity) leads consumers to draw inferences about their own focus on goal pursuit, increasing motivation when perceived goal progress was already high.

### "The Dynamics of Goal Revision: Updating the Discrepancy-Reducing Model of Self-Regulation."

*Chen Wang, University of British Columbia, Canada*
*Anirban Mukhopadhyay, Hong Kong University of Science and Technology, China*

Existing research on goal-directed behaviors has largely focused on striving towards static goals (e.g., Carver and Scheier 1981), with relatively little attention directed towards dynamic goal-setting and updating. However, as Fishbach and colleagues have demonstrated (Fishbach and Dhar 2005), goals are not always static. Rather, people frequently revise their goals upward or downward based on the discrepancies between their initial goals and subsequent achievements.

In this research, we generalize this model to goals that are dynamic, and propose that goals are updated every period based on the extent of achievement in the previous period. Based on this proposition, we incorporate an additional element–a "calibrator"–into Carver and Scheier's model. In our revised model, the goal-performance discrepancy serves not only as an input to the system as suggested by the original model, but also as the input to the goal calibrator. This goal calibrator is directed by an S-shaped response function which generates an updated goal for the next time period. This S-shaped function predicts the properties of *proportionality* and *diminishing sensitivity* for all goal-discrepancies, *failure aversion* for intrinsically motivated goals, and *satisficing* for extrinsically motivated goals.

Four experiments provide empirical support for our model. In Study 1, we manipulated discrepancy valence to be positive or negative, and provided hypothetical feedback for five successive time periods. Participants were to write down a savings goal and were then presented with a hypothetical performance outcome (e.g., you saved 15% more vs. less than your goal). Based on the feedback, they set their financial goal for the next month, and the next feedback was then presented. These procedures were repeated for five iterations. The performance outcomes ranged from 15% to 19%, always either positive or negative based on feedback condition. In support of our predictions, positive discrepancies resulted in continuous upward goal revision–savings targets for each month were higher than in the previous month. In contrast, negative discrepancies led to the maintenance of the original goal–savings targets stayed flat from month to month. Taken together, this experiment demonstrates (a) the existence of goal revision for self-set goals, and (b) the property of *failure aversion*.

Study 2 investigated effort exertion for positive versus negative discrepancies. We used a similar design, in the context of working out on the treadmill. Consistent with our hypotheses, we find that participants having positive discrepancies indicated the same amount of effort for each trial, whereas those with negative discrepancies indicated increasingly more effort to strive for the goal.

Study 3 further tested the characteristics of the S-shaped function by exploring the following features: proportionality, diminishing sensitivity, and failure aversion. Participants were presented a scenario in which they had a goal of burning 200 calories on the treadmill. The discrepancy was manipulated by giving hypothetical outcomes (burning 10 vs. 110 calories more vs. less). Next, participants established their calorie goal for the next day based on their performance. As predicted, consistent with the *proportionality* feature, large discrepancies resulted in greater goal revision than small discrepancies of the same valence. Further, discrepancies had a smaller marginal impact when they were more distant from the origin, demonstrating *diminishing sensitivity*. Finally, positive discrepancies led to larger goal revision than negative discrepancies of the same magnitude, highlighting *failure aversion*.

Study 4 tested *satisficing* for extrinsically motivated goals. In this study, we utilized a computerized anagram task. Participants were asked to set a goal for the first anagram (i.e., "to find __% of the possible solutions"). Manipulated feedback was presented after participants submitted their answers (i.e., 5% more vs. less than your goal). As predicted, participants with positive discrepancies initially maintained the original goal, but revised the goal upward as they kept receiving positive feedback. In contrast, those with negative discrepancies revised the goal downward based on the negative feedback. In sum, these experiments contribute to a greater understanding of multi-period consumer goal-directed behavior.

# Consumer Disposal Behavior: Retaining, Selling, Discarding, or Donating Used Products
Aaron Brough, Kellogg School of Management, Northwestern University, USA

## EXTENDED ABSTRACTS

### "To Have and To Hold? Marketing Implications of Consumers' Product Retention Tendency"
Kelly L. Haws, Texas A&M, USA
Rebecca Walker Naylor, Ohio State, USA
Robin A. Coulter, University of Connecticut, USA
William O. Bearden, University of South Carolina, USA

In this research, we introduce the concept of product retention tendency, defined as an individual's propensity to retain physical possessions. Per our conceptualization, consumers can fall anywhere on a continuum ranging from those who have no desire to "hang on to" their possessions and who therefore frequently dispose of things, to those who keep nearly all of their possessions and who do not like to discard anything. We argue that an individual's general tendency to retain physical possessions impacts not only their retention/disposal decisions, but also their acquisition- and consumption-related behaviors. We propose that consumers with a stronger product retention tendency are driven by the desire to avoid waste (reflected in their greater frugality, interest in creative reuse, and concern for the environment) and by their attachment to physical goods (including possession attachment and materialism). These characteristics influence how individuals with a strong (vs. weak) product retention tendency differentially respond to various marketing tactics (e.g., product/packaging design decisions and specific promotional strategies).

We draw upon relevant literature in marketing, consumer behavior, and psychology (e.g., Coulter and Ligas 2003; Frost et al. 2004; Lastovicka et al. 1999) to provide theoretical grounding for a nomological network for product retention tendency and related constructs, including compulsive hoarding. We then detail six studies (studies 1a-f) conducted to (1) develop a valid and reliable measure of product retention tendency (PRT), (2) establish discriminant validity between our construct of interest and clinical compulsive hoarding, and (3) assess the proposed relationships between the constructs in the nomological network. In accordance with our conceptualization, these studies also demonstrate that product retention tendency is associated with avoiding waste due to frugality, an interest in creative reuse, and concern for the environment, as well as with feeling connected to one's possessions because of possession attachment and materialism.

We then build upon insights from the nomological network of product retention tendency to discuss and hypothesize the influence of product retention tendency on consumers' acquisition- and consumption- related behaviors. We focus on waste avoidance motivations and reuse of product packaging in study 2 and on attachment motivations and the response to promotional offers in study 3.

In study 2 we expect that individuals who have a stronger (vs. weaker) product retention tendency will consider more alternative uses for product packaging because of their desire to avoid being wasteful. More specifically, we expect that the waste avoidance motivations of frugality, creative reuse, and environmental concern are the drivers of this behavior. As expected, a regression model with PRT as a continuous predictor variable revealed that participants with a stronger product retention tendency reported significantly more ways to reuse a glass mayonnaise jar (F(1, 398)=6.80, p<.01). Creative reuse fully mediates the relationship between PRT and the number of uses generated. Frugality and concern for the environment both partially mediate the relationship, as confirmed by significant

Sobel tests. Study 2 therefore demonstrates that the waste avoidance motivations in the nomological network help explain why consumers with a stronger (vs. weaker) product retention tendency respond differently to an opportunity to reuse product packaging. The results of study 2 suggest that managers can successfully target consumers with a stronger product retention tendency by using product packaging that is specifically designed to be reused by the consumer, perhaps even touting the potential for reuse as an added benefit of their offering.

In study 3, we draw on Okada's (2001) work on trade-ins to examine how differences in product retention tendency can impact response to two equally-valued promotional offers (i.e., a trade-in offer, in which a used good is "traded in" for a discount on a new good, vs. an equally-valued sale price offer on a new good). We predict that product retention tendency will moderate Okada's (2001) findings, which show an overall preference for the trade-in offer. Consistent with our expectations, we found a significant interaction between product retention tendency and camera offer condition (F(1, 201)=3.93, p<.05). Follow-up analyses revealed that participants with a weaker product retention tendency reported a greater likelihood of buying the camera because of the deal in the trade-in offer condition compared to the sale price offer condition (F(1, 201)=10.08, p<.01). In contrast, participants with a stronger product retention tendency, regardless of whether they were in the trade-in or the sale price condition, were equally likely to report that they would buy the camera because of the deal (F(1, 201)=.26, p>.10). We also found that the difference in response to trade-in versus sale price offers for consumers with a stronger versus weaker product retention tendency is mediated by consumers' emotional attachment to their possessions and their materialism. Our results suggest that Okada's (2001) findings may have been driven by consumers with moderate or weak levels of product retention tendency. For those with a stronger product retention tendency, both types of offer are attractive because of the motivating factors we identify, attachment to possessions and materialism.

Overall, our research seeks to draw attention to the area of product disposal and how such tendencies impact consumer responses to marketing tactics. Our studies provide examples of the many ways in which a consumer's attitude toward retention can affect their decision making behaviors through the waste avoidance and product attachment motivations.

## REFERENCES
Coulter, Robin A. and Mark Ligas (2003), "To Retain or Relinquish: Exploring the Disposition Practices of Packrats and Purgers," in *Advances in Consumer Research*, eds. Punam Anand Keller and Dennis Rook, Provo, UT: Association for Consumer Research, 38–43.
Frost, Randy O., Gail Steketee, and Jessica Grisham (2004), "Measurement of Compulsive Hoarding: Saving Inventory-Revised," *Behaviour Research and Therapy*," 42 (October), 1163–82.
Lastovicka, John L., Lance A. Bettencourt, Renee Shaw Hughner, and Ronald J. Kuntze (1999), "Lifestyle of the Tight and Frugal: Theory and Measurement," *Journal of Consumer Research*, 26 (June), 85–98.
Okada, Erica Mina (2001), "Trade-ins, Mental Accounting, and Product Replacement Decisions," *Journal of Consumer Research*, 27 (March), 433–46.

### "When Low Bids Win: Non-Price Competition among Buyers in Secondary Markets"
*Aaron R. Brough, Northwestern University, USA*
*Mathew S. Isaac, Northwestern University, USA*

A central aspect of marketing is how sellers compete for customers. Although price competition among sellers is prevalent, marketers recognized many years ago that customers also care about non-monetary factors. As a result, marketing literature has focused extensively on how sellers may successfully compete without lowering prices by differentiating themselves on dimensions such as location, brand, service, context, etc.

An area that has received less attention in the literature is how buyers compete for scarce goods. This neglect may be due to the assumption that sellers' pricing decisions are based on an aim to maximize profit (Monroe and Della Bitta 1978), and that therefore buyers compete exclusively on the basis of price (i.e., the highest bidder wins). Such an assumption may be particularly prevalent in the context of secondary markets, where sellers reveal a profit-motive by deciding to sell rather than keep, discard, or donate a used product. Furthermore, many second-hand exchanges are one-time transactions among relatively anonymous buyers, which incentivizes sellers to focus on profit-maximization.

In this research, we challenge the assumption that sellers of used goods are concerned exclusively with profit and argue that they may also care about non-monetary factors. We therefore predict that buyers of used goods may successfully compete with higher bidders by differentiating themselves on non-monetary dimensions. In particular, we focus on one non-monetary factor—buyer usage intent—and investigate how sellers' pricing decisions are influenced when prospective buyers communicate how they intend to use a product following a transaction. Building on diverse literatures which suggest a connection between a product and its owner (Argo, Dahl, and Morales 2008; Belk 1988; Thaler 1980), we attribute sellers' preferences regarding post-transactional product usage to a sense of product attachment that sellers feel towards their used goods. We test these predictions across three empirical studies.

Study 1 examines how sellers choose among two buyers who intend to use a product differently. 89 online participants were presented with a scenario in which they received offers from two buyers interested in purchasing a used piano. Buyer A planned to play the piano, but Buyer B planned to use the piano strictly for decoration. Participants were then presented with eleven pairs of offers from these two buyers in which the monetary amounts differed, and participants indicated for each pair to whom they would sell the piano. Results indicated that even for pairs where Buyer B offered a substantially higher amount (ranging from $500 to $4,000), many participants nevertheless preferred to sell to Buyer A. Whereas Study 1 demonstrates the effect of buyer usage intent on seller pricing decisions; Study 2 examines the role of product attachment intensity in driving this effect.

In Study 2, 100 online participants indicated the maximum amount they would be willing to accept (WTA) from each of two buyers with different usage intents. Participants were told that they originally intended to ask $500 for a wedding ring they were selling. After learning that a potential buyer planned to wear the ring to a costume party rather than use it for a marriage proposal, participants indicated WTA. They then encountered a second buyer who planned to use the ring for a marriage proposal and again indicated WTA. Finally, participants indicated their level of attachment to the ring using a scale which depicted differing degrees of overlap between themselves and the ring. Results showed that WTA of participants who felt weakly attached to the ring did not differ based on buyer usage intent. However, participants who felt strongly attached to the ring indicated a lower WTA from the buyer who planned to use the ring for a marriage proposal and a higher WTA from the buyer who planned to wear the ring to a costume party. These results are consistent with the notion that attachment influences the impact of buyer usage intent on seller pricing decisions. The next study examines the extent to which sellers regret a transaction after learning that actual product usage violated the seller's post-transactional preferences.

The objective of Study 3 was to provide additional evidence for the role of attachment by manipulating rather than measuring it. This was done by using hedonic versus utilitarian products, with the idea that participants would feel greater attachment to hedonic products than to utilitarian products. 142 undergraduates imagined that after selling a VHS tape which was originally purchased either for pleasure (hedonic) or for use in writing a term paper (utilitarian), they learned that the buyer had either watched the tape multiple times (proper usage intent) or recorded over its original content (improper usage intent). Participants were also informed that subsequent bidders had offered more money for the tape than the buyer to whom they sold it. Participants then indicated the extent to which they regretted selling to this buyer. Results showed that participants experienced greater regret after learning that a buyer had recorded over the VHS tape rather than watching it, but only when the tape was perceived to be a hedonic product.

Overall, this research contributes to the marketing literature by examining buyer-side competition. In particular, we suggest that like sellers, buyers may successfully engage in non-price competition. This insight has important implications for the pricing literature, which has focused primarily on how firms set prices and how consumers perceive and respond to those prices. In contrast, our work focuses on how consumers generate prices when selling used goods, and we identify product attachment as an important factor that influences seller pricing decisions in secondary markets.

### REFERENCES
Argo, Jennifer J., Darren W. Dahl, and Andrea C. Morales (2008), "Positive Consumer Contagion: Responses to Attractive Others in a Retail Context," *Journal of Marketing Research*, 45 (6), 690-701.
Belk, Russell W. (1988), "Possessions and the Extended Self," *Journal of Consumer Research*, 15 (2), 139-68.
Monroe, Kent B. and Albert J. Della Bitta (1978), "Models for Pricing Decisions," *Journal of Marketing Research*, 15 (3), 413-28.
Thaler, Richard (1980), "Toward a Positive Theory of Consumer Choice," *Journal of Economic Behavior & Organization*, 1 (1), 39-60.

### "Curb Your "Wastism": Interplay between the Abundance Mindset and Non-abundance Cues on Waste"
*Meng Zhu, Carnegie Mellon University, USA*
*Ajay Kalra, Rice University, USA*

Managing how much consumers waste has become an essential issue in maintaining sustainability of our society. Existing literature on waste holds the viewpoint that consumers are averse to waste due to their motivation to fully exhaust a product's residual value (e.g., Arkes 1996). We propose an additional "*Wastism*" perspective to examine consumer waste behavior at a non-conscious level. Specifically, we theorize that as mass production has become increasingly mastered by society (Riesman, 1950; Côté, 1993, 1996) people are in a default "abundance" mindset that emphasizes the need to seek convenience rather than conservation in consumption, which consequently leads to increased waste.

Building on the passive goal activation literature (e.g., Bargh et al. 2001; Laran and Janiszewski, 2008), we posit that subtle cues that highlight the non-abundance of resources (e.g., half-length pencil in a writing task) can trigger the goal to conserve. These cues can cause a shift away from the default abundance mindset and the tendency to seek convenience, therefore leading people to waste less in subsequent consumption, even when the consumption takes place in unrelated domains and utilizes different types of resources. Consistent with the passive goal-activation account, we find that this decrease in waste induced by non-abundance cues is attenuated when participants get a chance to conserve before the resource is provided (e.g., giving them a chance to help with an environmental-based charity as compared to an education charity). We also find that people with a chronic conservation goal are less susceptible to the influences of non-abundance vs. abundance cues.

Study 1 tests for the presence of a default abundance mindset and whether non-abundance cues can lead people to waste less resources in unrelated domains. Participants completed two purportedly unrelated tasks. In the first soft-drink sampling task, the experimenter poured the same quantity of drink into a sampling cup, but either took the bottle away after pouring the drink (non-abundance condition) or left the bottle on the desk (abundance condition). In the second task, participants were given a roll of wrapping paper and asked to gift wrap a box. In a third, control condition, participants proceeded to the second task directly. The length of wrapping paper utilized served as the dependent measure for the relative waste amount. Consistently with our prediction, the non-abundance cue lead subjects to waste relatively less resource (i.e., wrapping paper) in a subsequent unrelated task. Importantly, the length of wrapping paper utilized in the control condition was similar to that in the abundance condition, suggesting that people are naturally in an abundance mindset. Additionally, in support of our theorization, we found (with another group of participants) that participants in the control condition reacted to abundance words as quickly as those in the abundance condition, whereas participants in the non-abundance condition reacted more slowly.

Study 2 disentangles the effect of non-abundances cues on consumption quantity and waste quantity. In the first task, participants completed a figure drawing task, which randomly assigned them to either a non-abundance condition in which they were provided only a half-length pencil, or an abundance condition in which they were given a penholder holding a stack of regular pencils. In the second task, participants sampled three snacks and were told to rinse their mouth with water before each tasting. They were instructed to go to another desk in the room to get the water and then come back to their seat to finish the sampling task. The amount of water poured (i.e., the total amount of resource taken), the amount of water left in the cup (i.e., the waste amount) and the difference of the two (i.e., the consumption amount) were measured. The amount of water consumed was the same in both conditions, but as compared to the abundance condition, participants in the non-abundance condition took less water and wasted less. These results provide support for the proposed convenience-based explanation by demonstrating that non-abundance cues decreased waste because they reduced the amount of resource taken, rather than increasing the amount of resource consumed.

The last two studies seek support for the proposed goal-activation account. In both studies, we asked participants to evaluate the smell and color of a new detergent and provided them with a crystal cup. The amount of detergent subjects poured into the cup served as our waste measure as only a minimal amount is needed for evaluation. Specifically, Study 3 investigates whether people with a chronic conservation goal (high on the frugality scale) are

insensitive to the influence of non-abundance vs. abundance cues. As predicted, we found that a non-abundance cue as compared to an abundance cue (manipulated by offering participants a small or large quantity of ketchup in a prior sampling task) lead low frugality participants to pour less detergent; whereas high frugality participants poured very low amounts in both the abundance and non-abundance conditions. Finally, Study 4 tests whether giving people a chance to satisfy the activated conservation goal (manipulated by giving them a chance to help with an environmental charity vs. an education charity) influences the relationship between non-abundance vs. abundance cues (manipulated as in Study 1 by leaving or not leaving the bottle of a sample drink) and waste. Consistent with the goal-activation account, we found that the decrease in waste induced by the non-abundance cue disappeared only when participants got the chance to conserve in the environmental charity.

In contrast to the prevailing literature that people are averse to waste, we propose an additional "wastism" perspective to study consumer waste behavior at a non-conscious level. Our findings indicate the presence of a default abundance mindset. This default abundant mindset accentuates the need for convenience, which in turn increases waste of resources. Non-abundance cues in the environment can passively activate a conservation goal thereby decreasing waste even in unrelated domains. In support of this theorization, we find that giving participants a chance to conserve before the resource is provided can diminish the beneficial impact of non-abundance cues on conservation.

## REFERENCES

Arkes, Hal R. (1996), "The Psychology of Waste," *Journal of Behavioral Decision Making*, 9 (September), 213-24.

Bargh, John A., Peter M. Gollwitzer, Annette Lee-Chai, Kimberly Barndollar, and Roman Tro¨tschel (2001), "The Automated Will: Nonconscious Activation and Pursuit of Behavioral Goals," *Journal of Personality and Social Psychology*, 81(December), 1014–27.

Côté, James E. (1993), "Foundations of a psychoanalytic social psychology: Neo-Eriksonian propositions regarding the relationship between psychic structure and cultural institutions," *Developmental Review*, 13(1), 31–53.

Côté, James E. (1996), "Sociological perspectives on identity formation: the culture–identity link and identity capital," *Journal of Adolescence*, 19(5), 417-28.

Laran, Juliano and Chris Janiszewski (2009), "Behavioral Consistency and Inconsistency in the Resolution of Goal Conflict," *Journal of Consumer Research*, 35 (April), 967-984

Riesman, D. (1950), *The Lonely Crowd: A Study of the Changing American Character*. New Haven: Yale University Press.

### "Please, Accept My Kidney: Kidney Donors in African American Families"

*Naja Williams Boyd, Anka Behavioral Health, Inc., USA*
*Tonya Williams Bradford, Notre Dame, USA*

The gift of an organ represents a sacrifice (Mauss 1967) and typically is requested, highly specified, extensively investigated, and tightly managed by several members of the healthcare system. Kidney transplantation is the only solid organ transplant performed in which an individual is able to gift an organ to another human being and continue to live a healthy and substantially normal life. Kidney donation is a gift exchange that is extensively controlled, monitored, and managed by the market. A gift of a kidney may be desired by the donor, the recipient, and the recipient's loved ones, yet there are required intermediaries who make the final determination for the gifting process—a departure from our understanding of gifting in consumer research.

Through five extended case studies, we explore the experience of living African American kidney donors who have successfully donated a kidney to a loved one. Through the experiences of these donors, we seek to understand consumer gifting behavior in complex market-necessitated circumstances. We purposely study experiences of African American kidney donors because they are in high demand for African Americans End Stage Renal Disease patients who are less likely to be referred, placed on the national waiting list, or receive a transplant (Gadegbeku 2002).

As symbols, gifts represent relational ties and communicate expectations from the giver to the recipient (Belk, Wallendorf, and Sherry 1989; Caplow 1984). Gifts establish and maintain roles in social relationships (Otnes, Lowrey, and Kim 1993), fortify social bonds (Mauss 1967), alter relationships (Cheal 1988), and serve higher-order needs of love, self-esteem or self-actualization (Belk 1996; Offer 1997). For our organ donor informants, the desire to enable the health of their loved ones is a tangible—life-giving—symbol which is mediated and managed through the healthcare market. The trinity of giving, receiving, and reciprocating constitutes an exchange cycle that attracts others into an intimate, involved relationship with one another. Receiving an organ from a relative places the recipient in a state of owing a gift of comparable magnitude. In general, the recipient will never be able to repay the debt, a circumstance described as the "the tyranny of the gift (Fox and Swazey 2002)," though it may be the role of the market that obviates the very need for reciprocity in this form of gifting (Marcoux 2009). We find organ donation to loved ones may not always result in a process devoid of reciprocity, as the organ donor may be engaged in self-gifting.

In the complex gifting circumstance of kidney organ donation within African American families, we find six themes that reflect significant decision drivers for our informants: loss and abandonment; recipient's health; recipient resistance and reluctance; family support; healthcare provider optimism; and organ donation education. Themes of abandonment and loss resulted from experiences of previous losses in their respective families. One participant said she was aware of her own "selfishness" and another did not want to lose another parent if she could make the difference. Was the gift of the kidney an actual gift to the recipient or was it a self gift to the donor? The two may actually be one and the same.

Each informant stated that the health of the recipient was of paramount concern in their decision to donate: "It was devastating for me to see him on dialysis." Recipient reluctance was prevalent as donors sought to give their organ. Not all recipients are interested in receiving kidneys from loved ones, because they "didn't want to put them [the donors] through that…" One informant stated that he felt "it may be difficult for a sibling to ask another to donate because it's a sacrifice" and that his brother would feel responsible if something were to happen to him. Family support plays a significant role in the gifting decision process. One donor shares responses to her decision to donate: "Oh girl, are you out of your mind?!" "Do you realize that you are going under the knife?" Her perspective was that "most Black people do not give up their organs."

The role of the market is crucial to the successful culmination of organ donation. Once one donor made the decision to donate and the recipient's approval, they made a conscious choice to wait until a new transplant team was in place. The donor had not been impressed with the transplant surgeon on staff because of the way he handled the recipient's first transplant surgery. The gift-giver and recipient decided to wait until the existing team retired and the new team was in place. It was her belief that "you have to have a connection with whoever is going to be working with you." The

market also is involved in the education process. Donors became educated about the process from their work environments, medical providers, and websites. All gift-givers were willing to donate because they had knowledge and had become educated about living kidney donation.

A kidney is an extraordinary gift. People who give gifts want to know whether their gifts are appreciated and used for their intended purpose (Sherry 1983). Such expectations have a quality of self-interest and may develop into enmeshed relationships created by the donor toward the recipient. This leads to complications in the relationship for both parties, particularly for the recipient. Post-donation behavior will depend on the expectations of the donor when they made the decision to gift the kidney. Recipients may anticipate these feelings of obligation from the beginning; that may be the reason they prefer not ask a living relative to be a donor. Thus, relationships may be altered as a result of kidney donation (Ruth, Otnes, and Brunel 1999).

From the experiences of our informants, we find kidney organ donors may experience the gift of their kidney to a relative as a puritanic self-gift (Mick 1996) with the hopes of continuing a cherished relationship. As such, the gift of the kidney is both a gift and a self-gift which is reciprocated by the recipient through a continued affective relationship, and embraced by the donor as either reward or stress relief through the same which truly encapsulates the notion of the extended self (Belk 1988). We expand the notion of puritanic self gifts to encompass those where the task completion is the reinstatement of the desired status. In the case of kidney transplantation, task completion is that the kidney recipient engages in life fully without the constraints and limitations of end stage renal disease and the donor goes along, with one less kidney, for the ride!

## REFERENCES

Belk, Russell W. (1988), "Possessions and the Extended Self," *Journal of Consumer Research*, 15 (2), 139-60.
_____ (1996), "The Perfect Gift," in *Gift Giving: A Research Anthology*, ed. Cele Otnes and Richard Francis Beltramini, Bowling Green: Bowling Green Popular Press, 59-84.
Belk, Russell W., Melanie Wallendorf, and John F. Sherry, Jr. (1989), "The Sacred and the Profane in Consumer Behavior: Theodicy on the Odyssey," *Journal of Consumer Research*, 16 (1), 1-38.
Caplow, Theodore (1984), "Rule Enforcement without Visible Means: Christmas Gift Giving in Middletown," *American Journal of Sociology*, 89 (6), 1306-23.
Cheal, David (1988), *The Gift Economy*, Cambridge: University Press.
Fox, Renee Claire and Judith P. Swazey (2002), *The Courage to Fail: A Social View of Organ Transplants and Dialysis*, New Bruswick, NJ: Transaction Publishers.
Gadegbeku, Crystal (2002), "Racial Disparities in Renal Replacement," *Journal of the National Medical Association*, 94 (8), 45-56.
Marcoux, Jean-Sebastien (2009), "Escaping the Gift Economy," *Journal of Consumer Research*, 36 (4), 671-85.
Mauss, Marcel (1967), *The Gift.*, New York: Norton.
Mick, David (1996), "Self-Gifts," in *Gift Giving: An Interdisciplinary Anthology*, ed. Cele Otnes and Richard Beltrami, Bowling Green, KY: Popular Press, 99-120.
Offer, Avner (1997), "Between the Gift and the Market: The Economy of Regard," *The Economic History Review*, 50 (3), 450-76.

Otnes, Cele, Tina M Lowrey, and Young Chan Kim (1993), "Gift Selection for Easy and Difficult Recipients: A Social Roles Interpretation," *Journal of Consumer Research*, 20 (2), 229-44.

Ruth, Julie A., Cele C. Otnes, and Frederic F. Brunel (1999), "Gift Receipt and the Reformulation of Interpersonal Relationships," *Journal of Consumer Research*, 25 (4), 385-402.

Sherry, John F. (1983), "Gift Giving in Anthropological Perspective," *Journal of Consumer Research*, 10 (2), 157-68.

# The 'Nature' Of Life: How the Physical World Colors Impressions, Informs Decisions, and Shapes Who We Are

Joshua M. Ackerman, MIT Sloan School of Management), USA

Lawrence E. Williams, University of Colorado at Boulder, USA

## EXTENDED ABSTRACT

### "Haptic Experiences: A Touching Story of Impression Formation and Decision-Making"

*Joshua Ackerman, MIT Sloan School of Management, USA*

*Christopher C. Nocera, Harvard University, USA*

*John A. Bargh, Yale University, USA*

Touch serves a critical means of learning, communication, and developing social bonds, yet, despite the fact that tactile sensations are critical to both our intra- and interpersonal lives, touch remains perhaps the most underappreciated sense in behavioral research. Several researchers have begun to highlight the importance of touch within consumer domains (e.g., Peck and Childers 2003). Tactile cues can influence our conceptions about products, even when those cues are nondiagnostic for the actual qualities of the item (e.g., water seems to taste better from a firm bottle versus a flimsy bottle; Krishna and Morrin 2008). Why might our sense of touch direct our impressions about untouched (or untouchable) things?

One possibility is that sensorimotor experiences in early life form a scaffold for the development of conceptual knowledge, which is subsequently applied to novel events, situations and objects. This conceptual information is reflected in the use of particular psychological constructs such as metaphors. For example, grasping motions and feelings of warmth elicited by interpersonal touch may give rise to beliefs about holding and caring as expressed in the aphorism "the world is in our hands."

Building off work on metaphor priming, we propose that experiences with specific, object-related tactile qualities activate a haptic mindset such that touching objects triggers increased accessibility and application of associated concepts, even for unrelated impressions and decisions. We present 6 studies testing the role of 3 touch dimensions—weight, texture and hardness—in impression formation and decision-making.

*Weight*: The experience of weight, or heaviness, is metaphorically associated with concepts of seriousness and importance (e.g., "thinking about *weighty* matters,"). The physical experience of weight was manipulated by having participants hold either heavy or light clipboards. In Study 1, participants holding the heavy clipboard judged an academic job candidate as more serious about and better qualified for the position, but not as more likable. In Study 2, participants holding the heavy clipboard decided that important issues (e.g., air pollution standards), but not idiosyncratic issues (e.g., creation of universal electrical plug outlets), should receive more funding.

*Texture*: The experience of texture, or roughness, is metaphorically associated with the concepts of difficulty and harshness (e.g., "having a *rough* day,"). The physical experience of texture was manipulated by having participants complete either a rough or smooth puzzle prior to the main study DVs. In Study 3, participants completing a rough puzzle judged two people in an ambiguously-valenced interaction as displaying less coordinated (i.e., more difficult and harsh) behavior, but not less relationship familiarity. In Study 4, participants in an Ultimatum game offered lottery tickets to a 2nd person who could accept or reject the offer. Those completing the rough puzzle gave more tickets, which further analysis suggested

was compensatory behavior for perceptions of low coordination and not due to more cooperative inclinations.

*Malleability*: The experience of malleability, or hardness, is metaphorically associated with concepts of stability, rigidity and strictness (e.g., "*hard*-hearted"). The physical experience of hardness was manipulated both actively (Study 5) and passively (Study 6). In Study 5, participants examined one of two objects to be used in a magic act—a hard block of wood or a soft blanket—and then evaluated the personality of an ambiguously described employee. Participants who touched the hard wood judged the employee to be more rigid/strict, but not more or less positive on other traits (e.g., trusting, kind). In Study 6, participants sat in either hard wooden chairs or soft cushioned chairs while making two offers in a car-buying negotiation task. Participants sitting in the hard chair exhibited less change in price from 1st to 2nd offer, indicating reduced decision malleability.

In summary, six experiments showed that heavy objects trigger conceptions of importance, rough objects trigger conceptions of difficulty, and hard objects trigger conceptions of rigidity. First impressions are liable to be influenced by one's tactile surroundings, and control over these surroundings may be especially important for negotiators, pollsters, job seekers, and those interested in interpersonal communication.

### "Washing Away the Past with Cleaning Products: Of Dirty Mouths, Dirty Hands, and Post-Decisional Dissonance"

*Spike W. S. Lee, University of Michigan, USA*

*Norbert Schwarz, University of Michigan, USA*

Brushing our teeth, washing our hands, and taking showers are part of our daily routine. Their psychological effect goes far beyond cleaning our bodies. As a growing number of studies indicates, cleaning products remove more than stains, microbes, and contaminants—they also remove the guilt of past misdeeds, weaken the urge to engage in compensatory behavior (Zhong and Liljenquist 2006), and attenuate the impact of disgust on moral judgment (Schnall, Benton and Harvey 2008). These findings are usually conceptualized in terms of a "moral purity" metaphor that grounds abstract thought about morality in more concrete experiences of physical cleanliness. In natural language use, this metaphor is associated with the specific body parts involved in an immoral act, prompting speakers to refer, for example, to "dirty hands" or a "dirty mouth." This suggests that the specific motor-modality involved in an immoral act may figure prominently in the embodiment of the moral purity metaphor, potentially prompting people to purify the specific body part involved in the act. While this conjecture is compatible with the general canon of embodiment, the implied motor-modality specificity has not received attention and the embodiment of the moral purity metaphor has been treated as generic in previous research: washing one's hands (the only cleaning manipulation used to date) is assumed to restore purity independent of the specific body part involved in the "dirty" act.

Therefore, we conducted two experiments in which a transgression involved either only the hands ("manual modality") or only the mouth ("oral modality"). Experiment 1 coded for motor-modality in autobiographic memories of moral transgressions and Experiment 2 induced participants to lie on voicemail (involving the mouth) or email (involving the hands). As predicted, doing bad things with one's mouth increased the appeal (desire and willingness to pay) of mouthwash but not of hand-sanitizer; conversely, doing bad things with one's hands increased the appeal of hand-sanitizer but not of mouthwash. These converging findings indicate that the morality-purity link is specific to the motor-modality involved in moral transgressions.

Note, however, that metaphors involving physical cleanliness extend beyond moral issues. We may say, for example, that we "wipe our slate clean" to convey that we are ready to move on to new endeavors. If so, the use of cleaning products may not only restore moral purity but may metaphorically "wash away" traces of past behaviors that may have no particular moral implications. We tested whether physical cleansing can more generally reduce the impact of past actions, even actions without moral implications. Using a classic dissonance paradigm, we gave people a free choice between two similarly attractive music albums. After selecting one, they participated in a "product evaluation survey" that involved either simply examining a bottle of hand soap or actually washing one's hands with it. Finally, they provided another rating of the albums. Replicating the usual dissonance findings, the attractiveness of the chosen album increased, and the attractiveness of the rejected album decreased, after the choice. However, this was *only* observed when participants merely examined the soap. When participants tested the soap by washing their hands, their post-choice ratings were unaffected by the decision made, indicating that dissonance was "washed away."

In combination, these findings extend earlier research in several ways. First, they highlight that the metaphorical link between moral and physical purity is specific to the motor-modality used: if given a choice, consumers want to clean the tainted body part. Second, our findings highlight that the impact of physical cleansing extends beyond the domain of morality as has been previously assumed. Ongoing research addresses whether such cleansing effects are limited to past negative events (e.g., moral transgressions, poor choices) or also extend to the positive glow of competent and noble acts (e.g., being an eloquent salesperson, raising awareness of support to Haiti).

### "Embodied Real Estate: North-South Location Biases Housing Preference and Pricing"

*Brian P. Meier, Gettysburg College, USA*
*Julie J. Chen, Gettysburg College, USA*
*Arlen C. Moller, Northwestern University, USA*

People link abstract concepts to sensory experiences in metaphors to express preferences. One metaphor describes good and bad in terms of space. For example, good things are described as high ("her career is on the rise") while bad things are described as low ("he's on the bottom rung"). Research shows that when evaluating things, people unwittingly activate vertical perceptions in a metaphor-consistent manner (good=up; bad=down; Meier and Robinson 2004).

We examined an under-explored metaphor, north-south as up-down. Maps are typically constructed such that north is up and south is down despite the fact that north and south do not physically relate to vertical space. Frequent exposure to this representation may contribute to the tendency to describe north and south in vertical terms (e.g., "we're headed up north"; see Nelson and Simmons 2009). A consequence is that directions may have developed affective connotations (i.e., north represents "good"). For example, in some areas of the U.S., terms like "southie" or "movin' on up" suggest that northern areas of cities are more attractive than southern areas.

We predicted that a north-south affective bias has implications for an important decision context–real estate judgments. We hypothesized that people will perceive higher house prices and income among residents in northern areas of a city, and that people will prefer to live in northern areas as well.

*Study 1.* Sixty-six undergraduates (41 males) chose where to live in a fictional city. We created a city map that included lines around the city limits. Distances between north-south limits and west-east limits were equal. We told participants the map represents a city and the lines indicate the city limits. We asked them to imagine that they were moving to this city and could live anywhere, and to select a location on the map. We converted choices to a score that represented the distance from the north-south mid-point. Analyses revealed that participants' average choice was significantly north of the mid-point, $t(65)=2.15$, $p=.035$, $d=.27$.

*Study 2.* We hypothesize that people prefer to live in the north because they believe northern areas of a city have higher socioeconomic status (SES). The map from Study 1 was presented on paper. We randomly assigned 87 undergraduates (30 males) to one of two conditions in which we described either a High SES (wealthy) or Low SES (poor and unemployed) individual named Mr. Bennett. Participants drew an "x" on the map to indicate where they thought "Bennett" lived. We calculated position of the estimates for north-south and west-east locations and converted these into scores that indicated the distance from the mid-point. An ANCOVA examined the impact of condition on north-south estimate while controlling for west-east estimates. Estimates for the High SES person were further north than estimates for the Low SES person, $F(1,84)=32.75$, $p<.001$, partial $eta^2=.28$.

*Study 3.* We sought to determine if a north-south bias influences house prices. We collected data on house prices and locations for the 25 most populous cities in the U.S. We used a real estate website (Trulia.com) to find 50 houses in each city. We selected the first 50 listings for each city that included address, price, and square footage (1,250 data points). We found the latitude (north-south) and longitude (west-east) for each address using Geocoder.us. A partial correlation for each city was calculated between price and latitude (controlling for the quadratic, square footage, and longitude). The average Fisher's Z was .13, which was significantly greater than zero, $t(24)=1.96$, $p=.031$, $d=.40$, one-tailed. On average, housing prices support the north-south bias.

Our results reveal a surprising impact of north-south location on real estate preference and valuation. Embodied metaphor theory and research has revealed that cognition is grounded in metaphor, but the current findings move beyond laboratory-based social cognition by revealing the potential for such representations to influence behavior in contexts of significant financial importance.

### "I Am Where I Am: Physical Distance Fractures the Self"

*Alexandra Sedlovskaya, Yale University, USA*
*John A. Bargh, Yale University, USA*
*Lawrence E. Williams, University of Colorado at Boulder, USA*
*Valerie Purdie-Vaughns, Columbia University, USA*

Given the rapid pace of technological advances in telecommunication and transportation over the past century, people's lives commonly span large distances. Within the U.S., family networks extend across state boundaries, business is conducted in an increasingly global fashion, and students travel well beyond local confines to attend college. The boundaries of the average life space, defined as the sum of a person's intrapersonal, interpersonal, and ecological experiences (Lewin 1943), are arguably at their widest point in human history. What are the consequences of this heightened capability to live lives spanning large distances?

We propose that physical distance promotes fracturing of the self into distinct self-aspects. Support for this proposition stems from an emerging tradition that grounds people's psychological states in their physical environment (Williams, Huang and Bargh 2009). In this view, people's early childhood understanding of fundamental physical concepts, such as physical distance, facilitates the development of abstract concepts, such as interpersonal distance (Williams and Bargh 2008). Since the distinction between self-aspects involves psychological distance, greater physical distance should increase this distinction. For example, greater physical distance that students travel to attend university should increase the distinction they experience between school and home identities.

To examine this physical-self relationship, 46 university students were primed with either physical closeness or physical distance by plotting coordinates that appeared either close together or far apart on a Cartesian plane, thus allowing participants to perceive and engage in relevant motor actions (Williams and Bargh, 2008). To examine whether this physical distance cue altered the psychological distinction that students experience between their school and home identities, we next measured the speed with which participants indicated whether a series of traits best described them at school or at home, while controlling for their general speed of response. If people experience difficulty distinguishing between their school and home identities, then they should take more time to respond. We predicted that participants primed with physical distance would experience greater distinction between school and home identities and would thus be faster on this measure, compared to participants primed with physical closeness. Our results supported this prediction [$F(1, 41)=5.57, P=.02$], suggesting that physical distance strengthen the psychological distinction people draw between aspects of their identities.

Study 2 extended this finding by using a more ecologically valid operationalization of physical distance and by examining reported stress as a potential downstream consequence of self-fracturing. Study 2 employed the same response latency measure used in our first study, as well as the Perceived Stress Scale to measure stress at school. Physical distance was operationalized as the number of miles between students' university and their hometowns. Consistent with Study 1, data from 38 university students revealed that greater geographical distance was associated with shorter responses latencies, indicating greater distinction between school and home identities [$?=-.38, t(33)=-2.69, P=.01$], which was in turn associated with higher reported stress at school [$?=-.40, t(33) =-2.23, P=.03$].

In summary, the simple perception of and motor actions associated with physical distance increased the psychological bifurcation of the self into distinct self-aspects. This effect echoes recent demonstrations of how environmental cues can meaningfully affect people's judgments and decisions. Practically, this work suggests a psychological benefit of thinking locally (less identity fracturing, less stress), and encourages practitioners to recognize the power of local environs in shaping consumer identities.

## REFERENCES

Krishna, Aradhna and Maureen Morrin (2008), "Does Touch Affect Taste? The Perceptual Transfer of Product Container Haptic Cues," *Journal of Consumer Research,* 34(April), 807-818.

Lewin, Kurt (1943), "Defining the 'Field' at a Given Time," *Psychological Review*, 50 (3), 292-310.

Meier, Brian P., and Michael D. Robinson (2004), "Why the Sunny Side is Up," *Psychological Science*, 15 (4), 243-247.

Nelson, Leif D., and Joseph P. Simmons (2009), "On Southbound Ease and Northbound Fees: Literal Consequences of the Metaphoric Link between Vertical Position and Cardinal Direction," *Journal of Marketing Research*, 46 (6), 715-724.

Peck, Joann and Terry L. Childers (2003), "To Have and To Hold: The Influence of Haptic Information on Product Judgments," *Journal of Marketing,* 67(April), 35-48.

Schnall, Simone, Jennifer Benton, and Sophie Harvey (2008), "With a Clean Conscience: Cleanliness Reduces the Severity of Moral Judgments," *Psychological Science,* 19 (12), 1219-1222.

Williams, Lawrence E. and John A. Bargh (2008), "Keeping One's Distance: The Influence of Spatial Distance Cues on Affect and Evaluation," *Psychological Science,* 19 (March), 302-308.

Williams, Lawrence E., Julie Y. Huang, and John A. Bargh (2009), "The Scaffolded Mind: Higher Mental Processes Are Grounded in Early Experience of the Physical World," *European Journal of Social Psychology,* 39 (December), 1257-1267.

Zhong, Chen-Bo, and Katie Liljenquist (2006), "Washing Away Your Sins: Threatened Morality and Physical Cleansing," *Science,* 313 (September), 1451-1452.

# Moral Flexibility in Consumer Judgment and Choice
Dan Bartels, University of Chicago, USA

A. Peter McGraw, University of Colorado, Boulder, USA

## EXTENDED ABSTRACTS

### "Slam the Good Guys: Guilt Over Less Ethical Behavior Results in Denigration of Ethical Consumers"

*Julie R. Irwin, University of Texas, Austin, USA*

*Szu-Chi Huang, University of Texas, Austin, USA*

It has been suggested that observing others behaving ethically inspires admiration and "other-praising" (Algoe and Haidt 2009; Haidt 2001). We explore a less positive response to ethical others, especially among consumers who themselves have not behaved ethically. We examine the process by which behaving less ethically can result in "slamming" people who behave more ethically than we do, with the goal of preserving self-esteem.

Individuals gain self-esteem from thinking of themselves as moral and that they reconcile conflicts between their perceived morality and actual behavior in the direction of preserving self-esteem (Batson et al. 1999). Despite the motivation to perceive the self as highly moral, individuals frequently fail to carry out ethical behaviors in the market place. Many motivations, such as the desire to avoid reading about uncomfortable information (e.g., Ehrich and Irwin 2005) or the beliefs about moral tradeoffs (Luchs, Naylor, Irwin and Raghunathan in press), often lead consumers to avoid ethical information even when they care about the underlying issues.

Our project focuses on what happens after a consumer fails to act ethically (e.g., fails to seek out ethical information in order to make an informed ethical choice) in the market. We propose that after behaving less ethically, consumers denigrate other consumers who would have acted more ethically than they did. We show that guilt underlies these judgments, and that reducing guilt reduces the denigration. Furthermore, we show that the denigration reduces future ethical behavior.

In Study 1, participants chose between four pairs of jeans that differed on: style, price, manufacturer size and either manufacturers' labor practices (i.e., whether their factories employed children, the ethical condition) or manufacturers' delivery time (control condition). All of the attribute information was initially hidden and participants could choose to view the contents for two out of the four attributes before making their product choices. Thus, participants overwhelmingly chose to view price and style, not the fourth piece of information (labor practice or delivery time). We expected that only the participants in the ethical attribute condition would feel that their ethical self-view had been threatened from not choosing the fourth attribute. After choosing the attributes and the jeans, participants rated consumers who "ask about the labor practices used to produce their clothes (i.e., whether child labor was used) before buying them". Only a few participants viewed the fourth attribute; they were eliminated from the analysis. Our results supported our hypothesis of "slamming" the good guys: not viewing information about manufacturers' labor practices (vs. delivery time) resulted in significantly more unfavorable ratings of ethical others on both positive (e.g., fashionable and attractive) and negative (e.g., boring and preachy) characteristics.

In Study 2, participants could view the attribute value information for either one, two, or four (i.e., all) attributes before making product choices. We expected the two attribute condition to produce more threat than the other two conditions. Indeed, the denigration and self-esteem was statistically equivalent in the one and four/all attribute conditions. In addition, we measured self-esteem either right before or right after the (possible) denigration. Participants in the threatening two-attribute condition had significantly lower self-esteem prior to denigration, and were significantly more likely to denigrate ethical others. After denigrating others, self-esteem and ethical self-view were restored to the same level as groups who did not feel threatened, indicating that the denigration served its psychological purpose.

Study 3 tested our hypothesis using backpacks and a different ethical attribute (recycled content of materials). Participants could view information about one, two, or four (material, price, function, and recycled content) attributes. Participants made product choices and either evaluated ethical others or did not. In this study, in the "chance to denigrate" condition we allowed them to both rate others and to provide open-ended evaluation of "people who might check the recycling practices of the firms that make their backpacks". Also, at the end of the task all participants were invited to take a "Think Green" online pledge to sign up for e-newsletters about easy ways to be green. Both the open-ended responses and the ratings scales replicated the denigration results (i.e., more denigration in the threat condition). In addition, we also found that participants who were threatened (i.e., who were in the two-attribute condition) showed a significant difference in future ethical behavior depending on whether they were given the opportunity to denigrate. The more they denigrated others, the less likely they were to take the environmental pledge. In other words, denigration restored self-esteem to such an extent that it actually reduced future moral behavior.

Thus, consumers do not, at least in our context, respond with admiration to ethical behavior. Instead, they denigrate ethical consumers. We suggest that awe and other positive emotions may be more likely when guilt is absent; it may be easier to avoid denigration when self-esteem is not threatened.

### "Sweatshop Labor is Wrong Unless the Jeans are Really Cute: Motivated Moral Disengagement"

*Neeru Paharia, Harvard Business School, USA*

*Rohit Deshpandé, Harvard Business School, USA*

*Kathleen Vohs, University of Minnesota, USA*

We examine whether people may be motivated to morally disengage (Bandura 1991, 1999) in the presence of harmful attributes such as sweatshop labor when desire for a product is high. We show that moral disengagement can be driven by affective desire for a product. Mechanisms of moral disengagement may allow consumers to perceive their desire for products made with sweatshop labor to be consistent with their moral standards (Tsang 2002) enabling them to avoid dissonance (Festinger 1957). We demonstrate that levels of moral disengagement can be motivated by one's level of desire for a product made with sweatshop labor. Furthermore, we show a full mediated moderation where beliefs about sweatshop labor use moderates the impact of desirability on purchase intention, and moral disengagement mediates this process.

In experiment 1 participants were told about a hypothetical pair of jeans where sweatshop labor was either present or not. Participants were then asked about their desire for the jeans and answered questions on moral disengagement. We predicted that when sweatshop labor was present, there would be a stronger positive association between desire for a product and moral disengagement than when no sweatshop labor was present. In the *high sweatshop labor* condition participants first read: *Imagine that you are shopping and found the perfect pair of jeans. They look good on you and fit great. [A large amount of sweatshop labor was used to produce these jeans.]* In the *no sweatshop labor* condition the text in brackets was replaced by the following: *No sweatshop labor was used to produce these jeans.* Participants were first asked about their desirability for the jeans and then asked about moral disengagement. The moral disengagement measures were adapted from Bandura et al.'s (1996) original scale, and participants were asked to indicated how much the agreed or disagreed with the following four statements: 1. *The use of sweatshop labor is okay because otherwise those workers would not have jobs*; 2. *Without sweatshops poorer countries couldn't develop*; 3. *Buying clothes that are made with sweatshop labor is okay if it saves the consumer money because clothes are not affordable.*; and: 4. *The use of sweatshop labor is okay because companies must remain competitive and all other companies do it.* We found levels of moral disengagement to be significantly higher when desirability for a product was high and sweatshop labor was present. In the case where sweatshop labor was not present, there was no significant association between desirability and moral disengagement. Experiment 1 gives us cause to believe that moral disengagement may be motivated by one's desirability for a product.

In experiment 2, (in a 2X2 between subjects design) participants first read about the desirability of a hypothetical pair of Nike shoes. In the *high desirability* condition participants read: *Imagine that you own a pair of Nike running shoes. [The shoes retail for $175.00 and you got them at a 75% discount. You are extremely happy with these shoes.]* In the *low desirability* condition the text in brackets was replaced by the following: *The shoes retail for $175.00 and you got them at a 5% discount. You are satisfied with these shoes.* After answering this initial set of questions on desirability participants clicked through to the next page and were told about Nike's labor practices. In the *high sweatshop labor* condition participants read: *Imagine that you've just read an article that suggests that Nike [uses] sweatshop labor to make their shoes.* In the *no sweatshop labor* condition the text in brackets was replaced by: *does not use.* Participants then answered questions on moral disengagement, and asked about their beliefs about Nike's true use of sweatshop labor. Participants then answered a second set desirability questions that were identical to the first set. Finally participants were asked about purchase intention. We found that measures of moral disengagement were higher for *high desirability* products than for *low desirability* products when sweatshop labor was present; however we did not find this effect in the *no sweatshop labor* condition. Furthermore, we show a full mediated moderation where beliefs about high sweatshop labor use are associated with an *increased* purchase intention for high desirability products; however this effect does not hold for low desirability products.

In a follow up study we demonstrate the effects of moral disengagement can be attenuated when participants are put under cognitive load. More specifically, a positive association between one's desire for a product and level of moral disengagement disappears once participants are put under load. Such finding suggests that limiting one's cognitive resources may reduce desire-driven moral disengagement.

As we are confronted with conflicts between our desires, and our moral standards on nearly a daily basis it behooves us to carefully consider how our desires, in particular, drive us to morally disengage from harmful behavior. If our moral judgments vary based on our affective desires, any moral standards we may hold ourselves to are dubious at best, and desire-driven moral disengage-

ment may broadly contribute towards the tolerance of harm in our social and economic systems.

## "Choosing For the Right Reasons: Value-driven Reasoning in Consumer Choice"

*David Tannenbaum, University of California-Irvine, USA*
*Daniel M. Bartels, University of Chicago, USA*

Even if consumers do not always succeed in choosing outcomes that make them happier, healthier, or wealthier, they usually try their best to do so. In this way, most choices consumers make reflect a desire to maximize consequences. Some moral choices involving protected values, however, are more driven by proscriptions than by consequences (e.g., "do not allow companies to pollute for a fee, even if the fee helps reduce pollution"). In four studies, we examine how thinking about proscriptions and consequences may depend on the decision maker's initial preferences and on the situational context. We find that when presented with ethically-relevant information, consumers with a 'protected value' are both more *and* less consequentialist in their choices than consumers without protected values. Because PV consumers care deeply about the issue at hand, their choices vary based on what information they attend to (Bartels 2008) and what reasons are available for the choice (Shafir 1993).

In the first three studies, we presented participants with descriptions of each option's non-ethical attributes (e.g., workmanship and comfort ratings) and collected desirability ratings. Later, we presented them with ethically-relevant information (e.g., whether a desk used unsustainable rainforest wood) and assessed preferences for one option over the other.

Study 1 pitted an attractive product that used rainforest wood against a less attractive product that did not. The more attractive desk was described, depending upon condition, as constructed from rainforest wood that caused unmitigated harm to the environment ("Impoverished Harm") or from rainforest wood whose harm was mitigated through the planting of trees that resulted in a net gain for the environment ("Enriched Harm"). Only participants with a PV were likely to choose the more unattractive desk, and this was the case in both the Impoverished Harm and Enriched Harm conditions. When the choice context allows for one to honor a PV—with at least one option not causing harm to the rainforest—then subjects with PVs tend to choose on this basis, regardless of the consequences entailed and regardless of their initial preferences.

Study 2 was similar to Study 1, except now participants could choose only between the Impoverished and Enriched Harm conditions. Now, participants with a PV were most likely to choose the Enriched Harm option. When the choice context did not allow for honoring a PV—with both options caused some degree of harm—then subjects with a PV made more consequentialist choices than subjects without a PV, regardless of their initial preferences.

Study 3 examined if the previous two findings—that subjects with a PV can be both more and less consequentialist depending on the choice context—is the result of moral posturing or value-driven choice. A moral posturing account would explain this pattern by arguing that participants with a PV still wish to choose the more attractive desk (even if it causes more harm), but only have a reasonable excuse to do so in Study 2. A value-driven choice account would argue that participants with a PV will choose to not actively cause harm so long as they have the ability to do so (when they do not have that option, they will instead choose to maximize consequences). Study 3 was designed to pit these two accounts against each other. Participants now chose between three options: (i) a less attractive, No Harm option, (ii) a more attractive, Enriched Harm option, and (iii) a symmetrically-dominated very unattractive, very harmful option. Consistent with the value-driven choice account, participants with a PV tended to choose the No Harm option that honored their protected value even though they could justify choosing the more attractive, Enriched Harm option because it was both more attractive and caused less harm than the dominated option.

Our final study explored the role of reasons in explaining how participants made a value-driven decision. For Study 4, participants judged which of two companies was (depending upon condition) either more moral or more immoral. Similar to Study 2, one company's actions embodied Impoverished Harm and the other Enriched Harm. Subjects with a PV were more likely than non-PV subjects to both accept the enriched option as morally superior and reject it as morally inferior.

In sum, consumers with a PV are more likely than consumers without a PV to make use of ethical attribute information when presented with such information. If one or more options satisfies the proscription to do no harm—even if it is unattractive or other options might maximize consequences—they opt for the No Harm choice. If all available options cause some degree of harm, however, consumers with PVs maximize ethically-relevant consequences, regardless of their initial preferences. Consumers without a PV, however, choose according to their initial preferences.

### "Commercial Marketing with Communal Sentiments: Reframing Taboo Trade-offs in Religious Marketing"

*A. Peter McGraw, University of Colorado, Boulder, USA*
*Janet Schwartz, Duke University, USA*
*Philip E. Tetlock, University of California, Berkeley, USA*

While consumers typically expect businesses to profit from the marketing of goods and services, they believe that some organizations should be more focused on accomplishing communal goals than making a profit. When communally-focused organizations do use commercial marketing strategies, consumers react as though a taboo has been breached (Tetlock 2002). For example, consumers find it morally distressing to see churches using steadfast commercial-marketing strategies like advertising, rebranding, and outsourcing (e.g., McDaniel 1996). People will respond with a mix of moral outrage (condemn the perpetrators) and moral cleansing (distance oneself from the transgressors; Tetlock et al. 2000; McGraw, Tetlock, and Kristel 2003). This creates negative consequences for the organization; people stop using services or they spread negative word-of-mouth.

We investigate the ability of organizations to conceal or assuage taboo trade-offs. As a case study, we examine people's reactions to the use of marketing techniques by religious organizations. Churches compete with the secular world for the allegiance of worshipers, and churches are increasingly resorting to the same marketing techniques that corporations use to recruit, retain, and serve customers (e.g., Schlesinger and Mellado 1991, Symonds 2005). But not everyone finds these techniques acceptable; people can be horrified when churches use violent video games to recruit young people (Richtel 2007).

The project draws on work by McGraw and Tetlock (2005) that examines how rhetorical redefinitions (i.e., relational framing) change the perceived normative 'rules' at work for a strategy in order to assuage the unsettling nature of a taboo trade-off. We test the effectiveness of organizational justifications that reframe market interventions to have a communal focused (i.e., priorities and offerings based on cooperative and relationship-building principles; see Fiske 1991). If marketing techniques are rhetorically disguised through communal-focused endeavors, the church gets both market efficiency and loyalty. But if rhetorical disguises fail, market-based techniques may compromise the moral branding and sanctity of the church.

In Study 1a, we presented participants twelve marketing strategies that an organization was considering using. The strategies were pretested to vary along a continuum from communally-focused (e.g., provide child care for members) to market-focused (e.g., institute a rebranding strategy). We find that neither communal nor market focused strategies affected the judged acceptability of the marketing strategies used by a credit union, a secular market-driven organization. For a religious organization, however, judgments of acceptability were strongly influenced by the focus of the strategy. As the strategy became more communally focused as opposed to market focused the strategy was viewed as increasingly more acceptable. In Study 1b, we show that negative reactions to commercial marketing techniques by a church mediate people's desire to affiliate with the organization.

Study 2 investigated the effect of presenting communal-sharing justifications for market interventions conducted by a church. We found that distress with the Catholic Church's practice of outsourcing prayers to India due to a shortage of U.S. Priests was mitigated by invoking the shared world-wide communality of Priests, a justification that emphasizes the communal nature of the church across national boundaries. Reported distress in a market-pricing justification condition ("matching supply and demand in the market for prayer service, thus maximizing prayers and revenue generation") was no different than that of a control condition that featured no justification, which indicated that respondents spontaneously assumed and rebuffed the church's market-based intervention.

Study 2 also investigated who is most affected by communal justifications. We hypothesized that those who have the greatest moral stake in the organization would be most motivated to seize on the communal justification and thus show the greatest reduction in distress. We found that consumers who most regularly attend religious services were most persuaded by communal reframing justification.

In a third study, we demonstrate that moral outrage with outsourcing prayer was linked to moral contamination and not socially desirable responding. To do so, we drew on the Lady Macbeth effect, whereby people feel physically tainted by morally upsetting information and seek physical cleansing opportunities to symbolically cleanse themselves (Zhong and Liljenquist 2006). Indeed, respondents exposed to the outsourcing decision without a communal justification showed the greatest preference for cleaning products (e.g., Tide detergent) relative to non-cleaning products (e.g., post-it notes).

Marketing is commonly used to add value to consumer experience and build brand relationships. However, certain categories of marketing tactics appear to be disturbing to consumers when they believe the organization ought to be acting in communal ways. We show that distress with religious marketing is assuaged by simple rhetorical tactics that transform market actions into communal actions.

### REFERENCES

Bandura, A. (1991). Social cognitive theory of moral thought and action. In *Handbook of moral behavior and development: Theory, research, and applications,* W.M. Kurtines & J.L. Gewirtz (eds.) Hillsdale NJ: Erlbaum.

Bandura, A. (1999). Moral Disengagement in the Perpetration of Inhumanities. *Personality & Social Psychology Review, 3,* 193-

Bandura, A., Barbaranelli, C., Caprara, G.V., & Pastorelli, C. (1996). Mechanisms of moral disengagement in the exercise of moral agency" *Journal of Personality and Social Psychology, 71,* 364-374.

Batson, Daniel C., Elizabeth R. Thompson, Greg Seuferling, Heather Whitney, and Jon A. Strongman (1999), "Moral Hypocrisy: Appearing Moral to Oneself without Being So," *Journal of Personality and Social Psychology*, 77 (September), 525-37.

Baron, J., & Spranca, M. (1997). Protected values. *Organizational Behavior and Human Decision Processes, 70,* 1-16.

Bartels, Daniel M. (2008). Principled Moral Sentiment and the Flexibility of Moral Judgment and Decision Making, *Cognition, 108,* 381-417.

Bartels, D. M. & Medin, D. L. (2007). Are morally motivated decision makers insensitive to the consequences of their choices? *Psychological Science, 18,* 24–28.

Belk, R.W., Wallendorf, W.& Sherry J. (1989). The sacred and the profane in consumer behavior: Theodicy on the odyssey, *Journal of Consumer Research,* 16, 1-38.

Ehrich, K.R. & Irwin, J.R. (2005). Willful ignorance in the request of product attribute information. *Journal of Marketing Research, 42,* 266–77.

Festinger, Leon (1957), *A Theory of Cognitive Dissonance.* Stanford University Press, Palo Alto, CA.

Haidt, J. (2003). Elevation and the positive psychology of morality. In C. L. M. Keyes & J. Haidt (Eds.) Flourishing: Positive psychology and the life well-lived. Washington DC: American Psychological Association. (pp. 275-289).

Luchs, Michael, Rebecca Walker Naylor, Julie R. Irwin and Rajagopal Raghunathan. "The Sustainability Liability: Potential Negative Effects of Ethicality on Product Preference," *Journal of Marketing*, in press.

McDaniel, S. W. (1986). Church advertising: Views of the clergy and general public. *Journal of Advertising*, 15 (1), 24-9.

McGraw, A. P., Tetlock, P.E., & Kristel O.V. (2003). The Limits of Fungibility: Relational Schemata and the Value of Things. *Journal of Consumer Research, 30,* 219-29.

McGraw, A. P., & Tetlock, P.E. (2005). Taboo Trade-offs, Relational Framing and the Acceptability of Exchanges. *Journal of Consumer Psychology*, 15, (January) 2-15.

Richtel, M. (2007). Thou shall not kill, except in a popular video game at church. *New York Times.* Pg. A.1. October 7, 2007. New York, NY.

Schlesinger, L.A., & Mellado, J. (1991). Willow Creek Community Church. Cambridge MA: Harvard Business School Press.

Shafir, E. (1993). Choosing versus rejecting: Why some options are both better and worse than others. *Memory and Cognition, 21,* 546–546.

Symonds, W.C. (2005). Earthly empires: How evangelical churches are borrowing from the business playbook. *BusinessWeek*, 79-88. May 23, 2005.

Tetlock, P. E. (2002). Social Functionalist Frameworks for Judgment and Choice: People as intuitive politicians, theologians, and prosecutors. *Psychological Review, 109,* 451-71.

Tetlock, P.E., Kristel, O.V., Elson, B., Green, M., & Lerner, J. (2000) The Psychology of the Unthinkable: Taboo Trade-offs, Forbidden Base Rates, and Heretical Counterfactuals. *Journal of Personality and Social Psychology*, 78 (May), 853-870.

Tsang, J. (2002) "Moral rationalization and the integration of situational factors and psychological processes in immoral behavior," *Review of General Psychology* 6:25-50.

Zhong, C., & Liljenquist, K. (2006). Washing Away Your Sins: Threatened Morality and Physical Cleansing. *Science*, 313 (5792), 1451-52.

# Self-Identity Amplification: When (and How) Situations Promote Identity Congruent Behavior
Keri Kettle, University of Alberta, Canada

## EXTENDED ABSTRACTS

### "When do Consumers Bolster Their Preferences in the Face of Threat? The Role of Self-Construal and Collective Identity Activation"
*Katherine White, University of Calgary, Canada*
*Jennifer J. Argo, University of Alberta, Canada*
*Jaideep Sengupta, HKUST, China*

Marketers often link their brand with an aspect of consumer social identity. Pepsi attempts to link Pepsi Max with male gender-identity: "Maximum Taste, No Sugar, and Maybe Scorpion Venom. Pepsi Max, the First Diet Cola for Men," whereas Secret links its brand with female gender-identity: "Strong Like a Woman." Although marketers can link products with various aspects of consumer identity, the effectiveness of such a strategy may depend on other contextual factors. Recent research suggests that when consumers experience threat to one aspect of social identity (e.g., their gender identity or nationality), they sometimes avoid products associated with that identity (White and Argo 2009). The present research extends this previous work by identifying instances where consumers will strengthen their connection to, rather than avoid, the identity-linked product in response to social identity threat.

Drawing on social identity theory (Tajfel and Turner 1986) and self-construal theory (Singelis 1994), we predict that the impact of identity threat on product preferences is moderated by self-construal. The independent self is viewed as being autonomous, unique, and separate from other, whereas the interdependent self is viewed as more collectivistic, communal, and relational (Markus and Kitayama 1991). We propose and find that people with interdependent self-construals demonstrate more positive evaluations of identity-linked products when that social identity is threatened versus not threatened. Our framework proposes that this arises because people who are highly interdependent are particularly attuned to their social identities, and that identity threat primes/activates these multiple social identities. Interdependents are then able to draw on this repertoire of identities as a resource, and feel more positively about their multiple group memberships when under threat. In contrast, those with independent self-construals do not activate their identities in response to threat, but instead are motivated to enhance their individual self (Heine 2001). Consequently, independent people tend to avoid an identity-linked product when their social identity becomes threatened.

In study 1, we examined differences in self-construal by investigating differences between Asian (i.e., interdependent) and Caucasian (i.e., independent) Canadians. We exposed participants to negative (threat condition) or neutral information (neutral condition) regarding their university. Participants then completed the twenty statements task ("I am_____,") which was coded for statements related to social identities in general and university-identity in particular. The number of different reported identities were totaled and served as a measure for the degree to which multiple identities were activated. Participants then evaluated products that were matched for price and pretested as being related to university-identity or neutral (university book store vs. a restaurant gift certificate). Asian Canadians evaluated an identity-linked product more positively when threatened versus not threatened. In contrast, Caucasian Canadians evaluated identity-linked products more negatively when threatened

(vs. not threatened). These effects were mediated by the differential activation of multiple identities.

In study 2, we used a similar method to study 1, except that we assessed individual differences in self-construal (Singelis 1991) and measured the degree to which participants felt a sense of identification with their multiple social identities. Once again, interdependents (independents) evaluated an identity-linked product more positively (negatively) when threatened versus not threatened. These findings were mediated by feelings of identification to multiple social identities.

Study 3 investigated primed differences in self-construal (Brewer and Gardener 1996). The results support our framework by demonstrating that–in addition to demonstrating more positive evaluations of the focal identity when threatened–interdependents also show this bolstering effect for another aspect of identity, suggesting that multiple identities have been activated for more interdependent people (under threat).

Finally, in study 4 we further examined the underlying process by using a cross-national sample (Hong Kong vs. Canada, to represent interdependents vs. independents) and investigated the moderating role of affirmation type (self-affirmation, group affirmation, or no affirmation). The results show that, overall, interdependents demonstrate identity bolstering responses, whereas independents are more likely to show identity dissociating responses when the particular identity is threatened. Further, Hong Kong participants made more positive evaluations of the university identity-linked products under conditions of group affirmation as compared to conditions of no affirmation or self-affirmation. This suggests that for interdependents, group-affirmation enhances the ability to feel positively about a threatened group membership. Among independents, however, when under threat self-affirmation led to more positive university product evaluations as compared to no affirmation and group-affirmation. Thus, when under threat, independents are only able to evaluate the identity-linked product positively by affirming the individual self.

Taken together, the results across 4 studies highlight the conditions under which identity bolstering can occur and provide support for the notion that among interdependents, identity threat primes multiple identities which can have a buffering effect on social identity threat.

### "A Unified Theory of Consumer Response to Self-Threat"
*Justin Angle, University of Washington, USA*
*Mark Forehand, University of Washington, USA*

The self-concept–and its constituent associations–has powerful effects on behavior. Because consumers respond strongly when aspects of their self-concept are threatened, marketers routinely challenge components of the self-concept by introducing new negative information about a self-related group, or suggesting the consumer is an inadequate member of such a group. For example, Apple's "I'm a Mac, and I'm a PC" ads link computer choice to identity and suggest that PCs–and their owners–are dull, slow, complicated, and trouble-prone. We propose that consumer response to such identity threats depends on whether the threat targets the association of the self with the identity, or the association of the identity with positive valence. In addition, the strength of threat response is moderated by initial consumer self-esteem.

Recent work has shown that threats to the self can produce both identity-approach and identity-avoid behaviors. Consumers threatened with negative information about their social category tend to avoid products associated with that category (White & Argo 2009), avoid threatening social comparisons (Argo et al. 2006) and distance themselves from products related to dissociative outgroups (White & Dahl 2007). On the other hand, when a consumer's strength of association with a particular identity is threatened, an approach response is more likely as the consumer takes action to rectify threat (DeMarrée et al. 2007; Tetlock et al. 2000) and restore that self association (Gao et al. 2009).

Although these distinct research streams generate contrasting results, they identify processes that are less contradictory than they first appear. The negative information threats employed by White & Argo (2009) target a group associated with the consumer, and such group affiliations often act as resources protecting consumers from threat (Correll & Park 2005; Knowles & Gardner 2008). Although White & Argo provided evidence of this self-protection strategy in consumers for which group affiliation was important, they did not investigate how the negative information affects group associations or the importance of the group to one's self-concept. Similarly, the self-concept threats employed by Gao et al. (2009) are posited to shake the association of one's self with a group or attribute, yet these associations and any changes in them were not measured.

The present research develops a single theoretical framework to explain the apparently divergent findings of prior work, and offers predictions about how a variety of self-threat situations will influence consumer behavior. Building on the Unified Theory of Implicit Social Cognition (Greenwald et al. 2002), threat response is explained in terms of three types of implicit associations: self-esteem, self-group, and group-valence. Although prior investigations occasionally reference the importance of one or more of these associations, none of the research to date has actually measured them and assessed their influence on the self-threat response. We hypothesize that initial implicit self-esteem will predict strength of response to self-threat, such that people higher in self-esteem will exhibit stronger approach and avoidance tendencies.

The results of two experiments demonstrate this framework. Using a series of Brief Implicit Association Tests (BIATs), we show that consumers respond very differently to self-concept threats that target the association of the self with a given identity, as compared to threats that target the association of the identity with positivity. When the latter type of threat was encountered, the resultant avoidance effect was mediated by a weakening of the association of the threatened identity with positive valence. By contrast, when the former type of threat was encountered a weakening of the self-identity association mediated the expected approach response.

Together, these findings shed critical light on the processes driving consumer response to self-threat. In addition, the methodology employed in this research can contribute to a better understanding of relationships between the self, social groups, stereotypical attributes, and valence.

### "The Moderating Role of Self-Construal in Selective Self-Stereotyping"

*Linyun W. Yang, Duke University, USA*
*Tanya L. Chartrand, Duke University, USA*
*Gavan J. Fitzsimons, Duke University, USA*

Does it matter if someone stereotypes you? When a stereotyper inflicts harm on a target (e.g., denying a promotion, excluding from a social group), the answer is an obvious yes. Prior work has shown that individuals are selective in applying specific stereotypical traits to themselves in order to reconcile the conflicting goals of self-enhancement and group identification (Biernat et al. 1996; Pronin et al. 2004). Research has also shown that the effects of being stereotyped extend to domains where no overt harm occurs, such as by changing how the stereotyped individual views him or herself (Sinclair et al. 2006). The present research investigates the role that self-construal plays in determining individuals' self-evaluative response to being negatively stereotyped. We propose that self-construal moderates the way individuals address the stereotype and their motivation toward the stereotyper. These responses are reflected in targets' self-views in the form of selective self-stereotyping (assimilating toward the stereotype) or counter-self-stereotyping (contrasting away from the stereotype).

As stereotypes are multidimensional and contain numerous characteristics associated with a social group, individuals' self-views do not necessarily have to shift on all aspects of the stereotype. We posit that targets' self-evaluations change in a selective manner consistent with their self-construal orientations. That is, stereotype targets engage in selective self-stereotyping and leverage the multidimensionality of stereotypes in order to remain consistent with their attitudes toward the stereotyper. Rather than embracing or rejecting a stereotype in its entirety, stereotype targets alter their self-views on subsets of the stereotype. Targets' responses stem from their self-construals and thus determine whether they selectively assimilate toward or contrast away from the stereotype.

Self-construal refers to how individuals understand and define themselves in relation to the social environment (Markus & Kitayama 1991). People with interdependent self-construals see themselves as closely connected to the people in their social environment, whereas those with independent self-construals see themselves as distinct and separate from others. Research suggests that independent individuals are likely to contrast their self-evaluations away from stereotypes (Bry et al. 2007; Keller & Molix 2008; Stapel & Koomen 2001) and tend to respond in a hostile manner towards those who stereotype them (Pinel 2002; Wout et al. 2009). By contrast, interdependent individuals tend to assimilate their self-evaluations toward stereotypes and compensate for the stereotyper's negative expectations. In the present work, we find that one's response to the stereotype and the stereotyper shape how their self-evaluations shift in terms of stereotype-relevant traits.

In Study 1, we examined how interacting with a sexist male supervisor influenced interdependent and independent female participants. As independence increased, participants rated themselves lower on positive feminine traits and higher on negative masculine traits to contrast away from the female stereotype and to remain consistent with hostile feelings toward the supervisor. As interdependence increased, however, participants adopted the opposite strategy and rated themselves higher on positive feminine traits and lower on negative masculine traits. This served the dual purpose of remaining likeable to the supervisor but conforming to his stereotypical views of women.

In Study 2, using the self-evaluations of female participants, we examined whether the traits interdependent participants wish to embody are specific to the affiliation target. As predicted, we found that interdependent participants' self-evaluations changed depending on the affiliation target. When they imagined interacting with a colleague, interdependent participants increased their self-evaluations on feminine traits valued by the colleague, even though the traits were stereotype consistent. With a supervisor, interdependent participants did not decrease their self-evaluation ratings on masculine traits valued by the supervisor because doing so would compromise their self-image as it pertains to the supervisor. Independent individuals' self-evaluations, on the other hand, were not influenced by the interaction partner because they are less motivated to affiliate and less sensitive to the specific preferences of their interaction partners.

Our theory of selective self-stereotyping takes into account how individual differences in self-construal influence self-stereotyping in contrasting interpersonal contexts. This focus departs from previous research, which has generally focused on selective self-stereotyping where stereotype targets view themselves in a positive light. Furthermore, we contribute by examining selective counter self-stereotyping where individuals view themselves more negatively in order to respond to the stereotyper in a hostile manner.

### "The Signature Effect: Merely Signing One's Name Promotes Identity-Congruent Behavior"
*Keri Kettle, University of Alberta, Canada*
*Gerald Häubl, University of Alberta, Canada*

Your signature–the distinctive way in which you write your name–plays a vital role in your life. By simply signing your name on a document, you can commit to marriage, years of mortgage payments, or military service. Despite the importance of signatures, however, the influence of signing one's name on subsequent behavior has not been examined to date.

People associate their signature with their identity. They craft a signature that is unique (and thus difficult to forge) which they use to represent their identity in writing. We propose that signing one's name acts as a general self-identity prime, and thus promotes behavior congruent with the specific aspect of that self-identity that is afforded by the individual's current situation (Gibson 1977). We predict and demonstrate this phenomenon in five studies. In each study, participants were randomly assigned to either sign or print their own name on a blank piece of paper (ostensibly for a separate study about hand-writing) before entering into the focal situation.

The first two studies examine a domain with divergent schemas for women and men–food. As compared to men, women perceive that they are more prone to impulsive food consumption (Fredrickson et al. 1998). We hypothesized, therefore, that signing their name would promote impulsive food consumption among women, but would have no such effect on men. In Study 1, participants were given the opportunity to buy chocolates. Women who had signed their name bought more chocolate than those who had printed their name. By contrast, the amount of chocolate purchased by male participants was not affected by this manipulation. In Study 2, participants were offered free snack foods (carrots and pretzels) during a brief waiting period. As predicted, women who had provided a signature consumed more snacks than those who had printed their name, but male participants' snacking was not affected by whether they had signed or printed their name. Thus, the first two studies show that people who sign their name behave in a manner congruent with their gender identity.

Studies 3 and 4 investigate the relationship between how closely consumers associate their identity with a product domain and their engagement while shopping in that domain. Consumers who closely associate a product domain with their self-identity are engaged in that domain. Therefore, we hypothesized that signing their name would induce consumers who identify more (less) closely with a product domain to be more (less) behaviorally engaged when shopping in that domain. In study 3, participants searched for product attribute information prior to choosing from a set of products (cameras or dishwashers). As predicted, signing their name led participants who identify more (less) closely with the product domain to examine more (less) product information. In study 4, participants went to a retail store to choose a pair of running shoes. Signing their name induced participants who identify more (less) closely with running to spend more (less) time in the store and to try on more (fewer) pairs of shoes.

The final study tested our theoretical account by examining the effect of signing one's name on identity-signaling. After signing or printing their own name, participants identified a social group to which they either belonged (in-group condition) or did not belong (out-group condition), and then made choices in 19 product domains (Berger & Heath 2007). As predicted, signing their name promoted greater divergence from out-groups–and greater conformity with in-groups–in identity-relevant domains.

The present research is the first to show that merely signing one's name influences subsequent behavior in a predictable manner. Because consumers are often required to provide a signature (e.g., in a retail setting), our findings have important implications for both consumers and retailers.

# Globalcityscapes: Re-Reading Ethnicity in Movement

Eric Ping Hung Li, Quatar University, Quatar
Bernardo Figueiredo, University of New South Wales, Australia

## EXTENDED ABSTRACTS

### "Cityscapes and Migration: Encapsulating Acculturation in the Urban Collective Space"

*Luca M. Visconti, Università Bocconi, Italy*

Migration is structurally connected with the idea of movement. People leave a country, their houses, family members, and beloved objects to start elsewhere a new life and thus redefine their extended self (Belk 1988). Also, the employers in the countries of destination frequently appreciate migrant workers for their openness to geographical mobility given their weaker ties to a given place (Visconti 2007). Such flexibility better fits companies' territorial fast-moving needs and grants competitive advantage.

Despite the centrality of space in the construction of the migration experience, consumer acculturation studies have mostly interrogated migration in static fashion. The country of origin and of destination, as well as the cultures embedded in such loci, are crystallized, frozen, captured in a Polaroid snapshot, where they can be contrasted, scrutinized, mixed (Laroche, Kim, and Tomiuk 1998; Padilla 1980; Peñaloza 1994; Wallendorf and Reilly 1983).

From this perspective, it is arguable that migration studies have been so far dominated by the category of *time*. Time is surely a relevant dimension to capture the ongoing processes of cultural adaptation (Berry 1980), the learning of new languages and their symbolic nuances, the establishment of new social linkages, consumption practices, and meaningful experiences (Peñaloza and Gilly 1999).

Nonetheless, migration can be fruitfully understood also in the light of the category of *space*. Migrants enter territories, homes, marketplaces. They cross regions to settle down and reconnect with family members. The relevance of space in understanding culture and the relationships migrants establish with it are crystal clear in a world where cultural dynamicity and its deterritorialization are increasing (Craig and Douglas 2006).

However, a bunch of consumer studies dealing with migration and space is noteworthy. Transnationalism has come to the edge (Portes, Guarnizo, and Landolt 1999). Sometimes, transnational consumption experiences are mediated by the brands and remain within the sphere of imagination (Cayla and Eckhardt 2008). Other times, and more easily, transnationalism relates to real migration paths (Basch, Glick Schiller, and Szanton Blanc 1994) and openly interrogates the issue of place (Gupta and Ferguson 1997; Hannerz 1992).

Second, consumer researchers have documented the impact of globalization on the shaping of consumers' global identity (Üçok and Kjeldgaard 2006). Among others, Thompson and Tambyah (1999) highlight the tensions expatriates meet during their migratory process, in which nomadism and cultural adaptability contrast their loss of home.

In this paper, I look at space as *collective space*. Immigrants reach a new country, and their encounter is objectified through the encounter with a new city. Also, the city is a "shared land" in which migrants overcome the invisibility that the market and media sometimes generate. Being visible, they can reclaim a subject position and become active agents in/of their context of living. As noted by Kostof (1992, 123), public space is actually "a destination, a purpose-built stage for ritual and interaction." The city is a

collector of rival ideologies about the role that different dwellers have to express (Visconti et al., forthcoming).

From this viewpoint, understanding the way migrants live the city holds a terrific explanatory power about the processes of social inclusion, justice and equity, market and civic legitimation, and the power migrants have to cope with the contradictory stances posed by migration and the hosting culture.

This research is an ethnographic inquiry conducted in the city of Milan, Italy. The project is at an early stage of data collection. Three main typologies of neighbourhoods have been selected: i) areas dominated by migrant's dwellers belonging to a single ethnicity (mono-ethnic ghettoes); ii) areas appropriated by a prevalence of migrants from different ethnicities (multi-ethnic ghettoes); and, iii) areas of coexistence between autochthonous dwellers and migrants (dialogical areas). Sites of investigation span from citizens' dwellings (homes) to commercial spaces, and from profane recreational areas (e.g., parks, gardens, etc.) to sacred religious sites. Informants are involved both individually and jointly, in the form of families, religious communities, or associational groups.

This project aims at answering to a list of relevant questions. Do migrants feel part of the city they inhabit? How do they establish geographical, symbolic and emotional rooting in their cities? How do they feel about ethnic ghettoes or dialogical areas? Do they get involved in confrontations with other members of their neighbourhood? But also, how do they envision urban changes and to what extent do they feel legitimized to or interested in being part of this change?

Overall, my work extends our understanding of acculturation by reading it through the lens of collective space since the city should not be meant as a physical space only but also as a mental space (Park and Burgess 1984). As such, the city and the way dwellers live it mirror the existing social tensions, the identity projects of its inhabitants (Minowa, Visconti, and Maclaran, 2010), and the very fabric of acculturative practices.

### "Mobile Ethnicities In Global Cities"

*Bernardo Figueiredo, University of New South Wales, Australia*
*Eric Ping Hung Li, Qatar University, Qatar*

Moving beyond the traditional concept of ethnic migration and acculturation, our study aims to highlight the fluidity and mobility of ethnic representation in global cities (Bauman 2000). New forms of governance and market competition, along with the ever-increasing interaction between ethnic groups and ideologies alter the concept of nation and cities under the globalization discourse (Bhabha 1994; Appadurai 1996). The de-territorialization and re-territorialization of culturally diverse migrants not only challenges the traditional conceptualization of ethnicity which is associated with its geographic origin and historical roots, but also create a new order of global cities such as Toronto, New York, London, and Sydney (Sassen 1991). The construction of ethnic ghettos and expatriate regions illustrate the concept of multiplicity, diversity and complexity of the global city landscape. The co-existence of different groups from different ethnic and cultural backgrounds not only problematizes the form of and space for ethnic representations, but also forces different policy makers and cultural agents to create new strategies to ensure and maintain the harmony of the marketplace. Through comparing the commonalities and differences among mobile groups' experiences in different socio-cultural settings (expatriates in Sydney and immigrants in Toronto) our current study seeks to answer two research questions: (1) what is the role of global cities in organizing market-mediated ethnic relations and (2) how do ethnicities become resources for mobile consumers' identity projects in culturally diverse global cities? In order words, we are interested in studying the power relationships among different cultural agents in the construction of the "imagined" global cities (Anderson 1983; Pieterse 2007) and how individuals re-perform ethnicities within the global cultural supermarket (Mathews 2000).

Prior research on the movement of ethnic groups primarily focuses on acculturation and identity negotiation issues (e.g., Peñaloza 1994, Oswald 1999, Askegaard, Arnould and Kjeldgaard 2005; Üstüner and Holt 2007) but the impact of the mobilized group on the local cultures as well as the power relationships in facilitating the ethnic relations have been under-researched. The movement of ethnic groups, in many cases, challenges the structure and order of the city in a different way than they do in other contexts. In addition, the multiplicity and friction (Tsing 2005) of the various populations generate issues that related to market representation, ethnic identification and public policy. Also, literature on acculturation overlooks the creative and productive aspect of adaptation and representation in culturally diverse landscapes and the power of these landscapes in shaping consumption. Therefore research on the mutually constitutive inter-relationships between cultural practices in the construction of global cities and mobile identities is necessary.

In this study we adopted the multi-sited ethnographic method (Marcus 1998) to extend our understanding of the construction of "global cities" and the pattern of identity projects among mobile consumers (immigrants and expatriates) in two multi-ethnic global cities: Sydney and Toronto. The choice of cities was based on the fact that both rank among the top ten in ethnic diversity and welcome factor (Florida 2008). Moreover, both share public policies that openly aim to attract skilled labor (Salt 1997). By comparing the historical and socio-cultural development of these global cities we identified how a colonial past and government policies shape the construction of global city markets, and how different waves of immigration and migration re-construct the order and dynamic of the city. We also conducted participation observations, photographs and long interviews in order to have a better understanding of the identity projects and ethnic-related consumption practices among mobile groups in a naturalistic setting (Belk, Sherry and Wallendorf 1988). The multicultural background of the researchers together with the diversified cultural experiences of our informants allows us to triangulate our data from multiple sources and points of view.

Both Sydney and Toronto have experienced British colonial rule as well as successive waves of immigration in the past century, and the significant population changes underway in each means there is no numerically "dominant" group in either city. Our findings suggest that global cities provide a "stage" for performing multiplicity and diversity. Under the influence of multicultural policies and the organization of ethnicized space as well as the encouragement in preserving cultural uniqueness and mutual accommodation, consumers in Sydney and Toronto learn tolerance and open themselves to diversity, and are encouraged to preserve, display and exhibit their cultural practices. Ethnic-themed festivals, public policies that celebrate special ethnic holidays, the organization of neighborhoods, and ethnic-themed businesses highlight cultural differences within global city spaces and our findings demonstrate that the very meaning of ethnicity also undergoes a series of preservation, authentication, transformation and reinvention processes. As a result, ethnicity itself becomes a dynamic resource for mobile members

of all ethnic backgrounds. At the same time, different motilities use these resources in different ways according to their intention to stay and cultural knowledge. In order words, the structure and order of global cities, although different from one another, embody ideologies of mobility, of difference, and of multiple identities. This ideology becomes an important enabler of alternative identities (e.g. cosmopolitans) and alternative representations of the existing ones (e.g. diverse market-mediated representations of Chineseness).

This article supports a conceptualization of ethnicity and locality not in opposition to the global, but in relation to social, political, and cultural relationships that operate within and beyond these particular spaces. More specifically, our research extends current understanding on the role of global cities not only as culturally diverse landscapes, but as enablers of ethnic negotiations. It suggests that global cities are important arenas for revising and reinventing ethnic relations and ethnic symbols. Moreover, the history and organization of the city play defining roles in the identity construction of mobile ethnic groups. Thus, in an important extension to the consumer acculturation literature, this article shows that global cities are structured in a way that highlights mobility and integration and downplays assimilation.

### "The Role Of The Marketplace In The Immigrant Women's Negotiation Of Place Within The Dominated Space"
*Zuzana Chytkova, University of Pisa, Italy*

Most of the research regarding immigrant consumer acculturation has been carried out in environments with a long history and experience with immigration, such as the United States (Peñaloza 1994, Oswald 1999), United Kingdom (Jamal 2000, Lindridge, Hogg and Shah 2004), or Denmark (Askegaard, Arnould and Kjeldgaard 2005). However influential and important these studies, they concentrated on the immigrants' creative ethnic identity construction through the marketplace offerings in the contexts, in which the studied minority's culture was, in one way or another, commodified and marketed also to the mainstream. Such situation, then, creates a specific climate, in which there are certain legitimate ethnic identity positions created for the immigrants in and by the marketplace. It was, in fact, illustrated how, with time, the same marketers become influenced and changed by marketing to the ethnic minorities (and therefore more receptive and open towards the catered ethnic group), and how, for instance, English/Spanish bilingual advertisement legitimizes the Hispanics' presence in the American marketplace (Peñaloza and Gilly 1999). In such contexts, therefore, the space of the multicultural city can be seen as co-created by the dominant group and the ethnic minorities.

However, the immigration phenomenon is not confined to countries with a long tradition of accommodating differences. On the contrary, with the process of globalization, more First World countries become the destination of migrants from developing parts of the world. Given this premise, it becomes crucial to study the underlying conditions that allow for the accommodation of differences and the minimization of "otherness" within the multicultural spaces. One possible way to advance such knowledge is to study contexts in which the construction of such spaces is in its embryonic stage. In empirical contexts, in fact, in which the marketplace (and the society) is immature due to the recency of the immigration phenomenon, legitimate ethnic identity positions may not be offered. The common space, then, is not co-constructed, but rather constituted by the dominant group, as is the immigrants' place within the space. It is a question, then, if the immigrants in such setting still use the marketplace offerings to construct their hybrid ethnic identities, or if they are constrained to their "place" by the dominating discourses in a similar manner as proposed by Üstüner and Holt (2007).

The empirical context of the current study mirrors the above considerations, as it focuses on the Romanian female immigrants to Italy. Italy, traditionally a country of emigration and the source of workers for other European economies has not yet quite recovered from the "shock" of becoming the country of immigration some twenty years ago. As a result, multiculturalism or ethnic marketplace is still in diapers, especially outside the few big cities that could be considered as global. Italian companies, convinced by the media representation of immigrants as victims or delinquents (more than eighty percent of television and newspaper coverage on immigration in 2002) (Napolitano and Visconti 2007), do not consider them as feasible market segments. As a consequence, certain subjectivities are constructed in and by the marketplace. In the specific case of the food market serving the Romanian immigrants in Italy, for instance, the same organization of the marketplace where it is the small shops of Romanian propriety that cater to the Romanian community, but none of the mainstream distribution channels, creates a sort of subjectivity that evidently favors the self-perception of an "immigrant", rather than an integrated part of a multiethnic culture.

Yet, through the marketplace, the immigrant women also come into contact with the consumer culture representation of the modern woman, a woman that, through her consumption choices, can be whoever she wants to be (McDonald 2000). The representation of women in the consumer culture can be seen, and indeed has been criticized, as another discursive apparatus that constitutes female subjectivity in a certain way, more precisely as a gendered version of the neoliberal "enterprising consumer" (Catterall, Maclaren and Stevens 2005). The notion of the "enterprising self" is based on the economic and political liberalism that sees in a subject a self-defined, self-motivated individual that is free and able to decide what he wants and does what he can to reach it, assuming the responsibility for his own life (Slater 1997).

Based on depth interviews and video-registered cooking sessions with Romanian immigrants, I studied the way immigrant women use marketplace-originated symbolic resources to negotiate the subjectivities (places) ascribed to them within the dominant spaces. I concentrated on the practices of everyday life, namely cooking, as a means of resistance. Drawing on De Certeau's notion of consumption practices as "tactics" through which the "weak" appropriate the dominant "spaces" much as the reader appropriates the written text with his/her own imagination, I show how the immigrant women draw on the discourse of the "enterprising consumer" in its gendered alternative of the "modern just-do-it woman" and by doing so, they re-interpret the subject position of immigrant assigned to them.

The research shows that even when the "space" and the immigrants' "place" within it are constituted as a hegemonic structure by the dominating group, consumers are still able to make use of the symbolic resources offered by the marketplace to negotiate such identity positions. Further, it is illustrated how, with a growing cultural capital based on consumer culture knowledge and education, the immigrants make benefit of the marketplace symbolic resources in a more nuanced way, primarily by making use of what little multiethnic offerings the market provides in the construction of a cosmopolitan identity that allows them to take a reflexive distance from the dominated subjectivity assigned to them.

## "Ethnic Entrepreneurs: The Identity-Enhancing Tactics of Global City Consumption"

Ela Veresiu, Witten/Herdecke University, Witten, Germany
Markus Giesler, York University, Canada

How has consumer culture theory constructed migrant consumers? Below is a short collection of voices. Following the standard view, migrant consumers must

"not only cope with foreign languages, diverging cultural habits, and alternative markets, but also with multiple "ascriptive identities" (Horowitz 1975) and multifaceted national discourses and practices" (Luedicke and Giesler 2009)

"live in a society that undermines the building blocks of their identities: their ethnicities" (Özçaglar-Toulouse and Üstüner 2009)

"grapple with an alien mass-produced culture" (Üstüner and Holt 2007)

"struggle to extract a sense of real identity from acculturative experiences that are often anxiety provoking" (Askegaard, Arnould, and Kjeldgaard 2005)

"[be] fearful of being pigeonholed into stereotypes or fetishized into objects of curiosity" (Oswald 1999)

"confront a myriad of frustrating and seemingly intractable sociocultural barriers to getting inside the local culture" (Thompson and Tambyah 1999)

"[deal with] conflict and pressure to adjust to the way of life in the United States" (Peñaloza 1994)

Furthermore, migrant consumers are

"unable to engage with, let alone negotiate through the use of product consumption, daily interactions between South Asian and British White cultures (Lindridge and Dhillon 2005)

To conclude, migration is

"the emergency situation (economical crisis or the experience of the unknown upon arrival) (Chytkova and Özçaglar-Toulouse, 2010)

"not a simple process of integration but one that is highly contested and characterized by conflict" (Wamwara-Mbugua and Cornwell 2006)

"disempowering" (Chytkova and Özçaglar-Toulouse, 2010)

The existing theoretical picture on migrant consumption can be summarized as follows: Migrant consumers are suffering from adverse social circumstances due to the overwhelming challenge of negotiating competing identities and cultural practices in an unfamiliar sociocultural and market environment. Sedentary consumers, on the other hand, are generally more empowered due to their familiarity with the national context's sociocultural norms and market system. We characterize this view as the "struggling migrant" model.

To engage this dominant theoretical perspective, we studied migrant consumers of Roma ethnicity in three global cities. The Roma are commonly portrayed as a victimized ethnicity whose culture has been under constant threat by nation-state norms through centuries of official persecution, slavery, forced assimilation and attempted integration in all the countries that they migrated to (Belton 2005; Liégeois 1994; Petrova 2003). As a consequence, these migrant consumers should struggle the most.

As we interviewed the Roma consumers, we came to believe that the "struggling migrant" model fails to capture some of the most powerful identity-enhancing consumer tactics that are enabled in the context of global cities. Sociologist Saskia Sassen (2006, 316) has argued that "current conditions in global cities are creating not only new structurations of power but also operational and rhetorical openings for new types of political actors that may have been submerged, invisible, or without voice." Unlike other cities, the global city consists of a complicated and powerful nexus of economic, political, sociocultural, and infrastructural resources and structures that, when used effectively, enables citizens to establish a meaningful presence. Our consumer cultural addendum to this definition is that these resources and structures become the subject of consumption, and that this agentic consumption takes the shape of what we define as ethnic entrepreneurship.

To reveal ethnic entrepreneurship, we illustrate how our Roma migrants consume the available structures and resources of the global city in creative and often unexpected ways in order to support and enhance their ethnic identities. For example, the informants use the cities' advanced resources to create Roma organizations and community centers that provide an internal network of assistance, cultural solidarity and information exchange exclusively for Roma citizens. Similar to Belk and Paun's findings (1995, 2001) that "[Roma] survive by cleverness in adaptation, by finding viable economic niches," all of our informants pride themselves on being crafty businessmen, as well as highly flexible in their consumption of food, religion and clothing. However, upon closer inspection this seeming flexibility is a rhetorical device used to protect their core cultural identity from outsiders (the non-Roma), including us in the role of researchers. Furthermore they creatively integrate themselves in the global city's network in order to optimize their consumption of all available social services. We discuss these findings in detail and establish important interpretive boundary conditions by comparing Roma consumption and ethnic entrepreneurship in three different global cities.

In terms of methodological details, our study is part of a larger ethnographic and netnographic (Kozinets 2002) investigation of Roma consumers in Toronto, Pisa and Berlin. Our collection of ethnographic and consumer interview data was completed in the summer of 2009 and subsequently analyzed. The study intentionally spans three cities for the purpose of interpretive triangulation. Roma informants were solicited through Roma and activist websites, as well as Roma organizations. We conducted in-depth, semi-structured interviews with 29 Roma consumers, where everyday activities (e.g. housing, working, education, dress, religion, cooking, family and traveling) were discussed. In order to better understand the overall sociocultural and political environment of the respective global cities, we also interviewed national citizens, which were mainly solicited from anti-Roma websites and online discussion forums, as well as public officials across the social services, immigration, child welfare, and education sectors. The complete data set included 65 in-depth, semi-structured interviews, which ranged from 30 minutes to four hours in length, as well as 140 pages of online material, historical data, and media reports. A hermeneutic approach was used to analyze the data (Thompson 1997).

In conclusion, we combine our empirical findings with extant sociological research to trace the genealogy of the "struggling migrant" thesis in consumer culture research. We find that the "struggling migrant" thesis is an example of methodological nationalism. Critical sociologists define methodological nationalism as the assumption that the nation-state is the natural and necessary form of social, political and geographic organization in modernity (Beck 2000; Chernilo 2006; Wimmer and Schiller 2002). According to these scholars contemporary mainstream social theory has generally taken nationally bounded spaces and societies for granted, which overlooks other important human realities. For this reason, consumer theories on migration would not have predicted the important role of the global city as a strategic consumption resource in migrant consumers identity work. Our results offer new and important theoretical insights by presenting the empowered ethnic entrepreneur that creatively consumes the global city in order to reinforce his/her ethnic identity.

## REFERENCES

Anderson, Benedict (1983), *Imagined Communities: Reflections on the Origin and Spread of Nationalism*, London and New York: Verso.

Appadurai, Arjun (1996), *Modernity at Large: Cultural Dimensions of Globalization*, Minneapolis: University of Minnesota Press.

Askegaard, Søren, Eric J. Arnould, and Dannie Kjeldgaard (2005), "Postassimilationist Ethnic Consumer Research: Qualifications and Extensions," *Journal of Consumer Research*, 32 (June), 160–70.

Basch, Linda, Nina Glick Schiller, and Cristina Szanton Blanc, (ed.) (1994), *Nations Unbound: Transnational Projects, Postcolonial Predicaments, and Deterritorialized Nation-States*, Amsterdam: Gordon and Breach.

Bauman, Zygmunt (2000), *Liquid Modernity*, Cambridge: Polity.

Beck, Ulrich (2000), *What is Globalization?* Cambridge: Polity Press.

Belk, Russell (1988), "Possessions and the Extended Self," *Journal of Consumer Research*, 15 (2): 139-68.

_____, John F. Sherry, Jr., and Melanie Wallendorf (1988), "A Naturalistic Inquiry into Buyer and Seller Behavior at a Swap Meet," Journal of Consumer Research, *14 (March), 449-70.*

_____ and Magda Paun (1995), "Ethnicity and Consumption in Romania," in *Marketing in a Multicultural World: Ethnicity, Nationalism, and Cultural Identity*, eds. Janeen Arnold Costa and Gary J. Bamossy, Thousand Oaks, CA: Sage, 180-208.

Belton, Brian (2005), *Questioning Gypsy Identity: Ethnic Narratives in Britain and America*, CA: AltaMira Press.

Berry, John W. (1980), "Acculturation as Adaptation," in *Acculturation: Theory, Models, and Some New Findings*, ed. Amado M. Padilla, Boulder, CO: Westview Press.

Bhabha, Homi K. (1994), *The Location of Culture*, London: Routledge.

Cayla, Julien, and Giana M. Eckhardt (2008), "Asian Brands and the Shaping of a Transnational Imagined Community," *Journal of Consumer Research*, 35 (August): 216-30.

Chernilo, Daniel (2006), "Social Theory's Methodological Nationalism: Myth and Reality," *European Journal of Social Theory*, 9 (1), 5-22.

Craig, Samuel C., and Susan P. Douglas (2006), "Beyond National Culture: Implications of Cultural Dynamics for Consumer Research," *International Marketing Review*, 23 (3): 322-342.

Florida, Richard (2008), *Who's Your City : How the Creative Economy Is Making Where to Live the Most Important Decision of Your Life*, New York: Basic books.

Gupta, Akhil, and James Ferguson (1997), "Beyond "Culture": Space, Identity, and the Politics of Difference," in *Culture, Power, Place: Explorations in Critical Anthropology*, ed. Akhil Gupta and James Ferguson, Durham, NC: University Press, 6-23.

Hannerz, Ulf (1992), *Transnational Connections. Culture, People, Places*, London: Routledge.

Kostof, Spiro (1992), *The City Assembled: Elements of Urban Form Through History,* Boston, MA: Little Brown.

Kozinets, Robert V. (2002), "The Field Behind the Screen: Using Netnography for Marketing Research in Online Communities," *Journal of Marketing Research*, 39 (1), 61-73.

Laroche, Michel, Chankon Kim, and Marc A. Tomiuk (1998), "Italian Ethnic Identity and Its Relative Impact on the Consumption of Convenience and Traditional Foods," *Journal of Consumer Marketing*, 15 (2): 121-51.

Liégeois, Jean-Pierre (1994), *Roma, Gypsies, Travelers*, Strasbourg: Council of Europe Press.

Lindridge, Andrew, M., Margaret Hogg and Mita Shah. (2004), "Imagined Multiple Worlds: How South Asian Women in Britain Use Family and Friends to Navigate the "Border Crossings" Between Household and Societal Contexts," *Consumption, Markets and Culture*, 7 (3): 211-238.

Luedicke, K. Marius and Markus Giesler (2009), "Host Culture Responses to Brand-Related

Acculturation: Legitimation Struggles Between German and Turkish BMW Owners in Germany," in *Advances in Consumer Research*, Vol. 36, eds. Ann L. McGill and Sharon Shavitt, Duluth, MN: Association for Consumer Research, 135-138.

McDonald, Mary G. (2000), "Association and the making of postfeminism: The marketing of the women's national basketball," *International Review for the Sociology of Sport*, 35 (1): 35-47.

Marcus, George E. (1998), *Ethnography through Thick and Thin*, Princeton: Princeton University Press.

Mathews, Gordon (2000), *Global Culture/Individual Identity: Searching for Home in the Cultural Supermarket*, London and New York: Routledge.

Minowa, Yuko, Pauline Maclaran, and Luca M. Visconti (2010), "Researchers' Introspection for Multisited Ethnographers: A Xenoheteroglossic Autoethnography," *Journal of Business Research*, under submission.

Napolitano, Enzo M. and Luca M. Visconti (2007), "I target migranti," in *Stili migranti*, eds. Carla Fiorio, Enzo N. Napolitano and Luca M. Visconti, Biella.

Oswald, Laura R. (1999), "Culture Swapping: Consumption and the Ethnogenesis of Middle-Class Haitian Immigrants," *Journal of Consumer Research*, 25 (March), 303-18.

Özçaglar-Toulouse, Nil and Tuba Üstüner (2009), "How do Historical Relationships between the Host and Home Countries Shape the Immigrants' Consumer Acculturation Process?", in *Advances in Consumer Research,* Vol. 36, eds. Ann L. McGill and Sharon Shavitt, Duluth, MN: Association for Consumer Research, 16-19.

Padilla, Amado M. (ed.) (1980), *Acculturation: Theory, Models, and Some New Findings*, Boulder, CO: Westview Press.

Park, Robert E., and Ernest W. Burgess (1984 [1925]), *The City: Suggestions for Investigation of Human Behavior in the Urban Environment*, Chicago, IL: University of Chicago Press.

Peñaloza, Lisa (1994), "*Atravesando fronteras*/Border Crossings: A Critical Ethnographic Exploration of the Consumer Acculturation of Mexican Immigrants," *Journal of Consumer Research*, 21 (June), 32–54.

_____ and Mary C. Gilly (1999), "Marketer Acculturation: The Changer and the Changed," *Journal of Marketing*, 63 (July): 84-104.

Petrova, Dimitrina (2003), "The Roma: Between a Myth and the Future," *Social Research*, 70 (1), 111-61.

Pieterse, Jan Nederveen (2007), *Ethnicities and Global Multiculture: Pants for an Octopus*, Lanham: Rowman and Littlefield.

Portes, Alejandro, Luis E. Guarnizo, and Patricia Landolt (1999), "The Study of Transnationalism: Pitfalls and Promise of an Emergent Research Field," *Ethnic and Racial Studies*, 22 (2): 217-37.

Sassen, Saskia (1991), *The Global City: New York, London, Tokyo*. Princeton: Princeton University Press.

_____ (2006), *Territory, Authority, Rights: From Medieval to Global Assemblages*. Princeton: Princeton University Press.

Slater, Don (1997), *Consumer Culture and Modernity*, Cambridge: Polity Press and Blackwell Publishing.

Thompson, Craig J. (1997), "Interpreting Consumers: A Hermeneutical Framework for Deriving Marketing Insights from the Texts of Consumers' Consumption Stories," *Journal of MarketingResearch,* 34 (4), 438-56.

_____ and Siok Kuan Tambyah (1999), "Trying to Be Cosmopolitan," *Journal of Consumer Research*, 26 (December), 214-41.

Tsing, Anna Lowenhaupt (2005), *Friction: An Ethnography of Global Connection*, Princeton: Princeton University Press.

Üçok Mine, and Dannie Kjeldgaard, (2006), "Consumption in Transnational Social Spaces: A Study of Turkish Transmigrants, in *European Advances in Consumer Research*, ed. Karin Ekström and Helene Brembeck, vol. 7, Duluth, MN: Association for Consumer Research, 431-6.

Üstüner, Tuba and Douglas B. Holt (2007), "Dominated Consumer Acculturation: The Social Construction of Poor Migrant Women's Consumer Identity Projects in a Turkish Squatter," *Journal of Consumer Research*, 34 (June), 41-56.

Visconti, Luca M. (2007), *Diversity Management e Lavoratori Migranti: Linee Guida per la Gestione del Caso Italia*, Milan: Egea, BEA.

_____ , John F. Sherry Jr., Stefania Borghini, and Laurel Anderson, "Street Art, Sweet Art? Reclaiming the "Public" in Public Place," *Journal of Consumer Research*, forthcoming.

Wamwara-Mbugua, L. Wakiuru and T. Bettina Cornwell, 198, 198 (2006), "Immigrant Acculturation as a Dialogical Process", in *Asia-Pacific Advances in Consumer Research,* Vol. 7, eds. Margaret Craig Lees and Teresa Davis and Gary Gregory, Sydney, Australia: Association for Consumer Research, 192-193.

Wallendorf, Melanie, and Michael D. Reilly (1983), "Ethnic Migration, Assimilation, and Consumption," *Journal of Consumer Behavior*, 10 (December): 292-302.

Wimmer, Andreas and Nina Glick Schiller (2002), "Methodological Nationalism and the Study of Migration," *European Journal of Sociology*, 43 (2), 217-40.

# "How Close or How Far?" The Role of Perceived Goal Progress in Consumer Goal Pursuit

Minjung Koo, Sungkyunkwan University, Korea
Oleg Urminsky, University of Chicago, USA

## EXTENDED ABSTRACT

### "Stuck in the Middle: The Psychophysics of Goal Pursuit"

Andrea Bonezzi, Northwestern, USA
Miguel Brendl, Northwestern, USA
Matteo De Angelis, Luiss University, Italy

Achieving a goal often requires engaging in goal-consistent actions for a prolonged period of time. For example, losing weight requires sticking to a diet and resisting temptations to indulge for many months. The classic goal-gradient hypothesis (Hull 1932; see also Kivetz, Urminsky and Zheng 2006; Nunes and Dreze 2006) posits that motivation to reach a goal increases monotonically with proximity to the desired end-state.

In this research, we posit that motivation to reach a goal is not always a monotonic function of distance from the desired end-state. Specifically, we show that motivation to reach a desired end-state is higher when either far from the goal or close to the goal, and lower when halfway toward reaching the goal. We propose a psychophysical explanation that accounts both for this tendency to get "stuck in the middle" and for the classic goal-gradient pattern. In particular, we argue that motivation to engage in goal-consistent behavior is influenced by the perceived marginal value of progress granted by such behavior (Heath, Larrick and Wu 1999).

According to previous research, people monitor progress toward a goal in terms of distance from a standard of reference (Carver and Scheier 1998). Specifically, they can either use their initial state (i.e., their starting point) as the standard of reference, hence consider what they have achieved so far (e.g., to-date frame), or they can adopt the desired end-state as their standard of reference, hence consider what they still need to achieve (e.g., to-go frame), (Koo and Fishbach 2008). We suggest that people tend to adopt the initial state as the standard of reference when far from the goal and the final state as the standard of reference when close to the goal. Furthermore, consistent with the psychophysical power law (Stevens 2000), and the principle of diminishing sensitivity (Kahneman and Tversky 1979; Tversky and Kahnemen 1991), we suggest that the value of the same unit of progress decreases as the distance from the standard of reference adopted increases. For example, if the goal is to collect 100,000 frequent flier miles, flying 4,000 miles seems a lot when the account shows 5,000 miles (the standard) or when the account shows 95,000 miles (the standard being 5,000 miles to go). The same 4,000 miles, however, seem little when the account shows 50,000 miles because either standard yields a ratio of 4,000 to 50,000. Thus, "in the middle", when both standards of reference are far, an additional unit of progress is perceived to have less value, compared to when either close to the initial or to the final state.

Study One tested the hypothesis that motivation to engage in goal-consistent behavior is lower when about halfway toward reaching a goal. Participants read a scenario about a dieter, specifying her weight when she began dieting (200 lbs), the desired weight goal (140 lbs), and her current weight, varying between-subjects (190 lbs vs. 170 lbs vs. 150 lbs). Then they were told to imagine that the dieter was ordering from a restaurant menu offering many options, ranging from a very healthy but less tasty dinner (salad and fruit) to a very tasty but less healthy dinner (cheeseburger and cake). Participants then indicated on a scale from 1 (tasty dinner) to 9 (healthy dinner) which alternative they expected the

dieter to choose. Participants predicted the dieter would choose a less healthy (i.e. goal-inconsistent) dinner when halfway toward reaching her desired weight, compared to when she was either far from or close to her goal.

Study Two aimed at assessing how motivating an incremental unit of progress is perceived to be, as a function of the distance from the desired end-state. Respondents read a scenario describing a runner with a goal to run 10 miles. After running a certain distance, varying between-subjects (2 miles vs. 5 miles vs. 8 miles), he feels tired and feels he has the energy to run only about one more mile. Participants indicated on a scale from 1 (not motivated) to 9 (highly motivated) how motivated the runner would feel to keep running about one more mile. Participants thought the runner would feel less motivated to run an extra mile when halfway toward reaching his goal, compared to when he was either close to the beginning or close to the goal.

Study Three tested our theoretical explanation by explicitly manipulating the standard of reference used to monitor progress. Participants imagined they were enrolled in the frequent flyer program of Airline X, in which they could earn a free ticket after accumulating 25,000 miles. We manipulated the standard of reference adopted to monitor progress by informing participants of either how many miles they had already accumulated (4,000 vs. 12,000 vs. 21,000), or how many miles they still needed to reach the reward (21,000 vs. 12,000 vs. 4,000). Respondents then indicated the premium they would be willing to pay for an Airline X ticket that would earn them 3,000 miles, versus a $300 ticket from another airline that would earn them no miles. Specifically, they indicated how much more than $300 they would be willing to pay to fly with Airline X, thus adding 3,000 miles to those already accumulated (to-date), or deducting 3,000 miles from those they still needed (to-go). Respondents who were informed of how many miles they still needed to reach the reward were willing to pay most when close to the goal, less when halfway, and even less when far from the goal. Respondents who were informed of how many miles they had already earned were willing to pay a higher price when at the beginning and a lower price when halfway and near the end.

Across three experiments, we show that motivation to reach a goal is often higher when either far from the goal or close to the goal, and lower when halfway toward reaching the goal. We argue that this tendency to get *stuck in the middle* is due to the lower value an additional unit of progress is perceived to have when halfway toward reaching the goal.

### "The "Small Area" Effect: How Progress Monitoring Influences Participation in a Reward Program"

Minjung Koo, Sungkyunkwan University, Korea
Ayelet Fishbach, University of Chicago, USA

A large part of consumer behavior aims to achieve goals. Especially, in the context of reward programs, consumers invest a stream of efforts to earn future rewards. Previous literature has shown that their motivation to participate in and invest efforts to a reward program is largely driven by the perception of progress towards the goal (e.g., Carver and Scheier 1990; Kivetz, Urminsky and Zheng 2006; Nunes and Dreze 2006; Soman and Shi 2003).

This research introduces the "small area" effect, which demonstrates the role of proportional valuation of progress that each action would achieve towards goal attainment. By "area", we are referring to the size of goal progress that one can attend in terms of either accumulated progress to date or remaining progress to go (Koo and Fishbach 2008). For example, consumers can monitor their progress by counting the number of stamps collected so far versus stamps to be collected on a frequent-buyer card. We propose that the focus on the "small area" is more motivating than the focus on the "large area," because an additional action is seen as yielding greater progress when people compare it to a small (vs. large) number of actions. Specifically, we predict when the level of progress is low (less than 50%), the focus on accumulated progress to date would be more motivating than remaining progress to go. For example, for a consumer who has progressed up to 20% of goal attainment, focusing on 20% of progress that is already made (small area) would be more motivating more than focusing on 80% of progress more to go (large area). Conversely, when the level of progress is high (more than 50%), the focus on progress to go would be more motivating than progress to date. For example, for a consumer who has progressed up to 80% of goal attainment, focusing on 20% of progress more to go (small area) would be more motivating than focusing on 80% of progress that is already made (large area).

Three studies tested these predictions. Study 1 was a large-scale field experiment, in which we monitored over 1000 consumer purchases at a sushi restaurant. Customers were offered to enroll for free in a reward program of the restaurant, in which they had to make ten sushi meal purchases in order to earn a reward of free meal. To allow tracking of their purchases, members were required to carry a frequent sushi card. We manipulated the focus on accumulated progress to date versus remaining progress to go, by providing customers with a card on which a sushi-shaped stamp is added for each purchase (i.e., the visual focus is on the number of completed slots) versus a card on which a sushi-shaped stamp is removed for each purchase (i.e., the visual focus is on the number of remaining slots). We tracked 1) the number of purchases on their first visit (i.e., their level of goal progress); 2) whether they return during the promotion period (3 months); and 3) the number of purchases on their second visit. As expected, we found that as members made higher progress on their card on their first visit, the card that emphasized remaining (vs. accumulated) purchases was more motivating—that is, they were more likely to come back and made more purchases on their second visit. That is, emphasizing a small area was more motivating than a large area.

To further investigate the underlying process of the effect, study 2 extended the results to the context of a coffee reward program, in which we experimentally manipulated both the level of progress (30% vs. 70%) and the focus on accumulated vs. remaining purchases. As expected, we found that when the level of progress was low (vs. high), those with a coffee card that emphasized completed (vs. remaining) slots indicated higher willingness to participate in the program and greater anticipated progress by their next purchase, and vice versa. Important, we further found that the increase in anticipated progress mediated the effect of emphasizing the small area on willingness to participate in the program.

In our last study, we show that the focus on small area is more motivating than the focus on the large area only when people have a high desire to approach the goal end-state. That is, we predict that when people have a low desire to complete the goal (e.g., gift card), the small area effect would not hold because people do not draw higher proportional value from making progress toward the end-state. In study 3, we manipulated participants' desire to reach the end-state by employing two different reward programs at a bagel store—a regular "buy 10 get 1 free" reward card (high desire to reach the end-state) and a gift card that participants get discount for

10 purchases (low desire to reach the end-state). As predicted, we replicated previous effects in the reward card condition, whereas the effects were reversed in the gift card condition.

Taken together, these studies provide convergent evidence for the impact of importance of subjective evaluations of anticipated progress in goal pursuit. We believe that our findings have important theoretical and practical implications for motivation and goal behavior and for reward programs and marketing promotions.

### "Almost There? The Role of Absolute vs. Relative Error in Perceived Progress Towards an Accuracy Goal"
*Oleg Urminsky, University of Chicago, USA*

Recent research on goal progress has investigated the impact of people's perceptions of distance from a goal (e.g. Kivetz, Urminsky and Zheng 2006, Koo and Fishbach 2008). In this paper, we use the context of prediction accuracy to explore how people perceive differing degrees of progress to a goal. How do people determine when a prediction is closer to the accuracy goal (e.g. more or less accurate relative to the actual value)?

When people make a series of such assessments, the perceived discrepancy from the accuracy goal is primarily driven by attempting to assess and incorporate two salient pieces of information: the absolute and the proportional (percentage) error. Specifically, participants judgments exhibited what we term *quasi-proportionality*: the same absolute error will be evaluated as worse when the actual value is relatively small, while the same relative error will be evaluated as worse when the actual value is large. Furthermore, the relative weight on absolute vs. proportional distance in forming a distance judgment is systematically affected by the magnitude of the actual value. In particular, more weight is put on absolute error for large true values and more weight is put on proportional error for small true values.

In an initial study (N=40), which of a pair of election predictions is seen as more accurate is significantly affected by framing the outcomes in terms of the winning candidate's share (large true numbers) or the losing candidate's share (small true numbers), impacting how proportional errors are perceived.

In the second study, 111 participants evaluated a series of (16) pairs of predictions of different students' test scores, choosing the one they saw as more accurate. Participants' assessments exhibited quasi-proportionality, incorporating both absolute and proportional error, and the weights placed on each type of error in turn depended on the scale of the numbers (e.g. the average of the two actual values). The effects are shown not to be explainable by heterogeneity, not to vary based on beliefs about the distributions of scores and not to be affected by the participants' own mathematical ability.

The third study (N=116) extends the findings to three additional contexts: election outcomes, weather predictions and salesperson's outcomes. In particular, in assessing predictions of how many cars a salesperson will sell in a given time period, expressing the same rate expressed with small numbers over a shorter interval (one month) or with larger numbers over a longer interval (10 months) affects whether absolute errors or relative errors have more of an effect. When the same monthly rates for the sales predictions and outcomes are expressed as 10 month totals, participants place more emphasis in their judgments on absolute discrepancies relative (rather than proportional discrepancies).

The fourth study presented participants with a series of judgments designed specifically to distinguish between competing accounts of accuracy judgments. For example, in one task, 68% of participants evaluated a prediction of 20 vs. 24 actual as better than a prediction of 60 vs. 72 actual. In a separate task, only 36% of the participants evaluated a prediction of 68 vs. 72 actual as better than a prediction of 204 vs. 216 actual, a significant difference (p=.04). Note that in both tasks, the proportional errors are equal for both predictions (20% in the first task and 6% in the second task) while the absolute errors are the same in the first option for both tasks (12) and and in the second option for both tasks (4). Thus, neither proportional nor absolute distance can explain the pattern of choices. In contrast, quasi-proportionality (specifically the shifting-weights account of incorporating absolute and proportional discrepancies) was consistent with the findings. Furthermore, the patterns of choices could not be explained by the established view of the psychophysics of difference judgments (e.g. Marks and Cain 1972) or by a simple averaging model (Wright 2000).

The implications of the proposed account of accuracy judgment for choices among available agents are discussed. The implications of quasi-proportionality, beyond the specific context of accuracy goals, are discussed. In particular, perceptions of general goal progress are proposed to be governed by quasi-proportionality, such that the the perception of distance to the goal is determined by both absolute and relative distance remaining, with relative emphasis on absolute vs. relative determined by the scale of the numbers under consideration. The implications for motivation are discussed.

### "Can You" or "Will You": How Progress-Based Inferences Impact Motivation in Consumer Goal Pursuit

*Ying Zhang, University of Texas at Austin, USA*
*Szu-Chi Huang, University of Texas at Austin, USA*

A classical proposal in the study of goal pursuit is that people's motivational strength increases as they accumulates progress and approaches goal attainment (Hull 1932; Kivetz et al. 2006). Although it is well established that progress can have an impact on people's subsequent motivation, it is less clear whether the source of the progress would change its impact, and whether such influences would vary depending on one's relative positions in a pursuit. In the present research, we explore two different sources of motivation and propose that because people move from seeking information on goal attainability to information on goal value in the establishment of goal commitment as they progress toward achieving the goal, endowed and earned progress will have different impacts on individuals' motivation, depending on the stage of goal pursuit.

Specifically, low progress on attaining a certain goal raises the question of whether the goal is attainable. The amount of existing progress toward attaining the goal and the effort that people have expended on making that progress, in turn, indicate the difficulty of goal attainment. Compared with those who made progress without expending effort, people who have invested effort in achieving the same low level of progress would infer that the attainment would be more difficult, and thus be less motivated in further pursuit.

When the level of progress on achieving a goal is relatively high, however, people feel that the goal attainment is secured and would shift to focus on the value of the attainable goal. In these times, progress that is acquired through personal effort should be more motivating because it signals one's conscious commitment to pursuing the goal. In contrast, endowed progress carries little diagnostic information in terms of signaling goal value. Accordingly, we expect that when the progress on attaining a goal is high, progress that individuals have earned by expending effort (vs. endowed progress) should elicit greater motivation in further pursuit.

We test these hypotheses in four studies. In Study 1, we tested our hypothesis in two consumer loyalty program scenarios. We manipulated the type of progress by describing it either as made through personal effort, or as endowed without effort. We then manipulated the level of progress by describing it as either a large or small portion of what was needed for the final reward. We found

that when the progress level was low, participants whose progress was endowed (vs. earned) were more motivated to keep pursuing the goal despite inconveniences in accumulating points, but when the progress level on the program was high, those who made progress through personal effort (vs. endowed) expressed higher motivation.

In Study 2, participants completed a word-completion task and encountered a difficult question either at the beginning or toward the end of the task and progress that they accumulated before encountering the difficult question was either earned through their personal effort or was awarded by the computer. We found that among the participants with low progress, those who had made progress without expending effort persisted longer than did those who had invested effort to make the same amount of progress. Conversely, among the participants with high progress, those who had made the progress without expending effort persisted less than did those who had invested effort.

Study 3 tested our proposed mechanism and investigated whether it is indeed people's inferences at different stages of goal pursuit that influence their subsequent motivation. Participants in this study completed a word recognition task on computers and were made to listen to annoying noise when waiting for a question, either toward the beginning or approaching the end of the task. We further manipulated the progress type by convincing participants that the progress they had accumulated was either the result of their effort investment, or was given to them for free by the program. We then measured participants' persistence on waiting for the question under noise as well as the inference they made during the goal pursuit. We found that when the progress was low, participants with earned progress (vs. endowed progress) inferred lower attainability of the goal, and this inferred attainability decreased their persistence in waiting. When the progress on the task was high, however, participants with earned progress (vs. endowed progress) inferred greater value of the goal, and the higher inferred value further increased their persistence.

Finally, Study 4 used a field experiment to test our hypothesis in a real consumption context. In this study real customers at a local sandwich shop were given a loyalty card that required either a small or large number of additional purchases for a free meal, and they were led to believe that they received the initial progress on the card either because they had made past purchases at the shop (earned progress) or because the shop was running a general promotion (endowed progress). We found that although highlighting customers' efforts in making progress increased their subsequent purchase frequency when they were close to redemption, doing so at early stages of the program actually decreased their purchase frequency.

# Prosocial Behavior in the Field
Leif D. Nelson, University of California, USA
Lalin Anik, Harvard Business School, USA

## EXTENDED ABSTRACTS

### "Micro-financing Decisions"
*Jeff Galak, Carnegie Mellon University, USA*
*Deborah Small, University of Pennsylvania, USA*
*Andrew Stephen, INSEAD, France*

A recently-hyped effort to alleviate world poverty has emerged in the form of micro-financing, or small loans made to small businesses and entrepreneurs in developing countries. These types of loans have provided $25 billion in small collateral-free loans to the poorest of the poor. Given limited lending capital, a system of direct-to-borrower financing has been established to allow individuals to make uncollateralized loans to individuals and small businesses in need. This contemporary form of helping the poor has won favor because it appeals to economically-minded individuals who believe that supporting entrepreneurial endeavors will spur growth and thus do more good than traditional charitable giving (Yunus, 1999).

If micro-finance is indeed a more sensible solution to poverty, an important question is whether people who lend money are, in fact, behaving sensibly by making decisions that maximize social welfare. Recent research emphasizes the distorting impact of emotions on rational decision making. Much of this research focuses on choices for which the outcomes primarily affect the chooser's welfare. However, emotions can also bias decisions where the outcomes affect social welfare. For instance, when people donate to charity, emotional responses to victims and situations do not map onto to the gravest needs. Specifically, all else being equal, people are more likely to donate to a single individual than to a group of individuals (Kogut & Ritov, 2005a; Kogut & Ritov, 2005b). A single individual in need is more vivid and emotionally-compelling than multiple or statistical victims (Small & Loewenstein 2003; Small, Loewenstein, & Slovic, 2007). This is often sub-optimal because more people can benefit when resources are shared rather than concentrated on a single person.

Similarly, micro-finance loans to groups should be more beneficial than loans to individuals. However, our evidence suggests that lenders do the opposite. We analyzed micro-finance lending data from Kiva.org, a non-profit organization that links individual lenders and needy borrowers, who can be either individuals or groups. Lenders have full information about each loan request including information about the borrower(s) and the number of people in the borrower group. Lenders evaluate borrowers' requests and decide to whom and how much to lend (starting at $25). We analyzed 371,521 loans made to 23,024 borrowers (individuals or groups; size $M=1.37$, $SD=1.17$, min.=1, max.=20) between November 27, 2007 (the first day Kiva allowed group borrowers), and June 18, 2008.

We find two independent conclusions to support the contention that lenders are biased towards individual borrowers. First, we observe that it takes less time to fill a loan if it is requested by an individual. Second, we observe that as group size increases, the amount loaned (calculated as a proportion of the remaining loan available to fund) decreases non-linearly. As the size of the borrower group increased, loan sizes decreased exponentially. Hence, individual borrowers were more likely fund their loans faster and to receive larger loans than groups of borrowers acting as a consortium.

A second analysis on a similar data set revealed that lenders are more likely to lend to borrowers whose social distance is minimized (Flippen et al., 1996; Hewstone et al., 2002). After coders (on Amazon's mTurks system) parsed the names, gender, and occupation of 163,736 unique lenders, we were able to analyze the similarity between lenders and borrowers on these three dimensions (lender information was provided by Kiva.org). We observed a similarity effect for all three. Specifically, lenders were more likely to lend to borrowers who share their gender, occupation, and even, strikingly, the same first initial (Pelham et al., 2002). Though not specifically a bias, these results suggest that when lenders make decisions regarding whom to lend to, their decisions are influenced by factors other than optimal helping.

Because of the large volumes of money being distributed, as well as the gravity the problem of world poverty that micro-finance is purported to help solve, it is important to understand lending behaviors. Our evidence suggests a strong preference for (and perhaps bias toward) individual borrowers. This preference is apparent despite the logical argument that helping groups of individuals should be better both in terms of the number of people benefiting from the loan and the likelihood of successful loan repayment. Additionally, our evidence suggests that lender have a preference to lend borrowers who are similar to themselves, suggesting that loan distributions may be sub-optimal.

### "Social Preferences and Charitable Giving: How Pay-What-You-Want Pricing can Optimize Social Welfare"
*Ayelet Gneezy, University of California, San Diego, USA*
*Uri Gneezy, University of California, San Diego, USA*
*Leif D. Nelson, University of California, Berkeley, USA*

In 2007, *Radiohead*, an enormously popular British rock band, released its most recent album through their website and allowed their fans to download the album for any price they chose to pay (including $0). This pay-what-you-want (PWYW) pricing set of a cascade of media coverage, but relatively few certain answers to the most obvious questions: was the mechanism profitable and was it *more* profitable than a traditional release? If you let your customers pay as little as they want is there any reason that they would pay enough to make it a good decision?

We first considered these questions by seeking data from other companies who tried PWYW pricing. We received 15 months of download data from an independent artist who, like *Radiohead,* had released its album at PWYW (Study 1). Results indicated that the sale had an enormous influence on demand as over 600,000 people downloaded the album and generated nearly $1 million in revenue. Both figures dwarfed previous releases by the same artist. A second set of field data (Study 2), this time from a video game developer, told a similar story: in just two weeks the company saw more than 80,000 downloads, and nearly $200,000 in profits. Both were considerably more than a typical two week period for the company.

These data provided a sense that PWYW may be a profitable business strategy, but they did not necessarily provide evidence that it was a *better* business strategy than a more traditional alternative. By any traditional logic, PWYW would surely be considerably less profitable. We conducted a field experiment to try to answer this question (Study 3). A tour boat company photographed customers as they boarded the boat, printed the photos while the customers were at sea, and then posted them for sale at the point of disembarkation. The company traditionally sold the photos for $15, but during the

*Advances in Consumer Research*
*Volume 38, © 2012*

experiment some boats were randomly assigned to either a control condition ($15), a low-price condition ($5), or a PWYW condition. These three radically different prices were nearly identically profitable (with PWYW being slightly ahead of the other two). Even when given the opportunity to pay nothing for a novelty photo, people chose to pay enough to make it quite profitable for the firm. Most interestingly however, was the discovery that customers were *less* likely to purchase the photo at PWYW than they were at $5. We reasoned that this occurred because the social pressures of PWYW (e.g., "I don't want to look like a cheapskate.") drive people either to pay more or to not buy at all. Could the same social pressures be manipulated to drive prices even higher?

If people are concerned about looking fair in a traditional exchange, certainly they must feel doubly so when dealing with a charitable organization. We conducted a field study at a large amusement park (Study 4) in which participants (n=116,834) rode a rollercoaster-like attraction, were photographed during the ride, and later chose whether to purchase a print of the photo. A 2x2 between participants design crossed the photograph price (either the regular $12.95 price or PWYW) with a charitable giving promotion (either no charity or half of the revenue went to charity). Purchase rate was low and similar in the two fixed $12.95 treatments. PWYW increased purchase rates by an order of magnitude in PWYW with charity, and was twice as high again in PWYW without charity. However, people paid significantly more per photo when half of the revenues went to charity than with no charity ($t(3535)=43.24$, $p<.001$). PWYW, when combined with a charitable partner, was the most profitable condition for the company (by more than $50,000 a year) and it led to a substantial charitable surplus (nearly $1 million per year).

Pay-what-you-want pricing is certainly not for all firms, but as witnessed in these four studies, under the right circumstances it can lead to sustainable profitability and charitable giving.

## "The Counterintuitive Effects of Thank-you Gifts on Charitable Giving"

*George E. Newman, Yale University, USA*
*Y. Jeremy Shen, Yale University, USA*

Donations are one of the largest sources of revenue for most nonprofits and charities and, as a result, a great deal of research in psychology, economics, and marketing has explored what factors encourage charitable giving. In this paper we focus on the effectiveness of offering small 'thank-you' gifts, such as a pen, coffee mug, or tote bag, as means of soliciting charitable donations. Given the ubiquity of these kinds of requests (e.g., National Public Radio fund-drives) and the real-world consequences of their effectiveness (or ineffectiveness), it is critically important to directly investigate this issue. Yet, despite decades of research on the relationship between external incentives and altruistic behavior, whether such offers do in fact increase charitable donations is unclear.

As an initial test of people's lay beliefs, we asked adults to predict whether a thank-you gift (a pen bearing a PBS logo) would encourage people to donate more, less, or the same amount to public broadcasting compared to a donation request that did not offer a thank-you gift. The majority of participants (68%) predicted that thank-you gifts would *increase* donation amounts. Analogously, participants predicted that the group who was offered a thank-you gift would donate significantly more money than the group who was not.

In Study 2, a new group of adult participants were presented with the same materials as in Study 1. However, the presence or absence of a thank-you gift was manipulated between-subjects. In stark contrast to Study 1, participants who were simply asked for a donation (without any offer of a thank-you gift) were willing to donate significantly more than participants who were offered a thank-you gift. Moreover, the total amount of money donated was also higher in the no-gift condition than in the gift condition. Thus, despite people's predictions, the offer of a thank-you gift actually decreased donations both in terms of the average amount per individual as well as the total amount donated. Moreover, such counterintuitive patterns were not due to changes in beliefs about the importance of the charitable cause or to explicit beliefs about the influence of thank-you gifts.

Study 3 replicated this effect using actual donations, rather than hypothetical ones. In this experiment, participants were asked to donate a percentage of their winning from a lottery to the Save-the-Children foundation. Replicating the previous experiment, participants who were offered a thank-you gift, donated significantly less compared to participants who were simply asked for a donation.

One explanation this effect may be that participants inferred that the gift was undesirable because it was free (Kamins et al., 2009; Simonson et al., 1994). To test this possibility, Study 4 had three conditions: a desirable gift (a box of chocolate), an undesirable gift (an ugly tie), as well as a no-gift control. As expected, participants rated the chocolates as significantly more desirable than the tie. However, despite this difference in gift desirability, participants in the no-gift condition were willing to donate significantly more than participants in both the desirable-gift condition or the undesirable-gift condition. Donation amounts in the two gift conditions were not statistically different. Thus, the negative effect of thank-you gifts does not appear to be due to the undesirability of the gift offered.

An alternative explanation is that in assessing the value of the gift participants may have generated a relatively low value that anchored the subsequent amount participants were willing to donate. We tested this explanation by offering participants either an expensive gift (nice pen), an inexpensive gift (cheap pen), or a no-gift control. Despite the difference in gift value, however, participants in the no-gift condition were willing to donate significantly more than participants in either the expensive-gift or cheap-gift conditions. The two gift conditions were not statistically different. Thus, direct manipulation of the gift value within the same experiment did not alter donation amounts and in fact, we observed slightly higher donation amounts in exchange for a *less* (rather than more) expensive gift.

Study 6 examined the possibility that thank-you gifts reduce donation amounts because the external incentive undermines or "crowds out" participants' altruistic motivations (e.g., Deci, 1975; Lepper & Greene, 1980). To test this explanation the same gift (a cloth shopping bag, bearing the organization's logo) was framed as either something that could be used in a personally beneficial way (for shopping) or in a manner that benefited others (to increase awareness of the cause). As in previous studies, participants in the no-gift condition were willing to donate significantly more than participants in the benefit-to-self condition. However, consistent with the crowding out hypothesis, participants in the benefit-to-others condition also donated significantly more than participants in the benefit-to-self condition. Donation amounts in the no-gift condition and the benefit-to-others conditions were not statistically different. Thus, merely reframing the gift as consistent with altruistic goals attenuated the negative effect of thank-you gifts on donation amounts.

In sum, although people have the strong prediction that the offer of thank-you gifts should increase donations, such offers actually reduce charitable donations both in terms of the average amount donated per individual as well as the total amount donated. This effect is observed across a wide variety of charities and gifts types, regardless of whether the donations are hypothetical or real, the gift is desirable or undesirable, the charity is familiar or unfamiliar, or the gift is more or less valuable. Moreover, such patterns cannot solely be explained in terms of inferences about the charity's quality (e.g., either their efficacy or current wealth), the undesirability of the gift itself, or simple anchoring effects. Instead, results were consistent with the hypothesis that the offer of external incentives undermines or "crowds out" altruistic motivations.

### "The Prosocial Workplace: Prosocial Spending Improves Employee Satisfaction and Job Performance"

*Lalin Anik, Harvard Business School, USA*
*Michael I. Norton, Harvard Business School, USA*
*Lara B. Aknin, University of British Columbia, Canada*
*Jordi Quoidbach, University of Liège, Belgium*
*Elizabeth W. Dunn, University of British Columbia, Canada*

Recent surveys indicate that employee job satisfaction is at a twenty-year low in the United States (Conference Board, 2010)–perhaps because over the same time frame, Americans spend more and more of their time at work at the expense of devoting time to pursuits known to be linked to well-being, from forming social connections to engaging in prosocial acts such as volunteering (Schor, 1991). These findings, while seemingly aligned, also raise a puzzle: For many people, the line between work and social life is blurred, from spending time outside of the office with their friends from the office, to engaging fellow employees in prosocial behavior such as selling their daughter's Girl Scout cookies. We suggest that rather than forcing employees to make a losing tradeoff between social life and work life, employers can co-opt this tradeoff and focus instead on creating what we term a "prosocial workplace" by encouraging their employees to engage in prosocial behavior while at work. In two studies, we show that employers and employees alike can benefit by allowing employees to engage in prosocial spending–spending money on others instead of themselves–by providing them with money to spend on charities and on each other.

We base our interventions on recent research which demonstrates that individuals who spend money on others such as buying gifts for friends and donating money to charity–engaging in *prosocial spending*–are happier than those who spend on themselves (Dunn, Aknin, & Norton, 2008). We explore whether these individual benefits extend beyond the individual, conducting two field studies investigating whether prosocial spending lead to greater well-being, job satisfaction, and job performance. Indeed, previous research suggests that both happiness and prosocial behaviors are key predictors of success in the workplace. First, a large body of research demonstrates a link between people's overall well-being and their outcomes in many domains of life, including success at work (Boehm & Lyubomirsky, 2008; Lyubomirsky, King, & Diener, 2005). Second, several investigations have demonstrated that employees who chose to give money to an employee support program or engaged in helping behaviors in the workplace became more committed to their organization and performed better in their jobs (Bacharach, Bamberger, & Sonnenstuhl, 2001; Grant, 2008; Grant, Dutton, and Rosso (2008). We suggest that engaging employees in prosocial spending–encouraging them to spend money on others rather than on themselves–will therefore increase their individual well-being, their satisfaction with their jobs, and their actual performance at those jobs.

In Study 1, employees at an Australian company (*N*=179, 58% female) were randomly assigned to receive a $50 voucher or a $100 voucher that they could redeem online to donate to a charity of their choice; a control group of participants did not receive a voucher. We measured employees' overall well-being, as well as their satisfaction with their jobs, both prior to receiving the voucher and after redeeming it, approximately two weeks later. Compared to employees who did not receive a voucher, those who received a $100 voucher were significantly happier and reported higher job satisfaction.

But does this increase well-being and job satisfaction lead to better performance? In Study 2, we explored the impact of prosocial spending on the performance of two very different kinds of teams: Members of an intramural dodgeball league in Canada, and members of pharmaceutical sales teams in Belgium. For the dodgeball league, members of some teams were given $20 to spend on themselves (*personal spending*), while members of other teams were given $20 to spend on a teammate (*prosocial spending*). Similarly with the sales teams, members of some teams were given 15? to spend on themselves, while members of other teams were given 15? to spend on other members of their team. As we predicted, teams that had engaged in prosocial spending performed better than those that engaged in prosocial spending, across both samples. For the dodgeball league, prosocial spending teams showed an increase of the percentage of games won over the course of the season (moving from 50% to 81%) while those who engage in personal spending showed no improvement (50% to 43%). Similarly for sales teams, prosocial spending teams showed a significant increase in total sales after the intervention (going from an average of 3335? in sales to 3524?), while again personal spending teams did not improve (3928? to 3938?).

In sum, these studies demonstrate the positive impact of prosocial spending for organizations. We show that when employers build prosocial elements into the workplace by offering employees the opportunity to spend money on others–both their co-workers and those in need–both the employees and the company benefit, with increased job satisfaction, team performance, and revenues. Given that satisfaction with one's work is an essential component of people's overall well-being (Blustein 2008; Lucas, Clark, Georgellis, & Diener, 2004) and the previously mentioned decline in overall employee satisfaction, interventions that can improve both overall well-being and satisfaction may be timelier than ever.

# Will I Change My Emotion, Or Will It Change Me? Emotion Regulation and Emotional Processing in Consumer Behavior

Nicole M. Verrochi, University of Pennsylvania, USA

## EXTENDED ABSTRACTS

### "Will I Always Choose Champagne?: How Emotion Norms Shape Consumption Choices"

Eugenia Wu, Gavan Fitzsimons, Mary Frances Luce, Duke University, USA
Patti Williams, University of Pennsylvania, USA

Though emotion norms regarding when we should feel specific emotions and which emotions are appropriate to what situations provide a constant backdrop to everyday life, little research has examined how they might influence our consumption behavior. In this research, we begin to bridge that gap by exploring how emotion norms might encourage individuals to make nonintuitive consumption choices in an attempt to achieve or avoid specific emotional states. We focus specifically on how the emotion norm associated with feeling ashamed can lead individuals to make choices that are inconsistent with mood regulation and the hedonic principle. In particular, we propose that because shame is typically characterized by feelings of worthlessness and undeservingness (Tangney and Dearing, 2002), shame comes with an emotion norm that one does not deserve to feel positively. Furthermore, we suggest that this anti-positivity emotion norm, in combination with our basic desire to make hedonic choices and alleviate negativity (Gilbert, Wilson and Centerbar, 2003), leads ashamed individuals to prefer consumption products that elicit neither positive nor negative emotion but psychologically uncomfortable and aversive mixed emotions instead.

Study 1 validates that the emotion norm in shame is positivity avoidance. Participants were asked to rate how appropriate it would be for an individual who had done something he was ashamed about or sad about to engage in a series of positive and negative activities. Results revealed that individuals in the sad condition rated it as more appropriate for him to engage in mood-repair type activities relative to individuals in the shame condition. Thus, we find some confirmation that the emotion norm associated with shame is an avoidance of positivity.

In study 2, we examine how emotion norms might affect individuals' consumption choices. Participants were primed to feel shame or in a control condition and asked to allocate 100 points among a positive, a negative and a mixed emotion-eliciting novel. Results revealed that relative to the control condition, participants in the shame condition allocated fewer points to the positive novel option and more points to the mixed emotion option. Of note, the behavior of the shame condition individuals is in direct opposition to the classic mood repair findings and occurs despite the fact that mixed emotions are psychologically uncomfortable and aversive.

In study 3, we set out to provide further support for the existence of an emotion norm in shame and to rule out an alternative explanation for our effects. Participants were first asked to read a short paragraph that encouraged, discouraged or said nothing about relying on their sense of appropriateness to make decisions. Then, participants completed either a shame or neutral prime before allocating points across four novel options (positive, negative, neutral and mixed) and completing a measure of shame-proneness. Results revealed that shame condition consumers continued to divert their points from the positive to the mixed option, despite the presence of the neutral option. This result rules out the possibility

that ashamed participants chose the mixed emotion option because they expected the positive and negative components of the mix to cancel out and result in emotional neutrality. Furthermore, shame condition participants who were encouraged to rely on their sense of appropriateness allocated the most points to the mixed emotion option, suggesting that it is indeed emotional appropriateness that is driving our effects. Finally, these effects were moderated by individual differences in shame-proneness such that effects were exacerbated for individuals high in shame-proneness.

In study 4, we explore how the anti-positivity emotion norm in shame might lead individuals to prefer products that elicit specific combinations of mixed emotions over others. If emotion norms deter ashamed individuals from feeling purely positive emotions because they are undeserving, then we expect ashamed consumers would prefer mixed emotions where the positive component of the mix is other-focused rather than self-focused. Participants completed a shame or neutral prime and then allocated 100 points among novel options. In this study, the emotions characterizing the mixed emotion book were manipulated so that the focus of the positive and negative emotion components varied across conditions. The results of the study revealed that consistent with previous studies, shame condition participants allocated more points to the mixed option relative to control condition participants. Importantly, shame condition participants were especially likely to allocate points to the mixed option when the positive emotion component was other-focused rather than ego-focused. This result is consistent with the idea that positive other-focused emotions are more in line with the shame-related emotion norm than positive self-focused emotions.

Taken together, this work builds on and extends the existing research on motivated emotion, mixed emotion and emotion norms in 1) suggesting a novel reason for why individuals might seek out one emotional state or another 2) providing an explanation for why mixed emotion-eliciting products might succeed in the marketplace 3) demonstrating that not all negative emotions lead to hedonically driven behavior and 4) examining how this fundamental social structure influences consumption behavior.

### "Emotions and Motivated Reasoning: How Anger Increases and Shame Decreases Defensive Processing"

Adam Duhachek, Indiana University, USA
Da Hee Han, Indiana University, USA
Nidhi Agrawal, Northwestern University, USA

Consumer research in recent years has explored how emotional experiences impact consumer attitudes and behaviors. While most early research focused on the role of valenced affective states (i.e., positive or negative mood), recent research has begun to look at the role of specific discrete emotional states in information processing and persuasion. This literature on information processing has assumed that emotion driven consumers are either motivated to form accurate attitudes (e.g., Teidens and Linton 2001) or are driven to regulate their mood (e.g., Agrawal and Duhachek forthcoming).

In this paper, we examine how emotions impact the processing of consumers driven by defense motivation. In the persuasion literature, consumers have been shown to process messages in a defense motivated manner when they have a preference or an attitude towards a product and are exposed to preference consistent versus inconsistent information. Consumers tend to be receptive toward preference consistent information but tend to discount or ignore preference inconsistent information (e.g., Jain and Maheswaran 2000). The present research examines how emotions will impact the processing of such information.

Bringing together the literature on emotional appraisals with the work on defensive processing in the Heuristic Systematic Model, we draw novel predictions about how emotions will influence information processing. We contrast the two emotions of anger and shame and show that their appraisals determine their influence on the processing of preference inconsistent information. Both anger and shame arise from negative outcomes/situations, but diverge in who is held responsible for the negative outcome. Anger holds other people in a negative role where as shame casts the self in a negative light. In other words, anger say "I am right" where as shame could prompt "I am wrong." We suggest that these appraisals could serve as information when dealing with preference inconsistent information such that anger appraisals would prompt greater defensiveness against preference-inconsistent information where as shame would prompt an acceptance of ones' existing attitude being incorrect and hence an openness towards preference inconsistent information. We further show that, for high involvement products, individuals are able to 'correct' for the effects of these incidental emotions on their judgments.

Three studies examined how incidental anger and shame influence the processing of preference consistent versus inconsistent information. In all three studies, participants were first primed with either anger or shame. Then they were exposed to information about a brand that convinced them that the brand was better than another competing brand. After a filler task, they saw follow-up information about the brands that either reinforced their initial favorable opinion of the brand (i.e., preference consistent information) or conflicted with their existing favorable opinion (i.e., preference inconsistent information). While emotions had no effect on the processing of preference consistent information, they systematically affected the response to preference inconsistent information. Consistent with our predictions, anger increased resistance to preference inconsistent information where as shame led to an eagerness to accept preference inconsistent information. These effects manifested in attitude change (study 1) as well as cognitive responses (study 2) and only manifested under low involvement conditions (study 3).

Our findings contribute to research on emotion appraisal by showing that appraisals of self versus other blame can heighten or counteract defense motivation. We also extend the existing literature by identifying conditions emotional appraisals influence information processing (e.g., exposure to preference inconsistent information), when emotions have no effect on processing (e.g., exposure to preference consistent information), and when the effect of emotions on processing is corrected (e.g., high involvement conditions). Our finding that shame counteracts defensive processing by encouraging people to adopt preference inconsistent views makes a unique contribution to the literature on motivated reasoning and persuasion. While most past research has suggested that consumers tend indulge in motivated reasoning that helps them to maintain their preferred attitudes or helps them improve/maintain their existing emotion, we show that under some circumstances, emotions might work through appraisals to counteract or bolster the effects of such motivated reasoning. The implications of our findings for the literature on emotions, motivated reasoning, and persuasion will be discussed, as will the managerial implications for the placement of preference-inconsistent information.

### "Feeling Like My Self: Emotion Profiles and Identity"

*Nicole M. Verrochi, University of Pennsylvania, USA*
*Patti Williams, University of Pennsylvania, USA*

When do people want to change their emotional experience? Known as *emotion regulation*, individuals can self-manage their emotions by intervening in the ongoing emotional experience to adjust when, what, and how intensely they feel particular emotions (Gross 1998). Generally, people try to change their emotions when they feel bad, as when a person eats a chocolate bar after reading a sad story (Labroo and Mukhopadhyay 2009).However, there may be other reasons to experience emotions aside from simply "feeling good." Emotions do have hedonic components (Higgins 1997), but emotions are more than just valence—the appraisal dimensions and action readiness tendencies may be leveraged in assistance of other goals. Perhaps individuals will regulate their emotions in order to achieve goal-related benefits—even at the expense of feeling good (Cohen and Andrade 2004). The current work posits that there are associations between discrete emotions and specific social identities, and that individuals will choose to regulate emotion in order to maintain consistency between the active identity and the emotion experience. In this framework, emotions are integral to manifesting a given social identity, and thus can be used to achieve an identity-consistent experience.

Over the course of one pretest and four studies, this paper shows that there are associations between specific social identities and discrete emotions: giving rise to an *emotion profile* of each social identity. The pretest isolated two emotion profiles: athletes are associated with anger, but volunteers with sadness. In all studies, participants were first primed with either an athlete, volunteer or control identity. After activating the target identity, participants then experienced an emotion. In study 1, individuals exerted more effort when their emotion was consistent with their active identity, while in study 2 participants reported more positive attitudes and higher behavioral intentions for ads in which the emotion matched their identity.

While studies 1 and 2 established that individuals benefit from emotions which match the emotion profile of their active identity, Study 3 sought to evaluate whether individuals will actively manage their emotions in order to match their active emotion profile. Following the identity prime, participants engaged in an attention task which assessed emotion regulation. This task asked participants to quickly and accurately categorize the letter T, which was shown either right-side up or upside-down. Importantly, sad and happy pictures were interspersed within this perceptual task. As sadness is inconsistent with the athlete's emotion profile, participants with an active athlete identity should *divert* their attention away from sad pictures in order to avoid experiencing the inconsistent emotion of sadness. Volunteers, on the other hand, should *focus* their attention on the sad pictures, as they want to experience the identity-consistent emotion of sadness. This pattern of attention shifts was demonstrated: athletes were significantly slower and less accurate than volunteers when responding after sad pictures. No differences were found between athletes and volunteers following happy pictures. These results demonstrate individuals actively regulating their emotions to maintain consistency with the active emotion profile.

The final study presented participants with a product positioned as regulating their emotions: either enhancing or reducing emotional intensity. Again, participants were primed with an identity, and then emotions were induced via a film clip. Following the film, participants tried a beverage which was positioned as enhancing or reducing their emotional experience. As predicted, participants consumed (in grams) more of the beverage that aligned their emotions with the identity's emotion profile. For instance, athletes drank significantly more of the emotion *reducing* beverage when they were sad (inconsistent emotion), but more of the emotion *enhancing* beverage when they were angry (consistent emotion). This study both replicates the results of study 3 with consumption, and demonstrates that individuals will choose to experience an unpleasant emotion when it is valued by the active identity.

This research introduces emotion profiles, which constrain the emotions that are valid for each identity. This represents a new area of research, as well as suggests a new way in which the emotion regulation process may be initiated. Building on findings that demonstrate individuals approach products and enact behaviors which are identity-consistent, while avoiding those which are identity-inconsistent (White and Dahl 2007), this paper shows that individuals are motivated to regulate their emotions in identity-consistent ways. Specifically, people enhanced their experience of identity-consistent emotions, and reduced their experience of emotion profile-inconsistent emotions. This paper not only addresses a gap in the marketing literature by enriching our understanding of the concepts contained within an identity, but also provides an essential pre-condition to emotion regulation, furthering conceptualizations of the emotion management process. Beyond establishing that emotions are included within social identity structures, the current research suggests that identity-marketing appeals can be positioned as identity consistent without ever mentioning the salient identity, but rather by simply leveraging an emotion profile-consistent frame.

# Beyond Fluency: New Frontiers in Metacognition

Aner Sela, University of Florida, USA
Jonah Berger, University of Pennsylvania, USA

## EXTENDED ABSTRACTS

### "Getting to Know Is Getting to Like: Implicit Cognitive Progress Can Awaken Liking"

*Aparna A. Labroo, University of Chicago, USA*
*Ying Zhang, University of Texas—Austin, USA*
*Ayelet Fishbach, University of Chicago, USA*

The facial expressions of a loved one, the first tune of a favorite night comedy, or the immediate associations of a much-frequented restaurant are all examples of things that are readily accessible in memory and surface in the mind most easily. These familiar objects are also among the things that people instantly consider among the most pleasant and hold dearest in their hearts. On the other hand, the liking of certain other things, such as subtle jokes or novel music, might follow a different pattern of evaluation. Novel objects often appear odd at first, but given sufficient consideration, they become interesting and well liked, and a person's experience of increasing familiarity may account for one's positive evaluation.

Understanding factors that underlie evaluative judgment is a central concern of attitude research (Ajzen & Fishbein, 1980; Petty & Cacioppo, 1986), and several experiments now show that the ease of processing the target of evaluation is an important factor that affects evaluation (Reber, Schwarz, & Winkielman, 2004; Schwarz, 2004). It has been consistently demonstrated that people prefer targets that feel immediately familiar because their perceptual characteristics or their meaning is easy to process (Lee & Labroo, 2004; Lee 2002; Whittlesea, 1993; Zajonc, 1968). The focus of existing literature is on immediate response to a target stimulus and evaluation appears to capture a pleasantness-based affective response resulting from high immediate accessibility (Winkielman & Cacioppo, 2001).

We propose that there is a second, unexplored aspect of accessibility—a change in accessibility—which may affect evaluation of a target in later stages of processing. This is because in the processing of a target stimulus, recently changed accessibility is likely to be associated with feelings of cognitive progress, implicit learning, and interest (rather than pleasantness). Interest in a target builds or diminishes over time; it is high when change in accessibility is positive, but it is reduced when change in accessibility is constant. Changed accessibility is inconsequential when evaluation is immediate, and if that is the case, evaluation is based on an immediate, absolute accessibility (and pleasantness). In contrast, high accessibility is inconsequential in later stages of processing of a target which is instead more sensitive to changes in accessibility that mark cognitive progress.

This proposition is compatible with experiments that show that perceptual fluency might follow an inverted U-shaped pattern; specifically, moderately frequent prior exposure to a stimulus results in maximum liking, and overexposure leads to habituation and reduced interest with the stimulus (Bornstein, Kale, & Cornell, 1990; Lee 2001). But this proposition is also distinct from these past findings which presume that pleasantness and interest are on a continuum; we argue that fluency comprises of two distinct sources: immediate accessibility and pleasantness and a sense of implicit cognitive progress over time which reflects in interest. Immediate evaluation follows pleasantness; evaluation after a delay follows cognitive progress.

Two experiments tested these predictions that a change in accessibility influences the interest in a stimulus and changes in its positive evaluation after a delay. Experiment 1 (and a pilot experiment) demonstrated that the evaluation of target words that follow a typical prime decreases with delay because accessibility is constant over time and the evaluation of target words that follow an atypical prime increases with delay because accessibility increases. Experiment 2 demonstrated that the decrease (vs. the increase) in the evaluation of target words that follow a typical (vs. an atypical) prime corresponds to changes in interestingness rather than the pleasantness of the evaluated stimuli over time.

By focusing on changes in evaluation over time, this research shows that people's immediate response is different from their response to the same stimulus only a few seconds later. This research provides insight into how evaluation evolves over short periods of time and highlights its mercurial nature. Attitudes toward the same target are different depending on when response toward the target is evoked; attitudes build over a short delay and change substantially as more processing is added. *(Manuscript in preparation)*

### "Decision Quicksand: When Trivial Sucks Us In"

*Aner Sela, University of Florida, USA*
*Jonah Berger, University of Pennsylvania, USA*

Common wisdom suggests that people should spend more time and effort deliberating on important decisions (e.g., what 401k plan to use) than unimportant ones (e.g., what toothbrush to buy). However, we often find ourselves mired in trivial, everyday decisions, such as ordering at restaurants or buying flight tickets, and end up feeling that we spent similar or even larger amounts of time and effort than on decisions far more consequential. In such instances, choosing often becomes more difficult when we try to resolve it through deliberation (Dijksterhuis and Nordgren 2006; Wilson and Schooler 1991), as if sinking in quicksand. But while such experiences are quite common, our understanding of their underlying causes is limited.

We propose that metacognitive inference contributes to what we describe as "decision quicksand". Conflict of some degree is a defining property of choice, whether of important or trivial consequences. Our central premise is that people use the ease or difficulty experienced while making a decision as a cue to guide how much further time and effort to spend. We hypothesize that people hold naïve theories according to which more important decisions should be more difficult. Consequently, experiencing difficulty in choice may lead people to perceive the decision as more important which, in turn, increases the amount of time and cognitive effort they are motivated to expend on the decision (Alter et al 2007; Chaiken and Maheswaran 1994). We propose that this may lead to a vicious cycle whereby expending more effort further increases perceived importance and thus experienced difficulty.

Importantly, however, the influence of metacognitive experiences tends to be stronger the more the experience deviates from people's expectations (Schwarz 2004). Consequently, we predict that the tendency to spend more time and effort on difficult decisions would be more pronounced when the decision is perceived as unimportant, than when it is important. Because important decisions are expected to be difficult (Kivetz, Netzer, and Schrift 2009), the real-time experience of difficulty does not provide additional information. In contrast, decision difficulty should be more informative as a cue for decision importance when it is unexpected (cf. Maheswaran and Chaiken 1991).

We test these propositions in three experiments. In experiment 1, people chose between two flight options described using regular (fluent) or degraded (disfluent) font. In addition, the decision was described as either important (related to a business meeting) or relatively unimportant (visiting distant relatives). We measured how much time people spent before deciding and whether or not they would like to consider more options. Consistent with our prediction, when the decision was unimportant, people spent more time deliberating and were more likely to seek more options when the stimuli were disfluent (versus fluent). However, fluency did not have an effect in the important framing condition.

Experiment 2 manipulated decision difficulty through the number of difficult tradeoffs. People chose between two flight options, containing either few or many tradeoffs, and the task was again framed as either important or unimportant. In addition, we tested whether the effect of difficulty in the unimportant condition disappeared when difficulty could be attributed to a cause other than importance (by telling half the participants that people often find the task difficult). As predicted, increased decision difficulty led people to spend more time deliberating, but only in the unimportant framing condition and, ironically, more so in absolute terms than in the important framing conditions. Moreover, when people could attribute the difficulty to an unrelated cause, this effect disappeared, consistent with the notion that the effect of difficulty on deliberation resulted from misattribution.

Experiment 3 examines the progressive nature of "decision quicksand". After viewing the initial choice-set, as in experiment 2, participants were offered the opportunity to view more features for each option before making a selection. Compared to people who considered only the initial set, those who viewed the enhanced set spent increasingly more time considering the additional features, and this effect was more pronounced under unimportant than under important decision framing.

While prior research has shown that decision difficulty can lead people to defer choice (Dhar and Simonson 2003; Tversky and Shafir 1992), we show that choice difficulty can influence people's perceptions of the decision itself, through its role as a metacognitive cue. Especially in seemingly trivial decisions, this can have painful consequences for consumer decision making. *(Manuscript in preparation)*

### "Understanding Why People Sometimes Form Judgments and Decisions Too Hastily (Or How to Market a Political Candidate)"

*Adam L. Alter, New York University, USA*
*Daniel M. Oppenheimer, Princeton University, USA*
*Jeffrey C. Zemla, Rice University, USA*

People are frequently faced with the difficult task of deciding how much information to gather before settling on a decision or forming a judgment. Information gathering is a balancing act, because although people are motivated to form accurate conclusions about the world, they are also cognitive misers who prefer to think as little as possible about their decisions and judgments (Fiske & Taylor, 1991). Decades of research suggests that this introspective process is systematically flawed, and people frequently overestimate their understanding of focal events. To date, researchers have found this so-called *illusion of explanatory depth* (*IOED;* Rozenblit & Keil, 2002) when people assess their understanding of mechanical and natural processes (e.g., how bicycles and solar systems work). In this paper, we argue that people are prone to similar errors in many other domains—including political and consumer judgment and decision-making.

In four experiments, we sought to explain why this miscalibration in judgment occurs, and to show that this general mechanism explains why IOEDs occur in novel domains that researchers have not yet considered. Drawing on Construal Level Theory (Trope & Liberman, 2003), we argue that people consult inappropriate metacognitive cues (their sound understanding of the target's abstract properties—e.g., why a bicycle exists—rather than their poorer understanding of its concrete properties—e.g., how the bicycle's parts enable it to move). We also explain how these results inform marketing practices and enhance our understanding of consumer decision-making.

In Experiment 1, participants were primed to adopt either an abstract mindset or a concrete mindset. Participants in the concrete condition explained *how* three mundane processes occur, whereas participants in the abstract condition explained *why* the same three processes occur. As expected, participants in the abstract condition were significantly more likely than participants in the concrete condition to overestimate their understanding of processes like how a zipper works and how a bicycle lock works. We also administered a questionnaire that assessed how concretely or abstractly participants construed 13 everyday activities. A mediation analysis suggested that participants in the concrete construal condition showed a diminished IOED because they adopted a more concrete construal style.

The results in Experiment 1 were encouraging, but we were concerned that the construal prime was too similar to later questions that asked participants to assess their knowledge about the target process. Specifically, by asking them *how* certain processes worked, we had primed them to answer a subsequent question about *how* deeply they understood a mechanical process with greater accuracy. Accordingly, in Experiment 2, we used a second construal manipulation that was not at all related to the second phase of the experiment. Participants completed a construal manipulation questionnaire. The questionnaire listed 10 objects, and participants were asked to identify either a superordinate category to which the object belonged (inducing higher-level, abstract construal; e.g., a whale is a mammal or an animal) or a specific example of each object (inducing lower-level, concrete construal; e.g., an example of a whale is an orca or a baleen; adopted from e.g., Fujita & Han, 2009). Again, participants more profoundly overestimated their understanding of how the target processes worked in the abstract construal condition, when they were primed to attend to their knowledge of inappropriately abstract information.

Finally, in Experiments 3 and 4, we showed that the effect occurred in a novel domain: self-assessments of how well participants understood their favored 2008 Presidential Primary candidate's policies. Whereas participants who were induced to adopt an abstract construal style showed a strong IOED, participants who adopted a concrete mindset showed a significantly diminished IOED. Experiments 3 and 4 therefore demonstrated the IOED in a novel domain, suggesting that construal style is a domain-general mechanism that underpins the effect.

We conclude by considering how this construal-based mechanism might illuminate a range of social and judgment-based biases, and how marketers might promote fledgling political candidates and new products most effectively. *(Paper under review)*

### "Building Attitude Certainty to Promote Attitude Change"

*Joshua J. Clarkson, University of Florida, USA*
*Zakary L. Tormala, Stanford University, USA*
*Derek D. Rucker, Northwestern University, USA*

Imagine two individuals who hold equally favorable attitudes toward an object. Although these individuals have similar attitudes, they differ in attitude certainty. For example, perhaps because one individual has greater familiarity with the object, he or she feels more certain than the other. Intuitively, it is reasonable to expect that individuals who are certain of their attitudes will be more resistant to change than individuals who are uncertain of their attitudes. Similarly, an aspiring persuader generally would be advised to target the less certain individual, or to strategically undermine the more certain individual's certainty prior to delivering a message. Indeed, the conventional view of attitude certainty is that it is a metacognitive property of attitudes that makes them harder to change (see Tormala and Rucker 2007; Gross et al. 1995).

The current research asks whether this same metacognitive property might sometimes act as a *catalyst* rather than obstacle to change. That is, we posit that under some conditions, being certain of an attitude can actually make people more open to attitude change. We present a new perspective on attitude certainty—*the amplification hypothesis*—which suggests that rather than invariably strengthening attitudes, certainty amplifies the dominant tendency of a particular attitude in a particular situation. If a given attitude tends to be open to change in a given context, for instance, we propose that increasing attitude certainty will promote rather than obstruct this openness. If, however, an attitude tends to be resistant to change in some setting, increasing attitude certainty will increase this resistance, as in past research.

An extensive literature now highlights the conditions under which attitudes tend to be open rather than resistant to change. For example, all else equal, ambivalent attitudes tend to be more open to change than univalent attitudes (e.g., Visser and Mirabile 2004). Even among univalent attitudes, however, openness sometimes prevails. For instance, research on message position effects suggests that attitudes tend to be open to pro-attitudinal messages but resistant to counter-attitudinal messages (e.g., Lord et al. 1979; Petty and Cacioppo 1979). Yet even in the face of counter-attitudinal messages, attitudes are sometimes open. As an example, attitudes often show substantial change in the direction of counter-attitudinal attacks that match their cognitive or affective basis (e.g., Fabrigar and Petty 1999), whereas they tend to resist change toward messages that mismatch their basis. The present research explores whether increased attitude certainty might amplify rather than attenuate many of these classic effects.

In experiment 1, we orthogonally manipulated ambivalence and attitude certainty by presenting participants with evaluatively congruent or incongruent reviews of a new department store from a high or low credibility source. Following this information, we presented a persuasive message about the store and assessed attitude change in response to this message. Results indicated an interaction between congruence (univalence/ambivalence) and source credibility (high/low attitude certainty) on attitude change. When participants had univalent initial attitudes, they showed greater attitude change when the credibility manipulation induced low rather than high attitude certainty. When participants had ambivalent attitudes, however, they showed greater change when the credibility manipulation induced high rather than low certainty. Thus, certainty increased ambivalent attitudes' openness to change.

In experiment 2, we used a similar department store paradigm. In this study, however, we manipulated initial attitudes to be unambiguously positive or negative toward the store, manipulated attitude certainty using a priming procedure, and finally presented a persuasive message that was either pro- or counter-attitudinal. Results indicated an interaction. Participants who received a counter-attitudinal message changed more toward it when they were induced to have low rather than high certainty. In contrast, participants who received a pro-attitudinal message changed more toward it when they were induced to have high rather than low certainty. Thus, certainty increased univalent attitudes' openness to pro-attitudinal messages.

In experiment 3, we explored the effects of messages that matched or mismatched the basis of the target attitude. All participants were given initial positive affect-based attitudes toward a fictitious animal and were induced to hold this attitude with high or low certainty. Subsequently, participants received a negative message about the animal that was either cognitive or affective in tone. As predicted, we found an interaction between attitude certainty and the affective/cognitive tone of the message. Participants who received the mismatched (cognitive) message evinced greater attitude change under low compared to high certainty, whereas those who received the matched (affective) message showed greater change under high compared to low certainty. Thus, certainty increased affective attitudes' openness to matched (i.e., affective) counter-attitudinal messages.

*Discussion.* In summary, conventional wisdom and past research suggest that if a persuader seeks to change someone's attitude, he or she would benefit from first decreasing the target's attitude certainty. In contrast, the present research suggests that *increasing* attitude certainty can sometimes promote change. These findings are consistent with the amplification hypothesis, suggesting that under conditions in which attitudes tend to be open to change, increased certainty can augment this openness. Implications for our understanding of metacognitive factors in attitudes and persuasion are discussed. *(Completed manuscript)*

# Losing Control When We Least Expect It (and Surprising Ways to Get It Back!)

Kelly Goldsmith, Northwestern University, USA
Anastasiya Pocheptsova, University of Maryland, USA

## EXTENDED ABSTRACTS

### "Clouds on a Sunny Day: The Downside of Positive Mood for Goal Pursuit"

*Jordan Etkin, University of Maryland, USA*
*Francine Espinoza, ESMT, Germany*
*Anastasiya Pocheptsova, University of Maryland, USA*

A consistent finding in the literature is that positive mood is beneficial for goal pursuit and self-control. For example, happy mood signals a person to adopt an accessible goal and, consequently, one performs better on self-control tasks (Fishbach and Labroo 2007). However, previous research on the beneficial effects of positive mood primarily focuses on the pursuit of a single focal goal. Yet, consumers frequently pursue multiple goals simultaneously: An individual may wish to enjoy nice restaurants, lose ten pounds, spend time with family and exercise regularly. Multiple goal-pursuit often creates a self-control dilemma when pursuing one goal is seen to be in conflict with pursuing another goal (Fishbach and Dhar 2005). In these situations, individuals must exert self-control and distribute their efforts across the pursuit of many goals that are important to them. In this research we explore the role of positive affect in the pursuit of multiple goals.

We propose that in contrast to a beneficial effect of positive mood on the pursuit of a single goal, positive mood will have a detrimental impact on self-control when multiple goals compete for an individual's resources. We predict this happens because positive mood affects how individuals construe the relationships among their goals; by increasing perceived inter-goal conflict. Previous research has found that positive affect results in recognition of more, and more different, aspects or features of items (Isen et al. 1985; Isen, Daubman, and Nowicki 1987). When in positive mood, individuals are open to a larger diversity of information, giving rise to a greater recognition of differences and increasing the complexity and richness of a set (Kahn and Isen 1993). Applying these findings to the context of multiple-goal pursuit, we propose that positive mood will increase perception of the differences between goals and hence result in greater perceived inter-goal conflict. Increased goal conflict leads people to be less likely to engage in goal-consistent behaviors (Emmons and King 1988; Riediger and Freund 2004). Therefore, we propose that being in a positive mood while pursuing multiple goals will lead people to perceive greater differences among their goals, and the resulting increase in perceptions of inter-goal conflict will have detrimental effects for goal pursuit and self-control.

Across several studies, we find support for this proposition. In a pilot study, following a mood manipulation using a sad versus a happy video clip, participants were primed with three goals that had been pretested to be important for this population. We find that participants in a positive mood perceived significantly greater conflict among their goals than participants in a negative mood ($M_{happy}$=3.86 vs. $M_{sad}$=2.84). In study 1, following the same mood manipulation, participants were asked to list the three most important goals they were pursuing. We found that participants in a positive mood were less motivated (willing to devote less energy and work less intensely in pursuing their three most important goals) than participants in a negative mood ($M_{happy}$=4.28 vs. $M_{sad}$=4.75). Further, the effect of mood on self-control was mediated by perceived inter-goal conflict.

Goal conflict can be reduced by choice of multifinal means, which allows consumers to jointly pursue their conflicting multiple goals (Chun and Kruglanski 2005; Kopetz, Fishbach and Kruglanski 2010). However, in order for a multifinal mean to reduce inter-goal conflict, consumers must be able to recognize that the mean facilitates the attainment of more than one of their goals. If being in a positive mood highlights the differences between goals, we predict that happy consumers should be less likely to perceive any one mean as simultaneously serving the pursuit of more than one goal, thus making the means appear less multifinal (Zhang, Fishbach, and Kruglanski 2007). To test this, in study 2, after completing the mood and goal listing task as in Study 1, participants were asked to list means to achieve their goals and rate the extent to which the listed means served multiple goals. Consistent with our theorizing, participants in a positive mood perceived the means they listed as less multifinal than participants in a negative mood, who perceived their listed means as more likely to help them achieve more than one goal ($M_{happy}$=4.80 vs. $M_{sad}$=5.94). Importantly, mood did not influence the number of means generated.

To further explore the relationship between positive mood and means multifinality, in study 3 we examined whether explicitly providing participants with a multifinal mean would help reduce conflict for participants in a positive mood, thereby attenuating the detrimental effect of positive mood on motivation in multiple goal pursuit. After watching the sad versus happy videos, participants were primed with one or three goals as in the pilot study, and then were presented with an anagram task that was described as either unifinal (helping to achieve the first primed goal) or multifinal (helping to achieve all three primed goals). Motivation to pursue the primed goals was measured via the time participants persisted in the anagram task. We find that in the multiple goals condition participants in a positive (vs. negative) mood persisted less in the task when it was presented as being unifinal ($M_{happy}$=146.5 vs. $M_{sad}$=186.9), but they persisted more than participants in a negative mood when the task was described as multifinal ($M_{happy}$=221.4 vs. $M_{sad}$=162.1), supporting our prediction. Further, we found that participants in a positive (vs. negative) mood spent more time on the task when only one goal was primed, replicating the beneficial effect of positive mood for pursuit of one focal goal demonstrated in previous research ($M_{happy}$=197.1 vs. $M_{sad}$=159.6).

Taken together, our findings support the idea that positive mood leads to greater perceptions of inter-goal conflict, which, in turn, decreases consumers' motivation when pursuing multiple important goals. Though previous research suggests that positive mood improves self-control performance, we find that positive mood may have a detrimental impact on self-control when individuals pursue multiple goals. We also show that the choice of multifinal means attenuates this effect. Our findings contribute to the literatures on mood and self-regulation by expanding our understanding of the interplay between emotions and self-control in the context of multiple goals.

### "When Guilt Guides Us to the Lap of Luxury"

*Kelly Goldsmith, Northwestern University, USA*
*Margaret Gorlin, Yale University, USA*
*Ravi Dhar, Yale University, USA*

Consider a consumer who is choosing between two expensive pairs of shoes. Further imagine that prior to choosing a pair, she starts experiencing guilt. How would this consumer's guilt affect her choice? While it is now well established that guilt can serve a self-regulatory function, increasing self-control and inhibiting preference for more hedonic options (Amodio, Devine and Harmon-Jones 2007; Zemack-Rugar, Bettman and Fitzsimmons 2007) relatively little is known about how the activation of guilt will affect choices among indulgent options. For example, would this person be more or less likely to choose the more expensive pair of shoes in comparison to a person who was not feeling guilty?

This paper explores how a choice between two indulgent or luxury options is impacted when guilt is incidentally activated prior to the choice. Prior work has shown that unrelated emotions (i.e., guilt) may be carried over and affect behavior outside of awareness (Lerner and Keltner 2000; Lerner et al. 2004). We draw from research on guilt and behavioral decision theory to propose that when guilt is primed, consumers will experience an increased need to justify their decision (Dhar and Wertenbroch 2000; Kivetz and Simonson 2002; Okada 2005; Strahilevitz and Myers 1997). Because options providing maximum luxury may be easier to justify when they offer the consumer a special or unique peak experience (Dhar and Simonson 1999; Goldsmith and Dhar 2010; Kapner 2009) we argue that consumers primed with guilt will be *more* likely to choose the option in the set that offers maximum luxury (e.g., a more expensive special treat) than consumers for whom guilt is not activated. Thus we predict a counter-intuitive effect of guilt on choice: priming guilt can *increase* choice of more expensive, luxury options.

We test our predictions in four studies. Study 1 tests for our proposed effect. Using non-conscious guilt priming (sentence scrambles; Goldsmith, Kim and Dhar 2010), we manipulate if guilt is activated prior to a choice between two luxury goods (two entrée courses at a high priced restaurant), one being a more expensive and indulgent than the other (a higher priced entrée special). Supporting our central claim, we observed that priming guilt increased choice of the more expensive option ($P_{guilt}$ = 72%, $P_{control}$ = 53%, $p$< .05). Study 2 demonstrates an important boundary condition for this effect. By manipulating both guilt (versus control) and the product category (a choice between two indulgent chocolate bars versus a choice between two utilitarian highlighter sets), we show that guilt increases choice of the option offering maximum luxury only when the product category is associated with indulgence. In line with our predictions, we find choice of the more expensive chocolate bar increases with guilt ($P_{guilt}$ = 26%, $P_{control}$ = 9%, $p$=.02); however, guilt has no effect on choice of the more expensive highlighter set ($P_{guilt}$ = 6%, $P_{control}$ = 13%, $p$=n.s.d.; guilt * product category interaction: $p$=.04). These results help to rule out an alternate account for the pattern of results in Study 1 by demonstrating that guilt does not facilitate a mindset that reduces barriers to spending regardless of the product category (Huber, Khan and Dhar 2007), the effect is specific to product categories associated with indulgence, where the justification process is more likely to operate.

Testing for the mechanism behind this effect, Study 3 manipulates the salience of the justification for the more expensive good (e.g., quality ratings are provided and made focal to participants), and assesses how guilt and the salience of this justification affect consumers' interest in maximum luxuries. The results again demonstrate that guilt increases interest in maximum luxuries (dependent measure: a choice between two luxury hotel stays; $P_{guilt}$ = 71%, $P_{control}$ = 42%, $p$=.02). Additionally, we observe that when the justification for the maximum luxury is made salient to those in the control condition, there is an analogous effect on choice (choice of the maximum luxury increases significantly; $P_{control}$ = 62%, $p$< .05). As the effect of guilt and justification salience is non-additive, this suggests that those primed with guilt were already focused on the relevant justification for the maximum luxury, in line with our proposed theoretical account. Finally, Study 4 confirms that

these effects of guilt are counter-intuitive: when asked, consumers overwhelmingly predict that they would be *less* likely to choose the maximum luxury when guilt was activated ($p$< .01).

As the need for justification can affect consumer decisions and shift preference towards options that are supported by the best reasons, this research has clear implications for marketers seeking to maximize their understanding of consumer decision processes at the point of choice. Further, it extends what is currently known about the effect of guilt on consumer behavior, showing that guilt is not always associated with increased self-regulatory function: in the domain of luxury goods when the most salient justification may be maximum indulgence, guilt increases choice of maximum luxuries. We have two ongoing studies that are presently being run to further explore the process underlying this phenomenon. Specially, we seek to demonstrate: (1) that an increased desire to justify one's choice mediates the observed effects and (2) that the same guilt prime can lead to more (less) indulgent choices depending on the nature of the choice set (e.g., a choice between luxuries versus a choice between a luxury option and a utilitarian option). We hope that the current research will prompt future inquiry into this area.

## "Distance Makes the Will Grow Weaker: When Distance Hinders Self-Control"

*Lawrence Williams, University of Colorado—Boulder, USA*
*An Tran, University of Colorado—Boulder, USA*
*John Bargh, Yale University, USA*

Within the literature on judgment and choice, psychological distance and abstract thinking are often treated as interchangeable concepts. Construal level theory (CLT; Trope and Liberman 2003) provides a broad and powerful framework for accounting for the effects of temporal, social, and spatial distance on judgments, such that people in a psychologically distant (close) mindset think more abstractly (concretely), focus more of the desirability (feasibility) of action (Liberman and Trope 1998), and have an easier time deciding between options with nonalignable attributes (Malkoc, Zauberman and Ulu 2005). The success of CLT has resulted in an unintended consequence of limited exploration of the effects of psychological distance that are outside of the purview of the theory. The research described herein was designed to address that gap in knowledge.

It has been previously found that when people think abstractly, they become more committed to their self-control goals (Fujita, Trope, Liberman and Levin-Sagi 2006). For example, participants encouraged to think of why they pursue goals (priming high-level, abstract construal) persisted longer on a physical endurance task than participants who were encouraged to think about how they pursue goals (priming low-level, concrete construal). Also, people primed to think abstractly viewed potential temptations (that could interfere with self-control goals) more negatively, compared to people primed to think concretely.

Given the manner in which psychological distance and abstraction are intimately linked in the literature (e.g., Labroo and Patrick 2009), It would be tempting at this point to expect that psychological distance would produce the same effects on self-control as abstraction does, namely that psychological distance would help people accomplish their self-control goals. However, in addition to altering the level at which features of a decision context are construed, psychological distance should also influence the affective intensity of those features. There is an important, often-overlooked association between psychological distance and affective states. People in a distant mindset show reduced emotional intensity in their responses to emotionally evocative stimuli (Williams and Bargh 2008), and people who have emotionally intense experiences feel psychologically closer to those experiences (Van Boven, Kane, McGraw and

Dale forthcoming). In what follows, we experimentally examine the role distance plays in supporting people's capacity for self-control independent of changes in construal level, by examining their judgments of tempting foods (calorie estimates), and their choices.

In Study 1, participants were primed with physical distance or physical closeness by plotting points on a Cartesian plane. Participants in the physical distance condition plotted a set of points that were relatively far from each other on the Cartesian plane, whereas participants in the physical closeness condition plotted points that were relatively close to each other on the plane. This method was chosen to activate psychological distance versus closeness concepts without any contaminating co-activation of social concerns that might separately influence self-regulatory efforts. Furthermore, a separate study demonstrated that due to the absence of a self-referent in the priming task, using this method to activate distance (closeness) concepts does not produce corresponding changes in construal. Next, participants were asked to estimate the number of calories in five relatively unhealthy foods (chocolate bar, cheeseburger) and in five relatively healthy foods (apple, brown rice). We found that participants primed with distance viewed junk food as having fewer calories, compared to participants primed with closeness. In contrast to previous work demonstrating that abstract thinking promotes devaluation of tempting stimuli, these results suggest that psychological distance may attenuate the feeling that tempting foods are dangerous, perhaps making these unhealthy options seem more appropriate for consumption.

In Study 2, we hypothesized that if psychological distance attenuates the emotional features of the self-control decision context, then people in a distant mindset should be more committed to self-control when they are primarily experiencing feelings of pleasure associated with temptation, but should be less committed to self-control when they are primarily experiencing feelings of guilt associated with temptation. In this study, participants were first asked to recall either a time in which they felt particularly guilty when succumbing to temptation, or a time in which they felt particularly pleased when succumbing to temptation (between-subjects). Afterwards, participants were primed with either physical distance or physical closeness (using the same methodology used in Study 1). Finally, as thanks for participating in the study, participants were asked to choose between a chocolate cupcake and a (relatively healthier) granola bar. As predicted, we find that distance (vs. closeness) priming attenuated guilty feelings, undermining self-control and lead participants to choose the unhealthy cupcake more frequently. However, we also find that distance priming attenuated pleasurable feelings as well, thus bolstering self-control and leading participants in this condition to choose the healthier item more frequently.

This pattern of findings is informative for understanding how contextual factors help or hurt people's ability to exercise self-control. Furthermore, these investigations go a long way toward specifying when psychological distance and abstract thinking will produce similar versus dissociated effects on judgment and choice.

### "Defeating Depletion: How Self-control Can Increase Self-regulatory Resources

*Uzma Khan, Stanford University, USA*
*Amar Cheema, University of Virginia, USA*

Self-control is often viewed as an exhaustible resource. Consistent with this notion, past research on ego-depletion has shown that exerting self-control impairs the ability to control one's self later. Whereas a significant amount of research has examined the sources of ego-depletion, relatively little is known about how self-control resource can be replenished (Baumeister, Schmeichel&Vohs

2007). The current article fills this void by examining when exerting self-control may augment, rather than deplete, the self-regulation resources.

We propose that experiencing a self-regulation task that gets easier over time can replenish self-control resources rather than deplete them and can thus increase self-control on subsequent unrelated tasks. We posit that experienced ease in exerting self-control, such as when the difficulty of a task decreases over time, induces a sense of subjective vitality. Subjective vitality is the feeling of having energy available to the self (Ryan & Frederick 1997). The experience of vitality refers to energy that is perceived to emanate from the self and has an internal perceived locus of causality(Deci& Ryan 1985). Thus to the extent that people perceive themselves as getting better on an effortful self-regulation task-as suggested by decreasing experienced difficulty-it can increase the subjective experience of vitality. Experiencing subjective vitality can then counter the depleting effects of initial self-regulation and can increase, rather than decrease, self-control subsequently (Muraven et al. 2008).

Three studies provide support for our proposition. In Study 1, as a potentially depleting task participants solved 5 anagrams–either in an increasing or in a decreasing order of difficulty. Next, participants proceeded to an *e*-crossing task where they crossed as many *e*s in a passage of text as they could. To the extent that facing increasing difficulty requires great amount of self-control, participants who face anagrams in decreasing order of difficulty should be less depleted than those who solve the same anagrams in increasing order of difficulty. Thus, the former should persist longer in the subsequent task. Accordingly, participants who solved the anagrams in decreasing order of difficulty persisted longer on the e-crossing task ($M=536$ vs. $M=407$ seconds), $F(1,39)=4.42, p<.05$).

Study 2 tests whether exerting effort in a decreasing order of difficulty can increase self-control and whether this replenishing effect is greater than allowing people to rest after initial self-regulation. As a choice requiring self-control participants chose between a cookie and a plain yogurt (Khan &Dhar 2007). Prior to choosing between the snacks participants solved anagrams that served to deplete them. Participants were randomly assigned to four conditions. In the first condition participants solved three hard anagrams. In the second condition participants solved the same three hard anagrams and then solved four easy anagrams. In the third condition, after the hard anagrams participants were given a three minute break. Finally, in a control condition participants did not solve any anagrams but proceeded straight to the choice. Results showed that exertion of self-control (reflected by the choice share of yogurt) was significantly lower when participants only solved hard anagrams (32%) as compared to in the control condition (65%; $\chi^2 =3.95; p<.05$) suggesting that hard anagrams are indeed depleting. Moreover, the proportion exerting self-control was significantly higher when participants solved easy anagrams after solving the hard ones (86%) as compared to when they only solved the hard anagrams (32%; $\chi^2=12.18, p<.001$). In other words, while people solved fewer anagrams in the former condition they were more depleted as compared to those who solved the same anagrams plus some easy ones. Furthermore, the replenishing effect of a break after solving the hard anagrams was not significant, with 53% of participants exerting self-control in this condition vs. 32% for participants who only solved hard anagrams; $\chi^2=1.68; p=.19$. This rules out an account that easy anagrams serve as a break after the hard ones.

Purpose of Study 3 is threefold. 1) Replicate the effect in a clearly aversive domain. 2) Provide evidence of the subjective vitality based process 3) Test if the effect can be explained by positive affect or self-esteem changes that might ensue as self-regulation becomes easier over time. Study participants listened to 2 aversive sound clips-either in increasing or decreasing order of difficulty. Next, they completed a survey with measures of SV, mood, and self-esteem. Finally, participants completed an *e*-crossing. Results showed that compared to a control condition (where participants did not listen to any aversive sound), persistence on the *e*-crossing task significantly decreased after participants heard increasingly aversive sounds (*M*=492 vs. *M*=375 seconds; *t* (60)=2.68; *p*=.01). However, persistence on the e-crossing task significantly increased after participants heard decreasingly aversive sounds (*M*=492 vs. *M*=591, *t* (62)=-1.97; *p*=.05). These effects were mediated by the level of subjective vitality but neither positive mood nor self-esteem mediated the effect of initial task on subsequent persistence.

The findings contribute to the self-control and depletion literatures by showing how initial effortful self-regulation can increase, rather than deplete, subsequent self-control. Our studies suggest the importance of appreciating temporal patterns of self-regulation and examining *how* self-control is exercised and not just whether it is exerted or not. The results also have implications for the ordering of self-control targets that consumers set for themselves (e.g., weight-loss goals) or of tasks that are set for others (e.g., academic performance and sales targets), suggesting that in some contexts it may be useful to stack harder tasks up front relative to later in the sequence.

# Diffusion, Word of Mouth, and Social Epidemics: From Individual Psychology to Collective Outcomes

Jonah Berger, University of Pennsylvania, USA
Andrew Stephen, INSEAD, France

## EXTENDED ABSTRACTS

### "You Snooze You Loose: Comparing the Roles of High Activity and Connectivity in Information Dissemination over Online Social Networks"

*Andrew Stephen, INSEAD, France*
*Yaniv Dover, Hebrew University, Israel*
*Jacob Goldenberg, Hebrew University, Israel*

A rapidly growing trend among users of social media websites and online networks is to use these platforms not solely for the purposes of connecting with friends, but rather as tools for sharing information and digital content (e.g., links to videos on YouTube or news articles). What determines how widely a piece of information introduced into one of these networks will spread? Although there are a large number of potential drivers, we focus on factors related to the individuals who introduce or "transmit" the content in the first place, and individual psychology that could result in certain transmitter characteristics making information receivers more or less likely to retransmit, or pass on, information shared in online networks. Retransmission is a critical ingredient for information diffusing widely in this context.

Past literature has focused on so-called "hubs" or people in social networks with exceptionally high numbers of connections. E.g., when hubs adopt products diffusion processes tend to speed up. But are there other easily observable and measurable transmitter characteristics that could also play a role? An overlooked transmitter characteristic is simply how frequently they post content in a network. Psychologically, people who transmit more often may be perceived as being able to provide "fresher" content and, as such, their information may be more likely to be retransmitted since it is perceived as being more novel. A similar prediction is not possible for hubs; while they expose many people to information, this does not imply that their audience will be more likely to pass it on. This distinction suggests that, in the context of information sharing in online social networks, a transmitter's activity should at least play a role in driving information diffusion, perhaps more than their network connectivity.

We compare transmitter activity and connectivity to test this claim in three studies: an experiment, an agent-based simulation, and empirical analysis of a large link-sharing dataset from Twitter. Generally, we find that despite recent findings suggesting that hubs drive diffusion processes, we find that a transmitter's posting activity is at least as informative, if not more. First, in a laboratory study we tested whether people exposed to information in a Twitter- or Facebook-like online network were more or less likely to retransmit that information depending on the connectivity and activity of the transmitter who exposed them to the information. We found a positive main effect of activity (i.e., transmitters who post more frequently are more likely to have their information retransmitted) but no effect of connectivity (and no interaction). Mediation analysis showed that the activity effect on retransmission was mediated by a perception that the information transmitted by the more active transmitters was "fresher" and "newer." Second, in an agent-based simulation we built a formal model of information sharing and tested it in large, realistic simulated social networks. We varied where a given piece of information started spreading

(the seed node) and that node's connectivity and activity. We found that activity, not connectivity, was the critical driver of how widely information diffused. Third, we analyzed data from a random sample of approximately 2,500 Twitter users who we observed over 44 days. These users posted 114,711 tweets in this period, of which 21,430 (18.7%) contained URLs linking to outside-Twitter content. The diffusion of the content pointed to by these links was tracked and we examined how the extent of diffusion was affected by transmitters' connectivity (number of Twitter followers) and activity (average daily tweet posting rate). Consistent with the previous studies, we again found a strong positive effect of transmitter activity on extent of diffusion, but no effect of connectivity.

Taken together, these studies—employing three very different but complementary methodologies—show that transmitter content-posting activity is an important predictor of information diffusion in online social networks, and likely more important than how well connected these people are in the networks.

### "Early Adopters: Opinion Leaders or Opinion Keepers?"

*Sarit Moldovan, Technion, Israel*

Early adopters are believed to be essential to new product success as they ignite the diffusion process (Rogers, 1995). An important yet unresolved question is whether early adopters are opinion leaders. On the one hand, some studies show that early adopters are socially integrated and connected, show leadership, and are willing to volunteer information about products (e.g., Rogers 1995). On the other hand, the chasm theory claims that there is a break in communication between early adopters and the main market (Goldenberg, Libai, and Muller 2002; Moore 1999). If early adopters are opinion leaders then they should promote new products and accelerate the diffusion process. Why, in that case, is there a chasm?

This research uses a meta-analysis to propose a solution to this contradiction between the chasm theory and the studies that show that early adopters are opinion leaders. It shows that early adopters believe that they are opinion leaders, but although they are indeed communicative, they are not always influential. When the innovation is too radical and perceived as too risky, consumers may be reluctant to adopt it despite early adopters' w-o-m.

First, a meta-analysis on early adopters was employed to explore the correlation between early adoption and opinion leadership. The results confirmed a correlation between the two traits: $r=.28$ ($p<.01$). However, this correlation ranges between $r=-.39$ and $r=.82$, which indicates that there may be a moderator that affects this relationship.

Next, two meta-analyses on the characteristics of early adopters and opinion leaders were used to compare the similarities and differences between the two groups. Results indicate that there are many similarities between early adopters and opinion leaders. Both groups tend to be more confident, creative, risk-seeking and younger than the rest of the population. In addition, both groups show higher product knowledge, involvement and usage. Interestingly, both groups are also more communicative and influential than other consumers. This, once again, raises the question of why there is a chasm. The meta-analysis also showed some differences between early adopters and opinion leaders, confirming that these are two separate groups.

The next step was to search for possible moderators that can explain when early adopters act as opinion leaders and when they do not. Opinion leaders are reluctant to adopt radical innovations since they fear losing their leadership (Rogers 1995). It is therefore possible that early adopters of radical innovations lose their ability to influence others. These early adopters may think that they are opinion leaders because they spread w-o-m, but others may not be influenced. In that case early adopters will still be communicative but not as influential.

When early adopters are primed with radical innovations, or asked to recall their actual behavior after real product adoption, they may acknowledge that they are not as influential as they believed. We therefore explore whether early adopters' self-reported level of opinion leadership (communicativeness and influence) is moderated by (a) the type of scale that was used to measure early adoption (actual adoption of an innovation vs. a fictitious scenario), and (b) the product that was used as a stimulus in the study (high-risk/low-risk innovation).

The correlation between level of early adoption and level of influence was much higher in studies where early adopters were recognized using a self-reported early adoption scale, compared to studies where early adopters were recognized by stating that they have adopted a specific product ($r_{scale}$=.45; $r_{actual}$=.15, $F$=43.1, $p$<.01). This suggests that early adopters report themselves as highly influential when they have not adopted the target innovation, but acknowledge that their influence is much lower when they are asked about a specific product that they have adopted. The level of communicativeness was the same regardless of the early adoption scale used in the studies, suggesting that early adopters spread the word but not everyone follows. A similar effect was found when comparing the type of product used as a stimulus in the study. When early adopters were primed with a low-risk innovation they reported being more influential than when primed with a high-risk innovation ($r_{low-risk}$=.36, $r_{high-risk}$=.25; $F$=6.2, $p$<.02), while the level of their communicativeness remained the same.

The results were replicated in a lab experiment. Participants were primed using anagrams of words related to radical innovations (such as creative, pioneering, and unique) or to fruits. Early adopters reported that they are also opinion leaders when primed with fruit but not with innovation-related words ($r_{fruit}$=.57; $r_{innovations}$=.03, interaction term $b$=.34, $p$=.01).

## "Tie Strength and Need for Uniqueness Influences on Positive Word of Mouth"
*Amar Cheema, University of Virginia, USA*
*Andrew M. Kaikati, University of Georgia, USA*

An important factor driving word-of-mouth (WOM) information flows is social tie strength, which is represented by frequency of social contact and type of relationship (e.g. close friend, acquaintance). Prior research has identified contextual factors, including referral rewards (Ryu and Feick 2007) and information value (i.e., opportunity cost to an endorser; Frenzen and Nakamoto 1993), that impact positive WOM to weak vs. strong ties.

We aim to build upon this literature on WOM and tie strength. Across three studies, we investigate how an individual characteristic of the potential endorser (need for uniqueness, NFU) influences positive WOM for discretionary products to varying social ties. Consistent with Cheema and Kaikati (2010), we find that high-uniqueness individuals are less likely to generate positive WOM than low-uniqueness individuals. Prior research suggests that the disutility from decreased uniqueness (Snyder 1992) dissuades high-uniqueness individuals from recommending others to buy the product. However, the present research demonstrates that need for

uniqueness attenuates positive WOM *only* to strong ties and not to weak ties.

We propose that because consumers evaluate themselves more against close peers than socially distant individuals, adoption of unique products by close others may threaten their identity (Berger and Heath 2007), decreasing high-uniqueness endorsers' motivation to engage in WOM to close others. In contrast, product adoption by acquaintances and strangers is less likely to threaten one's identity, and in this case we expect that uniqueness will not affect WOM.

Consistent with this expectation, we find that among high-uniqueness individuals, positive WOM is more likely across weak ties than across strong ties. We find this moderation in within-subject surveys (study 1), a between-subjects experiment (study 2) and in analyses of real-world reports of WOM activity for two products (study 3).

Study 1 compares the within-subject likelihood of communicating positive WOM across strong (i.e. best friends), intermediate (i.e. classmate), and weak ties (i.e. another student), and measures chronic level of NFU. Participants imagine themselves in a scenario where they acquire a recently-launched cell phone (the Motorola KRZR), and rate their likelihood of telling another person positive things about it (1=not at all likely, 9=very likely). Results confirm a significant NFU x tie strength interaction. Univariate analyses reveal that high- (vs. low-) NFU respondents are less likely to engage in WOM to strong and intermediate ties, but not weak ties.

Study 2 replicates the study 1 effects using a between-subject design and a multi-item WOM measure. Participants imagine they own an Apple iPhone (study was conducted at time of the iPhone launch), and decide what to tell either a strong tie (best friend) or weaker tie (casual acquaintance) about it. The uniqueness x tie strength interaction supports our prediction–higher need for uniqueness significantly decreases positive WOM across strong ties but not across weak ties. Also, among high-uniqueness participants, WOM was greater to weak versus strong ties.

Study 3 examines real-world WOM data from BzzAgent. We compare WOM activity of agents across strong ties (e.g., best friends) and weaker ties (e.g., acquaintances, coworkers) for publicly- and privately-consumed products. The significant pattern of results in studies 1 and 2 is replicated for the public but not the private product, consistent with Cheema and Kaikati (2010).

The observation of increased WOM across weak versus strong ties is in contrast to prior research which finds that as a potential endorser's opportunity costs increase, "information is more likely to flow over strong than weak ties" (Frenzen and Nakamoto 1993, 372). This finding is also ironic, given the "strength of weak ties" in diffusing information (Granovetter 1973). In talking to weaker ties, consumers may contribute to macro-level information dissemination and to making possessions mainstream more quickly than if they restricted WOM only to strong ties.

## "What Do People Talk About and Why? How Product Characteristics and Promotional Giveaways Shape Word-of-Mouth"
*Jonah Berger, University of Pennsylvania, USA*
*Eric Schwartz, University of Pennsylvania, USA*

Why are certain products talked about more than others? Some movies get a great deal of buzz and some restaurants are the talk of the town, but what characteristics of products lead them to be talked about more? Further, word-of-mouth marketing companies often send consumers free products or gifts to encourage them to talk about the brand. But which types of giveaways actually increase buzz?

We examine psychological drivers of word of mouth, investigating how product characteristics and campaign giveaways shape what people talk about. While prior WOM research has focused on the impact of "special people" (i.e., influentials) or network structures, we focus on how the items themselves drive collective outcomes. One psychological factor that might influence whether people talk about a product is the amount of interest it evokes. But while it seems intuitive that people would talk more about interesting products than boring ones, this may not actually be true. Self-presentation (people want to see themselves as interesting) and memory biases (interesting topics are easier to remember) may lead people to *think* they talk more about interesting things, even if this is not actually the case. Further, given that interest fades, it is unclear whether more interesting products get more WOM overall (i.e., over time). Finally, to the degree that most conversations resemble idle chatter, what people talk about may be driven by what happens to come to mind than what is the most interesting. This points to the importance of conceptually-related cues in shaping WOM. Products that are cued more by the surrounding environment should be more accessible, leading them to be talked about more.

We investigate our questions in two ways: a model of an observational dataset and a large-scale field experiment. First, we analyze real WOM data from over 200,000 consumers in 330 buzz marketing campaigns (from BzzAgent). The data indicate how many times each person in each campaign talked about that particular product over an approximately ten week period. We examine WOM as a function of product characteristics and promotional giveaways. Groups of independent raters were given a description of each product and asked to rate them on either how interesting they were or how frequently they were cued by the environment. We also recorded the promotional giveaways sent to the agents (i.e., whether they received a free product, sample, coupon, or general gift as well as how many of each of these items). We use a hierarchical level model to control for unobserved individual differences and unobserved differences across product-campaign to test the relationships of interest.

Results indicate that while products that are cued more often were discussed more frequently, more interesting products did not get more WOM overall. Similar measures to interest (e.g., novelty, surprise, originality) yield the same results. Interest did predict WOM intentions in a separate sample, however, suggesting that people may think they will talk about more interesting things even if they do not actually do so. In addition, consistent our perspective, interest is related to WOM right after participants receive the product, but that this relationship fades over time. The relationship between WOM and cues, on the other hand, strengthens over time. Results also indicate which promotional giveaways are linked to WOM.

Second, building on the results of this statistical analysis, we conducted a large field experiment with random assignment across various US cities involving over 1,500 consumers. By directly manipulating the main psychological driver identified in the model (cues), we test its causal impact on word-of-mouth. We manipulated cues by manipulating the messaging different participants received during a BzzAgent campaign for the restaurant chain Boston Market. Half the agents received a message linking the product to a particular cue (dinner), while the other half received a control message. We also measured participants' prior associations between the brand and the cue to directly test whether cueing is driving any observed effects.

The results underscore the findings of the cross-campaign analysis; increasing the cues for a product, in this case, linking it to a usage situation that some participants did not already associate it with, increased WOM. Among participants who did not already associate Boston Market with dinner, linking the product to that cue led them to talk more about the brand.

Taken together, our findings sheds light on the psychological processes behind word-of-mouth, and provides insight into how companies can design more effective buzz marketing campaigns.

# The Dynamic Pursuit of Consumers' Social Identity Goals

Carlos J. Torelli, University of Minnesota, USA

## EXTENDED ABSTRACTS

### "American=Men? Gender and Cultural Dynamics in the Marketing of Male-Symbolic Brands to Women"

*Carlos J. Torelli, University of Minnesota, USA*
*Chi-yue Chiu, Nanyang Technological University, Singapore*
*Hean Tat Keh, Peking University, China*
*Nelson Amaral, University of Minnesota, USA*

Marketers are sensitive to gender differences in consumer preferences, as reflected by the development of brands that target a specific gender (e.g., Victoria's Secret for women). Some of these brands resonate strongly within the gender group they set out to target and become symbols of the group (or gender-symbolic brands) (Keller 1993). Yet, increasingly we find brands that try to leverage their equity by broadening their appeal to consumers of the opposite gender (e.g., Jockey women's underwear). Surprisingly, consumer research has little to say about the factors that contribute to a brand's success in bridging the gender divide. If any, recent research suggests unfavorable consumer responses to product-brand mismatch along the gender dimension of brand personality (Grohmann 2009), a finding that seems to recommend against marketing across the gender line.

The present research distinguishes between knowledge of consensual assumptions regarding the cultural symbolism of brands and personal agreement with these assumptions. Specifically, we propose that in the U.S., both men and women have high agreement on which brands can represent the two genders. More intriguingly, we argue that due to some socio-historical biases against women in the U.S., both men and women perceive a widespread consensus in American society that only male-symbolic brands are symbols of American culture. Analogous to previous research on "American=White" (Devos and Banaji 2005), we term this collective perception the "American=men" fallacy. We propose that how people act on and react to the "American=men" fallacy depends on their gender and extent of identification with their gender. Men, regardless of how much they identify with their own gender, would accept this perception as valid, and personally believe that only male-symbolic brands are symbols of American culture. Women, particularly those who identify strongly with their gender, personally disagree with the consensual perception and feel that female-symbolic brands should also be accepted as symbols of American culture.

We further suggest that women may like a male-symbolic brand via its association with the American identity. When this common in-group identity is salient, female consumers would tend to like male-symbolic brands that are symbols of America. However, when female consumers are made to feel "less American," they would tend to dislike male-symbolic brands that symbolize American culture. Because of the weak cultural associations of female-symbolic brands with the common American identity, cultural identification would have minimal effects on male consumers' liking for female-symbolic brands.

Study 1 tested the collectively perceived "American=men" fallacy. To test this hypothesis, we asked three different samples of participants from the two genders to rate the extent to which a large and varied group of brands (from pretests) symbolize American culture, men, and women (using the cultural symbolism scale, or CS, Torelli, Keh, and Chiu 2010). We found that brands that were rated more highly on male symbolism were also rated more highly on American culture symbolism ($r$ across all brands=.58, $p<.001$). In contrast, the correlation between American culture symbolism and female symbolism was significantly lower ($z$=3.22, $p<.005$) and not significantly different from zero, r=-.13, $p>.1$.

Study 2 investigated gender differences in consumers' personal agreement with the perceived consensus regarding the cultural symbolism of gender-symbolic brands. Participants from both genders rated three brands (male-symbolic, female-symbolic, or gender-neutral) on the extent to which they symbolized American culture from the perspective of an average American (perceived consensus), as well as from their own personal perspective (after a filler task). They also indicated their gender identification. Results showed that both men and women perceive a consensus in American society that only male-symbolic brands are symbols of American culture. However, men agreed with the consensual view regardless of their level of gender identification. In contrast, women with relatively low identification with their gender personally agreed with the cultural consensus that only male-symbolic brands are symbols of American culture, whereas women with relatively strong identification with their gender (although aware of the cultural consensus) personally felt that female-symbolic brands are also symbols of American culture.

In Study 3, we recruited two samples to investigate female consumers' evaluation of male-symbolic brands as a function of whether the "women=American" identity link is salient. We manipulated the "women=American" link in two ways. First, in sample 1, we increased the salience of a positive American identity to enhance women's identification with the common in-group identity. Next, in sample 2, we directly manipulated the salience of the link by highlighting women's contributions to American society versus the history of gender discrimination in the U.S. We measured brand evaluation and willingness to promote the brand. Results indicated that women evaluated a male-symbolic brand more favorably either when a positive American identity was salient or when women's contributions to America were highlighted. In contrast, they evaluated a male-symbolic brand less favorably when they were reminded of the exclusion of women from the common American identity.

### "Brand Preferences During Identity Transitions"

*Shirley Y. Y. Cheng, Hong Kong Baptist University, China*
*Sharon Ng, Nanyang Technological University, Singapore*
*Iris W. Hung, National University of Singapore, Singapore*

Brands are intimately related to self-identity—consumers like brands that match their active self-concepts (Aaker 1999) and use brands to tell others who they are (Escalas and Bettman 2005). Prior research has extensively studied brand preference when consumers have *stable* identities. However, how do *identity transitions* influence brand preference? This question remains largely unexplored despite its theoretical and practical relevance.

In face of an identity transition, consumers anticipate both the end of a current identity and the start of a future identity. Consumers may feel happy finishing an important life stage (e.g., finishing school). At the same time, they may feel upset about starting an uncertain future identity (e.g., starting work) and thus experience mixed emotions. This research seeks to understand brand preference in response to mixed emotions emerging from identity transitions.

We propose that some consumers are more likely than others to use brands for managing identity transitions. Those who consider their identity in their brand choice (i.e., *enactors*) would have an instrumental view of brand and identity construction. To them, identity-symbolizing brands can help in constructing their identity. So we hypothesize that when they feel mixed emotions about a transition, they would show a tendency to "move on"—their liking for brands that symbolize the expiring identity decreases but liking for brands that symbolize the new identity increases. However, for those who don't tend to consider identity issues when making brand choices (i.e., *non-enactors*), mixed emotions about identity transitions would have negligible effects on brand preferences. We tested this hypothesis and its underlying mechanism with undergraduate students, using graduation as the focal identity transition. In all four studies, we measured how much participants normally consider their student identity when they choose brands (i.e., levels of enactment) and use the rating as a continuous variable in the analyses.

In study 1, undergraduates first wrote an essay about how graduation makes them feel and rated the extent of mixed emotion they feel about graduation. Then, in an ostensibly unrelated study, the participants rated their liking for a student-brand (i.e., a brand that symbolizes student identity). As predicted, enactors' level of mixed emotion about graduation negatively correlated with liking of the student-brand. Whereas for non-enactors, mixed emotion did not correlate with their liking of the student-brand.

Study 2 provided evidence on the causal effects of feeling mixed emotions on enactors' tendency to "move on" in their brand preference. We manipulated participants' feeling toward graduation using a print ad on a photo-taking service for graduating students. The ad either portrayed graduation as a joyful or sentimental event; results confirmed that the sentimental ad elicited higher level of mixed emotion. Then, participants rated their reactions toward the student-brand relative to a work-brand (i.e., a brand that symbolizes work identity). As predicted, the mixed emotion manipulation decreased enactors' purchase intention, liking, and self-brand connection of the student-brand relative to the work-brand. The emotion manipulation did not affect responses of non-enactors.

We argued that enactors and non-enactors differ because enactors often use brand choice for constructing their identities. Thus, when dealing with the transition, enactors would find student-brands (vs. work-brands) less (vs. more) appealing. Inducing enactors to focus on preserving the expiring identity during identity transition (rather than constructing a new identity) should attenuate the effects of mixed emotion on brand preferences. We tested this hypothesis in study 3. Specifically, we manipulated the focus of identity management in two between-subject conditions. In the identity-preserving condition, participants read a description of a social networking platform that could help immigrants connect to people in their home country ("*Find your old friends from your home country! Savoring the old you!*"). In the control condition, participants read that the social networking platform could help immigrants connect to people in the new country ("*Make new friends in your new home! Creating the new you!*"). All participants were asked to imagine being an immigrant when reading the message. Then, in two ostensibly separate studies, participants rated mixed emotions about graduation and responses to the work-brand. Results in the control condition replicated the effects found in previous studies: Enactors who felt higher (vs. lower) level of mixed emotions preferred the work brand more (vs. less). More importantly, results in the identity-preserving condition supported our hypothesis. Priming the participants to focus on preserving an old identity attenuated enactors' tendency to "move on" in their brand preference—feeling mixed emotions did not increase their preference for the work-brand. This finding provides evidence on the proposed mechanism of enactors' "moving on" effect.

Lastly, we conducted a field study to examine whether enactors were indeed more likely to "move on" in their brand preference when they faced the real transition. We surveyed graduating seniors after they completed all their examinations. Results showed that for non-enactors and enactors who had not found a job, the more (vs. less) they miss being a student, the more (vs. less) they like a student-brand. However, for enactors who have already found a job, how much they miss student life no longer predicted liking for the student-brand. We reasoned that having a job at the time of the survey marked the actual transition from student identity to work identity. For enactors, having a job means that they have a new identity to enact, thus they moved on and their brand preferences dissociated from their feelings about student life.

## "I am Too Much of a Man to Be Artistic: Signaling Incompetence to Reduce the Threat of Being Associated with a Dissociative Group"

*Mohammed El Hazzouri, University of Manitoba, Canada*
*Sergio W. Carvalho, University of Manitoba, Canada*
*Kelley Main, University of Manitoba, Canada*

It is widely accepted that consumers often make consumption decisions in ways to protect their self-views. Previous research has shown that consumers are reluctant to use products that send negative cues (Banister and Hogg 2004) and avoid selecting products that are associated with dissociative reference groups, especially when the product is more symbolic in nature (White and Dahl 2006). Such actions are presumably driven by a desire to avoid the negative associations of the dissociative referent. However, in many real-life situations, people may not easily stay away from these negative associations. For instance, if a guy is just asked to wrap a gift for a co-worker, would he worry that doing so very neatly might be perceived by others as possessing the 'artistic' trait often associated with women? This research argues that, under certain conditions, such situations can be self-threatening and heighten the need to distance the self from undesirable associations, even by making oneself appears as incompetent.

Research on stereotype threat (e.g., Steele, Spencer, and Aronson 2002) suggests that people can feel a threat to the self when they become aware that their poor performance on a task can confirm the negative reputation associated with the groups they belong to. The presence of such threat seems to impair performance by introducing an additional pressure in order to disconfirm the negative stereotype (e.g., Aronson et al. 1999). We turn this relationship upside-down by extending the effects to the stereotype threat from the positive reputation associated with a dissociative reference group. We predict that when people's performance on a task can associate them with a dissociative reference group, they will also feel a threat to the self that leads to poorer performance. However, in this case, performing poorly is not driven by added pressure to *disconfirm* a negative stereotype, but instead by the desire to *confirm* that one does not fit the positive stereotype. Poor performance would signal that one does not possess the characteristic associated with the dissociative referent, and hence help dissociating from it.

Study 1 tested this prediction using a 2 (stereotype threat: present vs. absent) x 2 (gender: male vs. female) between subjects design. Participants were first primed with a positive stereotype of women: they are more artistic than men. In a subsequent, unrelated task, stereotype threat was manipulated by informing half of the participants that a gift-wrapping task they were about to do was designed to test the wrapping materials (stereotype threat absent) or to test their artistic ability (stereotype threat present). As expected, results demonstrated that stereotype threat significantly reduced performance for male but not for female participants. Further, results revealed a reduction in perceived competence, and performance satisfaction for men and not for women. No gender differences emerged when the stereotype threat was absent.

Study 2 was conducted to rule out the alternative interpretation that men's poorer performance may be driven by self-handicapping strategies (e.g., Steele and Aronson 1995) and not by the heightened dissociative needs argued here. Stone (2002) showed that when Caucasian athletes were threatened by the stereotype that Caucasians are incompetent in sports, they self-handicapped by practicing less before a sports-related task. Study 2 was similar to study 1, but the wrapping exercise was presented as a practice phase in which participants would have up to 8 minutes to practice before performing the main and more complicated gift-wrapping task (which did not occur). Results showed that male participants in the threat present condition took significantly more time to practice than those in the threat absent condition, presumably because doing so would signal their incompetence in terms of gift-wrapping (i.e., lack of artistic abilities). No effect of threat was found among female participants.

Study 3 was designed to more directly assess the notion that a desire to signal a lack of artistic abilities underlies men's poorer performance in the gift-wrapping task. We reasoned that men cued with their 'inartistic' nature should not exhibit these heightened needs, which in turn should mute the effects. We tested this proposition in a field study using a 2 (stereotype threat: present vs. absent) x 2 (inartistic cue: present vs. absent) between subjects design. Male participants were primed with the stereotype that females are more artistic than males, and were then told that gift-wrapping is either indicative or not of artistic ability. Men's inartistic nature was cued by having the experimenter replace a ribbon with an already made bow stating that males are not artistic enough to use a ribbon/no explanation was provided (present vs. absent). Study 1's results were replicated in the inartistic cue absent condition. In contrast, when cueing with men's inartistic nature, the stereotype threat present condition positively impacted participants' performance, perceptions of competence, and performance satisfaction. Interestingly, when inability was signaled, performance, perceived competence, and performance satisfaction reached the same level as when the stereotype threat was absent.

Our findings show that the prospect of being perceived as possessing the traits of a dissociative referent can be self-threatening, which in turn can trigger subsequent behavior aimed at confirming that one does not fit the stereotype of the undesirable group. To the extent that the barriers that separate gender and ethnic-based products become blurred (i.e., cross-marketing), the self-threat effects described here are likely to be more common. Our findings provide a framework to understand how consumers cope with such threats and adjust their behaviors to dissociate from undesirable social identities.

## "Substituting Brands with Social Behavior to Satisfy Identity Needs"

*Robert Kreuzbauer, Nanyang Technological University, Singapore*
*Chi-yue Chiu, Nanyang Technological University, Singapore*

People use brands to communicate important aspects of self-definition (Escalas and Bettman 2005). For example, a marketing professor might choose to wear for class a suit from a fashion label in order to signal distinctiveness from his students. Similarly, a college student might wear a T-shirt with the college's logo to signal connectedness with her institution. In both examples, brand usage provides the means to satisfy identity needs (e.g., distinctiveness and connectedness respectively). This research departs from prior work that explains how consumers use brands to achieve an optimal connectedness-distinctiveness balance (Berger & Heath 2007) and demonstrates that the mere act of being handed a brand can satisfy a salient distinctiveness (connectedness) need, and results in a reduced likelihood of expressing this need in a subsequent social task. This shows that consumers flexibly use brands and social behavior to satisfy social identity needs.

According to optimal distinctiveness theory (ODT, Brewer, 1991), individuals desire to attain an optimal balance of connectedness (belongingness) and distinctiveness *within* and *between* social groups and situations. These basic social needs can be flexibly satisfied through alternative means of attainment (e.g., by buying a product or by engaging in social activities, Kruglanski et al. 2002). Distinctiveness and connectedness needs are in constant opposition with each other. In most experimental conditions (cf. Brewer, 2003), situations that tilt self-categorization processes in one identity direction arouse the opposing need until the optimal point is reached again. This research uncovers an alternative mechanism for achieving optimal distinctiveness. We show that the balance between these two needs can also be achieved by satisfying the need for distinctiveness (or connectedness) through a brief encounter with a branded product, which consequently brings both needs back to an optimal level. We further show the flexible manner by which consumers can satisfy distinctiveness (or connectedness) needs. The mere act of being handed a low-involvement product (e.g., a branded tea-bag) associated with distinctiveness (connectedness) made people less interested to work alone (in a group). In other words, consumers can interchangeably use consumption and other social behaviors in order to restore the balance between distinctiveness and connectedness. Four experimental studies demonstrate the hypothesized effects.

The first two studies were set up to test these basic predictions. In study 1, participants were shown an advertisement about a tea-bag brand. The advertisement conveyed the notion that using the tea-bag brand would make a person feel distinctive. After seeing the advertisement, half of the participants were handed the same tea-bag shown in the advertisement (distinctiveness condition), whereas the other half were handed a different tea bag (control condition). We reasoned that receiving the "distinctive" tea-bag would help participants in the 'distinctiveness' condition to satisfy their need for distinctiveness more than those in the control condition. To assess this, after receiving the tea-bag, participants were presented with an ostensibly unrelated writing task in which they rated their willingness to work alone or in groups. Results showed that participants in the 'distinctiveness' condition were less willing to work alone than participants in the control condition were. Study 2 replicated the findings for a tea-bag brand associated with connectedness (instead of distinctiveness). In this case, participants who satisfied their need for connectedness when handed the tea-bag brand were less inclined to work in groups in the subsequent writing task.

The last 2 studies were designed to rule out an alternative interpretation of the findings based on possible 'disappointment' on the part of control participants handed a different (or 'wrong' bag), and to prime the target social need in a more controlled manner. Study 3 followed a procedure similar to that used in study 1. However, we first primed all participants with distinctiveness by presenting them with a set of related words and images. We also added two conditions in which participants read a neutral advertisement about the tea-bag brand. The design was then a 2 distinctiveness of tea-bag message (distinctiveness or neutral) X 2 tea-bag received (same in the ad or different). As expected, only participants handed the 'distinctive' (and same) tea-bag showed a decreased willingness to work alone compared to their counterparts handed a different bag, and also compared to those in the two 'neutral message' conditions that were handed the same or a different tea-bag. Study 4 replicated the findings with the same design, but using this time a tea-bag associated with connectedness. That is, participants who received the "connected" tea-bag brand were less willing to work in a group than participants in the other three conditions. Results from these two studies persisted after controlling for gender, mood and individual differences in the need for distinctiveness and belongingness.

In summary, our findings suggest that consumers' pursuit of identity goals is a dynamic process continuously shaped by their interactions with products. We show that people's interaction with a low-involvement product, such as a tea-bag, can trigger social identity needs that affect their subsequent social behaviors.

**REFERENCE LIST AVAILABLE UPON REQUEST**

# Making and Consuming Places: From Discrete Things to the Big Picture

Zeynep Arsel, Concordia University, Canada
Jonathan Bean, University of California-Berkeley, USA

## EXTENDED ABSTRACT

### "Interiority in Consumer Culture"

*Jeppe Trolle Linnet, University of Southern Denmark, Denmark*

This presentation considers an issue that lies close to sense of place (Sherry 2000), but has a more abstract dimension that manifests itself across physical spaces, social circles and symbolic structures: the relation between inside and outside, or interiority and exteriority.

Interiority is strongly exemplified by the experience of homeyness (McCracken 1989). It will be illustrated here by the Danish concept of *hygge*, on which I have done ethnographic research among families in Copenhagen. *Hygge* is a form of atmosphere (Pennartz 1999), which to most Danes denotes the essence of having a pleasurable, good time with other people in an informal spirit (Hansen 1980). In ways that resemble the anti-market normativity around home and family life, the families I have researched appreciate the experience of 'warm' sociality in contrast to the 'harder' and 'colder' interaction forms that characterize their professional life, the market economy, and public urban life. Yet this atmosphere is not limited to home or family life. The feeling of being in a well known, secluded space or even shelter, where intrusion from the outside world is experienced as a disturbance, also arises in commercial settings (Lugosi 2009) such as retailers and cafés. These '3rd places' are experienced as homey and authentic, often through the presence of close social ties among neighborhood, guests and staff.

Considering this phenomenon on a higher level of abstraction, symbolic and/or virtual structures without any material enclosure or social company to envelop the consumer can deliver this experience too. This is where the concept of interiority is worth exploring, as it concerns the experience of "inner space" as a form of identification and placement rather than a relation to spatial form (McCarthy 2005). Interiority is constructed through repetition, e.g. acts of routine behavior, cyclical changes in the environment, or the way humans create a sense of differentiation through symbolic or material structures. Branding is mentioned by McCarthy as one such practice, which through the repetition of stories, designs and other symbolic elements creates a sense of something well known, a bounded space that consumers step into through everyday acts of consumption. Technologies also interact with the human faculties of memory and imagination to create new forms of interiority, e.g. when the mobile phone "transport(s) its user to the memory of an interior" (McCarthy 2005: 122), effecting the form of public, semi-private behavior that has become a ubiquitous phenomenon in much of the world. If seen as a case of interiority, this might be a form of coziness on the go.

The concept of interiority is worth exploring because it suggests an analytical level where certain phenomena that otherwise seem separate become comparable. This might create a more holistic understanding of consumer culture. What can be learned about symbolic domains such as brands by thinking about their similarities to physical homes or a circle of friends, and vice versa? New product categories and brands offer forms of symbolic, material and social enclosure that are qualitatively new forms of community.

In terms of charting the historical development of consumer culture, interiority can alert us to the emergence and disappearance of spaces such as the gendered social spaces where either men or women would encounter only their own gender in equality-oriented Scandinavia (Frykman and Löfgren 1987). The concept of interiority can inspire one to consider whether the emergence of one form of space (or interior) is related to the disappearance of another.

In terms of consumers´ desire to try something new, e.g. to become part of a brand community, the concept of interiority is one way of considering the beckoning force of mystery that many closed structures possess, the seductive "desire to enter (as distinct from the actuality of entering) a 'space one might occupy'". Can a brand be managed on the basis of recognizing that humans are drawn to inner spaces, but also that they can only feel themselves located in an interior by speculating or fantasizing about the outer world? When seen through the lens of interiority, a boundary is a two-way membrane for the imagining of the exterior from the interior, and vice-versa–and thus for the presence of each in the other.

### "Networked Styles and Normalizing Taste Narratives"

*Zeynep Arsel, Concordia University, Canada*
*Jonathan Bean, University of California-Berkeley, USA*

Taste, the ability to identify and choose the legitimate, has been a fundamental modus of establishing and signifying social class distinctions (Bourdieu 1984). Yet, contemporary social theorists suggest that tastemaking no longer serves to maintain a social hierarchy that differentiates highbrow from lowbrow. Rather, tastes are fragmented (Featherstone 1991) subculturally bounded (Thornton 1996), or established through contextualized negotiation of meanings (Holt 1997). As a result, the power of traditional highbrow authorities has diminished (Johnston and Baumann 2007). Furthermore, individuals with higher cultural capital resources tend to break conventions and normative combinations of conventional styles and utilize a pastiche of high and low (Holt 1998). Within the concept of place, how do the material manifestations of taste such as styles referred to as "modern" or "traditional" as well as their sub-genres and hybrids (i.e. "shabby chic") emerge and become crystallized?

Our research demonstrates a process through which styles are normatively constructed through social networks. We argue that consumers are not nomadic postmodern mix-and-match artists who layer and imitate styles, but rather that they contribute to and help create coherent taste narratives that circulate in popular culture and serve as a distributed form of cultural authority. These narratives help consumers establish a sense of place by serving as a normative model for the right way of ordering objects in space, legitimizing preferences for particular arrangements and types, and, most significantly, by inviting, even requiring, consumers to create visual and textual representations of place in order to perpetuate the taste narrative.

Our empirical site, the popular home design blog Apartment Therapy [AT], started in 2004 and quickly grew to establish itself first as a web phenomenon and then as a serious competitor to now-defunct magazines such as Martha Stewart's Blueprint and Condé Nast's Domino (Green 2004). The effect of AT is like that of shelter or lifestyle magazines: it establishes a regime of visual and material order (Hand and Shove 2004). But unlike magazines, readers of the website participate in the creation of a taste narrative that prescribes a distinct way of creating place through organizing material objects and configuring practices within the home.

To show how consumers use the taste narrative for creating a sense of place in the home, we utilize longitudinal multi-method analysis. First, we analyze the blog content with special emphasis on normative discussions, advice seeking and contests. Second, we also include the spinoff book *Apartment Therapy: The Eight-Step Home Cure* (Gillingham-Ryan 2006) in this narrative analysis. We use the book to engage in an auto-ethnographic process of following the "cure" and transforming our homes. Third, we conduct interviews with participant-creators of the blog and individuals whose homes are featured in exemplary tours and competitions. We also incorporate participant observation in the production of the blog[1].

Our first finding highlights how tastemaking works in an increasingly fluid social hierarchy transformed by the adoption of new social technologies. We demonstrate that the participatory nature of new media enables a dialogical and collective process of tastemaking that sharply contrasts with the traditional models of cultural authority. While magazines have long used write-in features or visits to "actual homes" to relate ideas to readers (Keeble 2007), their core content is under direct editorial control and relies on the editors' position of authority. In contrast, the content of many of AT's popular post types —contests, "good questions," and house tours— comes from what would typically be thought of as the audience. We argue that these normative dialogues crystallize the boundaries of styles and instill a sense of normalcy in the participants while appearing ostensibly democratic. Our findings also show how the agency of cultural authority shifts between the collective and individual. Apartment Therapy engages with a corporate identity of "we," creating a master narrative which functions as a principle actor itself, again blurring the line between author and audience. Readers of the blog become a part of this "we" identity, commenting on posts, sending questions and content, and adapting similar narrative strategies to those employed by the "official" (i.e., paid) contributors. This "we" identity shifts the agency and authority to determine what is legitimate to the taste narrative instead of a specific individual or group. In this process we highlight the normative and exclusionary action of creating the AT archive (Derrida 1996). We argue that this taste narrative takes on jussive force (Bowker 2008).

With our presentation, we aim to highlight the changing dynamics of taste making in an increasingly participatory culture and show how homes are made through a collaborative process. Our contributions are twofold. First, we illustrate a relatively a new mode of taste formation through participatory media. Second, we show how closely bound the relationship between individual action and collective meaning can be, recapitulating the classic debate on structure and agency.

### "Materializing and Valorizing Cultural Capital: An Investigation of the "Cafe-scape" of a Gentrifying Neighbourhood"

*Yesim Ozalp, York University, Canada*

Cultural Capital of the artists is rubbed off the walls of neighborhood and is appropriated by the middle classes who are eager to accumulate both cultural and also economical capital. (Ley 2009)

Gentrification, investigated as a residential phenomenon for almost four decades, can also provide a social "lab" to study the "distinction" game played by retailers (Zukin and Kosta 2004). By investigating this distinction game, this study provides not only a context to provide a more dynamic account of cultural capital, one that goes beyond categorizing consumers into two levels (Low

Cultural Capital and High Cultural Capital, e.g. Holt 1998; Henry 2005); but also a more comprehensive method of accounting for consumption spaces that goes beyond narrative- or semiotics-based accounts of studying consumption spaces (cf. Sherry Jr. 1998).

Cultural capital, coupled with other forms of capital, is central to the position a subject occupies in a society (Bourdieu [1979] 1984). Its role in consciously or unconsciously shaping consumer preferences and processes has been investigated in Consumer Culture Theory (Holt 1998; Henry 2005). These studies, however, treat cultural capital as a "characteristic" or "trait" held by an individual. Even though this approach towards cultural capital clearly reproduces Bourdieu's lengthy analysis in *Distinction*, partially; it ignores the reconversion strategies mentioned in the same work. Bourdieu ([1979] 1984: 131-132) identifies two reconversion strategies in social space: vertical (movements within the same field) and transverse (a shift to another field). While vertical movements do not alter the composition of the assets (different capitals), transverse movements, such as those from the field of economic capital to the field of cultural capital, involve a transformation in the composition of assets. Although Bourdieu was more interested in the role of education and educational capital as well as structural transformations, the concept of transverse movements is critical in understanding consumption as a process of reconversion. In the microcosm of retail gentrification, retailers, through their use of space, provide knowledge of "authentic" tastes, "cool" places and "trendy" places to be, in exchange for the economic capital of their patrons. In constructing these ideals of authentic, cool, hip or trendy, retailers not only use their own sources of cultural capital (as identified by Bourdieu himself in the transformation of retail sector, [1978] 1984: 141) but also resources from the neighborhood's identity (Zukin and Kosta 2004). Naturally, this cycle of conversion also aims to produce more economic capital for the retailers themselves. Retail spaces mediate the transverse reconversion process between economic and cultural capital, providing a rich context that demonstrates how cultural capital is materialized and valorized.

In order to investigate how the transverse transformation is played out in the retail distinction game, it is essential to reframe the understanding of the concept of space in the CCT field. According to Lefebvre (1974/1991), social space is represented by a triad composed of the enactment of visions of planners and the businesses, the appropriation and representation of users, and the spatial practices through which the prior two are negotiated. In much CCT work, it is the social as well as the symbolic facets of consumption spaces that have attracted scholars' attention, and these concerns are frequently addressed separately (cf. Sherry Jr. 1998; Kozinets et al. 2004). These studies prioritize the agency and stories of consumers over those of producers and retailers, and specifically of a subset of consumers over the "mainstream" consumer. Nor has much attention been given to material objects and the space itself. However, as Lefebvre argues, space can be reduced neither to the symbolic and material work of any of the actors, nor to discourses or to institutions. Similarly, from an Actor-Network Theory perspective, space is constructed within a network of relationships between actants (Latour 2005). The social — e.g. interactions among residents of a neighbourhood — cannot create or define space — e.g. the neighbourhood — unless it is stabilized and woven with material such as houses, the retailscape, urban furniture, etc. (Murdoch 1998). Therefore, the complexity of how consumption spaces are constituted, embodied, enacted and represented can only be understood by looking beyond a group of consumers' representations or acts, to the space, the objects, the producers' symbolic strategies, and to other groups' representations and strategies.

---

[1] From 2007-2008, one of the authors of this paper (Bean) was a paid contributor to *Re-nest*, a website focused on green design which is affiliated with *Apartment Therapy*.

Employing ethnographic research techniques supported by visual and textual archival material, I investigated the "cafe-scape" of a gentrifying neighbourhood in Toronto. Looking at the aesthetics of space, objects, arrangements of objects, spoken and unspoken strategies and also consumers' interpretations, I will provide the details of four distinctive types of spaces, which I label *hybrid, retro, simple*, and *traditional*. For example, while the hybrid cafe-scape houses spatial practices of other retailers (e.g., displays with an appearance akin to those of jewelry stores), the *retro* cafe-scape stages objects which appeal to and to contribute to "bohemian" taste, characterizing the neighbourhood according to the promotional materials of condo developers. While some products (such as desserts) are sold as designed objects (artistic creations of a chef), other products enjoy being the object of a taste quest for "simple, not fancy", such as the case in the *simple* cafe-scape. Customers also play an important role in embodying the taste narratives of these consumption spaces. While knowing how to order a personalized coffee in a Starbucks may be valuable cultural capital for some, in many of the other cafes such capital is made inaccessible by restrictively limiting the menu to "pre-chosen" or "curated" ingredients, such as the case in *simple* or *traditional* cafe-scapes. While unpacking the network of relationships that construct these spaces, I will also show how these spaces utilize, produce, embody and categorize different sources of capital (e.g., cosmopolitan vs. local) and embody different movements of transverse reconversion (e.g., economic>cultural>economic vs. economic>cultural + social>economic).

## "Shangri-La, a Journey From an Imaginary Place to a Non-place"

*Rosa Llamas, University of León, Spain*
*Russell Belk, York University, Canada*

James Hilton's (1933) *Lost Horizon* is set in Shangri-La, a fictional paradise on Earth somewhere in the Himalayas. The myth of Shangri-La, a multi-ethnic community living a perfect life in an unblemished and wondrous natural enclave, enjoying harmony, longevity and supernatural powers, grew with the *Lost Horizon* screen version by Frank Capra (1937). Since then this imaginary paradise has been the object of Westerners' desires, sparking countless expeditions in the hope of finding it. Such a demand for utopian enclaves has yielded a number of pseudo-Shangri-Las blooming in the Himalayas. These Shangri-Las suffer from placelessness, the "casual eradication of distinctive places and the making of standardized landscapes that results from an insensitivity to the significance of place" (Relph 1976, ii) and are fostered by McDonaldized forms of tourism (Ritzer, 1998). In a bid to gain differentiation from this serial production of synthetic Shangri-Las, the PRC State Council announced a contest to assign Shangri-La's brand name to the "real" one. So, after decades of being a fantasy imaginaryscape, Shangri-La finally got some coordinates on Google Earth, which coincide with Zhongdian, a humble town in Diqing Tibetan Autonomous Prefecture, Yunnan Province (China).

The Shangri-La appellation allowed the town to ascend the status ladder, leaving behind its "life" as a modest village to become a paradisal tourist destination with world renown. Appearance was a key aspect in this transformation. The exotic, ethnic and sacred traits of Shangri-La (Kolås, 2004) were re-created in order to build a place to be consumed. These features combine material, spiritual and social place-making, an interwoven set of aspects that according to Sherry (2000) should be a focus of consumer researchers. Drawing on our observations and interviews with insiders (local and non-local players), we explore how paradise builders have enhanced or created these material, spiritual and social aspects in the making of Shangri-La as a placeless paradise.

The material issues in the still-under-construction Shangri-la include an international airport, museums, a temple with the biggest prayer wheel in the world, a renovated monastery, a reconstructed Old Town, and paved roads leading to natural attractions which are integral to marketing this tourist paradise. Fancy shops (offering a wide range of souvenirs ranging from fake yak skulls to local and imported crafts), restaurants (with hybridized menus offering yak burgers, Tibetan momos and pizza), soulless mega-hotels (like the Hotel Paradise), homestays at villagers' places, stupas and some stylized "local" constructions in the Old Town merge together in a superficially seductive appeal to exotic otherness. This combination, resembling a theme park or a "museumized" place, has led to one journalist to describe Shangri-La as a "Tibetan toy town" (MacGregor, 2002: quoted in Kolås, 2008).

During the Chinese Cultural Revolution (1966-1976) the Government erased every religious sign, but nowadays efforts are addressed to restoring and promoting Buddhist symbols whether in sacred or profane buildings. Buddhist iconography is present in the airport decór (Tibetan thangkas, bass prayer wheels and stupas) as well as in the mega-hotels (Tibetan Wheels of Life, thangkas and mandalas). Indeed, the main investments in Shangri-La are the new temple and the renovated Monastery, cardinal touristic attractions and integral to the town's Buddhist aestheticization. Captivated by the exotic allure of these photogenic symbols, tourists take pictures and spin the prayer wheels. Whether their function is sacred or aesthetic, Buddhist signs are a key contribution to the Disneyfication of Shangri-La.

The Shangri-La brand name has changed the ethnic distribution of the place. Indigenous people in their traditional clothing mix with laid-back Caucasians who have settled down in Shangri-La looking for a hip atmosphere, ambitious Han Chinese who have increased their numbers in town, and busloads of tourists armed with cameras. Tibetans are the main ethnic group but the region is very rich in terms of ethnic diversity. In this vein, the quaint ethnic villagers are part of the exotic rapture of Shangri-La, offering a more plural and colorful experience to suit Western Orientalist demands (Yan and Santos, 2009) by amusing the tourists and emphasizing fabled harmony.

Ancient craft techniques, shepherding and mushroom harvesting coexist with Internet cafes, shopping centers and tour groups. Old Buddhist rituals such as circumambulation of temples while whispering holy mantras mesh up with modern ones like following the touristic guide umbrella and dancing to recorded folk music in the town square each evening — a metaphor of harmony and solidarity. According to Relph (1976:141) "place is a fusion of human and natural order and any significant spatial center of a person or group's lived experience." Experiencing Shangri-La as an insider or outsider shapes different identities and meanings for different individuals and groups (Relph, 1976). We find a plurality of Shangri-Las: it is still Zhongdian for the natives, the "Lost Horizon" for Western travelers, "El Dorado" for Han Chinese businessmen, "just another touristic spot" for Chinese tourists and "Shangri-La" for Westerners living there.

Material, social and spiritual aspects guide Shangri-La's journey from a fictional place in the collective imagination to a placeless paradise in Yunnan Province. One of the manifestations of placelessness embodied by Shangri-La is "other-directedness", i.e., "places made up of a surrealistic combination of history, myth, reality and fantasy that have little relationship with a particular geographical setting" (Relph, 1976: 95). Shangri-La also suffers from "lack of human scale" or "gigantism" since it hosts the biggest prayer wheel in the world ("Fortunate Victory Prayer Wheel"), the largest white terrace in China (Baishui Terrace), the largest Tibetan monastery in Yunnan (Ganden Sumtseling Monastery) and the deepest gorge in the world (Tiger Leaping Gorge). Uniformity and standardization are also being adopted in Shangri-La with the construction of new roads, concrete squares and shopping centers and the cable cars and escalators that will likely dominate the future of the once pristine Paradise Lost.

## REFERENCES

Bourdieu, Pierre ([1979] 1984), *Distinction : A Social Critique of the Judgement of Taste*, Cambridge, Mass.: Harvard University Press.

Bowker, Geoffrey C. 2008. *Memory Practices in the Sciences*. MIT Press.

Derrida, Jacques. 1996. *Archive fever*. University of Chicago Press.

Featherstone, Mike. 1991. *Consumer Culture and Postmodernism*. 1st ed. Sage Publications Ltd

Frykman, Jonas and Orvar Löfgren (1987), *Culture Builders: A Historical Anthropology of Middle-Class Life*, New Brunswick; London: Rutgers University Press.

Gillingham-Ryan, Maxwell. 2006. *Apartment Therapy: The Eight-Step Home Cure*. Bantam.

Green, Penelope. 2004. "HABITATS/Bedford Street, Greenwich Village; It's Apartment Therapy, But Not on the Couch-New York Times." *The New York Times* http://tinyurl.com/yk7ao5a (Accessed February 23, 2010).

Hand, Martin, and Elizabeth Shove. 2004. "Orchestrating Concepts: Kitchen Dynamics and Regime Change in Good Housekeeping and Ideal Home, 19222002." *Home Cultures* 1:235-256.

Hansen, Judith Friedman (1980), *We Are a Little Land: Cultural Assumptions in Danish Everyday Life*, New York: Arno Press.

Henry, Paul C. (2005), "Social Class, Market Situation, and Consumers' Metaphors of (Dis)Empowerment.," *Journal of Consumer Research*, 31 (4), 766-78.

Hilton, James (1933), *Lost Horizon: A Novel,* New York: William Morrow.

Holt, Douglas B. 1997. "Poststructuralist Lifestyle Analysis: Conceptualizing the Social Patterning of Consumption in Postmodernity." *Journal of Consumer Research* 23:326.

Holt, Douglas B. (1998), "Does Cultural Capital Structure American Consumption?," *Journal of Consumer Research*, 25 (1), 1-25.

Johnston, Josée, and Shyon Baumann. 2007. "Democracy versus Distinction: A Study of Omnivorousness in Gourmet Food Writing." *American Journal of Sociology* 113:165-204.

Keeble, Trevor. 2007. "Domesticating modernity: Woman magazine and the modern home." http://eprints.kingston. ac.uk/804/ (Accessed February 23, 2010).

Kolås, Åshild (2004), "Tourism and the Making of Place in Shangri-La", *Tourism Geographies*, 6 (3): 262-278.

Kolås, Åshild (2008), *Tourism and Tibetan Culture in Transition: A Place Called Shangri-La*, London: Routledge.

Kozinets, Robert V., John F. Sherry Jr., Diana Storm, Adam Duhachek, Krittinee Nuttavuthisit, and Benet Deberry-Spence (2004), "Ludic Agency and Retail Spectacle.," *Journal of Consumer Research*, 31 (3), 658-72.

Latour, Bruno (2005), *Reassembling the Social : An Introduction to Actor-Network-Theory*, Oxford ; Toronto: Oxford University Press.

Lefebvre, Henri (1974/1991), *The Production of Space*, Oxford, UK ; Cambridge, Mass., USA: Blackwell.

Ley, David (2009), "Are There Limits to Gentrification?," *Presentation in Cities Centre, University of Toronto, October 19, 2009.*

Lugosi, Peter (2009), "The Production of Hospitable Space: Commercial Propositions and Consumer Co-Creation in a Bar Operation," *Space and Culture*, 12 (4), 396-411.

McCarthy, Christine (2005), "Toward a Definition of Interiority," *Space and Culture*, 8 (2), 112-25.

McCracken, Grant (1989), "Homeyness: A Cultural Account of One Constellation of Consumer Goods and Meanings," in *Interpretive Consumer Research*, ed. Elizabeth C. Hirschman, Provo, Utah: Association for Consumer Research, 168-83.

Murdoch, Jonathan (1998), "The Spaces of Actor-Network Theory," *Geoforum*, 29 (4), 357-74.

Pennartz, Paul J. J. (1999), "Home: The Experience of Atmosphere," in *At Home. An Anthropology of Domestic Space*, ed. Irene Cieraad, Syracuse, New York: Syracuse University Press, 95-106.

Relph, Edward C. (1976), *Place and Placelessness,* London: Pion.

Sherry Jr., John F. (1998), *Servicescapes : The Concept of Place in Contemporary Markets*, Lincolnwood, IL: NTC Business Books.

_____ (2000), "Place, Technology, and Representation," *Journal of Consumer Research*, 27 (2), 273-78.

Thornton, Sarah. 1996. *Club cultures:music, media, and subcultural capital*. Wesleyan University Press.

Yan, G., Santos, C.A. (2009), "China, Forever: Tourism Discourse and Self-Orientalism", *Annals of Tourism Research*, 36 (2), 295-315.

Zukin, Sharon and Ervin Kosta (2004), "Bourdieu Off-Broadway: Managing Distinction on a Shopping Block in the East Village," *City & Community*, 3 (2(June)), 101-1

# Consumers Behaving Badly

Maferima Touré-Tillery, University of Chicago, USA
Ayelet Fishbach, University of Chicago, USA

## EXTENDED ABSTRACTS

### "Recycling–A License to Waste?"

*Chen-Bo Zhong, University of Toronto, Canada*
*Nina Mazar, University of Toronto, Canada*
*Brendan Strejcek, (Unaffiliated)*

In the past few decades, conservation and environment protection have taken increasing significance in shaping public policy, corporate and marketing strategy, and individual consumer behavior. With more consumers expressing their environmental concerns through product choice (Laroche, Bergeron, & Barbaro-Forleo, 2001), companies are incentivized to integrate environmental and social issues into the production, packaging, and marketing of their products.

Of special interest is the recycling sector that involves manufacturing and marketing products using reusable content such as fiber, glass, and metal, preserving limited raw materials and reducing landfill wastes. The recycling industry has witnessed an impressive growth and has become a significant force of the economy: utilizing data from 1997 to 1999, the *U.S. Recycling Economic Information Study* reported that the recycling and reuse industry consists of approximately 56,000 establishments that employ over 1.1 million people, generate an annual payroll of nearly $37 billion, and gross over $236 billion in annual revenues. More and more products are advertised and marketed with the universal recycling symbol, highlighting their ecological friendliness.

In this paper, however, we propose a counterintuitive prediction that recycling products may actually *increase* the net use of raw materials. We argue that consumers feel licensed to use more of a product when they know that the product is made, in part or totally, of recycled materials. In addition, consumers do not typically engage in rational calculations on the percentage of recycled material to set limits on how much more of the recycled product they could consume compared to a comparable conventional product that will not result in a net increase of the use of raw materials. For example, if a brand of paper is made of 50% recycled material and 50% raw material, consuming 2 sheets of the recycled paper will result in the same amount of raw materials used as consuming 1 sheet of paper that is made of conventional (i.e. raw) material. If knowing that the paper is made of recycled materials licensed people to consume 3 sheets when they could have just used 1, this will result in a 50% increase of the use of raw materials. This is consistent with research in other domains showing that sampling healthy food (as opposed to tasty food) makes people hungrier afterwards and actually consumes more food later (Finkelstein & Fishbach, in press). We test this prediction in a controlled experiment.

Eighty-four undergraduate students were randomly assigned to one of three conditions: recycled paper vs. conventional paper with packaging vs. conventional paper without packaging. Participants were told that they were going to engage in an origami contest. They saw step-by-step instructions of a somewhat complex origami on the computer screen and were told that their goal was to successfully complete the origami as quickly as possible. Participants had 5 minutes to practice before the actual contest. They were told to grab as many sheets of paper from a nearby desk as they want for the practice. In the recycling paper condition, the stack of paper was wrapped in a paper package with the universal recycling symbol as well as a label indicating that the paper is made of 30% recycled content; in the conventional paper with packaging condition, the stack of paper was wrapped in a paper package without the symbol and any mentioning of recycled material; finally, in the conventional paper without packaging, the stack of paper was not wrapped in any packaging. In actuality, the same paper (conventional) was used in all 3 conditions. The sheets of papers used by participants in the practice session were recorded and used as dependent variable.

The result supported our prediction; participants in the recycled paper condition used about 22% more raw materials than those in the control conditions. This finding highlights the importance of a fuller understanding of consumer psychology in purchasing and consuming products made of recycled materials. Although people may prefer to buy recycled products, they may feel licensed to use more than needed, resulting in more waste than if they buy and consume conventional products.

### "When Psychological Closeness Creates Distance from One's Moral Compass"

*Francesca Gino, University of North Carolina at Chapel Hill, USA*
*Adam D. Galinsky, Northwestern University, USA*

Does feeling psychologically close to another person who acts unethically make one behave more or less dishonestly? Suppose you find out that a peer who shares your birth date is inflating her expense report or cheating on her taxes. How would you react to these dishonest behaviors? You might suppose that you would view them critically, judge the behaviors as harshly as an objective observer, and distance yourself from the individual with tainted morality. In this paper, we make the opposite prediction: We propose that if a person is psychologically connected to someone who engages in selfish or dishonest behavior, she may become vicariously motivated to justify that person's actions and thus more likely to behave unethically herself. We propose that even the subtlest of psychological connections, such as sharing the same birthday, can influence the likelihood that an individual will cross ethical boundaries.

Research has shown that people feel connected to others not only when they share a common group membership, but also when they share much subtler similarities. For example, people experience a sense of psychological closeness to another person when they share common attributes, such as a similar name or the same birthday.

As people grow closer, even when this closeness is just psychological, the line between self and other becomes blurred, leading to increased self–other overlap. This clouding of self and other is very common in close relationships and friendships, and can result from people's cognitive orientation or mindsets. For instance, people who construe the self as interdependent define themselves in terms of their groups' attributes (Brewer & Gardner, 1996). Similarly, individuals who dispositionally tend to take the perspective of others, or who are asked to do so, psychologically take on the characteristics of others (Galinsky, Ku, & Wang, 2008).

Even when subtle, these psychological connections create numerous vicarious possibilities. When people feel connected to others, they notice and experience others' emotions (Hatfield et al., 1994), including joy, embarrassment, and pain. More recently, Gunia, Sivanathan, and Galinsky (2009) found that a psychological connection between two decision makers leads the second decision maker to escalate commitment by investing further in a failing program orchestrated by the initial decision maker, even in the face of direct financial costs to the second decision maker. These findings suggest that psychological closeness blurs self-others boundaries, and thus can lead individuals to experience and behave more consistently with others' internal states.

In this paper, we examine the effects of feelings of psychological closeness on one's own ethical behavior. We suggest that a psychological connection to another individual who engages in selfish or dishonest behavior, however subtle, creates distance from one's own moral compass. We argue that, because of the psychological connection, one becomes vicariously motivated to justify the other person's selfish or unethical actions and to judge these actions as less morally problematic. We predict this should lead individuals who have formed a psychological connection with a wrongdoer to behave selfishly themselves—for example, by keeping more money for themselves when asked to share a fixed amount with others—or even dishonestly.

We observed a consistent pattern of results across five studies in which we measured people's intentions to behave selfishly or dishonestly, as well as their real behavior. Our results show that taking the perspective of a psychologically close person who behaved selfishly led people to report being more likely to behave selfishly themselves (Experiments 1 and 4), and that feelings of embarrassments mediated this effect (Experiment 4). Psychological closeness also led to higher levels of dishonesty in Experiment 2, in which we considered real, unethical behavior. We found that when participants shared attributes with a confederate who cheated, they were more likely to behave dishonestly by inflating their task performance and thus earned undeserved money. The same findings were replicated in a follow-up study in which we manipulated psychological closeness by activating an interdependent mindset through priming (Experiment 3). The results of Experiment 3 also show that people with an interdependent mindset view the selfish behavior of others as less unethical or wrong. Taken together, these studies provide convincing evidence that even subtle forms of psychological closeness lead individuals to vicariously justify the actions of the person they feel connected to and thus to be more likely to behave less ethically themselves.

Experiment 5 introduces the presence of out-group observers as an important moderator of the impact of psychological closeness. The results show that individuals respond differently to the selfish actions of a person to whom they feel psychologically close, depending on whether out-group observers are present or absent. When only in-group observers are present, feeling psychologically close to the wrongdoer increases one's own likelihood of acting selfishly. But when out-group observers are present, the opposite pattern occurs.

### "Taking Advantage of Future Forgiveness?–Licensing vs. Consistency Effects in the Context of Ethical Decision Making"

*Shahar Ayal, Duke University, USA*
*Francesca Gino, University of North Carolina, USA*
*Nina Mazar, University of Toronto, USA*
*Dan Ariely, Duke University, USA*

To many, the concept of confession is inextricably tied to the notion of forgiveness, which has recently become a topic of study for psychologists. This increased interest stems from the recognition that forgiveness represents an important response to a fundamental human challenge: how to maintain relations with others after harming them or being harmed by them (Fincham, Jackson, & Beach, 2005). Similarly, confession allows individuals to restore their

relationship with God in the case of the Catholic Church and open a new leaf in their moral account.

While prior work provides useful insights into the determinants and consequences of forgiving, it remains silent on the influence that expectations of forgiveness might have on individual behavior before and after making a confession. In this paper, we focus on a specific type of behavior: dishonesty, and test whether and how expected and received forgiveness through confession influences the likelihood to engage in dishonest behavior. Furthermore, we compare people's predictions to their real behaviors and explore the accuracy of their intuitions.

Prior research suggests that moral behaviors are figured into an implicit calculation of self-perception such that ethical behaviors boost one's moral self-image and transgressions dampen it (Jordan, Mullen, & Murnighan, 2009). Given that people typically care about morality and want to maintain a positive self-image but behaving morally often comes at a cost, people tend to be strongly motivated to engage in ethical behaviors if their moral self is threatened by a recent transgression; they are least likely to scrutinize the moral implications of their behaviors and to regulate their behaviors right after they experienced a boost from a good deed. For example, Carlsmith and Gross (1969) found individuals more likely to comply to help-requests after they violated moral rules.

Along similar lines, as individuals face ethical dilemmas, they can fall prey to the temptation to behave dishonestly, perhaps especially when they know their behavior will be forgiven and their moral violations "erased." That is, an expected future confession with its element of forgiveness might act as a moral offset that individuals can put into their current mental moral tap, and thus allows them to transgress even before the confession takes place without hurting their moral self-concept. This implies that an expected future forgiveness can license preceding unethical behaviors. Furthermore, dishonest behavior might be higher before than after an expected confession.

On the other hand, research on the consistency effect has found that drawing consumers' attention to moral standards could reduce dishonest behavior. For example, in studies conducted by Mazar, Amir & Ariely (2008) signing an honor code or recalling the Ten Commandments increased the saliency of one's own standards for honesty such that it subsequently increased honest behavior consistent with these standards. In line with this research, consumers will avoid dishonest behavior after receiving forgiveness and after the mentioning of a future confession. That is, the expectation of a confession might increase attention to morality and therefore result in behavior consistent with one's moral standards (i.e. decrease unethical behavior before and after the confession).

The predictions of the licensing and consistency effects were juxtaposed across three studies. In the first two studies we examined individuals' intuitive beliefs about the effects of both expected and received forgiveness on other people's likelihood to cheat. Study 1 showed that participants' adopted a cynical view of others, expecting strategic moral calculation. That is, participants predicted others to be more likely to cheat before rather than after an expected future confession. Study 2 extended the findings to test the influence of temporal distance. Similarly to the results of Study 1, participants predicted the likelihood of others to cheat to increase the closer a future confession, to drop right after the confession, and to increase again the further in the past the confession would be. Thus, participants predicted licensing before confession and consistency after confession with diminishing effectiveness of the latter over time.

Finally, Study 3 tested the effect of an expected confession on one's own dishonest behavior in a task in which participants had opportunities to cheat in order to earn more money. Interestingly, while we did find participants' dishonest behavior to decrease after (vs. before) an expected confession and to slowly increase again with distance from the confession (similar to the prediction results from Study 1 and 2), participants' dishonest behavior *before* the expected confession was lower than in a control condition where participants' did not know about the future confession.

Taken together, our findings suggest that individuals are much more concerned about their moral self-image and less strategic as their cynical view of humanity might suggest. We found that an expected confession does not license unethical behavior in the period leading to it, but rather produce beneficial effects on *honest* behavior. Thus, expecting forgiveness seems to act as a reminder of one's ethical standards leading consumers to act in consistency with these standards.

### "Slacking in the Middle: Relaxing Personal Standards in the Course of Goal Pursuit"

*Maferima Touré-Tillery, University of Chicago, USA*
*Ayelet Fishbach, University of Chicago, USA*

Goals often require the completion of a sequence of actions, such as students finishing a series of assignments to pass a class, or consumers with frequent buyer cards that require the purchase of a number of items to get a reward (e.g. free coffee). In the course of pursuing such goals, people decide how closely to follow their personal standards for each action, based on whether the benefits of relaxing these standards outweigh the costs. One such cost is the negative impact on self-image, as relaxing standards can signal to oneself that one has low standards. Indeed, people learn about themselves from their actions (Brehm and Festinger 1957; Koo and Fishbach 2008). Therefore, even when external costs are low, self-image concerns get in the way of relaxing standards. In the context of unethical behavior, Mazar et al (2008)showed that one way people resolve this internal conflict is by cheating "just a little bit": enough to benefit, but not enough to incur the costs to self-image. These findings are evidence that people behave in ways that allow them to present themselves *to themselves* in a positive light, and that actions serve as signals to the self.

We suggest that actions in the course of goal pursuit have differing signaling values for the self, and that relaxing standards on actions with low signaling value would minimize negative consequences on self-image. Previous research demonstrated significant order effects in sequences of information and events, with beginning and end being particularly important (Anderson 1965). Within this perspective, we propose that actions at the beginning and end of goal pursuit are stronger signals to the self of the true nature of the self than actions in the middle. Therefore, people protect their self-image by giving themselves a good first and last impression of themselves. Accordingly, we predict that people will be more likely to relax their standards in the middle of a sequence of goal-related actions than at the beginning/end.

Six studies confirmed our hypothesis in the contexts of ethical, performance and religious standards. In study 1, participants completed a word recognition task privately, and had the opportunity to cheat at the beginning/middle/end of the task, by claiming to know the meaning of a fake word. We found that a greater number of participants claimed to know a fake word (dishonest answer) when it appeared in the middle (vs. beginning/end) of the sequence. In study 2, we replicated this pattern using a less ambiguous form of dishonesty. In private, participants flipped a coin 10 times to assign themselves randomly to a series of 10 long vs. short proofreading tasks. We found that they were more likely to (falsely) report the favorable outcome of the coin flip (assigning themselves to the short passage) for tasks in the middle than for those at beginning/end. In

study 3, we replicated our findings in a more social context, where participants interacted with the experimenter throughout the task. They had the opportunity to take advantage of the experimenter's "forgetfulness" and get undeserved credit for a task that they did not do. We found that more participants accepted the undeserved credit for a task in the middle (vs. beginning/end) of the 7-task sequence. In study 4, we extended out findings to performance standards. Participants completed a shape-cutting task at their own pace. We found that out of the six shapes in the task, they cut the first/last shapes better than the middle ones. Study 5 was designed to examine underlying mechanisms by testing the idea that first/last (vs. middle) actions are stronger signals to the self. In the context of unethical behavior, we found that participants judged another person more harshly for cheating at the beginning/end (vs. middle) of goal pursuit. Because the mechanisms for judging the self mirror those for judging others, these findings suggest that people would think of themselves as more dishonest for cheating at the beginning/end (vs. middle) of pursuing a goal. Finally, with respect to meeting religious standards, study 6 found that participants were more likely to engage in the Hanukah ritual of lighting menorah candles on the first/last (vs. middle) nights of the 8-night Jewish holiday.

Taken together, these studies provide convergent evidence that people are more likely to relax their standards in the middle (vs. beginning/end) of a sequence of goal-related actions, because actions at the beginning/end (vs. middle) are stronger signals to the self of one's standards.

### REFERENCES

Anderson, N. H. (1965). Primacy effects in personality impression- Formation using a generalized order effect paradigm. *Journal of Personality and Social Psychology* 2(1): 1-9.

Brehm, J. and L. Festinger (1957). Pressures toward uniformity of Performance in groups. *Human Relations* 10(1): 85-91

Brewer, M. B., & Gardner, W. (1996). Who is this "we"? Levels of collective identity and self representations. *Journal of Personality and Social Psychology*, *71*, 83-93.

Carlsmith, J. M., & Gross, A. E. (1969). Some effects of guilt on compliance. *Journal of Personality and Social Psychology*, 11, 232-239.

Fincham, F. D., Jackson, H., & Beach, S. R. H. (2005). Transgression severity and forgiveness: Different moderators for objective and subjective severity. *Journal of Social and Clinical Psychology*, 24(6), 860-875.

Finkelstein, S. R. & Fishbach, A. (in press). When healthy food makes you hungry. *Journal of Consumer Research*.

Galinsky, A. D., Ku, G., & Wang, C. S. (2008). Perspective-takers behave more stereotypically. *Journal of Personality and Social Psychology*, *95*, 404-419.

Gunia, B. C., Sivanathan, N., & Galinsky, A. D. (2009). Vicarious entrapment: Your sunk costs, my escalation of commitment. *Journal of Experimental Social Psychology*, *45*(6), 1238-1244.

Hatfield, E., Cacioppo, J. T., & Rapson, R. L. (1994). Emotional contagion. *New York: Cambridge University Press*.

Jordan, J., Mullen, E., & Murnighan, J.K. (2009). On the pendulum of moral action: Contrasting effects of own and others' past moral behavior on future moral behavior. *Manuscript submitted for publication.*

Koo, M. and A. Fishbach (2008). Dynamics of self-regulation: How (un)accomplished goal actions affect motivation. *Journal of Personality and Social Psychology* 94(2): 183-195.

Laroche, M., Bergeron, J. & Barbaro-Farleo, G. (2001). Targeting consumers who are willing to pay more for environmentally friendly products. *Journal of Consumer Marketing*, 18:503-520.

Mazar, N., Amir, O., & Ariely, D. (2008). The dishonesty of honest people: A theory of self-concept maintenance. *Journal of Marketing Research*, 45, 633–644.

# Small Influences with BIG Consequences: Consumer Decisions in the Wild
Cynthia Cryder, Washington University in St. Louis, USA

## EXTENDED ABSTRACTS

### "Racial Preferences in Charitable Behavior Vary by Age of Recipient"

*Deborah Small, University of Pennsylvania, USA*
*Devin Pope, University of Pennsylvania, USA*
*Mike Norton, Harvard University, USA*

Decades of experimental research provide evidence about factors that influence charitable giving. Recent research in consumer behavior emphasizes characteristics of the description of the charity (Kogut & Ritov, 2005; Small & Verrochi, 2009) and characteristics of donation request strategies (Lui and Aaker, 2008; Shang & Croson, 2009) as crucial for understanding when charitable appeals succeed. Although this research is useful for isolating cause and effect relationships and for pinpointing psychological mechanisms, researchers and practitioners remain skeptical about the extent to which such effects persist in real charity markets, where the precise control of the laboratory is lacking. Thus examining factors that influence charitable donations in natural settings is an essential step for understanding the psychology of giving.

The present research utilizes data from an online charity that allows individuals to connect directly with classrooms in need. The charity's mission is to improve public education by empowering teachers to make changes and to enable citizens to be philanthropists. Public school teachers submit short proposals for needs for their classroom (e.g., microscope slides for biology class, violins for a school recital). Individuals browse proposals online and choose to give any amount. Once a project reaches its funding goal, the charity delivers the materials to the school.

Teachers can also include a picture that appears alongside their proposal—some 33% choose to do so. Given that vivid images tend to have a larger effect on judgment, memory, and behavior than pallid statistical information (Nisbett & Ross, 1980), posting a picture seems to be a wise strategy for a teacher requesting funds. Indeed, we find that proposals including a picture are 5% more likely to be funded than otherwise identical proposals. However, specific attributes of the pictures likely matter as well. For instance, Small and Verrochi (2009) found that when victim expressed sadness in a picture on a charity advertisement, people donated more than when the victim expressed happiness or neutral emotion. We expected that many other aspects of a picture may predict charitable giving choices.

Two features of a classroom in need that become particularly salient in the presence of a picture are the age of the students and their race. Given past research on stereotype activation (Devine, 1989), in-group preference in helping, and infrahumanization of African-Americans (Cuddy, Rock, & Norton, 2007), we expected that *for older children,* proposals containing pictures of Caucasian children would be more likely to be funded than those containing pictures of African-American children. However, we expected this common pattern to disappear or even reverse when the children are young because young African Americans will not be saddled by the same negative stereotypical associations as older children (e.g., Nosek et al., 2007).

We coded the race of the students in the pictures and used information provided in the proposal summary to ascertain the grade level of the students (either pre-K through 5th grade, or 6th through 12th grade). Our final sample includes 539 and 250 proposals that include a picture of African-American students in pre-K-5 and grades 6-12, respectively, and 894 and 332 proposals that include a picture of Caucasian students in preK-5 and grades 6-12, respectively.

We employ multivariate regression analysis to control for all other aspects of a proposal (amount of money being requested, type of project, poverty level, etc.) to isolate the causal effect of race and age and the interaction between race and age on the probability of a proposal being funded.

Overall, proposals with pictures of African-American students are funded 3.7% *more often* ($p=.06$) than otherwise similar Caucasian proposals. This general preference for African American classrooms—which runs counter to findings in much of the discrimination literature—could simply reflect the selective makeup of donors that participate in this particular online charity or the donors' assumptions regarding which classrooms benefit the most from their donation.

However, the simple comparison between donation rates by race masks an important underlying interaction of age and race. For young classrooms (pre-K-5), African-American proposals are funded at an even higher rate relative to Caucasian proposals: 6.7% higher. For older classrooms (grades 6-12), on the other hand, African-American proposals are funded 2.5% *less often* than otherwise similar Caucasian classrooms. Along with being economically large, this interaction effect is also statistically significant ($p=.03$).

In sum, we utilize donation data from a real charity to examine the subtle effects of the race and age of charity recipients on charitable donations. Future research will attempt to parse out different potential psychological mechanisms for the pattern of effects.

### "The Sunny Side of Giving"

*Cynthia Cryder, Washington University in St. Louis, USA*
*Roberto Weber, Carnegie Mellon, USA*

In 2008, charitable giving in the United States totaled over $300 billion dollars (Giving USA 2009). This is over 2% of Gross Domestic Product—a significant share. Despite the fact that charitable giving constitutes such a large portion of economic activity, the basic reasons why people give to others still are not firmly understood (e.g., Batson et al. 1981). Here, we test how an everyday environmental influence, sunshine, influences generosity.

Sunshine is associated with stock market trading (Hirschleifer and Shumway 2003), tipping (Cunningham 1979), and decisions about where to attend college (Simonsohn 2010). Sunshine's effect on behavior typically is attributed to mood; people consistently report being happier and more satisfied with their lives on sunny days as opposed to rainy days (Schwarz and Clore 1983).

Mood commonly is linked to generosity. Both positive and negative moods increase generosity compared to neutral moods. People who experience a mood-lifting event are more likely to help others than are people in a neutral state (Isen and Levin 1972). Similarly, people who are asked to recall a sad event are more likely to volunteer to help others than are people in a neutral state (Manuncia, Baumann and Cialdini 1984). Therefore, the prediction for how sunshine might influence giving is not clear. Prior works suggest that donations may increase with sunnier weather because sunny weather improves mood, while other prior works suggest that donations may decrease with sunnier weather because cloudy weather dampens mood. A curvilinear relationship in which both extremely sunny and extremely cloudy weather increase donations compared to average weather is also possible.

Here, we investigate two questions. First, does sunshine have a meaningful impact on charitable giving (and how large is that impact)? Second, if sunshine influences charitable giving, what type of influence does it have?

The dataset includes information for each U.S. contact made by a university phone fundraising team during 63 days in October-December of 2007 (N=5,224). Student fundraisers used standard university fundraising scripts throughout; they asked potential donors to update their contact information, thanked them for past support, told them about campus news, and finally requested a donation. Fifty-one percent of those answering donated nothing; forty-nine percent donated $1-$5,023 (of donations, Mean donation=$178.30, SD=$355.46, Median=$75). Dataset variables include call date, amount donated, contact's zip code, graduation year, and gender.

Based on zip code, we collected weather data for the contact's location on the call date and date before the call from Weather Underground (www.wunderground.com). Variables of interest included visibility distance and hourly cloud cover.

Linear regression models predicting amount donated based on clearness and visibility demonstrate robust effects. Controlling for gender, years since graduation (an age proxy), seasonal time trend (a "day" variable assigning each date a number, 1-63, corresponding with the day of data collection), and previous day clearness, we see that (completely) clear days as opposed to (completely) cloudy days are associated with an average $44.58 increase in donations per call ($b$=44.58, $t(3,990)$=3.79, $p$<0.0005). Similarly, a regression using the visibility variable and analogous controls, reveals that a one mile increase in visibility is associated with an average $9.53 increase in donations per call ($b$=9.53, $t(3,982)$=4.75, $p$<0.0005). Including a variable controlling for weather at callers' location did not significantly alter results, nor did including the first three digits of each contact's zip code as a fixed-effects location control. Squared terms for clearness and visibility were not statistically significant ($p$'s>0.25), suggesting no curvilinear influence of sunshine on giving. Coefficients for previous day sunshine are negative suggesting that sunshine contrast is important. Holding today's weather constant, it is easier to raise donation dollars today if yesterday was cloudy.

Logistic regressions in which the dependent variable indicated whether the potential donor donated or not showed no significant effects of clearness nor visibility. Thus, the effect seems to be that sunnier weather encourages people already giving to give more, not that sunnier weather encourages people who would give nothing to give something.

In sum, we see a robust and substantial positive effect of sunshine on charitable giving. The finding has important implications for fundraisers and donors, but also underscores the powerful influence of everyday environmental factors like weather on consequential decisions like in this case, decisions about giving resources to others.

### "The Effect of Providing Peer Information on Retirement Savings Decisions"

*John Beshears, Harvard University, USA*
*James J. Choi, Yale University, USA*
*David Laibson, Harvard University, USA*
*Brigitte C. Madrian, Harvard University, USA*
*Katherine L. Milkman, University of Pennsylvania, USA*

We report a field experiment evaluating a social norms marketing approach to influencing retirement savings decisions. Social norms marketing campaigns aim to encourage a behavior by informing individuals that the behavior is prevalent among their peers. We find some evidence that social norms marketing can increase savings rates, but our overall results suggest that social norms marketing may have limited power and can even produce boomerang effects.

Theoretical work suggests that an individual may mimic peers' actions because those actions signal information that is unavailable to the individual yet relevant to her payoffs. Empirical work shows that peer effects have a large impact in a range of settings (Goldstein, et al. 2005; Schultz, et al. 2007; Cialdini, et al. 1990; Kallgren, et al. 2000; Cialdini, 2003). Our paper joins the line of work that asks whether peer effects can be used to encourage desirable behaviors.

Our experiment was conducted at a large manufacturing company and included all U.S. employees ages 20-69 who were eligible for, but not participating in, the company 401(k) plan ("non-participants"), or who were participating in the plan at a before-tax contribution rate less than both their employer match threshold and 6% ("low savers").[1] These employees received letters encouraging them to enroll in or increase their contribution rate in the 401(k) plan. By checking a box on the letter and returning it to the company, employees could begin contributing 6% of their pay to the plan.

We randomly assigned employees to receive one of three types of letters: (1) a letter containing no peer information; (2) a letter offering information about the aggregate savings decisions of co-workers in the recipient's five-year age category (e.g., ages 25-29); or (3) a letter offering information about coworkers in the relevant ten-year age category (e.g., ages 20-29). For non-participating recipients in the peer information conditions, the letter stated the fraction of coworkers in the five-year or ten-year age category who were already enrolled in the plan. For low-saving recipients, the letter stated the fraction of plan participants in the five-year or ten-year age category who were already contributing at least 6% of pay. These peer information numbers were all greater than 70%.

We tracked contribution changes over two months following our mailing. We measured the effect of *presence* of peer information by comparing the extent to which employees in the peer information groups increased their contribution rates relative to the control group. We estimated the effect of *magnitude* of the peer information number that employees saw by exploiting: 1) variation generated by random assignment to different peer information as a result of differences in the 5-year and 10-year age categories and 2) age group boundary discontinuities.

Employees in our study naturally fell into four subpopulations: (1) unionized non-participants, (2) non-unionized non-participants, (3) unionized plan participants with low contribution rates, and (4) non-unionized plan participants with low contribution rates. We evaluate unionized employees separately from non-unionized employees because the latter were previously automatically enrolled in the retirement savings plan at a 6% contribution rate unless they opted out, while unionized employees were not subject to automatic enrollment. Prior research has found that automatic enrollment has a large impact on 401(k) enrollment, contribution rates, and asset allocations because employees often passively accept the default options (e.g., Madrian and Shea, 2001). Non-unionized employees who passively accepted the 6% contribution rate default did not receive letters. Therefore, among the four subpopulations who received a mailing, only unionized non-participants had never made an active 401(k) savings decision.

The effect of peer information in our experiment was mixed. Among non-unionized non-participants, exposure to peer information increased the likelihood of enrolling in the plan from 0.7% to

---

[1]The match threshold, which is the minimum employee contribution rate at which an employee receives all available employer matching contributions, varied from employee to employee. For many employees (including all non-unionized employees), it was equal to 6%.

3.4% (*p*<0.10). Among those non-unionized non-participants who received peer information, a one percent increase in the reported fraction of peer coworkers enrolled in the plan increased enrollment by 0.9 percent (*p*<0.10). However, the impact of peer information was reversed among unionized non-participants: the presence of peer information decreased the enrollment rate from 10.4% to 6.5% (*p*<0.05), and a one percent increase in the peer information number reduced enrollment by 1.8% (*p*<0.05). We find no statistically significant effects among either unionized or non-unionized participants with low contribution rates.

The negative response of unionized non-participants to peer information is somewhat surprising. This reaction is probably not due to learning that coworkers had a lower plan participation rate than expected, since the enrollment rate and contribution rate changes of unionized non-participants were also decreasing in the size of the peer information value they received.

### "Spurious! Implicit Egotism in Marriage and Moving Decisions: Lessons for Consumer Research"

*Uri Simonsohn, University of Pennsylvania, USA*

Multiple papers demonstrate the notion of *implicit egotism*: people like things more if these remind them of themselves. People like their initials, the numbers of their birthday, brands that resemble their names, etc… (see e.g., Anseel and Duyck 2008; Brendl, Chattopadhyay, Pelham and Carvallo 2005; Chandler, Griffin and Sorensen 2008; Nelson and Simmons 2007; Nuttin 1985; Pelham, Carvallo and Jones, 2005).

Several papers have taken this notion of implicit egotism and assessed whether it matters for big decisions.[2] Pelham, Mirenberg and Jones (2002) find that people are more likely than expected by chance to live in and move to streets, towns, and states that resemble their name, and to a town that contains a number from their birthday in their name (e.g., people born on February 2nd are disproportionately likely to live in "Two Oaks"). Jones, Pelham, Carvallo and Mirenberg (2004) find that people are disproportionately likely to marry others who share the initial of their last name, that share the exact same last name, and that have similar first names.

The current paper challenges the validity of all of the findings listed above. It does so by reanalyzing the same data sources used in the published articles and also looking at larger and cleaner sets. For every demonstration considered the name letter effect not only becomes statistically insignificant, it becomes very very close to zero. For example, for the first-name/marriage effect the original paper considers 12 names, 10 of which show a statistically significant effect. In my analyses, with a sample of 102,000 observations, none of the 12 names shows the effect and the average effect drops from 30%*** to 4% *ns*.

Here is a subset of the confounds documented in the paper:

1) Living in a city similar to one's last name: towns with names resembling last names (e.g. Smithville) are often founded by people with those last names. Smiths don't move to Smithville, they name the town where they already live Smithville. I conducted the analyses on the 10 largest cities in the US, where such reverse causality is implausible, and found a very precise 0 effect for name letter (e.g., people named York are not more likely to live in New York City).

2) Marrying someone with a similar last name: A small share of brides change their last names to their soon-to-be husbands'

names *before* marriage. Using public records I document a large number of people marrying each other, then divorcing, then marrying each other again. In the second marriage the bride has the groom's last name. Consistent with a measurement error explanation, I show that while exact last name matching are much more likely than would be expected by chance, very similar last names matching are not. E.g., a Gonzalez groom is twice as likely as would be expected by chance to marry a Gonzalez bride, but just as likely as expected by chance to marry a Gonzales bride.

3) Marrying someone with a similar first-name: Factors that influence the popularity of baby names (e.g., location, religion, fashionability of a given name over time, etc…) influence male and female versions of the name simultaneously. For example, the variation over time of the number of babies named Andrew and Andrea is *r*=.99. These factors influencing name popularity also influence who one marries (e.g., people marry others born around the same birth year). I show that if one uses as control names other people who have similar distribution of spouse choices the effect drops to 0 (intuitively, if one compares Andrews to other male names that were popular at the same time Andrew was, the effect goes to 0).

ACR this year is focusing on big picture issues. This paper raises big picture issues with respect to conducting psychological research outside the lab. Consumer research in the field is often apologetic about the non-experimental nature of the research but it falls short of employing state of the art techniques to analyze the data properly. The present paper exemplifies the shortcomings of such an approach. Economists routinely obtain convincing results from field data; should we not demand the same from our consumer researchers?

The paper also exemplifies the folly of arguing that if a paper contains multiple studies which a single explanation can account for, then we should not worry about the multiple alternative explanations for each of the studies, as the former is more parsimonious. Among other problems, this argument ignores the degree of freedom the authors possess in choosing which studies to run and which results to publish. The convincingness of evidence should be assessed on a study by study basis. Implicit egotism is the only explanation simultaneously consistent with all the studies reviewed above, and yet it cannot convincingly explain a single one of them.

---

[2]Two papers studying implicit egotism in real life decisions for small stakes are not affected by the confounds I discuss in the present paper, see (Chandler et al. 2008; Nelson and Simmons 2007).

# Layers of Feeling: Exploring The Complexity of Emotions

Iris W. Hung, National University of Singapore, Singapore
Anirban Mukhopadhyay, Hong Kong University of Science and Technology, China

## EXTENDED ABSTRACTS

### "Differentiating Between Simple and Complex Emotions: It's A Matter of Abstractness"

*Loraine Lau-Gesk, University of California, Irvine, USA*
*Joan Meyers-Levy, University of Minnesota, USA*
*Jesse R. Catlin, University of California, Irvine, USA*

Three studies demonstrate that emotions can vary in their construal level, ranging from fairly high-level abstract emotions to low-level concrete ones, and uncover process insights. Relational- (vs. item-specific) processing appears to underlie abstract (vs. concrete) emotions and their association with higher (vs. lower) construal levels. These findings are discussed in light of recent work on complex emotions.

The present research explores the possibility that emotions vary in their construal level, ranging from fairly high level abstract emotions to low level concrete ones. Drawing on construal level theory, we propose that higher level abstract (lower level concrete) emotions may entail mentally engaging in farther (closer) psychological distances (Liberman, Trope, and Stephan 2007). That is, emotions arising from appraisals that involve comparisons vis a vis a distant alternative are likely to be more abstract than those that involve comparisons with a proximal alternative. We suggest that certain complex emotions (Johnson-Laird and Oatley 1989; Ortony and Turner 1990), such as hope, pride, and awe, are likely to be fairly abstract because experiencing them requires that people compare their own situation to ones that are physically, socially, temporally, or hypothetically distant. For example, experiencing hope or pride involves a comparison with a distal expectation, ideal, or norm (Frijda, Kulpers and ter Schure 1990; MacInnis and de Mello 2005). By contrast, more concrete emotions include happiness, sadness, and fear since these arise from responses to more immediate situations and stimuli (i.e., close psychological distances; Liberman et al. 2007). Perhaps not surprisingly, these lower level, concrete emotions tend to be viewed as basic—feelings that are experienced universally from birth and in response to immediate needs (Ekman 1993; Plutchik 1981).

Study 1 explored whether emotions may indeed vary in their abstractness. We reasoned that people who experience more abstract versus concrete emotions should engage in a higher construal level and thereby should be more responsive to requests expressed at a higher versus lower construal level. Participants first wrote about an experience where they felt either proud or happy (i.e., abstract or concrete emotion). Subsequently they learned about a charity and were asked their willingness to make a donation—a request expressed at a high construal level, and to specify the precise amount they would donate—a request expressed at a low construal level. Participants also completed a BIF task, which directly assesses construal level (Vallacher and Wegner 1989). As expected, after participants had invoked the abstract emotion of pride versus the more concrete emotion of happiness, they were more willing to donate to the charity (a high level request) yet they committed a smaller dollar sum (a low level request). BIF results also showed after invoking pride versus happiness, participants construed data at a higher level.

Study 2 tests our theorizing more directly. Participants were randomly assigned to one of four conditions, where they experienced awe (abstract emotion) or happiness (concrete emotion)

through a writing task, or engaged in a laddering exercise that prompted lower or higher level construal. Participants then read a blog reviewing a new brand of chocolate chips. One blog reader's comments posted below the review described a recent experience at the target brand's store where a clerk who prepared a customized box of chocolate shortchanged the consumer. The box was either severely or slightly underweight. If abstract (vs. concrete) emotions correspond with higher (vs. lower) construal levels, then participants in these conditions should be sensitive to the degree of unethical behavior displayed by the clerk. Indeed, Eyal, Liberman and Trope (2008) found that a higher (vs. lower) construal level led people to respond more favorably to moral virtues and less favorably to moral transgressions. Thus, we expected participants who had experienced awe (vs. happiness) or whose laddering task induced a higher (vs. lower) level construal would be harsher in their judgments of the chocolate company. Supporting our theorizing, in both conditions where construal level was expected to be high (but not where it was low), evaluations were less favorable when unethical behavior was more versus less severe.

Study 3 explored yet another abstract emotion and examined its influence on creativity. Prior evidence indicates that the use of relational (but not item-specific) processing can elevate creativity (Friedman and Forster 2001). Particularly pertinent, however, theorists also suggest that relational processing may partially underlie abstract thought because relational thinking facilitates identification of commonalities, which fosters the production of higher level abstractions (Hunt and Einstein 1981). Based on this logic, we expected that among individuals who experience either the abstract emotion, hopefulness, versus a concrete emotion, happiness, performance on a creativity task is likely to vary depending on whether individuals also receive a priming task that incites either no particular processing type (i.e., control condition), item-specific processing, or relational processing. Assuming that relational processing truly contributes to abstract thinking, several hypotheses follow. First, under control conditions, creativity should be higher among participants who experience hopefulness versus happiness. In addition, creativity among those who experience the abstract emotion of hopefulness should be higher if they receive a control prime versus an item-specific prime, but their creativity should be higher still if they receive a relational prime. On the other hand, people who experience the concrete emotion of happiness should exhibit equal and relatively low levels of creativity regardless of receiving a control or item-specific prime, but their creativity should be enhanced if they receive a relational prime. Study 3, which was designed to test these hypotheses, offered some support for each of these predictions. Implications of our findings are discussed in light of recent work in construal level theory and complex emotions.

### "Benign Violations: Humor as a Mixed Emotional Experience"

*A. Peter McGraw, University of Colorado, Boulder, USA*
*Caleb Warren, University of Colorado, Boulder, USA*

Humor is frequently pursued by consumers and marketers but is not well understood by consumer researchers. We hypothesize that humor can be a mixed emotional experience. In five studies, we show that humor is aroused by benign violations and benign moral violations can elicit negative emotion as well as amusement.

Understanding humor is important for consumer research. Consumers seek humor in television, movies, and web content, while marketers attempt to deliver humor in feature entertainment (Martin 2007) and commercial interludes (Elpers, Mukherjee, and Hoyer 2004). Humor offers consumers hedonic benefits (Martin 2007) and helps attract attention and improve memory for marketing communications (Eisend 2009; Krishnan and Chakravarti 2003).

Although humor is typically considered a positive emotional experience (Gervais and Wilson 2005; Martin 2007), several theories suggest that humor requires some sort of violation, such as a threat, a norm breach, or taboo content (Freud 1928; Gruner 1997; Veatch 1998). Building on ideas proposed by humor theorists (Koestler 1964; Rothbart 1973; Veatch 1998), we hypothesize that humor is aroused by violations that simultaneously seem benign. Because a violation is a necessary condition to elicit humor, we suspect that successful humor attempts may be accompanied by negative emotion. Indeed, situations that encourage multiple interpretations often elicit mixed emotions (Larsen, McGraw, and Cacioppo 2001; Larsen et al. 2004; Andrade and Cohen 2007). Using marketing and consumer behaviors considered wrong, we test whether benign violations similarly elicit mixed emotions. Because moral violations typically cause disgust (Chapman et al. 2009) benign moral violations may cause amusement and disgust.

Study 1 investigates consumers' reactions to twelve morally questionable behaviors. For each scenario we constructed a control condition, describing a normal behavior, and a violation condition, describing a similar but potentially benign taboo behavior. In one scenario, for example, *Jimmy Dean* hires either a farmer (control) or a rabbi (violation) as a spokesperson for its pork products. Participants were more likely to respond to the violations with amusement (47% vs. 17%), disgust (58% vs. 10%), and mixed amusement and disgust (24% vs. 2%).

In Study 2 we observed behavioral responses rather than relying on self-report measures. An experimenter blind to condition was more likely to observe mixed emotional responses in participants' exposed to a violation, a man snorting his dead father's remains, than in participants exposed to a similar control behavior, a man burying his dead father's ashes (19% vs. 3%).

The remaining studies examine ways a behavior can be appraised as both a violation and benign. Benign violations may occur when one norm suggests the behavior is wrong but another salient norm suggests it is acceptable. Consequently, behaviors that are wrong according to one moral norm but acceptable according to another should elicit mixed emotions. Conversely, behaviors forbidden by both norms should elicit only negative emotions. In study 3, participants read an adapted scenario about a man rubbing his genitals against his pet kitten (Schnall et al. 2008). The behavior violates a norm against bestiality. We manipulated whether the behavior also was acceptable according to another norm based on harm. In the harmless condition, the kitten "purrs and seems to enjoy the contact." In the harmful condition, the kitten "whines and does not seem to enjoy the contact." Participants were equally disgusted by the two behaviors (94% vs. 94%). However, participants reported more amusement (61% vs. 28%) and mixed amusement and disgust (56% vs. 22%) in response to the harmless (vs. harmful) bestiality.

Consumers who are less committed to a moral norm have less at stake when that norm is violated. They may see the violation as benign and be both amused and disgusted. Conversely, consumers more committed to a moral norm should only be disgusted when that norm is violated. To test this hypothesis in Study 4, participants either read about a church (violation) or a credit union (control) that gives away a Hummer SUV as part of a promotion. Most consumers recognize that churches are sacred and should not be

governed by the same market-pricing norms as credit unions, which are secular (McGraw, Schwartz, and Tetlock 2010). However, only churchgoers are likely to be committed to this norm. As predicted, most non-churchgoers were both amused and disgusted by a church giving away a Hummer (69%). Churchgoers were also disgusted, but less likely to be amused (35%). There were no differences in the control condition.

Psychological distance may reduce the threat posed by a violation thereby making the violation seem benign and thus amusing. Study 5 tests this hypothesis by priming either far or near distance before exposure to a violation or a control scenario. After plotting points far from or near one another on a Cartesian plane (Williams and Bargh 2008), participants read a scenario adapted from Haidt and colleagues (1993) in which a man either *has sexual intercourse with* (violation) or *marinates* (control) a chicken before eating it. Compared to participants who plotted points close together, participants who plotted points far apart were significantly more likely to respond to the violation with amusement (73% vs. 39%) and with mixed emotions of amusement and disgust (64% vs. 28%). No differences were present in the control condition.

### "Choosing with Crying Smiles and Laughing Tears: The Dual Effects of Mixed Emotions on Variety Seeking"

*Jiewen Hong, Hong Kong University of Science and Technology, China*
*Angela Y. Lee, Northwestern University, USA*

This research examines the dual effects of mixed emotions on consumer variety seeking. Three experiments provide evidence that when people engage in affect regulation to reduce the conflicted feeling from mixed emotions, they seek less variety; however, people seek more variety when their focus is on the informational value of mixed emotions instead.

This research examines the influence of mixed emotions on decision making, and specifically, variety seeking. Following prior research (Ratner and Kahn 2002), variety seeking is conceptualized as the amount of variety chosen when selecting multiple items from a choice set on a single occasion. Building on the literature of affect regulation (e.g., Zillman 1988) and affect-as-information (e.g., Schwarz and Clore 1996), we argue that people's motivation to regulate their affect may prompt those who experience mixed emotions to narrow their scope of consideration when they attempt to reduce the feeling of conflictedness, which would in turn steer them toward committing to fewer options and seeking less variety. However, mixed emotions may also signal to people that they have multiple goals, which would in turn broaden their scope of consideration and lead to their seeking more variety.

Experiment 1 tested the dual effects of mixed emotions on variety seeking by manipulating the extent to which people feel conflicted from mixed emotions. The rationale is that if people experience conflictedness from mixed emotions, they are more likely to engage in affect regulation, which would in turn lead to less variety seeking. However, when people do not feel conflicted from mixed emotions, they are more likely to rely on mixed emotions as informational input, leading to more variety seeking. To vary whether people feel conflicted from mixed emotions, we manipulated participants' construal level: how abstractly or concretely they mentally represent information (Trope and Liberman 2003). We reason that mixed emotions would lead to less discomfort for those with high-level construals because they process information more inclusively and thus are better able to accommodate conflicts. Participants first completed a construal level manipulation in which they were asked to generate categories to which some objects belong (high-level construal induction), or exemplars of these objects (low-level construal induction; Fujita et al. 2006). Then they were asked to recall a mixed emotions life event (mixed emotions induction) or list activities from the past week (neutral induction). Finally, participants were asked to choose five M&M's from nine different colors of M&M's in any combination. Variety seeking was measured as the number of different colors of M&M's participants chose. As predicted, mixed emotions led to a feeling of conflictedness for participants primed with low-level construal, which in turn led to less variety seeking relative to the neutral control condition. The reverse occurred for those primed with high-level construals.

Experiment 2 tested the robustness of these findings by using a different method to operationalize affect regulation vs. affect-as-information. Participants first watched a video clip that either elicits mixed emotions or neutral affect. Then they were asked to perform a word fragment completion task to prime either a thinking or a feeling mindset. We reason that people are more motivated to reduce the conflicted feeling from mixed emotions when they focus on their feelings; but they should be more likely to draw inferences from their emotional state and incorporate it into their decision making when they focus on thinking. Finally, a similar measure of variety seeking as in Experiment 1 using candy bars was used. As hypothesized, we found that mixed emotions led to less variety seeking for participants primed to focus on feeling than the control, whereas the opposite occurred for those primed to focus on thinking.

The objectives of Experiment 3 were to provide convergent evidence by measuring participants' chronic inclination to regulate their affect, and to provide evidence for the mechanisms underlying the observed effects. Participants first completed a modified version of the Negative Mood Regulation Scale (Catanzaro and Mearns 1990) to measure their affect regulation tendency. The same emotion induction as in Experiment 2 was used. Participants were then asked to indicate how conflicted they felt and the extent to which they have multiple goals. To measure variety seeking, participants engaged in an actual choice task–they were asked to take 5 candy bars from 9 different bowls of candy bars. As predicted, results showed that mixed emotions led to less variety seeking among high affect-regulators compared to those in the control condition. Mediation analysis showed that this effect was driven by participants' feeling of conflictedness, providing evidence for the affect regulation mechanism. Conversely, mixed emotions led to more variety seeking among the low affect-regulators relative to the control, and this effect was mediated by participants' cognition of having multiple goals.

The current research adds to the mixed emotions literature by examining the influence of mixed emotions on consumer decision making via affect regulation and affect-as-information. It also adds to the literature on affect and decision making by demonstrating the unique affect regulation consequences and the informational property of mixed emotions, and identifying the conditions under which affect regulation vs. affect-as-information would occur.

### "Effects of Perspective-Taking on the Experience and Influence of Multiple Mixed Emotions"

*Iris W. Hung, National University of Singapore, Singapore*
*Anirban Mukhopadhyay, Hong Kong University of Science and Technology, China*

Mixed emotions may differ not only in valence, but also the extent to which they are hedonic vs. self-conscious. Four experiments examined the role of visual perspectives in the relative intensities of these mixed emotions, and their impact on effectiveness of emotion appeals of unrelated products that are subsequently encountered.

Consumers often experience mixed emotions when thinking about their decision or processing advertised situations about various real-life dilemmas. Would the use of different perspectives influence the way consumers interpret information described in these dilemmas, thereby affecting the relative intensity of mixed emotions and the effectiveness of emotional appeals? The present research examines two factors that might influence their responses in such situations. These are (1) the nature of the emotions (hedonic or self-conscious) that the advertisement elicits, and (2) the visual perspectives (whether they see themselves as actors or observers) that individuals use in appraising the advertisement.

Research in mixed emotions has focused on the simultaneous experience of mixtures of specific emotions (Larsen, McGraw, and Cacioppo 2001; Lau-Gesk 2005). In an impulse-buying situation, for example, one often feels both happy and guilty when deciding to buy (vs. not buy), and proud but sad when choosing not to buy (Mukhopadhyay and Johar 2007). These emotions not only differ in valence, but also in the extent to which they are hedonic (vs. self-conscious) in nature. Hedonic emotions such as happiness and sadness correspond to more immediate reactions toward an event, whereas self-conscious emotions such as pride and guilt correspond to more elaborate reactions toward that event (Giner-Sorolla 2001). Not much is known about the conditions that determine the relative intensities of hedonic vs. self-conscious emotions. We examine these issues in the context of self-control dilemmas. Specifically, we propose that the visual perspectives people employ in appraising a given self-control related situation can influence the relative intensities of the hedonic vs. self-conscious emotions they experience.

Jones and Nisbett (1972) suggest that the salience of information about the internal states of actors and observers differ in that actors tend to focus on circumstances involved in a given situation, whereas observers tend to focus on the actor in the situation. We propose that this difference in salience of information can lead to differences in emotional appraisals of the same event as perceived by actors and observers. We conjecture that when making a choice of a vice over a virtue, actors might experience a stronger feeling of more immediate emotions such as happiness than observers whereas observers who see themselves choosing a vice over a virtue might experience relatively stronger self-conscious emotions such as guilt. Further, based on an ease of processing account (Schwarz 2004), we suggest that these hedonic and self-conscious emotions could facilitate/undermine the processing of emotional appeals in advertising.

Four experiments support these propositions. Participants took either an actor's or an observer's perspective to process a choice that led to mixed hedonic and self-conscious emotions, and reported the emotions they felt (experiments 1-2). Regardless of the choice, actors [observers] indicated more intense hedonic [self-conscious] emotions than observers [actors].

Experiments 2 to 4 demonstrated that (1) the use of visual perspectives could influence the impact of emotions in advertising, and (2) this effect was mediated by the ease of processing of the emotional appeals. Participants viewed appeals that described a choice in a self-control dilemma (either choosing a virtue over a vice or a vice over a virtue) and an emotion that one could experience about this choice. The emotion described was positive self-conscious (pride), negative self-conscious (guilt), positive hedonic (happiness), or negative hedonic (sadness). Participants took either an actor or an observer perspective to process the appeal. Across experiments, we operationalized visual perspectives and emotion appeals in different ways to rule out alternative explanations. Specifically, participants recalled a previous self-control situation using an actor vs. observer perspective and then saw an ad for an unrelated product (experiment 2), had their visual perspective induced and then saw an ad that cued a related product (experiment 3), or had their visual perspective and emotion manipulated simultaneously by the same ad execution (experiment 4). Results consistently showed that the advertised product and the ad were evaluated more favorably when participants took an *actor* [*observer*] perspective than when they took an observer [*actor*] perspective to view a *hedonic* [*self-conscious*] emotion appeal. This effect was mediated by the ease of processing the emotional appeals, and was observed when the visual perspective was induced incidentally as well as integrally by the advertisement, and whether the advertisement was viewed subsequently or simultaneously.

Overall, results from these experiments shed new light on the role of situational factors (the nature of mixed emotions, and the use of visual perspectives to process events) in the experience and impact of mixed emotions on effectiveness of emotions appeals. Theoretical and practical implications will be discussed in the session.

SPECIAL SESSION

# Priming Susceptibility: The Role of the Self in Moderating Nonconscious Priming Effects

Heather Johnson, University of Maryland, USA
Amna Kirmani, University of Maryland, USA

## EXTENDED ABSTRACTS

### "The Role of the Self-Concept in Susceptibility to Priming Influences on Behavior"

*Dirk Smeesters, Erasmus University, The Netherlands*

Considerable research has demonstrated that behavior is influenced by construct accessibility, and there is rapidly growing evidence suggesting that susceptibility of the self-concept to influence can determine the susceptibility of individuals to primed constructs. In this presentation, we present several studies showing effects self-related processes can have in determining whether primed constructs will affect behavior.

A first factor that determines susceptibility to priming influences is the accessibility of the chronic self-concept. In the context of economic decision-making, two experiments tested whether participants with more accessible self-concept representations would be less likely to be influenced by primed constructs, but more likely to act in line with their chronic self-characteristics (Smeesters et al. 2009). Results of the first experiment showed that those who had highly accessible social value orientations acted in line with those self-representations and not with the primed constructs. Those who had less accessible social value orientations did *not* act in line with those self-representations, but rather acted consistently with the primed concepts. In a second experiment, the accessibility of the self-concept was manipulated. The primes affected participants whose self-concept was not made accessible by self-related words. However, when the accessibility of self-concept was increased, participants were no longer susceptible to the primed constructs.

A second factor that can determine susceptibility to priming influences is private self-consciousness. Past research on this dimension has found opposite effects: some demonstrated that private self-consciousness increased priming effects (Hull et al. 2002), whereas other showed that it decreased priming effects (Dijksterhuis and van Knippenberg 2000). Self-consciousness is a multifaceted construct containing two important dimensions: internal state awareness and self-reflectiveness (Wheeler, Morrison, DeMarree, and Petty 2008). Participants who score high on the internal state awareness factor of the private self-consciousness scale should be less susceptible to priming influences. Self-reflectiveness, on the other hand, might increase susceptibility to priming influences, as those who engage in self-reflection tend to process external feedback in terms of its implications for the self, thereby leading it to have greater effects on self-views and behavior (Wheeler et al. 2008). These predictions were tested in a study in which participants' scores on both internal state awareness and self-reflectiveness were measured (Wheeler et al. 2008). Results revealed independent interactions between primes and both internal state awareness and self-reflectiveness.

A third factor that can determine susceptibility to priming effects concerns the extent to which the context facilitates confusion of the primed content with one's actual self-views. When the context signals that a prime is "not me", it can diminish the prime's effect on behavior. In one experiment (Wheeler, Sleeth-Keppler, and Morrison 2010), non-Asian participants were subliminally primed with intelligence or not via a lexical decision task. Results indicated that the intelligence primes had an effect only when not preceded by Chinese characters, presumably because the Chinese characters signaled to non-Asian participants that the intelligence primes did not apply to them. In a follow-up study, participants

who identified or disidentified with math were subliminally primed with the elderly stereotype (or not). Either math symbols or a row of XXX served as forward and back masks to the priming stimuli. These results are consistent with the idea that the math symbols served as a signal as to whether the prime was self-relevant or not.

These studies contribute to a growing body of research showing the important role that the self-concept can play in prime-to-behavior effects and emphasize the importance of the self-concept in driving behavior.

### "Priming Susceptibility: The Moderating Role of Self-Brand Connection on Nonconscious Priming Effects"

*Heather M. Johnson, University of Maryland, USA*
*Amna Kirmani, University of Maryland, USA*

This paper proposes that self-brand connection serves an important moderator of priming effects. Self-brand connection reflects the extent to which a brand fits with one's self-concept (Escalas and Bettman 2005). Counter to prior research demonstrating main effects of nonconscious cue exposure, we predict an inverted U-shaped effect: consumers with a moderate level of self-brand connection to a target brand are more susceptible to a nonconscious prime's influence on their subsequent purchase intentions toward the target brand. For these individuals, a nonconscious prime renders related constructs accessible and this fluency effect will increase purchase intentions toward the product, consistent with main effects findings in the nonconscious priming literature (Berger and Fitzsimons 2008). However, consumers' high and low self-brand connection to a target brand shields them from influence of nonconscious cues.

In addition, we predict that consumers' self-brand connection to a competing brand also influences behavioral intentions toward a prime-congruent (target) brand after encountering a nonconscious prime related to that target brand. For example, if John has high self-brand connection to Nike he may be resistant to the influence of a Puma-related incidental cue on his propensity to purchase Puma. We show that this prediction holds, and interestingly that a nonconscious prime may even prompt individuals high in self-brand connection to a competing brand to express *decreased* purchase intentions toward the target brand.

Two experiments demonstrate the moderating effect. In the first study, we measured self-brand connection for both target (Puma) and competing brands prior to participants' encounter with a dog prime, and show that individuals with low or high self-brand connection are less susceptible to the prime. Study 2 employs a novel priming paradigm to provide generalizability to a different product domain, laptop computers. Participants again provided self-brand connection ratings for target (Apple) and competing brands in the category (e.g., Dell) and were exposed to an incidental cue related to the target brand (the flavor orange). We again show that by increasing the accessibility of the target brand for consumers moderate in self-brand connection, the prime can lead to increased purchase intentions, while consumers low or high in self-brand connection for the target or competing brands in the category do not express increased purchase intentions for the target brand. Interestingly—and importantly for marketing practitioners—we find that individuals with high self-brand connection for Dell express decreased purchase intentions for Apple laptops upon encounters with the Apple-related prime. These empirical findings extend recent main effect studies demonstrating a nonconscious prime's influence on purchase intentions by showing that consumers' susceptibility to these influences is based on self-brand connection.

## "The Effect of Action and Inaction Goal Primes on Consumers' Information Processing"
### *Juliano Laran, University of Miami, USA*

Action and inaction primes have been shown to influence motor output, such as doodling on a piece of paper and eating, and cognitive output, such as recall and problem solving (Albarracin et al. 2008). These primes can influence decision satisfaction, choice satisfaction, and ultimately the likelihood that consumers will be willing to perform behavior congruent with a marketer's intent (i.e., buy a given product). In other words, action and inaction primes make consumers more susceptible to performing *any* behavior intended by a marketer if the goal can be satisfied. I predict that priming of an action goal will make consumers willing to evaluate an increased amount of product information and be highly satisfied with the decision process when choice sets offer a lot of attribute information. Alternatively, priming of an inaction goal will make consumers willing to evaluate fewer pieces of product information and be highly satisfied with the decision process when choice sets offer only few pieces of attribute information. Satisfaction with the decision process may influence choice satisfaction and the likelihood to buy the chosen brand.

All studies were composed of three phases. In phase 1, participants were told that they would participate in a sentence recall test. Participants were exposed to ten sentences, which could be action-oriented (e.g., "you can do it"), inaction-oriented (e.g., "you deserve to relax"), or neutral, depending on the goal priming condition. In phase 2, an ostensibly unrelated study, participants were asked to make choice between two brands of digital cameras. In the low load condition, I presented information about 4 attributes, whereas in the high load condition, I presented information about 9 product attributes. In phase 3, participants were asked a series of questions, including satisfaction with the process of deciding which brand to choose and satisfaction with the chosen option. In study 1, participants in the action goal prime condition showed higher decision satisfaction when making a choice from a choice set offering high information load than when making a choice from a choice set offering low information load. Participants in the inaction goal prime condition showed higher decision satisfaction when making a choice from a choice set offering low information load than when making a choice from a choice set offering high information load. There was no influence of information load in the neutral prime condition. Choice satisfaction was found to be fully mediated by decision satisfaction. In a similar study, decision satisfaction also led to an increased likelihood that people would actually purchase the brand.

Study 2 examined whether these results would extend to actual behavior. Participants primed with an action goal were willing to donate more money to their favorite charity when a lot of information was presented. Participants primed with an inaction goal were willing to donate more money to their favorite charity when little information was presented. These results suggest that allowing people to process an amount of information congruent with a primed action or inaction processing goal makes them more susceptible to an external agent's influence outside of their awareness.

Study 3 manipulated goal achievement by having participants perform an action (i.e., solve GRE problems) vs. an inaction (i.e., close eyes and relax) task after being exposed to the goal primes. In the action (inaction) goal prime condition, after having performed an action (inaction) task, participants were more satisfied with the

decision process and showed higher likelihood of purchasing the chosen brand when the choice set offered low (high) information load.

## "Individual Susceptibility to Priming Effects"
### *Stacy Wood, University of South Carolina, USA*
### *Cait Poynor, University of Pittsburgh, USA*
### *Tanya Chartrand, Duke University, USA*

The purpose of this research is to test the susceptibility concept and identify the characteristics that would contribute to individual differences in susceptibility to priming (STP). While priming researchers would benefit from the creation of an STP scale because it would serve as a useful covariate, consumer behaviorists are likely to be interested in the concept of STP because of its implications for advertising efficacy. We posit that, counter to intuition, people who are both attentive to their environment and have a tendency to strong associational processing are those who are *most* susceptible to priming. Indeed, the mechanisms by which priming work suggest that primes require 1) physical (but not necessarily aware) exposure and 2) associative processing, suggesting two paths to priming susceptibility. We build on this conceptual development to generate a simple 6-item reflective STP measure. Three studies demonstrate that our STP index does predict the magnitude of an individual's response to a prime.

Study 1 demonstrates that priming individuals with concepts of the elderly (akin to the "walking to the elevator" study by Bargh, Chen, and Burrows [1996]) can influence susceptible consumers to "move slowly" in consumer domain, specifically in adversely affecting their attitude toward the speed of high tech product innovations. In study 1, we expose participants to a modified version of an "elderly prime and test the impact of this prime on responses to a survey about attitudes toward the speed of technological change; specifically, we predict that an elderly prime will serve to decrease reported attitudes toward speedy innovation. We anticipate that the STP index will moderate the effect of this prime, such that priming effects are strongest for those with higher STP.

Participants engaged in two ostensibly unrelated tasks that were, together, the focal task. In the first part of this task, participants filled out a survey that asked them to look at a list of brand names for products (e.g., Dasani water, Kleenex tissues) and to identify which brands they thought were American brands and which brands were Canadian brands. In the elderly prime condition, six fictional brand names were words associated with the elderly (e.g., Bingo cookies, Slow-Pour syrup). In the neutral condition, these words were replaced with unrelated words (e.g., Bell cookies, Sweet-Pour syrup). Participants then moved on to another separate survey about their attitudes about high tech products intended to tap into participants' attitude toward the pace of technological change.

We first created an STP index for each participant by averaging across the 6 STP items (?=0.76, M=5.57, SD=.74). We then analyzed the data using the STP index and the prime condition of the participant as predictors of attitudes towards technological change. The main effect of the prime (F(1, 151)=.14, p=.71) was not significant. However, there was a significant overall interaction of priming condition and STP scale score (F(1, 151)=4.08, p=.04). We then probed the nature of this interaction using spotlight analysis as suggested by Aiken and West (1991). This analysis indicates that the prime was ineffective for low and moderate STP individuals, who did not rate technology differently than did their unprimed counterparts (moderate: $M_{prime}$=4.92, $M_{no\ prime}$=4.85, F(1,151)=.14, p=.71; low: $M_{prime}$=4.77, $M_{no\ prime}$=5.09, F(1,151)=1.41, p=.49). However, among high STP individuals, the prime did have an effect. Higher STP individuals exposed to the elderly prime were significantly more likely to describe the pace of technological change as too fast (M=5.08) than those not exposed to the prime (M=4.61, F(1,151)=3.46, p=.05).

Studies 2 and 3 further support our hypotheses. Study 2 demonstrates that a subtle work-oriented prime can alter prime-susceptible college students to report increased intentions to study. Study 3 demonstrates that priming the concept of promotion versus prevention (Aaker and Lee 2006) within an advertisement can increase susceptible consumers' valuation of a promotion-congruent product attribute. These studies provide insight both into susceptibility to primes and to the nature of the prime itself: In some cases, the use of the index provides more nuanced interpretation of an apparently robust prime, showing that its overall effect is actually localized to only a subset of the population. In other cases, the use of the index allows a weak or marginally-significant aggregate effect of a prime to be understood as quite strong if only among a section of the sample.

## REFERENCES

Albarracín, Dolores, Ian M. Handley, Kenji Noguchi, Kathleen C. McCulloch, Hong Li, Joshua Leeper, Rick D. Brown, Allison Earl, and William P. Hart (2008), "Increasing and Decreasing Motor and Cognitive Output: A Model of General Action and Inaction Goals," *Journal of Personality and Social Psychology*, 95, 510-23.

Berger, Jonah, and Grainne Fitzsimons (2008), "Dogs on the Street, Pumas on Your Feet: How Cues in the Environment Influence Product Evaluation and Choice," *Journal of Marketing Research*, 45 (1), 1-14.

Chartrand, Tanya L., Joel Huber, Baba Shiv, and Robin J. Tanner (2008), "Nonconscious Goals and Consumer Choice," *Journal of Consumer Research*, 35 (August), 189-201.

Escalas, Jennifer Edson, and James R. Bettman (2005), "Self?Construal, Reference Groups, and Brand Meaning," *Journal of Consumer Research*, 32 (3), 378-389

Hull, Jay G., Slone, Laurie B., Karen B. Meteyer, and Amanda R. Matthews (2002), "The Non-consciousness of Self-Consciousness," *Journal of Personality and Social Psychology*, 83, 406–424.

Smeesters, Dirk, Vincent Y. Yzerbyt, Olivier Corneille, and Luk Warlop (2009), "When Do Primes Prime? The Moderating Role of the Self-Concept in Individuals' Susceptibility to Priming Effects on Social Behavior," *Journal of Experimental Social Psychology*, 45, 211–216.

Smeesters, Dirk, S. Christian Wheeler, and Aaron C. Kay (2010), "Indirect Prime-to-Behavior Effects: The Role of the Self, Others, and Situations in Connecting Primed Constructs to Social Behavior," *Advances in Experimental Social Psychology*, 42, 259-317.

Wheeler, S. Christian and Kenneth G. DeMarree (2009), "Multiple Mechanisms of Prime-to-Behavior Effects," *Social and Personality Psychology Compass*, 3, 566–581.

Wheeler, S. Christian, Kimberly R. Morrison, Kenneth G. DeMarree, and Richard E. Petty (2008). Does Self-consciousness Increase or Decrease Behavioral Priming Effects? It Depends," *Journal of Experimental Social Psychology*, 44, 882–889.

# When Do Goals Succeed Versus Fail? Effects of Consumer Beliefs on Self-Regulation
Claudia Townsend, University of Miami, USA

## EXTENDED ABSTRACTS

### "Choice as Magic: Using Current Consumption to Control Uncertain Future Outcomes"
Soraya Lambotte, University of Chicago, USA
Aparna A. Labroo, University of Chicago, USA
Ravi Dhar, Yale University, USA

We propose that people attempt to control the fate of uncertain future outcomes by being virtuous in their current consumption choices. When hoping for a positive outcome for which they feel responsible, or fearing a bad outcome due to chance, they reason, "If I am good, then good things will happen to me," and thus make virtuous current choices in an attempt to improve their potential position.

"If the conductor arrives before I count to seven, he (my fiancé) is alive."
~ Audrey Tatou as Mathilde, A Very Long Engagement (2004)

In waiting for important news over which you have no control, such as the review of a submitted paper, or a job offer, you may hope for the best, and fear the worse. That is, you may hope for a positive review, or an offer, and yet fear getting neither. In such a situation in which the end product is out of your hands, how might you respond? Would you decide to indulge yourself by going shopping, or eating unhealthy foods, or would you decide to be virtuous and exert restraint, and go exercise or do nothing of major consequence until all the results are in? And why should you modify your current consumption in any way, after all, the uncertain future outcome has nothing to do with the current consumption choices you are considering.

In the present research, we explore how people use their current consumption choices in an attempt to exert control over uncertain future outcomes. We look at why one may decide to engage in a virtuous choice over an indulgent one when making a current choice depending on one's perceived level responsibility for an uncertain future outcome and whether one is focused on hoping for the best or fearing the worst for the very same outcome. In particular, we find that people who generally have an indulgence goal, will show restraint and be virtuous by making healthy food choices in two cases: when they hope for a positive outcome for which they feel responsible, and when they fear a negative outcome for which they do not feel responsible. Specifically, in a 2 (responsibility: self vs. external) x 2 (outcome focus: hope vs. fear) x 2 (goal: indulgence vs. health) between-subjects design, participants were asked to recall a time during which they felt responsible for an outcome (vs. attributed to chance) that could go either way, as they hoped for the best or feared the worst. After this task, in an unrelated choice task, participants were asked to make a series of snack food choices, picking between healthy and unhealthy options. Those participants who felt responsible for the event described and hoped for the best, self-regulated, and made indulgence-goal inconsistent choices in an attempt to regulate fate. Conversely, participants who attributed the event to chance, indulged when they hoped for a good outcome, but showed restraint and were virtuous when they feared a bad outcome. This pattern of effects was only found among indulgent people, who by not indulging, could maintain their good fortune (in the case in which they felt responsible for a good outcome),

or improve their standing (in the case in which they feared a bad outcome due to chance). "If I am being good," the reasoning goes, "then good things will happen to me, and I will not tempt fate," and so in each of these cases, participants tried to improve their potential outcomes by being virtuous. Those with a health goal did not show a similar pattern of results, they generally made healthy choices in line with their overarching goal. To complement this finding, in a follow-up study, we further tested people's belief in magic, which leads them to be virtuous in their current choices when they want to improve or maintain their expected outcome. That is, when they feel responsible for a good outcome, or when they do not feel responsible for a bad outcome, they make virtuous current choices, so as not to tempt fate, and potentially demean or worsen their position in the future, as past research has shown that people hold the intuition that actions which tempt fate increase the likelihood of negative outcomes.

This research thus provides first evidence of how people use current choice to exert control over uncertain future outcomes. People who are generally indulgent use self-regulation as magic in order to try and improve the odds of a future outcome when hoping for the best and feeling responsible for the outcome, and when fearing the worst for an outcome one is not responsible for. Moreover, such behavior is mediated by feelings and perceptions of luck, such that people will engage increasingly in this self-regulatory behavior, the more they believe in luck and fear tempting fate.

### "Lay Theories of Obesity"
Brent McFerran, University of British Columbia, Canada
Anirban Mukhopadhyay, Hong Kong University of Science and Technology, China

Four experiments demonstrate that people mainly hold one of two different lay theories about what causes obesity: poor diet and lack of exercise. These lay theories influence food quantity decisions, and influencing their accessibility changes portion sizes chosen. Non-dieters are more likely to change behavior due to such interventions.

Consumers make over 200 food choices per day, and obesity has become a severe public health concern in many countries. Diet and exercise guides advocate numerous approaches to weight loss, variously implicating genetics, consumption, and exercise in explaining our expanding waistlines. While some authors point to sedentary lifestyles (Blair and Brodney 1999) or genetics (Comuzzi and Allison 1998), the strongest evidence implicates a marked increase in consumption of food and drink as the main driver of obesity (Young and Nestle 2002). Consumer researchers have investigated several factors that help explain this increase in eating. These include social influence (McFerran et al. 2010), regulatory focus (Sengupta and Zhou 2007), and recollections of prior instances of indulgence or restraint (Mukhopadhyay, Sengupta, and Ramanathan 2008). Of interest, recent research has demonstrated that consumers' food choices may be influenced by their lay theories, or naïve beliefs, such as those pertaining to self-control (Mukhopadhyay and Johar 2005) or emotions (Labroo and Mukhopadhyay 2009).

In this research, we take a more direct approach and examine the prevalence and consequences of lay theories about the causes of obesity itself, and demonstrate how they can profoundly influence consumers' food quantity decisions. Dar Nimrod and Heine (2010) report that people who believe that obesity is caused by genetic factors tend to eat more than those who believe it is caused by social reasons (Christakis and Fowler (2007). We extend this work by proposing that consumers have other, more prevalent lay theories of obesity: specifically, consumers largely believe that obesity is caused either by poor diet or by lack of exercise. Further, we predict that all else equal, those who believe that not exercising causes obesity eat more than those who believe that it is caused by a poor diet.

We tested our basic proposition in a survey of 100 Amazon.com users (N=100, 47% male, mean age 34). Respondents indicated what they thought was the primary cause of obesity: eating too much, not exercising enough, or genetics, and allocated 100 points among the options. Results indicated equal numbers of respondents sharing the diet and exercise lay theories (44 vs. 48); which was reflected in the points allocation (Ms=44.06 vs. 38.97). The genetics lay theory was far less prevalent (8 respondents, M=17.05). This is initial evidence supporting the prevalence of our lay theories of interest.

Study 2 tested whether lay theories about the relative importance of diet and exercise can actually affect consumption quantities. Participants were given a cup of chocolates while they filled out some unrelated questionnaires, including a measure assessing the relative weights of their lay theories of obesity. We found that those who believed that a lack of exercise was relatively more likely to cause obesity ate more chocolates from their given cups.

Study 3 aimed to establish the causal effects of these lay theories. Following Labroo and Mukhopadhyay (2009), participants read a paragraph, purportedly real research, which either stated that obesity is caused by diet or by exercise. As a second factor, they recalled a previous instance when they had resisted a tempting food or had succumbed to it (Mukhopadhyay et al. 2008). The order of the lay theory induction and the recall task was counterbalanced. Finally, they were presented with a hypothetical task involving making selections at an ice-cream parlor (McFerran et al. 2010). Results provided strong support for the role of lay theories as accessible cognitions in influencing eating quantity decisions. When the recall task came first, implying that lay theories were more accessible, those who had been primed with the exercise (versus diet) lay theory chose significantly more ice cream. When the recall task came second, those who read about the exercise theory chose smaller quantities, but only if they had recalled resisting.

Study 4 tested if certain types of individuals are more susceptible to lay theory inductions. Chronic dieters have a highly accessible goal of consumption restraint (Scott et al. 2008), and thus may be less likely to accept alternative lay theories. Unrestrained eaters have no such chronic preoccupation, and thus may be more likely to use other accessible cognitions (i.e., lay theories) to guide their behavior. Procedures followed the Study 3 lay theory first/succumb condition, except real consumption was measured (as in Study 2). Results revealed that dieters consumed the same amount regardless of whether the article claimed diet or exercise as the cause of obesity, but unrestrained eaters ate more if they had read the exercise article than the diet one.

Across four studies, we provide the first evidence that (a) people have mainly two different lay theories about what causes obesity (diet vs. exercise), (b) these lay theories guide actual food choices, (c) the accessibility of these lay theories can be influenced to change portion sizes, and (d) non-dieters are more likely to change behavior as a result of alternative lay theories. These results help answer the big picture question of what causes obesity, by explaining a large part of consumers' portion sizes.

## "Is making plans good for you? The Differential Impact of Planning on Behavior"
*Claudia Townsend, University of Miami, USA*
*Wendy Liu, UC San Diego, USA*

In four field studies we find that planning does not benefit everyone equally. Although making plans improves subsequent behavior when individuals consider their position positive in the relevant area, ironically making plans has a deleterious effect on actual behavior when decision-makers feel in poor standing in the relevant domain.

Both academic research and lay beliefs suggest that planning is advantageous for goal attainment and self-regulation (see for example Gollwitzer 1996, Schifter and Ajzen 1985). Yet, little is known about the emotional response to planning and how this may influence subsequent behavior. We consider that planning for self-regulation may produce emotional responses similar to those of positive self-statements and positive feedback which are not always constructive. While positive thinking and positive feedback are generally thought to improve mood and affect, there are instances when a boomerang effect can occur leading to worsened mood (Eisenstadt and Leippe 1994, Wood, Perunovic, and Lee 2009). The explanation is that when people feel that the feedback or positive statement is too positive and does not fit their self-conceptions, the discrepancy between their believed actual self and the idealized self as described by the feedback or statements becomes particularly salient. Like positive statements and feedback, by creating a plan one is, in essence, describing the acts of a possible future superior version of the self. If this possible future self as described in the plan is too different from one's perceived actual self then the plan may be outside the "latitudes of acceptance" and lead to psychological reactance (Sherif and Hovland 1961). We predict this will result in negative emotions such as stress which, in turn, likely might cause someone's actions to boomerang–and go in opposition to the proposed plan. Thus, while planning may be helpful for some, it may be harmful for those whose perceived self is dramatically different from the future self as described in the plan. The difference in these two selves promotes negative feelings such as stress leading to less goal-consistent behavior. Specifically, our hypothesis is that those who perceive themselves to be in good standing with respect to the relevant goal will be helped by planning with planning causing more goal-consistent behavior. Those who perceive themselves not to be in good standing are actually less likely to behave goal-consistently after planning than in the absence of planning. We examine this in four field studies.

In study 1 we consider the impact of planning on eating–whether planning one's diet has a positive or negative effect on subsequent snack choice. We find that those who perceive themselves as not overweight are aided by planning; planning decreases likelihood of selecting the unhealthy snack. However, those who perceive themselves as overweight are hindered by planning with planning increasing their likelihood of selecting the unhealthy snack. We also isolate the effect to planning in the relevant context, thus ruling out an explanation based on ego depletion (Baumeister, Bratslavsky, Muraven, and Tice 1998). Additionally, we examine the content of the plans and find that more and less confident people do not differ in the plans they make revealing that any differences in behavior are not due to plan content.

In study 2 we investigate the mechanism through which this occurs–how planning interacts with one's sense of security in the relevant area. We examine how planning makes people feel and whether one's emotional response to planning differs depending on perceived standing in the relevant area (overweight or not for our diet context). We find that for respondents who are not in good standing in the relevant domain planning calls attention to their deficit in the domain and accentuates how much demanding work they must accomplish in order to improve. Planning is, therefore, a stressful and upsetting task for them. In contrast, respondents in good standing do not find planning to be stressful or upsetting.

In the third study we use the same context of the impact of planning on eating, but also examine whether manipulation of perceived standing in the relevant area impacts behavior. A shortcoming of studies 1 and 2 is that self-perception is measured rather than manipulated and there may be a spurious correlation. In study 3 we manipulate whether someone feels in good or poor standing in the relevant area *after* the plans are made and, indeed, find this to affect the impact of planning as predicted.

In the fourth and final study, we consider the impact of planning in a different context–saving. We analyze consumers' use of the 2008 Economic Stimulus Tax Rebate and whether planning one's use of the money has a positive or negative effect on how it is spent. Study 4 replicates our original findings in another context and in several ways offers a more stringent test of our theory.

The findings presented in this research are relevant to numerous areas including work on goals, habits, self-regulation, and behavioral change. Implications on when and how planning should or should not be advocated are also discussed.

## "The Effects of Goal Breadth on Consumer Preferences"

*Eunice Kim, Yale University, USA*
*Ravi Dhar, Yale University, USA*

Broadly versus narrowly defining a goal affects choice. A series of studies demonstrates that individuals with a broader focal goal are more likely to choose a high price, high quality option over a low price, low quality option because broader goals decrease the consideration of the other relevant goals that shoppers have, such as the goal to be frugal.

While most of the goals research examines how a single goal affects choices and subsequent evaluations, in reality, individuals simultaneously maintain multiple goals that can interact to affect choices (Fishbach and Dhar 2005). Shah and Kruglanski (2002) state that for any given goal—a focal goal—individuals can also have other goals in that context, referred to as alternative or background goals, which can affect the pursuit of that focal goal. A question that arises is how focal and background goals interact to affect choice.

The current research examines how the breadth of the focal goal, whether it is broad (e.g. goal to buy clothes) or narrow (e.g. goal to buy jeans), influences the extent to which these other alternative or background goals are considered (e.g. goal to be frugal), and therefore leads to very different choice outcomes. To examine why and how the breadth of a focal goal might affect consumer choice, we rely on recent advances in a theory of goal systems by Kruglanski and his colleagues (2002). According to this framework, goals are described as an inter-related network of nodes. We propose that the setting of a broad focal goal leads to a spreading of activation to a greater number of related sub-goals and means. The activation of more sub-goals and means requires the consumption of more cognitive resources. This means that fewer resources remain for the consideration of other relevant background goals in any given context. The setting of a narrow focal goal, however, activates fewer related sub-goals and means, which leads to the consumption of fewer cognitive resources, and therefore leaves more resources for the consideration of other background goals. Thus, we propose that individuals who are assigned to a broad focal goal are less likely to consider other goals that are relevant to a shopping context, such as the goal to be frugal, than are individuals assigned to a narrow focal goal. As a consequence, those individuals assigned to a broad focal goal are more likely to choose the option that is best on the focal goal.

A series of studies test these hypotheses. These studies are generally composed of two parts. The first part is goal activation where participants are randomly assigned to either a broad or a narrow focal goal by imagining a broad focal goal (e.g. buy clothes) or a narrow focal goal (e.g. buy jeans) and writing about it. The second part is the choice task. Studies 1 and 2 find that individuals with a broad focal goal are more likely to choose a more expensive, higher-quality option compared to individuals with a narrow focal goal. In addition, these studies rule out two potential alternative accounts. The first account is that a broad goal might activate a more abstract mindset that focuses people on aspects of desirability (Liberman and Trope 1998). We address this by demonstrating that the effect of goal breadth on choice, unlike the effect of mindsets, does not carry over to all subsequent tasks but only applies to choices between goal-related options. A second alternative account is that a broad goal might call upon a larger mental budget that makes it easier to spend (Morewedge, Holtzman, and Epley 2007). We find, however, that even when participants are given a fixed budget, those with the broad focal goal are more likely to choose the high quality expensive option compared to those with the narrow focal goal.

The next set of studies examines the underlying mechanism. Study 3 shows that when participants with a narrow focal goal are subjected to a cognitive load task, which consumes cognitive resources, the competing background goal to be frugal becomes less accessible, and the difference in the preference for the higher priced option across goal breadth is attenuated. Studies 4a and 4b employ various methods, including a lexical decision task, to demonstrate that a broad focal goal increases the accessibility of various sub-goals and means, but decreases the accessibility of the goal to be frugal. Study 5 demonstrates that this effect may be bounded by the chronic activation of a frugality goal. Study 6 extends the effect of goal breadth beyond the domain of shopping to the domain of health and consumption. Lastly, Study 7 examines the intuitions held by people regarding the effect of goal breadth on consumer preferences.

We demonstrate that the breadth of a focal goal plays an important role in how multiple goals interact by influencing the extent to which background goals are considered in choice. Furthermore, these findings have implications for how consumers can set broad or narrow goals to aid in self-control.

# The Excluded Consumer: Impacts of Social Exclusion on Consumer Behavior
Yuwei Jiang, Hong Kong Polytechnic University, China

## EXTENDED ABSTRACTS

### "Lonely are the Brave: Effects of Social Exclusion on Consumer Risk-Taking"

*Echo Wen Wan, University of Hong Kong, China*
*Yuwei Jiang, Hong Kong Polytechnic University, China*
*Rod Duclos, Hong Kong University of Science and Technology, China*

Social exclusion, i.e., feeling ignored or rejected, is common in life (Baumeister et al. 2005; Williams 2007). Receiving a cold treatment from coworkers, being "dumped" by a significant other, getting evicted from a social organization are just a few examples of such unfortunate fate. The current research examines the impact of social exclusion on consumers' risk-taking in financial decision-making.

Previous research finds that experiencing social exclusion leads to feeling hurt, pain, and loneliness (Sommer et al. 2001). In turn, these feelings increase one's motivation to forge new social bonds (Maner et al. 2007). But how can one rebuild social connections after being rejected? According to Zhou, Vohs, and Baumeister (2009), ostracized individuals can use *money* to regain access to their social world and derive benefits from it once again. Building on this work, we predicted that consumers would respond to social exclusion by engaging in riskier but more lucrative investment opportunities.

To test this proposition, we invited participants in study 1 to play Cyberball (Williams et al. 2000), an online ball-tossing game intended to manipulate one's state of social inclusion versus exclusion. Next, in a seemingly unrelated study, subjects indicated their preference between two hypothetical gambles of equal expected utility (i.e., 20% chance of winning $800 vs. 80% chance of winning $200). As predicted, socially-excluded participants favored the riskier option more strongly than their included counterparts.

Though encouraging, study 1 leaves several questions unanswered. For instance, what is the directional impact of social exclusion on financial decision-making? I.e., does exclusion lead to riskier behavior (as theorized earlier), or does inclusion lead to preferring safer options? Furthermore, could affect (rather than social exclusion itself) be the real driving force behind our effect? After all, it is conceivable indeed that interpersonal rejection also leads to negative mood.

To answer these questions, we invited participants in study 2 to elaborate on one of four personal experiences. Per our theorizing, subjects in the first two conditions recalled a social experience where they felt either included or excluded (Pickett et al. 2004). To assess the directional impact of social exclusion, we added a control condition where participants recalled everything they ate and drank in the last 48 hours. Lastly, to rule out affect as an alternative explanation for our effect, we added a negative-mood condition where subjects recalled an instance during which they experienced physical pain (e.g., migraine, tooth ache). Next, in a seemingly unrelated gambling study, participants indicated their preference between two options of *un*equal expected utility (i.e., a 20% chance of winning $200 vs. a sure gain of $30). To make our task consequential, we bound participants in this study to their choice and paid them accordingly. As predicted, socially-excluded subjects exhibited stronger preferences for the riskier but more lucrative option than their counterparts in both the control and negative-mood conditions. Interestingly, socially-included

participants also differed from the latter two conditions, but in the *opposite* direction. I.e., included subjects exhibited strong risk aversion and preferred a sure gain of $30 over a more lucrative but uncertain gamble. These results replicate and extend those of study 1 in two ways: first, by contrasting the directional impact of social exclusion (vs. inclusion) on financial decision-making; second, by ruling out affect as an alternative mechanism for our effect. Indeed, while we readily concur that social exclusion is likely to be accompanied by negative mood, the latter (by itself) failed to replicate the effect documented across experiments.

From a theoretical perspective, our studies contribute to the literature by documenting and nuancing a new effect, that of social exclusion (vs. inclusion) on financial decision-making. Furthermore, by disentangling negative mood from social exclusion, these findings also shed light on the consequences proper to interpersonal rejection per se. Lastly, from a societal perspective, our results illustrate the significant impact that common experiences such as feeling rejected versus accepted can have on consumers' daily lives.

### "Does A Broken Heart Lead to an Empty Wallet? Exclusion Increases Willingness to Pay for Unappealing and Illegal Products"

*Nicole L. Mead, Tilburg University, The Netherlands*
*Roy F. Baumeister, Florida State University, USA*
*Kathleen D. Vohs, University of Minnesota, USA*
*Tyler F. Stillman, Florida State University, USA*
*Catherine D. Rawn, University of British Columbia, Canada*

Humans are a hyper-social species and have a fundamental need for positive social relationships. Consequently, people experience social exclusion as deeply aversive. How does social exclusion influence personal spending? Prior research suggests several possibilities, such as mimicking others' choices, impulse spending, and buying lovely gifts to relieve the sting of rejection and self-soothe. However, accumulating research suggests that the need to belong conforms to a specific pattern: when it is thwarted, people become motivated to affiliate with others. We therefore hypothesized that socially excluded people would use personal spending as a way to build social bonds. Specifically, in two experiments we tested whether social exclusion would increase willingness to consume products that were (1) expressly unappealing and (2) illegal and potentially harmful to the self when doing so could help commence or cement a social relationship.

In experiment 1, we tested whether social exclusion would increase participants' willingness to spend on an unfamiliar and visually unappetizing food item: chicken feet. To manipulate social exclusion, participants completed a personality test and received false feedback concerning how their personality would impact future social connections. Participants assigned to the exclusion condition were led to believe they could anticipate a life devoid of social connections whereas participant assigned to the acceptance condition were led to believe they could anticipate a life full of strong social connections.

After the manipulation, participants ostensibly shared information with their partner about their food preferences in preparation for the food-tasting task. In reality, participants received a sheet filled out by a same-sex confederate, which indicated that his or her favorite food was chicken feet. After viewing this information, participants were shown a slide show of four different foods from around the world (chicken feet, borscht, black pudding, and herring). They were asked to indicate their willingness to pay for each item, ostensibly because it would be used to determine which food item they would sample at the conclusion of the experiment.

However, before indicating willingness to pay, we varied whether preferences would be visible to the partner and whether participants had an opportunity to affiliate with the partner. This was done to ensure that increased willingness to spend on the chicken feet was a function of desire to affiliate rather than passive mimicry or conformity. In the public/interaction condition, participants were led to believe their spending intentions would be public and that they would sample the food item with their partner. In the private/interaction condition, spending intentions were not public but the joint tasting would take place. In the public/no interaction condition, spending intentions were visible but no joint tasting would take place. As predicted, exclusion only increased willingness to spend on the chicken feet when both spending intentions were made public and they had the opportunity to meet their partner, indicating that socially excluded people were not simply mimicking or conforming to their partner's preferences.

In experiment 2, we sought to extend the finding of experiment 1 to willingness to consume an illicit substance. First, participants were randomly assigned to recall a time in which they felt socially accepted, socially excluded, or when they were ill (negative non-social control). After the social exclusion manipulation, participants received one of two scenarios. Participants in the private condition imagined that one night, when they were home alone, they found some cocaine that had been left behind by a new friend. Participants in the public condition were asked to imagine that a new friend asked them to do cocaine with him or her when they were out at a party. All participants were asked to indicate how willing they were to try the drug. Results showed that, as compared to socially accepted and negative non-social control participants, socially excluded participants reported a higher willingness to use the cocaine, but only in the public condition. In the private condition, there was no difference in willingness or desire to use the cocaine as a function of the social exclusion condition. Additional analyses indicated that mood did not mediate the effect of social exclusion on increased desire to try the cocaine.

In sum, results from two experiments provide support for our hypothesis that socially excluded people use spending as a way to build new social bonds. The present studies suggest that the social motivation of affiliation has direct implications for consumption that are both theoretically and practically meaningful.

### "If I Ignore You, You Spend; If I Reject You, You Help: Different Types of Social Exclusion Threaten Different Needs and Produce Different Outcomes"

*Jaehoon Lee, University of Texas at San Antonio, USA*
*L. J. Shrum, University of Texas at San Antonio, USA*

Previous research suggests that social exclusion can produce two seemingly contradictory responses: antisocial responses such as aggression and prosocial responses such as conformity. One possible explanation for these contradictory outcomes is that different types of exclusion threaten different social needs. Exclusion can threaten social needs such as belonging, self-esteem, control, and meaningful existence, and reactions to restore threatened needs may drive either prosocial or antisocial responses. Individuals with relational needs (belonging and self-esteem) may behave prosocially because relational needs motivate them to be adaptive, whereas individuals with efficacy needs (control and meaningful existence) may behave antisocially because efficacy needs motivate them to increase visibility (Williams 2007). Research also suggests a distinction

between being rejected (explicit) and being ignored (implicit). Being rejected increases threats to relational needs such as self-esteem, whereas being ignored increases threats to efficacy needs such as meaningful existence (Molden et al. 2009). Taken together, the consequences of being rejected may be prosocial to be affiliative, but the consequences of being ignored may be antisocial to achieve immediate recognition. Moreover, some indirect antisocial behaviors may include the symbolic superiority over others (Baumeister et al. 1996), which may be achieved through consumption. Conspicuous consumption is a showy behavior intended to gain attention, and may provide the easiest and surest way of gaining immediate recognition, thereby satisfying efficacy needs. Thus, being ignored should increase conspicuous consumption (but not helping behavior). In contrast, being rejected should pose threats to relational needs, which should motivate individuals to engage in prosocial behaviors such as helping (but not conspicuous consumption).

Four experiments tested these propositions. Participants either wrote about (exp. 1-3) or imagined (exp. 4) an instance of either being rejected or being ignored or going grocery shopping, and then indicated their preferences for products with conspicuous vs. non-conspicuous brand logos and their helping intentions (operationalizations were varied). As expected, ignored conditions increased conspicuous consumption preferences but not helping intentions, whereas rejected conditions increased helping intentions but not conspicuous consumption preferences (exp. 1-4). Moreover, both sets of effects were greater for high than for low materialists (exp. 2). Materialistic values may be driven by *both* the needs to bolster self-esteem and bolster meaningful existence (Richins and Dawson 1992). Thus, materialism is a useful trait measure to serve as a proxy for need to bolster two different needs. However, when the underlying needs that are differentially threatened by being ignored versus being rejected were boosted prior to providing consumption and helping judgments, both social exclusion effects were eliminated. Specifically, under no-boost conditions, the effects of being ignored and being rejected were replicated. However, a self-esteem boost (exp. 3, 4) eliminated the effects of being rejected on helping intentions, but a power or meaningful existence boost did not, whereas a power (exp. 3) or meaningful existence (exp. 4) boost eliminated the effects of being ignored on conspicuous consumption preferences, but a self-esteem boost did not.

These studies provide evidence of social exclusion effects on consumption behavior, a topic that is relatively new to consumer behavior. In addition, the results provide a tentative explanation of inconsistent findings on the effects of social exclusion on pro- and anti-social behavior. Finally, the results provide important information regarding the motivations underlying both conspicuous consumption and helping behavior such as volunteering and charitable contributions.

### "The Effect of Social Exclusion on Consumers' Sensitivity to Construal Levels"

*Jing (Alice) Wang, University of Iowa, USA*
*Meng Zhang, Chinese University of Hong Kong, China*

Being excluded has been shown to have adverse effects on people's psychological and physical well-being, such as anxiety and depression, aggressive behavior, feeling cold and painful (e.g., Baumeister and Tice 1990). However, little research has examined whether social exclusion can impact people's sensitivity to differential mental representations, which in turn, may influence their decisions in subsequently encountered, seemingly unrelated tasks. The current research examines such a possibility. We hypothesize that relatively speaking, socially excluded people will be more sensitive to low-level construals (concrete, superordinate representations) and adopt a concrete, how-oriented thinking, whereas socially included people will be more sensitive to high-level construals (abstract, subordinate representations) and adopt an abstract, why-oriented thinking.

We draw our predictions on some interesting parallels observed between social exclusion and construal level. Specifically, prior research finds that people will focus more on proximal (distal) temporal distance when a low- (high-level) construal is induced or social exclusion (inclusion) is made salient; people's ability to exert self-control will be impaired (enhanced) when a low- (high-level) construal or a social exclusion (inclusion) is manipulated. Based on these lines of research, we propose an association between exclusion and a low-level construal, and inclusion and a high level construal. We tested our predictions in four experiments.

Experiment 1 used a product classification task. We propose that those who construe information at a high level would be more inclusive and use fewer categories to classify products than those who construe information at a low level. We first manipulated social exclusion using a method developed by Twenge et al. (2001). Specifically, participants were asked to fill out a personality questionnaire, and they received one of the three versions of bogus feedback concerning their future: they will be alone (exclusion), socially accepted (inclusion) or prone to accident (negative control). Then they were asked to perform two classification tasks. In each task, they placed a number of products into groups by writing down the items that belong together. As expected, the results showed that participants in future alone condition used more categories to classify both tasks than those in future belonging and accident prone conditions. The differences between the latter two conditions, however, were small and insignificant, indicating that negativity could not be an alternative explanation of the results.

Experiment 2 tested our prediction on consumers' evaluations of ads. It had a 2 (social: inclusion vs. exclusion) x 2 (product version: positive values associated with high-level construals, but negative associated with low level construals vs. positive values associated with low-level construals, but negative associated with high level construals) between subject design. We used a different method to manipulate social exclusion (Twenge et al. 2001). Specifically, participants were asked to form groups and were either be accepted or rejected by the confederate. Then in an unrelated task that followed, participants were asked to evaluate two ads of new products-a lotion and a drama-adopted from Kim et al. (2008). Significant interactions were found on both ads. As expected, socially rejected participants, as compared to socially included participants, reported a lower evaluation of the product which had positive high-level features, but a higher evaluation of the product which had positive low-level features.

Experiment 3 further tested our prediction on participants' chronic tendencies. We measured participants' chronic tendency to social exclusion (Russell 1996) and their chronic tendency to high/low construals (Vallacher and Wegner 1989). The results provide additional support for our hypothesis, showing that those who were lonelier tended to construe events at a lower level.

Finally, in the on-going experiment 4, we induced social exclusion by a brand scenario. Participants were asked to apply for a membership in a brand community club, and were informed later that their application was either accepted or rejected. The preliminary results showed that participants, who were excluded by the brand club, adopted a more single-minded thinking strategy in a later task. They were more successful in identifying details missing within a coherent visual whole than their counterparts who were included in the brand club. Collectively, these experiments provided converging evidence to our predictions in different decision domains, using different methods to operationalize social exclusion and construal levels.

## SELECTED REFERENCES

Kim, Kyeongheui, Meng Zhang, and Xiuping Li (2008), "Effects of Temporal and Social Distance on Consumer Evaluations," *Journal of Consumer Research*, 35 (December), 706-713.

Molden, Daniel C., Gale M. Lucas, Wendi L. Gardner, Kristy Dean, and Megan L. Knowles (2009), "Motivations for Prevention or Promotion Following Social Exclusion: Being Rejected Versus Being Ignored," *Journal of Personality and Social Psychology*, 96 (2), 415-431.

Sommer, Kristin L., Kipling D. Williams, Nathan J. Ciarocco, and Roy F. Baumeister (2001), "When silence speaks louder than words: Explorations into the interpersonal and intrapsychic consequences of social ostracism," *Basic and Applied Social Psychology, 23*, 227-245.

Twenge, Jean M., Roy F. Baumeister, Dianne M. Tice, and Tanja S. Stucke (2001), "If you can't join them, beat them: Effects of social exclusion on aggressive behavior," *Journal of Personality and Social Psychology*, 81(6), 1058-1069.

Williams, Kipling D. (2007), "Ostracism," *Annual Review of Psychology*, 58 (January), 425-452.

Zhou, Xin-Yue, Kathleen Vohs, and Roy F. Baumeister (2009), "The symbolic power of money: Reminders of money alter social distress and physical pain," *Psychological Science*, 20, 700-706.

# The Neglected Dimension of Affective States: New Findings on the Effects of Stress, Relaxation, Anxiety, and Arousal, on Consumer Behavior

Michel Tuan Pham, Columbia University, USA

## EXTENDED ABSTRACT

### "Decisions Under Distress: Stress Profiles Influence Anchoring and Adjustments"

*Karim Kassam, Carnegie Mellon University, USA*

Understanding how stress affects decision making is complicated by the fact that not all stress responses are created equal. Challenge states, for example, are characterized by efficient cardiovascular profiles, higher resource relative to demand appraisals, and are associated with approach motivation. Threat states, in contrast, involve less efficient cardiovascular profiles, higher demand relative to resource appraisals, and are associated with withdrawal motivation. We randomly assigned participants to social feedback conditions designed to engender challenge and threat states, as well as a control condition. Participants then completed an anchoring and adjustment questionnaire.

Anchoring and adjustment is a common mode of interaction of conscious and unconscious processing, we frequently make conscious adjustments to our beliefs, estimates and opinions based on information and social context. Following the stress manipulation, participants completed a number of trivia questions involving adjustment from self-generated anchors (e.g. What is the freezing point of vodka?). Adjustment from anchors on such questions has been shown to require conscious processing–participants generate intuitive answers they know to be incorrect but close to the right answer (e.g. 32 degF), and then serially adjust in the direction of the correct answer (Epley & Gilovich, 2001).

In order to engender challenge and threat stress responses, we used a modified version of the Trier Social Stress Task (Kirschbaum, Pirke, & Hellhammer, 1993)–a mock job interview consisting of speech and question-and-answer tasks. After application of physiological sensors, participants sat quietly for a 5-minute baseline period. Participants were then asked to imagine they were interviewing for a desirable job. They were given five minutes to prepare a speech describing their strengths and weaknesses, which they then delivered to two interviewers.

Previous research suggests that this stressor can engender challenge or threat states depending on the nonverbal feedback given by interviewers (Akinola & Mendes, 2008). Approximately thirty seconds into the speech, interviewers in the challenge condition began to express positive nonverbal feedback by nodding, smiling, and leaning forward. In the threat condition, interviewers expressed negative nonverbal feedback by shaking their heads, furrowing their brows, and crossing their arms. In the control condition, participants completed the same tasks but were alone in the experiment room. They were instructed that we were interested in physiological changes associated with delivering a speech, but we would not be watching them during the task. Immediately after the interview, all participants were given two minutes to provide their best guesses in response to nine anchoring and adjustment questions labeled "Trivia".

We found that type of stress, and not just the amount of stress, can have a significant impact on people's abilities to engage in cognitive tasks. Participants placed in a stressful situation with positive feedback cognitively adjusted more than those who experienced negative feedback, an effect that was mediated by cardiovascular (CV) reactivity. Those who exhibited CV responses consistent with challenge (increased cardiac output and decreased total peripheral resistance) showed greater cognitive adjustment than those who exhibited CV responses consistent with threat (decreased cardiac output and increased total peripheral resistance).

These findings have important implications for recent research showing incidental emotions can influence decision making. For example, anger has been shown to increase optimism and risk-taking relative to fear (Lerner & Keltner, 2000), and sadness affects people's willingness to buy and sell consumer goods (Lerner, Small, & Lowenstein, 2004). As work in this area continues to develop, it will be interesting to see if–like challenge and threat–the effects of emotion on decision-making can be indexed with *under the skin* responses.

### "Relaxation Increases Monetary Valuations"

*Michel Tuan Pham, Columbia University, USA*
*Iris W. Hung, National University of Singapore, Singapore*
*Gerald J. Gorn, Hong Kong University of Science and Technology, China*

Whether buying a house or considering whether to invest in the stock market, common wisdom holds that people should be relaxed and at ease. Relaxation is among the most important environmental states marketers try to create, whether in spas, hotel rooms, or restaurants. Yet, there is little consumer research on relaxation and the research that has been done has tended to focus on how states of relaxation affect reactions to print ads (c.f. Gorn et al. 1997; Bosmans & Baumgartner, 2005).

Our research documents an intriguing phenomenon. We find across six experiments that states of relaxation increase consumers' monetary valuations of products, compared to equally pleasant but less relaxed states. We interpret these findings as follows. Based on research suggesting that relaxation encourages broader thinking (Fredrickson & Branigan 2005), we propose that relaxed consumers have more global and abstract representations when assessing the monetary value of products than non-relaxed consumers. Research has also found (Liberman & Trope (1998) that individuals who have more abstract representations (higher-level construals) of goal-directed activities (e.g., going on a vacation in Mexico) focus more on the overall desirability of these activities (e.g., how appealing Mexico is), whereas individuals who have more concrete representations (lower-level construals) focus more on the feasibility of these activities (e.g., its cost). Linking these two streams of research together, we suggest that relaxation encourages a more abstract representation of the value of products, and this shifts the consumers' focus towards the general desirability of products and away from their more concrete characteristics. Because most consumer products (e.g., vacations, cameras) are inherently desirable, such a shift in representation results in products being valued more by more- relaxed consumers than by less-relaxed consumers. For example, in assessing the monetary value of a digital camera, a relaxed consumer would focus more on the overall desirability of owning the camera like the memories they can collect with it, and less on the concrete features of the camera itself like its size and weight. This shift in representation should result in relaxed consumers perceiving the camera to be more valuable than less-relaxed consumers.

Across six studies (total N=560), participants were induced into either a state of relaxation, or into an equally pleasant (but less relaxed) affective state using pre-tested videos. Next, as part of a supposedly unrelated study, they were asked to assess the monetary value of products. The results consistently showed that more-relaxed participants assigned greater monetary value to products than less-relaxed participants. This held true for the perceived prices they assigned to various products supposedly from a product catalogue (Studies 1 and 2), and for the maximum amount of money participants were willing to bid for a camera they were asked to imagine they were interested in and bidding on eBay for, and for their estimates of how much it was really worth (Studies 3 to 6).

Our reasoning was confirmed in Studies 4 to 6. For example, in Study 5 direct support for the proposed explanation was obtained through a priming manipulation of participants' levels of representation. If the effect of relaxation on monetary valuation is due to higher levels of representation, then the priming of an abstract level of thinking should amplify this effect by reinforcing relaxed individuals' tendency to represent the value of products at a higher level. Conversely, the priming of a lower level of construal should attenuate this effect. The results were supportive and further suggested that relaxed individuals inflate the monetary value of products. Using process measures of concrete versus abstract thinking, Study 6 further shows that relaxed consumers indeed have more abstract and less concrete representations of the products' value than less relaxed consumers.

Interestingly, across experiments 3-6, it was found that the bids of less- relaxed participants in the bidding experiments were generally close to the market value for the product. More-relaxed participants' estimates were however substantially higher than the market value, unless high-level construals were discouraged by the manipulations. Even though it is typically not in people's material interest to have inflated perceptions of the monetary value of products they might buy, our evidence suggests that they do nonetheless have them.

### "Focused on a Feeling or the Cause? The Regulation of Anxiety"

*Aparna A. Labroo, University of Chicago, USA*
*Derek D. Rucker, Northwestern University, USA*

Imagine that you are in the process of planning your annual vacation when your doctor calls. The results of a recent cholesterol test show deterioration and you feel anxious. How might you regulate your anxiety? Could simply browsing a brochure that makes you consider why your vacation will be calming help? Would completing an arm flexion exercise help? Given that neither the brochure nor the exercise addresses the problem that caused your anxiety, why should they have any effect on your current state? Would it matter whether your focus was on your anxious feelings or what caused the feelings: the test results?

Negative feelings typically result because of a problem and foster efforts to resolve the problem (Schwarz and Clore 1983). Thus, anxiety arising from a problematic test result could only be addressed by resolving the cause of those feelings. However, recent evidence suggests that anxiety is associated with a general avoidance orientation (Raghunathan and Pham 1999). According to this perspective, therefore, any outcome that fits with avoidance should be preferred, even though the outcome may not directly address what caused the anxiety. Thus, merely considering a calming vacation—an outcome associated with an avoidance orientation—or engaging in arm flexion exercises, which also simulate avoidance (vs. approach), might be beneficial. How might these two views be reconciled?

We propose that once negative feelings become activated, people can focus either on the problem that caused the feelings or on the negative feelings themselves. Focusing on the feelings activates a motivation to avoid threat or to approach reward, because all feelings are intrinsically tied to motivation. As a result, any positive outcome that fits with the general motivational state can mark symbolic progress and facilitate the regulation of the negative emotion. Only when individuals focus on the cause of their emotion, will actions that address the particular problem reduce their negative emotion.

Across five experiments, we first establish that when participants focus on feelings, both anxiety and calmness, considered by us in this research, correspond with an avoid-threat orientation whereas happiness, also considered by us, corresponds with an approach-reward orientation (Exp. 1). We then demonstrate that avoidance motivation intensifies over time when participants experiencing unresolved anxiety focused on feelings, but decays when they focused on the cognitive appraisals of the causal event, replaced by specific thoughts regarding the problem that evoked anxiety (Exp. 2). We next show that among anxious participants who focus on their general anxious feelings, avoidance motivation is reduced when they complete a short exercise in the interim that employs a motivational orientation that fits with that of the negative emotion (i.e., flex arm outward as if pushing a bad thing away vs. flex arm inward as if pulling a good thing; Exp. 3). Similar emotional benefit is not observed if participants focused on the causal event. Experiment 4 shows that participants who focused on feelings of anxiety rather than causal events, get emotional benefit from merely evaluating an outcome that fits with avoidance (calming vs. happy vacation ad), and perform better on a subsequent task known to benefit from positive feelings (e.g., the Remote Associates Test). A final experiment (Exp. 5) provides a dynamic measure of affect regulation. Anxious or non-anxious participants report their mood, they then read a happy or calming ad, and again report their mood. The data again suggest that a fit in avoidance orientation between the preexisting anxiety and the positive (calming) outcome is a basis for affect regulation, but only when people are focused on their feelings.

In summary, our results demonstrate that when consumers focus on their feelings (vs. causes), higher order motivational states are activated and merely considering any positive outcome compatible with the general motivational state can provide symbolic emotional benefit.

### "Arousal and Subjective Probabilities: An Alternative Interpretation of Wishful Thinking"

*Joachim Vosgerau, Carnegie Mellon University, USA*

Desirability bias denotes the tendency to judge desirable outcomes as more likely than undesirable outcomes. For example, in the classic study by Crandall, Solomon, and Kellaway (1955), participants were asked to predict random independent draws from decks of ten cards. Even though they knew that each deck contained 7 winning cards, they predicted drawing a winning card 89% of the time.

While such findings are typically interpreted as people suffering from a desirability bias, they actually don't show desirability bias at all. Knowing that the objective probability of a winning card is 70%, a rational decision maker would predict a winning card in 100% of the draws (thereby maximizing accuracy of prediction). So, compared to a rational decision maker, participants in the above experiment appear to be pessimistic or at least not accuracy-maximizing. Whatever is the case, they are certainly not overoptimistic.

Rather than always being too optimistic, I propose that the likelihood of an event may be judged by how aroused the stake-holder is. The greater the stake in the outcome, the more aroused will the stake-holder be, and the higher s/he will judge the likelihood of the outcome occurring or not occurring.

Study 1 employed a 2 (arousal vs. no arousal) x 2 (probability of occurrence vs. non-occurrence) between-subjects design. Half of the participants were asked questions such as "How likely do you think the Yankees will win the World Series?"; the other half was asked for the complementary probabilities. Arousal was manipulated by printing questionnaires on either pink or grey paper. As hypothesized, participants judged both outcomes (the Yankees winning and the Yankees not winning) as more likely in the arousal condition (pink paper).

In study 2, half of the participants were first asked to rate their arousal level, and subsequently to judge the likelihood of outcome occurrence or non-occurrence (outcome: participants won $5 when they got at least one 3 within four die-rolls, p=51.77%). The other half was first asked the likelihood question and then the arousal question. Misattribution of arousal to likelihoods was found as participants rated likelihoods higher before than after the arousal measures.

Study 3 employed a 2 (probability of outcome occurrence vs. non-occurrence) x 3 (stake in outcome: win a shot-glass vs. neutral vs. lose a shot-glass) between-subjects design. Half of the participants was asked how likely a computer, when rolling a die four times, would roll a 6 twice (p=11.57%). The other half was asked how likely the computer would not roll a 6 twice. As hypothesized, participants judged the probability of getting a 6 twice higher when they could win (M=19.77%) or lose a shot-glass (M=38.91%) than in the neutral condition (M=13.44%). Likewise, they judged the probability of not getting a 6 twice also higher in the win (M=72.32%) and the lose condition (M=61.79%) than the neutral condition (M=55.83%).

In study 4 German soccer fans imagined watching an upcoming match either live (more aroused) or taped (less aroused; Vosgerau et al. 2006, JCR). Fans were asked to indicate how likely their team (Stuttgart) was to win. When having the prospect of watching the match taped, Stuttgart was judged as equally likely to win/tie (M=52.40%) as to lose (M=51.36%). In contrast, for the live broadcast conditions, Stuttgart was rated as more likely to win/draw (M=58.48%) and also as more likely to lose (M=67.92%). Taken together, the four studies demonstrate that arousal (from having a stake in the outcome) can make consumers more optimistic and more pessimistic. Such optimism and pessimism call into question the ubiquity of wishful thinking.

# Embodied Consumption: Understanding Avatared Consumers

Haiyang Yáng, INSEAD, Singapore
Amitava Chattopadhyay, INSEAD, Singapore

## EXTENDED ABSTRACTS

### "Marketing to Avatars: The Impact of Virtual Embodiment on Consumer Self-Concept and Behavior"

*Haiyang Yáng, INSEAD, Singapore*
*Amitava Chattopadhyay, INSEAD, Singapore*

Hundreds of millions of people have entered three dimensional virtual worlds, interacting with each other and living out their digital second lives as avatars. Two streams of research shed light on the mechanism through which avatar embodiment may influence consumer self-concept. First, Aaker (1999) showed that self-concept is not a static and stable structure, but a malleable one. The content of the working self-concept depends on what has been invoked by the individual as a result of an experience, event, or situation at the given time (Markus and Kunda 1986). Second, people may make inferences about their own attitudes and values from observing their own behaviors, in a way similar to an outside observer (Bem 1972). These findings suggest that avatar embodiment experience may lead consumers to activate or form a working self-concept that is consistent with their avatar.

Consumer research provides ample evidence of the behavioral implications of the malleable-self. Mick and Buhl (1992) found that individuals under different self-concepts interpret advertisements differently. Aaker (1999) showed that situational cues can activate different personality traits, which, in turn, influence attitudes toward brands with different personality associations. These suggest that, if avatar embodiment results in changes in working self-concept, consumers may exhibit behavior consistent with the shifted working self-concept.

Furthermore, the research on close relationships (Aron et al. 1991) shows that individuals in close relationships tend to have highly overlapping mental representations of one another, and may confuse cognitions about a close other with cognitions about the self. The research on perspective-taking (Galinsky and Moskowitz 2000) demonstrates that perspective-taking may cause subjects to include mental representations of the target or target's group in their evaluations of themselves, leading subjects to evaluate themselves more in line with the perceived attributes of the target or target's group. Given that being embodied in an avatar may establish a close relationship between consumers and the avatar and enable them to take the perspective of the avatar, consumers, to the extent that they relate to the avatar, may view themselves as more in line with the avatar. That is, the shift in self-concept and change in behavior are moderated by the extent to which consumers identify with the avatar.

Finally, prior research has shown that people often are unaware of their mental processes and fail to realize external influences on their behaviors (Bargh 2002). In the context of avatar embodiment, consumers may not be consciously aware that they are identifying themselves with the avatar and incorporating the avatar's attributes into themselves. When, however, their identification with the avatar is made salient, consumers are likely to become aware of the influence of avatar embodiment and correct for it in their decision making.

To test our hypotheses, we developed two avatars that were identical in all aspects except the clothing. The first avatar (hereafter BizPerson) was dressed in business attire, whereas the second (hereafter Surfer) was dressed in surfer style. A pretest established that the avatars were perceived to be equally likable but significantly different on the images they projected.

In Experiment 1, participants were randomly assigned according to a 2 (avatar type: BizPerson vs. Surfer) x 2 (identification level: high vs. low) between-subject factorial design. Those in the high-identification condition (1) customized their avatar using a collection of business (surfer) style clothing items and (2) saw how the avatar looked using virtual mirrors. Through a yoked design, participants in the low-identification condition received avatars customized by those in the high condition. Embodied in their avatar, participants explored a virtual photo gallery, and then reported their self-concept and rated four photographs that were pretested to be congruent with the image of the Surfer. We found that, under the high-identification condition, participants' working self-concept shifted towards the projected image of the avatar they were embodied in; moreover, in comparison with those embodied in the BizPerson avatar, participants using the Surfer gave significantly higher ratings for the target photographs. When identification is low, however, we neither observed any significant differences in self-concept between the two avatar conditions, nor see any significant differences in the ratings of the target photographs.

In Experiment 2, we used a 2 (avatar type: BizPerson vs. Surfer) x 2 (identification awareness: before vs. after completing the dependent measures) between-subject factorial design. Those in the "before" awareness condition answered, prior to the dependent measures, a set of questions regarding the extent to which they identified with the avatar. The opposite was true for those in the "after" condition. The experimental procedure was identical to that of Experiment 1 except that (1) all participants customized their avatar, (2) we unobtrusively recorded participants' behavior in the virtual world and coded the amount of time they spent on the photographs, and (3) participants were also asked to experience a virtual vehicle that was modeled after a stereotypical surfer van. We found that those embodied in the Surfer avatar spent significantly more time looking at the target photos, and, when not made aware of their identification, rated the virtual van and its brand significantly higher.

Overall, the results of our experiments provided support for our hypotheses: when participants identified with their avatar, they formed self-conceptions consistent with the image of their avatar and had higher evaluations of the product congruent with the avatar. Moreover, the embodiment experience influenced behavior through a predominantly unconscious process. We are currently running additional experiments, aiming to show that the effects of avatar embodiment persist across worlds and can impact consumer decision making in the real world.

### "The Role of Context and Content on Recognition Accuracy in Virtual Worlds"

*Francesco Massara, IULM University, Italy*
*Thomas Novak, University of California, USA*

Virtual worlds such as Second Life, There.com and Blue Mars are three-dimensional, visually compelling, interactive environments inhabited by avatar representations of real world consumers. Such virtual worlds are beginning to be leveraged as platforms for consumer and marketing research (Novak 2010). An important question is the degree to which behavior occurring within virtual worlds is unique and different from behavior occurring outside the context of virtual worlds. For example, Bell, Castronova and Wagner (2009) have argued that research studies fielded within the context of a virtual world, rather than in an external context such as Web-based survey, prevent a break in immersion that might interfere with accurate recall of the virtual world environment. In general, however, there has been no formal consideration of how context (virtual world vs. Web survey) may interact with the form of information content (visual vs. text), and how the relationship of context and content may vary for different user tasks.

We consider distinctive aspects of virtual worlds for recognition tasks, for visual vs. text stimuli. As highly visual environments, virtual worlds are more likely to induce imagery processing, while Web browsers are more likely to induce discursive processing. When considering target stimuli that are either visual or text-based, this raises the question of whether a match or mismatch of context and content (i.e. assimilation or contrast effects) would be expected in recognition tasks.

We address this question in a series of three studies. Our first study, together with an extensive set of pretests, has been completed and uses a signal detection task (SDT) designed as a low elaboration recognition manipulation involving the shallow encoding of information. Hypotheses for our first study, with brief rationales, are as follows. H1. Recognition accuracy for visual stimuli will be greater than for text stimuli (the often demonstrated "picture superiority effect"). H2. Greater signal strength leads to greater recognition accuracy (at short exposure times there is not sufficient time to encode the information properly). H3. There will be an interaction of content and context. Response accuracy on stimulus recognition is higher for a text (visual) stimulus in a virtual world (web based) environment, and is lower for a text (visual) stimulus in a web based (virtual world) environment. (In virtual worlds the imagery processing system is used to process the context, so the alternative discursive system has greater resources for encoding the stimuli, leading to superior results for text. The reverse is true in Web based environments.) H4a: The interaction of content and context in H3 will be significant at high levels of signal strength (greater time is available for encoding). H4b: The interaction of content and context in H3 will be nonsignificant at low levels of signal strength (insufficient time is available for encoding).

In a 2x2x2 design we 1) administered an SDT either within the context of a virtual world (Second Life) or a Web browser, where we 2) presented a slideshow of either 40 visual or 40 text-based stimuli, where 3) signal strength was manipulated by presenting stimuli at relatively short (500ms, the shortest presentation time feasible in Second Life) or long (1500ms) exposure durations. After the slideshow, a second series of 40 stimuli was shown (20 that were presented before and 20 new) and respondents were asked to indicate if they recognized the stimuli from the first slideshow. Our primary dependent measure from this SDT was b, decisional criterion or bias, which is sensitive to content/context manipulations and which can be interpreted as the likelihood of good memories with respect to false memories. An additional dependent measure was d', which indicates the sensitivity of the respondent in recognizing previous information.

A total of 256 respondents completed Study 1. H1 was supported for sensitivity d' (p<.001) but not bias b, so that subjects were more sensitive towards pictures but not more accurate in recognizing them. H2 was supported for both sensitivity d' (p<.01) and bias b (p<.01) so that higher signal strength lead to greater recognition accuracy. For H3 we found supporting significant two-way interac-

tions between context and content on both sensitivity d' (p<.01) and bias b (p<.05). As predicted, means for b were higher in the virtual world context for text (M=1.75) than for pictures (M=1.45), while means were higher in the Web condition for pictures (M=1.61) than for text (M=1.20). H4a and H4b are supported in that the three way interaction was significant for bias b (p<.05). Further, at high (low) levels of signal strength the simple interaction effect of context and content was significant (not significant).

Thus, Study 1 demonstrates a contrast effect whereby text stimuli are recognized more accurately in virtual worlds, but visual stimuli are recognized more accurately in Web browsers. Mismatch between context and content improves recognition accuracy. Our second study will employ a manipulation requiring a deeper encoding of the stimuli, and hypothesizes an opposite interaction whereby an assimilation effect (i.e. match) improves recognition accuracy. Our third study will show pairs of matched pictures and text (semantic coherence) or mismatched pictures and text (semantic incoherence) to test the hypothesis that a contrast effect will be observed in the mismatched condition, but not in the matched condition. Together, this set of studies has important implications for response accuracy in contexts that vary in imagery vs. discursive processing, as well as the recall of marketing communications in virtual world vs. Web contexts.

## "Trust among the Avatars: Playing Trust Games in a Virtual World, with and without Textual and Visual Cues"

*Stephen Atlas, Columbia University, USA*
*Louis Putterman, Brown University, USA*

As experimentalists explore the potential of virtual worlds to provide a low-cost medium to study a diverse pool of subjects, exploration of established behavioral phenomena "in-world" provides value by both validating theory and establishing consistency of social norms across platforms. This investigation replicated the original Trust Game (Berg, Dickhaut and McCabe, 1995) paradigm (hereinafter BDM) in the virtual world, Second Life, with compensation comparable to "in-world" wages that are far below those of physical labs. The results reveal that baseline trust and reciprocity in the virtual lab is comparable to that of physical labs, suggesting that pro-social motivations extend to anonymous interactions while embodied in an avatar. We further found that pro-social behaviors in virtual worlds are heavily influenced but not eliminated by verbal and visual contextual cues and, in apparent contradiction with economists' expectations trust increases with age, employment and income among avatars.

Data was collected from 300 subjects from 39 countries. Among the first wave of in-world trust games, our lab is (to our knowledge) the first instance of a persistent economic experiment in a virtual world that eliminates interaction with the experimenter by automating recruitment, instruction, measurement and compensation. Further, this experiment appears to be unique in using payoffs commensurate with earnings from in-world jobs. As in-world wages are approximately one twentieth of the self-reported wage from real-world employment (55% of our subjects report holding a job in Second Life with hourly wages averaging L$170 per hour, corresponding with USD$0.65 per hour), we paid subjects a tenth of the amount paid by Fiedler et al. (in press) and by Chesney et al. (2009) without threatening incentive compatibility. Though subjects earned an average of L$177 (66 cents) for twenty minutes of involvement, 88% of respondents stated that the prospect of earning Lindens was "very important" or "moderately important" for their participation in the study.

The baseline treatment replicated the BDM trust game design. Subjects were endowed with L$100 (38 cents) and randomly assigned to be a first-mover or second-mover. The first decision maker chose to send an amount from their endowment; that amount was tripled and given to the second mover. This amount was in addition to their initial endowment, which is anonymously given to rule out a first-mover fairness motivation; (see Cox, 2004, for a review of this confound). The second mover could then anonymously send an amount to the first mover up to the tripled amount received. Equilibrium play assuming common knowledge of rationality and self-interested preferences is for the second mover to send nothing and, expecting this, the first mover sends nothing. In contrast, BDM and many replications reveal that a majority of first-movers and second-movers receiving money send positive amounts, a result widely interpreted as evidence of efficiency-enhancing social preferences wherein the first-movers trust and the second-movers exhibit reciprocity.

Evolutionary psychologists hold that social preferences are determined by innate predispositions that respond to environmental triggers (see Buss, 2008, for a review). One example is provided by Bateson, Nettle and Roberts (2006), who found that honor system payments were three times higher when the price list contained an image of human eyes than when it contained flowers. In this vein, we explored how virtual environmental stimuli influence trust and reciprocity through the inclusion of visual and verbal treatments. The visual treatments added optimistic and cautionary images to the baseline lab environment, while the textual treatments respectively added a cooperative and a competitive line to the instructions. To explore whether the visual and textual cues were mutually reinforcing, we also included treatments including the optimistic with cooperative cues and cautionary with competitive cues.

The baseline results reveal that first-movers sent on average 51.8% of their endowment, a finding remarkably similar to BDM (51.6%) and other replications in virtual and real labs. The smaller stakes, a more diverse subject pool and virtual environment in this case did not appear to impact average first-mover sending behavior. Mann-Whitney tests reveal that the differences within verbal treatments and visual treatments are each economically meaningful (close to a quarter of the total endowment size) and statistically significant ($p<0.05$). The combined treatments were not significantly different from the separated treatment effects. The second movers in the baseline treatment returned roughly half (50.7%) of the tripled amount received. This is considerably higher than the 33.3% necessary to make first-movers break even, higher than the 29.8% in BDM. Raw second-mover sending was predicted by treatment, but these effects disappeared after controlling for first-mover sending, indicating that the treatments did not influence reciprocity beyond its influence on trust.

The social preferences revealed by second-mover decisions resulted in a 42% return on trusting for the first-movers and in our virtual lab, trust facilitated a Pareto-superior allocation to the endowment. Our results highlight the potential advantages of experimentation in virtual worlds, including the potential to motivate subjects with lower incentives and to test the robustness of theories in an unconventional domain. Our experiment affirmed results from a brick-and-mortar laboratory setting and strongly support the notion that, social behaviors in virtual worlds, like the real world, are responsive to environmental cues.

## REFERENCES

Aaker, Jennifer L. (1999), "The Malleable Self: The Role of Self-Expression in Persuasion," *Journal of Marketing Research*, 36 (February), 45–47.

Aron, Arthur, Elaine N. Aron, Michael Tudor, and Greg Nelson (1991), "Close relationships as including other in the self", *Journal of Personality and Social Psychology*, 60, 241–253.

Bargh, John A. (2002), "Losing Consciousness: Automatic Influences on Consumer Judgment, Behavior, and Motivation," *Journal of Consumer Research*, 29 (September), 280–85.

Bateson, Melissa, Daniel Nettle and Gilbert Roberts (2006), "Cues of Being Watched Enhance Cooperation in a Real-World Setting," *Biological Letters* 2: 412-414.

Bell, M. W., Castronova, E., & Wagner, G. G. (2009), *Surveying the Virtual World: A Large Scale Survey in Second Life Using the Virtual Data Collection Interface (VCDI)*. June 12.

Bem, Daryl J. (1972), "Self-perception theory," in *Advances in Experimental Social Psychology*, L. Berkowitz, ed., New York: Academic Press.

Berg, Joyce, John Dickhaut, and Kevin McCabe (1995), "Trust, Reciprocity and Social History," *Games and Economic Behavior* 10: 122-42.

Buss, David (2008), *Evolutionary Psychology. The New Science of the Mind, 3rd Edition*. Boston: Allyn and Bacon.

Chesney, Thomas, Swee-Hoon Chuah and Robert Hoffmann (2009), "Trust in VCommerce: An Experimental Approach," mimeo, International Center for Behavioral Business Research, Nottingham University Business School.

Clifford, Stephanie (2009), "Yahoo Shows Search Ads with Images and Video," *The New York Times*.

Cox, James, (2004), "How to identify trust and reciprocity," *Games and Economic Behavior* 46: 260-81.

Debevec, Kathleen (1995), "Self-Referencing Measurement in Persuasive Communications," *Psychological Reports*, 77 (3, Pt 2), 1097-1098.

Edwards, Steven M., and Carrie La Ferle (2003), "Consumer Role-Taking: Enhancing the Online Experience," *Journal of Current Issues and Research in Advertising*, 25 (2), 45-56.

Fiedler, Marina and Ernan Haruvy, forthcoming, "The Lab versus the Virtual Lab and Virtual Field—An Experimental Investigation of Trust Games with Communication," *Journal of Economic Behavior and Organization* (in press).

Galinsky, Adam D. and Gordon B. Moskowitz (2000), "Perspective-taking: Decreasing stereotype expression, stereotype accessibility, and in-group favoritism," *Journal of Personality and Social Psychology*, 78, 708–724.

Markus, Hazel and Ziva Kunda (1986), "Stability and Malleability of the Self-Concept," *Journal of Personality and Social Psychology*, 51 (October), 858–866.

Mick, David Glen and Claus Buhl (1992), "A Meaning-Based Model of Advertising Experiences," *Journal of Consumer Research*, 19 (December), 317–338.

Novak, Thomas P. (2010), "eLab City: A Platform for Academic Research on Virtual Worlds," *Journal of Virtual Worlds Research*, April/May.

Perkins, Andrew, Mark R. Forehand, and Anthony Greenwald (2005), "Implicit Self-Referencing: The Self-Concept as a Source of Implicit Attitude Formation," Unpublished manuscript, Rice University, Houston, TX 77005.

Rogers, Timothy B., Nicholas A. Kuiper, and William S. Kirker (1977), "Self-reference and the Encoding of Personal Information," *Journal of Personality and Social Psychology*, 35, 677-88.

Sarvary, Miklos (2008), "The Metaverse: TV of the Future?" *Harvard Business Review*, 86(2). 30.

Shavitt, Sharon, and Timothy C. Brock (1984), "Self-Relevant Responses in Commercial Persuasion," In K. Sentis & J. Olson (eds.), *Advertising and Consumer Psychology.* New York: Praeger.

Zaichkowsky, Judith L. (1994), "The Personal Involvement Inventory: Reduction, Revision, and Application to Advertising," *Journal of Advertising,* 23 (4), 59-70.

# When is Disfluency Desirable? The Effects of Metacognitive Effort on Product Evaluations and Forecasting Behavior

Elise Chandon Ince, Virginia Tech, USA
Debora V. Thompson, Georgetown University, USA

## EXTENDED ABSTRACT

### "If it's Hard to Read, It's Worth It: When Metacognitive Effort Enhances Product Value"

*Debora V. Thompson, Georgetown University, USA*
*Elise Chandon Ince, Virginia Tech, USA*

Extensive research demonstrates that people's attitude toward a product becomes less favorable when product information is hard to process. Song and Schwarz (2008) showed that people misread the difficulty of reading a description of a target behavior as indicative of the difficulty of executing it. For instance, lowering the processing fluency of a description of an exercise routine or a cooking recipe significantly increased perceptions of required effort and skill and decreased one's willingness to engage in these tasks. Recent research (Pocheptsova, Labroo, and Dhar 2010) shows that in the context of special-occasion products, disfluency increases product attractiveness by making it appear unique or uncommon. Building on this research, we propose that disfluency has a positive effect on consumers' evaluative judgments in domains in which skill is an important driver of value. Consumers frequently hire professional agents or contract services because of their specialized skills and expertise. In such contexts, will product valuations increase when processing is less (rather than more) fluent? We examine this hypothesis in two studies.

In study 1, fifty-eight students were randomly assigned to either a low or high fluency condition. All participants were presented with a description of a service that helps students apply to graduate programs. After reading the information, participants provided their evaluations of the target service. Processing fluency was manipulated via background contrast (light blue font vs. black font). As expected, participants in the low fluency condition rated the service description as more difficult to read than participants in the high fluency condition. More interestingly, those in the low fluency condition reported higher willingness to pay ($191.2 vs. $76.4) for a one-subscription ($F(1,56)=3.7, p=.058$), and perceived greater value in the target service (5.0 vs. 4.1) than those in the high fluency condition ($F(1,56)=6.9, p<.05$). Lowering processing fluency increased participants' perceptions of how much expertise the target service provided. Notably, expertise ratings were a significant predictor of perceived service value ($\beta=.47, p<.01$).

Recent research indicates that disfluent stimuli are perceived as riskier because they are viewed as more novel/less familiar than fluent stimuli (Song and Schwarz, 2009). Thus, in study 2, we predicted that when an avoidance goal is made salient, disfluency will reduce consumers' valuations, despite its positive effect on skill inferences. One hundred and nine undergraduate students were randomly assigned to a 2 (goal: approach vs. avoidance) x 2 fluency (high vs. low) between subjects design. Participants were asked to imagine that they had relatives coming to visit and that they were searching for a restaurant for dinner on a Saturday evening. In the approach goal condition, participants read that they could be adventurous in their restaurant choice, as their relatives like trying new things. In contrast, in the avoidance goal condition, participants read that they should be conservative in their restaurant choice, as their relatives avoid trying new things. All participants then read a description of a local restaurant. The manipulation

of processing fluency was the same as in study 1. As expected, there was a significant goal by fluency interaction on participants' likelihood to select the restaurant ($F(1, 104)=8.3, p<.01$). While in the approach goal condition disfluency enhanced evaluations of the restaurant; this effect was reversed in the avoidance condition. Moreover, those in the low fluency condition expected the restaurant's chef to be more skilled ($F(1, 104)=3.9, p=.05$), and the restaurant to be more novel/less conventional than those in the high fluency condition ($F(1, 104)=5.6, p<.05$). In the approach condition, ratings of the chef's skills were a significant positive predictor of restaurant evaluations ($\beta=.41, p<.01$). In contrast, when avoidance goals were made salient, perceived novelty was a negative predictor of restaurant evaluations ($\beta=-.27, p<.07$), while the effect of perceived skill became nonsignificant ($\beta=.41, p<.01$).

A third study will test whether the positive effect of disfluency extends to domains in which convenience, rather than skill, is the primary benefit sought by consumers (e.g., home cleaning, laundry services, etc). We expect consumers' willingness to pay for such products or services to increase when they are described in a less fluent manner because of consumers' naïve theories about the amount of effort that is required to perform them. Overall, our findings point out to a different consumption domain in which experiences of disfluency can enhance consumers' evaluative responses.

### "Is What You Feel What They See?"

*Ted Matherly, University of Maryland, USA*
*Anastasiya Pocheptsova, University of Maryland, USA*

People frequently use products to express their identity and infer the identities of others. In this paper, building on the body of research on subjective experiences, we propose that people will use feelings of ease or difficulty of information processing when evaluating products that signal in-group or out-group identities.

A body of research on subjective experiences shows that these experiences can serve as information for decision-making, and that the interpretation of such experiences is context dependent. Ease of processing (fluency) is often interpreted to mean that a product is familiar, more common, and this perception leads to increased liking (Schwarz 2004). Recent research also illustrates that less fluent products are seen as less common and more unique. This leads to a preference for these products in consumption domains where uniqueness adds to the perceived value, such as special occasion goods (Pocheptsova, Labroo and Dhar 2010). Applying these findings to the context of identity signaling, we propose that less fluent products will be seen as better signals of identity compared to more fluent ones. People often use products to communicate about themselves to others. To ensure that these exchanges are effective, signaling products must effectively associate users with other people who have the same identity, as well as differentiate them from outsiders (Berger and Heath 2007). We propose that less fluent products will be more effective signals when one tries to differentiate an in-group from other groups, as low fluency would indicate that the product is less common and more unique.

In our first study, we tested the effect of fluency on the perception of signaling quality of a product. Participants imagined they were buying a t-shirt that was described as being very popular on their campus. Participants were presented with either a low or high fluency t-shirt, and rated its signaling quality of either a low or high fluency t-shirt. In addition, half of the participants read a short article describing their university's success in a sporting event against a rival school. This was designed to get participants to focus on associating with their university community rather than differentiating themselves from others. Consistent with our predictions, we find that the low fluency t-shirt was viewed as a better signal of one's identity compared to the high fluency t-shirt. However, when participants were motivated to identify with their university, they focused on the common usage of the product among group members, and fluency did not affect the perceptions of the signaling quality of the product.

The second study addresses the extent to which the desire to differentiate the self from others demonstrated in the first study affects the perception of processing ease or difficulty of signaling products. In this study, participants were shown an advertisement for a coffee mug that was described as popular among an in-group (their campus), an out-group (a rival school), or was generally popular (control). Consistent with the results of study 1, participants viewed the in-group mug advertisement as less fluent compared to the out-group and control conditions. This suggests that the perception of self-relevant identities as being more unique can carry over to affect perceptions of signaling products. Moreover, no significant difference in perceived fluency between the out-group and control conditions implies that the results were not driven by a desire to denigrate a disliked out-group, but instead were influenced by the participants' views of signals of their own identity.

By showing the role that fluency can play in identity communication, this research is the first to our knowledge to connect these two lines of research. Our results suggest that low fluency products are perceived as better identity signals because they are more unique and thus more effective in differentiating members from non-members. Further, peoples' beliefs about their uniqueness may carry over to affect their perceptions of the fluency of products that signal their identity.

## "Choice Difficulty Moderates Inferences about Preference Generalizability"

*Mary Steffel, University of Florida, USA*
*Chris Janiszewski, University of Florida, USA*
*Daniel M. Oppenheimer, Princeton University, USA*

Consumers may often draw upon choices as a source of information for gauging their preferences. Self-perception theory posits that people learn about their preferences by observing their own behavior (Bem, 1972). More recently, Bodner and Prelec (2003) have argued that people's choices signal something about their traits and dispositions to themselves and others.

Although the impact of choices on self inferences is well-documented, relatively little is known about the impact of the metacognitive experiences that accompany those choices. The present research explores how the metacognitive experience of choice difficulty impacts the inferences people make about the generalizability of their preferences. Holding all else constant, people who easily prefer one option to another are likely to have a stronger underlying preference for the features of the chosen option and are more likely to make similar choices in the future than people who struggle with the decision. Decision-makers who are asked to predict the likelihood that they will make similar choices in the future are likely to focus on extracting what information choice difficulty provides about their underlying preferences. They are likely to infer that the easier a choice feels, the stronger their underlying preferences, and the more likely they are to choose similar options in the future.

When choices feel difficult, decision-makers may infer that their underlying preference is weaker and that they are less likely to make similar choices in the future. The metacognitive experience when choices are difficult is likely to include competing emotions, preferences, motives, and values. Making salient a person's multiple motives and values may cast doubt on any one unified set of decision rules, set competing expectations for future behavior, and lead decision-makers to discount the diagnosticity of a particular choice for predicting their future choices. This may lead decision-makers to make less extreme predictions about their future behavior.

The inferences that people draw from choice difficulty are likely to be bounded by the perceived relevance of the current choice to choices in other domains, situations, or contexts. Thus, the inferences people draw may often be domain-specific. Additionally, the inferences people draw from choice difficulty may be limited to self versus social inferences. Observers do not have direct access to a decision-maker's feelings of choice difficulty and cannot be sure whether their own feelings of choice difficulty are representative of the individual whose preferences they are assessing. Observers, therefore, may place less diagnostic weight on choice difficulty as a cue for assessing a decision-maker's underlying preferences and predicting that person's behavior.

Study 1 examined the extent to which people would generalize their risk preferences from easy or difficult choices between low- and high-risk lotteries. Participants made a series of choices between lotteries that were constructed so that the low-risk options were always chosen. Choice difficulty was manipulated via relative attractiveness (i.e. the difference in relative value between the lotteries). Generalization was measured by asking participants to rate the likelihood that they would engage in risky behaviors in gambling, investment, and health/safety domains using the domain-specific risk attitude scale (Weber, Blais, & Betz, 2002). Participants rated themselves less likely to gamble at a casino, in a poker game, at a horse race, or at a sporting event when choices were easy than when they were difficult. Generalization was domain specific–choice difficulty did not impact the inferences participants made about their risk preferences in the investment or health/safety domains. This finding suggests that the inferences drawn from choices have to do with the specific content of those choices and the perceived relevance of that content to other domains, situations, or contexts. To explore whether preference generalization was limited to self versus social judgments, observers were instructed to review a previous participant's choices and predict the likelihood that the person would engage in risky behaviors in each of the three domains. Observers drew weaker inferences than did the decision-makers themselves. Furthermore, observers did not draw different inferences from easy choices versus difficult choices.

Study 2 utilized a fluency manipulation to vary choice difficulty while holding constant the actual relative value of the choice options. Fluency was manipulated by presenting choice options in an easy-to-read or difficult-to-read font. As in Study 1, decision-makers drew stronger inferences about their gambling risk preferences from easy choices than hard choices. These inferences were domain-specific and did not extend to social judgments.

Together, these studies show that people make less extreme generalizations about their preferences when choices feel difficult versus easy. Although easy choices engender confidence that similar options will be chosen in the future, this confidence may often be undiagnostic of actual choice behavior. Implications for accurately assessing preferences and predicting behavior will be discussed.

### "Debiasing Effect of Fluency on Linear Trend Prediction"

*Julie Huang, Yale University, USA*
*Hyunjin Song, Yale University, USA*
*John Bargh, Yale University, USA*

The assessment of future potential—that is, whether a certain event or characteristic will develop, continue, or stop over time—is a fundamental part of everyday judgments. For instance, people predict whether economic growth rates will continue or crash before they invest in the stock market, and employers predict whether a promising job candidate's career will continue to rise or eventually cease. Previous research has shown that people from Western cultures tend to predict that linear trends will continue into the future rather than change direction (Ji, Nisbett, & Su, 2001). The present research suggests processing disfluency can attenuate this heuristic by disturbing the feeling of momentum.

Processing fluency is the metacognitive experience of ease or difficulty associated with processing information and can be affected by incidental variables such as exposure duration, high or low figure-ground contrast, and easy or difficult-to-read fonts. Recent research identifies *simulation* as a mechanism underlying fluency effects. When people process information, they oftentimes mentally simulate the content; the nature of this simulation influences their subsequent judgments. For instance, people predict a task will require more time when the instructions are printed in difficult-to-read font than in easy-to-read font, presumably because simulation requires more time for the former (Song & Schwarz, 2008). Moreover, fluency increases liking for repeatedly presented stimuli (Zajonc, 1980); but blocking simulation of the presented oral stimuli (words) by chewing gum actually attenuates this traditional fluency effect (Topolinski & Strack, 2009).

These results suggest that judgments regarding a trend can be influenced by fluency. When people process information about a trend, fluency may lead to faster simulation of the trajectory, feeding the sensation of momentum, whereas disfluency may disrupt simulation and contribute to feelings of discontinuation. Therefore, we predicted that fluent processing of a trend will increase judgments that the trend will continue into the future. Specifically, we hypothesized that people who read descriptions of increasing or decreasing trends in easy-to-read font would be more likely to predict that the trend would continue into the future, compared to people exposed to difficult-to-read font.

In study 1, one-hundred thirty participants read a passage about a psychology professor's career trajectory from graduate student to assistant professor, including funding information. In each stage of his career he received one more grant. This vignette was presented in either an easy-to-read font (Arial) or a difficult-to-read font (Mistral). Afterwards, participants answered a question regarding career trend continuation, specifically, whether the professor would receive more grants in his next career stage (1=*Not at all likely*; 8=*Very likely*). An independent samples t-test revealed that participants who read the passage in an easy-to-read font predicted that the professor was more likely to continue getting more grants in his next career phase (*M*=7.08, *SD*=1.56), compared to participants who read the passage in a difficult-to-read font (*M*=6.14, *SD*=1.82), $t(126)=3.12$, *p rep*=.98, *d*=.56.

Study 1 suggests that processing fluency increases people's predictions that a trend will continue into the future. It could be argued, however, that processing fluency elicits positive affect (Zajonc, 1980), which results in a general positive: in this case, perceptions of a better career. To rule out this alternative hypothesis, Study 2 featured a decreasing career trajectory. Since decreasing career trends are negative in nature, if fluency increases judgments that negative career trends are more likely to continue, this will demonstrate that the effect is not merely driven by mood. In Study 2, one-hundred thirty-two participants read about a professor's career in either easy-to-read font (Arial) or difficult-to-read font (Mistral). In this version, however, the professor first received six grants and in each successive career stage, he received one fewer grant. Participants rated the likelihood that the professor would continue to receive *fewer* grants (using the same response scale from Study 1). Replicating the results from Study 1, we found that participants who read the passage in an easy-to-read font predicted that the professor would receive fewer grants in the future (*M*=5.14, *SD*=1.65) compared to participants who read a difficult-to-read font (*M*=4.55, *SD*=1.58), $t(126)=2.07$, *p rep*=.89, *d*=.37.

Two studies suggest that processing fluency influences people's perceptions of whether a trend will continue into the future. Every day, people derive predictions about the future across many domains including sports statistics, medical reports, weather patterns, and market performance. Varying the presentation of these materials through print clarity, background noise, or repeated exposure to news reports may influence public opinion regarding the future direction of a trend. Additional research may address these possibilities.

## REFERENCES

Bem, D. J. (1972). Self-perception theory. In L. Berkowitz (Ed.), *Advances in Experimental Social Psychology,* Vol. 6, San Diego, CA: Academic Press, 1-62.

Berger, Jonah, and Chip Heath (2007), "Where Consumers Diverge from Others: Identity Signaling and Product Domains," *Journal of Consumer Research,* 34, 121-134.

Bodner, R. & Prelec, D. (2003). Self-Signaling and Diagnostic Utility in Everyday Decision Making. In I. Brocas & J. D. Carillo (Eds.), *The Psychology of Economic Decisions.* New York, NY: Oxford University Press.

Ji, L.T., Nisbett, R.E., and Su, Y. (2001), "Culture, Change, and Prediction," *Psychological Science, 12,* 450-456.

Pocheptsova, Anastasya, Aparna Labroo, and Ravi Dhar, "Making Products Feel Special: When Metacognitive Difficulty Enhances Evaluation", *Journal of Marketing Research* (forthcoming).

Schwarz, Norbert (2004), "Meta-cognitive Experiences in Consumer Judgment and Decision Making," *Journal of Consumer Psychology*, 14, 332–348.

Song, Hyunjin and Norbert Schwarz (2008), "If It's Easy to Read, It's Hard to Do: Processing Fluency Affects Effort Prediction and Motivation," *Psychological Science,* 19 (10), 986-988.

Song, Hyunjin and Norbert Schwarz (2009), "If It's Difficult to Pronounce, It Must Be Risky: Fluency, Familiarity, and Risk Perception," *Psychological Science,* 20 (2), 135-138.

Topolinski, S. and Strack, F. (2009), "Motormouth: Mere Exposure Depends on Stimulus-Specific Motor Simulations," *Journal of Experimental Psychology: Learning, Memory, and Cognition, 35 (2),* 423-433.

Weber, E. U., Blais, A. R., and Betz, N. E. (2002), "A Domain-Specific Risk-Attitude Scale: Measuring Risk Perceptions and Risk Behaviors," *Journal of Behavioral Decision Making,* 15, 263-290.

Zajonc, R.B. (1980), "Feeling and Thinking: Preferences Need No Inference," *American Psychologist, 35,* 151–175.

# Expensive or Cheap? Reference Prices and Consumer Perception of Value

Aaron Brough, Northwestern University, USA

## EXTENDED ABSTRACTS

### "When Does Expensive Food Taste Better? Top-Down and Bottom-Up Processing in Price-Quality Inferences"

Manoj Thomas, Cornell University, USA
Vicki G. Morwitz, New York University, USA
Leonard Lodish, University of Pennsylvania, USA
Jin Seok Pyone, Cornell University, USA

It is widely accepted that price influences consumers' responses to marketplace offerings in two distinct ways. Price not only serves as a measure of economic sacrifice, but also influences consumers' inferences about the quality of the product. However, research has shown that the relationship between price and perceived quality is inconsistent; consumers sometimes consider a higher price as a signal of better quality, and sometimes do not. Several influential papers have presented different perspectives on when and why consumers use price as a signal of quality. The present research extends this body of work by suggesting that whether consumers use price as a signal of quality is contingent on the type of cognitive process they rely on to make inferences. We show that consumers tend to rely on two distinct types of cognitive processes to make inferences about quality: a top-down process based on prototype resemblance or a bottom-up process based on their belief about the correlation between price and quality. Under conditions of top-down processing, consumers begin with the representation of a prototypical high quality product in their mind, and make spontaneous inferences by comparing the new product to this mental prototype. Usually, a prototypical high quality product has a conjunction of positive attributes (i.e., attributes that are associated with high quality). Therefore, when the new product has a conjunction of positive attributes and thus resembles the prototype, they infer that the new product will have the same quality as the prototype and this spontaneous inference makes them more likely to consider a higher price as an indicator of better quality. Conversely, when the new product has one or more negative attributes and thus does not resemble the prototype, they do not consider a higher price as an indicator of better quality. Even when the new product has a higher price, they infer that since the new product does not resemble the prototype it will not have the same quality as the prototype. We refer to the tendency to inconsistently interpret price based on top-down processing as the prototype resemblance effect in price-quality inferences. Interestingly, this prototype resemblance effect does not manifest when inferences are based on bottom-up processing (i.e., based on their belief about the correlation between price and quality.)

As an illustrative example, consider the example of a consumer who is trying to infer the quality of food at two new restaurants in her city. Both restaurants have unimpressive decor. However, they differ on price. A typical meal at one of the restaurants costs $25 while at the other restaurant it costs $12. Will she consider the higher priced restaurant to have better quality food than the lower priced one, given that both restaurants have unimpressive decor? This consumers' inference will be contingent on the type of cognitive process she relies on to make the inference. If she relies on top-down processing, she will infer that the expensive restaurant will not have better quality food because it has unimpressive decor and thus does not resemble a prototypical high quality restaurant. In contrast, if she relies on bottom-up processing, she will infer that the expensive restaurant will have better food because price is positively correlated with quality.

Three experiments and a field study were conducted to examine the role of top-down and bottom-up processing in quality inferences. The studies presented in this article characterize how the activation of prototypes influences price-quality inferences. Although there is a rich literature on the role of prototype-based processing in consumer behavior (see Loken, Barsalou and Joiner 2007 for a recent review), and some researchers have examined the role of knowledge and beliefs in quality inferences (Baumgartner 1995; Kardes et al. 2004; Rao and Monroe 1988), we are not aware of any research that specifically examined the effects of prototype activation on price-quality inferences. The present research aims to remedy this omission. We address three specific questions in this research: (i) What is the structure of mental prototypes used in quality inferences (Study 1)? (ii) How do these prototypes influence consumers' interpretation of price (Study 2)? (iii) How do top-down prototype based inferences differ from inferences that are based on beliefs about the correlation between price and quality (Study 3)? We use response time data to examine whether consumers actually rely on their price-quality beliefs to make quality inferences. We show that participants' response times are influenced by prototype resemblance, but not by their price-quality beliefs. To the best of our knowledge, none of the previous studies have examined the patterns in response times and its implications for the theories of price-quality inferences. Further, we use data collected outside laboratory settings to empirically test which of the two modes of inferences is more pervasive in everyday quality inferences–the top-down process based on prototype resemblance or the bottom-up process based on beliefs about the correlation between price and quality. We analyze consumers' food quality ratings of 1,620 restaurants, and find that the dominant propensity is to rely on prototype resemblance. Finally, this study also contributes to the small but growing body of literature which suggests that a high price can play the role of a placebo and unconsciously influence consumers' actual product experiences (see Rao 2005; Shiv, Carmon, and Ariely 2005). The results from our field study, together with findings from placebo effect research (Shiv, Carmon, and Ariely 2005), suggest that when a restaurant with good décor charges a higher menu price, a consumer might actually experience the food to be of better quality. But when similar food at the same price is offered by a restaurant with mediocre décor, the consumer's experience might not be so favorable.

## References

Baumgartner, Hans (1995), "On the Utility of Consumers' Theories in Judgments of Covariation," *Journal of Consumer Research*, 21 (March), 634–43.

Kardes, Frank R., Maria L. Cronley, James J. Kellaris, and Steven S. Posavac (2004), "The Role of Selective Information Processing in Price-quality Inference," *Journal of Consumer Research*, 31(2), 368-74.

Loken, Barbara, Lawrence Barsalou, and Christopher Joiner (2008), "Categorization Theory and Research in Consumer Psychology: Category Representation and Category-Based Influence," in *Handbook of Consumer Psychology*, eds. C. P. Haugtvedt, Paul Herr, and Frank Kardes, 132-163.

Rao, Akshay and Kent B. Monroe (1989), "The Effect of Price, Brand Name, and Store Name on Buyers' Perceptions of Product Quality: An Integrative Review," *Journal of Marketing Research*, 26 (August), 351–57.

Shiv, Baba, Carmon Ziv, and Dan Ariely (2005), "Placebo Effects of Marketing Actions: Consumers May Get What They Pay For," *Journal of Marketing Research*, 42 (November), 383-93.

### "When Payless Meets Prada: Subtractive Judgments in Evaluating Product Bundles"

*Aaron R. Brough, Northwestern University, USA*
*Alexander Chernev, Northwestern University, USA*

Consumers often encounter combinations that include products from different price tiers. For example, retailers and manufacturers commonly bundle high- and low-priced products together, such as a computer with a printer or a sofa with an ottoman. Additionally, some combinations are formed coincidentally, such as when consumers place items from different price tiers into a shopping basket or purchase them in the same shopping episode. Despite its importance, the notion of how consumers determine their willingness to pay (WTP) for combinations is not well-understood.

Logically, estimating a bundle's overall value should involve adding the subjective value of each individual item. Some research assumes that bundle valuation is perfectly additive, such that WTP for a bundle is equal to the sum of WTP for its individual components (Bitran and Ferrer 2007). Empirical evidence shows that, in fact, WTP is often subadditive, such that the value of two items is discounted when they are evaluated together rather than separately (Cooke & Pecheux; Heeler et al. 2007). Regardless of the magnitude of this discount, conventional wisdom would suggest that the value of the bundle should be higher than the value of any individual item in the combination.

In contrast to prior literature documenting bundle valuation that is perfectly additive or subadditive, we identify conditions in which it is instead subtractive. That is, we show cases in which WTP for a combination is less than WTP for a single item in the combination, despite the fact that when evaluated individually, each item in the combination has positive utility for consumers. In addition, we propose a novel explanation for this subtraction effect and show that it cannot be explained by consumer expectations for quantity discounts or inferences that one of the bundle components is low-quality.

We argue that adding an inexpensive item to an expensive item decreases rather than increases WTP for the offering because of categorization. In particular, we argue that when items classified into opposite categories (e.g., expensive vs. inexpensive) are combined, the combination is perceived to be less extreme than its components (e.g., moderately expensive). Relying on this overall impression of the combination, individuals assign a lower numeric value to the combination than to the expensive item when articulating WTP. As a result, WTP for the combination is lower than WTP for the expensive item alone, despite the combination's objectively greater value.

We conducted four experiments to document the subtraction effect and examine its antecedents and consequences. Study 1 tests the proposition that individuals are less willing to pay for an expensive item when it is combined with an inexpensive item rather than evaluated alone. Across six product categories, online participants evaluated either an expensive item alone, an inexpensive item alone, or a combination that included the same expensive and inexpensive items presented to participants in the first two conditions. Results demonstrate the subtraction effect by showing that WTP for the

combination was lower than WTP for the expensive option alone in each of the six categories, as well as overall across categories.

Study 2 examines the role of impression formation in the subtraction effect by comparing WTP for a combination when items are presented side-by-side but evaluated either individually or as a combination. In particular, it shows that neither quality inferences nor expectations for quantity discounts can fully account for the subtraction effect. We predict that the subtraction effect is more likely to be observed when consumers evaluate the combination as a whole rather than evaluating each component of the combination in piecemeal fashion. As expected, mean WTP across categories was lower for the combination (when the offering was evaluated holistically) than for the expensive option alone (when the offering was evaluated in piecemeal fashion).

Study 3 provides further evidence that categorization causes the subtraction effect by documenting that this effect is attenuated when people focus on other attributes, such as functionality, rather than price. This study was similar to study 1, but in order to prompt categorization on a dimension other than price, half of the participants answered a question about the functionality of each product prior to articulating WTP. For example, when evaluating luggage, some participants were asked to indicate the expected size of the luggage relative to an average brand. As predicted, the subtraction effect was attenuated when participants focused on functionality rather than price.

Finally, Study 4 documents the role of categorization by showing that the subtraction effect is weaker when options are classified into the same category rather than opposite categories. We reason that introducing an extremely high reference price prior to evaluation should reduce the likelihood that expensive and inexpensive items are classified into opposite categories, since both items are likely to be perceived as inexpensive relative to the high reference price. Thus, participants estimated the likely price of a reference item prior to evaluating the target item(s) for each category. Reference items were selected such that participants would perceive the price to be relatively similar or extremely high compared to the prices of the target item(s). Consistent with our prediction, exposure to an extremely high reference price prior to evaluating the target option attenuated the subtraction effect.

Data from four studies offer converging support for the notion that adding an inexpensive item to an expensive one can decrease rather than increase the perceived value of an offering. This research has important managerial and theoretical implications. In particular, it suggests that bundling products from different price tiers may result in decreased revenue. Furthermore, it illuminates the role of categorization in value judgments, showing that changes in the qualitative classification of item(s) can impact numeric evaluation.

**References**

Bitran, Gabriel R. and Juan-Carlos Ferrer (2007), "On Pricing and Composition of Bundles," *Production & Operations Management*, 16 (1), 93-108.

Cook, Alan D. J. and Claude Pechex (working paper), "Subadditive Bundle Preferences and the Value of Variety"

Heeler, Roger M., Adam Nguyen, and Cheryl Buff (2007), "Bundles=discount? Revisiting complex theories of bundle effects," *Journal of Product & Brand Management*, 16 (7), 492-500.

### "The Effect of Shipping Fee Structure on Consumer Evaluations of Online Offers"

*Nevena T. Koukova, Lehigh University, USA*
*Joydeep Srivastava, University of Maryland, USA*
*Martina Steul-Fischer, University of Erlangen-Nuremberg, Germany*

*Long Abstract.* According to Forrester Research, online spending in the U. S. in 2008 was about $141 billion and should reach $156 billion in 2009. The growth in e-commerce as well as direct to consumer retailing has highlighted the importance of shipping fees. A critical decision is how to present these fees to consumers particularly when 30% of online shopping carts are abandoned due to shipping and handling surcharges (Jupiter Research 2006). Despite its importance to online and other direct retailers, only a few studies have examined the effects of shipping fees (cf. Lewis 2006; Lewis, Singh and Fay 2006; Schindler, Morrin and Bechwati 2005).

We investigate the effects of two common shipping fee structures–flat rate shipping and threshold based free shipping-on consumer evaluations of online offers. Drawing on the price partitioning literature (e.g., Hamilton and Srivastava 2008; Morwitz, Greenleaf and Johnson 1998), the basic premise is that separating the shipping fee from the product price makes the shipping fee more salient. Given that most evaluations are based on some standard of comparison (Kahneman and Tversky 1979), we propose that consumers use different referents to evaluate the shipping fees. Specifically, while the referent used to evaluate flat rate shipping is likely to be based on prior experience and/or knowledge and is somewhat imprecise, the natural referent used to evaluate threshold based free shipping is the possibility of free shipping that is more precise. A memory based referent requires more effort to access in the case of flat rate shipping whereas the stimulus based referent of free shipping in the case of threshold based free shipping is vivid and easily accessible. As such, given threshold based free shipping, order values below the threshold are coded as a loss whereas order values above the threshold are coded as a bonus or a quantity discount relative to the natural referent of free shipping. Our main prediction is that online offers will be evaluated less (more) favorably when the shipping structure is threshold based free shipping than flat rate shipping for order values below (above) the threshold for free shipping.

We report the results of five between-participants experiments which demonstrate that evaluations systematically vary as a function of shipping fee structure. Study 1a shows that compared with flat rate shipping, consumer evaluations are more favorable when an online offer has threshold based free shipping for order values above the threshold. The reverse is true for order values below the threshold for free shipping as the offer is evaluated less favorably with threshold based free shipping than with flat rate shipping. In addition, perceptions of shipping fee fairness mediate the effect of shipping fee structure and order value on offer evaluations. Study 1b demonstrates that the results are robust to the difference between order value and the threshold for free shipping. Specifically, consumer evaluations do not differ when the order value is just below the threshold (e.g., order value of $19.99 relative to a $25 threshold for free shipping) or significantly below the threshold (e.g., order value of $19.99 relative to a $75 threshold for free shipping).

Study 2 sheds more light on the underlying mechanism by examining the effect of shipping fee structure on consumer evaluations when an alternative referent is made salient. Our conceptualization suggests that making an alternative referent salient is likely to shift attention away from the shipping fee and reduce the reliance on the shipping fee referents, thus attenuating the effect of shipping fee structure on consumer evaluations. For example, an offer that is presented as a 20% discount off the regular price is likely to alter the focus of attention from shipping fee to the price discount. Consistent with the proposed mechanism, study 2 demonstrates that the effects of shipping fee structure are similar to those in study 1 in the absence of an alternative referent. However, there is no difference in consumer evaluations across the threshold based free shipping and flat rate shipping structures in the presence of an alternative salient referent, regardless of order value. These results highlight the shift in attention from the shipping fee and the associated referents in each of the two shipping fee structures to the price discount when it is made salient. Importantly, we rule out positive affect as an alternative explanation for the results.

Another question that this research investigates is whether the shipping fee structure affects consumer perceptions of the extent to which retailers use shipping fees to generate profits. Study 3 demonstrates that while participants are more likely to believe that the retailer is making profit in the threshold based free shipping condition than in the flat rate shipping condition for order values below the threshold, the reverse is true for order values above the threshold. With a flat rate shipping structure, since all consumers have to pay for shipping regardless of order value, the shipping fee is more likely to be viewed as the actual cost that the retailer incurs for delivery. With a threshold based free shipping structure, in the presence of the referent of free shipping, consumers are likely to believe that the retailer is using the shipping fee to generate profits.

Study 4 examines whether providing a justification for shipping fee structure and linking the shipping fee to the actual cost of delivery moderates the effect on evaluations of online offers as well as perceptions of shipping fees as generating profits. The results suggest that consumer evaluations as well as perceptions of shipping fees as generating profits do not differ across the flat rate and threshold based free shipping structures for all order values when a justification for the shipping fee is provided. The justification for the shipping fee and linking it to actual cost of delivery encourages consumers to view the shipping fee as the cost of doing business rather than as a loss or that the retailer is trying to making money on the shipping fee.

### References

Hamilton, Rebecca W. and Joydeep Srivastava (2008), "When 2+2 Is Not the Same as 1+3: Variations in Price Sensitivity Across Components of Partitioned Prices," *Journal of Marketing Research*, 45 (4), 450-61.

Jupiter Research (2006), *Retail Website Performance: Customer Reactions to a Poor Online Shopping Experience*, New York: JupiterKagan.

Kahneman, Daniel and Amos Tversky (1979), "Prospect Theory: An Analysis of Decision under Risk," *Econometrica*, 47 (March), 163-91.

Lewis, Michael (2006), "The Effect of Shipping Fees on Customer Acquisition, Customer Retention, and Purchase Quantities," *Journal of Retailing*, 82, 13-23.

Lewis, Michael, Vishal Singh, and Scott Fay (2006), "An Empirical Study of the Impact of Nonlinear Shipping and Handling Fees on Purchase Incidence and Expenditure Decisions," *Marketing Science*, 25, 51-64.

Morwitz, Vicki G., Eric A. Greenleaf, and Eric J. Johnson (1998), "Divide and Prosper: Consumers' Reactions to Partitioned Prices," *Journal of Marketing Research*, 35 (November), 453-63.

Schindler, Robert M., Maureen Morrin, and Nada Nasr Bechwati (2005), "Shipping Charges and Shipping Charge Skepticism: Implications for Direct Marketers' Pricing Formats," *Journal of Interactive Marketing*, 9, 41-53.

## "More than Just a Constraint: Budget Constraints Shape Preference"

Jeffrey *Larson, Brigham Young University, USA*
Ryan *Hamilton, Emory University, USA*

No matter their income or net worth, consumer purchases are all constrained by finite resources. Few consumer decisions are not affected by budget constraints. Despite its omnipresence in consumer decision making, research on the role of budget constraints on consumer decisions has been surprisingly limited. Heath and Soll (1996) and Ulkumen, Thomas, and Morwitz (2008) both focus on the mechanics of consumer budget setting and budget estimation, but devote less attention to how budgets impact consumer decision making. Hauser and Urban (1986) examine budget planning and show how budget constraints influence consumers' desire to maximize "bang for the buck."

While economists' notion of the hyper-rational agent has been sufficiently lambasted over the years, it is still universally accepted that consumers try to get the most for their money. While this effort is bound to be error-prone, consumers nevertheless attempt to assess the value of products relative to their price, and purchase the product that offers the most utility relative to the utility of the money exchanged. Extant theory posits that budget constraints should not play a role in the evaluation of a product's utility, but only in the evaluations of the relative price comparisons.

In contrast, we demonstrate that consumers' budget constraints affect even their evaluations of a product's desirability in two different ways. First, consumers tend to devalue products that are outside of their budget. Rather than recognizing that expensive products are superior to less expensive products (although perhaps not be worth the extra expense), consumers who are unable to afford a product convince themselves that expensive products are actually inferior. Second, consumers become sensitized to quality differences within the range of prices they are accustomed to shopping. For example, a woman accustomed to buying handbags in the price range of $50 to $100 would more readily notice the difference in quality between a $75 and a $95 handbag than between a $150 and $300 handbag.

To test our first proposition, we recruited 78 members of an online panel to participate in a study on product preferences. We told all participants to consider that they were planning to purchase an iPod nanoTM to exercise with. Participants were told that they had budgeted $170 for the purchase and had narrowed the decision down to one of two options—one with 8 GB storage for $133.99 or one with 16 GB storage for $159.95. They evaluated the desirability of each iPod nano on a 0 to 100 sliding scale and made a selection. In their evaluations of the products (in this and the following evaluations), they were asked to ignore price and only evaluate the product's desirability. After making this decision, participants were then told that they also wanted to purchase an armband to hold their iPod during exercise. Of course, their remaining budget for this decision depended on their previous iPod selection. Those who had selected the 8 GB nano had $36.01 remaining in their budget, while those who had selected the 16 GB nano had only $10.05 of their original budget remaining. The two armbands offered cost either $17.95 or $6.80. Thus, participants either had enough money in their budget for both or only for one of them. We hypothesized that those with only $10.05 would devalue the more expensive armband. Consistent with our prediction, the group with enough money remaining for either armband gave the cheaper armband an average rating of 58.8 and the more expensive armband a 64.9. The limited budget group, on the other hand, rated the cheaper armband a 67.6 and the more expensive armband a 57.5. The average difference in the two ratings was significantly different (p=.04, one-tailed).

To test our second hypothesis, that consumers become sensitized to quality differences within their budget range, we recruited 131 participants from an online panel for a study on product evaluations. To begin the survey, we asked each participant to report the most they had ever spent on a product from each of 10 product categories. Participants were then asked to rate five products, labeled with their actual online retail price, from several of these categories. Participants were also asked to rate the quality of each product in the set on a 0 to 100 sliding scale. Each person made these ratings for five products from four different product categories. All participants rated surround sound systems, sunglasses, and watches (the sunglasses and watches shown were gender-matched). Men further rated golf clubs, while women rated a set of handbags.

We hypothesized that participants' quality ratings would be sensitized to their budget range. We determined each participant's budget range from the most they had spent on the product category. If $100 was the most they had spent on a golf club, then their budget range must extend below and above $100. This reference value was matched to two products from the five products each participant rated. For example, we showed male participants golf clubs (all drivers) priced at $45, $87, $129, $171, and $213. A person who has spent at most $100 on a golf club should be sensitized to the difference between the $87 and $129 golf club such that the difference in quality between these two golf clubs is higher than between other clubs. Therefore, we modeled difference in quality ratings between each product and the product just above it. As expected, participants were more sensitive to quality differences in their budget range than between other products. The average difference in quality rating was significantly higher between the two product near the budget reference than between other products (p=.006).

If consumers desire to get the most for their money, they need to be able to reliably evaluate products. Based on findings from this research, product evaluations seem to be at least partially determined by consumer budgets; a factor which could prevent some consumers from maximizing utility.

## References

Hauser, John R. and Glen L. Urban (1986), "The value priority hypotheses for consumer budget plans," *Journal of Consumer Research*, 12 (4), 446-62.

Heath, Chip and Jack B. Soll (1996), "Mental budgeting and consumer decisions," *Journal of Consumer Research*, 23 (1), 40-52.

Ulkumen, Gulden, Manoj Thomas, and Vicki G. Morwitz (2008), "Will I spend more in 12 months or a year? The effect of ease of estimation and confidence on budget estimates," *Journal of Consumer Research*, 35 (2), 245-56.

# Strategic and Impulsive Allocation of Attention: Behavioral and Emotional Consequences

Suresh Ramanathan, University of Chicago, USA

## EXTENDED ABSTRACTS

### "Accentuate the Positive, Eliminate the Negative: Attention and Emotion Regulation"

Nicole M. Verrochi, University of Pennsylvania, USA
Patti Williams, University of Pennsylvania, USA

Individuals frequently manage their emotions, such as during a sad television commercial, looking at a soothing picture in a waiting room, or avoiding a plate of cookies at a party. In marketing, there is growing interest in understanding these emotion regulation processes and which strategies consumers use in various situations. Research (e.g., Gross 1998) has proposed five classes of emotion regulation strategies: situation selection, situation modification, attention deployment, cognitive change, and response modulation. To date, the bulk of research has focused on cognitive change and response modulation (Gross and Levenson 1993), while newer work has explored situation selection (e.g., Andrade and Cohen 2007). While each of these papers contributes to a deeper understanding of emotion regulation and its psychological components, certain strategies remain under-investigated.

This paper investigates attention deployment, whereby individuals strategically shift their attention toward or away from emotional stimuli to manage emotional experiences. Two studies demonstrate that people use attention shifts when presented with emotional stimuli, and a third shows that these changes in attention influence the intensity of experienced emotion, supporting an attention-based emotion regulation strategy.

Two studies tested whether individuals use attention shifts to regulate emotions when they encounter emotional stimuli. To examine these strategic attention shifts, a novel paradigm was created combining attention measures with emotional experiences. Attention was indexed by participants' accuracy as they identified rapidly presented targets. These measures captured whether the individual was focusing closely on the target or diverting attention away from it. Thus, participants were asked across many iterations to indicate whether a letter "T" was presented either upside-down or right-side-up as quickly as possible (the "T task"). Intermixed with the "Ts", participants were also exposed to a series of pictures. These pictures were from the International Affective Picture System (IAPS: Lang, Bradley and Cuthbert 2005), and reliably elicit emotional responses. The pictures appeared in the target location periodically throughout the study. Thus, if participants shift attention toward and away from emotional triggers, accuracy should change for the "Ts" which follow each emotional picture.

In the first study, participants were exposed to pictures that were positive (e.g., puppies) and negative (e.g., car crashes). Results showed that participants performed worse (lower accuracy) on the T task following negatively valenced emotional stimuli ($p < .001$). This suggests that individuals are diverting their attention away from the target when they encounter a negative stimulus, versus focusing their attention on the target when it was positive.

To test the influence of specific emotions on the efficacy of attention shifts, the second study involved a two-group design. The negative pictures were all either fearful (e.g., attacks) or sad (e.g., crying children) pictures. Research has shown differences between emotions of the same valence, such as fear and sadness; both are negative but fear is characterized by uncertainty and heuristic processing, while sadness is certain and engenders systematic processing (Tiedens and Linton 2001). In the fear condition, attention was unchanged across emotional stimuli ($p > .25$), but in the sad condition, performance worsened after a negative (sad) versus positive picture—as in study 1 ($p < .01$). This would suggest that in the sad condition, participants are strategically shifting their attention away from negative stimuli. However, for fearful stimuli, attention seems to remain focused on the target, reducing the likelihood that an individual could shift attention away from fearful stimuli. The results from studies one and two suggest that individuals naturally use attention shifts when encountering emotional stimuli, however certain negative emotions (fear) may be resistant to an attention-based emotion regulation strategy.

These two studies support attention as a key moderator of emotional experience, but do not connect these shifts to emotional experience. The third study captured this effect. Participants watched an emotional video clip (sad, fearful) under attention instructions. Participants were told to either focus on the faces of the actors (directing attention toward emotional cues) or on set design (diverting attention away from emotional cues). By manipulating participants' attention, the study assessed whether diverting attention away from emotional cues (versus directing attention toward) would reduce the intensity of emotion. Results show that within the sad condition, participants who directed their attention toward emotional cues (faces) experienced higher levels of sadness ($M=5.04$) than those who diverted attention away from emotional cues (scenes: $M=3.69$, $p<.05$). This pattern supports the hypothesized function of attention: when attention is directed onto emotional cues the intensity of emotion increases, but when attention is diverted away from these cues intensity decreases. For ratings of fear, however, the attention manipulation was non-significant ($p>.20$).

These studies demonstrate that individuals shift their attention in response to emotional stimuli, and that changes in attention influence the experience of emotion. Additionally, these results identify specific emotions which are more or less susceptible to regulation via attention deployment—an important boundary condition. Taken together, these studies certify that attention can be used to effectively manage emotional experiences, suggesting new directions for emotion regulation and consumer research.

### "Can We Help Consumers Make Healthier Food Choices? The Role of Product Associations"

Juliano Laran, University of Miami, USA
Marcus Cunha, University of Washington, USA

It is lunch time and Mary heads to the fast food restaurant near her office. She was about to order the usual Combo # 1, featuring a chicken sandwich and fries, when she notices that the restaurant introduced a second option, Combo # 2. This option features the same chicken sandwich available in Combo # 1and mixed greens salad. Mary likes fries and salad to the same extent, so what will determine whether she chooses Combo # 1 or Combo # 2? The choice might be explained by whether consumers feel they have made enough progress on a healthy eating goal recently (Fishbach & Dhar, 2005), by the amount of self-control resources available to consumers at the time of choice (Baumeister, Bratslavsky, Muraven, & Tice, 1998; Vohs & Faber, 2007), and by the most activated goal (i.e., healthy eating or indulgence) at the time of choice (Chartrand, Huber, Shiv, & Tanner, 2008)

Our research adds to the growing interest in understanding the role of presentation format on consumers' evaluations and choices of healthy vs. unhealthy food pairings (e.g., Fishbach & Zhang, 2008; Wilcox, Vallen, Block, & Fitzsimons, 2009). We propose that a mechanism of protection of associations can change the salience of each option in the scenario described above (Cunha, Janiszewski, & Laran, 2008; Kruschke, Kappenman, & Hetrick, 2005). We will show how this protection mechanism can contribute to understanding the process via which resources depletion and goal priming may operate as drivers of self control.

The Association Protection Mechanism. Consumers develop a large number of associations throughout their lifetime. For example, through repetition and co-occurrence, consumers learn that bacon and eggs, hamburger and Coke, tuna and mayonnaise go well together. Protecting these learned associations from interfering associations decreases cognitive costs and helps consumers more rapidly learn and adapt to their environment. The idea of protection of associations is grounded on attentional learning theory (Cunha et al., 2008; Cunha & Laran, 2009; Kruschke, 2001) and is predicted to occur when the cognitive system directs attention to information that can solve this potential conflict in the knowledge structure. Attention is then steered toward information that is useful in acquiring novel knowledge while still protecting prior knowledge.

For instance, when Mary first learned about Combo #1, featuring chicken sandwich and fries, there was no previous association between the food items and "Combo #1". Therefore, it is likely that both food items became associated with Combo # 1. When Mary became aware of Combo # 2, featuring chicken sandwich and salad, a conflict occurred (chicken sandwich partially defines Combo #1). Combo # 2 features a new food item (salad) that can facilitate the acquisition of new knowledge while preserving prior knowledge. Because reassessing and updating prior associations of Combo # 1 could be cognitively taxing, Mary can solve the conflict by simply shifting attention away from "chicken sandwich" and toward "salad" when presented with Combo # 2. As a result, "chicken sandwich" should become more strongly associated with Combo # 1 than with Combo # 2, whereas "salad" should become more strongly associated with Combo # 2 than "fries" are associated with Combo # 1. If Mary finds the chicken sandwich to be more desirable than the distinct items, she will judge Combo #1 to be more desirable overall. If she finds the distinct items to be more desirable than the chicken sandwich, she will judge Combo #2 to be more desirable overall.

The experiments involved the sequential presentation of food pairings followed by judgments of likelihood to consume each pairing. The sequential presentation was used to influence the strength of associations between food-items and their respective pairings. Study 1 shows that these associations may determine whether food choices are healthy or unhealthy. Study 2 shows that depleting consumers of their self-control resources affects their attentional capacity. As a consequence, we observe and amplification of the basic effect reported in Study 1. Study 3 and 4 show that the effect can be replicated using actual restaurant menus with a single exposure to the menus.

An important question stemming from our research is how policy makers and marketers can use our results? Policy makers can raise consumers' awareness of their tendency to protect associations so that they can more efficiently allocate attention when making choices with implications for consumer welfare. Legislators can also enforce that marketers design product displays, in a way that directs attention to specific options first, which will drive subsequent attention and choice.

### "A Decision-Path Model of Attention and Consideration at the Point of Purchase"
*Wesley Hutchinson, University of Pennsylvania, USA*
*Eric Bradlow, University of Pennsylvania, USA*
*Pierre Chandon, INSEAD, France*

Consumer behavior at the point of purchase is influenced by out-of-store memory-based factors (e.g., brand awareness and brand image) and by in-store attention-based factors (e.g., position and number of facings). In today's cluttered retail environments, creating memory-based consumer pull is not enough; marketers must also create "visual lift" for their brands—that is, incremental consideration caused by in-store visual attention. The problem is that it is currently impossible to precisely measure visual lift. Surveys can easily be conducted to compare pre-store intentions and post-store choices but they do not measure attention. They cannot therefore tell whether ineffective in-store marketing was due to a poor attention-getting ability—"unseen and hence unsold"—or to a poor visual lift—"seen yet still unsold". Eye-tracking studies have shown that eye-movements to brands displayed on a supermarket shelf are valid measures of visual attention, are correlated with brand consideration, and are influenced by POP marketing (Chandon et al. 2009; Russo and Leclerc 1994; Van der Lans, Pieters, and Wedel 2008). However, they have not provided a method for separating the effects of attention and memory on consumer decisions. They have also not shown that attention to a brand causes consideration, rather than memory for a brand to be considered causing visual search for that brand.

In this study, we show how eye-tracking data can be used to separate the effects of visual factors from memory-based factors as a determinant of brand consideration and hence to decompose a brand's consideration into its baseline and its visual lift. To achieve this goal, we develop a parsimonious decision-path model of visual attention and brand consideration.

The model is designed for simple eye-tracking data consisting of joint observations of the number of eye fixations provided by the study (zero, one, two, three, or at least four) and the consideration decision (yes or no) for each brand and consumer. We model the P-O-P decision making process as a sequence of events that alternate between sub-decisions to consider the brand and sub-decisions to make an eye fixation on the brand (see Figure 1). The first decision is a memory-based, pre-store consideration that is made before the brand is noticed. Next, consumers decide whether or not to look at the brand. If the brand is not fixated, no new information is acquired, and the consideration decision remains unchanged. If the brand is fixated, the new eye fixation provides a new opportunity to consider the brand. We assume that consideration is irreversible; that is, having considered a brand, consumers might choose to look at it again but they do not "un-consider" it. Of course, consumers may still decide not to buy the brand even though it is included in the consideration set. The model allows us to examine, first theoretically and then empirically, the effects of looks on consideration and the effects of POP activity on each of the attention and consideration decisions. First, the model shows that the conditional probability of consideration given fixation increases with the number of fixations, regardless of any marketing effects. Second, the model predicts that there are diminishing returns in the gain from each additional look. Third, we examine various models with asymmetries in attention and consideration probabilities, which allow us to examine whether people look more at brands already considered or whether facings change the "quality" of each look.

We applied this model to eye-movements and brand consideration data collected in collaboration with a leading eye-tracking company. We created a fractional factorial design which allowed us to test the effects of the number (4, 8, or 12) and location (which of four horizontal shelves and four vertical blocks) of shelf facings independently of any brand-specific effects using only 12 planograms. We recruited 384 adult shoppers and asked them to look at two categories (soap bars or pain relievers) and to make either consideration decisions while their eyes were being tracked. Each planogram includes the 11 top brands of the category and one brand unfamiliar to the participants. We obtained a total of 8,304 observations.

Our key findings for the soap category are that, out of an average consideration probability of 25%, 18% comes from pre-store consideration and 7% from in-store visual lift. For pain relievers, the average consideration was 24%, the average pre-store consideration was 11%, and the average visual lift was 13%. The higher visual lift for pain reliever was partly because, in this category, people are more likely to look at unconsidered brands (76%) than at already-considered brands (66%)—hence looks are more useful. In contrast, consumers were even slightly more likely to look at soap brands that they had already considered (79%) than at brands that they had not considered (76%). We also found that facings were particularly effective at attracting attention to unconsidered brands and that this effect was robust across the two categories. Finally, we found that facings slightly improved the quality of looks. Rather than simply providing another chance to toss the coin, looks caused by facings made the coin toss more likely to lead to consideration. This was particularly true for the first looks. Facings did not change the quality of looks after the fourth one. Further analyses looked at the effect of past purchase behavior. They found that visual lift is higher for regular users than for occasional users or for non users. On the other hand, the effects of facings were strongest for occasional users.

### "Sticky Desires or Tricky Self-Control? Dynamic Processes in Attentional Bias Towards Temptations"

*Suresh Ramanathan, University of Chicago, USA*
*Jun Lu, University of Chicago, USA*

A rich body of literature has looked at impulsive or indulgent behaviors through the lens of self-control, suggesting that such behaviors arise due to weakness of will or failures in self-control (Baumeister 2002). We propose an alternative view, suggesting a larger role for desires than previously thought. Specifically, we suggest that indulge tendency arises due to a strong attentional bias towards temptations that manifests in greater and more recurrent desires, particularly among impulsive individuls.

Previous literature has identified two types of attentional bias: *orientation bias* that results in spontaneous attraction towards stimulus and *engagement bias* that results in continued engagement with the stimulus. In three studies, we show that engagement bias better predicts people's yield to temptation and stems from people's tendency to approach temptations rather than a diminution in their ability to avoid. Furthermore, training impulsive individual to focus on stimulus inconsistent with their chronic goal can worsen the situation as their desire for temptation surges upon subsequent encounter.

Experiment 1 seeks to determine the nature of attentional biases towards temptations among impulsive vs. prudent people and whether indulgent behavior results from attentional bias. Participants first completed a scrambled sentence task that was either neutral or designed to activate the need for something sweet. They then engaged in a visual probe task (Bradley et al. 2002), in which participants were required to respond as quickly as possible to a small dot probe which was presented immediately after the display of a pair of pictures consisting one of dessert and one of healthy option. Picture pairs were presented for either 100 ms or 1250 ms

on the screen after a fixation cross that appeared for 500, 750 or 1250 ms at random. These were followed by a dot probe that appeared in one of the two positions and remained on screen till the respondent's response. Attentional bias scores were computed for each participant where positive values indicate greater vigilance for temptations. Positive values at the 100 ms exposure level indicate automatic visual orientation towards temptations, while those at the 1250 ms level indicate continued attention towards desserts even when the probe appeared in the position of the fruit. After the dot probe task, participants were given the opportunity to take cookies from a filled tray as an unrelated study. Finally, impulsivity was measured via the Consumer Impulsiveness Scale (Puri 1996) two weeks after the study. Results showed that impulsive individuals exhibited an orientation bias towards temptations. In addition, impulsive individuals who were primed with hedonic goal showed greater engagement with pictures of temptations. More importantly, those who exhibited the engagement bias took more cookies than those who exhibited orientation bias or no attentional bias, implying that engagement bias towards temptations leads to subsequent indulgent behaviors.

Experiment 2 examines the psychological processes underlying such attentional biases. In particular, we were interested in the dynamics of desire and avoidance towards the temptation in an attempt to determine whether indulgence is caused by strengthened desire or weakened avoidance. We changed the design of the dot probe task such that the dot probe would appear more frequently (90% of the trails) either at the location of the dessert picture or the fruit picture, thus manipulating attention in one direction. Subsequently, we measured desire-avoidance reactions towards a tempting chocolate snack on a 2-D grid by moving a mouse cursor continuously for 60 seconds. Participants indicated whether they felt little or a lot of desire and avoidance towards the snack right at the moment on two orthogonal dimensions. Using a new technique from dynamical psychology called Recurrence Analysis, we examined the trajectories followed by the time series for desires and avoidance, specifically looking for the extent to which the trajectories visited the same region in state space over time. Results confirmed that impulsive individuals who were manipulated to attend to desserts showed higher recurrence of desires and remained longer in a state of desire but not non-impulsive individuals, suggesting only impulsive individuals kept revisiting the same hedonic goal and were trapped in that goal state for a longer period of time. This phenomenon of trapped states is described in dynamical system theory as a "fixed point attractor" wherein individuals keep returning to a given state or goal despite occasional fluctuation (Carver 2004, Vallacher and Nowak 1999).

In experiment 3, we further explore how training attention engagement towards either towards temptation or healthy options can impact subsequent behavior when reward-seeking systems are activated at different time points. We followed the same procedure as in experiment 2 except that participants were additionally asked to sample a small piece of chocolate before or after the dot probe task. Sampling even a small bite of chocolate can cause activation of the reward-seeking system (Wadhwa et al. 2008). Results showed that impulsive individuals experienced higher recurrence of desire towards temptation when manipulated to attend to desserts if sampling before. More interestingly, impulsives experienced even higher recurrence of desire when they attended to healthy options first and then sampled a temptation. This data pattern suggests that reactance against goals inconsistent with their chronic goals may arise as a consequence of forced attention engagement on healthy options among impulsive individuals, hence training to focus on virtue can be a bad strategy to reinforce healthy behavior.

In summary, our research demonstrates that indulgent behavior exhibited by impulsive individuals is an immediate consequence of an engagement bias towards temptation that results in greater desires rather than weaker self-control. However, strengthened desire is not only limited to an elevated level of desire, but also extends to a more frequent recurrence of desire state and a longer trap time in that state. Forcing attention away from the temptation may backfire, resulting in higher recurrence of desire and consequently greater indulgence in impulsive individuals.

**References: Due to space limitations, references will be made available upon request.**

# Beyond Informational and Normative Influence: Conformity in Consumer Decision Making

Young Eun Huh, Carnegie Mellon University, USA
Joachim Vosgerau, Carnegie Mellon University, USA

## EXTENDED ABSTRACTS

### "Social Influence on Choice under Uncertainty"

*Young Eun Huh, Carnegie Mellon University, USA*
*Joachim Vosgerau, Carnegie Mellon University, USA*
*Carey Morewedge, Carnegie Mellon University, USA*

Choices are often made under uncertainty. While traveling abroad, for example, consumers often must choose among alternatives with information provided in a foreign unfamiliar language. Under such circumstances, one cue that decision-makers use is the choice of another decision-maker (e.g. a stranger at another table). In this research, we show that this cue is disproportionately weighted under conditions of uncertainty and investigate the underlying mechanisms of choice mimicry under uncertainty.

Social influence has been shown to play an important role in the decision making process (Childers and Rao 1992; Bearden and Etzel 1982; Campbell and Fairey 1989). The major paradigms in the social influence literature to explain social conformity have been normative influence and informational influence (Deutsch and Gerard 1955). Normative influence denotes the tendency to conform to the expectation of others. Informational influence denotes the tendency to accept information obtained from others (e.g., observation of others' behavior) as evidence about reality. We demonstrate that neither normative nor informational influence can explain choice mimicry under uncertainty. Alternatively, we propose the 'choice default' account. Under uncertainty, consumers trade off the effort of making a choice with the importance of making a correct decision. When the decision is of low importance, consumers simply follow others, but when it is of high importance, they expend the effort required to make a choice.

In Study 1, we tested whether participants would follow another decision-makers choice under uncertainty but not under certainty. The study consists of a 2 (prior choice: prior choice vs. no prior choice, a between-subjects factor) X 2 (product type: uncertain products vs. certain products, a within-subject factor) mixed design. All participants chose one tea from a set of two Korean teas (uncertain products, as our participants could not read Korean) and one tea from a set of two English breakfast teas (certain products) as remuneration for participating in the study. In the prior choice condition, participants followed a Caucasian confederate to the next room where the confederate first chose one of the two teas (Korean tea set and English tea set) and left the room. The participant was then left alone for making her choices. In the no prior choice condition, the participant went to the next room alone and made her choices. As hypothesized, more participants (79%) chose the Korean tea that was also chosen by the confederate compared to 56% who chose this tea in the no prior choice condition ((1)=4.66, p<.05). No such choice-mimicry was observed when participants chose among English teas (58% versus 51% in the control condition, (1)=.35, ns). Participants did not appear to mimic the confederate's choice under uncertainty because they believed that she was more knowledgeable—participants did not think that they would enjoy the Korean tea that they chose more than the Korean tea that they did not choose. However, participants thought they would enjoy the English tea that they chose more than the English tea that they did not choose. Thus, the observed choice-mimicry under uncertainty is not due to informational influence whereby participants believe

that the confederate's choice conveys information about the chosen options' utility.

In Study 2, we tested whether choice-mimicry under uncertainty is caused by normative influence. Participants choose one tea out of two Korean teas. In the absent-after-choice condition, the confederate chose a tea and left the room before participants chose a tea. In the present-after-choice condition, the confederate chose a tea and remained in the room while the participant chose a tea. In the control condition, participants chose a tea without observing the confederate's choice. Consistent with study 1, more participants chose the Korean tea that was also chosen by the confederate when the confederate left the room before participants made their choice (80% versus 48% in the control condition, (1)=3.86, p<.05). This choice mimicry, however, was reversed when the confederate remained in the room, as more participants chose the Korean tea that was not chosen by the confederate than in the control condition (only 17% followed the confederate's choice, (1)=4.18, p<.05). The results rule out the normative influence account of choice mimicry, which would predict more mimicry when the chooser makes the decision in the presence of others than in private.

In Study 3, we tested the choice default account in a 2 (choice stake: high stake vs. low stake) X 2 (prior choice: prior choice vs. no prior choice) between-subjects design. All participants were asked to choose among two different brands of Korean crackers. Participants in the low stake condition were told that they could take home their choice of cracker as remuneration for participating in the study. Participants in the high stake condition were told that they had to eat the crackers while in the lab. According to the choice-default account, choice-mimicry was expected in the low-stake but not the high-stake conditions. Consistent with the previous studies, in the low-stake conditions most participants chose the crackers that the confederate had chosen (78% versus 45% in the control condition, (1)=6.36, p=.01). This choice mimicry, however, was eliminated in the high stake conditions, as participants were no more likely to follow the confederate's choice compared to the control (41% vs. 48%, (1)=.58, ns).

Previous literature has demonstrated choice-mimicry under uncertainty due to either informational or normative influence. The current research demonstrates that choice-mimicry can also occur because consumers treat others' choices as defaults when they are not willing (or able) to exert mental effort to make their choice.

### "Seeing Ourselves in Others: Consumer Compliance with Recommendations Made by Ambiguous Agents"

*Rebecca Walker Naylor, Ohio State University, USA*
*Cait Poynor, University of Pittsburgh, USA*
*David A. Norton, University of South Carolina, USA*

Consumers often seek the influence of others when making product decisions. In these cases, social influence is explained by the information provider's expert status or the consumer's past experience (Gershoff and Johar 2006; Gershoff, Broniarczyk, and West 2001). However, many companies now present online reviews authored by individuals with whom a target consumer has no prior relationship, and which are often posted with no identifying information other than a user name. How does social influence operate when "influencers" are poorly identified, as opposed to known to be similar or dissimilar to the self?

We propose that in the absence of other information, consumers project their own characteristics onto an ambiguous individual. We argue that such "egocentric anchoring" occurs because the self constitutes the most psychologically proximate, accessible information source (Trope, Lieberman, and Wakslak 2007, Mussweiler 2003). Thus, consumers infer that an ambiguous other will be similar to themselves. As a result, these unidentified others exert relatively strong influence on preference and choice. However, since the self is an anchor, we also show that it can be adjusted. First, self-anchor effects can be moderated by making non-self-related cognitions more accessible. Second, directly disconfirming the hypothesis of similarity can also weaken the self-anchor and lower compliance with an ambiguous reviewer.

Four studies support the egocentric anchoring account and subsequent adjustment mechanisms. In study 1, participants read either a moderately positive or moderately negative restaurant review ostensibly written by another consumer. Participants saw either (1) no information about the reviewer (ambiguous reviewer condition), (2) information about a reviewer who was similar to the average student at their university (similar reviewer condition), or (3) information about a reviewer who was different from the average student at their university (dissimilar reviewer condition). Anticipated compliance was equivalent for ambiguous and similar reviewers. However, compliance with the recommendation was significantly lower for the dissimilar reviewer compared to the other conditions. Importantly, we show that these differences in compliance are mediated by participants' inferences of similarity to the reviewers. This pattern of effects held whether the review was moderately positive or moderately negative. Study 2 replicates this effect using a multi-product, multi-reviewer context.

Study 3 demonstrates that the egocentric anchor can be adjusted in this way, specifically, by making other-related cognitions more accessible. In this study, participants first described themselves (self prime) or the other people in the room with them (others prime). Next, participants read a restaurant review provided by one of the three types of reviewers (identical to the stimuli used in study 1). When self-related thoughts had been externally activated, there was again no difference in compliance with the recommendation between the similar and ambiguous reviewer conditions. However, when other-related thoughts had been made more acceptable, the self anchor was no longer adopted. Participants no longer assumed similarity with the ambiguous source, and, thus, were less likely to try the restaurant in the ambiguous versus similar reviewer condition.

A second way to prompt adjustment from an anchor is to directly disconfirm that the anchor provides an appropriate ground for inference-making. Study 4 shows that direct disconfirmation of the similarity hypothesis can also reduce reliance on the self-anchor. In this study, participants read reviews of an album on an online music review website, written by a similar, ambiguous, or dissimilar reviewer. Potential hypothesis-disconfirming information was given in the name of the website: www.CollegeMusic.com or www.AllMusic.com. The first website name was pretested to allow participants to believe the reviewer population was relatively homogeneous. In the homogeneous cue case, participants inferred similarity to and complied with the ambiguous reviewer at an equivalent level to the reviewer identified as similar, and more than the reviewer identified as dissimilar, suggesting reliance on the self-anchor as in prior studies. However, when participants saw the heterogeneous website name, this effect was attenuated, such that compliance was significantly higher for the identified similar reviewer than for the ambiguous and dissimilar reviewers.

In addition to providing theoretical insights regarding social influence and ambiguity, this work provides actionable advice for managers who allow consumers to post user-generated review content. Although managers of such sites may tend to err on the side of "more is better" in terms of reviewer identification, our research suggests that posting reviewer-identifying information along with a review may not be the best strategy in all cases. Rather, by constraining the amount of information a reviewer can provide, managers may be able to gain the benefits of similarity without raising the dangers associated with dissimilarity.

## "Social Treatment and Its Impact on Consumer Behavior"

*Monica Popa, University of Alberta, Canada*
*Jennifer Argo, University of Alberta, Canada*

Small-talk, ridicule, compliments, or insults are all type of social treatments that consumers commonly experience. In the present research we demonstrate that receiving a social treatment from one individual has implications for how the recipient of the treatment reacts toward other people in subsequent interactions. Furthermore, we find that the outcomes of social treatment are often counterintuitive. For example, we show that 'pay-it-forward' (the notion that a person who is treated well by someone should be nice toward others and conversely, a person who is treated badly may treat other people badly in turn) does not always occur; in fact, consumers often behave in the opposite manner. We offer a general theoretical framework that integrates previously fragmented investigations of social treatment (e.g., flattery, Campbell and Kirmani 2000; threat, Heatherton and Vohs 2000; teasing, Keltner et al. 2001) and reformulate context-specific explanations in terms of underlying dimensions.

Two dimensions of social treatment (affiliation: friendliness vs. hostility; and relevance for self-assessment: high vs. low) are predicted to interact in influencing consumers' behavior, and in particular consumers' socially-elevating behavior (i.e. behavior that requires a personal sacrifice and enhances the welfare of another person by providing material or psychological benefit). Receiving friendly versus hostile treatment is hypothesized to increase, through positive affect, consumers' likelihood to engage in socially-elevating behavior, but only when the treatment has low relevance for self-assessments. When relevance is high, social treatment's friendliness influences both affect and perceived self-efficacy in society. Affect and social efficacy act as opposing forces, because self-efficacy in society is predicted to have a negative effect, decreasing socially-elevating behavior. Furthermore, this research argues that the role of social efficacy becomes more prominent when the salience of the need for social connectedness is increased. The proposed relationships are tested in three studies.

Study 1 used a scenario-based methodology to examine the impact of receiving a social treatment from one shopper on a consumer's likelihood of helping another consumer pick up bags of scattered groceries. The social treatment was either compliment (friendly/high-relevance), small-talk (friendly/low-relevance), threat (hostile/ high-relevance) or grumble (hostile/ low-relevance). As predicted, in the case of low relevance the friendly treatment generated a higher likelihood to help than the hostile treatment. However, when social treatment was highly relevant, friendliness did not motivate consumers to be more helpful and in fact the opposite tendency was observed. Two follow-up experiments provided process evidence for affect and perceived social efficacy.

Study 2 used a field experiment to study how many people would pick up the tab for another shopper after receiving a social treatment. In the study each participant was given money to buy and consume products at a mall together with another participant (in actuality a confederate). During the purchase, the real participant received a social treatment from a customer standing behind them in the line-up. A significantly higher percentage of participants picked up the tab for the confederate after being treated with small-talk versus grumble. However, a significantly lower percentage of participants picked up the tab after being complimented versus threatened.

In study 3, also conducted at a mall, participants first received a task which primed either the need for social connectedness or the need for independence. They then made an individual purchase and were either complimented or threatened by a customer. When receiving cash back from the vendor, participants were overpaid by $1. The dependent variable was participants' reaction to the seller. As expected, consumers primed with social connectedness were significantly more willing to return the dollar after receiving the hostile (versus friendly) treatment. However, this effect was eliminated when the need for independence was primed.

Overall, this research extends the literature regarding social influences on consumer behavior. We show that social treatment (i.e. how the influencer treats the influenced person) is important and can have far-reaching behavioral consequences.

### "Feature Similarity, Popularity, and Cultural Success"
*Jonah Berger, University of Pennsylvania, USA*
*Eric Bradlow, University of Pennsylvania, USA*
*Alex Braunstein, Google, USA*

Some songs become hits while others languish and some products achieve blockbuster status while others are ignored. Why do certain things become more popular than others and how might the similarity between cultural items shape their success?

Some research has considered how item characteristics affect diffusion (i.e., innovations that are easier to try are adopted faster, Rogers 1995), but these perspectives tend to treat items as independent. While they recognize that "better" items (whether functionally superior or otherwise) tend to win out, they tend to ignore how the similarity between items might shape popularity. Take the example of first names. Might the popularity of other similar names help determine how popular a given name becomes? Might the future popularity "Karen," for example, be influenced not only by its current popularity, but also be the popularity of other names that start with a hard "K" sound, such as Carl, Katherine, and Katy?

Similar items may act as substitutes or complements. One possibility is that items with common features compete. If collective tastes are fixed (i.e., 25% of people like indie rock), then similar options being more popular should shrink the remaining audience and hurt the ability of another indie song to succeed. Alternatively, similarity to other items may help success. Exposure to a stimulus, or others choosing it, can increase liking or choice of that stimulus (i.e., same item effects, Zajonc 1968), but this increased favorability may also generalize to stimulus components (Gordon and Holyoak 1983; Monahan, Murphy, and Zajonc 2000). If that is the case, then people might prefer cultural items which share features with what they have been exposed to previously (i.e., cross item effects).

We examine cross item effects in the popularity of first names. We focus on first names for a number of reasons. First, there is relatively little influence of commercial effort (i.e., advertising) or technological advantage (names are essentially value neutral tokens). The absence of these other factors makes it easier to examine the relationship between phonetic similarity and cultural success. Second, given that people can choose whatever name they like, choice is unconstrained by producers who may have an incentive to make options similar over time (i.e., this years' televisions tend to look like last years).

To examine our research question, we analyze 100 years of data on the popularity of every first name in the US. We break each name up into its phonetic parts (Karen=K EH R AH N), and then look at the evolution of popularity of each of the 44 phonemes over time, based on their popularity both the past year and cumulatively the over 10 years prior. We do this for the phonemes at beginning and end of names as well as internal phonemes. Importantly, our analysis parcels out direct exposure effects. Thus we look at how the number of Karen's born one year relate to the popularity of the "K" sound the following year, outside of number of Karen's born that next year. We then aggregate these effects across all phonemes to look at the overall pattern.

Our results (1) suggest that social influence has cross item effects and (2) demonstrates the importance of such relationships for cultural success. Across all phoneme positions the more a phoneme is used in names one year, the more popular it will be in *other* names the following year. This relationship also holds for cumulative popularity over the ten years prior. Not surprisingly we also find that the more popular a name is one year the more popular it will be the next, but the cross-item effects persist even when controlling for such same item effects. These cross-item effects are strongest for phonemes that begin the name, consistent with the notion that this position should receive more stress. In addition, the coefficient on the quadratic terms of past popularity are negative, suggesting that too much popularity can lead to reduce future adoption.

These findings suggest a novel way in which social influence shapes popularity. Exposure to others choices not only affects whether people adopt that thing, but may also affect whether they adopt other things with common features. This has important implications for the way culture evolves. Things not only become popular based on their own characteristics, or whether they are better or worse than competing items, but may also be shaped by whether they share common features with what is currently popular.

SPECIAL SESSION

# Conspicuous Consumption in a Recession: Trends, Motivators, and Perceptions

Nailya Ordabayeva, Erasmus University, The Netherlands
Keith Wilcox, Babson College, USA

## EXTENDED ABSTRACTS

### "Conspicuous Consumption in a Recession: Toning it Down or Turning it Up?"

*Joseph C. Nunes, University of Southern California, USA*
*Xavier Drèze, University of California, Los Angeles, USA*
*Young J. Han, University of Southern California, USA*

Luxury goods that prominently display their brands are out. The recession has led wealthy consumers to adopt more subdued designs that reflect taste rather than signal status. At least that is what the pundits in the press would have you believe. The financial crisis has aimed a "death ray" at the ethos of conspicuous consumption according to the *New York Times*. "The muted, logo-free look is gaining traction as the standard-bearer for a new kind of luxury: subtle, long-lasting and recession proof," claims a report on the recession's impact on luxury by ad agency JWT.

Have consumers really toned it down? Reports about how conspicuous consumption is out of vogue are based on interviews with consumers and presumed experts; no data or scientific studies are cited. Ideally, researchers would track consumer behavior longitudinally documenting purchases and the use of luxury goods used to signal status both before and during a recession. This research takes a more practical albeit less direct approach.

We focus on luxury handbags, considered by the Chicago Tribune the "21st Century American woman's most public and pricey consumer craving." We examine data on product offerings collected from luxury handbag superpowers Louis Vuitton (LV) and Gucci, the world's top two luxury brands (Interbrand 2009), before and in the midst of the recession. We contrast what occurs with these two brands with what occurred at Hermès, a boutique brand concentrating on subtlety prior to the recession. If consumers are indeed demanding less conspicuous products, it would be reflected in these manufacturers' product lines and we should observe LV and Gucci offering more understated designs. Or, if firms do not tone down their products, we should observe a marked decrease in profitability as they fail to meet customer demand. This is not what we find.

Our research finds evidence that Louis Vuitton and Gucci have changed their product lines during the financial crisis to offer significantly more conspicuously branded products. These brands are far more prominently displayed on new product introductions when compared to those products withdrawn. Further, both brands simultaneously increased prices significantly. Louis Vuitton's new designer handbag line was priced an average of 31% higher than its product line one-and-one-half years earlier, while Gucci raised prices on 50% of those products the manufacturer did not remove, by 1% to 5%.

These tactics have not resulted in financial ruin. Profits for LVMH's fashion and leather goods rose from ?814 million in June 2007 to ?815 million in June 2008 and on to ?919 million in June 2009. The percentage of LVMH's revenues coming from the U.S. did not change between 2008 and 2009, remaining at 28%. The luxury goods division of PPR SA—the parent company of Gucci Group—recorded an increase in EBITDA from ?363 million in June 2008 to ?377 million in June 2009. Retail sales by Gucci, the division's flagship brand, were up 2.4%, led by an "extremely robust showing from leather goods."

In contrast, Hermès, which concentrated on understated designs before the recession, did not introduce more conspicuous products. This implies that desires amongst those consumers who sought understated designs prior to the recession did not change and many of those who do not exit the luxury goods market during a recession are still interested in logo-laden products, and perhaps even more so.

We posit a segmentation explanation based on consumers' need for status. Consumers low in their need-for-status don't use luxury goods to dissociate themselves from less well-to-do consumers (Han, Nunes and Drèze 2010). They bought quiet goods before the recession began, and they can reduce or postpone consumption without feeling their status is threatened. Hence Hermès, which caters exclusively to this customer segment, did not change its product line because doing so would be futile.

Conversely, high need-for-status consumers, who are also wealthy, use luxury as a mechanism to dissociate themselves from the have-nots. They feel a need to do this even in recessionary times, perhaps even more reinforcing that they are not impacted as much by the recession. This would shift demand for luxury goods toward loud products favored by this segment and encourage managers to alter the product lines accordingly. Hence, Louis Vuitton and Gucci steered their product introductions towards this segment and away from those that favor quieter displays.

Thus our data support the notion that those who are still in the market for luxury goods still like the loud products and are willing to pay a hefty sum for them. As with most platitudes, 2008-9 is not the first time that observers have predicted the downfall of conspicuous consumption and a rise in "conservative consumption." A general sentiment oft described is that consumers will economize out of necessity, but as incomes rise and frugality gives way to profligacy, consumers will eschew their wasteful ways of the past. Our findings suggest consumer researchers need to be certain conspicuous consumption has declined before saying it will never reclaim its previous place in consumer decision-making.

### "The Ironic Effects of Credit Card Balances and Credit Limits on Conspicuous Consumption"

*Keith Wilcox, Babson College, USA*
*Lauren Block, Baruch College, USA*

During the current economic crisis, consumers are facing sobering amounts of debt. In 2008, the average outstanding credit card balance per household was $10,679 (Nilson Report 2009) and approximately 13.9% of consumers' disposable income went to service credit card debt (U.S. Congress' Joint Economic Committee 2009). Additionally, the rising job losses are leading even those with good credit histories to incur unbearable amounts of credit card debt (Andrews 2009). Despite the staggering numbers virtually no research has examined how credit card debt affects consumer spending.

Previous research has documented a tendency by individuals to abandon a goal after failure (Cochran and Tesser 1996), particularly when goal failure represents a behavior that a person is trying to avoid. Because consumers try to avoid card debt, we suggest that carrying a balance makes consumers less focused on incurring credit card debt and subsequently increases spending. Moreover, we suggest this effect is strongest for people with high self-control. Because credit cards increase spending, and those with high self-control strategically avoid using payment mechanisms that increase spending (Raghubir and Srivastava 2009), prior to a balance being incurred, consumers with high self-control should be more focused on avoiding credit card debt. However, once a balance has been incurred, it signals goal failure, which increases their spending and shifts their preference towards high-priced luxury brands.

However, research suggests that the more resources individuals have available for consumption, the weaker the proportional impact of any one unit of consumption on one's overall resources (Morewedge et al. 2007). This suggests that the perceived magnitude of the failure from incurring a credit card balance may depend less on the actual value of the balance than on the proportional impact of the balance to the resources that are available on the credit card (i.e., the available credit). This also suggests another ironic effect: that the influence of an outstanding balance can be attenuated by increasing the available credit on the credit card, while holding the value of the balance constant. Thus, once a balance has been incurred, we propose that increasing the available credit should reduce the perceived magnitude of the failure and actually lower consumers' preference for luxury brands.

Four studies were conducted to test our predictions. In study 1, half of the respondents were told to imagine that they had $1,000 in their bank account and a credit card with a $1,000 credit limit and no outstanding balance. The remaining participants were instructed that they had a credit card with $1,500 credit limit and a $500 outstanding balance. Participants were asked to choose between two pairs of gender neutral sunglasses: a pair of Louis Vuitton sunglasses and a pair of Ray-Ban sunglasses. As expected, those with high self-control were more likely to purchase the Louis Vuitton sunglasses when they carried a balance compared to when they had no balance. No difference was observed for those with low self-control.

Study 2a replicated the basic findings of study 1 and provided evidence that the magnitude of the failure moderates the effect of a credit card balance on preference for luxury brands. Specifically, it shows that increasing the available credit reduces the magnitude of the failure and lowers conspicuous consumption for high self-control individuals. Study 2b, provides process level support for the effects found in Study 2a; specifically, we demonstrate that increasing the available credit reduces consumers' spending by making them more focused on debt avoidance.

Study 3 replicates the findings of previous studies while ruling out different inferences about wealth as an alternative explanation. Specifically, we provided respondents with two credit cards (a high available credit card and a low available credit card), but kept the total available credit and the outstanding balance between the two cards the same; we only manipulated which card carried the balance. We find that consumer spending depends on available credit on the credit card that carried the balance. Specifically, when the balance is carried on a card with low available credit, it increases the likelihood of purchasing a luxury product compared to when it was carried on the card with high available credit.

In this era of economic crisis and pending credit card regulation changes, it is important to better understand the factors that influence consumer spending and conspicuous consumption. Findings from the body of literature in this domain are often integrated into policy guidelines to aid and educate consumers to help them spend wisely and avoid debt. Future research that informs industry or regulatory guidance is encouraged.

## "Effects of Perceived Income Distribution, Equality, and Economy on Preferences for Conspicuous Consumption"
*Nailya Ordabayeva, Erasmus University, The Netherlands*
*Pierre Chandon, INSEAD, France*
*Daniel Goldstein, London Business School, UK*

It is widely believed that increasing income equality should reduce conspicuous consumption (Bagwell and Bernheim 1996). It is also believed that conspicuous consumption should drop in a recession, due to falling incomes and rising income equality (Moses 2008). Yet recent findings reported that boosting equality may backfire and increase conspicuous consumption among relatively poor consumers, as it allows those who consume to "leapfrog over" a larger portion of the population stacked in middle tiers (Ordabayeva and Chandon 2010). These arguments assume that consumers have an accurate perception of the income distribution and how it is changing. To correctly interpret them and to recommend effective strategies to reduce conspicuous consumption in a recession, it is important to test the role of perceptions. In this research, we examine the effects of perceived and actual income distributions on people's preferences for conspicuous consumption and test the roles of beliefs about equality and economy.

Specifically, we test whether conspicuous consumption is motivated by the perceived or the actual income distribution, income level or income rank, and examine how it changes depending on consumer beliefs about equality and economy. We predict that, due to its implications for social position, conspicuous consumption is predicted by income rank (i.e., position in the income distribution) rather than income level. Specifically, it is driven by rank in the local, rather than country-level, income distribution, consistent with social comparison theory (Festinger 1954). Further, because it is difficult to know the shape of the actual distribution, the effect of local rank should be moderated by perceived rather than actual distribution equality. Consistent with the "leapfrogging" hypothesis (Ordabayeva and Chandon 2010), high perceived equality should reduce conspicuous consumption among relatively rich consumers, but it should ironically boost conspicuous consumption among relatively poor consumers. We believe this ironic effect of equality could reverse when anticipating a recession.

In the first study, participants from a representative sample of US households used the Distribution Builder tool online (Goldstein, Johnson, and Sharpe 2008) to build the distribution of income that they believed was prevalent in the US. Afterwards they made three choices between inconspicuous and conspicuous consumption (renting an economy car vs. a premium car for a high school reunion, spending on necessities vs. luxuries if anticipating a salary bonus, saving on home decoration vs. home maintenance if anticipating an increase in expenses). We computed each participant's percentile in the perceived, country-level, state-level, and local area (core based statistical area)-level income distributions and GINI indices of the perceived and corresponding state- and local area-level income distributions. As predicted, percentile in the local income distribution predicted consumption decisions better than income level or percentile in the perceived, state- or country-level income distributions. The effect of local income rank was moderated by the GINI index of the perceived distribution. High perceived equality led to weaker preferences for conspicuous consumption among the top 50% of local earners, but it led to *stronger* preferences for conspicuous consumption among the bottom 50% of earners. Hence boosting perceived equality may indeed backfire for relatively poor consumers.

In the second study, we tested whether this ironic effect of equality would be similar in an economic expansion and a recession. This study was conducted in the lab, it focused on relatively poor consumers (who are at a higher risk of overspending) and actually provided the local distribution of a status product. The participants read that they were going on a beach vacation with their classmates and that they brought old unbranded sunglasses with them. At the beach, old sunglasses put them at the bottom (tier 5) of the distribution of sunglasses in their group, which led them to consider spending €90 on higher-status tier 3 sunglasses instead. The distribution of sunglasses was equal (with 15%, 25%, 15%, 40%, 5% of people in tiers 5-1) or unequal (with 15%, 15%, 15%, 40%, 15% in tiers 5-1), and the vacation was taking place in the time of an economic expansion or a recession (we provided basic facts about an expansion or a recession). The participants chose between spending €90 on tier 3 sunglasses and saving the money. As expected, when anticipating an expansion bottom-tier people were more likely to spend the money in the equal (vs. unequal) distribution. But anticipating a recession decreased their overall likelihood to spend, even more so in the equal distribution. A pilot study showed that this could be due to people's desire to fit in and to strengthen bonds with others in recessionary times. This showed that a recession may reduce the conspicuous consumption of relatively poor consumers, especially when equality increases at the same time.

Overall these findings improve our understanding of the macro-level and individual-level factors that drive conspicuous consumption. They show that merely changing people's beliefs about equality may be sufficient to shift their preferences for conspicuous consumption, which could be especially useful for increasing savings in this recessionary period.

## "Judging a Book by Its Cover: How Consumers Perceive Conspicuous Consumption by Others"

*Maura L. Scott, University of Kentucky, USA*
*Martin Mende, University of Kentucky, USA*
*Lisa E. Bolton, Penn State University, USA*

During tough economic times, consumers experience a heightened sensitivity to the level and type of conspicuousness of a seller (Williams 2008) and the source of affluence supporting the conspicuousness (Christopher et al. 2005). However, evaluation of others is highly context sensitive (Gawronski and Bodenhausen 2006) and differs depending on social settings (Gawronski, LeBel, and Peters 2007) and social roles enacted by targets (Barden et al. 2004). Consequently, we study how consumers–during the recession–perceive conspicuous consumption in commercial contexts. This research investigates how conspicuous consumption affects consumers' person perception of sellers, proposing that consumers infer personal characteristics from conspicuous consumption that, in turn, affect attitudes and behaviors toward the focal seller. Furthermore, we show how inferences consumers make about sellers' conspicuous consumption are moderated by the presence of a relationship and the nature of the commercial relationship.

Five studies–all conducted during the economic crisis–examine consumers' attitudes about sellers who engage in conspicuous versus modest consumption (e.g., level of caring, competence) and consumers' subsequent behavioral intentions. We demonstrate that in a communal (exchange) relationship, consumers perceive that sellers who engage in conspicuous versus modest consumption are less caring (more competent), which in turn drives less (more) favorable behavioral intentions. As a result, conspicuous consumption by sellers (such as service providers) affects consumer response (such as WOM and purchase intentions) in systematic ways—suggesting that firms may wish to use consumption cues to signal qualities in ways that improve their relationship building efforts with their customers.

Five studies provide support for the underlying psychological process while at the same time establishing boundary conditions on the phenomenon of interest. Studies 1 and 2 were a 2 (relational norm: communal/exchange) x 2 (conspicuous consumption: yes/no) between-subjects experiments. In study 1 scenarios, we manipulated relational norms based on relational norm definitions. In study 2, we manipulated relational norms by varying the profession of the seller (communal as medical doctor, exchange as financial advisor). We manipulated conspicuousness based on the seller's possessions (such as the watch, clothing, and car). We found that behavioral intentions decline when communal service providers engage in conspicuous consumption, while behavioral intentions increase under the exchange norm and the seller engages in conspicuous consumption.

Study 3 was a 2 (relational norm: communal/exchange) x 2 (conspicuous consumption: yes/ no) x 2 (customer relationship/ none). A three-way interaction in this study finds that the effects of conspicuous consumption on service provider attitudes depend critically on the existence of a provider relationship. The customer relationship makes salient relational norms, which translates to the attitude effects consistent with studies 1 and 2; in the absence of a buyer-seller relationship, the effects are not observed.

Study 4 examines the moderating role of the target's consumption focus (i.e., work-related or personal conspicuousness). Study 4 was a 2 (relational norm: communal/exchange) x 2 (conspicuous consumption: yes/no) x 2 (target's consumption: work-related/ personal) between-subjects experiment. The target's consumption factor examined whether the conspicuousness was reflected in business trappings (e.g., designer furniture, expensive equipment, etc.) or personal consumption (e.g., designer clothing, expensive car and watch). When conspicuous consumption is personal, the behavioral intentions are highly similar to prior studies; however, the behavioral intention effects were not significant for work-related conspicuous consumption—establishing a boundary condition on the impact of conspicuous consumption cues.

Study 5 was a 2 (relationship norm: communal/exchange) x 2 (source of affluence: luck/ earned) between-subjects experiment. The seller engaged in conspicuous consumption in all conditions. In the earned conditions, behavioral intentions are higher under exchange versus communal norms—consistent with the notion that earned income facilitates consumer inferences about competence (Christopher et al. 2005). In the luck conditions, behavioral intentions are higher under communal than exchange norms—which we argue occurs because the affect driven connection in a communal relationship creates a "luck may rub off" effect. More generally, the source of wealth is shown to be a boundary condition on consumers' responses to conspicuousness.

Our findings contribute to the literature by i) examining conspicuous consumption as perceived by others (rather than how and why consumers engage in such consumption), and ii) extending research on the importance of social and relational norms on consumer behavior in commercial contexts.

# Consumer Acculturation in an Age of Globalization: Critiques, Revisions and Advances

Dannie Kjeldgaard, University of Southern Denmark, Denmark

Marius K. Luedicke, University of Innsbruck, Austria

## EXTENDED ABSTRACTS

### "'Metacculturation': Cultural Identity Politics in Greenlandic Food Discourses"

Søren Askegaard, University of Southern Denmark, Denmark

Dannie Kjeldgaard, University of Southern Denmark, Denmark

Eric J. Arnould, University of Wyoming, USA

The majority of previous consumer research on ethnicity focuses on consumer acculturation by consumers who come from one (presumably homogeneous) consumer cultural context and acculturate to another (presumably homogenous) cultural context (Peñaloza 1994). The present article problematizes the relatively clear-cut dichotomy of home and host culture by exploring food consumption discourses from cooking literature and consumers' narrative in the context of Greenlandic consumers (Askegaard, Arnould & Kjeldgaard 2005; Kjeldgaard & Askegaard 2006). We argue that the articulation of ethnic identity through food consumption becomes a master trope of the definition of "Greenlandic", and that this articulation unfolds in and through a context of historically established (marketplace) mythologies of Danish and Greenlandic culture. Consequently, home as well as host cultures emerge as outcomes of the acculturation processes rather than antecedents thereof. We emphasize that this approach stands in marked contrast to standard assumptions in the acculturation literature, in which home and host are generally seen as antecedents to and not outcomes of the process. We argue that cultural reflexivity that is both a cause and a consequence of this discursive process represents a kind of cultural 'awakening.' This awakening is produced through the boundary drawing between food cultures; a reflexivity which represents an acculturation to being a carrier of a particular cultural identity. Since this is a second-order acculturation or, we have chosen the neologism 'metacculturation' as its denominator. In order to explore the dynamics of metacculturation among Greenlanders, we focus on food cultural consumption as it pertains to the establishment of identity among twenty Greenlandic migrants to Denmark and a sample from two high school classes totalling 12 young consumers in Greenland.

The socially informed perception of space and time appear as two fundamental and interrelated dimensions differentiating consumer experiences in the different cultural contexts. In the Greenlandic perspective, the spatial and temporal differences in social organization between Greenland and the Western world (represented by Denmark) are expressed in terms of a dichotomous distinction between nature and culture, Greenland representing the natural (space and time). These dimensions of nature and culture are reflected in a set of master tropes of a discursive definition and distinction of Greenlandic food culture that we elicit from our primary and secondary data. The close connection between the formulation of a Greenlandic identity and Greenlandic food culture is thus reflected in the data. Furthermore, the role of the cultural tropes ascribed to the colonial power (Denmark), in terms of food as well as more generally, are central for the formulation of a Greenlandic identity, both as a negative mirror image but also as a source for the cultural reflexivity generating the interest in the identity project in the first place. Consequently, the dynamic nature of food discourse shows us that the concept of authenticity can only exist as a perceptual construct on the basis of how a culture views its "self" and Others. In other words, we are witnessing an editing of 'authentic' food culture through processes of remembering and forgetting certain elements of the historical constitution of contemporary Greenlandic foodways.

Wilk (1996; 1999) discusses similar processes in his attempts to account for "cultural constructionism" in Belize and the grid of "global structures of common difference" that is containing this construction. But in Wilk's work, the acculturation processes into the notion of culture are more implicit, since he is focusing on various specific domains of the global structures of common difference, the beauty pageant (Wilk 1996) or the food cultural the creation of "real Belizean food" (Wilk 1999). Wilk, however, stops short of nominating the notion of culture itself a part of the overarching grid of global structures of common difference. Cultural boundaries are expressed, and therefore defined through the global structures, but culture and glocal cultural changes remain the boundary that contains these global structures and their manifest expressions

Summarizing, the concept of acculturation as it has been used in previous consumer research (Peñaloza 1994, Askegaard, Arnould & Kjeldgaard 2005, Holt and Üstüner 2007) as the negotiation of the tension experienced by having two (or more) cultural contexts of identification, becomes problematized when the notion of culture itself becomes a reflexive process (Askegaard, Kjeldgaard & Arnould 2009). Acculturation in this perspective is not just a matter of negotiating the tensions between host, home or 'third' cultures but it is also a matter of acculturation into the notion of culture itself. The notions of host and home cultures hence emerge as discursive outcomes of this culture of cultures rather than as building blocks of the acculturation process. We call this acculturation process into cultural reflexivity 'metacculturation'.

### "Consumer Acculturation and Competing, Countervailing Taste Structures"

Özlem Sandıkcı, Bilkent University, Turkey

Berna Tari, TOBB University of Economics and Technology, Turkey

Olga Kravets, Bilkent University, Turkey

Sahver Omeraki, Bilkent University, Turkey

Over the years conceptualizations of consumer acculturation process have moved from the "melting pot" model to a "postassimilationist" perspective Postassimilationist research (Askegaard, Arnould and Kjedgaard 2005; Oswald 1999; Penaloza 1994) challenged the linear acculturation model and conceptualized consumer acculturation as a dialogical process characterized by ongoing cultural negotiation and "culture swapping" (Oswald 1999). These studies revealed how consumers mix and match resources from the minority and dominant cultures and pursue hybrid identity projects as they integrate into their new environment. Recently, postassimilationist research has come under criticism for its bias toward studying contexts that are characterized by postmodern consumer culture which allows consumers to pursue hybrid identity projects (Ustuner and Holt 2007). Instead, Ustuner and Holt 2007 introduced "dominated consumer acculturation" model to account for the acculturation experiences of consumers in less developed countries. The authors argue that different sociocultural structures produce different patterns of consumer acculturation. In the case of less developed countries, immigrant consumers tend to have little economic, social and cultural capital; host consumer culture tends toward "an orthodox modern form" where tastes are rigidly defined by the upper social classes; and immigrants' culture tends to be in conflict with the ideologies of host culture (Ustuner and Holt 2007, 44). As a result, rather than individuated, hybrid modes of acculturation, immigrants collectively construct their identities as consumers either by reterrritorializing the minority culture or pursuing the dominant culture as a myth through ritualized consumption. Some, however, may fail to do either and experience "a shattered identity project" (ibid).

Our goal in this research is to contribute to this line of inquiry and further question some of the underlying assumptions in the theories of consumer acculturation. Specifically, we seek to draw attention to the following issue. Existing scholarship conceptualizes the dominant culture that consumers seek to (or fail to) acculturate as singular. Whether the focus is Haitians immigrated to the US, Greenlandic immigrants in Denmark, or peasants moved into urban Turkey, the host culture is characterized by a singular dominant consumer ideology and taste structure. This dominating culture is always in the shape of Western consumer ideology, be it in a localized version. Hence, little is known about how acculturation process unfolds when the host culture is characterized by multiple, co-existing, equally powerful, and competing taste structures and consumption ideologies (e.g., Sandıkcı and Ger 2010). We investigate this question through a qualitative study of Turkish rural to urban migrant women living in squatter dwellings in Istanbul and Ankara.

Similar to other developing countries, rural to urban immigration has been a key feature of Turkish history. Since 1950s, limited availability of non-agricultural work, increasing mechanization of farming, political turmoil, and difficulties in accessing to health and education pushed rural people to the cities. Given the insufficiency of public housing and high levels of unemployment, rural migrants typically settle in squatter houses located at the periphery of the big cities. For the Western urbanites or what Ustuner and Holt (2007) refer to as "*Batici*," squatter neighborhoods represent stigmatized ghettos and their residents the inferior and even threatening Other. The immigrants' multi-faceted alterity menaces *Batici*'s Western lifestyle that expresses a localized version of the global consumerist sensibilities coupled with a secular orientation. Western consumer goods and consumption practices, which have penetrated into Turkey after the adoption of neoliberal economic policies in the 1980s, constitute a key aspect of the urban modern middle-class ethos. However, since the 1980s, another global ideology has been increasingly influential in Turkey: Islamism. An important outcome of the Islamist movement has been the emergence of a new Islamist middle class (Sandıkcı and Ger 2010). According to the authors, "this new class owes its existence to the upward mobility and urbanization of the formerly rural, peripheral elites" and "now forms a parallel structure that competes with urban secular elites". Consumption practices of the Islamist middle class entails a new sense of hybrid aesthetics which is informed by Islamic as well as modern sensitivities.

Our analysis shows that the Islamist habitus provides a new set of resources for rural immigrants to draw from while pursuing their identity projects. Their accounts of migration-consumption experiences and practices suggest that Western secular consumer culture is not the only and dominating ideology that migrants have no choice but acculturate to. While our informants, similar to those of Ustuner and Holt, lack economic, social and cultural capital resources necessary to participate into the "*Batici*" lifestyle, they draw from resources provided by the Islamist habitus and acculturate into an Islamist yet modern urban lifestyle. Their consumption practices reflect pursuit of a hybrid identity project and empowerment through acquisition of new resources provided by the Islamist structure. Overall, our study indicates that host culture may not always be defined by a singular dominant culture and that different forms of hybridity may characterize acculturation processes and consumer identity accomplishments in less developed countries.

### "Acculturating Masculinity: Second Generation Turks Becoming Men"

*Nil Özçaglar-Toulouse, Université de Lille 2, France*
*Lisa N. Peñaloza, EDHEC Business School, France*

Previous work on consumer acculturation in the CCT tradition has emphasized the importance of situating consumption phenomena within contextual layers of history, colonial relations, and socio-economic difference between (Askegaard, Arnould, and Kjeldgaard 2005; Oswald 1999; Peñaloza 1994) and within nations (Kjeldgaard and Askegaard 2006; Üstüner and Holt 2007). Recent work addressing dimensions of gender has focused on women (Chytkova and Özçaglar-Toulouse 2009). Our work takes as its focus masculinity among second generation (Portes 1996) Turkish men in France. This topic is of particular relevance in the era of globalization. First, unlike the subordinated relations between Mexico (Peñaloza 1994a) and Haiti (Oswald 1999) with the U.S., and for Greenland in relation to Denmark (Askegaard, Arnould, and Kjeldgaard 2005), Turkey has never been colonized, and counts within its history the dominant status of the Ottoman Empire. Further, due to alliances with European nations in WWII, the widespread anti-colonial, anti-Western rhetoric characterizing the Middle East has not been as dominant here. And yet, like other minority groups studied, Turks are a minority in France, forming the largest immigrant group there and in several other nations within the European Union.

The theoretical framework brings together this previous work on consumer acculturation with that on gender and masculinity. Particularly useful is Butler's (1990) work emphasizing gender performance, as persons enact, reproduce, and challenge gender conventions in ways that transcend binary understandings of gender. Also useful is Connell's (1995) attention to economic institutions in legitimizing masculine ideals and practices. While drawing from this work, we emphasize the negotiations of gender in consumption as accommodated and reproduced in market cultural institutions (Holt and Thompson 2004).

The research entails on-going ethnographic study of 18 young men between the ages of 18 and 30. Interviews and observations were carried out in areas frequented by the young Turks in the suburbs of Lille and Paris. These suburbs are characterized by a high concentration of Turkish and Northern African minorities, under and unemployment, deindustrialisation and dense population similar to that documented by (Wacquant 2007). Among our research objectives are: 1) documenting ideals, norms, and practices of masculinity; 2) analyzing how the various cultural contexts—at home with their fathers and mothers, with friends and significant others in cafés, at work, dealings with France and Turkey, and various national and transnational media forms and institutions associated with each of these groups—come together in consumption ideals and practices associated with masculinity; and 3) addressing whether such contexts are converging in fashioning consumption ideals and practices favoring the homogenization of masculinity.

Our results derive four themes: becoming a father, not loitering in the street, protecting your honor, and conquering adversity. In articulating these themes, we emphasize a number of creative contradictions in the ways these young men navigate what it is to be a man in drawing upon idealized French fatherhood, relations with their girlfriends and mothers, Turkish history, and rural traditions in differentiating themselves from other minorities and their fathers. This research contributes to postassimilationist understandings of globalization by detailing the ways these young men forge distinctions from other minorities, it adds to understandings of consumer acculturation by documenting the processes and practices of second generation immigrants moving from a nation lacking a colonial past into a more subordinated, minority status; and finally this work contributes multicultural understandings of gender in elaborating how young Turkish men draw from multiple cultural domains in producing masculine ideals, norms and practices.

**"Broadening the Scope of Consumer Acculturation Theory"**
*Marius K. Luedicke, University of Innsbruck, Austria*

The existing body of consumer acculturation literature can broadly been divided into two parallel streams of research. The first stream, beginning around 1980, was predominantly concerned with assessing differences in immigrant/ethnic consumption behavior vis-à-vis the commercial mainstream (Desphande et al. 1986; Donthu and Cherian 1992; O'Guinn et al. 1986; Reilly and Wallendorf 1984; Saegert et al. 1985; Wallendorf and Reilly 1983). This insightful work produced significant knowledge on cultural consumption patterns, and illuminating preferences in emerging ethnic market segments that were, at the time, foreign to most marketers. The second stream, pioneered by Peñaloza in 1989, moved away from (literally) counting eggs to exploring immigrant consumers' identity projects and personal acculturation experiences. This body of work produced–and continues to produce–many important insights into the cultural complexities of consumer acculturation, including the troubling pushes and pulls from two socio-cultural systems, the wealth of despised and appreciated discourses and practices that migrants cope with, and the range of more or less integrative (and beneficial) outcomes of this process (Askegaard et al. 2005; Mehta and Belk 1991; Oswald 1999; Peñaloza 1989, 1994, 2007; Peñaloza and Gilly 1999).

The triple purpose of this presentation is (1) to revisit prior studies with respect to the conceptual and methodical paths that they have taken, (2) to show where these paths have begun to limit the scope of consumer acculturation research under globalizing cultural conditions, and (3) to propose an alternative model that highlights facets of consumer acculturation phenomena which have thus far receive little scholarly attention.

In particular, the author addresses three points of critique: an idea of consumer identity construction as a largely autarkic process of mixing and matching available cultural resources; a conceptualization of cultural resources as robust and largely independent of migrants' consumption practices; and a predominance of single-perspective (i.e. migrant-centric) ethnographic accounts as predominant sources of empirical insight. Based on this critique and on two influential and path-breaking studies of Thompson and Tambyah (1999) and Üstüner and Holt (2007), the author puts an alternative model of consumer acculturation forward for discussion that attenuates these critiques by conceptualizing consumer acculturation as a multi-directional, perpetuate process of cultural adaptation that focuses more on the discourses, practices, and resources that migrants and locals use for negotiating their intercultural relations (cf. Chrikov 2009; Chung and Fischer 1999).

Such an alternative lens may inspire consumer acculturation researchers to explore acculturation as mutual cultural adaptation embedded in an active and agentic network of observation, evaluation, and adaptation through consumption. In such a network, local and migrant consumers potentially observe the visible consumption practices of the respective others, evaluate these observations based on specific inter-cultural discourses and more general attitudes towards multiculturalism, religious diversity, or sharing of market resources (cf. Nagel 1994), and adjust their own consumption choices dependently.

In summary, a thus broadened field consumer acculturation theory may benefit from also taking intra- and inter-cultural discourses into (empirical) account that define local, national, and transnational (stereotypical) views about certain cultures, illuminate how consumers translate these meanings into practices of sharing or competing, and, potentially, reveal which discourses and consumption practices (i.e. cuisine, arts) may evoke integrative spirits where segregation prevails.

**REFERENCES**

Appadurai, Arjun (1996), *Modernity at Large. Cultural Dimensions of Globalization*, Minneapolis: University of Minnesota Press.
Askegaard, Søren, Eric J. Arnould and Dannie Kjeldgaard (2005), "Postassimilationist Ethnic Consumer Research: Qualifications and Extensions," *Journal of Consumer Research*, 32 (1), 160-70.
Askegaard, Søren, Dannie Kjeldgaard & Eric J. Arnould (2009), "Reflexive Culture's Consequences", in C. Nakata, ed., *Beyond Hofstede: Culture Frameworks for Global Marketing and Management,* Chicago: Palgrave Macmillan, 101-122.
Barth, Frederik (1969), *Ethnic Groups and Boundaries. The Social Organization of Culture Difference*, Bergen: Universitetsforlaget.
Berking, Helmuth (2003), "'Ethnicity is Everywhere': On Globalization and the Transformation of Cultural Identity", *Current Sociology*, 51 (3/4), 248-264.
Berry, John W. J (1980), "Acculturation as Varieties of Adaptation", in *Acculturation: Theory, Models and Some New Findings*, ed. Amado M. Padilla, Boulder, Colorado: Westview Press, 9-46.
_____ (2008), "Globalization and Acculturation", *Journal of Intercultural Relations*, 32, 328-336.
Chrikov, Valerie (2009), "Introduction to the special issue on Critical Acculturation Psychology," *International Journal of Intercultural Relations*, 33 (2), 87-93.
Chung, Ed and Eileen Fischer (1999), "Embeddedness: Socialising the "Social" Construction of Ethnicity," *International Journal of Sociology and Social Policy*, 19 (12), 34-55.
Chytkova, Zuzana and Ozcaglar-Toulouse, Nil (Forthcoming 2010), She, who has the spoon, has the power: Immigrant Women's Use of Food to Negotiate Power Relations, Advances in Consumer Research.
Connell, Raewyn (1995), Masculinities, Sydney, Australia: Allen & Unwin.
Cross, Gary (2000), *An All-Consuming Century: Why Commercialism Won in Modern America*, New York: Columbia University Press.
Desphande, Rohit, Wayne D. Hoyer and Naveen Donthu (1986), "The Intensity of Ethnic Affiliation: A Study of the Sociology of Hispanic Consumption," *Journal of Consumer Research*, 13 (September), 214-20.
Holt, Douglas and Craig J. Thompson (2004), Man-of-action heroes: The pursuit of heroic masculinity in everyday consumption, *Journal of consumer research*, 31, 425-440.
Kjeldgaard, Dannie & Søren Askegaard (2006), "The Glocalization of Youth Culture: The Global Youth Segment as Structures of Common Difference", *Journal of Consumer Research* vol. 33 (2), 231-247.

Metha, Raj and Russell W. Belk (1991) "Artifacts, Identity, and Transition: Favorite Possessions of Indians and Indian Immigrants to the United States", *Journal of Consumer Research,* 17 (March), 398-411.

Nagel, Joane (1994), "Constructing Ethnicity: Creating and Recreating Ethnic Identity and Culture," *Social Problems,* 41 (1), 152-76.

Oswald, Laura R. (1999), "Culture Swapping: Consumption and the Ethnogenesis of Middle-Class Haitian Immigrants," *Journal of Consumer Research,* 25 (4), 303-18.

Peñaloza, Lias (1994), "Atravesando Fronteras/Border Crossings: A Critical Ethnographic Exploration of the Consumer Acculturation of Mexican Immigrants," *Journal of Consumer Research,* 21 (1), 32-54.

Portes, Alejandro (ed.) (1996), *The New Second Generation,* New York, Russell Sage Foundation.

Reilly, Michael D. and Melanie Wallendorf (1984), "A Longitudinal-Study of Mexican-American Assimilation," *Advances in Consumer Research,* 11 735-740.

Roland Robertson (1992), *Globalization: Social Theory and Global Culture,* London: Sage.

Sandıkcı, Özlem and Guliz Ger (2010) "Veiling in Style: How Does a Stigmatized Practice Become Fashionable?" *Journal of Consumer Research,* (in press).

Üstüner, Tuba and Douglas B. Holt (2007), "Dominated Consumer Acculturation: The Social Construction of Poor Migrant Women's Consumer Identity Projects in a Turkish Squatter," *Journal of Consumer Research,* 34 (1), 41-55.

Wacquant, Loïc (2007), *Urban Outcasts: A Comparative Sociology of Advanced Marginality,* Cambridge, UK: Polity Press.

Wallendorf, Melanie and Michael D. Reilly (1983), "Ethnic Migration, Assimilation, and Consumption," *Journal of Consumer Research,* 10 (3), 292-302.

Wilk, Richard (1996), "Learning to be Local in Belize: Global Systems of Common Difference," in D. Miller, ed., *Worlds Apart: Modernity Through the Prism of the Local,* London: Routledge, 110-133.

Wilk, Richard (1999), ""Real Belizean Food": Building Local Identity in the Transnational Caribbean," *American Anthropologist,* 101(2), 244-255.

# The Construction of Celebrity in Contemporary Consumer Culture

Eileen Fischer, York University, Canada
Marie-Agnès Parmentier, HEC Montréal, Canada

## EXTENDED ABSTRACTS

### "The Construction of Ordinary Celebrity"

*John Deighton, Harvard University, USA*
*Leora Kornfeld, Harvard University, USA*

We compare four forms of "ordinary" celebrity, building on a comparison of Susan Boyle of Britain's Got Talent, Dave Carroll of United Breaks Guitars, Jill and Kevin of JK Wedding Dance, and the Balloon Boy hoax. In 1961, Boorstin characterized a celebrity as a person who is "famous for being famous," which Gabler (2006) termed an epitaph for any serious consideration of celebrity. But Boorstin's comments were more generative when he described celebrity as a "human pseudo-event," "manufactured for us" but lacking in substantiality, a "manifestation of our own hollowness." This perspective locates celebrity in the deficiencies of consumers, not the talents of the celebrated. Our paper uses celebrity as Boorstin does but offers a more complex view of the interplay between celebrity as manufactured for us and as manufactured by us.

In contrast to celebrity grounded in achievement, the ordinary celebrity's claim to fame rests on intrinsic ordinariness (Turner 2000). It is vested in performative claims to be an essential self plucked from obscurity by chance or fortune, rather than a cultivated, tutored or trained self transformed deliberately and calculatedly for motives invisible and therefore not entirely to be trusted. Ordinary celebrity is an element of success in several areas of market economies such as politics (Sarah Palin), religion (Joel Osteen) and sport (Dennis Rodman) and informs the narratives of entrepreneurs linked to brands like Orville Redenbacher popcorn and Wendy's hamburgers.

Ordinary celebrity has become more ubiquitous with the rise of video sharing sites like YouTube. We distinguish celebrity built on television from celebrity built on video sharing sites. We also draw distinctions among the generative processes based on two attributes: (1) whether the claim to celebrity is managed by an economic insurgent or an economic incumbent, and (2) whether the consumer initiates or responds to the claim of ordinary celebrity.

Traditionally media like television were considered carriers of power located in the State or commercial interests rather than as motivating ideological or economic forces in and of themselves (Turner 2006). The media were so-called because they mediated between the locations of power and their subjects. Turner contends that through the commercial success of reality television, media have become authors, not mere mediators, of cultural identity. In particular, reality TV produces an identity that celebrates the lack of exceptional talent or training, as long as people perform their ordinariness with some specificity or individuality. As media become economic actors with interests once the prerogative of the State and large corporations, the celebration of the ordinary becomes a profitable business strategy as much as an ideology.

We extend Turner's analysis by contending that in important respects YouTube, the dominant carrier of populist video content, benefits from the myth that media is an element of the center of the social (Couldry 2003). We argue that it (along with its parent, Google) shares the incentive to achieve cultural effects for economic interests. As has often been noted, however, YouTube differs from television in that it publishes user-generated content that is voted up or down by a massive, virtually global, democratic process. YouTube is, therefore, a house divided against itself. On one hand it operates an ideological system with power to serve incumbent economic and social interests. On the other hand it operates a system that empowers insurgent interests.

The first distinction in our typography of ordinary celebrity is between the interests of economic incumbents like large corporations and media groups (United Airlines and Sony Recorded Music in the cases we investigated,) and economic or social insurgents, the formerly powerless individuals now empowered as creators of content in pursuit of either economic power or social identity, such as wedding dancers Jill and Kevin or the parents of Balloon Boy. The second distinction has to do with whether consumers initiate or respond to the annunciation of celebrity and therefore to the claim of ordinariness. Media like YouTube allow the passive emergence of celebrity by a process of implicit voting or preferential attachment (Barabasi and Albert 1999). Thus it allows for what we have termed celebrity manufactured by us. In our work we place Jill and Kevin in this category. We contrast this with ordinary celebrity that is made for us, as in the case of Susan Boyle. We also highlight that the distinctions among the processes of construction of ordinary celebrity are not simply played out by responsive consumers. Our paper illustrates that consumers rely on but also defy broadcast media as each tries to control the production of ordinary celebrity.

### "Personal Blogging, Performance and the Quest for Fame"

*Zeynep Arsel, Concordia University, Canada*
*Xin Zhao, University of Hawaii-Manoa, USA*

The democratization in mass communication brought about by the participatory media (Jenkins 2006) opens new avenues to celebrity. Consider for example Julie Powell's crossover from a commoner to celebrity through her blog interlacing introspections on cooking Julia Child's recipes with glimpses of her marriage. Her chronicle formed the basis of the blockbuster movie Julie & Julia (Scott 2009). Estimates suggest there are 133 million blogs worldwide, with the number increasing by 1.4 new blogs per second (Technorati 2009). While stressing that not all bloggers want fame, our paper discusses how ordinary people seek to gain a discursive power and "a voice above others" (Marshall 1997) in the clutter of cyberspace by blogging (in most cases) about subject matters as mundane or trivial as cooking dinner. We frame blogging practice as an interactive performance through which the authors perform their lives in the eyes of the others and provide a dramaturgical analysis (Goffman 1959) of this practice.

Indisputably, the Internet produces new means for public self-presentation (Schau and Gilly 2003), and new avenues for research (e.g. Zhao and Belk's (2007) examination of blogs as channels for conspicuous consumption and Kozinets et al's (2010) study of narrative styles of word of mouth communicators in blogging networks). As yet, however, there is a theoretical void concerning performance in the production of blog content. This omission begs redress given that the social web features ever more specialized and dramatized blogs, a few of which garner fame and following by producing narratives on seemingly everyday consumption practices such as parenting (http://www.dooce.com/), cooking (http://smittenkitchen.com/), traveling (http://camelsandchocolate.com/), fashion (http://www.bryanboy.com/), gardening (http://www.yougrowgirl.com/), or running (http://runningat30.blogspot.com/). These blogs are not individualistic introspections, but are joint leisure activities that are shared among the blogger, his or her friends, and –if successful–

the stranger blog audiences. With our work, we aim to explore this under-theorized territory.

Our methodology incorporates both in-depth interviews and narrative analysis of blogs. We utilize a netnographic (Kozinets 2001, 2010) method to collect blog data. The blog entries are treated as consumers' retrospective and introspective narratives, through which they impose meanings on their daily activities and selectively underline particular aspects of consumption experiences (Thompson 1997). We juxtapose these narratives (the front stage) with the interview data to probe them about particular instances and stories and the underlying motives of representation (back stage). We also inquire about how bloggers imagine and construct their audiences through the comments left on their blogs or other monitoring processes. Our inquiry into the imagined audience further enables us to anchor the dramaturgical aspect of blogging processes and underscore the ways blog performances are shaped. As a supplemental data source, we also have collected interviews with famous bloggers from various media sources.

Our findings demonstrate how bloggers stylize the mundane and stage their lives to appeal to their audience in a dramatic fashion formulized by Goffman (1959) First, bloggers often seek to idealize (Goffman 1959) their mundane daily lives through weaving actual consumption experiences with readily available literary narratives, scripts and ideals. Blogging allows people to enact consumption fantasies encoded in popular culture rather than merely witnessing them. Second, bloggers continuously try to mystify their audiences to keep their audience involved and intrigued. Details about their lives are shared selectively, and contacts to the audience are regulated to maintain a social distance. By idealizing and mystifying consumption experiences, bloggers can conceal daily challenges thus enabling followers some escape from their own lived realties when they read and fantasize about bloggers' lives. By manipulating back stage and front stage selves, bloggers can instill different cultural meanings into their online persona.

Participatory media dilute the institutional structures through which fame is traditionally made. Our analysis of bloggers shows how consumers strive to gain a discursive voice and power (Marshall 1997) and manufacture a persona that could gain them celebrity status within relatively limited social networks or the greater cultural sphere. Whereas celebrities deploy scripted and readily available dramatic roles to fashion cultural meanings (McCracken 2005), bloggers create their own dramas and embellish their mundane activities through drawing upon a wide variety of cultural resources. We discuss the implications of our findings for theories of celebrity and self-representation and conclude our paper with further questions about the consumption of these blogs by their audiences and audience engagement with the celebrity blogger.

## "The Role of Brand Communities in the Construction of Celebrity"

*Marie-Agnès Parmentier, HEC Montréal, Canada*
*Eileen Fischer, York University, Canada*

Celebrities abound in our culture, as do writings on celebrity in the social sciences (e.g., Gamson 1994, Turner 2004). And while we know that consumers feel attachment to people who have acquired considerable celebrity we do not know why consumer make investments of attention and begin to feel attachments with those who as yet possess little or no fame. Given our cultural fascination with celebrity and its alleged democratization (e.g., Andrejevic 2002), it is timely to address this question. We focus in particular on an online brand community's attention and attachments to reality TV contestants.

Following others who examine celebrities in consumer research and cultural studies (e.g., Schickel 1985; Thomson 2006) we draw on relationship-focused theories to inform our understanding. However, our examination differs in two important ways. First, our focus is on relationships that develop between communities and individuals versus those between an individual consumer and a celebrity. Second, we focus on the formation of relationships between communities and those who possess little celebrity versus the evolution of relationships between fans and those who already possess a considerable level of fame (e.g., Tyra Banks).

As our goal is theory development, we use qualitative methods well suited to the purpose. Data was gathered through a 20 month netnography (Kozinets 2002) in the online brand community comprised of fans of America's Next Top Model (ANTM). In order to narrow down the dataset the material generated on one popular site (Television Without Pity), for contestants in one season ("Cycle" 9, Fall 2007) was collated. Out of the thirteen contestants who competed for the ANTM title that season, eight became the focus of our analysis: the four who generated the most attention in the community (e.g., posts and file size) and the four who generated the least from the moment threads for each contestant were created (August 26th 2007) to roughly three months after the season finale, and as the next cycle began (February 29th 2008). The analysis for this study follows the principles of grounded theory (Strauss and Corbin 1998). We engaged in open coding, axial coding, and constant comparison using Atlas ti software.

Our data analysis suggests that the formation of relationships with individuals under scrutiny by a community cannot be disentangled from the formation/maintenance of relationships between members of the community. That is, consumers forge relationships with some–but not all–contestants in the process of interacting with others who share an interest in this set of people who are vying for attention. To some extent, the visibility a contestant achieves and the meanings invested in that person are a by-product of the process of community practices such as communing, socializing, spoiling, and gossiping that have been identified in prior consumer and fan research (e.g., Baym 1999; Holt 1995; Jenkins 2006). Our analysis also reveals that the process of meaning creation for contestants is influenced both by what consumers perceive the focal individual to be or do and by what others with whom they are being compared are perceived as being or doing. That is, the pervasive practice of comparison with other contestants in current and prior cycles impacts visibility and meanings that a community attaches to a given individual. Another finding concern the dimensions along which a community's relationship with a contestant varies. One dimension is the extent to which the relationship features coaching: for some contestants, the community collectively provides advice about what she is doing wrong and right and about how she might further enhance her human potential. Another dimension is the extent to which the relationship features play: that is, some contestants garner considerable attention and differentiated meanings because the relationship between them and the community is a playful one that involves games such as coming up with the best metaphor to describe the individual's hairstyle, or competitive lampooning of the individual's character or demeanor. A third dimension is the extent to which the relationship features empathy: some contestants garner much greater sympathetic identification than do others. Our analysis links these relational dimensions to differences in the extent to which contestants achieve less measures of celebrity, within the community and beyond.

## "Above Celebrity: Maintaining Consumers' Experiences of Heritage-Based Fame"

*Cele Otnes, U. of Illinois at Urbana-Champaign, USA*
*Elizabeth Crosby, U. of Illinois at Urbana-Champaign, USA*
*Pauline Maclaran, Royal Holloway University of London, UK*

Consumers often seek connections to people possessing fame based on heredity, rather than on deeds. One example is the British Royal Family Brand (BRFB). Images and narratives pertaining to the BRFB are perpetuated through goods, services and experiences in myriad industries, and especially in tourism, media, and commemoratives/souvenirs. Balmer (2007) asserts the BRFB is "a global brand" (31). Its appeal extends from the Victorian Era, when one-fourth of the world's population and total land mass were under British rule (Aronson). BRFB images are highly mediated, and therefore often intermingle in discussions of glamour, manners and lifestyles. While it might be assumed that hereditary Royals are "only celebrities," they also resonate in ways achievement-based celebrities do not. As Balmer (2007) observes, monarchies as (human) brands possess an irresistible combination of five differentiating aspects: royal, regal, relevant, responsive, and respected.

In this paper, we explore two research questions: How do those responsible for orchestrating consumers' experiences with the BRFB perceive the Royals, vis-a-vis the notion of "celebrity?" How do these perceptions shape the ways stakeholders create and manage BRFB consumption experiences? Interviews were conducted with eight service providers England from April-August, 2005. (Follow-up interviews, for the purpose of member checks and updating providers' perspectives, are planned for summer 2010). Informants include three retailers, three journalists (including the founding editor of a global magazine devoted to royalty) and two senior employees of royal palace museums. The text from the 2005 interviews yielded over 280 typed pages of single-spaced text.

Our analysis reveals that with regard to the first question, no provider believes "celebrity" describes the BRFB. Rather, because the brand represents the heritage and history of others, providers believe most members deserve more respect and tolerance than "regular" celebrities (even as they acknowledge the human failings of individual Royals). Indeed, many providers evoke monikers such as "Saint," "Savior" and "Hero/Heroine," supporting these terms with narratives from past history or current events. Yet most also distinguish between this elevated stature of BRF members and the more celebrity-like stance of Princess Diana. One informant flatly states that BRF members "are not celebrities. They are way above that…all this celebrity bit comes from Diana…the Queen is hardly glamorous…if you see the queen as a celebrity [it] really cheapens everything…in the back of their [consumers'] minds, they know the history behind it all [the BRFB]." Another believes the moral duties of the BRFB distinguish them from celebrities: "…more is expected of the Royal Family…somebody said the Queen should have commented on such and such a crisis…So there is this expectation that the Royal Family be involved." However, our media informants also recognize (and acknowledge their role in perpetuating) an overlap in celebrity-like status of the BRFB, as media outlets are more invasive and the public is provided more access.

With regard to the second research question, we note providers use several strategies to help distance the BRFB from other celebrity-based human brands. First, they try to Connect the brand directly to consumers–e.g., by reminding them of the salience of the BRFB in their own lives. For example, one museum featured a "memory wall" where consumers left written remembrances of the memorable ways their lives had intersected with the BRFB. Providers also Enable consumers, by perpetuating aspects of the BRFB through narratives that support a distance from mere celebrities.

Providers also Sacralize the brand—supporting and offering narratives and displays that deify or differentiate the BRFB from other famous people. BRFB providers may also Teach, or reinforce the importance of the brand through history lessons, pageantry or narratives, to attract new BRFB admirers. Finally, unlike marketers of celebrities, providers Protect the brand by orchestrating consumers' experiences to focus more on positive aspects, and downplaying potentially tarnishing events or people. For example, although cheap porcelain exists that commemorates the BRFB, one informant only displays the finer variants. While he stocks lesser-quality goods, he hides them in a cabinet until a consumer requests those items. Interestingly (and perhaps counter-intuitively), journalists also use Protect in their daily or weekly coverage of the BRFB. Finally, providers also Aestheticize, by perpetuating the BRFB experience through sensory-laden activities (e.g., exhibitions and displays). Furthermore, they often actively discourage consumers from engaging in the lower-quality BRFB consumption (e.g., buying souvenirs from street vendors, or printing negative reviews of BRFB television programs). We explore these and other themes more fully in the paper.

# Psychological Aspects of Charitable Giving: Surprising New Insights About Benefactors, Beneficiaries, and the Giving Context

Eesha Sharma, New York University, USA

## EXTENDED ABSTRACTS

### "Cheapened Altruism: Discounting Prosocial Behavior by Friends of Victims"

Fern Lin, University of Pennsylvania, USA
Deborah A. Small, University of Pennsylvania, USA

Abundant research has investigated the factors and motivations causing charitable giving, but researchers have not explored folk psychological beliefs about its causes. This paper provides a first look at how people perceive charitable donors. The term charitable credit will refer to perceptions that a donor is a benevolent, charitable person whose prosocial behavior is driven by underlying altruistic qualities.

When are charitable donors given more or less credit for their donations? We believe that donors with a personal connection to the target cause, such as a relationship with a victim, are given less credit than donors without a personal connection because the personal connection cheapens the prosocial act. We theorize that even in the absence of potential material gain, these "friends of victims" are perceived as selfishly motivated and are thus given less credit for their donations. In other words, the perception of selfish motivation mediates the effect of a relationship with a victim on charitable credit. It follows that changing the perception of selfish motivation changes charitable credit and thus can moderate the effect of a relationship with a victim on charitable credit. That is, if friends of victims can undo the perceptions of selfish motivation, they can restore credit.

We propose two such moderators of the effect of relationship with a victim on charitable credit. First, giving to other unrelated charities makes the donation to the target cause indistinct, which should inhibit people from attributing the donation to selfish motivation. Second, stating an other-oriented reason for giving should also offset perceptions of selfish motivation.

Three studies support our theory. In all three, participants saw a profile of a donor to a leukemia charity who either lost a friend to the disease or who does not know any victims of the disease. Participants then rated the donor on four charitable traits and made three likelihood judgments about future charitable behaviors. These seven measures were averaged to form a composite charitable credit score.

In the first study, we confirm the basic hypothesis that when friends of victims donate to a charity that serves the cause that claimed their friend's life, they are given less credit for the donation compared to donors who do not know any victims.

The next study investigates if this effect is moderated by whether the donor also supports other unrelated charities. We predicted that donating to other charities reduces the diagnosticity of friendship with a victim on the donor's inherent charitable qualities because the donation to the same-misfortune charity is no longer distinctive; the relationship with a victim cannot account for the other charitable behavior. Additionally, we included a control condition in which participants received no information about the donor's relationship with a victim, allowing us to investigate whether the lower credit granted to friends of victims results from a credit loss to friends of victims (attributional discounting), a credit boost to donors who do not know any victims (attributional augmenting), or both. Among donors who donated only to the leukemia

charity, friends of victims were given the least credit, and donors who do not know any victims were given the most. In the control condition, charitable credit fell between the other two conditions. Among donors who gave to multiple charities, however, there was no credit difference between friends of victims, donors who do not know any victims, and the control condition. This pattern supports our prediction that distinctiveness moderates charitable credit and demonstrates that both attributional discounting and augmenting contribute to friends of victims being given less credit than donors who do not know any victims.

The third study examines a different moderator based on the donor's words, not actions. We expect that friends of victims who express an other-oriented motivation for donating restore the credit loss that results from their relationship with a victim. We also examine the mediating role of perceived selfish motivation. As in the previous studies, when donors did not provide a reason for donating, friends of victims were given less credit than donors who do not know any victims. When donors expressed an other-oriented reason for donating, however, this difference disappeared. In other words, expressing an other-oriented reason for donating moderates the effect of relationship with a victim on charitable credit. Measures of perceived selfish motivation followed the same pattern. A bootstrap confidence interval test confirmed that the moderating effect of an other-oriented reason on charitable credit acts indirectly through perceived selfish motivation.

To conclude, this research demonstrates that not all charitable actors are viewed as charitable, even when the donation presents no potential material gain. In particular, donors with a personal connection to a cause are given less charitable credit for their donations, for they are perceived as selfishly motivated. These donors can restore credit, however, by demonstrating other-oriented behavior and motivations.

### "I Give Therefore I Have: Charitable Donations and Subjective Wealth"

Zoë Chance, Harvard University, USA
Michael I. Norton, Harvard University, USA

Prosocial behavior is associated with a host of personal benefits. Helpers enjoy greater happiness (Dunn, Aknin and Norton 2008; Lyubomirsky, Tkach and Sheldon 2004); reduced mortality rates (Musick et al. 1999); less depression (Musick and Wilson 2003); better immune function (Post and Neimark 2007); and elevated dopamine levels (Bachner-Melman et al. 2005). Indeed, a longitudinal study of older adults (Brown et al. 2003), found that givers benefitted more than receivers. We suggest another important benefit of charitable behavior: Feelings of subjective wealth. How wealthy one feels is a function of objective and subjective inputs: current wealth level, income and expectations, gains and losses compared to a reference point, one's position in a wealth distribution, and psychological traits and states. As such, subjective wealth is malleable and may not always move in the same direction as objective wealth; our studies show that charitable donations–which decrease objective wealth–can increase feelings of subjective wealth.

We propose that philanthropy may have an unintentional self-signaling effect—when we observe ourselves making charitable donations, we infer we must be prosperous. Indeed, in a pilot study, we explored a romantic domain and found that men and women who spent more money on their Valentine reported feeling wealthier the next day, even holding monthly income and relationship satisfaction constant.

In Study 1, we tested the general relationship between giving and subjective wealth using a large national dataset. Some participants predicted how they would spend a hypothetical windfall, and others reported how they had actually spent real windfalls that year. For those who imagined receiving money, giving intentions were positively associated with subjective wealth. This association held up for those who had actually received extra money—feeling wealthy was associated with charitable giving, at all levels of wealth, and predicted donation behavior over and above the effects of income. These correlational data suggest that the feeling of subjective wealth may induce generosity, though the more intriguing interpretation, which we explore in our next studies, is whether causality also works in the reverse direction. In Study 2, we tested the impact of charitable giving on subjective wealth. Respondents were randomly assigned to one of five conditions; a control group (no donation) or one of four groups in a 2 (Real vs. Hypothetical) X 2 (Mandatory Donation vs. Self-Selection) between subjects design, in which some respondents donated $1 to a national or local charity. We found that all donors felt wealthier than the control group, whether donation was real or hypothetical, and whether they chose to donate or were required to. These findings are consistent with recent fMRI experiments showing that the reward centers of the brain are activated by donating money to charity in a similar way as receiving money for personal use (Moll et al. 2006), even when giving is mandatory (Harbaugh et al. 2007).

Study 3 explores the mechanism behind this giving/wealth relationship. According to Luks (1988), volunteers report experiencing a "helper's high" or physical sensation of calmness and warmth, associated with giving, with 43% of his sample reporting increased strength and energy. If, as we suggest, giving sends signals of resource abundance to the self, it follows that the boost in subjective wealth may be associated with strength or power. We measured feelings of power using the Sense of Power scale (Anderson and Galinsky 2006). Participants either received $1 to donate, $1 to spend on batteries, or no additional money. Givers reported feeling wealthier than spenders, and both felt wealthier than the control group. The group differences were fully mediated by feeling a sense of power, which affected the givers but not the spenders.

In sum, our current research shows that while decreasing objective wealth, giving money away can increase subjective wealth. We have gathered evidence in support of our self-signaling hypothesis, that we interpret charitable donations as signals of wealth and power, even when the donations are our own.

### "One vs. Many: The Effect of Efficacy and Entitativity on Charitable Giving"

*Eesha Sharma, New York University, USA*
*Vicki G. Morwitz, New York University, USA*

Given the ongoing economic crisis, donating money is increasingly difficult. The popular press notes that donors are (a) demanding more transparency from charities, (b) voicing growing interest in increasing their "philanthropic returns," and (c) seeking more efficient giving opportunities. An important factor for donors is their perceptions of whether they can help (Bendapudi, Singh, and Bendapudi 1996). Sometimes, making a small impact–helping "one" beneficiary–assures donors that they will make any impact at all. Because of this, people frequently donate to singular, identifiable victims vs. numerous statistical victims, and tactics employed by organizations such as Kiva (i.e., sponsor one specific microloan) and Heifer International (i.e., buy one heifer, one trio of rabbits, one flock of chicks) are effective.

Clearly, in terms of providing large-scale aid, mass donations to "one" are not as effective as mass donations to "many," and fundraising for one particular need is a less efficient use of advertising dollars than fundraising for large-scale needs. Still, a robust finding in the charity literature is that people prefer helping one vs. many beneficiaries, often because "one" is more tangible, concrete, and sympathy-provoking, whereas "many" blunt sympathy and caring (Jenni and Loewenstein 1997; Kogut and Ritov 2005a,b; Small and Loewenstein 2003). Still, just as numerous factors influence giving aside from purely altruistic ones, numerous factors also influence giving to one vs. many beneficiaries, aside from purely emotional ones (for a review, see Bendapudi et al., 1996). While specificity, tangibility, and the singularity of identified victims have received a significant amount of attention, with emotion as the underlying mechanism, we examine an alternative mechanism: efficacy.

Efficacy has been defined as the conviction that a person can successfully execute a behavior to produce a desired outcome (Bandura 1983). We propose that, over and above emotion, efficacy can significantly impact charitable giving. There are different forms of efficacy (e.g., self efficacy: "I can make a difference;" cause efficacy: "UNICEF can make a difference," program efficacy: "this initiative can make a difference," beneficiary efficacy: "the beneficiary can be helped") and thus there are various ways to increase perceptions of efficacy. Our studies focus specifically on self- and cause-efficacy. Through four studies, we examine the role of efficacy to understand (a) how one can increase giving to many and (b) situations in which it may hurt vs. help to focus on one vs. many. We then examine the role of entitativity (i.e., beneficiary cohesiveness, Campbell 1958) to demonstrate (a) how perceiving a collection of targets as an entity may or may not be beneficial and (b) that this relationship hinges on perceived efficacy.

Study 1a and b test whether people donate more to one vs. many, regardless of whether "one" refers to a singular beneficiary (i.e., one child) or a singular collection of beneficiaries (i.e., one village of many). As predicted, participants in study 1a donated more to one child vs. many children; we replicated this effect in study 1b for one village vs. many villages. We suggest that perceived efficacy generally tends to be low in giving contexts. By focusing on one manageable segment, benefactors have a stronger perceived ability to help. These perceptions in turn influence willingness to donate, over and above the influence of emotion. Thus, we replicated previous findings that people tend to donate more to one vs. many (Kogut and Ritov 2005a,b; Small and Loewenstein 2003; Burson et al., under review), and extend them by (a) demonstrating the robustness of the effect for a singular collection of beneficiaries and (b) suggesting efficacy as the underlying mechanism.

Study 2 tests whether increasing perceived efficacy boosts charitable giving to many relative to one. We hypothesized that providing feasibility, or "how to," information in a charitable appeal would influence the achievability of "making a difference," and would thereby increase giving to many vs. when no feasibility information was provided. Indeed, we observed a significant interaction between number of beneficiaries (one vs. many) and appeal focus (control vs. feasibility information) such that participants who did vs. did not receive feasibility information donated more toward many beneficiaries. Emotions measures were also collected but did not have a systematic influence on donations.

Study 3 uses a 3 x 2 between-subjects design which crosses a beneficiary scope (one vs. many vs. one of many) manipulation with an efficacy (higher vs. lower) manipulation. Including three beneficiary scope conditions allowed us to test efficacy as the mechanism underlying giving behavior to both a singular beneficiary (i.e., one child) and also a singular collection of beneficiaries (i.e., one village of many). As predicted, donation intentions toward one vs. many beneficiaries depended on whether efficacy was perceived as being higher vs. lower. Specifically, when efficacy was lower vs. higher, people preferred to donate to one (i.e., one child and one village of many children) vs. many. However, when efficacy was higher, participants donated more to many vs. one. We collected several other intentions measures (e.g., volunteering, joining a Facebook group, starting a club) and replicated the same patterns.

In study 4 (in progress), we manipulate beneficiary entitativity (i.e., cohesiveness) to examine how it impacts donations to one vs. many beneficiaries. Our preliminary results indicate that people give systematically more to a homogenous group of individuals, and that the mechanism underlying this result is perceived efficacy.

In summary, this work identifies ways of boosting giving to many, primarily by increasing perceived efficacy. We propose that: (a) generally, focusing on "one" (i.e., a singular beneficiary or a singular collection of beneficiaries) is an effective strategy to boost charitable giving, but (b) this is only effective when perceived efficacy is low; (c) when perceived efficacy is high, it is more effective to focus on many. Finally, since the effect of entitativity on giving is mediated by perceived efficacy, there may be instances in which perceiving many as a singular collection might hurt vs. help. In addition to its theoretical contributions, this work provides several practical implications, as there are numerous circumstances in which it is neither appropriate nor feasible to focus on "one."

### "Giving Against the Odds: When Highlighting Tempting Alternatives Increases Willingness to Donate"

*Kelly Goldsmith, Northwestern University, USA*
*Jennifer S. Danilowitz, Yale University, USA*
*Ravi Dhar, Yale University, USA*

Charitable giving is a large and important industry. Nearly 70% of all Americans gave to charity in 2006, creating a total of over a trillion dollars in revenue received by non-profits (Grabstats 2010). Despite the pro-social and personal benefits of charitable giving (Anik et al. 2009), the current economic crisis has caused many to reconsider making such donations. Thus the question of how to motivate charitable giving may be more relevant now than ever before. Prior research has identified certain factors that increase consumers' willingness to donate, such as one's information processing style (Liu and Aaker 2008; Reed, Aquino and Levy 2007) or mood (Hibbert et al. 2007; Small and Verrochi 2009). However, much of this work has focused on examining how such manipulations affect giving by influencing consumers' perceived relationship to the cause. In contrast, we propose that highlighting alternative ways to spend one's money can ironically increase consumers' willingness to donate by enhancing the self-signal the donation provides (Dhar and Wertenbroch 2010).

For example, imagine a consumer who is asked to make a small donation to the UNICEF. Prior to his decision, he sees a note which calls his attention to other ways his money could be used (e.g., purchasing a new hit song off of iTunes). How will his exposure to this alternative affect his likelihood of making the donation, in comparison to someone who did not see the note? As stated, we argue that making certain opportunities salient may be one way to increase charitable donations. While Frederick and colleagues (2009) have documented countless examples how salient opportunity costs generally reduce consumers' overall likelihood of purchase, other research suggests that bringing to mind certain opportunities may increase the self-signaling utility associated with an available option (here, the option to donate). Specifically, research

by Dhar and Werternbroch (2010) demonstrates that the self-signal one derives from any given choice is context dependent and can be affected by the non-chosen options available in the choice set. For example, these authors find that the over-all utility associated with a virtuous choice (e.g., a healthy apple) increases when that option is presented in a choice set where vices (e.g., tasty chocolates) are also available. Based on these findings we argue that simply making a hedonic opportunity salient in the context of a donation choice can increase the over-all utility consumers associate with the act of donating, specifically because the act of donating will send a more positive self-signal thereby increasing the utility from donating.

These hypotheses are tested in a series of lab and field experiments. In the two lab experiments, participants read a charity appeal asking them to make a donation (Experiment 1a: $50 to UNICEF; Experiment 1b: $75 to Hurricane Katrina Victims). Before reporting their willingness to donate to the charity, respondents in the hedonic opportunity salient conditions were reminded that for the same amount of money, they could indulge themselves with a hedonic reward (Experiment 1a: a silver Tiffany bookmark; Experiment 1b: a massage at a spa). Finally, all participants indicated their interest in making the donation (scale: 1–not at all interested to 9–very interested). The results supported our prediction. In both experiments, participants were more interested in donating when the hedonic opportunity was made salient as compared to the control condition (Experiment 1a: $M_{salient}=7.0$, $M_{control}=5.9$, p=.04; Experiment 1b: $M_{salient}=6.9$, $M_{control}=3.6$, p=.001).

The next two experiments test for these effects in actual choice scenarios where consumers were able to donate real money. Further, Experiment 2 was designed to rule out an alternate account for the observed results by showing that the pattern is specific to hedonic alternatives (as opposed to all alternatives). The self-signaling account implies an increase in utility only when indulgent options are rejected, since the positive self-signal results from denying oneself the hedonic (but not utilitarian) alternate opportunity. In Experiment 2 we manipulate if a hedonic versus a utilitarian alternative is made salient and compare their effects on donation to a control condition. Supporting our prediction, we observe the presence of a hedonic alternate substantially increased actual donation rates over the control condition ($P_{hedonic\ salient}=88\%$, $P_{control}=47\%$, p=.01). Further, as predicted, the utilitarian opportunity reduced donation rates as compared to the hedonic opportunity ($P_{utilitarian\ salient}=57\%$, p=.03) and approximated that of the control condition (p>.5). The final field experiment tests for convergent support for this phenomenon by investigating if the observed effect on monetary donations replicates when consumers are asked to donate their time. Participants received a charity appeal via email asking them to consider donating two hours of their time to help their local UNICEF chapter. The dependent measure was participants' choice to donate their time. For half of the participants, prior to the donation question, a hedonic opportunity was made salient ("Remember, it takes two hours of your time to watch the Season Finale of MTV's The Jersey Shore"). The results supported our prediction and the findings thus far. When the hedonic opportunity was made salient a significantly greater percentage of participants agreed to donate their time ($P_{salient}=32.1\%$, $P_{control}=11.8\%$, p=.023).

This research achieves several goals: we identify a subtle and practical means to increase charitable donation rates. Further, we extend what is currently known about opportunity costs and demonstrate when making such opportunities salient can actually increase spending. Our ongoing experiments are presently testing for self-signaling as the mechanism underlying these effects.

# Evolution, Consumer Behavior, and Decision-Making

Vladas Griskevicius, University of Minnesota, USA
Joshua Ackerman, Massachusetts Institute of Technology, USA

## EXTENDED ABSTRACTS

### "The Evolutionary Roots of Decision Biases: Erasing and Exacerbating Loss Aversion"

Yexin Jessica Li, Arizona State University, USA
Doug Kenrick, Arizona State University, USA
Vladas Griskevicius, University of Minnesota, USA
Steven Neuberg, Arizona State University, USA

From an evolutionary perspective, recurring biases such as loss aversion may reflect adaptive human heuristics. For example, because our ancestors lived in environments where it was difficult to obtain sufficient calories for survival, resource losses that could result in starvation matter more than gains. Consistent with this reasoning, loss aversion is a well-documented and robust finding in humans and other species.

Although a tendency toward loss aversion may initially appear to be a human universal, an evolutionary perspective suggests that organisms generally do not evolve domain-general biases. Instead, organisms manifest different biases in different evolutionary recurring domains (e.g., survival, reproduction, etc.) (Kenrick et al. 2009). We suggest that whereas loss-aversion is adaptive in the evolutionary critical domain of survival, loss aversion is unlikely to be adaptive in the domain of mating. Thus, whereas loss aversion should be exacerbated when survival-related motives are active, loss aversion may be erased when mating motives are activated.

Further consideration of human mating suggests that men are especially unlikely to be loss averse when motivated to pursue a mate. From an evolutionary perspective, men should tend to value an opportunity to mate more than women. Consistent with this reasoning, recent research shows that men's cognitions and behaviors are more attuned than women's to potential mating opportunities, leading men to downplay potential fiscal losses when mating opportunities are salient (Griskevicius et al. 2007). Thus, we predict that men should perceive gains and losses differently when thinking about mating. In particular, mating motives should spur men to underestimate the costs of losses and overestimate the benefits of gains.

In Study 1, we experimentally activated mating or control motives by having men and women read pre-tested stories (Griskevicius et al. 2007). Then, participants indicated how much money they would spend to gain or to avoid a drop in status. As predicted, men became significantly less loss averse in the mating condition compared to control, whereby men no longer showed loss aversion. For women, mating motives did not influence loss aversion.

In study 2, we examined how mating motives influenced loss aversion using a different methodology. After activating mating or control motives, participants indicated how happy or unhappy they would be if they lost or gained particular amount of money (Harinck, Van Dijk, Beest, and Mersmann 2007). For example, participants in the 'gain' condition were asked how happy or unhappy they would be if they found $50, $100, $200 and $400. As in the first study, mating motives erased loss aversion for men, meaning that men no longer showed this bias in the mating condition. Mating motives again did not influence loss aversion for women.

We earlier noted that loss aversion is likely to be an adaptation for solving survival challenges. Thus, we should observe the highest levels of loss aversion when individuals are motivated to protect themselves from danger. In Study 3, we activated either a self-protection motive or a control motive. Then, as in study 2, participants indicated how happy or unhappy they would be if they lost or gained particular amounts of money. Consistent with predictions, self-protection motives exacerbated loss aversion, leading both men and women to care significantly more about losses and care less about gains. This means that the bias toward loss aversion was strongest specifically when survival-related motives were salient.

Overall, these studies suggest that loss aversion is not a general universal human bias. Instead, this bias is highly sensitive to evolutionary critical contexts of survival and mating. Across studies, two evolutionary motives resulted in vastly different patterns in the relative valuation of gains versus losses. Specifically, because loss aversion likely evolved as an adaptation to survival challenges, we find that this decision bias is exacerbated when survival-related motives are salient (Study 3). However, loss aversion appears to be erased for men when the mating motives are salient (Study 1 and Study 2). More broadly, these findings suggest that evolutionary motives can alter decisional biases in ways that make functional sense in light of more general theories of evolution and cognition.

### References

Griskevicius, V., Tybur, J. M., Sundie, J. M., Cialdini, R. B., Miller, G. F. & Kenrick, D. T. (2007). Blatant benevolence and conspicuous consumption: When romantic motives elicit strategic costly signals. *Journal of Personality & Social Psychology,* 93, 85-102.

Harinck, F., Van Dijk, E., Beest, I. & Mersmann, P. (2007). When gains loom larger than losses: Loss aversion for small amounts of money. *Psychological Science,* 18, 1099-1105.

Kenrick, D.T., Griskevicius, V., Sundie, J.M., Li, Y.J. & Neuberg, S.L. (2009). Deep rationality: The evolutionary economics of decision-making. *Social Cognition, 27,* 764-785.

### "Ovulation, Female Competition, and Product Choice: Hormonal Influences on Consumer Behavior"

Kristina Durante, University of Minnesota, USA
Vladas Griskevicius, University of Minnesota, USA
Normal Li, Singapore Management University, USA
Sarah Hill, Texas Christian University, USA
Carin Perilloux, University of Texas Austin, USA

Much research has examined women's consumer behavior. For example, early research found that women have a high level of interest in shopping for fashion-related items. Women desire to stay up-to-date on fashion trends and purchase new items even when they are not dissatisfied with the products they already own. Women also tend to use clothing to enhance their mood and social self-esteem, and they are significantly more likely to go shopping to pass time, browse around, or just as an escape. However, research thus far has not examined whether women's consumption might be influenced by hormonal factors.

Emerging research in evolutionary biology shows that various aspects of women's psychology shift during the brief window within each monthly cycle when conception is possible. For instance, near ovulation, women prefer men who show classic biological indicators of male genetic fitness (e.g., facial symmetry, social dominance), are more motivated to cheat on their current romantic partners, have more favorable attitudes toward attending social gatherings, and desire to look sexier (e.g., Durante, Li and Haselton 2008; Gangestad and Thornhill 2008).

Drawing on this emerging theory and research, the current research tested the prediction that women's product choices shift toward products that enhance physical appearance at high fertility. We also examined whether ovulating women buy such products to appear sexier in an attempt to impress men or if ovulating women buy such products primarily in an attempt to outdo other attractive women.

Study 1 tested whether women at high fertility are more likely to choose sexier and more revealing clothing and accessories. In this study, women shopped for products using a simulated, online shopping website. Results showed that women's product choices shifted toward sexier and more revealing fashion items near ovulation. For example, ovulating women selected tops, skirts, and pants that were pre-rated to be more revealing and sexier. This shift occurred even though the women were not aware that they were currently ovulating.

The second study examined conditions that should exacerbate or suppress this ovulation effect. In Study 2, ovulating and non-ovulating women completed the same shopping task as in Study 1. However, prior to the shopping task, women were primed to think about one type of person: (1) attractive local women, (2) unattractive local women, (3) attractive local men, or (4) unattractive local men. Results showed that although women chose sexier and more revealing outfits when primed with attractive men, it did not make a difference whether the women were or were not ovulating. This finding suggests that the effects of ovulation on product choice are not predicated on mating motives directly. Instead, when women were primed with attractive female rivals, ovulation produced the largest effects on choice, leading ovulating women to choose much more sexy outfits and accessories. Findings support the notion that the ovulatory product-choice effect is predicated on same-sex competition with attractive rivals.

An additional study addressed the alternative possibility that simply priming attractive women, regardless of whether the women are viewed as potential rivals, would produce the ovulatory effect. Participants viewed photos of the same attractive women used in Study 2. However, whereas in Study 2 participants were told that the attractive women were local to the area (i.e., potential rivals), participants in the current study were told the women were not local. Results showed that ovulation had no effect on the percentage of sexy items that were chosen. Thus, women's ovulation-regulated desire for sexy items appears to be tied to the attractiveness of local, but not distant, same-sex others.

This theoretically driven and rigorous study of how hormones influence product choice marks the potential beginning of a new frontier in consumer research. The study of how biological factors such as hormones influence consumption has not only vast implications for linking consumer behavior with other disciplines (e.g., biology, animal behavior, anthropology, evolutionary psychology), it also presents a fruitful avenue for future research.

## References

Durante, Kristina M., Norman P. Li, and Martie G. Haselton (2008), "Changes in Women's Choice of Dress across the Ovulatory Cycle: Naturalistic and Laboratory Task-Based Evidence," *Personality and Social Psychology Bulletin,* 34 (November), 1451-1460.

Gangestad, Steven W., & Randy Thornhill (2008), "Human Oestrus," Proceedings of the Royal Society B, 275, 991-1000.

## "Peacocks, Porsches and Thorstein Veblen: Conspicuous Consumption as a Mating Signaling System"

*Jill Sundie, University of Houston, USA*
*Kathleen Vohs, University of Minnesota, USA*
*Vladas Griskevicius, University of Minnesota, USA*

Each year consumers spend hundreds of millions of dollars for conspicuous consumption products, often paying significant mark-ups to purchase premium brands (Han, Nunes and Drèze 2010). Previous work examining conspicuous consumption from an evolutionary perspective found that conspicuous product displays are linked to mating motives for men (Griskevicius et al. 2007). Men were motivated to conspicuously consume to impress women, while women were inclined to use other means (such as public displays of helping) to impress men. This research demonstrated one motive for purchasing luxury products (among men), but also raised additional theoretical questions about the links between men, mating, and conspicuous spending.

Conspicuous consumption is a risky spending pattern—for all but the wealthiest people, it involves trading off future financial security for frivolous indulgences today. As such, conspicuous spending may indicate financial irresponsibility and narcissism, characteristics generally not sought by women in a committed partner. Conspicuous spending is, however, one means for men to display risk-seeking and social dominance. Under what circumstances would women favor social dominance and risk-seeking in a mate (as conspicuous spending indicates) over financial security and cues to a man's willingness to share and invest his resources wisely within a committed partnership? An evolutionary perspective suggests that short-term (uncommitted) mating contexts may be one such set of circumstances.

Study 1 examined how mating motives influenced conspicuous consumption. Participants either read about attractive members of the opposite sex seeking dates (mating stimuli) or about possible housing options (control). Conspicuous consumption was measured via how a windfall gain was spent on various goods and services pre-rated for conspicuousness. Findings showed that men chronically seeking short-term partnerships were significantly more motivated to conspicuously consume in the mating versus the control condition, but more commitment-oriented men were not. Women, regardless of their interest in short-term vs. long-term partnerships, did not engage in more conspicuous consumption in the mating condition.

Study 2 examined how different active mating opportunities (long-term committed vs. short-term uncommitted) would influence men's desire to engage in conspicuous spending. After receiving either a short-term, long-term, or neutral prime, participants indicated how much they would spend on eight conspicuous products. Men with an interest in short-term partnerships spent more on conspicuous products (relative to the control condition) when *un*committed mating opportunities were salient, but not when committed partnership opportunities were salient. Neither commitment-oriented men, nor women, indicated they would spend more conspicuously in either mating condition.

Study 3 investigated whether conspicuous consumption would make a man more desirable to women as (a) a committed partner, and (b) as a short-term partner. Participants evaluated an opposite-sex target whose biography indicated he/she had just purchased either an expensive conspicuous car or a modest inconspicuous car. Men were rated significantly more desirable as a date if he had purchased a conspicuous car, but *not* more desirable for marriage. Female desirability did not vary with the type of car purchased for either relationship type. Further, the male target was perceived as significantly more likely to be seeking short-term, uncommitted partnerships if he purchased the conspicuous car.

Overall, we investigated conspicuous consumption signals by examining (1) which individuals send them, (2) which contexts trigger them, and (3) how observers interpret them. Two experiments demonstrated that conspicuous consumption is driven by men who are following a lower-investment (versus higher-investment) mating strategy, and is triggered specifically by short-term (versus long-term) mating motives. A third experiment showed that observers interpret such signals accurately, with women perceiving men who conspicuously consume as interested in short-term mating. Furthermore, conspicuous purchasing enhanced men's desirability as a short-term (but not as a long-term) mate. Overall, the current pattern of data suggests that flaunting status-linked goods to potential mates is not simply about displaying economic resources. Instead, conspicuous consumption appears to be part of a more precise signaling system focused on short-term mating.

### References

Han, Young Jee, Joseph C. Nunes and Xavier Drèze (2010), "Signaling Status with Luxury Goods: The Role of Brand Prominence," forthcoming at *Journal of Marketing*.

Griskevicius, V., J. M. Tybur, J. M. Sundie, R. B. Cialdini, G. F. Miller, and D. T. Kenrick (2007), "Blatant Benevolence and Conspicuous Consumption: When Romantic Motives Elicit Costly Displays," *Journal of Personality and Social Psychology*, 93, 85-102.

### "Evolutionary Goal Scaffolding: Building Social Motives on a Physical Foundation"

*Julie Huang, Yale University, USA*
*Joshua Ackerman, MIT Sloan School of Management, USA*
*John Bargh, Yale University, USA*

The current research begins with age-old question: Are superheroes lonely? More specifically, does having a power like invulnerability (in mere mortal terms, feeling safe from physical harm) heal the wounds of social exclusion? An evolutionary perspective suggests that this prospect may be more than pulp fiction. Modern models of hierarchical motivation suggest basic physical needs and goals, including hunger, warmth and safety, are evolutionarily more ancient than social needs and goals. Because evolution typically works through derived adaptation—building off of (and maintaining links to) pre-existing structures—it is possible that physical goal mechanisms acted as a mental scaffold for the development of social goal mechanisms. Indeed, evidence indicates that physical and social threat processing involve common neural and hormonal substrates. Both also produce states of mental withdrawal, lead people to devalue risky options, and trigger goals to restore feelings of safety through social connection (e.g., Epley et al. 2008; Griskevicius et al., 2009).

The evolved overlap between social and physical safety processing suggests a novel framework for studying consumer goal-pursuit. We propose that cues to physical safety may substitute for social safety cues, thereby completing active social goals. For example, social rejection elicits compensatory goals such as a desire to reconnect with friends or, failing that, a desire for indulgences like Ben & Jerry's. However, feelings of physical safety may satisfy these desires, restoring cognitive resources and de-biasing decisions. This cue substitutability would provide a means of connecting what are seemingly qualitatively different forms of goal-pursuit.

The current experiments provide some of the first research on how evolutionary goal scaffolding affects decision-making. We present three studies showing that responses to social rejection can be alleviated through simulations of physical safety.

Study 1 tested whether a physical safety manipulation interfered with responses from a prior rejection experience. Participants in two conditions recalled in detail a past experience with social exclusion. One group then received a guided visualization task in which they imagined having a superpower—being completely invincible from physical harm. The other group received no such instructions. A third comparison condition first received the superpower manipulation and then completed the exclusion recall task. All participants then responded to several indicators of negative affect. Participants who received the superpower prime after rejection reported less negative feelings than the other groups, suggesting that physical safety cues "turn off" rejection responses in goal-consistent fashion.

In Study 2, participants recalled either a past rejection experience or details about their last meal. Next, half of participants received the invincibility visualization, and the other half imagined having a different, but non-safety related, superpower—the ability to fly. All participants then completed established measures of social reconnection, the desire for which has been shown to strengthen after exclusion. "Flying" participants showed the expected greater desire to interact with friends, whereas "invincible" participants did not. Safety completely attenuated the rejection-control difference, again supporting a goal scaffolding framework.

Study 3 extended these findings to the realm of consumer product decisions. Participants recalled a rejection experience and then received either the flying or invincible superpower manipulation. They then reported their desire for both high status/image-related (e.g., fancy dinner, cosmetics) and low status/non-image-related (e.g., minivan, sofa) consumer products. Invincible participants desired image-related products more and non-image-related products less than participants who could fly. Thus, consumers may feel more freedom to acquire high status, flashy products when unconstrained by self-presentational, social reconnection concerns.

In summary, three studies show that responses to social rejection can be interrupted by processing cues to physical safety, consistent with an evolutionary goal scaffolding framework. This social-physical substitutability has important implications for researchers and marketers, the most significant being that consumer behavior applications need not focus purely on social goal modification, but may also benefit from changing perceptions of related physical needs.

### References

Epley, Nicholas, Scott Akalis, Adam Waytz and John T. Cacioppo (2008), "Creating Social Connection through Inferential Reproduction: Loneliness and Perceived Agency in Gadgets, Gods, and Greyhounds," *Psychological Science, 19*, 114-120.

Griskevicius, Vladas, Noah J. Goldstein, Chad R. Mortenson, Jill M. Sundie, Robert B. Cialdini and Douglas T. Kenrick (2009) "Fear and Loving in Las Vegas: Evolution, Emotion, and Persuasion," *Journal of Marketing Research, 46*, 384-395.

# From Evaluation to Compliance:
## Anthropomorphism and the Role of Loneliness, Trust, Uncertainty and Guilt
Hee-Kyung Ahn, University of Toronto, Canada

## EXTENDED ABSTRACTS

### "Once Bitten, Twice Shy: Differences in Social Efficacy Affect the Perceived Efficacy of Anthropomorphizable Products"

*Bart Claus, Catholic University Leuven, Belgium*
*Luk Warlop, Catholic University Leuven, Belgium*

Anthropomorphism as a practitioners' technique of imbuing brands with human-like qualities has longtime been used, and has proven to be efficient in the development of brand personality and brand relationships. Recent work by Aggarwal and McGill (2007) signals a shift in attention from brands towards anthropomorphic products. Additionally, anthropomorphization recently has been studied from a more phenomenological stance, with an interest in dispositional and situational drivers of anthropomorphization. Epley and colleagues (2007) found sociality motives to be one of the driving factors of anthropomorphization. Lonely people seek human company, which increases their susceptibility to anthropomorphize. The latter might lead to the inference that lonely consumers seek and prefer anthropomorphic products.

Loneliness can indeed be a motivator to reconnect to other people, and by extension to anthropomorphs. Loneliness then reflects a limited *quantity* of social interaction. However, loneliness is also often considered as the result of poor *quality* social interactions, i.e. negative social experiences. This kind of loneliness is caused by negative social experiences, not by the lack of social experiences. Although people may want to reconnect to others, social anxiety might influence their attitude towards new social contacts (Maner, DeWall, Baumeister, & Schaller, 2007).

In our research, we study whether attitudes that were originally directed towards humans, can spill over to non-human targets that are subject to anthropomorphization. With regard to anthropomorphization of products, we expect that lowered social efficacy will translate into lower a priori expectations towards the anthropomorph at hand. On the other hand, an unexpectedly successful interaction with an anthropomorph might bring relief to people's feelings of low social efficacy. We tested these inferences in several studies.

In Study 1, we found that people with a higher tendency to feel lonely indeed favor anthropomorphic products over nonanthropomorphic ones. However, people that were first submitted to an ostracism manipulation (Williams, Cheung, & Choi, 2000) showed the opposite effect, especially when they had a higher chronic tendency to feel lonely.

In Study 2, we this negative attitude. We again manipulated social efficacy between subjects, using the ostracism task. The product that had to be evaluated was an automatic vacuum cleaner, and we asked participants about their expectations about the efficacy of the product. We manipulated anthropomorphism by describing the product either in terms of its technical characteristics and product code "Samsung VC-RS60H", or in terms of more human traits and the friendlier name "Roomba". Results show that people's estimates of the product's efficacy were hampered by lower social efficacy–but only for anthropomorphs.

In study 3, we built on Leary et al.'s Sociometer Theory (Leary, Tambor, & Terdal, 1995), in assessing people's chronic efficacy in social interactions. We had participants evaluate the expected number of times they would 'guess' the same number as a number

generator, depicted either as an ordinary personal computer, or an anthropomorphic computer (manipulated similarly to earlier studies). Afterwards, a trait measure of self-esteem (Rosenberg, 1965) was administered. Results show that in the anthromorphization condition, trait self-esteem is positively related to people's estimation of future outcomes the product will deliver–more than in the control condition. This indicates that what is affected is people's belief in their own efficacy to interact with anthropomorphs.

Study 4 used a similar design as study 2, but with a digital picture frame as product stimulus. Control participants were told that this prototype contained sensors that adjusted the picture on display according to the atmosphere in its vicinity. Participants in the experimental condition were told that the frame was 'smart' and 'able to sense' the atmosphere. Participants then estimated the efficacy of the frame as part of a product evaluation survey. As in earlier studies, participants that had been ostracized stated lower beliefs in the efficacy of the frame, but only for the anthropomorphic description of the product. Subsequently the frame 'selected' one of the pictures. Using initial evaluations as a covariate, we found previously ostracized participants in the anthropomorphic condition to be most satisfied with the frame's selection performance.

In four studies, we used different operationalizations of anthropomorphism and different products. Using chronic gauges as well as momentary manipulations, we show that differences in social efficacy affect a priori evaluations of products more when these products are more readily susceptible to anthropomorphization. We also show that product sampling can overcome this effect. Our contribution is in demonstrating that social attitudes can bridge the gap towards non-human entities when anthropomorphization takes place.

### "Who or What to Believe: Trust and the Differential Persuasiveness of Anthropomorphized and Human Agents"

*Maferima Touré-Tillery, University of Chicago, USA*
*Ann L. McGill, University of Chicago, USA*

Current research on anthropomorphism suggests that people interact with anthropomorphized agents according to their generalized beliefs about people. Indeed, Epley et al. (2007) describe anthropomorphism as a specialized process of inductive inference in which knowledge about humans is used to make inferences about nonhuman agents. Aggarwal and McGill (2007) showed that consumers evaluate an anthropomorphized product more positively when it possesses characteristics congruent with the proposed human schema, if this schema is linked to positive affect.

In the present research, we investigate this question in the persuasion context by comparing messages from human sources to those from anthropomorphized entities. In persuasion, individual differences in interpersonal trust are particularly relevant: people low (vs. high) in interpersonal trust are harder to persuade because they generally believe that social agents are neither reliable nor credible (Rotter 1967). Based on the assumption that individuals use their knowledge about people when interacting with humanized objects, we should expect messages from anthropomorphized agents and human sources to elicit similar responses, such that individuals low in trust would be equally skeptical of both messages. We propose, however, that people who hold negative views about human nature (e.g. "people are not trustworthy"), might be motivated to perceive anthropomorphized agents in a more positive light (e.g. more trustworthy) than humans.

Epley et al (2008) found that dispositionally lonely people were more likely to anthropomorphize pets to satisfy their need for social connection. To us, these findings suggest that lonely people might be motivated to perceive humanized agents as more capable of providing social connectedness than real persons. Within this perspective, we propose that people low in interpersonal trust will perceive an anthropomorphized agent as more trustworthy than a human under similar circumstances. In the communication context, we predict that a message delivered by an anthropomorphized agent will be more persuasive to low trust individuals than one from a human source. As a result, behavioral intentions of people low in trust should align more closely with messages from anthropomorphized (vs. human) sources. However, people high in trust should respond similarly to anthropomorphized and human sources because they do not hold negative views about the trustworthiness of social agents.

In all studies, we measured trust using Rotter's (1967) interpersonal trust scale. In study 1, we tested our hypothesis in a health communication context. Participants read a message about a disease, including prevention information. The message was delivered by University authorities (human source), or by the disease itself (anthropomorphized source). We found that low trust participants were more fearful of the disease and more likely to comply with health recommendations when the source of the message was the anthropomorphized disease than when the source was human, suggesting greater perceived credibility for the "talking" disease. In the next two studies, we sought to replicate these findings for positive attitude objects to rule out the alternative explanation that low trust individuals transferred their fear of people onto the anthropomorphized agent. In study 2, participant saw a message delivered by a car advertiser (human source), or by the car itself (anthropomorphized source). The contents of the messages were identical, but low trust participants who read the message from the anthropomorphized (vs. human) source responded more positively to the car, and were more likely to buy it. Study 3 replicated these results: low trust participants preferred a fictitious brand of floss and were more likely to buy it when they read a message from the anthropomorphized (vs. human) source. Finally, study 4 demonstrated that for low trust individuals, the credibility of an anthropomorphized source is enhanced, not only for information pertaining to the source itself, but also for other pieces of information in the message. Participants read a message delivered by a fictitious dental floss advertiser or by the floss itself (Max Floss). The message from the advertiser objectified Max Floss and presented it as the best weapon against gingivitis. In the anthropomorphized source message, Max Floss presented itself as the reader's best ally against gingivitis. Participants low in trust felt more threatened by gingivitis when the message came from the anthropomorphized source (Max Floss) than when the source of the message was human. As expected, across all four studies, high trust participants responded similarly to messages from anthropomorphized and human sources.

Taken together, these studies provide convergent evidence that people low in interpersonal trust perceive anthropomorphized agents as more trustworthy than real persons in a similar context, and as a result are more persuaded by messages delivered by anthropomorphized (vs. human) agents.

## "Seeing Smiles: Consumers' Adoption of Anthropomorphized New Product"

*Lan Jiang, University of British Columbia. Canada*
*JoAndrea Hoegg, University of British Columbia. Canada*
*Darren W. Dahl, University of British Columbia. Canada*

It has become a common practice for marketers to design an anthropomorphized representation of a product or a brand. This strategy has also been widely used in the verbal descriptions of a product, i.e. using the personal pronouns instead of "it". Wetmore (1998) studied the phenomena of people befriending their cars and suggested that anthropomorphism helps individuals counteract the feelings of fear, threat or confusion with technology. Epley, Waytz and Caciopp (2007) further examined the motives underlying peoples' tendency to imbue nonhuman agents with humanlike characteristics, and one of them is the need to avoid uncertainty.

In this research, we seek to investigate whether consumers would be more likely to adopt humanlike new products. Launching new products is a risky task, since consumers are faced with high levels of uncertainty in understanding and applying new products in their lives. If the need to avoid uncertainty indeed drives an individual's tendency to desire anthropomorphized products, we should expect the strategy of anthropomorphizing products to be more effective for new products that entail higher uncertainty. Three lab experiments have been conducted to test this hypothesis.

In the first study, we pre-tested four products, two rated more uncertain than the others, and introduced them to the participants in either human or object terms. The two high-uncertainty products were a green printer and a concept phone, and the two low-uncertainty products were a nightlight and a scuba mask. The human version of the verbal descriptions included the phrases like "this little guy" and "eats your coffee dregs", while in the object condition these words were replaced by "this little machine" and "takes your coffee dregs". The study adopted a 2 (presentation: human vs. object) x 2 (uncertainty: high vs. low) mixed design. Analysis revealed an interaction effect of uncertainty and anthropomorphism. Participants rated the high-uncertainty products more favorably when they were presented in human versus object terms, but for low-uncertainty products there was no difference between two presentation formats. Participants also indicated a higher intention to adopt the high-uncertainty products when introduced in human rather than object terms, but no differences for low-uncertainty products.

Study 2 followed up the same design and further tested the hypothesis. A major difference of this study was that we manipulated the anthropomorphism visually, so in the anthropomorphism condition the images were professionally-morphed to possess more human features, such as smiley eyes or mouth. We kept the green printer and the nightlight, but for the ease of visual manipulation we replaced the concept phone with a bluetooth headset and used a pair of speakers to replace the scuba mask. Results from Study 2 further supported our hypothesis that anthropomorphism exerts stronger influences when people evaluate or plan to adopt new products that are high in uncertainty. Participants formed more favorable attitudes towards the green printer and the bluetooth when they were morphed to be humanlike, and indicated a higher intention to adopt. However, for low-uncertainty products, the ratings were equally favorable, regardless whether the images were original or morphed.

The main purpose of Study 3 was to test whether it is the feeling of familiarity generated by anthropomorphism that helps to alleviate the uncertainty and facilitate the comprehension, thus increasing the liking and adoption. We selected the green printer as our focal product and varied the uncertainty by either labeling it as "product #124-green printer" or "product #124". Visual morphing was used to manipulate the anthropomorphism. Consistent with the previous studies, a main effect of anthropomorphism emerged, where participants reported more favorably attitudes and behavioral intentions towards the green printer when the image featured a smiling face. More interestingly, we found an interaction between anthropomorphism and uncertainty. Participants indicated a preference for the anthropomorphized green printer, and this preference was stronger when the printer was labeled without a name. We further examined the familiarity measure, and the results followed the same pattern. Sobel test (Sobel 1982) confirmed the mediating role of familiarity in driving the effects of anthropomorphism.

In sum, we examined the effects of anthropomorphism, using both verbal and visual manipulations, on people's attitudes and adoption intentions towards the products and how uncertainty moderates the effects. The findings are consistent with our premise that people have a motive to avoid uncertainty and seek comprehension, and in consumption contexts anthropomorphism provides a solution when consumers are presented with new uncertain products. The human terms used to describe the products or the humanlike appearances increase the familiarity, and thus facilitate people's liking and adoption of them.

### "Guilt Driven Compliance by Anthropomorphized Social Causes"

*Hee-Kyung Ahn, University of Toronto, Canada*
*Hae Joo Kim, University of Toronto, Canada*
*Pankaj Aggarwal, University of Toronto, Canada*

Finding a cost-efficient and effective tool to enhance public welfare is important given that the U.S. state governments annually spend over 85 billion dollars on environmental and health issues (U.S. Census 2007). In the present research, we argue that adding anthropomorphic features to public policy campaigns can more effectively persuade consumers to comply with a social cause.

Particularly, we hypothesize that individuals will show more favorable behavioral intentions to comply with a public policy campaign when it depicts social causes with humanlike features than when these features are absent. To explain the underlying mechanism, we draw on literature in the interpersonal domain that associates helping behavior with feelings of guilt (e.g., Carlsmith and Gross 1969). Helping is an act of communion, and guilt is based on a threat to communion regardless of whether the relationship at stake concerns a close other or stranger (Baumeister, Stillwell, and Heatherton 1994). Applying this social principle to anthropomorphism, we predict that when individuals are faced with humanlike (vs. non-humanlike) agents, feelings of guilt will arise when contemplating the consequences of not complying, which consequently leads to increased compliance. Furthermore, we hypothesize that framing matters, such that information that intensifies (e.g., monetary penalty) or alleviates (i.e., monetary substitution) guilt will moderate the effect of anthropomorphism. Three studies were conducted to test these predictions.

In study 1, we examine the effect of anthropomorphism on compliance to an energy conservation campaign. Participants were assigned to either a control condition or an anthropomorphism condition. In the former (latter), participants were exposed to a campaign poster depicting a picture of a light bulb (with humanlike physical features) and a slogan written in a third-person (first-person) perspective. As predicted, behavioral intentions to comply with the energy conversation campaign were higher in the anthropomorphism condition than in the control condition.

In study 2, we replicate this effect in the context of a food waste recycling campaign. Participants were similarly exposed to a campaign poster with a waste bin depicted as a human in the anthropomorphism condition. Their control counterparts were exposed to the same poster in non-humanlike terms. In addition to measuring behavioral intentions of complying with the recycling campaign, we assessed participants' feelings of perceived guilt if they did not comply with the campaign. Once again, behavioral intentions to comply with the campaign were higher in the anthropomorphism condition than in the control condition. More importantly, we find that increased feelings of guilt partially mediated the effect.

In study 3 (in progress), we examine whether the framing of monetary information can moderate the effect of anthropomorphism on compliance. Participants are exposed to a food waste recycling campaign similar to study 2. In addition to an anthropomorphism manipulation, we manipulate the frame of monetary information included in the campaign poster such that it intensifies or alleviates feelings of guilt from not complying with the campaign. In the high guilt frame, the poster contains a warning for a financial penalty/fine if the participants do not recycle, "If you do not recycle, you have to pay $5." In the low guilt frame, the sentence is modified such that participants can avoid recycling by paying a small fee (i.e., "If you pay $5, you do not have to recycle."). When guilt is intensified by a monetary penalty we expect the compliance to be significantly greater than when the guilt is reduced by monetary substitution, showing the moderating effect of framing on feelings of guilt elicited by anthropomorphism.

To summarize, we find that campaign ads where social causes are anthropomorphized are more effective in heightening behavioral intentions to comply with the campaign compared to when the social causes contain no humanlike features. This effect was partially mediated by increased feelings of guilt upon considering the consequences of not complying with the public policy campaign. Moreover, information that can amplify or dampen feelings of guilt from not doing a prosocial act moderates the effect of anthropomorphism on compliance. Our findings contribute to the research on anthropomorphism by testing its effects in the domain of public policy and by identifying an underlying process of guilt. These findings have practical important implications for public policy makers who are concerned with improving the effectiveness of their prosocial messages. Additionally, they have practical implications for public policy makers whose concern is designing effective communication tools to increase prosocial behavior.

## REFERENCES

Aggarwal, P., and Ann L. McGill (2007), "Is That Car Smiling at Me? Schema Congruity as a Basis for Evaluating Anthropomorphized Products," *Journal of Consumer Research*, 34 (4), 468-79.

Baumeister, Roy F., Arlene M. Stillwell, and Todd F. Heatherton (1994), "Guilt: An Interpersonal Approach," *Psychological Bulletin*, 115 (March), 243-67.

Carlsmith, J. Merrill and Alan E. Gross (1969), "Some Effects on Guilt on Compliance," *Journal of Personality and Social Psychology*, 11 (March), 232-39.

Epley, Nicholas, Adam Waytz, and John T. Cacioppo (2007), "On Seeing Human: A three-Factor Theory of Anthropomorphism," *Psychological Review*, 114 (October), 864-86.

Epley, Nicolas., Adam Waytz, Scott Akalis, and John T. Cacioppo (2008), "When We Need a Human: Motivational Determinants of Anthropomorphism," *Social Cognition,* 26 (2), 143-55.

Leary, M. R., E. S. Tambor, K. Terdal, and D. L. Downs (1995), "Self-Esteem as an Interpersonal Monitor: The Sociometer Hypothesis," *Journal of Personality and Social Psychology*, 68 (3), 518-30.

Maner, J. K., C. N. DeWall, Roy F. Baumeister, and M. Schaller (2007), "Does Social Exclusion Motivate Interpersonal Reconnection? Resolving the "Porcupine Problem," *Journal of Personality and Social Psychology*, 92 (1), 42-55.

Rosenberg, M. (1965), *Society and the Adolescent Self-Image*, Princeton, NJ: Princeton University Press.

Rotter, J. B. (1967), "The New Scale for Measurement of Interpersonal Trust," *Journal of Personality and Social psychology*," 35 (4), 651-55.

Sobel, M. E. (1982), "Asymptotic Confidence Intervals for Indirect Effects in Structural Equation Models," In S. Leinhart (Ed.), *Sociological Methodology* (pp. 290?312), Jossey-Bass: San Francisco.

Wetmore, Jameson M. (1998), "Moving Relationships: Comparing the Corporate and Personal Practice of Naming Automobiles," *Interpreting the Automobile: Society of Automotive Historians/National Association of Automobile Museums Joint Conference*, Henry Ford Museum, Dearborn, Michigan, (September).

Williams, K. D., C. K. T. Cheung, and W. Choi (2000), "Cyberostracism: Effects of Being Ignored over the Internet," *Journal of Personality and Social Psychology*, 79 (5), 748-62.

# Having More: New Insights on the Impact of Numerosity on Consumer Decision Making
Haiyang Yáng, INSEAD, Singapore

## EXTENDED ABSTRACTS

### "Decisions Based on External versus Internal Cues: The Dual Effect of Attribute Quantity on Choice"
*Aner Sela, Stanford University, USA*
*Jonah Berger, University of Pennsylvania, USA*

People almost always consider some amount of attribute information when making decisions. They compare nutrition information when grocery shopping, examine compositions when choosing 401k plans, and contrast product features when selecting household goods.

But could the mere number of product attributes presented influence what type of option people choose? Some car-rental websites, for example, highlight only a few key features of each vehicle (e.g., make and model) whereas others list dozens of features under each option (e.g., cargo room, gas mileage, and various safety features). Product displays in stores may include just the basic facts (e.g., a smart-phone's weight and type of networks covered) or more detailed descriptions (e.g., applications, multimedia capabilities, and whether it has a camera). Might more exhaustive attribute lists lead people to favor efficient sedans over beefy roadsters, for example, or productivity- over fun-oriented smart-phones?

In a series of experiments, conducted in the field and the laboratory, we demonstrate that attribute quantity influences choice regardless of its content. We propose that, as the overall number of attributes increases, the focus of evaluation shifts from internal (i.e., experiential or memory-based cues) to external (i.e., stimulus-based) cues. Importantly, these different foci have different implications for choice under deliberate versus heuristic processing, such as with regard to the ubiquitous choice between hedonic and utilitarian options (e.g., Dhar and Wertenbroch 2000).

Under effortful deliberation, few attributes promote mental imagery (MacInnis and Price 1987), which tends to favor hedonics (Shiv and Huber 2000), whereas multiple attributes promote a more cognitive and analytical mode of thought (Peters and Slovic 2000) which highlights the appeal of utilitarian options (Rottenstreich et al. 2007). Under heuristic processing, however, fewer attributes promote reliance on accessible heuristics from memory, which often favor utilitarian options (Kivetz and Keinan 2006), whereas the presence of multiple attributes can be used as an external heuristic cue for practicality (Thompson et al. 2005) which tends to benefit hedonic more than utilitarian options (Nowlis and Simonson 1996).

Four experiments examine the dual role of attribute quantity in choice and explore underlying mechanisms. In experiment 1, four smart-phones (two described as "made for fun" and two as "made for work") were displayed on tables and passers-by were invited to select their preferred option. The options were described using either two or ten attributes. Next, participants completed the need for cognition scale. Consistent with our conceptualization, people higher in NFC were more likely to select a work phone in the ten-attribute condition and a fun phone in the two-attribute condition, but the opposite pattern emerged among people low in NFC.

Experiments 2 and 3, manipulated, rather than measured, participants' ability and motivation to deliberate. In addition, they used either all-hedonic (experiment 2) or all-utilitarian (experiment 3) attributes to demonstrate that the effects occur independently of attribute content. Consistent with experiment 1, participants who were encouraged to deliberate carefully selected more utilitarian options (work laptops and printers) as attribute quantity increased

continuously from 1 to 3 to 8 attributes. In contrast, participants under time pressure selected more hedonic options (gaming laptops and mp3 players) as attribute quantity increased. In addition, experiment 3 directly tested the underlying process behind these effects under both high and low deliberation. Specifically, the effect of attribute quantity under effortful deliberation was mediated by the extent of analytical thinking, whereas the effect under heuristic processing was mediated by the extent to which hedonic (but not utilitarian) options were perceived as practical.

Experiment 4 used thought-protocols to directly test the mediating role of shifting from memory- to stimulus-based evaluation. Participants were shown two utilitarian orthopedic backrests and two hedonic foot massagers, described using either 1 or 8 attributes. They were asked to write down their thoughts as they were considering which option to choose. Consistent with the hypothesized process, content analysis suggested that the effect of attribute quantity on option choice was mediated by the ratio of thoughts related to concrete, stimulus-based attributes relative to thoughts relating to people's internal experiences and memories.

In addition to shedding light on how attribute quantity affects what type of options consumers choose, this research makes two further theoretical contributions. First, dual process theories generally assume that under heuristic processing, increasing the number of attributes (or arguments) should increase option favorability, regardless of the type of option being evaluated. In contrast, we demonstrate that more attributes can have a differential effect on heuristic evaluation of hedonic versus utilitarian options. Specifically, we show that hedonic options benefit from attribute numerosity more than utilitarian ones. Second, dual process theories have assumed that heuristic cues, such as mere attribute quantity, influence evaluation under heuristic, but not under deliberative processing (e.g., Petty and Cacioppo 1984). In contrast, the present research suggests that seemingly irrelevant peripheral cues may in fact have a dual role in decision making, influencing evaluation under heuristic as well as deliberative processing, albeit in different ways.

### "The Effects of Emotional versus Cognitive Processing on Short-Term versus Long-Term Preference Consistency"
*Leonard Lee, Columbia University, USA*
*Song-Oh Yoon, Korea University, Korea*
*Dan Ariely, Duke University, USA*

A substantial body of research has established the benefits of conceptualizing the complex human mind as a dual-system model—the emotional system versus the cognitive system—in explaining a wide variety of human behavior (e.g., Loewenstein and O'Donoghue 2004). On the one hand, preferences based on deliberative processing and elaboration of relevant information has been shown to result in strong attitudes that are persistent over time and resistant to contextual changes (Krosnick and Petty 1994; Levin and Gaeth 1998). On the other hand, recent research suggests that too much cognitive processing can generate cognitive noise and degrade preferences stability across time (Lee, Amir, and Ariely 2009; Nordgren and Dijksterhuis 2009).

In this research, we seek to reconcile these two seemingly divergent sets of findings. Specifically, we propose that one moderating condition is the time frame over which decisions are made. Within a short time frame, people's emotional states remain relatively stable, and the holistic nature of emotional processing facilitates the making of consistent summary assessments of target stimulus, hence promoting preference stability; conversely, the analytical nature of cognitive processing can lead to more variations in stimulus assessments across time (e.g. changes in the specific attributes on which people focus) and generate greater preference inconsistency. When this time frame is extended, an opposite pattern may emerge: individuals might experience more fluctuations in their emotional states, which can impose a larger negative impact on preference stability than the cognitive noise inherent in deliberative processing.

In experiment 1, we adopted a 3 (processing-mode: emotion vs. cognition vs. control) x 2 (time-frame: short-term vs. long-term) between-subjects design. Participants were asked to rate the attractiveness of 10 electronic gadgets (each presented in the form of a picture and a brief description) in two different sessions (T1 and T2); these two sessions were separated by a 1-hour (1-week) gap in the short-term (long-term) condition. We manipulated participants' processing mode using a procedure adapted from Nordgren and Dijksterhuis (2009): participants in the *emotional* condition were instructed to evaluate the products based on their first impressions of and immediate emotional reactions toward them, whereas participants in the *cognitive* condition, on their cognitive deliberation and analysis of the products' pros and cons; participants in the *control* condition did not receive any specific processing-mode instructions. To minimize the possibility that participants evaluated the products at T2 simply based on their recalled evaluations at T1, we introduced two procedural-design elements. First, of the 10 products presented at each session, only 5 (target products) appeared in both sessions; the others were fillers. Second, different rating scales were used across the two sessions: a 0-100 scale at T1, versus a 13-point Likert scale (1: very unattractive, 13: very attractive) at T2.

The difference in participants' standardized ratings between the two sessions (to account for the different scales) was compared across conditions. A 2x3 ANOVA revealed a main effect of time frame, indicating that preference consistency was lower in the long-term than in the short-term condition. While there was no main effect of processing type on consistency, there was a significant time-frame X processing-mode crossover interaction. In the short-term condition, participants who evaluated the products based on their emotions were *more* consistent in their preferences compared to participants in both the cognitive and control conditions; consistency between the latter two conditions did not differ significantly. Conversely, in the long-term condition, participants in the emotion condition were *less* consistent in their preferences than those in the other two conditions (which, again, did not differ significantly.)

We replicated these results conceptually in experiment 2 using a more subtle approach to invoke different processing modes and to measure preference consistency over a more extended time frame in the long-term condition. This experiment was conducted online. Each participant was randomly assigned to one of four conditions in a 2 (product-representation: pictures vs. names) X 2 (time-frame: short-term vs. long-term) between-subjects design. Participants were first asked to study a set of ten electronic gadgets similar to the ones in experiment 1. Subsequently, they were shown all binary combinations of these products (45 pairs total) and asked to choose the one they preferred in each pair. Half the participants (short-term condition) had to make all their 45 choices in one sitting. In contrast, the other participants (long-term condition) made their choices over an extended period of time: after choosing from the first pair of products, they had to wait for a day before they received an email which directed them to a website to view and choose from the next pair of products; consequently, these participants made all their 45 product choices over more than 45 days. To manipulate processing mode, half the participants saw the products presented in the form of pictures during the product-choice stage, whereas the other half

saw the products in terms of their names. This manipulation was based on the notion that pictures tend to elicit greater emotional processing than names (Hsee and Rottenstreich 2004). To examine the degree of consistency in participants' choices, we compared the number of transitivity violations that participants made across conditions (Kendall and Babington Smith 1940). That is, given a set of any three products *A*, *B*, and *C*, a transitivity violation occurs when participants choose *A* over *B*, *B* over *C*, but *C* over *A*, hence leading to a (intransitive) preference cycle. The more violations participants made, the more inconsistent were their preferences.

A 2x2 ANOVA of the number of transitivity violations participants made revealed a similar pattern to that in experiment 1: there was a marginally significant main effect of time-frame, a significant interaction between time-frame and product-representation, but no main effect of product-representation. Again, whereas short-term participants who saw the products in terms of pictures made *fewer* transitivity violations than those who saw the products in terms of names, long-term participants who saw the products in terms of pictures made *more* transitivity violations.

Together, these results suggest that emotional processing and cognitive processing can have opposite effects on preference consistency depending on the amount of time between decisions.

### "When and Why Having More can Feel Worse than Having Less"
*Haiyang Yáng, INSEAD, Singapore*
*Ziv Carmon, INSEAD, France*

It is commonly believed that having more physical possessions (e.g., houses, furniture, cars) or engaging in more experiential consumptions (e.g., vacations, shows, dates) can bring more satisfaction. This belief is one reason consumers whose basic needs are satisfied, strive to and indeed consume more. In this research we propose that having more can dampen rather boost satisfaction, and offer an explanation for this phenomenon.

Whether an option is considered singularly or along with other options can significantly affect choices. For example, choosing between comparable options, rather than whether or not to choose one, can induce conflict and reduce choice probability of either option (Tversky and Shafir 1992). Building on such findings we propose that over the same duration, having multiple goods in the consumption set can be less satisfying if each good shares with other goods one or more features on which it is less attractive.

The notion that people often spontaneously contrast comparable objects at an early stage of cognitive processing and with minimal cognitive resources (see e.g., Wedell 1994) suggests that when consuming comparable goods, consumers may spontaneously contrast the consumption experiences. Consider, for example, a consumption set of two goods *X* and *Y*, each with two attributes $\alpha$ and $\beta$, and each yielding a similar level of overall satisfaction when consumed singularly over the same duration. When $\alpha_x$ is equal to $\alpha_y$ and $\beta_x$ to $\beta_y$, comparing *X* with *Y* is unlikely to lead to dissatisfaction; thus consuming both *X* and *Y* will produce higher satisfaction than just one of the goods. When $\alpha_x$ is larger than $\alpha_y$ and $\beta_x$ than $\beta_y$, the comparison, due to the shift in the reference point, may increase satisfaction derived from consuming *X* and decrease it for *Y*; but the total satisfaction derived will be higher than consuming only one of the goods. However, when $\alpha_x$ is greater than $\alpha_y$ but $\beta_x$ smaller than $\beta_y$, comparing *X* and *Y* can result in dissatisfaction, as both goods appear deficient on the respective dimensions. When the dissatisfaction is sufficiently large, consuming both goods can thus be less satisfying than consuming just one. Furthermore, given that consumers with a maximizing tendency regularly seek the best option (Schwartz et al. 2002) and that contrasting attributes makes the imperfections of both goods salient, maximizers more than satisficers, are likely to experience negative impact of having more.

We tested these predictions in two studies. In the first experiment, participants were randomly assigned to one of three consumption set conditions (good1, good2, or both). Building on Hsee and Leclerc (1998), we asked participants in the both-goods condition to imagine consuming two goods jointly (for possessions such as framed photographs) or sequentially (for experiential goods such as movies), and those in the single-good conditions to imagine consuming the one good; participants then indicated how satisfied they were overall with the consumption. As predicted, consuming both good1 and good2 jointly was less satisfying than consuming either one singularly. In experiment 2, we extend and replicate the prior experiments by assessing the consumption experiences with measures of pleasure equivalence (cf. Carmon and Ariely 2000; e.g., "How many M&M chocolate candies do you need to consume to achieve the same amount of pleasure"), and utilizing the Maximization Scale (Schwartz et al. 2002). As expected, we found a significant interaction effect—participants' maximization tendency significantly moderated the negative impact of having more. A field study examining consequences of having more possessions (e.g., houses, furniture, cars) or more experiences (e.g., vacations, shows, spouses, dates) in the 'real-world' is in progress.

To explore a boundary condition, we predicted that when participants elaborate on the difference between owning one versus both goods and thus assess the consumption more holistically, they will be less dissatisfied with having more. We tested this prediction in experiment 4. We asked a group of participants in the both-goods condition to rate how dissatisfied they would be if they didn't own one of the goods, before completing other dependent measures. As predicted, these participants reported a higher level of satisfaction than those did not receive the manipulation question.

Overall, the results of the four studies shed light on an explanation for the negative impact of having more, and establish a boundary condition on the link between consumption and satisfaction.

## "Set and Option Attractiveness as Moderators of the 'Too Much Choice' Phenomenon"

*Leilei Gao, Chinese, University of Hong Kong, China*
*Itamar Simonson, Stanford University, USA*

The "too much choice" phenomenon has received a great deal of attention in the past two decades. Large assortments were found to associate with greater decision difficulty, weaker preference, and greater likelihood of choice deferral (e.g. Iyengar and Lepper 2000; Schwartz 2004; Chernev 2003). In this research, we propose that the presence or absence of the "too much choice" phenomenon depends on the interplay between assortment size and the order in which consumers make the "whether to buy" and "which option to buy" decisions.

Large assortments generally represent situations where the choice set is attractive in general, but making a selection among options is rather difficult. Hence, if consumers are initially asked to select an option from the set, decision difficulty tends to reduce preference clarity and result in higher likelihood of choice deferral. However, in real-world purchase situations, consumers not only choose an option from a given assortment, they also consider whether or not to buy from the assortment (store). A typical purchase decision is twofold: "whether to buy" and "which option to buy". Although both decisions may be made simultaneously, sometimes the consumer first identifies an attractive option and then considers whether he or she actually needs it (a process that can be classified as a "select-buy" decision); in other situations, the consumer may

first make a tentative decision to buy and then focus on making a selection from the available options (a "buy-select" decision).

We propose that the degree of the initial emphasis placed on either the buy/no-buy or option selection decision is important, because these decisions tend to be driven by different criteria. When the option selection decision is considered first, the attractiveness of the option selected relative to the available alternatives is the main driver of the decision to buy. If the selection can be easily made (such as when the assortment size is small), then the consumer is more likely to purchase the option selected. Conversely, when the decision about whether to buy from a given set of options is emphasized initially, the consumer is likely to first "eyeball" the set to determine whether an attractive option is likely to be found within it. When a shopper engages in a more holistic processing of the set, it is the overall attractiveness of the option set, rather than the differences among the options within it, that is likely to loom large, with the identification of a specific choice left until later. Accordingly, any cues suggesting that the option set is generally attractive and contains options that may be worthy of selection (e.g. large assortment) are expected to increase the likelihood that the consumer will make a tentative or even irreversible commitment to purchase.

Study 1 was designed to test this basic proposition. Study participants were randomly presented with a large or small set (10 vs. 50 options) of jelly beans. In the select-buy sequence group, participants first selected a jelly bean flavor and then indicated whether they would prefer to receive one pack of jelly beans or $1 as a reward. Those in the buy-select sequence group were asked the same questions, but in reverse order. Our findings demonstrate that, the negative correlation between the number of options and choice likelihood is only observed when consumers focus initially on the option selection decision. Conversely, the probability of making a purchase is significantly enhanced as the number of options in the set increases when consumers focus initially on the decision whether to purchase.

Study 2 extended this investigation into a different product domain (i.e. chocolates) and employed a 2 x 2 between-subject manipulation of overall asset attractiveness and relative option attractiveness. In particular, beyond the large and small assortments presented to our participants, we created a third condition where products in the large assortment were grouped into meaningful categories to reduce selection difficulty; we also created a fourth condition where we blurred product information in the small assortment to increase selection difficulty. The results suggest that purchase likelihood is primarily determined by the overall attractiveness of a choice set when the "whether" question is emphasized early in the decision process, and by the relative attractiveness of the individual options within it when the "which" question is privileged. The greatest likelihood of a purchase occurs when both the overall set is attractive and making a selection is relatively easy.

Studies 3 and 4 extended our investigation to another important choice domain- the asymmetric dominance effect. Consistent with our general proposition and the earlier studies, the findings of studies 3 and 4 show that an initial focus on the decision whether to buy greatly reduces or eliminates the effect of asymmetric dominance in the choice set. Thus, the decision context and choice set context interact and are mutually dependent.

Finally, in a study to examine participants' thought protocols, we show that when asked to make an option selection decision, participants elaborated more on the relative attractiveness of individual options in the set. Conversely, following a "whether to buy" decision, participants' thoughts focused on more the overall attractiveness of the option set and their needs/wants for the product category. In addition, the decision "whether to buy" or "which one to buy" only affects the type of thoughts rather than the number of thoughts provoked by the purchase situation, hence providing further support to our hypotheses.

# The Self-Concept from Near and Far: Psychological Distance and the Consumer Self
Liad Weiss, Columbia University, USA

## EXTENDED ABSTRACTS

### "Understanding the "Self" in Self-Control: The Effects of Connectedness to Future Self on Far-Sightedness"

*Daniel M. Bartels, University of Chicago, USA*
*Kerry F. Milch, Columbia University, USA*
*Oleg Urminsky, University of Chicago, USA*

The exercise of self-control involves setting priorities and adhering to plans, even in the face of immediate temptations. Many decisions requiring self-control involve trading off consumption or happiness in the present or immediate future with consumption or happiness in the distant future. We posit that a crucial variable in such decisions is how a person views her distant future self (i.e., as a different person from her current self or as fundamentally the same person). In three studies, we show that how people view their future selves influences intertemporal preferences.

A decision maker is more closely linked to the person she will be tomorrow than to the person she'll be in 10 years, in terms of self-defining psychological properties, such as beliefs, values, and ideals. For this reason, she may prefer to allocate benefits to her more connected, sooner self at the expense of her less connected, later self. We propose that when people feel less psychologically connected to their future selves (e.g., because they foresee significant changes to the self), they will be less motivated to forego immediate benefits to provide long-term benefits for that future self, and we find that make "short-sighted" decisions over periods of time in which they anticipate the greatest changes in their identity. People who feel disconnected from the future self are more likely to choose so-called "vices" (options for which the short-run utility exceeds the long-run utility) over so-called "virtues" (options for which the long-term utility exceeds the short-run utility), and they engage in less responsible financial planning. They also tend to dehumanize that future self and indicate less willingness to take on burdens in the present to mitigate health risks in the distant future.

In Study 1, undergraduate participants read either that identity radically changes in early adulthood (especially during the college years), inducing a low degree of connectedness to their future self, or they read that the core features of one's identity are fixed in early childhood (and stable during college), inducing high connectedness to their future self. Participants were more likely to choose a lottery for a bookstore over bakery gift-certificate (e.g. virtue over relative vice) in the high-connectedness condition (after reading about the stability of their identity) than in the low-connectedness condition (after reading about how they would change).

In Study 2, we asked college seniors, who were about to graduate, how difficult it would be to generate either 2 or 10 reasons why their identity would not change as a result of college graduation. Participants in the 2-reasons condition, who found the task easier, inferred that their identity would be stable over time, yielding a greater sense of connectedness to their future self than for participants in the 10-reasons condition. The more highly connected participants in the 2-reasons condition then indicated that they would allocate more of their resources to those budgetary categories that they themselves separately judged to be the most responsible uses of money, suggesting a higher motivation to provide for the future self.

Study 3 was designed to learn more about how people view their future selves and how this relates to their willingness to engage in preventive health measures. We investigated how connectedness to a future self relates to the kinds of traits people ascribe to their future selves, and how this in turn impacts people's motivation to incur immediate costs for the sake of improved odds of long-term health. We found participants who felt disconnected from their future selves tended to "dehumanize" the future self. Using Haslam & Bain's (2007) measures of "human nature" traits, we found that people who felt disconnected from their future selves tended to characterize the future self as rigid, inert, and lacking in emotional warmth and depth. High connectedness between present and future selves and low dehumanization of the future self each predicted people's willingness to endure pain in the present (e.g., from a diagnostic procedure) in order to reduce the likelihood of negative health states (e.g., joint pain) experienced in old age.

Across these studies, we demonstrate that how we think of our future selves plays a fundamental role in how people approach the kind of tradeoff represented by self-control dilemmas–the tradeoff between immediate temptations and long-term benefits. We will also discuss how the effect of connectedness on self-control behaviors relates to other factors implicated in such choices, including salience of future outcomes, guilt and justification.

### "'In-self' and 'Out-self' Products: Assimilation and Contrast with Consumers' Traits"

*Liad Weiss, Columbia University, USA*
*Gita V. Johar, Columbia University, USA*

Marketers and researchers commonly ask consumers to evaluate branded products on different scales. To encourage truthful responses, product evaluators are often promised the product they evaluate as part of their compensation. Can the notion of keeping the evaluated product, in other words mere ownership, have a systematic effect on the assessment of specific brand traits such as creativity or sincerity?

The current research examines this question from a categorization perspective. We suggest and find that consumers sometimes act as if products they own are extensions of themselves. Consequently, when consumers get to keep a product, their view of it is directly affected by their perceptions of their own traits. However, these very same perceptions inversely affect the view of non-owned products. For example, consumers who perceive themselves as more (less) creative, evaluate products they keep as more (less) creative, but products that they don't keep as less (more) creative.

This effect is proposed to be an outcome of a categorization process. Previous research suggests that people classify others as in-group or out-group members. In-group members are considered to be an extended form of consumers' self-concept (e.g., Brewer 1991). Consumers are suggested to classify objects into two equivalent categories, in-self or out-self objects, as determined by object ownership. Owned objects become members of the in-self category, yet another extended form of the individual's self-concept (Belk 1988).

The self-concept can be a salient prime. Therefore, categorizing people or objects as members of one's self-concept (i.e., as in-group members or in-self objects) may affect the way they are evaluated. Categorization of a prime and a target together, commonly yields assimilation, namely a direct effect of the prime on target evaluation. However, exclusion of the prime from the target's category, may lead to its comparison with the target. This commonly yields contrast, namely, an inverse effect of the prime on target evaluation. In line with previous research on the effect of self concept on the evaluation of in and out group members, we predicted that self-view will directly (inversely) affect the evaluation of in-self (out-self) products.

This prediction was supported in two studies. In Study 1, participants first rated their own creativity. Then, after a filler task, they were asked to evaluate a pen. Half of the participants were promised the evaluated pen to keep. The rest were promised a luxurious mechanical pencil instead. All participants then received the same information about the pen, which was pretested to be perceived as moderately creative. Then, after trying the pen, participants rated how creative it was. As predicted, the interaction between ownership (keep/no-keep) and self-creativity ratings on pen creativity ratings was significant. The pen was rated as more creative by more creative individuals in the keep condition, and by less creative individuals in the no-keep condition.

In Study 2, differently from study 1, participants' perceptions of their own creativity were manipulated. This was achieved through an ease of retrieval manipulation. The rest of the procedure followed that of study 1. The dependent variable measured how likely it was that they would recommend the pen to "John" who was described as having different occupations that varied in their perceived creativeness (e.g., clerk as low and copywriter as high creativity occupations). As predicted, among participants in the keep condition, those in the high creativeness condition were more likely to recommend the pen to John if he was in a creative occupation. Conversely, among participants in the no-keep condition, those in the low creativeness condition were more likely to recommend the pen to John if he was in a creative occupation. There were no differences in recommendation to John if he was in a less creative occupation. To support our proposition that this effect was driven by the usage of the self-concept as a prime, we measured level of self consciousness. As expected, we find that the aforementioned interaction was stronger for individuals that are high (vs. low) on self-consciousness.

### "Opposing Selves: How American and Moral Identity Interact with the Psychology of International War to Undermine Charitable Giving to Foreign Civilians"

*Stephanie Finnel, University of Pennsylvania, USA*
*Americus Reed II, University of Pennsylvania, USA*
*Karl Aquino, University of British Columbia, Canada*

At the 2009 Nobel Prize ceremony, President Obama tried to promote his Afghanistan policy, using a strategy psychologists know to be effective: he encouraged people to morally disengage from (justify or excuse) the casualties of war (Aquino, Reed, Thau, and Freeman 2007). However, Obama has another goal: during his campaign, he said he wanted to double foreign aid. But if U.S. consumers are disengaged from the casualties of war, as Obama's speech encouraged, are they still likely to support charitable efforts that assist foreign civilians?

We propose that morally disengaging from the casualties of war often relates negatively to support for charitable efforts benefiting foreign civilians. By disengaging during war, consumers likely come to see themselves as more distant from foreign civilians, and hence they may be less helpful to foreign civilians in a subsequent, unrelated context (see Bushman and Anderson 2009).

However, if our effect really is driven by psychological distance between the self and foreign civilians, then it should become stronger when consumers are focused on an aspect of the self that amplifies this distance (e.g., American identity) but should become weaker when they are focused on an aspect of the self that attenuates this distance (e.g., moral identity). When American identity is activated, U.S. consumers likely perceive greater distance between themselves and foreign civilians. American identity may thus

reinforce disengagement: both are expected to decrease helpfulness toward foreign civilians. By contrast, moral identity, that is, consumers' views of themselves along traits commonly ascribed to moral exemplars (e.g., kindness), encourages concern for distant others (Aquino et al. 2007) like foreign civilians. Thus when moral identity is activated, U.S. consumers likely perceive less distance between themselves and foreign civilians. Moral identity may thus undermine disengagement: whereas disengagement is expected to decrease helpfulness toward foreign civilians, moral identity is expected to increase it. Therefore, we propose that disengagement during war is negatively related to support for charitable efforts benefiting foreign civilians, particularly when American (moral) identity is more (less) rather than less (more) central to the self and when American rather than moral identity is primed.

Study 1 tested this hypothesis with real donations. Participants first completed moral and American identity centrality scales (Aquino et al. 2007). Next they watched a slide show containing images from the Abu Ghraib prison scandal and completed a moral disengagement scale, which contains statements that justify harming others (e.g., "It is alright to fight to protect your friends.") (Aquino et al. 2007). Although this scale does not mention war, we expected participants to interpret it in the context of war, since it came just after the Abu Ghraib images.

Participants then received $4 and donated them as they pleased across three charities: (1) the United Services Organization, which aids American soldiers, (2) the Global Fund, which aids primarily foreign civilians, and (3) Amnesty International, which aids not only civilians but also soldiers and prisoners. We were interested in consumers' charitableness to foreign civilians so we focused on the Global Fund. Consistent with our hypothesis, more disengaged participants donated less to the Global Fund, particularly when their American (moral) identity was more (less) rather than less (more) central.

However, one could argue that the results emerged only because consumers explicitly traded off aiding foreign civilians against aiding Americans. Study 2 therefore presented the opportunity to aid foreign civilians separately, without reference to Americans. It also manipulated rather than measured identity activation.

Study 2 was a two-group (American versus moral identity prime) between-subjects design. Participants first completed a moral disengagement scale specific to war (e.g., "Military force is justified when a nation's economic security is threatened.") (McAlister, Bandura, and Owen 2006). Next they watched a slide show that primed either American or moral identity. Then, they sampled a bottled water whose manufacturer was purportedly donating a portion of its proceeds to the Global Fund. Finally, they rated the water's taste and their liking for the company's partnership with the Global Fund. Consistent with our hypothesis, we found that more disengaged participants liked the taste and the partnership less, but only when their American rather than moral identity was primed.

Therefore, reactions to war, along with aspects of the self salient during war, predict not only support for war (Aquino et al. 2007) but also support for seemingly unrelated charities benefiting foreign civilians. We believe this occurs because different aspects of the self can increase or decrease U.S. consumers' psychological distance to foreign civilians. Our findings illustrate how different aspects of the self can have opposing effects on charitable giving, and suggest that it may be hard to mobilize public support for both war and foreign aid, as Obama would like to do.

### "He or I Determines What or How: Effects of Visual Perspective on Perceived Self Change and Choice"
*Camille S. Johnson, Stanford University, USA*
*Dirk Smeesters, Erasmus University Rotterdam, The Netherlands*
*S. Christian Wheeler, Stanford University, USA*

Advertisements frequently prompt consumers to reflect on how they have changed over time. For example, the "Wild Thing" Viagra ad asks men to "remember that guy who used to be called 'Wild Thing,'" thereby prompting them to reflect on how their sexual behaviors have changed over time. How do people assess how much they have changed over time? How does this affect their choices?

The current studies test whether the visual perspective one adopts when assessing self-change over time (e.g. the first person actor's perspective versus the third person observer's perspective) can affect the extent of perceived change. We advance beyond prior research by providing evidence for a new mechanism by which visual perspective affects perceived self-change (i.e., reliance on retrieval content vs. ease) and by showing its implications for resulting self-views and choices.

We show that when visualizing their past selves from the third-person perspective, people use the content of their recollections in assessing self-change. We also show that when visualizing their past selves from the first-person perspective, people use their experiences of retrieval ease. Hence, visual perspective and aspects of the retrieval task interact to determine perceptions of self-change. We further demonstrate that perceptions of change affect behavior differently depending on whether people perceive they have changed positively or negatively over time. When people perceive positive change, they choose products that are consistent with that change, but when people perceive negative change, they choose products that are inconsistent with that change, presumably to repair their self-views.

In the first experiment, college participants wrote about how their intellectual abilities had either changed or remained stable from either the first-person or third-person perspective. They then indicated how much their intellectual abilities had changed, their current intellectual abilities, and their preference for intellectual vs. non-intellectual products. Results indicated that those who wrote about change (stability) from the third-person perspective perceived more change (stability), perceived themselves as more (less) intellectual, and were more (less) likely to choose intellectual products than those who estimated change from the first-person perspective.

Participants in this first study were instructed to generate as many instances as possible, thereby leading participants to generate extensive content with high perceived difficulty. To provide better evidence that the effects of perspective were driven by reliance on content vs. metacognition, we manipulated the difficulty of the task (via required number of examples). The task was similar to that in experiment one, except that participants were instructed to generate either two or eight examples of stability or change from the first- or third-person perspective. They then completed an open-ended measure of their self-views, estimated their self-change, and chose between intellectual and non-intellectual products. In the difficult (i.e., eight examples) condition, results replicated experiment one. Those who estimated eight examples of change (stability) from the third-person perspective perceived more (less) change, perceived themselves as more (less) intellectual, and were more (less) likely to choose intellectual products than those who estimated change (stability) from the first-person perspective, suggesting that the third-person perspective increased reliance on retrieval content. These results reversed in the easy (i.e., two examples) condition. Those who estimated two examples of change (stability) from the third-person perspective perceived less (more) change, perceived

themselves as less (more) intellectual, and were less (more) likely to choose intellectual products than those who estimated change (stability) from the first-person perspective, suggesting that the first-person perspective increased reliance on retrieval ease.

In our third experiment, we used an advertisement as our manipulation and tested our effects in a domain (i.e., healthy eating) in which our population expected negative change over time. College participants viewed an advertisement from the perspective of an eater or eater observer. The copy asked how the ad recipient was eating and said, "Think of two [eight] ways in which your eating habits have changed." Participants then estimated how their eating habits had changed over time and, at the experiment's conclusion, chose between an apple and candy bar. Results for perceived change conceptually replicated those from experiment two, except that perceived change was negative (i.e., participants who perceived change believed they ate worse than they used to). Choice results, however, were the opposite; people chose products inconsistent with perceived change. Those who perceived the greatest change (i.e., those who retrieved eight examples of change from the third-person perspective or two examples from the first-person perspective) choose healthier snacks, suggesting that snack choice was an attempt to repair self-perceptions of being an unhealthy eater.

### REFERENCES
Aquino, Karl, Americus Reed II, Stefan Thau, and Dan Freeman (2007), "A Grotesque and Dark Beauty: How Moral Identity and Mechanisms of Moral Disengagement Influence Cognitive and Emotional Reactions to War," *Journal of Experimental Social Psychology*, 43, 285-392.
Belk, Russell W. (1988), "Possessions and the Extended Self," Journal of Consumer Research, 15 (September), 139-68.
Brewer, M. B. (1991), "The Social Self-on Being the Same and Different at the Same Time," Personality and Social Psychology Bulletin, 17 (5), 475-82.
Bushman, Brad J., and Craig A. Anderson (2009), "Comfortably Numb: Desensitizing Effects of Violent Media on Helping Others," *Psychological Science*, 20(3), 273-277.
Haslam, N., & Bain, P. (2007). Humanizing the self: Moderators of the attribution of lesser humanness to others. Personality and Social Psychology Bulletin, 33, 57-68.

SPECIAL SESSION
# Doing Well and Doing Good:
## New Frontiers in Firm/Brand Perceptions and Perceptions of Social Good

Amit Bhattacharjee, University of Pennsylvania, USA

## EXTENDED ABSTRACTS

### "Is Profit Evil? Incentive Neglect and the Association of Profit with Social Harm"

Amit Bhattacharjee, University of Pennsylvania, USA
Jason Dana, University of Pennsylvania, USA
Jonathan Baron, University of Pennsylvania, USA

As sentiments arising from the current financial crisis illustrate, people often behave as if profit-seeking and social good are necessarily at odds. Narrative themes involving evil capitalists have been prevalent in literature and films from Shakespeare to the modern day (Ribstein 2009). However, economists have long noted that this association is carried too far, such that profit-seeking is seen as fundamentally in conflict with social welfare: an "ineradicable prejudice that every action intended to serve the profit interest must be anti-social by this fact alone (Schumpeter 1954 p. 234)."

We build on Caplan's (2007) notion of antimarket bias, which proposes that the benefits of the market mechanism in creating and rewarding value for society are systematically underestimated (Caplan and Cowen 2004). In other words, market transactions are regarded as mere transfers of wealth from the pockets of consumers to firms (Caplan 2007). Thus, profits may be perceived to indicate value being taken from consumers rather than provided to consumers—the opposite of what one might expect in a functioning market. Consistent with this theorizing, we show in three studies that consumers neglect the incentive properties of profit in rewarding value, and instead focus on the perceived intentions of organizations.

In study 1, participants either estimated or viewed actual profit figures for 32 US firms sampled from the Fortune 500 list and rated them on a number of dimensions of social good. Across firms, estimated profits were systematically far higher than actual profits, consistent with past findings of profit overestimation (e.g. Bolton Warlop and Alba 2003). More importantly, higher estimated profits were positively correlated with perceptions of social harm, unfair business practices, and a lack of value to society, but also with effectiveness in achieving organizational goals. Thus, even though higher profits are thought to indicate effectiveness in achieving firm objectives, those objectives are presumably seen as socially harmful and out of step with the objectives of society. This pattern also held for *actual* gross profits, suggesting that participants' perceptions were reasonably accurate, and actual revenues, suggesting that size and prominence may serve as a proxy for perceived profitability.

In order to eliminate pre-existing associations with particular firms and test these notions in a more tightly controlled setting, study 2 provided participants with descriptions of the business practices of hypothetical organizations across four different industries, varying only whether the organization was described as a for-profit corporation or a non-profit organization. After reading each scenario, participants rated the organization described on perceived social value and effectiveness. Consistent with study 1, even identically-described hypothetical organizations were seen as less valuable to society, yet more effective, when they were described as for-profit corporations (vs. nonprofit organizations). Thus, independent of actual profitability, merely being motivated by profits was enough to produce seemingly contradictory, simultaneous judgments of greater effectiveness and diminished value.

Study 3 sought to further explore perceptions of different types of businesses and consumers' focus on intentions. Participants rated types of firms across 42 industries on perceived profits, deservingness of these profits, value to society, source of these profits (i.e. whether they came at the expense of others), and the motives of those running the firms. Across industries, perceived profits were almost perfectly negatively correlated with the perceived social value the industry creates. Furthermore, higher perceived profits were associated with lesser perceived deservingness, less perceived value to society, and greater belief that these profits came at the expense of others. The only significant moderator of this correlation across individuals was the perceived motives of firms. Participants who did not exhibit this negative association of profits with social value tended to believe that businesses are motivated primarily by a desire to serve society or consumers. In other words, our participants believed that firms provide social value only when they intend to do so, not because profit-seeking encourages the creation of social value.

Together, our results suggest that consumers have little faith in the power of markets to create and reward value. Though even "base," self-interested profit-seeking should motivate firms to promote the common good (Caplan 2007), consumers neglect the incentive properties of profit and the workings of the market mechanism. Instead, they focus on the intentions of firms, associating a profit motive with social harm.

### "Non-Profits Are Seen as Warm and For-Profits as Competent: Firm Stereotypes Matter"

Jennifer Aaker, Stanford University, USA
Kathleen Vohs, University of Minnesota, USA
Cassie Mogilner, University of Pennsylvania, USA

In 2002, recent college graduate Charles Best started a philanthropic organization in the basement of his parents' home (Alter 2007). It consists of a Web site (DonorsChoose.org) that allows teachers to easily post requests for donations to fill specific pedagogical needs. Through donorschoose.org, requesters are not required to write in a heavy, formal grant-writing form (which is the norm when submitting aid requests); they can simply use plain language. For instance, a teacher in a high poverty district of New York City wrote to ask for "$1266 to purchase five laptop computers to help build the students' math and literacy skills."

Initially, outsiders were skeptical that the idea would work. In fact, MBA graduates from a prominent business school investigated the organization and declared that DonorsChoose.org was unlikely to stay in business. They even went so far as to withdraw a large gift tagged for the organization because they believed the non-profit's business plan was shabby. Seven years on, the organization is still afloat. DonorsChoose.org is, in fact, hugely successful, having won multiple awards and much acclaim.

We argue that the underlying story of donorschoose.org is a common one. The organization was perceived as caring and targeting a worthy cause, but as not possessing a high level of competency. This led to our inquiry into how people view non-profit and for-profit organizations. We proposed that people possess stereotypes of organizations merely based on the knowledge that a firm is a for-profit or not-for-profit.

People's judgments of other people often fall along two primary dimensions, namely how much they exude warmth and competence

(Judd James-Hawkins Yzerbyt and Kasima 2005). These two dimensions emerge in contexts as varied as split-second evaluations (Ybarra Chan and Park 2001), liked and disliked groups (Cuddy Fiske, and Glick 2007), employee hiring decisions (Casciaro and Lobo 2008), leadership qualifications (Chemers 2001), and romantic partner choices (Sinclair and Fehr 2005). The robustness of these two dimensions has led them to be deemed "fundamental" (Fiske Cuddy and Glick 2007). We examined whether warmth and competence color the way consumers view companies—in particular, non-profits and for-profits—and whether those judgments influence marketplace decisions. We then tested whether consumers' stereotypes can be altered to enhance perceptions of non-profits (since they lagged behind their for-profit counterparts on key metrics of marketplace appeal).

Across three experiments, we found that stereotypes do in fact exist for non-profit and for-profit organizations and that they predict crucial marketplace behaviors, such as likelihood to visit a website and willingness to buy a product from the organization. In experiment 1, participants viewed a description of a product made by a company whose URL ended with either dot-com (www.Mozilla.com) or dot-org (www.Mozilla.org). Results showed that consumers perceived the non-profit as being warmer than the for-profit, but as less competent. Relatedly, consumers perceived the non-profit as more needy, and the for-profit as more greedy.

In experiment 2, we used the same manipulation but with a different product and a different company (www.worldofgood.com vs. www.worldofgood.org), and in addition to measuring consumers' perceptions of the firm's characteristics, we measured consumers' intent to purchase a product from that firm. The results showed that although the non-profit was perceived to be more warm, consumers were more willing to buy a product offered by the for-profit because of perceptions of the company as more competent. Consequently, when perceived competence of the non-profit was boosted by an endorsement from a highly credible source (the *WSJ*, rather than *The Detroit Free Press*), we found that consumers were equally willing to buy from the non-profit as the for-profit. Furthermore, reconnecting with the participants one month after the initial study allowed us to see that the effect persists and impacts actual behavior (likelihood to have visited the firm's website since learning of it in the initial study).

In experiment 3, we showed that an even more subtle manipulation which boosts perceived competence (i.e., the implicit activation of money) can serve to increase consumers' willingness to buy from a non-profit. In identifying these stereotypes, our findings underscore the importance of framing firms as non-profits or for-profits (e.g., through the use of dot-org vs. dot-com internet domain names). To our knowledge, this research is the first to investigate whether stereotypes are used to evaluate non-profit and for-profit organizations, whether these stereotypes have downstream consequences on consumer behavior, and whether such stereotypes can be dispelled through marketing actions.

### "Can Luxury Brands Do Poorly by Doing Good? Brand Concepts and Responses to Socially Responsible Actions"

*Carlos Torelli, University of Minnesota, USA*
*Alokparna (Sonia) Monga, University of South Carolina, USA*
*Andrew Kaikati, University of Georgia, USA*

Though brands across a wide spectrum of industries actively communicate CSR messages, surprisingly little is known about how these efforts might interact with brand concepts and influence consumer outcomes. The current four studies fill this gap in the literature by: (1) identifying brand concepts that are spontaneously more compatible or incompatible with a CSR image, (2) document-

ing the unintended negative consequences from communicating the CSR actions of a brand with a CSR-incompatible concept, (3) uncovering the psychological processes underlying these unintended effects, and (4) devising branding strategies to offset them.

Brand concepts are brand-unique abstract images arising from particular combinations of attributes, benefits, and marketing efforts that translate these benefits into higher-order meanings (Park Milberg and Lawson 1991). Carefully crafted to distinctively appeal to target customers, brands concepts vary as much as people's self-relevant concerns and personalities (Aaker 1997). Communicating a brand's CSR actions can help marketers build a brand concept associated with a prosocial image (Brown and Dacin 1997). We argue that the results of such efforts depend on the compatibility of a brand's existing image with a prosocial one.

Prior research suggests that people's self-relevant concerns follow a circular structure in which some concerns are consistent, opposed to each other, or orthogonal (Schwartz 1992). Pursuing concerns linked to a high-order value dimension (e.g., status concerns linked to self-enhancement values) inhibits the pursuit of concerns linked to an opposing value dimension (e.g., prosocial concerns linked to self-transcendence values), but does not affect the pursuit of orthogonal value dimensions (e.g., openness or conservation; Maio et al. 2009). Because consumers use brands to fulfill their identity goals (Aaker 1999), this motivational structure should be reflected in spontaneous perceptions of incompatibility (compatibility) between prosocial and status (conservation or openness) images. In particular, information about CSR actions of a status brand should create confusion, diluting the brand image and decreasing brand evaluations. In contrast, no such effects are anticipated for conservation or openness brands.

We tested this proposition in experiment 1 using a fictitious brand in a 3 (brand concept: conservation/openness/status) X 2 (CSR information: present/absent) between-subjects design. Participants were given information consistent with the corresponding brand concept followed by CSR (vs. neutral) information. When exposed to CSR information, participants exhibited less favorable evaluations and brand image clarity for a status versus conservation or openness brand concept. In contrast, when the CSR information was absent, brand evaluations and perceptions of brand image clarity were similar across brand concepts. For the status brand concept, evaluations and clarity were less favorable when CSR information was present versus absent.

Experiment 2 extended these findings to a real luxury brand and investigated the role of people's preferences for status products (as an expression of their value orientation) on the evaluation of luxury brands engaged in CSR. We anticipated that people with status concerns, for whom the status affordances of a luxury brand are more self-relevant, should be more likely to exhibit the dilution effects found in experiment 1. We used a 2 (status concerns: low, high) x 2 (new brand information: CSR, control, openness) between subjects design. When exposed to CSR information, participants evaluated the luxury brand less favorably and perceived it less clearly in terms of a status image than those in a control condition, whose evaluations were based on their prior knowledge of the luxury brand. This was not the case for participants exposed to product information describing the brand in terms of stimulation values. In addition, these effects were stronger among individuals for whom status products are particularly self-relevant.

The last two experiments examined the process underlying the effect and explored ways to offset it through branding and communication practices. In experiment 3, we either encouraged participants to elaborate (or not) upon the congruity between prosocial and status images (e.g., by presenting examples of high-status persons who behave in prosocial ways). We replicated the previously documented effects in the no elaboration condition, in which participants relied on spontaneous perceptions of CSR-status incompatibility. However, when participants elaborated on the congruity between status and CSR, the effects dissipated.

Experiment 4 further investigated the reflexive nature of the effect and identified a sub-branding strategy as a viable option for offsetting it. Communicating the CSR actions of a luxury brand under a sub-brand strategy was more effective than doing so under a direct brand strategy. However, the favorable effect of the sub-branding strategy only emerged when participants had the resources available to reconcile the CSR and luxury images by sub-typing the information. When cognitive resources were insufficient, the sub-brand strategy failed to provide any benefit.

### "Are Inconsistent CSR Associations Always Detrimental? The Influence of Dialectic Thinking on Brand Perceptions"

*Alokparna (Sonia) Monga, University of South Carolina, USA*
*Zeynep Gürhan-Canli, Koç University, Turkey*
*Vanitha Swaminathan, University of Pittsburgh, USA*

The recent upsurge in CSR efforts reflects the belief that CSR is not only the *"right thing to do,* but also leads to *doing better* through its positive effects on customers and other stakeholders" (Bhattacharya and Sen 2004). In reality however, brands are finding it difficult to maintain a consistent image on CSR. For example, Starbucks is known for having good CSR record, yet it was involved in exploiting Ethiopian coffee growers (Wagner Lutz and Weitz 2009). Similarly, McDonald's has committed to reducing unhealthy trans-fats in its menu but the extent of such fats in its food varies from country to country (Wagner et al. 2009). BP, the oil company that positions itself as being environmentally friendly, started oil exploration in the Alaskan sands, attracting criticism from environmental groups (Macalister 2007). Furthermore, many brands that are now engaging in CSR were previously associated with a negative CSR record (e.g., oil companies; Yoon Gürhan-Canli and Schwarz 2006). Thus, many brands appear to be communicating inconsistent CSR associations to their consumers.

Prior research suggests that inconsistent brand associations can lead to negative consequences for the brand (Keller 2007; Loken and John 1993; Monga and John 2008). In this paper, we draw upon the literature on dialectic thinking to suggest that not all consumers are likely to be negatively affected by the inconsistent CSR information. Recent research suggests that dialectic thinkers appear to accept contradiction more easily than non-dialectic thinkers (Peng and Nisbett 1999). For example, dialectic thinkers appear to be more receptive to dialectical proverbs like, "sorrow is born of excessive joy." On the other hand, non-dialectic thinkers appear to like non-dialectical proverbs like "half a loaf is better than none." Dialectic thinkers are also more likely to resolve a social contradiction (e.g., a conflict between a mother and daughter) by accepting that both parties are correct (mother and daughter). In contrast, non-dialectic thinkers are more likely to choose one of the two parties as correct (e.g., mother or daughter). Thus, dialectic thinkers appear to be more favorably disposed to seeking out the middle ground and being more accepting of contradictory ideas (Peng & Nisbett, 1999).

By drawing upon this research, we predict that dialectic thinkers, who are more open to contradiction, are more likely to evaluate an inconsistent CSR brand more favorably than non-dialectic thinkers. Study 1 exposed participants (from an online consumer panel) to a news article about an oil company that was bad in CSR in the past and is now engaging in positive CSR activities (adapted from Yoon et al., 2006). A median split was used to identify dialectic and non-dialectic thinkers. Consistent with our expectations, dialectic thinkers, compared to non-dialectic thinkers, evaluated the brand more favorably and had higher behavioral intentions.

Prior research shows that dialectic thinking emerges when individuals fear being negatively evaluated by others. Consequently, those individuals conceal their views when they believe that they are in the minority. Thus, we expected that the nature of the decision context would affect responses to inconsistent CSR brands. In a public decision context, dialectic thinkers would respond more favorably to an inconsistent CSR brand than non-dialectic thinkers. However, in a private decision context, the difference would disappear. Study 2 employed a 2 (dialectic vs. non-dialectic) x 2 (public, private) between subjects design. The stimuli consisted of a car brand with positive CSR record partnering with a brand with a negative CSR record. As expected, we found that when the decision context was public, dialectic thinkers provided more favorable brand evaluations and behavioral intentions than non-dialectic thinkers. However, in a private decision context, the difference between dialectic and non-dialectic thinkers dissipated.

Prior research has distinguished between proactive and reactive CSR strategies (Wagner et al. 2009). Proactive strategies are those that consist of a positive CSR statement followed by a negative CSR behavior by the company. A reactive strategy consists of a negative CSR behavior by the company followed by a positive CSR statement. In study 3, we used a 2 (dialectic vs. non-dialectic) x 2 (proactive, reactive) between subjects design and found that purchase intention toward an inconsistent CSR brand was more favorable among non-dialectic thinkers than among dialectic thinkers when the strategy was proactive. However, no differences emerged in the reactive strategy. Taken together, our findings make important contributions to the areas of CSR, brand strategy, and consumer behavior.

# On the Psychology of Affective Forecasting: Inconsistency, Anticedents, and Consequences

Claire Tsai, University of Toronto, Canada
Min Zhao, University of Toronto, Canada

## EXTENDED ABSTRACTS

### "The Effects of Duration Knowledge on Forecasting Versus Actual Affective Experiences"

*Min Zhao, University of Toronto, Canada*
*Claire Tsai, University of Toronto, Canada*

Lay people predict that knowing the duration of an aversive episode would improve their experience, whereas knowing the duration of a pleasant episode would weaken their experience. The present research examines this intuition. We hypothesize that the lay prediction of the effect of duration knowledge is inconsistent with its actual effect. That is, rather than weakening the experiences, duration knowledge actually intensifies affective episodes experienced over time.

To understand how duration knowledge influences people's affective experiences, we need to consider how subjective experiences change over time. We draw on anticipated utility (AU) theory to develop our hypothesis. AU theory suggests that people derive enjoyment/pain from future events (savoring good things and dreading bad things) and the savoring/dreading intensifies as the events draw near (Elster & Loewenstein 1992). When an aversive episode is about to end, people savor the relief more. The positive feelings arising from anticipating the relief contrast with and worsen the on-going negative experience. Similarly, when a pleasant episode is about to end, people dislike the ending more. The negative feelings arising from anticipating the ending contrast with and enhance the on-going positive experience. As a result, duration knowledge decreases the evaluation of aversive episodes and increases the evaluation of pleasant episodes, thereby decelerating hedonic adaptation.

We tested this hypothesis in study 1 with a 2 (experiencer vs. predictor) x 2 (duration knowledge) x 2 (valence) between-subjects factorial design. Experiencers were asked to listen to a short song bite. Half of them were informed about the duration of the song (30 seconds), whereas the other half did not know the exact duration. The song was either recorded by the original singer (positive condition) or by an experimenter with a terrible voice (negative condition). Experiencers evaluated their pain/enjoyment both online and retrospectively. The results showed that the actual effect of duration knowledge was indeed the opposite of the lay predictions. Specifically, predictors indicated that duration knowledge would weaken their experience, rendering a positive event less enjoyable and a negative event more irritating. However, experiencers with duration knowledge actually rated the good song more positively and the bad song more negatively than those without duration knowledge. As expected, real-time rating of enjoyment showed that consistent with prior research on hedonic adaptation, when duration was unknown, the enjoyment leveled off quickly. In contrast, when duration was known, enjoyment became more intense towards the end of the song.

Similar evidence was obtained in study 2 (field study) where we further generalized our findings to relatively long experiences (45 minutes instead of 30 seconds). Study 2 fully replicated study 1.

Study 3 further tested the underlying mechanism and identified one boundary condition. The results showed that the duration knowledge effect was eliminated when a pleasant episode was followed by another pleasant episode. Presumably, matching the valence of the target event with the valence of the end of the event reduced the contrast between the on-going experience and the feelings arising from anticipating the end. However, if the duration information was unavailable, the presence of the second episode played a negligible role.

Our work contributes to research on affective forecasting and hedonic adaptation by identifying a circumstance in which the actual effect of duration knowledge contradicts people's intuition. Duration knowledge interrupts hedonic adaptation by intensifying affective experiences toward the end but people are in general unaware of this effect.

### "Belittling Can Be Flattering"

*Luxi Shen, University of Chicago, USA*
*Christopher K. Hsee, University of Chicago, USA*
*Jiao Zhang, University of Miami, USA*
*Xianchi Dai, Chinese University of Hong Kong, China*

Suppose that a person receives a guess at her monthly income. Imagine two alternative scenarios: In one scenario, the guess is higher than her actual monthly income (i.e., a flattering guess). In another scenario, the guess is lower than her actual monthly income (i.e., a belittling guess). Which guess will make her happier, the flattering guess or the belittling guess?

Both conventional wisdom and previous research on self-enhancement suggest that people feel happier about flattering guesses than belittling guesses. We, however, found that in certain situations belittling guesses can make people happier, which we call the belittling-is-pleasing effect here.

In one study, for example, we interviewed employees from various companies in China about their monthly salary. Most of these respondents earned about ¥5,000 per month. The interviewer guessed either that they made ¥7,500 per month (a flattering guess) or that they made only ¥2,500 a month (a belittling guess). Respondents receiving the belittling guess were significantly happier.

We propose a dual-route model of affective reactions to explain this belittling-is-pleasing effect. The central premise of our model is that a guess influences the listener's feelings through two routes, direct and indirect. Through the direct route, the guess indicates the truth. More positive guesses reflect better beliefs from others. Therefore, the better the guess, the happier the listener. Through the indirect route, the guess serves as a reference point by which the listener evaluates the actual value of what she possesses. Here, the better the guess, the less happy the listener is. For example, suppose that you make ¥5000 a month, but a friend guesses that you make ¥7,500 a month. You may treat ¥7,500 as a reference point, and in comparison, your actual income—¥5000—is relatively low and you feel annoyed and unhappy.

According to the dual-route model, the belittling-is-pleasing effect occurs when the indirect route is more prominent than the direct route. We identify two factors that influence the prominence of the indirect route: whether or not the listener knows the actual value being guessed at and whether she cares more about the consequences associated with the actual value or about others' impression. We propose that the belittling-is-pleasing effect is more likely to occur when the receiver knows the actual value being guessed at and cares more about the actual value than others' impressions.

The proposition was tested in a study in which we examined participants' affective reactions to a flattering guess versus a belittling guess at the bonuses they received. We manipulated both the knowledge of truth, whether the guess was received before or after the participants found out how much bonus they would receive, and the objective of seeking a high bonus, whether they needed the bonuses to make ends meet or they needed the bonuses to leave their friends an impression that their boss treated them well. In support of our proposition, we found that participants favored the belittling guess over the flattering guess only when they knew their actual bonuses and sought a high bonus for its own benefit.

In sum, our research shows a counterintuitive belittling-is-pleasing effect and specifies when it occurs. Our theory enriches existing literature on self-enhancement and impression formation, and yields practical implications for marketer-consumer relationships.

## "Motivated Underpinnings of the Impact Bias in Affective Forecasts"

*Eva Buechel, University of Miami, USA*
*Carey Morewedge, Carnegie Mellon University, USA*
*Joachim Vosgerau, Carnegie Mellon University, USA*

Affective forecasters exhibit an impact bias, whereby they overestimate the emotional reaction to future events. The impact bias has been shown to occur unintentionally, resulting from biases in attention and memory a failure to correctly anticipate hedonic adaptation, and erroneous lay theories about which features of events matter most. It is a robust bias. People not only overestimate the hedonic impact of events repeated once, they overestimate the hedonic impact of events they have experienced frequently.

Given its resistance to feedback, it seems worth examining whether the impact bias might persevere because it confers some benefit to forecasters. As anticipated and experienced emotions are potent sources of motivation, affective forecasters may exaggerate their forecasts to motivate themselves to produce desired outcomes.

This hypothesis makes three predictions, which were tested in four experiments. First, the impact bias should be greater for events of greater personal importance. In line with the first prediction, Study 1 found that the more hockey fans considered a hockey game to be personally important, the more likely they were to overestimate how happy they would be if their team won. (Previous research has shown that sports fans believe that they can personally control the outcome of sporting events).

Second, the hypothesis predicts that the extremity of affective forecasts should influence the effort expended to produce desirable outcomes. In Studies 2 and 3, low and high standards of comparison were used to induce contrast effects that experimentally manipulated the extremity of affective forecasts for desirable outcomes. Subsequent mental (Study 2) and physical effort (Study 3) expended to produce those outcomes were recorded. As predicted, participants first exposed to a lower standard made more extreme forecasts than did participants exposed to a higher standard, and consequently expended more effort to produce the desirable outcomes. As the extremity of forecasts mediated the effect of the contrast manipulation on mental and physical effort expended, Studies 2 and 3 suggest that extreme affective forecasts motivate forecasters to produce desired outcomes.

Third, forecasters should make more extreme forecasts when they believe they can influence an outcome than when they believe they cannot. This was tested in Study 4. Participants forecasted how happy they would feel if they won $5 in a die-roll before rolling the die, or after rolling the die (while the outcome of the roll was unknown). A separate condition experienced winning/not winning $5 after rolling a die. Participants who made forecasts before rolling the die predicted they would feel happier if they won than did participants who made forecasts after rolling the die. Participants

who experienced winning $5 also made less extreme forecasts, similar to participant who made the forecasts after rolling the die. Thus, participants made more extreme forecasts when they were able to influence an outcome that had yet to be determined than when it was determined but unknown or when it was experienced.

Errors in affective forecasting are often costly. They may lead patients to make medical decisions based on erroneous predictions of the impact that declines in their health will bring, partisanship among voters who overestimate the ineptitude of opposing parties, and so on. It is questionable, however, whether people would exercise, mend broken relationships, or spend late nights in the office if they accurately forecasted how easily they would adapt to sickness, solitude, and a larger income. This research is the first to suggest that errors in affective forecasting may confer some benefit-they may provide the motivation necessary to achieve the outcomes one desires.

## "Can Consumers Make Smarter Investment Decisions By Improving Their Affective Forecasting?"

*Karthik Easwar, Ohio State University, USA*
*Patricia West, Ohio State University, USA*

This research seeks to better understand how consumers' investment decisions can be improved by reducing the "affective forecasting error" (Kermer, Driver-Linn, Wilson and Gilbert, 2006; Gilbert & Wilson, 2000). Gilbert has shown that humans tend to misforecast their affective reactions to both good and bad events. For example, people predict that winning the lottery would significantly increase happiness and that losing a limb would permanently impair quality of life. However, these predictions have been shown to be wrong. Lottery winners are no happier than non-winners and amputees' reported quality of life rebounds more quickly than forecasted.

Psychological research examining the impact of goals on performance has demonstrated an interesting and relevant paradox. According to Garland (1984) people who set higher goals tend to perform better than those who set lower goals or no goal, yet feel worse about their performance.

Heath et al (1999) offer an explanation for this paradox. Like Gilbert's experiments, Heath's subjects read hypothetical vignettes about two individuals who were facing the same task (e.g., taking a test) but starting with different goals (e.g., hopes to get a score of 90 versus hopes to "do her best"). In the scenario, both individuals experienced the same outcome, sometimes exceeding the individual's goal and other times falling short of the goal. Subjects' forecasts of these individuals' affective states showed that goals serve as reference points dividing successes from failures, and that loss aversion and diminishing sensitivity also exist.

We strive to reduce loss aversion and thus improve the affective forecasting ability of individuals by giving them the opportunity to learn from their own or others past actions. We ask whether people can learn to correct for the affective forecasting error by experiencing it for themselves or receiving feedback on the discrepancies between their forecasts and actual feelings and if this frees them to be more risk-seeking.

Participants made a series of investment decisions and were paid based on the performance of the funds they select. Participants were randomly assigned to one of two conditions (see Fig. 1). Individuals in the *no experience* condition made a series of 24 investment decisions, using detailed information on nine actual mutual funds that varied in their level of risk. After each selection, participants were given their investment's performance (a range of predetermined outcomes in a random order) and asked to report their affective reaction.

Individuals in the *first-hand experience* condition predicted their affective response to 12 hypothetical outcomes. These differ from actual decisions in that the subjects are merely told the outcome for a given period and asked to respond to it, rather than go through the fund selection process. Following this, they made a series of 12 investment decisions as described above. After reporting their affective state, they received feedback on the discrepancy between their actual feelings and their forecasts from the hypothetical phase.

All participants engaged in a second phase of hypothetical outcome forecasting that was 10 periods long. Following this task, individuals made eight actual investment decisions. Again, the actual outcomes came from a pre-determined set. After each outcome, participants reported their affective state. These last responses were compared to the affective predictions reported to measure the size of participants' affective forecasting error. Contrary to previous literature, simple experience was enough to show significant improvement in affective forecasting. Over and above this, explicit feedback had a marginal effect of improving forecasting. The impact of improved forecasting on fund selection and risk-seeking is discussed. This suggests that practice makes perfect, and that even simulated practice could be beneficial to investment decisions.

# It's Not Only in the Mind: Physical Actions Steer Our Thoughts

Jiska Eelen, K.U.Leuven, Belgium
Aparna Labroo, University of Chicago, USA

## EXTENDED ABSTRACT

### "Sitting Position and Self-control"

*Joan Meyers-Levy, University of Minnesota, USA*
*Rui (Juliet) Zhu, University of British Columbia, Canada*
*Ravi Mehta, University of British Columbia, Canada*

Research on embodied cognition suggests that cognitive representations are fundamentally grounded in their physical context. A central tenet of this theory is that human cognition, including high-level conceptual processes (e.g., inferences and categorizations), relies not only on the brain's modal systems (e.g., vision) but also on actions (e.g., body movement; Barsalou 2008). One mechanism through which embodiment can influence cognition is through situated action (Barsalou et al. 2003). Specifically, repeated situations can become entrenched in memory as situated concepts. These situated concepts usually include sensory or motor states experienced in those situations. Thus, "victory" as a situated concept might include such embodiments as hand waving and hugging. On one hand, the activation of a situated concept can make salient its constituent sensory-motor states. On the other hand, the experience of such embodiments can trigger the situated conceptualization. In other words, sensory-motor states or embodiments are associated with situated conceptualization, such that priming one can trigger the other (Niedenthal et al., 2005).

Building on the above theorizing concerning embodied cognition, we examine whether certain body postures, specifically sitting positions, can affect individuals' inclination to exert self control. Prior research has found that when sitting in an upright versus a slumped manner, individuals experienced fewer feelings of helplessness when confronted with a frustrating task (Riskind and Cotay 1982), greater confidence about their thoughts (Brinol, Petty, and Wagner 2009), and greater feelings of pride upon succeeding in an achievement task (Stepper and Strack 1993). Based on observations like these, we hypothesize that individuals who maintain an upright versus slouched sitting position should exhibit greater self-control. The logic is that an upright body posture is usually associated with situations where people engage in activities that are virtuous and right. Thus, sitting in an upright position may prime individuals to do the right thing by engaging self-control, being modest, and choosing virtue versus vice. In contrast, a slouched position is often associated with situations where individuals feel relaxed and carefree. As such, maintaining a slouched position can trigger individuals to relax their rules, enjoy life, and thereby indulge more. A series of experiments were conducted to test our hypothesis.

Sitting position was manipulated in the same manner across our studies. Those in the upright condition were asked to "sit in an upright position... put your legs and feet together, lift up the upper part of your body so that your spine is very straight. Lift your shoulders and bring them back slightly, and do not lean against the back of the chair." In contrast, those in the slouched position were told to "sit in a relaxed position... put your legs and feet apart, about shoulder width. Drop your rib cage and curl your shoulders forward."

The first two studies tested our main hypothesis using different tasks. In study 1, participants were asked to complete a number of unrelated tasks. As they did so, they were offered a snack (i.e., some grapes). Self-control was assessed by the number of grapes individuals ate during the study session. As predicted, those in the upright sitting position ate fewer grapes compared to those in the slouched position. Study 2 conceptually replicated the main effect by demonstrating that when sitting upright, participants exhibited greater self-control by choosing less risky options.

In study 3, we extended our theorizing by proposing that different sitting positions might affect people's valuation of various types of products. Specifically, we anticipated that utilitarian products were likely to be valued more by those in the upright versus slouched sitting position, whereas the opposite should occur for hedonic products. Thus, this study employed a 2 (sitting position) X 2 (type of products) factorial design. Participants were asked to indicate highest price they would be willing to pay for a number of utilitarian and hedonic products. Results supported our theorizing, such that those in the upright (versus slouched) position were willing to pay significantly more for utilitarian products, yet the reverse was true for hedonic products. Study 4 offered evidence that the observed effects of sitting positions were sensation-based, and thus should be more salient among those who are more in tune with their bodily sensations.

To this point our findings have demonstrated that physical postures can affect behavior and product judgments. But could they also affect cognitive processes? That is, can sitting positions also affect people's thinking style? The last study sought to explore this idea. We posited that an upright sitting position might activate thoughts about self-control; in turn, this might prompt individuals to also think in a "controlled" manner. Consequently, these individuals should be less likely to think outside-of-the-box, and thereby exhibit lower creativity. A typical creativity task was employed in this study, and as predicted, individuals in the slouched versus upright position exhibited greater creativity.

### "Spreading Activation Model Reconsidered: Motor Action Can Result in Habit Spirals"

*Aparna A. Labroo, University of Chicago, USA*
*Jesper Nielsen, University of Arizona, USA*

In consumer psychology, the spreading activation model has been fundamental to understanding memory processes. The basic idea is that knowledge is represented in memory as a network of nodes and associative pathways between the nodes. When a part of the memory network is activated, activation spreads through the associative pathways to related concepts or nodes. The activation of any node can result from direct priming, or how frequently and recently that target concept was activated, or can result from indirect (associative) priming, or how frequently and recently associated concepts were activated, and the strength of association between the related and target concept. An important core assumption of the spreading activation model is that the spread of associations resides purely in the mind. In a departure from this basic assumption, in the current research we argue that cognition is for action, therefore (a) habits, good or bad, are stored in memory as cognitive structures, as things to be approached or avoided, as a whole, and (b) our own physical sensations or motor activities when merely exposed to a tempting bad habit can predispose us favorably toward that bad habit, but (c) most importantly, those positive associations evoked by one's motor actions can spread to other bad habits that reside within the habit structure, thus strengthening the tendency for an individual to not only adopt one bad habit but to essentially start on a downward spiral of becoming predisposed to multiple bad habits.

Recent research supports the idea that cognition is for action, and as a consequence, cognition is not an activity of just the mind alone, but is instead distributed across the entire interacting situation, especially one's body (e.g. Beer, 1995, pp. 182-183; Greeno & Moore, p. 49; Thelen & Smith, 1994, p. 17; Wertsch, 1998). In particular, motor actions that usually result from or accompany thought also facilitate accessibility to those very thoughts, and in this manner our bodies exert a powerful effect on our minds. For instance, standing upright results from and results in feeling powerful, holding a heavy weight can lead to "heavy" thinking, and writing with a dominant hand rather than the non dominant one can help validate ones thoughts. Similarly, approach actions can result in more favorable evaluations of a neutral target whereas avoidance actions can result in less favorable evaluations of a neutral target that one is exposed to at the time one is engaged in motor approach or avoidance. Building on these findings, in the current research we investigate whether given a particular exposure to a prime, can accompanying motor actions impact the strength of activation of the prime and of associated concepts, with a particular focus on the adoption and spread of bad habits.

Across three experiments we provide support for our propositions. We show that merely sitting on a chair that is leaning slightly forward (versus backward) when viewing acts of physical aggression predisposes a person to subsequently engage in greater financial risks (experiment 1), that moving ones head forward (versus backward) while examining a party CD can increase the amount a person binges on junk food (experiment 2), and that drawing marbles out of a box (versus dropping them into the box) while viewing sexy pictures of persons of the opposite sex can increase the consumption of sexy foods (dark chocolate) but reduce consumption of homey foods (grandmas cookies; experiment 3). Taken together, the data suggest that, a) habits are stored as cognitive structures in people's minds, and b) our bodies can control the activation and spread of associations to linked habits in those memory structures. Motor actions that simulate physical approach toward one bad habit not only can result in yearning for that bad habit but the positive associations towards that particular bad habit then spread to associated bad habits in memory, resulting in spirals of bad habits being adopted. Thus, the feeling that one is giving in to one bad habit can result in a person giving in to all kinds of other bad habits, and it is one's own unintended motor actions when considering a bad habit that contribute to the adoption or inhibition of other bad habits.

### "Embodied Preferences: How the Easiness of Grasping Objects Affects Their Liking"

*Jiska Eelen, K.U.Leuven, Belgium*
*Siegfried Dewitte, K.U.Leuven, Belgium*
*Luk Warlop, K.U.Leuven, Belgium*

When consumers shop in a store, they have no verbal lists of product features available for making choices, but they do observe physical products. That is why we investigate whether product presentations influence product preferences. Merely seeing a product activates an action tendency to grasp the product (Chao & Martin, 2000; Tucker & Ellis, 1998). Processing information about products that one can easily interact with is less effortful (Helbig, Graf, & Kiefer, 2006). In addition, it has been shown that fluent information processing of a stimulus increases its attractiveness (Reber, Winkielman, & Schwarz, 1998; Winkielman & Cacioppo, 2001). Hence, it could be hypothesized that products consumers can easily interact with will be liked more than products that are more difficult to interact with. Ping, Dhillon and Beilock (2009) have found preliminary evidence for this motor fluency effect. In three experiments we manipulate ease of interaction by the fit between the hand participants use for grasping products (right or left hand) and the orientation of products' handles (towards the right or left hand).

In a first experiment, we demonstrate that it is more difficult to interact with products oriented away from the hand used for grasping and that products oriented to the left suggest interacting with the left hand. Right-handed participants (N=18, 72% male) were shown one tool at the time on a table and were asked to move it with their dominant right hand to a shopping basket at their right side. For each participant, we created a percentage score that expressed how often products were grasped by their handle. We found that the tools were mainly grasped by their handle (M=93.72%), rather than by another part. If the handles were oriented towards the left hand and thus more difficult to grasp, the tools were grasped by their handle (M=89%) significantly less often than if the handles were oriented towards the right hand (M=98%, t(17)=-4.18, p<.001). We also found out that tools which were oriented towards the left were sometimes (mistakenly %) grasped with the left hand, whereas this never happened for tools with their handle towards the right (S=22.5, p<.01).

In a second experiment, participants had to select which of two tools, on a table in front of them, they would prefer to use. Right-handed participants (N=40, 40% male) indicated their preference by picking up the tool with their dominant hand and moving it to a box at their right side. Tool pairs were different products from the same product category (e.g. two different pizza cutters). One tool was easy to grasp, whereas the other tool was difficult to grasp. Overall, the easy-to-grasp-tools were chosen more often than the difficult-to-grasp tools (56%, Z=2.16, p<.05) . However there were large individual differences in the extent to which this motor fluency effect occurred.

In a third experiment, pictures of one easy and one difficult-to-grasp product were shown on a computer screen, simulating an online shopping environment. Participants indicated their preferred product by tapping on "D" (for the left product) or "K" (for the right product) on the keyboard. Half of all right-handed participants used their right hand to indicate their preference, whereas the other half used their left hand. After the choice experiment we measured participants' degree of right-handedness by means of a handedness scale. We predicted that if right-handers are flexible enough to capture environmental cues, using the left hand would lead to a preference for products oriented with its handle towards the left. For each participant (N=62, 23% male) we created a percentage score that expressed how often products oriented with its handle towards the right were chosen. The main effect for hand used was not significant (right hand: M=52%; left hand: M=46%), nor was the effect of right-handedness. However degree of right-handedness moderated the effect of the hand used (F(1,58)=15.51, p<.001). The interaction motor effect occurred for soft right-handers (M-1SD), but not for hard right-handers (M+1SD). Soft right-handers who used their right hand picked more products oriented towards the right than random (M=61%, p<.001) and soft right-handers who used their left hand picked more products oriented towards the left (M=39%, p<.05). Hard right-handers (M+1SD) showed no preference for particular product orientations, using their left (M=52%, p=ns) or right hand (M=43%, p=ns). Hence, our data suggest that the motor fluency effect only occurs for people who are not bounded by dexterity and construct their preference on-line on the basis of constraints by both their body (using left or right hand) and the environment (i.e. product presentation).

The present work about product preferences differs from prior consumer research by showing that consumers' physical interactions with products have an impact on decision making processes. Our findings indicate that information processing is flexible and situated. This implies that the fit between body characteristics and product presentations affect consumers' choices.

### "'On the One Hand, on the Other Hand': Motor Movements Activate the 'Balance' Goal"

*Spike W. S. Lee, University of Michigan, USA*
*Norbert Schwarz, University of Michigan, USA*

Life is a series of trade-offs and we often face situations that require a balancing of competing goals. The expression "on the one hand, on the other hand" is used to describe the weighing of pros and cons, strengths and weaknesses, or benefits and costs. It is often accompanied by a specific gesture: holding both hands palm-up and moving them alternately up and down, as though the two palms were balance pans on a scale. Pluses and minuses are thus compared by weighing what is "on the one hand" against what is "on the other hand."

While this may seem merely a convenient figure of speech, recent advances in cognitive science suggest otherwise. A growing body of work shows that human cognition is grounded in sensorimotor processes (Barsalou, 1999, 2008) and guided by metaphors that link abstract domains to more concrete ones (Lakoff & Johnson, 1980, 1999). For example, the abstract sense of comprehension of ideas is grounded in the more concrete sense of control and manipulation of objects (e.g., "I can finally grasp the idea"). The conceptual metaphor "Understanding Is Grasping" (Lakoff & Johnson, 1999, p. 54) explains why the same hand movement has no particular meaning when we hold the hands palm-down: An object can be grasped by the palm side, but not the back side of the hand. When an object sits atop the palm, it can also be weighed. The abstract sense of importance is embodied in the concrete sense of weight (Jostmann et al., 2009). Just as a balance weighs an object on one pan against another object on the other pan, the decision maker holds one idea (e.g., an attribute, an option) "on the one hand" and weighs its relative value against another idea "on the other hand." A sense of balance is conferred by the alternate up-and-down movements of both hands.

This analysis suggests that both hand movement and palm orientation are necessary to activate a sense of balance, resulting in three specific predictions. (1) The gesture of holding both hands palm-up and moving them alternately up and down should activate the goal to balance things out. (2) Holding the hands in the same position without moving them should not activate the goal. (3) Moving the hands, but with palms facing down, should also not activate the goal. Three experiments tested these predictions and showed that hand movements affect what people value (Experiment 1) and how they spend their time (Experiment 2) and money (Experiment 3).

*Experiment 1.* As part of an ostensible motor control task, participants (N=88) were induced to move their hands palm-up, or palm-down, or simply hold their hands stationary palm-up. While maintaining the gesture for 15 seconds, participants read a list of 10 values (balance in life, creativity, wealth, etc.) on a clipboard held by the experimenter, allegedly to save time. Afterwards, they ranked the values in order of personal importance (1=most important, 10=least important). As predicted, participants who had moved their hands palm-up ranked "balance in life" significantly higher (rank-out-of-10 M=2.94, SD=1.84) than those who had moved their hands palm-down (M=4.15, SD=2.71; planned contrast t(85)=2.06, p=.04; Cohen's d=0.52) or those who had rested their hands (M=4.18, SD=2.26; t(85)=2.15, p=.04, d=0.60). Ranks in the last two conditions were not significantly different, t(85)=.04, p=.97.

*Experiment 2.* While moving their hands palm-up or palm-down for 20 seconds, participants (N=80) thought about how to allocate their available time during a typical weekday to various activities (e.g., studying, hanging out with friends). Afterwards, they wrote down their allocations. Participants who moved their hands palm-up allocated time more evenly to work and leisure (M=50% for work-related activities, SD=22%) than those who moved their hands palm-down (M=40% for work-related activities, SD=23%), t(78)=2.18, p=.03, d=0.49.

*Experiment 3.* Preliminary data from Experiment 3 extended these findings from work-life balance to the emergence of compromise effects in consumer choice (Drolet, Luce, & Simonson, 2009). While moving their hands palm-up, or palm-down, or holding their hands stationary, participants (N=43) were asked to choose three products, each from three available options. Two were extreme options (e.g., speakers with high power and price, low power and price), one was a compromise option (medium power and price). Participants who moved their hands palm-up were more likely to choose compromise options than those who moved their hands palm-down or those who held their hands stationary (tau-c=.34, SE=.14, t=2.40, p=.02, for balancing vs. the other two gestures, which were not significantly different).

Hand movement and palm orientation together create a "balancing" gesture that has cognitive and motivational consequences: it activates the goal to balance things out, as reflected in differential value reports, time allocation intentions, and product choices. These findings combine insights from the embodiment and conceptual metaphor perspectives, lending support to the notion that abstract concepts and goals can be activated by motor movements. They highlight the importance of taking motion and orientation (e.g., Linkenauger et al., 2009) into account simultaneously. Lacking either component eliminates the balancing effect on values and choices. Implications for consumer decision making will be discussed.

# Beauty Beyond Affect: Positive and Negative Effects of Visual Attractiveness on Consumers' Judgments and Behaviors

Gratiana Pol, University of Southern California, USA

## EXTENDED ABSTRACTS

### "The A.I.R. Construct: The Processing Mechanism Underlying Aesthetics-Induced Consumer Behaviors"

*Gratiana Pol, University of Southern California, USA*
*C.W. Park, University of Southern California, USA*

It has long been recognized that beauty can exert a strong motivational influence on people. In a consumption context, aesthetically appealing products have been linked to favorable attitudes and higher purchase intentions as well as willingness to pay price premiums of up to fifty percent of a product's value. Yet after becoming the proud owner of a beautiful product–which often gets conspicuously displayed to the world–consumers sometimes become reluctant to actually use it for fear they might damage its pleasing visual appearance. What exactly could be driving these behaviors? Why do beautiful products motivate such responses in consumers?

A potential explanation suggested in the literature refers to the pleasure and positive mood elicited by beautiful objects, which may in turn explain the positive attitudes and behaviors triggered by attractive products. Yet mood alone may fail to account for why consumers place such a high value on aesthetics and why visual appeal sometimes has a downright anomalous impact on choice and usage behaviors. Currently there is an emerging view that consumers' responses to aesthetics differ from the low-level affective reactions typically associated with hedonic product attributes, yet we not know exactly how. We propose that a mechanism more complex than mood may represent that powerful and unique driving force behind beautiful products. This mechanism–which we call A.I.R. (Aesthetics-Induced Responses)–implies that appealing products engage us on three dimensions: affective, cognitive, and conative.

On an affective dimension, appealing products touch our hearts. One look at a beautiful object, and, similarly to looking at an attractive person, we can experience something akin to love-at-first-sight. We call this hot, emotion-laden response "spontaneous affect". On a cognitive dimension, beautiful products hold the promise of making us more attractive and socially desirable through possession. This effect–which is comparable to the social premium bestowed on us by having a good-looking partner–will be called "self-enhancement". Finally, on a conative (motivational) level, beautiful products elicit an immediate and powerful approach desire that manifests itself in a craving for sensory proximity. Not surprisingly, museums try to address this issue by asking viewers not to touch the displayed art. We call this motivational response "instantaneous approach". Together, these three dimensions of A.I.R. are believed to explain the effects of aesthetics on consumers' behaviors better than mood can.

We tested this assumption in an experiment in which we presented participants with the image and brief description of a highly attractive desktop computer. Participants then rated their mood, the A.I.R. measure, their behavioral intentions towards the computer, and their aesthetic impressions of the computer. The A.I.R. measure consisted of a 10-item scale which included the dimensions of spontaneous affect, instantaneous approach, and self-enhancement. Mood was measured using a validated scale that included both positively- and negatively-valenced items. We measured two types of behavioral intentions: those pertaining to simple consumption behaviors (such as buying a product) and those

pertaining to more complex and difficult-to-enact behaviors (such as delaying a purchase until the desired product becomes available).

A structural equation analysis indicated that the proposed model–with aesthetic impressions as independent variable, behavioral intentions as dependent variable, and the three-dimensional A.I.R. concept as mediator–provided a very good fit to the data, both for simple and for complex behaviors. In both cases, the direct path from aesthetics to behavioral intentions was not significant, indicating full mediation through A.I.R. However, when mood was used as a mediator instead of A.I.R., this path remained significant in each case, suggesting only a partial mediation through mood. This indicates that A.I.R. can explain the relationship between aesthetics and several types of consumer behaviors better than mood can, and thus represents a superior mediator. Aesthetics create decidedly more than just a mood effect, and thus go beyond the simple pleasure response typically associated with "hedonic" product attributes.

Additionally, we collected measures of the computer's perceived functionality, novelty/interestingness and status-signaling qualities and showed that, when these measures were entered into a model simultaneously with aesthetics and A.I.R., the path from aesthetics to A.I.R. remained significant, but none of the paths from the other measures to A.I.R. were significant. This indicates that the A.I.R. measure is directly driven by aesthetic impressions and is not a consequence of the functionality, novelty or status-signaling attributes of the attractive product.

Taken together, the present findings shed light on the powerful motivational force behind product aesthetics and allow us to better understand the unique processing mechanism through which aesthetics impact various consumer behaviors.

### "The Beauty Penalty: Too Sexy for the Job?"

*Meng Zhu, Carnegie Mellon University, USA*
*Joachim Vosgerau, Carnegie Mellon University, USA*
*Uri Simonsohn, University of Pennsylvania, USA*

Existing research has shown that physically attractive people benefit from various types of positive discrimination, from higher salaries, beneficial treatment in game shows, to more favorable offers in lab experiments. Explanations for this effect–called beauty premium–fall into two classes: taste-based explanations and statistical-based explanations. Taste-based explanations argue that beauty itself is valued by others but unrelated to productivity. Statistical-based explanations, in contrast, argue that beauty serves as a reliable indicator for productivity. For example, evolutionary accounts argue that both intelligence/fitness and beauty are inheritable characteristics. Since intelligent/fit men are more likely to mate with beautiful women, a positive correlation between beauty and productivity results. Recently, a third, belief-based explanation has been suggested, namely that beautiful people appear more confident, and since confident people are erroneously believed to be more productive, they are paid more.

We propose a slightly different belief-based explanation to account for the discrimination towards attractive people. Social psychology literature has shown that attractive people are not only perceived as more confident, they are also perceived as more sociable, dominant, and better adjusted than unattractive people. Given this validated positive link between beauty and perceived social skills, we conjecture that a beauty premium occurs for professions in which social skills are important, because people believe that beauty pays off in social interactions. In contrast, a beauty penalty occurs for professions that require analytical skills and extensive solitary training. This penalty effect is due to people believing that less attractive individuals incur higher costs in social interactions than attractive individuals, and are thus more likely than their attractive peers to engage in analytical activities and extensive training that do not require or may even inhibit social interactions. We test our explanation in three studies.

For Study 1 we selected 12 photos (3 of attractive and 3 of unattractive individuals of each gender) from a large set of working professionals. Respondents rated each photo along the dimensions of attractiveness, social and analytical skills. Consistent with our hypothesis, social and analytical skills were negatively correlated. Furthermore, individuals rated as more attractive were perceived to have better social skills but worse analytical skills.

Study 2 examined whether physical attractiveness would influence people's preference for service providers. In a separate pretest, we found that for lawyers (doctors), people judge social (analytical) skills to be relatively more important for career success. Thus, we expected participants to prefer attractive lawyers to plain-looking lawyers, but to prefer plain-looking doctors to attractive doctors. Further, we manipulated skill importance. We expected that preferences for attractive lawyers and plain-looking doctors would be attenuated when social and analytical skills are not important. Participants were asked to imagine that they either had a medical condition or needed to go to court to appeal a property tax estimate. They were then provided with the CVs and headshots of two equally qualified doctors/lawyers (one was attractive and the other was plain-looking) and asked to indicate which professional they would choose. Additionally, we manipulated the importance of analytical and social skills to be either high (kidney surgery or an $8,000 tax appeal) or low (getting a drug prescription or a $500 tax appeal). In support of our hypothesis, choice proportions did not differ when social/analytical skills were not important, but differed significantly when social/analytical skills were important. We found a beauty premium for social skills, as a majority of subjects selected the more attractive professionals in the legal case, and found a beauty penalty for analytical skills as a minority selected the more attractive professionals in the medial case.

In Study 3, we manipulated the requirement of social versus analytical skills within the lawyer profession. The procedures were similar to what we used for the lawyer condition in study 2, except for having 9 photo pairs within each professional's gender. Participants were told that they needed to hire a lawyer for a property tax reduction in the range of $6,000-9,000. Half of the participants were told that the lawyer needed to file a written appeal with the Board of Review (analytical skills condition), the other half was told that the lawyer needed to present their case in front of a jury (social skill condition). As hypothesized, we found a beauty premium for social tasks, as a majority of subjects in the jury-trial condition selected more attractive lawyers, but a beauty penalty for analytical tasks, as a minority did so for the paper-petition.

In conclusion, we demonstrate a beauty penalty effect, that is a negative discrimination against attractive service providers. Our results suggest that the beauty penalty might be as common as the beauty premium depending on whether social or analytical skills are required for the job. Further, our findings suggest that the beauty penalty versus premium cannot be explained by taste-based discrimination, as the same attractive persons are discriminated in favor of or against on tasks requiring different skills. Our results provide support for belief-based discrimination: People believe beauty pays off in social interactions, but hinders engagement and

training in analytical tasks. Whether people's beliefs that attractive people possess better social but worse analytical skills are indeed valid is an open question for future research.

## "The Good, the Bad, and the Ugly: Aesthetic Effects in Product Feature Judgments"

*JoAndrea Hoegg, University of British Columbia, Canada*
*Joseph W. Alba, University of Florida, USA*
*Darren W. Dahl, University of British Columbia, Canada*

Prior research examining the influence of product design on evaluation has demonstrated a powerful effect of aesthetics on overall liking and judgments in the absence of other information, but the question of whether aesthetics can influence judgments of objective feature information is unresolved. We address whether and how aesthetics might alter performance evaluations of specific product features. Specifically, we examine how consumers make functionality judgments when aesthetic information conflicts with feature performance information. In taking this approach, we also address what appears to be an implicit assumption in research and practice: that being attractive is always better than being unattractive. If consumers generally expect more attractive designs to perform better, when faced with conflicting functional and aesthetic cues, how does this violation of expectation impact judgment? We examine how consumers judge relative feature performance of two competing brands when both options possess conflicting cues (i.e., one is superior to the other on a performance attribute but inferior in attractiveness).

Three outcomes are possible. Given that the task is evaluation of relative performance of a functional feature, the normative outcome would be no effect of aesthetics. A second possibility is that feature judgments will be biased in the direction of the inferior but more attractive product due to a positive halo. A final possibility is that feature judgments will be biased in the direction of the less attractive product, reflecting a negative aesthetic effect. Assuming consumers recognize the inconsistency between their expectations and the observed pattern, they will attempt to resolve it, and in so doing may elaborate on the conflicting feature. Elaboration can render beliefs about an object more evaluatively consistent and lead to a polarized assessment. We test these possibilities in four studies.

*Study 1*. Participants were presented with fictitious *Consumer Reports* reviews for two brands, which were written so that one *target feature* was clearly superior to the other. We then manipulated whether these reviews were accompanied by pictures of the product designs. Half the participants saw only the two reviews; the other half saw the reviews accompanied by pictures of the product designs (presented side-by-side). One design was more attractive than the other. The more attractive design was paired with the review of the inferior feature, and the less attractive design was paired with the review of the superior feature. In addition we manipulated cognitive load by having participants memorize either a 2-digit or 11-digit number. The study conformed to a 2 (visual information: present vs. absent) x 2 (cognitive load: high vs. low) x 2 (product replicate: cookware vs. speakers) design. The key dependent measure was participants' judgment of which brand's target feature was superior. A rating of zero would indicate they thought the two brands were equal on the target feature. A positive rating would indicate they perceived the brand with the objectively superior feature (the unattractive design) to indeed be superior on the target feature. A negative rating would indicate they perceived the brand with the objectively inferior feature (the more attractive design) to be superior.

Analysis of relative judgments of the superiority of the target feature revealed a significant visual information X cognitive load interaction. Consistent with the negative aesthetic effect, we found that in the absence of cognitive constraints, participants seeing the pictures perceived the unattractive brand as *even better* on the target feature than did participants not exposed to pictures. This effect occurred only when participants had the cognitive capacity to consider the information. For participants who saw reviews and pictures, the addition of cognitive constraints moved the relative feature judgments in the direction of the more attractive design (inferior feature).

*Study 2.* In study 2 we manipulated the pairing of the visual and written information so that half the participants were presented with incongruent visual and written information as in the previous study, and half were presented with congruent visual and written information (i.e., attractive design paired with superior target feature, and less attractive design paired with inferior target feature). We also manipulated cognitive load. If consumers believe that attractive products perform better, evaluating a product where design and functionality conform to expectations (i.e., are congruent) should make processing easier, so people in the congruent conditions should not be affected by cognitive load. The procedure followed that of study 1.

Results indicated that when the picture and target feature were congruent, participants strongly favored the superior feature, regardless of cognitive load. However, when the picture and target feature were incongruent, participants favored the functionally superior (but aesthetically inferior) brand only when under low cognitive load. Moreover, when under low load, participants took more time to make their judgments when faced with incongruent rather than congruent information, supporting the inconsistency reconciliation explanation.

*Study 3.* In study 3 we investigated order as a potential boundary condition. Using the same incongruent pairings of design and reviews, we manipulated whether participants saw the visual and verbal information simultaneously or saw the pictures prior to reading the reviews. We found that when participants saw the designs of the competing brands prior to reading the reviews about them, the advantage for the unattractive product disappeared.

### "Blinding Beauty: How Unexpected Product Attractiveness Can Overpower Negative Information"

*Hanna Kim, Chungnam National University, China*
*Andreas Eisingerich, Imperial College, UK*
*Gratiana Pol, University of Southern California, USA*

Visual attractiveness can distort quality perceptions by making products appear significantly higher in quality than they actually are. What happens, however, if an attractive product is accompanied by less-than-stellar functionality information? Can beauty overpower such information, and if yes, when and through what psychological mechanism? The present study aims to answer these questions.

Building upon order effects theory, one can expect that, when an attractive product is paired with negative performance information–a violation of consumers' expectations–attractiveness may attenuate the negative impact of this information depending on whether the product's appearance is encountered before or after the functional information.

Recent research has indeed shown that, when the attractive product *picture* is presented *first,* it elicits an affect-based impression that can positively bias the subsequent processing of verbal information. This results in higher product quality evaluations than if the picture and functionality information were presented side-by-side. In real life, however, consumers sometimes receive information in the opposite order, meaning that they hear or read negative performance information about a product before actually

experiencing its attractive design. When one is then exposed to the appealing product, contrast theory predicts that the discrepancy between the low expectations induced by the negative information and the pleasantly surprising sight of the attractive design can magnify the positive impact of attractiveness on product evaluations. Thus, one can also expect consumers to form enhanced product quality evaluations when encountering the product *picture last* rather than simultaneously with functionality information. This order effect has not yet been examined.

To test whether product attractiveness will have a stronger positive impact when encountered *first* or *last*, we conducted a 2 (order: picture-first versus picture-last) x 2 (product performance: superior versus inferior) between-subjects study. Participants were presented with the picture of an attractive computer and fictitious consumer reviews depicting the computer as either superior (4.8 out of 5 stars) or inferior (2 stars) in performance. Half of the participants saw the computer image before the reviews, while the remaining participants saw the two in the opposite order. To ensure that the information was processed in the required order and to prevent recency effects, we asked participants to elaborate in writing on the first piece of information.

The results revealed an interaction between performance and order, such that, when the picture was presented first, product quality evaluations differed significantly between the superior- and inferior-performance conditions. However, when the picture was presented last, despite the rather large objective difference in product performance between the two conditions, consumers perceived the product to be just as high in quality in the inferior-performance condition as in the superior-performance condition. This suggests that, as predicted by contrast theory, when an attractive product is presented last, attractiveness can override negative performance information by positively distorting product quality evaluations. We call this the "blinding beauty" effect. In Study 2 we confirmed that this effect happens only for attractive and not unattractive products.

Study 3 aimed to confirm that the effect is indeed motivated by surprise and to elucidate the mechanism through which the effect occurs. Since consumers make quality judgments by combining both verbal and visual product information, their higher quality evaluations in the picture-last condition could have been formed through one of two possible processing mechanisms. First, given that the pleasantly surprising sight of an attractive product elicits positive affect, consumers could have distorted or even discounted the functional information encountered beforehand, which represents an affect-confirmation process. Alternatively, consistent with the inference-based view that people use visual design cues to form beliefs about unobservable product attributes, consumers could have drawn on the image to generate positive inferences about the product's quality, which often happens in the case of attractive products. This process should be intensified by attractiveness coming as a surprise, given that surprise-inducing stimuli enhance attention and elaboration. One would therefore expect an attractive product to trigger particularly favorable appearance-based quality inferences in the picture-last condition. By contrast, in the picture-first condition, the reduced surprise effect of attractiveness paired with the subsequent encounter of negative information may attenuate these positive inferences, resulting in lower picture-based product quality evaluations.

To verify the exact cause as well as the mechanism behind the blinding beauty effect, Study 3 employed a design similar to Study 1, and included several process measures. The results showed that the surprise induced by the attractive product image was indeed higher for picture-last than for picture-first participants. Visual recall measures further corroborated these findings by revealing that picture-last participants paid significantly more attention to the image than did picture-first participants, even though attractiveness perceptions–an alternative attention-enhancing variable–were identical between conditions.

When it comes to the processing mechanism associated with the surprise response, the product quality evaluations derived from the reviews as well as the reviews' credibility did not differ between the picture-first and picture-last condition, which argues against a mood-consistent distortion or discounting of the negative verbal information. In contrast, the quality perceptions inferred from the picture showed the same pattern as the surprise ratings, meaning that picture-last participants perceived the image as conveying higher product quality than did picture-first participants. Notably, since attractiveness ratings did not differ between conditions, a "beautiful-is-good" effect can be ruled out. Additionally, the quality inferred from the product image fully mediated the relationship between presentation order and overall quality evaluations, while verbal information-based quality perceptions did not.

Together, these findings suggest that when an attractive product is paired with inferior functionality information, showing the product picture last creates a strong surprise response that draws attention to the product appearance and can override the damaging impact of the functionality information. This "blinding beauty" effect can be best explained by consumers deriving superior product quality inferences from the attractive product design when encountering its picture last.

# Context Effects Revisited: New Antecedents, Moderators and Extensions
Selin A. Malkoc, Washington University in St. Louis, USA

## EXTENDED ABSTRACTS

### "The Middle Option Bias: Is the Compromise Effect Driven by a Response Order Effect"
Daniel Mochon, Yale University, USA
Shane Frederick, Yale University, USA

In the Compromise Effect an option gains choice share when an alternative is added to the choice set that makes this previously available option the middle one in the attribute space, and consequently the 'Compromise'. For example, in one study an average priced/average quality television was chosen more often relative to an expensive/high quality one when a cheap and low quality option was added to the choice set (Simonson 1989). This effect is generally attributed to the increased ease of justifying the compromise option (Simonson 1989), an aversion to extreme options (Simonson and Tversky 1992) and to inferences about the attributes themselves (Wernerfelt 1995).

One problem with many demonstrations of this effect is that they confound the position of the options in attribute space, with their position in physical space, since options are generally ordered by their attributes. For instance, in the above example, the televisions were ordered by price, and thus adding the cheap/low quality alternative made the 'Compromise' option the middle one in the response order as well.

Many studies have demonstrated that the order in which options are presented affects which one is ultimately selected (Krosnick 1999). For example, participants often show a primacy effect, where they are more likely to pick options presented earlier than those that appear later (Carp 1974). In this research we propose a new response order bias, which we label the 'Middle Option Bias' whereby participants are more likely to choose the second option presented when there are three rather than two options, independent of what the options might be. Consequently, we suggest that part of the Compromise Effect may be driven by the mere change in the 'Compromise' option's position on the survey, rather than its position in attribute space. In the first study we demonstrate the existence of this Middle Options Bias in a context where the options have no clear attributes, and therefore we would not expect any other context effects. In the second study we show how this bias can account for the Compromise Effect.

In the first study we tested the existence of the Middle Option Bias in a general context where the options don't have any attributes that can be ranked. This allows us to demonstrate this response order bias in a setting where other context effects should be absent. In this study, participants were told to imagine that they were in a contest where a ball would be drawn from an urn, and if they guessed the correct color, they won $10. They were told that the urn contained either 30 balls of each of 2 colors, or 30 balls of each of three colors, and were then asked to select the color they would guess. Participants were assigned to one of twelve conditions, based on a full factorial 2 Number of Options Presented (2 vs. 3) X 6 Order of the Options design. Thus each option appeared once in each position for both the two and three options conditions. We then examined how the order in which the options were presented affected their choice. In line with the Middle Option Bias, participants chose the second option presented more often when there were three options (42.1%) than when there were only two (34.0%). The increase in

the choice probability of the middle option relative to the first one was statistically significant ($p < .05$).

In the second study we tested whether the order in which the options are presented affects the magnitude of the Compromise Effect. In this study participants were asked to make choices in four domains, each domain appearing on a separate page in a random order. The number of options (2 vs. 3) and the order of these were manipulated between subjects. When focusing only on the two conditions with the order typically used in Compromise Effect studies (with the compromise option appearing second), the probability of choosing the 'Compromise' option was higher when there were three options than when there were two [54.5% vs. 39.1%; $p < .01$]. This effect however seems to be mainly driven by the fact that the 'Compromise' option is the middle response, rather than the fact that it is the middle one in attribute space. When we compare how often people choose the 'Compromise' option (the middle one in attribute space) independently of order–when averaging across the order manipulation–we find no Compromise Effect [45.0% vs. 44.6%, $p = .9$].

In these studies we suggested a new explanation for the Compromise Effect, where we argued that the effect might be driven by the order in which the options are presented, and not their position in attribute space. While we do not suggest that all of the Compromise Effect is driven by a response order effect, our findings do suggest that the effect may be much smaller than previously thought.

### "Between a Rock and a Hard Place: Desirability Based Attenuation of Attraction Effect"
Selin A. Malkoc, Washington University in St. Louis, USA
William Hedgcock, University of Iowa, USA
Steve Hoeffler, Vanderbilt University, USA

Many important decisions people face involve choosing between options that are undesirable — the proverbial "lesser of two evils." Consumers face budget or geographical constraints that lead to mostly undesirable consideration sets, yet a choice is necessary. We examine the role of desirability in the context of the attraction effect (Huber, Payne and Puto 1982). Based on negative information processing research, we argue that choosing from less desirable options will activate a more vigilant system, thus attenuating or eliminating the attraction effect. Conversely, when evaluating desirable options, heuristic processing is used, leading to attraction effect. Five studies found consistent support for our proposition.

In Experiment 1, we manipulated option desirability by employing an attribute space that varied from –10 to +10 for the rating of the product features (where a score of zero was considered average). The ratings on the desirable (undesirable) domain took positive (negative) values Participants chose a fitness club. Three choice sets were tested: (1) set {A, B}, where there was no decoy, (2) set {A', A, B}, where A asymmetrically dominated and (3) set {A, B, B'}, where B asymmetrically dominated. The analyses showed the attraction effect in the desirable domain, where choice of A was highest when A' (83%) was present, moderate when there was no decoy (64%) and lowest when B' was present (40%). As predicted however, presence or location of decoy had no effect in the undesirable domain (77%, 74% 64%).

To test the robustness and increase the generalizability of the effect, remaining studies manipulated desirability in unique, yet normatively familiar ways, without the use of negative signs. In Experiment 2, we used high and low attribute values to manipulate desirability. Participants chose a hotel from one of the two sets: {A', A, B} or {A, B, B'}. Results replicated study. When the options were desirable, we observed higher choice of A, when A' was present (73%) than when B' was present (36%). When they were undesirable however, there were no differences across conditions (54% vs, 47%).

In Experiment 3 manipulated desirability by setting a reference point for the attribute levels (industry average) and using geographical constraints to justify having a consideration set that falls above/below this point. Participants chose a frequent flyer program, where half of them saw options that were above industry average, whereas the other half saw options below the industry average. We found that the attraction effect persisted in the desirable domain (32% vs, 6%), but not in the undesirable domain (37% vs 30%).

In Experiment 4, we kept attribute values constant but varied participants' reference points (which served to make the exact same stimuli more or less desirable, depending on the prior reference point). Participants chose between two cell phone plans. These two plans were identical in desirable and undesirable domains. Instead the specifications of their current cell phone plan was manipulated to make these options appear more or less desirable. We found that when options were perceived to be more desirable, the attraction effect surfaced (76% vs, 39%), but was eliminated when the options were perceived as less desirable (63% 53).

In addition, Experiment 3 and 4 examined whether simply evaluating desirable versus less desirable options changed the post-choice regulatory focus and whether such changes could account for the asymmetry in the attraction effect. These studies ruled out regulatory focus as the process.

Experiment 5 used a positive and negative framing manipulation to change the perceptions of desirability. We kept the attribute values and the reference points constant, only altering how the attribute values were framed. Participants chose a humidifier, where the attributes were either framed positively (95% effective, returns permitted within 30 days), or negatively (5% ineffective, returns denied after 30 days). Once again, we found that attraction effect persisted in the desirable domain (73% vs, 38%), but not in the undesirable domain (64% vs. 54%). In this study, we also recorded participants' response latencies to test whether a processing shift can explain the desirability-based attenuation of the attraction effect. The mediation analysis indicate that the effect of (un)desirability on the attraction effect works through an increased processing while making the choice.

Lastly, we examined whether other context effects would also be susceptible to changes in the desirability of the set. To provide an initial test, a new study used the positive/negative attribute space manipulation from Study 1 and created two sets {A, B, C}, {B, C, D}. We find that share of B is higher when it is the compromise option (44%) than when it is the extreme (12%). However, this was not the case in the undesirable domain (8% vs. 14%). These results indicate that desirability of the choice set might be relevant for other context effects as well.

We provide evidence for the attenuation of the well-established attraction effect when choice involves less desirable alternatives, which is more commonplace with the current economic conditions. We suggest that the attraction effect (and other context effects) might be more malleable than previously thought of.

## "Preferences, Interrupted"

*Wendy Liu,* UCLA in UC San Diego, USA
*Jonathan Levav, Columbia University, USA*

In everyday life, decisions are often made in multiple stages due to interruptions or suspensions. For example, a consumer may be considering a purchase, but may be sidetracked for a while by other interests. In this paper we ask, what is the effect of such interruptions on preferences? Recent research (Liu 2008) shows that interrupting or postponing a decision can have a significant effect on decision outcome by changing the way people think about the decision. In particular, when thinking about a choice after a brief period of separation from initial exposure to the problem, thinking becomes more high-level and top-down, resulting in greater focus on high-level construal and less attention to low-level detail. Thus, people choose items that rate high on desirability (a high-level trait; Trope and Liberman 2000) rather than feasibility (a low-level trait). For instance, when choosing between a hiking trail that has beautiful scenery but is far away, and another that is plain but easily accessible, after an interruption people are more likely to choose the former option, compared to when the decision is not interrupted.

The current research builds on the growing interest in the dynamic course of decision making, and examines the effect of interruption on the degree of context-dependence in decisions. We find that interrupting decision-makers as they consider the option set attenuates the attraction effect, but increases the compromise effect. We propose that this occurs because interruption leads to a greater reliance on one's inherent, chronic preferences, rather than a construction of preferences based on contextual cues. Furthermore, this process shares similarities to the effect of thinking about the distant future, whereby the person focuses on the high-level construal of the problem.

In our studies we contrast two classic context effects: the compromise effect (Simonson 1989) and the attraction effect (asymmetric dominance; Huber, Payne and Puto 1982). Behavioral decision theory posits that choices are determined by two types of information concerning the options: preferences that exist in people's memory and responses to current contextual stimuli (Tversky and Simonson 1992). We propose that the two types of information correspond to different levels of "preference construal." Inherent preferences concern people's pre-stored attitudes toward objects. However, because memory is a limited resource, preferences for many objects is constructed rather than retrieved (Bettman, Luce and Payne 1998). We suggest that, as a result, retrieved preferences concern high-level dimensions of objects, such as the product's identity (e.g., its brand) or the identities of its main attribute dimensions. We associate these types of retrieved preferences with a "high level" of preference construal. In contrast, contextual information refers to specific relationships among the values contained in the decision situation, such as the attribute levels themselves. Since people typically do not have pre-sorted preferences regarding aspects such as attribute levels, they make decisions based on the relation between different attribute levels (e.g., dominance). We associate preferences that are based on this type of reasoning as reliant on a "low level" of preference construal. For example, in choosing between two computers, a high-level construal involves the identity of the attributes (e.g., the attributes of memory); a lower-level construal involves the values on these attributes (e.g., 2 GB for memory). We hypothesize that because the person processes at a higher level construal after a period of interruption in a decision, he/she will pay more attention to attribute identity, rather than relationships in attribute value after an interruption.

This hypothesis implies a different prediction for the attraction and compromise effects. The attraction effect relies on a perception of a peculiarity in attribute levels, namely, a dominance between values of one option. However, the attention to such a dominance relationship may be attenuated if a person's focus is on higher-level constructs such as the identity of the attribute dimensions, rather than attribute values. Consequently, we expect an interruption in decision making will reduce the attraction effect. This effect is confirmed in S1, where an interruption reduced the attraction effect in all categories.

On the other hand, the compromise effect is a result of feeling of conflict between two attribute dimensions. That is, if two attribute dimensions are both important to a decision (and both have reasonable attribute values), people may feel great conflict giving up value on either dimension, and as a result choose a middle ground where each value is at a middle level. We propose that when people pay greater attention to the higher level construal of attribute identity after an interruption, they are likely to feel even greater conflict between the attributes, and therefore be more likely to choose the compromise option. This prediction is borne out in S2 in 4 out of 4 categories.

A third experiment studies the mechanism underlying the interruption effect. Specifically, we find that temporal distance has a similar effect as decision interruption, attenuating the attraction effect, while increasing the compromise effect.

### "Choice Context from Distal Similarity Signals"

*Uzma Khan, Stanford University, USA*
*Ab Litt, Stanford University, USA*
*Itamar Simonson, Stanford University, USA*

When and how are we influenced by others' preferences and product recommendations? Trust, liking, closeness, and credibility of recommenders are likely important considerations. Another critical factor is how *similar* people feel they are to the recommender, e.g., in preferences, personality or beliefs (Simons et al., 1970). While similarity in choice-relevant preferences is a reasonable factor to consider in decision-making, we propose that people over-generalize similarity on one dimension to infer similarity in domains unrelated to the focal decision. For instance, a common taste in obscure art-house movies might be over-generalized to infer similarity in cell-phone preferences. Such distal *similarity signals* can exert important contextual influence in decision-making, influencing both choice and recommendation efficacy.

The "signal-value" of similarity cues and relative strength of associated context effects can depend on various factors, e.g., whether the signaled similarity is on a dimension important to one's self-identity, intensity or idiosyncrasy of the preference or characteristic, etc. For example, for a liberal individual, a review of a right-wing conservative book might have *high* signal-value, whereas that of kitchen utensils would have relatively *low* signal value. We examine whether distal similarity can serve as an influential contextual factor in decision-making by exploring similarity-induced asymmetric dominance (Huber et al., 1982). We show that varying the choice context established by different similarity signal permutations (high/positive vs. high/negative vs. low) can reverse and shift the asymmetric dominance effect.

Study 1: Participants chose a preferred digital camera from several options. Each option was recommended by another consumer, for whom participants were provided a sample product review in an unrelated domain. In the Control condition, they chose between two cameras, A and B, reciprocally dominating each other in mega-pixels and price, respectively. In two other conditions they chose between three cameras: A, B, and C. Option C here had the *same* objective specifications as B. A and B were recommended by consumers whose other reviews were of a calculator and kitchen utensil, respectively (low signal-value). In contrast, C was recommended by a consumer who previously reviewed a right-wing/conservative book (high signal-value), either positively (Pro-Conservative condition) or negatively (Anti-Conservative condition). For political liberals (who predominated in our sample),

the review in the Anti-Conservative condition was hypothesized to send a *positive* similarity signal, versus a *negative* (or dissimilarity) signal in Pro-Conservative condition.

Despite B and C having identical objective attributes, we hypothesized this similarity signal difference would influence relative preferences between these options. Consistent with this view, in Pro-Conservative condition the choice-share of B increased among the options {A,B,C} compared to the control choice-set {A,B}. The choice-share of A declined substantially compared to the control, whereas C was chosen by only one participant. Thus, camera-B asymmetrically dominated camera-C.

As evidence that this effect was due specifically to the unrelated preceding product review, in the Anti-Conservative condition we observed a reversal. Here, B's choice-share *decreased* and was below that of C, and A's choice-share also fell. This preference reversal between B and C combined with decline in A's share is consistent with C asymmetrically dominating B in this condition. As expected based on the nature of this similarity context, results were moderated by political liberalism

Study 2: An alternative account for Study 1 is that, instead of signaling similarly/dissimilalty, pro/anti-conservative reviews simply influenced how much participants *liked* that reviewer, which affected how participants evaluated that person's camera recommendation. Study 2 disentangled these factors by using a product review that induced liking of the reviewer but simultaneously signaled *dissimilarity*. We did so with a product review of a book on charitable giving, as part of which the reviewer revealed an extremely charitable lifestyle (e.g., dedication of 50% of annual income to charity). While such a person may be liked, their extreme nature (82% of participants reported donating 5% or less of annual income to charity) was hypothesized to cause dissimilarity to be inferred. The procedure was identical to Study 1's, though with only one {A,B,C} condition in which camera-C was recommended by the aforementioned extreme-charitable reviewer. Consistent with expectations, participants rated this reviewer as both more liked but more dissimilar to themselves than those who recommended camera-A and camera-B (for whom provided product reviews were of a calculator and kitchen utensil as in Study 1).

Supporting a similarity-based context effect (and opposite to a liking-based account) results were analogous to the Pro-Conservative condition in Study 1, i.e., a *dissimilarity* signal for C caused B to asymmetrically dominate it. Specifically, compared to the control choice-set {A,B}, the choice-share of B increased, that of A declined and C was chosen least frequently in the {A,B,C} choice-set condition. Moreover, individuals who chose B from the {A,B,C} choice-set reported lower perceived similarity between themselves and the charitable person than did those choosing A or C.

Conclusions. Results support an important role of distal similarity signals in establishing choice contexts, as observed here in inducing and reversing asymmetric dominance effects. When similarity between oneself and another is inferred, even in domains or dimensions unrelated to a focal decision, recommendations by that other person are more influential and likely to be heeded. These findings illustrate a novel way of influencing choices through contextual cues, and reveal an important moderator of the efficacy of product recommendations and potentially other forms of interpersonal influence.

### REFERENCES

Bettman, James R., Mary Frances Luce and John W. Payne (1998) "Constructive Consumer Choice Processes," *Journal of Consumer Research*, 25, 187-217.

Carp, Frances M. (1974), "Position Effects on Interview Responses," Journal of Gerontology, 29 (5), 581-87.

Huber, Joel, John W. Payne, and Christopher Puto (1982), "Adding Asymmetrically Dominated Alternatives: Violations of Regularity and the Similarity Hypothesis," Journal of Consumer

Research, 9 (June), 90-98.

Krosnick, Jon A. (1999), "Survey Research," Annual Review of Psychology, 50, 537-67.

Liu, Wendy (2008), "Focusing on Desirability: The Effect of Decision Interruption and Suspension on Preferences," Journal of Consumer Research, 35(4), 640-652.

Simons, Herbert W., Nancy N. Berkowitz, and R. John Moyer (1970), "Similarity, Credibility, and Attitude Change: A Review and a Theory," Psychological Bulletin, 73 (1), 1-16.

Simonson, Itamar (1989), "Choice Based on Reasons: The Case of Attraction and Compromise Effects," Journal of Consumer Research, 16 (September), 158-74.

Simonson, Itamar and Amos Tversky (1992), "Choice in Context: Tradeoff Contrast and Extremeness Aversion," Journal of Marketing Research, 29 (3), 281-95.

Trope, Yaacov and Nira Liberman (2000). Temporal construal and time-dependent changes in preference. Journal of Personality and Social Psychology,79, 876-889.

Wernerfelt, Birger (1995), "A Rational Reconstruction of the Compromise Effect: Using Market Data to Infer Utilities," Journal of Consumer Research, 21 (March), 627-33.

# In (or out of) Control: The Effect of Perceived Influence on Consumer Behavior, Decisions, and Satisfaction

Simona Botti, London Business School, UK

Leonard Lee, Columbia University, USA

## EXTENDED ABSTRACTS

### "Power and Spending on Oneself versus Others: From Psychological to Economic Value"

David Dubois, Northwestern University, USA

Derek D. Rucker, Northwestern University, USA

Adam D. Galinsky, Northwestern University, USA

Power—defined as asymmetric perceived control over resources or people— has been a central force in the study of organizational behavior. However, only recently has power been brought into marketing to understand consumer behavior. For instance, recent work suggested that states of powerlessness increase consumers' desire for products associated with status. This effect is argued to occur out of a desire to compensate for a lack of power via the demonstration of status to others.

The present work proposes that power, even for non-status products, can have a considerable effect depending on who a product is being bought for. Specifically, we hypothesize that psychological states of power and powerlessness can also provide information with respect to the *value* of one's self versus others.

Why would this occur? Based on work suggesting that increased power leads to greater value associated with one's own thoughts and goals, we hypothesize that a state of powerlessness accentuates one's feeling of dependence on others, making others more valued to an individual, consistent with work suggesting the powerless are better at taking the perspective of others and more sensitive to their immediate environment than the powerful. In contrast, a state of powerfulness signals that one is important and thus is of greater value.

If our hypothesis concerning differential value is correct, we propose that power should asymmetrically affect how much consumers are willing to spend on purchases for themselves versus others. When purchasing an item for another individual (e.g., gift certificates, chocolates), low-power individuals should spend more on the item than high-power individuals. However, when purchasing an item for themselves, this spending propensity should reverse: high-power individuals should spend more on the item than individuals in a state of low power. These ideas are tested across three experiments, using multiple power manipulations and dependent measures. In addition, we focus on relatively mundane objects, in order to avoid any status-seeking motive by low power participants.

In the first experiment, participants were randomly assigned to imagine themselves in a role of high power (i.e., a boss) or low power (i.e., an employee). Subsequently, as part of an ostensibly unrelated task, they indicated the amount they would spend on gifts (i.e., certificates for the movies, a casual restaurant) for themselves or another person. When purchasing items for themselves, high-power individuals were willing to spend more than low-power individuals. In contrast, when purchasing items for another person, low-power individuals were willing to spend more than high power individuals. Thus, the findings of experiment 1 support our differential value hypothesis.

In our second experiment we tested the hypothesis that the effects were dependent on people explicitly considering who would receive the gift. We hypothesized that when the recipient (self, other) was not made salient any effects of power would be attenuated.

Participants were assigned to low or high power via an episodic recall task. Subsequently, participants took part in a bidding study. Participants were told they would have an opportunity to bid on several objects (i.e., a mug, a t-shirt) and that they would be able to purchase the object if they bid more than an undisclosed reserve price. We randomly assigned participants to (a) bid on the object for themselves, (b) bid on the object for another person, or (c) no instructions on the target of the bidding. Replicating Experiment 1, when bidding on the object for themselves, high-power individuals bid higher than low-power individuals. In contrast, when bidding for another person, low-power individuals bid higher than high-power individuals. Finally, when the recipient of the object was not made salient, there were no differences in bidding behavior among low and high power participants.

The final experiment sought to provide evidence for the notion that it was the enhanced psychological value of others or one's self that led to the differential spending of high and low power individuals. Power was manipulated through a real hierarchical role whereby participants were assigned to take the role of an employee or boss in an upcoming task. It was made clear that in the upcoming interaction the boss (employee) had complete control (no control) over the employee (boss) in terms of how the task would be conducted. However, prior to this task, participants took part in a study on purchasing behavior. In this study, participants were randomly assigned to a task that allowed them to purchase a number of chocolates for themselves or another person. When participants were purchasing for themselves, individuals purchased significantly more chocolates when assigned to the high as opposed to low power condition. In contrast, when participants were purchasing for another person, individuals purchased more chocolates when assigned to the low as opposed to high power condition. In addition, mediation analyses revealed that high power increased self-importance and self-importance uniquely mediated the effects of power on spending on self. In contrast, low power increased dependence on others, and dependence on others uniquely mediated the effect of power on spending on others.

Overall, these studies support our proposition that perceived control, through power shifts the psychological value placed on oneself and others and consequently affect how much people are willing to spend on themselves or others.

### "Mere Influence Effect: When Motivation to Influence Drives Decision"

Xianchi Dai, Leilei Gao, Chinese University of Hong Kong, China

Baba Shiv, Stanford University, USA

People want to make sure that they live a meaningful life and they have control over the environment around them. One way to realize these dreams is to show that their actions can have some impact on others, the environment, and the world. We propose that this motivation to influence, independent of hedonic considerations of the choice options, can systematically affect decision making.

To demonstrate the *mere influence effect*, imagine a person is voting for one of two presidential candidates. In a close election, voting for the leading candidate (i.e., the slightly favored candidate as revealed by the poll) will most likely help to maintain the trend and increase the leading candidate's winning margin. If the person votes for the challenger (i.e. the slightly disfavored candidate), however, her vote could potentially be the "critical vote" that reverse the result. Voting for the challenger thus has a higher likelihood of making an influence. On the other hand, in a large-margin or one-sided election, it is highly unlikely to change the election result with one more vote for the challenger. Comparatively, voting for the leading candidate is an influence-maximizing action because the voter can at least entertain herself that she is on the winning side.

Based on the above reasoning, we predict that in a close competition, those who care more about influence are more likely than those who care less to vote for the challenger, whereas in a large-margin or one-sided election, the reverse would be true. More generally, we propose that the motivation to make an influence can systematically affect decision making independent of hedonic considerations of the choice options. We demonstrate the mere influence effect on decision making in four studies.

In the first two studies we showed that in a close competition higher motivation to influence leads to greater preference for slightly less favored option (by others). In study 1, participants were asked to vote for two traffic control programs varying in cost and effectiveness. We manipulated the influence potential of the voting results. We found that if the voting result was the sole determinant of which of the two traffic improvement programs to implement, participants were more likely to favor the slightly less supported program; whereas when the voting result was said be an unimportant piece of information for the policy makers, participants were equally likely to support both programs. Study 2 adopted the same context but manipulating influence by priming participants' need to influence. Those who were primed with high need to influence were more likely to favor the slightly less supported program than those low in this need.

Study 3 and 4 further demonstrated that the margins of the competition moderate the effect of need for influence on consumer preference. In study 3, participants were informed that $100 (real money) would be donated to a foundation to save endangered animal species and they were asked to vote for an animal species (from two candidates) as the beneficiary. Participants were further informed of the "voting statistics" based on previous participants' votes. Half of the participants were told that the supporting rates were 49% versus 51% for the two animals (a close competition), the other half were told 31% versus 69%. Our proposition was supported. In the small margin conditions (counterbalanced options), those who had stronger motivation to influence were more likely to vote for the less favored animal and the reverse was true in the large margin condition. In the final study we asked more than 2000 randomly selected senior citizens to recall their actual voting behavior in the past 4 US presidential elections. We also measured their individual levels of motivation for influence and other individual characteristics. Consistent with our theorizing, in the 1996 (Clinton vs. Dole) and 2008 (Obama vs. McCain) presidential elections, which we pretested (and were predicted by national polls) to be easy wins, those who had stronger motivation to influence were more likely to vote for the leading candidates; whereas in the 2000 (Bush vs. Gore) and 2004 (Bush vs. Kerry) presidential elections, which were predicted to be close games, those who had stronger motivation to influence were more likely to vote for the challenging candidates.

Overall, these studies support our proposition of the mere influence effect. The fact that people are motivated to influence others and the environment is consistent with a general psychological tendency of seeking control to cope in an uncertain world.

## "Control Deprivation and Compensatory Shopping"

*Charlene Y. Chen, Columbia University, USA*
*Leonard Lee, Columbia University, USA*
*Andy J. Yap, Columbia University, USA*

Control motivation is a dynamic and ubiquitous force that potentially reacts to everyday events. Violation of the basic need for control can provoke distress that initiates efforts to reassert control. Considering the abundance of opportunities people encounter in contemporary society to acquire goods and services, could consumer spending be an avenue via which control-deprived individuals attempt to recover their sense of control? This research examines whether control deprivation results in compensatory shopping behavior. In contrast with self-control that has been the focus of recent literature, "control" here refers to a more general notion involving control over external circumstances. We propose that people shop and spend more when they experience a weakened sense of control. This hypothesis runs counter to the view that control deprivation would engender passivity and withdrawal that could lead to reduced spending

Experiment 1 was designed to establish the effect of control deprivation on compensatory shopping in a field setting—a local supermarket. Regular shoppers (N=192) were recruited as they entered the store to participate in a short study in exchange for a $2-coupon. Before they commenced shopping, participants were randomly assigned to one of three conditions: they were asked to write about (1) an incident in which they had experienced a loss of control (LC condition), (2) one in which they had experienced a sense of control (HC condition), or (3) a typical day during the past month (baseline condition). After shopping, they handed their receipts to a research assistant to redeem the coupon.

Consistent with our hypothesis, LC participants spent significantly more than participants in both the HC and baseline conditions. Importantly, expenditure was not significantly different between the latter two conditions, thus indicating that control deprivation increased spending. Further analysis revealed that LC participants bought more items, particularly utilitarian products, than both the HC and baseline participants. However, the number of hedonic products purchased did not differ across conditions. To rule out the alternative explanation that differential spending across conditions was due to different emotions induced by the control manipulation, participants' writings were content analyzed by two independent raters for ten different affective states (i.e., anxious, fearful, sad, ashamed, frustrated, angry, disgusted, contented, happy, and excited). After controlling for these emotions (separately or in clusters through factor analysis), the control manipulation exerted the same effect on spending. Together, these results suggest that increased spending (particularly in potentially order-restoring utilitarian products) can serve as a strategy for individuals to regain a sense of control.

Experiment 2 was designed to conceptually replicate this effect within a controlled lab environment, while testing the underlying mechanism by relying on an individual-difference factor: need for cognitive closure (NFCC). Prior research has shown that, compared to low-NFCC individuals, high-NFCC individuals are more motivated to reach firm conclusions swiftly, and more averse toward ambiguity and unpredictability. Therefore, we expect high-NFCC individuals to be more sensitive toward control deprivation and to exhibit a higher tendency to compensate through spending when their sense of control is reduced.

In experiment 2, after completing the NFCC-Scale and a filler task, participants (N=60) were manipulated to experience either a momentary sense of control or not using the same recall task in experiment 1. As a token of our appreciation for their participation, they were then invited to shop at a store in the lab purportedly unrelated to the experiment. A variety of eight items comprising both hedonic and utilitarian products with prices ranging from $0.50-$5 (e.g., chocolates and school supplies) were offered for sale; participants were told that these products were experimental stimuli from previous studies sold at discounted prices. While each participant shopped, a research assistant (blind to the assigned conditions) recorded the number of items examined by the participant and rated the participant's involvement on a five-point scale.

As hypothesized, LC participants spent more than HC participants. LC participants also bought more utilitarian products than HC participants. In addition, LC participants examined more items in the store, and were more involved in the shopping process. Furthermore, there was a significant interaction effect between control and participants' NFCC scores. In particular, among high-NFCC participants, those in the LC group spent significantly more than those in the HC group. However, among low-NFCC participants, there was no significant difference in spending between both LC and HC participants. The interaction between control and NFCC also significantly predicted the number of utilitarian products purchased, with the pattern of interaction similar to that found for expenditure.

In sum, our findings demonstrate a compensatory mechanism that operates in response to control deprivation. In particular, shopping seems to serve as a strategy that individuals adopt when their sense of control is undermined. What remains uncertain however is which aspect(s) of the complex shopping process (e.g., browsing, selecting, spending, and consuming) help consumers regain their sense of control. Additionally, future research should also appraise the efficacy of consumer spending as a compensatory strategy. Specifically, personal control could be measured after spending to evaluate whether control is restored to initial levels before control deprivation.

**"Power and Choice: A Compensatory Theory of Control"**
*Simona Botti, London Business School, UK*
*M. Ena Inesi, London Business School, UK*

Research has shown that the provision and exercise of choice is an important means through which consumers experience control and its corresponding benefits, such as increased motivation, better mood, and greater satisfaction. More recent findings have demonstrated that choice is not always beneficial: Participants who chose one option from among undifferentiated alternatives were only as satisfied as those who were randomly assigned the same option, and participants who chose from among differentiated but undesirable alternatives were even more dissatisfied. While prima facie, these results seem to undermine the relation between choice and control, they actually provide additional evidence that the effects of choice on consumer well-being depend on the associated perceived control. When choosing among undifferentiated alternatives, participants felt less in control of the eventual quality of the outcome, which mitigated their satisfaction; when choosing among differentiated but undesirable alternatives they felt in control of an aversive outcome, blamed themselves for it, and experienced greater dissatisfaction.

Choice is not, however, the only way in which individuals can attain perceived control. The literature has suggested a theoretical link between control and power in that power has been defined as the capacity to control other people. Indeed, recent research has empirically proved that powerlessness leads to perceived loss of control and power to the experience of control.

Although choice and power both seem to provide a sense of control, their interactive effect on people's welfare has not been studied in prior research. What if people could achieve a sense of control both through the exercise of choice and the provision of power? We hypothesize a compensatory hypothesis for this interactive effect of power and choice according to which power and choice compensate for each other in satisfying people's need for control.

We tested this hypothesis in two studies. Study 1 investigated whether the absence of choice affects high-power participants less negatively than neutral-power participants. We used a recall task to either provide participants with a sense of power or leave them in a neutral state. Participants then engaged in an alleged second study, in which they imagined having dinner at a restaurant where they could choose their menu or where the chef had chosen a fixed menu. Participants indicated how much they liked the choice process they had experienced and how satisfied they thought they would be with the meal. Results support our compensatory hypothesis. High-power participants liked choosing their own meal as much as having the chef choosing it for them, whereas neutral-power participants liked choosing their own meal more than having the chef choose it for them. High-power participants also thought they would be as satisfied with the self-chosen meal as with the chef-chosen meal, whereas neutral-power participants thought they would be more satisfied with a self-chosen than with a chef-chosen meal. Providing further support to the idea that those in power were less affected by the loss of choice, high-power participants reported greater liking for the choice process and greater expected satisfaction than neutral-power participants in the chef-choice condition, but not in the self-choice condition.

Study 2 provided direct evidence of control as the mechanism for this compensatory effect. Following prior research, after manipulating power and choice we provided participants the opportunity to regain perceived control with an anagram task. We predicted that, relative to higher-power participants, lower-power participants would attempt to regain perceived control by persisting more on the anagram task when deprived of choice. Participants were first randomly assigned to a high- or low-power condition by telling them that they would simulate either the role of "Boss" or "employee" in an organization. Next, they participated in a taste-test for the snack options in their fictional organization's cafeteria. Participants in the choice condition chose which snack to eat, whereas those in the no-choice condition tasted a randomly selected snack. The last task was described as simulating a challenging situation at work consisting of unscrambling twenty anagrams which varied in difficulty (length). We measured persistence by recording how long participants spent on the last three anagrams, since persistence is most evident with fatigue. Consistent with prior literature, participants persisted longer on the final anagrams when they were randomly assigned a snack compared to when they had choice. The effect of choice was, however, weaker for high-power than for low-power participants: whereas the choice method significantly affected persistence in the low-power condition, it did not affect persistence in the high-power condition. Consistent with our theory, this interaction was stronger for the more difficult, 7-letter anagram, than for the easier, 3-letter anagram.

In summary, two studies support the hypothesis that choice and power compensate for each other in providing consumers with a sense of control. Lower-power participants were more sensitive toward a loss of choice than higher-power participants and, consistently, tried harder to regain control when deprived of choice.

# Adaptation Can Enhance Consumption Experiences

Young Eun Huh, Carnegie Mellon University, USA

Joachim Vosgerau, Carnegie Mellon University, USA

## EXTENDED ABSTRACTS

### "Thought for Food: Top-down Processes Moderate Sensory-Specific Satiation"

*Young Eun Huh, Carnegie Mellon University, USA*

*Carey Morewedge, Carnegie Mellon University, USA*

*Joachim Vosgerau, Carnegie Mellon University, USA*

Hedonic adaptation (Fredrickson and Loewenstein 1999) denotes the typically observed decline in pleasure when positive consumption experiences are repeated. In food consumption, it has been shown that consumption of a specific food leads to a decrease in liking of the food, without diminishing liking of foods not consumed. Such food specific adaptation is called sensory-specific satiation (Rolls, Rowe, and Roll 1982; Rolls, Rolls, Rowe, and Sweeney 1981). People typically react to sensory-specific satiation by switching to alternatives or consuming less (Herrnstein and Prelec 1991; McAlister 1982).

Whereas extant research on satiation has focused on the impact of initial consumption on the pleasure from subsequent consumption, this research focuses on the effect of imagined consumption on subsequent actual consumption. Mental imagery has been found to produce similar physiological responses (e.g., Brandt and Stark 1997; Huber and Krist, 2004), neurological processes (Kosslyn, Ganis, and Thompson 2001), and behavioral responses (e.g., Garcia, Weaver, Moskowitz, and Darley 2002; Woldmann, Healy, and Bourne 2007) as the actual consumption experience. If imagined consumption can act as a substitute for the sensory experience of consuming a food, imagining consuming a food should, like actual consumption of the food, lead to a decrease in its subsequent actual consumption. We investigated this possibility in five studies.

In study 1, participants were assigned to one of three conditions. In the control condition, participants imagined inserting 33 quarters into a laundry machine, one at a time. Participants in the small virtual consumption condition imagined inserting 30 quarters into a laundry machine and then imagined eating 3 M&M's. Participants in the large virtual consumption condition imagined inserting 3 quarters into a laundry machine and then imagined eating 30 M&M's (so in all conditions participants imagined 33 repetitive actions). After their imagination task, participants were given a bowl containing 40g of M&M's and ate as many M&M's as they would like to. Participants who imagined eating 30 M&M's ate significantly fewer M&M's than did participant who imagined eating 3 M&M's or no M&M's. Moreover, the amount of M&M's eaten in participants who imagined eating 3 M&M's or no M&M's did not significantly differ between conditions. These results suggest that imagined consumption of a food leads to virtual satiation rather than a whetting effect.

In study 2, we orthogonally manipulated imagined consumption experience (eating M&M's vs. inserting quarters into a laundry machine) and the amount of imagined consumption (3 M&M's/quarters vs. 30 M&M's/quarters) between-subjects. Participants who imagined eating thirty M&M's subsequently consumed fewer M&M's than participants who imagined eating three M&M's. No difference was found for respondents who imagined inserting thirty or three quarters into a laundry machine.

Study 3 employed a 2 (imagined consumption experience: eating M&M's vs. putting M&M's into a bowl) x 2 (amount of imagined consumption: 3 M&M's vs. 30 M&M's) between-subjects

design. As in the previous studies, participants who imagined eating thirty M&M's consumed significantly fewer M&M's than did participants who imagined eating three M&M's. The amount of M&M's eaten by participants who imagined putting 3 M&M's or 30 M&M's into a bowl did not differ. This finding demonstrates that virtual satiation is indeed caused by the imagined experience (consumption vs. putting M&M's into bowl) rather than the imagined stimuli (which were constant across experimental conditions).

An alternative explanation for the above results might be that participants who imagined eating many M&M's might have been primed to feel "full" and thus subsequently ate fewer M&M's. Study 4 ruled this out by employing a 2 (imagined consumption experience: eating M&M's vs. eating Gummi Bears) x 2(amount of imagined consumption: 3 M&M's/Gummi Bears vs. 30 M&M's/ Gummi Bears) between-subject design. Participants who imagined eating 30 M&M's ate fewer M&M's than participants who imagined eating three M&M's. Contrarily, participants who imagined eating 30 Gummi Bears ate more M&M's than those who imagined eating 3 Gummi Bears. These results demonstrate that imagined consumption induces sensory-specific satiation (as does actual food consumption) and not simply a feeling of being full.

Study 5 extended the findings to another food. Half of participants imagined eating 3 M&M's or 30 M&M's and the other half imagined eating 3 Cheese Cubes or 30 Cheese Cubes. Unlike the previous experiments, participants in Study 5 ate Cheese Cubes after their imagined consumption. Participants who imagined eating 30 Cheese Cubes ate less Cheese Cubes than those who imagined eating 3 Cheese Cubes. The amount of Cheese Cubes eaten by participants who imagined eating 3 M&M's or 30 M&M's did not differ.

The present research demonstrates that satiation can be induced without external stimuli through virtual consumption; thus, satiation is not only a consequence of physiological processes (a bottom-up process) but also involves cognitive "top-down" processes. We believe the foregoing research may help develop effective behavioral interventions to combat obesity. Thought suppression, a popular self-control method that many dieters use, has been shown to increase craving for the to be avoided food (Johnston, Bulik, & Anstiss 1999). Our research proposal examines whether the exact opposite may be most effective. Because people can habituate to a food by merely imagining eating it, willful and controlled imaginary consumption of foods that a dieter tries to avoid could be an effective way to decrease the appeal of, craving for, and intake of the food.

### "Motivated Taste Change for Diet Coke"

*Jason Riis, Harvard Business School, USA*

*Samuel McClure, Stanford University, USA*

While a number of studies have shown that changes in preference can occur with changes in consumption and exposure (Rozin, 1999), the question of whether taste change can be facilitated by motivation is more controversial (Loewenstein & Angner, 2003). Evidence for motivated taste change comes mostly from studies of dissonance, whereby people are thought to reduce negative feelings of disappointment by shifting their preferences to objects that happen to be in their possession (Brehm, 1956). In the present work, we investigate taste change that is motivated by concerns about health, and find that such concerns can influence awareness of taste change, and that this awareness has implications for future choice intentions.

The particular source of motivation that we investigate is the widespread concern about the health effects of sugared soda consumption. Obesity is considered by some public health experts to be the second leading cause of preventable death in America, and at least a third of American adults are attempting to lose weight (Kruger et al., 2004). Sugared sodas are thought to be one of the major contributors to the obesity epidemic, and diet sodas are rapidly gaining market share from sugared sodas.

Interestingly, many people claim that not only do they prefer diet soda because it is healthier, but that they also prefer the taste. In a pilot study with participants drawn from a paid, nationally representative panel, we found that 85% of the 120 frequent Diet Coke drinkers in the sample said that Diet Coke tasted better than regular Coke. More impressively, however, 70% of those who preferred the taste of Diet Coke said they used to prefer the taste of regular Coke. They also cited concerns about health and fitness, and not taste, as their original reason for switching to Diet Coke. These data are consistent with the possibility that concerns about health (i.e., motivation) led to an actual change in the liking of a product. Along these same lines, a recent Diet Coke ad even claims that, "It's the no calories that make it taste so good"

In the present studies we sought to test this possibility. In Study 1 we examined whether or not motivation is related to expectation of taste change. We hypothesized that it would be. People tend to be optimistic in their estimates of the likelihood of good outcomes (Weinstein, 1980). Since health-motivated people would be more likely to consider a taste improvement for a healthy product to be a good outcome, they should thus be more likely to expect this outcome to occur. This is indeed what we found. We asked 58 regular Coke drinkers to imagine that they were to drink Diet Coke daily for two weeks. The health-motivated participants predicted that their liking of Diet Coke would improve during such a trial, while the unmotivated participants predicted that they would come to like Diet Coke even less.

In Study 2 we actually examine taste change by exposing both motivated and unmotivated Coke drinkers to Diet Coke for two weeks. Based on previous mere exposure studies (e.g., Bertino et al., 1982, 1986), we expected blind taste tests to reveal increased liking of Diet Coke in both groups. In branded tests, however, we expected the groups to differ, with the motivated participants being more likely to report increased liking.

Participants were selected based on a pre-screening survey for heavy consumption of Coca Cola (mean of 3.8 cans per week) and for their level of concern about the effects of sugared soda on their health. Half of the participants were highly concerned (i.e., "motivated") and half were minimally concerned (i.e., "unmotivated"). The two groups did not differ in their soda consumption habits. Both groups were given a two week supply of Diet Coke, with the instruction to drink one can each day, and to refrain from drinking sugared soda. (Compliance, reported anonymously, was very high.) Participants were not asked about their expectations of taste change for fear that this would influence their subsequent reporting. Two kinds of taste tests were given, both at the beginning and end of the two week consumption period. In blind tests, participants drank several colas in clear, unlabelled plastic cups, and then rated the taste of each one on a 9 point scale (anchored at "dislike very much" and "like very much"). In "branded" taste tests, participants opened a can of Diet Coke, poured approximately one ounce into a clear plastic cup, tasted it, and then rated the taste using the same 9 point scale.

Both high-concern and low-concern participants revealed a large (4/5ths of a standard deviation) increase in liking of Diet Coke following the two-week consumption period. However, with the branded test, only the high concern participants revealed an increase in liking. Furthermore, the high concern subjects reported a greater increase in intention to purchase Diet Coke in the future. These results suggest that motivation for taste change may be independent of its actual occurrence, but that it may be required for awareness of its occurrence, and, importantly, for the intent to act on that taste change. The results do not isolate expectation as the mechanism of the motivational effect, although the results of Study 1 are consistent with this possibility.

### "Processing Fluency and Satiation"
*Jeff Galak, Carnegie Mellon University, USA*
*Joseph Redden, University of Minnesota, USA*

Consumers frequently consume products and experiences to the point where they no longer enjoy them, a process commonly referred to as "satiation" (Coombs and Avrunin 1977). This happens for a variety of stimuli ranging from the primarily physiological like food (Rolls, van Duijvenvoorde, and Rolls 1984) and sex (O'Donohue and Geer 1985), to the primarily non-physiological like music (Ratner, Kahn, and Kahneman 1999), television programs (Nelson, Meyvis, and Galak in press), art (Berlyne 1971), homes (Hsee et al. In Press), and cars (Frank 1999). In fact, satiation is often cited as a primary barrier to enduring happiness since, regardless of how satisfying a stimulus might be initially, that satisfaction tends to fade with repetition (Brickman and Campbell 1971).

One way to reduce unwanted satiation is to change the consumption experience. Prior work has shown that people satiate less when they consume slower (Galak, Kruger, and Loewenstein 2009), can more easily perceive the variety of an assortment being consumed (Kahn and Wansink 2004), or can subcategorize the consumption episodes (Raghunathan and Irwin 2000; Redden 2008). These approaches all act as preventive measures that slow satiation. In the present work, we instead explore remedies that can be used *after* satiation has occurred. If people can recover quickly and easily from a satiated state, then satiation poses a smaller problem for consumer enjoyment and happiness. In other words, people can fight satiation by either limiting it in the first place, or reversing it after the fact. We focus on the latter.

Past research has demonstrated that one antecedent to satiation is the degree to which an individual recalls past consumption experiences (Higgs 2002, 2008). We propose that while memory for past experiences is central in informing satiation, the subjective feeling of how much one has consumed is as, if not more, important. Specifically, we propose that when a person finds it particularly difficult to recall past consumption experiences, he or she will feel less satiated, as compared with someone who does not find the recall task difficult. For example, when a person attempts to recall many past consumption episodes, that recall task is subjectively difficult and he or she will feel like he or she has not consumed much—regardless of the fact that he or she may have recalled quite a number of past consumption episodes and thus should feel quite satiated. In contrast, a person who's task is to recall only a few past consumption episodes, will find the task relatively easy and thus infer that he or she has consumed a lot, leading to a heightened degree of satiation.

In Studies 1 and 2 we adapt the classic processing fluency paradigm from Schwartz et al. 1991. Participants recalled either the last 3 or 10 most recent television programs that they had seen (Study 1), or the last 2 or 6 times they consumed their favorite food (Study 2). We found that, presumably because it was subjectively more difficult to recall 10 television programs and 6 eating occasions, participants in the former conditions reported feeling less satiated even though they, in fact, recalled more instances.

In Study 3, satiation was induced in participants by exposing them to a photograph 20 times in a row (without explicit knowledge of how many times they were exposed to the photograph). Following this exposure and a short filler task, participants were asked to recall how many times they had seen the photograph with two different sets of response options created by adapting the paradigm from Schwartz et al. 1985. Participants in the *saw many (saw few)* condition answered the question with response options that ranged from "1-3 times" ("1-30 times") to "more than 15 times" ("more than 150 times"). Consistent with the first two studies, participants who were made to feel like they had seen the photo many times (*saw many*), felt more satiated than those who were made to feel like they had seen it few times (*saw few*). In summary, the subjective sense of how much one has consumed was a strong antecedent of satiation.

Across these three studies we demonstrate that feelings of satiation are malleable even after the consumption experience has ended and that they are informed based on the subjective sense of how much one has previously consumed.

## "The Role of Expectations in Unfolding Experiences"
*Jongmin Kim, Yale University, USA*
*Ravi Dhar, Yale University, USA*
*Nathan Novemsky, Yale University, USA*

Suppose you bought a present for your friend, and the store offered an option of gift wrapping at additional cost, or suppose your waiter in a restaurant suggested a glass of a special champagne before your meal. Would accepting these offers enhance the enjoyment of the gift or the meal, respectively? People generally believe that adding positive aspects to an experience will make the experience better. Therefore, we wrap gifts attractively to raise enjoyment of the gifts, and sometimes have a glass of champagne before a meal to make the experience better. Of course, adding positive features to the beginning of an experience can increase enjoyment of the experience, but it can also trigger unexpected effects. Positive moments early in an experience can establish high expectations against which the subsequent moments are compared, leading to a worse overall experience.

A large body of research has demonstrated that hedonic experiences can be contrasted with a prior expectation when there is a discrepancy between the expectation and the actual experience. Drawing from research on this expectation-disconfirmation model, we propose that adding positive moments early in an experience may result in lower satisfaction if subsequent moments in the experience do not meet the high expectations set by the early moments. For example, gift wrapping can decrease the liking of the gift, and great tasting champagne can detract from the rest of the dinner by establishing high expectations that are not met.

Study 1a examines people's lay beliefs about the effects of wrapping on evaluations of gifts. The results show that people believe gift wrapping increases liking of a gift regardless of the attractiveness of the gift (e.g. attractive DVD: the Lord of the Rings or unattractive DVD: Microcosmos documentary). Study 1b compares the enjoyment of wrapped and unwrapped presents to test the accuracy of the beliefs documented in study 1a. In study 1b, participants evaluated a hypothetical gift from a friend in a 2(wrapped vs. unwrapped) X 2(attractive vs. unattractive gift) between subjects design. Participants in the wrapped condition were told that their friend gave them a birthday present and were shown a picture of an appealing wrapped gift box. On the next page, participants imagined that they found a DVD set when they opened the wrapping. People in the unwrapped condition simply imagined that their friend gave them a DVD set as a present. Half of the participants in each condition were told the DVD set was the Lord

of the Rings (attractive condition) or Microcosmos documentary (unattractive condition). The results showed that for the attractive gift, participants showed a non-significant trend toward liking the gift more when it was wrapped compared to unwrapped. However, for the unattractive gift, participants liked the gift significantly *less* in the wrapped condition than the unwrapped condition. This result partially contradicts the lay beliefs in study 1a that gift wrapping raises evaluations of both attractive and unattractive gifts.

The result of Study 1b supports our proposition that appealing gift wrapping sets high expectation for the gift and can decrease the evaluation of unattractive gifts. In Study 2, we manipulate the level of expectations established by using both appealing and unappealing gift wrapping to test whether setting low expectations compared to high expectations can raise evaluations of unattractive gifts. Participants in Study 2 imagined that they received a birthday present and were shown a picture of either an appealingly or unappealingly wrapped gift box. Participants then imagined that they found the Microcosmos (unattractive) DVD inside the wrapping and evaluated the gift. The results showed that participants liked the gift *more* in the unappealing wrapped condition than the appealing wrapped condition. This result is consistent with our prediction that unappealing gift wrapping sets low expectations leaving recipients less likely to be disappointed with the unattractive gift.

Study 1a suggests that when people predict the impact of gift wrapping they do not incorporate the idea that gift wrapping establishes expectations against which the gift is compared. In Study 3, we examine whether erroneous prediction for gift wrapping documented in Study 1a can be corrected by providing a cue to think about expectations. Participants predicted the impact of gift wrapping in a 2 (cue vs no-cue) X 2(attractive vs. unattractive gift) between subjects design. All the participants were asked to consider receiving both an appealingly wrapped and an unwrapped present from a friend. Participants in the cue condition answered a question about when they would set a higher expectation for the gift between the two situations: receiving a wrapped vs. unwrapped gift. Participants in the no-cue condition were not asked such a question. Next, participants imagined that they found either the Lord of the Rings (attractive) or Microcomos (unattractive) DVD when they opened the wrapping. The results demonstrated that for the attractive gift, participants in both the cue and no-cue conditions believed that appealing gift wrapping would raise liking of the gift. For the unattractive DVD, however, providing a cue significantly changed participants' prediction. Participants in the cue condition were less likely to predict that gift wrapping will increase liking of the gift than those in the no-cue condition. This result suggests that people do not spontaneously consider expectation in prediction, but when their attention was drawn to expectations, they make more accurate predictions.

In summary, we find that appealing gift wrapping can decrease evaluations of a gift by setting high expectations. Using less appealing gift wrapping can actually set lower expectations and thereby enhance evaluations of a gift. However, people often fail to accurately predict this trend because they do not think about expectations spontaneously. Once reminded to consider expectations, however, people incorporate expectations into their predictions.

# Partners in Sustainability:
## Consumer Culture Theory Approaches to Personal and Social Transformation

Melea Press, University of Wyoming, USA
Robert V. Kozinets, York University, Canada

## EXTENDED ABSTRACTS

### "Social Media for Social Change: Sustainability-based Community in a Sustainable World"

*Robert V. Kozinets, York University, Canada*
*Frank-Martin, Belz,Technische Universität München, Germany*

As of 2010, the important role of social media in fostering and facilitating consumer engagement in political and marketing campaigns, and in facilitating other forms of activism are indelibly established. This presentation seeks to consolidate, broaden, and develop the view that social media and online communities can be useful sites of social betterment that consumer researchers should include in their studies.

We place our presentation in the context of sustainability concerns, and contribute to this literature by charting the intersections between social media and sustainable consumption. Overridingly, our concern is a practical one. How might online communities and their constituents help foster a more sustainable consumption style and a more sustainable consumer culture? This is a large question; in this session we aim to start the discussion by recognizing and connecting research streams, offering initial findings, and suggesting particular paths.

The presentation has three main sections. First, there is an overview of extant research on social media with a focus on the alleviation of social problems and the promotion of consumer behaviors that lead to self- or social betterment. Research in the area increasingly suggests that online communities act as locations for the personal and collective enactment of social betterment. Our necessarily broad and brief overview looks at three broad categories of social media-social connection: (1) altering institutional relationships, (2) offering emotional benefits, and (3) encouraging social involvement. We provide numerous references and pragmatic examples about these institutional, emotional, and social effects, across a variety of cases.

Next we consider the relationship of online communities –and online/offline community combinations—to issues of ecological orientation or sustainability. We explore how the role of local, involved, engaged communities has been increasingly invoked as the key to the transition to a more ecologically sustainable society. We are concerned with the specific and more generalizable role of intentional communities, which are widely viewed and held up publicly as a hotbed of political innovation and organized political influence.

We then offer initial observations and findings from netnographic and blended ethnographic/netnographic fieldwork on several of these communities in Europe and North America. Our initial findings regarding sustainability-oriented social media tell us four things. First, social media help consumers focus their awareness and attention together on particular options. Second, social media carry conservative values, in that they seek to foster more traditional forms of community. Third, online and offline media and community work together in new, important, and evolving ways. Finally, a "customizing" and "segmenting" of communal types of participation was evident in the diverse space of the Internet. As we continue to collect data and analyze it (the next stage of data collection is from June-September 2010), we expect these initial findings to deepen and broaden.

### "Transformative Outcomes of Identification Formation and Narrative Transparency"

*Melea Press, University of Wyoming, USA*
*Eric J. Arnould, University of Wyoming, USA*

Moving toward greater sustainability at any level of society (individual, community, institutional) involves transformations on an individual and collective level. Transformations have been discussed in literature on consumption communities, in policy literature, and in managerial literature. Furthermore, some have shown that the relationships built between constituents and organizations can be evocative and transformational (McAlexander, Schouten and Koenig 2002), yet the process of how these connections form has not been explored.

This presentation will look at both sides of identification formation, and how identification can lead individuals down the road towards meaningful connections with organizations, and ultimately to personal transformation, in this case towards more sustainable consumption patterns. From the constituent side, we will examine what drives these relationships to form and the value and behavior change that ensue. Then, from the organizational side, we look at what drives constituents toward the organization. We show that narrative (as opposed to measured) transparency and connection to long-standing cultural values provide a route for constituents to form meaningful relationships with organizations.

First, with data from constituents in two different contexts, we present a model of identification formation. The first data set contains 18 longitudinal interviews with members of a Community Supported Agriculture program, and the second data set contains 41 cross-sectional interviews with employees of an advertising agency. Using this new theoretical framework that brings together the concepts of identification formation and participation, we show three different modes of identification formation: Epiphany, Assimilation, and Exploration. We also show two conduits for participation, that is, through formal and informal means, and we reveal the role of productive consumption in personal transformation. We then demonstrate that when individuals identify with an organization, they take on the values of the organization as illustrated by individual behavior change.

Next, we use a third data set compiled from 50 Community Supported Agriculture websites to illustrate the importance of narrative transparency in expressing the values of the organizations to constituents. Transparency information is typically communicated through reporting of facts and figures. On CSA websites, we find that transparency is communicated through personal narrative, that is, through detailed and personal stories of activities on the farm. This data set also reveals the inadvertent way organizations connect to deeply held cultural values to build meaningful relationships with constituents, as well as legitimacy for the market form.

This research shows processes on both the constituent and the organization side of identification formation. It also shows how individuals transform their values and behaviors through closer relationships with model organizations.

**References**

McAlexander, James H., John W. Schouten, and Harold Koenig (2002), "Building Brand Community," *Journal of Marketing,* 66 (January), 38-54.

This page intentionally left blank.

*(Papers not presented at the conference)*

SPECIAL SESSION
# Partners, Masters, Friends, and Flings: Exploring the Multiple Roles of Brand Relationships

Vanitha Swaminathan, University of Pittsburgh, USA
Susan Fournier, Boston University, USA

## EXTENDED ABSTRACTS

### "Partners and Servants: Adopting Traits of Anthropomorphized Brands"

*Pankaj Aggarwal, University of Toronto, Canada*
*Ann L. McGill, University of Chicago, USA*

Research in social psychology has shown that automatic or non-conscious behavior may result from the activation of a social category. For example, Bargh, Chen, and Burroughs (1996) found that priming the construct of the 'elderly' led to participants walking more slowly since the elderly are strongly associated with the trait of being slow. Recent research by Fitzsimons, Chartrand, and Fitzsimons (2008) found that participants exposed to the Apple brand behaved more creatively, and those exposed to the Disney brand responded more honestly to questions compared to controls. These results are interesting in that they show that effects previously observed for social constructs replicate in the domain of brands.

In this research, we argue that one reason for this effect may be that the iconic brands studied by Fitszimons et al. (2008) were perceived much like people, that is, respondents may have anthropomorphized those brands. If this argument is correct, it implies that by anthropomorphizing brands, consumers open the door to "quasi social influences" in which brands elicit effects previously seen for responses to people. We examine this possibility by considering differences in the adoption of traits for brands that have been anthropomorphized or not. We assume that "trait adoption," a shorthand term for behaving in ways consistent with the characteristic of the brand, follows a motivational process such that the behavior adopted in response to brand exposure is goal-directed. To inform our theory, we rely on work by Cesario, Plaks, and Higgins (2006) who demonstrate that priming a social group triggers goals corresponding to people's desire for a successful social interaction. People adopt or reject a trait to the extent that the corresponding behavior achieves these interaction goals. Thus, priming 'elderly' led participants who like the category to walk more slowly, but if they disliked the category they walked faster presumably to get away (Cesario et al. 2006).

To test this framework, we propose two moderators of trait adoption for anthropomorphized (but not objectified) brands which determine the best route to achieve the goal of a successful social interaction. These moderators are liking for the brand, and perceived role for the brand—as a partner or as a servant. Consumers may adopt traits of anthropomorphized brands perceived as partners if they like them because in this case, trait adoption–acting the same way as the brand–promotes getting along with and helping the partner. By contrast, consumers reject traits of anthropomorphized partner brands if they dislike them because rejecting the trait pushes them away. Further, consumers reject traits of servant brands they like because successful interaction involves letting the servant "take care of the work." For example, consumers who see an anthropomorphized Volvo as a servant devoted to their safety may actually behave in riskier ways than those who see Volvo as a partner in safety. On the other hand, brands that are not anthropomorphized would not be affected by liking or role because the goals of successful social interaction are not triggered for objects, making the relevance and impact of these social factors inconsequential.

We test our proposed framework in three studies. In study 1, we consider two partner brands, Kellogg's and Krispy Kreme, near opposites on the healthy-unhealthy spectrum. Using an un-related dependent variable that taps into people's healthy (taking the stairs) or unhealthy (waiting for the elevator) behavior, we find consumers to be more likely to adopt the trait when they like the anthropomorphized brand, and reject the trait when they dislike it. In study 2, we consider two servant brands: Volvo (associated with safety) and Discovery Channel (associated with knowledge). We find consumers to be less likely to adopt the trait when they liked the anthropomorphized brand, and more likely to adopt the associated trait when they disliked it as evidenced by differences in unrelated tasks such as certainty equivalence for a risky gamble (Volvo) and responses to a set of SAT questions (Discovery Channel). In study 3, we manipulated perceived role of the brand, Volvo, under the pretext of testing two alternative advertising slogans that portrayed it either as a partner (works with you) or a servant (works for you). Results replicate the main effect in a more controlled environment.

This research is significant in its examination of an important yet an under-studied phenomenon in marketing–brand anthropomorphism. To our knowledge this is the first research that looks at the moderating effect of brand role on consumer's goals and subsequent behavior. Thus, this research contributes to an emerging literature that highlights the value of understanding how inanimate objects may extend into our social realm.

### "Bridging the Divide: Identity Expression with Brands Following a Self-Threat"

*Sara Loughran, University of Pittsburgh, USA*
*Vanitha Swaminathan, University of Pittsburgh, USA*

Since Belk (1988) introduced the concept of possessions "extending the self," a vast amount of research has confirmed that because consumers identify with objects, they use possessions to create and narrate their identities (Kleine, Kleine, and Allen 1995). In this research, we show that when individuals experience anxiety in their interpersonal relationships, they use objects and brands that assert their in-group identities as a way of coping, which leads to increases in the valuations of these objects and brands. Relationship anxiety is a function of an individual's view of self (Bartholomew and Horowitz 1991). Individuals with high relationship anxiety desire close relationships but yet are unsure about whether they can depend on others. They are characterized by a fear of rejection and abandonment and describe their most important interpersonal relationships in terms of jealousy, longing for reciprocation, and emotional highs and lows.

One way of coping with this anxiety is to gravitate towards objects and brands that help restore confidence in the social self (Gao, Wheeler, and Shiv 2009; Swaminathan, Stilley and Ahluwalia 2009). In study 1, undergraduate student participants (N=149) began by writing either about an anxious relationship they had experienced (relationship anxiety group)) or their average day (control group). Following this manipulation, respondents participated in a typical endowment effect experiment (Kahneman, Knetsch, and Thaler 1990), assuming the role of buyers and sellers of one of three ball point pens: one from their university (in-group good), one from a rival university (out-group good), or one that was non-descript (neutral good).

*Advances in Consumer Research*
*Volume 38, © 2012*

Comparing the selling prices for the in-group object, we find that those in the relationship anxiety condition had significantly greater selling prices than those in the control condition. In the out-group condition, a different pattern emerges. In the no relationship anxiety condition, the standard endowment effect occurs with participants reporting greater selling prices than buying. In the high anxiety condition, for the outgroup good, sellers and buyers did not report different prices from one another. It appears that relationship anxiety decreased selling prices for an out-group object. For the neutral good condition, we observed the classic endowment effect in both the control condition and the relationship anxiety condition. Relationship anxiety had no effect on either selling prices or buying prices of the neutral good.

In study 2, participants (N=261) in a nationally representative panel completed the same anxiety manipulation and then responded to a variety of questions regarding attitudes toward one of two given brands: DKNY (feminine) or Levi's (masculine). In this study, therefore, in-group/out-group was manipulated using the gender of respondents and the personality (masculinity/femininity dimension) of the brands. We first tested an ANOVA using social self-concept connection to the brands as our dependent variable. The interaction of anxiety and in-group was significant ($F(1, 253)=11.94, p<.001$). In the in-group brand condition, high anxiety lead to greater social self-concept connection compared to low anxiety. In the out-group brand condition, however, high anxiety lead to lower self-concept connection compared to low anxiety. We ran a similar ANOVA using willingness to pay for the brands as the dependent variable. Once again, only the interaction of in-group brand and anxiety was significant ($F(1, 250)=8.61, p<.01$). High anxiety led to greater willingness-to-pay for the in-group brand compared to low anxiety, and a lower willingness-to-pay for an out-group brand compared to low anxiety. Further analysis revealed that social self-concept connection mediated the effect of the interaction of in-group brand and anxiety on willingness-to-pay (Sobel's Z-score=1.97, $p<.05$). Implications of the findings for brand relationship theory will be discussed.

### "Brand Flings and the Transitional Self"
*Susan Fournier, Boston University, USA*
*Claudio Alvarez, Boston University, USA*

This study advances the brand relationship agenda by providing a phenomenological illumination of one unexplored relationship: brand flings (cf. Fournier 1998). As an analytic device, the research also contributes to brand relationship theory validation efforts by exploring the differences and similarities between brand and person-to-person flings.

Sixteen phenomenological interviews provide data for this investigation. Informants in half of the interviews discussed flings with brands; eight discussed flings with other people. Informants were men and women between the ages of 18-35. Gender was equally distributed to capture potential differences in how men and women experience flings. Informants were pre-recruited via telephone to ascertain their resonance with, and ability to discuss, the subject of human (brand) flings. A homework assignment instructed informants to select and bring to the interview "5-6 images that express your thoughts and feelings about having a fling with a (person/brand)." These images provided a structure around which the interviews unfolded. Interviews lasted from 2-3 hours, and were conducted by a mixed gender, 3-person team.

Our analysis suggests four emerging themes qualifying brand flings. Most characteristic is the emotionality of the fling experience. A deep sense of satisfaction and tremendous amount of excitement, passion, and enjoyment characterizes the playful brand

encounters that launch and sustain the fling. Secondly, some degree of obsession is embedded in the fling relationship, with significant investments of time, energy and attention dedicated to the brand. A third theme concerns a lack of rationality and sense of being out-of-control. Finally, a brand fling is temporary and time-bounded (though brand flings can recur). People experiencing brand flings are excited and obsessed but only for a while, after which time feelings and meanings taper almost unnoticeably as the person simply moves on. Our analysis highlights significant contrasts between brand flings and person-to-person flings. Person-to-person flings are most characteristically associated with freedom from commitment, and are surrounded by an aura of secrecy that derives from a sense of cultural taboo.

Collectively, thematic results support a role for brand flings that is analogous to the role played by transitional objects in psychoanalytic theories of child and adult development (Winnicott 1971). Brand flings open up a creative space in consumers' daily lives where people establish object relations that allow them to experiment playfully with different senses of self. Importantly, flings allow engagement with the concept of "not me," a pivotal idea in object attachment theory. Consumers have flings with brands they typically don't buy; brands not recognized as reflecting a known self. This separation from "the me" emerges as a fundamental goal of having a brand fling: to be taken out of ordinary life and away from the established self, if only for a brief moment or phase. Brand flings deliver squarely against Winnicott's (1971) idea of the "potential space" existing between the "me" and the "not-me" that forms as an individual develops and grows.

The transitional self activated via transitional brand flings is fundamentally different from other self conceptualizations explored in brand relationship research: ideal selves (Sirgy 1982), feared selves (Fournier 1998), and possible selves (Schouten 1991). Flings are simply not that consequential: the motivation to engage in flings comes less from one particular self image that is desired/feared/speculated than from the opportunity to leave the current self behind. "I am looking for a new excitement in something", as one informant explains. To a certain extent, what this "something" is doesn't matter much as long as it is new and different. Flings serve as transitional object relations that help consumers create and play with transitional selves.

This study supports brand flings as a relevant mechanism for consumer-brand engagement and provides a solid conceptual foundation for future research. The "potential space" filled by brand flings is a vital area in the mental life of the developing person. This finding is significant as prior research supports brands as replacements for under-realized interpersonal relationships, not valued relational objects in and of themselves. Research can explore the value of flings over partnerships in delivering brand attraction, willingness to pay, emotional commitment, and favorable brand experiences. The qualities of addiction and dependence evoked by transitional objects (Winnicott 1971) also suggest relationship maintenance in the face of stresses and strains. Transitional objects also serve as a defense against anxiety, and operate as soothing, comfort mechanisms in times of loneliness, deprivation or depressive moods, thus suggesting a role for brand flings as coping mechanisms when the anxious self is primed. Since transitional object relations occur at predictable developmental moments (e.g., the child becoming a separate individual, the teen becoming a young adult, the young adult becoming a parent), research can also investigate whether there exist productive, targetable periods for brand fling experiences along similar developmental lines.

### "Brand Are Like Friends: Goals and Interpersonal Motives Influence Attitudes Toward Preferred Brands"

*Christopher R. Long, Ouachita Baptist University, USA*
*Philip A. Gable, Texas A&M University, USA*
*Christina Albee, Ouachita Baptist University, USA*
*Courtney Boerstler, University of Oregon, USA*

The present series of studies suggest similarities between consumers' interpersonal relationships and brand relationships. Specifically, these studies demonstrate ways in which consumers draw closer to brands that facilitate specific goal pursuits, in the same way that consumers draw closer to acquaintances who facilitate such pursuits. Previous research has shown that when particular goals are activated, people feel closer to acquaintances who help them meet those goals (but not to other acquaintances; Fitzsimons and Shah 2008). In addition, research suggests that people tend to anthropomorphize products when those products symbolically address particular social deficit states (e.g., human-like products seem more human when people feel lonely; Epley et al. 2008). Building on this work, the present studies indicate how consumers evaluate preferred brands more positively when brand-relevant goals are activated and how this tendency is accentuated among consumers who have particular relational orientations (e.g., heightened belongingness needs or avoidant interpersonal attachment styles).

We performed three studies with college student participants. In Study 1, participants ($N=101$) completed the Need to Belong (NTB) scale, for which higher scores indicate increased investment in social acceptance (sample item: "I do not like being alone"). In addition, participants completed attitude measures targeting several popular shoe brands, including the brands they self-nominated in an earlier task as most helpful toward their goal of being healthy.

In Study 2, participants ($N=31$) completed an initial version of a subtle goal-priming task adapted from Fitzsimons and Shah (2008). This task required participants to unscramble sentences containing words related to healthiness (e.g., "active," "well") or, for control purposes, neutral words. Participants then completed attitude measures targeting several shoe brands, including the one that most facilitated their goal of being healthy. Shoe brands were self-nominated in an ostensibly unrelated earlier task.

In Study 3, participants ($N=49$) nominated a website which helped them achieve the goal of social connectedness and completed the Experiences in Close Relationships scale, comprising two subscales on which higher scores indicate greater attachment anxiety and attachment avoidance, respectively. Sample items include "I worry about being abandoned" (anxiety) and "I get uncomfortable when a romantic partner wants to be very close" (avoidance). One week later, in an ostensibly unrelated session, participants completed a goal priming task (similar to the task in Study 2) in which they were assigned to exposure to words implicating social connectedness (e.g., "associate," "community") or healthiness. Then, participants completed attitude measures targeting several brands and websites, including the websites they nominated one week earlier.

In Study 1, we found that NTB was positively related to feeling close to one's most helpful shoe brand ($r$, 86,=.33, $p=.02$) and negatively related to liking one's least helpful shoe brand, $r(24)=-.38$, $p=.05$. In Study 2, we found that participants primed with health-related words subsequently rated their self-nominated goal-relevant shoe brands as a better value than did participants who were primed with neutral words, means=6.75 vs. 5.94 on a 7-pt scale; $t(27)=2.54$, $p=.02$. In Study 3, we found that participants in the social connectedness prime condition felt closer to websites that helped them achieve social connectedness than did participants in the healthiness condition, means=5.84 vs. 4.58 on a 7-pt scale; $F(1, 47)=5.54$, $p=.01$. Likewise, attachment avoidance ($b*=-.29$,

$p=.04$) was predicted feelings of closeness, even while controlling for the priming effect ($b*=.28$, $p=.05$).

Studies 2 and 3 suggest similarities between processes governing consumers' relationships with goal-relevant people and with goal-relevant brands. In addition, Studies 1 and 3 indicate that individual differences in consumers' relational orientations can predict differences in consumers' brand attitudes. Our findings highlight the essential social character of consumers' brand representations in ways not documented by previous research. For researchers and practitioners, we see value in identifying similarities between motivational and dispositional forces regulating interpersonal relationships and those regulating brand relationships.

### REFERENCES

Aggarwal, Pankaj and Sharmistha Law (2005), "Role of Relationship Norms in Processing Brand Information," *Journal of Consumer Research*, 32 (3), 453-464.

Bartholomew, Kim and Leonard M. Horowitz (1991), "Attachment Styles Among Young Adults: A Test of a Four-category Model," *Journal of Personality & Social Psychology*, 61 (2), 226-44.

Bargh, John A., Mark Chen, and Lara Burrows (1996), "Automaticity of Social Behavior: Direct Effects of Trait Construct and Stereotype Activation on Action," *Journal of Personality and Social Psychology*, 71 (2), 230-244.

Belk, Russell W. (1988), "Possessions and the Extended Self," *Journal of Consumer Research*, 15 (2), 139-168.

Cesario, Joseph, Jason E. Plaks, and E. Tory Higgins (2006), "Automatic Social Behavior as Motivated Preparation to Interact," *Journal of Personality and Social Psychology*, 90 (6), 893-910.

Fitzsimons, Grainne M., Tanya L. Chartrand, and Gavan J. Fitzsimons (2008), "Automatic effects of Brand Exposure on Motivated Behavior: How Apple Makes You 'Think Different'", *Journal of Consumer Research*, 35 (1), 21-35.

Epley, Nicholas, Scott Akalis, Adam Waytz, and John T. Cacioppo (2008), "Creating Social Connection through Inferential Reproduction: Loneliness and Perceived Agency in Gadgets, Gods, and Greyhounds," *Psychological Science*, 19 (February), 114-120.

Fitzsimons, Gráinne M., and James Y. Shah (2008), "How Goal Instrumentality Shapes Relationship Evaluations," *Journal of Personality & Social Psychology*, 95 (August), 319-337.

Fournier, Susan (1998), "Consumers and Their Brands: Developing Relationship Theory in Consumer Research," *Journal of Consumer Research*, 24 (4), 343-373.

Fournier, Susan (2009), "Lessons Learned about Consumers' Relationships with their Brands," in D. MacInnis, C.W. Park and J. Priester (eds.), *Handbook of Brand Relationships*, NY: M.E. Sharpe.

Gao, Leilei, S. Christian Wheeler, and Baba Shiv (2009), "The "Shaken Self": Product Choices as a Means of Restoring Self-View Confidence," *Journal of Consumer Research*, 36 (1), 29-38.

Kahneman, Daniel, Jack L. Knetsch, and Richard H. Thaler (1990), "Experimental Tests of the Endowment Effect and the Coase Theorem," *Journal of Political Economy*, 98 (6), 1325-48.

Kleine, Susan Schultz, Robert E. Kleine, III, and Chris T. Allen (1995), "How is a Possession "Me" or "Not Me"? Characterizing Types and an Antecedent of Material Possession Attachment," *Journal of Consumer Research*, 22 (3), 327-343.

Sirgy, M. Joseph (1982). "Self-Concept in Consumer Behavior: A Critical Review," *Journal of Consumer Research*, 9(3), 287-300.

Swaminathan, Vanitha, Karen Page, and Zeynep Gürhan-Canli (2008), "My Brand or Our Brand: The Effects of Brand Relationship Dimensions and Self-Construal on Brand Evaluations," *Journal of Consumer Research*, 34 (August), 248-259.

Swaminathan Vanitha, Karen Stilley and Rohini Ahluwalia (2009) "When Brand Personality Matters: The Moderating Role of Attachment Styles", *Journal of Consumer Research*, 35 (6), 985-1002.

Winnicott, D. W. (1971), *Playing and Reality*, Harmondsworth, England: Penguin Books.

# It's Better to Give Than to Receive

Morgan Ward, University of Texas at Austin, USA
Susan Broniarczyk, University of Texas at Austin, USA

## EXTENDED ABSTRACTS

### "Ask and You Shall (Not) Receive: Choosing Between a Gift Registry Gift and Free Choice"

*Morgan K. Ward, University of Texas, Austin, USA*
*Susan Broniarczyk, University of Texas, Austin, USA*

Gift exchanges are complex transactions with relational and psychological implications for both giver and recipient. Givers strive to meet the needs and desires of the recipient with a gift that is both appealing and meaningful. When choosing a gift, the giver has three distinct goals: the item must 1) satisfy the recipient, and 2) reflect the relational intimacy between giver and recipient. The giver's task is complicated by the asymmetry of preference information between giver and recipient. Retailers have partnered to resolve this asymmetry in the form of gift registries, which provide perfect information about a recipient's preferences and preferred gifts to gift givers. However, while a registry reconciles the asymmetry, it may also constrain the giver from choosing a gift that signals relational intimacy.

We look at the circumstances in which givers are willing (vs. resistant) to choose from a registry. Our main hypothesis is that when choosing for a close (vs. distant) friend, the giver will discount the recipient's explicit preferences in favor of a gift that signals the giver's identity or the relationship between them. Further, we suggest that givers are more likely to make a free (vs. registry) choice for a close (vs. distant) friend, resulting in an increased likelihood of choosing a less desirable gift.

In Study 1, university staff members chose a gift for someone they knew in a professional setting and had rated on social closeness. Participants were presented with three lamps which had been pre-tested by a group similar to themselves. The pretest revealed that two lamps were equally liked and the third was significantly less liked than the others. Participants were told that the recipient had rated each of the three lamps either "good" or "excellent": the lamp liked the *least* in pretest was rated "excellent" by the recipient and the other two lamps (pre-tested as 'more liked') were rated "good" by the recipient. Thus, the recipient preferred one lamp and the givers preferred the other two. Givers chose a lamp to give to the recipient.

As predicted, givers indicating a closer relationship with the recipient were more likely to opt for one of their own preferred lamps (rated 'good' rather than 'excellent' by the recipient). Thus, we see evidence that givers are more likely to select a freely chosen gift and risk choosing something less liked when buying for a close friend.

In Study 2, we examine givers' specific strategies when choosing a gift for a close (vs. distant) friend. We primed givers with altruism (vs. no prime) as our presumption is that givers choosing for a close friend are motivated to choose something that will maximize the recipient's happiness. In order to manipulate social closeness between giver and recipient, close givers were told personal information (e.g. the recipient has "classic tastes") and distant givers were given no taste information about the recipient. The giver was then faced with three choices of lamps representing different aesthetic styles: classic, modern and plain. Pretests confirm that the modern lamp was the most preferred by givers, however, the plain lamp is designated by the recipient to be on the registry.

Thus, in this study setup, participants' preferences and recipients' expressed desires conflict, as givers know the recipient's registry choice but personally prefer the modern lamp. An added layer of complexity exists in close-friend conditions: the recipient has indicated the control lamp on the registry but the giver is aware that the recipient's tastes match the classic lamp. Thus, close givers perceive the wish list to be misaligned with the recipient's tastes while distant friends are unaware of his/her tastes.

The data reveal that distant givers display no effect of the altruistic prime. In both prime and no-prime conditions these givers' dominant strategy is to choose the registry lamp and secondarily, the modern lamp, which matches their own preferences. In close-friend conditions, the results are strikingly different. Givers in the no-prime condition again dominantly choose the registry gift. However, in the altruistic-prime condition, givers are equally likely to choose the registry lamp as the classic lamp.

It appears that when givers are focused on the goal of meeting recipients' needs (in altruistic conditions), they are more likely to achieve it when choosing for distant (vs. close) friends. Further, when choosing altruistically for close friends, givers appear to use their knowledge of the recipient to guide the choice rather than the recipient's explicit preferences.

In Study 3, we use a procedure similar to Study 2, to investigate givers' objectives in making a free-choice gift. In a 2 (Relationship Signaling: Signaling vs. Non Signaling) x 3 (Motivation Embodied by Gift: Explicit Recipient Preferences, Giver's Preferences, Relationship Intimacy) design, participants are told to imagine that they were exchanging gifts with friends who live far away using a "Secret Santa" paradigm. Importantly, participants are informed that after the gifts are given, their identity will be revealed (vs. not revealed) to the recipient, to remind the giver that s/he will (vs. not) receive attribution from the recipient for having chosen a well-liked gift. All participants are also told that the recipient has "classic tastes" and are faced with the same gift choices of lamps as described in Study 2.

The data reveal that givers make different choices when they receive (vs. do not receive) attribution from the recipient for the gift chosen: in the Relationship Signaling condition, givers were equally likely to choose from the registry as to choose the classic lamp, while in the Non-Relationship-Signaling condition, the registry choice was dominant. These results confirm that givers diverge from the registry to signal relational closeness rather than to match the recipient's inferred preferences.

These studies provide some insight into the paradox of gift-giving that well-intentioned givers are more likely to choose inappropriately for the people who matter to them most (i.e. close friends), as their needs to express themselves and the relationship supersede their goals of pleasing the recipient.

### "For You or For Me? How the Intended Recipient Influences the Customization Experience and Valuations of Customized Products"

*Leff Bonney, Florida State, USA*
*Kelly B. Herd, University of Colorado, USA*
*C. Page Moreau, University of Colorado, USA*

While recent interest in customization is growing among academics (e.g., Franke, Keinz, and Steger 2009; Moreau and Herd

2010), researchers have focused exclusively on consumers who are designing products for themselves. Many customization firms, however, are successfully positioning themselves as sources for unique gifts, enabling consumers to create custom products for others.

In two studies, we examine how the intended product recipient (self versus other) interacts with the level of design support provided (Study 1) and brand (Study 2) to influence customer's product reactions to customized products. Using participants drawn from the relevant target market, both studies involve real customization tasks undertaken on live web sites. Customized tote bags were selected as the product category for both studies and in both studies, participants were able make a several design decisions including size, fabric for three different sections of the bag (from a collection of 37 patterns and colors), and embroidered personalization.

In the first study, two factors were manipulated between participants: (1) the intended recipient (self vs. other) and (2) design support (present vs. absent). Design support was manipulated both in the instruction packet and on the website itself. Participants' self-assessed design skill was measured.

Following Irwin and McClelland (2003), design skill was treated as a continuous measure, and regression was used to test the effects of the independent variables on participants' expectations of their bags at the time of design. The results revealed a significant interaction between the two manipulated factors ($\beta$=1.09, t=2.84, $p$<.01) as well as a three-way interaction among all of the independent variables ($\beta$=-.16, t=-2.67, $p$<.01). An ANOVA was used to interpret the two-way interaction. When the tote bag was intended as a gift, the presence of design support significantly increased participants' expectations ($M_{Other, Support Present}$=8.2 vs. $M_{Other, Support Absent}$=7.7, contrast: $F(1, 41)$=4.06, $p$<.05). However, when the bag was intended for the participant herself, design support had little influence on expectations ($M_{Self, Support Present}$=7.5 vs. $M_{Self, Support Absent}$=7.5, contrast n/s). We also find that when the tote bag was intended as a gift, design support significantly reduced participants' anxiety-related negative emotions ($M_{Other, Support Present}$=2.7 vs. $M_{Other, Support Absent}$=3.7, contrast: $F(1, 41)$=4.69, $p$<.05) However, when the bag was intended for the participant herself, design support had little influence on these feelings ($M_{Self, Support Present}$=3.6 vs. $M_{Self, Support Absent}$=4.0, contrast n/s).

Approximately six weeks later, the bags arrived and willingness to pay measures (WTP) were taken. Interestingly, participants were willing to pay more for a bag designed for someone else rather than for themselves ($M_{Other}$=$28.11 vs. $M_{Self}$=$25.52). This main effect was qualified by the interaction. The presence of design support had a significant, positive influence on participants' WTP when the bag was for themselves ($M_{Self, Support Present}$=$27.03 vs. $M_{Self, Support Absent}$=$23.00) yet a negative influence when it was for someone else ($M_{Other, Support Present}$=$26.13 vs. $M_{Other, Support Absent}$=$30.58).

To determine whether participants differentially valued the effort they put into designing the bags, the correlation between self-reported effort and willingness to pay were assessed separately for those in the self and other conditions. There was a positive, significant correlation between effort and willingness to pay for those designing the product as a gift (r=.41, $p$<.05). For those designing the bag for themselves, the correlation was negative and non-significant (r=-.13, $p$ >.10).

In Study 2, no one received design support, participants did not expect to actually receive the bag they had designed, and the entire study was completed online. Both the intended recipient (self vs. other) and brand (present vs. absent) were manipulated between-participants in this 2x2 study. As a known brand (Vera Bradley) was used in the study, participants' attitude towards that brand was used as a covariate (see Moreau and Herd 2010) along with participants' self-reported design skill.

The results revealed a significant interaction between brand and the intended recipient (F(1, 75)=4.33, $p$<.05) on willingness to pay. The presence of the brand had a significant, positive effect on willingness to pay when the product was intended for the self ($M_{Self, No Brand}$=$30.05 vs. $M_{Self, Brand}$=$38.84, F(1, 36)=3.75, $p$=.05). However, when the product was intended as a gift, brand actually had a negative, but non-significant influence ($M_{Other, No Brand}$=$40.11 vs. $M_{Other, Brand}$=$35.41, F(1, 38)=1.46, n/s).

A similar ANOVA was used to test product expectations. The results reveal an interaction between brand and the intended recipient that was marginally significant (F(1, 75)=3.23, $p$=.07). Following the pattern observed for willingness to pay, brand had a significant, positive effect on expectations when the product was for the self ($M_{Self, No Brand}$=6.7 vs. $M_{Self, Brand}$=7.7, F(1, 36)=4.67, $p$<.05). However, when the product was intended as a gift, brand actually had a negative, but non-significant influence ($M_{Other, No Brand}$=7.7 vs. $M_{Other, Brand}$=7.3, F(1, 38)=.61, n/s).

We also find that when the tote was intended for the self, there was no significant correlation between time spent and willingness to pay (r=.02, n/s). However, when the tote was intended as a gift, this correlation was both positive and significant (r=.34, $p$<.05).

### "Give Them What They Want: The Benefits of Explicitness in Gift Exchange"

*Francesca Gino, University of North Carolina, USA*
*Francis J. Flynn, Stanford University, USA*

Gifts account for more than four percent of the typical household budget (Davis 1972; Garner & Wagner 1991), which suggests that gift-giving is a routine activity for most people. Nevertheless, research consistently shows that many individuals are poor gift-givers, often purchasing gifts that others would not choose to buy themselves (Waldfogel 1993) or focusing on the wrong criterion in attempting to select a meaningful gift (Flynn & Adams 2009). Thus, despite the fact that people spend a significant amount of time and money on gift-giving, their purchases often are less appreciated than they hope.

One means by which individuals attempt to facilitate gift exchange is by telling others explicitly what gifts they would like. To this end, people frequently organize registries for various occasions (e.g., baby showers, weddings) that list for potential gift-givers the items they should purchase. Is such transparency effective, or are gift-givers wary that gifts directly requested by the gift-recipient will not be appreciated as much? In anthropological studies, gift-giving is often described as a social exchange process, rife with symbolic meaning and interpersonal subtleties (e.g., Boas, 1895; Mauss, 1925). Accepting suggestions for gift purchases from the intended recipient could be interpreted as a sign that the giver does not know the recipient well enough to identify a meaningful gift, or does not wish to spend the time and effort needed to figure out what such a gift might look like.

Failures in gift-giving may reflect a problem in perspective-taking that afflicts many social exchanges. When predicting how others will evaluate their actions, people tend to focus too heavily on their own perspective (Epley, Savitsky, & Gilovich, 2002), and overestimate the extent to which others will share their point of view (Keysar, 1994; Van Boven, Dunning, & Loewenstein, 2000). Given this egocentric bias, gift-givers may fail to pay close attention to what a gift-recipient directly requests. Instead, they may believe that purchasing an unrequested item will signal a sincere concern for the recipient because they have gone out of their way to identify the gift. Yet, gift-recipients may be frustrated that the giver did not take note of the recipient's explicit suggestions. Indeed, gift recipients will likely report that gifts they requested are more thoughtful and considerate of their needs than those not requested because the former indicate that the giver is attentive and responsive.

In the present research we investigate the role of explicitness in gift-giving. In Study 1, we examine personal gift registries and ask people to consider how much they would appreciate an item purchased off the registry versus a highly similar item that was not listed. In Study 2, we consider registry and non-registry gift purchases and examine whether gift-recipients appreciate the gifts they request more than the gifts they do not, and whether gift-givers can account for this important difference. In Study 3, we attempt to highlight the underlying psychological mechanism for this failure in perspective taking: whereas gift-givers believe that requested gifts will appear less thoughtful and considerate than non-requested gifts, gift-recipients maintain the opposite belief. Finally, in Study 4, we consider a boundary condition for this effect—the number of gifts requested.

The results of our four studies demonstrate that gift-recipients are more appreciative of gifts chosen from a set of desired items than they are of alternative gift choices (Studies 1-3), but that gift-givers believe both types of gifts will be equally appreciated (Studies 2-3). We also show that when the recipient explicitly highlights his or her preferred gift, givers are receptive to such suggestions (Studies 4). Thus, while gift-givers often attempt to be more thoughtful by choosing a gift not included on a given list, they do not realize that sticking to the list will elicit stronger feelings of appreciation.

Our findings contribute to the literature on egocentric biases and perspective taking in social judgments. Prior work has found that people often fail to take others' perspectives into account and struggle to read their minds (Epley et al., 2004). We go beyond this point to investigate the impact of explicitness in one pervasive perspective-taking context: gift exchange. We find that even when gift-recipients provide a list of what they would like, givers fail to heed this clear-cut advice. Instead, gift-givers think it would be better to ignore the gift-recipient's explicit requests. It remains unclear whether gift-givers eventually learn to respond to gift-recipient's explicit cues, and thereby become better at eliciting appreciation. Gift-recipients are reluctant to reveal their true feelings of disappointment with the gifts they receive (Mauss, 1925). As a result, gift-givers may be left in the dark about their failed attempts to elicit appreciation and many may believe that their gift purchases are more effective in eliciting appreciation than is actually the case.

According to Webley, Lea, and Portalska (1983), "Gift-giving clearly fulfills an important social function and it is the act of giving…which is of prime importance, not the actual gift itself" (p. 237). Our results offer a different point of view—that whether the act of gift-giving counts may depend largely on whether or not the giver is attentive and responsive to the recipient's explicit suggestions when they are made available. Gift-givers would be wise to pay attention to gift registries, wish lists, and explicit requests from friends or significant others. Nevertheless, they often ignore such solicitations and underestimate the costs of doing so. Conversely, gift-recipients can help facilitate the gift-giving process by not only being more direct in making suggestions for gifts, but being more specific as well. Rather than put together one big "wish list," they should instead list one big wish.

## "Paying it Forward: Greed and Generosity in Upstream Reciprocity"

*Kurt Gray, Harvard University, USA*
*Adrian F. Ward, Harvard University, USA*
*Michael I. Norton, Harvard University, USA*

Paying it forward is a heart-warming notion, one that has long captured the attention of luminaries such as Ralph Waldo Emerson (1841) and Benjamin Franklin (1784) as well as laypeople (Hyde 2000). The concept is simple: A is kind to B, and B–rather than pay that kindness back to A–pays it forward to C. C then pays that kindness forward to D, and so on, creating a chain of goodwill. On any given day, however, people are the recipients of both generous and selfish acts from others. If people pay forward these negative behaviors as well, then selfish acts may similarly create chains of ill will. In this paper, we examine whether people are more likely to pay forward generosity or greed, and how being the victim of greed or the beneficiary of generosity drives subsequent behavior.

In our first experiment, we examined paying it forward in the domain of money. In one of four conditions, participants completed a dictator game, splitting $6 between themselves and an anonymous future receiver (give-only condition). In the three pay it forward conditions, participants were told that a previous dictator had completed the same game, with the participant as the receiver. They first learned how much money the previous dictator had given them–a greedy ($0/$6), equitable ($3/$6), or generous ($6/$6) split–and then acted as the dictator in another game, splitting an additional $6 between themselves and a different future receiver. As expected, participants in the greedy condition gave the least (M=$1.36), followed by those in the give-only condition (M=$2.40), followed by those in the equal (M=$3.38) and generous conditions (M=$3.71).

Paying it forward in the real world, of course, often involves more informal exchanges than the disbursement of cash; in any workplace, for example, there are both enjoyable and onerous tasks, and co-workers may divide this labor more or less equitably. Experiment 2 investigates if those who receive greedy (vs. generous) divisions of labor are more likely to pay forward their treatment, as well as the roles of affect and perceptions of fairness in mediating the extent to which participants paid behavior forward.

This experiment was similar to Experiment 1, except that instead of receiving and giving money, participants completed enjoyable and irritating tasks. The enjoyable task involved making free associations to words, while the irritating task involved circling vowels in passages of Italian prose. All participants were given a set of eight tasks–four good and four bad–and were told to complete any four of them and pass on the remaining four to a future participant. Participants could leave any combination of good versus bad tasks for future participants. One group of participants (give-only condition) simply completed four tasks and passed on the remainder. In the three pay it forward conditions, participants first learned that a previous participant had been asked to split these eight tasks, and had left them either a generous (completing all four bad tasks themselves and leaving the four good tasks for the participant), greedy (completing all four good and leaving all four bad tasks), or equitable split (completing two of each kind and leaving two of each kind). In these conditions, participants completed the four tasks that the previous participant had ostensibly left for them, then divided eight additional tasks (four good and four bad) between themselves and an unknown future participant. After completing the four tasks that the previous participant had left for them, participants indicated the extent to which they were feeling a variety of positive (e.g., happy) and negative (e.g., upset) affective states.

Replicating Experiment 1, participants in the greedy condition (M=1.04) gave significantly fewer good tasks than participants in all other conditions. The give-only gave the next least (M=1.67), though not significantly less than the equitable (M=1.95) or generous conditions (M=1.91). The equitable and generous conditions again did not differ from each other. The four conditions also differed significantly on negative affect, such that participants in the greed condition experienced significantly more negative affect than those in the other conditions. As we predicted, this incidental negative affect mediated the link between good tasks received and good tasks paid forward.

These results have both heartening and disheartening implications. We find that people do pass on some degree of kindness to others, but not to the same extent that they received it themselves. Thus the person who awakes to find his long driveway mysteriously cleared of snow and as a result holds the door for three seconds for a co-worker may feel he has "paid forward" a generous act, but the discount rate is sufficiently high that the perpetuation of this chain of good will likely ends there. On the other hand, the person who awakes to find his driveway blocked with snow from his neighbor's efforts to clear her own driveway may continue to pay forward bad deeds, creating a significantly longer chain of ill will.

# On The Psychology of Construal mindsets:
## Determinants & Consequences Of Concrete Thinking

Manoj Thomas, Cornell University, USA
Claire I. Tsai, University of Toronto, Canada

## EXTENDED ABSTRACTS

### "The Scale Effect: How Larger Measurement Units Shrink Perceived Size and Expand Mental Horizon"

Sam Maglio, New York University
Yaacov Trope, New York University

Maglio and Trope. When do people look at the world in fine-grained detail instead of in broad brushstrokes? And what are the consequences—both for visual perception and cognitive processing—of this small- versus large-scale distinction? We propose that a critical factor is the person's proximity to the target of judgment, that is, how psychologically close the object is to the person. A series of five studies suggest that smaller scale increases size estimates while also prompting more proximal timing estimates as well as a pattern of concrete thinking that generalizes to new targets.

How could perception fall prey to something as incidental as scale? Research on the clutter effect (Sadalla & Staplin, 1980) suggests that the presence of more distinct items (e.g., intersections crossed in a walk) increases perceived distance. We propose that smaller unit of measurement produces the same effect.

Are certain objects more likely to be measured in small scale? Construal level theory (Liberman & Trope, 2008; Trope & Liberman, 2003) points to one possibility: a person's psychological distance from a target. Those that are near (in time, space, or likelihood) are mentally construed according to their concrete, contextual features; more distal targets are construed in terms of their abstract, universal features. Of importance, distal (versus proximal) targets tend to be categorized into fewer categories (i.e., broader units) and described using more abstract language (Fujita, Henderson, Eng, Trope, & Liberman, 2006; Henderson, Fujita, Trope, & Liberman, 2006).

Study 1 tested two important predictions. First, a distal target should be measured using larger units relative to a proximal target. Second, this difference in unit size should give rise to differential clutter, producing different estimates of size. Thus, we presented participants with a piece of paper containing a straight diagonal line meant to represent a path to a grocery store that was either physically proximal or distal. Participants first created a single unit of measurement with which to subsequently measure the path. We found that those in the proximal condition estimated the line to look larger; this effect of condition was mediated by differences in scale size.

Our next studies directly manipulated scale to investigate its consequences for size perception as well as mental construal. Studies 2A and 2B provided participants with either a curved or straight line, respectively, and had them measure it using either millimeters, centimeters, or decimeters. The results indicated a linear increase in size perception with finer scale. In Study 3, participants who measured a curved line (meant to represent a road trip) using smaller scale not only indicated that it looked bigger but also that they expected it to happen sooner in the future (i.e., temporally proximal). Finally, Study 4 asked participants to measure a hallway in either feet or yards. Those measuring in feet estimated larger size and described a set of actions more concretely (versus abstractly) than those measuring in yards.

In sum, larger unit of measurement consistently elicited not only smaller visual estimates of size but also more abstract mental construal, characterized by judgments of temporal distance and high-level action identification. These effects were found both for the original target of measurement as well as for new, unrelated targets—evidence that large scale leads to big picture thinking.

### "Carry-Over Effects of Self-Control on Decision-Making: A Construal Level Perspective"

Echo Wen Wan, University of Hong Kong, China
Nidhi Agrawal, Northwestern University, USA

Wan and Agrawal. Past research has examined the effect of exerting self-control on subsequent decision-making from the resource perspective. Regulatory depletion theory (Vohs, Baumeister, and Tice 2008a) posits that exerting self-control leads to a temporary deficit in self-regulation resources and consequently harms subsequent self-control behavior such as the decision about unplanned purchase (Vohs and Faber 2007). The current research proposes a construal level driven complementary process through which regulatory depletion affects subsequent decisions.

Prior studies on regulatory depletion have shown that performing self-control leads to a heightened feeling of fatigue (e.g., Baumeister et al. 1998) that can increase the salience of current lack of resources (Agrawal and Wan 2009). Resources constitute the means of carrying out the action. Construal level theory (Trope and Liberman 2003) posits that individuals tend to adopt lower (vs. higher) levels of construal when considering the means of performing the action. Therefore, we propose that exerting self-control heightens a focus on resources that leads consumers to construe subsequent situations at lower levels, which will systematically prompt preferences for options with attractive lower-level construal features in their decision-making.

Five studies tested our propositions. Study 1 manipulated self-control with a letter-detecting task (Baumeister et al. 1998) and measured participants' construal levels (BIF, Vallacher and Wagner 1989). We found that participants with prior self-control scored lower than those without prior self-control, supporting our proposition that exerting self-control lowers construal levels. Studies 2–5 tested the effect of exerting self-control on subsequent judgments or choices that involved decision options varying in higher and lower construal level features: primary versus secondary features, temporal proximity versus distance, feasibility versus desirability.

In study 2, participants completed a continuous-choice task that manipulated self-control (Vohs et al. 2008b), and then indicated their intention of patronizing a restaurant described as either having attractive primary feature and non-attractive secondary feature (great food, mediocre view) or having attractive secondary feature and non-attractive primary feature (great view, mediocre food). Participants with prior self-control had greater dining intention than those without prior self-control when the restaurant offered an attractive secondary feature, supporting our proposition. Study 3 had participants first exert self-control or not in an emotion-control task (Muraven et al. 1998) and then actually choose between two calendars as the reward for their participation, one organized by week (temporal proximity) and another by month (temporal distance). A larger proportion of participants chose the weekly calendar (temporal proximity) when they exerted prior self-control than when they didn't. In study 4, participants completed a thought-listing task that manipulated self-control (Vohs and Faber 2007) and then chose between two hiking spots that varied in desirability (scene) and feasibility (transportation). As expected, a larger proportion of participants chose the park with high feasibility when they exerted prior self-control than when they didn't. Moreover, this effect was mediated by a focus on resources. Study 5 followed the same procedure as used in study 4 with one change: Half the participants were primed to adopt the higher-level construals ("why" mindset, Freitas, Gollwitzer, and Trope 2004) whereas the other half didn't (control). Results of study 4 were replicated in the control condition but were eliminated in the why mindset condition, suggesting that the effect of exerting self-control on subsequent choice was driven by the downward shift in construal levels.

This research contributes to the construal level literature by identifying self-control and regulatory depletion as an important trigger of construal level variation. It also extends the understanding of self-control and consumer decision by uncovering a new mechanism that complements the resource depletion theory in explaining the psychology of how self-control and depletion affect decision-making.

## "When Does Anticipating Regret Help Consumer Decision Making and When Does it Hurt?"
*Rebecca W. Hamilton, University of Maryland, USA*
*Debora V. Thompson, Georgetown University, USA*

Hamilton and Thompson. Avoiding regret is an important motivator in consumer decision making (Zeelenberg and Pieters 2007). For example, asking consumers to anticipate the regret they would experience if they made the wrong decision increases their willingness to pay more for a higher-priced brand of video player (Simonson 1992). It is not clear, though, whether considering anticipated regret helps consumers make more satisfactory purchase decisions because anticipated regret is often not a very accurate predictor of experienced regret.

In this paper, we focus on differences in the regret emotions that are anticipated and experienced. Research has shown that consumption experiences themselves can change the way consumers think about products because consumption experiences induce a more concrete mental construal than indirect experiences such as reading product descriptions (Hamilton and Thompson 2007). One key difference between anticipated regret and experienced regret is that anticipated regret is considered in prospect, while experienced regret is considered during or shortly after an experience. Construal level theory (Trope and Liberman 2000) proposes that the greater an individual's psychological distance from target events, the more abstractly these events will be represented. Thus, anticipated regret, which is considered in prospect, should feel more psychologically distant, evoking more abstract thought than experienced regret, which should evoke more concrete thought.

Notably, previous research has distinguished between two different kinds of regret: "hot" regret and "cold" or "wistful" regret (Gilovich, Medvec and Kahneman 1998; Kahneman 1995). Kahneman (1995) proposed that hot regret is a more short-term form of regret, which focuses on direct reactions to the outcome. In contrast, wistful regret is a more long-term form of regret, which focuses on counterfactual alternatives to the outcome. Using construal theory to link these two streams of research together, we propose that anticipated regret is more similar to cold regret, while experienced regret is more similar to hot regret.

In our research, we focus on this construal-based explanation for the gap between anticipated and experienced regret, and we conducted a series of three studies to examine the size of this gap and its effect on consumer decision making. In our first study, participants evaluated two different digital video players, an easy-to-use basic

model (high feasibility) and an advanced model with three times the number of features (high desirability). After choosing one of them, they answered several items designed to measure anticipated regret. Next, participants used their chosen product and answered items designed to measure experienced regret. Based on earlier research indicating that consumers tend to focus on the desirability of products prior to use but on the feasibility of products during consumption (Thompson, Hamilton and Rust 2005), we expected that participants would anticipate more regret when they chose the basic model, but actually experience more regret when they chose the advanced model.

As we had predicted, those who chose the basic model were more likely to anticipate regretting their choices than those who chose the advanced model. However, those who chose the advanced model were significantly more likely to regret their choices after using the product than those who chose the basic model. Notably, anticipated regret and experienced regret were not even significantly correlated (r=.09, p>.27).

In our second study, we replicated this misprediction of experienced regret in a new domain by having participants choose either a large or small set of art posters from which they would select their favorite poster for a raffle. We also measured emotions specific to hot regret and cold regret as well as anticipated and experienced regret.

In our third study, our goal was to see whether we could help participants make better choices by instructing participants to consider either hot regret or cold regret before choosing a product. We expected that those who considered hot regret emotions such as irritation and frustration before making their choice would be more likely to choose the basic product, experiencing more satisfaction and less regret after using the product. In contrast, those who considered cold regret emotions such as disappointment and longing for missed opportunities before choice were expected to be more likely to choose the advanced product.

As predicted, those who considered hot regret emotions prior to choice were more likely to prefer the basic player than those who considered cold regret emotions prior to choice. Notably, after using their chosen products, those in the hot regret condition evaluated them more favorably, indicated that they would be more likely to recommend it to others, and were marginally more satisfied with their choices than those in the cold regret condition. Considering hot regret before choosing between a basic and an advanced product seems to attenuate the "feature fatigue" effect (Thompson et al. 2005) demonstrated in previous research.

Taken together, these studies suggest that anticipated and experienced great differ not only quantitatively but also qualitatively. Because direct experiences with products shift consumers' construal levels from abstract to concrete, anticipating "hot" regret emotions can increase consumption satisfaction relative to anticipating "cold" regret emotions.

## "When Does Metacognitive Experience Influence Preference? The Moderating Role of Construal Mindset"
*Claire I. Tsai, University of Toronto*
*Manoj Thomas, Cornell University*

This paper explores how level of construal interacts with metacognitive experience to influence evaluative judgments. A large body of research has shown that consumers' judgments are not only based on the information content, but also on the ease or difficulty of processing the information content (Schwarz 2004; Alter and Oppenheimer 2009). In this paper, we suggest that the ease-of-processing effect is contingent on construal level. We hypothesize and find that people in a concrete-construal mindset are more likely to use ease of processing as an input for judgment. An abstract-construal mindset prompts them to ignore contextual; details that are not central to the judgment. Consequently, they are less likely to consider the subjective experiences of ease or difficulty under conditions of abstract-construal mindset.

The notion that abstract-construal mindset reduces consumers' tendency to use metacognitive experience as a cue is consistent with the process of abstraction as postulated by construal level theory (Trope and Liberman 2003). According to this theory, the concrete-construal mindset elicits lower-level construals that are concrete and contextualized representations which include subordinate and incidental features of events. In contrast, higher-level construals are schematic and decontextualized representations that extract the gist from the available information and omit contextual features. Since metacognitive experience is likely to be considered a contextual cue, consumers under abstract-construal mindset are likely to disregard their metacognitive experience while making judgments.

Study 1 showed that abstract-construal mindset mitigated the ease-of-processing effect demonstrated in extant literature. Participants first completed a task that evoked a concrete- or abstract-construal mindset. They then proceeded to the ostensibly unrelated main task and evaluated a fictitious brand of chocolate truffles based on either a clear (easy to process) or blurry (difficult to process) print advertisement. Participants assigned to the concrete-construal mindset liked chocolate less when the ad was blurry and difficult to process. In contrast, ease of processing did not affect liking for chocolate for participants assigned to abstract-construal mindset, confirming our hypothesis.

Since our primary interest in Study 1 was to test the moderating role of construal mindset, the information content was kept invariant across the conditions. However, a change in metacognitive experience might be accompanied by a change in the informativeness, a key determinant of judgment. How might construal mindset influence judgments in such situations? We investigated this issue in Study 2 and manipulated metacognitive experience by asking participants to generate either two or eight reasons for donating to a charitable cause (conserving polar bears). The results showed that abstract-construal mindset not only weakened the effect of metacognitive experience but also augmented the effect of information content, thereby reversing the effect of retrieval fluency. Study 2 expanded the findings by using a behavioral measure (donation) in a non-hedonic context and ruled out entitlement to consume as an alternative explanation. Although the consumption of hedonic products is often justified by effort (e.g., "If I exerted effort, I deserve to indulge"), it is unlikely that effort can be a justification for increased donation because donating to a charitable cause is not indulgent consumption. Study 3 further generalized the findings by replicating Study 2 (single-alternative) in a choice task (choosing between two paintings) and ruled out processing motivation as an alternative explanation.

Construal level theory posits the reason why ease of processing does not influence judgments in higher level construal is that subjective experiences are considered contextual and peripheral. If subjective experiences are deemed to be central to the task, then ease-of-processing effect will manifest even in higher level construal. We test this hypothesis in Study 4. Specifically, Study 4 showed that when feelings was described as a key determinant for judgment, ease of processing increased liking for chocolate for participants with abstract-construal mindset. These findings provide a clearer picture of when and why metacognitive experience affects evaluative judgments.

# The Prime of Your Life: The Big Picture of Small Influences
James A. Mourey, University of Michigan, USA
Carolyn Yoon, University of Michigan, USA

## EXTENDED ABSTRACTS

### "One Without the Other: The Effects of Priming Individual and Collective Mindset on Consumer Choice and Valuation"

*James A. Mourey, Univeristy of Michigan, USA*
*Carolyn Yoon, Univeristy of Michigan, USA*
*Daphna Oyserman, Univeristy of Michigan, USA*

What is peanut butter without jelly or bacon and lettuce without tomato? What would Ken be without Barbie? Is a shirt just a shirt or is it part of an outfit, completed with just the right tie, belt, and shoes? In some way, once a relationship is created among items, each alone feels incomplete and less desirable. If Ken without Barbie feels like a belt without a buckle, consumers should not want one without the other.

Priming individual- and collective-mindsets has been shown to influence cognitive processing style but, in the domain of marketing, the focus has been primarily on the influence of self-construal on interpersonal relationships. Mindsets are cognitive schemas that include content, procedures, and goals relevant to separating and decontextualizing, or connecting and contextualizing. Societies are likely to differ in whether a collective or an individual mindset is chronically accessible, but both mindsets are available to be used in every modern society so that the effects of mindsets can also be studied by priming a mindset or making it temporarily salient (Oyserman et al. 2009). When cued, mindsets influence the propensity to view objects in the world as either part of larger, related, and connected units (collective mindset), or as separate and discrete items (individual mindset). The current studies extend cultural mindset theory to predict the consequences of primed mindset for consumption of inter-product relationships, especially when consumption involves multiple sequential choices.

Although previous research has demonstrated the impact of salient mindsets on basic cognitive procedures (e.g., memory, visual and auditory processing) and on acceptance of brand extensions (Monga and John 2007), little is known about the consequences of salient mindsets on perceptions about products and services. We move beyond prior theorizing and research to predict that salient mindset will influence the extent that products and services are perceived as either related parts of a larger item unit or as separate units, and that these perceptions have consequences for willingness to consume partial sets and willingness to pay to complete such sets.

In three experiments we show that mindset priming influences both the relationships consumers perceive among products and their responsivity to these relationships. Consumers primed with collective-mindsets see more relationships among products than those primed with individual-mindsets, which leads to differences in initial product selection in a consumption context. Having made initial product selections, consumers primed with collective-mindsets are reluctant to break apart related items by consuming a partial set, whereas those primed with individual-mindsets do not exhibit such tendency. These differences influence the willingness to pay to complete sets, implying that the differences between the primed mindset groups are likely due to different valuations of relationships among items.

In our first study, we explore the proposed influence of mindset in the domain of snacks and beverages. As predicted, consumers primed with individual mindset primes exhibit a greater tendency to select obvious pairs of related beverage/snack combinations (e.g., milk and cookies, fitness water and a health bar) compared to collective mindset prime consumers who select beyond the obvious relationships and elaborate on the possibilities of relatedness among items (e.g., fitness water and cookies given their compensatory healthy/unhealthy relationships).

In our second study, we focus specifically on the differences between prime groups in their tendency to break up items perceived as being related, in this case cute puppy siblings. After making an initial puppy pair selection, participants are told they are only to have one puppy and must make one selection from all the puppies presented initially. As predicted, collective mindset prime consumers shift their selection to avoid breaking up sibling puppies while individual mindset prime consumers do not.

Our third study was conducted in the context of an online shopping experience, specifically that of Amazon.com. In addition to replicating the first two studies, the final study investigated whether the explicitness of the product presentation made a difference. We found that presenting products explicitly attenuates differences in the initial selection behavior between the prime groups. Additionally, a difference in the willingness-to-pay to restore partial sets emerged for collective mindset prime consumers who had selected to consume a partial set of products, suggesting that valuation of relationships drives the observed differences.

This work makes theoretical contributions with respect to the better understanding of the notion of situated cognition via individual- and collective-mindset priming, extensions beyond self-construal and processing, and differences in product relationship perceptions among consumers. Practical contributions with respect to product bundling, up-selling, cross-selling, and advertising or point-of-purchase displays are also discussed.

### "Playing misMatchmaker: The Impact of Matching versus MisMatching Brand Personalities in Incidental Brand Exposure"

*Keisha M. Cutright, Duke University, USA*
*Linyun Yang, Duke University, USA*
*Gavan Fitzsimons, Duke University, USA*
*Tanya Chartrand, Duke University, USA*

How often do you watch television where just one commercial is shown during the commercial breaks? When was the last time the commercial break on your favorite radio station was filled with the ad of just one brand? It is safe to say that such experiences are pretty rare; brands are generally surrounded by the messages of many other brands.

This research seeks to understand how exposure to more than one brand in a given context affects attitudes toward the focal brand. More specifically, we focus on whether being exposed to brands with 'matching' or 'mismatching' personality traits impacts attitudes toward the focal brand. Moreover, in light of consumers' inability to process all of the messages they encounter and their unwillingness to do so (as suggested by the rise of DVRs), we seek to understand how the impact of the brand environment differs based on whether people are attentive to the brands or are incidentally exposed to them.

Our hypothesis is that when consumers are incidentally exposed to brands, they prefer a focal brand more when it is paired with a brand with a mismatching personality than one with a matching personality. We argue that this is because being paired with a brand with a mismatching personality makes the focal brand appear more distinct and unique. We base this hypothesis on prior research demonstrating that (moderately) incongruent information often enhances individuals' attention and evaluations (e.g., Alden, Mukherjee, and Hoyer 2000; Lee and Mason 1999; Meyers-Levy and Tybout 1989). However, we do not expect this pattern to exist when people pay attention to the brand pairs and can therefore analyze the specific attributes of each brand more carefully.

In study 1, we tested the hypothesis that incidental exposure to mismatching brands leads to more favorable attitudes toward a focal brand than exposure to matching brands. Our focal brand was Dove chocolate, which we paired with a soft drink. After pre-testing several soft drinks, we found that Canada Dry is very similar in personality to Dove, while Mt. Dew is very different. In study 1, participants were asked to study faces in 20 photographs of individuals engaging in a variety of tasks. Unobtrusively embedded in four pictures were two brands. In one condition, participants were exposed to the two brands with matching personalities (Dove and Canada Dry). In the second condition, participants were exposed to the brands with mismatching personalities (Dove and Mt. Dew). Participants were then given a real choice between Dove and Ghirardelli chocolate. Analyses revealed that participants were more likely to choose Dove when it was paired with Mt. Dew than when it was paired with Canada Dry.

In study 2, we replicate study 1 while using a focal brand with traits different than those of the focal brand in study 1. We also wanted to demonstrate that our results hold for incidental exposure to brands, but not regular exposure. After watching the first two minutes of a clip from Discovery Channel's *Planet Earth* series, participants were shown two commercials (pre-tested to be similar in general, but very similar or very different in terms of the brands' personalities.) Specifically, one condition saw a Mt. Dew and a Hummer commercial (match), while the other condition saw the same Mt. Dew commercial paired with a Honda Pilot commercial (mismatch). Importantly, half of the participants watched the commercials at normal speed. The other half watched the commercials at 10x normal speed (i.e., the incidental exposure condition, similar to fast-forward speeds on DVR). As expected, when participants were exposed to the commercials incidentally, those who saw Mt. Dew paired with Honda (mismatch) were more willing to purchase Mt. Dew than those who saw Mt. Dew paired with Hummer (match). This pattern did not exist when participants viewed the commercials at regular speed. Moreover, preferences for other soft drinks were unaffected.

In study 3, our goal was to demonstrate that consumers also prefer a focal brand more when it is paired with a mismatching brand than when it is shown alone and to show this pattern is mediated by consumers' perceptions of the distinctiveness of the focal brand. The design of study 3 was similar to that of study 2; the only difference being that the condition in which participants watched the 'Mt. Dew and Hummer' commercials in study 2 was replaced with a 'Mt. Dew only' condition. As expected, participants in the incidental exposure condition rated Mt. Dew higher when it was paired with Honda Pilot than when it was seen alone. But, this was not true in the regular exposure condition, nor was it true for the other soft drink brands. Further, we found that the effect in the incidental exposure condition was mediated by participants' enhanced perceptions of the uniqueness of the Mt. Dew brand when it was shown with the Honda Pilot commercial.

Overall, these studies demonstrate that being paired with a brand with an opposite personality can enhance attitudes toward the focal brand, particularly under incidental exposure conditions.

This research allows us to take a broader perspective of how nonconscious exposure to brands impacts behavior by looking beyond the effects of an individual brand to exploring the environment in which it is situated. It also broadens our perspective of the impact of brand personalities. Not only do such dimensions affect individuals' evaluations of a focal brand itself, but they also impact attitudes toward other brands that the focal brand is associated with for just a short moment. Finally, this work suggests that marketers should consider responding to the increasing threat of DVRs by working strategically with media agencies to expose their brands with appropriately 'mismatching' brands.

## "Penny Wise Lb Foolish: From Ambition to Intemperance"

*Aparna A. Labroo, University of Chicago, USA*
*Sara Kim, University of Chicago, USA*

In 2008, with per capita income of over \$47,000, the USA comprised of some of the wealthiest and possibly the most ambitious people in the world. With over 74% of her population classified as obese, she was also one of the fattest, suggesting that she also comprised of some of the most intemperate people in the world. Much research is now establishing that ambition results in chasing material wealth but troublingly, material wealth does not make people happy; rather, it is investing in oneself that is the source of subjective well being. So why is it that ambitious people overinvest their efforts in the pursuit of material goods and under invest their efforts in the development of the self, the result being that they end up living increasingly intemperate but not happier lives?

In our research, we argue that one reason for this miscalibration is that mere reminders of ambition activate general reward seeking goals. This goal activation results in people who have been reminded of ambition: (a) investing additional effort to secure goal relevant indulgent or immediately rewarding outcomes, and more importantly (b) inferring from their own sense of effort while engaged in the pursuit of such indulgent and immediately rewarding outcomes that such outcomes must be more valuable than they actually are. Put simply, people reminded of ambition not only put effort to secure indulgent outcomes, but from their own sense of effort when engaged in securing such outcomes, they assign added value to such outcomes, leading to upward spirals of hedonism.

Thus, it is not just a general quest for rewards that is activated by ambition; rather, once this quest has been activated the subjective effort associated with a quest for rewards further enhances their perceived value. This latter prediction is in line with recent reports showing that because people associate effort with the pursuit of their most important goals, when engaged in the pursuit of any goal, they also see outcomes that are a means to goal attainment as more valuable when such outcomes are associated with a subjective sense of effort. In particular, building on self-perception theory which suggested that people infer their attitudes from their actions, Labroo and Kim (2009) demonstrated that people who were engaged in the pursuit of important goals (e.g., be a kind person) tended to infer that an outcome (donation to a particular charity, Kids-in-Danger) was more important to them when it was associated with subjective effort (its appeal employed slightly blurry versus clear font). By similar argument, if reminders of ambition might make people value decadent foods and actively channel their efforts into attaining such foods, then these individuals might also end up valuing decadent foods more when those foods are associated with a token effort, even subjective effort that in no way reflects a positive value of the outcome. Abstinence, and token reminders of abstinence, on the other hand, can result in upward spirals of wellbeing. Not only do such people start to reallocate their efforts towards the pursuit of activities that strengthen their inner core selves, but importantly, from their very own sense of effort while engaged in the pursuit of self strengthening outcomes, they infer added value of such outcomes. Ambition therefore feeds into and feeds out of intemperate living—that is, upward spirals result from reallocating effort to chase indulgence over self strengthening and additionally, inferring an enhanced value of such outcomes from a subjective sense of effort associated with the pursuit of such outcomes. And abstinence feeds into and is derived from ones subjective sense of effort to improve oneself.

Across three studies we provide evidence that (a) the ambition primed are more willing than non-ambition primed participants to exert real effort to attain indulgent outcomes, (b) that ironically, associating subjective effort (versus ease) to an indulgent outcome increases the valuation of that outcome among ambition-primed individuals but reduces the valuation of those outcomes among forsake ambition primed individuals, and (c) associating subjective effort (versus ease) to self-strengthening outcomes (e.g., yoga) reduces the valuation of that outcome among ambition-primed individuals but increases the valuation of those outcomes among forsake ambition primed individuals.

### "You're Cramping My Style: When Employee Appearance Leads to "Bad" Consumer Choices"
*Andrea Morales, Arizona State University, USA*
*Gavan Fitzsimons, Duke University, USA*
*Nancy Sirianni, Arizona State University, USA*
*Iana Castro-Nelson, Arizona State University, USA*

In an attempt to make purchase decisions they will be happy with, consumers rely on cues in retail and service environments, such as the appearance of employees, to help guide them to the right choices. This research examines the strong influence that employee appearance can exert on consumer choices, and while such a result has important practical implications, it is to be anticipated from a theoretical perspective given the growing number of papers demonstrating the powerful influence of activating or priming a context on consumer choices (e.g., Chartrand et al. 2008; Ferraro, Bettman and Chartrand 2009). What is perhaps most interesting and novel in our current work is the examination of the downstream consequences of this phenomenon. The focus of this research is on understanding how consumers subsequently feel if the appearance of an employee led them to choose a product that they might not otherwise have chosen.

For example, imagine walking into a retail store with the goal of purchasing a new business suit. As you explore the available options, a sales associate offers his assistance. You notice that he is formally dressed in black dress pants and shoes, a white long-sleeve oxford shirt and a navy blue tie. Based on his clothing, you infer that he is conservative, serious and perhaps a little old fashioned. You tell him what you are looking for and he provides you with an assortment of business suits. Will his traditional appearance have an effect on the type of suit that you eventually choose? Perhaps you were considering buying a less conventional, modern-style business suit. Does this idea now seem wrong to you? What type of suit do you buy and will you be happy once you've brought it home?

Following theory in impression formation and stereotype activation (Fiske, Lin and Neuberg 1999, Quinn, Macrae and Bodenhausen 2003), we propose that consumers who interact with an employee in a retail or service setting will categorize the employee based on observable cues derived from his or her overall physical appearance. Consumers will use this information to draw inferences about the employee's personality traits, goals and behaviors, and these inferences will have an impact on the choices consumers make in the presence of the employee. In order to make the right choice in the situation, all consumers will experience (either consciously or nonconsciously) pressure to choose in accordance to the presumptions they have made about the employee. Some consumers will then make a decision they believe the employee would make (behavioral assimilation), while others will choose to make a decision that does not conform (behavioral contrast) to the employee.

To understand how employee appearance can act as a contextual prime that influences both consumer choice and post-choice judgments, we conducted a series of experiments in which we manipulated the appearance of a confederate, who posed as an employee, to portray either formal or casual personal style during interactions with study participants. Our findings show that when a consumer perceives that he and an employee share similar traits, goals and behaviors, he makes his purchase decisions freely and is later satisfied with those choices. However, when a consumer perceives that he and the employee do not share similar traits, goals and behaviors, the consumer feels pressure to alter his behavior to conform to that of the employee. After the choice has been made, we find that consumers in the latter group experience lower levels of satisfaction (study 1) and higher decision regret (study 2) than those consumers who do not give in to the inferred pressure caused by the employee's appearance.

These results suggest that even though consumers conform out of a desire to meet informational, normative and self-concept goals (Cialdini and Goldstein 2004), making decisions in opposition to their natural choice tendencies leads to substantial negative downstream consequences. The tension between consumers' social interaction goals and their choice tendencies causes feelings of unrest. Therefore, consumers who disregard their own desires to make seemingly right choices based on employees' inferred traits, goals and behaviors later realize that they have made the wrong choices, which results in them experiencing negative consequences. While our results show that employee appearance can prime participants to make choices that they would not normally make, the novel contribution of our research is in providing an understanding of how consumers feel about those choices once they have been made. These findings contribute to our understanding of employee-consumer interactions as well as to the growing literature on contextual priming and consumption.

### [FULL REFERENCES OMITTED, BUT AVAILABLE UPON REQUEST.]

# Optimizing Corporate Social Responsibility Strategy:
## New Insights on the Impact of Csr on Consumer Behavior

Haiyang Yáng, INSEAD, Singapore
Amitava Chattopadhyay, INSEAD, Singapore

## EXTENDED ABSTRACTS

### "An Induction-Deduction Model of Consumer Inference: Implications for Selecting Optimal CSR Strategy"

*Haiyang Yáng INSEAD, Singapore*
*Amitava Chattopadhyay, INSEAD, Singapore*

People often act as "intuitive psychologists" in understanding the behaviors of others and use the observed behaviors to make inferences about general or abstract characteristics of the observed other (Heider 1958); these inferences are called inductions (Beike and Sherman 1994). Extant research has provided ample evidence that consumers frequently make inductive inferences based on firms' behaviors and form generalizations about firms (cf. Kardes et al. 2004). Furthermore, recent research indicates that these inferences are often formed spontaneously, requiring limited cognitive resources and without attention or awareness (cf. Uleman et al. 2008). For example, when consumers are exposed to the information that a firm donated millions of dollars to protect wildlife, they may spontaneously induce that the firm is environmentally responsible.

In addition to inductive inferences, consumers also engage in the opposite type of inference—deducing and predicting specific firm behaviors based on the generalizations they hold about the firm (Beike and Sherman 1994). Unlike inductive inferences that are often generated spontaneously, deductions require more deliberative reasoning and are less likely to be formed spontaneously (Rotello and Heit 2009). For instance, deliberative reasoning is likely required to deduce from the generalization that the firm is environmentally responsible, to that the food products manufactured by the firm are of superior quality.

Research on knowledge representation suggests that concepts are organized as conceptual webs, in which concepts are represented by nodes and relations among the concepts are represented by the link structure of the network (e.g., Goldstone 1996). Building on this literature, we define distance between two concepts as a function of the number of nodes that need be traversed to link the two concepts and the strength of the relations between these nodes (see Rada et al. 1989 for a similar definition). For example, the conceptual distance between MONKEY and BANANA is shorter than that between DEER and BANANA, because the concept of MONKEY can be directly linked to BANANA via a "eat" relation, whereas it requires intermediate nodes to link DEER to BANANA. Moreover, given that people assess how plausible a focal scenario is, using the principle of concept coherence—how well the scenario corresponds with their conceptual knowledge (e.g., Connell and Keane 2004), conceptual events that are closely related tend to be considered more plausible than ones that are far apart. For example, people are likely to judge events associated with MONKEY affecting BANANA as more plausible than events associated with DEER affecting BANANA. Thus, we posit that although different CSR actions can lead to similar inductive generalizations (e.g., the firm cares about wildlife; it's a good firm), actions that are perceived to be conceptually closer (e.g., protecting a species of monkey rather than deer) to the firm's product (e.g., banana) have a stronger impact on the deductive inferences about the product (e.g., taste, quality).

To test this hypothesis, we designed several pairs of CSR actions; each pair was pretested to ensure that (1) the CSR actions differ significantly in conceptual distance to a target product and (2) each CSR action leads to similar inductive generalizations about how likable and socially/environmentally responsible the firm is. Participants were shown the scenarios, each describing two firms pursuing either conceptually close or distant CSR actions, and were asked to decide which firm's product is superior on certain attributes and which they would purchase. As expected, significantly more participants favored the firm whose action is conceptually closer to the target product; for example, over 73% participants believed that the manufacturer aiding victims of tsunamis (vs. earthquakes) produces safer boats, the firm using wind-turbine generated (vs. solar) energy to reduce $CO_2$ emission manufactures aerodynamically superior planes, and the firm protecting the natural habit of a species of monkey (vs. deer) produces more tasty bananas.

Cognitions vary in their temporal stability; whereas factual details are forgotten most rapidly, generalizations are the most stable cognitions over time (Chattopadhyay and Alba 1988). The differences in accessibility between the specific details of CSR actions and inductive generalizations formed based on the actions are likely to impact consumer inference (Kardes et al. 2004). In memory-based tasks, consumers tend to rely on the more memorable, higher-order cognitions—generalizations (e.g., the firm cares about the environment; it's a good firm)—to make deductive inferences about the product. However, in stimulus-based tasks, consumer inference is influenced by not only the generalizations but also the specific details (conceptual distance). Thus, we predict that consumers can make significantly different deductive inferences about the product in stimulus- vs. memory-based tasks.

This hypothesis was tested in Experiment 2 using a 2 (conceptual distance: close vs. distant) x 2 (task type: stimulus- vs. memory-based) between-subject design. Participants were randomly assigned to evaluate one of two magazine ads about a consumer electronics firm's CSR initiative. The ads were identical in all aspects except the descriptions about what the firm's environmental action entailed—conceptually distant vs. close. Participants in the stimulus-based condition, were asked, with the ad present, to rate how much they liked the firm, the extent to which the firm is environmentally responsible, the extent to which the firm's products are energy efficient, and how likely they would purchase this firm's products. Those in the memory-based condition completed the same set of measures after a 24-hour delay. As expected, the generalizations, attitude, and perceived environmental friendliness, did not differ across the conditions. Nonetheless, a significant interaction effect was found for the inferences about the firm's product; without delay, those in the conceptually-close condition reported significantly higher energy efficiency and purchase likelihood ratings than those in the distant condition; with a delay, however, no difference was found.

Overall, the results of the experiments provided support for the theoretical model we proposed. We found that the conceptual distance between a firm's CSR action and its product can significantly impact consumers' inferences about the product, and that this inference can differ significantly in stimulus- vs. memory-based tasks. We are currently running two more experiments examining the moderating role of cognitive resources; these studies will provide additional support for our model by showing that those with high need-for-cognition (experiment 3) or more cognitive resources (experiment 4) are significantly more influenced by conceptual distance.

## "Self and Social Signaling Explanations for Consumption of CSR-Products"

*Aronte Bennett, Villanova University, USA*
*Amitav Chakravarti, New York University, USA*

Consumers frequently encounter, and buy products that have a CSR association (e.g., cell phones giving a portion of proceeds to cancer research). It is well documented that products with a CSR-association are extremely popular among consumers and consumers may even be willing to pay a premium for these products. However, what are some key motivations that underlie a consumer's decision to purchase these products? In our research, we find that consumers like CSR-associated products for two distinct reasons.

First, we find that consumers like the fact that these products send out highly visible, social signals regarding their benevolence. We find that a consumer's likelihood of adopting a CSR-associated product varies positively with the product's social signaling potential, even when that signaling potential is very subtly cued. Specifically, in three studies we manipulated the social signaling potential of the target product by (a) varying the suggested location of the product, as either for use in a private (i.e., bedroom) or a public (i.e., living room) living space, (b) describing the target product as being especially helpful either for social (i.e., entertaining friends) or for personal (i.e., indulging oneself) occasions, or (c) varying, literally, the visibility of the CSR-association of the target product (i.e., whether the CSR-association's trademark LIVESTRONG™ yellow color was easily, partly, or not visible). Across these three studies, our results indicate that when the products did not have a CSR association they were evaluated equally regardless of their social signaling potentials. However, when the products had a CSR-association, the products were evaluated more favorably in the high social signaling potential conditions than in the low social signaling potential conditions. In fact, low social signaling potential actually lead to lower evaluations than the ones in the control (no CSR association) conditions, thus indicating that consumers tended to devalue a CSR-associated product when it had a poor social signaling potential.

Consistent with this reasoning, in a fourth study we find that owners of a CSR-associated product tend to use it in ways that maximize its social signaling potential. The study showed that consumers prefer to use a CSR-associated product in a highly socially visible location (e.g., living room) rather than in a less socially visible one (e.g., bed room), a preference that did not occur for the equivalent, control products that did not have a CSR-association. Ironically, however, these attempts to send out social signals of their benevolence appear to be wasted since in a fifth study we find that consumers are not sensitive to these social signals. In other words, observers appear to be blind to consumers' attempts to consume CSR-associated products that have high social visibility.

Finally, we also find that consumers like the more private, self-signaling potential associated with the purchase of these products, even when a strong social signal is absent. Perhaps reassuring from a normative perspective, the ability to send social signals mattered less to consumers when they were explicitly reminded about the high self-signaling potential of CSR-associated products. These studies, using disparate manipulations and dependent measures, provide convergent findings. In sum, we find that the valuation of a CSR-associated product is jointly determined by its social and self-signaling potential.

## "Competing Through Corporate Social Initiatives: The Roles of Initiative Participation and Brand Trust"

*Shuili Du, Simmons College, USA*
*C.B. Bhattacharya, ESMT, Germany*
*Sankar Sen, CUNY, USA*

Defined broadly as "a commitment to improve [societal] well-being through discretionary business practices and contributions of corporate resources" (adapted from Kotler and Lee 2005), corporate social responsibility (CSR) occupies a prominent place on the global corporate agenda in today's socially conscious market environment. An increasing body of research has shown that there are multi-faceted business benefits companies can reap from engaging in CSR activities, such as more favorable product evaluation (Sen and Bhattacharya 2001), greater consumer loyalty and advocacy (Du, Bhattacharya and Sen 2007). According to a survey reported in McKinsey Quarterly (2009), companies are using CSR initiatives to build and strengthen their competitive position in the market. However, to the best of our knowledge, prior research on CSR has focused overwhelmingly on single brand contexts and therefore has excluded any potential effects of competition on the business returns to CSR.

Using the context of a challenger-leader competition, this research examines the efficacy of CSR initiatives as a challenger's competitive weapon against a market leader. We did a series of focus groups on participants and non-participants of a real-world corporate social initiative aimed at improving oral health among disadvantaged Hispanic communities. The initiative was undertaken by an oral care brand whose market share in the U.S. Hispanic segment was lagging behind its major competitor and hence was in a challenger position. Interviews with brand managers indicated that one of the business objectives in launching this social initiative was to gain market share in the Hispanic segment. The focus group study highlighted two factors that might affect consumers' reactions to the initiative, their participation (or not) in the challenger's initiative and their extant trust in the leader. More specifically, we find that consumers who had participated in the initiative described the challenger as more trustworthy (e.g., caring, trustworthy, angelical, and Latino-it is one of us) regardless of their trust in the leader. In contrast, the reactions of consumers who were merely aware of the initiative varied dramatically depending on their level of trust in the leader. Specifically, aware consumers who had high trust in the leader tended to question the sincerity of the challenger's CSR motives (e.g., *"they help the community to make a name for themselves and to gain popularity."*), or argue that the leader provided similar benefits to the community. On the other hand, aware consumers who were not emotionally attached to the leader embraced the challenger's social initiative (e.g., *"this means they care about our welfare and want us to get ahead."*) and displayed favorable reactions to the challenger's initiative similar to those of the participant consumers.

Based on the exploratory focus group study and prior research on relationship marketing, trust, and attributions, we developed a series of hypotheses which were then tested in a follow-up field survey in the same empirical context. Results from our survey provided support for our hypotheses regarding (1) the interactive effects of initiative participation (vs. awareness) and brand trust in the leader on consumer reactions to the challenger's initiative, (2) the mediating role of brand trust in cultivating consumer loyalty, and (3) the mediating role of CSR attributions in building brand trust.

Our research contributes to the literatures of CSR, trust, and competition. By looking at the real-world scenario involving a challenger brand trying to make inroads into the incumbent brand's turf, we are able to paint a more nuanced, realistic picture of the business returns to CSR compared to previous CSR research. As well, in light of extant thinking that a late entrant's superior marketing mix is often ineffective in the face of an incumbent brand's advantage (Bowman and Gatignon 1996; Shankar, Carpenter, and Krishnamurthi 1998), our research shows, for the first time, the late entrant's ability to leverage its CSR to overcome the incumbent advantage among not only participant consumers but also non-participant consumers who are aware of the CSR and whose trust in the incumbent is relatively low. Also importantly, our research points to the pivotal role of consumers' affective trust in the dynamics of challenger-leader competition. While the unique advantage of CSR in helping a challenger compete stems from the ability of such actions to engender trust amongst its desired consumers in a relatively short period of time, turning them into not just customers but champions, consumers' trust in the market leader represents the essential competitive barrier the challenger must overcome in order to win them over.

## "Can Corporate Social Responsibility Hurt New Brands?"

*Stefanie Rosen, University of South Carolina, USA*
*Stacy Wood, University of South Carolina, USA*

Corporate social responsibility (CSR) can be used as an effective marketing technique and in 2007 companies spent $4.4 billion on CSR (Lawrence and Mukai 2008). While many brands, new and established, engage in CSR activities, new brands are increasingly positioned as socially responsible options. For instance, a new brand on the market, Method, is positioned as an environmentally-friendly line of household cleaners. CSR, defined as a "company's status and activities with respect to its perceived societal obligations" (Brown and Dacin 1997, 68), can increase customer satisfaction with the company (Marin and Ruiz 2007) and enhance brand evaluations (Brown and Dacin 1997). However, recent research suggests that consumers perceive more ethical brands to be less effective (Luchs et al. 2008). Here, we investigate this "moral discount" and find that activities can potentially hurt new brands and that the type of "ethical element" (what we refer to as the CSR attribute) strongly influences this effect.

Attributes of a product can either be centrally tied to the product's use, i.e., intrinsic attributes, or peripherally related to the product, i.e., extrinsic attributes (Richardson, Dick, and Jain 1994). Consumers use both extrinsic and intrinsic attributes when making evaluations of a brand (Jacoby, Olson, and Haddock 1973). In regards to a CSR attribute, an example of an intrinsic attribute is earth-friendly ingredients and an example of an extrinsic CSR attribute is when the company donates money to a charity.

When a brand engages in a CSR campaign, the CSR attribute becomes an important piece of accessible information for consumers to use when evaluating a new brand. According to the accessibility-diagnosticity model, accessible information will be used as input into judgment if the information is perceived to be more diagnostic than other accessible inputs (Feldman and Lynch 1988). When accessible and diagnostic, consumers use memory-based information (Menon, Raghubir, and Schwarz 1995); however, this is only possible for established/familiar brands. Context-based information, information given during the time of the decision, is used when memory-based information is not accessible. With a new/unfamiliar brand, consumers cannot rely on previous associations of the brand and therefore, the context-based information of the CSR attribute becomes diagnostic. We predict that when context-based information is related to a typical extrinsic CSR attribute, e.g., donating money to a charity, consumers will fall prey to Luchs et al. (2008) 'ethical equals less effective' lay theory. Thus, we hypothesize that

compared to a non-CSR attribute, an extrinsic CSR attribute will decrease perceived brand effectiveness for an unfamiliar/new brand.

Since the physical makeup of a product does not change with an extrinsic CSR attribute, this type of attribute is generally easy to implement. However, many new brands are also focused around intrinsic CSR attributes (e.g., Method Cleaner). Thus, do consumers' perceptions of a new brand change when the CSR attribute is intrinsic versus extrinsic? We hypothesize that an intrinsic CSR attribute actually helps a new brand because the attribute becomes part of the contextual cues used to define the product. However, extrinsic CSR attributes do not provide the same depth of contextual information and therefore are not strong indicators of the product.

In study 1, we test our hypotheses and include a familiar/established brand as our control condition. The study was conducted among undergraduate students. Participants saw a picture of an acne medicine in one of six conditions in a 2 (brand: familiar vs. new) X 3 (attribute: extrinsic CSR attribute, intrinsic CSR attribute, no CSR attribute) between-subjects design. The first factor manipulated the brand of acne medicine (familiar brand, i.e., Clearasil, versus a new brand, i.e., Dermisa). The second factor manipulated the product's attribute (extrinsic CSR attribute, intrinsic CSR attribute, no CSR attribute). In the extrinsic CSR condition, the slogan stated "20% of All Profits Donated to Environmental Charities." In the intrinsic CSR attribute condition, the slogan stated "Made with All-Organic Ingredients." In the no CSR attribute condition, no CSR information was provided. Participants then responded to questions regarding the expected efficacy of the product. We conducted a 2 X 3 ANOVA with perceived effectiveness as the dependent variable. The results support our predictions; there is a significant Attribute X Brand interaction ($F(1,136)=3.13, p<.05$). Follow-up analyses in the new brand condition show the product that donates profits to charities is perceived to be significantly less effective than the product made with all-organic ingredients ($F(1,44)=8.74, p<.01$) and the product with no CSR information ($F(1, 38)=4.61, p<.05$). However, for the familiar (control) conditions, there are no differences among the products, regardless of the attribute type (all $p$'s >.14).

To examine our results across different segments of the population, study 2 was conducted among adults ($M_{age}=40$). Participants saw a household cleaner in one of six conditions in a 2 (brand: familiar vs. new) X 3 (attribute: extrinsic CSR attribute, intrinsic CSR attribute, no CSR attribute) between-subjects design. The first factor manipulated the brand of the cleaner (familiar brand, i.e., Lysol, versus a new brand, i.e., Dettol) and the second factor manipulated the product's attribute. As in study 1, the extrinsic CSR condition referred to making a donation, the intrinsic CSR condition referred to being made with all-organic ingredients, and the non CSR condition did not contain any CSR information. Participants were then asked questions regarding the expected efficacy of the cleaner. We conducted a 2 X 3 ANOVA with perceived effectiveness as the dependent variable. There is a significant Attribute X Brand interaction ($F(1,88)=3.21, p<.05$). For the new brand, the product that donates profits to charities is perceived to be significantly less effective than the product made with all-organic ingredients ($F(1,28)=10.87, p<.01$) and the product with no CSR information ($F(1,29)=7.89, p<.01$).

We conducted two more studies as product category replications, using candy bars and laundry detergent, respectively. The results of these two studies support the findings described above. Overall, this research demonstrates that, in promoting new socially responsible brands, managers should consider the type of CSR activity in which they engage.

# REFERENCES

Beike, Denise R. and Steven J. Sherman (1994), "Social Inference: Inductions, Deductions, and Analogies," in *Handbook of Social Cognition* (2nd ed., Vol. 1), R. S. Wyer and T. K. Srull, eds., Hillsdale, NJ: Lawrence Erlbaum Associates, Inc.

Bowman, Douglas, and Hubert Gatignon (1996), "Order of Entry as a Moderator of the Effect of the Marketing Mix on Market Share," *Marketing Science*, 15(3), 222-242.

Brown, Tom J. and Peter A. Dacin (1997), "The Company and the Product: Corporate Associations and Consumer Product Responses," *Journal of Marketing*, 61 (January), 68-84.

Chattopadhyay and Alba (1988), "The Situational Importance of Recall and Inference in Consumer Decision Making," *Journal of Consumer Research*, 15, 1-12.

Connell, Louise and Mark T. Keane (2004), "What Plausibly Affects Plausibility? Concept Coherence and Distributional Word Coherence as Factors Influencing Plausibility Judgments," *Memory & Cognition*, 32(2), 185-97.

Du, Shuili, C.B. Bhattacharya, and Sankar Sen (2007), "Reaping Relational Rewards from Corporate Social Responsibility: The Role of Competitive Positioning," *International Journal of Research in Marketing*, 24(3), 224-241.

Feldman, Jack M. and John G. Lynch Jr. (1988), "Self-Generated Validity and Other Effects of Measurement on Belief, Attitude, Intention, and Behavior," *Journal of Applied Psychology,* 73(August), 421-35.

Goldstone, Robert L. (1996), "Isolated and Interrelated Concepts," *Memory & Cognition*, 24(5), 608-628.

Heider, Fritz (1958), *The Psychology of Interpersonal Relations*, New York: Wiley.

Heit, Evan and Caren M. Rotello (2005), "Are There Two Kinds of Reasoning?" *Proceedings of the Twenty-Seventh Annual Conference of the Cognitive Science Society*.

Jacob, Jerry Olson, and Rafael Haddock (1973), "Price, Brand Name and Product Composition Characteristics as Determinants of Perceived Quality," *Journal of Applied Psychology*, 55 (December), 570-79.

Kardes, Frank R, Steven S. Posavac, and Maria L. Cronley (2004), "Consumer Inference: A Review of Processes, Bases, and Judgment Contexts," *Journal of Consumer Psychology*, 14 (3), 230-256.

Kotler, Philip, and Nancy Lee (2005), *Corporate Social Responsibility: Doing the Most Good for Your Company and Your Cause*, John Wiley & Sons, Inc.: Hoboken, NJ.

Lawrence, Steven and Reina Mukai (2008), "Foundation Growth and Giving Estimates: Current Outlook," http://foundationcenter.org/ gain knowledge/research/ pdf/fgge08.pdf.

Luchs, Michael G., Rebecca Walker Naylor, Julie R. Irwin (2008), "The Ethical Penalty: Consumers Believe that Product Ethicality is Negatively Related to Product Effectiveness," (*working paper*).

Marin, Longinos and Salvador Ruiz (2007), "I Need You Too!" Corporate Identity Attractiveness for Consumers and The Role of Social Responsibility," *Journal of Business Ethics*, 71(3), 245-60.

McKinsey Quarterly (2009), "McKinsey Global Survey Results: Valuing Corporate Social Responsibility," February.

Menon, Geeta, Priya Raghubir, and Norbert Schwarz (1995), "Behavioral Frequency Judgments: An Accessibility Diagnosticity Framework," *Journal of Consumer Research,* 22(September), 212-28.

Rada, R., H. Mili, E. Bicknell, and M. Blettner (1989), "Development and Application of a Metric on Semantic Nets," *IEEE Transactions on Systems, Man, and Cybernetics*, 19.

Richardson, Paul S., Alan S. Dick, Arun K. Jain (1994), "Extrinsic and intrinsic attribute effects on perceptions of store brand quality," *Journal of Marketing*, 58 (October), 28-36.

Sen, S. and Bhattacharya, C.B. (2001), "Does Doing Good Always Lead to Doing Better? Consumer Reactions to Corporate Social Responsibility," *Journal of Marketing Research*, 38 (May), 43-62.

Shankar, Venaktesh, Gregory S. Carpenter, and Lakshman Krishnamurthi (1998), "Late Mover Advantage: How Innovative Late Entrants Outsell Pioneers," *Journal of Marketing Research*, 35(1), 54-70.

# A Closer View of Online Reviews

Dilney Goncalves, INSEAD, France
Kurt Carlson, Georgetown University, USA

## EXTENDED ABSTRACTS

### "Effects of the Consumer Review Process on Attitude Formation and Communication"

*Stephen He, Georgia Institute of Technology, USA*
*Samuel Bond, Georgia Institute of Technology, USA*

The past decade has observed a dramatic increase in the use of consumer-generated content (CGC). Modern consumers are involved in creating, sharing, and reading content, and these behaviors have received increased attention from marketing practitioners and scholars. In particular, there has been a growing interest in the effects of product reviews on consumers' purchase behavior (Chevalier and Mayzlin 2006; Weiss, Lurie, and MacInnis 2008). However, very little research has focused on the effects of review writing on the writers themselves (c.f. Moore et al 2009). In order to address this need, the current paper considers a number of questions related to review writing and attitudes; in particular, we explore how the format of the review task affects the process of review writing and readers' comprehension of the review.

We start by assuming that a consumer has recently engaged in a consumption experience and holds some attitude toward the experience, however weakly formed. We consider two different scenarios, in which consumers write a text review either before or after reporting their attitude regarding the consumption experience. Our central argument is that these two scenarios generate fundamentally different motivations, which in turn dictate the reviewing process and downstream consequences. When the review task precedes any rating, reviewers are motivated to address the different views of unknown readers. This motivation leads to a more open-ended, unstructured review task that allows the reviewer to elaborate extensively on different aspects of the experience and his or her reactions towards them (Tetlock, 1989; Schlosser, 2005). Such an 'explorative unfolding' of information allows the consumer to bring to mind a wide variety of attitude-relevant information, resulting in attitude change.

A stark contrast exists when the reviewing task follows evaluation. In this case, reviewers who have already reported their attitude will feel committed to their rating and utilize their review to engage in "defensive bolstering" (Tetlock, 1989). However, individuals are generally poor at recognizing the reasons underlying their preferences (Nisbett and Wilson 1977), and this inability should lead reviewers to encounter difficulty generating sufficient support for their stated evaluations. In keeping with the principle of metacognitive inference (Schwarz, 2004), we suggest that this perceived difficulty may result in attitude moderation. Moreover, due to their one-sided, purposeful nature, text reviews written after a rating may not be very effective at conveying the authors' attitude to readers.

In a series of lab experiments, we examined hypotheses related to the two different cases above. A pretest utilizing various short animated movie clips revealed consistent attitude differences between participants who wrote a text review of a clip and participants who simply evaluated the movie. These pretest results provided initial evidence that the mere act of writing a text review changes reviewers' attitudes.

Study 1 explored the effect of task order on attitude change and actual review content. In the experiment, undergraduate participants (N=67) watched the target stimulus, a short animated movie clip, and were then given different instructions according to condition. Two factors were manipulated: task order and type of writing. Regarding the first factor, w*rite-then-rate* conditions completed the writing task and then rated the movie, while *rate-then-write* conditions completed the steps in the opposite order. Regarding the second factor, all participants were asked to generate either a *text review* of the movie or a *filler* (summarizing events of the preceding day). In a follow-up session occurring three weeks later, participants were reminded of the movie clip and asked to recall their evaluation.

Replicating our findings, analyses revealed that at t1, the mean attitude towards the movie was considerably lower for the *review-then-rate* condition than the other three conditions (which did not differ). At t2, this attitude remained basically unchanged. For the *rate-then-review* condition, not only was t2 attitude significantly lower than that of the control groups, but the absolute difference in attitudes between t1 and t2 was significant as well. These findings support our argument that even after initial assessment, attitude was moderated by the process of writing a text review.

In order to examine review content itself, we applied the Linguistic Inquiry and Word Count tool (Pennebaker and Francis ME 2001) to analyze reviews written by the two *text review* conditions. Among other findings, analyses revealed that the *review-first* group wrote significantly more words than the *rate-first* group, indicating more elaboration of the movie experience. In addition, the ratio of positive-to-negative word use was closer to one for the *review-first* group than the *rate-first* group, indicating that the writing of the former was more balanced. Finally, the *review-first* group made greater use of articles, suggesting a more objective writing style.

Study 2 examined how differences in review content influence readers' ability to infer the attitude of the reviewer. Among the reviews written by participants in Study 1, six each were selected from the *review-first* group and the *rate-first* group. Participants (N=68) were asked to read the reviews, estimate what ratings the authors assigned the movie clip, and report their confidence in these estimates.

Rating discrepancies were calculated by taking the absolute difference between a reader's estimated rating and the author's actual rating from Study 1. In support of our prediction, analyses indicated that rating discrepancies were lower for reviews written by the *review-first* group that for the *rate-first* group. Notably, participants were actually more confident in their estimates after reading reviews from the *rate-first* group, despite also being more inaccurate. Given the text analysis results reported above, it is likely that there balanced reviews of the *review-first* group seemed more ambiguous to the readers but actually conveyed the writers' opinion more effectively.

Overall, our results provide initial evidence that reviews written before vs. after global evaluation affect reviewers' attitudes in systematic ways, differ in terms of structure and content, and create different interpretations among downstream readers. These findings bear important implications for those researching the review-writing process, and also for marketing practitioners interested in utilizing consumer-created content.

**"The Ratings Paradox: Why We Prefer Reading Negative Reviews, But Then Subsequently Rate These Reviews as Less Useful"**

*Kurt Carlson, Georgetown University, USA*
*Abhijit Guha, Wayne State University, USA*

User reviews, on sites like REI and Amazon, have emerged as an important part of the consumer buying process. In fact, in a recent survey of undergraduate students, 78% of respondents reported that they read one or more user reviews before making an online product purchase. This percentage exceeded all other behaviors, which included talking to friends to get advice (58.5%), reading one or more expert reviews (35.4%), and visiting the store to see the product (20.7%).

User reviews typically include a rating (on a 1-5 scale), coupled with an explanation of the rating (the review) and a report on how useful the review was for previous readers of the review. The usefulness data is generated from those who answer yes or no to the question, "Was this review useful?" Prospective consumers can sort the reviews by valence (e.g., one-star vs. five-star) and by usefulness score (the average usefulness of the review, as reported by those who have previously read the review and answered the usefulness question).

If there is a relatively stable relationship between the number of people who read each review and the number who answer the usefulness question, then the total number of responses to the usefulness question can be used to assess which reviews are read more often. Those reviews with the greatest number of people who answered the usefulness question are those that were most read. When examining the useful ratings, we find the following pattern. Negative (one-star) user reviews are read more often than positive (five-star) reviews, but positive reviews are rated as more useful than negative reviews. We dub this the ratings paradox.

We propose that the ratings paradox can be explained as follows. Consumers who read online product reviews generally have a weak preference for one of the products. Empirical evidence supports this claim. In particular, respondents in a recent survey we conducted reported that (on average) 69.5% of the time that they read user reviews they had a preferred product in mind while reading the reviews. We propose that this preference drives consumers to seek negative reviews about the currently preferred product. It also causes consumers to bias their evaluations of negative reviews, making them subjectively neutral. Having distorted away their diagnosticity, negative reviews are rated as less useful than positive reviews.

We rely on a series of lab studies to test our theory. In the first study, participants (N=53) engage in a choice process involving two hotels. After reading some information about the hotels, participants are asked to report which hotel is leading the choice (i.e. which option they currently prefer). After reporting their leader, participants selected one user review they would like to read about the hotels. The reviews consisted of positive and negative user reviews for each hotel. Results reveal that participants exhibited a strong tendency to seek out the negative review about their weakly preferred hotel. Specifically, 70% participants wanted to read the negative review about their preferred hotel (significantly greater than chance, binomial $z=7.30$, $p<0.001$). Thus, consumers who have a weak preference sought negative reviews about their preferred product, a result that fits with our observation that negative user reviews are read more often than positive user reviews.

We next investigated why consumers rate negative reviews as less useful than positive reviews. We know that consumers who have a weak preference tend to bias the information they encounter to support this preferred option (Carlson 2006; Russo et al 1998). If consumers bias user reviews in this manner, then negative reviews

would be converted into less negative or possibly even neutral reviews. If subjectively seen as "near-neutral" by consumers, negative reviews would rightly be rated as less useful than positive reviews simply because they would be less subjectively diagnostic.

To examine this idea, we conducted two laboratory experiments using undergraduate participants from a US university. In the first experiment (N=60), participants examined one-star reviews and five-star reviews about some products (cameras, TVs, tents etc.) drawn from Amazon and REI. Online, only 18.9% rated the one-star reviews as useful, whereas 87.5% rated the five-star ratings as useful. Laboratory participants, who were not expected to have a preference for either product because they were not shown any information for the products rated the usefulness of the reviews exactly opposite. That is, 86.7% rated the one-star reviews as useful, whereas only 35.0% rated the five-star reviews as useful. These proportions were significantly different from each other ($z>2.5$, $p<0.05$).

We next conducted a laboratory experiment (N=44) to examine whether negative user reviews would be distorted to be subjectively perceived as near neutral. Half of the participants (N=21) were shown the hotel stimuli (described earlier) and were allowed to form a preference for one of the two hotels. Participants were then asked to choose between reading negative information about the preferred hotel or negative information about the other hotel. Consistent with Carlson and Guha (2009), 18 out of 21 chose to read negative information about the preferred hotel (significantly greater than chance, binomial $z=2.17$, $p<0.05$). Participants were then given the negative information they requested. The 18 participants who read the negative information about their preferred hotel rated this information as 4.55 (i.e., near-neutral) on a 1-9 scale, (where 1 indicated negative information and 9 indicated positive information). In contrast, a separate sample of 23 participants, who examined the negative information without first forming a hotel preference rated the negative information as 2.52 (i.e. closer to the negative end) on the same 1-9 scale (2.52 is less than 4.55; ($F(1, 40)=9.2$, $p<0.05$), evidencing distortion of negative information. In comparison, the two mean evaluations reveal a strong tendency for those with a preference to convert negative information into near neutral information.

In sum, we find consumers seek negative information about a preferred product and then bias that information making it seem less useful. This pattern of lab results is consistent with our finding that negative user reviews are read more often but rated as less useful, a finding we have dubbed the "ratings paradox."

**"What Determines Customers' Evaluation of Online Reviews? The Role of Review and Product Characteristics"**

*Simon Quaschning, Ghent University, Belgium*
*Mario Pandelaere, Ghent University, Belgium*
*Iris Vermeir, Ghent University, Belgium*

During the last years there has been a huge increase in available choice options for customers (Schwartz et al. 2002), a phenomenon called hyperchoice (Mick, Broniarczyk, and Haidt 2004). But confrontation with extensive options makes decision making more difficult (Schwartz et al. 2002), partly because customers feel more responsible for their choices (Mick et al. 2004). As a result consumers will experience more uncertainty (Anderson 2003). Being confronted with an extensive assortment size may be especially likely in an online context. In addition, products online are intangible which is an additional source of uncertainty (Eggert 2006). According to the uncertainty reduction theory (Berger, and Calabrese 1975), customers will engage in uncertainty reduction efforts to alleviate and eliminate risk caused by uncertainty and to maximize outcome value. Online customer reviews have become an important source of information and can play a prominent role in this process (Chevalier, and Mayzlin 2006). While previous research has mainly focused on the link between customer reviews and product sales (Chevalier, and Mayzlin 2006; Hu, Liu, and Zhang 2008), this study explores the use of customer reviews in a pre-decision context.

Confronted with an extensive number of alternatives, customers have to make a selection of considered products beforehand for which they subsequently engage in an online search. In an attempt to make an adequate decision, they may consult customer reviews. In the present study we investigate factors that influence customers' evaluation of the helpfulness of reviews. We focus on Amazon.com ratings of helpfulness of reviews. These ratings result from a two-step process. First, customers have to decide whether or not they will rate the helpfulness of a particular review. Second, if they decide to provide a rating, they will have to decide on a positive or negative rating. The current paper investigates whether and how these two decisions are affected by product and review characteristics, like whether the review was positive or negative, the number of words, the position of the review, whether the review is written by credible reviewer, the sales rank of a product, and the type of product.

Our data consists of both product features and customer review characteristics for 260 different products, of which 116 were books and 144 CD's, taken from the public website of Amazon.com. We collected information on the price, the position on the Amazon bestseller list (sales rank) and the number of reviews written for the product. We included products with different sales ranks, with groups ranked from 1 to 25, 101 to 125, 501 to 525, 1001 to 1025, 5001 to 5025 and 10001 to 10025. For each product we took a maximum of 20 reviews into our sample, which resulted in a total of 4229 reviews, of which 1664 (39,3%) were book reviews and 2565 were CD reviews (60,7%). For 40 products there were no reviews, so we did not include them in our analysis. For each review, we counted the number of words in the review, the position the review had on the website, whether it was a top 100–reviewer (i.e. credible reviewer), the score (ranging from 1 to 5) given by the reviewer to the product and also the number of customers that voted on the helpfulness and the percentage of voting customers that found it helpful. To explore which characteristics influence revealed customer appreciation we used multilevel regression analysis.

The present findings suggest that whether the review is positive or negative, its length and position, the reviewer credibility, the sales rank and the type of the product are important predictors for the review to get a helpfulness response by the reader. Whether this response is positive and thus indicating that the reader values this review or not depends on the sales rank (depending on the type of product), number of words and score given by the reviewer.

Customers are responding more to negative reviews, which presumably render them more uncertain about their inclinations to purchase, than to (moderately) positive reviews. At the same time, however, positive reviews are rated as more helpful than negative ones. While the former can be due to the fact that customers react more extensively to inconsistency, the latter can be explained by peoples' tendency to systematically prefer information that is consistent rather than inconsistent with their own standpoint (Festinger 1957). A quadratic relationship with review length shows that moderately long reviews are considered more helpful than short or long reviews. This represents a trade-off between a balanced message with different arguments and too much information. Regarding the position of a review, book reviews further down the website, which happen to be the older reviews, attract more responses. Reviews posted long after the product release will get less attention. For CD reviews, this position effect was not obtained. Consumers tend to

selectively pay more attention to reviews from top 100-reviewers, but no effect was found on the valence of the vote (helpful or not). Obviously, reviews for bestselling products attract more votes than reviews for products with low sales. However, reviews for products further down the sales ranking are perceived as more helpful. Indeed, they may be more unknown products, for which extra information can be more helpful. This relationship cannot be found for CD's. Finally, book reviews attract more votes regarding their helpfulness than CD reviews. Possibly, customers rely more on the opinions of others for books than for CDs. The latter are more subject to personal taste.

To conclude, our results show a significant effect of several product and review characteristics on the evaluation of online reviews. For future research it might be interesting to examine the influence of experts on the evaluation of negative reviews. Also an evaluation of the review content, such as objectivity, and its connection to the valuation of the review by the customer would be interesting. Finally, since we believe that the degree of uncertainty is essential to explain potential buyers' assessment of reviews, a further step would be to test this by manipulating the degree of uncertainty.

## "Anonymous and Unanimous: The Impact of Anonymity on Opinion Generalization"

*Dilney Goncalves, INSEAD, France*
*Amitava Chattopadhyay, INSEAD, Singapore*

People care about the opinion of others. In particular, the opinion of the majority is often regarded as representing the truth (e.g., Asch, 1951; Festinger, 1954). When consumers search information online, consumers may think that a given review presents a very general opinion about a product or she may think that the reviewer is an outlier and the opinion is very idiosyncratic. Since reviewers are self-selected, the distribution of reviews does not necessarily represent the distribution of opinions in the larger population (Xinxin & Hitt 2008). Thus, before making inferences about product quality, consumers are likely to make inferences about how general the opinion expressed in the review is. Weaver et al. (2007) have shown that people might use metacognitive experiences as information when judging the popularity of an opinion. They showed that more familiar opinions were considered more widespread than less-familiar opinions, even when familiarity was increased by incidental factors–like the number of times the same person expressed an opinion.

A fundamental difference between online word-of-mouth (e.g.: reviews) and traditional word-of-mouth lies in the fact that consumers receive opinions of strangers. More than unknown to the consumer, reviewers can be completely anonymous. We propose that anonymity can influence how general an opinion feels to the reader. In particular, we hypothesize that anonymous reviews will be judged more general than signed reviews.

We assume that people have experience with a variety of opinions, ranging from very idiosyncratic to very general ones. We further assume that opinions and people are linked in memory in a spreading activation network (Anderson, 1983). Thus, people have learned from experience that when an idiosyncratic opinion is activated in memory, activation spreads to the person linked to the opinion and it feels easy to associate person and opinion. Conversely, when a general opinion is activated, because it is connected to many more people, no particular person is easily associated with the opinion. As a result, it feels difficult to associate an opinion to any particular person when the opinion is widespread. We propose that people make the inverse inference: if it feels easy to associate a person to an opinion, then the opinion is probably idiosyncratic. Conversely, if it is difficult to associate a person to an opinion, then people judge the opinion to be more general. Although this is usually true, factors unrelated to the generality of an opinion can make it easier or more difficult to think of a person. One such factor is the presence of a name accompanying a review. Next, we describe three studies conducted in this research.

In study 1, we asked participants recruited online (N=251) to read and evaluate a consumer's opinion about a restaurant. After reading the opinion–which was negative –, participants were asked to estimate the percentage of the restaurant's customers who were dissatisfied. About half the participants saw an anonymous opinion. The other participants saw a signed opinion, which was exactly the same as the anonymous with the addition of a customer's name in the last line of text. In all studies, two names were used. Since there were no differences between the two name conditions and they were aggregated in all studies. The estimates of opinion generality supported our hypothesis: participants reading an anonymous complaint estimated that 53% of the restaurant's customers were dissatisfied while those reading a signed complaint estimated that 43% of customers were dissatisfied (p<.05).

To further test our process explanation and to examine whether knowledge about the population would eliminate it, we ran a second study. In this study, participants (N=338) read a restaurant review. Prior to reading it, though, participants were informed of the restaurant's average rating (high or low). The reviews were either positive or negative. Finally, reviews were either anonymous or signed–all factors manipulated between-subjects. After reading the review, participants were asked to estimate what percentage of consumers were as satisfied (dissatisfied) as the reviewer and to explain how they reached that estimate. A significant average rating x review valence showed that participants used the mean information and estimated greater agreement when the review was in line with the average (p<.001). More importantly to our hypothesis, a significant main effect of anonymity showed that its effect still persisted even when people had knowledge of the restaurant's average evaluation. Participants were more likely to make attributions to the reviewer when the review was signed (23.5%) than when the review was anonymous (11.5%; $\chi^2$=8.26; p<.05). Finally, a mediation test showed that attributions to the reviewer mediated the effect of anonymity on estimates of opinion generality.

In the third study, we examine the effect of reviewer anonymity on choice. Participants (N=183) were recruited online to participate in the study. They were randomly assigned to an anonymous- or signed-review condition. Participants read a scenario in which they had to buy a birthday present in a hurry. They were shown a gift-basket and a positive description of it. This was intended to generate a positive first impression of the gift-basket. Then, participants read a negative review which was either signed or anonymous. Participants decided whether or not they would buy the gift-basket and estimated the percentage of people who were dissatisfied with the gift-basket. After reading the negative review, participants were more likely to buy the gift-basket in the signed condition (18.2%) than in the anonymous condition (4.7%). This effect was mediated by estimates of opinion generality.

Our results provide evidence that anonymous opinions are considered more general than signed opinions. This is because it feels easier to associate an opinion to a particular person when the opinion is signed than when it is anonymous. As a result, people are also more likely to comply with anonymous reviews. Besides demonstrating a novel effect of anonymity in online reviews, this research contributes to and extends the literature on social influence and metacognitive experiences (e.g.: Schwarz, 2004; Weaver et al., 2007) and has direct implications for the design of websites.

# A Broad View of the Notion of Sensory Interaction

Aradhna Krishna, University of Michigan,USA
Joann Peck, University of Wisconsin-Madison, USA

## SESSION OVERVIEW

While much research in the area of sensory perception has been done in the areas of cognitive psychology and neuroscience, research on sensory marketing is relatively new with the first academic conference on the subject being organized in 2008. While the field is growing, most of the research in marketing thus far focuses on a single sense – both the antecedents and consequences of sensory perception. However, one sensory input may affect perception of another – for instance, smell may affect haptic perception as one of the papers show. Also, a second temporally distinct sensory input, even belonging to the same sense, may impact perception (and even memory) of the first by creating interference in perception and recall. This session explores the concept of sensory interaction with the four papers synergistically providing a good overview of the kinds of sensory interactions that may exist. The first three papers explore sensory interaction by a second input of the same sense where the interaction is more in the form of interference – the interference is at difference times in the first paper, and at the same time in the second and third papers. The fourth paper (and also the third) consider interference by a second sense.

More specifically, the first paper examines the notion of *retroactive interference*, i.e., sensory interference by a second stimuli after exposure to the primary stimuli – if one is first exposed to brand A with smell X and later exposed to brand A with smell Y (or brand B with smell X), what impact does it have on memory for brand A with smell X? The second paper examines the effect of *simultaneous (in time) interference* with a second input of the same sense that is incongruent with the first (subjects imagine one haptic object but actually feel another one that is haptically incongruent with the first). The third paper considers congruence of sensory inputs both from within and across senses. Specifically, it shows that an incongruent size change in one dimension (for example, if one physical dimension of a package is increasing when the two other dimensions are decreasing) as well as incongruence between vision and touch influence consumers' perception of volume change. The fourth paper also considers congruence of sensory inputs, in this case between two different senses, smell and haptics – it focuses on how a semantically congruent versus incongruent smell affect haptic perception (does a rough paper appear rougher when it has a masculine smell?).

Together, the papers provide a big picture overview of sensory interaction with a hope of growing the field in a broad new direction that has many possibilities for future research.

## EXTENDED ABSTRACTS

### Is Olfactory Memory Unique?

*Mimi Morrin, Rutgers University,USA*
*May Lwin, Nanyang Technological University, Singapore*
*Aradhna Krishna, University of Michigan,USA*

The sense of smell is of critical importance to humans, although it is often the most underrated of all the five senses (Martin, Apena, Chaudry, Mulligan and Nixon 2001). Perhaps not surprisingly, the sense of smell has received less attention from consumer researchers than have the visual and auditory sensory modalities. Yet interest in scent and its effects on consumer behavior is on the rise (e.g., Bone and Jantrania 1992; Bosmans 2006; Mitchell, Kahn and

Knasko 1995; Spangenberg, Crowley and Henderson, 1996). To date, consumer researchers have focused primarily on the conditions under which pleasant scents enhance product, store, and advertising evaluations as well as lingering and variety-seeking behaviors.

Considerably less consumer research has looked at the effects of scent on memory. The few studies that have been conducted provide some initial evidence to suggest that scent enhances recognition and recall of brand information (Morrin and Ratneshwar 2003), and that this information decays only minimally over time (e.g., Krishna, Lwin and Morrin, forthcoming). However, the precise nature of scent's ability to enhance memory is not well understood. Relevant research from the field of experimental cognitive psychology is limited in this respect as well. Indeed, a debate exists regarding whether or not olfactory memory possesses a special capacity to inhibit the forgetting process (Zucco 2003). Some researchers have suggested that olfactory memory possesses unique characteristics that render it distinct from memory based on information acquired from the other senses – specifically, that it is resistant to retroactive interference (Danthiir, Roberts, Pallier and Stankov 2001, Engen 1987). Others disagree (Koster, Degel and Piper 2002, Olsen, Lundgren, Soares and Johansson 2009, Walk and Johns 1984).

We contribute to the debate by exploring the effect of scent on consumer memory over time in a competitive market context. One hundred and twenty-nine undergraduates participated in the study which involved evaluating one or more brands of moisturizer. The study consisted of six different conditions: four interference groups and two non-interference groups. All participants were exposed to a hypothetical brand of moisturizer in the form of an advertisement and product sample at time 1. Two weeks later (at time 2), those in the interference groups were exposed to another moisturizer product (containing either the different brand name, a different scent, or both a different brand and different scent); those in the non-interference groups were exposed to nothing at this time. Two weeks later (at time 3), all participants' memories were tested.

In terms of unaided attribute recall for the first brand encountered, we find that, in the absence of competition, a scented moisturizer's attributes are much better recalled than are those of an unscented moisturizer (23% versus 12%, p < .01). This result demonstrates the basic memory-enhancing effects of product scenting. In all three of the scented interference conditions, participants' ability to recall the first brand's attributes was significantly lower than in the no-interference scented condition (all p's < .05). This result provides clear evidence of retroactive interference effects. The specific nature of the scented interfering material did not matter -- thus the second or interfering brand could have the same or a different name, and the same or a different scent. From these results we conclude that product scenting provides no special immunity to retroactive interference.

We also conducted an ANOVA on incremental aided attribute recall (i.e., additional items recalled when provided with a scent-based retrieval cue). Mean comparisons show that when participants were provided with a scented retrieval cue, they recalled a larger proportion of brand attributes (11%) if the brand had been scented and there was no interference, compared to all other conditions (0% to 7%, p's < .05). This result is another demonstration of the overall memory enhancing effects of product scenting. Interestingly, providing the scented retrieval cue produced more incremental recall in the three scented interference conditions than in the two unscented conditions (all p's < .05). This result demonstrates that, if provided with an adequate retrieval cue, in this case, the product's scent, much of the information that was retroactively interfered with can nevertheless later again be retrieved – suggesting that such information is available, if not always accessible, in long-term memory.

The pattern of results suggest that scent is indeed an effective memory enhancer, but it appears to be so not because scent-associated information is immune to later exposure to similar information – that is, not due to some special immunity from retroactive interference effects. Rather, it appears to be a function of enhanced olfactory encoding. These enhanced encoding effects were evident in two ways: a) in the fact that unaided recall was nearly double for scented versus unscented products (in the absence of competitive interference), and b) that incremental recall was generated by exposure to a scented retrieval cue even after exposure to the interfering material. Thus, olfactory memory processing can be considered unique or distinct from that based on the other sensory modalities not because the forgetting process is different, but because the encoding process is different. The difference in encoding may be due to a hippocampal resources advantages (Wixted 2004) or to the fact that olfactory information is coded more perceptually than is information from the other sensory modalities (Engen 1987).

### That's Not What I Feel:
### The Effect of Haptic Imagery and Haptic Interference on Psychological Ownership and Object Valuation
*Joann Peck, University of Wisconsin-Madison, USA*
*Victor Barger, University of Wisconsin-Madison, USA*
*Andrea Webb, University of Wicsonsin-Madison, USA*

Previous research has shown that consumers value objects more highly if they own them, a finding commonly known as the endowment effect (Thaler, 1980). This effect is not limited to legal ownership; psychological ownership, characterized by the feeling that something "is mine," also produces the endowment effect. One antecedent of psychological ownership is the ability of an individual to control an object by touching it. Peck and Shu (2009) show that when individuals are given the opportunity to touch an object (versus not), they report a greater sense of psychological ownership and value the object more highly.

If touch is not available, could the act of visualizing touch act as a surrogate? According to MacInnis and Price (1987), imaging is a resource demanding process in which sensory information is represented in working memory. Bone and Ellen (1992) conjecture that imagery "may involve sight, taste, smell and tactile sensations" (p. 93). Although research on imagery and the tactile system is limited (Klatasky, Lederman & Matula, 1993), there is some evidence for the interdependence of touch and visual imagery (Katz, 1925).

Since imaging requires cognitive resources and the effects of imagery are mediated by resource availability (Bone & Ellen, 1992; Unnava, Agarwal & Haugtvedt, 1996), blocking out perceptual distractions during imaging may enhance its effects. Unnava et al. (1996) found that when imagery and perception compete for the same resources, the positive effects of imaging are reduced. Similarly, Petrova and Cialdini (2005) found that difficulty in imagery generation can reverse the positive effects of imagery appeals. In some instances, consumer behavior researchers have instructed participants to close their eyes when imaging (e.g., Bone & Ellen, 1992; Keller & McGill, 1994 (Experiment 1); Petrova & Cialdini, 2005 (Study 3)), although this was not the focus of these studies. We hypothesize that closing one's eyes while imaging touching an object leads to greater psychological ownership and valuation than imaging touching an object when one's eyes are open.

An experimental study was designed to examine the effect of touch imagery on both psychological ownership and valuation. The design was a 4 (imagery/touch: imagery eyes closed, imagery eyes open, no touch no imagery, touch with no imagery) x 2 (product: Koosh ball, blanket), with the first factor manipulated between subjects, and the second factor varied within subjects. Three hundred and twenty-six individuals participated in the study.

Our first hypothesis predicted that when participants imaged touching the product with their eyes closed, both psychological ownership and valuation would be greater than when participants imaged with their eyes open. We found a main effect of touch/imagery for both psychological and valuation. For psychological ownership, both the touch condition and the touch imagery with eyes closed condition resulted in a significantly stronger sense of ownership than the touch imagery with eyes open condition and the no touch-no imagery condition. Interestingly, there was no significant difference in either psychological ownership or valuation between the touch imagery with eyes closed condition and the condition where actual touch was possible. For valuation as the dependent measure, the results were similar.

We next conducted a second study in order to examine the process in more detail. We hypothesized that when a person closes their eyes to imagine, they are focusing their cognitive resources which results in similar effects to actual touch. In the second study, we had participants imaging touching a product (as in Study 1) but we manipulated whether haptic interference was present and also whether the interference "fit" with the imagined object. The design of this study was a 2 (vision: eyes open, eyes closed) x 3 (haptic stimulus: none, congruent, incongruent) with both factors manipulated between subjects. Three hundred and eighty seven individuals participated and we were able to replicate our first hypothesis. We also found that when a person imagines with their eyes closed, the presence or absence of a haptic stimuli does not significantly impact haptic imaging unless the stimulus is incongruent with the product being imagined.

A final study currently being conducted delves deeper into both the process and the individual difference in Need for Touch (Peck and Childers 2003). While high NFT individuals are more influenced by positive sensory information, low NFT are more affected by negative haptic sensory information (Childers and Peck). In the current study, we examine positive and negative sensory interference by high and low NFT individuals.

### How do Consumers Estimate Product Downsizing and How Can they be Helped?
*Nailya Ordabayeva, Erasmus University*
*Pierre Chandon, INSEAD*

The supersizing of food portions and packages has been identified as one of the prime drivers of the obesity epidemic (Nielsen and Popkin 2003). Supersizing leads to overeating partly because consumers underestimate just how large supersized portions and packages are (Chandon and Wansink 2007; Krider, Raghubir, and Krishna 2001). Some food companies have started to offer downsized options on their menus (e.g., Ruby Tuesday, TGI Friday's "Right Portion Right Price" menu) but these initiatives have not be very successful because consumers are averse to portion downsizing. To help consumers better monitor their consumption and to help them choose smaller food portions, it is important to understand how consumers perceive package downsizing and to compare the effectiveness of informational, visual, and haptic de-biasing strategies.

Research in psychophysics has shown that estimations of object size follow an inelastic power function of actual object size (estimated size = $a \times$ actual size$^b$, where $b < 1$), meaning that people underestimate size increases (Stevens 1986). Research in market- ing has found that the underestimation of package size changes is even stronger when an object increases in all three spatial dimen- sions (height, width, and length) rather than in just one dimension (Chandon and Ordabayeva 2009). However, we don't know why these biases occur, how they can be reduced, and whether these biases, previously reported in the context of size increases, would be similar in the context of size decreases. In this research, we test attentional and computational sources of biased size perceptions, estimate several models of size change, and test informational, visual, and haptic strategies to improve the accuracy of consumers' size estimations in the context of package downsizing.

We hypothesize that people underestimate size decreases not just because they do not pay attention to the fact that the dimen- sions are changing but because they do not correctly integrate these changes (i.e., there are computational errors not just an attentional errors). We further hypothesize that estimations do not follow the normative model of size estimation which assumes that people multiply the changes in all of the three dimensions. Instead, we compare two models: an additive model which assumes that people just add the change in all of the three dimensions and a "surface area" model which assumes that people respond to changes in the surface area of the object instead of its actual volume.

These hypotheses imply that visual and informational strategies, such as drawing attention to individual dimensions and providing information about perceptual biases would not suffice to correct size estimations. They also predict that facilitating the computational problem by reducing the dimensionality of the size decrease (from 3D to 2D to 1D) or by allowing people to hold and weigh the product (and thus rely on haptic instead of just visual information) should improve the accuracy of size estimations. Another prediction of both the additive and surface models is that product downsizing would be more obvious when one dimension is decreased (1D downsizing) than when one dimension is actually increased while the other two are strongly decreased (elongated downsizing). Finally, because of the height/width illusion, we would expect that size estimations are more sensitive when it is the height of the object which is elongated rather than its width.

In study 1, participants saw four sizes (XL, L, M, and S) of rectangular candles and cylindrical candy boxes which decreased either in 1D (height only), 2D (width and length), or 3D. All participants were given the weight and price of the largest op- tion (XL) and were asked to estimate the weight and to provide their willingness to pay for sizes L, M, and S. Participants in the decomposition condition were also given the height, width and length of size XL and had to estimate the height, width, and length of the other sizes. This manipulation ensured that they would pay attention to the fact that more than one dimension may have been reduced. We found a strong underestimation bias on average (b = .85). Reducing the dimensionality of size decrease from 3D to 2D to 1D reduced and eliminated the bias (b = .67, b = .89, and b = 1.06), but drawing attention to individual dimensions did not. We also found that the additive model fit the data better than any other models. This shows that the errors are driven by computational errors and not by attention.

In Study 2, we used a similar design as in Study 1 but ma- nipulated whether the product was downsized in 1D or through elongation because it allows us to better compare the predictions of the additive and surface area models. In addition, some of the participants were asked to hold and weigh the products while others were given information about the feedback on their estimation ac- curacy in a prior similar task. A control group only saw the products visually and was given no feedback (just like in Study 1). Finally, we

manipulated the dominant dimension of the package by displaying the two products (soap bars or rectangular candles) either on their base (salient height) or on their side (salient width). As predicted, people noticed the size reduction more when only one dimension was changed than when the product was elongated (b = .81 vs. b = .23). Allowing people to touch and weigh the packs significantly improved estimation accuracy (b = .59 vs. b = .43). However, providing information and changing the dominant dimension of a package had no effect. Again, we found that the additive model fit the estimation data better than the alternative models.

In the third study, conducted in collaboration with a major consumer good company, we tested the effectiveness of elongated and 1D downsizing of dog food packages. The participants were all dog owners and were asked to choose between a regular-size pack of a competitor brand and a new downsized version of the company's product which was either downsized in 1D or elongated in height or width. As predicted, the choice share of the downsized pack was larger when the pack was downsized by elongation (57% for the height condition and 46% for the width condition) than when it was downsized in 1D (39%).

## The Semantic and Aesthetic Impact of Smell on Touch

*Cindy Caldara, University of Grenoble, USA*
*Ryan S. Elder, University of Michigan, USA*
*Aradhna Krishna, University of Michigan, USA*

The marketing literature has received a marked increase in scholarly attention devoted to the impact of sensory perception on consumer behavior (see Peck and Childers 2008). Not surprisingly, much of this exploration has shown the effects of the senses on consumer behavior in isolation from one another. Research on the impact of smell on memory (Morrin and Ratneshwar 2003), music on shopping behavior (Yalch and Spangenberg 2000), and touch on feelings of ownership (Peck and Shu 2009) highlight some of the fascinating results from this primary focus. Despite the need to continue exploring the impact of senses in isolation, the founda- tion now exists to support studies on the interaction of senses. We contribute to the literature on multisensory interactions by showing the sensory aesthetic (we define sensory aesthetics as the combined hedonically pleasing effects of sensory inputs) and semantic impact of smell on touch. Across two studies we show that the scent of a product can impact haptic perceptions, with these effects being moderated by the level of congruity between the sensory stimuli.

### Multisensory Interactions and Consumer Behavior

The overall neural representations of product experiences rely on a combination of all sensory inputs. Recent studies within consumer behavior have explored these cross-modal interactions, including touch and taste (Krishna and Morrin 2008), smell and sound (Matilla and Wirtz 2001), sound and vision (Russell 2002), vision and taste (Hoegg and Alba 2007), as well as multiple sensory inputs and taste (Elder and Krishna 2010). These cross-modal inter- actions between senses have important consequences on consumer perceptions and behavior.

The specific combination of smell and haptics has not received attention within the marketing literature despite the acknowledge- ment that both scent and touch in isolation greatly impact consumer behavior (e.g., Morrin and Ratneshwar 2000; Peck and Wiggins 2006). However, recent research within psychology provides pre- liminary evidence that these sensory inputs do interact. Dematte and colleagues (2006) show that scent can impact touch, wherein a positive scent leads to better fabric perceptions than an unpleasant scent. In addition to this overall halo effect of smell on touch, we anticipate that semantic associations of the scent, as well as the congruence of these associations and the tactile properties of the stimulus, will further affect perceptions of the product. Whether learned or automatic, scents are not devoid of meaning. Indeed, the meaning of scents can affect not only perceptions, but actual behavior (Holland et al. 2005). Our current work explores not the aesthetic impacts of smell on touch, as well as the importance of semantic congruence within cross-modal interactions. We exhibit our effects across two different dimensions of touch (texture, temperature), and using two sets of fragrances.

## Study 1

Study 1 explores the impact of semantic sensory associations and congruity. As we were interested in drawing semantic associations from the smell to the haptic experience, we needed to find a way to match the stimuli. The specific question to be addressed is whether a masculine or feminine smell can impact texture perceptions of paper matched for congruity (rough and smooth paper, respectively). We carefully pretested masculine and feminine smells, as well as rough and smooth paper for equal likeability as well as equal distances from the midpoint on a masculine/feminine scale.

*Design and Procedure.* Seventy-three undergraduate participants were randomly assigned to one of the four conditions. Each was given a scented piece of paper to evaluate. In contrast to the prior studies, participants were told to touch and also smell the fragrance on the paper. Following ratings of the smell, participants rated the overall texture of the paper.

*Results.* We found a significant main effect of texture ($p < .001$) as well as a significant interaction of paper type and smell on perceived texture of the paper ($p < .005$). Follow-up contrasts on the interaction revealed that within the smooth paper condition, the feminine smell lead to significantly smoother perceptions than the masculine smell. Similarly, in the rough paper condition, the masculine smell lead to significantly rougher perceptions than the feminine smell. The results support the semantic associations of smell as well as congruence effects. We show that scents do have meanings, and that these meanings can have a significant impact on other sensory inputs, such as touch.

## Study 2

In study 2, we replicate and extend the findings of study 1 on semantic congruence to a different dimension of touch, namely temperature. The specific question to be addressed is whether the feel or temperature of a smell can impact evaluations of haptic quality. We again pre-tested fragrances to be equal on overall likeability and familiarity, but to differ on perceived temperature of the smell. We ultimately selected pumpkin cinnamon as a warm smell and sea island cotton as the cool smell, and used therapeutic gel-packs (either hot or cold) as the product to be evaluated haptically.

*Design and Procedure.* We employed a 2 (fragrance: warm, cool) x 2 (gel-pack: warm, cool) between subjects design with overall evaluations as the dependent variable. Ninety-eight participants were instructed that they were to evaluate an aromatherapy hot/cold gel-pack. Each participant smelled the gel-pack and then placed the gel-pack on her hand for 15 seconds. Following this procedure, participants rated how well the gel-pack worked (very effective, very quickly, cooled/heated hand well).

*Results.* We find a significant main effect of gel-pack temperature, whereby the cold gel-pack is perceived as more effective than the warm gel-pack. More importantly, we also find our hypothesized interaction between gel-pack and fragrance temperature ($F(1, 94) = 8.49$, $p < .005$). Follow up contrasts reveal our anticipated effects as within the cold gel-packs, the cold smell leads to significantly higher evaluations than the warm smell. Similarly, within the warm gel-pack conditions, the warm smell led to significantly higher evaluations than the cool smell.

The results from study 2 replicate our findings from study 1 and add an additional dimension of touch (temperature). Furthermore, our findings explicate another instance where smell can lead to semantic associations that drive the evaluative consequences of congruence for haptic stimuli.

# Great Expectations: The Placebo Effect and Consumer Behavior
Eric Hamerman, Tulane University, USA
David Faro, London Business School, UK

## EXTENDED ABSTRACTS

### "Placebo Responses to Shaken Belief: Detrimental Impact of Consumer Choice on Product Efficacy"

*Baba Shiv, Stanford University, USA*
*Himanshu Mishra, University of Utah, USA*
*Ziv Carmon, INSEAD, France*

A large body of research documents the benefits of allowing people to control their fate by exercising choice over experiences they will undergo. In a particularly dramatic example, Langer and Rodin (1976) showed allowing nursing home residents an ability to choose among seemingly inconsequential options, such as on which of two possible dates they will watch a particular movie, dramatically improved both their well being and longevity. From a practical perspective, service providers and retailers are often encouraged to empower consumers to choose for themselves. We propose that such empowerment can backfire and impair the effectiveness of the chosen option. This prediction builds on the theories of Option Attachment (Carmon et al. 2003), and Placebo Effects of Marketing Actions (Shiv et al. 2005).

Research on Option Attachment suggests that empowering consumers to make choices involving significant conflict among the choice alternatives can lead to post-decision discomfort with the chosen option and an increase in the appeal of rejected options. And research on Placebo Effects of Marketing Actions shows that changes in consumer expectations about the effectiveness of products they are to consume can influence the actual efficacy of those products.

In light of those theories, we propose that choosing among choice alternatives can hurt expectations for, and confidence in, the efficacy of the selected option and as a result of a negative placebo effect lessen the actual efficacy of the chosen option.

The basic experimental paradigm was as follows. Participants were informed that some research has shown that caffeinated tea helps with having a focused brain, while tea with extracts from the chamomile flower (Chamomile tea) can calm the brain. However, the results of these studies are not completely definitive and, therefore, the purpose of this study is to examine the effectiveness of caffeinated tea versus chamomile tea. While participants were consuming the tea, they were shown a video purportedly to allow the ingredients to have their effects. After consuming the tea, they were asked to solve a series of word-jumble puzzles, with their goal being to solve as many puzzles as possible in the allotted 30 minutes.

The purpose of Experiment 1 was to document the basic effect and to show that conflict among the choice options is a significant cause of the effect. Our study design was a 2 (choice: participants chose vs. randomly assigned one of the options) x 2 (conflict: the choice options with conflicting vs. similar benefits). Analysis show that the number of puzzles solved was significantly lower in the choice condition than in the no-choice condition, but this was only true when the choice involved a conflict.

In Experiment 2, we sought further support for our option attachment explanation by asking one group of participants to list advantages and disadvantages of each choice alternative. Thus, the study design was a 2 (choice: participants chose vs. randomly assigned one) x (elaboration: before being asked to choose participants listed advantages and disadvantages of each option vs. this was not mentioned). As predicted we found a significant main effect

for choice as well as a significant interaction between elaboration and choice.

In Experiment 3, we sought a different way to evoke a debilitating effect of choice by manipulating participants' confidence in the quality of their choice by using a subtle handedness manipulation that has been shown to influence confidence. Specifically, in a separate study we asked participants to write either with their dominant or their non-dominant hand. Thus, the study design was a 2 (choice: participants chose vs. randomly assigned one) x (handedness: subjects were instructed to write with their dominant hand vs. subjects were instructed to write with their non-dominant hand). The results show the impact of choice as well as for the hand used to write affected the number of puzzles solved. We conclude by discussing the significant managerial and public policy implications of our findings.

### "Merely Accessible: Products May be Effective without Actual Consumption"

*David Faro, London Business School, UK*
*Monika Heller, London Business School, UK*
*Caglar Irmak, University of South Carolina, USA*

Imagine the following scenario. You wake up with a headache one morning, so on your way to work, you stop by the pharmacy and buy a headache medicine. You put the medicine in your bag and continue your journey to work. When you arrive, you are so busy that you do not take the medicine right away. Would the fact that you purchased the product and had access to it have a positive effect on your headache even though you did not actually consume the product? Would the mere fact that a solution was available and accessible to you suffice to relieve at least part of the problem?

In this paper, we provide evidence for this effect, which is to some extent reminiscent of the placebo effect. In a typical placebo study, a doctor gives a patient a pill that, unbeknownst to the patient, is only a sugar pill. Even though the pill has no inherent power to produce an effect, it has a genuine physiological effect on the patient. Placebo studies therefore show that an active ingredient need not be consumed to produce an effect (e.g., Geers et al. 2005; Irmak, Block, and Fitzsimons 2005; Shiv, Carmon, and Ariely 2005). In our study, we find that actual consumption may sometimes not be necessary either.

A pilot study was conducted following the first outbreak of swine flu in the UK in late 2009. We tested whether ease of access to Tamiflu (the main drug used in the prevention and treatment of swine flu), would affect participants' self-reports of immune system strength. Participants in an online pool first received basic information about swine flu. Then they received information about Tamiflu and were told that it functions similarly to the immune system by preventing the flu virus from entering body cells and by blocking the release of new copies of the virus. Participants in the high-accessibility condition, who were students, were told that college and university students (along with infants, schoolchildren, pregnant women, and the elderly) would be included in the priority groups to receive Tamiflu. Priority groups in the low-accessibility condition did not include college and university students. Participants then filled out a self-report of current immune system strength (which included items such as: How strong is your immune system in fighting viruses? How often do you get colds and flu? How are your energy levels? My immune system is ... very weak/very strong. My general health is … very bad/very good.) Participants in the high-accessibility condition reported their current immune system to be stronger. Moreover, their beliefs about the efficacy of Tamiflu in treating swine flu did not have a significant effect on the results. These results provided initial support for our contention that mere access to a remedy may bring about the claimed effects of the remedy.

In the next study, participants completed two separate concentration tasks. After the first task, participants in the experimental condition were told that coffee was available if they wanted it. On a table behind the participants were a thermos, cups, sugar/sweetener, and milk. In the control condition, coffee was not available and was not mentioned throughout the study. In a third condition aimed to rule out a priming explanation, coffee was mentioned as being available but then was not accessible during the study. The main dependent measure was participants' performance in a second reaction-time task. Participants saw a grid with empty check-boxes presented as a 10 x 10 matrix on a computer screen. We asked participants to click on as many boxes as they could in 20 seconds. We also collected self-reports of stress and perceived control, as well as expectations about coffee's efficacy in improving task performance. Results showed that performance in the coffee-available condition was significantly better than performance in the control and coffee-noted-but-unavailable conditions. Self-reports of stress, perceived control, and expectations about the efficacy of coffee did not show any significant effects.

These results, along with those of the pilot study, suggest that mere access to a product can be as effective as actual consumption and that this effect of accessibility is independent of expectations about product efficacy. Although perceived product efficacy did not have an effect on participants' performance in these experiments, accessibility to a beneficial product may enhance consumers' self-efficacy in accomplishing tasks related to the product's benefits and, as a result, improve task performance. If self-efficacy plays such a role in this process, we would expect to observe a stronger effect of accessibility on performance for participants with low self-efficacy.

Thus, in the final study, we tested the moderating effect of self-efficacy and examined the effect in a new setting. In the main task, participants solved word puzzles. Half the participants had access to a dictionary to which they could refer during the task if they wanted to do so. This was the manipulation of accessibility. For the manipulation of self-efficacy we used a typical procedure of positive or negative feedback in a preceding related task (e.g., Vancouver et al. 2002). Results indicated that for low-self-efficacy participants, the presence of the dictionary significantly improved performance in the word puzzles. For the high-self-efficacy participants we did not find such a difference. Whether participants made use of the dictionary did not change the results.

These results suggest that mere accessibility to a remedy increases consumers' self-efficacy and their task performance. In other words, under certain conditions, products can be effective without being consumed.

### "Two Wrongs Sometimes Make a Right: Task Difficulty in Nocebo and Placebo Treatments"

*Eric Hamerman, Tulane University, USA*
*Tor Wager, University of Colorado, USA*
*Gita V. Johar, Columbia University, USA*

The placebo effect is a robust phenomenon in the field of medicine that demonstrates how beliefs and expectations can impact treatment outcomes. When a patient expects to be cured, health often follows (Beecher, 1955). On the flip side, expecting poor health can lead to illness, which has been termed the "nocebo" effect (Benson, 1997; Hahn, 1997; Spiegel, 1997).

More broadly, negative outcomes tend to occur after individuals are presented with pessimistic suggestions, and vice versa. This is consistent with the idea that performance expectancies–whether positive or negative–are good predictors of actual performance (Wigfield & Eccles, 2000).

However, individuals will sometimes attempt to compensate for lower expectations by increasing their efforts (Fillmore & Vogel-Sprott, 1995; Harrell & Juliano, 2009). This paper attempts to address the issue of when people are most likely to engage in this compensatory response and reverse the nocebo effect.

In two studies, individuals are presented with an energy drink that is framed as either an "enhancement" (placebo treatment) or "impairment" (nocebo treatment) to performance. Additionally, the task which they are asked to perform is presented as either difficult or neutral. Both studies utilized a 2 x 2 between-subjects design, with factors of placebo treatment (placebo or nocebo) and task difficulty (difficult or neutral).

In Study 1, each participant completed a set of analytical reasoning questions (from the LSAT) as a baseline measure of performance, and then was given a placebo or nocebo treatment. In this case, the placebo treatment consisted of an energy drink purported to increase cognitive ability. The nocebo treatment was an energy drink that was said to have a side effect of decreasing cognitive ability. Subsequently, participants completed a second set of analytical reasoning questions, which was framed as either similar to–or more difficult than–the baseline questions.

The dependent variable was the change in number of questions answered correctly between the first and second set of analytical reasoning questions. Results indicated a significant interaction between placebo treatment and task difficulty. In the nocebo condition, framing the task as difficult (vs. neutral) led to a larger increase in performance versus the baseline. In the placebo condition, the results were reversed: a larger improvement in performance over the baseline occurred when the analytical reasoning problems were framed as neutral (vs. difficult).

In order to determine the mechanism by which nocebo respondents performed better when presented with a more difficult task, the experimental paradigm of Study 1 was replicated in Study 2, with a few important additions. After drinking the placebo or nocebo energy drink and being informed of the task difficulty, participants were asked to report their performance expectations, and then completed a threat-challenge scale that measured whether they appraised the analytical reasoning task as a threat or challenge.

Results indicated that in both the placebo and nocebo conditions, participants expected lower performance when the questions were described as difficult (vs. neutral). However, the performance results mirrored that of Study 1. Nocebo participants solved more problems when they were described as difficult (vs. neutral), while placebo respondents solved more problems when they were described as neutral (vs. difficult). As in Study 1, the interaction between placebo treatment and task difficulty was significant for performance.

Respondents were also asked how many additional questions they would be willing to answer at the close of the session for an additional payment. Nocebo participants reported that they would be willing to answer more questions when the questions were framed as difficult (vs. neutral); the reverse was true for the placebo respondents. This was the same interaction that occurred for performance, suggesting that differences in persistence and effort drove the changes in performance.

We hypothesized that the reason for the nocebo participants' performance improvement when faced with a difficult task was a compensatory response to a threatening situation. In support of this prediction, the self-reported measure of "threat" was found to be highest (compared to the other three conditions) in the case of a nocebo treatment combined with a difficult task.

## "Explaining the Crossmodal Influence of Color on Odor Identification Responses: An Expectations-Based Approach"

*Maya Shankar, Oxford University, UK*
*Chris Simons, Givaudan Flavors*
*Baba Shiv, Stanford University, USA*
*Samuel McClure, Stanford University, USA*
*Thuan K. Ngo, Oxford University, UK*
*Charles Spence, Oxford University, UK*

In tasks that require us to identify odors just on the basis of (orthonasal) olfactory cues, our performance is quite poor. In fact, we are only able to correctly identify roughly one third of familiar odors when these cues are presented in isolation (e.g., Engen & Ross, 1973; see Zellner et al., 1991, for a review). This is perhaps not so surprising, however, when one considers that under more naturalistic conditions, we rarely have to identify a substance without access to additional information from both higher level cognition and other sensory modalities (see de Araujo et al., 2005; Herz & von Clef, 2001; Zellner et al., 2001). As a result, we often look to the expectations generated by other sensory cues in order to help facilitate correct identification of odors. Crossmodal influences of this kind can help enhance and contribute to a more successful interpretation of those objects in the world around us (e.g., see Cardello, 2007, for a review).

One such cue comes from color. Previous research has shown that the color of a stimulus can generate salient expectations as to its likely properties and identity characteristics (Elliot et al., 2005). Critically, with regards to food and drink acceptance, Cardello (1994) asserts that expectations about the sensory or hedonic properties of food and drink can contribute just as much to a person's final assessments of a stimulus as the physiochemical properties of the food or drink itself (cf. Yeomans et al., 2008; see also Feather, 1982; Tolman, 1951). Given the significant implications of this assertion, it is somewhat surprising that little research has examined whether and in what ways expectations can influence sensory evaluations and identity judgments.

Thus, the current work examined one such unexplored relationship: namely, the role that color cues may play in our (orthonasal) identification of odors. More specifically, it explored the role of color as a generator of flavor-based expectations and the multitude of variables that may modulate whether these expectations exert a significant influence on our odor judgments.

In our procedure, participants were asked to identify–by smell–the flavor of drinks that varied in color. We found that respondents were likely to identify a flavor smell that was consistent with the color of the drink, even when the actual flavor differed. This was especially likely to occur when the discrepancy between the expected and actual flavors was small. We also collected self-reported data on consumer expertise, and found that this factor impacted participants' abilities to correctly identify flavors.

The contributions of this research are three-fold: 1) It introduces a novel methodology for properly measuring individuals' color-flavor associations and expectations prior to testing in order to control for individual differences; 2) It systematically examines variables that may mediate whether expectancy information influences participants' judgments of odor identity (and in the process, reveals that color can have differential effects on odor identification depending on a number of variables and experimental conditions); and 3) It accounts for the reported results by appealing to a categorical version of the Assimilation/Contrast Theory (Deliza & MacFie, 1992; Zellner et al., 1994). Critically, the model used to explain this data proposes that the confidence with which a participant views his or her color-based expectations may play just as big a role in mediating how participants use their expectations as the stimulus attributes themselves.

# "I Have a Feeling It Will Turn Out Fine":
## How Social and Emotional Factors Affect Risk Perception

Sara Kim, University of Chicago, USA
Ann L. McGill, University of Chicago, USA

## EXTENDED ABSTRACTS

### "Gaming with Mr. Slot or Gaming the Slot Machine? Power, Anthropomorphism, and Risk Perception"

*Sara Kim, University of Chicago, USA*
*Ann L. McGill, University of Chicago, USA*

Recent research in social psychology has begun to investigate factors that influence people's tendency to anthropomorphize non-human entities such as objects or animals (Epley et al. 2008). Consumer behavior researchers have been interested in how anthropomorphism in turn affects judgments and behavior (Aggarwal and McGill 2007). To date this work has primarily been interested in how anthropomorphism affects quality assessments and overall liking, and studies have contrasted evaluations of anthropomorphized and non-anthropomorphized products. The present research, by contrast, explores situations in which the same degree of anthropomorphism can color judgments differently depending on how people apply beliefs and expectations of social concepts such as power. Moreover, this research focuses on other types of judgments beyond liking, in particular, risk perception.

The central hypothesis of this research is that anthropomorphizing a product causes consumers to apply social expectations and beliefs they would not normally apply to an inanimate entity. For example, for consumers considering playing a slot machine, our hypothesis is that their perception of risk (and so their willingness to play) would depend on whether they see the machine as being human. If the product is not anthropomorphized, risk assessments should follow from nonsocial considerations. However, if the entity is anthropomorphized, risk assessments should follow from beliefs and expectations about human interaction, such as consumers' perceived social power over others, their degree of trust in others, their sense of personal need, and their view of others as kind or altruistic. Hence, anthropomorphism may have different effects depending on the model of social interaction brought to mind at the time of the decision.

In this sense, we can view the effect of anthropomorphism on risk assessment as a type of illusion of control. Previous research on illusory control shows that when a task has some characteristics that people associate with personal skill, individuals sometimes behave as if they can influence outcomes that are actually the result of pure chance (Langer 1975) This research proposes that anthropomorphism can also increase or decrease illusory control through the (mis-) application of social factors to outcomes that are based on chance. In this research, we focus in particular on the effect of perceived social power on risk assessments for anthropomorphized products.

In most social psychology studies, power is defined as an individual's relative controllability to change the states of others in accordance with his or her own will (Thibaut and Kelley, 1959). Further, the causal relationship between perceived power and feelings of control is bidirectional (Thibaut and Kelley, 1959). People believe they have more power over others when they have more control, and people believe they have more control when they feel more powerful. We propose that anthropomorphism increases application of power perception. That is, people who feel very powerful transfer this feeling of mastery to the anthropomorphized entity, believe they can control it, and so feel less risk. In contrast, people who are low in power feel at the mercy of the entity, and so feel greater risk.

In the first experiment, we showed that participants who felt powerful acted as if they had more control when they anthropomorphized the slot machine (lower risk perception). Anthropomorphism was manipulated by modifying the look of the machine so it appeared to have a face or not. Power was manipulated by asking participants to recall an incident in which they felt powerful or not. Powerful consumers who saw the machine as human were more willing to play a risk-related game, whereas the powerless acted as if they had less control over the outcomes when they anthropomorphized the slot (higher risk perception), decreasing willingness to play the game.

In the second experiment, we used skin cancer as a risk generating entity, a conceptual replication but also one which extends our investigation to a less pleasurable domain than gambling. Again we replicated the interactive effect between anthropomorphism and power on risk perception. In this study, anthropomorphism was manipulated by the message about the disease. In the high anthropomorphism condition, the disease was described as if it has evil intentions to hurt people. Power was manipulated as in the first study. Participants with low power perceived skin cancer as a more risky disease when it was highly anthropomorphized, whereas those with high power showed the opposite pattern. Moreover, this risk perception was positively correlated with liking of a sunscreen which can prevent skin cancer.

In the third experiment, we investigated the reverse effect that perceived risk affected people's tendency to anthropomorphize depending on their feelings of power. High risk (vs. low risk) increased anthropomorphism for people with low power, while low risk (vs. high risk) increased anthropomorphism for those with high power. Specifically, participants with low power were more likely to anthropomorphize the slot machine after losing than winning the game, whereas those with high power were more likely to anthropomorphize the slot after winning than losing the game. Theoretical implications pertaining to the power and anthropomorphism in judgments and preference construction and managerial implications regarding what managers might be able to do to change risk perception involving with products will be discussed. (843 words)

## References

Aggarwal, Pankaj and Ann L. McGill (2007), "Is That Car Smiling at Me? Schema Congruity as a Basis for Evaluating Anthropomorphized Products," *Journal of Consumer Research*, 34(December), 468-479.

Epley, Nicholas, Scott Akalis, Adam Waytz, and John T. Cacioppo (2008), "Creating Social Connection Through Inferential Reproduction: Loneliness and Perceived Agency in Gadgets, Gods, and Greyhounds," *Psychological Science*, 19(2), 114-120.

Langer, Ellen J. (1975), "The Illusion of Control," *Journal of Personality and Social Psychology*, 32 (2), 311-28.

Thibaut, John W. and Harold H. Kelley (1959), The Social Psychology of Groups, New York: Wiley.

### "Aesthetics as Impetus to Riskier Decision-Making"
*Claudia Townsend, University of Miami, USA*
*Suzanne Shu, University of California, Los Angeles, USA*

We investigate the psychological impact of aesthetics on decision-makers and how this affects propensity to engage in risky behavior. Previous research has shown that the aesthetics of a chosen object can influence a person's thoughts about themselves. Specifically, choice of highly aesthetic options can be a form of self-affirmation and have the same impact on subsequent behavior as does a self affirmation manipulation (Townsend and Sood 2009). Experimentally induced self-affirmation interventions can lead to positive outcomes such as overcoming confirmation bias and reduced defensiveness (e.g. Cohen, Aronson, and Steele 2000). Townsend and Sood (2009) find that people who choose a highly aesthetic product show subsequent reduced defensiveness, as though they had earlier engaged in self-affirmation. Using this prior literature as a starting point, we examine whether providing the consumer with a personal association with high aesthetics impacts subsequent decision-making and specifically risk taking. Given that association with highly aesthetic objects seems to be a source of self affirmation, we hypothesize that it will lead to both increased openness to arguments and riskier behavior. The increased risk taking that comes from association with aesthetic objects is consistent with recent findings that individuals with an induced or chronic greater sense of self engage in riskier behavior (Johnson 2000). The primary domain in which we test these predictions is financial decision making and investment in company stocks.

In study 1 we examine whether association with high aesthetics leads to riskier investment behavior. Using a student population we created an association with either high aesthetics or high functionality through hypothetical ownership in a company that either emphasizes aesthetics or functionality. We find that respondents who have previously been associated with high-aesthetics are more likely to invest in a hypothetical risky investment and also offer a higher minimum investment at which they would invest ($637.23 vs. $435.60) than respondents who have previously been associated with high functionality. Consistent with the theory that association with high aesthetics is self-affirming and impacts subsequent openness to arguments, participants who had been associated with the high aesthetics company found the pitch for the subsequent risky investment opportunity to be more convincing and reasonable than both the Control and Function-association participants. We also find that participants associated with aesthetics exhibit less risk aversion as measured through willingness to accept a risky gamble than respondents in the other two conditions.

In Study 2 we test this effect using a population with relevant expertise and real financial documents. We examine the investment behavior of respondents with a background in finance who, presumably, are more immune to irrelevant influences on their financial decision-making. Using pairs of actual published company annual reports matched by industry, respondents were told that they were owners of stock in either the companies represented by more aesthetic reports or by the less aesthetic reports within each pair (without explicit referral to aesthetics). After this association we presented respondents with the same risky investment decision and questions on willingness to engage in risky gambles as in study 1. The results confirmed the findings of study 1 revealing that association with high aesthetics leads to riskier investment behavior even among respondents with a background in finance who claim that the aesthetics of the report has no influence on their decisions. Moreover, we find that association with company annual reports alone can provide the aesthetic association needed to self-affirm and cause this effect.

Study 3 replicates the previous results and examines closely the process of self-affirmation through which this occurs. Respondents are told that they own stock in the companies with the aesthetic annual reports used in study 2. We then measure reduced defensiveness and openness to arguments, and show that the effect of high aesthetics on these measures is as strong as a self-affirmation condition, relative to a control group. It is this connection between high aesthetic design and the sense of the self that results in the increased risky behavior. Implications for this are discussed in the realms of self-affirmation theory, risk preferences, and decision-making. (665 words)

### References
Johnson, John C (2000), "Correlations of self-esteem and intolerance of ambiguity with risk aversion, *Psychological Reports*, 87(2), 534.
Townsend, C. and Sood, S. (2009). Self-Affirmation Through the Choice of High Design. UCLA working paper.

### "Negative Emotions and Health Messaging: Coping Efficacy and Message Framing Effects"
*Adam Duhachek, Indiana University, USA*
*Nidhi Agrawal, Northwestern University, USA*

Consumer research in recent years has explored how emotional experiences impact consumer attitudes and behaviors. While most research focused on the role of valenced affective states (i.e., positive or negative mood), recent research has begun to look at the role of specific discrete emotional states. A few studies have documented ways in which emotions might affect information processing and persuasion. The current research studies the emotions of shame and guilt in the context of public service messages related to binge drinking. We test the basic proposition that the specific negative emotions of shame and guilt, differ with respect to the efficacy appraisals underlying these emotions and these emotions are differentially responsive to gain versus loss message frames. Building off of theoretical work examining interactions between efficacy and message frame, we postulate the differential effectiveness of these messages are due to differences in the appraisal of coping efficacy, thereby contributing to the literature examining emotions and message framing effects.

Study 1 found that the low efficacy emotion of shame was compatible with a negative message frame, whereas the high efficacy emotion of guilt was compatible with a positive message frame. Not only did this compatibility result in increased persuasion in terms of binge intentions, but also with respect to individual perceptions of risk associated with excessive drinking. Study 2 examined the role of efficacy-based compatibility on subsequent resistance to information that runs counter to the health message. Those experiencing shame (guilt) and exposed to negative (positive) frames were better equipped to resist subsequent pro-alcohol information that ran counter to the health message. In both cases, these individuals were less willing to view alcoholic beverage recipes. Study 3 demonstrated that these compatible conditions resulted in increased efficacy as individuals in the shame (guilt) negative (positive) frames were more persuaded and held subsequently greater activation of the relevant coping strategy. Importantly, this coping strategy-related finding demonstrates the integral role of efficacy in interpreting the effects of message frame on persuasion. Study 4 sought additional evidence of the role of efficacy in driving these effects by testing a problem-focused coping empowerment mechanism to reverse the compatibility-effects of the low efficacy emotion of shame and negative frames. Those experiencing shame, a low efficacy emotion, responded to messages in ways similar to those experiencing the high efficacy emotion of guilt when they were empowered by problem-focused coping strategies.

This paper makes three main contributions to theory related to message frame and emotions as well as to the substantive domain of consumer health messaging. First, While past research has examined the effect of valenced affective states (positive versus negative mood) on message framing, we make a unique contribution by examining the effects of two discrete negative emotions on message framing. Second, we extend previous research on message frames by articulating an appraisal-based account of emotions that leads to discrepant predictions of message frame for two negative emotions. Finally, we demonstrate a mechanism through which low efficacy emotions can be empowered to mimic high efficacy emotions. This finding is among the first to provide evidence of a positive outcome resulting from a low efficacy emotion like shame. (519 words)

### "Uncertainty Exacerbates the Endowment Effect"

*Michael J. Liersch, New York University, USA*
*Yuval Rottenstreich, New York University, USA*
*Howard Kunreuther, University of Pennsylvania, USA*
*Min Gong, Columbia University, USA*

In standard endowment effect experiments, participants cannot lose their holdings. For instance, Knetsch (1989) gave participants either mugs or candy that they could keep or trade. Regardless of their choice, people walked away from the experiments with one of the items. However, actual endowments are often uncertain. For example, post-Madoff, investors worry their investments will disappear. In this paper, we examine how uncertainty impacts the reluctance to trade. Doing so is of practical significance and may also provide insight into the processes underlying the endowment effect.

In a baseline condition mirroring previous work, participants were endowed with either a mug or a box of highlighters, and given the opportunity to trade. We observed reluctance to trade. A second group of participants underwent the same procedure, but was told that after requested trades were completed, two coins would be flipped. One coin would determine whether participants holding mugs at the end of the experiment would keep their mugs (heads) or lose their mugs (tails); another coin would make the same determination for those endowed with highlighters. Compared to the baseline condition, reluctance to trade was significantly more pronounced when holdings were uncertain.

Researchers have recently suggested that feelings of attachment to an endowed item may underlie reluctance to trade (Strahilevitz and Loewenstein, 1998; Wolf et al., 2008; Johnson et al., 2009). Our results cast doubt on this notion. Because one should presumably be less attached to items that are only tentatively held, attachment accounts imply that certain endowment should yield more pronounced reluctance to trade than uncertain endowment.

It could be argued, however, that anticipatory regret of a "bad" trade engendered our results. For example, consider a mug holder who contemplates trading their mug for highlighters. Under certainty, the individual simply determines their preferences. However, under uncertainty, the individual might be highly averse to the possibility of losing their highlighters in the highlighter coin flip–especially if mug holders were to keep their mug in the coin flip. We ruled-out this possibility in a second uncertainty condition where a single coin was flipped to determine whether both mug and highlighter holders kept or lost their item. Importantly, the level of reluctance to trade was virtually identical in the one and two coin flip conditions.

We also examined whether uncertainty external to the items being traded might impact the reluctance to trade. Participants again received either a mug or highlighters, which they could trade; in addition, every participant received a Pack of Post-Its, which they could not trade. As expected, people were reluctant to make mug-highlighter trades. We then contrasted this baseline condition with two further conditions: A negative uncertainty condition, in which people could lose their Post-Its via a coin flip, and a positive uncertainty condition, in which people were initially endowed with a mug or highlighter and could win Post-Its via a coin flip. Reluctance to trade mugs and highlighters in the negative and positive uncertainty conditions was virtually identical to the baseline condition. Evidently, to increase reluctance to trade, uncertainty must be associated directly with the tradable items. Thus, we infer that anxiety or other affect arising from the mere presence of uncertainty was not responsible for increased endowment effects in our earlier uncertainty conditions.

In sum, it appears that uncertainty, as long as it is applied to the items to be traded, increases reluctance to trade. These findings indicate that notions of attachment cannot on their own account for endowment effects. Perhaps counter-intuitively, people may be more likely to hold onto their endowments, rather than trade, when holdings are uncertain. (597 words)

### References

Johnson, E., Hauble, G., & Keinan, A. (2007) Aspects of endowment: A query theory of loss aversion. Journal of Experimental Psychology: Learning, Memory, and Cognition, 33, 461-474.

Knetsch, J. (1989). The endowment effect and evidence of non-reversible indifference curves. American Economic Review, 79(5), 1277-1284.

Strahilevitz, M. & Loewenstein, G. (1998). The effect of ownership history on the valuation of objects. Journal of Consumer Research, 25(3), 276-289.

Wolf, J., Arkes, H., & Muhanna, W. (2008). The power of touch: An examination of the effect of duration of physical contact on the valuation of objects. Judgment and Decision Making, 3(6) 476-482.

# New Perspectives on Depletion: Expanding the Boundaries and Nature of Depletion
Nicole Mead, Tilburg University, The Netherlands

## EXTENDED ABSTRACTS

### "Exercising Self-Control Increases Approach Motivation"

*Brandon Schmeichel, Texas A&M University, USA*
*Cindy Harmon-Jones, Texas A&M University, USA*
*Eddie Harmon-Jones, Texas A&M University, USA*

Success at self-control is essential for several important aspects of life, from personal concerns such as losing weight and saving money to societal concerns such as reducing drug abuse and preventing violence. Self-control can be construed as a struggle between two competing forces: the force that motivates the expression of an impulse (i.e., impulse strength) versus the countervailing force that overrides the impulse (i.e., self-control strength).

The strength model of self-control posits that the inner mechanism for self-control operates on the basis of a limited resource or strength. The sufficiency of this strength for overriding behavior is determined in part by previous behavior. If the person has recently exercised self-control, then strength may be depleted and further efforts at self-control may be prone to failure.

However, the strength model is mute regarding the other element of the self-control struggle—the strength of the impulse that opposes the control mechanism. Given that both the motivation to act on an impulse and the capacity to control impulses jointly determine self-control outcomes, and given that self-control outcomes are determined in part by recent efforts at self-control, we hypothesized that recent efforts at self-control influence not only self-control strength, but also the motivation to act on impulse.

The present research tested the hypothesis that exercising self-control temporarily increases the strength of approach-motivated impulses. Results in support of this hypothesis would suggest that prior efforts at self-control affect subsequent behavior by increasing impulse strength. The research to be presented in this talk provides the first evidence that initial acts of self-control that have been shown to reduce self-control strength also increase approach-motivated impulse strength.

There are several specific behaviors (e.g., eating, aggression) that are driven both by the impulse that compels the behavior and by the inner mechanism that attempts to control the behavior. For these behaviors, it may be difficult to distinguish the contributions of impulse strength from the contributions of self-control strength. But other approach-motivated behaviors may be unrelated to self-control because the person has no interest or inclination to control them. To distinguish between approach-motivated impulse strength and self-control strength in the current work, we chose to study approach-motivated behaviors that are uninfluenced by self-control. We reasoned that, if exercising self-control causes an increase in approach-motivated behaviors that do not entail self-control, then we can be confident that exercising self-control temporarily increases approach motivation.

Study 1 found that prior efforts at self-control caused an increase in self-reported approach motivation. Study 2a identified a behavior—betting on low-stakes gambles—that is associated with approach motivation but not self-control, and Study 2b found that prior efforts at self-control cause an increase in low-stakes betting behavior. Last, Study 3 found that exercising self-control subsequently facilitates attention toward a reward-relevant symbol but not a reward-irrelevant symbol (Study 3), consistent with the view that self-control increases approach motivation.

Altogether, the current findings suggest that the strength model of self-control be amended to incorporate the other side of the self-control struggle—impulse strength. Prior acts of self-control may increase approach motivation in addition to reducing self-control strength. This amendment to the strength model expands our understanding of self-control failure and may help to explain why prior acts of self-control increase aggression, eating, drinking, profligate spending, and more.

### "Prisoners of Their Own Resources: Depletion in Parole Decision by Expert Judges"

*Shai Danziger, Ben Gurion University, Israel*
*Jonathan Levav, Columbia University, USA*
*Liora Avnaim, Ben Gurion University, Israel*

Highly experienced decision makers, such as judges, doctors, and government officials, often make sequential decisions in a single session. For example, parole board hearings, psychiatric release boards, university acceptance committees, and deportation hearings all involve sequential decisions of individual cases with results that carry significant implications both for the individuals under review as well as the public.

Previous work indicates that making successive decisions is mentally taxing (Vohs et al. 2008), and that decision fatigue leads to simplified decision making, such as accepting default options (Levav et al. 2010). We test whether highly experienced judges who make repeated decisions are susceptible to similar depletion effects.

A substantial body of evidence supports the assumption that experts' judgments are well-calibrated and that they are less susceptible than non-experts to the influence of contextual variables (e.g., Carlson and Bond 2006). Here we examine experts' "decision endurance." Since experts may decide more efficiently and may be mindful of extraneous influences on the quality of their decisions, are they more equipped to make better calibrated decisions over time?

We study parole rulings of expert judges as a function of the temporal order of the rulings. Specifically, we examined whether the probability of granting parole—a deviation from the less effortful option of rejecting parole and maintaining the status quo—decreases for decisions later in the case sequence. Also, following work by Gailliot and colleagues (2007), we examine whether food breaks that separate decision sessions can counteract the negative effects of choice and replenish depleted mental resources. In particular, we test whether cases considered immediately following a break are associated with a greater probability of release than cases considered immediately prior to the break.

Our data include 410 parole cases of Israeli criminals incarcerated for a variety of crimes of differing severity (e.g., theft, assault, rape). Highly experienced justices (N=13) consider 15-30 daily cases, in succession. Judges either grant or deny parole. Parole hearings, which continue from morning until early afternoon, are held in three sessions. A 30 minute break that includes a breakfast snack and an hour long lunch break separate the three sessions. The average case duration is approximately 11 minutes long, and does not vary by session.

Results of a logistic regression showed that the probability of granting parole was strongly affected by the temporal order of the rulings. Consistent with the view that choice taxes mental resources and that food and rest may replenish them, we find that parole likelihood is highest at the start of each session and that it gradually decreases throughout a session. The only other predictor variable that influenced the probability of granting parole was the number of times the prisoner had been incarcerated in the past.

The findings indicate that repeated judgments lead even experienced justices to prefer inaction and preference for the status quo (in this case imprisonment). Furthermore, it appears that these potentially detrimental effects of decision fatigue can be eliminated by a relatively simple intervention.

### "Lead Us Not Into Temptation: Depletion Does Not Require Individual Self-control Use"
*Joshua Ackerman, MIT, USA*

Research on the depleting effects of self-control has typically focused on intrapersonal causes and outcomes (e.g., engaging in thought suppression leads a person to spend more money on luxury goods). However, interpersonal cognition and neuroscience evidence suggests that the self-control actions of other people may elicit depleting effects *even in people who did not use self-control themselves*. This possibility would shed new light on the mechanisms that underlie self-control depletion and on the basic nature of depletion itself. In turn, these would provide new insight into social consumption experiences and the situations in which consumers are likely to benefit (or not) from the presence of other consumers.

Two possibilities emerge from the interpersonal processing literature. First, perceiving others may automatically prime similar cognitions and behaviors. Just as a laugh track can make a mediocre comedy more appealing, perceiving another's resistance of temptation may prime restraint in the perceivers (e.g., shopping with stingy friends may inspire less impulsive purchasing). An even more full-bodied outcome is suggested by research on mental simulation. Simulation occurs when actions and their downstream consequences are evoked purely through mental recreation of an event. Just as when we grimace watching someone else stub his/her toe, the simulation of one person's resistance may produce the consequences of self-control use—self-regulatory depletion.

Four studies demonstrate interpersonal consequences of self-control use for two important topics in consumer decision-making—(1) resistance to persuasive messages (Studies 1 and 2) and (2) time perception and impatience (Studies 3 and 4). In each study, I focus on the question: Is there depletion by proxy?

The availability of self-control resources predicts the ability to resist especially persuasive messages (Burkley 2008). In Study 1, participants first read a story about a waiter who came to work at a high quality restaurant without having eaten recently and thus had to exert self-control in order to resist eating food on the job (or else risk being fired). Subsequently, participants viewed an advertisement for a shaving razor that featured either strong or weak messages. The degree to which participants automatically simulated (took the perspective of) the waiter was measured. Automatic perspective-taking was positively associated with favorability towards the ad, primarily when the ad messages were strong, suggesting that participants were no longer able to effectively resist these persuasion attempts. Study 2 used a similar paradigm but actively manipulated perspective-taking. The second task in this study involved reading an essay that advocated changing the school grading system to one that participants initially disliked. Simulating the perspective of the hungry waiter in the first task completely eliminated the negativity towards the grading change and led to a doubling of support for this previously disliked system.

Depleted individuals have also been found to overestimate the passage of time and make more short-term decisions (Vohs and Schmeichel 2003). In Study 3, participants completed a temporal discounting measure after being exposed to another's self-control use. Those participants who simulated this self-control exhibited more impatience by discounting the future more strongly (i.e., preferring smaller, sooner rewards to larger, later ones). In Study 4, the actual time spent reading a self-control story was recorded along with participants' estimates of that time. Additionally, in a separate set of conditions, the waiter story was altered to involve a physically exerting, but self-control free, task. Participants who simulated the waiter's use of self-control believed that more time had passed than participants who either did not simulate mental self-control or those who mentally simulated physical exertion.

In summary, the results of four studies indicate that self-regulatory depletion can result even when people are not exposed to temptation themselves. These findings raise important theoretical questions for models of depletion that rely on the exhaustion of physical resources. They also suggest interesting consequences for consumers, as when shoppers who exert self-control to avoid buying luxury goods impair the self-control of friends who are shopping with them.

### REFERENCES
Burkley, Edward (2008), "The role of self-control in resistance to persuasion," *Personality and Social Psychology Bulletin*, 34, 419-431.
Carlson, Kurt A. and Samuel D. Bond (2006), "Improving preference assessment: Limiting the effect of context through pre-exposure to attribute levels," *Management Science,* 52(3), 410-421.
Fitzsimons, Gavan J. and Donald R. Lehmann (2005), "Reactance to recommendations: When unsolicited advice yields contrary responses," *Marketing Science,* 23 (1), 82-94.
Gailliot, Matthew T. and Roy F. Baumeister (2007), "The physiology of willpower: Linking blood glucose to self-control, *Personality and Social Psychology Review*, 11(4), 303-327.
Johnson, Eric J (2008), "Man, my brain is tired: Linking depletion and cognitive effort in choice," *Journal of Consumer Psychology*, 18 (1), 14-16.
Levav, Jonathan, Mark Heitmann, Andreas Herrmann, and Sheena S. Iyengar (2010), "Order in product customization decisions: Evidence from field experiments," *Journal of Political Economy*, in press.
Shiv, Baba and Fedorikhin Alexander (2002), "Spontaneous versus controlled influences of stimulus-based affect on choice behavior," *Organizational Behavior and Human Decision Processes,* 87 (2), 342-370.
Vohs, Kathleen D. and Brandon J. Schmeichel (2003), "Self-regulation and the extended now: Controlling the self alters the subjective experience of time," *Journal of Personality and Social Psychology,* 85, 217-230.
Vohs, Kathleen D., Roy F. Baumeister, Brandon J. Schmeichel, Jean M. Twenge, Noelle M. Nelson, and Dianne M. Tice (2008), Making choices impairs subsequent self-control: A limited-resource account of decision making, self-regulation, and active initiative," *Journal of Personality and Social Psychology,* 94, 883-98.

# Competitive Papers—Full

## The Effect of an Integrated Virtual Community on The Evaluation of an Online Store: Findings From an Internet Experiment

Peter Domma, Saarland University, Germany
Dirk Morschett, University of Fribourg, Switzerland
Hanna Schramm-Klein, University of Siegen, Germany
Joachim Zentes, Saarland University, Germany

### ABSTRACT:

We examined the impact of three characteristics of a virtual community within an online store on consumer evaluations of that store. In particular, we focused on the exertion of retailer influence, the quality of the virtual community and the degree of sociability. An Internet experiment with 477 participants using a professionally designed shopping Web site was conducted, confirming the influence of all three characteristics.

### INTRODUCTION

Forrester Research estimates that 74% of Europe's population will be online in 2011, and more than 176 million people will shop online (Dellner 2007). In addition, the use of the Web is changing dramatically. Applications that are summarized under the umbrella term "Web 2.0" used to refer to key concepts such as user empowerment and participation are changing the way consumers use the Web (Cheung, Lee and Rabjohn 2008). Implementing new strategies with regard to Web 2.0 will allow retailers to create competitive advantages. For example, a study by Brown, Tilton and Woodside (2002) showed that customers who participated in a virtual community (VC) provided by a Web site only accounted for about one-third of the visitors but generated two-thirds of the sales. As such, assessing the potential market opportunities in utilizing a VC becomes critical (Kim and Jin 2006).

As the topic of VCs is still at the early stages of research, there is little consensus regarding the definition of a VC (Kim and Jin 2006). Preece (2001) and Preece and Maloney-Krichmar (2005) identified a participatory design and employed the concepts of usability and sociability as the most important elements of a VC. A comprehensive literature review by Lee, Vogel and Limayem (2003) resulted in the working definition that VCs are cyberspaces supported by computer-based information technology centered upon communication and interaction of participants to generate member-driven content, resulting in relationships. The implementation of a VC can combine different aspects with various focuses, such as communities of transaction or communities of interest as described by Armstrong and Hagel III (1996); therefore, VCs can fulfill various types of human needs.

While research on the general concept of VCs is broad (Farquhar and Rowley 2006) and the implementation of a VC is acknowledged as an influential feature of business-to-consumer (B2C) Web sites, there is still a lack of studies investigating the influence of VCs on consumer perceptions of the transactional and relational qualities of a shopping Web site. Only a few exploratory studies have reported on the usefulness of a VC in an e-commerce context (Gupta and Kim 2004). Furthermore, the effects of different VC characteristics on consumer evaluations are widely unknown. We therefore identified three VC characteristics as influencing factors of consumer evaluations from prior literature and practical evidence. These include the exertion of influence by the operator (i.e., the retailer), the quality of the VC and the degree of sociability. We investigate the effects of these determinants on consumer perceptions of the transactional and relational qualities of a shopping Web site by means of an online experiment.

### EFFECTS OF VIRTUAL COMMUNITIES ON CONSUMER EVALUATIONS

We expect that the integration of a VC within the experimental shopping Web site to have a positive effect on consumer evaluations by improving their shopping experience and emotional reactions when visiting the online store. Past research has examined facets of consumer evaluation and acceptance of an information technology from two different perspectives (Dahui, Browne, and Wetherbe 2006). The first perspective, often called the transactional perspective, views a Web site as an information technology and thus focuses on cognitive factors such as perceived usefulness or perceived ease of use. A second perspective refers to the affective or relational components of a Web site such as perceived enjoyment. Recent literature has emphasized the importance of investigating the driving factors of Web site usage beyond cognitive factors, especially because of the changing nature of the Web (Loiacono, Watson, and Goodhue 2007).

Following the research that integrates the transactional and relational perspectives (Gefen and Straub 2004; Moon and Kim 2001), we conceptualize consumer evaluations using six constructs. The transactional perspective in our study includes the key antecedents of the intention to use a technology identified by the Technology Acceptance Model (TAM) (Davis 1989), namely, *Perceived Ease of Use (PEOU)* and *Perceived Usefulness (PU)*. As originally defined by Davis (1989, 320), PEOU refers to "the degree to which the prospective user expects the target system to be free of effort". With regard to e-commerce, PU of a Web site is "the extent to which an individual perceives a web-site to be useful in performing shopping tasks" (Kumar and Benbasat 2006, 428). We add Perceived Risk (PRisk) following Mitchell (1999) to comprise two components, namely, the perceived probability of a loss and the subjective evaluation of potential unfavorable consequences.

To capture the relational perspective of consumer evaluations, we consider three dimensions. *Perceived Social Presence (PSP)* is defined as to extent to which a medium is perceived to be warm if it conveys a feeling of human contact and sensitivity to the user (Hassanein and Head 2004). *Perceived Enjoyment (PEn)* refers to the extent to which the activity of using an information technology is perceived to be enjoyable, aside from performance consequences (Davis, Bagozzi, and Warshaw 1992). Following McMillan and Hwang (2002), this study defines Perceived Interactivity (PInt) as the extent to which users perceive the online store to enable (many-to-many) communication, to provide control (i.e., in terms of speed, navigation and content), and to respond to user requests.

### HYPOTHESES

The investigated determinants of consumer evaluations (i.e., VC characteristics) include the exertion of influence by the operator, the quality of the VC and the degree of sociability.

Concerning the *exertion of influence* on the VC by the operator, this can, on the one hand, be valued positively by members. For example, an operator can establish codes of behavior (i.e., netiquette or guidelines) to contain potential conflict (Leimeister, Sidiras, and Krcmar 2006). Andrews (2002) argued that operators must facilitate the formation of subgroups as well as reward and acknowledge member contributions. In these cases, a certain level of exertion of influence and contribution to the VC by the operator is needed to establish such structural patterns. The positive effect of a higher exertion of influence is supported by the literature on trust, which proposes that an organization must demonstrate its honesty, benevolence and competence to its members (Gefen 2000). In the context of a VC, the operator can show benevolence by being concerned for the welfare of the members of the VC; it can also demonstrate its competence if its contributions to the VC are significant and generate value (Flavián and Guinalíu 2006).

On the other hand, a very strong influence by the retailer will make consumers feel that the retailer tries to act in an opportunistic manner and exercises too much control (Flavián and Guinalíu 2006). The negative effect can be explained by the elaboration likelihood model (ELM) (Bhattacherjee and Sanford 2006) as a theoretical model of information adoption in computer-mediated communication (CMC) contexts. ELM posits that a message can influence people's attitudes and behaviors with source credibility acting as the peripheral influence (Cheung, Lee, and Rabjohn 2008). Source credibility refers to a message recipient's perception of the credibility of a message source; information provided by highly credible sources is perceived to be useful and reliable (Ko, Kirsch, and King 2005). In the context of CMC, user-generated content has found to be more credible than marketer-generated information (Bickart and Schindler 2001), which means that increasing the exertion of influence by the operator beyond a certain level will lead consumers to evaluate the credibility of information more negatively. Furthermore, reactance theory (Brehm 1966) implies that when people feel that their freedom to choose an action is threatened, they become motivated to reestablish the threatened freedom, which is the case in which content generated by the operator dominates the VC and consumers feel that the retailer acts in an opportunistic manner. Reactance theory also indicates that reactance must reach a certain intensity and thus surpass a threshold point for the perception of threat to take effect. These arguments indicate that a higher exertion of influence by the operator does not in every case lead to a more positive evaluation by the consumers and vice versa. Hence, we assume the effect of the exertion of influence to be nonlinear. This means that given a moderate exertion of influence and either a high or a low exertion, we expect a more positive evaluation from moderate exertion.

We propose that shifting intensity of the exertion of influence by the operator of the VC (i.e., the retailer) will have an effect on consumer PRisk because information from an independent third-party (e.g., other users) is perceived as more credible than information that comes directly from the retailer (Weathers, Sharma, and Wood 2007). We also propose an impact on consumer PU, since information provided by commercial sources is perceived as less useful, as well as on relational factors, that is, PEn and PInt. We expect the latter impact because too much influence by the operator hampers the sense of community among users and their perceived control over their community. Thus, we hypothesize:

*Hypothesis 1.1:* *Compared to a low exertion of influence, a moderate exertion of influence on the VC by the retailer will lead to (a) higher PU, (b) lower PRisk, (c) higher PEn and (d) higher PInt.*

*Hypothesis 1.2:* *Compared to a high exertion of influence, a moderate exertion of influence on the VC by the retailer will lead to (a) higher PU, (b) lower PRisk, (c) higher PEn and (d) higher PInt.*

As one of the most relevant factors of a VC, the literature highlights the depth, timeliness and quality of content (Farquhar and Rowley 2006). In a recent study by Leimeister, Sidiras and Krcmar (2006), content-related factors were ranked high in terms of relevance by VC members. As mentioned by Preece (2001), the volume, quality and timeliness of the information provided in a VC are factors that affect member engagement in the community, implying that those factors have a huge impact on the positive or negative evaluation by consumers of the VC. We therefore hypothesize a positive effect of high quality information on the perceived usefulness and ease of use. We also expect consumers to perceive the online store as more enjoyable if the depth, timeliness and quality of content are at high levels. As described by Koufaris (2002), product information searches can be fun-seeking experiences. We expect that the use of a comprehensive and lively virtual community can make the shopping experience more fulfilling and enjoyable. Based on our conceptualization of perceived interactivity (i.e., in terms of communication, control and response), we assume that the quality of the VC will affect the perceived possibility of communication as well as the perceived control over navigation and content. Referring to *VC quality*, we therefore hypothesize:

*Hypothesis 2:* *If the integrated VC is of high quality, consumers evaluate the online store more positively as compared to an online store in which the integrated VC is of low quality. In particular, they rate the online store more positively with respect to (a) PEOU, (b) PU, (c) PEn and (d) PInt.*

The impersonality of online retailing is still one of the major problems facing this distribution channel, which may be solved by the usage of Web 2.0 instruments. For example, a VC may help substitute for the personal treatment a consumer is given in bricks-and-mortar stores (Flavián and Guinalíu 2005). The term *sociability* relates to the development of software, policies and practices to support social interaction online (Preece 2001). One important determinant of success concerning sociability is the provision of information about community members, including, for example, what roles they are taking or how experienced they are (Preece 2001). We therefore assume that increasing sociability by adding more personal information on users will lead to a higher PSP.

The traditional concept of word-of-mouth as relating to personal sources of information takes the relational closeness between a decision maker and a recommendation source as its basis (Brown and Reingen 1987). With the advent of Web 2.0 and the integration of personal information on users within user-generated content, there is the possibility to implement such strong ties in the form of electronic word-of-mouth (eWOM). This can help to create a higher PU of online information and a lower PRisk in the buying decision.

The theory behind the effect of sociability on perceived enjoyment is based on literature that classifies information systems as hedonic (Heijden 2004). We act on the assumption that adding more social cues to the VC will move the nature of the information system toward a hedonic information system, which will be perceived as more enjoyable. Finally, based on the conceptualization of perceived interactivity, we expect a strong impact of sociability on the perceived possibilities to communicate with others:

*Hypothesis 3:*    *If the integrated VC provides a higher degree of sociability, then consumers evaluate the online store more positively as compared to an online store in which the integrated VC provides a lower degree of sociability. In particular, they rate the online store more positively with respect to (a) PU, (b) PRisk, (c) PSP, (d) PEn and (e) PInt.*

# METHOD

## Experimental Design

To test our hypotheses, we used a professionally designed fictitious online-shop. We chose to integrate two different areas into the VC. First, there was an area with a discussion forum, which has been identified as a popular feature of VC Web sites

(Pitta and Fowler 2005). Second, in order to address the aspects of a community of relationships and to manipulate sociability in the experiment, a user profiles section was added. Some screenshots illustrate the Web site and the VC (figure 1). All content within the online store and the VC has been sampled and adapted from real stores, discussion forums and virtual communities on the Web.

A laboratory 3x2x2 between-subject experiment was conducted. Given the need to control for shopping Web site and VC features, this design allowed us to isolate the effects of the different VC aspects on consumer responses.

*Exertion of influence.* Manipulation of factor 1 (exertion of influence: low/moderate/high) was achieved by varying the number of forum posts by an administrator. Note that the name and picture were chosen in a way that the association between the administrator and the retailer was obvious. In conditions with a low exertion of influence, the retailer did not appear in any forum post, whereas the discussion forum contained posts by the retailer in 50% of threads

## Figure 1: Sample screenshots

*Product page with hyperlink to the VC*        *Start page of the VC*

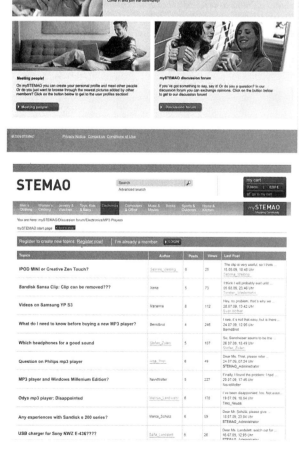

*Example from the user profile section*        *Discussion forum overview page*

for the moderate condition, and posts appeared in every thread for the high condition.

*VC quality.* The quality of information is evaluated in terms of information content, accuracy, format and timeliness (Cheung, Lee, and Rabjohn 2008). In our study, we focused on comprehensiveness as well as timeliness as grouped under the umbrella term "virtual community quality". To manipulate the virtual community quality (low/high), we varied the number of contributions to the discussion forum, the comprehensiveness of the content and the timeliness of contributions from group to group. The low quality setting contained very few threads with few posts within the threads; all entries were at least eight months old. We also manipulated the displayed number of views on the forum overview page.

*Sociability.* To manipulate the sociability (low/high) of the VC, a user profiles section was either present or absent within the VC. Depending on the experimental condition, the community start page contained a section to enter only the section with the discussion forum (conditions 1-6) or the discussion forum *and* the user profiles (conditions 7-12) or. Additionally, respondents who were assigned to conditions 7-12 also had the ability to follow hyperlinks on user aliases in the discussion forum. In the user profiles section, respondents had different ways of accessing the individual profiles (e.g., only the newest profiles or the full list of profiles could be viewed) and information on the profiled person, including profile picture, name, age, interests and his or her personal guestbook. All profiles were checked for plausibility (e.g., fit between age, gender and interest) and conformity with the cover story (e.g., language usage) in a pretest.

**Procedure**

To avoid participant awareness bias, we chose a non-forced exposure design and developed a cover story to avoid respondents guessing the actual purpose of the study and to induce the impression that they would be examining a portion of a real online store. After a short briefing on the experimental task (i.e., respondents were told to search for information about products in the online store and to choose one product), participants were forwarded to the overview page, which displayed the first three products, namely, mp3 audio players. From this page, participants were able to access the other overview pages as well as the individual product pages containing detailed information about the products. A button with a hyperlink to the VC (labeled "Find out more in our community") was present on the page header as well as at the end of every product page. Respondents were free to visit the VC. Participants who followed this link were lead to the VC. On every page of the VC, a link was avail-

able to return to the online store and the product pages. Respondents who did not enter the VC were assigned to the control group. After putting the selected product in the shopping cart and confirming their decision to purchase, respondents were forwarded to the online questionnaire. We first surveyed the dependent variables and then the variables for manipulation checks in order to avoid respondents recognizing the actual purpose of the study before answering the questions on the dependent variables.

**Measurement**

The dependent variables in this study were captured by an online questionnaire assessing constructs on a multiple-item seven-point scale (1=strongly disagree, 7=strongly agree). All measurement scales were pretested. To assess PEOU, we chose five reflective items based on Davis (1989) and Gefen, Karahanna and Straub (2003). The reflective five-item-scale for measuring PU was adopted from past applications of the TAM (Agarwal and Karahanna 2000; Davis 1989; Gefen, Karahanna, and Straub 2003). Both measurement models showed a high level of scale reliability; Cronbach's Alpha was .91 for PEOU and .93 for PU. We chose a reflective measurement approach for the dimensions of *PSP* (five indicators, Cronbach's Alpha = .97), all of which were adapted from validated constructs developed by Cyr et al. (2007). To capture *PEn*, we followed the conceptualization of Hassanein and Head (2005), Moon and Kim (2001) and van der Heijden (2004) (four indicators, Cronbach's Alpha = .92). Measures of sampling adequacy values (MSA) and factor loadings for the items of all scales exceeded .50; item-to-total correlations surpassed .40. As AVE for all reflective constructs mentioned above is greater than the squared correlation between that construct and any other construct, discriminant validity is confirmed.

PRisk was operationalized in a formative way to capture functional risk, financial risk as well as the risk of mispurchase (Cunningham 1967). None of the indicators revealed multicollinearity problems (all VIFs were well below 10; condition indices were all below 30). We also assessed nomological validity by analyzing bivariate correlations between the formative construct and a single item of trust, a construct that is closely related to PRisk and has been included as additional construct in the questionnaire. Bivariate correlations were strong and significant (r = .57, p < .001). The formative measure of PInt consists of a second-order formative factor composed of three components. Factor analysis of six items selected from past research on interactivity (Jee and Lee 2002) revealed three reflective components, namely, control, response and communication. Based on the theoretical work of McMillan and Hwang (2002), a formative construct of PInt was computed

**Table 1: Experimental conditions**

| Condition | Treatments | | |
|---|---|---|---|
| | Factor 1: exertion of influence (3) | Factor 2: VC quality (2) | Factor 3: sociability (2) |
| 1 | Low | Low | Low |
| 2 | Moderate | Low | Low |
| 3 | High | Low | Low |
| 4 | Low | High | Low |
| 5 | Moderate | High | Low |
| 6 | High | High | Low |
| 7 | Low | Low | High |
| 8 | Moderate | Low | High |
| 9 | High | Low | High |
| 10 | Low | High | High |
| 11 | Moderate | High | High |
| 12 | High | High | High |

from these three dimensions. None of the indicators revealed multicollinearity problems. Nomological validity was assessed by measuring bivariate correlations between the formative construct of PInt and a single item of interactivity, which also was included in the questionnaire. Bivariate correlations were highly significant ($r = .73$, p $< .001$).

## Sample and Manipulation Checks

The final dataset consists of 477 participants, of which 264 participants visited the VC and 213 did not. Respondents range in age from 16 to 65 years, with a mean age of 32.3 years. 50.3% of participants are female.

Manipulation checks were performed to control for the effectiveness of the treatments. To test for the perceived exertion of retailer influence on the VC, which was measured by a single item, an ANOVA analysis indicated that the three groups were significantly different ($F(2, 263) = 45.516$, $p < .001$). The results of post-hoc Scheffé tests confirmed that statistically significant differences existed between all groups. Manipulation of VC quality was checked with a variable that was characterized by three indicators, namely, the number of contributions to the message board (threads), the comprehensiveness of content (posts) and the timeliness of contributions. As intended, participants in the low quality sample perceived the VC as of lower quality ($M = 2.64$) than those in the high quality sample ($M = 4.69$, $F(1, 263) = 221.235$, $p < .001$). To ensure the successful manipulation of sociability, we removed those respondents from the dataset that were assigned to conditions including the presence of the user profiles section (high sociability) but reported that they did not see that particular part of the VC. Moreover, entering the VC at any point was observed by collecting participant identifications in a SQL database; respondents who actually visited the VC but reported to have not visited the VC were removed from the data set.

## RESULTS

The data was analyzed using a 3x2x2 MANCOVA due to the orthogonal between-subject design. Because past research showed a strong influence of *product involvement* and *Internet experience* on consumer behavior in an e-commerce setting, we included both as covariates. We first tested the overall null hypothesis as a screening analysis. The Wilks Lambda multivariate tests of overall group differences were all statistically significant for the main effects ($p < .001$). Regarding interaction effects, *exertion of influence* x *sociability* was found to be significant (Wilks´ Lambda: Multivariate $F =$

$1.899$, $p < .05$). Referring to factor 1, univariate between-subject tests showed that the exertion of influence was significantly related to PU, PRisk and PInt.

Contrast analysis reveals that statistically significant differences existed among all groups for PU (contrast estimate (c.e.) $_{\text{low vs. moderate}} = -.333$ with $p < .05$; c.e. $_{\text{moderate vs. high}} = .700$ with $p < .001$), PRisk (c.e. $_{\text{low vs. moderate}} = .297$ with $p < .05$; c.e. $_{\text{moderate vs. high}} = -.601$ with $p < .001$) and PInt (c.e. $_{\text{low vs. moderate}} = -.216$ with $p < .05$; c.e. $_{\text{moderate vs. high}} = .289$ with $p < .01$). All comparisons are in the expected directions. We therefore find support for hypotheses H1.1a, H1.1b, H1.1d, H1.2a, H1.2b and H1.2d. The results show that consumers tend to positively evaluate a moderate exertion of influence by the retailer, whereas a high influence leads to a negative effect on PU, PRisk and PInt. Moreover, respondents in the group with low exertion of influence also rated the online store to be less useful for shopping tasks and perceive a higher risk than respondents in the group with moderate exertion of influence. Furthermore, respondents evaluated the online store to be less interactive. As table 1 reveals, the exertion of influence does not have an effect on PEn, and therefore, hypotheses H1.1c and H1.2c must be rejected. Obviously, the exertion of influence mainly affects transactional factors, especially the risk perceived by respondents.

Because a significant interaction was found between the factors *exertion of influence* and *sociability* by multivariate testing, the main effects were qualified by this interaction. To further examine this interaction, we performed univariate tests and found the interaction to be significant only for PRisk. Even though the interaction effect size was small, apparently the presence of the user profiles section and the linking of aliases to profiles in the discussion forum have some alleviative effect on the negative impact of the high exertion of influence (figure 2).

Whereas respondents perceive a higher risk in purchasing from the online store in the group with high exertion of influence when the user profiles section is absent and sociability is low, this negative effect nearly disappeared when sociability was high and user profiles were present.

To test hypotheses H2, univariate F-tests showed that the high quality group ($M_{\text{PEOU}} = .528$; $M_{\text{PU}} = .369$; $M_{\text{PEn}} = .334$) scored significantly higher than the low quality group ($M_{\text{PEOU}} = -.105$; $M_{\text{PU}} = -.149$; $M_{\text{PEn}} = -.018$) with respect to PEOU, PU and PEn. There was no statistically significant difference between the two groups with respect to PInt. These findings supported hypotheses H2a, H2b and H2c, whereas H2d is rejected. The effect of VC quality

### Table 2: Univariate tests of hypotheses

| Independent variables | Dependent variables | Sum of Squares | df | Mean Square | F | Sig. | Partial η² | Observed Power [a] |
|---|---|---|---|---|---|---|---|---|
| Factor 1: Exertion of influence | PU | 21.353 | 2 | 10.677 | 10.136 | .000*** | .075 | .985 |
| | PRisk | 15.713 | 2 | 7.857 | 10.548 | .000*** | .078 | .988 |
| | PEn | 2.950 | 2 | 1.475 | 1.666 | .191NS | .013 | .349 |
| | PInt | 3.933 | 2 | 1.966 | 5.626 | .004** | .043 | .857 |
| Factor 2: VC quality | PEOU | 26.382 | 1 | 26.382 | 21.745 | .000*** | .080 | .996 |
| | PU | 17.594 | 1 | 17.594 | 16.703 | .000*** | .063 | .983 |
| | PEn | 8.126 | 1 | 8.126 | 9.175 | .003** | .035 | .855 |
| | PInt | 1.332 | 1 | 1.332 | 3.811 | .052NS | .015 | .494 |
| Factor 3: Sociability | PU | 3.755 | 1 | 3.755 | 3.564 | .060NS | .014 | .468 |
| | PRisk | 16.559 | 1 | 16.559 | 22.232 | .000*** | .082 | .997 |
| | PSP | 62.814 | 1 | 62.814 | 65.585 | .000*** | .208 | 1.000 |
| | PEn | 25.072 | 1 | 25.072 | 28.309 | .000*** | .102 | 1.000 |
| | PInt | 5.692 | 1 | 5.692 | 16.285 | .000*** | .061 | .980 |
| Factor 1 * Factor 3 | PRisk | 4.755 | 2 | 2.377 | 3.192 | .043* | .025 | .607 |

[a] computed using alpha = .05; *** p < .001, ** p < .01, * p < .05, NS not significant

**Figure 2: Joint effect of exertion of influence and sociability on PRisk**

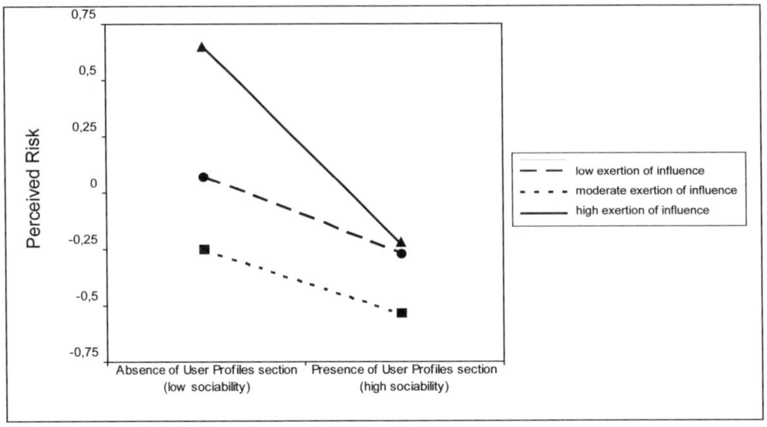

was highly significant for the transactional constructs of PEOU and PU, indicating that comprehensiveness and timeliness of content are effective components of consumer transactional evaluations. With regard to relational components, the results showed that the use of a comprehensive and lively VC makes the shopping task a more enjoyable experience. Further analyses supported hypotheses H3b, H3c, H3d and H3e. The comparison of the effects of high versus low sociability of the VC on PRisk, PSP, PEn and PInt were significant with large effect sizes for PSP and PEn. We found no support for hypothesis H3a ($F(1, 263) = 3.56$, $p > .05$); that is, the degree of sociability does not affect the perceived usefulness of the online store. Apparently consumers in an online environment tend to disregard the importance of tie strength (i.e., in terms of similarity, expertise and accessibility) as posited by traditional WOM theory, because the presence of user profiles does not lead to a higher PU. With regard to relational factors, the presence of user profiles (i.e., indicating high sociability) seems to be adequate to convey a feeling of human contact and warmth, thus increasing PSP. Moreover, the effect of changing the nature of the online store by adding the user profiles section is clear for PEn and PInt.

## IMPLICATIONS

This study investigated how to design an integrated VC within an online store with regard to different characteristics; thus, this study has various implications for marketers. First, retailers should pay attention to the exertion of influence on the VC. We showed that consumers tend to positively react to an increased exertion of influence by the retailer only to a certain point, beyond which an increasing exertion of influence leads to a negative effect on perceived usefulness, risk and interactivity. This effect seems to take the shape of an inverted U-form. However, online marketers may be able to compensate for the negative effect of a high exertion of influence by integrating user generated content areas and social cues within the shopping Web site, as there is a moderating effect of sociability on the effect of a higher exertion of influence with respect to perceived risk. Hence, e-retailers can, for example, boost sales with specific messages regarding new products or sales without consumer reactance if they simultaneously encourage a lively VC with a substantial number of social cues exchanged between members.

As indicated by past research, our study confirms that VC quality is also important in the e-commerce environment with

regard to transactional factors like perceived ease of use or usefulness as well as relational factors like perceived enjoyment. Only if consumers find the information they need and have the feeling that they are part of a vital community the positive effect of the VC appears. Finally, our investigation shows that the existence of the user profiles section of the VC has an enormous impact on relational factors of consumer evaluations of the online store such as perceived social presence or enjoyment, which is demonstrated by the large effect sizes. Referring to the rapid growth of this community type and its impact on the everyday lives of consumers, retailers can be recommended to provide these profiles in their VCs.

Our study provides evidence on re-embedding strategies that utilize social cues to infuse social presence through a Web interface, which can help to make the virtual interaction more similar to traditional shopping environments and thus lead to an enhanced online experience (Cyr et al. 2007). However, there was no effect of adding such social cues on perceived usefulness. This reveals an important difference between offline WOM and eWOM. Research on offline word-of-mouth emphasizes the importance of the closeness of relationship between the decision maker and the recommendation source. This closeness is determined by how the decision maker is able to evaluate similarity between the decision maker and the recommender as well as the expertise and credibility of the recommender. In our study, consumers tend to focus on the benefit of collective intelligence provided by user-generated content in a VC rather than on detailed information about particular recommendation sources.

## REFERENCES

Agarwal, Ritu and Elena Karahanna (2000), "Time Flies When You´re Having Fun: Cognitive Absorption and Beliefs About Information Technology Usage," *MIS Quarterly*, 24 (4), 665-94.

Andrews, Dorine C. (2002), "Audience-specific online community design," *Communications of the ACM*, 45 (4), 64-68.

Armstrong, Arthur and John Hagel III (1996), "The Real Value of ON-LINE Communities," *Harvard Business Review*, 74 (3), 134-41.

Bhattacherjee, Anol and Clive Sanford (2006), "Influence Processes for Information Technology Acceptance: An Elaboration Likelihood Model," *MIS Quarterly*, 30 (4), 805-25.

Bickart, Barbara and Robert M. Schindler (2001), "Internet Forums as influential sources of consumer information," *Journal of Interactive Marketing*, 15 (3), 31-40.

Brehm, Jack W. (1966), *A theory of psychological reactance*, Oxford: Academic Press.

Brown, Jacqueline Johnson and Peter H. Reingen (1987), "Social Ties and Word-of-Mouth Referral Behavior," *Journal of Consumer Research*, 14 (3), 350-62.

Brown, Shona L., Andrew Tilton, and Dennis Woodside (2002), "Online communities pay," *McKinsey Quarterly*, 19 (1), 17.

Cheung, Christy M. K., Matthew K. O. Lee, and Neil Rabjohn (2008), "The impact of electronic word-of-mouth: The adoption of online opinions in online customer communities," *Internet Research*, 18 (3), 229-47.

Cunningham, Scott M. (1967), "The Major Dimensions of Perceived Risk," in *Risk Taking and Information Handling in Consumer Behavior,* ed. Donald F. Cox, Boston: Boston University Press, 82-108.

Cyr, Dianne, Khaled Hassanein, Milena Head, and Alex Ivanov (2007), "The role of social presence in establishing loyalty in e-Service environments," *Interacting with Computers*, 19 (1), 43-56.

Dahui, Li, Glenn J. Browne, and James C. Wetherbe (2006), "Why Do Internet Users Stick with a Specific Web Site? A Relationship Perspective," *International Journal of Electronic Commerce*, 10 (4), 105-41.

Davis, Fred D. (1989), "Perceived Usefulness, Perceived Ease of Use, and User Acceptance of Information Technology," *MIS Quarterly*, 13 (3), 319-40.

Davis, Fred D., Richard P. Bagozzi, and Paul R. Warshaw (1992), "Extrinsic and Intrinsic Motivation to Use Computers in the Workplace," *Journal of Applied Social Psychology*, 22 (14), 1111-32.

Dellner, Tom (2007), "European e-commerce," *electronic Retailer magazine*, 4 (6), 46-53.

Farquhar, Jillian and Jennifer Rowley (2006), "Relationships and online consumer communities," *Business Process Management Journal*, 12 (2), 162-77.

Flavián, Carlos and Miguel Guinalíu (2005), "The influence of virtual communities on distribution strategies in the internet," *International Journal of Retail & Distribution Management*, 33 (6), 405-25.

_____, (2006), "Virtual Communities and E-Business Management," in *Encyclopedia of E-commerce, E-government, and Mobile Commerce,* ed. Mehdi Khosrow-Pour, Hershey: IGI Publishing, 1163-1168.

Gefen, David (2000), "E-commerce: the role of familiarity and trust," *Omega*, 28 (6), 725-37.

Gefen, David, Elena Karahanna, and Detmar W. Straub (2003), "Trust and TAM in Online Shopping: An Integrated Model," *MIS Quarterly*, 27 (1), 51-90.

Gefen, David and Detmar W. Straub (2004), "Consumer trust in B2C e-Commerce and the importance of social presence: experiments in e-Products and e-Services," *Omega*, 32 (6), 407-24.

Gupta, Sumeet and Hee-Wong Kim (2004) "Enhancing the Commitment to Virtual Community: A Belief and Feeling Based Approach," in *Proceedings of the AIS/ICIS 25th International Conference on Information Systems*, Washington DC, 99-111.

Hassanein, Khaled and Milena Head (2005), "The Impact of Infusing Social Presence in the Web Interface: An Investigation Across Product Types," *International Journal of Electronic Commerce*, 10 (2), 31-55.

Hassanein, Khaled S. and Milena M. Head (2004) "Building Online Trust through Socially Rich Web Interfaces," in *Proceedings of the Second Annual Conference on Privacy, Security and Trust (PST 2004)*, New Brunswick, 15-22.

Jee, Joonhyung and Wei-Na Lee (2002), "Antecedents and Consequences of Perceived Interactivity: An Exploratory Study," *Journal of Interactive Advertising*, 3 (1).

Kim, Hye-Shin and Byoungho Jin (2006), "Exploratory study of virtual communities of apparel retailers," *Journal of Fashion Marketing & Management*, 10 (1), 41-55.

Ko, Dong-Gil, Laurie J. Kirsch, and William R. King (2005), "Antecedents of knowledge transfer from consultants to clients in enterprise system implementations," *MIS Quarterly*, 29 (1), 59-85.

Koufaris, Marios (2002), "Applying the Technology Acceptance Model and Flow Theory to Online Consumer Behavior," *Information Systems Research*, 13 (2), 205-23.

Kumar, Nanda and Izak Benbasat (2006), "The Influence of Recommendations and Consumer Reviews on Evaluations of Websites," *Information Systems Research*, 17 (4), 425-39.

Lee, Fion S. L., Douglas Vogel, and Moez Limayem (2003), "Virtual community informatics: A review and research agenda," *Journal of Information Technology Theory and Application*, 5 (1), 47-61.

Leimeister, Jan Marco, Pascal Sidiras, and Helmut Krcmar (2006), "Exploring Success Factors of Virtual Communities: The Perspectives of Members and Operators," *Journal of Organizational Computing & Electronic Commerce*, 16 (3/4), 279-300.

Loiacono, Eleanor T., Richard T. Watson, and Dale L. Goodhue (2007), "WebQual: An Instrument for Consumer Evaluation of Web Sites," *International Journal of Electronic Commerce*, 11 (3), 51-87.

McMillan, Sally J. and Jang Sun Hwang (2002), "Measures of Perceived Interactivity: An Exploration of the Role of Direction of Communication, User Control, and Time in Shaping Perceptions of Interactivity," *Journal of Advertising*, 31 (3), 29-42.

Mitchell, Vincent Wayne (1999), "Consumer perceived risk: Conceptualisation and models," *European Journal of Marketing*, 33 (1/2), 163-95.

Moon, Ji Won and Young Gul Kim (2001), "Extending the TAM for a World-Wide-Web context," *Information & Management*, 38 (4), 217-30.

Pitta, Dennis A. and Danielle Fowler (2005), "Internet community forums: an untapped resource for consumer marketers," *Journal of Consumer Marketing*, 22 (5), 265-74.

Preece, Jenny (2001), "Sociability and usability in online communities: determining and measuring success," *Behaviour & Information Technology*, 20 (5), 347-56.

Preece, Jenny and Diane Maloney-Krichmar (2005), "Online Communities: Design, Theory, and Practice," *Journal of Computer-Mediated Communication*, 10 (4).

Rheingold, Howard (1993), *The virtual community: homesteading on the electronic frontier*, Reading: Addison-Wesley.

van der Heijden, Hans (2004), "User Acceptance of Hedonic Information Systems," *MIS Quarterly*, 28 (4), 695-704.

Weathers, Danny, Subhash Sharma, and Stacy L. Wood (2007), "Effects of online communication practices on consumer perceptions of performance uncertainty for search and experience goods," *Journal of Retailing*, 83 (4), 393-401.

# The Role of Perceived Review Credibility in the Context of Brand Equity Dilution Through Negative Product Reviews on the Internet

Silke Bambauer-Sachse, University of Fribourg, Switzerland
Sabrina Mangold, University of Fribourg, Switzerland

## ABSTRACT

In this paper, we examine effects of negative online product reviews on consumer-based brand equity as well as the role of review quality and perceived review credibility. The results of our study show that brand equity dilution increases with increasing review quality and that review credibility plays an important role.

## INTRODUCTION

A look at the historical development of the Internet as a source of product-specific information shows that, in a first phase, product-specific information was mainly provided by producers and retailers whereas a more recent phase is characterized by the trend that consumer-based product information in terms of product reviews, as a specific type of online word-of-mouth (WOM) communication, can be increasingly found in addition to company-based information. In the light of this trend, the finding that consumers are more susceptible to WOM communication than to company-based product information (Bickart and Schindler 2001; Herr, Kardes, and Kim 1991; Smith, Menon, and Sivakumar 2005; Trusov, Bucklin, and Pauwels 2009) leads to the assumption that consumer-based online product reviews have a comparatively strong impact on consumer behavior (Chatterjee 2001; Chevalier and Mayzlin 2006; Kiecker and Cowles 2001; Sen and Lerman 2007; Xia and Bechwati 2008). In addition, companies only spread positively valenced information, whereas consumers especially tend to share negative experiences with as many people as possible (Chatterjee 2001) and to look for negative product reviews because negative information is considered as more diagnostic than positive or neutral information and thus is weighted more heavily in judgments (Herr et al. 1991). Consequently, from a company's perspective, negatively valenced online product reviews are very harmful. Regarding the persuasiveness of online product reviews, it is important to consider that, over time, consumers have become more skeptical about consumer generated information that is provided on the Internet. This skepticism is due to news publications about Internet abuses (McKnight and Kacmar 2006) and the fact that people who provide information on the Internet are anonymous. In addition, the fact that such information is unfiltered (Cheung et al. 2009) and that marketers use the anonymity of the Internet to disguise their promotions as consumer recommendations or to pay people for writing negative online reviews about competitor products foster consumer skepticism.

Consequently, it is interesting to analyze whether effects of negatively valenced online product reviews generally exist or whether such effects depend on factors such as review quality and subjectively perceived review credibility. According to Park, Lee, and Han (2007), we refer to review quality as the relevance, understandability, sufficiency, objectivity, and persuasiveness of a review's content. Thus, high-quality reviews provide matter-of-fact information about product characteristics, whereas low-quality reviews are emotional, subjective and do not provide factual information. Perceived review quality is derived from the concept of source credibility which represents the extent to which a person who is processing the information provided by the source evaluates the source as being knowledgeable, qualified, experienced, trustworthy, and able to provide unbiased, objective information (Belch and Belch 2001).

In this paper, we consider the situation where consumers have the intention to purchase a specific product and visit opinion plat-

forms to learn about other consumers' evaluations of this product before making the final purchase decision. We only consider online product reviews posted on opinion platforms that are independent of producers or retailers because this is the most widely used type of online WOM communication (Hennig-Thurau et al. 2004). The target variable with regard to which we examine effects of online product reviews is consumer-based brand equity. Consumer-based brand equity corresponds to consumers' perceptions of a product's additional value that is generated by the brand name (Park and Srinivasan 1994) and is based on associations with the brand which are activated in response to the brand name (Krishnan 1996). These associations are composed of perceived brand attributes and brand benefits such as product quality (Keller and Lehmann 2006; Krishnan 1996). Since the late 1980s, brand equity has been one of the most important marketing concepts in both research and practice (Srinivasan, Park, and Chang 2005). Thus, the objectives of our research are to examine the effects of negative online product reviews on consumer-based brand equity in terms of brand equity dilution depending on review quality and to analyze the mediating role of perceived review credibility in the relation between review quality and brand value perceptions that are a pre-stage of brand equity. This paper adds to the existing body of research because studies on the link between negative online WOM communication and the dilution of consumer-based brand equity are scarce. Moreover, no study has examined in detail the role of perceived review credibility in the relation between review quality and consumer-based brand equity. In addition to addressing researchers, our paper addresses marketers by showing that online product reviews can have negative consequences for companies and by offering insights into the processes that underlie these effects.

## EMPIRICAL AND THEORETICAL BACKGROUND
### Previous Research on Review Quality and the Role of Perceived Review Credibility

Concepts such as message quality and perceived credibility have been subject to several studies in the field of offline communication (Dholakia and Sternthal 1977; Heesacker et al. 1983; Hovland and Weiss 1951-52; Jain and Posavac 2001; Nan 2009; Sternthal, Dholakia, and Leavitt 1978). However, as information processing in online environments differs considerably from offline information processing, we do not consider these studies in more detail. We will instead focus on research on effects of quality/perceived credibility of online product reviews.

In the field of online communication, only three studies cover review quality and/or perceived review credibility. Although none of these studies exactly examines the effects we are interested in, we will shortly summarize them because they still provide interesting aspects with regard to our study purpose. In a basic study, Park et al. (2007) investigated whether the quality of online product reviews can affect consumers' purchase intentions and found that this effect is significant. Note that this study did not include perceived review credibility and only examined effects of positive online product reviews. However, the findings of this study provide the notion that the quality of online product reviews plays an important role with regard to typical marketing response variables.

In another study, McKnight and Kacmar (2006) analyzed the role of perceived information credibility at the example of a legal advice website for consumers. Their results show that perceived

*Advances in Consumer Research*
Volume 38, © 2012

information credibility significantly mediates the relation between factors such as individual characteristics, technology affinity as well as the initial impression of the website, and the willingness to follow the provided legal recommendations. Note that this study did not test effects of consumer-based information, but effects of legal recommendations provided by experts and that this study does not cover negatively valenced information. However, the findings of this study are interesting with regard to our study purpose because they show the mediator effect of perceived credibility in the context of processing information that is provided on the Internet.

A study conducted by Cheung et al. (2009) has most in common with our research purpose. They examined the mediating role of perceived credibility in the relation between the argument strength of positively and negatively valenced online consumer recommendations and the intention to adopt the recommendation. They found that argument strength has a positive effect on perceived credibility which in turn positively influences the intention to adopt the recommendation. Starting from these findings, it is interesting to examine the mediating role of perceived credibility in the relation between review quality and more concrete consumer response variables such as brand value perceptions.

## Theoretical Background of Effects of Online Product Reviews on Consumer-Based Brand Equity and the Role of Review Quality and Perceived Review Credibility

In a first step, we will shortly discuss the concepts of brand equity and brand equity dilution. We refer to brand equity as a synonym for consumers' brand beliefs, attitudes and behaviorial intentions (Ailawadi, Lehmann, and Neslin 2003; Farquhar 1989; Keller and Lehmann 2006). According to Keller (1993), consumer-based brand equity describes the differential effect brand knowledge has on consumers' value perceptions of brands that are comparable with regard to their major attributes. Consumer-based brand value perceptions as a pre-stage of brand equity comprise aspects such as brand associations, perceived quality (Aaker 1991; Farquhar 1989; Keller 1993; Silverman, Sprott, and Pascal 1999; Washburn and Plank 2002) and aspects of consumer behavior such as purchase intentions and willingness to pay (Agarwal and Rao 1996; Faircloth, Capella, and Alford 2001; Yoo, Donthu, and Lee 2000). The concept of brand equity dilution reflects the idea that information processing can result in a revision of brand evaluations (Buchanan, Simmons, and Bickart 1999; Loken and Roedder John 1993; Roedder John, Loken, and Joiner 1998) through the weakening of important brand value perceptions. Such effects can result in lower purchase intentions (Pullig, Simmons, and Netemeyer 2006). Thus, in the context considered here, we refer to brand equity dilution as a revision of consumer-based brand value perceptions that differ across brand knowledge.

Note that brand equity and thus also brand equity dilution can only be examined on an aggregate level if brand knowledge is a between-subjects factor. Consequently, the below derived research hypotheses will contain brand equity as dependent variable if an analysis on an aggregate level is sufficient and brand value perceptions which constitute a pre-stage of brand equity as dependent variable if a more detailed analysis is needed.

In the following, we will first explain theoretically why online product reviews can have considerable strong effects on consumer-based brand equity. Afterwards, we will provide a theoretical explanation for the mediating role of perceived review credibility in the considered context.

In order to build up a theoretical framework for effects of negative online product reviews on brand equity we draw on previous studies on brand equity dilution in different fields of research such as brand extensions (Loken and Roedder John 1993; Milberg, Park,

and McCarthy 1997; Roedder John et al. 1998), retailing (Buchanan et al. 1999), and product-harm crises (Dawar and Pillutla 2000). A theoretical approach that can be found in this type of literature and that can be used to explain effects of negative online product reviews is the so-called search and alignment theory. According to this approach, consumers who initially have positive attribute-specific product information and then are faced with negative attribute-specific product information that challenges the initial impression, tend to revise this impression into the direction of the challenging information (Pham and Muthukrishnan 2002).

In our case, the initially positive attribute-specific product information translates into initially positive brand value perceptions that are due to the fact that consumers who are interested in buying a particular product have formed their intention to purchase the product on the basis of an initially positive evaluation of relevant product attributes. Furthermore, the negative information provided in online product reviews can be interpreted in terms of the negative attribute-specific product information because the authors of such reviews often report their experiences with a particular product in a very detailed way. Consequently, we explain effects of negative online product reviews on brand equity in terms of brand equity dilution as follows. Consumers who are faced with such online product reviews weight negative reviews more heavily than possibly also found positive ones. Processing negative online product reviews further means dealing with attribute-specific product information that is contrary to the initial brand value perceptions. Consequently, consumers are likely to revise their initial brand value perceptions into the direction of the negative online product reviews, which leads to brand equity dilution. The presented arguments lead to our first and basic research hypothesis:

Hypothesis 1:  Negative online product reviews have detrimental effects on consumer-based brand equity which occur in terms of brand equity dilution.

With regard to effects of review quality on consumer-based brand equity, we draw on literature in the field of effects of strong versus weak arguments. According to Petty and Cacioppo (1983), strong arguments provided in a message represent high message quality and lead to a stronger attitude change into the direction of the message than do weak arguments that correspond to low message quality. Consequently, we argue in our second hypothesis:

Hypothesis 2:  High-quality product reviews have stronger effects on consumer-based brand equity in terms of brand equity dilution than have low-quality product reviews.

The literature provides the following arguments with regard to the role of source credibility in the context of information processing. First, in computer-mediated communication, it is difficult to evaluate attributes such as attractiveness and physical appearance of the information source (Cheung et al. 2009) and thus, cues such as content credibility play a considerable role. Second, the cognitive response hypothesis (Greenwald 1968) proposes that when an issue is personally involving or relevant, people are more motivated to think about the information provided by a highly than by a less credible source. Moreover, attitudes are rather determined by argument quality if a message is presented by a highly credible source (Heesacker, Petty, and Cacioppo 1983).

In the context considered here, we focus on high-involvement products because especially in high involvement contexts, people are motivated to consult opinion platforms before making their purchase decisions. Thus, the arguments provided by the cognitive response hypothesis can be transferred to the context considered here as follows. The quality of negative online product reviews has an effect on perceived review credibility which in turn has effects on consumer-based brand equity. The latter effect can be explained by the fact that consumers are more motivated to think about the information provided in the online product review and to modify their brand value perceptions into the direction of the evaluation provided in the review if this review seems to be credible. These arguments lead to our third research hypothesis:

*Hypothesis 3:*    *Perceived credibility of a negatively valenced online product review mediates the relation between review quality and consumer-based brand value perceptions.*

## EMPIRICAL STUDY

### Test Products

We decided to use different test products to cover several product categories. Thus, we used one utilitarian (computer notebook), one hedonic (digital camera), and one hybrid product (a product with both utilitarian and hedonic features: multimedia mobile phone). We chose high-involvement products that were familiar to the respondents because especially such products are frequently subject to WOM communication (Ha 2002). This phenomenon can be explained by the fact that only in the case of high involvement, consumers are willing to process detailed product-related information and thus are motivated to write and look up online product reviews.

### Pretests

We conducted a first pretest to identify the average number of online product reviews people read on opinion platforms before making a purchase decision. In a university computer room, 20 test participants were asked to imagine that they intended to buy a specific product and then received the instruction to spend as much time as they would need in a real situation on an opinion platform to read as many reviews on this product as they thought to be appropriate.

Afterwards, people were asked to indicate the number of online product reviews they had read. The results show that on average, people read 2.6 reviews. Thus, we decided to use three reviews as test stimuli for the main study.

We conducted a second pretest to find high- and low-quality product reviews. In a first step, we looked at several opinion platforms to get an impression of the average length and the typical content of high- and low-quality product reviews on such platforms. We found that high-quality reviews usually have a length of about 350 words and contain attribute-specific information, whereas low-quality reviews have about half the length of high-quality reviews and rather express emotions. We then selected six negatively valenced online product reviews for each product (three reviews that we a-priori judged to be of high quality and three other reviews that we considered as low quality reviews) from a real opinion platform. In order to select the online product reviews, we used the criteria indicated by Belch and Belch (2001) and additionally considered the review quality ratings provided on the platform. The high-quality reviews we chose were more logical and persuasive and gave reasons based on specific facts about the product whereas the low-quality reviews we chose were emotional, subjective, did not offer any factual information, and simply provided a recommendation.

Thirty respondents participated in the pretest on perceived review quality. Each respondent rated the six online reviews for one of the products on the basis of five items that measured review quality (e.g., helpful/informative review, precise information, reviewer has a comprehensive knowledge etc.) on seven-point scales. The five single items were aggregated to an overall value for perceived review quality. The resulting mean values are shown in table 1.

A post-hoc analysis showed that the mean value differences among the online product reviews that were a-priori chosen as low-/high-quality reviews were not significant whereas the mean values of the low-quality reviews and the high-quality reviews differed significantly.

A third pretest was needed to prove that the chosen online product reviews were indeed judged as negatively valenced reviews. Thus, we asked another 30 people to participate in the negativity pretest.

### Table 1
### Results of the Pretest on Perceived Review Quality

| Review | A-priori assigned review quality | Perceived review quality | | |
|--------|---------------------------------|-------------------|---------------|--------------|
| | | computer notebook | digital camera | mobile phone |
| 1 | | 1.42 | 1.78 | 1.58 |
| 2 | low | 2.08 | 2.34 | 2.20 |
| 3 | | 1.52 | 1.68 | 1.54 |
| 4 | | 5.16 | 4.64 | 4.62 |
| 5 | high | 5.40 | 5.62 | 5.50 |
| 6 | | 5.86 | 5.84 | 5.96 |

### Table 2
### Results of the Pretest on Perceived Review Negativity

| Review | Review quality | Perceived review negativity | | |
|--------|---------------|-------------------|---------------|--------------|
| | | computer notebook | digital camera | mobile phone |
| 1 | | 6.10 ($t = 6.03$, $p < .001$) | 6.20 ($t = 8.82$, $p < .001$) | 6.30 ($t = 10.78$, p $p < .001$) |
| 2 | low | 6.40 ($t = 1.85$, $p < .001$) | 6.30 ($t = 7.67$, $p < .001$) | 5.60 ($t = 7.24$, $p < .001$) |
| 3 | | 5.70 ($t = 5.08$, $p < .01$) | 5.80 ($t = 6.19$, $p < .001$) | 6.40 ($t = 10.85$, $p < .001$) |
| 4 | | 5.90 ($t = 6.86$, $p < .001$) | 6.60 ($t = 15.92$, $p < .001$) | 6.50 ($t = 15.00$, $p < .001$) |
| 5 | high | 6.00 ($t = 9.49$, $p < .001$) | 6.40 ($t = 10.85$, $p < .001$) | 5.90 ($t = 6.04$, $p < .001$) |
| 6 | | 6.30 ($t = 10.78$, $p < .001$) | 6.00 ($t = 13.42$, $p < .001$) | 5.70 ($t = 7.97$, $p < .001$) |

Each participant was instructed to read the six reviews for one of the three test products (10 participants per test product) and to evaluate the negativity of each review using the item "the author has a very negative opinion of this product" (scale: 1 = "do not at all agree" to 7 = "totally agree"). The resulting mean values that are summarized in table 2 are significantly higher than the scale midpoint (one sample t-tests) and thus the online product reviews are perceived as being clearly negatively valenced.

The purpose of the fourth pretest was to identify brands about which consumers have more or less comprehensive brand knowledge. For each of the tested products (computer notebook, digital camera, mobile phone), we examined five existing brand names that were more or less known in the product category. We measured brand knowledge using several items that addressed the most important aspects of the brand knowledge concept. Each of the 45 participants of this pretest evaluated either the computer notebook brands, the digital camera brands, or the mobile phone brands on seven-point rating scales. The tested brand names and the mean values that resulted from the aggregation of the single items to an overall value for brand knowledge are shown in table 3.

We decided to select the brand names that were characterized by the lowest and the highest brand knowledge in the respective product category and thus chose the brand names Axxiv/Dell for computer notebooks, Sigma/Canon for digital cameras, and Glofiish/Nokia for mobile phones.

### Table 3
### Results of the Pretest on Brand Knowledge

| | | | | | |
|---|---|---|---|---|---|
| Computer notebook (*n* = 15) | Axxiv 1.07 | Packard Bell 3.00 | Acer 4.47 | Sony 6.60 | Dell 6.73 |
| Digital camera (*n* = 15) | Sigma 1.93 | Praktica 2.13 | Olympus 4.80 | Nikon 5.27 | Canon 6.73 |
| Mobile phone (*n* = 15) | Glofiish 1.13 | LG 2.47 | Samsung 4.67 | Sony 6.13 | Nokia 6.87 |

### Experimental Design and Measures

Our main study was based on a 2 (low/high review quality) x 2 (poor/comprehensive brand knowledge) x 3 (product type: utilitarian/hedonic/hybrid) between-subjects design. By testing utilitarian, hedonic and hybrid products in the study, we controlled for possible effects of product type.

In order to measure brand value perceptions as a pre-stage of consumer-based brand equity, we used the items shown in table 4 that we chose in accordance with existing literature (Aaker 1991; Agarwal and Rao 1996; Dawar and Pillutlar 2000; Keller 1993).

Furthermore, we measured perceptions of review credibility using four items ("I believe that the product reviews reflect the true experiences of these consumers", "the authors of these reviews are trustworthy", "these reviews are credible", and "if I had the intention to buy a product in this category, I would consider these reviews when making a purchase decision") according to the recommendations of Cheung et al. (2009) and got a coefficient alpha of 0.89. The high coefficient alpha values for brand value perceptions and perceived review credibility indicate that the chosen items are appropriate to reliably measure the concepts they were intended to measure.

Furthermore, we measured the respondents' perceptions of the general persuasiveness of online product reviews in order to examine whether the different experimental groups are comparable with regard to this variable. In order to do so, we used two items ("online product reviews have an impact on my purchase decisions", "before making important purchase decisions, I go to product review websites to learn about other consumers' opinions", 7-point rating scales), for which we identified a bivariate correlation of 0.56. As the alpha values and the correlation were sufficiently high, we calculated the overall values for the considered variables as mean values of the respective items.

In addition, we measured the perceived quality of the three presented online product reviews and brand knowledge in order to be able to do manipulation checks. We used the item "the reviews are helpful" (7-point scale) to check for review quality and the item "Please indicate your knowledge with regard to the brand [...]" based on a dichotomous scale ("poor knowledge" vs. "comprehensive knowledge") to check for brand knowledge. As perceived review quality and brand knowledge have already been subject to pretests, we decided to use these simplified measures to limit questionnaire length.

### Table 4
### Measures of Brand Value Perceptions

| Item | Coefficient alpha (measurement before WOM) | Coefficient alpha (measurement after WOM) |
|---|---|---|
| The [product] seems to be of high quality. I think that the [product] is reliable. I believe that the [product] is a high performance product. I like this [product]. I am interested in this [product]. I can imagine buying this [product]. I would recommend this [product] to my friends. I would prefer this [product] over others in this product category. | 0.93 | 0.97 |
| Note that we used seven-point rating scales ranging from 1 = totally disagree to 7 = totally agree | | |

## Sample and Procedure

Six hundred people participated in the main study (thus 50 people per experimental group). The sample consisted of 55% women and 45% men who were familiar with opinion platforms. The age of the participants ranged from 14 to 60 years, the average age was 25.8 years.

The procedure was as follows. The participants were instructed to imagine that they were planning to buy a product in the respective product category in the near future. Then, they were provided with a picture and a short description of the test product. Afterwards, we measured brand knowledge and a-priori brand value perceptions. Subsequently, the respondents were presented with three negative online product reviews. We varied the order of these reviews from respondent to respondent to counterbalance possible order effects. After having read the online product reviews, the participants were asked to answer the brand value perception scales for a second time. Then, the respondents had to indicate their perceptions of review credibility and to judge review quality. In a final step, the respondents were asked to indicate their perceptions of the general persuasiveness of online product reviews and to provide information about their age and gender.

## DATA ANALYSIS AND RESULTS

Before presenting the results of the main study, we prove that the experimental groups are comparable with regard to perceptions of general persuasiveness of online product reviews. An analysis of variance shows that the twelve groups that result from the experimental design described above do not differ with regard to perceptions of persuasiveness ($F = 0.53$, $p > .10$).

In the next step, we present the results of the manipulation checks for brand knowledge and perceived review quality. As both the brand knowledge manipulation and the brand knowledge measurement are dichotomous, we used a chi-square test. Ninety-four

percent of the respondents indicated poor knowledge about the brand that initially was chosen as a poor knowledge brand and 93% of the respondents agreed to have comprehensive knowledge about the brand that was intended to be the comprehensive knowledge brand ($X^2 = 450.75$, $p < .001$). Consequently, for the further analyses, we used the manipulated brand knowledge variable.

As perceived review quality was measured as a metric variable, we conducted an independent samples $t$-test with the manipulated review quality as independent variable and the perceived review quality as dependent variable. The results show that the reviews that were used as low-quality reviews were judged as significantly less helpful ($M = 3.86$) than the reviews that were used as high-quality reviews ($M = 5.55$, $t = 12.90$, $p < .001$). Therefore, the manipulated review quality variable was used for further analyses.

We now present the results of the main study that aimed to identify the numerical value of brand equity dilution depending on review quality and to examine the mediator effect of perceived review credibility in the relation between review quality and change in brand value perceptions as a pre-stage of brand equity. Based on the theoretical conceptualization, brand equity corresponds to the distance between a comprehensive-knowledge brand and a poor-knowledge brand. The value for this distance that represents brand equity was calculated as a difference by following the recommendations of Smith and Lusch (1976). Thus, we first calculated mean values of brand value perceptions before and after the contact with negative online product reviews, then the differences between comprehensive and poor brand knowledge, and finally the value of brand equity dilution as the difference of brand equity before and brand equity after the contact with the negative online product reviews. These calculations were done separately for low and high review quality. In order to judge whether the brand equity values are based on significant mean value differences and to evaluate brand equity dilution, we calculated independent samples $t$-test statistics. The results are shown in table 5.

### Table 5
### Brand Equity Dilution in the Case of Low and High Review Quality

| | Low review quality ($n = 300$) | | | | High review quality ($n = 300$) | | | |
| | VP | | E | test | VP | | E | test |
| | $K_c$ | $K_p$ | ($VP_{Kc} - VP_{Kp}$) | statistics | $K_c$ | $K_p$ | ($VP_{Kc} - VP_{Kp}$) | statistics |
|---|---|---|---|---|---|---|---|---|
| Before WOM | 4.99 | 3.99 | 1.00 | $t = 7.64$ ($p < .001$) | 5.10 | 3.95 | 1.15 | $t = 8.99$ ($p < .001$) |
| After WOM | 3.12 | 2.54 | 0.58 | $t = 4.02$ ($p < .001$) | 2.96 | 2.59 | 0.37 | $t = 2.53$ ($p < .05$) |
| Difference (before - after) | 1.87 | 1.45 | 0.42 | $t = 2.52$ ($p < .05$) | 2.14 | 1.36 | 0.78 | $t = 4.83$ ($p < .001$) |

Note: VP = brand value perceptions, E = brand equity, $K_c$/$K_p$ = comprehensive/poor brand knowledge

The results presented in table 5 show that the contact with negative online product reviews causes a significant brand equity dilution (low review quality: 0.42, high review quality: 0.78). This result that provides support for H1 shows the destructiveness of negative online product reviews with respect to consumer-based brand equity. The fact that brand equity dilution occurs implies that the deterioration of brand value perceptions is stronger in the case of comprehensive brand knowledge than in the case of poor brand knowledge. Thus, after the contact with negative online product reviews, the distance of brand value perceptions between the comprehensive knowledge brand and the poor knowledge brand is smaller than before. Thinking of findings of research on effects of traditional WOM communication that have shown that effects of WOM communication are weaker for comprehensive-knowledge brands than for poor-knowledge brands (Bone 1995; Sundaram

and Webster 1999), our finding might be surprising. However, an important difference between traditional and online WOM communication that provides an explanation for such a destructive effect of negatively valenced online product reviews even in the case of comprehensive brand knowledge is that traditional WOM communication means transmitting only one piece of information at one point in time whereas online WOM communication is much more voluminous in quantity and available for an indefinite period of time (Chatterjee 2001; Henning-Thurau et al. 2004).

The differentiation between low and high review quality further shows that brand equity dilution is significantly stronger in the case of high review quality ($t_{0.78-0.42} = 2.33$, $p < .05$). Thus, the results provide support for H2 and show that the danger of brand equity dilution as a consequence of the contact with negative online product reviews is much higher in the case of high quality reviews than in the case of low quality reviews.

In the second step of our analysis, we examined the mediator effect of perceived review credibility in the relation between review quality and the change in brand value perceptions. We did not use brand equity as dependent variable for this analysis because numerical values for brand equity can only be calculated on an aggregate data level whereas we needed data on the individual level to be able to accurately examine the mediator effect of perceived review credibility. Choosing brand value perceptions that constitute a pre-stage of the concept of brand equity should not pose a problem because in the first step of our analysis, we have shown that brand equity is calculated on the basis of brand value perceptions and thus both concepts are closely related. We used the SmartPLS procedure to determine the role of perceived review credibility in the relation between review quality and change in brand value perceptions. We estimated the model shown in figure 1.

The estimated path coefficients and the associated t-values as well as the factor loadings are summarized in table 6.

The significantly high factor loadings show that the chosen single items are appropriate to measure the model constructs. Furthermore, the estimated path coefficients are significant with plausible signs and thus provide support for the assumed relations. In more detail, the path coefficients indicate that a higher review quality leads to more positive perceptions of review credibility which in turn lead to a larger difference between brand value perceptions before and after the contact with negative online product reviews. Consequently, the data provide support for the assumed mediator effect of perceived review credibility and thus for the assumption of H3. As the differences have been calculated as brand value perceptions$_{before}$ – brand value perceptions$_{after}$, a larger difference means a stronger detrimental effect of negative online product reviews on brand value perceptions. Thus, the analysis has shown that perceptions of review credibility play an important role in the context of effects of negative online product reviews on brand value perceptions.

**FIGURE 1**
**PLS MODEL**

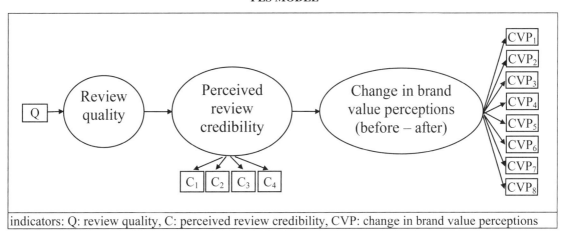

indicators: Q: review quality, C: perceived review credibility, CVP: change in brand value perceptions

**Table 6**
**Results of the PLS Analysis**

| Effect | Path coefficient | T-value |
|---|---|---|
| review quality à perceived review credibility | 0.42 | 4.77 |
| perceived review credibility à change in brand value perceptions | 0.34 | 3.93 |
| | Factor loading | T-value |
| perceived review credibility → $C_1$ | 0.81 | 18.64 |
| perceived review credibility → $C_2$ | 0.91 | 40.17 |
| perceived review credibility → $C_3$ | 0.91 | 44.67 |
| perceived review credibility → $C_4$ | 0.82 | 19.32 |
| change in brand value perceptions → $CVP_1$ | 0.80 | 15.51 |
| change in brand value perceptions → $CVP_2$ | 0.82 | 18.78 |
| change in brand value perceptions → $CVP_3$ | 0.82 | 17.64 |
| change in brand value perceptions → $CVP_4$ | 0.82 | 21.17 |
| change in brand value perceptions → $CVP_5$ | 0.84 | 19.90 |
| change in brand value perceptions → $CVP_6$ | 0.86 | 24.88 |
| change in brand value perceptions → $CVP_7$ | 0.86 | 27.18 |
| change in brand value perceptions → $CVP_8$ | 0.81 | 17.43 |
| indicators: Q: review quality, C: perceived review credibility, CVP: change in brand value perceptions | | |

## CONCLUSION

The starting point of this paper has been the observation that opinion platforms where consumers publish their product reviews become increasingly popular, from both the reviewers' and the readers' perspective. Moreover, both practical experience and previous research let assume that consumers are especially interested in writing and reading negative online product reviews. Additional important observations have been that such reviews vary considerably in quality and that consumers show an increasing skepticism toward online product reviews. Consequently, from a marketer's perspective, the questions arose which effects especially negatively valenced online product reviews might have on consumer-based brand equity, whether these effects exist for all negative product reviews or depend on review quality, and which processes underlie these effects. Therefore, it stood to reason to extend the existing body of research in the field of effects of online WOM communication which only consists of a small number of studies by introducing the concept of dilution of consumer-based brand equity as dependent variable, by examining possible effects of negative product reviews depending on review quality, and by shedding light on the processes that underlie these effects.

The findings of the empirical study show that negative online product reviews have considerable detrimental effects on consumer-based brand equity and that these effects increase with higher review quality. A more detailed analysis of the role of perceived review credibility shows that this variable mediates the relation between review quality and brand value perceptions that are a pre-stage of consumer-based brand equity.

Consequently, marketers should start considering such negative consequences that they might have neglected up to now when planning their communication strategies. Thus, marketers should continuously monitor the relation of high- and low-quality reviews on their brands that can be found on the most important opinion platforms. In addition, most of the leading opinion platforms provide information about the number of hits per review. Out of these two types of information, marketers can estimate the likelihood that potential customers will be faced with a comparatively large number of negatively valenced high-quality reviews. If this likelihood is considerably high, they should try hard to develop appropriate coping strategies.

## REFERENCES

Aaker, David A. (1991), *Managing Brand Equity: Capitalizing on the Value of a Brand Name,* New York: The Free Press.

Agarwal, Manok K. and Vithala R. Rao (1996), "An Empirical Comparison of Consumer-Based Measures of Brand Equity," *Marketing Letters*, 7 (3), 237-47.

Ailawadi, Kusum, Donald R. Lehmann, and Scott A. Neslin (2003), "Revenue Premium as an Outcome Measure of Brand Equity," *Journal of Marketing,* 67 (4), 1-17.

Belch, George E. and Michael A. Belch (2001), *Advertising and Promotion: An Integrated Marketing Communications Perspective*, New York: Mc Graw-Hill.

Bickart, Barbara A. and Robert M. Schindler (2001), "Internet Forums as Influential Sources of Consumer Information," *Journal of Interactive Marketing*, 15 (3), 31-40.

Buchanan, Lauranne, Carolyn J. Simmons, and Barbara A. Bickart (1999), "Brand Equity Dilution: Retailer Display and Context Brand Effects," *Journal of Marketing Research,* 36 (3), 345-55.

Chatterjee, Patrali (2001), "Online Reviews: Do Consumers Use Them?" *Advances in Consumer Research*, 28 (1), 129-33.

Chevalier, Judith A. and Dina Mayzlin (2006), "The Effect of Word of Mouth on Sales: Online Book Reviews," *Journal of Marketing Research*, 43 (3), 345-54.

Cheung, Man Yee, Chuan Luo, Choon Ling Sia, and Huaping Chen (2009), "Credibility of Electronic Word-of-Mouth: Informational and Normative Determinants of On-Line Consumer Recommendations," *International Journal of Electronic Commerce*, 13 (4), 9-38.

Dawar, Niraj and Madan M. Pillutla (2000), "Impact of Product-Harm Crises on Brand Equity: The Moderating Role of Consumer Expectations," *Journal of Marketing Research*, 37 (2), 215-26.

Dholakia, Ruby R. and Brian Sternthal (1977), "Highly Credible Sources: Persuasive Facilitators or Persuasive Liabilities?" *Journal of Consumer Research*, 3 (4), 223-32.

Faircloth, James B., Louis M. Capella, and Bruce L. Alford (2001), "The Effect of Brand Attitude and Brand Image on Brand Equity," *Journal of Marketing Theory and Practice,* 9 (3), 61-75.

Farquhar, Peter H. (1989), "Managing Brand Equity," *Marketing Research,* 1 (3), 24-33.

Greenwald, Anthony G. (1968), "*Cognitive Learning, Cognitive Response to Persuasion, and Attitude Change," in Psychological Foundations of Attitudes*, ed. Anthony G. Greenwald, Timothy C. Brock, and Thomas C. Ostrom, New York: Academic Press, 147-70.

Ha, Hong-Youl (2002), "The Effects of Consumer Risk Perception on Pre-Purchase Information in Online Auctions: Brand, Word-of-Mouth, and Customized Information," *Journal of Computer-Mediated Communication*, 8 (only available online).

Heesacker, Martin, Richard E. Petty, and John, T. Cacioppo (1983), "Field Dependence and Attitude Change: Source Credibility Can Alter Persuasion by Affecting Message-Relevant Thinking," *Journal of Personality*, 51 (4), 653-66.

Hennig-Thurau, Thorsten, Kevin P. Gwinner, Gianfranco Walsh, and Dwayne D. Gremler (2004), "Electronic Word-of-Mouth Via Consumer-Opinion Platforms: What Motivates Consumers to Articulate Themselves on the Internet?" *Journal of Interactive Marketing*, 18 (1), 38-52.

Herr, Paul M., Franck R. Kardes, and John Kim (1991), "Effects of Word-of-Mouth and Product-Attribute Information on Persuasion: An Accessibility-Diagnosticity Perspective," *Journal of Consumer Research*, 17 (4), 454-62.

Hovland, Carl I. and Walter Weiss (1951-52), "The Influence of Source Credibility on Communication Effectiveness," *Public Opinion Quarterly*, 15 (4), 635-50.

Jain, Shailendra P. and Steven S. Posavac (2001), "Prepurchase Attribute Verifiability, Source Credibility, and Persuasion," *Journal of Consumer Psychology*, 11 (3), 169-80.

Keller, Kevin L. (1993), "Conceptualizing, Measuring, and Managing Customer-Based Brand Equity," *Journal of Marketing*, 57 (1), 1-22.

Keller, Kevin L. and Donald R. Lehmann (2006), "Brands and Branding: Research Findings and Future Priorities," *Marketing Science*, 25 (6), 740-59.

Kiecker, Pamela and Deborah L. Cowles (2001), "Interpersonal Communication and Personal Influence on the Internet: A Framework for Examining Online Word-of-Mouth," *Journal of Euromarketing*, 11 (2), 71-88.

Krishnan, H. Shanker (1996), "Characteristics of Memory Associations: A Consumer-Based Brand Equity Perspective," *International Journal of Research in Marketing*, 13 (4), 389-405.

Loken, Barbara and Deborah Roedder John (1993), "Diluting Brand Beliefs: When do Brand Extensions Have a Negative Impact?" *Journal of Marketing*, 57 (3), 71-84.

McKnight, Harrison and Chuck Kacmar (2006), "Factors of Information Credibility for an Internet Advice Site," *Proceedings of the 39th Hawaii International Conference on System Science,* http://ieeexplore.ieee.org/stamp/stamp.jsp?arnumber=01579516&tag=1.

Milberg, Sandra J., Whan C. Park, and Michael S. McCarthy (1997), "Managing Negative Feedback Effects Associated With Brand Extensions: The Impact of Alternative Branding Strategies," *Journal of Consumer Psychology*, 6 (2), 119-40.

Nan, Xiaoli (2009), "The Influence of Source Credibility on Attitude Certainty: Exploring the Moderating Effects of Timing of Source Identification and Individual Need for Cognition," *Psychology & Marketing,* 26 (4), 321-32.

Park, Do-Hyung, Jumin Lee, and Ingoo Han (2007), "The Effect of On-Line Consumer Reviews on Consumer Purchasing Intention: The Moderating Role of Involvement," *International Journal of Electronic Commerce*, 11 (4), 125-48.

Park, Chan S. and V. Srinivasan (1994), "A Survey-Based Method for Measuring and Understanding Brand Equity and its Extendibility," *Journal of Marketing Research*, 31 (2), 271-88.

Petty, Richard E. and John T. Cacioppo (1983), "Central and Peripheral Routes to Persuasion: Application to Advertising," in *Advertising and Consumer Psychology*, ed. Larry Percy and Arch Woodside, Lexington, MA: Lexington Books, 3-23.

Pham, Michel Tuan and A. V. Muthukrishnan (2002), "Search and Alignment in Judgment Revision: Implications for Brand Positioning," *Journal of Marketing Research*, 39 (1), 18-30.

Pullig, Chris, Carolyn J. Simmons, and Richarg G. Netemeyer (2006), "Brand Dilution: When Do New Brands Hurt Existing Brands?" *Journal of Marketing*, 70 (2), 52-66.

Roedder John, Deborah, Barbara Loken, and Christopher Joiner (1998), "The Negative Impact of Extensions: Can Flagship Products Be Diluted?" *Journal of Marketing*, 62 (1), 19-32.

Sen, Shahana and Dawn Lerman (2007), "Why Are You Telling Me This? An Examination Into Negative Consumer Reviews on the Web," *Journal of Interactive Marketing*, 21 (4), 76-94.

Silverman, Steven N., David E. Sprott, and Vincent J. Pascal (1999), "Relating Consumer-Based Sources of Brand Equity to Market Outcomes," *Advances in Consumer Research*, 26 (1), 352-58.

Smith, Donnavieve, Satya Menon, and K. Sivakumar (2005), "Online Peer and Editorial Recommendations, Trust, and Choice in Virtual Markets," *Journal of Interactive Marketing*, 19 (3), 15-37.

Smith, Robert E. and Robert F. Lusch (1976), "How Advertising Can Position a Brand," *Journal of Advertising Research*, 16 (1), 37-43.

Srinivasan, V., Chan S. Park, and Dae R. Chang (2005), "An Approach to the Measurement, Analysis, and Prediction of Brand Equity and its Sources," *Management Science,* 51 (9), 1433-48.

Sternthal, Brian, Ruby Dholakia, and Clark Leavitt (1978), "The Persuasive Effect of Source Credibility: Tests of Cognitive Response," *Journal of Consumer Research,* 4 (4), 252-60.

Trusov, Michael, Randolph E. Bucklin, and Koen Pauwels (2009), "Effects of Word-of-Mouth Versus Traditional Marketing: Findings From an Internet Social Networking Site," *Journal of Marketing*, 73 (5), 90-102.

Washburn, Judith H. and Richard E. Plank (2002), "Measuring Brand Equity: An Evaluation of a Consumer-Based Brand Equity Scale," *Journal of Marketing Theory and Practice*, 10 (1), 46-62.

Yoo, Boonghee, Navee Donthu, and Sungho Lee (2000), "An Examination of Selected Marketing Mix Elements and Brand Equity," *Journal of the Academy of Marketing Science,* 28 (2), 195-211.

Xia, Lan and Nada N. Bechwati (2008), "Word of Mouse: The Role of Cognitive Personalization in Online Consumer Reviews," *Journal of Interactive Advertising*, 9 (1), 108-28.

# "Grandma's Fridge is Cool" –
# The Meaning of Retro Brands for Young Consumers

Andrea Hemetsberger, University of Innsbruck, Austria
Christine Kittinger-Rosanelli, University of Innsbruck, Austria
Barbara Mueller, University of Innsbruck, Austria

## ABSTRACT

This article addresses the question why young consumers favor retro brands although they had no consumption experience with the original counterpart. Interviews with young consumers revealed that retro brands are perceived to be special possessions which help young consumers coping with ambiguities in their search for identity. Retro brands are perceived as nostalgic and authentic objects reflecting continuity and discontinuity; retro brands help negotiating young consumers' individual identity and search for belongingness and are used as fashion icons that reflect young consumers' aspiration for social acceptance and non-conformism.

## THEORETICAL BACKGROUND

Literature has brought forward an abundance of explanations for the consumption of retro brand. Nostalgia has been the most prominent, so far. Holbrook and Schindler's view of nostalgia is closely related to what Davis (1979) was one of the first to distinguish among personal and communal nostalgia, where 'personal nostalgia' depicts a nostalgic feeling towards object-related experiences that have somehow been lost. Communal nostalgia occurs at the societal level and is often related to social turmoil, great depressions and other discontinuing moments in history.

Turner (1987) provided some additional thoughts on nostalgia that go beyond personal and communal nostalgia. He claims that nostalgia involves a sense of loss and decline, a melancholic vision of the contemporary world based on a perceived crisis in our civilization, a sense of loss of individual freedom and autonomy; and the idea of a loss of simplicity, authenticity and emotional spontaneity in a mass consumption culture. Similarly, Brown, Kozinets and Sherry (2003) found that retro brands allow referring to a particular past time and its ethos. Consumers, therefore, use retro brands to return to an imagined era of moral certainty.

As young consumers' lives are strongly determined by a search for identity and a period of conscious reflections on issues related to one's identity (Adamson, Hartman and Lyxell, 1999), identity formation and how individual and social identity go together in this critical period might provide another explanation for young consumers' liking of retro brands (Cooley, 1902; Mead, 1934; Erikson, 1968; Kroger, 1989; Mittal, 2006). It is our aim to find out how these quintessential questions are related to the meaning of retro brands for young consumers.

Our empirical work followed a 2-step process. First we identified young consumers who owned and liked retro brands using theoretical sampling (Glaser und Strauss 1967). In a second step we conducted narrative interviews (Schütze, 1987). A constant comparative method was applied for analysis (Charmaz, 2006).

## FINDINGS

Young consumers are also nostalgic. Although some of these feelings reflect derivative experiences with things owned by their grandparents or parents, young consumers do report about personal nostalgia through *memories from their childhood*, and *meaningful moments*, early experiences and habits that they had come to love. Retro brands are favored because they symbolize deep relationships but also when they help standing for one's own opinion and taste. Therefore, young consumers also alter traditional rituals that come with nostalgic brands and *re-interpret its meaning* for their own communal purposes. Retro brands also reflect communal nostalgia, *romanticizing the past and old values* but not in order to bring back the good old days but rather to set a counterpart to current societal developments that young consumers dislike. Retro brands help in this respect by their inherent stability and authenticity.

Our findings show that retro brands help overcome tensions between the defined inner self and the social roles that young consumers are beginning to take over (Mittal, 2006). Retro brands seem to work particularly well in expressing *personal values and attitude towards life* and the social self-concept (Sirgy, 1982), as they are considered as authentic, credible and expressive. Young consumers put particular emphasis on the differentiating elements of their favorite brands in order to underline their *individuality and personality* and at the same time draw a coherent picture of a young consumer's personality *for others to mirror*. Retro brands help communicate these values and also convey a particular aesthetic component.

Retro consumers commonly describe themselves as fashion-conscious and non-conformist, which marks retro brands as a symbol for fashion and style. Young consumers consider themselves as real non-conformists as all others go with the masses. Young consumers express this attitude by drawing a clear distinction among 'retros' and 'fashion victims' thus also strongly relating to his peer group and a certain communal spirit of like-minded consumers in search of autonomy. This way, retro brands allow young consumers to overcome the tension between non-conformity and social acceptance.

## DISCUSSION

Our research contributes to theory in many ways. First and most important, our findings show that retro brands do have deep meaning for young consumers. They provide meaning from a time perspective in that they embody history, childhood memory, nostalgia, and timelessness. At the same time, the discontinuities young consumers are facing in their lives, their striving for autonomy, their idealism that clashes with in-authenticities in contemporary political and market systems contributes to their choice of retro brands.

Retro brands are not just nostalgic objects for young consumers. They are consumed so as to define young consumers' self-concept at the crossroads of individual and social identity. Retro brands are identity-building in that they provide strong historical value systems to identify with. They have a high differentiating potential in that they are not marketed to the masses and embody authenticity and originality.

In a similar vein, retro brands are used to negotiate the distance-proximity tension in young consumers' lives (Adamson, Hartman and Lyxell, 1999). Young consumers' identity seeking processes are strongly related to processes of autonomy-seeking, which means distancing from particular values and societal developments, and social acceptance, which is necessary for any individual's psychological well-being. By successfully demonstrating autonomy, they fight established consumption patterns and gain acceptance among their peers as non-conformist consumption heroes.

## "Grandma's Fridge is Cool" – The Meaning of Retro Brands for Young Consumers

'Wow, this green grandma fridge is absolutely cool, Mum! Would be perfect for my new little apartment.' Mum agrees and smiles. This is quite common scenery, except that it seems quite counter-intuitive that mothers and their daughters are delighted by the same new, old-fashioned styles. As for mothers we can imagine that it would remind them of their childhood but what about their daughters?

Retro branding has become quite popular before and after the turn of the century and researchers recognized this (Brown, 2001). Most researchers base their assumptions and empirical accounts of retro brand consumption on feelings of nostalgia (Holbrook 1993; Holbrook and Schindler, 1989; 2003; Brown, Kozinets and Sherry, 2003). Some studies have related nostalgia to age and developmental changes that occur at a particular age. Davis (1979) was probably first to state that nostalgic feelings typically relate to times of adolescence and early adulthood in Western societies. Holbrook and Schindler (1989) and Schumann and Scott (1989) concordantly concluded from their studies that memories are structured by age whereby preferences typically peaked for things that were popular when individuals are in their early 20s. In stressing the role of experiences associated with objects that were common when one was younger, Holbrook and Schindler (1991) primarily provide explanations for the baby boom generation who have now grown old enough to have something to be nostalgic about. However, the question why their children or young consumers in general favor retro brands over others is yet to be studied. We define young adults as children of the baby boomer generation of Generation Y, who are between 20 and 30 years of age, tha age group that Holbrook and Schindler (1991) have studied, and exactly the formative period (Erikson, 1968) where first important independent life-changing choices are made.

As consumers of a younger age cohort have no experience with the original counterpart of a retro brand, nostalgia as an explanation for retro brand consumption seems counterintuitive. Yet, young consumers might be nostalgia prone, have childhood memories or derivative experiences stemming from their older relatives' stories and narratives. Furthermore, Davis (1979) contended that discontinuities in life, which are very common at the respective age, influence individuals' sense for continuity and the past.

In this article we try to go beyond obvious explanations of nostalgia and derivative experiences. We aim to research and theorize about the deeper meaning of retro brands for young consumers who had no consumption experience with the original brands. To this end we review the literature on retro branding and nostalgia. We introduce additional explanations for retro brand consumption and young consumers' identity development as a search field for explanation, and provide empirical insights into young consumers' narratives about their retro brands. In the discussion section we carve out the meaning of retro brands for young consumers' coping strategies with tensions in their identity search.

### RETRO BRANDS AND NOSTALGIA

Brown et al. (2003) defined Retro Branding as *"the revival or relaunch of a product or service brand from a prior historical period, which is usually but not always updated to contemporary standards of performance, functioning, or taste"* (Brown et al. 2003, 20). Retro brands combine designs from a prior period with innovative functionality thus creating a harmonious offer that unites the contemporary with the past. Usually marketers emphasize the nostalgic elements of retro brands, which are valuable sources of meaning for consumers. Retro brands include various forms of

relation to the past, ranging from exact reproductions of former brands (e.g.: Converse sneakers) to so called 'nostalgic' or 'vintage brands' that use designs from past times to technologically upgraded products with nostalgic designs (e.g.: the PT Cruiser and the VW New Beetle).

Particularly for older consumers, special possessions serve as materializations of memory and evoke a powerful sense of the past (Belk, 1991). Holbrook and Schindler (1989, 1994, 1996, 2003) intensely researched nostalgia and nostalgia proneness in various consumption contexts and related it to particular age cohorts. The authors define nostalgia as "A preference […] towards experiences associated with objects […] that were more common […] when one was younger…" (Holbrook and Schindler, 1991, 330). Via a process called nostalgic bonding, a consumer's history of consumption of particular brands during a critical period of preference formation can create a lifelong preference for those brands. Holbrook and Schindler (2003) were particularly interested in the baby boom generation and how they collectively memorize and celebrate their common history when they were in their early 20s (Holbrook and Schindler, 1989, 1993, 1994, 1996). Holbrook and Schindler's view of nostalgia is closely related to what Davis (1979) and Stern (1992) have described as 'personal nostalgia', a nostalgic feeling towards object-related experiences that have somehow been lost.

Relating these observations to young consumers in their early 20s, we can state that they are currently forming their preferences and nostalgic bonds with particular objects, rather than being nostalgic about preferred brands of their youth. However, Holbrook and Schindler (1993) found that some individuals are more nostalgia prone than others, where nostalgia proneness is independent from age-determined preferences. Furthermore, young consumers might refer to their childhood memories (Belk et al. 2003; Brown-La Tour, La Tour and Zinkhan, 2007) with brands that are preferred due to a sheer familiarity effect (Chaplin and Roedder John, 2005).

A second common facet of nostalgia refers to the collective memory of historical periods and styles that are commonly described as 'communal nostalgia' (Davis, 1979). Communal nostalgia occurs at the societal level and is often related to social turmoil, great depressions and other discontinuing moments in history. Stern (1992) has diagnosed a fin de siècle effect, which describes the tendency to retrospect as the turn of the century comes close. Communal or 'historical nostalgia', as depicted by Stern (1992), "expresses the desire to retreat from contemporary life by returning to a time in the past viewed as superior to the present." (Stern 1992, 13). In view of contemporary postmodern fragmentation, young consumers might well experience their upcoming life as adults as challenging and use retro brand consumption experiences as escape from unwanted societal developments and market hegemony and dive into the myths of past times. Movies and songs from the past are especially suited to serve this kind of temporary escapism from the disenchanted everyday life (Holbrook and Schindler, 1989, 1996).

### BEYOND PERSONAL AND COMMUNAL NOSTALGIA

Turner (1987) provided some additional thoughts on nostalgia. He claims that nostalgia involves a sense of loss and decline, a melancholic vision of the contemporary world based on a perceived crisis in our civilization, a sense of loss of individual freedom and autonomy; and the idea of a loss of simplicity, authenticity and emotional spontaneity in a mass consumption culture. In an attempt to summarize and differentiate Turner's writings, Kessous and Roux (2008) develop a semiotic square that describes different qualities and triggers of nostalgia, which could be long-lasting or just one significant event, reflecting two dimensions: 'continuity' and 'discontinuity'. Based on these dimensions they describe continuity as everyday past childhood memories as opposed to non-continuity which reflects transitional periods of ambiguity and unanchored identity. Discontinuity, on the other hand relates back to unique moments in life whereas non-continuity is related to traditional brand use for ritual occasions.

Brown, Kozinets and Sherry (2003) present yet another explanation for the success of retro brands, which is communal in its approach. Based on the philosophical concepts of allegory (symbolic stories), arcadia (a utopian sense of past worlds), aura (brand essence) and antimony (brand paradox), the authors found that retro brands allow referring to a particular past time and its ethos. The retro brand concretizes important symbolic elements of the past. Consumers, therefore, use retro brands to return to an imagined era of moral certainty. Retro brand consumers also emphasize the utopian and moral character of its fan communities. Retro brands which still exist as a brand story; that have a vital essence; are able to mobilize a utopian vision for a consumer cohort; and positively address opposing desires, are likely to constitute strong sources for consumer identity search.

As young consumers' lives are strongly determined by a search for identity and a period of conscious reflections on issues related to one's identity (Adamson, Hartman and Lyxell, 1999), identity formation in this critical period might provide another explanation for young consumers' liking of retro brands. Theories of understanding the self can be organized around two major themes: the self as a subject/object and the self in relation to others (Cooley, 1902; Mead, 1934). These major themes roughly reflect theories of individual and social identity, or the 'I' and the 'me' as depicted in current consumer behavior literature (Mittal, 2006), and how those identities are going together (Kroger, 1989). Erikson (1968) proclaimed the view that identity formation is a reciprocal process between the psychological interior of the individual and her/his socio-cultural environment. Especially in late adolescence and early adulthood, individuals consciously reflect on themselves as subjects and in relation to others. This identity formation process has many facets, one of them being related to existential questions and ideology. Adamson and Lyxell (1996) found that questions about the future, the meaning of life in general, death, and finally questions about one's own identity are the most crucial questions in late adolescence. It is our aim to find out how these quintessential questions are related to the meaning of retro brands for young consumers.

## METHOD

Our empirical work followed a 2-step process. First we identified young consumers who owned and liked retro brands using "theoretical sampling" as described in grounded theory (Glaser und Strauss 1967; Strauss und Corbin 1990). In our questionnaire we first presented a brief definition and examples for retro brands to ensure a shared understanding of retro brands. Participants then indicated on a 7-point-scale whether they owned retro brands and how much they liked them, in general and their own retro brands, in particular. We used snowball sampling to find appropriate informants, most of whom matched our criteria right away. Informants, who possessed retro brands, showed strong liking, and considered retro brands "very cool" or "cool" qualified for the main study. The final sample consisted of 5 female and 5 male respondents with an age range of 20 to 29 with varying professional backgrounds and a set of more or less well-known retro brands in fashion (Adidas and Puma retro fashion), cars (PT Cruiser, BMW Mini), motorbikes (Aprilia), beverages (Afri-Cola), entertainment and furnishing (wallpapers, lamps, and similar). Most of the respondents owned one to five retro or retro style brands.

In the second step we conducted narrative interviews (Schütze, 1987). We chose this qualitative and inductive approach to reveal meaning of retro brands to young consumers which has not yet been researched systematically. The interviewers used an open interview guideline, including photo-elicitation (Banks, 2007; Heisley und Levy 1991) and projective techniques (e.g. projective questioning, story completion, choice ordering, Haire 1950). A few days before the interview, respondents were equipped with a camera and invited to take pictures of their favorite retro brands. These pictures together with pre-selected pictures by the researchers were used during the interview to stimulate narratives and reveal meaning structures. Respondents were first, asked to talk about their relationship to their most favored retro brand, how they 'met', what kind of relationship they had, and how important they were for them. A second set of question related to the personality of the brand. In a subsequent set of questions, we asked respondents about reactions of their peers to their retro brands, before we turned to the respondents' opinions towards contemporary societal developments to uncover whether retro consumers are critical and past-oriented in that respect. The interviews took place at respondents' homes to ensure a natural setting. They lasted between 35 and 90 minutes and produced a total of 7h and 50 min. of information.

We tape-recorded the interviews and transcribed them verbatim. An idiographic analysis documented the individual retro-brand meanings based on personal and social backgrounds (Thompson, Locander and Pollio, 1989; 1994). To integrate and systematize themes and experiences in the individual cases we used "constant comparative analysis" (Strauss and Corbin, 1990; Charmaz, 2006) and the analysis software MaxQda.

## FINDINGS

Our interviews with young consumers reveal that the consumption of retro brands definitely entails feelings and experiences of nostalgia. However, nostalgia is not in the foreground but rather symbolizes a common striving among young adults that is related to their search for what is important in their lives. Retro brand consumption actually reflects young consumers' coping strategies, which helps balance their developing individuality with social attributions, their aspiration for stability and security with their attempts to flee the ordinary, and their aspiration for social acceptance and belongingness with anti-conformism. In the following, we will carve out these contradictions and discuss how retro brands help young consumers negotiating their developing identities within society.

### Continuity and discontinuity

Young consumers are also nostalgic. Although some of these feelings reflect derivative experiences with things owned by their grandparents or parents, young consumers do report about personal nostalgia through memories from their childhood, early experiences and habits that they had come to love. Continuity and discontinuity also reflects communal nostalgia, romanticizing the past and old values but not in order to bring back the good old days but rather to set a counterpart to current societal developments that young consumers dislike or protest against. Continuity and discontinuity are not contradictory but rather emanate from the deep desire for stability and security which they experienced in childhood, in times of accelerated pace of life and materialism, which young retro consumers opposed.

*Childhood and Derivative Brand Experience*

Young consumers' childhood memories are deeply influenced by grandparents, their houses, objects, and stories. These memories are engraved in their brains and provide feelings of warmth, security and comfort. As young consumers are confronted with more and more opportunities and freedom to construct their own life stories, they are also facing more uncertainties and feelings of insecurity. Retro brands have a history, reflect continuity in times of fast changes and are safely grounded in grandmother's wealth of experience (Kessous and Roux 2008).

> *"Yeah, and these old signs, they sure are beautiful [....]; over there we have these old Lindt chocolate signs and also Sarotti retro-signs, and this one how grandma cooked, from good old times and so on, [....]. Well you know, I mean this feeling of security: grandma is cooking for you and you are the hero in her world and you can wish for anything [....] somehow that is just cool..."*
> *(Daniel)*

Although young consumer never decided to consume these brands themselves, we know from Chaplin and Roedder John (2005) that children at the age 8-9 years connect to brands on a more concrete level related to their familiarity or ownership of the brand. They incorporate brands into their self on an un-reflected, highly affective basis. Young consumers also report about the memories of their parents as if those memories were their own. Through the deep empathic feelings with relatives and their narratives, young consumers seem to incorporate these derivative experiences into their own memory thus enriching brand meaning and its connection to the past.

### Meaningful Moments

Even if we consider young consumers' life times as being quite short, their memories and meaningful moments are by no means less intense. Meaningful moments do not need time to develop into nostalgia; similar to what Kessous and Roux (2008) described as discontinuity, young consumers refer to those unique reference points as a reason to favor retro brands. Our findings corroborate Davis' (1977) contention that those moments are connected with joyful experiences and mastery of life. Retro brands are favored because they symbolize relationships with good friends, exciting trips and parties, nice little gifts but also when they help standing for one's own opinion and taste. As young consumers are constantly exposed to social expectations, instances of successful emancipation from others' opinions mark their lives on their way to self-standing personalities. Retro brands help in this respect by their inherent stability and uncompromising idiosyncrasy.

### Re-interpretation of Traditional Objects of Bygone Times

As many contemporary brands have rather short life cycles, retro brands are symbols for continuity, reflecting long-lasting quality and historical heritage. Young consumers who like retro brands use them as stable anchors that reflect tradition and authenticity in a world of many materialistic, fake, and uninspiring objects. Respondents report about the genuine and superior quality and their trustful relationship with those brands. Furthermore, many retro brands are used for ritualistic practices among young consumers, which disconnect the brand from the mundane world. By ascribing retro brands the qualities of a genuine, disinterested object purified from persuasive marketing practices, those objects also become cult objects for young consumers. As Belk and Tumbat (2005) reported, cult brands often pass a period of deterioration (satanic myth) and resurrection (myth), which likens the development of many retro brands that gain cult status. Contrary to nostalgia based on non-discontinuity as described by Kessous and Roux (2008), young consumers do not pursue traditional acts and habits like their

ancestors but instead interpret those acts differently and use them for community-building rituals among young consumers.

### Romanticizing the Past and its Values

Retro brands not just represent tradition and lay the grounds for new interpretations of retro brands as cult objects; they also serve as powerful symbols of collective memory. Retro brands are not only perceived as authentic, they also embody past times and values of those times yet in a quite distorted manner. Even if young consumers are aware of some of their misperceptions, they nevertheless buy into the romantic view of the good old days as described by Davis (1979), in order to contrast it with what they feel is going in the wrong direction in contemporary society. As reported by Stern (1992), those romantic feelings are often based on idealized and imagined views of golden eras in order to transcend one's discrete existence in time, using retro brands as a sanctuary from contemporary meaninglessness, a transfiguration of the world of everyday consumption.

> *"A whole lot of families visit farms again, because they want to bring their children back to nature, they somehow want to get back to some place, back to something they consider to be better."*
> *(Carina)*

> *"Yeah, basically I think I was born too late anyway, ...well it is a certain feeling that you... not quite crave for the past, which sounds quite up the pole, because you were not even born then ... but you imagine that everything used to be a little more romantic then and they had only good music and fancy cars and that it would just be great to have it this way again. Well sure you don't want to have back everything, that's why you have a computer in your room. But at the same time, maybe by creating your own look, you want to get a little bit of that feeling."*
> *(Emily)*

Similar to Brown, Kozinets and Sherry's (2003) findings, consumers use traditional qualities of retro brands as reference to a past ethos thereby rebelling against contemporary developments. In absence of an own life history, this non-continuity tendency may relate to the current transitional period young consumers are living through, and their respective search for identity.

## Individual and social identity

Identity formation processes are full of troubles, uncertainties, but also successes and empowering moments. Our findings show that retro brands help overcome ambiguities between the defined inner self and the social roles that young consumers are beginning to take over (Mittal, 2006). Retro brands seem to work particularly well in expressing specific personality characteristics and the social self-concept (Sirgy, 1982), as they are considered as authentic, credible and expressive. Retro brands ease the task of finding one's own style as they remain stable, timeless, stay always true to themselves and, therefore, easy to hold on.

### Personal Values and the Art of Life

Late adolescence and early adulthood is the time for defining what young consumers want to achieve in life and how they want to live their lives. Early adulthood is a formative period as young adults usually make decisive decisions for their lives and form their attitudes and value systems. Respondents report about the art of living in a particular past period and relate to that in their descriptions of their attitude towards life and how they want to be seen. Retro brands help communicate these values and also convey a particular aesthetic component.

*„I am not a fan of all retro-products, but as it is, I hope that values from former times can be put across. I like most the music of the 60ies and 70ies, and I am super fond of bell-bottoms [......]; they also evoke former times and maybe other priorities that one can identify with, at least I can; and maybe you can also get that across."*
*(Finn)*

As demonstrated above, retro brands not only help depicting a person's attitudes and values; they also address and emphasize the differences between the contemporary social value system and that of a past era. Therefore, using retro brands is also a means of criticizing contemporary social values and thus self-definition (Mittal, 2006). Consuming retro brands is also expressive in that they reflect a consumer's particular way of life. According to the respondents they carry the aura of the respective decade that young consumers ascribe to the retro brand. Although some attributions are not accurate, young consumers favor those brands for the meaning ascribed to the respective time period.

*Emphasizing Individuality and Personality*
Particularly in times of identity formation and definition, young consumers are keen to act in a congruent manner in order to achieve a positive self-worth and approach their ideal self (Sirgy, 1982). An even stronger motivation to use retro brands for self definition is that they enable to differentiate from the masses. Young retro brand consumers put particular emphasis on the differentiating elements of their favorite brands; the fact that young consumers are usually early adopters of new fashion trends helps retro brand consumers sharpening the difference between themselves as retro style consumers and others, who buy into the persuasive tactics of the fashion industry.

*"[......] I am simply a person, who …. I mean I don't like it if … if everything is more or less the same,… if I cannot stand out with my belongings; not in the sense of standing above it, rather more to personify, to add a bit of character, that I can make a statement. I mean this car, according to my personal opinion, stands for more than a Polo [Volkswa-gen] and I simply enjoy that it is timeless."*
*(Anna)*

Paradoxically, and antithetical to typical youth brands, Anna emphasizes the stability and timelessness of her car that supports her need for individuality. Other respondents are creatively mixing and matching retro and more contemporary styles in an attempt to emphasize their creativity and uniqueness. Retro brands are often ascribed stronger personality characteristics than other brands. The historical aura of retro brands adds to this personality and enables young consumers to express a strong personality and to live in between times, a strategy to escape fragmentation and alleviate the boredom of contemporary life.

*Contrasting the "I" and the "Me"*
Young retro consumers like to contrast what they consider their individual personality with their social roles. Individuals steadily define themselves according to their own self-definition and their social roles, which often creates tensions (Mittal, 2006). Retro brands help bridge this gap in that they communicate continuity, authenticity,

originality, expressivity, and aesthetic design. As indicated above, they help the "I" to differentiate from the masses and at the same time draw a coherent picture of a young consumer's personality for others to mirror. For retro consumers early adulthood is also the time to emancipate from peer pressure and rather engage in constructing a reflected "I" that is mirrored in a social self-concept "Me", constructed with the help of favored retro brands.

*"Well, I think it heavily depends on age, let's say, if you are younger, you are completely dependent on your "peer group" … […] ,… you had to go by the group just to be cool, no matter if you yourself considered it cool. But very soon after you enter a stage where you realize, ok, they can tell me lots of sh…, they are not quite that awesome, now I make my own style, and then you start,… then I started to consider what do I want."*
*(Daniel)*

Mittal (2006) proposes three broad approaches to resolving the tension between self and social identity, namely switching reference group, educating others, or modifying consumption. Usually these strategies are adopting strategies to the social 'Me'. In the case of retro brands, consumers rather educate the others to bring the core self more to the forefront.

**Social acceptance and non-conformism**
Retro consumers commonly describe themselves as fashion-conscious and non-conformist, which marks retro brands as a symbol for fashion and style. Jana describes them as balanced and 'laid back' personalities, rather than whimsical early adopters of the various hype youth brands. By describing retro consumers as being different, young consumers do not want to portray themselves as conservative; on the contrary. They consider themselves as the real non-conformists as all others go with the masses but by consuming retro brands they act against hegemonic norms of consumption. As depicted above, retro brands shall help them adjusting the social self-concept to the reflected self identity. Yet social acceptance is still crucial. Without being accepted at some point, a non-conformist strategy would not work. Retro brand consumption is not to be thought of as resistive consumer behavior but rather as a successful attempt to resist conformity of fashion trends and taste.

*Non-Conformism*
Non-conformity through retro brand consumption has many facets. Non-conformity is demonstrated best by fashion and other conspicuous objects of consumption. Some young consumers report that they are bored by particular social norms in social arenas, such as professional life, and similar social situations. They simply like being different, a little provocative, and introduce a more casual look. Others emphasize the slightly anti-commercial meaning that comes with retro consumption as retro is 'recycled' design which is longer lasting. Julian expresses this unconventional attitude by drawing a clear distinction among 'retros' and 'fashion victims' thus also strongly relating to his peer group and a certain communal spirit of like-minded consumers in search of autonomy.

*"[......] with some products I sure have the feeling that you are sick of it after putting it on twice; you see it another ten times in the subway and then you are finally done with it; there is nothing individual left in it. This also happens to my friends, they are also rather relaxed people who do not bow to clichés, there is like no Polo-shirt-carrier with collars up or like the absolute "Mega-Fashion-Victim", well I´d*

*say just normal people and not–even if it might sound a bit
exaggerated–total victims of consumerism."*
*(Julian)*

Non-conformism is also strongly connected to the mix and match style of retro brand consumers. Mixing and matching is actually a strategy to get the best out of both in that young consumers avoid being trendy and mainstream but aspire to be authentic, bring the 'old charm' of retro brands to the foreground.

*Social Acceptance and Coolness*

The 'old charm' of retro brands often creates retro brand cults. The dramatic change of society in Germany, for instance, has brought forward a strong wave of 'Ostalgia', a nostalgic cult related to the bygone times of Eastern Germany (Eigler, 2004). Even if retro brands do not achieve cult status, they have the ingredients of being cool. As coolness is defined by the in-group, coolness cannot be created but is rather defined by young consumers. In the case of retro brands, our respondents emphasized that retro brands are cool but they would lose this attribute if they go mainstream. Thus, what is considered as cool in a younger age cohort that extensively consumes trendy retro brands is un-cool and unacceptable for young adults.

*"Especially those "Emos", all of them carrying Chucks,
they are all Chucks-zealot; or like these "tapered pants-
zealots" and the like. I mean there are some bands or
famous idols, who create certain styles that are readily
adopted by Teenies with maybe lower self esteem and they
think that is really cool. They jump on the bandwagon and
the industry is right there to seduce them 'hey, give us your
pocket money' […]."*
*(Daniel)*

Young consumers' coolness is inextricably interwoven with their striving for independence. This is exactly what unites them with other members of their age cohort. Gaining social acceptance means being non-conform, fighting mainstream. Hence, these findings point to the importance to discriminate among groups with different definitions of 'coolness' as being cool means belonging to a particular social group. This way, retro brands allow young consumers to overcome the tension between non-conformity and social acceptance.

## DISCUSSION

Our research contributes to theory in many ways. First and most important, our findings show that retro brands do have deep meaning for young consumers. They provide meaning from a time perspective in that they embody history, memory, nostalgia, and timelessness. Although young consumers often do not know the original counterparts of their favorite retro brands, they borrow from the collective memory, or gain derivative experience from parents' and grandparents' consumption habits. Contrary to their parents, young consumers experience retro brands in childhood rather than in their 20s, which is by no means less impactful on their emotional bonding with retro brands. The close-knit bonds with their families and the brands young consumers associate with family life strongly connect young consumers to original brands that later become their favorite retro brands. In connecting them with the 'safe haven' of family life they provide continuity in young consumers' lives. At the same time, the discontinuities young consumers are facing in their lives, their striving for autonomy, their idealism that clashes with in-authenticities in contemporary political and market systems contributes to their choice of retro brands.

Hence, retro brands, on the other hand, are not just nostalgic objects for young consumers. They are consumed so as to define young consumers' self-concept at the crossroads of individual and social identity. Retro brands are identity-building in that they provide strong historical value systems to, at least partly, identify with. They have a high differentiating potential in that they are not marketed to the masses and embody authenticity and originality. Therefore, retro brands enable young consumers to clearly communicate their identity for others to mirror. By defining retro brands as cool within the peer group, retro brands help coping with the ambiguity between 'the self' and 'the other' (Adamson, Hartman and Lyxell, 1999).

In a similar vein, retro brands are used to negotiate the distance-proximity tension in young consumers' lives (Adamson, Hartman and Lyxell, 1999). Young consumers' identity seeking processes are strongly related to processes of autonomy-seeking, which means distancing from particular values and societal developments, and social acceptance, which is necessary for any individual's psychological well-being. Combining new and old is a strong antidote to contemporary fashion dictates, used by young consumers to demonstrate autonomy. By successfully demonstrating autonomy, they fight established consumption patterns and gain acceptance among their peers as non-conformist consumption heroes.

Figure 1 summarizes how retro brands are consumed as expressive objects used for coping with tensions that are related to young consumers' life statuses.

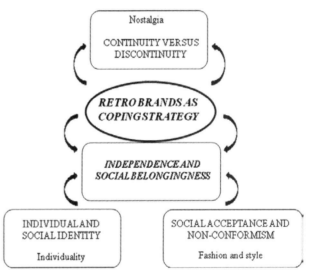

**Figure 1: Retro Brands as Coping Strategy**

Particularly in times of market turbulences and political promises of "change", retro brands constitute materializations of idealized forms of consumption for a particular young age cohort. Retro brands are pastiche forms of authentic, historical, value-laden objects that enchant contemporary technologically engineered and marketed objects. Retro brands are no less engineered and marketed than any other brand but they successfully serve young consumers' aspiration for continuity and stability in an age-related period of discontinuities and insecurity but also freedom to choose. At the same time and similarly paradox as Benjamin's antinomy (Brown, Kozinets and Sherry, 2003), retro brands are subject to the same fashion cycles as other fashion brands. They are perceived as highly individual and fashionable yet–contrary to new fashion brands–with retro brands individualized styles are created by young consumers, not just bought. It is the mix and match quality, the malleable historical context of retro brands that serves as a means of creating unique, fashionable artwork-like styles among young consumers.

## REFERENCES

Adamson, Lena, and Björn Lyxell (1996), "Self-concept and Questions of Life: Identity Development During Late Adolescence," *Journal of Adolescence*, 19 (6), 569-582.

Adamson, Lena, Sven G. Hartman and Björn Lyxell (1999), "Adolescent Identity – A Qualitative Approach: Self-concept, Existential Questions and Adult Contacts," *Scandinavian Journal of Psychology*, 40 (1), 21-31.

Banks, Marcus (2007), *Using Visual Data in Qualitative Research*, London: Sage Publications.

Belk, Russell W. (1990), "The Role of Possessions in Constructing and Maintaining a Sense of Past," *Advances in Consumer Research*, 17 (1), 669-676.

_____, Ger, Güliz and Søren Askegaard (2003), "The Fire of Desire: A Multisited Inquiry into Consumer Passion," *Journal of Consumer Research*, 30 (3), 326-351.

_____, Gülnur Tumbat (2005), "The Cult of Macintosh," *Consumption, Markets and Culture*, 8 (3), 205-217.

Brown, Stephen (2001), *Marketing - The Retro Revolution*. London: Sage Publications.

_____, Robert V. Kozinets und John F. Sherry Jr. (2003), "Teaching Old Brands New Tricks: Retro Branding and the Revival of Brand Meaning," *Journal of Marketing*, 67 (3), 19-33.

Braun-La Tour, Kathryn A., Michael S. La Tour and George M. Zinkhan (2007), "Using Childhood Memories to Gain Insight into Brand Meaning," *Journal of Marketing*, 71 (2), 45-60.

Chaplin, Lan Nguyen and Deborah Roedder John (2005), "The Development of Self-Brand Connections in Children and Adolescents," *Journal of Consumer Research*, 32 (1), 119-129.

Charmaz, Kathy (2006), *Constructing Grounded Theory – A Practical Guide Through Qualitative Analysis*, London: Sage Publications.

Cooley, Charles H. (1902), *Human Nature and the Social Order*, New York: Charles' Scribner's Sons.

Davis Fred (1977), "Nostalgia, Identity and the Current Nostalgia Wave," *Journal of Popular Culture*, 11 (2), 414-424.

_____ (1979), *Yearning for Yesterday: A Sociology of Nostalgia*, New York: The Free Press.

Eigler, Frederike (2004), "Jenseits von Ostalgie: Phantastische Züge in DDR-Romanen der Neunziger Jahre," *Seminar - A Journal of Germanic Studies*, 40 (3), 191-206.

Erikson, Erik H. (1968), *Identity: Youth and Crisis*, New York: W.W. Norton & Company, Inc.

Glaser, Barney G. und Anselm L. Strauss (1967), *The Discovery of Grounded Theory: Strategies for Qualitative Research*, Chicago: Aldine.

Haire, Mason (1950), "Projective Techniques in Marketing Research," *Journal of Marketing*, 14 (5), 649-656.

Heisley, Deborah D. und Sidney J. Levy (1991), "Autodriving: A Photoelicitation Technique," *Journal of Consumer Research*, 18 (3), 257-272.

Holbrook, Morris B. and Robert M. Schindler (1989), "Some Exploratory Findings on the Development of Musical Tastes," *Journal of Consumer Research*, 16 (1), 119-124.

_____ and Robert M. Schindler (1991), "Echoes of the Dear Departed Past: Some Work in Progress on Nostalgia," *Advances in Consumer Research*, 18 (1), 330-333.

_____ (1993), "Nostalgia and Consumption Preferences: Some Emerging Patterns of Consumer Tastes," *Journal of Consumer Research*, 20 (2), 245-256.

_____ and Robert M. Schindler (1994), "Age, Sex, and Attitude Toward the Past as Predictors of Consumers' Aesthetic Tastes for Cultural Products," *Journal of Marketing Research*, 31 (3), 412-22.

_____ and Robert M. Schindler (1996), "Market Segmentation Based on Age and Attitude Toward the Past: Concepts, Methods, and Findings Concerning Nostalgic Influences on Consumer Tastes," *Journal of Business Research*, 37 (1), 27-39.

_____ and Robert M. Schindler (2003), "Nostalgia for Early Experience as a Determinant of Consumer Preferences," *Psychology & Marketing*, 20 (4), 275-302.

Kroger, Jane (1989), *Identity in Adolescence. The Balance Between Self and Other*, London: Routledge.

Mead, George H. (1934), *Mind, Self and Society*, Chicago: University of Chicago Press.

Mittal, Banwari (2006), "I, Me, and Mine – How Products Become Consumers' Extended Selves," *Journal of Consumer Behaviour*, 5 (6), 560-562.

Schumann Howard and Jacqueline Scott (1989), "Generations and Collective Memory," *American Sociological Review*, 54 (), 359-381.

Schütze, Fritz (1987), *Das narrative Interview in Interaktionsfeldstudien*. Fernuniversität Hagen: Hagen.

Sirgy, M. Joseph (1982), "Self-Concept in Consumer Behavior: A Critical Review," *Journal of Consumer Research*, 9 (3), 287-300.

Stern, Barbara B. (1992), "Historical and Personal Nostalgia in Advertising Text: The Fin de Siècle Effect," *Journal of Advertising*, 21 (4), 11-22.

Strauss, Anselm L. and Juliet Corbin (1990), *Basics of Qualitative Research: Grounded Theory Procedures and Techniques*, Newbury Park, CA: Sage Publications.

Thompson, Craig J., Locander, William B. and Howard R. Pollio (1989), "Putting Consumer Experience Back into Consumer Research: The Philosophy and Method of Existential-Phenomenology," *Journal of Consumer Research*, 16 (2), 133-146.

Thompson Craig J., Howard R. Pollio und William B. Locander (1994), "The Spoken and the Unspoken: A Hermeneutic Approach to Understanding the Cultural Viewpoints That Underlie Expressed Consumer Meanings," *Journal of Consumer Research*, 21 (3), 432-452.

Will, Valerie, Douglas Eadie and Susan MacAskill (1996), "Projective and Enabling Techniques Explored," *Marketing Intelligence & Planning*, 14 (6), 38-43.

# Does Advertising Based on Gender Equality Work and Which Consumer Groups Should be Addressed?

Silke Bambauer-Sachse, University of Fribourg, Switzerland
Zoltan Horvath, University of Fribourg, Switzerland

## ABSTRACT

In this paper, we examine gender equality as one aspect of CSR that can be used for innovative image advertising. We identify two consumer groups that differ with regard to their internalization of gender equality and thus regarding their reactions to an image campaign that is based on gender equality.

## INTRODUCTION

A general trend in corporate communication is that companies increasingly move away from traditional communication messages that focus on exchangeable product attributes, which can easily be copied by competitors within the same industry. Instead, companies are increasingly looking for communication messages that are image-focused, unique, innovative and able to differentiate them from competitors (Kotler and Armstrong 2006). One such topic that companies increasingly cover in communication strategies is corporate social responsibility (CSR) (Brown and Dacin 1997). Corporate social responsibility refers to a company's status and voluntary activities with respect to its perceived societal obligations (Brown and Dacin 1997; Sen and Bhattacharya 2001). CSR activities are characterized by a long-term perspective and a proactive view of responsibility (McGee 1998). Aspects of CSR are for example environmental protection (e.g., environment friendly products, pollution control, recycling), customer orientation and care (responsibility for product safety), respecting business ethics, responsibility for economic development, community support (e.g., support of arts and health programs, educational and housing initiatives for the economically disadvantaged, generous/innovative giving), and employee support (e.g., job security, profit sharing, union relations, employee involvement, equal career opportunities for men and women) (Sen and Bhattacharya 2001).

Thus, announcing a corporate commitment to gender equality in terms of treating male and female employees equally could be part of a CSR communication strategy. Gender equality is given if equality between men and women is ensured in all areas including employment, work and payment. Despite broad and intensive efforts during the last decades, factual gender equality has not been realized to an acceptable extent in many European countries. Especially labor markets are often characterized by a clear gender-specific segregation. In addition, gender roles in private life do often not mirror the idea of gender equality. In many societies, women are still considered as being responsible for the family (Kirton and Green 2005; Mikkola 2005; Nentwich 2006; Royo-Vela et al. 2007).

Although talking about corporate commitment to gender equality in advertising strategies could be an innovative approach for an image advertising campaign that is built on CSR, gender equality has only been ascribed minor importance as a part of corporate communication strategies up to now (Grosser and Moon 2005). Consequently, the purpose of this paper is to pick out corporate commitment to gender equality (in terms of treating female and male employees equally) as one possible aspect of innovative image advertising and to identify different groups of consumers such advertising could be addressed to. The consumer group identification will be done on the basis of the extent of social internalization of gender equality as a personal norm because previous research provides the notion that the effectiveness of CSR strategies depends on the extent to which people within a society have internalized the concept that is subject to a certain CSR strategy as a personal norm (Lichtenstein, Drumwright, and Braig 2004; Osterhus 1997).

An examination of this research topic can add to the existing body of consumer research by considering an aspect of CSR that has not been analyzed in consumer research contexts before as well as by providing insights in characteristics of possible consumer segments that differ both with regard to the extent of internalization of gender equality as a personal norm and to their evaluation of relevant marketing response variables.

A practical benefit of our paper is that companies might have a higher motivation to pursue the implementation of gender equality with more effort than they have done in the past when they learn that they can profit from such measures in terms of generating positive consumer reactions by talking about the implementation in image advertising campaigns that address appropriate consumer groups. Moreover, our research will show that the communication of a clear commitment to gender equality to appropriate consumer groups can provide an added value for companies, which goes beyond satisfying increasing expectations from both government/legislation and society. Furthermore, motivating companies to go about implementing clear commitments to gender equality will lead to a stronger presence of this topic in both working and consumer life and hopefully finally to a stronger internalization of gender equality as a social and a personal norm.

## THEORETICAL BACKGROUND

### Basic Effects of Communicating a Clear Commitment to Gender Equality

As the commitment to gender equality is a part of CSR strategies, we draw on research in the field of CSR as well as on research in the field of gender equality to build up the theoretical background.

Literature on CSR indicates that high CSR efforts have positive effects on customer satisfaction, product evaluation, and corporate image (Brown and Dacin 1997; Lichtenstein, Drumwright, and Braig 2004). In addition, literature on social advertising provides the notion that communication strategies with a social dimension have positive effects on consumer response variables such as purchase intentions and attitudes toward the communication campaign (Drumwright 1996).

Although studies on gender-specific aspects have been conducted in different fields (e.g., Alreck, Settle, and Belch 1982; Chichilnisky, Hermann, and Frederiksen 2008; Gunkel et al. 2007; Hoeber 2007), no scientific studies exist on effects of communicating a clear commitment to gender equality in the context of corporate communication. However, several arguments coming from this stream of literature can be applied to our research. A first finding that might play a role is that brand gendering through stereotypical portrayal may alienate consumers and cause resentment and rejection of the brand, advertiser or media (Alreck, Settle, and Belch 1982). A more general interpretation of this finding is that stereotypical gendering may have negative effects. Put vice versa, a clear commitment to gender equality in the context of CSR strategies might at least avoid such negative effects on corporate image or even have positive effects. Other research has shown that men (women) do not necessarily ascribe major importance to traditionally stereotypical masculine (feminine) factors (Gunkel, Lusk, Wolff, and Li 2007).

Thus, this finding also supports the assumption of positive effects of communicating gender equality in the context of CSR strategies.

Literature on gender differences also provides a counter-argument. The notion that men often have difficulty accepting the gender changes that are occurring in their environment (Connell 2006) leads to the assumption of negative effects of communicating a clear commitment to gender equality.

The application of these contradictious findings to our research context leads to the assumption that openness to communication strategies that are based on gender equality might differ among consumers. Consequently, an analysis that aims to differentiate between several groups might lead to the identification of consumer groups that show very positive reactions to advertising strategies that are based on a clear commitment to gender equality and other groups that show less positive reactions to such strategies.

### The Role of the Internalization of Gender Equality

As it is the objective of this paper to pick out one specific dimension of CSR, namely gender equality, and to identify consumer groups on the basis of the internalization of gender equality as a personal norm, we will subsequently go more into the theoretical details of internalization in terms of transforming a social norm into a personal norm.

Social norms are characterized by perceptions about the nature and content of a prevailing social sentiment (Schwartz 1977). Individuals associate social norms with the importance of taking a specific action (Malhotra 2005). Thus, if the idea of treating women and men equally is considered as a social norm, people might associate this norm with the importance of implementing gender equality in daily life.

Internalization basically refers to the incorporation of a concept as part of one's own belief structure so that it becomes a personal norm (Kelman 1958; Lewis, Agarwal, and Sambamurthy 2003). In other words, internalization consists of transforming a social norm into a personal norm. In the context considered here, internalization can be referred to as the transformation of the concept of gender equality that is established as a social norm on a society level into a personal norm on the individual level.

According to Kelman (1958), individuals show different levels of changes in behavior as a consequence of an internalization of a social norm. These differences can be explained by different processes whereby individuals accept influence. The internalization of a specific idea and the behavior that is associated with this idea lead to satisfaction (Kelman 1958; Venkatesh and Davis 2000). Consequently, the internalization of a concept is closely associated with typical response variables that are subject to consumer research. Therefore, we argue that the internalization of gender equality might also be closely associated with other consumer response variables such as acceptability of an advertising campaign, interest in a company, or purchase intention when gender equality is used as an advertising topic. Therefore, we assume in our first research hypothesis:

**H1***: The higher the extent of internalization of the social norm of treating women and men equally, the higher are the acceptability of an advertising strategy that broaches the issue of gender equality, the interest in the company, and the purchase intention toward the products offered by this company.*

In order to make the idea of internalization more tangible, it is important to have a more detailed look at concepts that are related to internalization. As internalization means that a social norm is transformed into a personal norm, we will have a closer look at the concept of personal norms. According to Schwartz (1977) personal norms are mainly activated and translated into behavior by the awareness of consequences that are associated with a certain behavior. Awareness of consequences refers to whether someone is aware of the negative consequences for the case of not acting according to the internalized norm (Schwartz 1977). In the context considered here, the idea of awareness of consequences means that individuals are aware of negative consequences for the case of not adopting gender equality as a personal norm and implementing gender equality in their everyday life.

From the theoretical considerations presented above, we can derive two criteria upon which we will try to identify different consumer groups: the extent to which an individual has transformed a social norm into a personal norm and the awareness of consequences for the case of not behaving according to the norm. As people seem to be different with regard to these criteria, we argue in our second research hypothesis:

**H2***: Using the transformation of a social into a personal norm and the awareness of consequences as segmentation criteria will lead to the identification of at least two different segments of consumers.*

Applying the rationale that underlies hypothesis 1 to the context of hypothesis 2, we additionally assume:

**H3***: The segments that can be identified on the basis of the dimensions of internalization will differ significantly with regard to consumer response variables such as acceptability of an advertising strategy that broaches the issue of gender equality, interest in the company, and purchase intention toward the products offered by this company.*

## EMPIRICAL STUDY

### Study Overview

We conducted two empirical studies to cover two research purposes. The objective of the first study was to show that a relation between the internalization of gender equality as a personal norm and the evaluation of consumer response variables exists, thus to examine whether the dimensions of internalization determine consumer response variables such as purchase intention, interest in the company, and acceptability of gender equality as a topic of an advertising campaign. The objective of the second study was to identify different groups of consumers that differ with regard to the internalization of gender equality as a personal norm, to examine these groups in more detail with regard to demographics, and to analyze differences of these groups in their reactions to an advertising strategy that broaches the issue of gender equality.

As we used the same measures and the same procedure in both studies, we will describe these aspects first below and then present the results of the two studies.

## MEASURES

The statements used to measure the two dimensions of internalization (transformation of a social norm into a personal norm and awareness of consequences) were derived from literature in the fields of the internalization of norms (De Groot and Steg 2009; Osterhus 1997; Wall, Devine-Wright, and Mill 2007) and gender equality (Fletcher et al. 2007; Rubery et al. 2003). In order to measure the consumer response variables (purchase intention, interest in the company, and acceptability of gender equality as a topic of an advertising strategy), we created statements by looking at previous studies in consumer research where these variables have been operationalized (e.g., Brown and Dacin 1997; Webb and Mohr 1998). Table 1 gives an overview of the items we used to measure the respective variables and the alpha coefficients per variable and study. The alpha coefficients indicate that the respective items reliably measure the concept they were intended to measure. The sufficiently high alpha values allow for calculating the overall construct values as arithmetical means of the single indicators for each construct. These arithmetical means are used in the analyses presented subsequently.

## PROCEDURE AND SAMPLES

We created questionnaires that contained the measures shown in table 1 as well as age, gender, and educational qualification. In order to recruit the samples, we used official mailing lists of a Swiss university that contained the email addresses of students as well as of scientific and administrative staff to send out emails that informed about the purpose of one of the studies and provided a link to the respective questionnaire.

With regard to the generalizability of the results that were based on the samples described above, it is important to mention that Switzerland is generally characterized by a wide cultural diversity (Swiss Federal Statistical Office 2009). Moreover, especially Swiss

**Table 1**

Measures

| Variable | Item | | Coefficient alpha | |
|---|---|---|---|---|
| | | | study 1 | study 2 |
| Transformation of a social norm into a personal norm | I feel bad when I do nothing while other people take action against gender inequality. (T1) | | .79 | .80 |
| | I would do everything to prevent unequal treatment of women and men. (T2) | | | |
| | Each individual in our society is responsible if women and men are treated unequally. (T3) | | | |
| | Each individual should feel personally obliged to take actions to improve equal treatment of women and men. (T4) | | | |
| Awareness of consequences | If a society denies gender inequalities, this can lead to even higher inequality. (C1) | | .84 | .86 |
| | In my opinion, a sustainable implementation of gender equality can contribute to solving gender inequality problems such as gender pay gaps. (C2) | | | |
| | I think that ongoing gender inequalities can cause social tensions. (C3) | | | |
| | If children will be better educated in terms of gender equality, this will lead to a more tolerant generation. (C4) | | | |
| | I know that treating women and men unequally will foster discriminating tendencies in our society. (C5) | | | |
| Purchase intention | If a company's advertising campaign broached the issue of sus-tainnably implement-ting gender equality … | … I would be motivated to buy products from this company. (P1) | .91 | .91 |
| | | … this would have a positive effect on my purchase decision in favor of this company's products. (P2) | | |
| | | … this would positively influence my loyalty toward this company. (P3) | | |
| Interest in the company | | … I would become curious to learn more about this company. (I) | - | |
| Acceptability of gender equality as an advertising topic | | … I would recognize it as an interesting new advertising strategy. (A) | - | |

Note: the items were measured on 7-point rating scales ranging from 1 (do not at all agree) to 7 (totally agree)

universities are characterized by the fact that both administrative and scientific staff as well as students come from all over the world (Swiss Federal Statistical Office 2009). Consequently, the results coming from these data are not only Switzerland-specific, but can also be transferred to other countries.

### Results of study 1

Based on a sample of 186 questionnaires that we received in the context of the first study, we examined whether the extent of the internalization of gender equality can explain consumer response variables such as purchase intention, interest in the company, and acceptability of gender equality as a topic of an advertising strategy. Therefore, we conducted regression analyses with the two dimensions of internalization (transformation of a social norm into a personal norm and awareness of consequences)

as independent variables and the consumer response variables as dependent variables. The results of these regression analyses are summarized in table 2.

The results show that the dimensions of internalization have significantly positive effects on the three considered response variables and thus provide support for H1. Consequently, the more people have transformed the social norm of treating men and women equally into a personal norm and the more they are aware of positive consequences of implementing such a norm into daily life, the higher are their purchase intentions toward products of a company that broaches the issue of gender equality in its advertising campaign, the higher is their interest in such a company, and the more likely they are to accept gender equality as a topic of an advertising strategy.

## Table 2
### Effects of Internalization on Consumer Response Variables

| Independent variables | Dependent variables | | |
|---|---|---|---|
| | purchase intention | interest in the company | acceptability of gender equality as an advertising topic |
| Transformation of a social into a personal norm | $ß_1 = .62$ ($t = 7.04$, $p < .001$) | $ß_1 = .50$ ($t = 4.34$, $p < .001$) | $ß_1 = .60$ ($t = 5.32$, $p < .001$) |
| Awareness of consequences | $ß_1 = .48$ ($t = 5.09$, $p < .001$) | $ß_1 = .47$ ($t = 3.77$, $p < .001$) | $ß_1 = .43$ ($t = 3.51$, $p < .01$) |
| $R^2$ | .67 | .47 | .52 |

### Results of study 2

The data collection in the context of study 2 led to an initial number of 1209 questionnaires that were completely filled in. However, we had to exclude several questionnaires from the data analyses because they proved to contain inconsistent answers as will be further explained below.

In a first step, we used the initial data set that contained 1209 respondents and conducted a hierarchical cluster analysis (which is commonly used to determine the optimal number of clusters) based on the method "between-groups linkage" with the variables T1-T4 and C1-C5 (listed in table 1) as input variables. We used the heterogeneity coefficients from the agglomeration schedule to identify the optimal number of clusters. The relation between the heterogeneity coefficients and the number of clusters is shown in figure 1.

### FIGURE 1
### OPTIMAL NUMBER OF CLUSTERS

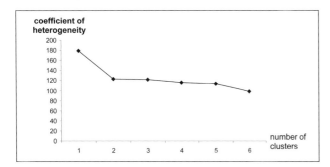

Figure 1 clearly shows that a two-cluster solution is optimal. Based on this notion, we used K-means cluster analysis (which is used for large samples) to assign the respondents to the clusters. In order to be able to identify respondents with inconsistent response patterns at the same time, we conducted two separate analyses, one based on the variables that were intended to measure the transformation of a social norm into a personal norm and one based on the variables that were used to measure the awareness of consequences. We then generated a cross-tab to examine to what extent each respondent was assigned to the same cluster when differentiating between the two factors. The cross-tab indicates that 87 (256) respondents who were assigned to cluster 1 (2) based on the extent of a transformation of a social into a personal norm were assigned to cluster 2 (1) based on their awareness of consequences. The fact that a person has been assigned to two different clusters based on two sets of cluster variables that are correlated means that this person has not provided consistent answers with regard to the two sets of variables. In our research context, such bias might come from a tendency to (inconsistently) provide socially desirable answers which is typical for such fields of research. Thus, we eliminated 343 people who provided inconsistent answers from our initial data set and were left with two clusters of which cluster 1 has more than double the size of cluster 2 (see table 3).

Based on the remaining data set of 866 respondents, we determined the cluster centers based on the person-to-cluster-assignment that resulted from the K-means cluster analyses. In order to examine the discriminatory power of the identified segments, we conducted independent samples t-tests for the cluster variables. The cluster centers and the t-test results are presented in table 3.

### Table 3
### Cluster Centers of the K-Means Procedure and t-Test Results

| Aspect | Item | Mean values | | t-test results |
|---|---|---|---|---|
| | | cluster 1 ($n = 618$) | cluster 2 ($n = 248$) | |
| Transformation of a social into a personal norm | T1 | 6.46 | 4.23 | $t = 20.27$ ($p < .001$) |
| | T2 | 5.04 | 2.46 | $t = 23.48$ ($p < .001$) |
| | T3 | 5.92 | 3.05 | $t = 29.13$ ($p < .001$) |
| | T4 | 5.75 | 3.23 | $t = 20.16$ ($p < .001$) |
| Awareness of consequences | C1 | 6.67 | 4.44 | $t = 19.29$ ($p < .001$) |
| | C2 | 6.60 | 4.22 | $t = 20.17$ ($p < .001$) |
| | C3 | 6.14 | 3.62 | $t = 21.43$ ($p < .001$) |
| | C4 | 6.47 | 4.22 | $t = 19.84$ ($p < .001$) |
| | C5 | 6.52 | 4.20 | $t = 18.95$ ($p < .001$) |

The highly significant t-values show that the two identified clusters can be clearly separated with regard to the cluster variables and thus provide support for H2. A look at the cluster centers shows that the extent of the internalization of gender equality is much higher in cluster 1 than in cluster 2. In order to make the resulting clusters more tangible, we additionally examined differences of the clusters with regard to age, gender, and education. The results of an independent samples t-test for age and chi-square tests for gender and education are shown in table 4.

The results of the age comparison show that people in cluster 1, which is characterized by a higher extent of internalization, are older on average (28.56 years) than people in cluster 2 (25.38 years). Although one might criticize that, descriptively, the age difference is not considerable, it can be stated, that these two age values characterize two different periods of life (people at the age of around 25 years are completing their education whereas people at the age of around 30 years are starting their professional lives and are founding a family). Moreover, cluster 1 is characterized by a clear dominance of women over men (81% vs. 19%), whereas in cluster 2, the percentage of men slightly dominates the one of women (55% vs. 45%). However, with regard to education, there are no significant differences between the two clusters. Thus, the extent of the internalization of gender equality obviously does not depend on education.

Finally, we analyzed whether the identified clusters differ with regard to the consumer response variables that have been used as dependent variables in the regression analyses of study 1 and that have also been measured in study 2. The mean values of these variables per cluster and the results of independent samples t-tests for the mean value differences are summarized in table 5.

The highly significant mean value differences of the considered variables show that cluster 1, which is characterized by a significantly higher extent of internalization is also characterized by significantly more positive reactions in terms of consumer response variables than is cluster 2. Thus, H3 is supported.

## CONCLUSION

The starting point of this paper has been the observation that CSR topics are becoming more and more popular in advertising campaigns and that many CSR-based advertising campaigns cover similar topics such as environmental protection. Consequently, the basic research interest that finally led to doing the studies presented above, was to find other CSR topics that might attract more attention and that could also be used in advertising campaigns. Therefore, from a consumer research perspective, we found it interesting to pick out gender equality as one rarely considered CSR topic and to examine whether the internalization of gender equality as a personal norm can be related to consumer reactions to an advertising strategy that is based on gender equality. Furthermore, we were interested in identifying different consumer segments based on the extent of the internalization of gender equality as well as in examining whether the identified segments differ with regard to typical consumer response variables such as acceptability of the advertising strategy, interest in the company, and purchase intention.

Consequently, we built up a new theoretical framework by bringing together literature from the fields of CSR/social advertising, gender equality and internalization in terms of the transformation of social into personal norms. Based on this theoretical framework, we conducted two empirical studies.

The findings of the first empirical study show that the extent of internalization (represented by the two dimensions transformation of a social into a personal norm and awareness of consequences) positively influences purchase intention toward the products of a company that broaches the issue of gender equality in its advertising campaign, the interest in such a company, and the acceptability of gender equality as a topic of an advertising strategy.

The results of the second study indicate that two consumer segments that differ significantly with regard to the aspects of internalization can be identified. The first segment has more than double the size of the second segment and it is characterized by a higher degree of internalization of gender equality. Thus, transferring

### Table 4
### Cluster Differences with Regard to Age, Gender and Education

| Variable | | Cluster 1 ($n$ = 618) | Cluster 2 ($n$ = 248) | Test results |
|---|---|---|---|---|
| Age | | 28.56 | 25.38 | $t = 5.06$ ($p < .001$) |
| Gender | male | 19% | 55% | $\chi^2 = 60.86$ ($p < .001$) |
| | female | 81% | 45% | |
| Education | secondary school | 3% | 2% | $\chi^2 = 2.41$ ($p > .10$) |
| | high school | 27% | 31% | |
| | college/university | 70% | 67% | |

Note: for gender and education, we report percentages because given the large difference in sample sizes, percentages are more meaningful than absolute values

### Table 5
### Cluster Differences with Regard to Consumer Response Variables

| Variable | Cluster 1 ($n$ = 618) | Cluster 2 ($n$ = 248) | T-test results |
|---|---|---|---|
| Purchase intention | 5.22 | 3.00 | $t = 20.44$ ($p < .001$) |
| Interest in the company | 5.42 | 3.47 | $t = 14.56$ ($p < .001$) |
| Acceptability as an advertising strategy | 5.40 | 4.00 | $t = 10.80$ ($p < .001$) |

these findings to a larger population means that about two thirds of people in a society have internalized the concept of gender equality as a personal norm to a considerable extent, whereas about one third of people in this society are characterized by a much lower degree of internalization. Furthermore, the results provide the notion that people who are characterized by a high degree of internalization of the concept of gender equality are older on average than people that rate lower on the internalization scale. An additional finding has been that the high-internalization segment is clearly dominated by women, whereas the low-internalization segment is slightly dominated by men. In addition, we found that education does not play a role with regard to the internalization of gender equality. Relating the identified clusters additionally to the consumer response variables that capture reactions to an advertising strategy that broaches the issue of gender equality provided the notion that the consumers in segment 1 responded much more favorably than did consumers in segment 2.

The managerial implications of our findings can be summarized as follows. First of all, our results have shown that it might be an innovative approach to base an image campaign on the CSR topic of gender equality because such a campaign might be accepted and would generate a higher interest in the company as well as positive effects on purchase intention. However, the results show at the same time that the target group addressed by such an advertising campaign should be carefully chosen. Only if the major target group is characterized by a high degree of internalization of gender equality, if it has an average age of about 28 years and consists mainly of female consumers, the reactions to such an advertising campaign will be favorable.

Starting points for future research could be to investigate in more detail the finding that gender equality does not depend on education as well as to examine possible effects of the respondents' country of origin because cultural aspects might also play a role in the considered context.

## REFERENCES

Alreck, Pamela L., Robert B. Settle, and Michael A. Belch (1982), "Who Responds to 'Gendered' Ads, and How?" *Journal of Advertising Research,* 22 (2), 26-32.

Brown, Tom J. and Peter A. Dacin (1997), "The Company and the Product: Corporate Associations and Consumer Product Responses," *Journal of Marketing,* 61 (1), 68-84.

Chichilnisky, Graciela and Elisabeth Hermann Frederiksen (2008), "An Equilibrium Analysis of the Gender Wage Gap," *International Labour Review,* 147 (4), 297-320.

Connel, Raewyn (2006), "The Experience of Gender Change in Public Sector Organizations," *Gender, Work and Organization,* 13 (5), 435-452.

De Groot, Judith I. M. and Linda Steg (2009), "Morality and Prosocial Behaviour: The Role of Awareness, Responsibility, and Norms in the Norm Activation Model," *Journal of Psychology,* 149 (4), 425-449.

Drumwright, Minette E. (1996), "Company Advertising With a Social Dimension: The Role of Noneconomic Criteria," *Journal of Marketing,* 60 (4), 71-87.

Fletcher, Catherine, Rebecca Boden, Julie Kent, and Julie Tinson (2007), "Performing Women: The Gendered Dimensions of the UK New Research Economy," *Gender, Work and Organization,* 14 (5), 449-450.

Grosser, Kate and Jeremy Moon (2005), "Gender Mainstreaming and Corporate Social Responsibility: Reporting Workplace Issues," *Journal of Business Ethics,* 62 (4), 327-340.

Gunkel, Maarjana, Edward J. Lusk, Birgitta Wolff, and Fang Li (2007), "Gender-specific Effects at Work: an Empirical Study of Four Countries," *Gender, Work and Organization,* 14 (1), 56-79.

Hoeber, Larena (2007), "Exploring the Gaps between Meanings and Practices of Gender Equity in a Sport Organization," *Gender, Work & Organization,* 14 (3), 259-280.

Kelman, Herbert C. (1958), "Compliance, Identification and Internalization Three Processes of Attitude Change," *Journal of Conflict Resolution,* 2 (1), 51-60.

Kirton, Gill and Annemarie Green (2005), "Gender, equality, and Industrial Relations in the 'New Europe': An Introduction," *European Journal of Industrial Relations,* 11 (2), 141-149.

Kotler, Philip and Gary Armstrong (2006), *Principles of Marketing,* New Jersey: Pearson.

Lewis, William, Ritu Agarwal, and Vallabh Sambamurthy (2003), "Sources of Influence on Beliefs About Information Technology Use: An Empirical Study of Knowledge Workers," *MIS Quarterly,* 27 (4), 657-678.

Lichtenstein, Donald R., Minette E. Drumwright, and Bridgette M. Braig (2004), "The Effect of Corporate Social Responsibility on Customer Donations to Corporate–Supported Nonprofits," *Journal of Marketing,* 68 (4), 16-32.

Malhotra, Yogesh and Dennis Galletta (2005), "A Multidimensional Commitment Model of Volitional Systems Adoption and Usage Behavior," *Journal of Management Information Systems,* 22 (1), 117-151.

McGee, John (1998), "Commentary on 'Corporate Strategies and Environmental Regulations: An Organizing Framework' by A.M. Rugman and A. Verbeke," *Strategic Management Journal,* 19 (4), 377-387.

Mikkola, Anne (2005), "Role of Gender Equality in Development - A literature review," *University of Helsinki Helsinki Center of Economic Research, Discussion Papers,* 1-44. http://ethesis.helsinki.fi/julkaisut/eri/hecer/disc/84/

Nentwich, Julia C. (2006), "Changing Gender: The Discursive Construction of Equal Opportunities," *Gender, Work and Organization,* 13 (6), 499-521.

Osterhus, Thomas L. (1997), "Pro Social Consumer Influence Strategies: When and How They Work?" *Journal of Marketing,* 61 (4), 16-29.

Royo-Vela, Marcelo, Joaquin Aldas-Manzano, Inés Küster, and Natalia Vila (2007), "Adaptation of Marketing Activities to Cultural and Social Context: Gender Role Portrayals and Sexism," *Sex Roles,* 58, 379-390.

Rubery, Jill, Damian Grimshaw, Colette Fagan, Hugo Figueiredo, and Mark Smiths (2003), "Gender Equality Still on the European Agenda, but for How Long?" *Industrial Relations Journal,* 34 (5), 477-497.

Sen, Sankar and C. B. Bhattacharya (2001), "Does Good Thing Always Lead to Doing Better? Consumer Reactions to Corporate Social Responsibility," *Journal of Marketing Research,* 38 (2), 225-243.

Schwartz, Shalom H. (1977), "Normative Influences on Altruism," *Advances in Experimental Social Psychology,* 10, 221-279.

Statistical Yearbook of Switzerland 2009 - Statistical Data in a Nutshell Swiss Federal Statistical Office FSO http://www.bfs.admin.ch/bfs/portal/en/index/ dienstleistungen/publikationen_statistik/statistische_jahrbuecher/stat__jahrbuch_ der.Document.76170.pdf

Thompson, Lindsay J. (2008), "Gender Equity and Corporate Social Responsibility in a Post-Feminist Era," *Business Ethics: A European Review,* 17 (1) 87-106.

Wall, Rob, Patrick Devine-Wright, and Greig A. Mill (2007), "Comparing and Combining Theories to Explain Proenvironmental Intentions," *Environment and Behaviour,* 39 (6), 731-753.

Web, Deborah J. and Lois Mohr (1998), "A Typology of Consumer Responses to Cause-Related Marketing: From Skeptics to Socially Concerned," *Journal of Public Policy & Marketing,* 17 (2), 226-238.

Venkatesh, Vishvanath and Fred D. Davis (2000), "A Theoretical Extension of the Technical Acceptance Model," *Management Science,* 46 (2), 186-204.

# Hiding in Plain Sight: 'Secret' Anorexia Nervosa Communities on YouTube™

Ekant Veer, University of Canterbury, New Zealand

## ABSTRACT

This research investigates the way in which online public forums are being utilized as a means of sharing ones experiences with Anorexia Nervosa. What is particularly fascinating as well as simultaneously being horrifying, is that many of these accounts are pro-anorexia and used as encouragement for other suffers to continue with their own eating disorders. With the ease of access to online video logging (vlogging) the role of the 'Vlogosphere' is growing in importance as a medium for public exhibitionism, even when the content of the posts are of an extremely sensitive nature. By adopting a netnographic research approach and Hermeneutic analysis method this research explores the role that personal video logs (vlogs) are being used as a means of public exhibitionism for five sufferers of Anorexia Nervosa. The findings show that the community that evolves around the sufferers act to maintain the vlogger's disease by encouraging her in her disorder and simultaneously defending her from attackers who disagree with her actions and vlogs.

## INTRODUCTION

The use of web logging (blogging ) and video logging (vlogging) as a means of self expression has increased exponentially in recent years (Nardi, Schiano, and Gumbrecht 2004) with the number of active blogs doubling every 6 months between 2003 and 2006 (Green 2007). Universal McCann estimate that 59% of internet users either read or own a blog of some form and 75% watch video clips online (Smith 2008). The potential that online media has as a portal for individual self expression appears limitless. This research focuses specifically on one aspect of online self expression many would define being stigmatized and outside mainstream consumer society. This research examines the way in which sufferers of Anorexia Nervosa use YouTube™ as a medium for expressing thoughts, fears, progress with their therapy, self identity, and other highly personal and sensitive topics to a relatively anonymous public audience with little control over the privacy of their posts.

Blood (2002) refers to a blog as a "coffee house conversation in text" (p.1) whilst other researchers define blogging by its format. Walker (2005) defines a blog as being a frequently updated web site consisting of dated entries in reverse chronological order so that the most recent post appears first. Blogs are typically posted by individuals having a personal or informal style and wish to produce an online diary (Walker 2005).

Some research has been done on the need for consumers to express their multiple selves through a variety of channels (Lee, Im, and Taylor 2008), whilst others have examined the motives behind 'online diaries' (Nardi et al. 2004). One area of interest in the literature is the need for stigmatized users to find ways of expressing themselves freely without judgment as a means of searching for belonging (Baumeister and Leary 1995). However, relatively little research has been conducted on the recent developments of video blogging and the motivations behind its use by internet users, with stigmatized identities such as Anorexia Nervosa. Therefore the research question presented here is: how does video blogging technology, and the community that it has created, motivate those with highly stigmatized identities, such as Anorexia Nervosa, to express their identity to complete strangers?

In achieving this aim we undertake a netnographic methodology (Kozinets 2002) to investigate five YouTube™ vloggers as they post their thoughts and feelings on the public forum. This research comprises data collected from vlogs themselves, viewer, and producer generated comments to specific vlogs and forum posts made by participants about their vlog posts. Hermeneutic analysis is used to explicate the underlying meanings associated with the vlogs as well as to derive a fuller understanding of the context in which the participants choose to adopt vlogging as a means of self expression. Preceding the findings and discussion is a brief review of the extant literature on exhibitionism its role in consumer culture.

## BACKGROUND
### Self-expression and exhibitionism

The notion of consumers having and expressing multiple selves is well founded in consumer research and psychology (Markus and Kunda 1986; McGuire et al. 1978; Onkvisit and Shaw 1987; Wylie et al. 1979). The pressure associated with public expectation can lead to self-impersonation and as such, it is argued that consumers carry an arsenal of different masks that reveal different aspects of our 'self' (Markus and Nurius 1986). This research focuses more on a specific form of self-expression, that of public exhibitionism of a self that is often stigmatized by mainstream society. Holbrook (2000) defines consumer exhibitionism as going hand in hand with consumer voyeurism. Exhibitionism, as used in this research, is the need for consumers to display, express, and expose a form of themselves (whether it is real or not) so that others (consumer voyeurs) may watch. It is the act of purposefully exposing a part of the self in order for it to be seen. Similar acts that may be concealed from others would not, in this case, be seen as exhibitionism. Therefore, had this research looked at the private diaries of Anorexia Nervosa sufferers for which the only audience is the writer, then the concept of exhibitionism would not be valid.

Much of the psychological literature on exhibitionism defines it as a deviant and abnormal act. The main bodies of research look at sexual exhibitionism and means of treatment (Marshall, Eccles, and Barbaree 1991; Zohar, Kaplan, and Benjamin 1994) and focus heavily on the irrational nature of the behavior. One interesting area of research looks at how sexual exhibitionism in adolescents may not be a psychological disorder, but rather a "strategic interaction" in a search for acceptance and engagement with others (Green 1987). This desire to interact through 'showing off' has been linked with an abusive history (Hold-Cavell 1985). More recently, Baslam (2008) shows that female exhibitionism may not necessarily be related to abnormal sexual deviancy but a "normative spectrum for pleasurably active sex seeking and pleasurable procreative desire and fantasy" (pp. 99). Baslan continues by describing how female exhibitionism can be designed not to interact, but to engage onlookers with a sense of envy and yearning, which further affirms the female performer in her role as exhibitionist (Baslam 2008). Again, although motives may be different, the purpose is to engage the voyeur in some way.

Beyond the sexual context of exhibitionism there remains a raft of literature on 'show off's that has not permeated into consumer research. Bal (1992) describes the use of displays in museums as a means of asserting dominancy of a culture. That is, by showing ones wares as a culture one is really showing off as to the superior nature of one culture over another. This notion of exhibitionism as a means of control, power, and even defence of ones identity is found in many contexts. Wilson and Daly's (1985) research on Detroit youth posits that violence in young men is often incited when a conflict in power exists between perceived competitors and such power struggles are further incensed when competitors show off their power, whether it be through their physical strength, peer support or weaponry. One could argue that such behaviors found throughout society, from the youth in city streets, to adults in halls of power. Showing off and exhibitionism are, in many cases, about control and power. The following section will look at the relationship between control, power and Anorexia Nervosa in young women.

**Anorexia Nervosa and Control**

Although the focus of this research is not the etiology of Anorexia Nervosa, it is important to understand some of the basic causes associated with the disorder if we are to fully understand the context associated with the participants in question (Palmer 1969). The DSM-IV classifies Anorexia as being an inability to maintain a healthy body weight combined with a fear of losing *control* over the sufferer's weight and becoming 'fat'. Sufferers often come from abusive and *controlling* families whereby nurturance is significantly lacking (American Psychiatric Association 2000). Although many treatment plans are effective if the sufferer is diagnosed in time, many are reluctant to undertake treatment as it does mean relinquishing *control* (American Psychiatric Association 2000). This theme of control is reiterated in a number of studies on anorexia. Indeed, Garner, Olmstead, and Polivy's (1983) eating disorder inventory includes subscales on both striving for effectiveness (desire to find methods or solutions that are effective in meeting necessary weight-loss goals) as well as idealized perfectionism (searching for a physical perfection, which may be a distorted reality of ones actual size), both items heavily related to control over one's physical self. Latterly, Morgan, Reid, and Lacey's (1999) measurement of eating disorders also puts a heavy emphasis on the impact of lost control with regard to the severity of the sufferer's condition. One of the earliest pieces of psychoanalytic work on Anorexia also notes that the nature of the disease is when a person "embarks on her [his] relentless pursuit of thinness and absolute control over her [his] body" (Sours 1974, p 567). It is clear that control over oneself, one's body, and a desire for self-control away from a parental control system are all key factors in understanding sufferers of the disease, which links openly with the desire for control by the exhibitionist. Although of significant interest, this research will not focus on understanding why some sufferers of Anorexia Nervosa choose to be exhibitionists whilst others do not – the focus here is to understand their behaviors and actions as exhibitionists. The following section outlines the methodology employed and the findings from the research.

## METHODOLOGY

This research utilized a netnographic approach (Kozinets 2002) as it offers significant advantages in this particular context. In particular it aids in researching sensitive subject areas as the researcher can covertly collect and analyse data without the vlogger feeling subjected to undue inquiry they may not be comfortable with (Langer and Beckmann 2005). This covert approach naturally raises issues of ethicality as participants may not wish their posts to be analysed and disseminated for public academic audiences. Netnography allows researchers to engage in stories presented on a freely available public forum without influencing the research participants. However, the nature of the posts and the research at hand on a public forum also allows the researcher (and anyone else surfing the web) to freely access the posts and ensure that ethicality is maintained as long as the participants is kept anonymous. As such, participants in this study will not be referred to by their actual user names and titles of posts will not be disclosed in this paper.

As much of the data being analysed is freely available on YouTube™ it was deemed appropriate to begin data collection by

finding participants [vloggers] who displayed characteristics akin to those suffering from Anorexia (Morgan et al. 1999). The search began by using search terms for "weight loss" which revealed a total of 212 individual vloggers. This search was then further refined with a search for "fast" or "fasting" which resulted in 13 individual vloggers being identified. By examining their initial posts all 13 displayed some characteristics of Anorexia, with 5 specifically mentioned that they have been diagnosed with the disorder. Although the other 8 vloggers may indeed be sufferers it would be imprudent of the researchers to assume the condition without formal psychoanalytic assessment of the vlogger by a specialist. As this is not available at this time these remaining 8 vloggers are not formally analysed as part of this study.

All five of the remaining vloggers were women aged between 20 and 31 at the time of analysis; however, logs made by diagnosed sufferers were identified by girls as young as 8 years old. Although a small proportion of Anorexia Nervosa suffers are male the sample here are all female. All of the women had a steady partner and either lived at home with their parents or with their partner and (and any children they may have). The netnography began by watching all the vlogs made by the five vloggers, transcribing text and copying any comments made by viewers or vloggers. In total, 249 vlogs were viewed ranging in length from 45 seconds to 15:13 minutes covering a range of topics. The number of views for each vlog varies from vlogger to vlogger. As an indication of the volume of data provided by the vlog creator [vlogger] and vlog voyeurs [viewer] the most prolific vlogger had created 92 vlogs, which were viewed over 190,000 times (as at January 2009) and had over 2,700 regular subscribers who were alerted to any new vlogs being posted. Although these numbers may pale in comparison to the millions of videos available online, it still shows an area of high usage and of importance to online community research.

For interpretation of the collected data a hermeneutic approach was adopted as it offers a greater insight of the stories being told by the vloggers by examining the underlying meanings and context associated with the stories (Palmer 1969; Thompson 1997). By adopting hermeneutic analysis the researcher requires an understanding of the personal history of the textual stories in order to help understand the meanings associated with the stories generated by respondents. This research will therefore look to understand historical notions of control from participants' perspectives and focus on their own processual desire for greater control through their YouTube™ vlogs. However, themes from other, interrelated subjects will also be drawn into the analysis as it is seen appropriate.

## FINDINGS

A number of themes emerged from the analysis of the data. However, due to the limited space associated with this submission we will only concentrate on three major themes, that of acceptance through self-validation, community and control. Other themes not discussed here include the vloggers' struggle with depression, anxiety, and validation. It is hoped these themes can be elucidated further in a future manuscript.

### Acceptance Through Self-Validation

Based on the data collected, YouTube™ seems to be providing those that suffer from Anorexia Nervosa the possibility to express their real selves as well as control the level of expression associated with the posts. YouTube™ provides vloggers with a space in which their identity can be expressed without fear of being unaccepted or misunderstood; something that these vloggers express is impossible outside this setting. Vloggers maintain a heavy control over their posts by enabling the right to delete posts that invalidate their expression or damage their identities. Many of the vloggers express that their fasting and Anorexia like behaviors are an important aspect of their lives and they feel unable to share it with those that matter to them the most. This indicates that they are fully aware of the controversy that surrounds their behavior but find that through the consumption of YouTube™, they do not risk the possibility of being unloved and unaccepted, as Vlogger A demonstrates here:

*" No one really understands what I go through, my parents would think I've gone crazy and send me to THAT clinic but it makes me feel so tired sometimes, and suppressed, and alone. They just don't understand what it feels like to want something so bad......thank you guys so much, I mean it... all my subscribers....it's nice to have someone that I can relate to and talk to....love you all and thanks for all your supportive messages... it's such a relief to finally be able to discuss this without people thinking that I'm a freak! " (Vlogger A, 31, engaged with one child – fasting for her wedding).*

Here Vlogger A offers a clear example of a need for belonging and validation (Baumeister and Leary 1995). When a lack of interpersonal belonging exists in real life for these vloggers they attempt to seek validation and belonging elsewhere. Some vloggers continue to build this need for belonging by further displacing themselves from their real life friends and families. Without a feeling of being understood by their friends and families and a deep sense of vulnerability, they crave the understanding of those on YouTube™. Therefore, as close relationships are formed on YouTube™, face to face relationships progressively diminish:

*"I have to spend time with my mother today....not only is she going to complain how I'm not eating but I have to actually have a CONVERSATION with her....I really don't want to go and want to spend time with you guys....what's the point anyway?! It's not like she is going to understand any of my problems or issues; she is just going to start crying and complaining that she doesn't know how to help me...I DON'T NEED HELP! What's wrong with her?! Anyway...I can't avoid going so I might as well and just have some form of civil conversation...I promise to let you guys know how it went and will be making a video soooon!" (Vlogger C, 24, living with long-term boyfriend - fasting to lose her "hips")*

The above not only shows the lack of enthusiasm towards face to face interaction but also reveals the closeness of the relationships formed online. The vloggers studied here all show a desire to spend time with their online viewers rather than with their families. This indicates that, YouTube™ users form online relationships that can be of more value than those formed over many years with their parents or partners as the vlogger finds themselves expressing their 'true' selves to online viewers, resulting in the formation of a stronger connection and therefore high levels of affection and closeness. This can be also shown in the specific videos made:

*"Just wanted to say hi to [name of viewer deleted], thank you for all your nice messages. You are so sweet. I saw recently that you're going through a bit of depression....you will be fine. You're amazing and such an inspiration to me. I hope you will pull through and I'm always here for you if you need to discuss anything. You have helped me stay motivated throughout my fasts and it's so sad when I see you upset. Please, PLEASE feel better soon.....hugs and kisses,*

*love you lots!" (Vlogger B, 22, living at home with parents – fasting to lose weight)*

These bonds with the viewing audience forms a sense of community online that the vloggers crave as a means of offering validation for their situation and endeavors to lose weight.

## Community

The more the vlogger engages with the YouTube™ community she has created the greater the ties between her online in-group and the weaker the ties with her offline friends and family (Batson et al. 1997; Tajfel 1982; Turner 1987). Such a creation results in greater reliance on YouTube™ itself and therefore provides a space whereby control of their identity becomes possible:

*"It's so nice to be able to talk to people who know what I'm going through...it's funny...I spend all day hiding having this eating disorder from people around me and getting stressed about it....and then on here you can actually talk so freely about it... YOU WANT PEOPLE TO KNOW! [Laughs]....I guess it's because you guys know what I'm on about...you won't just think oh my god she needs help... thanks sweethearts!" (Vlogger C, 24, living with long-term boyfriend - fasting to lose her "hips").*

Consequently, this reliance results in strong levels of attachment between users and therefore, the need for approval. All of these examples offer evidence of a need for community, acceptance and the exertion of control by the vlogger. Many of the vloggers admit their need for control stems from the lack of control they felt as they grew up:

*"It's not as if it's something I could have done anything about...HE was just a fucking monster now I think about it...HE was the one who did this to me and now HE's the one who thinks I'm a perfect angel...well it's not like that [long pause]. I couldn't change 'that' but I can change 'this'...this and NOW" [vlogger holds herself and squeezes stomach in so as to appear thinner] (Vlogger E, 21, living at home with parents – fasting to appear more attractive to a boy she likes).*

The historical context of the stories offers a greater insight into the way in which the vloggers use exhibitionism as an extension of their need for control, which is again, symptomatic of Anorexia Nervosa sufferers. Vloggers perceive their YouTube™ vlogs as being a portal to an identity and community where they are offered acceptance and protection from the reality of their everyday lives (Noble and Walker 1997; Turner 1964).

As previously discussed, results have shown that vloggers feel that YouTube™ is a place for self expression without judgment. Therefore, they feel at ease with expressing issues of concern and frustration that are related to their weight loss. It is the fact that such expression is directed at viewers that have similar interests and concerns that allows for high levels of support and encouragement in times of distress for the vlogger. Not only does such expression allow for a release of anxiety, but the support it generates allows the video bloggers to feel loved and cared about. This evidently allows for emotions of affiliation and belonging to be experienced:

*"I broke my fast today...I'm so angry with myself....IM A FAILURE!!! I ate so much....I'm so disappointed in myself.....WHY?!? I know this is probably boring for you, but I*

*need to get this feeling out!! I know you guys will under-stand....ITS SO FRUSTRATING!! I hope I haven't put on any weight! I don't want to step on the scales.....*" (Vlogger C, 24, living with long-term boyfriend - fasting to lose her "hips").

In response to this, a viewer commented:

"*Don't worry hunnie, we all have made mistakes. I know you are strong and can cope with this. Don't let it put you down, keep motivated. I swear you are such an inspiration to me and even though you feel really bad and like a disap-pointment, you are not! Keep up the fast and you will feel better, don't let yourself slip and most importantly remem-ber, we have ALL broken a fast at some time or another and what you did is normal. Love you and wish you the best*"

Participant C went on to thank the viewer in her next video:

"*Thank you so much for your comments!! It's nice that I can have someone to talk to that relates to my problems.... you made me feel a million times better, you're a sweet heart and I wish that your fast is going well! Thanks for caring!*"

All of these interactions aid the vlogger to exert greater strength and control over her situation and lead her further down the road of fasting as a means of losing weight. It is clear that the online communities offer much needed validation for these 'private' fasts and is only exaggerating the effects of the disease through greater need for control and greater desire to lose weight.

### Control

In order to control their identity without it being challenged, users tend to lie to friends and family about their eating disorder. In line with this they try just as hard to keep their video blogging activities a secret from those that know them:

"*... sorry....I have to keep my voice down....my parents are in the other room and they don't know about this video making...they would go really mad if they found out...and they would also find out a lot of things that I really don't want them to know, as you can imagine (sighs).....it's good that way......I get to have my own little world with you guys that's far away from the day to day crap*" (Vlogger D, 21, living at home - fasting to look beautiful).

The use of YouTube™ allows for strong levels of supportive interaction, but it also provides many of these women with a form of 'thinspiration' through the viewing of other similar online journals:

"*I was bored the other day...well I couldn't sleep....so I went on YouTube™ and watched some videos....I mean.... some of you girls are amazing...your so motivated and strong willed...I also watched a video on a fast and I decided that's what I need to do...so I'm starting a fast!!! Thanks for the inspiration (deleted word).....I realized how much weight you're losing and if you can do it....well it just gave me the motivation to try fasting*" (Vlogger A, 31, engaged with one child – fasting for her wedding).

This once again emphasises the strong sense of community provided by the consumption of YouTube™, but also shows how the vloggers engage with coping mechanisms to continue their in-dividual fasts. Conversely, when control is lost, the outcome often results in frustration, anger, depression, but also, more heightened levels of exhibitionism. This is shown by one vlogger's flamboyant outburst online after losing control of her fast:

"*...feeling like SHIT right now...really depressed...I mean, I weighed myself this morning and I've lost NOTHING!! NOTHING!!.....I'm just really frustrated, I know it's a bit silly but I just needed to get it out and I cant seem to sleep... ...I don't know...I guess this really has nothing to do with anything....I just wish I could zone out or disappear*"( Vlogger B, 22, living at home with parents – fasting to lose weight).

And again, the sense of frustration comes through with another vlogger, completely unrelated to the first but with a very similar narrative:

"*I am so fucking angry!!!! I weighed myself and nothing! NOTHING! (screams).......that's it I'm not going to post another video till I've lost some weight...this is just pathetic and I'm PATHETIC to watch.... I'm so sorry you guys... you've been so sweet to me and all I've done is let you down......just watch me I will loose the weight!*" (Vlogger E, 21, living at home with parents – fasting to appear more attractive to a boy she likes).

The frustration through lost control is symptomatic of suffer-ers of Anorexia Nervosa; however, their public, exuberant displays of anger are often not seen due to their fear of losing acceptance (Vitousek and Manke 1994). Sufferers are more likely to recluse from those not in favor of their behavior; but when a support network, such as the YouTube™ communities, exist, the vlogger is able to vent their emotional frustration and draw strength from viewer comments and responses to their situation.

### DISCUSSION

This research has looked at the role in which YouTube™ offers sufferers of Anorexia Nervosa the opportunity to seek acceptance, form communities of similarly minded supporters of their behav-ior and exert greater control over their lives. This research does not aim to offer an understanding for what may have caused their eating disorders nor does it offer contributions for understanding a cure for the disease. What this research is able to show is that technologically savvy consumers are able to find emotional catharsis through exhibitionist behaviors. The loss of control with one side of the vlogger's life is exaggerated with more and more extroverted presentations of self online. This is in line with Schau and Gilly's (1995) investigations into online presentational behavior and the desire to show one's self online in a way that may appeal to viewers. In this case the vloggers are presenting a sign that draws attention and sympathy from viewers, allowing the vloggers to further validate their decision to fast.

The findings here show that the expression of self using vlogs is a form of hyper-expression or exhibitionism compared with personal websites or even blogs. This could be indicative of a coping mechanism to generate validation for their actions and draw encouragement from the community they have created, or it is an extension of their disorder whereby a loss of control in one aspect of the vlogger's life leads to a need to gain of control by drawing attention to their plight through exhibitionism.

The paradox in this research lies with the fact that many of these sufferers act as though they are sharing their private thoughts in a private setting. The revelations of self they offer become more and more detailed and private in nature, similar to that of a private diary (Nardi et al. 2004), but in a public forum. The desire to exhibit themselves to the outside world, whilst still keeping their affliction hidden from their loved ones offers a significant area of interest for both consumer culture theorists and eating disorder therapists.

The Catharsis Hypothesis suggests that venting one's emotions can aid in alleviating the emotional anger or pain one is feeling (Feshbagh 1956). However, more recent evidence has shown that vented anger does not often relieve tension, but rather increases anger levels (Bushman 2002; Bushman, Baumeister, and Phillips 2001). But, it appears that when the vented emotions are subsequently validated by a strong community spirit to continue unhealthy behavior the vlogger reacts positively to the feeling of catharsis through the support she receives from YouTube™. This cathartic experience is thus harnessed as a means of mood repair. However, the result is a continuation of thoughts and behaviors that further validate the triggers of Anorexia Nervosa.

This research may offer more questions about vlogging behavior than it does answers, but it does highlight the need for awareness of the role that online communities play in self formation and self validation. What is known is that these women are suffering, but they are not suffering in silence and they are not suffering alone. The support rich environment offered by YouTube™ means that sufferers are able to be a 'validated self' and it is this 'self' that may continue to slowly kill them in the privacy of their webcams, computer screens and hundreds of thousands of online voyeurs.

## REFERENCES

American Psychiatric Association (2000), *Diagnostic and Statistical Manual of Mental Disorders*, Washington, DC: American Psychiatric Association.

Bal, Mieke (1992), "Telling, Showing, Showing-Off," *Critical Inquiry*, 18 (3), 556-94.

Baslam, Rosemary H. (2008), "Women Showing Off: Notes on Female Exhibitionism," *Journal of the American Psychoanalytic Association*, 56 (1), 99-121.

Batson, C. Daniel, Marina P. Polycarpou, Eddie Harmon-Jones, Heidi J. Imhoff, Erin C. Mitchener, Lori L. Bednar, Tricia R. Klien, and Lori Highberger (1997), "Empathy and Attitudes: Can Feeling for a Member of a Stigmatized Group Improve Feelings toward the Group?," *Journal of Personality and Social Psychology*, 72 (1), 105-18.

Baumeister, Roy F. and Mark R. Leary (1995), "The Need to Belong: Desire for Interpersonal Attachments as a Fundamental Human Motivation," *Psychological Bulletin*, 117 (3), 497-529.

Blood, Rebecca (2002), *The Weblog Handbook: Practical Advice on Creating and Maintaining Your Blog*, Cambridge, MA: Perseus Publishing.

Bushman, Brad J. (2002), "Does Venting Anger Feed or Extinguish the Flame? Catharsis, Rumination, Distraction, Anger, and Aggressive Responding," *Personality and Social Psychology Bulletin*, 28 (6), 724-31.

Bushman, Brad J., Roy F. Baumeister, and Colleen M. Phillips (2001), "Do People Aggress to Improve Their Mood? Catharsis Beliefs, Affect Regulation Opportunity, and Aggressive Responding," *Journal of Personality and Social Psychology*, 81 (1), 17-32.

Feshbagh, Seymour (1956), "The Catharsis Hypothesis and Some Consequences of Interaction with Aggressive and Neutral Play Objects," *Journal of Personality*, 24 (4), 449-62.

Garner, David M., Marion P. Olmstead, and Janet Polivy (1983), "Development and Validation of a Multidimensional Eating Disorder Inventory for Anorexia Nervosa and Bulimia," *International Journal of Eating Disorders*, 2 (2), 15-34.

Gilly, Mary C. (1995), "The Consumer Acculturation of Expatriate Americans," *Advances in Consumer Research*, 22, 506-10.

Green, D. (1987), "Adolescent Exhibitionists: Theory and Therapy," *Journal of Adolescence*, 10 (1), 45-56.

Green, Heather (2007), "With 15.5 Million Active Blogs, New Technorati Data Shows That Blogging Growth Seems to Be Peaking," in *Business Week*.

Holbrook, Morris B. (2000), "The Millennial Consumer in the Texts of Our Times: Experience and Entertainment," *Journal of Macromarketing*, 20 (2), 178-92.

Hold-Cavell, Barbara C. L. (1985), "Showing-Off and Aggression in Young Children," *Aggressive Behavior*, 11, 303-14.

Kozinets, Robert V. (2002), "The Field Behind the Screen: Using Netnography for Marketing Research in Online Communities," *Journal of Marketing*, 39 (1), 61-72.

Langer, Roy and Suzanne C. Beckmann (2005), "Sensitive Research Topics: Netnography Revisited," *Qualitative Market Research: An International Journal*, 8 (2), 189-203.

Lee, Doo-Hee, Seunghee Im, and Charles R. Taylor (2008), "Voluntary Self-Disclosure of Information on the Internet: A Multimethod Study of the Motivations and Consequences of Disclosing Information on Blogs," *Psychology & Marketing*, 25 (7), 692-710.

Markus, H. and P. Nurius (1986), "Possible Selves," *American Psychologist*, 41 (September), 954-68.

Markus, Hazel and Ziva Kunda (1986), "Stability and Malleability of the Self Concept," *Journal of Personality and Social Psychology*, 51 (4), 858-66.

Marshall, W. L., A. Eccles, and H. E. Barbaree (1991), "The Treatment of Exhibitionists: A Focus on Sexual Deviance Versus Cognitive and Relationship Features," *Behavior Research and Therapy*, 29 (2), 129-35.

McGuire, William J., Claire V. McGuire, Pamela Child, and Terry Fujioka (1978), "Salience of Ethnicity in the Spontaneous Self Concept as a Function of One's Ethnic Distinctiveness in the Social Environment," *Journal of Personality and Social Psychology*, 36 (5), 511-20.

Morgan, John F., Fiona Reid, and J. Hubert Lacey (1999), "The Scoff Questionnaire: Assessment of a New Screening Tool for Eating Disorders," *British Medical Journal*, 319 (December), 1467-68.

Nardi, Bonnie A., Diane J. Schiano, and Michelle Gumbrecht (2004), "Blogging as Social Activity, or, Would You Let 900 Million People Read Your Diary?," in *Proceedings of the 2004 ACM Conference on Computer Supported Cooperative Work*, Chicago, Illinois, USA: ACM, 222-31.

Noble, Charles H. and Beth A. Walker (1997), "Exploring the Relationships among Liminal Transition, Symbolic Consumption, and the Extended Self," *Psychology & Marketing*, 14 (1), 29-47.

Onkvisit, Sak and John Shaw (1987), "Self Concept & Image Congruence: Some Research and Managerial Implications," *Journal of Consumer Marketing*, 4 (Winter), 13-24.

Palmer, Richard E. (1969), *Hermeneutics: Interpretation Theory in Schleiermacher, Dilthey, Heidegger, and Gadamer*, Evanston: Northwestern University Press.

Smith, Tom (2008), "Wave 3: Power to the People, Social Media Tracker," http://www.universalmccann.com/Assets/wave_3_20080403093750.pdf.

Sours, John A. (1974), "The Anorexia Nervosa Syndrome," *The International Journal of Psychoanalysis*, 55 (567-576).

Tajfel, Henri (1982), "Social Psychology of Intergroup Relations," *Annual Review of Psychology*, 33 (1), 1-39.

Thompson, Craig J. (1997), "Interpreting Consumers: A Hermeneutical Framework for Deriving Marketing Insights from the Texts of Consumers' Consumption Stories," *Journal of Marketing Research*, 34 (November), 438-55.

Turner, John C. (1987), *Rediscovering the Social Group: A Self-Categorisation Theory*, Oxford: Basil Blackwell Ltd.

Turner, Victor (1964), "Betwixt and Between: The Liminal Period in Rites De Passage," in *Symposium on New Approaches to the Study of Religion*, ed. June Helm, Seattle: University of Washington Press, 4-20.

Vitousek, Kelly and Frederic Manke (1994), "Personality Variables and Disorders in Anorexia Nervosa and Bulimia Nervosa," *Journal of Abnormal Psychology*, 103 (1), 137-47.

Walker, Jill (2005), "Weblogs: Learning in Public," *On the Horizon*, 13 (2), 112-18.

Wilson, Margo and Martin Daly (1985), "Competitiveness, Risk Taking, and Violence: The Young Male Syndrome," *Ethology and Sociobiology*, 6 (1), 59-73.

Wylie, Ruth C., Peggy J. Miller, Susan S. Cowles, and Alice W. Wilson (1979), *The Self Concept*, Vol. Two, Lincoln: University of Nebraska Press.

Zohar, J., Z. Kaplan, and J. Benjamin (1994), "Compulsive Exhibitionism Successfully Treated with Fluvoxamine : A Controlled Case Study," *The Journal of Clinical Psychiatry*, 55 (3), 86-88.

# Sacred Places: An Exploratory Investigation of Consuming Pilgrimage

Leighanne Higgins, University of Strathclyde, UK
Kathy Hamilton, University of Strathclyde, UK

## ABSTRACT

In line with the growing commercialization of religion, this paper focuses on the consumption of sacred place within the context of the Christian pilgrimage. Theoretically, we raise the profile of place within consumer research and contribute to understandings of the relationship between the sacred and the profane.

## INTRODUCTION

The aim of this paper is to explore the religious consumption experience of pilgrims within sacred places. The interplay between economics and spirituality has been well documented within consumer research literature with regards to the sacralization of consumer culture (O'Guinn 1991, Kozinets 2001, Muniz and Schau, 2005). However, there is less research interest on the secularization of the sacred in relation to the commercialization of religion. We contribute to this research stream by exploring the context of the Christian pilgrimage.

Previous research on the interaction between the spiritual and the material has focused on people (O'Guinn 1991), possessions (Muniz and Schau 2005) and activities (Celsi, Rose and Leigh 1993, Arnould and Price 1993). Our focus brings the issue of place to the forefront, highlighting that place is central to our understandings and experiences. We begin by discussing the concept of pilgrimage to help contextualize the study.

## DEFINING PILGRIMAGE

The traditional definition of pilgrimage relates to "a physical and spiritual journey in search of truth, in search of what is sacred and holy" (Vulkonic 1996 cited in Timothy and Olsen 2006). This perspective prioritizes religious and spiritual fulfillment whereby pilgrims journey to a holy site where the earth and the divine are believed to meet. Within contemporary consumer culture the definition of pilgrimage has evolved to encompass more than holy sites alone. As Morinis (1992) suggested, a pilgrimage site can be any place where an individual finds enlightenment, clarity or happiness. Following this approach, pilgrimage can be discussed within the context of dark tourism to places like Auschwitz or celebrity pilgrimages such as a trip to Graceland.

Pilgrimage sites become sacralized because of events that have taken place there. In this paper we focus on Christian pilgrimage sites. For example, Lourdes in France is seen as one of the most celebrated Roman Catholic shrines in the world, with a yearly intake of approximately 5 million pilgrims, travelling to worship the apparition of the Virgin Mary in 1858. Similarly, Fatima in Portugal receives approximately a million pilgrims between May and October each year, honoring the apparition of the Virgin Mary to three children in 1917. A typical Christian pilgrimage involves processions, individual prayer, meditation, and collective worship during religious services.

Given the growing commercialization of religion, a consumption vocabulary surrounds Christian pilgrimage discourse. The pilgrim is increasingly viewed as a tourist and the pilgrimage site becomes the marketplace where hotels, souvenir shops, restaurants and tour operators all compete to attract the lucrative pilgrim consumer. In this respect, pilgrimage sites provide an overlapping of the sacred and the profane, offering an appropriate context to explore and seek understanding of the complex relationship between religion and consumerism.

## RELIGION AND RELIGIOSITY WITHIN CONSUMER CULTURE

Statistics point to the global decline of religious practice and belief. In Scotland, where the research was conducted, the 2001 population census found that thirty percent of the Scottish population had no religious affiliation whatsoever (Voas 2006). A similar trend is present in the USA with the "American Religious Identification Survey" discovering a nine percent drop in the number of citizens identifying themselves with a religion, and with Christianity seeing a twenty percent drop in following between the years 1990 and 2001 (Kosmin and Mayer 2001). In contrast, consumers are moving towards the production and reworking of their own religions (Scott and Maclaran 2009), implying that individual beliefs have more significance in everyday life than the social structures and institutions that support them. For example, in Ireland, despite falling Church attendance, Palmer and Gallagher (2007) argued that the ideology of religion remains important, thereby reinforcing the multidimensionality of religiosity. Religious institutions may have particular difficulty in appealing to younger age groups who seek innovative non-traditional approaches (Davis and Yip 2004). Equally, while we have witnessed a decline in traditional religious beliefs, there has been a proliferation of New Age spiritual thinkers, who according to Rindfleish (2005, 343) position New Age spirituality as ""social products" for consumption."

## SACRED CONSUMPTION

Following a Durkheimian approach, Belk, Wallendorf and Sherry (1989, 13) defined the sacred in contrast to the profane. They argued that sacred occurrences may be "ecstatic" and "self-transcending" and are often "aided by a social context involving fellow believers who also revere the object or experience." In opposition, the profane is "ordinary and lacks the ability to induce ecstatic, self-transcending, extraordinary experiences." However, research has acknowledged a blurring and narrowing of the boundaries between the sacred and the profane. This is evident through two parallel trends in relation to religion and consumption, first, the secularization of the sacred and second, the sacralization of the secular (Belk, Wallendorf and Sherry 1989).

The sacred experience is no longer confined to the religious arena, rather consumption activities offer the possibility of transcendence (Arnould and Price 1993, Celsi, Rose and Leigh 1993, Hamilton and Hewer 2009), filling the void left by the less central role of religion in everyday life. Shopping malls are seen as "cathedrals of consumption" that offer "enchanted settings" where consumers can gain a sense of community (Ritzer 2005, 7). Fans worship and imbue celebrities with god-like powers and fan clubs serve important social functions, facilitating sharing and bonding (O'Guinn 1991). "Cherished possessions" or "inalienable wealth" (Curasi, Price and Arnould 2004, 609) account for an important part of the self. The religiosity of brand communities highlights the transformation of seemingly profane and functional consumer goods into objects that offer emancipation and liberation (Muniz and Schau 2005). This use of religious themes and narratives in marketplace discussions points to "the continued presence, vitality, and relevance of religious connections" (Muniz and Schau 2005, 745). Through consumption practices "the material world can become the seat of the sacred again; consumption can become (re)ensouled" (Kozinets 2002, 32).

Equally, religious commercialization is growing as religious souvenirs, devotional objects, music and home decorations objectify the sacred (Ger and Wilk 2005) while religious theme parks merge the sacred and profane (O'Guinn and Belk 1989). Trends such as these draw attention to the expanding reach of market capitalism, supporting the idea of a consumer civilization (Campbell 2004).

## METHOD

This exploratory study was conducted in order to understand the experiences and opinions of visitors to Christian shrines. Ten one-to-one in-depth interviews formed the basis of data collection. A total of eight interviews were conducted with respondents who identified themselves as Christian and who had participated in a Christian pilgrimage. Access to five of the respondents was negotiated with the assistance of a parish priest from a local Catholic church. Following a snowball method, the parish priest then aided an introduction with a local Episcopalian minister which led to three further respondents. All of these respondents practiced their religion on a regular basis. Although not included in the current paper, we also conducted two interviews with respondents who identified themselves as Atheist. As shown in table 1, respondents were mixed in terms of gender and age.

The interviews were conducted in a social room within the Catholic Church hall and lasted up to 100 minutes. Interview topics focused on accessing the lived experience of respondents' understandings of pilgrimage. Discussion centered on defining pilgrimage, personal meaning of pilgrimage and the role of marketing in the pilgrimage experience. Interviews were audio-recorded and transcribed for data analysis. We adopted a hermeneutic approach to data analysis by first seeking an idiographic understanding of each transcript and second, seeking a holistic understanding by exploring common patterns and themes (Thompson, Pollio and Locander 1994).

## FINDINGS

The findings are presented in relation to three emergent themes; understanding pilgrimage, the social context, and pilgrimage as a consumption experience versus pilgrimage as a spiritual experience.

## UNDERSTANDING PILGRIMAGE

Belhassen, Caton and Stewart (2008) suggested that a fully comprehensive understanding of place cannot be obtained without consideration of physical environments, experiences and meanings. This provides an appropriate framework to deconstruct the meaning

**Table 1: Profile of Respondents**

| Pseudonym | Gender | Age | Occupation | Religious Belief | Pilgrimage Experience |
|-----------|--------|-----|------------|------------------|----------------------|
| Daniel | Male | 58 | Retired | Episcopalian | Jerusalem, Rome |
| David | Male | 53 | Taxi Driver | Catholic | Lourdes (several times) |
| Mark | Male | 18 | Student | Catholic | Lourdes (several times) |
| Robert | Male | 55 | Manager | Episcopalian | Lourdes (several times) |
| Fiona | Female | 51 | Clerical work | Catholic | Lourdes (once) |
| Isabelle | Female | 56 | Retired | Episcopalian | Lourdes, Walshingham |
| Katy | Female | 57 | House-wife | Catholic | Lourdes , Jerusalem |
| Penny | Female | 52 | House-wife | Catholic | Lourdes |

of pilgrimage and present this section of the findings. Although each aspect is discussed separately, it should be apparent that physical environment, experience and meaning are interrelated.

## PHYSICAL ENVIRONMENT

Given the centrality of place to the pilgrim experience, the aspects of physical location were frequently mentioned during interview discussions. For respondents, a pilgrimage site is somewhere that something "special" or "miraculous" has occurred. Put simply, it is "a holy site."

*Mark: "I feel that it has to have some type of spiritual core to it, some type of pull that makes people deem it as special enough to visit."*

*Daniel: "certain locations have this, what experts call, a numinous feel to it, where you actually feel when you are in a place that there is something special about it."*

Whilst the idea of specialness derives from shared social and cultural understandings relating to historical sacred occurrences, some referred to more personal events. For example, Mark considered his pilgrimage to Lourdes "as being one of the curers for my illness" reinforcing the powerful, self-transcendent nature of the sacred (Belk, Sherry and Wallendorf 1989). Irene described a pilgrimage as "a personal mission" while Katy commented:

*Katy: "I think it has to have something special to the individual. For me Lourdes is very special, not because I have seen huge miracles occurring there, but I truly believe that little miracles happen there every-day. And to see small children who are seriously ill and people seriously ill, but who still belief and smile, and laugh, that is humbling and puts life in perspective for you, makes you wonder what am I worrying for? So for me, that humbling aspect is a miracle in itself."*

Such social and personal understandings result in the pilgrimage site being viewed as "a place of worship," or "a place of prayer" where pilgrims can celebrate their faith in a spiritual centre.

Another key theme that emerged in relation to the physical environment was the way a pilgrimage must involve a "journey" and consequently, somewhere away from one's everyday domain. As Fiona commented, "a pilgrimage for me is travelling out with your normal environment and everyday life." For all of our respondents, the pilgrim had necessitated significant travel, normally involving a trip from the UK to continental Europe. However, further analysis of this idea reveals that the physical distance travelled is not the most important criteria of the journey:

*Katy: "I think the problem is we have got it into our minds that by going further afield we are making more of an effort, but I think that we all journey, and can all make good pilgrimages, as long as we set out and achieve the goal that we aimed for, no matter where we actually made the journey. I would not say you have to leave the county to make a pilgrimage, I mean it is all about a journey. And for some people it might be a hard journey just getting into the door of the church, or going to mass, so in that way yes I think for some it could be a pilgrimage. But for me mass, and prayer are my everyday norms, so going to Lourdes and other pilgrimage places, I feel helps me learn more about my faith and allows me to broaden my spiritual and faith journey."*

This further suggests that pilgrimages are individualistic experiences that involve a distancing from one's daily routines and realities. This physical distancing or escapism provides the additional benefit of time, or as one respondent puts it, "time for thoughts and prayer." Although from the above, it is evident that the physical environment is important, for many this is not the only or central aspect to a pilgrimage. Indeed, for some, the emotional journey becomes far more significant. This is explored further in the following section on the meanings of pilgrimage.

### MEANINGS

Given the personalized nature of pilgrimage, it can have many layers of meaning. Some see it as "enlightening," and a time for "spiritual growth in your inner faith." In this sense, it offers a reminder of the nature of existence:

*Daniel: "The basis of pilgrimage as far as I can understand it is the notion that our life on earth is transient, that we are all pilgrims in the sense that we have come, and we are moving and we are going, we cannot settle down here forever, we are on a pilgrimage. And the notion of going to holy places is to in a way, for many people anyway, is to bring that realization. .....to bring people to an awareness of the spiritual image of human existence."*

A common theme for many respondents was the potential of pilgrimage in relation to "the liberation of emotions." Particularly significant, was the idea of mixed emotions. While respondents mentioned "enjoyment," "pleasure" and "fulfilment," they also talked about "sacrifice," "effort," "tiredness," "exhaustion" and a "testing," "pushing" and "draining" of the self. Some respondents employ exchange terminology in an attempt to explain such mixed emotions. In other words, while the experience "can be quite exhausting both physically and mentally," this is "in exchange for spiritual fulfilment" and the achievement of other personal spiritual goals. As such, pilgrims are content to endure the "emotional cost" in order to reap individual benefits.

For some respondents it was this exchange aspect that differentiates a pilgrimage from a holiday:

*Mark: "there are times you will be in blasting heat and you think wow if I was on holiday I would be sunbathing or having a drink, but that is not why you're there, you're there to help the sick and to gain better spirituality yourself. So yes I agree there is and always should be a level of penance involved, I think that's what makes it worthwhile, and what separates normal holidays from pilgrimage."*

*Robert: "going on your holidays is solely to relax, but I think if you go on a pilgrimage you look to test yourself too, and it is not all about relaxing so I believe there is a level of penance and servitude involved."*

*Fiona: "A tourist is there to take pictures and do their nosy and see what the hype is and then move on, and to buy the tack, to buy the flashing Our lady and the huge tacky rosaries and all that. The pilgrim I feel is there for his or her purpose, you are there for your spiritual need, for you to take your time to pray the way you want to pray, to light your candles and all the things you want to do."*

Previous consumer research on experiential activities tends to adopt a positive tone in that they afford consumers the opportunity for relaxation, fun and pleasure (Goulding et al. 2008), and even in some cases a kind of flow experience (Celsi, Rose and Leigh 1993). In contrast, this study highlights the dual and complex nature of emotional release within the pilgrimage context. Alongside consumption and enjoyment, pilgrimages require "effort," "hard work" and "penance." These multiple meanings produce differential but complementing pilgrimage experiences, to which we now turn.

### EXPERIENCE

This section focuses on the various different roles played and performed by the pilgrim. These different roles can be partly explained by individual motivations behind the pilgrimage:

*Daniel: "In my case, when I go to a place it is more for historical reasons, more because I am interested in the history of religion, I am interested in where it comes from if you like, where its sources are, it was for this reason that I went to Jerusalem and Rome. It is maybe a bit idiosyncratic, I don't go for the usual reasons, I don't feel obliged to go as a kind of religious duty, I go out of interest to search out the underlying sort of historical meaning or truth behind the Christian faith."*

*Mark: "For me I have been to Lourdes as a member of the sick twice and as a helper once also. I feel that you get different things from the experience each time you go. When I went as a sick person, I found that it was meeting people and the generosity of people that moved me most, but as you go as a helper it changes as it is much more rigid and you have to do certain things. Making it more difficult at times, but also incredibly rewarding, as you know you are helping bring some peace to others who are now in a situation I was in before."*

The pilgrim site thus provides a stage where pilgrims are helpers, cultural and historical enthusiasts, worshippers or in search of healing.

Findings reveal that within the pilgrimage site, individuals often perform a dual role fluctuating between pilgrim and tourist. Despite these overlaps respondents are clear that "it is not by any means a holiday" and underlying motivation separate the pilgrim and the tourist.

Pilgrimages are often presented in a similar fashion as package holidays making it difficult to make a clear distinction between the two. We suggest that a distinction between journey and destination may be appropriate. Tourists consider the pilgrimage site as a destination, somewhere to explore while for pilgrims, the site is part of a journey. This calls to mind Belk, Ger and Askegaard's (2003) research on consumer desire. They argued that the journey towards aspirational consumption goals can be enjoyable in itself, sometimes outweighing the benefits that are achieved once the goal is realized. Within the context of pilgrimage, it is the journey itself that pilgrims value and in this respect it is pilgrims who gain the deepest satisfaction from the pilgrim site. This reinforces the need to think of place as comprising different elements; while the physical environment remains the same, individual experiences will differ (Belhassen, Caton and Stewart 2008).

## THE SOCIAL CONTEXT

Pilgrims can make their journey individually or as a part of an organized tour group, both of which provide slightly different experiences.

*Robert: "On your own you have the freedom to do as you wish meaning you can tailor your journey to suit you, your pilgrimage is to benefit you the way you want and need, extra prayer time, etc. But also on the organized trips you have more structure and routine, which can limit you, but you have comradeship, which can be nice and spiritual in its own way."*

Even those who make an individual pilgrimage are surrounded by other people, an issue that appeared to be central and "vital" to the pilgrimage experience for our respondents. Through a "common thirst for the some kind of spiritual reality," people from diverse nationalities and cultures are connected.

*Daniel: "I think it enhances or it should enhance the notion of human solidarity, and belonging and it should do away with the normal prejudices, like prejudices of race, etc..... I think that one of the great benefits of pilgrimage should be to see other people and realize that being human is what is important."*

*Isabelle: I also found that the mixing with the different nationalities was extremely rewarding and even though you don't speak the same language you all have a common understanding and can make yourself understood in the pilgrimage situation for you are there for the same purpose, searching and worshipping together.... I believe that it is about brotherhood and sisterhood, about realizing that we are all connected, about coming together."*

The idea of sharing a common purpose was something that several of the respondents mentioned. This creates a strong feeling of integration and togetherness and an environment where "there is so much love" and no barriers created by language or race. As Belk (2010) suggested, unlike economic exchange, such sharing helps to create a sense of community. The dissolution of boundaries between pilgrims creates a luminal state and strong evidence of communitas (Turner 1969).

While the common purpose often results in "a group of similarly minded people," pilgrimage also provides the opportunity to meet people with different religious beliefs and backgrounds. As Mark suggested, "there are so many that may not even come from a religious background, but they return year after year due to gaining something from the experience." Similarly, one of our respondents discussed an encounter with someone from a non-Catholic background:

*Penny/David: "one of the times I went to Lourdes, I met a man who was Grand Masonic Leader in Scotland, and he went just to see what all the hype was about at Lourdes, and felt so much passion and feeling when he entered the site, that he returned three times following from that, well he was on his fourth visit when I met him and he planned to return every year till as he put it 'God allowed.'"*

This provides an example of the way in which the pilgrimage site can incite the sharing of personal narratives creating unity even amongst strangers. To seasoned pilgrims, stories such as this serve to reinforce and confirm the miraculous and special nature of the pilgrimage site. Muniz and Schau (2005, 740) reported a somewhat similar situation in their investigation of the Apple Newton brand community where the telling of stories was identified as a form of "consumer magic." The emphasis on sociality contrasts with Palmer and Gallagher (2007) who found that the social support offered through religious institutions plays a less significant role in everyday life. Instead, it reinforces the importance of self-other relations with spatial environments.

## CONSUMPTION EXPERIENCE OR SPIRITUAL EXPERIENCE?

In this section we explore the interplay between religion and consumption, investigating whether respondents view pilgrim sites as truly sacred or if they have become contaminated by commercialization. Many of our respondents accepted that marketing, consumption and tourism are inevitable elements of pilgrimages and indeed, several simply explained marketing as an "everyday norm"

*David: "consumerism is a part of everyday life, so why would religion, which let's face it is a huge part of peoples' lives not also be included in this consumerism. It is just that when people think religion, they automatically believe it should be neutral from all changes, but it evolves and changes with life like everything."*

Nevertheless this does not appear to detract from the benefits of the pilgrimage and some even highlighted the resulting economic benefits of pilgrimage to towns surrounding the shrines. However, this perspective depends on the creation of certain boundary lines over which marketing cannot intrude. Several respondents discussed this idea in relation to Lourdes, arguing that as long as the grotto (where the visions of the Virgin Mary were seen) itself remains sacred, they do not object to commercialization outside the gates:

*Fiona: "to be honest at the grotto it is like another world, the grotto and the basilica is like another place completely, the minute you go through the gates it is the strangest thing, but it is almost like a presence enters you, and it stays with you throughout the domain, and it happens every time you go through the gates not just the first time. You see something different every time you go into the domain. They have managed to keep the bustle and tack of the commercial side of Lourdes away from the domain."*

Similarly, Penny suggested that "once you enter the domain, there is just so much relaxation, there is none of the bustle, or the buying and the selling." The movement from "busy streets" to "tranquility" allows for a change in mindset and complete absorption in the task at hand so that "you are not thinking about anything other than your faith and Our Lady." O'Guinn and Belk (1989) noted that visitors experienced a similar feeling of other-worldliness in Heritage Village, USA, the religious theme park, despite the presence of a shopping mall and other forms of entertainment. However, in the present study, findings suggest that the Christian pilgrim site can provide a complete and temporary escape from the marketplace as it is free from "tackiness" and "commercialization." In this respect, it can remain pure, outside the domain of contemporary consumer culture. Reminiscent of Belk's (2010, 730) conclusion on sharing, we can argue that an understanding of pilgrimage challenges "the encroachment of the perspective that all the world is a market and everything and everyone within it is an exchangeable commodity."

A few respondents discussed the way in which the surrounding consumer culture inadvertently contributed to a more intense pilgrimage experience:

*Daniel: "I believe that you just have to cling to your faith and ignore all the tackiness, and all the nonsensical things that happen around you whilst on your pilgrimage. I suppose you could say that is new form of penance in modern day pilgrimage that you have to eradicate from your mind, all the irrelevant things happening around you."*

Likewise, Irene concurred that an aim of pilgrimage is to "challenge myself to block out the everyday live and focus on my faith and religion." Others discussed more straight-forward benefits of the consumerist element, for example, some respondents appear to get enjoyment from the consumer environment that surrounds pilgrimage sites such as the opportunity to "go for dinner and maybe have a glass of wine or whatever with my friends." Others also like to shops for souvenirs:

*Isabelle: "I got a lot of enjoyment picking presents to take back for people in my church, you just had to watch where you went for them, obviously there are the tacky shops but there are also some really lovely and very spiritual shops which sell some lovely religious tokens."*

*Katy: "And I also think that brining back a small souvenir for people from a holy pilgrimage site can mean the world to the person, allows them to feel a part of that pilgrimage themselves and allows them to know they are thought about and loved."*

Souvenirs appear to provide a tangible memento or symbol of the journey both for the pilgrim or a way of spreading the sacredness to others. For some pilgrims, the opportunity to consume and relax is essential. Indeed one respondent argued that without escapism through the tourist market, "it would be torture." This supports the earlier discussion on the fuzzy boundaries surrounding the tourist and pilgrim roles.

## CONCLUSIONS

This paper focuses on the consumption of sacred place within the context of the Christian pilgrimage. In relation to theoretical contributions, we raise the profile of place within consumer research, addressing Sherry's (2000, 277) concern that consumption theory often neglects "place as a lived experience." Increased mobility, alongside technological advances, has resulted in a lack of embeddedness or indeed, placelessness appearing as a central feature of consumer culture (Cushman 1990). However, we demonstrate that place can have significant meaning in our lives, indeed, the spiritual and emotional release achieved by our respondents cannot be decontextualized from the physical places in which they occur. In this respect, place is central to our understandings and experiences.

We also contribute to understandings of sacred consumption, in particular the relationship between the sacred and the profane, discussions which have only a marginal place within consumer research literature (Arnould 2004). Much of the research in this area tends to focus on the sacralization process, whereby sacred and secular meanings intertwine as consumption extends far beyond a core commercial purpose. We attempt to redress this balance by exploring the issue of secularization and the way in which spiritual and religious meanings have become increasingly commercialized. We began this paper wondering if "consuming pilgrimage" was an appropriate phrase to use in the title. However, throughout the findings we have highlighted the fuzzy boundaries between the sacred and the profane and illustrated that places can combine both sacred and profane elements. We suggest that religion can have a place within consumer culture and that the presence of commercialization does not appear to reduce or dampen the religious or spiritual experience. Despite commercialization, pilgrimages still offer the opportunity to "transcend existence as a mere biological being coping with the everyday world" (Belk, Wallendorf and Sherry 1989, 2).

Place attachment theory is often considered in relation to our homes or places that we visit on a regular basis. However, through an examination of the physical environment, experiences and meanings of pilgrimage sites, we demonstrate how consumers can also experience strong attachment to places that are far from our place of residence yet places that are deemed to deserve reverence. Our findings reveal that the combination of sacred space and special activity or practices creates a sense of utopia (Maclaran and Brown 2005). Sacred sites place the consumer, providing a welcome feeling of belonging in light of the increasing displacement associated with consumer culture. Visiting such sites of enhancement can have important spiritual benefits. Within consumer culture theory there has been much debate surrounding rationality and emotion. We suggest that what is missing from this discussion is spirituality. As well as receiving functional and emotional benefits through consumption, spiritual benefits are also achievable. Indeed, as humans it could be argued that we need and seek some form of connection with the spiritual side of existence.

## REFERENCES

Arnould, Eric J. (2004), "Beyond the Sacred-Profane Dichotomy in Consumer Research", in *Advances in Consumer Research*, Vol. 34, ed. Barbara E. Kahn and Mary Frances Luce, Valdosta, GA: Association for Consumer Research, 52-54.

Arnould, Eric J. and Linda L. Price (1993), "River Magic: Extraordinary Experience and the Extended Service Encounter", *Journal of Consumer Research*, 20 (June), 24-44.

Belhassen, Yaniv, Kellee Caton, and William P. Stewart (2008), "The Search for Authenticity in the Pilgrim Experience", *Annals of Tourism Research*, 35 (3), 668-689.

Belk, Russell (2010), "Sharing", *Journal of Consumer Research,* 36 (Feb), 715-734.

Belk, Russell, Melanie Wallendorf and John F. Sherry (1989), "The Sacred and the Profane in Consumer Behavior: Theodicy on the Odyssey", *Journal of Consumer Research*, 16 (June),1-38.

Belk, Russell, Ger Güliz and Søren Askegaard (2003), "The Fire of Desire: A Multi-sited Inquiry into Consumer Passion", *Journal of Consumer Research*, 30 (December), 326-351.

Campbell, Colin (2004), "I Shop Therefore I Know that I am: The Metaphysical Basis of Modern Consumerism," in *Elusive Consumption,* ed. Karin Ekstrom and Helene Brembeck, Oxford, Berg, 27-44.

Celsi, Richard L., Randall L. Rose and Thomas W. Leigh (1993), "An Exploration of High-Risk Leisure Consumption through Skydiving", *Journal of Consumer Research*, 20 (June), 1-23.

Curasi, Carolyn Folkman, Linda L. Price and Eric J. Arnould (2004), "How Individuals Cherished Possessions Become Families' Inalienable Wealth", *Journal of Consumer Research*, 31(December), 609-622.

Cushman, Phillip (1990), "Why the Self is Empty: Towards a Historically Situated Psychology", *American Psychologist*, 45 (May), 599-611.

Davis, Teresa and Jeaney Yip (2004), "Reconciling Christianity and Modernity: Australian Youth and Religion," in Advances in Consumer Research, ed. Barbara E. Kahn and Mary Frances Luce, Valdosta, GA: Association for Consumer Research, 113-117.

Ger, Guliz and Richard Wilk (2005), "Religious Material Culture: Morality, Modernity, and Aesthetics," in *Advances in Consumer Research*, Vol. 32, ed. Geeta Menon and Akshay R. Rao, Duluth, MN: Association for Consumer Research, 79-81.

Goulding, Christina, Avi Shankar, Richard Elliott and Robin Canniford (2008), "The Marketplace Management of Illicit Pleasure", *Journal of Consumer Research*, 35 (Feb), 759-771.

Hamilton, Kathy and Paul Hewer (2009), "Salsa Magic: An Exploratory Netnographic Analysis of the Salsa Experience", in *Advances in Consumer Research* Vol. 36, ed. Ann L. McGill and Sharon Shavitt, Duluth MN: Association for Consumer Research, 502-508.

Kosmin, B.A. and E. Mayer (2001), *American Religious Identification Survey 2001,* New York, The Graduate Centre of the City University of New York.

Kozinets, Robert (2001), "Utopian Enterprise: Articulating the Meanings of Star Trek's Culture of Consumption", *Journal of Consumer Research*, 28 (June), 67-88.

Kozinets, Robert (2002), "Can Consumers Escape the Market? Emancipatory Illuminations from Burning Man", *Journal of Consumer Research*, 29, (June), 20-38.

Maclaran, Pauline and Stephen Brown (2005), "The Center Cannot Hold: Consuming the Utopian Marketplace", *Journal of Consumer Research*, 32 (Sept), 311- 323.

Morinins, Alan (1992) "Introduction: the territory of the anthropology of pilgrimage," in *Sacred Journeys: The Anthropology of Pilgrimage*, ed. Alan Morinis, Westport: Greenwood Press.

Muniz, Albert M. and Hope Schau (2005), "Religiosity in the Abandaned Apple Newton Brand Community', *Journal of Consumer Research*, 31, (March), 737-747.

O'Guinn, Thomas C. (1991), "Touching Greatness: The Central Midwest Barry Manilow Fan Club," in *Highways and Buyways: Naturalistic Research from the Consumer Behavior Odyssey,* Special Volumes, Association for Consumer Research, 102-111.

O'Guinn, Thomas C. and Russell W. Belk (1989), "Heaven on Earth: Consumption at Heritage Village, USA", *Journal of Consumer Research*, 16 (September): 227-238.

Palmer, Adrian and Damian Gallagher (2007), "Religiosity, Relationships and Consumption: A Study of Church Going in Ireland", *Consumption, Markets and Culture,* 10 (1), 31-49.

Rindfleish, Jennifer (2005), "Consuming the Self: New Age Spirituality as "Social Product" in Consumer Society", *Consumption, Markets and Culture*, 8 (4), 343-360.

Ritzer, George (2005), *Revolutionizing the Means of Consumption: Enchanting a Disenchanted World*, US: Pine Forge Press.

Scott, Linda and Pauline Maclaran (2009), "Roll your own" Religion: Consumer Culture and the Spiritual Vernacular", in *Advances in Consumer Research*, Vol. 36, ed. Ann L. McGill and Sharon Shavitt, Duluth, MN: Association for Consumer Research, 60-63.

Sherry, John F. (2000), "Place, Technology, and Representation", *Journal of Consumer Research*, 27 (Sept), 273-279.

Thompson, Craig J., Howard R. Pollio and Willam B. Locander (1994), "The Spoken and the Unspoken: A Hermeneutic Approach to Understanding the Cultural Viewpoints that Underlie Consumers' Expressed Meanings", *Journal of Consumer Research,* 21 (3), 432-452.

Timothy, D.J. & Olsen, D.H., (2006), 'Tourism, Religion & Spiritual Journeys', Chp.1, pg. 3, Routledge, Taylor & Francis Groups.

Turner, Victor (1969), *The Ritual Process: Structure and Antistructure*, Chicago: Aldine.

Voas, D. (2006) "Religious decline in Scotland: New Evidence on Timing and Spatial Patterns," *Journal for the Scientific Study of Religion*, 45 (1), 107-118.

# Consumer Reactions to Corporate Decisions to Outsource Labor Abroad

Silvia Grappi, University of Modena and Reggio Emilia, Italy
Simona Romani, Luiss Guido Carli, Italy

## ABSTRACT

This paper analyzes consumer reactions in the form of word of mouth communication to positive, negative, and hybrid (i.e. both positive and negative at the same time) CSR information. We also examine the mediating role of emotions in explaining these reactions, while controlling for the moderating role of consumer ethnocentrism.

*Fiat SpA, the Italian Turin-based car-manufacturer, is forging ahead with its decision to close its Termini Imerese plant in Sicily. Fiat's head of institutional relations has informed labor unions that the company has no intention of altering their plans to halt this facility's production after 2011. In fact, Fiat is currently in the process of gradually off-shoring production in countries where wage rates are a fraction of those in Italy, claiming that it is no longer competitive to keep the Termini Imerese plant going. The Italian government has held off on a decision regarding new "cash-for-clunkers" incentives, as the Minister for Industry insists that Fiat must maintain current levels of production and employment. Although Fiat does anticipate a "significant" drop in sales, its Chief Executive Officer stated that the company will not defer its plans and would fully agree with not renewing these incentives. The decision to close the Termini Imerese plant, which currently employs 1,658 full-time employees, is a model example of corporate decisions to outsource jobs abroad, which leave domestic workers in great difficulty, with no regard for the economical and social implications for that community, or indeed the whole country. In fact, this town is situated in Southern Italy where unemployment rates are extremely high and there are few alternatives available besides emigration. Fiat's essentially financially motivated decision has attracted much attention throughout Italy, especially because of the impact this is having and will continue to have on the workers and entire Termini Imerese community.*

Research available on consumers' responses to a company's Corporate Social Responsibility (CSR) record generally focuses on either positive or negative information. However, in the marketplace it is possible at times for consumers to be simultaneously exposed to different valenced CSR information on the same company in one or more domains.

This paper attempts to examine this situation with the aim of analyzing consumer reactions, in the form of word of mouth communication, to CSR information that is positive, negative, and hybrid – i.e. both positive and negative at the same time. In detail, we investigate the mediating role of emotions in explaining consumers' reactions to a company's CSR practices, controlling for the moderating role of consumer ethnocentrism.

The CSR context selected for the purposes of this study is the company decision to either source man-power from within the home market (positive CSR information) or totally/partially outsource these jobs abroad (negative/hybrid CSR information). The practice of outsourcing labor abroad has attracted much attention over recent years and been heavily criticized for the associated ethical issues. It is possible for consumers to perceive this choice as a sign of the ethical and/or moral commitment of the company to its home country; outsourcing sends a message to consumers that the company no longer supports the local or even national community and/or economy. Therefore, the locating of production abroad has CSR implications that can extend well beyond awareness on a local level and notably even come to backfire on the brand. Consumers may well conclude "Why should I sustain them? They don't support us anymore!"

## BACKGROUND AND CONCEPTUAL FRAMEWORK

Corporate Social Responsibility (CSR) is defined as a company's "status and activities with respect to its perceived social obligation" (Brown and Dacin 1997: 68). A number of studies show how information on CSR practices can influence consumer evaluations in terms of their attitude towards the company (Brown and Dacin 1997; Mohr and Webb 2005; Sen and Bhattacharya 2001; Sen, Bhattacharya, Korschun 2006), purchasing behavior (Sen and Bhattacharya 2001; Klein and Dawar 2004), and identification with the corporation (Sen and Bhattacharya 2001). It has also been demonstrated that consumers are more sensitive to irresponsible than responsible corporate behavior. In other words, we witness an asymmetric effect where doing bad harms more than doing good helps (e.g., Sen and Battacharya 2001, Battacharya and Sen 2004).

Although the extant research has examined the impact on consumer evaluations of either positive or negative CSR information as well as, more recently, the inconsistencies between a company's claimed CSR standards and their actual behavior (Wagner, Luz, and Weitz 2009), there is a lack of studies on reactions to hybrid CSR behavior (both responsible and irresponsible at the same time) and the possible role played by emotions in these responses. This paper introduces a conceptual framework to examine the specific consumer reaction of word of mouth to CSR behavior as well as taking into consideration the moderating role of individual ethnocentrism and mediating effects of emotions.

Corporate policy and practice on outsourcing jobs abroad provides an ideal context for investigating these effects. Companies are faced with the choice of either maintaining a domestic workforce in the aim of supporting the national economy (positive CSR behavior), or outsourcing domestic jobs abroad for opportunistic reasons (negative CSR behavior), or opting for a partial outsourcing of labor (hybrid CSR behavior).

In order to define these various CSR contexts it is possible to consider the literature on Country of Origin (CO) (Guran-Canli and Maheswaran 2000a, 2000b; Verlegh, Steenkamp and Meulenberg 2005), and, in particular, the critical distinction between the concept of country of design (CD) and country of manufacture (CM) (Ahmed and d'Astous 2008). Given that products can be designed in one country and manufactured or assembled in another, the CD and CM are both important elements in the analysis of responsible/irresponsible CSR behavior.

One factor that can play a key role in reactions to companies' outsourcing decisions is ethnocentrism. This expresses the point of view that the group to which one belongs is the center of everything (i.e. the home country) with all other groups (i.e. foreign countries) judged against this standard. Consumer ethnocentrism is the tendency to overestimate the quality of domestic products (Sharma, Shimp, and Shin 1995; Shimp and Sharma 1987) and favor products originating from one's own country over those imported (Ouellet 2007). The purchase of foreign products can be viewed as improper because it costs domestic jobs and harms the economy, or even as simply unpatriotic (Sharma, Shimp, & Shin, 1995; Shimp & Sharma, 1987).

Consideration should also be given to the mediating role of emotions in the relationship between CSR practices and consumer behavior. It is reasonable to expect that negative emotions play a central role in the CSR negative context, and likewise that positive emotions feature prominently in the CSR positive context, with both being associated in CRS hybrid contexts. An explanation for these responses may be found in the category of moral emotions. Morality can be defined as judgments that "must bear on the interest or welfare either of society as a whole or at least of persons other than the judge or agent" (Gewirth 1984: 978). Moral emotions are therefore those activated in moral contexts that prompt individual moral behavior, clearly connected to the interests of others (Haidt 2003). For the negative situation we have chosen to focus on the emotion anger, given that it is a typical reaction to unjustified insult and can be triggered on one's own or other's behalves (Haidt 2003), while for the positive context we concentrate on gratitude, in being a classic example of a positive valenced affect experienced in response to the benevolence of another. Gratitude is experienced especially when the recipient considers the benefits received as unexpected and/or costly to the "benefactor" (Tangney, Stuewig, and Mashek 2007).

## RESEARCH HYPOTHESES

We hypothesize that ethnocentrism plays a central role in moderating the overall effect of CSR practices on consumers' word of mouth behavior in contexts characterized by total or partial outsourcing of domestic jobs abroad (negative and hybrid CSR practices). Given that in these contexts ethnocentric consumers can perceive a threat to them as well as the group they belong to (home country), we predict that their evaluation of the company's decision is heavily influenced by their level of ethnocentrism.

**H1**: *The negative effect of the decision to outsource domestic jobs abroad (negative CSR practice) on consumers' word of mouth is moderated by consumers' ethnocentrism.*

**H2**: *The negative effect of the decision to partially outsource domestic jobs abroad (hybrid CSR practices) on consumers' word of mouth is moderated by consumers' ethnocentrism.*

We also predict that a company's decisions on outsourcing often give rise to moral emotions. Given that these choices closely relate to consumers' sense of national belonging and what they perceive to be in the interests of their country, we hypothesize that these moral emotions play a mediating role in the moderated effect between the "CSR practices–to–word of mouth" connection. We examine the role of the negative moral emotion of anger in the negative CSR context, and both anger and the positive moral emotion of gratitude in hybrid CSR contexts, where the appraisal of situations characterized by both positive and negative corporate practices can activate mixed feelings (Ruth, Brunel, and Otnes 2002).

**H3**: *The negative moral emotion of anger has a mediating role in the moderated negative effect of the decision to outsource domestic jobs abroad (negative CSR practice) on consumers' word of mouth.*

**H4**: *The moral emotions of gratitude and anger have a mediating role in the moderated negative effect of the decision to partially outsource domestic jobs abroad (hybrid CSR practices) on consumers' word of mouth.*

We can hypothesize that the role of ethnocentrism differs in the positive CSR context. In this case, the lack of a direct "threat" to domestic jobs would suggest an absence of the overall moderation of ethnocentrism. Here, we would expect the positive moral emotion of gratitude to have a mediating role in the "CSR practices–to–word of mouth" connection. Although we can expect ethnocentrism to have a reduced role in the positive context compared to that negative or hybrid, it may still have an influence on eliciting moral emotions and/or consumer actions.

**H5**: *The positive moral emotion of gratitude has a mediating role in the positive effect of the decision to support the national economy (positive CSR practice) on consumers' word of mouth. Consumers' ethnocentrism moderates this mediating process.*

## METHOD

The methodological approach adopted for testing the above hypotheses involves the use of an experimental design, conducted on Italian consumers. Pretests were conducted in order to select both the product and foreign country where the manufacture and/or design of the product is/are delocalized.

*Pretests.* First, subjects were asked to rate their overall level of knowledge of three different products chosen as representative of three diverse product categories (so as to ensure a wide range of initial possible options): a digital camera (electronic); a pair of sunglasses (fashion); and ceramic tiles (technical). In each pretest, performed separately on each of the products, the consumers rated their knowledge on a seven-point scale: sunglasses (n = 30; M = 4.00, std = 0.95); digital camera (n = 30; M = 3.57, std = 1.19); ceramic tiles (n = 30; M = 3.23; std = 0.94). In conclusion, the final product selected, with the highest level of knowledge among respondents, was sunglasses. Regarding the choice of foreign setting for the product's delocalized manufacture and/or design, we asked respondents to rate, on a seven-point scale, ten countries (Australia, Belgium, China, France, Japan, the UK, Morocco, Russia, Spain, and the USA) in terms of their ability in the manufacturing and, independently, design of the product (n = 30). The country selected, resulting as being considered the least skilled in both fields, was Morocco (M = 2.03, std = 1.10 as manufacturer; M = 1.33, std = 0.61 as designer). This choice is based on the need to put emphasis on the negative aspects of corporate behavior related to the outsourcing of labor (the company decision is motivated by purely economic motives and unrelated to workers' skills).

*Procedure and subjects.* In order to cover the relevant CSR contexts - (1) positive CSR: support of national economy (CD Italy/ CM Italy); (2) negative CSR: total outsourcing of domestic jobs abroad (CD Morocco / CM Morocco); (3) hybrid CSR: partial outsourcing of domestic jobs abroad (CD Italy / CM Morocco; CD Morocco / CM Italy) - and to test our hypotheses, we employed a 2 (CDs) × 2 (CMs) between-subjects design.

Initially, participants were provided with some background information about a fictitious company that produces and sells sunglasses, and then presented with a scenario of this company's CSR policies regarding support of the national economy. After reading this description, participants completed the relevant questionnaire, were debriefed and then thanked.

The participant group, randomly assigned to conditions, consisted of a sample of 339 consumers, both male (49.6%) and female (50.4%), with a mean age of 39. Of this sample, 70 questionnaires were collected for the control condition (without information on the company's outsourcing practices).

**Dependent variables.** All dependent variables were assessed using a scale from one to seven. First, subjects were asked to express the degree to which they felt given emotions based on the information they had just read, and then rate their intentions to practice word of mouth about the company. Subjects then responded to questions designed to measure their level of ethnocentrism and check for manipulation, and indicated their age and gender.

*Moral emotions.* Subjects were asked to express the degree to which they felt each of the given emotion descriptors on the basis of the information they had just read, using measures selected from the literature (Laros and Steenkamp 2005; Richins 1997; Shaver et al. 1987). The items used for anger are angry and very annoyed ($r = 0.94$), and for gratitude, thankful and feeling appreciation ($r = 0.78$). The items measuring the same emotions were averaged to form the emotions indexes.

*Consumer worth of mouth.* Subjects were asked to express their degree of agreement with various statements, aimed at measuring their intention to practice word of mouth: "I intend to recommend this company's products to friends, relatives, and acquaintances," "I intend to talk well of this company to friends, relatives, and acquaintances," and "I intend to mention this company to friends, relatives, and acquaintances" ($\alpha = 0.96$).

*Ethnocentrism.* Following Ouellet (2007), ethnocentrism was measured using four items selected from the CET scale (Shimp and Sharma 1987): "A good citizen does not buy foreign products," "It is not right to purchase foreign products because it puts us out of jobs," "We should purchase products manufactured in our country instead of letting other countries get rich off us," and "We should buy from foreign countries only those products that we cannot obtain within our own country" ($\alpha = 0.93$).

*Manipulation checks.* The final section of the questionnaire controls for manipulation, by asking respondents to recall where the product in question was designed and manufactured, and rate their perception of the company's CSR practices regarding outsourcing.

## RESULTS

A comparison was made between the experimental and control groups (Gurhan-Canli and Maheswaran 2000a), and no systematic effects were observed with gender and age as covariates.

*Manipulation checks.* Participants correctly recalled the product's CD and CM in each experimental condition. An ANOVA on the perception of the company's CSR practices (Tab. 1) revealed a clear differentiation between the four groups ($F(3, 265) = 68.56, p < .005$). Post hoc analysis revealed significant differences between the negative condition (CM Morocco / CD Morocco) and all the other (hybrid and positive) conditions; the positive condition (CM Italy / CD Italy) and all the other (hybrid and negative) conditions; and no differences between the two hybrid conditions (CM Morocco / CD Italy; CM Italy / CD Morocco) ($t = .421; p. = 0.67$).

**Table 1. Means (std deviations) of consumers' perceptions of the company's CSR practices**

|  | CD Italy | CD Morocco |
|---|---|---|
| CM Italy | 6.31 (0.85) | 4.19 (1.12) |
| CM Morocco | 4.27 (1.16) | 3.42 (1.45) |

Note – cell size ranges from $n = 59$ to $n = 70$

*Word of mouth.* First, we tested the bearing of CSR practices on consumers' word of mouth by comparing two groups: one corresponding exclusively to the control condition (with no information on the company's CSR practices); and a second, complete with all the other conditions. A t-test on the consumers' word of mouth index revealed that CSR decisions do indeed have a significant impact ($t = 5.34, P < .005$). An ANOVA on negative word of mouth revealed a great differentiation between the groups ($F(4, 334) = 50.28, p < .005$). Post hoc analysis revealed significant differences between the negative CSR condition (CM Morocco / CD Morocco) and all the other (hybrid and positive) conditions; the positive CSR condition (CM Italy / CD Italy) and all the other (hybrid and positive) conditions; and no differences between the two hybrid conditions (CM Morocco / CD Italy; CM Italy / CD Morocco) ($t = 1.38; p. = 0.17$).

We then tested our research hypotheses by analyzing the role of moral emotions in the "CSR practices–to–word of mouth" connection. Tables 2 and 3 present the resulting means and standard deviations of the dependent variable and moral emotions for each experimental condition.

**Table 2. Means (standard deviations) of word of mouth**

|  | CD Italy | CD Morocco |
|---|---|---|
| CM Italy | 5.73 (1.17) | 3.35 (1.40) |
| CM Morocco | 3.67 (1.33) | 2.85 (1.45) |
| Control group | 5.01 (1.44) | |

Note – cell size ranges from $n = 59$ to $n = 70$

**Table 3. Means (standard deviations) of moral emotions**

|  |  | CD Italy | CD Morocco |
|---|---|---|---|
| anger gratitude | CM Italy | 1.38 (.73) 5.32 (1.50) | 3.19 (1.97) 2.41 (1.59) |
| anger gratitude | CM Morocco | 2.71 (1.88) 2.96 (1.72) | 3.52 (2.24) 1.80 (1.08) |
| anger gratitude | Control group (no CO information) | 1.69 (1.14) 3.74 (1.81) | |

Note – cell size ranges from $n = 59$ to $n = 70$

In order to detect the role of moral emotions in explaining consumers' word of mouth within the experimental sets, we followed the approach of Muller, Judd, and Yzerbyt (2005) in analyzing the moderated mediation and mediated moderation processes. The relevant variables are: (1) the manipulated independent variable $X$ (the company's outsourcing policies: the product's CM and CD), indicating the different experimental conditions; (2) the outcome variable $Y$ (word of mouth), measuring the response of participants presumed to be affected by the treatment; (3) the mediating variables $Me$ (moral emotions), which are also responses expected to be influenced by the treatment; and (4) the continuously measured moderating variable, $Mo$ (ethnocentrism), an individual difference variable assumed to be unaffected by the treatment.

The *mediated moderation* process can only occur when moderation takes place. Given that the magnitude of the overall treatment effect on the outcome depends on an individual difference (in this case, ethnocentrism), then the question of mediated moderation is concerned with the mediating process that is responsible for that moderation. The *moderated mediation* process occurs if the mediating process responsible for producing the effect of the treatment on the outcome depends on the moderator variable value. Given that the moderator is an individual difference variable, in this case the mediating process that intervenes between the treatment and outcome varies according to people's different levels of ethnocentrism.

There are three models that underlie both these processes (Muller, Judd, and Yzerbyt 2005). The first assesses the moderation of the overall treatment effect:

$$Y = \beta_{10} + \beta_{11}X + \beta_{12}Mo + \beta_{13}XMo + \varepsilon_1 \qquad (1)$$

The second allows the treatment effect on the mediator to be moderated:

$$Me = \beta_{20} + \beta_{21}X + \beta_{22}Mo + \beta_{23}XMo + \varepsilon_2 \qquad (2)$$

And the third allows both the mediator's (partial) effect on the outcome and the residual effect of the treatment on the outcome, controlling for the mediator, to be moderated:

$$Y = \beta_{30} + \beta_{31}X + \beta_{32}Mo + \beta_{33}XMo + \beta_{34}Me + \beta_{35}MeMo + \varepsilon_3 \quad (3)$$

In all three models, $X$ and $Mo$ are uncorrelated and all the variables are centered at their mean, with the exception of the outcome (Muller et al. 2005). In distinct analyses for each moral emotion (gratitude and anger) we estimated models 1 through 3 to demonstrate mediated moderation and moderated mediation processes.

*Mediated moderation.* In model 1, we would expect $\beta_{13}$ to be significant, indicating overall treatment moderation; in models 2 and 3, either (or both) of two patterns should exist: both $\beta_{23}$ and $\beta_{34}$ and/or both $\beta_{21}$ and $\beta_{35}$ are significant. In addition, the moderation of the residual treatment effect $\beta_{33}$ should be reduced in magnitude compared with that of the overall treatment effect. In order to understand the mediated moderation effect, the following calculations prove useful:

the simple effects of treatment on the mediator (emotion) at values of one $SD$ above and below the moderator (ethnocentrism) mean score: $\beta_{21} + (\beta_{23} * \pm SD_{Mo})$ \qquad (4)

the simple effect of the mediator on word of mouth at values of one $SD$ above and below the ethnocentrism mean score: $\beta_{34} + (\beta_{35} * \pm SD_{Mo})$ \qquad (5)

the total indirect effects through the mediator (emotion), taking the product of the two simple effects (4) and (5) for each of the two ethnocentrism values

*Moderated mediation.* In model 1, we would expect $\beta_{11}$ to be significant, whereas not $\beta_{13}$. In models 2 and 3, either (or both) of two patterns should exist: both $\beta_{23}$ and $\beta_{34}$ and/or both $\beta_{21}$ and $\beta_{35}$ are significant. In consequence the residual treatment effect

should now be moderated, that is, $\beta_{33}$ may be significant, but this is not a necessary condition for establishing moderated mediation (Muller et al. 2005). It also proves useful to consider the following calculations:

the simple effects of the manipulation on the mediator (emotion) at one $SD$ above and below the moderator mean using the following equation: $\beta_{21} + (\beta_{23} * \pm SD_{Mo})$ \qquad (4)

the simple effect of the mediator on word of mouth at values of one $SD$ above and below the ethnocentrism mean score: $\beta_{34} + (\beta_{35} * \pm SD_{Mo})$ \qquad (5)

the total indirect effects through the mediator, taking the product of the two simple effects (4) and (5) for each of the two ethnocentrism values

the simple residual treatment effects at the two ethnocentrism levels: $\beta_{31} + (\beta_{33} * \pm SD_{Mo})$ \qquad (6)

Our findings, presented in Tables 4 and 5, demonstrate that consumers' ethnocentrism is capable of moderating the overall negative effect of corporate decisions regarding the total/partial outsourcing of domestic jobs abroad (negative/hybrid CSR practices) on consumers' word of mouth behavior, supporting H1 and H2.

We can also observe that, in the negative CSR context, the negative moral emotion of anger is capable of influencing word of mouth communication through a mediated moderation process, thus supporting H3. The effect of negative CSR practice on negative word of mouth interacting with the emotion of anger, is greater when the level of ethnocentrism is high (-0.57) compared to low (-0.39). After controlling for the mediator and its interaction with the moderator the residual direct effect of the manipulation on the outcome results as -0.57 (reduced from -0.63).

In the two hybrid CSR contexts both the moral emotions of gratitude and anger prove capable of affecting word of mouth through mediated moderation processes, thus supporting H4. In the first (CM Morocco / CD Italy), the effect of mixed CSR practices on word of mouth, interacting with the emotion of anger, is greater when the level of ethnocentrism is high (-0.46) compared to low (-0.04). After controlling for the mediator and its interaction with the moderator, the residual direct effect of the manipulation on the outcome is less moderated by ethnocentrism at -0.38 (reduced from -0.49). In the case of gratitude, the effect can also be seen to be greater when the level of ethnocentrism is high (-0.37) compared to low (-0.01), with the residual effect reduced from -0.49 to -0.41. In the second hybrid CSR context (CM Italy / CD Morocco), the effect on word of mouth interacting with the emotion of anger, is greater when the level of ethnocentrism is high (-0.62) compared to low (-0.14), with the residual effect reduced from -0.55 to -0.43. And again for gratitude the effect is greater when the level of ethnocentrism is high (-0.45) rather than low (-0.25), the residual effect is reduced from -0.55 to -0.49.

### Table 4. The mediated moderation and moderated mediation processes

| | Process | Emotions | |
| --- | --- | --- | --- |
| | | Gratitude | Anger |
| Set 1 – positive CSR (CM Italy / CD Italy) | $b_{13}$ = -.01, sig.=ns Moderated Mediation | $b_{21} \neq 0$ and $b_{35} \neq 0$ | No hypothesized effect |
| Set 2 – hybrid CSR (CM Italy / CD Morocco) | $b_{13}$ = -.55, sig.=.00 Mediated Moderation | $b_{23} \neq 0$ and $b_{34} \neq 0$ | $b_{23} \neq 0$ and $b_{34} \neq 0$ |
| Set 3 – hybrid CSR (CM Morocco / CD Italy) | $b_{13}$ =-.49, sig.=.00 Mediated Moderation | $b_{23} \neq 0$ and $b_{34} \neq 0$ | $b_{23} \neq 0$ and $b_{34} \neq 0$ |
| Set 4 – negative CSR (CM Morocco / CD Morocco) | $b_{13}$ = -.63, sig.=.00 Mediated Moderation | No hypothesized effect | $b_{23} \neq 0$ and $b_{34} \neq 0$ |

## Table 5. Simple and total effects in mediated moderation and moderated mediation processes

| | | High ethnocentrism | Low ethnocentrism |
|---|---|---|---|
| **Set 1 - CM Italy / CD Italy** | | | |
| Gratitude | simple effect of the manipulation on the mediator | 1.47 + (0.04*1.75) = **1.54** | 1.48 + (0.04*-1.75) = **1.40** |
| | simple effect of the emotion on WOM | 0.30 + (-0.04 * 1.75) = **0.23** | 0.30 + (-0.04 * -1.75) = **0.37** |
| | total indirect effect | 1.54 * 0.23 = **0.35** | 1.40 * 0.37 = **0.52** |
| | simple residual treatment effect | 0.17 + (0.04*1.75) = **0.24** | 0.17 + (0.04* - 1.75) = **0.10** |
| **Set 2 - CM Italy / CD Morocco** | | | |
| Gratitude | simple effect of the manipulation on the mediator | -1.36 + (-0.37*1.90) = **-2.06** | -1.36 + (-0.37*-1.90) = **-0.66** |
| | simple effect of the emotion on WOM | 0.30 + (-0.04 *1.90) = **0,22** | 0.30 + (-0.04 * -1.90) = **0.38** |
| | total indirect effect | -2.06 * 0.22 = **-0.45** | -0.66 * 0.38 = **-0.25** |
| Anger | simple effect of the manipulation on the mediator | 1.62 + (0.63*1.90) = **2.82** | 1.62 + (0.63*-1.90) = **0.42** |
| | simple effect of the emotion on WOM | -0.28 + (0.03 *1.90) = **-0.22** | -0.28 + (0.03 * -1.90) = **-0.34** |
| | total indirect effect | 2.82 * -0.22 = **-0.62** | 0.42 * -0.34 = **-0.14** |
| **Set 3 - CM Morocco / CD Italy** | | | |
| Gratitude | simple effect of the manipulation on the mediator | -0.82 + (-0.43*1.84) = **-1.61** | -0.82 + (-0.43*-1.84) = **-0.03** |
| | Simple effect of the emotion on WOM | 0.30 + (-0.04*1.84) = **0,23** | 0.30 + (-0.04 -1.84) = **0.37** |
| | total indirect effect | -1.61 * 0.23 = **-0.37** | -0.03 * 0.37 = **-0.01** |
| Anger | simple effect of the manipulation on the mediator | 1.10 + (0.53 *1.84) = **2.08** | 1.10 + (0.53 * -1.84) = **0.12** |
| | Simple effect of the emotion on WOM | -0.28 + (0.03*1.84) = **-0.22** | -0.28 + (0.03 * -1.84) = **-0.34** |
| | total indirect effect | 2.08 * -0.22 = **-0.46** | 0.12 * -0.34 = **-0.04** |
| **Set 4 - CM Morocco / CD Morocco** | | | |
| Anger | simple effect of the manipulation on the mediator | 1.86 + (0.37 *1.96) = **2.59** | 1.86 + (0.37 * -1.96) = **1.14** |
| | simple effect of the emotion on WOM | -0.28 + (0.03*1.96) = **-0.22** | -0.28 + (0.03 * -1.96) = **-0.34** |
| | total indirect effect | 2.59 * -0.22 = **-0.57** | 1.14 * -0.34 = **-0.39** |

In the positive CSR context, findings show that consumers' ethnocentrism is not capable of moderating the overall positive effect of the company decision to support the national economy on consumers' word of mouth. The moral emotion of gratitude results as affecting consumers' word of mouth through a moderated mediation process, and consumer ethnocentrism is capable of moderating this mediating process, thus supporting H5. In this context, the simple effects of the manipulation on the mediator gratitude, regardless of the ethnocentrism level, reveal that this emotion is increased (1.54 for high ethnocentrism; 1.40 for low ethnocentrism). We also calculated the simple effects of gratitude on word of mouth (0.23 for high ethnocentrism; 0.37 for low ethnocentrism). By taking the product of the two simple effects for each of the levels of ethnocentrism, we were able to calculate the overall indirect effect through gratitude (0.35 for high ethnocentrism; 0.52 for low ethnocentrism). The simple residual treatment effect for the high ethnocentrism condition is 0.24 and 0.10 for the low. These results reveal that the indirect effect, through the mediator, is greater when ethnocentrism is low rather than high. In fact, the experimental treatment has a greater effect on gratitude in the high rather than low ethnocentrism condition, whereas the effect of this emotion on word of mouth is stronger in the presence of low ethnocentrism.

## DISCUSSION

This research attempts to increase our understanding of consumer reactions in terms of word of mouth to different CSR decisions regarding the outsourcing of domestic jobs abroad, while taking account of the mediating role of positive and negative moral emotions and the moderating role of consumer ethnocentrism. Notably, our analysis of emotions and ethnocentrism is completely new in the CSR research field, and furthermore, we include a rare

examination of hybrid CSR contexts in addition to those typically positive and negative.

We are able to verify a model linking CSR practices to consumers' word of mouth behavior, adopting the approach of Muller, Judd, and Yzerbyt (2005) in analyzing the moderated mediation and mediated moderation processes. In the positive CSR context, the emotion gratitude proves important in explaining the impact of company practices on consumer word of mouth through a moderated mediation process, with ethnocentrism playing a significant role in influencing the effect of gratitude on the outcome. Subjects with high levels of ethnocentrism result as being less likely to engage in word of mouth compared to those with low levels. This would appear to suggest that the company decision to support the national economy in maintaining a domestic work-force is seen quite simply as fair practice and not worthy of particular "celebration" for highly ethnocentric individuals, whereas it is more note-worthy for those with low levels of ethnocentrism, making them more likely to engage in word of mouth about the company.

In the negative and hybrid CSR contexts (total/partial outsourcing of domestic jobs abroad), findings show that ethnocentrism does have a moderating role in the "CSR practices-to-word of mouth" connection. Notably, individuals with high levels of ethnocentrism result as having less intention of engaging in word of mouth compared to those with low levels. In the negative CSR context, the emotion anger proves important in explaining the moderated influence of company practices on consumer word of mouth behavior. In the two hybrid CSR contexts, both anger and gratitude play a mediating role in the moderated influence of company practices on consumer word of mouth. It is interesting to note a difference that emerges between these two hybrid contexts. In the case of Morocco as the CM and Italy as the CD, the negative effect on word of mouth for consumers with low levels of ethnocentrism is negligible, whereas in the reverse condition (CD Morocco / CM Italy) it is manifest, even for this group of subjects. The explanation for this possibly lies in the different consumers' perceptions of these two hybrid conditions. It appears that the outsourcing of design is perceived as a greater threat to the home country than manufacturing. The context used for analysis probably determines this specific result. The fact that Italy boasts a long tradition in fashion and design makes it possible to speculate that Italian consumers perceive the outsourcing of product design to Morocco as more negative than the manufacturing alone, and are thus more likely to react to it.

Another interesting result warranting further discussion concerns the presence of both positive and negative emotions in the hybrid contexts. How consumers act in the presence of mixed emotions remains an open issue in consumer research and marketing (Ruth et al. 2002). This situation can lead to inconsistent behavioral responses, but our findings suggest that consumers tend to reduce their intention to make word of mouth, overcoming the conflict and favoring the negative reaction. The only CRS context in which these mixed emotions are capable of inhibiting action in individuals with low levels of ethnocentrism is, as mentioned above, that where Morocco is the CM and Italy the CD. This preliminary evidence merits further examination in future research.

There are a number of intrinsic limits to this study which suggest possible directions for additional research. One such limitation regards our scenario-based approach, with participants giving their reactions to various descriptions of CSR practices under experimental conditions. It is likely that subjects pay more attention to these descriptions than if they had come across them in an everyday context such as a newspaper or magazine. Furthermore, respondents were prompted to express their emotional reactions and intentions regarding word of mouth immediately after reading these descriptions. Both these aspects suggest that the possible effect of CSR practices would be stronger in this artificial situation compared to in real life. Replicating this study under more natural conditions would undoubtedly provide a more conservative test. Another limitation relates to the fact that this paper focuses on a selected sub-area of CSR practices. The taking of other CSR domains into consideration would certainly broaden the perspective examined here. And lastly, future research on consumers' reactions to corporate outsourcing decisions from an intercultural and not purely Italian perspective would probably also prove to be of great relevance.

## REFERENCES

Ahmed, Sadrudin A. and Alain d'Astous (2008), "Antecedents, Moderators and Dimensions of Country-of-Origin Evaluations." *International Marketing Review,* 25 (1), 75-106.

Bhattacharya, C. B. and Sankar Sen (2004), "Doing Better at Doing Good: When, Why and How Consumers Respond to Corporate Social Initiatives," *California Management Review*, 47 (1), 9-24.

Brown, Tom J. and Peter A. Dacin (1997), "The Company and the Product: Corporate Associations and Consumer Product Responses," *Journal of Marketing*, 61 (January), 64-84.

Gewirth, Alan (1984) "Ethics," in the *Encyclopedia Britannica* 15th Edition (6). Chicago: Encyclopedia Britannica. 976-998.

Gurhan-Canli Zeynep and Durairaj Maheswaran (2000a), "Determinants of Country-of-Origin Evaluations," *Journal of Consumer Research*, 27 (June), 96-108.

Gurhan-Canli Zeynep and Durairaj Maheswaran (2000b), "Cultural Variations in Country of Origin Effects," *Journal of Marketing Research*, 37 (August), 309-317.

Haidt, Jonathan (2003) "The Moral Emotions," in *Handbook of affective sciences*, Richard J. Davidson, Klaus R. Scherer, and H. Hill Goldsmith, eds. Oxford: Oxford University Press. 852-70.

Klein, Jill and Niraj Dawar (2004), "Corporate Social Responsibility and Consumers' Attributions and Brand Evaluations in a Product–Harm Crisis," *International Journal of Research in Marketing*, 21 (3), 201-17.

Laros, Fleur J. M. and Jan-Benedict E. M. Steenkamp (2005), "Emotions in Consumer Behaviour: A Hierarchical Approach," *Journal of Business Research*, 58 (10), 1437-45.

Mohr, Lois A. and Deborah J. Webb (2005), "The Effects of Corporate Social Responsibility and Price on Consumer Responses," *Journal of Consumer Affairs*, 39 (1), 121-47.

Muller, Dominique, Charles M. Judd, and Vincent Y. Yzerbyt, (2005), "When Moderation is Mediated and Mediation is Moderated," *Journal of Personality and Social Psychology*, 89(6), 852-63.

Ouellet, Jean-Francois (2007), "Consumer Racism and Its Effects on Domestic Cross-Ethnic Product Purchase: An Empirical Test in the United States, Canada, and France," *Journal of Marketing*, 71(January), 113-28.

Richins, Marsha L. (1997), "Measuring Emotions in the Consumption Experience," *Journal of Consumer Research*, 24 (September), 127-46.

Ruth, Julie A., Frédéric F. Brunel, and CeleC. Otnes (2002), "Linking Thoughts to Feelings: Investigating Cognitive Appraisals and Consumption Emotions in a Mixed-Emotions Context," *Journal of the Academy of Marketing Science,* 30 (1), 44-58.

Sen, Sankar and C. B. Bhattacharya (2001), "Does Doing Good Always Lead to Doing Better? Consumer Reactions to Corporate Social Responsibility, " *Journal of Marketing Research*, 38 (May), 225-44.

Sen, Sankar, C. B. Bhattacharya, and Daniel Korschun (2006), "The Role of Corporate Social Responsibility in Strengthening Multiple Stakeholder Relationships: A Field Experiment," *Journal of the Academy of Marketing Science*, 34 (2), 158-66.

Shaver, Phillip, Judith Schwartz, Donald Kirson, and Cary O'Connor (1987), "Emotion Knowledge: Further Exploration of a Prototype Approach," *Journal of Personality and Social Psychology*, 52 (6), 1061-86.

Sharma, Subhash, Terence A. Shimp, and Jeongshin Shin (1995) "Consumer Ethnocentrism: A Test of Antecedents and Moderators," *Journal of the Academy of Marketing Science*, 23 (1), 26-37.

Shimp, Terence A. and Subhash Sharma, (1987), "Consumer Ethnocentrism: Construction and Validation of the CETSCALE," *Journal of Marketing Research*, 24 (August), 280-89.

Tangney, June P., Jeff Stuewig, and Debra J. Mashek (2007), "Moral Emotions and Moral Behavior," *The Annual Review of Psychology*, 58, 345-72.

Verlegh, Peter W. J., Jan-Benedict E.M. Steenkamp, and Matthew T.G. Meulenberg, (2005), "Country-of-Origin Effects in Consumer Processing of Advertising Claims," *International Journal of Research in Marketing*, 22(2), 127-39.

Wagner, Tillman, Richard J. Lutz, and Barton A. Weitz (2009), "Corporate Hypocrisy: Overcoming the Threat of Inconsistent Corporate Social Responsibility Perceptions," *Journal of Marketing,* 73 (November), 77-91.

# On Consuming Celebrities: The Case of the Kylie E-Community

Paul Hewer, Strathclyde University, UK
Kathy Hamilton, University of Strathclyde, UK

## ABSTRACT

In this paper, we seek to move beyond the standard endorsement and communications approach to celebrity so perceptively critiqued by McCracken (1989). To build upon the insights of O'Guinn (1991) and Penaloza (2004) gleaned from cultural analyis of the singular celebrity case through attention to computer-mediated fan communities. Our analysis reveals that celebrities offer consumers vital dreams of survival and escape achieved through consumer to consumer exchanges in the emerging digitalscape of online fan communities. Here celebrity functions as a form of collective therapy practiced through celebrity e-forums. In this way, we demonstrate how commercial domains are reappropriated and decommodified by fans as unique repositories for the exchange of empathetic understanding the collective display of affective emotional investments.

## INTRODUCTION

The labours of consumption operate in uncertain times; while stocks, shares and our beloved brands from yesteryear tumble and fall, those theories which purport to explain consumers as solely economic agents lose their appeal and credibility. Consumers lives, punctuated by news of the daily downturns of firms and organizations, seek other forms of solace and salvation. In this critical context of disenchantment the labours of consumption gains a more social and sacred character, enlivened and revitalized by the hyperreal vitality and presence of all manner of celebrity hopefuls. In this paper we seek to instigate a *celebrity turn* within consumer research and consumer culture theory (Arnould and Thompson 2005) to augment our understanding of consumers and the sacred character of the investments and identifications they make in celebrity culture. In this paper, we seek to move beyond the standard endorsement and communications approach so perceptively critiqued by McCracken (1989) and to build upon the insights of O'Guinn (1991) and Peñaloza (2004) gleaned from cultural analyses of the singular celebrity case. To advance such approaches we turn to the vital dreams of survival and escape which celebrities offer and the possibilities of transformation which they afford consumers in computer-mediated fan communities. As a context for this discussion we use the case of Kylie Konnect and Kylie forums to explore the vitality of consumer to consumer interactions - fan to fan conversations around the loved object (Ahuvia 2005) of Kylie.

On the face of it there would appear to be little of uniqueness about the case of Kylie[1]; little to merit concerted academic debate and discussion. But this would overlook the ingredients of Kylie which make her exactly the right context and imaginary resource for countless popular discussions on blogs and social networking sites centring upon the trials, tribulations and fascinations of celebrity affairs. In this paper we take seriously the vitality of such cyber interactions within contemporary culture to argue that consumer fascinations around the continuing appeal and resourcefulness of celebrities often resides in their storytelling potential; a potential

which accounts for the productive social aspects of those interactions where fans debate and come together over issues like their treatment by the media, their thwarted love affairs and music/fashion/celebrity appeal. In this respect we explore Kylie as a *loved object* (Ahuvia 2005); seeking to unpack the forms of love and sacralisation (O'Guinn and Belk 1989), that are made possible in consumer to consumer (fan to fan) celebrity brand communities (Muniz & O'Guinn 2001).

## THE CELEBRITY TURN

The turn to celebrity within consumer research is necessary to further contextualise and problematise consumer to consumer exchanges in the emerging digitalscape. The problem being that in writing about the pervasiveness of celebrity culture it is all too tempting to see them as simply existing at the level of the image; that is as flawless and airbrushed products of media representation and production. Such a perspective is evident within the celebrity endorsement literature which advocates the use of aspirational celebrities to help sell products (Silvera and Austad 2003). For us, it is necessary to go beyond such understanding to problematise celebrities as 'carriers of meaning', or 'role models' but from 'below' (Turner 2004). To instigate a grassroots cultural approach that considers them from the perspective of consumers themselves, to permit understanding of the significance they play in the consumption, but also production, of celebrity. Celebrity needs to be conceptualised as Cashmore and Parker suggest as: "a commodification of the human form, the epitome of economic fetishism. It is the process by which people are turned into "things," things to be adored, respected, worshipped, idolized, but perhaps most importantly, things which are themselves produced and consumed" (Cashmore and Parker 2003, 215). Such a perspective draws our attention to the types of investments consumers express and project upon celebrities, highlighting the everyday 'work' which consumers enact through their icons. Moreover, Maffesoli (2007) draws attention to the role of such persona within the tribal aesthetic: "They recreate what already exists...and it is by communing with their repeated stagings and identifying with them that we all...transcend ourselves and explode creatively, breaking free from our enclosures and throwing off the shackles of our small individual ids." (2007, 33).

Such promise of transcendence parallels research on sacred consumption (Belk, Wallendorf and Sherry 1989). Investments in consumption activities can transform seemingly profane consumer goods such as the Apple Newton into objects that offer potential for emancipation and liberation (Muniz and Schau 2005). Similarly, devotion to media brands such as Star Trek sometimes transcends mere entertainment to become a "profoundly motivating vision of the future" (Kozinets 2001, 77). In this way a religious metaphor becomes "adaptable in a consumer-centred world...[where] some of the same forces that drive many religions may drive the religiosity of brand communities (Muniz and Schau 2005, 746). Through such consumption practices we witness how "the material world can become the seat of the sacred again; consumption can [thus] become (re)ensouled" (Kozinets 2002, 32).

In establishing this point we seek in this paper to make explicit the character of consumers' investments in celebrity culture, but also the particular sacred appeal of celebrities to consumers. Sometimes as Jauss (cited by Marshall 1997, 69) reveals this connection is not only sympathetic or admiring, sometimes it is ironic and playful

---

1 We appreciate that to some to some audiences/markets, Kylie may be relatively unknown but since beginning her musical career in 1988, Kylie has enjoyed the success of 52 singles, 10 studio albums and countless awards and accolades including the prestigious BRIT, Grammy and MTV Europe music awards. For a fuller resume of her achievements we encourage readers to take a look at the wikipedia entry for Kylie as space restrictions prevent us from detailing these here.

but sometimes gains in momentum and investment, becoming associative (celebratory and participative) and even cathartic, so that fans gain a sense of emancipation from their affinity with the celebrity brand community.

Theoretically the notion of the 'fan' has previously been ascribed a type of passivity, defined in response to celebrity system (Jenkins 2006a). However, fans should be conceptualised as actively producing cultural meanings around celebrity (Peñaloza 2004; Grossberg 2005; Turner 2004); to embrace the move from a representational culture to a presentational culture where celebrities are reworked in terms of their value and utility by audiences and users (Marshall 2005). Celebrities, as Maffesoli suggests, exist as "Archetypes...[within] this creative unveiling...revelators trying to bring out what already exists." (Maffesoli 2007, 32). Similar to other consumer tribes, "fan communities move among corporate landscape, occupying them ideologically and affectively, 'poaching' and appropriating ideas, myths and memes, living with them, making them their own, and moving on" (Kozinets 2007, 195).

Writing about the 1920s star system, Firat and Dholakia (1998), comment that: "The people of fortune were celebrities and (almost) everyone wanted to know them, and to be acquainted (for most, of course, vicariously) with them. Celebrities, stars and others, who became the acquaintances of all, sold things.... ideas, values and attitudes." (1998, 47). Pringle in *Celebrity Sells* (2004) makes a similar point. And in this respect we witness how the marriage between celebrity culture, consumption and everyday life is firmly cemented and established. And as marriages go, it ain't a bad one since celebrities are part and parcel of consumer culture, their longevity and appeal expressive of the social forces which converge around the Entertainment-Marketing Complex (c.f C.W. Mills 1959).

Online fan communities are thus ideal platforms to explore the emerging participatory culture which is taking shape as people are learning how to live and collaborate within such knowledge communities (Jenkins 2006a, 2006b, 26). Kozinets (1997) suggests that identification with a virtual community of consumption depends largely on two factors, both we argue, are clearly evident in online fan communities. First is the relationship that the person has with the consumption activity. In comparison with other consumption contexts, experiences with celebrities involve a high level of intensity and emotion often appearing central to a fan's self-concept and indeed, the guiding heuristic is often a religious one as celebrities are said to perform some of the functions of gods who are worshipped by fans (O'Guinn 1991). In particular pop stars generate and instigate investments of time and energy as we are drawn "into affective and emotional alliances with the performers and with the performers' other fans" in search of "opportunities to make meanings of their social identities and social experiences that are self-interested and functional" (Frith 1987, 35-37). Second is the intensity of the social relationships and emotional interactions the consumer expresses and shares with other members of the virtual community. Given that fans are typically associated with cultural tastes that are denigrated by the dominant value system (Fiske 1992), the internet can thus provide a forum where the fan attempts to make up for an "absence of 'authentic' relationships... [a] perceived personal lack of autonomy, absence of community, incomplete identity, lack of power and lack of recognition" (Jenson 2002, 16-17).

In taking account of the social uses of celebrity, we do not deny that the celebrity is also "a manufactured commodity" that demands "commercially strategic" development (Turner 2004, 26). Here the commercial value of celebrity collides with, and feeds off, its cultural value to produce a regime of connections, investments

and effects. The challenge for marketers is to create a fusion between consumers; a fusion which begins with understanding the consumption rituals and practices which fans initiate (Sandvoss 2005; Hogg and Bannister 2000; Holt, 1995). For as, Taylor 1999, 161) suggests: "fans are not true cultists unless they pose their fandom as a resistance activity, one that keeps them one step ahead of those forces which would try to market their resistant taste back to them." So on the one hand, fans are seen as ideal consumers as their consumption habits can be highly predicted by the culture industry but they also express anti-commercial beliefs indicating a co-existence between commercial ideologies and commodity-completist practices (Hills 2002). The focus of our paper thus becomes to achieve a deeper understanding of online celebrity fan practices: What investments do they project upon celebrities through these e-forums? What significance does celebrity play in their lives? How is the celebrity brand re-imagined and reworked by fans in their communal exchanges?

## METHODOLOGY

To explore the richness and diversity of the emergent digitalscape demands a particular style of method. A methodology capable of taking seriously the social interactions and conversations consumers engage in through such new technologies. Our analysis took the form of a digital ethnography (Murthy 2008); and drew upon the insightful work of Kozinets (1997, 1998, 2001, 2002b) and Kozinets et al (2008). Such an approach provides researchers with "a window into naturally occurring behaviours", in relation to the "language, motivations, consumption linkages, and symbols of consumption-oriented online communities" (Kozinets 2002b, 62 & 70). Such "connected research" allows us to learn from social dynamics between participants (Schillewaert, De Ruyck and Verhaeghe 2009) as we increasingly witness a shift towards the "public display of private worlds" (Beer 2008, 624).

Textual and visual material in the form of conversations, images and blogs were thus collected through two online forums devoted to talk around Kylie (http://forums.kylie.com/ and http://kyliekonnect. com/). *Kylie.com* is an international forum with 15,687 registered users (as of 2/03/09). Over the 12 month period of our analysis 2052 discussion threads generating a total of 58,525 postings were made. The forum provides an arena for members to discuss Kylie's music, live appearances, TV appearances and press from around the world. *KylieKonnect* launched in November 2007 was the first artist social networking site for music fans. It allows members from around the world to create profiles, upload images and blogs; but also to connect and interact with other Kylie fans. The forum element[2] of the site is made up of 648 threads, totalling 8007 postings covering a variety of Kylie-related chat. Subsequent to the collection of this data, we attempted to code our material to organize our ideas into a set of thematic insights. These codes were based upon the collected material and the theoretical lens which surrounded our study. Analysis and interpretation was constructed around moving between individual postings, chunks of postings, entire discussion threads and the emergent understanding of the complete data set (de Valck 2007; Muniz and Schau 2005; Schau & Gilly 2003). Analysis of social interaction between participants in the form of naturally occurring discourse proved particularly insightful (Ritson and Elliott 1999). We adopted a number of techniques proposed by Wallendorf and Belk (1989) to establish the trustworthiness of the data including triangulation across researchers and forums, observation over time and negative case analysis. We also acknowledge that analysis is based on the communicative acts of only a small percentage of Kylie's fan base rather than the complete set of behaviours of all fans in the community (Kozinets 2002b). Our results are organized in terms of the follow-

---

2 Other elements of the site include a gallery of Kylie images and Kylie's latest blog (which by blog standards is highly commercial with the emphasis on updating fans on her latest performances, cds and perfume range); along with links to Kylie.com the official retail site where fans can view lyrics, download wallpaper, watch her performances and purchase CDs, DVDs, ringtones, widgets etc.

ing three themes: Exploring the Kylie community; the Othering of Kylie and finally, the theme of Knowing Kylie.

## UNPACKING THE KYLIE E-COMMUNITY

For O'Guinn (1991) the organising logic for celebrity worship is that of religion, as sometimes fans imbue celebrities with god-like powers and in this section we explore the ways in which the sacralisation of celebrity manifests itself on online fan communities like Kylie Konnect and the Kylie forum.

Members appear to emphasise the sense and awareness of themselves as being part of a brand community (Muniz & O'Guinn 2002; Muniz and Schau 2005). Fans in this respect talk of the role of the forum in social and sacred terms: *"As Kylie fans, we are here to share everything about her. As forum users, to critique as an audience of Kylie and other users' thoughts but as whole, we are here to support each other."* In terms of summing up and expressing the happenings of such forums we might concur with O'Guinn when he suggests: "They get together and talk, reminisce, and share one another's joys and sorrows... They gather in his[/her] name, but for each other." (1991, 8). The sense of camaraderie and the stress upon the value of forum membership is thus palpable, with members suggesting: *"I love KK* [Kylie Konnect] *it is the friendliest forum I have found anywhere and people here understand what you are saying and everything is taken as it is meant."* Moreover, they clarify the nature of the celebrity communion, one which transgresses global boundaries and traditional markers such as age and gender, rather as they affirm: *"it's not about age, it's about taste."* Here we see the promise of communitas in online fan forums; where communitas is pivotal to sacred consumption (Belk et al. 1989) and therein sometimes "consumption can become (re) ensouled" (Kozinets 2002a, 32).

The importance of the emerging digitalscape and the connections it makes possible is further emphasised when fans speak of how in their more mundane lives devotion to Kylie is not always met with such positive affirmation. For example, some forum members voiced their disappointment that their social contacts did not understand the appeal of Kylie: *"All of my friends hate her.... they don't understand how good she is live"*. Such awareness of the negative associations she brings forth in others, reveals the significance of the virtual forum as a space where such talk has little place. In this respect the e-forum provides a relief and platform to compensate for this absence of a Kylie community in their everyday lives (Jenson 1992)[3]. Instead, we witnessed a developing sense of shared taste and fellowship (O'Guinn 1989) that helps to explain the almost confessional character of many of the conversations around Kylie's appeal (c.f. Beer 2008 and Bauman 2007).

## THE OTHERING OF KYLIE

On the forums we witness the constant referencing to Kylie as akin to an *absent other* -where as an imaginary resource she makes possible threads of quasi-religious character and sentiment to be expressed. For example one of the forums sections is titled: *"Do we know whether Kylie is aware of our conversations?"* – responses ranged from the *"I can't say for sure if she checks in to see what her humble subjects are doing, but you never know...she could be here right now and we would be none the wiser.";* to the: *"I wonder does she even have a username"*. While some are sceptical about Kylie's presence, their questioning would suggest to us that they want to

believe that she is party to their conversations – overhearing their 'gifts' of praise and devotion which they offer through the forum.

In this respect we witness how participants seek to transform themselves and the sense of their own identities through the narratives they construct around their shared devotion and adoration to Kylie. For example, one of the sections is entitled: *Kylie is a new super hero?* Here we find creative renditions of authoring themselves through her appeal: *"Yes because she saves me from boredom and gets me all happy!"* to another fan who suggests:

> *"I wrote a story...about a Princess named Kylie that took place far into the future where the Earth is finally at peace and KYLIE is the heir to Earths thrown (sic). But then Evil arise from the depths of space and KYLIE has to become KYBORG (the thing she was dressed as at the beginning of the Fever Tour) to fight off the evil. It was kinda cheesy but still good."*

Forum members' expressions of their devotion to Kylie are littered throughout the forum. Two threads were particularly insightful: First, Kylie's 40th birthday in May 2008 was accompanied by the creation of a special area for postings of birthday wishes where expressions of gratitude dominated. Second, a thread titled: "What has Kylie done for you?" appeared to encourage the offering of survival and salvation tales (cf. Muniz and Schau 2005). For some, the appeal of her music runs deep and goes far beyond the derogatory view of it as 'pop' or mere 'entertainment'. Rather it generates strong emotional sentiment from fans keen to express their gratitude in relation to the help and comfort they gain from experiencing her music:

> *I just wanted to thank you for being such an inspiration for me, your beautiful voice is always like a light that shines even in the darkest places, and the most obscure moments of my life. I feel like i have no words to describe how happy your work makes me.*

Such sacralisation harks back to Belk's discussion of the domains of sacred consumption (1989); we witness how celebrities are through fans co-creation endeavours sometimes "set apart from others" (Belk 1989, 11): or, as another member echoes:

> *Thank- you for everything you have done for me, inspiring me and giving me courage to come through the most difficult part of my life. For that and for you being you and your music and everything about you, I love you.*

The forum in this instance enables us to glimpse the process of celebrity sacralisation in the making. In this way, expressions of 'love' were expressive of the emotional nature of the community (cf. Maffesoli 1996). For some, such declarations can be encouraged by feelings of sexual attraction towards Kylie; but for some treatment of Kylie as a 'loved object' (Ahuvia 2005) is perhaps generated through the affectual benefits that being a Kylie fan provides. As Rojek (2001, 52) suggests "the celebrity is an imaginary resource to turn to in the midst of life's hardships or triumphs, to gain solace from, to beseech for wisdom and joy". Here we see parallels with religious devotion (Muniz and Schau 2005) as fans employ the language and rhetoric of religious sentiment to express their reverence and respect for Kylie for fulfilling "a need to believe in something significantly more powerful and extraordinary than the self" (Belk, Wallendorf and Sherry 1989, 2). Or as one of her fans describes Kylie:

---

3 On the basis of our own participant observation (June 2008) we can suggest that her performances also represent a significant community gathering enabling disparate fans to come together and share their passions.

*For me she has not only been an inspiration, I loook up to her and see her as a role model, I think hr music is great and I love the personailty she lets us see. She has always been very special to me. Because I started having panic attacks when I 8, I had had them before but they came back when I was 8 that was the same time I became a fan and for me I think she was meant to come and help me and she has, she has been a support. She came when I needed her and it makes me feel happy when i see her because has not just been an idol but she has been a support.*

Seeing Kylie in such redemptive and enduring terms was a common theme amongst forum conversations. Many fans appreciate that she is not making the headlines for "driving too fast", "being drunk" "using drugs" or "doing other bad things". Fans, in this way, strive to distance Kylie from other less sacred celebrities, especially those who invite and encourage media speculation for their inappropriate or immoral behaviour. Rather Kylie becomes a sacred ideal in comparison to her profane rival celebrities (Pimentel and Reynolds 2004).

## KNOWING KYLIE WITHIN THE E-ECONOMY

In this section, we reveal how fans strive through their narratives to express their identifications with Kylie. Emblematic of this desire by fans are their attempts to collect Kylie memorabilia. Such collecting we argue permits fans to perpetuate and make tangible this sacredness (cf. Belk 1989, 21). For example, one of the most popular threads on the forum with a total of 2273 posts (as of 10/03/2009) was that devoted to "Your Kylie Collection". Discussions on this thread typically took the form of members 'listing' and displaying their collections to others members of her music, merchandising from posters to annuals etc, through such interactions we glimpse how fans attempt to make explicit the strength of their devotion through the ritual of collecting (Belk, 1989) but also through the act of constructing narratives and sharing those with others around their memorabilia we witness how the community imagines itself but also signifies the strength of its devotion within the e-community.

In this sense fans are keen to not only collect tangible objects which bring them closer to their heroes, but also to use the forums to strive for a proximity with others who share their own life-worlds and views. In this respect, what has touched audiences most is Kylie's recent battle with breast cancer (something that has inspired some of the songs from Kylie's most recent album). Fans appear to relate to Kylie on this level and the experience of her music then becomes an experience of identity formation in that "we absorb songs into our own lives and rhythm into our own bodies; they have a looseness of reference that makes them immediately accessible" (Frith 1996, 121). For fans, music and experience can become so intertwined that it is difficult to locate the music's meanings without talking about their own personal lives (Cavicchi 1998). This is in evidence through forum postings where fans narrate their own personal experiences of dealing with cancer. For example "*I lost my Mother last week to cancer and your wonderful "feel good" music did help me cope*" and "*I too have recently been dignosed with cancer; only being 33 years old... What I love about her is she still puts her diamonds and lippy on and if it's good enough for Kylie then it's good enough for me.*" For others, it extends beyond experiences with cancer, to also include coping with other illnesses.

*Kylie to me is a constant light in my life, i admire her so much, im proud to be a fan. at the moment she is helping me alot !! im having a big operation on 5th nov and right now*

*kylie and her music are keeping me together. ive been a fan for 20rys and kylie is in my heart for sure.* 😊

*On the 31st of March this year, I gave birth to stillborn twin daughters, 3 days before I was booked in for my c-section. Although the better days outnumber them now, I still have my bad days and listening to Kylie cheers me up a bit. Also, what I have been through and breast cancer are two completely different things, but I find it inspirational that Kylie has publicly been through a very dark time, and something that would have been very traumatic, and she did it with dignity and picked herself up and is back, better than ever. She is living, breathing proof that there is light at the end of the tunnel.*

As illustrated, fans have been dedicated followers of Kylie throughout her long career; such commitment is another key ingredient of sacred consumption (Belk et al. 1989). Kylie's music can be seen as having *transformative power* for fans and in this way it becomes part of the "care of the self" (DeNora 1999, 37). The religious theme is thus foregrounded and conventional thinking dictates that during times of illness people turn to religion to improve their emotional well-being or pray for healing and redemption. What we witness on the forum is fans putting their 'faith' in Kylie as an imaginary resource of hope, comfort and salvation, but also this connection enables them to link with like-minded others. De Nora (1999, 45) argues that "Music is a device or resource to which people turn in order to regulate themselves as aesthetic agents, as feeling, thinking and acting beings in their day-to-day lives." As one fan suggests, "*As for me personally, she changed my life completely, she made me believe in my own power, possibilities and dreams, in my own future - and she's done it just through her music, her behavior and just simply by being a real woman!*

The Kylie forum thus becomes a sacred space[4] wherein fans can come together to understand, make sense and manage the stress and anxieties that confront them in contemporary consumer culture. It is at these moments perhaps that communities take a 'sharing and caring' form (cf. Kozinets 2002a, 22).

It would be wrong, however, to suggest that all fans experienced the quasi-religious character of this style of devotion to Kylie, as the community is also noteworthy for its divergent character. For some fans, the appeal of Kylie is simply that of the enjoyment they receive from listening to her music, which provides "*lots and lots and lots of fun and entertainment*". While another suggested, "*she hasnt really done anything for me, she is only a singer nothing more than that to me. although some of her songs do make me happy when i feel sad, but thats all really.*" Another forum member was quick to agree "*Voice of reason once again. Second that.*" At times, Kylie's music can therefore be enjoyed as an end in itself, a hedonistic soundtrack to fun, dance and laughter, rather than as a means to some other personal or social goal (Holbrook 1987). Another noteworthy posting adopts a more critical stance towards such devotion suggesting that although it offers to many escapism, sometimes this may border on the "unhealthy":

---

4  It was Emile Durkheim who envisaged religion as the symbolic self-consciousness of society. Such a view places especial importance on the channels of communication with which society constructs itself. It was also Durkheim who confidently pronounced that "...If there is one truth that history teaches us beyond doubt, it is that religion tends to embrace a smaller and smaller sector of social life...this shows that there is a decreasing number of collective beliefs and sentiments which are both collective and strong enough to assume a religious character." (1987, 245). He did however draw our attention to the enduringness of such religious sentiment.

*Hmmm... I was half-tempted to go for the she hasn't done anything for me route, because, in all fairness, she hasn't. But I am in the mood to pay a kind of tribute to my younger years. Kylie kept me occupied during the hardest time of my life. I didn't have to think about my problems when I was being a "Kylie fan". Like a second identity I could escape to from real life. From this point, I know how unhealthy this was, and I also know it wasn't because it was Kylie, it could have happened with any celebrity. But it happened with her.*

Given these opposing and divergent uses - Kylie can be seen as a malleable and fragmented brand community. While some fans sacralise Kylie seeing her as possessing inspirational god-like qualities and seeking personalised meanings reflective of their own life experiences, others are more playful (dare we say postmodern) in terms of the ways they weave Kylie into the fabric of everyday life merely for fun and escapism.

## THE ALTERNATIVE THERAPIES FOR CONSUMING CELEBRITIES - DISCUSSION

In this paper we foreground what consumers share with other consumers on celebrity e-forums to demonstrate the sacred qualities of such spaces to highlight the consumption and identity 'work' that takes place through talk on celebrity mattering. Our analysis of the Kylie Brand Community reveals the forms of collective therapy and sacralisation being practiced on such celebrity e-forums. Here we might concur with Kozinets, who you might recall spoke of Star Trek as a, "moral compass around which fans centre their lives, one as all-encompassing as a religion." (2001, 77). Or even paraphrase Maffesoli to consider celebrity, through the sacred lens of religion which he defines as simply "that which unites us as a community" (1996, 38). To speak of consumers as fans places emphasis squarely upon Weber's concept of 'emotional communities' as ephemeral, changeable and ill-defined (cf. Maffesoli 1996, 12), and through attention to their illusive and ephemeral character we start to glimpse the extent to which celebrities are useful resources for rethinking ourselves and our forms of togetherness.

These commercial domains[5] are thus reappropriated and decommodified as 'inalienable' (cf Wallendorf and Arnould 1991) by fans as unique and cherished repositories for the exchange of forms of empathetic understandings and the collective display of affective emotional investments. Celebrities are then for consumers 'good to think with' (Levi-Strauss 1966), and the internet forums initiate a particular form of at-a-distance proximity between fans and on celebrities.

Moreover an unintended consequence of such proximity appears to be that they operate as *stages* for the construction of debates around celebrity, be they of an ethical, moral or sacred kind. Here we emphasise the narratives constructed and participation engendered around celebrities in such internet spaces. Spaces which make possible the emergence of identity, communal and transcendental value. But which also serve to make explicit to consumers the difficulties and tactics of negotiating ways of life within contemporary consumer culture. For as Dyer commented in the work *Heavenly Bodies* (1986), "the stars articulate what it is

to be a human being in contemporary society; that is, they express the particular notion we hold of the person, of the 'individual'." (quoted in Turner 2004: 104). Such a view suggests that sometimes celebrities be understood as 'moral beacons' (Porpora 1996, 210); or as Boorstin advocated, back in the 1960s: "receptacles into which we pour our own purposelessness." (*ibid*, 214). Here then we start to glimpse the importance of celebrities in an age of anxiety and uncertainty, without recourse to 'metanarratives' (Lyotard 1984; Firat and Venkatesh 1995); an age of "playing with the pieces of identity" (Baudrillard 1993); an age where as Marx prophetically pronounced "All that is solid melts into air" (cf. Berman 1983). In such a critical context of disenchantment our intense and emotional connection with celebrities, be it from afar or virtual means, starts to then make sense, for we witness how they permit us to enter into intense moral and social dilemmas. In some senses what is unique, in contrast to earlier eras, is the internet platform itself as a space wherein consumers weave and spin, through their interactions and narratives, their own 'threads' of significance (cf. Geertz 1973) which unite them and sometimes leads them into producing emergent understandings. Here we concur with Firat and Dholakia (1998) on the almost theatrical character of such spaces and spacings: "... instead of the stage, the backstage and the audience, the theater is composed only of the stage. All interaction across all dimensions – ecomomic, social, political – occur on this stage. This means that everyone is a player, an actor. On a stage, different groups of actors may be engaged in different interactions simultaneously. They all contribute to what is happening on the stage." (1999, 154-155). The value of such stages and the stagings therein, is revealed as a site wherein consumers "put them to work" (McCracken, 1989). And sometimes such consumption work is trivial and mundane, sometimes merely driven by distraction and diversion, but sometimes it becomes re-enchanting, and at other times it becomes playful and emancipative in character making possible catharsis. It is in such moments that the sacred character of such spaces is revealed – as communal spaces of revelation and insight.

In such commercial contexts, especially given the nature of the internet connection we witness how celebrity functions as a site for organizing social identity, a vessel for identity formation and group transformation. The liminality of celebrity thus takes centre-stage, for as Turner suggested: "In liminality people 'play' with the elements of the familiar and defamiliarise them" (1982, 27). And as a means for organizing identity (du Gay 2007), and for reorganizing such constituent parts, roles and characters, we might finally explore the value of what we might term celebrito-pias[6] – that is as a land of myth, magic and fairytale princes and princesses. The mythological space of celebritopia then presents itself to consumers as a neverending staging, a soap opera rich and ripe in potential for interaction, participation and collaboration. A neverending story of opportunity and possibility which punctuates our own more domestic, prosaic and profane everyday lives; an opportunity which in some senses renders our own lives and meanings as sharable; and a narrative which as we have sought to demonstrate provides our own lives with a sense of meaningfulness and sacralisation. When we start to see the social importance of celebritopias we see how celebrities are important sites for

5 See 1 above, but to save you the effort we note that Kylie Konnect is unashamedly commercial with the emphasis placed on updating fans on her latest performances, cds and perfume ranges); along with links to Kylie.com the official retail site where fans can view lyrics, download wallpaper, watch her performances and purchase CDs, DVDs, ringtones, widgets etc.

6 Here we might quote Porpora when he suggests: "Traditionally, heroes are the protagonists of myths – that is, metaphorical or figurative accounts that are addressed to the ultimate questions: Who are we? Where did we come from? Why are we here? Addressed to ultimate questions as they are, myths relate to a sacred plane of existence, a plane that transcends profane, everyday life. In the sacred plane, heroes personify transcendent ideals and transcendent visions of the good." (1996, 227)

the negotiation, revitalization and transformation of our public and private selves. Celebrity it would appear in its technological guise currently makes possible a space in our lives for sacredness to emerge, a space for innovation and interrogations to disturb and unsettle the eversame (cf. de Certeau 1984).

# REFERENCES

Ahuvia, Aaron C. (2005), "Beyond the Extended Self: Loved Objects and Consumers' Identity Narratives," *Journal of Consumer Research*, Vol.32, (1), June, pp. 171-184.

Bauman, Zygmunt (2007), *Consuming Life*, Polity, Cambridge.

Baudrillard, Jean (1993), *Baudrillard Live: Selected Interviews*. Routledge, London.

Belk, Russell; Wallendorf, Melanie and Sherry, John F. (1989), "The Sacred and the Profane in Consumer Behavior: Theodicy on the Odyssey", *Journal of Consumer Research*, Vol.16, June, pp.1-38.

Beer, David (2008), "Researching a confessional society", *International Journal of Market Research*, Vol.50, (5), pp.619-629.

Berman, Marshall (1983), *All That is Solid Melts into Air. The Experience of Modernity*. Verso, London

Cashmore, Ellis and Andrew Parker (2003), "One David Beckman? Celebrity, Masculinity, and the Soccerati," *Sociology of Sport Journal*, Vol.20, pp. 214-231.

Cova, Bernard (1997), "Community and consumption: towards a definition of the 'linking value' of product and services", *European Journal of Marketing*, Vol.31, (3), pp.297-316.

de Certeau, Michel (1984), *The Practice of Everyday Life*. Berkeley: University of California Press.

de Vlack, Kristine (2007), "The War of the eTribes: Online Conflicts and Communal Consumption," in *Consumer Tribes* eds. Bernard Cova, Robert V. Kozinets and Avi Shankar, Butterworth-Heinemann: Oxford, pp. 260-274.

du Gay, Paul (2007), *Organizing Identity*: Persons and Organisations 'after theory'. Sage, London.

Durkheim, Emile (1987), *Emile Durkheim: Selected Writings*, with an introduction by Anthony Giddens. Cambridge University Press, Cambridge.

Firat, Fuat A. and Dholakia, Nikhilesh (1998), *Consuming People: From Political Economy to theatres of consumption*. Routledge, London.

Firat, Fuat A. and Venkatesh, Alladi (1995), "Liberatory Postmodernism and the Reenchantment of Consumption", *Journal of Consumer Research*, Vol.22, December, pp.239-267.

Fiske, John (1992), "The Cultural Economy of Fandom," in *The Adoring Audience: Fan Culture and Popular Media*, eds. Lisa A. Lewis, Routledge, London, pp 30-49.

Frith, Simon (1987), "Towards an Aesthetic of Popular Music" in *Popular Music: Critical Concepts in Media and Cultural Studies*, ed. Simon Frith, Routledge, London, pp. 32-47.

_____ (1996) "Music and Identity". In *Questions of Cultural Identity* eds. Stuart Hall and Paul Du Gay, Sage, London, pp. 108-127.

Geertz, Clifford (1973), *The Interpretation of Culture*. Fontana.

Grossberg, Lawrence (2005), "Is there a fan in the house? The affective sensibility of fandom," in *The Celebrity Culture Reader*, ed. P. David Marshall, Routledge, London, pp. 581-590.

Hills, Matt (2002), *Fan Cultures*, Routledge, London.

Holt, Douglas (1995), "How Consumers Consume: a typology of consumption practices", Journal of Consumer Research, Vol.22, June, pp.1-16.

Hogg, Margaret K. and Emma N. Bannister (2000), "The Structure and Transfer of Cultural Meaning: A Study of Young Consumers and Pop Music" in *Advances in Consumer Research*, Vol 27, eds. Stephen J. Hoch and Robert J. Meyer, Provo, UT: Association for Consumer Research, pp. 19-23.

Ilikemusic.com (2008), "Kylie Launches Her Own Social Networking Site", www.ilikemusic.com/music_news/Kylie_Launches_Own_Social_Network_KylieKonnect-4264, accessed 13th February 2008.

Jenkins, Henry (2006a), *Fans, Bloggers and Gamers: Essays on Participatory Culture*, New York University Press, New York.

_____ (2006b), *Convergence Culture: Where Old and New Media Collide*. New York University Press, New York.

Jenson, Joli (1992), "Fandom as Pathology: The Consequences of Characterization," in *The Adoring Audience: Fan Culture and Popular Media*, eds. Lisa A. Lewis, Routledge, London, pp. 9-27

Kozinets, Robert V. (1997), "I Want To Believe": A Netnography of The X-Philes' Subculture of Consumption', *Advances in Consumer Research*, Vol.24, eds. Merrie Brucks and Deborah J. MacInnis, Provo, UT: Association for Consumer Research, pp. 470-475.

_____ (1998), "On Netnography: Initial Reflections on Consumer Research Investigations of Cyberculture", *Advances in Consumer Research*, Vol.25, pp. 366-371.

_____ (2001), "Utopian Enterprise: Articulating the Meanings of Star Trek's Culture of Consumption", *Journal of Consumer Research*, Vol.28, (1), June, pp. 67-88.

_____ (2002a), "Can Consumers Escape the Market? Emancipatory Illuminations from Burning Man", *Journal of Consumer Research*, Vol.29, (June), 20-38.

_____ (2002b), "The Field Behind the Screen: Using Netnography for Marketing Research in Online Communities", *Journal of Marketing Research*, Vol.39, (1), February, pp.61-72.

_____ (2007), "Inno-tribes: *Star Trek* as wikimedia" in *Consumer Tribes* eds. Bernard Cova, Robert V. Kozinets and Avi Shankar, Butterworth-Heinemann: Oxford, pp. 194-211.

Levi-Strauss, Claude (1966), *The Savage Mind*. University of Chicago Press, Chicago.

Lyotard, Jean-Francois (1984), *The Postmodern Condition*: A Report on Knowledge. Manchester University Press, Manchester.

McCracken, Grant (1989), "Who is the Celebrity Endorser? Cultural Foundations of the Endorsement Process," *Journal of Consumer Research*, Vol.16, (3), December, pp. 310-321.

Maffesoli, Michel (1996), *The Time of the Tribes: The decline of Individualism in Mass Society*, Sage, London.

_____ (2007), "Tribal Aesthetic" in *Consumer Tribes* eds. Bernard Cova, Robert V. Kozinets and Avi Shankar, Butterworth-Heinemann, Oxford, pp. 27-34.

Marshall, P. David (2005), "The Meanings of the Popular Music Celebrity: The Construction of Distinctive Authenticity" in *The Celebrity Culture Reader*, ed. P. David Marshall, Routledge, London, pp. 196-222.

Mills, C.W. (1959), *The Sociological Imagination*. Oxford University Press, New York.

Muniz, Albert M and O'Guinn, Thomas C. (2001), "Brand Community", *Journal of Consumer Research*, Vol.27, (4), March, pp. 412-423.

Muniz, Albert M. and Schau, Hope (2005), "Religiosity in the Abandaned Apple Newton Brand Community', *Journal of Consumer Research*, Vol.31, (4), March, pp. 737-747.

Murthy, Dhiraj (2008), "Digital Ethnography: an examination of the use of new technoloiges for social research", *Sociology*, Vol.42, (5), October, pp. 837-855.

O'Guinn, Thomas C. (1991), "Touching Greatness: The Central Midwest Barry Manilow Fan Club," in *Highways and Buyways: Naturalistic Research from the Consumer Behavior Odyssey,* Special Volumes, Association for Consumer Research, pp. 102-111.

_____ & Belk, Russell W. (1989), "Heaven on Earth: Consumption at Heritage Village, USA", *Journal of Consumer Research*, Vol.16, September, pp.227-238.

Peñaloza, Lisa (2004), "Consuming Madonna Then and Now: An Examination of the Dynamics and Structuring of Celebrity Consumption," in *Madonna's Drowned Worlds: New Approaches to her Cultural Transformations 1983-2003* eds. Santiago Fouz-Hernandez and Freya Jarman-Ivens, pp. 176-192.

Pimentel, Robert W and Reynolds, Kirsty E. (2004) "A Model for Consumer Devotion: Affective Commitment with Proactive Sustaining Behaviors", *Academy of Marketing Science Review*, Vol. 2004, pp.

Porpora, Douglas V. (1996), "Personal Heroes, Religion and Transcendental Metanarratives", *Sociological Forum*, Vol.11, (2), June, pp.209-229.

Pringle, Hamish (2004), *Celebrity Sells*. John Wiley and Sons, London.

Ritson, Mark and Elliott, Richard (1999), "The Social Uses of Advertising: An Ethnographic Study of Adolescent Advertising Audiences", *Journal of Consumer Research*, Vol. 26, December, pp. 260-277.

Rojek, Chris (2001), *Celebrity*, Reaktion Books, London.

Sandvoss, Cornel (2005), *Fans: The Mirror of Consumption*, Polity, Cambridge.

Schau, Hope and Mary C. Gilly (2003), "We are what we post? Self-presentation in Personal Web Space", *Journal of Consumer Research*, Vol.30, (3), December, pp.385-404.

Schillewaert, Niels, De Ruyct, Tom and Verhaeghe, Annelies (2009), "Connected Research: How Market Research can get the most out of Semantic Web Waves", *International Journal of Market Research*, Vol. 51 (1), pp. 11- 27.

Silvera, David H. and Austad, Benedikte (2003), "Factors predicting the effectiveness of celebrity endorsement advertisements", *European Journal of Marketing*, Vol.38, (11/12, pp.1509-1526.

Taylor, Greg (1999), *Artists in the Audience: Cults, Camp and American Film Criticism*, Princeton University Press, Princeton.

Turner, Graeme (2004), *Celebrity*, Sage, London.

Turner, Victor (1982), *From Ritual to Theatre: The Human Seriousness of Play*. New York: PAJ.

Wallendorf, Melanie and Belk, Russell W. (1989), "Assessing Trustworthiness in Naturalistic Consumer Research," in *Interpretive Consumer Research,* eds. E. C. Hirschman, Provo, UT: Association for Consumer Research, pp. 69-84.

Wallendorf, Melanie and Arnould, Eric (1991), "'We Gather Together': Consumption Rituals of Thanksgiving Day," *Journal of Consumer Research*, Vol.18, June, pp.13-31.

# Helping or hindering? Sibling interaction in child influence strategies

Ben Kerrane, Bradford University, UK
Margaret K. Hogg, Lancaster University, UK

## ABSTRACT

In this paper we explore the process of child influence, explicitly focussing on how sibling relationships ('sibship'), as one component of the family environment, shape the influence strategies which children direct towards their parents. Our findings point towards the ambivalent nature of sibling relationships, and suggest that sibling behaviours work to both help and hinder fellow siblings utilize influence strategies on their parents' consumption choices.

## INTRODUCTION

Understanding the influence that children exert in family consumption decisions remains a prominent area of concern for consumer researchers. Children influence up to $1.88 trillion of family expenditure globally (Lindstrom and Seybold, 2003), and yet we still lack a complete understanding of child influence processes (Cotte and Wood, 2004; Flurry, 2007). Whilst we do have a comprehensive account of the repertoire of strategies which children utilize in their attempts to get their own way from their parents, we know little about the motivations that lie behind strategy usage (Palan and Wilkes, 1997) or how contextual factors, such as the family setting and intra-family relationships, shape the influence strategies which children utilize (Cotte and Wood, 2004).

In this paper we specifically explore sibling relationships within the family setting. Sibling relationships have tended to be overlooked within existing consumer research (Cotte and Wood, 2004) which has usually focused on dyadic parent-child interaction. Our contribution is thus twofold. First we seek to better understand sibling relationships, which remain largely under explored in consumer research; and second, to investigate how sibling relationships shape the influence strategies which children employ within the family setting. Our study responds to Cotte and Wood's (2004) and Flurry's (2007) call for further research into the purchase influence of children in families, specifically by exploring how one aspect of the family environment (sibling interaction and relationships) affects the influence strategies that children employ.

### Child influence strategies: The research context

Research over the past forty years has established that *"purchase decisions within the family are not always the outcome of individual choice, but rather, family members influence each other"* (Hamilton and Catterall 2006, p.1032). The examination of children's influence strategies began with a study of cereal choices which identified that both the child's assertiveness and the mother's child-centeredness were central to a mother's susceptibility to her child's requests (Berey and Pollay 1968). In another study of cereal choice within a supermarket setting, children were more successful if they told their mothers to buy their preferred cereal, or if they demanded their choice, rather than if they simply asked their mother for it, or requested the item (Atkin 1978).

Another study specifically asked adolescents to write a series of essays entitled "How I get my way with my mother … father … best friend". Fifteen influence strategies were identified, sub divided by whether the strategies used were direct or indirect (Cowan, Drinkard and MacGavin 1984). Direct strategies included the use of more overt behaviours (asking, begging and pleading, telling or asserting, reasoning, demanding or arguing, stating importance, bargaining and persistence), whereas indirect strategies are believed to occur when *"the influencer acts as if the person on the receiving*

*end is not aware of the influence"* (Johnson 1976, p. 100). Indirect influence strategies included the use of negative affect (such as the use of crying, sadness and anger), positive affect (including the use of sweetness and innocence), verbal manipulation (often involving telling lies), eliciting reciprocity, using an advocate, evasion and laissez-faire (taking independent action, regardless) (Cowan *et al.* 1984). Adolescents directed more influence strategies towards their mothers than their fathers, and of those strategies directed towards mothers most involved the use of negative affect.

Examining explicitly the mother-child dyad, twelve child influence strategies were identified by Cowan and Avants (1988). These included: ask, bargain, show positive feelings, do as I please, show negative affect, persistence, beg and plead, perform good deeds, reason, cry and get angry. What is significant from this study is that strategies were related to the level of parental resistance that the children expected to encounter: high (anticipating non-compliance strategies e.g. beg and plead, cry) or low (autonomous strategies e.g. tell), and whether or not an equal power relationship existed between the parent and child (egalitarian strategies e.g. bargain and reason).

A study of the power strategies of popular and rejected black South African children identified four dimensions of influence strategies: direct and indirect influence strategies (as identified by Cowan *et al.* 1984), and bilateral and unilateral strategies (Bonn 1995). Falbo and Peplau (1980) had earlier identified the concept of bilateral and unilateral dimensions within influence strategies in their study of intimate relationships. Whereas bilateral strategies require the cooperation and responsiveness of the target (e.g. bargaining), unilateral strategies do not. Bonn (1995), through interviews with children involving hypothetical situations, identified a range of strategies, including persuasion, bargaining and compromise (bilateral, direct strategies); suggesting, ingratiating, and deception (bilateral, indirect strategies); sadness, crying and anger (unilateral, indirect strategies); and asking, threatening and coercion (unilateral, direct influence strategies). Rejected children often used unilateral influence strategies, frequently involving the use of aggression (Bonn 1995).

More recent work on adolescents and their parents identified four classes of influence strategies[1]: bargaining, persuasion, emotional, and request strategies (Palan and Wilkes 1997). In a diary study which applied Palan and Wilkes' (1997) influence strategy framework focussing on children's impact on innovative decision-making, children were subsequently found to employ persuasion strategies most often, followed by request and bargaining strategies (Götze, Prange and Uhrovska 2009). In only a few cases were children found to utilise emotion based strategies (Götze et al. 2009).

Lee and Collins (2000) and Lee and Beatty (2002), through videotaped recordings of family interactions during a simulated decision-making situation, recognised the potential for coalitions to form within families. Five main influence strategy types were identified: experience strategies (using experience and knowledge as a source of information to influence the outcome of a decision), legitimate strategies (which emphasise positional power and ste-

---

1 It should be noted that Palan and Wilkes (1997) identified seven influence strategies, although the latter three (expert, legitimate and directive) were strategies solely utilised by parents in response to their adolescent's use of an influence strategy.

reotypes), emotion strategies, bargaining strategies and coalition strategies (Lee and Collins 2000). Seven dimensions of children's direct influence strategies, ask nicely, bargain, show affection, just ask, beg and plead, show anger and con, have also been identified (Williams and Burns 2000). More recently the child influence strategies of justifying and highlighting the benefits of purchases, forming coalitions, compromising and remaining persistent, have also been documented (Thompson, Laing and McKee 2007).

In addition to the types of child influence strategies, a number of studies have also assessed children's influence on family decision processes in terms of the amount of influence children exert. Factors such as product classification and usage patterns (Belch *et al.* 1985; Shoham and Dalakas, 2003); the stage in the decision-making process (Szybillo and Sosanie 1977; Belch *et al.* 1985; Lee and Beatty 2002; Götze *et al.* 2009; Wang *et al.*, 2007); child demographics, such as age (John, 1999) and gender (Flurry 2007; Wang *et al.*, 2007); and family variables, such as family size (Jenkins 1979; Ahuja and Stinson 1993; Beatty and Talpade, 1994; Geuens, Mast and De Pelsmacker, 2002), income and social class (Ekström 2007; Jenkins 1979; Hamilton and Catterall, 2006; Moschis and Mitchell 1986; Lee and Beatty, 2002), and family type (Bates and Gentry 1994; Hall *et al.* 1995; Mangleburg and Grewal, 1999) are suggested to affect the amount of influence children exert.

Children appear to make informed choices about which influence strategy they will employ (Williams and Burns 2000). Their decisions are informed by the historical success or failure of utilizing such strategies in previous decision-making situations (Bao *et al.* 2007; Götze *et al.* 2009; Thompson *et al.* 2007). Ultimately, however, whilst we do know a great deal about the types of influence strategies which children utilize, and the amount of influence children have, we do not know how environmental variables (such as the family setting) shape the influence strategies which children direct towards their parents (Cotte and Wood, 2004). In this paper we explicitly focus on how sibling relationships, as one component of the family environment, shape the influence strategies which children utilize.

## METHODOLOGY

Phenomenological interviews (Thompson, Locander and Pollio 1989) were conducted with six families living in the North West of England, capturing the stories of twenty-nine family respondents. Following calls for family research which captures the dynamics of family purchase decision-making (Hamilton and Catterall 2006; Tinson and Nancarrow 2005) interviews were conducted with both children and their parents. In line with other interpretivist studies (see for instance Thompson and Troester 2002) purposive sampling (Miles and Huberman 1984) was used to identify and recruit a range of family types and not just nuclear family forms. Detailed profiles of the six families recruited are presented in Table 1. An emphasis on studying consumers in-depth necessitated a smaller sample size to be used to allow thick descriptions to emerge (Carrigan and Szmigin 2006) which is common for interpretivist consumer research.

The families were recruited partly through personal contacts; partly through placing online appeals for participants in family newspapers and publications; and partly by contacting relevant family organisations in the North West region. The interviews were conducted in the family home, usually in the kitchen at the dining table. Each family was visited between three and five times and interviews were conducted over a period ranging from four to twelve months. Respondents were first asked for their consent to participate in the research process, assured of anonymity, told about the purpose of the research and then asked for permission to record the conversations.

Consent was sought from parents and guardians to approach their children in order to then seek the children's consent to be involved in the data collection process (Mandell 1991). Methods by

**Table 1: Respondents' details**

| Family Pseudonym | Family Type/Comments | Parents/ Guardians | Working status of Parents/ Guardians | Children/ Ages | Number of interviews | Time period of interviews |
|---|---|---|---|---|---|---|
| Jones Family | Cohabiting couple headed family; Debbie and Paul are not married and have four children together | Debbie Paul | Childminder Plumber | Michael (14) Anna (12) Adam (9) Tina (7) | 5 | 11 months |
| Baldwin Family | Blended; Carole and Ray have one biological child together (Nina), and Jessica (Ray's step-daughter, Carole's biological child) also lives in the family home. Carole and Ray also have non-resident children from previous relationships | Carole Ray | Sales Assistant Plumber | Jessica (14) Nina (5) | 4 | 12 months |
| Harrison Family | Single parent family | Natalie | Unemployed | Mark Peters (21) David Peters (18) Luke Harrison (13) | 3 | 6 months |
| Francis/ Akua Family | Lesbian headed family | Fante Francis  Barbara Akua | Office Manager  Senior Civil Servant | Kwame Akua (19) Helen Akua (17) Ashanti Francis (5) Kaya Francis (3) | 3 | 4 months |
| White Family | Nuclear | Claire Brian | Administrator Sales Rep | Robert (12) Lee and Kevin (10) | 4 | 6 months |
| Bright Family | Blended | Pat Tom | Housewife Company Director | Zara (11) Jack (9) | 3 | 6 months |

which valid consent can be obtained from children were adhered to (Mason 2004). Recognising that children are potentially vulnerable research participants (Morrow and Richards 1996) the children were interviewed within the family home where an adult was always present, although not necessarily within earshot.

Interviews were tape recorded in full, lasted between 60 and 130 minutes, and were transcribed verbatim. The interviews with family members were conducted over three stages and explored themes such as family history, intra-family relationships and how family members got their own way. In stage one an interview was conducted with the parents/guardians. Following this initial interview, stage two involved interviews with the children. Given that children, particularly younger children, may feel uncomfortable in a one-on-one interview situation (Mayall 2001) the children were given the option to have another sibling present during their interview. Indeed in the second stage of the interviewing process the membership of the interviews was very fluid. Some children preferred to be interviewed individually, whereas in other families the children freely left and returned to the interview as other siblings joined and departed. Accordingly with some of the families one longer style visit was conducted with the children (comprising several shorter interviews with single and multiple children, often with overlapping attendance), whereas in other families the children preferred to have a much more contained interview. A semi participatory researcher role was adopted with the children (Mandell, 1991). Following this stage of interviewing, a final family group interview was conducted at stage three.

The interpretation of the interview texts was undertaken using a hermeneutical process (Thompson 1991; Thompson, Locander and Pollio 1990) which involved moving iteratively, back and forth between interview texts (within and across family cases) and the literature. Emerging themes in the data drove subsequent reading in the literature (Thompson 1996). Following hermeneutical principles (at the methodological level) a constant shift when reading between individual transcripts and the entire data set enabled a greater emergent understanding to develop in which elements of the part gave further meaning to the whole. Each family case was analysed on an idiographic basis which allowed for categorization of data from which larger conceptual classes emerged. These concepts were then compared across family cases, following Spiggle's (1994) initial steps for qualitative data analysis.

## FINDINGS

We have chosen to present, in a similar vein to Thompson (2005), two family cases which illuminate the global themes found across all the families in this study. Two family stories are used to emphasize the depth of the data which was collected and to show the complex and ambivalent nature of sibling relationships within the family setting. Our exploratory study highlights the ways in which children tried to help their siblings when they attempted to get their own way from their parents (*helping behaviours*, for example, expressing to parents the unfairness of not buying a product for a sibling; or voluntarily, or unwittingly, offering support to a sibling through coalition formation), and also the behaviours of siblings when they decided to counter the influence strategies of their brother(s)/sister(s) (*hindering behaviours*, such as using threats and violence to stop a child employing an influence strategy; or sabotaging their influence attempt). Primacy is placed on child accounts of sibling relationships.

Across each family story the children were aware that certain siblings within families were favoured by parents. Unequal parent-child relations, and parental favouritism of specific children, are suggested to be common characteristics of family life (McIntosh

and Punch 2009; Suitor et al. 2008) and this strongly emerged within our data. The siblings and parents alike highlighted within each family the children who were favoured by parents, which was particularly acute in the blended Baldwin family. Here Jessica Baldwin highlights her step-father, Ray's, favouritism of his biological child, Nina, supporting earlier research that step-parents often favour their biological children (Suitor *et al.*, 2008):

*Jessica: Nina. Yeah (..) she's their angel, she like, like gets all the time, she doesn't even have to ask for things, she just gets them from Ray, he buys her things all the time … It doesn't work like that for me (.) I have to put money to the things I want, or just go without, but I do try and work on them.*

A sense of the unfairness of parental favouritism emerged from the family stories which highlighted the relative ease with which certain siblings could influence their parents. Such ease antagonised the other siblings, particularly those siblings who felt that they had to work much harder in order to get their own way, as Anna Jones comments:

*Anna: It's so unfair. Michael gets everything, computer stuff, guitars, money to go out with his mates, Mum won't give me any extra money because I get my spends, and that's it.*

Michael Jones' preferential parental treatment results in volatile relationships between him and his fellow siblings, with parental differential treatment (PDT) giving rise to sibling rivalry and competitiveness amongst siblings (Tucker, McHale and Crouter 2005). Whilst PDT worked to help certain children influence their parents in attempts to get their own way (facing minimal parental resistance), it could also work to the disadvantage of the favoured children in relation to sibling interaction because PDT often represented an obstacle for certain children to overcome. Parental favouritism affected sibling relationships, as Michael Jones, described as his mother's "golden boy" by his father, explains:

*Michael: I suppose Mum does buy me more things (..) I can tell Anna's not happy about that, but what can I do? It's kind of a good thing, but a bad thing as well … yes I can get what I want from Mum, but I've got to watch my back a bit with Anna. She doesn't like it.*

Ultimately what emerges from the family stories is that parent-child relationships can affect sibling-sibling relationships, resulting in a spill-over of behaviours (i.e. that differing parent-child relations are manifest in, and shape, sibling-sibling relationships). Moreover, sibling-sibling relationships can also help or hinder a child's success in influencing parental decisions. Helping behaviours and hindering behaviours were evident amongst siblings in terms of facilitating or impeding another sibling's utilization of influence strategies on their parents.

### Sibling relationships and helping behaviours

Just as parent-child coalitions exist (Lee and Collins, 2000), sibling-sibling coalitions were also apparent (Thompson *et al.*, 2007) within each family story. Nina Baldwin, for example, frequently recognises the unfairness of her parent's resistance to her half sister's influence strategies. Fairness has been reported as a characteristic of sibling interaction and exchanges (McIntosh and

Punch, 2009), and Nina explains how she offers her help to Jessica in an effort to get her half-sister what she wants:

> *Nina: Mummy and Daddy just get me what I want (..) Jess doesn't get many things, so I help her ... I'll say to Mummy that I want something when really I don't, but it's for Jess.*

Nina likes spending time with her older half-sister, but frequently this is not reciprocated by Jessica. Although Jessica is often annoyed by Nina, with older siblings keen to distance themselves from younger siblings (Punch, 2008), Jessica does attempt to recruit Nina when utilizing an influence strategy directed towards her parents:

> *Jessica: I try just to ask them for things, but they're having none of it, they keep, they just say that I've had too much, and that they can't afford it. That's what they always say to me, we've got no money (..) but they get stuff for Nina, they buy her loads of stuff ... so I'll get Nina to ask them for things for me. They don't say no to her.*

Although Jessica is often annoyed by her half sister's actions and Nina's desires to spend time with her, Jessica also manipulates this relationship for her own gain – and recruits Nina to employ influence strategies on Jessica's behalf. Through promises to play with Nina and to spend time with her, which often do not materialise, Jessica recruits an ally who is skilled and successful in influencing her parents. Ultimately Nina's influence success and power is exploited by Jessica, and younger siblings are reportedly easily manipulated by older siblings in deal making situations (McIntosh and Punch, 2009). Such manipulation was also evident within the Jones family, with Michael's siblings often forming temporary coalitions with him to strengthen their chances of success when employing an influence strategy. Whilst his siblings report that they do not have a favourable opinion of Michael, largely because of PDT, they too recognise the minimal parental resistance that he faces when influencing their parents:

> *Anna: Michael's the good one, the favourite (.) the one that gets everything. He's dull, a swot, good at school. I don't hang out with him, I wouldn't (.) but then he's good to have on side if you want something from Mum and Dad.*

We feel that the above quotation is significant as it highlights the ambivalence and fluidity within sibling relationships (Edwards, Mauthner and Hadfield, 2005; Punch, 2008). Sibling relationships are far from static and fluctuate across contexts and influence strategy attempts, and are often manipulated and exploited by children to assist them in achieving their own ends. However, such manipulation is recognised by older siblings – and it does not always appear that they are totally duped by their fellow siblings into offering help – as Michael Jones comments:

> *Michael: I know what they're doing, I know that they want to use me so they can get something from Mum. But then I don't know when I might need them to help me get something (..) so I just go along with it, sort of bank it in case I need their help later.*

Tag-team sibling influence was also apparent. The Jones siblings discussed how they each took turns to help influence their parents buy products which they all wanted. Parents are more responsive to the influence of their children when multiple children argue for the purchase (Tinson and Nancarrow, 2007). Here Adam and Tina Jones discuss their actions when they approached their parents to get cable television:

> *Adam: We all wanted to get cable, so we just went on and on and on at them. We took it in turns to mither them*
> *Tina: We all helped to get that, everyone had at go (.) Michael helped, too, so we knew we would break them and get it because he wanted it*

Across the family stories, as Thompson *et al.* (2007) similarly report, the siblings did not formally or explicitly discuss the types of influence strategy that they would utilize. Rather the siblings used the influence strategy which they knew had proved to be most effective for them to use in the past. This lends support to the notion that children engage in a trial and error process to understand which strategy is most effective for them to utilize (Bao *et al.*, 2007):

> *Michael: I don't have to try too hard to get what I want (..) usually I just put my arms around Mum and tell her what I want. That usually does it.*

Ultimately siblings can work to help fellow siblings to get what they want from their parents. At times, however, younger children appeared to be easily manipulated by older children. Sibling relationships are often ambivalent, as Nina Baldwin comments. Here Nina highlights that although she does like her half-sister, and often freely offers her help to Jessica to influence their parents, at times the relationship between Nina and Jessica sours. It is at this point, as experienced by other siblings across the families, that violence is used to gain the 'help' of other siblings:

> *Nina: Sometimes I don't like Jessica, and Jessica doesn't like me. If she doesn't play with me I won't help her (.) she doesn't like that, and sometimes she says she'll hurt me if I don't help her, or she'll say she'll (..) she'll say she'll kick me if I don't help.*

Conflict is a common feature of sibship (Edwards et al., 2006). Violence was also a way in which siblings could hinder another child's utilization of an influence strategy, as the follow section describes.

### Sibling relationships and hindering behaviours

Threats of violence were also identified by the child respondents as ways in which siblings tried to block and hinder the use of influence strategies by their brother(s)/sister(s). Often siblings would tell one another what they were going to approach their parents for, before employing a given influence strategy. The siblings, however, were often very aware that their parents' resources were limited and that, because of this, there was a rush to be bought something first. Parents were also reported to justify non-compliance to their children's earlier influence strategies on the grounds of limited financial resources, as Palan and Wilkes (1997) also found, and so the children felt a heightened sense of urgency to get what they wanted before their siblings:

> *Jessica: The thing with Nina is that she gets all the time, she gets bought loads of things from Mum and Ray. I don't think that's fair, and when she comes to me saying that she's going to ask them for a new mobile or coat or whatever I try and stop her ... I might threaten her or something just to get her not to ask them. If she doesn't ask them for things then they can't use the excuse of having no money to me.*

Another related way in which children attempted to counter the influence strategies of their siblings was to directly emphasize to parents how often they [the parents] yielded to their sibling's influence strategies. This frequently concerned the children who the siblings felt were favoured the most by their parents due to PDT. As Anna Jones explains, Michael's success in influencing his mother and father antagonises her and her siblings, and as a result Anna stresses to her parents the unfairness and frequency with which they yield to Michael:

*Anna: Michael gets what he wants, he asks and he just gets, so that's when I say to Mum you bought him something last week (.) last time. I don't think she realizes how often she buys him things, so I let her know to stop him getting more stuff (..) I point it out to her, he shouldn't get anything else, it's not fair.*

Often multiple siblings would unite in larger families to highlight such unfairness to their parents, as Tina further explains:

*Tina: I think (..) I think if I just said it wasn't fair, that Michael gets things all the time Mum wouldn't believe me, not just me. But then if Adam and Anna says it too, then (.) then they believe us more.*

Siblings, either individually or in coalition with other siblings, would also attempt to sabotage the chances of their brother's or sister's influence success through suggesting to parents that buying him or her a given product would be a waste of their money. Such behaviour was obviously dependent on inter-sibling relationships and the quality of such relationships at a given point in time. Often siblings approached parents to cast a seed of doubt in their mind as to whether a child would use the requested product to block sibling influence attempts:

*Adam: I say to Mum and Dad that they won't use it, or they already have it (..) or that I know someone at school that has it, and they say it's no good (.) so don't get them it. I might not even know, but I say it to stop them getting things.*

A similar technique was also used by children to block and hinder the influence strategies employed by their siblings. Rather than deceive their parents, as the above extract illustrates, in some instances elder children would use the internet to research what their siblings were asking their parents for. Through the internet the children found negative information about the products that their siblings wanted, and used this information as a basis to inform their parents and sway their decisions. Here Jessica discusses using this technique when her younger half-sister asked her parents for a Nintendo DS™:

*Jessica: Nina wanted a pink DS (.) but I didn't want her to get one 'cos she gets too much. So I went online and found a bad review and showed it to Mum, I showed it to her, and told her that she'd get headaches using it, and she didn't buy it in the end.*

Rather than this being a selfless and supporting sibling act, we feel that Jessica acted in this way to stop her half-sister being bought an expensive item. Alongside Jessica feeling that Nina is bought too many things by her mother and step-father, Jessica is also aware that her parents have limited financial resources. Whilst children using the internet to gather information to support influence strategies is

documented elsewhere (Belch, Krentler and Willis-Flurry, 2005; Thomson and Laing, 2003), with parents responding favourably to children who are well informed, here siblings actively use the internet to gather information to hinder the influence strategies of their brother(s)/sister(s).

Again, the ambivalent nature of sibling relationships was also apparent in terms of hindering behaviours. Siblings who had once worked together to influence their parents would often work against each other in union with other siblings. Here Adam discusses a family decision of deciding where to eat out in which he united with his older brother, Michael, to get his own way. Adam often works in coalition with Tina and Anna to stop Michael getting his own way, but here Adam joined forces with Michael:

*Adam: Anna was on about us going to Nando's[2], but I didn't want to, I wanted a Chinese. Michael wasn't bothered where we went, so I got him to say he wanted a Chinese as well (.) I said he could lend my [computer] games, so in the end Mum said we should go for a Chinese.*

The above quotation from Adam again works to underline the ambivalent nature of sibling relationships, and also the power that certain children have within the family. In this decision making scenario Adam persuaded Michael to agree with his restaurant choice, with siblings often using products and monetary exchanges as currency to sway the decisions of other siblings (McIntosh and Punch, 2009), despite a volatile relationship existing between the brothers.

## DISCUSSION

Whilst we know a great deal about the types of influence strategies which children direct towards their parents, and the variables which affect the amount of influence that children exert in family consumption decision making, we do not have a thorough understanding of the *processes* of child influence itself. Our paper has attempted to fill an element of this gap by focussing attention on how one component of the family environment, sibling interaction and relationships, shapes the child influence process. Sibling relationships have largely been ignored by consumer researchers (Cotte and Wood, 2004) and sociologists alike (McIntosh and Punch, 2009), and our paper offers some insight into the ambivalent nature of sibship.

As our family stories suggest, sibling relationships are far from static, with sibling alliances and coalitions contested and negotiated by children, largely for their own gain. Within the Jones family, for example, Michael's strong relationship with his parents and the resulting parental differential treatment that he receives antagonizes his siblings, Anna, Tina and Adam. However, the siblings recognise Michael's strong position within this family, and the minimal parental resistance which Michael faces when utilizing influence strategies, and they will often work with Michael to bolster their own chances of influence success. Although Michael does not always lend his support to his siblings to strengthen their chances of influence success, he often does, largely because of the use of bribes (e.g. Adam's offer to Michael of lending Michael his computer games if Michael agreed with his choice of restaurant for the family meal) or because Michael feels he may need to recoup this help from his siblings at a later time.

Jessica Baldwin also recognises the ease in which her half-sister influences the decisions of her mother and step-father.

---

2 Nando's is a restaurant in the United Kingdom which specializes in chicken dishes

Despite Jessica being annoyed by her half-sister, with Nina enjoying spending time with Jessica and playing with her, Jessica will often attempt to recruit Nina to employ influence strategies on her behalf towards their parents. At times Nina will do this voluntarily, with Nina recognising the unfair parental resistance which Jessica faces when utilizing influence strategies. However, often Jessica will manipulate Nina into offering her help through threatening to hurt her if she doesn't, or making deals with her to encourage her to help (and these deals often do not materialize) when this relationship sours.

Children can help their siblings to get what they want from their parents through helping behaviours i.e. emphasizing to parents the unfairness of not yielding to a sibling's influence strategy; utilizing an influence strategy on parents on behalf of another sibling; or through working in coalition with siblings, either through their own free will or because they have been coerced into lending their support due to threats of violence. Largely we feel that these children chose to help a sibling because they expected to gain something back from doing so. The children reported that their parents responded well to displays of supposedly altruistic behaviour, and that selfless acts often resulted in material gain for the children (with parents rewarding such behaviour).

Children also displayed hindering behaviours, and would use violence; highlight to parents the unfairness of yielding to a child's influence strategy; form coalitions; and sabotage a child's chances of influence success (e.g. by informing parents that the item a child wants is not a good product, or that they wouldn't use it) to stop siblings getting their own way from their parents. The children were aware that their parents had limited financial resources, a feeling very much heightened given the current economic climate, and as such there was stiff competition amongst the siblings to get what they wanted first from their parents.

Siblings, therefore, can play an important role in helping or hindering the influence strategies which children utilize, offering insight into the process of child influence. Equally our study lends support to the notion that children utilize complex and sophisticated influence strategies in attempts to get what they want from their parents (Götze *et al.*, 2009; Thompson *et al.*, 2007). Whilst coalition formation has been documented elsewhere within family decision making (Lee and Collins, 2000), and in relation to sibling coalitions (see, for instance Thompson *et al.*, 2007), our study extends this body of literature by highlighting the fluidity of sibling coalition formation. Sibling coalitions appear ambivalent, and future research should further explore how such different coalition patterns form and re-form, coalescing around different family members and various combinations of influence strategies.

Our study was limited to examining the influence strategies children utilize on their parents, however scope also exists to explore the different ways in which children attempt to influence the behaviours of their siblings (intra-generational influence). The main focus of our paper was to explore how sibship affects child influence strategies, however we already have early findings that suggest that family type also affects the process (cf. Jessica's relationship with her step-father) which could be usefully explored further. Our paper has also, because of space constraints, focussed on the voice of siblings alone, although the stories and themes presented here through the voices of the children recruited are very much rooted in the accounts of family life from both children *and* parents. It is also recognised that the setting for the interviews was largely dictated by parents who initially granted access to their home. We also acknowledge that the family group interview could have produced socially acceptable results i.e. children may have felt constrained in this setting, and presented their family in a harmonious light, for example. However, an individual interview format was also offered to the children in an attempt to take account of such potential bias.

Opportunities exist to explore the influence strategies of children across a greater range of family types, and also to explore in further depth whether children direct different types of influence strategies towards different family members (e.g. siblings, grandparents, step-parents). Similarly opportunities exist to explore firstly, multiple family consumption sites (e.g. do children switch their use of influence strategy in different family settings, or homes); and secondly families of different cultures, in order to investigate whether such factors (as sibling relationships) also influence the choice processes involved in selecting which influence strategy to employ in families from different cultural settings.

## REFERENCES

Ahuja, R. D. and Stinson, K. M. (1993) Female-Headed Single Parent Families: An Exploratory Study of Children's influence in Family Decision Making. *Advances in Consumer Research*. Vol. 20, pp. 467-474.

Atkin, C. (1978) Observation of Parent-Child Interaction in Supermarket Decision-Making. *Journal of Marketing*. Vol. 42, pp. 41-45.

Bao, Y., Fern, E. F. and Sheng, S. (2007) Parental Style and Adolescent Influence in Family Consumption Decisions: An Integrative Approach. *Journal of Business Research*. Vol. 60, pp. 672-680.

Bates, M. J., and Gentry, J. W. (1994) Keeping the Family Together : How we Survived the Divorce. *Advances in Consumer Research*. Vol 21, pp 30 – 34.

Beatty, S. E. and Talpade, S. (1994) Adolescent Influence in Family Decision Making: A Replication With Extension. *Journal of Consumer Research*. Vol. 21 (2) pp. 332-341.

Belch, G. E., Belch, M. A. and Ceresino, G. (1985) Parental and Teenage Child Influences in Family Decision Making. *Journal of Business Research*. Vol 13, pp 163-176.

Belch, M. A., Krentler, K. A. And Willis-Flurry, L. A. (2005) Teen Internet Mavens: Influence in Family Decision Making. *Journal of Business Research*. Vol. 58, pp. 569-575.

Berey, L. A., and Pollay, R. W. (1968) The Influencing Role of the Child in Family Decision Making. *Journal of Marketing Research*. Vol 70 (2) pp 70 – 72.

Bonn, M. (1995) Power strategies used in conflict resolution by popular and rejected black South African children. *Early Child Development and Care*. Vol. 114, pp 39 – 54.

Carrigan, M. and Szmigin, I. (2006) 'Mothers of invention': Maternal Empowerment and Convenience Consumption. *European Journal of Marketing*. Vol. 40 (9/10) pp 1122-1142.

Cotte, J. and Wood, S. L. (2004) Families and Innovative Consumer Behaviour: A Triadic Analysis of Sibling and Parental Influence. *Journal of Consumer Research*. Vol. 31, pp 78 – 86.

Cowan, G. and Avants, S. K. (1988) Children's Influence Strategies: Structure, Sex Differences, and Bilateral Mother-Child Influence. *Child Development*. Vol. 59, pp 1303-1313.

Cowan, G., Drinkard, J. and MacGavin, L. (1984) The Effect of Target, Age, and Gender on use of Power Strategies. *Journal of Personality and Social Psychology*. Vol. 47, pp 1391-1398.

Edwards, R., Hadfield, L. and Mauthner, M. (2005) Children's Sibling Relationships and Gendered Practices: Talk, Activity and Dealing with Change. *Gender and Education*. Vol. 17 (5) pp. 499-513.

Ekström, K. (2007) Parental Consumer Learning or 'Keeping Up With Children'. *Journal of Consumer Behaviour*. Vol. 6, pp. 203-217.

Falbo, T. and Peplau, L. A. (1980) Power Strategies in Intimate Relationships. *Journal of Personality and Social Psychology*. Vol 38 (4), pp 618 – 628.

Flurry, L. A. (2007) Children's Influence in Family Decision-Making: Examining the Impact of The Changing American Family. *Journal of Business Research*. Vol. 60, pp. 322-330.

Geuens, M., Mast, G. and De Pelsmacker, P. (2002) Children's influence on family purchase behaviour:The role of family structure. *Asia Pacific Advances in Consumer Research*. Vol 5, pp 130 – 135.

Götze, E., Prange, C. and Uhrovska, I. (2009) Children's Impact on Innovative Decision Making: A Diary Study. *European Journal of Marketing*. Vol. 43 (1/2) pp. 264-295.

Hall, J., Shaw, M., Johnson, M. and Oppenheim, P. (1995) Influence of Children on Family Consumer Decision Making. *European Advances in Consumer Research*. Vol. 2, pp 45 – 53.

Hamilton, K. and Catterall, M. (2006) Consuming Love in Poor Families: Children's Influence on Consumption Decisions. *Journal of Marketing Management*. Vol. 22 (9-10), pp. 1031-1052.

Jenkins, R. L. (1979) The influence of Children in Family Decision Making: Parents' Perceptions. *Advances in Consumer Research*. Vol. 6, pp. 413-418.

John, D. R. (1999) Consumer Socialisation of Children: A Retrospective Look at Twenty-Five Years of Research. *Journal of Consumer Research*. Vol. 26 pp 183 – 213.

Johnson, P. (1976) Women and Power: Toward a Theory of Effectiveness. *Journal of Social Issues*. Vol. 32, pp 99-110.

Lee, C. K. C. and Beatty, S. E. (2002) Family Structure and Influence in Family Decision Making. *The Journal of Consumer Marketing*. Vol 19 (1) pp 24 – 39.

Lee, C. K. C. and Collins, B. A. (2000) Family Decision Making and Coalition Patterns. *European Journal of Marketing*. Vol. 34 (9) pp 1181 – 1198.

Lindstrom, M. and Seybold, P. B. (2003) *Brandchild*. London: Kogan Page.

Mandell, N. (1991) 'The Least Adult Role in Studying Children' In F. Waksler (Ed.) *Studying the Social Worlds of Children: Sociological Readings* (pp 38-59). London: Falmer Press.

Mangleburg, T. and Grewal, D. (1999) Family Type, Family Authority Relations, and Adolescents. Purchase Influence. *Advances in Consumer Research*. Vol. 26, pp 379-384.

Mason, J. (2004) 'The Legal Context' In S. Fraser, V. Lewis, S. Ding, M. Kellett and C. Robinson (Eds) *Doing Research with Children and Young People* (pp 43-58). London: Sage.

Mayall, B. (2001), "Conversations With Children Working With Generational Issues" In P. Christensen and A. James (Eds.) *Research With Children: Perspectives and Practices*, London: Falmer Press, pp. 120-135.

McIntosh, I. and Punch, S. (2009) Barter, Deals, Bribes and Threats: Exploring Sibling Interactions. *Childhood*. Vol. 16 (1), pp. 49-65.

Miles, M. B. and Huberman, A. M. (1984) *Qualitative Data Analysis: A Sourcebook of New Methods*. Beverly Hills: Sage.

Morrow, V. and Richards, M. (1996) The ethics of social research with children: An Overview. *Children and Society*. Vol. 10, pp 90 – 105.

Moschis, G. P. and Mitchell, L. G. (1986) Television Advertising and Interpersonal Influences on Teenager's Participation in Family Consumer Decisions. *Advances in Consumer Research*. Vol. 13, pp 181 – 186.

Palan, K. M. and Wilkes, R. E. (1997) Adolescent-Parent Interaction in Family Decision Making. *Journal of Consumer Research*. Vol. 24, pp 159 – 169.

Punch, S. (2008) 'You can do Nasty Things to your Brothers and Sisters without a Reason': Siblings' Backstage Behaviours. *Children and Society*. Vol. 22, pp. 333-344.

Shoham, A. and Dalakas, V. (2003) Family Consumer Decision-Making in Israel: The Role of Teens and Parents. *The Journal of Consumer Marketing*. Vol. 20 (2/3) pp. 238-251.

Spiggle, S. (1994) Analysis and Interpretation of Qualitative Data in Consumer Research. *Journal of Consumer Research*. Vol. 21, pp 491-503.

Suitor, J. J., Sechrist, J., Plikuhn, M., Pardo, S. T. and Pillemer, K. (2008) Within-Family Differences in Parent-Child Relations Across the Life Course. *Current Directions in Psychological Science*. Vol. 17 (5) pp. 334-338.

Szybillo, G. J. and Sosanie, A. (1977) Family Decision Making: Husband, Wife and Children. *Advances in Consumer Research*. Vol. 4, pp 46-49.

Thompson, C. J. (1991), May the Circle Be Unbroken: A Hermeneutic Consideration of How Interpretive Approaches to Consumer Research Are Understood by Consumer Researchers, *Advances in Consumer Research*, Vol. 18, pp. 63-69.

Thompson, C. J. (1996) Caring Consumers: Gendered Consumption Meanings and the Juggling Lifestyle. *Journal of Consumer Research*. Vol. 22, pp 388-407.

Thompson, C. J. (2005) Consumer Risk Perceptions in a Community of Reflexive Doubt. *Journal of Consumer Research*. Vol. 32, pp 235-248.

Thompson, E. S. and Laing, A. W. (2003), The Net Generation: Children and Young People, the Internet and Online Shopping, *Journal of Marketing Management*, Vol. 19, pp. 491-512.

Thompson, C. J. and Troester, M. (2002) Consumer Value System in the Age of Postmodern Fragmentation: The Case of the Natural Health Microculture. *Journal of Consumer Research*. Vol. 28 (4) pp 550-571.

Thompson, C. J., Locander, W. B. and Pollio, H. R. (1989) Putting Consumer Experience Back into Consumer Research: The Philosophy and Method of Existential-Phenomenology. *Journal of Consumer Research*. Vol. 16, pp 133 – 146.

Thompson, C. J., Locander, W. B. and Pollio, H. R. (1990), The Lived Meaning of Free Choice: An Existential-Phenomenological Description of Everyday Consumer Experiences of Contemporary Married Women, *Journal of Consumer Research*, Vol. 17, pp. 346-361.

Thompson, E. S., Laing, A. W. and McKee, L. (2007) Family Purchase Decision Making: Exploring Child Influence Behaviour. *Journal of Consumer Behaviour*. Vol. 6, pp. 182-202.

Tinson, J. and Nancarrow, C. (2005) The Influence of Children on Purchases: The Development of Measures for Gender Role Orientation and Shopping Savvy. *International Journal of Market Research*. Vol. 47 (1) pp. 5-27.

Tinson J. & Nancarrow C. (2007) GROwing Up: Tweenagers Involvement in Family Decision Making. *Journal of Consumer Marketing*. Vol. 24 (3) pp.160-170.

Tucker, C. J., McHale, S. M. and Crouter, A. C. (2005) Dimensions of Mothers' and Fathers' Differential Treatment of Siblings: Links with Adolescents' Sex Typed Personal Qualities. *Family Relations*. Vol. 52, pp. 82-89.

Wang, S., Holloway, B. B., Beatty, S. E. and Hill, W. W. (2007) Adolescent Influence in Family Purchase Decisions: An Update and Cross-National Extension. *Journal of Business Research*. Vol. 60, pp. 1117-1124.

Williams, L. A. and Burns, A. C. (2000) Exploring the Dimensionality of Children's Direct Influence Attempts. *Advances in Consumer Research*. Vol. 27, pp 64 – 71.

# Construction of Print Advertisement in the Context of Conceptual Coherence and Memory Distortion

Alicja Grochowska, Warsaw School of Social Sciences and Humanities, Poland
Andrzej Falkowski, Warsaw School of Social Sciences and Humanities, Poland

## ABSTRACT

Conceptual coherence of print advertisements and memory distortion of coherent-incoherent ads, considering brand familiarity is examined. The theoretical background are network models of the mind and theories of concepts. Results showed the significance of the coherence of ads in their resistance to memory distortion, examined in the backward framing paradigm.

## INTRODUCTION

**Construction of Print Advertisement in the Context of Conceptual Coherence and Memory Distortion**

It is important for marketers that their advertisements be well remembered and resistant to memory distortion. Consumers receive information about different products form different sources, for example from internet, the press, TV, or comparative advertisements created by competitors. One of the most important determinants of the effectiveness of an advertisement is its construction – in such a way that the structure of the ad is not sensitive to memory distortion. The goal of our research is to show that persuasive messages, such as print advertisements, are resistant to memory distortion only if they are conceptually coherent.

## CONCEPTUAL COHERENCE OF PRINT ADVERTISEMENT

Effects of information congruency versus incongruency in advertisements have been investigated in several empirical studies but the results are inconclusive. Discrepant results of the research on the memory and evaluation of ads in the context of (in)congruency seems to stem from different approaches to this problem.

Incongruency resulted in better evaluation and memory of an ad or product when (in)congruency between *different* marketing objects was investigated (e.g. ad-brand, product-celebrity, ad-magazine). Dahlén et al. (2005) found that ad-brand incongruency produced *more sophisticated* associations. However, it is worth noting that *similar* associations result in better memory of objects. Ad-brand incongruency had positive effects on credibility of ads, and product-celebrity mild incongruency had positive effects on product evaluation, but the memory has not been investigated in this context (Dahlen and Lange 2004; Lee and Thorson 2008). Dahlén et al. (2008) showed that ads placed in thematically incongruent media were better-remembered. It is worth noting that ads were incoherent with their external context and could draw consumers' attention (but incongruency *within* the ad has not been investigated). For example, an ad of automobile in a furniture magazine is incongruent and as a discrepant element it draws attention.

However, research in which (in)congruency *within* the advertisement or other marketing objects was investigated shows that congruent objects are better-remembered and evaluated (e.g. a dentist presenting a toothpaste). Incongruent objects are classified to the other category and it is hard to remember them. For example, Nedungadi and Hutchinson (1985) found that products classified into categories where they did not fit 'naturally' had more in common with contrasting categories and were far less typical, resulting in poor associations with the category concept and poor recall. According to Sujan and Bettman (1989) strong discrepancy of the focal attribute of the brand from the overall category schema, as compared to moderate discrepancy, resulted in higher recall of

discrepant features. The brand in the strongly discrepant condition was perceived as a distinct subtype. On the other hand, interproduct similarity was correlated positively with the number of common usages shared by the particular pair of products and negatively with the number of distinctive usages associated with the two products. Thus, the probability of recall of a category instance from memory was associated strongly with its typicality (Ratneshwar and Shocker 1991). Heckler and Childers (1992) found that unexpected and relevant information in the advertisement was remembered better than unexpected and irrelevant. One can say that relevant information is associated with the content of advertisement and is perceived as an integral part of an ad.

Findings presented above show that incongruency results in a better evaluation and memory of an advertisement when (in)congruency between *different* marketing objects is investigated (e.g. ad-brand, ad-magazine). However, congruent ads are better-remembered and evaluated when (in)congruency *within* the advertisement is examined. Congruent elements constituting an advertisement are associated with each other and easily recalled. We investigate the (in)congruency between different elements *within* the advertisement.

## THEORETICAL BACKGROUND

One may refer at this point to network models of the mind in which encoded information is stored in memory as a network structure, consisting of nodes representing concepts and links representing associations among concepts. The stronger associations among nodes, the easier connected pieces of information are retrieved (Anderson 1983; McClelland 1995). These findings are also confirmed by psychological theories of conceptual coherence (Murphy and Medin 1985) and theories of concepts (Smith 1995). One of the crucial theories explaining what makes a category seem coherent is Murphy and Medin's (1985) theory of conceptual coherence: Similarity of category members, correlated attributes, and knowledge about the word ('private theories'), as well as needs, goals are determinants of conceptual coherence. According to Murphy and Medin (1985) 'conceptual coherence derives from having a theory': representations of concepts are thought to be embedded in knowledge that embodies theories about the world. In further studies the importance of theories for conceptual coherence has been elaborated by Medin (1989), and Margoli (1999). Both authors provide additional evidence that the notion of similarity is too unconstrained to give an account of conceptual coherence, and that concepts are organized around theories. In this theoretical context the following issues are considered, and important for the present article: what makes a concept efficient, useful, and informative, and what makes a set of objects form a single category. In the marketing domain the conceptual coherence has been developing around the brand image. Lau and Phau (2007) carried out the research which showed that the mediating role of brand image fit between brand personality fit and dilution of brand affect is explained by using conceptual coherence theory.

Therefore, a coherence of print advertisement can be defined by the amount of similar associations provided by particular elements of an advertisement. These associations and their strength result from the knowledge about the advertisement. This means that the greater amount of similar associations between particular elements of the advertisement, the more coherent it is. According to this approach one may expect that the elements of an incoherent advertisement are remembered better when they are unusual and/or untypical but they can be remembered in *isolation* from other elements of the ad. On the other hand, memory is an active constructive process. Research conducted in the backward framing paradigm showed that information acquired *after* an experience can transform the memory of that experience. Postexperience information is most likely to distort memories when it is very similar to the actual experienced information (Braun et al. 1997, 2005). Thus, we can expect that coherent elements, strongly associated with each other, are more resistant to memory distortion than incoherent.

In Study 1 we propose the operationalization of the conceptual coherence of print advertisement. We also show the significance of brand familiarity in perceiving the coherence of ads. In Study 2 we demonstrate the importance of an advertisement coherence for its resistance to memory distortion, considering the moderating role of the brand familiarity.

## OPERATIONALIZATION OF CONCEPTUAL COHERENCE OF ADVERTISEMENT

According to network models of memory, the encoded information is stored in memory as a network structure, consisting of nodes representing concepts and links representing associations among concepts. The frequency with which a node is activated, as well as the duration with which activation spreads in the network, are also measures of connection strength (Anderson 1983; McClelland 1995). These assumptions about the network nature of the mind allow to operationalize the conceptual coherence of print advertisement. Shank's (1991) research showed that the extent to which a feature is associated with a category depends not only on the number of pairings of the feature with the category but also on the relative predictiveness of the feature for the category, which in turn illustrates the operation of a selectional process that determines the way in which the feature and the category are associated. This approach to the processes of categorization is a theoretical basis for operationalization of conceptual coherence of print advertisement. The strength of associations between particular elements of an advertisement is a measure of the ad's coherence. Kleine and Kernan's (1988) method of measuring 'consumption objects meaning' (affinity index) has been applied to analysis of conceptual coherence of print advertisement. In our research the effects of the coherence and memory distortion of advertisements are moderated by brand familiarity.

## BRAND FAMILIARITY AND PERCEPTION OF AD COHERENCE

Familiar brands are more easily detected in advertising clutter. Moreover, familiar brands are less affected by competing claims from other brands (Kent and Allen 1994; Pechmann and Stewart 1990) and have a more persuasive power of sources of claims (Snyder 1989). At the same time, consumers have well-established brand schemas for familiar brands, which leads them to expect a certain kind of communication from the brand (Campbell and Keller 2003; Dahlén and Lange 2004). Familiar brands have a well developed brand schema that may withstand incongruent information, whereas unfamiliar brand schemas are more sensitive to incongruency. Familiar brands are cognitively available and activate a wide area of an associative network. Thus, conceptual coherence of advertisements is moderated by brand familiarity. One can refer to the theory of conceptual coherence here (Murphy and Medin 1985): Knowledge of familiar brands, like knowledge, theories about the world, joins together elements of an advertisement in a consumer's mind.

**H1:** *Advertisements for familiar brands are perceived as more coherent than ads for unfamiliar brands: Advertisements for familiar brands elicit more similar associations between particular elements than ads for unfamiliar brands.*

The conceptual coherence of ads determines a way of storing information about an advertisement in memory. Coherent ads, as compared to incoherent, should be better remembered and more resistant to memory distortion.

## AD COHERENCE AND MEMORY DISTORTION

One of the important determinants of the effectiveness of an advertisement is a good memory for its elements. The advertisement is one of many sources of product information received by consumers. Coherent ads are better remembered: Particular elements of an advertisement are associated in a network in memory. Recalling one of its elements facilitates recalling other elements. On the other hand, memory can be distorted because of its constructive nature. That is why it is important for information in an advertisement to be resistant to memory distortion.

One of the most intriguing forms of memory distortion: when the memory of a previous experience with a product is altered by the actual information about the product, has been examined by Kathryn Braun-LaTour and colleagues (Braun and Zaltman 1997; Braun-LaTour and LaTour 2005) in the field of consumer behavior in the backward framing paradigm. An advertising misinformation effect was obtained for color memory of a previously seen candy bar wrapper (Braun and Loftus 1998). In other research, Braun found that a bad orange juice experience could be remembered as being better in retrospect if advertising were received after-the-fact. The advertising acted as a 'backward frame', altering how consumers remembered their sensory experience with the juice. In recall, consumers incorporated the language of the advertising to express their own experiences (Braun 1999). Moreover, advertising had an effect on how consumers remembered their past experiences. An autobiographical ad for Disney altered how consumers remembered their own childhood experiences – identifying Bugs Bunny as having been part of their original experience (Braun-LaTour et al. 2004).

In the same way any memory of a previously seen advertisement can be distorted by postexperience information. In this situation, it is not the memory of a previous experience with a product altered by actual experience with an ad but rather the memory of a previously experienced advertisement altered by the other sources of information. Thus, information presented after an experience alters how consumers remember their experience. The more similar the suggested post-experience activity is to what people actually experienced, the more likely source confusion may occur and result in memory distortion (McClelland 1995; Roediger and McDermott 1995). However, if pieces of information are strongly associated in memory networks, then they are more resistant to distortions. Therefore, one can expect that conceptually coherent advertisements are more resistant to memory distortion than incoherent ads. We examined to what extent brand claims in coherent ads are resistant to distortions in memory.

**H 2:** *Brand claims in coherent advertisements are more resistant to memory distortion than brand claims in incoherent ads.*

The effect of memory distortion of advertisements is moderated by brand familiarity as the research presented above has shown (Campbell and Keller 2003; Dahlén and Lange 2004).

**H 3:** *Advertisements for familiar brands are more resistant to memory distortion than ads for unfamiliar brands. The effect is moderated by the coherence of ads: A stronger resistance to memory distortion is expected for coherent than incoherent ads.*

## STUDY 1: CONCEPTUAL COHERENCE OF ADVERTISEMENT

### Participants, Material, and Procedure

Fifty undergraduates, aged 19-27 (*M* = 23.41) participated in each of four experiments (N=200). In each of experimental groups gender differences have been controlled (Males = 50%, Females = 50%).

*Stimuli.* Four series of print advertisements were used: (1) Ads for familiar brands of not expensive cosmetics: Eris, Ziaja, Dax, Dermika, Oxy; (2) Ads for unfamiliar brands of cosmetics: Carvella, Skin Wisdom, Eterna, Almey, Witch (these brands were unfamiliar in the country participants came from); (3) Ads for familiar brands of automobiles: Honda Accord, Volkswagen Golf Plus, Mercedes Class A, BMW 3 Series, Audi A6 Avant; (4) Ads for unfamiliar brands of automobiles: Yugo Tourer, Proton Plus, Avanti Alsa, Maruti Nerii, Hino Vant. The same ads were used for familiar and unfamiliar brands, only brand names have been changed in ads of cosmetics and brand names and product illustrations in ads of automobiles. Familiarity of all brands was checked in pretests: familiar brands were well known to all of 20 participants of the pretest, and unfamiliar brands were unknown to all of them. Each ad consisted of the following elements: the photograph, product illustration, brand claims, brand name, headline (Keller 1987). Advertisements for two different products (automobiles and inexpensive cosmetics) were used to be sure that the analyzed effects are replicable.

*Procedure.* Participants were asked to generate as many response words (associations) as they could in one minute, for each of five elements of the advertisement (the photograph, product illustration, brand claims, brand name, headline). This way, instructions referred to participants' 'private theories' of the advertisement, and associations essential for the advertisement were activated. The participants were asked to list their associations in the order that first came to mind. Each participant viewed one advertisement. Additionally, particular elements of the ad were presented on an instruction sheet. Finally, control questions were asked regarding participants' knowledge of advertising and the given brand.

## RESULTS

### Affinity Index as a Measure of Conceptual Coherence of the Print Advertisement

The strength of associations between particular elements of an advertisement was measured with the affinity index. The method of continued associations (Szalay and Deese 1978) provides a foundation from which to build such a measure. Affinities were derived from continued-association tasks. The affinity index value for each pair of elements in each ad was a measure of the conceptual coherence of the advertisement. Kleine and Kernan's (1988) methodology of measuring 'consumption objects meaning' has been applied to the analysis of the conceptual coherence of print advertisement. Affinity refers to the degree to which people see relations of any sort between any two stimuli and is operationalized as the amount of overlap between two response lists (the number of associations two objects have in common). Associations were generated to pictorial as well as verbal elements of the advertisement: all these elements constitute the advertisement and are perceived as a whole. Response words (associations) generated by participants were classified to particular semantic categories. For example, associations 'solid workmanship' and 'durable workmanship' for the brand name of Mercedes could be classified into the same category. These associations which first come to mind are the most readily available in memory and the most important for a subject (Tversky 1977). Since a participant's first responses are assumed to be more dominant (i.e., salient), each response is assigned a dominance score that is a measure of its relative salience. These scores were assigned according to Szalay and Deese's (1978) method: 6 to the first response produced by a participant, 5 to the second response, 4 to the third response, 3 to the fourth through seventh responses, 2 to the eighth and ninth responses, and 1 to each subsequent response. Dominance scores for common responses were summed up across subjects, for each element of the advertisement. This way, five lists of associations were prepared; one list for one element of the advertisement: for the photograph, product illustration, brand name, headline and brand claims. The sums of dominance scores for each element of the advertisement (diagonal values) were used for calculating the affinity index. Calculation of the inter-object affinity index involves summing up the dominance scores across the overlapping elements and across stimuli. This total is then divided by the sum of the total dominance scores of the objects being compared. The resulting index value is the proportion of the combined total dominance scores accounted for by the affinial relations. The index values could vary between 0 and 1 and increases in value as inter-object affinity increases. An example of affinity index between elements of the Honda Accord advertisement is presented in figure 1.

| Photograph | 237* | | | | |
|---|---|---|---|---|---|
| Product illustration | .495 a) | 238* | | | |
| Brand name | .349 | .361 | 227* | | |
| Headline | .411 | .337 | .237 | 186* | |
| Brand claims | .208 | .266 | .243 | .268 | 176* |
| | Photograph | Product illustration | Brand name | Headline | Brand claims |

* diagonal values; a) affinity index values

**FIGURE 1. AFFINITY INDEX BETWEEN ELEMENTS OF THE HONDA ACCORD ADVERTISEMENT**

The sum of the similarities for each of ten pairs of ad's elements was an index of the conceptual coherence of the advertisement. For example, an index of coherence for the Honda advertisement was: .495 + .349 + .411 + .208 + .361 + .337 + .266 + .237 + .243 + .268 = **3.175**

The higher value of the index the more coherent the advertisement is.

Four pairs of the most coherent versus the less coherent ads were selected for further analyses. For automobiles of familiar brands the most coherent was Honda Accord advertisement and the less coherent Mercedes Class A advertisement. Their equivalents for automobiles of unfamiliar brands were used: Yugo Tourer and Avanti Alsa, respectively. For cosmetics of familiar brands the most coherent was Oxy advertisement and the less coherent Dax

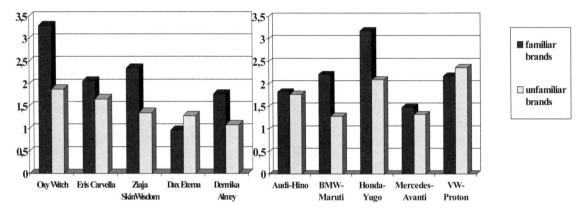

FIGURE 2. BRAND FAMILIARITY AND THE COHERENCE OF ADVERTISEMENT

advertisement. Their equivalents for cosmetics of unfamiliar brands were Witch and Eterna ads, respectively (figure 2).

The differences between the most coherent (Oxy/Witch and Honda/Yugo) and the less coherent (Dax/Eterna and Mercedes/Avanti) advertisements were tested in a one-way ANOVA. Affinity index values for ten pairs of ad's elements (see: figure 1) were used in the analysis of variance. The difference between the most coherent and the less coherent ads, of automobiles and cosmetics altogether, was significant: $F(1, 78) = 23.69$; $p = .00001$ (for automobiles: $F(1, 36) = 9.70$; $p = .0036$; for cosmetics: $F(1, 36) = 16.53$; $p = .00025$).

The differences in coherence of ads for cosmetics and automobiles were tested and turned out to be not significant: $F(1, 38) = .22$; $p = .65$. Thus, in further analyses ads for cosmetics and automobiles were analyzed in total.

**Brand Familiarity and the Coherence of Advertisement**

In order to verify hypothesis 1, repeated measurements (familiar-unfamiliar brand) in the analysis of variance were used. Ten indices of similarity for each ad (see: figure 1) were analyzed in ANOVA. Four ads were analyzed: the most and the less coherent for familiar and unfamiliar brand. According to hypothesis 1, advertisements for familiar brands were perceived as more coherent than ads for unfamiliar brands (figure 3).

The results showed that the effect of brand familiarity was statistically significant: $F(1, 39) = 6.43$; $p = .01$. Ads for familiar brands ($M = .226$) were perceived as more coherent than ads for unfamiliar brands ($M = .163$).

Although layouts of pairs of ads for familiar and unfamiliar brands were very similar, there were salient differences in the perceived coherence of ads.

An advertisement for familiar brand activates a schema – a representation of the brand. An associative network for a familiar brand is well developed and readily accessible in memory. Referring to the theory of conceptual coherence (Murphy and Medin 1985) one can say that knowledge of the brand like 'theory' joins together elements of the advertisement in the consumer's mind.

## STUDY 2: THE CONCEPTUAL COHERENCE OF ADVERTISEMENT AND MEMORY DISTORTION

In Study 2 the significance of the conceptual coherence of advertisement in memory distortion was examined. Advertisement's coherence and brand familiarity were taken into consideration as independent variables. Research was designed in the backward framing paradigm (Braun et al. 1997, 2005). After viewing a coherent versus incoherent print advertisement, participants were presented with a fragment of magazine article about the product they previously saw in the ad. The article acted as a 'backward frame', altering how consumers remembered brand claims from the ad.

## PARTICIPANTS, MATERIAL, AND PROCEDURE

Three hundred and twenty undergraduates aged 19-28 ($M = 21.76$) participated in the four experiments. In experiment 1 advertisements and magazine articles for cosmetics of familiar brands were used (N=80); in experiment 2 ads and magazine articles for cosmetics of unfamiliar brands (N=80), in experiment 3 ads and magazine articles for automobiles of familiar brands (N=80), and in experiment 4 advertisements and magazine articles for automobiles of unfamiliar brands (N=80). Gender differences in each of experimental groups have been controlled.

*Print Advertisements*. Four pairs of the most coherent versus the less coherent ads were selected from among the ads used in Study 1. For automobiles the most coherent was Honda Accord

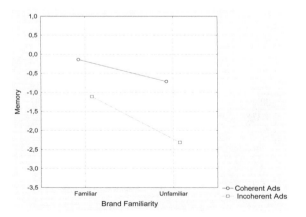

FIGURE 3. COHERENCE OF ADS FOR FAMILIAR AND UNFAMILIAR BRANDS

advertisement (its equivalent for unfamiliar brand: Yugo Tourer) and the less coherent Mercedes Class A advertisement (its equivalents for unfamiliar brand: Avanti Alsa). For cosmetics of familiar brands the most coherent was Oxy advertisement and the less coherent Dax advertisement. Their equivalents for cosmetics of unfamiliar brands were: Witch and Eterna, respectively.

*Postexperience Information.* Fragments of magazine articles prepared for the purpose of the experiment were used as post-experience information. Participants viewing advertisements of automobiles were presented with an article containing information of Honda Accord or Mercedes Class A as familiar brands or Yugo Tourer or Avanti Alsa as unfamiliar brands of automobiles, respectively. Participants viewing ads of cosmetics were presented with articles on Oxy or Dax as familiar brands or Witch or Eterna as unfamiliar brands of cosmetics.

*Measurement of Memory Distortion.* The strength of memory distortion was measured with a memory test consisting of 15 items (brand claims): 5 from the advertisement which participants were presented with, 5 from the magazine article-postexperience information, and 5 additional, not from the ad nor the article. Articles contained brand claims consistent with and similar to these in the advertisement. Additional brand claims were similar to these in the advertisement, too. Participants were asked to recognize which items came from the advertisement they viewed at the beginning of the experiment. Each correct response was scored with 1 point. The index of the memory of brand claims from the advertisement was: memory = brand claims from the advertisement - (brand claims from the magazine article + brand claims additional). This way, the highest score was 5 points and the lowest -10 points. Thus, the higher score, the less memory distortion of brand claims from the advertisement.

*Procedure.* The study was conducted in quasi-laboratory conditions. At the beginning of the experiment, participants were informed that they participate in the experiment on perception of the advertisement and that their attention and involvement during viewing ads is very important. Then participants were directed to either evaluate the merits of the advertised brand (brand-directed processing) or to judge the merits of the actual advertisement for the brand (ad-directed processing). Thus, each group of participants perceived ads in one of the two contexts. The context of ad perception had to be controlled because consumers never perceive ads 'in vacuo', but in one of these two contexts. Forty seconds were given to view each advertisement. Then participants solved a three-minute distraction task, a puzzle which had no relationship to the present experiment. Next, they were presented with a mock magazine article (postexperience information). Then, they solved another distraction task for three minutes. Finally, participants were asked to solve a memory test on brand claims (measurement of memory distortion).

## RESULTS

### Memory Distortion of Coherent and Incoherent Advertisements

At the beginning the differences in memory distortion between ads of automobiles and cosmetics were tested. The differences were not significant $F(1, 318) = .25$, $p = .62$, thus, in further analyses ads of cosmetics and automobiles were tested in total.

It was expected (H2) that brand claims in coherent advertisements are more resistant to memory distortion than brand claims in incoherent ads. The main effect of advertisement coherence in ANOVA was significant, $F(1, 318) = 23.33$, $p < .000001$ ($M = -.425$ for coherent ads and $M = -1.713$ or incoherent ads). This means that it is more difficult to distort memory of the coherent than incoherent advertisement. The greater amount of similar associations between particular elements of the advertisement, the better the advertisement is remembered and the less sensitive to memory distortion it is.

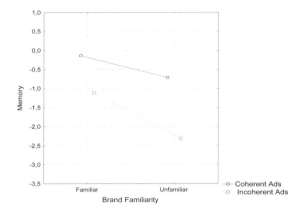

### FIGURE 4. MEMORY DISTORTION OF BRAND CLAIMS IN COHERENT AND INCOHERENT ADVERTISEMENTS

It can be seen in figure 4 that differences in the strength of memory distortion for incoherent advertisements for familiar and unfamiliar brands are salient, $F(1, 158) = 11.71$, $p = .0008$. However, in coherent ads such differences have not been observed, $F(1, 158) = 2.18$, $p = .14$. One can say that the memory of the advertisement and its resistance to memory distortion is determined by the coherence of its elements. Thus, one may refer to the theory of conceptual coherence (Murphy and Medin 1985): Elements of coherent ads are strongly associated with each other and more resistant to distortions.

### Brand Familiarity in Memory Distortion of Coherent and Incoherent Advertisements

According to hypothesis 3, it was expected that brand claims in advertisements for familiar brands are more resistant to memory distortion than brand claims in ads for unfamiliar brands. The one-way ANOVA showed that brand claims in ads for familiar brands ($M = -.625$) were less distorted than brand claims in ads for unfamiliar brands ($M = -1.513$), $F(1, 318) = 10.67$, $p = .001$. A stronger effect of resistance to memory distortion was expected for coherent than incoherent ads. Planned comparisons in the two-way ANOVA showed that in *coherent* advertisements the difference in memory distortion between familiar and unfamiliar brands was not significant: $F(1, 316) = 2.41$, $p = 0.12$. However, the effect was significant in *incoherent* ads: $F(1, 316) = 10.48$, $p = .001$. Ads for familiar brands $M = -1.113$) were less distorted than ads for unfamiliar brands ($M = -2.313$) (figure 5). It is worth noting that layouts of pairs of ads for familiar and unfamiliar brands were very similar, they differed *only* with the brand name (and product illustration in ads of automobiles).

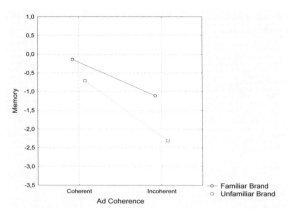

**FIGURE 5. MEMORY DISTORTION OF BRAND CLAIMS IN ADS FOR FAMILIAR AND UNFAMILIAR BRANDS**

Research showed that familiar brands are more easily detected in advertising clutter. Consumers have well-established brand schemas for familiar brands that may withstand incongruent information (Campbel and Keller 2003; Dahlén and Lange 2004).

Familiar brands are cognitively available and activate a wide area of an associative network. Thus, advertisements for familiar brands are less susceptible to memory distortion as compared to ads for unfamiliar brands. It is more difficult to bring false information into the memory of familiar than unfamiliar brands.

## FINAL REMARKS

The presented study, first of all shows rigorous methodology of research on the coherence of ads, sources of that coherence, and its importance for remembering the ads' content. This methodology, well grounded in the contemporary theories of cognitive psychology is, certainly, the stronger argument for accuracy of practical implications derived from the performed research.

First of all brand familiarity turned out to be an important determinant of an ad's coherence, that is, the ads of familiar brands appeared to be considerably more coherent than those of unfamiliar brands. According to Gestalt psychology or the prototype theory of concepts, familiar brands refer to the cognitive schema that is well established in memory. In this sense a coherent ad acquires the ideal features of a „good figure" (*pragnanz*) or prototype in which separate elements are tightly linked together. Unity achieved in this way is therefore closely related to the general tendency to perceive groupings of elements as an integrated entity. On the other hand it appears that coherent ads are less susceptible to memory distortion than incoherent ads. Such a result is compatible with psychological theories of conceptual coherence and concept formation which point at consolidated memory traces being resistant to distortion.

The essential, practical implication in regard to the creation of ads is to keep or strengthen their coherence. If the brand is familiar then its ad's coherence is intrinsically formed in the consumer's mind. At the same time the process activates psychological mechanisms of retrieving the prototype (good figure) of that product brand from memory. Some attempts to distort the memory of the ad by discrediting the familiar brand, say, in comparative negative ads, will fail because ads of familiar brands are resistant to distortions. The situation is completely different in the case of ads of unfamiliar brands, thus an effort should be put into keeping or strengthening the ad's coherence by carefully selecting it's elements. If the coherence is not protected then the ad can be easily distorted in consumer memory, for example in the marketing strategy of competitors who use comparative negative ads. Thus the product of an unfamiliar

brand may appear worse than as it was, in fact, advertised. To protect the ad's coherence is important, initially, to effectively cope with the competitors. Such protection is particularly important for unfamiliar or less known brands.

The results obtained suggest some practical implications for media communication. For example, when TV news are presented by a known presenter, a message is better-remembered and more persuasive; context is not important here. However, when the presenter is unknown, the background is important (coherent context). The results also show how to design a coherent advertisement or how to design an efficient ad for a new brand.

## REFERENCES

Anderson, John R. (1983), *The Architecture of Cognition*, Cambridge, MA: Harvard University Press.

Braun, Kathryn A. and Gerald Zaltman (1997), "Backward Framing Through Memory Reconstruction," Report No. 98-109 for Marketing Sciences Institute.

Braun, Kathryn A. and Elizabeth F. Loftus (1998), "Advertising's Misinformation Effect," *Applied Cognitive Psychology,* 12 (6), 569-91.

--------- (1999), "Postexperience Advertising Effects on Consumer Memory," *Journal of Consumer Research,* 25 (4), 319-34.

Braun-LaTour, Kathryn A., Michael S. LaTour, Jacqueline E. Pickrell, and Elizabeth F. Loftus (2004), "How and when Advertising Can Influence Memory for Consumer Experience," *Journal of Advertising,* 33 (Winter), 7-25.

Braun-LaTour, Kathryn A. and Michael S. LaTour (2005), "Transforming Consumer Experience. When Timing Matters," *Journal of Advertising,* 34 (3), 19-30.

Campbell, Margaret C. and Kevin L. Keller (2003), "Brand Familiarity and Advertising Repetition Effects," *Journal of Consumer Research,* 30 (September), 292-304.

Dahlén, Micael and Fredrik Lange (2004), "To Challenge or not to Challenge: Ad-brand Incongruency and Brand Familiarity," *Journal of Marketing Theory and Practice*, 12 (Summer), 20-35.

Dahlén, Micael, Fredrik Lange, Henrik Sjödin, and Fredrik Törn (2005), "Effects of Ad-brand Incongruency," *Journal of Current Issues and Research in Advertising,* 27 (Fall), 1-12.

Dahlén, Micael, Sara Rosengren, Fredrik Törn and Niclas Öhman (2008), "Could Placing Ads Wrong be Right? Advertising Effects of Thematic Incongruence," *Journal of Advertising,* 37 (Fall), 57-67.

Heckler, Susan E. and Terry L. Childers (1992), "The Role of Expectancy and Relevancy in Memory for Verbal and Visual Information: What Is Incongruency?'" *Journal of Consumer Research,* 18 (March), 475-92.

Keller, Kevin L. (1987). "Memory Factors in Advertising: The Effect of Advertising Retrieval Cues on Brand Evaluations," *Journal of Consumer Research*, 14 (3), 316-33.

Kent, Robert J. and Chris T. Allen (1994), "Competitive Interference Effects in Consumer Memory for Advertising: The Role of Brand Familiarity," *Journal of Marketing*, 58 (July), 97-105.

Kleine, Robert E. and Jerome B. Kernan (1988), "Measuring the Meaning of Consumption Objects: An Empirical Investigation," *Advances in Consumer Research,* 18, 311-24.

Lau, Kong Cheen and Ian Phau (2007), "Extending Symbolic Brands Using Their Personality: Examining Antecedents and Implications towards Brand Image Fit and Brand Dilution," *Psychology and Marketing,* 24 (May), 421-44.

Lee, Jung-Gyo and Esther Thorson (2008), "The Impact of Celebrity-Product Incongruence on the Effectiveness of Product Endorsement," *Journal of Advertising Research,* 48 (September), 433-49.

Margolis, Eric (1999), "What Is Conceptual Glue?," *Minds and Machines,* 9 (May), 241-55.

McClelland, James L. (1995), "Constructive Memory and Memory Distortions: A Parallel Distributed Processing Approach," in *Memory Distortion,* ed. Daniel Schacter, Cambridge, MA: Harvard University Press, 69-90.

Medin, Douglas L. (1989), "Concepts and Conceptual Structure," *American Psychologist,* 44 (December), 1469-81.

Murphy, Gregory L. and Douglas L. Medin (1985), "The Role of Theories in Conceptual Coherence," *Psychological Review,* 92 (July), 289-316.

Nedungadi, Prakash and J. Wesley Hutchinson (1985), "The Prototypicality of Brands: Relationships with Brand Awareness, Preference and Usage," *Advances in Consumer Research,* 12 (1), 498-503.

Pechmann, Cornelia and David W. Stewart (1990), "The Effects of Comparative Advertising on Attention, Memory, and Purchase Intentions," *Journal of Consumer Research,* 17 (September), 180-91.

Ratneshwar, S. and Allan D. Shocker (1991), "Substitution In Use and the Role of Usage Context in Product Category Structures," *Journal of Marketing Research,* 28 (August), 281-95.

Roediger, Henry L. III and Kathleen B. McDermott (1995), "Creating False Memories: Remembering Words not Presented in Lists," *Journal of Experimental Psychology: Learning, Memory and Cognition,* 21 (4), 803-14.

Shanks, David R. (1991), "Categorization by a Connectionist Network," *Journal of Experimental Psychology: Learning, Memory, and Cognition,* 17 (3), 433-43.

Smith, Edward E. (1995), "Concepts and Categorization," in *Thinking: An Invitation to Cognitive Science*, Vol. 3, ed. Edward Smith and Daniel Osherson, Cambridge, MA: The MIT Press, 3-34.

Snyder, Rita (1989), "Misleading Characteristics of Implied-Superiority Claims," *Journal of Advertising,* 18 (4), 54-61.

Sujan, Mita and James R. Bettman (1989), "The Effectiveness of Brand Positioning Strategies on Consumers' Brand and Category Perceptions: Some Insight from Schema Research," *Journal of Marketing Research,* 26 (November), 454-67.

Szalay, Lorand B. and James Deese (1978), *Subjective Meaning and Culture: An Assessment Through Word Associations*, Hillsdale, NJ: Erlbaum.

Tversky, Amos (1977), "Features of Similarity," *Psychological Review,* 84 (4), 327-52.

# Virtue, Vice, or Both? The Impact of Context-Induced Guilt on Choice and Consumption of Mixed Foods

Sabine Boesen-Mariani, Université Pierre Mendes France, Grenoble, France
Carolina Obino Corrêa Werle, Grenoble Ecole de Management and CERAG, UPMF, France

## ABSTRACT

Two studies using real choice settings demonstrate context influence on the choice and consumption of mixed foods (combining hedonic and utilitarian attributes). A hedonic context leads to the choice and reduced consumption of mixed foods for guilt-reducing reasons. A utilitarian context induces less guilt, and leads individuals to choose and consume more of the mixed foods. Priming guilt through nutritional information reverses these effects.

## INTRODUCTION

In their daily lives, consumers often confront decisions between hedonic and utilitarian options: for dessert, should I have a delicious chocolate cake or a healthy fruit salad? This kind of dilemma offers a typical example of the hedonic–utilitarian conflict widely studied in consumer behavior literature (for a review see Khan et al. 2005). Various researchers work to understand the consumption of hedonic and utilitarian products and the potential consequences of choosing one over the other (Khan et al. 2005). Yet few consumers choose simply between pure hedonic and pure utilitarian products, especially in the food industry. Rather, expanded choice sets in modern markets mean consumers often consider mixed products, such as such as ice cream, a pure hedonic product that offers low fat or extra calcium, which constitutes utilitarian attributes.

In two studies, we address consumers' choice and consumption of mixed foods according to the choice-set composition. Previous research notes the emotional consequences of deciding between a hedonic and a utilitarian option, in that choosing one or the other prompts mixed emotions (Chitturi et al. 2007). We therefore investigate the role of emotional activation in the choice of mixed foods. Wansink and Chandon (2006) show that "low-fat" nutrition labels reduce the guilt associated with the consumption of hedonic foods; emotion activation thus may be a determinant of choice and consumption. Mixed products may provide a balanced alternative that consumers prefer when they want to regulate their feelings, such as anticipated guilt (study 1).

We also gain some insight in the psychological reasons for the choice of mixed products in different contexts. We propose that presenting mixed food next to a pure hedonic option activates guilt, so the mixed food represents the appealing, guilt-regulating alternative. In contrast, a mixed product that appears beside a utilitarian option induces no guilt, so the choice of a mixed option should reflect pursuit of a hedonic goal. That is, the choice of the mixed food differs according to the context and reflects either the pursuit of pleasure or an attempt to regulate guilt (study 1).

Once they have chosen a mixed product, consumers must decide how much to consume. If the choice of the mixed product results from their trade-off between a hedonic and a mixed option, due to guilt activation, we suggest that the consumption will be reduced in order to address a high-priority goal. However, when the choice of the mixed product results from the trade-off with a pure utilitarian product, the context does not activate the guilt, the motivation is mainly hedonic, and the consumer feels free to eat a larger amount of the mixed option (study 1).

Finally, recent research suggests that low-fat labels can reduce anticipated guilt because they cause calorie misestimations (Wansink and Chandon 2006); consumers should be more likely to consume mixed foods because they perceive them as lower in calories and

fat. The presentation of nutrition information would give a more realistic idea of the guilt associated with each option in the choice set and therefore may attenuate the effect of the presentation context on the consumption of mixed products (study 2).

## CONCEPTUAL BACKGROUND

### Emotional Reactions to Hedonic and Utilitarian Products

According to Holbrook and Hirschman (1982), people consume products for two main reasons: (1) utilitarian reasons related to the function of the product or (2) hedonic reasons to achieve an affective experience. Hedonic consumption thus is driven by pleasure, emotions, and a sensation-seeking motivation, whereas utilitarian consumption derives from a desire to satisfy a basic need or accomplish a functional task through the practical, and instrumental characteristics of the product (Holbrook and Hirschman 1982). Although the hedonic option generates positive emotions, such as excitement and cheerfulness (Chitturi et al. 2007), its choice is harder to justify because it may have negative consequences in the long run (Hoch and Loewenstein 1991). Therefore, it also can engender negative emotions, such as guilt and anxiety (Giner-Sorolla 2001; Ramanathan and Williams 2007). That is, the consumption of a hedonic product raises mixed emotions: Consumers feel good because they achieve sensory pleasure, but they feel bad because they have succumbed to temptation (Macht and Dettmer 2006; Ramanathan and Williams 2007).

Traditionally, research on consumer decision-making (such as Shiv and Fedorikhin 1999) relies only two dimensions: affect (related of sensorial pleasure) versus cognition (related to the benefits of the products for consumers' health). However, research mentioned above suggests that the dimension related to affect could be formed by two sub-dimensions: positive reflecting the pleasure obtained by the consumption and a negative reflecting emotions such as guilt. Recent research such Wansink and Chandon (2006) and an exploratory study conducted by the authors suggests that a guilt-reducing motivation could determine choice and consumption of mixed products.

### Choice Context Effects and Activation of Emotions

Extant research indicates that the choice context can modify consumers' preferences and decision process (Bettman, Luce, and Payne 2008; Hsee et al. 1999). Different elements in the choice environment might activate different constructs in consumer memory and influence preferences and behaviors, as well as four specific systems: perceptual (e.g., stereotypes, traits), evaluative (i.e., attitudes), motivation (i.e., goals), and emotional (Bargh and Morsella 2009). Most research centers on the role of activated goals or traits to explain consumer choice and consumption (for instance: Fishbach et al. 2003; Sela, Berger, and Liu 2009; Wilcox et al. 2009). However, consistent with Bargh and Morsella's (2009) proposal, we suggest that the context activates certain emotions that determine the decision motivation. Specifically, we posit that certain contexts activate more guilt than do others and therefore lead to the choice of less hedonic products, in a sort of balance-seeking strategy (Zemack-Rugar et al. 2007).

When the mixed option appears together with a hedonic option (hedonic context), due to its evaluability the hedonic attribute is highlighted (Hsee et al. 1999). As mentioned earlier, hedonic attributes are not only associated to positive feelings such as pleasure but also to negative emotions such as guilt. Consequently, we propose that the hedonic choice-set activates guilt, and the mixed option provides a guilt-regulating mechanism.

Additionally, research on guilt shows that the presence of this emotion makes individuals prioritize utilitarian, long-term motivations (Baumeister and Exline 1999; Baumeister, Stillwell, and Heatherton 1995) and neglect short term motivations such as pleasure-seeking. Taking this into account, we suggest that in the hedonic context, consumers choose the mixed product to avoid feelings of guilt and the choice is driven by a utilitarian motivation. That is,

**H1:** *When the mixed product appears together with a hedonic product, the choice set activates guilt and leads to the choice of the mixed option (rather than the hedonic product) for utilitarian reasons in comparison with the utilitarian context.*

In contrast, when the mixed option appears with a utilitarian product (utilitarian context), the utilitarian attribute is highlighted, and the context does not activate the same amount of guilt. As a consequence, the choice of the mixed option is not driven by this emotion. The utilitarian context has, in fact, a liberating effect on individuals, encouraging them to indulge due to a health halo effect (Chandon and Wansink 2007a). The consumers will therefore choose the mixed option to satisfy a pleasure-seeking motivation. That is,

**H2:** *When the mixed product appears together with a utilitarian product, the choice set does not activate guilt and leads to the choice of the mixed option (rather than the utilitarian product) for hedonic reasons in comparison with the hedonic context.*

Wansink and Chandon (2006) also show that low-fat nutrition labels increase food consumption, because consumers increase their perceptions of the appropriate serving size. What happens to perceptions of serving size for mixed products presented together with pure hedonic versus pure utilitarian products? We believe it depends on the motivation behind the mixed product choice. Research on sequential choices indicates that when making similar decisions sequentially in a short period of time, people tend to commit to their first choice through a reinforcement mechanism (Dhar, Huber, and Khan 2007; Huber, Goldsmith, and Mogilner 2008). Therefore, if consumers choose a mixed product in a low-guilt context for hedonic reasons, they should take more of the mixed product to fulfill their pleasure motivation. However, if their choice is motivated by guilt-avoidance, they should tend to serve themselves a smaller portion to continue regulating or even eliminate their guilt. That is,

**H3:** *In a hedonic context, consumers serve themselves a smaller amount of the mixed product (compared to the utilitarian context).*

**H4:** *In a utilitarian context, consumers serve themselves a larger amount of the mixed product (compared to the hedonic context).*

**The Moderating Effect of Nutrition Information**

Previous research demonstrates that providing nutritional information influences perceptions, attitudes, intentions and consumption (Bui et al. 2008; Burton et al. 2006; Garg, Wansink, and Inman 2007; Howlett et al. 2009; Kozup et al. 2003), because most consumers lack of expertise in estimating the caloric content of foods. They generally underestimate caloric and fat content, especially for large meals (Chandon and Wansink 2007b), which might prompt a mistaken guilt-reducing perception, especially for mixed foods that use health-related claims and induce perceptions of lower caloric and fat content. If so, presenting the nutrition information for all options in the choice set should give consumers a more realistic perception. For mixed foods, the realistic perception may prime guilt especially in the utilitarian context were they are the more hedonic option. The guilt activation should alter the chosen product and amounts.

Specifically, we propose that in the hedonic context guilt is already activated by the characteristics of the choice set and presenting nutrition information only reinforces the presence of this emotion. However, in the utilitarian context guilt is previously absent, therefore, presenting nutrition information highlights guilt and has a strong impact on the amount consumed of the mixed option. As a result, consumers should moderate their consumption of mixed foods in the utilitarian condition with nutrition information to regulate their activated guilt. That is,

**H5:** *In the presence of a guilt prime (nutrition information), when the mixed product appears together with a utilitarian product, consumers serve themselves less of the mixed product to reduce their feelings of guilt (in comparison to the scenario without nutritional information).*

In the hedonic context, the presentation of nutrition information for both options should reinforce the guilt-reducing characteristics of the mixed food, because its calorie content is less than that of a hedonic food. Therefore, nutritional information in the hedonic context should lead to greater consumption of the mixed food, because the simple fact of choosing the mixed option may already reduce their activated guilt. Therefore,

**H6:** *In the presence of a guilt prime (nutrition information), when the mixed product appears together with a hedonic product, consumers serve themselves more of the mixed product (in comparison to the scenario without nutritional information).*

We use two experiments to test these hypotheses. First, we explore the impact of the choice context on the choice and consumption of mixed food (study 1). Then, we consider whether the provision of nutritional information might alter the consumption of the mixed option (study 2).

**STUDY 1**

For study 1, our objective is to test the effects of the presentation context on the evaluation, choice, and consumption of mixed foods. We have predicted that when the mixed food appears beside a hedonic product, the choice set activates guilt, prompts the choice of the mixed option for utilitarian reasons (H1), and leads to the consumption of a smaller amount of the mixed product to continue to regulate guilt (H3). We also argue that when the mixed product is in the same choice set as a utilitarian one, no guilt gets activated, which leads to the choice of the mixed option for hedonic reasons (H2) and the consumption of a large amount of the mixed product to obtain pleasure (H4). Study 1 tests these hypotheses.

## METHOD

Study 1 uses a one-factor, two-level (context of presentation: utilitarian option versus hedonic option) between-subjects design, and the 138 undergraduate student participants were randomly assigned to a condition. When they arrived for the study, the participants received a consent form and a participant number and then entered a second room, where they would receive a gift for their participation. In the second room, a research assistant explained that the participants could choose between two snacks. In the utilitarian context, the choice included "fine slices of oven-baked apple" (pure utilitarian product) and "light cocoa cookies enriched with cereal" (mixed product); in the hedonic context, they chose between "shortbread filled with melting chocolate" (pure hedonic product) and the same mixed product. The snacks in large plastic bowls appeared in a counterbalanced order, and participants used a scoop to serve themselves as much as they wanted of the chosen snack in a small plastic bag. The research assistant then identified the bag with the participant's number and explained that the next stage of the study would take place in the experimental lab, which people could not enter with food. Therefore, they would receive their snack at the end of the experiment. In the lab, participants first completed a lexical decision task (i.e., to measure the accessibility of concepts related to guilt, pleasure, and health), then a questionnaire with measures of their choice, motivations, evaluations of both the snack options, and participant's profile. While participants were completing this part of the study, a research assistant unobtrusively weighted the plastic bags content to calculate the caloric content of the amount of snack served. Finally, at the end of the experimental session, they received their snack bag, along with a debriefing of the study objectives, and were dismissed.

## STIMULI

Each participant considered two different snacks displayed in large plastic bowls and identified by a description (both descriptions contain similar numbers of words). The snacks represented real alternatives, which should increase the vividness of these options and intensify the affect experienced by the respondents (Shiv and Fedorikhin 1999). Although the pure utilitarian option (fine slices of oven-baked apple) was inspired by Shiv and Fedorikhin's (1999) research, French participants may consider a fresh apple a hedonic product (because it is refreshing), so we decided to use dried apple slices instead. The shortbread filled with melting chocolate provides the pure hedonic option because it contains typically hedonic ingredients (e.g., chocolate). Finally, the mixed option reflects our conceptualization of a hedonic product (cookie) to which we added utilitarian attributes (light and rich in cereals). A pilot study confirms these choices; the data are available from the authors on request. Because one of our dependent measures is the amount that each participant served him- or herself, the chocolate shortbread, cookies, and apple slices are better options than a whole apple or entire chocolate cake. Finally, the size and shape of each unit of the three options is similar (approximately 10 grams per unit), so these characteristics should not influence the participants' decisions.

## MEASURES

Each respondent first responded to the following prompt: "A few moments ago you made a choice from two options, fine slices of oven-baked apple (shortbread filled with melting chocolate) and the light cocoa cookies enriched with cereals. Please indicate below the option you chose." We confirmed these responses with the choice of snacks registered by the research assistant and find that the choices match across all respondents.

After the choice, in order to measure guilt activation in each context, we asked the participants to complete a lexical decision task on the computer. They considered a series of letter strings and decided, as quickly as possible, whether each letter string was a word. Each word appeared individually in the center of the screen and flashed very briefly. They classified the target letter strings as either words or nonwords, using the D and K keys. Each response was followed by a 1-second pause and then the next trial. After 10 practice trials, which included an equal number of words and nonwords, participants started the main lexical decision task, in which they classified 32 words (4 guilt-related words, 4 pleasure-related words, 4 health-related words, 4 neutral words, and 16 nonwords), which appeared for 50 ms each, followed by a white screen until the participants hit one of the keys, and then the next word. Participants exposed to the hedonic context (versus utilitarian context) should more readily identify words related to guilt, which would confirm the emotion activation effect. Because the latency of incorrect responses would be difficult to interpret, we use only correct responses in our subsequent analyses (Fazio 1990). To minimize the influence of outliers, we first transform all individual reaction times using a natural log transformation, then exclude any that exceed three standard deviations from the cell mean (Fazio 1990).

In line with Shiv and Fedorikhin (1999), we then asked the participants to indicate the basis of his or her choice on five seven-point items: "My choice of snack was driven by "my thoughts (1)/my feelings (7)," "my willpower (1)/my desire (7)," "the rational side of me (1)/the emotional side of me (7)," and "my head (1)/my heart (7)." The Cronbach's alpha for these items reach .89, and we therefore can average the responses to the five items to form a single index (i.e., Decision Basis). Each respondent also indicated, on seven-point scales, the extent to which hedonic, utilitarian, and guilt-reducing goals bore on their decision: "I was searching for pleasure," "I was seeking gratification.", "I was trying to avoid guilt," and "I was trying to make the best choice for my health".

Next, the participants indicated their familiarity with the different snacks, whether they have consumed this kind of snack, and if they thought these products were innovative. Finally, they indicated their gender, age, weight and height, when they had their last meal, if they were hungry, their knowledge about nutrition, their dietary restrictions (Herman and Polivy 1980), and several other self-perception measures. These measures serve as covariates in the various analyses and only those impacting the results are mentioned below.

## RESULTS

*Guilt activation.* Our hypotheses suggest that the hedonic context activates guilt and that this emotion leads to the choice of the mixed option for utilitarian reasons (H1). Conversely, in the utilitarian context, guilt is not activated and the choice of the mixed option (rather than the utilitarian product) for hedonic reasons (H2). The lexical decision task was used to verify the guilt activation. The results of this task show, as expected, that in the hedonic context, the words related to guilt are more accessible (smaller latency) than in the utilitarian context (528 vs. 544; $F(1, 67)= 6.89$, $p < .05$). These evidences show that in the hedonic context guilt is more accessible than in the utilitarian context[1]. Moreover, our analysis of other self-reported measures indicate that in the hedonic context, the choice of the mixed derives from the intention to avoid feeling guilty (guilt-avoidance motivation$_{mixed food choice}$=3.36; guilt avoidance motivation$_{hedonic food choice}$ = 2.48; $F(1, 57)= 5.47, p < .05$). However, in the utilitarian context condition, in accordance with hypothesis

---

1 The data on the accessibility of pleasure related words and health related words were no statistical significant

3, we find no difference in the guilt-reducing motivation among participants who choose the mixed products versus the utilitarian product (guilt-avoidance motivation$_{\text{mixed food choice}}$ = 3.23; guilt avoidance motivation$_{\text{utilitarian food choice}}$ = 2.94; $F(1, 58) = .26, p > .10$).

*Hedonic and Utilitarian Motivations for choice.* Consistent with previous research (Giner-Sorolla 2001; Zemack-Rugar et al. 2007), we find that the guilt activated by the choice context seems to induce a choice of the mixed product due to different motivations. In the hedonic context condition, guilt motivates participants to make a more reasoned choice; yet in the utilitarian context, they choose the mixed snack for affective reasons. Respondents who choose the mixed food rate their choice as reflecting affect in the utilitarian context (Decision Basis$_{\text{utilitarian context}}$ = 4.70) more than in the hedonic context (Decision Basis$_{\text{hedonic context}}$ = 3.73; $F(1, 73) = 9.89, p < .05$). In the same sense, participants choose the mixed food for their health in the hedonic context condition (health motivation$_{\text{utilitarian context}}$ = 2.55; health motivation$_{\text{hedonic context}}$ = 4.00; $F(1, 73) = 10.98, p < .05$), but they make this choice for pleasure in the utilitarian context (pleasure motivation$_{\text{utilitarian context}}$ = 4.19; pleasure motivation$_{\text{hedonic context}}$ = 3.50; $F(1, 73) = 5.73, p < .05$). These results are consistent with hypotheses 1 and 2, which suggest a more utilitarian motivation for the choice of the mixed product in the hedonic context and a more hedonic motivation guiding the choice of the mixed option in the utilitarian context.

*Testing the mechanism leading to the choice of the mixed option.* Additionally, to test the hypotheses 1 and 2, given the binary dependent variable, a logistic regression was conducted. The choice of the mixed option was coded as « 1 » and the choice of the others products was coded as « 0 ». Product terms were created by multiplying the independent variables (i.e., guilt and motivations). We examined the effects of guilt and hedonic and utilitarian motivation on the choice of snack in each of the context (hedonic and utilitarian). The results indicate that the interaction term between guilt and health motivation was a significant predictor of choice of the mixed option in the hedonic context (B=0.87; Wald = 11.41, $p < .05$) and in the utilitarian context the hedonic motivation was a significant predictor of choice of the mixed option (B= .604; Wald = 5.409, $p < .05$). The utilitarian motivation was also significant but helped to predict the choice of utilitarian option (B= -.435; Wald = 7.026, $p < .05$). These results of logistic regression allow us to confirm H1 and H2.

*Amount served.* Among participants who choose the mixed snack, those in the utilitarian context serve 54% more than those in the hedonic context (calories in amount served$_{\text{utilitarian context}}$ = 317.46; calories in amount served$_{\text{hedonic context}}$ = 206.16; $F(1, 74) = 3.86, p < .05$). These results align with the prediction of reinforcement between sequential choices (Huber et al. 2008) and therefore with hypotheses 3 and 4. When guilt is activated, the motivation for choosing the mixed food is utilitarian (in the hedonic context), people control themselves and take only a small amount. Yet, when guilt is absent, their motivation is hedonic (pleasure-seeking motivation in the utilitarian context) therefore they keep searching for pleasure and serve themselves more of the product.

## STUDY 2

With study 2, we test hypotheses 5 and 6 regarding the role of a guilt prime (nutritional information) in moderating the effect of the context on the choice of mixed products and the amount served. The presentation of a guilt prime should influence the amount of mixed food they served by participants, such that in the utilitarian context (H5), consumers should serve themselves less to avoid guilt and the hedonic context (H6), consumers serve themselves more because guilt was reduced by the choice of the mixed option.

## METHOD

Study 2 relies on a two-factor (context of presentation: with a utilitarian option versus with a hedonic option; guilt prime: nutritional information present versus absent) between-subjects design and the 121 undergraduate student participants were randomly assigned to a condition. The procedure, stimuli, and measures are similar to those in study 1, except that in the conditions with the guilt prime, we present nutritional information (caloric content, sugars, fat, and fiber) for both snack options available. In addition to the measures from study 1, we determine whether participants take into account the caloric content and the nutritional composition of the foods in their choice set, which serve as manipulation checks for the guilt prime. These items were averaged to form an index (alpha = .82).

## RESULTS

*Manipulation checks.* Participants exposed to nutritional information took into account the nutritional characteristics of the product when making their choice to a greater extent than did those who were not exposed to nutritional information ($M = 3.70$ versus $M = 3.00$; $F(1, 121) = 4.25$; $p < .05$). As we predicted, the presentation of nutrition information emphasizes the guilt associated with the choice in both contexts. Participants exposed to nutrition information declare more feelings of guilt after their choice ($M = 2.41$) than do those who received no exposure to nutritional information ($M = 2.00$; $F(1, 120) = 4,72, p < .05$) after controlling for dietary restrictions.

*Amount served.* In the hedonic context, the participants who see no nutritional information serve themselves fewer calories of mixed food ($M = 165.7$) than those in the utilitarian context ($M = 264.4$; $F(1, 31) = 6.76, p < .05$). These results are consistent with study 1. However, consumers exposed to nutritional information serve the same amount of the snack, independent of the presentation context (hedonic context = 202.7; utilitarian context = 186.2; $F(1, 33) = .19, p > .10$). Moreover, we find a decrease in the amount of mixed food served in the utilitarian condition when nutritional information appears (utilitarian context: no nutritional information = 264.4; nutritional information = 186.2; $F(1, 40) = 5.51, p < .05$). Consistent with our conceptualization, we find that presenting nutritional information attenuates the effect of the context of presentation on the amount of calories served among the participants who choose a mixed food. These results also indicate that the effect shown in study 1 is being driven by a guilt regulation. In the hedonic condition, however, the results are in expected direction (more consumption with nutritional information) but the difference is not statistically significant ($M_{\text{without information}} = 165.7$ versus $M_{\text{with information}} = 202.7$; $F(1, 24) = .80, p > .10$).

The presentation of nutritional information also influences the amount of mixed food served across conditions. Our analysis of the group of participants choosing the mixed food reveals that the effect observed in study 1 was reversed ($F(1, 40) = 4.63, p < .05$).

## GENERAL DISCUSSION

This research examines consumers' choice and consumption of mixed foods and the impact of the context (i.e., choice-set composition) and the presence of nutritional information on those choices. Prior research mainly studies consumers' reactions and behavior with regard to pure hedonic or utilitarian options; we instead focus on mixed options (i.e., a hedonic product that contains one or more utilitarian attributes).

Based on previous research (Giner-Sorolla 2001; Wansink and Chandon 2006), we claim that the mixed product can serve as a guilt reducing option but only in some situations. We suggest that depending on the choice-set composition, guilt can be activated or not and consequently determine the goal to be fulfilled (utilitarian related to health or hedonic related to pleasure, respectively). Additionally, as nutritional information can change the perception of a food product as well as intentions and consumption (Bui et al. 2008; Burton et al. 2006; Garg et al. 2007; Howlett et al. 2009; Kozup et al. 2003; Wansink and Chandon 2006), we suppose that the presence of nutritional information can activate guilt and reverse the choice-set composition effect described earlier. Through two studies (using real food choices) we demonstrate the role of guilt activation for the choice, and consumption of mixed products.

In study 1, we provide evidence that the context can activate guilt and this emotion influences both the motivation for the choice and the amount consumed of the mixed option. The hedonic context activates guilt and, in order to regulate this emotion, the choice of the mixed option is guided by a utilitarian motivation (i.e., health). Moreover, as a mean to reduce guilt, participants serve themselves a smaller amount of the mixed product. However, in a utilitarian context, we demonstrate that no guilt is activated and the choice and consumption of the mixed option are guided by hedonic motives. Additionally, our results show that these context effects are moderated by the presentation of nutritional information (study 2). More specifically, we found that, in the utilitarian context, consumers reduce their consumption of mixed option when nutritional information appears. This information primes guilt and leads to a reduction of the amount of mixed food consumed in the utilitarian context, reversing the overconsumption observed in study 1.

The results of these studies are consistent with the prediction that environmental stimuli (in that case, the choice-set composition) can activate the emotional system and motivational system that will consequently guide behavioral responses. In that sense, our results complement previous research (such as Fishbach et al. 2003; Wilcox et al. 2009) by putting forward the mediating role of emotion activation (i.e., guilt activation) when people are exposed to temptation. Specifically, the activation of guilt determines the goal to be pursued (hedonic or utilitarian). We empirically demonstrate an alternative path to the one suggested originally by Fishbach et al. (2003); the temptation can, in fact, activate guilt and this emotion will then determine the goal to be pursued. Our findings complement the research by Zemack-Rugar and colleagues (2007) by showing that the activated guilt influence the goals and these goals will then determine the consumers' decisions. Additionally, in our studies we employed different ways to activate guilt that are closer to real-world situations and could actually have an influence in decision making in the everyday consumer environment. We show that choice-set composition and nutritional information can activate guilt; previous research used instead more artificial ways to prime it (e.g., participants were subliminally primed with guilty emotion adjectives).

## IMPLICATIONS AND FUTURE RESEARCH

Our findings have important practical implications not only for brand managers but also for policy makers and consumers. For managers, our results indicate that positioning the mixed foods using a guilt-reducing argument can "speak to consumers". In fact, as Fabrigar and Petty (1999) show, persuasive arguments have to match the bases of the attitude toward the product. So, the usual health claims may not be enough to catch consumers; the emotional dimension also needs to be addressed. Moreover, our results help food manufacturers and retail store managers regarding display decisions. Our conclusions indicate that the mixed products sales could be increased by placing them in store shelves surrounded by utilitarian products rather than hedonic product, despite the risks of overconsumption. Moreover, our conclusions have also important

implications for policy makers and consumers assisting them in the context of obesity prevention. Previous research (Geyskens et al. 2007; Wansink and Chandon 2006) alerted to the fact that these mixed options could lead *de facto* to overconsumption. Our findings shed light on the circumstances in which consumers are more vulnerable to overconsumption indicating that placing mixed foods next to hedonic foods might be a good strategy for regulating their consumption. Likewise, our studies show that nutritional information may help consumers control their consumption of this kind of product when it appears in a utilitarian context.

Finally, this research suggests several further questions that additional research could address. First, we investigate the role of guilt activation in the context of choice related to mixed food products. As recent research shows (Keinan, Kivetz, and Netzer 2009), it also would be interesting to test and replicate these results with other mixed products (e.g., luxury clothes made with organic cotton). Second, in our studies the mixed products we used where hedonic product to which utilitarian attributes were added and removed (e.g., light cookies rich in cereals). Further research should explore consumers' reactions to and behavior toward different kinds of mixed products. An important question is whether there is difference between adding a utilitarian attribute (e.g., rich in calcium or fiber) versus removing a hedonic feature (e.g., fat or sugar free)? Similarly, we did not address in this research the fact that these products can have different degrees of "mixity" (more or less hedonic / utilitarian) and it could be relevant to explore the role of guilt in the decision process regarding these different types of mixed products. Third, it would be interesting to test the persistence of the context effects we find in this research and the guilt activation explanation using a more complex choice set (for instance, Sela et al. 2009).

## REFERENCES

Bargh, John A. (1997), "The Automaticity of Everyday Life," in *Advances in Social Cognition*, Vol. 10, ed. Robert S. Wyer, Mahwah, N J: Erlbaum, 1-61.

Bargh, John A. and Ezequiel Morsella (2009), "Unconscious Behavioral Guidance Systems," in *Then a Miracle Occurs: Focusing on Behavior in Social Psychological Theory and Research*, ed. Christopher R. Agnew, Donal E. Carlston, William G. Graziano and Janice R. Kelly, New York, NY: Oxford University Press, 89-118.

Baumeister, Roy F. and Julie Juola Exline (1999), "Virtue, Personality, and Social Relations: Self-Control as the Moral Muscle," *Journal of Personality*, 67 (6), 1165-94.

Baumeister, Roy F., Arlene M. Stillwell, and Todd F. Heatherton (1995), "Personal Narratives About Guilt: Role in Action Control and Interpersonal Relationships," *Basic & Applied Social Psychology*, 17 (1/2), 173-98.

Bettman, James R., Mary Frances Luce, and John W. Payne (2008), "Consumer Decision Making: A Choice Goals Approach," in *Handbook of Consumer Psychology*, ed. Curtis P. Haugtvedt, Paul M. Herr and Frank R. Kardes, New York, NY: Lawrence Erlbaum Associates, 589-610.

Bui, M. Y., Scot Burton, Elizabeth Howlett, and John Kozup (2008), "What Am I Drinking? The Effects of Serving Facts Information on Alcohol Beverage Containers," *Journal of Consumer Affairs*, 42 (1), 81-99.

Burton, Scot, Elizabeth H. Creyer, Jeremy Kees, and Kyle Huggins (2006), "Attacking the Obesity Epidemic: The Potential Health Benefits of Providing Nutrition Information in Restaurants," *American Journal of Public Health*, 96 (9), 1669-75.

Chandon, Pierre and Brian Wansink (2007a), "The Biasing Health Halos of Fast-Food Restaurant Health Claims: Lower Calorie Estimates and Higher Side-Dish Consumption Intentions," *Journal of Consumer Research*, 34 (3), 301-14.

_____ (2007b), "Is Obesity Caused by Calorie Underestimation? A Psychophysical Model of Meal Size Estimation," *Journal of Marketing Research*, 44 (1), 84-99.

Chartrand, Tanya L. (2005), "The Role of Conscious Awareness in Consumer Behavior," *Journal of Consumer Psychology*, 15 (3), 203-10.

Chitturi, Ravindra, Rajagopal Raghunathan, and Vijay Mahajan (2007), "Form Versus Function: How the Intensities of Specific Emotions Evoked in Functional Versus Hedonic Trade-Offs Mediate Product Preferences," *Journal of Marketing Research*, 44 (4), 702-14.

Dhar, Ravi, Joel Huber, and Uzma Khan (2007), "The Shopping Momentum Effect," *Journal of Marketing Research*, 44 (3), 370-78.

Fabrigar, Leandre R. and Richard E. Petty (1999), "The Role of the Affective and Cognitive Bases of Attitudes in Susceptibility to Affectively and Cognitively Based Persuasion," *Personality and Social Psychology Bulletin*, 25 (3), 363-81.

Fazio, Russell H. (1990), "A Practical Guide to the Use of Response Latency in Social Psychological Research," in *Review of Personality and Social Psychology*, Vol. 11, ed. Clyde A. Hendrick and Margaret S. Clark, Newbury Park, CA: Sage, 74-97.

Fishbach, Ayelet, Ronald S. Friedman, and Arie W. Kruglanski (2003), "Leading Us Not into Temptation: Momentary Allurements Elicit Overriding Goal Activation," *Journal of Personality and Social Psychology*, 84 (2), 296-309.

Garg, Nitika, Brian Wansink, and J. Jeffrey Inman (2007), "The Influence of Incidental Affect on Consumers' Food Intake," *Journal of Marketing*, 71 (1), 194-206.

Geyskens, Kelly, Mario Pandelaere, Siegfried Dewitte, and Luk Warlop (2007), "The Backdoor to Overconsumption: The Effect of Associating Low-Fat Food with Health References," *Journal of Public Policy & Marketing*, 26 (1), 118-25.

Giner-Sorolla, Roger (2001), "Guilty Pleasures and Grim Necessities: Affective Attitudes in Dilemmas of Self-Control," *Journal of Personality and Social Psychology*, 80 (2), 206-21.

Herman, C. P. and J. Polivy (1980), "Restrained Eating," in *Obesity* ed. A. Stunkard, Philadelphia: Saunders, 208-25.

Hoch, Stephen J. and George F. Loewenstein (1991), "Time-Inconsistent Preferences and Consumer Self-Control," *Journal of Consumer Research*, 17 (4), 492-507.

Holbrook, Morris B. and Elizabeth C. Hirschman (1982), "The Experiential Aspects of Consumption: Consumer Fantasies, Feelings, and Fun," *Journal of Consumer Research*, 9 (2), 132-40.

Howlett, Elizabeth A., Scot Burton, Kenneth Bates, and Kyle Huggins (2009), "Coming to a Restaurant near You? Potential Consumer Responses to Nutrition Information Disclosure on Menus," *Journal of Consumer Research*, 36 (2), forthcoming.

Hsee, Christopher K., George F. Loewenstein, Sally Blount, and Max H. Bazerman (1999), "Preference Reversals between Joint and Separate Evaluations of Options: A Review and Theoretical Analysis," *Psychological Bulletin*, 125 (5), 576-90.

Huber, Joel, Kelly Goldsmith, and Cassie Mogilner (2008), "Reinforcement Versus Balance Response in Sequential Choice," *Marketing Letters*, 19 (3/4), 229-39.

Keinan, Anat, Ran Kivetz, and Oded Netzer (2009), "Functional Alibi," in *Advances in Consumer Research*, Vol. 36, ed. Ann L. McGill and Sharon Shavitt, Duluth, MN: Association for Consumer Research, 27-30.

Khan, Uzma, Ravi Dhar, and Klaus Wertenbroch (2005), "A Behavioral Decision Theory Perspective on Hedonic and Utilitarian Choice," in *Inside Consumption: Frontiers of Research on Consumer Motives, Goals and Desires*, ed. S. Ratneshwar and David G. Mick, London: Routledge, 144-65.

Kozup, John C., Elizabeth H. Creyer, and Scot Burton (2003), "Making Healthful Food Choices: The Influence of Health Claims and Nutrition Information on Consumers' Evaluations of Packaged Food Products and Restaurant Menu Items," *Journal of Marketing*, 67 (2), 19-34.

Macht, Michael and Dorothee Dettmer (2006), "Everyday Mood and Emotions after Eating a Chocolate Bar or an Apple," *Appetite*, 46 (3), 332-36.

Okada, Erica Mina (2005), "Justification Effects on Consumer Choice of Hedonic and Utilitarian Goods," *Journal of Marketing Research*, 42 (1), 43-53.

Ramanathan, Suresh and Patti Williams (2007), "Immediate and Delayed Emotional Consequences of Indulgence: The Moderating Influence of Personality Type on Mixed Emotions," *Journal of Consumer Research*, 34 (2), 212-23.

Sela, Aner, Jonah Berger, and Wendy Liu (2009), "Variety, Vice, and Virtue: How Assortment Size Influences Option Choice," *Journal of Consumer Research*, 35 (6), 941-51.

Shiv, Baba and Alexander Fedorikhin (1999), "Heart and Mind in Conflict: The Interplay of Affect and Cognition in Consumer Decision Making," *Journal of Consumer Research*, 26 (3), 278-92.

Wansink, Brian and Pierre Chandon (2006), "Can Low-Fat Nutrition Labels Lead to Obesity?," *Journal of Marketing Research*, 43 (4), 605-17.

Wilcox, Keith, Beth Vallen, Lauren Block, and Gavan J. Fitzsimons (2009), "Vicarious Goal Fulfillment: When the Mere Presence of a Healthy Option Leads to an Ironically Indulgent Decision," *Journal of Consumer Research*, 36 (3), 380-93.

Zemack-Rugar, Yael, James R. Bettman, and Gavan J. Fitzsimons (2007), "The Effects of Nonconsciously Priming Emotion Concepts on Behavior," *Journal of Personality & Social Psychology*, 93 (6), 927-39.

# Body Beliefs Shape the Perceived Accuracy of Virtual Models

Ellen Garbarino, University of Sydney, Australia
Jose Antonio Rosa, University of Wyoming, USA

**ABSTRACT:**

The success of e-tailing highlights the need to understand how perceptions, including body-based beliefs, influence our interpretation of the virtual world. Using an Internet survey, we demonstrate women's body image discrepancy and body boundary aberration influence the perceived accuracy of virtual models, which in turn mediates their usage intentions.

## INTRODUCTION

The success of apparel sales online might come as a surprise to many who expected products for which consumption entails a high level of physical involvement would be hard to sell online (Yadav and Varadarajan 2005). Contrary to such expectations, apparel is one of the most dramatic success stories of online retailing, with double digit sales growth in recent years and the largest online sales revenue figures for all physical good (Mui 2007).

As sales volume and competition have increased, online retailers have relied on interactivity and personalization as powerful tools for online differentiation and success (Rust and Lemon 2001). Interactivity and personalization are valued for their ability to enhanced involvement, attitudes, and intentions (Fiore, Kim, and Lee 2005; Griffith, Krampf, and Palmer 2001; Kim and Forsythe 2008). Product visualization technologies, such as virtual models, offer some of the most intriguing tools for increasing interactivity and personalization. While product visualization tools have been shown to enhance the retail experience (Daugherty et al. 2008; Kim and Forsythe 2008), most research ignores the potential for individual differences to influence their effectiveness. In product categories with high body involvement, such as apparel, the effectiveness of product visualization may well depend on consumers' perceptions and beliefs about their physical body in ways that potentially limit the accuracy and effectiveness of virtual technologies. To explore this potential influence, we examine how two different belief systems about the body affect consumers' perception of virtual model accuracy and willingness to use them.

## BACKGROUND

### Product Visualization Technologies and Online Retailing

A number of researchers have explored the ability of product visualization technology to substitute for physical retail experiences. They find that 3D product visualization closely mimics the direct retail experience (Daugherty et al. 2008). 3-D representations have been found to increase psychological processing, involvement, enjoyment, and sense of being there (Li, Daugherty and Biocca 2001). However, this does not always translate into improved brand attitudes or purchase intentions (Li, Daugherty, and Biocca 2003; Westland and Au 1997). Conversely, other research finds that 3-D representations (i.e. virtual apparel models) improve attitudes towards retailers and the retail experience and increase purchase intentions (Daugherty et al. 2008; Fiore et al. 2005).

These conflicting findings may be the result of individual difference factors operating as moderators. A number of individual difference factors, including hedonic orientation (Fiore et al. 2005; Kim and Forsythe 2007), innovativeness (Kim and Forsythe 2008) and preferred level of stimulation (Daugherty et al. 2008), have been shown to moderate consumer responses to product visualization. We propose to explore how individual differences in consumer beliefs about their bodies might moderate the effectiveness of a product visualization tool. While the interrelationship between product visualization and body beliefs has received little attention, there is some evidence that body beliefs can influence consumers' online purchase intentions. Rosa et al. (Rosa, Garbarino, and Malter 2006) find that people's willingness to purchase apparel online is mediated by their involvement with apparel and their concern with fit, and that these mediators are in turn influenced by the consumers' beliefs about their bodies.

Virtual models simulate the visual aspects of traditional retail experiences, as partial replication of the more conclusive assessment of fit that comes from physically trying on garments. In contrast to traditional stores, however, where consumers can sensorially experience how the product looks and feels, the virtual experience involves an abstract perceptual process where one must mentally extrapolate the consumption experience from a 2-D caricature. The creation of such a mental representation does not merely draw on the consumers' perceptions of the product but also of the caricature and its ability to accurately represent their body as they perceive it. This more complex integration of product, digital rendering, and body information should make the interpretation of electronic representations susceptible to biases generated by the consumer's pre-existing notions about the shape, attractiveness, and adequacy of their bodies. In addition, given the impoverished information available in the Internet context, almost exclusively reliant on two-dimensional representations and text descriptions, it is reasonable to expect that consumers will rely more heavily on information they already hold when making product assessments in this context. Beliefs about one's body are among the sources of information consistently available, and hence likely to exert an exaggerated influence on consumers when shopping in the Internet's low information environment. It is expected that consumers who hold body beliefs that are not well calibrated to the objective reality of their bodies (e.g., see themselves differently than they appear to others) will carry this bias into their interpretation of the accuracy of virtual models, and hence relate differently to the sales tool.

## BODY BELIEFS

We focus on how two distinct types of beliefs that consumers hold about their bodies–body image discrepancy (Cash 1994; Cash and Szymanski 1995) and body boundary aberration (Fisher 1986)–affect the perception of a virtual model. Body image discrepancy (BID) is a cognitive evaluation of how well the appearance of various aspects of our body (e.g., hair, skin, muscle tone, body proportions, and weight) aligns with our ideals for those body parts (Cash 1994; Cash and Szymanski 1995). It is captured as a discrepancy between the consumers' perception of each body aspect (e.g., hair, skin, weight, body proportions, and muscle tone) and their ideals for that aspect, weighted for the importance of that aspect to the consumer (Cash 1994; Cash and Szymanski 1995). High body image discrepancy scores indicate a body image that differs from ideals.

Body boundary aberration (BBA) addresses the individual's sense of the location and stability of the edges of his or her body as a container (Fisher 1970, 1973). Most people recognize that they reside in a container, and that a boundary or edge separates them from the outside world. The alignment of this boundary with the skin surface, however, differs between persons, along with how well their boundary can withstand penetration. BBA occurs when an individual's sense of the location of that edge does not aligned with their skin surface, and when the individual perceives his or her body boundaries as threateningly susceptible to penetration (Fisher 1970,

1986). Initially noted and explored by neurologists in brain-damaged patients (e.g., Head 1926), BBA has also been studied in segments of the general population (Chapman et al. 1978; Fisher 1970, 1986), including consumers (Rosa et al. 2006). In general, perceived body boundary aligns with the skin surface, but it is possible for our sense of body containment to either move inward from the skin surface or extend beyond it to incorporate immediately adjacent objects in contact with the skin. Consumers whose boundaries extend beyond the skin surface sense objects adjacent to their skin (i.e., a tennis racket being held, apparel being worn) as integrated with their bodies, and experience a temporary sense of loss when physical contact ends. One common example of mild BBA is experiencing a general sense of nakedness and vulnerability when a habitually worn accessory (e.g., hat, bra, watch, or ring) is absent. Another example is experiencing an enhanced and generalized sense of power when wearing bold colors or tightly-woven dense fabrics (Fisher 1986). Body boundary aberration affects how people interact with products. Some consumers use products to reinforce their body boundaries (Fisher 1970, 1973), such as by driving autos that feel and sound impenetrable, and strategically choosing colors and fabrics that accentuate their boundaries. It has also been shown that consumers instinctively incorporate the shape and location of products into their body schemas and adjust their behavior accordingly, such as when without thinking they adjust their posture and movement to clear doorways when wearing tall head gear (Blakeslee 2004). BBA has been found to influence how people shop, and that consumers high on BBA are more willing to shop for apparel online (Rosa et al. 2006).

These constructs were chosen to represent different aspects of body belief; body image discrepancy as a consciously evaluative measure, and body boundary aberration as a perception with limited cognitive intrusion. Finding that body beliefs influence accuracy assessments, even when working with such distinct body beliefs, affirms the robustness of the phenomena. Using an online survey, we explore how these body beliefs influence consumer's assessments of virtual models and how their perceptions affect usage intentions.

## PROPOSED MODEL

Figure 1 depicts the proposed model of how body beliefs will influence consumer intentions to use virtual models. Because judgments of model accuracy are subjective, we believe they will be influenced by the consumer's body beliefs. Body image discrepancy is expected to have a negative influence on perceived virtual model accuracy. High body image discrepancy exists when consumers believe that aspects of their looks do not meet important standards, suggesting a more critical view of the self in the mirror. Discrepancies are likely to be more salient and influential for high body image discrepancy consumers, and given the evaluative nature of BID, it is reasonable to expect that the same critical eye that highlights discrepancies from the ideal when looking in the mirror will be used to assess the accuracy of any representation that purports to serve the same function. Consequently, body image discrepancy will have a negative relationship to virtual model accuracy.

The influence of Body Boundary Aberration (BBA) stems from the underlying uncertainty about body shape that BBA engenders. Body Boundary Aberration is expected to have a positive influence on the perceived accuracy of virtual models by virtue of the reassurance that comes from seeing a stand-alone representation of the self with unambiguous boundaries. High BBA consumers glean reassurance from seeing their boundaries well-defined, and we expect that a representation of self with well defined edges against a neutral and uniform background will be reassuring to consumers with high BBA.

Perceived model quality is defined as consumers' assessment of how effectively the model can represent how the clothing looks

and fits. It is expected to positively influence both their perception of how accurately the model can represent them and how likely they would be to use it. While we have no theoretical reason to expect that body image discrepancy and body boundary aberration influence quality assessments, we will test this assumption via alternative model testing. The inclusion of perceived model quality as an influence on accuracy assessments and usage intentions allows us to capture the variance in this endogenous variable and reduce the possibility of the paths from body beliefs being inflated by otherwise unaccounted for random variance. Both perceived accuracy and quality are expected to positively influence usage intentions.

**Figure 1: The Influence of Body Beliefs**

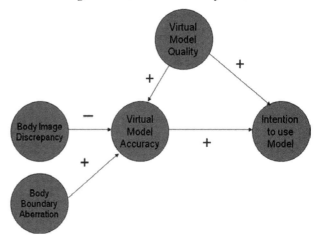

## METHODS

An online panel designed to represent the U.S Internet consumer population was used to collect a sample of female respondents (initial invites 8264; N=978; response rate 12%). Since women are the major purchasers of apparel on- and offline, only female consumers were used. This also avoids potential spurious influence due to gender differences in body beliefs (Rosa et al. 2006). The demographics of the sample closely match the U.S. Internet consumer population (ClickZ 2003; Pastore 2001). Average online consumer population versus average sample characteristics, respectively, were as follows: income – $49,800 versus $53,600; age – 41 years old versus 44; modal education – college graduate versus college graduate, websites visited per week – 13 versus 12; hours online per week – 6.2 versus 10. All U.S. states and the District of Columbia were represented in the sample. The respondents answered questions about their web usage, interest in apparel, online apparel purchase habits and basic demographics, most notably the respondent's height and weight which were used later to determine which virtual model they were shown. To avoid potential bias in weight responses, we reiterated that we had no way to know their identity and the importance of an honest answer for the integrity of the research. The results do not appear biased, since the weight/height ratio distribution of the sample closely parallels the U.S. distribution of women's weight and height, with a mean of weight/height ratio of 2.40 (as compared to the 2.20 of the national data; Halls 2000), median ratio of 2.30. Respondents were then shown a virtual model based on their body dimensions and wearing a classic black sheath dress in four positions, forward facing, backward facing and right and left side facing (see example in figure 2). The study uses a well-established personalized virtual model, My Virtual Model™; which uses the consumer's dimensions to create a virtual model that allows online shoppers to 'try-on' a wide array of apparel (see Nantel 2004 for a complete description). After viewing the model, respondents were asked to assess the quality and accuracy of the model, and their interest in using such a model in the future. Finally, they responded to BID and BBA items.

**Figure 2: Example My Virtual Model™ Stimuli**

Body image discrepancy (BID) was assessed using the scale developed by Cash and Szymanski (Cash and Szymanski 1995); respondents rate how well they match their ideals (i.e., 'actually are' against 'wish you were') on a 4-point scale (0 = exactly as I am - 3 = very unlike me) for eleven physical characteristics (see table 1 for items). In addition, respondents indicate the importance of these ideals (e.g., how important your ideal weight is to you) on a 4-point scale (0 = not important - 4 = very important). Using Cash's technique (Cash 1994), a composite score is computed for each characteristic by recoding all ratings of zero (0) for discrepancy and importance to -1, and multiplying the discrepancy rating and the importance rating for each characteristic. This procedure creates a single measure of BID that ranges from -3 to +9; with larger scores reflecting higher actual-to-ideal discrepancies on increasingly important ideals. The 11 items form a single factor ($\alpha$ =.81).

Body boundary aberration was assessed using a scale developed by Chapman et al. (1978), subjects responded to 49 statements on a 5-point Likert scale (1 - strongly agree to 5 - strongly disagree). The 10 items pertaining to BBA were interspersed, and later reversed scored such that higher scores signal higher BBA. The 10 items form a single factor ($\alpha$ =.87). The average of the ten items was used as a measure of BBA. The BBA scores are widely distributed; 1-1.99 (highest BBA) = 4%, 2-2.99 =14%, 3-3.99 =45%, 4-5 (lowest BBA) = 37%. As expected, the two body beliefs are not highly correlated (r =.11).

Perceived accuracy and quality of the model and future use intentions were captured on 7-point scales. Perceived accuracy of the model was assessed using two items designed to focus attention on the virtual model's body (not the face) and the ability of the model to represents the respondent's body. The items were 1) "Focusing on the body aspects, how much do you feel this model looks like you?" (very much like me – not at all like me), and 2) "How true a representation of you is this model?" (very accurate – very inaccurate). The two items are correlated .88. Perceived quality of the virtual model was captured by three items assessed on 7-point scales: 1) "How well does this representation demonstrate how the clothing would fit?" (very well – very poorly) , 2) "How well does this representation depict the clothing?" (very well – very poorly), and 3) "How would you judge the quality of this representation?" (very good – very poor), $\alpha$ = .93. The three perceived quality items were designed to focus on how well the model depicts the clothing, rather than how well it depicts the respondent. Intention to use the virtual model was captured by two items: 1) "How interested would you be in using such a model in your future apparel shopping?" (very interested – not at all interested), and 2) "How likely would you be

to use a model like this if it were available?" (very likely – not at all likely), r = .91. The three constructs show significant correlation, but no multicollinearity (Qual. – Accur. r = .52; Qual. – Use = r = .61; Accur. – Use r = .56).

Structural equation modeling with maximum likelihood estimation was used to test the relationships shown in figure 1. Correlations were allowed between single-item error terms for some measures of each of latent variable to account for measurement error. Means, standard deviations and correlations of the measures used in the SEM estimation are shown in appendix. Measurement and structural model estimates and model fit statistics are shown in table 1. Although not all body belief items loaded heavily on their hypothesized construct, all loadings were significant at the p<.000 level, and hence all items were retained to maintain the integrity of these established body belief measures.

## RESULTS

Although the $\chi 2$ goodness of fit statistic is significant ($\chi 2$ = 866.6 df =311, p=.00), as is common with large samples, our fit statistics meet the recommended levels (Hu and Bentler 1999); with the SRMR for the full model of .05, TLI of 0.95, NFI of 0.94, and RMSEA of 0.04, suggesting an acceptable fit for the measurement and structural model. All of the hypothesized structural relationships are statistically significant. Virtual model accuracy ($\gamma$= .315, p < .00) has a positive influence on consumer intentions to use virtual models. Moreover, Body Boundary Aberration has a positive influence on virtual model accuracy ($\gamma$ = .117, p < .00), supporting the notion that consumers high in BBA may consider renditions that highlight the body's edges more accurate. In contrast, Body Image Discrepancy ($\gamma$ = -.120, p = .00) has a negative influence on assessed virtual model accuracy, suggesting that consumer whose body attribute image differs substantially from their held ideals are less likely to consider virtual models accurate. As expected, quality perceptions have a positive influence on assessed virtual model accuracy ($\gamma$ = .507, p = .00) and intentions to use models ($\gamma$ = .486, p = .00). The SEM results affirm our expectations that body beliefs influence consumer assessments of the accuracy of virtual models even after accounting for quality perceptions.

Secondary SEM analyses were performed to confirm that the influence of body beliefs on consumer intentions to use virtual models is mediated by perceived accuracy and that body beliefs influence the perceived accuracy of virtual models and not their quality. In the first alternative model, perceived accuracy was retained in the model but the paths from body beliefs were redirected to consumer intentions to use virtual models. In this alternative model the paths from body beliefs (BID and BBA) to future use intentions are not significant, and goodness-of-fit deteriorates ($\Delta \chi^2$ = 265.6, df = 1, p = .000, $\Delta$SRMR = .03, $\Delta$TLI = -.03, $\Delta$NFI = -.03, $\Delta$RMSEA = .01). These results support the notion that body beliefs affect use intentions through their influence on assessment of virtual model accuracy. In the second alternative model, accuracy is again retained but the paths from body beliefs are redirected to quality of the virtual model. Again we find that the paths from body beliefs, this time from BID and BBA to quality, are not significant. Moreover, the overall goodness-of-fit is again less than for the proposed model ($\Delta \chi^2$ = 2359.0, df = 2, p = .000, $\Delta$SRMR = .07, $\Delta$TLI = -.20, $\Delta$NFI = -.18, $\Delta$RMSEA = .05). These results suggest that the influence of body beliefs on consumer intentions to use virtual models is not mediated by quality perceptions. Given the reduced goodness-of-fit of these alternative models, we conclude that the influence of body beliefs of consumer intentions to use virtual model is mediated by perceived accuracy.

**Table 1: Measurement and Structural Model Estimates and Fit Statistics**

| Measurement Model* | Stand. Coeff. | Stand. Error | Measurement Model* | Stand. Coeff. | Stand. Error. |
|---|---|---|---|---|---|
| **Body Image Discrep. α=.81** | | | **Body Boundary Aberration α=.87** | | |
| Weight[a] | .698 | | I have sometimes felt confused as to whether my body was really my own. [a] | .804 | .044 |
| Skin | .285 | .039 | I have had the momentary feeling that my body has changed shape. | .655 | .042 |
| Hair | .313 | .044 | Now and then when I look in the mirror, my face seems different from the usual. | .513 | .038 |
| Face | .436 | .041 | I have had the momentary feeling that things I touch remain attached to me. | .672 | .041 |
| Muscle | .728 | .044 | I have felt as if my body does not exist. | .735 | .038 |
| Body proportions | .759 | .038 | At least once, I have wondered if my body was really my own. | .705 | .036 |
| Height | .173 | .025 | I have felt as if I could not distinguish my body from other objects around me. | .707 | .042 |
| Chest | .463 | .043 | I can remember when it seemed as though one of my limbs took on an unusual shape. | .670 | .042 |
| Physical strength | .488 | .039 | I think it is possible that one of my arms or legs is disconnected from the rest of me. | .479 | .038 |
| Coordination | .499 | .040 | I have felt as if I am united with objects near me. | .316 | .044 |
| Overall appearance | .800 | .042 | | | |
| **Virtual Model Quality α=.93** | | | | | |
| How well depiction how clothing would fit [a] | .865 | | **Structural Model** | | |
| How well depict the clothing | .884 | .028 | Body Image Discrepancy à Accuracy of Virtual Model | -.120 | .022 |
| Judgment of general quality of representation | .859 | .026 | Body Boundary Aberration à Accuracy of Virtual Model | .117 | .054 |
| **Virtual Model Accur. ρ = .88** | | | Quality à Accuracy of Virtual Model | .507 | .046 |
| Model body looks like you [a] | .905 | | Quality à Intentions to Use | .486 | .046 |
| How true representation of you | .969 | .029 | Accuracy of Virtual Model à Intentions to Use | .315 | .031 |
| **Intentions to Use ρ = .91** | | | | | |
| Likely to use in the future [a] | .937 | | | | |
| Likely to use if available | .969 | .022 | | | |
| **Goodness of Fit[b]** | X²=866.6, df = 331, p = .00; SRMR=.05; TLI=.95; NFI=.94; RMSEA=.04 | | | | |

\* all significant p<.000

[a] = Loading value fixed at 1.000 for estimation purposes.

[b] = SRMR – Standardized Root Mean Squared Residual; TLI = Tucker-Lewis Indicator; NFI = Normed Fit Indicator; RMSEA = Root Mean Square Error of Approximation

## DISCUSSION

The study investigates the influence of body image discrepancy and body boundary aberration on consumer assessments of the accuracy of virtual models, and the subsequent influence that consumers' perceived accuracy has on their intentions to use such models. The findings argue for an important role for body beliefs in consumer response to the virtual models offered by online retailers. We find that body image discrepancy negatively influences assessments of virtual model accuracy. Consumers who have high discrepancy between held ideals and their self-image are more critical of the accuracy of virtual models and ultimately less likely to use such shopping tools. Moreover, consumers high in body boundary aberration find the models more accurate, and possibly more likely to make mistakes when making online purchases of apparel and using virtual models. This effect might be especially problematic because of earlier findings that high BBA consumers are more likely than low BBA consumers to shop for apparel online (Rosa et al. 2006). If high BBA consumers are concurrently more likely to shop for apparel online and misperceive virtual model accuracy to the positive, they may be among the consumers most likely to purchase apparel items that result in low satisfaction and higher returns to the online merchant.

Body boundary aberration is a little recognized shaper of consumer perceptions. Prior research found that body boundary aberration can influence concern with fit in electronic shopping environments (Rosa et al. 2006) and we find that it also influences the perceived accuracy of virtual models designed to diminish fit concerns. In contrast to body image discrepancy, however, body boundary aberration is not a factor that is easily addressed through reassuring commentary on a person's appearance and compliance with social standards, given its unconscious and hard-to-grasp nature. Body boundary aberration, in fact, may be better addressed through subtle manipulations of consumer sensitivity prior to exposing consumers to virtual representations of themselves, such as the bringing of body boundary perceptions to the foreground that arises when persons are exposed to a fractured mirror representation (Fisher 1986). Clearly, a better understanding of body boundary aberration is needed in consumer research, focusing in particular on how it may influence the perceptual mechanisms engaged in the processing on information and the development of mental representations. This will gain importance as information technology continues to expand the manner in which consumers are exposed to products and services, and encouraged to purchase.

Although consumers spend billions of dollars on apparel and other body-involving products, little research to date has focused on how consumers' attitudes toward their bodies affect consumption behavior. Our work contributes to the theoretical understanding of how body image can influence how consumers respond to technological driven shopping tools. It also contributes to the growing consumer literature addressing how the consumer's physical needs and preferences interact with limited information environment such as the Internet. In contrast to traditional in-store retailing, where the role of body beliefs may be attenuated by the ability to physically experience goods, in the online context such attitudes are likely to play a larger role in determining consumer behaviors because of the limited availability and low diagnosticity of online information. Our research demonstrates that how people see their bodies biases their response to tools that are explicitly designed to help them overcome the lack of physical product experience, and in turn influences how likely they are to use such tools in general. These findings highlight the importance of better understanding how people's pre-existing beliefs affect their responses to this new low body-information environment.

Several limitations in the study should be noted. The data were collected at a single point in time, and it is possible that cumulative practice with Internet shopping will alter these effects. It is hard to predict in what direction experience will have on the influence of body beliefs, given their noted complexity and subtlety, further affirming the need for more research. A limitation related to the indirect data collection method is the potential for misrepresenting the truth about one's body proportions. To minimize this effect we emphasized in the questionnaire both the importance of accurate reporting and the double-blind nature of the survey. However, it is still possible that people misrepresent their height and weight. Encouragingly, our data do not suggest deception by respondents, since the average weight/height ratio in our sample is actually slightly higher than the national averages while the other demographics are very much in line with them. Such limitations notwithstanding, our research has increased the field's understanding of how body beliefs such as body image discrepancy and body boundary aberration can influence consumer assessments of the accuracy of virtual models and their likelihood to use such tools, and moved the field toward a more complete understanding of the role body beliefs in consumer behavior.

## REFERENCES

Blakeslee, Sandra. (2004), "When the Brain Says, 'Don't Get Too Close'," The New York Times, (July 13, 2004).

Cash, Thomas F. (1994), "Body-Image Attitudes: Evaluation, Investment, and Affect," Perceptual and Motor Skills 78:3, pt2, 1168-1170.

_____ and Szymanski, Marcela L. (1995), "The Development and Validation of the Body-Image Ideals Questionnaire," Journal of Personality Assessment 64:3, 466-477.

Chapman, Loren J., Chapman, Jean P. and Raulin, Michael L. (1978), "Body-Image Aberration in Schizophrenia," Journal of Abnormal Psychology 87:4, 399-407.

ClickZ Stats Staff, (2003), "June 2003 Internet Usage Stats", ClickZ.com, Retrieved October 17th, 2009, from http://www.clickz.com/stats/big_picture/traffic_patterns/article.php/2237901

Daugherty, Terry, Li, Hairong, and Biocca, Frank (2008), "Consumer Learning and the Effects of Virtual Experience Relative to Indirect and Direct Product Experience," Psychology & Marketing, 25:7, 568-586.

Fiore, Ann Marie, Kim, Jihyun, and Lee, Hyun-Hwa (2005), "Effect of Image Interactivity Technology on Consumer Responses toward the Online Retailer," Journal of Interactive Marketing, 19:3, 38-53.

Fisher, Seymour (1970), Body Experience in Fantasy and Behavior, New York: Meredith Corp.

_____ (1973), Body Consciousness: You Are What You Feel. Englewood Cliffs, NJ: Prentice Hall.

_____ (1986), Development and Structure of the Body Image, vol. 1 and 2, Hillsdale, NJ: Lawrence Erlbaum Associates.

Griffith, David A.; Krampf, Robert F. and Palmer, Jonathan W. (2001), "The Role of Interface in Electronic Commerce: Consumer Involvement with Print versus On-line Catalogs," International Journal of Electronic Commerce, 5:4, 135-153.

Halls, Steven B. (2000), "Average Height and Weight Charts," Halls.md Health Calculators and Charts. Retrieved on 10/2/06 from http://www.halls.md/chart/height-weight.htm.

Head, H. (1926), Aphasia and Kindred Disorders of Speech. London: Cambridge.

Hu, Li-tze and Bentler, Peter M. (1999), "Cutoff Criteria for Fit Indices in Covariance Structure Analysis: Conventional Criteria versus New Alternatives," Structural Equation Modeling, 6:1, 1-55.

Kim, Jihyun and Forsythe, Sandra (2007), "Hedonic Usage of Product Visualization Technologies in Online Apparel Shopping," International Journal of Retail & Distribution Management, 35:6, 502-514.

_____ and _____ (2008a), "Adoption of Virtual Try-on Technology for Online Apparel Shopping," Journal of Interactive Marketing, 22:2, 45-59.

Li, Hairong, Daugherty, Terry, and Biocca, Frank (2003), "The Role of Virtual Experience in Consumer Learning," Journal of Consumer Psychology, 13:4, 395-407.

_____, _____, and _____ (2001), "Characteristics of Virtual Experience in Electronic Commerce: A Protocol Analysis," Journal of Interactive Marketing, 15:3, 13-30.

Mui, Ylan Q. (2007), "Online Sales Shift: Apparel Outpaced Computers in '06," Washingtonpost.com, http://www.washingtonpost.com/wpdyn/content/article/2007/05/13/AR2007051301263.html, accessed February 19th 2009.

Nantel, Jacques (2004), "My Virtual Model: Virtual Reality Comes into Fashion," Journal of Interactive Marketing, 18:8, 73-86.

Pastore, Michael (2001), "Online Consumers Now the Average Consumer," ClickZ.com, Retrieved October 17th 2009, from http://www.clickz.com/stats/big_picture/demographics/article.php/800201.

Rosa, Josa A., Garbarino, Ellen, and Malter, Alan J. (2006), "Keeping the Body in Mind: The Influence of Body Esteem and Body Boundary Aberration on Consumer Beliefs and Purchase Intentions," Journal of Consumer Psychology 16:1, 79-91.

Rust, Roland T. and Lemon, Katherine N. (2001), "E-Service and the Consumer," International Journal of Electronic Commerce 5:3, 85-101.

Westland, J. Christopher and Au, Grace (1997), "A Comparison of Shopping Experiences across Three Competing Digital Retailing Interfaces," International Journal of Electronic Commerce 2:2, 57-69.

Yadav, Manjit S. and Varadarajan, P. Rajan (2005), "Understanding Product Migration to the Electronic Marketplace: A Conceptual Framework," Journal of Retailing 81:2, 125-140.

## Appendix - Means, Standard Deviations, and Correlations for Measured Variables

| | Mean | SD | 1 | 2 | 3 | 4 | 5 | 6 | 7 | 8 | 9 | 10 | 11 | 12 | 13 | 14 |
|---|---|---|---|---|---|---|---|---|---|---|---|---|---|---|---|---|
| 1. BIQ Weight Composite | 3.89 | 3.52 | 1 | | | | | | | | | | | | | |
| 2. BIQ Skin | .146 | 2.67 | .08* | 1 | | | | | | | | | | | | |
| 3. BIQ Hair | 1.66 | 3.08 | .12** | .25** | 1 | | | | | | | | | | | |
| 4. BIQ Face | 1.26 | 2.66 | .17** | .34** | .35** | 1 | | | | | | | | | | |
| 5. BIQ Muscle Tone | 3.62 | 2.88 | .58** | .19** | .20** | .26** | 1 | | | | | | | | | |
| 6. BIQ Body Proportions | 3.37 | 3.03 | .68** | .10** | .18** | .23** | .60** | 1 | | | | | | | | |
| 7. BIQ Height | .04 | 1.74 | .09** | .14** | .10* | .22** | .07* | .10** | 1 | | | | | | | |
| 8. BIQ Chest | 1.64 | 2.97 | .26** | .16** | .28** | .27** | .29** | .36** | .12** | 1 | | | | | | |
| 9. BIQ Physical Strength | 1.99 | 2.65 | .28** | .16** | .20** | .23** | .39** | .32** | .06* | .28** | 1 | | | | | |
| 10. BIQ Coordination | 1.50 | 2.76 | .30** | .17** | .18** | .33** | .37** | .31** | .15** | .25** | .50** | 1 | | | | |
| 11. BIQ Overall Appearance | 3.02 | 2.70 | .59** | .26** | .26** | .34** | .55** | .61** | .14** | .37** | .41** | .42** | 1 | | | |
| 12. BBA Confused Body Own | 2.04 | 1.21 | .06* | .05 | .06 | .11** | .03 | .06 | .07* | .13** | .09** | .08* | .07* | 1 | | |
| 13. BBA Body Changed Shape | 2.49 | 1.34 | .05 | .09** | .08* | .10** | .06 | .03 | .04 | .11** | .03 | .08* | .03 | .55** | 1 | |
| 14. BBA Face Different | 3.04 | 1.25 | .01 | .15** | .12** | .16** | .07* | .04 | .04 | .11** | .08* | .12** | .07* | .43** | .45** | 1 |
| 15. BBA Touched Remains | 2.03 | 1.15 | -.03 | .06 | .04 | .06 | -.08* | -.07* | -.04 | .07* | .02 | .01 | -.08* | .53** | .48** | .31** |
| 16. BBA Body Doesn't Exist | 2.10 | 1.26 | .03 | .03 | .06 | .09** | .01 | .02 | .02 | .08* | .09** | .07* | .03 | .61** | .42** | .40** |
| 17. BBA Wonder Body Own | 2.39 | 1.36 | .09** | .04 | .03 | .05 | .02 | .06 | .03 | .11** | .03 | .05 | .08* | .68** | .48** | .40** |
| 18. BBA Dist From Objects | 1.88 | 1.09 | .03 | .04 | .01 | .09** | -.04 | .00 | .06* | .07* | .04 | .05 | .01 | .56** | .43** | .31** |
| 19. BBA Limb Unusual Shape | 2.05 | 1.19 | -.02 | .02 | .00 | .07* | -.03 | -.01 | .04 | .09** | .05 | .06 | -.02 | .47** | .47** | .31** |
| 20. BBA Arm/Leg Disconnect | 2.39 | 1.25 | .02 | .01 | .05 | .07* | .02 | .01 | .04 | .04 | .06 | .09** | .05 | .33** | .26** | .30** |
| 21. BBA United to Objects | 2.89 | 1.10 | -.03 | -.01 | .06* | .01 | -.02 | -.04 | -.02 | .09** | .05 | .01 | -.04 | .23** | .25** | .20** |
| 22. How Well Depicts Fit | 5.27 | 1.44 | .06 | -.07* | -.035 | -.06 | .04 | .03 | -.11** | -.01 | -.04 | -.02 | .01 | .05 | .08** | .06 |
| 23. How Well Depicts Clothes | 5.50 | 1.37 | .06 | -.09* | -.04 | -.05 | .05 | .01 | -.11* | -.01 | -.10** | -.03 | .01 | .01 | .05 | .04 |
| 24. Quality Representation | 5.62 | 1.27 | .06 | -.06 | -.04 | -.05 | .07* | .02 | -.09** | -.06* | -.08* | -.04 | .01 | -.01 | .03 | .02 |
| 25. Body Looks Like You | 3.83 | 1.91 | -.02 | -.09* | -.07* | -.05 | -.07* | -.10** | -.02 | -.11** | -.09** | -.05 | -.08* | .08** | .10** | .07** |
| 26. True Represent. of You | 3.77 | 1.80 | -.03 | -.07* | -.05 | -.03 | -.06* | -.09** | -.02 | -.09** | -.10** | -.05 | -.07* | .10** | .11** | .07** |
| 27. Like to Use in the Future | 5.24 | 1.83 | .04 | -.02 | -.02 | -.02 | .05 | -.01 | -.10** | -.04 | -.07* | -.03 | .03 | .05 | .08** | .14** |
| 28. Like to Use if Available | 5.32 | 1.86 | .05 | -.02 | -.02 | -.03 | .07* | .01 | -.09** | -.04 | -.07* | -.04 | .04 | .02 | .06 | .12** |

** Correlation is significant at the 0.01 level 2-tailed.    * Correlation is significant at the 0.05 level 2-tailed.

Appendix con't.

| | 15 | 16 | 17 | 18 | 19 | 20 | 21 | 22 | 23 | 24 | 25 | 26 | 27 | 28 |
|---|---|---|---|---|---|---|---|---|---|---|---|---|---|---|
| 1. BIQ Weight | | | | | | | | | | | | | | |
| 2. BIQ Skin | | | | | | | | | | | | | | |
| 3. BIQ Hair | | | | | | | | | | | | | | |
| 4. BIQ Face | | | | | | | | | | | | | | |
| 5. BIQ Muscle Tone | | | | | | | | | | | | | | |
| 6. BIQ Body Proportions | | | | | | | | | | | | | | |
| 7. BIQ Height | | | | | | | | | | | | | | |
| 8. BIQ Chest | | | | | | | | | | | | | | |
| 9. BIQ Physical Strength | | | | | | | | | | | | | | |
| 10. BIQ Coordination | | | | | | | | | | | | | | |
| 11. BIQ Overall Appearance | | | | | | | | | | | | | | |
| 12. BBA Confused Body Own | | | | | | | | | | | | | | |
| 13. BBA Body Changed Shape | | | | | | | | | | | | | | |
| 14. BBA Face Different | | | | | | | | | | | | | | |
| 15. BBA Touched Remains | 1 | | | | | | | | | | | | | |
| 16. BBA Body Doesn't Exist | .44** | 1 | | | | | | | | | | | | |
| 17. BBA Wonder Body Own | .40** | .56** | 1 | | | | | | | | | | | |
| 18. BBA Dist From Objects | .54** | .53** | .47** | 1 | | | | | | | | | | |
| 19. BBA Limb Unusual Shape | .48** | .38** | .43** | .61** | 1 | | | | | | | | | |
| 20. BBA Arm/Leg Disconnect | .30** | .41** | .33** | .37** | .35** | 1 | | | | | | | | |
| 21. BBA United to Objects | .38** | .20** | .20** | .26** | .23** | .15** | 1 | | | | | | | |
| 22. How Well Depicts Fit | .07* | .01 | .08* | .02 | .02 | -.02 | .10** | 1 | | | | | | |
| 23. How Well Depicts Clothes | .04 | .02 | .05 | .01 | .00 | -.01 | .09** | .77** | 1 | | | | | |
| 24. Quality Representation | .01 | -.01 | .03 | -.05 | .03 | -.01 | .04 | .73** | .77** | 1 | | | | |
| 25. Body Looks Like You | .10** | .07* | .09** | .12** | .08* | .03 | .05 | .42** | .35** | .38** | 1 | | | |
| 26. True Represent. of You | .12** | .05 | .07* | .11** | .08* | .02 | .06* | .47** | .41** | .43** | .88** | 1 | | |
| 27. Like to Use in the Future | .05 | .06 | .08* | .04 | .01 | .03 | .09** | .55** | .52** | .56** | .51** | .53** | 1 | |
| 28. Like to Use if Available | -.01 | .02 | .04 | -.01 | -.02 | .01 | .06* | .54** | .50** | .57** | .47** | .50** | .91** | 1 |

** Correlation is significant at the 0.01 level 2-tailed).   * Correlation is significant at the 0.05 level 2-tailed).

# Exploring the Everyday Branded Retail Experience-
## The Consumer Quest for 'Homeyness' in Branded Grocery Stores

Sofia Ulver-Sneistrup, Lund University, Sweden
Ulf Johansson, Lund University, Sweden

## ABSTRACT

This paper extends consumer culture theories of branded retail environments by analyzing the consumer experiences of the everyday site of the branded grocery store. The analysis suggests that McCracken's (1989) 'homeyness' framework succeeds to understand the orientations inflected in the everyday branded retail experience, as opposed to the 'mythotypic' (see Kozinets 2002) that explicates the power of the more spectacular. The implications for theoretical transferability in consumer research are discussed.

## INTRODUCTION

During the last decade the marketing management literature has paid a lot of attention to the growing impact of branded retail experiences on consumers, and especially to relationships in-between retailers' corporate, store and product brands (Ailawadi & Keller 2004; Burt & Carralero-Encinas 2002; Burt & Sparks 2000; Kotler 1973; Kumar & Kurande 2000; Kankurra & Kang 2007; Pine & Gilmore 1999; McGoldrick 2002; Moore, Fernie and Burt 2000 etc.). The majority of this literature focuses on branded grocery retailers, and quantitatively investigates specific factors that influence the preference of national or retailers' own brands (such as between store aesthetics and the evaluation of private brands (Richardson, Jain and Dick 1996), between quality and feature differentiation from the national brand (Choi, Chan, and Coughlan 2006), or the impact of retailer store image on private brand perception (Collins-Dodd and Lindley 2003)). These measuring exercises result in useful advice to retail managers regarding how to manage very specific components of the consumers' retail brand experience.

In contrast, in a quest for a more holistic understanding of the branded retail experience, consumer researchers inhabiting the marketing research tradition of consumer culture theory, CCT (Arnold & Thompson 2005), have begun to successively contribute to this domain of interest, or as Borghini et al (2009 p. 363) recently expressed it; "in the past few years, retail theory has developed a growing cultural orientation." This has been done by bringing in empirical data and analyzing it through cultural theory in order to understand what is really going on inside the branded retailers' stores from an overarching sociocultural perspective. Instead of testing relationships between already identified variables and factors, this growing cultural orientation has been able to offer cultural accounts that invent radically different concepts and ways to understand the retail brand experience as a whole and from a consumer-centric perspective. For example, Sherry (1998) found parallels to the narrative contents of certain mythologies in consumers' experience of the Nike Town and coined the expression 'brandscape', upon which Thompson and Arsel (2006) built their investigation of the Starbucks (anti)brand experience. Through ethnographic studies, Belk, Sherry and Wallendorf (1988) found dualistic opposites in their investigation of consumers' behavior at a swap meet, McGrath (1989) described consumer gift selection processes in a retail gift store, and McGrath et al. (1993) identified patterns of buyer-seller interactions and farmer/vendor behaviors in the periodic marketplace of a farmers' market. Kozinets et al. (2002) explored the mythological power of a themed flagship brandstore (*ESPN* in Chicago) where a flagship brandstore was defined as a retailer that (1) carries one brand only, (2) owns that brand, and (3) exists to build brand image

rather than make direct profit. Later, Kozinets et al. (2004) explored ludic behavior and identified elements of interagency between the themed brandstore and the consumers at the same spectacular venue. Building upon this themed flagship store framework, Borghini et al (2009) recently presented findings on retail ideologies at the American Girl Place, a themed brandstore claimed by the authors to be so experientially powerful due to its sophisticated play with many different ideological expressions in the same store.

Above examples of cultural analyses of consumer behavior in the physical marketplace provide fruitful insights regarding how consumers experience retailers' environments and branding efforts. However, although the found experiential elements probably can be readily applied to many themed flagship brandstores, to flee markets, swap meets and gift-stores, it is harder to see its transferability to retail sites of a more ordinary kind, e.g. the typical rationalized grocery store.

The grocery store is probably the most common retail experience of consumers in the western world, as it is part of people's everyday activities. Yet it has—despite large focus on the grocery retail brands (such as Tesco, Wholefoods and Carrefour) in more traditional marketing management literature—in the cultural domain of marketing been somewhat neglected in favor for far more spectacular retail brand experiences as seen above. As underlined by Kozinets et al. (2002, p.17); the primary intention of flagship brandstores is to "take the branding concept to an extreme level." But what about less extreme branded retail experiences? Which cultural constellations do consumers immerse when doing their regular everyday grocery shopping?

Thus, the contribution of this paper is to put cultural focus on a somewhat less extreme, yet branded, site; a site of the ordinary and everyday life—the grocery retailer —and to explore its more subtle brand representations through the experience of the consumer. This way, dimensions overarching the entire retailer brand experience (products, store, chain etc) that may be overlooked in the exploration of the spectacular and specific, may be unveiled.

### Branded Retail Experience in CCT

The research paradigm in which this investigation takes it departure is consumer culture theory, CCT where consumer experience and meanings have been the central focal point of analysis for more than twenty years (Arnould & Thompson 2005). Here the retail experience has predominantly been analyzed, as mentioned earlier, in terms of brandscapes, myths, narratives and ideologies. *Brandscapes* refer to "consumers' active constructions of personal meanings and lifestyle orientations from the symbolic resources provided by an array of brands" (Sherry 1998, p. 112) and a 'hegemonic brandscape' to " a cultural system of servicescapes that are linked together and structured by discursive, symbolic, and competitive relationships to a dominant (market-driving) experiential brand" (Thompson & Arsel 2004, p.632). Brandscapes are claimed to work as cultural models for consumers' behavior, identity-work and emotional experience on, but in terms of object of reference also off, the specific retail site, and the authors account for the cultural structure (global/local) and anti-branding discourses through which consumers experience these scapes.

Other concepts cultural scholars use to understand retail environment experiences are myths and ideologies that the narratives of these environments convey. *Retail ideology* is by Borghini et.al

(2009 p.365) defined as a "retail branding initiative and experience based upon a detailed representation of moral and social values, presented in an extensive and intensive manner through the physical environment and linked to actual moral action in the lives of involved consumers". They show how the retail environment of American Girl Place conveys narratives with strong ideological imperatives concerning femininity, motherhood and communality. Myths on the other hand "serve ideological agendas" (Thompson 2004) and can for example be spotted as archetypic characters (e.g. the protective man and the fragile woman), through storylines (e.g. the rise and fall of empires). Sensitive to these mythic constructions, Kozinets et al (2004) used Olson's (1999) ten characteristics (openendedness, verisimilitude, virtuality, negentropy, circularity, ellipticality, archetypical dramatis personae, inclusion, omnipresence and production values) of mythotypic (highly meaningful and emotionally generative symbols) narratives, to analyze ESPN Zone Chicago (a flagship brandstore for the ESPN sport network). They managed to show how spectacular brandstores could become experientially powerful to consumers by delivering on these mythotypic characteristics.

Above concepts make out important corner-stones in consumer culture research, as do concepts related to specific constellations of consumer goods and meanings found in sociocultural research generally. However, these prior conceptualizations of retail environments have largely ignored marketplaces of less mythotypic character, such as the ordinary branded grocery store. As these are probably the most frequent branded retail experiences consumers have on an everyday basis, its symbolic characteristics very likely differ from the mythotypic ones. In this paper we address this gap and propose an alternative analytical model for this everyday branded retail experience.

## ETHNOGRAPHIC METHODS

In consumer culture theory (CCT) the lived experience of consumers in the abstract and concrete "marketplace" is of most and common interest (Arnould & Thompson 2005; Thompson, Locander & Pollio 1989; Thompson, Pollio & Locander 1994). In our study, to capture these lived experiences various ethnographic methods (Elliott & Elliott 2003) were used with the aim to find spoken and unspoken meanings:

1. Semi-participant observations of the women shopping for groceries.
2. Unstructured interviews: After the shopping session, long interviews (McCracken 1988) lasting for about 2 hours, were conducted at the womens' homes.
3. Photo diaries: Each woman was given a disposable camera and a photo diary to fill in during five days over the course of one month. In each diary there were 40

questions and a request to take pictures corresponding to every question in the diary, hence in total at least 240 photos that came out of this exercise. Each question in the diary had a complementary question where the participant was instructed to describe what she has taken a picture of and why.

4. Artefact collection: All food shopping receipts and shopping lists of the household were also collected over the course of the diary month.

The women were instructed to send the diary, photos and receipts after a month, receiving a reward of 1000 Swedish kronor (approx 100 Euros) as compensation for their work.

The respondents were six Swedish women (see table 1), three from an urban area, and three from a suburban/rural area, aged 30-45 years. Three of these women were selected from a pool of approximately 50 women answering an add put up in a large award-winning grocery store with the ICA corporate brand and a local sub brand in the countryside in southern Sweden. These three women also lived in the countryside. The other three women lived in the city area of southern Sweden's largest town, Malmö, and were selected through the snowball method where we asked people to ask acquaintances' colleagues' friends' (etc) to contact the first author if they were interested in participating in the research project. Out of 30 interested, three were chosen based on certain criteria decided beforehand. The six women should belong to different quintiles of the middle-class and differing from each other in lifestyles, type of work engagements, and family constellations (alone with children or married with children), but should all have children living at home. This because the research project itself had a focus on retail brands and family shoppers.

When doing participant observations during grocery-shopping the first author came along to the store where "they most often go grocery shopping". However, in the photo diary they were asked to document and take pictures of other visits to other stores during the one-month period. All, except from one, visited many different grocery stores during this time but had one clear favourite for everyday shopping. This way we obtained sufficient variety in each individual's descriptions and experiences of different formats, chain and product brands, but could still immerse into the meaning structures of the retail environments they preferred the most. Every store that participants referred to in the diaries or interviews, the first author went to visit afterwards in order to see the environment with an ethnographer's own eyes, to better understand the experiences described by the informants.

The selected womens' identities were not necessarily bound up around being a mother (as is the case in Moisio, Arnould & Price (2004)) although two of the women's perhaps were more than the

## Table 1. Table of informants

| Pseudonym | Age | Sex | Site | Occupation | Education | Family Status |
|---|---|---|---|---|---|---|
| Hanna | 29 | F | Countryside Southern Sweden | Kindergarden teacher, temporarily home with baby | Child-caring | Married, one child age 1 |
| Madeleine | 41 | F | Countryside Southern Sweden | Researcher, natural sciences | PhD | Married, two children ages 6 and 9 |
| Stina | | | Countryside, Southern Sweden | Foster mother | High school | Married, one child + various foster children |
| Birgit | 30 | F | Larger town, Southern Sweden | Surgeon, temporarily home with children | Medical doctor | Married, two children ages 1 and 2 |
| Katrin | 38 | F | Larger town, Southern Sweden | Student and practitioner within HR | BA | Single, one child age 2 |
| Angelica | 38 | F | Larger town, Southern Sweden | Project manager | BA | Married, two children ages 7 and 9 |

other four. However, one may still argue that these women were all the main care-takers and family providers, in terms of grocery, whereby the theoretical analysis foremost can be said to have a valid transferability across other "providing" and "care-taking" consumer segments, rather than say women in single households or student dorms. Thompson (1996) called these "caring consumers" juggling in a shared system of conflicting ideologies regarding motherhood, feminism and professional careerism.

## 'HOMEYNESS' IN THE BRANDED RETAIL ENVIRONMENT

While hermeneutically moving back and forth between data and theory (Thompson, Pollio and Locander 1994; Thompson 1997) one specific cultural constellation, excellently described in the consumer cultural literature, namely that of 'homeyness', by Grant McCracken (1989), emerged as a readily applicable model to understand what could be discerned in the data analysis. Whereas Kozinets et al. (2002) analyzed the spectacular ESPN brandstore according to Olson's (1999) ten characteristics of mythotypes, as presented earlier, the more subtly branded retail environments in our investigation, turned out to be much better understood through McCrackens eight symbolic properties of 'homeyness' and how they act upon the environment: (1) *the diminutive property* (small and graspable, making places "good" to think because they are "easy" to think) makes it thinkable; (2) *the variable property* (inconsistent, non-linear, antiuniform/assymetrical, haphazard, made out of sudden passion and desire, far from anonymous calculation e.g. rubblestone) makes it real, (3) *the embracing property* (intimacy, layer on layer enclosing each other, a pattern of descending enclosure, encompassing e.g the ivy and the books, the "extraordinary intellectual geography for self-construction, memory walls, part-whole logic, takes *time* to accomplish) makes it cosseting, (4) *the engaging property* (welcoming, draws you in, openness, warmth, invites interaction and playfulness) makes it involving (5) *the mnemonic property* (historical character, significance of objects from the past, deeply personalizing the present circumstances, localized in time) makes it emplacing in time, (6) *the authentic property* (real, natural, personal nature, untouched by the calculated marketplace, "someone lives here") makes it emplacing in space, (7) *the informal property* (warm and friendly, humble, accessibility, not pretentious, puts people at ease) makes it reassuring and riskless, and finally (8) *the situating property* (the occupant takes on the properties of the surroundings and "becomes" a homey creature) makes it fully capturing.

Before moving forward to the findings, here is a short introduction to the corporate retail brands coming up in the empirical fieldwork; ICA, Willy's and Netto.

*ICA* is the biggest retail brand in Sweden, and thereby bigger than Coop and Axfood (owns the retail brand Willys) who are number 2 and 3. The Swedish competition authorities have many times warned that ICA is larger than the monopoly regulations allow but due to the franchise format ICA keeps on balancing on the critical 50% market share limit without getting penalties. To consumers in Sweden ICA is famous for its historical presence since the 1950's in almost every little village and town, its four different retail formats (ICA Nära, ICA Supermarket, ICA Kvantum, ICA Maxi) and not the least, their famous long-lived TV-commercial campaign consisting of the same actors since 2001 with soap opera story line and a new film every week. ICA has their own very successful private labels; ICA Selection (premium), I Love Eco (organic), ICA gott liv (Health), ICA-handlarnas (medium), and Euroshopper (budget). Approximately 20% of ICAs total sales is from private labels.

*Willys* is part of the Axfood Group and is famous for its large, low budget stores and supply. The stores are predominantly situated in the outskirts of city areas. They have a family owned background but were bought by Axfood in 2001. Axfood has since created private labels for Willys; Willys (medium /budget), Garant (organic) and Eldorado (budget) that make out approximately 20 % of total sales.

*Netto,* is also mentioned on several occasions by the respondents. It is a relavtively new medium-hard discount retailer concept on the Swedish market, with origins in Denmark. The Netto stores are often situated in central areas and offers to the Swedish audience a range of discount brands they don't see in other stores. They also have lines of baskets with goods quite atypical for concentrated grocery stores in central areas of the stores.

Below follows a categorization of our ethnographic observations and consumer experiences into these characteristics of homeyness. As the experience of a store in many aspects is a different one than of a home (where McCracken did his ethnographic study) we found that every property of homeyness could also complemented by a mythic theme, in terms of how the consumers filled these properties with aesthetic meanings. This meaning content was typically anchored in myths infused in consumer culture regarding the ideal place and the ideal foods. These complementing themes give aesthetic meaning to the homey properties and succeed the property theme in every headline. [Due to the limited space in this conference paper each characteristic doesn't go as deep as it would in a final journal paper].

### The Diminutive Property- The Family Ownership Myth

Entering the large *ICA Kvantum Anderssons* store in Södra Sandby, a small village on the countryside, is to an outsider like entering most large ICA stores in Sweden. It is quite large and has an open butcher space close to the meat counter. I visit this store with three of the respondents; Stina, Madeleine and Hanna, and even if the store is large the way they describe it is always in a way that emphasizes its diminutive characteristic. They call the store Bröderna Andersson, meaning "The Andersson Brothers". The store is famous in the larger local area for being well-taken care of by its small, tight family owners and exactly this family reference, rather than ICA reference, is central in observations, interviews and diaries from the participants regularly visiting this store. "I feel like home in this store. Everything is familiar and safe" says Madelelein and smiles. Also Sanna points at this emotional wellness character of ICA Kvantum Anderssons; "It would be a lie if I were to find anything negative in this store. Everything's perfect here. The staff is so nice, I always feel so good in this store and I'm never stressed when I'm here. It's top!". Hanna emphasizes this by saying that "I feel so safe her, and I know exactly what they have and don't have so [even if its more expensive] why go anywhere else when it's this great at home?" Thus, despite its relative largesse the store is experientially graspable, it is through experience *thinkable* to the informants. It does not have a diminutive character in terms of material environment, but in the consumers' minds it has become mentally small and graspable due to its familiarity and warmth.

I go (on different occasions) with Katrin and Birgit to *ICA Kvantum Malmborgs Erikslust* which is situated in a prosperous middle-class neighborhood in Malmö. The store is playfully infamous in Malmö as the "longest store in Sweden", and fair enough, yes it is both thin and long in its store layout. Both Katrin and Birgit comment on the unorthodox layout as "oddly narrow" but "funny". Sometimes "irritating" but more like an annoying sister than an unpleasant stranger. There is a love and hate relationship between my respondents and this pleasantly cramped store. Katrine says; "It is quite different that you really need to know which way you must walk not to bump into somebody, on the other hand bumping into someone can turn out to be quite amusing as well!". The smallness of the store creates an intimacy with other customers on a physical level, sometimes annoying but also a source of surprise and the spontaneous whims of life.

### The Variable Property- The Myth of Mediterranean Life

In the diaries where participants were asked to take pictures of the most inspiring parts of their stores/store experiences and also to describe in what way this was the case, the responses had a certain thing in common. They were all pictures of variable melanges of goods, for example of asymmetrical stacks of French, Italian, Portuguese, Swedish, and Danish cheeses; "Cheese lovers like myself fall head over heals over the grand cheese department. So many kinds—so many jummy cheeses! I quickly run pass them and save them for a more special occasion." Angelica writes about the cheese counter at *ICA Maxi Västra Hamnen* in Malmö. Other accounts on inspiring experiences relate to how the variety is presented, like the shelves with a wide variety of transparent bags with beans and olives, and Madeleine writes about the most inspiring counter at Bröderna Andersson—the cooked meats counter; "these entire chunks of salami and hams everywhere, I get this feeling of the open marketplace, the Mediterranean and other pleasant experiences".

The store aesthetics should offer asymmetrical layers on layers of various goods and brands to live up to this variability ideal, but must not break the rules *too* much; Madeleine, who loved the "Mediterranean" feel at *ICA Kvantum Andersson*, takes pictures of the aisle baskets at *Netto* and writes "It's complete chaos in this store. Tools and food in a terrible mess. I don't feel like home here, it's like being abroad".

### The Embracing Property- The Myth of a Loving Market

The diminutive property of is intensified by the embracing property. It has as McCracken writes "a pattern of descending enclosure". At *ICA Kvantum Malmborgs Erikslust* the long and narrow layout literally embraces the customer. She feels "cuddled with" as Katrin expresses it. The opposite is described by all respondents in diaries and interviews, illustrated with photos of empty cartons and shelves. Nothing irritates the respondents as much as when what they have planned to buy is out of stock. Especially if the store normally never is out of stock. As in Fournier's (1998) brand relationship thesis, where brands get anthropomorphized into humans with whom you can have loving and un-loving relationships, here someone you really trusted has betrayed you and it hurts more than if you had counted on it. It is a light shock.

An embrace can be further intensified through marketing tactics, e.g. by ICA's multichannel marketing. The respondents all refer to *ICA Buffé*, ICAs monthly magazine with recepies and inspiring images of happy dinner and lunch guests. To Angelica it is ICA Buffé that inspires almost all of her cooking, and *ICA Maxi Västra Hamnen* that inspires her most in store. That way ICA offers an embracive enclosure by providing inspiration from all directions.

### The Engaging Property- The Myth of Smalltown Friendliness

The intimacy offered by the diminutive property and the family ownership myth at *ICA Kvantum Andersson* not only feels like an embrace to the respondents, but it also engages them. Hanna and Madeleine both stop at the different counters to chat with the staff, to discuss new deliveries and to get advice for cooking. They also stop to taste at a corner where a store representative cooks meat balls from the store's own minced meat; "I trust ICA again, it could have happened to any of the retailers" Madeleine says (there had just been a national minced meat scandal connected to ICA where

some ICA retailers had been revealed to repack "old" meat in later date packages). Hanna, Madeleine, and Sanna take many pictures of the butcher's space of the store where the meat is cut up. They all express love for this "openness" which seems to draw them in through trustworthiness. The store involves its customers by bringing them into its own making, its core existence and family core, and gets engagement back.

### The Mnemonic Property- The Magic of the Past

Three of the respondents have childhood memories in relation to their everyday stores. "I live in the neighbourhood and when I was little my mum used to take me here, it was so exciting because the store is so long!" Birgit recalls about her childhood experiences at the *ICA Kvantum Malmborgs Erikslust*. "I've come here with mum since I was a baby, so I know exactly what I can get and not get. I feel safe with that" Hanna writes about *ICA Kvantum Andersson*.

Madeleine, who has been to *Netto* to by special protein rich pasta flour, shares one of the brand narratives she connects in relation to the Netto logo. "Scottish terriers always make me think of Netto, and even more of my youth when we went to Denmark to bargain. At Netto there are so many Danish products and brands, like for example cherry marmalade. Odd and exciting! In the brand line "O Sole Mio" there are some odd products, like they used to have dried cranberries. Fun!". In the case of Netto, Madeleine does not feel at home at all, as we saw earlier. However, she does find a home for Netto in pleasant memories from her youth, that through the magic power of nostalgia somehow compensates for this lack in spatial homeyness.

### The Authentic Property- The Myth of a Real and Genuine Market

The women in this investigation have all taken up on the mega trend of authenticity. Authenticity which usually is associated with the tastes of the high cultural capital class (Holt 1998; Ulver-Sneistrup 2008) has since the mainstream market picked up on this winning concept (Pine & Gilmore 2007) proliferated to the mass consumer of western consumer culture. There is a consistent idea of a dichotomy between real and unreal, where the real is considered more morally legitimate than the unreal. *ICA Kvantum Anderssons* get the role of the real and authentic in this investigation. Even if the store in no way is small like a local specialty shop (the stereotypical image of an authentic food market) it manages to play o myths narrating authenticity "here you see how they cut the meat and I mean that's so…nice" Sanna says. In fact, in every tale about ICA Kvantum Anderssons it is the story about meat cutting that is persistently told. Apart from the staff's friendliness and the fact that it is two brothers who own the store, the meat-cutting is the genuine proof that these people really love what they do, a prerequisite for true authenticity.

In contrast, Angelica has her roots in northern Sweden and writes that "I would love to buy mushrooms at the store but I just don't trust their origin. I always wait for my mum to come down with freshly picked mushrooms from the Northern Sweden's forests. That's the real thing!".

Authenticity emplaces a store in space, and if the origin is not seen (as the meat-cutting is at *ICA Kvantum Anderssons* or as the mushroom picker is to Angelica) the constellation of homeyness cannot be complete.

### The Informal Property- The Myth of the Humble Farmer

As has been abundantly clear in this paper, *ICA Kvantum Anderssons* is a retail case that scores high on every property of homey retail experience. The informal property is another one of these. This store puts its visitors at ease with its down-tuned but friendly approach to its customers. This in turn creates this embracive feel of well-being seen in many quotes earlier in this paper.

As all our respondents visited many different stores during the month of diary-writing we could compare through which categories they evaluated a shopping experience. In no other store than *ICA Kvantum Anderssons* was the staff mentioned, neither in interviews nor in diaries. It was as if there was no service staff. But at *ICA Kvantum Anderssons* the friendliness among the staff was mentioned at many occasions and in field observations casual conversations between staff and customers were seen at many occasions. Here are fieldnotes from the visit with Sanna:

*I am amazed how unpretentious Sanna is and that she is proud, rather than embarrassed, about admitting that she's been abroad once (and only once). How she so casually shares that she doesn't understand much of these new, international, "fashionable" products. When she asks one of the staff (I presume it is the store manager as I recognize him from the website), who is pottering around with the olive oil bottles, what kind of oil this "green liquid is" (olive oil), I expect him to reveal some kind of snobbish latent nature ("dear lord, have you never seen olive oil before??") towards Sanna. But instead he shines up like a sun and enthusiastically brings her with him into the universe of olive oil connaissance. He talks of sun, terroir and tree qualities. Of its sublime marriage with ripe tomatoes and parmeggiano cheese. Sanna looks entertained and inspired, however doesn't dare to buy that green liquid. But the man had an air of ease to him. The kind of air that makes people courageous to ask "dumb" questions without having to "lose face". Fieldnotes 11 November 2008*

This quality of accessibility and lack of risk comes with the property of informality, and must be mediated through social interaction, hence people, be it the service staff or the other customers. But it must not be *too* informal as we will see in the next paragraph.

**The Situating property- The Myth of Hermeneutic Transformation**

The last property of homeyness, that also makes this very experience complete, is the situating property. Here, the consumer experiences such involvement with her surroundings that she takes on its properties. She becomes part of the whole—a hermeneutic metamorphosis if you will. Although the experience at the everyday grocery retailer is far from spectacular, such subtle transformation may nevertheless take place. Especially this can be seen in the way respondents comment other customers in the store in the interviews and in the diaries. One can never fully immerse into one's surrounding and *become* homey if one does not identify with the surrounding customers. Katrin shares with me; "I feel so good in this store [*ICA Kvantum Malmborgs Erikslust*]. It's not stressful and everybody looks like they know and can afford to eat good food. I mean it is much nicer than say *Överskottsbolaget* [a hard discount store in a socially troubled neighbourhood in Malmö], ha ha. When I was there there two people were fighting. They had all kinds of technical aid, wheel chairs etc, but suddenly they were perfectly mobile! It's another breed of people there, not nice. But it's cheap. But I'm glad if I never have to go there again."

**DISCUSSION**

In this paper we have focused on the consumer experiences of branded spaces and environments where there is explicit branding-work going on a but on a radically less extreme level than in themed

flagship stores previously treated in the consumer cultural literature. Whereas the themed flagship brandstore is highly meaningful to a particular audience, and express a combination of "universal emotional states" such as "awe, wonder, purpose, joy and participation" (Kozinets et al 2002), the everyday branded retail environment expresses a somewhat more subdued, but yet very meaningful, experience. This experience turned out to be 'homeyness' among our care-taking grocery consumers.

'Homeyness' as conceptualized by McCracken (1989) is a *constellation* of cultural elements, creating a distinctive feeling of well-being. Hence, one cannot select one or the other specific factor, which the managerial retail literature often tends to do, that makes "the big difference," but it's the whole constellation of expressions that makes the everyday retail experience homey, and therefore inclusive. In addition, this experience can be even more seductive if each property plays on certain myths, supporting Kozinets et al (2002, 2004) and Borghini et al (2009), serving ideologies naturally succumbed in society. Here we could discern myths of the superiority of southern lifestyles, smaller town goodness and the personification of a loving market.

But why was it homeyness, and not, say, sexiness or cosmopolitanism, that encapsulated these consumers? There are probably many alternative explanations to this, but, in the culturally distinctive site of the everyday grocery store, one can imagine that consumers do not seek a transformative experience that fully blows their mind away. In fact, they are shopping for their family household and perhaps therefore need to have surroundings representing or at least supporting an ideal life at home. It is ideally a home outside home where the meanings of goods do not change despite being transported from the one site (shop) to the other (actual home).

One can also reason that the selection of the care-taking (providing for others at home) women in this study may have influenced this quest for homeyness. Do these women want homeyness more than, say men or women without families? McCracken (1989) found that differences could be found between lower and higher status groups (rather than between gender) where lower status groups were more apt to desire the homey atmosphere. A non-supporting pattern was present among Holt's (1998) low and high culture capital consumers where higher status groups preferred formal aesthetics and lower status groups pragmatic solutions, hence 'homeyness' was not an elaborated construct. In our investigation, five women belonged to a typical middle quintile of a large middle class, whereas one (Sanna) to a lower middle class, judging on education and parental background. That no difference was identified between these respondents in terms of homeyness would therefore imply that it very well may be a female, middle-class, local desire, but it may just as well be universally global, at least in the parts of the world that have "home" and "privacy" as cultural constructs in their meaning structures (Rybscynzki 1987). However, to get more comparable examples, this would have to be explored in future research.

This paper contributes to the consumer culture literature on retail by bringing in the culturally distinctive site of the everyday branded grocery store and thereby showing that other analytical models, than have been suggested for more spectacular arenas, are at play here; namely the cultural constellation of 'homeyness.' It also contributes to the more managerial retail literature in that it takes a cultural perspective, and giving this more holistic understanding of what is happening in the interaction between the consumer and the retailer brand, than more evidence based variable-focused work can do. The experience of homeyness consists of a complex but highly meaningful constellation of properties that can be intensified by the immersion into myths supporting the agendas of dominant, rather than emerging (which more spectacular arenas may strive for in their quest for overwhelming the consumer), ideology. Future research may concentrate on exploring further theoretical transferability options for the constellation of homeyness in branded retail environments across industrialized/less industrialized contexts, across gender, ethnicity and class. Homeyness may very well change character across settings, peoples and times, and there may also be contexts where other cultural constellations are of equal importance. However, in this investigation it stood clear that homeyness was highly meaningful as the fundament for the ideal everyday retail experience, and the lack of it was the fundament for avoidance. Or as Hanna so succinctly put it; "why go anywhere else when it's this great at home?".

## REFERENCES

Arnould, Eric J. and Craig J. Thompson (2005), "Consumer Culture Theory (Cct): Twenty Years of Research " *Journal of Consumer Research*, 31 (4), 868-82.

Ailawadi, Kusum L. and Kevin Lane Keller (2004), "Understanding Retail Branding: Conceptual Insights and Research Priorities," *Journal of Retailing*, 80 (4), 331-42.

Aaker,

Belk, Russell W., John F. Jr Sherry, and Melanie Wallendorf (1988), "A Naturalistic Inquiry into Buyer and Seller Behavior at a Swap Meet," *Journal of Consumer Research*, 14 (March), 449-70.

Belk, Russell W. (2000), "May the Farce Be with You: On Las Vegas and Consumer Infantilization," Consumption, Markets, and Culture, 4 (2), 101–23.

Borghini, S; Diamond, N; Koxinets, V.R.; McGrath, M.A.; Muniz, A.M.Jr.; Sherry, J.F Jr (2009), "Why Are Themed Brandstores So Powerful? Retail Brand Ideology at American Girl Place," *Journal of Retailing*, 85 (3), 363-75.

Burt, S. and Sparks, L. (2002), Corporate Branding, Retailing, and Retail Internationalization. *Corporate Reputation Review,* 5(2/3), 194-212

Burt, S. & Carralero-Encinas, J. (2000), 'The Role of Store Image in Retail Internationalization', *International Marketing Review,* 17(4/5), 433-453

Choi, S. Chan and T. Coughlan Anne (2006), "Private Label Positioning: Quality Versus Feature Differentiation from the National Brand," *Journal of Retailing*, 82 (2), 79-93.

Collins-Dodd, C. and T. Lindley (2003), "Store Brands and Retail Differentiation: The Influence of Store Image and Store Brand Attitude on Store Own Brand Perceptions," *Journal of Retailing and Consumer Services*, 10 (6), 345-52.

Elliott, Richard and Nick Jankel-Elliott (2003), "Using Ethnography in Strategic Consumer Research," *Qualitative Market Research: An International Journal*, 6 (4), 215-23.

Holt, Douglas B.(1998) Does Cultural Capital Structure American Consumption? *Journal of Consumer Research,* 25:1-25

Kamakura, Wagner A. and Wooseong Kang (2007), "Chain-Wide and Store-Level Analysis for Cross-Category Management," *Journal of Retailing*, 83 (2), 159-59.

Kotler, Philip (1973), "Atmospherics as a Marketing Tool " *Journal of Retailing*, 49 (4), 48-48.

Kumar, V.& Karande K (2000), "The Effect of Retail Store Environment on Retailer Performance," *Journal of Business Research*, 49 (2), 167-81.

Kozinets, Robert V., John F. Sherry Jr., Benet DeBerry-Spence, Adam Duhachek, Krittinee Nuttavuthisit, and Diana Storm (2002), "Themed Flagship Brand Stores in the New Millenium: Theory, Practice, Prospects," *Journal of Retailing*, 78, 17-29.

Kozinets Robert, V., F. Sherry John, Jr., Diana Storm, Adam Duhachek, and et al. (2004), "Ludic Agency and Retail Spectacle," *Journal of Consumer Research*, 31 (3), 658-72.

McCracken, Grant (1989), ""Homeyness": A Cultural Account of One Constellation of Consumer Goods and Meanings," in *Interpretive Consumer Research*, ed. Elizabeth C. Hirschman, Provo, UT: Association of Consumer Research, 168-83

McCracken, Grant (1988), *The Long Interview*, Vol. 13, Newbury Park, CA, USA: Sage.

McGrath, Mary Ann, John F. Jr Sherry, and Deborah D. Heisley (1993), "An Ethnographic Study of an Urban Periodic Marketplace: Lessons from the Midville Farmers' Market," *Journal of Retailing*, 69 (3), 280-319.

McGoldrick, Peter (2002), *Retail Marketing*, NY, US: McGraw-Hill Education.

Moisio, Risto, Eric J. Arnould, and Linda L. Price (2004), "Between Mothers and Markets: Constructing Family Identity through Homemade Food," *Journal of Consumer Culture*, 4 (3), 361-84.

Moore, M., Fernie, J. and Burt, S. (2000), "Brands without Boundaries", *European Journal of Marketing,* 34(8), 919-937

Pine, II, Gilmore, J and Joseph, B (2007) *Authenticity: What Consumers Really Want,* Harvard Business School Press, Boston: US

Pine, II, Joseph B. and James H. Gilmore (1999), *The Experience Economy: Work is Theatre and Every Business is a Stage,* Boston, MA: Harvard Business School Press.

Richardson, Paul, Arun K. Jain, and Alan Dick (1996), "The Influence of Store Aesthetics on Evaluation of Private Label Brands," *Journal of Product and Brand Management*, 5 (1), 19-28.

Rybczynski, Witold (1987), *Home: A Short History of an Idea*, London: Penguin Books.

Sherry, John F. Jr (1998), "The Soul of the Company Store- Nike Town Chicago and the Emplaced Brandscape," in *Servicescapes: The Concept of Place in Contemporary Markets*, ed. John F. Jr Sherry, Lincolnwood, IL, 109-46.

Schlosser, Ann E. (1998), "Applying the Functional Theory of Attitudes to Understanding the Influence of Store Atmosphere on Store Inferences," *Journal of Consumer Psychology*, 7 (4), 345-69.

Thompson, C & Arsel,, Z (2004) The Starbucks Brandscape and Consumers' (Anticorporate) Experience of Glocalization, *Journal of Consumer Research,* 31: 631-642

Thompson, Craig J. (1996), "Caring Consumers: Gendered Consumption Meanings and the Juggling Lifestyle," *Journal of Consumer Research*, 22 (March), 388-407.

Thompson, Craig J. (2004), "Marketplace Mythology and Discourses of Power," *Journal of Consumer Research*, 31 (1), 162-80.

Thompson, Craig J., William B. Locander, and Howard R. Pollio (1994), "The Spoken and the Unspoken: A Hermeneutic Approach to Understanding the Cultural Viewpoints That Underlie Consumers' Expressed Meanings," *Journal of Consumer Research*, 21 (December), 432-52.

Thompson, Craig J. (1997) "Interpreting Consumers: A Hermeneutical Framework for Deriving Marketing Insights from the Texts of Consumers' Consumption Stories," Journal of Marketing Research, 34 (November), 438–55.

Thompson, Locander and Pollio (1989) Putting Consumer Experience Back into Consumer Research: The Philosophy and Method of Existential-Phenomenology, Journal of Consumer Research, 16(2), 133-146

Ulver-Sneistrup, S. (2008) "Status Spotting", PhD thesis, Lund University Business Press

# An Exploration Into The Religious and Symbolic Meanings of Gendered Spaces in an Arab Gulf Home

Rana Sobh, Qatar University
Russell Belk, York University

## ABSTRACT

Houses are rich symbols representative of culture, self and identity (Marcus 1995). The current research provides a comparative perspective on Arab-Islamic (Qatari) and Western values as encoded in the home and use of spaces within it. Our ethnographic study involved observation and in-depth interviews with twenty four middleclass home-owning Qatari families living in Doha. We found gendered areas as well as visual and non-visual domains of privacy. Furthermore, we found a parallel between the home and the woman's body as these both relate to the notions of sanctity, purity, and reserve. Both also seem to embody and mediate global and local cultural controversies Qataris are subject to as a result of the increased influence of Western consumption patterns.

## INTRODUCTION

Houses are rich symbols representative of culture, self and identity (Marcus 1995). Differences in the use and sense of ownership of various spaces within the home by individual family members especially the adult males and females articulate social relations and define gender relationships in a particular society (Altman 1975). The home is conventionally understood as the foundation of the private sphere (Allan and Crow 1989). However, notions of privacy and separate public and private spaces within the home have emerged only within the last few hundred years (Tuan, 1982). Notions of private space are also encoded architecturally (Sommer 1969) and intimacy within the nuclear family is a concept that has grown as the presence of extended families sharing the same home has diminished (Rybczynski 1986).

While the home provides a more private space to the family compared to the public domain, it does not necessarily secure private spaces for individual family members from each other (Allan and Crow 1989). Such concepts have been extensively studied in the West, but little comparable work has been done in non-Western homes. Definitions of private and public spheres are different in Islam than those in Western paradigms. Privacy in the West refers to people's rights to non-intrusion and might be linked to the notion of individualism and individual rights to property. However, in the Arab-Islamic world, privacy is very much based on the notion of sanctity and concerns both women and the home (El Guindi, 1999). The current research provides a comparative perspective on Middle Eastern (Qatari) and Western values as encoded in the home and use of spaces within it. We found a parallel between the home and the woman's body as these both relate to the notions of sanctity, purity, and reserve. Both also seem to embody and mediate global and local cultural controversies Qataris are subject to as a result of the increased influence of Western consumption patterns. The domestic sphere seems to bind the past to the present.

We locate our research in the Gulf region and Qatar in particular where dramatic changes are occurring. Qatar and the Gulf States in general offer a context unique for several reasons: 1) Society requires strong adherence to traditional values and social norms, 2) There is an omnipresent awareness of Islam and religious values in shaping identities and informing behavior, 3)There is an abundance of financial resources available to locals and a significant growth of financial, educational, and media centers, and 4) There has been a significant dilution of local populations by the expatriates and guest workers who comprise more than 80% of local populations.

This influx of expatriates coupled with an influx of global mass media and other forms of popular culture resulted in the increasing adoption of Western lifestyles and tensions between the desire to embrace the modern and a desire to preserve local identity. Such tensions are reflected in many aspects of consumption including clothing (of both men and women),

## DATA COLLECTION AND ANALYISIS

Our ethnographic study involved observation and in-depth interviews with twenty four middleclass home-owning Qatari families living in Doha. Our sample involved families across different life stages (e.g., young married without children, families with young children, and families with older children). In addition, the researchers interviewed a Qatari architect, a real estate agent, and a religious scholar. Interviews lasted between 60 and 90 minutes. The interviews discussed meanings of home, favorite areas of the home, situations in which these spaces are used, favorite objects within the home, the meanings of these objects, and usage patterns by other family members, who makes decisions regarding home decorating in each room and how the house was selected or designed. As a stimulant for these interviews we used projective stimuli (e.g., metaphorical descriptions such as "If my home were an animal, it would be…) and visual elicitation (based on photographs of various areas of the home taken, with informant permission). Audio and video recordings of interviews and observations were made and transcribed. The analysis followed the logic of hermeneutic research in that we sought to identify shared cultural meanings underlying expressed meanings by individual consumers (Thompson, Pollio, and Locander 1994).

## HOME SANCTITY, PRIVACY, AND DIFFERENTIATED AREAS IN QATARI DOMESTIC SPACES

Qatari architecture and home design are influenced by characteristics inherent in Islam. For instance, because there is lack of emphasis on external appearance in Islam as compared to inner self, Islamic architecture generally focuses on interior space as opposed to the exterior space or façade. The dominant form of Islamic architecture is inward facing; the facade rarely gives an indication of the structure's richness of inner design. In other words, architecture must be experienced from within. Thus, a Muslim person should be simple in the facade of his home just as in his personal appearance; yet both should rich with faith, wisdom, and beauty inside. This is why in Qatar there is generally little variation between homes' facades compared to enriching and differentiated interior designs. However, this has been changing recently and the exteriors of new homes in Qatar are becoming more richly designed and differentiated. It is also evident that Qatari people are increasingly becoming extravagant in their appearances compared to a decade earlier (Sobh, Belk, and Gressel forthcoming).

### Privacy in Qatari Homes

The Qatari architecture in our study emphasized that the importance of inner spaces in Muslim architecture is also tied to an Islamic focus on privacy. There is much emphasis in Islam on the importance of respecting privacy for both males and females and on the sacredness of the home (Campo 1991). Surrounded by a simple facade, the courtyard which is the house's most private space is kept hidden. The inward design is used in traditional Arab Muslim homes including traditional Qatari homes. Such a courtyard house has high walls or facades and the courtyard or family spaces are in the back of the house, or at least not directly accessible from the front door. This design expresses the need to keep the public sphere from intruding or interfering with the family's privacy and the inner life. This is visually encoded by the sharp distinction between public and private spaces. Having an inward home structure that excludes and protects the private from the public is not only intended to protect family members' privacy, but also to protect neighbors' privacy.

*Abdullah (architect): Privacy and religious considerations have always been taken into consideration in Qatari homes. Qatari architecture reflects people's life style and values. Being respectful of Islamic religious values in Qatar, Bahrain, Saudi Arabia, the Middle East, Iran, and even Turkey has influenced architecture in these countries and regions. The difference lies in the building materials used. The architectural style in Qatar, Bahrain and Saudi Arabia is similar. There're a lot of windows but they are equipped with screens, like a woman with veil. She can see but cannot be seen. Even in Afghanistan, little openings in the face cover are used. The whole body is covered but there are two small openings for the eyes.*

So why are people's privacy, male or female, and the sacredness of their homes so highly emphasized in Islam? The Westerner's conception of privacy is coterminous with individualism, whereas the Middle Easterner's is not. Hurma (best translated to sanctity in English) denotes the concept closest to the notion of privacy in Arab-Islamic culture. What is private in Islam is any personal domain that should be concealed from others and within which individuals have freedom of action. In a spatial/physical sense, the home is par excellence a private space as well as the body or parts of the body that should be concealed in public '*Awra*'.

In Islam, intruding into a person's private space, trying to gain information about a sin an individual conceals behind a closed door of his/her home is itself considered a sin (Mottahaedeth and Stilt 2003). As such, people are completely free in the private space like home. But as soon as the person enters the public domain he/she constrained by the law prevalent in society with regard to clothing, eating and drinking, sexual behavior, and some forms of social conduct (Kadivar 2003).

The significant need for privacy within Qatari homes is also related to the concept of modesty in Islam. Modesty underpins the Muslim self and particularly the woman's self and her relation to private and public spaces and regulates gender relationships. Modesty (*haya'* in Arabic) is not limited to a person's dress in public (physical modesty); it is also reflected in speech, conduct and thoughts. Dress requirements have necessitated a unique convenient style whereby women's living quarters are separated from men's quarters so that they do not have to veil while in their homes, even if male guests are present elsewhere in the house.

While there are gendered areas within Western households (e.g., Chevalier 2002; Munro and Madigan 1999; Taylor 1999), there is a sharper distinctions and more formally drawn boundaries between men's and women's spaces as well as transitional spaces in moving from one gendered area to another within Arab Muslim homes. In all visited homes, the space designated as private was for the family (husband, wife and children) and close male relatives

from the *mahrem* category (those in a degree of sanguity precluding marriage), as well as female visitors. The public or communal areas were for men and their male visitors – *majles* (the place for sitting). These have separate entrances for males and females from the main street. Men's quarters emphasize openness to the public domain; their entrances are usually close to the street and the windows overlook the street, while the family or women quarters emphasize enclosure away from the public gaze; usually in the back of the house and are further separated from the street by high perimeter walls which visually encode a sharp distinction between private and public spaces. There is no permeability or internal link between these two domains which indicates that gender sociability is controlled and restricted (Farah and Klarqvist 2001).

## Non-visual Domains of Privacy

Our findings reveal that the concept of good smell is of great significance in Qatari homes as well as in other countries in the Arab Gulf. *Oud* – a very expensive type of wooden pieces is frequently burned in scentors to remove home odors, especially before and after receiving guests. The following quote illustrates the importance of smell in Qatari homes and the frequent use of *oud* to fumigate the house and prevent it from being contaminated with cooking smell as well as the presence of domestic helpers.

*Um Hussein: Because the number of dishes is large and there are the cooking smells. Our kitchen, the housemaid's room and washing room are isolated but are close to us so as to monitor what goes on. To prevent cooking smells from spreading we close the doors and use a ventilator. In addition, we always use incenses. They are nice to smell. Gulf people used them even in the past. I sometimes cook and I feel there is smell in my clothes and so incenses are needed. We also wash clothes every day, but the abaya is not washed every day [Thus it benefits from incense more].*

The significance of good smell in Qatari homes is inherent in the requirement of cleanness and purity (*taharah*) in the Islamic faith, both physical and spiritual. A good smell is associated with cleanness, angels, purity, good deeds and thus God's blessing and benediction. In contrast, bad smell is associated with what is dirty, the evil, bad deeds, and God's curse. A pleasant smelling person is considered pure and ready to enter a mosque, while someone who smells of food or other unpleasant odors is impure and contaminated.

Participants made statements associating perfuming and home fumigating with worshipping: "God will bless a man who washes himself, uses the best perfumes and dresses nicely, especially on Friday" (Saleh). "A smelly and dirty place will be vulnerable to devils and a scented place will be inviting to angels" (Rawdha).

Good smell is also an integral part of Arab hospitality rituals. Guests are traditionally welcomed for up to three days without question, but neither they nor the house should be contaminated by each others' presence. Not only the bedroom, but the entire house is sacred. The threshold of the door where the guest enters is a liminal space within which rites of transition (Gennep 1960) and rites of incorporation (Kanafani 1993) take place. In this case rites of transition (removing shoes, eating, and drinking coffee) transform what was profane into something sacred, with the threshold being the transitional space. The guest remains a stranger, even if they are a close relative or a friend, until they are incorporated into the host's home and thereby decontaminated and sacralized. In addition to fumigating the home before guests' arrival and departure, a special flask (*mrash*) is sometimes used for perfuming guests after eating and before leaving the house. Most visited homes, had a tray of scents and expensive perfumes used to create pleasant smelling spaces and people and to denote status and prestige of the hostess. Guests make ample use of these perfumes, placing certain scents on certain parts of the body. As Aubaile-Sallenave (2006) notes, these odors than become a part of the guests sacred "armor" as he or she goes out into the profane world.

The centrality of good smell in Qatari homes can as such be related to the strong value placed on privacy and home sanctity in Muslim home, as discussed earlier. There is a marked attempt to keep the smells of homes and guests from contaminating one another. Given the dry desert heritage of Bedouin predecessors in Qatar, Qataris use not only physical separation in rooms of the house, but various olfactory barriers and perfume and incense purifications rather than ablution rites to maintain purity. In a culture where water is at a premium, the use of perfume and incense is an important ritual. The separation of the exterior kitchen (and often the driver's and maid's quarters) from the home is another attempt to maintain the purity of the Qatari home.

### The Home: A Place for Freedom and Control for women

Our findings reveal that women dominate the family quarters in different ways. First, the wife or the female in charge in the household decides whom to allow in the home and whom not allow. For instance men from the non-mahrem category are generally not allowed. The husband and other male family members (sons) are expected to respect their mother and sisters' privacy and usually leave the home when they have female visitors. Having control of whom to allow and when to allow them gives women a sense of control over their domestic space and a sense of freedom within it. A home free from non-mahrem males is physically and symbolically liberating for women. Not only do they not have to bear the inconvenience of covering, but they can also show their ostentatious outfits, hair styles, jewelry and beauty to female guests to 'provoke their envy' and make statements about their status, taste and affinity for fashion.

*Mariam: My home is my kingdom. It's not big and others may consider it small. I wanted a small house with a good plan, reasonable size, easy to control. The important thing is to own my freedom, because we had been fed up with closed places. In many houses in Qatar, the swimming pool is indoors, i.e. without freedom. Ours is outdoors [i.e., not visible to neighbors], yet I enjoy both freedom and privacy in it.*
*Um Hussein: At home I feel in control and free. My favorite place to sit and spend time with my family is the family sitting room. It's comfortable from it I can monitor everything taking place within the house, children, husband and housemaids. I can call anyone from there. I can see and hear everyone from my place. I always sit at a strategic position by the window to monitor who comes in and who goes out during the day.*

The home thus appears to be an uncontrolled space for self expression as opposed to the more controlled public space. Women can move freely between rooms and different areas in the home. While people in all cultures experience, which is not necessarily to say enjoy, more privacy and freedom in their domestic environment, for Qatari women the freedom they experience in their homes is above and beyond the general sense of individual privacy that Westerners may enjoy in the domestic spaces. It is related to the convenience of gender privacy that reduces or eliminates the need

for bodily covering and modest self-presentation and conduct that is required of them in public.

*Abdullah: Qatari women control their households. This makes up for their lack of control outside. Yet, with a veil a woman can wear any make-up and type of dress underneath which also gives her a sense of freedom outside her home. The veil is like a mobile privacy for women.*

As emphasized by this Qatari architect, a woman's dominance of the domestic space diminishes as she moves out of her domestic space to enter the male dominated public sphere. Her sense of control and freedom within the public space is restricted. Nevertheless, women covering with the abaya, shayla, and sometimes a face cover in public creates a personal sense of privacy that a woman carries along with her as she moves into the public sphere. In many public domains like public schools, universities, banks, and hospitals, gender segregation is institutionalized to various degrees to accommodate women need for gender privacy. For instance, Qatar National University has different buildings for female and male students and public hospitals have different entrances for men and women and gender-differentiated waiting areas. Such attempts to control gender relationships in public through institutionalizing gender differentiated areas are an attempt by local governments to reach a compromise between ensuring respect of traditions and women's need for empowerment.

The religious scholar in our study explained how gender segregation in the home and public in the Gulf region is more of a local cultural practice than a religious requirement:

*Mutassim: Islam defines privacy between man and man, man and woman, woman and woman through the concept of Awra—body parts that can't be exposed or shown to others. This relationship is an important issue in Islam, which prohibits its encroachment. Islam does not impose full separation between men and women, as it is sometimes the case now. In fact, this is governed by cultural heritage, which is different in Egypt than in Syria or Lebanon, for instance. Shariaa does not impose full separation. On the contrary, during the Prophet's life, women took part in military expeditions and men and women ate together. Traditions are influential. Islam does not impose a specific space for a woman inside the home. Neither Christianity or Judaism does so. There is nothing in Islam that suggests that women and non mahrems or visitors can't sit and talk together. As I noted earlier, in the prophet Muhammad's era, women and men used to pray together and eat together. There was not the kind of separation we see nowadays in the Gulf society. As long as the woman observes Muslim dress code and manners, she can interact with men. Actually this is the purpose of the Muslim dress code for men and women. It aims to de-sexualize and prevents seduction so that they can interact (work, talk, study etc. together) without the possible drawbacks of such interaction.*

Nevertheless, the more traditional of our informants would never socialize together as two couples, for example. Only same sex gatherings took place within their homes. Although this obviously makes it difficult for young people to meet a potential husband or wife, the practice of arranged marriages and the off chance of a surreptitious meeting at a mall, co-educational university, or place of employment do provide opportunities to find partners.

While the home provides women in the family with gender privacy, bedrooms and parents' bedroom in particular, seem to be women's special safe heaven. The perception of the bedroom as the most private and exclusive place for the adult couple in the home is not exclusive to the Qatari culture (e.g., Chevalier 1999; Spain 1992). However, in Qatari homes, bedrooms and especially parents' bedrooms were found to be an especially sacred retreat for women. While some of the interviewees allowed the female researcher to see their bedrooms, many did not allow photos as they did for the rest of the house. Evidently the bedroom as an extension of self is an equally sensitive area as the body.

Maids usually have restricted access and some of participants prefer to clean their own bedrooms in order to prevent their room from being contaminated by their domestic helpers' presence. The bedroom for these women is not just a place to sleep, but a place to be themselves. Most of the female participants said that their bedroom is their most private space in the home and within it lie their favorite possessions and most sacred corner. This sacredness is by no means solely because of the intimate relationship between the husband and wife that takes place in it.

*Um Hussein: Bedrooms are never entered by strangers, sometimes not even by relatives. Visitors for the first time may be shown the house but bedrooms are private places inside the house and may not be entered by anybody.*

While bedrooms usually have a view of the courtyard or street, it is strictly one way—using mirrored window glass and in some cases mesherabia (filigree panels on windows) means that the woman can look out, but others may not see in. There is often a television, phone, and computer, so there is an indirect connection to the world outside. The woman's bedroom is the largest in the house and furnished to her taste, generally with chairs, sofas, a large bed, mirrors, lamps, and decorative flourishes. Many had large walk-in clothes closets, attached spa bathrooms, dressing rooms, makeup tables, and sometimes exercise equipment and a fireplace (decorative only, given the warm climate). There may be family photos, religious objects, and paintings. Oriental rugs and carpets are common on the floor. Inasmuch as women are excluded from many of the local mosques, it is not just metaphorically a sacred space, but also literally the place where the woman prays and worships.

*Mariam: I feel completely free and comfortable in my bedroom. When I'm not with my children, I prefer to be in my bedroom. I do my hair and nails, pray and recite the Quran there.*
*Um Hind: When I want to relax and have privacy and be on my own, I stay in my bedroom. My bedroom has a TV, a walk-in wardrobe, bathroom and Jacuzzi. I pray, reflect and recite the Quran in this private place.*

For these women their bedroom is a place where they can enact their most inner selves and perform spirituality. It is where they pray and recite Quran. As these participants suggest, the bedroom is not only for prayer, but also for reflection, for consolidating the self.

**The Home as a Place for Expression**

Besides being a place for freedom and control for women, the domestic space in Qatar is also used to make statements about taste and status. This is particularly the case in the design and furnishing of the female guest room, although such home features as elevators, swimming pools, and elaborate men's majleses also serve this purpose.

*Interviewer: If someone entered your house, what would be his/her impression about it?*
*Mariam: He/she would think we have a high style, and that while other people don't usually care for details, we do. Other people may pay the same amount but they don't get a fine home like this. It's a matter of how you utilize the budget... I'm proud of my home, mainly because I designed it.*

Even the quality of oud and other incenses used to perfume the home and guests make a difference. The outcome of a visit is usually evaluated based on the smell carried by the visitor and detected by others outside the host or hostess's home. The nicer the smell the higher the prestige of the absent hostess whose prestige and reputation are thereby extended (Kanafani 1983). Some participants noted that they would know the social class of the home owner from its oud smells as there are different types of oud scents and combinations that can be quite variable in price. This is different from western homes where only material objects (i.e. furnishing and design) convey meanings, denote status, and generate aesthetic experience. This may derive from the traditional Arab environment of desert with little water for use in cleaning and purification rituals, as has been common in the West (Shove 2003; Smith 2007). For men the home also appears to be a source of pride and fulfillment. It is a place of peace and safety for the family that the husband is expected to provide materially. Providing a home and being in charge financially are considered to be a husband's duty in Islam. It is related to the concept of *kiwama*--being in charge and responsible for the wife or women in the family. A woman, even if she has an income, has no obligation to spend it on the home or family.

*Interviewer: If your home were an animal. Which animal would it be?*
*Jamal: I'm fascinated with marine life. The whale is big, graceful and my home gives such [an] impression.*
*Abu Khalid: Though we don't like animals, a horse may represent it. It's strong and proud.*

Not only home design, but also furnishings were cited as points of pride. Furniture from Italy, fine oriental carpets, and original artwork were among the objects cited as being "unique." Likewise lush elaborate landscaping in the inner courtyard of one home made it hard to appreciate that it was located in an arid country of sand and deserts.

**The Men's *Majles*: A place for Pride and Honor**

The men's majles is a communal male space where the husband and other male family members, receive and entertain their male guests. It is a space that binds Qataris to their past and expresses cultural authenticity. It is the most prominent site for enacting Arab hospitality and a source of pride and honor that brings praise and supports the family or tribe reputation and prestige.

*Saleh: In [the] majlses I meet my friends and old classmates and cousins. [The] Majles is a place of prestige and a place of heritage. It has traditions surrounding it. It's large (6x10 meters) to accommodate as a large number of guests as possible. Not only is the size and magnificence of the majles important, it also brings honor and status to the host if many guests come, especially if they are prominent. Its significance is reflected in the type of treatment and generosity found in it, as well as implied cultural heritage. It's also reflected in the age of people present there [with older men being higher in status].*

People often have their meals on the floor and don't use chairs in the majles. Coffee has major importance in a majles. It's essential for hospitality. Guests are welcomed with incenses and *Oud*, Coffee is prepared from green grains following special rituals.

Objects and traditions from the Bedouin past are also an important part of the display in Qatari Majleses. We found that Qatari male favorite objects tend to be objects that represent a proud and prosperous heritage linked to the past and the traditions that are revered in the Arab Gulf region (e.g., heirloom swords, coffee pots, grandfather's photos) and these objects tend to be on prominent display for other men to see in the majles.

*Jassim: We have started to long for the past. You observe a lot of the old features in [the] Almannai [a prominent family with two majleses we visited] Majles: Old style doors and windows, rawashin [special places] where [they] display coffee pots, weapons, etc..*

Some would bring their falcons to the majleses they visit. When a falconer comes to majles with his falcon(s) he wants to demonstrate his skills in falconry. He also comes armed with his guns and daggers. Old swords and guns are currently used for decoration, together with other things used in the past such as the pump used in coffee-making. People used to express their pride in being a member of a specific tribe, family or district. [The] Majles in the Qatari and Gulf societies means honor. It's everything…. In the past tribal issues were discussed: politics, economics, etc.

Although the majles is an exclusive space for men, it could be occasionally used for a big women gathering. As such, the most public area in the domestic sphere can be temporarily converted to a women private sphere. This space mutability is inherent to the characteristic feature of the Islamic construction of space. For instance, a public space like a street can be temporarily altered into a private sacred space by occupying it for prayer by men or women (El Guindi 1999). The home could also be converted to a public space for women with the entrance of a man from the non-mahrem category.

### Embracing the Modern and Longing for the Traditional

Despite a cultural pride in Qatar's Bedouins and the Bedouin heritage of many Qataris, there is no doubt that contemporary conveniences are embraced as well. Land Rovers have replaced camels, homes and majleses have air conditioning and big screen televisions, and foods are prepared in kitchens equipped with all the latest conveniences. For these things are marks of status as much as links to past traditions and heritage are. The real estate agent in our study explained how the modern and the traditional co-exist:

*Agent: Now people like to have a beautiful garden, swimming-pool, Jacuzzi, marble, excellent decoration and central air-conditioning as well as an external majles and a separate space for a tent. People like to sit on the floor in the tent where they feel comfortable, while [the] majles is usually used for formal receptions. The tent is especially used in Ramadan. People prefer the tent during winter, listening to the sound of rain. Tents are air-conditioned now. It's a psychological need rooted n Qatari customs. To Qataris, tents may still be more beautiful than palaces! Even with the largest and finest majles, the tent is considered necessary. The tent is mainly for men. It is usually set up in the open space close to the house or within the house enclosure and is supplied with electricity. … Some families set up tents in the desert and some set up their tents close*

*to the sea. People like to go to the desert and if it rains wild plants grow and people enjoy the scenery.*

As noted by the real estate agent, tensions between the traditional and modern are evident in the configuration of homes and objects within them. Opulent two or three storey villas are replacing traditional, one story inward facing Qatari homes. Yet, many Qatari homes have an external Bedouin tent in their front yard usually used by male family members and their guests as part of a proud connection to prior roots. Although traditional furnishings like floor seating is increasingly being replaced by modern furniture in Qatari homes, some Qatari families still have a traditional space or corner in their homes with floor seating where family members sit and eat meals. Many Qatari families also have permanent tents in the desert where they go and spend the weekend away from the modern urban lifestyle in Doha. These and other examples show how Qataris embrace Western goods and symbols of modernity and at the same time use traditional goods and symbols as a way of preserving or reviving traditional roots. This process of creolization (Hannerez 1992) of blending the local with the global results in a new synthesis of consumption patterns with an increasing incorporation of modern, Western lifestyles and goods into traditional ways of life (Ger and Belk, 1996).

A part of the status of a family also comes from their membership in a prominent tribe. Although belonging to a prominent family can also still convey status in the West, in Qatari society family and clan reputations are more dependent on the moral reputations of family members. This is more similar to Asian notions of face than it is with Western concepts of new and old wealth. Conspicuous consumption, however is increasingly important in the Gulf as Qataris as well as Saudis, Emiratis, Bahrainis, Kuwaitis, and Omanis turn the inward focus of traditional housing more outward and as subtle signs of wealth (e.g., designer abayas, luxury watches, sunglasses, and purses, and expensive automobiles and SUVs become commonplace, even among teenagers. This part of Qatari culture is inflected by the combination of increased wealth and greater presence of global forces.

### DISCUSSION

At first glance it is tempting to see the simultaneous longing for the traditional in Qataris' preferences for traditional hospitality rituals, dress, tribal affiliation, high exterior walls around homes, and at least a room or corner with floor seating, as a reaction to the threat of too much foreign influence too quickly. There is some truth to this, but it is important to appreciate that it is given added emphasis by the status of Qataris as minorities in their own country. Coupled with a pan-Islamic embrace of overt Islamism in an era of various perceived and actual hostility to Muslims since September 11, 2001, there is a strong desire to assert a uniquely Muslim and Arab identity in Qatar and other Gulf States.

It is also tempting to see gender segregation in Qatari households as confining women to the home and veil. The public/private paradigm has been commonly used to describe gender segregation in an Arab- Islamic cultural space. However, we found that the privacy of family/women quarters give a woman a sense of freedom and mobility in the domestic space, just as bodily covering gives her a sense of freedom and mobility in the public space. The veil can be seen as a woman's mobile privacy that she transports with her as she moves from the private to the public sphere. *Hurma* is an Arabic term that refers at once to a woman or wife, to the sanctity of religious sites, and also to the sanctity of the home. In essence, it is that which is sacred and pure.

Without attempting to in any way suggest that Qatar is at an earlier stage of "development," it is also well to remember that similar degrees of gender segregation found in Qatari domestic spaces could be found in some Western spaces as recently as a century ago. Some even find that women's seclusion is more rooted in Western European traditions reflecting a "bourgeois conception of society" (Sciama 1993: 110). And as in the Gulf today, the ability to maintain gender segregation in the Western home was itself a demonstration of wealth and status.

The majles—is a space where roots and traditions are revived and where collective and tribal identities are enacted by men. However, the women's space is more expressive of individual identity and denotes personal status and wealth. Women's domain can be seen as an embodiment of individual identity, mobility and change, whereas men's domain can be seen as an embodiment of collective identify, stability and perseverance of roots. The majles has kept the horizontal traditional building architecture, design and furnishing whereas family homes are increasingly adopting a modern vertical structure (two or three storey villas) and use modern interior designs and furnishing. According to Tuan (1974), vertical elements of the landscape symbolize transcendence and evoke a sense of striving, while horizontal ones symbolize the ideal of roots identification and acceptance. The majles thus encompasses elements of stability and resistance to change, while women's space encompasses mobility and represents what is culturally changeable. Having both spaces in each Qatari household helps locals negotiate and reconcile the conflicting demands of modernity and tradition and to mediate the major social and cultural changes the country has been undergoing.

A similar dichotomy is seen in local personal adornment, where women's garments and grooming are becoming much more expressive while men's garments have changed little. The black, plain and modest abaya that Qatari women traditionally wear in public is increasingly assuming a modern fashionable appearance, accessorized with jewelry, designer handbags, and high heel shoes (Sobh, Belk, Gressel forthcoming). Whether in the configuration of their domestic spaces or appearance in the public space, women seem to capture the ambivalence and conflicting imperative of traditional norms and the temptations of the modern. Women carry the burden of their nation's culture and traditional norms but they also seem to carry change and transformation in their society; their challenge is to reconcile the two.

# REFERENCES

Allan, Graham and Crow, Graham (1989), *Home and Family: Creating the Domestic Sphere,* London: The MacMillan Press

Altman, Irwin (1975), *The Environment and Social Behavior: Privacy, Personal Space, Territoriality, Corwding*, Monterey, CA: Brooks/Cole.

Aubaile-Sallenave, Françoise (2006), "Bodies, Odors and Perfumes in Arab-Muslim Societies," in Jim Drobnick, ed., *The Smell Culture Reader*, Oxford: Berg

Campo, Juan E. (1991), *The Other Sides of Paradise: Explorations into the Religious Meanings of Domestic Space in Islam*, Columbia: University of South Carolina Press.

Chevalier, Sophie (1999), "The French Two-Home Project: Materialization of Family Identity," in Irene Cieraad, ed., *At Home: An Anthropology of Domestic Space*, Syracuse, NY: Syracuse University Press, 83-94.

Chevalier, Sophie (2002), "The Cultural Construction of Domestic Space in France and Great Britain," *Signs*, 27 (Spring), 847-856.

El Guindi, Fadwa (1981)," Veiling Infitah with Muslim Ethic: Egypt's Contemporary Islamic Movement," *Social problems*, 28 (4), 465-485.

El Guindi, Fadwa (1999), *Veil: Modesty, Privacy and Resistance*, NY: Berg

Farah, Eman. A and Klarqvist, Bjorn (2001) *Gender Zones in the Arab Muslim House". Conference proceedings, 3rd International Space Syntax Symposium.* Atlanta.

Gallagher, Winifred (2006), *House Thinking: A Room-by-Room Look at How We Live*, New York: Harper Collins.

Gennep, Arnold van (1960), *The Rites of Passage*, London: Routledge (original in French, 1909).

Ger, Guliz and Russell W. Belk (1996), "I'd Like to Buy the World a Coke: Consumption scapes of the "Less Affluent World," *Journal of Consumer Policy*, 19, 271-304.

Hannerz, Ulf (1992), Cultural complexity: Studies in the social organization of meaning. York: Columbia University Press.

Kadivar, Mohsen (2003), "An Introduction to the Public and Private Debate in Islam," Social Research, 70 (3), 659-680.

Kanafani, Aida S. (1993), *Aesthetics and Ritual in the United Arab Emirates: The Anthropology of Food and Personal Adornment among Arabian Women,* Beirut, Lebanon: American University of Beirut.

Marcus, Cooper. C (1995). House as a Mirror of Self: Exploring the Deeper Meaning of Home. Berkeley, CA: Conari Press.

Mottahedeth, Roy and Stilt, Kristne (2003), "Public and Private as Viewed Through The Work of Muhtasib," *Social Research*, 70 (3), 735-768.

Munro,Moira and Ruth Madigan (1999), "Negotiating Space in the Family Home," in Irene Cieraad, ed., *At Home: An Anthropology of Domestic Space*, Syracuse, NY: Syracuse University Press, 107-117.

Rybcyznski, Witold (1986), *Home: A Short History of the Idea*, New York: Viking Penguin.

Sciama, Lidia (1993), "The problem of privacy in Mediterranean Anthropology," in Shireley Ardener, ed, *Women and Space: Ground Rules and Social Maps,* pp.87-111. Oxford and Providence, RI: Berg.

Shove, Elizabeth (2002), *Comfort, Cleanliness and Convenience: The Social Organization of Normality*, Oxford: Berg.

Smith, Virginia (2006), *Clean: A History of Personal Hygiene and Purity*, Oxford: Oxford University Press.2007.

Sobh, Rana, Russell Belk, and Justin Gressel, "The Scented Winds of Change: Conflicting Notions of Modesty and Vanity among Young Qatari and Emirati Women," *Advances in Consumer Research*.

Sommer, Robert (1969), *Personal Space: The Behavioral Basis of Design*, Englewood Cliffs, NJ: Prentice-Hall.

Spain, Daphne (1992), *Gendered Spaces*, Chapel Hill, NC: University of North Carolina Press.

Taylor, Lawrence (1999), "Re-entering the West Room: On the Power of Domestic Spaces," in Donna Birdwell-Pheasant and Denise Lawrence-Zúñiga, ed., Oxford: Berg, 223-237.

Thompson, Craig J., Howard R. Pollio, and William B. Locander (1994), "The spoken and the unspoken: A Hermeneutic Approach to Understanding the Cultural Viewpoints That Underlie Consumers' Expressed meanings," Journal of Consumer Research, 21 (December), 432-453.

Tuan, Yi-Fu (1982), *Segmented Worlds and Self: Group Life and Individual Consciouness*, Minneapolis: University of Minnesota Press.

Tuan, Yi-Fu (1974), *Topohilia: A Study of Environmental Perception, Attitudes, and Values*, University of Minnesota: Prentice- Hall.

# Consumers' Attachment and Commitment to Brands and Media Titles: The role of Emotions

Rita Valette-Florence, IMUS & IREGE, France
Imene Becheur, Wesford School of Business, France
Virginie de Barnier, IAE Aix en Provence, France
Pierre Valette-Florence, IAE & CERAG, France

## ABSTRACT

In this research, we develop a new emotion scale that applies to both media titles and advertiser brands. The dimensions include a positive affective dimension, plenitude; a negative dimension fear; and a mixed dimension, possession, which includes a rather negative facet, envy, and a rather positive one, love. This research also studies the effects of emotions on affective relational variables, namely attachment and emotional commitment, and the potential mediating role of attachment on emotional commitment. Overall, results show a partial mediating effect of attachment between possession and commitment. Both fear and plenitude are complete mediators.

## INTRODUCTION

In this research, we develop a new emotion scale that applies to both media titles and advertiser brands. This research also studies the effects of emotions on affective relational variables, namely attachment and emotional commitment, and the potential mediating role of attachment on emotional commitment.

Considering the criticisms addressed to existing emotion scales, this study attempts to construct a new scale of emotions (applicable to advertiser brands and media brands) by combining elements of both Holbrook and Batra's (1987) and Richins's (1997) scales.

The qualitative study allowed us to collect emotion-type items that could describe magazines. and to verify the collected items and validate Richins's (1997) and Holbrook and Batra's (1987) scale items for magazines. Then, in our quantitative study, we relied on five media titles: *Le Monde* (national daily), *Télérama* (Television), *Elle* (Feminine), *Géo* (Tourism) and *L'Equipe* (Sport national daily), and four advertised brands: *Apple* (Computer), *Carte Noire* (Coffee), *Benetton* (Clothes) and *Ferrari* (Cars). After a series of analyses with CSA (covariance structure analysis) and PLS (partial least squares) (PLS) estimation model, we obtained a 10 variable solution, which clustered into three second-order dimensions: fear, possession, and plenitude. Some of these dimensions match those in Holbrook and Batra (1987) and Richins (1997), including scepticism, surprise, tranquillity, and envy, whereas other dimensions, such as distress, are new. The proposed scale therefore offers a specific measure of emotions that apply to both media titles and advertiser brands. The dimensions include a positive affective dimension, plenitude; the negative dimension fear; and a mixed dimension, possession, which includes a rather negative facet, envy, and a rather positive one, love.

The research model specifies relationships between emotions and two relational consequences, attachment and emotional commitment by magazine readers and brand consumers. We test the following hypotheses:

**H1**: *Fear has a negative impact on (a) attachment and (b) commitment toward the brand or magazine.*

**H2**: *Possession has a positive or negative impact on (a) attachment and (b) commitment toward the brand and magazine.*

**H3**: *Plenitude has a positive impact on (a) attachment and (b) commitment toward the brand and magazine.*

**H4**: *Attachment to the brand or magazine mediates the relationship between emotions and commitment to this brand or magazine.*

### Magazines

The fear dimension negatively influences attachment and commitment to magazines, in support of H1a and H1b. In contrast, plenitude has a positive impact on attachment and commitment toward magazines, in support of H3a and H3b. Possession negatively influences attachment and commitment to magazines, in support of H2a and H2b.

In the test of the model with attachment as an antecedent of commitment, the results indicate a partial mediating effect of attachment between possession and commitment. Both fear and plenitude are completely mediated by attachment, in support of H4. Globally, plenitude is the main determinant of attachment and commitment toward magazines. The negative influence of fear seems legitimate, whereas impact of possession is more paradoxical. This result suggests the need for a refined analysis for each magazine individually.

The mediating role of attachment for *Elle* is complete for plenitude and possession (the latter has a positive impact on attachment) and partial for fear. The path coefficient, though weaker, is statistically significant. More than 90 percent of the explicative power (i.e., contribution to R²) pertains to attachment, despite the partial mediation. This specific analysis of every press title also indicates that the negative influence of possession on all titles is due to the newspaper *Le Monde* (-.227)

### Brands

The impact of possession is positive on attachment and commitment. These results support recent findings regarding the concept of brand love (Albert, Merunka, and Valette-Florence 2008). Yet this mediating role is complete for brands. The influence of all second-order emotional dimensions on brand commitment is overrode by attachment.

As we did for media titles, it seems interesting to test the model with regard to each brand. For example, the analysis of Apple shows a complete mediating effect of attachment. Again, more than 90 percent of the explanatory power is due to the influence of attachment on commitment. In turn, the emotional commitment of Apple consumers to the brand occurs only if they are emotionally attached to the brand. The corresponding possession path coefficient for Apple is approximately .309 (.210 for all the titles). Further analyses of the direct impact of the possession first-order dimensions on attachment reveal that only the love dimension has a positive and significant influence (.314, .046 for envy). This result reemphasizes the role of brand love for Apple consumers (Albert et al., 2008).

An analysis of variance of the latent factor scores for the different brands and magazines assesses the differentiating power of the proposed scale. Results confirm the differentiating power of all scale dimensions. Love and surprise are the most differentiating dimensions.

Moreover, Duncan's test (not shown here to preserve space) identifies, for each dimension, the brands and magazines that have the same, different, or close profiles. The brands reflect various different means; for example, *Benetton* achieves a strong profile on fear, whereas *Apple* and *Carte Noire* score higher on possession (due to consumers' strong emotional commitment to *Apple* and the seduction-based advertising strategy of *Carte Noire*). In contrast, the magazine profiles are generally similar, except that *Elle* and *Géo* are stronger on love and envy. The informational character of *Le Monde* distinguishes it on all dimensions, and *L'Equipe* appears close to the other magazines.

Finally, in terms of their emotional proximity, *Apple* coexists better with *Géo* rather than *Le Monde*. However, only a study of *Apple* consumers who are also *Géo* or *Le Monde* readers could confirm this claim.

Emotional elements constitute the basis of the relationship between the consumer and brand, and various studies consider the length and content of that relationship (Hakansson 1982; Morgan and Hunt 1994). The relational paradigm insists on the attachment concept (Thomson, MacInnis, and Park 2005), which relates to emotional commitment (Chaudhuri and Holbrook 2001, 2002).

Such emotional reactions are among the various responses to advertising, though exposure to any media appears to provoke emotions (Murry and Dacin 1996). These emotions in turn affect people's intentions (Adelaar et al. 2003). But does this link mean that the medium used to promote a brand also influences the audience's emotional reaction? For example, if a consumer experiences certain emotions and feels attached to a brand, does that person also feel emotions and attachment to the magazine in which an ad for the brand appears? On a more general level, this study investigates a critical question: Is it legitimate to apply the same emotion scale to brands and to specific media titles? The answer is important on both theoretical and managerial levels. This research also examines the extent to which emotions influence attachment and emotional commitment towards press titles and commercial brands.

The remainder of this article first describes the development of a new emotion scale that applies for both press titles and commercial brands. Then, it presents a research model that modelizes the influence of emotions on attachment and emotional commitment, along with the test of the mediating effect of attachment. Finally, the findings, limitations, and further research opportunities appear in the conclusion.

## 1. A new emotion scale

We first underline the importance of emotions in consumer-brand relationships. Then, we review the existing emotion scales. After developing a new scale that assesses emotions elicited while reading a magazine, or consuming a brand, we show its superiority over existing emotion scales.

### *1.1. Importance of emotions in consumer-brand relationships*

"Emotions are ubiquitous in marketing: They influence information processing, mediate responses to persuasive appeals, measure the effects of marketing stimuli, initiate goal setting, enact goal-directed behaviours, and serve as ends and measures of consumer welfare" (Bagozzi, Gopinath, and Nyer 1999, 202). Zajonc (1980) and Zajonc and Markus (1982) furthered recognition of the importance of emotional reactions, prompting the elaboration of a new approach described as "experiential" (Holbrook and Hirschman 1982).

For the defenders of this approach, consumption represents an experience and therefore entails a range of emotional reactions, including feelings, sensations, emotions, and so on. These theorists also argue that emotions influence information processing, stimuli evaluations, and satisfaction. In particular, Westbrook and Oliver (1991) identify three emotional responses as important antecedents of satisfaction with newly purchased automobiles: pleasant surprise, interest, and hostility. Oliver (1992) expands these determinants of satisfaction to include positive affect (interest and joy) and negative affect (anger, disgust, contempt, shame, guilt, fear, sadness), as well as disconfirmation beliefs (Bagozzi, Gopinath, and Nyer 1999).

### *1.2. Previous emotion measurements*

This research study focuses on measuring emotions linked to consumption. The consumption emotion scale (CES) proposed by

Richins (1997) can capture emotions during consumption experiences, and recent studies show that the CES applies in a French context (Ferrandi, De Barnier, and Valette-Florence 2003).

This scale may be appropriate for measuring emotions during brand consumption, but advertising pages in publications, such as magazines, also may affect emotions, whether directly or indirectly, and therefore the readers' emotions toward the subsequently consumed brand. Approximately 30 percent of magazine pages contain advertising or publicity, so other measurement scales may be necessary or beneficial in this context.

Measures that assume discrete emotions suggest that emotions belong to identifiable and independent categories (Aaker, Stayman, and Vezina 1988; Batra and Holbrook 1990; Batra and Ray 1986). Those that adopt a continuous approach instead imagine that emotions combine two or more dimensions (Holbrook and Batra 1987). The discrete approach suffers two important limitations, in the sense that, first it cannot identify relations between basic emotions and therefore cannot investigate combinatory effects, and second, no general agreement exists regarding basic emotions or listings of emotions, which makes it difficult to synthesize any results.

Considering these criticisms, this research adopts a continuous approach to emotions.

Among the existing emotion scales, the standardized emotion profile (SEP) scale by Holbrook and Batra (1987) seems to offer the best and most valid measure of emotional reactions stimulated by exposure to printed advertising stimuli. In comparison with other scales, it provides the double advantage of a precise factorial structure and easily understandable items. In addition, French magazines such as *Géo* and *Elle* correspond better to the emotions measured by Holbrook and Batra's scale, whereas dailies such as *Le Monde* or magazines like *Capital*, which include less intrusive advertising, might register better with Richins's measured emotions.

Based on Holbrook and Batra's (1987) and Richins's (1997) scales, this study attempts to develop a new emotion scale for commercial brands and press titles.

### *1.3. Scale development*

The scale construction process consists of two parts: a qualitative study and a quantitative study, with exploratory and confirmatory factor analyses.

**Qualitative studies**

From a managerial point of view, magazines are brands. However, magazines also entail some particularities when presented as brands. Therefore, the scale development process must generate groups of items related to the emotions activated when people read magazines to identify any missing items from prior scales.

Focus groups provide an effective means for doing so (Edmunds 1999), because they combine social interaction and group influence phenomena. Following Derbaix and Poncin (2005), this step includes projective and classical qualitative studies that explore respondents' conscious and subconscious minds.

The qualitative study consists of two steps. First, the "discovery step" attempted to collect emotion-type items that could describe magazines. Second, the confirmation step (classical method) intended to verify the collected items and validate Richins's (1997) and Holbrook and Batra's (1987) scale items for magazines. Both expert analyses and synonym checking confirmed that the retained items could all be regrouped into Holbrook and Batra's and Richins's scales.

**Quantitative study**

The selection of publications was based on the number of printings in France, as well as the possibility that the titles would induce

## Table 1: Scale's structure and validity

| Measure variables | interpretation | CSA First order parameters estimation | CSA T test | CSA Convergent validity | PLS Convergent validity | CSA Reliability | PLS Reliability |
|---|---|---|---|---|---|---|---|
| Sad | Irritation | 0.666 | 23.199 | 0.553 | 0.692 | 0.787 | 0.870 |
| Angry | | 0.807 | 38.470 | | | | |
| Irritated | | 0.751 | 31.371 | | | | |
| aggrieved | Fright | 0.756 | 34.845 | 0.635 | 0.724 | 0.874 | 0.913 |
| tense | | 0.814 | 45.453 | | | | |
| Worried | | 0.795 | 41.630 | | | | |
| Affraid | | 0.820 | 46.968 | | | | |
| Suspicion | Scepticism | 0.661 | 23.775 | 0.684 | 0.778 | 0.864 | 0.913 |
| Scepticism | | 0.901 | 59.183 | | | | |
| Mistrust | | 0.896 | 58.018 | | | | |
| Humiliated | Distress | 0.805 | 43.638 | 0.605 | 0.680 | 0.884 | 0.914 |
| Ashamed | | 0.826 | 48.339 | | | | |
| Unhappy | | 0.768 | 36.653 | | | | |
| Embarrassed | | 0.747 | 33.574 | | | | |
| Depressed | | 0.740 | 32.497 | | | | |
| Envious | Envy | 0.776 | 23.636 | 0.603 | 0.787 | 0.752 | 0.880 |
| Jealous | | 0.777 | 23.676 | | | | |
| Romantic | Love | 0.810 | 44.749 | 0.624 | 0.690 | 0.891 | 0.917 |
| Sentimental | | 0.666 | 24.511 | | | | |
| In love | | 0.870 | 61.394 | | | | |
| Sexy | | 0.873 | 62.559 | | | | |
| Warm-hearted | | 0.707 | 28.619 | | | | |
| Calm | Tranquillity | 0.788 | 28.516 | 0.741 | 0.865 | 0.85 | 0.927 |
| Peaceful | | 0.928 | 35.138 | | | | |
| Joyful | Joy | 0.717 | 30.681 | 0.705 | 0.759 | 0.922 | 0.940 |
| Happy | | 0.905 | 87.936 | | | | |
| Content | | 0.877 | 71.518 | | | | |
| Enthusiastic | | 0.875 | 70.283 | | | | |
| Satisfied | | 0.809 | 47.156 | | | | |
| Thankful | Thankfulness | 0.643 | 20.746 | 0.526 | 0.680 | 0.768 | 0.864 |
| Respected | | 0.728 | 27.550 | | | | |
| Comforted | | 0.797 | 35.549 | | | | |
| Astonished | Surprise | 0.778 | 32.486 | 0.614 | 0.728 | 0.825 | 0.889 |
| Surprised | | 0.881 | 43.416 | | | | |
| Amazed | | 0.679 | 23.616 | | | | |

| First order dimensions | Interpretation | CSA Second order parameters estimation | CSA T test | CSA Convergent Validity | PLS Convergent Validity | CSA Reliability | PLS Reliability |
|---|---|---|---|---|---|---|---|
| Irritation | Fear | 0.905 | 45.185 | 0.729 | 0.707 | 0.913 | 0.906 |
| Fright | | 0.964 | 66.323 | | | | |
| Scepticism | | 0.605 | 17.965 | | | | |
| Distress | | 0.896 | 52.987 | | | | |
| Envy | Possession | 0.603 | 13.301 | 0.49 | 0.668 | 0.654 | 0.794 |
| Love | | 0.785 | 19.798 | | | | |
| Tranquillity | Plenitude | 0.604 | 16.187 | 0.561 | 0.6 | 0.83 | 0.854 |
| Joy | | 0.902 | 45.405 | | | | |
| Thankfulness | | 0.875 | 34.171 | | | | |
| Surprise | | 0.548 | 13.899 | | | | |

**Figure 1: Emotions scale**

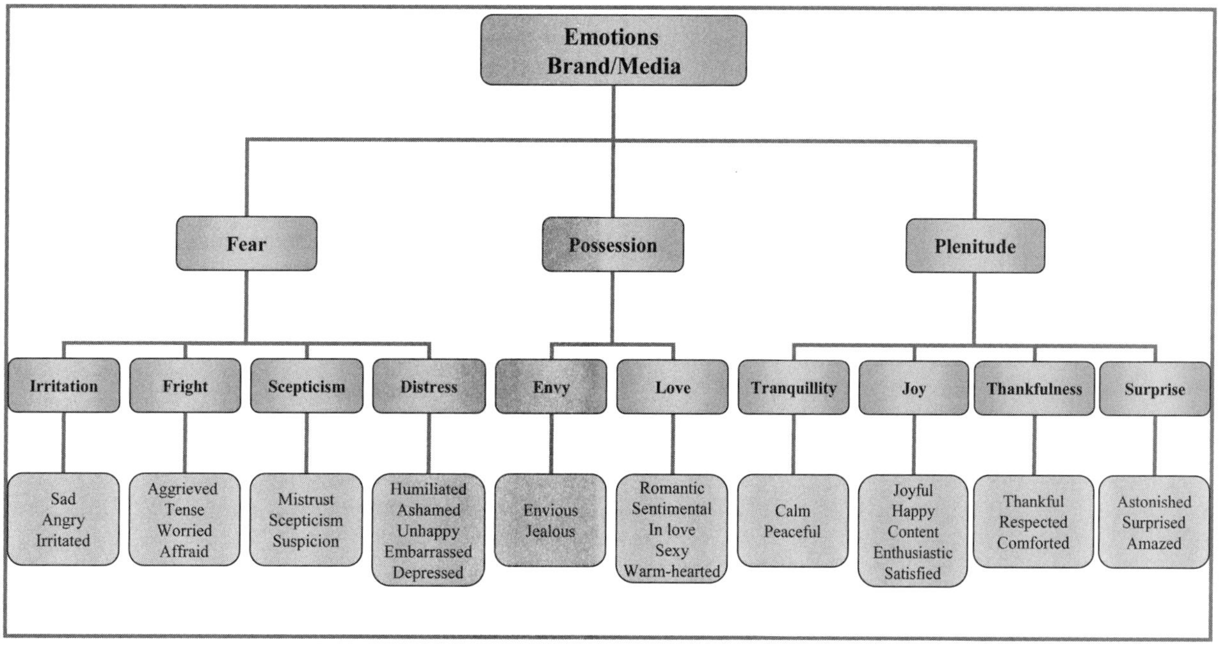

different emotions, such as "fear" or "interest" (the daily newspaper *Le Monde*), "sadness" or "joy" (sport magazine *L'Equipe*), and "jealousy" (fashion magazine *Elle*). All in all, we relied on five media titles: *Le Monde* (national daily), *Télérama* (Television), *Elle* (Feminine), *Géo* (Tourism) and *L'Equipe* (Sport national daily)

The selection of advertised brands includes well-known brand names that would induce a wide range of emotions. For example, *Carte Noire* (a very famous coffee brand in France) likely provokes "sentimentality" or "romanticism". In that survey, we selected four brands, namely *Apple* (Computer), *Carte Noire* (Coffee), *Benetton* (Clothes) and *Ferrari* (Cars).

Respondents were either brand consumers (to support measures of the impacts on attachment and brand commitment) or brand experts (to build a reliable emotion scale). The questionnaire included items from our newly developed emotion scale, as well as from Lacoeuilhe's attachment scale (2000) and Fullerton's emotional commitment scale (2003). The convenience, non representative sample (498 respondents) contains a range of social and professional classes and age groups.

Two types of confirmatory factor analyses validate the scale's structure, namely, a classical covariance structure analysis (CSA) and a partial least squares (PLS) estimation model (Tenenhaus et al., 2005). Considering the non-normality of the measurement variables and the relatively small size of the sample, these analyses relied on a systematic bootstrap procedure (500 replications for CSA and 250 replications for PLS). The CSA approach tests and validates the adequacy of the model according to the fit indexes recommended in the literature (Hu and Bentler 1998). The root mean squared error of approximation (RMSEA) is .0565; the goodness-of-fit (GFI) and adjusted goodness-of-fit (AGFI) indices are .914 and .895, respectively. In the PLS model, the GoF (goodness of fit) index proposed by Tenenhaus et al. (2005) reaches .821 for internal GoF and .997 for external GoF. This model therefore is satisfactory, because GoF is close to 1.

Convergent validity, reliability, and discriminant validity tests consider the specific quality of each scale's dimension. As Table 1 shows, all t-tests in the CSA are significant. The loadings also are important, and the extracted variance is greater than 50 percent (close to .50 for "possession") (Fornell and Larcker 1981). The reliability of every latent variable, according to Joreskog's coefficient, is satisfactory,

particularly for second-order dimensions. All 10 variables clustered into three second-order dimensions: fear, possession, and plenitude.

Finally, a series of sequential tests that compare free with constrained models (i.e., correlations between two latent variables fixed to 1) confirm that the free models exhibit better fit with the data, in support of discriminant validity (also proved for the PLS model). These results confirm a 10-dimensional first-order structure and a three-dimensional second-order structure (Figure 1). Some of these dimensions match those in Holbrook and Batra (1987) and Richins (1997), including scepticism, surprise, tranquillity, and envy, whereas other dimensions, such as distress, are new.

The proposed scale therefore offers a specific measure of emotions that apply to both media titles and advertiser brands. We also checked by means of a multi-group confirmatory factor analysis that the scale structure remained invariant between press titles and commercial brands. This result confirms the universal nature of emotions, which don't depend on the domain of inquiry. Overall, the dimensions include a positive affective dimension, plenitude; the negative dimension fear; and a mixed dimension, possession, which includes a rather negative facet, envy, and a rather positive one, love.

Finally, by means of series of discriminant analyses, we compared the predictive power of our new emotion scale with than of Richins (1997) and Holbrook and Batra (1987). For all three scales, we used PLS latent scores as independent predictive variables, and six of the studied brands (*Apple, Carte noire, Elle, Le Monde, L'equipe,* and *Geo*) as the dependent variable. Results show that the new developed scale outperform the two other scales as for the overall classification rate (namely 56 percent vs. 51 percent for Holbrook and Batra's scale, and 50 percent for Richins's scale).

## 2. The effects of emotions on attachment and emotional commitment

McQueen, Foley, and Deighton (1993) illustrate the emotional development between brands and consumers with the notion of attachment, which can lead to brand commitment. Moreover, Chaudhuri (2006) underlines the importance of affect, which binds the antecedents of emotions to their manifestations, such as attachment and commitment, considered as two key brand relational variables (Thomson, MacInnis, and Park, 2005).

*2.1 Relational variables*

The relational perspective shows that attachment linked to attitudinal loyalty and brand commitment is now considered as an independent construct with its own measures (Thomson, MacInnis, and Park, 2005; Lacoeuilhe 2000). In the marketing field, brand attachment reportedly results from nostalgic connections with life events or image congruence (real or ideal) between the consumer and brand (Lacoeuilhe 2000). Attachment represents a strong emotional relation to the brand (Aaker and Fournier 1995), which one can define as a strong, interactive and lasting psychological and emotional relation between consumer and brand that can be manifested by dependency and friendship.

Lacoeuilhe's (2000) definition also considers brand attachment "*a psychological variable that translates a lasting and changeless emotional relation (separation is painful) towards brand and that expresses a relation of psychological closeness to it.*" This author therefore argues that emotions, though similar to attachment, differ from it, in that emotions are more intense, shorter, and related to an event's nature, whereas attachment is a long-term, evaluative reaction. This study adopts both Lacoeuilhe's (2000) definition and his four-item measurement scale, rather than Thomson and colleagues' (2005) attachment scale, which includes items linked to emotions such as love.

Early commitment studies in the organizational field (Meyer and Allen 1991; Mowday, Steers, and Porter 1979) include a measurement scale based on three dimensions: emotional commitment, cognitive or calculated commitment, and normative commitment (Allen and Meyer 1990a, 1990b). Various researchers apply this concept to marketing, particularly in the field of relationship marketing (Bansal, Irving, and Taylor 2004; Fullerton 2003, 2005; Gundlach, Achrol, and Mentzer 1995; Morgan and Hunt 1994). In this research, we define commitment as a firm's willingness to support a relation with the brand. This study focuses particularly on emotional commitment, which reflects the degree of involvement and identification with the organization (Meyer and Allen 1991), which in turn leads to a sense of membership. In marketing, it leads to consumer loyalty, because commitment causes a favourable attitude toward the brand, along with an intention to re-purchase it (Fullerton 2005). According to Fournier (1998), consumers develop relations with the brands they use. In this sense, commitment creates the benevolent will to sustain a satisfactory relationship over the long term, which involves accepting short-term, necessary sacrifices and creating obstacles to the dissolution of the relationship.

Fullerton (2005) also argues that commitment constitutes the heart of such relationships, because it leads customers to develop positive affect toward the brand. For example, in consumption communities, consumers share or feel positive emotions toward the object of consumption, both on their own and together with the community members. (McAlexander, Kim, and Roberts, 2003). Finally, emotional commitment relates closely to the expressive function of brands, a source of emotions and feelings. Consequently, this research assesses the impact of emotions activated when people consider a brand or read a publication on their attachment and emotional commitment to those brands and media titles.

*2.2. Research model & Hypotheses*

The research model tests the effects of emotions on affective relational variables, namely attachment and emotional commitment, and the potential mediating role of attachment on emotional commitment. Strong relations between consumers and brands underlie schemata and emotion-laden memories. In effect, interactions between consumers and objects lead to strong emotions, which create strong attachments toward those objects (Thomson, MacInnis, and Park 2005). Therefore, emotional items from prior attachment scales, such as emotional, delighted, passionate, or cheerful (Lacoeuilhe 2000; Thomson, MacInnis, and Park 2005) should characterize attachments toward the brand. These

emotions are positively valenced, in that they reflect a positive, nice, and intense evaluation of the object (brand) (Lazarus 1991; Roseman 1991). Indeed, brands create emotional attraction and have the capacity to activate strong feelings, emotions, and pleasure. Therefore, emotions should affect brand attachment positively.

In social psychology, Simpson et al. (2007) show that positive emotions affect positively attachment to one's partner, whereas negative emotions affect it negatively. Similarly, positive emotions should reinforce emotional attachments to the brand or publication, whereas negative emotions should influence them negatively. The effect of possession may be mixed, because this dimension consists of two first-order variables, one positive (love) and one negative (envy) (Pines and Friedman 1998; Richins 1997).

Therefore, positive (negative) emotions should favour (inhibit) commitment toward the brand or magazine. In turn,

**H1**: *Fear has a negative impact on (a) attachment and (b) commitment toward the brand or magazine.*

**H2**: *Possession has a positive or negative impact on (a) attachment and (b) commitment toward the brand and magazine.*

**H3**: *Plenitude has a positive impact on (a) attachment and (b) commitment toward the brand and magazine.*

The intensity of an emotional attachment with an object may be associated the consumers' willingness to abandon their immediate interests to promote a stronger relationship with the object (Thomson, MacInnis, and Park 2005). That is, "*Consumers' brand emotional attachment predicts their commitment towards this brand and their willingness to make financial sacrifices in order to acquire it*". Lacoeuilhe (2000) also considers attachment a determinant of commitment toward brand, with an emphasis on the importance of dissociating calculated commitment from emotional commitment. Emotional commitment appears more likely to explain the effect of attachment on customer loyalty to brand. Therefore,

**H4**: *Attachment to the brand or magazine mediates the relationship between emotions and commitment to this brand or magazine.*

Figure 2 summarizes these hypotheses.

*2.3. Methodology & results*

To test our model, we used a PLS approach (Tenenhaus et al., 2005). The GoF index reaches .832 for press titles, and .829 for commercial brands. All in all, the total predictive power of attachment, at 49.1 percent and 52.5 percent for magazines and brands, respectively, is much less than that of emotional commitment. Specifically, commitment's predictive power reaches 71.1 percent for magazine readers and 86.3 percent for brand consumers. This result further suggests that brand consumers are more attached and committed to their brands than are magazine readers. Further analyses of *Elle* magazine and the Apple brand, discussed subsequently, support this result.

**Press titles**

In Figure 3, the path coefficients appear in red. The fear dimension negatively influences attachment and commitment to magazines, in support of H1a and H1b. In contrast, plenitude has a positive impact on attachment and commitment toward magazines, in support of H3a and H3b. Possession negatively influences attachment and commitment to magazines, in support of H2a and H2b.

**Figure 2: Research model**

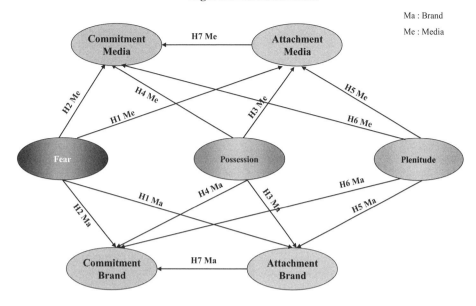

**Figure 3: Path coefficients for media**

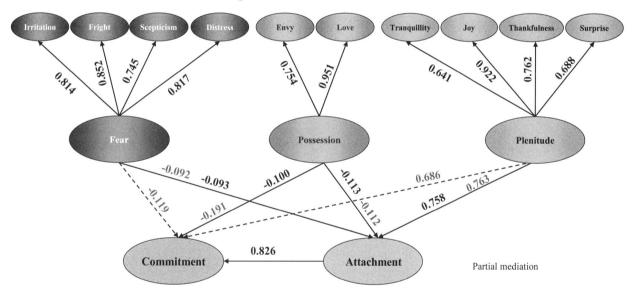

In red : Path coefficients after bootstrap with attachment on one side and commitment on the other side

In black : Path coefficients after bootstrap with attachment antecedent of commitment

In the test of the model with attachment as an antecedent of commitment (path coefficients in black) (Lacoeuille 2000), the results indicate a partial mediating effect of attachment between possession and commitment. Specifically, possession still has a direct influence on commitment to the magazine.

Both fear and plenitude are completely mediated by attachment, in support of H4. Globally, plenitude is the main determinant of attachment and commitment toward magazines. The negative influence of fear seems legitimate, whereas impact of possession is more paradoxical. This result suggests the need for a refined analysis for each magazine individually.

The mediating role of attachment for *Elle* is complete for plenitude and possession (the latter has a positive impact on attachment) and partial for fear. The path coefficient, though weaker, is statistically significant. More than 90 percent of the explicative power

(i.e., contribution to $R^2$) pertains to attachment, despite the partial mediation. This specific analysis of every press title also indicates that the negative influence of possession on all titles is due to the newspaper *Le Monde* (-.227)

**Commercial brands**

Similar to the magazine model, the hypotheses receive validation for brands (path coefficients in red in Figure 4). The impact of possession is positive on attachment and commitment. These results support recent findings regarding the concept of brand love (Albert, Merunka, and Valette-Florence 2008).

Yet this mediating role is complete for brands. The influence of all second-order emotional dimensions on brand commitment indirectly goes through attachment (Figure 4).

**Figure 4: Path coefficients for brands**

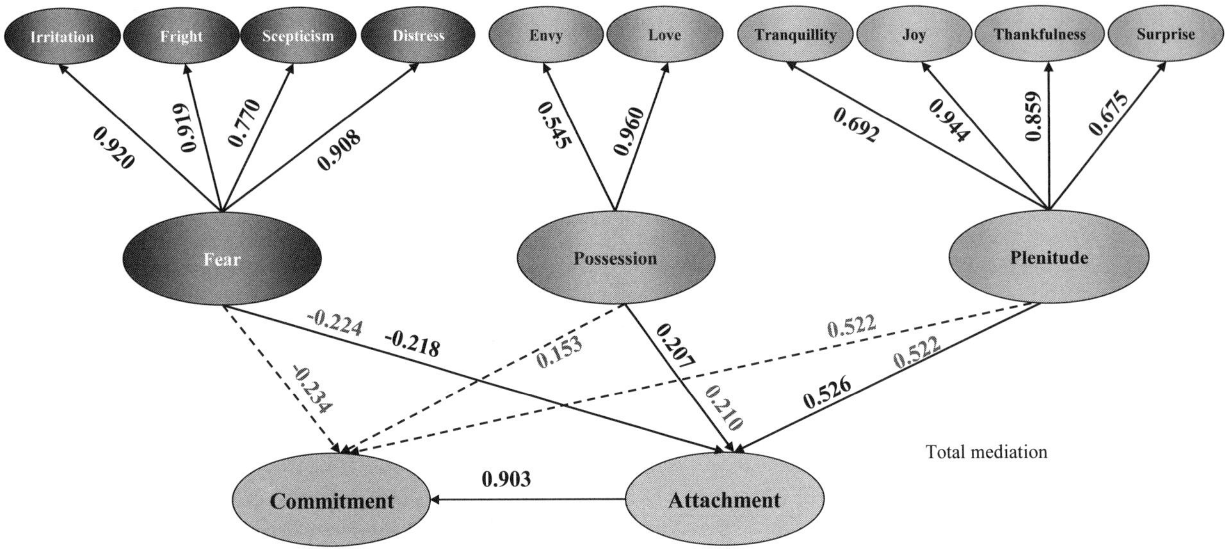

In red : Path coefficients after bootstrap with attachment on one side and commitment on the other side
In black : Path coefficients after bootstrap with attachment antecedent of commitment

As we did for media titles, it seems interesting to test the model with regard to each brand. For example, the analysis of Apple shows a complete mediating effect of attachment. Again, more than 90 percent of the explanatory power is due to the influence of attachment on commitment. In turn, the emotional commitment of Apple consumers to the brand occurs only if they are emotionally attached to the brand. The corresponding possession path coefficient for Apple is approximately .309 (.210 for all the titles). Further analyses of the direct impact of the possession first-order dimensions on attachment reveal that only the love dimension has a positive and significant influence (.314, .046 for envy). This result reemphasizes the role of brand love for Apple consumers (Albert et al., 2008).

**Commercial brands & press title profiles**

Because the purpose of this research also involves the operational appeal of the proposed emotion scale, this section confirms the strong differentiating power of this scale. Table 2 shows the results of latent factor scores variance analysis for the different brands and magazines. They confirm the differentiating power of all scale dimensions. Love and surprise are the most differentiating ones.

Moreover, Duncan's test (not shown here to preserve space) identifies, for each dimension, the brands and magazines that have the same, different, or close profiles. The brands reflect various different means; for example, *Benetton* achieves a strong profile on fear, whereas *Apple* and *Carte Noire* score higher on possession (due to consumers' strong emotional commitment to *Apple* and the seduction-based advertising strategy of *Carte Noire*). In contrast, the magazine profiles are generally similar, except that *Elle* and *Géo* are stronger on love and envy. The informational character of *Le Monde* distinguishes it on all dimensions, and *L'Equipe* appears close to the other magazines.

Figure 5 reveals that consumers perceive irritation, fear, scepticism, and distress as less predominantly emotional traits, but that surprise, thankfulness, love, tranquillity, and especially joy are the most important emotional traits. Consumers' emotional brand profiles are identical to their emotional magazine profiles, though some differences appear, especially for the second-order dimensions of fear, which consists of fright, scepticism, irritation, and distress. These dimensions have greater impacts on magazines than on brands, whereas all the other dimensions, especially love, are more important for brands than for magazine titles.

**Table 2: Variance analyses, F-tests (p < .05)**

| Dimensions | Love | Surprise | Joy | Scepticism | Fright | Irritation | Envy | Thankfulness | Tranquillity | Distress |
|---|---|---|---|---|---|---|---|---|---|---|
| F | 17,44 | 8,09 | 7,18 | 5,95 | 5,74 | 5,10 | 4,41 | 4,37 | 3,36 | 2,92 |

Finally, in terms of their emotional proximity, *Apple* coexists better with *Géo* rather than *Le Monde* (Figure 6). However, only a study of *Apple* consumers who are also *Géo* or *Le Monde* readers could confirm this claim.

**4. Discussion, limitations & future research**

This research attempts to confirm that brands generate emotions, which could constitute the basis of an affective route (emotions–attachment–emotional commitment). This research also reveals that specific media titles, as brands, can prompt emotions. An empirical approach creates and validates an emotion scale applicable to both

brands and media titles that outperforms existing emotion scales (Holbrook and Batra 1987; Richins 1997).

In addition, the test of the research model reveals the partial or total mediating effect of attachment on emotional commitment, as well as the role of positive (plenitude) and negative (fear) emotions on attachment and emotional commitment for each brand and media title studied. Moreover, the validated emotions scale suggests a variety of applications. Brand and media managers now have a new, qualitative instrument with real action levers that they can use to enhance customer's attachment and commitment towards brands. Measuring the emotions provoked while reading a magazine title and assessing their coherence with the emotions activated by exposure

Figure 5: Brands and magazine profiles

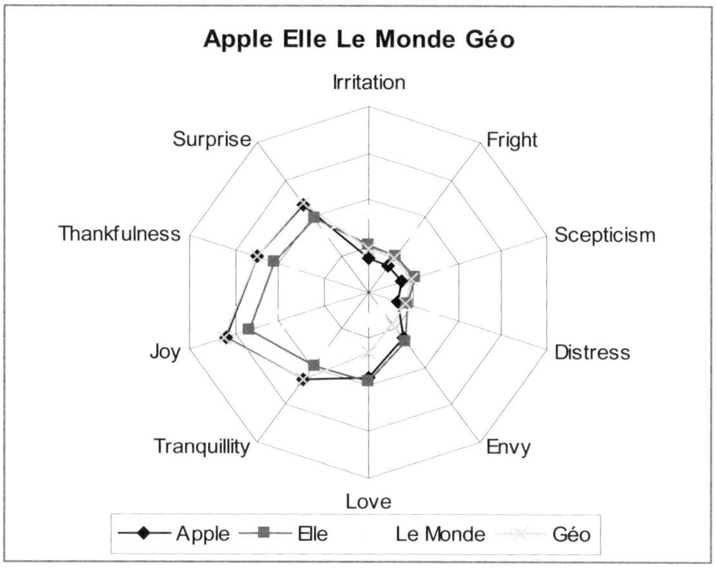

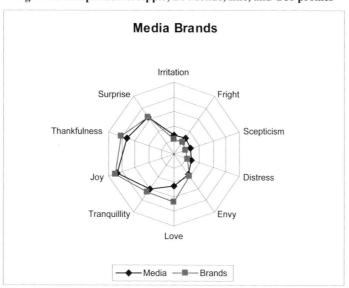

Figure 6: Comparison of Apple, Le Monde, Elle, and Géo profiles

to advertised brands offers a valid measure of the qualitative affinity between media titles and brands. Finally, managers should opt for strategies that emphasize the positive emotions activated during brand consumption or media reading to compete better.

As usual, this research suffers from several limitations, including the small sample size and questions of its representativeness. Other affective relational concepts, such as brand love (Albert, Merunka and Valette-Florence, 2008) or identification (Escalas, 2004) also could have been integrated into our model. Additional research therefore should attempt to advance understanding of the emotional qualitative affinity between brands and media (i.e., when people are both brand consumers and media readers). It also will be important to test various publications and media categories, including different forms such as radio and television. This extension could suggest better and more precise media selections for advertisers.

Another interesting avenue for future research would be to explicitly test that the media context of a given ad may lead to different emotions, and hence to changes in attachment and commitment. In addition, an experiment could show that the same ad may elicit different feelings or emotions when printed in different outlets. For instance, it could be interesting to compare Ab and Aad for an *Apple* ad incorporated within *Elle* vs. *Geo*.

## REFERENCES

Aaker, David A., Douglas M. Stayman, and Richard Vezina (1988), "Identifying feelings elicited by advertising", *Psychology & Marketing*, 5 (1), 1-16.

Aaker, Jennifer L., and Susan M. Fournier (1995), "A brand as a character, partner, and person: three perspectives on the question of brand personality," *Advances in Consumer Research,* 22, 391-395.

Adelaar, Thomas, Susan Chang, Karen M. Lancendorfer, Byoung-kwan Lee, and Mariko Morimoto (2003), "Effects of media formats on emotions and impulse buying intent," *Journal of Information Technology*, 18 (4), 247-266.

Allen, Natalie J., and John P. Meyer (1990), "The measurement and antecedents of affective, continuance and normative commitment to the organization," *Journal of Occupational Psychology*, 63, 1-18.

Albert, Noel, Dwight Merunka, and Pierre Valette-Florence (2008), "When consumers love their brands: Exploring the concept and its dimensions," *Journal of Business Research*, 61 (10), 1062-1075.

Bagozzi, Richard P., Mahesh Gopinath, and Prashanth U. Nyer (1999), "The role of emotions in marketing", *Journal of the Academy of Marketing Science*, 27 (2), 184-206.

Ball, Dwayne and Lori H. Tasaki (1992), "The role and measurement of attachment in consumer behaviour," *Journal of Consumer Psychology*, 1, 155-72.

Bansal, Harvir S., Gregory P. Irving, and Shirley F. Taylor (2004), "A Three-Component Model of Customer Commitment to Service Providers," *Journal of the Academy of Marketing Science*, 32 (3), 234-50.

Batra, Rajeev and Morris B. Holbrook (1990), "Developing a typology of affective responses to advertising," *Psychology & Marketing*, 7 (1), 11-25.

Batra, Rajeev and Michael L. Ray (1986), "Affective responses mediating acceptance of advertising," *Journal of Consumer Research*, 13 (2), 234-249.

Belk, Russel (1988), "Possessions and the extended self," *Journal of Consumer Research*, 15 (3), 139-61.

Berscheid, Ellen, and Elaine Walster (1978), *Interpersonal Attraction*, MA : Addison-Wesley.

Chaudhuri, Arjun (2006), *Emotion and Reason in Consumer Behavior*, Oxford: Elsevier.

Chaudhuri, Arjun and Morris B. Holbrook (2001), "The chain of effects from brand trust and brand affect to brand performance: The role of brand loyalty.", *Journal of Marketing*, 65, 81-93

Chaudhuri, Arjun and Morris B. Holbrook (2002), "Product-class effects on brand commitment and brand outcomes: the role of brand trust and brand affect," *Brand Management*, 10 (1), 33-58.

Derbaix, Christian and Ingrid Poncin (2005), "La mesure des réactions affectives en marketing: Évaluation des principaux outils," *Recherche et Applications en Marketing*, 20 (2), 55-76.

Edmunds, Holly (1999), The Focus Group Research Handbook, Chicago, IL: NTC Business Books and American Marketing Association.

Escalas, Jennifer (2004), « Narrative processing building consumer connections to brands," *Journal of Consumer Psychology*, 14 (1/2), 168-80

Ferrandi, Jean-Marc, Virginie De Barnier, and Pierre Valette-Florence (2003), "Emotions and Advertising : A Preliminary Test of Richins'Consumption Emotion Set" *Summer Marketing Educators' Conference*, 319-324.

Fornell, Claes and David F. Larcker (1981), "Evaluating structural equation models with unobservable variables and measurement error", *Journal of Marketing Research*, 18 (1), 39-50.

Fournier, Susan M. (1998), "Consumers and their brands: developing relationship theory in consumer research," *Journal of Consumer Research*, 24 (4), 343-373.

Fullerton, Gordon (2003), "When does commitment lead to loyalty?", *Journal of Service Research*, 5 (4), 333-44.

Fullerton, Gordon (2005), "The Impact of Brand Commitment on Loyalty to Retail Service Brands Canadian," *Journal of Administrative Sciences*, 22 (2), 97-110.

Gundlach, Gregory T., Ravi S. Achrol, and John T. Mentzer (1995), "The structure of commitment in exchange," *Journal of Marketing*, 59 (1), 78-92.

Hakansson, Hakan (1982), International Marketing and Purchasing of Industrial Goods: An Interaction Approach, New York: John Wiley & sons.

Holbrook, Morris B. and Rajeev Batra (1987), "Assessing the role of emotions as mediators of consumer responses to advertising", *Journal of Consumer Research*, 14 (3), 404-420.

Holbrook, Morris B. and Elizabeth C. Hirschman (1982), "The experiential aspects of consumption: Consumer fantasies, feelings, and fun", *Journal of Consumer Research*, 9 (2), 132-140.

Hu, Li-Tze and Peter M. Bentler (1998), "Fit indices in covariance structure modelling: Sensitivity to underparameterized model misspecification," *Psychological Methods*, 3, 424-453.

Lacoeuilhe, Jérôme (2000), "L'attachement à la marque: Proposition d'une échelle de mesure," *Recherche et Applications en Marketing*, 15 (4), 61-77.

Lazarus, R. S. (1991), Emotion and Adaptation, New York: Oxford University Press.

McAlexander, James H., Stephen K. Kim, and Scott D. Roberts (2003), "Loyalty : the influences of satisfaction and brand community integration," *Journal of Marketing Theory and Practice*, 11 (4), 1-11.

McQueen, Josh, Carol Foley, and John Deighton (1993), "Decomposing a brand's Consumer Franchise into Buyer Types", in *Brand equity and Advertising*, David Aaker and Alexander Biel, eds. NJ: Hillsdale: Lawrence Erlbaum Associates, 235-45.

Meyer, John P., Natalie J. Allen, and Ian R. Gellatly (1990), "Affective and Continuance Commitment to the Organization : Evaluation of Measure and Analysis of Concurrent and Time-lagged Relations," *Journal of Applied Psychology*, 75 (6), 710-20.

Morgan, Robert M., and Shelby D. Hunt (1994), "The Commitment-trust Theory of Relationship Marketing," *Journal of Marketing*, 58, 20-38.

Mowday, Richard T., Richard M. Steers, and Lyman W. Porter (1979), "The measurement of organizational commitment," *Journal of Vocational Behavior*, 14, 224-247.

Murry, John P. and Peter A. Dacin (1996), "Cognitive moderators of negative-emotion effects: Implications for understanding media context", *Journal of Consumer Research*, 22, 439-447.

Oliver, Richard L. (1992), "An investigation of the attribute basis of emotion and related affects in consumption: Suggestions for a stage-specific satisfaction framework," *Advances in Consumer Research*, 19, 237-244.

Pieters, Rik G. M. and W. Fred Van Raaij (1988), "Functions and management of affect: Application to economic behaviour," *Journal of Economic Psychology*, 9, 251-282.

Pines, Ayala M. and Ariella Friedman (1998), "Gender differences in romantic jealousy," *Journal of Social Psychology*, 138 (1), 54-71.

Richins, Marsha L. (1997), "Measuring emotions in the consumption experience," *Journal of Consumer Research*, 24 (2), 127-146.

Roseman, Ira J. (1991), "Appraisal determinants of discrete emotions", *Cognition and Emotion*, 5, 161-200.

Simpson, Jeffrey A., W. Andrew Collins, Sisi Tran, and Katherine C. Haydon (2007), Attachment and the Experience and Expression of Emotions in Romantic Relationships: A Developmental Perspective, *Journal of Personality and Social Psychology*, 92, 2, 355-367.

Tenenhaus, Michel, Vincenzo Esposito Vinzi, Yves-Marie Chatelin, and Carlo Lauro (2005), "PLS path modeling," *Computational Statistics & Data Analysis*, 48, 159-205.

Thomson, Matthew, Deborah J. MacInnis, and C. Whan Park (2005), « Les liens attachants : mesurer la force de l'attachement émotionnel des consommateur à la marque, » *Recherche et Applications en Marketing*, 20 (1), 79-98.

Vanhuele, Marc (1994), "Mere exposure and the cognitive-affective debate revisited", *Advances in Consumer Research*, 21, 811-821.

Westbrook, Robert A. and Richard L. Oliver (1991), "The dimensionality of consumption emotion patterns and consumer satisfaction," *Journal of Consumer Research*, 12 (June), 84-91.

Zajonc, Robert B. (1980), "Feeling and thinking: Preferences need no inferences," *American Psychologist*, 35, 151-175.

Zajonc, Robert B. and Hazel Markus (1982), "Affective and cognitive factors in preferences," *Journal of Consumer Research*, 9, 123-131.

# Consumer's Perceived Control
## A Critical Review and a Research Agenda

Renaud Lunardo, Troyes Champagne School of Management, France

## ABSTRACT

The inconsistent results about the influence of perceived control on consumer behavior raised questions regarding its conceptualization and the need to consider desire for control when modeling its influence. This paper presents a review of past research on perceived control and offers a propositional agenda for further research.

## INTRODUCTION

There is virtual consensus among researchers that individuals' understanding of how much control they can exert over their behavior has been shown to affect how they behave and how they evaluate themselves and the environment (Rotter 1966). Despite the term "control" has been used and defined in a multitude of ways, it is often referred to as "the belief that one can determine one's own internal states and behavior, influence one's environment, and/or bring about desired outcomes" (Wallston et al. 1987, 5). As such, perceived control has been studied in a wide number of fields, from psychology to medicine (Skinner 1996). It has been demonstrated to be an important driver of behavior, resulting in more performance of behavior. For instance, in the field of psychology, empirical evidence testing prominent theories, including the theory of reasoned action (Fishbein 1967) and the learned helplessness model (Seligman 1975), has shown that perceived control exerts a significant influence on human well-being (Langer and Rodin, 1976), task performance (Geer, Davison, and Gatchel 1970), anxiety (Staub, Tursky and Schwartz 1971) and stress (Lazarus and Folkman 1984; Paterson and Neufeld 1995).

It was not until the 1990s that perceived control made its first appearance in consumer-related studies (Hui and Bateson 1991). Relying on Mehrabian and Russell's (1974) approach to environmental psychology by conceptualizing perceived control as an affective response to the environment – the emotion of dominance – the study of perceived control in consumer research intensified with the emergence of emotions as a component of the consumer experience (Holbrook and Hirschman, 1982) and new conceptualizations of servicescapes (Bitner 1992). Despite a high criticism of the most frequently used perceived control measure – the Dominance subscale of the PAD (Mehrabian and Russell 1974) – inclusion of perceived control in consumer research continued unabated.

However, significant perceived control findings in consumer research have sometimes been rare or contradictory, leading some suggest that the inclusion of perceived control in consumer research is unproductive and should be abandoned (Russell and Pratt 1980; Yani-de-Soriano and Foxall 2006). Several reasons have emerged to explain the lack of significant findings. For example, some have suggested that the problems may come from the inappropriate use of terms resulting in conceptual ambiguity.

Given these concerns, the purpose of this paper is to present a thorough review of consumer behavior studies in the marketing literature that have examined perceived control. The review is grounded in the theoretical models from several fields, from social psychology to marketing, with the specific goal of providing a framework to address the question: "To what extent are differences in perceived control useful in explaining meaningful variations among consumer behaviors?" Addressing this question will help clarify whether enthusiasm or skepticism about perceived control research in consumer behavior is warranted, and, if warranted, what direction(s) future research should take.

## PERCEIVED CONTROL AS A PSYCHOLOGICAL CONSTRUCT

A wide set of different terms, signifying essentially the same thing, have been used over the course of perceived control research. The perceived control construct has been called by "many different things, including, besides control, self-directedness, choice, decision freedom, agency, mastery, autonomy, self-efficacy, and self-determination" (Rodin 1990, 1). Meanwhile, as the definition has broadened, the precision of the meaning has lessened, leading to a surprising heterogeneity among the constructs researchers use to describe perceived control (Skinner 1996). Thus, a literature review is needed to provide a clear and unambiguous definition of the subject under analysis. With respect to this particular literature review, it requires not only understanding what perceived control is, but also understanding how it is related to, yet different from, other control terminology.

Contributing to the inconsistent use of terminology is the fact that the term "control" is not similarly treated in both psychology and marketing. In psychology, the history of research on perceived control is a long one, involving many different general theoretical frameworks and a host of specific constructs, including locus of control, causal attributions, and self-efficacy (Skinner 1995). From Rotter's (1966) general social learning theory came the construct of locus of control (LOC), which refers to people's perceptions about whether or not their behaviors are reliably linked to outcomes. An internal locus of control is the belief that they are, and an external locus of control is the belief that they are not. Despite hundreds of studies dealing with the influence of the LOC on behavior, theorists have pointed out that perceptions of control may not only result from the contingency between their actions and the outcomes, but also from the explanation one gives for why that is so. In other words, it is not uncontrollability per se, but the attributions individuals make for a perceived noncontingency between actions and outcomes that influence behavior (Weiner et al. 1972). Thus, locus of control and causal attributions are quite similar by both referring to control in terms of subjective beliefs about the extent to which certain causes lead to success and failure. However, they must not be confounded since they differ in terms of stability. Indeed, the causes to which individuals attribute events can be arrayed along three main dimensions: internality, stability and controllability, and while locus of control only relies on the dimension of internality, attribution relies also on stability. During the attribution process, the more an outcome is attributed to stable causes, the greater the weight that will be given to that outcome in determining predictions for the future.

Although in both of the preceding conceptualizations perceptions of control are products of external conditions (here, the degree of contingency between actions and outcomes), they also can refer to individual actions. In this case, perceived control results from individual efforts to achieve a goal (White 1959). These perceptions of control are sometimes referred to as feelings of efficacy (Bandura 1977). Self-efficacy appears to be similar to the perceived behavioral facet of control, one of the three facets of control identified by Averill (1973) who distinguished between behavioral, cognitive, and decisional control. Referring here to "the availability of a response which may directly influence or modify the objective characteristics of a threatening event" (286-287), it can also refer to the ease or difficulty of performing a behavior, or to the confidence in one's ability to perform, as in the Theory of Planned Behavior (Ajzen 1991, 2002). In a review of papers that have assessed perceived control, Ajzen (2002, 6) highlights that a common operationalization is "for me to perform behavior x would be very easy / difficult". When also reviewing papers that contrasted self-efficacy and perceived control, self-efficacy is frequently operationalized as "for me to engage in behavior x would be easy/difficult", which is the same as the definition of perceived control. As noted by Ajzen (2002), perceived behavioral control and self-efficacy are quite similar since both are concerned with perceived ability to perform a behavior, leading to a considerable conceptual overlap in the operationalizations of both the constructs of self-efficacy and perceived control. Thus, a challenge to addressing the question of the role of perceived behavioral control concerns the imprecision with which this construct and self-efficacy are used in research. It seems clear that most researchers tend to use these terms interchangeably, even if they have distinctive qualities.

Despite those numerous conceptualizations discussed in psychology, perceived control is in marketing surprisingly often referred to as an emotion. In contrast with conceptualizations that see control as a durable learning process – such as the LOC – the perceived control literature in consumer research explicitly defines control in terms of dominance, an affective response to the environment (Mehrabian and Russell 1974). As such, dominance represents "the extent a person feels powerful vis-a-vis the environment that surrounds him" (Russell and Mehrabian 1976, 6), ranging from extreme feelings of lack of control upon one's surroundings to feelings of being influential and powerful, or in control. In other words, the positive pole is defined as the disposition to assume the lead, to take control, and to direct or influence others. The opposite pole represents the disposition to submit to authority, to follow orders and to comply with demands (Lorr 1991). People experience control in a particular setting when they feel that the environment facilitates goal achievement, whereas they feel a lack of control when the environment prevents them from achieving their goals (Lunardo and Mbengue 2009; Ward and Barnes 2001).

## PERCEIVED CONTROL: AN IMPORTANT DRIVER OF CONSUMER BEHAVIOR

The Theory of Learned Heplnessness (Seligman 1975) and the Theory of Planned Behavior (Ajzen 1991, 2002) have widely been used in psychology to explain the consequences of control on behavior. They both posit that a perception of control can motivate individuals to engage in a behavior. As a result of the use of these theories, a large body of theory and evidence is available to show that perceived control is a powerful predictor of emotions and behavior. The purposes of this section are to draw upon these theories and marketing research to identify antecedents of perceived control and to demonstrate how perceived control can motivate consumers to engage in a behavior.

### Perceived Control as the Consequence of Predictability, Choice and Crowding

Existing literature suggests that the most prominent antecedents of perceived control are predictability and choice (Skinner 1996). In fact, some theorists so strongly believe that these constructs are antecedents of control that they have labeled them predictive control and decisional control.

The ability to predict events in the environment has been found to be important for the comfort and safety of organisms. Predictability refers to being informed about things, anticipating what may happen, feeling certain about the outcome, or anticipating potential problems (Troup and Dewe 2002). Existing evidence in psychol-

ogy shows that the ability to predict events increases feelings of control and in turn reduces tension or anxiety (Staub et al. 1971). In consumer research, Holt (1995) has showed how predictability of action by spectators in professional Baseball enhances perceptions of control: by predicting action on the field, spectators enhance the perception that they are involved in the game's production and so how they interject some control over the game.

Unlike predictability, choice as an antecedent of perceived control has been studied in research examining the mediating role of perceived control on the effect of density and choice on consumer's emotional feelings during the service encounter (Hui and Bateson 1991). As found out by the authors from an experiment including two service settings, a bank and a bar, results showed that when consumers have choice (the perception that an outcome is caused by a person's own decision, Hui and Bateson 1991, 175), it increases decisional control and results in positive outcomes, leading authors to conclude that "perceived control is a powerful concept in explaining the consumer's reactions to consumer density in the service environment" (182). Other studies also demonstrate that consumer choice in the traditional retail setting results in more consumer's perceived control (Chang, 2006). However, studies indicate that the relationship between choice and perceived control is complex, and that giving control through more choice may not be as desirable as it seems at first. For instance, Wathieu et al. (2002) suggest that choice can be considered a predictor of perceived control only if the consumer has the ability to specify and adjust the choice context.

In a more setting-specific point of view, perceived control has also been seen as resulting from density. Because density can facilitate or obstruct desired behaviors, it can determine the individual's perceptions of crowding which in turn negatively affect perceived control (Schmidt and Keating 1979; Hui and Bateson 1991). A study conducted by Langer and Saegart (1977) showed that those negative effects of crowding can be reduced by information that give individuals cognitive control of the situation. In contrast to the negative relationship between perceived crowding and perceived control, the sign of the relationship between density and perceived control can vary according to settings. For instance, Hui and Bateson (1991) found out that in a bank setting, high density is associated with lower perceived control, while in a bar setting it is associated with higher control. Such results give support to the assumption that perceived control can be used to explain the emotional and behavioral effects of density according to settings.

### The Wide Range of Effects of Perceived Control on Consumer's Behavior

Perceived control in psychological research has been found to exert influence on a wide set of responses. As noted by Skinner (1996, 556), "when people perceive that they have a high degree of control, they exert effort, try hard, initiate action, and persist in the face of failures and setbacks (…). When people perceive control as impossible, they withdraw, retreat, escape, or otherwise become passive; they become fearful, depressed, pessimistic, and distressed." Briefly, it is acknowledged that when people are exposed to uncontrollable environments, they exhibit a variety of negative behavioral responses. In contrast, when they believe that they can personally control the environment, their performance is less affected.

As a multidimensional concept, perceived control in consumer research has been related to many constructs. When referring to the LOC, it has been found to have a significant influence on search (Srinivasan and Tikoo 1992), internals perceiving greater benefits to search and find the purchase process less stressful. It also has influence of the service encounter evaluation: when customers perceive the cause of service failure to be within the control of the firm, they will be more dissatisfied than when the firm is perceived to have less control (Leong, Ang and Hui Lin Low 1997; Van Raaij and Pruyn 1998).

Despite studies referring as perceived control through the LOC or through the more specific perceived behavioral facet (Kidwell and Jewell 2003; Lwin and Williams 2003; Nysveen, Pedersen and Thorbjornsen 2005; Kang et al. 2006), the largest segment of consumer research on perceived control refers to dominance, especially in retail and service setting literatures. Perceived control has been found to have an impact on consumer self-confidence (Bearden, Hardesty and Rose 2001), pleasure (Hui and Bateson 1991), mood, involvement (Ward and Barnes 2001), satisfaction (Wathieu et al. 2002; Navasimayam and Hinkin 2003) and intention to behave (Mathur 1998). In retail studies involving either crowding (Dion 2004; Van Rompay et al. 2008) or arousal (Lunardo and Mbengue 2009) as aversive stimuli, perceived control has also been proved to be related to stress and coping strategies. Results show that no simple relationship exists between perceived control and stress, along with Averill (1973, 300-301) who suggested that "the stress-inducing or stress-reducing properties of personal control depend upon the meaning of the control response for the individual".

Although significant results have been found out, two major criticisms can be raised. First, studies rely on measures of dominance that have been rejected by several researchers due to lack of psychometric qualities. Second, quite surprisingly, studies investigating the effect of control do not consider if the control is actually desired by consumers. The next section addresses these issues.

## THE NEED FOR FURTHER RESEARCH

Given that perceived control is not well understood, and often misunderstood, there is a pressing need for further research. The remainder of this article sets forth a series of issues that collectively can serve as the foundation for a perceived control research agenda. Two main future research directions are presented. The first relates to the conceptualization and operationalization of perceived control, the second to the need to consider individual differences in the desire for control. These issues impact the theoretical framework within which future studies will be designed.

### Beyond Perceived Control as an Emotion in Consumer Research: Interests and Limitations

Although the dominance has proved useful in the contexts for which it was developed, several limitations in its application to the consumer research must be recognized. It is our position and the position of other authors (Russell and Pratt 1980; Yani-de-Soriano and Foxall 2006) that dominance is not always an appropriate operationalization of the perceived control concept. This conclusion is based on four main considerations, all relying on that perceived can not only be viewed as an emotion.

First, in the wide range of usages of the expression "perceived control", it is often referred to as a belief. According to Skinner (1995), the term "belief" is appropriate since it is open to revision. Beliefs can refer to the future or the past, and be used at any level of generality from the most situation specific to the most global. Since emotions are transient phenomena, they cannot refer to such beliefs, and thus can not refer to perceived control.

Second, when defined as an emotion, perceived control is not seen global but rather context specific, and would differ according to contexts. As such, it can only refer to specific situations and not at a more general level. Thus, while general consumer's perceived control should be able to predict tendencies, consumer's dominance would only predict more specific responses.

Third, Clore, Ortony, and Foss (1987) excluded from the domain of emotion those descriptors that refer to subjective evaluations of people. However, in the psychological literature, perceived control widely refers to subjective evaluations. For instance, locus of control can be seen as subjective beliefs about the extent to which certain causes lead to success and failure, and perceived behavioral control refers to the subjective evaluation of being able to adopt a behavior. Thus, if subjective evaluation can not be conceptualized as emotions, nor can perceived control.

Fourth, when perceived control is considered an emotion, researchers use the 6-item dominance subscale of the Mehrabian and Russell's (1974) PAD model (Pleasure-Arousal-Dominance). Notwithstanding its popularity and widespread application, the dominance subscale has been subjected to a number of theoretical and operational criticisms (Yani-de-Soriano and Foxall 2006). Two main problems regarding the use of dominance as a measure of perceived control remain unresolved. First, as mentioned by Yani-de-Soriano and Foxall (2006), Russell (1978) did not found support for dominance. About 46% of the variance in dominance could be predicted from the other two emotions (pleasure and arousal), leading to consider dominance as confounded with pleasure. This overlap between dominance and pleasure makes dominance be in the PAD the factor that contributes the least to variance in approach-avoidance behavior, accounting only for 14% of the total variance while pleasure accounted for 27% and arousal for 23%. Those problems have led numerous researchers to eliminate the semantic differential format (Babin and Darden 1995), to delete items from the original scale to replace them by ad hoc items (Donovan and Rossiter 1982), to create their own scale (Hui and Bateson 1991), or even to delete the variable in their study (Donovan et al. 1994). Second, the validity of the scale in assessing emotional responses to other stimuli, as interpersonal aspects of shopping, is not assumed (Yani-de-Soriano and Foxall 2006).

Thus, the conceptualization of perceived control as dominance poses research directions. It does not capture the complex nature of the perceived control concept, and its measure has not been proven of quality. However, operationalizing perceived control not as dominance but as a multidimensional concept would also pose research directions. First, because of the multiplicity of perceived control constructs, people may have complex understandings of the many facets of control. Thus, in terms of measurement, researchers should be explicit in their assessments of control if they want to operationalize their constructs successfully. For instance, researchers may be willing to use items like "Did you have any control over outcome Y?" or "To what extent did you feel you had control over outcome Y". Such measures may result in answers that reflect different constructs, such as perceptions of control, a sense of effectiveness, or even, when the outcome is negative, feelings of responsibility or self-blame (Skinner 1996). Thus, researchers should precise if they aim at measuring global or specific dimensions of perceived control. To cope with this problem, researchers may use one of the different measures of facets of perceived control. Among the three distinct dimensions of perceived control identified by Averill (1973), behavioral and cognitive controls are dimensions for which a scale already exists. Regarding perceived behavioral control, Ajzen (2002, 6) provides a list of scales for which the internal consistencies or reliabilities range from 0.61 to 0.90. Concerning cognitive control, Faranda (2001) developed a 7-item, two-dimensional and reliable scale (a dimension of self-control with an alpha of 0.82 and a dimension of informational control with an alpha of 0.93). To date, only the decisional dimension cannot yet be measured due to a lack of measure of quality. This analysis of marketing studies that assessed perceived control suggests that it is possible to obtain reliable and valid measures of perceived control, but this is not assured and care must be taken in the formative stages of the research to explicitly formulate what form of perceived control the researchers aims at measuring.

**Does Everybody Want to Control? The Need to Include Individual Differences Variables in the Desire for Control**

Not all individuals react identically to issues of personal control. Although most individuals have a strong desire to obtain control over important environmental outcomes, individual differences in the motivation for control exist. As noted by Burger (1989), consumers may sometimes not desire feeling in control over specific situations. This desire for control has been defined as "a stable personality trait reflecting the extent to which individuals generally are motivated to control events in their lives" (Burger 1985, 1520). As pointed out by Burger and Cooper (1979), these individual differences in the motivation for control should help account for variation in behavior. According to them, individuals high in the desire for control are more assertive, decisive, active, and seek to influence others when such influence is advantageous. They prefer to avoid unpleasant situations or failures by manipulating events to ensure desired outcomes. On the contrary, indivudals low in the desire for control are generally nonassertive, passive, indecisive, and are less likely to attempt to influence others and may prefer that many of their daily decisions be made by others.

In consumer research, desire for control has been shown to affect behavior, especially when linked to locus of control. For instance, in a lottery context, because individuals with an internal locus think they have the ability to affect the outcomes of events in their lives, they are more likely to perceive ability to influence lottery outcomes by choosing winning numbers. As a result, they are more likely to continue to play a lottery in the face of losses (Sprott, Brumbaugh and Miyazaki 2001).

However, only a few researchers included desire for control in their studies. For example, in the study of the impact of human and spatial density on the consumer's emotional and behavioral responses, only the study of Van Rompay et al. (2008) among a wide number of studies on this topic (Dion 2004; Eroglu and Harrell 1986; Eroglu and Machleit 1990; Eroglu, Machleit and Chebat 2005; Machleit, Eroglu and Mantel 2000) explicitly included the desire for control to explain the influence of control. The authors showed that the effects of human and spatial density vary with consumers' desire for control: consumers high in desire for control react to high human density with negative affect and less approach behaviors, whereas consumers low in desire for control do not respond with negative affect. Not explicitly including the desire for control construct but the motivational orientation, Lunardo and Mbengue (2009) found out similar results in a study examining the impact of perceived control on shopping behavior. Since utilitarian consumer behavior has been described as task related, the authors suggest that utilitarian-oriented consumers prefer stores in which the environmental stimuli enhance their feeling of control. From a field study, their results showed that for highly utilitarian-oriented consumers, a perception of lack of control leads to an increase in stress, while this effect is not exhibited for low utilitarian-oriented shoppers.

## CONCLUSION

Even though widely discussed, perceived control is not well understood, and the term itself is often abused and misused. In psychology, the expression "perceived control" can either refer to locus of control, self-efficacy or the multidimensional concept of perceived control. Such a case in which the same term is used to refer to very different constructs is confusing, and may lead to ambiguous results in research. In consumer behavior, researchers mostly rely on Mehrabian and Russell's (1974) dominance, the extent to which an individual feels in control over his environment. By defining perceived control in this manner, the definition can be used by retailers for which the influence of the store environment on consumer's perceived control can be of great importance. However, problems related to this conceptualization still exist. Thus, the purpose of this paper was to outline an agenda for further research around the theme of consumer's perceived control.

Two future research directions were presented, one dealing with the emotional conceptualization of control, the other addressing the need to include individual differences in the "desire for control". Considering the issue of measure, future research should address an underestimated aspect of perceived control in consumer research, the discriminant validity of the construct. Research should explore how perceived control differs from a number of similar constructs already under scrutiny in consumer behavior, such as self-confidence, or persuasion knowledge. The development of scales aiming at measuring perceived control over specific stimuli also warrants consideration. This would allow perceived control to be included in consumer research to explain how marketing stimuli may lead to a feeling of being controlled offers an interesting area for additional research. In retailing research, it would lead to a better understanding of the conditions under which atmospheric stimuli such as music, color or scents may increase consumer's feeling of being controlled by the retailer through the atmosphere. This issue is especially important considering the numerous stimuli used by retailers to control consumer's behavior in the servicescapes (Bitner 1992).

Considering the individual differences in the desire for control, Von Rompay et al. (2008) found that desire for control moderates the effects of human and spatial density on perceived control, which in turns affects consumer's behavior. It would be of interest to determine whether consumers with higher desire for control, as compared to those with lower levels of desire for control, are more willing to adopt approach-behavior when feeling in control over other stimuli than density in retail settings. Further, the effect of stimuli in online settings could be investigated to get a deep understanding on their effects on perceived control and behavior.

## REFERENCES

Ajzen, Icek (1991), "The Theory of Planned Behavior," *Organizational Behavior and Decision Human Processes*, 50 (2), 179–211.

Ajzen, Icek (2002), "Perceived Behavioral Control, Self-Efficacy, Locus of Control, and the Theory of Planned Behavior," *Journal of Applied Social Psychology*, 32 (4), 665–83.

Averill, James R. (1973), "Personal Control over Aversive Stimuli and its Relationship to Stress," *Psychological bulletin*, 80 (4), 286–303.

Babin, Barry J. and William R. Darden (1995), "Consumer Self-Regulation in a Retail Environment," *Journal of Retailing*, 71 (1), 47–70.

Bandura, Albert (1977), "Self-Efficacy: Toward a Unified Theory of Behavioral Change", *Psychological Review*, 84 (2), 191–215.

Bearden William O., David. M. Hardesty, and Randall L. Rose (2001), "Consumer Self-Confidence: Refinements in Conceptualization and Measurement," *Journal of Consumer Research*, 28 (1), 121–34.

Bitner, Mari-Jo. (1992), "Servicescapes: The Impact of Physical Surroundings on Customers and Employees," *Journal of Marketing*, 56 (2), 57–71.

Burger, Jerry M. (1985), "Desire for Control and Achievement-Related Behaviors," *Journal of Personality and Social Psychology*, 48 (6), 1520–33.

Burger, Jerry M. (1989), "Negative Reactions to Increases in Perceived Personal Control," *Journal of Personality and Social Psychology*, 56 (2), 246–56.

Chang, Chia-Chi (2006), "When Service Fails: The Role of the Salesperson and the Customer," *Psychology & Marketing*, 23 (3), 203–24.

Clore, Gerald L., Andrew Ortony, and Mark A. Foss (1987), "The Psychological Foundations of the Affective Lexicon", *Journal of Personality and Social Psychology*, 53 (4), 751–66.

Dion, Delphine (2004), "Personal Control and Coping with Retail Crowding," *International Journal of Service Industry Management*, 15 (3), 250–63.

Donovan, Robert J. and John R. Rossiter (1982), "Store Atmosphere: An Environmental Psychology Approach," *Journal of Retailing*, 58 (1), 34–57.

Donovan, Robert J., John R. Rossiter, Gilian Marcoolyn, and Andrew Nesdale (1994), "Store Atmosphere and Purchasing Behavior," *Journal of Retailing*, 70 (3), 283–94.

Eroglu, Sevgin A. and Harrell, G. D. (1986), "Retail Crowding: Theoretical and Strategic Implications," *Journal of Retailing*, 62 (4), 346–63.

Eroglu, Sevgin A and Karen A. Machleit (1990), "An Empirical Study of Retail Crowding: Antecedents and Consequences," *Journal of Retailing*, 66 (2), 201–21.

Eroglu, Sevgin A., Karen A. Machleit, and Jean-Charles Chebat (2005), "The Interaction of Retail Density and Music Tempo: Effects on Shopper Responses," *Psychology & Marketing*, 22 (7), 577–89.

Faranda, William T. (2001), "A scale to Measure the Cognitive Control Form of Perceived Control: Construction and Preliminary Assessment," *Psychology & Marketing*, 18 (12), 1258–81.

Fishbein, Martin. (1967), *Readings in Attitude Theory and Measurement*, New York, John Wiley & Sons Inc.

Geer, James H., Gerald C. Davison, and Robert I. Gatchel (1970), "Reduction of Stress in Humans through Nonveridical Perceived Control of Aversive Stimulation," *Journal of Personality and Social Psychology*, 16 (4), 731–38.

Holt, Douglas B. (1995), "How Consumers Consume: A Typology of Consumption Practices," *Journal of Consumer Research*, 22 (1), 1–16.

Hui, Michael K. and John E.G. Bateson (1991), "Perceived Control and the Effects of Crowding and Consumer Choice on the Service Experience," *Journal of Consumer Research*, 18 (2), 174–84.

Kang, Hyunmo, Minhi Hahn, David R. Fortin, Yong J. Hyun, and Yunni Eom (2006), "Effects of Perceived Behavioral Control on the Consumer Usage Intention", *Psychology & Marketing*, 23 (10), 841–64.

Kidwell, Blair and Robert D. Jewell (2003), "An Examination of Perceived Behavioral Control: Internal and External Influences on Intention," *Psychology & Marketing*, 20 (7), 625–42.

Langer, Ellen J. and Judith Rodin (1976), "The Effects of Choice and Enhanced Personal Responsibility for the Aged: A Field Experiment in an Institutional Setting," *Journal of Personality and Social Psychology*, 34, 191–98.

Langer, Ellen J. and Susan Saegart (1977), "Crowding and Cognitive Control," *Journal of Personality and Social Psychology*, 35, 3, 175–82.

Lazarus, Richard S. and Susan Folkman (1984), *Stress, Appraisal and Coping*, New York: Springer.

Lunardo, Renaud and Ababacar Mbengue (2009), "Perceived Control and Shopping Behavior: The Moderating Role of the Level of Utilitarian Motivational Orientation," *Journal of Retailing and Consumer Services*, 16 (6), 434–41.

Lorr, Maurice (1991), "A redefinition of dominance," *Personality and Individual Differences*, 12 (9), 877–79.

Lwin, May O and Jerome D. Williams (2003), "A Model Integrating the Multidimensional Developmental Theory of Privacy and Theory of Planned Behavior to Examine Fabrication of Information Online, *Marketing Letters*, 14 (4), 257–72.

Machleit, Karen A., Sevgin A. Eroglu and Susan Powell Mantel (2000), "Retail Crowding and Shopping Satisfaction: What Modifies this Relationship?," *Journal of Consumer Psychology*, 9 (1), 29–42.

Mathur, Anil (1998), "Examining Trying as a Mediator and Control as a Moderator of Intention-Behavior Relationship," *Psychology & Marketing*, 15 (3), 241–59.

Mehrabian, Albert and James A. Russell (1974), *An approach to environmental psychology*, Cambridge, AM: M.I.T. Press.

Navasimayam Karthik and Timothy R. Hinkin (2003), "The Customer's Role in the Service Encounter: The Effects of Control and Fairness," *Cornell Hotel and Restaurant Administration Quaterly*, June, 4 (3), 26–36.

Nysveen, Herbjørn, Per E. Pedersen, and Helge Thorbjornsen (2005), "Intentions to Use Mobile Services: Antecedents and Cross-Service Comparisons," *Journal of the Academy of Marketing Science*, 33 (3), 330–46.

Rotter Julian B. (1966), "Generalized Expectancies for Internal versus External Control of Reinforcement," *Psychological Monographs: General and Applied*, 80 (1), 1–28.

Paterson, Randy J. and Richard W. Neufeld (1995), "What are my Options?: Influences of Choice Availability on Stress and the Perception of Control," *Journal of Research in Personality*, 29, 145–67.

Rodin, Judith (1990), "Control by any Other Name: Definitions, Concepts, and Processes", In J. Rodin, C. Schooler, and K. W. Schaie (Eds.), *Self-directedness: Cause and effects throughout the life course*, Hillsdale, NJ: Erlbaum, 1–15.

Russell, James A. (1978), "Evidence of Convergent Validity on the Dimensions of Affect," *Journal of Personality and Social Psychology*, 36 (10), 1152–68.

Russell, James A. and Mehrabian Albert (1976), "Some Physical Effects of the Physical Environment," In *Experiencing the Environment*, ed. Wapner S, Cohen S, Kaplan B, New York: Plenum, 5–33.

Russell, James A. and Geraldine Pratt (1980), "A Description of the Affective Quality Attributed to Environments," *Journal of Personality and Social Psychology*, 38 (2), 311–22.

Schmidt, Donald E. and John P. Keating (1979), "Human Crowding and Personal Control: An Integration of Research," *Psychological Bulletin*, 86 (4), 680–700.

Seligman, Martin E. P. (1975). *Helplessness: On Depression, Development, and Death*, San Francisco: Freeman.

Skinner, Ellen A. (1995), *Perceived Control, Motivation, and Coping*, London: Sage Publication.

Skinner, Ellen A. (1996), "A Guide to Constructs of Control," *Journal of Personality and Social Psychology*, 71 (3), 549-71.

Sprott, David E., Anne M. Brumbaugh and Anthony D. Miyazaki (2001), "Motivation and Ability as Predictors of Play Behavior in State-Sponsored Lotteries: An Empirical Assessment of Psychological Control," *Psychology and Marketing*, 18 (9), 973–83.

Srinivasan, Narasimhan and Surinder Tikoo (1992), "Effect of Locus of Control on Information Search Behavior", *Advances in Consumer Research*, Vol. 19, ed. John F. Sherry, Jr. And Brian Sternthal, UT: Association for Consumer Research, 498–504.

Staub, Ervin, Bernard Tursky and Gary E. Schwartz (1971), "Self-Control and Predictability: Their Effects on Reactions to Aversive Stimulation," *Journal of Personality and Social Psychology*, 18 (2), 157–62.

Troup, Carolyn and Philip Dewe (2002), "Exploring the Nature of Control and its Role in the Appraisal of Workplace Stress," *Work & Stress*, 16 (4), 335–55.

Van Raaij, Fred, and Ad ThH Pruyn (1998), "Customer Control and Evaluation of Service Validity and Reliability," *Psychology & Marketing*, 15 (8), 811–32.

Van Rompay, Thomas J. L., Mirjam Galetzka, Ad T. H. Pruyn and Jaime Moreno Garcia (2008), "Human and Spatial Dimensions of Retail Density: Revisiting the Role of Perceived Control," *Psychology and Marketing*, 25 (4), 319–35.

Wallston, Kenneth A., Barbara Strudler Wallston, Shelton Smith, and Carolyn J. Dobbins (1987), "Perceived Control and Health," *Current Psychological Research & Reviews*, 6 (1), 5–25.

Ward, James C. and James W. Barnes (2001), "Control and Affect: The Influence of Feeling in Control of the Retail environment on Affect, Involvement, Attitude, and Behavior," *Journal of Business Research*, 54 (2), 139–44.

Wathieu, Luc, Lyle Brenner, Ziv Carmon, Amitava Chattopadhyay, Klaus Wertenbroch, Aimee Drolet, John Gourville, A.V. Muthukrishnan, Nathan Novemsky, Rebecca Ratner, and George Wu (2002), "Consumer Control and Empowerment: A Primer," *Marketing Letters*, 13 (3), 297-305.

Weiner, Bernard, Heinz Heckhausen, Wulf-Uwe Meyer, and Cook R.E. (1972), "Causal Ascriptions and Achievement Behavior: A Conceptual Analysis of Effort and Reanalysis of Locus of Control," *Journal of Personality and Social Psychology*, 21 (2), 239–48.

White, Robert W. (1959), "Motivation Reconsidered: The Concept of Competence," *Psychological Review*, 66 (5), 297–333.

Yani de Soriano, Mirella. and Gordon R. Foxall (2006), "The Emotional Power of Place: The Fall and Rise of Dominance in Retail Research," *Journal of Retailing and Consumer Services*, 13 (6), 403–16.

# Exploring Consumer Forgiveness In Service Failures

Yelena Tsarenko, Monash University, Australia
Yuliya Strizhakova, Rutgers University, USA

## ABSTRACT

Despite the significant increase in service failures, little attention is given to understanding the notion of consumer forgiveness. Drawing upon 15 in-depth interviews with consumers across three service industries, we discuss three main discourses of consumer forgiveness. Our research offers a novel perspective on the way consumers frame and interpret unsatisfactory service incidents.

## INTRODUCTION

Instances of services failures have become more abundant and severe in recent years, resulting in traumatizing experiences for consumers. Companies dealing with failures utilize their best PR practices to mitigate public criticism; however, much less attention is given to consumers and their experience of failures in such circumstances. Specifically, the question that business practice and research has been largely neglecting is: how do consumers forgive service providers for their mistakes? Although forgiveness has attracted a growing line of inquiry within such fields as psychology, moral development, philosophy, psychotherapy and political studies (Mellor, Bretherton, & Firth, 2007; Rosser, 2008; Shriver, 1995), consumer forgiveness still remains largely unexplored.

What stands behind such a familiar and at the same time elusive concept as forgiveness? There are various conceptualizations of forgiveness; yet, no accepted definition has been consistently adopted. One definition of forgiveness proffered by Enright, Gassin and Wu (1992) states: "as the injured party ceases fighting against the other and gives him or her the unconditional gift of acceptance as a human being, the former is said to be forgiving" (p.101). Forgiveness is understood to be a process of decreasing "inter-related negative resentment-based emotions" (Malcolm & Greenberg, 2000), associated with "motivation/behavior" (McCullough, Sandage, & Worthington, 1997) and "cognition" (DiBlasio, 1998) and is predominantly studied as one of the ways by which individuals respond to stress.

There is a general consensus that forgiveness is a complex process that evolves over time rather than a straightforward response to an incident. It forms a part of the life cycle of an incident that involves many steps (Thoresen, Harris, & Luskin, 1999).The main component of this complex process of forgiveness is the transformation of negative emotions, although debates exist about the extent of this transformation (Exline, Worthington Jr., Hill, & McCullough, 2003). Forgiveness is also regarded as an intended, deliberate activity and not merely a dissipation of negative emotions (Karremans & Aarts, 2007; McCullough, Fincham, & Tsang, 2003), driven by decreased intentions to avoid the offender and seek revenge and by increased good-will toward the transgressor. The main motivational drive of forgiveness lies within the offended party: it is one's intention to rediscover self and reclaim the future for oneself (Holloway, 2002). Forgiveness is also distinct from forgivingness: the former is a transgression-driven process, whereas the latter is one's general predisposition to forgive. In addition, the complexity of the forgiveness process varies based on the type of relationship, the nature of a transgression and steps undertaken by a transgressor to seek forgiveness.

The primary goal of our research is to explore the role of consumer forgiveness with a deeper focus on how consumers understand, conceptualize and practice forgiveness in business settings. Even though we situate consumer forgiveness within the broader process models of forgiveness discussed above, we contribute to prior research by examining forgiveness as a distinct consumer process. Specifically, we develop a theoretical framework of consumer forgiveness by identifying three idiosyncratic discourses of consumer forgiveness. Discourses reflect the social and political aspects of language and subjectivity as well as influence an individual's interpretation of the world and its phenomena (Bristor & Fischer, 1993). Drawing upon in-depth interviews with 15 victims of service failures, we highlight three interpretive meanings – self-healing, reconciliation, and disappointment – that guide consumer discourses of forgiveness. Not only does our research bring the concept of forgiveness to the consumer domain, but also, and most importantly, it develops distinct interpretations of *consumer forgiveness*, derived from the nature of provider-consumer relationships and marketplace constraints. The three discourses of consumer forgiveness identified in our research provide a basis for the theory of consumer forgiveness and have vital implications for future academic research and managerial practice

## METHOD

Data was collected through in-depth interviews with informants recruited by a market research agency. The screening criterion for the interview was that participants had experienced a service failure at least six months prior to the interview. Service failures were drawn from three service sectors with a varying complexity and risk factors for consumers: healthcare, finance and retail sectors. A total of 15 in-depth interviews were conducted: fourteen interviews in the healthcare, thirteen interviews in the finance sector and seventeen in the retail sector. Written consent was obtained prior to the interviews; all interviews were audiotaped and documented by a professional transcription service.

The sample selected for our study was configured to provide a contribution to the generalization of the theory rather than to satisfy statistical principles. The process of recruiting additional respondents ended when theoretical saturation was achieved (Strauss & Corbin, 1998). Recognizing that human feelings, cognitions and motives are complex and ambiguous, the interview process required special preparation and structure to maximize the value of elicited information (McCracken, 1988). To avoid priming our interviewees on the subject of forgiveness, we constructed the dialogue in such as way as to gradually arrive at the topic of forgiveness. Each interview started with some general stories of consumer preferences and dislikes that allowed informants to naturally move to the second stage of the discussion, i.e., their experience of a service transgression. Interviewees exposed details of a negative encounter from its beginning to a resolution or its ongoing 'limbo' state. In some instances, satisfactory transgression resolution either did not exist or was not possible to achieve. The next stage of the interview involved a dialogical encounter between the interviewer and interviewee to obtain an understanding of the concept of forgiveness and its meaning and interpretation (Schwandt, 2000). To achieve such an understanding, we aimed to elicit a conceptualization of forgiveness that was produced by the informants (rather than reproduced as a normative conceptualization) through a detailed conversation with informants about the feelings and emotions they experienced when facing issues in their daily lives. Because respondents were not primed in advance to discuss 'forgiveness', the ensuing conversations about emotions and forgiveness very often prompted them to share personal and sometimes very private accounts of situations in which they had offered or withheld forgiveness or had sought (successfully or otherwise) forgiveness from another party. This approach enabled participants to produce an account of 'forgiveness' according to the particular interpretation and meaning they ascribed to the concept.

Preliminary analyses were undertaken after documenting the initial verbatim transcripts to inform and modify subsequent interviews. This process involved assessment of transcripts to gain an insight into the scope of the content and emerging themes. Initially, two researchers independently read, reflected upon, and conducted a preliminary interpretation of concepts derived from the transcripts. Subsequently, after extensive discussions, a detailed data analysis and classification of categories were carried out using NVivo 8.0. Themes and concepts that had emerged were subsequently refined for axial coding. We undertook an iterative process that involved consulting multidisciplinary literature on forgiveness and interpreting the concepts and themes constructed by participants.

## FINDINGS

Individuals' striving for an emotional balance and harmony guides their trajectory of forgiveness. Boundary conditions that are pertinent to business settings (e.g. extended service recovery, ease of switching to another service provider, allocation and distribution of power in the business relationship, etc.) shape and determine the way in which consumers deal with transgressions. In this section, we highlight similarities and emphasize differences in the process of consumer forgiveness by elaborating on three idiosyncratic discourses of consumer forgiveness.

### The Discourse of Self-Healing

The discourse of self-healing suggests that self is a dynamic concept that is central to internal organizing principles of psychological functioning (Wilson, 2006). In the modern, fast-paced, hyper-active Western society, filled with stress and constant uncertainty, self-healing courses and mediation programs have attracted an unprecedented interest (Askegaard & Kjeldgaard, 2008). The popularity of these self-healing courses stems from a biological desire for self-preservation and survival. It also explains why many informants approach forgiveness as a healing process which does not always result in a restoration of relationships with service providers, but rather has an enormous self-healing impact upon the injured party.

*I read a lot of books on positive thinking and self help and there're hundreds of books at home. So in the books they sort of say that if you forgive others, you can forgive yourself because you're only hurting yourself and I realise that "well, hang on, that's true" because they're probably running off doing their own thing in their own life and not thinking two thoughts about you. But you're here two years later with things that are holding you back...so even if you don't get that apology, you have to do a bit of work and say "I'm hurting myself here" because you're not setting yourself free.[Linda]*

Linda's statement succinctly summarizes three prevailing aspects of the self-healing discourse of forgiveness: the injured party's strong internal focus on self-healing, an unsatisfactory outcome with the transgressor, and the salient role of spirituality. Many informants concur that forgiveness is inextricably intertwined with the healing process. Susan, a physiotherapist, offers her professional perspective on the healing virtue of forgiveness when discussing

her dealings with an insurance company that refused coverage of some medical expenses.

*I suppose you can say that I have forgiven it; I've just let it go. When people don't forgive, they get very bitter and hold on to negative feelings or thoughts, which can become destructive. Life's too short to be holding negative anger. People get really bitter and I know from a health perspective with my industry that a lot of illnesses and disease can come if people bottle things up and store it inside and get angry and don't forgive and let go. [Susan]*

She acknowledges her expectations of the service recovery and emphasizes the fact that no recovery was offered in her case.

*Nothing was given to me. They didn't address the fact that this girl told me the wrong information and it was her first day. She sort of acknowledged that but didn't say "I'm sorry". There was actually no apology. [Susan]*

Many informants agree that the forgiveness process is a result of an internal motivation to maintain positive physical and psychological well-being. Forgiveness emerges as pursuant to mending the consequences of harm. The self-healing power of forgiveness is evident in Karen's account of dealing with her mother's hospice care. It resonates with her other strategies in life driven by the same goal of self-preservation, such as her active engagement in water aerobics and other exercises, the value she places on slimming and toning, and growing her own vegetables.

*I think it's better for you to forgive. I think because if you don't forgive after a while, you will make yourself into a harder person ... but I don't always put that into practice but that's what I think. I think first of all you get angry and then you think to yourself, it's better for you if you can forgive. I think you have a better type of life if you can forgive people and realise that everybody has got their business.[Karen]*

Karen's discourse is filled with juxtapositions of the self-healing virtue of forgiveness with reflections on how hard it is for her to arrive at forgiveness. Karen has learned to forgive but it does not come naturally to her. She also believes that being "a happy person" makes people forgive easier.

Informants who express the self-healing discourse of forgiveness often emphasize that spiritual/ religious beliefs and practices are central to their attitudes, motivations and behaviors when dealing with stressful service failures. For example, Sandra who faced a dilemma with the return of merchandise recognizes that it is easier for her to forgive now than it was several years ago.

*It's a little bit easier for me the last few years, because I'm a member of a religion which is called [...]. It's one of the spiritual teachings that you don't hold things against another person and you actually try to find out the reason in yourself. [Sandra]*

The post-injury phase and the question of how to deal with the transgression lead to an introspective analysis of one's internal state that includes values, desires, beliefs, and emotions. At this point, one's system of organization of self is challenged; i.e., an individual faces the dilemma of finding the meaning of self in a stressful encounter and initially seeks remedies to maintain or preserve the status quo. However, as the stressful encounter unfolds, the process of reconstruction of self begins. Such notions as self-worth and self-confidence are at a crossroads, marking a new stage of rediscovering self. In light of this, the self has the capacity to change the existing situation either via positive transformations or by engaging in self-defeating or self-destructive behaviors. Forgiveness often becomes the only remedy, the only self-healing tool when a customer's stress is not appropriately addressed by the provider.

**The Discourse of Reconciliation**

The second discourse of forgiveness reflects consumer reconciliation of experienced negative emotions with justifications for the transgression. In other words, reconciliation is an internal process driven by one's emotional states and cognitive elaborations rather than an external reconciliation between parties. It should further be noted that forgiveness, while not equivalent to reconciliation between parties can, in some instances, promote it. In this case, forgiveness as a coping strategy helps to reduce stressful reactions to a transgression and may increase one's motivation to pursue relationship-constructive actions toward the offender.

> Well, it [forgiveness] means that I've got a compassion-ate side to me or an understanding side to me, things aren't just black and white, things can be grey. Because I understood the overall situation. You can't blame one person, unless it was a personal fault or they did something on purpose. That's when I don't like it, but if they simply forgot something, well, that's human. Yes, everyone has emotional problems and just because I was treated badly on one occasion doesn't mean that I wouldn't use them again. I'm not like that. [Frank]

Frank's statement summarizes several salient aspects of forgiveness as reconciliation of self and the transgression: attribution of blame for the transgression, cognitive elaborations on the transgression, and the role of one's personality in this process. As evident from Frank's account, forgiveness is achieved by understanding and weighing all possible causes for the wrong and accepting that wrong was unintentional. Frank maintains a broader perspective on his mishap with a malfunctioning new TV set that cost him extra money to have delivered to his house and back to the retailer for the repair: the failure was a result of a combination of factors that extended beyond one person's negligence. Frank does not attribute blame for the mishap to the retailer or the manufacturer. Controlling his impulse to respond to the service failure with an emotional response and engage in name-calling the transgressor, Frank combats his negative feelings and replaces them with cognitive elaborations that reflect his intention to internally reconcile the issue. In reconciling his anger with the transgressor's role in the incident, Frank recognizes the role of human factors in the service failure; however, he is not quick to jump to the conclusion that his relationship with the service provider is over. He takes a balanced approach whereby he controls his emotion and is trying to keep the situation in perspective.

The discourse of forgiveness as reconciliation is particularly prominent among informants who discuss their experiences with transgressions in the healthcare industry. On the one hand, hospital overcrowding and nursing understaffing have been frequently cited as a classic area of service failures where problems can only be exacerbated (Berry & Bendapudi, 2007). On the other hand, the nature of health services is involuntary; in itself healthcare is already associated with greater uncertainty, fear and vulnerability. In addi-

tion, the stakes of errors are very high and may be life-changing. This apparent controversy influences the way individuals differ in their attribution of blame. While some are ready to pursue litigation, others attempt to transform their negative experience and take a more balanced approach in their evaluation.

> I forgive because I know people are human and I know they don't have enough funding, I know they don't have much money and I know that a lot of them are doing the best they can do but when you – I think a lot of people can forgive but you don't forget; it stays with you so if it happens again, it's always there and it's always that worry that you're going to get stressed; are they going to look after my kids?[Carol]

Despite forgiving, informants in the health industry are not capable of forgetting the incidents because of the very high stakes of such errors. Unless constrained by insurance or geographic location, most informants do not envision seeking future services with providers at fault. Carol's discourse is filled with reconciling themes: empathy for the provider driven by her knowledge and respect for the doctors and anxiety about her future with the provider. Similar to many other informants, Carol reconciles the transgression and forgives the provider both cognitively and emotionally; however, her behavior toward the provider is likely to remain avoidant because of the experienced high stakes of the transgression. Carol's excerpt reveals not only the ubiquitous nature of forgiveness in modern life, but also separates forgiveness as a motivational process, distinct from forgetting.

The most complex cognitive elaboration on the provider failure is found in Sharon's account:

> I just need some answers and I respect you [surgeon] enough to provide that in a way that I can understand. So yeah, it wasn't going anywhere making me feel with the intent to degrade his ability or his knowledge or his experience. It wasn't that at all because we're talking about one of the most prominent brain surgeons in the state, I guess. It was more his attitude wasn't very nice but at the end of the day, I think he respected me for that and we had a nice sort of – we understood each other. I think he respected me for taking him on but not on a professional level otherwise I would never have done it. [Sharon]

Sharon's family was shocked when her father had a stroke during his surgery that left him half-paralyzed. In order to come to grips with and comprehend that trauma, Sharon and her family needed a detailed explanation of what had happened during the surgery. However, the elicited information was clouded by medical jargon without any proper acknowledgment of their loss. In her account of forgiveness, Sharon faced the dilemma of having to acknowledge the skills and expertise of the surgeon while challenging his interpersonal skills and his attitude to the members of patient's family. Despite the surgeon's apparent lack of empathy and the transactional nature of the business relationship, Sharon was attempting to relinquish her self-righteous and judgmental attitude that separates the injured party from the transgressor (Exline, Campbell, et al., 2004; Tangney, 2002).

In thinking about forgiveness, our informants often discussed their understanding of the positions of the transgressors, which in Amy's case comes from her observation and contemplation of the positions of the service providers:

*But then again, the customer probably doesn't under-
stand what they've [personnel] been through in the day.
I think that a lot of customers do feel like they're the only
customer and they expect to be treated like they're the
only person but I suppose well, they're supposed to be
serving you or whatever and maybe people have got a
right to feel a bit special but then some people expect too
much, I think [Amy]*

Amy is able to empathize with the pharmacy and its personnel
in particular, despite the loss of her prescription. Being sick and
elderly, she felt very frustrated with her situation but she made a
conscious attempt to remain positive and retain some compassion
and understanding of the service personnel. In other words, she
was reconciling her frustration with the failure with her empathetic
feelings toward the provider.

**The Discourse of Disappointment**

Some consumers projected feelings of disappointment with
service providers at large onto a given failure; hence, one failure
resonated with a spectrum of failures they expected from providers
and resulted in lowered negative emotions. Consumer forgiveness in
such cases is driven by one's disappointment with the whole service
provider system and is achieved through cognitive elaborations
that compare an individual incident with one's expectations of the
general social system. In other words, metaphorically, forgiveness
as disappointment is "when goodness goes beyond virtue and evil
beyond vice" (Arendt, 1963).

*I went back [to the lab] and it was convenient and I
did forgive. I thought it's happened once, okay, they
probably didn't fulfil my obligations of how I would
have rectified the situation, but then I didn't have high expectations of them being a health provider. I'm not really
happy with the health care. On the other side, I probably
need them more than they need me. So it's a little bit different so hence going back and forgiving them and to be
honest, I'm glad that I did. [Irene]*

Consumer discourse of forgiveness as disappointment was
driven by a feeling of inequitable power between self and the "big
institution", marketplace constraints and an astute sense of betrayal.
Irene's path to forgiveness lies in a web of ambiguous thoughts
driven by her disappointment with the whole healthcare system.
Because of a mix-up of blood test results, she was given a false
positive diagnosis that caused anxiety and fear. She had to undergo
the whole process all over again. Undoubtedly, Irene questioned the
accuracy of results each subsequent time. Moreover, she was sent an
invoice at home stating that she had to pay $80 for this test which
was supposed to be covered through the government-sponsored
healthcare system. Irene acknowledges the mishap, but further
elaborates that recovery did not meet her standards. However, she
did not have high expectations; instead she replaced them with her
diminished view of the importance of the system. Forgiveness stems
from Irene's disappointment with the whole system and her greater
need of this particular service provider in contrast to her own value
to the provider. In Irene's statement, it is evident that forgiveness
is a highly motivational process which occurs as an integration of
strategies designed to produce a desired outcome but this motivational process is marked by an asymmetrical relationship and
market constraints rather than by gracious and dignified feelings.

In the passage below, Brett who did not receive an appropriate
explanation about fees on his account describes his forgiveness of
a financial institution as a "selfish act". His disappointment with
the banking system resonates with broader consumer descriptions
of banking services: traditional and ordinary but, as Arendt (1963)
puts it, "banality evil". Financial institutions are services where
customers often feel alienated, unprotected and without much
control over their relationships with them. The provider-customer
inequality is further aggravated by the sheer size and monetary
power of these establishments.

*...but it's just a small guy fighting a big bank. I didn't feel
like I was treated as an individual. They don't have to
fight for your, um - loyalty, I suppose and retention.
I've forgiven for sure - selfish once again, you know,
okay, but if I've had a bad experience, I'm going to tell
people through conversation. I wouldn't recommend them
to go to that - that shop, that branch, whatever. But I'd
forgive only on a monetary, selfish way. I mean, I've still
got my credit card with them and the savings account
with them, you know. So I've probably forgiven the bank
indirectly. [Brett]*

The impersonal service that is provided when consumers
do not feel valued or cared about is largely a norm rather than an
exception, it is a default mode of operandi underlying the asymmetry in this relationship (La Caze, 2008; Young, 1997). While
service provider-customer relationships remain unproblematic,
there is no explicit need to re-evaluate the positions of each party.
Once the conflict emerges, the differences between parties become
more salient and their positions become more diverging. Such a
state leaves the consumer with little to no choice but to embrace
forgiveness as a defensive mechanism to retain their own human
side. Brett considers his forgiveness as a selfish behavior, emphasizing the monetary, not emotional, value of his forgiveness (i.e.,
his ability to continue using the credit card and earning interest on
a savings account).

Assessment of market constraints, particularly in the health
service industry where the number of options is relatively limited,
forces consumers to embrace forgiveness in light of their needs.
Jane explicitly states that she not only contemplates forgiveness
but also her preparedness for further patronage of this particular
hospital. This sense that you need the service more than the service
needs you dominates the approach of how consumers forgive the
service failure.

*I can forgive and I will consider going back there be-
cause there's not many other hospitals to go to. [Jane]*

In contrast, Harry's path to forgiveness is driven by his disappointment with the whole banking system and is overshadowed with
the feeling of betrayal. His debit card was not returned by an ATM
machine in a foreign county and his bank was not able to replace
it in a timely manner, leaving him only with one credit card but no
access to his bank account on a multi-country trip

*When I was overseas when I needed them the most –
that's what I said to her "when I needed you the most,
you let me down" so it would have been nice to have the
bank help me when I needed them. I'm still banking with
them and I've been banking with them for a very long
time as well, so I haven't decided to take my business
elsewhere. I think I would only be replacing them with*

*pretty much the same thing because it's probably the same. So obviously, I've forgiven. [Harry]*

Harry doubts the efficiency of other financial institutions. He does not see the point of replacing one "locked-in" relationship with another one of the same quality and value. Harry declares his forgiveness; however, this is no more or less than a discrepancy-reduction strategy.

## DISCUSSION

Consumer forgiveness is a complex process that involves emotional transformations, cognitive elaborations and behavioral expressions. Through three distinct discourses, we show how consumers intrinsically deal with negative incidents in their consumption practice. Affective, cognitive and behavioral aspects of forgiveness are untangled through delineating three main discourses of forgiveness as self-healing, reconciliation and disappointment. Discourses unveil how consumers construct, understand, and interpret their forgiveness process.

Our findings demonstrate that consumer forgiveness, apart from being internal, is a highly motivational process that is influenced by both internal and external forces. For example, self-healing and reconciliation are driven by internal motives when consumers rely on internal strength, values and beliefs in their accounts of forgiveness. The influence of the service provider is important but not essential in order for consumers to forgive. These discourses at large correspond with both emotional and unconditional forgiveness in psychological research (Worthington, 2006). Self-healing discourse is associated with the way consumers replace their negative emotions with neutral or positive ones, regardless of the actual problem resolution. In a similar vein, reconciliation is aimed at one's emotions and the incident at hand. Reconciliation of negative emotions elicited by the transgression and their transformation into more empathetic feelings occurs through extensive cognitive elaborations, attribution of blame, and appreciation of a personal factor in which the offended party steps beyond the transgression in an attempt to justify it. It is based upon available body of knowledge on human mistakes and their causes. Hence, the discourse of forgiveness as reconciliation is characterized by elaborated cognitive processes that reconcile one's negative affective states with one's humanity to understand why mistakes happen in the first place.

Finally, the discourse of disappointment is likely to be unique and relevant to institutional relationships: it is driven by marketplace constraints, a sense of betrayal and a perceived asymmetry of the relationship. Consumer forgiveness stems from a resonance of one transgression with an overall view on business relationships that are shaped by inequality and betrayal. In contrast to other discourses of forgiveness, forgiveness as disappointment does not result in any positive emotions, but rather, reduces immediate anger and frustration with less negative disappointment. Forgiveness emerges as an individual's survival response to external constraints and institutional powers rather than as an internal virtue.

It should be noted that although in this study discourses of consumer forgiveness are presented as distinctive interpretive frameworks, in reality more than one discourse may shape the consumer forgiveness process. Service failure contexts, marketplace constraints, and individual differences impact the salience of each discourse in individual accounts. Overall, by situating our research within broader process models of forgiveness in psychology and applying the discourse analysis methodology to our interviews, we are able to highlight the multi-faceted nature of consumer forgiveness and provide a foundation for future theoretical advances in this new frontier.

## REFERENCES

Arendt, H. (1963). *Eichmann in Jerusalem: A Report on the Banality of Evil*: London: Faber.

Askegaard, S., & Kjeldgaard, D. (2008). *The Global Myth of "Me": Self-actualization and Identity Practices in the Contemporary Global Consumptionscape* Paper presented at the Advances in consumer research.

Berry, L. L., & Bendapudi, N. (2007). Health Care: A Fertile Field for Service Research. *Journal of Service Research, 10*(2), 111-122.

Bristor, J., & Fischer, E. (1993). Feminist Theory and Consumer Research. *Journal of Consumer Research, 19*(March), 518-536.

DiBlasio, F. A. (1998). The use of decision-based forgiveness intervention within intergenerational family therapy. *Journal of Family Therapy, 20*(1), 77-94.

Enright, R. D., Gassin, E. A., & Wu, C.-R. (1992). Forgiveness: a developmental view. *Journal of Moral Education, 21*(2), 99-114.

Exline, J. J., Worthington Jr., E. L., Hill, P., & McCullough, M. E. (2003). Forgiveness and Justice: A Research Agenda for Social and Personality Psychology. *Personality and Social Psychology Review, 7*(4), 337-348.

Holloway, R. (2002). *On forgiveness: how can we forgive the unforgivable?* Edinburgh: Canongate.

Karremans, J. C., & Aarts, H. (2007). The role of automaticity in determining the inclination to forgive close others. *Journal of Experimental Social Psychology, 43*(6), 902-917.

La Caze, M. (2008). Seeing Oneself through the Eyes of the Other: Asymmetrical Reciprocity and Self-respect. *Hypatia, 23*(3), 118-135.

Malcolm, W. M., & Greenberg, L. S. (2000). Forgiveness as a process of change in individual psychotherapy. In M. E. McCullough, K. I. Pargament & C. E. Thoresen (Eds.), *Forgiveness: Theory, Research, and Practice* (pp. 179-202). New York: Guilford Press.

McCracken, G. D. (1988). *The Long Interview*. Newbury Park CA: Sage Publications.

McCullough, M. E., Fincham, F. D., & Tsang, J.-A. (2003). Forgiveness, forbearance, and time: The temporal unfolding of transgression-related interpersonal motivations. *Journal of Personality and Social Psychology, 84*(3), 540-557.

McCullough, M. E., Sandage, S. J., & Worthington, E. L., Jr. (1997). *To forgive is human: How to put your past in the past*: Downers Grove, IL: InterVarsity Press.

Mellor, D., Bretherton, D., & Firth, L. (2007). Aboriginal and non-aboriginal Australia: the dilemma of apologies, forgiveness, and reconciliation. *Peace and Conflict: Journal of Peace Psychology, 13*(1), 11-36.

Rosser, A. (2008). Neo-liberalism and the politics of Australian aid policy-making. *Australian Journal of International Affairs, 62*(3), 372 - 385.

Schwandt, T. A. (2000). Three epistomological stances for qualitative inquiry: Interpretivism, Hermenutics, and Social Constructionism. In N. K. Denzin & Y. S. Lincoln (Eds.), *Handbook of qualitative research* (pp. 189-213): Sage Publications, Inc.

Shriver, D. W. (1995). *An ethic for enemies: forgiveness in politics*. New York: Oxford University Press.

Strauss, A. L., & Corbin, J. M. (1998). *Basics of Qualitative Research. Second Edition*: Newbury Park CT, Sage Publications.

Thoresen, C. E., Harris, A. H. S., & Luskin, F. (1999). Forgiveness and Health: An unanswered question. In McCullough M., Pargament K. & Thoresen C. (Eds.), *The Frontiers of Forgiveness: Conceptual, Empirical, and Clinical Perspectives*. New York: Guilford Press.

Wilson, J. P. (2006). *The posttraumatic self: restoring meaning and wholeness to personality*: New York: Routledge.

Worthington, E. L. (2006). *Forgiveness and reconciliation: theory and application*: New York : Routledge.

Young, I. M. (1997). *Intersecting voices: Dilemmas of gender, political philosophy, and policy*: Princeton, N.J.: Princeton University Press.

# Big Ideas on the Contribution of Brands to Consumers' Lives

Sandy Bulmer, Massey University, New Zealand
Margo Buchanan-Oliver, University of Auckland, New Zealand

## ABSTRACT

Concepts from adjacent fields are used to show that brands contribute to feelings of belonging to national communities. We propose that national identity is a significant, overlooked form of community. Studies of brands and national identity have clear potential for adding new insights into how consumers use brands.

## INTRODUCTION

Brands are ubiquitous. It is almost impossible for consumers to avoid exposure to brands via traditional advertising media, publicity/public relations activities or in-store display and promotional programs. Furthermore, new digital models of communication are extending the reach of brands into consumers' lives through social media, user generated content, brand websites, advergames, e-mail based viral marketing, SMS and mobile marketing etc. Despite being pervasive, brands are not usually considered to affect society in any significant way. Certainly, brands are not commonly credited with contributing to productive and enabling forces within society, and in the popular media little is heard about any positive contributions that brands make to society in general. Indeed, for many consumers, admitting that brands have social use or cultural relevance is tantamount to declaring moral bankruptcy and intellectual shallowness.

Within consumer research literature, there is still much to be learned of what consumers DO with brands, and the experiential dimensions of brands are poorly understood. Many scholars and researchers deploying diverse methodologies have contributed to understanding concepts of branding (see, for example, Aaker 1991; Fournier 1998; Kapferer 1997; Keller 2003; Muñiz and O'Guinn 2001; Schouten and McAlexander 1995). Fournier's landmark article on consumer-brand relationships (1998) boosted the process of addressing these issues. Nevertheless, the contribution of brands to the lives of consumers—and the communities they are part of—is under-researched, although concepts of community have been popular amongst consumer researchers in the past 15 years (Arnould and Price 2000; Cayla and Eckhardt 2008; Cova 1997; Fournier 1998; Kates 2004; Kozinets 2002; Mathwick, Wiertz, and de Ruyter 2008; Muñiz and O'Guinn 2001; Schau, Muñiz, and Arnould forthcoming; Thompson 2005).

New forms of community enabled by technology, such as online brand communities, have been documented (Cova and Pace 2006; Muñiz and Schau 2005). These exemplify the kinds of imagined communities originally described by Benedict Anderson in his reflections on the origin and spread of nationalism (Anderson 1983). Anderson developed his ideas based on the impact of print media, particularly newspapers, and added to Marshall McLuhan's media thesis that widely disseminated standardized stories, consumed in common, serve to unite people (McLuhan 1962).

The power of mass media to both constitute nations and draw communities together is widely accepted in cultural studies, political science, journalism and mass-communication literature (Askew and Wilk 2002; Frosh 2007; Millard et al. 2002; Moreno 2003; Prideaux 2009). These researchers are in no doubt that advertising produces nationalism and informs the process of conceptualizing a nation. In essence, other literatures suggest that advertisements contribute to national identity. However, researchers in consumer research and marketing have not yet made the logical extension of this argument. If brands typically sponsor such advertisements, then

how do brands affect national identity? And why might national identity matter to marketers and consumer researchers anyway?

A popular position taken by observers is that national identity is an irrelevant construct nowadays, since many consumers (at least in advanced economy countries) have an external focus and global outlook. Globalization commentators such as Stalnaker (2002) suggest that national identity is an outmoded concept and posit that today's urban consumers belong to a global class not limited by race or dominated by national identity, but by what they like, what they want, and what they are willing to pay for. However, others suggest that the very processes of globalization are partly responsible for an apparent increase in the importance and significance of ethnic and national identities. Paradoxically, consumers have multiple allegiances, simultaneously belonging to a stateless global class and having a heightened sensibility of national identity.

Multiple quests by consumers for local, trans-national and global identities are explained by the post-modern perspective. Firat and Dholakia (2004) suggest that the chaotic fragmented lives that people lead give rise to a desire for meaning and substance. "The consumer transforms from someone who belongs to a culture, society or a lifestyle to someone who actively negotiates one or more communities—an active cultural constructor" (Firat and Dholakia 2004, 10). According to this view, national identity is a dynamic collaboration between community members that is not reliant on tradition but is built using resources from the imagined present. It is assumed that people hold multiple identities and utilize each as required, so that simultaneous membership of nations within nations, ethnic and racial groups is not discounted. There is no necessity to commit oneself to a single way of being; individuals will take on various identities at different times and situations as it suits their needs.

Ethnic and national identities are key elements in social identity and categorization today, essential for maintaining self-respect, belonging, a sense of security and giving people meaning in their lives. In some national communities there is a long established and confident sense of national identity. In these communities national identity is not necessarily subject to widespread commentary but, as Billig (1995) suggests, reference to national identity may be so embedded, familiar and continual that it is not consciously registered.

A review of the literature in several specialist journals devoted to the study of nations and identity including *National Identities, Nationalities Papers: The Journal of Nationalism and Ethnicity* and *Social Identities: Journal for the Study of Race, Nation and Culture* points to numerous contemporary contexts where national identity is being actively negotiated and is relevant and important. Clearly, many national communities struggle with their unique identity, possibly grappling with issues of colonization and indigenous populations, recent establishment and linkages with other nations or economic communities, ethnic diversity and the effects of biases in immigration policies—in this we include the European Union countries and others once part of the USSR and Yugoslavia, many African nations and countries such as Australia, Canada and New Zealand which are part of the (British) Commonwealth.

National identity is a creditable and relevant contemporary form of identification. Furthermore, a well developed and strong sense of national identity has the power to be a productive and enabling force within society providing positive social capital with benefits such as improved cooperation with others, improved information flows and more effective, better functioning government and other democratic institutions (Aldridge 2002). With this in mind, government policy makers in many countries are actively looking for opportunities of building social capital by way of developing some shared sense of national identity and common talking points. The 'Picturing America' Program made available to schools and libraries across the United States through the National Endowment for the Humanities (NEH) is one such initiative. In other countries strategies such as 1) better funding public service broadcasting and the development of local programming and 2) expanding and enhancing the museum and library sectors to develop insights into national identity (including digital strategies for creation, preservation and protection of content) have been deployed in an attempt to assist community members to define who they are, what they believe in, and why they live in the place that they do. Ultimately, these strategies are underpinned by the provision of relevant narratives and imagery and by facilitating discourse within society—a default role that is played by brand communications.

In addressing the conference theme of big phenomena that are of real importance to consumers' lives, we present an argument that consumers use brands in hitherto unrecognized ways. We utilize conversations in other branches of social science to assist in drawing the reader's attention to an aspect of consumer experience that has not been considered in our field, despite the clear potential for adding insight (Deighton et al. 2010). The strategy of "poach[ing] and cross-fertiliz[ing] ideas, methods, and contexts from a variety of theoretical conversations that differentially address core topics" has much to recommend it as "theoretical insights and constructs from one paradigmatic conversation are reconceptualized and reworked in relationship to a different paradigmatic vernacular" (Arnould and Thompson 2005, 869). Our claim is that brands, through their marketing communications, contribute to important personal and collective identities, and to feelings of belonging to over-arching communities such as national communities. We provide support for the proposition that national identity is a significant but overlooked form of community and suggest that future studies relating to brands and national identity have clear potential for adding insight into the broad question of what consumers do with brands, particularly concerning brands as the focus of advertisements.

## THEORETICAL BACKGROUND
### Consumption, Symbolism and Experiences

Consumption, and the cultural symbolism surrounding it, is inextricably linked with aspects of self-identity and other dimensions of community, as has been shown in the consumer research literature for many years. Consumption is essentially a symbolic activity (Douglas and Isherwood 1979) and goods are consumed, in part at least, for the role they play in mediating and communicating meaning. The meanings assigned to goods whether simple or complex, perform a major function in key social and psychological activities such as identity formation, the maintenance of kin relations, belongingness and class structure (Jackson 2004). Consumption practices designed to enable communication between consumers are common to all social groups and communities. Social signaling is at the heart of consumption rituals such as those observed at special occasions, such as weddings (Otnes and Scott 1996), and in everyday activities, such as drinking a favored brand of beer with friends (Pettigrew 2002). Image management through consumption is maintained through scripted behaviors that hold special meaning for the participants and unique consumption practices ranging from gift giving to the use/wearing of particular objects and clothing (Otnes and Scott 1996).

The brands one consumes help define the self and therefore can help in the quest to be someone different and to be part of a group (Schouten and McAlexander 1995). The depth and power of the consumed brand's symbolic meaning within a social group can be seen when teenagers insist on wearing particular branded trainers that symbolize their desired personality, characteristics and reference group affiliation (Chaplin et al. 2005). Similarly, within the Harley Davidson owners' group (HOG), brand consumers authenticate their identity by performing a role and sharing experiences within a particular community of consumption (Schouten and McAlexander 1995). Furthermore, through their stories and symbolism, brands can assist communities other than those whose focus is consumption, helping in the outward expression and celebration of key values (Kates 2006).

Brands are experienced in many different ways and live as stories in the minds of consumers which contribute to "the range of identities that people can use to think of themselves" (Cayla and Eckhardt 2008, 226). According to Elliott and Wattanasuwan's (1998) model of Consumption and the Symbolic Project of the Self, brand purchase and usage experiences (lived experiences of brands) are complemented by brand advertising and other types of brand marketing communications (mediated experiences of brands). It is this mediated experience of the brand and indirect consumption, via storied audio/visual representations that we now focus on. For the purposes of this paper the argument we develop refers to brand advertising. However, other types of brand marketing communications are also anticipated to impact on national identity, especially publicity and sponsorship programs.

### Brands as Resources

Brand communications are intended by producers, not only to provide information but, to enhance the direct experience of brand purchase and usage. Underpinning this view of advertising is the understanding that meaning is co-created. Using insights obtained from cultural anthropology McCracken (1986) advanced the view that advertising works by bringing the product and a representation of the culturally constituted world together in an advertisement, emphasizing the importance of the societal context that an advertisement is embedded in. The advertising consumer completes the work of the advertising producer and is the final author of the brand advertisement (McCracken 1986); thus consumers actualize the meaning of advertisements (presupposing that they make assumptions and have the knowledge to make texts meaningful) (Mick and Buhl 1992). The process of advertising meaning co-creation, mediated by the influences of the social and individual realm, is dependent on the consumer's unique life experiences and plans, and the uses they have for the interpreted meaning (Ritson and Elliott 1995).

One of the ways that mediated brand experiences are able to supplement consumption is by providing a scripted story or by articulating loosely constructed thoughts about a brand (Elliott and Wattanasuwan 1998). While we certainly do not suggest that consumers always accept the narratives provided (and indeed they may reject the brand stories developed by advertising agencies), these advertising stories are conceptualized as a resource that the consumer can use for her/his own purposes (Elliott and Wattanasuwan 1998). Furthermore, if mass media are used in a brand's marketing communication program, then advertising stories become a common resource that is available to everyone in an advertising audience, as Ritson and Elliott described in their study of adolescents (1999); consuming advertising is a joint, communal activity.

## Linking Value

Ongoing social interactions and communal events have been shown to be facilitated within groups of advertising consumers (Ritson and Elliott 1999). Advertisements can provide a focal point for consumer to consumer contact that is valued for reasons beyond product recommendation, decision-making and the purchasing process. The concept of social connections, the establishment and/ or reinforcement of bonds between individuals, facilitated by marketing activities has also been highlighted by Cova (1997) and this approach is encompassed by Consumer Culture Theory (Arnould and Thompson 2005). Consumer culture necessarily implies a role for brands in creating and re-creating a sense of self, personal purpose and belonging. Cova (1997) introduced the idea of the linking value of products and services that in some way permit and support social connections between consumers and forge feelings of solidarity through the pursuit of common consumption interests. Cova and Cova note, "such linking value is rarely intentionally embedded in the use value of the product/service concept, yet it is a quality that merits our careful attention" (2001, 70).

Brand advertising provides the means for uniting consumers within communities, providing a focal point for consumer to consumer contact and for imagining belonging to a community of individuals linked through commonality of some sort. The combination of Elliott and Wattanasuwan's (1998) concept of mediated experiences of brands as resources, and Cova's (1997) linking value, provides a neat framework for the argument that identity projects and community connections are supported by brands as experienced through marketing communications. That is, the literature provides a theoretical basis for the claim that brand advertising has a linking value in communities. Furthermore, the linking value extends beyond word-of-mouth effects, product recommendations and assistance in the decision-making/purchasing process. Brand marketing communications have a vital role to play in striking a chord within the isolated consumer, connecting people with each other through the "lifestyles, stories, experiences, and emotions" conveyed (Leach 2000, 18).

## Community

Connections between people are central to the ideas of community, and as discussed earlier, the construct of community is well-established in consumer research studies. Communities are social groups that help define an individual within society—community implies a consciousness of kind where there is a collective sense of difference from others not in the community. Consumer research publications have focused on many notions of community, including brand communities (Muñiz and O'Guinn 2001), new communities (Goulding, Shankar, and Elliott 2002), virtual communities (Mathwick et al. 2008), and the struggle for self and community (Arnould and Price 2000). However, there has been little published regarding national communities and the linkages between consumers who share the same national identity, despite strong evidence that membership of national communities remains a matter of relevance, as discussed earlier.

## National Identity

National identity refers to a shared perception of self within a national community, and is characterized by the belief that there are commonalities which unite members of a nation (Kirloskar-Steinbach 2004). National identity is not just about shared culture; it is about the feeling of belonging (Grimson 2010). This social phenomenon assists individuals to understand their place in the world and necessarily emphasizes similarities and differences between people. National identity is not a fixed view, but one that is an act

of imagination, such that it is most unlikely that a group of fellow community members will imagine exactly the same thing—there is "no such thing as the one and only national identity" (de Cillia, Reisigl, and Wodak 1999, 154). Thus, within a nation and amongst different generational cohorts, various national identities develop which claim to express the same national past but in fact envisage it in different ways.

National identity is flagged in everyday life and is embodied in habits of thinking and using language (Billig 1995). In effect, it is a dynamic collaboration between community members that is not reliant on tradition but is built from usable pasts (Brooks 1915) and the imagined present (Humphrey 2004; Spangler 2002; Squire 1996). As Denny et al. (2005, 20) suggest "only through the imaginations and activities of many can the idea of a nation and national culture be achieved". Without even realizing it, brand owners contribute to national identity through the provision of usable pasts and visions of the imagined present in advertisements.

The concept of usable pasts was first introduced in the book 'America's Coming of Age' to capture the move towards reconstructions of history that served to unite the nation, emphasizing defining moments of the past (Staples 2003). More recently, usable past has been conceptualized as what we ought to elect to remember, signaling the "desire to make sense of national experiences in ways that unify rather than separate us" (Carnegie Council 2001). Conscious attempts to draw a nation together in this way are seen in the official commissioning of murals, statues and other monuments in public spaces, postage stamps, coins, anthems and flags that serve to make visible the myths, historical memories and common mass culture.

Construction of the nation also occurs through media culture and especially through cinema; national identity may be apprehended in the narratives, iconography and recurring motifs of popular culture (Elsaesser 2005). The term national cinema is used to distinguish the cinema tradition and style of a country (in contrast with Hollywood and the cinema of the United States). In addressing how national cinema expresses national identity in the French context, Hayward (2005) proposes seven typologies—Narratives (where the narrative is an adaptation of an indigenous text); Genres (certain types are characteristic of particular nations); Codes and Conventions (production practices become typical); Gesturality and morphology (intonations, attitudes and postures are rooted in a nation's culture); The star as sign (actors embody national cultural codes); Cinema of the centre and of the periphery (mainstream, heartland cinema in one country contrasts with its less conventional, avant-garde and narrow-interest films); Cinema as the mobilizer of the nation's myths and of the myth of the nation (the texture of society is reflected in cinema as political, social and economic changes occur). On a more compressed scale, brand advertisements (especially television commercials) also provide these types of stories and imagery, reflecting society and commonly held values, showcasing beloved geographic locations and personalities, and highlighting myths and representations of the way we are and used to be—utilizing the unifying experiences of a nation.

We know advertising is culturally anchored and the idea that society is reflected by advertising is not new—although Elliott (1997, 291) notes that the extent to which "advertising reflects reality or actually creates it is problematic." We further note that brand communications are embedded with visual representations and narratives which form part of the visual landscape (Schroeder 2002; Schroeder and Salzer-Mörling 2006). However, our argument is not that culture is shown in advertisements. We posit that consuming brand advertisements that offer imagery and stories that in some way reflect the nation, contributes to the feeling of belonging to that collective. Consuming brand advertising is a widespread community practice that affects national identity.

## Social Identities

Having presented the argument that brands affect national identity we now discuss the self and the construction of personal and social identities, the I/we negotiations of consumer identity projects. Self-concept refers to a person's own mental image or perception of her/himself as an object; each person holds numerous perceptions regarding their personal existence and each perception is integrated with the others (Reed 2002). Individuals are motivated to keep a positive self-image, assimilating new ideas and excluding old ones, in a continuous process of self-concept development. Thus, self-concept is not static; individuals engage in perpetual re-construction of identity as a result of social experience (Mead 1934).

The self is socially constructed; we understand ourselves in relation to others around us, and because of the similarities or differences between ourselves and others. Schroeder and Salzer-Mörling, in discussing brand culture, note that rather than being 'authentic, coherent and deep," selfhood can be construed as being "constructed, contingent and performed" (2006, 121). Sense of self evolves and develops, both consciously and in an automatic or unconscious fashion, throughout the lifetime and is not present at birth (Mead 1934). Activities and interactions with other individuals in society are essential to the development of self (Mead 1934). The young adult attempts to validate the simple series of factual events that have shaped the self so far and to craft a meaningful life-story; as a child matures s/he begins to "discover the self through story in historical and biographical terms" (Cardillo 1998). Interaction with a wider range of society also presents opportunities for a wider range of the self to become apparent.

Selfhood is one of many identities, including gender and ethnicity, which is neither fixed nor timeless. Jenkins' thesis, building on the foundational sociological and social anthropological works of Mead, Goffman and Barth, is that the "self is an ongoing, simultaneous synthesis of (internal) self definition and the (external) definitions of oneself offered by others" (Jenkins 1996, 20). Identity exists and is maintained through relational processes of interconnectedness (Barth 1969). There is an ongoing to and fro process of constructing and re-negotiating identity according to the responses of others within society, which Jenkins calls the internal—external dialectic of identification. Membership of multiple social groups leads to the existence of not one, 'personal self', but rather several selves according to the Theory of Social Identity, developed by Tajfel and Turner (1979). Various social situations trigger an individual to think, feel and act according to their personal, family or national level of self (Turner et al. 1987).

## Using Brand Resources to Negotiate Identities

Consumers of brand resources are bricoleurs—that is to say, in constructing stories and identities they pick and choose, drawing on a wide range of things that happen to be available (Lévi-Strauss 1962). This type of thinking and development of ideas involves manipulating and making resourceful use of materials, irrespective of their original purpose. Further explanation of this is given by Ritson and Elliott (1995, 1036) who present a view of the advertising audience "as not passive, homogenous receivers of ads containing pre-specifiable, intended meanings but as active co-creators of meaning who display an ability to read, co-create then act on polysemic meanings from ads that they view." Consumer use and interpretation of advertising is idiosyncratic and uncontrollable and research shows that consumers' interpretations of advertisements are more wide ranging than intended by advertising creators (Phillips 1997).

Advertisements are assemblages of resources, drawing on words, pictures, movement, sounds and colors which refer to cultural texts, pre-existing knowledge about products and consumption practices, long running campaigns and historical precedents in advertising, cultural myths, other tacit cultural knowledge and utilize language derived rhetorical devices (McQuarrie and Mick 1996). Images, stories and other fragments of advertisements provide resources used by consumers as they negotiate their identities. Brands provide triggers for thinking about how I see myself, how others see themselves, how I feel I have something in common with others, how we have a sense of shared experiences and feelings about the nation. A disjointed group of individual consumers can recognize themselves as individuals and as part of a nation; they can imagine the national community because they recognize shared feelings of commonality and belonging.

Brands, through their marketing communications offer views of what we as a nation did, what we value, who we honor, where we consider special places, and what characteristics as individuals we share. They are a pervasive source of ideas that allow us to imagine and negotiate I/we, our internal self identity but also more overarching types of social identities, including national identity. (We acknowledge that this argument is not limited to national identity and is relevant to all sorts of social identities, tribes and communities. However, one of the purposes of this paper is to put the focus on national identity as an under-researched form of identity that is surprisingly relevant in contemporary society).

Many brands unwittingly incorporate elements of myth into brand marketing communications. We note also the reported deliberate and cynical use of existing cultural myths, not as a component of an advertisement but, as an entire brand foundation in a few exceptional cases (Holt 2006). Some advertisements are not very rich in resources for national identity projects, but the use of visual coding and recognizable national and cultural markers in brand advertising is widespread in some product/service types and is more apparent in some nations. Nostalgia is one type of appeal that is often rich in elements of a mythic golden age—referring to imagined moments of peace, harmony, stability, and prosperity. Although the mythic components do not necessarily communicate the main message enunciated in a brand advertising brief, there is clear evidence of myths in many marketing communications—see, for example, the study of Wal-Mart advertising flyers (Arnold, Kozinets, and Handelman 2001).

In summary, we have presented an argument that others in different disciplines know that advertisements affect national identity. We have argued that national identity is a relevant contemporary form of identification and a construct worthy of further investigation. Overall, we have taken a consumer experience perspective and focused on examining the literature regarding how the brands that are the sponsors of advertisements affect national identity. Conceptualizations of the linking value of brands, brands as resources, the provision of usable pasts, socially constructed identities and the advertising consumer as bricoleur have been employed in the construction of our case.

## DISCUSSION AND CONCLUSION

We stated at the beginning of this paper that brands have not been credited with contributing to productive and enabling forces within society, and yet there is evidence that brands contribute to national identity and that strong national identity is a stabilizing force that contributes a sense of security and meaning to consumers' lives. The idea that brands, through their marketing communications, might be useful to consumers in negotiating and imagining a national community is new and raises many interesting questions.

It also poses new opportunities for brand owners and their advertising agencies as they consider how they might be more sensitive to consumption experiences and consumer uses of brand advertising.

Creatives and others involved in the process of developing advertisements would benefit from utilizing more socio-cultural readings of brands as resources and understanding elements of national identity that are central to a national community. So far, most brands have only unwittingly contributed to national identities. A more informed and deliberate approach might be of real benefit to both consumers and brand owners. Government agencies and organizations such as the Carnegie Council have already understood the benefit of utilizing a usable past in drawing a nation together. The construct of a usable past is contingent on the times and mores, and subject to change. If advertisers were to understand which parts of usable past could be used or conceived as being usable at any particular time, that would also benefit brands. Some studies have been reported that analyze advertisements from an expert perspective (Arnold et al. 2001). However, we believe that more research into consumer responses to advertisements, conceived as assemblages that act as resources in the construction and negotiation of national identity, would also be useful.

Feelings of belonging to a collective that shares advertising consumption experiences and holding a strong sense of national identity are important to many consumers throughout the world today, yet these dimensions of consumer experience have not been examined in the consumer research literature. The contribution of this paper is in tying together concepts from the literatures of history, sociology, cultural studies, film, television, and media—which are purely conceptual but have importance and potency—with marketing and consumer research on brands, communities and identities. The unique perspective we offer combines all these concepts, and moves forward by considering the insights on national identity and brands from the point of view of the consumer.

We believe that our big idea on the contribution of brands to consumers' lives has the potential to stimulate new and useful insights in consumer research. The ideas articulated in our paper (cross-fertilized by concepts from several other disciplines) offer many opportunities for future research. Further studies should be undertaken to answer questions such as: What is the relationship between national identity and the brands that are advertised? What are the mechanisms by which brands affect national identity? How do consumers experience national identity in brand advertisements? There are broad questions to be answered regarding the role that the entire range of a brand's marketing communication program plays in creating value for consumers and for brands. More work is needed to address the role of brand marketing communications in offering fragments which form part of the wider social milieu of resources that surround consumers and contribute to identity projects. Such research would add to the clarification of what consumers do with brands.

Research into the relationship between communications and national identity might include mapping those elements that provide the richest resources for national identity in different countries. A catalogue of the most significant elements (visual, aural and behavioral) that contribute to national identity would offer marketing communicators useful insights into the potential links that could be made between brands, consumers and their national identity. Obtaining consumer insights into how well a brand's communications conform to expectations of what national identity is would be of use to marketers. Studies might also consider the types of stories that are most effectively employed by communications that contribute significantly to national identity.

The practitioner relevance and contribution of such future studies would be to provide a clearer understanding of how aspects of marketing communications can impact on brand value; to contribute towards better understanding global brand advertising; to generate insights that make for improved brand marketing communications experiences that resonate with aspects of national identity and to provide insights for brand owners into leveraging brands further though intensifying brand messages and enhancing consumer reception. Finally, we suggest that this new perspective is particularly relevant to US brands as they look outside their own borders and seek to understand the power of their brands in other national markets.

## REFERENCES

Aaker, David A (1991), *Managing Brand Equity*, New York: Free Press.

Aldridge, Stephen (2002), "Social Capital," http://ec.europa.eu/employment_social/knowledge_society/docs/aldridge.pdf.

Anderson, Benedict (1983), *Imagined Communities: Reflections on the Origin and Spread of Nationalism*, New York: Verso.

Arnold, Stephen J, Robert V Kozinets, and Jay M Handelman (2001), "Hometown Ideology and Retailer Legitimation: The Institutional Semiotics of Wal-Mart Flyers," *Journal of Retailing*, 77 (2), 243-71.

Arnould, Eric J and Linda L Price (2000), "Authenticating Acts and Authoritative Performances: Questing for Self and Community," in *The Why of Consumption: Contemporary Perspectives on Consumer Motives, Goals and Desires*, ed. Srinivasan Ratneshwar, David Glen Mick and Cynthia Huffman, London; New York: Routledge, 140-63.

Arnould, Eric J and Craig J Thompson (2005), "Consumer Culture Theory (CCT): Twenty Years of Research," *Journal of Consumer Research*, 31 (March), 868-82.

Askew, Kelly and Richard R Wilk (2002), *Anthropology of Media: A Reader*, Oxford: Blackwell Publishers.

Barth, Fredrik (1969), *Ethnic Groups and Boundaries: The Social Organization of Culture Difference*, London: Allen & Unwin.

Billig, Michael (1995), *Banal Nationalism*, London: Sage Publications.

Brooks, Van Wyck (1915), *America's Coming-of-Age*, Whitefish, MT: Kessinger Publishing.

Cardillo, Maren (1998), "Intimate Relationships: Personality Development through Interaction During Early Life," http://www.personalityresearch.org/papers/cardillo.html.

Carnegie Council (2001), "The Search for a Usable Past," http://www.cceia.org/resources/articles_papers_reports/716.html.

Cayla, Julien and Giana Eckhardt (2008), "Asian Brands and the Shaping of a Transnational Imagined Community," *Journal of Consumer Research*, 35 (August), 216-30.

Chaplin, Lan Nguyen, Deborah Roedder John, Dawn Iacobucci, and Laura Peracchio (2005), "The Development of Self-Brand Connections in Children and Adolescents," *Journal of Consumer Research*, 31 (June), 119-29.

Cova, Bernard (1997), "Community and Consumption: Towards a Definition of The "Linking Value" Of Products or Services," *European Journal of Marketing*, 31 (3/4), 297-316.

Cova, Bernard and Véronique Cova (2001), "Tribal Aspects of Postmodern Consumption Research: The Case of French in-Line Roller Skaters," *Journal of Consumer Behaviour*, 1 (1), 67-76.

Cova, Bernard and Stefano Pace (2006), "Brand Community of Convenience Products: New Forms of Customer Empowerment – the Case "My Nutella the Community"," *European Journal of Marketing*, 40 (9/10), 1087-105.

de Cillia, Rudolf, Martin Reisigl, and Ruth Wodak (1999), "The Discursive Construction of National Identities," *Discourse & Society*, 10 (2), 149-73.

Deighton, John (2010), "Broadening the Scope of Consumer Research," *Journal of Consumer Research*, 36 (6).

Denny, Rita M, Patricia L Sunderland, Jacqueline Smart, and Chris Christofi (2005), "Finding Ourselves in Images: A Cultural Reading of Trans-Tasman Identities Issue," *Journal of Research for Consumers* (8), http://www.jrconsumers.com/academic_articles/issue_8?f=5736.

Douglas, Mary and Baron Isherwood (1979), *The World of Goods: Toward an Anthropology of Consumption*, New York: Basic Books.

Elliott, Richard H and Kritsadarat Wattanasuwan (1998), "Brands as Symbolic Resources for the Construction of Identity," *International Journal of Advertising*, 17 (2), 134-44.

Elliott, Richard H (1997), "Existential Consumption and Irrational Desire," *European Journal of Marketing*, 34 (3/4), 285-96.

Elsaesser, Thomas (2005), *European Cinema. Face to Face with Hollywood*, Amsterdam: Amsterdam University Press.

Firat, A Fuat and Nikhilesh Dholakia (2004), "Theoretical and Philosophical Implications of Postmodern Debates: Some Challenges to Modern Marketing," http://www.cba.uri.edu/offices/dean/workingpapers/documents/TheoreticalAndPhilosophicalImplicationsOfPostmodernDebatesSomeChallengesToModernMarketing.pdf.

Fournier, Susan M (1998), "Consumers and Their Brands: Developing Relationship Theory in Consumer Research," *Journal of Consumer Research*, 24 (March), 343-73.

Frosh, Paul (2007), "Penetrating Market, Fortifying Fences: Advertising, Consumption, and Violent National Conflict," *Public Culture*, 19 (3), 461- 82.

Goulding, Christina, Avi Shankar, and Richard Elliott (2002), "Working Weeks, Rave Weekends: Identity Fragmentation and the Emergence of New Communities," *Consumption, Markets & Culture*, 5 (4), 261-84.

Grimson, Alejandro (2010), "Culture and Identity: Two Different Notions," *Social Identities*, 16 (1), 61-77.

Hayward, Susan (2005), *French National Cinema*, Oxford: Routledge.

Holt, Douglas B (2006), "Jack Daniel's America: Iconic Brands as Ideological Parasites and Proselytizers," *Journal of Consumer Culture*, 6 (3), 355-77.

Humphrey, Michael (2004), "Lebanese Identities: Between Cities, Nations and Trans-Nations," *Arab Studies Quarterly*, 26 (1), 31-50.

Jackson, Tim (2004), "Consuming Paradise - Unsustainable Consumption in Cultural and Social-Psychological Context," www.env.leeds.ac.uk/~hubacek/leeds04/1.2Consuming%20 Paradise.pdf.

Jenkins, Richard (1996), *Social Identity*, London: Routledge.

Kapferer, Jean Noël (1997), *Strategic Brand Management: Creating and Sustaining Brand Equity Long Term* (2nd ed.). London; Dover, N.H.: Kogan Page.

Kates, Steven M (2004), "The Dynamics of Brand Legitimacy: An Interpretive Study in the Gay Men's Community," *Journal of Consumer Research*, 31 (September), 455-64.

--- (2006), "Researching Brands Ethnographically: An Interpretive Community Approach," in *Handbook of Qualitative Research Methods in Marketing*, ed. Russell W Belk, Cheltenham: Edward Elgar, 94-105.

Keller, Kevin Lane (2003), "Brand Synthesis: The Multidimensionality of Brand Knowledge," *Journal of Consumer Research*, 29 (4), 595-600.

Kirloskar-Steinbach, Monika (2004), "National Identity: Belonging to a Cultural Group? Belonging to a Polity?" *Journal for the Study of Religions and Ideologies*, 8 (1), 31-42.

Kozinets, Robert V (2002), "Can Consumers Escape the Market? Emancipatory Illuminations from Burning Man," *Journal of Consumer Research*, 29 (June), 20–38.

Leach, Grant (2000), "Beyond Branding: Enter the Dream Society," *Marketing*, 19 (6), 18-19.

Lévi-Strauss, Claude (1962), *The Savage Mind (La Pensée Sauvage)*, Chicago: The University of Chicago Press.

Mathwick, Charla, Caroline Wiertz, and Ko de Ruyter (2008), "Social Capital Production in a Virtual P3 Community," *Journal of Consumer Research*, 34 (April), 832-49.

McCracken, Grant (1986), "Culture and Consumption: A Theoretical Account of the Structure and Movement of the Cultural Meaning of Consumer Goods," *Journal of Consumer Research*, 13 (June), 71-84.

McLuhan, Marshall (1962), *The Gutenberg Galaxy: The Making of Typographical Man*, London: Routledge and Kegan Paul.

McQuarrie, Edward F and David Glen Mick (1996), "Figures of Rhetoric in Advertising Language," *Journal of Consumer Research*, 22 (March), 424-38.

Mead, George Herbert (1934), *Mind, Self & Society from the Standpoint of a Social Behaviorist*, Chicago: The University of Chicago Press.

Mick, David Glen and Claus Buhl (1992), "A Meaning-Based Model of Advertising Experiences," *Journal of Consumer Research*, 19 (December), 317-38.

Millard, Gregory, Sarah Riegel, and John Wright (2002), "Here's Where We Get Canadian: English-Canadian Nationalism and Popular Culture," *American Review of Canadian Studies*, 32 (1), 11-34.

Moreno, Julio (2003), *Yankee Don't Go Home! Mexican Nationalism, American Business Culture, and the Shaping of Modern Mexico, 1920-1950*, Chapel Hill, NC: University of North Carolina Press.

Muñiz, Albert M and Thomas C O'Guinn (2001), "Brand Community," *Journal of Consumer Research*, 27 (March), 412-32.

Muñiz, Albert M and Hope Jensen Schau (2005), "Religiosity in the Abandoned Apple Newton Brand Community," *Journal of Consumer Research*, 31 (March), 737-47.

Otnes, Cele and Linda M Scott (1996), "Something Old, Something New: Exploring the Interaction between Ritual and Advertising," *Journal of Advertising*, 25 (1), 33-50.

Pettigrew, Simone (2002), "A Grounded Theory of Beer Consumption in Australia," *Qualitative Market Research: An International Journal*, 5 (2), 112-22.

Phillips, Barbara J (1997), "Thinking into It: Consumer Interpretation of Complex Advertising Images," *Journal of Advertising*, 26 (2), 77-87.

Prideaux, Jillian (2009), "Consuming Icons: Nationalism and Advertising in Australia," *Nations and Nationalism*, 15 (4), 616-35.

Reed, Americus (2002), "Social Identity as a Useful Perspective for Self-Concept-Based Consumer Research," *Psychology and Marketing*, 19 (3), 235-66.

Ritson, Mark and Richard H Elliott (1995), "A Model of Advertising Literacy: The Praxiology and Co-Creation of Advertising Meaning," in *24th European Academy of Marketing Conference*, Vol. 1, ed. Michelle Bergadaa, Cergy-Pontoise, France: ESSEC, 1035-54.

--- (1999), "The Social Uses of Advertising: An Ethnographic Study of Adolescent Advertising Audiences," *Journal of Consumer Research*, 26 (December), 260-77.

Schau, Hope Jensen, Albert M Muñiz, and Eric J Arnould (forthcoming), "How Brand Community Practices Create Value," *Journal of Marketing*.

Schouten, John W and James H McAlexander (1995), "Subcultures of Consumption: An Ethnography of the New Bikers," *Journal of Consumer Research*, 22 (June), 43-61.

Schroeder, Jonathan E (2002), *Visual Consumption* London: Routledge.

Schroeder, Jonathan E and Miriam Salzer-Mörling (2006), *Brand Culture*, London: Routledge.

Spangler, Matthew (2002), ""A Fadograph of a Yestern Scene": Performances Promising Authenticity in Dublin's Bloomsday," *Text and Performance Quarterly*, 22 (2), 120–37.

Squire, Shelagh J (1996), "Literary Tourism and Sustainable Tourism: Promoting 'Anne of Green Gables' in Prince Edward Island," *Journal of Sustainable Tourism*, 4 (3), 119-34.

Stalnaker, Stan (2002), *Hub Culture: The Next Wave of Urban Consumer*, Singapore: John Wiley & Sons.

Staples, Shelley (2003), "Negotiating the Racial Mountain," http://xroads.virginia.edu/~MA03/staples/douglas/home.html.

Tajfel, Henri and John C Turner (1979), "An Integrative Theory of Intergroup Conflict," in *The Social Psychology of Intergroup Relations*, ed. William G Austin and Stephen Worchel, Monterey, CA: Brooks/Cole., 33-47.

Thompson, Craig J (2005), "Consumer Risk Perceptions in a Community of Reflexive Doubt," *Journal of Consumer Research*, 32 (September), 235-48.

Turner, John C, Michael A Hogg, Penelope J Oakes, Stephen D Reicher, and Margaret S Wetherell (1987), *Rediscovering the Social Group: A Self-Categorization Theory*, Cambridge, MA: Blackwell.

# Consuming Label Information in Product Series
Lin Huang, University of Michigan, USA

## ABSTRACT

This research examines the psychological avenues in processing extrinsic numerical cues and its verbal counterpart in the context of product series evaluation, which is affected by the mere choice of product labels on a newer generation with the membership being indexed either numerically or verbally. A theoretical model is proposed to account for this "label effect" which posits that numerical labels activate an expectancy mode to unconsciously search outward for information compatible with the expected product specification, while equivalent descriptive labels activate a self-fit mode to unconsciously search inward for incidental goals congruent with the anticipated product experience.

## INTRODUCTION

Consumers are known to attend to extrinsic cues, such as brand names, during consumption experiences (Dodds et al., 1991) and are sensitive to the presentation format of such marketing information (Biehal and Chakravarti, 1982; Levin and Gaeth, 1988), sometimes in a nonconscious manner (Fitzsimons and Shiv, 2001; Shiv et al., 2005; Chartrand, 2005; Chartrand et al., 2008). Therefore, the manufacturer's decision to assign a brand name or a label to a product in general is certainly strategic (Keller, 1993; Robertson, 1989; Pavia and Costa, 1993). A manufacturer typically carries a line of related products (a product series) as a result of innovations over time. Subsequently, when naming a product from a later generation in this series, the manufacturer oftentimes adopts the original brand name of its predecessor from an earlier generation to take advantage of the established brand equity, and adds a new component to index membership. This new component in the brand name is mostly seen in either numerical forms (e.g., Airbus 320, 330, 380; Acrobat Reader 7, 8, 9) or descriptive/verbal[1] forms (e.g., Nike Air Max *Light* preceded by Nike Air Max).

While the use of this umbrella branding strategy is deliberate, the choice between a numerical and an equivalent descriptive form seems more idiosyncratic and largely interchangeable, at least as seen in the eyes of the consumers. One of the best illustrations of such perceived random choice in naming schemes comes from the Microsoft Windows OS series. The latest generation Windows 7, released in 2009, only surprisingly has its most immediate predecessor in terms of the same numerical naming scheme back in 1990 (Windows 3). During almost two decades in between, several descriptive names, among others, were dragged to fill in the seemingly odd blanks (e.g., Windows XP, Windows Vista). Please note that I am not claiming that manufacturers are always reckless in choosing between numerical and descriptive naming schemes for their product series. It is only that the decision criterion behind such choices, which may or may not be effective, is usually unknown to consumers and researchers alike. The focus of this research, however, is to understand how consumers process numerical and (equivalent) verbal information, and the resulting patterns in judgment and evaluation. In the end, manufacturers should be more able to design appropriate brand names for a product series if they have such additional knowledge about consumers at hand.

I contend that consumers have a consistent yet nonconscious pattern in processing the inter-product information (such as innovation) embedded in an extrinsic cue, whether such information is conveyed through numerical or verbal components in product series brand names. Specifically, numerical information in a product series brand name (henceforth *numerical label*) activates an expectancy mode in which consumers nonconsciously search outward for product specifications compatible with the expected outcome; and verbal information in a product series brand name (henceforth *descriptive label*) activates an self-fit mode in which consumers nonconsciously search inward for motivational constructs (such as goals) congruent with the anticipated product experience.

## ALPHA-NUMERIC BRANDING AND COMPARATIVE JUDGMENT

To motivate the discussions of including a numerical or descriptive (verbal) component in a product series label, I draw theoretical background from the literatures on alpha-numeric branding and comparative judgment. First, there is a small cohort of research studying optimal brand name design. Robertson (1989) provides a list of desirable brand name characteristics based on phonetic and semantic appeals. More specifically, research shows that consumers perceive alpha-numeric brand names favorably (Boyd, 1985; Pavia and Costa, 1993; King and Janiszewski, 2009) whenever appropriate. Alpha-numeric brand name is defined as "a (brand) name that contains one or more numbers" (Pavia and Costa, 1993), equivalent to the term of *numerical label* adopted in this research. People are known to interpret number information through multiple cognitive channels, such as stereotyping of certain "good" or "bad" numbers (Simmons and Schindler, 2003) and classical conditioning of certain "special" numbers (Goodman and Irwin, 2006) without relying on the conscious belief in the associative systems. Therefore, using numbers in brand names has proved its theoretical relevance. Pavia and Costa (1993) opt for an exploratory research via focus groups to identify common reactions towards alpha-numeric brand names. They find respondents generally agree that alpha-numeric brand names are suggestive of product series and are more appropriate for functional/technical products than for fun/sensual products. However, the authors do not specify the cognitive foundations behind their findings. More recently, King and Janiszewski (2009) find that certain numbers are favored more than others due to the differences in metacognitive experiences of fluency. Therefore, brands with such numbers are evaluated more favorably than those who do not.

Then, it should be noted that the product series paradigm used in this present research has its root from the law of comparative judgment (Thurstone, 1927), which focuses on measuring the perceived intensity of stimuli through pairwise comparisons rather than measuring the standalone physical properties. In this spirit, a product is judged by its membership in a product series rather than just by its own features. Hsee and colleagues started a line of research on separate and joint evaluations of product options (please see Hsee et al. 1999 for a review) which posits that some types of product features are easier to evaluate than others in a joint evaluation mode. This finding speaks for an interesting class of preference reversal effects. The inter-product relation within a product series, such as innovation, is inherently easier to evaluate in a joint evaluation mode (i.e., joint evaluation across product generations). So the use of this product series paradigm should predict novel (and potentially different) patterns of preferences compared to the use of a single-product paradigm.

Given the product series paradigm, it is natural to go beyond *numerical labels* (i.e., alpha-numeric brand names) and include *descriptive/verbal labels* into the model, since it is also a widely

---

1 Henceforth, "*verbal*" and "*descriptive*" are used as equivalent terms.

accepted candidate to denote membership in a product series. In this research, I define this descriptive component in the product label as an adjective quantifier, such as [brand name] *Elite Edition* or [brand name] *Xtra*. Previous research that explicitly contrasts the use of numerical and verbal information is scarce. The most relevant work in this line focuses on the memory representation and distortion of such information (Viswanathan and Childers, 1996). They study the product attribute domain where either numerical or verbal information is used to express magnitude (e.g., *10* calories versus *low* calories) and find that numerical attribute information is more prone to memory distortion and is therefore easier to deviate from its original representation than numerical information. Then, they conclude that numerical information is generally more preferable for memory tasks (such as recall or recognition) than its verbal counterpart. They also argue that numerical information does not have meaning by itself unless being compared against each other while verbal information is inherently descriptive.

## NONCONSCIOUS CONSUMPTION OF EXPECTANCY AND FIT

Previous research on cognitive elaboration suggests that peripheral cues are less important in persuasion when there is sufficient motivation or ability to process the true merits of the stimulus (Petty and Cacioppo, 1986). However, there is also ample evidence that, holding the physical consumption constant, the consumption of information (such as the information embedded in peripheral/extrinsic cues) can redirect the whole consumption experience (Shiv et al., 2005; Ariely and Levav, 2000; Morales and Fitzsimons, 2007). To generalize the role of consuming information, Ariely and Norton (2009) propose a *conceptual consumption* account to pin down this independent effect "over and above utility from physical consumption". The conceptual consumption account posits that consumers may forgo positive physical consumption or choose negative physical consumption when the information compatible with certain psychological avenues becomes available. Two such psychological avenues that are most relevant to this present research are *expectancy* and *regulatory fit*.

There has been lots of evidence that expectancy can influence consumptions and this stream of research in psychology/marketing is analogous to the medical research on the placebo effect of medical treatments (please see Price et al. 2008 for a review). Shiv et al. (2005) study the placebo effect of price and find subjects who consume an energy drink bought at a discounted price perform worse on a follow-up puzzle solving task compared to those who consume the same drink at a regular price. They propose that the expectancy on the price-quality association leads to this effect. Besides price, brand is also documented as a stimulus that alters expectancy. Allison and Uhl (1964) find that consumers believe their favorite brand beer tastes better when they see the brand displayed, however they report it tastes just the same as any other beer when there is no brand information.

As for regulatory fit, it is natural to view it as a class of conceptual consumption because this is basically a metacognitive experience of feeling right and all metacognitive experiences involve "the interplay of declarative and experiential information" (Schwarz, 2004 & 2006). Higgins and colleagues study the regulatory fit effect in a set of research, positing that the fit is experienced when there is a manner of decision making (e.g., eager or vigilant) that sustains the goal orientation (e.g., promotion/prevention focus). Avnet and Higgins (2006) explore the use of feelings/reasons as psychological equivalence to the use of explicitly manipulated (eager/vigilant) manners. Borrowing from Viswanathan and Childers (1996), it is consistent in this present research to deduce that numerical labels are

perceived as reason-intensive while descriptive labels are perceived as feeling-intensive; meanwhile, the incidental goal priming in the present research for the shrift/prestige focus (see Chartrand et al., 2008) is induced through an item listing task adapted from Idson et al. (2000) & Cesario et al. (2004). I use the "unrelated studies" paradigm (Avnet and Higgins, 2006) in this present research so the goal priming is seemingly unrelated to label conditions in order to allow the possibility of nonconscious processes. Finally, it should be noted that the automated choice of a psychological avenue (expectancy/fit) in conceptual consumptions is situational and dependent on the availability of relevant information (Schwarz, 2006), such as the numerical/verbal cues in the present research.

Interestingly, both classes of conceptual consumption may be potentially experienced in a nonconscious manner. Shiv et al. (2005) find that the expectancy on price-quality association is processed out of the awareness of consumers. Analogously, Jones et al. (2002) find the fit between the preference for letters used in self name and self-esteem level is experienced unconsciously. Extant research on nonconscious goals (Chartrand et al., 2008; Chartrand, 2005; Fitzsimons et al., 2002; Fitzsimons and Shiv, 2001; Janiszewski and van Osselaer, 2005) suggests that incidental goals can be activated by extrinsic cues, such as brand names. Although consumers are generally aware of the outcome of the goal once it is fulfilled, they can be nonconscious of the source and/or process of this goal. Also, certain metacognitive experiences (such as fit or fluency) may actually be due to nonconscious processes (Fitzsimons et al., 2002). The nonconscious property is examined through extensive debriefing (Chartrand, 2005) and/or mediation tests (Shiv et al., 2005). The present research focuses on the latter, but collects some qualitative evidence as well.

### Hypotheses

Taken together, the number processing, conceptual consumption, and nonconscious goal literatures provide the following insights for this present research. First, numerical labels are easier to compare against each other due to the fact that numbers are inherently ordinal. In the product series paradigm, numerical labels facilitate direct specification comparison across product generations, where the gains in utility (or, innovations) are distributed along declarative (utilitarian) dimensions. However, descriptive/verbal labels are easier to trigger subjective interpretation of an anticipated product experience due to the fact that adjective quantifiers are inherently descriptive. In the product series paradigm, descriptive labels help appreciate the gains in utility (or, innovations) that are distributed along experiential (hedonic) dimensions. This distinction in innovation judgment due to labels shall become blurred when the numerical or descriptive information in the labels becomes less diagnostic.

*Hypothesis* **1a:** *Consumers judge a product belonging to a product series with numerical labels more favorably when the judgment is on the utilitarian dimensions. They judge descriptive labels more favorably when the judgment is on the hedonic dimensions.*

*Hypothesis* **1b:** *The judgment shall converge once the numerical or descriptive information in the labels becomes less diagnostic.*

Second, a natural conjecture from the above hypotheses is that the label effect shall be moderated by the type of product messages available to consumers (presumably during various chances of exposures to marketing campaigns). To be specific, declarative product messages that meet expectations of certain product specification improvement shall be more appreciated when paired with numerical labels. On the flip side, experiential product messages that meet an incidental goal orientation shall be more appreciated when paired with descriptive labels.

*Hypothesis 2:*    *Consumers prefer a product belonging to a product series with numerical labels when they observe declarative product information. They prefer descriptive labels when observing experiential product information.*

Third, since labels are basically extrinsic cues, consumers may be unaware of this information in forming judgment. They can be clueless if they ever use this information or how to use such information. In the product series paradigm, they can be unaware of the changes in expectancy (in the case of numerical labels) or feeling right (in the case of descriptive labels) that is attributable to labels. Alternatively, consumers might also consciously and intentionally make inferences from the labels like they typically make from many product features. I hypothesize that:

*Hypothesis 3:*    *Consumers engage in a nonconscious processing of certain extrinsic cues, particularly product series labels.*

And finally, this present research aims to pin down the psychological factors that are likely to influence this label effect. Based on previous findings on expectancy and regulatory fit (e.g., Shiv et al., 2005; Avnet and Higgins, 2006), expectancy strength and incidental goal priming are two promising candidates for this purpose and I will further elaborate on these in the respective experiments. Here, I hypothesize that:

*Hypothesis 4:*    *Consumers prefer a product belonging to a product series with numerical labels when they are in a high expectancy strength condition (versus a low expectancy strength condition); Expectancy strength has no effect on descriptive labels.*

*Hypothesis 5:*    *Consumers prefer a product belonging to a product series with descriptive labels when they are primed with a prestige orientation. They prefer numerical labels when primed with a thrift orientation.*

## STUDY 1

The goal of study 1 was to test the hypothesis that numerical labels lead to different product series judgment compared to descriptive labels, depending on whether the judgment is on the utilitarian or hedonic dimensions (hypothesis 1a). Participants were asked to state their judgment on a new generation automobile belonging to an automobile series with either a numerical label or a descriptive label to index its generation. Each participant made judgment on both utilitarian and hedonic measures. It was expected that participants in the numerical label condition would judge this new generation automobile more favorably on utilitarian measures while those in the descriptive condition would judge the automobile more favorably on the hedonic measures.

### Design and Procedure

Study 1 used a between-subject manipulation of the label conditions (numerical, descriptive). One hundred and fifteen undergraduate students from a large Midwestern university participated in this study for course credit. Participants were invited into a behavioral lab and were told that the study investigated "product design in the automobile industry". They were instructed that a fictitious model XYZ is a popular automobile model made by an anonymous automobile manufacturer. Now the manufacturer is in the process of designing a new generation of this model. For the participants in the numerical condition, they were instructed that the manufacturer is to market the new generation as model XYZ 2 and put it into production next year. For the participants in the descriptive condition, everything was similar except that they were instructed that the new generation will be marketed as XYZ *SE (Special Edition)*. No other information was given to the participants.

Then the participants were instructed that, at this stage, the public knew very little about this new generation automobile and they were asked to offer their best intuitive guess on this new model by using 7-point scales (1 = *strongly disagree* and 7 = *strongly agree*) on the following statements – "The new model is *fun*"; "The new model is *entertaining*"; "The new model is *exciting*"; "The new model is *well designed*"; "The new model is *functional*"; and "The new model is *practical*". The order of these statements was randomized. "Fun", "entertaining" and "exciting" statements were designed to make hedonic judgment. And "well designed", "functional" and "practical" statements were designed to make utilitarian judgment. Finally, the participants were asked how likely they would like the new model by a 7-point scale (1 = *least likely* and 7 = *most likely*) and they were invited to write down their other free thoughts about the new model (if there was any).

### Results

The results from three utilitarian statements (well-designed/functional/practical) were combined to form a utilitarian measure (Cronbach's $\alpha = .93$) and the results from three hedonic statements (fun/entertaining/exciting) were combined to form a hedonic measure (Cronbach's $\alpha = .95$). The data were analyzed using a one-way between-subject ANOVA with the label as the between-subject factor. The main effect of the label on the utilitarian measure was significant ($F(1, 113) = 25.22, p < .001$), and the main effect of the label on the hedonic measure was also significant ($F(1, 113) = 7.86, p < .05$). Participants in the numerical label condition judged the new model more favorably on the utilitarian measure ($M = 4.96$) than participants in the descriptive label condition ($M = 4.02; t(113) = 3.73, p < .001$). In contrast, participants in the descriptive label condition judged the new model more favorably on the hedonic measure ($M = 5.28$) than participants in the numerical label condition ($M = 4.76; t(113) = 1.97, p < .05$).

*Supplemental Analysis.* When using a more inclusive judgment variable "like", it turned out that the label effect was insignificant ($F(1,113) = 2.17, p > .10$). In fact, participants liked the new model similarly, no matter they were in the numerical label condition ($M = 4.93$) or in the descriptive label condition ($M = 4.59; t(113) = 1.47, p > .10$).

### Discussion

Study 1 demonstrates that consumers have more favorable utilitarian judgment on the product series using numerical labels. And they have more favorable hedonic judgment on the product series using descriptive labels. This pattern provides evidence in support of hypothesis 1a. Since there was no other product information available in this study except for the label condition itself, the resultant effect should be clearly attributable to the label manipulations. The findings in this study are generally in line with Pavia and Costa (1993) where they posit that functional or technical products are more appropriate to use alpha-numeric brand names than fun or sensual products.

Interestingly, the label effect is insignificant on the inclusive judgment variable "like" when this "like" is not projected onto a more specific hedonic or utilitarian dimension. This finding confirms that people have no hardwired preferences for either kind of label when used in a product series. In other words, neither numerical nor descriptive labels have an absolute advantage over its counterpart in terms of the holistic preferences. However, study 1 suggests that different types of labels are indeed advantageous on different facets of preferences. The next question is, naturally, what might be the relevant information that is more conducive to utilitarian (versus hedonic) judgment when a numerical (versus descriptive) label is used in a product series?

## STUDY 2

Study 1 found that consumers favor product series with numerical labels during utilitarian judgment and favor descriptive labels during hedonic judgment. If this is so, it is then possible to identify a particular type of informative product message that is conducive to a particular dimension of judgment. The goal of study 2 was two folded. First, I wanted to test the hypothesis that consumers prefer a product series with numerical labels when they have access to the declarative product message. On the flip side, they prefer descriptive labels when having access to the experiential product message (hypothesis 2). Second, I wanted to additionally test the hypothesis that consumers make use of the product series label information in a nonconscious manner (hypothesis 3). Participants were asked to state their preference for the sequel to an animation movie. The membership of the sequel in this movie series was indexed either with a numerical label or with a descriptive label. Unlike the generic brand in study 1, here I used an actual movie title. It was expected that the participants in the numerical label condition would favor the sequel more than those in the descriptive label condition when they were presented with declarative movie information on its plot; and participants in the descriptive label condition would favor the sequel more than those in the numerical label condition when they were presented with experiential movie information on 3D enhancement.

### Design and Procedure

Study 2 used between-subject manipulations on both factors - the label conditions (numerical, descriptive) and the movie information conditions (declarative message on plot, experiential message on 3D enhancement). Two hundred and fifty-six undergraduate students from a large Midwestern university participated in this study for course credit. Participants were invited into a behavior lab and were told that the study was to investigate consumer preferences for the sequel of *Up*, a 2009 American computer-animated film.

For the participants in the numerical label condition, they were told that the sequel will be named as *Up 2*. For those in the descriptive label condition, they were told that the sequel will be named as *Up: Russell's Special Mission*. For the participants in the declarative message condition, they were told that "Pixar recently announced that the screen writer of *Up* will write the sequel. And the studio plans to bring back the producing team from *Up*. The voice actors for the two main characters will reprise their roles in the sequel." For those in the experiential message condition, they were told that "the sequel will be one of the world's most expensive animation movies and will be the first full-length movie in the history to use the latest Digital 3D IMAX technology, which can

significantly improve the 3D viewing experience especially for viewers sitting closer to the screen, a major unsatisfying problem for many traditional 3D movies)".

Participants were randomly assigned to one of the four combinations of these conditions. They provided responses on 7-point scales for two dependent measures: "liking of the sequel", and "the intention to watch this sequel". Additionally, I recorded data on two covariate measures: "how do you like animation movies in general (on a 7-point scale)", and "have you watched the original title *Up* before? (binary)".

Finally, I did two things for the nonconscious process hypothesis. One was to design a mediation test adapted from Shiv et al. (2005). At the end of the study, I asked the participants to rate how relevant that they felt the name of the sequel was to their preferences of the sequel on a 7-point scale ranging from 1 ("not at all relevant") to 7 ("very relevant"). The rationale was that if the participants were nonconscious of this process, this relevance measure should not mediate the effects of the independent variables on the dependent measures. The other thing that I also did was to ask the participants to write down their thoughts on the potential hidden agenda of this study (if there was any) or any other thoughts about this study in general. This was not as rigorous as the extensive debriefing proposed by Chartrand (2005), but was designed as a mini version to accommodate administrative constraints during the study.

### Results

The data were analyzed using a two-way between-subject ANCOVA with the label and message as the two between-subject factors and with the two covariate measures as mentioned earlier. The label by message interaction was significant as expected ($F(1, 249) = 59.54$, $p < .001$) for the "liking" dependent measure and ($F(1, 249) = 54.18$, $p < .001$) for the "intention to watch" dependent measure. Furthermore, participants in the numerical label condition liked the sequel more when they were presented with declarative messages ($M = 4.48$) than with experiential messages ($M = 3.57$; $t(134) = 2.81$, $p < .005$). On the flip side, participants in the descriptive label condition liked the sequel more when they were presented with experiential messages ($M = 4.50$) than with experiential messages ($M = 3.49$; $t(118) = 3.71$, $p < .001$). With the "intention to watch" dependent measure, I also got the similar crossover pattern. Specifically, participants in the numerical label condition were more likely to watch the sequel when they were presented with declarative messages ($M = 4.31$) than with experiential messages ($M = 3.41$; $t(134) = 2.73$, $p < .01$). In contrast, participants in the descriptive label condition were more likely to watch the sequel when they were presented with experiential messages ($M = 4.20$) than with experiential messages ($M = 3.26$; $t(118) = 3.30$, $p < .001$). Additionally, "watched the original title before" was the only significant covariate on the "intention to watch" dependent measure ($F(1, 249) = 73.83$, $p < .001$). No other covariates were significant in any other cases.

*Nonconscious Processing.* As discussed earlier, I used a mediation approach to address this issue. Recall that at the end of the study, I asked the participants to rate how relevant that they felt the name of the sequel was to their preferences of the sequel on a 7-point scale ranging from 1 ("not at all relevant") to 7 ("very relevant"). Had the participants been conscious of this process, this relevance measure should have mediated the effects of the independent variables on the dependent measures. Sobel tests on both dependent measures failed to support such mediations (Sobel $z = .32$, $p = .37$ for the "liking" dependent measure; Sobel $z = .28$, $p = .38$ for the "intention to watch" measure). This result suggests the nonconscious processing hypothesis. Additionally, on the hidden

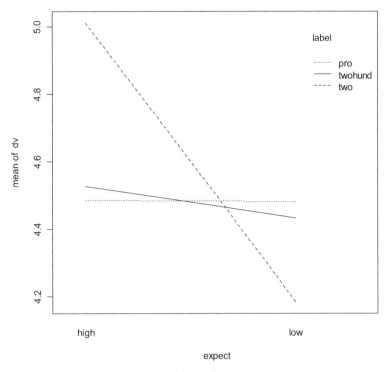

**Figure 1**

agenda thoughts elicitation task, none of the participants correctly guessed the purpose of this study or suggested that their preferences were resultant of the sequel name. This also provides another piece of evidence that the participants were unaware of the process.

## STUDY 3

Study 3 was designed to focus on the expectancy mode and address three issues. First, I wanted to test the hypothesis that the numerical label effect is stronger when consumers have a strong expectation (that an improved specification in the new generation leads to gains in utility) than when they have a mild expectation. This prediction should not hold for the descriptive label effect (hypothesis 4). Second, I wanted to test the hypothesis that numerical labels are evaluated similarly as descriptive labels whenever the numerical information becomes less diagnostic for comparative judgment (hypothesis 1b). And third, I wanted to continue investigating the nonconscious nature of the label effect (hypothesis 3). Participants were asked to state their preference for a new model of portable media player from the family of such players. The membership of this new model in its family was indexed with a typical (diagnostic) numerical label, an atypical (non-diagnostic) numerical label, or a descriptive label.

### Design and Procedure

Study 3 used between-subject manipulations on the two factors – the label conditions (typical numerical, atypical numerical, descriptive) and the expectancy strength conditions (high, low). Three hundred and six national adult samples from an online paid subject pool were recruited for this study. They were told that the study was meant as a survey for portable media player designs and read the following instructions – "Creative Labs is a portable media player producer with a strong foothold in European and Asian markets. Its flagship player, Creative ZEN, was released in 2008. It was the world's first 32 GB flash memory based player. Now the company's top priority is to get a more substantial market share in North America where it plans to launch a successor to the popular

Creative ZEN next year. This next generation player will set a new world record of 64 GB capacity with an additional SDHC card slot for even bigger storages".

The participants were then instructed that the new generation player would be marketed as Creative ZEN *2* (for typical numerical label condition), Creative ZEN *200* (for atypical numerical label condition), or Creative ZEN *Pro* (for descriptive label condition). Meanwhile, the expectancy strength conditions were manipulated as suggested in Shiv et al. (2005). Particularly, participants in the high expectancy strength condition were instructed that "according to a preliminary marketing analysis, the new features in this next generation player will *definitely* help attract *significant* attention from a *large* number of North American consumers". Those in the low expectancy strength condition were instructed that "according to a preliminary marketing analysis, the new features in this new generation player *might* help attract *some* attention from *certain* North American consumers".

Participants were randomly assigned to one of the six combinations of these conditions. They provided responses on 7-point scales for a set of three dependent measures: "liking of the new player", "intention to buy the new player", and "worth recommending the new player to friends". I also use 7-point scales for a set of three utilitarian statements as I did in study 1 and collected data on routine demographic covariates as I did in study 2. For the nonconscious process hypothesis, the data collection procedures were similar to study 2 where I used a relevance scale for the mediation test and a mini debriefing for qualitative evidence. However, the relevance scale in this study was designed as more nuanced in that I did not ask for the relevance of label per se; instead, I asked for the relevance of the expectancy to the preference – "How relevant that you feel the preliminary marketing analysis was to your preference for this new player?" This change should make the relevance scale less susceptible to demand artifacts and more straightforward to identify if the non-consciousness of interest was due to the nonconscious process of expectancy.

## Results

The data were analyzed using a 3 (typical, atypical numerical labels & descriptive label) by 2 (high & low expectancy strengths) factorial between-subject ANOVA. The demographic covariates turned out insignificant and were eventually dropped in the analysis. The three dependent variables ("liking of the new player", "intention to buy the new player", and "worth recommending the new player to friends") were combined to form a preference measure (Cronbach's α = .85). Consistent with study 1, the three utilitarian statements ("well-designed", "functional", and "practical") were combined to form a utilitarian measure (Cronbach's α = .91). The main finding was that the label by expectancy strength interaction was significant as expected $(F(2,300)) = 3.48, p < .05)$ for the preference measure. Particularly, participants in the typical numerical label condition prefer the new player more $(M = 5.01)$ than those in the atypical numerical label condition $(M = 4.53; t(101) = 1.65, p < .1)$ or those in the descriptive label condition $(M = 4.49; t(104) = 1.97, p < .05)$ when they had high expectancy strengths (Note: the difference between the latter two means was insignificant; $t(115) = .21, p = .84$). Besides, the only significant preference change between high and low expectancy strengths happened in those assigned to the typical numerical condition $(M_{high\,expect} = 5.01, M_{low\,expect} = 4.18; t(85) = 2.71, p < .01)$. There were no significant preference changes in the remaining two label conditions $(p$'s $> .65)$ between high and low expectancy strengths.

*Nonconscious Processing.* The results were consistent with study 2 in support of the nonconscious hypothesis. As discussed earlier, I used a modified relevance scale for the mediation test. Recall that at the end of the study, I asked the participants to rate how relevant that they felt the preliminary marketing analysis was to their preferences of the new player on a 7-point scale ranging from 1 ("not at all relevant") to 7 ("very relevant"). Had the participants been conscious of the role of expectancy, this relevance measure should have mediated the effects of the independent variables on the dependent measure. A Sobel test failed to support such mediations (Sobel $z = -.10, p = .39$). This result suggests the nonconscious processing of expectancy. Additionally, on the hidden agenda thoughts elicitation task, none of the participants correctly guessed the purpose of this study or suggested that their preferences were resultant of the marketing analysis. This also provides another piece of evidence that the participants were unaware of the role of expectancy.

## Discussion

Study 3 demonstrates that consumers prefer a product series with (diagnostic) numerical labels when they have high expectancy strength. Expectancy strength has no effect on descriptive labels or (non-diagnostic) numerical labels alike. This pattern provides evidence in support of hypothesis 4 in that numerical labels (rather than descriptive labels) distinctly activate an expectancy mode as a psychological avenue to process extrinsic cues. The resultant effect is stronger when the expectancy of a specification-induced outcome is stronger (for instance, in the high expectancy strength condition, the marketing analysis speculated that the new player would be hugely successful due to specification improvement over the older generation).

The fact that the non-diagnostic (atypical) numerical labels were treated as if they were descriptive labels supports hypothesis 1b. The diagnosticity of the numerical information in this product series paradigm is simply the sufficiency of the input for a comparative judgment task.

Finally, study 3 also confirms the nonconscious process prediction in hypothesis 3. This is consistent with the finding in study 2. Particularly, I find that consumers handle the expectancy of a specification-induced outcome in a nonconscious manner, which is in line with the finding in Shiv et al. (2005) that consumers process price-quality associations unconsciously. Next, I switch gears to study regulatory fit as the other psychological avenue to process extrinsic cues and perform an analogous process analysis with respect to nonconscious goals.

## STUDY 4

Study 4 was designed to complement study 3, and focused on investigating the role of regulatory fit as another means (versus expectancy) to process extrinsic cues. There were two purposes for this study. First, I wanted to test the hypothesis that a product series with a descriptive label is preferred when consumers are primed with a prestige focus. In contrast, a numerical label is preferred when they are primed with a thrift focus (hypothesis 5). And second, I wanted to continue investigating the nonconscious processing perspectives (hypothesis 3) and I focused on the aspect of nonconscious goals in this study.

### Design and Procedure

Study 4 used a between-subject design with two factors – the label conditions (numerical, descriptive) and the goal priming conditions (thrift, prestige). Two hundred and twenty-seven national adult samples from an online paid subject pool were recruited for this study.

At the beginning of the study, the participants were randomly primed with a thrift or prestige goal through an item listing task suggested by Idson et al. (2000) & Cesario et al. (2004). For participants in the prestige priming condition, they were given the following instructions – "Suppose you get your dream job and you are in great financial conditions, how you would spend your money in the next five years to make you feel happy and fulfilling? Please list five such spending". For those in the thrift priming condition, the instruction was – "Let's think broadly about the future. What might be your most concerned financial problems or general economic situations in the next five years? Please list five such concerns". Then, the participants were assigned to a short unrelated filler task to help set up the "unrelated studies" paradigm (Avnet and Higgins, 2006), which better allowed the possibility of processing nonconscious goals because the goal priming was seemingly separate from the later label conditions.

Next, the participants were told that they were invited to take a survey for e-book reader designs with the following instructions – "Kindle is an e-book reader developed by Amazon. The original Kindle was released in November 2007. It was sold out on the first day and the device remained out of stock until April 2008. Earlier this year, Amazon just released a new generation of Kindle. This next generation Kindle model had a trendy facelift with an overall thickness of mere .36 inches". They were then instructed that the new generation was marketed as Kindle *2* (for the numerical label condition), or Kindle *DX* (for the descriptive label condition).

Participants were therefore randomly induced into one of the four label-by-prime conditions. The types of dependent variables collected were analogous to study 3. The setup on the non-consciousness investigation was also analogous to study 3, except that the wording in the relevance scale was modified to examine the nonconscious goals – "How relevant that you feel your hypothetical future financial well-beings were to your preference for this new Kindle model?"

## Results

The data were analyzed using a two-way between-subject AN-COVA with the label and goal priming as the two between-subject factors and with a scale covariate ("how do you feel a consumer electronic product representative of you being who you are?") that turned out marginally significant ($p = .06$). Analogous to study 3, the three preference variables were combined to form a preference measure (Cronbach's $\alpha = .90$) and the three hedonic statements were combined as a hedonic measure (Cronbach's $\alpha = .97$). I found the label by goal prime interaction was significant as expected ($F(1, 220) = 6.24$, $p < .05$) on the preference measure. Particularly, when primed with a prestige goal, the participants preferred descriptive labels more ($M = 4.60$) than numerical labels ($M = 4.12$; $t(104) = 1.72$, $p < .1$). However, I did not find the predicted crossover pattern with the thrift goal priming. It turned out that when primed with a thrift goal, the participants had similar preferences between numerical ($M = 4.26$) and descriptive label conditions ($M = 3.91$, $t(119) = 1.35$, $p = .18$). Moreover, the preference for numerical labels was insensitive to the goal priming ($p = .51$).

*Nonconscious Processing.* Recall that at the end of the study, I asked the participants to rate how relevant that they felt your hypothetical future financial well-beings were to their preferences of the new Kindle model on a 7-point scale ranging from 1 ("not at all relevant") to 7 ("very relevant"). Had the participants been conscious of the role of goal priming, this relevance measure should have mediated the effects of the independent variables on the dependent measure. A Sobel test failed to support such mediations (Sobel $z = .22$, $p = .38$). This result suggests the nonconscious goal hypothesis. Additionally, on the hidden agenda thoughts elicitation task, none of the participants correctly guessed the purpose of this study or suggested that their preferences were resultant of the earlier item listing task for the goal priming.

## Discussion

Study 4 partially supports hypothesis 5 in that descriptive labels are indeed advantageous under the prestige priming. But there is no parallel pattern for the numerical labels under the thrift priming. In fact, a new product generation indexed with the numerical label is insensitive to goal priming in general. Although all these results do suggest that that descriptive labels (rather than numerical labels) distinctly activate a fit mode as a psychological avenue to process extrinsic cues (e.g., when primed with a prestige goal, consumers may feel right to interpret the descriptive label, such as *DX* (deluxe) in this study; and such an interpretation is facilitated by the portrayal of the trendy thin look in the product message), the lack of the crossover pattern for the numerical label under the thrift priming is somehow surprising.

Previous literature posits that there is "feeling right (i.e., fit)" when the reason-intensive stimulus (such as the numerical label) sustains a thrift focus, or when the feeling-extensive stimulus (such as the descriptive label) sustains a prestige focus. Subsequently, the conceptual consumption of such a stimulus becomes more favorable when this "fit" is met (Avnet and Higgins, 2006; Viswanathan and Childers, 1996; Chartrand et al., 2008). In this study, the effect due to descriptive-label-prestige-goal fit is congruent with the previous literatures. However, the lack of the effect under numerical-label-thrift-goal fit is probably due to the fact that, within a product series paradigm, the numerical label is not sufficient to sustain a thrift goal. In a single-product paradigm, recall that the numerical information in the brand name suggests a number-magnitude-quality association, and may provide a basis of justification for purchase. For example, seeing the number *57* in Heinz *57* sauce may make the consumer feel the product has good quality and therefore like it more when

she has a need for thrift. However, the numerical information has very different roles in the product series paradigm where it suggests membership in a particular product generation and may no longer sustain a thrift goal (unless this number information is accompanied by a declarative product message that suggests a utilitarian product specification improvement to meet the need for thrift, which was not the case in this study). That being said, this interesting finding that the numerical label tends to be irresponsive to goal priming remains consistent with the focal conclusion that numerical and descriptive extrinsic cues activate distinct psychological avenues – expectancy and fit, respectively – to process such information.

Like the results in the previous study, study 4 also confirms the nonconscious process prediction in hypothesis 3. Particularly, I find that the incidental goal priming is processed in a nonconscious manner, which is in line with the rich literature on nonconscious goals (Chartrand et al., 2008; Chartrand, 2005; Fitzsimons et al., 2002; Fitzsimons and Shiv, 2001).

## GENERAL DISCUSSION

This research mainly attempts to contribute to three theoretical topics. The first issue concerns the conceptualization of distinct processing patterns between parallel information sources. Schwarz (2006) proposes that cognitions are inherently situational and adaptive. The findings in this present research are consistent with this theorizing in that when consumers face the numerical labels in a product series, they are hardwired to distinctly activate an expectancy mode to search outward for information on the expected product specification improvement. When they face the parallel descriptive labels, they are instead hardwired to distinctly activate a fit mode to search inward for incidental goals that facilitate the interpretation of the anticipated product experience. Meanwhile, the experimental results here suggest that a numerical extrinsic cue is not conducive to a regulatory fit pathway while a descriptive extrinsic cue is not conducive to an expectancy pathway.

This research furthers the understanding of the conceptual consumption account (Ariely and Norton, 2009) since the pattern here speaks for a *distinctness* property between competing conceptual consumption classes. Therefore, it may be interesting to investigate in the future what causes the compatibility between certain types of information and certain classes of conceptual consumption. Correspondingly, it is advisable to study other sources of parallel information that are capable of activating distinct conceptual consumption modes.

The second theoretical issue concerns nonconscious processing of extrinsic cues. This research offers evidence in support of the perspective that extrinsic cues may be processed unconsciously and certain metacognitive experiences have their nonconscious foundations (e.g., Fitzsimons et al., 2002; Chartrand et al., 2008). Particularly, this research identifies the nature of the non-consciousness in the label effect. I find that consumers are unaware of the activation of this nonconscious process because they cannot identify the label as a source of the process. Moreover, consumers are oblivious of the process itself – they cannot tell that either the expectation on the specification-induced outcome (when they are in the expectancy mode) or the incidental goal (when they are in the fit mode) is the actual force behind this process.

The third theoretical issue concerns the consumption of inter-product concepts. Even within the school of the conceptual consumption research, I argue that the inter-product concepts are very under-researched. The efforts have been disproportionally focused on a single-product paradigm to study how the extrinsic cues for this product (e.g., price, brand) lead to various psychological effects. However, the same extrinsic cues could lead to different predictions when used in a product series paradigm where there is a whole new class of (inter-product) concepts, such as innovation. In summary, the *distinctness*, *non-consciousness*, and *interdependence* properties in consuming information have significant merits on their own and warrant further attentions from the academia and the practitioners alike.

## REFERENCES

Allison, Ralph I. and Kenneth P. Uhl (1964), "Influence of Beer Brand Identification on Taste Perception," *Journal of Marketing Research*, 1:36–39.

Ariely, Dan and Jonathan Levav (2000), "Sequential Choice in Group Settings: Taking the Road Less Traveled and Less Enjoyed," *Journal of Consumer Research*, 27:279–90.

Ariely, Dan and Michael Norton (2009), "Conceptual Consumption," *Annual Review of Psychology*, Vol. 60: 475-499.

Avnet, Tamar and E. Tory Higgins (2006), "How Regulatory Fit Affects Value on Consumer Choices and Opinions," *Journal of Marketing Research*, 43:1–10.

Biehal, Gabriel and Dipankar Chakravarti (1982), "Information-Presentation Format and Learning Goals as Determinants of Consumers' Memory Retrieval and Choice Processes," *Journal of Consumer Research*, 8:4, 431.

Boyd, Colin D. (1985), "Point of View: Alpha Numeric Brand Names," *Journal of Advertising Research*, 25 (October/November), 48-52.

Cesario, Joseph, Heidi Grant, and E. Tory Higgins (2004), "Regulatory Fit and Persuasion: Transfer From 'Feeling Right'," *Journal of Personality and Social Psychology*, 86 (March), 388–404.

Chartrand, Tanya L. (2005), "The Role of Conscious Awareness in Consumer Behavior," *Journal of Consumer Psychology*, 15 (3), 203–10.

Chartrand, Tanya L., Joel Huber, Baba Shiv, and Robin J. Tanner (2008), "Nonconscious Goals and Consumer Choice," *Journal of Consumer Research*, 35:2, 189-201.

Dodds, William B., Kent B. Monroe, and Dhruv Grewal (1999), "Effects of Price, Brand, and Store Information on Buyers' Product Evaluations," *Journal of Marketing Research*, Vol. 28, No. 3, 307-319.

Fitzsimons, Gavan J., J. Wesley Hutchinson, Patti Williams, Joseph W. Alba, Tanya L. Chartrand, Joel Huber, Frank R. Kardes, Geeta Menon, Priya Raghubir, J. Edward Russo, Baba Shiv and Nader T. Tavassoli. (2002), "Non-Conscious Influences on Consumer Choice," *Marketing Letters*, 13.3 (August): 269(11).

Fitzsimons, Gavan J., and Baba Shiv (2001). "Nonconscious and Contaminative Effects of Hypothetical Questions on Decision Making," *Journal of Consumer Research*, 28(2), 224–238.

Goodman, Joseph K. and Julie R. Irwin (2006), "Special Random Numbers: Beyond the Illusion of Control," *Organizational Behavior and Human Decision Processes*, 99 (March), 161-74.

Hsee, Christopher K., George F. Loewenstein, Sally Blount, and Max H. Bazerman (1999), "Preference Reversals between Joint and Separate Evaluations of Options: A Review and Theoretical Analysis," *Psychological Bulletin*, Vol 125(5), 576-590.

Idson, Lorraine Chen and E. Tory Higgins (2000), "How Current Feedback and Chronic Effectiveness Influence Motivation: Everything to Gain Versus Everything to Lose," *European Journal of Social Psychology*, 30 (July–August), 583–92.

Janiszewski, Chris and Stijn M. J. van Osselaer (2005), "Behavior Activation is not Enough," *Journal of Consumer Psychology*, 15(3), 218-224.

Jones, John T., Brett W. Pelham, Matthew C. Mirenberg, and John J. Hetts (2002), "Name Letter Preferences are Not Merely Mere Exposure: Implicit Egotism as Self-regulation," *Journal of Experimental Social Psychology*, 38 (March), 170-77.

Keller, Kevin Lane (1993), "Conceptualizing, Measuring, and Managing Customer-Based Brand Equity," *Journal of Marketing*, Vol. 57, No. 1 (January), 1-22.

King, Dan and Chris Janiszewski (2009), "Affective Responses to Numbers," *working paper*.

Lastovicka, John L., Lance A. Bettencourt, Renee Shaw Hughner, and Ronald J. Kuntze (1999), "Lifestyle of the Tight and Frugal: Theory and Measurement," *Journal of Consumer Research*, Vol 26; Number 1, 85-98.

Levin, Irwin P., and Gary J. Gaeth. (1988). "How Consumers are Affected by the Framing of Attribute Information Before and After Consuming the Product," *Journal of Consumer Research*, 15 (December), 374–378.

Morales, Andrea C., and Gavan J. Fitzsimons (2007), "Product Contagion: Changing Consumer Evaluations through Physical Contact with "Disgusting" Products," *Journal of Marketing Research*, 44:272–83.

Pavia, Teresa M. and Janeen A. Costa (1993), "The Winning Number: Consumer Perceptions of Alpha-numeric Brand Names," *Journal of Marketing*, 57 (July), 85-98.

Petty, Richard E. and John T. Cacioppo (1986), "The Elaboration Likelihood Model of Persuasion," *Advances in Experimental Social Psychology*, Volume 19, 123-205.

Price, Donald D., Damien G. Finniss, and Fabrizio Benedetti (2008), "A Comprehensive Review of the Placebo Effect: Recent Advances and Current Thought," *Annual Review of Psychology*, 59:565–90.

Robertson, Kim (1989), "Strategically Desirable Brand Name Characteristics," *Journal of Consumer Marketing*, 6 (Fall), 61-71.

Schwarz, Norbert (2004), "Metacognitive Experiences in Consumer Judgment and Decision Making," *Journal of Consumer Psychology*, 14:332–48.

Schwarz, Norbert (2006), "Feelings, Fit, and Funny Effects: A Situated Cognition Perspective," *Journal of Marketing Research*, Vol 43(1), 20-23.

Shiv, Baba, Ziv Carmon, and Dan Ariely (2005), "Placebo Effects of Marketing Actions: Consumers May Get What They Pay For," *Journal of Marketing Research*, 42:383–93.

Simmons, Lee C. and Robert M. Schindler (2003), "Cultural Superstitions and the Price Endings Used in Chinese Advertising," *Journal of International Marketing*, 11 (2), 101-11.

Thurstone, L. L. (1927), "A Law of Comparative Judgment," *Psychological Review*, Vol 34(4), 273-286.

Viswanathan, Madhubalan and Terry L. Childers (1996), "Processing of Numerical and Verbal Product Information," *Journal of Consumer Psychology*, Vol. 5, No. 4, 359-385.

# Approaching God: Proxy and Proximity of Brand Heroes to the Brand Community
Toni Eagar, Australian National University, Australia

## ABSTRACT
An ethnographic exploration of a brand community and their hero was conducted to understand the outcomes of greatness through proxy and proximity. Proxy allowed an idealized mythology of the hero to form, which was enhanced by the possibility of proximity. However, proximity can expose the hero's feet of clay.

## INTRODUCTION

Narratives form a central component to brand communities, where story telling by and about the community form identity and mythology. Included in these narratives is the heroic figure that brings success to the brand through the conquering of the commercial world. However, there is a difference between achieving reflected greatness through the proxy of the brand and attempting to achieve greatness through proximity to the hero (Schau and Muniz 2007). This paper contrasts the Schau and Muniz (2007) findings of proxy being the dominant method for approaching the hero with a community that desires both. The tension between proxy and proximity is explored and the impact on community narratives is outlined. For marketers the management of proximity encounters between the community and the hero becomes important as the hero in the flesh can reveal feet of clay.

## THE HEROISM OF THE BRAND HERO

Not all employees of a brand are heroes; this paper focuses on those that have been identified by the community for their special association with the brand, product and community. The definition of a hero is somewhat fluid but it is a person, either real or fictional "who has given his or her life to something bigger than oneself" (Campbell 1988, p.123). The hero narrative generally revolves around a figure that either experiences trials and attains a physical deed through performing an act of courage or who has a revelation and through a spiritual deed learns to experience the supernatural. In either heroic narrative the hero sacrifices something of themselves for the benefit of society. The role of these heroic tales is to provide the steps that the ordinary man can take to be "liberated from his personal impotence and misery and be endowed (at least temporarily) with an almost superhuman quality" (Jung 1964, p.79). So the tales of heroes are for the purpose of giving the ordinary human being the hope or the method of becoming more than their current condition. In a sense the hero is a social archetype of the desired perfect citizen as the hero embodies or becomes those aspects that a society admires most.

The study of comparative mythology has established a common myth structure for the narratives of heroes. Jung (1964) proposed that the traditional hero myth structure had the following basic story line:

1. The hero has a humble birth
2. Early proof of superhuman strength
3. A rapid rise to prominence or power
4. A triumphant struggle with the forces of evil
5. The hero suffers the fallibility through the sin of pride
6. The hero falls through betrayal or makes a 'heroic' sacrifice in death

The above basic story of the hero encapsulates the role of the hero as more than human, the basic role of the hero in ridding society of a negative element, be it evil, monsters or sin, and the ultimate destruction or sacrifice of the hero. In Jung's psychological perspective the role of these heroic symbols is to strengthen the ego and make a person feel they are or can be more than their current self. Campbell (1949, 1988) takes a similar perspective of the role of hero myths to individual psychology but he expands on the hero myth narrative through what he terms the monomyth (Campbell 1949). The monomyth is the formula of separation – initiation – return, where:

> "A hero ventures forth from the world of common day into a region of supernatural wonder, fabulous forces are there encountered and a decisive victory is won, the hero comes back from this mysterious adventure with the power to bestow boons on his fellow man" (Campbell 1949, p.23)

For the brand hero this would be encompassed with the hero leaving the non-commercial world of the ordinary man and entering the marketplace and overcoming the competitive forces and the negative aspect of 'the opposition' and either creating the brand to bring forth to the brand community or increasing the brand's success or value which is considered a boon by the community. The brand hero monomyth narrative reads:

> A brand hero ventures forth from the non-producer world of the consumer into the unknown and inexplicable world of the commercial producer where fabulous forces of the market are encountered and a decisive victory is won over other brands. The brand hero then delivers the brand and its value to the brand community.

This commercialization of the world in which the hero enters is a reflection of the norms of modern society and as such the attributes that the brand hero embraces are those of market success and is entrenched in the capitalist paradigm of the free market that seeks success over the competition (Csapo 2005).

An alternate view to the synthesization of modern worship as discussed above is the study of the sacred in what would appear to be the profane setting of consumption (Belk, Wallendorf, and Sherry 1989). The underlying assumption of this perspective is that consumption has become a secular ritual through which transcendent experience is sought (Belk et al. 1989; Hirschman and Holbrook 1982; Muniz and Schau 2005; O'Guinn and Belk 1989; Schouten, McAlexander, and Koenig 2007; Wallendorf and Arnould 1988). This research has indicated that with the rise of individualism and the move away from formal religions in modern society, individuals are using consumption practices and purchases to attain the sacred and achieve transcendence (Belk et al. 1989; Schouten et al. 2007). The marketplace has become central to society, so the heroes of the market are as appropriate figures of worship as those from history.

## PROXY VERSUS PROXIMITY OF THE BRAND HERO

The tribal perspective has seen the consideration of mythology and religiosity in stigmatized (Kozinets 2001; Muniz and Schau 2005) and non-stigmatized brand communities (Schau and Muniz 2007). In one of the closest references to brand heroes found in the literature Schau and Muniz (2007) discuss the impact of Tom Petty on the values, myths and rituals enacted by the brand community of Tom Petty and the Heartbreakers (TPATH). Their work focused on the similarities across brand communities and proposed that a brand community did not need to be marginalized or stigmatized for magico-religious myth and ritual to manifest. This work highlights the idealized nature in which Tom Petty is held as "god by proxy not proximity". The TPATH community represent and actively defend the ideas that Tom Petty displays; this identity is built on the ideas of temperance, family, friends, the environment, anti-commercialism and the USA. These ideals result in the community defending Tom Petty against claims that contradict this persona, such as claims of infidelity and drug use. There is also enforcement of the norms of community behavior, restricting or reprimanding references to sexually explicit material or drug references besides alcohol and marijuana. This is a clear indication that the idealized version of the brand hero becomes a model of correct behavior and core to the identity of the brand community.

The other key finding from the study of TPATH is the distinction of the relationship between the brand hero as a god by proxy rather than proximity. The authors distinguish between the proxy role which views brand hero as god and as source of greatness as it is bestowed through the brand's product versus the proximity role which seeks greatness through contact. The brand community seeks greatness through camaraderie with the product which is a crucial difference in the motivation of brand community members and celebrity worshippers. This paper extends Schau and Muniz's work by comparing a community seeking proxy with a community that has the tension of seeking both proxy and proximity.

## METHOD

Qualitative methods were applied, using both a grounded theory approach, particularly the principles of building theory from data through constant comparison and theoretical sampling (Glaser and Strauss 1967), and ethnography, and its concern for culturally based patterns of behavior (Goulding 2005). These were considered the most appropriate method as mythological narratives about the brand hero were constantly generated, negotiated and perpetuated by the brand community. Using Nvivo the analysis method applied was to open-code data, build categories and through systematic comparison develop theoretical constructs and relationships. Data gathering involved an embedded ethnographic study of three online forums, 25 real world interviews, 30 online interviews, attendance at a three-day convention, and three book-signing events, as well as informal community meet-ups in Australia, the UK, and Germany.

The investigation was conducted in the Discworld brand community, with Terry Pratchett as the author of the Discworld books representing the brand hero. Discworld is a fantasy-comedy series that has sold over 40 million books worldwide. There are 38 books in the series, which is aimed at an adult readership. While, the researcher had read some of the Discworld books prior to the commencement of this study they were not involved in the brand community. Discworld was selected because of the nature of book marketing, with limited use of advertising, the marketing efforts of the author, including book signings and readings, and the strong, long-running brand community. The brand community's greater access to the brand hero provided the opportunity to explore the narratives that emerged from the community's stories and encounters with Terry Pratchett.

## FINDINGS

### The Brand Community

The most central tenet of the Discworld community's identity is that they are the one's that "get it". This is tied to the core value of the Discworld brand, "the joke", which will be discussed in the following section. For community members being one of those that understand the value of Discworld mean that are, in a sense, more educated, smarter, and have a more sophisticated sense of humour than those that do not read Discworld. This is a way of differentiating fans from non-fans but it also relates to how fans see themselves as somehow similar to the brand hero.

"What's a normal fan of Pratchett? I don't … I know most of my family and a whole range of people. I think the only thing you can say about a Terry Pratchett fan is that most of them have above average IQ's, it's about the only thing I can think of to say about Terry Pratchett fans" (David, Social Network, Personal Interview)

David saw others that would 'get it' as being of above average intelligence. His friend Chris described David as an 'intellectual snob' for this statement but others have expressed a similar view of Discworld fans. Sharon described Discworld fans as:

"We are intelligent, literate and social people" (Sharon, AusDWCon attendee, Personal Interview)

As can be seen from the quotes regarding how the community perceives other Discworld fans there are clear indicators that the community perceive themselves to be 'intelligent' and 'literate'. Those people interviewed that had attended real-life Discworld events such as book singings, public lectures or conventions, stated that they thought that the other people in attendance were like themselves with one respondent referring to the people at a Pratchett signing as; "People in the queue? Very much like the people I was hanging around with at the time the nerdy geeky uni type" (Judy, Social Network, Personal Interview).

### The Brand

The core value that the community identified with the Discworld brand was "the joke". This is associated with the nature of the Discworld story. Discworld is predominantly a satire in a fantasy setting; there are many references to real world ancient and modern history, as well as, puns, word plays and the twisting of the everyday or expected language forms. These many references to the real world as a basis for "the joke" mean that the reader has to be aware of the real world reference in order to get the Discworld joke.

"You can read it on so many levels depending on what you actually know about the world, its history and things like that. You actually understand different stuff. So, you can read a different book that you haven't read for years and get different things in it because over that time you've grown yourself. And it makes fun of the world. It makes fun of everything of things that people think are so important and sort of puts it in perspective. I like the fact that it makes fun of everyone. At the same time there's a note of seriousness in it too…

"He took things that really happened in history, like to the witches and things like that, there's stuff about witchcraft except the witch trials instead of burning witches at the stake its actually this fantastic time when they all [witches] got together and had fun and compared spells and stuff." (Alison, Personal interview)

This understanding of the real world that is used to create "the joke" forms an important aspect of the interpretive function of the community. "The joke" was a recurring theme in how the Discworld community saw themselves and also as how they viewed Terry Pratchett. There was a strong element that he created and continues Discworld to share "the joke" rather than for commercial motivations. This narrative proved to be problematic when the community came into proximity with the brand hero, commercial motivations were Terry Pratchett's feet of clay.

## The Brand Hero

The perception of Terry Pratchett as the mythical hero of the brand community versus the profane self-promoter with his own agenda was heavily influenced by the proximity of Pratchett to the community member. There is a great tension between being perceived as accessible with the disappointment in meeting the hero to find that he does not fit the mythology. This adds an additional dimension to Schau and Muniz's (2007) religiosity through proxy rather than proximity. In the Discworld case it was found that while community member's desired greatness through proxy, they also desired a certain level of proximity. This section will explore the community reactions to the perception of proximity, actual proximity and how this influences the narratives of Terry Pratchett as a sacred and as a profane figure.

Besides the proxy narratives there was evidence that proximity played an important role in the creation of the hero narratives and perceptions of sacredness. The transcendent religious experience of the brand hero was most strongly experienced in the convention setting where Pratchett was present. This communal interaction with Pratchett was the basis for many of the narratives of his accessibility. The accessibility myth relies on interpretations of proximity that if Pratchett was nearby community members could approach him in conversation. Terry Pratchett was considered a credible Discworld community member because he would behave just like any other fan at community events.

> "Now, the question is, why does he do it? Why give up three days of precious free time to spend them in a field with people who would buy your books anyway? Even if it did increase sales, the amount would be a drop in the ocean compared to what he's selling already. So I'm left with the notion that he enjoys it. He walks around, chatting to fans, occasionally being photographed but not, I hope, being hassled too much. He doesn't appear to have an entourage (we saw him walking down from the top barn to his car on Sunday morning, presumably to pick up something) or to have any security worries (if he had any 'minders', they were very well hidden) and because he acts like a 'regular person', that's how he gets treated. It might be that he feels he 'owes' it to the fans to turn up at events like this. In the Q&A, he was asked whether he was going to be at the Australian Convention, and after saying that the date had been changed a couple of times already, he said that whatever date it finally ended up on, he'd be there, because "they've gone to so much trouble" (and that he never misses a chance to go to Australia). I don't know of any author with a comparable level of sales who gives so much time to keeping fans happy."" (Diane L, alt.fan.Pratchett, 05.08.2005)

For this Discworld brand community member they perceive that Terry Pratchett is motivated by enjoyment of fan contact rather than by commercial concerns. In her mind this gives added credibility and appeal to Pratchett as a brand hero. The 'regular person' aspect of his credibility presents a persona that the brand community is able to identify as someone similarly committed to the community and the brand. The brand community perceived that they and the brand hero were working together for the benefit of the brand.

Another example was at the AusDWCon Pratchett sat with up to 50 attendees in conversation outside of the formal sessions. These conversations ranged from the shepherds hut that Pratchett had built as his library to the various ancient sites of interest around England, such as the Long Man, and the White Horse, which are referred to in Discworld books. The conversation I witnessed at the convention lasted for 2 hours and is not the only reported interaction between Pratchett and the community, with mentions being made of long interactions in bars and pubs at other events. These examples create and reinforce narratives of the hero's accessibility and approachability. These are values that the Discworld community believes to be part of their ethos, with inclusive practices such as only using proper English instead of netspeak in online interactions. Proximity in communal interactions provides evidence of Pratchett's character and has formed an important basis for heroic mythology and community ethos. However, proximity can have negative consequences which will be discussed next.

The issue that proximity to Pratchett raises is around the revelation of the hero as profane and ordinary. There were two instances within the Discworld community that illustrated the dangers of proximity between members and the hero. The first relates to Pratchett making rude comments to a respondent at a book signing, the second was an attendant at the AusDWCon who after a small group discussion with Pratchett was disillusioned with the market motives that underlied his behavior. These incidences indicate that there are issues with proximity leading to the hero revealing himself as profane rather than mythic.

The first incident that revealed the issues of proximity between the hero and the community was in an interview with Judy, who describes meeting Terry Pratchett twice, the first in a large group setting for a public lecture and the second in a book signing. The book signing meeting was quite confrontational, she described it in the following way:

> "At that particular signing I also got a Discworld magic cards signed. I was playing Discworld magic deck, I don't know if you know them…it is just a card game basically of dungeons and dragons sort of thing…. Cardboard, expensive bits of cardboard. Anyway there's an orangutan card there's a wizards card and a Terry Pratchett thing. When I gave them to him to be signed he was quiet scathing about the amount of money people spent on silly pieces of cardboard."

The second meeting at a book signing event was also perceived as negative.

> "The one with the cards which I said he was quite scathing about silly card games the way people spent masses amounts of money on etc. And the other was probably entirely my fault I got up to the table and hadn't really been thinking "what can I say to this man", I got to the table put the books down and foolishly made a reference to banana daiquiris. He says 'couldn't people come up with something original' or something like that. He was a fraction rude so like his books, but as a person I find him quiet abrasive."

Judy's experience with Terry Pratchett indicates an antithesis to the open and friendly hero figure described in previous narratives. For her he was scathing, rude and abrasive. Interestingly these apparently negative character flaws were justified by their reflection in "the joke" at the core of the brand. So in this case if the hero is perceived as negative this is what makes their contribution to the brand so special. Also, evident in Judy's description of the meeting with Pratchett is the need to think about and plan the interaction prior to the event. This was reflected in a number of respondents who felt intimidated by the pressure of the formal meeting situation that book signings provided. Community members didn't want to appear gushing or clichéd but wanted to express their appreciation for the books. Many described their encounters as brief:

"What happened, I went up said "I'm a big fan" he said "Thank you" and I got my books signed." (Chris, Personal interview)

Others described wanting to meet Pratchett in a more informal setting, with the implication that both parties could more accurately represent themselves. There was also a sense that a long informal "chat" with Pratchett would in some way validate them as an interesting and therefore worthy individual.

"I guess it would be cool to just run into him by accident. Like, you know, in a pub or something and wind up talking and it's a situation where he could genuinely walk away and say I've had enough of talking to you but didn't. So if you actually were able to hold you own in a real life conversation with him that would be cool because, like, I said I think of his intellect as being, you know, somewhere up there, you know. So having a real life conversation with him would be cool." (Tegan, Personal interview)

This respondent sees an informal meeting as being on a more level playing field where it is an opportunity to match intellects with Pratchett. Where the formal book signing meeting seems to attract the community, with most respondents attending one, there is a desire or the fantasy for the personal meeting between equals. The formal meetings, especially the book signing events, place the hero and the community within prescribed roles. It would seem that these roles do not sit comfortably with either party, with Pratchett appearing occasionally abrasive and fans uncomfortable with appearing gushing and deferential. So for the community the ideal form of proximity is in an idealized informal scenario rather than the stilted actual interactions available.

The second negative outcome that proximity caused was to draw attention to the commercial motives of the hero. These were in conflict with the mythology and the community's values. This proved to be an area of conflict between the commercial-based mythology of the hero bringing success to the brand in the market and the belief that the hero does this out of love of the brand and affinity for the community. The second encounter that was reported as negative was where the perception of Pratchett's motives as love and affinity was undermined. Vanessa an attendee at the AusDW-Con was one of a few attendees who won the opportunity to meet with Terry Pratchett in a small group meeting. She describes the experience as disillusioning:

"You have all sorts of ideas about what Terry's going to be like. But I was disappointed. Terry Pratchett really is in it for Terry Pratchett." (Vanessa, informal conversation at a post-AusDWCon meet-up)

For Vanessa the meeting with Pratchett undermined her idealized ideas of who he was as a person with the reality that he is motivated by his own desire for commercial success. Within this encounter lies a central problem of the community – hero relationship, it is idealized myth couched within a commercial and profane environment. This tension between the fantasy and the reality can be exposed when the community is placed within proximity of the hero.

A certain level of positive proximity can create and reinforce myths about a hero, as approachable and as having affinity for the community. The wrong kind of proximity, or a negative encounter, can expose feet of clay and bring the hero back into the real-world and a profane commercial 'sell out'. In this context the idea of Pratchett 'selling out' was in the belief that he was motivated by money rather than a love of the brand and a kinship with the fans. The Discworld community wants to believe that he loves what he does, from writing the books to meeting the fans. The commercial side is a by-product of this love rather than the motivation for it.

## DISCUSSION

For the brand hero their role is to provide a norm of behaviour for the community to aspire to and replicate and to reflect back to the community the qualities that they believe themselves to possess. The heart of the impact of the brand hero in brand communities is in the co-creation of identity, where Terry Pratchett is "intelligent, literate and well-mannered"; the brand community believes itself to reflect those qualities. In reinforcement, Pratchett tells them that they reflect these qualities also. For the brand hero to be effective they must continue to embody these qualities or risk the undermining of the core of the community's ethos. This is a major challenge as the hero is a commercial figure, up against a community who believes them to be motivated by non-commercial objectives and who is ultimately human. The feet of clay that the community does not want to see is the commercial imperative of the modern brand hero.

For brand communities the touching of god through proxy is a process of negotiating identity, where the brand hero reflects the ideal identity and provides an outline for members to achieve the same ideal state. In the case of the brand community this ideal state is in getting "the joke" and in being intelligent enough to match the joke's creator. This sense of identity is not reliant on actual interactions with the brand hero. However, the sense of community is enhanced when there is the possibility of brand hero proximity. So in this case the greatness of the proxy was improved by the hope of proximity, which is the first tension that exists between proxy and proximity. For marketers, the issue becomes how much access to allow between brand heroes and the community where the hero is seen as accessible but retains their mythology.

The dangers of proximity were also found with the brand hero revealing that instead of being the idealized inclusive and nice figure of the mythology he can be abrasive and rude. This encounter formed a negative impression for the respondent of the hero. This was relayed to her friends who when I spoke to them they were all familiar with her experience. While they were familiar with the incident they seemed to not believe it, the community members were unwilling to attribute an actual negative encounter over their idealized idea of the hero. For Judy she explained Pratchett's behaviour as a reflection of "the joke", so rather than negatively effecting her perception of the brand it reinforced her reasons for liking Discworld. This suggests that isolated negative encounters do not eclipse idealized mythologies of the hero. More research is needed into when and how many negative brand hero experiences cause a shift in a positive idealized brand hero myth.

Another important issue found when brand community members came into proximity with the brand hero was in the realization of the community that the brand hero is a commercial figure. The brand hero forms an intersection between the market imperatives of the brand and the non-commercial religiosity of the brand community. While the mythology of the brand hero is couched in the marketplace the assumption of the community is that their motivation is non-commercial. Within the Discworld community there is the belief that Pratchett is motivated by a love of the brand and a respect for the community. Proximity with the brand hero may reveal that they are motivated by market forces or self-promotion. The ongoing tension for communities and brand heroes is in their desire for the celebration of ownership while balancing alternate motivations for profit (Muniz and O'Guinn 2001; Muniz and Schau 2005). This tension between marketers need to make profits and brand communities' desire for a non-commercial magico-religious experience has been recognized in previous research (Muniz and Schau 2005; Schau and Muniz 2007). Unlike previous research that has considered the commercial nature of the products, this study has focused on the perceived marketization of the brand's creators and managers. In brand community settings marketers need to minimize proximity that highlights the commercial nature of the brand hero.

## LIMITATIONS AND FUTURE RESEARCH

The current study explores the issues with encountering brand hero greatness through proxy and proximity. While proxy builds an idealized mythology of the hero, proximity can create a sense of affinity with the community. However, this proximity can have negative outcomes in revealing the hero's feet of clay and the unwelcome reminder market motives. There is a need for more research into the balance between proxy and proximity, what are the optimal amounts and is there a qualitative difference in the types of proximity. For instance, the Discworld community has the option of book signing events, conventions, online and real-world question and answer sessions. Marketers would be better able to manage the relationship between the community and hero if there was more information about the effectiveness of the different encounters.

Limitations exist in this study as it explores only one fan community that has one brand hero. Other brand communities will have multiple brand heroes that have different functions within the brand. For instance, a football team has the players, coaches, and management who may be considered heroes of the brand. These different types of heroes may form alternate relationships with the community with different expectations as to ideal behaviors. Comparing the expectations of ideal brand hero behaviors would reveal the underlying drivers of commercial heroic mythology. It is in understanding the heroic that we can form an understanding of community aspirations.

## REFERENCES

Belk, Russell W., Melanie Wallendorf, and John F. Jr. Sherry (1989), "The Sacred and the Profane in Consumer Behavior: Theodicy on the Odyssey," *Journal of Consumer Research*, 16, 1-38.

Campbell, Joseph (1949), *The Hero with a Thousand Faces*, Novato, California: New World Library.

--- (1988), *The Power of Myth*, New York: Doubleday.

Csapo, Eric (2005), *Theories of Mythology*, Oxford: Blackwell Publishing.

Hirschman, Elizabeth C. and Morris B. Holbrook (1982), "Hedonic Consumption: Emerging Concepts, Methods and Propositions," *Journal of Marketing*, 46, 92-101.

Jung, Carl G., ed. (1964), *Man and His Symbols*, London: Penguin books.

Kozinets, Robert V. (2001), "Utopian Enterprise: Articulating the Meanings of Star Trek's Culture of Consumption," *Journal of Consumer Research*, 28 (June), 67-88.

Muniz, Albert M. Jr. and Thomas C. O'Guinn (2001), "Brand Community," *Journal of Consumer Research*, 27 (March), 412-32.

Muniz, Albert M. Jr. and Hope Jensen Schau (2005), "Religiosity in the Abandoned Apple Newton Brand Community," *Journal of Consumer Research*, 31 (4), 737-47.

O'Guinn, Thomas C. and Russell W. Belk (1989), "Heaven on Earth: Consumption at Heritage Village, USA," *Journal of Consumer Research*, 16, 227-38.

Schau, Hope Jensen and Albert M. Jr. Muniz (2007), "Temperance and Religiosity in a Non-Marginal, Non-Stygmatized Brand Community," in *Consumer Tribes*, ed. Bernard Cova, Robert V. Kozinets and Avi Shankar, Oxford: Elsevier, 144-62.

Schouten, John W., James H. McAlexander, and Harold F. Koenig (2007), "Transcendent Customer Experience and Brand Community," *Journal of the Academy of Marketing Science*, 35 (3), 357-68.

Wallendorf, Melanie and Eric J. Arnould (1988), ""My Favourite Things": A Cross-Cultural Inquiry into Object Attachment, Possessiveness, and Social Linkage," *Journal of Consumer Research*, 14, 531-47.

# The Attractiveness of New Zealand as a University Study Destination: A COO Study of Chinese Students

Sussie Celna Morrish, University of Canterbury, New Zealand
Jia Guo, Xi'an Xiang Rui Real Estate Co. Ltd., China

## ABSTRACT

The development of global markets and the growth of international trade have increased interest in COO effects on consumers' perceptions and intentions but traditionally focused on goods more than services (such as providing international education). This study develops a model of COO factors affecting choices of study destination. Using in-depth interviews with Chinese students intending to study overseas, it finds that COO variables influencing their evaluation include: reputation, language, economic, social, legal, and geographic factors.

## INTRODUCTION

Country of origin (COO) effects refers to how consumers perceive products coming from a particular country (Roth and Romeo, 1992). From a marketing perspective, COO may strengthen or weaken a product's position (Srikatanyoo and Gnoth 2002). In general, COO has been used as a country stereotype, an extrinsic cue to product attributes, and a halo/summary constructs. While it is widely acknowledged that COO plays an important role in information processing and has an impact on product evaluations (Al-Sulaitu and Baker 1998), there has been limited research on COO effects on choice of services. The increasing importance of global trade in services urges marketers to gain insights into the underlying factors considered by consumers when evaluating services. Given that services are typically characterized by significant interpersonal contact, complexity, divergence, and customization than other products, its quality attributes cannot be perceived, felt or possessed in advance. For example, the quality of higher education may vary distinctly from country to country, year to year, class to class, lecturer to lecturer, and student to student (Patterson, Romm and Hill 1998). In particular, international tertiary education (ITE) is a high involvement service that requires high costs, personal relevance, and time for international students' decision making (Gray 1991). As global trends within the field of higher education have brought new competitors (Ivy 2001), it is extremely important for international educational institutions, to understand how international students evaluate and choose service providers in order to maintain their competitive advantage and develop distinctive images.

## BACKGROUND LITERATURE

COO effects refer to how consumers perceive products originating from a particular country. Since first studied (Schooler 1965), numerous practical and theoretical implications of COO effects have made it one of the most fruitful areas in marketing research. In many cases it has been found to play a more important role in foreign product evaluations than price and brand (Wall, Liefeld and Heslop 1991). From a marketing perspective, COO has important strategic implications for firms manufacturing and exporting products because it is a way to differentiate products from competitors especially in their promotional campaigns and packaging or brand decisions (Papadopoulos, 1993). From a consumer's perspective, COO affects not only the evaluation of product quality, but most importantly the likelihood of purchase.

Like many other extrinsic cues, COO may become part of a product's total image to reduce potential risks. Reierson (1966) suggests that while consumers have preconceived notions about foreign products, attitudes are really national stereotypes. Country stereotyping has been found to be universal with studies showing that developing countries receive unfavorable judgments of their product quality because consumers have biased stereotyping information of their country's images (Nagashima 1977; Nes and Bilky 1993). Consumers are different in the extent to which they use country stereotypes (Chiou, 2003) given that perceptions regarding products from a given country seem positively correlated with the degree of the source country's economic development, stability of political climate and the perceived similarity with its belief system (Wang, 1978).

Roth and Romeo (1992) report that consumers from certain countries have different beliefs regarding products made in a given country compared with consumers from other countries but tend to evaluate their own countries' products comparatively more favorably than that of foreigners (Nagashima 1970). Some researchers however found that the impact of COO on product evaluation is moderated by the consumer's prior knowledge of product categories and their ability to analyze and elaborate the product information (Chiou 2003). Thus, increasing consumer knowledge and awareness could have positive COO effects.

Demographic variables also play a role in differences in COO effects. For example, there is a tendency for older consumers to rate foreign products relatively higher than would younger consumers; female consumers evaluate foreign products more favorably than male consumers; and consumers with a high level of education have more favorable attitudes towards foreign products than those with limited education (Schooler 1965). Wang (1978) found that consumers with a higher income level favor foreign products more than those with lower income.

An often raised criticism of early COO studies is their reliance on a single cue context whereby COO is the only available information that respondents rely on for product evaluations. This is of course problematic given that a real-life purchasing situation is more complex and often involves multiple cues that help consumers' decision-making. Agrawal and KamaKura (1999) in fact suggest that the impact of COO as a single cue may be weaker in real world situations. Another criticism of early COO studies relates to sample selection where students were usually the main participants. Further, Bilkey and Nes (1982) observed that COO effects were often studied under a controlled experiment environment where respondents were given only verbal descriptions of products, with no sample or visual representation. There has also been a primary focus on COO effects on product evaluation and nationality differences in the consumption of a product in more developed countries (Bilkey and Nes 1982). Reliability and validity were seldom demonstrated in earlier studies and it was not until the 1990s that scholars began to address these concerns (Papadopoulos 1993).

Although studies indicate that COO does indeed affect product evaluations both in general and in specific classes, types of products, and brands (Javalgi, Cutler and Winans 2001), these had mainly focused on goods. Very few studies have investigated the way consumers react to the country of origin of a service and whether COO has a similar effect on service evaluation. Overall, there has been a very few studies that have examined the impact of COO effects on the consumption and evaluation of services, and most of these studies examined consumers' perceptions towards services in western or developed countries (Al-Sulaiti and Baker 1998).

## COO Effects on Evaluation of Services

Despite the importance of global trade in services, relatively few studies have considered COO issues on international services. For this reason, Javalgi, et al. (2001) reviewed the literature that specifically applies to services. They identified three primary categories of studies namely: a) core services, such as medical care or travel services; b) supplementary services provided to enhance the value of a product, such as a warranty or guarantee; or c) cross-national service comparisons, where services produced and consumed in individual countries are compared. Extant literature suggests that findings of COO research also apply to services whereby COO does appear to be an important informational cue for consumers of services. Javalgi, et al. (2001) suggest that the relationship between COO and services appears to be similar to the relationship between COO and manufactured products. For example, COO was found to have effects in specific service areas such as European ski vacations (Ofir and Lehman 1986), choice of opthalmology service providers (Harrison-Walker 1995), retail services (Lascu and Giese 1995) and airline selection (Al-Sulaiti and Baker 1997; Bruning 1997). Overall, these studies report that COO is more important when brand names are not well known (Ofir and Lehman 1986), but less important when price is a consideration (Al-Sulaiti and Baker 1997; Bruning 1997). There is also a perception that offerings in more developed countries such as Germany are better than in less developed ones like Mexico (Lascu and Giese 1995), where prices are expected to be discounted. While perceptions of quality are higher for foreign carriers (Al-Sulaiti and Baker (1997), consumers are quite happy to switch to another nation's carrier if there were price or service advantages Bruning (1997).

Ahmed and Johnson (2002) examined COO and brand effects on consumers' evaluations of cruise lines. They found that COO effects played a more important role than brand effects for quality and attitude ratings, while brand was more significantly correlated with purchase intentions. Therefore, a positive country image is necessary to bring about a positive attitude and a favorable image of service providers.

However, it is questionable whether the findings from studies of core services by COO are directly applicable to international tertiary education. Consequently, it is essential to understand the unique characteristics of international tertiary education in order to explore the impact that COO has on the evaluation of New Zealand universities.

## Export Education in New Zealand

New Zealand export education has been a rapidly growing industry that has brought and continues to bring many economic, educational and cultural benefits to the country and its educational institutions. The total economic benefits to New Zealand position the industry in fourth place, between the export values of the timber and fishing industries (Asia-NZ 2000 Foundation of New Zealand 2003). International students attending New Zealand educational institutions are the main mode of New Zealand export education services. New Zealand educational institutions consider it strategically desirable to strive to increase the number of international students (Smith and Rae 2006).

The export education industry is a sustainable 'green' export, which fits well with New Zealand's vision of developing a knowledge-based economy. International students can potentially contribute to New Zealand's economic and social development, and its future trade opportunities (Asia-NZ 2000 Foundation of New Zealand). According to New Zealand international enrolments, the overall economic contribution of the international education sector including tuition fees paid, living costs for students, and multiplier factors for the wider economy amounted to $2.21 billion in 2004, $2.034 billion in 2005 and $1.9 billion in 2006 (NZ Ministry of Education 2007).

From an academic perspective, New Zealand's international relationships are further strengthened through educational partnerships. New Zealand research benefits from increased international collaboration, funding, and commercialization. There is greater uptake of New Zealand educational intellectual property and services overseas. International education is also well linked with other New Zealand business activities. Additionally, the New Zealand export education industry is estimated to have created up to 20,000 jobs (NZ Ministry of Education 2007).

## Competitors in the Global Market

In the more globalized world of tertiary education, New Zealand is an active and visible player with several strengths in the area of internationalization (Goedegebuure 2007). When compared to its main competitor nations, New Zealand appears to have a heavy weighting towards onshore delivery of education for international students. In other words, its focus is on students who travel to New Zealand and live in the country in order to study (Education NZ 2005). New Zealand is an attractive destination for international students because it is English-speaking and perceived as clean, green, and increasingly important these days, safe. New Zealand's education system is considered to be of a high standard, and it is a cheaper destination to complete a bachelor's degree (in relation to tuition fees and living costs,) than Australia, the UK, Canada and the US (Asia-NZ 2000 Foundation of New Zealand 2003). Five countries received 60% of all foreign students in 2006 – the United States (23%), the United Kingdom (12%), Germany (11%), France (10%) and Australia (7%).

The numbers of students worldwide seeking education outside of their home country is expected to grow from 1.8 million students in 2000 to 7.2 million by 2025 (Bohm et al. 2002). New Zealand is ranked third in terms of growth in international students, and is second only to Australia in terms of export earnings from foreign students as a percentage of total export earnings from services (Patterson 2005). New Zealand international enrolments indicate that in 2006 the majority of international tertiary students came from the three main North Asian countries: China, Japan, and South Korea (69%), followed by Europe (9%) and North America (7%). Most Asian enrolments were in undergraduate courses (51%), as were most North American enrolments (57%). European enrolments had the highest proportion of postgraduate courses (27%). China dominates enrolments in universities (55%) and other public tertiary institutions (46%). Since the peak in 2002, there has been a 40 % decline in Chinese enrolments to 31,905 in 2006. This decline has usually been ascribed to factors like negative publicity, due partly to the high-profile failure of a number of private education providers in New Zealand. There has been much greater competition from other countries for Chinese students (notably universities in Australia, United Kingdom, and Canada), a greatly increased provision of tertiary education opportunities in China, and an increase in costs due to the rising value of the New Zealand dollar (NZ Ministry of Education 2007).

## COO and NZ Education Services

Compared with the purchase of manufactured products, services tend to be more heterogeneous, more intangible, and more difficult to evaluate than manufactured products. Consumers may rely more on COO in evaluating services, where purchase and consumption are usually simultaneous and where they constitute a higher risk for consumers (Ahmed and Johnson, 2002). This is especially the case for international tertiary education. Heterogeneity makes it difficult to control and standardize the quality of education. Intangibility makes it difficult to display or communicate the quality of education service to prospective students (Mazzarol, 1998). Consequently, students find it difficult to evaluate the quality of education in advance of their purchase and consumption.

Tertiary education has become less nationally and more internationally oriented (Srikatanyoo and Gnoth 2002) and only a handful of studies have been conducted on the marketing of education within international markets (Mazzarol 1998). Existing literature that has examined the decision-making process of prospective international students has tended to focus on the study of factors relating to the institution itself, ignoring the influence of the country of origin (Cubillo, Sanchez and Cervino 2006).

In view of the findings from Srikatanyoo and Gnoth (2002), prospective students may evaluate the quality of international tertiary education by using the image of host country. It is important to explore how international students perceive New Zealand as a study destination, and how its universities are influenced by its country-specific factors. Further analysis of the determining factors in the decision-making process of the prospective international students would allow educational institutions, as well as national governments interested in attracting international students to strengthen their image, to minimize their perceived weaknesses, and hence, to increase the possibility of being chosen as a destination for international tertiary education.

**Decision-making Process**

The decision to study abroad is one of the most significant and expensive initiatives that students may ever undertake (Mazzarol 1998). Because of high costs and the complex decision, students are involved in deep purchase consideration. Many models of decision-making in relation to high involvement purchases suggest that consumers make a decision by moving through the three stages, namely problem recognition, information search, and alternative evaluation. Theoretically, this is applicable to educational choice, too (Engel Kolatt and Blackwell 1995). *Problem recognition* occurs when international students realize that they need to study abroad (Pimpa 1999). The most common reasons motivating students to study overseas are to gain an internationally recognized qualification, to improve their English and communication skills, to experience Western culture, and to get permanent residence (Davey 2005). Previous study suggests that this stage becomes more complex after students make the decision to go abroad. They start to consider problems like which country to go to, which university to choose, and what subjects to study. They may deal with these three problems all at once (Patterson et al. 1998).

Prospective students usually *search information* of countries, universities, and courses from both personal sources (parents, relatives, friends, agents) and non-personal sources (newspaper and television advertisements, international education fairs). A number of studies suggest that recommendations from family or friends who have previously experienced a similar type of service are the most important information sources since they can reduce risk for a high involvement purchase and provide clarification and feedback for consumers (Pimpa 1999). Comparably, students rely less on non-personal sources (e.g. mass media) than on word-of-mouth communication. *Alternative evaluation* is the last stage in the consumer decision-making process. Hill, et al. (1992) found that engaging in alternative evaluation, the customer organizes the information gathered from the search stage, chooses appropriate criteria, and compares various alternatives according to their recog-

nized needs. In this case, each student's decision criteria may vary from another because of different individual motivations and needs.

**Factors Influencing Choice of Destination**

The literature indicates that the choice of destination for studying overseas depends on many different factors. Mazzarol and Soutar (2002) found that the most important determinants for student's choice of a particular host country are knowledge and awareness of the host country, recommendations from friends and relatives, the cost of education and living, the local environment, social links and geographic proximity, and other institutional factors, such as the recognition of the academic qualifications and the quality of the institution's staff. In their study of international students' decision-making process, Cubillo, et al. (2006) identified four factors influencing the preferential choices of prospective students: personal reasons, country image effect, institution's image and program evaluation. Both studies suggest that country image played an important role in the choice of a study destination. Bourke (2000) found that prospective students tend to choose a country first, and then select an institution. Srikatanyoo and Gnoth (2002) indicate that while country image may directly influence student's attitudes towards its academic institutions, students' beliefs about the institutions may also change their perceptions of a country.

In relation to the selection of a particular host institution, the most important variables include the quality and *reputation of the institution*, the recognition of the institution's qualifications, and the quality of the institution's expertise and teaching faculty (Mazzarol and Soutar 2002). Further, Price, et al. (2003) found that teaching and studying facilities also influence the image of the institution. Moreover, Mazzarol (1998) suggests that the ability to offer a broad range of courses and programs plays an important role as well.

**Country Image and Education Quality**

Previous studies show that the country's image affects the evaluation of education services (Lawley, 1998; Srikatanyoo and Gnoth, 2002; Cubillo et al., 2006). Since the country's image is assumed to be the first factor that consumers consider in product evaluation, it plays a much more important role than other factors which influence the evaluation of a product or service (Wall, Liefeld and Heslop 1991). *Language* is an important COO consideration with English being one of the dominant languages in global communication, business, and science. For many Asian students, international study is an opportunity to improve English proficiency and skills. English speaking countries therefore become popular choices. Additionally, *cost* is considered an important factor that influences student destination choice (Mazzarol and Soutar 2002) as well as safe environment (Mazzarol, et al. 2001) and visa/residency regulations (Davey 2005). Mazzarol, et al. (2001) also found that Chinese students who choose to study in New Zealand and Australia are more likely to be influenced by geographic proximity than other students who choose different host countries. In addition, students from other Asian countries are also attracted to New Zealand due to geographic motivations (Malcolm, Ling and Sherry 2004).

## METHODOLOGY

The overall research goal is to explore COO effects on the choice of an international education provider. Since the research question of interest is how international students evaluate and choose the country and institution when making the decision to study abroad, previous research is used to guide the factors and issues explored in this study. We deemed qualitative research an appropriate method to obtain insights into the motivation, emotional, attitudinal, and personality factors that influence decision-making.

Telephone interviews were conducted with ten Chinese students (five males and five females) from three major cities (Bei Jing, Shang Hai, and Cheng Du) in China. Eight of them were still in China and had the intention to go overseas for tertiary education; another two were currently studying in middle school and high school in New Zealand. An interview protocol was designed consisting of open ended questions to allow interviewees to expand on their answers.

# RESULTS

## Problem Recognition

The participants were asked to reflect on the reasons on wanting to study overseas. Even though they each have distinctive motivations for studying abroad, in general, these motivations fall into four categories: 1) belief that a qualification from international tertiary institutions enjoys world-class recognition, 2) to get an independent life experience and obtain a better perspective and understanding of the world, 3) international qualification may help them to gain work experience and benefit their future career and 4) improve their English proficiency and communication skills.

## Information Search

Beside the country they had already applied to, they were asked to indicate the other countries they had actively considered in this process. Five countries, U.S., U.K., Canada, Australia, and New Zealand, were mentioned. Students searched information of these countries and relevant institutions from both personal and non-personal sources. The most often-used source was personal sources, such as recommendations from families and friends. These students trusted word-of-mouth information more than information from non-personal sources, a finding consistent with literature. As the purchase of international tertiary education is a high-risk decision making process, students were willing to spend a large amount of time and effort for information search. They would rely on information from people who had real experiences and their feedback in order to reduce possible risks. Some non-personal sources used by students include the internet, intermediary agents, TV programs, education fairs and books. Information from these sources was less powerful than personal information because the students believe they were commercially promoted. However, the main function of media information is to provide preliminary impressions of countries or institutions and then direct students to personal source for further confirmation.

## Alternative Evaluation

Six out of ten students chose New Zealand as their study destination after comparing all possible options. Those who did not choose New Zealand preferred to study in the US. Of main concern however is the US visa requirement. Failing this, UK and Canada would be their second choice. The findings indicate that lack of knowledge and awareness of New Zealand is a universal phenomenon for most of the students, who had not considered this country on their initial list or as the preferred destination. The level of knowledge by the two students who already studied in New Zealand at secondary school was obviously higher than that of the other eight. Their living and studying experiences generated for them a positive perception of New Zealand, specifically as a quality education provider, its relatively lower costs, ease of getting a visa and so on.

Understandably, a majority believes that a country's economic development level was related to its educational level. Therefore, the US and UK were their first preference. In general, the most frequently-mentioned factors in selecting the alternative countries

are costs, language of the host country, the university's reputation, visa application, and work opportunities.

## Factors Influencing Destination Choice

Students who chose to study in New Zealand regarded the relatively lower costs of studying and living, world-recognized universities, English speaking country, safe society, the ease of getting a visa, and the opportunity of finding part-time jobs as the most significant factors in their decision. Of secondary importance were: geographic environment and lifestyle and enjoyment. We capture these factors in a COO-based model in Figure 1.

Although six out of ten students who participated in the in-depth interviews chose New Zealand as their final destination, nine students had considered other countries as their most preferred destination in the beginning. Among these, the US and UK were always considered first for overseas study. Students held positive perceptions of these two countries as quality education providers. They believed that large countries have a longer history of good educational background, world-class universities, and higher academic standard. All the participants suggested that they only considered English-speaking countries as their study destination. The major economic issues of concern to students are expensive tuition fees that are significantly higher than domestic rates and living expenses. Unless students are offered scholarships or the students' families are wealthy, the cost of studying overseas is always a serious concern for prospective students. More than half the participants who would like to study in the US or the UK in the beginning finally changed their mind and chose New Zealand as their study destination because of the higher costs in those other two countries.

While some students did not consider safety as a major decision issue, parents were more concerned about it. As a result, being safe is a fundamental consideration for students who intend to pursue education abroad especially for families of female students in this study. They believe that safety is very important and it was the reason for them to choose New Zealand in the end.

Life style and enjoyment in the host country did not appear to be important to most of these students. They generally believe that living in a country with different life style in not an issue because they were going abroad to have different life experience and they could get used to new things very fast. Secondly, it would always be good to have entertainment, but they preferred not to have much of it because the reason to go overseas was mainly for study. Their parents believed that New Zealand was calm and relaxing and the US by comparison has lots of temptations.

Eight out of ten students have considered the difficulty of applying for a visa, an important factor in their final decision. Some students gave up their preferred countries (e.g. US and Canada) because it was too difficult to get a visa or some of them had been rejected several times. In comparison, they thought it was easier to get a visa to New Zealand, a factor that puts New Zealand in a favorable position to attract students. Half of the participants indicated that while the natural environment of the host country is not the most important factor, it still plays a role in evaluating alternatives in overseas tertiary study. Thus, countries which have a clean and beautiful environment are more attractive than others.

## Institution and Moderating Factors

Recognition of qualifications acts as the most important criterion for students to choose a university. All of them emphasized that a qualification from a world-famous university is desirable for future work opportunities therefore qualifications need to be recognized both internationally and by future employees. University ranking

**Figure 1: COO Model**

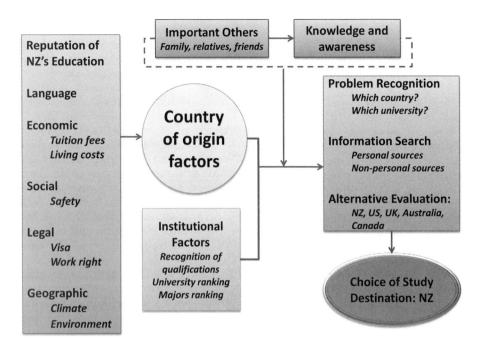

is perceived to be desirable such that studying in a world famous university will make it easier for students to find a job in China after graduation. In addition, the ranking of majors is also deemed important because they realize the overall ranking of a university is not necessarily equal to the quality of a certain major offering. Therefore, they chose the major first and then the university next.

Knowledge and awareness of New Zealand and its institutions as well as the influence of other important people moderated the final choice of destination. Except for the two students with good knowledge of New Zealand, the information on New Zealand was generally sourced from friends and agents.

## CONCLUSION, IMPLICATIONS AND CONTRIBUTION

This study does not aim to draw definitive conclusions. Rather it serves to provide valuable insights of how COO factors affect the choice of international tertiary education in a New Zealand context. The findings of this study suggest that country reputation, language, economic, social, legal, and geographic factors play significant roles in evaluating alternative countries as a study destination. Students are concerned most about the recognition of their qualification, cost of studying and living, the safety of the host country, and difficulties of visa application. Their family and friends influence their knowledge and awareness of the host countries and eventually the final choice of study destination.

This study fills a much-needed gap in the literature relating to how COO affects consumer's evaluation of services, in this case, international tertiary education. It identified country-specific factors that might influence the prospective international students' perception and choice of study destination, and developed a conceptual model of how Chinese students select New Zealand to pursue their overseas study. This was based on both relevant literature and the findings from interviews.

The rapid development of international tertiary education requires that we understand the characteristics of the market it tries to tap. This study will be important to academics, administrators and practitioners who are involved in international tertiary education. The conceptual model may help achieve an understanding of the true characteristics of the Chinese study abroad student market, and develop appropriate strategies to enhance the image of New Zealand's education quality. The findings will also benefit institutions by contributing to the use of their competitive advantages for international student recruitment.

There are two significant limitations to this study that prevent generalization of these findings to broader contexts. First, this study has focused on a modest sample of Chinese students and reflects only one destination country. Students from other countries living under different social contexts may show differences in the primary beliefs that affect their decision-making in regard to their choice of overseas study destination. Second, participants were interviewed using qualitative methods, whereas the use of quantitative methods, inferential statistical analysis, and longitudinal studies might have revealed further details.

The marketplace for international tertiary education is dynamic and will change over time. Therefore, further work should also consider conducting a cross-nation study of other overseas destinations, and selecting participants from different source countries to comprehend the decision-making stages and the variety of types of international students.

## REFERENCES

Ahmed, Z. U., Johnson, J. P., Chew, P. L., Tan, W. F., & Ang, K. H. (2002). Country-of-origin and brand effects on consumers' evaluations of cruise lines. *International Marketing Review*, *19*(3), 279-302.

Al-Sulaitu, K. I., & Baker, M. J. (1997). *Qatari consumers' perceptions and selections of domestic vs. foreign airline services* (Working Paper Series, 97/7). University of Strathclyde, Department of Marketing.

Al-Sulaiti, K. L., & Baker, M. J. (1998). Country of origin effects: A literature review. *Marketing Intelligence and Planning, 16*(3), 150-199.

Asia-NZ 2000 Foundation of New Zealand. (2003). *The export education industry: Challenges for New Zealand.* Retrieved August 16, 2007, from http://www.asianz.org.nz/research/exporteducation

Bilky, W. J., & Nes, E. (1982). Country of origin effects on product evaluation. *Journal of International Business Studies, 8*(1), 89-99.

Bourke, A. (2000). A model of the determinants of international trade in higher education. *The Service Industries Journal, 20*(1), 110-138.

Bruning, E. R. (1997). Country of origin, national loyalty and product choice. *International Marketing Review, 14*(1), 59-74.

Chiou, J. (2003). The impact of country of origin on pretrial and posttrial product evaluations: The moderating effect of consumer expertise. *Psychology and Marketing, 20*(10), 935-954.

Cubillo, J. M., Sanchez, J., & Cervino, J. (2006). International students' decision-making process. *International Journal of Educational Management, 20*(2), 101-115.

Davey, G. (2005). Chinese students' motivations for studying abroad. *International Journal of Private Higher Education, 2,* 16-21.

Education New Zealand. (2005). *Offshore education stocktake and analysis.* Retrieved August 10, 2007, from http://www.educationnz.org.nz/indust/eeip/OffEdFinalRpt281105.pdf

Engel, J. F., Kollatt, D. T., & Blackwell, R. D. (1995). *Consumer behavior,* (6th ed.). Harcourt, Brace Jovanovich Publishers, Sydney.

Goedegebuure, L., Santiago, P., Fitznor, L., Stensaker, B., & Steen, M. (2007). *Thematic review of tertiary education: New Zealand country note.* Retrieved September 6, 2007, from http:// www.oecd.org/dataoecd/11/52/38012419.pdf

Gray, L. (1991). *Marketing education.* Open University Press, Buckingham.

Harrison-Walker, L. J. (1995). The relative effects of national stereotype and advertising information on the selection of a service provider. *Journal of Services Marketing, 9*(1), 47-59.

Hill, C., Romm, T., & Patterson, P. (1992). *The pre-purchase decision making process experienced by overseas students in Australia: A longitudinal, retrospective Study.* In 6th Australia and New Zealand Marketing Conference. University of Western Sydney.

Ivy, J. (2001). Higher education institution image: A correspondence analysis approach. *International Journal of Educational Management, 15*(6/7), 276-282.

Javalgi, R. G., Cutler, B. D., & Winans, W. A. (2001). At your service! Does country of origin research apply to services? *Journal of Services Marketing, 15*(7), 565-582.

Lascu, D. N., & Giese, I. (1995). Exporting country bias in a retailing environment: Implications or retailer country of origin. *Journal of Global Marketing, 9*(1/2), 41-58.

Lawley, M. (1998). *Choice of destination in international education: A cross national model.* Unpublished doctoral dissertation, The University of Southern Queensland, Toowoomba.

Mazzarol, T. (1998). Critical success factors for international education marketing. *International Journal of Education Management, 12*(4), 163-175.

Mazzarol, T., & Soutar, G. N. (2002). "Push-pull" factors influencing international student destination choice. *International Journal of Educational Management, 16*(2), 82-90.

Mazzarol, T., Soutar, G. N., Smart, D., & Choo, S. (2001). *Perceptions, information and choice: Understanding how Chinese students select a country for overseas study.* Australia Education International, Canberra.

Nagashima, A. (1970). A comparison of Japanese and U.S. attitudes toward foreign products. *Journal of Marketing, 34,* 68-74.

Nagashima, A. (1977). A comparative "made in" product image survey among Japanese businessmen. *Journal of Marketing, 41,* 95-100.

Ness, E., & Bilky, W. J. (1993). A multiple-cue test of country of origin theory. In Papadopoulos, N., & Heslop, L. A. (Eds.), *Product-country images: Impact and role in international marketing* (pp.179-185). New York: International Business Press.

New Zealand Ministry of Education. (2007). *The international education agenda: A strategy for 2007-2012.* Retrieved September 6, 2007, from

http://www.minedu.govt.nz/web/downloadable/dl11950_v1/11950-ie-agenda-final-download-100807.pdf

Ofir, C., & Lehman, D. R. (1986). Measuring images of foreign products. *Columbia Journal of World Business, Summer,* 105-109.

Papadopoulos, N. (1993). What product and country images are and are not. In Papadopoulos, N., & Heslop, L. A. (Eds.), *Product-country images: Impact and role in International marketing* (pp.3-38). New York: International Business Press.

Patterson, G. (2005). Collaboration/Competition Crossroads: National/Supranational Tertiary Education Policies on a Collision Course. *Tertiary Education and Management, 11,* 355-368.

Patterson, P., Romm, T., & Hill, C. (1998). Consumer satisfaction as a process: A qualitative, retrospective longitudinal study of overseas students in Australia. *Journal of Professional Services Marketing, 16*(1), 135-157.

Pimpa, N. (1999). Decision making stages and types of international students: The case of Chinese students in Australia. *Marketing Higher Education, 13*(3), 69-81.

Pimpa, N. (2003). The influence of family on Thai students' choices of international education. *International Journal of Educational Management, 17*(5), 211-219.

Price, I., Matzdorf, F., Smith, L., & Agahi, H. (2003). The impact of facilities on student choice of university. *Facilities, 21*(10), 212.

Reierson, C. (1966). Are foreign products seen as national stereotypes? *Journal of Retailing, 42,* 33-40.

Roth, M. S., & Romeo, J. B. (1992). Matching product category and country image perceptions: A framework for managing country-of-origin effects. *Journal of International Business Studies, 23*(3), 477-497.

Schooler, R. D. (1965). Product bias in the central American common market. *Journal of Marketing Research, 11*(2), 394-397.

Schooler, R. D. (1971). Bias phenomena attendant to the marketing of foreign goods in the U.S. *Journal of International Business Studies, 2*(1), 71-80.

Smith, L. M., & Rae, A. N. (2006). Coping with demand: Managing international student numbers at New Zealand universities. *Journal of Studies in International Education, 10*(1), 27-45.

Srikatanyoo, N., & Gnoth, J. (2002). Country image and international tertiary education. *Journal of Brand Management, 10*(2), 139-146.

Wall, M., Liefeld, J., & Heslop, L. A. (1991). Impact of country of origin cues on consumer judgments in multi-cue situations: A covariance analysis. *Journal of the Academy of Marketing Science, 19*(2), 105-113.

Wang, C. (1978). *The effect of foreign economic, political and cultural environment on consumers' willingness to buy foreign products.* Unpublished dissertation, Texas A & M University.

# The Emperor's New Clothes: Are We Seeing our Subjects Clearly?

Simone Pettigrew, University of Western Australia, Australia

## ABSTRACT

Referencing consumption-related themes in popular music, this paper playfully and provocatively suggests that transformative consumer research could boldly refuse to adopt the underlying assumptions of much previous consumer research and instead consider an alternative interpretation of the consumer.

## INTRODUCTION

Imagine that we could forget our roles as scientists commissioned with identifying and measuring constructs relating to consumer behavior. Imagine that we could forget our duties as educators where we teach students to view consumption through the lens of theoretical concepts and profit maximization. If we could look at consumption through uninitiated eyes, what would we see? Would everything we behold support our learned interpretations, or is it possible that the metaphorical emperor, our consumer as king, would no longer be swathed in layers of fine clothes but instead appear naked to us? In other words, would the consumer whom we primarily depict as an agentic decision-making unit turn out to be a bewildered and put-upon individual who has a vague awareness of his or her subordination in the marketplace but lacks the knowledge and skills to redress the situation?

It is difficult to adopt a tabula rasa perspective retrospectively, but perhaps if we accessed views on consumption that are offered up in contexts outside of laboratories and formal interviews we could tap into different interpretations that provide alternative views on how consumption 'works' in consumers' everyday lives. Increasingly, consumer researchers are turning to the Internet and social media for insights, but there is an older medium that has been long communicating attitudes about consumption and its role in society. For decades, popular music has been an avenue for consumers to make statements about their relationships with specific consumer goods and the marketplace in general. With the occasional use of lyrics from some of these songs as a loose framework, this paper playfully and provocatively suggests that transformative consumer research could boldly refuse to adopt the underlying assumptions of much previous consumer research and instead consider the implications of an alternative interpretation of the consumer. Given that the task of TCR is to engage in "investigations that are framed by a fundamental problem or opportunity, and that strive to respect, uphold, and improve life in relation to the myriad conditions, demands, potentialities, and effects of consumption" (Mick 2006, p2), the perspective adopted in relation to the role of the consumer will be critical in ensuring that research results achieve their potential to improve consumer welfare.

## I AM A WEAPON OF MASSIVE CONSUMPTION AND IT'S NOT MY FAULT, IT'S HOW I'M PROGRAMMED TO FUNCTION
### LILY ALLEN, "THE FEAR", 2009

In most consumer behavior research, consumers are viewed as active (as opposed to passive) in their consumption decisions (e.g., Baumeister, Sparks, Stillman, and Vohs, 2008; McCracken 1990; Wallendorf and Arnould 1988; Wright 2002). According to this perspective, consumers are able to make complex consumption decisions with a view to meeting their functional and symbolic needs (Baumgartner 2002; Hirschman and Thompson 1997; Holt 1995). Consumers are described as thinking, feeling subjects who imbue

the consumption process with many different levels of meaning (Tetreault and Kleine 1990). They are seen to be self-directed in their consumption projects (McCracken 1987), choosing alternatives that will maximize their happiness and wellbeing (Thompson and Troester 2002). Throughout this process, they actively employ products in the fashioning of their self-determined self-images (Holt 1995; McCracken 1990). Consumption is viewed as an enjoyable activity that can be appreciated in its own right as well as being a means to an end (Belk 1996).

Based on assumptions of agency and rationality, this prevailing view considers consumers to be largely in control of their own identity projects (Elliott 1997; Schau, Gilly, and Wolfinbarger 2009). The use of objects to assist in the construction and maintenance of the self-concept is seen as a conscious, controllable process in which consumers engage to maximize their satisfaction (McCracken 1989; Walker and Olson 1997). This enables them to shop for a self-identity much as they would for a consumer good (Hirschman and Thompson 1997). In this scenario, consumers deliberately consider symbolism in their consumption decisions and make informed choices about which self out of numerous optional selves they wish to communicate at a particular point in time (Hirschman and Thompson 1997; McCracken 1990).

But what if Lily Allen is on to something? What if today's consumers are effectively programmed to consume at high levels and in ways that are largely beyond their individual control? Could growing up in a materialistic environment (Giddens, Schermer, and Vernon 2009) and exposure to more than 3,000 advertisements per day (Kalkbrenner 2004) result in consumers being effectively programmed to abide by the requirements of the marketplace, whether they want to or not?

While less frequently explicitly articulated in the consumer behavior literature, Lily's idea of programmed consumption can be found in numerous accounts of consumer behavior that attribute decisions and activities to elements other than consumers' conscious decision-making processes. Repetition of messages, unintended exposure to advertising, and associative learning are recognized as producing lasting effects that circumvent consumers' conscious barriers to persuasion (Ajzen 2001; Bettman Luce, and Payne 1998; Fitzsimons, Chartrand and Fitzsimons 2008; Shapiro 1999; Shimp, Stuart, and Engle 1991; Tybout and Artz 1994). In addition, over the years researchers have identified age, gender, social class, stage of the family life cycle, personality traits, mood, aspects of the physical environment, methods of information presentation, time pressures, marketing communications, situational factors, other social actors, and broad cultural forces as having significant impacts on consumer behavior (Bearden, Hardesty, and Rose 2001; Bettman et al. 1998; Klein and Lansing 1955; Lury 1996; Mick 2008; O'Guinn and Faber 1989; Raghunathan, Pham, and Corfman 2006; Wallendorf and Arnould 1988). These factors are largely beyond consumers' direct control and therefore can be expected to exert influence over consumption decisions and activities in ways that reduce consumers' agency. Other factors, such as existing product knowledge, are only partially under the consumer's direct control but are also influential (Celsi and Olsen 1988). This begs the question: To what extent can behavior be considered volitional in the wake of so many influencing variables? How much 'space' is left for truly individual, conscious, and deliberate consumption decisions?

## YOU KNOW THAT WE ARE LIVING IN A MATERIAL WORLD AND I AM A MATERIAL GIRL
### *MADONNA, "MATERIAL GIRL', 1984*

Madonna sensitizes us to the tendency for individuals to adapt their behaviors in accordance with the requirements of the external environment in order to survive and thrive. While advertisements might be promoting different products, it is possible that in aggregate they are advocating a culture of acquisitiveness (Tybout and Artz 1994), which in turn prevents the visualization or contemplation of alternative lifestyles (Waide 1987). In this situation, the healthy doses of skepticism towards advertising often attributed to consumers (e.g., Kivetz 2005; Scott 1990) are of less relevance because the consumer culture produces an overall orientation to consumption that is unconsciously assimilated.

Murray (2002) has outlined in detail how symbolic meanings resident in consumer goods are pre-determined by the capitalist system. Consumption codes are assimilated from childhood onwards, resulting in an internalized set of consumption priorities that typically prevents consumers from recognizing the pre-programmed nature of their desires. Any resistance only occurs within the system and is merely cosmetic. The result, according to Murray, is consumers who are merely participating in the construction of a reality that has been pre-determined and thus are unwittingly reinforcing the prevailing market system (see also Baudrillard 1988; Firat and Dholakia 1998).

In recent years there has been an increasing focus in consumer research on consumer creativity (Burroughs and Mick 2004; DeBerry-Spence 2008; Moreau and Dahl 2005). In this research stream, the ways in which consumers manipulate meanings and craft individual assortments of objects are seen to be confirmation of their ability to control their consumption behaviors in deliberate ways that are meaningful and satisfying. However, the strategies that have been interpreted by consumer researchers as masterly and creative could be considered reactive and compromised if they are viewed as consumer responses to market-produced tensions (Murray 2002). This is particularly the case where the role of such strategies is to reduce negative emotions rather than to maximize positive outcomes (Luce et al. 2001).

## OH LORD, WON'T YOU BUY ME A MERCEDES BENZ? MY FRIENDS ALL DRIVE PORCHES, I MUST MAKE AMENDS
### *JANIS JOPLIN, "MERCEDES BENZ", 1971*

As appreciated by Janis, conformity pressures place substantial limits on consumer agency. The instinctive need to create and maintain meaningful relationships with others ensures humans are tuned in to the expectations of other consumers (Cialdini and Goldstein 2004). To effectively achieve their desire for social fit, consumers are compelled to continually monitor the consumption behaviors of others and of themselves (Firat 1994). They observe others' consumption behaviors and reactions to their own consumption choices, and through these monitoring processes they attempt to conform to socially-prescribed forms of consumption (Hormuth 1990; Lury 1996). Advertising can encourage this behavior by alerting people to the ridicule or rejection they may experience if they consume inappropriately (Waide 1987).

Similarities in consumption patterns at the societal level demonstrate that sociocultural forces are very effective in prescribing behavior (Firat and Dholakia 1982). Consumers continually attempt

to utilize the most appropriate behavioral models for their social grouping(s) (Firat 1991), with any differences in behaviors the likely result of differences in "cultural expertise" (Roth and Moorman 1988, p403). Bourdieu (1984) notes that the taste structures taught to members of subcultures form cultural capital that provides an unconscious guide to decision making. The result is that apparent extensive choice in consumer markets conceals the reality that alternatives are constrained at the macro level to a relative few that are socially and culturally acceptable (Csikszentmihalyi and Rochberg-Halton 1981; Droge, Calantone, Agrawal, and Mackoy 1993). Individual differences in behaviors between consumers are considered to be negligible at the macro level of analysis (Firat and Dholakia 1982; Levy 1981).

## SQUARE-CUT OR PEAR-SHAPED THESE ROCKS DON'T LOSE THEIR SHAPE DIAMONDS ARE A GIRL'S BEST FRIEND
### *MARILYN MONROE, "DIAMONDS ARE A GIRL'S BEST FRIEND", 1953*

Marilyn's emphasis on diamonds over relationships reflects the view that objects can be more constant and reliable than people. The withering of the social structures and growing anonymity of most modern marketplaces have been described as resulting in an empty self that is insatiable for consumer goods that fail to satisfy because they cannot replicate the fulfillment that comes with satisfying human relationships (Cushman 1990). In contexts where relationships are superficial, consumers can be highly dependent on consumption for communication, to the point that they have no choice but to employ products in their social interactions (Firat and Dholakia 1998; Hormuth 1990). Consumers have an underlying awareness that they judge others and in return are judged according to their consumption behaviors (Firat 1995). This results in a heightened need to possess certain types of products to facilitate image management (Baudrillard 1988; Pettigrew 2001).

Another consequence of the relative anonymity of modern societies is the need to present oneself differently in different contexts (Firat 1995; Lury 1996). Although most consumers are more comfortable with a stable sense of self, this is difficult to achieve in a social environment that requires them to perform multiple and sometimes competing roles. Attempts to synthesize competing aspects of self can be unsustainable and result in ongoing effortful identity work for the individual (Ahuvia 2005).

Other complications can also occur in the process of integrating objects into the extended self. The individual wishes to feel unique in consumption, thus supposedly selecting objects that are somehow special or unique (Csikszentmihalyi and Rochberg-Halton 1981; Hirschman and Thompson 1997). Paradoxically, the objects selected are often mass-produced and common to many other consumers (Hormuth 1990). Consumers are encouraged to believe that their consumption assortments are distinctive and constitute genuine expressions of individuality (Baudrillard 1988; Firat 1991). For some analysts, this belief is legitimate as small differences in product combinations are considered to be adequate to claim uniqueness (Murphy and Miller 1997). However, others consider it a form of self-delusion as small differences only camouflage the over-riding similarity between the consumption patterns of individuals (Droge et al. 1993).

# I'VE LOOKED AT LIFE FROM BOTH SIDES NOW FROM UP AND DOWN, AND STILL SOMEHOW IT'S LIFE'S ILLUSIONS I RECALL, I REALLY DON'T KNOW LIFE AT ALL
*JONI MITCHELL, "BOTH SIDES NOW", 1969*

Joni's description of extensive experience failing to provide definitive answers about the nature of life resonates with the TCR task of attempting to address intractable problems that have resisted resolution despite much effort to understand and address them. We need to acknowledge that existing knowledge structures, and especially the dominant assumptions of consumer agency, will constrain our activities in this area of research (Murray and Ozanne 1991). As Joni alludes to above, if we're not careful our attention will be drawn to the illusions on show (our emperor's clothes) rather than the underlying substance.

Consumer researchers are often located in marketing or management schools, and as such these researchers typically approach consumption from the perspective that market-based consumption is a liberating, enjoyable, and largely optional pastime in which individuals engage at their discretion. This interpretation justifies the activities of marketers and the academics who assist them in their quest to generate profit from the marketplace. However, adopting a TCR perspective calls for a different approach to consumer research and its intended uses. In particular, it highlights the defensive position of consumers in modern markets and the need to empower them to improve their position relative to other actors in the marketplace (Atherton and Wells 1998). The relatively small amount of attention given to consumer empowerment in the consumer behavior literature has focused on the potential for consumer education to assist individuals in achieving their goals and protecting their interests in the market place (Bazerman 2001; Luce et al. 2001; Wathieu et al. 2002; Wright 2002). It is suggested that consumer education should commence early in life and constitute a formalized component of the school curriculum (Benn 2002; Ringold 2002). The underlying belief is that education will assist consumers to act more rationally and thereby enhance their welfare (Atherton and Wells 1998; Bazerman 2001).

Some researchers have pointed to the failure of consumer education initiatives in the past to illustrate that education alone cannot be the answer (Loewenstein 2001). In the case of alcohol consumption, for example, past studies have shown that supply-side factors such as limiting access through minimum age stipulation, restricting store opening hours, and enforcing price increases have been more effective at modifying demand than attempts to educate consumers about the dangers of excessive consumption (Bentzen, Eriksson, and Smith 1999; Wagenaar et al. 2000). At a different level, Seitz (1972) argued that consumer education is inherently futile in dynamic marketplaces where the number of products available is large and growing and where organizations have infinitely more resources at their disposal to obtain and analyze market information. According to this view, consumers will always be in catch-up mode and as a result the power distribution will remain permanently unequal, leaving consumers vulnerable to the actions of those with dominant market power.

Given the inadequacies of education as an all-encompassing path to consumer empowerment, other realms of influence must also be considered if consumers are to be empowered beyond their current position in the marketplace. The important role of social and cultural forces points to the need to address these factors, but they are extremely difficult to change. Influencing the sociocultural environment via upstream initiatives is thus one of the greatest challenges facing transformative consumer researchers. Choices must be made about which aspects of the sociocultural environment to target and how they will be modified. A first step may be to focus on assisting public policy makers to empower consumers through the development and implementation of consumer-focused regulations and legislation (Hollander, Keep, and Dickinson 1999). Some consumer researchers are already active in this area (e.g., Friedman 1998; Karpatkin 1999; Sommer 1994). Such an approach would acknowledge the limited abilities of individual consumers to change the environments in which they live and recognize the necessity of political intervention to achieve large-scale changes (Benn 2002; Seitz 1972). This approach would respond to Murray and Ozanne's (1991) call for consumer researchers to actively attempt to change social structures to improve consumers' lives. However, upstream initiatives are still likely to face difficulties in achieving consumer empowerment due to the ability of commercial lobby groups to effectively protest government initiatives that have the capacity to diminish their market power (Pal and Byrom 2005).

Another alternative would be to tame the consumer culture of some of its materialistic ways. The enormity of this task is overwhelming, but just as government-induced cultural change has been effective in the past (such as is currently occurring in the area of attitudes to the environment in many countries), there is potential to alter consumers' attitudes regarding their ideal lifestyles. For example, it is theoretically possible for public service announcements (PSAs) to be increased in number to equal or even eclipse commercial advertising. PSAs could actively encourage consumers to create meaning in their lives without an over-reliance on goods and services, such as by cultivating those personal virtues that are ultimately more fulfilling and being less concerned with accumulation (Waide 1987). Of course, such an approach would require decisions relating to which values and virtues should be prioritized, an inherently difficult and contentious task.

A further option is to use our skills and expertise to assist consumer associations and activist groups in achieving their goals. These groups attempt to address the imbalance of market power between consumers and organizations by representing consumers in general and disadvantaged consumers in particular (Karpatkin 1999). Alliance with such groups would allow consumer researchers access to those who have some ability to communicate with and resolve issues for individual consumers and groups of consumers. Such an alliance could also empower consumer groups to interact with governments and industry lobby groups on a more equal footing.

To conclude, researchers seeking to transform consumers' lives in positive and enduring ways may need to step back from current conceptualizations of the consumer that emphasize agency and rational decision-making. Instead, it may be productive to take a more critical view that explicitly recognizes the many and varied forces impacting both researchers' and consumers' interpretations of the consumption process. Stripping back the layers of previously learned and implicitly accepted understandings may hold the key to generating new answers to age-old questions.

## REFERENCES

Ahuvia, Aaron (2005), "Beyond the Extended Self: Loved Objects and Consumers' Identify Narratives," *Journal of Consumer Research*, 32 (1), 171-84.

Ajzen, Icek (2001), "Nature and Operation of Attitudes," *Annual Review of Psychology*, 52, 27-58.

Atherton, Margaret and Juliet Wells (1998), "Consumer Education: Learning for Life," *Consumer Policy Review*, 8 (4), 127-31.

Baudrillard, Jean (1988), *Jean Baudrillard: Selected Writings*, ed. Mark Poster, Stanford: Stanford University Press.

Baumeister, R. F., Sparks, E. A., Stillman, T. F., & Vohs, K. D. (2008), "Free will in consumer behavior: Self-control, ego depletion, and choice," *Journal of Consumer Psychology*, 18, 4–13.

Baumgartner, Hans (2002), "Toward a Personology of the Consumer," *Journal of Consumer Research*, 29 (2), 286-92.

Bazerman, Max H. (2001), "Consumer Research for Consumers," *Journal of Consumer Research*, 27 (4), 499-504.

Bearden, William O., David M. Hardesty and Randall L. Rose (2001), "Consumer Self-Confidence: Refinements in Conceptualisation and Measurement," *Journal of Consumer Research*, 28 (1), 121-134.

Belk, Russell W. (1996), "On Aura, Illusion, Escape and Hope in Apocalyptic Consumption," in *Marketing Apocalypse: Eschatology, Escapology and Illusion of the End*, eds. S. Brown, J. Bell, and D. Carson, London, Routledge, 87-107.

_____, Guliz Ger and Soren Askergaard (2003), "The Fire of Desire: A Multisited Inquiry into Consumer Passion," *Journal of Consumer Research*, 30 (3), 326-51.

Benn, Jette (2002), "Consumer Education Considerations and Perspectives," International *Journal of Consumer Studies*, 26 (3), 169-77.

Bentzen, Jan, Tor Eriksson, and Valdemar Smith (1999), "Rational Addiction and Alcohol Consumption: Evidence from the Nordic Countries," *Journal of Consumer Policy*, 22 (3), 257-79.

Bettman, James R., Mary F. Luce and John W. Payne (1998), "Constructive Consumer Choice Processes," *Journal of Consumer Research*, 25 (3), 187-217.

Bourdieu, Pierre (1984), *Distinction: A Social Critique of the Judgement of Taste*, London: Routledge and Kegan Paul.

Burroughs, James E. and David G. Mick (2004), "Exploring Antecedents and Consequences of Consumer Creativity in a Problem-Solving Context," *Journal of Consumer Research*, 31 (2), 402-11.

Celsi, Richard L. and Jerry C. Olson (1988), "The Role of Involvement in Attention and Comprehension Processes," *Journal of Consumer Research*, 15 (2), 210-24.

Cialdini, Robert B. and Noah J. Goldstein (2004), "Social Influence: Compliance and Conformity," *Annual Review of Psychology*, 55, 591-621.

Csikszentmihalyi, Mihaly and Eugene Rochberg-Halton (1981), The Meaning of Things, Domestic Symbols and the Self, New York: Cambridge University Press.

Cushman, Philip (1990), "Why the Self is Empty," *American Psychologist*, 45 (5), 599-611.

DeBerry-Spence, Benét (2008), "Consumer Creations of Product Meaning in the Context of African-Style Clothing, *Journal of the Academy of Marketing Science*, 36, 395–408.

Droge, Cornelia, Roger Calantone, Madhu Agrawal and Robert Mackoy (1993), "The Strong Consumption Culture and its Critiques: A Framework for Analysis," *Journal of Macromarketing*, 13 (2), 32-45.

Elliott, Richard (1997), "Existential Consumption and Irrational Desire," European *Journal of Marketing*, 31 (3/4), 285-96.

Firat, A. Fuat (1991), "The Consumer in Postmodernity," in *Advances in Consumer Research*, Vol. 18, eds. Rebecca H. Holman and Michael R. Solomon, Provo, UT: Association for Consumer Research, 70-75.

_____ (1994), "Gender and Consumption: Transcending the Feminine," in *Gender Issues and Consumer Behaviour*, ed. Janeen A. Costa, Thousand Oaks: Sage, 205-28.

_____ (1995), "Consumer Culture or Culture Consumed?" in *Marketing in a Multicultural World*, eds. Janeen A. Costa and Gary J. Bamossy, California: Sage, 105-25.

_____ and Nikhilesh Dholakia (1982), "Consumption Choices at the Macro Level," *Journal of Macromarketing*, 2 (2), 6-15.

_____ (1998), *Consuming People: From Political Economy to Theaters of Consumption*, London: Routledge.

Fitzsimons, Gráinne M., Tanya L. Chartrand, and Gavan J. Fitzsimons (2008), "Automatic Effects of Brand Exposure on Motivated Behavior: How Apple Makes You 'Think Different'," *Journal of Consumer Research*, 35, 21-35.

Friedman, Monroe (1998), "Coping with Consumer Fraud: The Need for a Paradigm Shift," *Journal of Consumer Affairs*, 32 (1), 1-12.

Giddens, Justine, L., Julie A. Schermer, and Philip A. Vernon (2009), "Material values are largely in the family: A twin study of genetic and environmental contributions to materialism," *Personality and Individual Differences*, 46, 428–431.

Hirschman, Elizabeth C. and Craig J. Thompson (1997), "Why Media Matter: Toward a Richer Understanding of Consumers' Relationships with Advertising and Mass Media," *Journal of Advertising*, 26 (1), 43-60.

Hollander, Stanley C., William W. Keep, and Roger Dickinson (1999), "Marketing Public Policy and the Evolving Role of Marketing Academics; A Historical Perspective," *Journal of Public Policy & Marketing*, 18 (2), 265-69.

Holt, Douglas B. (1995), "How Consumers Consume: A Taxonomy of Consumption Practices," *Journal of Consumer Research*, 22 (1), 1-16.

Hormuth, Stefan E. (1990), *The Ecology of the Self*, Cambridge: Cambridge University Press.

Kalkbrenner, P. (2004), Advertising Damages Mental Health, Portland Independent Media Centre, http://portland.indymedia.org/en/2004/06/290078.shtml, accessed 28 February 2010.

Karpatkin, Rhoda, H. (1999), "Toward a Fair and Just Marketplace for All Consumers: The Responsibilities of Marketing Professionals," *Journal of Public Policy and Marketing*, 18 (1), 118-22.

Kivetz, Ran (2005), "Promotion Reactance: The Role of Effort-Reward Congruity," *Journal of Consumer Research*, 31 (4), 725-36.

Klein, Lawrence R. and John B. Lansing (1955), "Decisions to Purchase Consumer Durable Goods," *Journal of Marketing*, 20 (2), 109-32.

Levy, Sidney J. (1981), "Interpreting Consumer Mythology: A Structural Approach to Consumer Behavior," *Journal of Marketing*, 45 (3), 49-61.

Loewenstein, George (2001), "The Creative Destruction of Decision Research," *Journal of Consumer Research*, 28 (3), 499-505.

Luce, Mary F., James R. Bettman and John W. Payne (2001), "Consequences of Trade-Off Difficulty," *Monographs of the Journal of Consumer Research*, University of Chicago Press.

Lury, Celia (1996), *Consumer Culture*, New Brunswick: Rutgers University Press.

McCracken, Grant (1987), "Advertising: Meaning or Information?" in *Advances in Consumer Research*, Vol. 14, eds. Melanie Wallendorf and Paul Anderson, Provo, UT: Association for Consumer Research, 121-24.

_____ (1989), "Who is the Celebrity Endorser? Cultural Foundations of the Endorsement Process," *Journal of Consumer Research*, 16 (3), 310-21.

_____ (1990), Culture and Consumption, USA: Indiana University Press.

Mick, David G. (2006), "Meaning and Mattering through Transformative Consumer Research," in *Advances in Consumer Research*, Vol. 33, eds. Cornelia Pechmann and Linda L. Price, Duluth: Association for Consumer Research, 1-4.

_____ (2008), "Degrees of Freedom of Will: An Essential Endless Question in Consumer Behavior, *Journal of Consumer Psychology*, 18, 17–21.

Moreau, Page C. and Darren W. Dahl (2005), "Designing the Solution: The Impact of Constraints on Consumers' Creativity," *Journal of Consumer Research*, 32 (1), 13-22.

Murphy, Patricia L. and Carol T. Miller (1997), "Post Decisional Dissonance and the Commodified Self-Concept: A Cross-Cultural Examination," *Personality and Social Psychology Bulletin*, 23 (1), 50-62.

Murray, Jeff B. (2002), "The Politics of Consumption: A Re-Inquiry on Thompson and Haytko's (1997) "Speaking of Fashion"," *Journal of Consumer Research*, 29 (3), 427-40.

_____ and Julie L. Ozanne (1991), "The Critical Imagination: Emancipation Interests in Consumer Research," *Journal of Consumer Research*, 18 (2), 129-44.

O'Guinn, Thomas C. and Ronald J. Faber (1989), "Compulsive Buying: A Phenomenological Exploration," *Journal of Consumer Research*, 16 (2), 147-57.

Pal, J. and J. Byrom (2005), "More than one Bite of the Cherry: A Study of UK Grocery Retailers' Attempts to Influence the Retail Planning Policy-Making Process," *Journal of Public Affairs*, 5 (2): 136-149.

Pettigrew, Simone (2001), "King or Pawn? The Role of the Australian Beer Drinker," *Journal of Research for Consumers* (www.jrconsumers.com), 2.

Raghunathan, Rajagopal, Michel T. Pham and Kim P. Corfman (2006), "Informational Properties of Anxiety and Sadness, and Displaced Coping," *Journal of Consumer Research*, 32 (4), 596-601.

Ringold, Debra J. (2005), "Vulnerability in the Marketplace: Concepts, Caveats, and Possible Solutions," *Journal of Macromarketing*, 25 (2), 202-14.

Roth, Martin S. and Christine Moorman (1988), "The Cultural Content of Cognition and the Cognitive Content of Culture: Implications for Consumer Research," in *Advances in Consumer Research*, Vol. 15, ed. Michael J. Houston, Provo, UT: Association for Consumer Research, 403-10.

Schau, Hope J., Mary C. Gilly, and Mary Wolfinbarger (2009), "Consumer Identity Renaissance: The Resurgence of Identity-Inspired Consumption in Retirement," *Journal of Consumer Research*, 36, 255-76.

Scott, Linda (1990), "Understanding Jingles and Needledrop: A Rhetoric Approach to Music in Advertising," *Journal of Consumer Research*, 17 (2), 223-36.

Seitz, Wesley D. (1972), "Consumer Education as the Means to Attain Efficient Market Performance," *Journal of Consumer Affairs*, 6 (2), 198-209.

Shapiro, Stewart (1999), "When an Ad's Influence is Beyond Our Conscious Control: Perceptual and Conceptual Fluency Effects Caused by Incidental Ad Exposure," *Journal of Consumer Research*, 26 (1), 16-36.

Shimp, Terence A., Elnora W. Stuart and Randall W. Engle (1991), "A Program of Classical Conditioning Experiments Testing Variations in the Conditioned Stimulus and Context," *Journal of Consumer Research*, 18 (1), 1-13.

Sommer, Robert (1994), "Serving Two Masters: Center for Consumer Research at the University of California, Davis, 1976-1992," *Journal of Consumer Affairs*, 28 (1), 170-86.

Tetreault, Mary A. and Robert E. Kleine III (1990), "Ritual, Ritualised Behaviour, and Habit: Refinements and Extensions of the Consumption Ritual Construct," in *Advances in Consumer Research*, Vol. 17, eds. Marvin E. Goldberg, Gerald Gorn, and Richard W. Pollay, Provo, UT: Association for Consumer Research, 31-8.

Thompson, Craig J. and Maura Troester (2002), "Consumer Value Systems in the Age of Postmodern Fragmentation: The Case of the Natural Health Microculture," *Journal of Consumer Research*, 28 (4), 550-71.

Tybout, Alice M. and Nancy Artz (1994), "Consumer Psychology," *Annual Review of Psychology*, 45, 131-39.

Wagenaar, A. C., D. M. Murray, John P. Gehan, Mark Wolfson, Jean L. Forster, Traci L. Toomey, Cheryl L. Perry, and Rhonda Jones-Webb (2000), "Communities Mobilizing for Change on Alcohol: Outcomes from a Randomized Community Trial," *Journal of Studies on Alcohol*, 61 (1), 85-94.

Waide, John (1987), "The Making of Self and World in Advertising," *Journal of Business Ethics*, 6 (2), 73-9.

Walker, Beth A. and Jerry C. Olson (1997), "The Activated Self in Consumer Behaviour: A Cognitive Structure Perspective," in *Research in Consumer Behavior*, Vol. 8, ed. Russell W. Belk, London: JAI Press, 135-71.

Wallendorf, Melanie and Eric J. Arnould (1988), "'My Favourite Things': A Cross-Cultural Inquiry into Object Attachment, Possessiveness, and Social Linkage," *Journal of Consumer Research*, 14 (4), 531-47.

Wathieu, Luc, Lyle Brenner, Ziv Cameron, Amitava Chattopadhyay, Klaus Wertenbroch, Aimee Drolet, John Gourville, A.V. Muthukrishnan, Nathan Novemsky, Rebecca K. Ratner and George Wu (2002), "Consumer Control and Empowerment: A Primer," *Marketing Letters*, 13 (3), 297-305.

Wright, Peter (2002), "Marketplace Metacognition and Social Intelligence," *Journal of Consumer Research*, 28 (4), 677-82.

# Men, Bags and The City - Male's Adoption of Non-Traditional Gender Aesthetics

Ralf Weinberger, University of Innsbruck, Austria
Andrea Hemetsberger, University of Innsbruck, Austria

## ABSTRACT

This article studies male's overt consumption of non-traditional gender aesthetics. Phenomenological interviews revealed that consumers use these items to build a unique aesthetic gender identity. Consumers apply strategies of differentiation and contrasting to safeguard their aesthetic individuality and set themselves apart from communal forms of consumption.

## INTRODUCTION

"Look, this guy carries a handbag…" Whereas several years ago such a whisper would have led to surprised glances at the guy with the handbag, men carrying handbags in cities are not that much of a surprise anymore. Rather, when taking a walk through cities one can see an increasing number of men carrying handbags in their hands, in the crook of their arms or draped over one shoulder. Uninformed observers may ask themselves "Aren't handbags for women? ..... Have guys become the new gals?"

In recent years males have been increasingly in researchers' foci, since males started to participate in what we denominate here as non-traditional gender aesthetic consumption. We define non-traditional gender aesthetic consumption as forms of aesthetic consumption which break with long held aesthetic conceptions of a certain gender in Western societies. Since the advent of the metrosexual trend (Simpson, 2002), different studies researched such male consumption practices intended for the stylistic and aesthetic display. Changes on the macro-social, social and individual level, caused a reshaping of male identities (Schroeder and Zwick, 2004; Simpson, 2002; Patterson and Elliott, 2002; Nyeck et al, 2002).

Schroeder and Zwick (2004) and Patterson and Elliott (2002) argue that advertising portrayals of men led to a renegotiation of male identities in society. Bakewell et al. (2006) regard women's emancipation and the gay liberation movement as impacting factors on the increasing aesthetic discourse among men. Subcultural communities and peer groups also set boundaries of male's legitimate consumption of grooming products (Rinallo, 2007; Nyeck et al, 2002). An increased male narcissism (Sturrock and Pioch, 1998, Ourahmoune and Nyeck., 2008), rebellions against societal conventions (Nyeck et al., 2002) or transitional lifetimes (Ourahmoune and Nyeck, 2008) were found to be influencing factors on males' embellishing consumptions. However, particularly heterosexual males still fear stigmatization and engage in avoidance behavior (Ourahmoune and Nyeck, 2008, Kimmel and Tissier-Desbordes, 1999). Non-traditional gender aesthetic items go beyond male narcissism, beauty rituals, and new male aesthetics as norms of gendered consumption seem to be relevant here as well. Furthermore, fear of stigmatization and avoidance behavior runs counter overt displays of non-traditional gender objects as fashion items and aesthetic statements of male consumers. We draw on Nietzsche (1969), Featherstone (2004) and Venkatesh and Meamber's (2008) assertion that, by consuming in a non-traditional manner, consumers are creating their lives and selves as aesthetic identity projects.

We aim to research and theorize about deeper seated individual meanings of non-traditional gender aesthetic consumption for consumers' identity projects as well as consumers' patterns of aesthetic consumption. We start with a literature review on aesthetic consumption and identity construction. Following the empirical data we elaborate the relevance and meanings of non-traditional gender aesthetic consumption for consumers. In the discussion section we work out deviations from present knowledge in the literature and present strategies consumer undertake to manage aesthetic identity projects.

## AESTHETIC THEORY

Aesthetics is often perceived as an ambiguous concept of meanings of the beautiful, which can either relate to experiences, sensory characteristics, the arts, or consumption activities (Venkatesh and Meamber, 2008). In this article we understand aesthetics as consumer's interpretation, evaluation and meaning production, which define the beauty of consumption items. We use Nietzsche's contribution as a theoretical introduction into aesthetic theory. Nietzsche's nihilism, the denial of objectivity and persistent truth, renders aesthetics into the sphere of the individual and its interpretations and meaning creations. Nietzsche claims that people are active producers of their (aesthetic) worlds and realities (Welsch, 1997). Aesthetics is understood as being formed by people's individual perception, understanding and interpretation of the world.

Postmodernism resumes this notion of the subjectivity in aesthetics. Aesthetics and Postmodernism are particularly closely tied together, since Postmodernism is inter alia born out of fundamental aesthetic changes, such as the collapse of the boundaries between art and everyday life, between high art and the mass/popular culture or an overall promiscuity of styles (Featherstone, 2004). A postmodern approach to aesthetics deems that aesthetics is mixed and strongly interrelated with aspects of the everyday lives, where facets of the political and social life, popular arts or everyday aesthetic issues, such as environmentalism, fashion, and lifestyles, are constituted by aesthetics. A Postmodern aesthetic understanding also implies a plurality of styles and diverse aesthetic notions that exist next to each other, without claiming that a particular style is more important or meaningful (Welsch, 1997).

Featherstone (2004) argues that the consumer culture contributes heavily to an ongoing aestheticization quest of people. People constantly consume and strive for new styles and tastes in order to construct different lifestyles. Consumers aspire aesthetically constructed lifestyles, since aesthetics is the only principle, which still holds in a world where norms and conceptions are in flux. Since modern conventions of "right and wrong" behaviors or styles macerated, people need to individually make sense of what they consider as beautiful and aesthetic (Featherstone, 2004, Welsch, 1997, Firat and Venkatesh, 1995). This aestheticization trend is particularly lived out in urban areas by a young middle class, who is usually more active in the stylization of their lives. The urban context provides people with a style plurality from which they can individually make use of. Aestheticization manifests itself in accumulations of expressive goods such as clothing, furniture, in bodily alterations, and other aesthetic projects, which help people demonstrate their individuality and aesthetic differentiation (Featherstone, 2004; Firat and Venkatesh, 1995; Veryzer, 1995).

Venkatesh and Meamber (2008) argue that consumers are constantly seeking aesthetics in their everyday consumption, highlighting the centrality of aesthetics for people's lives. Venkatesh and Meamber (2008) further contend that aesthetics in people's lives and in consumption practices impact not only on people's taste formations, but also on their emotions and feelings, which are central for people's identity formation. Based on these findings, Venkatesh and Meamber (2008) conceive consumers as aesthetic subjects, who use meanings of various aesthetics in their identity creations (Thompson and Hirschmann, 1995, Venkatesh and Meamber, 2006). Non-traditional gender aesthetics add to identity creations, which is not limited to the adoption of styles, or to idiosyncratic consumption styles but derives much of its meaning from 'gendered' consumption. Gender aesthetics are playfully mixed and matched so as to define one's gender identity on the continuum between femininity and masculinity.

## CONSUMER GENDER IDENTITY PROJECTS

Thompson and Haytko (1997) define identity as a sense of the consumer of who s/he is, which is constantly (re)defined, negotiated and created. In contrast to the postmodern identity conception (Firat and Venkatesh, 1995) or the empty self concept (Cushmann, 1990), we assume that consumers actively construct identity narratives in which personal histories and conceptions of the social and cultural environment are interwoven. Consumers refer to market offerings by negotiating meanings and symbols via which they further develop their identity narratives. Nevertheless, consumers try to forge a coherent, if diversified identity narrative (Arnould and Thompson, 2005; Schau and Gilly, 2003; Thompson and Hirschmann, 1995).

Consumption patterns and objects provide people with means to create not only desired, utopian identities, but also to foster the development of consumer's individual identity narratives (Kozinets, 2001). In the case of transitional life episodes, for instance, consumption objects, such as loved objects also help people to give meaning to these episodes or/and to stay "true" to their own identity. Similarly, certain consumption objects stand for specific personal meanings to which people refer to and by which they construct their subjective individual identity narratives (Ahuvia, 2005). Consumption objects also serve the purpose of socializing and categorization (Holt, 1995). Furthermore, recent research has shown that consumption is also deeply interlinked with individual's self-understanding of their gender identity.

Fischer and Arnould (1994) define gender identity as the extent to which people think of themselves as masculine or feminine. Connell (2002) conceives gender as a project, where personal and society's gender understandings are negotiated. Patterson and Elliott (2002) assume that males are currently reevaluating their gender identity understandings since advertising increasingly promotes the groomed, slim and sexy male, attributes which were formerly regarded as feminine. Nyeck et al. (2002) found that the extent of consuming non-traditional gender aesthetics also depends upon the different gender identity understandings of gays and straights. Males consume these items either to blend into their reference or peer groups, thus adhering to the reference groups' gender understandings or to rebel against gendered conventions and norms of society. In a similar vein, Rinallo (2007) concludes that peer groups of males set boundaries of legitimate male consumption behaviors. Ourahmoune and Nyeck (2008) found that males participate in clandestine consumption to overcome stigmatizations and social sanction due to their deviation from their peer's or society's gender conception. Male's gender identity understandings are in flux, which is why males have become more involved in their aesthetic appearance. However, males still use non-traditional gender aesthetic items primarily to hide bodily imperfections or to act out their narcissistic needs (Ourahmoune and Nyeck, 2008; Nyeck et al, 2002). These findings run counter empirical observations of overt, public display of traditionally feminine items, such as handbags, which are neither hidden, nor just serve to compensate imperfections or narcissistic needs. It is the aim of our study to address this specific form of non-traditional gender aesthetics consumption and its role in male's identity narratives.

## METHOD

Our empirical study followed a two step process. First, male handbag wearers were observed and approached online, or personally approached on the streets in urban areas. Our purposive sample followed the principles of snowball sampling (Patton, 1991). However, snowball sampling turned out problematic as handbag users rarely knew other handbag consumers. Hence, we adapted our methodology accordingly and followed the technique of criterion sampling (Patton, 1991) which focused a male handbag usage and did not address other characteristics such as e.g. sexual orientations. People, who agreed to participate in our study were asked to write a diary over a period of 2.5 to 3 weeks in which they were asked to write freely about their usage of handbags (Alaszewski, 2006). In addition, informants were asked to take pictures of items of which they particularly liked for their design. In total, 14 participants took part in our study. All of them live in urban areas in Central Europe, with ages ranging from 25 to 42.

In a second step we conducted phenomenological interviews (Thompson et al, 1989) with the participants at their homes or in their offices if participants did not feel comfortable being interviewed at home. Informant's home and office styles were also observed. We chose phenomenological interviews to learn about the participants' experiences with non-traditional gender aesthetics and to reveal the deeper meanings of non-traditional gender aesthetics consumption. The interviews started with broad general questions about consumers' lives and then focused on their experiences with aesthetics and non-traditional gender aesthetics. Secondly, we asked for other experiences with other non-traditional gender aesthetics to reveal the overall importance of non-traditional gender aesthetic consumption to their lives. Subsequently, our questions focused on perceived societal changes and on a self estimation of masculine and feminine traits. We asked about other people's reactions to the participant's usage of non-traditional gender aesthetic consumption to reveal stigmatization experiences and behaviors. Additionally, a set of questions aimed at the identification of situations when appearance and style are particularly important to the informants.

**Table 1: sample characteristics**

| | |
|---|---|
| Interview 1: Daniel, teacher, 29 | Interview 8: Patrick, designer, 30 |
| Interview 2: Marcus, company owner, 28 | Interview 9: Simon, editor, 31 |
| Interview 3: Steve, student, 25 | Interview 10: Marc, student, 25 |
| Interview 4 : Robert, student, 27 | Interview 11: Oliver, make up artist, 24 |
| Interview 5: Peter, hairdresser, 29 | Interview 12: Richard, social worker, 27 |
| Interview 6: Thomas, employee, 28 | Interview 13: Nico, self employed, 35 |
| Interview 7: Michael, employee, 42 | Interview 14: Lukas, student/ marketer, 28 |

Diaries were not only used to identify important usage situations of handbags but also stimulated stories and narrations about experiences with non-traditional gender aesthetics and about the informant's general aesthetic preferences. Photo-elicitation (Heisley and Levy, 1991) also helped with eliciting relevant stories of non-traditional gender aesthetic consumption.

Interviews lasted between 1h 30 min and 2h 45 min and accounted to a total of a bit less than 30 hours of information. The interviews were transcribed and accounted to 290 single spaced pages of interview transcription. A hermeneutic-phenomenological analysis according to the principles of phenomenological analysis by Thompson et al. (1989) was conducted. An idiographic analysis documented the individual life stories and meaning of non-traditional gender aesthetics. Integrative analysis revealed similarities and differences and allowed us to formulate themes, and relate them to processes of identity construction and differentiation through aesthetic consumption.

## FINDINGS

### Defining individual gender identity through non-traditional gender aesthetics

The findings revealed that the male handbag usage is not a singular, restricted activity, but it joins the ranks of a personal history of activities related to non-traditional gender aesthetic consumption. Male handbag consumption and usage is merely a continuation of such consumption activities and starts as a search for an aesthetic gender identity.

*"In the past it was more colorful, more flashy, also items from the women's collection. Well, my favorite designer in the 1990's was Helmut Lang. I changed between a woman's trousers with a sash ... and also the tops were all for women when I went out"*
*(Simon)*

*"[…] or make up, I also used make up back then and that kind of stuff […] even as a child and I always wore handbags. Male bags, those real ...men bags, like the Freitag ones, I never wore them."*
*(Patrick)*

These verbatims demonstrate that consumers used non-traditional gender aesthetics already in their youth and teenage years when these items were not at all advertised in the media (Schroeder and Zwick, 2004). We assume that a history with non-traditional gender aesthetics facilitates an easier adoption of other or further non-traditional gender aesthetic consumption activities in their later lives. Gendered forms of consumption usually follow a certain path until they become part of an individual's self understanding. The meaning of non-traditional gender aesthetics consumption is not homogenous and changes over the course of lifetime. Some meanings may become dominant for the individual consumer during a specific phase of life. Other meanings may add to the overall pattern of consuming non-traditional gender aesthetics as a part of their aesthetic life project.

*Coming out phase*

While Ourahmoune et al. (2008), Rinallo (2007) or Nyeck et al. (2002) highlight the distinction between a heterosexual and homosexual involvement, usage, and personal history with non-traditional gender aesthetics, our findings contradicted these results. Both, heterosexual and homosexual males were equally involved in non-traditional gender aesthetic consumptions, yet the purpose of these consumption activities is different between gay and straight males. Gay informants heavily use non-traditional gender aesthetics for their coming out.

*B: sparkling, colorful skirts for males... very, very much so, yes; and deliberately taking them to the countryside to go out. Yes, yes,*
*A: for what purpose?*
*B: To show that this here is a gay guy.*
*(Daniel)*

*B: […] then it happened very quickly - my coming out phase. Flashy, wrap around skirts, I was bleached blond […] I also wore handbags then, well such nylon ones.*
*A: What did you want to express here?*
*B: that I was gay.... apparently...*
*(Simon)*

During this coming out phase non-traditional gender aesthetics help gay males not only to demonstrate their sexual orientation, but also assisted them to define themselves as gay and to negotiate a gay identity during a time when gayness is a central topic for them. As the next respondent demonstrates, these non-traditional gender aesthetics can also fulfill a social-political purpose during the coming out phase. Using non-traditional gender aesthetics is a public statement to the public that being gay is not a problem, and normal.

*"[…] I am different, I am gay, I am that obviously gay; look, you can all notice that I am gay, because I don't have a problem with that. I publically demonstrate that I don't have a problem with it. That everyone, the world may know it."*
*(Daniel)*

During the coming out phase respondents also reported that non-traditional gender aesthetics are extensively consumed and applied as the gay scene offers a liminal zone for such activities and aesthetics. When this coming out phase is over, the extent of the usage of non-traditional gender aesthetics often decreases. Hence, we assume that non-traditional gender aesthetics for gay males is also a coping strategy with these turbulent times of defining one's own sexual orientation on the one hand, and dealing with publicity on the other hand.

*Urban change and freedom*

Some respondents mentioned that they were more heavily involved in this form of consumption when they either moved to a city (Ourahmoune and Nyeck, 2008) or started to spend most of their time there. Here, the contrast between the city and countryside, where the respondents felt constrained in their possibilities, becomes apparent.

*A: You mentioned that you wanted to move to a bigger city, why was that?*
*B: I don't know, I am just like that. A lot of people say "Listen Alex, you just belong to a big city". In the village I was always the odd duck, and therefore I thought that I needed to go to a big city […] well and I was being looked at in an odd way. Particularly when you are not coming from a big city, where there are different people like you. And that is why I am feeling quite comfortable here.*
*(Oliver)*

The city liberates and provides freedom to act out one's own identity and to consume products, such as non-traditional gender aesthetics, which would render the individual as the odd one out on the countryside. However, respondents also used non-traditional gender aesthetics to symbolize their transition from the rural area to the city and to establish a stark contrast to the rural social environment. Non-traditional gender aesthetics are used as a strong sign of a genuine urban lifestyle identity.

*"For a country bumpkin, XXXX was a metropolis par excellence. Then it was also to show your friends from the countryside "look I have been to the city and I have become really city-like", because I wear glittering clothes...."*
*(Daniel)*

*Individual gender understanding*

The responses concerning the gender understandings of the respondents supported the notions that male identity conceptions are currently changing drastically (Ourahmoune and Nyeck, 2008, Schroeder and Zwick, 2005). On a continuum contrasting of what the individual respondent connects with masculinity on the one hand and femininity on the other hand, informants rated themselves as being somewhere in between the masculine – feminine continuum. In describing themselves, respondents also referred to attributes which they used to describe femininity.

*"Yes, well, probably something in between a bit. Yes, because, since I am not embodying what I consider as masculine, yes, well I am rather ... a bit androgynous."*
*(Simon)*

*"Puh, I would say somewhere in between these two. Well in between these two, I don't hope that I am appearing too feminine, but I also don't feel the need to appear too masculine...."*
*(Marc)*

These findings also highlight that the respondents, gay and straight, do not have a problem to incorporate feminine traits into their self understanding. Heterosexual and homosexual males do equally not try to neglect them and spoke freely about aspects of their identity which could be rated as feminine. Male's gender identity understandings are not set in opposition to feminine attributes but rather combine attributes of both genders into their aesthetic identity.

*(Non)stigmatized*

In contrast to the results by Kimmel and Tissier-Desbordes, (2000), Ourahmoune and Nyeck (2008) or Rinallo (2007) that non-traditional gender consumption behaviors are stigmatized and that males, in particular heterosexual males, enact avoidance behaviors due to fears of social sanctions such as ridicule, our study rather supports the opposite. Informants are quite bold in their public display of non-traditional gender aesthetics and did not fear social sanctions or stigmatization. Several informants, heterosexual as well as homosexual, already experienced some forms of sanctions such as name calling or ridicule, but instead of avoiding carrying non-traditional gender aesthetic items, they vehemently defend their individual identity project.

*B: "why are you running about with a bag like a fairy?"*
*A: Who said that?*
*B: These were close acquaintances.*

*A: And what did you think when you heard that?*
*B: Bite me! [laughs]*
*A: So would you abstain from using the bag?*
*B: No. No. No. No. When I need it, then I need it. I am not here to ... satisfy any aesthetic or social requirements of other people.*
*(Nico)*

Not only did the informants not refrain from using non-traditional gender aesthetic objects when they experienced social sanctions but some also reported that they actively fight against such ridicule. Although the participants were sampled in urban areas of different population size (from 130.000 inhabitants to 1.3 million), larger urban areas are not different in that regard. Nevertheless, respondents reported that such social sanctions are quite rare.

Stigmatizations and social sanctions do occur, however our study did not support previous findings of avoidance behavior and fear of stigmatization. Also heterosexual's fear of being judged as gay (Ourahmoune and Nyeck, 2008) was not supported, which gives rise to the assumption that non-traditional gender aesthetics consumption is rather a deliberate, bold statement of one's uniqueness and individuality as a male consumer.

**Constructing aesthetic individuality**
*Uniqueness and Otherness*

Non-traditional gender aesthetics facilitate differentiation from others and from mainstream consumption. Respondents report a particularly strong desire to demonstrate their otherness within their surrounding social environment. Non-traditional gender aesthetics provide the means to construct a unique individuality even at the odds of being totally out of fashion, or far ahead of any fashion trends.

*"I even have more extreme ones[watches], the one is pink with turquoise and has in the centre a diamond, which is rotating, such a... everyone would think that I am nuts. No one would wear anything like that."*
*(Steve)*

*"The lacquered shoes, the bags, be it the normal shoulder bag or the handbag, doesn't matter, because no one in my environment wears any bags like that. Ahm sunglasses, huge Dior sunglasses, Ray Ban, whatever, ahm jewellery, ...everything that the XXX newspaper is spreading as styling tips, that is, yes, well, that is for people who do not want to draw attention, these are people who are satisfied with what society tells them to do. I am different."*
*(Robert)*

Apart from the creation of aesthetic boundaries from the surrounding environment (Featherstone, 2004), individuals thereby also negotiate their individual need for attention or blending in. Using non-traditional gender aesthetics does not only facilitate differentiation, but due to this purposeful public display individuals draw attention to themselves as aesthetic subjects. Yet throughout the interviews it became obvious that non-traditional gender aesthetics are not geared at provoking others. Rather, respondents emphasize their aspiration to differentiate themselves from the masses. Individuals sort of participate in a tightrope walk between catching attention and blending into contexts such as events, job environment or leisure time activities. They also indicated that they did not have a history of provocation, oftentimes not even during puberty or teenage years.

*"I am a person who needs a tremendous lot of attention. Ahm … probably that's also one of the reasons why I am dressed like this and buying those things. Not to boost my ego, but to … simply…I am against this group thinking, this collective thinking. Ahm I am rather, I was born as an individual and I don't need to be like everyone else. That means that I also don't need to please everyone."*
*(Robert)*

Non-traditional gender aesthetics help people create their self as non conformist. Respondents repeatedly judge the mainstream as negative from which they want to distance themselves. Perceived narrow-mindedness, constrained thinking or collectivism were noted characteristics of their environment from which the individuals want to (aesthetically) distance themselves. Hence, respondents in most cases were the only ones in their environment to carry handbags and only few knew other males who used handbags. Informants also did not participate in handbag consumer communities. None of the informants would be active or know about handbag communities as this would run counter to their deep inner aspiration to be unique; different; interesting.

*Self branding*

In a similar vein, people use non-traditional gender aesthetics for the purpose of "self branding". They purposefully display their handbags and /or extravagant outfits to portray themselves as unique and to generate a lasting impression. Self branding with non-traditional gender aesthetics means to ease the identification and recognition of people at social events, or in business situations. This form of self branding was particularly widespread among individuals who run their own (fashion) business.

*"Yes, there are always looks and laughter that he has his bag with him that's an identifying feature […] yes, people know you because you always have the bag with you […]"*
*A: How is that…?*
*"Actually that's pleasant, positive. And it supports the brand. Hm… the ego"*
*(Marcus)*

*"I also wear one from my collection in the evening when I go out, then I wear the clutch I have my business cards, the cigarettes, the money and the cell phone and that is often the first topic when I am talking. With the rich women, when they ask me where I got that great bag from then I say "from my own collection" and you strike up a conversation like that."*
*(Patrick)*

Here, non-traditional gender aesthetics are used in a business context for self branding and for branding the business. Hence, non-traditional gender aesthetics are part of the fashion system, and are used to demonstrate uniqueness and innovativeness.

*"You get attention in certain circles and you develop an own brand and it is prototypical for someone that he always appears like that, that's important […]", Marcus).*

In this context the personal identity project coalesces with the company purpose and serves to build a strong (self and corporate)

brand identity. Individuals purposefully select the appropriate handbag and outfit to draw attention to their specific business idea.

*Contrasting*

Individuals create their own aesthetic identity by consuming aesthetically unique or exceptional items. When a certain style, which they liked at the onset, is taken over by several people, the same style can become unaesthetic to them.

*"The funny thing is that there are products that are beautiful in my opinion and which I like, but when a lot of people wear them, they become ugly."*
*(Steve)*

*"I would say indeed that I would not wear something that a lot of people are wearing. If there are one or two then it is okay […]"*
*(Thomas)*

Consumers actively search for styled products, such as clothes which few other people consume. This quest for consumer individuality is not restricted to fashion but is also to be found in other areas of aesthetic consumption, such as food or hairstyles. It can even pervade a consumer's whole consumption behavior, where items are actively avoided as soon as other people possess them.

*A: when did you start to search for your very own style?*
*"it started… it has actually always been like that that I always wanted the items that others did not have."*
*(Steve)*

This aesthetic life projects are not restricted to consumption in a narrow sense. For certain consumers this aesthetic striving is central to their lives and extends into other life areas, such as their choice of partners or friends.

*"I have to admit that the particular look - being particular, also applies to my girlfriends. [A: yes?] Well I don't like normal girlfriends; they are too boring for me. They need to be special in a way. I had completely different types. But they always draw attention. They always stand out."*
*(Steve)*

Another way to achieve one's aesthetic goals is not by avoiding consuming mass aesthetics but by avoiding items that are in fashion. Instead of using purchased fashion items, they are stowed away until it is out of fashion and other people do not use or wear it. Individuality becomes the dogma of consumption, even at the expense of not being able to use new fashion items and being totally out of fashion.

*"Right, it will become old and shabby and then in ten years no one will wear such a thing, but it is classic enough to look okay and in ten years I can wear it. No one will wear a thing like that and then it will just be fine"*
*(Nico)*

One way of understanding the desire for individuality is that respondents feel an intrusion into their private sphere when other people are similarly dressed or have similar aesthetic understandings.

*"When there is a point where you are converging, and clothes are one example of that, then you need to deal with this person and this may cause, well not anxieties, because nothing is happening, but ah... well.. it's a strange feeling"*
*(Richard)*

Similar to the striving for uniqueness and otherness, contrasting serves the need for individuality. Contrasting, though, goes beyond just using non-traditional gender items, and is psychologically distinct. Whereas uniqueness supports the extended self, contrasting helps delineating individual identity from collective identity and sameness.

Non-traditional gender aesthetic consumers also had recurring aesthetic styles in their consumption behaviors. Thus we assume that consumers have certain aesthetic styles according to which they, inter alia, choose products and base their consumption decisions on. However, this does not mean that consumers have only one specific style but they deliberately choose different ones, which they can use to contrast their aesthetic style with others. In an aesthetic context, respondents evaluate authenticity based on mass consumption of items (=unauthentic) or on individually used, unique products. Aesthetic authenticity can be achieved when very few or no other people possess the same items, or are unable to copy a particular aesthetic style mix. Whereas Beverland (2005) contends that authenticity is socially constructed, our findings rather indicate that non-traditional gender aesthetics serve the purpose of highly individualized aesthetic authentication.

## DISCUSSION

The findings of our study contribute to theory in at least two important ways. First, they show that consumers use non-traditional gender aesthetic items to deal with important life projects, such as the negotiations of gay, of urban and of gendered self understandings and to create a unique and authentic self. Our study highlights that rather consumer's gender identity than their sexual orientation influences non traditional gender aesthetic consumption. Second, by contrasting consumption behavior and styles with those of others and emphasizing otherness, respondents also contrast the current emphasis of communal forms of consumption in consumer research. Instead, they highlight the necessity to redress the balance between highly individual and highly communal forms of consumption.

Our findings address motivations and strategies to achieve individuality by participating in individual aesthetic identity projects. Consumers of non-traditional gender aesthetics demonstrate a particularly high need to deviate from common, mass consumption. Similar to Nietzsche's (1969) and Featherstone's (2004) notion of the individual aesthetic self, individuality is expressed by a constant quest for uniqueness and otherness and the creation of an authentic, inasmuch individual, aesthetic identity. For this purpose consumers pursue different strategies to aesthetically escape commoditization. One strategy refers to the creation of distinct consumption activities by public display of non-traditional gender aesthetic items. Contrary to prior findings (e.g. Ourahmoune and Nyeck, 2008, Kimmel and Tissier-Desbordes, 1999) stigmatization is not an issue, as being different is the prime motivator for non-traditional gender aesthetics.

A further strategy is the creation of aesthetic contrasts. People create contrasts in their personal, individual styles so as to emphasize otherness. Furthermore, contrasts are created through the application of diverse styles to facilitate an aesthetic break from the ordinary. A third strategy relates to the individualization of consumer objects. Consumers either remove parts, redesign or olden consumer articles to distinguish themselves from the masses.

Contrasting is also used to negotiate consumers' individual place in society. Rather than provoking and standing out at any rate, they try to style themselves appropriately (e.g. not in tutu for opera) to contexts and occasions. However, within this context dependent aesthetic range, aesthetic individuality is emphasized through non-traditional gender aesthetics. By contrasting context-dependent with non-traditional consumption, individuals sharply distinguish themselves from others.

Three different indicators also support our assumption that non-traditional gender aesthetics are a highly individual rather than communal form of consumption. First, snowball sampling technique could not be successfully applied to recruit interview partners and respondents frequently mentioned the individuality of their aesthetic behavior. Second, to our knowledge participants did not participate in internet communities of male handbag wearers. Third, a lacking of a consciousness of kind (Muniz and O'Guinn, 2001) became obvious in respondents narratives. Male handbag users rather emphasized their uniqueness and striving to set themselves apart from the masses. Based on these indicators, we may conclude that non-traditional gender aesthetics are a genuinely individual life project which runs counter communal forms of consumption in brand communities (Muniz and O'Guinn, 2001). When items, which consumers judge as expressive for their individual aesthetic identity, are copied or become fashionable, their aesthetic identities are endangered. Consumers, again, seek to contrast communal forms of mass aesthetics by seeking for the non-traditional. Interestingly, non-traditional gender aesthetics does not oppose social norms or communal forms of consumption in a resistive manner but rather seeks to authenticate a unique and distinct aesthetic gender identity.

## REFERENCES

Ahuvia, Aaron C. (2005), "Beyond the extended self: loved objects and consumers' identity narratives," *Journal of Consumer Research*, 32 (1), 171-184.

Alaszewski, Andy (2006), *Using Diaries for Social Research,* London: Sage Publications.

Arnould, Eric J. and Craig J. Thompson (2005), "Consumer Culture Theory (CCT): Twenty Years of Research," *Journal of Consumer Research*, 31(4), 868- 882.

Bakewell, Cathy, Vincent-Wayne Mitchell and Morgan Rothwell (2006), "UK Generation Y male fashion consciousness," *Journal of Fashion Marketing and Management*, 10(2),169-180.

Beverland, Michael, B. (2005), "Crafting Brand Authenticity: The Case of Luxury Wine," *Journal of Management Studies*, 42(5), 1003–30.

Connell, Raewyn (2002), *Gender,* Oxford: Polity Press

Cushman, Philip (1990) "Why the self is empty," *American Psychologist*, 45(5), 599-611.

Featherstone, Mike (2004), *Consumer Culture and Postmodernism*, London: Sage Publications.

Firat, Fuat and Alladi Venkatesh (1995), "Liberatory Postmodernism and the Reenchantment of Consumption," *Journal of Consumer Research*, 22(3), 239–267.

Fischer, Eileen and Stephen J. Arnold (1994) "Sex, Gender Identity, Gender Role Attitudes, and Consumer Behavior", *Psychology & Marketing,* 11(2), 163-182.

Heisley, Deborah D. und Sidney J. Levy (1991), "Autodriving: A Photoelicitation Technique," *Journal of Consumer Research*, 18 (3), 257-272.

Holt, Douglas B. (1995), "How Consumers Consume: A Typology of Consumption," *Journal of Consumer Research*, 22 (1), 1-16.

Kimmel, Allan J. and Elisabeth Tissier-Desbordes (2000), "Masculinity and Consumption: A Qualitative Investigation of French and American Men", *Proceedings of the 5th International Conference on Gender and Marketing,* Schroeder, Jonathan and Celes C. Otnes (eds.), Association for Consumer Research, Chicago, 23-24, June 2000, 1-17.

Kozinets, Robert V. (2001), "Utopian Enterprise: Articulating the Meaning of Star Trek's Culture of Consumption," *Journal of Consumer Research*, 28(1), 67–89.

Muniz, Albert M. and Thomas C. O'Guinn, (2001), "Brand Community," *Journal of Consumer Research*, 27(4), 412-432.

Nitzsche, Friedrich (1969), Die Geburt der Tragödie, Frankfurt: Ullstein

Nyeck, Simon, Elyette Roux and Florence Dano (2002), "Les hommes, leur apparance et les cosmetique: approche semiotique," www.iae-aix.com/fileadmin/files/cerog/wp/637.pdf 14.10.2007.

Ourahmoune, Nassima and Simon Nyeck (2008), "Male consumers entering the private sphere: an exploratory investigation of French male involvement, practices and interaction around lingerie for men consumption," *Proceedings of Latin American Advances in Consumer Research*, Acevedo, Claudia R., Hernandez, Jose Mauro C., Lowrey, Tina M. (eds.), 2, Association for Consumer Research.

Patterson, Maurice and Richard Elliott (2002), "Negotiating Masculinities: advertising and the inversion of the male gaze," *Consumption, Markets and Cultures*, 5(3), 231-246.

Patton, Michael, Q. (1991), *Qualitative Evaluation and Research Methods*, Newbury Park: Sage Publications.

Rinallo, Diego (2007) "Metro/Fashion/Tribes of men: Negotiating the Boundaries of Men's Legitimate Consumption", in *Consumer Tribes: Theory, Practice and Prospects*, edited by Covas B., Kozinets, R., Shankar A. (2007) Butterworth-Heinemann.

Simpson, Marc (2002), "Meet the Metrosexual", *Salon.com*, 22 July.

Schau, Hope J. and Mary C. Gilly (2003), "We Are What We Post? Self-Presentation in Personal Web Space," *Journal of Consumer Research*, 30 (3), 385- 404.

Schroeder, Jonathan E., and Detlev Zwick (2004), "Mirrors of masculinity: representations and identity in advertising images," *Consumption, Markets and Culture*, 7(1), 21-52.

Sturrock, Fiona and Elke Pioch (1998), "Making himself attractive: the growing consumption of grooming products,*" Marketing Planning & Intelligence*, 15 (5), 337-343.

_____ and Diana L. Haytko, (1997), "Speaking of fashion: Consumer's Uses of Fashion Discourses and the Appropriation of Countervailing Cultural Meanings," *Journal of Consumer Research*, 24(1), 15-40.

_____ and Elizabeth C. Hirschman (1995), "Understanding the Socialized Body: A Poststructuralist Analysis of Consumers' Self-Conceptions, Body Images, and Self-Care Practices," *Journal of Consumer Research*, 22 (2), 139–53.

_____ Williams Locander and Howard R. Pollio (1989), "Putting consumer experience into consumer research: the philosophy and method of existential-phenomenology," *Journal of Consumer Research*, 16 (2), 133-146.

Venkatesh, Alladi and Laurie A. Meamber (2006), "Arts and aesthetics: marketing and cultural production," *Marketing Theory*, 6 (1), 11-39.

_____ and Laurie A. Meamber (2008), "The aesthetics of consumption and the consumer as an aesthetic object," *Consumption, Markets & Culture*, 11(1), 45-70.

Veryzer, Robert (1995), "The Place of Product Design and Aesthetics in Consumer Research," *Advances in Consumer Research*, 22, 641-645.

Welsch, Wolfgang (1997), *Undoing Aesthetics*, London: Sage Publications.

# Do Foreign Brand Preferences Lead to Counterfeiting? Cross-Country Insights

Bernhard Swoboda, Trier University, Germany
Karin Pennemann, Trier University, Germany
Markus Taube, Mercator School of Management, Germany
Dirk Morschett, University of Fribourg, Switzerland

## ABSTRACT

Foreign brand preferences matter when explaining consumers' counterfeiting behavior. The study examines the indirect impact of foreign brand preferences on purchase intention toward counterfeits for developing and developed countries. These impacts are moderated by price consciousness and integrity. Results show that price consciousness is more crucial in developing countries.

## INTRODUCTION

Many international companies selling branded goods suffer losses of up to 10% of their revenue due to counterfeits (Business Standard 2009). Not only is consumers' demand diverted, but counterfeits also devalue the genuine foreign brand and thus jeopardize the brand's equity (Green and Smith 2002). Now that 'Louis Vuitton' handbags are sold for ten dollars at the wayside, the unique brand's style appears on thousands of consumers, undermining the foreign brand's exclusiveness. Counterfeits are a cheap way to embellish oneself with admired symbols. However, the way in which consumers' illicit behavior is driven by foreign brand preferences is unclear. Foreign brand preferences have been investigated in the context of the country-of-origin (COO) effect, which is related to the country's level of economic development (Bilkey and Nes 1982). Foreign products from developed countries are preferred to products from developing countries (Ger, Belk, and Lascu 1993). Especially in developing countries, quality and prestige are ascribed to foreign brands (Batra et al. 2000). Thus, not only foreign brands, but also counterfeits allow consumers to display status brands, but without paying a premium price (Grossman and Shapiro 1988) when choosing the latter. Chuchinprakarn (2003) shows that taste for Western products and materialism predict the use of counterfeits.

The purpose of this paper is to analyze the relation between foreign brand preferences and purchase intention toward counterfeits. Such a cross-country investigation broadens the understanding of consumer behavior and gives insights for actions implemented internationally that are aimed at tackling companies' losses caused by counterfeits. We examine whether or not foreign brand prefer- ences (FBPs) indirectly impact the purchase intention toward counterfeits (PItC) through attitude toward counterfeits (AtC) and attitude toward originals (AtO). As the most crucial antecedents for purchasing and against purchasing counterfeits, price consciousness (PC) (Bloch, Bush, and Campell 1993) and integrity (IN) (Ang et al. 2001) are tested as moderators. In detail, we examine the following research questions:

1. Do FBPs indirectly impact PItC?
2. Does the impact differ between developing and developed countries?
3. Is the impact moderated by price consciousness and integrity?
4. Are there different strengths between developed and developing countries for those moderating effects?

The remainder of this study is organized as follows: referring to the theory of reasoned action, we derived hypotheses linking FBPs and PItC indirectly through AtC and AtO. Beside this basic model, additional moderators are tested which stimulate and impede the purchase of counterfeits. The analysis is based on consumer data from China, Romania, and Germany, applying multi-group structural equation modeling. Results are presented and discussed before limitations and further research are addressed.

## CONCEPTUAL FRAMEWORK AND HYPOTHESES

The conceptual model underlying our research is twofold (see Figure 1). Firstly, we build upon the work of Batra et al. (2000) and Ger et al. (1993) when outlining how FBPs are indirectly linked with PItC. Based on the theory of reasoned action (Ajzen and Fishbein 1980), we focus on the basic model indirectly linking FBPs and PItC through AtC and AtO. Secondly, we outline the moderating variables of country, price consciousness, and integrity.

### Foreign Brand Preferences

Consumers base their purchasing decisions on intrinsic as well as extrinsic information cues. Extrinsic cues (e.g. brand name, brand's COO) are used especially when intrinsic cues are not immediately accessible (Jacoby, Olsen, and Haddock 1971).

**Figure 1: Conceptual Framework**

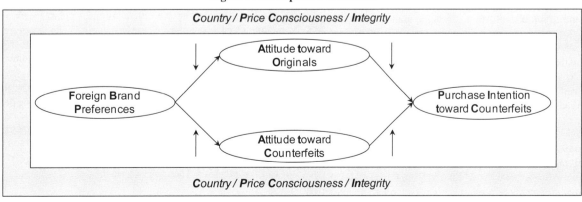

Consumers' preferences for foreign brands are strongly linked to the COO effect, which has been studied intensively in academic literature (for literature reviews see Bilkey and Nes 1982; Peterson and Jolibert 1995; Verlegh and Steenkamp 1999). Schooler (1965) showed that consumers evaluate identical products differently when the products' COO is varied. Thus, the brand's origin serves as a cue for product evaluation (Bilkey and Nes 1982; Han 1989), as well as for social status and prestige (Batra et al. 2000). Foreign brands, especially Western brands in developing countries, have a positive effect on brand attitudes (Ger et al. 1993). This has become apparent in developing countries like China and Romania, where - in times of communism - foreign brands had restricted market access (Ger et al. 1993). Since the rapid influx of foreign brands in developing countries (Walters and Samiee 2003), foreign brands' origin is mainly associated with developed countries and therefore used as extrinsic cue for brand evaluation.

## Counterfeits

As mentioned previously, not only foreign brands, but also counterfeits allow consumers to display status brands, but without paying a premium price (Grossman and Shapiro 1988). Thus, counterfeits are the cheap way to embellish oneself with admired symbols. Following Lai and Zaichowski (1999) and Cordell, Wongtada, and Kieschnick (1996), counterfeits are illegally made products that copy a trademark, but are typically of lower quality and price. Research findings show that consumers' purchase intention is influenced by their attitude toward counterfeits (De Matos, Ituassu, and Rossi 2007), which in turn is affected by object-related factors, such as brand image, price, and COO (Bian and Moutinho 2008; Bloch et al. 1993; Chakraborty, Allred, and Bristol 1996), as well as by psychographic factors, such as moral beliefs and materialism (Wee, Tan, and Cheok 1995; Wilcox et al. 2009). Materialism and the taste for Western products predict the use of counterfeits (Chuchinprakarn 2003), thereby taste is described as the concept of brand preferences and materialism.

## Theory of Reasoned Action

The conceptual model is based on the theory of reasoned action (Ajzen and Fishbein 1980) whereupon a person's attitude predicts behavioral intention, which in turn predicts actual behavior. In their study of drug consumption, Bentler and Speckart (1997) found that attitude is a more accurate predictor for intention than for actual behavior. We therefore apply this attitude-intention relationship to our model, which also uses criminal intention as an outcome variable. This outcome variable PItC is explained by AtC on the one hand and by AtO on the other. Cronan and Al-Rafee (2008) and Cordell et al. (1996) showed that AtC affects consumers' PItC. Although AtO has received less attention in the literature, it is not necessarily less important when explaining consumers' PItC. Consumers' choice between the original (genuine brand) and the counterfeit is influenced, for example, by the genuine brand's equity (Yoo and Lee 2005) or the consumers' fairness (Ang et al. 2001) toward the original. Consumers' behavioral intention is based on the attitude toward the behavioral options to buy the original or the counterfeit.

As mentioned above, there are common drivers, such as materialism (Wilcox et al. 2009) and conspicuous consumption (Phau and Teah 2009; Wang and Chen 2004), that link FBPs with PItC. Since brands offer an identity, consuming of brands is motivated by achieving status and social prestige (Eastman, Goldsmith, and Flynn 1999). Foreign brands carry symbolic meanings of quality and social status which have been widely acknowledged in developing countries (Batra et al. 2000). "Counterfeiting unbundles the status and quality aspects of a product" (Grossman and Shapiro 1988, 82), thus consumers holding FBPs are supposed to favor genuine

brands on the one hand or counterfeits on the other. Summing up, we hypothesize:

*Hypothesis* $_{1\text{-Basic}}$: *The stronger the consumers' FBPs, the more positive their AtO.*
*Hypothesis* $_{2\text{-Basic}}$: *The stronger the consumers' FBPs, the more positive their AtC.*

*Hypothesis* $_{3\text{-Basic}}$: *The more positive the consumers' AtO, the lower their PItC.*

*Hypothesis* $_{4\text{-Basic}}$: *The more positive the consumers' AtC, the higher their PItC.*

## Moderating Effects

A **moderator** addresses the question of 'when' a variable most strongly predicts or causes an outcome variable (Fraizer, Tix, and Barron 2004). It can be hypothesized that the relations of the basic model vary across the context variable country, as well as across the psychographic antecedents price consciousness and integrity. Including these moderators in the basic model will give a deeper understanding of 'when' consumers who prefer foreign brands favor either the original or the counterfeit.

*Differences between developed and developing countries.* Bilkey and Nes (1982) extracted several differences between developed and developing countries from prior research and suggested a positive relationship between the level of economic development and product evaluations. A significant body of research has studied products' COO in developing countries, where their origin serves as a symbol for status and therefore suggests overall quality (Batra et al. 2000). This has been examined for developing countries such as China (Sklair 1994), where "everything foreign had an automatic cachet" (Sklair, 269), as well as for Romania, where "status goods are nearly inevitably foreign" (Ger et al. 1993, 104). Developing countries provide an environment where interpersonal relationships play an important role (Ger et al. 1993) and status mobility is high (Kottak 1990, 49). Thus, in developing countries, foreign brands are used to display status and to participate in the global consumer culture (Venkatesh and Swamy 1994, 207). Studies in Western developed countries show that foreign brands were favored only when product quality was perceived as superior (Knight 1999; Gürhan-Canli and Maneswaran 2000). One can suggest that foreign brands are not automatically a signal of quality and prestige for consumers in developed countries.

*Hypothesis* $_{1\text{-4-C}}$: *The suggested paths differ between developed and developing countries.*

*Price consciousness.* From a consumer's point of view, a price premium signals prestige and exclusiveness. While prices are kept high, the brand is available exclusively to a special customer group that can afford to pay a premium. Counterfeits are alternatives for consumers with limited purchasing power. According to Bloch et al. (1993, 31), "people buy counterfeits because they are getting prestige without paying for it." Price consciousness can be defined as "the degree to which the consumer focuses exclusively on paying low prices" (Lichtenstein, Ridgway, and Netemeyer 1993) and has been shown to be crucial in explaining consumers' purchase intention toward counterfeits (Albers-Miller 1999; Bloch et al. 1993; Cordell et al. 1996). Thus, we assume that:

*Hypothesis* $_{1\text{-4-PC}}$: *The suggested paths differ between consumers with high and low price consciousness.*

*Integrity.* While price is discussed predominantly in the literature on what drives the purchase of counterfeits, integrity is a much investigated variable that prevents consumers from purchasing counterfeits. Ang et al. (2001) found integrity to be the best predictor for attitude toward piracy. Lawful-minded consumers who place importance on ethical standards have a less favorable attitude toward piracy (Ang et al. 2001). Also Kwong et al. (2003) found that ethical belief has the highest impact on attitude toward piracy. Integrity refers to lawful and moral beliefs. According to Kohlberg's (1976) moral competence theory, individuals' intentions are affected by their personal sense of justice. Cordell et al. (1996) found that lawfully guided consumers are less likely to purchase counterfeits. Therefore we assume that:

Hypothesis ₁₋₄₋ᵢₙ: *The suggested paths differ between consumers with high and low integrity.*

*Price consciousness and country differences.* Several studies (e.g. Watchravesringkan, Yan, and Yurchisin 2008) examine cross-country differences in price perception. According to the economic disparity of the countries of investigation, consumers' price consciousness might be influenced by the home country's level of economic development. Consumers from developing countries are more price conscious (Fan and Xiao 1998) than consumers from developed countries. Thus, we assume:

Hypothesis ₁₋₄₋c*PC: *The suggested paths are moderated by the country's economic development and consumers' price consciousness.*

*Integrity and country differences.* When investigating counterfeiting, national legal settings and public policies are highly relevant as antecedents for lawful attitudes and intentions (Cordell et al. 1996). Comparing the countries of investigation, they differ in their tradition of trademark protection. Thus public visibility and acceptance of counterfeiting differ between the countries. In contrast to the developing countries, developed countries such as Germany have long-established trademark legislation (Germany since 1874). Generally speaking, law and social norms are related: norms can be a source of or a substitute for law (Posner 1977). In view of the

**Table 1: Sample Characteristics**

| | Chinese sample | | Romanian sample | | German sample | |
|---|---|---|---|---|---|---|
| | Male | Female | Male | Female | Male | Female |
| 16-24 | 7.3% | 8.7% | 9.0% | 8.6% | 6.9% | 6.9% |
| 25–49 | 27.9% | 27.9% | 22.0% | 21.6% | 22.6% | 21.1% |
| 50–64 | 10.7% | 9.9% | 10.0% | 11.3% | 10.4% | 10.9% |
| Over 64 | 5.3% | 2.4% | 7.1% | 10.4% | 9.6% | 11.7% |
| Total | N = 700 | | N = 700 | | N = 700 | |

**Table 2: Country Indicators**

| Countries | China | Romania | Germany |
|---|---|---|---|
| Inhabitants (millions) | 1,325.6 | 21.5 | 82.1 |
| GDP (2008 in USD millions) | 3,860,039 | 200,071 | 3,652,824 |
| GDP per capita (2008 in USD) | 2,913.23 | 9,305.63 | 44,492.37 |
| Percentage of total trading volume of counterfeits/pirated goods | 79% | < 1% | < 1% |
| Trademark Legislation (since) | 1982 | 1996 | 1874 |

**World Trade Organization 2008; U.S. Customs and Border Protection 2009.**

**Table 3: Measurements: Operationalization and Reliability**

| **Foreign Brand Preferences (FBPs)** (α = .807; AVE = .667) **Reference** | |
|---|---|
| I prefer to buy foreign brands if I want to give the product away as a gift. | Adopted from Staack and Schramm (2005) |
| When I invite friends, I try to offer foreign brands. | |
| I choose foreign brands because they are cool and hip. | |
| It's best to buy foreign brands because they are of high quality. | |
| **Attitude toward Originals (AtO)** α = .625; AVE = .596) | Adapted from Wang et al. (2005) and Ang et al. (2001) |
| I want to support the brands I like. | |
| If I cannot distinguish between the original and counterfeit, I won't buy any of them. | |
| I always choose brands because they grant a guarantee. | |
| **Attitude toward Counterfeits (AtC)** (α = .676; AVE = 727) | Adapted from Ang et al. (2001) |
| Because fashion changes so fast, I would not mind buying fake brands. | |
| I buy fakes because they copy the newest version of the brand which is not available here. | |
| **Purchase Intention toward Counterfeits (PItC)** | Adapted from Ajzen and Fishbein (1980) |
| I intend to purchase counterfeits in fashion and clothing. | |
| **Price Consciousness (PC)** (α = .713; AVE = .776) | Adapted from Huang, Lee and Ho (2004), developed by Lichtenstein et al. (1993) |
| I am willing to pay a premium for my favorite brand (r). | |
| Generally I am willing to pay more for brands (r). | |
| **Integrity (IN)** (α = .670; AVE = .771) | Adapted from Ang et al. (2001) |
| It is illegal to buy fakes. | |
| It is immoral to buy fakes. | |
| GFI= . 982; AGFI = .966; TLI=.948; CFI=.965; RMSEA=.051; c2=196.678 (d.f.= 30); c2/d.f.=6.556 | |
| α = Cronbach's Coefficient Alpha; AVE = Average Variance Explained. | |

facts, we assume that consumers in developed countries are more lawfully and morally guided toward counterfeits than consumers from developing countries. Thus, we hypothesize:

*Hypothesis* $_{1\text{-}4\text{-}C*IN}$: *The suggested paths are moderated by the countries' economic development and integrity.*

## EMPIRICAL STUDY AND MAIN RESULTS
### Sample Design

Some 2700 face-to-face interviews were conducted in three urban areas in China, Romania, and Germany. Random samples of 700 questionnaires per country were included in the analysis to compare equal sized country samples, as can be seen in Table 1. The survey was based on quota sampling modeled on age and sex, according to the national distribution of the population.

Anonymity was assured and an explanation was given on how counterfeits should be understood according to Lai and Zaichowski (1999) and Cordell, Wongtada, and Kieschnick (1996). In order to enhance the generalizability of the study (Alden, Steenkamp, and Batra 1999), we chose the countries of investigation according to their level of economic development. Based on the GDP per capita, China and Romania are among the developing countries, whereas Germany belongs to the developed countries, as illustrated in Table 2.

### Measurements

The measurements were drawn from established scales using five-point Likert-type scales.

The dependent single item measure PItC asks about clothing and fashion goods, thus our results are limited to this product category. We performed confirmatory factor analysis (CFA) to verify the measurement (Gerbing and Anderson 1988,) as can be seen in Table 3.

In addition to the classic tests for checking validity and reliability (e.g. Fornell and Larcker's 1981 procedure for assessing discriminant validity), verification of equivalence and measurement invariance are especially important in cross-cultural studies. Firstly, we applied the forward translation and back translation method to ensure semantic equivalence (Berry 1980). In a second step, assessment of the content-related equivalence, i.e. measurement invariance, was conducted in three checking stages (Steenkamp and Baumgartner 1998): tests for configural, metric, and scalar invariance. According to Cheng and Rensvold (2002), partial scalar invariance is largely confirmed for all constructs between the countries, as illustrated in Table 4.

### Method

The analysis is based on multi-group structural equation modeling. Three moderating factors are tested within the model: (1) country, (2) price consciousness, and (3) integrity. The first moderator includes China and Romania as developing countries and Germany as developed country. The latter two moderators were conducted by splitting each country sample into two groups according to their mean: high versus low price consciousness and high versus low integrity.

The moderating factors price consciousness and integrity are compared using the model fit ($\chi^2$/d.f., AIC, and MECVI) to access which moderator is most crucial. Absolute fit measures like Chi-Square/degrees of freedom judge a model per se, without any alternative, and are not sufficient criteria in our case. Akaike Information Criterion (Akaike 1987) and Maximum Likelihood ECVI (Browne and Cudeck 1989, 1993) are based on information

### Table 4: Measurement Invariance Testing

| Countries | | $c^2$ | $\Delta c^2$ (p-value) | CFI $\Delta$CFI | TLI $\Delta$TLI | RMSEA $\Delta$RMSEA |
|---|---|---|---|---|---|---|
| Model 1 | Configural invariance | 340.726 | - | .947 (-) | .926 (-) | .035 (-) |
| Model constrained | Intercepts and factor loadings constrained | 1742.896 | 1402.17 (.000) | .652 (.295) | .633 (293) | .078 (.043) |
| Model 2 | Metric invariance (partly freed) | 390.229 | 49.503 (.000) | .938 (.009) | .920 (-.006) | .036 (.001) |
| Model 3 | Scalar invariance (partly freed) | 398.174 | 57.448 (.019) | .937 (.010) | .920 (-.006) | .036 (.001) |

### Table 5: Results based on SEM–Basic Model

| No moderator – basic model n = 2100 | | | | | | |
|---|---|---|---|---|---|---|
| H$_{1\text{–Basic}}$ | FBPs à AtO (supported) | .220 | *** | H$_{3\text{–Basic}}$ | AtO à PItC (supported) | -.564 | *** |
| H$_{2\text{–Basic}}$ | FBPs à AtC (supported) | .157 | *** | H$_{4\text{–Basic}}$ | AtC à PItC (supported) | .494 | *** |

GFI= .978; AGFI = .963; TLI=.941; CFI=.958; RMSEA=.055; c2=233,170 (d.f.=32); c2/d.f.=7.287
* p<.1; ** p<.05; *** p<.01; n.s. = not significant.

### Table 6: Results based on SEM–Country

| Country as a moderator | | China (n=700) | | Romania (n =700) | | Germany (n=700) | | c2–Difference | | |
|---|---|---|---|---|---|---|---|---|---|---|
| | | | | | | | | CN vs. RO | CN vs. GE | RO vs. GE |
| H$_{1\text{–C}}$ | FBPs à AtO (rejected) | .169 | *** | .707 | *** | .043 | n.s. | 44.031*** | 3.597* | 54.370*** |
| H$_{2\text{–C}}$ | FBPs à AtC (rejected) | .244 | *** | .021 | n.s. | .310 | *** | 8.657*** | .812 n.s. | 11.041*** |
| H$_{3\text{–C}}$ | AtO à PItC (rejected) | -.189 | ** | -.571 | *** | -.549 | *** | 12.512*** | 9.490*** | .034 n.s. |
| H$_{4\text{–C}}$ | AtC à PItC (rejected) | .427 | *** | .570 | *** | .622 | *** | 1.868 n.s. | 3.532*** | .288 n.s. |

GFI= .969; AGFI = .946; TLI=.926; CFI=.947; RMSEA=.035; c2=486.234 (d.f.=96); c2/d.f.=3.549
* p<.1; ** p<.05; *** p<.01; n.s. = not significant.

theory and used when choosing between different models with non-nested data, as in our case.

## Results

Our basic model using no moderating factor is accepted. The results (Table 5) reveal that proposed impacts are significant and signs are correct. However, the model fit Chi-Square/degrees of freedom (7.287 > 2.5) exceeds the threshold (Hinkin 1995), but Comparative Fit Index (.958) and Root Mean Square Error of Approximation (.055) are within the acceptable range (Brown and Cudeck 1993).

Adding country as a moderator to the basic model, the results (Table 6) show that eight out of twelve paths within the county comparison differ significantly. However, there was no evidence that developed and developing countries differ significantly from each other. Hypotheses 1-C to 4-C are rejected because we found differences between the developing countries.

Examining the results of the moderating factor price consciousness, hypothesis 1-PC is rejected , but hypotheses 2-PC, 3-PC, and 4-PC can be partly supported: Hypotheses are supported for Romania, but not for Germany, and only hypothesis 2-PC for China. Investigating the results of the moderating factor integrity, hypothesis 1-IN is supported for China and hypothesis 2-IN is supported for Germany.

For Romania, there were no significant differences found between individuals scoring high in integrity versus those scoring low.

The findings of the moderating effect of country and price consciousness ($H_{1-4-C*PC}$), as well as country and integrity ($H_{1-4-C*IN}$), revealed that differences between developed and developing countries regarding the moderators price consciousness and integrity can be rejected.

Nevertheless, we found interesting results when comparing these two moderator models: We tested the moderators country and price consciousness, as well as country and integrity, within competing models to access which model achieves the best model fit. The model applying country and price consciousness as moderators (Table 7) reveals a better model fit than the model incorporating country and integrity as moderators ($\Delta\chi^2(0) = 55.395$; $\Delta$ AIC = 55.395; $\Delta$ MECVI =.026).

Finally, we also tested other plausible rival models (Steenkamp, Batra, and Alden 2003) which achieve a poorer model fit. When testing reverse causal direction, the model fit reveals a significant 22% poorer model fit ($\chi^2(32) = 299,789$, p < .001, RMSEA = .063, CFI = .944, TLI = .921) compared to our proposed basic model ($\Delta\chi^2(0) = 66.619$). Additionally, we provide strong support for the indirect impact of FBPs on PItC. Modeling the direct effect of FBPs on PItC,

### Table 7: Results based on SEM–Price Consciousness

| Price Consciousness (PC) as a moderator | | China (n=700) | | Romania (n =700) | | Germany (n=700) | | c2-Difference | | |
|---|---|---|---|---|---|---|---|---|---|---|
| | | | | | | | | CN vs. RO | CN vs. GE | RO vs. GE |
| $H_{1-C*PC}$ | FBPs à AtO (PC$_{low}$) (rejected) | .081 | n.s. | .328 | *** | .073 | n.s. | 5.951** | .008 n.s. | 5.060** |
| $H_{2-C*PC}$ | FBPs à AtC (PC$_{low}$) (rejected) | .202 | *** | -.243 | *** | .293 | *** | 19.967*** | .759 n.s. | 21.782*** |
| $H_{3-C*PC}$ | AtO à PIC (PC$_{low}$) (rejected) | -.283 | ** | -.612 | *** | -.479 | * | 2.063 n.s. | .955 n.s. | .304 n.s. |
| $H_{4-C*PC}$ | AtC à PIC (PC$_{low}$) (rejected) | .349 | *** | .839 | *** | .592 | *** | 10.167*** | 2.738* | 2.440 n.s. |
| $H_{1-C*PC}$ | FBPs à AtO (PC$_{high}$) (rejected) | .092 | n.s. | .491 | *** | -.090 | n.s. | 8.870*** | 2.997* | 18.447*** |
| $H_{2-C*PC}$ | FBPs à AtC (PC$_{high}$) (rejected) | .463 | *** | .262 | ** | .396 | *** | 2.271 n.s. | .292 n.s. | .930 n.s. |
| $H_{3-C*PC}$ | AtO à PItC (PC$_{high}$) (supported) | -.138 | n.s. | -.201 | *** | -.568 | *** | .238 n.s. | 6.962*** | 6.171* |
| $H_{4-C*PC}$ | AtC à PItC (PC$_{high}$) (rejected) | .553 | ** | .424 | *** | .636 | *** | .750 n.s. | .278 n.s. | 3.248* |
| | | | | | | | | c2-Difference PC$_{low}$ vs. PC$_{high}$ | | |
| | | | | | | | | China | Romania | Germany |
| $H_{1-PC}$ | FBPs à AtO (rejected) | | | | | | | .017 n.s. | 1.148 n.s. | 2.382 n.s. |
| $H_{2-PC}$ | FBPs à AtC (partly supported) | | | | | | | 6.638*** | 15.729*** | .692 n.s. |
| $H_{3-PC}$ | AtO à PItC (partly supported) | | | | | | | .714 n.s. | 4.809** | .199 n.s. |
| $H_{4-PC}$ | AtC à PtIC (partly supported) | | | | | | | 1.620 n.s. | 9.317*** | .098 n.s. |

AIC=706.993; MECVI=.342; GFI=.961; AGFI=.933; TLI=.918; CFI=.942; RMSEA=.024; c2=430.839 (d.f.=192); c2/d.f.=2.244
* p<.1; ** p<.05; *** p<.01; n.s. = not significant.

### Table 8: Results based on SEM–Integrity

| Integrity (IN) as a moderator | | China (n=700) | | Romania (n =700) | | Germany (n=700) | | c2-Difference | | |
|---|---|---|---|---|---|---|---|---|---|---|
| | | | | | | | | CN vs. RO | CN vs. GE | RO vs. GE |
| $H_{1-C*IN}$ | FBPs à AtO (IN$_{high}$) (rejected) | .076 | n.s. | .603 | *** | .104 | n.s. | 16.711*** | .099 n.s. | 15.109*** |
| $H_{2-C*IN}$ | FBPs à AtC (IN$_{high}$) (rejected) | .314 | *** | .086 | n.s. | .139 | n.s. | 3.509* | 1.981n.s. | .151 n.s. |
| $H_{3-C*IN}$ | AtO à PItC (IN$_{high}$) (rejected) | -.311 | * | -.499 | *** | -.601 | *** | .632n.s. | 1.159 n.s. | .264 n.s. |
| $H_{4-C*IN}$ | AtC à PItC (IN$_{high}$) (rejected) | .324 | *** | .532 | *** | .615 | *** | 2.204 n.s. | 4.448* | .249 n.s. |
| $H_{1-C*IN}$ | FBPs à AtO (IN$_{low}$) (rejected) | .246 | *** | .784 | *** | -.065 | n.s. | 22.758*** | 10.245*** | 45.393*** |
| $H_{2-C*IN}$ | FBPs à AtC (IN$_{low}$) (rejected) | .186 | *** | -.038 | n.s. | .433 | *** | 5.390** | 7.112*** | 16.397*** |
| $H_{3-C*IN}$ | AtO à PItC (IN$_{low}$) (rejected) | -.139 | n.s. | -.630 | *** | -.419 | *** | 13.904*** | 4.426** | 1.812 n.s. |
| $H_{4-C*IN}$ | AtC à PItC (IN$_{low}$) (rejected) | .531 | *** | .604 | *** | .533 | *** | .194 n.s. | .000 n.s. | .274 n.s. |
| | | | | | | | | c2-Difference IN$_{high}$ vs. IN$_{low}$ | | |
| | | | | | | | | China | Romania | Germany |
| $H_{1-IN}$ | FBPs à AtO (partly supported) | | | | | | | 3.755* | 1.201n.s. | 2.596 n.s. |
| $H_{2-IN}$ | FBPs à AtC (partly supported) | | | | | | | 2.056n.s. | .959n.s. | 5.308** |
| $H_{3-IN}$ | AtO à PItC (rejected) | | | | | | | .706n.s. | .674n.s. | .801 n.s. |
| $H_{4-IN}$ | AtC à PItC (rejected) | | | | | | | 1.701n.s. | .272n.s. | .252 n.s. |

AIC=762.234; MECVI=.368; GFI= .956; AGFI = .925; TLI=.910; CFI=.936; RMSEA=.027;
c2=486.234 (d.f.=192); c2/d.f.=2.532
* p<.1; ** p<.05; *** p<.01; n.s. = not significant.

the rival model fit ($\chi^2(31)$ = 231,531, p < .001, RMSEA = .056, CFI = .958, TLI = .936) shows a poorer Root Mean Square Error of Approximation, Comparative Fit Index and Tucker-Lewis Index, in addition to a non-significant different model fit ($\Delta\chi^2$ (1) = 1.639, n.s.). Based on these results, our proposed basic model is supported.

## DISCUSSION

### Theoretical Implication

Huang et al. (2004) called for further research investigating the relationship between price consciousness and attitude toward gray market goods. Pursuing this call, the present study reveals insights in the importance of price consciousness and integrity as moderating factors combining two streams of research: foreign brand preferences and counterfeits. After evaluation of the competing models that differ in terms of their moderator, the results indicate the best model fit for the model incorporating country and price consciousness. These results are in line with Bloch et al. (1993), who found that people purchasing counterfeits rely heavily on price. In addition, the competing model using country and integrity as moderators examines the antecedent that was previously found to have the highest impact in lowering PItC (Ang et al. 200; Kwong et al. 2003), but in the present study achieves a slightly poorer model fit than the model incorporating country and price consciousness. Especially in Romania, as a developing country, price consciousness plays a crucial role. The impact of FBPs on AtC was not only moderated in strength, but also in direction. For individuals that score low in price consciousness, FBPs impact negatively AtC ($\beta$ = -.243, p < .001), whereas for their peers that score high in price consciousness, FBPs impact positively AtC ($\beta$ = .262, p < .05). For China, the moderating effect can be confirmed for only one path, and in Germany for no path. We conclude that price consciousness in such developing countries influences consumer behavior much more than values and norms, like integrity. In Romania, people scoring high or low on integrity did not significantly differ from each other in the proposed relationships. This could not be observed for developed countries, such as Germany, where consumers that score high in integrity have FBPs that lead less to a positive AtC than the FBPs of consumers scoring low in integrity. Thus, integrity in developed countries serves as an inner state that averts a positive AtC, which cannot be observed for developing countries.

Moreover, the findings show that the moderators differ in strength between the countries, but these differences are not due to their economic development alone. Differences might be derived from inherent country-specific patterns, such as cultural differences. The Chinese culture has emphasized the sharing of one's developments with the society. The Chinese understanding of copying and its honor to the master differs from Western beliefs (Swinyard, Rinne, and Keng Kau 1990).

### Managerial Implications

Apart from such a theoretical contribution, some interesting insights from a manager's point of view can be drawn from this study. In China and Romania, there are insufficient legal regulations to constrain a rising appreciation for the society's integrity that might disregard counterfeiting. For such regulations, firms must work hand in hand with local authorities. Once counterfeiting is socially disregarded, especially in such collectivistic societies, counterfeits will not be used any more to display status and prestige. Thus, brands' investments should not only target the brand and its intangible value, but also its physical uniqueness, which makes cost-effective counterfeiting difficult.

### Limitations and Further Research

Our study does have some limitations: In the dependent variable PItC, we ask about clothing and fashion goods, which constrains the results to this product category. Further research should investigate other product categories and especially additional countries to generalize and broaden the results. Although country differences appeared to be significant the data set should be extended to discover the relevance of countries' level of economic development. Examining the influence of culture, further studies should include a direct measurement for cultural dimensions to state culture-specific hypotheses. This might shed some light on the country differences discovered. We also suggest a revision of measurement to include at least four items in order to obtain more scope for eliminating items that have no cross-cultural equivalent.

## REFERENCES

Ajzen, Icek and Martin Fishbein (1980), *Understanding Attitude and Predicting Behavior*, Englewood Cliffs, N.J: Prentice–Hall.

Alden, Dana L., Jan-Benedict E.M Steenkamp, and Rajeev Batra (1999), "Brand Positioning through Advertising in Asia, North America and Europe: The Role of Global Consumer Culture," *Journal of Marketing*, 63 (January), 75-87.

Albers-Miller, Nancy D. (1999), "Consumer Misbehaviour: why people buy illicit goods," *Journal of Consumer Marketing*, 16 (3), 273–87.

Akaike, Hirotugu (1987), "Factor analysis and AIC," *Psychometrika*, 52 (September), 317–32.

Ang, Sween Hoon, Peng Sim Cheng, Elison A.C. Lim, and Siok Kuan Tambayah (2001), "Spot the difference: consumers respond toward counterfeits," *Journal of Consumer Marketing*, 18 (3), 219–35.

Batho, John (2009), "Anti-Counterfeiting 2009–A Global Guide," *World Trademark Review*, Special Issue, 1–216.

Batra, Rajeev, Venkatram Ramaswamy, Dana L. Alden, Jan-Benedict E.M. Steenkamp, and S. Ramachander (2000), "Effects of Local and Nonlocal Origin on Consumer Attitudes in Developing Countries," *Journal of Consumer Psychology*, 9 (2), 83–95.

Belk, Russell (1985), "Materialism: Trait Aspects of Living in the Material World," *Journal of Consumer Research*, 12 (December), 265–80.

Berry, John W. (1980), "Social and cultural change," in *Handbook of cross-cultural psychology*, Harry C. Triandis and Richard Brislin, eds. Boston: Allyn & Bacon, 211–79.

Bian, Xuemei and Luiz Moutinho (2009), "An investigation of determinants of counterfeit purchase consideration," *Journal of Business Research*, 62 (March), 368–78.

Bilkey, Warren J. and Erik Nes (1982):, "Country-of-Origin Effects on Product Evaluations," *Journal of International Business Studies*, 13 (Spring/Summer), 89–99.

Bloch, Peter H., Ronald F. Bush, and Leland Campbell (1998), "Consumer 'accomplices' in product counterfeiting: a demand side investigation," *Journal of Consumer Marketing*, 10 (4), 27–36.

Bentler, Peter M. and G. Speckart (1979), "Models of attitude-behavior relations," *Psychological Review*, 86, 452–64.

Browne, Michael W. and Robert Cudeck (1989), "Single sample cross-validation indices for covariance structures," *Multivariate Behavioral Research*, 24 (October), 445–55.

--------- (1993), "Alternative ways of assessing model fit," in *Testing Structural Equation Models*, Kenneth A. Bollen and J. Scott Long, eds. Newbury Park CA: Sage.

Chakraborty, Goutam, Anthony Allred, Ajay Singh Sukhdial, and Terry Bristol (1997), "Use of Negative Cues to Reduce Demand for Counterfeit Products" in *Advances in Consumer Research,* Vol. 24, eds. Merrie Brucks and Deborah J. MacInnis, Provo, UT: Association for Consumer Research, 345-49.

Cheung, Gordon W., and Roger W. Rensvold (2002), "Evaluating Goodness-of-Fit Indexes for Testing Measurement Invariance," Structural Equation Modeling , 9 (April), 233–55.

Chuchinprakarn, Supanat. (2003) "Consumption of Counterfeit Goods in Thailand: Who Are the Patrons?" in *European Advances in Consumer Research Vol.* 6, eds. Darach Turley and Stephen Brown, Provo, UT: Association for Consumer Research, 48-53.

Cordell, Victor V., Nittaya Wongtada, and Robert L. Kieschnick Jr. (1996), "Counterfeit purchase intentions: Role of lawfulness attitudes and product traits as determinants," *Journal of Business Research*, 35 (January), 41–53.

Cronan, Timothy Paul and Sulaiman Al Rafee (2008), "Factors that influence the intention to pirate software and media," *Journal of Business Ethics*, 78 (April), 527–45.

De Matos, Celso Augusto, Cristiana Trindade Ituassu, and Carlos Alberto Vargas Rossi (2007), "Consumers attitude toward counterfeits: a review and extension," *Journal of Consumer Marketing*, 24 (1), 36–47.

Eastman, Jacqueline K., Ronald E. Goldsmith, and Leisa Reinecke Flynn (1999), "Status Consumption in Consumer Behavior: Scale Development and Validation," *Journal of Marketing Theory and Practice*, 7, 41–52.

Fan, Jessie X. and Jing J. Xiao (1998), "Consumer Decision Making Styles of Young Adult Chinese" *Journal of Consumer Affairs,* 32 (Winter), 275–94.

Fornell, Claes and David F. Larcker (1981), "Evaluating structural equation models with unobservable variables and measurement error," *Journal of Marketing Research*, 18 (February), 39–50.

Ger, Güliz, Russell W. Belk, and Dana-Nicoleta Lascu (1993), "The development of consumer desire in marketizing and developing economies," in *Advances in Consumer Research,* **Vol. 20**, ed. L. McAllister and M.L. Rothschild, Provo, UT: Association for Consumer Research, 102–107.

Gerbing, David W. and James C. Anderson (1988), "Structural Equation Modeling in Practice: A Review and Recommended Two Step Approach," *Psychological Bulletin*, 103 (3), 411–423.

Green, Robert T. and Tasman Smith (2002), "Executive Insights: Countering Brand Counterfeiters," *Journal of International Marketing*, 10 (4), 89–106.

Grossman, Gene M. and Carl Sharpio (1988), "Foreign counterfeiting of status goods," The *Quarterly Journal of Economic*, 103 (February), 79–100.

Gürhan-Canli, Zeynep and Durairaj Maheswaran (2000), "Cultural Variations in Country of Origin Effects," *Journal of Marketing Research*, 37 (August), 309–17.

Fraizer, Patrica A., Andrew P. Tix, and Kenneth E. Barron (2004), "Testing Moderator and Mediator Effects in Counseling Psychology Research," *Journal of Counseling Psychology*, 51 (1), 115–34.

Han, Min C. (1989), "Country Image: halo or summary construct," *Journal of Marketing Research*, 26 (May), 222–29.

Hinkin, Timothy R. (1995), "A Review of Scale Development Practice in the Study of Organizations," *Journal of Management*, 21 (5), 967–88.

Huang, Jen-Hung, Bruce C.Y. Lee, and Shu Hsun Ho (2004), "Consumer attitude toward gray market goods*," Journal of Consumer Marketing*, 21 (6), 598–614.

Jacoby, Jacob, Jerry C. Olson, and Rafael A Haddock (1971), "Price Brand name, and Product Consumption characteristics as determinants of perceived quality," *Journal of Applied Psychology*, 55 (December), 570–579.

Kohlberg, Lawrence (1976), "Moral stages and moralization: the cognitive development approach," in *Moral Development and Behavior*, ed. T. Lickona, New York: Holt, Rinehart & Wilson, 31–53.

Kottak, Conrad P. (1990), "Culture and economic development," *American Anthropologist*, 92 (September), 723–31.

Knight, Gary A. (1999), "Consumer Preferences for Foreign and National Brands," *Journal of Consumer Marketing*, 16 (2), 151–62.

Kwong, Kenneth K., Oliver H. M. Yau, Jenny S. Y. Lee, Leo Y. M. Sin, and Alan C. B. Tse. (2003), "The Effects of Attitudinal and Demographic factors on Intention to Buy Pirated CDs: The Case of Chinese Consumers," *Journal of Business Ethics*, 47 (October), 223–35.

Lai, Kay Ka-Yuk and Judith Lynne Zaichowski (1999), "Brand imitation: do Chinese have different views?," *Asia Pacific Journal of Management*, 16 (August), 179–92.

Lichtenstein, Donald R., Ridgway, Nancy M., and Richard G. Netemeyer (1993), "Price Perceptions and Consumer Shopping Behavior: A Field Study," *Journal of Marketing Research*, 30 (May), 234–45.

Peterson, Robert A. and Alain J. P. Jolibert (1995), "A Meta-Analysis of Country-of-Origin Effects," *Journal of International Business Studies*, 26 (4), 883–900.

Phau, Ian and Min Teah (2009), "Devil wears (counterfeit) prada: a study of antecedents and outcomes of attitudes towards counterfeits of luxury brands," *Journal of Consumer Marketing*, 26 (1), 15–27.

Posner, Richard A. (1997), "Social Norms and the Law," *American Economic Review*, 87 (May), 365–69.

Schooler, Robert D. (1965), "Product Bias in the Central American Common Market," *Journal of marketing Research*, 2 (November), 394–97.

Sklair, Leslie (1994), "The cultural ideology of consumerism in urban China," *Research in Consumer Behavior*, 7, 259–92.

Staack, Thorsten; Schramm, Matthias (2005), "Evolving brand preferences: The Case of China–an empirical study", IAMA Conference June 25, 2005.

Steenkamp, Jan-Benedict E. M. and Hans Baumgartner (1998), "Assessing measurement Invariance in Cross-National Consumer Research," *Journal of Consumer Research*, 25 (June), 78–90.

Swinyard, William R., Heikki Rinne, and Ah Keng Kau (1990), "The Morality of Software Piracy: A Cross-Cultural Analysis," *Journal of Business Ethics*, 9 (August), 655–64.

Ozsengul, Tugrul (2009), "Counterfeit products dog FMCG companies too," Business Standard, January 18.

U.S. Customs and Border Protection (2009), Intellectual Property Rights, Washington, D.C., Government Printing Office.

Verlegh, Peter W. J. and Jan-Benedict E. M. Steenkamp (1999), "A review and meta-analysis of country-of-origin research," *Journal of Economic Psychology*, 20 (October), 521–46.

Venkatesh , Alladi. and Suguna Swamy (1994), "India as an emerging consumer society–A cultural analysis," in *Research in Consumer Behavior*, Vol. 7, eds. Clifford. J. Schulz, II, Russel. W. Belk, and Guliz Ger, Greenwich, CT: JAI. 193–223.

Walters, Peter G.P. and Saeed Samiee (2003), "Marketing Strategy in Emerging Markets: The Case of China," *Journal of International Marketing*, 11 (1), 97–106.

Wang, Cheng Lu and Zhen Xiong Chen (2004), "Consumer ethnocentrism and willingness to buy domestic products in a developing country setting: testing moderating effects," *Journal of Consumer Marketing*, 21 (6), 391–400.

Wang, Fang, Hongxia Zhang, Hengjia Zang, and Ming Ouyang (2005), "Purchasing pirated software: an initial examination of Chinese consumers," *Journal of Consumer Marketing*, 22 (6), 340–51.

Watchravesringkan, Kittichai T., Ruoh-Nan Yan, and Jennifer Yurchisin (2008), "Cross-Cultural invariance of consumers′ price perception measures–East Asian perspective," *International Journal of Retail & Distribution Management*, 36 (10), 759–79.

Wee, Chow-Hou, Soo-Jiuan Tan, and Kim-Homg Cheok (1995) "Non-price determinants of intention to purchase counterfeit goods," *International Marketing Review*, 12 (6), 19–46.

Wilcox, Keith, Hyeong Min Kim, and Sankar Sen (2009), "Why do consumers buy counterfeit luxury brands?," *Journal of Marketing Research*, 46 (2), 247–59.

World Trade Organization (2008), "Trade Profiles," http://stat. wto.org/CountryProfile/ WSDBCountryPFReporter.aspx?Language=E.

*Yoo, Bonghee* and Seung-Hee *Lee (2005), "Do Counterfeits Promote Genuine Products?,"* Hofstra University, Hempstead, NY.

# Gamerz: A Videographic Study of Hardcore Xbox 360 Game Players

João Fleck, Universidade Federal do Rio Grande do Sul, Brazil
Stefânia Almeida, Pontifícia Universidade Católica, Brazil
Marlon Dalmoro, Universidade Federal do Rio Grande do Sul, Brazil
José Mazzon, Universidade de São Paulo, Brazil

## ABSTRACT

We utilized a videographic approach to analyze and understand the peculiarities of video game consumption in the context of hardcore players that interact in Microsoft Xbox 360 virtual communities. The results allowed us to infer that the virtual experience and the online interaction are key elements presently in the consumption of games.

## INTRODUCTION

The dawn of the video games era is linked to consoles such as Atari and Nintendo 8-bit in the decade of the 1980s (Shankar and Bayus 2003); however, the explosive growth in sales of this equipment is more recent. From 1996 to 2007, video games sales presented a growth of 700% and in 2008, in the United States, the games industry made a profit of $21.3 billion (Matthews 2009).

The growth of the games market is a result of the considerable improvement in the quality of consoles and systems. Since the 1980s, games producers have released new gaming systems, at five years interval on average, satisfying the desire of consumers that search constantly for more potent games (Clements and Ohashi 2005). It is also noticeable that the advent of the internet in the gaming world has altered the ways in which the interaction occurs, not only among consumers but also among consumers and the producers (Evans et al. 2001). Games with online interaction present an exponential growth and win popularity, including computer games, online games, and video games. These kinds of games are usually multiplayer allowing users to fantasize and to be entertained through interaction in a virtual world (Hsu and Lu 2004).

This virtual gaming world results in a new social and marketable structure with the sprouting of virtual communities of consumption. In these communities, the commitment and the trust can be considered as supporting the relationship structure amongst consumers themselves and also between the consumers and the organization, because the active members tend to be loyal and engaged to the product (McAlexander, Schouten, and Koenig 2002; Algesheimer and Dholakia 2006).

In the video gaming industry, consoles are the mainstream and they represent a mature and competitive market (Williams 2002). This competition allows consumers to develop an optional loyalty. One of the leading companies in consoles is Microsoft with the Xbox/Xbox 360 platform (Matthews 2009). This product already has solid market participation, representing 18.6% of the video game market in 2007 and more than 100 million consoles sold (Orry 2008). Besides the configuration of virtual communities around its product, the Xbox has a hedonic nature: its consumption is involved in stories, myths and rituals, and games are an entertainment product to group consumption. Since the dawn of the video game era, the consumption forms of these products have gone through profound changes, especially regarding the interconnection of players through the internet and the formation of virtual communities. Having this new scenery as our premise, our goal is to understand and analyze the peculiarities of video games consumption from the perspective of hardcore players that interact in a virtual community of Microsoft Xbox 360. We believe that our results are pertinent, because the study focused on users highly involved with the product and also due to our interpretative approach that allowed the reaching of broader results.

## THE GAMES, THE GAMERZ, THE SOCIAL INTERACTION, AND THE FORMATION OF VIRTUAL COMMUNITIES

Online games are a type of entertainment based on the web and on IT. They are multiplayer games that allow the users to fantasize and to be entertained, more specifically the role-playing ones, that are similar to Multi-User Dungeons (MUDs) based on text, and are a hybrid of adventure games and chat. The online players appreciate friendlier interfaces and multimedia effects that are available on traditional MUDs. Besides, the internet allows virtual players to fulfill a series of roles in the fantasy world, interact with others and even to create their own virtual worlds (Hsu and Lu 2004).

According to Mendenhall, Napomuceno and Saad (2010), the characters in games can be analyzed as a form of escapism, because they have abilities that are incongruent with human biology such as the ability to fly. The escapism of virtual games leads to users completely immerse in their cyberspace activities, which characterizes a flow experience (Shin and Kim 2008).

In the flow state, the consumer experiences a sensation of happiness, followed by a feeling of trust and a desire for exploration. A consumer in a flow state also may have his vision of the passing of time distorted, once there is no temporal pressure conducting the specific activity that gives a positive feedback. As a result of this process, the time allocated for such activity tends to increase exponentially (Chou and Ting 2003).

According to Csikszentmihalyi (1991), the flow experience can be defined as the "the holistic experience that people feel when they act with total involvement". In the vision of Hsu and Lu (2004), this definition suggests that flow consists of four components: control, attention, curiosity and intrinsic interest. When they experience a flow state, people remain absorbed in the activity, their senses are focused on the activity itself, they lose consciousness, and they feel in control of the environment. Using similar reasoning, Hoffman and Novak (1996) characterize the flow state on the web as a cognitive status that occurs during virtual experience, involving: (1) high levels of ability and control, (2) high levels of challenge and activation; and (3) focused attention. This experience is also elevated due to interactivity and telepresence. In an analysis of the virtual gaming world, Hsu and Lu (2004, p.857) defined flow as "an extremely enjoyable experience, where an individual engages in an online game activity with total involvement, enjoyment, control, concentration and intrinsic interest".

According to Holt (2000), players evaluate video games based on the fact that they provide a flow experience or not. To Chen (2007), the majority of current video games include flow components, delivering a sensorial and instant feedback, and offering clear objectives that the player reaches through specific abilities. Accordingly, a well designed game transports the players to their personal flow zones, arousing genuine feelings of joy and happiness (Chen 2007). The flow experience, social norms and attitudes explains approximately 80% of intentions of online gaming (Hsu and Lu 2004).

Regarding norms and social influences in virtual interactions, Hsu and Lu (2004) argued that interpersonal interaction among players leads to the creation of virtual communities that may increase the business value through the propitiated participation and the loyalty of users. Using the same reasoning, Schubert and Ginsburg (2000) considers virtual communities as social aggregations that emerge on the internet when a sufficient number of individuals carry discussions for a sufficient period, with a sufficient human feeling, to develop networks of personal relationships in the virtual space. In the view of Dholakia, Bagozzi, and Pearo (2004), consumers encounter and interact online for the purpose of reaching personal objectives, as well as objectives shared with other members. Therefore, the aim of virtual communities is to create value and knowledge to all its members (Bagozzi and Dholakia 2002). One of the advantages of such communities for consumers is that they recognize others as themselves (McWillian 2000). In this way, virtual communities can be understood as networks of interpersonal bonds that provide sociability, support, information, belongingness, and social identity. Also, it is important to emphasize that this communities are "becoming defined socially and not spatially" (Wellman 2005, p.53).

According to Ellemers, Kortekaas and Ouwerkerk (1999) and Bagozzi (2000), social identity is formed by three elements: (1) a cognitive component, formed based on the consciousness of belonging to the group (also defined as self-categorization); (2) an emotional or affective component, created from the sense of emotional involvement with the group and the affective commitment; and (3) an evaluative component, created by the connotation of positive or negative value connected to the feeling of belonging to the group, in other words, the self-esteem based on the group. It is important to highlight that the process of self-categorization accentuates similarities among the individuals and other group members as well as dissimilarities between non-members.

People tend to choose activities that are congruent with the salient aspects of their identities, as well as to support institutions that represent these identities (Ashforth and Mael 1989). They tend to find organizations attractive when their social identities are perceived with a sense of distinction. The higher the level of involvement of a person with an organization, the higher the level of attractiveness the organizational identity over this individual will be (Dutton, Dukerich, and Harquail 1994). A strong identification with an organization makes the cooperative behavior towards group members to be elevated due to: (1) the sense of trust and reciprocity in the community, (2) the higher social attraction among group members and (3) the presentation of a favorable image of the organization for himself and for others (Dutton et al. 1994).

In the view of Hsu and Lu (2004), when players play virtually, the interaction with other users creates a connection of continually growing strength. In that sense, usability through dialogue and social interaction, access and connection is the key to the successful management of a gaming online community (Hsu and Lu 2004). The key to success is the desire of consumers to interact among them, keeping an active community. One of the main difficulties to create and sustain a virtual community of any size is the time, energy and the commitment of consumers around one specific brand or product. This tends to occur only if the brand or product is really a determinant of the lifestyle of consumers, passion or hobby (Achrol and Kotler 1999).

## METHOD

In this study we used an interpretative approach through the accomplishment of in-depth filmed interviews with hardcore players of Microsoft XBOX 360. The interviews were held inside the Microsoft headquarters in Brazil, in an event that assembled members of one of the largest Xbox communities of users in the world, the Portalxbox. We conducted eight in-depth interviews applying an 18 question semi-structured questionnaire with questions regarding two main themes – communities and gaming. The choice of the subjects is due to their profound involvement with the Microsoft console as well as their active participation in the Portalxbox community. The interviews were transcribed and analyzed, afterwards we edited a 42 minute videography, and, based on this videography we re-analyzed the data for this paper. In consonance with the pragmatic perspective, to interpret the data gathered, we used discourse analysis following the guidance of Pêcheux (1969).

In the past, consumer behavior researchers had the tendency to minimize or simply to ignore the importance of the audiovisual aspect of their studies (Kozinets and Belk 2006). However, this atmosphere is changing. The use of videographies as a research method in marketing academic studies is being disseminated recently. In the consumer behavior area, we can cite the studies of Smith, Fisher and Cole (2007), Kimura and Belk (2005) and Bengtsson, Ostberg and Kjeldgaard (2005) among others.

The filmed interview has strong advantages over the one that is audio-recorded or directly transcribed (Belk and Kozinets 2005). It allows the researcher to analyze the body language of the interviewee and also to analyze the tone of a determined answer, generating a better content analysis. According to Spanjaard and Freeman (2006), the videography allows a bigger understanding and richer results than conventional in-depth interviews.

Another advantage of the videographic technique is that it opens more interpretative venues than the written analysis (Smith et al. 2007). Regarding consumer behavior research it is a given fact the visual information are cognitively more complex than textual, and that the learning is facilitated when information is presented in a varied form. Therefore, studies that combine visual and textual elements are more comprehensive for knowledge dissemination (Heisley 2001).

Using the same reasoning, Sherry and Schouten (2002) inferred that one of the most convincing advantages of the validity of this method is its ability to engage the audience in a multisensory set of materials, facilitating the gain of knowledge, not only cognitive, but also emotional and resonant. Last but not least, the videography allows that a study initially intended for the academic audience reaches a broader audience, working as a bridge between the academia and the world outside its boundaries.

## RESULTS

To advance on the understanding on videogames and their hardcore players, specifically the users of Xbox 360, we now present the analysis of the eight filmed interviews. It is important to consider that the respondents José, Maurício and Paulo are the administrators and the creators of the community. The other subjects are active users.

### THE BEGINNING OF EVERYTHING

The video games industry had its boom in the decade of 1970. In the first development phases, the industry was characterized by very low performance consoles, until 1974, when Sears released the Atari Pong, pioneering a new market. In 1977, the popular Atari Video Computer System was released, creating a new gaming concept. According to the interviewees, the video game culture is directly linked to Atari, since these was the first console of several gamers.

In the beginning, playing video games was susceptible to prejudice and even taboo. In the view of our informants some prejudices endures until today. Maurício comments that, when he started to play, he used to it hidden from his parents:

[...] at that time there was some prejudice [...] even today there still is some [...] but at that time existed not only prejudice, but also some tales, like the one that said that the video game damages the television... so, when my parents went out, we used that free time to play and since then I've been playing [...] since the Atari I had almost all the video games consoles [Maurício]

Another taboo related to games consumption highlighted by the interviewees is the fact that it is related to a childish entertainment. One informant talks about these taboos, especially in the view of his fathers and how they considered video games as something meant for children and that adults playing would be a sign of regression to childhood.

However, it is noticeable that since the acquisition of the first console, the interviewees evolved along with the games industry of games – the childish play stayed behind and the systems evolved to become an entertainment form full of diverse meanings. We observed that the majority of our subjects tried to follow the evolution of the video games industry – when a new product was released, they bought it, and experimented new forms of play. However, in front of the diversity of options aroused preferences related to games forms, types and brands. In the view of the interviewees, specific functionalities of the Xbox strengthen the preference for this console.

Therefore, the Xbox community consists in an attribute for the users of the Microsoft console. The online interaction enabled by the *Live* environment of the Xbox 360 conquered users since its releasing, what is noteworthy, given the fact that Microsoft had no tradition in video games.

The Xbox online environment enabled the creation of bonds among users and generated affinity to the brand. The integration promoted by *Live* results in virtual communities that imply in value for the product given the participation that the environment creates and users loyalty, an outcome of identification with the product, because this congregates users with mutual interest around one community.

## SOCIAL BONDING

The social relationships that are developed in the Xbox 360 made the video game more than just a gaming environment. It became an interaction environment, developing social bonding and emotion sharing. This new dynamics provided by the console, attract consumers to beyond the game, as for instance, the online chat, that even can became more important than the game itself:

You can ask several players why they turned their video games on the past week and several of them will tell that they did so just to chat [Bruno]

It is also noticeable the strength of the friendships that are created in *Live*, especially due to the sharing of references, as in the solving of doubts regarding the games. This social interaction sometimes even surpasses the technical questions of a game, for instance, the low graphic quality being minimized due to a good interaction environment. Also, it even surpasses the dissatisfaction with the console itself:

I already lost a console due to its defects and I bought another due to the friends that I've made [...] I have more contact with the friends that I've made in the Xbox than with my so-called physical friends [Alessandro]

It is obvious the extension of the utility of the game as a tool of social interaction. This interaction is a tendency of current video games, making the game a social experience and not an individual one. Allied to that, through the formation of communities, the interaction with other users creates a connection of continually growing strength.

Talking about this belongingness feeling regarding the community – that even utilizes a common language – the interviewees emphasized the fact that on the moment that the game became a social experience, this experience is transposed beyond the playing moment. Due to the involvement in the online games communities, the user encounters commonalities with other users that are interested in sharing feelings towards the game. The socialization through the communities creates the opportunity to performing activities online and offline, information exchange, recommendation and knowledge dissemination.

The involvement with the game became a fundamental element of its consumption. One informant even mentioned that, in his view, to quantify the game consumption nowadays it is impossible just to take into account the time that the player is playing, but how much time in life of a player is related to the game. Commonly, it is perceivable that the users play daily, with a signifying increase of gaming time during the weekends. The concern regarding the excess of time dedicated to the game is constant in their lives, even with some self-imposed limits.

One interesting discovery is that the interviewees consider the game as a healthy form of spending their time, an escape valve and not an addiction:

[...] I simply love it [...] today I play more as an escape valve of the real life, the work, the stress, the financial difficulties [Felipe].

Games nowadays demand a bigger dedication, because they are becoming more complexes and requiring more gaming time. In this way, it is possible to observe a thin line that separates being a hardcore gamer and an addict gamer. The interviewees demonstrated concern regarding being in the limit of addiction and not to exchange real life for the digital one, using reasons to justify their long time of use as well as the complacency of people of their social circle outside the game.

## MARKET COMPETITION

The video game market is a multimillionaire industry. Currently, in the configuration of this market, three companies are predominant: Microsoft, with the Xbox 360, Sony, with the Playstation 3 and Nintendo, with the Wii.

In this market configuration, the Xbox 360 and the Playstation 3 are preferred by hardcore players, and both platforms have a similar quality, while the Nintendo Wii is preferred by casual players:

I place the Wii in a relatively inferior level, precisely due to the fact that it has a different focus [...] it is a casual console. You invite some friends over, you take that controllers and shake them. It's a group experience that can be boring individually [Fábio].

Among the differences in consoles, the subjects also emphasized the option of playing online existent in the Xbox 360 and in the Playstation 3, that is not available on the Wii. On the other hand, one interviewee analyzed that the Nintendo console is directly towards a different social interaction, the one that happens physically. The

Wii is considered a product directed to have fun with friends, in a reunion or a party.

We noticed that the users consider the three main options of consoles available in the market to be in two distinct segments. While the Xbox and the Playstation is directed at the hardcore gamer, that demand more complex and long games, with better graphic quality, the Wii satisfy casual gamers that use it as a tool to have fun, mainly with friends.

These differences are confirmed in the games. In the view of the gamers, the Playstation and the Xbox titles have similarities in their libraries and also similar characteristics and quality. The Wii, however is highlighted to have a broader games library, however, with worst games and a stronger focus on games for children.

The Playstation 3 and the Xbox 360 are consoles with similar characteristics. Given the fact that they are directed at a hardcore audience, the companies choose not to do announce in the traditional mass media, while Nintendo use it to publicize the Wii. Due to the focus on the casual user, the promotion of the Wii helps to boost its sales, while the other consoles rely on their network of users to spread the word on their product, generating a positive effect on their consumption.

This element distinguishes even more the difference among the profile of users. In the case of video games, the relationship of the users to the brand is heightened, especially due to the community that it is formed around the product, once that, in this interaction they recognize others as themselves and the formation of a group. In this way, products directed towards a large-scale of users, such as Xbox and Playstation, the building of a network of users guarantees a relationship with the brand and the perenniality of the product consumption.

## GAME EXPERIENCE

Games are designed in a way that make consumers feel so strongly involved with them to the point that they perceive the games as reality (Mendenhall, Nepomuceno, and Saad 2010). The insertion in the gaming environment incorporates feelings of the real life in the virtual environment. The experience suppresses passions, desires and dreams:

[...] driving games are my favorites, they suppress my desires [...] I strongly value the immersion that outcomes from the game [...] in the moment you turn your TV volume up, you feel yourself as if you were a driver [Bruno]

[...] my biggest passion are cars and the video game is a form of living, at least partially, this passion, because I don't have the money to afford a high performance car, so at least I can drive one virtually [Fábio]

Conversely, the experiences provided by the game are also transposed to outside the virtual world. One subject mentioned that the simulation games brings several elements from reality, as for instance, the racing games in which you have to adjust your car to improve its performance and that they are very similar to the real competition environment. Consequently, the gamers end up searching for information on the real racing environment in order to apply them in the game.

In the view of the interviewees, the consumption experience provided by the video game takes the gamer on a travel to a parallel world and to forget everything else. This is a characteristic of the post-modern consumer in the conception of Firat and Dholakia (1998). The immersion in consumption experiences that differ from the quotidian that enables the opportunity to experience lifestyles different from the ones daily lived and difficult to bare. These experiences enables the creation of an imaginary in a world of fantasy beyond the real one, creating their own virtual worlds that up to a point may be incongruent with the human abilities.

The experience enabled by the game also arouses memories associated with determined moments of life, as well as feelings and emotion for the players. These feelings are aroused not only by the gaming context, but also by sound and visual effects that are part of the game; especially when they aggregate elements of interactivity:

[...] this is a game that I consider to be a great art, as if it were a film. They managed to create such a unique gaming environment that you end up involved in it, wanting or not, you will be involved with the story and it is very difficult to turn off and go to sleep [...] when that specific music plays, it boost up your energy, not your character's but your own [Renato]

The stimulation of feelings and emotions proportionate to the players a flow experience. During a flow experience an individual act with total involvement with the experience, having in mind anything except overcoming a determined challenge. The diverse element existent in current games, such as music and interactive elements, allied to the fast growing competence of game developers have enabled more intense flow experiences through means of greater demands of learning and high levels of challenge, strengthening constantly the playing desire.

This desire can even overcome the individual rationality in front of what is socially accepted, generating behaviors that are strange even for the gamers themselves. Several interviewees talked about situations in which they felt the urge to play.

A newly released game arrived in the afternoon at work and then you went out to play. It's nothing that will compromise your work performance, but you manage somehow to flee from work to enjoy the new game [Alessandro]

It is clear that the gamers have an exorbitant consumption desire, having the constant need to immediately have in their hands the latest version of their favorite games. But in their conception, this attitude are not characteristics of addiction, because a gamer would only be and addict in the moment that he started to bring emotions from the game to the real world.

The consumption experience is connected to social interaction. In the analysis of the interviews we observed that actions such as stay up all night playing is a social moment, in which, the interaction with the friends group has a great amount of importance. One subject mentioned that the social group creates the propitious environment for the gaming consumption, eliminating possible apprehensiveness and prejudices from others, in other words, during the game, everyone, no matter how different they may be, is sharing the same experiences, probably with a similar intensity.

## FINAL DISCUSSION

Our goal in this study was to analyze and understand the peculiarities of video game consumption in the view of hardcore gamers that interact in Xbox 360 virtual communities. We used an interpretative approach through a videography to capture the nuances of this form of consumption.

Based on what was aforementioned, we may conclude that the interaction and the insertion in a specific environment such as the one that exists in the current generation of video games (Playstation

3 and Microsoft Xbox 360) has consequences on the feelings and emotions of players through mechanisms such as social interaction, imaginary construction and flow experience. Nevertheless, the virtual communities that sprout from the online environment aggregate and enhance several artifacts in the use of video games.

The video games – that were initially produced with the objective of entertain solely individuals, or sometimes groups, as long as they were in the same place – evolved in the last years to became one of the main tools of social interaction, creating strong bonds among users, sometimes even stronger than the physical ones. In the view of our informants, we can infer that gone are the days in which video games were an individual entertainment, now it is the era in which they became a social interaction tool.

This form of entertainment, once considered to be designed for children, finds today its main target among youngsters of A and B classes, reaching a profitability of US$18 bi in the year of 2007 only in the U.S. (Matthews 2009). This figure is even more impressive if we compare it to the profitability from the movies industry in the U.S. in the same period: US$ 9.6 bi (MPAA 2007).

The characteristics that we use in the present study do not allow us to extrapolate its results and are limited to players of Microsoft Xbox 360. New researches should be conducted along with hardcore players of other consoles or of PC games, aiming at understanding similarities and differences among platforms. We also instigate others to conduct consumer behavior videographies, given its power to capture non-verbal elements that may help in broadening the scope of the studied phenomenon.

Last but not least, it is important to emphasize that leisure, play and entertainment are themes of high importance nowadays and in order to offer a greater comprehension on these sub-areas more researches should be carried, aiming not only at understanding the consumer experience but also using this understanding to support advances in the production side that fulfill the desire of consumers.

## REFERENCES

Achrol, Ravi S. and Kotler, Philip (1999), "Marketing in the Network Economy," in *Journal of Marketing*, 63 (Special Issue), 146-63.

Algesheimer, Rene and Dholakia, Utpal M. (2006), "The Long-Term Effects of Joining and Participating in Customer Communities," in *Unpublished Working Paper*. Rice University, Houston, TX.

Ashforth, Blake E. and Mael, Fred. (1989), "Social Identity Theory and the Organization," in *The Academy of Management Review*, 14(1), 20-39.

Bagozzi, Richard P. (2000), "On the Concept of Intentional Action in Consumer Behavior," in *Journal of Consumer Research*, 27 (December), 388-96.

Bagozzi, Richard P. and Dholakia, Utpal M. (2002), "Intencional Social Action in Virtual Communities," in *Journal of Interactive Marketing*, 16(2), spring, 2-21.

Belk, Russel and Kozinets, Robert (2005), "Videography in marketing and consumer research," in *Qualitative Market Research*: an international journal. 8(2), 178-86.

Bengtsson, Anders, Ostberg, Jacob, and Kjeldgaard, Dannie (2005), "Prisoners in paradise: subcultural resistance to the marketization of tattooing," in *Consumption, Markets and Culture*, 8(3), 261-74.

Chen, Jenova (2007), "Flow in Games (and Everything Else)," in *Communications of the ACM*, 50(4), 31-34.

Chou, Ting-jui and Ting, Chih-Chen (2003), "The Role of Flow Experience in Cyber-Game Addiction," in *Cyberpsychology and Behavior*, 6(6), 663-75.

Clements, Matthew T. and Ohashi, Hiroshi (2005), "Indirect Network Effects and the Product Cycle: Video Games in the U.S. 1994-2002," in *Journal of Industrial Economics*. 53(4), 515-42.

Csikszentmihalyi, Mihaly (1991). *Flow, the Psychology of Optimal Experience*, Harper and Row, New York.

Dholakia, Utpal M., Bagozzi, Richard P., and Pearo, Klein L. (2004), "A Social Influence Model of Consumer Participation in Network-and small-group-based Virtual Communities," in *International Journal of Research in Marketing,* 21(3), 241-63.

Dutton, Jane, Dukerich, Janet. M., and Harquail, Celia V. (1994), "Organizational Images and Member Identification," in *Administrative Science Quarterly*, 39(2), 239-63.

Ellemers, Naomi, Kortekaas, Paulien, and Ouwerkerk, Jaap (1999), "Self-categorization, commitment to the group and group self-esteem as related but distinct aspects of social identity," in *European Journal of Social Psychology*, 29(2-3), 371-89.

Evans, Martin G., Wedande, Gamini, Ralston, Lisa, and Hul, Selma (2001), "Consumer Interaction in Virtual Era: Some Qualitative Insights," in *Qualitative Market Research,* 4(3), 150-59.

Firat, A. Fuat and Dholakia, Uptal M. (1998), *"Consuming People: From Political Economy to Theatres of Consumption,"* London, UK: Routledge.

Heisley, Deborah D. (2001), "Visual research: current bias and future direction," in *Advances in Consumer Research*, 28(1), 45-6.

Hoffman, Donna and Novak, Thomas (1996), "Marketing in Hypermedia Computermediated Environments: conceptual foundations," in *Journal of Marketing*, 60(3), 50–68.

Holt, R (2000). *Examining Video Game Immersion as a Flow State*. B.A. Thesis, Department of Psychology, Brock University, St. Catharines, Ontario, Canadá.

Hsu, Chin-Lung and Lu, Hsi-Peng (2004), "Why do people play on-line games? An extended TAM with social influences and flow experience." in *Information and Management*, 41(7), 853–68.

Kimura, Junko and Belk, Russell W. (2005), "Christmas in Japan: globalization versus localization," in *Consumption, Markets and Culture,* 8(3), 325-38.

Kozinets, Robert and Belk, Russell (2006), "Camcorder society: quality videography in consumer research," in *Handbook of qualitative research methods in marketing*, vol. 1, ed. Russell W. Belk, Cheltenham, UN and Northampton, MA: Edward Elgar Publishing, 335-44.

Matthews, Matt (2009), *"NPD: Behind the Numbers,"* http://www.gamasutra.com/view/feature/3906/npd_behind_the_numbers_december_.php.

McAlexander, James, Schouten, John, and Koenig, Harold (2002), "Building Brand Community," in *Journal of Marketing*, v. 66(January), 38-54.

McWillian, Gil. (2000), "Building Stronger Brands through On-line Communities," in *Sloan Management Review*, 41(3), 43-54.

Mendenhall, Zack, Nepomuceno, Marcelo V., and Saad, Gad (2010), "Exploring video games from an evolutionary psychological perspective," in *Encyclopedia of E-Business Development and Management in the Global Economy,* Vol. 1, ed. In Lee, Hershey: Igi Global.

MPAA - Motion Picture Association of America (2007), *"Entertainment Industry Market Statistics,"* http://www.mpaa.org/.

Orry, James (2008), "*XBOX 360 leads 2007 market share by value*," http://www.videogamer.com/news/10/02/208-7223

*Pêcheux,* Michel (1969), "*Analyse automatique du discours*," Paris: Dunod.

Schubert, Petra and Ginsburg, Mark (2000), "Virtual Communities of Transaction: The Role of Personalization in Electronic Commerce," in *Electronic Markets Journal,* 10(1), 45-55.

Shankar, Venkatesh and Bayus, Barry (2003), "Network Effects and Competition: An Empirical Analysis of the Home Video Game Industry," in *Strategic Management Journal*, 24(4), 375-84.

Sherry, John F. and Schouten, John W. (2002), "A role for poetry in consumer research," in *Journal of Consumer Research,* 29(2), 218-34.

Shin, Dong-Hee and Kim, Won-Young (2008), "Applying the Technology Acceptance Model and Flow Theory to Cyworld User Behavior: Implication of the Web 2.0," in *Cyberpsychology and Behavior,* 11(3), 378-82.

Smith, Scott, Fisher, Dan, and Cole, S. Jason (2007), "The lived meanings of fanaticism: understanding the complex role of labels and categories in defining the self in consumer culture," in *Consumption, Markets and Culture,* 10(2), 77-94.

Spanjaard, Daniela and Freeman, Lynne (2006), "Tread Softly: Using videography to capture shopping behavior," in *Advances in Consumer Research, Asia Pacific, Vol. 8,* Duluth, USA.

Wellman, Barry (2005), "Community: From Neighborhood to Network," *Communications of the ACM*, 48(10), 53-5.

Williams, Dmitri. (2002) "Structure and Competition in the U.S. Home Video Game Industry", in *The International Journal on Media Management.* vol. 4, 1, 41–54.

# "Fine Feathers Make Fine Birds" – Community Brands and Branded Communities

Roland Schroll, University of Innsbruck, Austria
Andrea Hemetsberger, University of Innsbruck, Austria
Johann Füller, University of Innsbruck, Austria

## ABSTRACT

This article introduces the concept of branded communities. A qualitative study of Apache, an Open Source software community, revealed that creative communities not only create brands but have become brands themselves. We conclude that we should incorporate branded communities and their members in an extended theory of brands and branding.

## ACKNOWLEDGEMENTS

We would like to thank Sally Khudairi and the Apache community for their support, for their willingness to serve as interview partners, and the kind reception at the ApacheCon 2009.

## INTRODUCTION

Consumers create brands. With the diffusion of network technologies, consumer innovation and creation is taking on new forms that are radically transforming the nature of consumption and production, branding and meaning creation. This paper elaborates on the notion of many well-recognized scholars that the predominant branding concept needs to catch up with reality and that our current understanding of brands is ripe for review (Holt 2002; Kozinets 2002; Pitt et al. 2006; Prahalad and Ramaswamy 2004b). Especially in the last decade of the previous century technological innovations, such as the mobile phone, the Internet and social software portals such as Facebook, have fundamentally changed our lifestyles and created opportunities for collaboration, participation in the market system, and sharing (Belk 2010; Giesler 2006; Kozinets, Hemetsberger, and Schau 2008; von Krogh et al. 2008).

Similarly, for brands and branding new opportunities arise. Due to an increasing availability of worldwide communication and production capabilities and a general revival of community and tribes in our postmodern society (Cova 1997; Maffesoli 1996), communities are given the means to create community brands (Füller, Lüdicke, and Jawecki 2007) and become brands in and of themselves that members as well as consumers identify with. Meanwhile, grassroots community activities have taken on institutionalized forms of communal production, such as the Open-source organization and the Apache Foundation, and gradually developed into the realm of marketing and branding.

Linux and Apache are well known examples where community members not only develop their software but also create strong brands (Pitt et al. 2006). Community-driven brands like Apache – comprising the leading open source web server and other software products, or Mozilla with their main sub-brands Firefox, Thunderbird, Sunbird, and many others, are initiated, created, owned, and driven by user communities and not by companies and their marketing departments. Community brands, in general, are gaining momentum. They emerge in a wide range of consumer goods as well. Members of consumer communities, for example interested in gaming, skiing, or beer-brewing create, brand, and market their own products - games, skies, or beer, respectively (Kozinets et al. 2008). Those brands create significant brand value. Recent research in this area has studied the value of community brands as compared to commercial brands (Füller et al. 2007), and how brand community practices create value (Schau, Muniz and Arnould 2009).

However, how communities are creating brands and the value of the community itself is yet to be studied.

To this end, we first problematize traditional views of brands and brand creation, and argue that theories of co-creation and customer integration fall short to explain the dynamics of branded communities. Second, we aim to show that communities have taken over important brand functionalities typically fulfilled by brands. By introducing the concept of branded communities we argue that creative communities have become brands in themselves, offering significant meaning for members and non-members alike. Based on our findings, we discuss community brands and branded communities in the context of existing theory and theorize on how community brands may impact markets currently dominated by company brands.

## BRANDS AND BRANDING
### From proprietary towards open brands

Over the years, brands had transformed from simple markers of identification attached to products to complex social phenomena (Berthon et al. 2007; Mühlbacher et al. 2006). Furthermore, as brands are increasingly perceived as cultural agents that are also expected to give back to the society and fulfill civic obligations (Holt 2002). According to Holt (2002), it is this recurring mismatch between the predominant branding concept and consumer's expectations which results in an ongoing advancement of brands and branding. It is the inefficiency of the predominant branding paradigm, which creates the necessity for brands and branding to move it one step further. However, consumers according to Holt "are revolutionary only insofar as they assist entrepreneurial firms to tear down the old branding paradigm and create opportunities for companies that understand emerging new principles." (Holt 2002, 89). Holt's view implies that consumers depend on branding efforts of corporations. Only then the advancement of brands and branding under corporate control will continue.

One exception to this is the Open Source (OS) movement. Pitt et al. (2006) argue that, in relation to the Open Source movement, brands and branding are moving towards a fourth and final phase, in which brands will provide the same functions for consumers, but it is unclear which benefits these brands provide for 'producers'. This does not mean that profit-seeking corporations cannot benefit from OS brands but rather that some of the traditional functions of brands for producers, such as financial incentives, vanish when brands are nonproprietary (Pitt et al. 2006). Indeed, the proliferation of information and communication technologies, together with the re-emergence of new forms of communities (Cova 1997; Maffesoli 1996), challenges the predominant understanding of the roles of corporations in building brand value. For instance, the benefit of reducing consumer's search costs is challenged by the increasing availability of search technologies. Similarly, the risk of buying the wrong product or brand is reduced by the open access to other consumer's reviews and ratings. Many of the benefits brands provided in terms of risk reduction and limitation of search costs proved very valuable at a time when communication and sharing was limited. In an open environment, such as the Internet, sources of brand value have changed (Schau et al. 2009).

## Active Consumers and the Brand

Recently, the active role of the consumer in the creation process of brand meaning has attracted scholars' attention. While traditionally the consumer was ascribed a rather passive role, the advantage of integrating the consumer as a co-creator of value has been stressed by several scholars (Payne et al. 2009; Prahalad and Ramaswamy 2004a; Vargo and Lusch 2004). A recent study shows that „where consumers are given large degrees of freedom to create or co-create with organizers, they feel authenticity, a type of soulfulness and meaning, and they respond with enthusiasm, energy, and action" (Sherry, Kozinets, and Borghini 2007, 30). Today, it is widely accepted that consumers can and often do shape, appropriate, and co-create the meaning of commercial brands (Cova and Pace 2006; Kozinets et al. 2004; Muniz and Schau 2005; Thompson and Arsel 2004; Thompson, Rindfleisch, and Arsel 2006). Producers may develop and introduce a brand on the marketplace, but consumers and other stakeholders, then, may modify its meaning in unexpected ways. Consumers may openly denunciate brands (Klein 2000), challenge the producer-intended meaning (Kates 2004; Thompson et al. 2006), decide upon legitimate brand ownership (Kirmani, Sood, and Bridges 1999), or even hijack a brand (Muniz and Schau 2005; Wipperfürth 2005).

Despite the influence consumers have on existing brands, an increasing desire among consumers to interact with the market in new ways has been observed (Cova and Rémy 2007; Szmigin, Carrigan, and Bekin 2007). Modernity has widely alienated workers from production processes (Slater 1997), workers lost ownership of the products they produced (Bocock 1993). This is a profound detachment of work from workers. Following Marx, the process of production is an important means for self-expression and advancement (Marx, Engels, and Arthur 1970), which led consumers to act out their creativity within their own private domain. New media technology has fundamentally altered consumers' possibilities to create and has taken much of the constraints of organized, de-enchanted work. Producers' lack of willingness to give off control and integrate the consumer in the production process resulted in the emergence of new, emancipated consumption communities. These communities have a strong influence on existing brands, as shown above, but more importantly, they can also become active players on the market themselves (Thompson and Coskuner-Balli 2007).

It is our aim to carve out the specific idiosyncrasies of community brands and branded communities. Communities as developers of brands are a very recent phenomenon which has not yet been studied. Hence, if we are to study the value of those community brands we first need to explore how the community perceives their brand; whether they think of their creations as a brand at all; and how they describe the inner values of the brand of itself and in comparison with other non-community brands. To this end, we researched a prominent and successful 'creative crowd', members of the Apache Foundation and its contributor community.

## METHOD

For our study we applied qualitative-inductive methodology (Denzin and Lincoln 1994) in order to gain rich insights into the phenomenon studied (Creswell 1998; Maxwell 2005). First, we identified informants from the Apache foundation using "theoretical sampling" as described in grounded theory literature (Glaser and Strauss 1967; Strauss and Corbin 1990). All together 12 interviews were conducted. All of our respondents were between 29 and 48 years of age and male due to the predominance of male community members. We only interviewed community members, since we were interested in the brand's and the community's development and were dependent on first hand information of people inside the community.

In order to look at the phenomenon from different perspectives, respondents were chosen based on several criteria. Degree of community involvement was the first criterion. While some respondents took over central roles within the community (e.g. President of the ASF), others were only loosely connected to the community through their day-time job. Four of the interviewees have either founded their own company based on Apache products or were working for such a company. Second, we looked at the duration of community involvement. While four of the respondents were members of the initial Apache Group or involved with the software shortly after and thus community members since the very beginning, others could not look back on such a long history of community membership. The status role respondents held in the community was a third criterion. While nine out of the 12 interviewees were members of the Apache Software Foundation, four respondents additionally were members of the Board of Directors, which has the social oversight over the communities' development. Other roles of respondents included project chairman, documentation contributor, Vice President for conference planning, and simple code committers (see Table 1 for interviewee profiles).

We used a semi-structured interview guide composed of four parts. Interviewees were first asked to introduce themselves and report about their commitment and current role within the Apache community. In a second part we asked for the respondents' view of the historical development of the community. The main part of the interview revolved around Apache as a brand; whether community members perceived it as a brand; about the uniqueness of Apache as a brand; their motives to contribute; and the perceived overall meaning of Apache. Finally, we focused on the relationship of the Apache brands with other brands such as Microsoft, as well as possible future developments of the community and the brand.

All interviews took place at the „ApacheCon Europe", the official conference of the Apache Software Foundation. The conference provided a perfect context to interview prominent community members in their natural setting of discussing strategically important future perspectives of Apache. The interviews lasted between 35 and 90 minutes and produced a total of 7h and 50 min. of information. We tape-recorded the interviews and transcribed them verbatim. The interviews were content-analyzed and interpreted until theoretical saturation (Goulding 2002) was achieved. Typical verbatims were selected to demonstrate our main findings.

## FINDINGS

### The meaning of the Apache brand

At first sight, the Apache brand does not differ from any commercial brand. In this part of the paper we describe the brand's social, symbolic, and commercial value and demonstrate that the community itself embodies a great part of the Apache brand value. An important aspect of the brand's social value is its ability to connect like-minded people, create a sense of community, and provide a platform for exchange as the following statements demonstrate:

> *"It's an immediate connection that we have ... So when I meet someone now there is little chance that we actually have commonality on the project we are involved with. But we are part of that larger community and there is an immediate connection." (Steven)*

In this regard Apache is not very different from many commercial brands which also create a sense of community among members, such as for instance Harley Davidson. However, in contrast to many other brand communities, it is not the product which is at the centre of the Apache community. The "community over code" principle present in the community demonstrates that it is the community and the social relations between members which are valued above everything else; or as the following interviewee put it:

> " ... there is this slogan that the community is more important than the code. And that's more than a slogan. If there are technical decision there is a real effort to resolve the community issues before solving the code issues. It's interesting to see these folks putting aside technical issues in favor of interpersonal issues." (Steven)

In contrast to Apache, many other OS communities did not survive,

> "...because they did not put community first. This is where Apache has got it right. They talk about the community ... and then the code. ... That's one reason why Apache survived ..." (Peter)

The importance of the community and the social relations between the individual members fits well to Cova (1997)'s notion that the link is more important than the thing, and further corroborates Schau et al.'s (2009) notion of value creation through community practices. In their search of meaningful relationships to others consumers are increasingly looking for brands, which enable them to connect with others and enable them to engage in meaningful activities.

> "...there is also a community of experts within the Microsoft community. But I definitely think that we have the upper hand in terms of giving something back to society ... our software can make a difference in life and I believe that is more Apache than it is Microsoft." (Thomas)

It is evidenced here that the Apache brand has much more to offer than many commercial brands; much more than just functional and hedonic benefits. The Apache brand derives much of its meaning from the motivation to give something back to society and thus find meaning in life. Being a member of the Apache community is not just a personal expression of preferences and social belongingness. The Apache brand can be seen as a lifetime partner, a valuable companion for one's identity construction and something that is worth living for. This idealistic and ethical notion is hardly found in traditional, commercial brands. Whereas the value of many commercial brands becomes evident in specific situations, such as the reduction of search costs in a shopping situation or the display of a specific personality in a social situation, the value of the Apache brand is less static and not only tied to specific moments in time. The brand stands for a life-time project which enables community members to constantly derive meaning from. It is primarily the connectedness and this self-transcending quality that differentiates community brands from commercial endeavors.

## Personal Branding - The value of community membership

Most commercial brands just need to be bought in order to provide symbolic and social value; membership in brand communities is usually just a matter of brand ownership and expertise. However, in the case of the Apache brand it is a bit more complex. The community has installed a strict member selection process, which does not only demand significant effort on the side of potential members but also gives the community control over who is being associated with the brand and with whom the brand is associated with.

> "It's very hard to become a committer. You need to show quality over a long period of time and also show commitment to the community. So there is this process in place that guarantees the quality. That is also important to us. We do not want to constantly check everything." (Justin)

> "You contribute and at some point someone tells you: ‚Ok, become one of us!' And that's it." (Chris)

> "... the way the people become members is through peer recognition. You have to contribute for a certain amount of time and then someone might nominate you for membership and as the members we vote on that membership." (Steven)

Membership has to be earned by excellent contributions and commitment. The only way to become a member is by acceptance of the existing members. During their first involvement with the community, not only their work is under constant review but also their personality to determine whether they fit the community and the so called "Apache Way".

> "But I think what is difficult is to teach the new committers the 'Apache Way', the way you have to behave when you are in a project." (Chris)

The „Apache Way" does not only guarantee that projects are executed in a specific way but also safeguard the special community culture by teaching new members how to behave. While many commercial brands have to deal with a rather heterogeneous user group and the resulting conflict about who is a legitimate brand owner and who is not, this is different with the Apache brand. As the brand cannot be separated from the individual community member it is essential for the brand that the right people are chosen to represent the brand. The brand is the community, and the individual members are the brand. What the brand stands for is not prescribed but rather evolves through everyday community interaction, communal practices, andthe behavioral patterns of its members.

A series of benefits arise from the member selection process described above. These benefits result from the fact that group membership and thus brand association is not open to everyone, as it is the case with most commercial brands, but rather a number of qualities need to be fulfilled in order to be accepted as a member.

> "The other side of the brand is personal branding. The fact that I am a member of the Apache Software Foundation opens lots of doors." (Bill)

> "... they said: 'You are just a contractor, we do not care what you say!' Then I sent an e-mail using my apache.org account and afterwards all the technical guys came to me and said: 'Oh you work for Apache. You said something yesterday?' So it changes perception." (Chris)

As the above statements demonstrate, being associated with the Apache community does carry a lot of value in the IT area. Community membership can be transformed into individual assets in the workplace and beyond. This strict and extensive process of becoming a community member upholds the high status and prestige associated with Apache. Referring to Simmel (1906), especially in communities with restricted access, membership is perceived as more valuable. The prestige and status associated with membership of the Apache community manifest itself in various situations, such as for instance during job interviews.

*"... there are stories, like people going to job interviews and mentioning that they are a community member... It makes the people listen, because it does carry some value." (Roland)*

Just as with commercial brands, members make us of the Apache brand to communicate their identity. However with most commercial brands, use of a specific brand does only provide limited information about the true personality of the brand owner. One might wear designer shoes in order to be perceived as classy or elegant, however the receiver of the message has only limited possibilities to check for the validity of these claims. Due to the members selection process this is somehow different with the Apache brand. The receiver of the message can draw conclusions on the person's behavior and skills, his sub-cultural background, work ethics and morality. Hence, not only the *community brand* creates value for its creators and users but also membership in the *branded community* of Apache, in particular.

## DISCUSSION

This paper explores the phenomenon of community-created brands using the example of Apache, an open-source software community well known for its expertise in programming and its market-leading web server. Our findings contribute to theory in at least two important ways. First, we were able to show that brand development is not restricted to managerial strategy and action but in reality emerges as a grassroots activity of communities. Contrary to commercial brands, community branding processes naturally evolve as side effect of the communities' natural, everyday activities. Freely available software can be monetized. Apache's market share and the amount of sponsorship for Apache demonstrate its market value. Second, voluntary community work pays back in a number of ways, which are beneficial and of enormous value for the community, the individual, and society at large.

In the case of Apache, every community member is able to and actually engages in communicating about the brand and community identity. Every single member becomes a marketer of the Apache brand. As identification with and self-expression through Apache membership is much stronger for community members than for employees of traditional companies, Apache members turn out to be true and credible evangelists of the Apache brand. Additionally, the Apache foundation gives some guidance to members how to communicate, thus ensuring that the values of the Apache community brand are passed on. This stands in stark contrast to profit-oriented companies where usually not all employees consider themselves being ambassadors of their brands. The Apache foundation constitutes a platform where all members actively contribute to the brand. In companies brands are usually crafted and executed by marketing departments, or even outsourced to agencies. The average employee plays a minor role and is often a rather passive stakeholder. Admittedly, brands as Apache are not faced with pricing or distribution issues as the brand is distributed via the Internet and for free. Hence the community concentrates on product development and market communication tasks. Yet, they provide a role model for authentic and sustainable brand buzz and cult as depicted by Holt (2002) and others.

In addition to the unique brand building process, Apache offers an attractive and unique brand meaning and value for its members and non members to identify with. Apache stands for high quality software and a group of very knowledgeable, highly intellectual,

self-motivated computer geeks who aim to write the best software. The prestige and status granted from outsiders manifests this position. Community values, such as "community over code", demonstrate their orientation towards the human element, which is solidly based in community philosophy. The genuine belief in what they are doing, their independence and non-commercial interest considerably enhance credibility and authenticity. As Apache is not following the dominant market logic of increasing revenue and profit it is not forced to run after quantitative growth but rather concentrates on fulfilling user expectations. With community brands consumers are able to escape the branding mill of commercial brands who try to exploit the brand's value by attracting more and more customers thus diluting the brand's power as a source of identification for its consumers. Instead, as we have shown above, the Apache brand carefully selects its members and thus determines who is associated with the brand and who represents the brand. On the one hand this increases the value of community membership and on the other hand endows the community with some control over how the brand is perceived. This stands in contrast to many commercial brands, where brand association is largely determined through the market.

Previous research (Schau et al. 2009) already demonstrates that brand community practices create value. However the value created in these communities can almost exclusively be retrieved inside the community and is mostly limited to the consumption of the brand. Our study contributes to research in this area by showing that brand community practices can also create value outside of the community and in contexts not related to consumption situations, for instance on the job market. Due to careful member selection processes, Apache community membership equals a strong 'employer brand'. Also in traditional brand communities issues evolving around members or brand user selection in the form of brand user legitimacy struggles can be observed (Kirmani et al. 1999). As communities such as Apache do not only provide desired meanings as citizen artists, but also provide consumable products, they may become true alternatives to commercial and profit-oriented organizations, and build a new form of self-organized and volunteer-based organization, not only in terms of product innovation but also in terms of branding.

Recognizing the concept of community-created brands, we can draw several implications. Similar to the concept of community-based and user-based innovation we touch on new community-based marketing approaches that may emerge by trying to leverage the value of community brands. Like open innovation concepts are trying to leverage the creativity and innovative capabilities of users for new product development, open marketing concepts are able to leverage the branding activities of communities. Community brands are much more organic and holistic entities, marketed by the community, by its sponsors and users in a process of constant mutual exchange of economic, financial, social, emotional and intellectual value. Consumers' ability and capability to do so pose new challenges onto commercial brands in terms of authenticity and customer proximity.

Community brands have radically changed our view of brands and branding. The phenomenon of community brands shows that the concept of brands and branding is not limited to the product domain and that it is much better described as a complex social phenomenon including community membership into a new understanding of contemporary branded communities.

## REFERENCES

Belk, Russel (2010), "Sharing," *Journal of Consumer Research*, 36 (February), 715-734.

Berthon, Pierre, Morris B. Holbrook, James M. Hulbert, and Leyland F. Pitt (2007), "Viewing Brands in Multiple Dimensions," *MIT Sloan Management Review*, 48 (2), 37.

Bocock, Robert (1993), *Consumption*, New York, NY: Routledge.

Cova, Bernard (1997), "Community and Consumption: Towards a definition of the "linking value" of product or services," European *Journal of Marketing*, 31 (3/4), 297-316.

Cova, Bernard and Stefano Pace (2006), "Brand Community of Convenience Products: Now Forms of Customer Empowerment - the Case ‚My Nutella the Community'," *European Journal of Marketing*, 40 (9/10), 1087-105.

Cova, Véronique and Eric Rémy (2007), "I Feel Good - Who Needs the Market? Struggling and Having Fun with Consumer Driven Experiences," in *Consuming Experience*, ed. Antonella Carù and Bernard Cova, New York, NY: Routledge, 17-33.

Creswell, John W. (1998), *Qualitative Inquiry and Research Design: Choosing Among Five Traditions*, Thousand Oaks, CA: Sage Publications.

Denzin, Norman K. and Yvonne S. Lincoln (1994), "Introduction: Entering the Field of Qualitative Research," in *Handbook of Qualitative Research*, ed. Yvonne S. Lincoln and Norman K. Denzin, Thousand Oaks, CA: Sage Publications, 1-17.

Füller, Johann, Marius K. Lüdicke, and Gregor Jawecki (2007), "How Brands Enchant: Insights from Observing Community Driven Brand Creation " in *Annual North American Conference*, ed. Association for Consumer Research, Memphis, USA.

Giesler, Markus (2006), "Consumer Gift Systems," *Journal of Consumer Research*, 33 (2), 283-90.

Glaser, Barney G. and Anselm L. Strauss (1967), *The Discovery of Grounded Theory: Strategies for Qualitative Research*, Hawthorne, NY: Aldine de Gruyter.

Goulding, Christina (2002), *Grounded Theory: A Practical Guide for Management, Business and Market Researchers*, London, UK: Sage Publications.

Hemetsberger, Andrea and Christian Reinhardt (2006), "Learning and Knowledge-Building in Open-Source Communities: A Social-Experiential Approach," *Management Learning*, 37 (2), 187-214.

_____ (2009), "Collective Development in Open-Source Communities: An Activity Theoretical Perspective on Successful Online Collaboration," *Organization Studies*, 30 (9), 987-1008.

Holt, Douglas (2002), "Why Do Brands Cause Trouble? A Dialectical Theory of Consumer Culture and Branding," *Journal of Consumer Research*, 29 (June), 70-90.

Kates, Steven M. (2004), "The Dynamics of Brand Legitimacy: An Interpretive Study in the Gay Men's Community," *Journal of Consumer Research*, 31 (2), 455-64.

Kirmani, Amna, Sanjay Sood, and Sheri Bridges (1999), "The Ownership Effect in Consumer Responses to Brand Line Stretches," *Journal of Marketing*, 63 (1), 88-101.

Klein, Naomi (2000), *No Logo,* London, UK: Harper Collins.

Kozinets, Robert V. (2002), "Can Consumers Escape the Market? Emancipatory Illuminations from Burning Man," *Journal of Consumer Research*, 29 (1), 20-38.

Kozinets, Robert V., John F. Sherry, Diana Storm, Adam Duhachek, Krittinee Nuttavuthisit, and Benét Deberry-Spence (2004), "Ludic Agency and Retail Spectacle," *Journal of Consumer Research*, 31 (December), 658-72.

Kozinets, Robert V., Andrea Hemetsberger, and Hope J. Schau (2008), "The Wisdom of Consumer Crowds: Collective Innovation in the Age of Networked Marketing," *Journal of Macromarketing*, 28 (4), 339-54.

Maffesoli, Michel (1996), *The Time of the Tribes*, London, UK: Sage Publications.

Marx, Karl, Friedrich Engels, and Christopher J. Arthur (1970), *The German Ideology*: International Publishers Co.

Maxwell, Joseph A. (2005), *Qualitative Research Design: An Interactive Approach*, Thousand Oaks, CA: Sage Publications.

Mühlbacher, Hans, Andrea Hemetsberger, Eva Thelen, Christine Vallaster, Rudolf Massimo, Johann Füller, Clemens Pirker, Robert Schorn, and Christine Kittinger (2006), "Brands as Complex Social Phenomena," in *Proceedings of the Thought Leaders International Conference on Brand Management*, Birmingham.

Muniz, Albert M. and Hope J. Schau (2005), "Religiosity in the Abondened Apple Newton Brand Community," *Journal of Consumer Research*, 31 (March), 737-47.

Payne, A, K Storbacka, P Frow, and S Knox (2009), "Co-Creating Brands: Diagnosing and Designing the Relationship Experience," *Journal of Business Research*, 62 (3), 379-89.

Pitt, Leyland F., Richard T. Watson, Pierre Berthon, Donald Wynn, and George M. Zinkhan (2006), "The Penguin's Window: Corporate Brand from an Open-Source Perspective," *Journal of the Academy of Marketing Science*, 34 (2), 115-27.

Prahalad, Coimbatore K. and Venkatram Ramaswamy (2004a), *The Future of Competition: Co-Creating Unique Value with Customers*, Boston, MA: Harvard Business School Press.

Prahalad, Coimbatore K. and Venkatram Ramaswamy (2004b), "Co-Creating Unique Value with Customers," *Strategy & Leadership*, 32 (3), 4-9.

Schau, Hope J., Albert M. Muñiz, and Eric J. Arnould (2009), "How Brand Community Practices Create Value," *Journal of Marketing*, 73 (5), 30-51.

Sherry, John F, Robert V. Kozinets, and Stefania Borghini (2007), "Agents in Paradise - Experiential Co-Creation through Emplacement, Ritualization, and Community," in *Consuming Experience*, ed. Antonella Carù and Bernard Cova, *New York, NY: Routledge*, 17-33.

Simmel, Georg (1906), "The Sociology of Secrecy and of Secret Societies," *American Journal of Sociology*, 11 (4), 441-98.

Slater, Don (1997), *Consumer Culture and Modernity*, Cambridge, UK: Polity Press.

Strauss, Anselm L. and Juliet M. Corbin (1990), *Basics of Qualitative Research: Techniques and Procedures for Developing Grounded Theory*, Newbury Park, CA: Sage Publications.

Szmigin, Isabelle; Marylyn Carrigan, and Caroline Bekin (2007), "New Consumption Communities and the Re-Enabling of 21st Century Consumers," in *Consumer Tribes*, ed. Bernard Cova, Robert V. Kozinets, and Avi Shankar, Oxford, UK: Elsevier, 296-311.

Thompson, Craig J. and Gokcen Coskuner-Balli (2007), "Countervailing Market Responses to Corporate Co-Optation and the Ideological Recruitment of Consumption Communities," *Journal of Consumer Research*, 34 (2), 135-52.

Thompson, Craig J. and Zeynep Arsel (2004), "The Starbucks Brandscape and Consumers' (Anticorporate) Experiences of Glocalization," *Journal of Consumer Research*, 31 (December ), 631-42.

Thompson, Craig J., Aric Rindfleisch, and Zeynep Arsel (2006), "Emotional Branding and the Strategic Value of the Doppelgänger Brand Image," *Journal of Marketing*, 70 (January), 50-64.

Vargo, Stephen L. and Robert Lusch (2004), "Evolving to a New Dominant Logic for Marketing," *Journal of Marketing*, 68 (January), 1-17.

von Krogh, Georg, Sebastian Spaeth, Stefan Haeflinger, and Martin Wallin (2008), "Open Source Softwares: What We Know (and Do Not Know) About Motives to Contribute," in *DIME Working Papers on Intellectual Property Rights 38*.

Wipperfürth, Alex (2005), *Brand Hijack: Marketing without Marketing*, New York, NY: Portfolio.

# What Happens between the Memory Option and the Stimulus Option?
## Attribute Valence and Information Retrieval in Mixed Choice

Mauricio Palmeira, Monash University, Australia
Shuoyang Zhang, Colorado State University, USA
Shanker Krishnan, Indiana University, USA

## ABSTRACT

Previous research on mixed choice has focused on attractive options and suggested a conservative bias. The current study investigates the role of attribute valence and shows in three experiments that consumers tend to prefer the stimulus option when the options are described by attractive attributes and the memory option when they are described by negative attributes. Further, the preference patterns can be explained by consumers' imperfect memory retrieval.

## INTRODUCTION

Unlike the ideal scenarios often seen in decision making experiments, consumers usually do not have all the options presented in their consideration set at the same time. Instead, consumers often find themselves in mixed choice settings, in which the information of a certain brand is directly observable, while that of another brand is available only in memory. For instance, when Lynda visits Sears, finds a viable washer/dryer combo, continues to search in Lows for alternatives, and ends up seeing another qualified combo, she must rely on the information in memory of the previously considered option in order to compare with the physically present one. This type of scenario has been described as mixed choice (Lynch and Srull 1982), as opposed to solely stimulus-based choice, where all the information about brands or attributes is directly observable at the time of choice, or solely memory-based choice, where all the information must be recalled from memory and not physically present. Mixed choice is very common in the marketplace because the range of products one store can carry is very limited, especially for products that imply high financial risks (Alba, Marmorstein, and Chattopadhyay 1992).

Among the handful of studies that have examined mixed choice, (Alba et al., 1992; Biehal and Chakravarti 1983, 1986; Dick, Chakravarti, and Biehal 1990; Lynch, Marmorstein, and Weigold 1988), most has relied exclusively on choice tasks involving brands with attractive attributes and largely ignored the ones with unattractive attributes. This somewhat narrow focus is understandable given that in advertising and marketing context it is prevalent to emphasize on the positive features. However, consumers with limited resource in real life often find themselves in situations where they face the choice between two undesirable options. For example, first time home buyers Sam and his wife Carol can only afford houses in a certain price range even after both taking multiple part-time jobs. They have to take a relatively older house in a less than ideal neighbourhood in order to take advantage of the tax credit before its deadline. Therefore, they must decide whether to select the open house that just came to the market today or the previous house that they remembered from an earlier visit. Apparently constrained by time, money, and energy, consumers may have to choose between the bad options when the good ones are simply not available. Further, consumers may use the comparison between the undesirable attributes as their strategy in considering the tradeoffs and choosing products that are similar in terms of positive attributes.

The current research adds to the body of mixed choice research by investigating the role of attribute valence in consumers' preferences on both positive and negative tasks. Valence has been shown to play an important role in shaping theories of consumer behavior (e.g. Ahluwalia 2002; Brenner, Rottenstreich, Sood, and Bilgin 2007; Dhar and Simonson 1992; Nicolao, Irwin, and Goodman 2008). We predict that consumers' choice pattern is contingent upon the valence of attributes used to describe the options in the consideration set. Specifically, consumers are more likely to prefer the stimulus option over the memory option when they are described by attractive attribute, which is consistent with the conservative bias suggested in prior research (Alba et al. 1992; Biehal and Chakravarti 1983, 1986). In contrast, consumers are more likely to prefer the memory option over the stimulus option when the options are described by negative attributes. This is because consumers' inability to recollect the complete information of the memory option decreases the extremity of either positive or negative attribute. Therefore the imperfect memory makes the positive memory option less positive, leading consumers to prefer the stimulus option; and makes the negative memory option less negative, leading them to prefer the memory option.

In the next section we elaborate on how attribute valence may influence consumer preference in mixed choice through memory imperfection. We then test the hypotheses and the mechanism in three experiments using different mixed choice scenarios. We conclude by discussing the findings and directions for future research.

Biehal and Chakravarti (1983) represents the first formal investigation of situations in which information of different options in a consideration set is partly externally available and partly in one's memory. They found that when consumers did not have the perfect memory for all the aspects of a previously encountered brand, they tended to favor the fully observable brand, often leading to suboptimal choices. Specifically, they attribute the differences in choice outcomes to the differences in memory accessibility induced by manipulating learning goals at information encoding. Alba et al. (1992) referred to this finding as a conservative bias. In their examination, they found that this tendency to "overvalue" externally present information at the time of choice can be reversed when characteristics of the alternatives lead to a superior retrospective evaluation. Specifically, when abstract claims or a large number of attributes are used, consumers form superior evaluations about the memory brand, because abstract beliefs and number of arguments are easier to recall than detailed attribute information.

The current research investigates the role of attribute valence in mixed choice and suggests that consumers' choice pattern is contingent upon the valence of attributes used to describe the options in the consideration set that that the preference pattern is explained by imperfect memory retrieval. Specifically, we predict that consumers are more likely to prefer the stimulus option over the memory option when they are described by attractive attribute, which is consistent with the conservative bias suggested in prior research (Alba et al. 1992; Biehal and Chakravarti 1983, 1986). In contrast, consumers are more likely to prefer the memory option over the stimulus option when the options are described by negative attributes. This is because consumers' inability to recollect the complete information of the memory option decreases the extremity of either positive or negative attribute. Therefore the imperfect memory retrieval makes the positive memory option less positive, leading consumers to prefer the stimulus option; and makes the negative memory option less negative, leading them to prefer the memory option.

# EXPERIMENT 1

Experiment 1 provides an initial investigation into the effects of attribute valence in a mixed choice situation. Participants read information about two used cars described either in terms of attractive or unattractive features. We reasoned that while participants have full information about the stimulus option, they have only imperfect information about the memory option. By that we mean that participants can only recall some, but not all the features of the memory option. When options are described in terms of attractive features, not remembering some of the features decrease the relative attractiveness of the memory option, as participants would see fewer reasons to choose it. This in turn should lead to a preference for the stimulus option. Conversely, when options are described by unattractive features, this imperfect recollection actually helps the memory option, as it gives fewer reasons to reject it. In this case, participants can see all the unattractive features of stimulus option, but can only access some of the unattractive features of the memory option.

## Stimuli and pre-test

One-hundred and twelve business undergraduate students from a large Midwestern University evaluated the attractiveness or unattractiveness of 15 fifteen possible features of a used car. Half of the participants were asked to consider they were buying a car in a tight budget and evaluated how much each of the negative features presented (e.g., "the passenger door does only open from the inside," "the heater is very weak and helps very little in winter," "there is a crack in the windshield (but no leak)") would bother them in a nine point scale from "1-would not bother me at all" to "9-would be a complete deal breaker." The other half considered a series of positive features (e.g., "it has a sliding glass sunroof," "the painting has a beautiful finish") and rated how much each would please them on a nine point scale from "1-I wouldn't mind at all" to "9-This would be really good".

Based on these ratings, we created two profiles for attractive used cars, each described by six desirable features (all averages between 5.0 and 7.5). Conversely, we combined two sets of six undesirable features (all averages between 5.0 and 7.5) to create two unattractive used car profiles. The complete stimuli are presented in the Appendix.

In the attractive cars condition, participants were told that the car was a little beyond their budget, but it had a series of nice features. In the unattractive cars condition, participants were told that they were on a tight budget and despite these inconveniences, their mechanic had guaranteed that the car would last at least until they graduated.

## Method

*Design.* We employed a 2 (features attractiveness: positive vs. negative) x 2 (order of presentation: A→B vs. B→A) between-subject design.

*Participants and Procedure.* Eighty-nine business undergraduate students from a large Midwestern University completed this experiment in partial fulfillment of a course research requirement. The experiment was conducted on computer stations using the Medialab interface. Participants were directed to a computer station to complete the experiment and randomly assigned to one of the four conditions. Participants read a scenario in which they were asked to consider the purchase of a used car. They read the description of the first car at their own pace and clicked to continue to an unrelated study, which served as a filler task for our experiment. After completing the filler task, which took approximately 10 minutes, participants were presented with a second used car and asked to make a choice between the option they saw in the beginning of the session and the one presented at the time of choice. Finally, they were asked to type all they could remember about the first alternative.

## Results

We ran a logit model to predict choice of alternative A using valence of features and order of presentation (i.e. whether option A was presented first or second) as independent factors. There was a marginally significant effect for valence ($X^2(1) = 2.93$, p = .087) and marginally significant effect for order ($X^2(1) = 3.10$, p = .078). More importantly, we found a significant interaction ($X^2(1) = 9.65$, p < .01), indicating that the effect of order is moderated by valence of the attributes.

In order to understand the nature of this moderation, we looked at choice pattern in each set. In the attractive features condition, replicating the finding of previous research (Alba et al. 1992; Biehal and Chakravarti 1983), we found a tendency to prefer the stimulus option, as the choice share of option A increased from 50% when it was the memory option to 63% when it was the present option (consequently the share of option B increased from 37% to 50% as it shifted from memory to present). In other words, on average, a stimulus option was chosen 57% of the times. This difference however, failed to reach significance ($\chi^2(1) = .73$, n.s.). More importantly, in the unattractive features condition, we found support for our hypothesis. The choice share of option A shifted from 37% when it was the stimulus option to 84% when it was the memory option ($\chi^2(1) = 14.77$, p < .01). Thus, on average, a memory alternative was chosen 74% of the time.

In order to be able to attribute this pattern to memory, as opposed to mere order of presentation, we turned to the analysis of the free recall measure. If our theory is correct, we should find stronger effects for those with worse memory. For each set, we counted the number of items recalled by each participant and created two groups based on a median-split. Those in the poor memory group (n = 44) recalled up to 2 features, while those in the good memory group (n = 45) recalled 3 or more features. For each set, we ran a logit model using order and recall group as independent factors. For the attractive set, we found a significant interaction ($\chi^2(1) = 3.83$, p < .05) between order and recall, indicating that participants with better memory behaved differently than those with worse memory. Specifically, in the good memory group (n = 26), only 40% of participants chose the stimulus option, while 70% of those in the poor memory group (n = 15) did the same, suggesting that those with worse memory are more likely to choose a stimulus option. Order of presentation had no effect ($\chi^2(1) = .41$, n.s.) and there was a marginal main effect for recall group, which has no theoretical significance ($\chi^2(1) = 2.81$, p = .094). For the unattractive set, we fail to find an interaction between order and recall group ($\chi^2(1) = .13$, n.s.).

## Discussion

Results from our first experiment provided initial support for our hypothesis about the role of attribute valence on mixed choice. We hypothesized that a preference for a stimulus option observed in previous research would only manifest when attributes were attractive, while the reverse would occur when attributes were unattractive. Consistent with our hypothesis, our data showed a strong preference for the memory option in the unattractive set (74%). Results from the attractive set were consistent with those observed in previous research, indicating a preference for the stimulus option. However, our analysis based on memory performance failed to establish the role of memory in the unattractive set, as those with poor memory were just as likely to choose the memory option as those with good memory. In addition, we found evidence for the role of memory, as the tendency to prefer the stimulus option only manifested in the group with poor memory.

## EXPERIMENT 2

We designed Experiment 2 with two goals. First, we sought to replicate the choice pattern obtained in Experiment 1 using a different choice category. Second, the initial experiment only showed evidence for the role of memory in the attractive set condition. In this second experiment, we looked for the corresponding evidence for the unattractive set.

### Stimulus and pre-test

For this experiment, we used a set of jobs as the stimuli. We believe this is a relevant consumer behavior context to the extent that successful companies try to market themselves to prospective employees that face a choice between two or more jobs. This category has also been used in previous consumer behavior research (Brenner et al. 2007, Tversky and Kahneman 1991) and provides a good test for the generalizability of the effect.

We followed the same procedure used in Experiment 1 pretesting the stimuli. Participants evaluated the attractiveness or unattractiveness of fifteen possible features of a job they would take upon graduation. Based on these ratings, we created two sets of profiles. As in Experiment 1, none of the profiles was completely attractive or completely unattractive. In the unattractive set, each job was described by five unattractive features, but it had a nice salary. The attractive set on the other hand, was described on five attractive features, but had a lower salary. All options are described in the Appendix.

### Method

*Design.* We employed a 2 (valence of features: attractive vs. unattractive) x 2 (order of presentation: A→B vs. B→A) between-subject design.

*Participants and Procedure.* Eighty-three business undergraduate students from a large Midwestern University completed this experiment in partial fulfillment of a course research requirement. The experiment was conducted on computer stations using the Medialab interface. Participants were directed to a computer station to complete the experiment and randomly assigned to one of the four conditions. Participants read a scenario in which they were about to graduate and were considering a choice between two job offers. They read the description of the first job at their own pace and clicked to continue to an unrelated study, which served as a filler task for our experiment. After completing the filler task, which took approximately 10 minutes, participants were presented with a second job offer and asked to make a choice between the option they saw in the beginning of the session and the one presented at the time of choice. After this selection, participants were asked to type as much as they could remember about the first offer.

### Results

Following the analysis of Experiment 1, we ran a logit model to predict choice of A using order and valence as the predictors. As hypothesized, we found a significant interaction effect between order and valence ($\chi^2(1) = 12.11$, p < .001). The effect of valence was marginally significant ($\chi^2(1) = 3.11$, p = .078) and there was no effect for order ($\chi^2(1) = .66$, n.s.).

In the attractive features set, the choice share of option A increased from 33% to 60% as it shifted from memory to present ($\chi^2(1) = 3.16$, p = .075), representing an average of 63% choice share for the stimulus option. In the unattractive features set, the pattern was reversed: the choice share of option A shifted from 43% when it was the present option to 86% when it was the memory option ($\chi^2(1) = 10.50$, p < .01). Thus, on average, the memory option received 71% of the choices. These results replicate those of Experiment 1 showing the conservative bias for attractive features, but the reverse for the unattractive ones.

As in Experiment 1, we coded the number of items participants recalled and performed a median-split to create two groups for each set. Participants that recalled fewer than 3 features were considered the poor memory group (n = 37), whereas those that recalled 3 or more made up the good memory group (n = 46). For each set, we ran a logit model using recall group, order and their interaction as the predictors. In the attractive set, we found a significant interaction ($\chi^2(1) = 11.16$, p < .001). Participants in the good memory group (n = 17) selected the stimulus option only 57% of the time, compared to an 88% selection from the poor memory group (n = 24). There was also significant main effect for order ($\chi^2(1) = 6.12$, p < .05), indicating an overall tendency to prefer the stimulus option, and a main effect of recall group ($\chi^2(1) = 5.28$, p < .05), which has no theoretical significance. For the unattractive set, although there was a tendency for a stronger effect in the poor memory group compared to the good memory group (77% vs. 88%), the interaction failed to reach significance ($\chi^2(1) = .92$, n.s.).

### Discussion

Experiment 2 had two purposes. First, it aimed to provide a test of our hypothesis in a new context, namely choice between job offers. Results replicated those observed in experiment 1. That is, participants tend to prefer the stimulus option over the memory option when considering attractive attributes; where as they tend to prefer the memory option when considering unattractive attributes. Second, we sought evidence that poor memory for the initial option was driving the effect in both sets. As in Experiment 1, we found evidence of it for the attractive features set, as only those in the poor memory group (recall below median) displayed the effect. However, in the unattractive features set, the predicted pattern was not significant.

Although our first two experiments showed a strong reversal in the conservative bias, we have yet to demonstrate the role of memory. In addition, there is an important alternative explanation that deserves attention. As we reasoned before, in a mixed choice scenario, consumers have full information about the stimulus option, but unless one has perfect memory, there is only limited information about a memory option. This asymmetry of information may be interpreted as a choice between a safe option, for which all information is available, and a risky one for which only partial information is available. In fact, the term "conservative bias" given by Alba et al. (1992) to the pattern obtained by Biehal and Chakravarti (1983) suggests a risk avoidance interpretation of the phenomenon.

In the development of prospect theory, Kahneman and Tversky (1979) showed that individuals tend to be risk averse in the domain of gains, but risk seeking in the domain of losses. If participants interpret a mixed choice situation as a risky decision, this pattern of risk aversion and risk seeking would lead to the exact same pattern that we observed in our experiments. When consumers face a choice between attractive features, they are assumed to be choosing in the domain of gains, and therefore should be risk averse and choose the safe option, which would be the stimulus option in our study. However, when consumers face a decision involving negative features, they should be risk seeking and prefer safe option, which would be the memory option. Although our hypothesis stays the same, this could be an alternative explanation. We examine this risk-based explanation in the next experiment.

## EXPERIMENT 3

We designed Experiment 3 with three goals in mind. First, we wanted to test the risk-based alternative explanation. Second, we sought to obtain evidence for the role of memory in the negative set that was not shown in the previous experiments. To that end, we decided to use recognition task as a more sensitive memory measure as opposed to the free recall used in Experiments 1 and 2. In addition, we doubled the sample size to make sure that there would be enough power for the analysis. Third, we wanted to provide further test of generalizability using a different choice category.

### Stimulus and pre-test

Thirty-seven business undergraduate students from a large Midwestern University completed this experiment in partial fulfillment of a course research requirement. The procedure followed those of Experiments 1 and 2 with participants evaluating 15 positive and 15 negative characteristics of apartments that they would be renting. Based on these ratings we created two attractive profiles, which were described on seven positive features, but had the disadvantage of being expensive. Conversely, two unattractive profiles were created in which each apartment had seven undesirable features, but had a good price. All descriptions are presented in the Appendix.

### Method

*Design.* We employed a 2 (features attractiveness: positive vs. negative) x 2 (order of presentation: A→B vs. B→A) between-subject design.

*Participants and Procedure.* One-hundred and ninety-two business undergraduate students from a large Midwestern University completed this experiment in partial fulfillment of a course research requirement. Participants were directed to a computer station to complete the experiment and were randomly assigned to one of the four conditions. Participants read a scenario in which they had just graduated and were moving to a big and expensive city. They were looking for an apartment, but didn't have much time. They were presented with the description of the first apartment, which they read at their own pace. They then continued to the next unrelated study, which took approximately 10 minutes and served as a filler task for our experiment. After completing the filler task, participants read the description of the second apartment. In the next screen, while they could still read the description of the second apartment, participants were asked to choose one of the two apartments that they have seen. After that, as a test of the risk explanation, participants rated their agreement with the following statements on a seven-point scale: "choosing the first option is riskier," "choosing the first option involves more uncertainty," and "choosing the second option is safer." Then, participants were asked to explain what went through their minds as they made their choice. Finally, participants performed a recognition task. In a series of 13 screens, we randomly presented the seven attributes that were used to describe the first apartment and the six foil attributes that were not used to describe either apartment. Participants were asked to indicate whether each attribute described the first apartment and their confidence on a five-point scale: "1-completely confident it is true;" "2-somewhat confident it is true;" "3-completely unsure;" "4-somewhat confident is false;" "5-completely confident it is false".

## Results

*Choice.* As in Experiments 1 and 2, we ran a logit model to predict choice of A using order and valence as the independent variables. As predicted, we found a significant interaction between order and valence ($\chi^2(1) = 22.54$, $p < .001$). None of the main effects were significant (order: $\chi^2(1) = .33$, $p > .70$; valence: $\chi^2(1) = .70$, $p > .40$).

Despite our efforts to create equally attractive options in each set through the pre-test, there was clear preference for option B in each set. In extreme cases, an unbalanced set, in which one option is much more attractive than another, decreases the power of any manipulation due to the formation of strong preferences. Choice effects are easier to detect when options are perceived as similarly attractive, so that experimental manipulations can tip preferences one way or the other. However, we note that although this unbalance may decrease the power of our experiment, it does not affect the conclusions from our analyses, as we are not interested in the overall preference for a given option, but how this preference differs when it is the memory option versus when it is the stimulus option.

In the attractive features set, we found that the choice share of option A increased from 12% to 39% as it shifted from memory to present ($\chi^2(1) = 9.73$, $p < .01$), representing an average of 64% choice share for the stimulus option. In the unattractive features set, the pattern was reversed: the choice share of option A shifted from 15% when it was the present option to 47% when it was the memory option ($\chi^2(1) = 12.94$, $p < .01$). In other words, a memory option received 66% of the choices. These results replicate the pattern observed in the previous experiments.

*Memory.* We computed a recognition index by summing the scores for the true attributes, subtracting the scores for the false attributes and inverting the sign of the score. A person with a perfect memory should be completely confident that attributes that described the first option are true, and completely confident that attributes that do not describe the first option are false. Therefore, this person should answer "1-completely confident it is true" for all seven attributes of the memory option and "5-completely confident it is false" for every false attribute. This person would have a score of 1 x 7 (7 real attributes) – 5 x 6 (6 foil attributes) = -23. We invert the sign of the score, so that better memory coincides with higher scores. A perfect memory gets a score of 23. On the other extreme, a person that was completely confident and wrong in all attributes would get a score of $-(5 \times 7 - 1 \times 6) = -29$. In our data, the scores ranged from -11 to 23 with a median of 12.

For each set we ran a model using order and the recognition score to predict choice of option A. In the attractive features set, consistent with the pattern obtained in our previous experiments using free recall, we found a significant interaction between memory and order ($X^2(16) = 35.99$, $p < .001$). More importantly, in the unattractive features set, we also obtained a significant interaction ($X^2(16) = 34.76$, $p < .001$). We can illustrate the nature of this interaction comparing the group with recognition score below the median to the group with scores above the median. In the attractive features set, 56% of participants in the good memory group (n = 44) preferred the stimulus option compared to 70% from the poor memory group (n = 45). In the unattractive features set, the memory option was preferred by only 56% of those in the good memory group (n = 50), compared to 74% of those from the poor memory group (n = 43).

*Risk statements.* We used four statements to capture the extent to which participants viewed this situation as a risky decision. Participants rated their agreement on seven-point scales and we tested whether the average was significantly different from the midpoint of the scale. For each statement in each set, we mean-centered the answers and ran an ANOVA using order as the independent factor. For ease of exposure, we report the means using the original seven-point scales.

In the attractive features condition, there was no support for a risk perspective. On average, participants disagreed that "choosing the first option is riskier" (M = 3.55, F(1,88) = 10.81, p < .01) and displayed no significant tendency for the other two statements ("choosing the first option involves more uncertainty", M = 3.84, F(1,88)=1.09, p>.3; "choosing the second option is safer", M=4.13, F(1,88) = .89, p >.3 ). In every analysis, the order was significant, which means that in addition to considering whether an option was the memory or the stimulus one, participants' answers were also affected by the specific alternative. All answers were consistent with the higher attractiveness of option B, which as discussed before has no theoretical value. As indicated, the analyses reported here control for this difference in attractiveness.

In the unattractive features condition, there was also no support for a risk perspective. In all three statements, the average was not significantly different from the midpoint of the scale ("choosing the first option is riskier," M = 3.84, F(1,92) = 1.10, p > .29; "choosing the first option involves more uncertainty," M = 3.89, F(1,92) = .38, p >.50). There was a marginally significant disagreement with one statement ("choosing the second option is safer," M = 3.74, F(1,92) = 2.89, p = .092), which is also not consistent with a risk interpretation. Order was significant for all statements except for "choosing the second option is safer," but as discussed before, this has no theoretical relevance.

**Discussion**

Results from Experiment 3 successfully replicate the pattern observed in the previous experiments using apartment as a new category for the mixed choice situation. In other words, participants are more likely to choose the stimulus option rather than the memory option when they are exposed to options described by attractive attributers, while the reverse would occur when attributes were unattractive. This experiment further strengthened our hypothesis from four aspects. First, it served as another test of our hypothesis in a new context, namely choice between job offers, and replicated the findings observed in experiments 1 and 2. Second, it provides further evidence that poor memory for the initial option was driving the effect in both attractive and unattractive sets. Moreover, using a more sensitive memory measure (recognition), this experiment showed significant evidence for the role of memory in the unattractive features set, which we had not found in previous experiments using free recall. Last but not least, the results in support of our memory-based hypothesis rejected the alternative risk-based explanation. We asked participants to rate their agreement with statements that framed the decision as a risky choice. The results showed that there was no tendency of agreement with any of the statements. Therefore, we conclude that there is no support for a risk-based explanation.

**Conclusion**

Across the three experiments, we find converging evidence for our hypothesis that in a mixed choice situation, failure to recall specific features affects choice in a systematic way. If participants fail to recall positive features, their evaluation deteriorates and there is a tendency to favor a stimulus alternative. Conversely if participants cannot recall negative features, their evaluation improves and the memory option is favored. We further established the memory-based mechanism and suggest the preference pattern is driven by imperfect information retrieval. Specifically, consumers with good memory are less likely to demonstrate the conservative bias when choosing from options with attractive features and less likely to

demonstrate the reversed bias when choosing from options with unattractive features. In other words, consumers with good memory are less likely to prefer the stimulus option than those with poor memory in the attractive set; they are also less likely to prefer the memory option than those with poor memory in the unattractive set.

As suggested by Feldman and Lynch (1988), information accessibility is determined by a range of different factors, such as the time delay, the level of interference, message elaboration, and motivation to process the information. Future research could consider how these factors influence the retrieval process and the preference pattern. For example, because information retrieval is largely determined by the cues in the environment in making a particular decision (Lynch and Srull 1982; Tulvinig and Psotka 1971), there is a possibility that providing cues may induce a different preference pattern. In the current study, memory quality was measured as a personal trait. Future research could employ retrieval cues as a manipulation of enhanced memory. It is likely that participants who were exposed to the pictures of the choice set may tend to retrieve more information from memory and exhibit less conservative bias comparing with those who were not exposed to the pictures. What's more, Biehal and Chakravarti (1986) showed that information that was processed more was recalled more accurately in a subsequent cured recall test. In other words, brand-attribute information that receives more processing is remembered better. Future research could manipulate the memory accuracy by having participants engage in more or less information processing when they are exposed to the memory option.

**REFERENCES**

Ahluwalia, Rohini (2002) "How Prevalent is the Negativity Effect in Consumer Environments?" Journal of Consumer Research, 29 (September), 270-279.

Alba, Joseph W., Howard Marmorstein, and Amitava Chatto-padhyay (1992) "Transitions in Preference Over Time: The Effects of Memory on Message Persuasiveness," Journal of Marketing Research, 29 (November), 406-416.

Biehal, Gabriel and Dipankar Chakravarti (1983), "Information Accessibility as a Moderator of Consumer Choice," Journal of Consumer Research, 10 (June), 1-14.

Biehal, Gabriel and Dipankar Chakravarti (1986), "Consumers' Use of Memory and External Information in Choice: Macro and Micro Perspectives," Journal of Consumer Research, 12 (March), 382-405.

Brenner, Lyle, Yuval Rottenstreich, Sanjay Sood and Baler Bilgin (2007), "On the Psychology of Loss Aversion: Possession, Valence, and Reversal of Endowment Effect," Journal of Consumer Research, 34 (October), 369-376.

Dhar, Ravi and Itamar Simonson (1992), "The Effect of the Focus of Comparison on Consumer Preferences," Journal of Marketing Research 29 (November), 430–441.

Dick, Alan, Dipankar Chakravarti, and Gabriel Biehal (1990), "Memory-Based Inferences during Consumer Choice," Journal of Consumer Research, 17 (June), 82-93.

Kahneman, Daniel and Amos Tversky (1979), "Prospect Theory: An Analysis of Decision under Risk," Econometrica, 47 (March), 263-292.

Lynch, John G., Jr. and Thomas K. Srull (1982), "Memory and Attentional Factors in Consumer Choice: Concepts and Research Methods," Journal of Consumer Research, 9 (June), 18-37.

Lynch, John G., Jr., Howard Marmorstein, and Michael F. Weigold (1988), "Choice From Sets Including Remembered Brands: Use of Recalled Attributes and Prior Overall Evaluations," Journal of Consumer Research, 15 (September), 169-184.

Nicolao, Leonardo, Julie R. Irwin and Joseph K. Goodman (2008), "Happiness for Sale: Do Experiential Purchases Make Consumers Happier than Material Purchases?" Journal of Consumer Research, 36 (August), 188-198.

# APPENDIX

## USED CARS (EXPERIMENT 1) ATTRACTIVE FEATURES SET

**Option A**
- It is quite fuel efficient for its category.
- It comes with very classy trim and interior design.
- It has a sleek and modern style.
- It comes with one year free subscription of satellite radio.
- It has a sliding glass sunroof.
-

**Option B**
- There is a lot of storage space in the trunk.
- The acceleration is short and smooth.
- It has a video monitor for reverse driving.
- The painting has a beautiful finish.
- It comes with a 100,000 mile warranty and road-side service.

## USED CARS (EXPERIMENT 1) UNATTRACTIVE FEATURES SET

**Option A**
- The passenger's door only opens from the inside.
- The heater is very weak and helps very little in winter.
- The radio works, but it doesn't play CDs.
- The paint fell off on a few spots on the hood.
- The window does not close properly and you have to push it with your hand for it to fit in the frame.

**Option B**
- The engine is not very powerful.
- There is a crack in the windshield (but no leak).
- It is burning some oil, requiring you to add oil more frequently.
- It takes a long time for the air conditioning to take effect.
- The car trembles at high speed.

## JOB OFFERS (EXPERIMENT 2) ATTRACTIVE FEATURES SET

**Option A**
- The company is located in a nice area where the weather is always sunny and pleasant.
- The working hours are very flexible. You can decide when you want to start and finish your work day as long as you accomplish the 8 hours.
- You will have 14 days of paid vacation every year and it is accumulative across years. It is up to you how you want to allocate it.
- The company frequently offers training and consulting programs in order to develop your long-term career.
- Employees are encouraged to think creatively.
- There are opportunities to work overseas for those interested in it.

**Option B**
- The company is located in a very safe neighborhood. Transportation to and from work is very convenient.
- Your office will be located in a central area of the city, close to bars, restaurants, and health clubs.
- Employees never do overtime or work on weekends.
- It is a growing company. Many of the recent hires are in your age group. You have the option of joining a mentoring program designed for the new comers.
- Most people in the upper management were promoted within the company.
- The job offer package also offers a very good retirement plan.

## JOB OFFERS (EXPERIMENT 2) UNATTRACTIVE FEATURES SET

**Option A**
- The company is located in a small town, which is more than an hour away from any metropolitan area.
- The weather is quite rainy and cloudy.
- Due to the nature of the industry, your work hours are fixed from 5am-2pm and have little flexibility.
- You have 7 days of paid vacation every year and it is not accumulative across years.
- The decision making in this company seems to be very centralized.
- There is a strong and rigid hierarchy, so there wouldn't be much contact with upper management.

**Option B**
- The company is located in a not very safe neighborhood. Robberies are not uncommon in the area.
- Winters are long and very cold.
- Employees tend to do a lot of overtime are often expected to work on weekends.
- The company does not tend to provide much training or career development.
- The company has no policy regarding retirement plan.
- There doesn't seem to be many people in your age group.

## APARTMENTS (EXPERIMENT 3) ATTRACTIVE FEATURES SET

**Option A**
- There is beautiful park nearby.
- There are plenty of good restaurants in the area.
- The apartment is in a new and modern building.
- Virtually no outside noise can be heard when the windows are shut.
- There is free high speed wireless Internet.
- The apartment receives plenty of natural light.
- The living room is spacious and well illuminated.

**Option B**
- The apartment has a nice view to a lake.
- All kitchen appliances are new.
- Public transportation to this area is very convenient.
- The bedroom is very spacious.
- Most neighbors are young professionals like you.
- The building has a well equipped gym.
- The apartment is in a beautiful and renovated building.

## APARTMENTS (EXPERIMENT 3) UNATTRACTIVE FEATURES SET

**Option A**
- The apartment is in the 4th floor and there are no elevators in the building.
- The street has very poor lighting.
- It is a long commute from your work.
- There are no restaurants nearby.
- The street is very busy and noisy.
- The living room gets almost no sun light.
- There are no grocery stores nearby.

**Option B**
- The apartment only has a view to an internal patio.
- The heater is not strong enough to completely warm up the place.
- One of your neighbors plays trumpet during the day.
- The kitchen has very few cabinets.
- Traffic is intense in the area.
- The water pressure in the shower is somewhat low.
- It has two very small bedrooms, instead of a good sized one.

# Introducing the WOM Transmitter in Generational Word of Mouth:
## Why Consumers Refuse to Transmit Positive or Negative Word of Mouth

Florian Dost, ESCP EUROPE Campus Berlin, Germany
Jens Sievert, ESCP EUROPE Campus Berlin, Germany
Martin Oetting, TRND.com, Germany

## ABSTRACT

Taking a transmitter's perspective, this study identifies reasons to refuse word of mouth (WOM) transmission, creates a category system and analyzes the influence of either positive or negative WOM. We show that the transmission of negative WOM is refused more often, a result which is mainly driven by social constraints.

## INTRODUCTION

Word of mouth (WOM) has become increasingly popular, both among marketing academics and marketing practitioners. While academics tend to focus on the generation of WOM (Oetting 2009), the excitement of practitioners more relates to the fact that WOM is spread by transmission. The rationale behind this is that network effects, also called contagion or viral effects, create powerful and potentially costless benefits, as WOM spreads across multiple generations of communicators (Carl, Libai and Ding 2008). However, knowledge on the individual processes of transmission is scarce. Moreover knowledge on why consumers might choose not to transmit and thus inhibit network effects is missing. Research on the WOM transmitter has been largely neglected on an individual level: Most previous studies on transmission focus on a network perspective (Bass 1969; Coleman, Katz and Menzel 1957). Additionally most past research is about successful WOM communication only. This is particularly surprising as it is already known that WOM transmission is a deliberative process (Banerjee & Fudenberg 2008), which implies that a transmitter will not only reason his decision to transmit but also might reason against it. Transmission refusal is therefore a key in understanding transmission process.

Moreover, despite extensive literature on positive and negative WOM, it is not known how WOM valence might influence whether WOM gets transmitted at all.

This study aims at exploring this gap by answering the following research questions:

1. What are reasons for a transmitter to refuse WOM transmission?
2. Do PWOM and NWOM have a different impact on transmission refusal?
3. If so, what are the reasons for this different impact of PWOM and NWOM?

Our study is mainly explorative in nature. Taking the perspective of the WOM transmitter, we aim at identifying and categorizing the reasons for transmission refusal. In order to do so, precise definition and clarification of terms are mandatory, followed by a review of relevant literature, the study design and then the study results. Implications are presented at the end of the paper.

## WORD OF MOUTH TRANSMISSION
### Word of Mouth, Positive and Negative Word of Mouth

Word of mouth is "a process of personal influence, in which interpersonal communications between a sender and a receiver can change the receiver's behavior or attitudes" (Sweeney, Soutar and Mazzarol 2008, 345). We additionally introduce a third party to the sender and the receiver which we call "the transmitter". We will explain why we do so in the subsequent section.

Throughout this paper we will use the term 'WOM impact' to describe any effect that is caused by WOM and the term WOM topic when referring to the actual content of the WOM message. When referring to the tone of the WOM message, we will restrict this to WOM valence. Most researchers divide WOM according to its valence into positive word of mouth (PWOM) and negative word of mouth (NWOM). We will also use this distinction.

### WOM Transmission and Transmitter's Perspective

Unlike most prior WOM research we will take the perspective of the so-called WOM "transmitter", an intermediary of WOM. WOM transmission occurs when a WOM message generated by a sender is received by a transmitter and then passed on to another receiver. The transmitter himself acts on a dual role as he is first a receiver and then a sender. The WOM roles of sender, transmitter and receiver are shown in figure 1. We take the transmitters' perspective for two reasons. First, the unique feature of WOM is that WOM is frequently transmitted. This is known as contagion, viral, or cascade effect (Coleman et al.1957). Secondly, prior research has focused on dyadic WOM between sender and receiver. While this approach is useful when describing the antecedents of original WOM generation (sender) or the impact of WOM (receiver), it implies that the mere transmission of the WOM would be actually a generation of new WOM by the former receiver.

Taking the transmitter's perspective incorporates existing knowledge on WOM generation, but also allows for a simple WOM transmission as in the case of viral campaigns.

**FIGURE 1**
**The Roles of WOM Sender, Transmitter and Receiver**

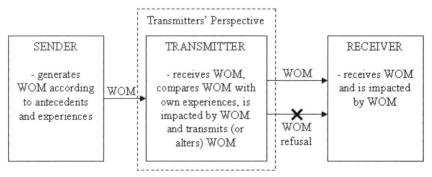

# LITERATURE REVIEW
## Reasons for WOM Transmission

A broad body of literature focuses on transmission processes, such as diffusion studies (Bass 1969) or studies on social contagion (Coleman et al. 1957). However the focus is on aggregate measures and network characteristics, neglecting the individual processes (Bansal and Voyer 2000). Only few works provided some insights into individual WOM transmission processes. Most important is that the transmitter's decision to engage in WOM transmission is deliberate (Banerjee and Fudenberg 2004; Stephen and Lehmann 2009). WOM is transmitted because it can lead to potential social benefits but it also involves risks if transmitted WOM is incorrect, not helpful, or not wanted. Therefore WOM transmission is selective (Stephen and Lehmann 2009). Transmission depends on the motivation or willingness of the transmitter to share WOM (Granovetter 1973; Frenzen and Nakamoto 1993). Moreover, it is particularly surprising that most research is about successful WOM communication only, implying that transmission refusal occurs in the absence of these antecedents. The fact that transmission refusal might be caused by particular reasons is neglected.

## The Impact of WOM

WOM has an influence on the receiver's perceptions and therefore can lead to changes in judgment and likelihoods of choice (Arndt 1967; Fitzgerald Bone 1995). Regarding brand or product attitude, this is mainly due to an impact in reducing perceived risk (Roselius 1971). Consequently, WOM has a larger impact on consumers' attitudes in riskier categories

Regarding WOM valence, PWOM and NWOM are usually seen as closely similar behaviors (East, Hammond, and Lomax 2008). In contrast, Sweeney et al. (2008) argue that PWOM and NWOM are not homogenous in impact as people vary in their reaction to PWOM and NWOM

Marketers usually believe that NWOM is more common and has more impact than PWOM (East, Hammond, and Wright 2007). Still, there is an ongoing debate on the effect of WOM valence (East et al. 2008; Stephen and Lehmann 2009): Some works (e.g. Arndt 1967) support that NWOM might have a larger impact than PWOM. In contrast, East et al. (2008) state that the positive effect PWOM exerts on purchase probability is larger than the negative impact NWOM exerts on purchase probability. Other studies find that positive and negative information have much the same impact size on brand attitudes (Ahluwalia, Burnkrant, and Unnava 2000; Ahluwalia 2002). However, these works do not refer specifically to an impact on WOM transmission. We have to distinguish between the WOM impact on receiver's attitudes and the WOM impact on WOM transmission (Merton 1968). Therefore we will turn to the underlying explanations for different impacts of PWOM and NWOM. We should also note that any impact on a receiver is somehow intertwined with the impact on transmission. This transmitted impact is often referred to as „ripple effect"(Gremler and Brown 1999; Sweeney et al. 2008; Oetting 2009), a multiplication effect of WOM that is not part of the current study.

Skowronski and Carlston (1989) find that negative information has a stronger impact on judgment than positive information and is therefore more persuasive. One reason for a greater diagnostic value of negative information is its rarity, compared to positive information (Anderson 1965; Chevalier and Mayzlin 2003; Mizerski 1982). Also, people prefer diagnostic information to more accessible ones (Lynch, Marmorstein, and Weigold 1988). With social desirability effects favoring recall of positive information (Fisher 1993), PWOM gets more accessible and is thus less preferred.

Given a higher diagnostic value of NWOM, we should expect that NWOM is more likely to be transmitted. However, social desirability may also let consumers avoid NWOM (Rosen and Tesser 1972), resulting in higher rates of NWOM transmission refusal.

Another explanation for the impact dominance of NWOM is the attribution effect (Mizerski 1982). Consumers attribute an adversary motive to positive information. They think for example that positive information might be arranged. Now one would expect PWOM to result in more transmission refusal. However, attribution is not by definition restricted to positive information. Our research questions refer to that overall ambiguity.

## Antecedents of WOM Generation and Transmission

Research on WOM antecedents is restricted to WOM generation. While generated WOM starts with the sender as a reaction to any antecedent, transmitted WOM is passed on or altered after the event of received WOM. However, as the transmitter is also a sender, we argue that antecedents of original WOM generation may also influence WOM transmission.

*Valence as Antecedent.* Satisfaction and dissatisfaction are the main sources for PWOM and NWOM, respectively (Richins 1983). Dissatisfied consumers produce more WOM than satisfied consumers (Hanna and Wosniak 2001; Silverman 1997). A contradictory finding says that satisfied customers outnumber dissatisfied customers (Mittal and Lassar 1998). Still, East et al.(2007) show that in general, PWOM exceeds NWOM. We therefore also propose a higher occurrence of PWOM than WOM:

Proposition 1: PWOM occurrence exceeds NWOM occurrence.

Also Anderson (1998) states that WOM generation is higher for dissatisfied consumers and that extremely satisfied or dissatisfied consumers spread WOM most. Remarkably, about 80% consumers that were neither satisfied nor dissatisfied still engage in WOM generation of the more extreme cases. This is a general tendency for WOM generation or engagement that is not explained by satisfaction or dissatisfaction. According to Mangold, Miller, and Brockway (1999), satisfaction or dissatisfaction account for only 12% of all WOM generation, whereas over 50% relate to the need for WOM activity. In all, research fails to explain how valence direction relates to WOM generation while it is obvious that valence strength seems just to be one influence on WOM generation among many. Given this dominance of other reasons, such as a need for WOM activity, we expect and propose fewer transmission refusals than transmissions:

Proposition 2: There are fewer WOM transmission refusals than WOM transmissions.

*Intrapersonal Antecedents.* De Matos' and Rossi's (2008) meta-analysis on antecedents of WOM generation reveals that apart from satisfaction, key antecedents of WOM generation are brand or product loyalty, quality, commitment, perceived value,and trust. Most of these factors are intrapersonal to the transmitter. We would expect to see reasons for WOM transmission refusal that are related to such intrapersonal antecedents.

*Interpersonal Antecedents.* Other antecedents such as trust or source credibility lie in the transmitter's perception of the sender. These perceptions can be influential in a WOM context (Bansal and Voyer 2000; Fitzgerald Bone1995). Therefore it is likely that perceptions such as the WOM need of the receiver assumed by the transmitter (Mangold et al.1999) are influential. Another antecedent is the type of relationship between sender and transmitter. Numerous studies have shown an effect of tie strength. The stronger the tie strength the more likely it is that this relationship will be used for WOM communication (Brown and Reingen 1987), and more WOM occurs between close ties such as friends or relatives.

Literature also states an explicit influence of weak ties on WOM transmission (Granovetter 1973). However this explicit influence is not relevant for our study, as it refers to a network perspective, arguing that weak ties foster the wider spread of WOM by means of larger relationship distances. Still we expect to find reasons for transmission refusal that relate either to the transmitter's perceptions of the sender or the receiver's needs or to the closeness of the relationship. As close relationships incorporate intimacy and trust we additionally expect that matters of privacy play a role in transmission refusal.

*Message related Antecedents:* It is known that the style, power, and content of WOM can have an influence on the receiver (Dichter 1966; Herr, Kardes, and Kim 1991). Therefore these WOM message characteristics may be crucial for the decision whether to transmit or not.

*Context related Antecedents:* Time constraints were found to have an effect on WOM generation (Sweeney et al.2008). But to our knowledge there are no studies on an effect of WOM place. However, we expect reasons that refer to context.

## RESEARCH METHOD
### Data Collection and Sample Structure

We collected data using an online questionnaire. Respondents were asked to remember an actual, recent WOM incident and to state details such as topic, category, WOM channel and type of relationship. Perceived WOM valence was measured as the average on three seven-point scale items (Cronbachs Alpha: .94). Respondents were then asked to state whether they would transmit this WOM. Any respondent to refuse WOM transmission was asked to state his top of mind reasons for doing so. The questionnaire was presented to about 200,000 members of a German panel in winter 2009. The panel is one of the biggest professional marketing communities in Europe and specialized in WOM marketing. A total of 31,173 respondents from Germany, Austria, and Switzerland returned the questionnaire resulting in a response rate of about 16% in two weeks.

Because the panel is especially aware of WOM related topics and has conducted several studies with professionally managed WOM, a careful but rigid data cleansing was mandatory with respect to the data validity and generalizability of our results. The elimination was done by an excessive search for all relevant brand or product names, including all spelling mistakes, in all open questions, to excluded any cases related to professional campaigns. Furthermore all cases with incorrect, or incomplete data (any missing values) were removed from the dataset. Regarding valence, the few respondents stating an average of exactly 4.0, and thus perfectly neutral WOM, were also excluded as we could not put them into one group or the other without risking bias.

The mean age of the remaining 19,648 respondents was 29 years (s.d. = 9.10), with a gender distribution of 74.9% female and 25.1% male. Therefore the sample structure was not representative for the German population but neither age nor gender had a main effect on transmission behavior, confirming the general suitability of the sample structure for our study.

### Procedure of Data Analysis

The focus of our research is on the analysis of the open-ended question dealing with the reasons for transmission refusal. We aim at developing a categorization system inductively extracted from the 2,254 textbox answers in order to gain deeper insights into consumers' barriers for transmission of either positive or negative WOM as well as underlying mechanisms of WOM transmission behavior. We took the steps of Mayring's (2000) framework for inductive category development. This procedure is in line with the reductive processes in psychological text processing (van Dijk 1980)

After having defined a scope of research derived from theoretical background and research question (step 1) the material was coded and paraphrased by two independent coders. Then, categories (for details see next section) were formulated (step 2). After having coded 30% of the material, we revised the category scheme (step 3), and in a feedback loop the new categories were applied to the whole material (step 4). Inter-coder differences were always solved by discussion. We then reduced our scheme to main categories (Miles and Huberman 1994; Strauss and Corbin 1990) and coded the material again (step 5). Intra-coder consistency in a final loop check was 97.8%, and simple inter-coder percentage of agreement (Bettman and Park 1980) was 91.2%. The results of the described process were the following main categories: intrapersonal reasons, interpersonal reasons, situation or context related reasons and message or topic related reason. Based on this category scheme, we analyzed relative frequencies of the different subcategories (step 6).

## RESULTS
### Intrapersonal Reasons

*Missing Relevance of Product or WOM Topic to the Transmitter.* Some respondents stated that they are generally not interested in this brand, product, or WOM topic. Exemplary respondent answers are: "Because I'm not interested." "Because I don't need that product."

*Missing Judgment Ability.* Some respondents said that they were not able to evaluate the product, brand, or WOM topic because of too little experience or because of lack of knowledge. Exemplary respondent answers are: "Because […] I couldn't check the product myself." "Because I did not try it for myself and I do not recommend anything I do not know."

*Product or WOM Topic Dislike.* Some respondents disliked the product, brand, or WOM topic. Exemplary respondent answers are: "Because I disliked the taste of it." "The product failed to enthuse me after I tested it."

*Alternative Product or WOM Topic Favorite.* Some respondents expressed their preference or loyalty to another brand, product, or WOM topic as a reason to refuse WOM transmission. Exemplary respondent answers are: "Because I use very good products myself." "Because I am against constantly changing my provider."

*Judgment Differences.* Some respondents said that they hold opposite experiences or attitudes about the brand, product, or WOM topic. Exemplary respondent answers are: "Because my own experience is otherwise." "Because it was a one time event, bad luck."

*Received Information was Forgotten.* Some respondents stated that they were inattentive or had forgotten relevant information. Exemplary respondent answers are: "Because I did not listen well enough." " Because I have forgotten so much."

*No WOM Motivation.* Some respondents said that they did not have a reason to transmit or they expressed missing motivation. Exemplary respondent answers are: "Because I don't want to." "Because I don't have a reason for this." "I don't feel like it."

### Interpersonal Reasons

*Missing Perceived Relevance to Potential Receiver.* Some respondents stated that they do not perceive an interest in the product, brand or WOM topic by anyone who could serve as a potential receiver. Exemplary respondent answers are: "I don't know anyone who would be interested in it." "Because no one I know would buy the product."

*Interpersonal Barriers.* Some respondents said that it was a conversation about private or personal topics, internal information, or private or business secrets and nobody else should or needs to know. Exemplary respondent answers are: "It was about something very private." "It was only intended for myself." "Family matter." "Because it should stay between us."

*Missing Credibility.* Some respondents perceived the sender or the product, brand or WOM topic as not reliable or credible. Some even assumed hidden motives. Exemplary respondent answers are: "Because I don't know if it's true." "He was too pushy."

*Solicitation Expected.* Some respondents said that they are only willing to transmit WOM if a potential receiver requests the information. Exemplary respondent answers are: "As long as nobody asks me about it, I will not carry it further." "Somebody has to ask me."

*Uncertainty about Receiver's Benefit.* Some respondents expressed their concerns that they cannot judge on the receiver's taste or preferences. Exemplary respondent answers are: "Because everybody will rate this differently." "I don't like it, someone else might."

*Facilitate Own Experiences.* Some respondents stated that everybody should make his own experiences. Exemplary respondent answers are: Everybody should get his own view on it." "Because everybody should make his own experiences."

## Reasons Attributed to Situation or Context

*Missing Opportunity.* Some respondents said that they had not found the time or opportunity to spread WOM. Some would only talk about the topic if it's appropriate and of relevance to the conversation. Exemplary respondent answers are: "No time." "I will only talk about it if a conversation touches the topic."

*Information Saturation.* Some respondents said that all people they know already knew about the product, brand or WOM topic. Exemplary respondent answers are: "Because everyone I know owns one for himself."

## Reasons Attributed to the Message or Topic

*Not Convinced by Received WOM.* Some respondents stated, that they were not convinced. Usually it was not obvious whether this related to the topic, the sender, the message or anything else. Exemplary respondent answers are: "Because I was not convinced." "Because the information was not convincing to me."

*Doubted Applicability to Receiver.* Some respondents said that the product, brand or WOM topic is tailored to specific needs or is only applicable in specific contexts. Exemplary respondent answers are: "It is a very special product." "Very specific information." "Because it is a local offer."

*Missing Novelty.* Some respondents stated that the brand, product, or WOM topic was either too old or not available any-

more. Exemplary respondent answers are: "Because the article is outdated." "It was nothing new."

## Other Reasons

Categories that received only minor counts were summarized to "Other" and are as such presented here in shorter form. We deliberately set the threshold for this category at below 1% of all counts. Additionally this category includes all not interpretable answers. The categories were: *Negative WOM attitude* (some respondents had specific opinions about positive or negative WOM that let them to transmission refusal), *replace with own experience* (some respondents said that they had own experience and would transmit them instead)

*relevant information was omitted* (some respondents said that relevant information was missing when WOM was received or that it was to general) *missing self credibility* (some respondents stated the fear of not being a reliable source to spread the WOM), *self solicitated* (few respondents said that they specifically asked for information themselves), and *don't know/error* (this last category subsumes all respondents who stated that they don't know as well as all cryptic or otherwise non interpretable answers).

## Descriptive WOM Results

After having described and categorized the reasons for WOM transmission refusal in a qualitative way, the following results aim to draw a more quantitative picture.

As expected the total occurrence of NWOM was relatively low in respect to PWOM, thus confirming the findings of East et al. (2007) and our proposition 1. Also the total occurrence of not transmitted WOM was relatively low with 11.5% of all WOM transmitters not willing to transmit, thus confirming proposition 2. Still a first interesting finding to potential differences of PWOM and NWOM regarding transmission refusal is the relatively large share of NWOM incidents. A Pearson chi-square test revealed the difference as highly significant ($\chi^2(1, 19648) = 306.42$, p < .001) but according to Cramer's V the association is not a very strong one (Cramer's V = .125).

## Frequencies of Transmission Refusal Results

All frequencies of categories are shown in table 2. The number of counts (2,254) is slightly different from the number of refusing respondents (2,261) because some respondents provided several answers and others provided none. The three most common reasons for refusal were: (1.) the transmitter has a low interest in the WOM topic (Missing Relevance of Product or WOM Topic, 16.0%), (2.)

**Table 1**
**Counts of Transmitted and Not Transmitted WOM by WOM Valence**

| | PWOM | NWOM | Total WOM |
|---|---|---|---|
| Transmitted WOM | | | |
| Absolute Counts | 16270 | 1117 | 17387 |
| (Relative to Column) | (89.6%) | (74.6%) | (88.5%) |
| Not Transmitted WOM | | | |
| Absolute Counts | 1881 | 380 | 2261 |
| (Relative to Column) | (10.4%) | (25.4%) | (11.5%) |
| Total | | | |
| Absolute Counts | 18151 | 1497 | 19648 |
| (Relative to Column) | (100%) | (100%) | (100.0%) |
| (Relative to Row Total) | (92.4%) | (7.6%) | (100.0%) |

the transmitter perceived the relevance or interest of potential receivers as low (Missing Perceived Relevance to Potential Receiver, 14.8%), and (3.) the transmitter felt not able to judge or evaluate the WOM topic (Missing Judgment Ability, 11.1%). Intrapersonal reasons were most common, followed by interpersonal reasons. Keeping in mind the little research on interpersonal reasons in a WOM context, this is of surprisingly high importance. Specifically, the transmitter's perceptions of the receiver seem to be important while at the same time being neglected by previous research, thus potentially guiding future research. The same applies to situation and context factors which seem to be of importance (Missing Opportunity, 9.2%; Information Saturation, 5.8%), although prior research largely neglected them as antecedents, too.

Regarding the differences of PWOM and NWOM we find support for the notion that NWOM is perceived as being more relevant or diagnostic (Missing Perceived Relevance to Potential Receiver: PWOM, 15.8% vs. NWOM, 9.9%). NWOM therefore seem to be less susceptible to time constraints in conversation (Missing Opportunity: PWOM, 9.8% vs. NWOM, 6.0%), and is faster perceived as being saturated (Information Saturation: PWOM, 5.4% vs. NWOM, 7.8%).

In line with prior research, we also observe that NWOM is more easily recalled (Received Information was Forgotten: PWOM, 2.5% vs. NWOM, 0.8%). However, the differences of PWOM and NWOM within the important interpersonal category indicate that the spread of NWOM is socially more constrained, supported by the category 'negative WOM attitude' (not shown in table 2: PWOM, 0.6% vs. NWOM, 2.3%) and typical respondent statements in this

category ("You should not talk about bad memories." "I just tell about positive things."). Prior research supports the notion that people may avoid NWOM because of potential social undesirability (Rosen and Tesser 1972), or because NWOM is relatively scarce, implying the risk of social inconformity (Moscovici 1985; Burnkrant and Cousineau 1975). The latter is strongly supported by our data: For example, respondents are less willing to take the risk of transmitting a negative message they do not approve of than a positive message (Judgment Differences: PWOM, 1.7% vs. NWOM, 9.1%). In the case the transmitter already has a negative conviction, he will more likely transmit NWOM than without such a conviction (Product or WOM Topic Dislike: PWOM, 7.2% vs. NWOM, 2.6%). Furthermore missing credibility should then be more relevant for NWOM than for PWOM transmission (Missing Credibility: PWOM, 3.3% vs. NWOM, 7.3%).

To further verify that NWOM transmission is socially constrained, we should expect that tie strength moderates the importance of some reasons of transmission refusal. While the differences in relative frequencies are generally low, however the three criteria with the largest differences do all reflect the tie strength' influence. As expected, transmission refusal due to missing relevance for the next receiver is higher for close ties (Relevance to Receiver Perceived as Missing: weak tie, 12.6% vs. strong tie, 16.1%) and nearly similar regarding WOM valence. Perceived sender credibility is also lower for weak ties (Missing Credibility: weak tie, 9.0% vs. strong tie, 1.1%) and not different in terms of WOM valence. However, the most interesting effect is seen on transmission refusal due to judgment differences. In support of the social conformity principle,

**Table 2**
**Not Transmitted WOM by Category and WOM Valence**

| | PWOM | | NWOM | | Total WOM | |
|---|---|---|---|---|---|---|
| | Abs. Count | % of Col. | Abs. Count | % of Col. | Abs. Count | % of Col. |
| Missing Relevance of Product or WOM Topic | 299 | 16.0% | 62 | 16.1% | 361 | 16.0% |
| Missing Perceived Relevance to Potential Receiver | 296 | 15.8% | 38 | 9.9% | 334 | 14.8% |
| Missing Judgment Ability | 213 | 11.4% | 38 | 9.9% | 251 | 11.1% |
| Missing Opportunity | 184 | 9.8% | 23 | 6.0% | 207 | 9.2% |
| Product or WOM Topic Dislike | 135 | 7.2% | 10 | 2.6% | 145 | 6.4% |
| Information Saturation | 100 | 5.4% | 30 | 7.8% | 130 | 5.8% |
| Interpersonal Barriers | 80 | 4.3% | 30 | 7.8% | 110 | 4.9% |
| Missing Credibility | 62 | 3.3% | 28 | 7.3% | 90 | 4.0% |
| Judgment Differences | 32 | 1.7% | 35 | 9.1% | 67 | 3.0% |
| Not Convinced by Received WOM | 48 | 2.6% | 10 | 2.6% | 58 | 2.6% |
| Doubted Applicability to Receiver | 44 | 2.4% | 5 | 1.3% | 49 | 2.2% |
| Received Information was Forgotten | 46 | 2.5% | 3 | 0.8% | 49 | 2.2% |
| No WOM Motivation | 43 | 2.3% | 4 | 1.0% | 47 | 2.1% |
| Alternative Product or WOM Topic Favorite | 41 | 2.2% | 1 | 0.3% | 42 | 1.9% |
| Missing Novelty | 36 | 1.9% | 5 | 1.3% | 41 | 1.8% |
| Solicitation Expected | 30 | 1.6% | 7 | 1.8% | 37 | 1.6% |
| Uncertainty about Receiver's Benefit | 21 | 1.1% | 14 | 3.6% | 35 | 1.6% |
| Facilitate Own Experiences | 14 | 0.7% | 17 | 4.4% | 31 | 1.4% |
| Other | 145 | 7.8% | 25 | 6.5% | 170 | 7.5% |
| (Thereof Don't know/Error) | (88) | (4.7%) | (11) | (2.9%) | (99) | (4.4%) |
| Total | 1869 | 100% | 385 | 100% | 2254 | 100% |

the higher risk by NWOM than by PWOM is more severe when the relationship is close (Judgment Differences weak tie 4.3% vs. strong tie 11.8%).

## CONCLUSION

We developed a category system for reasons to refuse WOM transmission, comprising intrapersonal, interpersonal, context–related, and topic-related reasons as categories. We identified the most important reasons for transmission refusal, including the transmitter's perception of the receiver and context factors that have so far been neglected in WOM research. Further research should go into more detail with respect to these categories. We additionally replicated the larger occurrence of PWOM as previously found by East et al. (2007). Moreover, we confirmed that the refusal of WOM transmission is relatively scarce (transmission refusal rate below 10% of all WOM incidents). Still, there is a highly significant influence of WOM valence on WOM transmission. We then identified reasons for the different influence of WOM valence. This supported the notion that NWOM is perceived as being more relevant or diagnostic. Furthermore, we showed that social constraints are more related to the transmission of NWOM than of PWOM. We were able to argumentatively validate this finding using the moderating effect of tie strength on the social constraints proposition. This finding adds to the debate about differences of PWOM and NWOM in respect to their effects and may provide an additional explanation on the relative scarcity of NWOM occurrence. Social constraints are a topic with few related studies in WOM literature. But given the potential influence, this is another path for future research.

Marketing managers might be delighted to hear that NWOM is more susceptible to transmission refusal. But our key contribution is the categorized system of transmission refusal. The particular merit lies in a differentiated picture of the drivers for transmission refusal reasons for PWOM and NWOM which could be used to gain detailed insights into why PWOM campaigns might fail or to tailor specific marketing measures to fight NWOM.

For example, to minimize transmission refusal in a PWOM campaign, managers should engage in increasing the perceived topic relevance to the transmitter. This can be achieved by a variety of traditional communication measures that focus on generating awareness and need. In order to tackle missing judgment ability as a reason for transmission refusal, one should focus on informative communication as collateral measure.

## REFERENCES

Ahluwalia, Rohini, Burnkrant, R. E., & Unnava, H. R. (2000), "Consumer response to negative publicity," *Journal of Marketing Research*, 37 (May), 203-14.

Anderson, N. H. (1965), "Averaging versus adding as a stimulus combination rule in impression formation," *Journal of Personality and Social Psychology*, 2 (July), 1-9.

Anderson, E. W. (1998), "Customer satisfaction and word of mouth," *Journal of Service Research*, 1(-), 5-17.

Arndt, Johan (1967), "The role of product-related conversations in the diffusion of a new product," *Journal of Marketing Research*, 4 (August), 291-95.

Banerjee, Abhijit and Fudenberg, Drew (2004), "Word-of-Mouth Learning" *Games and Economic Behavior*, 46(1), 1-22.

Bansal, H. S. and Voyer, P. A. (2000), "Word-of-mouth processes within a services purchase decision context," *Journal of Service Research*, 2 (November), 166 – 77.

Bass, Frank (1969), "A New Product Growth Model for Consumer Durables," *Managent Science*, 15(5), 215-27.

Bettman, James R. and Park, C. Whan (1980), "Effects of Prior Knowledge and Experience and Phase of the Choice Process on Consumer Decision Processes: A Protocol Analysis," *Journal of Consumer Research*, 7 (December), 234-48.

Brown, Jacqueline J. and Reingen, Peter H. (1987), "Social ties and word-of-mouth referral behaviour," *Journal of Consumer Research*, 14(3), 350-62.

Burnkrant, Robert E. and Cousineau, Alain (1975), "Informational and Normative Social Influence in Buyer Behavior," *Journal of Consumer Research*, 3 (December), 206-15.

Carl, Waler J., Libai, Barak and Ding, Adam (2008), "Measuring the Value of Word of Mouth" ARF Audience Measurement 3.0 Conference, June 24-25, N.Y.

Chevalier, Judith A. and Mayzlin, Dina. (2003), "The effect of word of mouth on sales: Online book reviews," *Journal of Marketing Research*, 44(3), 345-54.

Coleman, James, Katz, Elihu and Menzel, Herbert (1957), "The Diffusion of an Innovation Among Physicians," *Sociometry*, 20( 4), 253-70.

Dichter, E. (1966), "How word or mouth advertising works," *Harvard Business Review*, 44(1), 147-60.

De Matos, Celso A. and Rossi, Carlos A.V. (2008), "Word-of-Mouth Communications in Marketing: A Meta-Analytic Review of the Antecedents and Moderators," *Journal of the Academy of Marketing Science*, 36, 578-96.

East, Robert, Hammond, Kathy and Lomax, Wendy (2008), "Measuring the Impact of Positive and Negative Word of Mouth on Brand Purchase Probability," *International Journal of Research in Marketing*, 25(3), 215-24.

East, R., Hammond, K. A. and Wright, M. (2007), "The relative incidence of positive and negative word of mouth: A multi-category study," *International Journal of Research in Marketing*, 24(2), 175-84.

Fisher, R. F. (1993), "Social desirability bias and the validity of indirect questioning," *Journal of Consumer Research*, 20 (September), 303-13.

Fitzgerald Bone, P. (1995), "Word-of-mouth effects on short-term and long-term product judgments," *Journal of Business Research*, 32, 213-23.

Frenzen, Jonathan K. and Nakamoto, Kent (1993), "Structure, Cooperation, and the Flow of Market Information," *Journal of Consumer Research*, 20 (December), 360-75.

Granovetter, Mark S. (1973), "The Strength of Weak Ties," *American Journal of Sociology*, 78(6), 1360-80.

Gremler, Dwayne D. and Browne, Stephen W. (1999), "The Loyalty Ripple Effect: Appreciating the Full Value of Customers," *International Journal of Service Industry Management*, 10(3), 271-15.

Hanna, N. and Wosniak, R. (2001), *Consumer Behaviour: An Applied Approach*, N.J.: Prentice Hall.

Herr, Paul. M., Kardes, Frank. R. and Kim, John. (1991), "Effects of word-of-mouth and product attribute information on persuasion: An accessibility-diagnosticity perspective," *Journal of Consumer Research*, 17 (March), 454-62.

Lynch, J. G., Marmorstein, H. and Wingold, M. F. (1988), "Choices from sets including remembered brands: Use of recalled attributes and prior overall evaluations," *Journal of Consumer Research*, 15 (September).

Mangold, W. G., Miller. F. and Brockway, G. R. (1999), "Word-of-mouth communication in the service marketplace," *Journal of Services Marketing*, 13(1).

Mayring, Philipp. (2000), "Qualitative Content Analysis", _Qualitative Social Research Forum_, 1(2), http://www.qualitative-research.net/fqs-texte/2-00/2-00mayring-e.htm.

Merton, Robert K. (1968), _Social theory and social structure_, N.Y.: Free Press.

Miles, M. B. and Huberman, A. M. (1994), _Qualitative Data Analysis: An Expanded Source Book_, Thousand Oaks, CA: Sage.

Mittal, B. and Lassar, W. M. (1998), "Why do customers switch? The dynamics of satisfaction versus loyalty," _The Journal of Services Marketing,_ 12(3).

Mizerski, R. W. (1982), "An attributional explanation of the disproportionate influence of unfavourable information," _Journal of Consumer Research,_ 9(1).

Moscovici, Serge (1985), "Social Influence and Conformity," in _Handbook of Social Psychology_, ed. George Lindzey and Eliot Aronson, N.Y.: Random House.

Oetting, Martin (2009), _Ripple Effect: How Empowered Involvement Drives Word of Mouth_, Wiesbaden: Gabler.

Richins, M. (1983), "Negative word of mouth by dissatisfied customers: A pilot study," _Journal of Marketing,_ 47(1).

Rosen, Sidney and Tesser, Abraham (1972), "Fear of negative evaluation and the reluctance to transmit bad news," _Journal of Communication,_ 22 (June), 124-41.

Roselius, Ted (1971), "Consumer Rankings of Risk Reduction Methods," _Journal of Marketing_, 35 (January), 56-61

Silverman, G. (1997), "How to harness the awesome power of word of mouth," _Direct Marketing,_ 60(7).

Skowronski, Jone J. and Carlston, Donal E. (1989), "Negativity and extremity biases in impression formation: A review of explanations," _Psychological Bulletin,_ 105(1).

Stephen, Andrew T. and Lehmann, Donald R. (2009), "Why Do People Transmit Word-of-Mouth? The Effects of Recipient and Relationship Characteristics on Transmission Behaviors," Working Paper, Columbia University.

Strauss, A. L. and Corbin, J. (1990), _Basics of Qualitative Research: Grounded Theory, Procedures and Techniques,_ Newbury Park, CA: Sage.

Sweeney, Jillian C., Soutar, Geoffrey N. and Mazzarol, Tim (2008), "Factors influencing word of mouth effectiveness: receiver perspectives," _European Journal of Marketing_, 42(3/4), 344-64.

van Dijk, Teun A. (1980), _Macrostructures_, Hillsdale, N.J.: Erlbaum.

# Giving Advice to Others: The Role of Social Distance

Yu Hu, Salem State College, USA

## ABSTRACT

This research examines the effects of social distance on interpersonal advising behavior. We propose that when an advice is based on a decision's desirability and feasibility attributes, the social distance between the advisor and the advisee would affect how the advisor evaluates the relative importance of those decision attributes, and consequently it would lead the advisor to offer different advice to different advisees. Specifically, this research demonstrated in two studies that although a decision's desirability attributes are judged by the advisor as more important than feasibility attributes, this difference is more evident when the advice is offered to a distant social relation (e.g., strangers) than a close social relation (i.e., best friends); a decision's feasibility attributes have more influence only when the advice is given to a close relation than to a distant one.

## INTRODUCTION

We often seek advice from or give advice to other people—we trust others' advice on important life decisions; we also believe the advice we give to others is based on our best judgments. But ironically, empirical evidence has repeatedly shown that people who give advice to others often make different decisions for themselves (e.g., Jones, Schulz-Hard, and Frey 2005; Kray 2000). This self-other discrepancy has been demonstrated across many decision-making domains, including risk prediction (Hsee and Weber 1997), reward preference (Heath 1999), medical decision (Zikmund-Fisher 2006), and job selection (Kray and Gonzalez 1999). Despite the consistent finding, to date, researchers have primarily focused on the self-other comparison, and very few empirical studies have examined the conditions under which advisors would adapt their advice to suit different advice recipients. For example, would a physician recommend the same treatment regime to a new patient and to a close friend, if both of them display the same symptom? Would it be possible that he'd recommend an aggressive one for the new patient and a conservative one for his friend, or vice versa? If yes, then why? The goal of the present research is to investigate advice recipients' influence on interpersonal advising behavior.

From an advisor's perspective, there are many ways to characterize the advisee, such as gender, age, experience, attitude, etc. In this research we choose to focus on the *social distance* between the adviser and the advisee, a choice based on the reasoning and evidence that social distance or interpersonal relation is a dominating factor that guides human social interaction (Clark and Mill 1979; Heider 1958; Sahlins 1972). Psychologically and physically, people are closer to their spouses or friends than to their co-workers or casual acquaintances, and the influence of social distance (or relationship strength) on cognition and behavior has been shown in a variety of consumer domains (e.g., Frenzen and Nakamoto 1993; Kim, Zhang, and Li 2008). Adding to this literature, the present research proposes that social distance could affect how advisors evaluate other people's decision situations and consequently alters how they give decision advice to others. Specifically, we argue and found that the distinct effect of social distance in advising is that it could change the adviser's evaluation and judgment of a decision's feasibility concerns. In the next session, we first present literature examining the social distance effect on interpersonal perception and information processing, which will then be followed by our prediction of the social distance effect on the advisor's differential weighting of decision attributes.

## SOCIAL DISTANCE EFFECT

To examine the influence of social distance on interpersonal advising behavior, we turn to the conceptual framework proposed by the Construal Level Theory (CLT, Trope and Liberman 2003). In simplicity, CLT articulates how psychological distances—time, space, social relation, or probability—influence individuals' mental representations of related objects, events or behavior (e.g., other people's actions or decisions): the greater the perceived psychological distance, the more likely are the perceivers to form high-level (e.g., abstract) rather than low-level (e.g., detailed) construal of the objects or the events. In other words, CLT predicts that people's mental representations of other people's actions can take different forms: for close social relations, people are more likely to use concrete, detailed, contextualized features (i.e., low-level construal) to construe the target person's action; for distant social relations, people are more likely to use abstract, simple, primary, generalized features (i.e., high-level construal).

Although CLT literature has mainly focused on the effects of temporal distance, there are studies that have examined the effects of social distance on construal levels (e.g., Kim, Zhang, and Li 2008; Liviatan, Trope, and Liberman 2008; Smith and Trope 2006). Most germane to the current research, Liviatan et al (2008) predicted and found that social distances induced by perceived interpersonal similarity changed people's construal of similar and dissimilar individuals, even when the same information about those individuals were presented. These different representations, in turn, had influenced people's judgments about similar and dissimilar others' decisions. In one of Liviatan et al (2008)'s study, the subjects gave more decision weight to lower-level, secondary decision attributes for similar (vs. dissimilar) target person's decision, and consequently, they also made different decisions for the target person because of the differential weighing of decision's secondary attributes. Additional evidence of the social distance effect can be found in the studies of interpersonal power relations. For example, Smith and Trope (2006) demonstrated that elevated power in social relations increases the perceived distance one feels from others. As a consequence, people with power consequently adopt a high level construal of their low power counterpart, which makes them process other's information in a more abstract fashion and base their judgments about other more on low-level, secondary information. Extending those existing CLT studies on social distance effect, this present research uses a different operationalization of the social distance—the interpersonal relationship strength exhibited between close and distant social relations—to examine how social distances between the advisor and the advisee would change the advisor's processing of the advisee's decision situation and would consequently affect the advisor's advice given to the advisee.

## DECISION DESIRABILITY AND FEASIBILITY

When deciding on whether to take or advice other to take an action, the decision-maker or the adviser has two main concerns: the desirability concern, which focuses on the potential outcome of the action (i.e., reasons to commit to the action) and the feasibility concern, which focuses on the implementation process of the action (i.e., means to carry out the action), (Bandura 1982; Fischhoff 1999; Gollwitzer 1990). A job position, for example, might promise high salary and generous benefits (i.e., desirability); meanwhile, applying for the job might include a lengthy application process and multiple interview trips (i.e., feasibility). A job decision-maker would assess the importance of these two concerns before reaching a decision. And, when it comes to advising on other's job decision, assessing these concerns becomes more challenging in that the adviser has to evaluate the implementation and consequences of the decision on behalf of the advisee. Will the adviser favor the job's desirability features more than the feasibility ones, or vice versa? As we elaborate later, we predict that the perceived social distance between the adviser and the advisee would influence whether the adviser assigns different evaluative weights to the desirability and feasibility concerns of the action.

According to the CLT research (e.g. Liberman and Trope 1998), desirability concerns are viewed as the high-level construals of a decision action; feasibility concerns the low-level construals of a decision action. CLT further predicts that the greater psychological distance from the decision-maker to the target action, the more influential is the desirability considerations than the feasibility considerations. For example, from a temporal distance perspective, Liberman and Trope (1998) demonstrated that purchase decisions for the near future (i.e., close psychological distance) was more likely to be affected by product feasibility concerns, whereas distance future purchase decision was more likely to be influenced by product desirability concerns. Hence, linking the evidence of temporal distance effects on information processing with the recent advances in the CLT research on the social distance dimension, it is reasonable to propose that, when evaluating decision situations and giving advice to social partners, advisors would assign disproportionate weights to either the desirability or feasibility considerations, under the influences of the perceived social distances between the advisor and the advisee.

What Liberman and Trope (1998) and Liviatan et al (2008) did not extricate in their studies was the comparative importance of a decision's desirability and feasibility attributes when those are considered together: in Liberman and Trope (1998; study 2 and 3), desirability and feasibility attributes were evaluated in isolation while temporal distances were manipulated. However, in many everyday situations, giving advice usually requires the advisor to simultaneously consider both types of attributes, so it is empirically important to examine how psychological distances would affect the advisor's joint evaluation of a decision's desirability and feasibility attributes. Building on the CLT's findings, we predict that when considered together for a decision or advice, desirability would have more influences than feasibility. More important, under the influence of social distance, the desirability's dominance is greater when the decision is related to a distance social relation, whereas feasibility should become more important when the decision is related to a close social relation. That is to say, for a casual acquaintance, the advisor would base his advice mostly on the high-level, desirability attributes; for a close friend, the advisor would be more likely to be influenced by the low-level, feasibility attributes. Formally:

*Hypothesis 1:*     *Decision advice offered to a distant social partner (e.g., casual acquaintances) would be influenced more by the decision's desirability concerns than its feasibility concerns,*

*Hypothesis 2:*     *Decision's feasibility concerns would have greater influence when the advice is offered to a close social partner (e.g., best friends) than to a distance social partner.*

State differently, we expect that when advising a distant advisee, the advisor tends to focus on the desirability considerations and is less likely to be concerned about the feasibility aspects of the

advice; comparatively, when advising a close advisee, the advisor tends to pay more attention to the feasibility aspects of the advice. But It is worth noting that we do not expect that the advisor would see a decision's feasibility features as more important than the desirability ones when the advice is offered to a close friend—Our prediction only specifies that the advisor would assign more weight to the decision's feasibility concerns when the advisee is a close social relationship partner, as compared to a socially distant advisee.

Two lab experiments were conducted to test the research propositions. Study 1 assessed the importance ratings participants attached to a job decision's desirability and feasibility information for distant and close social relationship partners. In Study 2, we directly examined the advice offered to those two different social relations. The research methods used in the studies benefited both from several aforementioned CLT studies (Liberman and Trope 1998; Liviatan et al 2008) and from the priming research of interpersonal relationship (e.g., Fitzsimons and Bargh 2003). As a whole, besides its focal proposition, this research introduces a new and effective experimental paradigm to the study of social distance and its effects on consumers' information processing and behavior.

## STUDY 1

This study was designed to test the hypothesis that when giving decision advice to other people, advisors tend to attach different importance weights to a decision's feasibility and desirability considerations. Specifically, it's predicted that desirability considerations should play a greater role for a distance advisee, while feasibility considerations should play a greater role for a close advisee. In the study, participants were first randomly assigned to two relationship groups (best friend vs. stranger) by an imagination task modeled after a procedure used by Fitzsimons and Bargh (2003). Immediately after the priming, participants were asked to act on behalf of the target person to provide importance ratings on a job offer's desirability and feasibility attributes.

### Procedure

Fifty five undergraduate students participated in this lab experiment in exchange for extra course credit. Upon arrival, they were given a survey booklet allegedly used to study how college students interact with their peers. Used as a priming task adopted from Fitzsimons and Bargh (2003), the survey consisted of a set of questions designed to activate a mental representation either of a best friend or a stranger. It first asked participants to take a moment to bring to mind either a stranger that they had met in class in the current semester or one of their best friends on campus. They were asked to provide the first name of the person they imagined, if they knew, and then to describe their latest conversation with the person. In order to strengthen the priming effect, in the best friend condition, the questionnaire asked two additional questions: (1) "Briefly describe two things this best friend has done for you that make you think it is worthwhile to have a friend like him/her;" (2) "Describe one situation in detail in which your best friend did something for you that made you think it is really worthwhile to have a friend like him/her?" In the stranger condition, the priming question simply asked the participants to describe one situation that they interacted with a stranger.

### Decision Description, Dependent Measure, Manipulation Check

Immediately following the priming questions, participants were told that the person they had just imagined was deciding whether to accept a job offer. They were then instructed to evaluate the job offer on behalf of the target person. The job was briefly described in the booklet in a random order of ten job related features: Five were related to the desirability considerations of a job decision (i.e., salary, promotion, interest, working hours, job security) and the other five were related to the feasibility considerations (i.e., application complexity, interview procedure, interview location, training period, job relocation requirement). A pilot study using the same subject pool confirmed the intended perception of desirability and feasibility concerns of the ten features. After reviewing the job information, participants were asked in the next page to indicate, in order for the target person to make a good decision, how important it is for him to have some additional information about each job feature. To highlight the advising role, it was reminded to the participants that they were making a judgment for the target person, not for themselves. The importance rating measure used an 11-point scale, ranging from *Not important at all* (0) to *Very Important* (10). To assess the success of social distance manipulation, at the end of the experiment, participants indicated how close they felt to the imagined person at a 9-point scale ranging from "Not at all" to "Very much". As expected, participants rated the imagined best friend closer to themselves (M = 7.41) than the stranger (M = 2.82, p < .01). Before they were debriefed and dismissed, participants were given an open-ended question to estimate the true research purpose of the study, and content analysis did not reveal any meaningful suspicion.

## Results

A 2 (Target Person: best friend vs. stranger) X 2 (Job Feature Type: desirability vs. feasibility) mixed ANOVA with target person as between-subjects factor and job feature type as within-subjects factor was performed on participants' importance ratings. The main effect of feature type was significant, indicating both of the two groups were able to discriminate between desirability and feasibility concerns and they preferred the desirability attributes more than the feasibility ones (M = 9.36 and 6.75, respectively; p < .05). More important, the results showed the expected interaction between job feature type and target person, p < .01, $\eta^2$ = .17, indicating that the perceived importance of desirability and feasibility considerations is a function of the relationship between the advisor and advisee. As expected, the perceived importance of feasibility considerations decreased when the advisor and advisee were close friends ($M_{best friend}$ = 7.39 and $M_{stranger}$ = 6.11); but somewhat unexpectedly, the best friend group also gave greater importance ratings to the desirability features ($M_{stranger}$ = 9.8 and $M_{best friend}$ = 8.77), which might be attributed to the lack of motivation for the participants in the stranger group. But, overall, this study confirmed the hypothesized role of social distance in advising behavior: although a decision's desirability attributes were perceived by the advisor as more important than its feasibility attributes, this difference was more apparent when the advising decision was related to strangers than to best friends. That is to say, when giving advice to others people, the advisor attaches greater importance to desirability concerns when the advisee is a distance social partner and feasibility concerns play a greater role in close relationship advising than in distant relationship advising.

Notwithstanding these confirming results, this study has two apparent drawbacks. First, the priming procedures could simply heightened the involvement or motivation of the participants in the best friend group, which might explain why those subjects rated the feasibility attributes more important than those in the stranger group did. Second, this study did not examine whether the importance rating was predictive of the advisor's actual advising behavior. A second study was conducted to address these issues.

## STUDY 2

Study 1 has showed that social distance between the advisor and advisee can change how advisors perceive the relative importance of desirability and feasibility decision features. The present study was designed to test whether the different importance perception can in fact influence how advisors give advice. After the same priming procedure as in Study 1, participant was asked to act on behalf of the target person to evaluate a job position and express the likelihood that they would recommend the job to the target person. The job information was selected from the aforementioned ten job features in Study 1 and two versions of the job were created: Job 1 had two positive desirability features and one negative feasibility feature; Job 2 had two positive feasibility features and one negative desirability feature. We expect that Job 1 would be preferred across relationship groups and, more important, a job's feasibility features would have more influences on advice offered to a close friend than to a stranger.

## Procedure

Eighty two undergraduate students participated in this lab experiment in exchange for extra course credit. Upon arrival, they were given the similar survey booklet used in Study 1, which, in its first part, contained the same relationship priming procedure and manipulation checks, which were successful and will not be discussed further. After the priming, participants were told that the target person was considering a job offer. What followed was the description of the target job position and choice likelihood measure. Participants were randomly assigned to the two job groups and were asked to express the likelihood (a 7-point scale, ranging from 1, *Not at all likely* to 7, *Very likely*) that they would recommend the target person to accept the job offer. Like in Study 1, before answering the likelihood measure, participants were reminded that they were making a judgment for the target person, not for themselves. In addition, participants in both experimental groups were asked to carefully evaluate the information and make a best judgment on behalf of the target person, a measure that was intended to remove the possible motivation differences between the two groups.

## Results

A 2 (Target Person: best friend vs. stranger) X 2 (Job Type: most positive desirability [Job 1] vs. most positive feasibility [Job 2]) ANOVA was performed on participants' recommendation likelihood rating. As expected, job type main effect was found: participants preferred the job with most positive desirability features over the one with most positive feasibility features (M = 5.47 and 5.01; p < .01), replicating the finding of desirability superiority in Study 1. And there was a significant interaction between job type and target person type, F(1, 80) = 12.87, p < .01). Post hoc simple effect analysis of target person revealed that the job with all positive desirability features and one negative feasibility feature was disliked more by the best friend group than by the stranger group ($M_{best friend}$ = 5.1 and $M_{stranger}$ = 5.84; p < .01), confirming the hypothesized overweighing of feasibility concerns by the close relation advisors. There was no significant difference between these two groups on the job with all positive feasibility features ($M_{best friend}$ = 4.95 and $M_{stranger}$ = 5.06; NS). However, only participants in the stranger group liked the job with all positive desirability features significantly more than the other job, $M_{job1}$ = 5.84 and $M_{job2}$ = 5.06; p < .05. Together, these results clearly indicate that, when giving advice to others, decision's feasibility features exerted more influences on the advisor's preference of the job for best friends than for strangers; when advising strangers, desirability considerations are the ones that count.

## GENERAL DISCUSSION

The goal of this research is to investigate the role of social distance on interpersonal advising behavior. We argue that when an advice is based on a decision's desirability and feasibility concerns, the social distance between the advisor and the advisee would affect how the advisor evaluates the relative importance of those concerns, and consequently it would lead the advisor to offer different advice to advisees of different social relations. Borrowing heavily from the seminal Construal Level Theory (Trope and Liberman 2003) and its empirical findings (e.g., Liberman and Trope 1998, Liviatan et al 2008), we reason that social distance changes the advisor's construal of the advisor's decision situation in the following way: a distant advisee's decision is construed with higher level abstraction, whereas a close advisee's decision is construed with higher level of concreteness. As a consequence of this information processing difference, the advisor assigns different evaluative weights to a decision's desirability and feasibility concerns in that a decision's desirability concerns are high-level construal and feasibility concerns are low-level construal. Put these propositions into an advising context, this current research predicts that decision advice offered to a distant social partner (e.g., casual acquaintances) would be influenced more by the decision's desirability concerns than its feasibility concerns; a decision's feasibility concerns would have greater influence when the advice is offered to a close social partner (e.g., best friends) than to a distance social partner.

Two studies tested the research hypothesis. Study 1 assessed the importance ratings advisors assign to a job decision's desirability and feasibility information for distant and close social relations. Participants were first randomly assigned to two relationship groups (best friend vs. stranger) by an imagination task. Immediately afterwards, they were asked to act on behalf of the target person to provide importance ratings on a job offer's desirability and feasibility attributes. The results indicated that while the job's desirability was deemed more important than its feasibility by both the experimental groups, advisors for their best friends gave more importance ratings to the job's feasibility attributes. In other words, when the advisee is a close social relation, advisors consider not only why the advisee should or should not take the action (i.e., desirability), they also take into consideration how the advisee could carry out the action (i.e., feasibility); when advising a distant social relation, the advisors only focus on the desirability concerns.

In Study 2, we directly compared the advice participants made to different social relations. Two versions of a job description were created: Job 1 had two positive desirability features and one negative feasibility feature; Job 2 had two positive feasibility features and one negative desirability feature. As expected, participants preferred the job with most positive desirability features (Job 1) over most positive feasibility features (Job2). More relevant, only the participants in the best friend group exhibited significant doubt about the job with one negative feasibility feature (Job 1), which echoed the finding from Study 1 that the importance of a decision's feasibility attributes is greater when the decision is related to a close social partner than to a distant one. Hence, taken together, two studies confirmed the dominant role of a decision's desirability considerations in distant relation advising and the stronger role of feasibility considerations in close relation advising.

The intended contribution of this research is to demonstrate the effects of advisees in the interpersonal advising behavior. Past research on this topic has focused exclusively on the decision differences between advising others and deciding for oneself. Expanding this literature, two studies reported here show that the social distances between the advisor and the advisee would influence how the advisor evaluate decision attributes and consequently affect what advice the advisor offers to different advisees. For future research, we suggest to replicate the current findings by testing the advisee effects with other psychological dimensions. For instance, would the physical distance between the advisor and the advisee have the same effect as the social distance does? In other words, what are the differences between face-to-face advising and long distance advising? What about temporal distance? Would it be different if the decision happens tomorrow or next year? And how would this temporal distance interact with social distance? As we can see, many intriguing research projects await us. Bon voyage.

## REFERENCE

Bandura, Albert (1982), "Self-Efficacy Mechanism in Human Agency," *American Psychologist*, 37 (February), 122-47.

Clark, Margaret S. and Judson Mills (1979), "Interpersonal Attraction in Exchange and Communal Relationships," *Journal of Personality and Social Psychology*, 37 (January), 12-24.

Fischhoff, Baruch (1992), "Giving Advice: Decision Theory Perspectives on Sexual Assault", *American Psychologist*, 47 (April), 577-88.

Fitzsimons, Gráinne M. and John A. Bargh (2003), "Thinking of You: Nonconscious Pursuit of Interpersonal Goals Associated with Relationship Partners", *Journal of Personality and Social Psychology*, 84 (January), 148-63.

Frenzen, Jonathan, and Kent Nakamoto (1993), "Structure, Cooperation and the Flow of Market Information," *Journal of Consumer Research*, 20 (December), 360-75.

Gollwitzer, Peter M. (1990), "Action Phases and Mind-Sets," in *Handbook of Motivation and Cognition: Foundations of Social Behavior*, Vol. 2, ed. Tory Higgins and Richard M. Sorrentino, New York: Guilford, 53-92.

Heath, Chip (1999), "On the Social Psychology of Agency Relationships: Lay Theories of Motivation Overemphasize Extrinsic Incentives," *Organizational Behavior and Human Decision Processes*, 78 (April), 25-62.

Heider, Fritz (1958), *The Psychology of Interpersonal Relations*. New York: Wiley.

Hsee, Christopher K. and Elke U. Weber (1997), "A Fundamental Prediction Error: Self-Others Discrepancies in Risk Preference," *Journal of Experimental Psychology: General*, 126 (1), 45-53.

Jonas, Eva, Stefan Schulz-Hardt, and Dieter Frey (2005), "Giving Advice or Making Decisions in Someone Else's Place: The Influence of Impression, Defense, and Accuracy Motivation on the Search for New Information," *Personality and Social Psychology Bulletin*, 31 (July), 977-90.

Kim, Kyeongheui, Meng Zhang, and Xiuping Li (2008), "Effects of Temporal and Social Distance on Consumer Evaluations," *Journal of Consumer Research*, 35 (4), 709-713.

Kray, Laura J. (2000), "Contingent Weighting in Self-Other Decision Making," *Organizational Behavior and Human Decision Processes*, 83 (September), 82-106.

Kray, Laura J. and Richard Gonzalez (1999), "Differential Weighting in Choice versus Advice: I'll Do This, You Do That," *Journal of Behavioral Decision Making*, 12 (3), 207-217.

Liberman, Nira and Yaacov Trope (1998), "The Role of Feasibility and Desirability Considerations in Near and Distant Future Decisions: A Test of Temporal Construal Theory," *Journal of Personality and Social Psychology*, 75 (1), 5-18.

Liviatana, Ido, Yaacov Trope, and Nira Liberman (2008), "Interpersonal Similarity as a Social Distance Dimension: Implications for Perception of Others' Actions," *Journal of Experimental Social Psychology*, 44 (5), 1256-69.

Sahlins, Marshall (1972), *Stone Age Economics*, Chicago: Aldine Atherton.

Smith, Pamela K. and Yaacov Trope (2006), "You Focus on the Forest When You're in Charge of the Trees: Power Priming and Abstract Information Processing," *Journal of Personality and Social Psychology*, 90 (4), 578-96.

Trope, Yaacov and Nira Liberman (2003), "Temporal Construal," *Psychological Review*, 110 (July), 403-21.

Zikmund-Fisher, Brian J., Brianna Sarr, Angela Fagerlin, and Peter A. Ubel (2006), "Matter of Perspective: Choosing for Others Differs from Choosing for Yourself in Making Treatment Decisions," *Journal of General Internal Medicine*, 21 (June), 618-22.

# 'No Longer, But Not Yet' – Tweens and the Mediating of Liminal Selves Through Metaconsumption

Kevina Cody, Dublin Institute of Technology, Ireland
Katrina Lawlor, Dublin Institute of Technology, Ireland
Pauline Maclaran, Royal Holloway, University of London, UK

## ABSTRACT

Using the anthropological theory of liminality as a lens of analysis, the following paper outlines specific elements of a research project exploring the consumer culture of a liminal group – tweens. The lived experience of a tween is explored using a multi-method approach incorporating personal diaries, in-depth interviews and accompanied shopping trips. Outcomes of one aspect of this longitudinal research project – the theory of metaconsumption - are presented, suggesting an important divergent theoretical path from the 'effects' - dominated consumer socialization approach to researching young people and their relationships with consumption. We conclude that those in a shadowed reality, those social neophytes no longer children but not yet teens engage with consumption practices and spaces particular to those who must exist mid-way between two spheres of identity. Thus this shadowed reality, this socially indiscernible identity belies agentive consumption and active engagement with signifiers of a duality of mediated selves.

## INTRODUCTION

Marketing theory and research, in particular the vibrant tendril of consumer culture and consumer behavior research embodies a kaleidoscopic essence of cross-disciplinary infusion and hybridism. The origins of interpretive consumer research as outlined for example by Tadajewski, (2006), as well as contemporary theorizations (e.g. Arnold and Thompson, 2005) and empirical advancements (e.g. Kozinets, 2001) have been shown to embrace ontologies far beyond the scope of marketing's seminal mantras (e.g. Kotler et al, 2008). Rather than consequently exist as a diluted pseudo-discipline, consumer research has thrived in its plurality, with the work of those who seek to investigate and theorize upon the symbiosis between meaningful ways of life and the symbolic marketplace visibly nourished and revitalized by contributions from social sciences such as psychology, anthropology and sociology.

This paper attempts to harness one such untapped reservoir of potential empirical and theoretical advancement; the anthropological theory of liminality, attesting to the potential of this theoretical framework as a lens of analysis for consumption practices but also offering a divergent avenue of exploration and theorization in relation to consumer socialization. The interstices of socio-cultural organization have proved sources of fascination and powerful theory development in the fields of anthropology, sociology and psychology (e.g. Van Gennep, 1961; Turner, 1974; 1978; 1988; Freud, 1950; Foucault, 1977). Douglas (1966: 137) writes that within society, 'there is energy in its margins and unstructured areas'. Consumer culture research has hitherto acknowledged the fruitfulness of transitional phenomena, spaces and places, as well as the experiences of the individual or group in flux and evolution (e.g. Davies & Fitchett, 2004; Maldonado & Tansuhaj, 1999; Gentry, 1997; Schouten, 1991). But it is the heart of this transition that has evaded exploration, slipped beneath the radar of interest. The farthest realms of the threshold may inevitably beckon, but the interim must be experienced to enact the resolution so often the focus of researcher's attentions. For many, the threshold is their current reality, their centre of nowhere.

This research focuses on the premise that for those whose sense of self is ambiguous, vague or blurred by the experience of standing mid-way between two symbolically-loaded social spheres of interaction, belonging to neither, but embedded in both, consumption practices and relationships with consumption take on a new meaning, a divergent core. Focusing specifically on the pre-adolescent or tween, who has come to represent the epitome of a categorical anomaly, a socio-cultural miasma (James, Jenks and Prout, 1998; Cook, 2004a), we set out to explore and theorize upon the dynamics of these liminars' relationships with and through goods and their associations. This paper presents one of the theoretical conclusions of this longitudinal research project – the theory of metaconsumption – which explores consumption within the tweens' liminal shadow of activity and regeneration which prepares these social neophytes for entry into a teenage world.

## EVERYTHING AND NOTHING – THE THEORETICAL FRAMEWORK OF LIMINALITY

Defined by Turner & Turner (1978: p.249) as 'the state and process of mid-transition in a rite of passage', a 'moment in and out of time' (Turner, 1969: p.96), the liminal phase of a transition, represents an instance of incompleteness, when the liminars (the ritual subjects in this phase) 'elude or slip through the network of classifications that normally locate states and positions in cultural space' (Turner, 1969: p.95). Understanding the attributes of liminal entities also serves to illustrate the core ideologies of the theory. One such attribute is structural and social invisibility, seclusion from the spheres of everyday life (Turner, 1967). In addition, ideologies of liminal theory espouse characteristics such as tabula rasa, symbolization of concurrent degeneration and gestation or parturition (Turner, 1967), heteronomy, silence, equality and obscurity.

Turner's (1967, 110) 'invitation to investigators of culture to focus their attention on the phenomena and processes of mid-transition' has resulted in contrasting disciplines welcoming liminality and its constituent dimensions into their midst to enrich an understanding and analysis of many phases of cultural change. Several bodies of literature forming a hybridism of theoretical perspectives with liminality unite around a core trope of illness and loss (e.g. Little et al, 1998; Gough, 2005, Jones et al, 2007). In the context of these studies, the theoretical framework of liminality has added credence to instances where alliance with social categories and social structures is suspended and irrelevant. Anderson (2003), Campbell et al (2005), Landzelius (2001) and Waskul (2005) have engaged with contextual specificities such as implantable cardioverter defibrillators (ICDs), advertising, incubated pre-term babies and internet personas respectively in their integration of this anthropological theory of structural anomalies.

Contexts as disparate as place and space (Pritchard & Morgan, 2006; Matthews et al, 2000), performance (Dunne, 2002; Rill, 2006; Brown, 2007; Hooker, 2007), and Postmodernity (Bhabha, 2004; Zukin, 1991; Bettis, 1996) also highlight the infusion and contribution of many areas of socio-cultural research with ideologies of the liminal, adding vividness and analytical depth to contemporary lived experiences of socio-cultural evolvement and disruption.

## LIMINAL CONSUMPTION

But what of liminal consumption? Have the ideologies of interim states been used as a lens of analysis for consumption practices and behaviours? Within interpretive consumer research's current brand of organization and theorization, CCT, liminal theory has been relatively underutilized as a theoretical lens through which to understand the consumption practices of those betwixt and between social categories or states of being. Schouten (1991) represents the inaugural integration of this anthropological perspective on mid-transition with individual consumption practices. Despite introducing a link between liminality and consumption, the overall emphasis of Schouten's (1991) research is divided between self-concept theories, role transitions, rites of passage and liminal ideologies. This multi-theoretical focus implies that less in-depth insights of specifically liminal consumption behaviours are garnished. Schouten (1991, 422) himself concludes that 'little is yet known about the consumption behaviours of liminal people'.

Despite focusing on a proposed relationship between liminal transitions, symbolic consumption and the extended self, the work of Noble & Walker (1997) gravitates around the notion of transitions as opposed to the state of liminality itself and additionally utilizes a positivist framework and quantitative methodology to align with its dissemination in predominantly psychologically oriented fields of inquiry.

Several other studies have approached the phenomenon of consumption in a liminal state (Hogg et al, 2004; Landzelius, 2001; Pavia & Mason, 2004). Although generating fascinating insights in their own right, these studies commonly relegate the liminal to a constituent dimension of a wider terrain of focus. It appeared that Schouten's (1991) cry to rally the troops towards explorations of this potential reservoir of symbolic meaning and consumer experiences had been relegated to the margins of interpretive consumer research. Thus this research aimed to explore the interweaving of consumption and identity amongst those whose sense of self is as much about past as future; selves that are embedded in what was, but concurrently gravitating towards what is to come.

## METHODS

In order to explore the interaction of liminal lived experiences and tween consumption practices, there were several methodological considerations and implications. Firstly, cognizant of the inherent ideologies of liminality, an instance of time deemed fundamentally disruptive or ambiguous in the life of a pre-adolescent was selected so as to capture lived experience of 'betwixt and between' at its most lucid. Therefore, a longitudinal study of a year was undertaken spanning the participants' final months of primary school and early months of secondary education in two Irish cities[1]. Three main sites of access were utilized; drama schools, personal contacts and primary schools.

Second, in line with Richardson's (1994) conceptualization of multiple methods within the interpretive domain as 'crystallization', this year-long exploratory research project was interjected at various points by a constellation of data collection techniques. A focal point of Richardson's (1994) theorization is the premise that 'what we see depends on the angle of our repose' (p.523). Five data collection methods were employed; namely in-depth interviews (which were conducted at two separate intervals), personal diaries, accompanied shopping trips, e-collages and researcher diaries. Each method was chosen so as to reflect a divergent angle of repose on the lived experience and consumption practices of a liminar. However, due to space constraints, only interview data will be integrated into this paper.

---

1    These stages of education correspond to junior and senior high school in the United States

Analysis of such a myriad set of data collection techniques required a specific combination of rigor and creativity. In line with the work of Strauss and Corbin (1998), a grounded theory process of analysis was used which proved 'mechanistic and indeterminate in roughly equal portions' (McCracken, 1988: p.41). Following this process of analysis which inherently involves stages of memo writing, axial coding and selective coding, core categories were developed around which the other categories and constructs revolved and offered explanatory power (Spiggle, 1994). This process of data analysis culminated in a stage of data interpretation in the manner of 'a hermeneutic circle' (Arnold and Fischer, 1994: p.63).

## RESEARCH FINDINGS AND ANALYSIS

The following section details one of the central findings of the first phase of data collection – during the last months of primary school – the theory of metaconsumption. Although the main focus of this paper is the metaconsumption theorized as reflective of the consumption practices engaged with by the liminal tweens, it is necessary to briefly ground this theory in the context in which it emerged. This contextual grounding lays the foundation for the emergence of the metaconsumption theory.

## THE LIMINAL TWEEN

As discussed throughout the literature review, the theoretical framework of liminality (Turner, 1967; 1969; 1974) was utilized as a prism for interpreting the cultural and social categorization of these ambiguously located beings. Due to space constraints there will be a brief delineation of one of the component concepts of the notion of the liminal tween; clashing age perceptions. This and many other instances of liminality that emerged throughout the data add empirical credence to the social invisibility experienced by these 'betwixt and between' girls. This sense of being socially imperceptible would emerge as a focal point for the metaconsumption strategies engaged with by these interstitial consumers.

### Clashing Age Perceptions

Established within the specific elements of Turner's (1967) theorization of liminality is acknowledgement of the ambiguity and indeterminacy that embodies the experience of one who exists as a miasma of socio-cultural categorization and perceptions. One of the most overtly liminal components of the tween identity was the tension experienced between their own conceptualization of how others in society should react to them versus the reality of their social positioning. Testament to the theorization that these girls are no longer, but not yet, their social and personal categorizations were often at odds with one another resulting in an acute sense of social invisibility and often darkness for the girls. Their sense of impending immersion into a teen sphere of social interaction was not matched with others' behaviors' towards them.

In the following interview excerpt, Elaine informs me that although she is given the responsibility of caring for her own brother and sister, many people outside of her family would consider her age far too young to be held responsible for their children. However she is quick to point out that she herself does not hold the same view.

E: *'but I am far more mature than a lot of 13 year olds I know…I think it is more to do with the fact that people hear 12 years old and they think oh that's too young to babysit children…*

K: *'and when do you think they would be okay with it…. other people'*

E: *'I think at about 14 or 15 it is more acceptable, by other people, to be babysitting for children'*

Here Elaine finds herself grappling with her own sense of personal development and the views of those who ascribe to the wider social implications of age-aligned development, socialization and consequent competencies. She exists awkwardly at the threshold of what is deemed acceptable socially and how she considers herself personally; blurring boundaries, confusing classification.

In this marketplace example, Rachel highlights the tension she experiences between her own sense of distance from a child-like persona but concurrently other peoples' conceptualization of her as far removed from the realms of teen consumer autonomy.

K: 'and how do you decide what to buy….when you're shopping'

R: 'well probably like….when my mother's coming down town with me…and it's like oh this is lovely and she calls over the shop assistant…then I feel like such a child and I'm like oh no I hate that and she's like oh yea this is lovely, try this on….and I'm like oh no…I hate this outfit…like I hate the pants or something… and then you know the way you wouldn't want to say it in front of the shop assistant and then you're just like…oh okay I'll try it on'

Rachel's experience with the sales assistant exemplifies her occupation of or location in a category lacking boundaries or clarification and as a result her developing sense of autonomy and independence resides uncomfortably beside society's attempts to classify her as a child. Although understanding herself as a competent, self-knowing consumer, this is not how others behave towards her. Thus Rachel's experience of shopping results in a clashing of subjectivities owing to her existence as a 'betwixt and between' (Cook, 2004), exemplifying an interim subjectivity, a liminal self.

## THE EGOCENTRIC TWEEN

The incorporation of a theoretical perspective from the field of psychology was an emergent development following initial data analysis. Elkind's (1967) notion of egocentrism is considered by those specializing in the field of adolescent psychology, to be an under-researched idea, with constructive potential for anyone attempting to theorize on the lived experiences of young adolescents (Elliot & Feldman, 1990). In essence, Elkind's theory centres on the advanced cognitive capabilities of those approaching adolescence status in particular their increased ability to incorporate the perspectives of others into their own way of thinking and understanding themselves and the world around them. What differentiates adolescents however, and perhaps most pertinent to this research, is the tendency of this group to over-generalize and believe themselves to be the focus of most other people's attention all of the time akin to an 'imaginary audience' (Elkind, 1967).

Amanda's interview illustrates vividly her tendency to incorporate an imagined audience into her developing self-system. She explains that the impending move to secondary school has meant divesting herself of any stationary that would be considered young or child like, in the hope of avoiding what she imagines would be certain disdain and ridicule from her new class mates.

K: 'what else did you have to buy for secondary school?'

A: 'yea like I used to have all these little parers[2] and little fancy girly parers but then I was like I'd probably get into trouble…. people would be like 'why do you have that'…so I went for a plain pencil parer'…

K: 'what would people think if you have a plain pencil parer?'

A: 'if you had a big girl sittin up on the table they might be like hmmmmm…baby….

Here Amanda is using the imagined reactions of her peers to alter her consumption repertoire and future buying habits. It is almost like how she envisages her class-mates reacting to her display of consumption objects, is harnessed and utilized as a gauge for what will be suitable to bring along to secondary school. At this point in time, Amanda has not yet experienced the social environs of secondary school at first hand. However her advancing cognitive abilities have allowed her to consider the perspective of those girls she has yet to meet, albeit to an exaggerated degree. Even something as seemingly unrelated to social judgments and ridicule as the theft of her MP3 player is reflective of the egocentric nature of Amanda's developing self.

A: 'I nearly made myself sick thinking about it….i dunno why I got so upset about it….'

K: 'was it to do with losing your zen…or that it was robbed by someone….'

A: 'I dunno…I guess it was a bit of both….i just dunno….i just cracked….i imagined everyone will think I can't look after stuff…'

In this example it appears that what had unsettled Amanda so much following the theft of her MP3 player was less to do with the physical void of the item but more with what she imagined the incident conveyed to others about her ability to be responsible for her possessions. Egocentrically, she believes this mishap to be the sole focus of others' attentions.

## METACONSUMPTION

As outlined above, the liminars' lived experiences are characterized by social ambiguity, categorical invisibility and an overt preoccupation with how they appear in the eyes of those around them. It emerged throughout the data analysis that despite their conveyed annoyance at their status as social non-descripts, their shadowed realities were a vital resource. As evidenced in the data, various consumption strategies were being utilized by the tweens in order to paradoxically evade definite categorization via consumption owing to their egocentric tendencies and fear of social reprisal, prior to a more assured and competent entry into teenager-hood. But concurrently these strategies enable the tweens to tentatively participate in the consumer culture towards which they know their imperatives must be oriented if they are to be accepted by friends and envisaged onlookers.

Regardless of contextual application, the pre-fix 'meta' denotes 'something of a higher or second-order kind' (OED, 2009). A relatively recent consideration within the domain of cognitive analysis is that of second order thinking; or 'thinking about thinking' (Keating, 1990). Metacognition is frequently studied within the realm of psychology as 'the ability to monitor one's own cognitive abilities and activity for consistency, for gaps in information that need to be filled' (Keating, 1990: p75). This theory appeared to have potential for application within the domain of this instance of consumer research. When re-appropriated to analyze the emergent consumption practices of these liminal tweens, the theory of metaconsumption emerged as a viable theoretical process. Fundamentally metaconsumption was envisaged as involving a variety of second order consumption practices; or consumption about consumption. Specifically these metaconsumptive practices focused on consumption mastery, regulation & monitoring of consumption experiences & knowledge for gaps that need to be filled, as opposed to tangible marketplace experiences.

During this liminal existence, these metaconsumption strategies, as will be outlined, served to realize the main preoccupation of a tween; remaining covertly active. It appears to be one of the primary preoccupations of the liminal experience, the main product of this ambiguous, obscure interval. Eluding definite categorization as either child or teen, the tweens channel this cultural anonymity into preparing for one of the most socially pertinent roles of their lives thus far; becoming a teenager. These metaconsumption strategies, as will be delineated, allow the girls to paradoxically both evade definite categorization via consumption prior to a more assured

2    Parer is an Irish slang word referring to pencil sharpener

and competent entry into teenager-hood but also enables them to tentatively participate in the consumer culture towards which their imperatives must be oriented.

Prior to outlining a selection of metaconsumption strategies, it is necessary to theoretically position metaconsumption in relation to consumer behavior research extant in the area of young consumers and consumption practices.

## CONSUMER SOCIALIZATION – A DIVERGENT PATH?

Despite the fact that 'a consumer culture of childhood stands as a ubiquitous fixture in public life' (Cook, 2004b: p1), there are few theoretical accounts of young people's specific negotiations and 'styles of agency' (James and Prout, 1996: p47) as they mediate the intricacies of their lived experiences and social contexts within contemporary consumer culture. Within the realm of children's consumer culture theorists, Martens et al (2004: p161) contend that 'relatively little is known about how children engage in practices of consumption or what the significance of this is to their everyday lives and broader issues of social organization.' The most widely accepted view amongst contemporary sociologists is that this subordinate theoretical positioning has its origins in the paradigm which has dominated the sociology of children and consequently consumer behavior studies with children, for decades; Developmentalism. Disseminated widely by the work of Piaget (e.g. 1955), the child is envisaged as an incomplete work in progress, evolving along a trajectory of cognitive capacity to a point of adult competence. Fundamentally this paradigm relegates the child's social world to inconsequentiality.

Within the sociology of childhood, these paradigmatic specificities became manifest in the form of socialization theory (e.g. Coley, 1998; Harris, 1995; Maccoby, 1992). In part due to its suggestion of the potential to influence or intervene at various stages of development (Gunter & Furnham, 1998; Mills, 2000) the theory of socialization has been applied to consumer research of children via a myriad of studies and theoretical advancements (John, 1999). The term consumer socialization was first introduced to the field of consumer behaviour by Ward (1974) and defined as: 'the processes by which young people acquire skills, knowledge, and attitudes relevant to their functioning as consumers in the marketplace' (p: 2). John (1999) presents the most comprehensive and thorough delineation of literature and theoretical developments in the consumer socialization of children, providing structure and summary to an increasingly expansive area of research. The recognition of brand names and advertising (e.g. Hogg et al, 1998; Achenreiner & John, 2003; Chaplin & John, 2005), and the influence of particular 'socialization agents' on children's growth as consumers (e.g. Dotson & Hyatt, 2005; Grant & Stephen, 2005; Ekstrom, 2007) represent the core focus of research in this area.

In other words, as represented in figure 1, children's evolving relationships with consumption have been predominantly conceptualized under the mantle of 'effects research'. However burgeoning research within children's consumer culture studies have begun an attempt to embrace an alternative perspective on young peoples' interactions and relationships with consumption practices.

For example Cook's (2008) concept of 'commercial enculturation' attempts to capture the 'variety of ways children come to know and participate in commercial life' (Cook, 2008: p9) by shifting the focus to 'how consumption and meaning, and thus culture, cannot be separated from each other but arise together through social contexts and processes of parenting and socializing with others.' (Cook, 2008: p9). Thus commercial enculturation espouses the notion that a more insightful perspective can be gained by view-

ing children as not so much socialized into becoming one kind of specific consumer as they are seen entering into social relationships with and through goods and their associations. There have been several key studies, as listed in figure 1, which align with such a perspective on children's interactions with consumption orienting from the premise that traditional theorizations via consumer socialization theory obscure fruitful ways of seeing consumer behaviour 'in expansive & nuanced ways' (Cook, 2008: p11). Thus from 'the effects' perspective consumption practices and the role of the consumer engage with fairly limited spheres of interaction, and are 'tied to market transactions, brand & products' (Cook, 2008: p11).

The metaconsumption practices outlined below highlight not a concrete socialization process of liminal tween to secure teenager, but rather an intricate interweaving of relationships between consumption and identities - past, present and future- as these social neophytes mediate the intricacies of their interstitial positioning.

### Brand Apathy

The nexus of the metaconsumption strategy is thus the maintenance of an unobtrusive, yet concurrently burgeoning site of consumption, which the liminal period appears to represent for these girls. Several strategies had at their core the notion that any activity, which wrenched the girls from the comfort of their categorical ambiguity and assign them to either a child or teen status before they feel prepared, is detrimental. One concept reflective of the tweens' striving towards consumption practices that facilitate preservation of their social anonymity, for fear of premature emergence before their imagined audience, is brand apathy. Pervasive throughout the first interview data is a definite reluctance by the girls to express an alignment with or affinity to branded products for fear of making an error conducive to social exclusion and ridicule. Contrary to the abundant secondary research in this area (e.g. Siegal et al, 2004; Lindstrom, 2003b; McNeal, 1992), the girls displayed a noticeable reticence when a discussion of brands and their importance to them arose.

In this example Nicola dismisses the notion that brands are important to her, but acknowledges that 'some people' like to revolve their consumption patterns around them.

**K:** *'so do you think brands matter to people your age?'*

**N:** *'well some people do...like they have to get all the brand.... it doesn't matter to me'*

**K:** *'does it not...so what's important to you'*

**N:** *'just kind of if I like the top or not.'*

At this stage, she is still a novice when it comes to buying her way into the teen/consumption dialectic. By refusing to commit to an engagement with brand labels, she is not expected to know anything about them and thus cannot err in her discourse around brands and consumption. Her social status cannot be allocated and she can remain in the interstices of categorisation until such a time when she is equipped with enough social-kudos oriented information to emerge.

Another metaconsumption strategy seemingly utilized in order to convey a purposeful apathy about branded items is price preoccupation. There are numerous examples throughout the first interview data, which suggest that reverting to the reliable utilitarian justification of 'because non-branded things are cheaper', allays the possibility that their incompetence with consumer culture will be brought to notice.

Two excerpts from Rachel's interview add credence to the notion that apathy or resistance toward acknowledging the centrality of brands to their lived experiences is a strategic defense mechanism often couched in a fixation on value for money, designed to protect the shadow side of their being, their liminal regeneration.

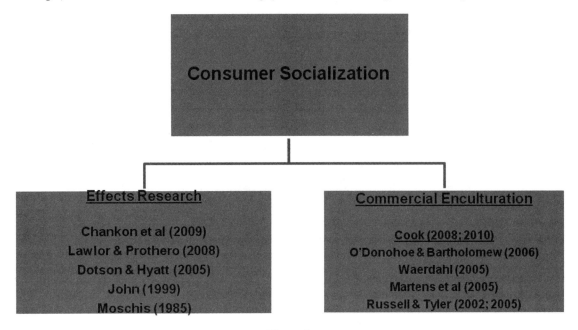

**Figure 1**

K: *'and do you think brands matter to people in your class.... well not just your class...but your friends....do ye talk about brands at all?'*

R: *'amm....not really....the main place that we go is penneys[3].... coz it's so cheap and it actually does have some nice clothes and stuff...and they just have everything at a really cheap price... and say if you went into somewhere else...like where would you go... am...really expensive like Pauls or somewhere....and you'd see the same string top or the same jumper for like fifty euro and like the one you could get in penneys would be like fifteen or twenty...'*

In this first passage, Rachel's attitude is analogous to the other tweens, in that she justifies her supposed detachment from branded goods by referral to the value for money at non-branded stores. However just minutes later, Rachel recalls the experience of buying a new outfit for her confirmation a couple of months previously.

K: *'and what other shops would you go to....say if you went in with your mum?'*

R: *'well radical[4] I bought my confirmation outfit in.'*

K: *'what kind of outfit did you get?'*

R: *'well I got these grey bench combats....they're really nice and I got this tee-shirt and I love it I wear it all the time...and I got a bench hoody....and am its really cool you can put on the sleeve you can put your thumb through a little hole in it...its really cool... and I got my runners[5] there as well....they're van.'*

It appears therefore that Rachel's earlier expressed indifference to brands is not consistent with her behaviour. In this instance, when her mother's financial agency enters the equation, and Rachel has had a tangible experience with a brand, Rachel's priorities change and the non-branded shop doesn't get a mention. Rather she manages to list two big brands in her purchases. Surely if the non-branded store is such good value, her mother's financial resources would have gone a long way further? Clearly Rachel's interview, visible

---

3    Penney's is a discount clothing and accessories store in Ireland

4    Radical is a store in Ireland which stocks branded clothing and footware

5    Runners is Irish slang for trainers/sneakers

in part through this inconsistency, suggests that indifference is a defense mechanism. Expressing a detachment from the world of labels, logos and symbolism is less important a goal when resources not available to the neophyte materialize.

**Parody**

Cognizant of the fact that the core of the metaconsumption strategy is its focus on existing without exhibiting, I was made aware of yet another component of this strategy during the accompanied shopping trips. This strategy centred on the agentive dimension of this liminal shadow in which the tweens exist; consumption strategies that evinced monitoring and acquiring of information and competencies needed when the time came to lead their liminal cocoon and embrace young teen identity.

During these shopping trips, the ambiguity and ensuing tension that the girls experienced in many of the shops seemed to stem from their recurring misallocation as a group or social category. At times the shops we visited were so beyond the realm of possibility for these girls on every level, while concurrently other stores evinced notions of a former childhood self that they were eager to forsake. In other words, it was palpable throughout these trips, that expressing interest in particular items was a risky, value-laden endeavor. Signaling interest in an item deemed 'inappropriate' in any dimension appeared to represent social suicide. I soon realized that these weren't just shopping trips, but opportunities to manage, protect and accumulate the knowledge that was expected of them as young, female consumers.

The concept of parody emerged as a means through which the girls could openly experiment with possible signifiers and configurations of consumption, but maintain a distance from any personal reflections ensuing because of these experiments at the same time. It allowed them to exist without exhibiting. During the shopping trip with three tweens for example, I witnessed firsthand the use of this strategy. On entering one particular store, the girls picked up random tops and skirts claiming 'this is so you' or 'this is my dream outfit'. I only realized after chatting to the girls later on, that this was a statement of sarcasm meant to denote that something was not to their taste and they weren't at all genuine in their sentiments. However although it was not genuine admiration they espoused, expressing opinions or preferences couched in parody or mockery, protects the girls' vulnerability at a time when their level of consumer experience is limited.

**The Fake Facilitators**

This concept refers to the conclusion that many of the girls chose to forsake a preoccupation with having the genuine brand and instead focused on manipulating and utilizing the sign value even associated with counterfeit versions to assert a provisional foot into the world of teen consumption. Therefore although many of the 'brands' they possess are in fact fakes, these products nonetheless facilitate a participation in a version of consumer culture, however diluted. This strategy allows for an engagement with the imperatives that dominate teen consumption but concurrently does not demand the resources only attributed to those of a more defined societal categorization such as finances, life experience or definite market place allocation. In this example, Katie is taking me through some of the possession in her room, including a fake Von-Dutch cap. Interestingly she herself points out that it is a fake.

**K:** 'What other brands do you use?'

**KL:** 'von dutch...I got those in Majorca...they have lasted me two years now'

**K:** 'wow...and do you have any other von dutch stuff....do you know much about the brand?'

***Katie roots underneath her bed***

**K:** 'ooh a cap...do you wear that much'

**KL:** 'yeah...its fake von dutch...but it's still von dutch'

What Katie seems to mean here is that to others, it still appears to be Von Dutch, or at the very least she is appearing to others to be engaging with the brands that form the appropriate staple diet of any normative teen. The important thing for Katie then is appearances rather than authenticity. Appearances maintains the shadow side of their being so that they can incur as little anticipated social ridicule as possible while they experiment with the intricacies of the teen persona/consumption dialectic.

Rachel also displayed an affinity for the non-authentic version of some well-known brands.

**K:** *(reading diary)...Louis Vitton is one of my favourite designers. I love his bags....so which one is yours?'*

**R:** 'well I got the both of them off my next door neighbour (laughs), she got them...

**K:** 'what do you like about those bags?'

**R:** 'I think they look really cool...and I don't mind of they're fake...because no-one really knows'

Rachel here articulates the key element of the fake facilitator concept, as a metaconsumption strategy. Counterfeit products allow the liminal tweens, despite their lack of agency as a socially ambiguous category, to engage with a desirable facet of consumer culture; the repository of symbolic meaning and social implications behind the Louis Vitton logo. Although the use of fake brands is not a consumption practice limited to this age group, the role that these brands play in the lived experience of a liminal tween is significant towards understanding how consumption is enacted during a time of social invisibility.

## DISCUSSION

This paper has described some of the constituent elements of metaconsumption; the proposed theorization of the liminars' consumption practices and a suggested diversion from 'the effects' perspective on young consumers' socialization. Being neither a child consumer nor a teen purchaser implies that there exists a gap between the self they were and the self they long to be and

the liminal status that ensues. In addition, advancing cognitive capacities instill the tweens with a flagrant sense of trepidation regarding their neophyte-like social standing and potential public transgressions. Consequently they long to reside in the shadowed side of being, attempting to learn, monitor and accumulate socially oriented consumer knowledge, but all the while protect and maintain the anonymity that shields them from social scrutiny and insinuations. This intense period of second order consumption practices, or 'consumption focused on consumption' aligning oneself with the nuances and mores of the social sphere which will help sculpt their entry into teenager-hood, provides examples of a myriad consumption strategies and practices which further a theorization of liminal beings and their consumption practices. In addition, metaconsumption advances the burgeoning area of children's consumer culture research which attempts to explore the mediation of socio-cultural hierarchies and boundaries by young people via their relationships with consumption.

Thus this desire to exist without exhibiting is the core characteristic of the liminal existence and subsequently the theory of metaconsumption has an integral role in its manifestation. For example, the visible propensity of the tweens to convey decided apathy and even resistance towards branded consumption with the variant but related strategy of price preoccupation, was reflective of an effort to preserve the unspecific nature of their social categorization. Not committing to a brand meant not committing to an (unfinished) teen identity. This theoretical conclusion stands in stark contrast to the prevalent literature on branded consumption, whether conceptually, theoretically or managerially oriented (Lindstrom, 2003; McDougall & Chantrey, 2004; Elliot & Leonard, 2004) that convey brand-oriented consumption as a transparently positive and desired facet of tween consumer culture.

However it is equally as intrinsic to the liminal existence that this period of time is not entirely static. As theorized by Douglas (1966, p.137) in relation to interstitial existences 'there is energy in the margins and unstructured areas'. A degree of agency must become part of the metaconsumptive practices of the tween if they are to progress towards the essence of their teen identity (Jenks, 2003). Thus the concepts of the fake facilitators and parody encapsulate the covert but fervent accumulation of consumer-oriented knowledge and experience that concurrently embodies the liminar's 'betwixt and between' existence. For example, parody, akin to the foundational premise of the other metaconsumption strategies is both an enabling and a protective mechanism in that it facilitates the tweens' engagement with the appearance of teen consumerism but yet safeguards the anonymity necessary to prevent premature alignment with a teen identity that they are ill prepared for.

Cognizant of the tweens' concurrent engagement with and detachment from consumption practices, the liminal period is proposed to represent a fruitful darkness (Turner, 1967, p110). Akin to understudies waiting in the wings anxiously ingesting as much information as possible in order to better prepare themselves for the biggest performative role of their lives to date – which as of yet is just out of sight – the fructile chaos of the fruitful darkness facilitates a private rehearsal for what will eventually be a very public performance. The metaphor of the fruitful darkness embodies the concurrent darkness and energy, the restorative obscurity that epitomizes the liminars' experiences with consumer culture within the interstices of socio-cultural categorization. Although at times the tweens appear passive or nonchalant about many of the signifiers of teen culture, this passivity appears to belie a fervent task. Turner (1967, p.102) similarly theorized when he claimed that during the liminal period 'his apparent passivity is revealed as an absorption of powers which will become active after his social status has been redefined…'

## CONCLUSION

Schouten's (1991: p422) assertion that 'little is yet known about the consumption behaviours of liminal people' was one which had been tentatively approached amongst those exploring the intricate and fascinating interweaving of self and consumption. Research had been instigated and conclusions drawn in relation to consumers and transitions without in-depth focus of that interim period when transition is midway and individuals exist on a threshold blurring past, present and future. As articulated by Turner (1974: p13) it is 'in this gap between ordered worlds that almost anything may happen'. In addition, studies of young consumers and their interactions with consumption have been stifled by a fixation on 'effects' approaches to the detriment of interpretive explorations of the social relationships which emerge between young people and various realms of consumer culture and practices, cognizant of the boundaries and hierarchies which constitute their social world. There are many other areas within consumer culture theory which would reap the rewards of considering the liminal; that threshold existence which embodies both light and dark, stillness and energy, ambiguity and focus. Those experiencing the mid-state of transition have received sparse attention in the field of consumer research. This paper has begun addressing this dearth and by doing so has attested to the potential of the liminality theory itself.

'The Liminal status is a fructile chaos, a storehouse of possibilities, not a random assemblage but a striving after new forms and structures, a gestation process'.
(Turner & Bruner, 1986: p42)

## REFERENCES

Achenreiner, G. B. & John Roedder, D. (2003) 'The meaning of brand names to children: a developmental perspective'. *Journal of Consumer Psychology*. Vol 13 (3):205-219

Anderson, C. C. (2003), *Phenomology of Implantation: The Liminal Body and the Implantable Cardioverter Defibrillator*, Unpublished Doctoral Dissertation, Griffith University.

Arnold, S. J. and Fischer, E. (1994), 'Hermeneutics and Consumer Research', *Journal of Consumer Research*, 21 (1), 55-70.

Arnould, E. J. and Thompson, C. J. (2005), 'Consumer Culture Theory (CCT): Twenty Years of Research, *Journal of Consumer Research*, 31 (4), 868-882.

Bettis, P. J. (1996), 'Urban Students, Liminality and the postindustrial context', *Sociology of Education*, 69 (2), 105-125.

Bhabha, H. K. (2004), *The Location of Culture*, New York: Routledge.

Brown, K. B. (2007), 'Introduction: Liminality and the social location of musicians', *Twentieth Century Music*, 3 (1), 5-12.

Campbell, N., O' Driscoll, A. & Saren, M. (2005), 'Cyborg Consciousness: A Visual Culture Approach to the Technologised Body', In: Ekstrom, K. M. & Brembeck, H. (Eds). *Proceedings of the European Advances in Consumer Research Conference*, Gothenburg, Duluth, MN: Association for Consumer Research.

Chaplin, L. N. & John Roedder, D. (2005) 'The development of self-brand connections in children and adolescents'. *Journal of Consumer Research*. Vol 32 (1):119-129

Coley, R. L. (1998), 'Children's socialization experiences and functioning in single mother households: the importance of fathers and other men', *Child Development*, Vol 69 (1): 219-230.

Cook, D. T. (2004a), 'Beyond either/or', *Journal of Consumer Culture*, 4 (2), 147-153.

Cook, D. T. (2004b) *The Commodification of Childhood*. Durham & London: Duke University Press.

Cook, D. T. (2008), 'Commercial Enculturation: Moving beyond Consumer Socialization', *Accepted for the 3rd Child and Teen Consumption Conference, Norwegian Centre for Child Research, Trondheim, Norway.*

Davies. A. & Fitchett, J. A. (2004), 'Crossing Culture: A multimethod enquiry into consumer behaviour and the experience of cultural transition', *Journal of Consumer Behaviour*, 3 (4), 315-330.

Dotson, M. J. & Hyatt, E. M. (2005). 'Major Influence Factors in children's consumer socialisation'. *Journal of Consumer Marketing*. Vol 22 (1):35-42

Douglas, M. (1966), *Purity and Danger: An Analysis of the concepts of pollution and taboo*, London: Allen Lane.

Dunne, M. (2002), 'Resolving a paradox through liminality', *Journal of Popular Film and Television*, 29 (4), 182-189.

Ekstrom, K. M. (2007). 'Parental Consumer learning or keeping up with the children'. *Journal of Consumer Behaviour*. Vol 6 (4):203-217

Elkind, D. (1967), 'Egocentrism in Adolescence', *Child Development*, 38 (4), 1025-1034.

Elliot, G. R. and Feldman, S. S. (1990), 'Capturing the Adolescent Experience'. In Elliot, G. R. and

Feldman, S. S, eds. *At the Threshold: The Developing Adolescent*, US: Harvard University Press.

Elliot, R. and Leonard, C. (2004), 'Peer Pressure and poverty: exploring fashion brands and consumption symbolism among children of the British poor', *Journal of Consumer Behaviour*, 3 (4), 347-359.

Foucault, M. (1977), *Language, Counter-Memory, Practice* (contains the 1963 essay 'Preface to Transgression'), New York: Cornell University Press.

Freud, S. (1950), *Totem and Taboo*, New York: Routledge & Kegan Paul Ltd.

Gentry, J. W. (1997), 'Life-Event transitions and Consumer Vulnerability', *Advances in Consumer Research*, 24 (1), 29-31.

Gough, A. (2005), 'Body/Mine: A Chaos Narrative of Cyborg Subjectivities and Liminal Experiences', *Women's Studies*, 34 (3-4), 249-264.

Grant, I. J. & Stephen, G. R. (2005) 'Buying behaviour of "tweenage" girls and key societal communicating factors influencing their purchasing of fashion clothing' *Journal of Fashion Marketing and Management*. Vol 9 (4):450-467

Gunter, B. & Furnham, A. (1998). *Children as Consumers: A psychological analysis of the young people's market*. London: Routledge.

Harris, J. R. (1995), 'Where is the child's environment? A group socialization theory of development', *Psychological Review*, Vol 102 (3):458-489.

Hogg, M. K., Curasi, C. F. &Maclaran, P. (2004), 'The (Re-) Configuration of Production and Consumption in empty nest households/families', *Consumption, Markets and Culture*, 7 (3), 239-259.

Hogg, M.K., Bruce, M., Hill, A.J. (1999), "Brand recognition and young consumers", *Advances in Consumer Research*, Vol. XXVI pp.671-4.

Hooker, L. (2007), 'Controlling the liminal power of performance: Hungarian scholars and Romani musicians in the Hungarian folk festival', *Twentieth-Century Music*, 3 (1), 51-72.

James, A. Jenks, C. & Prout, A. (1998), *Theorizing Childhood*, Cambridge: Polity Press.

James, A. & Prout, A. (1996), 'Strategies and Structures: Towards a New Perspective on children's experiences of family life' , IN M. O'Brien and J.Brannen (eds) Children in Families: Research and Policy, London: Falmer Press

Jenks, C. (2003), *Transgression*, London: Routledge.

Jenks, C. (2005), *Childhood*, New York: Routledge.

John Roedder, D. (1999). 'Consumer socialisation of children: A retrospective look at twenty-five years of research'. *Journal of Consumer Research*. Vol 26 (3):183-13

Jones, K. T., Zagacki, K. S. and Lewis, T. V. (2007), 'Communication, liminality and hope: the September 11th Missing Person Posters', *Communication Studies*, 58 (1), 105-121.

Keating, D. P. (1990), 'Adolescent Thinking'. In Elliot, G. R. and Feldman, S. S, eds. *At the Threshold: The Developing Adolescent*, US: Harvard University Press.

Kotler, P., Armstrong, G., Wong, V. and Saunders, J. (2008), *Principles of Marketing 5th European Edition*, London: Financial Times/Prentice Hall

Kozinets, Robert V. (2001), "Utopian Enterprise: Articulating the Meanings of Star Trek's Culture of Consumption," Journal of Consumer Research, 28 (June), 67-88

Landzelius, K. M. (2001), 'Charged Artifacts and the Detonation of Liminality: Teddy-Bear Diplomacy in the Newborn Incubator Machine', *Journal of Material Culture*, 6 (3), 323-344.

Lindstrom, M. (2003), *Brand Child*, London: Kogan Page Limited.

Little, M., Jordens, C. F., Paul, K., Montgomery, K. and Philipson, B. (1998), 'Liminality: A major category of the experience of cancer illness', *Social Science & Medicine*, 47 (10), 1485-1494.

Maccoby, E. E. (1992), 'The role of parents in the socialization of children: an historical overview', *Developmental Psychology*, Vol 28 (6):1006-1017.

Maldonado, R. & Tansuhaj, P. (1999), 'Transition Challenges in Consumer Acculturation: Role Destabilization and Changes in Symbolic Consumption*, Advances in Consumer Research*, 26 (1), 134-140.

Martens, L, Southerton, D. & Scott, S. (2004) 'Bringing children (and parents) into the sociology of consumption: towards a theoretical and empirical agenda'. *Journal of Consumer Culture* Vol 4 (2):155-181

Matthews, H., Taylor, M., Percy-Smith, B. and Limb, M. (2000), 'The unacceptable flaneur: the shopping mall as a teenage hangout', *Childhood*, 7 (3), 279-294.

McCracken, G. (1988), *Culture and Consumption*, Bloomington: Indiana University Press.

McDougall, J. and Chantrey, D. (2004), 'The making of tomorrow's consumer', *Young Consumers*, 5 (4), 8-18.

McNeal, J. U. (1992), *Kids as Customers: a handbook of marketing to children*, New York: Lexington Books.

Mills, R. (2000). 'Perspectives of Childhood'. In Mills, J. & Mills, R. eds. *Childhood Studies: A reader in perspectives of childhood*. London: Routledge.

Noble, C. H. and Walker, B. A. (1997), 'Exploring the relationships among liminal transitions, symbolic consumption and the extended self', *Psychology & Marketing*, 14 (1), 29-47.

Pavia, T. M. and Mason, M. J. (2004), 'The Reflexive Relationship between consumer behaviour and adaptive coping', *Journal of Consumer Research*, 31 (2), 441-454.

Piaget, J. (1955). *The Child's Construction of Reality*. London: Routledge and Kegan Paul.

Pritchard, A. and Morgan, N. (2006), 'Hotel Babylon? Exploring hotels as liminal sites of transition and transgression', *Tourism Management*, 27 (5), 762-772.

Richardson, L. (1994), 'Writing: A Method of Inquiry', In Denzin, N. K. and Lincoln, Y. S, eds. *Handbook of Qualitative Research*, Thousand Oaks, CA: Sage.

Rill, B. (2006), 'Rave, Communitas and Embodied Idealism', *Music Therapy Today*, 7 (3), 648-661.

Schouten, J. W. (1991), 'Selves in Transition: symbolic consumption in personal rites of passage and identity reconstruction', *Journal of Consumer Research*, 17 (4), 412-425.

Siegal, D. L., Coffey, T. J. and Livingston, G. (2004), *The Great Tween Buying Machine: Capturing your share of the multibillion dollar tween market*, US: Dearborn Trade Publishing.

Slater, D. (1997), *Consumer Culture and Modernity*, Oxford, UK: Polity Press.

Spiggle, S. (1994), 'Analysis and Interpretation of Qualitative Data in Consumer Research*, Journal of Consumer Research*, 21 (3), 491-503.

Strauss, A. and Corbin, J. (1998), *Basics of Qualitative Research*, California: Sage.

Tadajewski, M. (2006) 'Remembering Motivation Research: Toward an Alternative Genealogy of Interpretive Consumer Research', *Marketing Theory* 6(4): 429-466.

Turner, V. W. & Bruner, E. M. (Eds) (1986). *The Anthropology of Experience*, Urbana: University of Illinois Press.

Turner, V. W. & Turner, E. (1978), *Image and Pilgrimage in Christian Culture: Anthropological Perspectives*, New York: Columbia University Press.

Turner, V. W. (1967), *The Forest of Symbols: Aspects of Ndembu ritual*, Ithaca: Cornell University Press.

Turner, V. W. (1969), *The Ritual Process: Structure and Anti-Structure*, Ithaca: Cornell University Press.

Turner, V. W. (1974), *Dramas, fields and metaphors: symbolic action in human society*, Ithaca: Cornell University Press.

Van Gennep, A. (1961), *The Rites of Passage*, US: Chicago University Press.

Ward, S. (1974) 'Consumer Socialisation'. *Journal of Consumer Research*. Vol 1 (1):1-14

Waskul, D. D. (2005), 'Ekstasis and the internet: liminality and computer-mediated communication', *New Media & Society*, 7 (1), 47-63.

Zukin, S. (1991), *Landscapes of Power: From Detroit to Disneyworld*, London: University of California Press Ltd.

# Personality and Sustainable Consumption: An Application of the 3M Model

Ricardo Teixeira Veiga, UFMG, Brazil
Juliane Almeida Ribeiro, UFMG, Brazil

## ABSTRACT

The personality traits that predict sustainable consumption are investigated, adopting the 3M model as theoretical framework. Altruism seems to be a trait consistently useful to predict ecologically-correct purchase, resources saving, and recycling. Consumerism only seems to be useful to explain variance in resources saving.

## INTRODUCTION

The increase of consumption in a global scale is a consequence of the extraordinary increase in the human population in the twentieth century, of the intensified urbanization and of the industrialization in most countries (Penna 1999). The obsession for economical growth and consumption is a reflection of the spreading of the development ideology, inherent to capitalism (Baudrillard 1998). The environmental problems resulting from that are acute and potentially catastrophically, for they tend to worsen. Deforestation, pollution, the destruction of ecosystems and biodiversity, global warming and others, are concrete activities that show the human influence on the planet.

It is necessary to raise people's awareness about their negative impact on the environment and about the importance of their assuming an active role regarding nature conservation and quality of life in the long run, through the engagement in an ecologically responsible lifestyle and way of consuming.

Authors like Fraj and Martinez (2007) and Straughan and Roberts (1999) show some optimism when remembering that the general concern about human consumption as a sustainable factor has increased. Nevertheless, the spreading of ecological consciousness has been occurring in a slow rhythm, especially in countries of late industrialization. In Brazil, for example, only one in three consumers is worried about separating garbage for recycling, buying organic products and/or produts made with recycled material, avoiding water and energy waste or to perform other types of ecologically conscious behaviors (Akatu 2006).

So, it is important to deepen the researches about sustainable consumption, aiming at the elaboration of educational programs and social intervention that make consumers in general, more sensitive to ecological issues.

When investigating the relation between personality traits and ecologically conscious consumption, this research adopts the 3M Model of Motivation and Personality (Mowen 2000) as theoretical frame, in order to identify effective ways to persuade people to consume with ecological responsibility.

In the next section, we will present a brief literature review about ecologically conscious consumption. Based on this review and on the consumer behavior concept, we come up with a sustainable consumption concept that is integrated to the theoretical framework and to the research hypothesis.

## THEORETICAL BACKGROUND

Consumers have been aware of the need to buy in a socially responsible way and to demand from the companies adequate ecological behaviors. There was an increase in ecological awareness during the twentieth century and the changing of the environmental issue into an strategic priority to citizens, countries and organizations (Straughan & Roberts 1999). According to the authors, many companies have been trying to act in a more relevant way, doing more than just implementing processes of clean production, but

engaging in ecological activities on behalf of sustainable development. In a more skeptical perspective, Peattie (2001) argues that the ecological engagement of the companies is a way of dealing with consumers that ask for a bigger responsibility towards nature conservation.

From the 1980's on, because of a greater worry about the consumption impact on the environment, the concept of "green consumer" has been consolidated. Together with the emergence of this consumer segment, a "green market" expanded to a considerable rate in the developed countries (Schlegelmilch, Bohlen and Diamantopoulos 1996; Follows and Jober 2000; Peattie 2001), since a reasonable part of the consumers were willing to pay more for goods which were made regarding a greater care for nature. For example, a survey made by Mintel, concluded that 27% of English adults were willing to pay 25% more for green products (Prothero 1990 apud Schlegelmilch, Bohlen and Diamantopoulos 1996), whereas a research made by J. Walter Thompson suggested that 82% of North-American would pay 5% more for this kind of product (Peattie, op. cit.). Furthermore, as a group, the green products gained a market share of 20% and, in specific categories, of 30% (Kohl 1990 apud Follows and Jobber 2000).

Nowadays, although there are still many challenges in order to develop a sustainable market, there are indications that it is potentially big and profitable (Mintu-Wimsatt and Bradford 1995; Tucker 1980 apud Wergin 2009). According to the company of marketing research called Mintel International Group, in 2006 the green market had a turnover of 200 billion dollars, and it is supposed to grow more in the future. There are also evidences that the consumers are becoming more inclined to have ecologically conscious behaviors: according to Ottman (1993), 70% of the North-American consumers declared that the fact that the products they bought were in recyclable packages affected their buying decisions, whereas in Brazil, 74% of the consumers stated their intention of buying products that do not degrade the environment (Mansur, Arini and Ferreira 2008).

Some investigations done during the 1970's (Kassarjian 1971; Kinnear, Taylor, and Ahmed, 1974; Webster 1975) were already about identifying and analyzing the values, attitudes and behavior of ecologically conscious consumers, as well as explore means of reaching them more efficiently (Schaefer and Crane 2005).

Fraj and Martinez (2007) discuss three perspectives adopted along the years for the study of ecologically conscious consumers. Firstly, these researchers were interested in understanding these consumers behavior according to demographic and socio-economic measures (e.g., Vining and Ebreo, 1990, Bhate and Lawler, 1997, Daniere and Takahashi, 1999, Fraj et al., 1999, Fraj and Martinez, 2003). Later on, a new field of studies considered the amount of information and knowledge that people had regarding environmental problems and issues (e.g., Arnutnoth and Lingg, 1975, Ramsey and Rickson, 1976, Grunert and Kristnesen, 1992). A third approach used psychographic variables, that included values, lifestyle, personality traits and attitudes (e.g., Batson et al., Granzine and Olsen, 1991, Ramanaiah et el., 2000), to trace the profile of ecologically conscious consumers.

Although the marketing focus of ecologically conscious consumption is related to the trading of ecologically right products, that is, those with a minimum or none negative environment impact (Ottman 1993; Roberts 1996; Peattie 2001; Fraj and Martinez 2007), this research assumes that sustainable consumption (SC) must be widely understood. It must also include the search for a means of reducing the consumption of materials and energy, buying organic foods, buying goods that are produced in the local place, active participation in recycling, promoting the use of mass transportation and economy of resources (Halkier 1999 *apud* Connolly and Prothero 2008).

In fact, sustainable consumption must be also understood in the consumer behavior perspective, defined by Solomon (2002, p. 24) as "the study of the processes involved when individuals or groups select, buy, use or dispose products, services, ideas or experiences in order to satisfy necessities and desires".

Based on this definition and on the review about ecologically conscious consumption, we propose to conceptualize sustainable consumption as: " the search for ecologically-correct products, the preference for corporations and organizations actively engaged in environment conservation, the using of materials and equipment up to the end of its service life, the saving of resources such as water and energy, the reusing, whenever possible, the right destination of materials to recycling and the propensity to a lifestyle with a smaller negative environment impact".

The perspective adopted, aimed at complementing the previous studies, proposing a concept of sustainable consumption tied to the whole consumption cycle (acquisition, use and discharge) and coherent to the concern about saving the natural resources and support companies and institutions that are ecologically responsible. It is a way of consumption according to a less consumerist lifestyle, and, consequently, with a less negative environmental impact.

As in the long run, the objective of our research is to influence people so that they consume in a more sustainable way, we used the 3M model as framework, because identifying personality traits and associating them to sustainable consumption behavior, can set a base to elaborate messages that stimulate this behavior through the activation of these traits (Mowen and Harris 2003).

The 3M - a Meta-theoretical Model of Motivation and Personality

In this research, we employ the 3M Model that integrates control theory, evolutionary psychology principles, and elements of the hierarchical trait theories (Mowen 2000). This model provides a four-level structure to organize traits, based on an integrated account of how personality traits interact with situations to influence feelings, thoughts, and behaviors. The 3M Model has been employed as the theoretical model to investigate the trait antecedents of many types of behavior, including aggressive and distracted driving (Bone and Mowen 2006), credit card misuse among college students (Pirog III and Roberts 2007) and consumer competitiveness (Mowen 2004).

The 3M Model proposes that personality traits are arranged into a four-level hierarchy based upon their abstractness. Elemental traits are at the most abstract level and are enduring, cross-situational dispositions that arise from genetics and early learning history (Mowen 2000). The model proposes eight elemental traits, which should be included as control variables in the hierarchical model: openness to experience, conscientiousness, extroversion/introversion, agreeableness, emotional instability, need for body resources, need for material resources, and need for arousal. Based on works by Buss (1988) and Zuckerman (1979), Mowen suggested the addition of the last three elemental traits, extending the set of personality traits of the five-factor model (McCrae and Costa 1997). *Need for body resources* and *need for material resources* are traits strictly concerning self-preservation.

Compound traits are at the next level of the hierarchy. They are defined as cross-situational dispositions, that emerge from the interplay of elemental traits, culture, and the individual's learning history (Mowen 2000). In the present study, we investigate two

compound traits: general self-efficacy (Mowen 2000) and altruism (Stern 2000).

Compound traits were based on literature. Empirical results show that a belief in one's own capacity of succeeding in performing tasks, irrespective of chance, influence the engagement in ecologically-oriented behaviors (e.g. Bodur and Sarigöllu 2005). But self-efficacy is a compound trait linked to personal control and has a crucial role in the performance of tasks (Mowen, 200). Besides, self-efficacy influences the performance of types of behavior which demand commitment and persistence to overcome difficulties (Bandura 1977 *apud* Mowen 2000). So, we propose general self-efficacy as antecedent of sustainable consumption.

Altruism can be understood as value or personality trait. There are many studies which found relationship among altruism, concern with environment, and ecologically-oriented behavior (e.g., Granzin and Olsen 1991; Dietz *et al.* 1998; Karp 1996; Stern and Dietz 1994; *apud* Stern 2000), if we understand altruism as a personal orientation which surpasses selfishness, individualism, competitiveness, and the predominant interest in the immediate social circles. In the present research, we conceptualize altruism as a compound trait and propose that it is also antecedent of sustainable consumption.

At the third level of hierarchy are situational traits, which result from combinations of elemental traits, compound traits, as well as the effects of situational environment (Mowen 2000). The situational trait investigated in this study is consumerism.

At the most concrete level in the hierarchy are superficial traits, which represent enduring dispositions to act within category-specific contexts (Mowen 2000). Superficial traits have a strong behavioral component. They result from the combined effects of elemental, compound, situational traits, and the press of the specific situational context. Based on the concept of sustainable consumption, we propose ecologically-oriented purchase, resources saving and recycling as superficial traits in this research. Figure 1 shows the hierarchical model employed in the present research.

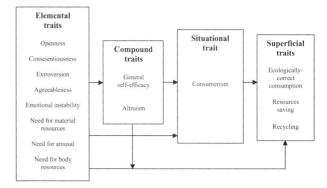

**Figure 1. The research hierarchical model**

Situational and superficial traits were defined at the exploratory stage of the research by factor analyzing a 24-item scale of sustainable consumption (SC) as defined in the present research. Source of items were other scales, literature (e.g., a scale of consumerism was provided by De Young 2000) and personal judgment. By using principal component analysis and orthogonal rotation (varimax), we retained only 13 items to operationalize consumerism, ecologically-correct purchase, resources saving and recycling. We selected the non-ambiguous items which loaded more strongly on the respective factors. As a result, factor unidimensionality was reached. See table 1 for more information.

## Table 1
## Situational and Superficial Traits Resulted of Exploratory Analysis

| Factor | Variable | Item-total correlation | Item description |
|---|---|---|---|
| **Consumerism (*)** | | | |
| Cronbach's alpha = .62 | i6 | .42 | I wear clothes that are in fashion. |
| AII = .35 | i8 | .43 | I have the most modern electronic gadgets and consumer goods. |
| | i17 | .44 | I have luxury items and conveniences available in our society. |
| **Ecologically-correct purchase (**)** | | | |
| Cronbach's alpha = .75 | i4 | .48 | I vote for politicians who support the environmental causes. |
| AII = .50 | i12 | .58 | I stop buying from companies which doesn't show concern for the protection of the environment. |
| | i14 | .66 | I change my brand preferences to support companies that show more concern for the protection of environment. |
| **Resources saving (**)** | i16 | .45 | I let television and computer on even when not using them. |
| Cronbach's alpha = .62 | i21 | .29 | I turn off the taps when soaping or washing dishes. |
| AII = .35 | i22 | .51 | I let lights on without need. |
| **Recycling (**)** Cronbach's alpha = .94 AII = .80 | i2 i11 i20 i23 | .86 .91 .80 .89 | I separate metal objects (e.g. cans) for recycling. I separate glass (e.g. beer bottles) for recycling. I separate paper for recycling. I separate plastic packaging (e.g. plastic bottles, plastic bags etc.) for recycling. |

Notes: AII – Average inter-item correlations; (*) situational trait; (**) superficial trait.

## HYPOTHESES DEVELOPMENT

As recommend by Mowen (2000), all eight elemental traits were include in the research model as control variables. Proposed relationships among elemental traits and traits of other hierarchical levels are based on literature and logical analysis.

According to Borden and Francis (1978) people more concerned about environment tend to be more mature, responsible, sociable, and conscientious then the ones who are not concerned. Fraj and Martinez (2006) say that ecologically-correct consumers have higher scores in measures of extroversion (sociability), amiability and consciousness. Ramanaiah et al. (2000) found that the traits openness to experience and agreeability were more significant to distinguish consumer segments with high and low scores in environmental responsibility. Monteiro et al. (2008) observe that people who are more agreeable, creative and conscientious are more likely to strive for a balance between nature and modern life. As ecologically-correct purchase, resources saving and recycling are traits which show care for the environment, the following hypotheses were proposed:

*Hypothesis$_{1a}$:* *Conscientiousness is positively related with ecologically-correct purchase.*

*Hypothesis$_{1b}$:* *Conscientiousness is positively related with resources saving.*

*Hypothesis$_{1c}$:* *Conscientiousness is positively related with recycling.*

*Hypothesis$_{2a}$:* *Openness to experience is positively related with ecologically-correct purchase.*

*Hypothesis$_{2b}$:* *Openness to experience is positively related with resources saving.*

*Hypothesis$_{2c}$:* *Openness to experience is positively related with recycling.*

*Hypothesis$_{3a}$:* *Agreeability is positively related with ecologically-correct purchase.*

*Hypothesis$_{3b}$:* *Agreeability is positively related with resources saving.*

*Hypothesis$_{3c}$:* *Agreeability is positively related with recycling.*

*Hypothesis$_{4a}$:* *Extroversion is positively related with ecologically-correct purchase.*

*Hypothesis$_{4b}$:* *Extroversion is positively related with resources saving.*

*Hypothesis$_{4c}$:* *Extroversion is positively related with recycling.*

As in the long run sustainable consumption is oriented towards saving natural resources and protecting the environment in order to guarantee survival, we predicted the following relationships:

Hypothesis$_{5a}$:      The need for body resources is positively related with ecologically-correct purchase.

Hypothesis$_{5b}$:      The need for body resources is positively related with resources saving.

Hypothesis$_{5c}$:      The need for body resources is positively related with recycling.

As Straughan and Roberts (1999) state that altruism and self-efficacy seem to be personality traits typical of ecologically-correct consumers, we proposed the following hypothesis about compound traits:

Hypothesis$_{6a}$:      Altruism is positively related with ecologically-correct purchase.

Hypothesis$_{6b}$:      Altruism is positively related with resources saving.

Hypothesis$_{6c}$:      Altruism is positively related with recycling

Hypothesis$_{7a}$:      General self-efficacy is positively related with ecologically-correct purchase.

Hypothesis$_{7b}$:      General self-efficacy is positively related with resources saving.

Hypothesis$_{7c}$:      General self-efficacy is positively related with recycling

Consumerism can be understood as the search for conveniences of modern society and continuous interest in new or innovative products (De Young 2000). We assume that four elemental traits are related with consumerism:

Hypothesis$_{8a}$:      Openness to experience is positively related with consumerism.

Hypothesis$_{8b}$:      The need for arousal is positively related with consumerism.

Hypothesis$_{8c}$:      The need for body resources is positively related with consumerism.

Hypothesis$_{8d}$:      The need for material resources is positively related with consumerism.

As consumerism is essentially self-oriented we assume that there must be a negative association between consumerism and altruism:

Hypothesis$_{6d}$:      Altruism is negatively related with consumerism.

De Young (2000) did not find any correlation between consumerism and ecologically-correct consumption. Nevertheless, we assume that there is an association, so we proposed hypotheses of negative association among consumerism and the superficial traits concerning sustainable consumption.

Hypothesis$_{9a}$:      Consumerism is negatively related with ecologically-correct purchase.

Hypothesis$_{9b}$:      Consumerism is negatively related with resources saving.

Hypothesis$_{9c}$:      Consumerism is negatively related with recycling.

Finally, some hypotheses concerned relationships among compound and elemental traits. According to meta-analysis, Mowen (2000) concluded that with the exception of the need for material resources trait, all elemental traits were significant predictors of general self-efficacy. In the case of altruism, we decided to test correlation with all eight elemental traits.

Hypothesis$_{10}$:      General self-efficacy is related with all the elemental traits, except with the need for material resources trait.

Hypothesis$_{11}$:      Altruism is related with all the eight elemental traits.

## METHOD

College students of different undergraduate courses of the same university were surveyed. We obtained 512 valid questionnaires over a 2 week-time period. The mean age was 22.8 years, and 50.1 per cent were women. The four-page survey contained measures of the traits under investigation and also demographic measures. Consistent with prior research on the 3M Model, the survey was arranged such that respondents answered items in their order in the hierarchical model, starting by responding to the elemental traits items. Elemental traits items were taken from Monteiro et al. (2008). Compound traits (general self-efficacy and altruism) were respectively taken from Mowen (2000) and Schultz (2000). De Young (2000) provided items to measure consumerism, and the other sustainable consumption items were also taken from literature and personal judgment. Five-point scales were used for all variables.

Exploratory data analysis was carried out by employing SPSS version 17. The problem of missing data was almost negligible as only 0.2% of item data were missing. Their distribution was considered as completely at random (MCAR Litte's test: chi-square = 197.976, d.f. = 207, p = .662). So, multiple data imputation was adopted to get a complete data set. Variables did not exhibit univariate normality, according to Kolmogorov-Smirnov tests.

The sample was randomly split in two subsamples. The biggest one (n = 312) was used to operationalize the constructs associated to sustainable consumption (consumerism, ecologically-correct purchase, resources saving and recycling), and to select single items to represent the elemental traits and the best indicators of compound traits (altruism and general self-efficacy). The smallest subsample (n = 200) was used to estimate the research hierarchical model.

**Table 2**
**Accounted Variances and Significant Effects in the Full Hierarchical Model**

| Trait | Accounted Variance | Non-sig. Predictor | Significant Predictor | t | P |
|---|---|---|---|---|---|
| **Altruism** | 39% | | **Agreeability** | 3.85 | *** |
| **(Alt.)** | | | **Openness** | 1.77 | 0.08 |
| | | | **Conscienc.** | 2.54 | 0.01 |
| | | | **Material.** | -2.73 | 0.01 |
| | | | **Body res.** | 2.77 | 0.01 |
| | | | **Instability** | -2.24 | 0.03 |
| | | Arousal | | | |
| | | Extroversion | | | |
| **General self-efficacy** | 18% | | **Agreeability** | 2.84 | 0.01 |
| **(GSE)** | | Openness | | | |
| | | | **Conscienc.** | 3.25 | 0.00 |
| | | Body res. | | | |
| | | Instability | | | |
| | | | **Arousal** | 2.00 | 0.05 |
| | | Extroversion | | | |
| **Consumerism** | 43% | | **Alt.** | -2.08 | 0.04 |
| **(Consum.)** | | Openness | | | |
| | | | **Material.** | 5.21 | *** |
| | | Body res. | | | |
| | | Arousal | | | |
| **Ecologically-correct** | 38% | Agreeability | | | |
| **purchase** | | | **Alt.** | 4.12 | *** |
| **(ECP)** | | GSE | | | |
| | | Openness | | | |
| | | Conscienc. | | | |
| | | Consum. | | | |
| | | Body res. | | | |
| | | Extroversion | | | |
| **Resources saving** | 26% | Agreeability | | | |
| **(RS)** | | | **Alt.** | 1,96 | 0,05 |
| | | | **GSE** | 2,06 | 0,04 |
| | | Openness | | | |
| | | Conscienc. | | | |
| | | | **Consum.** | -2,32 | 0,02 |
| | | Body res. | | | |
| | | Extroversion | | | |
| **Recycling** | 16% | | **Agreeability** | -2,15 | 0,03 |
| **(Recyc.)** | | | **Alt.** | 2,82 | 0,01 |
| | | GSE | | | |
| | | Openness | | | |
| | | Conscienc. | | | |
| | | Consum. | | | |
| | | Body res. | | | |
| | | Extroversion | | | |

## RESULTS

First of all, the measurement model was assessed. All traits were included. In the case of elemental traits, only a single item represented each trait. Although chi-square is significant, RMSEA and the incremental fit statists were satisfactory in general ($\chi^2$ = 304.3, df = 241, $p$ < 0,01, $\chi^2$ / df = 1.3, CFI = 0.96, TLI = 0.94, NFI = 0.84, RMSEA = 0.036). Composite reliability were all at least 0.65, except for altruism (CR = 0.57). Additionally, coefficient alphas for all constructs were all above 0.60, except for altruism ($\alpha$ = 0.59). Bivariate correlations among constructs were not above 0.60, so discriminant validity was assumed.

A full mediation model was employed in order to assess the predicted hypotheses. The fit statistics of this model were satisfactory ($\chi^2$ = 330.6, df = 259, $p$ < 0,01, $\chi^2$ / df = 1.3, CFI = 0.96, TLI = 0.94, NFI = 0.83, RMSEA = 0.037). Accounted variance and significant effects are shown on Table 2.

Altruism, whose accounted variance is 39%, is significantly predicted by six elemental traits (except for need for arousal and extroversion), whereas only three of the seven hypothesized elemental traits were significant predictors of general self-efficacy (accounted variance = 18%). As expected, altruism is a significant predictor of ecologically-correct purchase, resources saving, and recycling. Also, the hypothesis of a negative association effect of altruism on consumerism is supported. General self-efficacy predicts significantly resources saving. But, contrary to expected, neither ecologically-correct purchase nor recycling is significantly predicted by self-efficacy. Accounted variance in consumerism is 43%, and this construct has a negative effect on resources saving, and is significantly predicted by need for material resources, an elemental trait. But no significant effects were detected between consumerism and the other two superficial traits.

Accounted variance in ecologically-correct purchase is 38%, but only altruism is a significant predictor of this superficial trait. No elemental trait is a significant predictor of resources saving. But, as expected, altruism and general self-efficacy are significant predictors of resources saving. The model accounted for 26% of the variance in resources saving. Of the superficial traits, only recycling is significantly predicted by one of the elemental traits hypothesized (agreeability). Recycling, whose accounted variance is only 16%, is also predicted by altruism, as mentioned before.

## DISCUSSION, IMPLICATIONS AND FUTURE RESEARCH

Our research aimed to investigate the traits antecedents of sustainable consumption, operationalized as three superficial traits: ecologically-correct purchase, resources saving, and recycling. Based on the literature review, we proposed that sustainable consumption is negatively related with consumerism, and positively related with general self-efficacy and altruism. We also predicted associations of theses constructs with elemental traits.

Corroborating the point of view of Straughan and Roberts (1999), altruism, a compound trait, seems to be a trait consistently useful to predict sustainable consumption, because it is a significant predictor of ecologically-correct purchase, resources saving, and recycling. Consumerism only seems to be useful to explain variance in resources saving. Besides altruism, agreeability (an elemental trait) is a significant predictor of recycling. Resources saving has self-efficacy as a significant predictor, besides altruism and consumerism.

In the present research, taken into account the mediating effect of consumerism, self-efficacy and altruism, no elemental trait, with the exception of agreeability, seems to have a significant direct effect on constructs associated to sustainable consumption. (In fact,

no substantial increase in accounted variance of superficial traits was obtained in a partial mediation model in which paths were run from all the elemental traits to consumerism, ecologically-correct purchase, resources saving, and recycling.)

Nevertheless, six elemental traits are significant predictors of altruism: agreeability ($t$ = 3.75, $p$ < 0.001), openness to experience ($t$ = 1.77, p < 0.10), conscientiousness ($t$ = 2.54, $p$ < 0.05), need for material resources ($t$ = -2.73, $p$ < 0.05), need for body resources ($t$ = 2.77, $p$ < 0.05), and emotional instability ($t$ = -2.24, $p$ < 0.05).

In order to enhance sustainable consumption, altruism should be encouraged. Surprisingly, altruism seems to be predicted not only by traits associated to agreeableness, but also by traits concerning self preservation. So, persuasive communication aimed to promote sustainable consumption could strengthen the importance of preserving the environment and natural resources as a means of collective survival. On the other hand, reduction of consumerism could be associated to a natural tendency to save natural resources if we succeed in discouraging materialism.

Future research should deepen the investigation of the relationship between personality and sustainable consumption. Scales of sustained consumption should be improved. Other traits, such as value consciousness, could be included in the research hierarchical model. A panel of consumers could be surveyed in order to get data from people more representative of the population in general. The inclusion of demographic variables would also be useful to assess their relevance as predictors of sustainable consumption.

## ACKNOWLEDGMENTS

We thank very much FAPEMIG ("Fundação do Apoio à Pesquisa do Estado de Minas Gerais") for financial support for preparation and presentation of this work. We also thank two ACR's anonymous reviewers for helpful comments on an earlier draft of the article.

## REFERENCES

Akatu, Instituto (2006), "Como e por que os consumidores brasileiros praticam o consumo consciente?" http://www.akatu.org.br/akatu_acao/publicacoes/perfil-do-consumidor.

Balderjahn, Ingo (1988), "Personality variables and environmental attitudes as predictors of ecologically responsible consumption patterns," *Journal of Business Research*, 17, 51-56.

Baudrillard, Jean (1998), *The consumer society: miths and structure,* London: Sage.

Bodur, Muzaffer and Emine Sarigöllü (2005), "Environmental sensitivity in a developing country," *Environment and Behavior*, Vol. 37, No. 4, 487-510.

Bone, Sterling A. and John C. Mowen (2006), "Identifying the traits of aggressive and distracted drivers: a hierarchical trait model approach," *Journal of Consumer Behavior*, 5: 454-64.

Borden, Richard J. and Janice L. Francis (1978), "Who cares about ecology? Personality and sex differences in environmental concern," *Journal of Personality*, Vol. 46 (1), 190-203.

Connolly, John and Andrea Prothero (2008), "Green Consumption: life-politics, risk and contradictions," *Journal of Consumer Culture*, Vol. 8(1), 117-45.

De Young, Raymond (2000), "Expanding and evaluating motives for environmentally responsible behavior," *Journal of Social Issues*, Vol. 56, N. 3, 509-26.

Follows, Scott B. and David Jobber (2000), "Environmentally responsible purchase behavior: a test of a consumer model," *European Journal of Marketing*, Vol. 34, N. 5/6, 723-46.

Fraj, Elena and Eva Martinez (2006), "Influence of personality in ecological consumer behavior," *Journal of Consumer Behavior*, Vol. 5, May-June, 167-81.

—————————————— (2007), "Ecological consumer behavior: an empirical analysis," *International Journal of Consumer Studies*, 31, 26-33.

Kassarjian, Harold H. (1971), "Incorporating Ecology into Marketing Strategy: The Case of Air Pollution," *Journal of Marketing*, Vol. 35, July, 61-65.

Kinnear, Thomas C.; James R. Taylor and Sadrudin A. Ahmed (1974), "Ecologically Concerned Consumers: who are they?" *Journal of Marketing*, Vol. 38, 20-24.

Mansur, Alexandre; Juliana Arini and Thais Ferreira (2008), "Compre Verde: como nossas compras podem ajudar a salvar o planeta," *Época,* N. 515, 65-70.

Monteiro, Plínio Rafael R.; Ricardo T. Veiga; Marlusa Gosling and Márcio A. Gonçalves (2008), "Personalidade e Consumo Ecologicamente Consciente," *FACES*, Vol. 7, Abr./Jun, N.2, 30-49.

Mowen, John C. (2000), *The 3M Model of Motivation and Personality: theory and empirical applications to consumer behavior,* Boston, MA: Kluer Academic Publishers.

—————————— (2004), "Exploring the trait of competitiveness and its consumer behavior consequences," *Journal of Consumer Psychology*, 14(1&2): 52-63.

—————————— and Harris EG (2003), "The MDPS Method of message theme development: a new tool for managers", *Journal of Consumer Marketing*, 20(12): 1045-1066.

Ottman, Jacquelyn. A. (1993), *Marketing Verde,* São Paulo: Makron Books.

Peattie, Ken (2001), "Towards Sustainability: The Third Age of Green Marketing," *The Marketing Review*, 2, 129-46.

Penna, Carlos G. (1999), *O estado do planeta: sociedade de consumo e degradação ambiental,* Rio de Janeiro: Record.

Pirog III, Stephen F. and James A. Roberts (2007), "Personality and credit card misuse among college students: the mediating role of impulsiveness", *Journal of Marketing Theory and Practice*, Vol. 15, N.1, 65-77.

Ramanaiah, Nerella V.; Michael A. Clumpe and Patrick J. Sharpe (2000), "Personality profiles of environmentally responsible groups," *Psychological Reports*, (1), August: 176-8.

Schaefer, Anja and Andrew Crane (2005), "Adressing Sustainability and Consumption," *Journal of Macromarketing*, Vol. 25, June, N. 1, 76-92.

Schlegelmilch, Bodo B.; Greg M. Bohlen and Adamantios Diamantopoulos (1996), "The link between green purchasing decisions and measures of environmental consciousness," *European Journal of Marketing*, Vol. 30, N. 5, 35-55.

Schultz, P. W. (2000), "Empathizing with nature: The effects of perspective taking on concern for environmental issues". *Journal of Social Issues,* 56, 391-406.

Solomon, Michael R. (2002), *O comportamento do consumidor*: *comprando, possuindo e sendo,* 5ª edição. Porto Alegre: Bookman.

Stern, Paul C. (2000), "Toward a coherent theory of environmentally significant behavior," *Journal of Social Issues*, Vol. 56, N. 3, 407-24.

Straughan, Robert D. and James A. Roberts (1999), "Environmental segmentation alternatives: a look at green consumer behavior in the new millennium," *Journal of Consumer Marketing,* Vol. 16, N. 6, 558-75.

Webster Jr., Frederick E. (1975), "Determining the characteristics of the socially conscious consumer," *Journal of Consumer Research,* Vol. 2, December, 188-96.

Wergin, Rand E. (2009), "The frugal and the environmentally concerned: who are they, what do they do, and how do you influence them?" Unpublished dissertation, Faculty of the Graduate College of Oklahoma State University, Oklahoma City, USA.

# Competitive Papers——Extended Abstracts

## A Complex Account of Service Recovery: Subtle Efforts to Remedy Subtle Service Failure

Fang Wan, University of Manitoba, Canada
Pingping Qiu, Monash University, Australia
L. J. Shrum, University of Texas at San Antonio, USA

### EXTENDED ABSTRACT

Service failure and recovery are complex and dynamic constructs (Bonifield and Cole 2007). However, most existing literature focused on blatant and outrageous service failure (Bonifield and Cole 2007; O'Donohoe and Turley 2007) and the role of strong and outward emotions such as anger in service failure and recovery (Bonifield and Cole 2007; O'Donohoe and Turley 2007). Our research explores an understudied area—the effectiveness of recovery strategies in a subtle service failure situation that involves a passive negative emotion embarrassment. Drawing on research on embarrassment (Grace 2007; Keltner and Buswell 1997) and goal automaticity (Bargh 2002; Leary 1995), we identify that even perfectly friendly and personalized service encounter can fail when it violates contextually activated social goals. More importantly, we propose that in such a situation with a subtle service failure, the effectiveness of various recovery efforts is impacted by subtle cues such as types of recovery strategy, awareness of the recovery efforts and time of service evaluation. Three experiments are reported to demonstrate the impact of these subtle cues in ameliorating the service experience.

In Study 1, we identified a service setting with a subtle failure. Specifically, we examined a personalized service scenario in which the server unintentionally discloses the customers' privacy (i.e., reminding the customer of their previous unhealthy food choice in a restaurant) and jeopardize their contextually activated social goals (i.e., impression management goal when dining with a date for the first time plus health goal if the date is a fitness instructor). By conducting a 2 (personalization: high vs. low) by 3 (social goal: dining with a friend, a date, a date as a fitness instructor) between-subjects experiment with restaurant dining scenarios, we identified that even high-personalized service may cause subtle service failure (evoke felt embarrassment and incur negative service evaluation) if this service unintentionally violates the customer's contextually driven social goals. The subtle service failure scenario (high personalization and dining with date as fitness instructor) identified in this study is utilized in the following experiments.

In Study 2 we examined whether the server or customer is the recovery initiator will make the service recovery more effective. As research on embarrassment suggests that either the person who feels embarrassed or the others who evokes the embarrassing situation can relieve the felt embarrassment (Miller and Leary 1992; Miller 1995)(Miller 1995). We designed strategies with the server (or self) initiating an attempt to mitigate the transgression: "Well, you (or I) may like trying something else today." We further argue that high awareness of server's recovery efforts can exacerbate the attention paid to the previous service failure and can incur more negative attributions about the server, making recovery efforts futile (Kelley 1972; Main et al. 2007). We tested the hypothesis with a 2 (remedy initiator: self vs. server) x 2 (awareness of the remedy effort: high vs. control) between-subjects design, plus a no-remedy control condition. We manipulated awareness of the recovery efforts by measuring responses to the self or the server's recovery attempts either before (high awareness condition) or after (control

condition) service experience related measures. ANOVA analyses yielded significant interaction effects, supporting our hypotheses.

Study 3 further explores the effectiveness of recovery efforts by examining the different recovery strategies a server can take, as well as the role of time lag. Based on service recovery (Hoffman, Kelley, and Rotalsky 1995) and embarrassment literature (Keltner and Buswell 1997), we designed two types of server's recovery strategies, explicit (directly correcting the transgression) versus implicit (offering a free coupon—distracting the attention). In addition, according to emotion regulation (Gross et al. 2007) and interpersonal relationship literature (Fletcher and Clark 2002), we argued that distraction (implicit recovery) may help reduce the felt embarrassment and enhance service evaluation in the short run. However, with a time lag, the explicit recovery (confronting the issue) can be more effective in helping reduce felt embarrassment, and therefore, ameliorate the service experience. In this study, a 2 (explicit vs. covert recovery) by 2 (immediate vs. delayed service evaluation) between-subject design was adopted to test the hypothesis. ANOVA findings supported our hypotheses.

Taken together, our research examines the subtle service failures and recoveries that involve a passive emotion such as embarrassment. Theoretically, service failure, recovery, and emotions are complex and dynamic processes that may vary dramatically from one situation to another (Bonifield and Cole 2007). We provide nuances of a complex interaction between subtle recovery efforts and consumers' perceptions and subsequent reactions. To service managers, the most important message is that service delivery can be personalized but can not be done at the cost of revealing sensitive information. When embarrassing service encounter is incurred, recovery strategies vary depending on whether a short-term or long-term oriented goal is adopted by service managers. In a short run, implicit strategies such as incentives can be effective. But in a long run, explicit strategies are more effective.

### REFERENCES (SELECTED)

Bargh, John. A. (2002), "Losing Consciousness: Automatic Influences on Consumer Judgment, Behavior and Motivation," *Journal of Consumer Research*, 29, 280-285.

Bearden, William. O. and Michael J. Etzel (1982), "Reference Group Influence on Product and Purchase Brand Decisions," *Journal of Consumer Research*, 9(September), 183-194.

Bonifield, Carolyn and Catherine Cole (2007), "Affective Responses to Service Failure: Anger, Regret, and Retaliatory Versus Conciliatory Responses," *Marketing Letters*, 18 (1), 85-99.

Boshoff, Christo (1997), "An Experimental Study of Service Recovery Options," *International Journal of Service Industry Management*, 8 (2), 110.

Edelmann, Robert J. (1981), "Embarrassment: The State of Research," *Current Psychological Reviews,* 1(May-August), 125-138.

_____ (1987), *The Psychology of Embarrassment*, Chichester, UK: Wiley.

Esterlami, Hooman and Peter De Maeyer (2002), "Customer Reactions to Service Provider Overgenerosity," *Journal of Service Research*, 4(February), 205-216.

Fletcher, Garth and Clark (2002), *Blackwell Handbook Of Social Psychology: Interpersonal Processes,* Wiley-Blackwell.

Friestad, Maria and Peter Wright (1994), "The Persuasion Knowledge Model: How People Cope with Persuasion Attempts," *Journal of Consumer Research*, 21(June), 1-31.

Goodwin, Cathy (1993), "A Conceputalization of Motives to Seek Privacy for Non-Deviant Consumption," *Journal of Consumer Psychology*, 1(3), 261-84.

Grace, Debra (2007), "How Embarrassing! An Exploratory Study of Critical Incidents Including Affective Reactions," *Journal of Service Research*, 9 (February), 271-84.

Gross, James J. and Ross A. Thompson (2007), "Emotion Regulation: Conceptual foundations," in James J. Gross (ed.), *Handbook of Emotion Regulation,* New York: Guilford Press.

Grubb, Edward L. and Barbra L. Stern (1971), "Self-Concept and Significant Others," *Journal of Marketing Research*, 8(August), 382-85.

Keltner, Dacher and Brenda N. Buswell (1997), "Embarrassment: Its Distinct Form and Appeasement Functions," *Psychological Bulletin,* 122(November), 250-70.

Kelley, Harold H. (1972), "Attribution in social interaction," in *Attribution: Perceiving the Causes of Behavior*, eds. Edward E. Jones, David E. Kanouse, Harold H. Kelley, Richard E. Nisbett, Stuart Valins, and Bernard Weiner , New Jersey: General Learning Press, 1-26.

Leary, Mark R. (1995), *Self-Presentation: Impression Management and Interpersonal Behavior,* Dubuque, IA: Brown Communications.

Main, Kelley J., Darren Dahl, and Peter R. Darke (2007), "Deliberate and Automatic Bases of Suspicion: Empirical Evidence of the Sinister Attribution Error," *Journal of Consumer Psychology*, 17(1), 59-69.

McCullough, Michael E., Frank D. Fincham, and Jo-Ann Tsang (2003), "Forgiveness, Forbearance, and Time: The Temporal Unfolding of Transgression-Related Interpersonal Motivations," *Journal of Personality and Social Psychology*, 84(March), 540-57.

Midgley, David F. (1983), "Patterns of Interpersonal Information Seeking for A Symbolic Product," *Journal of Marketing Research,* 20(February), 74-83.

Miller, Rowland S. (1995), "On the Nature of Embarrassability: Shyness, Social Evaluation, and Social Skills," *Journal of Personality,* 63(June), 315-39.

Mittal, Banwari and Alfried M. Lassar (1996), "The Role of Personalization in Service Encounters," *Journal of Retailing*, 72 (1), 95-109.

Modigliani, Andre (1968), "Embarrassment and Embarrassability," *Sociometry,* 31(September), 313-26.

O'Donohoe, Stephanie and Darach Turley (2007), "Fatal Errors: Unbridling Emotions in Service Failure Experiences," *Journal of Strategic Marketing*, 15 (1), 17-28.

Parrott, W. Gerrod and Stephanie F. Smith (1991), "Embarrassment: Actual vs. Typical Cases, Classical vs. Prototypical Representations," *Cognition and Emotion*, 5(September-November), 467-88.

Schlenker, Barry R. (1980), *Impression Management: The Self Concept, Self Identity, and Interpersonal Relations*, Monterey, CA: Brooks/Cole.

Tedeschi, James T. (1981), *Impression Management Theory and Social Psychological Research*, New York: Academic.

# How Low Can I Go? The Comparative Effect of Low Status Users on Buying Intentions

Edith Shalev, Technion, Israel
Vicki Morwitz, New York University, USA

## EXTENDED ABSTRACT

Imagine the following scenario: you are considering a subscription to a well established scientific journal. The journal is highly respectable and its readers are known to be intellectually curious and intelligent. On your way to the office, still undecided, you come across a maintenance worker who is sitting on a bench and avidly reading the latest issue of the scientific journal. How might such an observation effect your subscription decision? Will it increase or decrease your likelihood of subscribing to this journal?

The literature on social influence suggests that consumers from a low socio-economic class are not ideal influencers, at least not of premium brands. Empirical research profiles the "influential" as more educated than average (Boster, Serota, Andrews, & Carpenter, 2009; Row, 2004) and theoretical research (e.g. Berger & Heath, 2008; White & Dahl, 2006) suggests we are positively influenced by those who are similar to us or who are members of an aspirational reference group. Since consumers of premium brands typically do not aspire to be members of a low status group, it is unlikely that they will be positively influenced by actual members of that group. If anything, they would probably become less interested in products that low status users have chosen.

The current work questions this basic premise and reexamines the ways in which the observation of a low-status consumer using a particular product might influence the purchase intentions of an observer. We use the term "*observer*" to denote a consumer, who currently does not own the target product, and who observes another consumer using the product. While previous research that has investigated this question has taken a reference group perspective, we develop an alternative framework based on social comparison theory. In contrast to previous findings, we show that, under certain circumstances, observers are *more* likely to emulate the choices of *low status* than high status users–a phenomenon we call "*the low status user effect*".

Our analysis begins with the notion that products serve a socially symbolic function (Belk, 1988; Grubb & Hupp, 1968; Levy, 1959). For example, using new technological products may signal high levels of innovativeness; eating organic foods may signal high levels of health consciousness; and subscribing to scientific journals may signal high levels of intellectual curiosity. We hereby define the "*focal trait*" of a product as a human trait, that users of that product would be expected to have at high levels. Given our earlier examples, the focal traits for new technological product, organic foods, and scientific journals would be innovativeness, health awareness and intellectual curiosity, respectively.

Intuitively, we would expect under most circumstances that low-status consumers would have low levels of the focal trait of a premium product. In fact, their mere usage of a premium product is likely to be surprising. An observer might be surprised by a low status consumer reading the scientific journal if he associates high levels of intellectual curiosity with high education and socio-economic status.

In this research, we posit that the observation of a low-status person using a premium brand elicits an attribution process whereby the observer attempts to reconcile the gap between his expectations and his observation of the low-status user's product choice. The observer might reconcile his expectation and his observation by reasoning that the low status user, and therefore people in general, are, higher on the focal trait than he previously thought.

This account evokes a social comparison process (Festinger, 1954) whereby the observer re-evaluates his own relative standing on the focal trait and concludes that it is lower than previously estimated. In response to the ego-threat posed by this notion and in order to restore his expected relative standing on the focal trait, the observer purchases the target product (Gao, Wheeler, & Shiv, 2009). Ironically, this process leads consumers to emulate the purchase behavior of individuals they may under other circumstances not wish to be associated with. Our research establishes this low status user effect across different product categories, including apparel, MP3 players, and WiFi detectors.

We further show that, like other social comparison processes, this effect is sensitive to the importance of the focal trait to the observer (Tesser, 1988) and the confidence that the observer has about his standing on the focal trait (Kruglanski & Mayseless, 1990; Morse & Gergen, 1970).

# Consumer Response to Spokesperson's Race: A Research Synthesis of Racial Similarity Effects in Advertising

Ioannis Kareklas, University of Connecticut, USA
Maxim Polonsky, University of Connecticut, USA

## EXTENDED ABSTRACT

Following the civil rights movement, minorities were increasingly being portrayed in both television and print advertisements. Many researchers responded by investigating how White and African American consumers evaluate advertisements featuring models of different races. Some researchers examined how White consumers respond to advertisements featuring African American models (e.g., Bush, Gwinner, and Solomon 1974; Bush, Hair, Jr., and Solomon 1979; Hoon and Ramaprasad 2006; Whittler and DiMeo 1991). Others assessed the advertising evaluations of African American consumers in response to ads featuring either White or African American models (e.g., Choudhury and Schmid 1974; Green 1999; Simpson et al. 2000; Whittler 1989; Whittler and Spira 2002). A third set of studies examined the advertising evaluations of both majority and minority consumers in response to integrated advertisements, featuring both White and African American models in the same ad (e.g., Barban 1969; Cagley and Cardozo 1970; Guest 1970; Perkins, Thomas, and Taylor 2000; Schmid 2000; Stafford, Birdwell, and Van Tassel 1970; Szybillo and Jacoby 1974). The majority of extant findings suggest that consumers respond more favorably to ads that feature spokespersons of the same race as them (for a review, see Whittler 1991).

## The Current Review

Using meta-analytic procedures we summarize extant advertising findings related to the effects of racial similarity (vs. dissimilarity) between source and participants. Furthermore, we investigate the conditions under which consumers may prefer racially similar (vs. dissimilar) endorsers, by examining various study characteristics (e.g., geographic region where data was collected), the demographic profile of participants, the methodological aspects of the studies (e.g., medium in which advertisements were presented), as well as additional variables of conceptual importance in this domain (e.g., the level of participants' ingroup identification). We focus on the evaluations of African American and White consumers exposed to advertisements featuring either racially similar or dissimilar endorsers. Our synthesis includes 84 statistically independent data sets, each of which was treated as the meta-analysis unit. Collectively, these studies span forty years of research work in this domain, ranging from 1969 to 2009, and include data from a total of 9,496 participants (3,232 African Americans and 6,264 Whites).

## Computation of Effect Sizes

The effect size metric selected for the analysis was the standardized mean difference (g), defined as the difference between the advertising evaluation means for participants exposed to majority spokespersons (i.e., White models) and those exposed to minority spokespersons (i.e., African American models), divided by their pooled standard deviation (see Hedges and Olkin 1985). As defined, an effect size with a positive (negative) sign implies that participants exposed to majority spokespersons exhibited more positive (negative) advertising evaluations than participants exposed to minority spokespersons.

## Major Findings

We found that participants of both races evaluated ads featuring same-race spokespersons more favorably than ads featuring different-race models. Specifically, using fixed-effects assumptions, the weighted mean effect size for studies with African American participants was: $d_+=-.53$ (CI=-.60, -.45, k=36), and for studies with White participants the weighted mean effect size was: $d_+=.15$ (CI=.10, .20, k=48).

*Effect of Participant Characteristics.* The gender composition of samples was significantly related to $d$s for African American studies ($\beta=.44$, $p<.001$), but not for studies with White participants ($\beta=.09$, $p=.24$). Specifically, the weighted mean effect size for studies with male African American participants, $d_+=-1.31$ (CI=-1.53, -1.09, k=36) was almost seven times as large as that of studies with female African American participants, $d_+=-.19$ (CI=-.31, -.08, k=36). The mean age of participants was also significantly related to $d$s for African American studies ($\beta=.17$, $p<.01$), but not for studies with White participants ($\beta=.03$, $p=.73$). Specifically, younger African American participants were much more in favor of their ingroup ($d_+=-.68$, CI=-.81, -.55, k=36) than older African American participants ($d_+=-.31$, CI=-.48, -.14, k=36).

*Effect of ingroup identification.* The level of participants' ingroup identification was significantly related to $d$s. This effect was larger for studies with White participants ($\beta=.57$, $p<.001$), than for studies with African American samples ($\beta=.40$, $p<.001$). Participants of both races reported a larger preference for ads featuring same race spokespersons when they identified highly with their ingroup, than when they had a low level of ingroup identification. Specifically, the weighted mean effect size, $d_+=-.95$ (CI=-1.12, -.78, k=8), for studies with African American participants that were high in ingroup identification is more than twice as large as that observed for participants with low levels of ingroup identification, $d_+=-.41$ (CI=-.58, -.24, k=8). Similarly, the weighted mean effect size, $d_+=.64$ (CI=.48, .81, k=8), for studies with White participants who were high in ingroup identification is more than four times as large as that observed for participants with low levels of ingroup identification, $d_+=.15$ (CI=-.01, .31, k=8).

*Effect of Major African American Events.* We tested the effect of the valence of major events in Black history during the year of data collection on effect sizes. Major African American events were significantly related to $d$s for studies with African American participants ($\beta=.20$, $p<.001$), but not for studies with White participants ($\beta=.05$, $p=.52$). Major historical events during the year of data collection which had favorable outcomes for African Americans (e.g., the Voting Rights Act of 1965) were associated with a greater preference for ads featuring Black models ($d_+=-.61$, CI=-.69, -.52, k=7) than were negative events such as the assassination of Martin Luther King, Jr. in 1968, which were associated with a lower preference for ads featuring Black models ($d_+=-.34$, CI=-.47, -.20, k=29) supporting our third hypothesis.

# REFERENCES
(Articles Included In The Meta-Analysis Are Denoted
With An Asterisk)

*Aaker, Jennifer L., Anne M. Brumbaugh, and Sonya A. Grier (2000), "Nontarget markets and viewer distinctiveness: The impact of target marketing on advertising attitudes," Journal of Consumer Psychology, 9 (3), 127-40.

*Appiah, Osei (2001), "Ethnic identification on adolescents' evaluations of advertisements," Journal of Advertising Research, 41 (5), 7-22.

*Avery, Derek R., Morela Hernandez, and Michelle R. Hebl (2004), "Who's watching the race? Racial salience in recruitment advertising," Journal of Applied Social Psychology, 34 (1), 146-61.

*Barban, Arnold M. (1969), "The Dilemma of" Integrated" Advertising," The Journal of Business, 42 (4), 477-97.

*Block, Carl E. (1972), "White backlash to negro ads: Fact or fantasy?," Journalism Quarterly, 49 (Summer), 258-62.

*Brumbaugh, Anne M. and Sonya A. Grier (2006), "Insights from a 'failed' experiment: Directions for pluralistic, multiethnic advertising research," Journal of Advertising, 35 (3), 35-46.

*Brunel, Frédéric F., Brian C. Tietje, and Anthony G. Greenwald (2004), "Is the Implicit Association Test a Valid and Valuable Measure of Implicit Consumer Social Cognition?," Journal of Consumer Psychology, 14 (4), 385-404.

Bush, Ronald F., Robert F. Gwinner, and Paul J. Solomon (1974), "White consumer sales response to black models," Journal of Marketing, 38 (2), 25-29.

*Bush, Ronald F., Joseph F. Hair Jr., and Paul J. Solomon (1979), "Consumers' level of prejudice and response to Black models in advertisements," Journal of Marketing Research, 16 (3), 341-45.

*Cagley, James W. and Richard N. Cardozo (1970), "White response to integrated advertising," Journal of Advertising Research, Vol. 10 (2), 35-39.

*Choudhury, Pravat K. and Lawrence S. Schmid (1974), "Black models in advertising to Blacks," Journal of Advertising Research, 14 (3), 19-22.

*David, Prabu, Glenda Morrison, Melissa A. Johnson, and Felecia Ross (2002), "Body image, race, and fashion models: Social distance and social identification in third-person effects," Communication Research, 29 (3), 270-94.

*DelVecchio, Devon and Ronald C. Goodstein (2004), "Moving beyond race: The role of ethnic identity in evaluating celebrity endorsers," in Diversity in advertising: Broadening the scope of research directions, Jerome D. Williams and Wei-Na Lee and Curtis P. Haugtvedt, Eds. Mahwah, New Jersey: Lawrence Erlbaum Associates, Publishers.

*Deshpande, Rohit and Douglas M. Stayman (1994), "A tale of two cities: Distinctiveness theory and advertising effectiveness," Journal of Marketing Research, 31 (1), 57-64.

*Forehand, Mark R. and Rohit Deshpande (2001), "What we see makes us who we are: Priming ethnic self-awareness and advertising response," Journal of Marketing Research, 38 (3), 336-48.

*Fullagar, Clive and Julian Barling (1983), "Social learning theory: A psychological approach to advertising effectiveness?," South African Journal of Psychology, 13 (1), 18-22.

*Green, Corliss L. (1999), "Ethnic evaluations of advertising: Interaction effects of strength of ethnic identification, media placement, and degree of racial composition," Journal of Advertising, 28 (1), 49-64.

*Guest, Lester (1970), "How negro models affect company Image," Journal of Advertising Research, 10 (2), 29-33.

Hedges, Larry V. and Ingram Olkin (1985), Statistical Methods for Meta-Analysis. Orlando, FL: Academic Press.

*Hoon, William (2005), "Effects of model race/ethnicity on responses to print advertising: Do popular culture identification and prejudice make a difference?," doctoral dissertation, Department of Mass Communication and Media Arts, Southern Illinois University at Carbondale.

*Hoon, William and Jyotika Ramaprasad (2006), "Effects of Model Race/Ethnicity on Responses to Print Advertising: Do Popular Culture Identification and Prejudice Make a Difference?," presented at the 2006 Annual Conference of the International Communication Association, Dresden, Germany.

* Kareklas, Ioannis (2009), "Consumer Response to Spokesperson's Race: A Quantitative Review and Extension of Racial Similarity Effects in Advertising," doctoral dissertation, School of Business, University of Connecticut.

*Lai, Hsiu-chen Sandra, Zoe Tan, and Marye Tharp (1990), "Receiver prejudice and model ethnicity: Impact on advertising effectiveness," Journalism Quarterly, 67 (4), 794-803.

*Martin, Brett A. S., Christina Kwai-Choi Lee, and Feng Yang (2004), "The influence of ad model ethnicity and self-referencing on attitudes: Evidence from New Zealand," Journal of Advertising, 33 (4), 27-37.

*Muse, William V. (1971), "Product-related response to use of black models in advertising," Journal of Marketing Research, 8 (1), 107-09.

*Perkins, Lesley A., Kecia M. Thomas, and Gail A. Taylor (2000), "Advertising and recruitment: Marketing to minorities," Psychology & Marketing, 17 (3), 235.

*Qualls, William J. and David J. Moore (1990), "Stereotyping effects on consumers' evaluation of advertising: Impact of racial differences between actors and viewers," Psychology & Marketing, 7 (2), 135-51.

*Raspberry, Patricia Dodson (1997), "Racial cues, involvement and advertising: An information processing perspective," doctoral dissertation, Department of Psychology, University of Michigan.

*Schlinger, Mary J. and Joseph T. Plummer (1972), "Advertising in black and white," Journal of Marketing Research, Vol. 9 (2), 149-53.

*Schmid, Jill Diane (2000), "White backlash revisited: Consumer response to model's race in print advertisements," doctoral dissertation, Department of Communication, University of Washington.

*Simpson, Eithel M., Thelma Snuggs, Tim Christiansen, and Kelli E. Simples (2000), "Race, homophily, and purchase intentions and the black consumer," Psychology & Marketing, 17 (10), 877-89.

*Stafford, James E., Al E. Birdwell, and Charles E. Van Tassel (1970), "Integrated advertising—white backlash?," Journal of Advertising Research, 10 (2), 15-20.

*Sullivan, Ryan Dabo (2004), "A study measuring product-related reactions to the use of black models in advertising," M.S., Oklahoma State University.

*Szybillo, George J. and Jacob Jacoby (1974), "Effects of different levels of integration on advertising preference and intention to purchase," Journal of Applied Psychology, 59 (3), 274-80.

*Tolley, B. Stuart and John J. Goett (1971), "Reactions to Blacks in newspaper ads," Journal of Advertising Research, 11 (2), 11-17.

*Wang, Xiao and Laura M. Arpan (2008), "Effects of race and ethnic identity on audience evaluation of HIV public service announcements," Howard Journal of Communications, 19 (1), 44-63.

*Whittler, Tommy E. (1991), "The effects of actors' race in commercial advertising: Review and extension," Journal of Advertising, 20 (1), 54-60.

*_____ (1989), "Viewers' Processing of Actor's Race and Message Claims in Advertising stimuli," Psychology & Marketing (1986-1998), 6 (4), 287.

*_____ and Joan DiMeo (1991), "Viewers' reactions to racial cues in advertising stimuli," Journal of Advertising Research, 31 (6), 37-46.

*_____ and Joan Scattone Spira (2002), "Model's race: A peripheral cue in advertising messages?," Journal of Consumer Psychology, 12 (4), 291-301.

*Williams, Jerome D., William J. Qualls, and Sonya A. Grier (1995), "Racially exclusive real estate advertising: Public policy implications for fair housing practices," Journal of Public Policy & Marketing, 14 (2), 225-44.

# Measuring Associations Across Cultures: A Comparison of Best-Worst and Rating Methods

Julie Anne Lee, University of Western Australia, Australia
Geoffrey N. Soutar, University of Western Australia, Australia
Timothy M. Daly, University of Akron, USA

## EXTENDED ABSTRACT

One of the major issues in cross-cultural research is that of response bias. Significant cross-cultural response biases have been attributed to extreme (i.e., using the end points of a scale) and acquiescent (i.e., yea-saying) response patterns. The current standard in cross-cultural research is to address potential response biases post data collection, using one of the several standardization methods recommended for such purposes (e.g., Hofstede, 1980; Schwartz, 1992; Van de Vijver and Leung, 1997). However, the danger of this strategy is that substantive cross-cultural differences may be removed (Van Hemert, Van de Vijver, Poortinga, and Georgas, 2002). Unfortunately, few studies have proposed or examined proactive solutions to avoid this, which has meant response bias continues to be a major unresolved problem (Campbell, 1996). This issue may be compounded in research involving East-Asian samples, as a large number of cross-cultural studies have reported fewer negative correlations in East-Asian than in Western samples. Although this has been attributed to East Asians' dialectical thinking, which recognizes a duality in all things, it is unclear whether any of the suggested duality might be attributable to response bias due to the reliance of ratings scales in cross-cultural research.

Best-worst scaling (BWS; Finn and Louviere, 1992) is a relatively new measurement method that has the potential to reduce response bias. It has been suggested BWS can reduce potential problems commonly produced by ratings scales in three major ways, including improving lexical equivalence of anchoring terms, eliminating the need to use numerical anchors and removing response style effects (Lee, Soutar and Louviere, 2007; 2008). In terms of response style effects, BWS does not allow respondents to consistently use the middle or extreme points, as they are asked to choose the most distinct pairs within each of a set of statements. To date, however, BWS's measurement ability has not been assessed against more traditional rating scales in cross-cultural contexts. Thus, the major aim of this study was to compare and contrast results obtained in a cross-cultural context using BWS with those obtained by traditional ratings scales.

As nomological validity is often lower in East Asian than in Western countries (e.g., Wong et al., 2003), the study also examined whether such problems can be reduced by the use of BWS, especially when there are expected negative relationships. In order to operationalize this, the current study examined a set of expected positive and negative correlations between Schwartz's (1992) personal values, which is the most widely used values measure in cross-cultural research, and tourism benefits in the United Kingdom (UK) and South Korea (SK) using the different response formats. The relationships between personal values and tourism benefits were chosen to reflect measures that should show less duality than personality and traits.

Data were collected from members of commercial online panels in the UK and SK. The samples were chosen from online panel members aged between 18 and 65 years, who were permanent residents of their country and resided in the Greater London area in the UK and the Greater Seoul area in SK. The samples were screened to include international travelers, who do not work in advertising, marketing research or the tourism industries. Schwartz's (1992) values were measured using either the traditional 57-item Schwartz Value Survey (SVS; see Schwartz and Littrell, 2005) in a rating scale format, or the newer Schwartz Values Best-Worst Survey (SVBWS; Lee et al., 2008). The SVS was also standardized using the mean-centering approach suggested by Schwartz (1992), producing the SVSc. Each of these three values measures were used to compute the focal higher order dimensions of Openness-to-change and Conservation. Travel benefits (developed in conjunction with Tourism Western Australia) were also measured in both a ratings scale format and a BWS format. Sample sizes ranges from 201 to 242.

The results showed that, overall, each of the three method combinations (SVWBS-Benefits BWS; SVS-Benefits Rating; SVSc-Benefits Rating) produced the expected positive associations in both the UK and SK. The only exceptions being that the SVSc-ratings combination in SK did not produce a significant positive association between OC and *experience a different culture*, or CO and *safe and secure*.

However, the results were very different in terms of the predicted negative associations. Only the SVBWS-BWS combination produced all of the expected negative associations in both the UK and SK. The SVSc-rating combination produced the three expected negative associations in the UK, but only one in SK. The SVS-rating combination failed to produce a single predicted negative association in either the UK or SK. Indeed, this method resulted in counter-intuitive significant *positive* associations between CO and *step into the unknown* and CO and *experience a different culture*. Further, the average expected negative correlations were significantly (p<0.05) higher for the SVBWS-BWS combination than for the SVS-rating combination in both the UK and SK, but only marginally (p<0.10) higher than for the SVSc-rating combination in SK.

In summary, the BWS combination was the only method that produced all of the expected positive and negative correlations in both the UK and SK. Further, the BWS combination was the only combination not to have a significant difference between the expected correlations in the UK and SK. Finally, the BWS combination worked significantly better than the SVS combination for SK, and marginally better than the SVSc combination, but importantly, *without* the post hoc standardization of scores that may remove both substantive and response bias. As such, cross-cultural researchers should consider using the BWS approach when collecting data, especially in East Asian cultures. The BWS approach has several advantages for cross-cultural researchers, as the BWS task produces metric scores that are equivalent across cultures and do not need to be standardized, issues with lexical equivalence are reduced, the BWS does not use numbers, which can often have different meanings in certain cultures and the BWS task is simple for respondents, and takes much less time to complete than do equivalent rating scale tasks.

## REFERENCES

Bagozzi, R. W., Wong, N., & Yi, Y. (1999). The role of culture and gender in the relationship between positive and negative affect. *Cognition and Emotion, 13*(6), 641-672.

Brislin, R. W. (1970). Back-translation for cross-cultural research. *Journal of Cross Cultural Psychology, 1*, 185-216.

Campbell, D. T. (1996). Unresolved issues in measurement validity: An autobiographical overview. *Psychological Assessment, 8*, 363-68.

Finn, A., & Louviere, J. J. (1992). Determining the appropriate response to evidence of public concern: The case of food safety. *Journal of Public Policy and Marketing, 11*, 19–25.

Fischer, R. (2004). Standardization to account for cross-cultural response bias. *Journal of Cross-Cultural Psychology, 35*, 263-282.

Hofstede, G. H. (1980). *Culture's Consequences: International Differences in Work-Related Values*. Beverly Hills, CA: Sage.

Hofstede, G. H. (2001). *Culture's Consequences* (2nd ed.). Thousand Oaks, CA: Sage.

Johnson, T., Kulesa, P., Cho, Y. I. K., & Shavitt, S. (2005). The relation between culture and response styles: Evidence from 19 countries. *Journal of Cross-Cultural Psychology, 36* (2), 264-277.

Lee, J. A., & Kacen, J. (1999). The relationship between independent and interdependent self-concepts and reasons for purchase. *Journal of Euromarketing, 8* (1/2), 83-99.

Lee, J. A. & Soutar, G. N. (2010). Is Schwartz's Value Survey an interval scale, and does it really matter? *Journal of Cross-Cultural Psychology*, 41(1), 76-86.

Lee, J. A., Soutar, G. N., & Louviere, J. J. (2007). Measuring values using best-worst scaling: The LOV example. *Psychology & Marketing, 24* (12), 1043-1058.

Lee, J. A., Soutar, G. N., & Louviere, J. J. (2008). The best-worst scaling approach: An alternative to Schwartz's Values Survey. *Journal of Personality Assessment, 90*, 335–347.

Little, T. D. (1997). Mean and covariance structures (MACS) analyses of cross-cultural data: Practical and theoretical issues," *Multivariate Behavioral Research, 32 (1),* 53-76.

Peng, K. & Nisbett, R. E. (1999). Culture, dialectics, and reasoning about contradiction. *American Psychologist, 54,* 741-754.

Peng, K., Ames, D., & Knowles, E. (2001). Culture, theory and human inference: Perspectives from three traditions. In D. Matsumoto (Ed.), *The Handbook of Culture and Psychology*. Oxford, UK: Oxford University Press.

Schwartz, S. H. (1992). Universals in the content and structure of values: Theoretical advances and empirical tests in 20 countries. In M. Zanna (Ed.), *Advances in Experimental Social Psychology (Vol. 25*, pp. 1–65). New York: Academic Press.

Schwartz, S. H. (1994). Are there universal aspects in the content and structure of values? *Journal of Social Issues, 50*, 19–45.

Schwartz, S. H. & Bardi, A. (2001). Value hierarchies across cultures. *Journal of Cross-Cultural Psychology, 32*, 268-290.

Schwartz, S. H., & Littrell, R. (2005). Draft users manual. Retrieved January 4, 2007, from http://www.crossculturalcentre.homestead.com.

Smith, P. B. (2004). Acquiescent response bias as an aspect of cultural communication style. *Journal of Cross-Cultural Psychology, 35*, 50–61.

Van de Vijver, F., & Leung, K. (1997). *Methods and Data Analysis of Comparative Research*. Thousand Oaks, CA: Sage.

Van Hemert, D. A., Van de Vijver, F. J. R., Poortinga, Y. H., & Georgas, J. (2002). Structure and score levels of the Eysenck Personality Questionnaire across individuals and countries. *Personality and Individual Differences, 33*, 1229–1249.

Wong, N., Rindfleisch, A., & Burroughs, J. E. (2003). Do reverse-worded items confound measures in cross-cultural consumer research? The case of the Material Values Scale. *Journal of Consumer Research, 30*, 72-91.

# A Prognosis on Consumerism

Can Uslay, Chapman University, USA
Gokeen Coskuner-Balli, Chapman University, USA

## EXTENDED ABSTRACT

Despite its obvious importance for marketers, policy-makers, and consumers, there is a dearth of research on the *future of* the consumerism movement in the post-modern society. It has been well established in consumer behavior and sociology literature that minorities and sub-cultures are influential in driving mainstream culture in future generations (Clark 2003; Etzioni 1987; Giesler 2008). In order to anticipate the future of consumerism, we conduct an exploratory analysis of the emerging consumer movements and trends. The effort results in a startling discovery: regarding all four basic consumer rights that were granted back in the sixties, a growing minority of consumers have expectations that are in figurative contrast with what the regulators and in some cases marketers had intended. These consumers do not necessarily want to be safe, heard, informed, or be forced to choose.

In this article, we identify, discuss, and exemplify the reasons why these consumers are resenting, and at times opposing current regulation and/or marketing practices regarding their rights. We posit that consumerism will be transformed dramatically in the coming few decades as first individual consumers, next marketers, and ultimately the government adapts to this post-modern societal transformation.

## The End of Consumerism (The Way We Know It)

*The Right to be NOT Safe.* There have been impressive developments to enhance the safety of consumer goods, yet there are an increasing number of consumers that do not want to be safe. Their motivations can vary drastically, but the resulting action is the same: these consumers would rather take risk than be safe about their consumption. In the past couple of decades the number of consumers who participate in extreme sports have exploded in growth (Celsi et al. 1993; Tomlinson 2004). There are consumer demanding they be allowed to take medication without having to wait for the completion of lengthy experimental trials and the FDA approval process (Conko 2008). Some consumers want a unique experience minimizing, and at times undermining western medicine and treatments. For example, natural childbirth with midwives at home instead of with doctors and hospitalization (and frequently C-section (Declercq, Menacker, and MacDorman 2005) has been gaining ground.

*The Right to be NOT Informed.* There have been advancements with regard to regulation to provide consumers with more and accurate information regarding their options, yet there are an increasing number of consumers that would rather be disturbed less, and in some cases not be informed at all. Consumers are being bombarded by an excessive array of marketing messages every day. Many of these marketing activities simply represent wasteful or dumb marketing (Sheth and Sisodia 2006). The promotion bombardment continues to intensify, and the opt-out procedure to avoid marketing remains confusing and cumbersome. Nevertheless, the FTC initiated Do Not Call list apparently struck a chord with the consuming public (more than 157 million phone numbers have been enrolled in the program (FTC 2008)). Currently, consumer groups across the US are working to pass municipal/state resolutions in support of a Do Not Mail registry to stop junk mail but Federal action is not expected anytime soon (Sullivan 2009).

*The Right to be NOT Heard.* There are an increasing number of consumers that would rather be not heard. These consumers and their advocates believe that their privacy is being trampled upon by the marketers that collect information and then share these with third parties for profit or for access to other databases (Zwick and Knott 2009). The Center for Digital Democracy and the U.S. Public Interest Research Group recently filed a complaint against several behavioral online advertising networks that track and record the surfing patterns of unaware consumers (Tynan 2007). Internet advertising through behavioral tracking is a cause for controversy since consumer information can be collected, compiled, and sold secretly, all done without reasonable safeguards.

*The Right to NOT Choose.* The service and product providers have been putting their efforts enhance the variety of goods available to consumers. Yet there are at least two groups of growing number of consumers that would rather simplify the process, and in many cases not be faced with a choice at all. The first group feels that there are just too many choices out there. They do not think that 285 varieties of cookies, and 275 types of cereal in an ordinary supermarket are necessary (Botti and Iyengar 2006). Even from the marketer perspective, this clutter represents wasteful product development and less effective sales outcomes (Iyengar and Lepper 2000) in addition to less satisfied consumers (Carmon et al. 2003; Schwartz et al. 2002). The second group would like to ignore choices altogether (or making a choice to circumvent hyperchoice), favoring subscription based business models where the cost is not directly tied to a specific purchase allowing experimentation and sampling. For example, these consumers would like to subscribe to music databases to sample a variety of music of different genre without the limitations of paying per album or song.

## Conclusion

Freud (1930) argued that the modern consumer traded her *personal freedom* for *economic security*. In contrast, Bauman (1998, 1999) argued that the *post-modern consumer* was ready to reclaim and enjoy her personal freedom to consume at the expense of her economic security (also see Tester 2004). In retrospect, we think both theses were partially supported. Our attempt provides interesting insights into how consumers deal with this alleged paradox between security and freedom in the post-modern society. Interestingly, we suggest and our analysis alludes that the post-modern consumer may opt for *economic and personal freedom* at the expense of economic security, and at times personal safety. To facilitate this, it has been argued that "[m]arketing doesn't need reform; it needs restraint" (Brown 1995; 2006, 63). It remains to be seen if this will be primarily in the form of self-restraint, imposed upon, or both.

## REFERENCES

Aaker, David A. and George S. Day (1982), *Consumerism: Search for the Consumer Interest*, New York, NY: The Free Press.

Acohido, Byron (2009), "Hackers Breach Heartland Payment Credit Card System," *USA Today*, January 20.

Alba, Joseph, John Lynch, Barton Weitz, Chris Janiszewski, Richard Lutz, Alan Sawyer and Stacy Wood (1997), " Interactive Home Shopping: Consumer, Retailer, and Manufacturer Incentive to Participate in Electronic Marketplaces," *Journal of Marketing*, 3 (July), 38-53.

Bauman, Zygmunt (1998), *Work, Consumerism, and the New Poor*, Buckingham, UK: Open University Press.

_____ (1999), *In Search of Politics*, Stanford, CA: Stanford University Press.

Bell, M. and W. Emory (1971), "The Faltering Marketing Concept," *Journal of Marketing*, 35(October), 37-42.

Belk, Russell (2006), "Out of Sight and Out of Our Minds: What of Those Left Behind by Globalism," in *Does Marketing Need Reform?* Sheth and Sisodia ed., Armonk: M.E. Sharpe, 209-16.

Bettman, James R., Mary Frances Luce, and John W. Payne (1998), "Constructive Consumer Choice Processes," *Journal of Consumer Research*, 25 (December), 187-217.

Bianco, Anthony (2004), "The Vanishing Market," *Business Week*, July 12, 60.

Binswanger, Mathias (2006), "Why Does Income Growth Fail to Make us Happier?: Searching for the Treadmills Behind the Paradox of Happiness," *Journal of Socio-Economics*, 35 (April), 366-81.

Blanck HM, MK Serdula, and C. Gillespie (2007), "Use of Non-prescription Dietary Supplements for Weight Loss is Common Among Americans," J Am Diet Assoc, 107(3): 441-47.

Bloom, Paul and Stephen A. Greyser (1981), "The Maturing of *Consumerism*," *Harvard Business Review*; 59(6), 130-39.

Botti, Simona and Sheena S. Iyengar (2006), "The Dark Side of Choice: When Choice Impairs Social Welfare," *Journal of Public Policy&Marketing*, 25 (Spring), 24-38.

Brown, Stephen (1995), *PostModern Marketing*, New York, NY: Routledge.

Bush, J. (2004), *Consumer Empowerment and Competitiveness*, National Consumer Council, London.

Buskirk, R. H., and J. T. Rothe (1970), "Consumerism—An Interpretation," *Journal of Marketing*, 34 (October), 61-65.

Carmon, Z. K. Wertenbroch and M. Zeelenberg (2003), "Option Attachment: When Delibrating Makes Choosing Feel Like Loosing," *Journal of Consumer Research*, 30(1), 15-29.

Celsi, Richard, Randall Rose, and Thomas Leigh (1993),"An Exploration of High-Risk Leisure Consumption through Skydiving," *Journal of Consumer Research*, 20 (June), 1-21.

Clark, David (2003), "The Death and Life of Punk, The Last Subculture 1", in *The Post-Subcultures Reader*, David Muggleton, Rupert Weinzierl eds., Oxford, Berg.

Coleman, Ellen (2007), "Weight Loss Supplements to Watch (and Watch Out For),"*Today's Dietitian*, 9 (August), 10.

Conko, Gregory (2008), "Sick Patients Need Cutting-Edge Drugs," *The Wall Street Journal*, August 23.

Dahl, Jonathan (2009), *1,001 Things They Won't Tell You: An Insider's Guide to Spending, Saving, and Living Wisely*, Workman Publishing Company: New York.

Darke, Peter and Robin Ritchie J. B. (2007), "The Defensive Consumer: Advertising Deception: Defensive Processing, and Distrust," *Journal of Marketing Research*, 44(Feb), 114-27.

Declercq Eugene, Fay Menacker, Marian MacDorman (2005), "Rise in "No Indicated Risk" Primary Caesareans in the United States, 1991-2001: Cross Sectional Analysis," *British Medical Journal*, 330, 71-72.

Deighton, John (1996), "The Future of Interactive Marketing," *Harvard Business Review*, 74 (November-December), 151-62.

_____ (1998), "The Right to be Left Alone," *Journal of Interactive Marketing*, 12(2), 2-4.

_____ (2004), "The Presentation of Self in the Information Age," *Harvard Business School Marketing Research Papers*, No. 04-02.

Drucker, P. F. (1969), "The Shame of Marketing," *Marketing Communications*, 297(Aug), 60-4.

Elgin, Duane (1993), *Voluntary Simplicity: Toward a Way of Life That Is Outwardly Simple, Inwardly Rich*, New York, NY: William Morrow and Company, Inc.

Etzioni, Amitai (1987), "Entrepreneurship, Adaptation and Legitimation: A Macrobehavioral Perspective, *Journal of Economic Behavior and Organization*, (8): 175-89

_____ (1998), "Voluntary Simplicity: Characterization, Select Psychological Implications, and Societal Consequences", *Journal of Economic Psychology*, Vol. 19 No.5, pp.619-43.

_____ (2004), "The Post Affluent Society," *Review of Social Economy*, 62(September), 407-420.

Fasig, Lisa Biank (2009), "For Consumers, Less Choice Means Better Selection: Retailers are Reducing Variety to Boost Productivity," *Business Courier of Cincinnati*, July 17.

Federal Trade Commission (2008), "Do Not Call Registrations Permanent and Fees Telemarketers Pay to Access Registry Set," http//:www.ftc.gov/opa/2008/04/dncfyi.shtm, April 10.

Fiore, David C. (2003), "Injuries Associated with Whitewater Rafting and Kayaking," *Wilderness Environ. Med*, 14 (Winter), 255-60.

Fletcher, Dan (2009), "A Brief History of Spam," *Times*, November 2.

Foxman, E. R. and P. Kilcoyne (1993), "Information Technology, Marketing Practice, and Consumer Privacy: Ethnical Issues," *Journal of Public Policy&Marketing*, 12(Spring), 106-19.

Freud, Sigmund (1930), *Civilization and Its Discontents*, ed, by M, Masud R, Khan and trans, by James Strachey (London: The Hogarth Press and the Institute of Psycho-Analysis, 1973).

Gaski, J. F., and Etzel, M. J. (2005) "National Aggregate Consumer Sentiment Toward Marketing: A Thirty-year Retrospective and Analysis," *Journal of Consumer Research*, 31(March), 859-867.

Gaskin, Ina M. (2002), *Spiritual Midwifery*, 4th edition, Summertown, TN: Book Publishing Co.

Gates, Bill (2003), "Why I Hate Spam," *The Wall Street Journal*, June 23. [available at http://www.microsoft.com/presspass/ofnote/06-23wsjspam.mspx] (access Jan 20, 2010).

Giesler, Marcus (2008), "Conflict and Compromise: Drama in Marketplace Evolution," *Journal of Consumer Research*, 34 (April), 739-53.

Goodwin, Cathy (1991), "Privacy: Recognition of a Consumer Right," *Journal of Public Policy and Marketing*, 10 (Spring), 149-66.

Griffin, Drew and David Fitzpatrick (2009), "U.S. Patients Try Stem Cell Therapies Abroad," CNNHealth.com, June 2 (last accessed Jan 12, 2009). [available at http://www.cnn.com/2009/HEALTH/06/02/stem.cell.therapy/]

Gross, Grant (2007), "Privacy Groups Call for Do-Not-Track List," *PCWorld*, October 31.

Grover, Varun, Jaejoo Lim, and Ramakrishna Ayyagari (2006), "The Dark Side of Information and Market Efficiency in E-Markets," *Decision Sciences*, 37(3), 297-324.

Humphreys, Ashlee (2010), "Megamarketing: The Creation of Markets as a Social Process," *Journal of Marketing*, 74(March), forthcoming.

Iyengar, S. S. and M.R. Lepper (2000), "When Choice is Demotivating: Can One Desire Too Much of Good Thing?" *Journal of Personality and Social Psychology*. 79(6), 995-1006.

Jaffe, Daniel L. (2005), "An Interview with the Federal Trade Commission Chairman," *The Advertiser*, October, 18-28.

Kaikati, Andrew M. and Jack G. Kaikati (2004), "Stealth Marketing: How to Reach Consumers Surreptitiously," *California Management Review*, 46 (Summer), 6-22.

Keegan, Paul (2009), "How Car Sharing Start-up Zipcar is Cranking Up a Transportation Revolution," *Fortune*, September 14, 42-52.

Kennedy, John F. (1962), "Special Message to the Congress on Protecting the Consumer Interest," available at [http://www.jfklink.com/speeches/jfk/publicpapers/1962/jfk93_62.html] (Jan 6, 2010).

Kotler, Philip (1972), "What Consumerism Means for Marketers," *Harvard Business Review*, 50, 48–57 (May–June).

Lee, Byung-Kwan and Wei-Na Lee (2004), "The Effect of Information Overload on Consumer Choice Quality in an On-Line Environment," *Psychology&Marketing*, 21March, 159-83.

Leonard-Barton, Dorothy (1981), "Voluntary Simplicity Lifestyles and Energy Conservation," *Journal of Consumer Research*, 8 (December), 243-52.

Malhotra, Naresh K. (1984), "Reflections on the Information Overload Paradigm in Consumer Decision Making," *Journal of Consumer Research*, 10 (March), 436-440.

Mick, David Glen, S. M. Broniarczyk and J. Haidt (2004), "Choose, Choose, Choose, Choose, Choose, Choose, Choose: Emerging and Prospective Research on the Deleterious Effects of Living in Consumer Hyperchoice," *Journal of Business Ethics*, 52 (June), 207-11.

Nader, Ralph (1959), "The Safe Car You Can't Buy," *The Nation*, New York, N.Y., Apr. 11, 188:310-12.

_____ (1965), Unsafe at Any Speed *The Designed-In Dangers of The American Automobile*, Grossman Publishers, New York LC

*OC Weekly* (2009), "The Rolling Paper: Your Guide to Medical Marijuana," December 11-17, 15(15), 1-28.

Ramasastry, Anita (2005), "Tracking Every Move You Make: Can Car Rental Companies Use Technology to Monitor Our Driving?" *FindLaw*, (http://writ.news.findlaw.com/ramasastry/20050823.html) (last access on April 4, 2007).

Rayport, Jeffrey F. (2008), "Where is Advertising Going? Into 'Stitials," *Harvard Business Review*, May, 18-9.

Reibstein, David J. (2002), "What Attracts Customers to Online Stores, and What Keeps them Coming Back?," *Journal of the Academy of Marketing Science*, 30 (September), 465-73.

Rosenberg, Adams (2009), "CDT Statement on Facebook's New Privacy Settings," http//: www.cdt.org, December 9.

Schor, Juliet B. (1999), *The Overspent American: Why We Want What We Don't Need*, New York, NY: Perenial.

Schultz, Ray (2006), "Canadian Telemarketers Face Jail," *Direct*, 18(7), 21.

Schwartz, B. (2004), *The Paradox of Choice: Why More is Less*, Harper Collins: New York.

_____, A. Ward, J. Monte, S. Lyubomirsky, K. White and D. R. Lehman (2002), "Maximizing Versus Satisficing: Happiness is a Matter of Choice," *Journal of Personality and Social Psychology*, 83(5), 1178-97.

Shankar, Avi, Helene Cherrier and Robin Canniford (2006), "Consumer Empowerment: a Foucauldian Interpretation," *European Journal of Marketing*, 40(9/10), 1013-30.

Sheth, Jagdish N., and N. J. Mammana (1974), "Recent Failures in Consumer Protection," *California Management Review*, 16(3), 64-72.

_____ and Rajendra Sisodia (2006), *Does Marketing Need Reform?* Armonk: M.E. Sharpe.

_____ ,_____ , and Adina Barbulescu (2006), "The Image of Marketing," in *Does Marketing Need Reform?* Sheth and Sisodia ed., Armonk: M.E. Sharpe, 26-36.

Staelin, Richard (1978), "The Effects of Consumer Education on Consumer Product Safety Behavior," *Journal of Consumer Research*, 5(June), 30-40.

Steinberg, Brian (2007), "Ads Keep Spreading, But Are Consumers Immune?" *Advertising Age,* 78(46).

_____ and Suzanne Vranica (2004), "The Ad World's Message for 2005: Stealth," *The Wall Street Journal*. (Eastern edition). Dec 30, B.1.

Straver, W. (1977). The international consumerist movement: Theory and Practical Implications for Marketing Strategy, *European Journal of Marketing*, 11, 93-117.

_____ (1978). The Consumerist Movement in Europe: Challenges and Opportunities for Marketing Strategy, *European Journal of Marketing*, 12(4), 316-25.

Sullivan, Elizabeth A. (2009), "Play By the New Rules," *Marketing News*, December 30, 5-9.

Tester, Keith, (2004), *The Social Thought of Zygmunt Bauman*, New York, NY: Palgrave MacMillan.

Thompson, Craig J (2002), "Consumer Value Systems in the Age of Postmodern Fragmentation: The Case of the Natural Health Microculture," *Journal of Consumer Research*, 28 (March), 550-70.

_____ and Maura Troester (2002), "Consumer Value Systems in the Age of Postmodern Fragmentation: The Case of the Natural Health Microculture," *Journal of Consumer Research*, 28 (March), 550-71.

_____ (2005), "Consumer Risk Perceptions in a Community of Reflexive Doubt," *Journal of Consumer Research*, 32 (September), 235-47.

_____ and Gokcen Coskuner-Balli (2007a), "Countervailing Market Responses to Corporate Co-optation and the Ideological Recruitment of Consumption Communities," *Journal of Consumer Research*, 34 (August), 135-52.

_____ and_____ (2007b), "Enchanting Ethical Consumerism: The Case of Community Supported Agriculture," *Journal of Consumer Culture*, 7(3), 275-303.

Tomlinson, Joe (2004). *Extreme Sports: In Search of the Ultimate Thrill*. Hove: Firefly Books.

Truett, Richard (2006), "U.S. Decides On Rules For 'Black Box'," *Automative News Europe*, 11(18), 27.

Tynan, Dan (2007), "Watch Out For Online Ads That Watch You," *PC World*, 25(March), 26.

Westman, A, M. Rosen, P. Berggren, U. Bjornstig (2008), "Parachuting from Fixed Objects: Descriptive Study of 106 Fatal Events in BASE Jumping 1981–2006," *British Journal of Sports Medicine*, 42, 431-36.

Williamson, Jed (2009), *Accidents in North American Mountaineering 2009*, Golden, CO: American Alpine Club Press.

Woosley, Ben and Mark Schulz (2010), *Credit Card Statistics, Industry Facts, Debt Statistics*, Creditcards.com Survey, June 2007. [available at http://www.creditcards.com/credit-card-news/credit-card-industry-facts-personal-debt-statistics-1276.php] (Jan 20, 2010).

Zwick, Detlev and Janice Denegri Knott, (2009), "Manufacturing Consumers," *Journal of Consumer Culture*, 9(2), 221-247.

# Iconoclasm, Autotelicity, Narcissism, and COOL Beyond Distinction

Soonkwan Hong, Michigan Technological University, USA

## EXTENDED ABSTRACT

Distinction as an imperative of consumer culture and a prerequisite for postmodern self-identity has been widely recognized and discussed by theorists ever since the homogenization of consumers in modernity provoked individuals to seek a distinct identity (e.g., Bourdieu 1984; Holt 1998; Jameson 1991). This subsumption of distinction under consumer identity project, which also manifests as an unprecedentedly important part of consumer culture, necessitates consumers' proactive devotion to distinction-making (Firat and Venkatesh 1995) and thus interests consumer researchers. Nevertheless, the extant literature on distinction tends to stay within the normative boundary of distinction that all can conceive, perceive, simulate, and emulate, with a slight exception as to gender and sexual-orientation issues (e.g., Kates 2002, 2004).

In order to contribute to the advance of the theories relevant to distinction as a recursive topic of consumer culture, this study employs a context that facilitates the understanding of novel styles of making distinction. The X Games event is selected as the context for the theorization of "hyper-distinction," which seems quite evident in the extreme locale. As extreme sports participants display self-fulfilling characteristics of socio-cultural "distancing" from others in the context, newly emerged "freestyle" and "no string attached" distinctions become palpable. It is also frequently quoted that the followers of extreme sports are defying not only gravity but also social standards. This constant distinction-making that is to contrast with mainstream culture, establishment, social structure, and hegemonic brands ultimately brings much attention and value to the extreme sports event, as a culturally and theoretically rich context for this study of distinction and the dynamics in consumer culture.

Following grounded theory approach, this study employs a multi-sited and multi-layered approach, often used in consumer culture theory literature (e.g., Giesler 2006; Kjeldgaard and Askegaard 2006; Kozinets 2001, 2002; Kozinets and Handelman 2004; Schau and Gilly 2003). The multi-layered approach for this study involves ethnographic in-depth interview (primary data source), fieldnotes, participant observation, videotaping, and photographs.

Among many possible forms that autotelic and/or narcissistic consumption praxes can take, extreme sports participants employ iconoclastic, self-complacent, and intrinsic(cool hunting) methods to make distinction. Extreme sports participants appear to pursue autotelic self-identity that is less negotiated and more asserted than what theories have by far codified (cf., Giesler 2008; Kates 2002; Kjeldgaard and Askegaard 2006; Sandikci and Ger 2010; Thompson and Haytko 1997). Distinction in extreme sports context, in which "mild and naïve" distinctions become worse than "no distinction," may be seen as the extreme case of "the cult of the self." In order to turn the blurred line between self and others to a bolder one, consumers perform narcissistic practices with less concern about reflexivity of the self (cf., Finkelstein 1991; Giddens 1991). The narcissism consumers in the context take for granted is their ultimatum to others that prevents unwanted overlaps of self-identity. Narcissism for those consumers is the mode of being that is not a pathological anomaly, but a purely cultural choice for cultivating the self as Giddens (1991, 81) states, "we have no choice but to choose." The extracted themes of distinction indicate possibilities of presenting distinctiveness to the outside of the self without staying within the normative boundary.

Consumers who freely improvise and still display nuanced hipness are distinct in the context. Socio-cultural background is neither questioned nor relevant. Unlike some macro (national) and global(ized) contexts in which the logic and practice of distinction-making have been studied (e.g., Holt 1998; Ustuner and Holt 2010), in the relatively micro and more culturally defined context, consumers appear to unleash themselves from the rigid cultural propositions and schemata. Because Bourdieu (1984, 1990) is not a determinist, there is always a room for consumer agency, not subjectivity, even though the habitus is all-pervasive. In practice, perhaps consumers have to be a subject with minimal consumer agency in certain contexts wherein habitus is less malleable, but they can be rule-breakers in some contexts (i.e., X Games) that encourage agentic contribution to cultural progress (cf. Bourdieu 1990). Thus, some research has to follow in order to better understand how consumers perceive the boundary between the two possibly distinct types of context. Research on how consumers maneuver within the field of distinction that connotes different levels of plasticity of the habitus will also provide a theoretical insight for consumer researchers.

"Trickling-up" cultural penetration and proliferation are of particular interest. The hipness and cool invented and spread by a group of people (i.e., extreme sports athletes and participants), who socio-politically represents almost the opposite of "high-cultural-capital" consumers, are now the dominant form of distinction in many contexts. The encroachment of the culture from the "bottom of the pyramid" upon the historical role of cultural capital, which has been operating as the most important currency for distinction, is widely observed and rapidly developing. The Winter Olympic Games' acceptance of some events (i.e., ski cross and half pipe) created by rebellious and yet cool people, who originally ridiculed the elitism in the sports, clearly shows how the logic can be upside down.

The consumers who portray a cool persona and practice natural hipness are comparable to the consumers in the past who enjoyed their high cultural capital. Although cool may not be something to be explained, analyzed, and theorized, it will be thought-provoking if research explores different facades of cool in different context to see if a similar manifestation of cool in a context can be transferred to the other. Cool as distinction in the context of X Games seems well-received in many other contexts as marketers strived to transplant the cool to brands and trends. However, the grass-roots types of distinction (cool), found in this study, is very far from what is usually targeted by marketers and consumers because they present extremity and essentialism. The distinction inflation promoted in such a context may hinder the co-optation as business culture, and therefore it protects the distinction from commercialization. In that case, what would be hyper-co-optation of hyper-distinction like?

## REFERENCE

Arnould, Eric J., Linda L. Price and Risto Moisio (2006), "Making Contexts Matter: Selecting Research Contexts for Theoretical Insights," in *Handbook of Qualitative Research Methods in Marketing*, ed. Russell W. Belk, Northhampton, MA: Edward Elgar Publishing Ltd., 106-128.

Arnould, Eric J. and Melanie Wallendorf (1994), "Market-Oriented Ethnography: Interpretatioin Building and Marketing Strategy Formulation," *Journal of Marketing Research*, 31 (November), 484-504.

Askegaard, Søren, Eric J. Arnould, and Dannie Kjeldgaard (2005), "Postassimilationist Ethnic Consumer Research: Qualifications and Extensions," *Journal of Consumer Research*, 32 (June), 160-170.

Baudrillard, Jean (1975), *The Mirror of Production*, St. Louis, MI: Telos Press.

_____ (1981), *For a Critique of the Political Economy of the Sign*, St. Louis: Telos.

_____ (1983), *Simulations*, New York: Semiotexte.

Belk, Russell W. (1988), "Possessions and the Extended Self," *Journal of Consumer Research*, 15 (September), 139-68.

Barthes, Roland (1972), *Mythologies*, trans. Annette Lavers, London: Cape.

Bauman, Zygmunt (1991), *Modernity and Ambivalence*, Cambridge: Polity Press.

Beverland, Michael B. and Francis J. Farrelly (2010), "The Quest for Authenticity in Consumption: Consumers' Purposive Choice of Authentic Cues to Shape Experienced Outcomes," *Journal of Consumer Research*, 36 (February), 838-856.

Bourdieu, Pierre (1984), *Distinction: A Social Critique of the Judgment of Taste*, Cambridge, MA: Harvard University Press.

_____ (1990), *The Logic of Practice*, CA: Stanford University Press.

Brewer, Marilynn B. (1991). "The social self: On being the same and different at the same time," *Personality and Social Psychology Bulletin*, 17, 475-482.

Bonsu, Samuel K. and Russell W. Belk (2003), "Do Not Go Cheaply into That Good Night: Death Ritual Consumption in Asante Ghana," *Journal of Consumer Research*, 30 (June), 41–55.

Bouchet, Dominique (1995), "Marketing and the Redefinition of Ethnicity," in *Marketing in a Multicultural World*, ed. Janeen Costa and Gary Bamossy, Thousand Oaks, CA: Sage, 68–104.

Charters, Steve (2006), "Aesthetic Products and Aesthetic Consumption: A Review," *Consumption, Markets and Culture*, 9 (September), 235-255.

Elliott, Richard (1998), "A Model of Emotion-Driven Choice," *Journal of Marketing Management*, 14, 95-108.

Epp, Amber M. and Linda L. Price (2008), "Family Identity: A Framework of Identity Interplay in Consumption Practices," *Journal of Consumer Research*, 50-70.

Feldman, Martha S. (1995), *Strategies for Interpreting Qualitative Data*, Thousand Oaks, California, Sage Publications.

Finkelstein, Joanne (1991), *The Fashioned Self*, Cambridge, MA: Polity Press.

Firat, A. Fuat and Alladi Venkatesh (1995), "Liberatory Postmodernism and the Reenchantment of Consumption," *Journal of Consumer Research*, 22 (December), 239-267.

Foucault, Michel (1988), Technologies of the Self, in *Technologies of the Self*, ed. Luther H. Martin, Huck Gutman, and Patrick H. Hutton, Amherst: The University of Massachusetts Press.

Frank, Thomas (1997a), *The Conquest of Cool*, Chicago: The University of Chicago Press.

_____ (1997b), "Why Johnny Can't Dissent," in *Commodify Your Dissent*, ed. Thomas Frank and Matt Weiland, New York: W.W. Norton, 31-45.

Giddens, Anthony (1991), *Modernity and Self-Identity*, Stanford, CA: Stanford University Press.

Giesler, Markus (2006), "Consumer Gift Systems," *Journal of Consumer Research*, 33 (September), 283-290.

_____ (2008), "Conflict and Compromise: Drama in Marketplace Evolution," *Journal of Consumer Research*, 34 (April), 739-753.

Glaser, Barney G. and Anselm L. Strauss (1967), *The Discovery of Grounded Theory: Strategies for Qualitative Research*, Hawthorne, NY: Aldine Transaction.

Grubb, Edward L. and Harrison L. Grathwohl (1967), "Consumer Self-Concept, Symbolism, and Market Behavior: A Theoretical Approach," *Journal of Marketing*, 31 (October), 22-27.

Heath, Joseph and Andrew Potter (2004), *Nation of Rebels: Why Counterculture Became Consumer Culture*, New York: HarperCollins.

Hetada, Sherif (1998), "Dollarization, Fragmentation, and God," in *The Cultures of Globalization*, ed. Fredric Jameson and Masao Miyoshi, Durham and London: Duke University Press.

Holt, Douglas B. (1998), "Does Cultural Capital Structure American Consumption?" *Journal of Consumer Research*, 25 (June), 1–26.

_____ (2002), "Why Do Brands Cause Trouble? A Dialectical Theory of Consumer Culture and Branding," *Journal of ConsumerResearch*, 29 (June), 70–90.

Jameson, Fredric (1991), *Postmodersim, or, The Cultural Logic of Late Capitalism*, Duke University Press.

Kates, Steven M. (2002), "The Protean Quality of Subcultural Consumption: An Ethnographic Account of Gay Consumers," *Journal of Consumer Research*, 29 (December), 383–99.

_____ (2004), "The Dynamics of Brand Legitimacy: An Interpretive Study in the Gay Men's Community," *Journal of Consumer Research*, 31 (September), 455-464.

Kellner, Douglas (1989), *Jean Baudrillard: From the Marxism to Modernity*, Baltimore, MD: The Johns Hopkins University Press.

Kjeldgaard, Dannie and Søren Askegaard (2006), "The Glocalization of Youth Culture: The Global Youth Segment as Structures of Common Difference," *Journal of Consumer Research*, 33 (September), 231-247.

Knobil, Marcel (2002), "What Makes a Brand Cool? Market Leader," *Journal of the Marketing Society*, 18, 21-25.

Kozinets, Robert V. (2001), "Utopian Enterprise: Articulating the Meaning of *Star Trek*'s Culture of Consumption," *Journal of Consumer Research*, 28 (June), 67–89.

_____ (2002), "The Field Behind the Screen: Using Netnography for Marketing Research in Online Communities," *Journal of Marketing Research*, 34 (February), 61-72.

Kozinets, Robert V. and Jay M. Handelman (2004), "Adversaries of Consumption: Consumer Movements, Activism, and Ideology," *Journal of Consumer Research*, 31 (December), 691–704.

Luedicke, Marius K., Craig J. Thompson, and Markus Giesler (2010), "Consumer Identity Work as Moral Protagonism: How Myth and Ideology Animate a Brand-Mediated Moral Conflict," *Journal of Consumer Research*, 36 (June), Forthcoming.

McCracken, Grant (1989), " 'Homeyness': A Cultural Account of One Constellation of Consumer Goods and Meanings," in *Interpretive Consumer Research*, Elizabeth C. Hirschman, ed. Provo, UT: Association for Consumer Research, 168-185.

_____ (2008), *Transformations: Identity Construction in Contemporary Culture*, Bloomington, IN: Indiana University Press.

Miller, Daniel (1987), *Material Culture and Mass Consumption*, New York, NY: Basil Balckwell.

Muniz, Albert M., and Thomas C. O'Guinn (2001), "Brand Community," *Journal of Consumer Research*, 27 (March), 412-432.

Murray, Jeff B. (2002), "The Politics of Consumption: A Re-Inquiry on Thompson and Hayko's (1997) "Speaking of Fashion"," *Journal of Consumer Research*, 29 (December), 427-440.

Nancarrow, Clive and Pamela Nancarrow (2007), "Hunting for Cool Tribes," in *Consumer Tribes*, ed. Bernard Cova, Robert V. Kozinets, and Avi Shankar, Jordan Hill: Oxford, UK: Butterworth-Heinemann.

Oswald, Laura R. (1999), "Culture Swapping: Consumption and the Ethnogenesis of Middle-Class Haitian Immigrants," *Journal of Consumer Research*, 25 (March), 303–18.

Penaloza, Lisa (2001), "Consuming the American West: Animating Cultural Meaning at a Stock Show and Rodeo," *Journal of Consumer Research*, 28 (December), 369–98.

Postrel, Virginia (2003), *The Substance of Style: How the Rise of Aesthetic Value is Remaking Commerce, Culture, and Consciousness*, New York: HarperCollins.

Pountain, Dick and David Robins (2000), *Cool Rules: Anatomy of an Attitude*, London: Relation Books.

Ricoeur, Paul (1995), *Oneself as Another*, trans. Kathleen Blamey, Chicago: University of Chicago Press.

Sandikci, Ozlem and Guliz Ger (2010), "Veiling in Style: How Does a Stigmatized Practice Become Fashionable," *Journal of Consumer Research*, 37 (June), Forthcoming.

Schau, Hope Jensen and Mary C. Gilly (2003), "We Are What We Post? Self-Presentation in Personal Web Space," *Journal of Consumer Research*, 30 (December), 385–404.

Schau, Hope Jensen, Mary C. Gilly, and Mary Wolfinbarger (2009), "Consumer Identity Renaissance: The Resurgence of Identity-Inspired Consumption in Retirement," *Journal of Consumer Research*, 36 (August), 255-276.

Sennett, Richard (1977), *The Fall of Public Man*, Cambridge: Cambridge University Press.

Simmel, Georg ([1904] 1957) , "Fashion," *American Journal of Sociology,* 62 (May) , 541–558.

Slater, Don (1997), *Consumer Culture and Modernity*, Malden, MA: Blackwell Publishing.

Smith, Scott, Dan Fisher, and S. Jason Cole (2007), "The Lived Meanings of Fanaticism: Understanding the Complex Role of Labels and Categories in Defining the Self in Consumer Culture," *Consumption, Markets, and Culture*, 10 (June), 77-94.

Snyder, C. R. and Howard L. Fromkin (1977), "Abnormality as a Positive Characteristic: The Development and Validation of a Scale Measuring Need for Uniqueness," *Journal of Abnormal Psychology*, 86 (October), 518-527.

Spiggle, Susan (1994), "Analysis and Interpretation of Qualitative Data in Consumer Research," *Journal of Consumer Research*, 21 (December), 491-503.

Thompson, Craig J. (1997), "Interpreting Consumers: A Hermeneutical Framework for Deriving Marketing Insights from the Texts of Consumers' Consumption Stories," *Journal of Marketing Research*, 34 (4), 438-56.

——— (2004), "Marketplace Mythologies and Discourses of Power," *Journal of Consumer Research*, 31 (June), 162–80.

Thompson, Craig J. and Diana L. Haytko (1997), "Speaking of Fashion: Consumers' Uses of Fashion Discourses and the Appropriation of Countervailing Cultural Meanings," *Journal of Consumer Research*, 24 (June), 15–42.

Thompson, Craig J. and Zeynep Arsel (2004), "The Starbucks Brandscape and Consumers' (Anti-corporate) Experiences of Glocalization," *Journal of Consumer Research*, 31 (December), 631–42.

Thornton, Sarah (1995), *Club Cultures: Music, Media and Subcultural Capital*, Cambridge, Polity Press.

Tian, Kelly Tepper, William O. Bearden, and Gary L. Hunter (2001), "Consumers' Need for Uniqueness: Scale Development and Validation," *Journal of Consumer Research*, 28 (June), 50-66.

Turner, Victor (1982), *From Ritual to Theatre: The Human Seriousness of Play*, New York: PAJ.

Üstüner, Tuba and Douglas B. Holt (2010), "Toward a Theory of Status Consumption in Less Industrialized Countries," *Journal of Consumer Research*, 37 (June), Forthcoming.

Vignoles, Vivian. L., Xenia Chryssochoou., & Glynis M. Breakwell (2002), "Sources of distinctiveness: Position, difference and separateness in the identities of Anglican parish priests," *European Journal of Social Psychology*, 32, 761-780.

# Conceptions of Consumption in Consumer Culture Theory: A Dynamic Framework

Ahir Gopaldas, York University, Canada

## EXTENDED ABSTRACT

Presidential addresses to the *Association of Consumer Research*, from the first published (Pratt 1974) to the most recent (Janiszewski *forthcoming*), and editorial statements in the *Journal of Consumer Research*, from the first (Frank 1974) to the most recent (Deighton 2005), regularly assert that what anchors the field of consumer research is not a theoretical perspective but a substantive domain called consumption. Thus, unsurprisingly, the field houses several conceptions of consumption. Consumption is conceived of as utility maximization in an economic perspective, as information-processing in a cognitive-psychological perspective, as decision-making in a behavioral-economic perspective, as structuration in a sociological perspective, as meaning-making in a cultural-anthropological perspective, and as goal seeking, identity management, need fulfillment, and want negotiation among numerous other conceptions. There is nothing intrinsically wrong with any of these conceptions so long as one does not reify these conceptions. Conceptions are images, models, or ways of perceiving. Conceptions are neither true nor false; rather, conceptions are more or less useful. It is futile to seek a universal best conception; instead, one must determine which conceptions of a phenomenon are valuable across different sets of circumstances, or inversely, which sets of circumstances substantiate the value of different conceptions (Lewis and Grimes 1999; Morgan 1980; Weick 1989).

*Scope.* In a historical period when the consumer research community is home to over a thousand researchers and over a dozen annual conferences and dedicated journals, the field is simply too vast and varied to fit all of its working conceptions of consumption into a single essay. One functional way to manage the issue of scope is to choose one sub-field of consumer research as a boundary condition. There are three established sub-fields of consumer research, consumer culture theory (CCT), consumer decision making (CDM), and consumer information processing (CIP), and one growing field of transformative consumer research (TCR) (Arnould and Thompson 2005; Hudson and Ozanne 1988; Johar, Maheswaran, and Peracchio 2006; Loken 2005; MacInnis and Folkes *forthcoming*; Mick 2008; Simonson et al. 2001). The decision making and information processing conceptions of consumption lie at the foundations of CDM and CIP respectively, though each of those sub-fields also host variations of those conceptions (Newell and Broder 2008). By contrast, conceptions of consumption lie at the frontiers of CCT research. A tacit assumption among CCT researchers is that because there can be no universal conception of consumption across contexts, perspectives, or times, there should be no ruling conception in CCT either. Rather, CCT researchers often try out multiple conceptions during the course of a single study and debate the merits of various conceptions across a stream of literature (Arnold and Fischer 1994; Holt 1995; Spiggle 1994). It is precisely because conceptions of consumption are contested and evolving in CCT that it is theoretically valuable to focus our attention on this sub-field.

*Conceptions.* This essay could have been framed as *analogies*, *images*, *interpretations*, *models*, *metaphors*, or *theories* of consumption, or even *concepts* or *conceptualizations* of consumption. Our preference for *conceptions* of consumption is based on a few heuristics and on early reviews. *Conception* is not as superficial as *image* but not as deep as *theory*. Though all conceptions discussed in this essay have generated substantial insight for marketing theory or practice, not all conceptions have produced full-fledged theories as of yet. *Conception* does not carry as much disciplinary baggage as some of the other terms do. For example, while some cultural anthropologists and cognitive scientists have documented the function and power of *metaphor* in human culture and cognition (Lakoff and Johnson 1980), many theorists and practitioners overlook *metaphor* as a mere rhetoric matter owing to the term's association with literature. Unlike *concept*, the terms *conception* and *conceptualization* clearly evoke not only the cognitive product but also the cognitive process that produces it. Furthermore, reviewers of an early draft of this essay misconstrued *concepts of consumption* to be concepts within consumption theory rather than conceptualizations of the consumption phenomenon, as we intended. Finally, the hexa-syllabic *conceptualization* proved too cacophonous for many readers. In sum, we prefer *conception* because it communicates both cognitive process and product, at an appropriate level of theoretical maturity, without associative or aural excess.

*Organization.* Our ongoing objective is to map conceptions of consumption along informative dimensions of differentiation. Owing to the space constraints in this forum, it is not possible to discuss each of the dimensions and each of the conceptions in the detail that each deserves. However, it is possible to identify and partially illuminate some of the major dimensions and major conceptions in a condensed tabular form. The first section delineates the dimensions of differentiation that are useful in sorting through alternative conceptions of consumption. The second section itemizes major conceptions of consumption and explicates them along relevant dimensions. Thereafter, distinguishing characteristics of our framework are discussed and recommendations for future research and theory building are proffered.

# Same Destination, Different Paths: The Effect of Observing Others' Divergent Reasoning on Choice Confidence

Cait Poynor, University of Pittsburgh, USA
Rebecca Walker Naylor, The Ohio State University, USA
Kelly L. Haws, Texas A&M University, USA

## EXTENDED ABSTRACT

After Barack Obama's victory in the 2008 presidential election, strategists convened to analyze John McCain's loss. Pundits generally grouped McCain's supporters into two camps: Moderates, who appreciated McCain's centrist libertarianism, and Conservatives, who valued his social and fiscal conservatism. Both groups together made up the American center (Kass 2008). The fact that these groups supported McCain could have bolstered the confidence of individuals in either group that they had chosen the correct candidate, thus enhancing McCain's chances of victory. Interestingly, however, this failed to occur. Rather, divergence in perceptions of the importance of various issues among Conservatives may have led to fragmentation within the Republican party (Rodgers 2008), increasing McCain's vulnerability among what should have been his base. Could observing others' *divergent perceptions of importance of reasons* for a *convergent choice* have undermined the confidence of McCain's supporters in their choice of candidate? More generally, can the observation of divergent assessments of the relative importance of potential reasons for making a convergent choice have such a strong influence on individuals' choice confidence? Certainly, social influence research shows that observing others' behavior can have a strong influence on our own (Burnkrant and Cousineau 1975; Escalas and Bettman 2003; Park and Lessig 1977). We contend, however, that convergence or divergence of choice does not fully explain the influence that observing others can have on one's own choice confidence.

Rather, our results suggest that when an observed other's justification for making the same choice as our own does not correspond with our justification, choice confidence can be undermined. In other words, when individuals disagree on how important different reasons should be in justifying a choice, their reasoning is divergent even if their choice is convergent. We argue that in such cases the importance prescribed by observed others to possible reasons for making a given decision is seen as highly diagnostic in determining the validity of our own choice. When others rely on reasons we consider relatively trivial, it throws into question the validity of our decision process and decreases confidence in our choice. By contrast, reasoning related to divergent choices is not perceived to be as directly diagnostic in evaluating our own choice. In these cases, we propose that the applicability of others' behaviors will be discounted and our choice confidence will not be adversely affected.

We therefore propose a framework which recognizes that both observed choice and reasoning may either converge or diverge with an observer's own. Reasoning is a key element in evaluating the validity of a thought process (Simonson and Nowlis 2000). As such, models of reason-based choice assume that individuals choose by considering the reasons for choosing one alternative versus the other (Shafir, Simonson, and Tversky 1993). That is, consumers believe that good choices are based on good reasons and that good reasons will lead to good choices (Barber, Heath, and Odean 2003). Seeing someone choose what we do based on the same reasoning that drove us to choose it (i.e., perfect choice and reasoning convergence) should be doubly affirming–we have convergent support for our choice and know that we made it well. However, we propose that knowing that someone else has differ-

ent justifications for a choice can be quite damaging to our choice confidence, particularly if the choices are convergent. We propose that an individual consumer who observes another making the same choice s/he does will see the underlying reasoning of the observed other as highly diagnostic in determining the validity of his/her own choice. Therefore, the consumer will question his/her choice if the reasoning of the observed other for making the same choice diverges from his/her own.

We also predict that observing divergent reasoning for the same choice may shake confidence more so than does observing another consumer making a completely different choice. Unexpected reasoning attracts more attention and elaboration than does expected reasoning (Greenwald and Sakumura 1967; Simonson and Nowlis 2000). Divergent reasoning for a shared choice is likely to be less expected than is any reasoning related to divergent choice–while shared choices promote tendencies to anchor on one's own thought processes as the norm, divergent choices may cue consumers to recognize heterogeneity among those around them (Gilovich, Savitsky, and Mevec 2000) and, therefore, to be less surprised if they report divergent reasoning. The direct applicability of divergent reasoning to convergent choice behavior will also make it more persuasive than reasoning related to a different option (Goldstein, Cialdini, and Griskevicius 2008). Thus, we anticipate that individuals will question the validity of their decision processes more when faced with reasoning relevant to their own choice versus reasoning irrelevant to that choice.

Results from two studies demonstrate the circumstances under which an observed other's choice and reasoning for choice will impact one's own choice confidence. Specifically, in study 1, we use the context of political decision making to demonstrate that while observing convergent choice and reason ranking evokes the greatest confidence in our own choice, observing someone make a convergent choice based on divergent reason ranking actually undermines confidence such that confidence in choice is decreased compared to when the observed other chooses a different alternative. This effect, however, only exists when choices are framed in terms of selection rather than rejection, highlighting the difference in the diagnosticity of reasons for liking versus disliking an alternative (Gershoff, Mukherjee, and Mukhopadhyay, 2007). Study 2 suggests that the effects we predict and demonstrate on choice confidence are most likely to emerge when individuals anticipate having to defend the validity of their decisions (e.g., in a public setting), and that these effects are attenuated when no public revelation or discussion is anticipated.

# Perceptual Prominence Effects in Consumer Choice

Sehoon Park, Sogang University, Republic of China
Moon-Yong Kim, Dongguk University, Republic of Korea
Se-Hyuk Park, The College of William and Mary, USA

## EXTENDED ABSTRACT

One of the most important and robust context effects is the attraction, or asymmetric dominance, effect that was first described by Huber, Payne, and Puto (1982). Although most research on context effects, including that on the attraction effect, has explored how context can influence relatively deliberate analytic processes, recent research by Hamilton, Hong, and Chernev (2007) has examined how context can affect intuitive choice processes. Hamilton and colleagues found that in the context of the attraction effect, adding fully dominated options that change the perceptual characteristics of the decision set can make one option (i.e., the non-dominating option) perceptually focal, increasing its likelihood of being chosen due to the perceptual focus effect and decreasing the strength of the attraction effect. That is, contrasting the perceptual focus effect and the attraction effect, they found that the preference for asymmetrically dominating options decreased in the presence of a perceptually focal option.

In the current research, however, we examine consumer choice as a function of the perceptual similarity of options at the attribute level in a two-attribute decision set. In particular, adding to the findings of the attraction effect by Hamilton et al. (2007), we examine a scenario in which a binary decision set is extended by adding asymmetrically dominated frequency or range decoys that change its perceptual characteristics, thus increasing the prominence of one of the attributes in the decision set and generating a perceptual prominence effect at the attribute level. In this context, we propose that perceptual prominence at the attribute level may either decrease or increase the choice share of the target depending on the added decoys' location in the set (frequency vs. range), which will, in turn, moderate the strength of the attraction effect; the attraction effect is attenuated in the frequency decoy condition, whereas the attraction effect occurs in the range decoy condition. Further, we propose that the perceptual prominence effect at the attribute level and its subsequent impact on the attraction effect in frequency and range decoy conditions will be a function of the type of processing (by attribute vs. by group) affecting consumers' decision procedures, such as lexicographic or dominance procedures; the proposed effects are more pronounced in the by-attribute condition, whereas the effects are mitigated in the by-group processing condition.

In experiment 1, participants consisted of 250 students from a large university in a metropolitan area, and they were randomly assigned to one of five experimental conditions. Participants in the first condition were presented with a binary set of options described on two attributes (set AB), such that option A was superior on attribute 2 and option B was superior on attribute 1. Asymmetrically dominated decoys were positioned according to the different decoy placement strategies (i.e., frequency or range). Participants in the second condition chose from a three-option set in which a third, asymmetrically dominated frequency option (C) had been added to the core set (set ABC), while participants in the third condition chose from a three-option set where a third, asymmetrically dominated range option (C') had been added to the core set (set ABC'). Participants in the fourth condition chose from a five-option set where two additional asymmetrically dominated frequency options (D and E) were included along with the three-option set, ABC (set ABCDE). Participants in the fifth condition chose from a five-option set where two additional asymmetrically dominated range options (D' and E') were added to the three-option set, ABC' (set ABC'D'E'). All attributes were rated on a 100-point scale, with 100 as the best. The choice sets were designed so that options C, D, and E (C', D' and E') all shared a common attribute value on attribute 2 (attribute 1) with option B. Thus, option A was the only option with a dissimilar attribute value on one attribute, and it was a perceptually focal option in the choice set. Following the methodology established by Hamilton et al. (2007), once assigned to an experimental condition, participants were asked to select one option from each of two choice sets (cell phones and MP3 players). The experimental findings showed that (1) the attraction effect occurs when an asymmetrically dominated decoy is added to a binary (core) set, irrespective of the decoy location; and that (2) when three additional asymmetrically dominated options (one asymmetrically dominated option and two newly-introduced asymmetrically dominated options) are added to the binary set, the attraction effect can be attenuated in the frequency decoy condition, while the attraction effect can still occur in the range decoy condition.

In experiment 2, participants consisted of 200 students from a large university in a metropolitan area. They were given a choice task involving five-option decision sets that consisted of a digital camera and vitamin water. As in experiment 1, the attribute values of digital cameras and vitamin water were rated on a 100-point scale. Participants were randomly assigned to the conditions of a 2 (processing type: by attribute vs. by group) x 2 (location of decoy: frequency vs. range) factorial design. In the by-attribute processing condition, the choice sets included horizontal lines separating attribute values in each row, as in Hamilton et al.'s (2007) experiment. In the by-group processing condition, the choice sets included vertical lines separating a group of options and a lone option, which encourages by-group processing. The experimental findings supported the prediction that the observed perceptual prominence effect is indeed contingent on the type of processing; that is, the perceptual prominence effect at the attribute level and its subsequent impact on the attraction effect in frequency and range decoy conditions are more pronounced in the by-attribute processing condition, whereas the effects are mitigated in the by-group processing condition.

Taken together, we extended the research done by Hamilton et al. (2007) by positing that perceptual prominence at the attribute level that has been induced by changing the perceptual characteristics of a choice set can either decrease or increase the choice share of the target depending on the location of the added decoys (frequency vs. range) in the set, which will moderate the strength of the attraction effect. Moreover, we provided additional support for the perceptual prominence effect at the attribute level in choice by showing that effects are moderated by the type of processing (by attribute vs. by group) facilitating consumers' decision procedures, such as lexicographic or dominance procedures.

# REFERENCES

Bettman, James R., Mary Frances Luce, and John W. Payne (1998), "Constructive Consumer Choice Processes," *Journal of Consumer Research*, 25 (December), 187-217.

Brenner, L., Y. Rottenstreich, and S. Sood (1999), "Comparison, Grouping, and Preference," *Psychological Science*, 10 (3), 225-229.

Coupey, Eloise (1994), "Restructuring: Constructive Processing of Information Displays in Consumer Choice," *Journal of Consumer Research*, 21(June), 83-99.

Frederick, Shane and Leonard Lee (2008), "Attraction, Repulsion and Attribute Representation," *Advances in Consumer Research*, Vol. 35, Angela Y. Lee and Dilip Soman (eds.), Memphis, TN: Association for Consumer Research, 122-124.

Ha, Young-Won, Sehoon Park, and Hee-Kyung Ahn (2009), "The Influence of Categorical Attributes on Choice Context Effects," *Journal of Consumer Research*, 36 (October), 463-477.

Hamilton, Ryan P., Jiewen Hong, and Alexander Chernev (2007), "Perceptual Focus Effects in Choice," *Journal of Consumer Research*, 34 (August), 187-199.

Hogarth, Robin M. (1982), *Judgment and Choice*, New York: John Wiley & Sons.

Huber, Joel, John W. Payne, and Christopher Puto (1982), "Adding Asymmetrically Dominated Alternatives: Violations of Regularity and the Similarity Hypothesis," *Journal of Consumer Research*, 9 (June), 90-98.

Kahneman, Daniel and Amos Tversky (1979), "Prospect Theory: An Analysis of Decision Risk," *Econometrica*, 47, 265-291.

Luce, Mary Frances (1998), "Choosing to Avoid: Coping with Negatively Emotion?Laden Consumer Decisions," *Journal of Consumer Research*, 24 (March), 409–434.

Luce, Mary Frances, John W. Payne, and James R. Bettman (1999), "Emotional Trade-Off Difficulty and Choice," *Journal of Marketing Research*, 36 (May), 143-159.

Lurie, Nicholas H. and Charlotte H. Mason (2007), "Visual Representation: Implications for Decision Making," *Journal of Marketing*, 71 (January), 160-177.

March, James G. (1978), "Bounded Rationality, Ambiguity, and the Engineering of Choice," *Bell Journal of Economics*, 9 (2), 587-608.

Mourali, M., U. Bockenholt, and M. Laroche (2007), "Compromise and Attraction Effects under Prevention and Promotion Motivations," *Journal of Consumer Research*, 34 (August), 234-247.

Parducci, Allen (1974), "Contextual Effects: A Range-Frequency Analysis," in *Handbook of Perception, Volume II*, eds. L. Carterette and M. P. Friedman, NY: Academic Press, 127-141.

Payne, J., J. Bettman, and E. Johnson (1993), *The Adaptive Decision Maker*, Cambridge University Press, Cambridge, England.

Sen, Sankar (1998), "Knowledge, Information Mode, and the Attraction Effect," *Journal of Consumer Research*, 25 (June), 64-77.

Simonson, Itamar (1989), "Choice Based on Reasons: The Case of Attraction and Compromise Effects," *Journal of Consumer Research*, 16 (December), 158-174.

Simonson, Itamar and Amos Tversky (1992), "Choice in Context: Trade-off Contrast and Extremeness Aversion," *Journal of Marketing Research*, 29 (August), 281-296.

Simonson, Itamar, Stephen Nowlis, and Katherine Lemon (1993), "The Effect of Local Consideration Sets on Global Choice Between Lower Price and Higher Quality," *Marketing Science*, 12, 357-377.

Sood, S., Y. Rottenstreich, and L. Brenner (2004), "On Decisions That Lead To Decisions: Direct and Derived Evaluations of Preference," *Journal of Consumer Research*, 31, 17-25.

Tversky, Amos (1977), "Features of Similarity," *Psychological Review*, 84, 327-352.

Tversky, Amos and Itamar Gati (1978), "Studies of Similarity," in *Cognition and Categorization*, Eleanor Rosch and Barbara Lloyd, eds., Hillsdale, NJ: Lawrence Erlbaum Associates, 79-98.

Tversky, Amos, Shmuel Sattath, and Paul Slovic (1988), "Contingent Weighting in Judgment and Choice," *Psychological Review*, 95 (3), 371-384.

# Coloring Decisions: The Effect of Red and Blue Colors on Consumer Behavior

Rajesh Bagchi, Virginia Tech, USA

Amar Cheema, University of Virginia, USA

## EXTENDED ABSTRACT

Colors play an important role in affecting our perceptions. They form an integral part of our daily lives, influencing our interactions with other individuals and with inanimate objects. Colors are ubiquitous in consumer contexts. Identical products are often sold in different colors or with different colors of packaging. Shopping mall walls, aisles, and displays use multiple colors. Web site backgrounds and product displays use varied colors. Colors are integral in advertisements and in company logos. In spite of its importance, however, little is known about how color affects consumer behavior (Elliot et al. 2007).

The literature on animal behavior suggests that red signals vigor and dominance among animals and induces aggression (Andersson et al. 2002; Cuthill et al. 1997). Similarly, physiological studies of human responses to color reveal that exposure to red versus blue colors increases irritability and decreases patience (Bellizzi, Crowley, and Hasty 1983). In laboratory studies using retail scenarios, Bellizzi and colleagues (Bellizzi et al. 1983; Bellizzi and Hite 1992) find that although warm colors (red, yellow) attract more attention, these colors are less likely to lead to purchases relative to cool colors (green, blue). However, prior studies are inconclusive about whether these color differences affect individual-level aggression in social contexts, and whether colors influence consumers' willingness-to-pay.

The present research investigates the influence of red versus blue colors on aggression in social settings and on consumers' willingness-to-pay in auctions and negotiations. In doing so, we seek to make two important contributions. First, we explicitly test the proposition that red enhances aggression relative to blue in social situations (study 1). Second, and more importantly, we investigate how color influences consumers' monetary transactions (studies 2-4). In study 2 we show that red induces more aggressive bidding relative to blue in laboratory auctions with real money. In study 3 we analyze data from eBay auctions and demonstrate that these effects also manifest in real-world settings. Finally, in study 4 we investigate the role that color plays in negotiations and demonstrate that red induces more aggressive negotiation relative to blue.

## Summary of Findings

We find that red induces greater aggression relative to blue, while blue increases patience relative to red in social settings (study 1). We also demonstrate the effect of color on aggression in auctions (studies 2-3) and negotiations (study 4). In auctions, buyers attempt to "win" the auctioned product by outbidding other potential competitors. In such instances, aggression induces bidders to offer higher bid jumps (Sinha and Greenleaf 2000). Correspondingly, we find that buyers offer higher bid jumps when a product is sold using a red background relative to when it is sold using a blue background. We demonstrate these effects in auctions conducted in the lab with real money (study 2) as well as in eBay auctions (study 3).

In contrast, in negotiations, where a buyer negotiates one-on-one with a seller, aggression typically entails eliciting unilateral concessions from the opponent (Ganesan 1993). In price negotiations, a more aggressive buyer would try to reduce the buying price. As expected, we find that red color reduces buyers' willingness-to-pay relative to blue colors. We also find that buyers negotiating the purchase of the red product report a lower likelihood of being persuaded to increase their willingness-to-pay than do people who see the blue product (study 4). This likelihood of persuasion measure mediates the effect of color on willingness-to-pay. These results are consistent with those of Bellizzi and Hite (1992) who find lower purchase incidences with red colors relative to blue in a scenario study conducted in a lab.

## Implications

We find that red induces greater aggression in consumer purchase contexts, such as in auctions and negotiation settings, relative to blue. In auction settings, aggression leads to higher bids, and bidders who see red (vs. blue) pay more. Thus, bidders are worse off (but sellers are better off) in auctions with red (vs. blue) listings. In contrast, in negotiation settings, red reduces buyers' willingness-to-pay. Thus, buyers are better off (but sellers are worse off) in negotiations where buyers see red (vs. blue). These results are consistent with the findings of Bellizzi and Hite (1992), who find that red colors reduce purchase incidences relative to blue.

Our findings provide a possible explanation, demonstrating that red reduces buyers' willingness-to-pay as well as buyers' willingness to be persuaded to consider higher prices relative to blue. Thus, our results document conditions where red may be beneficial as well as detrimental from the seller's perspective.

## REFERENCES

Andersson, Staffan, Sarah R. Pryke, Jonas Ornborg, Michael J. Lawes, and Malte Andersson (2002), "Multiple Receivers, Multiple Ornaments, and a Trade-Off Between Agonistic and Epigamic Signaling in a Widowbird," *The American Naturalist*, 160, 683–91.

Bellizzi, Joseph A., Ayn E. Crowley, and Ronald W. Hasty (1983), "The Effects of Color in Store Design," *Journal of Retailing*, 59 (1), 21-45.

Bellizzi, Joseph A. and Robert E. Hite (1992), "Environmental Color, Consumer Feelings, and Purchase Likelihood," *Psychology and Marketing*, 9 (5), 347-63.

Cuthill, Innes C., Sarah Hunt, Colette Cleary, and Corinna Clark (1997), "Colour Bands, Dominance, and Body Mass Regulation in Male Zebra Finches (Taeniopygia guttata)," *Proceedings of the Royal Society B: Biological Sciences*, 264, 1093–99.

Elliot, Andrew J., Markus A. Maier, Arlen C. Moller, Ron Friedman, and Jorg Meinhardt (2007), "Color and Psychological Functioning: The Effect of Red on Performance Attainment," *Journal of Experimental Psychology: General*, 136 (1), 154-68.

Ganesan, Shankar (1993), "Negotiation Strategies and the Nature of Channel Relationships," *Journal of Marketing Research*, 30 (May), 183-203.

# Brands and Impulsive Desire: Implicit Brand Processing Biases Incidental Decision-Making

Philip Harris, The University of Melbourne, Australia
Carsten Murawski, The University of Melbourne, Australia

## EXTENDED ABSTRACT

This study examined whether implicit brand processing can impact on decision-making for incidental rewards. Findings indicated a bias towards impulsive choices of incidental rewards following subconscious brand logo exposure. Findings of the study were linked with the effect of a generalized affective-motivation mechanism cued by favored brand exposure.

## Introduction

Recent research has indicated that subliminal brand presentation may influence goal-directed behaviour, even without conscious awareness of the stimulus (Chartrand, Huber, Shiv, & Tanner, 2008; Fitzsimons, Chartrand, & Fitzsimons, 2008). In addition, recent neuroimaging insights support the proposal that favored brands act as reward cues that moderate decision-making (e.g. Plassmann, Kenning, Deppe, Kugel, & Schwindt, 2008; Schaefer & Rotte, 2007). Additionally, recent theory discussing motivated goal pursuit distinguishes two separate reward-related components of goal-related behaviour: a status linked with specific goal-pursuit states, and also a non-specific status which motivates behaviour towards or away from a reward cue (Kent. C. Berridge, Robinson, & Aldridge, 2009; Martin Veltkamp, Aarts, & Custers, 2009). Together, these insights may have important consequences for brand theory. Brand responses may impact on behaviour via reward-related processing in parallel with activation of brand-related schema in the absence of conscious processing. Furthermore, the impact of brand processing on decision-making may occur not only by moderating the salience of goal-linked attitudes, but also by activating non-specific valence-linked motivational states. In this research we sought to examine these processes. We examined whether: 1). implicit brand processing can impact on incidental decision-making, and 2). whether implicit processing primed by brands provides an impulsive bias on decision-making processes.

## Conceptual Development

Insights from neurobiological research provide the basis for the intriguing possibility that implicit brand processing may impact on decision-making not only via implicit goal-linked processes, but also by influencing the contribution of the affective-motivational system towards decision-making. Following subliminal priming with favored brands, we anticipated that reward-based decision-making subserved by a non-specific motivational process would show greater influence of impulsivity than decisions that are less exposed to the influence of the affective-motivational system. Furthermore, as motivational states primed by reward cues may bias incidental decisions (Li, 2008; Van den Bergh, Dewitte, & Warlop, 2008; Wilson & Daly, 2004), an initial experimental hypothesis (H1) proposed that subconscious priming by brands linked with reward value would motivate impulsive choices for incidental rewards. In view of evidence linking impulsivity with faster task responses (Ramanathan & Menon, 2006), a second experimental hypothesis (H2) proposed that response times for choices of incidental rewards would be reduced when subconsciously primed by brands linked with reward value.

## Method

One hundred and eighty-three undergraduate college students participated in a computer-based temporal discounting task which offered a series of choices between an immediate reward of $20 and a reward of higher value to be paid at one of six possible delays (1, 10, 21, 55, 90 180 days). Each choice was preceded by the subliminal presentation (16 ms, pre- and post-masked) of one of four priming image types: brand logos (Apple or Windows); smiling faces, or household objects which served as a baseline condition. Participants completed the discounting task four times, once for each of the priming image types. The principal dependent variable was the subjective value assigned to delayed rewards when subliminally primed by each of the four image types. Following the discounting task, participants completed a five-item brand affect scale which incorporated seven-point ratings of brand salience, brand affective value, brand ownership, desire to own brand products, and intention to purchase branded products within the next six months. A post-hoc recognition task assessed participants' recognition of stimuli used in the main experimental task.

## Results

Brand affect scale ratings for Apple were significantly higher than for Windows overall, $t(183)=3.83$, $p=.0001$. A logistic model was fitted to participants' choices in order to investigate the relationship between decision parameters (reward amount, reward delay, and priming condition) and response time on the one hand, and choice on the other. Compared to decisions made following a neutral prime, 'Now' decisions were significantly more likely following brand primes ($b_{Apple}=-.0703$, p<0.05; $b_{Windows}=-.0566$, p<0.10). These data provide support H1. In a second model, the probability of choice of a 'Now' reward decision was higher when response times were lower ($b_{ResponseTime}=-.0648$, p<0.01) and when decisions were primed with the Apple or Windows logos. ($b_{Apple}=-.0667$, p<0.05; $b_{Windows}=-.0666$, p<0.05). This data demonstrates that impulsive choices are significantly associated with faster responses and support H2. Panel regression models fitted to response times indicated that incidental reward choices following brand and smile primes were associated with faster response times than when following a neutral prime ($b_{Apple}=-.0582$, p<0.01; $b_{Windows}=-.0636$, p<0.01), and that the reduction in responses time following a brand prime was directionally strongest when choosing immediate rewards ($b_{Apple}=-.1021$, p<0.01; $b_{Windows}=-.0613$, p<0.10). These data provide further support for H2. Finally, logistic models of choice revealed that that incorporation of response times in a choice model increased the predictive power of the model, and thus revealed participants' preferences.

## Discussion

Our results indicate that the affective value associated with a brand may impact on unrelated decision-making processes. Following presentation of brand logos, participants were more likely to choose an immediate reward, and to do so more quickly than when primed by a neutral stimulus. Further, participants did not explicitly recognize presentation of brand logos in the discounting task, indicating that the effects of brand presentation on decision-making occurred without conscious awareness of the priming episode.

Questionnaire responses indicated significantly stronger brand affect ratings linked with Apple than with Windows brands. Linking these explicit questionnaire responses with decision data, we note that stimuli with affective value have been demonstrated to impact on the extent that delayed rewards are discounted (Van den Bergh, et al., 2008; Wilson & Daly, 2004). Further, neuroimaging research indicates that immediate reward choices reflect greater relative contributions of neural systems associated with affective processing (McClure, Ericson, Laibson, Loewenstein, & Cohen, 2007; McClure, Laibson, & Cohen, 2004). In view of these findings, we propose that in the current research, a favored brand may have primed generalized affective processes underlying decision-making mechanisms.

Response time data support this proposal. When primed by a favored brand, preference for immediate rewards was strongly associated with faster response-times for immediate reward choices but less so for delayed choices. Furthermore, a prediction model incorporating both choice and response times demonstrated that response time data improve the predictive power of a model that links brand priming with subsequent reward choices.

In parallel with research demonstrated that affective primes may provide an incidental impulsive bias on reward-linked decision-making, the current study provides initial evidence that brand logos may also provide a subconscious motivational bias on incidental decisions. We tentatively propose that a bias towards impulsive incidental reward choices reflects the effect of a generalized affective-motivation mechanism cued by favored brand exposure.

# Opportunity Costs Neglect in the Tradeoff between Time and Money

Subimal Chatterjee, Binghamton University, USA
Dipankar Rai, Binghamton University, USA
Timothy Heath, ESSEC Business School, France

## EXTENDED ABSTRACT

Recent research suggests that when consumers tradeoff between price and quality, they may not spontaneously consider the opportunity cost of money in their decision-making. For example, Frederick, Novemsky, Wang, Dhar, and Nowlis (2009) show that in a choice between a 32 gigabyte iPod for $399 and a 16 gigabyte iPod for 299, the choice of the cheaper iPod increased from 37% to 71% when its price was reframed from "spend $299" to "spend $299 and save $100" (Page 555). The authors suggest that consumers tend to confine their thoughts to the information that marketers provide to them, and seldom bother to "fill in the logical consequences of their choice" (Frederick et al. 2009, Page 554) unless marketers explicitly remind them to do so. The purpose of our paper is to extend Frederick et al.'s (2009) research to investigate if consumers spontaneously account for opportunity costs of time along with money when they have to tradeoff between these two fungible currencies.

Although both time and money are fungible currencies, research suggests that figuring out the next best use of time may be more difficult than figuring out the next best use of money. For example, Okada and Hoch (2004) observe that the opportunity cost of time is more ambiguous than the opportunity cost of money. LeClerc, Schmitt, and Dube (1995) point out that time, unlike money, is less transferrable since time cannot be stored, and planning how to make the best use of time is perhaps even more important than planning how to make the best use of money. Consequently, frames that sensitize consumers to the opportunity cost of time could be more powerful than frames that sensitize consumers to the opportunity cost of money.

In one experiment, we asked ninety-five undergraduate students (58 females) to imagine that they were on vacation and waiting in line to purchase a train ticket that would take them to a ski resort. They had a choice between a slower train (Train A; 3 hours, $10 ticket price) and an express train (Train B: 45 minutes, $26 ticket price). After reading the scenario, the participants reported their likelihood of selecting each train (9-point scale, 9.0=Very Likely, 1.0=Very Unlikely), and the train that they would select (A, or B). We randomly assigned the participants to one of three experimental conditions. In the "money" condition, we reminded participants that taking the slower train would save money ("select Train A, and save $16"). In the "time" condition, we reminded participants that taking the express train would save time ("select Train B, and save 2 hours and 15 minutes of travel time"). In the "control" conditions, we did not sensitize them to either saving time or saving money ("select Train A or Train B").

Sensitizing the participants to the opportunity cost of time significantly increased the choice of the express train, from 59% in the control condition to 81% in the "time" condition ($\chi_1^2$ = 3.74, p=.05). The significant increase in the likelihood of selecting the express train (M's of 5.97 and 7.77; $F(1,55)=7.30, p<.01$) was coupled with a significant decrease in the likelihood of selecting the slower train (M's of 5.07 and 3.19; $F(1,55)=8.32, p<.01$). Sensitizing the participants to the opportunity cost of money, however, decreased the choice of the slower (and cheaper) train, instead of increasing it (from 41% in the control condition to 21% in the "money" condition;

$\chi_1^2$ = 3.21, p=.07). While there was no change in the likelihood of selecting the express train (M's of 5.97 and 6.76; $F(1,58)<1$), there was a significant reduction in the likelihood of selecting the slower train (M's of 5.07 and 3.53; $F(1,58)=4.61, p=.04$).

We speculate that, in the context of vacation travel time, consumers may be more inclined to save time than money, and generally prefer the faster train. Therefore, a "time" frame "fits" with the consumers' natural inclination, and gives them a "just right" feeling about their choice (see Aaker and Lee, 2006). However, the "money" frame tries to enhance the appeal of the disliked option, locking consumers in a prevention mindset and making them avoid that option (Malkoc, Hoeffler, and Hedgcock, 2008). We tested this prediction in a follow-up experiment, with an iPod Touch as the focal product. Our pretests indicated that consumers generally consider saving money more important than saving time in the context of an iPod purchase.

In the second experiment, we asked eighty-seven undergraduate students (57 females) to imagine that they could buy an iPod Touch either from Store A ($199.99; 5-minute drive) or from Store B ($129.99 with a student discount; 80-minutes drive). We randomly assigned the participants to one of three experimental conditions. In the "money" condition, we reminded participants that choosing Store B saved them money ("select Store B and save $70"). In the "time" condition, we reminded participants that choosing Store A saved them driving time ("select Store A and save an hour and fifteen minutes of driving time). In the "control" conditions, we did not sensitize them to either saving time or saving money ("select Store A or Store B"). Sensitizing the participants to the opportunity cost of money significantly increased the choice of the cheaper (but more distant) store from 56% in the control condition to 82% in

the "money" condition ($\chi_1^2$ = 4.58, p=.03). However, sensitizing the participants to the opportunity cost of time did not affect the choice of the nearer (but more expensive) store. The store choice decreased from 44% in the control condition to 34% in the "money"

condition ($\chi_1^2$ < 1).

Our research extends that of Frederick et al. (2009) and suggests that when consumers tradeoff between time and money, they do not spontaneously consider the opportunity costs of either of these currencies. However, they come into the decision with some sense of what matters more to them, saving time or saving money. For example, saving money may matter more than saving driving time in the context of an iPod Touch purchase. Therefore, sensitizing consumers to the opportunity cost of money favors the selection of the cheaper iPod (entailing a longer drive time), but sensitizing them to the opportunity cost of time does not bias them towards the more expensive iPod (even though the drive time is less). Conversely, saving time may matter more than saving money in the context of a vacation. Consequently, sensitizing consumers to the opportunity cost of time favors the selection of the faster (but more expensive) train, but sensitizing them to the opportunity cost of money does not bias them towards the slower (but cheaper) train.

# Strategy Compatibility: The Time versus Money Effect on Consumer Decision Making

Lei Su, The Chinese University of Hong Kong, China
Leilei Gao, The Chinese University of Hong Kong, China

## EXTENDED ABSTRACT

Consider a consumer who wants to buy a piece of furniture at IKEA. She needs to spend money on the purchase and delivery. She also spends time visiting the store, searching for the product, waiting for delivery, and assembling the furniture at home. Despite the well-known adage that "time is money", recent research suggests that time and money are fundamentally distinct resources and that people evaluate and allocate them in different manners (Leclerc, Schmitt, and Dube 1995; Soman 2001; Zauberman and Lynch 2005). In this study, we focus on the influence of activating time versus money on consumers' evaluation strategies. We show that priming time versus money during a purchase leads to the greater use of alternative-based evaluation strategies, whereas priming money leads to the greater use of attribute-based evaluation strategies. As a result, consumers display systematic preference reversals across several choice contexts.

## Research Hypotheses

Time and money are two fundamentally distinct resources, and the distinction is enhanced through the different roles they play in our daily lives. On the one hand, time is independent of human effort, can cannot be inventoried. Time can be measured but not compared because its value depends on how people use it, and its opportunity cost is difficult to judge (Frederick 2009; Okada, Mina, and Hoch 2004). The evaluation of time is discretionary, and people tend to focus on the intrinsic value of spending time doing something. This ambiguity and context dependency prevents extensive comparisons across different scenarios of using time, and induced people to evaluate time according to the alternatives for which it could be used. As a consequence, time is associated with holistic information processing. On the other hand, money is created specifically for exchange and is thus fungible–its units can be substituted for each other. Consumers are also trained to compare value and utility in monetary transactions and emphasize the relative value of spending money. And consumers even tend to automatically adopt these market norms for activities that involve money (Ariely, Gneezy, and Haruvy 2008). The value of money is then judged by more explicitly measurable standards, and consumers can easily compare the value of money across transactions. We propose that the concept of money is associated with comparative information processing.

Consistent with the notion that a given concept can not only activate semantic features but also dynamic properties such as forms of behavior and goals related to that concept (Bargh, Chen, and Burrows 1996; Dijksterhuis et al. 2000), we propose that when time is activated, consumers are more likely to adopt alternative-based strategies with greater emphasis on attributes compatible with holistic evaluation. Conversely, priming money activates the greater use of attribute-based strategies whereby consumers focus more on those attributes that are compatible with comparative evaluation. We tested this general proposition in a series of four experiments.

## Method and Results

Experiment 1 was conducted to test the time versus money preference reversal between options superior in verbal and numerical attributes. Time or money was activated by asking participants to note whether time or money expenditure was involved in acquiring an electronic product. The results across three scenarios reveal that verbal (vs. numerical) attributes tend to weigh more in activation of time (vs. money).

In experiment 2, we examined preference shifting between options superior in alignable and nonalignable attributes. We extended our test to experiential products. In addition, the manipulation of time or money priming was achieved by asking participants to list thoughts related to time or monetary expenditure. The results across different product categories consistently demonstrate that nonalignable (vs. alignable) attributes weigh more in activation of time (vs. money).

In experiment 3, we showed that the well-known prominence effect is enhanced after the activation of money but alleviated after the activation of time. Furthermore, a more rigorous test of the time versus money effect was achieved by only activating the concepts of time and money in general.

To further demonstrate the decision process after the activation of different concepts, Mouselab was used in experiment 4. The results show that time (vs. money) induces consumers to employ alternative-based (vs. attribute-based) strategies in subsequent decision tasks. The aforementioned preference reversals are mediated by the different decision strategies.

To summarize, in four studies involving binary choices in various categories, we show that the activation of time (vs. money) leads to a greater likelihood of choosing options that feature more verbal (vs. numerical) attributes, nonalignable (vs. alignable) attributes, and relatively less (more) important attributes. In addition, mediation analyses and a process-tracing procedure provided further evidence that the time vs. money preference reversal was due to the different decision strategies employed. Simply making people think about time versus money (in general) can shift their decision criteria and lead to systematic preference reversals.

## REFERENCES

Ariely, Dan, Uri Gneezy, and Ernan Haruvy (2008), "On the Discontinuity of Demand Curves around Zero: Charging More and Selling More," *Advances in Consumer Research*, 35, 38.

Bargh, John A., Mark Chen, and Lara Burrows (1996), "Automaticity of Social Behavior: Direct Effects of Trait Construct and Stereotype Activation on Action," *Journal of Personality and Social Psychology*, 71 (2), 230-44.

Dijksterhuis, Ap, Henk Aarts, John A. Bargh and Ad van Knippenberg (2000), "On the Relation Between Associative Strength and Automatic Behavior," *Journal of Experimental Social Psychology*, 531-44.

Frederick, Shane, Nathan Novemsky, Jing Wang, Ravi Dhar and Stephen Nowlis (2009), "Opportunity Cost Neglect," *Journal of Consumer Research*, 36 (December), 553-61.

Leclerc, France, Bernd H. Schmitt, and Laurette Dube (1995), "Waiting Time and Decision Making: Is Time like Money?" *Journal of Consumer Research*, 22 (June), 110-19.

Okada, Erica Mina and Stephen J. Hoch (2004), "Spending Time versus Spending Money," *Journal of Consumer Research*, 31 (September), 313-23.

Soman, Dilip (2001), "The Mental Accounting of Sunk Time Costs: Why Time is not like Money," *Journal of Behavioral Decision Making*, 14 (3), 169-85.

Zauberman, Gal and John G. Lynch Jr. (2005), "Resource Slack and Propensity to Discount Delayed Investments of Time versus Money," *Journal of Experimental Psychology: General*, 134 (1), 23 -37.

# The Impact of Price on Preference Consistency over Time

Ki Yeon Lee, University of Toronto, Canada
Min Zhao, University of Toronto, Canada

## EXTENDED ABSTRACT

Past research has shown that consumers have inconsistent preference over time in interdisciplinary areas such as behavioral decision making (e.g., Thaler 1981), self-control (e.g. Rachlin 1995), and delay of gratification (e.g., Mischel, Shoda, and Rodriguez 1989). Construal-level theory (CLT, Liberman and Trope 1998; Trope and Liberman 2000, 2003) proposes that people' preference is time-dependent due to their tendency to focus on different aspects of future events depending on the time frame. People put more weight on the desirability-related aspect of a distant future event and like options with high desirability, whereas they focus more on the feasibility-related aspect of a near future event and prefer options with high feasibility (Trope and Liberman 2003). As a result of this inconsistent preference over time, consumers might regret their choice, have lower satisfaction and not redeem their committed choice (Soman 2003). Thus, knowing how to overcome this preference inconsistency is crucial for both consumers and marketers.

How can consumers overcome their preference inconsistency? Prior research has demonstrated some moderators which help people overcome their inconsistency such as practicing or planning distant-future tasks in full detail (Gollwitzer 1999; Trope and Liberman 2003), switching their attention away from the concrete qualities of the immediate temptation and focus on its abstract qualities in the long term (Baumeister and Heatherton 1996; Hoch and Lowenstein 1991; Mischel, Shoda and Rodriguez 1989), and using two different mental simulations—process vs. outcome simulations (Zhao, Hoeffler, and Zauberman 2007). Our research extends research on preference consistency over time and proposes that introducing price information or simply increasing people's price sensitivity leads to preference consistency over time due to the increased importance perception of product quality. We report findings from four experiments to support our predictions.

To test our proposed predictions, experiment 1 used two software packages from Zhao et al. (2007). We manipulated the prices of software packages as free of charge, $10, or $200. We replicated prior literature, illustrating that people have inconsistent preference over time for a free product (i.e., a higher preference for higher-desirability (feasibility) option in the distant (near) future). However, having price information (e.g., $10 and $200) increased preference towards the higher-desirability option in the near future which led to preference consistency over time.

Experiment 2 aimed to generalize our findings to a different consumption situation (i.e., the choice of a desk) and test the mediating role of perceived quality importance. Again, we found that preference inconsistency obtained from no price conditions was overcome in the price conditions. Furthermore, our mediation analyses revealed that the perceived quality importance mediated the interactive effect of time and price on relative preference between two options.

The objective of experiment 3 was to address an alternative process for the intertemporal preference consistency with price. One possible account is the pain of paying (Prelec and Loewenstein 1998; Rick, Cryder, and Loewenstein 2008). One may argue that when people see the price information of a product, they might feel painful by realizing how much they have to pay to obtain the product. And it is this pain of paying that led to a desire to get the best features to make up for the cost. If this were true, the effect of price information on preference consistency over time should vanish if we remove the pain of paying. To test this idea, we used a scenario of winning a prize (e.g., a digital camera) from a lottery rather than paying for it themselves. Even for the prize product, we still found the intertemporal choice and preference consistency in price conditions as opposed to no price conditions. As long as people know the price of product, whether they purchase the product or obtain it as a prize does not matter. This finding suggests that the driver of the intertemporal preference consistency is not the pain of paying.

Although we replicated the effect of price on intertemporal preference in different product domains throughout experiments 1 to 3, one may still claim that giving the same price information for two different products is problematic. Experiment 4 intended to address this issue by having participants to be sensitized to price, instead of providing a specific price. To manipulate price sensitivity, we used two surveys—purchase history (e.g., listing their purchase items and prices) and price surveys (e.g., indicating their WTPs for three products). We expect that this manipulation would make participants more sensitive to price and cause them to process the descriptions of products in a similar way as they have price information. Thus, even though they do not have the price information of the target products (i.e., restaurants), we believe, the price sensitivity manipulation will give rise to intertemproal preference consistency. The results of experiment 4 showed that participants who were sensitized to price were more likely to be consistent in their choice and preference over time than those who were not.

Taken together, our findings showed that including price information leads to preference consistency across near future and distant future. Across four experiments, we obtained the same results in different product domains (e.g., software, desk, digital camera, and restaurant), and showed increased perception of quality importance as the underlying mechanism. Further, we demonstrated that this effect held for an extremely low or high price (experiment 1), just a regular price (experiment 2), a price that people actually didn't need to pay out of their own pocket and thus did not incur personal pain of paying (experiment 3), or when no specific price information was even given other than the fact that people's price sensitivity was increased (experiment 4).

We believe that this research make several important contributions. First, it contributes to extend our understanding of the underlying mechanism for inducing preference or choice consistency over time by demonstrating that price information itself or price sensitivity helps people make consistent decision, which may reduce their regret from their choice and increase their satisfaction. Second, contrary to previous literature on framing effects in pricing which has shown preference reversals, this research illustrates a positive role of price by making people consider desirability information (e.g., the quality of a product) even if the decision is for near future. Thus, price information can be a useful cue which induces decision consistency over time.

**REFERENCES**

Ainslie, George and Nick Haslam (1992), "Self Control" in *Choice Over Time*, ed. George Loewenstein and John Elster, New York: Russell Sage Foundation, 177-209.

Anderson, Eric T. and Duncan Simester (2003), "Effects of $9 Price Endings on Retail Sales: Evidence from Field Experiments," *Quantitative Marketing and Economics*, 1 (1), 93-110.

Baron, Reuben M. and David A. Kenny (1986), "The Moderator-Mediator Variable Distinction in Social Psychological Research: Conceptual, Strategic, and Statistical Considerations," *Journal of Personality and Social Psychology*, 51 (6), 1173-82.

Baumeister, Roy F. and Todd F. Heatherton (1996), "Self-Regulation Failure: An Overview," *Psychological Inquiry*, 7, 1-15.

Gerstner, Eitan (1985), "Do Higher Prices Signal Higher Quality?," *Journal of MarketingResearch*, 22 (2), 209-15.

Gollwitzer, Peter M. (1999), "Implementation Intentions: Strong Effects of Simple Plans," *American Psychologist*, 54, 493-503.

Heath, Timothy B., Subimal Chatterjee, and Karen R. France (1995), "Mental Accounting and Changes in Price: The Frame Dependence of Reference Dependence," *Journal of Consumer Research*, 22 (June), 90-97.

Hoch, Stephen J. and George F. Loewenstein (1991), "Time-inconsistent Preferences and Consumer Self-Control.," *Journal of Consumer Research*, 17 (March), 492-507.

Kirmani, Amna and Akshay R. Rao (2000), "No Pain, No Gain: A Critical Review of the Literature on Signaling Unobservable Product Quality," *Journal of Marketing*, 64 (2), 66-79.

Liberman, Nira and Yaacov Trope (1998), "The Role of Feasibility and Desirability Considerations in Near and Distant Future Decisions: A Test of Temporal Construal Theory," *Journal of Personality and Social Psychology*, 75 (1), 5-18.

Loewenstein, George. (1996), "Out of Control: Visceral Influences on Behavior," *Organizational Behavior and Human Decision Processes*, 65 (March), 272-92.

Malkoc, Selin. And Gal Zauberman (2006), "Deferring Versus Expediting Consumption: The Effect of Outcome Concreteness on Sensitivity to Time Horizon," *Journal of Consumer Research*, 43 (November), 618-27.

Mischel, Walter, Yuichi Shoda, and Monica L. Rodriguez (1989), "Delay of Gratification in Children," *Science*, 244 (4907), 933-38.

Mishra, Himanshu, Arul Mishra, and Dhananjay Nayakankuppam (2006), "Money: A Bias for the Whole," *Journal of Consumer Research*, 32 (March), 541-49.

Plassmann, Hilke, John O'Doherty, Baba Shiv, and Antonio Rangel (2008), "Marketing Actions Can Modulate Neural Representations of Experienced Pleasantness," *Proceedings of the National Academy of Sciences*, 105 (3), 1050-54.

Prelec, Drazen and Duncan Simester (2001), "Always Leave Home Without It: A Further Investigation of the Credit-Card Effect on Willingness to Pay," *Marketing Letters*, 12 (1), 5-12.

Prelec, Drazen and George Loewenstein (1998), "The Red and the Black: Mental Accounting of Savings and Debt," *Marketing Science*, 17 (1), 4-28.

Rachlin, H. (1995). Self-Control: Beyond Commitment. *Behavioral and Brain Sciences*, 18, 109-59.

Rao, Akshay R. and Kent B. Monroe (1989), "The Effect of Price, Brand Name, and Store Name on Buyers' Perceptions of Product Quality: An Integrative Review," *Journal of Marketing Research*, 89 (3), 351-57.

Rick, Scott I., Cynthia E. Cryder, and George Loewenstein (2008), "Tightwads and Spendthrifts," *Journal of Consumer Research*, 34 (April), 767-82.

Soman, Dilip (1998), "The Illusion of Delayed Incentives: Evaluating Future Effort-Money Transactions," *Journal of Marketing Research*, 35(4), 427-37.

_____ (2003), "The Effect of Time Delay on Multi-Attribute Choice," *Journal of Economic Psychology*, 25 (2), 153-75.

Thaler, Richard. (1981), "Some Empirical Evidence on Dynamic Inconsistency," *Economics Letter*, 8 (3), 201-7.

Thomas, Manoj, Sucharita Chandran and Yaacov Trope (2007), "The Effects of Information Type and Temporal Distance on Purchase Intentions," *Working Paper*.

Trope, Yaacov and Nira Liberman (2000), "Temporal Construal and Time-Dependent Changes in Preference," *Journal of Personality and Social Psychology*, 79 (6), 876-89.

_____ (2003), "Temproal Construal," *Psychological Review*, 110 (3), 403-21.

Wathieu, Luc and Marco Bertini (2007), "Price as a Stimulus to Think: The Case for Willful Overpricing," *Marketing Science*, 26 (1-2), 118-29.

Zauberman, Gal and John G. Lynch (2005), "Resource Slack and Propensity to Discount Delayed Investments of Time Versus Money," *Journal of Experimental Psychology: General*, 134 (1), 23-37.

Zeithaml, Valarie A. (1988), "Consumer Perceptions of Price, Quality, and Value: A Means-End Model and Synthesis of Evidence," *Journal of Marketing*, 52 (3), 2-22.

Zhao, Min, Steve Hoeffler, and Gal Zauberman (2007), "Mental Simulation and Preference Consistency over Time: The Role of Process- Versus Outcome-Focused Thoughts," *Journal of Marketing Research*, 44 (3), 379-88.

# Bending Arms, Bending Discounting Functions. How Motor Actions Affect Intertemporal Decision-Making

Bram Van den Bergh, Erasmus University Rotterdam, The Netherlands
Julien Schmitt, Loughborough University, UK
Siegfried Dewitte, K. U. Leuven, Belgium
Luk Warlop, Catholic University Leuven, Belgium

## EXTENDED ABSTRACT

Many consumer decisions involve trading off costs and benefits over time. For example, a consumer may think about replacing a two-year-old car with a shiny new model, rather than driving his old car and saving for retirement. A dieter may find that a fattening chocolate cake is irresistible in the short run, although a fruit salad is more beneficial in the long run. In making such decisions, consumers trade off long run and short run benefits. The factors that influence intertemporal choice receive increasing attention from marketing scholars (e.g., Malkoc and Zauberman 2006; Zauberman et al. 2009) because a better understanding of intertemporal preferences is critical to gain a better understanding of numerous consumption decisions.

Our research examines the effect of bodily feedback from motor actions on intertemporal tradeoffs. We test whether the enactment of basic motor actions, such as extending or flexing one's arm, affects intertemporal decision-making. More specifically, we conjecture that somatic motor actions associated with "approach" lead to present-biased preferences. That is, flexing your elbow may cause you to spend now rather than to save for later or may lead you to prefer chocolate cake over fruit for dessert. Prior research suggests that bodily positions are able to influence attitudes: Simply by pairing stimuli with arm flexion (where the motor action is directed toward the self) or arm extension (where the motor action is directed away from the self), rudimentary attitudes can be established (Cacioppo, Priester, and Berntson 1993). We conjecture that the effects of arm positions extend beyond attitude formation. In this research, we propose that the effects of somatic activity, such as flexing or extending your arm, generalizes beyond attitude formation and affects intertemporal choices between smaller, sooner and larger, delayed monetary rewards (hypothesis 1).

In the *pilot study*, we found that consumers using a shopping basket (i.e., arm flexion) are more likely to purchase vice products (i.e., products providing immediate benefits) at the cash register of a retailer than consumers using a shopping cart (i.e., arm extension). Because of the correlational nature of the pilot study, we designed 4 follow-up experiments to demonstrate the causal path that leads from arm flexion to present-biased preferences. In the experimental studies, participants pressed one of their hands against the table: In the arm flexion (extension) condition, participants put the palm of one of their hands under (on) the table and press upward (downward). In *study 1A*, participants showed a greater preference for vice options relative to virtues (e.g., camping versus studying over the weekend) in the arm flexion condition than in the arm extension condition. In *study 1B*, participants had a greater preference for smaller, earlier rewards (e.g., ?67 tomorrow vs. ?85 in 70 days) in the arm flexion condition than in the arm extension condition. These studies demonstrate that somatic activity associated with approach leads to a preference for immediate over delayed benefits (i.e., present-biased preferences)

Prior research suggests that increasing desire in one domain (e.g., sex, cookies, heroin, cigarettes,…) can affect intertemporal choices in an unrelated domain (e.g., money) (Field et al. 2006; Giordano et al. 2002; Van den Bergh, Dewitte, and Warlop 2008). That is, upon an increase in desire, consumers might want anything rewarding (Wadhwa, Shiv, and Nowlis 2008). This is consistent with recent neuroscientific evidence demonstrating that many rewards are processed similarly in the brain (Breiter et al. 2001; Montague, King-Casas, and Cohen 2006): Indeed, the same dopaminergic reward circuitry of the brain is activated for a wide variety of different reinforcers (Camerer, Loewenstein, and Prelec 2005). That is, a similar set of brain reward regions responds in common to very distinct categories of reward—for example, beautiful female faces and erotic stimuli activate the classical reward circuitry associated with drug and monetary rewards (Aharon et al. 2001). We propose that somatic activity, through arm flexion contraction, activates this general neurological system processing rewards and affects intertemporal choice as a consequence (hypothesis 2). We demonstrate in *study 2* that the effect of arm flexor contraction on present-biased preferences is moderated by the sensitivity of the brain circuitry processing rewards: Only when the Behavioral Approach System is sensitive enough to be activated by somatic actions, impatience is observed.

In addition, we test whether the effect of arm flexion on present-biased preferences relies on the learned association between arm flexor contraction and the activation of the neurological reward system. A lifetime of experience of motor actions paired with differential evaluative outcomes has established an association between arm flexion and approach orientation (Cacioppo et al. 1993). In the absence of a learning process, the association between arm flexion and approach is most likely not established (hypothesis 3). We hypothesize that actions of the nondominant arm have established fewer higher-order associations between motor actions and evaluative outcomes than actions of the dominant arm. In *study 3*, we are able to confirm that the effect of arm flexion on preference for immediate gratification is restricted to reward system activation by means of the dominant arm.

These studies demonstrate that task-irrelevant somatic activity is able to influence intertemporal decision making: Simply flexing one's arm leads to present-biased preferences. To our knowledge, this is the first research (1) demonstrating effects of somatic activity on economic decision making, (2) that demonstrates that the effect of arm flexor contraction is dependent on the sensitivity of the general reward system, and (3) investigating the role of conditioning as the causal mechanism fostering higher order associations between motor actions of the arm and evaluative outcomes. A limitation of the present research is that we have only focused on the role of arm flexion and the reward system. A complementary set of studies might well be carried out to investigate the consequences of arm extension and the potential role of the punishment system (Carver and White 1994; Gray 1987, 1990; Torrubia et al. 2001). Future research could investigate whether arm extension makes individuals more likely to buy insurances (i.e., avoiding negative outcomes) or affects the choice between a smaller, immediate fine and a larger, delayed fine.

# REFERENCES

Aharon, Ithzak, Nancy Etcoff, Dan Ariely, Chris F. Chabris, Ethan O'Connor, and Hans C. Breiter (2001), "Beautiful Faces Have Variable Reward Value: Fmri and Behavioral Evidence," *Neuron*, 32 (3), 537-51.

Breiter, Hans C., Itzhak Aharon, Daniel Kahneman, Anders Dale, and Peter Shizgal (2001), "Functional Imaging of Neural Responses to Expectancy and Experience of Monetary Gains and Losses," *Neuron*, 30 (2), 619-39.

Cacioppo, John T., Joseph R. Priester, and Gary G. Berntson (1993), "Rudimentary Determinants of Attitudes: Ii. Arm Flexion and Extension Have Differential Effects on Attitudes," *Journal of Personality and Social Psychology*, 65 (1), 5-17.

Camerer, Colin, George Loewenstein, and Drazen Prelec (2005), "Neuroeconomics: How Neuroscience Can Inform Economics," *Journal of Economic Literature*, 43 (1), 9-64.

Carver, Charles S. and Teri L. White (1994), "Behavioral Inhibition, Behavioral Activation, and Affective Responses to Impending Reward and Punishment: The Bis/Bas Scales," *Journal of Personality and Social Psychology*, 67 (2), 319-33.

Field, Matt, Mary Santarcangelo, Harry Sumnall, Andrew Goudie, and Jon Cole (2006), "Delay Discounting and the Behavioural Economics of Cigarette Purchases in Smokers: The Effects of Nicotine Deprivation," *Psychopharmacology*, 186 (2), 255-63.

Giordano, Louis A., Warren K. Bickel, George Loewenstein, Eric A. Jacobs, Lisa Marsch, and Gary J. Badger (2002), "Mild Opioid Deprivation Increases the Degree That Opioid-Dependent Outpatients Discount Delayed Heroin and Money," *Psychopharmacology*, 163 (2), 174-82.

Gray, Jeffrey A. (1987), "Perspectives on Anxiety and Impulsivity: A Commentary," *Journal of Research in Personality*, 21 (4), 493-509.

_____ (1990), "Brain Systems That Mediate Both Emotion and Cognition," *Cognition & Emotion*, 4 (3), 269-88.

Malkoc, Selin A. and Gal Zauberman (2006), "Deferring Versus Expediting Consumption: The Effect of Outcome Concreteness on Sensitivity to Time Horizon," *Journal of Marketing Research*, 43 (4), 618-27.

Montague, P. Read, Brooks King-Casas, and Jonathan D. Cohen (2006), "Imaging Valuation Models in Human Choice," *Annual Review of Neuroscience*, 29, 417-48.

Torrubia, Rafael, César Avila, Javier Molto, and Xavier Caseras (2001), "The Sensitivity to Punishment and Sensitivity to Reward Questionnaire (Spsrq) as a Measure of Gray's Anxiety and Impulsivity Dimensions," *Personality and Individual Differences*, 31 (6), 837-62.

Van den Bergh, Bram, Siegfried Dewitte, and Luk Warlop (2008), "Bikinis Instigate Generalized Impatience in Intertemporal Choice," *Journal of Consumer Research*, 35 (1), 85-97.

Wadhwa, Monica, Baba Shiv, and Stephen M. Nowlis (2008), "A Bite to Whet the Reward Appetite: The Influence of Sampling on Reward-Seeking Behaviors," *Journal of Marketing Research*, 45 (4), 403-13.

Zauberman, Gal, B. Kyu Kim, Selin A. Malkoc, and James R. Bettman (2009), "Discounting Time and Time Discounting: Subjective Time Perception and Intertemporal Preferences," *Journal of Marketing Research*, 46 (4), 543-56.

# What to *Acquire* and What to *Forfeit*: The Effect of Decision Task and Product Type on Consumers' Choice between Promotion and Prevention Appeals

Tilo Chowdhury, Quinnipiac University, USA
Camelia Micu, Fairfield University, USA

## EXTENDED ABSTRACT

### Motivation

Consider Nina and Kaitlin, who need to replace their current DVD players. The two girls face different decision choices: Nina got a gift card from her relatives that she decided to use towards the purchase of a new DVD player (acquisition task), whereas Kaitlin got two DVD players from her relatives as a gift and she needs to decide which she will return (forfeiture task). In this decision task, they are both seriously considering two brands whose advertisements emphasize different strengths. One brand claims to "enhance one's entertainment needs in life," whereas the other claims to "prevent any boredom in life." The former claim reflects a promotion-based message (Higgins 1997), involving a strategy that maximizes presence of a positive outcome, whereas the latter claim reflects a prevention-based message, involving a strategy that maximizes avoidance of a negative outcome. Considering the hedonic nature of DVD players and the different nature of their decision tasks, which brand would each prefer?

In the current research, we bring together multiple theoretical perspectives to investigate how individual consumers' relative brand preferences for promotion (vs. prevention) messages change based on the decision task (acquisition vs. forfeiture) and product type (hedonic vs. functional) via two experimental studies. Our work is distinguished from previous research on decision task effects and regulatory focus in several ways. First, to our knowledge, this is the first research ever indicating which type of regulatory focus message individuals prefer in different purchase situations (acquisition versus forfeiture), depending on the type of product (hedonic versus utilitarian), within the same product category. Second, despite the recent work done by Dhar and Wertenbroch (2000), there has not been much follow up research done in the acquisition and forfeiture area. Our work extends acquisition and forfeiture decision situations in a new context, giving rise to a variety of interesting questions for researchers to investigate with regards to brand preferences. Finally, although a significant body of work has contributed to understanding post-ad exposure effects of message's regulatory focus, it is noteworthy that research to-date has not examined how consumers' evaluations are affected by direct experience with the product. Our work is designed to assess the impact of product trial on choice (Study 1), as well as to examine the role of individuals' need for touch (Peck and Childers 2003; Study 2) on these assessments.

### Conceptualization

Regulatory focus theory (Higgins 1997), proceeding from the fundamental principle that people approach pleasure and avoid pain, distinguishes between two modes of motivation and self-regulation termed as promotion and prevention goals or foci (Higgins, 1997; 1998). Building on regulatory focus theory, researchers have proposed that advertising persuasion might also depend on a message characteristic called "message's regulatory focus," which could also be promotion-oriented or prevention-oriented. According to Aaker and Lee (2001), when individuals' regulatory goals match the message frames in terms of regulatory orientation (i.e., when there is goal compatibility), more positive persuasive effects result. Research extended the notion of compatibility to the context of purchasing hedonic versus utilitarian products. Chernev (2004) suggests that hedonic products may help individuals attain promotion goals, whereas utilitarian products help them attain prevention goals. Building on these findings, Micu and Chowdhury (2010) show that prevention (vs. promotion) focus messages are more preferred for utilitarian products, whereas for hedonic products, the reversed effect is true. We expect these findings to be differentially affected by the *decision task* and provide our rationale below.

Our focus on differences between acquisition and forfeiture choices is motivated by research on loss aversion that demonstrates an asymmetry in evaluations depending on the direction of the proposed trade, that is, whether a good is acquired or forfeited relative to the consumer's current state (Kahneman, Knetsch, and Thaler 1990); indicating consumers are more likely to experience more risk aversion in the forfeiture than in the acquisition condition. Further, according to Sanna (1996), consumers are more likely to engage in prefactual thinking when they have to forfeit an item (i.e., upward prefactual; comparison with more preferred alternatives) than when they have to acquire an item (i.e., downward prefactual; comparison with less preferred alternatives). Also, upward prefactual thinking induces negative emotions because one is about to be worse off than before (Roese 1997; Sanna 1999). To the extent that forfeiture situations spontaneously trigger upward comparisons that highlight negative affective consequences, consumers are motivated to minimize the anticipated negative emotions.

For hedonic products, the negative emotions experienced in forfeiture conditions are amplified by the feelings of guilt associated with the purchase of hedonic products, which is perceived as being decadent and involving self-gratification (Khan, Dhar, and Wertenbroch 2005). Further, research on regulatory focus indicates that a promotion focus prompts the use of relatively risky strategies, whereas a prevention focus is associated with the use of more conservative strategies. Thus, to minimize the perception of risk, as well as the negative emotions spontaneously triggered in a forfeiture (vs. acquisition) condition, consumers will choose a prevention focused message. Examined from the other direction, the acquisition (vs. forfeiture) condition should make the promotion focused appeal more valued. Although previous research indicating that promotion (vs. prevention) appeals are preferred for hedonic products has not manipulated decision task, the scenarios in those studies resemble an acquisition situation (see Micu and Chowdhury 2010).

Further, we assume that utilitarian products relative to hedonic products do not evoke much hedonic thoughts irrespective of whether the consumer is acquiring or forfeiting; instead it should primarily evoke more utilitarian thoughts focused towards the product quality/value etc. Unlike hedonic products, utilitarian products are not perceived as being decadent and involving self-gratification (Khan, Dhar, and Wertenbroch 2005) and are not associated with guilt and consequently individuals buying utilitarian products should be relatively less risk averse, irrespective of whether they are forfeiting or acquiring the product; hence they should not differ significantly in their preferences for promotion vs. prevention-oriented messages.

Furthermore, when consumers experience the products, we expect the post-ad exposure effects hypothesized above to disappear. Indeed, previous research indicates that pre-trial advertising does not impact consumers' evaluations of highly diagnostic products (as those used in our study) if advertising and trial provide consistent (e.g., positive) information (Hoch and Ha 1986; Kempf and Smith 1998). However, an individual's need for touch is a key variable that explains the way individuals respond to product experience (Peck and Childers 2003). Thus, we expect the effects hypothesized above to be moderated by individuals' need for touch, specifically, for hedonic products, when given the opportunity to explore the product, for forfeiture conditions, low (vs. high) NFT individuals will prefer more prevention focus messages. However, for acquisition conditions, there will be no significant differences in message preference for varying levels of need for touch. Further, in case of functional products, individual need for touch will not interact with decision task.

## Methodology and Findings

In study 1, 121 undergraduate student participants were randomly assigned to one of the four experimental conditions: 2 (decision task: acquisition versus forfeiture) X 2 (product type: hedonic versus utilitarian). Participants took part individually in a brand decision task on a PC equipped with a high-speed Internet connection. After reading the given decision task scenario for a specific product type, participants were exposed to two different brand advertisements (one promotion oriented and one prevention oriented; order randomized) in the same product category. After examining the ads, they indicated their relative brand preferences and then they answered some questions regarding their task motivation, thought measures, manipulation checks, and demographics. Study 2 procedure was very similar to study 1 (112 undergraduate students). Thus, the main differences in study 2 were: individual need for touch measures and actual thought protocols were collected and individuals made their brand choice after having the opportunity to touch and visually see the two brands.

Results from study 1 confirm that individuals faced with an acquisition (vs. forfeiture) decision task engage in more hedonic thoughts and do prefer a more promotion vs. prevention oriented brand message and this is mainly true for buying hedonic products. Also, results from study 2 provide support that an individual's need for touch attenuate the effects of decision task on relative brand message preferences, only in case of hedonic (not, functional) products.

# Mixing It Up: The Effects of Cognitive Contrasting on Cognitive Resource Availability and Advertisement Recall

Ryan S. Elder, University of Michigan, USA
James A. Mourey, University of Michigan, USA

## EXTENDED ABSTRACT

Resource depletion theory is predicated on the idea that cognitive resources are finite and limited. Thus, tasks involving cognitive effort tap into this finite pool of resources and, in doing so, leave fewer resources available for subsequent tasks requiring cognitive effort (Engle et al. 1995, Baumeister et al. 1998). These effects have been shown with self-regulation and self control in the domains of dieting and emotion regulation (Vohs and Heatherton 2000), avoiding impulse purchases (Vohs and Faber 2007), and resisting persuasive messages (Wheeler, Briñol, and Hermann 2008). Additionally, recent research has extended these findings in to the domain of choice (Poceptsova et al. 2008).

The prior literature, therefore, displays the robust findings that a task that utilizes cognitive resources will lead to fewer cognitive resources in a subsequent task. However, the malleability and replenishing of these resources has received less attention. In their self-control strength model, Muraven and Baumeister (2000) show that even self-control failure could lead to stronger self-control in the long-term suggesting that the resource pool could, in fact, increase over time. Furthermore, findings in cognitive neuroscience exhibit the brain's flexibility in addressing the need for cognitive resources through a feedback loop involving the dorsolateral prefrontal cortex and the anterior cingulate cortex (MacDonald et al. 2000).

We propose that the malleability of cognitive resources will be greatest when a series of tasks oscillate between levels of difficulty, therefore disrupting the feedback loop and causing the brain to plan for this uncertainty in resource need by increasing resource availability. Therefore, individuals presented with tasks placing inconsistent (vs. consistent) demands on cognitive resources will have greater (fewer) cognitive resources available for subsequent tasks. Following the oscillation in task difficulty, we anticipate that the resulting increase in cognitive resources will lead to heightened recall of advertising information contained within the series of tasks. Finally, we anticipate that an explicit measure of cognitive resource availability will mediate the relationship between task consistency and advertising recall.

## Study 1

The purpose of the initial study is to show the fundamental idea that a series of tasks placing either consistent or inconsistent demands on cognitive resources will produce differences in the availability of cognitive resources available for a subsequent task.

Our study design is a 2 (first task: easy or hard) x 2 (second task: easy or hard) between subjects design. One hundred and twenty-one participants were told they would be solving a series of math questions for the GMAT®. Each participant answered six questions that were either all hard, all easy, alternating beginning with hard or alternating beginning with easy. Following the six math questions, participants were given an anagram task, which is our measure of cognitive resources. Specifically, we focus on the time they spent solving the anagrams (Muraven, Tice, and Baumeister 1998).

Our primary dependent variable of interest is the time participants spent solving the anagrams. Neither the main effect of first task difficulty nor the effect of second task difficulty is significant; however, we do get a significant interaction between first and second task difficulty ($p<.05$). Examining the means we see that on average,

participants in the alternating conditions spent significantly more time on the anagram tasks than those in the consistent conditions ($M_{alternating}=266.82, M_{consistent}=194.96$). Thus, as predicted, alternating task difficulty leads to a higher availability of cognitive resources than does maintaining consistency.

## Study 2

With study 2, we seek to replicate the effects of study 1 in an advertising context. Additionally, although the phenomenon found in study 1 was theorized to be due to cognitive resource availability, this underlying process was not explored in the initial study.

The design for study 2 closely mirrored that of study 1, except that the second, fourth, and sixth task was to view an advertisement. The first, third, and fifth task in the sequence was a math question from study 1. We manipulated advertisement difficulty by varying the typeface used to convey product relevant information (Sung and Schwarz 2008). In sum, we used a 2 (math question: easy, difficult) x 2 (advertisement: easy, difficult) between subjects design.

One hundred participants completed the study, moving between the math questions and the advertisements. In addition to the questions from study 1 (and the anagram task), following the task sequence participants reported their current enjoyment of performing difficult tasks. This was captured as a more explicit measure of cognitive resource availability. They then proceeded to answer questions regarding the advertisements they had seen earlier, including any specific information they recalled.

An analysis on time spent on the anagram task reveals only a significant interaction of the two factors, replicating our findings from study 1. More importantly, we also get the hypothesized two-way interaction on advertising recall. The means exhibit the hypothesized relationship as participants in the contrasting conditions recalled significantly more information than those in the consistent conditions ($p <.01$; $M_{contrasting}=4.96$, $M_{consistent}=3.41$).

Our explicit measure of cognitive resources (current enjoyment from performing difficult cognitive tasks) also revealed only the significant interaction with participants in the contrasting conditions, reporting significantly more enjoyment than in the consistent conditions. Indeed, this measure partially mediates the relationship between cognitive contrasting and recall. (Sobel z =1.77, $p< .08$).

## Study 3

Study 3 was designed to replicate the findings from study 1 and study 2 with a direct manipulation of cognitive resources (cognitive load). Participants memorized either a 10 or 2 digit number and then proceeded to view the advertisements, and complete the anagram task, as well as report their current enjoyment of difficult tasks.

As in studies 1 and 2, an analysis on our implicit measure of cognitive resources (time spent on anagrams) reveals the hypothesized interaction as participants in the contrasting conditions spent significantly more time on the anagram tasks than those in the consistent conditions. Similar significant interactions were present for our explicit measure of cognitive resources (p<.05), and advertisement recall (p<.05). As in study 2, the explicit measure of cognitive resources mediates the relationship between cognitive contrasting and recall(Sobel z=1.97, $p<.05$)

# REFERENCES

Anand, P. and B. Sternthal (1988), "Strategies for Designing Persuasive Messages: Deductions from the Resources Matching Hypothesis," in Patricia Cafferata and Alice Tybout (eds.), Cognitive and Affective Responses to Advertising, Lexington, Mass. 135-60.

Baumeister, Roy F. (2002), "Yielding to Temptation: Self-control Failure, Impulsive Purchasing, and Consumer Behavior," *Journal of Consumer Research,* 28 (4), 670–76.

Baumeister, Roy F., M. Muraven, and D.M. Tice (2000), "Ego depletion: a resource model of volition, self-regulation, and controlled processing," *Social Cognition*, 8, 130-150.

Baumeister, Bratslavsky, Ellen, Mark Muraven, and Dianne M. Tice (1998), "Ego Depletion: Is the Active Self a Limited Resource?" *Journal of Personality and Social Psychology,* 74 (5), 1252–65.

Bosmans, Anick, Rick Pieters, and Hans Baumgartner (2010), "The Get Ready Mind-Set: How Gearing Up for Later Impacts Effort Allocation Now," *Journal of Consumer Research*, June 2010.

Bruyneel, Sabrina, Siegfried Dewitte, Kathleen D. Vohs, and Luk Warlop (2006), "Repeated Choosing Increases Susceptibility to Affective Product Features," *International Journal of Research in Marketing,* 23 (2), 215–25.

Courtney, Susan M., Laurent Petit, José Ma. Maisog, Leslie G. Ungerleider, and James V. Haxby (1998), "An area specialized for spatial working memory in human frontal cortex," *Science*, New Series, Vol. 279, No. 5355 (Feb.), pp. 1347-1351.

Engle, R.W., A.R.A. Conway, S.W. Tuholski, and R.J. Shisler (1995), "A resource account of inhibition," *Psychological Science*, 6, 122-125.

MacDonald, Angus W., Jonathan D. Cohen, V.A. Stenger, and Cameron S. Carter (2000), "Dissociating the role of the dorsolateral prefrontal and anterior cingulate cortex in cognitive control," *Science*, 288, 1835-1838.

Muraven, Mark R. and Roy F. Baumeister (2000), "Self-regulation and Depletion of Limited Resources: Does Self-control Resemble a Muscle?" *Psychological Bulletin,* 126 (2), 247–59.

Muraven, Mark, D.M. Tice and R.F. Baumeister (1998), "Self-control as limited resource: regulatory depletion patterns," Journal of Personality and Social Psychology 74.

Richeson, Jennifer, Abigail A Baird, Heather L Gordon, Todd F Heatherton, Carrie L Wyland, Sophie Trawalter, and J Nicole Shelton (2003), "An fMRI investigation of the impact of interracial contact on executive function," *Nature Neuroscience*, Vol. 6, Num. 12, 1323-1328.

Schacter, Daniel L., Gagan S. Wig, and W. Dale Stevens (2007)."Reductions in Cortical Activity Due to Priming," *Current Opinion in Neurobiology,* Vol. 17, 171–76.

Schmeichel, Brandon. J. (2007), "Attention Control, Memory Updating, and Emotion Regulation Temporarily Reduce the Capacity for Executive Control," *Journal of Experimental Psychology: General*, 136 (2), 241–55.

Vohs, Kathleen D., Roy F. Baumesiter, Brandon J. Schmeichel, Jean M. Twenge, Noelle M. Nelson, and Dianne M. Tice (2008), "Making Choices Impairs Subsequent Self-Control: A Limited-Resource Account of Decision Making, Self-Regulation, and Active Initiative", Journal of Personality and Social Psychology, forthcoming.

Vohs. Kathleen D. and Todd F. Heatherton, "Self-Regulatory Failure: A Resource-Depletion Approach," *Psychological Science*, Vol. 11, No. 3 (May, 2000), pp. 249-254.

Wheeler, S. Christian, Pablo Briñol, and Anthony D. Hermann, "Resistance to persuasion as self-regulation: Ego-depletion and its effects on attitude change processes," *Journal of Experimental Social Psychology*, Vol. 43, Iss. 1, January 2007, pp. 150-156

# Devaluation and Fluency Effects of the Depth Position of a Non-focal Image on Image Evaluation

Sangdo Oh, University of Illinois, USA
Sukki Yoon, Bryant University, USA
Patrick Vargas, University of Illinois, USA

## EXTENDED ABSTRACT

People live and consume in the three-dimensional (3D) world. Yet most prior research into consumers' perception of advertising has been limited to just two physical dimensions: horizontal and vertical. Presently we examine an under-studied topic—how the position of an image on a third dimension—depth—influences consumers' evaluation of an image. Consumers encounter numerous images appearing in various points on the depth dimension: billboards are erected near and far alongside the highway; cereal boxes on promotion are displayed near and far in the aisles of a grocery store.

Consumers often encounter marketing messages that are placed outside their focal point (Ferraro, Bettman, & Chartrand, 2009). For example, suppose that a consumer is reading the news online and notices an image that is transparently superimposed on the headline and appears to be nearer than the headline (the depth dimension operating in a 2D environment).[1] Or consider someone playing a 3D Tetris game when an image suddenly appears either nearer or farther than the target. Given that the reader or gamer has focused attention on the task-relevant target—a headline to read or a shape to match—would they evaluate the image differently depending on whether the image appears nearer or farther than the target? Would this depth position effect vary for consumers who are trying to read or trying to play a game when the encounter occurs? Does the image, itself, matter (e.g., meaningless abstract or brand logo)?

Marketers enjoy one potential advantage when they place an image in front of, rather than behind, a focal target: the image has direct, upfront exposure. But this advantage also has a potentially threatening flip side: viewers might be irritated by an ad's invasiveness. A practical dilemma, then, is whether the advertiser should go with the foreground position for better exposure, or the background position for less intrusiveness (Edwards, Li, & Lee, 2002). Although marketers recognize that question is important, the literature has been silent on this point. In the virtual world, particularly, this question is even more pressing because technology enhances advertisers' abilities to introduce images in the foreground and background of web pages. Unfortunately, the psychological consequences of the depth position of visual stimuli are largely unknown. The present research is the first, to the best of our knowledge, to explore this question.

Although no direct evidence has indicated whether the position of stimuli on the depth dimension produces different evaluations of an image, two contrasting predictions may be deduced from the extant literature: devaluation and fluency effects (e.g., Raymond et al. 03 vs. Janiszewski and Chandon 2007). We test these rival hypotheses in Experiment 1 in a 2D setting and in Experiment 2 in a 3D setting.

H1.1. *The Devaluation Hypothesis*: A foreground image relative to the attentional focus will be evaluated more negatively than a background image.

H1.2. *The Fluency Hypothesis*: A foreground image relative to the attentional focus will be evaluated more positively than a background image.

Furthermore, we question whether the depth position effect (H1) would be contingent on (1) whether a consumer is in the conceptual or perceptual information processing (H2), and (2) whether the distracting image is a meaningless abstract or a brand logo (H3).

H2. When the focal and non-focal stimuli elicit different processing modes, foreground stimuli should be evaluated more favorably than background stimuli.

H3. When focal and non-focal stimuli elicit similar processing modes, foreground stimuli should be evaluated more negatively than background stimuli.

## EXPERIMENT 1

Participants in the foreground image condition were exposed to a set of abstract patterns that were transparently superimposed in front of the target words; participants in the background image condition were exposed to the same set of abstract patterns that were transparently superimposed behind the target words.

Participants in the foreground image condition ($M_{front}$ = 4.66) exhibited a higher degree of favorability toward all abstract figures than did participants in the background image condition ($M_{behind}$ = 3.75). This results support the fluency hypothesis (H1.2) but not the devaluation hypothesis (H1.1) in a simulated 2D setting.

## EXPERIMENT 2

We tested H2 and H3 in a 2 (Image Position: Front vs. Back) x 2 (Task Nature: Word Recognizing vs. Arrow Matching) x 2 (Distracter Type: Abstract vs. Logo) factorial design.

The results from Experiment 2 showed that when perceptual distractors (abstract figures) and target objects appeared together in different positions on the depth dimension, the fluency effect (i.e., higher favorability for the nearer-than-target image over the farther-than-target image) emerged among participants in the conceptual processing mode (i.e., the task-distractor mismatch), but the devaluation effect (i.e., lower favorability for the nearer-than-target image over the farther-than-target image) emerged among participants in the perceptual processing mode (i.e., the task-distractor match). However, when participants saw conceptual distractor (brand logos) instead of perceptual distracters (abstract figures), the devaluation effect emerged in the conceptual processing mode, but no such effect, if not a reversal, emerged in the perceptual processing mode.

The findings are theoretically and practically important in several ways. First, they shed light on how the conceptual or perceptual natures of a task determine the depth position effects of an image in a 3D setting. Second, the findings show that the relationship between the depth position of an image and the nature of a primary task is contingent on the type of image that appears. Third, the findings offer marketers principles to adopt and ways to improve their understanding of what they should show and where they should show it on the depth dimensions of reading- and gaming-oriented websites.

Although the depth dimension is a 3D-relevant concept, it could still play a role, as we see in this example, in influencing one's perception in a 2D setting.

# When White Space Is More than Burning Money: Economic Signaling Meets Visual Commercial Rhetoric

John Pracejus, University of Alberta, Canada
Thomas O'Guinn, University of Wisconsin-Madison, USA
Douglas Olsen, Arizona State University, USA

## EXTENDED ABSTRACT:

When White Space Is More than Burning Money: Economic Signaling Meets Visual Commercial Rhetoric

The pioneering work of Nelson (1970, 1974, & 1978) brought forth the idea that under certain conditions high advertising expenditures can inform consumers about particularly high product quality, even if consumers never actually see any of the advertising. While this mechanism of action for the economic analysis of advertising is widely accepted, there are few demonstrations of consumers inferring quality from advertising elements which suggest "burning money". One set of studies show that ad repetition can lead to inferences of quality (Kirmani, 1997; Moorthy & Hawkins, 2005) or ad size (Kirmani, 1990; Homer 1995). As Moorthy and Hawkins (2005) pointed out, ad frequency effects are thoroughly confounded with mere exposure effects leaving the role of signaling in doubt for those studies that manipulated frequency. This limitation effectively leaves ad size as the only advertising variable purported to indicate product quality to consumers through a burning money signal.

Both Kirmani (1990) and Homer (1995) manipulated ad size in their studies. Surprisingly, however, both studies also manipulated the amount of white space in the ads. Given this, it is possible that large ads did not signal quality to consumers via inferences about market power. An alternative explanation for the behavioral effects of white space proposed by Pracejus, et al. (2006) holds that in North America, white space is a well-known and widely understood trope in the lexicon of modern visual commercial rhetoric, which developed from specific historical moments during the late 1950's and Early 1960's when advertising and commercial design were strongly influenced by the minimalist movements taking place in art.

Given these two potential ways white space can influence consumers, two studies were conducted. Study one contrasts white space against ad size. If the economic signaling explanation is correct, there should be little difference between these two expensive and extravagant advertising techniques. Study two compares the effect of white space across cultures. If the economic signaling explanation is correct, there should be little difference in the impact of white space across cultures.

## Study 1

*Participants.* One hundred and eighty-four undergraduate students at a North American university.

*Design and Stimuli.* Three ad conditions (full-page, low white space; full-page, high white space; and, 1/5th page low white space) were used, with 2 product category replicates for each ad (furniture and mutual funds). Participants were told they would view an ad for Hastings (furniture/clothing) that would run in, a British newspaper.

*Dependent Variables.* After viewing the ad for 30 seconds, participants responded to 10 statements about Hastings along a seven-point, 1= "Strongly Disagree" and 7="Strongly Agree" scale. Eight of these statements were from Pracejus, et al. (2006). Attitudes and purchase intentions were also taken.

## Results

For cases where the type of the advertisement differed, contrasts were conducted to examine the source of the difference. The impact of ad size alone can be assessed through contrasting the 1/5th page ad with the full page, low white space ad. Here, the only significant impact of ad size is on the item *Hastings has considerable market share* ($F=14.71$, $p<.001$). This is in keeping with the expectations of the burning money signaling theory.

When the 1/5th page ad was compared with the full page, high white space ad, however, we observed significant increases in beliefs about Hastings in 6 out of 8 of the specific meanings expected to be conveyed by white space, as well as significant increases in attitudes and purchase intentions.

## Study 2

The second way the rhetorical account can be distinguished from the burning money account is cross culturally. if the socio-historical account is accurate, we should expect a different—weaker, narrower—impact of white space on consumers outside of the North American context. To explore the role of culture and social history on the meanings conveyed to consumers through the use of white space in advertising we compared responses to white space across groups with different social histories.

*Participants.* 260 undergraduate students 130, at a university in North American, and 130 at a university in Hong Kong.

*Design and Stimuli.* A 2 (product category) x 2 (high/low white space) x 2 (country of residence) between-subjects design. All advertisements contained a picture of a clock, accompanied by a logo for a fictitious brand (Hastings), along with ambiguous copy like that used in Study 1. Exposure and cover story and dependent variables were similar to study1.

## Results

The impact of white space on brand perceptions varied significantly by country. After mean centering by country and product class , an ANOVA revealed a significant interaction of white space and country of residence on quality, risk, prestige, trust, and overall brand attitude. The interaction was also marginally significant on expensive ($F=3.7$, $p>.055$) and leadership ($F=3.4$, $p>.06$). So, for nearly every meaning associated with the social history of white space, its impact was principally dependent on culture.

For North American participants, white space significantly increased perceptions of quality, low risk, prestige, trust, and leadership. It also significantly increased overall brand attitude and purchase intention. For the Hong Kong participants, however, white space only significantly influenced perceived market share ($F=5.29$, $p<.023$). It also marginally impacted expense ($F=3.57$, $p<.061$) and trust ($F=3.25$, $p>.074$). However, for both of these measures, the impact of white space was in the opposite direction to the North American participants. That is, low white space was marginally predictive of the brand being expensive and trustworthy.

## General Discussion

Whereas white space in an ad can imply that the advertiser is a large company much like a large ad does, it does not only mean the company has money to burn. In North America, it turns out that white space in ads implies much more about the brand.: quality, prestige, trust, etc. In Hong Kong, white space only implied a large market share. This is convincing evidence that the rhetorical account adds substantially to our understanding compared to economic signaling alone.

## REFERENCES

Bagwell, K. (2007). The economic analysis of advertising. In M. Armstrong & R. Porter (Eds.), *Handbook of industrial organization* (vol. 3) (pp. 1701–1844). Amsterdam: North Holland.

Becker, G. S. ,& Murphy, K. M. (1993). A simple theory of advertising as a good or bad. *Quarterly Journal of Economics, 108*, 941-964.

Homer, P. M. (1995). Ad size as an indicator of perceived advertising costs and effort: The effects on memory and perceptions, *Journal of Advertising, 24*(4), 1-12.

Kirmani, A. (1990). The effect of perceived advertising costs on brand perceptions. .*Journal of Consumer Research, 17,* 160-171.

Kirmani, A. (1997),.Advertising repetition as a signal of quality: If it's advertised so much, something must be wrong. *Journal of Advertising, 26* (3), 77-86

Kirmani, A., & Wright, P. (1989). Money talks: Perceived advertising expense and expected product quality. *The Journal of Consumer Research, 16* (3), 344-353

Milgrom, P., & Roberts, J. (1986). Price and advertising signals of product quality..*Journal of Political Economy, 91* (4), 796-821.

Moorthy, S., & Hawkins, S. A. (2005). Advertising repetition and quality perception. *Journal of Business Research, 58* (3), 54– 360

Nelson, P. (1970). Information and consumer behavior. *Journal of Political Economy, 78*, 311-329.

Nelson, P. (1974). Advertising as information. *Journal of Political Economy, 82,* 729-754.

Nelson, P. (1978). Advertising as information once more. In D.C. Tuerck (Ed.) *Issues in advertising: The economies of persuasion*, Washington, D.C.: American Enterprise Institution.

Orzach, R., Overgaard, P. B., & Tauman, Y. (2002). Modest advertising signals strength. *RAND Journal of Economics, 33*, 340-358

Pracejus, J. W, Olsen, G. D., & O'Guinn, T. C. (2006). How nothing became something: white space, rhetoric, history, and meaning. *Journal of Consumer Research, 33* 82-90

Schmalensee, R. (1978). A model of advertising and product quality. *Journal of Political Economy, 86*, 485-503.

Van de Vijver, F. & Leung, K. (1997). *Methods and data analysis for cross cultural research.* Thousand Oaks: Sage.

# The Confluence of Ideologies in Consumption Activities

Lindsay McShane, Queen's University, Canada

## EXTENDED ABSTRACT

Globalization has facilitated the transfer of cultural activities across borders such that consumers in Western societies increasingly engage in activities and use products that have roots in other cultures. As consumers adopt these products and participate in these activities, they draw on elements from their own culture rather than fully embracing the product/activity in its traditional form, along with its existing cultural underpinnings. For example, while yoga has philosophical roots in India (Eliade 1973), Western consumers only selectively draw on elements of this ancient practice and instead engage in a revised form of yoga that also reflects local cultures (Marowetz 2007). This adaptation is particularly interesting given these activities/products often embody ideological values that lie in stark contrast to the capitalist ideology of Western societies. For instance, given the centrality of transcendence in yoga, consider the divergent views across Eastern and Western philosophies of the relationship between technology and transcendence. Western consumers are quite adept at uniting their "infatuation with technological advance" with their "spiritual quest for transcendence" (Sherry 2000, p. 276). In fact, Western consumers rely heavily on technology to advance several capitalist ideals (e.g., freedom, efficiency, control) and are accustomed to drawing on technological resources to enhance consumption experiences and achieve goals (Kozinets 2008; Simpson 2003). In contrast, Eastern philosophy adopts an experiential and internally-driven worldview of transcendence (Gould 1991a). Eastern philosophy demands the rejection of the external world (i.e. material possessions), stating that this is necessary to becoming attuned with your inner self and achieving connectedness with the universe (Eliade 1973). Yet, Western consumers seamlessly integrate ancient practices into the capitalist marketplace such that the fusion of Eastern philosophies with Western ideology has become ubiquitous in culture. This paper seeks to enrich our understanding of the lived experience of consumers who negotiate these ideological conflicts and to examine why they may choose to immerse themselves in these conflicts.

To develop a rich understanding of the consumers' lived experience as they engage in activities and use products that blend disparate ideologies, I conducted six phenomenological interviews with yoga practitioners in Western cultures. The interviews, which ranged from 60 to 90 minutes, were initiated with a grand-tour question yet remained largely unstructured so that participants could steer the interview. Probing questions, adapted to the language of the participant, were asked as needed to facilitate a fulsome discussion. While the confluence of ideologies is relevant across numerous consumer activities, yoga is a particularly rich context in which to examine the phenomenon. *With historical roots in India, yoga refers to "any ascetic technique or any meditation method" (Eliade and Trask 1970, p.3). The focus is on achieving nirvana, a state of nothingness that contrasts with the materialist orientation of Western societies (Ojha 1999). Yet, d*espite these philosophical roots that seem antithetical to capitalism, yoga has been incorporated into Western society. American consumers buy technical yoga clothing and mats, engage in yoga forums and retreats, purchase yoga videos, join yoga studios and subscribe to yoga magazines (Morawetz 2007; Moran 2006). The interviews suggest that consumers are aware of the disparate worldviews that they are uniting in constructing their Westernized yoga practice. The participants actually held strong normative views of yoga and wrestled with the notion that their yoga practice diverged from these normative views. Interestingly, the gap between their yoga practice and normative yoga appeared to stem from the use of technology and its underlying values. In fact, a dominant theme across interviews was the conflicting presence of technology as both a liberator and constraint. Consumers used technological resources extensively to enhance their yoga experience (e.g., to engineer an ideal environment), yet were so dependent on these technological resources that they felt constrained by these same liberating resources. For example, because the interviewees depended on certain external resources (e.g., music, temperature, DVDs) to achieve instrumental goals, they were no longer self-sufficient and instead dependent on these resources. Thus, central to understanding the consumers' lived experience is the contradictory relationship with technology. Technology at once liberates them from constraints (e.g., time) and yet constrains them from achieving their normative views of yoga.

The interviews also shed light on why consumers may choose to immerse themselves in these ideological conflicts. It appears that one reason consumers may do so is to authenticate their hedonistic pursuits. For instance, participants framed traditional Western forms of exercise (e.g., aerobics), which focus solely on physical benefits with little meaning behind the movements, as more shallow and superficial. Thus, unable to authenticate their hedonic needs through exercise routines that align with capitalist ideology, consumers may endeavour to do so by engaging in activities that have socio-historic roots in non-capitalist systems of philosophy. In a sense, consumers seem to use the inherent conflict associated with these activities to their advantage, reworking the Eastern ideology of individual transcendence to authenticate their practice while also satisfying hedonic needs. By co-opting cultural elements from Eastern philosophy, consumers can lend authenticity to their consumption experience without sacrificing hedonic pursuits such as comfort, efficiency and enjoyment.

This paper extends the literature in two important ways. First, whereas previous work notes that certain people turn to Eastern health solutions in rejection of Western scientific practices (Thompson 2004), this study notes that one reason consumers may instead engage in activities from Eastern cultures to authenticate their individual hedonistic pursuits. Second, this study suggests that consumers draw on ideological discourses not only to craft their identities (Denzin 2001; Hebdige 1979; Holt 2002; Holt and Thompson 2004) but also to construct meaningful consumption experiences. Broadly speaking, this paper enriches our understanding of the consumer's lived experience as they participate in activities that embody ideological conflicts. Despite the inherent contradictions in the activities, which seems to stem, in part, from a conflicted relationship with technology (i.e., technology as liberator and constraint), consumers are able to draw on Eastern ideologies to authenticate their hedonic pursuits and craft an authentic consumption experiences. In doing so, consumers demonstrate how they can fluidly bring together seemingly disparate ideological elements into their daily consumption activities.

## REFERENCES

Arnould, Eric J. and Craig J. Thompson (2005), "Consumer Culture Theory (CCT): 20 Years of Research," *Journal of Consumer Research*, 31 (4), 868-881.

Brigham, Mark and Lucas D. Introna (2007), "Invoking politics and ethics in the design of information technology: undesigning the design," *Ethics and Information Technology*, 9, 1-10.

Davis, Erik (1998), *Techgnosis: Myth, Magic and Mysticism in the Age of Information*, New York: Three Rivers.

Eliade, Mircea (1973), *Yoga: Immortality and Freedom*. Bollingen Series LVI. Trans. Willard R. Trask. Princeton: Princeton UP.

Firat, A. Fuat and Alladi Venkatesh (1995),"Liberatory Postmodernism and the Reenchantment of Consumption," *Journal of Consumer Research*, 22 (December), 239-67.

Gould, Stephen J. (1991a), "An Asian Approach to the Understanding of Consumer Energy, Drives and States," in *Research in Consumer Behavior*. Vol. 5, ed. Elizabeth C. Hirschman, Greenwich, CT: JAI, in press.

_____ (1991b), "The Self-Manipulation of My Pervasive, Perceived Vital Energy through Product Use: An Introspective-Praxis Perspective," *Journal of Consumer Research*, 18 (September) 194-207.

Grayson, Kent and Radan Martinec (2004), "Consumer Perceptions of Iconicity and Indexicality and Their Influence on Assessments of Authentic Market Offerings," *Journal of Consumer Research*, 31(2) 296-312.

Harris, John G. (1999), *Gnosticism: beliefs and practices*, Published by Sussex Academic Press, 224 pages.

Hebdige, Dick (1979), *Subculture: The Meaning of Style*, London: Routledge.

Hoeller, Stephan A. (2002), Gnosticism: New Light on the Ancient Tradition of Inner Knowing, U.S: Quest Books.

_____ , "The Gnostic World View: A Brief Summary of Gnosticism" www.gnosis.org (Accessed April 1, 2009).

Holt, Doug (2002), "Why do Brands Cause Trouble? A Dialectical Theory of Consumer Culture and Branding," *Journal of Consumer Research*, 31 (June), 162-180.

_____ and Craig Thompson (2004), "Man-of-Action Heroes: The Pursuit of Heroic Masculinity in Everyday Consumption," *Journal of Consumer Research*, 31(September) 425-440.

King, Karen L. (2005), *What is Gnosticism?* Harvard University Press, U.S.

Kozinets, R.V. (2008), "Technology/Ideology: How Ideological Fields Influence Consumers' Technology Narratives," *Journal of Consumer Research*, 34 (April), 865-881.

Margolis, Joseph (2003), "Technology and the Aesthetics of Embodiment," in *Technology and Cultural Values*, ed. P.D. Hershock, M. Stepaniants, R. Ames, University of Hawaii Press. U.S, 443-447.

Moran, Susan (2006), Meditate on This: Yoga is Big Business, New York Times, Published December 28, 2006.http://www.nytimes.com/2006/12/28/business/28sbiz.html

Morawetz, Zoe (2007), Piracy & Other Yoga Controversies: Fitness Trends meets Spiritual Tradition, May 31, 2007. http://yogapilates.suite101.com/article.cfm/piracy_other_yoga_controversies

Noble, David F. (1999), *The Religion of Technology: The Divinity of Man and the Spirit of Invention*, New York: Penguin.

Ojha, Ashok (1999) "Yoga: Is Therapy Good Without the Philosophy," *The Journal of Online Education*, Edition 99, Ed. Julia Keefer, New York University.

Pierce, Troy "What do you Believe," December 25, 2005. http://gnoscast.blogspot.com/2005/12/what-do-you-believe.html.

Simpson, Lorenzo C. (1995), *Technology Time and the Conversations of Modernity*. Routledge. United States.

Sherry Jr., John F. (2000), "Place, Technology, and Representation," *Journal of Consumer Research*, 27 (September) 273-278.

"What is Technology" Technically Speaking, The National Academies http://www.nae.edu/nae/techlithome.nsf/weblinks/KGRG-55A3ER.

Thompson, Craig. J. (2004) "Marketplace Mythology and Discourses of Power," *Journal of Consumer Research*, 31 (June) 162-180.

Thompson, Craig J., William B. Locander, and Howard R. Pollio (1989), "Putting Consumer Experience Back into Consumer Research: The Philosophy and Method of Existential-Phenomenology," *Journal of Consumer Research* 16 (September), 133-146.

# Beyond Consumer Boundaries: A Conceptual Model for Understanding the Consumer Role and its Impact on Behavior

Jodie Whelan, Richard Ivey School of Business, Canada

## EXTENDED ABSTRACT

Despite the prevalence of the consumer role and the existence of a discipline devoted to studying the consumer, little is known about the consequences of being a consumer. The relevant empirical findings, though indirect and scattered, seem centered on the effects of living in hyperchoice and on making choices (Mick, Broniarczyk, and Haidt 2004; Schwartz et al. 2002; Vohs et al. 2008a). As a field, we have yet to explore whether the consequences of being a consumer extend further, "perhaps degrading key aspects of human psychology, including moral character" (Mick et al. 2004, 207) and penetrating non-consumer domains. Furthermore, little is known about the consumer role in general. The actual norms, expectations, values, and behaviors that define the consumer role have yet to be specified. Until we understand everything this role entails, we cannot begin to fathom its consequences on the individual. Thus, the purpose of this article is to provide a conceptual framework for exploring the consumer role and its potential spillover into non-consumer domains. Using nine theoretical propositions, I outline how individuals transition into the consumer role; how behavior may be altered by the consumer role; and when and why the consumer role may spillover into non-consumer domains.

Role theory began as a theatrical metaphor. Like actors playing specific roles, human beings behave in ways that are different and predictable depending on the context and the role they occupy (Biddle 1986). Role theory is not new to marketing; however, it has yet to be applied to the *consumer* level (see Wilson and Bozinoff 1980 for a comprehensive overview of role theory and marketing). The study of role-related problems is most frequent in management studies and gender/family studies, where the primary focus seems to be how individuals transition between work roles and home roles (Ashforth, Kreiner, and Fugate 2000; Burr 1972).

Like any other role, the consumer role begins with a role-relevant cue (proposition 1). Cues specific to the consumer role could include such things as a salesperson, a store, an ad on TV, and even money. Whether cues are successful at triggering consumer role entry will depend on the degree of role integration (i.e., the existence of role boundaries; Ashforth et al. 2000) and the strength of the situation. I propose that, for most North Americans, the consumer role is highly integrated with other daily roles (propositions 2 and 3); thus, consumer role entry is likely to be mindless and automatic—all that is required is a role-relevant cue. Furthermore, even if individuals have created idiosyncratic boundaries around the consumer role (i.e., voluntary simplifiers), consumer role entry will still be automatic if the situation is strong enough (i.e., context-appropriate; proposition 4).

The next three propositions concern consumer role definition. They are all based on the assumption that, because these expectations or behaviors are so common to consumer experiences, they have become ingrained in the consumer role and detached from their original sources. Subsequently, being in the consumer role is all that is required to experience their effects—the usual antecedents are no longer necessary. Specifically, I propose that the consumer role triggers materialistic values (proposition 5), engenders a sense of entitlement (proposition 6), and provides feelings of empowerment (proposition 7). While the propositions concerning materialism and entitlement have direct behavioral implications, empowerment is viewed more as a benefit of the consumer role. This distinction is important when considering why and how the consumer role is likely to spillover into non-consumer domains.

While these consequences may be acceptable in a consumer context, they could be extremely inappropriate and even harmful in other situations. Consider materialism. We know that high materialism leads to increased possessiveness and nongenerosity (Belk 1985). Though this may be advantageous while shopping, how could it impact behavior in non-consumer contexts? Will a mom in the consumer role be less responsive to her children's needs and more focused on her own desires? Consider entitlement. Will a student in the consumer role feel entitled to above-average marks—after all, he is *paying* for his education?

Given the frequency and mindlessness with which individuals can enter the consumer role and the unique benefits it can provide, I believe spillover is highly probable. Spillover occurs when the consumer role is active in an inappropriate context, and it can happen for two different reasons. As we become more practiced at enacting a role, transitioning is likely to become more automatic and more mindless (Ashforth and Fried 1988); thus, encountering a role-relevant cue could lead individuals to enter the consumer role without any regard for whether or not such behavior is appropriate (proposition 8). This will be most likely to occur when the consumer role is highly integrated; if the role is highly segmented, boundaries should prevent mindless entry when in an inappropriate context.

Proposition 8 details how spillover can occur due to dysfunctional role entry. Proposition 9 focuses on role exit. Though highly integrated roles should be easy to transition in and out of, individuals may be reluctant to exit a role when they are good at performing it and/or the role is extrinsically rewarding and intrinsically satisfying (Kohn and Schooler 1983). For some, the consumer role may be the only role in their lives that provides respect, courtesy, and attendance to their needs (Wänke 2009); thus, even though a different role may be more suitable, individuals may be unwilling to exit the role. The consumer role and its role-relevant behaviors persist even though they may no longer be appropriate.

Fully understanding the consumer role and its impact on both consumer and non-consumer domains will provide new and valuable insight into both individual- and societal-level behavior. We have long acknowledged that we are a society of consumers–it's about time we move beyond consumer boundaries and begin to explore everything else this entails.

## REFERENCES

Aggarwal, Pankaj (2004), "The Effects of Brand Relationship Norms on Consumer Attitudes and Behavior," *Journal of Consumer Research*, 31 (June), 87-101.

Ashforth, Blake E. and Yitzhak Fried (1988), "The Mindlessness of Organizational Behaviors," *Human Relations*, 41 (4), 305-29.

Ashforth, Blake E., Glen E. Kreiner, and Mel Fugate (2000), "All in a Day's Work: Boundaries and Micro Role Transitions," *The Academy of Management Review*, 25 (3), 472-91.

Belk, Russell W. (1984), "Three Scales to Measure Constructs Related to Materialism: Reliability, Validity, and Relationships to Measures of Happiness," in *Advances in Consumer Research*, Vol. 11, ed. Thomas Kinnear, Provo, UT: Association for Consumer Research, 291-97.

_____ (1985), "Materialism: Trait Aspects of Living in the Material World," *Journal of Consumer Research*, 12 (December), 265-80.

473                                     *Advances in Consumer Research*
                                        *Volume 38, © 2012*

Berger, Arthur Asa (2005), *Shop 'Til You Drop: Consumer Behavior and American Culture*, Lanham, MD: Rowman & Littlefield Publishers, Inc.

Biddle, B. J. (1986), "Recent Developments in Role Theory," *Annual Review of Sociology*, 12 (1), 67-92.

Boyd III, Henry C. and Janet E. Helms (2005), "Consumer Entitlement Theory and Measurement," *Psychology and Marketing*, 22 (March), 271-86.

Burr, Wesley R. (1972), "Role Transitions: A Reformulation of Theory," *Journal of Marriage and the Family*, 3 (August), 407-16.

Burroughs, James E. and Aric Rindfleisch (2002), "Materialism and Well-Being: A Conflicting Values Perspective," *Journal of Consumer Research*, 29 (December), 348-70.

Chaplin, Lan Nguyen and Deborah Roedder John (2007), "Growing up in a Material World: Age Differences in Materialism in Children and Adolescents," *Journal of Consumer Research*, 34 (December), 480-93.

Cooper, William H. and Michael J. Withey (2009), "The Strong Situation Hypothesis," *Personality and Social Psychology Review*, 13 (1), 62-72.

Freund, Julien (1969), *The Sociology of Max Weber*, New York: Vintage.

Friestad, Marian and Peter Wright (1994), "The Persuasion Knowledge Model: How People Cope with Persuasion Attempts," *Journal of Consumer Research*, 21 (June), 1-31.

Fromm, Erich (1955), *The Sane Society*, New York: Rinehart and Winston.

Henry, Paul C. (2005), "Social Class, Market Situation, and Consumers' Metaphors of (Dis)Empowerment," *Journal of Consumer Research*, 31 (March), 766-78.

Heyman, James and Dan Ariely (2004), "Effort for Payment: A Tale of Two Markets," *Psychological Science*, 15 (11), 787-93.

Higgins, E. Tory (1987), "Self-Discrepancy: A Theory Relating Self and Affect," *Psychological Review*, 94 (3), 319-40.

Holt, Douglas B. (2002), "Why Do Brands Cause Trouble? A Dialectical Theory of Consumer Culture and Branding," *Journal of Consumer Research*, 29 (June), 70-90.

Iyengar, Sheena S. and Mark R. Lepper (2000), "When Choice Is Demotivating: Can One Desire Too Much of a Good Thing?," *Journal of Personality and Social Psychology*, 79 (6), 995-1006.

Kohn, Melvin L. and Carmi Schooler (1983), *Work and Personality: An Inquiry into the Impact of Social Stratification*, Norwood, NJ: Ablex.

Malhotra, Naresh K. (1984), "Reflections on the Information Overload Paradigm in Consumer Decision Making," *Journal of Consumer Research*, 10 (March), 436-40.

McNeal, James U. (1964), *Children as Consumers*, Austin, TX: University of Texas Bureau of Business Research.

Mick, David Glen, Susan M. Broniarczyk, and Jonathan Haidt (2004), "Choose, Choose, Choose, Choose, Choose, Choose, Choose: Emerging and Prospective Research on the Deleterious Effects of Living in Consumer Hyperchoice," *Journal of Business Ethics*, 52 (June), 207-11.

Mischel, Walter (1977), "The Interaction of Person and Situation," in *Personality at the Crossroads: Current Issues in Interactional Psychology*, ed. David S. Magnusson and Norman S. Endler, Hillsdale, NJ: Lawrence Erlbaum, 333-52.

Otnes, Cele, Tina M. Lowrey, and Young Chan Kim (1993), "Gift Selection for Easy and Difficult Recipients: A Social Roles Interpretation," *The Journal of Consumer Research*, 20 (September), 229-44.

Raskin, Robert and Howard Terry (1988), "A Principal-Components Analysis of the Narcissistic Personality Inventory and Further Evidence of Its Construct Validity," *Journal of Personality and Social Psychology*, 54 (5), 890-902.

Schor, Juliet B. (1998), *The Overspent American: Why We Want What We Don't Need*, New York: Basic Books.

Schwartz, Barry, Andrew Ward, John Monterosso, Sonja Lyubomirsky, Katherine White, and Darrin R. Lehman (2002), "Maximizing Versus Satisficing: Happiness Is a Matter of Choice," *Journal of Personality and Social Psychology*, 83 (5), 1178-97.

Solomon, Michael R. (1983), "The Role of Products as Social Stimuli: A Symbolic Interactionism Perspective," *Journal of Consumer Research*, 10 (December), 319-29.

Solomon, Michael R., Carol Surprenant, John A. Czepiel, and Evelyn G. Gutman (1985), "A Role Theory Perspective on Dyadic Interactions: The Service Encounter," *The Journal of Marketing*, 49 (Winter), 99-111.

Turner, Ralph H. (1990), *Life as Theater: A Dramaturgical Sourcebook*, New York: Walter de Gruyeter, Inc.

Vohs, Kathleen D., Roy F. Baumeister, Brandon J. Schmeichel, Jean M. Twenge, Noelle M. Nelson, and Dianne M. Tice (2008a), "Making Choices Impairs Subsequent Self-Control: A Limited-Resource Account of Decision Making, Self-Regulation, and Activie Initiative," *Journal of Personality and Social Psychology*, 94 (May), 883-98.

Vohs, Kathleen D., Nicole L. Mead, and Miranda R. Goode (2008b), "Merely Activating the Concept of Money Changes Personal and Interpersonal Behavior," *Current Directions in Psychological Science*, 17 (3), 208-12.

Wänke, Michaela (2009), "What's Social About Consumer Behavior?," in *Social Psychology of Consumer Behavior*, ed. Michaela Wänke, New York, NY: Psychology Press, 3-18.

Ward, Scott (1974), "Consumer Socialization," *Journal of Consumer Research*, 1 (2), 1-14.

Wathieu, Luc, Lyle Brenner, Ziv Carmon, Amitava Chattopadhyay, Klaus Wertenbroch, Aimee Drolet, John Gourville, A. V. Muthukrishnan, Nathan Novemsky, Rebecca K. Ratner, and George Wu (2002), "Consumer Control and Empowerment: A Primer," *Marketing Letters*, 13 (August), 297-305.

Wilson, David T. and Lorne Bozinoff (1980), "Role Theory and Buying-Selling Negotiations: A Critical Overview," in *Marketing in the 1980's*, ed. Richard P. Bagozzi, Chicago: American Marketing, 118-21.

# Where to from Here? A Comparison of the Meanings Designed Into Three Public Spaces.

Jan Brace-Govan, Monash University of New South Wales, Australia

## EXTENDED ABSTRACT

This paper challenges the commonly presented view in marketing that space is open to negotiation and that meanings emerge from individual experiences within spaces. Instead the role of space in conveying specifically created or designed meanings is explored and suggested as a research area with potential.

Drawing from anthropology, Sherry (1998) noted that the spaces people shopped in had an effect on the shopping experience. Thus open air markets were different to the enclosed shopping mall and others examined meanings for shoppers (Sandicki and Holt 1998) and the immersed experience of bridal salons (Otnes 1998). Kozinets and colleagues uncovered the spectacular consumption space provided by ESPN Zone t (Kozinets et al 2002, 2004), while Maclaran and Brown (2005) considered the literary metaphor of utopia to discuss a reconstruction of a shopping space. Other consumer culture research explored the joint production of space through events like the rodeo (Penaloza 2001) and the fantasy world of Rocky Mountain men (Belk and Costa 1998) and Star Trek (Kozinets 2001). In this research the self-expression and self-transformation that were part of the immersed imaginings of consumers was key. Overall though, in these studies the co-creative and dialogic elements of consumer experiences within these spaces was the focus of the research. That spatial elements had a joint part to play is not the issue here. Instead the focus is shifted to space as a means to convey specific meanings that were selected by the designer.

Specifically this project explored whether the intended design of physical open space, such as public gardens, was understood and experienced as intended by consumers. A great deal of marketing relies on the visuality of consumption to comprehend advertisements, web sites, and other means of communication (Schroeder 2002). And the marketing discipline has expended quite some effort on understanding this feature of human consumption. However, little attention has been paid to the vista, or the visual display that is a designed open space. If the agenda of environmental sustainability is to gain any ground then the visual aspects of our landscape will become increasingly important both as a means of gauging the extent of the sustainability agenda, and also as a way in which to represent in public the values of "being green". This initial, exploratory study is a first step on this journey into a research sphere that is expected to be substantial. As such the paper is not intended to offer closure but instead begin to open up questions that need to be examined in much greater depth.

## Method

A modified grounded theory method was adopted and was appropriate given the exploratory nature of this investigation. In this process a preliminary literature was used to direct the initial engagement of the project and devise research questions. The ensuing stages were selected through analysis of the findings from the previous steps. This generated further research questions, established criteria for the selection of suitable sites and created related and relevant interview questions (Goulding 2005). After developing an understanding of each site through literature and other secondary information, interviews were taken with 15 informants relevant to each public space. Interviews were transcribed verbatim and the text was analysed for themes through open and axial coding (Goulding 2005). As each example space builds from the analysis of the previous space, the findings for each section of the project will be presented separately at first. A comparison across all three will draw the threads of the argument together. A short closing discussion identifies the ensuing research question(s) that informed the selection of the next space and its relevant informants. [Images included in the presentation.]

*Recreational Space provided within a real estate development.* In all six interviewees confirmed the symbolism presented in marketing materials that suggested the recreational site encouraged feeling of escaping the hustle and bustle of the city and created the sensation of an oasis. Although these consumers had all chosen to engage with this space so their agreement was unsurprising, the point for this first example was that the intention of the designers was indeed upheld.

*Cultural Space provided by a migrated group to celebrate their culture.* This example asked, what is the consumer experience when there is a distinct difference between the symbolism from which the space is designed and the symbolism in which the consumer is living? A public garden created by the Chinese community as a gift was the next example. Five informants were quizzed about their understanding of the Chinese garden's symbolism. Three were first generation Chinese and two were second generation Chinese. There were no differences in their views about Chinese gardens and their experience of them. All five enjoyed the gardens as a place of recovery and respite reflecting the intention of the garden design. However, there were differences in their understandings of the symbolism. This raised the question about the extent to which visual information can convey ideological density

## Communal Space Provided as a Community Garden

Community gardens have existed for several decades and there are well known examples in New York, Boston (Barlett 2005) and around the UK. Interestingly this space presented a visual mayhem of the individualized plots and the overall impression of disaggregation in terms of vista was a strong contrast to the consistency of the singular design of the previous examples. Nonetheless, the space as a whole presented quite a clear picture as the encompassing and welcoming community that it claimed to be and thus achieved a collective symbolic representation above and beyond the individualized plots. Four interviewees discuss how their activism engages with politicians and corporations, thus opening up the co-optation of this space to the politicians and corporations to utilize in their branding.

The final discussion is formed around the function, structure and aesthetic of the space (Schroeder 2002) to suggest that the disjunctions in understanding here need further research in particular around sustainability, politics (Mansvelt 2009) and brand image.

Thank you to Michelle Dichmann, Peta McIver, Jun Yao, and Ringo Teng for their assitance and enthusiasm. However, they are not responsbile for the current interpretation; this is all my own.

## REFERENCES

Barlett, Peggy (2005), *Urban Place. Reconnecting with the Natural World*, Cambridge, MA.: The MIT Press.

Belk, R.W. and Costa, J. (1998) 'The Mountain Man Myth: A contemporary consuming fantasy', *Journal of Consumer Research* 25 (3): 218-240.

Goulding, Christina, (2005), "Grounded Theory, Ethnography and Phenomenology", *European Journal of Marketing*, 39, (3/4), 294-308

Kozinets, Robert, John Sherry, Jr., Storm, Diana., Duhachek, Adam., Nuttavuthisit, Krittinee. and DeBarry-Spence, Benet. (2004) Ludic Agency and Retail Spectacle, *Journal of Consumer Research*, 31, (3), 658-

Kozinets, Robert, John Sherry, Jr., Storm, Diana., Duhachek, Adam., Nuttavuthisit, Krittinee. and DeBarry-Spence, Benet. (2002), "Themed Flagship Brandstores in the New Millenium: Theory, Practice, Prospects", *Journal of Retailing* 78 (1), 17-29.

Kozinets, Robert, (2001) Utopian Enterprise: Articulating the Meanings of Star Trek's Culture of Consumption, *Journal of Consumer Research*, 28 (1), 67-88.

Maclaran, Pauline, and Stephen Brown, (2005), "The Center Cannot Hold: Consuming the Utopian Marketplace", *Journal of Consumer Research* 32 (2), 311-323.

Mansvelt, Juliana (2009), "Geographies of Consumption: Engaging with Absent Presences", Progress in Human Geography, 1-10.

Otnes, Cele. (1998) 'Friend of the Bride–and then some: Roles of the Bridal Salon during wedding planning', in Sherry, J. (ed.) *Servicescapes: The concept of place in contemporary markets.* Lincolnswood, IL: NTC Business Books: 229-258.

Peñaloza, L. (2001) Consuming the American west: Animating cultural meaning and memory at a stock show and rodeo, *Journal of Consumer Research* 28 (3): 369-99.

Peñaloza, L. (1999) 'Just Doing It: Consumer agency and institutional politics at Niketown', *Consumption, Markets and Culture* 2 (Spring): 337-400.

Sandicki, O. and Holt, D. (1998) 'Malling Society: Mall, consumption practices and the future of public space', in Sherry, J. (ed.) *Servicescapes: The concept of place in contemporary markets.* Lincolnswood, IL: NTC Business Books: 305-336.

Schroeder, J. (2002), *Visual Consumption.* London and New York: Routledge.

Sherry, J. (1998) *Servicescapes: The concept of place in contemporary markets,* Lincolnwood, Illinois: NTC Business Books.

Turner, T. (2010), *Asian gardens 3000 BCE to 2000 CE ,* Routledge, London

# Learning to be Cosmopolitan

Bernardo Figueiredo, University New South Wales, Australia
Julien Cayla, University of New South Wales, Australia

## EXTENDED ABSTRACT

Cosmopolitanism refers to a perspective that considers that all individuals are citizens of the world. In recent years, it has received considerable research attention from consumer researchers (Cannon and Yaprak 2002; Cleveland, Laroche, and Papadopoulos 2009; Holt 1998; Thompson and Tambyah 1999). These studies recognize the overarching influence of cosmopolitanism as an important shaper of consumption in the global arena, which moderates and mediates many consumer attitudes and values. Despite the fact that consumer researchers agree that cosmopolitanism has a profound impact on consumer behavior, they have not explained how consumers acquire such dispositions.

There is a dearth of studies in the literature which investigate the process of becoming cosmopolitan. Current literature focuses on the relationship between cosmopolitanism and other consumer dimensions such as ethnocentrism and materialism (Cleveland et al. 2009), and fails to the dynamic nature of the construct itself. Thompson and Tambyah (1999), in one of the few studies that view cosmopolitanism as a dynamic process, point out that the expatriate informants of their study are neither completely cosmopolitan nor completely local, but rather aspiring to cosmopolitanism. The authors offer extensive ideographic data on masculine and feminine narratives present in expatriate discourses and relate them to the postcolonial economy. However, they cannot explain why some expatriates can adopt cosmopolitan ideals while others cannot. The literature lacks explanations on how consumers learn to be cosmopolitan. Therefore, this article aims to fill that gap by answering the following questions: *How do consumers learn to be cosmopolitan and what are the implications of that for consumer research?*

In our first section we differentiate among four types of cosmopolitanism in the literature: a) *philosophical cosmopolitanism*, a moral and political standpoint that seeks universal rights and global justice; b) *analytical cosmopolitanism*, an investigative tool and solution for problems created by the second modernity (Beck); c) *banal cosmopolitanism*, concrete processes of diversification and complexification of the world; and d) *ideological cosmopolitanism*, a set of neoliberal ideas historically linked to the growth of capitalism and therefore promoting values of mobility, fluidity, individuality, and flexibility. This research addresses the last two types of cosmopolitanism. In other words, we want to know how the cosmopolitan ideology is learned and how it integrates with diversification of the world.

We chose transnational mobile professionals (Bardhi 2004) as our research context, as the literature and travelling patterns indicate a high possibility of finding cosmopolitans among this group. The research took place in Sydney, Australia, a multicultural city that attracts expatriates from all over the world. We conducted 17 in-depth interviews with 11 transnational mobile professionals. Informants were asked to describe their life trajectories and explain their motivations for living in different countries. The identification of major life themes and life projects (Mick and Buhl 1992) together with processes of comparison, dimensionalization, and integration in categories relevant to the processes related to transnational mobility and the reproduction of cosmopolitanism.

Our findings show that cosmopolitanism, as an ideology of dominant classes, reinforces ideals attached to flexibility, adaptability, mobility, and diversity that provide transnational professionals with extra motivation for moving and seeking new and different places. Cosmopolitans process these novel experiences as opportunities for self-development and for exercising mobility skills valued by dominant classes. For cosmopolitans, mobility becomes a means of building up competencies, which are necessary in the competitive capitalist arena. These competencies involve the ability to orchestrate knowledge, experiences, and stories from different places and transform them in resources that are reprocessed as social, cultural or economic capital.

Cosmopolitan ideology, as a set of practices and skills, must be learned. As demonstrated here, it is by experiencing cosmopolitanism in a prolonged manner, through social institutions (e.g.: family, schools, workplaces) that especially convey cosmopolitan ideals, that mobile professionals acquire it in an embodied form. However, institutionalized cosmopolitanism is not accessible to everyone. These competencies are class based and represent a form of global-cultural capital that is not accessible to all. Transnational mobile consumers who have little contact with institutionalized forms of cosmopolitanism cannot incorporate embodied forms of cosmopolitanism. As a result, they do not learn how to be cosmopolitan. Moreover, they tend to interpret their mobile experiences in very different ways from those who are more cosmopolitan; rather, they see it as difficult and painful, which only reinforces their class position.

The performance of cosmopolitan practices allows individuals to highlight the benefits of their mobility and underplay the problems caused by it in a way that creates opportunities for capital accumulation and reproduction of the status quo. They actively consume cultural differences and display these differences as assets, which sets them apart from the less travelled. Their cosmopolitan identities are not linked to the objects themselves but to the way they organize consumption practices and objects. These creative uses of consumption products and experiences function as authenticating acts (Arnould and Price 2003) that transform personal agency into cosmopolitan self-narrative. These acts however are only meaningful to the extent they can be used to differentiate the performer from the others.

Explaining cosmopolitanism as an ideology which moves through global dimensions of cultural capital has many implications for consumer research. First, it becomes clear that cosmopolitanism is not accessible to everyone, which implies that underlying the debate around cosmopolitanism in the marketplace, there should be an awareness of how the society is stratified. Second, we use caution when inferring democratization of the marketplace, as different objects and experiences will be filtered differently, depending on the level of embodied cosmopolitanism one has. Third, according to the data, cosmopolitanism as an ideology seems to be adopted by people from different parts of the world, which suggests some isomorphism of structures present in different countries. In analytical terms, this is good because it creates a platform of comparison between marketplaces, in the so-called global structures of common differences (Wilk 1995) Fourth, pointing out the modes in which cosmopolitanism exists (institutionalized, embodied, and objectified) creates constructs that can be further used to explain relationships between consumption and cosmopolitan ideology in the marketplace.

## REFERENCES

Arnould, Eric J and Linda L Price, eds. (2003), *Authenticating Acts and Authoritative Performances*, London: Routledge.

Cannon, Hugh M and Attila Yaprak (2002), "Will the Real-World Citizen Please Stand Up! The Many Faces of Cosmopolitan Consumer Behavior," *Journal of International Marketing*, 10 (4), 30-52.

Cleveland, Mark, Michel Laroche, and Nicolas Papadopoulos (2009), "Cosmopolitanism, Consumer Ethnocentrism, and Materialism: An Eight-Country Study of Antecedents and Outcomes," *Journal of International Marketing*, 17 (1), 116-46.

Holt, Douglas B. (1998), "Does Cultural Capital Structure American Consumption?," *Journal of Consumer Research*, 25 (1), 1-25.

Mick, David G. and Claus Buhl (1992), "A Meaning-Based Model of Advertising Experiences," *Journal of Consumer Research*, 19 (3), 317-38.

Thompson, Craig J. and Siok K. Tambyah (1999), "Trying to Be Cosmopolitan," *Journal of Consumer Research*, 26 (3), 214-41.

Wilk, Richard (1995), "Learning to Be Local in Belize: Global Systems of Common Difference," *Worlds Apart: Modernity Through the Prism of the Local*, 110-31.

# Evidence for Two Faces of Pride in Consumption: Findings From Luxury Brands

Brent McFerran, University of British Columbia, Canada
Karl Aquino, University of British Columbia, Canada
Jessica Tracy, University of British Columbia, Canada

## EXTENDED ABSTRACT

What is it that consumers feel when they adorn themselves with products that speak in the silent language of luxury, exclusiveness, and extravagance? Undoubtedly, one of the emotions experienced in such situations is pride. The *Oxford English Dictionary* defines pride as "a high or overweening opinion of one's own qualities, attainments, or estate, which gives rise to a feeling and attitude of superiority over and contempt for others." This definition is consistent with ancient Greek and Biblical thought condemning "excessive pride," or "hubris". However, recent research in psychology (e.g., Tracy and Robins 2007) has identified two distinct facets of pride.

The first cluster (authentic pride) includes words such as "accomplished" and "confident," and fits with the pro-social, achievement-oriented conceptualization of pride. The second cluster (hubristic pride) includes words such as "arrogant" and "conceited," and fits with a more self-aggrandizing, egotistical conceptualization. If people prone to experiencing hubristic pride are motivated to self-aggrandize and inflate an artificially positive sense of self, then they may be particularly motivated to consume luxury brands. Luxury brands convey a sense of status, wealth, and achievement (Chadha and Husband 2006; Mandel, Petrova, and Cialdini 2006), and thus may be a shorthand way of informing others (and the self) of one's high status, accomplishments, and even perfection. For such persons, luxury brand purchases can bolster their self-image in the absence of authentic achievement. They may use the purchase and display luxury brands as one way of maintaining these artificially inflated self-representations. In contrast, individuals prone to experiencing authentic pride should have less need for luxury brands, given that it is tied to actual hard work and achievements.

Study 1 employed a one factor design where 214 participants were randomly instructed to write a story about themselves in an episodic recall task (e.g., Galinsky, Gruenfeld, and Magee 2003) where they felt either snobbish (hubristic pride condition), accomplished (authentic pride condition), or a typical day (control condition). Results revealed that those primed with hubristic pride exhibited a significantly greater willingness to pay extra for luxury brands (M=3.47) than those primed with authentic pride (M=2.91, p=.03), or those in the control group (M=2.88, p=.02). The latter two conditions did not differ statistically. However, this study does not rule out the possibility that hubristic pride results in a generalized heightened desire to purchase *all* products, and treats each of the pride facets as only induced feelings, when research shows they are also chronic, dispositional states as well (Tracy and Robins 2007).

Study 2 utilized a survey design with 149 participants. All completed the Tracy and Robins (2007) Authentic and Hubristic pride scales, followed by unrelated items, and then their desire to purchase 3 luxury brands (Rolex, Lexus, Armani) as well as 3 non-luxury brands from the same category (Timex, Hyundai, Old Navy). Results showed that while hubristic pride was positively related to a desire to purchase luxury brands ($\beta$ =.42, p=.02), the relationship between trait authentic pride and a desire to acquire luxury brands was not significant ($\beta$ =.30, p>.20). When the brands were non-luxury, however, the relationship between hubristic pride and a desire to consume disappeared ($\beta$ =.11, ns), and again there was no relationship between authentic pride and a desire to consume ($\beta$ =-.09, ns).

Study 3 examined each facet of pride as a consequence, rather than an antecedent, of consumption. We tested the possibility that consumers will be more likely to experience a heightened feeling of hubristic pride from consuming a luxury rather than a non-luxury equivalent of the same product. However, their feelings of authentic pride should not be as strongly influenced by the brands they consume. 120 participants completed a survey that utilized a 2(brand: luxury vs. non-luxury) x 2(pride: authentic vs. hubristic) mixed experimental design, with the first factor manipulated between subjects and the second a repeated measures factor. The first factor was manipulated using an episodic recall task, where participants wrote a brief story about themselves involving a luxury (or non-luxury) brand. Results revealed the predicted brand x pride interaction (p=.01). Consistent with our hypothesis, while authentic pride was not affected by whether the product was a luxury (M=4.99) or non-luxury brand (M=4.69), people felt significantly more hubristic pride when they wrote about themselves consuming a luxury (M=3.24) than a non-luxury (M= 2.22) brand (p<.001).

Finally, Study 4 investigates the possibility that observers infer authentic and hubristic pride in others as a result of the product choices they make. We also propose that when people infer that a consumer experiences heightened hubristic pride, they may consequently assume that the consumer is also less prosocial. This prediction is based on the link between hubristic pride and various anti-social qualities (Tracy et al. 2009). 52 females participated in a study where they read a story actually completed by a former undergraduate student about her life in 5 years time, which was manipulated to contain a number of luxury or non-luxury brands. A mixed design ANOVA revealed the predicted brand x pride interaction (p<.001). Inferences of authentic pride were not affected by whether the products owned by the story's author were luxury (M=5.69) or non-luxury brands (5.73), but participants inferred that the author felt significantly more hubristic pride when she consumed luxury (M=4.10) rather than non-luxury (M=2.65) brands (p<.001). Results also showed that participants in the luxury condition judged the author to possess fewer pro-social personal qualities (concern for others/generous/ a good person/ cares for the environment) (M=3.79) than those in the non-luxury condition (M=4.46) (p<.01), and that hubristic (but not authentic) pride mediated the relationship between the other's brand choices and their social attractiveness.

This research provides the first evidence of the two-faced nature of pride in consumption settings. Further, we show that pride can serve as both an antecedent and consequence to consumption, provide the first evidence of which we are aware that people's inferences of others' pride experiences are shaped by their consumption preferences. Furthermore, these inferences are associated with decreased attribution of prosocial personal qualities in the consumer.

## REFERENCES

Chadha, Radha and Paul Husband (2006), *The Cult of the Luxury Brand: Inside Asia's Love Affair With Luxury*, London, UK: Nicholas Brealey International.

Galinsky, Adam D, Deborah H. Gruenfeld and Joe C. Magee (2003), "From Power to Action," *Journal of Personality and Social Psychology*, 85 (3), 453-466.

Mandel, Naomi, Petia K. Petrova, and Robert B Cialdini (2006), "Images of Success and the Preference for Luxury Brands," *Journal of Consumer Psychology*, 16 (1), 57-69.

Tracy, J. L., Joey T. Cheng, Richard W. Robins, & Kali Trzesniewski (2009), "Authentic and Hubristic Pride: The Affective Core of Self-Esteem and Narcissism," *Self and Identity*, 8 (2), 196-213.

Tracy, Jessica L. and Richard W. Robins (2007), "The Psychological Structure of Pride: A Tale of Two Facets," *Journal of Personality and Social Psychology, 92*, 506-525.

# Affective Sensory Regulation: A Framework for Understanding Affect Regulation via Sensory Regulation

Dan King, University of Florida, USA

## EXTENDED ABSTRACT

The author integrates emerging findings in the affective neurobiology and physical regulation literatures to propose *Affective Sensory Regulation*, a parsimonious framework to account for how consumers use physical sensations as visceral indicators in the process of affect regulation, causing them to prefer different kinds of products under different states. Using neural theories on how physical sensory perception is linked to affective circuits, it is proposed that different affective states induce different temperature tones, weight tones, speed tones, and brightness tones. First, affective states can have different temperature tones. Loneliness feels cold whereas frustration and anger feel hot; hence consumers under these states unconsciously prefer different products with different thermoregulatory tones. Second, affective states can have different weight tones. Anxiety and guilt feel heavy and relief feels light, hence consumers under these states prefer perceptually light soups when anxious, whereas consumers prefer rich soups when relieved. Third, affective states have different speed tones. Fear and anger have fast sensory-motor tones, whereas loneliness and despair have slow sensory-motor tones, hence consumers prefer advertising materials with different speed tones under different states. Fourth, affective states have different brightness tones. Interest has a bright tone, whereas pessimism has a dark tone, hence consumers prefer bright advertising materials when they are experiencing interest, whereas consumers prefer dark advertising materials when they are experiencing pessimism. The article also explores under what conditions consumers wish to maintain their affective temperature, weight, or brightness tones (even when they are aversive), and under what conditions consumers wish to change their affective temperature, weight, or brightness tones (even when they are pleasant).

# Dissociating Positive Emotions of Hope and Hopefulness and their Differential Impact on Consumer Financial Risk-Taking: A Functional Magnetic Resonance Imaging Study

Martin Reimann, University of Southern California, USA
Gergana Y. Nenkov, Boston College, USA
Deborah MacInnis, University of Southern California, USA
Maureen Morrin, Rutgers University, USA
Antoine Bechara, University of Southern California, USA

## EXTENDED ABSTRACT

The construct of hope has captured the interest of researchers in numerous fields, including psychology (Snyder 1994), sociology (Desroche 1979), medicine (Taylor 2000), theology (Moltmann 1983) as well as consumer and marketing research (e.g., Agrawal and Menon 2009; MacInnis and De Mello 2005; Passyn and Sujan 2006). As an emotion experienced in relation to future outcomes, hope has considerable relevance to understanding motivation and decision-making. This is so because choices are often guided by future outcomes individuals hope will happen. Without a doubt, the incorporation of future goals and outcomes is central to appraisal theories of emotion, which regard hope as an emotion emanating from appraisals of goal-congruent and desired outcomes whose future occurrence is appraised as uncertain but possible. Moreover, like other future-oriented emotions, such as fear, hope may be associated with distinct areas of brain activation, adding to our knowledge of emotion-brain-behavior linkages. Despite the potential value of the hope construct, however, hope is a relatively understudied emotion (Lazarus 1991).

Prior research on hope reveals subtle but important differences in the definition of hope. Appraisal theories of emotion (Frijda, Kuipers, and Ter Schure 1989; Roseman 1991; Smith and Ellsworth 1985) characterize hope as an emotion that arises from assessments of outcomes viewed as compatible with one's goals (i.e., goal-congruent), yearned for (i.e., desirable), and uncertain but possible. Characterizing hope along these appraisal dimensions is useful as it helps to distinguish hope from other emotions such as fear, disgust, pride, and happiness, as well as from potentially related constructs like expectation, involvement, wishing, and faith (MacInnis and Chun 2007). Although the aforementioned appraisals characterize the emotion of hope, hope has not been consistently defined in the literature (MacInnis and Chun 2007; MacInnis and De Mello 2005). Specifically, although various definitions entail the above-noted appraisal dimensions, definitional variants have emphasized different appraisal dimensions.

The current research addresses this issue and contributes to the literature in several important ways. First, we contribute to the emerging *literature on hope* by conceptually and empirically differentiating two positive emotions, "hope" and "hopefulness," which are oftentimes used interchangeably. This differentiation clarifies definitional inconsistencies in the literature on hope. These constructs entail the same underlying appraisals described above, but they involve *variation* on different appraisal dimensions. *Hope* varies with the degree of yearning for (or desirability of) a future outcome. *Hopefulness*, in contrast, varies with the degree to which the future outcome is seen as more (vs. less) likely (hence is seen as less (vs. more) uncertain), and is defined as the extent to which one appraises a goal-congruent and yearned possible outcome as more or less likely (or less vs. more uncertain). With this construct, what varies is not how much the goal-congruent outcome is yearned for, but rather how certain or uncertain the goal-congruent outcome is appraised to be. People become more (or less) hopeful about a yearned for and possible goal-congruent outcome as *likelihood estimates* of the outcome rise (or decline).

Second, we show that distinguishing hope and hopefulness is important because these constructs have distinct effects on consumer financial decision-making. We demonstrate this distinctiveness here by showing their unique effects on *decision-making under risk*.

Third, we contribute to the literature on the *neural underpinnings of emotions* (Damasio 1994, 1999), showing that hope and hopefulness activate distinct areas of the brain when consumers make financial decisions involving risk. We find that hope is linked to activation of the insula, the prefrontal cortex, and anterior cingulate, areas of the brain previously linked to yearning and risk aversion. Hopefulness, in contrast, is linked to activation of the nucleus accumbens, globus pallidus, and caudate, brain regions previously linked to appraisals of likelihood and risk taking behavior.

In the present study, we found that hope and hopefulness recruit different neural processes when anticipating financial choice. We observed distinct neural patterns of activation for the two emotions; patterns which are consistent with our framework and past literature. These results further establish the notion that hope and hopefulness are discrete constructs that are differentially related to risk-taking.

We add to past research on the neural underpinnings of discrete emotions. Our results suggest that two emotions—hope and hopefulness— indeed have distinct neural patterns. While increased activation in the insula, the prefrontal cortex (particularly, the medial frontal gyrus), and the anterior cingulate was identified when participants were hoping, in states of hopefulness increased activations were found in the nucleus accumbens, the globus pallidus, and the caudate as well as decreased activation was identified in the prefrontal cortex (in particular, the gyrus rectus). These findings extend prior research by shedding more light on discrete emotions, their neural mechanisms, and behavioral effects on consumer financial decision making.

## REFERENCES

Agrawal, N. and G. Menon (2009), "Harboring Hopefulness and Avoiding Anxiety: The Role of Uncertain Emotions in the Effectiveness of Health Messages," Northwestern University, Evanston, IL.

Damasio, Antonio R. (1994), *Descartes' Error: Emotion, Reason, and the Human Brain*, New York, NY: Putnam.

— (1999), *The Feeling of What Happens: Body and Emotion in the Making of Consciousness*, Chicago, IL: Harcourt.

Desroche, H. (1979), *The Sociology of Hope*, Boston, MA: Routledge/Thoemms Press.

Frijda, N. H., P. Kuipers, and E. Ter Schure (1989), "Relations among Emotion, Appraisal, and Emotional Action Readiness," *Journal of Personality and Social Psychology*, 57 (2), 212-28.

Lazarus, R. S. (1991), *Emotion and Adaptation*, New York, NY: Oxford University Press.

MacInnis, D. J. and H. E. Chun (2007), "Understanding Hope and Its Implications for Consumer Behavior: I Hope, Therefore I Consume," *Foundations and Trends in Marketing*, 1 (2), 97-189.

MacInnis, D. J. and G. E. De Mello (2005), "The Concept of Hope and Its Relevance to Product Evaluation and Choice," *Journal of Marketing*, 69 (1), 1-14.

Moltmann, J. (1983), *Theology of Hope*, London: SCM Press.

Passyn, K. and M. Sujan (2006), "Self-Accountability Emotions and Fear Appeals: Motivating Behavior," *Journal of Consumer Research*, 32 (4), 583-89.

Roseman, I. J. (1991), "Appraisal Determinants of Discrete Emotions," *Cognition & Emotion*, 5 (3), 161-200.

Smith, C. A. and P. C. Ellsworth (1985), "Patterns of Cognitive Appraisal in Emotion," *Journal of Personality and Social Psychology*, 48 (4), 813-38.

Snyder, C. R. (1994), *The Psychology of Hope*, New York, NY: Free Press.

Taylor, J. D. (2000), "Confronting Breast Cancer: Hopes for Health," in *Handbook of Hope: Theory, Measures, and Applications*, ed. C. R. Snyder, New York, NY: Academic Press, 355-71.

# Neural Structures of Emotional Responses to Television Commercials: A Functional Magnetic Resonance Imaging Study

Feng Shen, Saint Joseph's University, USA
Jon Morris, University of Florida, USA

## EXTENDED ABSTRACT

No study to date has directly compared the discrete and dimensional approaches of emotional responses to advertising from a neurobiological perspective. We took the initiative to address this issue, and discovered a prefrontal-temporal cortical circuitry that corresponded to a pleasure-arousal response system in modeling emotions in television commercials.

## INTRODUCTION

A rich consumer behavior literature indicates that emotion in advertising can be classified into a spectrum of discrete categories or identified in a multidimensional space, and preference is given to the dimensional approach, more specifically the pleasure-arousal-dominance (PAD) model (Mehrabian and Russell 1974). The most important support for the dimensional approach comes from Havlena and Holbrook's (1986) consumption experience study. Havlena and Holbrook (1986) found that the PAD dimensions exhibited higher reliability and validity in explaining consumption-related emotions than did the emotion categories from Plutchik's (1980) Emotion Profile Index. Nevertheless, this evidence turned out to be quite tenuous when Richins (1997) noted that emotional experiences with consumption were significantly different from emotional responses to advertising.

The advent of cognitive neuroscience brings consumer behavior researchers an unprecedented opportunity to reassess many of the important topics in marketing (Yoon, Gonzalez, and Bettman 2009). This article is the beginning of a process to reinvestigate the relative advantages between the discrete and dimensional emotion models in advertising with neuroimaging technology, particularly functional magnetic resonance imaging (fMRI).

## LITERATURE REVIEW AND HYPOTHESES

In essence, the concept of discrete emotions reflects a Darwinian approach to emotions, which seeks evolutionarily fundamental emotions to define all emotional experiences (Darwin 1872/1965). According to this approach, there is a finite set of basic emotions that are innate to all human beings across various cultures and development stages, and certain pattern or combination of these basic emotions results in the experience of emotion (Plutchik 1980). Nevertheless, the status of an emotion as basic is often proposed on grounds, such as frequency-related salience in Western culture and levels in an emotional hierarchy, that are irrelevant to whether the emotion is biologically or psychologically primitive (Ortony and Turner 1990).

Despite all these concerns over the validity of this approach, a majority of the current neuroimaging studies still focuses on identifying distinctive brain activations for each basic emotion (Posner, Russell, and Peterson 2005). It turned out that one basic emotion can activate multiple brain regions and one brain region can be activated by multiple basic emotions, so it could be largely futile to seek an exact link between one brain region and one basic emotion (Barrett and Wager 2006). Furthermore, studies of the discrete approach essentially require respondents to recognize stimuli as belonging to certain emotion categories (Mackay 1980). This requirement itself produces neural activities that contaminate natural brain responses to emotions.

A better framework of emotional response in the brain should be a system perspective that endeavors to identify hardwired neural circuitry for emotional response systems rather than individual emotions (Ortony and Turner 1990). This neural circuitry should be composed of a set of brain regions activated by both sensory experience and information processing of emotional stimuli, and the exact structure of the circuitry varies by the characteristics of a stimulus (Barrett and Wager 2006).

The dimensional approach to emotions or the PAD model conceptually fits this alternative system perspective. Compared to the discrete approach, the PAD model essentially posits an emotional response system composed of three dimensions, and all individual emotions can be quantitatively identified with their positions along the three dimensions (Mehrabian and Russell 1974). Previous research suggests that three brain regions, the amygdala, prefrontal cortex and temporal cortex, are likely to be associated with emotional responses to television commercials. Together with findings at the gyrus level of these regions (Decety and Chaminade 2003; Morris et al. 1998; Morris et al. 1996; Morris, Scott, and Dolan 1999), it was hypothesized:

**H1:** Emotional responses to television commercials activate the amygdala, prefrontal cortex, and temporal cortex.

**H2:** The inferior frontal gyrus and middle temporal gyrus are activated by the pleasure dimension of the emotional responses.

**H3:** The superior frontal gyrus and superior temporal gyrus are activated by the arousal dimension of the emotional responses.

## EMPIRICAL EVIDENCE

Our arguments above led to a recent neuroimaging study with our colleagues in neuroscience (Morris et al. 2009). Respondents watched television commercials inside of a scanner, and their emotional responses included both BOLD signals recorded through fMRI and self-reported feelings on the pleasure, arousal and dominance dimensions.

Our analysis indicated activation of the prefrontal and temporal cortices by both pleasure and arousal. But we were unable to find activation in the amygdala. Hypothesis 1 was partially supported. Further investigation of the activations in the prefrontal and temporal cortices led to the selection of the bilateral inferior frontal gyri and bilateral middle temporal gyri for the pleasure dimension. Hypothesis 2 was supported. We were also able to identify the bilateral middle frontal gyrus and right superior temporal gyrus for the arousal dimension, but the activation of the superior frontal gyrus was insignificant. Hypothesis 3 was partially supported.

## DISCUSSION AND CONCLUSION

No study to date has directly compared the discrete and dimension approaches to emotions in advertising from a neurobiological perspective. We took the initiative to address this issue, and discovered a prefrontal-temporal cortical circuitry that corresponded to a pleasure-arousal response system in modeling emotions in television commercials.

Neuroscientists traditionally use sensory stimuli without or with limited social cues in imaging studies on emotion. Our selection of television commercials substantially enriches this line of research. Brain systems are known to function differently depending on the characteristics of social stimuli (Hietanen et al. 2006), and these differences can be further explained at the behavioral level by social contextual research from advertising scholars (Forehand, Deshpandé, and Reed 2002). Our research can also lead to a paradigm shift in neuroscience. Although an increasing number of researchers are questioning the concept of basic emotions and the existence of distinct brain regions of these emotions, these researchers did not provide enough empirical evidence to support an alternative model and the discrete approach still dominates the neuroimaging research of emotion. We advocate the use of the dimensional PAD model, and our preference is supported by the successful identification of the prefrontal-temporal cortical circuitry of the pleasure-arousal response system.

# How the Order of Information About an Experiential Product Impacts Affective Evaluation

Keith Wilcox, Babson College, USA
Anne Roggeveen, Babson College, USA
Dhruv Grewal, Babson College, USA

## EXTENDED ABSTRACT

In three experiments, this research demonstrates that when favorable product information is presented before sampling an experiential product it leads to an assimilation effect and more positive affective evaluations. However, when favorable information is presented after sampling it results in a contrast effect and more negative affective evaluations.

Numerous studies have demonstrated that product information, such as its price or brand name, learned prior to experiencing a product can affect consumers' expectations, which can, in turn, influence their product evaluations (Klaaren, Hodges and Wilson 1994). Less is known, however, how learning such information after the initial product experience affects consumers' evaluations. This current research examines whether product information learned before or after sampling an experiential product will lead to differences in consumers' evaluation of the experience.

Experiential products have affective, sensory and informational components (Nowlis and Shiv 2005). Importantly, when consumers sample experiential products, the affective component carries more weight than the informational component (Biswas, Grewal and Roggeveen 2010). One of the key differences between these components is that the affective and sensory components are based on reactions that arise from the experience and occur automatically; whereas the informational component is based on controlled processes (Nowlis and Shiv 2005). Based on assimilation and contrast theory (e.g., Stapel and Winkielman 1998), we expect the automatic formation of affective evaluations to result in differences in affective evaluations when information is received before or after a product is experienced.

One of factor that decides whether contextual information results in assimilation or contrast is how distinct the information is from the target being judged (Stapel and Winkielman 1998). Distinctness is often determined by the extent to which the information is evaluated with the target being judged or presented separate from the evaluation. For example, Martin and Seta (1983) showed that if descriptions of two persons were given and participants were asked to read about both before forming their evaluations, the impression of the target person was assimilated towards the contextual person. In contrast, when participants were asked to form separate evaluations of the target person and the contextual person, the impression of the target was contrasted with the context. This is because the separate evaluations lead the context to serve as a comparison standard when judging the target.

For somatosensory experiences if information is received prior to experiencing the product, then we expect assimilation of the experience towards the product information. This is because, knowing that they will be experiencing the product immediately, people are not expected to judge the product on the product information alone. Instead, judgments are expected to occur after both the product information and the experience have occurred resulting in judgments being assimilated towards the contextual information. However, if product information is received after the experience, then we expect contrast to occur for affective judgments. This is based on the fact that affective judgments occur automatically (Nowlis and Shiv 2005). After experiencing the good, the consumer is expected to automatically think about how much they liked the taste. This will lead subsequent contextual information to be distinct from the experience and serve as a comparison standard.

More formally, we hypothesize that when product information is presented before sampling an experiential product, it will result in an assimilation effect such that consumers' affective evaluations of the experience will by more (less) favorable when the information signals a good (poor) experience. However, when the same information is presented after sampling, it will result in a contrast effect for affective evaluations such that consumers' affective evaluation of the experience will be less (more) favorable when the information signals a good (poor) experience.

We test this prediction in three studies. In study 1, participants were asked to sample a piece of chocolate before or after being told the chocolate was from either Switzerland (favorable experience) or China (unfavorable experience). Even though the sampled chocolate was the same in all conditions, consistent with an assimilation effect, participants' affective evaluation was higher when they thought the chocolate was from Switzerland (vs. China) prior to sampling. Interestingly, and in line with our prediction, when the country-of-origin was presented after sampling, but before the formal evaluation, participants' affective evaluation was higher when they thought the chocolate was from China (vs. Switzerland).

The second study replicated the findings using price as the product information. Specifically, we found that when price was presented prior to sampling, participants' affective evaluation was higher when they thought the chocolate was expensive (vs. inexpensive). However, when the price was presented after sampling participants' affective evaluation was higher when they thought the chocolate was inexpensive (vs. expensive). Interestingly, when participants were given a price discrediting cue, price had no effect on participants' evaluations.

In the third study, we only focused on the after sampling conditions. However, instead of presenting participants with information about the chocolate, we made an enjoyable chocolate experience salient. The results, replicated those in the previous studies. Specifically, we found that when an enjoyable experience was made salient after sampling, participants rated the chocolate more negatively, compared to when a less enjoyable product experience was made salient.

These results have important implications for both retailers and market researchers who are actively engage in sampling programs in a host of sensory categories ranging from food, beverages, videos, music and perfumes. More specifically, for high-end products, our results suggest that it is important to convey that information (e.g., price, brand, country-of-origin) prior to the participant sampling the merchandise. The reverse order would be preferable for products that have less favorable cues (e.g., a wonderful tasting chocolate that is made in China).

## REFERENCES

Biswas, Dipayan, Grewal, Dhruv, Roggeveen, Anne (2010), "How the Order of Sampled Experiential Products Affects Choice," *Journal of Marketing Research*, forthcoming.

Klaaren, Kristen J., Sara D. Hodges and Timothy D. Wilson (1994), "The Role of Affective Expectations in Subjective Experience and Decision-Making," *Social Cognition*, 12(2), 77-101.

Martin, Leonard L. and John J.Seta (1983), "Perceptions of Unity and Distinctiveness as Determinants of Attraction," *Journal of Personality and Social Psychology*, 44, 755-64.

Nowlis, Stephen and Baba Shiv (2005), "The Influence of Consumer Distractions on the Effectiveness of Food-Sampling Programs," *Journal of Marketing Research*, 42 (2), 57-168.

Stapel, Diederik A. and Piotr Winkielman (1998), "Assimilation and Contrast as a Function of Context-Target Similarity, Distinctness, and Dimensional Relevance," *Personality and Social Psychology Bulletin*, 24 (6), 634-46.

# Your Life or Your Money:  Threat Revision in Response to Taboo Trade-offs

Adriana Samper, Duke University, USA
Janet Schwartz, Duke University, USA

## EXTENDED ABSTRACT:

Consumer-driven healthcare is increasingly relied upon as a strategy to curb rising healthcare costs. A key assumption is that by making consumers both more aware of cost, the healthcare market will become more efficient. However, this rationale fails to consider that consumers often reject trade-offs that treat "sacred values," such as health and life, as fungible entities that can be traded for money (Fiske and Tetlock 1997). In reality, such taboo trade-offs often lead to moral outrage (Tetlock et al. 2000) and evoke negative emotion (e.g., Haidt and Algoe 2004). In fact, given the opportunity, people are motivated to avoid taboo trade-offs altogether (Tetlock, 2003). In this research, we show price transparency has the unintended consequence of influencing consumers' risk perceptions, and does so in a manner distinct from other contexts that involve risk but not taboo trade-offs. Consistent with consumers' desire to avoid negative emotion (Luce 1998), we propose that, when facing high prices for health goods, consumers avoid making complete trade-offs between health and money by downplaying the perceived threat of disease.

To first test this hypothesis we presented a web-based sample of adults with a short passage about a new vaccine for the H1N1 pandemic. Participants were told that the vaccine would cost them either $10 or $250 and were then asked to rate the seriousness of the H1N1 threat (perceived threat). Participants in the $250 condition rated the perceived threat significantly lower than those in the $10 condition, demonstrating that price influences the perceived threat of a negative health event.

In Study 2, we examined whether this pattern was driven by a reluctance to confront taboo trade-offs by asking people about perceived threats at different price points across "taboo" (health) and "non-taboo" (electronics) domains. We also examined the extent to which threat perceptions were influenced by whether or not consumers were responsible for the cost. A web-based sample of adults participated in this 2 (price: low ($10) vs. high ($250)) vs. x 2 (payer: self vs. insurance) x 2 (domain: sacred (health) vs. secular (electronics)) experiment. Participants read either a similar passage about the threat of H1N1 flu from Study 1 or a passage about the threat of electronics damage due to strong summer thunderstorms. They were told that the vaccine (high powered surge protector) was available for either $10 or $250 and that this preventive product was either covered or not covered by insurance. Participants then rated how serious they perceived the threat of H1N1 flu (storm-induced electronics damage) to be and the extent to which they felt that the price for the vaccine (surge protector) was fair.

The results revealed a 3-way interaction on both perceived threat and price fairness. While those in the H1N1 flu condition downgraded the perceived threat from $10 to $250 (regardless of payer), those in the electronics damage condition only downgraded the threat when they bore the cost themselves. In fact, individuals in the electronics damage condition directionally increased the perceived threat when insurance took on the cost. Perceived price fairness revealed a similar pattern of results whereby individuals in the H1N1 condition found the $250 cost marginally more fair if insurance was paying, while individuals in the electronics condition found the $250 to be significantly more fair if insurance was paying. Further analyses examining the impact of price on perceived threat in the insurance conditions (isolating responses to those of the mere comparison between the health (consumer) good and money) revealed a significant moderated mediation, whereby the perceived fairness of the trade-off mediated the effect of price on

perceived threat in the health insurance condition, but not in the electronics insurance condition. These results suggest that the perceived unfairness of making a trade-off between health and money leads to a reduction in perceived threat. Thus, in the sacred health domain, any price information leads to risk revision, while in the secular consumer goods domain, risk revision only occurs when individuals are paying out of pocket.

Finally, in Study 3, we extended this work to disease screening and examined how high price may move beyond threat to impact health care consumption. A web-based sample of female participants participated in this 2 (payer: self vs. insurance) x 2 (price: $800 vs. $15) experiment. Participants were informed that due to recent evidence questioning the effectiveness of mammograms for women under 50, to imagine that insurance coverage for the test had changed. As a result, an upcoming mammogram would cost $800 ($15) and would (not) be covered by insurance. Participants then rated the perceived seriousness of the threat of breast cancer, as well as the likelihood of getting a mammogram. As in Study 2, results revealed only a main effect of high price reducing perceived threat relative to low price, regardless of payer. For perceived likelihood of getting a mammogram, however, the results revealed a significant payer by price interaction. Reflecting the current reality, individuals were more likely to get a mammogram when the cost was covered by insurance than when it was paid of out of pocket. However, within the insurance conditions, individuals were less likely to get a mammogram if the cost was $800 covered by insurance than if it were $15 covered by insurance. These results suggest that high price of screening reduces both the perceived threat of illness and the likelihood of getting screened. This takes place regardless of payer, such that high prices, regardless of who pays, affect perceptions of risk and the willingness to consume healthcare.

Taken together, these findings have important implications for communications and price transparency in consumer health decisions. We see that high price may actually lead to falsely deflated threat of illness as well as reduced consumption of care, independent of who is paying for the care. Given upcoming changes that may take place in the health care space involving increased price transparency as well as increased health care coverage, it is important to understand the potential influences of these changes on risk perceptions and behavior to improve consumer health decisions and outcomes.

# Promoting the Effective Use of Counterfactual Generation to Tackle Negative Consumption

Candy K. Y. Ho, Hong Kong Baptist University, Hong Kong, China
Jessica Y. Y. Kwong, The Chinese University of Hong kong, China

## EXTENDED ABSTRACT

Negative consumption (e.g., having a car accident or missing a flight), like negative life events, are inevitable to consumers. To help consumers to tackle negative consumption is therefore imperative to consumer research. This research explores how the generation of counterfactual thoughts may help consumers to tackle negative consumption.

Counterfactual thoughts are imaginations of how the negative consumption might have turned out differently. Extant literature suggests that certain types of counterfactual thoughts appear more helpful to tackle negative consumption than the others. Specifically, recent research (Ho and Kwong 2009) has made a distinction between counterfactuals that are process-focused (i.e., thoughts that focus on the process or actions that might have led to a better consumption outcome) or outcome-focused (i.e., thoughts that elaborate on the benefits that might have brought by the better consumption outcome). It is demonstrated that while process-focused counterfactuals better help consumers to tackle problems with the consumption, outcome-focused counterfactuals induce stronger negative feelings. These findings establish that, by generating process- but not outcome-focused counterfactuals, consumers can learn how to tackle negative consumption without hurting their feelings. Importantly, however, research to date has not addressed how we may promote generating process- but not outcome-focused counterfactuals.

In this research, we aim to identify the factors that promote the generation of process- and outcome-focused counterfactuals. First, we propose that consumption repeatability, or how likely consumers expect they will be in similar consumption situations again, will promote the generation of process- but not outcome-focused counterfactuals. Consumers who perceive the consumption situation to be more repeatable are more motivated to find out the ways of getting better outcomes (Markman et al. 1993). This increased motivation is likely to promote the generation of process-focused counterfactuals, which provide information on what corrective actions might have led to a better outcome. This corrective information will help consumers to pursue better outcomes next time they are in similar consumption situations. Outcome-focused counterfactuals, however, focus on how much better off consumers would have been had they had a better outcome. These elaborations do not provide corrective information and therefore do not serve the motivation to excel. Therefore consumption repeatability is expected to increase the amount of process- relative to outcome-focused counterfactuals generated by consumers.

Second, we argue that outcome closeness will promote the generation of outcome- but not process-focused counterfactuals. Outcome closeness relates to how close consumers perceive they have missed a better consumption outcome. Compared with those who missed by a great deal, consumers who missed closely a better outcome are likely to have a stronger belief that they should have got that outcome (Kahneman and Varey 1990). Thus they are more likely to elaborate on how better off their consumption outcome would have been. Elaborations of this kind amount to outcome-focused counterfactuals. These consumers, however, who assume that they have got a better outcome, should pay less attention to the means to getting that outcome. Therefore, outcome closeness is proposed to increase the amount of outcome- relative to process-focused counterfactuals generated by consumers.

In addition, this research also examine whether consumption repeatability and outcome closeness would influence consumers' ability to tackle negative consumption and the role the amount of process- and outcome-focused counterfactuals played in it. It is predicted that consumption repeatability will increase consumers' ability to solve consumption problems and that such effect will be driven by the relative amount of process-focused counterfactuals it induces. Similarly, we predict that outcome closeness will intensify negative feelings and that such effect will be driven by the relative amount of outcome-focused counterfactuals it induces.

We conducted an experiment to test these predictions. The experiment used a 2 (consumption repeatability) x 2 (outcome closeness) between-subjects design. The participants, who were undergraduate students, were asked to participate in a game to win prizes. The study manipulated consumption repeatability (no-repeat vs. repeat) by telling the participants that they would play the game three times (the repeaters) or one time (the non-repeaters). Winners would receive real prizes. However, the game was set such that all participants lost in the first time they played. Outcome closeness (far-miss vs. close-miss) was manipulated by varying how close the participants might have won the game in the first round, such that the close-missers missed the chance to win more closely than did the far-missers. After playing the game once, the participants generated counterfactuals related to their losing in the game and reported their feelings about losing in the game.

In addition, be unknown to the non-repeaters, they were also invited to play the game one more time at the end of the study. The study compared the second round performances of the repeaters and that of the non-repeaters.

Supporting our predictions related to consumption repeatability, results indicated that: (1) the repeaters (vs. the non-repeaters) reported a higher proportion of process- to outcome-focused counterfactuals; (2) the repeaters outperformed the non-repeaters in the second round of game, and this differential performance was explained by the relative amount of process-focused counterfactuals they generated. Similarly, consistent with our predictions related to outcome closeness, we found that: (1) the close-missers (vs. the far-missers) reported a higher proportion of outcome- to process-focused counterfactuals; (2) the close-missers (vs. the far-missers) felt more negative about losing in the game, and such difference was mediated by the relative amount of outcome-focused counterfactuals they generated.

To conclude, this research show that (1) consumption repeatability increases the amount of process- relative to outcome-focused counterfactuals consumers generated, which in turn increases consumers' ability to tackle problems in a subsequent consumption, and that (2) outcome closeness increases the amount of outcome-relative to process-focused counterfactuals consumers generated, which in turn intensifies consumers' negative feelings about the current outcome. These findings implies we can promote the generation of process-focused counterfactuals, those that help tackle problems, while suppressing the generation of outcome-focused counterfactuals, those that are painful to consumers. We believe this knowledge is important to consumer well-being because this helps consumers to draw useful lessons from imaginations that are not painful and saves them from repeatedly experiencing negative consumption outcomes.

# Angels and Demons: The Differential Effects of Less Threatening Food Temptations on Consumption

Nina Belei, Maastricht University, The Netherlands
Kelly Geyskens, Maastricht University, The Netherlands
Caroline Goukens, Maastricht University, The Netherlands
Jos Lemmink, Maastricht University, The Netherlands

## EXTENDED ABSTRACT

This research examines whether and under which conditions less threatening food temptations (e.g., heart-healthy chips and low-fat chips) are effective in promoting food intake control. We demonstrate the differential effects of temptations with health references and temptations with low-fat references.

## Conceptualization

Literature provides conflicting findings regarding the effects of food temptations on consumers' abilities to control their food intake. While it was generally accepted that tempting food cues trigger self-control failure, recent research suggests that temptations may have the potential to enhance self-control if the temptations exceed a critical level of threat (Fishbach, Friedman, and Kruglanski 2003; Geyskens, Dewitte, Pandelaere, and Warlop 2008). Yet, instead of increasing the perceived level of threat of food temptations (e.g., by making food enticements even more alluring), health organizations continue to encourage the dissemination of less threatening food alternatives.

Our research examines whether and under which conditions food temptations for which the perceived level of threat is reduced are effective in promoting food intake control. In a series of experiments we compare the effects of hedonic food with low-fat references to hedonic food with health references. In contrast to low-fat hedonic food alternatives stressing the reduced amount of something 'bad' (e.g. less fat), healthier versions of hedonic food often directly refer to a long-term health goal, thereby emphasizing the 'good' aspects of the food. In line with prior research, we expect that low-fat references on highly tempting, yet unhealthy food lead to self-control failure expressed in overconsumption of that food. Contrarily, when an unhealthy yet tempting food is made less threatening by making an explicit link to consumers' long-term health goals, we expect self-control to be enhanced, as a result of the activation of a health goal. This, in turn, should induce health-goal relevant behavior, which is reflected in decreased consumption of the food in question, as well as of other unhealthy food. Moreover, this activated health goal should result in an increased consumption if it results from health references for an inherently healthy food.

## Studies

In a first study (N=109) we examine whether healthier (versus low-fat) versions of hedonic food decrease (versus increase) actual food consumption. The results reveal that only temptations with a direct link to consumers' long-term health goals lead to a significant decrease in actual food consumption, thereby effectively enhancing self-control. We observe the same increase in actual consumption as was found by Wansink and Chandon (2006) for hedonic food with low-fat references. In a second study (N=130), we show that the decreased consumption of healthier hedonic food appears to be driven by an increased activation of one's health goals triggered by the health reference on the food. Seeing healthier versions of hedonic food through the lens of the activated health goal leads to less consumption of this food because it remains unhealthy in nature and thus does not contribute to attaining the activated health goal. Contrarily, no such health goal activation was found for hedonic food with low-fat references implying that the increased consumption of low-fat hedonic food alternatives seems to be attributable to an implicit license to eat often associated with low-fat food. We continue with focusing on the dynamics of health references on hedonic food and demonstrate in a third study (N=62) that we find the same effects of healthier temptations when consumers subsequently consume another food item of the unhealthy product category. We replicate this effect in study 4a (N=55) and 4b (N=52) in which we switch from hedonic food to hedonic beverages. To finally challenge the robustness of the underlying mechanism, we conducted a fifth and final study (N=84), in which we show that health references on healthy food are able to increase the consumption of that healthier food.

## Summary and Contribution

Together, the results illustrate the differential effects of low-fat references and health references on hedonic food. Both low-fat references and health references aim at making the respective food appear less threatening to consumers' long-term goals. Yet, we demonstrate the counter effect of health references in that instead of reducing the level of threat of the healthier hedonic food, the activation of a health goal lets consumers reassess the food as being helpful to attain the activated health goal or not. As the healthier hedonic food still remains unhealthy in nature, it is considered as inappropriate for attaining the activated health goal. Consequently, consumers eat less of it than they would of a regular version of a hedonic food. Thereby, our study provides clarity on the question to what extent the recent hedonic food alternatives promoted by health organizations are successful in stimulating more healthy eating patterns. Our study contributes to existing literature in that we provide evidence that also a less threatening food temptation can increase self-control if the food is directly linked to a long-term health goal. As such, we complement the research by Fishbach et al. (2003) by demonstrating that the combination of a less threatening food temptation with a health reference enhances self-control as well. Our findings have strong implications for food manufacturers in that we show that the strategy to offer healthier alternatives of inherently unhealthy food might end up having a counter effect as consumers will be careful in not eating too much of such food. In contrast, we demonstrate that adding health references on inherently healthy food can increase consumption up to 50 %, implying that food manufacturers would reap benefits if they remind consumers on the healthiness of inherently healthy food. For public policy makers our findings imply that not all marketing efforts aimed at decreasing the level of threat of unhealthy, yet tempting food have negative consequences for consumers' eating patterns. While we again show the detrimental effects of low-fat references on food intake, we demonstrate the positive outcomes of health references in terms of consumption regardless of whether they are put on unhealthy or healthy food. As such, stressing the positive, healthy aspects of food appears to be an effective strategy for promoting more healthy eating patterns.

**References**

Coelho Do Vale, Rita, Rik Pieters, and Marcel Zeelenberg (2008), "Flying under the radar: Perverse Package Size Effects on Consumption Self-Regulation," *Journal of Consumer Research*, 35 (October), 380-90.

Critser, Greg (2003), *Fat Land: How Americans became the fattest People in the World*. New York: Mariner/Houghton Mifflin.

Fazio, Russell H. (1990), "A practical guide to the use of response latencies in social psychological research," in *Review of personality and social psychology*, C. Hendrick and M.S. Clark, eds. Vol. 11. Newbury Park CA: Sage.

Ferguson, Melissa J. (2008), "On becoming ready to pursue a goal you don't know you have: Effects of nonconscious goals on evaluative readiness," *Journal of Personality and Social Psychology*, 95 (6), 1268-94.

Ferguson, Melissa J. and J. A. Bargh (2004), "Liking is for doing: Effects of goal pursuit on automatic evaluation," *Journal of Personality and Social Psychology*, 88, 557-72.

Fishbach, Ayelet, Ronald S. Friedman, and Arie W. Kruglanski (2003), "Leading us not unto temptation: Momentary allurements elicit overriding goal activation," *Journal of Personality and Social Psychology*, 84, 296-309.

Geyskens, Kelly, Siegfried Dewitte, Mario Pandelaere, and Luk Warlop (2008), "Tempt me just a little bit more: The effects of prior food temptation actionability on goal activation and consumption," *Journal of Consumer Research*, 35 (December), 600-10.

National Institutes of Health (2004), "*Weight Loss and Nutrition Myths*," accessed January 2010, www.win.niddk.nih.gov/publications/myths.html#dietmyths).

Nestle (2002), *Food Politics: How the Food Industry Influences Nutrition and Health*. Berkley: University of California Press.

Raghunathan, Rajagopal, Rebecca Walker Naylor, and Wayne D. Hoyer (2006), "The unhealthy=tasty intuition and its effects on taste inferences, enjoyment, and choice of food products," *Journal of Marketing*, 70 (October), 170-84.

Wansink, Brian and Pierre Chandon (2006), "Can "low-fat" nutrition labels lead to obesity?" *Journal of Marketing Research*, XLIII (November), 605-17.

# The Obesity Superhighway: An I³ Theory Analysis of Unhealthy Food Consumption

Eli Finkel, Northwestern University, USA
Kenneth Herbst, Wake Forest University, USA
Gráinne Fitzsimons, Duke University, USA

## EXTENDED ABSTRACT

This paper approaches obesity from a psychological perspective, exploring the circumstances under which people eat moderately versus excessively when they confront an unexpected opportunity to consume fattening, unhealthy food. In this paper, we introduce a novel meta-theory designed to provide a process-oriented, integrative framework for organizing these risk factors.

According to I³ Theory (pronounced "I-Cubed Theory"), individuals will overeat unhealthy food when Instigating triggers are strong, Impelling forces are strong, and Inhibiting forces are weak. (The underlined vowels represent the three Is in I³ Theory.) *Instigating triggers* are situational events or circumstances that induce a behavioral inclination toward unhealthy consumption (e.g., the degree to which the consumer is focused on the viscerally enticing aspects of the food or whether the presence of other people triggers moderate versus excessive consumption). *Impelling forces* consist of factors that strengthen the consummatory craving individuals experience in response to an instigating trigger (e.g., hunger or liking for the food). *Inhibiting forces* consist of factors that increase the likelihood that consumers will override the craving to eat the food rather than to act upon this craving (e.g., plentiful self-control resources or an imminent life event for which the consumer wishes to look relatively thin). According to I³ Theory, risk factors predict unhealthy consumption not only on their own, but also in interaction with risk factors from the other I³ Theory categories. Unhealthy consumption is most extreme when instigating triggers and impelling forces are strong and inhibiting forces are weak.

In this paper, we examined the effects of two different instigating triggers, one impelling factor, and one inhibiting factor. The instigating trigger in Study 1 (conducted in a supermarket) was whether consumers were assigned to think about the food (cinnamon rolls) in terms of its appealing gustatory (visceral) properties or in terms of its nongustatory (non-visceral) basic ingredients (Mischel, Shoda, and Rodriguez 1989). The viscerality manipulation was effective. Shoppers in the visceral condition ate significantly more grams of cinnamon roll than did shoppers in the focused nonvisceral condition and the no-instructions condition.

To test I³ Theory, we predicted grams of cinnamon roll eaten from the viscerality manipulation, self-reported hunger and depletion, all two-way interactions, and the three-way interaction. Consistent with predictions, the Viscerality x Hunger x Depletion interaction effect was significant. Simple effects tests revealed that the Hunger x Depletion interaction effect was not significant in the nonvisceral condition, but it was significant in the visceral condition. Follow-up simple effects tests revealed that, within the visceral condition, the association of hunger with grams eaten was not significant for shoppers who were not feeling depleted, but it was significant and positive for shoppers who were. It seems that shoppers in the visceral condition remained capable of resisting the craving to eat excessively as they became hungrier—unless their self-control resources were depleted.

The instigating trigger in Study 2 (conducted in the lab) was whether consumers witnessed other people (confederates) consume Peanut m&m's with or without exuberance (Nisbett and Storms 1974). We also manipulated the impellor (hunger) and the inhibitor (depletion) (Schmeichel 2007; Vohs and Faber 2007) using a new unhealthy food (Peanut m&m's).

All three manipulations were effective and powerful. Participants in the strong modeled exuberance condition ate significantly more than did participants in the weak modeled exuberance condition. Participants assigned to the hungry condition ate significantly more than did participants assigned to the nonhungry condition. In addition, participants assigned to the depletion condition ate significantly more than did participants assigned to the nondepletion condition.

To test I³ Theory, we predicted grams of Peanut m&m's eaten from the three experimental manipulations, all two-way interactions, and the three-way interaction. Consistent with the Study 1 results, the Modeled Exuberance x Hunger x Depletion interaction effect was significant. Simple effects tests revealed that the Hunger x Depletion interaction effect was not significant in the weak modeled exuberance condition, but it was significant in the strong modeled exuberance condition. Follow-up simple effects tests revealed that, within the strong modeled exuberance condition, the effect of hunger on grams eaten was not significant for participants in the nondepleted condition, but it was significant and positive for participants in the depleted condition. Consumers in the strong modeled exuberance condition remained capable of resisting the craving to eat excessively as they became hungrier—unless their self-control resources were depleted.

Taken together, the results of Studies 1 and 2 speak to the power of I³ Theory to generate novel approaches to the study of unhealthy food consumption. These two studies demonstrate that hungry people are likely to indulge in unhealthy consumption when faced with an instigating trigger, but only when their self-control resources are depleted.

## REFERENCES

Baumeister, Roy F., Todd F. Heatherton, and Dianne M. Tice (1994), *Losing Control: How and Why People Fail at Self-Regulation*, Academic: New York.

Baumeister, Roy F., Kathleen D. Vohs, and Dianne M. Tice (2007), "The Strength Model of Self-Control," *Current Directions in Psychological Science*, 16 (6), 351-55.

Schmeichel, Brandon J. (2007), "Attention Control, Memory Updating, and Emotion Regulation Temporarily Reduce the Capacity for Executive Control," *Journal of Experimental Psychology (General)*, 136 (2), 241-55.

Mischel, Walter, Yuichi Shoda, and Monica L. Rodriguez (1989), "Delay of Gratification in Children," *Science*, 244 (4907), 933-38.

Nisbett, Richard E., and Michael D. Storms (1974), "Cognitive and Social Determinants of Food Intake," In *Thought and Feeling: Cognitive Alternation of Feeling States*, ed. Harvey London and Richard E. Nisbett, Aldine: Chicago, 190-208.

Stroebe, Wolfgang (2008), *Dieting, Overweight, and Obesity: Self-Regulation in a Food-Rich Environment*, American Psychological Association: Washington, DC.

U.S. Department of Health and Human Services, Centers for Disease Control and Prevention, National Center for Health Statistics (2009), with special feature on the health of young adults http://www.cdc.gov/nchs/data/hus/hus08.pdf.

Vohs, Kathleen D., and Ronald J. Faber (2007), "Spent Resources: Self-Regulatory Resource Availability Affects Impulse Buying," *Journal of Consumer Research*, *33* (4)*, 537-47.

Vohs, Kathleen D., and Todd F. Heatherton (2000), "Self-Regulatory Failure: A Resource-Depletion Approach," *Psychological Science*, *11* (3), 249-54.

Wansink, Brian (2006), *Mindless Eating: Why We Eat More Than We Think*, Bantam: New York.

World Health Organization (2000), *Obesity: Preventing and Managing the Global Epidemic*, Geneva.

# The Influence of Front-of-Pack Nutrition Labels on Consumers' Food Choices at the Point of Purchase and the Point of Consumption

Joerg Koenigstorfer, Saarland University, Germany
Andrea Groeppel-Klein, Saarland University, Germany
Friederike Kamm, Saarland University, Germany

## EXTENDED ABSTRACT

Front-of-pack labels on food products commonly feature on major food manufacturers' products. Grunert and Wills (2007, 385) state that they are an attempt to provide consumers "with information about the nutrition content of individual food products, in order to enable consumers to choose nutritionally appropriate food." The goal of this article is to assess whether front-of-pack nutrition labeling is effective in stimulating healthy food choices. This is highly relevant for two reasons: First, most buying decisions with respect to food items are conducted habitually or impulsively and take just a few seconds, with little or no cognitive control (Hoyer 1984; Moorman 1996; Rook 1987). Thus labels have to be designed to attract consumers' attention and provide them with clear information. Second, past attempts to trigger healthier choices by providing additional information on the packages–such as back-of-pack labeling, nutrition or health claims–were either unsuccessful or even counterproductive in stimulating healthier food selection and consumption (Balasubramanian and Cole 2002; Roe, Levy, and Derby 1999; Wansink and Chandon 2006).

As part of our investigation, we carried out an initial qualitative study aimed at analyzing both conscious and unconscious, habitualized aspects of consumers' food choices with respect to different front-of-pack nutrition labeling schemes. In the study we employed a projective photo-elicitation technique. This method was chosen for three reasons: to assess differences in the use of nutrition labels at the point of purchase and the point of consumption; to reduce the social desirability bias (Rook 2006); and to investigate unconscious aspects of human behavior (Kassarjian 1974; McClelland, Koestner, and Weinberger 1989). We took photographs of ten families at different stages of the family lifecycle at both the point of purchase (during a shopping trip made by the main person responsible for meal planning) and the point of consumption (during a family meal at home). We used selected photos as stimuli for photo elicitation and conducted autodriving interviews, which we recorded and analyzed using a holistic approach. Four themes emerged from the data: perceived time pressure at the point of purchase; the relevance of nutrition information for making inferences with regard to the healthiness and tastiness of products; consumers' trust in nutrition information; and their use of this information at the point of purchase or point of consumption. The results show that nutrition labels influence consumers' food choices only at the point of purchase, if at all; people generally disregard them when preparing and eating a family meal at home. At the point of purchase, people appreciate labels, particularly those that provide precise information about the main nutrients without overly limiting their freedom of choice. Examples of such systems are Guideline Daily Amount systems (GDA systems).

In a second study, we investigated the effectiveness of two different labeling schemes in stimulating healthy food choices at the point of purchase: the traffic light color-coded (TL) GDA and the monochrome (MC) GDA systems–both of which were characterized as particularly helpful systems by consumers in study 1. We proposed six hypotheses about consumer decision-making processes, relating to the awareness and automatic processing of labels, the degree to which labels permit accurate information processing, the direct effect of labels on actual choices, and determinants of future choices. A laboratory experiment examining actual product choices for ready meals with 209 participants shows that TL-GDA systems generate higher awareness and tend to more positively impact healthy product choices than MC-GDA systems, but only if consumers are aware of the label. Although nutrition labels are not the main reason for choosing a product, consumers refer to labels employing the TL-GDA system more often than to those using the MC-GDA system. Consumers also find it somewhat easier to interpret labels that use the TL-GDA system, especially in forced exposure conditions. Study 2 extends previous attempts to compare different nutrition labeling systems (Feunekes et al. 2008; FSA 2009a; Jones and Richardson 2007; Kelly et al. 2009; Kümpel Nørgaard and Brunsø 2009; van Kleef et al. 2007) by analyzing actual product choices in close-to-real-life environments and minimizing the tendency to evoke socially desired responses.

In the two studies we focus on nutrition labels and showed that two types of GDA systems impact on consumers' food choices, making them more likely to choose a lower-calorie diet. In reality, however, we need to consider a range of other marketing factors when evaluating the potential of front-of-pack nutrition labeling for supporting healthy diets. These factors include the store environment, product prices, package and portion sizes, shapes and other front-of-pack stimuli such as images of slim models and athletes. We also need to consider consumers' emotions and cognitions relating to food, such as their tendency to regulate their affect, self-control and conscious or subconscious goal conflicts. Nevertheless, the results of our study provide both insights into the relevance of front-of-pack nutrition labeling and important directions for future research.

# To Think or Not to Think: The Effect of Cognitive Deliberation on Social Norm Influence

Vladmir Melnyk, Wageningen University, The Netherlands
Erica van Herpen, Wageningen University, The Netherlands
Arnout Fischer, Wageningen University, The Netherlands
Hans C. M. van Trijp, Wageningen University, The Netherlands

## EXTENDED ABSTRACT

Marketers have realized the potential of social norms to influence consumers' attitudes and preferences, and use norms frequently in marketing campaigns (Berkowitz 2005). Consumers can process norm information at different levels of cognitive deliberation. Sometimes their thinking is inhibited by, for example, time pressure or fatigue, whereas at other times consumers may freely and actively think about social norms. As the depth of deliberation is often seen as key to attitude change (Petty, Haugtvedt, and Smith 1995), it is likely that this will also affect the influence of social norms.

Despite a large body of research on social norms and on the role of cognitive deliberation in persuasion little is known about the effect of cognitive deliberation on social norms messages, and whether this influence differs between injunctive and descriptive norms. The effect of cognitive deliberation on different norm formulations is particularly interesting because it can explain a fundamental difference between injunctive and descriptive norms. This study thus provides an understanding about how and why social norms influence decision making, and focuses on the role of cognitive deliberation.

Social norms can be formulated in two distinct ways: (1) through giving information about the behavior of other people — descriptive norms (what most people do), and (2) through highlighting social rules–injunctive norms (what ought to be done). Descriptive norms are generally supported by the belief of consumers that others act in an effective way (Cialdini 2006), and therefore in a process of deliberation consumers are likely to come up with arguments in favor of the behavioral patterns observed in others. In contrast, injunctive norms contain an explicit request of what one should do. These norms do not convey information about behavioral effectiveness, and therefore can stimulate both thoughts in favor and against the behavior. For example, consumers may perceive an injunctive norm as a limitation of their freedom to choose and while deliberating on this injunctive social norm, they are more likely to come up with reasons which would help to overcome this request (Mann and Hill 1984). Thus the effect of cognitive deliberation would be different, and even opposite for the two norm formulations.

The experimental study (N=1010) had a 2 (norm formulation: injunctive vs. descriptive) x 3 (cognitive deliberation level: cognitive load vs. control vs. cognitive deliberation) between subject design and a two level measured factor (belief in the content of the message: non-believers vs. believers). Formulation of the social norm was manipulated in a fictitious short newspaper article entitled "Study among Dutch consumer", which promoted either a descriptive norm ("Yes, I always buy environmentally-friendly processed potatoes"), or an injunctive norm ("Everybody should buy environmentally-friendly processed potatoes"). Participants in the cognitive load condition were instructed to count how many times the whole-word "the" was used in the newspaper article, thus preventing deliberation on the message and social norm content. Participants in the control condition were provided with the newspaper text without any instructions that might influence their cognitive deliberation level. In the cognitive deliberation condition participants were asked to carefully read the text of the newspaper article and think about its content.

To test the types of thoughts that the different social norms activate, an open question was added, asking participants to list all the thoughts that they had in separate boxes. Subsequently, participants were asked to answer a number of questions about their attitudes and purchase intentions towards environmentally-friendly processed potatoes.

Results showed that when consumers have limited cognitive capacity to process a normative message their attitudes and intentions are less in favor of the advocated behavior, compared to when they can process the message without cognitive limitations. Furthermore, and interestingly, the effect of cognitive deliberation depends on norm formulation. Cognitive deliberation on a descriptive norm makes attitudes and intentions more congruent with the normative message, whereas deliberation on injunctive norms has a negative effect on attitudes and intentions in favor of the advocated behavior. Cognitive deliberation appears to suppress either negative or positive thoughts depending on norm formulation. In particular, deliberation suppresses negative thought for descriptive norms and suppresses positive thought for injunctive norms.

Our study has several implications. First, it reveals a fundamental difference between descriptive and injunctive norms and explains the different effect of cognitive deliberation between these. This effect is not due to the *number* of thoughts, but is fully mediated by the difference in *valence* of the thoughts that each norm formulation triggers. Second, norm formulation can influence the thought generation process, which is in line with the reasoning that, depending on information characteristics, cognitive deliberation can produce thinking that is biased either in favor or against (e.g., when reactance is instilled) an advocated position (Petty and Briñol 2008). By switching the formulation of a persuasive message from injunctive to descriptive it is possible to partially compensate for or even reverse the effect of cognitive deliberation. Therefore when using descriptive norms one should make sure that it is used in situations where consumers are stimulated to deliberate upon this norm message. In contrast, messages using injunctive norms should be simple and straightforward to avoid cognitive deliberation upon this message. Third, consumers who are cognitively loaded in the process of reading a social norm message are less susceptible to social norm influence. Future research may shed light on how and to what extent this can be generalized to situations in which consumers are cognitively depleted prior to reading the message (compared to cognitively loaded while reading the message).

This study increases our understanding of the influence of social norms on decision making by showing how the level of cognitive deliberation with which norms are being processed in combination with norm formulation affects the influence of social norms on both attitudes and purchase intentions.

## REFERENCES

Berkowitz, Alan D. (2005), "An Overview of the Social Norms Approach," in *Changing the Culture of College Drinking: A Socially Situated Health Communication Campaign*, ed. Linda C. Lederman and Lea P. Stewarts, Creskill, NJ: Hamptom Press, 193–214.

Cialdini, Robert B. (2006), *Influence: The Psychology of Persuasion*, New York: Collins Business Essentials.

Mann, Millard F. and Thomas Hill (1984), "Persuasive Communications and the Boomerang Effect: Some Limiting Conditions to the Effectiveness of Positive Influence Attempts," *Advances in Consumer Research*, 11, 66-70.

Petty, Richard E. and Pablo Briñol (2008), "Psychological Processes Underlying Persuasion: A Social Psychological Approach," *Diogenes*, 55 (1), 52-67.

Petty, Richard E., Curtis P. Haugtvedt, and Stephen M. Smith (1995), "Elaboration as a Determinant of Atttitude Strength: Creating Attitudes That Are Persistent, Resistent, and Predictive of Behavior," in *Attitude Strength: Antecedents and Consequences*, ed. Richard E. Petty and Jon A. Krosnick, Mahwah, N.J.: Lawrence Erlbaum Associates, 93-130.

# Out of Sight, Out of Mind: On the Irrational Side of Egocentrism in Social Comparisons

Steven Chan, New York University, USA
John Chambers, University of Florida, USA
Justin Kruger, New York University, USA

## EXTENDED ABSTRACTS

Social comparisons are common in everyday life. Whether comparing their intelligence with other students, their chances of winning a round of Texas Hold'em against other gamblers, their likelihood to contract a virus versus peers, or their ability to succeed with a startup venture relative to other entrepreneurs, people are interested in knowing their standing relative to others (Festinger 1954). Fearing they may not be as academically gifted as their peers, students expend less effort studying and ultimately do worse in school (Marsh and Parker 1984). Expecting that their business is more likely to survive in a competitive marketplace than other new businesses, entrepreneurs invest more and are more confident of their chances of success (Camerer and Lovallo 1999; Moore and Cain 2007). And convinced that they are less vulnerable to sexually transmitted diseases, people may take fewer precautions than advised (Menon, Block, and Ramanathan 2002).

Yet, as often as people compare themselves with others, a wealth of research suggests that those comparisons are systematically biased. Most people believe that they are more happy, conscientious, socially skilled, and generous than the average person, and less neurotic, impatient, and immoral (see Alicke 1985; Campbell 1986). They do so in defiance of simple laws of probability that state that not everyone can be better than average. They are overconfident in competitions, believing that they have a greater chance of winning than their competitor(s) (Windschitl, Kruger, and Simms 2003; Moore and Kim 2003).

Initially, researchers suggested that these tendencies reflected a fundamental motivation to see oneself in the most favorable light possible (Taylor and Brown 1988; Alicke 1985). However, more recent work suggests that people occasionally see themselves in a less positive light (Chambers and Windschitl 2004). Although people believe that they are above-average in their ability to perform easy tasks such as riding a bicycle and operating a computer mouse, for instance, they believe they are below-average in their ability to perform difficult tasks such as riding a unicycle or programming a computer (Kruger 1999). Similarly, although they see themselves as having above-average chances of experiencing common desirable outcomes like finding a quarter lying on the ground, they believe they have below-average chances of experiencing rare desirable outcomes like finding a $50 bill lying on the ground (Chambers, Windschitl, and Suls 2003; Kruger and Burrus 2004).

Evidence now suggests that when people compare themselves with others, they myopically focus on their own strengths and abilities and pay less attention to the (equally relevant) strengths and abilities of the comparison group (Chambers et al. 2003; Klar and Giladi 1999; Kruger 1999). We suspect, however, that all is not equal. We suggest that the self receives the lion's share of the attention because it is the self. Specifically, we propose that social comparisons are not merely myopic, but egocentric. After all, representations of the self are some of the most accessible representations that people possess. Conceptual representations become more accessible the more they are activitated (Higgins and Bargh 1987; Srull and Wyer 1979), and we spend considerably more time thinking about ourselves than we do about others. This leads to the fairly straightforward prediction that people are likely to egocentrically focus on their own strengths and achievements more than the strengths and achievements of others when they compare

the two. And yet, despite nearly a decade of research on the topic (including many with "egocentrism" in the title), there are no data that explicitly rule in egocentrism.

The present research was designed to provide the first unequivocal evidence of egocentrism in social comparisons. We present three studies. In Study 1, we show that information about the self is brought to mind more quickly than information about others, and that difference mediates the magnitude of bias in social comparisons. In Study 2, we manipulated participants' accessibility of the comparison group by changing the salience of the competitor while holding information about that competitor constant. Participants predicted their chances of beating a competitor on a trivia game comprised of easy and difficult categories. Path analyses revealed that participants based their predictions on their own knowledge of the trivia category more than on their competitors' knowledge of the category. However, that effect was attenuated when participants had a constant reminder of their competitor with a simple photograph. Finally in Study 3, we demonstrate that the mode of competition matters in highlighting the salience of competitors. Participants who played a game directly against their opponent (head-to-head) exhibited less egocentric bias than those who played through an intermediary (the computer).

Whether comparing their event chances, abilities, or entrepreneurial success, people tend to overweight self-assessments and underweight assessments of the comparison group, giving rise to both above- and below-average effects. Although much prior work has identified egocentrism as the cause of this myopia, very little work explicitly rules in egocentrism. In the present work, we show that comparisons are indeed egocentric. We demonstrated not only that self-information comes to mind more rapidly than information about a comparison group, but that those for whom self-information is especially accessible tend to be most myopic in their comparisons (and as a result, see themselves as most above- and below-average). Furthermore, we showed that increasing the salience of the comparison group led to corresponding decreases in egocentrism and above- and below-average comparisons. As a key implication from this research, we emphasize that changing the context of social comparison or competition, by simply highlighting the presence of the other or competitor (without changes in amount or quality of information) can alone diminish the degree of comparison bias. As for the theoretical take away, these results suggest that a major reason why comparisons are myopic is that others are simply "out of sight" and "out of mind."

## REFERENCES

Alicke, Mark D. (1985), "Global Self-Evaluation as Determined by the Desirability and Controllability of Trait Adjectives," *Journal of Personality and Social Psychology, 49 (6)*, 1621-1630.

Camerer, Colin and Dan Lovallo (1999), "Overconfidence and Ex-cess Entry: An Experimental Approach," *American Economic Review, 89* (March), 306-318.

Campbell, Jennifer D (1986), "Similarity and Uniqueness: The Effects of Attribute Type, Relevance, and Individual Differences in Self-Esteem and Depression," *Journal of Personality and Social Psychology, 50*, 281-294.

Chambers, John R. and Paul D. Windschitl (2004), "Biases in Social Comparative Judgments: The Role of Non-Motivated Factors in Above-Average and Comparative-Optimism Effects. *Psychological Bulletin, 130*, 813-838.

Chambers, John. R., Paul D. Windschitl, and Jerry Suls (2003), "Egocentrism, Event Frequency, and Comparative Optimism: When What Happens Frequently is 'More Likely to Happen to Me'," *Personality and Social Psychology Bulletin, 29*, 1343-1356.

Festinger, Leon (1954), "A Theory of Social Comparison Processes," *Human Relations, 7 (2)*, 117-140.

Higgins, E. Tory and John A. Bargh (1987), "Social Cognition and Social Perception," *Annual Review of Psychology, 38*, 369-425.

Klar, Yechiel and Eilath E. Giladi (1999), "Are Most People Happier Than Their Peers, or Are They Just Happy?" *Personality and Social Psychology Bulletin, 25*, 585-594.

Kruger, Justin (1999), "Lake Wobegon be Gone! The "Below-Average Effect" and the Egocentric Nature of Comparative Ability Judgments," *Journal of Personality and Social Psychology, 77 (2)*, 221-232.

Kruger, Justin and Jeremy Burrus (2004), "Egocentrism and Focalism in Unrealistic Optimism (and Pessimism)," *Journal of Experimental Social Psychology, 40 (3)*, 332-340.

Marsh, Herbet W. and John W. Parker (1984), "Determinants of Student Self-concept: Is it Better to be a Relatively Large Fish in a Small Pond Even if You Don't Learn to Swim as Well?" *Journal of Personality and Social Psychology, 47(1)*, 213-231.

Menon, Geeta, Lauren Block and Suresh Ramanathan (2002), "We're at as Much Risk as We're Led to Believe: Effects of Message Cues On Judgments of Health Risk," *Journal of Consumer Research, 28* (March), 533-549.

Moore, Don A. and Tai G. Kim, (2003), "Myopic Social Prediction and the Solo Comparison Effect," *Journal of Personality and Social Psychology, 85(6)*, 1121-1135

Moore, Don A. and Daylain M. Cain (2007), "Overconfidence and Underconfidence: When and Why People Underestimate (and Overestimate) the Competition," *Organizational Behavior and Human Decision Processes, 103(2)*, 197-213.

Sobel, Michael E. (1982) "Asymptotic Intervals for Indirect Effects in Structural Equations Models," in *Sociological Methodology*, ed. S. Leinhart, San Francisco: Jossey-Bass, 290-312.

Srull, Thomas K. and Robert S. Wyer Jr. (1979), "The Role of Category Accessibility in the Interpretation of Information about Persons: Some Determinants and Implications," *Journal of Personality and Social Psychology, 37 (10)*, 1660-1672.

Taylor, Shelley E. and J.D. Brown (1988), "Illusions and Well-Being: A Social Psychological Perspective on Mental Health," *Psychological Bulletin, 103*, 193-210.

Windschitl, Paul D., Kruger, Justin, and Ericka N. Simms (2003), "The Influence of Egocentrism and Focalism on People's Confidence in Competitions: When What Affects us Equally Affects Me More," *Journal of Personality and Social Psychology, 85 (3)*, 389-408.

# Revisiting Contexts of Socialization: Friendship Group as the Consumer Socialization Context

Cagri Yalkin, King's College, London, UK
Richard Elliott, Bath School of Management, UK
Ekant Veer, University of Canterbury, New Zealand

## EXTENDED ABSTRACT

The aim of this study is to explore the role of friendship groups as the context of socialization and to provide an account of the actual use of fashion goods in the consumer socialization process. It draws on recent reviews in socialization (Harris 1999), which suggests a re-examination of the role of the environment in consumer socialization. This work suggests studying what consumer knowledge, skills, and competence means for consumers in different contexts (Cook 2004) and that the actual use and consumption of goods need to be featured in consumer socialization studies (Ekström 2006). It also suggests that talking and emotional sharing is a significant part of women's friendships and that these friendships take place against the backdrop of an activity (Sheehy 2000). In light of this recent work, this thesis studies consumer socialization in the female friendship groups' by qualitatively inquiring about their consumption and use of fashion.

As Wooten (2006) pointed out, consumer culture theory (CCT) (Arnould and Thompson 2005) approaches to consumer socialization have the potential to "advance knowledge of consumer socialization by illuminating aspects of social life that influence the acquisition of consumption motives and values" (p.196). As CCT is proposed as a framework to help study socio-cultural, experiential, symbolic, and ideological aspects of consumption, this approach could prove useful in the study of consumer socialization, whose symbolic, experiential, and ideological aspects have more or less been understudied.

Furthermore, Ekstr?m (2006) points out the insufficient coverage of the use and consumption of goods in consumer socialization studies. John's (1999) review of 25 years of consumer socialization research provides insight into the categories of findings in the bulk of these studies. The findings are generally about children's advertising knowledge, transaction knowledge (products, brands, shopping, and pricing), decision-making skills and strategies, purchase requests and negotiation strategies, and consumption motives and values. One of the more insightful studies is Peracchio's (1992) study which examines learning abilities and concludes that young children are able to gain knowledge equivalent to that of older children when the experiment materials and response formats are congruent with their encoding and retrieval abilities. Others include John and Whitney's (1986) study which suggests that older children use more sophisticated processing skills and strategies than younger children as they get more information and experience in the marketplace, and Belk et al.'s (1982) study which dealt with the development of consumption symbolism in children. These three studies have adopted experimental methods. Hence, with the exception of Banister and Booth's (2003) study on the formation of children's likes and dislikes, the consumer socialization literature has mainly adopted quantitative studies. Especially thick descriptions of how young consumers gain symbolic skills, knowledge, and competencies are missing from the children's and adolescents' accounts of consumer socialization (see John 1999).

Cook's (2004) discussion of commodification of childhood and the transformation of the child into the individualized consumer is noteworthy in that it reflects a summary of the accumulated research in consumer socialization: "Consumer socialization studies need to consider what competence means for consumers in different contexts and should not be limited to focusing on utilitarian outcomes and effectiveness. There is a need to feature social as well as market relationships in consumer socialization research. In other words, to show how people use products and services in negotiating relationships with others as well as how the market is incorporating these relationships" (p.149).

Finally, Webley and Lea (1993, p.461) note that researchers should not focus on "how do children come to understand the economic world of grown-ups" but that rather they should ask "how do children solve the economic problems they are faced with" (Webley and Lea 1993, p.461). Together, Cook's (2004) suggestion that researchers need to explore what competence means for young consumers in different contexts, and that there is a need to take into account social relationships when studying consumption and Webley and Lea's (1993) suggestion that researchers should ask how do children solve the consumption-related problems they are faced with constitute the gaps that warrant attention in order to advance the consumer socialization studies. Hence, non-family environment or the outside-of-home context needs to be taken into account and the research question is: *What is the role played by the non-family environment, particularly in the form of a friendship group, in consumer socialization?*

Analysis and interpretation of the data collected through focus groups and interviews with 12 to 16 year-old adolescents revealed that the information flow in friendship groups leads to communication, which serves as the key catalyst of consumer socialization. The friendship group, furthermore, emerged as the site where the socialization process took place, as suggested by Harris (1995; 1999). Adolescents are able to strengthen both rational and symbolic skills within their friendship groups by participating in the background act of 'going shopping' and by talking about consumption related issues, hence enabling them to operate as successful consumers in the marketplace. The gendered consumer identity is also negotiated within the context of shopping, consuming fashion, and marking individuality versus belonging in one's friendship group. Finally, the data analysis revealed that the adolescents surrealize the images in fashion communications as a way to resists such advertisements.

# Variety For Nothing

Mauricio Mittelman, Universidad Torcuato Di Tella, Argentina & COPPEAD Graduate School of Business, Brazil
Amitava Chattopadhyay, INSEAD, Singapore
C. Miguel Brendl, Northwestern University, USA

## EXTENDED ABSTRACT

When choosing multiple items from a product category, people often seek variety in order to achieve a goal (e.g., to get stimulation). But not always. In this work we propose that sometimes people seek variety for no reason other than to merely satisfy an urge to make different choices. In other words, when choosing multiple items from a product category, not only do people seek variety in the choice outcome, but they also do in the choice process—defined here as the series of individual choices needed to carry out the overall choice. Our argument builds on Drolet's (2002) results. She has shown that consumers tend to vary their use of decision rules because of a favorable valuation of the decision change itself. That is, sometimes consumer choices are not based on the valuation of the choice options, but instead reflect an urge to adopt a different decision rule (e.g., to choose an intermediate option rather than to choose the cheapest option). Likewise, we propose that consumers tend to choose different items because of a favorable valuation of making a different choice itself. That is, consumers' variety-seeking is not necessarily driven by any benefit associated with a set of varied items, but instead may reflect an urge to make different choices. Making a different choice, like applying a different decision rule, is intrinsically satisfying.

The hypothesis above suggests an important corollary. Suppose that when choosing multiple items from a product category, people do not make a series of choices but instead make a single choice. It follows from our hypothesis that people who choose items one-by-one (i.e., a series of choices) will seek more variety than people who choose items all-at-once (i.e., a single choice). When choosing items one-by-one, people may seek variety in the choice process by making subsequent choices different from previous ones. Not so when choosing items all-at-once, because in that case there is only a single choice. As a consequence, in all-at-once choices people may seek variety in the choice outcome only, whereas in one-by-one choices people may seek variety both in the choice outcome and in the choice process. We report two studies supporting these two hypotheses.

In study 1, participants whose first choice was of a high-variety set of candies sought less variety by choosing low-variety sets more often than those whose first choice was of a low-variety set of candies (63% and 17%, respectively; $\chi^2(1)=13.61$, $p<.001$).. They did so because they sought variety in the choice process by making a second choice different from the first choice. As a consequence, they got *less* varied candies than they could get otherwise—had they made the second choice identical to the first choice, they would have chosen a set of more varied items. Beyond supporting the main hypothesis, this result showed that people could in fact be much eager to seek variety in the choice process than in the choice outcome. In study 2, participants who composed their bouquet of roses choosing their roses one-by-one selected mixed-color bouquets more often than those who picked up a pre-arranged bouquet choosing their roses all-at-once (70% and 48%, respectively; $\chi^2(1)=4.80$, $p<.05$), a result that supports the corollary.

This work has two important implications. Theoretically, it offers a novel explanation for why people often seek too much variety (Kahn and Ratner 2005). We propose that people's choice of varied items can be driven by an urge to seek variety in the choice process (i.e., to make different choices) rather than by an urge to seek variety in the choice outcome (i.e., to choose different items). Differently from what has been proposed so far, our results thus suggest it is not that people may miscalculate how much variety they want. Rather, people may not make any calculation at all. For example, Read and Loewenstein (1995) reported that students who chose snacks to be received in the future later regretted choosing too many different snacks. Our explanation suggests that these students did not miscalculate their snack preferences in the future. Instead, they may not have thought much about their preferences, chose too many different candy snacks because they sought variety in the choice process, and later found out they would have been better off if they had chosen their most-preferred option.

Practically, this work suggests that consumers may behave differently depending on how sellers make their products available. Specifically, it suggests that people are more likely to choose varied items when selecting individual units than when selecting whole assortments. When selecting individual units, people may seek variety in the choice process by making subsequent choices different from previous ones. Not so when selecting whole assortments, because in that case there is only a single choice. As a consequence, people may seek variety in the choice outcome when selecting whole assortments, whereas people may seek variety both in the choice outcome and in the choice process when selecting individual units. This idea explains the common market practice of offering packs of identical items, which is otherwise difficult to explain given the plenty of evidence that people are avid variety-seekers.

In conclusion, this research shows that people need no reason to seek variety. Sometimes preference for variety stem from a desire to make different choices, not from a desire to choose different items.

# Social Networks and the Value of Collaborative User-Generated Content

Sam Ransbotham, Boston College, USA
Gerald Kane, Boston College, USA
Nicholas Lurie, Georgia Institute of Technology, USA

## EXTENDED ABSTRACT

User-generated content is a valuable resource for many firms. Examples include product reviews that affect product search, choice, and sales (Chevalier and Mayzlin 2006; Dellarocas, Zhang, and Awad 2007; Mayzlin and Moe 2009), consumer-created ads that generate brand excitement (Kozinets, Hemetsberger, and Schau 2008), and user-developed information that drives traffic to websites that depend on advertising. Although much user-generated content is created by individuals, an increasing amount is developed by groups of people working collectively. This includes the wiki websites Wikia and Wikipedia, where contributors work together on articles; virtual worlds such as Second Life and World of Warcraft, where participants create shared objects and spaces and perform shared tasks (Hemp 2006); and citizen journalism websites like CNN's iReport, where amateur reporters create content that drives advertising viewership. All of these involve collaborative user-generated content, which may be distinguished from individually created content through characteristics such as concurrent editing of the same content, the need to reach consensus given constraints about what to include and what not to include, and final output that is often substantially different from the original contributions made by individuals.

We propose that the social networks that result when individuals work with others to generate multiple sources of user-generated content are important determinants of the market value of that content. We assess market value through viewership since viewership is a primary determinant of the revenue that advertisers obtain from user-generated content. We focus on three dimensions of the social networks involved in the creation of collaborative user-generated content: (1) the size of the network (i.e., the number of distinct contributors to the user-generated content), (2) the strength of the network (i.e., the intensity with which collaborators work on multiple other sources of user-generated content), and (3) the richness of the network (i.e., the relative importance of other user-generated content on which collaborators work). We further argue that the effects of these network characteristics in increasing the market value of collaborative user-generated content should be greater for newer relative to older content, since collaborative content is likely to stabilize over time.

We test our hypotheses by applying social network analysis (SNA) to Wikipedia's Medicine Wikiproject, examining how social network characteristics affect the market value of user-generated content. Medical information is an increasingly important and valuable type of user-generated content (Fox and Jones 2009). We downloaded the full text history of 2,026,992 revisions of 14,088 articles by 40,479 unique contributors within the Medicine Wikiproject as of March 2009 to construct a 174,800 observation monthly panel. Controlling for article topic, links to other content, and other factors that may affect the market value of user-generated content, our data provide unique insights into the role of social networks in the creation of user-generated content. Results demonstrate a curvilinear relationship between the number of distinct contributors to content and its market value. We also find that content created by stronger and richer social networks of contributors generate more valuable content. These social network effects are stronger for newer user-generated content with the exception of network strength, which has a stronger impact on increasing market value as content ages.

## REFERENCES

Chevalier, Judith A. and Dina Mayzlin (2006), "The Effect of Word of Mouth on Sales: Online Book Reviews," *Journal of Marketing Research*, 43 (August), 345-54.

Dellarocas, Chrysanthos, Xiaoquan (Michael) Zhang, and Neveen F. Awad (2007), "Exploring the Value of Online Product Reviews in Forecasting Sales: The Case of Motion Pictures," *Journal of Interactive Marketing*, 21 (4), 23-45.

Fox, Susannah and Sydney Jones (2009), "The Social Life of Health Information," in *Pew Internet & American Life Project*, Washington, DC: Pew Research Center.

Hemp, Paul (2006), "Avatar-Based Marketing," *Harvard Business Review*, 84 (6), 48-56.

Kozinets, Robert V., Andrea Hemetsberger, and Hope Jensen Schau (2008), "The Wisdom of Consumer Crowds: Collective Innovation in the Age of Networked Marketing," *Journal of Macromarketing*, 28 (4), 339-54.

Mayzlin, Dina and Wendy W. Moe (2009), "The Impact of Consumer Reviews on Consumer Search and Firm Profits," in *Advances in Consumer Research*, Vol. 37, ed. Margaret C. Campbell, J. Jeffrey Inman and Rik Pieters, Duluth, MN: Association for Consumer Research, forthcoming.

# Tell the Truth: The Effects of Disclosure in Word-of-Mouth Marketing

Lisa Abendroth, University of St. Thomas, USA
James Heyman, University of St. Thomas, USA

## EXTENDED ABSTRACT

During the past two decades, marketers have implemented a variety of stealth marketing tactics that deliver product messages surreptitiously (Kaikati & Kaikati, 2004). Word-of-mouth (WOM), which previously existed as an organic product discussion between friends, was hijacked along the way as marketers began incenting everyday people to talk about brands with other consumers. The technique's usage grew (PQ Media, 2009) as it proved effective at generating sales (Godes and Mayzlin, 2009; Ryu and Feick, 2007). However, it simultaneously gathered scrutiny for being deceptive and unethical (Kennett and Matthews, 2008) as agents often failed to disclose their material connection to the marketer, even when instructed to do so (Ahuja, Michels, Walker, and Weissbuch, 2007; Carl, 2008). In response, the WOMMA, and more recently the FTC (2009), developed guidelines that WOM agents must disclose material connections with the brand, but it is still too soon to tell how much compliance they will obtain (Baar, 2009). The goal of this research is to gain a better understanding of how disclosure of the agent-brand relationship affects WOM recipients' thoughts, feelings, and purchase intentions as compared to seemingly organic WOM. Is honesty really the best policy?

There is a general sense among marketers and agents that disclosure undermines the effectiveness of the recommendation (Ahuja et al., 2007; Carl, 2008; Creamer, 2005; Kaikati and Kaikati, 2004; Kennett and Matthews, 2008). Disclosure is believed to turn turn everyday conversations into commercial messages, causing consumers to engage their persuasion defenses, doubt that the agent is sincere, and therefore discount his or her recommendation (Campbell and Kirmani, 2000; Friestad and Wright, 1994; Verlegh, Verkerk, Tuk, and Smidts, 2004). While we agree with this logic, we argue that the consumers' reactions also depend on how and when they learn about the agent-brand relationship. We argue that if the agent discloses the relationship during the conversation, consumers' reactions are likely to be less negative, and perhaps even positive, compared to a situation where disclosure occurs incidentally after the WOM incident. While there have been two papers on the timing of disclosure, during vs. after the WOM incident (Carl, 2008; Tuk, Verlegh, Smidts, and Wigboldus, 2009), neither paper compares this known, incented WOM to seemingly organic WOM. To truly gauge the effect of disclosure that marketers are worried about, we extend the disclosure research by comparing disclosure during and after the WOM incident to seemingly organic WOM where the consumer has no information that such a relationship exists. At the same time, we examine whether the effect of disclosure is moderated by the strength of the tie between the consumer and agent, strong or weak.

Experiment 1 (N=86) used a latin-square design with agent (friend, stranger) manipulated between subjects, disclosure (none, later, during) manipulated within subjects, and product (cell phone, energy drink, and movie) manipulated within-subject and counterbalanced such that each group saw a different disclosure-by-product combination. The products and brands used as stimuli were selected based on a pre-test (N=23). As expected, later disclosure reduced attitudes towards the agent and product, but surprisingly had no effect on purchase intentions. Meanwhile, the ethical and legal approach of disclosure during the conversation increased purchase intent while simultaneously reducing attitude toward the agent and having no effect on attitude toward the product. Participants viewed friends as more sincere and were more likely to act on their recommendations, which is consistent with Godes and Mayzlin (2009) and Tuk et al. (2009). However, the consumers' relationship with the agent did not interact with disclosure, suggesting that tie strength does not moderate the effect of disclosure on effectiveness.

Experiment 2 (N=64) had only friends as agents and manipulated disclosure (none, later, during) and product (cell phone, energy drink) between-subjects to eliminate possible contrast effects from seeing multiple disclosure conditions. We also added measures on feelings (deceived or informed) and perceptions of the conversation (unethical, clever, and typical). Compared to seemingly organic WOM, we replicated the finding that disclosure during helped purchase intent, while disclosure after had no effect on behavioral intentions, though intermediate attitudinal measures were affected. We also identified three attitudinal measures that appeared to mediate the effect of disclosure on purchase intentions. While it was not surprising that attitude toward the product had a strong influence on purchase intent, the more interesting finding was that feeling informed as a result of the conversation also positively influenced purchase intent, while finding the agent to be sincere and credible had a negative effect on purchase intent.

In summary, the big picture finding is that ethical and legal disclosure of the agent-brand relationship can be beneficial for both marketers and agents, while a failure to disclose that gets uncovered later can have a backlash effect. These results support recent FTC guideline changes that mandate disclosure, which will ultimately protect consumers from stealth marketing approaches.

## REFERENCES

Ahuja, R.D. , Michels, T.A., Walker, M.M., & Weissbuch, M. (2007). Teen perceptions of disclosure in buzz marketing. *Journal of Consumer Marketing*, 24(3), 151-159.

Baar, A. (2009). FTC puts onus on marketers, not bloggers. *MediaPost*, 9/14/09.

Bone, P. F. (1995). Word-of-mouth effects on short-term and long-term product judgments. *Journal of Business Research*, 32(3), 213-223.

Brown, J. J. & Reingen, P. H. (1987). Social ties and word-of-mouth referral behavior. *Journal of Consumer Research*, 14(3), 350-362.

Campbell, M. C., & Kirmani, A. (2000). Consumers' use of persuasion knowledge: The effects of accessibility and cognitive capacity on perceptions of an influence agent. *Journal of Consumer Research*, 27(1), 69-83.

Carl, W. J. (2004). What's all the buzz about? Everyday communication and the relational bias of word-of-mouth and buzz marketing practices. *Marketing Communications Quarterly*, 19(4), 601-634..

Carl, W. J. (2008). The role of disclosure in organized word-of-mouth marketing programs. *Journal of Marketing Communications*, 14(3), 225-241.

Chevalier, J. A., & Mayzlin, D. (2006). The effect of word of mouth on sales: Online book reviews. *Journal of Marketing Research*, 43(3) 345-354.

Creamer, M. (2005). Is buzz marketing illegal? *Advertising Age*, 76(40), 6.

Federal Trade Commission (2009). FTC publishes final guides governing endorsements, testimonials: Changes affect testimonial advertisements, bloggers, celebrity endorsements. *FTC Press Release*, 10/5/09.

Feick, L. F., & Price, L. L. (1987). The market maven: A diffuser of marketplace information. *Journal of Marketing,* 51(1), 83-97.

Friestad, M. & Wright, P (1994). The persuasion knowledge model: How people cope with persuasion attempts. *Journal of Consumer Research,* 21(1), 1-31.

Gatignon, H. & Robinson, T. S. (1986). An exchange theory model of interpersonal communications. In R. J. Lutz (Ed.), *Advances in Consumer Research, Volume 13* (534-538). Provo, UT: Association for Consumer Research.

Godes, D., & Mayzlin, D. (2004). Using online conversation to study word-of-mouth communication. *Marketing Science,* 23(4), 545-560.

Godes, D., & Mayzlin, D. (2009). Firm-created word-of-mouth communication: Evidence from a field test. *Marketing Science,* 28(4), 721-739.

Grewal, R., Cline, T. W., & Davies, A. (2003). Early-entrant advantage, word-of-mouth communication, brand similarity, and the consumer decision-making process. *Journal of Consumer Psychology*, 13(3), 187-197.

Kaikati, A. M., & Kaikati, J. G. (2004). Stealth marketing: How to reach consumers surreptitiously. *California Management Review*, 46(4), 6-22.

Kennett, J., & Matthews, S. (2008). What's the buzz? Undercover marketing and the corruption of friendship. *Journal of Applied Philosophy*, 25(1), 2-18.

Mayzlin, D. (2006). Promotional chat on the internet. *Marketing Science,* 25(2) 155-163.

PQ Media (2009). Despite worst recession in decades, brands increased spending on word-of-mouth marketing 14.2% to $1.54 billion in 2008. *PQ Media Press Release*, 7/29/09.

Reingen, P. H. & Kernan, J. B. (1986). Analysis of referral networks in marketing: Methods and illustration. *Journal of Marketing Research,* 23(4), 370-378.

Rosen, E. (2000). *The Anatomy of buzz: How to create word of mouth marketing.* New York: Random House.

Ryu, G. & Feick, L. (2007). A penny for your thoughts: Referral reward programs and referral likelihood. *Journal of Marketing,* 71(Jan), 84-94.

Samson, A. (2006). Understanding the buzz that matters: negative vs. positive word of mouth. *International Journal of Marketing Research*, 48(6), 647-657.

Tuk, M. A., Verlegh, P. W. J., Smidts, A., & Wigboldus, D. H. J. (2009). Sales and sincerity: The role of relational framing in word-of-mouth marketing. *Journal of Consumer Psychology,* 19(1), 38-47.

Verlegh, P. W. J., Verkerk, C., Tuk, M. A., & Smidts, A. (2004). Customers or sellers? The role of persuasion knowledge in customer referral. In B.E. Kahn & M. F. Luce (Eds.), *Advances in Consumer Research, Volume 31* (304-305). Duluth, MN: Association for Consumer Research.

# The Impact of Shopping the Right Way: The Influence of Fit between Mindsets and Shopping Orientations on Product Evaluations and Willingness to Pay

Oliver B. Büttner, Zeppelin University, Germany
Arnd Florack, Zeppelin University, Germany
Anja S. Göritz, University of Würzburg, Germany

## EXTENDED ABSTRACT

In retailing, value for consumers is created not only by the offered products, but also by the shopping experience. Kaltcheva and Weitz (2006), for instance, found that music played in a store that fits the shopping orientation of the consumers affects the pleasantness of the shopping experience and the intentions to visit a store and to make purchases. In this article, we argue that it is not only a fit between the store environment and shopping orientations that has value for consumers, but also the fit between mindsets of cognitive procedures applied during shopping and shopping orientations. In line with research on regulatory fit theory (Higgins et al. 2003), we assume that consumers "feel right" when mindsets that are active during shopping match the way consumers prefer to shop. We suppose that this feeling right spreads to the evaluations of products and strengthens the willingness to purchase an appealing product, and to pay a higher price for such a product.

Research on regulatory fit has found that when people are able to pursue a goal in a way that sustains their regulatory orientation, they "feel right" and enjoy the action more (Freitas and Higgins 2002). Moreover, the value from feeling right may spill over to the outcome of the process, resulting in a more positive evaluation of products and persuasive appeals, as well as in a higher willingness to pay (Avnet and Higgins 2003, 2006; Cesario, Grant, and Higgins 2004; Higgins et al. 2003). Regulatory fit effects, however, have not been examined for a regulatory orientation that is especially important at the point of purchase: consumers' shopping orientation. Two fundamental shopping orientations can be distinguished: a utilitarian shopping orientation and a hedonic shopping orientation (cf. Babin et al. 1994; Kaltcheva and Weitz 2006). Under a utilitarian shopping orientation, consumers consider shopping a task to be done and they are satisfied when they accomplish their mission as efficiently as possible. In contrast, hedonic shoppers focus on experiencing pleasure from the process of shopping itself.

We assume that these two shopping orientations entail different mindsets (Gollwitzer and Bayer 1999). We argue that shopping under a hedonic orientation draws on cognitive procedures that constitute a deliberative mindset, and that shopping under a utilitarian orientation draws on the cognitive procedures of an implemental mindset. This assumption is supported by a study using verbal protocols on shoppers' in-store experience (Büttner 2008).

In line with regulatory fit theory (Higgins et al. 2003), we assume that consumers experience regulatory fit when the active mindset provides cognitive procedures that support how consumers usually shop. Hedonic shoppers will experience regulatory fit when in a deliberative mindset; utilitarian shoppers will experience regulatory fit when in an implemental mindset. When consumers are confronted with attractive products, regulatory fit (non-fit) increases (decreases) the value they attribute to the product. As a consequence, consumers are more tempted by the offer and are willing to pay higher prices. Hence, hedonic shoppers are more tempted by the offer and are willing to pay higher prices when in a deliberative mindset than when in an implemental mindset. Utilitarian shoppers are more tempted and willing to pay higher prices when in an implemental mindset than when in a deliberative mindset. We examined these assumptions in three experiments.

In Study 1, we examined the assumption that a fit between consumers' chronic shopping orientation and activated mindset increases their susceptibility to persuasive communication in a point-of-purchase setting. We applied a 2 (chronic shopping orientation: utilitarian vs. hedonic) X 2 (deliberative vs. implemental mindset) between-subjects design ($N=66$). We measured chronic shopping motivation using a seven-item scale and manipulated active mindset by the personal problem versus project paradigm (e.g., Gollwitzer, Heckhausen, & Steller, 1990). Results from moderated regression support the fit hypothesis. Utilitarian shoppers were more willing to taste the product in an implemental mindset; hedonic shoppers were more willing to taste the product in a deliberative mindset.

Study 2 and 3 used the same design and the same measure for chronic shopping motivation, but different scenarios and mindset manipulations. In Study 2 ($N=140$), we manipulated participants' mindset by either writing down the pros and cons of buying a new car (deliberative mindset), or by listing five important steps when planning to buy a new car (implemental mindset) (Dhar, et al., 2007). A product-sampling scenario followed the mindset manipulation. As expected, we found that a fit between chronic shopping orientation and active mindset increased consumers' desire to consume the offered product and increases the price that consumers were willing to pay for the product.

In Study 3 ($N=62$), mindsets were evoked by either writing down the pros and cons of preparing an Italian dinner (deliberative mindset), or by naming the five most important steps when preparing an Italian dinner (implemental mindset). In a subsequent impulse-purchasing scenario, we found support for the fit hypothesis: utilitarian shoppers were more willing to pay a premium in an implemental mindset; hedonic shoppers were more willing to pay a premium in a deliberative mindset.

Overall, we established the fit effect between activated mindset and chronic shopping orientation across three studies. Utilitarian shoppers were more tempted by products encountered at the point of purchases and were willing to pay higher prices when in an implemental mindset. Hedonic shoppers, on the other hand, were more tempted and were willing to pay a higher price when in a deliberative mindset. These findings extend research on regulatory fit: while Higgins et al (2003) speculated about fit effects concerning mindsets, this link had not yet been empirically demonstrated. Moreover, the studies contribute to research on mindset effects on consumer behavior. Our findings suggest that these effects, such as the shopping momentum effect (Dhar et al. 2007), are moderated by consumers' shopping orientation. Concerning practical implications, our results suggest that retailers' persuasive attempts at the point of purchase as well as consumers' strategies to shield themselves against unwanted purchases are more effective when they are tailored to consumers' chronic shopping orientation.

## REFERENCES

Avnet, Tamar and E. Tory Higgins (2003), "Locomotion, Assessment, and Regulatory Fit: Value Transfer from 'How' to 'What'," *Journal of Experimental Social Psychology*, 39 (5), 525-30.

_____ (2006), "How Regulatory Fit Affects Value in Consumer Choices and Opinions," *Journal of Marketing Research*, 43 (1), 1-10.

Babin, Barry J., William R. Darden, and Mitch Griffin (1994), "Work and or Fun: Measuring Hedonic and Utilitarian Shopping Value," *Journal of Consumer Research*, 20 (4), 644-56.

Büttner, Oliver B. (2008), "Tracing Cognitive Processes at the Point of Purchase: The Validity of Concurrent and Retrospective Verbal Reports," in *Marketing Landscapes: A Pause for Thought, Proceedings of the 37th EMAC Conference 2008*, ed. Keith J. Perks and Paurav Shukla, Brighton, UK: European Marketing Academy.

Cesario, Joseph, Heidi Grant, and E. Tory Higgins (2004), "Regulatory Fit and Persuasion: Transfer from 'Feeling Right.'," *Journal of Personality and Social Psychology*, 86 (3), 388-404.

# The Effect of Construal Matching on Consumers' Evaluative Judgments

Susanna Y. N. Wong, The Chinese University of Hong Kong, China
Jessica Y. Y. Kwong, The Chinese University of Hong Kong, China

## EXTENDED ABSTRACT

Construal level theory (CLT) posits that psychological distance, defined as the distance of an event from the perceiver's direct experience, can be specified in four dimensions: temporal distance, spatial distance, social distance and hypotheticality (or probability) (Liberman, Trope, and Stephan 2007). Research to date has focused on the premise that as the psychological distance of a product increases, its evaluations are more influenced by its primary, essential, high-level features, as compared with its secondary, peripheral, low-level features (Liviatan, Trope, and Liberman 2008; Todorov, Goren, and Trope 2007; Trope and Liberman 2000). As an extension of CLT, we propose a construal matching effect in which psychological distance influences evaluations of a product independent of its features.

Specifically, we propose that there is a greater degree of match when the product is psychologically distant, or close, in various dimensions. For example, a gift to be purchased in a few months' time for a casual acquaintance involves a temporally distant future as well as a socially distant person, and is said to have a good match in its psychological distances (i.e., the gift is psychological distant in both dimensions). Similarly, a gift to be purchased in a few days' time for a good friend involves a temporally close future and a socially close person, and hence is also said to have a good match in its psychological distances. Conversely, there will be a poor match when the product is psychologically distant in one dimension, but close in another dimension. Thus, a gift to be purchased in a few months' (few days') time for a good friend (causal acquaintance) is said to have a poor match in its psychological distances, as it involves a temporally distant (close) future yet a socially close (distant) person.

We further hypothesize that a product with a greater match in psychological distances will be evaluated more favorably. Since the more psychologically remote an object is, the higher the level it is construed (Liberman et al. 2007), a match in the psychological distances implies a consistency in the construal level of the object along each dimension. For instance, a temporally remote purchase for a casual acquaintance will be construed primarily with high-level features along the temporal and social dimensions. This requires activating a relatively small set of features and thus is cognitively less demanding. Conversely, a poor match implies that different dimensions call for different levels of construal. For instance, a temporally remote purchase for a good friend will necessitate representations of both high- and low-level features simultaneously. This involves activating a relatively large set of features and thus requires greater mental efforts.

In prior investigations on the phenomenal feelings of meta-cognitive experiences, ease in processing product information leads to a sense of feeling right (or feeling appropriate) about the product (Lee and Aaker 2004; Reber, Schwarz, and Winkielman 2004). This feeling right yields enhanced evaluations of the product, as people misattribute such experience to a higher quality of the product. Because of the lower cognitive demand in comprehending its information, this research suggests that people are more likely to feel right about a product when it has a greater match in psychological distances. This will stimulate a more favorable evaluation of the product. In other words, a product would be evaluated more favorably when it has a greater match in psychological distances. Further, the feeling right experienced in processing its information would mediate such effect.

We assessed our ideas using scenario experiments that undergraduate students participated for cash reimbursement. Study 1 tested the effect of the match in psychological distances on product evaluations. In the scenario, participants would depart for a trip five days later (near future condition) or nine months later (distant future condition) and considered a hotel for their trip from a choice set of three hotels (high base probability condition) or 15 hotels (low base probability condition). Here the base probability pertained to the chance for a particular hotel being chosen, which was much higher in the 3-hotel choice set (i.e., 1/3) than in the 15-hotel choice set (i.e., 1/15), given that the participants had no idea about any of the hotels. Then, participants were given information of a hotel from their choice set and asked to evaluate the hotel. Consistent with our proposed construal matching effect, participants who would depart five days later evaluated the hotel more favorably when the hotel was from a 3-hotel versus 15-hotel choice set. Yet, participants who would depart nine months later evaluated the hotel more favorably when the hotel was from a 15-hotel versus 3-hotel choice set. These results support our idea that a greater match in psychological distances could enhance product evaluations.

Study 2 was conducted to explore the mechanism underlying the proposed construal matching effect. In the scenario, participants considered a CD as a gift for their good friend (socially close gift recipient) or a casual acquaintance (socially distant gift recipient). They were asked to read a review of the CD. The author of the review acted as the influencer in participants' decision to purchase the CD and was described as a student from participants' university (socially close influencer) or a working adult (socially distant influencer). Results showed that participants who read a review written by a socially close (distant) influencer evaluated the CD more favorably when their gift recipient was socially close (distant) versus distant (close). More importantly, the feeling right participants experienced in processing the review mediated the interactive effect of the social distances of gift recipient and influencer on evaluation of the CD. These findings support our idea that the feeling right aroused in the process of evaluation drives the enhanced evaluations under construal matching.

In sum, we proposed and demonstrated a construal matching effect that a product is evaluated more favorably when it has a greater match in psychological distances. While previous research on psychological distances focuses on how product features shape consumers' evaluations, our proposed construal matching effect is driven by the feelings generated from the processing of product information.

## REFERENCES

Baron, Reuben M. and David Kenny (1986), "The Moderator?Mediator Variable Distinction in Social Psychological Research: Conceptual, Strategic, and Statistical Considerations," *Journal of Personality and Social Psychology*, 51 (December), 1173–82.

Brown, Jacqueline J. and Peter H. Reingen (1987), "Social Ties and Word-of-Mouth Referral Behavior," *Journal of Consumer Research*, 14, (December), 350–62.

Cesario, Joseph, Heidi Grant, and E. Tory Higgins (2004), "Regulatory Fit and Persuasion: Transfer from 'Feeling Right'," *Journal of Personality and Social Psychology*, 86 (March), 388–404.

Clore, Gerald L. (1992), "Cognitive Phenomenology: Feelings and the Construction of Judgment," in *The Construction of Social Judgments*, ed. Leonard L. Martin and Abraham Tesser, Hillsdale, NJ: Erlbaum, 133–64.

Eyal, Tal, Nira Liberman, Yaacov Trope, and Eva Walther (2004), "The Pros and Cons of Temporally Near and Distant Action," *Journal of Personality and Social Psychology*, 86 (6), 781–95.

# Message Framing of Health Communications: Effects on Pap Exam Attitude and Intention

Laurie Balbo, Grenoble University, France
Elizabeth Pomery, Yale University, USA
Marie-Laure Gavard-Perret, Université Pierre mendes France, CERAG, France
Peter Salovey, Yale University, USA

## EXTENDED ABSTRACT

### Introduction

From a marketing point of view, authors recognize the potential consumer research has for the study of health (Moorman, 2002). To date, articles related to health marketing exist (Maheswaran and Meyers-Levy, 1990; Block and Keller, 1995; Ragubir and Menon, 1998; Cox and Cox, 2001; Chandran and Menon, 2004; Keller 2006) but the needs for researchers and practitioners to better understand health related behaviors draws our attention and interest to the study of health communications.

Health communication has been defined as "the study and use of communication strategies to inform and influence individual and community decisions that enhance health [...] Another area is the dissemination of health messages through public education campaigns that seek to change the social climate to encourage healthy behaviors, create awareness, change attitudes, and motivate individuals to adopt recommended behaviors." (Healthy People, 2010). The costs of health care and the consequences of some diseases (cancer, obesity, AIDS) has risen the question of individuals education regarding prevention, detection and treatment (Latimer et al., 2008).Because of their impact on peoples' decision to engage health behaviors (Gerend and Shepherd, 2007), health communications are of the interest of researchers.

### Conceptual Background

In their meta-analysis, Latimer et al. (2008) highlighted different message tactics that showed evidences in motivating people to engage in health-protective behaviors. One is the framing of health messages. The literature on the framing effect concept (Tversky and Kahneman, 1981; 1986) within health communications (Meyerowitz and Chaiken, 1987; Rothman et al., 1993) suggests that the wording of a health message associated with a recommendation can be a reason for a communication's effectiveness (Meyerowitz and Chaiken 1987; Rothman et al., 1993).The fundamental aspect of this theory is that people respond differently to the same problem if it is positively or negatively framed. Health messages can be framed to highlight potential benefits associated with engaging in a particular behavior (gain-framed messages), or to highlight potential costs resulting with failing to engage in the behavior (loss-framed messages). Early research on health message framing compared the relative influence of gain- and loss-framed messages in leading to different attitudes, intentions and behaviors. While some authors underline the effectiveness of gain-framed messages (Rothman et al., 1993; Detweiler et al., 1999; Apanovitch et al., 2003; Keller et al., 2003) others (Meyerowitz and Chaiken, 1987, Banks et al., 1995, Block and Keller, 1995, Schneider et al., 2001) report similar findings for loss-framed messages. These mixed results inspired researchers to further explore the conditions under which gain- and loss-framed messages are more efficient.

One approach gives attention to the function of the behavior promoted to understand the frame that will be more efficient. Detection behaviors (which represent the efforts to screen and stop the development of a specific illness, e.g. mammography can reveal the presence of breast cancer), are viewed as more risky than prevention behaviors (that enable people to increase their control over and

improve their health, e.g. eating fruits and vegetables every day to stay healthy). On the postulate of prospect theory (Tversky and Kahneman, 1981; 1986), authors (Rothman et al., 1993; Rothman and Salovey, 1997) proposed that "the function served by a health behavior can be a reliable heuristic for whether people construe a behavior as a relatively risky or safe course of action" (Rothman et al., 2006, p.205): gain-framed messages are more efficient in promoting prevention behaviors, whereas loss-framed messages are more efficient in promoting detection behaviors.

Even if this rule has received some supports in the literature (Detweiler et al., 1999; Kiene et al., 2005; Gerend and Shepherd, 2007), a new stream of research seeks to explore "the optimal conditions for using gain-and loss-framed messages, looking beyond categories such as prevention versus detection" (Latimer et al., 2007). Some researchers postulate that the perception an individual has about a behavior is more predictive than the category to which this behavior belongs. This recent hypothesis has received little attention and partial support in the literature (Rothman et al., 1999; Rivers et al., 2005).

We were interested in testing this hypothesis; so we predicted that fitting message framing with perceived behavior function will result in more favorable attitude (H1) and greater intention to follow recommendation (H2).

The literature on health related behaviors posits individuals' perception of vulnerability as one of the most important construct (e.g. Health Beliefs Model, Rosentsock, 1974; Protection Motivation Theory, Rogers, 1975). We were also interested in exploring how perceived vulnerability (i.e. the perceived likelihood to experience the undesirable consequences embedded in the message by not taking action) could moderate the effects of message framing and perceived behavior function on attitude (H3) and intention (H4).

### Method

To test our hypotheses, we run an experimentation as a full-factorial between-subjects design with two levels of message framing (gain vs loss) and two levels of perceived behavior function (prevention vs detection). Four pamphlets were designed to recommend women to get an annual Pap exam in order to examine cervical changes that can result in cervical cancer. Two hundred and nine females of at least 18 years of age ($M_{age}$=35, 76; $SD_{age}$=11, 82) were recruited to participate in this online experiment.

### Results

Analyses revealed that the message framing by perceived behavior function interaction had an effect on attitude and intention toward the recommendation. While perceived behavior function had no effect in the gain conditions, it had the predicted effect in the loss conditions with participants having more favorable attitude and higher intention when exposed to a message that described a Pap exam as a detection behavior.

Regarding the moderation of perceived vulnerability, as predicted we found that under non-fit conditions (gain-detection and loss-prevention), that is to say, when the frame used in the message is not the most relevant according to the level of risk induced by the targeted behavior, participants that thought that they could contract cervical cancer in their lifetime had higher intention to get an annual Pap exam. However, the present data suggests that perceived vulnerability does not moderate the interaction between message framing and perceived behavior function on attitude toward the recommendation.

# REFERENCES

Apanovitch A.M., McCarthy D. and Salovey P. (2003), "Using message framing to motivate HIV testing among low income, ethnic minority women", *Health Psychology*, 22, 1, 60-67.

Banks S. M., Salovey P., Greener S., Rothman A. J., Moyer A., Beauvais J. and Epel E. (1995), "The Effects of Message Framing on Mammography Utilization", *Health Psychology*, 14, 2, 178-184.

Block L. G. and Keller P. A. (1995), "When to Accentuate the Negative: The Effects of Perceived Efficacy and Message Framing on Intentions to Perform a Health-Related Behavior", *Journal of Marketing Research*, 32, 2, 192-203.

Chandran S. and Menon G. (2004), "When a Day Means More Than a Year: Effects of Temporal Framing on Judgments of Health Risk", *Journal of Consumer Research*, 31 2, 375-389.

Cox D. and Cox A. D. (2001), "Communicating the Consequences of Early Detection: The Role of Evidence and Framing", *Journal of Marketing*, 65, 3, 91-103.

Detweiler J.B, Bedell B.T., Pronin E. and Rothman A.J. (1999), "Message framing and sunscreen use: gain framed messages motivate beach-goers", *Health Psychology*, 18, 2, 189-196.

Gerend M. A. and Shepherd J. E. (2007), Using Message Framing to Promote Acceptance of the Human Papillomavirus Vaccine, *Health Psychology*, 26, 6, 745-752.

Keller A.P (2006), "Regulatory Focus and Efficacy of Health Messages", *Journal of Consumer Research*, 33, 1, 109-114.

Keller A.P., Lipkus I.M. and Rimer B.K (2003), "Affect, Framing and persuasion", *Journal of Marketing Research*, 40, 1, 54-64.

Kiene S.M., Batra W.D., Zelenski J.M. and Cothran D.L. (2005), "Why are you bringing up condoms now? The effect of message content on framing effects of condom use messages", *Health Psychology*, 24, 3, 321-326.

Latimer A.E., Salovey P. and Rothman A.J. (2007), "The effectiveness of gain-framed messages for encouraging disease prevention behavior: Is all hope lost?" *Journal of Health Communication*, 12, 7, 645-649.

Maheswaran D. and Meyers-Levy J (1990), "The Influence of Message Framing and Issue Involvement", *Journal of Marketing Research*, 27, 3, 361-367.

Meyerowitz B. E. and Chaiken S. (1987), "The Effect of Message Framing on Breast Self-Examination Attitudes, Intentions, and Behavior", *Journal of Personality & Social Psychology*, 52, 3, 500-510.

Moorman, C. (2002), "Consumer Health under the Scope", *Journal of Consumer Research*, 29, 1, 152-158.

Raghubir P. and Menon G. (1998), "AIDS and Me, Never the Twain Shall Meet: Factors Affecting Judgments of Risk", *Journal of Consumer Research*, 25, 1, 52-63.

Rivers S.E., Pizarro D.A., Schneider T.R., Pizarro J. and Salovey P. (2005), "Message framing and Pap test utilization among women attending a community health clinic", *Journal of Health Psychology*, 10, 67-79.

Rogers R. W. (1975), "A protection motivation theory of fear appeals and attitude change", *Journal of Psychology*, 91, 93-114.

Rosenstock I. (1974), "Historical Origins of the Health Belief Model", *Health Education Monographs*, 2, 4, 175-183.

Rothman A.J., Bartels R.D., Wlaschin J. and Salovey P. (2006), "The strategic use of gain- and loss-framed messages to promote healthy behavior: How theory can inform practice", *Journal of Communication*, 56, 202-221.

Rothman A. J., Martino S. C., Bedell B. T., Detweiler J. B. and Salovey P. (1999), "The systematic influence of gain- and loss-framed messages on interest in and use of different types of health behavior", *Personality and Social Psychology Bulletin*, 25, 1355–1369.

Rothman A.J. and Salovey P. (1997), "Shaping perception to motivate healthy behavior: the role of message framing", *Psychology Bulletin*, 121, 1, 3-19.

Rothman A.J., Salovey P., Antone C., Keough K. and Drake M.C. (1993), "The influence of message framing on intention to perform health behaviors", *Journal of Experimental and Social Psychology*, 29, 408-433.

Schneider T. R., Salovey P., Apanovitch A. M., Pizarro J., McCarthy D., Zullo J. and Rothman A. J. (2001), "The Effects of Message Framing and Ethnic Targeting on Mammography Use Among Low-Income Women", *Health Psychology*, 20, 4, 256-266.

Tversky A. and Kahneman D. (1981), "The framing of decisions and the psychology of choice", *Science*, 211, 4481, 453-458.

Tversky A. and Kahneman D. (1986), "Rational Choice and the Framing of Decisions", *Journal of Business*, 59, 4, 251-278.

U.S. Department of Health and Human Services (2000), *Healthy People 2010: Understanding and Improving Health*, 2nd ed. Washington, DC: U.S. Government Printing Office.

# Consumer Victimization: A Psychological Contracts Perspective

Hyokjin Kwak, Drexel University, USA
Anupam Jaju, George Mason University, USA
Marina Puzakova, Drexel University, USA

## EXTENDED ABSTRACT

According to the Oxford English Dictionary (2009), victimization entails cheating, swindling, or defrauding an individual, making them a victim and causing them to suffer inconvenience, discomfort, and annoyance either deliberately or through misdirected attentions. Consumer victimization occurs when firms exploit their consumers. Much of the consumer affairs literature focuses on the economic and physical consequences victimization has on consumers. In this paper, a psychological contract model is introduced to explain how victimization develops and its implications for consumers' reactions.

Psychological contracts represent the perceived reciprocal obligations that consumers believe that they have with a given company. It consists of the beliefs the parties hold regarding the terms of the informal exchange agreement. While expectations and psychological contracts are related concepts, researchers suggest that the two constructs are not equivalent with one another (Rousseau 1990). Expectations can take a number of forms ranging from an individual's probabilistic beliefs regarding the likelihood that a given behavior will have a given outcome, to their normative beliefs regarding the appropriate behaviors required in a given situation (Oliver 1980; Rousseau and Parks 1993). These expectations, however, may not be contractual in nature if promises are absent. As such, psychological contracts differ from the general notion of expectations in part because psychological contracts are promissory and reciprocal (Rousseau 1990).

When the ratio of benefits provided by the organization in relation to the benefits promised matches the ratio of contributions provided by the consumer in relation to the contributions promised by him or her, the contract is perceived as being fulfilled (Morrison and Robinson 1997). If, on the other hand, this relationship becomes unbalanced, the contract is breached. That is, psychological breach refers to consumers' cognitions that a company failed to fulfill its obligations in a manner commensurate with consumers' contributions. The psychological contract model differs from the expectations-dissatisfaction model, in part due to the inclusion of the concept of violation. This model incorporates a sense of relationship and trust, not seen in other models, and can be used to understand the existence of continued future relationships (Turnley and Feldman 1999). Violation involves not only the experiences of unmet expectations, but also something deeper and more emotional (Rousseau 1989, 1995). As per Rousseau (1989), violation is a feeling or perception of betrayal and strong emotional distress, where the individual experiences anger, bitterness and wrongful harm. In essence, violation involves anger, disappointment, and frustration stemming from the perceived betrayal and mistreatment by the firm. Elaborating on Rousseau's definition, we suggest that psychological contract violation can be interpreted as a measure of victimization. Victimization by definition suggests that an individual is being mislead, defrauded, or taken advantage of (Oxford English Dictionary 2009). Thus, following Rousseau's definition, when a seller is perceived as intentionally not fulfilling their obligations to a buyer, the buyer will feel mislead or taken advantage of, manifesting itself in perceptions of violation.

We explore consumers' possible behavioral reactions when the company fails to (intentionally/unintentionally) live up to its obligations (i.e., breach, violation) as perceived by the consumer. We expect that the violation of psychological contract will lead to consumers' retaliatory behavior (i.e., switching, direct and third-party

complaining). Using SEM, we test our model across three different threats to consumers' well-being (i.e., economic, physical, social). Our experimental data show that consumers' perceptions of breach lead to higher perceptions of psychological contract violation, and violation in turn leads to higher incidences of consumer retaliatory behavior (i.e., switching, complaining). Our results also showed that not all breaches are created equal. When examining the results across the three threat conditions, we found that the associations between breach and violation were typically stronger for social threats and weaker for economic threats. In support of hypothesis two, the perceived intentionality of the unmet obligations also moderated the associations between breach and violation in the physical and social threat conditions, but not the economic condition. While perceptions of breach are lower in the social threat conditions, when social threats do occur and are perceived as intentional they would be more surprising and unsettling, producing greater negative reactions and, consequently, stronger retaliatory behaviors than was seen with economic threats. Finally, the current research outlines theoretical implications and future directions of scientific inquiry. For instance, we suggest that outcome assessments (e.g. magnitude of the breach, nature of the breach), social and formal contracts (e.g. legal obligations, written contracts, type of exchange) may influence consumers' perceptions of victimization. When examining the effects of violation on participants' retaliatory behavior it will be informative to take into account the influence of investment and perceptions of alternatives. Overall, we show how consumers' interpretation process can influence their reactions to firms' breach, and how the magnitude of their retaliation may vary with the type of threat they experienced.

## REFERENCES

Oxford English Dictionary (2009), ed. John Simpson. Second ed. Oxford: Oxford University Press.

Bechwati, Nada Nasr and Maureen Morrin (2003), "Outraged Consumers: Getting Even at the Expense of Getting a Good Deal," *Journal of Consumer Psychology*, 13 (4), 440-53.

Crocker, Jennifer and Lora E. Park (2004), "The Costly Pursuit of Self-Esteem," *Psychological Bulletin*, 130 (3), 392-414.

Dykman, Benjamin M. (1998), "Integrating Cognitive and Motivational Factors in Depression: Initial Tests of a Goal-Orientation Approach," *Journal of Personality and Social Psychology*, 74 (1), .139-59.

Folkes, Valerie S. (1984), "Consumer Reactions to Product Failure: An Attributional Approach," *Journal of Consumer Research*, 10 (March), 398-410.

Gelbrich, Katja (2009), "Anger, Frustration, and Helplessness after Service Failure: Coping Strategies and Effective Informational Support," *Journal of Academy of Marketing Science*, in press.

Grégoire, Yany and Robert J. Fisher (2006), "The Effects of Relationship Quality on Customer Retaliation," *Marketing Letters*, 17 (January), 31-46.

_____ (2008), "Customer Betrayal and Retaliation: When Your Best Customers Become Your Worst Enemies," *Journal of the Academy of Marketing Science*, 36, 247-61.

510

*Advances in Consumer Research*
*Volume 38, © 2012*

Grégoire, Yany, Thomas M. Tripp, and Renaud Legoux (2009), "When Customer Love Turns into Lasting Hate: The Effects of Relationship Strength and Time on Customer Revenge and Avoidance," *Journal of Marketing*, 73 (November), 18-32.

Jones, E. E. and R.E. Nisbett (1980), "The Actor and the Observer: Divergent Perceptions of the Causes of the Behavior," in *Attribution: Perceiving the Causes of Behavior*, ed. D. E. Kanouse E. E. Jones, H. H. Kelley, R. E. Nisbett, S. Valins and B. Weiner. Morristown, NJ: General Learning Press, 79-94.

Kelly, Harold H. and John W. Thibaut (1978), *Interpersonal Relations: A Theory of Interdependence*, New York: Wiley.

Lazarus, Richard S. and Susan Folkman (1984), *Stress, Appraisal, and Coping*, New York: Springer.

McColl-Kennedy, Janet R. and Beverley A. Sparks (2003), "Application of Fairness Theory to Service Failures and Service Recovery," *Journal of Service Research*, 5 (February), 251-66.

McQuitty, Shaun, Adam Finn, and James B. Wiley (2000), "Systematically Varying Consumer Satisfaction and Its Implications for Product Choice," Academy of Marketing Science Review, Vol. 10, Available at:http://www.amsreview.org/articles/mcquitty10-2000.pdf

Moorman, Christine, Gerald Zaltman, and Pohit Deshpande (1992), "Relationships Between Providers and Users of Marketing Research: The Dynamics of Trust Within and Between Organizations," *Journal of Marketing Research*, 29 (August), 314-29.

Morrison, Elizabeth W. and Sandra L. Robinson (1997), "When Employees Feel Betrayed: A Model of How Psychological Contract Violation Develops," *Academy of Management Review*, 22 (1), 226-56.

_____ (2004), "The Employment Relationship from Two Sides: Incongruence in Employees' and Employers' Perceptions of Obligations," in *The Employment Relationship: Examining Psychological and Contextual Perspectives*, eds. Jacqueline A.-M. Coyle-Shapiro and Lynn M. Shore and M. Susan Taylor and Lois E. Tetrick. Oxford: Oxford University Press, 161-80.

Oliver, Richard L. (1980), "A Cognitive Model of the Antecedents and Consequences of Satisfaction Decisions," *Journal of Marketing Research*, 17 (November), 460-69.

_____ (1989), "Processing of the Satisfaction Response in Consumption: A Suggested Framework and Research Propositions," *Journal of Consumer Satisfaction, Dissatisfaction and Complaining Behavior*, 2, 1-16.

Robinson, Sandra L. (1996), "Trust and Breach of the Psychological Contract," *Administrative Science Quarterly*, 41 (December), 574-99.

Robinson, Sandra L. and Elizabeth W. Morrison (2000), "The Development of Psychological Contract Breach and Violation: A Longitudinal Study," *Journal of Organizational Behavior*, 21 (5), 525.

Rousseau, Denise M. (1989), "Psychological and Implied Contracts in Organizations," *Employee Responsibilities and Rights Journal*, 2 (June), 121-39.

Rousseau, Denise M. and J. McLean Parks (1993), "The Contracts of Individuals and Organizations," in *Research in Organizational Behavior*, Vol. 15, eds. L. L. Cummings and B. M. Staw. Greenwich, CT: JAI Press, 1-43.

Rousseau, Denise M. and Martin M. Greller (1994), "Human Resource Practices: Administrative Contract Makers," *Human Resource Management*, 33 (Fall), 385-401.

Rousseau, Denise M. (1995), *Psychological Contracts in Organizations: Understanding Written and Unwritten Agreements*, Thousand Oaks, CA: Sage Publications.

_____ (2001), "Schema, Promise and Mutuality: The Building Blocks of the Psychological Contract," *Journal of Occupational and Organizational Psychology*, 74 (November), 511-41.

Rousseau, Denise M. (1990), "New Hire Perceptions of Their Own and the Employer's Obligations," *Journal of Organizational Behavior*, 11 (389-400).

Schein, Edgar H. (2001/1965), *Organizational Psychology*, New Jersey: Englewood Cliffs.

Schlenker, Barry R., Beth A. Pontari, and Andrew N. Christopher (2001), " Excuses and Character: Personal and Social Implications of Excuses," *Personality and Social Psychology Review*, 5 (1), 15-32.

Schneider, Benjamin and David E. Bowen (1999), "Understanding Customer Outrage and Delight," *Sloan Management Review*, 41 (Fall), 35-45.

Turnley, William H. and Daniel C. Feldman (1999), "A Discrepancy Model of Psychological Contract Violations," *Human Resource Management Review*, 9 (3), 367-86.

Ward, James C. and Amy L. Ostrom (2006), "Complaining to the Masses : The Role of Protest Framing in Customer-Created Complaint Web Sites," *Journal of Consumer Research*, 33 (December), 220-30.

Zajonc, Robert B. (1980), "Feeling and Thinking: Preferences Need No Inferences," *American Psychologists*, 35, 151-75.

Zeelenberg, Marcel and Rik Pieters (2004), "Beyond Valence in Customer Dissatisfaction: A Review and New Findings on Behavioral Responses to Regret and Disappointment in Failed Services," *Journal of Business Research*, 57, 445-55

# Can Biases About the Future Push Consumers to Act? Effects of Affective Forecasting on Consumer Procrastination

Lily Lin, University of British Columbia, Canada
Timothy Silk, University of British Columbia, Canada

## EXTENDED ABSTRACT

Behavioral economics classifies procrastination as present-biased preference. This perspective implies that people are insufficiently forward-looking and that procrastination occurs as a consequence of failing to appreciate that repeated decisions to postpone today's tasks will result in a lack of progress in the long term (Akerlof 1991). A logical extension of this perspective suggests that manipulations that encourage forward-looking behavior may de-bias present-bias preference. The proposed research introduces affective forecasting as a means of manipulating forward-looking behavior in an attempt to mitigate procrastination.

Procrastination applies to a wide range of consumer contexts with important consequences, such as completing tasks on time to obtain financial rewards or avoid penalties (e.g., tax returns, financial investments, etc.), and meeting purchasing deadlines for gift-giving occasions (e.g., birthdays, Christmas, Valentine's day, etc.). Research on procrastination suggests that people are likely to procrastinate due to factors such as task aversiveness and perceived effort required for a given task (Anderson 2003). Numerous individual difference variables can also contribute to procrastiantion (Steel 2007). Research in this domain, however, is largely silent on mediating variables that may motivate action. For example, research has yet to examine whether limitations in people's self-knowledge (e.g., inability to accurately predict one's future emotional states) can influence procrastination.

Affective forecasting refers to predictions people make about their future emotional states. Research in this domain has consistently demonstrated an effect termed the "impact bias" whereby "forecasters" tend to overestimate the intensity and duration of their reactions to future events compared to "experiencers" who experience the same events but do not engage in affective forecasts. (Gilbert et al. 1998). Importantly, the impact bias has been shown to be stronger for negative emotions (e.g. regret) than for positive emotions (e.g. happiness) (Wilson and Gilbert 2003). While the majority of research in affective forecasting has focused on the identification of these biases, little empirical work has looked at how these biases might influence people's actions. That is, most work has focused on the forecasts themselves and research has yet to examine whether the motivation to avoid such negative states in the future might encourage individuals to take action to change their environment. Therefore, the main motivation behind this research is to examine the behavioral consequences of affective forecasting by looking at its influences on procrastination.

The current research examines the effects of affective forecasts on people's progress in three consumer contexts. Three studies track changes in consumers' progress, stress, and other emotional responses over time to identify underlying mechanisms that influence procrastination. We observe that consumers who make affective forecasts overestimate the negative emotions associated with procrastination. This impact bias motivates consumers to avoid forecasted negative states by initiating and completing tasks earlier than non-forecasters. Further, we find that issuing implicit and explicit warnings about the negative consequences of procrastination are largely ineffective at motivating action. Findings suggest that the underlying process that takes place during affective forecasts is unique and does more than serve a mere warning function.

Experiment 1 examined the relationship between affective forecasting and consumers' progress on holiday shopping. Longitudinal data was collected over a one-month period to assess changes in participants' affective forecasts and progress on their holiday shopping lists. One month prior to the holiday gift exchange season, 44 undergraduates were randomly assigned to either the "forecaster" or "experiencer" condition. Following the lab session, participants were contacted periodically and asked to complete six additional online diaries. As predicted, forecasters were found to significantly overestimate the intensity of negative emotions (stress, unhappiness, and perceived difficulty) they would feel in the future. Results also showed that forecasters initiated and completed tasks earlier than experiencers and made greater progress over time.

Experiment 2 examined the relationship between affective forecasting and consumers' progress toward Valentine's Day shopping. The complexity of the task was decreased in this study because participants only needed to shop for one individual. Additionally, a shorter two-week time frame was examined in order to test if similar effects would be observed over a shorter period of time. In essence, we were curious to know whether the effects observed in Experiment 1 would manifest themselves in a less complex task with potentially higher consequences over a shorter period of time. The overall design and basic methodology were similar to Experiment 1. Fifty-six undergraduates in romantic relationships were randomly assigned to either the "forecasters" or "experiencers" condition. Following the lab session, participants were contacted asked to complete 3 additional online diaries. As in Experiment 1, the forecasters overestimated intensity of their future negative emotions, initiated and completed tasks earlier than experiencers, and made greater progress over time.

The purpose of Experiment 3 was to examine whether affective forecasting essentially operates as a mere warning function. Specifically, we aimed to investigate whether the process that occurs when making affective forecasts differs from being warned about how one will feel in the future if they procrastinate. To test this,169 undergraduates participated in a consumer-themed scavenger hunt modeled after the TV reality show *The Amazing Race*. Participants were given two weeks to complete a series of five tasks which required them to take a photograph of various retail stores in the local area and upload the photographs to a website that tracked each participant's progress over time. Participants were randomly assigned to the "forecasters", "experiencers", "implicit warning", or "explicit warning" condition. The manipulations for the forecasters and experiencers conditions were similar to the first two studies. Those in the implicit warning condition were warned that they would feel negative emotions if they were to procrastinate, and were told to act accordingly. Those in the explicit warning condition received the same warning and were explicitly told that such negative emotions could be avoided by not procrastinating and starting the task right away. Forecasters again exhibited an impact bias and a higher proportion of forecasters completed the race by the deadline. Issuing implicit and explicit warnings about the negative consequences of procrastination were largely ineffective at motivating action, suggesting that the underlying process that takes place during affective forecasting does more than serve a mere warning function.

# REFERENCES

Akerlof, George (1991), "Procrastination and Obedience," *American Economic Review,* 81 (2), 1-19.

Anderson, Christopher J. (2003), "The Psychology of Doing Nothing: Forms of Decision Avoidance Result From Reason and Emotion," *Psychological Bulletin,* 129, 139-67.

Ariely, Dan and Klaus Wertenbroch (2002), "Procrastination, Deadlines, and Performance: Self-Control by Precommitment," *Psychological Science,* 13 (3), 219-24.

Baron, Rueben M. and David A. Kenny (1986), "The Moderator-Mediator Variable Distinction in Social Psychological Research: Conceptual, Strategic and Statistical Considerations," *Journal of Personality and Social Psychology,* 51 (6), 1173-1182.

Blunt, Allan K. and Timothy Pychyl (2000), "Task Aversiveness and Procrastination: A Multi-Dimensional Approach to Task Aversiveness Across Stages of Personal Projects," *Personality and Individual Differences,* 28 (1), 153-67.

Dunn, Elizabeth W., Timothy D. Wilson, and Daniel T. Gilbert (2003), "Location, Location,

Location: The Misprediction of Satisfaction in Housing Lotteries," *Personality and Social Psychology Bulletin,* 29 (11), 1421-32.

Finkenauer, Catrin, Marcello Gallucci, Wilco W. van Dijk, and Monique Pollmann (2007), "Investigating the Role of Time in Affective Forecasting: Temporal Influences on Forecasting Accuracy," *Personality and Social Psychology Bulletin,* 33 (8) 1152-66.

Gilbert, Daniel T., Elizabeth C. Pinel, Timothy D. Wilson, Stephen J. Blumberg, and Thalia P. Wheatley (1998), "Immune Neglect: A Source of Durability Bias in Affective Forecasting," *Journal of Personality and Social Psychology,* 75 (3), 617-38.

Greenleaf, Eric A. and Donald R. Lehmann (1995), "Reasons for Substantial Delay in Consumer Decision Making," *Journal of Consumer Research,* 22 (2), 186-99.

Liberman, Nira, Yaacov Trope, Sean M. McCrea, and Steven J. Sherman (2007), "The Effect of Level of Construal on the Temporal Distance of Activity Enactment," *Journal of Experimental Social Psychology,* 43 (1), 143-49.

MacInnis, Deborah J. and Vaness M. Patrick (2006), "Spotlight on Affect: Affect and Affective Forecasting in Impulse Control," *Journal of Consumer Psychology,* 16 (3) 224-31.

Morewedge, Carey K., Daniel T. Gilbert, and Timothy D. Wilson (2005), "The Least Likely of Times: How Remembering the Past Biases Forecasts of the Future," *Psychological Science,* 16 (8), 626-30.

Steel, Piers (2007), "The Nature of Procrastination: A Meta-Analytic and Theoretical Review of Quintessential Self-Regulatory Failure," *Psychological Bulletin,* 133 (1), 65-94.

Tice, Dianne M. and Roy F. Baumeister (1997), "Longitudinal Study of Procrastination, Performance, Stress, and Health: The Costs and Benefits of Dawdling," *Psychological Science,* 8 (6), 454-58.

Tice, Dianne M., Ellen Bratslavsky, and Roy F. Baumeister (2001), "Emotional Distress Regulation Takes Precedence Over Impulse Control: If You Feel Bad, Do It!," *Journal of Personality and Social Psychology,* 80 (1), 53-67

Vohs, Kathleen D., Roy F. Baumeister, Brandon J. Schmeichel, Jean M. Twenge, Noelle M. Nelson, and Dianne M. Tice (2008), "Making Choices Impairs Subsequent Self-Control: A Limited-Resource Account of Decision Making, Self-Regulation, and Active Initiative," *Journal of Personality and Social Psychology,* 94 (5), 883-98.

Wilson, Timothy D. and Daniel T. Gilbert (2003), "Affective Forecasting," in *Advances in Experimental Social Psychology,* Vol. 35, ed. Mark Zanna, Elsevier, New York, 345-411.

# The Effects of Circular and Linear Time Orientations on Personal Savings Estimates and Savings Behavior

Leona Tam, Old Dominon University, USA
Hanie Lee, Rice University, USA
Utpal Dholakia, Rice University USA

## EXTENDED ABSTRACT

A low personal savings rate has been an important concern from economic, social and policy standpoints, especially as the U.S. savings rate dipped into negative territory in 2005 (Guidolin and Jeunesse 2007) and remained there until unease from the recent economic down turn brought it back up to positive levels in the fourth quarter of 2009 (BEA 2010). Nevertheless, there is still a wide range in personal savings rates across consumers. Some consumers are able to save a significant amount of their incomes, whereas others can barely make it from paycheck to paycheck. Moreover, such differences cannot be explained solely by differences in income (e.g., Masson, Bayoumi and Samiei 1998). It is therefore important to examine factors affecting personal savings of consumers. Prior research has shown that the temporal frame such as length of duration and delay used in decision making is crucial to personal finance tasks (e.g., Ulkumen, Thomas, and Morwitz 2008; Tam and Dholakia 2010).

We examined effects of circular and linear time orientation on personal savings estimates and savings behavior. The distinction between circular and linear time orientation originates from people's view of life. Under a linear time orientation, there is a past, present, and future, and time is separable into discrete compartments and moves toward the future in a linear fashion. Under the circular time orientation, in contrast, time is not perceived as a straight line stretching from the distant past to the far future, but rather, it is seen as a circular system in which the same events are repeated according to some cyclical pattern (Graham 1981). The "discrete compartment of time" view in the linear time orientation results in a difference in how much people focus on the future versus the present. Individuals under a linear time orientation are more future oriented and less present oriented than those under circular time orientation (Bergadaa 1990). Linear and circular time orientations also differ in how goals are approached.

Based on the three different characteristics between linear and circular time orientation, (1) the overall progression in life, (2) a future versus present orientation, and (3) a planning mind set, one would expect to see higher savings rate from people with a linear time orientation than a circular time orientation because linear time orientation is expected to put a stronger emphasis on future retirement needs and enable formulation of more concrete plans to accumulate personal savings. Future goals should determine present actions and people with linear time orientation should plan for the future and thus behavior in the present should be based on making forward progress towards achieving long-term goals. Yet, in reality, many empirical surveys show that people that tend to adopt a linear time orientation save much less than those who tend to adopt a circular time orientation (Horioka and Wan 2008; Caillois and McKeon, 1963).

We draw on Resource Slack Theory (Zauberman and Lynch 2005) and Construal Level Theory (Liberman and Trope 1998) to explain this anomaly and to better understand the effects of circular and linear time orientations on savings estimates and personal savings. Theoretically, resource slack as operationalized by future optimism and level of construal of the savings task are likely to be affected by time frames for which savings estimates are given. In the context of saving behavior, Resource Slack Theory suggests that people think they will be able to save more in the distant future than the near future because of the notion of future optimism. Future optimism is expected to result in a higher estimate of saving for distant future time periods than near future time periods. Linear time orientation is more future oriented and circular time orientation is more present oriented. When future optimism affects personal savings estimates, we expect higher savings estimates to result from linear time orientation than circular time orientation. However, once specific savings plan (e.g., saving 10% of paycheck) is set, a circular time orientation that has lower level of future optimism and focuses on tasks on hand could save actually more than linear time orientation.

Construal Level Theory posits that temporal distance changes decision makers' responses to future events by changing the way they mentally represent those events (Trope and Liberman 2003) and provides useful insights into the role of savings task construal under linear and circular time orientation. This theory suggests that in the case of circular time orientation, decision makers think of saving activities and estimation tasks more concretely using lower level construal, in comparison to linear time orientation where personal savings is considered in more long term progress with higher level construal. Consequently, under circular time orientation, people would be thinking of more specific ways in which they will be able to save money and sticking to the more mundane savings activities set for each paycheck. Construal of the savings task in detailed, concrete (vs. abstract) terms for circular time orientation is expected to lead to a greater personal savings when compared to linear time orientation.

For these reasons, we expected circular time orientation would result in higher level of savings estimates and actual personal savings. Two longitudinal experimental studies were conducted. Study 1 found that people who applied circular time savings method provided higher personal savings estimates and indeed saved more in reality, compared to people who applied linear time savings method. Study 2 tested future optimism and construal level as mediators in the effects of circular and linear time orientation on personal savings estimates and savings behavior. Study 3, using a longitudinal method, is currently underway.

## REFERENCES

Aaker, Jennifer L. (2006), "Delineating Culture," *Journal of Consumer Psychology*, 16(4), 343-347.

Bergadaa, Michelle M. (1990), "The Role of Time in the Action of the Consumer," *Journal of Consumer Research*, 17(December), 289-302.

Briley, Donnel A. and Jennifer L. Aaker (2006), "Bridging the Culture Chasm: Ensuring That Consumers are Healthy, Wealthy, and Wise," *Journal of Public Policy and Marketing*, 25(1). 53-66.

Bureau of Economic Analysis (BEA, 2010), "Growth Moderates in the Fourth Quarter," http://www.bea.gov/newsreleases/national/pi/2010/pdf/pi1209_fax.pdf.

Caillois, Roger and Nora McKeon (1963), "Circular Time, Rectilinear Time," *Diogenes*, 11(1), 1-13.

Chen, Haipeng, Sharon Ng, and Akshay R. Rao (2005), "Cultural Differences in Consumer Impatience," *Journal of Marketing Research*, 42(August), 291-301.

Croson, Rachel, Femida Handy, and Jen Shang (2009), "Keeping Up with the Joneses: The Relationship of Perceived Descriptive Social Norms, Social Information, and Charitable Giving," *Nonprofit Management & Leadership*, 19(4), 467-489.

Graham, Robert J. (1981), "The Role of Perception of Time in Consumer Research," *Journal of Consumer Research*, 7(March), 335-342.

Guidolin, M., & La Jeunesse, E. A. (2007). The decline in the U.S. personal saving rate: Is it real and is it a puzzle? *Federal Reserve Bank of St. Louis Review, 89,* 491-514.

Horioka, Charles Yuji and Junmin Wan (2008), "Why Does China Save So Much?" in *China, Asia, and the New World Economy*, ed. Barry Eichengreen, Yung Chui Park, and Charles Syplosz, Oxford University Press, p.371-392.

Masson, Paul R., Tamim Bayoumi and Hossein Samiei (1998), "International Evidence on the Determinants of Private Saving," *World Bank Economic Review*, 12, 483-501.

Tam, Leona and Utpal M. Dholakia (2010), "Delay and Duration Effects of Time Frames on Personal Savings Estimates and Behavior," Working Paper, Rice University.

Trope, Yaacov and Nira Liberman (2003), "Temporal Construal," *Psychological Review,* 110(3), 403-421.

Ulkumen, Gulden, Manoj Thomas, and Vicki G. Morwitz (2008), "Will I Spend More in 12 Months or a Year? The Effect of Ease of Estimation and Confidence on Budget Estimates," *Journal of Consumer Research*, 35(August), 245-256.

Yamada, Yako and Yoshinobu Kato (2006), "Images of Circular Time and Spiral Repetition: The Generative Life Cycle Model," *Culture & Psychology*, 12(2), 143-160.

Zauberman, Gal and John G., Jr. Lynch (2005), "Resource Slack and Propensity on Discount Delayed Investments of Time Versus Money," *Journal of Experimental Psychology: General,* 134, 23-37.

# Hate the Wait? Why Customers Who Wait Longer Buy More

Alan D. Cooke, University of Florida, USA
Nira Munichor, The Hebrew University of Jerusalem, Israel

## EXTENDED ABSTRACT

Delays are an abhorred but inescapable element of shopping. Scholars have sought to understand the effects of waiting on consumer reactions, and to find ways to manage waiting with the goal of mitigating negative reactions usually elicited by a wait (e.g., Carmon, Shanthikerumar, and Carmon 1995; Maister 1985; Zhou and Soman 2003). Surprisingly, however, little research examines how waiting might influence subsequent purchase behavior. Researchers have examined intentions to revisit the store or to spread word-of-mouth about the retailer (e.g., Gorn et al. 2004; Hui, Dube, and Chebat 1997), but have not addressed the effects that waiting may have for purchases during the trip. Our research is aimed at bridging this gap; it reveals the counterintuitive impact of waiting time on subsequent purchase behavior.

While waiting duration is assumed to have considerable influences on consumer behavior, the exact nature of those influences is still a puzzle. Available literature portrays contradicting findings with regard to the impact of wait time on consumers (e.g., Hornik 1984; Hui and Tse 1996; Munichor and Rafaeli 2007; Taylor 1994), which may hint at the complex nature of the effects of wait-time on consumers. On the one hand, consumers typically regard prolonged waits as distasteful, which may result in lower purchase levels. On the other hand, the process of waiting and cognitions about the nature and reasons for the prolonged wait may affect both beliefs about the goods and/or the process by which consumers determine purchase quantities, potentially resulting in a counterintuitive increase in purchases that are made following the wait (such as those made in counter-service restaurants).

Experiment 1 tested the effect of waiting time on the number of items chosen to be consumed subsequently, using a computer-based consumption task. Participants were asked to evaluate the presentation skills of some speakers based on a series of videos. We asked them to choose which of two types of videos to watch (lectures or stand-up comedy), and then manipulated the amount of time they had to wait before choosing the specific videos to watch. The number of videos chosen served as our primary dependent variable.

We found that, although participants perceived a longer wait as more annoying than a shorter wait, they also chose to watch more videos. Thus, when made to wait before a choice, people choose more if made to wait longer. This result occurs despite, or possibly because of, the additional frustration resulting from the wait.

Experiment 2 further tested whether the positive relationship between wait time and purchase amount results from people who waited longer believing the goods to be more attractive, a social signaling account. Participants went through a procedure similar to that used in experiment 1. Social signaling was manipulated through instructions; participants in the signaling condition were told that their wait time was dependent on other people's choices, whereas participants in the no-signaling condition were told that their wait time was dependent only on the speed of the network.

Again, participants perceived a longer wait as more annoying than a shorter wait. Further, a significant effect of the interaction between time and signaling on the number of chosen videos was found. When participants were told that their wait time was dependent on other people's choices, they chose more videos following a longer wait than following a shorter wait. When participants were told that their wait time was dependent on network connectivity, however, the opposite pattern emerged. These results support the hypothesis that social signaling underlies the positive effect of

wait time on purchase amount. When wait time is perceived to be the product of others' preferences, such that a longer wait signals greater product's popularity, people choose more items following a longer, rather than a shorter wait. When wait-time is perceived to be independent of other people's choices, however, longer waits lead to fewer items chosen.

In summary, the current work shows that longer waits produce subsequent *increased* purchase when waiting time serves as a social signal about the value of the items. This study contributes to the investigation of the effects of waiting on subsequent actual behaviors, and sheds light on the psychological mechanisms that underlie these effects. Our results undermine the commonly held view that waiting can only damage firms' bottom lines, and shows that some effects of waiting time may take a counterintuitive form. Our findings therefore may carry important implications for the management of queues and waiting, and may also make customers more aware of the non-trivial influences that a wait may exert on their behavior. Our research also contributes to the development of behavioral theory by revealing the direct and indirect relationships between the process of waiting and other common consumer behaviors. We also discuss the role that cognitive dissonance and self-control depletion may play in causing people who have waited longer to consume more.

## REFERENCES

Antonides, Gerrit, Peter C. Verhoef, and Marcel van Aalst (2002), "Consumer Perception and Evaluation of Waiting Time: A Field Experiment," *Journal of Consumer Psychology*, 12 (3), 193-202.

Aronson, Elliot (1997), "Back to the Future," *The American Journal of Psychology*, 110, 127-37.

Banerjee, Abhijit V. (1992), "A Simple Model of Herd Behavior," *The Quarterly Journal of Economics*, 107 (3), 797-817.

Baumeister, Roy F. (2002), "Yielding to Temptation: Self-Control Failure, Impulsive Purchasing, and Consumer Behavior," *Journal of Consumer Research*, 28 (4), 670-76.

Baumeister, Roy F., Erin A. Sparks, Tyler F. Stillman, and Kathleen D. Vohs (2008), "Free Will in Consumer Behavior: Self-Control, Ego Depletion, and Choice," *Journal of Consumer Psychology,* 18, 4-13.

Cameron, Michaelle A., Julie Baker, Mark Peterson, and Karin Braunsberger (2003), "The Effect of Music, Wait-Length Evaluation, and Mood on a Low-Cost Wait Experience," *Journal of Business Research*, 56, 421-30.

Carmon, Ziv and Daniel Kahneman (1996), "The Experienced Utility of Queuing: Experience Profiles and Retrospective Evaluations of Simulated Queues," working paper, Fuqua School, Duke University, NC 27708.

Carmon, Ziv, George J. Shanthikerumar, and Tali F. Carmon (1995), "A Psychological Perspective on Service Segmentation Models: The Significance of Accounting for Consumers' Perception of Waiting and Service," *Management Science*, 41 (11), 1806-815.

Chevalier, Judith A. and Dina Mayzlin, (2006), "The Effect of Word of Mouth on Sales: Online Book Reviews," *Journal of Marketing Research*, 43, 345-54.

Cialdini, Robert B. (1985), "Persuasion Principles," *The Public Relations Journal*, 41 (October), 12-6.

Clemmer, Elizabeth C. and Benjamin Schneider (1993), "Managing Customer Dissatisfaction With Waiting: Applying Social-Psychological Theory in a Service Setting," in *Advances in Services Marketing and Management*, 2, ed. Teresa A. Swartz, David E. Bowen, and Stephen W. Brown, Greenwich, CN: JAI Press Inc., 213-29.

Dellaert, Benedict G. C. and Barbara E. Kahn (1999), "How Tolerable Is Delay? Consumers' Evaluations of Internet Web Sites Sfter Waiting," *Journal of Interactive Marketing*, 13, 41-54.

Evangelist, Shane, Badger J. J. Godwin, Joey Johnson, Vincent Conzola, Robert Kizer, Stephanie Young-Helou, and Richard Metters (2002), "Linking Marketing and Operations: An Application at Blockbuster, Inc.," *Journal of Service Research*, 5 (2), 91-100.

Festinger, Leon (1957), *A theory of cognitive dissonance*. Evanstone, IL: Row, Peterson

Goldenberg, Jacob, Barak Libai, Sarit Moldovan, and Eitan Muller (2007), "The NPV of Bad News," *International Journal of Research in Marketing*, 24, 186-200.

Gorn, Gerald J., Amitava Chattopadhyay, Jaideep Sengupta, and Shashank Tripathi (2004), "Waiting for the Web: How Screen Color Affects Time Perception," *Journal of Marketing Research*, XLI (May), 215-25.

Grewal, Dhruv, Julie Baker, Michael Levy, and Glenn B. Voss (2003), "The Effect of Wait Expectations and Store Atmosphere Evaluations on Patronage Intentions in Service-Intensive Retail Stores," *Journal of Retailing*, 79, 259-68.

Hellofs, Linda L. and Robert Jacobson (1999), "Market Share and Customers' Perceptions of Quality: When Can Firms Grow Their Way to Higher Versus Lower Quality?" *Journal of Marketing*, 63 (January), 16-25

Hershey, John C., David A. Asch, Thi Thumasathit, Jacqueline Meszaros, and Victor V. Waters, (1994) "The Roles of Altruism, Free Riding, and Bandwagoning in Vaccination Decisions," *Organizational Behavior and Human Decision Processes* 59 (2), 177-87.

Hornik, Jacob, (1984), "Subjective vs. Objective Time Measures: A Note on the Perception of Time in Consumer Behavior," *Journal of Consumer Research*, 11 (June), 615-18.

Hornik, Jacob and Dan Zakay (1996), "Psychological Time: The Case of Time and Consumer Behavior," *Time & Society,* 5(3), 385-97.

Hui, Michael K., Laurette Dube, and Jean-Charles Chebat (1997), "The Impact of Music on Consumers' Reactions to Waiting for Services," *Journal of Retailing*, 73 (1), 87-104.

Hui, Michael K. and David K. Tse (1996), "What to Tell Consumers in Waits of Different Lengths: An Integrative Model of Service Evaluation," *Journal of Marketing*, 60, 81-90.

Hui, Michael K. and Lianxi Zhou (1996), "How does Waiting Duration Information Influence Customers' Reactions to Waiting for Service?" *Journal of Applied Social Psychology*, 26 (19), 1702-717.

Katz, Karen L., Blaire M. Larson, and Richard C. Larson (1991), "Prescription for the Waiting-in-Line Blues: Entertain, Enlighten, and Engage," *Sloan Management Review*, 32 (2), 44-53.

Koo, Minjung and Ayelet Fishbach (forthcoming),"A Silver Lining of Standing in Line: Queuing Increases Value of Products," in *Journal of Marketing Research.*

Kumar, Piyush (2005), "The Competitive Impact of Service Process Improvement: Examining Customers' Waiting Experiences in Retail Markets," *Journal of Retailing*, 81 (3), 171-80.

Larson, Richard C. (1987), "Perspectives on Queues: Social Justice and the Psychology of Queueing," *Operations Research*, 35 (6), 895-905.

Leather, Phil, Diane Beale, Angeli Santos, Janine Watts, and Laura Lee (2003), "Outcomes of Environmental Appraisal of Different Hospital Waiting Areas," *Environment and Behavior*, 35 (6), 842-69.

Leclerc, France, Brendt Schmitt, and Laturette Dube (1995), "Decision Making and Waiting Time: Is Time Like Money?" *Journal of Consumer Research*, 22 (June), 110-19.

Maister, David H. (1985), "The Psychology of Waiting Lines," in *The service encounter: managing employee/customer interaction in service businesses*, ed. John A. Czepiel, Michael R. Solomon and Carol Suprenant, Lexington, MA: Lexington Books.

Miller, Elizabeth G., Barbara Kahn, and Mary Frances Luce (2008), "Consumer Wait Management Strategies for Negative Service Events: A Coping Approach," *Journal of Consumer Research*, 34 (5), 635-48.

Minton, Hannah (2008), "Waiting and Queuing in the Check-In Hall: An Ethnographic Study of Queuing and Waiting for Check-In Services at Manchester Airport," *Airport Management*, 2 (3), 249-64.

Munichor, Nira and Anat Rafaeli (2007), "Numbers or Apologies? Customer Reactions to Telephone Waiting Time Fillers," *Journal of Applied Psychology*, 92 (2), 511-18.

Muraven, Mark and Roy F. Baumeister (2000), "Self-Regulation and Depletion of Limited Resources: Does Self-Control Resemble a Muscle?" *Psychological Bulletin*, 126 (2), 247-59.

Osuna, Edgar E. (1985), "The Psychological Cost of Waiting," *Journal of Mathematical Psychology*, 29, 82-105.

Rafaeli, Anat, Greg Barron, and Keren Haber (2002), "The Effect of Queue Structure on Perceptions," *Journal of Service Research*, 5 (2), 125-39.

Raz, Ornit and Eyal Ert (2008), "Size Counts: The Effect of Queue Length on Choice Between Similar Restaurants," paper presented at the Association for Consumer Research Conference, Memphis, TN.

Rose, Gregory M., Matthew L. Meuter, and James M. Curran (2005), "On-Line Waiting: The Role of Download Time and Other Important Predictors on Attitude toward E-Retailers," *Psychology & Marketing*, 22 (2), 127-51.

Schmitt, Bernd H., Laurette Dube, and France Leclerc (1992), "Intrusions Into Waiting Lines: Does the Queue Constitute a Social System?" *Journal of Personality and Social Psychology*, 63 (5), 806-15.

Schwartz, Barry (1975), *Queueing and Waiting: Studies in the Social Organization of Access and Delay*, Chicago: University of Chicago Press.

Selvidge, Paula R., Barbara Chapparo, and Gregory T. Bender (2002), "The World Wide Wait: Effects of Delays on User Performance," *International Journal of Industrial Ergonomics*, 29 (1), 15-20.

Simonsohn, Uri and Dan Ariely (2005), "Ebay's Happy Hour: Non-Rational Herding in Online Auctions," working paper, Wharton, PA 19104.

Soman, Dilip (2002), "The Mental Accounting of Sunk Time Costs: Why Time is Not Like Money," *Journal of Behavioral Decision Making*, 14 (July), 169-85.

Taylor, Shirley (1994), "Waiting for Service: The Relationship between Delays and Evaluations of Service," *Journal of Marketing*, 58 (2), 56-69.

Veeraraghavan, Senthil K. and Laurens G. Debo, (2007) "Customer Herding in Services with Waiting Costs," working paper available at SSRN: http://ssrn.com/abstract=1030562

Vohs, Kathleen D., Roy Baumeister, Brandon J. Schmeichel, Jean M. Twenge, Noelle M. Nelson, and Dianne M. Tice (2008), "Making Choices Impairs Subsequent Self-Control: A Limited-Resource Account of Decision Making, Self-Regulation, and Active Initiative, *Journal of Personality and Social Psychology*, 94 (5), 883-98.

Vohs, Kathleen D. and Ronald J. Faber (2007), "Spent Resources: Self-Regulatory Resource Availability Affects Impulse Buying, *Journal of Consumer Research*, 33, 537-47.

Whitt, Ward (1999), "Improving Service by Informing Customers About Anticipated Delays," *Management Science*, 45 (2), 192-207.

Zakay, Dan and Jacob Hornik (1991), "How Much Time Did You Wait in Line? A Time Perception Perspective," Working Paper No. 20/91: The Israel Institute of Business Research, Tel-Aviv University, Tel-Aviv 69978, Israel.

Zhou, Rongrong and Dilip Soman (2003), "Looking Back: Exploring the Psychology of Queuing and the Effect of the Number of People Behind," *Journal of Consumer Research*, 29, 517-30.

＿＿＿＿ (2008), "Consumers' Waiting in Queues: The Role of First-Order and Second-Order Justice," *Psychology & Marketing*, 25 (3), 262-79.

Zohar, Eti, Avishai Mandelbaum, and Nahum Shimkin (2002), "Adaptive Behavior of Impatient Customers in Tele-Queues: Theory and Empirical Support," *Management Science*, 48 (4), 566-83.

# Effect of Temporal Units on Duration Sensitivity

Ashwani Monga, University of South Carolina, USA
Rajesh Bahchi, Virginia Tech, USA

## EXTENDED ABSTRACT

Because individuals usually prefer to receive rewards sooner rather than later, they want to be compensated for delays. For example, while holding a certificate of deposit (CD) that is about to mature and yield cash, an investor may be willing to delay the CD's maturity date, but only in return for an additional amount at the end. Moreover, the acceptable amount is likely to be higher if the maturity date is delayed by, say, 6 months rather than 3 months. The amount is likely to depend on individuals' duration sensitivity—the extent to which they are sensitive to a prospective change in the time of CD maturation. The current research demonstrates that duration sensitivity depends on the units employed to express durations. We show that sensitivity to delays expressed in larger units such as months (3 vs. 6) might be different from delays expressed in smaller units such as days (90 vs. 180).

Our arguments are based on a confluence of two different streams of research: numerosity (Pelham, Sumatra and Myaskovsky 1994), which offers insights into how people respond to numbers of differing magnitudes; and construal-level theory (Vallacher and Wegner 1987; 1989), which provides guidance on how events and actions can be construed at concrete or abstract levels. The starting point of our thesis is that a duration has two components: a number and a unit. For instance, a duration of 6 months is composed of the number "6" and the unit "months." If the units of a duration are changed, the numbers need to be changed as well in order to keep the duration objectively equivalent. That is, as units become smaller (e.g., from month to day), the associated numbers become larger (from 6 to 180). This inverse relationship between units and numbers is central to our arguments. We conduct a series of studies, primarily in the context of Certificates of Deposit, because such financial products do not have complex characteristics and provide a relatively simple template to cleanly test our predictions. This approach is consistent with prior research (e.g., LeBoeuf 2006) that has relied on Certificates of Deposit to study issues related to time discounting. In our studies, we explore conditions that facilitate a focus on units versus numbers, with consequent implications for duration sensitivity. We show that duration sensitivity is sometimes higher for larger units (months, rather than days), but, at other times, it is higher for smaller units (days, rather than months).

Our results have practical implications. For instance, when banks decide on the amount of money that they would need to offer in return for extending a CD, they need to consider how individuals would react to duration differences expressed in different units. Similarly, if online bookstores observe insensitivity between, say, a 2-day versus a 4-day delivery, they might be better off using the latter, which is likely to save costs.

Our results are also important from a theoretical standpoint. The idea that objective and subjective time durations are different has been long known to researchers in different disciplines, including consumer research (Hornik 1984). However, the notion that subjectivity of time might be determined by the units used to express durations has not been considered earlier. If duration sensitivity changes with units, as we propose in this article, it would have implications for a variety of areas, but particularly the area of time discounting, which refers to individuals having a strong bias toward the present rather than the future. It has recently been shown that this phenomenon can be attributed to individuals' sensitivity to duration (Kim and Zauberman 2009; Zauberman et al. 2009).

Our results on duration sensitivity imply that time discounting might also depend on temporal units. Our results also contribute to research on numerosity, which shows that people use the magnitude of numbers as a heuristic to make various judgments (Pelham et al. 1994). While people do indeed rely on the magnitude of numbers on some occasions, we show that they might ignore numbers at other times, and instead rely on the magnitude of the associated units. Finally, our results contribute to research on construal-level theory (Trope and Liberman 2000). We decompose a duration into different elements that have different levels of construal, and demonstrate consequent implications for duration sensitivity.

## REFERENCES

Hornik, Jacob (1984), "Subjective vs. Objective Time Measures: A Note on the Perception of Time in Consumer Behavior," *Journal of Consumer Research*, 11 (June), 615-618.

Kim, B. Kyu, and Gal Zauberman (2009), "Perception of Anticipatory Time in Temporal Discounting," *Journal of Neuroscience, Psychology, and Economics*, 2 (2), 91-101.

LeBoeuf, Robyn A. (2006), "Discount Rates for Time Versus Dates: The Sensitivity of Discounting to Time-Interval Description," *Journal of Marketing Research*, 43 (February), 59-72.

Pelham, Brett W., Tin Tin Sumarta, and Laura Myaskovsky (1994), "The Easy Path from Many to Much: The Numerosity Heuristic," *Cognitive Psychology*, 26 (April), 103-133.

Trope, Yaacov, and Nira Liberman (2000), "Temporal Construal and Time-Dependent Changes in Preference," *Journal of Personality and Social Psychology*, 79 (6), 876-889.

Vallacher, R. R., and D. M. Wegner (1987), "What Do People Think They're Doing? Action Identification and Human Behavior," *Psychological Review*, 94, 3-15.

Vallacher, R. R., and D. M. Wegner (1989), "Levels of Personal Agency: Individual Variation in Action Identification," *Journal of Personality and Social Psychology*, 57, 660-671.

Zauberman, Gal, B. Kyu Kim, Selin A. Malkoc, and James R. Bettman (2009), "Discounting Time and Time Discounting: Subjective Time Perception and Intertemporal Preferences," *Journal of Marketing Research*, 46 (August), 543-556.

# When Biasing Cues Improve vs Bias Quality Judgments

Wouter Vanhouche, Lessius University College, Belgium
Stijn van Osselaer, Erasmus University Rotterdam, The Netherlands

## EXTENDED ABSTRACT

Recent research demonstrates that quality judgments made at the time of repeat purchase can be more accurate, as opposed to less, when those quality judgments had been biased at the time of trial (e.g. when the price is high but quality low), compared to when quality judgments had never been biased (Vanhouche and van Osselaer 2009). This phenomenon was dubbed "the accuracy-enhancing effect of biasing cues" and could easily be taken as evidence for consumers' updating of pre-existing price-quality beliefs. Such an interpretation might seem reasonable given some specific task characteristics in the paradigm used by Vanhouche and van Osselaer—e.g. the easiness of the rules to be learned and the non-ambiguous quality feedback—but would be at odds with most of the literature which documents scant rule updating (Pechmann and Ratneshwar 1992; Broniarczyk and Alba 1994; Lichtenstein and Burton 1989).

The current research replicates the accuracy-enhancing effect of biasing cues (Study 1) and uncovers the mechanism behind it (Study 2). Even though rule updating seemed to have been possible or even likely, the results indicate that consumers use the initially biasing cue as an extra powerful memory cue to retrieve the quality level of individual previously experienced price-quality points. In other words, the accuracy-enhancing effect of biasing cues is driven by an exemplar based process rather than a rule based process. In addition, the pre-existing price-quality belief had remained unchanged. It was not updated.

As a result, quality judgments of not previously experienced products remained biased (Study 3) even though participants could have learned that, "at least in this particular context", price did *not* positively predict quality. In other words, the accuracy-enhancing effect does not generalize easily to situations in which the prices and brands at time of repeat purchase are different than during trial, indicating that pre-existing price-quality beliefs remain powerful and influential.

The broader implication may be that consumers use different processes to judge the quality of products they have versus have not tried before. The exemplar-based process helps them to quickly learn to avoid specific products they had a bad experience with. The rule-based process is updated much more conservatively and seems hardly affected by a few rule-inconsistent experiences. This conservativeness may be highly functional by providing stability in quality judgment (McClelland, McNaughton, and O'Reilly 1995), but may also represent a dysfunctional failure to learn from experience, as if rule-inconsistent experiences are picked up by the exemplar-based system (and used to correctly evaluate the specific, previously-experienced, rule-inconsistent products in the future) but are totally ignored by the rule-based process. In that case, Brehmer's (1980) conclusion about learning, "in one word: not from experience," may indeed apply. But it only applies to rules and judgments about products we have not tried before. Luckily, consumers also have an exemplar-based process that very effectively helps them to avoid the berries that made them sick when they tasted them, or that high-priced orange juice that tasted like vinegar.

## REFERENCES

Brehmer, Berndt (1980), "In One Word: Not From Experience," *Acta Psychologica, 57,* 117-39.

Broniarczyk, Susan M. and Joseph W. Alba (1994a), "Theory versus Data in Prediction and Correlation Tasks," *Organizational Behavior & Human Decision Processes,* 57 (January), 117-139.

Lichtenstein, Donald R. and Scott Burton (1989), "The Relationship between Perceived and Objective Price-Quality," *Journal of Marketing Research,* 26 (November), 429-443.

McClelland, James L., Bruce L. McNaughton, and Randall C. O'Reilly (1995), "Why there are Complementary Learning Systems in the Hippocampus and Neocortex: Insights from the Successes and Failures of Connectionist Models of Learning and Memory," *Psychological Review,* 102 (3), 419-57.

Pechmann, Cornelia and S. Ratneshwar (1992), "Consumer Covariation Judgments: Theory or Data Driven?" *Journal of Consumer Research,* 19 (December), 373-386.

Vanhouche, Wouter and Stijn M.J. van Osselaer (2009), "The Accuracy-Enhancing Effect of Biasing Cues," *Journal of Consumer Research,* 36, 317-327.

# Catching More Flies with Vinegar:
## The Ironic Effect of Product-Specific Search Cost on Consumer Choice

Xin Ge, University of Northern British Columbia, Canada
Gerald Häubl, University of Alberta, Canada
Neil Brigden, University of Alberta, Canada

## EXTENDED ABSTRACT

This paper introduces the hypothesis that making it harder for consumers to find out about a product can actually result in greater preference for it. The results of three experiments demonstrate this phenomenon and illuminate the mental mechanisms that underlie the ironic effect of product-specific search cost on consumer choice.

In purchase decisions, search costs often vary across alternatives even for a single consumer. For example, a consumer might be in a convenience store and observe that the store only carries a few brands of chips. The consumer might know that a grocery store nearby carries several additional brands. For this consumer, at this moment, the brands that are only available at the grocery store have a relatively higher search cost associated with them. The consumer would have to expend additional resources in order to acquire more information about these brands and to have an opportunity to purchase them. The question of how such differential search costs might influence consumer choice is the focus of the present research.

Economic theory suggests that the cost of search is a key determinant of the extent of consumer search activity such that one should stop searching when the expected marginal benefit no longer exceeds the marginal cost of search (Ratchford 1982; Rothschild 1974; Weitzman 1979). There is no economically rational reason for search costs to influence the decision making process once search is complete. This combined with the fact that adding a differentially higher search cost to an alternative will decrease the number of consumers who are exposed to that alternative, leads to the conclusion that a higher search cost can only reduce market share.

We propose that higher search costs can ironically increase market share because these costs do influence decision making after the search phase. Bastardi and Shafir demonstrated that a piece of information favoring an alternative became more influential once searched for (1998). Similarly, having incurred an additional cost to see and potentially purchase an alternative, a consumer might be more inclined to purchase that alternative. We propose two mechanisms that jointly contribute to this effect: (1) the acquisition of information about a product for which search cost is comparatively high might increase a consumer's commitment to that product in line with a sunk cost fallacy and (2) choices might be influenced by a self-perception process whereby consumers use their own search behavior, and in particular the effort they have expended to acquire information about a product of high search cost, as a basis for making inferences about their preference for that alternative.

Search costs, once incurred become "sunk" or irretrievable and should therefore not affect choice. The final product choice should be based only on whatever information about the alternatives themselves is available to the consumer when making the choice. However, behavioral research has revealed a greater tendency to continue an endeavor once an investment in money, time, or effort has been made in connection with it, and this phenomenon has been termed the "sunk cost fallacy" (Arkes and Blumer 1985). We hypothesize that "sunk" search costs influence choices in the same way increasing a consumer's tendency to choose options for which additional search costs have been incurred.

Self perception theory argues that an individual uses observations of her own behavior to make inferences about her own attitudes (Bem 1967, 1972). Therefore, consumers who observe themselves choosing to pay additional search costs to view an alternative might infer that they have a relative preference for the higher search cost alternative over the alternative that was available without additional cost.

To test these hypotheses we conducted three experiments. In each experiment participants saw one alternative (the Competitor), and had the option of incurring an additional search cost to see and potentially purchase a second alternative (the Target). Search cost was operationalized as distance (Experiment 1), keystrokes (Experiment 2) and money (Experiment 3). Experiments 1 and 3 involved consequential choices while experiments 2 used hypothetical choices. Across all experiments the alternatives that served as the Target and the Competitor were counterbalanced.

Across all three experiments the Target alternative, which had a higher search cost, earned a significantly greater share of participant choices than the Competitor. Experiment 1 demonstrates the basic effect in a consequential choice for granola bars. Participants were initially presented with one flavor of granola bar. They could either take that bar or they could walk across the room to see a second flavor (the first flavor was also present across the room). Participants preferred the second flavor. Experiment 2 used an online shopping task involving six product categories. Participants were assigned to either an equal search cost or differential search cost condition. Participants in the differential search cost condition preferred the alternative with the higher search cost while no preference existed for the same alternatives when search costs were equal. Experiment 3 involved consequential choices for gambles. This experiment demonstrated that even when search cost was recoverable, participants preferred the alternative with the larger search cost. This result suggests that sunk costs are not sufficient to explain the effect and that self-perception also contributes.

## REFERENCES

Arkes, Hal R. and Catherine Blumer (1985), "The psychology of sunk cost," *Organizational Behavior and Human Decision Processes*, 35 (February), 124-140.

Bastardi, Anthony and Eldar Shafir (1998), "On the pursuit and misuse of useless information," *Journal of Personality and Social Psychology*, 75 (July), 19-32

Bem, Daryl J. (1967), "Self-perception: An alternative interpretation of cognitive dissonance phenomena," *Psychological Review*, 74 (3), 183-200.

Bem, Daryl J. (1972), "Self-perception theory," *Advances in Experimental Social Psychology*, 6, 1-62.

Ratchford, Brian T. (1982), "Cost-benefit models for explaining consumer choice and information seeking behavior," *Management Science*, 28 (February), 197-212.

Rothschild, Michael (1974), "Searching for the lowest price when the distribution of prices is unknown," *Journal of Political Economy*, 82 (4), 689-711.

Weitzman, Martin L. (1979), "Optimal search for the best alternative," *Econometrica*, 47 (3), 641-654.

# The Effect of Scarcity on Product Evaluation

Seung Yun Lee, McGill University, Canada
Ashesh Mukherjee, McGill University, Canada

## EXTENDED ABSTRACT

Marketers often use scarcity to influence consumers, with announcements such as "hurry, limited quantities", "until stocks last," or "few tickets left for this event." Past research indicates that scarcity generally has a positive effect on product evaluation, because consumers infer that scarcity is a consequence of high demand for the product, which in turn arises from superior value offered by the product[1,2]. In the present research, we argue that consumers can also make a second type of inference about scarcity–namely that scarcity is perceived as a signal of manipulative intent on the part of marketers to increase demand for the product. For example, it is possible for marketers to artificially restrict the quantity of product being offered in a given retail outlet or sales territory, and thus send a false signal of popularity among consumers. In summary, therefore, we argue that two kinds of inferences are possible when consumers are faced with scarcity: value inference and manipulative intent inference. Greater the value inference, the more positive would be the effect of scarcity on product evaluation; the greater manipulative intent inference, the less positive would be the effect of scarcity on product evaluation. Based on this framework, we specify four moderators, namely persuasion knowledge, frequency of exposure to scarcity claims, decision reversibility, and cognitive load that influence the interpretation of scarcity as value or manipulative intent, and hence the effect of scarcity on product evaluation.

Study 1 focused on persuasion knowledge, defined as individuals' knowledge about persuasion tactics[3,4]. We argued that when salience of persuasion knowledge is high, consumers are likely to think about why the marketer is using scarcity claims. This questioning of marketers' motives, in turn, is likely to prompt inferences that the scarcity is a manipulative intent designed to boost demand. And greater these inferences about manipulative intent on the part of marketers, the less positive will be the effect of scarcity on product evaluation. In contrast, when salience of persuasion knowledge is low, consumers are likely to fall back on the inference that scarcity implies value. Consequently, scarcity will have a stronger positive effect on product evaluation when salience of persuasion knowledge is low. Participants in this study were told that they were participating in two independent experiments. The first experiment manipulated salience of persuasion knowledge using a priming procedure validated in previous research[4]. The second experiment presented participants with a hypothetical retail scenario, which included an ad for a wristwatch. The ad manipulated scarcity, in terms of limited quantities. The dependent variable of product evaluation was measured by a single item, nine-point scale for purchase intent and an item assessing willingness to pay (WTP). Inferences about scarcity were measured by coding thought listings from study participants after they evaluated the target product. We predicted and found that scarcity increased purchase intent and WTP when salience of persuasion knowledge was low, but not high. Consistent with our hypothesis, 61% of participants under the high salience of persuasion knowledge condition perceived scarcity as a manipulative intent to increase sales, as compared to only 29% of participants under the low salience of persuasion knowledge condition.

Study 2 focused on frequency of exposure to scarcity claims. We argued that the individuals who are exposed to many (compared to few) scarcity claims, i.e., high frequency of exposure, are more likely to interpret scarcity claims as a signal of manipulative intent. For example, consider an individual who is reading a magazine where several ads contain statements such as "Hurry, few items left in stock" and "Only a limited number of products released". Seeing repeated use of scarcity claims, individuals may wonder if these claims are really manipulative techniques used by marketers to increase sales. To the extent individuals see scarcity as a signal of manipulative intent, the positive effect of scarcity on product evaluation will be weakened. In contrast, when frequency of exposure to scarcity claims is low, consumers are less likely to infer manipulative intent, and hence scarcity would have a stronger positive effect on product evaluation. Participants in this study were told that they were participating in two independent experiments. In the first experiment, frequency of exposure was manipulated in the magazine by inserting scarcity claims into either one ad (low frequency) or four ads (high frequency). In the second experiment, the participants were asked to rate a new line of sunglasses available through an online shopping website. A printout of the online shopping webpage manipulated scarcity using limited quantities of the product. We developed a two-item scale to measure the inference of scarcity claims as a manipulative intent: "The ad was being honest about the number of sunglasses available for sale" and "The ad tried to artificially increase sales by mentioning the number of sunglasses available for sale." This two-item scale was adapted from the six-item scale measuring inferences of manipulative intent validated in past research[5]. We predicted and found that scarcity increased purchase intent and WTP when frequency of exposure to scarcity claims was low, but not high. Consistent with our hypothesis, respondents were more likely to perceive scarcity as a manipulative intent when frequency of exposure was high, compared to low.

Study 3 focused on decision reversibility, defined as the ability to undo a purchase decision[6]. We argued that when a scarce product is unconditionally refundable ("30-day unconditional money-back guarantee"), individuals are likely to interpret scarcity as a signal of product value. This is because a money back guarantee indicates that the seller is confident about product quality[7]. As a result, the "scarcity=value" inference should be highlighted, and scarcity should have a positive effect on product evaluation. In contrast, if a scarce product cannot be refunded once purchased (e.g., "All sales are final"), such low reversibility protects sellers from the consequences of selling defective items. Consequently, scarcity with low reversibility should highlight manipulative intent on the part of marketers, which is likely to reduce the effect of scarcity on product evaluation. As in Study 2, participants were asked to rate a new line of sunglasses available through an online shopping website. A printout of the online shopping webpage manipulated scarcity using limited quantities of the product validated in past research[8]; reversibility was manipulated by a sign saying either "All sales are final" or "30 day unconditional money-back guarantee." We predicted and found that scarcity increased purchase intent and WTP when decision reversibility was high, but not low. Consistent with our hypothesis, respondents were more likely to perceive scarcity as a manipulative intent when decision reversibility was low, compared to high.

Study 4 focused on cognitive load. Drawing inferences about hidden marketing tactics behind a persuasive message are likely to require cognitive capacity. Thus we argued that when cognitive load is low, consumers possess sufficient mental capacity to draw inferences about hidden marketing tactics behind a persuasive

*Advances in Consumer Research*
*Volume 38, © 2012*

message. In this case, consumers are likely to think about why the advertiser has created the ad with scarcity claims. This questioning of marketers' motives, in turn, is likely to prompt inferences that marketers are using scarcity to manipulate consumers into buying the product. Such inference of manipulative intent can dilute value inference, and hence reduce the positive effect of scarcity on product evaluation. In contrast, when cognitive load is high, consumers do not have the cognitive capacity to engage in inferential processing. In this case, consumers are likely to fall back on the simpler and less effortful inference, namely value inference, and hence scarcity would have a positive effect on product evaluation. Participants in this study were told that they were participating in two independent experiments. In the first experiment, cognitive load was manipulated by asking participants to memorize either a seven-digit number (high cognitive load condition) or a two-digit number (low cognitive load condition)[9]. In the second experiment, participants were asked to rate wines available through an online shopping website. A printout of the online shopping webpage manipulated scarcity using limited quantities of the wine products. We predicted and found that scarcity increased purchase intent and product choice when cognitive load was high, but not low. In addition, respondents were more likely to perceive scarcity as a manipulative intent when cognitive load was low, compared to high.

In summary, the four studies reported herein make a theoretical contribution by identifying a new psychological mechanism (i.e., *why*) and corresponding boundary conditions (i.e., *when*) of scarcity, a tool that is widely used in marketing communications.

## REFERENCE

Lynn, M. (1989). Scarcity effects on value: Mediated by assumed expensiveness? *Journal of Economic Psychology*, *10*, 257-274.

Cialdini, R. B. (2001). *Influence Science and Practice*. Allyn and Bacon *(4ᵗʰ eds)*.

Friestad, M. and Wright, P. (1994). The Persuasion Knowledge Model: How People Cope with Persuasion Attempts. *Journal of Consumer Research*, *21* (June), 1-31.

Campbell, Margaret C. and Kirmani, Amna (2000). Consumers' Use of Persuasion Knowledge: The Effects of Accessibility and Cognitive Capacity on Perceptions of an Influence Agent. *Journal of Consumer Research, 27* (June), 69-83.

Campbell, Margaret C. (1995). When Attention-Getting Advertising Tactics Elicit Consumer Inferences of Manipulative Intent: The Importance of Balancing Benefits and Investments. *Journal of Consumer Psychology,* 4 (3), 225-254.

Tsiros, M. and Mittal, V. (2000). Regret: A Model of Its Antecedents and Consequences in Consumer Decision Making. *Journal of Consumer Research, 26*, 401-417.

Boulding, W. and Kirmani, A. (1993). A Consumer-Side Experimental Examination of Signaling Theory: Do Consumers Perceive Warranties as Signals of Quality? *Journal of Consumer Research, 20*, 111-123.

Jung, Jae Min. and James J. Kellaris (2004). Cross-National Differences in Proneness to Scarcity Effects: The moderating Roles of Familiarity, Uncertainty Avoidance, and Need for Cognitive Closure. *Psychology and Marketing, 21* (9), 739-753.

Gillbert, D. T., and Osborne, R. E. (1989). Thinking Backward: Some Curable and Incurable Consequences of Cognitive Busyness. , *Journal of Personality and Social Psychology, 57 (6),* 940-949.

# Until the Dust Settles: Why an Economic Downturn Promotes Consumer Spending Strikes and How to Overcome This

Jaione Yabar, Tilburg University, The Netherlands
Rik Pieters, Tilburg University, The Netherlands
Diederik A. Stapel, Tilburg University, The Netherlands

## EXTENDED ABSTRACT

This research examines the "dust settling effect," that consumers' feelings of uncertainty about the future state of the economy activate an automatic inaction tendency which leads to a tendency to stop and postpone spending, even if the uncertain future does not have direct personal financial consequences, and even if the uncertain future may actually hold positive financial implications. The dust settling effect has been speculated upon by economic psychologists at least since the Great Depression of the 1930s, but not yet studied empirically among consumers. The dust settling effect may lead to self-fulfilling prophecies and thus have grave implications for the economy at large. Then, uncertainty about the future economy leads to spending strikes by consumers that actually create or worsen the feared crisis. Thus, the present research investigates consumers´ apparent tendency to wait until the economic dust settles, even when the dust does not block the own eyes. In addition, it examines a potential strategy to overcome uncertainty-invoked spending strikes, namely stimulating feelings of anticipated regret of inaction.

Economic downturns can have severe negative effects for large groups of consumers due to income loss or reduced investments. However, they can also have positive side effects and generate advantageous purchase opportunities in particular for those consumers who do not face direct income drops by the crisis, for instance, because retail prices drop and deep promotions are used by firms to stimulate sales. Still, recent industry studies suggest that even consumers with sufficient resources and without direct economic threats reduce their spending when a crisis hits (BCG, 2009, TNS 2009). This seems to reflect an automatic tendency to stop spending in times of general uncertainty. Then, consumers may miss opportunities to take advantage of changed market conditions. Besides, widespread consumption cutbacks by consumers may aggravate the economic crisis in depth and duration

Research on consumer coping during economic hardships (e.g., Kelley & Scheewe, 1975; Shama, 1981) has focused on the behavior of consumers who were actually directly affected through reduced financial resources (unemployment, lost investments and savings). As a result, we know surprisingly little about the influence of an economic crisis on those consumers who are not directly negatively affected by it, and this group may be the largest even under the severest downturns. The economic psychologist Katona (1975) offered the postponement hypothesis that "during a recession, as well as during inflation, most people, irrespective of whether or not they are directly affected, have a sense of reduced certainty and reduced security and hence spend less". Although there is indirect and macro evidence for the hypothesis, direct evidence obtained from consumers is not available. The present research tests the hypothesis. However, we extend and build on the idea in two important ways. First, we will argue and show that dust settling effects occur even when the uncertainty feelings concern potential gains, such as winning a lottery. Second, we examine one specific strategy to overcome the dust settling effect, namely activating consumers' anticipated regret of inaction

Uncertainty is an aversive state that motivates behaviors aimed at reducing it. Theories on decision-making under uncertainty have suggested that a dominant mechanism to cope with uncertainty is to actively gain full information and understanding. Thus, these theories imply that uncertainty leads to action. But individuals may not always try to actively reduce uncertainty by searching information and taking action. Uncertainty can be attributed to the external world or to the individual's state of knowledge (Kahneman and Tversky 1982). When uncertainty feelings are about the external world and beyond personal control, collecting additional information may not be possible or may not help to reduce uncertainty, as those feelings do not refer to individual knowledge. Research on the omission bias in emotion research, for instance, has found that people tend to remain inactive under uncertainty. Organizational decision theories have also shown the role of postponement in managing of uncertainty. This and other research suggests that inaction rather than action is at the core of the uncertainty.

Building on this, we propose that with uncertainty in the economic environment, consumers´ spending decisions are driven by an inaction tendency, regardless of the consequences of the economic uncertainty for their personal situation (hypothesis 1). Moreover, given the influence that emotions exert on behavior and the importance of uncertainty resolution for human behavior (Loewenstein, Weber, Hsee, and Welch 2001), we hypothesize that even when the uncertainty implies potential gains and not losses, perceived uncertainty leads to focus on not-spending. (hypothesis 2). Finally, since consumers attempt to minimize regret rather than risk (Bell 1982; Zeelenberg and Pieters 2004), we propose that evoking future regret of something consumers' failed to do will help reduce this inaction focus of uncertain consumers (hypothesis 3).

Four studies tested these predictions. Study 1 documented the natural tendency to stop spending during times of economic uncertainty even when the uncertainty does not have direct personal financial implications (hypothesis 1). Study 2 found that uncertainty, even when it concerns potential gains (and not losses) –such as winning a lottery prize -, also invokes a not-spending focus (hypothesis 2). Study 3 ruled out that the sheer valence of the emotions, positive-negative, rather than uncertainty, and that active-saving rather than not-spending, account for the findings. The study revealed that uncertainty feelings, and not specific emotions (happiness, hope, anger or fear), lead consumers to not-spend rather than to actively save money. Finally, Study 4 tested one mechanism to overcome the inaction effects of uncertainty and encourage consumers to spend, namely evoking future regrets of inaction. After showing participants a news item about consumers´ future regrets of action [inaction] during an economic downturn, those participants told about future inaction regrets spent more money and overcame their inaction tendency. Jointly the findings reveal that uncertainty about future economic situations, even if consumers are not directly affected, and even if they may entail gains, promote spending strikes. These can be routed by activating anticipated inaction regret. In this way, the present research identifies how consumers' self-fulfilling prophecies about economic downturns arise and can be broken.

## REFERENCES

Bar-Anan, Y., Wilson, T.D., and Gilbert, D.T. (2009). The feeling of uncertainty intensifies affective reactions. *Emotion*, 9 (1), 123-127.

Bell, D.E. (1982). Regret in decision making under uncertainty. *Operations Research*, 30 (5), 961-981.

Bettman, J.R. (1979). *An information processing theory of consumer choice*, Reading, MA: Addison-Wesley.

Boston Consulting Group (2009). Winning consumers through the downturn. *Boston Consulting Group April 2009*.

Cryder, C.E., Lerner, J.S., Gross, J.J. and Dahl, R.E. (2008). Misery is not miserly: sad and self-focused individuals spend more. *Psychological Science*, 19 (6), 525–530.

Euromonitor (2009). FMCG and the recession–how are consumers of food, drink and tobacco products responding? *Euromonitor International*.

Heath, C. & Tversky, A. (1991). Preference and belief: Ambiguity and competence in choice under uncertainty. *Journal of Risk and Uncertainty*, 4, 5-28.

Kahneman, D. and Tversky, A. (1982). Variants of uncertainty. *Cognition*, 11, 143-157.

Katona, G. (1975). *Psychological Economics*. New York: Elsevier.

Kelley, E.J. and Scheewe, L.R. (1975). Buyer behavior in a stagflation/shortages economy. *Journal of Marketing*, 39, April, 44-50.

Keppe, H.J. and Weber, M. (1995). Judged knowledge and ambiguity aversion. *Theory and Decision,* 39, 51-77.

Krugman, P. (2009). *The return of depression economics and the crisis of 2008*. New York: The New York Times.

Lanzetta, J.T. and Driscoll, J.M. (1968). Effects of uncertainty and importance on information search in decision making. *Journal of Personality and Social Psychology*, 10 (4), 479-486.

Lerner, J.S. and Keltner, D. (2000). Beyond valence: toward a model of emotion-specific influences on judgment and choice. *Cognition and Emotion*, 14 (4), 473-493.

Lipshitz, R. and Strauss, O. (1997). Coping with uncertainty: A naturalistic decision-making analysis. *Organizational Behavior and Human Decision Processes,* 69 (2), 149-163

Loewenstein, G. (2000). Emotions in economic theory and economic behavior. *The American Economic Review*, 90 (2), 426-432.

Loewenstein, G., Weber, E.U., Hsee, C.K. and Welch, N. (2001). Risk as feelings. *Psychological Bulletin*, 127, 267-286.

Shama, A.(1981). Coping with staglation: Voluntary simplicity. *Journal of Marketing,* 45 (3), 120–134.

Simonson, I. (1992). The influence of anticipating regret and responsibility on purchase decisions. *Journal of Consumer Research*, 19, 105-118.

Slovic, P., Finucane, M., Peters, E. and MacGregor, D.G. (2002). The affect heuristic, in T.Gilovich, D.Griffin and D.Kahneman (Eds.), *Heuristics and Biases: The Psychology of Intuitive Judgement*. New York: Cambridge University Press.

Smith, C.A. and Ellsworth, P.C. (1985). Patterns of cognitive appraisal in emotion. *Journal of Personality and Social Psychology*, 48 (4), 813-838.

Tversky, D. and Kahneman, A. (1973). Availability: A heuristic for judging frequency and probability. *Cognitive Psychology,* 5, 207-232.

Urbany, J.E., Dickson, P.R. and Wilkie, W.L. (1989). Buyer uncertainty and information Search. *Journal of Consumer Research*, 16 (2), 208-215.

Van den Bos, K. (2001). Uncertainty management: The influence of uncertainty salience on reactions to perceived procedural fairness. *Journal of Personality and Social Psychology*, 80 (6), 931-941.

Van den Bos, K., Euwema, M., Poortvliet, P., and Maas, M. (2007). Uncertainty management and social issues: Uncertainty as an important determinant of reactions to socially deviating people. *Journal of Applied Social Psychology*, 37, 1726–1756.

Yang, B., Burns, N.D. and Backhouse, C.J. (2004). Management of uncertainty through postponement. *International Journal of Production Research,* 42 (6), 1049-1064.

Zeelenberg, M., and Pieters, R. (2004). Consequences of regret aversion in real life: The case of the Dutch postcode lottery. *Organizational Behavior and Human Decision Processes*, 93, 155–168.

# Effect of Attribute Change on Preference Modification

Ataollah Tafaghodi Jami, University of Utah, USA
Himanshu Mishra, University of Utah, USA

## EXTENDED ABSTRACT

This paper uses dual-systems of processing to explain why people, who detect an attribute change in their choice set, choose the option with the highest (lowest) absolute change when the change is positive (negative). Three studies provide support for the proposed account and reject other alternative explanations.

Imagine that a grocery store sells Kellogg's Special-K in two package sizes: 10 oz. for $2.50 and 15 oz. for $3.75. John buys Special-K, and since the unit price for each pack is the same, he is indifferent between either of the packs. Recently, he noticed that Kellogg's is offering bonus packs with the purchase of Special-K—a 10 oz. pack plus 4 oz. for $2.50, and a 15 oz. pack plus 6 oz. for $3.75. Which package would John prefer now? Based on his past preference, one might predict that he would be indifferent between both packages as unit price is still the same across both of them. Contrary to this prediction, we find that he would no longer be indifferent and would prefer the bigger package over the small package. We call this phenomenon the Detection of Change Effect (DCE), where people, who were indifferent between two options before the change, later prefer the option with a higher magnitude of change when the change is positive (desirable), and the option with a lower magnitude of change when the change is negative (undesirable).

The preliminary evidence of the DCE was found through a study in which participants were randomly assigned to a two cell between-participant experimental design, and presented with a choice between two breakfast cereals. In the control condition, participants were asked to choose between two packages of cereal (i.e., package A: 12 oz. for $4; and package B: 18 oz. for $6). Note that the unit price for both packages was 33 cents/oz. In the "positive change" condition, participants were first given information akin to the information given to the control condition participants. Then, they were told that the company had introduced some changes by adding smaller bonus packages to the original ones (Package A: 12 oz. plus 4 oz. for $4; and package B: 18 oz. plus 6 oz. for $6). Note that the unit price for the new packages was 25 cents/oz. Then, the participants were asked to choose the option that they preferred to buy.

In the control condition, participants chose the smaller package slightly more than the bigger package (package A: 59.5%, package B: 40.5%). However, in the positive change condition, participants preferred the bigger package more than the smaller one (package A: 35.7%, package B: 64.3%) which was significantly different from the control condition ($\chi^2$ (1)=4.77, $p<.03$).

Why do people prefer the option with a higher absolute change? Research has shown that people use two modes of processing (known as System 1 and System 2) for making a decision (Kahneman 2003). System 1 is known for its automatic judgments and heuristic-based decision making whereas System 2 produces more deliberative responses toward a stimulus (Kahneman 2003). While System 1 and 2 are often working simultaneously and independently, research has shown that the outcome of one system can interact with the other system which results in a biased mental representation (Mishra et al. 2007). Following this literature, we propose that people, who perceive an attribute change, use System 2 to compare the original and changed options and to find out how much the original options have changed. Then, when they want to evaluate the changed options, System 1 uses the outcome of System 2 (i.e., the difference between the original and the changed options)

and the bigger-is-better heuristic to form the preference toward the option with the highest absolute amount of change. Since the bigger-is-better heuristic was mainly observed on the gain side (i.e., when people receiving something), it is expected that people use the bigger-is-worse heuristic when they are comparing losses. Therefore, we expect that when there is a negative attribute change (i.e., when quantity is reduced or price is increased), people choose the smaller box over the larger one since they want to avoid the bigger loss.

There are three alternate accounts that can also explain the results of the preliminary study. These three accounts are the value-of-free products (Shampanier, Mazar, and Ariely 2007), Increasing Proportional Sensitivity (IPS) (Prelec and Lowenstein 1991), and the general law of demand (Marshall 1895). According to these accounts, participants in the preliminary study chose the bigger cereal box because either they assigned higher value to the bonus box as a free product (the value-of-free product), or changing the weights of boxes, regardless of knowing about the original options, improved the importance of the weight attribute in decision making (IPS), or increasing the weight of boxes reduced the unit price (price per weight) and consequently increased the demand for the product (the general law of demand).

The aim of study 1 and 2 was to provide more evidence for the main account and to assess the efficacy of the three alternate accounts. Study 1 supported our proposition for the negative attribute change as it showed that participants chose the option with lowest amount of change when the change was negative. This pattern was not predicted by the value-of-free-product account since no additional product was offered in this case. Moreover, study 1 ruled out the IPS account as it showed that the preference for the bigger option depended on knowing about the original options and detecting the change.

Study 2 supported our proposed account as it showed that directing participants' attention toward the differences between the original and changed options increased the DCE. Also, the second study ruled out the general law of demand as an alternate account since the results showed that directing participants' attention toward the unit price eliminated the DCE. Finally, in the third study, with the help of Process Dissociation Procedure (PDP), we provided empirical evidence that showed and contrasted the role of System 1 and System 2 in the DCE.

In sum, these findings suggest that people's response to an attribute change is not their mere reaction to the new magnitude of the changed attribute. In other words, they do not evaluate a weight of 12 oz. plus 4 oz. similar to a weight of 16 oz. But, they use the additional information that they have (i.e., the magnitude of the attribute before the change) to evaluate the changed product.

## REFERENCES

Chandon, Pierre and Nailya Ordabayeva (2009), "Supersize in One Dimension, Downsize in Three Dimensions: Effects of Spatial Dimensionality on Size Perceptions and Preferences," *Journal of Marketing Research*, 46 (6), 739-53.

Chapman, Gretchen B. and Jennifer R. Winquist (1998), "The magnitude effect: Temporal discount rates and restaurant tips," *Psychonomic Bulletin and Review*, 5 (1), 119-23.

Evans, Jonathan St B. T. (2008), "Dual-Processing Accounts of Reasoning, Judgment, and Social Cognition," *Annual Review of Psychology*, 59 (1), 255-78.

Ferreira, Mario B., Leonel Garcia-Marques, Steven J. Sherman, and Jeffrey W. Sherman (2006), "Automatic and Controlled Components of Judgment and Decision Making," *Journal of Personality and Social Psychology*, 91 (5), 797-813.

Gigerenzer, Gerd and Daniel G. Goldstein (1996), "Reasoning the Fast and Frugal Way: Models of Bounded Rationality," *Psychological Review*, 103 (4), 650-69.

Jacoby, Larry L. (1991), "A process dissociation framework: Separating automatic from intentional uses of memory," *Journal of Memory and Language*, 30 (5), 513–541.

Kahneman, Daniel (2003), "A perspective on judgment and choice: mapping bounded rationality," *The American Psychologist*, 58 (9), 697–720.

Kahneman, Daniel and Shane Frederick (2002), "Representativeness Revisited: Attribute Substitution in Intuitive Judgment," in *Heuristics and Biases*, ed. T. Gilovich, D. Griffin and Daniel Kahneman, New York: Cambridge University Press, 49–81.

Krider, Robert E., Priya Raghubir, and Aradhna Krishna (2001), "Pizzas: Pi or Square? Psychophysical Biases in Area Comparisons," *Marketing Science*, 20 (4), 405.

Krishna, Aradhna (2006), "Interaction of Senses: The Effect of Vision versus Touch on the Elongation Bias," *Journal of Consumer Research*, 32 (4), 557-66.

Marshall, Alfred (1895), *Principles of Economics* (3rd ed.). New York: Macmillan and Co.

Mishra, Himanshu, Arul Mishra, and Dhananjay Nayakankuppam (2007), "Seeing through the Heart's Eye: The Interference of System 1 in System 2," *Marketing Science*, 26 (5), 666-78.

Prelec, Drazen and George Loewenstein (1991), "Decision Making Over Time and Under Uncertainty: A Common Approach," *Management Science*, 37 (7), 770-86.

Scott-Brown, Kenneth C., Mark R. Baker, and Harry S. Orbach (2000), "Comparison Blindness," *Visual Cognition*, 7 (1-3).

Shampanier, Kristina, Nina Mazar, and Dan Ariely (2007), "Zero as a Special Price: The True Value of Free Products," *Marketing Science*, 26 (6), 742-57.

Shen, Hao and Robert S. Wyer Jr. (2008), "Procedural Priming and Consumer Judgments: Effects on the Impact of Positively and Negatively Valenced Information," *Journal of Consumer Research*, 34 (5), 727-37.

Silvera, David H., Robert A. Josephs, and R. Brian Giesler (2002), "Bigger Is Better: The Influence of Physical Size on Aesthetic Preference Judgments," *Journal of Behavioral Decision Making*, 15 (3), 189-202.

Strack, Fritz, Leonard L. Martin, and Norbert Schwarz (1988), "Priming and Communication: Social Determinants of Information Use in Judgments of Life Satisfaction," *European Journal of Social Psychology*, 18 (5), 429-42.

# Evaluating Ratio Data and the Role of Consumer Processing Mode: Can Analytical Processing Bias Judgments?

Dipayan Biswas, Bentley Unversity, USA
Patricia Norberg, Quinnipiac University, USA
Donald Lehmann, Columbia University, USA

## EXTENDED ABSTRACT

Consumers often encounter information presented in the form of ratios (Peters et al. 2007; Silverblatt 2009), and they are sometimes required to compute the averages of multiple pieces of data in ratio formats. Commonly encountered ratios in daily activities include laundry detergent information given as loads per container (LPC), fitness equipment information regarding calories burned per minute (CPM) of exercise, and vehicle speed information in miles per hour (MPH). In this research, we examine how computing averages for multiple pieces of data in such ratio formats might bias consumer judgments. Equally importantly, we also examine how processing mode might moderate the effects of ratio formats on consumer averaging judgments.

There has been limited research on how consumers process ratio information (with Denes-Raj and Epstein 1994, Hsee et al. 2003, Larrick and Soll 2008, and Raghubir and Greenleaf 2006, being notable exceptions), and no study has examined how consumer judgments might be biased when they are computing averages of multiple pieces of data in different ratio formats. Further, no study has examined the moderating effects of consumer processing modes in this context. Thus, the present research examines the potential for bias when computing averages, and examines the moderating effects of consumer processing mode (Studies 1 and 3) and cognitive capacity (Study 2). We find an interesting paradoxical result–analytical (vs. heuristic) processing accentuates the bias when processing certain ratio data, and likewise higher cognitive capacity reduces the judgment accuracy for certain ratio data. Finally, we identify alternative data formats that can potentially reduce consumer judgment biases.

People tend to process numerical information in a linear fashion (Brousseau, Brousseau, and Warfield 2002). Such linear arithmetic processing is likely to lead to erroneous judgments when evaluating inverse ratio data (i.e., where the focal variable is in the denominator). Specifically, for inverse ratios (like LPC, CPM, or MPH), the appropriate mathematical computation to use would be a harmonic mean. However, consumers are instead likely to employ the linear arithmetic mean, leading to biased judgments.

Study 1 examined how consumers compute the average rate of calories burned across multiple exercise routines (or fitness machines) with information given in a commonly used format of calories burned per minute, or CPM (see Zeni, Hoffman and Clifford 1996), versus an alternative format of minutes taken per calorie (MPC). Study 1 also examined the moderating effects of consumer processing mode (analytical versus heuristic) (e.g., Alter et al. 2007; Kahneman and Frederick 2002). Under analytical processing, a consumer is more likely to rely on mathematical calculations, and therefore more likely to compute the linear arithmetic mean across the multiple pieces of ratio data. In contrast, under heuristic processing, an equivalent of a random choice between the options would be more likely. Hence, analytical (versus heuristic) processing of the data would magnify the proportion of erroneous judgments. Therefore, we propose that when consumers are computing averages across multiple pieces of data in CPM format, analytical (vs. heuristic) processing will paradoxically increase judgment inaccuracy. However, when consumers are computing averages across multiple pieces of data in MPC format, analytical (vs. heuristic) processing will increase judgment accuracy.

Study 1 was a 2 (type of data format for calorie burning rate: calories per minute vs. minute per calorie) X 2 (processing mode: analytical vs. heuristic) between-subjects experiment (N=114). The results of study 1 supported our hypothesis that when computing averages across multiple pieces of data in inverse ratio formats (such as CPM), consumers are prone to make erroneous judgments. Study 1 also showed that such erroneous judgments for ratio data are likely to get enhanced when consumers are making judgments under analytical (than heuristic) processing mode.

Study 2 extended the findings of study 1 by examining a different context using the scenario of a decision-maker choosing between two route options with speed data in miles per hour (MPH), and the moderating effects of cognitive capacity. Study 2 showed that different levels of cognitive capacity lead to a similar pattern of results as processing mode. That is, paradoxically, when consumers exert greater effort in analyzing the given options and employ mathematical computations to a greater extent under high (vs. low) cognitive capacity, their judgments become more inaccurate/biased.

Study 3 had three objectives. First, it replicated the potential bias in computing of averages of ratios in the context of laundry detergent usage. Second, it examined how presenting ratio information through a medium (e.g. Hsee et al. 2003) such as price per load might reduce consumer judgment bias. Third, while in Study 1 processing mode was manipulated, Study 3 measured processing mode as an inherent personality trait (Pacini and Epstein 1999). Study 3 was a 2 (type of data format for laundry detergent: loads per container vs. Dollar per load) X 2 (processing mode: analytical vs. heuristic) between-subjects experiment (N=144). The results of Study 3 again highlighted how an inverse ratio format like LPC, which is commonly used, can bias consumer judgments when computing averages of multiple pieces of data; the judgment bias can be reduced by presenting the data with the help of a medium, such as price per load. Study 3 also demonstrated that analytical (vs. heuristic) processing tendency increases consumer judgment biases with the LPC format, but lead to more accurate judgments with DPL format.

In sum, the results of three experiments highlight how some commonly used ratio formats might bias consumer judgments when they are computing averages. Equally interestingly, analytical processing or higher cognitive capacity can reduce judgment accuracy when consumers attempt to compute the mean of multiple data pieces in certain ratio formats such as CPM, MPH, or LPC. The bias can be corrected if the data are presented in alternative formats of MPC or DPL, which are conducive to linear mathematical processing.

# Covariation Learning, Quality Expectation and Product Valuation Under Homoscedastic and Heteroscedastic Uncertainty

Bart de Langhe, Erasmus University Rotterdam, The Netherlands
Stefano Puntoni, Erasmus University Rotterdam, The Netherlands
Ann L. McGill, University of Chicago, USA
Stijn van Osselaer, Erasmus University Rotterdam, The Nethelands

## EXTENDED ABSTRACT

Over the past four decades, a substantial amount of research has been conducted to study how people acquire cue-outcome relations, including literature on contingency learning (Allan 1993; van Osselaer et al. 2004), covariation judgments (Baumgartner 1995; Pechmann and Ratneshwar 1992), category representations (Erickson and Kruschke 1998), and function learning (DeLosh et al. 1997; Juslin et al. 2008) . Despite the important insights gained into how humans detect systematic cue-outcome associations against a background of uncertainty, no research has investigated if cue-outcome learning depends on whether the degree of uncertainty is the same (i.e., homoscedastic) or varies (i.e., heteroscedastic) across different ranges of the cue. To illustrate this distinction in the nature of randomness, consider consumers' price-quality beliefs for restaurants. Prior research on cue-outcome learning assumes no differences between a *homoscedastic* world where high-end restaurants display the same medium level of variance in quality as do inexpensive restaurants and a *heteroscedastic* world where quality can vary wildly among inexpensive restaurants but instead tends to be consistently high among high-end restaurants.

According to linear statistical theory, the correlation coefficient is a function of overall error variance and it is not affected by where, in the range of the cue, the uncertainty is located (Cohen et al. 2003). Therefore, if the overall cue-outcome association strength (i.e., the correlation coefficient) is the critical input for covariation inferences (e.g., Brehmer 1973), then the nature of the error (homoscedastic vs. heteroscedastic) may not matter, as long as the overall level of uncertainty remains the same. However, the distinction between homoscedastic and heteroscedastic uncertainty may be crucial if covariation judgments are in fact influenced by local variations in cue-outcome association strength (i.e., local correlations).

The current research proposes that (a) local correlations are taken into account when expressing overall judgments of covariation and (b) that local correlations are influenced by the nature of outcome uncertainty (heteroscedastic vs. homoscedastic). We theorize that homo- versus heteroscedasticity determines the perception of local correlations according to a two-step process. The first step entails a statistical nonlinear decreasing effect of error variance on local correlations (Doksum et al. 1994), whereas the second entails a psychophysical nonlinear increasing effect of objective correlation on perceived correlation (Jennings et al. 1982). The result of this process is that, all else being equal, the reduction in error variance in the low uncertainty range of heteroscedastic environments has a disproportionately large impact (relative to the impact of the increase in error variance in the high uncertainty range) on perceived local cue-outcome association strengths.

The first two experiments in this paper establish that heteroscedastic error variance, relative to homoscedastic error variance, results in more extreme judgments of cue-outcome association strength. In Study 1, we presented participants with cue-outcome pairs in tabular format and asked them to judge the overall cue-outcome association strength. We manipulated homo- versus heteroscedasticity within-participants via an elaborate procedure that varies across tables the nature of the error while holding constant other factors that may influence judgments of covariation (overall cor-relation, regression slope, intercept of the regression, mean, etc.). To avoid that any effect of homo- versus heteroscedasticity could be attributed to the existence of prior theories about the association between cue and outcome, we used X and Y as cue-outcome labels in this first study (e.g., Baumgartner 1995). The results show that overall judgments of cue-outcome association strength are more extreme when error variance is heteroscedastic.

In Study 2, participants learned first about the prices and quality scores of several brands in a fictive product category. Homo- versus heteroscedastic uncertainty about quality was manipulated between-participants. Subsequently, we asked participants to indicate to what extent they thought it was difficult to predict quality at different price levels (to measure the perceived local correlations). The results show that participants found it less difficult to predict quality in the low uncertainty range of the heteroscedastic condition than in the homoscedastic condition, while there was no difference between the high uncertainty range of the heteroscedastic condition and the homoscedastic condition. This study shows that error variance has a nonlinear decreasing impact on the perceived local correlations.

Two additional experiments attest to the managerial importance of these findings by establishing systematic differences in product quality expectations and product valuation between homoscedastic and heteroscedastic environments. Study 3 shows that quality expectations are more sensitive to price under heteroscedastic outcome uncertainty than under homoscedastic outcome uncertainty. When heteroscedasticity is manipulated by increasing uncertainty at higher price levels, participants in the homo- and heteroscedastic condition expect similar quality for low-priced brands. However, for higher-priced brands, participants in the heteroscedastic condition expect higher quality than participants in the homoscedastic condition.

Finally, Study 4 investigates consumers' product ratings (value for money) when they are provided with objective information about product price and quality. If, compared to participants in a homoscedastic condition, participants in a heteroscedastic condition with increasing variance over the price range expect higher quality for higher-priced products, they should also rate a high-priced product with a specific quality to be of less value for money. The findings confirm this prediction.

## REFERENCES

Aiken, Leona S. and Stephen G. West (1991), *Multiple Regression: Testing and interpreting interactions*. Newbury Park, CA: Sage.

Allan, Lorraine G. (1993), "Human Contingency Judgments-Rule-Based or Associative," *Psychological Bulletin*, 114 (3), 435-48.

Baumgartner, Hans (1995), "On the Utility of Consumers Theories in Judgments of Covariation," *Journal of Consumer Research*, 21 (4), 634-43.

Bjerve, Steinar and Kjell Doksum (1993), "Correlation Curves-Measures of Association as Functions of Covariate Values," *Annals of Statistics*, 21 (2), 890-902.

Brehmer, Berndt (1973), "Single-Cue Probability Learning as a Function of the Sign and Magnitude of the Correlation between Cue and Criterion," *Organizational Behavior and Human Performance*, 9, 377-95.

Cohen, Jacob, Patricia Cohen, Stephen G. West, and Leona S. Aiken (2003), *Applied Multiple Regression / Correlation Analysis for the Behavioral Sciences (3rd ed.)*. Mahwah, NJ: Lawrence Erlbaum Associates, inc.

DeLosh, Edward L., Jerome R. Busemeyer, and Mark A. Mc-Daniel (1997), "Extrapolation: The sine qua non for abstraction in function learning," *Journal of Experimental Psychology: Learning Memory and Cognition*, 23 (4), 968-86.

Doksum, Kjell, Stephen Blyth, Eric Bradlow, Xiao-Li Meng, and Hongyu Zhao (1994), "Correlation Curves as Local Measures of Variance Explained by Regression," *Journal of the American Statistical Association*, 89 (426), 571-82.

Einhorn, Hillel J., Don N. Kleinmuntz, and Benjamin Kleinmuntz (1979), "Linear Regression and Process-Tracing Models of Judgment," *Psychological Review*, 86 (5), 465-85.

Erickson, Michael A. and John K. Kruschke (1998), "Rules and exemplars in category learning," *Journal of Experimental Psychology: General*, 127 (2), 107-40.

Hagafors, Roger and Berndt Brehmer (1983), "Does Having to Justify One's Judgments Change the Nature of the Judgment Process?," *Organizational Behavior and Human Decision Processes*, 31, 223-32.

Jennings, Dennis L., Teresa M. Amabile, and Lee Ross (1982), "Informal Covariation Assessment: Data-based versus Theory-based Judgments," in *Judgment under Uncertainty: Heuristics and Biases*, Daniel Kahneman and Paul Slovic and Amos Tversky, Eds. New York: Cambridge University Press.

Juslin, Peter, Linnea Karlsson, and Henrik Olsson (2008), "Information integration in multiple cue judgment: A division of labor hypothesis," *Cognition*, 106 (1), 259-98.

Kalish, Michael L., Stephan Lewandowsky, and John K. Kruschke (2004), "Population of linear experts: Knowledge partitioning and function learning," *Psychological Review*, 111 (4), 1072-99.

Karelaia, Natalia and Robin M. Hogarth (2008), "Determinants of linear judgment: A meta-analysis of lens model studies," *Psychological Bulletin*, 134 (3), 404-26.

Lane, David M., Craig A. Anderson, and Kathryn L. Kellam (1985), "Judging the Relatedness of Variables: the Psychophysics of Covariation Detection," *Journal of Experimental Psychology: Human Perception and Performance*, 11(5), 640-649.

Lewandowsky, Stephan, Michael L. Kalish, and S. K. Ngang (2002), "Simplified learning in complex situations: Knowledge partitioning in function learning," *Journal of Experimental Psychology: General*, 131 (2), 163-93.

Olsson, Anna-Carin C., Tommy Enkvist, and Peter Juslin (2006), "Go with the flow: How to master a nonlinear multiple-cue judgment task," *Journal of Experimental Psychology: Learning Memory and Cognition*, 32 (6), 1371-84.

Pechmann, Cornelia and S. Ratneshwar (1992), "Consumer Covariation Judgments-Theory or Data Driven," *Journal of Consumer Research*, 19 (3), 373-86.

Rao, Akshay R. and Kent B. Monroe (1989), "The Effect of Price, Brand Name, and Store Name on Buyers Perceptions of Product Quality-an Integrative Review," *Journal of Marketing Research*, 26 (3), 351-57.

Sheets, Charles A. and Monroe J. Miller (1974), "The Effect of Cue-Criterion Function Form on Multiple-Cue Probability Learning," *American Journal of Psychology*, 87 (4), 629-41.

van Osselaer, Stijn M. J., Chris Janiszewski, and Marcus Cunha (2004), "Stimulus generalization in two associative learning processes," *Journal of Experimental Psychology: Learning Memory and Cognition*, 30 (3), 626-38.

# Affective Evaluations Are More Ordinal

Michel Tuan Pham, Columbia University, USA
Olivier Toubia, Columbia University, USA
Claire Lin, Columbia University, USA

## EXTENDED ABSTRACT

There is growing evidence that affective responses provide an alternative means of assessing value. We advance the hypothesis that, compared to the cognitive system, the affective system assesses value in a relatively more ordinal (less cardinal) fashion. We base this hypothesis on the rationale that our ancestral affective system was originally meant to support behavioral choices, which requires primarily ordinal (rather than cardinal) assessments. The relatively greater "ordinality" of the affective system helps explain various apparent biases in affective judgments of value, such as their greater reference-dependence and scope-insensitivity (see Pham, 2007).

Support the ordinality-of-affect hypothesis was obtained across three studies involving both outcome and process-level data. First, affective assessments of value have more ordinal distributions than more cognitive assessments of the same targets. Second, process-level data indicate that, when asked to assess evaluative targets based either on feelings or on cognitive assessments, affect-oriented participants tend to evaluate targets jointly as if ordinally ranking them, whereas cognition-oriented participants tend to evaluate each target separately. Finally, affect-oriented participants appear to have stronger memory for rank-order information than cognition-oriented participants.

The purpose of the first study was to provide process-level evidence that the affective system assesses values in a more ordinal fashion. Participants were shown the pictures of target individuals of the opposite sex and asked to rate them either as potential dates (a more affective assessment) or as potential teammates for a project (a more cognitive assessment). (Previous studies and pretests had shown that these instructions indeed varied the reliance on affective vs. cognitive information.) As predicted, participants assessing the targets as potential dates tended to generate their own order to rate these targets, suggesting that relative ordering of the targets was an important consideration to these affect-oriented participants. In contrast, participants assessing the targets as potential teammates tended to simply follow the order in which the targets where presented, suggesting that the relative ordering of the targets was less important to these cognition-oriented participants. In addition, compared to participants in the potential teammates (cognition) condition, participants in the potential dates (affect) condition had more accurate memory for the relative location of the pictured target individuals, suggesting that comparisons across targets were more likely in the potential date (affect) condition. Finally, compared to participants in the potential teammates (cognition) condition, participants in the potential dates (affect) condition re-ranked the targets more consistently, suggesting than relative ranking was a more important determinant of their assessments. These process results suggest that affect-oriented participants tended to evaluate the targets jointly as if ordinally ranking them, whereas cognition-oriented participants tended to evaluate these targets separately.

The purpose of studies 2a and 2b was to document a previously unrecognized property of affective evaluations that logically follows from the proposition that affective evaluations are more ordinal. Specifically, if affective evaluations are indeed generated by an ordinal, rank-ordering process, people making affective evaluations should tend to distribute targets more uniformly along the full evaluative scale. We call this phenomenon *distributive scale use*, which we demonstrate both in a field study and in a lab study.

In the field study, men and women participants took part in a "speed-dating" event in which they had a series of "mini-dates" with opposite-sex participants. After each date, each participant rated the other person in terms of physical attractiveness, a presumably more affective judgment, and intelligence, a presumably more reason-based judgment. Individual-level analyses of these ratings revealed that ratings of attractiveness indeed exhibited more distributive scale use—that is, had more ordinal distributions across potential dates—than ratings of intelligence, which had more interval-scale-like distributions.

Another lab study replicated and generalized these in the context of responses to magazine pictures. Compared to the field study, more direct measures of affective versus cognitive evaluative responses were obtained by instructing respondents to record either the pleasantness of the feelings elicited by each picture or the judged quality of each picture using previously validated instructions (Pham, Cohen, Pracejus, and Hughes, 2001). More refined distributions of the two types of responses were additionally obtained by increasing both the number of target stimuli (pictures) and the number of levels of responses on which they could be assessed (a 1-100 real-time electronic dial-turning scale). Again, individual-level analyses of these responses revealed that feelings elicited by the pictures had more ordinal distributions than the judged quality of these pictures, which had more interval-scale-like distributions.

Overall, the results of these three studies are consistent with the hypothesis that the affective system of valuation is more ordinal and more attuned to rank-order information than the cognitive system of evaluation.

## REFERENCES

Pham, Michel Tuan (2007), "Emotion and Rationality: A Critical Review and Interpretation of Empirical Evidence," *Review of General Psychology*, 11 (2), 155-78.

Pham, Michel Tuan, Joel B. Cohen, John W. Pracejus, and G. David Hughes (2001), "Affect Monitoring and the Primacy of Feelings in Judgment," *Journal of Consumer Research*, 28 (2), 167-88.

# When one culture meets another:
## The impact of culturally (mis)matched thinking styles on self-regulation

Minkyung Koo, University of Illinois, USA
Sharon Shavitt, University of Illinois, USA
Ashok K. Lalwani, University of Texas at San Antonio, USA
Yifan Dai, University of Illinois, USA
Sydney Chinchanachokchai, University of Illinois, USA

## EXTENDED ABSTRACT

It is well documented that Westerners tend to engage in analytic thinking whereas Asians tend to engage in holistic thinking (Nisbett, Peng, Choi, & Norenzayan, 2001). Although a great deal of research has revealed various antecedents and consequences of cultural differences in thinking styles, little attention has been paid to the consequences of engaging in culturally mismatched thinking styles. We hypothesized that culturally mismatched thinking styles impact the self, particularly one's regulatory resources. Self-regulation refers to "the self's capacity to alter its own states and responses" or limited resources similar to strength or energy (Baumeister, 2002). In three studies, we provide evidence that culturally mismatched thinking styles can be an important source of self-regulatory depletion and thus can impair subsequent evaluation and further actual consumption behaviors. Our findings indicate the effects are generalizable to real-life settings and therefore have significant implications for creating advertisements and forecasting their effects on audiences of differing ethnicities and cultural backgrounds.

Study 1 tested the hypothesis that a mismatch between one's culturally dominant thinking style and a situationally induced thinking style can impair self-control. Participants from both individualistic (e.g., Caucasian) and collectivistic (e.g., Asian, Hispanic) cultural backgrounds were recruited. Half of the participants in each cultural background were assigned to an analytic task condition: they were shown a picture in which 11 embedded objects were to be found (Monga & John, 2007). The rest of the participants were assigned to the holistic task condition, in which they were shown the same picture but with an instruction to focus on the background. Subsequently, participants' self-regulation was measured using a self-control scale (Tangney, Baumeister, & Boone, 2004).

As hypothesized, a significant interaction emerged between the participants' cultural background (individualists vs. collectivists) and their primed thinking styles (analytic vs. holistic). In the analytic condition, individualists scored significantly higher on self-control than did collectivists. In contrast, in the holistic condition, collectivists scored higher on the self-control scale than individualists.

These findings suggest that a culturally mismatched thinking style can deplete self-regulatory resources. However, it can be argued that those participants in the matched condition may have experienced a greater degree of fluency while doing the task and that this led to more favorable judgments about themselves compared to those in the mismatched condition. In other words, the disfluency experiences associated with culturally mismatched thinking styles may have affected participants' perceived ability to engage in self-control.

Study 2 was designed to pit these two explanations (depletion vs. disfluency) against each other. Participants were induced to think either analytically or holistically using the same procedures as in Study 1. They were then given a description of one of two cereal bars (a delicious but unhealthy chocolate cereal bar vs. a healthy but less delicious multi-grain bar) and were asked to rate their evaluation and likelihood of buying the described food item. Finally, participants' chronic thinking styles were measured using the Analysis-Holism Scale (Choi, Koo, & Choi, 2007).

Processing fluency is known to increase the perceived familiarity with and fondness for a stimulus (e.g., Reber, Winkielman, and Schwarz, 1998). Therefore, if a mismatched task creates a sense of disfluency, participants' evaluation of the tempting food and evaluation of the less tempting one should not differ. Instead, those in the matched (vs. mismatched) condition should evaluate whichever food they were shown more positively. In contrast, if a culturally mismatched task leads to depletion, participants in the mismatched condition should evaluate the tempting option more positively than the less tempting option.

Supporting the depletion explanation, a significant interaction was found between the type of experience (matched vs. mismatched with one's chronic thinking style) and the type of food (chocolate bar vs. multi-grain bar) both in evaluation and purchase likelihood. Participants in the mismatched condition evaluated the chocolate bar more positively than the multi-grain bar and also reported a greater purchase likelihood for the chocolate bar than for the multi-grain bar. Those in the matched condition did not differ in their evaluation or purchase likelihood as a function of the type of food.

Study 3 examined the managerial implications of the effect of culturally mismatched experiences using a real-world situation and measuring participants' actual consumption behavior. In a field study, which was introduced to the participants as a consumer study, participants were given a set of mock ads and asked to evaluate them. Each ad included a picture of individual chocolates or candies of different colors and shapes arranged in the shape of different objects such as a house and a tree. Participants in the analytic condition were asked to describe what made each piece distinct, and those in the holistic condition were asked to describe what shape the individual pieces make as a whole. Analytic thinkers were expected to have a harder time finding the figure than holistic thinkers because analytic thinkers in general tend to focus on details whereas holistic thinkers tend to focus on the big picture (Nisbett et al., 2001). Subsequently, participants were guided to a popcorn tasting study in which they were given an opportunity to sample as much popcorn as they wanted. The amount of popcorn they served themselves was our measure of self-regulation.

Consistent with the previous two studies, a significant interaction between culture (individualistic vs. collectivistic) and the type of task (analytic vs. holistic) emerged. Individualists took more popcorn when they had to find an overall figure than when they had to focus on individual chocolates in the ads. The opposite was the case for collectivists.

Overall, the three studies showed converging evidence that engaging a culturally mismatched thinking style is depleting and can impair a person's self-regulatory performance. This was evidenced on a self-control scale, on food evaluation, and on actual snack consumption. The findings suggest that (mis)matches to one's cultural thinking styles are an important set of experiences impacting one's self-regulatory resources. Indeed, people of certain ethnicities, nationalities, and backgrounds can experience self-regulatory depletion (and increased temptation) merely through exposure to ads or activities that require them to think in an unfamiliar way.

# REFERENCES

Baumeister, Roy F. (2002). Yielding to Temptation: Self-control failure, impulsive purchasing, and consumer behavior. *Journal of Consumer Research,* 28, 670-676.

Baumeister, R. F., Schmeichel, B. J., & Vohs, K. D. (2007). Self-regulation and the executive function: The self as controlling agent. In A. W. Kruglanski & E. T. Higgins (Eds.), *Social Psychology: Handbook of Basic Principles* (2nd ed., pp. 516-539). New York: Guilford Press.

Choi, I., Koo, M., & Choi, J. A. (2007). Individual differences in analytic versus holistic thinking. *Personality and Social Psychology Bulletin,* 33(5), 691-705.

Converse, P. D., & DeShon, R. P. (2009). A tale of two tasks: reversing the self-regulatory resouce depletion effect. *Journal of Applied Psychology,* 94, 1318-1324.

Monga, A. B., & John, D. R. (2007). Cultural Differences in Brand Extension Evaluation: The Influence of Analytic versus Holistic Thinking. *Journal of Consumer Research,* 33(4), 529-536.

Nisbett, R. E., Peng, K., Choi, I., & Norenzayan, A. (2001). Culture and systems of thought: Holistic versus analytic cognition. *Psychological Review,* 108(2), 291-310.

Reber, R., Winkielman, P. & Schwarz, N. (1998). Effects of perceptual fluency on affective judgments. *Psychological Science,* 9, 45-48.

Tangney, J.P., Baumeister, R.F., & Boone, A.L. (2004). High Self-Control Predicts Good Adjustment, Less Pathology, Better Grades, and Interpersonal Success. *Journal of Personality,* 72, 271-324.

# Just This Once: Perceptual Distortion Entitles Consumers to Indulge

Bert Weemaes, K. U. Leuven, Belgium
Siegfried Dewitte, K. U. Leuven, Belgium
Luk Warlop, Catholic University Leuven, Belgium

## EXTENDED ABSTRACT

Three experimental studies show that perceived differences between current and future choice situations reduce food intake self-regulation in the current choice. We demonstrate that the effect occurs because, in response to a currently available food temptation, consumers perceptually differentiate the current choice situation from future choice situations allowing them to indulge without threatening their long-term goal.

This work examines how relating a current food temptation to future food temptations influences the current decision to indulge. Specifically, it looks at the impact of perceived dissimilarity between current and future choice situations on the current decision.

In itself, the long-term consequences of consuming a few potato chips, a single burger, or a frappuccino may not sufficiently motivate consumers to abstain from the immediate pleasure of consuming them (Gilbert et al. 2004; Read, Loewenstein, and Rabin 1999). Still, consumers do not always follow the logic that marginal amounts of vice consumption will only have marginal effects on their weight or health. Instead, they translate higher-order goals into guidelines for behavior by implicitly forming overgeneralized decision rules (Amir and Ariely 2007; Amir, Lobel, and Ariely 2005). For instance, a consumer who holds a weight goal may implicitly form the rule "not to eat fattening food."

Indulging in a frappuccino right now causes a negligible weight gain but, more importantly, the mere act of choosing against one's implicit rule causes people to make inferences about themselves (Khan, Dhar, and Wertenbroch 2005). Thus, the decision whether to indulge in the current choice situation is influenced by what this choice tells consumers about their future choices (Huffman, Ratneshwar, and Mick 2000).

This framework implies that consumers may be able to justify current indulgence if they can perceive the current situation as different from future choice situations. Combining the findings that temptations motivate consumers to construct justifications to indulge without harming goals or rules (Cheema and Soman 2006; Poynor and Haws 2009) and that ambiguous stimuli are assimilated to consumers' current motive (Balcetis and Dunning 2006), we suggest that a currently available food temptation (e.g. the opportunity to have a burger now) may distort consumers' perception such that consumption appears justifiable.

We predict that consumers differentiate current from future food temptations by depicting the current and future choice situations as dissimilar. We hypothesize that doing so can even be triggered by trivial (i.e. non-diagnostic) differentiation cues. Establishing the current choice situation as dissimilar from future choice situations in turn leads to increased current indulgence. Two studies tested these predictions.

Study 1 demonstrates the effect by manipulating a nondiagnostic differentiation cue. Participants were given the opportunity to indulge in a small, presently available food temptation (M&Ms©). Before they decided whether or not to indulge in this temptation, they were explicitly provided with a future reference point in the form of a second temptation that was to follow later on in the experimental session In the Classic-Classic (CC) condition participants were given the opportunity to eat from a small amount of Classic M&Ms currently in front of them while they expected to get a large bowl of Classic M&Ms later. The Halloween-Classic (HC) condition offered the opportunity to consume a small amount of "Halloween M&Ms" (colored black and orange) while expecting to receive a large bowl of Classic M&Ms later. A mirrored Classic-Halloween (CH) condition was also added. Relative to the CC condition, we found that tempted participants were likely to eat if a subtle, non-diagnostic differentiating cue was present (HC and CH conditions). Presumably, the differentiation cues allowed participants to more easily construe the current choice as different from future decisions, increasing the likelihood that tempted individuals chose to indulge.

Study 2 exposes the proposed process using an experimental-causal-chain design (Spencer, Zanna & Fong, 2005). Study 2A aims to show that currently available food temptations cause consumers to perceptually differentiate the current choice situation from future choice situations. Study 2B provides the causal chain's second part: perceiving current and future choice situations as dissimilar increases indulgence in the current choice.

Participants in the large-amount-later condition of 2A received a small serving of sweet pepper flavored potato chips. They were told that would receive a second temptation later that consisted of a large amount of salt flavored potato chips. As a comparison point, we included a second, baseline condition with neither a currently available food temptation nor the expectation of a second temptation. We also included a control condition: the small-amount-later condition was identical to the large-amount-later condition, but participants were told that the second temptation consisted of a small amount of salt chips. We used a multidimensional scaling (MDS) approach to observe participants' perceptions of a two-dimensional product space (Kruskal and Wish 1978). Aggregate consumption would be threatening to the long-term goal by exceeding a critical limit only in the large-amount later condition (do Vale, Pieters, and Zeelenberg 2008; Gilbert et al. 2004). We expected and found that, relative to the baseline condition, the large-amount-later (but not the small-amount-later) condition would start to perceive products that differ among the flavor dimension (the dimension in which the sweet pepper and salt potato chips differ) as more dissimilar. Large-amount-later participants perceptually set the current and future choice situations apart.

Study 2B manipulated dissimilarity while keeping products identical across conditions, ruling out a variety seeking explanation. We selected sweet pepper chips (current temptation) and sweet pepper encrusted peanuts (future temptation) as stimuli. We examined whether participants decided to eat from a small amount of sweet pepper chips, while they expected to receive a large bowl of sweet pepper encrusted peanuts later in the experimental session. Before participants had the opportunity to consume the sweet pepper chips, the latter were suggested to be more dissimilar from (vs. similar to) the encrusted peanuts through a task that repeatedly depicted products of the two consumption phases as belonging to a different (vs. the same) product-group. Indulgence increased when a cue, allowing participants to more easily perceive the current and future choice situations as different, was emphasized (vs. suppressed).

People often sincerely intend to avoid having too many tasty frappuccinos or delicious burgers. Still, they stray from their long-term goals more frequently than they would like (Hoch and Loewenstein 1991). Our findings imply that one of the reasons for this phenomenon may be that consumers unwittingly undermine their good intentions by spontaneously and repeatedly distorting their perception of the current choice situation.

## REFERENCES

Amir, On and Dan Ariely (2007), "Decisions by Rules: The Case of Unwillingness to Pay for Beneficial Delays," *Journal of Marketing Research*, 44 (1), 142-52.

Amir, On, Orly Lobel, and Dan Ariely (2005), "Making Consumption Decisions by Following Personal Rules," in *Inside Consumption: Frontiers of Research on Consumer Motives, Goals, and Desires*, ed. S. Ratneshwar and David G. Mick, London and New York: Routledge Press, 86-101.

Balcetis, Emily and David Dunning (2006), "See What You Want to See: Motivational Influences on Visual Perception," *Journal of Personality and Social Psychology*, 91 (4), 612-25.

Cheema, Amar and Dilip Soman (2006), "Malleable Mental Accounting: The Effect of Flexibility on the Justification of Attractive Spending and Consumption Decisions," *Journal of Consumer Psychology*, 16 (1), 33-44.

do Vale, Rita Coelho, Rik Pieters, and Marcel Zeelenberg (2008), "Flying under the Radar: Perverse Package Size Effects on Consumption Self-Regulation," *Journal of Consumer Research*, 35 (3), 380-90.

Gilbert, Daniel T., Matthew D. Lieberman, Carey K. Morewedge, and Timothy D. Wilson (2004), "The Peculiar Longevity of Things Not So Bad," *Psychological Science*, 15 (1), 14-19.

Hoch, Stephen J. and George F. Loewenstein (1991), "Time-Inconsistent Preferences and Consumer Self-Control," *Journal of Consumer Research*, 17 (4), 492-507.

Huffman, Cynthia, S. Ratneshwar, and David Glen Mick (2000), "Consumer Goal Structures and Goal Determination Processes: An Integrative Framework " in *The Why of Consumption: Contemporary Perspectives on Consumer Motives, Goals and Desires*, ed. S. Ratneshwar, David Glen Mick and Cynthia Huffman, London and New York: Routledge, 11-35.

Khan, Uzma, Ravi Dhar, and Klaus Wertenbroch (2005), "A Behavioral Decision Theoretic Perspective on Hedonic and Utilitarian Choice " in *Inside Consumption: Frontiers of Research on Consumer Motives, Goals, and Desires*, ed. S. Ratneshwar and David G. Mick, London and New York: Routledge, 144-65.

Kruskal, Joseph B. and Myron Wish (1978), *Multidimensional Scaling*, Newbury Park, CA: Sage.

Poynor, Cait and Kelly L. Haws (2009), "Lines in the Sand: The Role of Motivated Categorization in the Pursuit of Self-Control Goals," *Journal of Consumer Research*, 35 (5), 772-87.

Read, Daniel, George Loewenstein, and Matthew Rabin (1999), "Choice Bracketing," *Journal of Risk and Uncertainty*, 19 (1-3), 171-97.

# Healthy Satiation: The Role of Satiation in Having Effective Self Control

Joseph Redden, University of Minnesota, USA
Kelly Haws, Texas A&M University, USA

## EXTENDED ABSTRACT

The present research merges perspectives from past research on satiation and self-control. We study how satiation may serve to enhance self-control in the domain of food consumption. Past research has shown that people tend to satiate on a variety of products and experiences. Interestingly, satiation is most typically viewed negatively, as something that needs to be overcome through a variety of mechanisms such as variety seeking (Ratner, Kahn, and Kahneman 1999), use of more detailed levels of categorizations (Redden 2008), among other things. In the present research, we examine the potential positive effects of satiation. Specifically, we examine circumstances under which various levels of satiation beneficially impact self-control related behaviors.

We define satiation as the decline in pleasure with repeated consumption (Coombs and Avrunin 1977; Redden 2008). Research regarding the "hedonic treadmill" (Brickman and Campbell 1971) suggests that we continually seek to have new experiences in order to simply keep our current level of happiness from declining. Such perspectives suggest that reducing satiation will provide benefits to the consumer. However, hedonic treadmill aside, could it be that the human tendency to satiate actually serves a very useful purpose in goal-driven behavior?

Consider for example, the abundance of cookies, candies, and other tempting desserts readily available during the holiday season. Might some people simply get their fill of such indulgences more quickly than others, and therefore have fewer holiday pounds to shed in the aftermath? Presumably, they enjoy such indulgences as much as the next guy, but perhaps they more quickly feel satisfied with the experience? In the present research, we examine how self-control and decreases in the enjoyment of a consumption opportunity may interact to contribute to "healthy" satiation. After establishing the basic effect, we examine differences in product type and a potential process explanation for our results in a series of three studies.

In study 1, we establish a link between inherent self-control and predicted satiation on an ambiguous stimulus. The 73 adult participants were provided with a description of pretzels, and were then asked to indicate how much they would enjoy the first, fifth, and tenth handful of these pretzels. Separately, their inherent self-control was assessed using the 13-item version of the general self-control scale (Tangney et al. 2004). Results indicated that the decreases in enjoyment from the first bite to both the fifth and tenth bites were more dramatic for consumers higher in self-control. In other words, they predicted that they would satiate more quickly on the pretzels. We note that initial levels of enjoyment did not differ based on self-control.

In study 2, we test the role that product type might play in influencing rates of satiation. We theorize that the consumption of virtuous products should not be perceived to negatively influence long-term goals because such products do not elicit the same level of temptation for immediate gratification or threat to achievement of long-term outcomes (Wertenbroch 1998). As such, differences in rates of satiation based on one's level of self-control will be enhanced for products viewed as more vice in nature. To test this prediction, 175 adult consumers were asked to consider either a set of three relatively healthy desserts or three relatively unhealthy desserts. Our results indicate that high self-control consumers tend to enjoy healthier desserts more initially, but satiate at the same rate as low self-control consumers with repeated consumption. In contrast, high self-control people find unhealthy desserts to be just as enjoyable the first time they have it, but they get satiated much faster. This overall interaction illustrates that the type of product matters, and that high self-control individuals appear to satiate more quickly when it is healthy to do so, but not when it is less beneficial to do so.

Finally, in study 3 we examine actual consumption as well as the underlying process for our effects. Specifically, we propose that the reduction in liking or desire that high self-control individuals exhibit for ambiguous or unhealthy alternatives can be explained by the enhanced monitoring or attention that they pay to their consumption experiences. This leads to an enhanced recognition that their enjoyment of the stimulus has decreased. We used a natural between subjects manipulation of healthiness (based on pretesting) and presented 215 students with either a set of three candy bars or a set of three granola bars. Three options were given in order to ensure that participants would have a reasonable level of liking for the selected product (thereby providing "room" for decreased enjoyment). Our primary measures of satiation in this study included anticipated recovery time (i.e., how soon they would want the snack again) and desire to have the snack again the next day. In addition, after a filler task, we presented them with another serving of their chosen snack and we measured their actual consumption. Self-control was once again assessed separately from the main study. As in study 2, a significant interaction emerged. For healthy snacks, the recovery time had a negative relationship with self-control, indicating that high self-control individuals expected to recover from satiation on healthy snacks faster than those low in self-control. For unhealthy snacks, the data showed the opposite pattern as high self-control individuals tended to expect longer recovery times. Similar patterns were found for the desire to eat tomorrow and actual consumption of a second serving of the snack. Additional analysis demonstrates that the attention paid to consumption mediates the relationship between the self-control X snack type interaction and all three of our dependent measures.

In conclusion, we suggest that differences in satiation rates may help explain why some people find it easier to exhibit self-control than others. In particular, people high in self-control will get satiated faster with unhealthy foods and less so with relatively healthy foods. We suggest that this is explain in part by the attention that high in self-control pay to their consumption quantity when consuming an unhealthy food that helps them recognize their reduction in desire.

## REFERENCES

Brickman, Philip and Donald T Campbell (1971), "Hedonic Relativism and Planning the Good Society," *Adaptation-Level Theory,* ed, M. H, Appley, New York: Academic Press, 287-302.

Coombs, Clyde H. and George S. Avrunin (1977), "Single-Peaked Functions and the Theory of Preference," *Psychological Review,* 84 (2), 216-30.

Ratner, Rebecca K., Barbara E. Kahn, and Daniel Kahneman (1999), "Choosing Less-Preferred Experiences for the Sake of Variety," *Journal of Consumer Research,* 26 (1), 1-15.

Redden, Joseph P. (2008), "Reducing Satiation: The Role of Categorization Level," *Journal of Consumer Research,* 34 (February), 624-34.

Tangney, June P., Roy F. Baumeister, and Angie Luzio Boone (2004), "High Self-Control Predicts Good Adjustment, Less Pathology, Better Grades, and Interpersonal Success," *Journal of Personality*, 72 (April) 271-322.

Wertenbroch, Klaus (1998), "Consumption Self-Control by Rationing Purchase Quantities of Virtue and Vice," *Marketing Science*, 17 (4), 317-37.

# Saying No to Tattoos and Yes to Safe Sex: Ego-Depletion May Help Boost Self-Regulation

Monika Lisjak, Northwestern University, USA
Angela Y. Lee, Northwestern University, USA

## EXTENDED ABSTRACT

A large body of research shows that exercising control over one's impulses and other inner processes in one domain leads to subsequent impairments in self-regulation in other domains, a phenomenon that has been referred to as ego-depletion (Baumeister et al.1998; Muraven, Tice and Baumeister 1998). Existing literature finds that ego-depletion has negative consequences for the individual and the society, such as overeating, overspending and violence. In this research we suggest that ego-depletion may also lead to some beneficial outcomes. More specifically, we suggest that ego-depletion leads to a strategic reallocation of the diminished regulatory resource to increase vigilance. That is, depleted people pay more attention to negative information and are less likely to engage in risky behaviors.

A resource model has been proposed to explain the ego-depletion effect (Baumeister et al. 1998; Muraven et al. 1998). According to this model, all acts of self-regulation draw on a common pool of resource that is limited. After exerting self-control in one domain, people have less resource available to engage in subsequent self-regulation. Recent findings suggest that effects of ego-depletion do not reflect a complete loss of the capacity to self-regulate; rather the effects are due to attempts to conserve the diminished resource–a highly adaptive strategy to prevent a complete loss of self-regulatory ability. The objective of this paper is to more systematically explore the adaptive nature of the ego-depletion effect.

It is commonly accepted that people engage in vigilant processes, which are highly functional for survival. Research shows that negative stimuli are detected faster than positive stimuli (Dijksterhuis and Aarts 2003), and that people pay more attention to negative as opposed to positive information (Pratto and John 1991). And adaptive vigilant processes are thought to underlie people's general tendency to assign more value to negative than positive information (Kahneman and Tversky 1984).

Drawing from this functional perspective, we suggest that ego-depletion leads to a strategic reallocation of the diminished regulatory resource to increase vigilance. We posit that depleted individuals pay more attention to negative information and are less likely to engage in risky behaviors compared to their non-depleted counterparts. We tested our hypothesis in four experiments.

Experiment 1 was designed to examine the effect of ego-depletion on the recognition of concepts associated with vigilance. We first manipulated ego-depletion by using the Stroop task. Following established procedures (Pocheptsova et al. 2009) we presented participants with color words displayed in a font that mismatched the word (e.g., the word "green" written in yellow). Participants assigned to the control condition were instructed to indicate the semantic meaning of the color word (green), while participants assigned to the depletion condition were asked to indicate the font color of the word (yellow). Next, participants completed a lexical decision task. Participants were randomly presented with words and non-words and were asked to identify whether the letter string represented a word or a non-word. Some of the words were neutral (e.g., blouse) while other were vigilance-related words (e.g., safety), negative other-focused words (e.g., brutal), negative self-focused words (e.g., lonely), positive words (e.g., happy), and self-related words (e.g., mine). The results showed that depleted participants were slower at recognizing neutral words than non-depleted participants. However, depleted participants were faster than non-depleted

participants at recognizing vigilance-related words and negative other-focused words after controlling for baseline responses. No difference in response time was observed for the other target words.

In experiment 2 we investigated the effect of ego-depletion on the persuasiveness of messages that promote risky behavior. We first manipulated ego-depletion by using the "cross-off-the-letter" task (Wan and Sternthal 2007). Control participants were asked to cross-off all instances of the letter "e" that appeared in a text. Depleted participants were asked to cross-off all instances of the letters "a" and "e" when several criteria were met. Then, participants read a persuasive message about tattooing and reported their interest in learning more about tattooing. As predicted, we found that depleted participants reported lower interest in learning more about tattooing than their non-depleted counterparts.

The objective of experiment 3 was to investigate the effect of ego-depletion on the intentions to engage in risky behaviors. We first manipulated depletion by using the "cross-off-the-letter" task. Then, we presented participants with a scenario in which they had to decide whether to engage in unprotected sex with an attractive acquaintance. We found that depleted participants reported lower intention to engage in a sexual intercourse than non-depleted participants.

Our final experiment was designed to rule out the potential rival explanation that depleted people are less likely to act; that is, they prefer inaction rather than action. Another objective was to examine whether perceived risk may moderate the effect. We first manipulated ego-depletion using the same cross-off-the-letter task as in study 2 and 3. Then, we asked participants to read a message about hepatitis testing (Hong and Lee 2009). Half of the participants read a high perceived risk message, while the other half read a low perceived risk message. Next, participants reported their intention to get tested for hepatitis. As expected, among participants in the low perceived risk condition those who were depleted indicated greater intentions to get tested than those in the control condition. Depletion had no effect on participants in the high perceived risk condition.

Taken together, these findings suggest that the ego-depletion may strengthen self-regulation through greater vigilance. More broadly, this research provides novel insights in the nature and the adaptive value of the ego-depletion effect.

## REFERENCES

Baumeister, Roy F., Ellen Bratslavsky, Mark Muraven, and Dianne M. Tice (1998), "Ego Depletion: Is the Active Self a Limited Resource?" *Journal of Personality and Social Psychology*, 74 (May), 1252–65.

Muraven, Mark, Dianne M. Tice, and Roy F. Baumeister (1998), "Self-Control as Limited Resource: Regulatory Depletion Patterns," *Journal of Personality and Social Psychology*, 74 (3), 774–89.

Dijksterhuis, Ap and Henk Aarts (2003), "On Wildebeests and Humans: The Preferential Detection of Negative Stimuli," *Psychological Science*, 14 (January), 14–18.

Hong, Jiewen and Angela Y. Lee (2008), "Be Fit and Be Strong: Mastering Self-Regulation Through Regulatory Fit," *Journal of Consumer Research*, 34 (February), 682–695.

Kahneman, Daniel and Amos Tversky (1984), "Choices, Values, and Frames," *American Psychologist,* 39 (April), 341–350.

Pocheptsova Anastasiya, On Amir, Ravi Dhar and Roy F. Baumeister Amir (2009), "Deciding Without Resources: Psychological Depletion and Choice in Context," working paper.

Pratto, Felicia and Oliver P. John (1991), "Automatic Vigilance: The Attention-Grabbing Power of Negative Social Information," *Journal of Personality and Social Psychology*, 61 (May), 380–91.

Wan, Echo Wen and Brian Sternthal (2008), "Regulating the Effects of Depletion through Monitoring," *Personality and Social Psychology Bulletin*, 34 (1), 47–60.

# You Save, I Save, You Spend, I Spend: The Moderating Role of Deliberative Mindsets on Mental Budgeting by Social Comparison

Karen Stilley, University of Pittsburgh, USA
Karen Page Winterich, Pennsylvania State University, USA
Gergana Y. Nenkov, Boston College, USA

## EXTENDED ABSTRACT

How much should you be saving? How much is too much to spend? Though many consumers may not know how much to save or spend, we know that American consumers tend to save too little and spend too much (Kostigen 2007). Perhaps attempts to change these behaviors have been futile due to the extent to which social comparisons influence consumers' evaluations of their own behaviors, thereby altering subsequent behaviors (Festinger 1954). In two studies, we examine the moderating impact of deliberative mindsets on consumers' reactions to social comparison saving and spending information.

Though consumers use mental budgets, the exact amount that should be allocated to each budget category is somewhat ambiguous (Thaler 1999). In situations where the correct behavior is unclear, individuals tend to conform to the behavior of referent others (i.e., Asch 1956; Bernheim 1994). Festinger's (1954) theory of social comparison states that individuals compare themselves and their behaviors to those of others to better understand themselves. An upward comparison (a comparison to someone or something which is better than the current self or object) tends to result in a negative self-evaluation, often resulting in changes in behavior (Argo et al. 2006; Suls et al. 2002), or increasing savings. In contrast, a downward comparison (a comparison to someone or something which is worse than the current self or object, respectively) tends to result in a positive self-evaluation (Wills 1981) such that individuals tend to maintain their behavior, or maintain savings.

Inferring "correct" behavior from social comparisons can have detrimental consequences for savings. Thus, we seek to understand when the positive impact of upward social comparison information could be increased. To do so, we utilize Gollwitzer's (1990) deliberative mindsets which results in consumers being more open-minded to peripheral information such as social comparison information (Fujita et al. 2007). When consumers are more open-minded to this information, the threat associated with an upward comparison increases, thereby resulting in increased savings. While these individuals will also be more open-minded to the downward comparison information, deliberative mindsets also tend to increase generation of counterfactuals which leads to a decreased susceptibility to information framing effects (Nenkov et al. 2009) such that they should not decrease savings allocation. Two studies test this theorizing.

The first study was a 2 (Social Comparison Information: Upward vs. Downward) X 2 (Mindset: Control vs. Deliberative) X 2 (Consumer Susceptibility to Interpersonal Influence (CSII): High vs. Low) between-subjects design with the informational dimension CSII from Bearden et al. (1989) measured as a continuous variable ($\alpha$=.68). We examine the moderating role of CSII in this study to provide greater support for our theorizing such that the moderating role of deliberative mindsets should only exist for those with low CSII, or those who do not tend to pay attention to social comparison information.

Participants first read a scenario and indicated what amount of their monthly internship income to they would allocate to savings. Then they completed either a deliberative or control mindset prime (Gollwitzer 1990), received social comparison information for the average college student savings in a hypothetical newspaper article

($450/high vs. $50/low), and reported their savings allocation again before completing a variety of measures including the CSII scale.

Supporting our theorizing, we find a significant three-way interaction between social comparison information, mindset prime, and CSII on final savings allocation while controlling for initial savings allocation. For those low in CSII, the effect of the social comparison information is qualified by the mindset prime such that those in the upward social comparison condition with a deliberative mindset reported greater savings allocations than those in the control group. A reverse pattern emerged for the downward social comparison condition, with the mindset prime leading to marginally lower final savings than the control condition. For those with high CSII, the social comparison information and mindset prime interaction was not significant such that there were no differences in savings allocation between mindset conditions. Additionally, social comparison-related thoughts mediate the moderating effect of CSII, deliberative mindset, and social comparison information on final savings allocation.

These results indicate that among those with low CSII, the deliberative mindset prime led to a larger *increase* in savings following an upward comparison, which is consistent with our theorizing. These results are particularly important given America's current economic crises and the American consumer's tendency to engage in detrimentally low amounts of savings (Nannie 2005). What if, however, individuals are provided with an upward social comparison for spending? In a spending frame (instead of a savings frame), individuals will focus on the positive aspects of spending such as enjoyment and status (Tversky and Kahneman 1981). Therefore, individuals are likely to be threatened by an upward spending comparison, thereby displaying an increased tendency to spend.

Study 2 tested the effect of deliberative mindset and social comparison information on spending as theorized above. Deliberative mindset was primed similar to Study 1. Then participants read an article for a "memory study" that contained social comparison information regarding average college student spending in a particular product category ($400 high, upward/$100 low, downward condition). Last, participants evaluated an advertisement for designer handbags (females; designer watches, males) and reported their likelihood of buying one of these designer goods priced at $278.

As hypothesized, we found a significant interaction of social comparison information and mindset prime on likelihood to purchase (i.e., spending intentions). Those with an upward comparison in the deliberative mindset (vs. control) condition indicated significantly greater spending intentions. In contrast, deliberative mindset did not have a significant impact on spending for those in the downward social comparison condition. These results indicate that the deliberative mindset prime can result in *increased spending (i.e., likelihood to purchase a designer handbag or watch)* for an upward comparison. Self-importance of savings mediates the effect of deliberative mindset and social comparison information on spending.

Taken together, we find that a deliberative mindset increases the reliance on upward social comparison information. While beneficial for enhancing consumer savings, such comparisons could be detrimental in the realm of consumer spending. Clearly, marketers, public policy officials, and consumers alike need to consider the pervasive impact of social comparison information on consumers' behaviors, particularly when one may be elaborating on potential consequences.

# Flocks, Herds, and Families: The Influence of Victim-Unitization on Charitable Giving

Katherine Burson, University of Michigan, USA
Robert Smith, University of Michigan, USA
David Faro, London Business School, UK

## EXTENDED ABSTRACT

Charitable donations are often insensitive to the number of victims. Six studies show that people donate more to multiple victims if those victims are perceived as a single coherent unit. Because this occurs due to an increased emotional response, unitizing negative victims actually decreases donations.

People react strongly to images, names, and personal stories of individual victims. However, when it comes to helping large numbers of victims, charitable and emotional reactions are typically muted. Two patterns of findings have been documented. First people are "scope insensitive." When asked how much money they would donate to save 2,000, 20,000, or 200,000 migrating birds from drowning in oil ponds, people indicated they would give only slightly more to save 200,000 birds than to save 2,000 birds (Desvousges et al. 1993). Second, people show a "singularity effect": They donate more to help a single child identified with a photo and a name than to help several children (Kogut & Ritov, 2005a, b). Thus, though tragedy often occurs on a large scale and requires action that takes the quantity of victims into account, both the scope insensitivity and singularity effect literatures suggest that it is in these cases that reactions are often most muted.

The singularity effect is driven by an increase in sympathy and concern for a single individual. Previous research has suggested that people react more strongly to individual victims than multiple victims because single units are perceived as more internally consistent than multiples (Kogut & Ritov, 2005b). Individuals are perceived as more coherent entities, or "entitative," than disaggregated groups, which causes their salient attributes to be perceived as psychologically coherent. This in turn makes trait judgments more extreme for individuals than for groups. However, groups can also be entitative; those that are presented with higher coherence and unity receive more extreme judgments than those that are not (Hamilton & Sherman, 1996; Mishra, 2009; Geier, Rozin, & Doros, 2006).

We hypothesize that perceiving multiple victims as a single unit increases the coherence of their defining attributes. When those victims are defined by positive attributes, perceived favorability, sympathy, and concern should increase when these multiple victims are unitized. This will then lead to an increase in donations. However, by the same logic, unitizing will not always lead to a more favorable response than disaggregated victims. Any victims with unfavorable defining attributes should be judged as more unfavorable when presented as a unit (see Mishra, 2009 for a product-related example of this). Thus, sympathy and concern should be diminished when unfavorable victims are unitized and donations should suffer in turn.

In this article we show that people can react more strongly to a large number of victims if they are perceived as a single, coherent unit. In 3 studies, we manipulate the quantity of victims and their perceived unity. In Study 1, participants made hypothetical donations to save 2,000, 200,000, or a flock of 200,000 birds. Though participants' donations were not different for 2,000 and 200,000 birds, donations were significantly higher for a *flock* of 200,000 birds than the disaggregated 200,000 birds. This effect was replicated when perceived unity was affected through priming of global processing instead of semantically describing the birds as a flock. In Study 2, hypothetical donations were made to save 1, 200 or a herd of 200 gazelles. Similar results were observed, and could be explained by participants' emotional reaction to the manipulation. As in study 1, the effect was replicated with a unitization prime.

Study 3 involved actual donations. Though donations were lower for 6 disaggregated children than for a single child, donations were significantly higher when the same six children were said to belong to one unit. As entitativity research would predict, this effect held only for children with positive traits. In fact, the pattern reversed for unfavorable children: Donations were lower for the family of 6 child prisoners than the disaggregated 6 child prisoners. Participants' feelings of sympathy and concern explain these effects. Additionally, unitizing multiple favorable victims increases their perceived favorability, while unitizing multiple unfavorable victims decreases their perceived favorability.

These results show that the singularity effect is much more general than originally thought. Single victims are just one example of a unit. The process of increased sympathy and concern that underlies the assessment of a single victim also extends to unitized multiple victims. Therefore, these results suggest a simple way to increase prosocial behavior toward multiple victims. However, there is also an unfortunate effect to unitizing some victims. We show that unitization reduces perceived favorability and prosocial behavior toward some less favorable victims. In these cases, sympathy and donations are higher if the multiple victims are presented as disaggregated.

## REFERENCES

Desvousges, William H., F. Reed Johnson, Richard W. Dunford, Sara P. Hudson, K. Nicole Wilson, and Kevin J. Boyle (1993), "Measuring Natural Resource Damages with Contingent Valuation: Tests of Validity and Reliability," in *Contingent Valuation: A Critical Assessment*, ed. Jerry A. Hausman, Amsterdam: North Holland, 91-164.

Geier, Andrew B., Paul Rozin, and Georghe Doros (2006), "Unit Bias: A New Heuristic That Helps Explain the Effect of Portion Size on Food Intake," *Psychological Science,* 17 (June), 521–5.

Hamilton, David L. and Steven J. Sherman (1996), "Perceiving Persons and Groups," *Psychological Review,* 103 (April), 336–55.

Kogut, Tehila and Ilana Ritov (2005a), "The "Identified Victim" Effect: An Identified Group, or Just a Single Individual?" *Journal of Behavioral Decision Making,* 18 (July), 157–67.

_____ (2005b), "The Singularity Effect of Identified Victims in Separate and Joint Evaluations," *Organizational Behavior and Human Decision Processes,* 97 (July), 106–16.

Mishra, Arul (2009), "Influence of Contagious versus Noncontagious Product Groupings on Consumer Preferences," *Journal of Consumer Research,* 36 (June), 73–82.

# The Drunken Idiot Bias: Consuming Alcohol Can Reduce Perceived Intelligence

Scott Rick, University of Michigan, USA
Maurice Schweitzer, University of Pennsylvania, USA

## EXTENDED ABSTRACT

What we consume often conveys information about who we are. Consumers often select products to signal favorable aspects of their identity (Belk 1988; Berger and Heath 2007). Additionally, observers often infer aspects of a target's personality based on what the target chooses to consume (Calder and Burnkrant 1977). These inferences are not totally unfounded: observers can often draw reasonably accurate personality inferences based on possessions (Gosling 2008).

Intelligence, in particular, can often be accurately estimated based on minimal cues (Borkenau and Liebler 1993). However, irrelevant cues, such as warmth (Cuddy 2009; Fiske et al. 2002), can bias perceptions of intelligence and competence. We examine whether a different cue–alcohol consumption–is treated as diagnostic of intelligence even when it is not.

Specifically, we experimentally examine whether consuming alcohol can reduce the perceived intelligence of the person consuming it, in the absence of any actual reduction in cognitive performance, a mistake we term the 'drunken idiot' bias. In order to detect a drunken idiot bias, we experimentally unconfound alcohol consumption and cognitive performance. That is, we manipulate whether confederates appear to be consuming alcohol, but hold their cognitive performance constant across conditions. Any difference in perceived intelligence across conditions is a mistake attributable to the observation of alcohol consumption.

We hypothesize that the drunken idiot bias is a misapplication (or more specifically, an over-application) of a heuristic or 'lay theory' that is grounded in reality and often correct. At sufficiently large doses, alcohol impairs attention, general cognitive functioning, and short-term memory, particularly on the ascending limb of the blood alcohol curve (e.g., Jones and Vega 1972; Steele and Josephs 1990).

Because alcohol consumption and diminished cognitive performance frequently co-occur, we anticipate that observing alcohol consumption will increase the accessibility of the concept of diminished intelligence, which will in turn color perceptions of people of ambiguous intellect. The prediction is based largely on semantic network models of memory, which posit that concepts that co-occur frequently (e.g., *tiger* and *stripes*) are stored close to one another in memory. When one concept is activated, closely related concepts tend to become more accessible via a spreading activation process (Collins and Loftus 1975). Concepts or categories that are particularly accessible tend to act as lenses through which ambiguous stimuli are subsequently perceived (e.g., Higgins, Rholes, and Jones 1977).

Thus, we predict that observing alcohol consumption will bring to mind the concept of diminished intelligence, which will in turn color perceptions of people of ambiguous intellect. We utilized four experiments to examine whether the drunken idiot bias exists, to explore its implications, and to rule out alternative explanations. In Experiment 1A, participants evaluated photographs of confederates either holding a beer or holding no drink. Confederates were perceived as significantly less intelligent when holding a beer, but no less likeable, suggesting alcohol selectively reduces perceived intelligence.

To control for the act of consumption, and to examine whether the bias generalizes across different types of alcohol, Experiment 1B elicited perceptions of a confederate drinking wine, Coke, or nothing. Consistent with Experiment 1A, confederates were per-ceived as significantly less intelligent when consuming wine than when consuming soda or when consuming nothing.

Because the judgments in Experiment 1 were made in the absence of context, it is difficult to definitively determine whether observers were actually making a "mistake." Additionally, it is difficult to determine whether people believe that consuming alcohol leads to diminished intelligence or whether people believe diminished intelligence leads to the selection of alcohol (or perhaps both). Experiment 2 addressed these limitations by utilizing confederates who were actually attempting to make intelligent, persuasive arguments, and by manipulating whether confederates chose their own beverage or had it selected for them. Specifically, a confederate made videotaped arguments in favor of comprehensive exams for undergraduates while drinking either Coke or a beer. We also varied whether participants believed that the confederate chose their own drink, or whether the experimenter selected the drink. Confederates were perceived as significantly less intelligent and persuasive when they were consuming alcohol, regardless of whether they chose to consume it. The results suggest that the bias results from the over-application of a heuristic suggesting that consuming alcohol diminishes cognitive performance.

We next explored whether the drunken idiot bias could have important professional consequences. In Experiment 3, real-world managers viewed a hypothetical job interview held over dinner and evaluated the hireability and intelligence of the candidate. We manipulated the drinks ordered by the candidate (wine or soda) and the manager (wine or soda). The real-world managers viewed candidates as significantly less intelligent and hireable when consuming alcohol than when consuming soda, even when the manager was also drinking alcohol.

Participants in Experiments 1-3 were sober, but typically evaluations of people drinking alcohol will be made by evaluators who are themselves drinking alcohol. Because people who are not currently drinking alcohol may fail to understand how they would view the world when they are drinking (cf. Loewenstein 1996), in Experiment 4 mildly intoxicated MBA students, playing the role of bosses, interviewed job candidates (confederates) who were either drinking alcohol or soda. Consistent with Experiments 1-3, candidates were viewed as significantly less intelligent and hireable when consuming alcohol, suggesting that the drunken idiot bias is not an artifact of a cold-to-hot empathy gap.

Experiment 5 examined whether people in a position to be evaluated anticipate the drunken idiot bias. Specifically, we presented MBA students about to go on the job market with a hypothetical job interview that manipulated the boss's drink choice (alcohol, soda, or unknown). Participants were then asked what they would order if they were the job candidate. If prospective candidates anticipate the drunken idiot bias, we should observe minimal selection of alcohol across conditions. Instead, one-quarter of participants ordered alcohol when the boss's drink choice was unknown, and this figure nearly tripled when the boss ordered alcohol first. Thus, candidates generally do not appear to anticipate the drunken idiot bias.

## REFERENCES

Belk, Russell W. (1988), "Possessions and the Extended Self," *Journal of Consumer Research*, 15 (2), 139-68.

Berger, Jonah and Chip Heath (2007), "Where Consumers Diverge from Others: Identity Signaling and Product Domains," *Journal of Consumer Research*, 34 (2), 121-34.

Borkenau, Peter and Anette Liebler (1993), "Convergence of Stranger Ratings of Personality and Intelligence with Self-Ratings, Partner Ratings, and Measured Intelligence," *Journal of Personality and Social Psychology*, 65 (3), 546-53.

Calder, Bobby and Robert Burnkrant (1977), "Interpersonal Influence on Consumer Behavior: An Attribution Theory Approach," *Journal of Consumer Research*, 4 (1), 29-38.

Collins, Allan M. and Elizabeth F. Loftus (1975), "A Spreading-Activation Theory of Semantic Processing," *Psychological Review*, 82 (6), 407-28.

Cuddy, Amy J. C. (2009), "Just Because I'm Nice, Don't Assume I'm Dumb," *Harvard Business Review,* 87, 24.

Fiske, Susan T., Amy J. C. Cuddy, Peter Glick and Jun Xu (2002), "A Model of (Often Mixed) Stereotype Content: Competence and Warmth Respectively Follow From Perceived Status and Competition," *Journal of Personality and Social Psychology*, 82 (6), 878-902.

Gosling, Samuel D. (2008), *Snoop: What your stuff says about you.* New York: Basic Books.

Higgins, E. Tory, William S. Rholes and Carl R. Jones (1977), "Category accessibility and impression formation," *Journal of Experimental Social Psychology*, 13 (2), 141-54.

Jones, Ben M. and Arthur Vega (1972), "Cognitive Performance Measured on the Ascending and Descending Limb of the Blood Alcohol Curve," *Psychopharmacology,* 23 (2), 99-114.

Loewenstein, George (1996), "Out of Control: Visceral Influences on Behavior," *Organizational Behavior and Human Decision Processes*, 65 (3), 272-92.

Steele, Claude M. and Robert A. Josephs (1990), "Alcohol Myopia: Its Prized and Dangerous Effects," *American Psychologist,* 45 (8), 921-33.

# The Effect of Schadenfreude on Choice of Conventional versus Unconventional Options

Thomas Kramer, Baruch College, CUNY, USA
Ozge Yucel-Aybat, Baruch College, CUNY, USA
Loraine Lau-Gesk, University of California, Irvine, USA

## EXTENDED ABSTRACT

"Mr. Borovina is indulging in what seems to be the summer's favorite guilty pleasure – delighting in others' misfortune, or schadenfreude. Between Martha Stewart, Michael Ovitz, L. Dennis Kozlowski, Kenneth Lay and Jeffrey Skilling, and Samuel D. Waksal, there is plenty of misfortune going around, and, as it turns out, plenty of delight."

St. John (2002)

Although others' fortunes often make us feel happy, and their misfortunes sad, as the above quote from the *New York Times* illustrates, sometimes it is others' hardships and troubles rather than their good luck that delight us and give us joy. Another recent instance of such malicious joy, or schadenfreude, includes coffee drinkers rejoicing at Starbucks' financial woes and its subsequent decision to close down 600 of its stores: "I'm so happy; I'm so not a Starbucks person," says one aficionado of small independent cafes (Wulfhorst 2008). Persuasive messages may also often seek to elicit schadenfreude. For example, the recent "more bars in more places" AT&T advertising campaign featured comical situations in which misfortunes (such as a house destroyed by an exploding deep-fried frozen turkey) befall cell phone owners because they had made the wrong choice of cell phone service and could hence not be reached in time to avert the calamity.

Yet, even though schadenfreude is often discussed in the popular press and may indeed arise in many situations, it has received surprisingly little attention in the psychological and marketing literatures. Schadenfreude, or pleasure in others' misfortunes (Heider 1958), is a socially reprehensible emotion that is elicited through social comparison in response to others' failure (Feather and Sherman 2002; Foster 1972). Research has started to examine empirically the antecedents of schadenfreude, including envy (Smith et al. 1996; Sundie et al. 2009), liking (Hareli and Weiner 2002), resentment (Feather and Nairn 2005; Feather and Sherman 2002), and deservingness (Brigham et al. 1997; van Dijk et al. 2005). Importantly, findings have confirmed the role of deservingness in the relationship between misfortune and schadenfreude (Feather 1994, 1999). Van Dijk et al. (2005), for instance, showed that the more others were responsible for their misfortune, the more the misfortune was perceived to be deserved, which in turn increased the level of schadenfreude experienced.

Overall, although extant research has thus demonstrated the ubiquity of schadenfreude and some of the conditions under which schadenfreude is elicited, if, how, and under which conditions schadenfreude can impact everyday choices has not been explored. For example, does the experience of schadenfreude have a systematic impact on the choice likelihood of safe over risky options? Clearly, others' unfortunate decisions will not elicit the same level of schadenfreude for all choices alike. Based on our proposition that others' choices that go against the norm are perceived as more deserving of misfortune, we expect not only that greater levels of schadenfreude are experienced when others' choices of unconventional (vs. conventional) options turn out badly, but also more crucially, that the experience of schadenfreude systematically increases the choice likelihood of conventional options, such as compromise or safe options.

Study 1 establishes that others' unfortunate choices of unconventional, hedonic (vs. utilitarian) and risky (vs. safe) options elicit greater feelings of schadenfreude. In a follow-up study we then rule out social acceptance to expressing schadenfreude for unfortunate unconventional choices as a possible alternative explanation. In study 2, we demonstrate that incidental schadenfreude, as opposed to happiness, results in greater choice likelihood of a conventional, compromise option. A conceptually similar preference pattern emerges when comparing schadenfreude with sadness: decision-makers feeling schadenfreude, as opposed to sadness, are more likely to choose a conventional, safe option than an unconventional, risky option. Finally, Study 3 offers process insights. Specifically, the relatively greater choice share of conventional options following the experience of schadenfreude appears to be driven by decision-makers' interpretation of schadenfreude as information regarding the options they should choose. That is, if schadenfreude serves an informational function regarding the options individuals should choose, then its experience should no longer be informative if its informational value is discredited (Schwarz and Clore 1983; Pham 1998). Following Raghunathan et al. (2006), we discredit the informational value of schadenfreude for half the subjects in study 3 by making its source salient, and find that schadenfreude increases the choice share of the conventional option only when subjects were not aware of the source of their affect.

## REFERENCES

Brigham, Nancy L., Kimberly A. Kelso, Mark A.. Jackson, and Richard H. Smith (1997), "The Roles of Invidious Comparisons and Deservingness in Sympathy and Schadenfreude," *Basic and Applied Social Psychology,* 19, 363-80.

Feather, N. T. (1994), "Attitudes toward High Achievers and Reactions to their Fall: Theory and Research Concerning Tall Poppies," *Advances in Experimental Social Psychology,* 26, 1-73.

Feather, N. T. and Katherine Nairn (2005), "Resentment, Envy, Schadenfreude, and Sympathy: Effects of Own and Other's Deserved and Undeserved Status," *Australian Journal of Psychology,* 57, 87-102.

Feather, N. T. and Rebecca Sherman (2002), "Envy, Resentment, Schadenfreude, and Sympathy: Reactions to Deserved and Undeserved Achievement and Subsequent Failure," *Personality and Social Psychology Bulletin,* 28, 953-61.

Foster, George M. (1972), "The Anatomy of Envy: A Study in Symbolic Behavior," *Current Anthropology,* 13, 165-202.

Hareli, Shlomo and Bernard Weiner (2002), "Dislike and Envy as Antecedents of Pleasure at Another's Misfortune," *Motivation and Emotion,* 26, 257-77.

Heider, Fritz (1958), *The Psychology of Interpersonal Relations.* New York: Wiley.

Pham, Michel T. (1998), "Representativeness, Relevance, and the Use of Feelings in Decision Making," *Journal of Consumer Research*, 25, 144-59.

Raghunathan, R., Michel T. Pham, and Kim P. Corfman (2006), "Informational Properties of Anxiety and Sadness, and Displaced Coping," *Journal of Consumer Research,* 32, 596-601.

Schwarz, Norbert and Gerard L. Clore (1983), "Mood, Misattribution, and Judgments of Well-being: Informative and Directive Functions of Affective States," *Journal of Personality and Social Psychology*, 45, 513-23.

Smith, Richard H., Terence J. Turner, Ron Garonzik, Colin W. Leach, Vanessa Urch-Druskat, and Christine M. Weston (1996), "Envy and Schadenfreude," *Personality and Social Psychology Bulletin,* 22, 158–68.

St. John, W. (2002). Sorrow so sweet: A guilty pleasure in another's misfortune. *New York Times*, August 24, B7.

Sundie, Jill M., James C. Ward, Daniel J. Beal, Wynne W. Chin, and Stephanie Geiger-Oneto (2009), "Schadenfreude as a Consumption-Related Emotion: Feeling Happiness about the Downfall of Another's Product," *Journal of Consumer Psychology,* 19, 356-73.

van Dijk, Wilco W., Jaap W. Ouwerkerk, Sjoerd Goslinga, and Myrke Nieweg (2005), "Deservingness and Schadenfreude," *Cognition and Emotion*, 19, 933-39.

Wulfhorst, Ellen (2008), "Some Coffee Fans Get Grim Delight in Starbucks Woes," http://www.reuters.com/article/domesticNews/idUSN0437926720080706?sp=true.

# Sadness and Consumption: The Attenuating Role of Choice

Nitika Garg, University of Mississippi, USA
Jennifer Lerner, Harvard University, USA

## EXTENDED ABSTRACT

Research on incidental emotion has discovered the pervasive tendency of emotions to carry over from one situation to another, coloring behavior in unrelated tasks (for reviews, see Forgas, 1995; Isen, 1993; Keltner and Lerner, 2009). For some time now, researchers have been paying closer attention to the influence of emotion on consumption and have hinted at a possible relationship between the two. One of the most curious carry-over examples involves sadness and consumption. First, its effects depart from what one would predict based on emotional valence. The standard prediction of a valence-based model would be that any negative emotion, including sadness, should trigger generalized negative valuation of, say, a new product. The idea is that a negative state leads one to perceive the world in negative ways. While disgust, another negative emotion, fits that predicted pattern, sadness does not. Sadness triggers positive valuation of new products, as measured by willingness to pay (Lerner et al., 2004). A second curious aspect of sadness and consumption is that the carry-over effect drives consumption behavior across diverse domains. In the domain of eating, for example, sadness (relative to happiness) leads to increased consumption of tasty, fattening food products, such as buttered popcorn and M&M candies (Garg et al., 2007). In the domain of monetary transactions, sadness (relative to a neutral state) leads to increased amount spent to purchase items (Lerner et al., 2004). Importantly, these undesirable consumption effects of sadness typically occur without awareness by those in the sad state; they also typically occur even when the sadness-eliciting events have no rationally-justifiable relation to the consumption choices at hand (Cryder et al., 2008). Thus, the increased consumption represents more than typical, conscious attempts at "consumer therapy." Rather, it represents unbidden and undesirable behavior.

Understanding how to attenuate the undesirable effects of sadness on consumption is an important issue. Individuals do not want to pay more or over-consume when they are sad; yet they do so. In the present research, we seek to examine whether increasing decision makers' sense of individual control and decreasing their sense of helplessness would moderate the carry-over effects. Although a few studies have now documented carry-over effects of sadness on consumption (i.e., spending and eating), we do not know of any study that has discovered ways to significantly attenuate its effect on consumption. More generally, we examine both the robustness of the effect of sadness on consumption and its moderating and mediating factors.

As discussed earlier, sadness has been associated with conscious or unconscious attempts at mood repair (e.g., Raghunathan and Pham, 1999; Schwarz and Clore, 1983). Given the underlying themes of loss and helplessness associated with sadness (Frijda, Kuipers, and ter Schure, 1989; Keltner and Lerner, 2009; Lazarus, 1991) as well as the pattern of compensatory consumption, could sadness' effect on consumption be attenuated by providing individuals greater individual control and diminished helplessness?

An opportunity to choose a hedonic (i.e., rewarding) gift, rather than merely being given one, may attenuate the otherwise robust carry-over effect. A long line of research on perceived control and choice suggests that individuals prefer choice (vs. no-choice) because of its link to self-determination and sense of control (Averill, 1973; Langer, 1975). Thus, because choice might give individuals some semblance of control and therefore alleviate the helplessness that is typically concomitant with sadness, we expect that choice will attenuate sadness' effect. We test this idea across two studies with different dependent variables of interest. Study 1 focuses on the more established relationship between sadness and food consumption (e.g., Garg et al., 2007; Tice et al., 2001), and Study 2 examines the lesser-known effect of sadness on monetary transactions, such as willingness to pay for a new product (e.g., Lerner et al., 2004).

Study 1 established three key points: (1) that sadness elevates self-reports of helplessness in response to the emotion-inducing situation; (2) that this increased helplessness mediates the sadness-consumption effect; and (3) that inducing a sense of control (via the provision of choice) attenuates sadness' effect. Study 2 also established three key points: (1) that sadness' effect replicates not only in food consumption but also in purchasing consumption; (2) that different kinds of sadness inductions (writing versus video watching) both produce sadness' carry-over effect; and (3) that the timing of receiving the good (pre- or post- emotion induction) is not responsible for the effect of choice (control) on attenuation of sadness' effect.

Overall, the studies provide critical insight into the underlying mechanism relating sadness and consumption, and extend prior work by discovering a key moderator and a key mediator. Specifically, giving sad individuals a choice about what they can receive, rather than simply giving them a good, determined whether sadness' effect was attenuated. Our data suggest that this occurs because having a choice confers a sense of individual control, which counteracts the sense of helplessness associated with sadness. Now that we better understand the sadness-consumption relationship, such undesirable effects as spending or eating too much when one is sad can hopefully be reduced with strategic interventions. As part of the larger discussion about emotions and their effects on decision making, our research suggests that the underlying 'appraisal theme' of an emotion might be the key to understanding and managing its effects.

## REFERENCES

Averill, J.R. (1973). Personal control over aversive stimuli and its relationship to stress. *Psychological Bulletin*, 80, 286-303.

Baron, R. M., and Kenny D. A. (1986). The moderator-mediator variable distinction in social psychological research: Conceptual, strategic and statistical considerations. *Journal of Personality and Social Psychology*, 51, 1173-1182.

Becker, G.M., DeGroot, M.H., and Marschak, J. (1964). Measuring utility by a single-response sequential method. *Behavioral Science*, 9, 226-232.

Cryder, C.E., Lerner, J.S., Gross, J.J., and Dahl, R.E. (2008). Misery is not miserly: Sad and self-focused individuals spend more. *Psychological Science*, 19, 525-530.

Forgas, J.P. (1995). Mood and judgment: The affect infusion model (AIM). *Psychological Bulletin*, 117, 39-66.

Frijda, N. H., Kuipers, P., and ter Schure, E. (1989). Relations among emotion, appraisal, and emotional action readiness. *Journal of Personality and Social Psychology*, 57, 212-228.

Garg, N., Inman, J.J., and Mittal, V. (2005). Incidental and task-related affect: A re-inquiry and extension of the influence of affect on choice. *Journal of Consumer Research*, 32, 154-159.

Garg, N., Wansink, B., and Inman, J.J. (2007). The influence of incidental affect on consumers' food intake. *Journal of Marketing*, 71, 194-206.

Higgins, E.T., Idson, L.C., Freita, A.L., Spiegel, S., and Molden, D.C. (2003). Transfer of value from fit. *Journal of Personality and Social Psychology*, *84*, 1140-1153.

Isen, A. M. (1993). Positive affect and decision making: Handbook of emotions. New York, NY: Guilford Press, pp. 261-277.

_____ (2001). An influence of positive affect on decision making in complex situations: Theoretical issues with practical implications. *Journal of Consumer Psychology*, 11, 75-85.

Johnson, E. J., and Tversky, A. (1983). Affect, generalization and the perception of risk. *Journal of Personality and Social Psychology*, 45, 20-31.

Keltner, D. and Lerner, J. S. (2009). Emotion. The Handbook of Social Psychology (5th edition), New York: McGraw Hill.

Keltner, D., Locke, K.D., and Audrain, P.C. (1993). The influence of attributions on the relevance of negative feelings to personal satisfaction. *Personality and Social Psychology Bulletin,* 19, 21-29.

Keppel, G., and Zedeck, S. (1989). *Data analysis for research designs: Analysis of variance and multiple regression/correlation approaches.* New York, NY: W. H. Freeman and Co, Publishers.

Langer, E.J. (1975). The illusion of control. *Journal of Personality and Social Psychology*, 32, 311-328.

Lazarus, R.S. (1991). *Emotion and adaptation.* London, UK: Oxford University Press.

Leith, K. P., and Baumeister, R. (1996). Why do bad moods increase self-defeating behavior? Emotion, risk taking and self-regulation. *Journal of Personality and Social Psychology,* 71, 1250- 1267.

Lerner, J.S., Goldberg, J. H., and Tetlock, P.E. (1998). Sober second thought: The effects of accountability, anger, and authoritarianism on attributions of responsibility. *Personality and Social Psychology Bulletin,* 24, 563-574.

Lerner, J.S., and Keltner, D. (2000). Beyond valence: Toward a model of emotion-specific influences on judgment and choice. *Cognition and Emotion*, 14, 473-493.

_____ (2001). Fear, anger and risk. *Journal of Personality and Social Psychology*, 81, 146-159.

Lerner, J.S., Small, D.A., and Loewenstein, G. (2004). Heart strings and purse strings: Carry-over effects of emotions on economic transactions. *Psychological Science,* 15, 337-341.

Raghunathan, R., and Pham, M.T. (1999). All negative moods are not equal: Motivational influences of anxiety and sadness on decision making. *Organizational Behavior and Human Decision Processes*, 79, 56-77.

Schwarz, N., and Clore, G.L. (1983). Mood, misattribution, and judgments of well-being: Informative and directive functions of affective states. *Journal of Personality and Social Psychology*, 45, 513-523.

Smith, C.A., and Ellsworth, P.C. (1985). Patterns of cognitive appraisal in emotion. *Journal of Personality and Social Psychology*, 48, 813-838.

Tice, D.M., Bratslavsky, E., and Baumeister, R.F. (2001). Emotional distress regulation takes precedence over impulse control: If you feel bad, do it! *Journal of Personality and Social Psychology*, 80, 53-67.

Tiedens, L.Z., and Linton, S. (2001). Judgment under emotional uncertainty: The effects of specific emotions on information processing. *Journal of Personality and Social Psychology*, 81, 973-988.

Wansink, B., Cheney, M.M., and Chan, N. (2003). Exploring comfort food preferences across gender and age. *Physiology and Behavior*, 79, 739-747.

# Ambiguity of Direct Experience and Product Specification Effects on Consumer Choice

Sehoon Park, Sogang University, Republic of Korea
Moon-Yong Kim, Dongguk University, Republic of Korea
Se-Hyuk Park, The College of William and Mary, USA

## EXTENDED ABSTRACT

Consumers often resort to indirect experiences with products, such as reading product specifications, to make purchasing decisions. In particular, quantitative specifications such as megapixels for digital cameras, wattage ratings for stereos, cotton counts for sheets, calorie counts for cookies, and sun protection factors for sunscreens, among others, can provide useful information for potential buyers to predict their consumption experience with the products that they may purchase (Hsee, Yang, Gu, and Chen 2009). With respect to the effects of quantitative specifications on consumer behavior, recent research by Hsee et al. (2009) showed that even when consumers can assess the quality of a product through direct experience, their purchasing decisions are susceptible to the influence of superfluous quantitative specifications, even meaningless ones.

In the current research, we extend the findings of Hsee et al. (2009) by identifying the conditions under which the effects of quantitative specifications on consumer choice would be strong or weak when direct experiences are either available or not available. We propose that the effects of specifications on choice are not constant under all circumstances; that is, under certain conditions, specifications fail to have a significant effect on choice, whereas under other circumstances, specifications may have a significant effect on choice. This proposition implies the moderating influence of the ambiguity of direct experience on the specification effects. It is doubtful that the observed specification effect in experiments by Hsee et al. (2009) would also be found when the direct product experience is unambiguous because prior research (e.g., Ha and Hoch 1989; Hoch and Ha 1986; Wooten and Reed 1998) has suggested that other information about a product is of limited use to a consumer who has an unambiguous experience with that product. Hoch and Ha (1986, experiment 1) found that advertising did not affect evaluations for participants who had an unambiguous product experience following message exposure. Similarly, specifications may not influence consumers' own evaluations of a product if they have an unambiguous experience with it.

Study 1 examined whether the effects of quantitative specifications on consumer choice vary depending on the format of specifications when direct experiences are unavailable. The participants consisted of 200 students from a large university in a metropolitan area. In the absence of direct product experience, two factors--the specification format (total-dot specification vs. diagonal-dot specification) and the level of the ambiguity of direct product experience (unambiguous vs. ambiguous)--were manipulated between subjects, and they were randomly assigned to one of four cell conditions. The participants were asked to imagine that they were shopping for a TV and had narrowed their choice to two models (A and B). The participants could not directly view and experience the sharpness of the images from the TV screens. Instead, only the specification information (i.e., price and sharpness (resolution)) on the two TV models was offered to the participants. The participants were presented only with the specifications for image quality indexed by dot counting (total or diagonal) reflecting the high- or low-ambiguity of direct experience. Finally, based on the specification information alone, the participants under the high-ambiguity and low-ambiguity conditions were asked to choose between the two models with different levels of sharpness (resolution). The experimental results indicated that the format of specifications (i.e., total-dot specification vs. diagonal-dot

specification) could influence choice outcomes, irrespective of the level of the ambiguity of direct experience.

Study 2 examined how the ambiguity of direct product experience moderates the effects of specifications on consumer choice when direct experiences are available. The participants consisted of 300 students from a large university in a metropolitan area. As in study 1, the participants were asked to imagine that they were shopping for a TV in the market and had narrowed their option to two models, A and B. In study 2, however, the participants could directly view and experience the sharpness of the images from the two TV models. That is, in the presence of direct product experience, two factors--the ambiguity of direct product experience (unambiguous vs. ambiguous) and the specification format (no specification/total-dot specification/diagonal-dot specification)—were manipulated between subjects, and they were randomly assigned to one of six cell conditions. The image quality (sharpness) of each TV model was represented as photos of TV screens. We made certain adjustments to make the differences in image quality relatively clear or ambiguous; that is, we made the image of Model A (vs. Model B) in the unambiguous condition look much better, whereas we made the image of Model A (vs. Model B) in the ambiguous condition look comparable. As in Hsee et al.'s (2009) study, sharpness was either unspecified or specified in terms of the total number of dots or in terms of the number of diagonal dots. Finally, the participants were asked to choose between Model A and Model B. The experimental results suggested that neither the availability of specifications nor the method by which specifications are presented affects consumer choice when direct experience is unambiguous (vs. ambiguous). That is, specification effects were found to be moderated by the ambiguity of one's experience with a product.

Taken together, we extend the work of Hsee et al. (2009) by positing that the ambiguity of direct experience moderates the effects of specifications on choice when direct experiences are available. Furthermore, the results of our study with respect to the interaction between direct product experience and indirect experience (i.e., specifications) are consistent with those of previous studies (e.g., Ha and Hoch 1989; Hoch and Ha 1986; Wooten and Reed 1998), and the current study contributes to the literature by investigating how multiple factors interact to influence product preference and evaluations. From a managerial perspective, the present results imply that marketers can emphasize the difference between options by presenting the same underlying attribute information in a different specification format. In addition, when consumers can directly experience the consequences of using the products under consideration, marketers need to know how ambiguous the direct product experience is to better understand the effects of specification on consumer choice.

## REFERENCES

Baylis, G. C. and J. Driver (1992), "Visual Parsing and Response Competition: The Effects of Grouping," *Perception & Psychophysics*, 51, 145-162.

Camerer, C. and M. Weber (1992), "Recent Developments in Modeling Preferences: Uncertainty and Ambiguity," *Journal of Risk and Uncertainty*, 5, 325-370.

Deighton, John (1984), "The Interaction of Advertising and Evidence," *Journal of Consumer Research*, 11 (December), 763-770.

*Advances in Consumer Research*
*Volume 38, © 2012*

Duncan, J. and G. W. Humphreys (1989), "Visual Search and Stimulus Similarity," *Psychological Review*, 96, 433-458.

Ellsberg, D. (1961), "Risk, Ambiguity and the Savage Axioms," *Quarterly Journal of Economics*, 75, 643–669.

Feldman, J. M. and J. G. Lynch (1988), "Self-Generated Validity and Other Effects on Measurement on Belief, Attitude, Intention and Behavior," *Journal of Applied Psychology*, 73, 421-435.

Frisch, D. and J. Baron (1988), "Ambiguity and Rationality," *Journal of Behavioral Decision Making*, 1, 149-157.

Ha, Young-Won and Stephen J. Hoch (1989), "Ambiguity, Processing Strategy, and Advertising-Evidence Interactions," *Journal of Consumer Research*, 16 (December), 354-360.

Hamilton, Rebecca W. and Debora Viana Thompson (2007), "Is There a Substitute for Direct Experience? Comparing Consumers' Preferences after Direct and Indirect Product Experiences," *Journal of Consumer Research*, 34 (December), 546-555.

Heath, Chip and Amos Tversky (1991), "Preference and Belief: Ambiguity and Competence in Choice under Uncertainty," *Journal of Risk and Uncertainty,* 4, 5-28.

Herr, P.M., F. R. Kardes, and J. Kim (1991), "Effects of Word-of-Mouth and Product-Attribute Information on Persuasion: An Accessibility-Diagnosticity Perspective," *Journal of Consumer Research*, 17, 454-462.

Ho, J. L., L. R. Keller, and P. Keltyka (2001), "Managers' Variance Investigation Decisions: An Experimental Examination of Probabilistic and Outcome Ambiguity," *Journal of Behavioral Decision Making*, 14 (4), 257-278.

Hoch, Stephen J. (2002), "Product Experience is Seductive," *Journal of Consumer Research*, 29 (December), 448-454.

Hoch, Stephen J. and John Deighton (1989), "Managing What Consumers Learn from Experience," *Journal of Marketing*, 53 (April), 1-20.

Hoch, Stephen J. and Young-Won Ha (1986), "Consumer Learning: Advertising and the Ambiguity of Product Experience," *Journal of Consumer Research*, 13 (September), 221-233.

Hsee, Christopher K., Fang Yu, Jiao Zhang, and Yan Zhang (2003), "Medium Maximization," *Journal of Consumer Research*, 30 (June), 1-14.

Hsee, Christopher K., J. Zhang, F. Yu, and Y. Xi (2003), "Lay Rationalism and Inconsistency between Predicted Experience and Decision," *Journal of Behavioral Decision Making*, 16, 257-272.

Hsee, Christopher K., Yang Yang, Yangjie Gu, and Jie Chen (2009), "Specification Seeking: How Product Specification Influence Consumer Preference," *Journal of Consumer Research*, 35 (April), 952-966.

Kempf, D. S. and R. E. Smith (1998), "Consumer Processing of Product Trial and the Influence of Prior Advertising: A Structural Modeling Approach," *Journal of Marketing Research*, 35 (3), 325-338.

Krider, Robert E., Priya Raghubir, and Aradhna Krishna (2001), "Pizzas: ϖ or Square? Psychophysical Biases in Area Comparisons," *Marketing Science*, 20 (4), 405-425.

Kwong, Jessica Y. Y. and Kin Fai Ellick Wong (2006), "The Role of Ratio Differences in the Framing of Numerical Information," *International Journal of Research in Marketing*, 23 (4), 385-394.

Mooy, Sylvia C. and Henry S. J. Robben (2002), "Managing Consumers' Product Evaluations through Direct Product Experience," *Journal of Product and Brand Management*, 11 (7), 432-444.

Muthukrishnan, A. V. and Frank R. Kardes (2001), "Persistent Preference for Product Attributes: The Effects of the Initial Choice Context and Uninformative Experience," *Journal of Consumer Research*, 28 (June), 89-104.

Quinlan, Philip T. and Richard N. Wilton (1998), "Grouping by Proximity or Similarity? Competition between the Gestalt Principles in Vision," *Perception*, 27 (4), 417–430.

Smith, Robert E. and William R. Swinyard (1982), "Information Response Models: An Integrated Approach," *Journal of Marketing*, 46 (Winter), 81-93.

Smith, Robert E. and William R. Swinyard (1983), "Attitude-Behavior Consistency: The Impact of Product Trial versus Advertising," *Journal of Marketing Research*, 20 (August), 257-267.

Tversky, Amos (1977), "Features of Similarity," *Psychological Review*, 84, 327-352.

Tversky, Amos and Itamar Gati (1978), "Studies of Similarity," in *Cognition and Categorization*, Eleanor Rosch and Barbara Lloyd, eds., Hillsdale, NJ: Lawrence Erlbaum Associates, 79-98.

Wooten, David B. and Americus Reed II (1998), "Informational Influence and the Ambiguity of Product Experience: Order Effects on the Weighting of Evidence," *Journal of Consumer Psychology*, 7 (1), 79-99.

# To Do, to Have, or to Share:
## The Value of Experiences Over Material Possessions Depends on the Involvement of Others

Pater Caprariello, University of Rochester, USA
Harry Reis, University of Rochester, USA

## EXTENDED ABSTRACT

Recent evidence suggests that spending money on experiences makes people happier than spending money on material goods. We propose and test the hypotheses that experiences take place with others more often than not, and that it is the social aspect of experiences that provides value relative to material goods.

Scholars have long questioned how having money affects happiness (Diener, Suh, Lucas, & Smith, 1999; Howell & Howell, 2008). However, little research has examined how *spending* money on different kinds of purchases affects happiness. Those who have distinguished between types of purchases have focused their distinctions on varieties of tangible, material goods (e.g., Dhar & Wertenbroch, 2000), at the exclusion of intangible, experiential purchases, which may have comparable but distinct benefits (Sears, Le Bel, & Dube, 2004).

Van Boven and Gilovich (2003) provided the first empirical test of the effects of buying "life experiences" versus tangible, material goods on happiness. Their data (and those from Nicolao et al.'s, 2009, replication) consistently supported the hypothesis that experiences make people happier than material objects. However, we propose that there may be a key hidden variable in this research: More often than not, experiences involve others, an influential source of happiness (Baumeister & Leary, 1995; Reis & Gable, 2003). Furthermore, Dunn, Aknin, and Norton (2008) showed that spending money on others better promotes happiness than spending money on oneself. Therefore, spending money to do things with others should make people happier than material objects or to do things alone. Conversely, spending money to do things alone should make people *less* happy than material objects.

In Study 1, 33 participants viewed a list of 12 hypothetical experiences and were asked to imagine they "chose to do the following activities," to "picture yourself doing each of them," and to "describe each experience in about three sentences." No other instructions were given. Two coders, blind to hypotheses, viewed the list of spontaneous descriptions and rated each for a social reference (0="other people were not clearly part of the person's experience," 1="other people were clearly part of the person's experience;" $\alpha$=.88). Across all descriptions, 179 (49%) were spontaneously described as involving other people. Overall, these results support our assumption that experiences tend to be social insofar as that without any prompting by us, participants spontaneously described many of the experiences in terms of doing things with others nearly half the time. Although there was variability in the degree to which experiences were depicted socially, it seems that including others is a naturally accessible component of most experiences.

In Study 2, 327 participants were randomly assigned to pick between 1 of 2 kinds of purchases–between material objects and social experiences, material objects and solitary experiences, solitary and social experiences, and material objects and experiences in which the presence of others was not explicitly stated. When comparing material purchases to social experiences, participants were significantly more likely to pick the social experience, $M$=.64, $\chi^2(1)$=73.61, $p$<.001, and to indicate it would make them happier, $M$=.70, $\chi^2(1)$=151.36, $p$<.001. When comparing material purchases to solitary experiences, participants were significantly *less* likely to pick the solitary experience, $M$=.37, $\chi^2(1)$=65.97, $p$<.001, and to indicate it would make them happier, $M$=.38, $\chi^2(1)$=54.22, $p$<.001.

When comparing material purchases to ambiguous experiences, participants were equally like to pick both, $M$=.51, $\chi^2(1)$=.68, $p$=.41, but were significantly more likely to indicate that experiences would make them happier, $M$=.60, $\chi^2(1)$=35.74, $p$<.001. Finally, when comparing solitary to social experiences, participants were significantly more likely to pick the social experience, $M$=.82, $\chi^2(1)$=411.00, $p$<.001, and to indicate it would make them happier, $M$=.85, $\chi^2(1)$=465.08, $p$<.001. These results make clear that sharing experiences with others is necessary for deriving happiness from the experience.

In Study 3, as part of a representative panel study, 1,424 German respondents were given definitions of material, solitary, and social purchases, asked to think of a time that they spent money on each kind, reported how happy each of the purchases made them on a scale from 1 (*Neutral*) to 5 (*Exceptionally Happy*), and ranked the 3 purchases in terms of happiness. Consistent with hypotheses, social experiences were rated as making people the happiest ($M$=3.55), material purchases the next happiest ($M$=3.33), and solitary experiences the least happiest ($M$=3.24), $F(2, 2286)$=32.59, $p$<.001, $\chi^2$=.03. On average, social experiential purchases were ranked higher ($M$=1.71) than material purchases ($M$=2.12) and solitary experiences ($M$=2.17), $\chi_r^2(2)$=187.80, $p$<.001. No interactions between happiness ratings and demographic variables were statistically significant, indicating that these effects were not moderated by demographic niche. Thus in Study 3 we again reversed Van Boven and Gilovich's (2003) effect, by showing that solitary experiences made people *less* happy than material possessions, whereas social experiences made people more happy. Furthermore, participants described the effects on happiness of spending their own money on actual purchases, rather than hypothetical purchases. The results suggest that when you remove others from the experience, its value and potential for providing happiness drops relative to material possessions and social experiences.

These results are consistent with recent data showing that spending money on others makes people happier than spending money on oneself (Dunn et al., 2008). Although evidence suggests that merely reminding people of money distances the self from others (Vohs, Mead, & Goode, 2006), overcoming a self-reliant mindset to spend money to do things with others, rather than to have things, may be an important outlet for promoting sustainable happiness (Lyubomirsky, Sheldon, & Schkade, 2005). Theoretically, these findings hint that social interaction itself may be a "conceptual commodity" that people are motivated to purchase to increase happiness, above and beyond the motivation to acquire life experiences per se (Ariely & Norton, 2009).

## REFERENCES

Ariely, D., & Norton, M. (2009). Conceptual consumption. *Annual Review of Psychology, 60,* 475-499.

Baumeister, R., & Leary, M. (1995). The need to belong: Desire for interpersonal attachments as a fundamental human motivation. *Psychological Bulletin, 117,* 497-529.

Dhar, R., & Wertenbroch, K. (2000). Consumer choice between hedonic and utilitarian goods. *Journal of Marketing Research, 37,* 60-71.

Diener, E., Suh, E. M., Lucas, R. E., & Smith, H. L. (1999). Subjective well-being: Three decades of progress. *Psychological Bulletin, 2,* 276–302.

Dunn, E., Aknin, L., & Norton, M. (2008). Spending money on others promotes happiness. *Science, 319,* 1687-1688.

Howell, R., & Howell, C. (2008). The relation of economic status to subjective well-being in developing countries: A meta-analysis. *Psychological Bulletin, 134,* 536-560.

Lyubomirsky, S., Sheldon, K., & Schkade, D. (2005). Pursuing happiness: The architecture of sustainable change. *Review of General Psychology, 9,* 111-131.

Nicolao, L., Irwin, J., & Goodman, J. (2009). Happiness for sale: Do experiential purchases make consumers happier than material purchases? *Journal of Consumer Research, 36,* 188-198.

Reis, H.T., & Gable, S.L. (2003). Toward a positive psychology of relationships. In C.L. Keyes & J. Haidt (Eds.), *Flourishing: The positive person and the good life.* (pp. 129-159). Washington, DC: American Psychological Association.

Sears, D., Le Bel, J., & Dube, L. (2004). Differentiating hedonic consumption on the basis of experiential qualities and emotional make-up. *Advances in Consumer Research, 31,* 358-361.

Van Boven, L. & Gilovich, T. (2003). To do or to have? That is the question. *Journal of Personality and Social Psychology, 85,* 1193-1202.

Vohs, K., Mead, N., & Goode, M. (2006). The psychological consequences of money. *Science, 314,* 1154-1156.

# When Rewards Backfire: Customer Resistance to Loyalty Programs

Dominique Roax, Université paris-Sud 11, France
Mariem El Euch Maalej, IRG-Université Paris-Est, France

## EXTENDED ABSTRACT

Customer loyalty represents a critical issue for firms that try to create enduring relationships with their customers, which helps explains the multiplicity and diversity of loyalty programs (Palmatier et al. 2006). However, most existing research indicates that the success of these programs is questionable and that their effects have only limited scope (Dowling and Uncles 1997; O'Brien and Jones 1995; Sharp and Sharp 1997). Prior studies note the relative ineffectiveness of loyalty programs but, owing to behavioural methods they use, they leave in the dark the possible reasons for negative assessments. Besides, staying at a general level, very few qualitative approaches consider the causes of potential negative perceptions of loyalty programs and the marketing practices on which they are based (Fournier, Dobscha, and Mick 1998; O'Malley and Prothero 2004).

In the light of scarce information about perceptions of loyalty programs, which represent main tools of relationship marketing, this study explores the negative elements perceived by customers that may lead them reject membership in such programs. Using an exploratory study of 15 customers who resisted joining a loyalty program, this research attempts to answer three questions: What reasons do they give to explain their refusal? What is their aim exactly? What individual and situational characteristics might influence these justifications?

Entry into loyalty programs primarily is motivated by a gain or use that the consumer expects to attain. However, research provides widespread evidence of the effect of autoselection, which poses the crucial question of how retailers can attract occasional and not only regular customers who are naturally loyal to a particular point of sale. Besides, questions about privacy and discrimination raise concerns about loyalty programs (Wendlandt and Schrader 2007). In addition, other factors are likely to provoke customer resistance to loyalty programs, such as perceived attempts by the seller to influence them, the level of engagement required, and subsequent appeals to which members are subjected (O'Malley and Prothero 2004). As Friestad and Wright (1994) suggest, consumers' "metacognition" about persuasion mechanisms may increase their perception of influence attempts thus hampering their will to participate in relationship marketing. This article thus explores how practically consumers negotiate their refusal to join loyalty programs and what reasons they put forward to support their decision. We seek to understand whether this resistance follows from previous bad experiences and what situational and/or psychological antecedents play a part in customers' refusal. In this respect, we investigate individual characteristics that are likely to influence consumer resistance and have not been addressed in previous studies.

Because of the extent, novelty, and lack of prior investigation into this issue, this study adopts a qualitative, in-depth approach, based on the analysis of discourses by 15 informants who have refused loyalty cards, including free ones offered by retailers. Five informants had never possessed a card, and the other 10 owned one or two that they had never used. Because age appears to influence the informants' cognitions, this study adopts a homogeneous split, based on the average age of the sample, 47 years, which matches the median that falls between 22 and 70 years. It seemed equally important to vary the size of the households and the family structure, which both influence the amount and nature of purchases. The approximately two-hour respondent interviews were recorded, transcribed, and analyzed sequentially, which allowed for control of the progressive development of themes and provided a guideline for choosing subsequent profiles. Four resistance themes emerge from the discourses: the unacceptable invasion of privacy that programs impose; shifts of interpersonal frames of reference and domestic values being unduly appropriated by the marketing sphere; suspected dishonesty of companies; and perceptions of the poor value of the programs, such that the rewards do not compensate for the overall inconvenience.

The results suggest reasons that consumers might refuse loyalty cards, which, except the perceived unbalance between rewards and nuisances, have less to do with the content of the scheme itself than to what such programs represent in relation to the marketplace. The informants are recalcitrant about such forms of loyalty because customer–company relationship appears as a commercial strategy, whose hidden profit objective is masked by rhetorical discourse and fallacious methods. This resonates with O'Malley and Prothero's (2004) contribution but extends it two ways: firstly, it shows that informants' alleged resistance do not solely derives from previous bad experiences and feelings about the program, but from an extended sympathy for more vulnerable customers who may be victims of companies' interests; secondly, it accounts, other than plain rejection of loyalty card, for various resistant behaviours that are less discernible but possibly more detrimental to firms, such as opportunist and disloyal behaviours. Our findings also show that informants have developed a "marketplace metacognition" (Friestad and Wright 1994) that influences their perceptions of the consumer society and the loyalty devices that companies use to capture them. This knowledge makes them circumspect in their responses to every attempt used by companies to create a relationship. The perception of a mismatch between the "Market World" and the "Domestic World" or "Civil World" (Boltanski and Thévenot 2006), as well as the psychological reactance, need for cognition and cynicism that characterize this group of consumers, play key roles in their refusal. As a consequence for practitioners, relational approaches are inappropriate for these consumers and a better strategy would be to maintain a transactional orientation toward them. In addition, the informants' inferences about corporate dishonesty and unethical practices suggest the need for more transparency, respect, and ethics, as well as the more moderated and timely use of marketing techniques. The possible consequences of consumer resistance also suggest many avenues for further exploration. Because of their metacognition about market function, customers who resist loyalty programs may develop other negative perceptions of companies' practices. Their more general tendency to doubt the allegations of the firms and disloyalty toward ads, offers and labels represent additional areas that could benefit from further development of this research.

## REFERENCES

Boltanski, Luc and Laurent Thévenot (2006), *On Justification. The Economies of Worth*, Princeton, NJ: Princeton University Press.

Dowling, Graham R. and Mark Uncles (1997), "Do Customer Loyalty Programs Really Work?" *Sloan Management Review*, 38 (Summer), 71-82.

Fournier, Suzan, Suzan Dobscha, and David Glen Mick (1998), "Preventing the Premature Death of Relationship Marketing," *Harvard Business Review*, 76 (January/February), 42-51.

Friestad, Marian and Peter Wright (1994), "The Persuasion Knowledge Model: How People Cope with Persuasion Attempts," *Journal of Consumer Research*, 21 (June), 1-31.

O'Brien, Louise and Charles Jones (1995), "Do Rewards Really Create Loyalty?" *Harvard Business Review*, 73 (May/June), 75-82.

O'Malley, Lisa and Andrea Prothero (2004), "Beyond the Frills of Relationship Marketing," *Journal of Business Research,* 57 (November), 1286-94.

Sharp, Byron and Anne Sharp (1997), "Loyalty Programs and their Impact on Repeat-Purchase Loyalty Patterns," *International Journal of Research in Marketing*, 14 (December), 473-86.

Wendlandt, Mark and Ulf Schrader (2007), "Consumer Reactance Against Loyalty Programs," *Journal of Consumer Marketing,* 24, 293-04.

# Consumption as Contaminating Innocence: A Study of Children's Birthday Parties

Laura Jennings, Monash University, Australia
Jan Brace-Govan, Monash University, Australia

## EXTENDED ABSTRACT

Are children's birthday parties occasions for material abundance and the embrace of commercialism? A study of Australian mothers finds it not to be so. Consumption is to be managed to ensure it does not contaminate the innocence of childhood—especially in such a special context as a birthday party.

## BACKGROUND

Birthday parties represent the most personal celebration of all annual celebrations (McKendrick, Bradford, and Fielder 2000) and serve to both individuate children and socialise them into larger groups (Shamgar-Handelman and Handelman 1991; Weil 1986). Despite the apparent simplicity and fun of children's birthday parties, they are multi- textured, multi-layered events (Schoonmaker 2006) that have offered researchers opportunities to study family ritual and socialisation (Otnes, Nelson, and McGrath 1995), gender socialisation (Otnes and McGrath 1994), rites of passage (Weil 1986), income-constrained celebration consumption (Lee, Katras, and Bauer 2009), and the consensual processes surrounding motherhood (Clarke 2007). In addition, the Australian children's birthday party industry is conservatively valued at AU$200 million and is part of the US$20 trillion that women spend globally per year (Silverstein and Sayre 2009). Given that younger children's parties are family celebrations which concentrate on children and build broader social ties, their organisation and orchestration is usually completed by mothers (Clarke 2000). Thus, the context of birthday parties offers marketing researchers the opportunity to study how a mother's consumption intersects and frames her own and her family's identity (Thomsen and Sorensen 2006) and her enactment of this identity. In understanding birthday parties as enactments of ideology or public performances by mothers (Goffman 1959), a broader understanding of their significance can be gained.

## METHOD

To understand the cultural, family and individual influences on women as they planned and navigated their child's birthday party, this research was designed to develop a deeper understanding of the forces at play for women in the public performance of their role as mother. In-depth, face-to-face interviews were conducted with eight mothers of children who were between five and seven years at their most recent birthday party. Variation across the sample was sought in relation to child's age, school attended, birth order, and child's gender. Semi-structured interviews were used to discuss cultural, family, and individual influences on mothers as they recollected how they planned and navigated their children's birthday parties. Goffman's (1959) performance theory was used as the analytical lens to understand the actions of the mothers and directly addresses Fisk and Grove's (1996) call to apply the drama metaphor more broadly in marketing. It also moves marketing literature about children's birthday parties beyond the ritual frame.

## FINDINGS

The children's birthday parties were all complex social and personal events where mothers celebrated and demonstrated an intimate understanding of their children and also maintained her and her child's social networks. Through this, the birthday parties provided a significant social space in which the women performed their identities as a mother to herself, her child, her family, friends, and the broader community. They represented a celebration of the individual child and a time of reflection for the mothers.

Media, children's schools, memories from childhood, and reference groups did not merely present different options or provide recommendations for children's parties, they also provided a normative framework and created a social discourse of good mothering (Banister and Hogg 2007). To be a good mother, the mothers enacted three ideologies—the mother's love was shown through the personalisation of the party to her child, the children were made to feel special with a focus on non-material means, and childhood was protected by the mothers so it could be fun, innocent and simple. For the mothers in this research, birthday parties were also occasions where commercial consumption activities, consumer socialisation of children, and teaching children the importance of relationships over and above materialism (Miller 1997) intersected.

In orchestrating their children's birthday parties, the mothers were hostesses, directors, protectors, event planners, friends, family members, and mothers of the birthday child. The complexity and number of roles each mother assumed made this an involved and consuming performance for the mothers and caused them all a level of anxiety which had to be managed. The two key roles played by the mothers were director and teacher at their children's birthday parties. As directors they used consumption to assist in staging the best party possible, and as educators they sought to educate their children as consumers and thus protect their children from being exploited through commercialism (Cook 2008).

## DISCUSSION

The mothers all purchased goods or services in the course of organising and orchestrating their children's birthday parties, and they did so with both themselves and their child in mind (Cook 2008). Importantly, consumption was representative of interpersonal care (Thompson 1996) and was used and viewed by these mothers more as an "expression of relationships (rather) than some mindless materialism" (Miller 1997, 75) as it was used to socialise children (Otnes and McGrath 1994) and to demonstrate love through intimate knowledge of their needs and likes. By personalising their children's birthday parties, the mothers also used consumption to define their and their family's identity (Clarke 2000) and demonstrate their position in consumer culture (Schoonmaker 2006). Importantly, this personalisation of the birthday party through consumption and other acts was viewed as the opposite to the commodified birthday parties that were offered by venues such as commercial play centres. Whilst consumption was a tool in enacting the mothers' ideologies, its use and type was constrained by each mother's individual commodity frontier (Hochschild 2003). Each mother defined this frontier individually and uniquely. It was the responsibility of the mothers to set limits on the level of "commercial violation" (Hochschild and Machung 1989, 284) into the home and party and determine the commodity frontier.

Excess commercialism is generally felt to intrude upon the sanctity of childhood through either exploiting children or forcing them to mature early as consumers in order to be able to successfully navigate the efforts of marketers (Cook 2008). The mothers in this study educated their children as consumers through gift exchange processes and demonstrated that birthday parties are a celebration of 'togetherness', rather than material consumption. Mothers are re-affirming the importance of birthday parties as family rituals (Otnes et al. 1995) and events to forge community togetherness (Schoonmaker 2006).

## REFERENCES

Banister, Emma N. and Margaret K Hogg (2007), "The Self-Determination Processes of New Mothers," paper presented at the European Advances in Consumer Research Special Session, Milan.

Clarke, Alison J. (2000), "Maternity and Materiality: Becoming a Mother in Consumer Culture," in *Consuming Motherhood,* ed. Janelle S. Taylor, Linda L. Layne and Danielle F. Wozniak, London: Rutgers University Press, 55-71.

_____ (2007), "Making Sameness: Mothering, Commerce and the Culture of Children's Birthday Parties" in *Gender and Consumption: Domestic Cultures and the Commercialisation of Everyday Life,* ed. Emma Casey and Lydia Martens, Burlington, VT: Ashgate, 79-95.

Cook, Daniel T. (2008), "The Missing Child in Consumption Theory," *Journal of Consumer Culture,* 8 (2), 219-243.

Fisk, Raymond P. and Stephen J.Grove (1996), "Applications of Impression Management and the Drama Metaphor in Marketing: An introduction," *European Journal of Marketing,* 30 (9), 6-12.

Goffman, Erving. (1959), *The Presentation of Self in Everyday Life,* New York: Anchor Books.

Hochschild, Arlie R. and Anne Machung (1989), *The Second Shift,* New York: Avon Books.

Hochschild, Arlie R. (2003), *The Commercialization of Intimate Life: Notes from Home and Work,* Los Angeles, CA: University of California.

Lee, Jaerim, Mary Jo Katras, and Jean W. Bauer (2009), "Children's Birthday Celebrations from the Lived Experiences of Low-Income Rural Mothers," *Journal of Family Issues,* 30 (4), 532-553.

McKendrick, John H., Michael G. Bradford, and Anna V. Fielder (2000), "Time for a Party!: Making Sense of the Commercialisation of Leisure Space for Children," in *Children's Geographies: Playing, Living, Learning,* ed. Sarah L. Holloway and Gill Valentine, London: Routledge, 100-116.

Miller, Daniel (1997), "How Infants Grow Mothers in North London," *Theory, Culture & Society,* 14 (4), 67-88.

Otnes, Cele and Mary Ann McGrath (1994), "Ritual Socialisation and the Children's Birthday Party: The Early Emergence of Gender Differences," *Journal of Ritual Studies,* 8 (1), 73-93.

Otnes, Cele, Michelle Nelson and Mary Ann McGrath (1995), "The Children's Birthday Party: A Study of Mothers as Socialization Agents," *Advances in Consumer Research,* 22, 622-627.

Schoonmaker, Sarah (2006), "Piece of Cake: Children's Birthday Celebrations and Alternatives to Consumer Culture," *Sociological Focus,* 39, 217-234.

Shamgar-Handelman, Lea and Don Handelman (1991), "Celebrations of Bureaucracy: Birthday Parties in Israeli Kindergartens," *Ethnology,* 30 (4), 293-312.

Silverstein, Michael J. and Kate Sayre (2009), "The Female Economy," *Harvard Business Review,* September, 46-53.

Thompson, Craig J. (1996), "Caring Consumers: Gendered Consumption Meanings and the Juggling Lifestyle," *Journal of Consumer Research,* 22 (March), 388-407.

Thomsen, Thyra U. and Elin B. Sorensen (2006), "The First Four-Wheeled Status Symbol: Pram Consumption as a Vehicle for the Construction of Motherhood Identity," *Journal of Marketing Management,* 22 (9/10), 907-927.

Weil, Shalva (1986), "The Language and Ritual of Socialisation: Birthday Parties in a Kindergarten Context," *Man,* 21, 329-341.

# Changes in Relationship Closeness: A Turning Point Analysis

Gary Daniel Futrell, Florida State University, USA

## EXTENDED ABSTRACT

Spending on relationship marketing programs has grown exponentially since the early 1980's as managers have adopted the premise that investments in relationship marketing build stronger relationships and improve financial performance by creating loyal customers that spread positive word-of-mouth, make repeat purchases, and are willing to pay price premiums (Pine, Peppers, and Rogers 1995). Researchers and managers alike have made relationship marketing a top priority. Yet research in this field has often yielded mixed results, and managers readily admit that they have experienced only limited success and often question the ability to translate relationship marketing theory into practice (Band 2009). Numerous calls have been made for greater understanding about relationship building. Price and Arnould (1999, p. 38) caution that, "charging ahead with relational programs without an understanding of what marketing relationships can and cannot be puts the cart before the horse."

By utilizing a novel research technique, this research investigates marketplace relationships between customers and service providers. Turning point analysis (borrowed from the communications literature) is used here to investigate how *relationship closeness*, a key factor in relationship building, changes over the course of a marketplace relationship.

Closeness is often the characteristic referred to when differentiating strangers, acquaintances, friends and intimates. Collins and Feeney (2004, p. 164) define closeness as "the degree to which relationship partners are cognitively, emotionally, and behaviorally interdependent with one another." That is, the degree to which individuals influence one another's outcomes and depend on one another to meet social, emotional, and physical needs. It is the process that underlies many relationship phenomena and is proposed as the primary construct by which a relationship should be assessed (Berscheid, Snyder, and Omoto 1989). Several relational constructs have been proposed in the marketing literature as key elements for relationship assessment. Among the most commonly cited are: attachment, commitment, bond, relationship strength, relationship satisfaction, and relationship quality. A study by Jones, Ranaweera, and Bansal (2009) suggests that there is significant overlap in meaning among these constructs and that both researchers and consumers see little difference among them. These constructs directly or indirectly use closeness as a key dimension. For example, relationship quality has been conceptualized as relationship commitment (Jones et al. 2009). Commitment, in turn, has been conceptualized as attachment and closeness (Garbarino and Johnson 1999).

A qualitative study was undertaken in an effort to gain greater understanding about what events trigger a change in relationship closeness between consumers and service providers. The research question of interest for this study is "what events characterize changes in closeness throughout the history of a consumer's relationship with a service provider?" The method of investigation, turning point analysis, is a new technique in the marketing research. This research method has proven to provide insight into critical events that affect closeness, as well as how relationships change over time. The following section provides an overview of the use of turning point analysis in relationship research. This is followed by a discussion of the methods used for this study, results and conclusions.

Fourteen participants were interviewed separately using the retrospective interview technique (Baxter and Bullis 1986). They were asked to think of a specific service professional that they are currently using, have used at least three times, and have patronized for at least 12 months. The concept of relationship closeness was defined for the participant and they were asked to rate on a scale from 0 to 10 (with 0 being the lowest possible score and 10 being the highest), how "close" they felt to the service provider currently and when they first used the service provider. In accordance with Collins and Feeney (2004) closeness was defined as "the degree to which individuals influence one another's outcomes and depend on one another to meet social, emotional, and physical needs." Using a preprinted graph with 0 to 10 marked on the Y-axis to indicate closeness, the author then completed the graph by plotting the months on the X-axis. The participant was oriented to the graph, and asked to plot their level of closeness when they first used the service provider and currently. Participants were then asked to recall and plot "all of the times when there were changes in the closeness you fell toward the service provider." Participants were asked to describe the nature of the event that affected the relationship, how they felt about the event and how they altered their behavior. After discussion of each plotted turning point, the participant was asked to connect the prior point to the most recently drawn point and explain how the line represents the change in relationship. This procedure was repeated as the participant moved from left to right across the x-axis. After completing the graph, the participant was asked to review the graph and consider the initial instruction and discussion about the relationship. The participant was allowed to make any changes and provide any additional information that they felt relevant. The participant was debriefed and thanked.

Turning points were coded by the researcher and similar turning points were grouped together. Several themes emerged based on the data analyzed in this study: economic salience, community connection, and insider knowledge. The first category, economic salience occurs when, through the actions of the service provider, the customer is reminded that the relationship is an economic arrangement. Results from the study suggest that customers feel less close when they are reminded that the relationship is a marketplace arrangement. The second category, community connection, occurs when the customer discovers that the service provider has ties to the community. Closeness increases when, for example, the customer learns that the service provider is a member of a local civic organization, school or church.

The final category, insider knowledge, refers to when the customer learns personal information about the service provider's family or business. Customer's feeling of closeness increases upon meeting or learning personal information about the service provider's family members.

In addition to the findings of this qualitative study, this research provides evidence that turning point analysis and RIT are viable methods of investigation and data analysis in consumer behavior research.

## REFERENCES

Aron, Arthur P., Debra. J. Mashek, and Elaine N. Aron (2004), "Closeness as Including Other in the Self," in *Handbook of closeness and intimacy*, ed. Debra. J. Mashek and Arthur Aron, Mahwah, NJ: Lawrence Erlbaum Associates, Inc., 27-41.

Band, William (2009), "Risk-Proofing Your CRM Initiative," *Customer Relationship Management*, 13 (3), 12.

Baxter, Leslie A. and Connie Bullis (1986), "Turning Points in Developing Romantic Relationships," *Human Communication Research*, 12 (4), 469-93.

Berscheid, Ellen, Mark Snyder, and Allen M. Omoto (1989), "The Relationship Closeness Inventory: Assessing the closeness of interpersonal relationships," *Journal of Personality and Social Psychology*, 57 (5), 792-807.

_____ (2004), "Measuring Closeness: The Relationship Closeness Inventory (R C I) Revisited," in *Handbook of closeness and intimacy*, ed. Debra. J. Mashek and Arthur Aron, Mahwah, NJ: Lawrence Erlbaum Associates, Inc., 81-101.

Bock, Timothy and John Sergeant (2002), "Small sample market research," *International Journal of Market Research*, 44 (2), 235-44.

Collins, Nancy L. and Brooke C. Feeney (2004), "An Attachment Theory Perspective on Closeness and Intimacy," in *Handbook of closeness and intimacy*, ed. Debra. J. Mashek and Arthur Aron, Mahwah, NJ: Lawrence Erlbaum Associates, Inc., 163-87.

Duck, Steve (1990), "Where Do All the Kisses Go? Rapport, Positivity, and Relational-Level Analyses of Interpersonal Enmeshment," *Psychological Inquiry*, 1 (4), 308-09.

_____ (2007), *Human Relationships*, Los Angeles: Sage Publications.

Duck, Steve W. and H. K. A. Sants (1983), "On the origin of the specious: Are personal relationships really interpersonal states?," *Journal of Social and Clinical Psychology*, 1 (1), 27-41.

Flandez, Raymund (2009), "Entrepreneurs Strive to Turn Buzz Into Loyalty — Companies With Cult Status Push Array of Giveaways and Contests to Build Long-Term Business From First Rush of Success," *Wall Street Journal*, Jul 21, 2009, B4.

Fournier, Susan, Susan Dobscha, and David Glen Mick (1998), "PREVENTING THE PREMATURE DEATH OF RELATIONSHIP MARKETING," *Harvard Business Review*, 76 (1), 42-51.

Garbarino, Ellen and Mark S. Johnson (1999), "The Different Roles of Satisfaction, Trust, and Commitment in Customer Relationships," *Journal of Marketing*, 63 (2), 70-87.

Golish, Tamara D. (2000), "Changes in closeness Between adult children and their parents: A turning point analysis," *Communication Reports*, 13 (2), 79-97.

Griffin, Abbie and John R. Hauser (1993), "The Voice of the Customer," *Marketing Science*, 12 (1), 1.

Huston, TL, CA Surra, NM Fitzgerald, and RM Cate (1981), "From Courtship to Marriage: Mate Selection as an Interpersonal Process," in *Personal Relationships 2: Developing Personal Relationships*, ed. Steve Duck and Robin Gilmore, New York: Academic Press.

Jones, Tim, Chatura Ranaweera, and Harvir Bansal (2009), "Relational Confusion," in *Academy of Marketing Science 2009 Annual Conference*, Baltimore, MD.

Kellas, Jody Koenig, Dawn Bean, Cherakah Cunningham, and Ka Yun Cheng (2008), "The ex-files: Trajectories, turning points, and adjustment in the development of post-dissolutional relationships," *Journal of Social & Personal Relationships*, 25 (1), 23-50.

Kelley, Harold H. (2002), *Close relationships*, Clinton Corners, NY: W.H. Freeman & Company.

Mashek, Debra. J. and Arthur P. Aron (2004), "Introduction," in *Handbook of closeness and intimacy*, ed. Debra. J. Mashek and Arthur Aron, Mahwah, NJ: Lawrence Erlbaum Associates, Inc., 1-6.

O'Brien, Louise and Charles Jones (1995), "Do Rewards Really Create Loyalty?," *Harvard Business Review*, 73 (3), 75-82.

Oracle (2009), "Create Enduring Customer Relationships," in *[Brochure]*, Redwood Shores, CA.

Palmatier, Robert W., Rajiv P. Dant, Dhruv Grewal, and Kenneth R. Evans (2006), "Factors Influencing the Effectiveness of Relationship Marketing: A Meta-Analysis," *Journal of Marketing*, 70 (4), 136-53.

Parks, Malcom R. (1997), "Communication Networks and Relationship Life Cycles," in *Handbook of personal relationships: theory, research, and interventions*, ed. Steve Duck, Chichester, West Sussex, England: John Wiley & Sons Ltd, 351-72.

Perman, Stacy (2009), *In-N-Out Burger: A Behind-the-Counter Look at the Fast-Food Chain That Breaks All the Rules*, New York: HarperBusiness.

Peterson, Robert A. (1995), "Relationship marketing and the consumer," *Journal of the Academy of Marketing Science*, 23 (4).

Pine, B. Joseph, Don Peppers, and Martha Rogers (1995), "Do You Want to Keep Your Customers Forever?," *Harvard Business Review*, 73 (2), 103-14.

Prager, Karen J. and Linda J. Roberts (2004), "Deep Intimate Connection: Self and Intimacy in Couple Relationships," in *Handbook of closeness and intimacy*, ed. Debra. J. Mashek and Arthur Aron, Mahwah, NJ: Lawrence Erlbaum Associates, Inc., 43-60.

Price, Linda L. and Eric J. Arnould (1999), "Commercial Friendships: Service Provider—Client Relationships in Context," *Journal of Marketing*, 63 (4), 38-56.

Starr, Michael, Lior Arussy, Rachel Yurowitz, and Michael Blackmire (2009), "2009 Customer Experience Management Benchmark Study," Rochelle Park, NJ: Strativity Group, Inc.

Starzyk, Katherine B., Ronald R. Holden, Leandre R. Fabrigar, and Tara K. MacDonald (2006), "The personal acquaintance measure: A tool for appraising one's acquaintance with any person," *Journal of Personality and Social Psychology*, 90 (5), 833-47.

Tax, Stephen S., Stephen W. Brown, and Murali Chandrashekaran (1998), "Customer Evaluations of Service Complaint Experiences: Implications for Relationship Marketing," *Journal of Marketing*, 62 (2), 60-76.

Verhoef, Peter C. (2003), "Understanding the Effect of Customer Relationship Management Efforts on Customer Retention and Customer Share Development," *Journal of Marketing*, 67 (4), 30-45.

Zaichkowsky, Judith Lynne (1985), "Measuring the Involvement Construct," *Journal of Consumer Research*, 12 (3), 341-52.

Zaltman, Gerald (1996), "Metaphorically speaking," *Marketing Research*, 8 (2), 13-20.

Zeithaml, Valarie A., Leonard L. Berry, and A. Parasuraman (1996), "The Behavioral Consequences of Service Quality," *Journal of Marketing*, 60 (2), 31-46.

# Revisiting The Subculture:
## Fragmentation of The Social and The Venue for Contemporary Consumption

Emre Ulusoy, University of Texas-Pan American, USA
A. Furat Firat, University of Texas-Pan American, USA

## EXTENDED ABSTRACT

Although, subcultures have traditionally been defined mostly on the bases of nationality, ethnicity, religion, and class distinctions and thus people have been categorized and compressed into given, stable and clearly demarcated categories based on traditional and modern lineages, with the cultural turn from the modern to the postmodern, it is observed that people have the potential and vision for generating their own categories and, therefore, do not need to obey or try to fit in these predetermined, static categories with boundaries. People have begun to construct and structure cultural identities more often on the basis of their personal choices. The very idea of stable, coherent subcultures as distinct entities with recognizable boundaries has thus been challenged. Instead the focus is on the fluid, heterogeneous, taste-based, fragmented, and transitory nature of so-called postmodern subcultures.

Thus, subcultures have come to provide a venue for people to find anchors and feel empowered to generate more dynamic, fluid and organic identities and modes of life. Subcultures have also grown to be venues for consumers to not only perform their personal lifestyle choices, but to also respond to an alienating and objectifying individualism by constructing collective identities using activities, including music, style, and ideology. On the one hand, subculture is perceived as a meaningful alternative to a dominant culture, therefore, not a direct challenge to the dominant institutions in our lives. On the other hand, alternative lifestyle practices and creating venues for expression for alternative ways of being can also be considered to be a resistance to the dominant system of meanings and values.

When humanity lost faith in the emancipation potential of science and the progress of modernity, the grand narratives of modernity have waned and the social is fragmented. No longer the grand narratives of modernity but multiple, fragmented narratives that we observe in subcultures tend to be employed to practice fragmentation and dispersion. Postmodern subculture identities are multiple and fluid. They are constituted through consumption and are the new sources of identity, as well as the new signifiers of difference. Consumers do not have to worry about contradictions among their selected subcultural identities for there are only ephemeral attachments to a variety of styles.

In the fragmentation process, one form or style does not dominate over or eliminate all others. Instead, different styles work as a catalyst for fragmentation, in which consumers are willing to experience and sample the different styles and cultural artifacts. A postmodernist sensibility recognizes the fact that various subculture groups will have preferences for different and multiple ways of being and living rather than cling to or claim the superiority of just one. Therefore, fragmentation gains strength in postmodernism by having tolerance for differences and multiplicity; without any judgmental assessment in terms of superiority and inferiority. However, in order for these fragmented life modes to work, community is required since consumers can only achieve meaning and existence through participation in or construction of communities, thus enabling experiences of varied (sub)cultures, styles, and modes of being. In sum, contemporary subcultures are the consequence of the fragmentation of society and the means for producing the meaningful experiences that are sought in life, as well as for producing selves or self images within these experiences. Human beings transform from relatively passive consumers into active producers in the venues of subcultures whereby they are empowered.

Music is a core element or artifact of subcultural phenomena that is set apart from other arts and activities due to its transcendent popularity over the others and its highly permeated position in everyday life. Music is proposed as a producer of people and experiences rather than simply a reflection. Subcultural identities are created and developed through active participation in the production and consumption of music. Music works as a means of facilitating the entry of a subculture as well as diffusing it. Music provides this resource for subcultures because not only can members utilize it easily but also because it has a culturally integrative potential to integrate individuals with the group. Music and live performances, as a form of cultural expression and cultural artifact, play a key role in generating subcultural identity and collective experience.

The forms of resistance have transformed in step with the epochal changes in human history. Rebellion was the dominant form of resistance in traditional culture where forces beyond humanity were believed to control human destiny. With modernity, confrontation became the dominant form of resistance in which discontent could be confronted with the goal of changing the world. However, with the waning of modernity, presentation is substituting confrontation as the dominant form of resistance. There are no claims of fundamentals, but the universe we encounter is seen as what has been culturally constructed, providing people greater license to present possible and potential modes of living and being in the world. In sum, subcultures present core meanings of resistance, but then offer venue for individuals to customize their subcultural identity. Subcultures are consumers' own sites of being by resisting imposed meanings while producing their own. Self-creativity through resistance, mixing styles, music, and ideologies, which offer aesthetic avenues and thereby greater texture for immersing into and experiencing life becomes the preferred presentational mode.

We have attempted to explain the reasons for the growth and multiplication, through fragmentation, of subcultures as the sites of much future consumption. We identified two key forces in the development and growth of subcultures: The cultural impulse for fragmentation and the change to presentational forms of resistance; two forces that impel each other. We have also identified the means most conducive to helping the trend toward fragmentation and presentation: Music. Consequently, what we find is a continual multiplication of subcultures, as different members of an initial subculture find purpose in presenting a different, even if in nuance, mode of organizing and experiencing life to produce meaningful and substantive moments.

# In Pursuit of Balanced Perspective on Consumer Agency and the Power of the Social: Discourse Theory of Laclau and Mouffé for Consumer Research

Hyun Jeong Min, University of Utah, USA
Debra Scammon, Univesity of Utah, USA

## EXTENDED ABSTRACT

The debate of consumers as agents versus dupes has been widely discussed in the literature of social sciences and consumer research (Arnould 2007; Schor 2007). Consumer images of single minded, status seeking (Veblen 1979) individual or the helpless, manipulated consumers in the Frankfrut School's theorization gave way to a view of "consumers as motivated, discerning, even demanding in their relationship to the producers of cultural texts, products, and advertising" (Schor 2007, 23). However, if zooming out to the more macro level of actions, we can see that the structuring power of the social is still working strong. To accommodate the need to balance between consumer agency and structuring power of the social, we draw on the discourse theory of Laclau and Mouffe.

Laclau and Mouffe's discourse theory sees all reality as discursively constituted and in principle it is legitimate to use discourse analytical tools to analyze all aspects of the world including physical reality such as the body and the material world (Jørgensen and Phillips 2002). Their analysis rejects the distinction between discursive and non-discursive practices. Instead it affirms that every object is constituted as an object of discourse and that any distinction between what are usually called linguistic and behavioral aspects of social practice is an incorrect distinction (Laclau & Mouffe 1985) because the boundary between the linguistic and the non-linguistic in a certain social practice is not clear (Laclau and Mouffe 1987). They propose that discourses fix meanings in certain ways and therefore exclude all other possible meanings through hegemonic closures and that the discursive constructions appear as natural through myths about society and identity. According to Laclau and Mouffe (1985), no discourse is a closed entity but it is constantly being transformed through contact with other discourses. Different discourses, each of which represents particular ways of talking about and understanding the social world, are emerged in a constant struggle with one other to achieve hegemony, fixing the meanings in their own way (Jørgensen and Phillips 2002; Laclau and Mouffe 1985).

Although Laclau and Mouffe are mostly interested in more abstract discourses, the idea that these discourses are created, maintained and changed in diverse everyday practices is implied in their theory (Jorgensen and Philips 2002). Especially their concepts including nodal points, articulation, and the logic of equivalence and difference have potentials to be used effectively in detailed empirical analysis to answer the questions such as how each discourse constitutes knowledge and reality, identities and social relations.

By drawing on the discourse theory of Laclau and Mouffe, consumer researchers can have a means to balance between consumer agency and socio-political forces structuring consumption. In consumer research, the term discourse has been examined in relation to the construction of consumption narratives (Thompson & Haytko 1997; Murray 2002; Kozinets 2008) and mainly focused on the linguistic performances of consumers. By concentrating on consumer narratives, consumer's agency in consumer culture was emphasized while the influence of structural forces was under-investigated. Another problem of looking at discourse in the context of consumer narrative construction is that concrete practices of consumption are missed in the discussion of consumer behaviors. Concrete practices of buying clothes, putting things together to make an ensemble, and accessorizing only exist in the narratives of consumers. Considering that a consumer's narrative is also an act of representation (Hall 1997), consumer researchers need to understand how certain consumption practices and the narratives about them are produced in the socio-political context beyond the relationship of specific consumption behaviors to consumer's life project and life theme.

As another benefit of utilizing discourse analysis consumer researcher can overcome the limitation of thematic analysis. Consumers' narratives have usually been analyzed according to hermeneutic or phenomenological approaches and these approaches are mainly interested in the text-content relationship and therefore overlook the discursive conditions of production, diffusion, and reception of complex discursive configurations (Sitz 2008). However, the hermeneutic circle approaches used for discourse analysis may raise a problem by treating quotes from transcribed interviews as thematic evidence of discourse although the quotes should be analyzed as the evidence of local production of discourse (Cloyes 2007). In fact, Foucault was deeply critical of the conventional notion of the subject as the independent, authentic source of action and meaning. He challenges the privileged position of the subject in relation to meaning. Subjects may produce particular texts, but they are operating within the limits of the discursive formation of a particular period and culture (Hall 1997). Another problem in using thematic analysis for discourse analytic studies arises from the loss of the detail and discursive subtlety of the original (Antaki et al. 2002). Discourse analysis is more concerned with 'parole,' which pertains to the particular acts of utterance, rather than 'langue,' which refers to underlying rule-governed structure of language. Therefore summarizing data into several themes may lose sight of the subtle ways that the 'I' as author construct stories with the character 'I' to produce certain effects, which can be the justification of his or her consumption choice or impression management in the interaction with researchers.

In this vein, discourse theory of Laclau and Mouffe (1985) suggests specific strategies to overcome the drawbacks of using thematic analysis in researching discursive aspects of consumption behaviors. Their work is not strictly methodological texts (Cloyes 2004), the concepts in their theorization provide useful guidelines to study discursive formation in consumer culture.

## REFERENCES

Antaki, Charles, Michael Billig, Derek Edwards, and Jonathan Potter (2002), "Discourse Analysis Means Doing Analysis: A Critique of Six Analytic Shortcomings," in *Discourse Analysis Online*, Vol. 1.

Arnould, Eric J. (2007), "Should Consumer Citizens Escape the Market?," *Annals of the American Academy of Political and Social Science*, 611 (1), 96-111.

Belk, Russell W., John F. Sherry, and Melanie Wallendorf (1988), "A Naturalistic Inquiry into Buyer and Seller Behavior at a Swap Meet," *Journal of Consumer Research*, 14 (4), 449-70.

Bourdieu, P. (1990). *The Logic of Practice*. Cambridge: Polity Press.

Chouliaraki, Lilie and Norman Fairclough (1999), *Discourse in Late Modernity : Rethinking Critical Discourse Analysis*, Edinburgh: Edinburgh University Press.

Cloyes, Kristin G. (2004), "The Politics of Mental Illness in a Prison Control Unit: A Discourse Analysis," Ph.D., University of Washington, Washington.

Crystal, David (1985), *A Dictionary of Linguistics and Phonetics*, Oxford [Oxfordshire] ; London: B. Blackwell in association with A. Deutsch.

Davies, Bronwyn and Rom Harré (1990), "Positioning: The Discursive Production of Selves," *Journal for the Theory of Social Behaviour*, 20 (1), 43-63.

Edgar, Andrew and Peter R. Sedgwick (1999), *Key Concepts in Cultural Theory*, London ; New York: Routledge.

Fairclough, Norman (1992), *Discourse and Social Change*, Cambridge, UK: Polity Press.

Finlayson, Alan. (1999), Chapter 3: Language. In Fidelma. Ashe, Alan. Finlayson, Moya. Lloyd, Ian. MacKenzie, James. Martin, & Shane. O'Neil (Eds.), *Contemporary social and political theory: An introduction*, pp. 47-68. London: Open University Press.

Firat, A. Fuat and Alladi Venkatesh (1995), "Liberatory Postmodernism and the Reenchantment of Consumption," *Journal of Consumer Research*, 22 (3), 239-67.

Foucault, Michel (2000), "The Subject and Power," in *Power: Essential Works of Foucault, 1954-1984, Volume Iii*, ed. James D. Faubion, New York: The New Press.

Gee, James Paul (1999), *An Introduction to Discourse Analysis : Theory and Method*, London ; New York: Routledge.

Hall, Stuart (1997), *Representation : Cultural Representations and Signifying Practices*, London: Sage.

Halliday, M. A. K. (1978), *Language as Social Semiotic : The Social Interpretation of Language and Meaning*, London: E. Arnold.

_____ (1985), *An Introduction to Functional Grammar*, London ; Baltimore, Md., USA: E. Arnold.

Hardin, Pamela K. (2001), "Theory and Language: Locating Agency between Free Will and Discursive Marionettes," *Nursing Inquiry*, 8 (1), 11-18.

Harvey, David (1996), *Justice, Nature and the Geography of Difference*, Cambridge, Mass.: Blackwell Publishers.

Hebdige, Dick (1991), *Subculture : The Meaning of Style*, London ; New York: Routledge.

Holt, Douglas B. and Craig J. Thompson (2004), "Man-of-Action Heroes: The Pursuit of Heroic Masculinity in Everyday Consumption," *Journal of Consumer Research*, 31 (2), 425-40.

Jørgensen, Marianne and Louise Phillips (2002), *Discourse Analysis as Theory and Method*, London; Thousand Oaks, Calif.: SAGE Publications.

Kozinets, Robert V. (2001), "Utopian Enterprise: Articulating the Meanings of Star Trek's Culture of Consumption," *Journal of Consumer Research*, 28 (1), 67-88.

Kress, Guther (2001). From Saussure to critical sociolinguistics: The turn toward a social view of language. In M. Wetherell, S. Taylor & S. J. Yates (Eds.), *Discourse theory and practice: A reader*, pp.29-38. London: Sage.

Laclau, Ernesto (1990), *New Reflections on the Revolution of Our Time / Ernesto Laclau ; [Translated by Jon Barnes]*, London: Verso.

_____ (1996), *Emancipation(S)*, London: Verso.Laclau, Ernesto and Chantal Mouffe (1985), *Hegemony and Socialist Strategy : Towards a Radical Democratic Politics*, London: Verso.

_____ (1987), "Post-Marxism without Apologies," *New Left Review*, 16 (2), 28.

McAlexander, James H., John W. Schouten, and Harold F. Koenig (2002), "Building Brand Community," *Journal of Marketing*, 66 (1), 38-54.

O'Guinn, Thomas (2000), "Touching Greatness: The Central Midwest Barry Manilow Fan Club," in *The Consumer Society Reader*, ed. Juliet Schor and Douglas Holt, New York: The New Press.

Outhwaite, W., & Bottomore, T. (Eds.). (1993). *The Blackwell Dictionary of Twentieth-Century Social Thought*. Oxford, UK: Blackwell.

Schor, Juliet B. (2007), "In Defense of Consumer Critique: Revisiting the Consumption Debates of the Twentieth Century," *Annals of the American Academy of Political and Social Science*, 611, 16-30.

Sherry Jr, John F. (1990), "A Sociocultural Analysis of a Midwestern American Flea Market," *Journal of Consumer Research*, 17 (1), 13-30.

Sitz, Lionel (2008), "Beyond Semiotics and Hermeneutics: Discourse Analysis as a Way to Interpret Consumers' Discourses and Experiences," *Qualitative Market Research: An International Journal*, 11 (2), 15.

Smith, Jennifer L. (2007), "Critical Discourse Analysis for Nursing Research," *Nursing Inquiry*, 14 (1), 60-70.

Thompson, Craig J. and Diana L. Haytko (1997), "Speaking of Fashion: Consumers' Uses of Fashion Discourses and the Appropriation of Countervailing Cultural Meanings," *Journal of Consumer Research*, 24 (1), 15-42.

Thompson, Craig J. and Elizabeth C. Hirschman (1995), "Understanding the Socialized Body: A Poststructuralist Analysis of Consumers' Self-Conceptions, Body Images, and Self-Care Practices," *Journal of Consumer Research*, 22 (2), 139-53.

Torfing, Jacob (1999), *New Theories of Discourse : Laclau, Mouffe, and ¿ *I¿ *Ek*, Oxford, UK ; Malden, Mass.: Blackwell Publishers.

Veblen, Thorstein (1979), *The Theory of the Leisure Class*, New York: Penguin Books.

Wrangel, Claes (2007), "Towards a Modified Discourse Theory Pt. 1: Laclau's "Empty Signifier"," http://thatsnotit.wordpress.com/2007/05/03/towards-a-modified-discourse-theory-pt-1-laclaus-empty-signifier/.

# Forget Negotiation: The Non-Dialectical Model of Identity Project By Extreme Sports Participants

Soonkwan Hong, Michigan Technological University, USA

## EXTENDED ABSTRACT

Consumer culture theory views identity project as a process and a practice through and by which consumers' cultural bricolage of the self is embodied and enacted in negotiation with the hegemonic market influences, such as globalization, brands, and gendered consumption environment (Arnould and Thompson 2005; Askegaard et al. 2005; Epp and Price 2008; Holt 2002; Kates 2002; Kjeldgaard and Askegaard 2006; Oswald 1999; Üstüner and Holt 2010). Accordingly, negotiation, compromise, reconcilement, cooperation, and rapprochement have thus far been the preferred (in fact, almost required) methods to present idiosyncratic identities (Giesler 2008; Holt 2002; Kozinets et al 2004; Thompson and Coskuner-Balli 2007; Thompson and Tian 2008).

The received view of identity negotiation, however, has overlooked other possibilities (forms) of consumer-market power relations (see Foucault 1980 for power relation) that are palpable and facilitate non-negotiated and thus dialectic-absent identity projects. Hence, this study first seeks to illuminate a context wherein consumers perform purely self-fulfilling identity projects with less concern about social consequences of such existential endeavor (cf., Marino 2004). Second, it is of importance to re-examine the current view of authentic self-identity *vis-a-vis* the continuously inculcated notion of fragmentation of self (cf. Ahuvia 2005), as identity negotiation becomes less germane to a certain context.

The annual X Games event is selected as the research context. The counter-mainstream ethos of extreme sports represents the sub-cultural or countercultural values that underpin the events (Quester, Beverland, and Farrelly 2006). The deliberate "distancing" from mainstream culture, establishment, social structure, and hegemonic brands brings much attention and value to the extreme sports event, as a culturally and theoretically rich context for this study of non-negotiated identity project. The event is still a carnivalesque-like paradoxical consumption festival through which authenticity becomes commercialized; resistance to the market is intermingled with or even acclimatized to the profit-driven practices; and consumers act multiple roles as they face subcultures/mainstream cultures, conformists/rebels, and co-optation/countervailing forces.

Thirty phenomenological interviews, as the primary data source, were conducted (Thompson 1990). Observations were recorded using fieldnotes, videotapes, and photographs in order to easily utilize them for the following analyses and interpretations. Overall, 581 photographs were taken, and approximately 172 minutes of video recording was conducted. Following Thompson (1997), a creative, playful, subjective, and yet substantially translative hermeneutics is expected to yield meaningfully interpreted and theoretically contributing themes of non-negotiated identity project, based on consumers' transformative ideologies and performances.

Consumers' signification process for non-negotiated identity is represented mostly by creativity, reminiscence (memory or nostalgia), personalization, unusual experience, relationship-orientation, experimentation, and, especially, being outdoors as the first priority for extreme sports participants. It is an observation that "being outdoors" is not only the inception, but also the quintessence of the signification process.

There were six convergent themes identified from the semiotic clustering. Each of the themes represents a distinct (non-negotiated) way in which consumers engage in the sense-making of their lives in relation to (at times in opposition to) social norms, enticing marketing influence, pseudo-authentic cultural materials, and conformity-ridden socio-cultural environment.

It is noteworthy that a new context can promote a theoretical divergence. In contrast to the Burning Man project that only guarantees temporary and geographically-bounded sanctions to such an anti-market endeavor, X Games unleash the consumers from cultural and normative dogma, which have constrained consumers to discontinue pursuing non-negotiated identities in other spaces (i.e., home and work) after the duration of such events. Evidently, some extreme sports participants continuously work on their authentic non-negotiated identity. Thus, research that specifically discusses some contexts in which consumers opt to be a true agent with no or little concern about inter-agential conflict will move the current theoretical outlook of consumer agency forward. Moreover, when more of such contexts are found to exist and become more common than before, the boundary conditions should be identified. In other words, it is of importance to study when the supposedly incessant pursuit of non-negotiated identity fostered in the context is ceased.

The "dialectical model of branding" (Holt 2002) can be revisited as well. When consumers practice non-negotiated identity project, the dialectics in the domain of branding become less explanatory. That is, consumers do not necessarily need to symbolically rely on or respond to the brands they constantly face in the market. Authenticity of the brands does not concern them as they can totally "dis-necessitate" brands for their identity narratives, which may be more coherent without any brand. There are some exemplary grassroots brands widespread in snowboards and outdoor equipment industry. A group of handful individual fanatics and supporters of snowboarding have launched their own brand in order not to negotiate with the brands identities and personalities developed by marketers and other consumers. Research should address this type of "no logo" praxes that are not as direct or perceptible as boycott, anti-consumption, consumer terrorism or "culture-jamming" (Lasn 2000) but still transforming the current consumer culture.

Perhaps all the simulations and emulations in the identity narratives by signifying consumers are not to contest or escape the market system but to revitalize the inertia in the market. The context of X Games and the participants appear to propose a new way to enjoy symbiosis between consumers and the market as the context promotes "hyper-authenticity" and individuals take advantage of it to survive, as contemporary consumers, without dialectics. It will be, however, of more interest to observe and theorize how marketers respond to the extreme presentations of self-identity without any trace of negotiation. Can (will) they still co-opt them?

## REFERENCEs

Ahuvia, Aaron C. (2005), "Beyond the Extended Self: Loved Objects and Consumers' Identity Narratives," *Journal of Consumer Research*, 32 (June), 171-184.

Arnould, Eric J. and Linda L. Price (1993), "River Magic: Extraordinary Experience and the Extended Service Encounter," *Journal of Consumer Research*, 20 (June), 24-45.

Arnould, Eric J. and Craig J. Thompson (2005), "Consumer Culture Theory (CCT): Twenty Years of Research," *Journal of Consumer Research*, 31 (March), 868-882.

Arnould, Eric J. and Melanie Wallendorf (1994), "Market-Oriented Ethnography: Interpretatioin Building and Marketing Strategy Formulation," *Journal of Marketing Research*, 31 (November), 484-504.

Askegaard, Søren, Eric J. Arnould, and Dannie Kjeldgaard (2005), "Postassimilationist Ethnic Consumer Research: Qualifications and Extensions," *Journal of Consumer Research*, 32 (June), 160-170.

Barthes, Roland (1972), *Mythologies*, trans. Annette Lavers, London: Cape.

Baudrillard, Jean (1975), *The Mirror of Production*, St. Louis, MI: Telos Press.

_____ (1981), *For a Critique of the Political Economy of the Sign*, St. Louis: Telos.

_____ (1983), *Simulations*, New York: Semiotexte.

Belk, Russell W. (1988), "Possessions and the Extended Self," *Journal of Consumer Research*, 15 (September), 139-68.

Belk, Russell W. and Janeen Arnold Costa (1998), "The Mountain Myth: A Contemporary Consuming Fantasy," *Journal of Consumer Research*, 25 (December), 218-40.

Bonsu, Samuel K. and Russell W. Belk (2003), "Do Not Go Cheaply into That Good Night: Death Ritual Consumption in Asante Ghana," *Journal of Consumer Research*, 30 (June), 41-55.

Bouchet, Dominique (1995), "Marketing and the Redefinition of Ethnicity," in *Marketing in a Multicultural World*, ed. Janeen Costa and Gary Bamossy, Thousand Oaks, CA: Sage, 68-104.

Caillois, Roger (1961), *Man, Play, and Games*, New York: Free Press.

Celsi, Richard, Randall Rose, and Thomas Leigh (1993), "An Exploration of High-Risk Leisure Consumption through Skydiving," *Journal of Consumer Research*, 20 (June), 1–21.

Cherrier, Hélène and Jeff B. Murray (2007), "Reflexive Dispossession and the Self:

Constructing a Processual Theory of Identity," *Consumption, Markets and Culture*, 10 (March), 1-29.

Emerson, Robert M., Rachel I. Fretz, and Linda L. Shaw (1995), *Writing Ethnographic Fieldnotes*, London, UK: University of Chicago Press.

Epp, Amber M. and Linda L. Price (2008), "Family Identity: A Framework of Identity Interplay in Consumption Practices," *Journal of Consumer Research*, 50-70.

Feldman, Martha S. (1995), *Strategies for Interpreting Qualitative Data*, Thousand Oaks, California, Sage Publications.

Foucault, Michel (1980), *Power/Knowledge: Selected Interviews and Other Writings 1972-77*, ed. Colin Gordon, New York: Pantheon.

Gergen, Kenneth J. (1991), *The Saturated Self*, New York, NY: Basic Books.

Giddens, Anthony (1991), *Modernity and Self-Identity*, Stanford, CA: Stanford University Press.

Giesler, Markus (2008), "Conflict and Compromise: Drama in Marketplace Evolution," *Journal of Consumer Research*, 34 (April), 739-753.

Glaser, Barney G. and Anselm L. Strauss (1967), *The Discovery of Grounded Theory: Strategies for Qualitative Research*, Hawthorne, NY: Aldine Transaction.

Grayson, Kent and Radan Martinec (2004), "Consumer Perceptions of Iconicity and Indexicality and Their Influence on Assessments of Authentic Market Offerings," *Journal of Consumer Research*, 31 (September), 296-312.

Holt, Douglas B. (1995), "How Consumers Consume: A Typology of Consumption Practices," *Journal of Consumer Research*, 22 (June), 1-16.

_____ (1997), "Poststructuralist Lifestyle Analysis: Conceptualizing the Social Patterning of Consumption," *Journal of Consumer Research*, 23 (March), 326-50.

_____ (1998), "Does Cultural Capital Structure American Consumption?" *Journal of Consumer Research*, 25 (June), 1-26.

_____ (2002), "Why Do Brands Cause Trouble? A Dialectical Theory of Consumer Culture and Branding," *Journal of ConsumerResearch*, 29 (June), 70-90.

Horkheimer, Max. and Adorno, Theodor W (1976), *The Culture Industry: Enlightenment as Mass Deception*, New York, NY: Continuum International Publishing Group.

Hughes, Glyn (2004), *SportCo: Branding, Management Culture, and Subjectivity in U.S. Sports Media*, Doctoral Disseration, University of California, Santa Babara.

Kates, Steven M. (2002), "The Protean Quality of Subcultural Consumption: An Ethnographic Account of Gay Consumers," *Journal of Consumer Research*, 29 (December), 383-99.

Kjeldgaard, Dannie and Søren Askegaard (2006), "The Glocalization of Youth Culture: The Global Youth Segment as Structures of Common Difference," *Journal of Consumer Research*, 33 (September), 231-247.

Kozinets, Robert V (2001), "Utopian Enterprise: Articulating the Meaning of *Star Trek*'s Culture of Consumption," *Journal of Consumer Research*, 28 (June), 67-89.

_____ (2002) "Can Consumers Escape the Market? Emancipatory Illuminations from Burning Man" *Journal of Consumer Research*, 29 (June), 20-38.

Kozinets, Robert V., John Sherry Jr., Diana Storm, Adam Duhachek, Krittinee Nuttavuthist, and Benet DeBerry-Spence (2004), "Ludic Agency and Retail Spectacle," *Journal of Consumer Research*, 31 (December), 658-72.

Lasn, Kalle (1999), *Culture Jam: How to Reverse America's Suicidal Consumer Binge-And Why We Must*, New York: HarperCollins.

Leach, Edmund (1976), *Culture and Communication*, Cambridge: Cambridge University Press.

Levy, Sidney J. (1959), "Symbols for Sale," *Harvard Business Review*, 37(July-August), 117-124.

_____ (1981), "Interpreting Consumer Mythology: A Structural Approach to Consumer Behavior," *Journal of Marketing*, 45 (Summer), 49-61.

Lury, Celia (2001), *Consumer Culture*, Cambridge: Polity Press.

Mannings, Peter. K (1987), *Semiotics and Fieldwork*, Newbury, CA: Sage.

Marino, Gordon (2004), *Basic Writings of Existentialism*, New York: Modern Library.

Maclaran, Pauline and Stephen Brown (2005), "The Center Cannon Hold: Consuming the Utopian Marketplace," *Journal of Consumer Research*, 32 (September), 311-323.

McCracken, Grant (1988), *The Long Interview*, Newbury Park, CA: Sage.

Mick, David Glen (1986), "Consumer Research and Semiotics: Exploring the Morphology of Signs, Symbols, and Significance," *Journal of Consumer Research*, 13 (September), 196-213.

Mick, David Glen, James E. Burroughs, Patrick Hetzel, and Mary Yoko Brannen (2004), "Pursuing the Meaning of Meaning in the CommercialWorld: An International Review of Marketing and Consumer Research Founded on Semiotics," *Semiotica*, 152 (1-4), 1-74.

Murray, Jeff B. (2002), "The Politics of Consumption: A Re-Inquiry on Thompson and Hayko's (1997) "Speaking of Fashion"," *Journal of Consumer Research*, 29 (December), 427-440.

Oswald, Laura R. (1999), "Culture Swapping: Consumption and the Ethnogenesis of Middle-Class Haitian Immigrants," *Journal of Consumer Research*, 25 (March), 303-18.

Peirce, Charles Sanders (1998), *Collected Papers of Charles Sanders Peirce*, ed. Charles Hartshorne, Paul Weiss, and Arthur Blank, 8 vols., Bristol: Thoemmes.

Pine, Joseph II and James H. Gilmore (1999), *The Experience Economy*, Boston: Harvard Business School Press.

Quester, Pascale, Michael Beverland, and Francis Farrelly (2006), "Brand-Personal Values Fit and Brand Meanings: Exploring the Role Individual Values Play
in Ongoing Brand Loyalty in Extreme Sports Subcultures," *Advances in Consumer Research*, 33, 21-27.

Rinehart, Robert E. (2008), "Exploiting a New Generation: Corporate Branding and the Co-optation of Action Sport," in *Youth Culture and Sport: Identity, Power, and Politics*, ed. Michael D. Giardina and Michele K. Donnely, New York: Routledge, 71-90.

Saussure, Ferdinand de (2000), *Course in General Linguistics*, trans. Roy Harris, Peru, IL: Open Court.

Schau, Hope Jensen, Mary C. Gilly, and Mary Wolfinbarger (2009), "Consumer Identity Renaissance: The Resurgence of Identity-Inspired Consumption in Retirement," *Journal of Consumer Research*, 36 (August), 255-276.

Schouten, John W. (1991), "Selves in Transition: Symbolic Consumption in Personal Rites of Passage and Identity Reconstruction," *Journal of Consumer Research*, 17 (March), 412-425.

Sherry, John F. (2000), "Place, Technology, and Representation," *Journal of Consumer Research*, 27 (September), 273-278.

Thompson, Craig J. (1990), "The Lived Meaning of Free Choice: An Existential-Phenomenological Description of Everyday Consumer Experiences of Contemporary Married Women," *Journal of Consumer Research*, 17 (December), 346-61.

_____ (1997), "Interpreting Consumers: A Hermeneutical Framework for Deriving Marketing Insights from the Texts of Consumers' Consumption Stories,"
*Journal of Marketing Research*, 34 (4), 438-56.

Thompson, Craig J. and Diana L. Haytko (1997), "Speaking of Fashion: Consumers' Uses of Fashion Discourses and the Appropriation of Countervailing Cultural Meanings," *Journal of Consumer Research*, 24 (June), 15-42.

Thompson, Craig J. and Maura Troester (2002), "Consumer Value Systems in the Age of Postmodern Fragmentation: The Case of the Natural Health Microculture," *Journal of Consumer Research*, 28 (March), 550-71.

Thompson, Craig J. and Gokcen Coskuner-Balli (2007), "Countervailing Market Responses to Corporate Co-optation and the Ideological Recruitment of Consumption Communities," *Journal of Consumer Research*, 34 (August), 135-152.

Thompson, Craig J. and Kelly Tian (2008), "Reconstructing the South: How Commercial Myths Compete for Identity Value through the Ideological Shaping of Popular Memories and Coutermemories," *Journal of Consumer Research*, 34 (February), 595-613.

Thornton, Sarah (1995), *Club Cultures: Music, Media and Subcultural Capital*, Cambridge, Polity Press.

Tian, Kelly and Russell W. Belk (2005), "Extended Self and Possessions in the Workplace," *Journal of Consumer Research*, 32 (September), 297-310.

Turner, Victor (1974), "Liminal to Liminoid in Play, Flow and Ritual: An Essay in Comparative Symbology," *Rice University Studies*, 60 (3), 53-92.

Üstüner, Tuba and Douglas B. Holt (2010), "Toward a Theory of Status Consumption in Less Industrialized Countries," *Journal of Consumer Research*, 37 (June), Forthcoming.

Zolfagharian, Mohammad Ali.and Jordan, Ann.T. (2007), "Multiracial identity and art consumption", in Belk, R.W. and Sherry, J.F. (Eds), *Consumer Culture Theory*, Elsevier, Oxford, pp. 343-67.

# Construal and Categorization: Impacts of Psychological Distance on Brand Extensions

Fang-Chi Lu, University of Iowa, USA
Dhananjay Nayakankuppam, University of Iowa, USA

## EXTENDED ABSTRACT

The topic of brand extension has been pervasively studied in the fields of marketing and consumer psychology. Previous research suggested that brands and their affiliated products are represented in memory as different categorical representations, and consumers use those mental representations to assign a new product or service to a certain category, and draw inferences about it (Loken et al., 2002). Categorical representations are flexible and malleable, and the likelihood of category inferences depends on the similarity or match between the representation of the existing brand category and the representation of a new category member (i.e. Meyvis & Janiszewski, 2004; Cowley & Mitchell, 2003). The higher the match between the extension product and its parent brand category, the more likely beliefs and attitudes typical to the parent brand will be ascribed to the extension.

Recently, Ahluwalia's research (2008) showed a consumer's self-construal influences the perceived fit of an extension and thus, a brand's stretchability. Interdependent self-construal leads to a superior ability to uncover relationships between an extension and its parent brand, and thus is likely to enhance the perceived fit and acceptance of an extension.

The construal level theory (CLT) proposed by Liberman and Trope (1998) suggested that the chronically-built association between psychological distance and abstraction in cognition results in the tendency to construe objects/events with more high (low)-level, abstract (concrete) features when they are psychologically distant (near). Categorization itself is hieratical and with different levels of abstractness; one could construe less or more inclusive categories of objects, depending on the level of construal being used to represent the objects. Greater psychological distance leads to a more inclusive categorization (Liberman et al., 2002).

On the basis of this literature, we propose that psychological distance also enhance the stretchability of a brand extension. Psychological distance will influence the levels of construal people use to represent an extension, its categorization, and the likelihood of category inferences from existing brand category to the extension. Specifically, when a brand extension is represented at a higher, more abstract, and superordinate construal level, it is more likely to be included in the existing brand category, leading to greater category inferences. We report the results of four experiments that examined our propositions.

In Study 1, construal level was manipulated by temporal distance of brand extensions. Participants were presented with a series of brand extensions (four brands and each had eight proposed extensions) which were suggested to be introduced in either near or distant future, and then reported their attitude toward the extensions. A control group was asked to evaluate the consistency of those extensions to their affiliated parent brands. A median-split was performed on these consistency measures to categorize the extension into low and high consistency group. Fifty-eight undergraduate students participated in this study. Results showed extensions represented in distant future were evaluated more favorably than the ones in the near future. Furthermore, the interaction between temporal distance and consistency suggested that the psychological distance effect was greater for low consistency extensions than high consistency ones.

To increase generalizability, different brand extensions were used in Study 2. Furthermore, another psychological distance dimension was included to manipulate construal level. Study 2 is a 2(psychological distance: near vs. far) X 2 (distance type: temporal vs. spatial) mixed design with construal level as between-subjects factor and distance type as within-subjects factor. Forty-seven undergraduate students participated in this study. They were presented with eighteen hypothetical extensions (three brands, each with six extensions), suggested to be introduced either in the near (distant) future or in the US (a foreign country). For each brand, half of the extensions were manipulated by temporal distance and the other half was by spatial distance. Participants then reported their attitude toward each extension. Results of study 2 again supported our hypothesis. When extensions were introduced in either distant future or spatially distant, participants evaluated the brand extensions more favorably. And the effect of psychological distance remained regardless of brands, extensions, and distance type.

Study 3 is to examine the mediation effect of perceived similarity (fit). The design of study 3 is similar to study 2, except that one more brand and six more extensions were included, and measures of brand attitude as well as perceived similarity (fit) were included because previous research suggested that brand attitude effect on brand extension evaluation is also mediated by fit. One hundred undergraduate students participated. Results replicated the findings of study 1 and 2, and extended previous studies by demonstrating that the influence of psychological distance on brand extension evaluation was mediated by the perceived similarity (fit) (Sobel's test: $p_{1\text{-}tailed}$=0.01).

Study 4 adopted a 2 (temporal distance: far vs. near) x 2 (social distance: far vs. near) between-subject design to examine the potential interplay between different dimensions of psychological distance. Participants were presented with ten domestic (US-based) vs. foreign (foreign country of origin) brand extensions to be introduced in temporally near vs. distant future. We matched the brands in terms of their product class and brand strength. It's assumed that although all the brands are available in the US markets, foreign brands should be perceived more socially distant than domestic brands. Results showed a significant social distance main effect on liking and purchase intention toward brand extension, and a marginal significant two-way interaction effect on purchase intention.

Taken together, the findings across four studies shed light on the linkage between construal level theory and categorization theory, and their application on brand extension. The categorization and evaluation of a new product extension is influenced by its psychological distance, especially when the extensions are inconsistent with the parent brands. The present study contributes to the brand extension literature by providing construal level as another route to understand the potential of brand stretchability, and how a brand extension is perceived, and its likelihood of acceptance by consumers. This study also extends previous research by examining the effect of other psychological distance dimensions (spatial and social) and their interplay on brand extension evaluation.

## REFERENCES

Aaker, D. and Keller, K. L. (1990). Consumer evaluations of brand extensions. *Journal of Marketing*, 54, 27-41.

Ahluwalia, R. (2008). How far can a brand stretch? Understanding the role of self-construal, *Journal of Marketing Research, 45*, 337-350.

Barone, M. J. and Miniard, P. W. (2002). Mood and brand extension judgments: asymmetric effects for desirable versus undesirable brands. *Journal of Consumer Psychology*, 12(4), 283-291.

Barone, M. J., Miniard, P. W., and Romeo, J. B. (2000). The influence of positive mood on brand extension evaluations. *Journal of Consumer Research*, 26, 386-400.

Bless, H. and Schwarz, N. (1999). Context effects in political judgement: assimilation and contrast as a function of categorization processes. *European Journal of Social Psychology*, 28(2), 159-172.

Bottomley, P. A. and Holden, S. J. S. (2001). Do we really know how consumers evaluate brand extensions? Empirical generalizations Based on secondary analysis of eight studies. *Journal of Marketing Research*, 38(4), 494-500.

Boush, D. M. and Loken, B. (1991). A process-tracing study of brand extension evaluation. *Journal of Marketing Research*, 18, 16-28.

Cowley, E. and Mitchell, A. A. (2003). The moderating effect of product knowledge on the learning and organization of product information. *Journal Consumer Research*, 30, 443-454.

Dhar, R. and Kim, E. Y. (2007). Seeing the forest or the trees: implications of construal level theory for consumer choice. *Journal of Consumer Psychology*, 17, 96-100.

Eyal, T., Liberman, N., Trope, Y., and Walther, E. (2004). The pros and cons of temporally near and distant action. *Journal of Personality and Social Psychology*, 86, 781-795.

Farquhar, P. H., Han, J. Y., Herr, P. M., and Ijiri, Y. (1992). Strategies for leveraging master brands. *Marketing Research*, 4, 32-43.

Fujita, K., Eyal, T., Chaiken, S., Trope, Y., and Liberman, N. (2008). Influencing attitudes toward near and distant objects. *Journal of Experimental Social Psychology*, 44, 562-572.

Henderson, M. D., Fujita, K. F., Trope, Y., and Liberman, N. (2006). The effect of spatial distance on social judgment. *Journal of Personality and Social Psychology*, 91, 845-856.

Herr, P. (1989). Priming price: prior knowledge and context effects. *Journal of Consumer Research*, 16, 67-75.

Herr, P., Farquhar, and Fazio, R. (1996). Impact of dominance and relatedness on brand extensions. *Journal of Consumer Psychology*, 5(2), 135-159.

Higgins, E. T. (1996). Knowledge activation: accessibility, applicability, and salience. In E. T. Higgins & A. Kruglanski (Eds.), *Social Psychology: Handbook of basic principles* (pp. 133-168) .New York: Guilford.

Higgins, E. T., Bargh, J. A., and Lombardi, W. (1985). Nature of priming effects on categorization. *Journal of Experimental Psychology: Learning, Memory, and cognition*, 11, 59-69.

Jones, C. R. M., and Fazio, R. H. (2008). Associative strength and consumer choice behavior. In Haugtvedt, C. P., Herr, P. M., & Kardes, F. R. (Ed.), *Handbook of Consumer Psychology* (pp.437-459). New York: Psychology Press.

Kardes, F. R., Posavax, S. S., Cronley, L. C., and Herr, P. M. (2008). Consumer inference. In Haugtvedt, C. P., Herr, P. M., & Kardes, F. R. (Ed.), Handbook of Consumer Psychology (pp.165-191). New York: Psychology Press.

Kim, J. and Wilemon, D. (2002). Sources and assessment of complexity in NPD projects. *R&D Management*, 33 (1), 16-30.

Lee, A. Y. and Sternthal, B. (1999). The effects of positive mood on memory. *Journal of Consumer Research*, 26, 115-128.

Loken, B., Barsalou, L. W., and Joiner, C. (2008). Categorization theory and research in consumer psychology. In Haugtvedt, C. P., Herr, P. M., & Kardes, F. R. (Ed.), *Handbook of Consumer Psychology* (pp.133-163). New York: Psychology Press.

Loken, B., Joiner, C., and Peck, J. (2002). Category attitude measures: exemplar as inputs. *Journal of Consumer Psychology*, 12 (2), 149-161.

Liberman, N., Sagristano, M. D., and Trope, Y. (2002). The effect of temporal distance on level of mental construal. *Journal of Experimental Social Psychology*, 38, 523-534.

Liberman, N. and Trope, Y. (1998). The role of feasibility and desirability considerations in near and distant future decisions: a test of temporal construal theory, *Journal of Personality and Social Psychology*, 75(1), 5-18.

Liberman, N., Trope, Y., and Stephan, E. (2007). Psychological distance. In A. W. Kruglanski & E. T. Higgins (Eds.) *Social Psychology: Handbook of Basic Principles*. New York: Guilford Press.

Liberman, N., Trope, Y., and Wakslak, C. (2007). Construal level theory and consumer behavior. *Journal of Consumer Psychology*, 17(2), 113-117.

Liviatan, I., Trope, Y., and Liberman, N. (2008). Interpersonal similarity as a social distance dimension: implications for perception of others' actions. *Journal of Experimental Social Psychology*, 44 ,1256-1269 .

Meyers-Levy, J. and Tybout, A. M. (1989). Schema congruity as a basis for product evaluation. *Journal of Consumer Research*, 16, 39-54.

Meyvis, T. and Janiszewski, C. (2004). When are broader brands stronger brands? An accessibility perspective on the success of brand extensions. *Journal of Consumer research*, 31(2), 346-357.

Monga, A. B., and John, D. R. (2007). Cultural differences in brand extension evaluation: the influence of analytic versus holistic thinking, *Journal of Consumer Research, 33*, 529-536.

Murphy, G. L., and Medin, D. L. (1985). The role of theories in conceptual coherence. *Psychological Review*, 92, 289-316.

Park, C. W., Milberg, S., and Lawson, R. (1991). Evaluation of brand extensions: the role of product feature similarity and brand concept consistency. *Journal of Consumer Research*, 18, 185-193.

Ratneshwar, S., Barsalou, L. W., Pechmann, C., and Moore, M. (2001). Goal-derived categories: the role of personal and situational goals in category representations. *Journal of Consumer Psychology*, 10(3), 147-158.

Rosch, E. (1975). Cognitive representation of semantic categories. *Journal of Experimental Psychology*, 104(3), 192-233.

Singer, J. D. (1998). Using SAS PROC MIXED to fit multilevel models, hierarchical models, and individual growth models. *Journal of Educational and Behavioral Statistics*, 24(4), 323-355.

Smith, P. K., and Trope, Y. (2006). You focus on the forest when you're in charge of the tree: power priming and abstract information processing. *Journal of Personality and Social Psychology*, 90(4), 578-596.

Taylor, S. E. (1981). The interface of cognitive and social psychology. In J. H. Harvey (Ed.), *Cognition, social behavior, and the environment*. Hillsdale, NJ: Lawrence Erlbaum Associates.

Thomas, M., Chandran, S., and Trope, Y. (2006). The effects of temporal distance on purchase construal. Unpublished manuscript, Cornell University.

Trope, Y. and Liberman, N. (2000). Temporal construal and time-dependent changes in preference. *Journal of Personality and Social Psychology*, 79(6), 876-889.

Trope, Y., Liberamn, N., and Wakslak, C. (2007). Construal levels and psychological distance: effects on representation, prediction, evaluation, and behavior. *Journal of Consumer Psychology*, 17, 83-95.

Wakslak, C. J., Trope, Y., Liberman, N., and Alony, R. (2006). Seeing the forest when entry is unlikely: probability and the mental representation of events. *Journal of Experimental Psychology: General*, 135, 641-653.

Waldman, M. R., Holyoak, K. J., and Fratianne, A. (1995). Causal models and the acquisition of category structure. *Journal of Experimental Psychology: General*, 124(2), 181-206.

Wank, M., Bless, H., and Schwarz, N. (1998). Context effects in product line extensions: context is not destiny. *Journal of Consumer Psychology*, 7 (4), 299-322.

# Top 10 or #10?: How Positional Inferences Influence the Effectiveness of Category Membership Claims

Mathew S. Isaac, Northwestern University, USA
Kent Grayson, Northwestern University, USA

## EXTENDED ABSTRACT

When making advertising claims, marketers routinely highlight their product's membership in a ranked list (e.g., a top 10 list) in an attempt to enhance perceptions of the product. The present research shows that touting a product's membership in an elite list can sometimes backfire on marketers and lead to *less* favorable consumer evaluations of their product. Specifically, I claim that when consumers make positional inferences by attempting to estimate a product's specific rank in a list, product evaluations will be negatively affected. In this research, I explain when positional inferences occur and why they adversely influence evaluations of a target.

My research focuses on lists in which all members are arranged ordinally, such that each member has a specific rank or position in the set. Marketers often highlight their product's inclusion in such lists at the broad category level (e.g., "top 10," "25 best") without disclosing their product's exact rank. As a result, consumers may often be aware of a product's presence in a ranked list without knowing its *specific* position in the list. If consumers receive category membership information about a target, they often integrate this new information into their evaluation of the target at the category level. For example, learning that a specific item has been ranked among the top 10 products of its type is likely to bolster evaluations of the item since its inclusion in an elite set presumably carries positive associations. Rather than relying solely on broad category-level information to inform their evaluations, consumers may also attempt to *infer* a target's precise position within the list. In the above example, learning that a product has been ranked in the top 10 may motivate some consumers to make a positional inference regarding the exact rank of the product within the set.

When consumers estimate a target's rank based on category membership information, I propose that they tend to infer a rank relatively close to the lower bound (i.e., the least desirable value) of the category. This phenomenon, which I label the Category Floor Tendency (CFT), can be explained by consumer reliance on communication norms. As a result of the CFT, I predict that evaluations of a target will generally be *less* favorable when consumers estimate the target's specific rank within the category rather than relying on category-level information. Across three experiments, I provide evidence of a systematic CFT and show how this particular positional inference diminishes evaluations of a target. I also demonstrate two ways in which cognitive elaboration influences whether consumers make positional inferences altogether.

Participants in experiment 1 learned that a target product had been included in an elite numerically bounded category (e.g., a top 10 list). I then manipulated the presence or absence of positional inferences by explicitly instructing (or not instructing) participants to consider the specific rank of the target prior to making their evaluation. Consistent with my predictions, I found that reflecting on a target's specific position within a ranked list has an adverse effect on subsequent evaluations. I also produced direct evidence that the CFT is responsible for the negative impact of positional inferences on target evaluations. Participants who estimated a rank closer to the category floor evaluated the target less favorably than those who estimated a rank that is farther from the floor (i.e., more favorable).

In experiment 2, I showed that increasing the likelihood of elaboration by using unconventional category floors (e.g., top 19, 21) fosters positional inference-making. Consumers who were explic-

itly prompted (versus who were not prompted) to make positional inferences evaluated a target *less* favorably when they encountered conventional category claims (top 20). However, unprompted and prompted evaluations of a target did not differ if the target was a member of an unconventional category (top 19, 21). This difference suggests that consumers are more likely to make unprompted positional inferences when they encounter unconventional category claims than when they encounter conventional category claims.

In experiment 3, I demonstrated that engaging in qualitatively different forms of elaboration also impacts whether positional inference-making occurs. Specifically, level of construal (i.e., how abstractly or concretely stimuli in the environment are represented) determined whether a consumer processed a category membership claim at the broad category level or embarked on a search for ordinality. I found that consumers who had been explicitly prompted (versus who had not been prompted) to make positional inferences evaluated a target *less* favorably if they were at high levels of construal. However, unprompted and prompted evaluations of a target did not differ if consumers were at low levels of construal. This difference suggests that consumers are more likely to make unprompted positional inferences at low levels of construal than at high levels of construal.

This research broadens our understanding of numerical cognition, which has examined the information processing of numerical values but has largely ignored numerically bounded categories. I contribute to this literature by showing how consumers evaluate products that are defined by their membership in a numerically bounded category. In addition to documenting a systematic positional inference that consumers make (i.e., the CFT) when encountering a claim of membership within a ranked list, I identify two moderators of this effect. I demonstrate that quantitative and qualitative dimensions of cognitive elaboration determine if consumers engage in unprompted positional inference-making altogether. As another contribution to the numerical cognition literature, I provide evidence that the numerical conventionality of category floors determines whether positional inference-making occurs. Additionally, this research also enriches our understanding of categorization by exploring a structurally distinct type of category (i.e., a ranked list) that has been understudied. Despite the ubiquity of ranked lists, very little academic research has previously explored how consumers process information about categories in which members are organized ordinally.

Although I have focused exclusively on ranked lists in this paper, the applications of my research are considerably broader. When evaluating a target, consumers may base their evaluation of the target on category-level information or they may attempt to seek out individuating information about the target. Using ranked lists, my research seeks to understand when consumers seek out individuating information rather than relying more generally on category-level information. This objective is shared by researchers studying impression formation, person perception, and stereotyping, who are all interested in the antecedents of categorical thinking (and the stereotypical judgments which follow). Given our common objective, my findings may be highly relevant to these other domains. For example, based on the results of my third experiment, one could extrapolate that high levels of construal result in greater reliance on stereotypes. Future research might investigate whether the insights derived from numerically bounded categories transfer to social judgments, which may be somewhat more motivational and less cognitive in nature.

## REFERENCES

Agrawal, Nidhi and Echo Wen Wan (2009), "Regulating Risk or Risking Regulation? Construal Levels and Depletion Effects in the Processing of Health Messages," *Journal of Consumer Research*, 36 (3), 448-62.

Bergreen, Laurence (1994), *Capone: The Man and the Era*, New York: Simon and Schuster.

Dehaene, Stanislas and Jacques Mehler (1992), "Cross-linguistic Regularities in the Frequency of Number Words," *Cognition*, 43 (1), 1-29.

Dijkstra, Majorie, Heidi E. J. J. M. Buijtels, and W. Fred van Raaij (2005), "Separate and joint effects of medium type on consumer responses: a comparison of television, print, and the Internet," *Journal of Business Research*, 58 (3), 377-86.

Fazio, Russell H. (1995), "Attitudes as Object-Evaluation Associations: Determinants, Consequences, and Correlates of Attitude Accessibility," in *Attitude Strength: Antecedents and Consequences*, ed. Richard E. Petty and Jon A. Krosnick, Mahwah, NJ: Erlbaum, 247-82.

Fazio, Russell H., Martha C. Powell, and Paul M. Herr (1983), "Toward a Process Model of the Attitude-Behavior Relation: Accessing One's Attitude upon Mere Observation of the Attitude Object," *Journal of Personality and Social Psychology*, 44 (4), 723-35.

Fishbein, Martin and Icek Ajzen (1975), *Belief, Attitude, Intention, and Behavior: An Introduction to Theory and Research*, Reading, MA: Addison-Wesley.

Fiske, Susan T. and Mark A. Pavelchak (1986), "Category-Based versus Piecemeal-Based Affective Responses: Developments in Schema-Triggered Affect," in *Handbook of Motivation and Cognition: Foundations of Social Behavior*, Vol. 1, ed. Richard M. Sorrentino and E. Tory Higgins, New York: Guilford Press, 167-203.

Freitas, Antonio L., Peter Gollwitzer, and Yaacov Trope (2004), "The Influence of Abstract and Concrete Mindsets on Anticipating and Guiding Others' Self-Regulatory Efforts," *Journal of Experimental Social Psychology*, 40 (6), 739-52.

Freitas, Antonio L., Peter Salovey, and Nira Liberman (2001), "Abstract and Concrete Self-Evaluative Goals," *Journal of Personality and Social Psychology*, 80 (3), 410-24.

Fujita, Kentaro, Yaacov Trope, Nira Liberman, and Maya Levin-Sagi (2006), "Construal Levels and Self-Control," *Journal of Personality and Social Psychology*, 90 (3), 351-67.

Gioia, Dennis A. and Kevin G. Corley (2002), "Being Good Versus Looking Good: Business School Rankings and the Circean Transformation From Substance to Image," *Academy of Management Learning and Education*, 1 (1), 107-20.

Grice, H. Paul (1975), "Logic and Conversation," in *Syntax and Semantics 3: Speech Acts*, ed. Peter Cole and Jerry L. Morgan, New York: Academic Press.

Hatschek, Keith (2002), *How to Get a Job in the Music Industry*, Vol. 2, Boston, MA: Berklee Press.

Kahneman, Daniel and Dale T. Miller (1986), "Norm Theory: Comparing Reality to Its Alternatives," *Psychological Review*, 93 (2), 136-53.

Kim, Hakkyun and Deborah Roedder John (2008), "Consumer Response to Brand Extensions: Construal Level as a Moderator of the Importance of Perceived Fit," *Journal of Consumer Psychology*, 18 (2), 116-26.

Liberman, Nira, Michael D. Sagristano, and Yaacov Trope (2002), "The Effect of Temporal Distance on Level of Mental Construal," *Journal of Experimental Social Psychology*, 38 (6), 523-34.

Meyer, Wulf-Uwe, Michael Niperl, Udo Rudolph, and Achim Schützwohl (1991), "An Experimental Analysis of Surprise," *Cognition and Emotion*, 5, 295-311.

Meyers-Levy, Joan and Alice M. Tybout (1989), "Schema Congruity as a Basis for Product Evaluation," *Journal of Consumer Research*, 16 (1), 39-54.

Moyer, Robert S. and Thomas K. Landauer (1967), "Time Required for Judgments of Numerical Inequality," *Nature*, 215 (5109), 1519-20.

Nisbett, Robert E. and Lee Ross (1980), *Human Inference: Strategies and Shortcomings of Social Judgment*, Englewood Cliffs, NJ: Prentice-Hall.

Rosch, Eleanor (1978), "Principles of Categorization," in *Cognition and categorization*, ed. Eleanor Rosch and Barbara B. Lloyd, Hillsdale, NJ: Erlbaum, 27-47.

Schindler, Robert M. and Patrick N. Kirby (1997), "Patterns of Rightmost Digits Used in Advertised Prices: Implications for Nine-Ending Effects," *Journal of Consumer Research*, 24 (2), 192-201.

Schützwohl, Achim (1988), "Surprise and Schema Strength," *Journal of Experimental Psychology: Learning, Memory, and Cognition*, 24, 1182-99.

Shadish, William R., Thomas D. Cook, and Donald T. Campbell (2002), *Experimental and Quasi-Experimental Designs for Generalized Causal Inference*, Boston: Houghton Mifflin.

Smith, Pamela K. and Yaacov Trope (2006), "You Focus on the Forest When You're in Charge of the Trees: Power Priming and Abstract Information Processing," *Journal of Personality and Social Psychology*, 90 (4), 578-96.

Sperber, Dan and Dierdre Wilson (1986), *Relevance: Communication and Cognition*, Oxford: Basil Blackwell.

Thomas, Manoj and Vicki G. Morwitz (2005), "Penny Wise and Pound Foolish: The Left Digit Effect in Price Cognition," *Journal of Consumer Research*, 32, 154-64.

———— (2009), "Heuristics in Numerical Cognition: Implications for Pricing," in *Handbook of Research in Pricing*, ed. Vithala Rao: Edward Elgar Publishing, 132-49.

Trope, Yaacov and Nira Liberman (2003), "Temporal Construal," *Psychological Review*, 110 (3), 403-21.

Tybout, Alice M. and Nancy Artz (1994), "Consumer Psychology," *Annual Review of Psychology*, 45 (1), 131.

Vallacher, Robin R. and Daniel M. Wegner (1989), "Levels of Personal Agency: Individual Variation in Action Identification," *Journal of Personality and Social Psychology*, 57 (4), 660-71.

Wegener, Duane T., John Downing, Jon A. Krosnick, and Richard E. Petty (1995), "Measures and Manipulations of Strength-Related Properties of Attitudes: Current Practice and Future Directions," in *Attitude Strength: Antecedents and Consequences*, ed. Richard E. Petty and Jon A. Krosnick, Mahwah, NJ: Erlbaum.

# When Seeing Many Types of Wine Makes You More Sensitive to Technological Threats: Unrelated, Prior Categorizations and Reactions to Change

Amitav Chakravarti, New York University, USA
Christina Fang, New York University, USA
Zur Shapira, New York University, USA

## EXTENDED ABSTRACT

Detecting change is a fundamental, all-pervasive cognitive activity. It forms the core of many cognitive activities, such as visual, auditory, olfactory, and tactile discrimination tasks, similarity judgments, and categorization. Naturally then, the ability to detect a change, to accurately assess the magnitude of the change, and to react to the change in a commensurate fashion, is of critical importance in many substantive domains (Massey and Wu 2005, Rensink 2002), ranging from medical decisions, business investment decisions, and face recognition, to air traffic control. Thus, it is important to understand factors that systematically affect people's ability to detect change. To that end, we document a simple, yet novel effect: people's reactions to a change (e.g., visual change, or technology change), are systematically affected by the categorizations they encounter in an unrelated, prior task (e.g., how a wine store categorizes its wines).

Before surmising about reactions to change, it is important to consider, more generally, how exposure to many, narrow (vs. few, broad) categorizations might affect an individual's information processing. First, an individual who is exposed to a detailed environment with many, narrow (vs. few, broad) categories, should be cued to the notion that objects differ from each other in many different ways, and will fine tune her cognitive apparatus accordingly, using more (vs. less) dimensions to perceive and evaluate objects (e.g., see Barsalou 1993, Linville 1982). Further, as long as the subsequent context does not cue the need for cognitive reorganization, the recently tuned cognitive apparatus will likely be used, as is, for the next task at hand (e.g., see Bargh and Chartrand 2000, Smith and Branscombe 1987, Mullen, Pizzuto, and Foels 2002, Ülkümen, Chakravarti, and Morwitz (forthcoming)). Therefore, in a subsequent, unrelated task, an individual previously exposed to narrow (broad) categorizations is likely to continue to employ and discern relatively many (fewer) dimensions.

This brings us to the more specific question: how would such an individual react to a change that she subsequently encounters? Theoretically, there are two distinct possibilities. If the *perceptual* system alone is affected, then people previously exposed to many, narrow (few, broad) categorizations should have a more (less) sensitive perceptual encoding system, one that is attuned to processing incoming perceptual stimuli on relatively many (fewer) dimensions. Such people, therefore, should detect and *perceive* more (less) change, subjectively, when they encounter a subsequent change. In this case, then, prior exposure to unrelated, narrow (broad) categorizations will lead to stronger (weaker) reactions to a given change.

In contrast, if the *evaluative* system is affected, then prior exposure to many, narrow (few, broad) categorizations should encourage decision makers to *evaluate* the subsequent change more (less) carefully, using many (few) dimensions. The use of many (few) dimensions to evaluate the presented change should lead to perceptions of a relatively small (large) change, since the presented change would have to satisfy multiple (fewer) criterion in order to be deemed a significant enough change. Thus, in this case, prior exposure to narrow (broad) categorizations will lead to weaker (stronger) reactions to a given change. The question of which of these two conjectures is likely to prevail, is an empirical one, one which we leave our studies to answer.

Across four different studies, we find that unrelated, prior exposure to narrow (vs. broad) categorizations improves decision makers' ability to detect a visual change (study 1) and leads to stronger reactions to a given change (studies 2-4). These differential reactions occur because the prior categorizations, albeit unrelated, alter the extent to which the subsequently presented change is perceived as either a relatively large change or a relatively small one.

Each experiment comprised two, ostensibly unrelated studies. The first task was used to administer the prior categorization manipulation and the second task was used to record reactions to a presented change (Figure 1). We began by looking at how these prior categorizations affect a person's ability to detect a presented visual change, using well-established stimuli from the "change-blindness" paradigm (study 1). We then went on to looking at judgments that are contingent on people's subjective reactions to a presented change (studies 2-4). Specifically, we assessed their reactions to an innovative new technology that loomed in the horizon. A pretest was used to verify that the new technologies were perceived to be relatively innovative.

We operationalized the fine grained nature of the decision context in multiple ways. In some instances participants answered preference questions presented either on relatively simple 3-point semantic differential scales, or on more differentiated 7-point ones. In other instances, participants are incidentally exposed to the same set of products that have been grouped either in a coarse-grained manner (e.g., movies classified as comedy or drama movies), or in a fine-grained manner (e.g., movies classified as comic action, dark comedy, romantic comedy, courtroom drama, historical drama, or melodrama movies). Irrespective of the nature of the manipulation, we find a very similar pattern of carryover effects.

The manipulations used show that even incidental exposure to narrow-broad categorizations can have a systematic effect on change detection, and reactions to change. Interestingly, the effects are not attributable to differential involvement, confidence, familiarity, knowledge, mood, and task completion times. Taken together, these findings suggest the interesting possibility that decision makers can become more discerning, even in the absence of having exerted any extra effort. Given that category structure is a ubiquitous feature of many decision environments, our work constitutes an important first step in documenting how seemingly innocuous categorizations might affect a decision maker's reactions to change.

## REFERENCES

Bargh, John A, and Tanya L. Chartrand (2000), "The Mind in the Middle: A Practical Guide to Priming and Automaticity Research," in *Handbook of Research Methods in Social and Personality Psychology*, ed. Harry T. Reis and Charles M. Judd, New York, NY: Cambridge 253-285.

Barsalou, Lawrence W. (1993), "Flexibility, Structure, and Linguistic Vagary in Concepts: Manifestations of A Compositional System of Perceptual Symbols," in *Theories of Memory*, ed. Alan F. Collins and Susan E. Gathercole, Hillsdale, NJ: Erlbaum, 29-101.

Linville, Patricia W. (1982), "The Complexity-Extremity Effect and Age-Based Stereotyping," *Journal of Personality and Social Psychology*, 42 (February), 193-211.

Massey, Cade and George Wu (2005), "Detecting Regime Shifts: The Causes of Under and Overreaction," *Management Science*, 51 (6), 932–947.

Mullen, Brian, Pizzuto, Carmen and Rob Foels (2002), "Altering Intergroup Perceptions by Altering Prevailing Mode of Cognitive Representation: 'They Look Like People'," *Journal of Personality and Social Psychology*, 83 (6), 1333-1343.

Rensink, Ronald A. (2002), "Change Detection," *Annual Review of Psychology*, 53, 245–77.

Smith, Eliot R., and Nyla R. Branscombe (1987), "Procedurally Mediated Social Inferences: The Case of Category Accessibility Effects," *Journal of Experimental Social Psychology*, 23 (September), 361-382.

Ülkümen, Gülden, Chakravarti, Amitav, and Vicki G. Morwitz (forthcoming), "The Effect of Exposure to Narrow versus Broad Categorizations on Subsequent Decision Making and Information Processing," *Journal of Marketing Research*.

# Does Exposure to Concept Products Affect Judgment of Marketed New Products?

Irene Scopelliti, Bocconi University, Italy
Paola Cillo, Bocconi University, Italy
David Mazursky, The Hebrew University of Jerusalem, Israel

## EXTENDED ABSTRACT

In some industries, it is a common practice to develop prototypes that are very innovative and that are loosely coupled with the actual product that is subsequently marketed. These prototypes are referred to as *concept products*, and are usually exhibited at trade shows and at industry events. They typically feature technical functionalities that are very innovative, sometimes too advanced to be implemented on large scale production, and are typically characterized by an extreme design, often too futuristic to be featured by marketable versions without substantial adaptations and moderations.

By means of theories on the effects of exaggeration and on structural alignment, we argue that exposure to the design and functionalities of concept products may affect consumer evaluation of marketed products. Specifically, we predict a positive effect of exposure to a visually exaggerated concept product on the judgment of the marketed product (H1): when a novel design is preceded by exposure to its exaggerated form, i.e., the concept product, exaggeration may attract subjects' attention to the distinctive features of the design more than in the case of exposure to a non-exaggerated exemplar (Rhodes, Brennan and Carey 1987; Mauro and Kubovy 1992; Rhodes and Tremewan 1996). Moreover, the emphasis on the distinctive features of the design provided by exaggeration is feasible to leave a stronger trace in subjects' implicit memory. This trace may eventually enhance the ease in elaborating those features when subjects encounter other exemplars, more moderate, of the same design, thus enhancing their evaluation. We expect, however, that functional exaggeration of the concept product moderate such effect (H2): On the one hand, we expect that exposure to an exemplar featuring very high (extreme) levels of performance on a given functional feature may set a new standard for the judgment of other exemplars on that same feature, causing a contrast effect that hurts the judgment of the other exemplars (Herr, Sherman and Fazio 1983; Herr 1986). On the other hand, however, the occurrence of such contrast effect is contingent upon the degree of context-target similarity, i.e., occurs only both the priming (concept product) and target (marketed product) are judged as belonging to the same category (Stapel and Winkielman 1998). An exaggerated design (high visual exaggeration) may favor the perception of the concept product as less thematically or temporally related, thus reducing the contrast effect due to the concept product exaggerated functionalities on the judgment of the moderate target product.

Concept products may feature different degrees of visual and functional alignment with their respective marketed versions. For instance, firms may invest in developing and promoting a very advanced technological feature within a concept project, but then implement and promote different features in the moderate marketed version. Similarly, they can develop very innovative and futuristic designs for their concept products, but then base the actually marketed products on different and less disruptive designs. We argue that the visual alignment between the concept product and the marketed product influences negatively the judgment of the marketed product (H3), since it activates a 'thematic link' between the two objects in consumers' mind. The more the two products are visually aligned, the higher likelihood that they are judged as belonging to the same category and thus compared in terms of functionalities. Once this link is activated, it leads to an implicit comparison between the technical features of the concept product and those of the marketable product. In the case in which the concept product features high functional alignment with the marketable product, then the very high (extreme) levels of performance on the technical functionalities are likely to influence negatively the evaluation of the marketable product, since the latter typically features more moderate levels of performance on those same technical functionalities than the former. However, it may be that the concept product features different technical functionalities (low functional alignment) than the marketable car. Therefore, it is less easy for consumers to compare the features of the concept product with those of the marketable products, since non-alignable differences are harder to compare than alignable differences (Markman and Gentner 1996; Gentner and Markman 1993). In such case, consumers would be less likely to be influenced by the extreme performance of the concept product when they evaluate the marketable product (H4).

Results of two experimental studies using concept cars and cars as stimuli support our hypotheses and show that i) exposure to a visually exaggerated concept product positively affect the judgment of a moderate product featuring a similar design, and moderates the negative effects of the concept product functional exaggeration; ii) the degree of functional alignment between a concept product and a marketed product negatively affects the judgment of the marketed product upon exposure to the concept product, with this effect being moderated by the degree of visual alignment between the concept product and the marketed product. Our results contribute to shed light on the role of concept products on the evaluation of marketed products, thus emphasizing a different way in which the use of design in the initial stages of new product development may enhance new product performance.

# Choosing versus Rejecting: How Power Shapes our Decision Strategies

Mehdi Mourali, University of Calgary, Canada
Anish Nagpal, University of Melbourne, Australia

## EXTENDED ABSTRACT

When deciding among several alternatives, consumers may proceed by choosing (selecting, including) the most attractive option. Alternatively, they may adopt a decision strategy of rejecting (eliminating, excluding) the unattractive options. The literature on task framing investigates whether choosing and rejecting are two sides of the same coin. The principle of task invariance requires that decision makers should arrive at the same conclusion about product choice regardless of whether they reject or choose from the same finite set. However, past research has shown that the principle of task invariance does not always hold, and that decision outcomes are sensitive to which decision strategy consumers adopt (e.g., Park, Jun, and MacInnis 2000; Shafir 1993). Prior research has focused primarily on the consequences of framing a decision as either a choosing task or a rejecting task. However, much less in known about the circumstances under which consumers are more inclined to choose versus reject. Initially, Shafir (1993) noted that choosing might be the more preferred strategy relative to rejecting. Conversely, Ordonez, Benson, and Beach (1999) concluded that the norm during screening tasks seems to be to reject the bad options rather than to screen in the good ones. Later investigations, however, revealed that the natural process for screening choice options is dependent on the characteristics of the decision task. Levin et al. (2001), for instance, found that people are more likely to favor an inclusion strategy when the task is positive (e.g., hiring employees), while preferring a rejection strategy when the task is negative (e.g., firing employees).

The present research goes beyond the influence of task characteristics, and examines the role of power–a consumer characteristic– in determining the preferred decision strategy. It also investigates the interactive effect of power and task frame on consumer satisfaction with the chosen option. Building on the approach/inhibition theory of power (Keltner et al. 2003), we hypothesize that activation of the behavioral approach system would make choosing a more natural strategy than rejecting for powerful consumers, whereas activation of the behavioral inhibition system would make rejecting a more natural strategy than choosing for powerless consumers. Indeed, activation of the behavioral approach system results in greater attention to potential rewards and positive outcomes. This should lead powerful consumers to favor a decision strategy that accentuates the choice options' positive features, which is more typical of a choosing strategy (Shafir 1993). In contrast, activation of the behavioral inhibition system heightens the perception of threat in the environment. Further, a focus on threats and negative outcomes is likely to emphasize the choice options' negative features. Since negative features tend to be weighted more heavily under rejection instructions than under choosing instructions (Shafir 1993), we predict that powerless consumers are likely to prefer rejecting over choosing decision strategies.

Consistent with our predictions, study 1 found that a heightened sense of power increases preference for choosing versus rejecting. Further, high power consumers were more satisfied with their choices when they adopted a choose strategy than when they adopted a reject strategy. Conversely, low power consumers were more satisfied with their choices when they adopted a reject strategy than when they adopted a choose strategy.

In study 2, we investigated the moderating role of responsibility. We argued that a heightened sense of responsibility would raise the perceived constraints that a powerful individual feels which, in turn, would lead to reduced approach-related tendencies and reduced preference for choosing versus rejecting. Our data showed that the effect of power on decision strategy indeed disappeared when consumers' sense of responsibility was made salient. We also found that a high sense of responsibility makes both high and low power consumers more satisfied with their choices after adopting a reject strategy than after adopting a choose strategy.

## REFERENCES

Keltner, Dacher, Deborah H. Gruenfeld, and Cameron Anderson (2003), "Power, Approach, and Inhibition," *Psychological Review*, 110 (April), 265-84.

Levin, Irwin P., Carolyn M. Prosansky, Daniel Heller, and Brad M. Brunick (2001), "Prescreening of Choice Options in "Positive" and "Negative" Decision Making Tasks," *Journal of Behavioral Decision Making*, 14 (4), 279-93.

Ordonez, Lisa D., Lehman Benson III, & Lee Roy Beach (1999), "Testing the Compatibility Test: How instructions, accountability, and anticipated regret affect pre-choice screening of options," *Organizational Behavior and Human Decision Processes*, 78 (1), 63-80.

Park, C. Whan, Sung Youl Jun, and Deborah J. MacInnis (2000), "Choosing What I Want versus Rejecting What I Do Not Want: An Application of Decision Framing to Product Option Choice Decisions," *Journal of Marketing Research*, 37 (2), 187-202.

Shafir, Eldar (1993), "Choosing versus Rejecting: Why Some Options are both Better and Worse than Others," *Memory and Cognition*, 21 (4), 546-56.

# How Objective and Subjective Mental Resources Influence Task Performance: Testing the "I Worked Hard, I Must Be Depleted" Hypothesis

Anick Bosmans, Tilburg University, The Netherlands
Rik Pieters, Tilburg University, The Netherlands
Hans Baumgartner, Pennsylvania State University, USA

## EXTENDED ABSTRACT

At the end of an extensive shopping trip or after a complicated decision task, we should be depleted. We worked hard, so we must be tired, not? How will this influence how much resources we will allocate to a subsequent task?

We test the hypothesis that resource allocation to a task depends not only on the actual amount of resources available for a task, but also on consumers' inferences about the amount of resources available. More specifically, we propose and test the idea that inferences about the resource demands of preceding tasks (regardless of that task's actual demands) affect the amount of resources that will be allocated to a subsequent task. When people believe that a preceding task was difficult, they will allocate fewer resources to a subsequent (unrelated) task and task performance on this task will thus detoriate, compared to when people believe that the preceding task was easy.

Of course, resource allocation to a task depends on the demands set by that task (Locke and Latham 1990), and on the amount of resources the consumer has available for that task. When a demanding preceding task has depleted one's pool of mental resources, insufficient resources will be available for subsequent tasks and task performance will decrease (Ackerman and Kanfer 2009; Baumeister et al. 2008; Vohs et al. 2008).

Research on the effects of resource scarcity has mainly focused on the objective amount of mental resources available (i.e., how many resources one actually has available), but little is known about whether and how beliefs about resource availability (i.e. how many resources one assumes to have available for a task) affect resource allocation to a current task. This is surprising, because most people find it difficult to determine how much mental resources were consumed in the past (Ackerman and Kanfer 2009) or will be required for a future task (Fennema and Kleinmutz 1995; Garbarino and Edell 1997). Because people find it difficult to assess their objective resources, they may instead rely on their ideas about subjective resources when allocating resources to a task.

The results of three studies in which we manipulate perceived task demands but keep the actual task demands constant support our "I worked hard, I must be depleted" hypothesis. In a first study we asked participants to write a short essay about a task they had executed in the recent past that was either easy and simple or complex and difficult, thereby manipulating the salience of preceding task demands. In a control condition, we simply asked participants to write an essay about the physical environment they were currently in. Consistent with the "I worked hard, I must be depleted" hypothesis, we observed that participants consulted less information about a new product in a subsequent task when they were first asked to write about a difficult task performed in the near past, compared to when they were asked to write about an easy task or about the physical environment.

In a second study we tested our proposed hypothesis under different conditions of actual and perceived depletion. We asked participants to work on an anagram task for either one or ten minutes (thereby manipulating actual depletion levels). In both conditions, participants were led to believe that the anagram task was either easy or difficult (thereby manipulating perceived depletion levels). Afterwards, task performance on a subsequent (unrelated) task was

measured. We observed that, as long as actual depletion levels were low, people inferred the amount of resources available for a task from the perceived difficulty level of the preceding (anagram) task. That is, when people believed that the preceding task was difficult, they felt more depleted and allocated fewer resources to a subsequent task compared to when they believed that the preceding task was easy.

In study 3, we tested the hypothesis that people would be less likely to infer available resources from the perceived demands of a preceding task when both tasks appear dissimilar. Indeed, when we explicitly instructed participants that both tasks drew on different psychological processes and resources, the amount of resources consumed in the past was no longer informative when assessing the amount of resources available for a subsequent task and the "I worked hard, I must be depleted" effect disappeared.

In sum, we observed that resource allocation to a current task does not only depend on the actual amount of resources available for that task, but is also a function of the inferences that people make about the amount of resources they assume to have available. Characteristics of the context, such as the perceived ease or difficulty of a preceding task, can inform people about how many resources they can allocate to subsequent tasks. These findings reveal the great flexibility in resource allocation that consumers have and show that resource depletion is not necessarily an objective phenomenon. Our studies show that not only the actual level of resource depletion, but also consumers' naïve theories about when they should or should not be depleted determine subsequent task performance.

## REFERENCES

Ackerman, Phillip L. and Ruth Kanfer (2009), "Test Length and Cognitive Fatigue: An Empirical Examination of Effects on Performance and Test-Taker Reactions," *Journal of Experimental Psychology: Applied*, 15(2), 163-181.

Baddeley, Alan D. and Graham J. Hitch (1974), "Working Memory", in *The Psychology of Learning and Motivation: Advances in Research and Theory*, ed. Gordon A. Bower, vol. 8, New York: Academic Press, 47-90.

Baumeister, Roy F., Ellen Bratslavy, Mark Muraven, and Dianne M. Tice (1998), "Ego Depletion: Is the Active Self a Limited Resource?" *Journal of Personality and Social Psychology*, 74 (June), 1252-65.

Bosmans, Anick, Rik Pieters, and Hans Baumgartner (2010), "The Get Ready Mind-Set: How Gearing Up for Later Impacts Effort Allocation Now," *Journal of Consumer Research*, in press

Carver, Charles S. and Michael F. Scheier (1998), *On the Self-Regulation of Behavior*, New York: Cambridge University Press.

Dweck, Carol S. (2002), "Beliefs that Make Smart People Dumb," in *Why Smart People Can Be so Stupid*, ed. Robert J. Sternberg, New Haven, CT: Yale University Press, 24-41.

Fennema, M.G. and Don N. Kleinmuntz (1995), "Anticipations of Effort and Accuracy in Multiattribute Choice," *Organizational Behavior and Human Decision Processes*, 63 (July), 21-32.

Garbarino, Ellen C. and Julie A. Edell (1997), "Cognitive Effort, Affect, and Choice", Journal of Consumer Research, 24 (September), 147-58.

Heatherton Todd F. and Janet Polivy (1991), "Development and Validation of a Scale for Measuring State Self-Esteem," *Journal of Personality and Social Psychology*, 60 (June), 895-910.

Iyengar, Sheena S. and Mark R. Lepper (2000), "When Choice is Demotivating: Can One Desire Too Much of a Good Thing?" *Journal of Personality and Social Psychology*, 79, 995-1006.

Locke, Edwin A. and Gary P. Latham (2006), "New Directions in Goal-Setting Theory," *Current Directions in Psychological Science*, 15 (October), 265-8.

Martijn, Carolien, Petra Tenbült, Harald Merckelbach, Ellen Dreezens, and Nanne de Vries (2002), "Getting a Grip on Ourselves: Challenging Expectancies about Loss of Energy after Self-Control," *Social Cognition*, 20 (December), 441-60.

Molden, Daniel C. and Carol S. Dweck (2006), "Finding "Meaning" in Psychology: A Lay Theories Approach to Self-Regulation, Social Perception, and Social Development," *American Psychologist*, 61 (April), 192-203.

Martin, Leonard L., David W. Ward, John W. Achee, and Robert S. Wyer (1993), "Mood as Input: People Have to Interpret the Motivational Implications of Their Moods," *Journal of Personality and Social Psychology*, 64 (March), 317-26.

Moller, Arlen C., Edward L. Deci, and Richard M. Ryan (2006), "Choice and Ego-Depletion: The Moderating Role of Autonomy," *Personality and Social Psychological Bulletin*, 32 (August), 1024-36.

Muraven, Mark, Dikla Shmueli, and Edward Burkley (2006), "Conserving Self-Control Strength," *Journal of Personality and Social Psychology*, 91 (September), 524-37.

Muraven, Mark and Elisaveta Slessareva (2003), "Mechanisms of Self-Control Failure: Motivation and Limited Resources," *Personality and Social Psychological Bulletin*, 29 (July), 894-906.

Norman, Don and Tim Shallice (1986), "Attention to Action: Willed and Automatic Control of Behavior," in *Consciousness and Self-Regulation: Advances in Research and Theory*, ed. Richard Davidson, Gary Schwartz, and David Shapiro, vol. 4, New York: Plenum Press, 1-18.

Pham, Michel Tuan (1998), "Representativeness, Relevance, and the Use of Feelings in Decision Making," *Journal of Consumer Research*, 25 (September), 144-59.

Schwarz, Norbert and Gerald L. Clore (1983), "Mood, Misattribution, and Judgments of Well-Being: Informative and Directive Functions of Affective States," *Journal of Personality and Social Psychology*, 45 (September), 513-23.

Tice, Dianne M., Roy F. Baumeister, Dikla Shmueli, and Mark Muraven (2007), "Restoring the Self: Positive Affect Helps Improve Self-Regulation Following Ego Depletion," *Journal of Experimental Social Psychology*, 43, 379-84.

Vohs, Kathleen D. and Ronald J. Faber (2007), "Spent Resources: Self-Regulatory Resource Availability Affects Impulse Buying," *Journal of Consumer Research*, 33 (March), 537-547.

Vohs, Kathleen D., Brandon J. Schmeichel, Noelle Nelson, Roy F. Baumeister, Jean M. Twenge, and Dianne M. Tice (2008), "Making Choices Impairs Subsequent Self-Control: A Limited-Resource Account of Decision Making, Self-Regulation, and Action Initiative," *Journal of Personality and Social Psychology*, 94 (5), 883-98.

Vidulich, Michael and Christopher D. Wickens (1986), "Causes of Dissociation Between Subjective Workload Measures and Performance: Caveats for the Use of Subjective Assessments," Applied Ergonomics, 17 (December), 291-6.

Webb, Thomas L. and Paschal Sheeran (2003), "Can Implementation Intentions Help to Overcome Ego-Depletion?" *Journal of Experimental Social Psychology*, 39 (May), 279-86.

Yeh, Yei-Yu and Christopher D. Wickens (1988), "Dissociation of Performance and Subjective Measures of Workload," *Human Factors*, 30 (February), 110-20.

# Inhibition Spill-Over: Sensations of Peeing Urgency Lead to Increased Impulse Control in Unrelated Domains

Mirjam Tuk, University of Twente, The Netherlands
Debra Trampe, University of Groningen, The Netherlands
Luk Warlop, Catholic University Leuven, Belgium

## EXTENDED ABSTRACT

People often encounter decision situations in which they have to choose between an option that is on the short term more rewarding and attractive, and another option that is on the long term the more beneficial one, like choosing between going out for dinner tonight versus saving money for retirement. When people follow their impulses (prefer the more immediate option) and when people resist impulsive input (and opt for the more long-term beneficial option), has been an important topic of previous research (e.g., Vohs 2006). Recent research adds to this domain by providing evidence for the existence of a general reward system (Briers et al. 2006; Van den Bergh, Dewitte, and Warlop 2008). When people's desire for a reward is triggered (e.g., by the sight, smell or taste of rewarding stimuli), their desire for any kind of reward increases, rather than only their desire for stimuli that are directly linked to the aroused state. For example, exposing people to a consumption sample of a tasty food does not only increase their desire for food, but also their desire for other rewarding goods (like beverages and a holiday).

In the current research, we argue that inhibitory signals are domain unspecific. Recent neurological research (Berkman, Burklund, and Lieberman 2009) suggests that inhibitory signals in the motor, cognitive and affective domain share the same neurological network. Berkman and colleagues argue for the relative efficiency of such a network from a neurological point of view. However, a side-effect of such a shared network is the possibility that inhibitory signals are not completely domain specific, but can spill-over to other domains and result in an unintentional increase in inhibitory signals in unrelated domains as well. Berkman et al. provide neurological evidence for inhibition spill-over effects. We aim to provide evidence for inhibition spill-over from a behavioral point of view. We argue that inhibitory signals from one domain can spill-over and result in more impulse inhibition in unrelated domains. One important physiological condition that largely relies on inhibitory signals is bladder control. As the bladder becomes increasingly full, the impulse (immediate voiding) has to be inhibited until an appropriate place and time. This inhibition occurs during most parts of the day, and is relatively automatized since an early age. Griffiths and Tadic (2008) show that the inhibitory signal stems from the Anterior Cingulate Cortex (ACC), which is also one of the brain areas identified as an important part of the general inhibition network. In the current research, we argue that increased inhibitory signals due to increased bladder control will spill-over to unrelated domains and result in increased impulse control.

In the first study, we manipulate peeing urgency by means of a water drink test approximately one hour upfront. After one hour passed, respondents engaged in an intertemporal choice task (adapted from Li 2008). They were asked to choose eight times between either a smaller but sooner reward, or a later but larger reward. Foregoing a smaller but more immediate reward in order to obtain a later, but larger reward requires impulse control. Manipulation checks showed significant differences in reported peeing urgency. In line with our expectations, respondents more often chose for the later larger reward when they had to pee more urgently.

In the second study, we show that sensitivity of the Behavioral Inhibition System (BIS) moderates this effect. BIS is known to be involved in response inhibition and punishment avoidance (e.g.,

Carver and White 1994). In line with our expectations, peeing urgency had a stronger effect on intertemporal patience for people with a relatively sensitive BIS compared to people with a relatively insensitive BIS.

In study 3, we examined whether the inhibition system can also be triggered by exogenous cues. We primed half of the respondents with the concept of peeing, which we expected to induce an increase in peeing urgency. In line with this reasoning, we found that the peeing prime induced an increase in reported peeing urgency, which subsequently significantly influenced intertemporal patience. Mediation analysis was significant.

Finally, in study 4 we show that increased peeing urgency also impacts performance on a task that stongly relies on inhibition, namely switching abilities in a stroop task (Stroop 1935). When people had to pee relatively more urgently, they could more easily switch between two tasks (word naming versus color naming), indicating that they were relatively better in inhibiting the previously learned behavior (which interferes with the currently required behavior after switching between two tasks).

The results of these four studies provide support for inhibition spill-over effects. With this research, we contribute to recent neurological research suggesting that people possess a general inhibition system (Berkman et al. 2009), by providing behavioral data that suggests in the same direction. This suggests that inhibition spill-over effects are not only of neurological nature, but also show itself in human behavior. Furthermore, this research contributes to the current knowledge about impulse control. We show that increased impulse control can be the unintentional side-effect of increased inhibition in an unrelated domain (e.g., bladder control). We provide evidence for inhibition spill-over effects on an intertemporal choice task which is quite deliberative in nature, but also on a task relying more on automatic responses, namely response times on a stroop task. This suggests that inhibition spill-over is a relatively automatic process. The current research suggests that impulse control does not necessarily rely on an energy consuming resource that can become depleted after previous acts of self-control, but can also be a by-product of inhibitory signals in a completely unrelated domain.

## REFERENCES

Berkman, Elliot T., Lisa Burklund, and Matthew D. Lieberman (2009), "Inhibitory Spillover: Intentional Motor Inhibition Produces Incidental Limbic Inhibition Via Right Inferior Frontal Cortex," *Neuroimage*, 47 (2), 705-12.

Briers, Barbara, Mario Pandelaere, Siegfried Dewitte, and Luk Warlop (2006), "Hungry for Money-the Desire for Caloric Resources Increases the Desire for Financial Resources and Vice Versa," *Psychological Science*, 17 (11), 939-43.

Carver, Charles S. and Teri L. White (1994), "Behavioral-Inhibition, Behavioral Activation, and Affective Responses to Impending Reward and Punishment-the Bis Bas Scales," *Journal of Personality and Social Psychology*, 67 (2), 319-33.

Griffiths, Derek and Stasa D. Tadic (2008), "Bladder Control, Urgency, and Urge Incontinence: Evidence from Functional Brain Imaging," *Neurourology and Urodynamics*, 27 (6), 466-74.

Li, Xiuping P. (2008), "The Effects of Appetitive Stimuli on out-of-Domain Consumption Impatience," *Journal of Consumer Research*, 34 (5), 649-56.

Stroop, John R. (1935), "Studies of Interference in Serial Verbal Reactions," *Journal of Experimental Psychology*, 18, 643-62.

Van den Bergh, Bram, Siegfried Dewitte, and Luk Warlop (2008), "Bikinis Instigate Generalized Impatience in Intertemporal Choice," *Journal of Consumer Research*, 35 (1), 85-97.

Vohs, Kathleen D. (2006), "Self-Regulatory Resources Power the Reflective System: Evidence from Five Domains," *Journal of Consumer Psychology*, 16 (3), 217-23.

# Body Beliefs Shape the Perceived Accuracy of Virtual Models

Ellen Garbarino, University of Sydney, Australia
Jose Antonio Rosa, University of Wyoming, USA

## EXTENDED ABSTRACT

Apparel is one of the big success stories of online retailing, with double digit sales growth in recent years (Mui 2007). As competition has intensified, online retailers have begun to rely on product visualization technologies, such as virtual models. While product visualization tools have been shown to enhance the retail experience (Daugherty, Li, and Biocca 2008; Kim and Forsythe 2008), most research ignores the potential for individual differences to influence their effectiveness. In high body-involvement categories, such as apparel, the effectiveness of product visualization may depend on consumers' perceptions and beliefs about their physical body in ways that potentially limit its accuracy and effectiveness.

To explore the influence of body beliefs, we surveyed women consumers to examine how two different body belief systems affect their perception of virtual model accuracy and willingness to use them. We focus on how two distinct types of body beliefs–body image discrepancy (Cash 1994; Cash and Szymanski 1995) and body boundary aberration (Fisher1986). Body image discrepancy (BID) is a cognitive evaluation of how well the appearance of various aspects of our body (e.g., hair, muscle tone, body proportions, and weight) aligns with our ideals for those body parts (Cash 1994; Cash and Szymanski 1995), weighted for the importance of that aspect. Body boundary aberration (BBA) addresses the individual's sense of the location and stability of the edges of his or her body (Fisher 1970, 1973). The alignment of the body boundary with the skin surface differs between persons. BBA occurs when an individual's sense of the location of that edge does not align with their skin surface (Fisher 1970, 1986). It is possible for our sense of body containment to either move inward from the skin surface or extend beyond it to incorporate immediately adjacent objects. One example of mild BBA is the sense of nakedness and vulnerability when a habitually worn accessory (e.g., hat, bra, watch, or ring) is absent. Another example is the enhanced sense of power when wearing bold colors or tightly-woven dense fabrics (Fisher 1986).

Body image discrepancy should negatively influence perceived virtual model accuracy. High body image discrepancy exists when consumers believe that aspects of their looks do not meet important standards, suggesting a more critical view of the self in the mirror. This same critical eye should be used to assess the accuracy of any representation that purports to serve the same function as a mirror.

Body Boundary Aberration is expected to have a positive influence on the perceived accuracy of virtual models by virtue of the reassurance that comes from seeing a stand-alone representation of the self with unambiguous boundaries. High BBA consumers glean reassurance from seeing their boundaries well-defined, and we expect that a representation of self with well defined edges against a neutral and uniform background will be reassuring to consumers with high BBA.

Perceived model quality captures how effectively the model can represent how the clothing looks and fits. It is expected to positively influence both their perception of how accurately the model can represent them and how likely they would be to use it. Both perceived accuracy and quality are expected to positively influence usage intentions.

Using an online panel, a sample of 978 women consumers was collected. The demographics closely match the U.S. Internet consumer population (ClickZ 2003). The respondents answered questions about their web usage, interest in apparel, online apparel purchase habits and demographics, including height and weight.

Respondents were then shown a virtual model based on their body dimensions. After viewing the model, respondents assessed the quality (3 item α =.93) and accuracy (2 items r =.88) of the model, and their interest in using such a model in the future (2 items r = .91). Finally, they responded to BID and BBA items.

Body image discrepancy (BID) was assessed using the scale developed by Cash and Szymanski (Cash and Szymanski 1995); respondents rate how well they match their ideals on eleven physical characteristics and indicate the importance of each aspect. The 11 items form a single factor (α =.81) with higher score indicating higher BID.

Body boundary aberration was assessed using a scale developed by Chapman et al. (Chapman, Chapman, and Raulin 1978), subjects responded to 49 statements with 10 BBA items interspersed. The 10 items form a single factor (α =.87), with higher scores signifying higher BBA. The BBA scores are widely distributed; 1-1.99 (highest BBA) = 4%, 2-2.99 =14%, 3-3.99 =45%, 4-5 (lowest BBA) = 37%. As expected, the two body beliefs are not highly correlated (r =.11).

The structural equation model shows an acceptable level of fit (SRMR of .05, TLI of 0.95, NFI of 0.94, and RMSEA of 0.04) with all of the hypothesized relationships as expected and statistically significant. Virtual model accuracy ($\gamma$ = .315, p < .00) has a positive influence on consumer intentions to use virtual models. Body Boundary Aberration has a positive influence on virtual model accuracy ($\gamma$ = .117, p < .00), consistent with the idea that consumers high in BBA consider renditions that highlight the body's edges more accurate. In contrast, Body Image Discrepancy ($\gamma$ = -.120, p = .00) has a negative influence on assessed virtual model accuracy, suggesting that consumer whose body image differs substantially from their held ideals are less likely to consider virtual models accurate. As expected, quality perceptions have a positive influence on assessed virtual model accuracy ($\gamma$ = .507, p = .00) and intentions to use models ($\gamma$ = .486, p = .00). The SEM results affirm our expectations that body beliefs influence consumer assessments of the accuracy of virtual models even after accounting for quality perceptions.

Additional SEM analyses show that the effects of body beliefs on model usage intentions are fully mediated by their influence on perceived accuracy. All alternative models lead to substantial reductions in model fit, supporting that the influence of body beliefs on intentions to use virtual model is mediated by perceived accuracy.

## REFERENCES

Blakeslee, Sandra. (2004), "When the Brain Says, 'Don't Get Too Close'," The New York Times, (July 13, 2004).

Cash, Thomas F. (1994), "Body-Image Attitudes: Evaluation, Investment, and Affect," Perceptual and Motor Skills 78:3, pt2, 1168-1170.

_____ and Szymanski, Marcela L. (1995), "The Development and Validation of the Body-Image Ideals Questionnaire," Journal of Personality Assessment 64:3, 466-477.

Chapman, Loren J., Chapman, Jean P. and Raulin, Michael L. (1978), "Body-Image Aberration in Schizophrenia," Journal of Abnormal Psychology 87:4, 399-407.

ClickZ Stats Staff, (2003), "June 2003 Internet Usage Stats", *ClickZ.com,* Retrieved October 17th, 2009, from http://www.clickz.com/stats/big_picture/traffic_patterns/article.php/2237901

Daugherty, Terry, Li, Hairong, and Biocca, Frank (2008), "Consumer Learning and the Effects of Virtual Experience Relative to Indirect and Direct Product Experience," *Psychology & Marketing*, 25:7, 568-586.

Fiore, Ann Marie, Kim, Jihyun, and Lee, Hyun-Hwa (2005), "Effect of Image Interactivity Technology on Consumer Responses toward the Online Retailer," Journal of Interactive Marketing, 19:3, 38-53.

Fisher, Seymour (1970), Body Experience in Fantasy and Behavior, New York: Meredith Corp.

_____ (1973), Body Consciousness: You Are What You Feel. Englewood Cliffs, NJ: Prentice Hall.

_____ (1986), Development and Structure of the Body Image, vol. 1 and 2, Hillsdale, NJ: Lawrence Erlbaum Associates.

Griffith, David A.; Krampf, Robert F. and Palmer, Jonathan W. (2001), "The Role of Interface in Electronic Commerce: Consumer Involvement with Print versus On-line Catalogs," International Journal of Electronic Commerce, 5:4, 135-153.

Halls, Steven B. (2000), "Average Height and Weight Charts," *Halls.md Health Calculators and Charts*. Retrieved on 10/2/06 from http://www.halls.md/chart/height-weight.htm.

Head, H. (1926), Aphasia and Kindred Disorders of Speech. London: Cambridge.

Hu, Li-tze and Bentler, Peter M. (1999), "Cutoff Criteria for Fit Indices in Covariance Structure Analysis: Conventional Criteria versus New Alternatives," Structural Equation Modeling, 6:1, 1-55.

Kim, Jihyun and Forsythe, Sandra (2007), "Hedonic Usage of Product Visualization Technologies in Online Apparel Shopping," *International Journal of Retail & Distribution Management*, 35:6, 502-514.

_____ and _____ (2008a), "Adoption of Virtual Try-on Technology for Online Apparel Shopping," *Journal of Interactive Marketing*, 22:2, 45-59.

Li, Hairong, Daugherty, Terry, and Biocca, Frank (2003), "The Role of Virtual Experience in Consumer Learning," *Journal of Consumer Psychology,* 13:4, 395-407.

_____, _____, and _____ (2001), "Characteristics of Virtual Experience in Electronic Commerce: A Protocol Analysis," *Journal of Interactive Marketing,* 15:3, 13-30.

Mui, Ylan Q. (2007), "Online Sales Shift: Apparel Outpaced Computers in '06," Washingtonpost.com, http://www.washingtonpost.com/wpdyn/content/article/2007/05/13/AR2007051301263.html, accessed February 19th 2009.

Nantel, Jacques (2004), "My Virtual Model: Virtual Reality Comes into Fashion," *Journal of Interactive Marketing,* 18:8, 73-86.

Pastore, Michael (2001), "Online Consumers Now the Average Consumer," *ClickZ.com*, Retrieved October 17th 2009, from http://www.clickz.com/stats/big_picture/demographics/article.php/800201.

Rosa, Josa A., Garbarino, Ellen, and Malter, Alan J. (2006), "Keeping the Body in Mind: The Influence of Body Esteem and Body Boundary Aberration on Consumer Beliefs and Purchase Intentions," Journal of Consumer Psychology 16:1, 79-91.

Rust, Roland T. and Lemon, Katherine N. (2001), "E-Service and the Consumer," International Journal of Electronic Commerce 5:3, 85-101.

Westland, J. Christopher and Au, Grace (1997), "A Comparison of Shopping Experiences across Three Competing Digital Retailing Interfaces," International Journal of Electronic Commerce 2:2, 57-69.

Yadav, Manjit S. and Varadarajan, P. Rajan (2005), "Understanding Product Migration to the Electronic Marketplace: A Conceptual Framework," Journal of Retailing 81:2, 125-140.

# Satisfaction in the Context of Customer Co-Production:
## A Behavioral Involvement Perspective

David Hunt, University of Wyoming, USA
Stephanie Geiger Oneto, University of Wyoming, USA
Philip Varca, University of Wyoming, USA

## EXTENDED ABSTRACT

Customer satisfaction has a decades-long history of research in marketing. Scholarly interest has been sustained by evidence that satisfaction leads to loyalty (Suh and Yi 2006), efficiency of promotional programs (Luo and Homburg 2008), and financial performance (Anderson, Fornell, and Mazvancheryl 2004; Fornell, Mithas, Morgeson, and Krishnan 2006).

Against this backdrop of the established importance of satisfaction, marketing appears to be undergoing a paradigm shift from goods dominant logic to services-dominant logic (S-D Logic: Vargo and Lusch 2008; Vargo and Lusch 2004). That is, marketing scholars and practitioners have shifted their focus from tangible resources, to intangible resources, the co-creation of value, and relationships (Vargo and Lusch 2004). A cornerstone of S-D Logic is the assumption that consumers are integrated in value creation from the initial stages of design through the entire usage life of a product (Lusch, Vargo, and O'Brien 2007).

This development reflects a dramatic shift in researchers' interest in consumer behaviors that occur after a market transaction to consumer behaviors that are wholly integrated throughout production and consumption. This wholly integrated role of consumers likely is not devoid of implications for consumers' evaluations of their experiences with goods. The influence of behaviors on a broad range of experiences is well established (Fishbein and Ajzen 1975). However, despite evidence that behaviors influence attitudes and despite the increasing emphasis on customer value creation, research has not addressed the degree to which behavioral engagement in value creation activities relates to customer satisfaction.

The present study aims to address this gap by examining the extent to which behavioral commitment to value creation is associated with satisfaction with the product. Our study differs from past studies in that we examine how behavioral variables, as opposed to attitudinal variables, relate to customer satisfaction outcomes. Satisfaction studies grounded in an attitudinal perspective are limited in the degree to which they can explain how the behavioral demands of customer value creation relate to satisfaction.

The produce product category reflects a market landscape where some consumers are presented with choices between traditional market channels or less traditional channels that require greater customer co-production. Understanding why consumers pursue and remain within alternative market channels has obvious implications for marketing practice. However, a conceptual framework for understanding these consumer decisions is a necessary prerequisite for developing generalizable practices. We argue here that dissonance theory is an apt framework for examining the co-production effects that occur in non-traditional market channels.

The purpose of this paper is to add to the current research on consumer satisfaction by 1) using CSAs as a context to test Vargo and Lusch's (2004) service dominant logic, 2) offering an initial conceptual frame for understanding consumer satisfaction in this CSA context; 3) developing a framework for further research and practical steps for increasing the market for alternative food channels such as CSAs.

In order to test our theoretical framework, data were collected in three urban areas using a stratified random sample design. Respondents were randomly recruited from zip codes found to have a high concentration of CSA locations. One-hundred ninety-eight individuals, serving on a panel at a large marketing research firm, completed an online survey. Results showed several significant differences between CSA and non-CSA members. First, CSA users were found to have greater levels of satisfaction with their vegetables than traditional grocery shoppers. Second, CSA members reported more behavioral involvement in food-related activities than traditional supermarket shoppers. Third, the relationship between CSA membership and product satisfaction was found to be mediated by behavioral involvement in food-related activities. Finally, this mediated effect is more robust with time. In other words, continued behavioral involvement increases the likelihood of continued CSA membership and increases in product satisfaction.

Our findings suggest that the relationship between greater customer co-production and greater satisfaction can be explained by a dissonance-reduction framework. The effort demanded from co-production produces dissonance that is reduced by strong feelings of satisfaction with the product. These findings are consistent with the inherent value from co-production suggested by Vargo and Lusch (2004). Lusch, Vargo, and O'Brien (2007) argue that consumers add value to product experiences through both pre-purchase co-production and post-purchase consumption activities. That is, consumers collectively create value through both co-production and value-in-use activities (Merz, He, and Vargo 2009). By demonstrating significant relationships between satisfaction and both commitment to co-production and behavioral involvement in the product category, our study provides empirical support for both types of value-adding activities proposed by service-dominant logic theorists.

## REFERENCES

Anderson, E. W., Fornell, C., & Mazvancheryl, S. (2004). Customer satisfaction and shareholder value. *Journal of Marketing*, 68(October), 172-185.

Fishbein, M & Ajzen, I. (1975). *Belief, attitude, intention, and behavior: An introduction to theory and research*. Reading, MA: Addison-Wesley.

Fornell, C., Mithas, S., Morgeson, F. V., & Krishnan, M. S. (2006). Customer satisfaction and stock prices: High returns, low risk. *Journal of Marketing*, 70(January), 3-14.

Lusch, R. F., Vargo, S. L., and O'Brien, M. (2007). Competing through service: Insights from service-dominant logic. *Journal of Retailing*, 83(1), 5-18.

Luo, X. & Homburg, C. (2008). Satisfaction, complaint, and the stock value gap. *Journal of Marketing*, 72(July), 29-43.

Suh, J. C. & Yi, Y. (2006). When brand attitudes affect the customer satisfaction-loyalty relation: The moderating role of product involvement. *Journal of Consumer psychology*, 16(2), 145-155.

Vargo, S. L. & Lusch, R. F. (2004). Evolving to a new dominant logic for marketing. *Journal of Marketing*, 68(January), 1-17.

# The Impact of Emotions on Customers' Perception of Website Atmospheric Cues: An Empirical Cross-Cultural Investigation

Ebrahim Mazaheri, Concordia University, Canada
Marie-Odile Richard, University of Montreal, Canada
Michel Laroche, Concordia University, Canada

## EXTENDED ABSTRACT

Eroglu, Machleit and David (2001) categorized the environmental cues into two groups: high- and low-task relevant cues. They defined high-task relevant cues as all the site descriptors on the screen which facilitate the consumer's shopping goal attainment and low-task relevant cues as the ones that are "relatively inconsequential to the completion of the shopping task" (p. 180).

Previous research has studied the importance of site atmospheric cues such as site informativeness and entertainment (e.g. Davis, Wang, Lingridge, 2008; Hausman and Siekpe, 2009; Richard, 2005). It has been suggested that these site atmospheric cues influence customers variables such as website attitudes, involvement, flow, and purchase intentions (Hausman and Siekpe, 2009; Richard and Chandra, 2005). Surprisingly, the impact of emotions is often ignored in customers' evaluation of site atmospheric cues. The purpose of this research is twofold: First, consistent with Zajonc's (1980) theory of emotions we propose that the customers' emotions arise upon the initial Internet experience, which influence other affective and cognitive variables. As a result, we investigated the impacts of emotions on customers' perception of site high-task and low-task relevant atmospheric cues. Then, following the Stimulus-Organism-Response (SOR) framework developed by Mehrabian and Russell (1972) and previous literature, we hypothesize the impacts of customers' perception of site atmospheric cues on other consumer variables such as site attitudes and site involvement, and purchase intention.

Second, the attempt was made to compare the proposed model between two cultures: Chinese and Canadian. Given the wide reach of Internet and the fact that culture does impact the customers' responses to store atmospherics (Davice, Wang, and Lindridge, 2008); it is crucial to explore the role of culture in customers' reactions to the online store atmospherics. Based on Hofstede's (1991) cultural value dimensions, we hypothesized that the impact of high- and low- task relevant cues on customer variables vary across the two cultures.

For testing the hypotheses, 8 service industries were chosen: hotels, online bookstores, dental services, banks, vacation destination, restaurants, financial investments and plastic surgery. We selected four websites four dental services, two sites for online bookstores, four sites for restaurants, two sites for financial investments, four sites for hotels, four sites for plastic surgery, three sites for vacation destinations and two sites for banks. The subjects were randomly assigned to one of the twenty five websites. They were exposed to a real website of a service company and were asked to surf the site and collect information

Data were collected online using a computer lab in a large Northeastern university. After elimination, the data consist of 234 Chinese (54% female and 46% male) and 350 Canadian (58% female and 42% male). The majority of the respondents were undergraduate students (98.3% of Chinese and 98.9% of Canadian) between the age of 18 to 24 (75% of Chinese and 80% of Canadian).

The results of multi-group analyses in EQS strongly supported the overall model. Emotions strongly impacted the customers' perception of high- and low-task relevant cues in both cultures. Customers' perceptions of site atmospheric cues influenced customers' attitudes toward the site and site involvement; which in turn impacted purchase intentions. Moreover, the result suggested that the impacts of low-task relevant cues on site attitudes and site involvement are stronger for Chinese customers compared to their Canadian counterparts. On the other hand, customers' perceptions of high-task relevant cues on site attitudes and involvement was found to be stronger for Canadian customers compared to their Chinese counterparts.

## REFERENCES

Davis L., Wang S., and Lindridge A. (2008). Culture influences on emotional responses to on-line store atmospheric cues. *Journal of Business Research,* 61, 806-812.

Eroglu, S. A., Machleit, K. A., and Davis, L. M. (2001). Atmospheric qualities of online retailing: A conceptual model and implications. *Journal of Business Research,* 54 (2), 177-184.

Hausman, A.V. and Siekpe, J.S. (2009). The effect of web interface features on consumer online purchase intentions. *Journal of Business Research,* 62, 5-13.

Hofstede, G. (1991). *Cultures and Organizations: Software of the Mind.* New York: McGraw-Hill.

Mehrabian, A., and Russell, J. A. (1974). The basic emotional impact of environments. *Perception Motor Skills,* 38, 283-301.

Richard, M.-O. (2005). Modeling the impact of internet atmospherics on surfer . *Journal of Business Research,* 58(12), 1632-1642.

Richard, M.-O., and Chandra, R. (2005). A model of consumer web navigational : Conceptual development and application. *Journal of Business Research,* 58(8), 1019-1029.

Zajonc, R. B. (1980). Feeling and thinking: Preferences need no inferences. *American Psychologist,* 35(2), 151-175.

# A Meta-analysis on the Effectiveness of Publicity versus Advertising

Martin Eisend, European University Viadrina, Germany
Franziska Küster-Rohde, Free University Berlin, Germany

## EXTENDED ABSTRACT

This study tries to provide an answer to the question whether and when publicity (versus advertising) is more or less effective. For this purpose, we investigate the trade-off between enhanced credibility effects (due to third-party endorsement) and negative effects of recipients' exposure to negative information (due to lack of control over media content by the advertiser) by means of a meta-analysis.

Three models are applied in the literature to explain the effects of publicity versus advertising. The source credibility model shows that highly credible sources are viewed as more trustworthy and generate more attitude change than low-credibility sources. The information processing model assumes that intentional exposure to news and publicity enhances the number of cognitive responses. Publicity, compared to advertising, also lends greater salience to information. Enhanced information processability can produce positive responses towards the message and the product being evaluated. The information evaluation model assumes that publicity in comparison to advertising will not only lead to enhanced processing, it is also likely that the increase is higher for negative than for positive information. Negative information is also more salient. That leads to more thorough processing of negative information than positive information, which directly impacts object evaluation.

The literature search for the meta-analysis covered the period from 1971 (the publication year of a study that is considered the first empirical study on the topic) up to and including 2009. Only studies that investigated the impact of marketing-oriented publicity versus advertising on recipients concerning the following dependent variables were considered: attitude towards message, attitude towards brand, cognitive responses (total, positive, and negative), message processing, purchase/behavioral intention, source credibility, recall, and recognition. This search resulted in 30 independent samples with 257 effect sizes that could be included in the meta-analysis. The effect size metric selected for the analysis is the correlation coefficient; higher values of the coefficient indicate a stronger effect of marketing-oriented publicity over advertising on outcome variables. The meta-analytic integration procedures were performed taking a random-effects perspective. The integration of the correlations uses variance weights in order to consider the varying sample sizes of the studies. Furthermore, measurement errors were corrected by considering reliability coefficients of the dependent and independent variables. Weights for multiple measures were considered as well. Study moderator variables are used as predictors in a regression model in order to explain the heterogeneity of the effect sizes of dependent variables that are based on a sample of at least twenty effect sizes. Furthermore, a structural model analysis was performed. The suggested models include seven variables in total. That is, 28 off-diagonal cells have to be filled in order to produce the input of the correlation matrix for structural equation modeling. Hence, in addition to the results of the effect size integration, the studies were searched for further statistical measures reporting the relationship between the dependent variables.

The meta-analytic results show that marketing-oriented publicity (compared to advertising) has a positive effect on all dependent variables. The structural models show an acceptable fit. All coefficients are significant and indicate the assumed direction in the models. That is, marketing-oriented publicity versus advertising enhances source credibility, total, positive, and negative cognitive responses. Both source credibility and total cognitive responses

enhance attitude towards message, which enhances attitude towards brand. Positive cognitive responses enhance and negative cognitive responses reduce attitude towards brand. Attitude towards brand enhances purchase/behavioral intention. The total effects show that the source credibility path explains most of the variance in the dependent variables brand attitudes and purchase/behavioral intention; the effect is about twice as strong as the effect of the information evaluation model, and about five times as strong as the total effect of the information processing model. The moderator model showed that the effect of publicity versus advertising on positive cognitions and on source credibility decreases significantly for known versus unknown products. If we replace the coefficients in the model with the coefficients for the subgroups of known versus unknown products the results indicate a moderator effect. For unknown products, the total effects become stronger. For known products, however, the total effects become negative with the negativity effect increasing and the source credibility effect even reversing due to a superior effect of advertising over marketing-oriented publicity.

The results of the meta-analysis support the effect of publicity over advertising that is due to a source credibility effect, an information processing effect, and an information evaluation effect. While the last effect is an overall negative effect, both other paths show a positive effect, with the source credibility effect being about twice as strong as the negative effect due to evaluation of negative information. The results show that the trade-off between credibility and control is in favor of the credibility of the source. This effect is moderated by prior product knowledge, though. The described relationship holds and even becomes stronger for unknown products. However, the effect changes for known products where the total effect of the source on dependent variables becomes even negative. These results show that marketing-oriented publicity versus advertising is superior for products where consumers lack prior knowledge. Indeed, most studies that have investigated and supported the positive effects of media coverage refer to product innovations, product pre-announcements, or products with which most consumers are not yet familiar. The meta-analytic results further contribute to the research on the negativity effect as triggered by publicity, because they support this effect but also show that an overall evaluation of publicity effects needs to take different effect paths into account in order to produce an overall effect on consumers. By introducing prior knowledge as an important moderator for the negativity effect, the findings show that the negativity effect can be outweighed by a positive source credibility effect in case consumers do not yet know a product.

# Bounded Defensive: Advertising Deception, Deception Knowledge, and Meta-cognitive Expectancies

Guang-Xin Xie, University of Massachusetts Boston, U.S.A.
David M. Boush, University of Oregon, U.S.A.
Courtney N. Boerstler, University of Oregon, U.S.A.

## EXTENDED ABSTRACT

Advertisers often emphasize positive product attributes and promise superior value. When consumers' experience falls short of expectations, the perceived discrepancies are often ascribed to advertising deception (Russo et al. 1981). Using the framework of the Persuasion Knowledge Model (Friestad and Wright 1994), we propose that consumers' deception knowledge and meta-cognitive expectancies influence their attitudes toward ads and brands in two ways: while the expected seriousness of the consequences of being misled aggravates the negative effect of deception, the optimistic tendency to trust the claims attenuates this effect.

### Experiment 1

Experiment 1 employed a 2 (deception knowledge: more salient vs. less salient, between) x 2 (high- vs. low-stake, between) x 2 (high- vs. low- deceptiveness ads, within) mixed design. Participants (N=133) were asked to carefully evaluate six print advertisements (pre-tested) presented on PC screens. For each ad, they were asked to identify the brand name first, and then answered attitudinal questions on 9-point scales. Deception knowledge salience was manipulated by the priming instructions at the beginning of the questionnaire. The one-page instructions described the nature of deception knowledge, common deceptive tactics, and cues to detect advertising deception. Participants in the control condition were not primed. The seriousness of expected consequences and deceptiveness were manipulated by having the participants view different types of print ads. In the high-stake condition (more serious consequences), the participants rated six ads: three were high in deceptiveness and three were low in deceptiveness (within-group). This was repeated in the low-stake condition (less serious consequences).

Participants in the primed condition (M=5.17) rated the ads as more deceptive than those in the unprimed condition (M=4.61), $F(1, 130)=4.23, p=.032$. The interaction between manipulated deceptiveness and deception knowledge salience was not significant, $F(1, 130)=.38, p=.35$. But the deceptiveness had a significant negative impact on attitude toward the ads: the attitude (M=3.35) was more negative toward high-deceptiveness ads than low- deceptiveness ads (M=4.62), $F(1, 128)=75.22, p<.001$. The interaction between deceptiveness and high- vs. low-stake situation was significant: the negative attitude (M=2.84) was significantly stronger toward the deceptive than non-deceptive ads (M=4.83) in the high-stake condition, $F(1, 130)=38.93, p<.001$. In the low-stake condition, however, attitude toward deceptive ads (M=4.60) was not significantly different from non-deceptive ads (M=4.64), $F(1, 130)=.02, p=.89$.

### Experiment 2

The purpose of Experiment 2 (N=176) is to examine the effect of optimistic expectancy and need for cognition in relation to the outcome expectancy of deception. We followed the same procedure as that in Experiment 1. In addition, the optimistic expectancy scale was asked for each advertisement, and participants also completed the Need for Cognition (NFC) scale (Cacioppo et al. 1984) at the end. Structural equation modeling was used to test mediation/moderation effects following the methods suggested by Judd et al. (2001). In the best-fit model, the expected seriousness of consequences moderated the effect of advertising deceptiveness on attitude toward ads. The moderation effects of all other exogenous variables were not significant at $p < .05$. In comparison, the attitude differences toward brands differed significantly across the average, the difference of optimistic expectancy in high- and low-deceptiveness ads conditions, as well as the individual difference in NFC. The proposed moderation effect was found in the attitude towards the brands, but not in the attitude toward advertisements.

The results suggest that optimistic expectancy can function as both a moderator and mediator of the attitude difference toward brands between high- and low-deceptiveness ads. The advertised claims (deceptive or not) may have caused more optimistic expectancy, which in turn, leads to less negative attitude toward the advertised brands.

### Discussion

In two experiments, we demonstrate that consumer deception knowledge and expectancies may not only undermine advertising effectiveness as widely acknowledged, but also regulate the effect of deceptiveness in favor of the advertised brands. The salience of deception tactics schema can significantly increase the perceived deceptiveness of ads but the salience does not necessarily lead to more negative attitude toward the ads. More interestingly, the optimistic expectancy can be both a moderator and mediator for the negative effect of advertising deception on attitude toward the brands. A possible explanation is that the optimistic expectancy serves two functions. The mediation effect occurs because expectancy is a significant motivating factor in favor of the brands (but not the ads). In comparison, the moderation effect occurs as a result of individual difference in the extent to which consumers would like to think positively about the brands. Even when the advertised claims are perceived more deceptive, those with more optimistic expectancy would have less negative attitude toward the brands.

## REFERENCES

Cacioppo, John T., Richard E. Petty, and Chuan Feng Kao (1984), "The Efficient Assessment of Need for Cognition," *Journal of Personality Assessment*, 48 (3), 306-07.

Friestad, Marian and Peter Wright (1994), "The Persuasion Knowledge Model: How People Cope with Persuasion Attempts," *Journal of Consumer Research*, 21 (1), 1-31.

Judd, Charles M, David A. Kenny, and Gary H. McClelland (2001), "Estimating and Testing Mediation and Moderation in Within-Subject Designs," *Psychological Methods*, 6 (2), 115-34.

Russo, J. Edward, Barbara L. Metcalf, and Debra Stephens (1981), "Identifying Misleading Advertising," *Journal of Consumer Research*, 8 (2), 119-31.

# Match-Up Effects Happen for a Reason: The Impact of Activating Persuasion Knowledge on Endorser Effectiveness

Leen Adams, Hogeschool-Universiteit Brussel, Belgium
Maggie Geuens, Ghent University, Belgium
Tina Tessitore, Ghent University, Belgium

## EXTENDED ABSTRACT

An experiment was set up to clarify the when and why of endorser effectiveness. We found that match-up effects are more likely in case of high than low activation of persuasion knowledge (advertising vs. product placement) due to differences in perceptions of fit. The depth of processing did not contribute…

The use of endorsers is a common ad tactic. Research on endorser effectiveness has put forward the match-up hypothesis which states that the message conveyed by the image of the endorser and of the product should converge (Kahle and Homer 1985). However, the results of empirical studies testing this hypothesis are inconclusive. Therefore, researchers started to investigate moderators.

For example, Kang and Herr (2006) recently showed that the depth of processing and/or the sensitivity to source biases moderate the impact of endorsers on persuasion. More specifically, in case of heuristic processing and/or in case of low sensitivity to source biases, endorsers merely serve as cues, whereas in case of in-depth processing and/or in case of high sensitivity to source biases, the link between the source and the product becomes important and match-up effects on persuasion arise.

Although prior studies already tested moderators related to the depth and the type of processing, they did not examine the relative weight of each antecedent in the formation of match-up effects yet. The contribution the current research would like to make is to integrate the different prior perspectives and further clarify the conditions in which match-up effects can be expected and why in particular.

Therefore, we turn to the Persuasion Knowledge Model (PKM) of Friestad and Wright (1994). Research built on the PKM shows that the depth of processing only explains skeptical responses to persuasion to the extent that it also leads to a more intense activation of PK (Campbell and Kirmani 2000). Based hereupon, we predict that the activation of PK, rather than the mere depth of processing, drives the perception of the level of product-endorser fit, and as such, determines the persuasiveness of product-endorser combinations used in marketing campaigns.

Additionally, we also look into the role of specific perceptions of tactic appropriateness next to the more general perceptions of persuasive intent (i.e., activation of PK), as the results of Kang and Herr (2006) also indicate that a product-endorser match generally leads to highly favorable attitudes, even after an endorser bias is primed. This is counter-intuitive given the assumption that the activation of PK leads to resistance to persuasion and thus, to unfavorable responses (Campbell and Kirmani 2000). However, concerning the latter, Wei, Fischer, and Main (2008) showed that the activation of PK only had a strong negative impact on evaluations when respondents perceived the stimulus to be inappropriate. So, perceptions of tactic appropriateness also seem to determine consumer responses to persuasion attempts.

Therefore, we set up an experiment with a 2 (level of product-endorser fit: non-fit vs. fit) x 2 (level of PK activation: high vs. low) x 2 (depth of processing: high vs. low) between-subjects design in the context of promoting foods as healthy by means of healthy-looking endorsers. We also measured perceived product-endorser fit and perceived appropriateness of the persuasion attempt to test whether they mediate match-up effects on persuasion.

To investigate the impact of depth of processing, we implemented a distraction task (Williams, Fitzsimons, and Block 2004). To manipulate the level of PK activation, we used TV ads versus product placements (Balasubramanian, Karrh, and Patwardhan 2006). Within these formats, real-life stimuli showing either congruent (i.e., healthy model and healthy food) or incongruent product-endorser (i.e., healthy model and unhealthy food) combinations were sought. To prevent confounds, we set out standards for content and execution style and selected several (i.e., four) stimuli per condition (Jackson, O' Keefe, and Jacobs 1988). An online pretest with our target group (i.e., female respondents between 18 and 26 years old) showed that the selected stimuli contained the intended level of product-endorser fit.

In the main experiment, run in a lab, 252 young females participated. In two seemingly independent studies, we first randomly exposed them to one of the 16 stimuli, whether or not accompanied by the distraction task, and then asked stimulus related questions (attitudes and attention). A second study with filler and target questions concerning product considerations and purchase intentions followed. Finally, we incorporated questions about mediators, manipulation checks and covariates.

As predicted, we found that in a clear persuasive context, the difference between a product-endorser fit and a non-fit was clearly perceived, which led to a significantly more favorable attitude towards the congruent versus the incongruent stimulus and towards the accompanying endorser. Moreover, the congruent combinations were perceived to be more appropriate than the incongruent ones, also partially explaining the match-up effects. In a context in which the persuasive intent was less obvious, there was no significant difference in perception of product-endorser fit. As a result, no match-up effects were found.

As such, we demonstrated the usefulness of the PKM for the endorsement domain (Friestad and Wright 1994). Based on this model, we were able to clarify the type of processing that leads to the perception of a match versus a mismatch between products and endorsers, and as such, extend prior research (Kang and Herr 2006). Further research could study whether the perception of product-endorser fit and the perceived appropriateness of a product-endorser combination are independent concepts and examine their relative contribution.

Despite the contributions of this study, we did not find the same results on product related responses as on ad related responses. However, prior research has encountered the same issue (Till and Busler 2000). Explanations could be found in the differences between these dependent measures, as, for example, they tend to result from a different type of processing (i.e., rational vs. emotional, conscious vs. unconscious).

The current study also suffers from the limitation that we used ads versus product placements to manipulate PK activation. We controlled for several potential confounds (e.g., type of creative strategy: transformational and positive), but from a theoretical point of view, this was not the cleanest manipulation. Further research could, therefore, manipulate PK activation in a more conservative way. However, using several real-life stimuli has the advantage that they enhance the external validity of the results.

## REFERENCES

Balasubramanian, Siva K., James A. Karrh, and Hemant Patwardhan. (2006), "Audience Response to Product Placements: An Integrative Framework and Future Research Agenda," *Journal of Advertising*, 35(3), 115-41.

Campbell, Meg C. and Amna Kirmani. (2000), "Consumers' Use of Persuasion Knowledge: The Effects of Accessibility and Cognitive Capacity on Perceptions of an Influence Agent," *Journal of Consumer Research*, 27(1), 69–83.

Friestad, Marian and Peter Wright. (1994), "The Persuasion Knowledge Model: How People Cope With Persuasion Attempts," *Journal of Consumer Research*, 21(1), 1-31.

Jackson, Sally, Daniel J. O'Keefe, and Scott Jacobs. (1988), "The Search for Reliable Generalizations About Messages: A Comparison of Research Strategies," *Human Communication Research*, 15(1), 127-42.

Kahle, Lynn R. and Pamela M. Homer. (1985), "Physical Attractiveness of the Celebrity Endorser: A Social Adaptation Perspective," *Journal of Consumer Research*, 11(4), 954-61.

Kang, Yong-Soon and Paul M. Herr. (2006), "Beauty and the Beholder: Toward an Integrative Model of Communication Source Effects," *Journal of Consumer Research*, 33(1), 123-30.

Till, Brian D. and Michael Busler. (2000), "The Match-up Hypothesis: Physical Attractiveness, Expertise, and the Role of Fit on Brand Attitude, Purchase Intent and Brand Beliefs," *Journal of Advertising*, 29(3), 1-13.

Wei, Mei-Ling, Eileen Fischer, and Kelley J. Main. (2008), "An Examination of the Effects of Activating Persuasion Knowledge on Consumer Response to Brands Engaging in Covert Marketing," *Journal of Public Policy and Marketing*, 27(1), 34-44.

Williams, Patti, Gavan J. Fitzsimons, and Lauren G. Block. (2004), "When Consumers do not Recognize "Benign" Intention Questions as Persuasion Attempts," *Journal of Consumer Research*, 31(3), 540-50.

# Mere Proactivity Effects of Sales-related Service Offerings: A Field Experiment

Walter Herzog, WHU-Otto Beisheim School of Management, Germany
Mike Hammerschmidt, University of Mannheim, Germany

## EXTENDED ABSTRACT

Excellent post-sales services are considered to be an effective strategy for stimulating customer loyalty. However, as relationships evolve, customers' repurchase intentions become increasingly salient making so-called pre-sales services for existing customers an important feature of relationship marketing. For example, a car dealer might offer the opportunity to test drive a new car in temporal proximity to a prospective repurchase decision (Bhattacharya and Bolton 2000). To the best of our knowledge, pre-sales services have been the subject of scientific inquiry only in the context of customer acquisition but not in the context of relationship marketing. Pre-sales services like product trials can either be provided reactively, i.e. in response to customer requests, or they can be provided proactively, i.e., the firm takes the initiative to contact customers and offer the product trial (Challagalla, Venkatesh, and Kohli 2009). Despite the enormous relevance of pre-sales services in the repurchase phase of a customer's buying process, it is not clear if suppliers should really offer these services proactively or remain with their traditional reactive strategy. In the present paper, we answer this question for product trials by existing customers.

At first glance, a positive effect of a proactive strategy could be fully attributed to the fact that some customers (so-called "compliers") are encouraged to test the product, which in turn enhances their loyalty. This argument implies that the effect of proactively offering a product trial on customer loyalty is completely mediated by the customer's increased probability to experience the product (Jo 2008). However, we propose that this argument neglects that "the mere act of a supplier proactively reaching out to customers" (Challagalla et al. 2009, 73) produces psychological and behavioral effects above and beyond the effects of using the service (product trial). More specifically, we argue that there are two mere proactivity effects: First, a proactive strategy results in a significant proportion of customers rejecting the offer as they do not have interest in a product trial (so-called "never-takers"). We argue that never-takers, who do not test the product independent of any company activities, are likely to perceive the offer as an intrusive tactic which undermines their loyalty (Deci, Koestner, and Ryan 1999). Second, there are customers trying the product independent of the company's strategy ("always-takers"). We assume that always-takers, due to their intrinsic interest in the product, are likely to perceive a firm proactively and voluntarily offering product trials as likeable and empathic (Palmatier et al. 2009), which should increase their loyalty.

Our hypotheses are tested by means of a large-scale field experiment with more than 3000 customers of a car manufacturer. The experiment consisted in proactively offering a test drive to a randomized set of customers by means of a personalized invitation by their respective car dealers (proactive condition) and withholding the offer from the remaining customers (reactive condition), i.e. the latter group could conduct a self-initiated test drive under the very same conditions. Our analysis combines experimental, psychometric, and behavioral data. We used the principal stratification approach (based on Rubin's Causal Model) to estimate the effect of proactive strategy on repurchase behavior via relationship satisfaction with the car dealer and brand loyalty for the three latent customer classes or "principal strata": compliers, always-takers, and never takers (Jo and Muthén 2001; Frangakis and Rubin 2002). The identification of principal stratification models requires the inclusion of covariates predicting class membership (Mealli and Rubin 2002). In this study, we consider perceived value of test-driving, perceived importance

of the brand, age, gender, price of the current car, and number of purchased cars of the brand.

For compliers we find that a proactive product trial strategy initiated by the dealer directly boosts brand loyalty-creating a direct upstream spillover to the aggregated manufacturer level-and indirectly enhances brand loyalty via increasing dealer satisfaction, i.e. creating an indirect upstream spillover. The increased brand loyalty in turn enhances repurchase probability. Therefore, at a first glance, the predominant goal of dealers' proactive strategies could be to encourage customers to use a service (product trial) that they would otherwise not use. However, this focus neglects the fact that compliers only account for a very small proportion of the customer base and hence exclusively targeting this group hinders the deployment of economies of scale. Moreover, it neglects that–against intuition–significant effects can also occur for customers whose service usage decision is independent from dealers' actions (always-takers and never takers).

In support of our hypotheses, we not only find significant proactivity effects for compliers but also for always-takers and never takers, i.e. we find *mere* proactivity effects. Specifically, we find that for never-takers and always-takers satisfaction with the dealer fully mediates the proactivity-brand loyalty link, i.e. we only observe indirect upstream spillovers. With respect to always-takers, by providing proactive offers the dealer can not only enhance customer evaluations for the own business but indirectly facilitates the generation of favourable manufacturer-related evaluations although the manufacturer does neither provide nor control the proactive offerings. For the never-takers, we find that the frustration following a proactive (i.e. intrusive) action is not only targeted to the dealer but subsequently also to the brand.

It has to be noted that the observed positive dealer- and brand-related effects for the always-takers are exclusively caused by proactively offering a service that is used anyway by the consumer, i.e. it is the incremental effect of mere proactivity beyond and above the effect of using the offered test drive. At the other hand, the negative response of never takers to a proactive strategy (negative mere proactivity effect) is exclusively caused by the unsolicited offer of a service that they would never use.

## REFERENCES

Bhattacharya, C. B. and Ruth N. Bolton (2000), "Relationship Marketing in Mass Markets," in *Handbook of Relationship Marketing*, ed. Jagdish N. Sheth and Atul Parvatiyar, Thousand Oaks, CA: Sage, 327-54.

Challagalla, Goutam, R. Venkatesh, and Ajay K. Kohli (2009), "Proactive Postsales Service: When and Why Does It Pay Off?" *Journal of Marketing*, 73 (March), 70-87.

Deci, Edward L., Richard Koestner, and Richard M. Ryan (1999), "A Meta-Analytic Review of Experiments Examining the Effects of Extrinsic Rewards on Intrinsic Motivation," *Psychological Bulletin*, 125 (6), 627-68.

Frangakis, Constantine E. and Donald B. Rubin (2002), "Principal Stratification in Causal Inference," *Biometrics*, 58 (March), 21-29.

Jo, Booil (2008), "Causal Inference in Randomized Experiments With Mediational Processes," *Psychological Methods*, 13 (December), 314-36.

Jo, Booil and Bengt O. Muthén (2001), "Modeling of intervention effects with noncompliance: A latent variable modeling approach for randomized trials," in *New developments and techniques in structural equation modeling*, ed. George A. Marcoulides and Randall E. Schumacker, Mahwah, NJ: Lawrence Erlbaum Associates, 57-87.

Mealli, Fabrizia and Donald B. Rubin (2002), Discussion of "Estimation of Intervention Effects with Noncompliance: Alternative Model Specifications" by Booil Jo, *Journal of Educational and Behavioral Statistics*, 27 (Winter), 411-15.

Palmatier, Robert W., Cheryl Burke Jarvis, Jennifer R. Bechkoff, and Frank R. Kardes (2009), "The Role of Customer Gratitude in Relationship Marketing," *Journal of Marketing*, 73 (September), 1-18.

# Conflicting Selves and the Role of Possessions: Exploring Transgenders' Self-Identity Conflict

Ayalla Ruvio, Temple University, USA
Russell Belk, York University, Canada

## EXTENDED ABSTRACT

While the notion of possessions as an extension of the self has received extensive research attention (e.g. Belk 1988; Hirschman and Labarbera 1990), most of the literature has focused on possessions as reflecting a holistic self or specific aspects of the self (e.g., uniqueness). However, according to Erikson (1956), conflicts between different aspects of their self-identity are experienced by all individuals throughout their lifetime. Though some argue that possessions play an important role in cases of self-conflict (Csikszentmihalyi and Rochberg-Halton 1981), there have been very few studies on this subject. Taking a qualitative approach, this study seeks to understand the role possessions play in the formation, development, coping and resolution of the conflict between different selves using an extreme example of gender identity conflict--transgendersim.

Since gender is one of the most defining characteristics of the self (Gagne, Tewksbury and McGaughey 1997; Rudacille 2006), incongruencey between gender identity and one's genital configuration leads to a gender identity conflict. The establishment of gender identity occurs during early childhood, becomes an internalized aspect of one's self and is virtually immutable. Transgender people experience a gender identity conflict which compels them to develop an alternative gender identity and enact a gender presentation that does not coincide with their sex (Gagne et al. 1997). In this study, using grounded theory analysis and interpretation of five in-depth, unstructured interviews with male-to-female transgenders, we explore the way transgenders utilize material possessions in negotiating their gender conflict. We assert that insights gathered from these extreme cases of self-conflict can educate us about more common or usual behaviors (Katz 1998).

The formation of an alternative gender identity requires transgenders to cross over either temporarily or permanently from one sex/gender category to another (Gagne et al. 1997; Lev 2004). In Western society, dominated by the binary perceptions of gender, the act of crossing over challenges the cultural and structural social order, exposing the person to social sanctions. Several multiple stage developmental models have been used to describe this process, building on Erikson's (1956) social development theory.

Our findings are consistent with Gagne et al.'s (1997) integrative model. In its first stage, **conflict emergence,** our informants experienced transgendered feelings, but have not labeled them as such. This stage occurs during childhood, and our informants reported feeling that something was wrong with them (Bockting and Coleman 2007; Katz 1998). The gendered meaning of possessions (such as clothing and toys) raised their feelings to the level of conscious awareness. Possessions also defined the boundaries of socially accepted behaviors. While using possessions the "wrong way" (e.g., a boy wearing a skirt) resulted in acts of correction or punishment from others in an attempt to address the "problem", at the same time they allowed the informants to engage in initial cross-gender socialization.

**Identity exploration**, the second stage, involved an extensive information search in an effort to label the source of the conflict as well as reach out to similar others. Our informants reported building a parallel world that enabled them to practice the performance of their new identity. Possessions (e.g., a secret cosmetics box) helped them segregate their conflicting identities, and thus, minimize and control their conflict.

In the third stage, **coming out to one's self**, our informants coped with and internalized the meaning of their new transgender identity ("this is who I am"). Possessions played different roles in the variety of coping strategies utilized (Lazarus and Folkman 1984) such as denial (dressing like their original sex), acceptance (dressing according to their alternative gender identity), and self-control (keeping their alternative gendered possessions private). However, in order to resolve the conflict, transgerders had to accept and build their alternative gender identity and develop its public presentation ("to pass").

In the fourth stage, **coming out to others**, the participants disclosed their transgender identity to significant others (spouses, family, friends), and often experienced rejection as a result (Lev 2004). Passing in this stage was not enough for them as they felt the need to present a convincing public image of cross-gender identity. As part of the new self, possessions were presented as embedded in the new gender identity.

Striving to find their "true" identity, most of our informants reached the final stage of **conflict resolution.** They explored various identities in an attempt to achieve a coherent identity in which transgenderism was only a part. Decisions regarding to what extent to cross over (e.g., have full surgery, just take hormones, etc.) were made in order to finalize their private and public identity. Possessions were no longer perceived as a means to project gender identity but as a means to express a new congruent self-identity.

Our study can be viewed in the context of the over arching theory of the extended self. The findings indicate that a person's process of dealing with self-conflict is reflected in the use of possessions. As the conflict evolves, the role of possessions changes. They surface the conflict to the level of consciousness, are part of the coping process, and reflect the conflict's resolution and the eventual formation of a new self-identity. We posit that our findings can be generalized to many other self-conflicts such as those involving athleticism, overt sexiness, and class affiliation, thereby contributing to the literatures on transgenders and the extended self.

## REFERENCES

Belk, Russell W. (1988), "Possessions and the extended self," *Journal of Consumer Research*, 14 (September), 139-168.

Csikszentmihalyi, Mihaly and Eugene Rochberg-Halton (1981), *The Meaning of Things: Domestic Symbols and the Self*. Cambridge University Press

Erikson, Erik H. (1968), *Identity: Youth and Crisis*. New York: Norton.

Gagne, Patricia, Richard Tewksbury and Deanna McGaughey (1997), "Coming out and crossing over: Identity formation of proclamation in the transgender community," *Gender and Society*, 11(4), 478-508.

Hirschman, Elizabeth C. and Pricilla A. Labarbera (1990), "Dimensions of possession importance," *Psychology and Marketing*, 7(3), 215-233.

Katz, Steven M. (1998), *Twenty Million New Customers: Understanding Gay Men's Consumer Behavior*. New York: The Haworth Press,.

Lazarus, Richard S. and Susan Folkman (1984), *Stress, Appraisal, and Coping*. New York: Springer.

Lev, Arlene (2004), *Transgender Emergence: Therapeutic Guidelines for Working with Gender-Variant People and Their Families*. New York: The Haworth Clinical Practice Press.

Rudacille, Deborah (2006), *The Riddle of Gender: Science, Activism, and Transgender Rights*, New York: Pantheon.

# Conflicting Imperatives of Modesty and Vanity Among Young Women In The Arabian Gulf

Rana Sobh, Qatar University, Qatar
Russell Belk, York University, Canada
Justin Gressel, University of Texas-Pan American, USA

## EXTENDED ABSTRACT

Muslim women's clothing is a visible form of public consumption, and has been the subject of much debate within social science literatures. A large body of work has looked at the diverse meanings and connotations of the Muslim veil and the practice of *hijab* (observing Muslim women's dress code) in many Muslim countries including Egypt (e.g., El-Guindi, 1999b), Turkey (Sandikci and Ger, 2007; Secor, 2002; Gole, 2002), Mali (Shultz, 2007), Cote D'Ivoire (leBlanc, 2000), Indonesia (Jones 2003), South India (Oseall and Osealla, 2007), and London (Tarlo, 2007b). However, the black abaya within oil-rich Gulf countries is embedded in a different contemporary local context and is increasingly associated with status and wealth (Abaza, 2007). Young Muslim women's dress in the Gulf States of Qatar and United Arab Emirates (UAE) is both emotionally and politically charged.

The Gulf States are unique for several reasons: 1) There is a distinct and strong ethos of traditional dress for both men and women, 2) There is an omnipresent awareness of Islam and religious values in shaping identities and informing behavior, 3) There has been a rapid increase in wealth due to petrodollars, and 4) There is a dramatic presence of foreigners from both Western and Non-Western cultures, such only around 17% of Qatar residents are Qataris and 16% of Emirates residents are Emirati. The latter conditions create a situation unique in the immigration literature in which there is pressure for the locals to acculturate to the immigrant rather than the more normal reverse situation. Locals increasingly fear the dissolution of their ethnic identity and therefore strive to emphasize their authenticity and ethnic affiliation distinction through wearing ethnic dress but also through other consumption styles such as extravagant conspicuous and luxurious consumption that foreigners in general cannot afford. Furthermore, the main acculturative agent in our context is not the dominant host culture as opposed to the minority or immigrant culture, but rather the forces of globalization and more specifically transnational Western consumer culture and its underpinning ideology that fundamentally conflicts with the local religious and patriarchal principles. Hence, new clothing styles and adornment practices are increasingly adopted by young women in the region and reflect the conflicting forces of Western values that emphasize display of women's beauty and sexuality in the public sphere and traditional values requiring modesty and promoting a virtuous public domain. The abaya itself has been gradually reinvented and has evolved from being a concealing garment that hides women's sexuality and beauty in public to an embellished fashionable, trendy haute couture garment that enhances beauty and reveals sexuality, all supposedly without undermining the local look. We propose to understand the dynamics underlying conflicting imperatives of modesty and vanity and to probe the ambivalence inherent in such performative constructions of identity and conceptions of the self as well as explore how young women negotiate and reconcile resulting tensions.

In-depth interviews were conducted with twenty four middle class university students in business from Qatar University (12) and American University of Sharjah (12). The informants ranged in age from 17 to 22. In addition to interviews, all researchers used observations of clothing and adornment practices in public places by young women (e.g., university, malls, restaurants) and the female researcher observed clothing and adornment practices in private spaces as well (homes, social gatherings, fashion shows, weddings and other women's parties). Projective techniques were used and consisted of showing participants a set of stimulus pictures of girls wearing different types of abayas and using adornment practices across the spectrum from vain to modest.

Our findings reveal that young women resolve conflicting tensions between the conflicting imperatives of the transnational consumer ideology and traditional local values through a number of appropriation and adaptation processes. Informants construct idiographic meanings of prevalent religious, cultural and fashion discourses informed by the two conflicting ideologies. They negotiate dominant values in the Western ideology, adopting and adapting some while resisting and rejecting others. They appropriate global fashion trends to create local glamorous fashion trends and symbolically charged clothing practices that give them a sense of uniqueness and superiority over expatriates and foreigners. In effect they out-global the global consumer culture representatives, at least in some respects. Young women also enact Western style identities in uncontrolled spaces and settings such as in women-only gatherings and gender segregated spaces where tensions between the traditional and modern and the modest and vain are alleviated.

While accepting and acknowledging the local value systems, they manipulate and reinterpret some of the meanings to justify their clothing practices and condemn those of others. Regardless of their degree of religiosity, Islam was used by all informants to justify their clothing practices whether vain, modest or somewhere between the two extremes. Informants negotiate their need for beauty display in public within the Islamic discourses of beauty and the legitimacy of good self-presentation and enjoyment of life.

Besides, young women seem to reconcile opposing pressures by injecting Western symbols such as designer names and fashion trends and patterns into traditional garments in order to rejuvenate and bestow modernity on them. This reinvention of tradition gives them a feeling of connection with the youth consumer culture and engagement in the world of fashion while still maintaining connections to local traditions that they are proud of. The purpose of wearing the abaya is also manipulated to be more aligned with Western ideologies and beauty discourses. Ironically, the abaya is interpreted by locals as a camouflage garment that makes them look taller and thinner, hence enhancing their beauty and hiding their body imperfections, tendencies which are in accordance with Western fashion discourses. Playing with meanings and altering the original uses and meanings of the abaya can be interpreted as unintentional resistance (Ger and Belk 1996) of the local hegemony emphasizing social conformity and as an affirmation of young women's power in managing their appearances and enacting their identities in public. Following Blumer (1969), the abaya fashion seems to help young women mediate cultural contractions they are subject to in some Arab Gulf countries and to adjust in a disciplined and orderly way to their fast moving society to help cope with the major social changes their countries have been undergoing as a result of globalization.

# REFERENCES

Abaza, Mona (2007), "Shifting Landscapes of fashion in Contemporary Egypt", *Fashion Theory*, 11(2/3), 281-289.

Abu Odeh, Lama (1993), "Post-Colonial Feminism and the Veil: Thinking the Difference", *Feminist Review*, 43 (Spring), 26-37.

Al-Albani, Mohammed Nasr Adeen (2002), *The Jilbab and the Muslim Woman in the Qur'an and Sunnah* [Jilbab almaraa el Muslimah fi al Kitab wa Assunnah], Dar Es Salam.

Al-Qaradawi, Yusuf (1995), *The Lawful and the Prohibited in Islam* [Al-Halal Wal-Haram Fil Islam], Translators Kamal El-Helbawy, M Moinuddin Siddiqui, Syed Shukry, KUWAIT, Al Faisal Press.

Alsanea, Rajaa (2007), *Girls of Riyadh*, New York: The Penguin Press

Appadurai, Arjun (1990), "Disjuncture and Difference in the Global Economy," in *Global Culture: Nationalism, Globalization, and Modernity*, ed. Mike Featherstone, London: Sage, 295–310.

Arnould, Eric J. and Linda L. Price (2000), "Authenticating Acts and Authoratative Performances: Questing for Self and Community," in *The Why of Consumption*, ed. S. Ratneshwar, David G. Mick, and Cynthia Huffman, London: Routledge, 140–63.

Askegaard, Søren, Eric J. Arnould, and Dannie Kjeldgaard (2005), "Postassimilationist Ethnic Consumer Research: Qualifications and Extensions," *Journal of Consumer Research*, 32 (June), 160-70.

Balasescu, Alexandru (2007), "Haute Couture in Tehran: Two Faces of an Emerging Fashion Scene," *Fashion Theory*, 11 (2/3): 299-318.

——— (2003), "Tehran Chic: Islamic headsarves, Fashion Designers, and New Geographies of Modernity", *Fashion Theory*, 7 (1), 39-56

Belk, Russell W. (1988), "Possessions and the Extended Self," *Journal of Consumer Research*, 15 (2), 139-168.

——— (1991), "The Ineluctable Mysteries of Possessions,: *Journal of Social Behavior and Personality*, 6 (6, June), 17-55.

——— (2003), "Shoes and Self,"*Advances in Consumer Research*, Vol. 29, Punam Anand Keller and Dennis Rook, eds., Valdosta, GA: Association for Consumer Research, 2003, 27-33.

——— and Janeen Arnould Costa (1998), "The Mountain Man Myth: A Contemporary Consuming Fantasy,' *Journal of Consumer Research*, 25 (December), 218-240.

——— , Güliz Ger, and Søren Askegaard (2003), "The Fire of Desire: A Multi-Sited Inquiry into Consumer Passion," *Journal of Consumer Research*, 30 (December), 326-351.

Bennett, Andy (1999), *Popular Music and Youth Culture: Music, Identity, and Place*, London: Palgrave.

Bier, Kurt (1986), "Justification in Ethics," in *Justification Nomos XXVII*, J. Roland Pennock and John Chapman, ed., New York: New York University Press, 3-27.

Blumer, Herbert (1969), "Fashion: From Class Differentiation to Collective Selection," *Sociological Quarterly*, 10 (Spring), 275-291.

Boulanouar, W. Aisha (2006), "Dressing for Success: A background to Muslim Women's Clothing", *New Zealand Journal of Asian Studies*, 2 (12),135-157.

Clunas, Craig (2004), *Superfluous Things: Material Culture and Social Status in Early Modern China*, Honolulu: University of Hawaii Press.

Crockett, David and Melanie Wallendorf (1998), "Sociological Perspectives on Imposed School Dress Codes: Consumption as Attempted Suppression of Class and Group Symbolism," *Journal of Macromarketing*, 18 (Fall), 115-131.

El Guindi, Fadwa (1981), "Veiling Infitah with Muslim Ethic: Egypt's Contemporary Islamic Movement", Social Problems. 4 (April), 465-485.

El Guindi, Fadwa(1999), "Veiling Resistance", *Fashion Theory*, 3(1), 51-80.

Fabricant, Stacey M. and Stephen J. Gould (1983), "Women's Makeup Careers: An Interpretive Study of Color Cosmetics Use and 'Face Value'," *Psychology and Marketing*, 10 (November/December), 531-548.

Forsythe, Sandra, Mary F. Drake, and Jane H. Hogan (1985), "Influence of Clothing Attributes on Perception of Personal Characteristics," in *The Psychology of Fashion*, Michael Solomon, ed., Lexington, MA: Lexington Books, 267-277.

Ger, Guliz and Russell W. Belk (1996), "I'd Like to Buy the World a Coke: Consumptionscapes of the "Less Affluent World," *Journal of Consumer Policy*, 19, 271-304.

Gibson, Pamela (2000), "Redressing the Balance: Patriarchy, Postmodernism and Feminism," in *Fashion Cultures: Theories, Explorations and Analysis*, Stella bruzzi and Pamela Gibson, ed., London: Routledge, 349-362.

Giesler, Markus, Marius K. Luedicke, and Berrin Ozergin (2009), "American Self-Enhancement Culture and the Cyborg Consumer: Consumer Identity Construction Beyond the Dominance of Authenticity", in *Advances in Consumer Research*, 36, Duluth, MN : Association for Consumer Research, 72-75.

Gole, Nilufer (2002), "Islam in Public: New Visibilities and New Imageries", *Fashion Theory*, 14 (1), 173-190

Greenwalt, Kurt (1986), "Distinguishing Justifications from Excuses," *Law and Contemporary Problems*, 49 (Summer), 89-108

Hannerz, Ulf (1987). The world in creolisation. *Africa*, 57, 546-559.

——— (1992), *Cultural complexity: Studies in the social organization of meaning.* York: Columbia University Press.

Hobsbawm, Eric and Terence Ranger, ed. (1983), *The Invention of Tradition.* Cambridge: Cambridge University Press.

Holt, Douglas B. (1997), "Poststructuralist Lifestyle Analysis: Conceptualizing the Social Patterning of Consumption in Postmodernity," *Journal of Consumer Research*, 23 (December), 326–50.

——— (1998), "Does Cultural Capital Structure American Consumption?" *Journal of Consumer Research*, 25 (June), 1–25.

Huntington, Samuel P. (1993), "The Clash of Civilizations?" *Foreign Affairs*, 72 (3), 22-49.

Jones, Carla (2007), " Fashion and Faith in Urban Indonesia", **Journal** 11 (2/3), 211-232.

Joy, Annamma and Venkatesh Alladi (1994), "Postmodernism, Feminism, and the Body: The Visible and Invisible in Consumer Research," *International Journal of Research in Marketing*, 11 (June), 333–357.

Lakoff, George and Mark Johnson (1999), *Philosophy in the Flesh: The Embodied Mind and Its Challenge to Western Thought*, New York: Basic Books.

LeBlanc, M. Natalie (2000), "Versioning Womanhood and Muslimhood: Fashion and the Life Course in Contemporary Bouake, Cote D'Ivoire", Africa. 70(3), 442-480.

Mabro, J. (1996), *Veiled Half-Truths: Western Travellers' Perceptions of Middle Eastern Women,* London: I.B. Tauris & Co., Ltd..

McCracken, Grant (1988), *Culture and Consumption: New Approaches to the Symbolic Character of Consumer Goods and Activities*, Bloomington, IN: Indiana University Press.

Moors, Annelies (2007), "Fashionable Muslims: Notions of Self, Religion, and Soceity in San'a," *Fashion Theory*, 11(2/3), 319-346.

Mule, Pat and Diane Barthel (1992), "the return of the veil: Individual Autonomy vs. Social Esteem," *Sociological Forum,* 7(2), 323-332.

Murphy, Robert F. (1964), " Social Distance and the Veil," *American Anthropologist*, 66 (December), 1257-1274.

Osealla, Caroline and Osello, Filippo (2007), "Muslim Style in South India". *Fashion Theory*, 11 (2/3), 233-252.

Oswald, Laura R. (1999), "Culture Swapping: Consumption and the Ethnogenesis of Middle Class Haitian Immigrants," *Journal of Consumer Research*, 25 (March), 303-18.

Owen, John, (1806), *The Fashionable World Displayed*, New York: J. Osborn.

Peiss, Kathy (1998), *Hope in a Jar: The Making of America's Beauty Culture*, New

Ruby, F. Tabassum (2006), "Listening to Voices of Hijab", *Women's Studies International Forum*, 29, 54-66.

Kuchler and Daniel Miller, Oxford: Berg, 61-82,.

Sandikci, Ozlem and Ger, Guliz (2007), "Constructing and Representing the Islamic Consumer in Turkey". *Fashion Theory*, 11 (2/3), 189-210.

Scott, Marvin B. and Stanford B. Lyman (1968), "Accounts," *American Sociological Review*, 33 (February), 46-61.

Secor, J. Anna (2002), "The Veil and Urban Space in Istanbul: Women's Dress Mobility and Islamic Knowledge." *Gender, Place and Culture*, 9(1): 5-22.

Schama, Simon (1997), *An Embarrassment of Riches: An Interpretation of Dutch Culture in the Golden Age*, New York:Vintage.

Shaheen, Jack G. (2001), *Reel Bad Arabs: How Hollywood Vilifies a People*, Northampton, MA: Interlink.

Shultz, E. Dorothea (2007), "Competing Sartorial Assertions of Femininity and Mali Identity in Mali," *Fashion Theory*, 11(2/3), 253-280.

Simmel, Georg. (1904). "Fashion." *International Quarterly,* 10 (October), 130-155.

———— (1957), "Fashion," *American Journal of Sociology*, 62, 541-558.

Solomon, Michael (1986), "Deep Seated Materialism: The Case of Levi's 501 Jeans," in *Advances in Consumer Research*, 13.

Stonely, Peter (1999), "The Fashionable World Displayed: Alcott and Social Power," *Studies in American Fiction*, 27 (1), 21.

Tarlo, Emma (2007), "Hijab in London: Metamorphosis, Resonance and Effects", *Journal of Material Culture*, 12(2), 131-156.

Üstüner, Tuba and Douglas B. Holt (2007), "Dominated Consumer Acculturation: The Social Construction of Poor Migrant Women's Consumer Identity Projects in a Turkish Squatter," *Journal of Consumer Research*, 34 (June), 41-56.

# Mixed Origins, Diverse Preferences: Consumption Compromises in Contemporary Homes

Samantha N. N. Cross, Iowa State University, USA
Mary C. Gilly, University of California, Irvine, USA

## EXTENDED ABSTRACT

This research examines everyday food consumption relationships and compromises in contemporary bi-national and mono-national homes. In this study, a bi-national household consists of spouses from differing countries of origin (e.g., China and the U.S.), whereas a mono-national household has partners from the same country of origin. Building on the studies and methodological approaches of Fournier (1998) and Coupland (2005), this study seeks to further our understanding, as researchers and consumers, of the significance of food purchases and food consumption patterns in bi-national homes. To better understand food consumption practices in the home, this research uses a combination of interviews, observation and photographic documentation to take a deeper look at the contents of consumers' food storage areas. The following research questions are asked: 1) How are consumption compromises manifested in bi-national and mono-national families in the context of everyday food consumption? 2) What symbolic role does food play in the formation and maintenance of the individual and collective identities within the bi-national family unit?

The findings suggest that everyday food purchases and consumption behavior in participant families can be indicators of relative influence and negotiation in the household. Food is a key cultural expression (Alba 1990, Mintz and Du Bois 2002, Peñaloza 1994) and offers an opportunity to examine household consumption in a new context: bi-national families. Aspects of Miller's (1998) theory of shopping as essentially about sacrifice, and ultimately about relationships, are seen to be applicable when examining the trade-offs that take place between spouses in the participating households, with differing implications for consumption compromises, depending on the type of household.

We find that compromise happens not at the individual purchase level as the family decision making literature assumes, but over time and in response to other decisions. When cultures interact within the confines of the family, consumption decisions take on meaning beyond simply what is purchased and why. There is a blending process taking place in bi-national families, as well as an alternative type of juggling–juggling of consumption preferences based on cultural differences. The usual compromises spouses face are amplified when one spouse is an immigrant to the native spouse's homeland. Household member preferences are seen to be very specific, yet there are a host of constraints to satisfying those preferences, both internal and external to the household. The specificity of the preferences and the impact of the constraints vary depending on the type of household. In bi-national families, there seem to be greater constraints on preferred consumption, but there is also considerable effort expended to mitigate those constraints. The limited accessibility to immigrants' food choices results in greater shopping effort and stockpiling, with the native spouse also seeking out opportunities for the immigrant spouse to connect to their country of origin through food.

For members of bi-national homes, especially for immigrant household members, preferred food items were more than just sustenance or even desired treats, but links to home, identity and a vital aspect of maintaining access to both cultures within the family unit. Substitutability of preferred products was not a desired option or even a considered option at all. Stockpiling in these homes is based not just on price and bulk (Mela et al. 1998, Wansink and Deshpande 1994), but also on availability of the preferred items for the immigrant spouse. Food consumption is shown to be a manifestation of negotiated influence and compromise between the immigrant and native spouses, with the bi-national family unit providing a unique setting for harmony, resourcefulness, ingenuity and ultimately enhanced food consumption experiences.

Implications are drawn for the family decision making literature and consumer/brand relationships. Conflict and negotiated compromise are seen to be manifested not through major purchase decisions, but through everyday food consumption decisions. The analysis demonstrates that while there are clear similarities between mono-national and bi-national households, there are also key differences in everyday consumption experiences. This research highlights the importance of considering household characteristics and cultural diversity within the home as key factors in better understanding family decision making and consumption.

This study also augments the findings of researchers such as Fournier (1998) and Coupland (2005), by showing that partners who were born and raised in different countries, and even in different regions within the U.S., expend maximum effort to satisfy their specific consumption preferences. Participants expressed aversion to substitution, an aversion often intensified after a less than positive substitution experience. In several cases brand preferences seemed to be strengthened after substitution and then substitution at the same brand or preference level was no longer an option. These findings have implications for brand relationships when there's limited accessibility and advocate future research on the effect of accessibility and substitution on brand preference and loyalty.

The findings also emphasize the paradox within the home to build the collective unit versus the effort to retain the individual identities of the spouses. Compromise in food consumption choices and offerings is both a means of achieving harmony and a manifestation of respect for what each culture has to offer. The bi-national family is an aggregate entity, but an entity with a role and requirements that transcend those of the family members of which it is composed. Individual preferences are both encouraged and contained, as the bi-national household as a unit accommodates, unifies and eventually develops into a distinct entity that is greater than the sum of its founding partners.

## REFERENCES

Alba, Richard (1990), *Ethnic Identity,* New Haven, CT: Yale University Press.

Coupland, Jennifer C. (2005), "Invisible Brands: An Ethnography of Households and the Brands in Their Kitchen Pantries," *Journal of Consumer Research*, 32 (1), 106-18.

Fournier, Susan (1998), "Consumers and Their Brands: Developing Relationship Theory in Consumer Research," *Journal of Consumer Research,* 24 (4), 343-73.

Mela, Karl F., Kamel Jedidi and Douglas Bowman (1998), "The Long-Term Impact of Promotions on Consumer Stockpiling Behavior," *Journal of Marketing Research*, 35 (2), 250-262.

Miller, Daniel (1998), *A Theory of Shopping*, Ithaca, NY: Cornell University Press.

Mintz, Sidney W. and Christine M. Du Bois (2002), "The Anthropology of Food and Eating," *Annual Review of Anthropology*, 31, 99-119.

Peñaloza, Lisa (1994), "Atravesando-Fronteras Border Cross-ings-a Critical Ethnographic Exploration of the Consumer Acculturation of Mexican Immigrants," *Journal of Consumer Research,* 21 (1), 32-54.

Wansink, Brian and Rohit Deshpande (1994), "Out of Sight, out of Mind": Pantry Stockpiling and Brand-Usage Frequency," *Marketing Letters*, 5 (1), 91-100.

# Globalization Tug-of-War: Consumption as a Site of Conflict

Aliakbar Jafari, University of Strathclyde, UK
Christina Goulding, Wolverhampton Business School, UK

## EXTENDED ABSTRACT

Over the past two decades, consumer researchers have taken timely steps in uncovering the complexities associated with globalization and their findings have delicately supported some of the key debates on the globalization of consumption culture; that is, 'consumptionscapes' (Ger and Belk 1996) and the proliferation of identities via the commodification of consumer goods (Friedman 1994). Based on their key contributions, the existing seminal studies could fall within at least three thematic categories: 1) addressing Wilk's (1995) notion of 'global structures of common difference' (Askegaard and Kjeldgaard 2002; Kjeldgaard and Askegaard 2006) 2) addressing Robertson's (1992) proposed concept of 'glocalization' (Kjeldgaard and Ostberg 2007) 3) addressing consumers' 'identity salience' (Kjeldgaard 2009; Sandikci and Ger 2002; Thompson and Arsel 2004; Russell and Russell 2006).

These studies have genuinely enriched the consumption culture literature on globalization; yet, they focus mainly on Western or, at least, secular contexts in which consumers are viewed as emancipated individuals whose 'liberatory consumption' choices (Firat and Venkatesh 1995) provide them with a broad array of opportunities to exploit a choice of lifestyles. None of these studies has investigated consumers' interactions with globalization in a non-secular society, widely disciplined according to a set of non-secular socio-cultural and political ideologies. Moreover, these investigations have generally examined the *contents* and *consequences* of globalization. That is, they have analyzed either the ways by which consumers use the global *contents* (market resources) to create meanings (i.e., identities) or the ways these people react to the *manifestations* of globalization (e.g., brandscapes and global styles). Therefore, the processes in which "tensions between local and global meanings systems and institutions" (Arnould and Thompson 2007, 12) occur have been considerably overlooked in consumer research. It is these traits that underpin our study as we analyze the *mechanisms* of the global-local interactions.

We present an analysis of 'cultural globalization' (Appadurai 1990; Ger and Belk 1996) in order to examine consumption practices and lifestyle choices of young adult individuals in Iran, a society in which globalization is highly contested and problematic. In so doing, we analyze the *processes* in which the consolidating forces of the local socio-cultural and political context clash with the dynamics of cultural globalization and tackle individuals' 'self-actualization' projects (Giddens 1991). Iran offers an interesting context to study such issues because reposed on theories of cultural imperialism (Mattelart 1994), globalization is populistically demonized as an invasive project of neo-colonialism (Czinkota and Ronkainen 2001).

Given the paucity of research in Iran, the complexities associated with the sensitivity of the topic and political situation of the country, we embarked on an inductive theory building process using in-depth interviews, participatory observation and memo writing. Following Glaser and Strauss (1967), we analyzed our data (collected from Tehran and Karaj over a period of six months) through a systematic process of constant comparison.

Our findings indicate that through its influx, cultural globalization has produced a strong basis of 'knowledge' (Kim 2005) for Iranian youth. It has generated an excess of 'signs', 'images', 'meanings', 'lifestyles', and 'identities' (Nijman 1999; Friedman 1994) whereby reflexivity, as a way of 'self-analysis' and 'self-confrontation' (Beck 1994) is fostered. We theorize this reflexivity as a 'virtual intercultural learning' process and present two conceptual models to demonstrate how in 'confrontation with other cultures' (Ger 1998), young Iranians compare and contrast themselves with other people around the world. Reading consumer practices against the socio-cultural and political background of Iran, we discuss that this kind of reflexivity becomes extremely problematic in society. Reflexivity, as Archer (2007) states, depends on a 'subject-object' relationship. That is, whilst the subjects (agents) aspire to shape their lives based on their own tastes and needs, their life-design projects depend on the "objectivity of their social circumstances which, through their own descriptions, will encourage them to follow one course of action rather than another" (Archer 2007, 34). The examination of such interplay between social structure and agency (Giddens 1994) suggests that these individuals' critical vision is rejected in Iran. Whilst these young people seek to subjectively define their own intended lives based on a large number of sources (offered to them by cultural globalization), the objectivity of their socio-cultural context acts as a deterring force. Although such restraints are also rooted in the society's mindset (concatenated with history and tradition), they are strongly related to the grand narratives of the state that forces them to believe that their culture is unrivalled. We acknowledge the fact that such ideology (exaggeration of identity) is not an exclusive characteristic of Iranian society as it is indicative of an 'imagined community' (Anderson 1983). Yet, what becomes paradoxical in this case is the obvious opposition of this mentality with the solid teachings of Islam explicitly stated in the Holy Koran.

Scrutinizing our informants' consumption practices in the context of a political/ideological Islam, we argue that quite contrary to common belief (i.e., globalization threatens Islamic values), Islam itself fuels globalization as it essentially deems 'self-reflexivity' a progressive human practice. Also, reflecting on Islam as a 'discursive tradition' (Wong 2007), we discuss that unlike other Islamic societies (e.g., Turkey and Malaysia) where political secularity has provided a relatively tolerant state-citizen relationship, the state's political ideology of Islam in Iran has resulted in discrepancies between the state's objective structure and the citizens' subjective agencies. Consequently, consumption has become a problematic site of socio-cultural conflict; one in which consumers' very personal life practices are extensively affected by the state's omnipresent social policies. Therefore, the real clash happens to be not merely between the local and global institutions, but between the local and local systems of meanings because globalization only acts as a catalyst. Based on our findings, we propose our conceptual models as useful analytical tools to systematically investigate consumers' multiple interactions with global and local dynamics in other societies as well.

# Negotiating the Boundary between the Self and the Other: Individuation and Association through Socially-visible Brand Use

Heather Schulz, University of Texas at Austin, USA
Patricia Stout, University of Texas at Austin, USA

## EXTENDED ABSTRACT

Recent research in consumer culture theory has focused on the role of the brand as an instrument in the interpretation of social interactions. In this paper, we expand this stream of research be examining how consumers use socially-visible brands to create and communicate their identity. Here we define a socially-visible brand as a brand located on or near an individual's body that is visible to another individual in the public atmosphere. Socially-visible brand use is centered on the everyday and even mundane brands all consumers use during their daily routines. It is argued that socially-visible brands are a strategic tool consumers can use for impression management. Socially-visible brands offer identity cues to others about one's self-concept, but they also assist in the bonding relationships one has with others. Overall, socially-visible brands serve in the identity negotiation process between an individual and society.

We briefly explain how three social psychology theories, namely social identity theory, self-verification theory, and impression management theory, juxtapose with consumer culture theory in general and self-extension theory in particular. The goal is to impart a framework for understanding the interaction of people, their possessions, and society. Every individual faces the conflicting task of connecting with other individuals in pro-social interactions (i.e., association), while at the same time maintaining a comfortable boundary so the individual self remains intact (i.e., individuation). The individuation side of this self-other boundary negotiation has been discussed in previous consumer research literature topics such as a "consumer's need for uniqueness," "counter-conformity" (Tian, Bearden, and Hunter 2001), and "identity signaling" (Berger and Heath 2007). The association side of this self-other boundary negotiation has also been discussed in several ways, but can best be described as communal consumption. This can occur at the dyadic level (Argo and Main 2008; Ramanathan and McGill 2007; Tanner, Ferraro, Chartrand, Bettman, and Van Baaren 2008) and at the reference group level (Epp and Price 2008; Escalas and Bettman 2005; Luna, Ringberg, and Peracchio 2008; White and Dahl 2007).

Social identity theory argues that one's personal identity (the individual self) and one's social identities (the collective selves) combine to form one's total identity (Hogg 2003). Through the process of identity negotiation, people maintain social group membership and distinctiveness. Swann (1987) argued that people engage in identity negotiations in order to obtain "existential security" (p. 1039). Individual self-concepts are the lens people use to understand their world and their place in the world. They desire stable self-concepts, and engage in activities that will provide them with feedback from others confirming their self-concept. He called this process "self-verification." One technique utilized by individuals during times of incongruence is impression management (Goffman 1959). During this process, individuals attempt to exert control over the perceptions others may have of them. Using a theatric metaphor, Goffman explained how people put on shows for one another by managing their impression through the use of social cues.

Self-extension theory describes the items used during impression management, which can include setting, clothing, appearance, words, and nonverbal actions. In terms of mass communication, self-extension theory looks at how consumers use the possession of specific brands in order to express their identity (Belk 1988).

The symbolic meanings attached to brands are cultural markers. Therefore, if one is able to possess that brand, one can indirectly possess that cultural meaning. Therefore, during impression management, socially-visible brands are a tool utilized to create one's identity for the self and to communicate one's identity to others.

Forty-one informal face-to-face interviews were conducted with graduate and undergraduate students at a university in the southwestern U.S. Most of the interviews lasted about 30 minutes. The structure for the interview protocol consisted of asking respondents about the individual and social aspects of their identity, top-of-mind brand awareness, the specific brands they own for socially-visible items such as clothes, shoes, sunglasses, etc., and the socially-visible brands the respondent was currently wearing.

From these interviews, a Boundary Negotiation Framework is presented that can be used as a guide to gain a better understanding of how individuals use socially-visible brands in order to develop their self-concept and various levels of social identity. The results show how people use socially-visible brands in order to associate with other individuals, reference groups, and society as a whole during interpersonal interactions. Using this Boundary Negotiation Framework, individuation and associations interactions can be analyzed at the dyadic, reference group, and societal level. This Boundary Negotiation Framework can be utilized in the future to analyze post-purchase behavior of consumers with their socially-visible brands. In addition, advertisers can use this framework while crafting their branding and communication strategies.

## REFERENCES

Argo, Jennifer J. and Kelley J. Main (2008), "Stigma by Association in Coupon Redemption: Looking Cheap because of Others," *Journal of Consumer Research*, 35 (December), 559-572.

Belk, Russell W. (1988), "Possessions and the Extended Self," *Journal of Consumer Research*, 15 (September), 139-168.

Berger, Jonah and Chip Heath (2007), "Where Consumers Diverge from Others: Identity Signaling and Product Domains," *Journal of Consumer Research*, 34 (August), 121-134.

Epp, Amber M. and Linda L. Price (2008), "Family Identity: A Framework of Identity Interplay in Consumption Practices," *Journal of Consumer Research*, 35 (June), 50-70.

Escalas, Jennifer Edson and James R. Bettman (2005), "Self-Construal, Reference Groups and Brand Meaning," *Journal of Consumer Research*, 32, 378-389.

Goffman, Erving (1959), *The Presentation of Self in the Everyday Life*. Garden City, NY: Doubleday & Company, Inc.

Hogg, Michael (2003), "Social Identity. In *Handbook of Self and Identity*, ed. Mark Leary and June Tangey, New York: The Guilford Press, 304-332.

Luna, David, Torsten Ringberg, and Laura A. Peracchio (2008), "One Individual, Two Identities: Frame Switching among Biculturals," *Journal of Consumer Research*, 35 (August), 279-293.

Ramanathan, Suresh and Ann L. McGill (2007), "Consuming with Others: Social Influences on Moment-to-Moment and Retrospective Evaluations of an Experience," *Journal of Consumer Research*, 34 (December), 506-524.

Swann, Jr., William B. (1987), "Identity Negotiation: Where Two Roads Meet," *Journal of Personality and Social Psychology*, 53 (6), 1038-1051.

Tanner, Robin J., Rosellina Ferraro, Tanya L. Chartrand, James R. Bettman, and Rick Van Baaren (2008), "Of Chameleons and Consumption: The Impact of Mimicry on Choice and Preferences," *Journal of Consumer Research*, 34 (April), 754-766.

Tian, Kelly Tepper, William O. Bearden, and Gary L. Hunter (2001), "Consumers' Need for Uniqueness: Scale Development and Validation," *Journal of Consumer Research*, 28 (June), 50-66.

White, Katherine and Darren W. Dahl (2007), "Are All Out-Groups Created Equal? Consumer Identity and Dissociative Influence," *Journal of Consumer Research*, 34 (December), 525-536.

# Copycats as Uncertainty Reducing Devices

Femke van Horen, University of Cologne, Germany
Rik Pieters, Tilburg University, The Netherlands
Diederik A. Stapel, Tilburg University, The Netherlands

## EXTENDED ABSTRACT

Purchase decisions are often made under conditions of varying uncertainty regarding product quality. When the context induces such uncertainty, consumers tend to seek additional information to reduce these feelings. Copycat brands may benefit under these circumstances.

Copycats imitate the trade-dress of a leading brand in order to leverage the positive associations that the latter has in the mind of the consumer (Loken, Ross, and Hinkle 1986; Zaichkowsky 2006). Research has demonstrated that consumers generally dislike blatant copycats, especially when these are blatant and awareness of the imitation strategy is high (Van Horen, Pieters and Stapel 2009; Warlop and Alba 2004, study 4). Surprisingly little is however known about the circumstances under which consumers actually *like* blatant copycats even when fully aware that the copycat is imitating. The extant research has focused on how package similarity influences copycat evaluation and purchase, but has not yet tested the potential influence of contextual factors on evaluation and choice of copycats. In the current research, we posit and show that copycat evaluation is critically dependent on contextually induced uncertainty.

Consumers are often faced with uncertainty about product quality when choosing between competing brands. Uncertainty refers to situations in which consumers do not know which choice to make (Lipshitz and Strauss 1997, Muthukrishnan and Kardes 2001). When feeling uncertain, consumers are likely to search for signals to assess quality in order to reduce these feelings of uncertainty. Information about the price, packaging, and brand image can then serve as such signals (Dawar & Parker, 1994; Kirmani & Rao, 2000). As copycats imitate the trade-dress of leading national brands and packaging is an important component of stored product knowledge, imitation can activate knowledge associated with the leader brand and serve as a signal. Thus, when consumers are uncertain about the quality of products and are looking for familiar cues to guide them in decision-making, copycats may be able to profit most. However, when consumers feel certain about the quality of products and do not need to rely on familiar cues, copycats may be interpreted negatively. When consumers are aware that a copycatting strategy is being used, similarity may be perceived as a intentional ploy to mislead consumers about product quality (Campbell and Kirmani 2000; Warlop and Alba 2004).

Three studies demonstrate that consumers systematically prefer copycats to visually differentiated products when the situation induces feelings of uncertainty about the quality of products, whereas the reverse is true when the situation induces feelings of certainty. In addition, we show that the positive evaluation of copycats in uncertainty inducing situations is due to consumers' reliance on familiar cues that signal quality. Two situations are explored that are likely to induce different levels of uncertainty. The first, more explicit, situation is when people are abroad as compared to being at home. When consumers are visiting another country and are unacquainted with the available brands, they are likely to feel uncertain about product quality. A second, more subtle situation is store-type. As compared to high-end stores, the quality of products at discounters is more variable and perhaps lower, which should activate consumers' feelings of uncertainty.

Study 1 tested the influence of being abroad or at home on copycat evaluation and choice. Participants were either instructed to imagine being in Being, China, or in their home country, looking for a coffee shop. Next, they evaluated a copycat logo, which was a clear imitation of the "Starbucks" logo and a visually differentiated logo that did not share any similarities with the Starbucks logo. Further, they were asked to indicate whether their evaluation of the coffee shops was guided by familiar cues. In support of the hypothesis, copycat evaluation was dependent on country-induced uncertainty: when people imagined to be in a foreign country, the copycat was evaluated more positively and chosen more often than the visually differentiated product, whereas the opposite pattern emerged when people imagined to be in their home country. These results were mediated by reliance on familiar cues and were not due to source confusion. Study 2 tested whether the same effects appeared when uncertainty was manipulated through store-type. Half of the participants were asked to imagine doing shopping in a typical discount store, whereas the other half in a typical high-end store. Then, they were asked to evaluate a copycat chocolate bar ("Milka" look-alike) as compared to a visually differentiated brand. The results reveal that–compared to a visually differentiated product–a copycat was evaluated more positively in a discounter, than in a high-end store. These effects were shown not to be due to source confusion. In study 3 uncertainty was directly manipulated, instead of indirectly through specific situations, to provide further support for the idea that uncertainty is the key factor. Two packages (a copycat and a visually differentiated product) were created within the product category "Energy drinks". In the uncertainty (certainty) condition participants were asked to imagine doing shopping in an unknown (well known) supermarket, in which they were uncertain (certain) about the quality of the products. Again, participants were asked to evaluate both energy drinks and to make a choice. As predicted the copycat energy drink was evaluated more positively and chosen more often when uncertainty was induced than when certainty was induced. These results provide direct support for the underlying "uncertainty reduction" mechanism.

These results contribute to the literature on trademark infringement in several ways. First, the present research is, to our knowledge, the first to demonstrate that, besides package similarities, the specific shopping situation critically determines copycat evaluation and choice. This underlines the importance of moving beyond the similarities between copycat and leader brand in package design to understand copycat effects. Furthermore, it shows that even when fully aware and thus "not tricked", consumers may still prefer and choose copycats to reduce feelings of uncertainty. Hence, whereas consumers generally prefer differentiated brands to copycats, the reverse holds under conditions of uncertainty.

## REFERENCES

Campbell, Margaret C. and Amna Kirmani (2000), "Consumers' Use of Persuasion Knowledge: The Effects of Accessibility and Cognitive Capacity on Perceptions of an Influence Agent," Journal of Consumer Research, 27 (1), 69-83.

Dawar, Niraj and Philip Parker (1994), "Marketing Universals: Consumers' Use of Brand Name, Price, Physical Appearance, and Retailer Reputation as Signals of Product Quality," *Journal of Marketing*, 58 (2), 81-95.

Foxman, Ellen R., Darrel D. Muehling, and Phil W. Berger (1990), "An Investigation of Factors Contributing to Consumer Brand Confusion," *The Journal of Consumer Affairs*, 24 (1), 170-89.

Kapferer, Jean Noel (1995), "Brand Confusion: Empirical Study of a Legal Concept," *Psychology & Marketing*, 12 (6), 551-69.

Kirmani, Amna and Akshay R. Rao (2000), "No Pain, No Gain: A Critical Review of the Literature on Signaling Unobservable Product Quality," *Journal of Marketing*, 64 (2), 66-79.

Lipshitz, Raanan and Orna Strauss (1997), "Coping with Uncertainty: A Naturalistic Decision-Making Analysis," *Organizational Behavior and Human Decision Processes*, 69 (2), 149-63.

Loken, Barbara, Ivan Ross, and Ronald L. Hinkle (1986), "Consumer ''Confusion'' of Origin and Brand Similarity Perceptions," *Journal of Public Policy & Marketing*, 5, 195-211.

Muthukrishnan, A. V. and R. Kardes Frank (2001), "Persistent Preferences for Product Attributes: The Effects of the Initial Choice Context and Uninformative Experience," *Journal of Consumer Research*, 28, 89-104.

Warlop, Luc and Joseph W. Alba (2004), "Sincere Flattery: Trade-Dress Imitation and Consumer Choice," *Journal of Consumer Psychology*, 14 (1&2), 21-27.

Zaichkowsky, Judy L. (2006), *The Psychology Behind Trademark Infringement and Counterfeiting*, New Jersey: Lawrence Erlbaum Associates, Inc.

# Reputable Brand Names can Improve Product Efficacy

Moty Amar, Ono Academic College & Duke University, USA
Dan Ariely, Duke University, USA
Maya Bar-Hillel, The Hebrew University, Israel
Ziv Carmon, INSEAD, France
Chezy Ofir, The Hebrew University, Israel

## EXTENDED ABSTRACT

Common sense suggests that the efficacy of products should be a function of how they are designed and produced. Brand names, on the other hand, can presumably only influence expectations and subjective assessments of efficacy. However, we illustrate that the brand name that products carry can also influence rather than merely reflect objective efficacy. We thereby extend Shiv, Carmon, and Ariely's (2005) pioneering work on placebo effects of marketing actions, to a different type of marketing action (branding), study it with several new types of tasks, less likely to be influenced by voluntary control. In particular, across four experiments, each conducted in carefully controlled conditions, we show that attaching a prestigious brand name to a product can boost the performance of those who consume the product.

In experiment 1, participants repeatedly held the same titanium framed eyeglasses bearing either a prestigious or the less prestigious brand name in one hand, then held one of several paperweights each weighing slightly less or slightly more than the eyeglasses with no cue to its weight in the other hand, then judged which was heavier—the eyeglasses or the paperweight. Several aspects of the experimental design made it difficult to be insincere, thus reducing the likelihood of demand effects. As predicted, results showed that participants underestimated the true weight of the frame bearing the prestigious brand name more frequently and overestimated its weight less frequently, suggesting that the glasses seemed lighter when they bore the more prestigious brand.

In experiment 2, all participants first drank a cup of the same chamomile tea that was described as soothing to body and mind, which carried either a prestigious brand name or a less prestigious one. After a few minutes they were asked to complete as many puzzles as they could during a limited timeframe. As predicted, results showed that participants whose tea bore the more prestigious brand name gave more correct answers and fewer incorrect answers than those whose tea bore the less prestigious brand name.

In experiment 3, all participants faced a glaring light and were asked to read printed words as accurately and as quickly as they could, receiving compensation proportional to their performance. As predicted, those wearing sunglasses bearing a reputable brand name were able to read more quickly and with fewer errors than those wearing sunglasses bearing a less reputable brand name but were otherwise identical. Note that there are two ways that a participant who believes he or she is wearing quality sunglasses might perform better, to fulfill the expectation caused by the prestigious brand name. One is to try harder. That could account for the smaller number of errors, but not for the faster rate. Since both were recorded, willful effort seems to be ruled out. The other is to contract the pupil more, thus cutting out more glare. But our experimenters were instructed to make sure that participants did not do this. More importantly, inasmuch as the pupil is under voluntary control, it seems that putting one's faith in one's sunglasses would lead to the opposite inclination: One need not contract one's pupil as much when one has effective sunglasses as when one does not. Whatever happens in this task, then, is not trivial.

In experiment 4, all participants wore the same pair of earmuffs said to reduce noise while assisting in hearing conversations, bearing either the prestigious brand name or a less prestigious one. They listened to a recording of an announcer reading a list of 62 unrelated words, read on the background of a very loud and noisy construction site and were asked to identify the words as they heard them. As predicted, participants whose earmuffs bore the more prestigious brand name identified more words correctly and fewer words incorrectly than those whose earmuffs carried the less prestigious brand name. Note that in this task it is not clear what a motivated participants could do in order to improve performance over a less motivated participant.

Altogether, this paper illustrates that in addition to coloring preferences and expectations the commercial reputation that is embodied in brand names can also influence objective efficacy in a manner that is difficult to attribute to volitional effort. The results can have significant managerial and public policy implications. As one example, firms may be able to boost the efficacy of their products by attaching more reputable names to them. Analogously, the findings suggest that generic medications may in fact not be as effective as branded ones, putting into question the common practice of substituting one for the other.

# Guilt Appeals in Green Advertising: Influences of Issue Proximity and Environmental Involvement

Chun-Tuan Chang, National Sun Yat-sen University, Taiwan
Yu-Kang Lee, National Sun Yat-sen University, Taiwan
Ting-Ting Chen, National Sun Yat-sen University, Taiwan

## EXTENDED ABSTRACT

With increasing public concern about the environment and corporate social responsibility on environmental sustainable development, the 1990s was declared the decade of environmentalism (Drumwright, 1994; Kangun, Carlson, and Grove, 1991). Consequently, recent studies have begun to examine potential factors that might affect the effectiveness of green marketing campaigns and how consumers respond to green marketing initiatives (e.g., Chan, 2000; Obermiller, 1995; Schuhwerk and Lefkof-Hagius, 1995). One influential variable that has been identified to determine the success of green marketing is its advertising (e.g., Karna et al., 2001). Emotional appeals are widely used to "cut through the clutter" and arouse persuasive communication. Among them, guilt appeals are identified as popular, especially in the contexts related to public service announcement.

This article contributes to this evolving stream of research by applying guilt appeals in green marketing campaigns to demonstrate that guilt appeals are not equally persuasive in all conditions, and can be influenced by the impacts of issue proximity and environmental involvement. A fictitious product, leftover-grounds printer, was developed as the test product. An experiment with 2 (advertising appeal: guilt appeal vs. positive appeal) X 2 (issue proximity: low vs. high) X 2 (environmental involvement: low vs. high) factorial design was conducted. The first two factors were manipulated and the final one was measured. Therefore, four experimental versions were produced. Participants were randomly assigned to one of the conditions above. After successful manipulation checks, a series of analysis of variance were conducted to examine proposed hypotheses.

The results indicate that focusing on the comparison between guilt and positive appeals may be overly simplistic. Indeed, the findings presented here establish that the influence of guilt appeals on consumer response is relatively complex and contingent on issue proximity and environmental involvement. Three observations are noteworthy.

*First*, in terms of the relative effects of issue proximity, this study shows systematic effects on consumer responses by comparing low and high issue proximity. High proximity made a difference in advertising effectiveness; a local issue, as opposed to a foreign issue in a less familiar region, yielded more favorable evaluation and higher behavioral intention. This perspective is conceptually consistent with social impact theory and signaling theory. The reason could lie in the notion that the local community is more salient to consumers—regardless of the advertising appeal. No differences are found between a guilt and positive appeal in advertising effectiveness of high-proximity issue. This idea does not suggest, however, firms only address local issues and neglect global or foreign issues because advertising appeal may not be a concern in their advertising campaign when presenting a local issue. When an issue is perceived as less proximal, the tactic of guilt appeal allows a firm to enhance consumers' attitudes toward the product and purchase intention.

*Second*, that effects of advertising appeal are contingent on environmental involvement is noteworthy. This construct delineates the boundary conditions for the guilt appeals on persuasion. A guilt appeal works for those with low environmental involvement.

Compared with individuals with low environmental involvement, those with high environmental involvement are less likely to be not influenced by the advertising appeals. The results are consistent with the observation by Schuhwerk and Lefkoff-Hagius (1995). The study here also echoes that guilt can generate negative responses and disrupt the advertiser's intended objectives as well (Cotte et al., 2005; Shrum et al., 1995).

*Third*, the effectiveness of guilt and positive appeals depends on issue proximity and environmental involvement simultaneously. Instead of blindly applying any type of advertising appeal, advertisers should pay particular attention to perceived proximity of the environmental issue and consumers' individual differences in environmental involvement. When facing individuals with low environmental involvement, the guilt appeal performed better than the positive appeal in promoting an issue with high proximity. Thus, when dealing with a problem people regard as relatively important or about which they are self-relevant, the impact of guilt appeal may offer advantages. As Schuhwerk and Lefkoff-Hagius (1995) note that consumers pay attention to external cues such as how an ad is framed when they do not possess strong beliefs about the environment. Alternatively, when concern for the issue is low (low issue proximity), no differences of advertising effectiveness between a guilt and positive appeal can be found. Because of weak impetus to process the message and less well-developed green product schema, the less involved consumers may not be able to identify the differences between the two appeals. When facing highly involved consumers, the guilt appeal was more persuasive than the positive appeal in promoting a less proximal issue. However, this observation appears to be reversed when the ad was presented to less involved consumers. The guilt appeal may offer a redundant warning, or worse, cause a boomerang effect. Consistent with prior work on involvement and skepticism about advertisers' environmental claims, environmentally involved individuals may engage in more effortful and elaborative processing and discount the received information. In such cases, the positive appeal is preferable. The implication is that advertisers must be careful not to arouse guilt feelings through the ads. If such care is not taken, a backlash may occur whereby the consumers develop negative attitudes toward the promoted product. In any event, advertisers are advised to adopt a situational perspective by taking the possible interaction effect among advertising appeal, issue proximity, and environmental involvement.

Findings from this investigation are informative both theoretically and pragmatically. This study contributes to the academic literature and industry by increasing our understanding of guilt appeals in a green marketing context by proposing issue proximity and environmental involvement as factors that moderate the relationships between guilt appeal and consumer responses toward the promoted product. The findings underscore the importance for green marketers to learn more about whether guilt appeals work, and in turn describe how practitioners can avoid negatively toward guilt appeals. The present research should serve as a starting point for entry into this under-researched area.

599

*Advances in Consumer Research*
*Volume 38, © 2012*

# Metaphors in Advertising: Cognitive Flexibility Matching Perspective

Kyung-Jin Kim, The University of Suwon, Korea
Jongwon Park, Korea University Business School, Korea

## EXTENDED ABSTRACT

Prior research suggests that a metaphor in advertising can have a positive effect on evaluations of the target product (McQuarrie and Phillips 2005; Moreau, Markman, and Lehmann 2001). However, the effect tends to be restricted to the metaphors which are easy to interpret (Gregan-Paxton and John 1997; Roehm and Sternthal 2001). Yet, it is common that companies employ complicated, idiosyncratic, and difficult metaphors in their advertising. This discrepancy can be resolved, however, if we consider both the level of cognitive flexibility required to process the metaphor and the level of individuals' actual cognitive flexibility at the time of metaphor processing as determinants of the effectiveness of a metaphor.

The present research proposes a cognitive flexibility matching hypothesis that the match between the required and actual level of cognitive flexibility is a key determinant of the metaphor's effectiveness. That is, when the level of cognitive flexibility necessary to comprehend a metaphor matches the level of individuals' actual cognitive flexibility at the time of metaphor processing, using the metaphor in an ad could be beneficial for evaluations of the target product. When the individuals' actual cognitive flexibility is either below or above the required level to process a metaphor, however, using the metaphor could be detrimental.

To test this proposition, we borrow from research based on temporal construal theory that a distant-future perspective (vs. a near-future perspective) increases individuals' cognitive flexibility momentarily (Forster et al. 2004; Trope and Liberman 2003). Based on this, we hypothesize that a difficult metaphor, compared to its easier version or a literal message counterpart, can lead to more favorable product evaluations when people consider the target product for a distant-future purchase, but would produce less favorable evaluations when they consider it for a near-future purchase. To put it differently, an increase in temporal distance is expected to increase the effectiveness of a difficult metaphor, but to decrease the effectiveness of an easy metaphor.

These hypothesized (diametrically opposite) effects were confirmed in five experiments in which participants evaluated a target product described by either a difficult meteor, an easier version of the metaphor, or its literal message counterpart, while considering the message for a possible purchase of an advertised product either next day (near-future condition) or next year (distant-future condition). Moreover, the effects generalized over different products and metaphors and were evident regardless of whether the level of difficulty of a metaphor was manipulated by employing different versions of a metaphor, by varying individuals' knowledge to process a metaphor, or by varying their mood state.

Experiment 1 demonstrated that a difficult metaphor, compared to a literal message that has a same implication of the metaphor, led to a more favorable evaluation of the target product in the distant future condition, whereas this difference was reversed in the near future condition. Experiment 2 replicated these results and in addition showed that a difficult metaphor was more effective than an easy metaphor as well in the distant future condition, whereas this difference was reversed in the near future condition. Experiments 3a, 3b, and 3c investigated the role of individuals' knowledge to process the metaphor and found that a (difficult) metaphor was more effective for low-knowledge individuals than for high-knowledge individuals when the product decision was made for a distant future, whereas the difference was reversed when the decision was made for a near-future. Similarly, Experiment 4a and 4b demonstrated that a (difficult) metaphor was more effective for individuals in the positive mood condition than for those in the negative mood condition when the product was evaluated for purchase in the distant future, whereas the difference was reversed when the product was considered for a near-future purchase. Finally, experiment 5 assessed the level of comprehension about the metaphor based on participants' thought protocols. A mediation test confirmed that the effect of temporal distance on the effectiveness of a difficult metaphor was mediate by its influence on the extent to which participant actually comprehended the meaning of the metaphor.

Thus, collectively, results from five experiments provide consistent evidence for our cognitive flexibility matching hypothesis. At the same time, the research identifies moderators (product knowledge and mood state) for the diametrically opposite effects observed in the experiments. Theoretical and managerial implications of these findings are discussed.

## REFERENCES

Donnelly, C. M. and M. A. McDaniel (1993), "Use of Analogy in Learning Scientific Concepts," *Journal of Experimental Psychology: Learning, Memory, and Cognition*, 19 (4), 975-987.

Forster, Jens, Ronald S. Friedman, and Nira Liberman (2004), "Temporal Construal Effects on Abstract and Concrete Thinking: Consequences for Insight and Creative Cognition," *Journal of Personality and Social Psychology*, 87 (2), 177-189.

Gregan-Paxton, J. and D. R. John (1997), "Consumer Learning by Analogy: A Model of Internal Knowledge Transfer," *Journal of Consumer Research*, 24 (December), 266-284.

Hirt, Edward R., Erin E. Devers, and Sean M. McCrea (2008), "I Want to Be Creative: Exploring the Role of Hedonic Contingency Theory in the Positive Mood–Cognitive Flexibility Link," *Journal of Personality and Social Psychology*, 94 (2), 214–230.

Isen, Alice M., Kimberly A. Daubman, and Gary P. Nowicki (1987), "Positive Affect Facilitates Creative Problem Solving," *Journal of Personality and Social Psychology*, 52 (June), 1122-1131.

Jaffe, F. (1988), "Metaphor and Memory: A Study in Persuasion," (Doctoral Dissertation, Northwestern University) *Dissertation Abstracts International*, 49, p. 2311.

Kats, A. N., Paivio, A., and M. Marschark (1985), "Poetic Comparisons: Psychological Dimensions of Metaphoric Processing," *Journal of Psycholinguistic Research*, 14 (4), 365-383.

Lakoff, G. and M. Johnson (1980), *Metaphor We Live By*, Chicago: University of Chicago Press.

Liberman, Nira and Yaacov Trope (1998), "The Role of Feasibility and Desirability Considerations in Near and Distant Future Decisions: A Test of Temporal Construal Theory," *Journal of Personality and Social Psychology*, 75, 5–18.

Marschark, M. and R. Hunt (1985), "On Memory for Metaphor," *Memory & Cognition*, 13, 413-424.

McQuarrie, E. F. and B. J. Phillips (2005), "Indirect Persuasion in Advertising," *Journal of Advertising*, 34 (2), 7-20.

Moreau, C. P., A. B. Markman and D. R. Lehmann (2001), ""What Is It?" Categorization Flexibility and Consumers' Responses Really New Products," *Journal of Consumer Research*, 27 (March), 489-498.

Murray, N., H. Sujan, E. R. Hirt, and M. Sujan (1990), "The influence of Mood on Categorization: A Cognitive Flexibility Interpretation," *Journal of Personality and Social Psychology*, 59, 411–425.

Richards, I. A. (1981), *The Philosophy of Rhetoric, Philosophical Perspectives on Metaphor*, Minnesota: University of Minnesota Press.

Roehm, M. L. and B. Sternthal (2001), "The Moderating Effect of Knowledge and Resources on the Persuasive Impact of Analogies," *Journal of Consumer Research*, 28 (September), 257-272.

Sopory, Pradeep and James Price Dillard (2002), "The Persuasive Effects of Metaphor," *Human Communication Research*, 28 (3), 382-419.

Trope, Yaacov and Nira Liberman (2003), "Temporal Construal," *Psychological Review*, 110 (3), 403-421.

Whaley, B. (1991), "Toward a Comprehensive Model of Analogy in Persuasion: A Test of the Persuasive Role of Analogy," (Doctoral Dissertation, Purdue University) *Dissertation Abstracts International,* 53, p. 20.

# Testing Phonetic Symbolism Effects on Brand Name Preference for Bilinguals Across Multiple Languages

L. J. Shrum, University of Texas at San Antonio, USA
Tina M. Lowrey, University of Texas at San Antonio, USA
Dawn Lerman, Fordham University, USA
David Luna, Baruch College, USA
Min Liu, University of Texas at San Antonio, USA

## EXTENDED ABSTRACT

Good brand names can enhance memorability, create favorable images, and increase preference for the products, and are an important component in building brand equity (Aaker 1996; Keller 1993). When investigating the construction of the brand names, researchers found that not only the semantic meaning, but also phonetic symbolism, which refers to a non-arbitrary relation between sound and meaning, may influence brand preference (Klink 2000). In its simplest form, phonetic symbolism suggests that phonemes (the smallest unit of sound) can convey meaning apart from their configuration in words or syllables. Research on the relation between phonetic symbolism and brand name preference has shown that brand name preference and brand attitudes are more positive when the fit between phonetic symbolism and the product attributes is maximized. Although previous research has been successful at documenting phonetic symbolism effects in brand names, the processes underlying these effects have remained elusive. First, as some critics have pointed out, phonetic symbolism effects do not necessarily occur spontaneously, but only when specific dimensional judgments (e.g., size, shape, brightness) are elicited (Bentley and Varon 1933), suggesting that the effect may be a methodological artifact. Second, the effects that have been obtained with determining the meaning of foreign words (e.g., matching pairs of antonyms in a foreign language with comparable English antonyms; Brown, Black, and Horowitz 1955) are eliminated if both sets of stimulus words are in languages foreign to the participants (Maltzman, Morrisett, and Brooks 1956). Besides, there are in fact some reasons to think that phonetic symbolism effects would not hold for some forms of language. For example, in the Chinese written language, there are important differences in how alphabetic and logographic word representations are processed (Schmitt, Pan, and Tavassoli 1994; Tavassoli 2001), and there is considerable debate as to whether phonetic information in logographic characters can even be activated prior to some semantic activation (Chua 1999; Zhou 1978).

The goal of this paper is to extend previous research on the existence of phonetic symbolism and its application to brand naming by testing the generalization of these findings across languages, and testing the extent to which fluency may moderate the phonetic symbolism effects. On the one hand, if the phonetic symbolism effects are indeed universal (Ultan 1978), fluency may have little effect. On the other hand, research shows that form and meaning in a second language, even for fluent bilinguals, are not as tightly connected as for a first language (Luna and Peracchio 2001). If so, then we would expect to see weaker effects for less fluent second-language learners.

Three experiments were conducted to determine the extent to which phonetic symbolism effects are spontaneous and generalizable to other languages, and the extent to which non-native speakers are influenced by second-language fluency. In experiments 1–3, Spanish-, French- and Chinese-speaking participants who were fluent in English expressed preferences between brand name pairs that differed only in their primary vowel sound (front vs. back), and did so as a function of product category (2-seater convertible, knife, 4 X 4 vehicle, hammer). In addition, Chinese-speaking participants

received brand name stimuli that were constructed using either alphabetic letters or logographic symbols in order to test possible differences in the two presentations. Our focal hypothesis was that preference for front versus back vowel sound words as brand names would vary as a function of product category: front vowel sound words should be preferred over back for 2-seater convertible and knife, and back vowel sound words should be preferred over front for 4 X 4 vehicle and hammer. Note that the elicitation of a brand name preference for each product category does not directly elicit a judgment regarding concepts such as size, speed, or sharpness (cf. Bentley and Varon 1933). Rather, the predicted effects should be noted only if participants form perceptions of these concepts spontaneously and then apply them to their preference judgments. The results of the ANOVA indicated that there was a significant interaction between vowel sound and product category as we predicted, whereas the effect of experiment was not significant. These findings indicate that phonetic symbolism effects are robust across the different languages and cultures we tested, including logographic representations in Chinese. The results also show that these general relations were for the most part unaffected by whether participants completed the experiment in their native language or a foreign language, and were also unaffected by their proficiency in that language.

The studies we have presented make a number of contributions to the consumer behavior literature, but they also contribute to the more general fields of cognitive psychology and psycholinguistics. We replicate the phonetic symbolism effects noted in previous studies (Lowrey and Shrum 2007; Yorkston and Menon 2004), but also show that a) these effects generalize to languages other than English, b) generalize to languages in which presentation is non-alphabetic (logographic), c) hold for second-language as well as first-language participants, d) these latter effects are observed regardless of level of proficiency of participants, and e) the effects are spontaneous rather than a function of being elicited by the research method.

## REFERENCES

Aaker, David A. (1996), *Building Strong Brands*, New York: The Free Press.

Bentley, Madison and Edith J. Varon (1933), "An Accessory Study of 'Phonetic Symbolism'," *American Journal of Psychology*, 45 (January), 76-86.

Brown, Roger W., Abraham H. Black, and Arnold E. Horowitz (1955), "Phonetic Symbolism in Natural Languages," *Journal of Abnormal & Social Psychology*, 50 (3), 388-93.

Chua, Fook Kee (1999), "Phonological Recoding in Chinese Logograph Recognition," *Journal of Experimental Psychology: Learning, Memory, and Cognition*, 25 (July), 876-91.

Keller, Kevin L. (1993), "Conceptualizing, Measuring, and Managing Customer-Based Brand Equity," *Journal of Marketing*, 57 (January), 1-22.

Klink, Richard R. (2000), "Creating Brand Names With Meaning: The Use of Sound Symbolism," *Marketing Letters*, 11 (1), 5-20.

Lowrey, Tina M. and L. J. Shrum (2007), "Phonetic Symbolism and Brand Name Preference," *Journal of Consumer Research*, 34 (October), 406-14.

Luna, David and Laura A. Peracchio (2001), "Moderators of Language Effects in Advertising to Bilinguals: A Psycholinguistic Approach," *Journal of Consumer Research*, 28 (September), 284-95.

Maltzman, Irving, Lloyd Morrisett, Jr., and Lloyd O. Brooks (1956), "An Investigation of Phonetic Symbolism," *Journal of Abnormal & Social Psychology*, 53 (September), 249-51.

Schmitt, Bernd H., Yigang Pan, and Nader T. Tavassoli (1994), "Language and Consumer Memory: The Impact of Linguistic Differences between Chinese and English," *Journal of Consumer Research*, 21 (December), 419-31.

Tavassoli, Nader T. (2001), "Color Memory and Evaluations for Alphabetic and Logographic Brand Names," *Journal of Experimental Psychology: Applied*, 7 (June), 104-11.

Ultan, Russell (1978), "Size-Sound Symbolism," in *Universals of Human Language*: *Vol. 2*: *Phonology*, ed. Joseph H. Greenberg, Charles A. Ferguson, and Edith. A. Moravcsik, Stanford, CA: Stanford University Press, 525-68.

Yorkston, Eric A. and Geeta Menon (2004), "A Sound Idea: Phonetic Effects of Brand Names on Consumer Judgments," *Journal of Consumer Research*, 31 (June), 43-51.

Zhou, Y.-G. (1978), "To What Degree are the "Phonetics" of Present-Day Chinese Characters Still Phonetic?" [In Chinese], *Zhongguo Yuwen*, 146, 172-77.

# What Makes Things Cool? How Autonomy Influences Perceptions of Coolness

Caleb Warren, University of Colorado, USA
Margaret C. Campbell, University of Colorado, USA

## EXTENDED ABSTRACT

Coolness is a socially desirable trait often pursued by consumers and marketers (Belk, Tian, and Paavola 2008; Dar Nimrod et al. 2008; Kerner and Pressman 2007). Both people and brands can become cool, although it is not well understood how this occurs. Leading theories suggest that coolness comes from conforming to behaviors desired within a particular subculture (Danesi 1994; O'Donnell and Wardlow 2000; Thornton 1996) or by quickly mimicking the behaviors of other cool people (Gladwell 1997; Lupiono-Misdom and de Luca 1998). These theories, however, provide an incomplete explanation because they do not account for the origins of coolness nor do they explain how coolness diffuses across subcultures.

Building on prior work in cultural studies, sociology, and psychology (Frank 1997; Heath and Potter 2004; Pountain and Robins 2000), we hypothesize an alternative way people and brands can become cool: display bounded autonomy from mainstream society. In other words, we suspect that people and brands can become cool by going their own way, rather than following society's conventions. We test this hypothesis in three experiments.

Autonomy cannot be directly observed. Rather, it must be inferred by observing the extent to which a person or brand adheres to society's norms. People and brands that resist or ignore these norms will likely be seen as more autonomous than people and brands that conform. Consequently, we hypothesize that rebellion and uniqueness will influence perceptions of autonomy, which will influence perceptions of coolness.

Our first study tests whether people who are more rebellious and unique are perceived to be cooler than people who are less rebellious and unique. Furthermore, we test whether these effects are mediated by perceived autonomy. Participants read descriptions of target people who either described themselves as fairly rebellious or not rebellious and fairly unique or not unique. Rebellion and uniqueness were fully crossed and manipulated between-subjects. For example, one target person was either described as "not afraid to go against the grain" or "careful not to go against the grain," depending on whether the participant was in the high or low rebellion condition, respectively. After reading the descriptions, participants rated their perceptions of the target person's autonomy and coolness. As expected, target people who seemed more rebellious were considered cooler than target people who seemed less rebellious ($M = 6.9$ vs. $4.6$). Uniqueness had a similar effect ($M = 6.8$ vs. $4.8$). Importantly, both main effects were mediated by perceptions of autonomy.

Next we investigate whether the relationship between autonomy and perceptions of coolness is strictly increasing or curvilinear. Social norms exist in part to prevent destructive, anti-social behavior (Rousseau 1994). Consequently, we suspect that showing extreme levels of autonomy by completely disregarding these norms will not be seen as cool. Thus, the relationship between autonomy and perceived coolness will likely be curvilinear: perceived coolness will initially increase with displays of autonomy, but will begin to decrease as displays of autonomy become too extreme.

Individuals differ in terms of the extent to which they value autonomy and, consequently, the amount of autonomy they will consider acceptable. Individuals higher in counterculturalism, an ideology centered on the belief that societal institutions promote widespread conformity while repressing individuality, will likely value autonomy more than individuals lower in counterculturalism. Consequently, we hypothesize that the level of autonomy considered cool–i.e., the point at which the curvilinear function between autonomy and perceived coolness peaks–will be higher for consumers higher in counterculturalism.

Our second study tests whether the relationship between autonomy and perceived coolness is curvilinear, and whether the amount of autonomy considered cool varies depending on counterculturalism. Participants read about a target person who was described as displaying either a low (e.g. "she rarely would assert her independence"), moderate (e.g. "she occasionally would assert her independence"), high (e.g. "she often would assert her independence"), or extreme (e.g. "she always would assert her independence) level of autonomy. Participants rated perceived coolness of the target person and completed a scale measuring their level of counterculturalism. As hypothesized, perceived coolness initially increased as autonomy increased from a low to moderate level, but decreased as autonomy moved from a high to extreme level. Additionally, however, participants higher in counterculturalism considered higher levels of autonomy cooler than participants lower in counterculturalism.

Our third study explores when consumers will desire cool brands. Because displays of autonomy lead to perceptions of coolness, we suspect that consumers can use cool brands to signal an autonomous identity. Individualistic consumers will want to signal their autonomy, and hence will be most likely to prefer cool brands, when their identity as an autonomous individual has been threatened (Brewer 1991; Gao, Wheeler, and Shiv 2009).

In this study we test whether American consumers whose autonomous identity has been threatened are more likely to prefer cool brands. We threatened the autonomous identity of some participants by making them feel undifferentiated from others by priming their interdependent self (e.g., Aaker and Lee 2001). Subsequently, participants indicated whether they preferred a cool winter hat brand (i.e., one displaying bounded autonomy) or an uncool winter hat brand (i.e., one displaying low autonomy). Participants primed with an interdependent self were more likely to select the cool hat brand (68%) than participants primed with an independent self (44%). Desire to express autonomy was higher for participants primed with an interdependent self, and this measure mediated the effect of the self-construal prime on brand preference.

Following subcultural norms and mimicking cool people are not the only ways to become cool. People and brands can also become cool through displays of bounded autonomy. Identifying autonomy as an additional antecedent of perceived coolness suggests where coolness originates and how cool trends diffuse across subcultures. Things first become cool when they are seen as autonomous from mainstream society and cool trends typically diffuse from outsider subcultures and consumers higher in counterculturalism to more mainstream subcultures and consumers lower in counterculturalism. Our research suggests that consumers and brands that want to be cool should be rebellious and unique, but be careful not to go too far.

## REFERENCES

Aaker, J. L. and A. Y. Lee (2001), ""I" Seek Pleasures And "We" Avoid Pains: The Role of Self-Regulatory Goals in Information Processing and Persuasion," *Journal of Consumer Research*, 28, 33-49.

Baron, R. M. and D. A. Kenny (1986), "The Moderator Mediator Variable Distinction in Social Psychological Research-Conceptual, Strategic, and Statistical Considerations," *Journal of Personality and Social Psychology*, 51, 1173-82.

Belk, Russell W., Kelly Tian, and Heli Paavola (2008), "Consuming Cool: Behind the Unemotional Mask," Working Paper, Toronto: York University.

Berger, Jonah and Chip Heath (2007), "Where Consumers Diverge from Others: Identity Signaling and Product Domains," *Journal of Consumer Research*, 34, 121-34.

Brewer, Marilynn B. (1991), "The Social Self-on Being the Same and Different at the Same Time," *Personality and Social Psychology Bulletin*, 17, 475-82.

Brooks, David (2000), *Bobos in Paradise: The New Upper Class and How They Got There*, New York: Simon and Schuster.

Chartrand, T. L. and J. A. Bargh (1999), "The Chameleon Effect: The Perception-Behavior Link and Social Interaction," *Journal of Personality and Social Psychology*, 76, 893-910.

Cialdini, Robert B., C. A. Kallgren, and R. R. Reno (1991), "A Focus Theory of Normative Conduct: A Theoretical Refinement and Reevaluation of the Role of Norms in Human Behavior," *Advances in Experimental Social Psychology*, 24, 201-34.

Danesi, Marcel (1994), *Cool: The Signs and Meanings of Adolescence*, Toronto ; Buffalo, N.Y.: University of Toronto Press.

Dar-Nimrod, Ilan, I. G. Hansen, T. Proulx, and D. R. Lehman (2008), "Where Have You Gone James Dean? An Empirical Investigation of Coolness," Working Paper, University of British Columbia.

Frank, Thomas (1997), *The Conquest of Cool: Business Culture, Counterculture, and the Rise of Hip Consumerism*, Chicago: University of Chicago Press.

Gao, Leilei, S. Christian Wheeler, and Baba Shiv (2009), "The 'Shaken Self': Product Choices as a Means of Restoring Self-View Confidence," *Journal of Consumer Research*, 36, 29-38.

Gladwell, Malcolm (1997), "The Coolhunt," *The New Yorker*, 11.

Grossman, Lev (2003), "The Quest for Cool," *Time*, 162.

Heath, Joseph and Andrew Potter (2004), *Nation of Rebels: Why Counterculture Became Consumer Culture*, New York: HarperCollins.

Hirschman, Elizabeth C. (1993), "Ideology in Consumer Research, 1980 and 1990-a Marxist and Feminist Critique," *Journal of Consumer Research*, 19, 537-55.

Hogan, Patrick Colm (2001), *The Culture of Conformism: Understanding Social Consent*, Durham: Duke University Press.

Hollander, E. P. (1958), "Conformity, Status, and Idiosyncrasy Credit," *Psychological Review*, 65, 117-27.

Jones, Edward E. and Keith E. Davis (1965), "From Acts to Dispositions–The Attribution Process in Person Perception," *Advances in Experimental Social Psychology*, 2, 219-266.

Kerner, Noah and Gene Pressman (2007), *Chasing Cool: Standing out in Today's Cluttered Marketplace*, New York: Atria.

Leland, John (2004), *Hip, the History*, New York: Ecco.

Lupiono-Misdom, Janine and Joanne de Luca (1998), *Street Trends: How's Today's Alternative Youth Cultures Are Creating Tomorrow's Mainstream*, New York: Collins.

Mailer, Norman (1957), *The White Negro*, San Francisco: City Lights Books.

Markus, Hazel Rose and Barry Schwartz (2010), "Does Choice Mean Freedom and Well-Being?" *Journal of Consumer Research*, Forthcoming.

McCracken, Grant (1986), "Culture and Consumption-a Theoretical Account of the Structure and Movement of the Cultural Meaning of Consumer-Goods," *Journal of Consumer Research*, 13, 71-84.

Milgram, Stanley (1963), "Behavioral-Study of Obedience," *Journal of Abnormal Psychology*, 67, 371.

Nancarrow, Clive, Pamela Nancarrow, and Julie Page (2002), "An Analysis of the Concept of Cool and Its Marketing Implications," *Journal of Consumer Behaviour*, 1, 311-22.

O'Donnell, Kathleen A. and Daniel L. Wardlow (2000), "A Theory on the Origins of Coolness," *Advances in Consumer Research*, 27, 13-18.

Oyserman, D. and S. W. S. Lee (2008), "Does Culture Influence What and How We Think? Effects of Priming Individualism and Collectivism," *Psychological Bulletin*, 134, 311-42.

Pountain, Dick and David Robins (2000), *Cool Rules: Anatomy of an Attitude*, London: Reaktion.

Rousseau, Jean-Jacques (1994), *Discourse on the Origin of Inequality*, Oxford: Oxford University Press.

Ryan, R. M. and E. L. Deci (2000), "Self-Determination Theory and the Facilitation of Intrinsic Motivation, Social Development, and Well- Being," *American Psychologist*, 55, 68-78.

Tian, Kelly Tepper, William O. Bearden, and Gary L. Hunter (2001), "Consumers' Need for Uniqueness: Scale Development and Validation," *Journal of Consumer Research*, 28, 50-66.

Thornton, Sarah (1996), *Club Cultures: Music, Media, and Subcultural Capital*, Hanover, NH: University Press.

# How Asking "Who Am I?" Affects What You Buy: The Influence of Self-Discovery on Consumption

Eugenia Wu, Cornell University, USA
Keisha Cutright, Duke University, USA
Gavan Fitzsimons, Duke University, USA

## EXTENDED ABSTRACT

Are you an introvert or an extravert? A dreamer or a realist? Tools that ask and answer such questions are becoming a ubiquitous part of our lives, seeking to serve a universal thirst for self-discovery. Stores like Nordstrom and Bloomingdales offer color consultations to shoppers so they can learn whether "summer" or "winter" colors are better for them. Gyms offer fitness assessments to help consumers understand what type of exerciser they are and which activities they should be doing to reach their fitness goals. Self-help books abound which profess to help consumers learn about the self.

Consumers' drive towards self-discovery makes sense–the better we understand ourselves, the better decisions we can make. Interestingly, the process of discovering and defining the self can also be seen as a way of placing constraints on the self. If you are Type A, you cannot also be Type B. For individuals who are sensitive to the prospect of limitations, the findings from self-discovery may be particularly likely to be viewed as a constraint on who they can be. Thus, these individuals may reject such findings. We hypothesize that individuals characterized by an independent self-construal (for whom the act of defining the self is inconsistent with their conception of the self as an indefinable whole), as well as individuals who are highly reactant, will reject the findings of self-discovery and make consumption choices inconsistent with them, even as they actively seek to learn about themselves. Conversely, individuals who are characterized by interdependent self-construals and are low in reactance should accept the findings of self-discovery and incorporate such into their consumption decisions.

In study 1, participants completed a "personality quiz" consisting of personality items, IQ questions, and Singelis' (1994) Self-Construal Scale. Participants were either told that they were better than 70% of students in competence and better than 95% in excitement, or that they were better than 95% of students in competence and better than 70% in excitement. As the dependent measure, participants chose between Business 2.0 (low competence/high excitement) or Consumer Reports (high competence/low excitement) magazines. As expected, interdependents were more likely to choose Business 2.0 (low competence) when they received low competence feedback. They were more likely to choose Consumer Reports (high competence) when they received high competence feedback. In contrast, independents were more likely to choose Consumer Reports (high competence) when they received low competence feedback and Business 2.0 (low competence) when they received high competence feedback. Thus, interdependents made choices that were consistent with the self-information they received while independents made decisions that were inconsistent.

In study 2, we further explore the idea that self-knowledge can be constraining by demonstrating that individuals who are known to react against constraints (i.e., highly reactant individuals) also react against the limiting nature of self-knowledge. Participants first made a series of selections between pairs of products. Product pairs could consist of two branded products, two generic products or one branded and one generic product. Participants were then assigned to one of two feedback conditions. In the 'brand conscious' condition, participants read that they were more brand conscious than the average consumer. In the 'not brand conscious' condition, they read that they were less brand conscious than the average

consumer. Participants then made a second series of choices between branded and generic products. As expected, highly reactant individuals chose fewer brands when told that they were more brand conscious than others, and more brands when told that they were less brand conscious than others. Individuals low in reactance, however, chose more brands when told that that they were more brand conscious than others, and fewer brands when told that they were less brand conscious.

While the results of studies 1 and 2 reveal that in response to self-discovery findings, independents conduct themselves like high reactants and that interdependents behave like low reactants, we aimed to show a more direct link between self-construal and reactance in study 3. We expected independents to report increased levels of state reactance in response to the limitations inherent in self-discovery findings relative to interdependents. We further expected feelings of state reactance to mediate the relationship between self-construal and subsequent choice. Participants first completed the same product choice quiz described in study 2 Before being primed to be independent or interdependent (Brewer and Gardner, 1996). Next, participants read that they were more brand conscious than average, less brand conscious than average, or received no information at all. Participants who received feedback then answered four questions about their feelings of reactance toward the information (Lindsey 2005). Finally, all participants made choices between a second series of brands and generics. As expected, independents made product choices that were inconsistent with the self-knowledge they received while interdependents made choices consistent with their self-information. Importantly, reactance mediated the relationship between self-construal and brand choice as independents reported stronger feelings of reactance, regardless of the type of feedback.

Overall, studies 1-3 suggest that certain individuals may view self-knowledge as constraining, and that this may lead to some unexpected consequences for consumer behavior. Specifically, we find that independents and high reactants reject self-discovery findings and make consumption choices inconsistent with them even as they actively seek to learn about themselves. Thus, this research provides a key theoretical refinement in terms of when individuals will seek and yet reject self-discovery findings and establishes how this has significant consequences for consumption. We also contribute to research suggesting that individuals use consumption to enhance and express the self, especially when threatened (Gao, Wheeler, and Shiv 2009). We show that individuals' conceptualization of the self will determine how they use consumption to express the self in the face of feedback. This research also brings together the reactance and self-construal literatures in a novel way, offering new insights regarding when and why they exert similar effects on consumers' choices. Moreover, our results have important practical implications: Consumers' innate desire for self-discovery may be one need that marketers should be wary of fulfilling, as it may lead to surprising and unintended consequences.

## REFERENCES

Brewer, Marilynn B. and Wendi Gardner (1996), "Who Is This
We"? Levels of Collective Identity and Self Representations,"
*Journal of Personality and Social Psychology*, 71, 83-93.

Gao, Leilei, S. Christian Wheeler, and Baba Shiv (2009), "The "Shaken Self": Product Choices as a Means of Restoring Self-View Confidence," *Journal of Consumer Research*, 36 (1), 29-38.

Lindsey, Lisa L. Massi (2005), "Anticipated Guilt as Behavioral Motivation," *Human Communication Research*, 31 (4), 453-81.

Singelis, Theodore M. (1994), "The Measurement of Independent and Interdependent Self-Construals," *Personality and Social Psychology Bulletin*, 20 (5), 580-91.

# Distracted by the Man in the Mirror: Focusing Attention on the Outside Body Reduces Responsiveness to Internal Signals in Food Intake

Evelien van de Veer, Wageningen University, The Netherlands
Erica van Herpen, Wageningen University, The Netherlands
Hans C. M. van Trijp, Wageningen University, The Netherlands

## EXTENDED ABSTRACT

In Western societies, an increasing number of people is overweight or obese (WHO 2004). At the same time, media increasingly emphasize thinness ideals and outward appearance (Wiseman et al. 1992). In the current study, we test the relation between focusing on outside appearance and food consumption. More specifically, we hypothesize that focusing on the outside of the body impedes internal body cues to have an effect on food consumption.

A wealth of literature shows how internal cues, external cues and psychological states separately influence food intake (Wansink 2004), yet little is known on whether and how these cues and psychological states interact. Our study extends this work by examining consumers' responsiveness to internal satiety cues in different psychological states. To do so we assess how capable consumers are of compensating for previous food intake rather than looking at an absolute amount of food intake at a single point in time. One of the psychological states that has been found to stimulate food intake is distraction. Whereas it has been repeatedly demonstrated that distraction increases food intake within the consumption episode (e.g. Bellisle, Dalix and Slama 2004), there is some recent evidence that the effects of distraction may go beyond the consumption episode in affecting subsequent consumption (Higgs and Woodward 2009). We build on this work and, drawing on self-objectification theory, propose that focusing on outward appearance is a distractor that hinders individuals in compensating for previous food intake.

Self-objectification has been defined as the process whereby individuals observe themselves from a third-person perspective and regard their body as an object instead of as a subject (Fredrickson and Roberts 1997). Appearance focus is a manifestation of self-objectification. Fredrickson et al. (1998) found that a state of self-objectification, had detrimental effects on task performance due to a limited availability of cognitive resources. Based on the same reasoning, self-objectification theory predicts that focusing on outward appearance reduces responsiveness to bodily cues. Initial evidence indeed shows that self-reported measures of self-objectification and responsiveness to bodily cues are negatively related (Daubenmier 2005). However, using self-report measures of these constructs seems problematic. In the current study we have therefore tested this prediction assessing actual consumption.

In a pilot study we tested and showed that exposure to a mirror induces in participants a focus on public observable parts of the body, but not on private parts of the body. Thus, the use of a mirror appears to be a good manipulation of an outward appearance focus. In an experiment we subsequently tested the effects of an outward appearance focus on consumers' ability to compensate for the caloric content of previous food intake. Participants were served either a high caloric milkshake or a low caloric milkshake and were either seated in front of a mirror or not. In a second part of the experiment, participants evaluated neutral video fragments with a bowl of M&M's placed next to their screens. At the end of the experiment, participants' M&M consumption was assessed.

The effects of appearance focus and caloric content of the milkshake were assessed for the likelihood of M&M consumption and for the amount of M&M consumption. The results showed that the likelihood of starting to eat M&M's was influenced by the caloric content of the milkshake: When participants had previously been served a high caloric milkshake, they were less likely to start consuming M&M's. Interestingly, the effect that the caloric content of the milkshake had on the amount of consumption, was qualified by whether an appearance focus was induced in participants. Under control conditions, participants compensated for the caloric content of the milkshake by consuming fewer M&M's when previously served a milkshake of high caloric content than when served a low caloric milkshake. However, when participants were induced to focus on their outward appearance, the effect of caloric content on M&M consumption was (marginally) significant in the opposite direction. That is, participants consumed more M&M's when they had previously consumed a high caloric milkshake than a low caloric milkshake, indicating counterregulation rather than compensation of previous food intake.

The current study makes a number of contributions to the literature on cues affecting eating behavior. As our findings demonstrate that an appearance focus reduces the extent to which individuals are able to compensate for their previous intake, this indicates that the psychological state a consumer is in affects the influence of internal cues on consumption. This extends previous work that has looked mostly at how internal cues, external cues and psychological states separately affect food intake. The current findings provide insight into how a psychological state and internal physiological cues can jointly affect consumption. We have done so by looking at compensation for previous intake, rather than at absolute amounts of food intake. How well individuals are able to compensate for previous food intake under different psychological states, may also provide an understanding of when individuals are able to counteract the negative influences that a range of external cues and psychological states have on consumption levels (Wansink 2004). Finally, our findings suggest that future research may benefit from assessing both initiation of consumption and the amount of consumption, as our findings indicate that they may be affected by different processes.

This study has implications for consumers who regularly focus on their looks to monitor and regulate the potential harmful consequences of food consumption on body appearance. Our findings show that the effect may be counterproductive: Focusing on the outer body diminishes the power of internal satiety cues to regulate food consumption. This could result in a pattern where consumers overeat, gain weight and subsequently focus even more on their looks. On a broader level, the thinness and beauty ideals that are conveyed through commercials and other media may also foster an attentional focus on outward body appearance. These have the potential of negatively affecting healthy eating patterns as they may exert their effects within consumption contexts such as TV commercials, shopping malls or cinema's.

# Bandwagon, Snob and Veblen Effects in Luxury Consumption

Minas Kastanakis, ESCP Europe, UK
George Balabanis, Cass Business School, UK

## EXTENDED ABSTRACT

### Conceptualization

Many years ago Leibenstein (1950) highlighted the importance of "signaling effects" on consumption, which means that the utility derived from a product is enhanced or decreased due to the fact that "others" are purchasing and consuming it or due to the fact that the product bears a higher or lower price tag. In marketing it was taken for granted that "people buy luxuries to impress": most of consumer research has implicitly assumed that luxuries are consumed for social signaling purposes (Kapferer, 2006; Dubois, Laurent, and Czellar, 2001). However, there is a scarcity of empirical support to this claim. This study tries to plug this gap by providing empirical support to the possible antecedents of three luxury consumption effects. It aims to improve the existing theoretical understanding of the psychological antecedents and signaling behavior of luxury consumption.

Specifically, a veblen effect arises when consumer preference for a good increases as a direct function of its price; a snob effect when preference for a good increases as its quantity in the market is decreased; and a bandwagon effect is observed where consumer preference for a good increases as the number of people buying it is increased. As Vigneron and Johnson (1999) have pointed out, these effects are particularly observed in luxury product markets.

Research on luxuries' consumption has led to recent evidence (Tsai, 2005) that calls for a distinction between socially and personally-oriented luxury consumers (Wiedmann, Hennigs, and Siebels, 2007). The origins of these two orientations can be traced in an individual's self-concept. Some individuals focus more on the "internal domain" and their self-related goals or needs (independent self-concept); while others are more concerned about the inter-personal domain, the reaction of others and their external "persona" (inter-dependent self-concept). This literature (Wong and Ahuvia, 1998) advocates that consumers with an independent self show a more personal orientation in the way that they consume luxuries (focusing on their hedonic, utilitarian and self-communication goals) whereas consumers with inter-dependent self care more for the social impact of such consumption (the three investigated effects).

The existing work has not paid sufficient attention to the social effects (i.e., the bandwagon, snob, and veblen effects). It is not clear how exactly the self orientations impact on the consumption of luxuries. Against the previous background, this study proposes that these effects are driven by both an independent and an inter-dependent self-concept (they are both personally and socially-driven behaviors) and that a number of relevant traits act as mediators between the self-concept(s) and the signaling behavior.

With the help of the literature and qualitative exploratory research (interviews with managers of luxury products) the following four traits emerge to be related to the bandwagon, snob and veblen effects: need-for-uniqueness, vanity, status-seeking, and susceptibility to interpersonal influence.

Need-for-uniqueness (NFU) is "the trait of pursuing differentness relative to others through the acquisition, utilization and disposition of consumer goods" (Tepper, Bearden and Hunter, 2001). NFU is positively related to both independent and inter-dependent self concepts and is hypothesized to be an antecedent of both snob and veblen effects, while negatively related to a bandwagon effect.

Vanity (Netemeyer, Burton, and Lichtenstein, 1995) has a physical and an achievement dimension. Vanity is hypothesized to be positively related to both independent and inter-dependent self concepts. In addition vanity is an antecedent of a veblen effect (i.e., expensive luxuries), a snob effect (i.e., rare luxuries) and a bandwagon effect (i.e., through consumption of popular luxuries) as well.

Status-seeking is defined as the "process by which individuals strive to improve their social standing trough the conspicuous consumption of products that confer and symbolize status" (Eastman, Goldsmith, and Flynn, 1999). It reflects a social orientation and it is hypothesized to be positively related to the inter-dependent self (and negatively to the independent self). In addition, using the same argumentation line, status-seeking is hypothesized to be an antecedent of the veblen, snob and bandwagon effects.

Consumer susceptibility to interpersonal influence, refers to the need to "identify with or enhance one's image in the opinion of significant others" through relevant consumption (Bearden, Netemeyer, and Teel, 1989). This trait reflects a social orientation and, as such, is hypothesized to be positively related to the inter-dependent self (and negatively to the independent self). It is an antecedent of the bandwagon effect and it is negatively related to snob effect.

### Method

Data were collected by the "drop and collect" survey method in a probability sample of 431 consumers of luxuries in London. Three mediated structural models with the following variables were estimated: (independent and inter-dependent) self-concepts as antecedents (exogenous variables), need-for-uniqueness, status-seeking, vanity and susceptibility to interpersonal influence as mediators, and bandwagon, snob and veblen behavior(s) as outcome variables.

### Major Findings

Bandwagon behavior is mostly influenced by inter-dependence. Managers who want to position their products as popular luxuries should focus-with this order-on enhancing their products' projected status (status from popularity/conformity), normative (fit-in) messages, and (physical) vanity/attractiveness appeal; while avoiding "stand-out" (avoidance of similarity) messages.

Snob behavior is mostly influenced by independence. Managers who want to position their products as exclusive luxuries should focus-with this order-on status derived from exclusivity, creating an aura of scarcity and uniqueness, and (physical) vanity/attractiveness appeal; while avoiding conformity (fit-in) messages.

Veblenian behavior is marginally influenced by inter-dependence. Managers who want to boost consumption of their luxury products using (very expensive) price-signaling should focus-with this order-on communicating messages coherent with the traits of these target consumers: status messages (status from prestige-pricing since, for the purely conspicuous consumer, the satisfaction comes from audience reaction to the wealth displayed), (physical) vanity/attractiveness appeals, as well as on scarcity and uniqueness messages based on creative counter-conformity.

These results contribute to understanding in depth the antecedents behind the signaling behavior of consumers of luxury goods. This behavior is both personally meaningful and socially driven. These findings provide practical help to managers in a) segmenting their markets, and b) evaluating and predicting the reaction of consumers to changes in their offerings and communication campaigns.

# REFERENCES

Alston, W. P. (1975), "Traits, Consistency and Conceptual Alternatives for Personality Theory", *Journal for the Theory of Social Behavior*, 5, 17-48.

Amaldoss, W. and Jain, S. (2005), "Conspicuous Consumption and Sophisticated Thinking", *Management Science*, 51 (10), 1449-1466.

Bagozzi, R.P. and Heathenon, T. F. (1994), "A General Approach to Representing Multifaceted Personality Constructs: Application to State Self-Esteem", *Structural Equation Modeling*, 1, 35-67.

Bagwell, L. S. and Bernheim, B. D. (1996), "Veblen effects in a theory of conspicuous consumption", *American Economic Review*, 86 (3), 349.

Baron, R. M. and Kenny, D. A. (1986) "The Moderator-Mediator Variable Distinction in Social Psychological Research: Conceptual, Strategic and Statistical Considerations", *Journal of Personality and Social Psychology*, vol. 51 (6), pp. 1173-1182.

Bearden, W. O., Netemeyer, R. G. and Teel, J. E. (1989), "Measurement of Consumer Susceptibility to Interpersonal Influence", *Journal of Consumer Research*, 15, 473-481.

Belk, R. W. (1988), "Possessions and the extended self", *Journal of Consumer Research*, 15, 139-168.

Braun, O. L. and Wicklund, R. A. (1989), "Psychological antecedents of conspicuous consumption", *Journal of Economic Psychology*, 10 (2), 161.

Brioschi, A. (2006), "Selling Dreams: The Role of Advertising in Shaping Luxury Brand Meaning", in *Brand Culture*, eds. Schroeder, J. E. and Salzer-Mörling, Routledge: Oxon.

Byrne, B. N. (2001), *Structural Equation Modelling with AMOS*, NJ: Lawrence Erlbaum Associates.

Chao, A. and Schor, J. B. (1998), "Empirical Tests of Status Consumption: Evidence from Women's Cosmetics", *Journal of Economic Psychology*, 19, 107-131.

Chaudhuri, H. R. and Majumdar, S (2006), "Of Diamonds and Desires: Understanding Conspicuous Consumption from a Contemporary Marketing Perspective", *Academy of Marketing Science Review*, 2006 (11), http://www.amsreview.org/articles/chaudhuri09-2006.pdf

Coelho, P. R and McClure, J. E. (1993), "Toward an Economic Theory of Fashion", *Economic Inquiry*, Oxford University Press, 31(4), 595-608.

Corfman, K. P., Lehmann, D. R and Narayanan, S. (1991), "Values, utility, and ownership: Modeling the relationships for consumer durables", *Journal of Retailing*, 67(2), 184-204.

Corneo, G. and Jeanne, O. (1997), "Conspicuous Consumption, Snobbism and Conformism", *Journal of Public Economics*, 66, 55-71.

Coulter, R.A., Price, L.L. and Feick, L. (2003), "Rethinking the origins of involvement and brand commitment", *Journal of Consumer Research*, 30 (2), 151-182.

Dubois, B., Laurent, G., Czellar, S. (2001), "Consumer rapport to luxury: analyzing complex and ambivalent attitudes", *Working Paper 736, HEC School of Management*, Jouy-en-Josas.

Dubois, B. and Duquesne, P. (1993), "The Market for Luxury Goods: Income versus Culture", *European Journal of Marketing*, 27 (1), 35.

Dubois, B. and Laurent, G. (1994), "Attitudes Towards the Concept of Luxury: an Exploratory Analysis", in *Asia-Pacific Advances in Consumer Research*, eds. Siew Meng Leong and Joseph A. Cote, Singapore, 1 (2), 273-278.

Duesenberry, J. S. (1949), *Income, Saving and the Theory of Consumer Behavior*, Harvard University Press, Cambridge.

Eastman, J. K., Goldsmith, R. E. and Flynn, L. R. (1999), "Status Consumption in Consumer Behavior: Scale Development and Validation", *Journal of Marketing Theory and Practice*, 7 (3), 41-51.

Ellis, J.B. and Wittenbaum, G.M. (2000), "Relationships between self-construal and verbal promotion", *Communication Research*, 27, 704-722.

Eysenck, H. J. (1990), "Biological Dimensions of Personality", in *Handbook of Personality: Theory and Research*, ed. L. A. Pervin, New York: Guilford.

Goffman, E. (1959), *The Presentation of Self in Everyday Life*, Garden City, NY: Doubleday.

Gudykunst, W.B. and Lee, C.M. (2003), "Assessing the validity of self-construal scales", *Human Communication Research*, 29, 2, 253-274.

Hansen, F. (1998), "From lifestyle to value systems to simplicity", *Advances in Consumer Research*, 25, 181-195.

Jaramillo, F. and Moizeau, F. (2003), "Conspicuous Consumption and Social Segmentation", *Journal of Public Economic Theory*, 5 (1), 1-24.

Johansson-Stenman, O. and Martinsson, P. (2006), "Honestly, Why Are You Driving a BMW?", *Journal of Economic Behavior and Organization*, 60, 129-146.

Kapferer, J.-N. (1997), "Managing Luxury Brands", *Journal of Brand Management*, 4 (4), 251-60.

Kapferer, J.-N. (1998), "Why are we seduced by luxury brands?", *Journal of Brand Management*, 6 (1), 44-49.

Kapferer, J.-N. (2006), "The Two Business Cultures of Luxury Brands", in *Brand Culture*, eds. Schroeder, J. E. and Salzer-Mörling, Routledge: Oxon.

Kline, Rex B. (2005), *Principles and Practice of Structural Equation Modelling*, 2nd ed., NY: Guilford Press.

Leibenstein, H. (1950), "Bandwagon, Snob, and Veblen Effects in the Theory of Consumers' Demand", *Quarterly Journal of Economics*, 64, 183-207.

Markus, H. and Kitayama, S. (1991), "Culture and the Self: Implications for Cognition, Emotion, and Motivation", *Psychological Review*, 98, 224-53.

Mason, R. (1981), *Conspicuous Consumption: A Study of Exceptional Consumer Behavior*, New York: St. Martin's Press.

Mason, R. (1984), "Conspicuous Consumption: A Literature Review", *European Journal of Marketing*, 18 (3), 26.

McDonald, R. P. and Ho, M. H. (2002) "Principles and Practice in Reporting Structural Equation Analyses", *Psychological Methods*, vol. 7, pp. 64-82.

Nail, P. R. (1986), "Toward an Integration of Some Models and Theories of Social Response", *Psychological Bulletin*, 100, 190-206.

Netemeyer, R. G., Burton, S. and Lichtenstein, D. R. (1995), "Trait aspects of vanity: measurement and relevance to consumer behavior", *Journal of Consumer Research*, 21 (4), 612.

Podsakoff, P. M., Mac Kenzie, S. B., Lee, J. Y. and Podsakoff, N. P. (2003) "Common Method Biases in Behavioral Research: A Critical Review of the Literature and Recommended Biases", *Journal of Applied Psychology*, vol. 88 (5), pp. 879-903.

Richins, M. L. and Dawson, S. (1992), "A consumer values orientation for materialism and its measurement: Scale development and validation", *Journal of Consumer Research*, 19 (3), 303.

Shrout, P. E. And Bolger, N. (2002), "Mediation in Experimental and Non-Experimental Studies: New Procedures and Recommendations", *Psychological Methods*, vol. 7 (4), pp. 422-445.

Schumacker, R. E. and Lomax, R. G. (2004), *A Beginners Guide to Structural Equation Modelling*, 2nd ed., New York: Taylor and Francis Group.

Singelis, T. M. (1994), "The Measurement of Independent and Interdependent Self-Construals", *Personality and Social Psychology Bulletin*, 20, 580-91.

Solomon, M. R. (2006), *Consumer Behavior: Buying, Selling and Being*, Prentice Hall, New Jersey.

Tepper, K. T., Bearden, W.O. and Hunter, G. L. (2001), "Consumers' Need for Uniqueness: Scale Development and Validation", *Journal of Consumer Research*, 28 (1), 50.

Tepper, K. T. and McKenzie, K. (2001) "The Long-Term Predictive Validity of the Consumers' Need for Uniqueness Scale", *Journal of Consumer Psychology*, 10 (3), 171-193.

Triandis, H. C. (1989), "The Self and Behavior in Differing Cultural Contexts", *Psychological Review*, 96, 506-20.

Tsai, S. (2005), "Impact of personal orientation on luxury-brand purchase value", *International Journal of Market Research*, 47 (4), 429-454.

Veblen T. (1899), *The Theory of the Leisure Class*, Macmillan: New York.

Vigneron, F. and Johnson, L. W. (1999), "A Review and a Conceptual Framework of Prestige-Seeking Consumer Behavior", *Academy of Marketing Science Review, 1999 (1)*, http://www.amsreview.org/articles/vigneron01-1999.pdf

Wiedmann, K-P., Hennigs, N. and Siebels, A. (2007), "Measuring Consumers' Luxury Value Perception: A Cross-Cultural Framework", *Academy of Marketing Science Review*, 2007 (7), http://www.amsreview.org/articles/wiedmann07-2007.pdf

Wong, N. Y and Ahuvia, A. C. (1998), "Personal taste and family face: Luxury consumption in Confucian and Western societies", *Psychology and Marketing*, 15 (5), 423-441.

Wong, N. Y. C. and Zaichkowsky, J. L. (1999) "Do counterfeits devalue the ownership of luxury brands?", *Journal of Product and Brand Management*, 9 (7), 485-497.

# The Power of Positive Thinking: Asymmetrical Affective Perseverance in Consumer Brand Judgments

Brent Coker, University of Melbourne, Australia

## EXTENDED ABSTRACT

Consumers update their attitudes towards brands as new information in encoded. For example, when reading online reviews about hotels or restaurants when booking a holiday, consumers will adjust their attitude in line with the positivity or negativity of the reviews being read. In many situations, the valence of information encoded about a product or service is mixed. It is rare for instance for online hotel reviews to be consistently positive or negative; there are always some patrons who appear to have had a more positive or more negative experience with the hotel than the majority. From a big picture standpoint, the issue of how consumers form attitudes towards products and services from reading online reviews raises the more general issue of how consumers adjust their attitudes when information describing the quality of product or service is mixed. The goal of this research therefore is to explore how consumers update their attitudes towards products and services when information encountered during decision making is of opposite valence.

Conventional wisdom would suggest that if a consumer has a favorable attitude towards a brand, which is then contested by negative information, the consumer will have control over their judgments and adjust their evaluation accordingly. For example, a consumer may hear a rumor about a brand, which they later find to be untrue. Similarly, when a consumer encodes positive information contesting previously encoded negative information, they will also have control over their judgments and adjust their evaluations accordingly. The present research argues however that consumers are less successful at adjusting their attitudes in a positive to negative direction than they are at adjusting their attitudes in a negative to positive direction. Specifically, this research proposes a theory of asymmetric affective perseverance, whereby positive attitudes continue to contaminate judgments towards a brand when replaced by negative attitudes, but negative attitudes do not. This leads to the paradoxical finding that consumers' attitudes towards a brand are positively skewed if they encode positive information before negative information, than if they encode the same information in the opposite order.

This research further finds that this asymmetrical perseverance of affect is contingent on trend of information over time, and that it only occurs when information is deeply encoded. When trend information is available, such as when positive reviews are old, and negative reviews are recent, the pattern of results is reversed, and the nature of asymmetric affective perseverance is muted.

The phenomenon of asymmetric affective perseverance is attributed to people's relative difficulty in shifting their attitude in a positive to negative direction, than in a negative to positive direction. Anecdotally, the concept of denial in psychiatric literature describes a similar cognitive process. A person given bad news will often experience the protection mechanism of disbelief, deferral, and dismissal before a relatively negative affective state sinks in (Lubinsky 1994). In contrast, the shift from relative despair to happiness is often instantaneous, and has a stronger effect on imagined outcomes than negative factors. In general, human beings prefer to remain optimistic and are more willing and hopeful towards adopting a positive outlook than remaining in a relative state of negativity. The asymmetry in attitude adjustment pertaining to brands is demonstrated in two studies comprised of four experiments.

The first study demonstrates asymmetric perseverance of positive affect in two hypothetical brand evaluation exercises. Experiment one documents the existence of positive contamination when a positive attitude is replaced by a negative attitude, with an absence of negative contamination when the attitude replacement is from negative to positive. Experiment two further documents asymmetrical attitude replacement, finding the same effect when attempts by participants to adjust attitudes to a relative state of ambivalence are unsuccessful after participants are told the positive information that shaped their attitude was false.

The second study investigates the mechanisms underlying asymmetric affective perseverance. Specifically, experiment 3 further tests the theory by demonstrating how asymmetric perseverance of affect is contingent on time trend information. In a simulated task of evaluation based on online reviews, it is assumed that a consumer should be more forgiving of a brand if negative reviews are relatively old, and have been replaced by more recent positive reviews. This pattern should suggest improvement, and therefore less likelihood of regret. The results suggest attenuation of positive contamination when trend information is available. Finally, experiment four lends support to the theory by showing that asymmetrical affective perseverance appears to be a function of cognitive elaboration.

From a big picture standpoint, our theory is interesting because it sheds light on how consumers form attitudes towards brands, when influenced by oppositely valenced information. Our theory is also interesting because it explains inconsistent findings in psychology literature about attitude replacement, which is also relevant to how consumers form brand judgments. Although some research has found that people are successful at discounting previously formed judgments (Golding et al. 1990), other research has found that invalidated information may continue to contaminate future judgments, without the subject being aware (Bekerian and Bowers 1983; Greenwald and Banaji 1995; Lindsay and Johnson 1989).

# Mood Matching: The Importance of Fit between Moods Elicited by TV Programs and Commercials

Joseph Lajos, HEC Paris, France
Nailya Ordabayeva, Erasmus University Rotterdam, The Nethelands
Amitava Chattopadhyay, INSEAD, Singapore

## EXTENDED ABSTRACT

Previous consumer research suggests that TV viewers have more favorable attitudes toward commercials when they are in a happy mood than when they are in a sad mood. Research has demonstrated this effect with moods induced by commercials themselves (Batra and Stayman 1990; Derbaix 1995; Edell and Burke 1987; Holbrook and Batra 1987) and with moods induced by TV programs in which the commercials are embedded (Goldberg and Gorn 1987; Mathur and Chattopadhyay 1991). This research has revealed two main effects. All else equal, TV viewers like commercials more when (1) they induce happy moods rather than sad moods, and (2) they are embedded in programs that induce happy moods rather than sad moods. These effects are important since attitude toward the ad ($A_{Ad}$) reliably influences brand attitudes and purchase intentions (MacKenzie, Lutz, and Belch 1986; Madden, Allen, and Twible 1988; Miniard, Bhatla, and Rose 1990; Mitchell and Olson 1981; see Brown and Stayman 1992 for a review), and is the single best predictor of an ad's ability to influence sales (Haley and Baldinger 1991). However, previous research has not examined whether commercials that induce a happy mood elicit more favorable responses compared to those that induce a sad mood, irrespective of whether the mood induced by the program is positive or negative. This is the focus of our research.

In this paper, we propose that when TV viewers watch a program that establishes a mood, they expect to continue experiencing that mood throughout the duration of the TV viewing experience. We draw on research on mood as input to role fulfillment evaluation processes (Martin et al. 1997) to hypothesize that TV viewers have more favorable attitudes toward commercials that support moods established by programs than toward those that break established moods. Our hypothesis leads to the novel prediction that, during a sad program, TV viewers will like sad commercials more than happy commercials.

The results of experiment 1 support our hypothesis. In the experiment, we find that participants liked two sad commercials significantly more when they followed sad program clips than when they followed happy program clips, and liked two happy commercials more when they followed happy program clips than when they followed sad program clips, albeit not significantly so.

A key finding of experiment 1 is that, under some conditions, viewers may actually have more favorable attitudes toward commercials when they are aired during sad programs than when they are aired during happy programs. This finding may initially seem to be at odds with mood as information theory (Schwarz and Clore 1983, 1988), which proposes that people use their momentary affective states as information when making judgments and evaluations, for example by asking "how do I feel about it?" Mood as information theory thus predicts that people will evaluate stimuli more favorably when they are in a positive mood than when they are in a negative mood. However, we assert that the apparent contradiction between our predictions and those of mood as information theory can be reconciled by noting that role fulfillment evaluations are based on an expectation comparison process. Specifically, we hypothesize that role fulfillment evaluation theory makes accurate predictions when people are likely to have mood expectations, whereas mood as information theory makes accurate predictions when people are unlikely to have mood expectations.

The results of experiment 2 support this hypothesis. In the experiment, we find that, following a sad program clip, viewers who focused on their mood during the TV watching experience liked sad commercials more than happy commercials, whereas viewers who were distracted from their mood during the experience liked happy commercials more than sad commercials. Furthermore, we find that a second focus manipulation administered after, rather than during, the TV viewing experience, did not affect viewers' evaluations, thus providing further evidence that a difference in expectations underlies the aforementioned results.

Our research contributes to theory and practice in three ways. First, we use role fulfillment evaluation theory to identify an effect that is at odds with the recommendations of previous research on the attitudinal effects of moods induced by TV programs and commercials. Second, we identify mood expectations during the experience as a moderating variable, allowing us to reconcile our main result with those of extant research. Third, our results provide guidance to advertising managers who seek either to select a program during which to air existing commercials, or to produce commercials that will be aired during a particular program. Our suggestion that sad commercials can be more effective when aired during sad programs than during happy programs seems to go against common advertising practice. According to Mathur and Chattopadhyay (1991), several major organizations have policies that prohibit advertising during sad programs. Consistent with this, news articles report that many groups have pulled their commercials from sad programs. Based on our findings, we believe that advertising managers should reassess the usefulness of scheduling some commercials during sad programs.

## REFERENCES

Batra, Rajeev and Michael L. Ray (1986), "Affective Responses Mediating Acceptance of Advertising," *Journal of Consumer Research*, 13 (September), 234-49.

Batra, Rajeev and Douglas M. Stayman (1990), "The Role of Mood in Advertising Effectiveness," *Journal of Consumer Research*, 17 (September), 203-14.

Bergkvist, Lars and John R. Rossiter (2007), "The Predictive Validity of Multiple-Item Versus Single-Item Measures of the Same Constructs," *Journal of Marketing Research*, 44 (May), 175-84.

Bower, Gordon H. (1981), "Mood and Memory," *American Psychologist*, 36 (2), 129-48.

Bower, Gordon H. and Paul R. Cohen (1982), "Emotional Influences in Memory and Thinking: Data and Theory," in *Affect and Cognition*, ed. Margaret Clark and Susuan Fiske, Hillsdale, NJ: Erlbaum, 291-331.

Brown, Steven P., Pamela M. Homer, and J. Jeffrey Inman (1998), "A Meta-Analysis of Relationships between Ad-Evoked Feelings and Advertising Responses," *Journal of Marketing Research*, 35 (February), 114-26.

Brown, Steven P. and Douglas M. Stayman (1992), "Antecedents and Consequences of Attitude Toward the Ad: A Meta-Analysis," *Journal of Consumer Research*, 19 (June), 34-51.

Burke, Marian Chapman and Julie A. Edell (1989), "The Impact of Feelings on Ad-based Affect and Cognition," *Journal of Marketing Research*, 26 (February), 69-83.

Derbaix, Christian M. (1995), "The Impact of Affective Reactions on Attitudes Toward the Advertisement and the Brand: A Step Toward Ecological Validity," *Journal of Marketing Research*, 32 (November), 470-79.

Edell, Julie A. and Marian Chapman Burke (1987), "The Power of Feelings in Understanding Advertising Effects," *Journal of Consumer Research*, 14 (December), 421-33.

Gardner, Meryl P. (1985), "Mood States and Consumer Behavior: A Critical Review," *Journal of Consumer Research*, 12 (December), 281-300.

Goldberg, Marvin E. and Gerald J. Gorn (1987), "Happy and Sad TV Programs: How They Affect Reactions to Commercials," *Journal of Consumer Research*, 14 (December), 387-403.

Gorn, Gerald J., Marvin E. Goldberg, and Kunal Basu (1993), "Mood, Awareness, and Product Evaluation," *Journal of Consumer Psychology*, 2 (3), 237-56.

Haley, Russell I. and Allan L. Baldinger (1991), "The ARF Copy Research Validity Project," *Journal of Advertising Research*, 31 (2), 11-32.

Higgins, E. Tory and William S. Rholes (1976), "Impression Formation and Role Fulfillment: A 'Holistic Reference' Approach," *Journal of Experimental Social Psychology*, 12, 422-35.

Holbrook, Morris B. and Rajeev Batra (1987), "Assessing the Role of Emotions as Mediators of Consumer Responses to Advertising," *Journal of Consumer Research*, 14 (December), 404-20.

Isen, Alice M. (1984), "Toward Understanding the Role of Affect in Cognition," in *Handbook of Social Cognition*, ed. Robert S. Wyer and Thomas K. Srull, Hillsdale, NJ: Erlbaum, 179-236.

Isen, Alice M., Thomas E. Shalker, Margaret Clark, and Lynn Karp (1978), "Affect, Accessibility of Material in Memory, and Behavior: A Cognitive Loop?" *Journal of Personality and Social Psychology*, 36 (1), 1-12.

MacKenzie, Scott B., Richard J. Lutz, and George E. Belch (1986), "The Role of Attitude Toward the Ad as a Mediator of Advertising Effectiveness: A Test of Competing Explanations," *Journal of Marketing Research*, 23 (May), 130-43.

Madden, Thomas J., Chris T. Allen, and Jacquelyn L. Twible (1988), "Attitude Toward the Ad: An Assessment of Diverse Measurement Indices under Different Processing Sets," *Journal of Marketing Research*, 25 (August), 242-52.

Martin, Leonard L., Teresa Abend, Constantine Sedikides, and Jeffrey D. Green (1997), "How Would I Feel If...? Mood as Input to a Role-Fulfillment Evaluation Process," *Journal of Personality and Social Psychology*, 73 (2), 242-53.

Mathur, Mahima and Amitava Chattopadhyay (1991), "The Impact of Moods Generated by Television Programs on Responses to Advertising," *Psychology & Marketing*, 8(1), 59-77.

Miniard, Paul W., Sunil Bhatla, and Randall L. Rose (1990), "On the Formation and Relationship of Ad and Brand Attitudes: An Experimental and Causal Analysis," *Journal of Marketing Research*, 27 (August), 290-303.

Mitchell, Andrew A. and Jerry C. Olson (1981), "Are Product Attribute Beliefs the Only Mediator of Advertising Effects on Brand Attitude?" *Journal of Marketing Research*, 18 (August), 318-32.

Murry, John P. Jr., John L. Lastovicka, and Surendra N. Singh (1992), "Feeling and Liking Responses to Television Programs: An Examination of Two Explanations for Media-Context Effects," *Journal of Consumer Research*, 18 (March), 441-51.

Russell, James A. (1979), "Affective Space is Bipolar," *Journal of Personality and Social Psychology*, 37, 345-56.

_____ (1980), "A Circumplex Model of Affect," *Journal of Personality and Social Psychology*, 39, 1161-178.

Schwarz, Norbert and Gerald L. Clore (1983), "Mood, Misattribution, and Judgments of Well-Being: Informative and Directive Functions of Affective States," *Journal of Personality and Social Psychology*, 45 (September), 513-23.

_____ (1988), "How Do I Feel About It? The Information Function of Affective States," in *Affect Cognition and Social Behavior*, ed. Klaus Fiedler and Joseph Forgas, Lewinston, NY: Hogrefe, 44-62.

Srull, Thomas K. (1983), "The Impact of Affective Reactions in Advertising on the Representation of Product Information in Memory," in *Advances in Consumer Research*, Vol. 10, ed. Richard Bagozzi and Alice Tybout, Ann Arbor, MI: Association for Consumer Research, 520-25.

Wang, Jing and Bobby L. Calder (2006), "Media Transportation and Advertising," *Journal of Consumer Research*, 33 (September), 151-62.

Watson, David and Auke Tellegen (1985), "Toward a Consensual Structure of Mood," *Psychological Bulletin*, 98, 219-35.

Woll, Stanley B., David G. Weeks, Carolyn L. Fraps, Joe Pendergrass, and Mary A. Vanderplas (1980), "Role of Sentence Context in the Encoding of Trait Descriptors," *Journal of Personality and Social Psychology*, 39 (1), 59-68.

Wyer, Robert S. Jr. (1970), "The Prediction of Evaluations of Social Role Occupants as a Function of the Favorableness, Relevance, and Probability Associated with Attributes of These Occupants," *Sociometry*, 33 (1), 79-96.

# How Mood Moderates the Effect of Context on Product Judgments

Davy Lerouge, Tilburg University, The Netherlands
Yana Avramova, Tilburg University, The Netherlands
Diederik A. Stapel, Tilburg University, The Netherlands

## EXTENDED ABSTRACT

Does a restaurant serve meals that are sufficiently large? Is a 640M 2.5GH laptop at $1300 attractive? How one perceives, evaluates, and judges a product is not only driven by characteristics of the product itself, but also by the context the product is presented in. The size of a gastronomic nouvelle cuisine meal may look ridiculously small on an oversized plate, but sufficiently large when served on a normal sized plate (Wansink and van Ittersum 2006; Wansink, van Ittersum, and Painter 2006). And the same notebook is typically perceived as more attractive when it is the middle option in a choice set than when it is an extreme option (Simonson 1989; Simonson and Tversky 1992). As pervasive and robust as context effects are, however, we predict that mood critically determines the extent to which consumers take the context into consideration when making product judgments.

Our prediction is mainly based on the assumption that mood alters attentional scope as such that positive mood broadens attentional scope to both the target product and context and negative mood narrows attentional scope to the target product only. First support for this assumption is provided by studies using perceptual tasks that contain both broad and narrow visual features. These studies consistently found that happy individuals focused more on the broad feature and sad individuals focused more on the narrow features (Basso et al. 1996; Frederickson and Branigan 2005; Gasper and Clore 2002). In addition, other studies in which participants are asked to focus on a central target and ignore flanking distracters showed that sad participants were less affected by the distracting context stimuli and therefore performed better compared to happy participants (Fenske and Eastwood 2003; Rowe, Hirsh, and Anderson 2007). Finally, Schmitz, Rosa, and Anderson (2009) provided neuroscientific evidence illustrating that mood alters visual cortical responses, such that negative affect decreases and positive affect increases the scope of early perceptual encoding in a visuospatial task.

So, previous research suggests that attentional scope is fundamentally influenced by mood. Therefore, it seems reasonable to predict that happy consumers will rely more and sad consumers were rely less on the context when making product judgments compared to consumers who are in a neutral mood state. We provided support for this prediction with three studies testing the effect of different mood manipulations on a variety of context effects that have been previously observed in consumer behavior.

In the first study, we employed the perceptual contrast effect (based on the Ebbinghaus Illusion task) to find initial evidence for the notion that mood moderates the extent to which product judgments are affected by the context. After we induced mood, we asked participants to estimate the size of a target product (apples, coke cans, bottles of liquid laundry detergent, peanut butter jars) that was surrounded by either larger or smaller versions of the target product. Consistent with our predictions, size estimations of positive mood participants were significantly more and those of negative mood participants were significantly less affected by the surrounding stimuli than those of neutral mood participants. In other words, happy participants were more and sad participants were less susceptible to the Ebbinghaus illusion than neutral mood participants.

In study 2 and 3 we further tested the effect of mood on two well-known and robust context effects in consumer behavior: the attraction (or asymmetric dominance) effect and the compromise effect. Consistent with our assumption that positive (negative) mood results in more (less) attention to the other products in the choice set, we found that positive (negative) mood resulted in stronger (weaker) attraction and compromise effects compared to the neutral control condition.

Together the current studies provide strong evidence that positive mood strengthens and negative mood eliminates the effect of context on product judgments and refute a depth of processing account as alternative explanation. Instead, we argue that our effects are driven by a shift in attentional scope with positive mood promoting broader attention to both the target and the context and negative mood focusing attention on the target. Study 3 indeed illustrated that the effect of mood on context dependence was fully mediated by attentional scope.

We believe that the effect of mood on context dependence may have ample implications for consumers and decision makers. As long as there is a target product to be judged and a context in which it is presented, the pattern we proposed should hold strong. We would speculate that a sales assistant who is trying to trick us into buying a product by comparing it to a ridiculously overpriced alternative, or a product's television ad featuring poignant music and heart-warming scenes will be more successful if we are in a good, than in a bad mood. Our findings suggest that being happy can make us more susceptible to persuasive communication that relies on the power of context. However, being happy can also be pretty useful. Looking at the top and bottom (and left and right) shelves in the supermarket can save you money, and make you discover new and potentially better product alternatives.

## REFERENCES

Basso, Michael R., Bruce K. Schefft, M. Douglas Ris, and William N. Dember (1996), "Mood and global-local visual processing," *Journal of International Neuropsychological Society*, 2 (3), 249-55.

Fenske Mark J. and John D. Eastwood (2003), "Modulation of focused attention by faces expressing emotion: Evidence from flanker tasks," *Emotion*, 3 (4), 327-43.

Fredrickson, Barbara L. and Christine Branigan (2005), "Positive emotions broaden the scope of attention and thought-action repertoires," *Cognition and Emotion*, 19 (3), 313-32.

Gasper, Karen and Gerald L. Clore (2002), "Attending to the Big Picture: Mood and Global Versus Local Processing of Visual Information," *Psychological Science*, 13 (1), 34-40.

Rowe, G., J. B. Hirsh, A. K. Anderson, and Edward E. Smith (2007), "Positive Affect Increases the Breadth of Attentional Selection," *PNAS Proceedings of the National Academy of Sciences of the United States of America*, 104 (1), 383-88.

Schmitz, Taylor W., Eve De Rosa, and Adam K. Anderson (2009), "Opposing influences of affective state valence on visual cortical encoding," *The Journal of Neuroscience*, 29 (22), 7199-207.

Simonson, Itamar (1989), "Choice Based on Reasons: The Case of Attraction and Compromise Effects," *Journal of Consumer Research*, 16 (2), 158-74.

Simonson, Itamar and Amos Tversky (1992), "Choice in Context-Tradeoff Contrast and Extremeness Aversion," *Journal of Marketing Research*, 29 (3), 281-95.

Wansink, Brian and Koert van Ittersum (2006), "The Visual Illusions of Food: Why Plates, Bowls and Spoons Can Bias Consumption Volume," *FASEB Journal*, 20 (4), A618-A618, Part 1.

Wansink, Brian, Koert van Ittersum, and James E. Painter (2006), "Ice Cream Illusions: Bowl Size, Spoon Size, and Serving Size," *American Journal of Preventive Medicine*, 31 (3), 240-43.

# Responses to Animal Anthropomorphism in Advertising Based on Character Similarity to Humans

Paul M. Connell, Stony Brook University, USA

## EXTENDED ABSTRACT

Throughout civilization, people have imbued creatures from the natural world with human traits and motivations. Marketers have capitalized on this tendency by creating a plentitude of anthropomorphic animal mascots for a variety of products and services. Yet, research examining anthropomorphism on consumer behavior is sparse. The purpose of this research is to understand which types of animals are portrayed anthropomorphically most often in marketing communications (based upon their perceived similarity to humans) and how consumers' attitudes are affected by such anthropomorphism.

Anthropomorphism is the process of assigning real or imagined human characteristics, intentions, motivations, or emotions to nonhuman objects, often motivated by explaining and understanding the behavior of those nunhuman agents (Epley, Waytz, and Cacioppo 2008). People do this with a seemingly unending array of things, including brands and television characters, to the extent that they sometimes form parasocial relationships with them (Fournier 1998; Russell, Norman, and Heckler 2004). Instead of leaving it up to individuals to anthropomorphize objects of consumption, marketers often create advertising mascots with the express intent of imbuing them with personality characteristics, in a sense anthropomorphizing the brand for the consumer (Aaker 1997).

Individuals help to make sense out of their world by organizing things in categories. Each category and subcategory has mental prototypes. Objects are stored in memory around these prototypes by both their similarity to the prototype and their similarity to other items in the category (Tversky 1977). People seem to be particularly adept at categorizing animals. Henley (1969; see also Tversky 1977) devised a study asking participants to rate the similarity of 30 familiar animals to each other. The results were plotted on a cognitive map where the animals that were perceived to be most similar to each other were closer to one another (i.e., closer in psychological distance) on the cognitive map. While Henley (1969) interpreted this cognitive map as having two axes of size and ferocity, one could also interpret this cognitive map as indicating each animal's similarity to human beings. I characterize these animals as highly similar to humans (e.g., non-human primates such as monkeys and gorillas), moderately similar to humans (e.g., carnivorous animals such as lions and wolves as well as rodents and rodent-like animals such as rabbits), and relatively dissimilar to humans (e.g., hoofed mammals such as horses, goats, and deer). Results from a pilot study support this categorization.

A large body of research has converged on the finding that people like similar others, possibly due to an increased motivation to process information about close others (Aron, Aron, Tudor, and Nelson 1991). The foundational work in this literature stream was built on attitude similarity (Byrne 1971; Byrne, Clore, and Smeaton 1986; Heider 1958). This research has been subsequently extended to domains such as similarity in personality traits (Tesser and Campbell 1980; Tesser and Paulhus 1983) and biological characteristics (Chen and Kenrick 2002). Miller and colleagues (1998) found that even trivial similarities, such as a shared birthday, cause people to view others more favorably. In extending this similarity-attraction principle to animal images, the most obvious prediction would be that high-similarity animals would be viewed more positively than moderate-similarity animals, which would in turn be viewed more positively than low-similarity animals. Furthermore, all types of animals should be viewed more positively when presented in anthropomorphic form due to heightened levels of similarity to humans.

However, researchers have found that construal level can moderate the relationship between similarity and attraction. Less similar objects, because they are psychologically more distant, are construed at higher, more abstract levels (Liviatan, Trope, and Liberman 2008). Likewise, higher similarity leads to lower-level, more concrete construals. Thus, it is possible that nonanthropomorphic images of all animals would be assigned more abstract representations, such as "animal." Therefore, due to lower similarity to humans among all animal types in nonanthropomophic portrayals, there may be little or no preference for highly similar animals over less similar animals. However, because greater similarity leads to more concrete construals with more focus on secondary features, it is possible that anthropomorphizing animal images increases salience to the differences between the high, moderate, and low similarity animals, thus leading to differences in preference for anthropomorphic images but no preference among nonanthropomorphic images.

Additionally, Chen and Kenrick (2002) found that increasing similarity for outgroup members can have a more powerful effect on liking than increasing similarity for ingroup members. The authors argue that these effects are driven by lower levels of baseline similarity, and thus liking, in outgroups. Thus, enhancing similarity leads to a positive violation of expectations and increased attraction that does not occur for ingroups, whose baseline similarity is already high. In the context of this research, relatively dissimilar animals would have lower baseline similarity to humans, whereas moderately animals would have higher baseline similarity to humans, and highly animals would have the highest baseline similarity to humans. Therefore, it is possible that relatively dissimilar animals would benefit more from anthropomorphism than moderately similar animals, which would in turn benefit more from anthropomorphism than highly similar animals.

The purpose of this research is to explore how anthropomorphized animal images are used in marketing communications and how consumers respond to them based on their similarity to humans. Findings of content analyses indicate that animals that are perceived to be moderately similar to humans are more frequently used as anthropomorphic mascots than animals that are either highly similar or relatively dissimilar to humans. However, results from an experimental study indicate that, while participants are indifferent between animal types when they are presented nonanthropomorphically, relatively dissimilar animals gain the most in terms of attitude favorability when presented anthropomorphically. I argue that these results are driven by a lower level of baseline similarity to humans in the nonanthropomorphic form. Thus, enhancing similarity to humans via anthropomorphism leads to positive violation of expectations and enhanced attraction toward relatively dissimilar animal images. Consequently, animals that are relatively dissimilar to humans might be underutilized as anthropomorphic spokescharacters.

# Brand Anthropomorphization: A Homocentric Knowledge Activation Perspective

Marina Puzakova, Drexel University, USA
Hyokjin Kwak, Drexel University, USA
Trina Larsen Andreas, Drexel University, USA

## EXTENDED ABSTRACT

We describe a four-stage process of brand anthropomorphization, which begins with primary cognition and proceeds through secondary cognition stages. Two types of anthropomorphized brands perceptions are formed–one that is transient and one that lasts longer. Stronger forms of brand anthropomorphization, going beyond brand personality attribution (e.g., weaker forms), exist.

Consumers' perceptions of brands as human may have important implications in the area of branding. At present, we do not know much about the process that influences the degree to which consumers perceive brands as complete human beings. Social science researchers have considered anthropomorphization an automatic psychological process that does not vary among individuals, and marketing researchers who have explored the notion of humanized brands (e.g., brand personality), have also considered the process as a chronically occurring consumer judgment (Fournier 1998). However, the anthropomorphization theory introduced by Epley et al. (2007) posits that the tendency to anthropomorphize objects is a phenomenon varying in strength depending on different domains, contexts, and individual differences.

This research contributes to the literature in the following three manners. First, we fill a gap in the marketing literature by extending consumers' perceptions of brands as fully human, instead of as merely possessing personality traits. We show that consumers consciously report their anthropomorphic perceptions of brands and behave toward them as if they, in fact, possess human traits. Second, we go beyond the idea that anthropomorphism is explained by the qualities of the target (i.e., morphological features of a product (Aggarwal and McGill 2007)) and show that the characteristics and motivations of perceivers are an important component of the process of anthropomorphization. Third, we introduce a process of brand anthropomorphization. Finally, we delineate the outcomes of the brand anthropomorphization process for consumer behavior.

Deriving our argument from related research in social and neuropsychology, and from the results of in-depth interviews (8 focus-group interviews (n = 21) and three one-to-one in-depth interviews), we posit that the process consists of two phases: a) primary cognition and b) second-order cognition. In the first phase, we argue that the concurrent activation of human knowledge (i.e., highly accessible and salient brand personality attributions) and a strong emotional arousal triggered at a specific moment of consumer-brand interaction make individuals anthropomorphize brands. Amygdala, the neural structure in the brain, participates in both emotional processing and complex social judgments, including anthropomorphism (Heberlein and Adolphs 2004). Thus, the processing of social information and emotionally arousing stimuli are causally related. In fact, we observed that respondents experienced strong emotional arousal at their first encounters with brands, and, concurrently, they possessed accessible social (e.g., brand personality) knowledge about the brands that they perceived in human terms. A less stable initial perception of anthropomorphized brand (AB) is formed at the end of the primary cognition stage.

In the secondary-order cognition (metacognition) stage, a more enduring perception of AB is formed. At the metacognition phase, individuals evaluate their initial judgment and identify their thoughts as favorable or unfavorable (Petty et al. 2007). When consumers find that their AB perceptions are favorable or desirable, they will be motivated to refine their existing thoughts of afferent AB. We define the refinement process of afferent AB as the process through which consumers engage in more complex attribution of human capabilities to the initial afferent AB judgment. The relevant literature and the results of in-depth interviews have shown that AB refinement agents such as sociality motivation, effectance motivation, and brand love-dependency operate as drive states which facilitate the perception of brands as human. In turn, high cognitive capacity leads to the correction of the initial perception of brand as a transient human to the perception of brand as a commercial entity.

In the refinement stage, we find that consumers project mind, intentions, emotions, and spirit to brands. Consumers also show signs of parental solicitude by viewing their brands as little brother or son. That is, individuals feel the desire to treat a brand with the same social conventions that they would give to another human. The fourth stage ends with the formation of stable, long-lasting perception of brand as a human. Finally, AB perceptions have important theoretical and practical implications. Specifically, consumers who anthromorphize their brands trust the brands more, expect higher performance, forgive the brands' transgressions as they would forgive a friend, care for them with parental solicitude, and are willing to spend extra for brands' accessories. Brands also consciously affect consumers' manner to behave. Deeper understanding of the nature of anthropomorphic brand judgment presents rich material for more effective marketing communications.

This is an exploratory, qualitative study, and future research should further empirically test the process presented across a wider variety of respondents. We believe that the theory of anthropomorphism may be extended by incorporating the activation of not only human knowledge structures but also self-knowledge representations. We also believe that there are additional avenues for future examination regarding how specific marketing communication efforts may impact consumers' perceptions of brands as empathic or moral and, subsequently, influence further inferences regarding brands in human terms.

## REFERENCES

Aaker, Jennifer L. (1997), "Dimensions of Brand Personality," *Journal of Marketing Research*, 24, 347-56.

Adler, A. and C. Brett (1998), *Social Interest: Adler's Key to the Meaning of Life*, Oxford, United Kingdom: Oneworld Publications.

Aggarwal, Pankaj (2004), "The Effects of Brand Relationship Norms on Consumer Attitudes and Behavior," *Journal of Consumer Research*, 31 (June), 87-101.

Aggarwal, Pankaj and Sharmistha Law (2005), "Role of Relationship Norms in Processing Brand Information," *Journal of Consumer Research*, 32 (December), 453-64.

Aggarwal, Pankaj and Ann L. McGill (2007), "Is This Car Smiling at Me? Schema Congruity as Basis for Evaluating Anthropomorphized Products," *Journal of Consumer Research*, 34 (December), 468-79.

Birtchnell, J. (1988), "Defining Dependency," *British Journal of Medical Psychology*, 61, 111-23.

Cacioppo, John T., Richard E. Petty, and C. Kao (1984), "The Efficient Assessment of Need for Cognition," *Journal of Personality Assessment*, 48, 306-07.

Cheney, D. and R. Seyfarth (1990), *How Monkeys See the World*, Chicago: University of Chicago Press.

Daly, M. and M. Wilson (1999), "Special issue: Stepparental Investment," *Evolution & Human Behavior*, 20, 365-66.

Dawes, R. and M. Mulford (1996), "The False Consensus Effect and Overconfidence: Flaws in Judgment or Flaws in How We Study Judgment?," *Organizational Behavior and Human Decision Processes*, 65, 201-11.

Deshpande, Rohit (1983), "'Paradigms Lost:' On Theory and Method in Research in Marketing," *Journal of Marketing*, 47 (Fall), 101-10.

Epley, Nicholas, Adam Waytz, Scott Akalis, and John T. Cacioppo (2008), "When We Need a Human: Motivational Determinants of Anthropomorphism," *Social Cognition*, 26 (2), 143-55.

Epley, Nicholas , Adam Waytz, and John T. Cacioppo (2007), "On Seeing Human: A Three-Factor Theory of Anthropomorphism," *Psychological Review*, 114 (4), 864-86.

Fitzsimons, Grainne M., Tanya L. Chartrand, and Gavan J. Fitzsimons (2008), "Automatic Effects of Brand Exposure on Motivated Behavior: How Apple Makes You "Think Different"," *Journal of Consumer Research*, 35 (June), 21-35.

Fournier, Susan (1998), "Consumers and Their Brands: Developing Relationship Theory in Consumer Research," *Journal of Consumer Research*, 24, 343-73.

Gardner, W. L. and M.L. Knowles (2008), "Love Makes You Real: Favourite Television Characters Are Perceived as "Real" in a Social Facilitation Paradigm," *Social Cognition*, 26 (2), 156-68.

Gilmore, George W. (1919), *Animism or Thought Currents of Primitive Peoples*, Boston: Marshall Jones Company.

Gray, H. M., K. Gray, and D.M. Wegner (2007), "Dimensions of Mind Perception," *Science*, 315, 619.

Greenebaum, Jessica (2004), "It's a Dog's Life: Elevating Status from Pet to "Fur Baby" at Yappy Hour," *Society and Animals*, 12 (2), 117-35.

Grégoire, Yany, Thomas M. Tripp, and Renaud Legoux (2009), "When Customer Love Turns into Lasting Hate: The Effects of Relationship Strength and Time on Customer Revenge and Avoidance," *Journal of Marketing*, 73 (November), 18-32.

Grohmann, Bianca (2009), "Gender Dimensions of Brand Personality," *Journal of Marketing Research*, 46 (1), 105-19.

Harris, Lasana T. and Susan T. Fiske (2008), "The Brooms in Fantasia: Neural Correlates of Anthropomorphizing Objects," *Social Cognition*, 26 (2), 210-23.

Harter, S. (1978), "Effectance Motivation Reconsidered: Towards a Developmental Model," *Human Development*, 21, 34-64.

Haslam, Nick (2006), "Dehumanization: An Integrative Review," *Personality and Social Psychology Review*, 10 (3), 252-64.

Heberlein, Andrea S. and Ralph Adolphs (2004), "Impaired Spontaneous Anthropomorphizing Despite Intact Perception and Social Knowledge," *The National Academy of Sciences of the USA*, Vol. 101, ed. James L. McGaugh. 7487-91.

Higgins, E. T. (1996), "The "Self Digest": Self-Knowledge Serving Self-Regulatory Functions," *Journal of Personality and Social Psychology*, 71, 1062-83.

Kassarjian, Harold H. (1971), "Personality and Consumer Behavior: A Review," *Journal of Marketing Research*, VIII (November), 409-18.

Keller, Kevin Lane (1993), "Conceptualizing, Measuring, and Managing Customer-Based Brand Equity," *Journal of Marketing*, 57 (January), 1-22.

_____ (2002), *Branding and Brand Equity*, Cambridge, MA: Marketing Science Institute.

_____ (2003), "Brand Synthesis: The Multidimensionality of Brand Knowledge," *Journal of Consumer Research*, 29 (March), 595-600.

Kruglanski, A.W. and D.M. Webster (1996), "Motivated Closing of the Mind: "Seizing" and "Freezing"," *Psychological Review*, 103, 263-83.

Ng, Sharon and Michael J. Houston (2006), "Exemplars or Beliefs? The Impact of Self-View on the Nature and Relative Influence of Brand Associations," *Journal of Consumer Research*, 32 (March), 519-29.

Petty, Richard E., Pablo Brinol, Zakary L. Tormala, and Duane T. Wegener (2007), "The Role of Metacognition in Social Judgment," in *Social Psychology: Handbook of Basic Principles*, eds. Arie W. Kruglanski and E. Tory Higgins. 2nd. ed. New York: Guilford Press, 254-84.

Pickett, Cynthia, Wendi. L. Gardner, and Knowles Megan (2004), "Getting a Cue:The Need to Belong and Enhanced Sensitivity to Social Cues," *Personality and Social Psychology Bulletin*, 30 (September), 1095-107.

Pincus, Aaron L. and Michael B. Gurtman (1995), "The Three Faces of Interpersonal Dependency: Structural Analysis of Self-Report Dependency Measures," *Journal of Personality and Social Psychology*, 69 (4), 744-58.

Santelli, Alexander G., C. Ward Struthers, and Judy Eaton (2009), "Fit to Forgive: Exploring the Interaction Between Regulatory Focus, Repentance, and Forgiveness," *Journal of Personality and Social Psychology*, 96 (2), 381-94.

Shimp, Terence A. and Thomas Madden (1988), "Consumer-Object Relations: A Conceptual Framework Based Analogously on Sternberg's Triangular Theory of Love," *Advances in Consumer Research* Vol. 15, ed. M. Houston. Provo, UT: Association for Consumer Research, 163-68.

Sung, Ja-Young, Lan Guo, Rebecca E. Grinter, and Henrik I. Christensen (2007), *"My Roomba is Rambo": Intimate Home Appliances*, Berlin: Springer/Heidelberg.

Watson, John J. (1979), *Nursing: The Philosophy and Science of Caring*, Boston: Little Brown.

# Emotional Anthropomorphism: What Kind of Face Sits Well on a Car's Frontal Appearance?

Jan R. Landwehr, University of St. Gallen, Switzerland
Bernd Weber, University of Bonn, Germany
Andreas Hermann, University of St. Gallen, Switzerland

## EXTENDED ABSTRACT

While there is an increasing body of research on the effects product design and its aesthetics unfold on consumers' behavior (e.g., Bloch 1995; Chitturi et al. 2007, 2008) the specific aspect of anthropomorphism as a guideline for designers has only attracted scattered attention in the scientific study of product design (Aggarwal and McGill 2007). This is astonishing since it is well known that the human face posses an evolutionary highly relevant stimulus configuration that is processed faster and with more attention than most other stimuli in the environment (Mondloch et al. 1999). Both these characteristics constitute basic marketing aims (Pieters and Wedel 2004).

Although scientific insights into the specific mechanisms underlying anthropomorphism are only scattered, this concept seems nevertheless to enjoy at least in the domain of car design a high popularity among practitioners. In a detailed exploration of several car designs and based on interviews with car designers Welsh (2006) for example reaches the conclusion that in practice the analogy between human faces and car fronts is a widespread source for inspiration and used by almost all car makers as an orientation for their designs. While it is appealing to rely on this simplified heuristic and go ahead with designing anthropomorphized cars, it nevertheless leaves open some questions that are both from a theoretical as well as from a practical point of view critical. The present research is aimed at providing insights into detailed aspects of anthropomorphizing on a process level and employs the neuroscientific method of fMRI to shed light on the involved mental processes. Answers to three major questions regarding the specifics of anthropomorphism are intended to be answered by the present research endeavor.

First, whether the reference to human faces is suited to guide a company's design strategy or whether it is just a scientific construct that is pulled on the shapes that actually unfolds its effect independently of any emotional interpretation. We found evidence in the neuronal activation pattern that the perception of car and human faces leads to a considerable correspondence in neuronal activity which suggests more of an effect for anthropomorphism than a simple descriptive metaphor that conveys placement and shape of the car's features. Our findings suggest that people do indeed see cars as having facial expressions in a way that goes beyond simple descriptive metaphor.

Second, the question whether different kinds of faces (male vs. female) are equally suited to serve as an inspiration to design a product with the aim of increasing its liking. We found that liking of car faces and female faces can be traced back to similar patterns of activation in the reward circuit while male faces are (at least by male participants) judged on a different basis. In addition to the insight that there are many different kinds of faces and one is well advised to think about anthropomorphism in a more detailed way, this finding also offers some initial hints for the clarification of the underlying motives for a peoples' preference for certain car designs. In particular, one can clarify whether people are searching for a design that allows them to express themselves in a desired way; thus, literally using the car front as a kind of mask for themselves or whether they simply strive for the most attractive or aesthetically appealing design, respectively. Because car fronts activate the reward circuit in a similar way as female faces do, it is unlikely that our exclusively male participants are willed to use a car as a way to express themselves. In contrast, as men like female faces better than male faces, are longer looking to them and appreciate them according to their attractiveness (Levy et al. 2008), the similarity in processing indicates that car fronts cause a feeling of reward directly due to attractiveness and not mediated by semantic associations.

Finally, the third question asks for the best liked combination of friendliness and aggressiveness in a car's front. Our findings allow the recommendation to give the grille a friendly expression whereas the headlights should rather look aggressive. From a theoretical perspective it is very interesting to notice that this preference pattern was found both in the reward circuit as well as in the observed behavioral pattern. This points to the conclusion that this specific combination of emotions unfold a rather direct impact on preference without complex or sophisticated mental processes mediating this relationship. That is, people seem to have an initial preference for this combination of emotions rather than having to think intensively about the potential meaning of these emotions. Further research is however needed to clarify the exact nature of the underlying mental mechanism to better understand this result.

Cars do have a face–this is the answer to the central question posed at the outset of this research project. The remarkable similarity in processing human faces and car fronts indicates that the anecdotic evidence gathered by Welsh (2006) has a substantial basis and is suited to serve as a valuable source for inspiration when it comes to design a new car front. This result enables a more intense application of insights gathered in the domain of human facial attractiveness and, thus, to tap so far unused potentials. Especially proportions that constitute an attractive female face seem to be suited to optimize a car's front to please the eyes of the beholder.

# Product Involvement vs. Product Motives as Moderators of the Effects of Ad-evoked Feelings: An Analysis of Consumer Responses to 1,100 TV Commercials

Maggie Geuens, Ghent University and Vlerick Leuven Gent Management School, Belgium
Michel Tuan Pham, Columbia University, USA
Patrick De Pelsmacker, University of Antwerp, Belgium

## EXTENDED ABSTRACT

Many studies have shown that ad-evoked feelings have a positive influence on consumers' brand attitudes (e.g., Brown, Homer and Inman 1998; Burke and Edell 1989, Holbrook and Batra 1987). While these effects of ad-evoked feelings thus seem well established, three things are striking: (1) the limited pool of ads in each study, raising issues of selection bias (e.g., Aaker, Stayman and Hagerty 1986, Burke and Edell 1989, Stayman and Aaker 1988), (2) the fact that unknown brands are often used (e.g., Burke and Edell 1989, Derbaix 1995, Miniard et al. 1991), and more importantly, (3) the fact that product category effects are not considered, even though academics and advertising practitioners generally assume that the effectiveness of emotional advertising appeals depends on the product category (e.g., Adaval 2001, Batra and Stephens 1994, Johar and Sirgy 1991, Malhotra 2005, Morris et al. 2002, Rossiter, Percy and Donovan 1991). The purpose of this research is to revisit the role of feelings on brand evaluations using a much more comprehensive and representative set of existing commercials (addressing the issue of potential selection bias, fictitious ads and unfamiliar brands) and testing whether these effects depend—as previous experimental lab research would suggest—on the level of involvement and the type of motives, hedonic versus utilitarian, associated with the product category.

Although a dual role of affect has been theorized by several researchers in the sense that ad-evoked feelings automatically transfer to brand attitude under low involvement, whereas under high involvement feelings are assumed to impact brand attitudes by biasing brand cognitions (e.g., MacInnis and Park 1991, Miniard et al. 1991, Petty et al. 1993, Olsen and Pracejus 2004), other researchers suggest that emotional advertising works better for low than for high involvement products (e.g., Lautman and Percy 1984, Morris et al. 2002, Rossiter et al. 1991). Indeed, it is a classic prediction of dual-route models of persuasion such as the ELM (Petty and Cacioppo 1986) that feelings should have lower influence on persuasion under conditions of high elaboration likelihood than under conditions of low elaboration likelihood. Our studies will test whether this theoretical prediction holds when the source of involvement comes from the product category being advertised rather than from an external manipulation, as in typical persuasion research.

Another stream of research on the effects of affective states in consumer judgments and decisions suggests that affect is more likely to be relied upon when consumers have hedonic motives than when they have utilitarian motives (Pham 1998)—a finding that has been replicated in multiple subsequent studies (e.g., Adaval 2001, Yeung and Wyer 2004). According to a feeling-as-information explanation (Schwarz and Clore 1983, 2007; Pham 1998), this is because feelings are perceived to be more relevant in light of hedonic/experiential motives than in light of instrumental motives. This finding raises the question of whether similar moderating effects would occur in typical advertising exposure settings when the type of motives comes not from an external manipulation (as in previous studies) but simply from the product category being advertised.

Therefore, previous experimental laboratory research makes very clear predictions about the moderating effects of involvement and types of motives on the effects of feelings on attitudes and evaluations. However, it is not clear whether these predictions would

hold in typical ad exposure settings where the primary source of involvement or type of motives is not an experimental manipulation, but merely the product category being advertised. The purpose of this research is thus to submit these two lab-derived theoretical predictions to a large-scale "external reality check."

Study 1 examines how the emotions evoked by 413 TV commercials (featuring 294 different brands across 93 different product categories) influence the brand evaluations of a representative set of 907 adult consumers. Each respondent evaluated a set of about 20 commercials and each commercial was evaluated by 40 to 60 respondents. After seeing each commercial, respondents rated their (1) attitude toward the ad (Aad) (3 items, $\alpha$=.96), (2) their cognitive assessments of the ad's content (2 items, $\alpha$=.90), and (3) their attitudes toward the advertised brand (Ab) (2 items, $\alpha$=.86). These Aad, cognitive assessments (CogAss), and Ab responses were averaged across respondents for each ad to form 413 aggregate ad-level dependent-variable observations. The emotional content of each ad was assessed on a 15-item emotional scale by an independent group of 12 judges who were blind to the study's hypotheses ($\alpha$=.97). To control for the possibility that ratings of emotional responses to the ads may reflect some other aspects of the ads, such as their originality or creativity, the same 12 judges also rated all the ads in terms of their originality (5 items, $\alpha$=.99). Finally, the 93 product categories represented in the ads were coded by another set of six judges. This second set of judges were given the names of the product categories and asked to rate them on 5 'product category involvement' items ($\alpha$=.94) and 5 'utilitarian/hedonic product motive items' ($\alpha$=.95). Inter-judge reliabilities were high for all items and for all judges.

The results of a series of regressions show that, even after controlling for respondents' Aad and cognitive assessments of the ad and for the ads' originality, the emotional content of the ads had a significant positive influence on consumers' brand attitudes ($\beta$=.236, t=4.93, p<.001). Further, the results suggest that, contrary to what one would predict based on a peripheral-route explanation of affective influences, the effects of emotions on brand attitudes did not depend on the level of involvement associated with the product category ($\beta_{\text{Emotion x Involvement}}$=.014, t<1). However, the effects of emotions on brand attitudes were significantly moderated by the type of motivation associated with the product categories ($\beta_{\text{Emotion x Hedonic}}$=.112, t=3.03, p<.01).

A second study was carried out (1) to assess the robustness and generalizeability of the first study's findings, and (2) to address a limitation of the first study by controlling for brand familiarity effects. To this end a different set of 687 TV commercials were evaluated by a different sample of 427 consumers, keeping the design and methodology largely identical to Study 1. This time the impact of the emotional content of the ad on consumers' brand attitudes was fully mediated by Aad. However, the results concerning the product category motivational factors remained identical as in Study 1. Again product involvement did not and utilitarian/hedonic product motive did moderate the impact of emotional ad content on brand evaluations. The latter finding is consistent with recent theoretical suggestions that the selective reliance on feelings as a function of their relevance is quite flexible (Pham 2004).

# REFERENCES

Aaker, D. A., Stayman, D. M. and Hagerty, M. R. (1986), "Warmth in Advertising-Measurement, Impact, and Sequence Effects", *Journal of Consumer Research, 12*(4), 365-381.

Adaval, Rashmi (2001), "Sometimes it just feels right: The differential weighting of affect-consistent and affect-inconsistent product information", *Journal of Consumer Research, 28*(1), 1-17.

Batra Rajeev, Stephens Debra (1994), "Attitudinal effects of ad-evoked moods and emotions: The moderating role of motivation", *Psychology and Marketing*, 11 (3), 199-215.

Brown, S. P., Homer, P. M. and Inman, J. J. (1998), "A meta-analysis of relationships between ad-evoked feelings and advertising responses", *Journal of Marketing Research, 35*(1), 114-126.

Burke, M.C. and Edell, J. A. (1989), "The Impact of Feelings on Ad-Based Affect and Cognition", *Journal of Marketing Research, 26*(1), 69-83.

Derbaix, C. M. (1995), "The Impact of Affective Reactions on Attitudes toward the Advertisement and the Brand-a Step toward Ecological Validity", *Journal of Marketing Research, 32*(4), 470-479.

Holbrook, M. B. and Batra, R. (1987), "Assessing the Role of Emotions as Mediators of Consumer Responses to Advertising", *Journal of Consumer Research, 14*(3), 404-420.

Johar J S., Sirgy M. Joseph (1991), "Value-expressive versus utilitarian advertising appeals: When and why to use which appeal", *Journal of Advertising,* 20(3), 23-33.

Lautman M.R. and Percy L. (1984), "Cognitive and affective responses in attribute based versus end-benefit oriented advertising", In: T.C. Kinnear, editor. *Advances in Consumer Research*, vol. 10, Provo, UT: Association for Consumer Research, 11-17.

MacInnis D.J., Park C.W. (1991), "The differential role of characteristics of music on high-involvement and low-involvement consumers processing of ads, *Journal of Consumer Research*, 18(2), 161-173.

Malhotra, Naresh K. (2005), "Attitude and affect: new frontiers of research in the 21st century", *Journal of Business Research*, 58:477-482.

Miniard, P. W., Bhatla, S., Lord, K. R., Dickson, P. R. and Unnava, H. R. (1991), "Picture-based persuasion processes and the moderating role of involvement", *Journal of Consumer Research,* 18(1), 92-107.

Morris, J.D., Woo, C., Geason, J.A. and Kim, J. (2002), "The Power of Affect: Predicting Intention", *Journal of Advertising Research*, 42(3), 7–17.

Olsen G.D., Pracejus J.W. (2004), "Integration of positive and negative affective stimuli", *Journal of Consumer Psychology*, 14(4), 374-384.

Petty, R.E. and Cacioppo, J.T. (1986), "The Elaboration Likelihood Model of Persuasion", *Advances in Experimental Social Psychology*, 19, 123–205.

Petty, R.E., D.W. Schumann, S.A. Richman and A.J. Strathman (1993), "Positive Mood and Persuasion: Different Roles for Affect Under High and Low Elaboration Conditions", *Journal of Personality and Social Psychology*, 64, 5-20.

Pham, M. T. (1998), "Representativeness, relevance, and the use of feelings in decision making", *Journal of Consumer Research,* 25(2), 144-159.

Pham, M. T. (2004), "The Logic of Feeling", *Journal of Consumer Psychology, 14*(4), 360-369.

Rossiter John R., Percy Larry, Donovan Robert J. (1991), "A better advertising planning grid", *Journal of Advertising Research,* 1991, 31October/November), 11-21.

Schwarz, N. and Clore, G. L. (1983), "Mood, Misattribution, and Judgments of Well-Being-Informative and Directive Functions of Affective States", *Journal of Personality and Social Psychology, 45*(3), 513-523.

Schwarz, N. and Clore, G. L. (2007), "Feelings and Emotional Experiences", in A. W. Kruglanski and E. T. Higgins (Eds.), *Social Psychology: Handbook of Basic Principles* (Second ed., pp. 385-407): Guilford.

Stayman, D. M. and Aaker, D. A. (1988), "Are All the Effects of Ad-Induced Feelings Mediated by Aad", *Journal of Consumer Research, 15*(3), 368-373.

Yeung, C.W.M. and Wyer, R.S. (2004), "Affect, appraisal, and consumer judgment", *Journal of Consumer Research, 31*(2), 412-424.

# The Variety Paradox. Why LESS Evokes MORE

Anne Klesse, Massricht University, The Netherlands
Caroline Goukens, Maastricht Univeristy, The Netherlands
Kelly Geyskens, Maastricht University, The Netherlands
Ko de Ruyter, Maastricht University, The Netherlands

## EXTENDED ABSTRACT

### Conceptualization

Nowadays, consumers are used to being spoilt with choice: Most retailers offer an abundance of product variants since they acknowledge that consumers prefer stores that provide large assortments. Some stores, however, (strategically) form an exception. For instance, convenience stores trade fulfilling consumers' need for convenience against their wish for variety. Accordingly, choice is limited to one or two kinds per product category. In this research we examine whether consumers behave differently when facing low-variety assortments compared to high-variety assortments. In particular, we intend to find out whether they will include more variety in their subsequent choices to make up for the perception of limited choice triggered through low-variety assortments.

Although consumer researchers have extensively studied the effects of assortment breadth on choice making (Chernev 2003; Gourville and Soman, 2005; Iyengar and Lepper, 2000; Kahn and Wansink, 2004; Sela et al., 2009), they have focused on choice-specific effects within the assortment. They neglected general motivational effects that are triggered through looking at the assortment, linger on, and influence subsequent decisions from different choice sets. We know from psychological research that providing choices determines consumers' feelings of autonomy (Deci and Ryan, 2000). Being able to choose from various options enables consumers to express themselves as individuals (Kim and Drolet, 2003) and boosts happiness (Patall, 2008). On the contrary, situations perceived as restricting one's option to choose freely arouse reactance (Brehm, 1966), a motivational state that triggers behavior aimed at reasserting one's personal freedom (Wicklund, 1974).

Accordingly, we propose that low-variety assortments trigger the perception of limited choice and evoke reactance. Once the motivational state of reactance is aroused consumers are increasingly interested in behavior that functions as a means to regain their freedom. Levav and Zhu (2009) showed that spatially confined consumers engage in more variety seeking in order to reassure their personal freedom. Thereby, they demonstrated that variety seeking behavior constitutes a means to deal with reactance. Hence, we predict that low-variety assortments trigger subsequently more variety seeking than high-variety assortments since they evoke the need to offset the perception of limited choice.

### Studies

The validity of this prediction is tested in five studies. In the first study (N=94) we manipulated the variety that participants saw before making a subsequent, seemingly unrelated choice. They saw either three (low variety) or eight (high variety) different chips flavors. Afterwards, they chose five snacks out of a five item choice set as a reward for their participation. We measured variety seeking behavior through the number of different snacks that participants chose. Consistent with our hypothesis participants sought significantly more variety after seeing the low-variety assortment than after seeing the high-variety assortment.

The objective of study 2 (N=68) was to test the robustness of the effect by varying the nature of the stimuli. We used a print advertising depicting chocolate. Second, we kept the overall number of items equal across conditions: both advertisings showed twelve chocolate bars and differed only in the variety of different flavors they showed (3 vs. 12). The results confirmed our previous finding: Participants who saw the low-variety advertising sought significantly more variety.

We use reactance theory to explain the underlying process of our finding. The objective of study 3 (N=67) was to test the effect of reactance directly by measuring participants' chronic reactance tendencies. As predicted participants' chronic reactance tendency interacts with the variety manipulation. This suggests that reactance is the underlying psychological factor driving the effect. The effect of the variety manipulation was accentuated for highly reactive individuals and attenuated for weakly reactive individuals.

We claim the perception of limited choice to be responsible for evoking more variety seeking. The objective of study 4 was to test this by deliberately manipulating the perception of limited choice. Hence, this study made use of three conditions: one low-variety condition and two high-variety conditions. One of the high-variety conditions (high-confined) showed some items crossed out indicating that they are no longer available. This evokes the perception of limited choice. The results showed that participants in the low-variety and high-confined condition did not significantly differ from each other in their variety seeking behavior. However, both sought significantly more variety than the high-variety condition. This implies that the perception of limited choice is responsible for evoking a heightened need for variety.

While the previous studies demonstrate the effect in laboratory conditions, study 5 intended to replicate our findings in a real purchase context, i.e. the coffee shop at the university. One day we put up advertisings showing a low-variety of pastries in the while on another day we used advertisings showing a high-variety of pastries. We compared students' variety seeking behavior on the two days. Thereby, we defined variety seeking not as taking several different products but as trying out something special. Students tried out significantly more special coffees when they saw the low-variety advertising while they chose more normal coffee kinds when they saw the high-variety advertising.

### General Discussion

Across five studies we show that facing low-variety assortments compared to high-variety assortments evokes subsequently more variety seeking. This is grounded in reactance theory: Low-variety evokes the perception of limited choice and triggers reactance. Accordingly, consumers experience the heightened need to reassure their threatened freedom and engage in variety seeking behavior.

Our findings hint at a 'variety paradox'. Although retailers offer high-variety to cater consumers' needs for variety, less variety is more effective in triggering subsequent variety seeking. Our findings provide some interesting guidelines for retailers and convenience stores: It is important to acknowledge that assortment variety triggers motivational states which prevail and affect consumers' subsequent behavior. For instance, in stores where the assortment is limited facing the first shelves evokes the perception of limited choice and triggers consumers to seek more variety. These stores could cater this need by providing more variety in the following shelves or offering specialities, new or lesser known brands. Consumers' desire to express themselves through their choice will increase the likelihood of choosing several different items or trying out new products.

# REFERENCES

Aiken, Leona S. and Stephen G. West (1991), Multiple Regression: Testing and Interpreting Interactions, Thousand Oaks, CA: Sage.

Boatwright, Peter, and Joseph C. Nunes (2001), "Reducing Assortment: An Attribute-Based Approach", *Journal of Marketing*, 65 (3), 50-63.

Brehm, Jack W. (1966), A Theory of Psychological Reactance, New York: Academic Press.

Chernev, Alexander (2003), "When More is Less and Less is More: the Role of Ideal Point Availability and Assortment in Consumer Choice", *Journal of Consumer* Research, 30 (2), 170-183.

Chernev, Alexander and Leigh McAllister (2005) "Product Assortment and Variety-Seeking in Consumer Choice", *Advances in Consumer Research*, 2005, 32 (1), 119-121.

Clee, Mona A. and Robert A. Wicklund, (1980), "Consumer Behavior and Psychological Reactance", *Journal of Consumer Research*, March, 6 (4), 389-405.

Deci, Edward L., and Richard M. Ryan, (1985), Intrinsic Motivation and Self-Determination in Human Behavior, New York: Plenum Press.

Deci, Edward, L. and Richard M. Ryan (2000), "Self-Determination Theory and the Facilitation of Intrinsic Motivation, Social Development, and Well-Being", *American Psychologist*, 55 (1), 68-78.

Dijksterhuis, Ap et. al. (1998), "Seeing One Thing and Doing Another: Contrast Effects in Automatic Behavior", *Journal of Personality and Social Psychology*, 75 (4), 862-871.

Godek, John, Yates J. Frank, and Auh Seigyoung (2001), "Customization Decisions: The Roles of Assortment and Consideration", *Advances in Consumer Research*, 28 (1), 396.

Goukens, Caroline, Siegfried Dewitte, Mario Pandelaere, and, Luk Warlop (2007), "Wanting a Bit(e) of Everything: Extending the Valuation Effect to Variety Seeking", *Journal of Consumer Research*, 34 (October), 386–394.

Gourville, John T. and Dilip Soman (2005) "Overchoice and Assortment Type: When and Why Variety Backfires", *Marketing Science*, 24 (3), 382–395.

Herrmann, Andreas, Mark Heitmann, Robert Morgan, Stephan C. Henneberg, and Jan Landwehr (2009), "Consumer Decision Making and Variety of Offerings: The Effect of Attribute Alignability", *Psychology & Marketing*, 26 (4), 333-358.

Hong, Sung-Mook and Salvatore Faedda (1996), "Refinement of the Hong Psychological Reactance Scale", *Educational and Psychological Measurement* 56 (1), 173-82.

Hoch, Stephen J., Eric T. Bradlow, and Brian Wansink, (1999), "The Varity of an Assortment", *Marketing Science*, 18 (4), 527-546.

Huffman, Cynthia and Barbara E. Kahn (1998), "Variety for Sale: Mass Customization or Mass Confusion?", *Journal of Retailing*, 74 (4), 491-513.

Iyengar, Sheena S. and Mark R. Lepper (2000), "When Choice is Demotivating: Can One Desire Too Much of a Good Thing?", *Journal of Personality and Social Psychology*, 79 (6), 995-1006.

Kahn, Barbara E. (1995), "Consumer Variety-Seeking among Goods and Services", *Journal of Retailing and Consumer Services* 2 (Fall), 139-148.

Kahn, Barbara E. and Andrea Morales (2001), "Choosing Variety" In: Hoch, Stephen J., Howard C. Kunreuther, and Robert R.Gunther (Eds.), Wharton on Marketing Decisions (63-77). New York: John Wiley & Sons.

Kahn, Barbara E. and Brian Wansink (2004), "The Influence of Assortment Structure on Perceived Variety and Consumption Quantities", *Journal of Consumer Research*, 30 (March), 519-533.

Kim, Heejung S. and Aimee Drolet (2003), "Choice and Self-Expression: A Cultural Analysis of Variety Seeking", *Journal of Personality and Social Psychology*, 85 (August), 373-382.

Kim, Heejung S. and Aimee Drolet (2009), "Express Your Social Self: Cultural Differences in Choice of Brand-Name versus Generic Products", *Personality and Social Psychology Bulletin*, 35 (12), 1555-1566.

Levav, Jonathan and Rui J. Zhu (2009), "Seeking Freedom through Variety", *Journal of Consumer Research*, 36 (4), 600-610.

Maimaran, Michal and Christian S. Wheeler (2008), "Circles, Squares, and Choice: The Effect of Shape Arrays on Uniqueness and Variety Seeking", *Journal of Marketing Research*, 45 (6), 731-740.

Markus, Hazel, R. and Barry Schwartz (2010), "Does Choice Mean Freedom and Well Being?", *Journal of Consumer Research* (forthcoming)

Patall, Erika A., Harris Cooper, and Jorgianne Civey Robinson (2008), "The Effects of Choice on Intrinsic Motivation and Related Outcomes: A Meta-Analysis of Research Findings", *Psychological Bulletin*, 134 (2), 270-300.

Pogressive Grocer (2004), "Independents Report: Dollar Wise", http://www.progressivegrocer.com/progressivegrocer/esearch/article_display.jsp?vnu_content_id=1000649432

Progressive Grocer (2008), "When Small is Big", http://www.progressivegrocer.com/progressivegrocer/esearch/article_display.jsp?vnu_content_id=1000649429

Ratner, Rebecca K. and Barbara E. Kahn (2002), "The Impact of Private versus Public Consumption on Variety-Seeking Behavior", *Journal of Consumer Research*, 29 (2), 246-257.

Sela, Aner, Jonah Berger, and Wendy Liu (2009), "Variety, Vice and Virtue: How Assortment Size Influences Option Choice", *Journal of Consumer Research*, 36 (6), 941-951.

Wicklund, Robert A. (1974), Freedom and Reactance, Potomac, MD: Erlbaum

# The Impact of Assortment Variety on Inferences and Purchase Intentions

Chrissy Mitakakis, Baruch College, USA
Thomas Kramer, Baruch College, USA

## EXTENDED ABSTRACT

Consumer inferences play an important role in marketing (see Kardes, Posavac, and Cronley 2004 for a review). For example, consumers often use observable product attributes to judge unobservable ones, such as inferring product quality based on its price (e.g., Huber and McCann 1982), warranty period (Srivastava and Mitra 1998), or country of origin (Teas and Agarwal 2000). However, although research has shown that consumers may indeed often rely on observable attributes or the overall product evaluation (e.g., Broniarczyk and Alba 1994) when evaluating products, we currently do not know if, or more specifically, under which conditions, consumer inferences of product quality are based on retailers' assortment variety. This lack in the literature is even more surprising given that assortment variety differs greatly across stores.

Based on our proposition of the existence of a lay theory suggesting that retailers with larger product assortment variety cannot know much about the quality of any one product and hence offer lower quality product selections overall, we identify a "jack-of-all-trades-master-of-none" inference strategy as a tool employed by consumers when evaluating a product. That is, although normatively quality perception of a product should not differ according to the variety of other noncomparable products sold in the store, we propose that consumers are likely to rely on the degree of variety of a retailer's assortment for quality inferences, which in turn will drive purchase likelihood. Furthermore, because we expect that the "jack-of-all-trades-master-of-none" inference requires cognitive resources, purchase likelihood and quality perceptions based on this lay theory should be limited to those consumers with available cognitive resources.

To examine the proposed lay theory consumers have regarding the presence of noncomparable products, we investigated the effects of the size of the assortment of noncomparable products in the purchase environment on consumers' evaluations of a target product. For our first study, we told participants that they were shopping for a toothbrush that was found in an assortment with either three or twenty noncomparable products (such as household cleaners, food items, etc.). Since we expect the proposed inference strategy to be employed only when consumers have the cognitive resources to do so, we also varied some participants' cognitive resources with a cognitive load task. After the presentation of the hypothetical shopping scenario, we assessed participants' likelihood of purchasing that product. Our results support the hypotheses that consumers use a "jack-of-all-trades-master-of-none" inference strategy, and thus are more likely to purchase a product when it is found in a small (vs. large) assortment variety. However, as hypothesized, this effect occurs only with participants who have the cognitive resources available.

We extend our findings with our second study, and also demonstrate that use of the "jack-of-all-trades-master-of-none" inference is moderated by the level of comparability of other products in the assortment. More specifically, participants were told that they were shopping for a notebook that was found in an assortment of either three or twenty comparable or noncomparable products. Similar to study 1, we also varied participants' cognitive resources. Consistent with our hypothesis, we found that the extent of comparability of the other products in the assortment moderated consumers' use of the "jack-of-all-trades-master-of-none" inference.

In our third study, we sought to find process evidence for our proposed inference strategy, and to demonstrate that differences in quality perceptions drive the effect of assortment variety on purchase likelihood. We told participants that they were shopping for a digital camera that was found in an assortment variety of either three or twenty noncomparable products. In addition to purchase intentions, we also examined participants' quality perceptions of the digital camera. Analyses show that quality perceptions drive the effect of assortment variety on purchase intentions. In particular, participants were more likely to purchase the digital camera and had higher quality perceptions of the digital camera that was part of a small (vs. large) assortment variety. Quality perceptions fully mediated the effect of assortment variety on purchase likelihood.

In sum, we were able to provide evidence for a "jack-of-all-trades-master-of-none" inference strategy that consumers use. We found that consumers use this inference when evaluating products that are found in assortments of noncomparable products, suggesting that is it variety, and not size, of the assortment that drives this lay theory. We showed that consumers were more likely to purchase an item when it was found in a small (vs. large) assortment variety. Since we argued that use of this inference would require cognitive resources, we did not expect to find this inference to be utilized when consumers were under cognitive restraint. Furthermore, we provide evidence that it is the level of comparability of the other items in the assortment, and not merely the size of the assortment variety itself that drives consumers to use the "jack-of-all-trades-master-of-none" inference. Lastly, we provide support that shows how the relationship between assortment variety and purchase intent is mediated by consumers' quality perceptions.

## REFERENCES

Baker, Julie, A. Parasuraman, Dhruv Grewal, and Glenn B. Voss (2002), "The Influence of Multiple Store Environment Cues on Perceived Merchandise Value and Patronage Intentions," *Journal of Marketing Research*, 66 (April), 120-41.

Baron, Reuben M. and David A. Kenny (1986), "The Moderator-Mediator Variable Distinction in Social Psychological Research: Conceptual, Strategic, and Statistical Considerations," *Journal of Personality and Social Psychology*, 61(6), 1173-82.

Bettman, James R., and Sujan, Mita (1987), "Effects of Framing on Evaluation of Comparable and Noncomparable Alternatives by Expert and Novice Consumers," *Journal of Consumer Research*, 14(September), 141-54.

Broniarczyk, Susan M. and Joseph W. Alba (1994), "The Role of Consumers' Intuitions in Inference Making," *Journal of Consumer Research*, 21 (December), 393-407.

Chernev, Alexander and Gregory Carpenter (2001), "The Role of Market Efficiency Intuitions in Consumer Choice: A Case of Compensatory Inferences," *Journal of Marketing Research*, 38 (August) 349-61.

Cronley, Maria L., Steven S. Posavac, Tracy Meyer, Frank R. Kardes, and James J. Kellaris (2005), "A Selective Hypothesis Testing Perspective on Price-Quality Inference and Inference-Based Choice," *Journal of Consumer Psychology*, 15(2), 159-69.

Hansen, Chris J. and George M. Zinkhan (1984), "When Do Consumers. Infer Product Attribute Values?" *Advances in Consumer Research*, 11, 187-92.

*Advances in Consumer Research*
*Volume 38, © 2012*

Huber, Joel and John M. McCann (1982), "The Impact of Inferential Beliefs on Product Evaluations," *Journal of Marketing Research,* 19, 324-33.

Johnson, Michael D. (1984), "Consumer Choice Strategies for Comparing Noncomparable Alternatives," *Journal of Consumer Research*, 11 (December), 741- 53.

Kahn, Barbara and Brian Wansink (2004), "The Influence of Assortment Structure on Perceived Variety and Consumption Quantities," *Journal of Consumer Research*, 30 (March), 519-33.

Kardes, Frank R., Steven S. Posavac, and Maria L. Cronley (2004), "Consumer Inference: A Review of Processes, Bases, and Judgment Contexts," *Journal of Consumer Psychology*, 14 (3), 230-56.

Menon, Geeta, and Priya Raghubir (2003), "Ease-of-Retrieval as an Automatic Input in Judgments: A Mere Accessibility Framework?," *Journal of Consumer Research*, 30 (September), 230-43.

Mogilner, Cassie, Tamar Rudnick, and Sheena S. Iyengar (2008), "The Mere Categorization Effect: How the Presence of Categories Increases Choosers' Perceptions of Assortment Variety and Outcome Satisfaction," *Journal of Consumer Research*, 35 (August), 202-15.

Rao, Akshay and Kent B. Monroe (1988), "The Moderating Effect of Prior Knowledge on Cue Utilization in Product Evaluations," *Journal of Consumer Research*, 15(September), 253-64.

Srivastava, Joydeep and Anusree Mitra (1998), "Warranty as a Signal of Quality: The Moderating Effect of Consumer Knowledge on Quality Evaluations," *Marketing Letters*, 9 (4), 327-36.

Teas, R. Kenneth and Sanjeev Agarwal (2000), "The Effects of Extrinsic Product Cues on Consumers' Perceptions of Quality, Sacrifice, and Value," *Journal of the Academy of Marketing Science*, 28 (2), 278-90.

Tellis, Gerard J. and Gary G. Gaeth (1990), "Best-Value, Price-Seeking and Price Aversion: The Impact of Information and Learning on Consumer Choices," *Journal of Marketing*, 54 (April), 34-45.

# Improving the Power of Switching Intent to Predict Actual Switching Behavior-A Construal Level Theory Perspective

Yu-chen Hung, National University of Singapore, Singapore
Catherine Yeung, National University of Singapore, Singapore
Jochen Wirtz, National University of Singapore, Singapore

## EXTENDED ABSTRACT

Recent research has shown that repurchase intent is often not a good predictor of actual repurchase. A number of reasons for this discrepancy have been suggested in the literature, but have not been examined empirically. We propose that one critical distinction between switching intention and actual switching is that the former is a response to a hypothetical situation, whereas the latter is an action that is actually carried out. Recent behavioral research on construal level theory (CLT, see Trope and Liberman 2007 for a review) shows that when an event feels psychologically far away (e.g., when the event is going to happen in the distant future, is socially distant, or is hypothetical), people tend to focus on "central" aspects of the event–i.e., aspects that give direct implications to the desirability of the event. According to CLT, these aspects constitute the "higher level construal" of the event. On the other hand, when an event feels psychologically near (e.g., when it is going to happen in the near future, is socially near, or when is not hypothetical), people tend to focus on aspects that are associated with the procedures involved in carrying out the action (e.g., practicality, feasibility considerations). These aspects constitute the "lower level construal" of an event.

We first conducted a longitudinal study surveying cell phone service subscribers of all three providers in a city state. This approach allowed us to measure satisfaction and other attitudinal variables and switching intent in one period, and subsequently observe actual switching behavior in the next period. The survey was conducted in six waves over a 24 months period.

Monetary switching costs (e.g., penalties for switching during a contractual period) and non-monetary switching costs (e.g., the hassle of going to the service provider to cancel the contract, signing up for a new contract, potentially changing cell phone number) feature highly in switching cell phone service switching. Based on CLT, we expect that monetary switching costs, which are closely related to the desirability of switching, constitute a higher level construal, whereas non-monetary costs constitute a relatively lower level construal of switching. According to CLT, consumers are likely to focus on desirability-related aspects and underestimate the importance of other feasibility-related considerations when they respond to hypothetical situations–to this extent, monetary costs, but not non-monetary costs, are likely to serve as a basis for their response to intention questions. Moreover, non-monetary costs will be taken into account only when consumers consider carrying out actual switching.

The findings of our longitudinal study confirm this hypothesis, to the extent that the non-monetary switching cost main effect and its interaction effect with satisfaction are insignificant in predicting switching intent. However, for actual switching behavior, the non-monetary switching costs effects explain more variance than the equivalent effects of monetary switching costs. This finding suggests that while non-monetary switching costs are important determinants of actual switching behavior, they may not be taken into consideration when consumers report their switching intention.

We then conducted a series of experiments to directly test the CLT and demonstrate how the consideration of non-monetary costs can be facilitated when consumers respond to intention questions. Specifically, recent research has shown that process simulation (i.e., asking respondents to visualize the step-by-step process of carrying out a certain action) highlights the feasibility-related aspects of an event and encourages a lower-level construal of the event (Zhao, Hoeffler and Zauberman 2007) . We therefore predicted and found that when process simulation is employed in surveys, it can potentially reduce the inconsistency between responses to intention measures and actual switching behaviors. Our findings suggest the possibility of an unobtrusive administration of this procedure in surveys that will improve the predictive power of intention measures of actual switching behavior. These findings have potential applications beyond the immediate switching behavior application to any intent-actual behavior measurement context.

## REFERENCE:

Liberman, N., Trope Y., and Stephan, E. (2007), "Psychological distance," In A. W. Kruglanski and E. T. Higgins (Eds), *Social Psychology: Handbook of Basic Principles*, New York: Guilford Press.

Zhao, Min, Steve Hoeffler and Gal Zauberman(2007), "Mental Simulation and Preference Consistency over Time: the Role of Process-versus Outcome-Focused Thoughts. " *Journal of Marketing Research*, Aug, 379-388

# Can Thinking Abstractly Help Choosing From Large Assortments?

Jing Xu, Peking University, China
Zixi Jiang, Peking University, China
Ravi Dhar, Yale University, USA

## EXTENDED ABSTRACT

A visit to the supermarket attests to the large assortment or variety in almost any product category. Recent research shows findings for the negative effects of assortment size and relies on the assumption that choosing from large assortments involves making more trade-offs among the competing advantages and disadvantages and thus making decision makers generally worse off. Prior research has shown that an increase in the assortment size is accompanied with an increase in choice difficulty, and consequently a decrease in choice satisfaction (Chernev 2006; Iyengar and Lepper 2000).

Besides number of options in the assortment, choice conflict depends on whether the attribute differences among assortment options are seen as linked to competing goals or seen as servicing the same goal. Specifically, a consumer may experience greater conflict when the options in an assortment are seen as more dissimilar and being linked to different goals. This is because the more dissimilar are the alternatives to each other, the more distinct dimensions are considered and compared and require more difficult trade-offs to be made (Shugan 1980). On the contrary, a consumer may find choice less difficult to make when the attributes of the assortment options are seen as servicing the same objective and options appear to be more similar to one another. Thus, holding constant the assortment options, changes in similarity perception could affect levels of difficulty and satisfaction experienced in the choice process. This paper examines how changes in mental representation of choice options in large assortments affect similarity perceptions, and subsequently influence choice difficulty and outcome satisfaction. We propose that when choosing from large assortments, consumers who represent the options at a higher level are likely to engage in higher-level, alternative-based evaluations and perceive alternatives in a single category as serving the same higher order goal and thus more similar and substitutable to one another. In contrast, consumers who represent options at a lower level will focus on lower-level, feature-based trade-offs and perceive alternatives as attaining different competing sub-goals and thus more dissimilar and unsubstitutable to one another. This reliance on feature level comparisons heightens the level of conflict and choice difficulty experienced when choosing from large assortments. Here, we stress that similarity perceptions of options in a large assortment made by different levels of representations are construed at different levels. Specifically, whereas a higher level of representation finds options in a single category more similar in terms of serving the same consumption goal and providing similar benefits, a lower level of representation perceives options as more dissimilar to one another with respect to the attribute level difference.

Therefore, we hypothesize that when choosing from a large assortment, individuals who represent assortment options at a higher level experience less choice difficulty and more satisfaction with the chosen option than those who represent options at a lower level. Consistent with our proposition, three experiments demonstrated that, when facing large assortments, participants activated with a higher level of representation found options in an assortment more similar to one another, experienced less difficulty while choosing, and reported greater satisfaction with the chosen option than those activated with a lower level of representation.

Experiment 1 tests the effect of mental representations of the choice set on choice difficulty and satisfaction in a real choice scenario involving small versus large assortments. Experiment 1 found that, when facing a large assortment, consumers who represent options at a lower level find options more dissimilar to one another and competing for different sub-goals. As a result, they considered more distinct dimensions, made more comparisons, and consequently experienced more difficult trade-offs. On the other hand, representing options at a higher level makes the options in large assortment seen as more similar, less diversified, more substitutable in satisfying the same consumption goal, and consequently experiences less conflict and less difficult trade-offs. Indeed, our meditated moderation analysis show that perceived similarity among options mediated the moderating effect of mental representation of options on assortment size and choice difficulty.

To provide a stronger test of our argument, we next explicitly manipulate the perceived similarity among options in Experiment 2 and Experiment 3. Experiment 2 manipulates perceived similarity with same-colored plates vs. different-colored plates for candy options. Since different-colored plates highlights the differences among options, consumers with lower level of representation in such condition perceive greater dissimilarities among choice options and engage in more trade-off comparisons than when candies displayed in same-colored plates. Consequently, consumers with lower level of representation experience greater degree of difficulty and less satisfaction with the chosen outcome when candies displayed in different-colored plates than in same-colored plates.

Experiment 3 manipulates perceived similarity with assortment structure. Whereas choosing from feature-based categories highlights the differences among options and would lead to more trade-off difficulty and less satisfaction, choosing from benefit-based assortments focuses on the similarities among options and would lead to less choice difficult and greater satisfaction with choice outcome. The results show that choice difficulty experienced by consumers with a lower level of representation is mitigated when perceived similarity among items increases in benefit-based assortment structure. As options are perceived as more similar to one another in a large assortment, they are seen as more substitutable and servicing the same consumption goal.

The present paper contributes to the existing literature in two important ways. First, our research provides new insights into the ways in which levels of mental representations affect choice making process and choice consequences in large assortments. Second, we provide new perspective of the role of similarity perceptions in comparisons and choice process. Particularly, we show that different levels of representation construe similarity perceptions differently. Our results also provide important implications for marketers. Although recent research on assortment size has generally concluded that large assortments lead to increased choice difficulty and decreased satisfaction, marketers can improve choosers' experience and satisfaction with large assortments by altering the level at which assortment options are represented.

# Price-Based Expectations

Ayelet Gneezy, University of California at San Diego, USA
Uri Gneezy, Univeristy of California at San Diego, USA

## EXTENDED ABSTRACT

Consumers often lack the time, training, or inclination to judge the quality of a product. Consequently, to infer quality, they seek simpler alternative signals (cf. Aaker 1991), such as the product's country of origin, how heavily it is promoted (Raghubir 1998), or, most relevant to the current paper, its price.

Considerable evidence demonstrates that consumers judge higher-priced products to be of higher quality (Riesz 1979; Huber and McCann 1982; Gerstner 1985; Rao and Monroe 1989). It appears that our pleasure from consuming products like wine does not depend only on our sensors (e.g., smell, taste), but also on extrinsic attributes such as price or brand name.

One way in which prices can affect quality judgment is through expectations. For example, prices have been shown to produce placebo effects such that discounted products are less effective than regular-priced products (e.g., Shiv, Carmon, and Ariely 2005; Waber, Shiv, Carmon, and Ariely 2008). Participants in these experiments assigned higher efficacy to the fully priced product, hence the placebo effect. In line with these findings, we can reasonably assume individuals tasting wines are following the same reasoning: having relatively high expectations when tasting highly priced wines.

In a between-participants design, we asked three groups of participants in Experiment 1 to indicate how much they expected to like our 2004 Cabernet Sauvignon before asking them to taste it, based only on price ($10, $20, or $40) and appearance. We find that expectations were positively correlated with price.

What will the effect of high expectations be after tasting the wine? Expectations Confirmation Theory (ECT, Oliver 1977, 1980) conjectures that the interaction between expectations and perceived or actual performance leads to post-purchase satisfaction. If a product meets one's expectations, satisfaction will follow. However, if a product falls short of expectations, the consumer is likely to be dissatisfied (Oliver 1980; Spreng et al. 1996).

One way to consider expectations here is as a reference level in which people are loss averse and the environment determines endogenously the reference point they use (Ko˝szegi and Rabin, 2006). By this account, a person's reference point is the rational expectations she held in the recent past about outcomes that are consistent with optimal behavior given expectations. In the language of our Experiment 1, the model predicts that higher prices will increase peoples' expectations that will be subsequently used as a reference point.

Moving to a dynamic set up (Ko˝szegi and Rabin, 2009), higher prices should create higher expectations, and consumers would judge the realization (taste of the wine) relative to this reference point. If the wine meets or exceeds the high expectation, an individual will evaluate a wine using the price-quality heuristic, assigning higher ratings for higher-priced wines. In contrast, if the wine quality falls short of the expectations, we expect tasters to be disappointed and give the wine a lower rating. Since higher prices result in higher expectations, the likelihood of disappointment increases with price.

To test this prediction, in Experiment 2, we gave six different groups of participants the opportunity to taste and rate the wine. Three groups tasted the lower-quality Cabernet Sauvignon, whereas the other three groups tasted the higher-quality Cabernet Sauvignon (a pretest confirmed the wines' quality). Participants were informed that the wines were available for purchase in the winery, for $10, $20, or $40. Consistent with past research, the higher the price of the high quality wine (2005), the higher the participants rated it. In line with the above predictions, the responses of participants tasting the lower quality wine produced a negative correlation between price and quality.

The results of Experiment 1 and Experiment 2 suggest that high prices create high expectations, and that these expectations serve as a reference point in subsequent quality judgments. When a product meets (or exceeds) expectations, quality judgments are high, but when a product falls short of expectations, quality judgments drop.

Experiment 3 provides a direct test of the degree to which participants' expectations are met under each price-quality combination. We asked participants in this experiment to first taste the wine under the same six conditions as in Experiment 2. Then each participant indicated what they thought about the wine: "disappointing," "meets expectation," or "exceeds expectations." The results support our predictions: the good wine met expectation, and disappointment in the low quality wine increased with price.

Even if consumers' appreciation of a product is positively correlated with its price, demand will not necessarily increase. Often consumers approach the winery with a budget constraint, so even if a higher price makes the wine tastier, actual sales may not increase. Recently, Heffetz and Shayo (2009) investigated the relationship between price, inferred quality and demand by disentangling the price-quality effect from the budget-constraint effect. Their findings show that prices do affect the stated willingness to pay. When they considered actual demand, however, quality-judgment elasticities were smaller than budget-constraint elasticities, and hence, in line with standard assumptions, the demand function was downward sloping.

How should wine sellers use our empirical findings when pricing their products? The most appropriate way to test the effect of expectation confirmation on demand is by conducting a field study in a real business. To the best of our knowledge, ours is the first demonstration of the effect the price-quality heuristic has on demand in an actual market setting. In the winery we study, despite the noticeable difference in quality between the 2004 and 2005 wines, the owner of the winery was planning to price the new wine at $10 also, primarily because sales were slow and he did not want to scare customers away (the experiment was conducted during the summer of 2009). Before introducing the higher-quality wine, the owner agreed to experiment with different prices.

We offered winery visitors one of the Cabernet Sauvignon as part of the six wines they tasted (we never had the 2004 and 2005 present at the same time). On different days, the wines' prices varied: $10, $20, or $40. The dependent variables were the number of bottles of Cabernet Sauvignon sold in each of the six treatments, and the profits to the winery. We find downward-sloping demand for the lower-quality wine. For the higher-quality wine, however, more people bought the wine at $20 than at $10.

## REFERENCES

Aaker, David A. (1991). Managing Brand Equity: Capitalizing on the value of a brand name. New York: The Free Press.

Allison, Ralph I. and Kenneth P. Uhl (1964). Influence of beer brand identification on taste perception. *Journal of Marketing Research*, 1 (August), 36-39.

Brochet, Frédéric (2001). Tasting. A study of the chemical representations in the field of consciousness. Working paper, General Oenology Laboratory, Talence Cadex, France.

Erdem, Tulin and Joffre Swait (1998). Brand equity as a signaling phenomenon. *Journal of Consumer Psychology*, 7 (2), 131-57.

Gerstner, Eitan (1985). Do higher prices signal higher quality? *Journal of Marketing Research*, 22 (May), 209-15.

Goldsteina, Robin, Johan Almenbergb, Anna Dreberc, John W. Emersond, Alexis Herschkowitscha, and Jacob Katza (2008). Do more expensive wines taste better? Evidence from a large sample of blind tastings. *Journal of Wine Economics*, 3 (Spring), 1-9.

Heffetz, Ori, and Moses Shayo (2009). How large are non-budget-constraint effects of prices on demand? *American Economic Journal: Applied Economics*, 1(4): 170-99.

Hodgsona, Robert T. (2008). An examination of judge reliability at a major U.S. wine competition. *Journal of Wine Economics*, 3 (2), 105-13.

Huber, Joel and John McCann (1982). The impact of inferential beliefs on product evaluations. *Journal of Marketing Research*, 19 (August), 324-33.

Janiszewski, Chris and Stijn M.J.Van Osselaer, (2000). A connectionist model of brand-quality associations. *Journal of Marketing Research*, 37 (August), 331-50.

Koszegi, Botond and Mathew Rabin (2006). A model of reference-dependant Preferences. *Quarterly Journal of Economics*, 1221(4), 1133-65.

Koszegi, Botond and Mathew Rabin (2009). Reference-dependent consumption plans. *American Economic Review*, 99 ( 3), 909-36.

McClure, Samuel M., Jiam Li, Damon Tomlin, Kim S. Cypert, Latané M. Montague, and P. Read Montague (2004). Neural correlates of behavioral preference for culturally familiar drinks. *Neuron*, 44 (October), 379-87.

Oliver, Richard L. (1977). Effect of expectation and disconfirmation on post exposure product evaluations - An alternative interpretation. *Journal of Applied Psychology*, 62(4), 480.

Oliver, Richard L. (1980). A cognitive model of the antecedents and consequences of satisfaction decisions. *Journal of Marketing Research*, 17 (November), 460-69.

Plassmann, Hilke, John O'Doherty, Baba Shiv, and Antonio Rangel (2008). Marketing actions can modulate neural representations of experienced pleasantness. *Proceedings of the National Academy of Sciences*, 105, 1050-54.

Raghubir, Priya (1998). Coupon value: a signal for price? *Journal of Marketing Research*, 35(3), 316-24.

Rao, A.R. and Monroe, K.B. (1989). The effect of price, brand name, and store name on buyers' perceptions of product quality: an integrative review. *Journal of Marketing Research*, 36, 351-57.

Riesz, Peter C. (1979). Price-quality correlations for packaged food products. *Journal of Consumer Affairs*, 13 (Winter), 236-47.

Shiv, Baba, Ziv Carmon, and Dan Ariely (2005). Placebo effects of marketing actions: consumers may get what they pay for. *Journal of Marketing Research*, 42, 383-93.

Spreng, Richard A., Scott B. MacKenzie, and Richard W. Olshavsky (1996). A reexamination of the determinants of consumer satisfaction. *Journal of Marketing*, 60 (July), 15-32.

Waber, Rebecca L., Baba Shiv, Ziv Carmon, and Dan Ariely (2008). Commercial features of placebo & therapeutic efficacy. JAMA: *The Journal of the American Medical Association*, 299 (9), 1016-17.

Weil, Roman L. (2001). Parker v. Prial: The death of the vintage chart. Chance 14(4), 27-31.

Weil, Roman L. (2005). Analysis of Reserve and regular bottlings: why pay for a difference only the critics claim to notice? *Chance*, 18(3), 9-15.

# Deep Discount or Free? The Effects of Price Promotion on Willingess to Pay

Mauricio Palmeira, Monash University, Australia
Joydeep Srivastava, University of Maryland, USA

## EXTENDED ABSTRACT

Research on price promotions has shown that when a free product is bundled together with another product, consumers reduce their willingness to pay for the free product when it is not being offered for free (Kamins, Folkes and Fedorikhin 2009; Raghubir 2004). For example, when a pizzeria offers free bread sticks with the purchase of a pizza, consumers expect to pay less for bread sticks on a subsequent visit when the promotion is no longer in effect. Raghubir (2004) reasoned that when a product is offered as a free gift, consumers infer that the cost of the product is low and lower their willingness to pay for it when it is not in promotion.

In the current research, we examine promotions in which a product is offered for a low price–but not free–with the purchase of another product. If a free offer reduces consumers' reservation price through inferences regarding the cost of the product, it follows that the impact of a promotion that allows a purchase for a reduced price should be a function of the magnitude of the promoted price. In this sense, free, or zero price, would be an extreme example of the application of this inference. In other words, compared to a situation in which a product is promoted for free, when a product is promoted for a price greater than zero, consumers should infer a higher cost. In turn, we should expect that this type of promotion would have a smaller impact on consumers' willingness to pay on subsequent purchases.

Research on several aspects of human psychology has shown that zero is used in a qualitatively different manner than other numbers, often causing discontinuity in the transition from small numbers to zero (Heyman and Ariely 2004; Kahneman and Tversky 1979; Shampanier, Mazar and Ariely 2007). This literature suggests that zero is a special number and the effect of price promotions on subsequent purchase occasions may not be a direct function of magnitude of the discount. We propose that the value of the required purchase is used as an anchor when consumers estimate their reservation prices. In addition, when a product is not offered for free, but for a low price, consumers will also use this low price as an anchor. While a product can't possibly cost zero, it can conceivably have a low price. Thus, we argue that zero will not be used as an anchor to estimate the price of a product, but a low price will. In this case, the reservation price of a free product will have only one anchor (value of the required purchase), while the reservation price of a product promoted for a value greater than zero will have both the required purchase and the promoted price as anchors.

Our reasoning leads to an interesting effect: a low price can lower reservation prices further than a zero price. Referring back to our opening example, we expect that a promotion that offers bread sticks for free with the purchase of a pizza will have a smaller impact on reducing consumers' willingness to pay for bread sticks on subsequent visits, than one that offers bread sticks for a low price, like one dollar with the purchase of a pizza. Consistent with an anchoring mechanism, as the promoted price increases, reservation prices also increase and eventually are superior to those of the free condition. Therefore, we predict a discontinuity in the relationship between promoted product price and reservation price at zero, such that a zero price will lead to higher reservation prices than a low price.

Our hypothesis was tested in two studies. In our first study, 164 participants answered a series of questions about two promotional advertisements. Participants were randomly assigned to one of four conditions: control, free, 50 cents and 2 dollars. Thus, the between-subject manipulation was the type of promotion (if any) that was offered with the purchase of a product. In the control condition, participants were informed about the price of a product (pizza and tomato sauce), but no mention was made to the price of the promoted product (bread sticks and spaghetti). For both products, we found that participants in the free condition were willing to pay more for the promoted products when they were not in promotion than participants in the 50 cents condition. For bread sticks, even a two-dollar price lead to lower WTP than a free price. For both products, expected quality was not affected by the price manipulation.

In study 2, we manipulated two factors: type of promotion (free vs. low price) and price of the required purchase (medium vs. high). Participants were randomly assigned to four conditions and asked to consider that they were looking for a gift for a friend who loved wine and to state how much they would be willing to pay for a wine thermometer. Participants also answered a few questions related to their expectations of quality. We found main effects for required purchase price and promotion type. More importantly, we found a significant interaction, as the WTP of a free product was significantly affected by the price of the main purchase, whereas the WTP of a low price product was not. Together, these studies offer support for our hypothesis.

## REFERENCES

Heyman, James, and Dan Ariely (2004), "Effort for Payment: A Tale of Two Markets," *Psychological Science*, 15(11), 787-793.

Kahneman, Daniel and Amos Tversky (1979), "Prospect Theory: An Analysis of Decision Risk," *Econometrica*, 47, 265-91.

Kamins, Michal A., Valerie S. Folkes and Alexander Fedorikhin (2009), "Promotional Bundles and Consumers' Price Judgments: When the Best Things in Life Are Not Free," *Journal of Consumer Research*, 36 (December), 660-670.

Raghubir, Prya (2004), "Free Gift with Purchase: Promoting or Discounting the Brand?" Journal of Consumer Psychology, 14 (1&2), 181-185.

Shampanier, Kristina, Nina Mazar and Dan Ariely (2007), "Zero as a Special Price: The True Value of Free Products," Marketing Science, 26 (November), 742-57.

# Europoly Money: The Impact of Currency Framing on Tourists' Spending Decisions

Priya Raghubir, New York University, USA
Vicki Morwitz, New York University, USA
Shelle Santana, New York University, USA

## EXTENDED ABSTRACT

In January 1999, 12 countries decided to adopt the Euro at a given exchange rate: Belgium, Germany, Greece, Spain, France, Ireland, Italy, Luxembourg, the Netherlands, Austria, Portugal and Finland. In all of these countries, except Ireland, the nominal prices of goods were lower in Euros than they were in the prior local currency. From January 1999 onwards, the 12 participating countries included prices in Euros along with the prices in their local currencies. The legal tender of Euro was introduced on January 1, 2002, and countries gradually ended the circulation of their existing national currencies. There was a dual circulation period until the changeover was complete, during which time both the new Euro and the old national currency remained in circulation. By the end of February 2002, all 12 countries had discontinued the use of their local currency. However, to help people translate prices from one currency into the other, in many countries, a reverse pricing communication system was adopted: Prices were displayed in Euro terms, with the local national currency conversion shown just below. It was expected that, over time, consumers would become accustomed to thinking in Euro terms, and would no longer require the local currency reference as an aid. This paper examines whether that assumption was well founded.

We investigate how framing a price in two nominally different (but economically identical) currencies affects consumer-spending decisions based on the predictions of the "money illusion," a tendency to over-weight nominal values relative to real values (cf. Shafir, Diamond, & Tversky, 1997). Prior research has shown that the money illusion influences spending in foreign currencies: People under spend when one unit of their home currency buys multiple units of the foreign currency and overspend in the reverse situation (Raghubir & Srivastava, 2002). We extend this line of research by examining how sequential and simultaneous exposure to multiple currencies, that is exposure to a price in French Francs and in Euros, affects consumers' price magnitude perceptions and spending. The primary theoretical contribution of this paper is to show that when multiple nominal values are available, then the manner in which people integrate them can lead to "money illusion" biases, and that these individual level effects have economic consequences with implications for consumer welfare, public policy, and the prices that companies can charge.

We first examine the impact of sequential exposure to foreign currencies on price perception and intended spending. We propose that people will perceive prices in Euros to be cheaper if they are first exposed to a currency whose face value is larger than the Euro (DM $2 \cong €1$) than if they are first exposed to a currency whose face value is smaller than the Euro (£$0.5 \cong €1$). A one-way ANOVA on the total cost of a hypothetical shopping basket using three levels of prior currency exposure (DM, £ or Irish Punt 1=€1) was significant ($F$ (2, 48)=9.96, $p<.01$). As predicted, those in the UK £ condition overestimated the cost of their shopping basket ($M$=€89.78 vs. Actual=€46.96, Control Irish Punt=€52.13), whereas those in the German DM condition underestimated it ($M$=€33.47).

The second experiment examines the impact of simultaneous exposure to two foreign currencies. We propose that people anchor on the nominal value of the currency that is more salient and display the "money-illusion" effect, even when the original currency is available to them in the context. We provided people prices in two currencies: Euro and French Franc highlighting one and providing

the second as a reference: €$_{FF}$ or FF€. Study participants rated their likelihood of purchasing 13 different products including toiletries and clothing, using the cover story that they had to shop due to their baggage being misplaced by an airline. A repeated measures ANOVA on the purchase intentions for the thirteen items showed that people are likely to spend more when the frame is €$_{FF}$ versus FF€ ($M$€$_{FF}$=2.24 vs. $M_{FF}$€=1.87, $F$ (1, 22)=3.55, $p<.05$), and are also likely to consider a larger set of items ($M$€$_{FF}$=5.60 vs. $M$$_{FF}$€=3.62, $F$ (1, 22)=4.49, $p<.05$). Study 3 examines the external validity of these effects. We analyzed tourist receipts data from 1993–2008 for 10 of the 12 countries that adopted the Euro (excluding Ireland as the exchange rate is in the opposite direction, and Luxembourg due to data unavailability) compared to a set of six comparable countries that did not: UK, Denmark, Iceland, Norway, Sweden, and Switzerland. To control for country differences and overall trend in tourism expenditures, we included GDP, CPI, population, and unemployment numbers for the year as predictor variables along with whether or not the country had adopted the Euro (0=not, 1=yes), the number of years prior to or subsequent to the introduction of the Euro (e.g., 1993=-9, 2002=0, 2008=6), as well as the interaction between these two variables. The regression was significant ($R^2_a$=.73, $F$ (8, 196)=66.24, $p<.01$), with the interaction term positive and significant ($\beta$=4433.93, $t_{196}$=2.64, $p<.05$). The positive and significant interaction implies that tourism receipts were higher after the Euro introduction in 2002 for those countries that adopted the Euro as compared to those who did not, controlling for overall trend and other differences across Euro and non-Euro countries.

To summarize, we show that while presenting prices in multiple currency frames could lead to a gradual adaptation to the new Euro currency standard as demonstrated by Marques and Dehaene (2004), it may not be sufficient. Results of our laboratory experiments determined that there was a systematic error in the price magnitude perceptions of the same unfamiliar currency due to differences in prior exposure to another currency (experiment 1), and when prices were presented in more than one currency (experiment 2), suggesting that providing both currencies simultaneously is not adequate at attenuating money-illusion effects.

## REFERENCES

Cannon, Edmund S. and Giam Pietro Cipriani (2006), "Euro-Illusion: A Natural Experiment," *Journal of Money, Credit and Banking, 38(5)*, 1391-1403.

Desmet, Pierre (2002), "A Study of the Potential Effects of the Conversion to Euro. *Journal of Product and Brand Management, 11(3)*, 134-46.

Gamble, Amelie, Tommy Gärling, John Charlton, and Rob Ranyard (2002), "Euro-Illusion: Psychological Insights into Price Evaluations with a Unitary Currency," *European Psychologist, 7(4)*, 302-11.

Gamble, Amelie, Tommy Gärling, Daniel Västfjäll, and Agneta Marell (2005), "Interaction Effects of Mood Induction and Nominal Representation of Price on Consumer Choice. *Journal of Retailing and Consumer Services, 12*, 397-406.

Gaston-Breton, Charlotte and Pierre Desmet (1999), "Perceived Effects of Psychological Price Thresholds According to the Monetary Unit," Paper presented at the Second Annual Conference of Pricing Research, Fordham University, New York, New York.

Jonas, Eva, Tobias Greitmeyer, Dieter Frey, and Stefan Schulz-Hardt (2002), "Psychological Effects of the Euro—Experimental Research on the Perception of Salaries and Price Estimations," *European Journal of Social Psychology*, *32(2)*, 147-69.

Kooreman, Peter, Riemer Faber, and Heleen M.J. Hofmans (2004), "Charity Donations and the Euro Introduction: Some Quasi-Experimental Evidence on Money Illusion," *Journal of Money, Credit, and Banking*, *36*, 1121-24.

Kühberger, Anton and Alexander Keul (2003), "Quick and Slow Transition to the Euro in Austria: Point of Sale Observations, and a Longitudinal Panel Survey," Paper presented at the Euro-Workshop (IAREP), Vienna, Austria.

Lemaire, Patrick and Mireille Lecacheur (2001), "Older and Younger Adults' Strategy Use and Execution in Currency Conversion Tasks: Insights from French Franc to Euro and Euro to French Franc Conversions," *Journal of Experimental Psychology: Applied*, *7(3)*, 195-206.

Marini, Giancarlo, Alessandro Piergallini, and Pasquale Scaramozzino (2007), "Inflation Bias After the Euro: Evidence from the UK and Italy," *Applied Economics, 39*, 461-70.

Marques, J. Frederico and Stanislas Dehaene (2004), "Developing Intuition for Prices in Euros: Rescaling or Relearning Prices?" *Journal of Experimental Psychology: Applied*, *10(3)*, September, 148–55.

Mussweiler, Thomas and Fritz Strack (2004), "The Euro in the Common European Market: A Single Currency Increases the Comparability of Prices," *Journal of Economic Psychology*, *25(5)*, 557-63.

Mussweiler, Thomas and Birte Englich (2003),"Adapting to the Euro: Evidence from Bias Reduction," *Journal of Economic Psychology*, *24(3)*, 285-92.

Raghubir, Priya and Joydeep Srivastava (2002), "Effect of Face Value on Product Valuation in Foreign Currencies," *Journal of Consumer Research*, *29*, 335-47.

Ranyard, Rob, Carole Burgoyne, Gabriela Saldanha, and David Routh (2003), " Living With the Euro but Thinking in Punts? A Preliminary Report of Experiences in the Republic of Ireland," Paper presented at the Euro-Workshop (IAREP), Vienna, Austria.

Romani, Simona and Daniele Dalli (2002),"Effects of the Transition from Lira to Euro on Buyers' Product Evaluations," Paper presented at the EMAC conference, Braga, Portugal.

Shafir, Eldar, Peter Diamond, and Amos Tversky (1997), "Money Illusion," *Quarterly Journal of Economics*, *112(2)*, 341-74.

United Nations Environment Programme (2005), "Economic Impacts of Tourism." http://www.uneptie.org/pc/tourism/sust-tourism/economic.htm, February 8, 2005.

World Tourism Organization (2005), "WTO World tourism barometer," 3(1), Madrid: World Trade Association, 1-4.

# Framing and Sales Promotions: Understanding the Characteristics of Present and Prospective Consumers

Fei Lee Weisstein, University of Texas-Pan American, USA
Kent Monroe, University of Illinois, USA

## EXTENDED ABSTRACT

Economic-based literature suggests that charging loyal customers a higher price than prospective customers would lead to greater profits if loyal customers are comparatively more price insensitive than prospective customers (Chen 1997; Chen, Narasimhan, and Zhang 2001; Taylor 2003). Behavioral research, however, shows that when targeted promotions occur, loyal customers perceive higher unfairness and betrayal when they know that they paid higher prices than non-loyal customers (Feinberg et al. 2002). Targeted promotions may generate a side effect by making the targeted segment salient as potential comparison others to those consumers who are not offered the promotions. Other consumers (e.g., loyal customers) will necessarily be at a price disadvantage in relation to the targeted segment (e.g., prospective customers). In particular, loyal customers, knowing that they paid higher prices, exhibit higher perceived unfairness than prospective customers (Tsai and Lee 2007). Loyal customers often perceive that they are entitled to an equal or even a lower price since they invest comparatively more than prospective customers in the firms (Cox 2001). These different conclusions from marketing research raise an interesting and important question: what is the effect of sales promotion framing on consumers' perception of price fairness across different customer segments (regular vs. prospective)? Recently, a study showed that price framing, presenting the same price offer or price change in various formats, may reduce consumers' negative reactions even when consumers know that they paid higher prices than other people (Lee and Monroe 2008). However, the study did not examine whether using price framing to minimize consumers' negative perceptions can be implemented across different customer segments. This research contributes to consumer research by showing that using different price promotion framing tactics can induce price-disadvantaged consumers to have different transaction perceptions and subsequently increase their perceived price fairness across different customer segments and promotion deal comparisons of different magnitudes.

The prediction that consumers generally would prefer segregated gains more than reduced losses in their buying decisions was first proposed by Thaler (1985). Diamond and Sanyal (1990) later confirm that sales promotions framed as gains are chosen more often than promotions framed as reduced losses. Their study finds that consumers perceive promotions of equivalent financial magnitude framed as gains as better value than those framed as reduced losses. We propose that for assumed less price sensitive and more emotionally attached regular customers, they would be more attracted to a reward promotion (e.g., free gift) framed as a separate extra gain than discount promotion framed as a reduced monetary loss. The additional reward may generate an exclusiveness effect that loyal customers may feel more special than other customers who do not receive any rewards. On the other hand, if prospective customers are more price sensitive and less emotionally attached to the firm, they would be more attracted to a discount promotion (e.g., pure price reduction) framed as a reduced monetary loss.

Using two experiments, we examined whether the effect of sales promotion framing can successfully reduce consumers' negative perceptions of targeted pricing across different customer segments and deal comparison situations. Participants first read a short scenario asking them to consider buying a notebook computer from their all-time favorite and frequently visited online store or an online store that they had never patronized before. All participants were presented the same notebook computer web page with the same product but with a different sales promotion framing format. Participants were randomly assigned to either the control or various framing conditions. After all participants indicated their willingness to buy the notebook computer, they were told that a friend recently bought the same notebook computer from the same online store for a much lower price. Finally, participants were asked to evaluate the dependent measures on nine-point scales.

In both two studies, price discount and reward framing, compared to an equivalent financial offer without any framing tactics, successfully increased consumers' perceived transaction dissimilarity, which subsequently increased their perceived price fairness. The results confirmed that the degree of perceived transaction similarity is highly related to perception. In addition, price promotion framing tactics work differently across different customer segments. Our findings suggest that regular customers perceived significantly higher price fairness when they received a price promotion that was framed as a reward than as a discount. On the other hand, prospective customers perceived significantly higher price fairness when they received a promotion that was framed as a discount than as a reward. Previous studies suggest that retailers should treat regular customers better since they would be more upset when they learn that prospective customers received a better deal than they did. We propose an alternative explanation that price-disadvantaged regular customers' negative price unfairness perception might also be influenced by the easiness of comparing their own transaction to other individuals' transactions. Our research findings suggest that price-disadvantaged customers' negative perceptions toward targeted pricing can be mitigated by not only using different price promotion presentation formats but also giving different levels of promotion to different customer segments so that the offers will be less comparable.

# Consumer's Motivation of Counterfeit Consumption in China

Felix Tang, Hang Seng School of Commerce, China
Vane-Ing Tian, The Chinese University of Hong Kong, China
Judith Lynne Zaichkowsky, Simon Fraser University, Canada

## EXTENDED ABSTRACT

Economic-based literature suggests that charging loyal customers a higher price than prospective customers would lead to greater profits if loyal customers are comparatively more price insensitive than prospective customers (Chen 1997; Chen, Narasimhan, and Zhang 2001; Taylor 2003). Behavioral research, however, shows that when targeted promotions occur, loyal customers perceive higher unfairness and betrayal when they know that they paid higher prices than non-loyal customers (Feinberg et al. 2002). Targeted promotions may generate a side effect by making the targeted segment salient as potential comparison others to those consumers who are not offered the promotions. Other consumers (e.g., loyal customers) will necessarily be at a price disadvantage in relation to the targeted segment (e.g., prospective customers). In particular, loyal customers, knowing that they paid higher prices, exhibit higher perceived unfairness than prospective customers (Tsai and Lee 2007). Loyal customers often perceive that they are entitled to an equal or even a lower price since they invest comparatively more than prospective customers in the firms (Cox 2001). These different conclusions from marketing research raise an interesting and important question: what is the effect of sales promotion framing on consumers' perception of price fairness across different customer segments (regular vs. prospective)? Recently, a study showed that price framing, presenting the same price offer or price change in various formats, may reduce consumers' negative reactions even when consumers know that they paid higher prices than other people (Lee and Monroe 2008). However, the study did not examine whether using price framing to minimize consumers' negative perceptions can be implemented across different customer segments. This research contributes to consumer research by showing that using different price promotion framing tactics can induce price-disadvantaged consumers to have different transaction perceptions and subsequently increase their perceived price fairness across different customer segments and promotion deal comparisons of different magnitudes.

The prediction that consumers generally would prefer segregated gains more than reduced losses in their buying decisions was first proposed by Thaler (1985). Diamond and Sanyal (1990) later confirm that sales promotions framed as gains are chosen more often than promotions framed as reduced losses. Their study finds that consumers perceive promotions of equivalent financial magnitude framed as gains as better value than those framed as reduced losses. We propose that for assumed less price sensitive and more emotionally attached regular customers, they would be more attracted to a reward promotion (e.g., free gift) framed as a separate extra gain than discount promotion framed as a reduced monetary loss. The additional reward may generate an exclusiveness effect that loyal customers may feel more special than other customers who do not receive any rewards. On the other hand, if prospective customers are more price sensitive and less emotionally attached to the firm, they would be more attracted to a discount promotion (e.g., pure price reduction) framed as a reduced monetary loss.

Using two experiments, we examined whether the effect of sales promotion framing can successfully reduce consumers' negative perceptions of targeted pricing across different customer segments and deal comparison situations. Participants first read a short scenario asking them to consider buying a notebook computer from their all-time favorite and frequently visited online store or an online store that they had never patronized before. All participants were presented the same notebook computer web page with the same product but with a different sales promotion framing format. Participants were randomly assigned to either the control or various framing conditions. After all participants indicated their willingness to buy the notebook computer, they were told that a friend recently bought the same notebook computer from the same online store for a much lower price. Finally, participants were asked to evaluate the dependent measures on nine-point scales.

In both two studies, price discount and reward framing, compared to an equivalent financial offer without any framing tactics, successfully increased consumers' perceived transaction dissimilarity, which subsequently increased their perceived price fairness. The results confirmed that the degree of perceived transaction similarity is highly related to perception. In addition, price promotion framing tactics work differently across different customer segments. Our findings suggest that regular customers perceived significantly higher price fairness when they received a price promotion that was framed as a reward than as a discount. On the other hand, prospective customers perceived significantly higher price fairness when they received a promotion that was framed as a discount than as a reward. Previous studies suggest that retailers should treat regular customers better since they would be more upset when they learn that prospective customers received a better deal than they did. We propose an alternative explanation that price-disadvantaged regular customers' negative price unfairness perception might also be influenced by the easiness of comparing their own transaction to other individuals' transactions. Our research findings suggest that price-disadvantaged customers' negative perceptions toward targeted pricing can be mitigated by not only using different price promotion presentation formats but also giving different levels of promotion to different customer segments so that the offers will be less comparable.

# Purchase Intention Toward Counterfeits–Antecedents And Consequences From Culturally Diverse Countries

Bernhard Swoboda, Trier University, Germany
Karin Pennemann, Trier University, Germany
Markus Taube, Mercator School of Management, Germany
Cristian Dabija, Babes-Bolyai University, Romania

## EXTENDED ABSTRACT

### Introduction

The sale of counterfeit products accounted for up to 9% of the world trade volume, amounting to an increase of 10,000% in the past two decades (IACC 2009). Since firms manage their brands internationally across many markets, marketers should understand how the antecedents' impacts on consumer behavior vary across countries. Even counterfeiting is a cross-national phenomenon; its antecedents have rarely been investigated cross-nationally.

Brand manufacturers of illegally copied brands sustain damage: the brand's equity is jeopardized and the consumer's demand is diverted into gray markets (Green and Smith 2002). Nevertheless, Nia and Zaichkowski (2000) note that the majority of consumers "did not believe that counterfeits decrease the demand for original, luxury brand name products" (Nia and Zaichowski 2000, 494). Commuri (2009) states that the impact of counterfeiting on consumers of genuine goods (originals) is little-noticed. Thus, a further investigation is needed on counterfeits' impact on originals.

In their literature review, Eisend and Schuchert-Güler (2006) note antecedents related to the person, such as demographics, antecedents related to the product, such as price, social as well as cultural context, and also purchase situation, which all stimulate the purchase of counterfeits. They emphasize a more solid theoretical grounding for further studies and call for cross-cultural investigations to illuminate potential differences between the antecedents (Eisend and Schuchert-Güler 2006).

The purpose of the following study is to examine antecedents of purchase intention toward counterfeits (PItC) and its influence on consumers' willingness to pay for the original (WtPO).

### Conceptual Framework

To develop the conceptual model, we draw firstly upon the theory of planned behavior (Ajzen 1991), secondly on the adaptation-level theory (Helson 1964), and thirdly focus on the moderating effect of country specifics.

Armitage and Conner (2001) achieved a higher explained variance for intention using the theory of planned behavior instead of the theory of reasoned action. Following the theory of planned behavior, we first hypothesize the impact of subjective norm of socially legitimate (counterfeit) behavior, and secondly hypothesize the impact of perceived behavior control, defined as the ease of access to counterfeits, on purchase intention toward counterfeits (PItC). Additionally we hypothesize the impact of novelty seeking, perceived risk, integrity, and fairness toward the original on purchase intention toward counterfeits (PItC).

We refer to Helson's (1964) adaptation-level theory linking PItC to willingness to pay for the original (WtPO). According to this theory, exposure to formerly perceived stimuli serves as a reference by which stimuli perceived later are judged. As noted by Cordell, Wongtada, and Kieschnick (1996), counterfeits are sold at a lower price, thus we hypothesize a negative impact of PItC on WtPO.

We suggest that culture (i.e. collectivism, uncertainty avoidance, Confucian values, and holistic thinking), economic development (GDP per capita) and trademark legislation serve as context

factors. Thus, consumer behavior in the counterfeit context and its antecedents' impacts are proposed as varying across countries.

### Method

Our sample included 700 face-to-face consumer interviews in each country of investigation. Enhancing the generalizability of the study (Alden, Steenkamp, and Batra 1999), we chose China, Romania and Germany as countries of investigation in view of their differences in economic development, culture, and trademark legislation, where we note a considerable variation, to make our hypothesis more suitable for generalization (van de Vijver and Leung 1997). In addition to validity and reliability confirmation, we also confirmed partial scalar invariance of the measurement in comparing country samples (Steenkamp and Baumgartner 1998). Since we operationalized PItC as a formative measurement to include the main product categories that are counterfeited, we applied the partial least squares approach for its handling of formative and reflective measurement models and its less stringent assumptions concerning the distribution of variables and error terms (Hensler, Ringle, and Sinkovics 2009). The structural model was estimated for each country, and differences in path coefficients were tested for significance (Keil et al. 2000).

### Findings and Discussion

Our study pursues the call of Eisend and Schuchert-Güler (2006) for a better theoretical grounding and a cross-cultural investigation in further studies on the counterfeit context, and the call of Commuri (2009) for an examination as to how counterfeits impact genuine brands.

Applying the theory of planned behavior (Ajzen 1991), we examine the antecedents' impact on PItC and reveal that country specifics, such as culture, economic development and Confucianism, matter when investigating consumers' illicit behavior. Such a cross-country investigation amplifies the understanding of consumer behavior and thus provides insights for internationally implemented actions that are aimed at tackling companies' losses caused by counterfeits.

In China, where Confucian values are a strong cultural trait, Fairness to the genuine brand does not lower PItC, whereas in Western countries it does. Thus Fairness, which has not been discussed previously in the counterfeit context, matters as an antecedent of PItC when investigating societies where Confucian values are not common. The Asian understanding of copying and of honoring one's master differs from Western beliefs and has its roots in the Confucian set of values and ethical norms

Integrity has no significant/negative impact for developing countries, such as China and Romania, where trademark law was only established quite recently and its implementation is somewhat sporadic. Recently, China has aligned its legal framework within the international intellectual property rights treaty and is still revising its trademark legislation. Since laws and norms are related, a cross-national legal alignment is of increasing importance.

Subjective Norms do legitimate counterfeiting behavior and have a higher impact on PItC for collectivistic countries, such as China and Romania, than for individualistic countries. Popular endorsers and opinion leaders are a means of increasing consumers' awareness of negative outcomes affecting brand manufacturers, as well as society at large. Once counterfeiting is socially disregarded, especially in collectivistic societies, counterfeits will not be used any more to display status and prestige.

Following the adaptation-level theory (Helson 1964), we show that the availability of typically low-priced counterfeits lower the reference price for genuine brands in the consumer's mind. Especially in Romania, brand manufacturers seem to be jeopardized by the visibility level of counterfeits.

## REFERENCES

Ajzen, Icek. (1991), Theory of planned behavior. *Organizational Behavior and Human decision Processes*, 50 (December), 179-211.

Alden, Dana L., Jan-Benedict E.M Steenkamp, and Rajeev Batra (1999), "Brand Positioning through Advertising in Asia, North America and Europe: The Role of Global Consumer Culture," *Journal of Marketing*, 63 (January), 75-87.

Armitage, Christopher J. and Mark Conner (2001), "Efficacy of the Theory of Planned Behaviour: A meta-analytic review," *British Journal of Social Psychology*, 40 (December), 471-99

Commuri, Suraj (2009), "The Impact of Counterfeiting on Genuine-Item Consumers' Brand relationships," *Journal of Marketing*, 73, 86–98.

Cordell, Victor V., Nittaya Wongtada, and Robert L. Kieschnick Jr. (1996), "Counterfeit purchase intentions: Role of lawfulness attitudes and product traits as determinants," *Journal of Business Research*, 35 (January), 41-53.

Eisend, Martin, and Pakize Schuchert-Güler (2006), "Explaining counterfeit purchase: A review and preview," *Academy of Marketing Science Review*, 12, 1-21.

Green, Robert T. and Tasman Smith (2002), "Executive Insights: Countering Brand Counterfeiters," *Journal of International Marketing*, 10 (4), 89-106.

Helson, Harry (1964), "Current trends and issues in adoption-level theory," *American psychologist*, 19 (1), 26-38.

Henseler, Jörg, Christian M. Ringle, and Rudolf R. Sinkovics (2009). The use of partial least squares path modelling in international marketing. *Advances in International Marketing*, 20, 277-319.

IACC (2009), "Get Real–The Truth About Counterfeiting," http://www.iacc.org/counterfeiting/ counterfeiting.php.

Keil, Mark, Bernard C. Y. Tan, Kwok-Kee Wei, Timo Saarinen, Virpi Tuunainen, and Arjen Wassenaar (2000), "A cross-cultural study on escalation of commitment behavior in software projects," *MIS Quarterly*, 24 (June), 299–325.

Nia, Arghavan, and Judith Lynne Zaichowsky (2000), "Do counterfeits devalue the ownership of luxury brands?," *Journal of Product and Brand Management*, 9 (7), 485-97.

Steenkamp, Jan-Benedict E. M. and Hans Baumgartner (1998), "Assessing measurement Invariance in Cross-National Consumer Research," *Journal of Consumer Research*, 25 (June), 78-90.

# Opinion Seeking In Consumer Networks

Seung Hwan (Mark) Lee, University of Western Ontario, Canada
June Cotte, University of Western Ontario, Canada

## EXTENDED ABSTRACT

The importance of social communication in explaining consumer behaviour has been highlighted across a wide variety of research streams (e.g., Childers 1986). What is known from prior research is that consumers tend to rely on their social networks (e.g., like a network of friends) as resources for product information, evaluations, and recommendations to make better purchase decisions (Brown and Reingen 1987; Gershoff, Broniarczyk, and West 2001). Given the importance of social networks in the consumer's search process, it is surprising that research has largely ignored the effect of consumer's position in a social network on opinion seeking behavior. Studies in this domain have generally ignored the possibility that *where* a consumer is located within a social network may influence the degree to which that consumer seeks opinions from others. For instance, will the opinion seeking behavior of a consumer be any different if he is strategically connected to others in the network versus if he is not strategically connected? Will a consumer increase her propensity to seek out opinions knowing she is in a better network position to reach those who could help her with her information search? These research questions suggest that as a discipline we do not have a thorough understanding of how network positions influences the opinion seeking behavior of consumers. Therefore, our research focuses on both the structural properties of the social network (network centrality), and the outcomes of those relational characteristics (e.g., how the social links affect opinion seeking behavior).

Opinion seeking is the act of searching out advice from other consumers (Flynn et al. 1996). Our research investigates how occupying a certain network position affects the extent to which consumers seek the opinions *of others*, as well as the extent to which consumers are approached *by others* for their opinions. One of the ways in which individuals can occupy such an advantageous position is to become *central* in a network (Lee, Cotte, and Noseworthy 2010). Network centrality is measured by examining the number of direct relationships an individual has with others, or by assessing the extent to which an individual links otherwise unconnected cliques or individuals (Freeman 1979). Thus, centrality can be defined by the number (quantity) of ties or the configuration (strategic location) of ties. In this paper, we focus on two common measures of network centrality: degree centrality and betweenness centrality.

Occupying a central position, through either degree or betweenness centrality, reflects greater social capital (Burt 2000). Individuals located in central positions have unique social advantages; they can take advantage of their network structure for information and resources (Coleman 1990). We propose that those who are centrally located in a network will exhibit a greater tendency to seek opinions than those who are on the periphery of the network. By tendency, we mean the frequency with which central people approach others for their opinions. In addition, we propose that central individuals are more likely to be approached for opinions than those residing in the periphery.

To test our theory, we conducted two network studies using social network analysis. One of the main strengths of social network analysis is that it enables researchers to locate the structural position of individuals in a network (Lee et al. 2010). In study 1, we examine a brand community made of primarily young adults. We measure an individual's opinion seeking behavior for a *product* associated with the brand community. In study 2, we extend our theory to a different type of a social network (a seniors' social club), and measure opinion seeking behaviors for a *service* associated with this club.

The results of two field studies provide strong support the positive association between network centrality and opinion seeking, as well as, network centrality and opinions sought. With regards to degree centrality, out-degree centrality was positively related to both opinion seeking measures. However, this was not the case for in-degree centrality. The results support the notion that people who rated themselves as central (social perception) were associated with having higher opinion seeking tendencies, while people who were central (as rated by others) did not have higher opinion seeking tendencies. In contrast, for the opinions sought measure, a positive relationship was found for in-degree centrality, but not for out-degree centrality.

With regards to betweenness centrality, the data reveals positive relationship with both opinion seeking and opinions sought. Results from the two field studies reveal that those occupying a high betweenness position are most likely to take advantage of their brokering opportunities to seek opinions from others; but it also opens up opportunities for others to seek opinions from them. This is an important finding because it emphasizes the social benefit (i.e. increased opportunity to seek out diverse information) from occupying a betweenness central position. However, it is possible that they may also face social costs or burdens as others may come to depend on them for information.

Concluding, this research contributes to the literature by recognizing that there are unique opportunities and advantages of occupying a central position in a social network. Overall, the findings suggest that centrality is positively related to both opinion seeking and opinion approachability. We have firmly demonstrated the importance of both the number of social ties and the position of those ties in the flow of opinions through a social network. Future researchers can continue to advance on this understanding in both face-to-face and online social networks and communities. The growth in peer-to-peer technologies is fuelling growth in virtual social networks, and the opinion-seeking and opinion-sharing that attend those communities.

# The Flow of Cosmetic Routines in Iran

Aliakbar Jafari, University of Strathclyde, UK
Pauline Maclaran, Royal Holloway, University of London, UK
Babak Taheri, University of Strathclyde, UK

## EXTENDED ABSTRACT

Conceptualizing consumption as an experiential process rather than solely a cognitive purchasing behavior (Holbrook and Hirschman 1982; Bloch 1982; Hawkins et al. 1983; Bloch and Bruce 1984), in the past three decades, researchers have addressed "consumers' subjective and emotional reactions to consumption objects" (Holt 1995, 2). Among a variety of dimensions of consumption as experience (e.g., emotional, experiential, hedonic, aesthetic) (Holbrook and Hirschman 1982; Belk et al. 1989; Celsi et al. 1993), autotelic consumption has gained momentum in studying recreational activities in which consumption becomes 'an end in itself' (Csikszentmihalyi 1975). That is, consumers' deep involvement with the object of consumption results in their self-defined form of recreation, pleasure, and flow experience (Csikszentmihalyi 1975, 1992; Bloch and Bruce 1984).

Within consumer research, Csikszentmihalyi's concept of 'flow' has been acknowledged as an important part of autotelic consumption, usually associated with various leisure activities such as games (Holbrook et al. 1984), aesthetic appreciation (Joy and Sherry 2003), sports (Holt 1995; Sherry et al. 2005), extraordinary experiences such as skydiving (Celsi et al. 1993; Celsi 1992) or white water rafting (Arnould et al. 1999), gambling (Cotte 1997), and even online search experience behaviors (Mathwick and Rigdon 2004). Noticeably, although Csikszentmihalyi (1975, 1992) highlights opportunities for finding flow in non-leisure activities, and perhaps due to the cultural turn's emphasis on identity issues, the more mundane aspects of everyday life have been overlooked in the literature on autotelic consumption. Neither has his point about flow's context-dependency triggered any cross-cultural research, particularly in non-Western societies. Our present study addresses these gaps in the literature and scrutinizes consumption of cosmetics as an everyday life practice among young adult women in Iran.

In our study, first, we were inspired by the fact that with a population of only 70 million (25 million women under the age of 35), Iran achieved the seventh rank in global markets for consumption of cosmetics and toiletries in 2007 (Euromonitor, 2008). Also, given the recent political interpretations of Iranian women's excessive consumption of make-up (as either a silent rebellion against the political ideology of the Islamic Republic or a sign of Western decadence), we were motivated to explore the potential symbolic meanings (McCracken 1988; Schouten 1991) embedded in these individuals' consumption of cosmetics. Although our non-participatory observations and memos provided us with a pool of ideas, through our in-depth interviews with 15 young adult women (aged between 21 and 32) in Tehran and Karaj, we gained a deep understanding of our informants' consumption practices. Our data analysis followed a systematic process of constant comparison in terms of searching for similarities and differences (Glaser and Strauss 1967).

Quite contrary to our expectations, our emergent findings revealed that our informants' make-up practices were less to do with identity construction (Schouten 1991; Merskin 2007; Thompson and Haytko 1997; Askegaard et al. 2002; Reynolds et al. 1977; Bloch and Richins 1992; Brownmiller 1984; Ragas and Kozlowski 1998; Peiss 1990) and more to do with a total immersion in the experiential and creative aspects of make-up use and as a way to uplift their tired spirits in a monotonous environment. Despite facing various challenges, including frequent stigmatization on account of their often excessive use of make-up, our informants derived high levels of satisfaction from their make-up routines.

The consumption of cosmetics, as our study reveals, is a way of sustaining wellbeing for those women who have less exciting lives. They use their body as an immediate natural environment (Tuan 1997) and a great potential source of joy (Csikszentmihalyi 1992; Stebbins 1977, 2009). Their 'escapist' (Hirschman 1983) engagement with make-up as a source of 'flow' provides them with a sense of solace, pleasure, and creativity (Holbrook and Hirschman 1982; Bloch and Bruce 1984). In the absence of extrinsic satisfaction and appreciation from their society (Csikszentmihalyi 1992; Bloch and Bruce 1984), they continue to engage in their make-up rituals on a daily basis. Although they do not necessarily believe that make-up makes them more beautiful or relate its use to their self-esteem, they still experience 'significant mood changes' (Celsi 1992). For them, flow (i.e., application of make-up) becomes its own reward and offers intrinsic satisfaction (Bloch and Bruce 1984) and brings feelings of serenity and ecstasy. Yet, for these women, the real challenge of flow experience lies not in the task itself (i.e., consumption of cosmetics) (Csikszentmihalyi 1975) but in the *consequences* of accomplishing the task, which are related to the dominant cultural order of their society (Jafari and Goulding 2008). Generally speaking, excessive use of make-up is frowned upon in Iran. The state views it as an un-Islamic behavior and a sign of Western decadence. Therefore, women with heavy make-up are labeled as '*street women*' and are usually stopped and advised by the morality police. Likewise, conservative families do not approve of their female members' excessive use of make-up as it signals lack of dignity. Such women are also more susceptible to sexual harassment.

Despite all these problems, these individuals accomplish the task of wearing make-up with determination. They feel more "alert, concentrated, happy, satisfied and creative" (Csikszentmihalyi and LeFevre 1989, 816). The 'activation energy' embedded in their autotelic experience (Csikszentmihalyi 1975) focuses them in total absorption on the task in hand to the exclusion of all else around them. Although they know that make-up will do little to change their situation in real life, they can escape into a fantasy world for some part of the day. They give themselves up to the processes of its application, losing themselves in the creative play and artistry that these processes facilitate without giving much thought to final outcomes.

Based on our findings from this context, we stress that changing socio-cultural dynamics in contemporary societies give rise to new forms of autotelic consumption which need to be investigated. By extending the application of autotelic consumption to very mundane life practices, we also emphasize that flow is context-bound and what may lead to flow for one person in a particular socio-cultural context may not necessarily hold true across different socio-cultural environments.

# Caught Between a Rock and a Hard Place: Adult Children's Consumption of Care Services for Their Elderly Parents

Aimee Huff, University of Western Ontario, Canada
June Cotte, University of Western Ontario, Canada

## EXTENDED ABSTRACT:

There is no shortage of anecdotal or scholarly evidence that adult children experience stress as they engage in care decisions for their elderly parents. However, adult children are often conflicted when faced with the task of translating their respect and love for their parents into actual decisions about care. That is, the tasks of choosing and using elder care services are not straightforward or unproblematic for adult children.

The purpose of this paper is to theoretically account for the stress experienced by adult children by attending to the underlying cultural influences on elder care consumption. We take the position that adult children are consumers of elder care services because they are (typically) caregivers for their parents; adult children can choose to provide the requisite care themselves, or to consume commercial services that provide care. The marketplace for elder care services has responded to the care-giving needs of adult children by offering a variety of care options, ranging from in-home visits to assisted living facilities to long-term nursing care. However, although the need for elder care services is often inevitable and the marketplace offers a number of solutions, many children find the experience of making care decisions traumatic and stressful.

It is critical that we acknowledge that we are examining only a sub-set of elder care decisions–those made by the adult children–and, in doing so, we implicitly strip agency from the elderly parents. Certainly, many seniors make their own decisions about care, and others make decisions in conjunction with their children. In this paper, we choose to focus on the experiences of adult children who play the lead roles in decisions about their parents care. We use the context of making care decisions for an elderly parent to reveal how consumers experience stress in the marketplace, and, therefore, do not seek to imply that elder care decisions are the sole responsibility of adult children.

The context of elder care is particularly revealing of consumption-related stress because it often does not involve one specific decision. Rather, elder care consumption involves a cycle of major and minor decisions as various care services are chosen, used, and then deemed inappropriate. Further, adult children typically want to do what is best for their parents, yet are torn between a desire to keep parents safe (from physical harm, etc.) and a desire to respect their parents' wishes to live as independently as possible. However, being physically and cognitively self-sufficient can become problematic as we age, and many children find themselves worried about their parents on a host of issues including mobility and physical safety, diet and medication, hygiene, finances, and social interaction. Further, many children experience significant lifestyle changes as their parents become more dependent on them to provide and manage their care. This can result in children feeling torn between their responsibilities to their parents and to their own spouses and children.

In this paper, we use data gathered from depth interviews with adult children to examine these tensions and to reveal how they are experienced. We find evidence of two dominant tensions in our informants' narratives. The first is a general awareness that it is not possible to respect a parent's wishes to live independently *and* to ensure that s/he is receiving the "proper" level of care. The second tension revolves around an awareness that it is not possible to fulfill the obligations of actively managing a parent's care needs *and* to maintain independence from the parent. We suggest that adult children experience stress as an outcome of these tensions, and we find that stress is characterized by guilt, exhaustion, and anxiety.

We also discuss the cultural ideologies of autonomy and active care management, and suggest how they are related to the context of elder care. Autonomy encompasses the strong cultural value placed on being independent individuals. In the context of elder care, the independence of both parties (i.e., the adult and the child) becomes compromised as the parent's need for care becomes apparent. Active care management encompasses the broad, pervasive expectation that adult children will employ an active, managerial approach to their parents' care by taking all steps necessary to ensure health and safety.

In our interpretation, we propose that the tensions arise as adult children encounter these two distinct cultural ideologies, which can have opposing implications for elder care consumption. That is, in the context of elder care, consumers experience tensions across their individual interpretations of the cultural ideologies because these interpretations push them in different directions in terms of consumption. The outcome of these tensions is stress, as adult children feel torn between the different levels of care that would satisfy them and that would satisfy their parents.

The theoretical contribution of this research is that it demonstrates that consumers are not always able to satisfactorily resolve tensions between their interpretations of cultural ideologies. Prior research has demonstrated that consumers can appropriate discrepant ideological positions and discourses to effectively negotiate personalized consumption meanings and shape their individual consumption behavior. In this paper, we build on this extant work, and we suggest that a particular consumption context can link seemingly unrelated cultural ideologies such that consumers are unable to negotiate an acceptable outcome, and that inability to negotiate the discrepancy can result in stress. Further, we demonstrate that marketplace solutions to consumer needs can, in fact, problematize and complicate consumption; in the context of choosing and using elder care services, many adult children are unable to negotiate disparate ideologies and are therefore unable to reach a satisfactory consumption outcome.

# Inalienable Wealth and Trauma Resolution: An Explanation of Genealogy Consumption

Andrew Lindridge, Open University, UK

## EXTENDED ABSTRACT

Inalienable wealth has been defined as possessions that are intentionally kept within a close group, with previous research focussing on certain possessions taking on behavioural dynamics of guardianship or temporal orientation (Curasi, Price and Arnould, 2004; Price, Arnould and Curasi, 2000). These perspectives, however, have focussed on possessions becoming a contested area arising from issues of ownership and wanting to maintain and perpetuate cherished meanings associated with products. However, this perspective is from a living individual wanting and willingly seeking out ways to engage with later generations by perpetuating these memories. This paper aims to understand how the living create inalienable wealth by seeking out possessions and information from previous ancestral generations (including photographs, sharing ancestral data, visiting places and historical documents), even though there may be no living, emotional, linkage between the generations concerned. We will argue that peoples motivations to undertake genealogical consumption reflects not only cultural and societal changes but a fundamental need by individuals to use genealogy consumption for, conscious and unconscious, resolution of personal and inter-generational traumas.

The antecedents of genealogical consumption were explored using a Consumer Culture Theory perspective that focussed on the individual's self-identity and their cultural context. Western culture has been identified to varying levels with individualism, referring to a cultural system that emphasises the rights of the individual over the community and attributed to declining levels of family orientation and, from a British context, declining levels of religiousness (Halman, 1996; *.*, 2005). Previously individualism has been attributed to materialism, reflecting wider dissatisfaction within an individual's life (Burroughs and Rindfleisch, 2002; La Barbera and Gurhan, 1997). However, the failure of possessions, and hence materialism, to lead to personal happiness may be reflective of a deeper, personal, crisis, within the individual. This crisis, we argue, motivates the consumer to seek resolution through alternative possession meanings, i.e. obtaining inalienable wealth through genealogy. The motivation for these behaviours we argue can be identified with personal and inter-generational trauma, i.e. inherited from previous generations.

Inter-generational trauma can be identified from two perspectives. First, the psycho-analytical perspective argues that trauma is inherited by the child from the parent preventing the child from developing their own, unique, personality, consequently, resulting in inter-generational trauma (Abraham and Torok, 1994; Praeger, 2003). The second distinct research field draws upon sociological studies, which argues that each generation occupies a particular social location, allowing for social experiences to be refracted and made meaningful. However, failure by the individual to identify with and belong to that period of time ensures that they remain traumatized and instead focused on historical experiences and events (Dilthey, 1924; Mannheim, 1928/1972).

The methodology involved a four year immersion into the genealogical consumption arena, covering the period January 2006 to January 2010, including access to a variety of genealogical data and consumption arenas. The sampling procedure employed was theoretical, relational and discriminative. To achieve this, only participants who were related to the researcher were interviewed, regardless of whether this connection was within his wider extended family or from several generations back. This was assessed by participants having a *.* surname appear within their respective genealogical lineage. All the participants were approached via a genealogy website producing a sample group consisting of eight people, aged from 48 to 67, living in Australia or Britain. Participants were interviewed with open-ended, grand tour style questions exploring various inter-related themes including: the participants' reasons for their genealogy research, how they engaged with historical records (including their personal meaning for the participant) and their immediate family histories. During the interview process the author probed participants to explore in greater depth personal experiences, family myths, stories and traumas, opinions and thoughts and how this was reflected in their genealogy research.

The interviews were then transcribed, analyzed to identify emergent themes. Finally to ensure reliability and validity the findings were reviewed and discussed with the help of two academic reviewers–one a consumer behaviorist, the other a qualified psychotherapist.

The findings supported the notion that participants were using genealogy as a means of creating a sense of identity in response to their irreligious, lack of materialistic traits and need to seek out a community and wider sense of family. Genealogy offered then an opportunity to substantiate and maintain a sense of identity through creating inalienable wealth through genealogical consumption. Participants discussed how they collected, shared and exchanged ancestral documents, photographs, and stories, often leading to meetings and trips to shared ancestral locations. These engagements offered an opportunity for a reconstruction of a sense of family and inter-connectedness. The need to seek information from the past is reflective of the sociological perspective of inter-generational trauma.

From a psycho-analytical perspective, only one participant did not discuss a personal and /or inter-generational trauma that had motivated them to undertake genealogical research. Personal traumas ranged from loss of a father, unwanted divorce or a wider need to understand their world, whilst inter-generational trauma included stories of slavery, death in child birth and loss of aristocratic titles and lands. Participants by seeking out ancestral documents, stories and myths provided an opportunity to explore, understand and resolve the cultural, economic and social aspects of their inherited trauma.

Genealogy then presented opportunities for participants to seek out and develop the cues, materials and prompts for the individual to recall particular events to the extent of creating memories that they may never have experienced. These memories were then actively shared and sought out amongst participants and genealogical communities providing a needed and sought affirmation of their self-identity. Commemorative and other related memory symbols (such as documents and photographs) become then symbolic to the participants because of their ability to elicit a reaction from individuals; a reaction identifiable with and developing further previous work into inalienable wealth by Curasi, Price and Arnould's (2004) and Price, Arnould and Curasi's (2000). The genealogical community based upon a shared ancestor offered opportunities for intimacy, creating social networks and resolution of personal and inherited traumas but also a means to achieve autonomy and independence.

## REFERENCES

Abraham, Nicolas and Torok, Maria (1994), *The Shell and the Kernel,* 1. Rand, Nicholas T. (Ed.) Chicago, IL: University of Chicago Press.

Burroughs, J. Rindfleisch (2002), "Materialism and well-being: A conflicting values perspective", *Journal of Consumer Research*, 29 (3): 348-370.

Curasi, Carolyn F., Price, Linda L. and Arnould, Eric J. (2004) "How Individuals Cherished Possessions Become Families' Inalienable Wealth," *Journal of Consumer Research*, 31(3): 609-622.

Dilthey,Wilhelm (1924), *Gesammelte Schriften*, Leipzig: Treubner, cited in Schorske, Carl (1978), "Generational tension and culture change: reflection on the case of Vienna", *Daedalus*, 107 (4): 111-122.

Halman, Loek (1996), "Individualism in Individualized Society– Results from the European Values Surveys", *International Journal of Comparative Sociology,* XXXXVII (3):195-214.

La Barbera, Priscilla and Gurhan, Zeynep (1997), "The Role of Materialism, Religiosity and Demographics in Subjective Well-Being", *Psychology and Marketing*, 14 (1): 71-97.

Mannheim, Karl (1928), "*The Problem of Generations*" 101-138, in Altbach, Philip J. and Laufer, Robert S. (Eds) (1972), "*The New Pilgrims: Youth Protest in Transition*", Jed McKay and Company, New York.

Praeger, Jeffrey (2003), "Lost childhood, lost generations: the intergenerational transmission of trauma", *Journal of Human Rights*, 2 (2): 173-181.

Price, Linda L., Arnould, Eric J. and, Curasi, Carolyn F. (2000), "Older Consumers' Disposition of Special Possessions," *Journal of Consumer Research*, 27 (Sep.): 179-201.

_____ (2005), 'Religiosity and the construction of a cultural-consumption identity', *Journal of Consumer Marketing*, vol. 22, no. 3, pp. 142-152.

# The Defensive Trust Effect: Consumers' Defensive Use of Belief in a Just World to Cope with Decision-Generated Threat

Andrew Wilson, St. Mary's College of California, USA
Peter Darke, York University, Canada

## EXTENDED ABSTRACT

The Defensive Trust Effect: Consumers' Defensive Use of Beliefs in a Just World to Cope with Decision-Generated Threat

Consumers cope with many threats in the course of buying, consuming, and interacting with marketers. Previous research has examined how consumers cope with the threat of negative emotions (Yi and Baumgartner 2004), potentially misleading persuasion attempts (Campbell and Kirmani 2000; Darke and Ritchie 2007), and difficult decisions (Luce 2005; Luce, Payne, and Bettman 1999). Decision-making is inherently threatening to consumers; both in terms of their goal to make accurate decisions (Luce, Bettman, and Payne 1997), and also their goals of maintaining self-esteem and self-presenting as competent deciders (Janis and Mann 1977; Luce 2005). This research introduces a previously unexamined coping strategy consumers engage–termed *defensive trust coping*–in which consumers fall back on positive world beliefs to re-construe the situation as one in which they can and should trust marketing agents.

Drawing on just world theory (Hafer and Begue 2005; Lerner 1980), positive illusions research (Taylor and Brown 1988, 1994) and cognitive experiential self theory (CEST; Epstein and Pacini 1999), we develop theory that specifies psychological mechanism and situational moderators. Just world theory specifies that individuals are motivated to perceive the world as a place where they get what they deserve (Lerner 1980; Lerner and Simmons 1966). This belief is more strongly held by some individuals than others (Rubin and Peplau 1975). BJW functions as a healthy coping mechanism that helps individuals adapt to their own potential misfortunes (i.e. I am a good person, I deserve good outcomes, so I will get good outcomes; Furnham 2003; Hafer and Begue 2005). Our research views BJW as a type of positive illusion (Taylor and Brown 1988, 1994), which operates through consumers' trust judgments of marketing agents. Past research suggests that consumers typically respond negatively to threat by becoming less trusting of marketers (Campbell and Kirmani 2000; Darke and Ritchie 2007) (Slovic, Flynn, and Layman 1991). In contrast, our model predicts that high-BJW consumers respond to decision-generated threats by falling back on their BJW as a coping resource, leading to buffering–or even positive–effects on trust judgments. The result of four experiments support our conception and predictions.

Exp 1 used choice as a manipulation of threat, with post-choice serving as the high threat condition. Pre (post) choice participants responded to an adapted seven-point trust scale (Delgado-Ballester 2004) before (after) choosing between the two cameras. BJW was measured as a continuous variable using seven items from an established scale (Dalbert 1999). Participants imagined an interaction with a retail salesperson culminating in the salesperson recommending one digital camera over another. Moderated multiple regression analysis (Aiken and West 1996) revealed a significant choice-stage x BJW interaction (β .259, $t$=2.422, $p<.05$), such that high-BJW participants (+1 SD) trusted the salesperson more [Predicted Value ($PV$)=4.46] than low-BJW (-1SD; $PV$=3.58), but only in the post-choice stage, when decision-generated threat was high. A mediation test (Baron and Kenny 1986), using coded thought listings of valanced thoughts as a mediator, supported the assumption that defensive trust coping operates through a relatively pre-conscious process, in that it did not require cognitive elaboration.

Exp 2 examined conditions wherein consumers experience threat both pre- and post-choice. Consumers experience conflict in the pre-decision phase when choice alternative are not differentiable, because they cannot find a reason on which to base their choice (Shafir et al. 1993). A non-differentiable choice set was inserted into the scenario described for Exp 1. Under this form of decision conflict, high-BJW consumers again trusted a retail salesperson more ($PV$=5.01) than low-BJW ($PV$=3.73; β=.429, $t$=4.428, $p<.001$), across both decision phases.

Exp 3 further extended the findings in three important ways: 1) an experimental priming manipulation of BJW provided causal evidence for the effects, 2) a cognitive load manipulation provided further evidence that defensive trust coping operates through a pre-conscious process, and 3) a manipulation of ulterior motive established a boundary condition of the effects, such that they were extinguished under ulterior motive.

Exp 4 provided clearer evidence of the defensive nature of the effect by manipulating the level of decision-generated orthogonally along two dimensions, material consequence and psycho-social threat. Material consequence threat was manipulated by instructions to half the participants that a draw would award some participants the actual digital camera chosen. Psycho-social threat was manipulated by assigning half the participants to role of buyer (high-threat), and the other half to observer (low-threat). Exp 4's protocol differed from the earlier studies in that participants shopped for a digital camera on an actual electronic retailer website. The salesperson interaction occurred through an instant messaging (IM) software protocol that ensured a plausible, but controlled, salesperson interaction. The main result was a marginal BJW x consequence x role interaction (β=.113, $t$=1.904, $p$=.058), such that high-BJW participants in the buyer role/real consequence condition trusted more ($PV$=5.13) than all other conditions ($PV's$ from 4.46 to 4.60).

This research makes a number of contributions to our understanding of the ways in which consumers cope with decision threat. For instance, whereas extant research on consumer coping has focused on conscious coping strategies (Duhachek 2005; Duhachek and Iacobucci 2005; Duhachek and Oakley 2007), we extend this pursuit by examining a new coping strategy that focuses on a just world belief, which seems to defend consumers against threat without the need for conscious awareness. Moreover, in contrast to extant research (Campbell and Kirmani 2000; Darke and Ritchie 2007; Slovic et al. 1991) which shows threat generally has negative effects on trust, we identify conditions under which threat can actually lead to positive effects on consumer trust of marketers. Although this pattern is somewhat counterintuitive, it is nonetheless predicted by the proposed model of defensive consumer coping.

## REFERENCES

Aiken, L.S. and S.G. West (1996), *Multiple Regression: Testing and Interpreting Interactions*, Thousand Oaks, CA: Sage.
Baron, R. M. and D. A. Kenny (1986), "The Moderator Mediator Variable Distinction in Social Psychological-Research-Conceptual, Strategic, and Statistical Considerations," *Journal of Personality and Social Psychology*, 51 (6), 1173-82.

Brehm, J. W. (1956), "Postdecision Changes in the Desirability of Alternatives," *Journal of Abnormal and Social Psychology*, 52 (3), 384-89.

Campbell, M. C. and A. Kirmani (2000), "Consumers' Use of Persuasion Knowledge: The Effects of Accessibility and Cognitive Capacity on Perceptions of an Influence Agent," *Journal of Consumer Research*, 27 (1), 69-83.

Dalbert, C. (1999), "The World Is More Just for Me Than Generally: About the Personal Belief in a Just World Scale's Validity," *Social Justice Research*, 12, 79-98.

Darke, P. R. and R. J. B. Ritchie (2007), "The Defensive Consumer: Advertising Deception, Defensive Processing, and Distrust," *Journal of Marketing Research*, 44 (1), 114-27.

Delgado-Ballester, E. (2004), "Applicability of a Brand Trust Scale across Product Categories," *European Journal of Marketing*, 38 (5/6), 573-92.

Duhachek, A. (2005), "Coping: A Multidimensional, Hierarchical Framework of Responses to Stressful Consumption Episodes," *Journal of Consumer Research*, 32 (1), 41-53.

Duhachek, A. and D. Iacobucci (2005), "Consumer Personality and Coping: Testing Rival Theories of Process," *Journal of Consumer Psychology*, 15 (1), 52-53.

Duhachek, A. and J. L. Oakley (2007), "Mapping the Hierarchical Structure of Coping: Unifying Empirical and Theoretical Perspectives," *Journal of Consumer Psychology*, 17 (3), 218-32.

Epstein, S> and R.Pacini (1999), "Some Basic Issues Regarding Dual-Process Theories from the Perspective of Cognitive-Experiential Self-Theory," in *Dual Process Theories in Social Psychology*, ed. S. Chaiken and Y. Trope, New York and London: The Guilford Press, 462-82.

Furnham, A. (2003), "Belief in a Just World: Research Progress over the Last Decade," *Personality and Individual Differences*, 34, 795-817.

Hafer, C. L. and L. Begue (2005), "Experimental Research on Just-World Theory: Problems, Developments, and Future Challenges," *Psychological Bulletin*, 131 (1), 128-67.

Janis, I. L. and L. Mann (1977), *Decision Making: A Psychological Analysis of Conflict, Choice, and Commitment*, New York, NY (US): Free Press.

Lerner, M. J. (1980), *The Belief in a Just World: A Fundamental Delusion*, New York: Plenum Press.

Lerner, M. J., D. T. Miller, and J. G. Holmes (1976), "Deserving and the Emergence of Forms of Justice," in *Advances in Experimental Social Psychology* Vol. 9 ed. L. Berkowitz and E. Walster, New York: Academic Press., 133–62

Lerner, M. J. and C. H. Simmons (1966), "Observers Reaction to Innocent Victim-Compassion or Rejection," *Journal of Personality and Social Psychology*, 4 (2), 203-10.

Luce, M. F. (2005), "Decision Making as Coping," *Health Psychology*, 24 (4), S23-S28.

Luce, M. F., J. R. Bettman, and J. W. Payne (1997), "Choice Processing in Emotionally Difficult Decisions," *Journal of Experimental Psychology-Learning Memory and Cognition*, 23 (2), 384-405.

Luce, M. F., J. W. Payne, and J. R. Bettman (1999), "Emotional Trade-Off Difficulty and Choice," *Journal of Marketing Research*, 36 (2), 143-59.

Main, K. J., D. W. Dahl, and P. R. Darke (2007), "Deliberative and Automatic Bases of Suspicion: Empirical Evidence of the Sinister Attribution Error," *Journal of Consumer Psychology*, 17 (1), 59-69.

Rubin, Z. and L. A. Peplau (1975), "Who Believes in a Just World?," *Journal of Social Issues*, 31 (3), 65-89.

Slovic, P., J.H. Flynn, and M. Layman (1991), "Perceived Risk, Trust, and the Politics of Nuclear Waste," *Science*, 254 (5038), 1603-07.

Taylor, S. E. and J. D. Brown (1988), "Illusion and Well-Being-a Social Psychological Perspective on Mental-Health," *Psychological Bulletin*, 103 (2), 193-210.

— (1994), "Positive Illusions and Well-Being Revisited-Separating Fact from Fiction," *Psychological Bulletin*, 116 (1), 21-27.

Yi, S. W. and H. Baumgartner (2004), "Coping with Negative Emotions in Purchase-Related Situations," *Journal of Consumer Psychology*, 14 (3), 303-17.

# When Does an Attack to the Brand Call for Action? The Role of Self-Brand Connection and Implicit Self-Esteem

Monika Lisjak, Northwestern University, USA
Angela Y. Lee, Northwestern University, USA
Wendi L. Gardner, Northwestern University, USA

## EXTENDED ABSTRACT

In the modern marketplace consumers are often exposed to negative brand information. Existing research shows that brand commitment, which reflects consumers' desire to have a particular brand, influences how people respond to negative brand information. After reviewing negative brand information, low commitment consumer revisit their attitude toward the brand downward, whereas high commitment consumers tend to counterargue the negative information and resist attitude change (Ahluwalia, Burnkrant and Unnava 2000). More recent research shows that brand commitment is influenced by the extent consumers identify and connect with the brand (Escalas and Bettman 2003). In this paper, we suggest that to understand how consumers respond to negative brand information, it is important to examine the interplay between their connection with the brand and their implicit self-esteem.

Research suggests that consumers who are connected with a brand include the brand in their self-concept (e.g., Belk 1988; Escalas and Bettman 2003). Seminal work by W. James (1890) suggests that when objects are incorporated in the self, they elicit the same emotional responses and behaviors as the self. Therefore, an attack to the brand is analogous to an attack to the self. When people are attacked, they use an arsenal of defensive strategies to maintain a positive self-evaluation. Research shows that when participants cope with threats by affirming important aspects of the self, they are no longer defensive (Steele and Liu 1983; Tesser and Cornell 1991), suggesting that different defensive strategies are substitutable for one another. People also defend more when the self is activated (Steele, Spencer and Lynch 1993).

People's defensive responses are influenced by their self-esteem. Research suggests that implicit self-esteem, which is an automatic evaluation of the self, buffers people against threats (e.g., Spalding and Hardin 1999; Greenwald and Farnham 2000). Following a threat to the self, people with low implicit self-esteem become defensive, whereas those with high self-esteem are not.

By building on these findings, we suggest that consumers who are connected with a brand will defend the brand when it is under attack. More importantly, we predict that consumers' defensive responses will be accentuated among those with low implicit self-esteem when their self-concept is activated. Finally, we predict that their defensive response will dissipate if they have the opportunity to self-affirm. We tested these predictions in three experiments.

In experiment 1, we first measured participants' implicit self-esteem by using the name-liking measure (Gebauer et al. 2008). Then, we assessed the connection participants had with Starbucks by using the self-brand connection scale (Escalas and Bettman 2003). Next, participants were randomly assigned to write an essay that either activated or not the self. Finally, participants were presented with an unfavorable editorial about the Starbucks and asked to report how their attitude toward the brand might have changed. Consistent with past research we found a main effect of self-brand connection, whereby participants who felt connected with Starbucks were less likely to devalue the brand after reading the negative editorial. This effect, however, was qualified by the three-way interaction between self activation, self-brand connection and implicit self-esteem. When the self was not activated, participants' self-brand connection negatively predicted attitude change; whereas implicit self-esteem had no effect. However, when the self was activated, participants' self-brand connection and their implicit self-esteem jointly influenced attitude change. In particular, participants with low implicit self-esteem who felt connected with Starbucks reported more favorable attitudes toward the brand. We replicated these findings in a follow-up experiment using the implicit association test (IAT; Karpinski and Steinman 2006) as a measure of implicit self-esteem.

The objective of experiment 2 was to provide converging evidence for our predictions by using a different brand (Facebook) and to investigate the underlying process. We first assessed participants' implicit self-esteem and their connection with Facebook by using the same measures as in experiment 1. Participants then wrote an essay that activated (or not) the self. Next, participants read a negative editorial about Facebook. Finally, participants were asked to report their attitude change and respond to some process measures. Similar to experiment 1, the results revealed a significant effect of self-brand connection, which was qualified by the three-way interaction. When the self was not activated, no effect was significant. However, when the self was activated, participants with low implicit self-esteem had a more favorable attitude toward Facebook compare to their high implicit self-esteem counterparts. Participants' net positive brand thoughts partially mediated the effect.

In our final experiment, we examined whether affirming the self might dissipate the defensive response of low implicit self-esteem individuals. As in experiment 1, participants first filled in a measure of implicit self-esteem and reported their self-brand connection with Starbucks. To activate the self, participants were asked to write a brief essay. Next they were asked to read a negative editorial about Starbuck. After reviewing the editorial, half of the participants were affirmed while the other half were not. Finally, participants were asked to report their attitude change toward Starbucks. We found a main effect of self-brand connection, which was further qualified by the three-way interaction. When participants were not affirmed, we replicated the results from previous experiment. That is, participants with low implicit self-esteem who were connected with Starbucks boosted their brand attitude. However, when participants were affirmed, low implicit self-esteem participants who felt connected with Starbucks did not defend the brand. It seems that it is possible to buffer low-implicit self-esteem participants against self-threats by making them feel good about themselves.

This research demonstrates the importance of examining the interplay between consumers' connection with the brand and their implicit self-esteem when trying to gain a better understanding of how people respond to negative brand information. After receiving negative brand information, low implicit self-esteem consumers who are connected with the brand defend the brand as they would defend the self.

## REFERENCES

Ahluwalia, Rohini, Robert E. Burnkrant, and Rao H. Unnava (2000), "Consumer Response to Negative Publicity: The Moderating Role of Commitment," *Journal of Marketing Research*, 37 (May), 203-214.

Belk, Russell W. (1988), "Possessions and the Extended Self," *Journal of Consumer Research*, 15 (September), 139-168.

Escalas, Jennifer Edson and James R. Bettman (2003), "You Are What They Eat: The Influence of Reference Groups on Consumers' Connections to Brands," *Journal of Consumer Psychology*, 13 (3), 339-348.

Gebauer, Jochen E., Michael Riketta, Philip Broemer, and Gregory R. Maio (2008), "How Much Do You Like Your Name? An implicit measure of global self-esteem," *Journal of Experimental Social Psychology*, 44 (September), 1346-1354.

Greenwald, Anthony G. and Shelly D. Farnham (2000), "Using the Implicit Association Test to Measure Self-Esteem and Self-Concept," *Journal of Personality and Social Psychology*, 79 (December), 1022-1038.

James, William (1890), *"The Principles of Psychology,"* Vol. 1, New York: Henry Holt.

Karpinski, Andrew and Ross B. Steinman (2006), "The Single Category Implicit Association Test as a Measure of Implicit Social Cognition," *Journal of Personality and Social Psychology*, 91 (July), 16-32.

Spalding, Leah R. and Curtis D. Hardin (1999), "Unconscious Unease and Self-Handicapping: Behavioral Consequences of Individual Differences in Implicit and Explicit Self-Esteem," *Psychological Science,* 10 (November), 535-539.

Steele, Claude M. and Thomas J. Liu (1983), "Dissonance Processes as Self-Affirmation," *Journal of Personality and Social Psychology*, 45 (July), 5-19.

Steele, Claude M., Steven J. Spencer, and Michael Lynch (1993), "Self-Image Resilience and Dissonance: The Role of Affirmational Resources," *Journal of Personality and Social Psychology*, 64 (June), 885-896.

Tesser, Abraham and David P. Cornell (1991), "On the Confluence of Self-Processes," *Journal of Experimental Social Psychology*, 27 (November), 501-526.

# "Keeping It Real": Marketing Implications of Brand Authenticity

Melissa Minor, University of Florida, USA
Robyn LeBoeuf, University of Florida, USA

## EXTENDED ABSTRACT

Although there is evidence in the literature that being authentic provides benefits to the firm, most, if not all, of these conclusions have been drawn from depth interviews or other qualitative work. What is missing is experimental evidence that perceptions of brand or product authenticity provide other benefits to the firm. Using an experimental approach, this paper demonstrates that authenticity is a malleable facet of the brand, and provides evidence that consumers' perceptions of a brand's authenticity affect other brand-related cognitions such as quality perceptions and willingness to pay. This paper also shows the potentially ironic consequences of fostering authenticity.

Although many definitions of authenticity have been offered in the literature, this paper will focus on two main sources of authenticity: inherent qualities of the object and consumers' subjective judgments about the brand. In general, offerings that are natural, handmade, simple and/or based in fact are generally considered by consumers to be more authentic (Groves 2001; Boyle 2003; Munoz, Wood and Solomon 2006; Beverland 2005; Potter 2008). Consumers also make subjective judgments about the authenticity of a product using contextual information such as information about the brand's image and its marketing. Summarized in Gilmore and Pine's (2007) *Polonius Test*, brands are considered to be authentic if they are "true to self" and/or "are what they say they are". Being "true to self" means that a brand is perceived as existing because of the passion of its founder–not simply for monetary gain. On the other hand, "being what you say you are" means that to be authentic, a company or offering must live up to its own promises–there must be truth in advertising.

While much attention has been given to the importance of authenticity to the consumer, limited attention has been paid to the benefit (or detriment) being authentic has for the firm. The extant literature provides some evidence that judgments of authenticity have the potential to have a direct and indirect impact on consumers' search for information, consideration set formation and, ultimately, choice (Chalmers 2007; Groves 2001). While existing work suggests that consumers' perceptions of authenticity may affect inferences consumers make about the brand, it does not address the types of inferences that consumers make. We hypothesize that consumers will infer that more authentic brands are also higher in quality, and that they will be willing to pay more for these products. Additionally, to the extent that consumers believe that authentic products are more "real" than inauthentic products, we hypothesize that consumers will be more confident in the inferences they make about authentic products than inauthentic products.

In studies 1a and 1b, authenticity was manipulated by informing participants that authentic and inauthentic brands were owned by large corporations. Revealing this information should cause consumers to doubt the authenticity of the authentic brands, because the discrepancy between the images and motives of the authentic brands and their parent corporations should bring into doubt whether the authentic brands truly are who they say are, a key component in perceptions of authenticity. Measures of authenticity perceptions, product quality, willingness to pay and attitude confidence were taken both before (Time 1) and after (Time 2) the corporate ownership information was revealed. Study 1a and 1b revealed that perceptions of authenticity do affect other brand-related cognitions. At Time 2, after reading of the authentic brands' corporate parents, participants' reported lower perceptions of authenticity of quality,

decreased willingness to pay, and less confidence in their attitudes. The drops in quality perceptions, willingness to pay, and attitude confidence were fully mediated by participants' lower perceptions of brand authenticity. However these results were unique to the authentic focal brands. The inauthentic brands actually benefited from their connection to a large parent corporation. At Time 2, perceptions of authenticity, product quality, and willingness to pay increased among the inauthentic brands.

While studies 1a and 1b, and previous work on brand authenticity, seem to suggest that increased authenticity is uniformly positive for the brand, might there be situations where a brand's authenticity could be detrimental? In study 2, we are interested in determining how authentic brands weather brand transgressions, and if perceptions of the brand following the transgression are affected by the type of transgression committed. Although all transgressions should be detrimental to any brand, we hypothesize that some transgressions will be especially harmful for authentic brands. Specifically, we hypothesize that a transgression directly related to the basis of an authentic brand's authenticity will be more damaging for the authentic brand than an equivalent transgression would be for another brand.

In study 2, participants were given information about an authentic or inauthentic brand and were then informed that this brand had committed one of three types of transgressions (moral, generic, or dangerous ingredient). While each transgression should be damaging to any brand, we hypothesize that the ingredient transgression will be especially damaging to the authentic brand (Burt's Bees) because the transgression undermines its authenticity (all-natural ingredients). As hypothesized, following the moral and generic transgressions, both the authentic and inauthentic brands' quality perceptions were damaged to a similar degree. However, following the ingredient transgression, the authentic brand's quality perceptions were damaged significantly more than the inauthentic brand's. This drop in quality perceptions was fully mediated by the decrease in participants' perceptions of the authentic brand's authenticity.

Drawing on the importance of "being what you say you are" in consumers' judgments of brand authenticity, we presented three studies that demonstrate positives and negatives of brand authenticity. Our findings show that consumers perceive more authentic brands to be higher in quality and suggest that they may also be willing to pay more for them. Additionally, consumers' confidence in their opinions about brands is directly tied to the extent to which they perceive those brands to be authentic. However, despite these advantages, we also demonstrated that authenticity can harm the brand if the brand commits a transgression that undermines its authenticity. Additionally, these studies demonstrate ways in which consumers' perceptions of a brand's authenticity can be manipulated.

## REFERENCES

Aaker, Jennifer, Susan Fournier, and S. Adam Brasel (2004), "When Good Brands Do Bad," *Journal of Consumer Research*, 31 (June), 1-16.

Beverland, Michael B. (2005), "Crafting Brand Authenticity: The Case of Luxury Wines," *Journal of Management Studies* V. 42, Issue 5, 1003-1029.

_____, Adam Lindgreen and Michiel W. Vink (2008), "Projecting Authenticity through Advertising: Consumer Judgments of Advertisers' Claims," *Journal of Advertising*, vol. 37, no. 1, pp. 5-15.

Boyle, David (2003). *Authenticity: Brands, Fakes, Spin and the Lust for Real Life.* Flamingo: Hammersmith, London.

Caruana, Robert, Adnrew Crane and James A. Fitchett (2008), "Paradoxes of Consumer Independence: A Critical Discourse Analysis of the Independent Traveler," *Marketing Theory*, Vol. 8(3): 253-272.

Chalmers, Tandy (2007), "Advertising Authenticity: Resonating Replications of Real Life," Unpublished Manuscript. University of Arizona.

Chhabra, Deepak (2005), "Defining Authenticity and Its Determinants: Toward an Authenticity Flow Model", *Journal of Travel Research*, v. 44 (August), 64-73.

Costa, Janeen Arnold and Gary J. Bamossy (1995), "Perspectives on Ethnicity, Nationalism and Cultural Identity," in *Marketing in a Multicultural World,* ed. Janeen Arnold Costa and Gary J. Bamossy, Newbury Park, CA: Sage, 3-25.

Elliott, Richard and Andrea Davies (2006), "Symbolic Brands and Authenticity of Identity Performance," in eds. Jonathan E. Schroeder and Miriam Salzer-Morling's *Brand Culture.* New York: Routledge, pp. 155-170.

Gilmore, Joseph and B.J. Pine (2007). *Authenticity: What Consumers Really Want.* Boston, MA: Harvard Business School Press.

Grayson, Kent and Radan Martinec (2004), "Consumer Perceptions of Iconicity and Indexicality and Their Influence on Assessments of Authentic Market Offerings," *Journal of Consumer Research*, Vol. 31 (Sept.): 296-312.

Groves, Angela M. (2001), "Authentic British Food Products: A Review of Consumer Perceptions," *International Journal of Consumer Studies*, 25 (3), 246-254.

Heynen, Hilde (2006), "Questioning Authenticity," *National Identities*, 8 (3), 287-300.

Holt, Douglas B. (1998), "Does Cultural Capital Structure American Consumption?" *Journal of Consumer Research*, 25, 1-25.

_____ (2002), "Why Do Brands Cause Trouble? A Dialectical Theory of Consumer Culture and Branding," *Journal of Consumer Research*, 29, 70-90.

Hughes, Michael (2000), "Country Music as impression management: A meditation on fabricating authenticity," *Poetics*, 28, 185-205

Judd, Charles M., David A. Kenny, and Gary H. McClelland (2001), "Estimating and Testing Mediation and Moderation in within-Participant Designs," *Psychological Methods*, 6 (June), 115-134.

Munoz, Caroline L., Natalie T. Wood and Michael R. Solomon (2006), "Real or blarney? A Cross-cultural investigation of the perceived authenticity of Irish pubs," *Journal of Consumer Behaviour*, 5: 222-234.

Penaloza, Lisa (2001), "Consuming the American West: Animating Cultural Meaning and Memory at a Stock Show and Rodeo," *Journal of Consumer Research*, 28, 3 (Dec), 369-398.

Peterson, Richard A. (2005), "In Search of Authenticity," *Journal of Management Studies*, 42:5 (July), 1084-1098.

Potter, Andrew (2008), "Can One Be Authentic without Being a Snob?" *Maclean's*, 121 (22)

Thompson, Craig J. and Siok Kuan Tambyah (1999), "Trying to Be Cosmopolitan," *Journal of Consumer Research*, 26 (Dec), 214-241.

Wallendorf, Melanie, Joan Lindsey-Mullikin, and Ron Pimentel (1998), "Gorilla Marketing: Customer Animation and Regional Embeddedness of a Toy Servicescape," in Sherry, ed. (1998), 147-198.

# Motivated Consumer Innovativeness: Concept, Measurement and Validation

Bert Vandecasteele, Lessius University College and Ghent University, Belgium
Maggie Geuens, Ghent University and Vlerick Leuven Gent Management School, Belgium

## EXTENDED ABSTRACT

Since the early seventies, several researchers have tried to predict consumers' innovative buying behavior by means of different scales intended to measure innovativeness as a personality trait. However, most previous research disregards the consumer-product relation (Gatignon and Robertson 1985; Goldsmith and Flynn 1992) and ignores the different motivation sources. By constructing a new Consumer Innovativeness scale which incorporates a diversity of underlying goals and motivations for buying an innovation, we take the notion of product-consumer interactions in Consumer Innovativeness one step further: Consumers differ not only in level of innovativeness (i.e., personality trait of consumers) but also in type of innovativeness (i.e., motivations to buy the innovation).

Consumer innovativeness is "the tendency to buy new products in a particular product category soon after they appear in the market and relatively earlier than most other consumers in the market segment" (Foxall, Goldsmith, and Brown 1998, 41). This personality trait should provide an explanatory basis for innovative buying behavior, however, predictive validity still is problematic with the existing innovativeness scales (Im, Bayus, and Mason 2003). By including a wider spectrum of motivations, we are able to construct an innovativeness scale that performs better both in terms of content validity and predictive validity. Moreover, it may help marketing researchers and managers to identify and reach the motivated innovative consumer for their innovation more effectively.

We base our conceptualization on general motivation, goal and value taxonomies (Ford and Nichols 1987; Schwartz 1992) and can conclude that at least four motivational dimensions are of importance for Consumer Innovativeness: (1) Functionally Motivated Consumer Innovativeness (fMCI) is Consumer Innovativeness motivated by the functional performance of innovations which focus on task management and accomplishment improvement. (2) Hedonically Motivated Consumer Innovativeness (hMCI) is Consumer Innovativeness motivated by an affective or sensory stimulation and gratification. (3) Socially Motivated Consumer Innovativeness (sMCI) is Consumer Innovativeness motivated by the self-assertive social need for differentiation. And finally, (4) Cognitively Motivated Consumer Innovativeness (cMCI) is Consumer Innovativeness motivated by stimulation of the mind. These four motives often recur in general consumer behavior literature (Rossiter and Percy 1997; Sweeney and Soutar 2001), innovativeness literature (Arnould 1989; Fisher and Price 1992; Simonson and Nowlis 2000; Voss, Spangenberg, and Grohmann 2003) or different innovativeness scales (Baumgartner and Steenkamp 1996; Roehrich 1994; Venkatraman and Price 1990), however, hardly any innovativeness scale has been developed that includes a wider array of potential consumer motives.

We develop a 20-item 4-dimensional MCI scale based on a combination of eight studies (with about 2,600 respondents in total).

We start with an item pool of 254 items, based on literature review, existing Consumer Innovativeness scales, exploratory interviews and an exploratory quantitative study with 279 respondents who had to indicate to what extent 135 human motives (Chulef, Read, and Walsh 2001) are applicable to the purchase of innovations. Based on expert and consumer judgments of all items, taking content validity, representativeness, dimensionality, comprehensibility, and unambiguousness into account, 90 items remain. These 90 items are included in an online survey with 452 respondents. Based on principal component analyses and confirmatory factor analysis taking scale development procedures of Netemeyer, Bearden, and

Sharma (2003) into account, we can reduce the pool to 30 items, and can confirm the 4 MCI factors. These factors prove to possess high internal validity, sufficient discriminant validity, composite reliability, and average variance extracted. Furthermore, the 4-factor correlated model results in an acceptable overall fit and proves to be the best model. Moreover, we can prove convergent validity with Roehrich's (1994) Hedonic and Social Consumer Innovativeness scale, and discriminant validity with Baumgartner and Steenkamp's (1996) Exploratory Acquisition of Products scale and Eysenck, Eysenck, and Barrett's (1985) Extraversion scale.

We further refine the scale with a new survey including the 30 MCI items. Based on similar procedures, we have to remove 10 extra items, resulting in the 20 final MCI items. Again, the fit indices indicate a good model, which outperforms other models. In addition, MCI proves to be stable over time, as we can prove test-retest reliability. Moreover, MCI is not sensitive to social desirability bias.

Finally, an innovativeness scale also needs to predict innovative consumer behavior in everyday life. We check this with two studies: First, a predictive validity study is set up with fictitious innovations, which are manipulated towards the four innovativeness motivations. Moreover, as we add two existing general innovativeness scales to the survey, we can verify whether MCI performs better in predicting innovative behavior than existing scales. Second, we have another study with a list of existing innovations. Both studies prove that there is a unique relation between each motivation dimension and the attitude, the buying intentions or buying behavior of consumers regarding innovations that satisfy these specific functional, hedonic, social or cognitive needs. Moreover, we prove that MCI predicts innovation buying behavior better than the traditional Cognitive and Sensory Innovativeness scale of Venkatraman and Price (1990), and the recently developed Global Consumer Innovativeness scale of Tellis, Yin, and Bell (2009).

To conclude, this four-dimensional Consumer Innovativeness scale consisting of a hedonic, functional, social, and cognitive dimension is useful for several reasons. First, the eight studies show that the dimensionality, reliability, convergence, discriminant, and predictive validity of MCI prove satisfactory. Second, MCI measures more than existing Consumer Innovativeness scales: (1) MCI not only measures the intensity of Consumer Innovativeness, but also its origin. (2) MCI keeps the middle ground between existing general innovativeness scales, which are unimpressive in predicting innovative buying behavior, and the domain-specific innovativeness of Goldsmith and Hofacker (1991), which is product-specific and thus not very practical, leading to a better performance in terms of predicting innovative behavior. (3) Moreover, MCI disproves the general consensus that younger people are more innovative than older people: Older people are as innovative as younger people as far as functional innovations are concerned. As most existing innovativeness scales focus on hedonic and social innovativeness, and older people are less hedonically and socially motivated to buy innovations, these scales are not able to capture the innovativeness of older people.

## REFERENCES

Arnould, E. J. (1989), "Toward a broadened theory of preference formation and the diffusion of innovations-Cases from Zinder-province, Niger-Republic," *Journal of Consumer Research, 16*(2), 239-67.

Babin, B. J., W. R. Darden, and M. Griffin (1994), "Work and or Fun: Measuring Hedonic and Utilitarian Shopping Value," *Journal of Consumer Research, 20*(4), 644-56.

Ballard, R. (1992), "Short forms of the Marlowe-Crowne social desirability scale," *Psychological Reports, 71*, 1155-160.

Baumgartner, H. and J.-B. E. M. Steenkamp (1996), "Exploratory consumer buying behavior: Conceptualization and measurement," *International Journal of Research in Marketing, 13*(2), 121-37.

Bruner, G. C., K. E. James, and P. J. Hensel (2001), *Marketing Scales Handbook: A Compilation of Multi-item Measures. Volume III*, Chicago: American Marketing Association.

Chesson, D. (2002), *The Impact of Value Systems on Consumer Innovativeness across Three Countries in the Asian Pacific Region.* PhD Dissertation.

Chulef, A. S., S. J. Read, and D. A. Walsh (2001), "A hierarchical taxonomy of human goals," *Motivation and Emotion, 25*(3), 191-232.

Churchill, G. A. (1979), "Paradigm for Developing Better Measures of Marketing Constructs," *Journal of Marketing Research, 16*(1), 64-73.

Citrin, A. V., D. E. Sprott, S. N. Silverman, and D. E. Stem Jr (2000), "Adoption of Internet Shopping: The Role of Consumer Innovativeness," *Industrial Management and Data Systems, 100*(7), 294-300.

Cotte, J. and S. L. Wood (2004), "Families and Innovative Consumer Behavior: A Triadic Analysis of Sibling and Parental Influence," *Journal of Consumer Research, 31*(1), 78-86.

Daghfous, N., J. V. Petrof, and F. Pons (1999), "Values and Adoption of Innovations: a Cross-Cultural Study," *Journal of Consumer Marketing, 16*(4/5), 314-31.

DeVellis, R. F. (2003). *Scale Development: Theory and Applications* (2nd ed.). Thousand Oaks, CA: Sage.

Dickerson, M. D. and J. W. Gentry (1983), "Characteristics of Adopters and Non-Adopters of Home Computers," *Journal of Consumer Research, 10*(2), 225-35.

Eysenck, S. B. G., H. J. Eysenck, and P. Barrett. (1985), "A revised version of the psychoticism scale," *Personality and Individual Differences, 6*(1), 21-9.

Fisher, R. J. and L. L. Price (1992), "An investigation into the social-context of early adoption behavior," *Journal of Consumer Research, 19*(3), 477-86.

Ford, M. E. and C. W. Nichols (1987), "A taxonomy of human goals and some possible applications," in *Humans as Self-constructing Systems: Putting the Framework to Work*, ed. M.E. Ford and D. H. Ford, New York: Erlbaum, 289-311.

Fornell, C. and D. F. Larcker (1981), "Evaluating structural equation models with unobservable variables and measurement error," *Journal of Marketing Research, 18*(1), 39-50.

Foxall, G. R., R. E. Goldsmith, and S. Brown (1998), *Consumer Psychology for Marketing*, London: Thomson.

Gatignon, H. and T. S. Robertson (1985), "A propositional inventory for new diffusion research," *Journal of Consumer Research, 11*(4), 849-67.

Goldsmith, R. E. and L. R. Flynn (1992), "Identifying innovators in consumer product markets," *European Journal of Marketing, 26*(12), 42-55.

Goldsmith, R. E. and C. F. Hofacker (1991), "Measuring consumer innovativeness," *Journal of the Academy of Marketing Science, 19*(3), 209-21.

Hardesty, D. M. and W. O. Bearden (2004), "The use of expert judges in scale development: Implications for improving face validity of measures of unobservable constructs," *Journal of Business Research, 57*(2), 98-107.

Hirschman, E. C. (1980), "Innovativeness, novelty seeking, and consumer creativity," *Journal of Consumer Research, 7*(3), 283-95.

Hirschman, E. C. (1984), "Experience seeking-a subjectivist perspective of consumption," *Journal of Business Research, 12*(1), 115-36.

Huffman, C., S. Ratneshwar, and D. G. Mick (2000), "Consumer Goal Structures and Goal-Determination Processes," in *The Why of Consumption,* Ed. S. Ratneshwar, D.G. Mick, and C. Huffman, New York: Routledge, 9-35.

Im, S., B. L. Bayus, and C. H. Mason (2003), "An Empirical Study of Innate Consumer Innovativeness, Personal Characteristics and New-Product Adoption Behavior," *Journal of the Academy of Marketing Science, 31*(1), 61-73.

Joseph, B. and S. J. Vyas (1984), "Concurrent Validity of a Measure of Innovative Cognitive Style," *Journal of the Academy of Marketing Science, 12*(2), 159-75.

Le Louarn, P. (1997), "La tendance à innover des consommateurs: Analyse conceptuelle et proposition d'une échelle de mesure," [The tendency to consumer innovativeness: Conceptual analyses and proposal of a measurement scale], *Recherche et Applications en Marketing, 12*(1), 3-20 (in French).

Leavitt, C. and J. Walton (1975), "Development of a scale for innovativeness," *Advances in Consumer Research, 2*(1), 545-52.

Lynn, M. and B. D. Gelb (1996), "Identifying Innovative National Markets for Technical Consumer Goods," *International Marketing Review, 13*(6), 43-57.

Manning, K. C., W. O. Bearden, and T. J. Madden (1995), "Consumer innovativeness and the adoption process," *Journal of Consumer Psychology, 4*(4), 329-45.

Midgley, D. F. and G. R. Dowling (1978), "Innovativeness-concept and its measurement," *Journal of Consumer Research, 4*(4), 229-42.

Midgley, D. F. and G. R. Dowling (1993), "A longitudinal-study of product form innovation-the interaction between predispositions and social messages," *Journal of Consumer Research, 19*(4), 611-25.

Netemeyer, R. G., W. O. Bearden, and S. Sharma (2003), *Scaling procedures-Issues and applications.* Thousand Oaks, CA: Sage.

Oppenheimer, D. M., T. Meyvis, and N. Davidenko (2009), "Instructional Manipulation Checks: Detecting Satisficing to Increase Statistical Power," *Journal of Experimental Social Psychology, 45*, 867-72.

Ostlund, L. E. (1974), "Perceived innovation attributes as predictors of innovativeness," *Journal of Consumer Research, 1*(2), 23-9.

Richins, M. L. (2005), "What Consumers Desire: Goals and Motives in the Consumption Environment," in *Inside Consumption: Consumer motives, goals, and desires*, Ed. S. Ratneshwar and D. G. Mick, New York: Routledge, 340-48.

Roehrich, G. (1994), "Innovativités hédoniste et sociale: Proposition d'une échelle de mesure," [Hedonic and social innovativeness: A measurement scale], *Recherche et Applications en Marketing, 9*(2), 19-42 (in French).

Roehrich, G. (2004), "Consumer innovativeness-Concepts and measurements," *Journal of Business Research, 57*(6), 671-77.

Roehrich, G., P. Valette-Florence, and J.-M. Ferrandi (2003), "An exploration of the relationship between innate innovativeness and domain specific innovativeness," *CERAG*, 02-11.

Rogers, E. M. (2003), *Diffusion of innovations*, New York: The Free Press.

Rossiter, J. R. (2002), "The C-OAR-SE procedure for scale development in marketing," *International Journal of Research in Marketing*, *19*(4), 305-35.

Rossiter, J. R. and L. Percy (1997), *Advertising Communications and Promotion Management*, London: McGrawHill.

Schwartz, S. (1992), "Universals in the Content and Structure of Values: Theoretical Advances and Empirical Tests in 20 Countries," *Advances in Experimental Social Psychology, 25*, 1-65.

Sheth, J. N., B. I. Newman, and B. L. Gross (1991), "Why we buy what we buy: A theory of consumption values," *Journal of Business Research*, *22*(2), 159-70.

Simonson, I. and S. M. Nowlis (2000), "The role of explanations and need for uniqueness in consumer decision making: Unconventional choices based on reasons," *Journal of Consumer Research*, *27*(1), 49-68.

Steenkamp, J.-B. E. M. and H. Baumgartner (1992), "The role of optimum stimulation level in exploratory consumer-behavior," *Journal of Consumer Research*, *19*(3), 434-48.

Steenkamp, J.-B. E. M., F. Hofstede, and M. Wedel (1999), "A cross-national investigation into the individual and national cultural antecedents of consumer innovativeness," *Journal of Marketing*, *63*(2), 55-69.

Steiger, J. H. (1980), "Tests for Comparing Elements of a Correlation Matrix," *Psychological Bulletin*, *87*(2), 245-51.

Sweeney, J. C. and G. N. Soutar (2001), "Consumer perceived value: The development of a multiple item scale," *Journal of Retailing*, *77*(2), 203-20.

Tellis, G. J., E. Yin, and S. Bell (2009), "Global consumer innovativeness: Cross-country differences and demographic commonalities," *Journal of International Marketing, 17*(2), 1-22.

Tian, K. T., W. O. Bearden, and G. L. Hunter (2001), "Consumers' Need for Uniqueness: Scale Development and Validation," *Journal of Consumer Research, 28*(1), 50-66.

Uhl, K., R. Andrus, and L. Poulsen (1970), "How Are Laggards Different? An Empirical Inquiry," *Journal of Marketing Research, 7*(1), 51-4.

Venkatraman, M. P. (1991), "The impact of innovativeness and innovation type on adoption," *Journal of Retailing, 67*(1), 51-67.

Venkatraman, M. P. and L. L. Price (1990), "Differentiating between cognitive and sensory innovativeness: Concepts, measurement, and implications," *Journal of Business Research*, *20*(4), 293-315.

Voss, K. E., E. R. Spangenberg, and B. Grohmann (2003), "Measuring the Hedonic and Utilitarian Dimensions of Consumer Attitude," *Journal of Marketing Research, 40*(3), 310-20.

This page intentionally left blank.

*(Papers not presented at the conference)*

This page intentionally left blank.

*(Papers not presented at the conference)*

# Innovation Aesthetics: The Relationship between Category Cues, Categorization Certainty and Newness Perceptions

Miranda Goode, University of Western Ontario, Canada
Darren W. Dahl, University of British Columbia, Canada
C. Page Moreau, University of Colorado at Boulder, USA

## EXTENDED ABSTRACT

Research suggests a disconnect between what marketers deem to be new and innovative versus what consumers actually perceive (Gourville 2006). Many factors may contribute to this, however, we investigate the factor that has significant potential to first attract a consumer to a new product, the product's visual aesthetic design. Despite the capacity for innovative product design to elevate a company's success in the marketplace, there has been little attempt to determine how this may influence newness perceptions. It is acknowledged that "product newness is a vital selling point," (Bloch 1995) and "widely respected" (Moreau and Dahl 2005), and visual design is often a central focus of new product managers; yet when considered together, there is limited insight into the factors that underlie their relationship. While research on innovation adoption has identified factors that influence consumer preferences, the majority of the studies assume product newness to be objectively perceived and appreciated by participants. In contrast, we introduce a unique perspective of consumer response to new products by examining newness perceptions as a dependent variable that is inherently comparative, highly subjective and dependent on the certainty of underlying categorization processes. By utilizing a categorization framework to examine the relationship between innovative visual aesthetics and newness, we are also able to provide support for the role of categorization certainty, a type of certainty that may account for the somewhat surprising subjectivity of newness perceptions.

The relation between innovative visual aesthetics and newness perceptions has not been well defined. There are at least two reasons for this. First, studies on new products have typically made visual product information non-essential in the evaluation of an innovation by not providing product pictures and focusing participants explicitly on written descriptions of a product's non-visual features, functionality, and benefits (e.g., Alexander et al. 2008; Castano et al., 2008; Hoeffler 2003; Lajos et al. 2009). Second, research investigating consumer response to design has used products that do not deviate visually in any substantial way from typical category members (Cox and Cox 2002; Page and Herr 2002; Veryzer and Hutchinson 1998). In contrast, our focus is on innovative visual aesthetics. When the exterior of a product differs significantly from known category members, identifying the product's category may be difficult, uncertain or impossible. With the innovative Roomba vacuum, for example, even if consumers were provided with the product's category, uncertainty in the vacuum label may arise because its design is drastically different from that of a prototypical vacuum. It is this uncertainty in a new product's categorization that we predict will explain the influence of innovative aesthetics on newness perceptions.

We define categorization certainty as the level of confidence an individual has in their categorization of a product. This parallels a construct in attitude persuasion, thought confidence (Petty, Brinol, and Tormala 2002). Similar to how thought confidence is proposed to influence attitudes, we propose that how certain a consumer is in the categorization of a product will influence newness perceptions. The source of categorization uncertainty may vary. For instance, Gregan-Paxton et al. (2005) and Lajos et al. (2009) explored categorization uncertainty associated with products that possess features and functionality from different categories. We build on this, by explicitly defining and measuring categorization certainty

and its independent effect on newness perceptions in response to innovative aesthetics. Specifically, we predict that when categorization certainty is low (high), an aesthetically innovative new product will be rated as less (more) new (hypothesis 1).

When faced with innovative product design, consumers will first seek to identify the new product's category. Innovative aesthetics may make categorization difficult and reliance on all available category cues will be necessary to identify a product's category with certainty. In our attempt to isolate the effect of innovative visual aesthetics on newness perceptions, we treat product function and brand name as additional sources of category information or cues, as these may be processed in addition to visual aesthetics to confirm a product's categorization. Thus, we anticipate that when additional diagnostic category cues are available, the more certain consumers will be in a product's categorization and the newer they will perceive an innovative product. We predict that categorization certainty will mediate the influence of category cues on newness perceptions (hypothesis 2).

In studies 1 and 2, we manipulated the availability of supplemental category cues, during exposure to a new product, to examine how additional category information affects the relation between categorization certainty and newness perceptions. In study 1, the number of category cues available to participants was manipulated through the presence or absence of a brand name on the product's exterior. In study 2, category cue level was manipulated by having participants either view a picture of a new product or a video demonstration. Support for both hypotheses was found in studies 1 and 2. In study 3, we contrasted two products from the same category, through a manipulation of design prototypicality, to further demonstrate that innovative visual aesthetics exacerbates the negative effect of categorization uncertainty on newness perceptions.

Prior investigations have not defined or isolated the effect of categorization certainty on judgements, like newness perceptions, that occur early in the new product adoption process, nor examined the role of visual aesthetics and availability of category cues as antecedents to categorization uncertainty. We demonstrate that if a consumer cannot categorize a new product with certainty, as can happen with innovative aesthetic design, a product's newness is likely to be underappreciated. Our findings do not imply that product designers should be conservative in the visual design of their new products. In fact, Verganti (2006) points out that radical innovations actually tend to have longer commercial success, higher margins and increased consumer receptivity. Rather, our findings suggest that there is a potential danger in letting consumers self select and validate a new product's category membership. Consistent with Verganti (2006), our research emphasizes the importance of "preparing the public" for "ground-breaking products". When introducing new products with innovative visual aesthetics, this preparation should come through the careful and deliberate disclosure of a product's category membership.

## REFERENCES

Alexander, D. L., Lynch Jr., J. G., and Wang, Q. (2008). As time goes by: Do cold feet follow warm intentions for really new versus incrementally new products. *Journal of Consumer Research*, 45 (June), 307-19.

Bloch, P. H. (1995). Seeking the ideal form: Product design and consumer response. *Journal of Marketing*, 59 (July), 16-29.

Castano, R., Sujan, M., Kacker, M., and Sujan, H. (2008). Managing consumer uncertainty in the adoption of new products: Temporal distance and mental simulation. *Journal of Marketing Research*, 45 (3), 320-36.

Cox, D. and Cox, A.D. (2002). Beyond First Impressions: The effects of repeated exposure on consumer liking of visually complex and simple product designs. *Journal of the Academy of Marketing Science*, 30 (2), 119-30.

Gourville, J. T. (2006). Eager sellers stony buyers: understanding the psychology of new product adoption. *Harvard Business Review*, 84 (6), 98-106.

Gregan-Paxton, J., Hoeffler, S., and Zhao, M. (2005). When categorization is ambiguous: Factors that facilitate the use of a multiple category inference strategy. *Journal of Consumer Psychology*, 15 (2), 127-40.

Hoeffler, S. (2003). Measuring preferences for really new products. *Journal of Marketing Research*, 40 (4), 406-20.

Lajos, J., Katona, Z., Chattopadhyay, A., and Sarvary, M. (2009). Category activation model: A spreading activation network model of subcategory positioning when uncertainty is high. *Journal of Consumer Research*, 36 (June).

Moreau, C. Page and Darren W. Dahl (2005), "Designing the Solution: The Impact of Constraints on Consumers' Creativity," *Journal of Consumer Research*, 32 (June), 13-22.

Page, C. and Herr, P. M. (2002). An investigation of the processes by which product design and brand strength interact to determine initial affect and quality judgments. *Journal of Consumer Psychology*, 12 (2), 133-47.

Petty, Richard E., Pablo Brinol, and Zakary L. Tormala (2002), "Thought Confidence as a Determinant of Persuasion: The Self-Validation Hypothesis," *Journal of Personality and Social Psychology*, 82 (5), 722-41.

Verganti, R. (2006). Innovating through design. *Harvard Business Review*, 84 (12), 114-22.

Veryzer, R. W. JR. and Hutchinson, J. W. (1998). The influence of unity and prototypicality on aesthetic responses to new product designs. *Journal of Consumer Research*, 24 (March), 374-94.

# You Get What You Pay for But I Don't: Effect of Construal Level on The Price-Quality Relationship

Dengfeng Yan, Hong Kong University of Science and Technology, China
Jaideep Sengupta, Hong Kong University of Science and Technology, China

## EXTENDED ABSTRACT

Consider the following scenario: you observe that a friend has bought a well-designed, attractive bag for a surprisingly low price. What inference would you draw regarding the quality of that bag: high quality (because of its attributes such as design and materials) or low quality (because of the low price)? And would your quality inference be any different given a perspective shift–namely, would you be more or less inclined to assess quality on the basis of price if it were a bag you had bought yourself? Alternately, suppose you were evaluating the quality of a product for immediate use as compared to future use–when would you give greater weight to the product's price, as opposed to its attributes, when forming your judgment of quality?

In seeking to answer questions such as the above, this paper addresses the key issue of how consumers form inferences regarding product quality; and in particular, the extent to which they base these inferences on price as opposed to product attributes. The current research builds on construal level theory (Trope, Liberman, and Wakslak 2007) to propose a key contingency as to when the influence of price on quality perceptions may be diminished or enhanced. The central idea is that price has greater impact on consumers' quality judgments of psychologically distant vs. nearer purchases, with the reverse being true for the impact of product attributes. The concept of psychological distance subsumes several dimensions, such as interpersonal distance (e.g., whether an inference is drawn on the basis of one's own or another's behavior) and temporal distance (whether an inference has to do with the immediate or distant future). Thus, invoking construal level theory allows us to provide a unified answer to the seemingly disparate questions raised in the opening paragraph as to how price may influence quality perceptions in different scenarios.

### Theoretical Background

Findings from the construal theory literature suggest that abstract information, compared with concrete information, tends to exert more impact on representations and judgments of psychologically distant events, while the reverse holds when the focal judgment is about psychologically near events (e.g., Liberman and Trope 2000). We argue that this premise contains direct implications for how quality inferences are formed in different situations. Compared to specific, concrete product attributes, price can be thought of as a more abstract, general cue, especially with regard to its implications for quality. One reason for the relatively more abstract nature of the price cue has to do with it being a universal component for practically all products; thus, the price-quality heuristic itself represents a generalized abstraction of a consumer's many observations and experiences. In contrast, the diagnosticity of attributes is usually specific to different product categories (e.g., hard disk capacity can be used to infer computer quality, but is inapplicable to judgments about cars; on the other hand, the physical attractiveness of the packaging is often used for quality judgments of food items, but less so for computers). Indeed, the idea that the price-quality belief is an abstract "theory" while product attributes are more concrete "data" has been widely adopted in previous consumer research (Baumgartner 1995; Broniarczyk and Alba 1994). In light of this distinction, and given the preceding arguments arising from construal level theory, it follows that:

Consumers' reliance on price for making quality inferences will be enhanced when the judgment is psychologically relatively distant. Information relating to product attributes, on the contrary, will be utilized more when the quality judgment is psychologically closer.

### Studies

A series of five experiments provided convergent support for these predictions. The first three experiments used the "self" vs. "other" interpersonal dimension to operationalize psychological distance.

The first study looked exclusively at the influence of price on quality judgments. Participants were asked to predict the quality of a series of products whose prices (high vs. low) were given; they were told either that the purchase had been made by themselves ("self" condition, representing low psychological distance) or by others ("other" condition, representing high psychological distance). Experiment 2 assessed quality inferences after manipulating both price and the favorability of product attributes. Specifically, we asked participants to judge the tastiness of a dish of fried rice, on the basis of two cues: its price, and its physical attractiveness. In Experiment 3, we sought to replicate the previous findings obtained on quality assessments (Experiments 1 and 2) using a selection paradigm. Instead of simply being asked to make a quality judgment based on information about a single product, participants were asked to indicate which of two yogurts was tastier: one that was expensive and had an unattractive package, while the other was presented as being cheap but attractive. Experiment 4 then operationalized psychological distance through a different (temporal) dimension. Finally, experiment 5 provided strong support for the posited mechanism by directly manipulating construal level. In line with our hypotheses, and across different product categories, results across from all of these studies showed that participants relied more on price than on product attributes when predicting product quality from an "other" vs. a "self" perspective; in contrast, the weight accorded to product attributes followed the reverse pattern. It is noteworthy that convergent support for our predictions was obtained across a variety of product categories, different dependent variables (single-option quality judgments as well as the choice paradigm used in experiment 3), pre- and post purchase scenarios, and several different manipulations of construal level, including two different dimensions of psychological distance (interpersonal and temporal) as well as the direct manipulation used in experiment 5.

# How Does Construal Level Influence Donations to Individuals and Organizations

Danit Ein-Gar, Tel-Aviv University, Israel
Liat Levontin, Interdisciplinary Center (IDC) Herzliya, Israel

## EXTENDED ABSTRACT

The current research explores the interacting effect of individuals' construal level and the donation target (i.e., person or organization) on willingness to donate time and money.

According to findings from research on construal level (CLT, Trope & Liberman 2003), individuals' cognitive mindset influences the way they process information and, as a result, their preferences and behaviors. It is argued that psychologically proximal events are mentally represented via low level construal, while psychologically distant events are mentally represented through high level construal (e.g. Trope & Liberman 2003; Chandran & Menon 2004; Bar-Anan, Liberman & Trope 2006; Trope, Liberman & Wakslak 2007).

We suggest that a donation campaign may be processed differently depending on its psychological distance from the audience. For example, a campaign calling for immediate donations is more likely to be processed with a low level of construal while a campaign that is expected to be launched in the future is more likely to be processed with high level construal due to the differences in time distance. Also, a campaign for poor elderly people launched at a university campus is more likely to be processed by students via a high level of construal while a campaign for students in financial need is more likely to be processed via low level construal due to differences in social distance.

We hypothesize that individuals led to adopt a low-level construal mindset will be more willing to donate to a specific, rather than general, donation target. A campaign focused on a specific donation target, that is, on a particular individual in need, fits with low level construal representation because it focuses on specific categories, details and context-dependent information. On the other hand, individuals led to adopt a high construal mindset will be more inclined to donate to a general, rather than personal, donation target. That is so because a campaign focused on a general donation target, such as a charitable organization, fits with high level construal processing, as it focuses on broader categorization, general descriptions, and de-contextualized information.

## STUDY 1

Expectancy and value are two components of the motivational force (Vroom, 1964). Thus, donations are based on the expectancy that a campaign will be successful and on the value of the campaign. We suggest that the fit between level of construal and the campaign message's personalization level increases both expectancy and value.

One hundred and thirty two participants were randomly assigned to one of four conditions in a 2 (construal level) x 2 (personalization) design.

*Personalization*: Participants were either asked to help an underprivileged boy (personal) or to assist under-privileged children who stay in care centers (non-personal) with their school assignments.

*Construal level*: Participants were either told that the campaign was expected to be launched in the next month (low level) or at the beginning of the next year (high level).

As expected, two-way interactions were found such that in the low construal condition, participants indicated a higher expectancy that the campaign would be successful and assigned more importance to it when the message was personalized. Conversely, in the high construal condition, participants demonstrated higher expectancy and attributed more importance to the campaign when the message was non-personalized (Expectancy: $F_{(1,128)}$=3.23, p=.05; Value: $F_{(1,128)}$=4.33, p<.05).

## STUDY 2

In Study 2 we investigated that the fit between level of construal and the campaign message's personalization level increases participants' willingness to donate time.

One hundred and twenty two participants were randomly assigned to one of four conditions in a 2 (construal level) x 2 (personalization) design.

*Personalization*: Participants were either asked to help an immigrant settle-in (personal) or to help at an absorption center (non-personal).

*Construal level*: Participants were either told that the campaign focuses on helping immigrant students (low level), or that it focuses on helping elderly immigrants (high level).

Finally, participants were asked how many hours they were willing to give per month and how many months they would be willing to volunteer as well as report their expectancy and campaign importance.

As expected, under low construal participants were more willing to contribute time when the message was personalized. Conversely, under high construal participants were more willing to donate time when the message was non-personalized (Hours: $F_{(1,118)}$=5.16, p<.05; Months: $F_{(1,118)}$=4.27, p<.05).

Furthermore, replicating the results of Study 1, the cross over interaction was found significant for both expectancy ($F_{(1,118)}$=6.17, p<.05) and value ($F_{(1,118)}$=3.92, p =.05)

## STUDY

Time and money are processed differently (Zauberman and Lynch 2005, Malkoc and Zauberman 2006; Liu and Aaker 2008). Specifically, when thinking about time, compared to money, people are more susceptible to biases in decision-making. The current study seeks to demonstrate that the fit effect also occurs in willingness to donate money.

Three hundred and fifty eight participants were randomly assigned to one of six conditions in a 2 (construal level) x 2 (personalization) x 2 (gender) design.

*Personalization*: Participants were either asked to help a person injured in a car accident (personal) or to assist in the department for rehabilitating individuals injured in car accidents (non-personal).

*Construal level*: When a potential donor's gender is congruent with the target's gender, information will be processed more with low level construal due to high psychological proximity than when gender is incongruent. Therefore, participants' gender was coded. Match conditions (e.g. male participant and male target) were coded as the low level condition while discordant conditions were coded as the high level condition.

Finally, participants were asked how much money they were willing to donate.

As expected, a three-way interaction was found ($F_{(1,350)}$=4.64, p<.05). Men were willing to donate more money to injured men in the low construal condition when the message was personalized. When the message was not personalized, men were willing to donate more money to injured women under the high construal condition. The same effect was found for women.

## REFERENCES

Bar-Anan, Y., Liberman, N. & Trope, Y. (2006). The Association Between Psychological Distance and Construal Level: Evidence From an Implicit Association Test. *Journal of Experimental Psychology: General,* 135, 609-622.

Chandran, S. & Menon G. (2004). When a day means more than a year: Effects of temporal framing on judgments of health risk. Journal of consumer research, 31,

Liu, W. & Aaker, J. (2008). The Happiness of Giving: The Time-Ask Effect. *Journal of Consumer Research,* 35, 543-557.

Malkoc, S. & Zauberman, G. (2006). Deferring versus Expediting Consumption: The Effect of Outcome Concreteness on Sensitivity of the Time Horizon. *Journal of Marketing Research,* 43 (November), 618–27.

Trope, Y. & Liberman, N. (2003). Temporal Construal. *Psychological Review,* 110(3), 403–421.

Trope, Y., Liberman, N. & Wakslak, C. (2007). Construal Levels and Psychological Distance: Effects on Representation, Prediction, Evaluation, and Behavior. *Journal of Consumer Psychology* 17(2), 83–95.

Vroom, V. H. (1964). *Work and Motivation.* New York: Wiley.

Wakslak, C. & Trope, Y. (2009). The Effect of Construal Level on Subjective Probability Estimates. *Psychological Science,* 20( 1), 52-58.

Zauberman, G. & Lynch, J.G. (2005). Resource Slack and Propensity to Discount Delayed Investments of Time Versus Money. *Journal of Experimental Psychology: General,* 134(1), 23-37.

# Socially Conscious Consumption and Civic Engagement: Mobilizing Collective Concern through Private Interest

Lucy Atkinson, University of Texas at Austin, USA

## EXTENDED ABSTRACT

Consumer culture is often criticized for the deleterious effects it is assumed to have on civic connectedness and concern for the social good. The rising trend of socially conscious consumption, such as buying fair-trade products, offers a challenge to this view of consumer behavior. However, little research exists empirically testing the relationship between socially conscious consumption and civic and political engagement. The modest amount of research that does explore these connections is largely conceptual and assumes a negative relationship, with consumer preferences winning out over civic ones.

The research outlined here challenges these shortcomings. Using a series of depth interviews, I demonstrate that pro-social consumer orientations can have a positive influence on civic and political engagement. Accepted wisdom among critics of consumer-motivated civic involvement holds that this consumer orientation fosters individualism and self-interest at the expense of a collective focus, and that it redirects civic action away from the political realm to the corporate arena. The concern is that politically motivated consumers will be civic-minded only to the degree that their own issues can be resolved and will avoid collective action at resolving more generalized societal issues. The data, which were collected using an existential-phenomenological approach, suggest such fears may be overstated. Among socially conscious consumers, marketplace behaviors offer a viable and meaningful springboard to political engagement. It is by attending to private, individual concerns that consumers address moral and ethical issues at the collective level. Socially conscious consumption taps into and encourages a kind of enlightened self-interest whereby concern for the self, as expressed through consumption, breeds concern for the collective.

This study draws on Soper's (2008) notion of the alternative hedonist to understand how socially conscious consumers relate their private consumer practices to their public citizenship practices. It relies on a series of depth interviews with socially conscious consumers aimed at understanding the meanings they ascribe to their consumer choices. These meanings are uncovered through existential-phenomenological interviewing and hermeneutic analysis (Craig J. Thompson, 1997; Craig J. Thompson, Locander, & Pollio, 1989).

To explore the consumption as politics thesis, a group of white, middle-class, college-educated consumers who self-identify as socially conscious were interviewed using the E-P approach about their consumer practices and motivations. Literature about socially conscious consumption indicates that socially conscious consumers tend to be middle class, well-educated and white, as they are the individuals likely to have both the means and the opportunity to engage in socially conscious consumption.

Informants were recruited from a small Midwestern city in two phases: first, through the researcher's extended social network and second, through these informants' social networks. In total, eight informants were interviewed over the course of two months in spring 2009. Although all informants were white and middle class, they represent a relatively diverse group in terms of ages, occupations, genders and family structure. Six of the interviews took place in the informants' home, one took place in the researcher's home and one took place in a coffee shop. They were all semi-structured and lasted between 35 and 85 minutes, yielding 80 pages of transcribed interview notes. The interview format was informed by the E-P approach advocated by Thompson, Locander and Pollio (1989). As such, although the researcher relied on a brief interview guide, the interviews were allowed to develop freely and naturally.

The results here expand on Soper's framework by offering an explanation of the process behind the self-interested attention to the wider social good. Specifically, it is proposed that consumers engage in a process of making pleasurable compromises and trade offs. Socially conscious consumers reap a number of benefits (beyond the simple acquisition of material goods or services) by engaging in prosocial consumption. Across each informant interview, four particular and interrelated themes emerged: socially conscious consumption as authentic, as socially embedding, as empowering and as self-actualizing. For each of the socially conscious consumers interviewed, the reasons behind certain consumer choices were clearly energized by personal concerns, such as family health. And while broader social concerns–such as the environment, animal rights–played into their consumption calculus, individuals did not differentiate between these different collective concerns nor did they prioritize one over the other. These collective benefits were thought of as a package and working toward them was part and parcel of enacting their own self-interest. This self-interest was tempered through a process of compromises and trade offs that were rationalized as enjoyable and pleasurable.

Each informant noted how their consumption choices entailed a degree of effort and sacrifice, but these sacrifices were made willingly. Rather than focus on the cost, both literal and figurative of leading a socially conscious consumption lifestyle, the informants concentrated on the enjoyment such compromises brought. By reframing the extra effort as a source of potential pleasure to another possible benefit, the informants were able to reconcile the burdensome side of prosocial consumption with the self-interested, private motivations that underpinned it.

Work by Hirschman and Holbrook (1982) offers insight into how consumers might transform consumption costs into benefits. Hirschman and Holbrook argue that commodities should not be thought of simply in terms of their utilitarian or functional attributes–as object entities–but as subjective symbols. Consumers engage in hedonic consumption when they impart subjective meanings to objects and incorporate emotion into their consumer practices. This emotional aspect muddies the simple cost-benefit analysis that rationalizing consumers are assumed to make but also explains why consumers will make decisions that are not always the easiest or most cost effective.

Instead of focusing on the problematic aspect of the consumption act ("the store is difficult to get to" or "I can't eat strawberries in January"), the informants emphasized the potential joy ("the store delights my senses" or "depriving myself of strawberries makes them taste that much sweeter when I can eat them"). One informant underscores this mental readjustment when she says: "We don't feel like we're sacrificing anything really. It's all a gain." By understanding the informants' consumption practices through an "alternative hedonist" lens it is possible to understand how socially conscious consumers privilege their private desires while also benefiting the collective good.

## REFERENCES

Atkinson, L. (2009). *Politics by other means: Marketing, consumption and engagement.* Unpublished Dissertation, University of Wisconsin—Madison Madison.

Barnett, C., Cafaro, P., & Newholm, T. (2005). Philosophy and ethical consumption. In R. Harrison, T. Newholm & D. Shaw (Eds.), *The Ethical Consumer* (pp. 11-24). London: Sage.

Brooker, G. (1976). The Self-Actualizing Socially Conscious Consumer. *The Journal of Consumer Research, 3*(2), 107-112.

Brunori, G. (2007). Local food and alternative food networks: a communication perspective. [article]. *Anthropology of Food*(6), 430.

Cafaro, P. (2001). Economic Consumption, Pleasure, and the Good Life. *Journal of Social Philosophy, 32*(4), 471-486.

Hirschman, E. C., & Holbrook, M. B. (1982). Hedonic Consumption: Emerging Concepts, Methods and Propositions. *The Journal of Marketing, 46*(3), 92-101.

Kozinets, R. V., & Handelman, J. (1998). *Ensouling Consumption: A Netnographic Exploration of The Meaning of Boycotting Behavior.* Paper presented at the Advances in Consumer Research, Provo: UT.

Maslow, A. (1968). *Toward a Pyschology of Being* (2nd ed.). New York: Van Nostrand Reinhold.

Moore, O. (2006). Understanding postorganic fresh fruit and vegetable consumers at participatory farmersâ?™ markets in Ireland: reflexivity, trust and social movements. *International Journal of Consumer Studies, 30*(5), 416-426.

Sassatelli, R. (2006). Virtue, Responsibility and Consumer Choice: Framing Critical Consumerism. In J. Brewer & F. Trentmann (Eds.), *Consuming Cultures, Global Perspectives: Historical Trajectories, Transnational Exchanges.* Oxford: Berg.

Soper, K. (2007). Re-thinking the 'Good Life': The citizenship dimension of consumer disaffection with consumerism. *Journal of Consumer Culture, 7*(2), 205-229.

Soper, K. (2008). ALTERNATIVE HEDONISM, CULTURAL THEORY AND THE ROLE OF AESTHETIC REVISIONING. *Cultural Studies, 22*(5), 567-587.

Thompson, C. J. (1997). Interpreting consumers: A hermeneutical framework for deriving marketing insights from the texts of consumers' consumption stories. *Journal of Marketing Research, 34*(4), 438.

Thompson, C. J. (2007). A Carnivalesque Approach to the Politics of Consumption (or) Grotesque Realism and the Analytics of the Excretory Economy. *The ANNALS of the American Academy of Political and Social Science, 611*(1), 112-125.

Thompson, C. J., Locander, W. B., & Pollio, H. R. (1989). Putting Consumer Experience Back into Consumer Research: The Philosophy and Method of Existential-Phenomenology. *The Journal of Consumer Research, 16*(2), 133-146.

Zavestoski, S. (2002). The Social-Psychological Bases of Anticonsumption Attitudes. *Psychology & Marketing, 19*(2), 149-165.

# Fabricating "Green" Meaning: An Empirical Examination of the Role of Indexical and Iconic Cues to Authenticity

Douglas Ewing, University of Cincinnati, USA
Chris Allen, University of Cincinnati, USA
Randall Ewing, Ohio Northern University, USA

## EXTENDED ABSTRACT

Extant consumer concerning authenticity has imbued the literature with numerous definitions and conceptualizations of authenticity but little in the way of theory about its antecedent/consequent processes (cf. Leigh, Peters, and Shelton 2006). The present research attempts to bring authenticity into the lab and pursue the phenomenon in a unique way. We draw on research in semiotics (e.g. Grayson and Martinec 2004; Hoshino 1987; Mick 1986, 1998) and test explicit hypotheses about how indexical and iconic cues influence judgments about brands in a context of "green" consumption.

Indexical cues are attributes of an object that provide a spatio-temporal and/or verifiable link to a reference point (Grayson and Martinec 2004). Their presence provides overarching validation that a consumption object has the appropriate characteristics and abilities to bear a "green" meaning. Assuming that individuals recognize the connection suggested by a "green" indexical cue, they will be more likely to judge an object as having an authentic "green" meaning leading to increased beliefs that it is "green," thus yielding more favorable attitudes (Fishbein and Ajzen 1975; Lutz 1977).

Iconic cues are qualities that suggest "schematic fit" with expectations for an authentic object but lack an externally-verifiable reference point or "correspondence of fact" (Mick 1986). These cues emphasize general congruence with a consumer's idiosyncratic, internal frame of reference (Grayson and Martinec 2004; Leigh et al. 2006). Provided an individual has some expectations, he/she should judge an object as more authentic to the extent that there is matching between expected and observed iconic cues. As with indexical cues, this should have positive effects on both "green" beliefs and brand attitudes. However, given the straightforward meaning validation provided by a singular indexical cue, it seems plausible that these stronger cues will have a greater effect on beliefs and attitudes.

The efficacy of both indexical and iconic cues is likely to vary according to relevant characteristics of their associated product. One very basic product quality is whether it is an infrequently purchased durable or a more frequently purchased non-durable. Durable goods tend to have more features and be larger purchases in terms of cost, both of which may incline consumers to desire more information and engage in a more extended search (e.g. Brucks 1985). Thus, it is conceivable the information provided indexical and iconic cues will be less effective for a durable versus a non-durable.

Beyond predicted effects of indexical and iconic cues and a differential effect between durable and non-durable goods, a general assertion of this conceptualization is that semiotic cues enable a consumer to validate a "green" product meaning. This "green" meaning should lead to specific beliefs about a product as well as more positive attitudes. Hence, the effect of the indexical and iconic cues on brand attitude likely operates through brand beliefs (Ajzen 2008).

These general predictions were tested in a 2 (Indexical Cue: Green/Non-Green) x 2 (Iconic Cue: Green/Non-Green) x 2 (Product Type: Consumable/Durable) within-subjects design (n=140). Participants evaluated 8 durable or non-durable brands based on visuals and text information embodying indexical and iconic cues.

The indexical cue manipulation took the form of recognizable labels or co-brands intended to verify the target quality of "green." The iconic cue manipulation comprised elementary information about such features as product composition or usable life to signal the target quality of "green." The product type manipulation took the form of consumables versus durables. Each participant evaluated 4 consumable brands (2 laundry detergents and 2 batteries) and 4 durable brands (2 desktop computers and 2 car tires).

Participants reported their brand attitudes and beliefs via a 7-point semantic differential scale. Attitude items were favorable/unfavorable, pleasant/unpleasant, and good/bad. The belief items of primary interest were green/not green, thrifty/wasteful, and natural/artificial. Additional items belief items were collected to make memory-based comparison more difficult. The dependent variables retained for subsequent analyses were attitude and green-belief for each brand represented by a mean-centered sum of respective items. The data were analyzed with linear mixed models using maximum likelihood estimation to account for potential non-independence across ratings.

Results indicate that indexical cues and iconic cues had significant effects on green beliefs. Participants had more favorable green beliefs and attitudes when indexical and iconic cues signaled a "green" quality. Indexical cues were stronger than iconic cues in affecting green beliefs but not brand attitude. In addition to the cue types alone, results suggested that changes in green beliefs and attitudes towards durables were less sensitive to indexical cues and iconic cues than were consumables. A mediation analysis indicated that green beliefs fully mediated the effect of indexical cues and partially mediated the effect of iconic cues on brand attitude.

Overall, indexical cues had a more robust effect on green beliefs and attitudes and that these effects of both cue types are stronger upon consumables versus durables. Furthermore, the effectiveness of these semiotic cues varies according to a basic durable/non-durable distinction among products and green beliefs fully or partially mediate the effects of indexical and iconic cues manipulations on brand attitudes. Hence, it can be said that indexical cues and to a lesser extent iconic cues activate spontaneous inferences that manifest as new beliefs and corresponding brand attitudes. In addition, the pattern of results generally in line with predictions provides evidence that iconic versus indexical cues can be systematically manipulated to affect authenticity judgments. Taken together, the results provide evidence supporting a meaning validation process as the basis of authenticity judgments.

This research conceptualizes authenticity judgments in familiar terms for consumer researchers; that is, as a process involving spontaneous inferences about specific brand beliefs that then effect brand attitudes. Viewed this way, it is possible to bring authenticity phenomena into the laboratory and construct a nomological network to guide theory building. This research represents a first step on that path. Supplementing extant, interpretive research on authenticity with disciplined theory building represents a meaningful opportunity to inform the debate in a substantive domain where there is broad researcher and practitioner interest.

# REFERENCES

Ajzen, Icek (2008), "Consumer Attitudes and Behavior," in *Handbook of Consumer Psychology*, ed. Curtis P. Haugtvedt, Paul Herr and Frank R. Kardes: Routledge, 525-48.

Asimov, Eric (2007), "The Power in the Case: Old Ways, New Beer," *New York Times*.

Belk, Russell W. and Janeen Arnold Costa (1998), "The Mountain Man Myth: A Contemporary Consuming Fantasy," *Journal of Consumer Research*, 25 (3), 218-40.

Beverland, Michael B. and Francis J. Farrelly (2010), "The Quest for Authenticity in Consumption: Consumers' Purposive Choice of Authentic Cues to Shape Experienced Outcomes," *Journal of Consumer Research*, 36 (February), 838-56.

Beverland, Michael B., Adam Lindgreen, and Michiel W. Vink (2008), "Projecting Authenticity Through Advertising: Consumer Judgments of Advertisers' Claims," *Journal of Advertising*, 37 (1), 5-15.

Brewer, Marilynn (1988), "A Dual Process Model of Impression Formation," in *Advances in Social Cognition*, Vol. 1, ed. Thomas K. Srull and Robert S. Wyer, Hillsday, NJ: Erlbaum.

Brown, Stephen, Robert V. Kozinets, and John F. Sherry, Jr. (2003), "Teaching Old Brands New Tricks: Retro Branding and the Revival of Brand Meaning," *Journal of Marketing*, 67 (3), 19-33.

Brucks, Merrie (1985), "The Effects of Product Class Knowledge on Information Search Behavior," *Journal of Consumer Research*, 12 (June), 1-16.

Calder, Bobby J. and Alice M. Tybout (1987), "What Consumer Research Is..." *Journal of Consumer Research*, 14 (1), 136-40.

Fishbein, Martin and Icek Ajzen (1975), *Belief, Attitude, Intention, and Behavior: An Introduction to Theory and Research*, Reading, MA: Addison-Wesley.

Fiske, Susan T. and Mark A. Pavelchak (1986), "Category-based Versus Piecemeal-based Affective Responses: Developments in Schema-triggered Affect," in *Handbook of Motivation and Cognition: Foundations of Social Behavior*, ed. Richard M. Sorrentino and E. Tory Higgins, New York: Guilford Press, 167-203.

Gilmore, James H. and B. Joseph Pine, II (2007), *Authenticity: What Consumers Really Want*, Boston: Harvard Business School Press.

Grayson, Kent and Radan Martinec (2004), "Consumer Perceptions of Iconicity and Indexicality and Their Influence on Assessments of Authentic Market Offerings," *Journal of Consumer Research*, 31 (September), 296-312.

Grewal, Rajdeep, Raj Mehta, and Frank R. Kardes (2004), "The Timing of Repeat Purchases of Consumer Durable Goods: The Role of Functional Bases of Consumer Attitudes," *Journal of Marketing Research*, 41 (1), 101-15.

Hoshino, Katsumi (1987), "Semiotic Marketing and Product Conceptualization," in *Marketing and Semiotics*, ed. Jean Umiker-Sebeok, Berlin: Mouton de Gruyter.

Kardes, Frank R. (1996), "In Defense of Experimental Consumer Psychology," *Journal of Consumer Psychology*, 5 (3), 279-96.

Kardes, Frank R., Steven S. Posavac, Maria L. Cronley, and Paul M. Herr (2008), "Consumer Inferences," in *Handbook of Consumer Psychology*, ed. Curtis P. Haugtvedt, Paul M. Herr and Frank R. Kardes, New York: Erlbaum, 165-91.

Kilbourne, William E. (1995), "Green Advertising: Salvation or Oxymoron?," *Journal of Advertising*, 24 (2), 7-19.

Kleine, Robert E., III and Jerome B. Kernan (1991), "Contextual Influences on the Meanings Ascribed to Ordinary Consumption Objects," *Journal of Consumer Research*, 18 (December), 311-24.

Kozinets, Robert V. (2002), "Can Consumers Escape the Market? Emancipatory Illuminations from Burning Man," *Journal of Consumer Research*, 29 (1), 20-38.

Leigh, Thomas W., Cara Peters, and Jeremy Shelton (2006), "The Consumer Quest for Authenticity: The Multiplicity of Meanings Within the MG Subculture of Consumption," *Journal of the Academy of Marketing Science*, 34 (4), 481-93.

Loken, Barbara, Lawrence W. Barsalou, and Christopher Joiner (2008), "Categorization Theory and Research in Consumer Psychology: Category Representation and Category-Based Inference," in *Handbook of Consumer Psychology*, ed. Curtis P. Haugtvedt, Paul M. Herr and Frank R. Kardes, New York: Erlbaum, 133-63.

Lutz, Richard J. (1977), "An Experimental Investigation of Causal Relations among Cognitions, Affect, and Behavioral Intention," *Journal of Consumer Research*, 3 (4), 197-208.

Mick, David Glen (1986), "Consumer Research and Semiotics: Exploring the Morphology of Signs, Symbols, and Significance," *Journal of Consumer Research*, 13 (September), 196-213.

Mick, David Glen (1998), "Semiotics in Marketing and Consumer Research: Balderbash, Verity, Pleas," in *Consumer Research: Postcards From the Edge*, ed. Stephen Brown and Darach Turley: Routledge, 244-56.

Peugh, James L. and Craig K.' Enders (2005), "Using the SPSS Mixed Procedure to Fit Cross-sectional and Longitudinal Multilevel Models," *Educational and Psychological Measurement*, 65 (5), 717-41.

Rose, Randall L. and Stacy L. Wood (2005), "Paradox and the Consumption of Authenticity through Reality Television," *Journal of Consumer Research*, 32 (September), 284-96.

Schouten, John W. and James H. McAlexander (1995), "Subcultures of Consumption: An Ethnography of the New Bikers," *Journal of Consumer Research*, 22 (1), 43-61.

Schuhwerk, Melody E. and Roxanne Lefkoff-Hagius (1995), "Green or Non-Green? Does Type of Appeal Matter When Advertising a Green Product?," *Journal of Advertising*, 24 (2), 45-54.

Shrum, L.J., John A. McCarty, and Tina M. Lowrey (1995), "Buyer Characteristics of the Green Consumer and Their Implications for Advertising Strategy," *Journal of Advertising*, 24 (2), 71-82.

Thompson, Craig J., Aric Rindfleisch, and Zeynep Arsel (2006), "Emotional Branding and the Strategic Value of the Doppelganger Brand Image," *Journal of Consumer Research*, 70 (January), 50-64.

Webster, Frederick E., Jr. (1975), "Determining the Characteristics of the Socially Conscious Consumer," *Journal of Consumer Research*, 2 (3), 188-96.

Weinberger, David (2008), "Authenticity: Is It Real or Is It Marketing?," *Harvard Business Review*, 86 (3), 33-43.

Wheaton, Belinda and Becky Beal (2003), "'Keeping It Real' Subcultural Media and the Discourses of Authenticity in Alternative Sport," *International Review for the Sociology of Sport*, 38 (2), 155-76.

Wright, Tom (2008), "False 'Green' Ads Draw Global Scrutiny," *The Wall Street Journal*.

# The Dark Side of Product Attachment: An fMRI Study of Reactivity of Users and Non-Users to Addictive Advertising Cues

Dante Pirouz, University of Western Ontario, Canada
Connie Pechmann, University of California at Irvine, USA
Paul Rodriguez, UC San Diego, USA

## EXTENDED ABSTRACT

Advertising is a ubiquitous and pervasive environmental cue. The average consumer, for example, is exposed on average to three thousand ads per day (Schwartz 2004). Under normal circumstances, consumers choose which advertising cues to attend to both consciously and non-consciously (Bargh 2002; Grunert 1996). However for consumers, environmental cues may elicit a unique type of response affecting decision making and driving behavior (Bernheim and Rangel 2004). The aim of this research is to explore how environmental cues affect addictive product users and non-users using the brain imaging technique developed in neuroscience functional magnetic resonance imaging (fMRI) for cue-exposed users and non-users.

A great deal of debate, both in the literature and among advertisers and public policy makers, centers on how environmental cues influence people to engage in risky and addictive behaviors (Pollay 1986; Pollay et al. 1996a). Marketers and manufacturers argue that advertising and promotional materials offer consumers brand options and information that enhance the consumer's ability to make choices (Gilly and Graham 1988; Goldberg et al. 2006), while researchers and public health officials argue that there is a strong correlation between detrimental behavior and exposure to marketing for addictive products (Pollay 1986; Pollay et al. 1996b). There remain unanswered questions regarding how users and non-users respond to this type of stimulus. In addition, there are conflicting indications of how craving elicited by cues impacts cognitive processing, including cognitive depletion leading to impulsivity outside the addictive substance domain. Given the ongoing debate there is a need for a better understanding of the underlying psychological and physiological mechanisms that drive the reactive response to advertising cues by users and non-users.

The research question addressed in this research is whether environmental cues–namely cigarette advertising–cause a reactive response in the form of increased craving in users or non-users resulting in downstream impulsive behavior as a result of cognitive resource depletion. The study uses functional magnetic resonance imaging (fMRI) to examine the underlying neural response to addictive (cigarette) advertising versus non-addictive (non-cigarette) advertising in users (smokers) and non-users (non-smokers). Brain imaging data have been collected from 10 current, daily smoker and 10 non-smokers for this study. This study was a 2 (user type: smoker vs. non-smoker) x 2 (cue type: addictive ad cue vs. non-addictive ad cues) design using a 3T fMRI scanner.

A long history of addiction studies demonstrates how drug cues elicit craving via reactivity to the cue (for reviews see Carter and Tiffany 1999; Childress et al. 1993; Stritzke et al. 2004). There has also been evidence of attentional bias toward addictive cues in users (Robinson and Berridge 2003; Robinson and Berridge 2001; Robinson and Berridge 1993). Some studies have shown that this response may result in increased attentional bias and increased arousal (Bradley et al. 2004; Drobes 2002; Johnsen et al. 1997; Mogg and Bradley 2002; Munafo et al. 2003). However other studies have found that addictive product users, when exposed to these cues, may have an ability to inhibit the craving response and its effects (Artiges et al. 2009; Goldstein et al. 2007a; Stippekohl et al. 2010; Volkow and Fowler 2000; Volkow et al. 2010). On the other hand, non-users have been shown to be largely unaffected by exposure to addictive cues (Due et al. 2002; Tapert et al. 2003). However, research on the uptake of addictive products by new users points to evidence that addictive product cues, such as advertising, do indeed have an effect on non-users (Altman et al. 1996; Pierce et al. 1991). Thus there remains a debate in the literature as to whether advertising enhances or attenuates the craving response in users and how it ultimately affects non-users.

This brain imaging data indicates neural activation of brain regions that are related to craving and self-control in smokers and non-smokers. For example, there is differential activation in regions associated with craving including the amygdala and the thalamus. Regions associated with self-control including the dorsolateral prefrontal cortex and anterior cingulate cortex are also differentially activated with significant deactivation in smokers exposed to cigarette ads. The results show significant differential activation for non-users when exposed to addictive ad cues versus non-addictive ad cues. In addition, the results show a different effect when users are exposed to addictive ad cues versus non-addictive ad cues. They demonstrate that a cue reactivity response elicits significant activation in brain regions associated with craving in both non-users and users. There is also significant activation in regions associated with cognitive resource depletion for non-users as a result of the increased craving activation. This may be due to the fact that non-users underestimate the effect of this type of advertising, assuming that because they do not smoke, there ads are not targeted directly to them. However, because these non-users have not built up the ability to resist the tempting urge response generated by the addictive product ads, brain regions necessary in order to resist the temptations are activated. Interestingly there is significant deactivation in brain regions of users associated with self-control indicating inhibition of the cognitive resource depletion possibly as a way for users to cope with stimuli that they feel is targeting towards them and an urge response for which they feel they cannot satisfy at that moment.

## REFERENCES

Altman, D. G., D. W. Levine, R. Coeytaux, J. Slade, and R. Jaffe (1996), "Tobacco promotion and susceptibility to tobacco use among adolescents aged 12 through 17 years in a nationally representative sample," *Am J Public Health*, 86 (11), 1590-93.

Artiges, Eric, Emmanuel Ricalens, Sylvie Berthoz, Marie-Odile Krebs, Jani Penttilä, Christian Trichard, and Jean-Luc Martinot (2009), "Exposure to smoking cues during an emotion recognition task can modulate limbic fMRI activation in cigarette smokers," *Addiction Biology*, 14 (4), 469-77.

Bærentsen, Klaus B., Hans Stødkilde-Jørgensen, Bo Sommerlund, Tue Hartmann, Johannes Damsgaard-Madsen, Mark Fosnæs, and Anders C. Green (2010), "An investigation of brain processes supporting meditation " *Cognitive Processing*, 11 (1), 57-84.

Bailey, Steffani R., Katherine C. Goedeker, and Stephen T. Tiffany (2010), "The impact of cigarette deprivation and cigarette availability on cue reactivity in smokers," *Addiction*, 105 (2), 364-72.

Baker, Timothy B., Elsimae Morse, and Jack E. Sherman (1986), "The motivation to use drugs: A psychobiological analysis of urges," in Nebraska Symposium on Motivation Vol. 34.

Beauregard, Mario, Johanne Levesque, and Pierre Bourgouin (2001), "Neural Correlates of Conscious Self-Regulation of Emotion," _J. Neurosci._, 21 (18), 165RC-.

Binder, J. R., J. A. Frost, T. A. Hammeke, P. S. F. Bellgowan, S. M. Rao, and R. W. Cox (1999), "Conceptual Processing during the Conscious Resting State: A Functional MRI Study," _Journal of Cognitive Neuroscience_, 11 (1), 80-93.

Bradley, B., M. Field, K. Mogg, and J. De Houwer (2004), "Attentional and evaluative biases for smoking cues in nicotine dependence: component processes of biases in visual orienting," _Behavioural Pharmacology_, 15, 29-36.

Brody, Arthur L., Mark A. Mandelkern, Richard E. Olmstead, Jennifer Jou, Emmanuelle Tiongson, Valerie Allen, David Scheibal, Edythe D. London, John R. Monterosso, Stephen T. Tiffany, Alex Korb, Joanna J. Gan, and Mark S. Cohen (2007), "Neural Substrates of Resisting Craving During Cigarette Cue Exposure," _Biological Psychiatry_, 62 (6), 642-51.

Carter, Brian L. and Stephen T. Tiffany (2001), "The Cue-Availability Paradigm: The Effects of Cigarette Availability on Cue Reactivity in Smokers," _Experimental & Clinical Psychopharmacology_, 9 (2), 183-90.

_____ (1999), "Meta-analysis of cue-reactivity in addiction research," _Addiction_, 94 (3), 327-40.

Carter, Cameron S., Todd S. Braver, Deanna M. Barch, Matthew M. Botvinick, Douglas Noll, and Jonathan D. Cohen (1998), "Anterior Cingulate Cortex, Error Detection, and the Online Monitoring of Performance," _Science_, 280 (5364), 747-49.

Childress, A.R., A.V. Hole, R.N. Ehrman, S.J. Robbins, A.T. McLellan, and C.P. O'Brien (1993), "Cue reactivity and cue reactivity interventions in drug dependence," _NIDA Res Monogr._, 137, 73-95.

Childress, Anna Rose, A. Thomas McLellan, and Charles P. O'Brien (1986), "Conditioned responses in a methadone population : A comparison of laboratory, clinic, and natural settings," _Journal of Substance Abuse Treatment_, 3 (3), 173-79.

Cohen, Jonathan D., Matthew Botvinick, and Cameron S. Carter (2000), "Anterior cingulate and prefrontal cortex: who's in control?," _Nat Neurosci_, 3 (5), 421-23.

Critchley, H. D., R. N. Melmed, E. Featherstone, C. J. Mathias, and R. J. Dolan (2001), "Brain activity during biofeedback relaxation: A functional neuroimaging investigation," _Brain_, 124 (5), 1003-12.

David, Sean P., Marcus R. Munafò, Heidi Johansen-Berg, Stephen M. Smith, Robert D. Rogers, Paul M. Matthews, and Robert T. Walton (2005), "Ventral Striatum/Nucleus Accumbens Activation to Smoking-Related Pictorial Cues in Smokers and Nonsmokers: A Functional Magnetic Resonance Imaging Study," _Biological Psychiatry_.

Dehaene, Stanislas, Michael I. Posner, and Don M. Tucker (1994), "Localization of a Neural System for Error Detection and Compensation," _Psychological Science_, 5 (5), 303-05.

Drobes, David J. (2002), "Cue Reactivity in Alcohol and Tobacco Dependence," _Alcoholism: Clinical and Experimental Research_, 26 (12), 1928-29.

Due, Deborah L., Scott A. Huettel, Warren G. Hall, and David C. Rubin (2002), "Activation in mesolimbic and visuospatial neural circuits elicited by smoking cues: Evidence from functional magnetic resonance imaging," _American Journal of Psychiatry_, 159 (6), 954-60.

Ehrman, Ronald, Steven Robbins, Anna Childress, and Charles O'Brien (1992), "Conditioned responses to cocaine-related stimuli in cocaine abuse patients," _Psychopharmacology_, 107 (4), 523-29.

George, Mark S., Raymond F. Anton, Courtnay Bloomer, Charlotte Teneback, David J. Drobes, Jeffrey Lorberbaum, Ziad Nahas, and Diana J. Vincent (2001), "Activation of Prefrontal Cortex and Anterior Thalamus in Alcoholic Subjects on Exposure to Alcohol-Specific Cues," _Arch Gen Psychiatry_, 58, 345.

Gilly, Mary C. and John L. Graham (1988), "A Macroeconomic Study of the Effects of Promotion on the Consumption of Infant Formula in Developing Countries," _Journal of Macromarketing_, 8 (1), 21.

Gloria, Rebecca, Lisa Angelos, Hillary S. Schaefer, James M. Davis, Matthew Majeskie, Burke S. Richmond, John J. Curtin, Richard J. Davidson, and Timothy B. Baker (2009), "An fMRI investigation of the impact of withdrawal on regional brain activity during nicotine anticipation," _Psychophysiology_.

Goldberg, Marvin E., Ronald M. Davis, and Anne Marie O'Keefe (2006), "The role of tobacco advertising and promotion: themes employed in litigation by tobacco industry witnesses," _Tob Control_, 15 (suppl_4), iv54-67.

Goldstein, R. Z., D. Tomasi, S. Rajaram, L. A. Cottone, L. Zhang, T. Maloney, F. Telang, N. Alia-Klein, and N. D. Volkow (2007a), "Role of the anterior cingulate and medial orbitofrontal cortex in processing drug cues in cocaine addiction," _Neuroscience_, 144 (4), 1153-59.

Goldstein, Rita Z., Nelly Alia-Klein, Dardo Tomasi, Jean Honorio Carrillo, Thomas Maloney, Patricia A. Woicik, Ruiliang Wang, Frank Telang, and Nora D. Volkow (2009), "Anterior cingulate cortex hypoactivations to an emotionally salient task in cocaine addiction," _Proceedings of the National Academy of Sciences_, 106 (23), 9453-58.

Goldstein, Rita Z., Nelly Alia-Klein, Dardo Tomasi, Lei Zhang, Lisa A. Cottone, Thomas Maloney, Frank Telang, Elisabeth C. Caparelli, Linda Chang, Thomas Ernst, Dimitris Samaras, Nancy K. Squires, and Nora D. Volkow (2007b), "Is Decreased Prefrontal Cortical Sensitivity to Monetary Reward Associated With Impaired Motivation and Self-Control in Cocaine Addiction?," _Am J Psychiatry_, 164 (1), 43-51.

Goldstein, RZ and ND Volkow (2002), "Drug addiction and its underlying neurobiological basis: neuroimaging evidence for the involvement of the frontal cortex," _Am J Psychiatry_, 159 (10), 1642-52.

Hahn, Britta, Thomas J. Ross, Yihong Yang, Insook Kim, Marilyn A. Huestis, and Elliot A. Stein (2007), "Nicotine Enhances Visuospatial Attention by Deactivating Areas of the Resting Brain Default Network," _J. Neurosci._, 27 (13), 3477-89.

Inzlicht, Michael and Jennifer N. Gutsell (2007), "Running on Empty: Neural Signals for Self-Control Failure," _Psychological Science_, 18 (11), 933-37.

Johnsen, Bjorn Helge, Julian F. Thayer, Jon C. Laberg, and Arve E. Asbjornsen (1997), "Attentional bias in active smokers, abstinent smokers, and nonsmokers," _Addictive Behaviors_, 22 (6), 813-17.

Kerns, John C., Jonathan D. Cohen, Angus W. MacDonald Iii, Raymond Y. Cho, V. Andrew Stenger, and Cameron S. Carter (2004), "Anterior Cingulate Conflict Monitoring and Adjustments inControl," *Science*, 303 (5660), 1023-26.

Knoch, Daria and Ernst Fehr (2007), "The Right Prefrontal Cortex and Self-Control," *Annals of the New York Academy of Sciences*, 1104 (1), 123-34.

Lancaster, J.L., M.G. Woldorff, L.M. Parsons, M. Liotti, C.S. Freitas, L. Rainey, P.V. Kochunov, D. Nickerson, S.A. Mikiten, and P.T. Fox (2000), "Automated Talairach Atlas Labels for Functional Brain Mapping," *Human Brain Mapping*, 10, 120-31.

Lancaster, Jack and Peter Fox (2008), "*Talairach Daemon*." San Antonio, TX.

Lane, Richard D., Eric M. Reiman, Beatrice Axelrod, Lang-Sheng Yun, Andrew Holmes, and Gary E. Schwartz (1998), "Neural Correlates of Levels of Emotional Awareness: Evidence of an Interaction between Emotion and Attention in the Anterior Cingulate Cortex," *Journal of Cognitive Neuroscience*, 10 (4), 525-35.

Li, Chiang-shan Ray and Rajita Sinha (2008), "Inhibitory control and emotional stress regulation: Neuroimaging evidence for frontal-limbic dysfunction in psycho-stimulant addiction," *Neuroscience & Biobehavioral Reviews*, 32 (3), 581-97.

Liddle, Peter F., Kent A. Kiehl, and Andra M. Smith (2001), "Event-related fMRI study of response inhibition," *Human Brain Mapping*, 12 (2), 100-09.

Mazoyer, B., L. Zago, E. Mellet, S. Bricogne, O. Etard, O. Houdé, F. Crivello, M. Joliot, L. Petit, and N. Tzourio-Mazoyer (2001), "Cortical networks for working memory and executive functions sustain the conscious resting state in man," *Brain Research Bulletin*, 54 (3), 287-98.

McKiernan, Kristen A., Jacqueline N. Kaufman, Jane Kucera-Thompson, and Jeffrey R. Binder (2003), "A Parametric Manipulation of Factors Affecting Task-induced Deactivation in Functional Neuroimaging," *Journal of Cognitive Neuroscience*, 15 (3), 394-408.

Meyer, Roger E. (1988), "*Conditioning Phenomena and the Problem of Relapse in Opioid Addicts and Alcoholics*," in Learning Factors in Substance Abuse, Barbara A. Ray (Ed.). Washington, DC: NIDA.

Mogg, Karin and Brendan P. Bradley (2002), "Selective processing of smoking-related cues in smokers: manipulation of deprivation level and comparison of three measures of processing bias," *Journal of Psychopharmacology*, 16 (4), 385-92.

Munafo, Marcus, Karin Mogg, Sarah Roberts, Brendan P. Bradley, and Michael Murphy (2003), "Selective Processing of Smoking-Related Cues in Current Smokers, Ex-Smokers and Never-Smokers on the Modified Stroop Task," *J Psychopharmacol*, 17 (3), 310-16.

Park, Mi-Sook, Jin-Hun Sohn, Ji- A. Suk, Sook-Hee Kim, Sunju Sohn, and Richard Sparacio (2007), "Brain substrates of craving to alcohol cues in subjects with alcohol use disorder," *Alcohol Alcohol.*, 42 (5), 417-22.

Payne, Thomas J., Patrick O. Smith, Lois V. Sturges, and Sharon A. Holleran (1996), "Reactivity to smoking cues: Mediating roles of nicotine dependence and duration of deprivation," *Addictive Behaviors*, 21 (2), 139-54.

Pierce, John P., David M. Burns, Elizabeth Whalen, Bradley Rosbrook, Donald Shopland, and Michael Johnson (1991), "Does Tobacco Advertising Target Young People to Start Smoking? Evidence from California," *Journal of the American Medical Association*, 272 (8), 608-11.

Pollay, Richard W (2005), "*The Richard Pollay Tobacco Advertising Collection at Roswell Park Cancer Institute*."

Pollay, Richard W. (1986), "The distorted mirror: Reflections on the unintended consequences of advertising," *Journal of Marketing*, 50 (2), 18-36.

Pollay, Richard W., S. Siddarth, Michael Siegel, Anne Haddix, Robert K. Merritt, Gary A. Giovino, and Michael P. Eriksen (1996a), "The last straw? Cigarette advertising and realized market shares among youths and adults," *Journal of Marketing*, 60 (2), 1.

Pollay, Richard W., S. Siddarth, Michael Siegel, Anne Haddix, Robert K. Merritt, Gary Giovino, and Michael P. Eriksen (1996b), "The Last Straw? Cigarette Advertising and Realized Market Share Among Youths and Adults, 1979-1993," *Journal of Marketing*, 60 (2), 1.

Potenza, Marc N., Marvin A. Steinberg, Pawel Skudlarski, Robert K. Fulbright, Cheryl M. Lacadie, Mary K. Wilber, Bruce J. Rounsaville, John C. Gore, and Bruce E. Wexler (2003), "Gambling Urges in Pathological Gambling: A Functional Magnetic Resonance Imaging Study," *Archives of General Psychiatry*, 60 (8), 828-36.

Raichle, Marcus E., Ann Mary MacLeod, Abraham Z. Snyder, William J. Powers, Debra A. Gusnard, and Gordon L. Shulman (2001), "A default mode of brain function," *Proceedings of the National Academy of Sciences of the United States of America*, 98 (2), 676-82.

Richeson, Jennifer A., Abigail A. Baird, Heather L. Gordon, Todd F. Heatherton, Carrie L. Wyland, Sophie Trawalter, and J. Nicole Shelton (2003), "An fMRI investigation of the impact of interracial contact on executive function," *Nature Neuroscience*, 6 (12), 1323-28.

Robinson, Terry E. and Kent C. Berridge (2003), "Addiction," *Annual Review of Psychology*, 54, 25-53.

_____ (2001), "Incentive-sensitization and addiction," *Addiction*, 96, 103-14.

_____ (1993), "The neural basis of drug craving: an incentive-sensitization theory of addiction," *Brain Research Reviews*, 18 (1993), 247-91.

Sayette, Michael A. and Michael R. Hufford (1994), "Effects of Cue Exposure and Deprivation on Cognitive Resources in Smokers," *Journal of Abnormal Psychology*, 103 (4), 812-15.

Shulman, Gordon L., Julie A. Fiez, Maurizio Corbetta, Randy L. Buckner, Francis M. Miezin, Marcus E. Raichle, and Steven E. Petersen (1997), "Common Blood Flow Changes across Visual Tasks: 11. Decreases in Cerebral Cortex," *Journal of Cognitive Neuroscience*.

Sinha, Rajita, Cheryl Lacadie, Pawel Skudlarski, and Bruce E. Wexler (2004), "Neural Circuits Underlying Emotional Distress in Humans," *Annals of the New York Academy of Sciences*, 1032 (Biobehavioral Stress Response: Protective and Damaging Effects), 254-57.

Stippekohl, Bastian, Markus Winkler, Ronald F. Mucha, Paul Pauli, Bertram Walter, Dieter Vaitl, and Rudolf Stark (2010), "Neural Responses to BEGIN- and END-Stimuli of the Smoking Ritual in Nonsmokers, Nondeprived Smokers, and Deprived Smokers," *Neuropsychopharmacology*.

Stritzke, Werner G.K., Mary Jo Breiner, John J. Curtin, and Alan R. Lang (2004), "Assessment of Substance Cue Reactivity: Advances in Reliability, Specificity, and Validity," *Psychology of Addictive Behaviors*, 18 (2), 148-59.

Tapert, Susan F., Gregory G. Brown, Sandra S. Kindermann, Erick H. Cheung, Lawrence R. Frank, and Sandra A. Brown (2001), "fMRI measurement of brain dysfunction in alcohol-dependent young women," *Alcoholism: Clinical & Experimental Research*, 25 (2), 236-45.

Tapert, Susan F., Erick H. Cheung, Gregory G. Brown, Frank R. Lawrence, Martin P. Paulus, Alecia D. Schweinsburg, M J Meloy, and Sandra A Brown (2003), "Neural response to alcohol stimuli in adolescents with alcohol use disorder," *Archives of General Psychiatry*, 60 (7), 727-35.

The FIL Methods Group (2006), "*SPM5 Manual.*" London, UK: Functional Imaging Laboratory, Wellcome Department of Imaging Neuroscience.

Turkkan, Jaylan S., Mary E. McCaul, and Maxine L. Stitzer (1989), "Psychophysiological Effects of Alcohol-related Stimuli: II. Enhancement with Alcohol Availability," *Alcoholism: Clinical and Experimental Research*, 13 (3), 392-98.

van Veen, Vincent and Cameron S. Carter (2002), "The anterior cingulate as a conflict monitor: fMRI and ERP studies," *Physiology & Behavior*, 77 (4-5), 477-82.

Volkow, Nora D. and Joanna S. Fowler (2000), "Addiction, a Disease of Compulsion and Drive: Involvement of the Orbitofrontal Cortex," *Cereb. Cortex*, 10 (3), 318-25.

Volkow, Nora D., Joanna S. Fowler, Gene-Jack Wang, Frank Telang, Jean Logan, Millard Jayne, Yeming Ma, Kith Pradhan, Christopher Wong, and James M. Swanson (2010), "Cognitive control of drug craving inhibits brain reward regions in cocaine abusers," *NeuroImage*, 49 (3), 2536-43.

Yang, Zheng, Jun Xie, Yong-Cong Shao, Chun-Ming Xie, Li-Ping Fu, De-Jun Li, Ming Fan, Lin Ma, and Shi-Jiang Li (2008), "Dynamic neural responses to cue-reactivity paradigms in heroin-dependent users: An fMRI study," *Human Brain Mapping*, 9999 (9999), NA.

# Subliminal Prime-to-Behavior Effects

Hélène Deval, Dalhousie University, Canada
Bruce E. Pfeiffer, University of New Hampshire, USA
Frank R. Kardes, University of Cincinnati, USA

## EXTENDED ABSTRACT

A wide variety of consumer judgments, decisions, and behaviors occur automatically, or without conscious awareness or intention (Bargh 2002, 2007; Dijksterhuis 2010; Dijksterhuis, Smith, Van Baaren, & Wigboldus, 2005; Wyer 2008). Many different situational cues prime or activate consumer goals and traits in a nonconscious manner. Our research contributes to the understanding of prime-to-behavior effects by: (a) investigating the influence of subliminal goal primes and trait primes, (b) demonstrating that subliminal goal and trait prime-to-behavior effects are influenced by different moderating variables, and (c) investigating the influence of subliminal goal primes and trait primes related to money.

Prior research on subliminal priming has demonstrated that subliminal goal primes are influential only when the goal is already active (e.g., Strahan, Spencer, and Zanna 2002). Theoretically, however, the influence of subliminal trait primes on behavior should not depend on goal activation. Instead, the Active-Self model suggests that the influence of trait primes on behavior should depend on the extent to which these primes alter self-perceptions via selective processing of self-relevant information or on the extent to which these primes expand the self-concept (Wheeler, DeMarree, and Petty 2007). Both of these processes are influenced by individual differences in self-monitoring, or the extent to which consumers attempt to control their behavior to influence the impressions that others form of them (Snyder 1974). High self-monitors adapt their behaviors to their social environments, whereas low self-monitors behave consistently across situations.

Although prior research has shown that trait prime-to-behavior effects are often greater for low self-monitors than for high self-monitors (DeMarree, Wheeler, and Petty 2005), Wheeler et al. (2007) suggest that trait primes should have a greater influence on high self-monitors when social norms are invoked or when ought primes are activated. In addition, because the attitudes of high self-monitors frequently serve the social-adjustive function (Lavine and Snyder 2000), trait primes pertaining to the social-adjustive function should have a greater influence on high than on low self-monitors. Money frequently serves a social-adjustive function because money can be used to impress others (a self-presentational strategy) or to attain goals without assistance from others (the self-sufficiency principle; Vohs, Mead, and Goode 2006). Further, a strong association between money and consumption behavior has been illustrated in prior research. Briers et al. (2006) demonstrated that money related-supraliminal primes increased the consumption of candies.

In two experiments, we show that subliminal priming of goals and traits influence consumption behavior in goal-consistent and trait-consistent ways. Subliminal goal primes were influential only when a relevant goal was already active, regardless of individual differences in self-monitoring. Conversely, subliminal trait primes were more influential when self-monitoring is high rather than low, regardless of the level of goal activation.

In study 1, we predicted that subliminally priming hungry participants with either money related trait primes (rich and millionaire) or goal related primes (spend and money) would increase the amount of food eaten when compared to participants in the neutral prime condition (stone and picture). The effectiveness of the subliminal goal primes should depend on whether the goal is already active. Since all participants were instructed to arrive at the study in a hungry state, all participants in the goal prime condition

were expected to eat more than those in the control condition. In contrast, since trait primes influence self-perception, they should have a greater effect on high self-monitors than on low self-monitors. As a result, we predicted that the level of self-monitoring would moderate the eating behavior of those in the subliminal trait prime condition in such a way that high self-monitors would eat more than low self-monitors.

All participants were asked not to eat anything and not to drink anything but tea, coffee, or water for at least 3 hours prior to the study. The subliminal primes (goal, trait, or neutral) were imbedded in a lexical decision task (LDT). Following the LDT, participants were asked to perform a taste test in which they evaluated two types of candy. They were instructed to eat as much as they wanted in order to comparatively evaluate the two types of candy. Following the taste test, participants completed the 18-item Self-Monitoring Scale (Snyder and Gangestad 1986) and performed a subliminality check to insure the integrity of the priming manipulation

The primary dependent variable was the amount of candy eaten by the participants during the taste test. To test our hypotheses, we submitted this measure to a hierarchical regression analysis using the prime conditions, the self-monitoring score, and their interactions as predictors. As expected, the presence of both goal and trait primes had a significant positive main effect on the amount of candies eaten. Further, the interactions revealed that participants in the trait prime condition ate more candies as self-monitor scores increased. Self-monitoring had no influence on participants in the goal prime condition.

Study 2 was designed to replicate that effect from study 1 as well as demonstrate that goal primes but not trait primes depend on whether the goal is already active at the time of priming. The primary difference in the procedure between study 1 and study 2 was the addition of a cookie taste test to manipulate satiation. Participants in the satiated condition performed the cookie taste test at the beginning of the study before the LDT and candy taste test. Participants in the hungry condition performed the cookie taste test after the LDT and candy taste test.

Consistent with study 1, participants in the trait prime condition ate more candies as self-monitor score increased, but self-monitoring had no effect on participants in the goal prime condition. Also, consistent with our predictions, participants in the goal prime condition ate more candies when they were hungry than when they were satiated, but satiation had no effect on participants in the trait prime condition.

Both these experiments contribute to the existing literature by providing further support for the strong cognitive link between money and consumption, extending prior findings from supraliminal priming to subliminal priming, and demonstrating that trait and goal primes operate under different boundary conditions.

## REFERENCES

Bargh, John A. (2002), "Losing Consciousness: Automatic Influences on Consumer Judgment, Behavior, and Motivation," *Journal of Consumer Research,* 29 (2), 280-285.

Bargh, John A. (Ed.) (2007), *Social Psychology and the Unconscious: The Automaticity of Higher Mental Processes*, New York: Psychology Press.

Bargh, John A., Mark Chen, and Lara Burrows (1996), "Automaticity of Social Behavior: Direct Effects of Trait Construct and Stereotype Activation on Action," *Journal of Personality and Social Psychology*, 71, 230-244.

Briers, Barbara, Mario Pandelaere, Siegfried Dewitte, and Luk Warlop (2006), "Hungry for Money: The Desire for Caloric Resources Increases the Desire for Financial Resources and Vice Versa," *Psychological Science*, 17 (11), 939-943.

Callan, Mitchell, J., Aaron C. Kay, James M. Olson, Novjyot Brar, and Nicole Whitefield (2010), "The Effects of Priming Legal Concepts on Perceived Trust and Competitiveness, Self-Interested Attitudes, and Competitive Behavior," *Journal of Experimental Social Psychology*, 46, 325-335.

Chartrand, Tanya L., Joel Huber, Baba Shiv, and Robin J. Tanner (2008), "Nonconscious Goals and Consumer Choice," *Journal of Consumer Research*, 35, 189-201.

Cohen, Jacob, Patricia Cohen, Stephen G. West, and Leona S. Aiken (2003), "Applied multiple regression/correlation analysis for the behavioral sciences" (3rd ed. ed.), Mahwah, N.J, L. Erlbaum Associates.

DeMarree, Kenneth G., S. Christian Wheeler, and Richard E. Petty (2005), "Priming a New Identity: Self-Monitoring Moderates the Effects of Nonself Primes on Self-Judgments and Behavior," *Journal of Personality and Social Psychology*, 89 (5), 657-671.

Dijksterhuis, Ap (2010), "Automaticity and the Unconscious," in *Handbook of Social Psychology*, Fifth Edition, eds. Susan T. Fiske, Daniel T. Gilbert, and Gardner Lindzey (Vol. 1, pp. 228-267), Hoboken, NJ: Wiley.

Dijksterhuis, Ap, Henk Aarts, John A. Bargh, and Ad van Knippenberg (2000), "On the Relation Between Associative Strength and Automatic Behavior," *Journal of Experimental Social Psychology*, 36, 531-544.

Dijksterhuis, Ap, Pamela K. Smith, Rick B. van Baaren, and Daniel H. J. Wigboldus (2005), "The Unconscious Consumer: Effects of Environment on Consumer Behavior," *Journal of Consumer Psychology,* 15 (3), 193-202.

Dijksterhuis, Ap, and Ad van Knippenberg (1998), "The Relationship Between Perception and Behavior, or How to Win a Game of Trivial Pursuit," *Journal of Personality and Social Psychology*, 74, 865-877.

Feinberg, Richard A. (1986), "Credit Cards as Spending Facilitating Stimuli," *Journal of Consumer Research*, 13, 348-356.

Fitzsimons, Grainne M., Tanya L. Chartrand, and Gavan J. Fitzsimons (2008), "Automatic Effects of Brand Exposure on Motivated Behavior: How Apple Makes You 'Think Different'," *Journal of Consumer Research*, 35, 21-35.

Kay, Aaron C., S. Christian Wheeler, John A. Bargh, and Lee Ross (2004), "Material Priming: The Influence of Mundane Physical Objects on Situation Construal and Competitive Behavioral Choice," *Organizational Behavior and Human Decision Processes*, 95, 83-96.

Lavine, Howard, and Mark Snyder (2000), "Cognitive Processes and the Functional Matching Effect in Persuasion: Studies of Personality and Political Behavior," in *Why We Evaluate: Functions of Attitudes*, eds. G. R. Maio and J. M. Olson, Mahwah, NJ: Erlbaum, 97-131.

Sela, Aner, and Baba Shiv (2009), "Unraveling Priming: When Does the Same Prime Activate a Goal versus a Trait?" *Journal of Consumer Research*, 36 (3), 418-433.

Snyder, Mark (1974), "Self-Monitoring of Expressive Behavior," *Journal of Personality and Social Psychology*, 30, 526-537.

Snyder, Mark, and Steven W. Gangestad (1986), "On the nature of self-monitoring: Matters of assessment, matters of validity," *Journal of Personality and Social Psychology*, 51, 125-139.

Strahan, Erin J., Steven J. Spencer, and Mark P. Zanna (2002), "Subliminal Priming and Persuasion: Striking While the Iron is Hot," *Journal of Experimental Social Psychology*, 38, 556-568.

van Strien, Tatjana., Jan E.R. Frijters, Gerard P. A. Bergers, and Peter B. Defares (1986), "The Dutch Eating Behaviour Questionnaire (DEBQ) for assessment of restrained, emotional and external eating behavior," *International Journal of Eating Disorders*, 5, 747–755.

Vohs, Kathleen D., Nicole L. Mead, and Miranda R. Goode (2006), "The Psychological Consequences of Money," *Science*, 314, 1154-1156.

Wheeler, S. Christian, and Jonah Berger (2007), "When the Same Prime Leads to Different Effects," *Journal of Consumer Research*, 34, 357-368.

Wheeler, S. Christian, Kenneth G. DeMarree, and Richard E. Petty (2007), "Understanding the Role of the Self in Prime-to-Behavior Effects: The Active-Self Account," *Personality and Social Psychology Review*, 11 (3), 234-261.

Wheeler, S. Christian, Kimberly Rios Morrison, Kenneth G. DeMarree, and Richard E. Petty (2008), "Does Self-Consciousness Increase or Decrease Priming Effects? It Depends," *Journal of Experimental Social Psychology*, 44, 882-889.

Wyer, Robert S., Jr. (2008), "The Role of Knowledge Accessibility in Cognition and Behavior: Implications for Consumer Information Processing," in *Handbook of Consumer Psychology*, eds. Curtis P. Haugtvedt, Paul M. Herr, and Frank R. Kardes, New York: Psychology Press.

# Revealing an Advertising Myth: How Supportive is Editorial Support?

Claas Christian Germelmann, Saarland University, Germany
Andrea Groeppel-Klein, Saarland University, Germany

## EXTENDED ABSTRACT

In public relations and marketing, positive media articles about companies or brands are considered to be "gold standard". Yet, other than what has been learned from anecdotal evidence, little is known about their success with consumers. In two experimental studies we thus focus on two critical questions:

Does coupling positive news stories with advertisements leverage ad memory and attitudes toward the advertised brand?

Could coupling advertisements and editorial content actually backfire and damage brand and/or media brand image?

### Research on Effects of Editorial Content on Brands in Consumer Research

Positive news stories about companies or brands are often deemed to be more effective in influencing attitudes than advertisements (Jo 2004; Putrevu 2005; Çelebi 2007). This has been explained by the higher credibility of editorial content due to a lack of "manipulative intent" (Hallahan 1999). Only a few studies deal explicitly with ads and editorial content about a brand in the same medium. Loda and Coleman (2005) and Micu (2005) tested whether sequencing of the same message presented either as an ad or as news has an impact on persuasion. Both established mildly positive effects of supporting ads with positive news stories. However, the studies lacked realistic contexts and relied solely on forced exposure procedures in which subjects were asked to examine the stimulus material closely and didn't have the chance to avoid exposure altogether.

### Repetition and "Memory Trace Refreshment" Effects on Brand Recall

From the perspective of memory research, coupling means repeating a brand message. Information that is perceived successively from two different sources (ad and news), and thus in two different contexts, leaves more "memory traces" to facilitate retrieval than information presented in only one context. Thus:

H1: If a positive editorial report about a brand appears in the same medium as an advertisement for the brand ("article/advertisement coupling"), consumers' recall of the brand will be higher than if the editorial report were to appear alone.

### Effects of Supporting Ads with News Stories on $A_{Brand}$

The mere exposure effect suggests that repeated exposure should lead to a more positive attitude toward the object (Zajonc 1968). Familiarity of the message is increased by repetition in both ad and news story, and coupling multiple sources leads to a "truth effect" (Roggeveen and Johar 2002). Based on these theories, a positive effect on $A_{Brand}$ could be hypothesized.

Expecting a positive effect is based on the assumption that consumers do not notice the connection between a news story and an ad at all (due to typical low-involvement situations). If consumers *do* consciously notice the connection, or if they just feel that there might be manipulative intent behind the editorial support, a negative effect can be hypothesized. Friestad and Wright (1994; 1995) posited that consumers possess knowledge about persuasion strategies used in advertising. The use of such knowledge typically requires cognitive processing of messages. However, even when consumers are not willing or able to elaborate on persuasive messages, it is possible that they would unconsciously draw on former experiences of perceived manipulation by editorial support. Such "tacit" knowledge about manipulative or covert ad strategies can work as a readily available quick heuristic that could alert consumers to intended manipulation. MacKenzie and Lutz (1989) pointed to the fact that, in low-involvement situations, an attitude can be shaped not only by the features offered but also by the advertising context. However, we focus first on $A_{Brand}$ since we are interested in natural exposure situations in which $A_{Ad}$ may not be the best indicator of immediate ad effectiveness (Coulter and Punj 1999). Weighing all arguments, we find stronger theoretical bases for a negative effect of couplings:

H2: If a positive news story about a brand appears in the same medium as an advertisement for the brand, consumers' attitudes toward the brand will be more negative than if the news story were to stand alone.

### The Persistence of Editorial Support Effects Over Time

Most studies on persistence of attitudes are based on the sleeper effect, positing that negative evaluations caused by the message source (in our case, the coupling of ad and news story) can phase out over time. However, two critical conditions for such an effect are not met here: the discounting cue "editorial support", from which consumers could gather possible vested interests, is not conveyed beforehand, and the ability or motivation to think about the message and its context is usually low in standard media exposure situations. In such low-involvement situations, a second contact with the brand by way of supportive editorial support (e.g., in the course of a second survey), which was evaluated negatively after the first contact, could even trigger a reinstatement effect which could intensify the negative affective reaction to the ad itself and to the brand. Thus:

H3: If a positive news story about a brand appears in the same medium as an advertisement for the brand, after two weeks, consumers' attitudes toward the brand and to the ad will be more negative than if the news story were to stand alone.

### The Problem of Realistic Experimental Designs in Advertising Research

Experimental designs in advertising and media research differ from natural settings in two ways. In the first place, the stimuli often lack realistic contexts. Secondly, the typical paradigm in experimental advertising effectiveness research uses forced exposure, and this creates a risk that consumers start hypothesis-guessing and potentially adapt their behavior accordingly. Forced exposure provides no opportunity for non-selection of the medium, thus ruling out ad avoidance and making ad and ad context processing generally more likely than in biotic media contact situations (Schuman and Thorson 1990). Consequently, in a pretest, we tested for the effects of exposure in experimental research on editorial support by comparing forced exposure with quasi-biotic exposure (where consumers know that they take part in a study but they are not informed that the stimuli are part of the design).

### Key Findings

Our two studies show that news stories consistently do *not* improve the impact of ads on *brand image*. On the contrary, over time, the image of $A_{Brand}$ deteriorates due to the coupling, and H3

669

finds support. When consumers' active involvement with the medium is low, $A_{Brand}$ deteriorates if the ad receives editorial support (H2 is supported). Thus, we presume to have observed a peripheral or heuristic process to be at work. In both studies we found a positive effect of coupling ad and news story on recall, thus confirming H1. However, the second study shows that this result can also be achieved by adding a reminder spot to a commercial break, because familiarity seems to be the reason for the improved recall rather than a multiple source effect.

From a methodological perspective, the forced exposure designs commonly used in advertising research run the risk of exaggerating positive evaluations of $A_{Brand}$. On the other hand, forced exposure experiments tend to downplay the memory effects.

# Market Scarcity and Persuasion: An Information Congruity Perspective

Feng Shen, Saint Joseph's University, USA

## EXTENDED ABSTRACT

In advertising theory and practice, atypicality is considered to be an effective creative strategy to break through the clutter, and to boost ad evaluations and memory for the ad and brand (Heckler and Childers 1992; Smith and Yang 2004). However, research on this issue is limited (Smith and Yang 2004). Moreover, most advertising research used long and forced ad exposures of up to thirty seconds or longer to investigate advertising processing and effectiveness (reviewed by Meyers-Levy and Malaviya 1999), whereas attention to ads is much shorter in practice, typically a few seconds or less (Pieters and Wedel 2004). It remains unclear whether the positive effects of atypicality carry over to these much shorter durations. In fact, considering people's basic need for certainty (Loewenstein 1994), there is reason to believe that the effects of atypicality may be different at shorter exposures.

The present research focuses on information processing within the first exposure to the ad, from 100 ms onwards. Motivated to identify the stimuli they are exposed to, people attempt to identify the ads that they encounter, i.e., what they are for. In three experiments, we show that, depending on the typicality of the ad, this identification process can take different forms over the course of a single exposure, which in turn influences how evaluations develop over time (experiment 1 and 2), the attention devoted to the ad (experiment 3), and subsequent memory (experiment 2).

Typical ads display objects and scenes that are expected for the advertised category (Mervis and Rosch 1981), such as a car in a car ad. The product category of these ads is rapidly identified and with certainty in 100 ms or even less ("Ha, it's a car ad"; Pieters and Wedel 2009), and this identification certainty contributes to an immediately positive ad evaluation (Loken and Ward 1990). Additional information that becomes available after the first glance confirms the immediate identification, leaving the ad evaluation at relatively high levels of positivity, until boredom eventually befalls these ads. We distinguish two types of atypical ads, hereafter referred to as "atypical" and "typical-other" ads. Atypical ads display objects and scenes that do not immediately bring up a product category, leading to identification uncertainty ("What is that ad for?"). This negatively affects the initial ad evaluation. When exposure to the ad continues, additional information and cognitive integration contribute to ad comprehension reducing identification uncertainty ("Aha, it's a car ad"). This increased certainty is appreciated, leading to a positive updating of the evaluation. Finally, typical-other ads display objects and scenes that are typical for another category, such as a lady misting her face in a car ad. These ads are initially identified with certainty ("Ha, it's a fragrance ad"), which is liked. However, new information that becomes available during exposure disconfirms the initial identification, which needs to be revised ("Oh no, it is a car ad"). This need to revise one's initial identification may lead to confusion and requires more cognitive effort, which is disliked and leads to a downward adjustment of the initially positive evaluation.

Thus, typicality determines the identification process—identification confirmation (typical), identification disconfirmation (typical-other) or uncertainty reduction (atypical)—which has predictable effects on how ad evaluations are updated within a single exposure. In addition, it influences attention and memory, and we predict different effects depending on whether recall or recognition performance is assessed. Typical ads do not retain attention well, since they are immediately identified and additional processing does not provide much "new" information. However,

because a connection between the ad and the advertised category is immediately established upon exposure, and the ad category serves as a useful retrieval cue (Goodman 1980), they are recalled well, even after brief exposures. Recall performance of atypical ads, in contrast, is relatively poor after brief exposures, but strongly improves when additional processing leads to ad comprehension (Bransford and Johnson 1982). Because atypical ads cannot be immediately identified, they retain attention longer, such that memory should be good. In case of typical-other ads, rapidly identified inconsistencies between the initial identification and newly processed information motivate people to prolong attention to the ad. However, recall performance remains relatively poor for these ads despite additional time attending, because of source-confusion (Roediger and McDermott 2000). Recognition performance, in contrast, is poor after very brief exposures for all three ad types, but strongly improves with additional time attending (Loftus and Bell 1975), except for typical ads, that remain relatively difficult to discriminate from other ads. Due to their typicality, these ads appear familiar regardless of whether they were presented or not, increasing false recognition (Silva, Groeger, and Bradshaw 2006).

We tested and found support for our predictions about the dynamic identification, evaluation and memory processes within a single exposure in experiments 1 and 2, where we systematically varied the exposure duration of ads between-conditions from 100 ms (which is less than a single eye fixation) up to 10 seconds (cf. Donders 1868). Finally, support for the prediction that atypical and typical-other ads retain attention longer than typical ads was provided in experiment 3, where participants freely viewed a large set of ads. These findings are the first to provide insights into the rapid advertising processes from 100 ms onwards. They reveal that the effects of typicality critically depend on the exposure duration, and require revision of the idea of atypicality as a universal creative strategy to improve advertising effectiveness. Although we observe the benefits of atypical ads, we also find that their effectiveness crucially depends on their ability to retain the consumer's attention. Typical ads, in contrast, do not require such sustained attention in order to develop positive ad evaluations and memory traces for the ad and brand. Moreover, we argue for careful consideration of the type of atypicality, since typical-other ads failed on almost all accounts in the present research. We believe that the proposed theory and methodology are applicable to other situations where initial feelings may be rapidly updated, and point to repeated ad exposures as a relevant area of future research.

## REFERENCES

Bransford, John D. and Marcia K. Johnson (1972), "Contextual Prerequisites for Understanding: Some Investigations of Comprehension and Recall," *Journal of Verbal Learning and Verbal Behavior*, 11, 717-726.

Donders, F.C. (1868), "On the Speed of Mental Processes," *Acta Psychologica: Attention and Performance*, 30, 412-431.

Goodman, Gail S. (1980), "Picture Memory: How the Action Schema Affects Retention," *Cognitive Psychology*, 12, 473-495.

Heckler, Susan E. and Terry L. Childers (1992), "The Role of Expectancy and Relevancy in Memory for Verbal and Visual Information: What is Incongruency?" *Journal of Consumer Research*, 18 (March), 475-92.

Loewenstein, George (1994), "The Psychology of Curiosity: A Review and Reinterpretation," *Psychological Bulletin*, 116 (1), 75-98.

Loftus, Geoffrey R. and Susan M. Bell (1975), "Two Types of Information in Picture Memory," *Journal of Experimental Psychology: Human Learning and Memory*, 104 (2), 103-113.

Loken, Barbara and James Ward (1990), "Alternative Approaches to Understanding the Determinants of Typicality," *Journal of Consumer Research*, 17, 111-26.

Mervis, Carolyn B. and Eleanor Rosch (1981), "Categorization of Natural Objects," *Annual Review of Psychology*, 32, 89-115.

Meyers-Levy, Joan and Prashant Malaviya (1999), "Consumers' Processing of Persuasive Advertisements: An Integrative Framework of Persuasion Theories," *Journal of Marketing*, 63 (Special Issue), 45-60.

Pieters, Rik and Michel Wedel (2004), "Attention Capture and Transfer in Advertising: Brand, Pictorial, and Text-Size Effects," *Journal of Marketing*, 68, 36-50.

_____ (2009), "Gist in a Glance: Determinants of Immediate Advertising Identification," *Unpublished manuscript*, Tilburg University.

Roediger, Henry L. and Kathleen B. McDermott (2000), "Distortions of Memory," in Endel Tulving and Fergus I.M. Craik (eds.), *The Oxford Handbook of Memory*, Oxford, UK: Oxford University Press, 149-62.

Silva, Mariana M., John A. Groeger, and Mark F. Bradshaw, "Attention-Memory Interactions in Scene Perception," *Spatial Vision*, *19 (1)*, 9-19.

Smith, Robert E. and Xiaojing Yang (2004), "Toward a General Theory of Creativity in Advertising: Examining the Role of Divergence," *Marketing Theory,* 4 (1/2), 31-58.

# Generation Y's Representations of Who They Are and How They Give

Caroline Urbain, University of Nantes, France
Marine Le Gall-Ely, ICI, Université de Bretagne Occidentale, France
Christine Gonzalez, LEMNA Université de Nantes, France

## EXTENDED ABSTRACT

The emergence of each successive generation raises new questions on the transmission, continuity and rupture of social behaviors (work, consumption, daily life…). Also referred to as the *E-generation*, *Net Generation* or *Millennial Generation*, the generation Y is composed, in the western world, of individuals born between the late 1970s and the mid 1990s who grew up with the excesses of the consumer society and amidst the astounding development of the information society. This generation takes the social and societal transformations of the 1960s and 1970s for granted, or even considers them obsolete, and is immersed in growing debates on ecology, the harmful effects of globalization and tomorrow's uncertainties (Allain, 2009). Socialized in a world in profound mutation, it is made up of young adults liable to develop new and unexpected solidarity and giving representations and practices.

In the face of the emergence of these new lifestyles and mindsets, and of growing debate over monetary donation collection methods, how should associations and charities approach this generation? This question brings out two preliminary lines of investigation which are the focus of this research:

How do the individuals of this generation define themselves?
How do they represent giving?

Several conceptions of giving emerge from the human and social sciences literature: an instrument of power for the giver (Mauss, 1923-1924), of domination (Weiner, 1992) making the receiver dependent, or even alienated (Testart, 1982), a sacrifice (Lévinas, 1987, 1995), a deprivation, an impossibility (Derrida, 1991), a purely disinterested, altruistic gesture, a free exchange but which creates links, obligations, debts (Mauss, 1923-1924; Lévi-Strauss, 1949; Titmuss, 1970; Sahlins, 1972; Godbout and Caillé, 1992). This polysemy shows that giving is both a collective and an individual phenomenon which is represented by a wide range of practices (Authors, 2009b). Our work is assimilated with the comprehensive research trend which has developed within Consumer Culture Theory (Arnould and Thompson, 2005). Giving is thus regarded as a system (Sherry 1983) and revolving aroud consumption (Giesler, 2006 ; Marcoux, 2009).

Our research focus on social representations (SR), known as allowing individuals to interpret reality in their physical and social environment and direct their behaviors and social relations (Abric, 1994). SR studies can mobilize different methodological approaches (Viaud and Roussiau, 2002; Doise, Clemence and Lorenzi-Cioldi, 1993). The free association technique, already employed in marketing (authors, 2009a), was selected for this study. This technique "consists, based on an induction word (referring to the object of the SR), of asking the informant to provide all the words, expressions or adjectives which come to mind" (Abric, 1994).

In order to answer the research questions, an exploratory quantitative study was conducted on a convenience sample of 276 individuals born between 1979 and 1991 (people belonging to Generation Y aged 18 plus as they were presumed to have autonomous giving practices). In French language, the questionnaire began with the following open question: "*Generally speaking, what does the term giving evoke for you?*", in response to which informants were asked to provide five words. It carried on to cover giving practices, exchange behavior, entourage, knowledge of associations, to finish with questions on identity (sex, age…), including "*give five words which come to mind to describe your generation*". The free associations generated were analyzed with the software EVOC2005.

These results show both an individualistic Generation Y and a very mobile generation seeking links which is united around technology and the consumer society. This generation is not marked by collective events (as previous generations may have been). Festivity appears to be a structuring element.

Over and above this specificity, Generation Y givers and non-givers express convergence in their representations of giving:

- A vision of giving which is becoming institutionalized: associations and volunteering are terms which structure the representation.
- The strong presence of a relationship with others: at the center or close to the representation we find the notions of solidarity, sharing, aid, charity and gifts.
- A freely consenting act: a free gesture, or a gesture belonging to a gratuitous approach, which reflects an individualist dimension.

Illness is the prominent element against which giving can be mobilized: it appears first, far ahead of poverty for instance. This risk is no doubt conveyed by the media more frequently than ecological risks or natural disasters (telethon, AIDS, cystic fibrosis…) and is more easily associated with the person's close entourage.

Givers and non-givers have a pragmatic vision of giving: the objects of giving of blood, money and organs are central elements of the representation. Nevertheless, non-givers insist upon this functional component (blood and money are quoted significantly more). One hypothesis is the media coverage of giving blood or money, non-givers thus expressing a "media-broadcast" vision of giving (they more frequently employ the term *telethon*). Furthermore, givers show a collective apprehension of giving, seen as a system, while, in an emerging trend, non-givers have a more personal vision.

Finally, two results are worth emphasizing. First, the almost complete absence of terms expressing a negative vision of giving. Secondly, the notions of constraint and commitment were rarely touched upon. This conception of giving is distant from the notion of obligation presented in the literature on the subject (Sahlins, 1972; Sherry, McGrath and Levy, 1993; Marcoux, 2009). This representation of giving is coherent with the way in which Generation Y describes itself: turned towards others, free, largely unconcerned with notions of duty and effort. Commitment and investment must undoubtedly be a pleasure.

From a managerial point of view, these results are the first to shed light on the factors liable to cause members of this generation to give : use of social networks such as Facebook or Twitter, use of factors such as pleasure, festivities and efficiency to encourage them to adhere to causes and actions rather than recourse to guilt and duty, encourage them to "work for the association" using their skills to improve its offer.

# Exploring the Everyday Branded Retail Experience-
# The Consumer Quest for 'Homeyness' in Branded Grocery Stores

Sofia Ulver-Sneistrup, Lund University, Sweden
Ulf Johansson, Lund University, Sweden

## EXTENDED ABSTRACT

This paper extends consumer culture theories of branded retail environments by analyzing the meanings that experiences of the everyday site of the branded grocery store hold for consumers. In consumer culture theory (CCT) (Arnould & Thompson 2005), despite a growing interest in branded retail environments, little interest has been paid to the ordinary and everyday experience of the grocery store. While this site has been the predominant focus in more evidence-based consumer marketing research (e.g. Burt & Carralero-Encinas 2002; Choi, Chan and Coughlan 2006; Collins-Dodd & Lindley 2003; McGoldrick 2002; Richardson, Jain and Dick 1996), in CCT, marketplaces of more spectacular character have made out the arenas of investigation (Borghini et al 2009; Kozinets et al 2004, 2002; Thompson & Arsel 2004; Sherry 2008). Among these the development of the concept 'themed flagship brandstore' (Kozinets et al 2002, 2004; Borghini et al. 2009) is of extra interest for our investigation, as it looks at the mythological appeal in the physical as well as symbolic structure of the store. However, as the symbolic properties of such spectacular brand venues were understood as constellations of mythotypic characteristics, creating "awe" and other intense sensations among its consumers, another cultural constellation was highly likely needed to understand the more ordinary, but yet meaningful, ideal consumer experience of the everyday branded grocery store. Noting the growth of heavily branded grocery retail chains with their accompanying private brands, some of these sites may in the future live up to the epithet brandstore, but is it the same symphony of impressions sought, in these venues for everyday visits, as it is in more entertainment-heavy brand arenas?

Using ethnographic data collection methods (photo-diaries, participant observations, long interviews, artifact collections) we studied the grocery shopping habits and life at home among six Swedish middle-class working women with children during a month in the fall of 2008. Through diligent and time-consuming hermeneutic data analysis, where we iteratively moved between data and theory (Thompson et al 1994), we found that Grant Mc-Cracken's (1989) cultural account of the properties making out the experience of 'homeyness' was readily applicable to our consumers' experiences of the ideal branded grocery retailer. In addition, the eight properties of 'homeyness'—the diminuitive, the variable, the embracing, the engaging, the mnemonic, the authentic, the informal, and the situating—were infused with meanings in marketplace myths through which the meaning structure of homeyness was intensified. Such marketplace myths could be fantasies about the *bella viva* around the Mediterranean, the romantization of the simple life and the humble farmer etc.

The properties of 'homeyness' and myths inflected in the consumers' everyday retail experience were of a more subdued, less mind-blowing, kind than the mythotypic emotional state conveyed by Kozinets et als (2002, 2004) and Borghinis (2009) themed brandstores. Yet, highly meaningful. These consumers held strong ties to their favorite grocery retailer brand where the 'homeyness' constellation, despite its seemingly subdued character, executed power over these women that went beyond mere convenience. Still, in terms of retail brand ideology, where the immersion into marketplace myths supports the agendas of ideologies (Thompson 2004) the myths conveyed in these everyday marketplaces rather supported unreflected dominant ideologies, than paradigm-breaking

and emerging ideology which more spectacular arenas may strive for in their quest for an overwhelming consumer experience. Thus, the powerful and distinctive experience of homeyness demands an ideology-neutral surrounding supported by marketplace-crafted myths.

We discuss the alternative understanding of the data had we selected another group of respondents. Additional research is needed to see if and how the constellation of homeyness is applicable in other national, gender, class, ethnic and lifestyle contexts. Hence, the conceptual implications of our analysis for consumer research concern on one hand the possible transferability and appropriation of the specific constellation of 'homeyness' to other important consumer cultural contexts, and on the other hand more generally the importance for consumer cultural researchers to not primarily always aim for the spectacular but also direct their eyes towards experiences of the more ordinary, yet culturally rich, kind.

## REFERENCES

Arnould, Eric J. and Craig J. Thompson (2005), "Consumer Culture Theory (Cct): Twenty Years of Research " *Journal of Consumer Research*, 31 (4), 868-82.

Ailawadi, Kusum L. and Kevin Lane Keller (2004), "Understanding Retail Branding: Conceptual Insights and Research Priorities," *Journal of Retailing*, 80 (4), 331-42.

Aaker,

Belk, Russell W., John F. Jr Sherry, and Melanie Wallendorf (1988), "A Naturalistic Inquiry into Buyer and Seller Behavior at a Swap Meet," *Journal of Consumer Research*, 14 (March), 449-70.

Belk, Russell W. (2000), "May the Farce Be with You: On Las Vegas and Consumer Infantilization," Consumption, Markets, and Culture, 4 (2), 101–23.

Borghini, S; Diamond, N; Koxinets, V.R.; McGrath, M.A.; Muniz, A.M.Jr.; Sherry, J.F Jr (2009), "Why Are Themed Brandstores So Powerful? Retail Brand Ideology at American Girl Place," *Journal of Retailing*, 85 (3), 363-75.

Burt, S. and Sparks, L. (2002), Corporate Branding, Retailing, and Retail Internationalization. *Corporate Reputation Review,* 5(2/3), 194-212

Burt, S. & Carralero-Encinas, J. (2000), 'The Role of Store Image in Retail Internationalization', *International Marketing Review,* 17(4/5), 433-453

Choi, S. Chan and T. Coughlan Anne (2006), "Private Label Positioning: Quality Versus Feature Differentiation from the National Brand," *Journal of Retailing*, 82 (2), 79-93.

Collins-Dodd, C. and T. Lindley (2003), "Store Brands and Retail Differentiation: The Influence of Store Image and Store Brand Attitude on Store Own Brand Perceptions," *Journal of Retailing and Consumer Services*, 10 (6), 345-52.

Elliott, Richard and Nick Jankel-Elliott (2003), "Using Ethnography in Strategic Consumer Research," *Qualitative Market Research: An International Journal*, 6 (4), 215-23.

Holt, Douglas B.(1998) Does Cultural Capital Structure American Consumption? *Journal of Consumer Research,* 25:1-25

Kamakura, Wagner A. and Wooseong Kang (2007), "Chain-Wide and Store-Level Analysis for Cross-Category Management," *Journal of Retailing*, 83 (2), 159-59.

674
*Advances in Consumer Research*
*Volume 38, © 2012*

Kotler, Philip (1973), "Atmospherics as a Marketing Tool " *Journal of Retailing*, 49 (4), 48-48.

Kumar, V.& Karande K (2000), "The Effect of Retail Store Environment on Retailer Performance," *Journal of Business Research*, 49 (2), 167-81.

Kozinets, Robert V., John F. Sherry Jr., Benet DeBerry-Spence, Adam Duhachek, Krittinee Nuttavuthisit, and Diana Storm (2002), "Themed Flagship Brand Stores in the New Millenium: Theory, Practice, Prospects," *Journal of Retailing*, 78, 17-29.

Kozinets Robert, V., F. Sherry John, Jr., Diana Storm, Adam Duhachek, and et al. (2004), "Ludic Agency and Retail Spectacle," *Journal of Consumer Research*, 31 (3), 658-72.

McCracken, Grant (1989), ""Homeyness": A Cultural Account of One Constellation of Consumer Goods and Meanings," in *Interpretive Consumer Research*, ed. Elizabeth C. Hirschman, Provo, UT: Association of Consumer Research, 168-83

McCracken, Grant (1988), *The Long Interview*, Vol. 13, Newbury Park, CA, USA: Sage.

McGrath, Mary Ann, John F. Jr Sherry, and Deborah D. Heisley (1993), "An Ethnographic Study of an Urban Periodic Marketplace: Lessons from the Midville Farmers' Market," *Journal of Retailing*, 69 (3), 280-319.

McGoldrick, Peter (2002), *Retail Marketing*, NY, US: McGraw-Hill Education.

Moisio, Risto, Eric J. Arnould, and Linda L. Price (2004), "Between Mothers and Markets: Constructing Family Identity through Homemade Food," *Journal of Consumer Culture*, 4 (3), 361-84.

Moore, M., Fernie, J. and Burt, S. (2000), "Brands without Boundaries", *European Journal of Marketing,* 34(8), 919-937

Pine, II, Gilmore, J and Joseph, B (2007) *Authenticity: What Consumers Really Want,* Harvard Business School Press, Boston: US

Pine, II, Joseph B. and James H. Gilmore (1999), *The Experience Economy: Work is Theatre and Every Business is a Stage,* Boston, MA: Harvard Business School Press.

Richardson, Paul, Arun K. Jain, and Alan Dick (1996), "The Influence of Store Aesthetics on Evaluation of Private Label Brands," *Journal of Product and Brand Management*, 5 (1), 19-28.

Rybczynski, Witold (1987), *Home: A Short History of an Idea*, London: Penguin Books.

Sherry, John F. Jr (1998), "The Soul of the Company Store- Nike Town Chicago and the Emplaced Brandscape," in *Servicescapes: The Concept of Place in Contemporary Markets*, ed. John F. Jr Sherry, Lincolnwood, IL, 109-46.

Schlosser, Ann E. (1998), "Applying the Functional Theory of Attitudes to Understanding the Influence of Store Atmosphere on Store Inferences," *Journal of Consumer Psychology*, 7 (4), 345-69.

Thompson, C & Arsel,, Z (2004) The Starbucks Brandscape and Consumers' (Anticorporate) Experience of Glocalization, *Journal of Consumer Research,* 31: 631-642

Thompson, Craig J. (1996), "Caring Consumers: Gendered Consumption Meanings and the Juggling Lifestyle," *Journal of Consumer Research*, 22 (March), 388-407.

Thompson, Craig J. (2004), "Marketplace Mythology and Discourses of Power," *Journal of Consumer Research*, 31 (1), 162-80.

Thompson, Craig J., William B. Locander, and Howard R. Pollio (1994), "The Spoken and the Unspoken: A Hermeneutic Approach to Understanding the Cultural Viewpoints That Underlie Consumers' Expressed Meanings," *Journal of Consumer Research*, 21 (December), 432-52.

Thompson, Craig J. (1997) "Interpreting Consumers: A Hermeneutical Framework for Deriving Marketing Insights from the Texts of Consumers' Consumption Stories," Journal of Marketing Research, 34 (November), 438–55.

Thompson, Locander and Pollio (1989) Putting Consumer Experience Back into Consumer Research: The Philosophy and Method of Existential-Phenomenology, Journal of Consumer Research, 16(2), 133-146

Ulver-Sneistrup, S. (2008) "Status Spotting", PhD thesis, Lund University Business Press

# Rituals in Transition: Reciprocal Pig Feasts in Northeastern Rural China

Ann Veeck, Western Michigan University, USA
Hongyan Yu, Sun Yat-sen University, China
Gregory Veeck, Western Michigan University, USA

## EXTENDED ABSTRACT

With the rapid globalization and urbanization occurring in many parts of the world, many celebratory rituals that have been practiced for generations are likely to become extinct in upcoming years. Examining rural traditions in transitional communities offers an opportunity to understand how ritual activities communicate social standing and provide structure to economic processes. At what point do the benefits secured through long-standing rituals cease to be worth the sacrifice of time, labor, and money necessary to participate in the traditions? Answering this question can not only provide increased understanding of the practice of rituals, but offer insight into the effects of economic development and privatization.

Research on ritualistic acts has shown that ceremonies and celebrations serve to initiate, strengthen, or reproduce social ties (Driver 1991; Marshall 2000; Mathwick, Wiertz, de Ruyter 2008). Consonant with this theme, a number of consumer culture theorists have approached some consumption activities as ritualistic practices that serve to maintain social cohesion (e.g. Belk and Costa 1998; Bonsu and Belk 2003; Wallendorf and Arnould 1991). The social solidarity nurtured through ceremonies makes the instrumental and symbolic value of these ritual events akin to similar benefits derived from gift giving (Belk 1976; Ruth, Otnes, and Brunel 1999; Sherry 1983; Wooten 2000), with ritual ceremonies functioning as "gift systems" (Geisler 2006). In rural settings, in which the roles of producer and consumer are tightly interwoven, ritual ceremonies can serve to establish embedded economies that operate independently from capitalist markets via norms of reciprocity and trust (Gouldner 1960). Some theorists argue that communal activities involving private citizens, such as ceremonies and celebrations, which produce an abundance of social capital, can help to create civil societies, which, in turn, provide individuals some protection from the vagaries of the external market and the state (Edwards and Foley 1998; Fukuyama 2002; Woolcock 1998).

With this theoretical backdrop, this research examines the annual pig roasts, hosted by Chinese families in Jilin Province during the Spring Festival (lunar New Year). Our fieldwork included sixteen in depth interviews conducted with farm families over the course of two summers. During the first trip, made during the summer of 2008, we conducted in depth interviews with nine families in Zhenlai County, located in western Jilin Province approximately 250 kilometers northwest of Changchun, the provincial capital of Jilin. The first round included five families in the township of Dongping, and four families in the township of Momoge. During the second trip, made during the summer of 2009 and using a slightly revised interview guide, in depth interviews were conducted with an additional seven families in Jiutai County, just fifty kilometers northeast of Changchun. These interviews included three families in the township of Lianhua and four in the townships of Longjiapo. The two counties represent two quite different conditions of rural economic development, with per capita income about twice as high for residents of Jiutai County as for Zhenlai County.

Each of the families we interviewed, following a long-standing rural tradition in northern China, raises pigs throughout the year and then slaughters the pig during the period shortly before Spring Festival and cooks part of it to host a feast for friends and relatives. Via the descriptions and interpretation of the pig feasts by farmers, we learned that these annual ceremonies have provided an important role in stabilizing and maintaining rural societies through the generation of social capital (Bourdieu 1984; Coleman 1988; Putnam 2000). The pig feasts have served to establish and reinforce a social network of relatives and friends that can be relied upon for assistance throughout the year (Kipnis 1997; Yan 1994). We identified four kinds of social capital—identity, moral, emotional, and instrumental—that have provided distinctive, but interrelated, benefits to the participants of the social gatherings.

In less-developed Zhenlai County, the pig feast ritual continues to be practiced by every household that we encountered and appears to continue to provide an important purpose in affirming an informal market that serves to collectivize tasks that are necessary for survival in rural villages. In wealthier, better-connected Jiutai County, the pig feast ritual is no longer uniformly practiced. Even the households that continue to engage in the tradition do not all feel it is necessary to commit the time and labor necessary to sustain this ritual on an annual basis. As Jiutai County is becoming more economically developed, alternative means to acquire social capital have emerged, and a formal economic system is developing that operates to perform many of the activities (e.g. loans, farm tasks, house building) that previously might have been executed with the help of an informal social network.

The decrease in the practice of the pig feast in Jiutai County raises some broader issues related to globalization, modernization, and capitalization, including potential support for western theory that ties modernization to individualization (e.g. Beck 1992; Giddens 1991) and substantiation of a link between reciprocal feasts and egalitarian societies (Durrenberger 2008). Given the prevalence of ceremonies involving ritual transaction in most societies, this research suggests the usefulness of studying the rise and fall of rituals to gain greater understanding of the rules and meanings of rituals within the larger social and economic order (Arnould and Thompson 2005).

# Cultural In-betweeness and Migrant Identity: Recreating Culture in Online Thirdspaces or Heterotopias

Teresa Davis, University of Sydney, Australia

## ABSTRACT

This Cyberethnographic (Robinson and Shulz 2009) study follows migrant women living over 3 continents Beginning with Babha's (1994) "thirdspace" and cultural hybridity; this examines disjunctive notions of place, 'other space' and time. Foucauldian heterotopia is offered as an explanation of this 'Other Space' and as a metaphor for migrant experience.

# Opportunity or Challenge?
# The Impact of Exposure to Similar Extensions on the Extensions of Late Movers

Hakkyun Kim, Concordia University, Canada
Sharon Ng, Nanyang Technological University, Singapore

## EXTENDED ABSTRACT

This research examines how consumers evaluate brand extensions in the context of rivalry and competition. Specifically, unlike the extant literature, which has investigated consumers' responses to extensions with isolated market situations, the current research investigates how consumers use their knowledge of previous similar brand extensions when generating evaluations toward similar extensions from follower brands. Because any market is shared by multiple competitors, and because consumers can be exposed to competitors' actions, it may be wrongful to assume that consumers will generate new product evaluations solely based on fit perceptions (i.e., how well an extension matches the parent brand). Rather, consumers who have been exposed to similar brand extension examples may use this cue when evaluating similar extensions of other brands. Thus, this research intends to extend the consumer brand extension model by incorporating consumer knowledge into the market situation, which is assumed to be a more realistic approach.

Motivated by the importance of considering rivalry and competition situations, this research draws on consumer learning by the analogy model (Gregan-Paxton and John 1997), which posits that consumers attempt to understand and form preferences toward something unfamiliar and new by relating it to something familiar. Such relational reasoning involves a process by which people transfer their knowledge of a well-known base to a lesser-known target. Moreover, the driving force behind this knowledge transfer via analogical reasoning is the perceived similarity between the base and the target (Moreau, Markman, and Lehmann 2001; Roehm and Sternthal 2001). For instance, when faced with a generic drug, consumers may be unsure about its performance. However, these people may predict how it will work when they are informed that generic drugs have the same active ingredients as the original formulation, and they rely on their knowledge about branded counterparts.

Such a human tendency to learn about and evaluate new targets hints at the possibility that consumers can base their evaluations on prior examples that they know. For instance, when evaluating Mercedes motorcycles, consumers may rely on how good (or bad) BMW motorcycles have been, since the BMW brand is similar to the Mercedes brand, and since consumers are aware of the performance of BMW motorcycles. Therefore, we reason that consumers who have knowledge of prior similar extensions (e.g., BMW entering the motorcycle category) may generate evaluations on new extensions from other brands by relying on such a prior example, but not necessarily on the extension fit perception. Extending the notion that consumers do not generate evaluative judgments in a vacuum, this research proposes that consumers may have other evaluative input on which they can rely more than perceived fit. To be more specific, we show that the performance of prior similar extension exemplars can be a factor more diagnostic than perceived fit. Furthermore, we expect that such an influence of prior examples (success or failure) will become greater as the base and the target brands are similar to each other. Therefore, we hypothesize that the degree of perceived similarity between brands will moderate the impact of prior extensions on consumer responses toward a new similar extension from a different brand.

Two experiments were conducted to test the above hypotheses. Experiment 1 aimed to assess whether prior success or failure of similar brand extensions influences consumers' responses to similar types of subsequent brand extensions by other brands. To accomplish this goal, we employed a 2 (Prior Example: Success, Failure) x 2 (Fit Level: High, Moderate) between-subjects design and measured participants' evaluations of a new product idea from the BMW brand when the performance of a similar type of extension from the Mercedes-Benz brand varied. Providing support for our hypothesis, participants in the prior failure condition (i.e., those who were reminded that the same type of products introduced by the Mercedes-Benz brand failed) evaluated a moderate-fit extension (sunglasses) from the BMW brand less favorably than participants in the prior success condition (i.e., those who were reminded that the same type of products introduced by the Mercedes-Benz brand succeeded). However, there was no difference between prior failure and success conditions in terms of brand extension evaluations toward a high-fit extension (tires). This pattern of evaluations reflects relational reasoning involving a process by which people transfer their knowledge of a well-known base (prior examples) to a lesser-known target (a new extension).

In a follow-up study, we replicated these findings using a different set of brands and extensions. More importantly, we further investigated the moderating role of the perceived similarity between brands. The results from experiment 2 confirmed our premise that the transfer of knowledge is further facilitated as the similarity perception increases. Specifically, by using simple slope tests on extension evaluations when the perception of similarity was centered at 1 standard deviation above and below the mean, we found that only among participants who perceived these two brands as similar to each other (i.e., +1 SD above case), was the interaction between prior example and fit level significant, thus replicating our previous findings. Therefore, these findings supported our prediction about the moderating role of the perceived similarity between pioneer and follower brands.

Taken together, these findings add to an emerging stream of research that explores the contextual differences in consumer responses to brand extensions. In addition, the managerial implications from the current research can be important in that the first-movers (extending a new branding category for the first time) have to spend a great deal of resources to convince consumers to adopt new products from their brands, while other followers can gain an advantage by strategically following (or not following) trails of pioneer moves. Therefore, the results of the current research imply the possibility of free-riding in a competitive market structure: second-movers had better simply follow the successful route of the first-movers, and first-movers (who should avoid free-riders) have to build uniqueness of their own brands in order to disconnect them from their followers.

## REFERENCES

Aaker, David A. and Kevin Lane Keller (1990), "Consumer Evaluations of Brand Extensions," *Journal of Marketing*, 54 (1), 27-41.

Barone, Michael J., Paul W. Miniard, and Jean B. Romeo (2000), "The Influence of Positive Mood on Brand Extension Evaluations," *Journal of Consumer Research*, 26 (March), 386-400.

Boush, David M and Barbara Loken (1991), "A Process-Tracing Study of Brand Extension Evaluation," *Journal of Marketing Research*, 28 (1), 16-28.

Boush, David M., S. Shipp, Barbara Loken, E. Gencturk, S. Crockett, E. Kennedy, B. Minshall, D. Misurell, L. Rochford, and J. Strobel (1987), "Affect Generalization to Similar and Dissimilar Brand Extensions," *Psychology & Marketing*, 225-37.

Broniarczyk, Susan M. and Joseph W. Alba (1994), "The Importance of the Brand in Brand Extension," *Journal of Consumer Research*, 31 (May), 214-28.

Gentner, Dedre (1983), "Structure Mapping: A Theoretical Framework for Analogy," *Cognitive Science*, 7, 155-70.

_____ (1989), "The Mechanisms of Analogical Transfer," in *Similarity and Analogical Reasoning*, ed. S. Vosniadou and A. Ortony, Cambridge: Cambridge University Press, 199-241.

Gregan-Paxton, Jennifer and Deborah Roedder John (1997), "Consumer Learning by Analogy: A Model of Internal Knowledge Transfer," *Journal of Consumer Research*, 24 (December), 266-84.

Keller, Kevin Lane (2002), "Branding and Brand Equity," in *Handbook of Marketing*, ed. B. A. Weitz and R. Wensley, London: Sage, 151-78.

Kim, Hakkyun and Deborah Roedder John (2008), "Consumer Response to Brand Extensions: Construal Level as a Moderator of the Importance of Perceived Fit," *Journal of Consumer Psychology*, 18 (2), 116-26.

Loken, Barbara and Deborah Roedder John (1993), "Diluting Brand Beliefs: When Do Brand Extensions Have a Negative Impact?," *Journal of Marketing*, 57 (3), 71-84.

Monga, Alokparna Basu and Deborah Roedder John (2007), "Cultural Differences in Brand Extension Evaluation: The Influence of Analytic Versus Holistic Thinking," *Journal of Consumer Research*, 33 (March), in press.

Moreau, C. Page, Arthur B. Markman, and Donald R. Lehmann (2001), "'What Is It?' Categorization Flexibility and Consumers' Responses to Really New Products," *Journal of Consumer Research*, 27 (March), 489-98.

Mortimer, Ruth (2003), "Fool's Gold for Marketers?," *Brand Strategy*, 168 (February), 20-22.

Ng, Sokling and Michael J. Houston (2006), "Exemplars or Beliefs? The Impact of Self-View on the Nature and Relative Influence of Brand Associations," *Journal of Consumer Research*, 32 (March), 519-29.

Oakley, James, Adam Duhachek, Bala Balachander, and S Sriram (2008), "Order of Entry and the Moderating Role of Comparison Brands in Brand Extension Evaluation," *Journal of Consumer Research*, 34 (February), 706-12.

Roehm, Michelle L. and Brian Sternthal (2001), "The Moderating Effect of Knowledge and Resources on the Persuasive Impact of Analogies," *Journal of Consumer Research*, 28 (September), 257-72.

Völckner, Franziska and Henrik Sattler (2006), "Drivers of Brand Extension Success," *Journal of Marketing*, 70 (April), 18-34.

# Perceived Entitativity and Accessibility-Diagnosticity As Moderators of Reciprocal Extension Effects

Joseph W. Chang, Paul R Jackson, Yung-Chien Lou

## EXTENDED ABSTRACT

### Conceptualization

Social cognition research has paid considerable attention to the influence of two characteristics of social groups on how they are perceived (e.g., Crawford, Sherman, and Hamilton 2002; Lickel, Hamilton, Wieczorkowska, Lewis, Sherman and Uhles 2000), namely variability and entitativity. As the cognitive processes underlying the evaluations of objects and subjects are common (Loken 2006), it is expected that at least some influences on the perception of social groups apply also to the perception of family brands, which suggests that the feedback effects of brand extensions on high- and low-entitative family brands may also be disproportionate. However, relatively little empirical research has investigated this important issue. Therefore, in addition to categorical similarity and perceived variability, this study moves a further step to examine how family brand entitativity mediates feedback extension effects on its subsequent family brand evaluations. Crawford and colleagues (2002) proposes the model of group-level trait transference (GLTT; Figure 1) to discuss the influence of individual members on the group and other group members. In the GLTT model, perceived entitativity serves as a pre-determinant of a three-stage information processing: trait abstraction (or trait inference), stereotyping (or group impression formation), and trait generalization (or trait transference). As with social groups, the attribute transference across brand extensions is more likely to occur for high-entitative family brands and induces asymmetric effects on family brand evaluations. Given the same quality of brand extensions, high-entitative family brands shall be more favorably evaluated than low-entitative family brands because perceivers make more extreme judgments and form more disproportional polarized impressions on high-entitative groups (Hamilton and Sherman 1996; Sherman et al. 1999). Therefore, a high- (vs. low-) entitative family brand is more favorably evaluated (Hypothesis 1). Based on the cue-diagnosticity model (Skowronski and Carlston 1987), as extreme cues receive more weight on impression formation (e.g., Anderson 1981), the diagnostic cue of positive extension information is perceived as more extreme to, and will have more positive impacts on, a low-entitative family brand, which yields extremity and positivity biases (e.g., Skowronski and Carlston 1987). In contrast, the diagnostic cue of negative extension information is perceived as more extreme to, and will have more negative impacts on, a high-entitative family brand, which yields extremity and negativity biases. In other words, a low-entitative (or moderate-quality) family brand is expected to be more significantly enhanced by positive extension information, whereas a high-entitative (or high-quality) family brand is expected to be more significantly diluted by negative extension information. This result yields asymmetric (or disproportionate) impacts of positive and negative extension information on family brand evaluations, which is likely mediated by the prior perceived entitativity of family brands. Hence, low- (vs. high-) entitative family brands are more significantly enhanced by positive extension information (hypothesis 2), whereas high- (vs. low-) entitative family brands are more significantly diluted by negative extension information (hypothesis 3).

### Method

Two studies were conducted to examine the hypotheses under highly and lowly accessible conditions respectively. For the first study (the high accessibility condition), following previous research (e.g., Loken and John 1993), two fictitious XXX (high-entitative) and YYY (low-entitative) family brands in Consumer Reports' format were portrayed representing high- and low-entitative family brands respectively. Anti-cavity toothpastes and pain relievers were selected as similar and dissimilar brand extensions respectively based on a pre-test which requested respondents to list possible similar and dissimilar brand extensions of the hypothesized family brands. The research design of the second study was similar to the first study, except intervening tasks were added to manipulate the low accessibility of brand extension information. The accessibility of extension information was manipulated by varying the intervening material between the experimental treatment of extension information and family brand evaluations. The intervening materials were confusing tasks designed to decrease the accessibility of experimental treatments (e.g., Feldman and Lynch 1988) including a filler task and a confusing task.

### Major findings

The study's results indicated that, when extension information was highly accessible, family brand images were enhanced and diluted by positive and negative extension information respectively, regardless of the categorical similarity of brand extension and the perceived entitativity of family brand. However, while both high- and low-entitative family brands were enhanced and diluted by positive and negative extension information respectively, the dilution and enhancement effects on high-entitative family brands were different from those on low-entitative family brands. High- (vs. low-) entitative family brands were more significantly diluted by negative extension information (H2), whereas low- (vs. high-) entitative family brands were more significantly enhanced by positive extension information (H3). The asymmetric result was caused by the polarization effect of perceived entitativity on family brand evaluations. Based on the GLTT model, attribute transference should be more significant for high-entitative family brands. The abstracted attributes of high-entitative family brands transferred across brand extensions and, eventually, associated with each individual brand extension. The strongly associated attributes across brand extensions amplified consumers' impressions about the attributes of high-entitative family brands and led to the result that high-entitative family brands were more favorably evaluated (H1). The research results of the second study paralleled the first study. However, by comparisons, highly accessible positive extension information was more diagnostic and, thus, more enhancive than lowly accessible extension information on family brand evaluations, while highly and lowly accessible negative extension information yielded similar dilution effects on family brand evaluations. In conclusion, except the factor of categorical similarity, the determination about the dilution and enhancement of brand extension information on family brands pretty much depended on the cue-diagnosticity of extension information, rather than the accessibility.

## REFERENCES

Ahluwalia, Rohini and Zeynep Gurhan-Canli (2000), "The Effects of Extensions on the Family Brand Name: An Accessibility-Diagnosticity Perspective," *Journal of Consumer Research*, 27 (December), 371-381.

Anderson, N. H. (1981), *Foundations of Information Integration Theory*. New York: Academic Press.

Brewer, M. B. (1988), "A Dual Process Model of Impression Formation," in *Advances in Social Cognition*, Vol. 1, T. K. Srull and R. S. Wyer, eds. Hillsdale, NJ: Erlbaum.

Brewer, M. B. and A. S. Harasty (1996), "Seeing Groups as Entities: The Role of Perceiver Motivation," in *Handbook of Motivation and Cognition*, Vol. 3, E. T. Higgins and R. M. Sorrentino eds. New York: Guilford Press, 347-370.

Campbell, D. T. (1958), "Common Fate, Similarity, and Other Indices of the Status of Aggregates of Persons as Social Entities," *Behavioral Science*, Vol. 3, 14-25.

Crawford, M. T., S. J. Sherman, and D. L. Hamilton (2002), "Perceived Entitativity, Stereotype Formation, and the Interchangeability of Group Members," *Journal of Personality and Social Psychology*, 83 (5), 1076-1094.

Feldman, Jack M. and John G. Lynch (1988), "Self-Generated Validity and Other Effects of Measurement on Belief, Attitude, Intention, and Behavior," *Journal of Applied Psychology*, Vol. 73 (August), 421-435.

Fiske, S. T. and S. L. Neuberg (1990), "A Continuum of Impression Formation, from Category-Based to Individuating Processes: Influences of Information and Motivation on Attention and Interpretation," in *Advances in Experimental Social Psychology*, Vol. 23, M. P. Zanna, ed. New York, NY: Academic Press, 1-74.

Gaertner, L. and J. Schopler (1998), "Perceived Ingroup Entitativity and Intergroup Bias: An Interconnection of Self and Others," *European Journal of Social Psychology*, 28, 963-980.

Gurhan-Canli Z (2003), "The effect of expected variability of product quality and attribute uniqueness on family brand evaluations," *Journal of Consumer Research,* 30, 105-114.

Hamilton, D. L. and S. J. Sherman (1996), "Perceiving Persons and Groups," *Psychological Review*, Vol. 103, 336-355.

Hamilton, D.L., S.J. Sherman, and J.S. Rodgers (2003), "Perceiving the groupness of groups: Entitativity, homogeneity, essentialism, and stereotypes," in Yzerbyt V, Judd CM, and O. Corneille (Eds). *The Psychology of Group Perception: Contributions to the Study of Homogeneity, Entitativity, and Essentialism*. Philadelphia, PA: Psychology Press, 39-60.

Lickel, B., D. L. Hamilton, G. Wieczorkowska, A. C. Lewis, S. J. Sherman, and A. N. Uhles (2000), "Varieties of Groups and the Perception of Group Entitativity," *Journal of Personality and Social Psychology*, Vol. 78, 223-246.

Loken B (2006), "Consumer psychology: Categorization, inferences, affect, and persuasion," *Annual Review of Psychology,* 57 (January), 453-485.

Loken, Barbara and Deborah Roedder John (1993), "Diluting Brand Beliefs: When Do Brand Extensions Have a Negative Impact?" *Journal of Marketing*, Vol. 57 (July), 71-84.

Milberg, S.J. and F. Sinn (2008), "Vulnerability of global brands to negative feedback effects," *Journal of Business Research* 2008, 61(June), 684-690.

Rosch, E. (1978), "Principles of Categorization", In *Cognition and Categorization*, E. Rosch and B. B. Lloyd, eds. Hillsdale, NJ: Erlbaum, 27-48.

Salinas, E.M. and J.M.P. Perez (2009), "Modeling the brand extensions' influence on brand image," *Journal of Business Research,* 62(January), 50-60.

Sherman, S. J., D. L. Hamilton, and A. C. Lewis (1999), "Perceived Entitativity and the Social Identity Value of Group Membership," in *Social Identity and Social Cognition*, D. Abrams and M. Hogg, eds. Oxford, UK: Blackwell, 80-110.

Skowronski, John J. and Donal E. Carlston (1987), "Social Judgment and Social Memory: The Role of Cue Diagnosticity in Negativity, Positivity, and Extremity Biases," *Journal of Personality and Social Psychology*, Vol. 52(4), 689-699.

# Can Brand Commitment be Harmful to the Brand? The Moderating Role of Psychological Contracts

Sekar Raju, Iowa State University, USA
Kalpesh Kaushik Desai, State University of New York at Binghamton, USA
H. Rao Unnava, Ohio State University, USA
Nicole Montgomery, College of William and Mary, USA

## EXTENDED ABSTRACT

Research on brand commitment has typically focused on the benefits that commitment provides in protecting the brand when brand failures occur (e.g., Ahluwalia 2007; Ahluwalia, et al. 2000; Raju and Unnava 2008). However, recent research has found that committed consumers may pose risks for brands, especially when brand failures occur. Researchers have found that when a brand fails to live up to some expected standard, committed consumers under certain circumstances are likely to retaliate, seek revenge, and change from loving the brand to hating it (Aaker, Fournier, and Brasel 2004; Gregoire, Tripp, and Legoux 2009). A possible reason that consumers in strong relationships turn around and retaliate against something they love might have to do with the belief that in such relationships the other partner (in our case, the brand) is obligated to them more than in weak relationships (Ward and Ostrom 2006).

We suggest that it is not the failure itself but the nature of the failure that leads consumers to support or not support the brand. That is, we propose that failures that violate perceived pacts or "psychological contracts" between the consumer and the brand create a greater likelihood of retaliation, while failures that do not violate such perceived pacts lead to support for the brand. The term psychological contract refers to the beliefs that a consumer has about the reciprocal obligations that exist between the consumer and the brand. These beliefs are based on perceived promises that the consumer deems the brand has made to them in return for their patronage of the brand (Rousseau 1989).

We argue that consumers committed to a brand are voluntarily restricting their consideration set by being psychologically tied to a brand and excluding other brands (Raju and Unnava 2005). Because committed consumers give up something, they are likely to believe that the brand owes them more than consumers who are less committed (Gregoire et al. 2009). Because committed consumers saddle brands with this reciprocal obligation, we propose that committed consumers are likely to have many more items in their psychological contract with the target brand compared than less committed consumers.

H1: Committed consumers will report more items in their psychological contracts than less committed consumers.

Further, if committed consumers believe that the brand is contractually obligated to perform at some level and it fails to do so, they will view the failure as a breach of the contract. However, as reviewed earlier, others have found that brand commitment also offers brands a buffering effect from negative information (Ahluwalia et al. 2000). We resolve this apparent discrepancy in the literature by arguing that committed consumers feel betrayed only when the brand failure relates to a feature that is part of the psychological contract (henceforth called "in-contract"). When the brand failure relates to a feature that is outside the psychological contract (henceforth called "out-of-contract"), we expect that the buffering effects of commitment will occur. In contrast, less committed consumers do not have as strong a tie to the brand as committed consumers; therefore, we do not anticipate any differences in their responses to a brand failure regardless of whether they classify the failure as in-contract or out-of-contract

H2: Committed consumers will rate in-contract violations less favorably than out-of-contract violations.
H3: Less committed consumers will rate both in-contract and out-of-contract violations unfavorably.

## Study 1

The objective of this study is to demonstrate that consumers who are more versus less committed to a brand will exhibit differences in the contents of their psychological contracts with a preferred brand. Participants either high or low in commitment to an existing brand in each of the two categories (online store and bank) participated (n=201). For each category, participants were asked to provide the name of their preferred brand, after which they were presented with the list of promise items obtained from a pretest. For each item on the list, respondents were asked to report the extent to which their preferred brand promised them each item using a four-point scale obtained from Conway and Briner (2005).

Consistent with the idea that psychological contracts exist and their contents differ for high versus low commitment consumers, the analysis revealed a different pattern of results for high versus low commitment participants for online stores and banks. Specifically, a larger percentage of high versus low commitment consumers indicated that their preferred brand either strongly suggested the promise of the item or explicitly promised the item in writing or verbally.

## Study 2

This study directly tests whether a violation of an item in the psychological contract versus outside of the psychological contract results in different effects for high and low commitment consumers. A 2 (commitment: high or low) x 2 (contract item violation: in-contract vs. out-of-contract) between-participants design was implemented.

Participants were presented with a description of a barbershop/hair salon that included a brand failure (i.e., unexpected price increase) and to two filler consumption descriptions. The primary dependent variable was their evaluation of a fictitious competitive barbershop/salon.

Our expectation was that high commitment consumers would evaluate the competitive brand more favorably if their preferred brand's failure pertained to an item in-contract versus out-of-contract. However, we expected low commitment consumers to evaluate the competitive brand equivalently, regardless of their inclusion of the violation item in their contract. Consistent with our expectations, this analysis revealed a significant interaction $(F (1, 205)=4.46, p<.05)$. Low commitment participants that reported that "competitive prices" was not an item in their contract $(M=5.39)$ evaluated the competitive brand equivalently to participants that reported that the item was part of their contracts $(M=5.23, t (103)=0.68, p>.1)$, supporting H3. However, high commitment participants evaluated the new brand more favorably when the violation item was included in their contract $(M=5.37)$ versus not perceived as part of their psychological contract $(M=4.81, t (104)=2.30, p<.05)$, supporting H2.

The results of the two studies support the idea that the nature of the brand failure-whether it is in-contract or out-of-contract has a major role to play in determining whether committed consumers support or respond negatively to a brand failure.

# Got to Get You into My Life: Do Brand Personalities Rub Off on Consumers?

Ji Kyung Park, University of Minnesota, USA
Deborah Roedder John, University of Minnesota, USA

## EXTENDED ABSTRACT

Consumers often use brands as an instrument to create a more positive self-image. In particular, brands with appealing personalities, such as Cartier (sophisticated) and Harley-Davidson (adventurous), are particularly useful for consumers wanting to enhance a self-image in line with a brand's personality (Escalas and Bettman 2003). In this research, we ask the question, "*Does using a brand with an appealing personality enhance the way consumers view themselves?*" Prior research documents that consumers often prefer and choose brands in an effort to affirm and enhance their sense of self, but what happens when consumers actually have an opportunity to use these brands?

We propose that *only* consumers with certain implicit theories view brand experiences as opportunities to signal that they possess the same appealing traits as the brand, and *only* these consumers actually perceive themselves more positively after a brand experience. Implicit self-theories are lay beliefs people hold about the malleability of their personalities. Two types have been identified: entity versus incremental theory (Dweck 2000). Individuals who endorse incremental theory ("incremental theorists") view their personal qualities as something they can enhance through their own direct efforts at self-improvement. In contrast, individuals who endorse entity theory ("entity theorists") view their personal qualities as something they cannot improve their own direct efforts. Instead, they seek out opportunities to signal their positive qualities to the self or others. We predict and find that entity theorists (not incremental theorists) are responsive to the signaling value of brands with appealing personalities. They use a brand associated with an appealing personality to signal that they possess the same appealing personality as the brand, resulting in more positive self-perceptions.

## Study 1: Does Victoria's Secret Make You Feel Better-Looking?

Consumers at a local shopping mall were asked to use a Victoria's Secret shopping bag (*brand experience*) or a plain pink shopping bag (*no brand experience*) during their shopping trip. This setting provided an initial test of our proposition in a natural environment where consumers could experience the signaling value of a brand through a common activity of carrying a shopping bag. Victoria's Secret was selected because of its appealing brand personality, associated with traits such as good-looking, feminine, and glamorous. Implicit beliefs about personality were measured (Implicit Persons Theory Measure: Levy et. al. 1998) prior to the shopping trip, with self-perceptions regarding personality traits (including those associated with Victoria's Secret) measured after the shopping trip.

After carrying the Victoria's Secret shopping bag (vs. plain pink shopping bag), entity theorists perceived themselves to be better-looking, more feminine, and more glamorous. However, incremental theorists were not influenced by their brand experience. Differences between these groups were not evident for personality traits unconnected to the Victoria's Secret brand, which rules out response biases, general affective states, and contextual factors as possible alternative explanations.

## Study 2: Why Are Entity Theorists More Affected by Brand Personalities?

Study 2 extends prior findings by: (1) manipulating implicit self-theories to rule out the possibility that individuals who endorse entity or incremental theories may also vary on other dimensions that influence response to brand experiences; and (2) examining the mediating process for why entity theorists, but not incremental theorists, are affected by brand experiences. Female undergraduate students were asked to participate in treasure hunt. To collect items during the treasure hunt, they used a Victoria's Secret shopping bag or a plain pink shopping bag. After using the shopping bag, participants were asked about their self-perceptions on traits associated with Victoria's Secret, and were also asked how much they used Victoria's Secret as signals of one's identity.

The results replicated the findings from study1. Further, a mediation analysis revealed that relative to incremental theorists, entity theorists are more responsive to the signaling value of the Victoria's Secret brand experience and this difference mediates the influence of implicit self-theory on self-perceptions.

## Study 3: Can Entity Theorists Recover From Self-threats Using Brand Personalities?

Entity theorists view personal qualities as something that they cannot directly improve through their own direct efforts. Dweck and her colleagues suggest that such pessimistic thinking about self-improvement reduces emotional and psychological resources available to cope with negative feedback on personal qualities. In study 3, we examined whether or not entity theorists can recover a threatened self through experiences with a brand associated with an appealing personality in a threat-related domain. After receiving negative feedback on a GRE test, participants were asked to use either a MIT pen or a regular pen, and then completed the self-perception measure.

The results showed that entity theorists recovered negative self-views after brand experiences; they perceived themselves to be more intelligent, harder-working, and more of a leader after using the MIT pen (vs. the regular pen).

## Summary

We identify implicit self-theories as an important moderator of the influence of brand experiences on consumer self-perceptions. Only entity theorists view use a brand associated with an appealing personality to signal that they possess the same appealing personality as the brand, resulting in more positive self-perceptions.

## REFERENCES

Dweck, Carol S. (2000), Self-Theories: Their Role in Motivation, Personality and Development, Philadelphia: Psychology Press.

Escalas, Jennifer E. and James R. Bettman (2003), "You Are What They Eat: The Influence of Reference Groups on Consumers' Connections to Brands," Journal of Consumer Psychology, 13 (3), 339-48.

Levy, Sheri R., Steven J. Stroessner, and Carol S. Dweck (1998), "Stereotype Formation and Endorsement: The Role of Implicit Theories," Journal of Personality and Social Psychology, 74 (6), 1421-36.

# It's all about THE GREENS: Conflicting Motives and Making Green Work

Kelly Haws, Texas A&M University, USA
Karen Page Winterich, Pennsylvania State University, USA
Rebecca Walker Naylor, Ohio State University, USA

## EXTENDED ABSTRACT

Consumers frequently encounter decisions regarding whether to purchase environmentally-friendly products in place of more traditional products (e.g., reusable vs. plastic grocery bags, non-toxic, biodegradable cleaners). While there has been an increasing emphasis on green attributes of products in the marketplace, the potential goal conflicts of engaging in environmentally-friendly purchases are not well understood. We seek to determine how to identify green consumers, whom we define as those with a tendency to consider the environmental impact of their purchase and consumption behaviors, and distinguish their preferences from those of non-green consumers to aid the marketing of green products, considering both product positioning and product pricing.

Though there have been several efforts at identifying green consumers (e.g., Antil 1984; Roberts 1995; Webb, Mohr, and Harris 2008; Webster 1975 over the last few decades, such efforts have led to rather complex and often dated measures. We present a parsimonious, yet valid measure of green consumer attitudes, enabling managers and marketers to better determine potential responses to green-related efforts based on their consumer base. In doing so, we focus on characteristics of consumers that might provide underlying motivations for green consumption. Specifically, we expect those who are more green to be more conscientious of their monetary resources and more careful users of physical resources.

*Study 1.* We first develop a simple six-item measure to succinctly capture green attitudes. We find our measure correlates positively with socially responsible consumption behavior (r=.69; Antil 1984) and negatively with environmental claims skepticism (Mohr et al. 1998) and hindrances to buying green (adapted from Harris Interactive 2008). A separate follow-up study using an adult panel further validates the GREEN measure.

We also assess the relationship of green attitudes with both monetary and nonmonetary resources. Regarding monetary resources, consumers demonstrating a higher level of GREEN were also found to be more frugal, more self-controlled, and more value and price conscious suggesting that consumers who express green attitudes are also quite sensitive to the wise use of financial resources. For physical resource consumption, product retention tendency and use innovativeness were positively related to GREEN, suggesting that consumers with strong green attitudes are also reluctant to discard of possessions and likely to find new ways to use existing possessions.

*Study 2.* We examined the extent to which GREEN predicted behavioral intentions and product choice. Measuring GREEN three weeks in advance of reported behaviors and choice, results indicated participants choosing a reusable grocery bag (green option; n=99) had a higher average green score than those choosing the pens (non-green option; M=4.23 vs. 3.70, F(1, 235)=11.68, p<.001). GREEN was also positively correlated (r=.73) with reported likelihood of engaging in eight green behaviors such as recycling (adapted from Straughan and Roberts 1999).This study provides evidence that our simple measure of GREEN predicts behavioral intentions and actual behaviors.

*Study 3.* Though high GREEN consumers conserve monetary and physical resources, they also value environmentally-friendly products. Goldsmith and Dhar (2008) state that green products can be positioned based on two distinct dimensions: self benefits (gentle on your skin) or earth benefits (save the planet). If costs are equal, consumers with higher green attitudes are likely to be more concerned with earth (vs. self) benefits.

To test the effect of benefit framing, students responded to the 6-item green scale and were later asked to view an advertisement for a new natural dish washing liquid and indicate their purchase likelihood. The benefits of the product were described as leaving your dishes clean and shiny and helping to protect and soothe your skin (self benefits) or as posing no threat of harm to the environment and contributing to a healthier planet (earth benefits).

Results revealed an interaction such that the earth (vs. self) framing increased purchase likelihood among consumers high in GREEN whereas purchase likelihood did not differ among low GREEN consumers regardless of benefit framing. For GREEN consumers, positioning a green product with earth benefits is more effective than positioning with benefits for oneself, which may be of particular importance to marketers who may decrease green purchases if they attempt to capture a larger share of the market by emphasizing self benefits.

*Study 4.* In our final study, we directly examine the inherent conflict between the economic and the green motivations of consumers by examining environmental products with a price premium. Though we anticipate that green consumers will be more accepting of price premiums than will nongreen consumers, products that meet goals of both greenness and frugality will be most favorably received by consumers pursuing these multiple goals.

Student participants completed the 6-item GREEN scale in a battery of unrelated items and then completed the main study a week later. The main study consisted of a one-factor (price premium: none vs. 20% premium for more green product) between-subjects design. Participants were shown two laundry detergents which were identical except that one received an excellent environmental score whereas the alternative product received an average environmental rating. In the no premium condition, the two products were the same price, whereas in the price premium condition, the green product (high rating) was listed at 20% higher. Respondents indicated which of the two products they preferred on a 9-point scale.

Results indicated, as expected, an interaction of GREEN and price premium condition such that GREEN consumers are more likely to prefer premium-priced green products than are non-GREEN consumers. However, both GREEN and non-GREEN consumers significantly prefer the equally-priced green option. The significant decline in the price premium condition, even among GREEN consumers, demonstrates their value on both environmental and economic goals. Though important to equalize price of green products as much as possible, these results indicate there is a segment of consumers willing to pay the premium for green.

Clearly, understanding the multiple motivations underlying consumers' decisions regarding green products will help managers better market their environmentally-friendly alternatives. Furthermore, theoretical insights are provided by considering the goal conflict inherent in valuing green products while valuing conservation of monetary resources.

## REFERENCES

Antil, John H. (1984), "Socially Responsible Consumers: Profile and Implications for Public Policy," *Journal of Macromarketing*, 5 (2), 18-39.

Goldsmith, Kelly and Ravi Dhar (2008), "Getting Gold by Going Green: The Importance of Fitting the Message to the Mindset," *Advances in Consumer Research*. 36, eds. Ann L. McGill and Sharon Shavitt, Duluth, MN: Association for Consumer Research.

Mohr, Lois A., Dogan Eroglu, and Pam Scholder Ellen (1998), "The Development and Testing of a Measure of Skepticism Toward Environmental Claims in Marketers' Communications," *Journal of Consumer Affairs,* 32 (1), 30-56.

Roberts, James A. (1995), "Profiling Levels of Socially Responsible Consumer Behavior: A Cluster Analytic Approach and its Implications for Marketing," *Journal of Marketing Theory & Practice,* 3 (4), 97-118.

Straughan, Robert D. and James A. Roberts (1999), "Environmental Segmentation Alternatives: A Look at Green Consumer Behavior in the New Millenium," *Journal of Consumer Marketing*, 16 (6), 558-575.

Webb, Deborah J., Lois A. Mohr, and Katherine E. Harris (2008), "A Re-Examination of Socially Responsible Consumption and Its Measurement," *Journal of Business Research*, 61 (2), 91-98.

Webster, Frederick E. Jr. (1975), "Determining Characteristics of the Socially Conscious Consumer," *Journal of Consumer Research*, 2 (3), 188-196.

# Green Requests: Issue Importance and Compliance with Assertive Language

Ann Kronrod, Ben-Gurion University, Israel
Amir Grinstein, Ben-Gurion University, Israel
Luc Wathieu, ESMT, Germany

## EXTENDED ABSTRACT

### Background

While any request limits the freedom of the addressee (Brown and Levinson, 1987), assertive language is even more restricting, as it leaves the addressee an even smaller option for refusal (Searle, 1969; Vanderveken 1990). Consequently, as it is shown in previous research, assertive message phrasings typically decrease compliance with the message, compared with non-assertive messages (e.g., Dillard and Shen 2005; Edwards, Li, and Lee 2002; Quick and Considine 2008). However, some counterintuitive findings (e.g. Buller, Borland, and Burgoon 1998) imply that compliance with assertive language can be elevated in situations of higher issue importance.

We show this general phenomenon, employing the example of messages which relate to environmental behavior. Issue importance plays a great role in consumer's reaction to environmental campaigns because environmental issues bear a non-personal character and therefore are generally less close to the consumer's heart. While the common finding is that assertive environmental messages result in low compliance (e.g., Lord 1994; Shrum, Lowrey, and McCarty 1994), many environment-related issues are being promoted aggressively through assertive messages such as "*Use only what you need!*"–the Denver water economy campaign.

We suggest that issue importance not only diminishes non-compliance with assertive messages, but even leads to higher compliance with assertive messages than with non-assertive ones. The key reason for this suggestion is that when an issue is important, an assertive message supports one's attitude, while a non-assertive request may have the opposite influence as it implies a non-serious attitude toward the issue. Thus, we hypothesize that when an issue is considered important and the message is assertive, the fit between message phrasing and consumer's attitude leads to higher compliance. A non-assertive message in this situation would contradict consumer's ends and yield lower compliance. However, if an issue is not deemed important, a non-assertive message would be a higher fit than and assertive one, resulting in higher compliance with a non-assertive message.

## METHOD

### Study 1–Field Study

The purpose of the study was to measure compliance with an assertive versus a non-assertive ad as an effect of issue importance. To meet our hypothesis we created a 2 (assertiveness) by 2 (issue importance) design in the following way:

Assertiveness manipulation: We placed two sponsored links in Google Adwords advertising system, calling viewers to sign a petition to save the Mediterranean Sea: one assertive (*You must save the Mediterranean Sea!*) and one non-assertive (*You could save the Mediterranean Sea.*)

Issue importance conditioning: Two types of search words were identified: Sea-related (e.g. Mediterranean Sea pollution) and General (e.g. knitting machines). We relied on the assumption that people who type a sea-related search word deem higher importance to sea pollution than people who type in a general word.

We then compared the number of clicks on each of the ads, following a general or a sea-related search word. In line with our prediction, we found significantly higher ratio of clicking the assertive ad after typing in a sea related search word, and significantly higher clicking on the non-assertive ad after typing in a general search word.

### Studies 2 and 3

In order to support our socio-linguistic explanation which involves issue importance, we conducted two studies which were similar in their 2 by 2 design, but different in type of behavior and in operationalization.

Study 1 used an assertive and a non-assertive message regarding an important (water economy) and an unimportant (recycling plastic containers) issue for the specific society we examined (www.hh-law.co.il). Participants (N=102) were exposed to a short and simple message, which was either assertive or non-assertive and related either to water economy or to recycling plastic containers. The assertive message read: "*You must economize water/recycle plastic containers.*" The non-assertive message read: "*It's worth economizing water/recycling plastic containers.*" After reading the message participants filled out a questionnaire which measured issue importance and compliance intention. Results revealed a significantly higher compliance intention with the assertive message vs. a non-assertive message calling for water economy. As predicted, for recycling messages there was no difference in compliance intentions between people who read an assertive and a non-assertive message.

Study 2 manipulated issue importance by addressing two different groups: low issue importance (students of Business school, N=53) vs. high issue importance (students of Agriculture and Environment, N=52). Assertiveness was manipulated using the recycling related materials from Study 1. Our results showed an interaction for assertiveness and issue importance: while for Business students there was no difference in compliance as an effect of assertiveness, Environment students showed significantly higher compliance intentions with an assertive recycling message than with a non-assertive one.

### Study 4

We hypothesized that the effect of compliance with an assertive message can be created by temporarily elevating issue importance. This is an important point because of its practical implications. In this study we temporarily elevated issue importance using a clip about air pollution. Participants (N=146) were divided into two groups: one group first completed a general environmental issue importance questionnaire, then saw the clip, and then completed an air-pollution issue importance questionnaire and compliance intention questions. The second group filled out all three measures in a row.

Results: While the groups did not differ in general environmental issue importance, the group that saw the clip showed significantly higher air-pollution issue importance. This evidence implies that issue importance can indeed be temporally elevated. Further, the group that saw the clip revealed significantly higher compliance intention with the assertive pollution message than with the non-assertive message, while the group that did not see the clip revealed no difference in compliance intention. These results suggest that even a temporarily elevated issue importance can affect compliance with assertive environmental messages.

## Summary

When compliance is the goal, issue importance appears to be a central variable in determining message phrasing. This is true not only for environmental issues, but also in health related promotion (e.g. sunscreen usage), and possibly even in encouraging the public to pay taxes regularly. We therefore hope to further explore this general and straightforward mechanism of the influence of issue importance on perception of assertive requests.

## REFERENCES

Albarracin, Dolores, Joel Cohen B., and Taren Kumkale G. (2003), "When Communications Collide With Recipients' Actions: Effects of Post-Message Behavior on Intentions to Follow the Message Recommendation," *Personality and Social Psychology Bulletin*, 29 (July), 834-45.

Archakis, Argiris and Papazachariou, Dimitris (2008), "Prosodic Cues of Identity Construction: Intensity in Greek Young Women's Conversational Narratives," *Journal of Sociolinguistics*, 12(5), 627-47.

Buller, David B., Ron Borland, and Michael Burgoon (1998), "Impact of behavioral intention on effectiveness of message features: Evidence from the Family Sun Safety Project," *Human Communication Research*, 24(3), 433-53.

Chandran, Sucharita and Vicki Morwitz G. (2005), "Effects of Participative Pricing on Consumers' Cognitions and Actions: A Goal Theoretic Perspective," *Journal of Consumer Research*, 32(2), 249-60.

Clark, Anne R. (1993) "The Impact of Cost of Compliance, Deservingness of Aid, and Directness of Request on Reactions to the Request," *The Southern Communication Journal*, 58(3), 215-26.

Clark, *Thomas* (1998), "The Impact of Candid versus Legally Defensible *Language* on the Persuasiveness of *Environmental* Self-Assessments," *The Journal of Business Communication*, 35(3), 368-83.

Cleveland, Mark, Maria Kalamas, and Michel Laroche (2005), "Shades of Green:

Linking Environmental Locus of Control and pro-Environmental Behaviors," *The Journal of Consumer Marketing*, 22(4), 198-212.

Dillard, James P. and Shen, Lijiang (2005), "On the Nature of Reactance and Its Role in Persuasive Health Communication," *Communication Monographs, 72*, 144-168.

Edwards, Steven M., Hairong Li, and Joo-Hyun Lee (2002), "Forced Exposure and Psychological Reactance: Antecedents and Consequences of the Perceived Instrusiveness of Pop-Up Ads," *Journal of Advertising*, 31(Fall), 83-95.

Fazio, Russ H. (1995), "Attitudes as Object-Evaluation Associations: Determinants, Consequences, and Correlates of Attitude Accessibility," In R. E. Petty J. A. Krosnick (Eds.), Attitude Strength: Antecedents and consequences (pp. 247-82). Hillsdale, NJ: Erlbaum.

Goldstein, Noah J., Robert Cialdini B., and Vladas Griskevicius (2008), "Norms to Motivate Environmental Conservation in Hotels," *Journal of Consumer Research*, 35(3), 472-82.

Grandpre, Joseph, Eusebio Alvaro M., Michael Burgoon, Claude Miller H., and John Hall R. (2003), "Adolescent Reactance and Anti-Smoking Campaigns: A Theoretical Approach," *Health Communication*, 15, 349-66.

Granzin, Kent and Janeen Olsen (1991), "Characterizing Participants in Activities Protecting the Environment: A Focus on Donating, Recycling, and Conservation Behaviors," *Journal of Public Policy and Marketing*, 10(2), 1-27.

Grinstein, Amir and Nisan, Udi (2009), "Demarketing, Minorities and Marketing Attachment," *Journal of Marketing*, 73(2), 105-122.

Lakoff, Robin T. and Sachiko Ide (eds.), *Broadening the Horizon of Linguistic Politeness*. (Pragmatics and Beyond New Series, 139). Amsterdam/Philadelphia: John Benjamins, 2005.

Levin, Irwin P., Sandra Schneider L., and Gary Gaeth J. (1998), "All Frames Are Not Created Equal: A Typology and Critical Analysis of Framing Effects," *Organizational Behavior and Human Decision Processes*, 76(2), 149-88.

Lindsey, Lisa L. Massi (2005), "Anticipated Guilt as Behavioral Motivation: An Examination of Appeals to Help Unknown Others through Bone Marrow Donation," *Human Communication Research*, 31(4), 453-81.

Lord, Kenneth R. (1994), "Motivating Recycling Behavior: A Quasiexperimental Investigation of Message and Source Strategies," *Psychology and Marketing*, 11(September), 341-59.

Marshall, *Heather M., Amber* Reinhart M., *Thomas* Feeley H., Frank Tutzauer, and Ashley Anker (2008), "Comparing College Students' Value-, Outcome-, and Impression-Relevant Involvement in Health-Related Issues," *Health Communication*, 23(2), 171-83.

Mills, Margaret (1993), "On Russian and English Pragmalinguistic Requestive Strategies," *Journal of Slavic Linguistics*, 1(1), 92-115.

Mittal, Banwari (1995), "A Comparative Analysis of Four Scales of Consumer Involvement," Psychology and Marketing, 12(7), 663-82.

Quick, Brian L. and Considine, Jennifer R. (2008), "Examining the Use of Forceful Language When Designing Exercise Persuasive Messages for Adults: A Test of Conceptualizing Reactance Arousal as a Two-Step Process," *Health Communication*, 23(September), 483-91.

Quick, Brian L. and Stephenson, *Michael T.* (2007), "Further Evidence That Psychological Reactance Can Be Modeled as a Combination of Anger and Negative Cognitions," *Communication Research*, 34(3), 255-76.

Shrum, L. J., Tina Lowrey M., and John McCarty A. (1994), "Recycling as a Marketing Problem: A Framework for Strategy Development," *Psychology and Marketing*, 11(4), 393-417.

Tsuzuki, Masaki, Miamoto Setsuko, and Zhang Qin (1999), "Politeness Degree of Imperative and Question Request Expressions: Japanese, English, Chinese," *Sixth International Colloquium on Cognitive Science*-ICCS99-proceedings.

Zhao, Guangzhi and Cornelia Pechman (2007), "The Impact of Regulatory Focus on Adolescents' Response to Antismoking Advertising Campaigns," *Journal of Marketing Research*, 44(4), 671-87.

# Green and Guilt Free: The Role of Guilt in Determining the Effectiveness of Environmental Appeals in Advertising

John Peloza, Simon Fraser University, Canada
Jingzhi Shang, Simon Fraser University, Canada
Katherine White, University of Calgary, Canada

## EXTENDED ABSTRACT

Virtually every product available on the market can boast at least some environmentally-friendly attributes. But consumer response to marketers' positioning their offerings on the basis environmental attributes–so-called *green marketing*–is relatively unstudied, and has produced equivocal results. Consumers' concern for the environment does not predict responsiveness to green marketing, or marketing communications that positions itself on the basis of environmental attributes (Schuhwerk and Lefkoff-Hagius 1995). One promising stream of research examines the role of marketing communications in stimulating consumer demand for green products. However, the efficacy of green marketing strategies remains equivocal (e.g., Kangun, Carlson and Grove 1991; Montoro-Rios, Luque-Martinez and Rodriguez-Molina 2008) and research examining how consumers can be motivated to engage in environmentally friendly actions is relatively understudied (Goldstein, Cialdini and Griskevicius 2008).

In this article we examine the process by which the implicit anticipation of guilt leads consumers to make product selections in favor of marketing communications that highlight environmentally-friendly attributes. While previous research has examined explicit guilt appeals that directly induce consumer guilt, we find that the increased prominence of environmental information in advertising is itself enough to alleviate consumer guilt in situations where guilt has been implicitly activated. Across three studies we find that consumers respond most positively to environmental appeals when the product category is hedonic in nature, when the setting is public, and when relevant social norms are activated. We find evidence that green marketing can be successful in guiding consumer choice, and that this effect is mediated through anticipatory guilt.

Study 1 used brands in a hedonic category (Chocolate: Mars and Cadbury) and utilitarian category (Soap: Dove and Ivory), each positioned via a green appeal or a performance-based appeal (e.g., taste, cleansing ingredients). Information in each appeal was held constant. The design of either appeal was based on color, images and prominence given to environmental attributes.

Participants (n=99) in the hedonic category responded more positively to the green appeal (74% chose the brand promoted through a green appeal versus 26% for the brand that used a performance-based appeal). Those in the utilitarian category responded more to the performance-based appeal (67% versus 33% for the green appeal), $\chi^2(1)=22.365$, $p<.001$. Mediation analysis to test for the role of anticipatory guilt confirms that the preference for the green appeal is based on implicit guilt related to the product category. To test for mediation through anticipatory guilt, first guilt was regressed on the product category, which was significant ($\beta=-1.996$, $t=-10.269$, $p<.001$). Next, the product choice (choice corresponding to either the green or performance-based appeal) was regressed on guilt using logistic regression, which was also significant ($\beta=-1.904$, Wald=26.124, $p<.001$). Product choice was regressed on product category, which was also significant ($\beta=-2.070$, Wald=20.456, $p<.001$), and finally product choice was regressed on both product category and guilt. Product category was no longer significant ($\beta=1.029$, Wald=1.565, $p=.211$) while guilt was highly significant ($\beta=-2.239$, Wald=22.388, $p<.001$). A Sobel test (Baron and Kenny 1986) was significant as well, $z=4.583$, $p<.001$.

Study 2 (n=119) uses the presence of others as the basis for stimulating anticipatory guilt and promoting response to green marketing appeals. Two brands of granola bars (Kellogg's and Quaker) were used, and offered to participants through either a green or performance-based appeal. Participants viewed the ads and selected products either alone or as part of a small group. As expected, those in the group condition favored the green appeals (68% versus 32% selection based on the performance-based appeal). In the alone condition, appeals were equally successful (49% green versus 51% performance-based), $\chi^2(1)=4.518$, $p=.034$.

Mediation analysis again confirms the role of anticipatory guilt in the preference for green appeals. The regression of guilt on setting (group versus alone) was significant ($\beta=-.427$, $t=-2.63$, $p=.01$), as was the regression of product choice (product corresponding to either the green or performance-based appeal) on guilt ($\beta=-.831$, Wald=10.671, $p=.001$). Product choice was regressed on setting, which was also significant ($\beta=.803$, Wald=4.452, $p=.035$), and finally product choice was regressed on both product category and guilt. Product category was no longer significant ($\beta=.570$, Wald=2.01, $p=.156$) while guilt was highly significant ($\beta=-.771$, Wald=8.95, $p=.003$). The Sobel test was significant as well, $z=2.052$, $p=.02$.

In study 3 (n=111) we manipulate the relevant social norms and seek to either stimulate perceived expectations to respond to a green appeal, or give participants "permission" to choose a product based on performance-based (i.e., self-serving) appeals. The same brands of granola from study 2 were used, but prior to the experiment participants were primed with the relevant social norm (White and Peloza 2009). As expected, green appeals were more successful in the environmental norm prime condition (64% versus 36%) but in the product performance prime, participants responded to the performance-based appeal 57% of the time, $\chi^2(1)=5.020$, $p=.025$.

Mediation analysis again confirms the role of anticipatory guilt in participants' product selection. The regression of guilt on norm manipulation (environmental versus product performance) was significant ($\beta=-.818$, $t=-4.309$, $p<.001$), as was the regression of product choice (choice corresponding to either green or performance-based appeal) on guilt ($\beta=-.526$, Wald=7.318, $p=.007$). The regression of product choice norm manipulation was significant ($\beta=.854$, Wald=4.943, $p=.026$), and finally, product choice was regressed on both product category and guilt. Product category was no longer significant ($\beta=.534$, Wald=1.653, $p=.199$) while guilt was significant ($\beta=-.433$, Wald=4.471, $p=.034$). The Sobel test was significant as well, $z=2.689$, $p=.003$.

## REFERENCES

Auger, Pat, Timothy Devinney, Jordan Louviere, and Paul Burke (2008), "Do Social Product Features Have Value to Consumers?" *International Journal of Research in Marketing*, 25 (3), 183-91.

Auger, Pat and Timothy Devinney (2007), "Do What Consumers Say Matter? The Misalignment of Preferences with Unconstrained Ethical Intentions," *Journal of Business Ethics*, 76 (4), 361-83.

Baron, Reuben M. and David A. Kenny (1986), "The Moderator-Mediator Variable Distinction in Social Psychological Research: Conceptual, Strategic, and Statistical Considerations," *Journal of Personality and Social Psychology*, 51 (6), 1173-82.

Basil, Debra Z., Nancy M. Ridgway and Michael D. Basil (2006), "Guilt Appeals: The Mediating Effect of Responsibility," *Psychology & Marketing*, 23(12), 1035-54.

Baumeister, Roy F., Harry T. Reis, and Phillipe A.E.G. Delespaul (1995), "Subjective and Experiential Correlates of Guilt in Daily Life," *Personality And Social Psychology Bulletin*, 21 (12), 1256-68.

Baumeister, Roy F., Arlene M. Stillwell, and Todd F. Heatherton (1994), "Guilt: An Interpersonal Approach," *Psychological Bulletin*, 115, 243-67.

Burnett, Melissa S. and Dale A. Lunsford (1994), "Conceptualizing Guilt in the Consumer Decision-Making Process," *Journal of Consumer Marketing*, 11 (3), 33-43.

Cotte, June, Robin A. Coulter and Melissa Moore (2005), "Enhancing or Disrupting Guilt: The Role of Ad Credibility and Perceived Manipulative Intent," *Journal of Business Research*, 58, 361-68.

Coulter, Robin A. and Mary Beth Pinto (1995), "Guilt Appeals in Advertising: What Are Their Effects?" *Journal of Applied Psychology*, 80 (6), 697-705.

Dahl, Darren W., Heather Honea and Rajesh V. Manchanda (2005), "Three Rs of Interpersonal Consumer Guilt: Relationship, Reciprocity, Reparation," *Journal of Consumer Psychology*, 15 (4), 307-15.

Dahl, Darren W., Heather Honea, and Rajesh V. Manchanda (2003), "The Nature of Self-Reported Guilt in Consumption Contexts," *Marketing Letters*, 14(3), 159-71.

Ellen, Pam Scholder, Joshua Lyle Wiener, and Cathy Cobb-Walgren (1991), "The Role of Perceived Consumer Effectiveness in Motivating Environmentally Conscious Behaviors," *Journal of Public Policy & Marketing*, 10 (2), 102-17.

Gardner, Meryl Paula (1983), "Advertising Effects on Attributes Recalled and Criteria Used for Brand Evaluations," *Journal of Consumer Research*, 10, 310-18.

Goldstein, Noah J., Robert B. Cialdini and Vladas Griskevicius (2008), "A Room With A Viewpoint: Using Social Norms to Motivate Environmental Conservation in Hotels," *Journal of Consumer Research*, 35, 472-82.

Huhmann, Bruce A. and Timothy P. Brotherton (1997), "A Content Analysis of Guilt Appeals in Popular Magazine Advertisements," *Journal of Advertising*, 26 (2), 35-45.

Kallgren, Carl A., Raymond R. Reno, and Robert B. Cialdini (2000), "A Focus Theory of Normative Conduct: When Norms Do and Do Not Affect Behavior," *Personality and Social Psychology Bulletin*, 26, 1002-12.

Kangun, Norman, Les Carlson and Stephen J. Grove (1991), "Environmental Advertising Claims: A Preliminary Investigation," *Journal of Public Policy & Marketing*, 10 (2), 47-58.

Kivetz, Ran and Itamar Simonson (2002), "Earning the Right to Indulge: Effort as a Determinant of Customer Preferences Toward Frequency Program Rewards," *Journal of Marketing Research*, 39, 155-70.

Krebs, D.L. (1970), "Altruism—An Examination of the Concept and a Review of the Literature," *Psychological Bulletin*, 73, 258-302.

Montoro-Rios, Francisco Javier, Teodoro Luque-Martinez, and Miguel-Angel Rodriguez-Molina (2008), "How Green Should You Be: Can Environmental Associations Enhance Brand Performance?" *Journal of Advertising Research*, 547-63.

Okada, Erica Mina (2005), "Justification Effects on Consumer Choice of Hedonic and Utilitarian Goods," *Journal of Marketing Research*, 42, 43-53.

Park, C. Whan, Bernard J. Jaworski, and Deborah J. MacInnis (1986), "Strategic Brand Concept-Image Management," *Journal of Marketing*, 50 (4), 135-45.

Schuhwerk, Melody E. and Roxanne Lefkoff-Hagius (1995), "Green or Non-Green? Does Type of Appeal Matter When Advertising a Green Product?" *Journal of Advertising*, 24(2), 45-54.

Shavitt, Sharon (1990), "The Role of Attitude Objects in Attitude Functions," *Journal of Experimental Social Psychology*, 26 (2), 128-48.

Shrum, L.J., John A. McCarty and Tina M. Lowrey (1995), "Buyer Characteristics of the Green Consumer and Their Implications for Advertising Strategy," *Journal of Advertising*, 24(2), 71-82.

Strahilevitz, Michal and John G. Myers (1998), "Donations to Charity as Purchase Incentives: How Well They Work May Depend on What You Are Trying to Sell," *Journal of Consumer Research*, 24(4), 434-46.

Wansink, Brian and Pierre Chandon (2006), "Can 'Low-Fat' Nutrition Labels lead to Obesity?" *Journal of Marketing Research*, 43, 605-17.

Wertenbroch, Klaus (1998), "Consumption Self-Control by Rationing Purchase Quantities of Virtue and Vice," *Marketing Science*, 17(4), 317-37.

White, Katherine and John Peloza (2009), "Other-Benefit Versus Other-Self-Benefit Marketing Appeals: Their Effectiveness in Generating Charitable Support," *Journal of Marketing*, 73 (4), 109-24.

# Trust of the Virtual eWOM Reviewer and the Role of Gendered Self-Construal

Shahana Sen, Columbia University, USA

## EXTENDED ABSTRACT

### Summary of the Paper

Previous research has found that compared to men, women are significantly more likely to consider eWOM consumer reviews as informative, and report that they are more likely to use these in their decision-making. Women also exhibit the negativity bias, viz. find reviewers of negative eWOM significantly more trustworthy than those who write positive reviews, in comparison with men. We investigate the role of gender differences in consumers' self-construals in influencing these attitudes towards the virtual reviewers writing the eWOM consumer reviews. We find that the differences in a person's relational-interdependent self-construal is an underlying reason leading to this gendered difference in the trust of a virtual eWOM reviewer.

### Conceptualization

Based on our research and the extant literature, we propose two hypotheses relating to the effect of gender on the trust of eWOM reviewers. In our first hypothesis, we propose how this relationship between gender and trust of the reviewer may be moderated by review valence and the type of product being reviewed. We draw from previous research (Sen and Lerman 2007; Sen (*forthcoming*)) and propose that women will more likely exhibit the negativity bias than men, and moreover, be more likely to trust a virtual reviewer writing a negative review for a utilitarian product than for a hedonic product. To investigate the process of this gendered difference, we explore the role played by the subject's relational-interdependent self-construal (RISC), since literature in social psychology has demonstrated that many gender differences in cognition, motivation, emotion, and social behavior may be explained in terms of men's and women's different self-construals (e.g., Sherif 1982; Banaji & Prentice, 1994; Baumeister 1998; Greenwald & Pratkanis, 1984; Markus & Wurf, 1987).

### Method

A 2 (*Gender*: male, female) x 2 (*Review valence*: negative, positive) x 2 (*Product type:* hedonic, utilitarian) between-subjects experiment was conducted. Proposition 1 was tested using linear regression. Subjects' relational-interdependent self-construal (RISC) was measured using the scale developed by Cross et al. (2000), and used to test mediation of the effect of gender on the trust of an eWOM reviewer by the subject's RISC score (Proposition 2). The mediation was tested by using the 3 step regression analysis suggested by Baron and Kenny (1986).

### Major Findings

We found support for our mediated moderation model in Proposition 2 which posited that relational-interdependent self-construal (RISC) would mediate the effect in Proposition 1 and would be the reason behind the gender differences in trust of the virtual reviewer. Our finding is consistent with Cross and Madson (1997)'s view that individuals' self facilitates their engagement in and adaptation to the environments, and we believe that in the case of women, their higher RISC motivates them to adapt their attitudes or behavior to the virtual reviewer, to ensure a smooth and harmonious interaction (e.g., having trust in the motivations of the virtual reviewer.)

# Conversations Sell: How Dialogical Judgments and Goals Underpin the Success of Viral Videos

T. E. Dominic Yeo, University of Cambridge, UK

## EXTENDED ABSTRACT

The potential for online videos to command widespread attention without the need for extensive resources or interference from traditional media gatekeepers has attracted millions of professionals and consumers alike to put up videos on media-sharing sites like YouTube in the hope that they will go viral. Highly successful viral videos can command a large following, obtain substantial media coverage, and may spawn a slew of remixes that feeds on their popularity. But viral phenomena are fraught with uncertainty. Without a clearer understanding of the forces driving individuals to pass on viral contents or engage in word-of-mouth communications about them, explicit efforts to stimulate buzz through deliberate viral attempts run the risk of backfiring.

This paper illustrates an approach to explicate virality by examining how individuals make sense of a viral phenomenon, and engage in interpersonal communication about it. Successful viral videos are typified by their phenomenological attributes—people typically mention a viral video by first talking about the elements for its popularity or about the attention it receives. In this way, a highly significant quality for virality is based on how the video becomes elaborated within the group it is popular with. What people find salient, meaningful and useful about the video, and the degree to which these knowledge structures are commonly shared within the group are fundamental to the communicative success of the video.

The present research examines the emergence of collective meaning of a viral video within a given socio-cultural context, and from which to form hypotheses and make predictions concerning individuals' choices and actions associated with it. Using the example of the "Bus Uncle" viral video?a man covertly filmed on a camera phone reviling a fellow Hong Kong bus passenger for interrupting his call?three studies were conducted to elicit participants' goals, judgments and collective meaning-making of the phenomenon. The case helps to exemplify the socio-cultural aspects of consumers' participation in viral phenomena, the nature of user-generated content, and the psychological mechanism of 'virality.'

The first two studies were conducted with local participants in Hong Kong. In Study 1, a laddering questionnaire was used to elicit participants' goals for viewing the Bus Uncle video and the linkages between these goals. Using means-end chain analysis, the structure of the viewing goals and their linkages was mapped. In Study 2 participants were asked to sort newspaper comments obtained from local press coverage of the phenomenon. The sorted comments were then subjected to multidimensional scaling (MDS) to uncover participants' common conceptual space and judgments. To elucidate contextual differences in the representations of the phenomenon, Study 3 replicated the procedures in Study 2 with British participants in the U.K.. Using a geometric analytical procedure, the concordance between the knowledge structures obtained from the MDS analysis of the two samples was tested.

Study 1 showed that the desire for common conversation topics among friends was the most salient goal for viewing the video. Study 2 revealed that participants' interpretations of press coverage on the video were guided by their judgments of whether the issues mentioned would make good conversations. These judgments converged with a relevant set of goals for viewing the video, suggesting that participants' interpretations were motivated by their goals. When Study 2 was replicated in Study 3, judgments that serve dialogical purposes in the out-group sample were notably missing.

This paper proposes that a video becomes a viral phenomenon when it is sufficiently elaborated within a social group and shared ideas begin to emerge. The ability to make conversations about the video is arguably the most proximal determinant in this process. Tracing the goals and linkages that preceded this goal can illuminate the process that leads a video to virality. The studies show that salient aspects of individuals' representations of viral videos do not arise from item characteristics but correspond to the relationships between people and the item, and the events represented by these relationships. They also reveal that the role of media coverage in facilitating a video going viral was not in raising the salience of any particular issue but in helping people understand what went on.

The findings suggest that the buzz and virality arising from the video were attributable to participants' goals to create and negotiate social relationships through conversations with others in their social group. The need for personal judgments about the video becomes extenuated when participants were initially drawn to the video owing to others' recommendations or to a lesser extent because it was widely talked about. In such circumstances, participants would rely on the judgments of others provided that their superordinate goal was to create conversation topics. This point to the importance of examining consumers' goal-directed behaviors when seeking explanations for the persuasiveness of word-of-mouth communication.

## REFERENCES

Bangerter, Adrian and Chip Heath (2004). "The Mozart effect: Tracking the evolution of a scientific legend," *British Journal of Social Psychology*, 43 (December), 605-623.

McAdams, Dan P. (1995). "What do we know when we know a person?," *Journal of Personality*, 63 (September), 365-396.

Moscovici, Serge (1963). "Attitudes and Opinions," *Annual Review of Psychology*, 14 (January), 231-260.

_____ (1973). "Introduction," in *Health and illness: a social psychological analysis*, ed. Claudine Herzlich, London, England: Academic Press.

Penenberg, Adam L. (2009). *Viral Loop: The Power of Pass-it-on*. London, England: Sceptre.

Wagner, Wolfgang and Nicky Hayes (2005). *Everyday Discourse and Common Sense: The Theory of Social Representations*. New York, NY: Palgrave Macmillan.

# When Electronic Recommendation Agents Backfire

Joseph Lajos, HEC Paris, France
Amitava Chattopadhyay, INSEAD, Singapore
Kishore Sengupta, INSEAD, Singpore

## EXTENDED ABSTRACT

Online nutrition retailers offer consumers an enormous selection of highly nutritious foods, drinks, and dietary supplements. For a novice health and fitness enthusiast, deciding which of these categories of products are likely to be helpful, and then choosing individual products within those particular categories, can be confusing, even when only a few options are available. For example, when selecting a nutrition bar, consumers may consider a diverse array of product attributes, including Calories, fat content, fiber content, glycemic index, protein to carbohydrate ratio, protein quality, and vitamin and mineral content, among others. Typically, the product that is best for a given consumer will depend on a variety of individual factors as well, such as age, eating patterns, exercise frequency and intensity, gender, and strength and weight goals, among others.

This example illustrates how the increasing selection of products and product features available in the marketplace, and especially online, has increased the complexity of many purchase decisions. Since consumers do not want more choices per se, but rather the more customized options that expanded choice can bring (Pine, Peppers, and Rogers 2005), it follows that the attractiveness of the expanded choice set offered by internet retailers depends on the ability of consumers to sort through it efficiently (Alba et al. 1997).

Product recommendation websites assist consumers in making complex purchase decisions in diverse product categories. These websites provide electronic recommendation agents that first ask users questions about individual factors and their preferences for product attributes, and then rate available products on the basis of their responses. The goals of these agents include improving decision quality and increasing satisfaction (West et al. 1999).

Although previous research has extensively examined the influence of electronic recommendation agent use on decision quality (e.g., Haubl and Trifts 2000), far less research has examined effects on satisfaction. Furthermore, those papers that have examined satisfaction have primarily focused on satisfaction with the choice process (e.g., Bechwati and Xia 2003), rather than on satisfaction with the choice itself. However, choice satisfaction is important to marketers, since it has been shown to influence attitudes and purchase intentions (Oliver 1980).

In this paper, we examine how use of an electronic recommendation agent for nutrition bars impacts consumers' choice satisfaction, attitudes, and purchase intentions over a period of one to two weeks, the time frame in which repurchase decisions for nutrition bars are typically made.

We conducted an experiment within the nutrition bar product category. The experimental design had two between-subjects conditions (recommendation agent vs. control). People recruited outside a behavioral laboratory near a large, urban university were assigned to one of the conditions and asked to examine descriptions of eight brands of nutrition bars (four of which were relatively utilitarian, and four of which were relatively hedonic) and to select one of these brands to sample at home. At the conclusion of the in-lab portion of the experiment, participants received a package containing five sample bars of the brand that they had selected. Then, one week later, they received an email that contained a link to an online follow-up survey that assessed their satisfaction with the brand as well as their attitudes, purchase intentions, and other measures of interest.

Based on Wilson et al.'s classic finding that when people carefully analyze the reasons underlying their decisions they become biased to overweight utilitarian considerations and underweight hedonic considerations (see Wilson and Dunn 1985), we predicted that participants in the agent condition would be more likely to choose one of the four relatively utilitarian brands compared to participants in the control condition. The data supported this prediction. The data also revealed that although the total amount of time that participants spent examining the brands did not differ between the two conditions (suggesting that participants in the agent condition did not blindly follow the recommendations provided to them), across these conditions participants who ultimately selected a utilitarian brand spent more time on average examining the brands than did those who ultimately selected a hedonic brand, consistent with the notion that utilitarian choices result from more intensive processing than do hedonic choices (Shiv and Fedorikhin 1999).

The data further revealed that, in addition to influencing participants' brand choices, use of an electronic recommendation agent reduced their satisfaction with the chosen brand. This is consistent with Wilson et al.'s (1993) finding that analyzing reasons can reduce post-choice satisfaction. Furthermore, the data revealed that among participants in the agent condition satisfaction was lower among those who chose a utilitarian brand than among those who chose a hedonic brand, whereas among participants in the control condition satisfaction did not differ between those who chose a utilitarian or hedonic brand. These findings suggest that the observed decrease in satisfaction among participants who used an agent resulted from the utilitarian bias that was induced by interacting with the agent. It seems that after some time had passed participants' decision bases returned to their normal levels, leading those who had selected a utilitarian brand after interacting with the agent to regret their choice.

We observed this same pattern of results with a rich set of additional dependent variables, including participants' taste ratings, their likelihood of purchasing the chosen brand, and their likelihood of recommending the chosen brand to a friend.

In a planned second study, which we will conduct before ACR, we will attempt to rule out alternative explanations based on the content of the agents' recommendations. In the study, participants who use an agent will either receive a set of recommendations that, unbeknownst to them, has been generated randomly, or, after providing their responses to the agents' questions, will receive a message saying that the recommendation agent server has malfunctioned and that the brands will therefore be displayed randomly.

By showing that including a product in an electronic recommendation agent can have negative consequences, our results give a word of caution to managers. In particular, our results suggest that marketers who manage relatively utilitarian brands within product categories in which both hedonic and utilitarian brands are established should be especially cautious. Although agents might help increase short-term sales of such products by leading consumers to overweight utilitarian product attributes and underweight hedonic product attributes, this boost may come at the cost of long-run profitability due to consumers' reduced satisfaction with their choices and a resulting decline in repurchasing behavior.

## REFERENCES

Alba, Joseph, John Lynch, Barton Weitz, Chris Janiszewski, Richard Lutz, Alan Sawyer, and Stacy Wood (1997), "Interactive Home Shopping: Consumer, Retailer, and Manufacturer Incentives to Participate in Electronic Marketplaces," *Journal of Marketing*, 61 (July), 38-53.

Bechwati, Nada Nasr and Lan Xia (2003), "Do Computers Sweat? The Impact of Perceived Effort of Online Decision Aids on Consumers' Satisfaction with the Decision Process," *Journal of Consumer Psychology*, 13 (1&2), 139-48.

Bergkvist, Lars and John R. Rossiter (2007), "The Predictive Validity of Multiple-Item Versus Single-Item Measures of the Same Constructs," *Journal of Marketing Research*, 44 (May), 175-84.

Darke, Peter R., Amitava Chattopadhyay, and Laurence Ashworth (2006), "The Importance and Functional Significance of Affective Cues in Consumer Choice," *Journal of Consumer Research*, 33 (December), 322-8.

Deighton, John (1984), "The Interaction of Advertising and Evidence," *Journal of Consumer Research*, 11 (December), 763-770.

Dhar, Ravi and Klaus Wertenbroch (2000), "Consumer Choice Between Hedonic and Utilitarian Goods," *Journal of Marketing Research*, 37 (February), 60-71.

Fitzsimons, Gavan J. and Donald R. Lehmann (2004), "Reactance to Recommendations: When Unsolicited Advice Yields Contrary Responses," *Marketing Science*, 23 (1), 82-94.

Haubl, Gerald and Kyle B. Murray (2001), "Recommending or Persuading? The Impact of a Shopping Agent's Algorithm on User Behavior," in Michael P. Wellman and Yoav Shoham (eds.), *Proceedings of the 3rd ACM Conference on Electronic Commerce*, New York, NY: Association for Computing Machinery, 163-70.

_____ and _____ (2003), "Preference Construction and Persistence in Digital Marketplaces: The Role of Electronic Recommendation Agents," *Journal of Consumer Psychology*, 13 (1&2), 75-91.

Haubl, Gerald and Valerie Trifts (2000), "Consumer Decision Making in Online Shopping Environments: The Effects of Interactive Decision Aids," *Marketing Science*, 19 (1), 4-21.

Kmett, Carla M., Hal R. Arkes, and Steven K. Jones (1999), "The Influence of Decision Aids on High School Students' Satisfaction with Their College Choice Decision," *Personality and Social Psychology Bulletin*, 25 (10), 1293-1301.

Mandel, Naomi and Eric J. Johnson (2002), "When Web Pages Influence Choice: Effects of Visual Primes on Experts and Novices," *Journal of Consumer Research*, 29 (September), 235-45.

Millar, Murray G. and Abraham Tesser (1986), "Effects of Affective and Cognitive Focus on the Attitude-Behavior Relation," *Journal of Personality and Social Psychology*, 51 (2), 270-6.

_____ and _____ (1989), "The Effects of Affective-Cognitive Consistency on the Attitude-Behavior Relation," *Journal of Experimental Social Psychology*, 25, 189-202.

Moldovan, Sarit, Jacob Goldenberg, and Amitava Chattopadhyay (2006), "What Drives Word-of-Mouth? The Roles of Product Originality and Usefulness," *MSI Working Paper* 06-111.

Oliver, Richard L. (1980), "A Cognitive Model of the Antecedents and Consequences of Satisfaction Decisions," *Journal of Marketing Research*, 17 (November), 460-9.

Payne, John W., James R. Bettman, and Eric J. Johnson (1993), *The Adaptive Decision Maker*, Cambridge, UK: Cambridge University Press.

Pine, B. Joseph II, Don Peppers, and Martha Rogers (1995), "Do You Want to Keep Your Customers Forever?" *Harvard Business Review*, 73 (March-April), 103-14.

Reeves, Marina M. and Sandra Capra (2003), "Predicting Energy Requirements in the Clinical Setting: Are Current Methods Evidence Based?" *Nutrition Reviews*, 61 (April), 143-51.

Rossiter, John R. (2002), "The C-OAR-SE Procedure for Scale Development in Marketing," *International Journal of Research in Marketing*, 19 (December), 305-35.

Russo, J. Edward (1977), "The Value of Unit Price Information," *Journal of Marketing Research*, 14 (May), 193-201.

Schwartz, Barry (2000), "The Tyranny of Freedom," *American Psychologist*, 55 (1), 79-88.

Shiv, Baba and Alexander Fedorikhin (1999), "Heart and Mind in Conflict: The Interplay of Affect and Cognition in Consumer Decision Making," *Journal of Consumer Research*, 23 (December), 278-92.

Shugan, Steven M. (1980), "The Cost of Thinking," *Journal of Consumer Research*, 7 (September), 99-111.

Swaminathan, Vanitha (2003), "The Impact of Recommendation Agents on Consumer Evaluation and Choice: The Moderating Role of Category Risk, Product Complexity, and Consumer Knowledge," *Journal of Consumer Psychology*, 13 (1&2), 93-101.

Thompson, Debora Viana, Rebecca W. Hamilton, and Roland T. Rust (2005), "Feature Fatigue: When Product Capabilities Become Too Much of a Good Thing," *Journal of Marketing Research*, 42 (November), 431-42.

Todd, Peter and Izak Benbasat (1999), "Evaluating the Impact of DSS, Cognitive Effort, and Incentives on Strategy Selection," *Information Systems Research*, 10 (4), 356-74.

West, Patricia M., Dan Ariely, Steve Bellman, Eric Bradlow, Joel Huber, Eric Johnson, Barbara Kahn, John Little, and David Schkade (1999), "Agents to the Rescue?" *Marketing Letters*, 10 (3), 285-300.

Widing, Robert E. II and W. Wayne Talarzyk (1993), "Electronic Information Systems for Consumers: An Evaluation of Computer-Assisted Formats in Multiple Decision Environments," *Journal of Marketing Research*, 30 (May), 125-41.

Wilson, Timothy D. and Dana S. Dunn (1985), "Effects of Introspection on Attitude-Behavior Consistency: Analyzing Reasons versus Focusing on Feelings," *Journal of Experimental Social Psychology*, 22, 249-63.

Wilson, Timothy D., Douglas J. Lisle, Jonathan W. Schooler, Sara D. Hodges, Kristen J. Klaaren, and Suzanne J. LaFleur (1993), "Introspecting About Reasons Can Reduce Post-Choice Satisfaction," *Personality and Social Psychology Bulletin*, 19 (3), 331-9.

Winter, Joysa (2008), "Energy Bars: Will they Return to their Glory Days?" *Functional Ingredients*, (accessed March 5, 2008), [available at http://www.functionalingredientsmag.com].

Zajonc, Robert B. and Hazel Markus (1982), "Affective and Cognitive Factors in Preferences," *Journal of Consumer Research*, 9 (September), 123-31.

Zhang, Shi and Gavan J. Fitzsimons (1999), "Choice-Process Satisfaction: The Influence of Attribute Alignability and Option Limitation," *Organizational Behavior and Human Decision Processes*, 77 (3), 192-214.

# Balance as an Embodiment of Parity

Jeffrey Larson, Brigham Young University, USA
Darron Billeter, Brigham Young University, USA

## EXTENDED ABSTRACT

Philosophers and linguists have long postulated that metaphorical language is more than a simple cultural construction, but reflects deeper cognitive relationships (Aristotle, circa 335 BCE). According to research on embodied cognition, our understanding of abstract concepts is grounded in physical experience (Lakoff & Johnson, 1999). New, unfamiliar, abstract concepts are understood through metaphorical association with familiar, physical activities in a process known as "scaffolding" (Williams, Huang, & Bargh 2009). Because language utilizes neural systems that were developed for other purposes, the activation of motor behavior can similarly activate the deeper cognitive associations that are scaffolded onto that motor behavior. Similarly, activation of an abstract concept can activate the motor regions of the brain upon which it was scaffolded.

We examine the balance metaphor, which has not been experimentally demonstrated to exhibit multi-modal influence. Balance is one of the earliest developing and most pervasive physical metaphors (Zaltman & Zaltman, 2008). Beginning in early childhood, people learn through repeated experiences the importance of maintaining physical balance. To bipedal mammals, balance is so fundamental for well-being that balance and anxiety disorders share neuronal circuitry and commonly co-occur (Balaban & Thayer, 2001; Furman & Jacob, 2001). As a learner encodes the actions required to obtain balance, they are also encoding other relevant information from the learning context. One of the important ways that a standing person obtains balance is by equalizing the weight placed across both feet. In the learning process, the concept of balance and the need for evenness are encoded concurrently, creating a strong mental association between these two concepts.

The neural connection between physical balance and the more abstract concept of evenness or parity is evidenced by many metaphoric phrases from the English language. Accountants "balance the ledger" while chemists "balance equations." Fair-minded individuals ascertain "both sides of the story", and someone in control of her emotions is said to be "even-tempered." (Many of these metaphors are similar in other languages.) These idioms are best understood in the guise of a twin-pan balance scale evaluating opposing abstract states. The balancing apparatus reaches equilibrium when both pans hold equal portions. Similarly, accounts are balanced when they reflect equal parts debits and credits, while truth is ascertained when opposing viewpoints are weighed against each other.

These balance-based metaphors arise because of the strong neural connections between balance and parity that are encoded during infancy. Exposure to balance metaphors causes concurrent activation of the neural systems governing balance and the neural systems governing cognitions about parity, which strengthens the association (Lakoff & Johnson, 1999). Repeated exposure to symbolic representations of balance, for example the twin-pan balance scale and the yin and yang symbol, also reinforces the link between balance and parity.

Given this link between the neural systems governing balance and more abstract thoughts on parity, we expect that experiencing physical balance should consequently access the mental representation of the balance metaphor, which is closely associated with the need for parity, and thereby influence choice. Engaging in physical balance activities should activate instinctual desires *for* balance, and thereby enhance the desirability of metaphorically balanced choice options. Specifically, activation of physical balance should increase the desire for choice options that offer some form of parity.

In four studies, we activate physical balance through a variety of means and observe a consistent increase in the choice share of options that offer various forms of parity. In study 1, participants played one of three games on the Wii Fit™ while simultaneously responding to a verbal survey administered by a research assistant that was blind to the hypotheses of the study. Two of these games (Yoga and Penguin Slide) activated significantly more thoughts on physical balance than the neutral (Jogging) condition. Participants selected a printer and a car from a set of three choice options that included a compromise choice. Participants in the Yoga and Penguin Slide conditions demonstrated an increased selection of both a compromise printer (M=40% vs. M=23%) and a compromise car (M=55% vs. M=38%). The pooled test was significant (z=1.99, p=.05).

In study 2, physical balance is activated through mental simulation. Participants performed a fifteen second mental simulation of either walking across a balance beam in perfect balance, walking across a balance beam with poor balance, or swinging around a high bar. Those in either of the two balanced beam conditions selected the compromise computer (M=66% and M=63%) more often than those in the high bar condition (M=45%, z=2.04, p=.04). The results suggest that the strength of activation of balance metaphor is not dependent on the kind of physical activation, unbalanced or balanced. Furthermore, the results indicate that the activation of the association between balance and parity occurs even when balance is activated through mental simulation.

In study 3, the balance metaphor is activated through supraliminal exposure to balance symbols. In the balance condition, the four corners of the web survey displayed a crude silhouette of a balance (see Figure 2). In the control condition, no picture was shown. The survey asked participants to make six meal choices; each choice set showed two meals, with one meal being more balanced than the other (offering greater parity across food groups). In the balance condition, participants chose the balanced meal 68% of the time as opposed to only 56% of the time for the control. A logistic regression on meal choices showed that condition assignment was significant, t(399)=2.3, p=.02.

Finally, study 4 activates semantic representations of the balance metaphor. We asked half the participants to write for three minutes about a time when their life felt "out of balance". These participants choose the compromise computer more often (*M*=83%) than those who wrote about their typical day (*M*=50%), z=2.15, p<.05.

Across four studies, we activate balance a number of ways and demonstrate that such activation consistently leads to an increase in the choice of options that offer parity.

## REFERENCES

Aristotle, *The Poetics* (circa 335 BCE).

Balaban, C.D., Thayer, J.F. (2001). Neurological bases for balance-anxiety links. *Journal of Anxiety Disorders*, 15, 53-79.

Furman, J.M., & Jacob, R.G. (2001). A clinical taxonomy of dizziness and anxiety in the otoneurological setting. *Journal of Anxiety Disorders*, 15, 9-26.

Lakoff, G., & Johnson, M. (1999). *Philosophy in the Flesh*. New York, NY: Basic Books.

Williams, L.E., Huang, J.Y. & Bargh, J.A.(2009). The scaf-
    folded mind: Higher mental processes are grounded in early
    experience of the physical world. *European Journal of Social
    Psychology*, 39, 1257-1267.
Zaltman, G. & Zaltman, L. (2008). *Marketing metaphoria: What
    deep metaphors reveal about the minds of consumers*. Cam-
    bridge, MA: Harvard Business Press.

# Staying Warm in the Winter: Seeking Psychological Warmth to Reduce Physical Coldness

Yan Zhang, National University of Singapore, Singapore
Jane Risen, University of Chicago, USA

## EXTENDED ABSTRACT

On a cold, snowy night, there is nothing better than sitting by the fire and drinking a hot cup of cocoa. It is a basic human drive to seek physical warmth when feeling cold. This research explores whether there also exists a drive to seek psychological warmth when feeling cold. On a cold, snowy night, are people especially interested in having a romantic dinner with a loved one or a phone conversation with a dear friend? More broadly, we ask: When people are physically cold, are they motivated to engage in psychologically warm activities?

Psychologically warm events are positive experiences that promote a feeling of social connection. Recent research on embodied cognition suggests that a link exists between physical warmth and psychological warmth (IJzerman & Semin, 2009; Williams & Bargh, 2008; Zhong & Leonardelli, 2008). For instance, people perceive a target individual to be "warm" (e.g., kind and charitable) when they are holding a hot cup of coffee (Williams & Bargh, 2008), they perceive themselves to be socially close to others when they are in a warm room (IJzerman & Semin, 2009), and they report feeling physically cold when they are socially excluded (Zhong & Leonardelli, 2008).

In this research we suggest that psychological warmth, like physical warmth, is perceived as a means of reducing the feeling of coldness. As a result, people are more interested in engaging in psychologically warm activities when they are physically cold. This argument goes beyond the "metaphor" or "priming" domain of embodied cognition research. Instead of asking whether activities will be perceived as psychologically warmer or colder, we focus on the goal-oriented nature of the phenomenon and test whether feeling cold motivates people to seek psychological warmth. We suggest psychological warmth and physical warmth are two means for satisfying the same goal of reducing a feeling of coldness.

Study 1 supports the basic prediction by showing that cold participants are especially interested in psychologically warm activities. Specifically, participants who completed a questionnaire outside in the cold in a Midwestern city's winter showed more interest in warm events than in non-warm activities, but those who completed the study inside a heated building were equally interested in warm and non-warm activities. Study 2 extends the work to real-world behavior. Beginning a romantic relationship is perhaps the most powerful tool for forging social connection. We find that participants are more likely to start relationships in cold weather than end them. In Study 3, we primed people either with the goal of reducing physical coldness or the concept of coldness. The results showed that priming people with the goal of reducing physical coldness led to greater interest in both physically and psychologically warm events (relative to non-warm events), but priming people with the concept of coldness did not, suggesting that it is the motivation to reduce coldness that is central to people's interest in warm events. Finally, in Study 4, to test whether psychological warmth and physical warmth are two means for satisfying the same goal of reducing a feeling of coldness, we asked participants to fill out the same questionnaire as in Study 1 either outside in the cold or inside a heated building. However, half of the participants were reminded that they would step into a heated building momentarily. We replicated the results of Study 1 in the no-reminder condition, showing that people showed greater interest in psychologically warm events if they were feeling physically cold than if they were not feeling cold; but this increased interest in psychologically warm events is reduced when participants were reminded that their motivation to reduce coldness will be met through physical means, indicating that psychological warmth and physical warmth are two means for satisfying the same goal of reducing a feeling of coldness.

Our findings support the argument that while people satisfy their physical goals through physical means, the mapping between mind and body also leads them to satisfy their physical goals through psychological means. This research adds to the growing body of work supporting a theory of embodied cognition, and specifically to work suggesting that the mental concepts of psychological warmth and social connection are deeply rooted in the sensorimotor experience of physical warmth. In addition, the present work goes beyond demonstrating a conceptual mapping between the physical sensation of warmth and the psychological experience of warmth. It highlights the role of goals and motivation in the link between the mind and the body. We find that the link leads people to satisfy their physical goal with actions that could satisfy the matching psychological goal. Namely, when people are motivated to reduce physical coldness, they show interest in events that promote psychological warmth.

# The Influence of Mirror Decoration on Food Taste

Ataollah Tafaghodi Jami, University of Utah, USA
Himanshu Mishra, University of Utah, USA

## EXTENDED ABSTRACT

Recent studies show an alarming increase in obesity in the United States with 74.1% of the population over 15 years old considered overweight (Streib 2007). Various organizations are dealing with this issue and trying different weight-loss strategies such as low-carbohydrate diets, physical exercises, fat burning or appetite reducing pills, and fat removal surgeries. At the same time, others are looking for more self-driven ways of controlling obesity by changing people's eating habits and introducing standards of healthy eating. The aim of these standards is to promote eating of healthy foods and prevent unhealthy eating practices. Emphasizing by media and many food producers through calorie or fiber intake, smaller portions, and reduced fat or fat-free products, standards of healthy eating have been widely accepted. However, there are still many people who do not follow these standards though they believe that it is harmful for them.

One of the critical aspects of unhealthy foods, which attracts people's attention and convince them to choose it over a healthy option, is the taste of unhealthy foods. Research has shown that regardless of the actual taste, considering a food as less healthy makes it more tasty (Raghunathan, Naylor, and Hoyer 2006). Thus, making an unhealthy food less tasty could potentially reduce its consumption and help people to practice healthy food consumption. Therefore, in this research, we investigated the possibility of making unhealthy foods less tasty without changing their ingredients.

Past research has shown that self-focused people tend to compare themselves with standards of correctness (Duval and Wicklund 1972), and experience positive affect when they act in concert with standards, and negative affect when they act in opposition to standards (Duval, Silvia, and Lalwani 2001). The person who feels the positive or negative affect does not immediately know why he or she has such feelings (Oatley and Johnson-Laird 1996). Moreover, research has shown that self-focused people tend to attribute positive events to self and negative events to external factors (Duval, Silvia, and Lalwani 2001).

Since mirror, as a self-awareness enhancing tool, can be used as a decorative item in many food consumption settings, this research examined if, and under what conditions, eating a food product in front of a mirror affects its taste perception. According to the reviewed literature, it is expected that eating a healthy or an unhealthy food in front of a mirror generate positive or negative feelings since standards of healthy eating are widely accepted. Therefore, we propose that if people consume their food in a room decorated with mirrors compared to a room without mirrors, they will attribute the positive affect of eating a healthy food internally to self and the negative affect of eating an unhealthy to the food taste as an external factor.

The first study was designed to provide empirical evidence for the proposed effect of mirror decoration on food taste. We used fruit salad and chocolate cake to represent healthy and unhealthy foods. Results confirmed our expectations and showed that participants gave a lower overall taste evaluation to the chocolate cake when they consumed it in front of mirror compared to the no-mirror condition. However, the taste evaluations of the fruit salad were not significantly different between the mirror and no-mirror conditions.

Study 2 and 3 investigated two factors moderating the effect of mirror decoration on food taste. Research has shown that people must perceive themselves responsible for acting against standards in order to experience the negative feelings (Duval, Silvia, and Lalwani 2001). Accordingly, the second study showed that when participants did not perceive themselves to be responsible for eating the unhealthy food (i.e., when they think that there is no choice and they have to do it), they did not give a lower evaluation to the taste of the unhealthy food in the mirror condition compared to the no-mirror condition.

Research has also found that simplicity of the connection between cause and effect is an important factor for the attribution system; and people tend to attribute the effects to the most plausible causes (Duval, Silvia, and Lalwani 2001). Therefore, we expected that introducing a more plausible cause for the negative affect would move the attribution of discomfort away from the unhealthy food taste. Study 3 supported this expectation and showed that when we introduced music as a more plausible cause of the negative affect, participants did not evaluate the taste of the unhealthy food to be lower in the mirror condition compared to the no-mirror condition.

In sum, this research contributes to the extant body of literature on the self-awareness theory by demonstrating the link between the self-awareness and the attribution of feelings induced by the self-standards comparison system. At a practical level, results of this research suggest that mirror decoration can be used in food consumption settings to decrease unhealthy eating practices as mirrors make the consumption of an unhealthy food less pleasant.

## REFERENCES

Baumeister, Roy F. (1995), "Self and Identity: An Introduction," in *Advanced Social Psychology*, ed. A. Tesser, New York: McGraw-Hill, 50-97.

Beaman, Arthur L., Bonnel Klentz, Edward Diener, and Soren Svanum (1979), "Self-Awareness and Transgression in Children: Two Field Studies," *Journal of Personality and Social Psychology*, 37 (10), 1835-46.

Carmon, Ziv, Klaus Wertenbroch, and Marcel Zeelenberg (2003), "Option Attachment: When Deliberating Makes Choosing Feel Like Losing," *Journal of Consumer Research*, 30 (1), 15-29.

Cohen, Jerry L., Nancy Dowling, Gregory Bishop, and William J. Maney (1985), "Causal Attributions: Effects of Self-Focused Attentiveness and Self-Esteem Feedback," *Personality and Social Psychology Bulletin*, 11 (4), 369-78.

Diener, Edward and Mark Wallbom (1976), "Effects of Self-Awareness on Antinormative Behavior," *Journal of Research in Personality*, 10 (1), 107-11.

Duval, Thomas Shelley and Paul J. Silvia (2002), "Self-awareness, probability of improvement, and the self-serving bias," *Journal of Personality and Social Psychology*, 82 (1), 49-61.

Duval, Thomas Shelley, Paul J. Silvia, and Neal Lalwani (2001), *Self-awareness & causal attribution: a dual systems theory*, Boston: Kluwer Academic Publishers.

Duval, Thomas Shelley and Robert A. Wicklund (1972), *A Theory of Objective Self-Awareness.*, New York: Academic.

Federoff, Nancy A. and John H. Harvey (1976), "Focus of Attention, Self-Esteem, and the Attribution of Causality," *Journal of Research in Personality*, 10 (3), 336-45.

Gibbons, Frederick X. (1978), "Sexual Standards and Reactions to Pornography: Enhancing Behavioral Consistency through Self-Focused Attention," *Journal of Personality and Social Psychology*, 36 (9), 976-87.

Gross, James J. (1998), "The Emerging Field of Emotion Regulation: An Integrative Review," *Review of General Psychology*, 2 (3), 271-99.

Heider, Fritz (1944), "Social Perception and Phenomenal Causality," *Psychological Review*, 51 (6), 358-74.

Heider, Fritz (1958), *The Psychology of Interpersonal Relations*, New York: Wiley.

Ickes, William John, Robert A. Wicklund, and C. Brian Ferris (1973), "Objective Self Awareness and Self Esteem," *Journal of Experimental Social Psychology*, 9 (3), 202-19.

Kelley, Harold H., (1973), "The processes of causal attribution," *American Psychologist*, 28, 107-128.

Kivetz, Ran and Yuhuang Zheng (2006), "Determinants of Justification and Self-Control," *Journal of Experimental Psychology: General*, 135 (4), 572-87.

Oatley, Keith and Philip N. Johnson-Laird (1996), "The communicative theory of emotions: Empirical tests, mental models, and implications for social interaction," in *Striving and feeling: Interactions among goals, affect, and self-regulation*, L. L. Martin and A. Tesser, Eds. Mahwah, NJ: Erlbaum.

Raghunathan, Rajagopal, Rebecca Walker Naylor, and Wayne D. Hoyer (2006), "The Unhealthy=Tasty Intuition and Its Effects on Taste Inferences, Enjoyment, and Choice of Food Products," *Journal of Marketing*, 70 (4), 170-84.

Reber, Rolf, Norbert Schwarz, and Piotr Winkielman (2004), "Processing Fluency and Aesthetic Pleasure: Is Beauty in the Perceiver's Processing Experience?," *Personality and Social Psychology Review*, 8 (4), 364-82.

Scheier, Michael F., Allan Fenigstein, and Arnold H. Buss (1974), "Self-Awareness and Physical Aggression," *Journal of Experimental Social Psychology*, 10 (3), 264-73.

Sentyrz, Stacey M. and Brad J. Bushman (1998), "Mirror, Mirror on the Wall, Who's the Thinnest One of All? Effects of Self-Awareness on Consumption of Full-Fat, Reduced-Fat, and No-Fat Products," *Journal of Applied Psychology*, 83 (6), 944-49.

Shiv, Baba and Alexander Fedorikhin (1999), "Heart and Mind in Conflict: The Interplay of Affect and Cognition in Consumer Decision Making," *Journal of Consumer Research*, 26 (3), 278-92.

Silvia, Paul J. (2002), "Self-Awareness and Emotional Intensity," *Cognition & Emotion*, 16 (2), 195-216.

Silvia, Paul J., and Crandall, Christian S. (2007), "*Attribution and perceptual organization: Testing Heider's approach to spontaneous causal thinking*" Manuscript submitted for publication.

Silvia, Paul J. and T. Shelley Duval (2001), "Objective Self-Awareness Theory: Recent Progress and Enduring Problems," *Personality and Social Psychology Review*, 5 (3), 230-41.

Streib, Lauren (2007), "World's Fattest Countries," (accessed February 22, 2010), [available at http://www.forbes.com/2007/02/07/worlds-fattest-countries-forbeslife-cx_ls_0208worldfat.html].

Wicklund, Robert A. and Shelley Duval (1971), "Opinion Change and Performance Facilitation as a Result of Objective Self-Awareness," *Journal of Experimental Social Psychology*, 7 (3), 319-42.

Williamson, Donald A., Eric Ravussin, Ma-Li Wong, A. Wagner, A. Dipaoli, Sinan Caglayan, Metin Ozata, Corby Martin, Heather Walden, Cheryl Arnett, and Julio Licinio (2005), "Microanalysis of Eating Behavior of Three Leptin Deficient Adults Treated with Leptin Therapy," *Appetite*, 45 (1), 75-80.

# Boundary Conditions for Copy Complexity Enhancement Effects

Tina M. Lowrey, University of Texas at San Antonio, USA
Youngseon Kim, University of Texas at San Antonio, USA

## EXTENDED ABSTRACT

Five experiments investigated copy complexity, length, level of involvement, medium, task attention, and reading level on persuasion. Experiments 1 and 2 investigated involvement, complexity, and length. Experiment 3 investigated involvement, complexity, and medium. Experiments 4 and 5 investigated reading level and task attention as boundary conditions.

## EXPERIMENT 1

Experiment 1 involved a 2 (simple/moderately complex copy) X 2 (short/long) manipulation of direct mail pieces. Complexity should impact the persuasiveness of the offer but length should not (although this is a null prediction, it is important to demonstrate that complexity, isolated from length, exerts effects on persuasion). Motivation should also exert a main effect on order intentions (high involvement participants will have greater intentions than low involvement participants). Motivation should also moderate the effect of complexity. An interaction between complexity and involvement is expected, such that intentions will be greatest for those high in involvement exposed to complex versions.

Independent variables included complexity, involvement, and length. Involvement was a self-reported measure on two nine-point scales, with higher numbers indicating greater involvement. The two scales correlated significantly ($.63$; $p=.000$), so were averaged, and then dichotomized ($M=5.46$). The dependent variable was order intention on a nine-point scale (higher numbers indicated greater order intention).

Participants were 85 college students who provided informed consent to participate. Participants participated in groups of 12, seated at cubicles in a laboratory. Participants read the direct mail offer, then received the measurement booklet. Upon completion, the participants were debriefed and were free to leave.

A 2 (simple/moderate copy) X 2 (short/long) X 2 (low-/high-involvement) ANOVA was conducted. Complexity contributed to order intentions, as expected. Those who received the complex versions had higher intentions to order ($M=2.98$) than those who received the simple versions ($M=2.05$; $F(1,83)=3.99$; $p<.05$). There was also a main effect for involvement, as expected, such that those who reported high levels of involvement were more likely to order than those low in involvement (2.96 vs. 2.04; $F(1,83)=3.78$; $p<.05$). Length did not contribute to order intentions, consistent with expectations.

Involvement moderated the impact of complexity on order intentions, as expected. High involvement participants who received the complex offer had higher order intentions than all other participants ($F(1,81)=9.24$; $p<.005$). Thus, complexity had a positive impact on those high in involvement. The expected results were obtained, but order intentions were quite low.

## EXPERIMENT 2

Given this negative response, Experiment 2 used a more interesting item (otherwise, the replication was identical). Participants were 103 college students participating for extra credit.

Experiment 2 replicated Experiment 1—complexity exerted a main effect on intentions (moderate=5.00 vs. simple=3.77; $F(1,85)=6.23$; $p<.05$). Involvement also exerted a main effect (high=5.57 vs. low=3.36; $F(1,85)=23.48$; $p<.001$). Length had no effect. The pattern of results for the interaction between involve-

ment and complexity was as expected, and was significant ($p<.05$). Highly involved participants exposed to moderate copy had higher intentions to order than all other participants.

## EXPERIMENT 3

Experiment 3 involved a 3 (simple/moderate/complex copy) X 2 (print/broadcast medium type) manipulation for the same item from Experiment 2. The addition of radio was intended to test the hypothesis that the persuasiveness of copy in commercials will decrease as copy gets beyond moderate complexity. An interaction between complexity, medium, and involvement (identical to procedures in Experiments 1 and 2) was expected.

Participants were 241 college students participating for credit in the same laboratory. Participants were randomly assigned to a cubicle with a computer monitor, which showed a randomly pre-selected condition. Participants in the print conditions read the offer on the screen and responded to the questionnaire. Participants in the radio conditions listened to the commercial on headsets and responded to the questionnaire. Six print and six radio versions were prepared, adding a very complex version. Order intentions were measured on a five-point scale.

There was no main effect for complexity but there was one for involvement (high=2.91 vs. low=2.16; $F(1,239)=6.42$; $p<.05$). The interaction between medium, complexity, and involvement was also marginally significant ($F(2,239)=2.37$; $p<.10$). For those high in involvement exposed to the print version, complexity enhanced persuasion (even at the highest level of complexity), but for those high in involvement exposed to the radio version, complexity had a deleterious effect on persuasion.

## EXPERIMENT 4

Experiment 4 involved a 3 (simple/moderate/complex copy) X 2 (item offered) within-subject design, measured reading level, and included an instructional manipulation check (IMC [Oppenheimer, Meyvis, and Davidenko 2009]). An interaction between complexity, reading level, and involvement was expected.

Participants were 93 college students participating for credit in the same laboratory. Participants were randomly assigned to a cubicle with a computer monitor, which showed a randomly pre-selected condition from Experiment 3 (print only). Order intentions were measured on a five-point scale. Participants engaged in a non-timed distraction task between presentation of the two offers.

There was no main effect for complexity, reading level, or involvement for the first offer. All but two participants passed the IMC. The interaction between complexity, reading level, and involvement was not significant ($p>.10$). The results for the second offer were difficult to interpret. Given the distraction task was non-timed, the low number of errors on the IMC, and the low cell size, Experiment 5 was conducted to replicate the basic design with a timed distraction task and a higher sample size.

## EXPERIMENT 5

Experiment 5 replicated Experiment 4, but with a timed distraction task. An interaction between complexity, reading level, and involvement was expected. Participants were 117 college students participating for credit in the same laboratory.

There were no main effects for complexity or reading level, but there was one for involvement, such that those who reported high levels of involvement had greater order intentions than those at low levels of involvement (3.19 vs. 2.60; $F(1,116)=5.64$; $p<.05$). Again, errors on the IMC were quite low. The interaction between medium, complexity, and involvement was not significant ($p>.10$). It would appear that, at least for college student participants, neither reading level nor task attention serve as boundary conditions.

## REFERENCES

Anand, Punam, and Brian Sternthal (1990), "Ease of Message Processing as a Moderator of Repetition Effects in Advertising," *Journal of Marketing Research*, 27 (August), 345-353.

Bradley, Samuel D., and Robert Meeds (2002), "Surface-Structure Transformations and Advertising Slogans: The Case for Moderate Syntactic Complexity," *Psychology & Marketing*, 19 (July-August), 595-619.

Chebat, Jean-Charles, Claire Gelinas-Chebat, Sabrina Hombourger, and Arch G. Woodside (2003), "Testing Consumers' Motivation and Linguistic Ability as Moderators of Advertising Readability," *Psychology & Marketing*, 20 (July), 599-624.

Craik, Fergus I. M., and Robert S. Lockhart (1972), "Levels of Processing: A Framework for Memory Research," *Journal of Verbal Learning and Verbal Behavior*, 11, 671-684.

Denbow, Carl J. (1975), "Listenability and Readability: An Experimental Investigation," *Journalism Quarterly*, 52 (2), 285-290.

Flesch, Rudolph (1951), *How to Test Readability*, New York: Harper and Brothers.

Gunning, R. (1968), *The Technique of Clear Writing*, New York: McGraw Hill.

Lowrey, Tina M. (1998), "The Effects of Syntactic Complexity on Advertising Persuasiveness," *Journal of Consumer Psychology*, 7 (2), 187-206.

Lowrey, Tina M. (2006), "The Relation Between Script Complexity and Commercial Memorability," *Journal of Advertising*, 35 (3), 7-15.

Lowrey, Tina M. (2008), "The Case for a Complexity Continuum" in *Go Figure: New Directions in Advertising Rhetoric*, eds. Edward F. McQuarrie and Barbara J. Phillips, Armonk, NY: ME Sharpe, 159-177.

McQuarrie, Edward F., and David Glen Mick (1996), "Figures of Rhetoric in Advertising Language," *Journal of Consumer Research*, 22 (March), 424-438.

Oppenheimer, Daniel M., Tom Meyvis, and Nicolas Davidenko (2009), "Instructional Manipulation Checks: Detecting Satisficing to Increase Statistical Power," *Journal of Experimental Social Psychology*, 45, 867-872.

Peracchio, Laura A., and Joan Meyers-Levy (1997), "Evaluating Persuasion-Enhancing Techniques From a Resource-Matching Perspective," *Journal of Consumer Research*, 24 (September), 178-191.

Petty, Richard E., and John T. Cacioppo (1986), Communication and Persuasion: Central and Peripheral Routes to Attitude Change, New York: Springer-Verlag.

# Color Harmony and Aesthetic Self-Design: Empirical Tests of Classical Theories

Xiaoyan Deng, Ohio State University, USA
Sam Jui, New York University, USA
Wesley Hutchinson, University of Pennsylvania, USA

## EXTENDED ABSTRACT

In this paper, we aimed at identifying and testing principles that can explain and predict color harmony perception. Color harmony is a function of distance between colors in the color space. We first briefly described different models of color space and reviewed the color harmony literature, based on which we summarized three classic principles of color harmony (i.e., identity, similarity, and contrast) that were relatively well-accepted in this literature. Because the coordinate system underlying the classic color solids does not provide a straightforward distance metric to represent color similarity or difference (i.e., do not satisfy perceptual uniformity), we adopted the theoretical background of a more recent, alternative coordinate system (i.e., CIELAB coordinate system), which was designed to approximate human vision thereby provides a straightforward distance metric for color perception. We then reviewed prior empirical tests of classic color harmony theories that are similar to the principles we summarized. Some of these tests were conducted using the classic cylindrical coordinate system, others using the modern CIELAB color space. Nevertheless we found that these tests generate mixed results.

For our own test of the color harmony principles we adopted a unique and realistic context: aesthetic self-design of an athletic shoe (which has seven areas: base, secondary, swoosh, accent, lace, lining, and shox). This specific type of self-design task is especially suitable for testing color harmony principles because, first, the task environment allows for interactive color harmony judgment and, second, color harmony plays a major role in consumers' decision. Based on this context, we proposed hypotheses about the relationships between the observed frequencies of color combinations in self-designed athletic shoes and color distance for identity, similarity, and contrast. Further, we hypothesized that a "small palette" can meet the need for color harmony if it is indeed determined by identity (if a single color is used repeatedly then less colors are needed in the palette) or contrast (colors that are mutually complementary spread evenly in the color space and the number of such colors is limited).

Results from our empirical tests provide evidence for our hypotheses. First, the principle of identity was supported for color pairs involving minor shoe areas (e.g., swoosh, lace, lining, and shox). Second, the principle of similarity was supported for the two major shoe areas (i.e., base and secondary). Third, the principle of contrast was supported for color pairs involving a major and a minor shoe area (e.g., base-lining, base-shox). Finally, the "small palette" hypothesis was also supported as the number of colors actually used in self-designed athletic shoes was smaller than the number expected based on assumption of statistical independence.

Taking these results together, we can picture the color coordination strategy consumers use during the self-design process, in which they make seven sequential color decisions for base, secondary, swoosh, accent, lace, lining, and shox (ordered as such). First, they pick a color for base according to their own preference. Second, anchoring on the base color, they choose a secondary color that is similar to that of base. Third, when making color decisions for the remaining five minor areas, consumers tend to use the same color for most of these areas, and this color oftentimes is a color contrasting to the base color. Taking into account the relative area of the seven shoe components, this strategy leads to a harmonious design where large areas define the overall color scheme of the shoe while small areas deviate from the basic scheme and "spice up" the overall design. This shows that when coordinating multiple colors, consumers are guided by intuitions about color harmony and their intuitions are consistent with the principles of identity, similarity, and contrast.

The identification and confirmation of several robust principles of color harmony provide some practical insights for managers of aesthetic self-design programs. First, these well-defined principles can be used as guidelines to design the color palettes. Second, the number of colors included in the color palettes can be greatly reduced therefore the size of the solution space of the self-design configurator can be largely reduced as well. Third, based on color harmony principles, the configurator can be designed to generate automatic recommendations to the user regarding her color choice. Last but not least, although in this paper we implicitly assume that most people prefer color harmony, those who are fond of disharmonious color combinations can also benefit from our research findings. Online product configurators include a simple survey about personal color taste to categorize their customers and, for some of them, provide "clashing" color palettes.

# When *I* becomes *We*: Interpersonal Ties in Product Co-Creation

Adriana M. Boveda-Lambie, RIT, USA
Ruby Roy Dholakia, URI, USA

## EXTENDED ABSTRACT

Customer knowledge has been extensively discussed in terms of objective and subjective knowledge, where subjective knowledge is what the individual perceives s/he knows and objective knowledge is what they truly know (Alba & J. W. Hutchinson, 2000). Knowledge exerts a significant and fundamental influence on customer decision-making; customers' decisions vary as a function of what they think they know (Moorman, Diehl, Brinberg, & Kidwell, 2004). In the case of choosing to co-create, it is their subjective knowledge about their perceived competence that will drive the process.

Customers can use their social networks as an external memory, blending the social and cognitive seamlessly into a social hard drive holding vast amounts of information (Ward & Reingen, 1990). Viewed under the service-dominant logic definition of co-creation (Lusch & Vargo, 2006), social networks are part of the customer's operant resources, which means the customer can tap into them to co-create value. Companies have used the Internet to give customers the opportunity to engage in the production process (Xie et al., 2008).

Even with access to Internet, people seem to prefer turning to other people for information (Cross & Sproull, n.d.; Levin & Cross, 2004). In other words, a customer facing a perceived lack of competence to complete a task will seek what s/he needs from other individuals (Arias, Eden, Fischer, Gorman, & Sharff, 2000; Salomon, 1993).

H1: Customers with higher (*lower*) perceived competence are more likely to engage (*not engage*) in co-creation

H2: Customers engaging in individual co-creation will have higher perceived competence than those engaging in collaborative co-creation

H3: Customers engaging in collaborative co-creation will elicit partners with higher perceived competence

The willingness to engage in co-creation requires a strong degree of product involvement (Bendapudi & Leone, 2003). Customers will not only need to use their knowledge but must also be willing to invest their time, which is a scarce and premium resource for most (Etgar, 2006, 2008). In addition, involvement with the product category and the brand itself can determine their choice to co-create since customer's product involvement can lead to increased perception of attribute differences, greater product importance and greater commitment (Howard & Sheth, 1968; Zaichkowsky, 1985). When product differences are perceived to be of greater importance, customers can be more willing to get involved in co-creation and dispense the required effort and time (Etgar, 2008). If under low involvement individuals involve in minimal searches while high involvement results in extensive searches then it follows that involvement would also moderate the amount of time a customer is inclined to spend on his/her purchase–in this case, in co-creation.

H4: Customers with higher (*lower*) product involvement are more likely to engage in co-creation (*not engage in co-creation*).

Marketers are increasingly interested in how consumers use products and brands to build and maintain a social identity, and previous studies have emphasized that self brand congruence alone can determine consumer choice (Malhotra, 1988). Brands, as social objects, are socially constructed and imbued with meaning, and customers actively engage in that creation using brands as bridges towards or fences against other people (Douglas & Isherwood, 1979; Escalas & Bettman, 2003, 2005; Muniz & O'Guinn, 2001). Research on brand communities shows that customers can use commercial offerings (brands) and brand associations as ways to create and further their self-image and shape their reality (Schau & Gilly, 2003). Co-creation may be seen as a way of self-expression through production of their own products and experiences, and taking pride while strengthening their self-identity and fulfillment (Holt, 1995). Customers engaging in co-creation have a tendency to take ownership and pride in their co-creation.

H5: Customers who choose to engage in co-creation will develop stronger self-brand associations.

## Methodology

Two-hundred and forty students from a large northwestern and southeastern university participated in an the online survey, where they read a pretested scenario to make one of three decisions: (1) purchase what is available at the store (2) engage in individual co-creation or (3) engage in collaborative co-creation . A final sample size of 233 students was attained. Participants were aged 21–22 (58.3%) and between 18 -21 years of age (41.8%). Gender was evenly distributed with 53% males and 47% females. There was no university effect on the main dependent variables ($F_{(2,232)}$=.65, $p$=.52; Levene$_{(2,232)}$=1.08, $p$=.34).

Competence was significantly different across co-creation groups ($F_{(2,229)}$=30.10, p<.01, $w^2$=.16) with participants' perceived competence highest among those choosing individual co-creation ($M_{IndCC}$=7.18, $SD$=1.47; $M_{CollCC}$=6.38, $SD$=1.64; $M_{NoCC}$=5.15, $SD$=2.07). These results support H1 and H2.

The competence of participant's selected tie(s) was significantly higher ($t_{(49)}$=4.94, $p$<.01) than participants' competence ($M_{Participant}$=6.35, $M_{Tie}$=7.33), supporting H3.

Involvement was not significantly different across co-creation groups ($F_{(2,232)}$=1.19, $p$=.31) although it noted some directional results with those choosing Coll CC having higher involvement ($M$=5.90) than participants choosing IndCC ($M$=5.69) or purchasing at the store ($M$=5.74). Therefore H4 was not supported.

There were significant differences (L=.815, $p$<.01; $F_{(1,228)}$=51.65) between the SBB ($M_{SBB}$=3.75, $SD$=1.53) and SBA ($M_{SBA}$=4.55, $SD$=1.66).

SBB and SBA were significantly different across groups ($F_{(2,228)}$=20.683, $p$<.01), with those choosing IndCC ($M_{SBB}$= 3.75, $M_{SBA}$=4.93) and CollCC (($M_{SBB}$=3.85, $M_{SBA}$=4.84) having significantly higher *after* brand associations ($p$<.01), supporting H5.

## Discussion

The results reported bring new challenges for companies wanting to implement co-creation strategies. First, they need to consider a customer's ability. The companies interface with the customer must be easy or make customers feel competent to take on the task at hand.

Second, companies must consider the possibility that customers will not be acting alone, and this can affect not only their relationship with the individual customer but also gives the company the opportunity to present themselves to a new set of customers–those invited to help.

# REFERENCES

Alba, J. W., & Hutchinson, J. W. (2000). Knowledge calibration: What consumers know and what they think they know. *Journal of Consumer Research, 27*(2), 123-156.

Arias, E., Eden, H., Fischer, G., Gorman, A., & Sharff, E. (2000). Transcending the individual human mind: Creating shared understanding through collaborative design. *ACM Transactions on Computer Human-Interaction, 7*(1), 84-113.

Bendapudi, N., & Leone, R. P. (2003). Psychological implications of customer participation in co-production. *Journal of Marketing, 67*(January 2003), 14-28.

Bettencourt, L. A. (1997). Customer voluntary performance: Custoemrs as partners in service delivery. *Journal of Retailing, 73*(3), 383-406.

Bloch, P. H., & Richins, M. (1983). A theoretical model for the study of product importance perceptions. *Journal of Marketing, 47*(3), 69-81.

Bughin, J., Johnson, B. C., & Miller, A. (2008). *Distributed co-creation: The next wave in innovation.* Digital Content Services. McKinsey.

Bughin, J., Schellekens, M., & Singer, M. (2007). *Tapping into the power of digital co-creation: Learning from virtual worlds.* Digital Content Services. McKinsey.

Celsi, R. L., & Olson, J. C. (1988). The role of involvement in attention and comprehension processes. *Journal of Consumer Research, 15*(2), 210-224.

Cross, R., & Sproull, L. (n.d.). More than an answer: Information relationships for actionable knowledge. *Organization Science, 15*(4), 446-462.

Dellaert, B. G., & Stremersch, S. (2005). Marketing mass-customized products: Striking a balance between utility and complexity. *Journal of Marketing Research, 42*(May 2005), 219-227.

Douglas, M., & Isherwood, B. (1979). *The world of goods: Towards an anthropology of consumption.* New York: Basic Books.

Escalas, J. E., & Bettman, J. R. (2003). You are what they eat: The influence of reference groups on consumers' connections to brands. *Journal of Consumer Psychology, 13*(3), 339-348.

Escalas, J. E., & Bettman, J. R. (2005). Self-construal, reference groups, and brand meaning. *Journal of Consumer Research, 32*(December), 378-389.

Etgar, M. (2008). A descriptive model of the consumer co-production process. *Journal of the Academy of Marketing Science, 36*(1), 97-108.

Etgar, M. (2006). Co-production of services: A managerial extension. In *The service-dominant logic of marketing: dialog, debate and directions* (pp. 128-138). New York: M. E. Sharpe.

Fischer, G. (2005). *Distances and diversity: Sources for social creativity.* ACM Press.

Fischer, G., Giaccardi, E., Eden, H., Sugimoto, M., & Ye, Y. (2005). Beyond binary choices: Integrating individual and social creativity. *International Journal of Human-Computer Studies, 63*, 482-512.

Franke, N., & Reisinger, N. (2003). Remaining within cluster variance: A meta-analysis of the "Dark" Side of cluster analysis. Working Paper, Vienna Business University.

Gruner, K. E., & Homburg, C. (2000). Does customer interaction enhance new product success? *Journal of Business Research, 49*(1), 1-14.

Hemetsberger, A. (2003). *When consumers produce on the internet: The relationship between cognitive-affective, socially-based, and behavioral involvement of prosumers.* University of Insssbruck, Austria.

Holt, D. B. (1995). How consumers consume: A typology of consumption practices. *Journal of Consumer Research, 22*(1), 1-16.

Howard, J., & Sheth, J. (1968). *Theory of buyer behavior.* New York: J. Wiley & Sons.

Humphreys, A., & Grayson, K. (2008). The intersecting roles of consumer and producer: A critical perspective on co-production, co-creation and prosumption. *Sociology Compass, 2,* 1-16.

Levin, D. Z., & Cross, R. (2004). The strength of weak ties you can trust: The mediating role of trust in effective knowledge transfer. *Management Science, 50*(11), 1477-1490.

Lusch, R. F., & Vargo, S. L. (2006). Service-dominant logic: Reactions, reflections and refinements. *Marketing Theory, 6*(3), 281-288.

Malhotra, N. K. (1988). Self concept and product choice: An integrated perspective. *Journal of Economic Psychology, 9,* 1-28.

Moorman, C., Diehl, K., Brinberg, D., & Kidwell, B. (2004). Subjective knowledge, search locations, and consumer choice. *Journal of Consumer Research, 31*(3), 673-680.

Muniz, A. M., & O'Guinn, T. C. (2001). Brand community. *Journal of Consumer Research, 27*(March), 412-432.

O'Hern, M. S., & Rindfleisch, A. (2007). A typology of customer co-creation. In *2007 Winter Educators Conference.* San Diego, CA: American Marketing Association.

Prahalad, C. K., & Ramaswamy, V. (2004). Co-creation experiences: The next practice in value creation. *Journal of Interactive Marketing, 18*(3), 5-14.

Salomon, G. (1993). *Distributed cognitions: Psychological and educational considerations.* Cambridge, UK: Cambridge University Press.

Schau, H. J., & Gilly, M. (2003). We are what we post? Self-presentation in personal web space. *Journal of Consumer Research, 30*(3), 385-400.

Von Hippel, E. A. (2005). *Democratizing innovation.* Cambridge, MA: MIT Press.

Ward, J. C., & Reingen, P. H. (1990). Sociocognitive analysis of group decision making among consumers. *Journal of Consumer Research, 17*(December), 245-262.

Xie, C., Bagozzi, R., & Troye, S. V. (2008). Trying to prosume: Toward a theory of consumers as co-creators of value. *Journal of the Academy of Marketing Science, 36*(1), 109-122.

Zaichkowsky, J. L. (1985). Measuring the involvement construct. *Journal of Consumer Research, 12*(3), 341-352.

# The Distortion of "Objective" Scales: A Theory of Context Effects in Sequential Judgments

Shane Frederick, Yale University, USA
Daniel Mochon, Yale University, USA

## EXTENDED ABSTRACT

We propose that even on so called "objective" scales (e.g. pounds, calories, meters, etc.), many contextual effects, such as anchoring, are often best interpreted as scaling effects–reflecting changes in the use of the response scale rather than a change in respondents' perception of the focal stimulus. We present a theory which details how prior responses act as comparative standards for the interpretation and use of other numbers on that scale.

In support of our theory of scale distortion, we first show that a contextual stimulus only affects subsequent judgments that share the response scale. In our first demonstration, we randomly assigned 467 picnickers to one of three conditions. One group judged only the weight of a giraffe in pounds. A second did this after first judging the weight of a raccoon in pounds. The third group was like the second, except that they raccoon's weight on a 7-point heaviness scale.

The giraffe estimates averaged 1254 pounds among the group who made only that judgment, but just 709 pounds among those who first judged a raccoon's weight in pounds. Thus, the presence of the raccoon in the judgmental sequence induced a pronounced assimilation effect when judgments of its heaviness were rendered in units identical to the target judgment. However, when judged on a subjective heaviness scale (from 1 to 7), the raccoon judgment had no effect on estimates of the giraffe's weight (which averaged 1265 pounds).

The second set of studies also implicate a pure scaling effect, by showing that contextual manipulations which affect the target response have no influence on conceptually affiliated judgments of the target stimulus rendered on different scales. All participants then estimated three features of a giraffe: its weight (in pounds), its height (in feet), and its weight relative to a grand piano, on a seven point scale. Half of the 218 respondents made only these judgments. The other half had first estimated the weight of a raccoon in pounds. Again, the giraffe was judged to weigh less by those who had first judged the weight of a raccoon [760 pounds vs. 1117 pounds], but, notably, the raccoon had no appreciable effect on conceptually affiliated estimates rendered on other scales.

The final two studies bear further hallmarks of scale distortion: In one, a total of 157 participants recruited from an online survey site examined a list of fifteen animals ordered by weight, from very small (mouse) to very large (elephant) and were asked to select the one whose average adult weight was closest to 1000 pounds. Half of the participants estimated the weight of an average adult wolf before making this judgment while the other half did not. As predicted, estimating the weight of a (comparatively light) wolf increased the perceived size of the animal corresponding to '1000 pounds.' Respondents in the "wolf" condition selected animals whose true weight averaged 2170 pounds, whereas those in the control condition selected animals whose true weight averaged 1385 pounds.

In the second study, a total of 206 students were given a brief paper and pencil survey which listed thirteen food items ordered from least caloric (hard-boiled egg) to most caloric (Burger King Whopper with cheese) and were asked to select the item closest to 400 calories. Half of the participants first estimated the number of calories in an average apple before making this judgment, while the other half did not.

The conceptual replication succeeded. Prior estimates of the number of calories in an apple appeared to increase participants' perception of what '400 calories' means. Respondents in the "apple" condition picked items that were significantly more caloric [M=394] than respondents in the control condition [M=330]. Unlike previous studies 1 and 2, in which the numeric contrast effects specified by our theory manifest as assimilation effects in the responses (since a smaller number of units will seem adequate to represent the mass of a giraffe), here the proposed numeric contrast effects are transmitted directly to the overt response.

In summary, we suggest that objective scales may be susceptible to the same sorts of response scale effects that plague the interpretation of subjective scales. Though judgments on objective scales (such as pounds) are markedly affected by preceding judgments, we find no evidence that this effect is accompanied by a corresponding change in the underlying representation of the judged stimulus. Thus, we propose that the presence of contextual effects on objective scales *cannot* be assumed to reflect changes in the mental representation of the target stimulus, and that response scale effects play a much larger role in these results than is customarily acknowledged. Our findings resurrect the challenge of distinguishing representational effects from response language effects across a broad array of judgments where that distinction formerly seemed secure.

# Effects of Alphanumeric Brand Names: A Selective Anchoring Perspective

Dengfeng Yan, Hong Kong University of Science and Technology, China
Rod Duclos, Hong Kong University of Science and Technology, China

## EXTENDED ABSTRACT

Airbus A330, 7-Up, Coke Zero, Miss Sixty: these are just a few examples of the many brands and products featuring numbers in their name. Given the astronomical and ever growing budgets spent today on brand-building advertising, this research examines whether the presence of seemingly innocuous numbers in brand names bears any impact on consumers. More specifically, we focus our efforts on understanding how and when alphanumeric brands names (i.e., those containing both letters and numbers) may influence consumer judgments.

Building on anchoring theory, our central proposition is that consumers may use the number contained in alphanumeric brands as an anchor which can subsequently bias either up- or downward their appreciation of a product's price, weight, volume, etc.

We qualify this proposition, however, by arguing that such anchoring effect should occur mostly when (a) the numeric component of a name appears *relevant* for the judgment at hand, and (b) consumers evaluate attributes on the basis of *heuristics* (rather than systematic deliberation).

## THEORETICAL BACKGROUND

Across industries, marketers dedicate nowadays colossal sums of money (i.e., billions of dollars in the US alone) to branding activities. Not surprisingly, academic research focusing on brand naming has soared in the last two decades (Klink 2000; Schmitt et al.1994; Zhang and Schmitt 2001). Interestingly, much of this research focuses primarily on linguistics (e.g., understanding the interplay between morphemes, sounds, and the mental images they trigger in consumers). But despite this rich work, little research examines the impact of alphanumeric brand names on consumer behavior and decision-making. In one of a few exceptions, Pavia and Costa (1993) found that alphanumeric brand names are more suitable for technically complex, manufactured items (e.g., stereos, computers, cameras) and/or unemotional, formulated products such as vitamin-oriented cereals.

Drawing from anchoring theory and previous work in psychology and BDT, we propose that consumers may sometimes derive product information from alphanumeric brand names, regardless of the original meaning of the latter. That is, consumers use alphanumeric brand names as self-generated anchors to infer unknown product attributes. For example, consumers may assume that the Airbus A330 has roughly 330 seats, even though its name has little to do with seat capacity.

For this anchoring effect to occur, however, we argue that at least two conditions should be met. First, consumers must perceive the numeric component of the brand name as *relevant* to the attribute under consideration (e.g., "330" in the Airbus example should appear relevant to the number of seats in the aircraft). Second, consumers must process information heuristically (i.e., superficially) rather than systematically. In the next section, we report four studies aimed at testing our anchoring hypothesis and its boundary conditions.

## EXPERIMENTS

Study 1 aimed to demonstrate our basic proposition that the number contained in alphanumeric brand names can indeed function as an anchor and subsequently bias consumers' judgments. To this end, we randomly assigned participants to one of two conditions (Boeing B767 vs. Airbus A330) and asked them to estimate the number of seats in their aircraft. As predicted, subjects in the Boeing condition believed their aircraft had more seats than their counterparts in the Airbus condition.

Seeking to extend these results and test our first boundary condition, we randomly assigned participants in study 2 to two new conditions (Sprite vs. 7-Up) and asked them to estimate the price, volume, launch year, calories, and vitamin content of their drink. Whereas both products sell for approximately HK$5 in Hong Kong (i.e., the country where this study was run), subjects in the 7-Up condition estimated their drink to be more expensive (and closer in price to HK$7) than their counterparts in the Sprite condition. Importantly, however, the two groups did not differ on any other dependant variable. These results further confirm our anchoring proposition and shed light on the first boundary condition hypothesized earlier: I.e., for anchoring to occur, consumers must perceive the numeric component of the brand name (e.g., "7") as related to the attribute under consideration.

Building on the "relevance" argument aforementioned, we asked participants in study 3 to review information about one of two MP3 players (named M-200 vs. M-900) before estimating the price of the product. To test our second boundary condition, we manipulated participants' processing style (heuristic vs. systematic) by manipulating the order and lay-out of our study materials. As predicted, subjects in the M-900 condition perceived their product to be more expensive. This anchoring effect was reduced, however, when subjects processed information systematically.

Study 4 mirrored study 3 with the exception of the processing-style manipulation. To extend our results, we adopted here a classic cognitive-load manipulation known to reliably favor heuristic vs. systematic processing. While rehearsing an 8- vs. 2-digit number for an alleged memory task, participants estimated the price of one of two MP3 players (cf. study 3). As expected, subjects in the M-900 condition perceived their product to be more expensive. Yet, this effect vanished in the low cognitive-load (i.e., systematic-processing) condition.

## DISCUSSION

This research examines how and when seemingly innocuous alphanumeric brand names (e.g., 7-Up, Coke Zero) can bias a variety of consumer judgments (e.g., price estimates) by anchoring them either up- or downward. In four experiments, we find that consumers do indeed utilize the numbers contained in alphanumeric brand names as self-generated anchors to infer ostensibly relevant product attributes. For this effect to occur, however, consumers must process information heuristically, not systematically.

These findings provide new theoretical insights to two distinct lines of research. First, our results contribute to the brand-naming literature by proposing another mechanism through which numeric brand names can influence consumer judgment. Indeed, compared to prior work, our conceptualization is more general and therefore could be applied to a variety of numbers, product classes, and cultures. Second, our findings contribute to the psychology and BDT literatures by showing that anchoring can occur automatically (i.e., without the need for explicit or heavy-handed manipulations). As such, our studies suggest that anchoring might be more pervasive in consumer's daily life than previously assumed.

# Whether You Win or Whether You Lose: The Differential Risk of Priming the Deliberative and Affective Systems in On-line Auctions

Yael Steinhart, University of Haifa, Israel
Michael Kamins, Stony Brook University, USA
David Mazursky, The Hebrew University of Jerusalem, Israel
Avi Noy, University of Haifa, Israel

## EXTENDED ABSTRACT

Consumers' decision processes are generally influenced by both emotional and cognitive systems (Damasio 1994; Lee, Amir and Ariely 2009; Loewenstein and O'Donoghue 2004). For example, Loewenstein and O'Donoghue (2004) have developed a comprehensive two-system model in which a person's behavior is the outcome of an interaction between a *deliberative system* that assesses options with a broad, goal-based cognitive perspective and the *affective system* that encompasses emotions such as fear and is primarily driven by affective states that are currently activated.

The present research examines the role of the two-system model as a basis for further understanding the loss aversion phenomenon (Kahneman and Tversky 1979). This is important because the marketing literature has paid relatively scant attention to the question of how the deliberative system influences loss aversion. Overall, the marketing literature has focused to-date almost solely on the affective system.

We posit that each system has an opposite effect on the perception of loss aversion and therefore on the price bidders will be willing to pay for a given product. The direction of effect is contingent on the expected outcomes of the auction. In the case that the affective system is activated, bidders are proposed to pay higher prices when they are primed to anticipate losing the item rather than winning it. That is, the fear of losing the item is expected to override the joy of winning and consequently enhance the willingness to pay. On the other hand, when the deliberative system is made more accessible, bidders should pay higher prices if the potential of winning is made salient as opposed to losing. In this case, priming the goals of winning the auction, increases the cognitive focus on the product benefits, and therefore makes the perceived risk of losing the item less acceptable.

The first study manipulated two between-subject factors, thus creating a two (winning vs. losing outcome expectation) by two (affective vs. deliberative orientation) matrix. Its findings demonstrated the contradicting effects of the two-model system and the expected outcomes of the auction in determining the price bid for the product as well as the perceived risk of losing the item. The perceived risk of losing was also found to mediate the interactive effect of one's winning expectation and the two-model system on the placed bid.

The second study confirmed our expectations in terms of the placed bid, in a field setting. The field study was conducted on eBay over the period of four months. It consisted of four different conditions of actual auctions of the identical product, in which we activated either the affective or deliberative system and the type of outcome expectation via the product description.

The third study examined the robustness of the proposed effect when priming the winning or losing orientation in an unrelated prior task. This study is extremely important because it shows that one's success or failure in environmental tasks can have a behavioral effect on subsequent totally unrelated tasks. Findings supportive of our hypotheses would present the tantalizing suggestion that the way one sees oneself through the looking glass (i.e., as a "winner" or as a "loser") may have important implications in terms of which orientation is appropriate to use in inducing task specific behavior. Specifically, this study manipulated ones perception of performance

in a game through winning or losing points when completing a task by deciphering jumbled brand names. After this task, subjects were then subsequently asked to participate in an auction. Hence, a winning or losing orientation was independently induced prior to participation in the auction rather than win or loss expectations for the auction itself.

In future research, it would be interesting to examine the effect of expected outcomes on different types of products: emotional oriented products (such as a wedding ring) and cognitive oriented products (such as a scientific book). It is likely to assume that the type of product may differentially prime the influence of cognition and/or affect in the two model system and possibly make it easier to observe field effects. It will also be interesting to explore the association between this research and the regulatory focus stream of research. This research stream suggests that consumers are driven by either the prevention orientation (e.g. their duties, obligations, and responsibilities) or the promotion orientation (e.g., their hopes, aspirations, and dreams) (Higgins 1997, Freitas and Higgins 2002).

From a practical perspective, this research offers marketers simple and effective tools for activating the loss aversion effect among consumers. It shows that inserting a short note within the product description from a deliberative or affective perspective regarding the possible outcomes of winning or losing the product, can have a dramatic influence on the consumers' decision processes and behavior.

# Can I Correct My Errors without Knowing?: The Effect of Nonconscious Priming of a Target Attribute on Judgmental Errors

Ki Yeon Lee, University of Toronto, Canada
Andrew Mitchell, University of Toronto, Canada

## EXTENDED ABSTRACT

*Attribute substitution* (Kahneman and Frederick 2002) has been used to explain why people rely on heuristics and show biases. Attribute substitution occurs "when an individual assesses a specified target attribute of a judgment object by substituting another property of that object—the heuristic attribute—which comes more readily to mind" (p53). Substituting the target attribute with the heuristic attribute inevitably introduces systematic errors because these two attributes are different. What would happen if the target attribute is more accessible by subliminally priming words related to the target attribute? We expect that people are less likely to make the errors because the target attribute is made more accessible. The purpose of the present research is to examine whether and how subliminal priming of a target attribute can reduce the errors (e.g., base-rate neglect) and whether this correction process elicited by nonconscious priming requires cognitive resources, which implies the involvement of reasoning.

Experiment 1 examines whether the subliminal priming of a target attribute can correct judgmental errors by using the Kirkpatrick and Epstein (1992)'s jelly beans task which shows the *ratio-bias (RB) phenomenon*. The RB phenomenon refers to "the perception of the likelihood of a low-probability event as greater when it is presented in the form of larger (e.g., 10-in-100) rather than smaller (e.g., 1-in-10) numbers" (Pacini and Epstein 1999, p303). This phenomenon is attributed to a tendency to focus on the frequency of the numerator (i.e., heuristic attribute) instead of the overall probability (i.e., target attribute). Selecting one of two trays that offer equal probabilities is, in itself, not a judgmental error. However, the preference for a 9% over a 10 % probability is (Denes-Raj and Epstein 1994).

In experiment 1, participants were asked to choose one of two trays from which they could participate in a lottery where they could win $50 if they drew a red jelly bean: tray A (10% tray) containing 1 red and 9 white beans and tray B (9% tray) containing 9 red and 91 white beans. Since the target attribute is the 'objective probability' of drawing a red bean, if participants choose a tray based on the target attribute instead of the number of red jelly beans, they should be more (less) likely to choose the 10% tray (the 9 % tray).

Participants were randomly assigned to either a control or a target attribute priming condition. The priming task was disguised as a perception task. Words related to the objective probability (e.g., probability, proportion) were *subliminally* (i.e., 20 ms) shown to participants depending on the priming conditions. The primed words were masked by a string of letters (e.g., addick). Participants were asked to identify whether each string of letters presented on a computer screen contained two vowels or not. After finishing the perception task, participants were asked to complete the next task—the jelly beans task. They were asked to indicate their own preference between the two trays on a five-point scale. Next, they were asked to choose which tray they wanted to draw from for a real drawing.

We found main effects of attribute priming in self-preference scale and tray choice. Participants primed with the target attribute were more likely to prefer the correct 10 % tray than those who were not primed. Consistent with this result, participants primed with the target attribute chose the 10 % tray significantly more than those who were not primed.

Experiment 2 extends the findings in Experiment 1 to a different judgmental bias, base-rate neglect by using an analogue of the engineer-and-lawyer problem (Kahneman and Tversky 1973). In the engineer-and-lawyer problem, people are given the base rate of engineers (e.g., 30 engineers out of 100 individuals) and the description of a person (e.g., typical characteristics of an engineer such as having no interest in political and social issue and spending time in home carpentry). Although the base-rate of engineers in a given sample is very low (e.g., 30%), people's estimation of the probability that a person is an engineer is much higher (e.g., 80%) than the base rate due to their tendency to rely on the description of the person rather than the base rate. The base-rate neglect in probability judgment is problematic because it induces people to violate the fundamental Bayesian rule of statistical prediction.

The procedures in experiment 2 are similar to those in experiment 1. We used Betsch et al. (1998)'s professor-and-non-professor item. Participants were randomly assigned to either a control or a target attribute priming condition. After finishing the priming task, participants were given a description of a person. They were told that this description was one of a survey sample which contained 17.6 % professors and 82.4 % non-professors. Their task was to rate the probability that the person is a professor given description of the person and the base rate.

We found that participants primed with the target attribute were more likely to estimate the probability to be lower (closer to the base rate of professors) than those who were not primed. This finding provides further evidence that subliminally priming the target attribute reduced the judgmental error.

Experiment 3 examines whether the process of correcting judgmental errors requires the involvement of System 2 by manipulating cognitive load. Since the processes of System 1 are automatic and effortless whereas those of System 2 are slow and effortful, if System 2 is involved in the correction process, a high cognitive load should interfere with this correction process which is facilitated by subliminally priming the target attribute.

The procedures in experiment 3 are similar to those in experiment 2 except the manipulation of cognitive load. Participants were randomly assigned to a 2 (target attribute priming: no priming vs. target attribute priming) x 2 (cognitive load: low vs. high load) between-subjects design. We manipulated cognitive load by asking participants to memorize either a 2- or 9-digit number. To rule out the alternative explanation of mood effect, we measured their mood using PANAS scale (Watson, Clark, and Tellegen 1988).

Our manipulation check was successful in that participants found it more difficult to memorize the 9- than the 2-digit number. In the low cognitive load conditions, participants primed with the target attribute were more likely to estimate the probability to be lower (closer to the base rate) than those who were not primed. However, in the high cognitive load conditions, participants' probability estimates were equally high (far from the base rate). This finding implies that cognitive busyness impairs the process of correcting the bias (i.e., the base-rate neglect). We ruled out the alternative account by showing no differences in the PANAS scale as a function of cognitive load. The findings of experiment 3 suggest that System 2 is involved in the process of correcting judgmental errors.

These studies provide evidence for the idea that priming the target attribute *nonconsciously* can reduce judgmental errors. We believe that this research is important for two reasons: First, it contributes to extend our understanding of the underlying mechanism for reducing judgmental errors by demonstrating that not only explicit/conscious methods but also *implicit/nonconscious method* (i.e., priming a target attribute) can reduce the judgmental errors. Second, it shows that the process of correcting judgmental errors requires cognitive resources, which implies the involvement of System 2.

## REFERENCES

Agnoli, Franca (1991), "Development of Judgmental Heuristics and Logical Reasoning: Training Counteracts the Representativeness Heuristic," *Cognitive Development*, 6, 195–217.

Agnoli, Franca and David H. Krantz (1989), "Suppressing Natural Heuristics by Formal Instruction: The Case of the Conjunction Fallacy," *Cognitive Psychology*, 21, 515–50.

Bargh, John A. (1990), "Auto-Motives: Preconscious Determinants of Thought and Behavior," in *Handbook of motivation and cognition*, Vol. 2, ed E. Tory Higgins and Richard M. Sorrentino, New York: Guilford Press, 93–130.

Bargh, John A, and Tanya L. Chartrand (1999), "The Unbearable Automaticity of Being," *American Psychologist*, 54, 462–79.

Betsch, Tilmann, Glenn-Merten Biel, Claudia Eddelbüttel, and Andreas Mock (1998), "Natural Sampling and Base-Rate Neglect," *European Journal of Social Psychology*, 28, 269–73.

Bodenhausen, Galen V. (1990), "Stereotypes as Judgmental Heuristics: Evidence of Circadian Variations in Discrimination," *Psychological Science*, 1(5), 319–22.

Camerer, Colin F. and Robin Hogarth (1999), "The Effects of Financial Incentives in Experiments: A Review and Capital-labor-production Framework," *Journal of Risk and Uncertainty*, 19, 7–42.

Chartrand, Tanya L. and John A. Bargh (1996), "Automatic Activation of Impression Formation and Memorization Goals: Nonconscious Goal Priming Reproduces Effects of Explicit Task Instructions," *Journal of Personality and Social Psychology*, 71, 464–78.

Cosmides, Leda and John Tooby (1996), "Are Humans Good Intuitive Statisticians After All?: Rethinking Some Conclusions of the Literature on Judgment under Uncertainty," *Cognition*, 58, 1–73.

Denes-Raj, Veronika and Seymour Epstein (1994), "Conflict between Intuitive and Rational Processing: When People Behave against Their Better Judgment," *Journal of Personality and Social Psychology*, 66, 819–29.

Epstein, Seymour (1994), "Integration of the Cognitive and the Psychodynamic Unconscious," *American Psychologist*, 49(8), 709–24.

Evans, Jonathan St. bt and David E. Over (1996), *Rationality and Reasoning*, Hove, UK: Psychology Press.

Gabrielcik, Adele and Russell H. Fazio (1984), "Priming and Frequency Estimation: A Strict Test of the Availability Heuristic," *Personality and Social Psychology Bulletin*, 10, 85–89.

Gigerenzer, Gerd and Daniel G. Goldstein (1996), "Reasoning the Fast and Frugal Way: Models of Bounded Rationality," *Psychological Review*, 103(4), 650–69.

Gigerenzer, Gerd and Ulrich Hoffrage (1995), "How to Improve Bayesian Reasoning without Instruction: Frequency Formats," *Psychological Review*, 102, 684–704.

Gilbert, Daniel T. (2002), "Inferential Correction" in *Heuristics and Biases*, ed Gilovich, Thomas, Dale Griffin, and Daniel Kahneman, New York: Cambridge University Press, 167–84

Gilbert, Daniel T. and J. Gregory Hixon (1991), "The Trouble of Thinking: Activation and Application of Stereotypic Beliefs," *Journal of Personality and Social Psychology*, 60, 509-17.

Kahneman, Daniel (2002, December), "Maps of Bounded Rationality: A Perspective on Intuitive Judgement and Choice," Nobel Prize Lecture, Retrieved January 11, 2006, from http://nobelprize.org/nobel_prizes/economics/laureates/2002/kahnemann-lecture.pdf.

_____ (2003), "A Perspective on Judgment and Choice: Mapping Bounded Rationality," *American Psychologist*, 58, 697–720.

Kahneman, Daniel and Shane Frederick (2002), "Representativeness Revisited: Attribute Substitution in Intuitive Judgment," in *Heuristics and Biases*, ed Gilovich, Thomas, Dale Griffin, and Daniel Kahneman, New York: Cambridge University Press, 49–81.

_____ (2005). "A Model of Heuristic Judgment", in *The Cambridge Handbook of Thinking and Reasoning*, ed. K.J. Holyoak and R.G. Morrison Cambridge, U.K.: Cambridge University Press, 267–93.

Kahneman, Daniel and Amos Tversky (1972), "Subjective Probability: A Judgment of Representativeness," *Cognitive Psychology*, 3, 430–54.

_____ 1973), "On the Psychology of Prediction," *Psychological Review*, 80 (4), 237–51.

Kirkpatrick, Lee A. and Seymour Epstein (1992), "Cognitive-Experiential Self-Theory and Subjective Probability: Further Evidence for Two Conceptual Systems," *Journal of Personality and Social Psychology*, 63, 534–44.

Krull, Douglas S. (1993), "Does the Grist Change the Mill? The Effect of Perceiver's Goals on the Process of Social Inference," *Personality and Social Psychology Bulletin*, 19, 340–8.

Liberman, Akiva M. (2001), "Exploring the Boundaries of Rationality: A Functional Perspective on Dual Models in Social Psychology," in *Cognitive Social Psychology: The Princeton Symposium on the Legacy and Future of Social Cognition*, ed. G. B. Moskowitz, Mahwah, NJ: Erlbaum, 291–304.

Nisbett, Richard E., David H. Krantz, Christopher Jepson, and Ziva Kunda (1983), "The Use of Statistical Heuristics in Everyday Inductive Reasoning," *Psychological Review*, 90, 339–63.

Pacini, Rosemary and Seymour Epstein (1999), "The Interaction of Three Facets of Concrete Thinking in a Game of Chance, *Thinking and Reasoning*, 5, 303–25.

Pacini, Rosemary, Francisco Muir, and Seymour Epstein (1998), "Depressive Realism from the Perspective of Cognitive-Experiential Self-Theory," *Journal of Personality and Social Psychology*, 74, 1056–68.

Pontari, Beth A. and Barry R. Schlenker (2000), "The Influence of Cognitive Load on Self-Presentation: Can Cognitive Busyness Help as well as Harm Social Performance?" *Journal of Personality and Social Psychology*, 78, 1092–108.

Sloman, Steven A. (1996), "The Empirical Case for Two Systems of Reasoning," *Psychological Bulletin*, 119, 3–22.

Stanovich, Keith E. and Richard F. West (2000), "Individual Differences in Reasoning: Implications for the Rationality Debate," *Behavioral and Brain Sciences*, 23, 645–726.

_____ (2002), "Individual Differences in Reasoning: Implications for the Rationality Debate," in *Heuristics and biases*, ed Gilovich, Thomas, Dale Griffin, and Daniel Kahneman, New York: Cambridge University Press, 421–40.

Tversky, Amos, and Daniel Kahneman (1973), "Availability: A Heuristic for Judging Frequency and Probability," *Cognitive Psychology*, 5, 207–32.

_____ (1974, September 27), "Judgment under Uncertainty: Heuristics and Biases," *Science*, 185, 1124–31.

_____ (1983), "Extensional vs. Intuitive Reasoning: The Conjunction Fallacy in Probability Judgment," *Psychological Review*, 90, 293–315.

Watson, David, Lee A. Clark, and Auke Tellegen (1988), "Development and Validation of Brief Measures of Positive and Negative Affect: The PANAS scale," *Journal of Personality and Social Psychology*, 54, 1063–70.

Wegner, Daniel M., Ralph Erber, and Sophia Zanakos (1993), "Ironic Processes in the Mental Control of Mood and Mood-Related Thought, *Journal of Personality and Social Psychology*, 65, 1093–104.

Yamigishi, Kimihiko (1997), "When a 12.86% Mortality Is More Dangerous than 24.14%: Implications for Risk Communication," *Applied Cognitive Psychology*, 11, 495–506.

Zukier, Henri and Albert Pepitone (1984), "Social Roles and Strategies in Prediction: Some Determinants in the Use of Base-Rate Information," *Journal of Personality and Social Psychology*, 47, 349–60.

# Attainment Versus Maintenance Goals: Differences in Cognitive Processing and Goal Attractiveness

Antonios Stamatogiannakis, INSEAD, France
Amitava Chattopadhyay, INSEAD, Singapore
Dipankar Chakravarti, Johns Hopkins University, USA

## EXTENDED ABSTRACT

Consumers and firms across many domains (e.g., dieting, saving, exercising) use goals to regulate behaviour. For example, HSBC offers the "Premier Investor Savings" account, which requires the maintenance of a $25000 minimum balance, but at the same time offers higher interest rates with higher balances.

Depending on the relation between the actual and the desired state of the goal, these goals are classified in two categories: Attainment and maintenance goals. Attainment goals are those for which the actual state differs from the desired state (e.g., increase your balance to get a higher interest rate). Maintenance goals are those for which the actual and the desired states coincide, but there is a time difference between the present and the goal time horizon (e.g., maintain your balance to be eligible for this savings account).

Given the mixed use of these two goal types, it is surprising that we know very little on how attainment and maintenance goals compare with each other. Recent comparisons between these two goal types revealed that people are overoptimistic for attainment goals, but not for maintenance goals. As a result, attainment goals are perceived as easier than objectively easier maintenance goals (Stamatogiannakis, Chattopadhyay and Chakravarti 2010).

This paper adds to the above results in two important ways. First, it investigates the content of thoughts triggered by attainment versus maintenance goals, and tests whether it can account for differences in the perceived difficulty. We predict that people will tend to focus on the comparison between the actual and the desired state more for attainment goals, relative to maintenance goals. As a result, they will be overoptimistic for attainment goals' achievement (Dunning 2007), and will perceive them as easier (Stamatogiannakis et al. 2010).

Second, it examines whether attainment or maintenance goals are more attractive.. Easier and more achievable goals are more attractive (Kruglanski et al. 2002). We predict therefore that attainment goals will be more attractive than maintenance goals, because they are perceived as easier.

To test these two predictions we examine in depth the open ended responses collected by Stamatogiannakis et al. (2010), and we conduct two scenario based experiments. In all three studies goal type (attainment vs. maintenance) is manipulated between participants. Scenarios about weight, GPA, daily working out time, money, and weekly sales goals are used.

Stamatogiannakis et al. (2010) asked participants to rate goal difficulty and list their thoughts on what would make goal achievement more or less likely. To uncover differences in thoughts generation between attainment and maintenance goals, we did an in-depth analysis of these thoughts. These were coded across two dimensions, valence and content. In valence coding, each thought was categorised as favorable (i.e., a success thought), unfavorable (i.e., a failure thought), or neutral (i.e., unrelated thought) for goal achievement. In content coding, each thought was categorised as related or not to the following: effort/ motivation put for goal achievement, the person pursuing the goal, goal context, specific plans for goal achievement, and goal level. Finally, statements related to the goal level were further categorised depending on whether they involved a comparison between the actual and the desired state, or not.

The results suggest that attainment goals evoke more thoughts comparing the actual and the desired state, and more plan-related

success thoughts, but less context-related failure thoughts relative to maintenance goals. Only the first mediate the effects of goal type on difficulty.

The next two experiments examine effects of goal type on goal attractiveness. We predicted that attainment goals will be more attractive than maintenance goals, because they are perceived as easier.

Experiment one uses a 2 x 2 between participants design. Some participants judged maintenance goals and some attainment goals. Further (to draw attention to possible goal difficulties), the action required for goal achievement was explicitly stated only for some of the participants. Goal attractiveness and difficulty were the dependent measures. The goal type x required action interaction was significant for both. When no action was provided, attainment goals were seen as more attractive and easier than maintenance goals. However, when attention was directed to required action, the two goal types were seen as equally attractive and difficult. The interaction on attractiveness ratings was mediated by the difficulty ratings.

Experiment two uses a 2 x 2 x 2 between participants design. Some participants judged maintenance goals and some attainment goals. Further (to draw attention to possible goal difficulties), some participants rated only goal attractiveness, but some rated goal difficulty before that. Finally the difficulty question was negatively framed (i.e., "How difficult?") for some of the participants, but positively framed (i.e., "How challenging?") for others. The goal type x attractiveness question order interaction effect on attractiveness was significant. Attainment goals were judged as more attractive than maintenance goals when the attractiveness question was asked first. However, when the difficulty question was asked first, drawing attention to goal difficulty, the results reversed. Finally, difficulty framing did not moderate the above result.

To conclude, this paper adds to previous literature comparing attainment with maintenance goals. It demonstrates that maintenance goals evoke more contextual interference thoughts, but attainment goals evoke more success plans and actual-desired state comparison thoughts. The latter cause attainment goals to be perceived as easier and more attractive than maintenance goals. Effects on goal attractiveness are attenuated or even reversed, when consumer attention is drawn to possible difficulties for goal achievement.

## REFERENCES

Dunning, David (2007), "Prediction: The Inside View," in *Social psychology: Handbook of basic principles (second edition)*, eds. Arie W. Kruglanski, and E. Tory Higgins, NY: Guilford, 69-90.

Kruglanski, Arie, James Y. Shah, Ayelet Fishbach, Ron Friedman, Woo Young Chun, and David Sleeth-Keppler (2002), "A Theory of Goal Systems," *Advances in Experimental Social Psychology*, 34, 331-78.

Stamatogiannakis, Antonios, Amitava Chattopadhyay, Dipankar Chakravarti (2010), "Maintenance versus Attainment Goals: Why People Think it Is Harder to Maintain their Weight than to Lose a Couple of Kilos", in *Advances in Consumer Research*, Vol. 37, eds. Margarett C. Campbell, J. Jeffrey Inman, and Rik Pieters, Duluth, MN: Association for Consumer Research.

# Maintenance versus Attainment Goals:
## Influence of Self-Regulation Goal Type on Goal Pursuit Behaviors

Napatsorn Jiraporn, State University of New York at Binghamton, USA
Kalpesh Kaushik Desai, State University of New York at Binghamton, USA

## EXTENDED ABSTRACT

The extant goal literature has focused mainly on *attainment goals,* in which the desired state is positively discrepant from the current state, but has neglected the *maintenance goals,* in which the current state is equal to or better than the desired state. This casts doubt on whether the implications of findings from the literature can apply to the challenges related to maintenance goals. We addresses these gaps by contrast the two goal types and examine the mechanisms underlying each of them. Our findings suggest that consumers in the two groups are attracted to different self-regulation strategies. Therefore, firms can provide different products for consumers in these two groups.

What differentiate maintenance goals from attainment goals? First, by their definitions, the two goal types differ in the distance between the current and the desired states. Second, the two goal types differ in the clarity about temporal ending of goal pursuit (H1). In case of an attainment goal, achieving the desired state suggests end of goal pursuit. However, in case of a maintenance goal, there is less clarity about the temporal ending because the current state is already better than the benchmark. Moreover, some maintenance goals are to be pursued over long term such as health-related goals (e.g. exercise goal) so these goals are not temporally bound.

Moreover, the two goal types differ in their underlying mechanisms. We propose that maintenance goals activate retrospective (vs. prospective) thought because maintenance goals indicate the past actions of consumers were good enough. In contrast, attainment goals activate prospective thought because attainment goals suggest that the past actions did not bring about the desired state so consumers focus more on future actions (H2). Moreover, maintenance goals trigger more process-focused (vs. outcome-focused) thinking while attainment goals trigger more outcome-focused thinking (H3). The reason is that thoughts in retrospection tend to have richer context (Van Boven, Kane, & McGraw 2009) and make consumers think at more concrete (vs. abstract) level. Thoughts at concrete level involve feasibility aspects and process of means to goal but thoughts at abstract level focus on consequences of means or goal (Liberman & Trope 1998; Trope & Liberman 2003). Hence, when considering goal pursuit strategies, maintainers tend to focus more on processes of the strategies whereas attainers focus more on outcomes of the strategies.

The two underlying mechanisms lead to different goal pursuit behaviors. First, we predict that maintainers will construct smaller consideration set of goal pursuit strategies than attainers (H4). This is because maintainers' retrospective thoughts constrain them with reality (Van Boven et al 2009) and prevent them from choosing strategies that are less practical. Consistently, process-focused thinking makes maintainers consider only strategies with easier implementation process. In contrast, attainers are less constrained by reality and more outcome-driven so they consider any strategies which appear to deliver satisfactory outcomes.

Furthermore, based on the difference in clarity about temporal ending of the two goal types, maintainers will prefer strategies that require less (vs. more) effort because the temporal ending of their goal pursuit is not clear. On the other hand, attainers might be more willing to exert higher effort as they perceive that the goal pursuit is more temporally bound (H5a). In addition, the outcome-focused thinking might make attainers prefer strategies that require higher

effort because they rely on 'instrumentality heuristics', naïve belief that higher effort leads to better outcome (Labroo & Kim 2009). Along the same line, we predict that maintainers prefer a disaggregated framing of strategy implementation (e.g. exercise 15 minutes for 6 days per week) than an aggregated framing (e.g. exercise 45 minutes for 2 days per week) (H5b). This is because maintainers might perceive the former as easier to implement.

In three studies, the two goal types were manipulated. All three studies successfully established that maintenance goals are characterized with less clear temporal (H1). Study 1 with a 2 (maintenance vs. attainment goal) x 2 (domain replicates) between-subject design (n =225) tested the consideration set size hypothesis in two goal domains, cholesterol and money saving. The results were consistent across two domains and showed that maintainers considered fewer strategies than attainers ($M_{Maintainers}$ = 3.61 vs. $M_{Attainers}$ = 4.12, ($F(1, 207) = 4.16, p < .01$). Thus, our H1 & H4 were supported.

Study 2 (n = 56) replicated the results of Study 1 with stronger measures of psychological processes. The analysis revealed that attainers engaged more in prospective than prospective thoughts ($M_{Retro}$ = 4.44 vs. $M_{Pro}$ = 5.10, $t(28) = 2.14, p < .05$) but maintainers engaged in thoughts in both time frames. Thus, H2 was partially supported. Further analysis showed that attainers engaged more in outcome-focused thinking than process-focused thinking ($M_{Proc}$ = 4.56 vs. $M_{Out}$ = 5.25, $t(28) = 3.28, p < .01$) but maintainers did not differ between the two thinking styles. Thus, H3 was also partially supported. We added measures of whether consumers consider old versus new strategies. The results indicated that maintainers considered both old and new strategies but attainers tended to consider new strategies ($M_{Old}$ = 4.31 vs. $M_{New}$ = 4.93, $t(28) = 1.98, p = .06$).

Study 3 (n = 28) tested our effort-related hypothesis (H5) with a 2 (maintenance vs. attainment goal) x 2 (aggregated vs. disaggregated framing) design with framing as within-subject factor. The results revealed that maintainers evaluated a disaggregated framing (workout 15 minutes for 6 days per week) more positively than an aggregated framing (workout 45 minutes for 2 days per week) ($F(1, 25) = 2.85$, $M_{disagg}$ = 5.08 vs. $M_{agg}$ = 4.78, $p < .1$). In addition, maintainers rated the former as less effortful than the latter ($M_{disagg}$ = 3.36 vs. $M_{agg}$ = 5.36, $t(11) = 2.97, p < .05$). However, attainers did not differ in their attitude between the two framings. Thus, H5 was partially supported.

Across three studies, the results showed robust supports that maintenance goals differ from attainment goals in characteristics, underlying processes, and pursuit behaviors. The research helps managers recognize that consumers striving different goal types are not homogenous and distinct marketing strategies are needed to serve the two consumer groups.

## REFERENCES

Bagozzi, Richard and Dholakia, Utpal (1999), "Goal Setting and Goal Striving in Consumer Behavior," *Journal of Marketing*, 63, 19-32

Baumgartner, Hans and Pieters, Rik (2007), "Goal-directed Consumer Behavior: Motivation, Volition, and Affect," in *Handbook of Consumer Psychology*, eds. Haugtvedt, Curtis P; Herr, Paul M; and Kardes, Frank R., New York, Psychology Press, 367-392

Blaszczynski, Alex and Lia Nower (2002), "A Pathways Model of Problem and Pathological Gambling," *Addiction*, 97, 487-499

Brownell, Kelly D., G. Alan Marlatt, Edward Lichtenstein, and G. Terence Wilson (1986), "Understanding and Preventing Relapse," *American psychologist*, 41 (7), 765-82.

Brodscholl, Jeff; Kober, Hedy; and Higgins, Tory (2007), "Strategies of Self-Regulation in Goal Attainment Versus Goal Maintenance," *European journal of social psychology*, 37 (4), 628 – 648

Chartrand, Tanya L., and John A. Bargh (2002), "Nonconscious Motivations: Their Activation, Operation, and Consequences," in *Self and Motivation: Emerging Psychological Perspectives*, ed. Abraham Tesser, Diederik A. Stapel, and Joanne V. Wood, Washington, DC: American Psychological Association, 13-41

Fishbach, Ayelet and Dhar, Ravi (2005), "Goals as Excuses or Guides: The Liberating Effect of Perceived Goal Progress on Choice," *The Journal of consumer research*, 32 (3), 370

Gaine, Graham and La Guardia, Jennifer (2009), "The unique contributions of motivations to maintain a relationship and motivations toward relational activities to relationship well-being*," Motivation and emotion*, 33 (2), 184-202

Gilbert, Daniel T., Carey K. Morewedge, Jane L. Risen, and Timothy D. Wilson (2004), "Looking Forward to Looking Backward," *Psychological Science-Cambridge*, 15, 346-50

Gollwitzer, Peter M. (1999), "Implementation intentions: Strong effects of simple plans," *American Psychologist*, 54, 493-503

Gourville, John (1998), "Pennies-A-Day: The Effect of Temporal Reframing on Transaction Evaluation," Journal of Consumer Research, 24 (March), 395-408

Hertel, Andrew W.; Finch, Emily A.; Kelly, Kristina M.; King, Christie; Lando, Harry; Linde, Jennifer A.; Jeffery, Robert W.; Rothman, Alexander J. (2008), "The impact of expectations and satisfaction on the initiation and maintenance of smoking cessation: An experimental test," *Health Psychology,* 27(3S), S197-S206

Labroo, Aparna & Kim, Sara (2009), "The "instrumentality" heuristic: Why metacognitive difficulty is desirable during goal pursuit," *Psychological Science, 20,* 127–134

Liberman, N., & Trope, Y. (1998), "The role of feasibility and desirability considerations in near and distant future decisions: A test of Temporal Construal Theory," *Journal of Personality and Social Psychology, 75,* 5-18

Phelan, Suzanne; Hill, James; Lang, Wei; Dibello, Jullia; and Wing, Rena (2003), "Recovery from Relapse among Successful Weight Maintainers," *American Journal of Clinical Nutrition, 78*(6), 1079-1084

Stamatogiannakis, Antonios; Chattopadhyay, Amitava, and Chakravarti, Dipankar (2009), "Maintenance versus Attainment Goals: Why People Think it Is Harder to Maintain their Weight than to Lose a Couple of Kilos," in *Advances in Consumer Research* 2009

Taylor, Shelley E., Lien B. Pham, Inna D. Rivkin, and David A. Armor (1998), "Harnessing the Imagination: Mental Simulation, Self-Regulation, and Coping," *American psychologist*, 53, 429-39.

Trope, Yaacov, & Liberman, Nira (2000), "Temporal construal and time-dependent changes in preference," *Journal of Personality and Social Psychology,*79, 876–889

-------- (2003). Temporal construal theory of time dependent preferences. In J. Carillo, I. Brocas, & J. D. Carrill (Eds.), *The psychology of economic decisions: Rationality and well-being* Oxford, England: Oxford University Press

Van Boven, Leaf, Kane, Joanne., and McGraw, A.Peter (2009) "Temporally asymmetric constraints on mental simulation: Retrospection is more constrained than prospection" In K. Markman, W. Klein, & S.Shur (Eds.), *The Handbook of Imagination and Mental Simulation*. (pp. 131-150) Psychology Press.

Tversky, Amos and Derek J. Koehler (1994), "Support Theory: A Nonextensional Representation of Subjective Probability," *Psychological review*, 101 (4), 547-66.

# Squeezing a Dry Towel: Reducing Consumers' Optimistic Prediction Biases

Kyeong Sam Min, University of New Orleans, USA
Hal Arkes, Ohio State University, USA

## EXTENDED ABSTRACT

Consumers tend to be optimistic in predicting when they will complete an upcoming activity. Optimistic predictions are often more problematic than pessimistic predictions, because they not only delay other planned projects, but they also make consumers use unexpected additional resources to complete the current project. Even though research to date has proposed various bias reduction aids in the context of optimistic time predictions (e.g., Roy, Christenfeld, and McKenzie 2005), many of them were not empirically supported or earned only mixed support. The purpose of this paper is to propose and test new debiasing strategies that help to reduce consumers' optimistic prediction biases.

One of the possible causes of the optimistic prediction bias is that individuals overestimate the likelihood of the occurrence of a chain of events in completing a project. As shown in the explanation bias literature (e.g., Hirt, Kardes, and Markman 2004), people tend to view a particular outcome as more likely to occur if they have explained a sequence of steps required to complete the project. Because individuals often base their judgments upon the information that is readily available, the project that has been explained is more accessible and thus gets higher likelihood estimates. Thus consumers who can easily simulate the sequence of an event may be optimistic in concluding that the event is likely to take place soon.

Drawing upon the literature in judgment and decision making, we argue that the magnitude of planning difficulty effects will be mitigated when an individual planner's accountability increases, a planner write a pessimistic scenario, or a planner is led to believe that ease is bad. First, accountable individuals tend to thoroughly process the information and do not heavily rely upon heuristics such as ease of generation (e.g., Tetlock, Lerner, and Boettger 1996). Thus, we predicted that the influence of planning difficulty on optimistic prediction bias would be weaker when individuals' *accountability* for their prediction outcome was high, rather than low. Second, following up Sanna and Schwarz (2004), we predicted that individuals' optimistic prediction bias would be smaller when it was easy, rather than difficult, to generate a *pessimistic* scenario about an upcoming event. Third, building upon Briñol, Petty, and Tormala (2006), we predicted that experiencing ease in generating an optimistic scenario would reduce optimism when people interpreted *ease* of generation to be *bad*, rather than good.

Using "real world" planning activities, each of these predictions were tested across three experiments, respectively. In Experiment 1 we examined how planning difficulty would influence individuals' optimistic prediction biases. We also tested the role of accountability as a debiasing aid. People who were engaged to be married were first asked to identify one of their pre-wedding activities that would be completed soon. Then they were told to describe how they would complete the activity by writing about it in relatively easy or difficult steps. They were also assigned to one of two accountability conditions. Next the participants estimated the time that the target activity would be completed and then evaluated their planning processes. Lastly, participants reported their actual completion times when they were contacted 10 days after the predicted deadline of the chosen activity. As predicted, people who were engaged to be married made more realistic time estimates for the project completion when they were asked to write a relatively difficult, rather than easy step, optimistic scenario. However, unlike our prediction, accountability did not play any moderating role. Each individual in the high accountability condition seemed to have been less susceptible to our accountability instruction because his or her responses would be ultimately examined by the experimenter as well as the other member of the couple. In Experiment 2 we tested how planning difficulty would interact with scenario type: optimistic versus pessimistic. As predicted, the planning difficulty effect shown in Experiment 1 was qualified by the type of scenario that people generated. The optimistic prediction bias decreased when individual planners generated the difficult, as opposed to the easy, optimistic scenario or when individuals generated the easy, as opposed to the difficult, pessimistic scenario. In Experiment 3 we tested how planning difficulty would interact with shoppers' interpretation of the feeling of ease. As expected, the planning difficulty effect was qualified by the subjective meaning of ease. Planners who generated a difficult, rather than an easy, optimistic scenario were less likely to exhibit the optimistic prediction bias when they positively interpreted the feeling of ease. In contrast, planners who generated an easy, rather than a difficult, optimistic scenario were marginally less likely to exhibit the optimistic prediction bias when they negatively interpreted the feeling of ease.

In sum, across three experiments using "real world" planning activities we found support for two important debiasing aids. We hope our new debiasing strategies will not only help illuminate the processes behind the optimistic prediction bias but will also assist all of us in making more realistic plans.

## REFERENCES

Briñol, Pablo, Richard E. Petty, and Zachary L. Tormala (2006), "The Malleable Meaning of Subjective Ease," *Psychological Science,* 17, 200-06.

Buehler, Roger, Dale Griffin, and Michael Ross (1994), "Exploring the 'Planning Fallacy': Why People Underestimate Their Task Completion Times," *Journal of Personality and Social Psychology*, 67, 366-81.

Buehler, Roger, Johanna Peetz, and Dale Griffin (2010), "Finishing on Time: When Do Predictions Influence Completion Times?" *Organizational Behavior and Human Decision Processes,* 111, 23-32.

Fitzsimons, Gráinne M. and Ayelet Fishbach (in press), "Shifting Closeness: Interpersonal Effects of Personal Goal Progress," *Journal of Personality and Social Psychology.*

Hansen, William B., Linda M. Collins, C. Kevin Malotte, C. Anderson Johnson, and Jonathan E. Fielding (1985), "Attrition in Prevention Research," *Journal of Behavioral Medicine,* 8, 261-75.

Hirt, Edward R., Frank R. Kardes, and Keith D. Markman (2004), "Activating a Mental Simulation Mind-Set Through Generation of Alternatives: Implications for Debiasing in Related and Unrelated Domains," *Journal of Experimental Social Psychology*, 40, 374-83.

Kahn, Barbara E., Mary Frances Luce, and Stephen M. Nowlis (2006), "Debiasing Insights from Process Tests," *Journal of Consumer Research*, 33, 131–38.

Kahneman, Daniel and Amos Tversky (1979), "Intuitive Prediction: Biases and Corrective Procedures," *TIMS Studies in Management Science*, 12, 331-27.

Kruger, Justin and Matt Evans (2004), "If You Don't Want To Be Late, Enumerate: Unpacking Reduces the Planning Fallacy," *Journal of Experimental Social Psychology*, 40, 586-98.

Lilienfeld, Scott O., Rachel Ammirati, and Kristin Landfield (2009), "Giving Debiasing Away: Can Psychological Research on Correcting Cognitive Errors Promote Human Welfare?" *Perspectives on Psychological Science*, 4, 390-98.

Newby-Clark, Ian R., Michael Ross, Roger Buehler, Derek J. Koehler, and Dale Griffin (2000), "People Focus on Optimistic Scenarios and Disregard Pessimistic Scenarios While Predicting Task Completion Times," *Journal of Experimental Psychology: Applied*, 6, 171–82.

Roy, Michael M., Nicholas J. S. Christenfeld, and Craig R. M. McKenzie (2005), "Underestimating the Duration of Future Events: Memory Incorrectly Used or Memory Bias?" *Psychological Bulletin*, 131, 738-56.

Sanna, Lawrence J. and Norbert Schwarz (2004), "Integrating Temporal Biases: The Interplay of Focal Thoughts and Accessibility Experiences," *Psychological Science,* 15, 474-81.

Schwarz, Norbert, Herbert Bless, Fritz Strack, Gisela Klumpp, Helga Rittenauer-Schatka, and Annette Simons (1991), "Ease of Retrieval as Information: Another Look At the Availability Heuristic. *Journal of Personality and Social Psychology*, 61, 195-202.

Tetlock, Philip E., Jennifer S. Lerner, and Richard Boettger (1996), "The Dilution Effect: Judgmental Bias, Conversational Convention, or a Bit of Both? *European Journal of Social Psychology*, 26, 915-34.

Tormala, Zachary L., Richard E. Petty, and Pablo Briñol (2002), "Ease of Retrieval Effects in Persuasion: A Self-Validation Analysis," *Personality and Social Psychological Bulletin*, 28, 1700-12.

Tversky, Amos Derek J. Koehler (1994), "Support Theory: A Nonextensional Representation of Subjective Probability," *Psychological Review,* 101, 547-67.

Ülkümen, Gülden, Manoj Thomas, and Vicki G. Morwitz (2008), "Will I Spend More in 12 Months or a Year? The Effect of Temporal Frames on Budget Estimates," *Journal of Consumer Research*, 35, 245-56.

Yates, J. Frank, Elizabeth S. Veinott, and Andrea L. Patalano (2003), "Hard Decisions, Bad Decisions: On Decision Quality and Decision Aiding," in *Emerging Perspectives on Judgment and Decision Research,* ed. Sandra L. Schneider and James Shanteau, Cambridge, UK: Cambridge University Press, 13-63.

# When Small Steps Become Big Leaps: Goal-Consistency Judgments and the Illusion of Goal Progress

Andrea Bonezzi, Northwestern University, USA
Alexander Chernev, Northwestern University, USA

## EXTENDED ABSTRACT

Goals play a central role in driving consumers' mental processes and ultimate behaviors. Whether consciously held (Bagozzi & Dholakia, 1999; Locke & Latham, 1990), or activated outside of awareness (Bargh & Chartrand, 1999; Chartrand & Bargh, 1996) goals act as motivational drives (Gollwitzer, 1999) prompting people to engage in actions functional to achieving the desired end-state.

An important aspect of achieving a goal involves monitoring progress toward the desired end-state. Monitoring goal-progress plays a fundamental role in regulating consumer behavior by informing individuals about the contribution of each action to reaching the desired end-state.

In line with this idea, monitoring goal-progress has been conceptualized as a process involving comparing a behavioral outcome with a relevant standard of reference (Carver & Scheier, 1998). For example, one can adopt either the initial or the final state as the standard of reference and monitor goal-progress by considering either what has been achieved so far, or what still needs to be achieved (Koo & Fishbach, 2008). Consequently, perceived goal progress is typically measured by asking participants to indicate on a Likert scale the extent to which a particular decision contributes to advancing toward an active goal (Fishbch & Dhar, 2005; Louro, Pieters, & Zeelenberg, 2007). We refer to such judgments as *degree-of-progress* evaluations.

Building on previous research we propose that often people evaluate progress toward a goal by judging whether their actions are consistent with the active goal (i.e., "Will this help me reach my goal?"). For example, a person who is trying to save money could evaluate progress toward the goal by judging whether dining at home rather than at a restaurant is consistent with the goal to save money, without accurately considering how much money he is actually saving. We refer to such judgments as *goal-consistency* judgments.

Goal-consistency judgments are frequently triggered both by external and internal constraints. Often, the choice task induces people to categorize actions as consistent or inconsistent with an active goal. For instance, people are often bounded to choose the best option among the available ones. Moreover, due to limited mental resources, people often tend to simplify judgments by employing mental shortcuts, simplifying rules and heuristics (Tversky & Kahneman, 1974). Previous research has argued that one simplifying approach to judgment involves categorical or qualitative thinking (Rozin, Ashmore, & Markwith, 1996). Thus, people engage in categorization to easily make sense of the complexity of the world (Allport, 1954; Fiske & Taylor, 1991).

Does engaging in goal-consistency judgments influences degree-of-progress evaluations? In this research, we argue that consumers focused on goal-consistency are likely to overestimate the degree-of-progress granted by an action that provides a marginal contribution toward reaching a desired end-state. We test the proposition that goal-consistency judgments influence goal-progress evaluations in a series of four experiments.

In Experiment 1 we show that goal-consistency judgments lead to overestimating goal-progress. We test this basic proposition across three domains, representing three different goals: saving money, controlling calorie intake and caring for the environment. We find that respondents making goal-consistency judgments overestimated goal-progress compared to respondents not focusing on goal-consistency. This effect was directionally consistent across all three domains.

In Experiment 2 we provide further evidence for the phenomenon and show that the goal progress overestimation is not a function of progress valence. In particular, we show that goal-consistency judgments lead to overestimating the movement toward a goal produced by a goal-consistent action, as well as the movement away from a goal produced by a goal-inconsistent action.

In Experiment 3 we identify boundary conditions and show that the influence of goal-consistency judgments on goal-progress evaluations is a function of the magnitude of actual progress. In particular, goal-consistency judgments lead to overestimating goal-progress only when the actual progress is marginal, but not when the actual progress is large.

Finally, in Experiment 4 we show that goal-consistency evaluations can be spontaneously triggered by the choice task. In particular we show that a series of goal-consistent choices is perceived to yield more progress than a single choice producing the same final result.

Overall, the four experiments reported in this research offer converging evidence for the proposition that goal-consistency judgments bias goal-progress evaluations. In particular, we show that consumers focused on goal-consistency are likely to overestimate the degree-of-progress granted by an action that provides a marginal contribution toward reaching a desired end-state. Our results point to the importance of investigating how different strategies consumers use to monitor progress toward a goal might create the illusion of goal-progress and eventually backfire.

## REFERENCES

Allport, G. W. (1954). *The nature of prejudice*: Oxford, England: Addison-Wesley.

Bagozzi, R. P., & Dholakia, U. (1999). Goal setting and goal striving in consumer behavior. *Journal of Marketing, 63*(Special Issue), 19-32.

Bargh, J. A., & Chartrand, T. L. (1999). The unbearable automaticity of being. *American Psychologist, 54*(7), 462-479.

Carver, C. S., & Scheier, M. F. (1998). *On the self-regulation of behavior*. New York, NY US: Cambridge University Press.

Chartrand, T. L., & Bargh, J. A. (1996). Automatic activation of impression formation and memorization goals: Nonconscious goal priming reproduces effects of explicit task instructions. *Journal of Personality and Social Psychology, 71*(3), 464-478.

Fishbach, A., & Dhar, R. (2005). Goals as Excuses or Guides: The Liberating Effect of Perceived Goal Progress on Choice. *Journal of Consumer Research, 32*(3), 370-377.

Fiske, S. T., & Taylor, S. E. (1991). *Social cognition* (2nd ed.). New York: McGraw-Hill.

Gollwitzer, P. M. (1999). Implementation intentions: Strong effects of simple plans. *American Psychologist, 54*(7), 493-503.

Koo, M., & Fishbach, A. (2008). Dynamics of self-regulation: How (un)accomplished goal actions affect motivation. *Journal of Personality and Social Psychology, 94*(2), 183-195.

Locke, E. A., & Latham, G. P. (1990). *A theory of goal setting & task performance*. Englewood Cliffs, NJ US: Prentice-Hall, Inc.

Louro, M. J., Pieters, R., & Zeelenberg, M. (2007). Dynamics of multiple-goal pursuit. *Journal of Personality and Social Psychology, 93*(2), 174-193.

Rozin, P., Ashmore, M., & Markwith, M. (1996). Lay American conceptions of nutrition: Dose insensitivity, categorical thinking, contagion, and the monotonic mind. *Health Psychology, 15*(6), 438-447.

Tversky, A., & Kahneman, D. (1974). Judgment under uncertainty: Heuristics and biases. *Science, 185*(4157), 1124-1131.

# Film Festival 2010

## The Last Picture Show

*Russell Belk and Robert Kozinets, York University*

Unlike the movie theater in Peter Bogdanovich's *The Last Picture Show*, the 2010 ACR Film Festival will not be the last. But after 10 years of co-chairing the Festival, we have turned over the reigns to the very capable hands of Marylouise Caldwell and Paul Henry. Over the past 10 years we have seen videographic consumer research grow, mature, and ripen into something quite amazing. Both the quality and quantity of consumer research videos have grown over this period. The North American ACR Film Festivals have shown more than 125 films and the ACR Conferences in Europe, Latin America, and the Asia Pacific have developed their own exciting and locally-flavored Film Festivals as well.

From its inception, the North American festival itself has always had strong international representation among filmmakers and topics. If one of the challenges of consumer ethnography is to make the strange familiar and the familiar strange, consumer videography has excelled in meeting this challenge. Many of these films have found their way into classrooms and a number of them have been included in special DVD issues of several journals as well as into print journal article and chapter form. With its origins in an ACR Special Session in 2000, the Film Festival is now an ACR institution. We hope that no one could imagine a future ACR that did not offer researchers the option of representing our knowledge of consumer in an audio-visual format. As industry increasingly embraces videographic techniques for representing consumer realities and portraying their marketing research findings, it is useful for our field to follow suit and, in many ways, lead the charge towards finding new, rich forms for understanding the consumer.

The format of video and video editing over this period has been non-linear and digital throughout the past decade. Technologies have evolved and have driven the costs of video storytelling down to quite affordable levels. Thanks to the conference chairs, at the 2010 ACR Film Festival we not only had trailers available on the conference hotel CCTV, but also on the conference web site. For the upcoming Beijing ACR Conference in 2011 we will be receiving and reviewing (jurying) Film Festival entries on the Internet. ACR Films over the past decade have gone from standard definition analog VHS tapes to high definition DVDs. Camcorders have become smaller, cheaper, and more sophisticated. Digital still photography cameras are no longer so still. These technologies have also become ubiquitous as even the convergent technologies of mobile phones are capable of capturing high definition video. And editing equipment and software that would have been prohibitively expensive for the individual videographer two decades ago is now inexpensive or included free with computer operating systems and cameras. But it is not just technologies that have changed, so have the skills of filmmakers. We don't mean by this that the ACR videos have been produced by film school graduates (although a few have), but rather that ACR members have learned from practice, by watching other ACR films, through videos on YouTube, Vimeo, and similar sites, and from occasional consumer videography workshops and classes. Over the past decade, we have witnessed dramatic improvements in the quality of Consumer Research Videography as a field. We have been fortunate to watch as several stars of the field emerged and excelled in this medium.

The medium of video has allowed experimentation with different ways of representing consumer behavior. Resulting films have varied from two and one-half minutes to ninety minutes. They have represented consumption on every continent. No doubt the medium is best used when there is behavior to be shown rather than the talking heads of interviews. Many of these stories are allowed to unfold without much narration or voice-over, but "voice-of-god" storytelling has not disappeared. Much more use is now made of video montages, quick-cuts, music, and other cinematic devices for sustaining audience interest and managing the pace and flow of the video. These techniques too have evolved and kept pace with what's on TV and what's on the Internet. Some films have had amusing topics and approaches while others have been deadly serious. Interestingly, both of these extremes have resulted in award-winning films.

We have had a People's Choice Award from the first ACR Film Festival, but over the past six years we have also had a Juror's Award. The latter award also has a monetary prize, thanks to the generosity of Gary Bamossy, Alladi Venkatesh, the Center for Consumer Culture, and the University of California, Irvine. The criteria for evaluating submitted films and the Juror's Award have also evolved over the first decade of ACR Films. We have described these criteria in several papers (Belk 2006; Belk and Kozinets 2006a, 2006b; Kozinets and Belk 2005). They include the "Four Ts" of topical, theoretical, theatrical, and technical considerations.

This year's ACR Film Festival showed ten films out of 19 submitted for a 53 percent acceptance rate. The films are a good example of the geographic and cultural diversity noted above. The films focus on consumption phenomena in Botswana, Brazil, China (Tibet), Japan, Qatar, and the United States, with filmmakers from Australia, Brazil, Canada, Japan, Norway, Qatar, Spain, and the U.S. As noted in the abstracts below, the topics were equally diverse, ranging from Twitter, videogamers, and World of Warcraft to Green Consumption, AIDS in Africa, Beer in Montana, Japanese tea ceremonies, Arab Gulf homes, and Shangri-La.

This year for the first time, both the People's Choice Award and the Juror's Award went to the same film: "Walk the Talk, Talk the Walk," by Marylouise Caldwell, Ingeborg Kleppe, and Stephen Watson. Congratulations go to these filmmakers for their powerful and moving film about a competition for positive role models for HIV positive men in Botswana. It is fitting that we should turn over the film festival at this time in its history to one of its top award-winning film-makers. We are looking forward to the next decade of successful ACR Film Festivals.

*Advances in Consumer Research*
*Volume 38, © 2012*

# BRIEF ABSTRACTS

### Beer Country
*Caroline Graham Austin, Montana State University, USA*

Since the first settlers arrived at the St. Mary's mission in the mid-19th century, Montanans have loved beer --- they love making it, sharing it, talking about it, and drinking it. In this film, we investigate the historic, economic, cultural and aesthetic values that make Montana America's own Beer Country.

### Retweet: A Digital Meditation on the Power of Twitter
*Donna Hoffman, University of California, Riverside, USA*
*Thomas P. Novak, University of California, USA*

The phenomenal growth of Twitter, a popular microblogging application, is testament to consumers' desires to instantaneously connect with other consumers. Though many deride the seeming meaningless of the "twitter stream," consumers are putting the application to use in surprisingly potent ways. This video offers a brief reflection on the recursive power of Twitter.

### Talk The Walk, Walk the Talk
*Marylouise Caldwell, University of Sydney, Australia*
*Ingeborg Kleppe, Norwegian School of Economics and Business Administration*
*Stephen Watson, e+b media, University of Sydney, Australia*

This documentary shows how HIV+ people in Botswana radically transform themselves from AIDS victims to become public role-models of Positive Living, a health life-style that prolongs infected people's lives and prevents them from infecting others and reinfecting themselves. They learn to deal with stigma, ignorance and limited social or financial support.

### Tea for Two: Luxury in Japanese Tea Ceremony
*Hiroshi Tanaka, Chuo University, Japan*
*Junko Kimura, Hosei University, Japan*

This study aims to anatomize the mechanism of luxury generation in the Japanese tea ceremony. Based on detailed interviews, we found that (1) Teamwork, (2) Theme-orientation, and (3) Game, are the three key concepts which depict the interactions between host and the guests and thus lead to generate sense of luxury.

### Is Green?
*Gary Bamossy, Georgetown University, USA*
*Basil Englis, Berry College, USA*

This film examines consumers' reactions to the marketing practices of "Green Washing" –representing products as being environmentally friendly in ways that result in consumers feeling confused, skeptical, and cynical about those claims, and more generally, about the green movement towards sustainable consumption practices. The public discourse around "environmentally friendly" offerings is becoming increasingly contentious, socially divisive, and politicized, and this film explores these dynamics.

### Domains of Privacy in Arab Gulf Homes
*Sobh Rana, Qatar University, Qatar*
*Russell Belk, York University, Canada*

Globalization has both ameliorating and exacerbating effects on traditional cultural patterns. Based on ethnographic fieldwork over a three-year period, we analyze how local Islamic cultures affect consumption and marketing amid this swirl of new influences.

### Paradise Lost: The Making of Shangri-La
*Russell Belk, York University, Canada*
*Rosa Llamas, University of León, Spain*

Once upon a time, there was a peaceful Himalayan Fairyland that was a Garden of Eden, an earthly Paradise, and a Heaven on Earth. Its name was Shangri-La. And now the harried city dweller can vacation there. In 2002 the county of Zhongdian in China's Yunan Province changed its name to Shangri-La. Based on fieldwork in 2009, we consider the positive and negative effects of this bid to attract tourists and transform the local economy.

### Sustainability: A New Consumer Movement
*Adam Schmidt, Saint Joseph's University, USA*
*Thomas Ferraro, Saint Joseph's University, USA*
*Diane M. Phillips, Saint Joseph's University, USA*

Consumers define sustainability in different ways and enact a variety of different behaviors to construct, maintain, and enhance their sustainable lifestyles. Further, those resulting multi-dimensional lifestyles are clearly personal. They tap into deeply held values, connect to communities, and evoke strong emotions. Sustainability is a new consumer movement.

## Gamerz
*João Fleck, Universidade Federal do Rio Grande do Sul, Brazil*
*Stefânia Almeida, Pontifícia Universidade Católica, Brazil*
*Utpal Dholakia, Rice University, USA*
*José Mazzon, Universidade de São Paulo, Brazil*

We aimed at analyzing and understanding the peculiarities of video game consumption interviewing hardcore players that interact in Microsoft Xbox 360 virtual communities. The results allowed us to infer that the virtual experience and the online interaction are key elements presently in the consumption of games.

## World of Warcrafters
*João Fleck, Universidade Federal do Rio Grande do Sul, Brazil*
*Carlos Rossi, Universidade Federal do Rio Grande do Sul, Brazil*
*Rodrigo Segabinazzi, Universidade Federal do Rio Grande do Sul, Brazil*
*Getúlio Reale, Universidade Federal do Rio Grande do Sul, Brazil*
*Diego Costa, Universidade Federal do Rio Grande do Sul, Brazil*
*Marco Martins, Universidade Federal do Rio Grande do Sul, Brazil*

We aimed at understanding, through a videographic study, what caused the reputed online game, World of Warcraft, to become such a phenomenon of consumption. Our results indicate that the involvement of players results from the achievement of goals, through the manipulation of an avatar that cooperates with others to compete.

## References
Belk, Russell (2006), "You Ought to be in Pictures: Envisioning Marketing Research," *Review of Marketing Research*, Vol. 3, Naresh Malholtra, ed., Armonk, NY: M.E. Sharpe, 193-205.
Belk, Russell and Robert Kozinets (2006a), "Camcorder Society: Quality Videography in Consumer and Marketing Research," in Russell Belk, ed., *Handbook of Qualitative Research Methods in Marketing,* Cheltenham, UK: Edward Elgar, 335-339.
Belk, Russell and Robert Kozinets (2006b), "Videography," in *Sage Dictionary of Social Research Methods*, Victor Jupp, ed., Thousand Oaks, CA: Sage, 318-322.
Kozinets, Robert and Russell Belk (2005), "Videography in Marketing and Consumer Research," *Qualitative Market Research*, 8 (2), 141-183.

# Roundtable Summaries

ROUNDTABLE

## Neuroscience, Marketing, and Vulnerable Consumers: Integrative Approaches to Advancing Theory and Social Welfare

**Chairs:**
Dante Pirouz, University of California, Irvine, USA
Ab Litt, Stanford University, USA
Baba Shiv, Stanford University, USA

**Participants:**
James R. Bettman, Duke University, USA
June Cotte, University of Western Ontario, Canada
Adam Craig, University of South Carolina, USA
Angelika Dimoka, Temple University, USA
Laurette Dubé, McGill University, Canada
William Hedgcock, University of Iowa, USA
Todd A. Hare, California Institute of Technology, USA
Ming Hsu, University of California, Berkeley, USA
Uma Karmarkar, Stanford University, USA
Theo Noseworthy, University of Western Ontario, Canada

## Extended Abstract

***Topic and Motivation.*** Two exciting recent developments in consumer research have been the burgeoning use of *decision neuroscience* to explore unanswered questions about consumer psychology and behavior, and *transformative consumer research* taking the express aim of investigating and improving personal and collective well-being. For the former, an ongoing undertaking has been the identification of explanatory niches in which neuroscience can most offer major conceptual advances above and beyond behavioral approaches alone. In contrast, the task of transformative consumer researchers is to identify important questions for consumer welfare, and integrate diverse research strands to best answer those questions and yield new insights.

This roundtable centers on a topic that ideally melds these goals of both movements, one that is both a core issue in transformative research and that can be studied with unique and essential depth using neuroscientific techniques: the effects of marketing actions on *vulnerable and at-risk consumers*, and the consumption patterns exhibited by these individuals. Vulnerable consumers are defined as individuals who have personal or situational disadvantages in the marketplace that can create negative outcomes for either themselves or for society as a whole. These vulnerable consumers include age segments such as children, adolescents, and the elderly; those suffering from addiction and substance-abuse problems; and those with behavioral control problems in other domains such as spending money, gambling, eating and weight management, and even problematic overuse of the internet and video games. Vulnerable consumers also include those compromised by medical conditions, including neurological damage, deficits, or disorders, or by medications and medical interventions meant to deal with such conditions.

Such consumers often exhibit distorted patterns of consumption within and across domains, and unusual susceptibility to various types of marketing actions. The typical consumer is exposed to numerous marketing messages every day. Under normal circumstances, consumers are generally able to process which to attend to and which to filter out in order to successfully regulate their overall consumption. However, this is often not the case for vulnerable and at-risk consumers. Consequently, an area of critical importance in transformative research and its public policy applications is the protection of vulnerable and at-risk consumers from the adverse effects of products and their marketing.

Neuroscientific techniques can provide detailed and direct insight into the most basic biological, pharmacological, and psychophysiological mechanisms responsible for the deficits and risk factors characterizing vulnerable consumers. Such efforts can leverage much existing research regarding neurological changes over the lifespan, effects of specific brain impairments, and how different neural circuits predict, adapt to, and develop sensitivity and tolerance to specific stimuli. As such, they can reveal much about the nature, fundamental bases, and underlying conceptual constructs and interactions responsible for diverse decision-maker vulnerabilities. Doing so in a manner informed by theories and conceptual constructs from behavioral research, decision neuroscientists can contribute distinctively to the construction of more enlightened and biologically informed policy viewpoints and recommendations. Thus, revealing the bases of consumer vulnerabilities is an area where decision neuroscience has clear promise and value to consumer research overall and transformative consumer research in particular, in terms of both generating novel conceptual insights and revealing key results for consumer well-being.

This roundtable will be a chance to discuss these possibilities for advancing theory and social welfare, and to develop interesting and promising new research directions from behavioral, neural, and integrative perspectives. We have drawn together a diverse panel of experts in neuroscience, decision research, and transformative consumer research, who are eager to explore these questions and issues regarding vulnerable consumers. Several specific issues already identified to be discussed are:

1. How research should be conducted and communicated when it has both clinical and managerial antecedents and consequences.

2.  Identifying vulnerable consumer groups that can be most effectively studied and whose well-being has most potential for improvement by integrating neural and behavioral approaches.

3.  Discussion of past experiences of panel members who have researched various vulnerable consumer groups using behavioral and neural techniques—what was found, and what couldn't be ascertained but is important to further explore.

4.  How findings from disparate areas may be best communicated both to researchers in distal fields, and more broadly in order to influence critical public policy issues.

5.  The most promising conceptual and methodological frontiers for studying vulnerable consumers, both in terms of specific populations deserving deeper study, and novel or integrative approaches with high potential for revealing important new insights.

### Interested and Likely-to-Benefit Audiences

A wide range of attendees would benefit from attending this roundtable. Those interested in transformative consumer research, clinical consumer research, public policy, and consumer well-being would find this roundtable illuminating and informative regarding results from a burgeoning consumer research sub-field with particular relevance to key questions of interest. In addition, those working in neuroeconomics and decision neuroscience, as well as the larger community of consumer researchers who recognize the growing importance and promise of neuroscientific approaches and results, would also find this roundtable valuable for identifying novel consumer domains in which neuroscientific investigation could offer important insights.

To a large degree, each of these groups is only infrequently exposed to the discoveries and approaches of the other. Hence, a key benefit of this roundtable is in bringing these groups together in active discussion.

### Facilitating Pre-Conference Discussions

The roundtable organizers are committed to fostering vigorous informal discussion amongst participants prior to the conference. We plan to facilitate such discussions primarily using either the ACR Knowledge Exchange forum or through moderated e-mails. Prior to the conference participants will be encouraged to develop and share with the group discussion points of most interest to them, as well as informal summaries of relevant research they have been conducting themselves or are interested in learning more about through discussions. All such materials will be collated by the organizers as needed and distributed to the group, and interactions regarding the issues, questions, and research results brought to the fore will be both encouraged and actively initiated by the organizers. Through these pre-conference efforts we hope to maximize the value and meaningfulness of the session itself.

ROUNDTABLE

# Barbara Stern's Legacy to Consumer Research

**Chairs:**
Cristel Antonia Russell, University of Auckland, New Zealand
Stephen J. Gould, Baruch College, USA

**Participants:**
Aaron Ahuvia, University of Michigan, Dearborn, USA
Barbara Olsen, SUNY Old Westbury, USA
Brett Martin, Queensland University of Technology, Australia
Craig Thompson, University of Wisconsin, USA
David Mick, University of Virginia, USA
Ed Mcquarrie, University of Santa Clara, USA
Eileen Fischer, York University, Canada
Eric Arnould, University of Wyoming, USA
Gita Johar, New York University, USA
Jennifer Escalas, Vanderbilt University, USA
Jonathan Schroeder, University of Exeter, UK
Laurie Meamber, George Mason University, USA
Margo Buchanan-Oliver, University of Auckland, New Zealand
Mark Ritson, Melbourne Business School, Australia
Marla Royne Stafford, University of Memphis, USA
Michael Mulvey, University of Ottawa, Canada
Sandy Bennett, University of Auckland, New Zealand
Steven Kates, Simon Fraser University, Canada

**Extended Abstract**

The purpose of the roundtable is to review and discuss the contributions of Barbara Stern's literary approach to the field of consumer research. Participants who have worked with Barbara will provide a brief review of her contributions in key areas and solicit participant discussion around each topic. The discussion of Barbara's legacy has already begun in email exchanges between roundtable participants and the co-organizers. We have created a Barbara Stern listserv'. Once the roundtable is accepted, an online forum will be activated on the ACR website so that anyone will be able to post comments and thoughts. The proposal incorporates contributions from others who, while unable to attend this year's conference, have shared how Barbara Stern's work influenced their own research. These scholars will contribute to the discussion via the online board, pre- and post- conference.

In Barbara Stern fashion, the proposal begins with an etymological analysis of the word legacy. Legacy is something transmitted from the past. It is also defined as a gift and this second meaning is just as suited to describe Barbara's contributions to the field of consumer research. Gifted herself, she gifted us with novel insights and theoretical perspectives from English literature. In organizing this roundtable, we solicited statements from scholars who knew Barbara and/or her work. Some worked directly with her, all found her work inspirational. The purpose of the gathering will be to review and uphold her thriving legacy to consumer research.

Barbara's pioneering contributions to consumer research are best stated in Morris Holbrook's words: "she transformed the possibilities for interpretive work in marketing research. By virtue of her training and experience in critical analysis–her ability to draw on a wealth of literary material not available to the typical marketing scholar–Barb infused her research with an authoritative command of interpretive methods not heretofore found in our discipline… She has incorporated key ideas from feminism, has made a case for advertising as a species of drama, has applied influential taxonomic and structural models borrowed from the basic discipline, and has even ventured forth into an exploration … of deconstructionism …. she loads her critical approach with insights into the meaning of consumption and other marketing-related phenomena. These discoveries make her work a constant challenge–and joy–to read … one is constantly impressed by the high level of originality, imagination, creativity, and wisdom that she has brought to her work." (Holbrook 2009, 6).

The roundtable will proceed as an open discussion guided by the topics brought up in pre-conference discussions amongst participants. Since the exchange has already begun, emerging topics are listed here, using or paraphrasing (or quoting but unattributed) the participants' own words in describing Barbara's contributions to themselves personally and to the field as a whole.

*Literary Theory.* Barbara's work brought to light the centrality of the humanities in general and literary approaches to the study of marketing in particular. She covered such topics as the uses of literary devices (allegory, personae, rhetorical irony) in advertising and the relationship of literary criticism to consumer research. In her breakthrough article (JM 1988) Barbara compared advertising to medieval allegory in that it provides didactic instruction to consumers. In 1989 (JCR), she introduced us to the role literary criticism can play in consumer research, etching out the different schools and how they focus on different elements, including author, reader and text (e.g., reader response, genre analysis, deconstruction). She then playfully applied deconstruction to Joe Camel (JCR 1996) in a subversive, destabilizing reading to reveal how his behavior hovers in undecidability (*différance*) between various gendered-sexualities including dominant masculinity, repressed male homosexuality and implied femininity.

*Advertising.* Barbara's research offered new insights into the study of advertising text and narrative. She transformed our understanding, for instance, of the traditional communications model in advertising (source, message, recipient) by treating advertising as crafted text rather than as mere everyday speech as the model implies (JA 1994).

*Feminism.* Barbara was an "embodiment of the kind of feminist who opened up opportunities for others both because of her exemplary scholarship and because of her supportiveness of specific individuals" (female participant). She was "a true 2nd wave feminist as well as having overcome a bad marriage and all the obstacles professional women faced in the 60s. She was pretty fearless" (male participant). This topic will undoubtedly lead to lively discussion about feminism and how it has been manifested in the marketing academy. In 1993 (JCR), Barbara introduced us to feminist-deconstructive reading of ads suggesting that consumers engage in gendered reading such that males and females exhibit different reading styles.

*Pluralism.* Barbara believed that pluralistic research projects drawing from different paradigmatic strengths (Kuhn 1962; Laudan 1984) contributed to each other (Lakatos 1978) in fruitful knowledge exchanges. She viewed the humanities as a source of theoretical insights and hypotheses testable by empirical methods but, although she was intrigued by experimental research, she had no background in it. She walked the talk of synergy between humanities theory and scientific method (Geertz 1988; Holbrook 1987), collaborating with researchers with complementary background to hers in experimental design (e.g., Escalas and Stern 2003).

*Likely Audience.* Seasoned and novice consumer researchers will benefit from attending this session. We anticipate that the discussion will evolve more generally from Barbara Stern's legacy of literary criticism to more general ways in which theory advances and the contribution of other disciplines to consumer research.

## Selected References

Geertz, Clifford (1988), *Work and Lives: The Anthropologist as Author*, Stanford, California, Stanford University Press.

Escalas, Jennifer Edson and Barbara B. Stern (2003), "Sympathy and Empathy: Emotional Responses to Advertising Dramas, "*Journal of Consumer Research*, 29 (March), 566-578.

Holbrook, Morris B. (1987), "What Is Consumer Research?" *Journal of Consumer Research,* 14 (June), 128-132.

Holbrook, Morris B. (2009), "In Memoriam–Barbara B. Stern," *Marketing Theory*, 9(1), 5-7.

Hunt, Shelby D. (1989), "Naturalistic, Humanistic, and Interpretive Inquiry: Challenges and Ultimate Potential," in *Interpretive Consumer Research*, ed. Elizabeth C. Hirschman, Provo, UT: Association for Consumer Research.

Kuhn, Thomas S. (1962), *The Structure of Scientific Revolutions*, Chicago: University of Chicago Press.

Lakatos, Imre (1978), *The Methodology of Scientific Research Programs*, Cambridge, England: Cambridge University Press.

Laudan, Larry (1984), *Science and Values*, Berkeley: University of California Press.

Stern, Barbara B. (1988), "Medieval Allegory: Roots of Advertising Strategy for the Mass Market," *Journal of Marketing*, 52 (July), 84-94.

Stern, Barbara B. (1989), "Literary Criticism and Consumer Research: Overview and Illustrative Analysis," *Journal of Consumer Research*, 16 (3), 322-334.

Stern, Barbara B. (1993), "Feminist Literary Criticism and the Deconstruction of Ads: A Postmodern View of Advertising and Consumer Responses," *Journal of Consumer Research*, 19 (March), 556-566.

Stern, Barbara B. (1994), "A Revised Communication Model for Advertising: Multiple Dimensions of the Source, the Message, and the Recipient," *Journal of Advertising*, 23 (June), 5-15.

Stern, Barbara B. (1995), "Consumer Myths: Frye's Taxonomy and the Structural Analysis of Consumption Text," *Journal of Consumer Research*, 22 (September), 165-185.

Stern, Barbara B. (1996), "Deconstructive Strategy and Consumer Research: Concepts and Illustrative Exemplar," *Journal of Consumer Research*, 23 (September), 136-147.

Stern, Barbara B. (1998), 'Narratological Analysis of Consumer Voices in Postmodern Research Accounts', in B.B. Stern (ed.) *Representing Consumers: Voices, Views and Visions*, London: Routledge, 55-82.

# The Evolving Definition of Rationality

**Chair:**
Rajagopal Raghunathan, University of Texas at Austin, USA

**Participants:**
Christopher Hsee, University of Chicago, USA
Michel Tuan Pham, Columbia University, USA
Ming Hsu, University of California at Berkeley, USA
J. Edward Russo, Cornell University, USA
Itamar Simonson, Stanford University, USA
Dan Ariely, Duke University, USA
Eduardo B. Andrade, University of California at Berkeley, USA

## Extended Abstract

The concepts of rationality and utility are irrevocably intertwined, since rationality is generally defined and conceived as utility maximizing behavior (e.g., Edwards 1954). Thus, to understand what rationality means, it is important to understand what utility means.

From a classical economist's perspective, utility can be taken to mean whatever it is that an individual (or a group) wishes to maximize. In this view, even the so-called "dark" consumption behaviors—such as addiction to drugs or alcohol (Solomon 1980), the inability to save sufficient money for the future (Thaler and Shefrin 1992), or the inability to prevent oneself from compulsive shopping (Rook 1987)—can be conceived as rational. As such, many scholars interested in examining these types of (dark) behaviors have been careful to avoid characterizing these types of behaviors as irrational, and prefer, instead, to use less loaded terms such as, *time-inconsistent preferences*, or *myopia* to refer to them (e.g., Hoch and Loewenstein 1991).

If utility can mean anything and everything, however, the concept of rationality is rendered meaningless, since *any* judgment or decision could be considered rational. To circumvent this conceptual impasse, one yardstick that has often been applied is whether the judgment/decision in question conforms to logic (Kahneman 1994); in this view, people are rational if their "beliefs, judgments, choices and actions respect certain standards of logic" (Pham 2007, p. 156). For instance, judgments or decisions that do not satisfy transitivity (Birnbaum 2008) or do not sufficiently account for base-rates (Bar Hillel 1980) would be considered irrational. But is conformance to norms of logic alone enough? Some scholars appear to think so; for instance, Sharif and Leboeuf (2002, p. 492) note that "the predominant theories of rationality are predicated on notions of consistency"; thus, in the eyes of these scholars, even behaviors that would be considered patently irrational by lay-people (e.g., addiction to drugs or extreme impulsivity) could be construed as rational so long as these behaviors are, in some logically justifiable way, consistent and coherent.

Other scholars, however, have taken a different stance: by implicitly equating utility to subjective well-being or happiness, they appear amenable to characterizing judgments/decisions that diminish emotional positivity—even if they are logically justifiable—as sub-rational (e.g., Thaler and Sunstein 2008). This perspective, of equating utility to emotional well-being, also appears to be echoed in the work of some other scholars (e.g., Hsee et al. 2003; Wilson and Schooler 1991), in as much as they portray the more (vs. less) enjoyable options as being superior, even though the choice of other options may be logically defendable.

A third perspective on rationality adopts a societal-level lens through which judgments and decisions are evaluated; in this view, judgments/decisions that maximize societal (vs. individual) well-being are rational. This, so-called, "ecological" perspective of rationality (e.g., Miller 2009; Haidt 2001, 2007) would characterize judgments/decisions that serve the higher-purpose of enhancing the utility of the society or group to which the decision-maker belongs as rational, even if these judgments/decisions come at a cost to the decision-maker himself.

One framework that could prove useful in clarifying the pros and cons of subscribing to a particular definition of utility (and, therefore, rationality), is that offered by Kahneman and his colleagues (e.g., Kahneman Wakker and Sarin 1997). These researchers distinguish between two types of utilities—decision and experienced utility—where decision-utility refers to the "wantability" of options whereas experienced utility refers to the amount of pleasure (minus pain) provided by them. Thus, an option that provides higher levels of pleasure (minus pain) would be the rational choice from the perspective of an individual aiming to maximize experienced utility, and yet be sub-rational from the perspective of someone interested in concerns other than just enjoyment. For example, some people may attach great importance to making choices that appear (to oneself or to others) as justifiable (e.g., Simonson 1989), and to such people, the hedonic superiority of an option may not guarantee its choice.

The primary objective of this session is to provide clarity on the various ways in which rationality and utility have been conceptualized and to shed light on the subtle (and not-so-subtle) ways in which these conceptualizations differ. As a result of such clarity, we expect the audience to be able to judge for themselves the pros and cons of adopting different perspectives of utility and rationality. Time permitting, the panelists in the session may also discuss other related questions, including the following: (1) What is the role of consciousness in making rational judgments or decisions, that is, could a decision be rational if it were made sub-consciously (*a la* Dijksterhuis 2004)? Or is it necessary for the decision-agent to have been conscious of the process underlying the calculation of utilities?, (2) What is the role of stability of preferences, and to what extent is the assumption of stability of preferences valid (Ariely, Loewenstein and Prelec 2003)?, and (3) When are preferences constructed and when do they appear to be based on inherent tastes (Simonson 2008)?

The session is expected to have broad appeal, since assessing the quality of a judgment or decision (whether one refers to such assessments by the use of the term rationality) is central to all of consumer research.

# Compliments, Critiques, and Consumption: The Effects of Word-of-Mouth Valence and Social Ties on Peer Advice in Socially-Embedded Settings

**Chair:**
Renee Gosline, MIT Sloan School of Management, USA

**Participants:**
Breagin Riley, Syracuse University, USA
Kent Grayson, Northwestern University, USA
Aronte Bennett, Villanova University, USA
Tiffany White, University of Illinois, Urbana-Champaign, USA
David Dubois, Northwestern University, USA
Jeff Lee, Harvard Business School, USA
Lora Harding, Northwestern University, USA
Omar Woodham, Syracuse University, USA

## Extended Abstract

The concepts of rationality and utility are irrevocably intertwined, since rationality is generally defined and conceived as utility maximizing behavior (e.g., Edwards 1954). Thus, to understand what rationality means, it is important to understand what utility means.

From a classical economist's perspective, utility can be taken to mean whatever it is that an individual (or a group) wishes to maximize. In this view, even the so-called "dark" consumption behaviors—such as addiction to drugs or alcohol (Solomon 1980), the inability to save sufficient money for the future (Thaler and Shefrin 1992), or the inability to prevent oneself from compulsive shopping (Rook 1987)—can be conceived as rational. As such, many scholars interested in examining these types of (dark) behaviors have been careful to avoid characterizing these types of behaviors as irrational, and prefer, instead, to use less loaded terms such as, *time-inconsistent preferences*, or *myopia* to refer to them (e.g., Hoch and Loewenstein 1991).

If utility can mean anything and everything, however, the concept of rationality is rendered meaningless, since *any* judgment or decision could be considered rational. To circumvent this conceptual impasse, one yardstick that has often been applied is whether the judgment/decision in question conforms to logic (Kahneman 1994); in this view, people are rational if their "beliefs, judgments, choices and actions respect certain standards of logic" (Pham 2007, p. 156). For instance, judgments or decisions that do not satisfy transitivity (Birnbaum 2008) or do not sufficiently account for base-rates (Bar Hillel 1980) would be considered irrational. But is conformance to norms of logic alone enough? Some scholars appear to think so; for instance, Sharif and Leboeuf (2002, p. 492) note that "the predominant theories of rationality are predicated on notions of consistency"; thus, in the eyes of these scholars, even behaviors that would be considered patently irrational by lay-people (e.g., addiction to drugs or extreme impulsivity) could be construed as rational so long as these behaviors are, in some logically justifiable way, consistent and coherent.

Other scholars, however, have taken a different stance: by implicitly equating utility to subjective well-being or happiness, they appear amenable to characterizing judgments/decisions that diminish emotional positivity—even if they are logically justifiable—as sub-rational (e.g., Thaler and Sunstein 2008). This perspective, of equating utility to emotional well-being, also appears to be echoed in the work of some other scholars (e.g., Hsee et al. 2003; Wilson and Schooler 1991), in as much as they portray the more (vs. less) enjoyable options as being superior, even though the choice of other options may be logically defensible.

A third perspective on rationality adopts a societal-level lens through which judgments and decisions are evaluated; in this view, judgments/decisions that maximize societal (vs. individual) well-being are rational. This, so-called, "ecological" perspective of rationality (e.g., Miller 2009; Haidt 2001, 2007) would characterize judgments/decisions that serve the higher-purpose of enhancing the utility of the society or group to which the decision-maker belongs as rational, even if these judgments/decisions come at a cost to the decision-maker himself.

One framework that could prove useful in clarifying the pros and cons of subscribing to a particular definition of utility (and, therefore, rationality), is that offered by Kahneman and his colleagues (e.g., Kahneman Wakker and Sarin 1997). These researchers distinguish between two types of utilities—decision and experienced utility—where decision-utility refers to the "wantability" of options whereas experienced utility refers to the amount of pleasure (minus pain) provided by them. Thus, an option that provides higher levels of pleasure (minus pain) would be the rational choice from the perspective of an individual aiming to maximize experienced utility, and yet be sub-rational from the perspective of someone interested in concerns other than just enjoyment. For example, some people may attach great importance to making choices that appear (to oneself or to others) as justifiable (e.g., Simonson 1989), and to such people, the hedonic superiority of an option may not guarantee its choice.

The primary objective of this session is to provide clarity on the various ways in which rationality and utility have been conceptualized and to shed light on the subtle (and not-so-subtle) ways in which these conceptualizations differ. As a result of such clarity, we expect the audience to be able to judge for themselves the pros and cons of adopting different perspectives of utility and rationality. Time permitting, the panelists in the session may also discuss other related questions, including the following: (1) What is the role of consciousness in making rational judgments or decisions, that is, could a decision be rational if it were made sub-consciously (*a la* Dijksterhuis 2004)? Or is it necessary for the decision-agent to have been conscious of the process underlying the calculation of utilities?, (2) What is the role of stability of preferences, and to what extent is the assumption of stability of preferences valid (Ariely, Loewenstein and Prelec 2003)?, and (3) When are preferences constructed and when do they appear to be based on inherent tastes (Simonson 2008)?

The session is expected to have broad appeal, since assessing the quality of a judgment or decision (whether one refers to such assessments by the use of the term rationality) is central to all of consumer research.

ROUNDTABLE
# Walking the Work-life Tightrope

**Chair:**
Raj Raghunathan

**Participants:**
Darren Dahl, University of British Columbia, Canada
Kelly Haws, Texas A&M University, USA
Gita Johar, Columbia University, USA
Aparna Labroo, University of Chicago, USA
Rhiannon MacDonnell, University of Calgary, Canada
Himanshu Mishra, University of Utah, USA
Vicki Morwitz, New York University, USA
Joseph Nunes, University of Southern California, USA
Stijn van Osselaer, Erasmus University Rotterdam, The Netherlands
Deborah Small, University of Pennsylvania, USA

**Extended Abstract**

Although the economists' assumption, that "more of a good thing is better" has come under increasing scrutiny and criticism in recent years—for example, it has been shown not to be true for many things, including jam (Iyengar and Lepper 2000), TV channels, and babies (personal experience 2010)—, it seems to be true for at least one thing: happiness. We all want to be as happy as we can be, and the happier we are, well, the happier we feel! But, what does it take to be happy?

According to Freud, the two biggest determinants of happiness are: (1) satisfaction with work and, (2) satisfaction with love. So, the more productive we are at work, and the greater the sense of intimacy/belongingness we have with our chosen social circle (which includes our partner, kids and friends), the happier we are likely to be. But, given that being productive at work and maintaining a healthy social-life take time, effort and (sometimes) money, and given that we have a limited pool of these resources, it can be a challenge to maintain a good work-life balance. So, how do we decide how much resource to allocate to work vs. family vs. friends?

This is a tough nut to crack, as most of us (especially those with kids) have found out the hard way. Some of us decide to allocate more resources to family/friends, only to feel bad that we haven't been as productive as we could have been. (And those pesky, super-productive single colleagues don't help!) Others decide to devote more resources to work, only to feel socially isolated and miserable.

In sum, the challenge of leading a happy life—through an ideal mix of "work" and "love"—presents an optimization problem that is more challenging than the health-care problem currently facing the US government (some may disagree with us on this, but we have anecdotal and apocryphal data to back our stance). So, who better to turn to, than the elite set of marketing faculty who have it all—productivity at work, a great family life, an intimate circle of friends, and more! Yes, our esteemed panel members lead enviable, "happily now (vs. ever after)" lives because they have hit the work-life balance sweet-spot!

But, before you let that tinge of envy (which is no doubt creeping up your spine) develop into a full-blown bout of uncontrolled jealousy, let me assure you that the happy position in which our panelists find themselves wasn't easy to achieve. They had to endure a long, harrowing period of struggle, with periodic attacks of spasmodic back pain, carpal tunnel syndrome, thou-art-neither-here-nor-there syndrome and spontaneous spousal spurnment. (Some of these are new diseases.)

But, despite all the hardships that they had to endure to painfully assimilate their pearls of wisdom, the panelists are eager to share their perspectives on this important topic (bless their hearts!). Each panelist will spend about 5-8 minutes first, outlining their preferred solution to the "work-life balance dilemma". In the course of doing so, they will share their views on a number of issues, including the following:

What are some creative ways by which one can have "one's cake and eat it too" (i.e., be productive at work and enjoy a healthy social life)? Who are some people who stand out as good exemplars of maintaining a good "work-life" balance and what are their strategies?

Should the allocation of resources vary depending on where (in which stage) one is? For instance, should one devote more resources to work (vs. social life) before tenure, and more to social life (vs. work) after having kids?

For those who have chosen to devote more time to family (vs. work), how can they cope with feelings of inadequacy that comes with a (hopefully temporary!) dip in productivity?

For those who have chosen to devote more time to work (vs. family), how can one get "one's groove back" (i.e., develop and maintain healthy social relationships)?

Are there any resources (e.g., books, agencies) that can help us out with this issue?

Once the panelists have had a chance to share their perspectives, the floor will be opened to a question and answer session, which is expected to last about 30 minutes.

The session is expected to have broad appeal, since most of us value both our work life and our social life. The session will be particularly valuable for junior faculty (and PhD students) with an active social/family life.

# Roundtable
## Green, Ethical, Sustainable Consumption

**Chair:**
Andrew Gershoff, University of Texas at Austin, USA

**Participants:**
Susan Dobscha, Bentley College, USA
Amitav Chakravarti, New York University, USA
Julie Irwin, University of Texas at Austin, USA
Karen Page Winterich, Pennsylvania State University, USA
Michael Luchs, William and Mary, USA
Bram Van den Bergh, Erasmus University Rotterdam, The Netherlands
Rebecca Walker Naylor, Ohio State University, USA
Kelly Haws, Texas A&M University, USA
Vladas Griskevicius, University of Minnesota, USA

## Extended Abstract

Over the last decade there has been a steady increase in sales and consumer interest of environmentally friendly, ethically produced, and so-called sustainable products (Freedonia 2009). Mainstream manufacturers and retailers such as Walmart, Home Depot, P & G, and General Electric have increased their offerings of products labeled "green" and they have altered many business practices in order to decrease or offset their impact on the environment.

Research on consumer attitudes and response to green, ethical, and sustainable marketing has also begun to take root in a number of important directions, especially as it becomes apparent that despite positive attitudes toward such products, in many product categories consumers still don't buy or use them (Luchs, Naylor, Irwin, Raghunathan 2010; UNEP 2005). As a result, questions of when and why these products will be adopted have been on the forefront. For example, a number of researchers have explored questions associated with the traits and indicators of consumers who tend to be green consumers (Haws, Winterich, Naylor 2010; Webb, Mohr, and Harris 2008). Others have asked about consumer response to the real or inferred trades-offs that consumers must make between the green benefits of the products and other primary benefits of the products (Luchs et al. 2010). In addition, many researchers have begun to uncover a potential dark side associated with purchase of green products. For example Ehrich and Irwin (2005) found that consumers may intentionally avoid leaning about a product's negative ethical connections in order to protect a favored status of a preferred product. Others have shown that a licencing effect appears to occur with either the purchase of green products or beliefs about one's own past green behavior. This may result in consumers becoming *less likely* to make subsequent green purchases, and may even be more likely to engage in other immoral or selfish behavior (Becker-Olsen, Bennett, Chakravarti 2010; Mazar and Zhong 2010). Finally, even when people do purchase green products, the benefits they seek may not be associated ethical, nor altruistic goals. Instead, the decision to purchase a green product may be driven by a goal of signaling status (Griskevicius, Tybur, and Van den Bergh 2010).

Although a respectable body of knowledge in green and sustainable consumer behavior has clearly been established, this area is still both young enough and important enough to society to merit further inquiry. Rather than simply reviewing the work that has been completed thus far, the purpose of this roundtable will be to discuss and develop key questions and research priorities for future study of green, sustainable, and ethical marketing. At least nine recognized researchers this area have agreed to attend and contribute. Toward developing these research priorities, a number of areas for discussion have been proposed.

One area for consideration is consumer response to the way in which green and sustainable benefits are introduced and manifest in the products they consume. For example, products may become more green in a number of ways. First, manufacturing and transportation methods may be used by a company to reduce any negative impact on the environment or society but these changes may not alter the product or consumer experience in any way. Second, materials used in the product or package may have a reduced impact on natural resources either by reducing material use, reusing materials, or using alternative materials. These methods may have an impact on the environment, but it may be affect the product experience as well. Third, design of products may be altered so that when used the products have less impact on the environment by reducing their energy consumption or pollution. Finally, products may be designed so that when they are disposed of they have less impact on the environment. Each of these methods may result in a similar impact on the environment, but they may differ in consumer reactions. For instance, tangible and observable aspects of the greenness of products may lead to inferences that the product is less effective in other ways, which may reduce demand, yet it may facilitate public signaling of the purchase, which could increase demand through perceived benefit to status (Griskevicius et al. 2010). Further, even unobservable changes may influence demand for green products depending on where in the consumption stream the change has occurred. For instance, upstream improvements toward the greening of a product (i.e. alterations in manufacturing transportation processes) may be perceived as more desirable than downstream benefits because the greening of the product has already taken place when the consumer makes the purchase decision, while downstream changes (i.e. alterations in design that improve efficiency during use of disposal) may be perceived as more desirable than upstream benefits because they allow the consumer to be a cooperative player in the green benefit being realized.

While aspects of the product may be one area for consideration of key research objectives, a second area is in aspects of consumers' identities. Recent work suggests that people have many identities, or self-construals, that may be activated at different times, leading to differences in motivations, information processing, and behaviors (Oyserman 2009). Such identity activation may be important for facilitating consumer compliance with behaviors and purchase of products that benefit a common good, rather than their own self interest. In other domain this has been shown to be effect. For example, identity congruent appeals have been shown to be effective for influencing decisions to exercise and to reduce alcohol and drug use (Martin and Leary 2001; Werch 2007, 2008).

The session is expected to have a very broad appeal as research in this area continues to take off. Further, the questions posed in this line of research also dovetail with many other areas of research including the role of emotions in decision making, common goods decisions, attitude formation and change, and self presentation. As a result it is expected that this session will draw both attendees immediately interested in green, ethical and sustainable marketing, as well as those interested in these varied, yet influential, research topics.

## References

Becker-Olsen, Karen, Aronte Bennett, and Amitav Chakravarti (2010), "The Green-Self Paradox: An Examination of Licensing Effects In Green Behavior," presented at the Society for Consumer Psychology Conference, St. Pete Beach, Florida

Ehrich, K., and J. Irwin (2005), "WIllful Ignorance in the Request for Product Information," *Journal of Marketing Research*, 42 (Aug. 2005), 266-277.

Freedonia (2009), "Green Building Materials to 2013," *Study 2459*, February.

Griskevicius, Vladas , J. M. Tybur, and B. Van den Bergh, (in press), "Going Green to Be Seen: Status, Reputation, and Conspicuous Conservation," *Journal of Personality and Social Psychology*.

Haws, Kelly, Karen Page Winterich, and Rebecca Naylor (2010), "It's all about THE GREENS: Conflicting Motives and Making Green Work," Working Paper.

Luchs, Naylor, Irwin, Raghunathan (in press), The Sustainability Liability: Potential Negative Effects of Ethicality on Product Prefrerence," *Journal of Marketing*.

Mazar, N. & Zhong, C. B. , "Do Green Products Make Us Better People?" *Psychological Science* (in press)

Martin, K. A., & Leary, M. R (2001), "Self-Presentational Determinants of Health Risk Behavior Among College Freshmen," *Psychology and Health*, 15, 1-11.

Oyserman, D. (2009). "Identity-Based Motivation: Implications for Action-Readiness, Procedural-Readiness, and Consumer Behavior," *Journal of Consumer Psychology*, 19, 250-260.

United Nations Environment Programme (UNEP) (2005), Talk the Walk: Advancing Sustainable Lifestyles through Marketing and Communications. *UN Global Compact and Utopies*.

Webb, Deborah J., Lois A. Mohr and Katherine E. Harris (2008), "A Re-examination of Socially Responsible Consumption and its Measurement," *Journal of Business Research*, 61, (February), 91-98.

Werch, Chudley E. (2007). "SPORT: A brief program using image to influence drug use and physical activity." *Health Education & Behavior*, 34(2), 275-276.

# Roundtable
## Developing a Dissertation Idea

**Chair:**
Eduardo B. Andrade, University of California, Berkeley, USA

**Participants:**
Clayton Critcher, Cornell University, USA
Jeff Galak, Carnegie Mellon University, USA
Chris Janiszewski, University of Florida, USA
Peter McGraw, University of Colorado, USA
Tom Meyvis, New York University, USA
Leif D. Nelson, University of California, Berkeley, USA
Joseph P. Simmons, Yale University, USA
Stacy Wood, University of South Carolina, USA

**Extended Abstract**

To generate a dissertation idea is a daunting task. Those who have gone or are going through this process know it well. Interestingly, there is unfortunately little discussion about (1) how PhD students (should) develop their dissertation ideas and (2) how professors (should) involve themselves in the process. This roundtable is meant to address this issue. Specifically, it will discuss descriptive and normative aspects related to: research topics of interest, hypothesis generation, faculty involvement, and differences between psychology and marketing departments.

*Choosing an Area of Interest Within Consumer Research.* Given its interdisciplinary approach, consumer research topics can vary dramatically. After being exposed to wide range of areas, how does a student decide on a topic of interest? Moreover, how much is the choice process influenced by intrinsic vs. extrinsic considerations (e.g., passion for the area vs. whom to work with vs. likelihood of publication)? How to balance these two aspects? How variation is there between schools and between students? Are there specific rules of thumb to be followed?

*Selecting a Specific Idea/Hypothesis.* Once a research area is identified, how does the student identify a novel research question and a testable research hypothesis? Are there specific strategies to facilitate this process?

*Faculty involvement.* How much should the faculty adviser be involved? The answer to this question is hotly debated. Should faculty contribute to idea generation or should they merely step back? How should students navigate the considerable cultural differences between universities?

*Psychology/Consumer Research.* The fact that many marketing professors have been trained in psychology also raises the question on whether or not the preceding topics vary systematically depending on the nature of the faculty adviser's personal training. Where systematic differences exist, is there room for identifying a strategy that synthesizes the best tactics from both?

In short, this roundtable will shed light into the different strategies employed by individuals, departments, and disciplines, in the generation and consolidation of a dissertation idea. We hope to attract the interest of senior and junior faculty, and, most importantly, doctoral students.

# Understanding Prosocial Behavior Among Consumers and Organizations

**Chair:**
Michal Strahilevitz , Golden Gate University, USA

**Participants:**
David Mick, University of Virginia, USA
Deborah Small, Wharton School of Business, USA
Carlos J. Torelli, University of Minnesota, USA
Andrew M. Kaikati, Terry College of Business, University of Georgia, USA
Kelly Goldsmith, Kellogg School, Northwestern University, USA
Michael Norton, Harvard School of Business, USA
Nicole Verrochi, University of Pittsburg, USA
Sankar Sen, Zicklin School of Business, Baruch Colege/CUNY, USA
Sergio Carvalho, University of Manitboa, Canada
Karen Page Winterich, Pennsylvania State University, USA
Christopher Olivola, Cognitive, Perceptual and Brain Sciences, University College London, UK
Ekant Veer, University of Canterbury, New Zealand
Susan Dobscha, Bentley University, USA
Uri Simonsohn, Wharton School of Business, USA
Wendy Liu, U.C. San Diego, USA
Stacy Wood, University of South Carolina, USA
Aronte Bennett, Villanova University, USA
Andrea Scott, Pepperdine University, USA
Jing (Alice) Wang, University of Iowa, USA
Lalin Anik, Harvard School of Business, USA
Shuili Du, Simmons College School of Management, USA
Stefanie Rosen, University of South Carolina, USA
Zoe Chance, Harvard School of Business, USA
Aditi Grover, Plymouth State University, USA
Susan Harmon, Pacific Lutheran University, USA
Diane Martin, University of Portland, USA

## Extended Abstract

The interest in prosocial behavior has increased in the last few years as consumers seek greater meaning in their everyday lives. Many companies and consumers are paying attention to the impact their choices have on society at large, and an increasing number of consumer behavior scholars have begun to look at the causes and consequences of prosocial behavior among consumers and organizations.

This roundtable will appeal broadly to those scholars interested in the factors influencing different types of prosocial behavior as well as the effects of different types of prosocial behavior on consumers' lives. Beyond this, it will also appeal to those interested in research examining the effects of prosocial behavior on the part of organizations and the effects of CSR on both employees and consumers. Our relatively large panel of committed attendees purposely includes scholars from a diverse mix of methodological backgrounds as well as a broad range of topics relating to understanding the causes and effects of prosocial behavior. Researchers on our panel are doing research on many important subjects that fit under the "prosocial" umbrella. These include exploring factors affecting charitable giving and volunteerism, the effects of charitable behavior on consumer welfare and satisfaction, cause marketing, sustainability and green consumer behavior, how prosocial activities within organizations affect employee morale and job satisfaction, and the many factors influencing consumer responses to corporate social responsibility (including the type of CSR, the nature of the product, the nature of the consumer, the communication strategy, and prior CSR activities by the organization). Our panel includes scholars with diverse backgrounds and interests, so that we can learn from each other and foster a community that keeps the big picture in mind, rather than focusing on one type of research methodology or paradigm.

We aim to encourage dialogue before, during and after the roundtable. This will include identifying key areas of current research, discussing potential synergies between different streams of work, identifying directions for future research and discussing the challenges of doing research in this area. Due to the huge appeal of this topic to many scholars with diverse perspectives, we hope to not only attract a wide range of scholars from different backgrounds and interests, but also to help foster a community that will continue to be active even after ACR 2010 has passed. Due to the diverse backgrounds of those on our panel, this roundtable will be of interest to both qualitative and experimental researchers. The topics covered will be relevant to those interested in broadening our theoretical understanding of prosocial behavior, those dedicated to doing research with prosocial benefits (TCR), and those focused on managerial implications. Indeed, many on our panel are dedicated to doing research that addresses all three of these goals.

While many of our confirmed participants are impressive, we are particularly happy to have David Mick, who is considered by many to the be the founder of the currently active Transformative Consumer Research community. In his ACR presidential address several years ago, Mick described transformative consumer research as "consumer research in the service of quality of life" (Mick 2006, p. 3). This roundtable will appeal to a large portion of the TCR community, but will also attract a range of scholars who are not (currently) part of the TCR group. One of the "big picture" questions we will address in our discussion is whether or not it is prosocial to study prosocial behavior. Obviously, prosocial behavior is not always motivated by purely by altruistic motives. Indeed, researchers our panel have demonstrated a connection between prosocial behavior and happiness (Liu and Aaaker 2008; Dunn Aknin and Norton 2008), while others have identified the effectiveness of appealing to rather selfish status-seeking motives to encourage seemingly prosocial behavior in certain contexts (Torelli, Monga, and Kaikati, 2010). More and more, nonprofits are focused not only on helping the causes they support, but also on keeping their donors and volunteers feeling appreciated and happy, if not downright entertained (Strahilevitz 2010). Still, understanding that prosocial behavior is not always motivated purely by a desire to help others can still help us to encourage actions that benefit society. Given the importance and "bigness" of these topics, we will ask David Mick to briefly speak on the potential value of doing research in this area, with a focus on work that is both rigorous in terms of theory, but also potentially helpful in terms of service to society. We will also, as a group, briefly discuss strategies for promoting the value of research on prosocial behavior within a business school setting.

Before and after the conference, continued dialogue will be facilitated via a combination of email exchanges (facilitated by the roundtable chair), postings on the ACR Knowledge Exchange Forum, and postings on our newly created FaceBook group "Prosocial Consumer Research." The FaceBook group is open to any scholar interested in research in this area, but will begin with invitations to the roundtable participants. In our pre-ACR dialogue, we will develop a plan for organizing breakout sessions focusing on issues such as factors affecting consumer responses to CSR, causes and consequences of different types of prosocial behavior by consumers, the prosocial nature of research on prosocial behavior, and the challenges that come with research in this area.

## References

Dunn, Elizabeth, Lara B Aknin and Michael I. Norton, "Spending Money on Others Promotes Happiness," *Science* (2008).

Liu, Wendy and Jennifer Aaker, "The Happiness of Giving: The Time-Ask Effect," *Journal of Consumer Research* (2008).

Mick, David Glen (2006), "Presidential Address: Meaning and Mattering through Transformative Consumer Research," *Advances in Consumer Research*, 33, 1-4.

Strahilevitz, Michal, (in press) "A Model Comparing the Value of Giving to Others to the Value of Having More for Oneself: Implications for Fundraisers Seeking to Maximize Donor Satisfaction," in *The Science of Giving: Experimental Approaches to the Study of Charity*. Oppenheimer, D.M., & Olivola, C.Y. (eds.). New York: Taylor and Francis.

Torelli, Carlos, Alokparna Basu Monga, and Andrew M. Kaikati, Does It Hurt to Communicate the Good Deeds of a Luxury Brand? Power Concerns and Attitudes toward Luxury Brands Positioned on Social Responsibility, presented at the Society for Consumer Psychology, 2010, St Petersburg Florida.

# Working Paper Abstracts

## The Impact of Preannouncements and Rumors on Consumer Evaluations

Jun Wang, Delft University of Technology, The Netherlands
Maria Sääksjärvi, Delft University of Technology, The Netherlands
Erik-Jan Hultink, Delft University of Technology, The Netherlands
Tripat Gill, University of Ontario Institute of Techology, Canada

In the contemporary high-tech markets, products are rarely launched unexpectedly, as new product preannouncements have become common practice (Kohli, 1999; Lilly and Waters, 1997). Besides new product preannouncements, or "formal, deliberate communication" (Eliashberg and Robertson, 1988), informal communication, such as rumors, often take place prior to the launch of a new product. Rumors provide signals on the incoming new product and together with preannouncements develop market anticipations (Schatzel and Calantone, 2006) and build prior-to-launch expectations of the forthcoming new product (Nagard-Assayag and Manceau, 2001).

Rumors have become especially important due to the internet, in which rumors spread quickly through online-blogs and various websites. The most active participants of online-blogs often are lead users and early adopters (Dorge, Stanko and Pollite, 2010), who play an important role in new product adoption (Rogers, 1962). Despite their increasing importance, the role of rumors in new product adoption has received little research attention (Kamins, Folkes, Perner, 1997). The present two studies explore the impact of rumors and preannouncements on consumer evaluations of new high-tech products. Specifically, we investigate the role of two factors–(1) type of innovation (incremental versus radical) and (2) extent of ambiguity of the rumors–on the consumer curiosity and purchase intentions towards high-tech innovations. We propose that rumors stimulate consumer curiosity towards a new product, which subsequently influence consumers purchase intension. In addition, we hypothesize that rumors about a radical innovation involve more novel content that could create greater curiosity than that about an incremental innovation.

Study 1 used a content analysis to explore both preannouncements and rumors about two types of innovations: radical versus incremental innovations. We selected the iPhone as a radical innovation as it was the first touch-screen mobile phone that radically changed how consumers interact with their Smartphones. Sony's PlayStation 3 was chosen as the incremental innovation as it was an improvement over the previous two generations of the PlayStation gaming consoles. We followed the preannouncements and rumors about these two innovations through press releases and blogs from credible sources. As rumors are mainly transmitted through blog postings, we chose Engadget and Gizmodo as the main research sites because of their consistently high ratings, popularity and focus on new product information (Dorge, Stanko, Pollitte, 2010).

We collected a sample of 49 postings on the iPhone (1999–2007) and 47 postings on the PlayStation 3 (1999–2006). We analyzed the content as well as the timing of these postings. The content of the postings was classified based on the core elements of the marketing mix: namely, content related to product (including product name and performance features), price, distribution and promotion. The majority of the content was related to the product (iPhone: 80%, PlayStation 3=79%). There were more discussions on the price of PlayStation 3 (16%) than that of the iPhone (6%). Nearly a quarter of the postings discussed launch timing (iPhone 18%, PlayStation 3: 26%), while only a few mentioned distribution (iPhone: 4%, PlayStation 3: 4%) and promotional programs (iPhone: 2%, PlayStation 3: 4%). An analysis of the timing revealed that the rumors started well in advance of the company's official preannouncement. Rumors on Apple's iPhone and Sony's PlayStation 3 started eight and six years, respectively, before the two companies officially preannounced the product releases. One major difference between the preannouncements of the two products was the ambiguity of the information. Apple remained ambiguous in their responses to rumors. It did not discuss product specifics before the official announcements. In contrast, Sony's executives responded to rumors and made specific comments about the product features in the press.

In Study 2, we decided to further investigate the effect of ambiguity of rumors on consumer curiosity and purchase intention. We used a 2x2 between-subjects design manipulating product innovativeness (radical innovation versus incremental innovation) and rumor ambiguity (ambiguous rumor versus unambiguous rumor). Consumer curiosity served as a mediator and the dependent variable was purchase intention. We collected data from 71 participants aged between 18 and 42, who first read a rumor about a new product, and we measured their extent of curiosity about the product. Subsequently, they read an official preannouncement about the product by the firm, and we measured their purchase intentions. The type of innovation (radical versus incremental) and the ambiguity of the rumor (ambiguous versus unambiguous) was manipulated in the scenarios read by the participants.

We found a significant effect of product innovativeness on consumer curiosity [$F(1,69)=25.612$, $p<0.001$]. The mean score on curiosity towards the radical innovation (M=5.026, SD=0.877) was significantly higher than that for the incremental innovation (M=3.888, SD=1.019), $t(69)=5.061$, $p<0.001$. Rumor ambiguity did not have a significant influence on curiosity [$F(1,69)=0.067, p=0.797$]. We further found an interaction between product innovativeness and rumor ambiguity leading to a positive effect on consumer curiosity (F=8.242, $p<0.01$). Respondents have stronger curiosity towards the radical innovation in an ambiguous rumor (M =5.253, SD=0.718) than the radical innovation in an unambiguous rumor (M=4.800, SD=0.978). Conversely, respondents are more curious about the incremental innovation in an unambiguous rumor (M=4.244, SD=0.866) than that in an ambiguous rumor (M=3.460, SD=1.051). Finally, we found that consumer curiosity had a positive effect on purchase intention (regression coefficient=0.456, $p<0.001$).

The results of our two studies suggest that new product rumors spread much earlier than the official preannouncements, indicating that consumers' first impressions of a new product are formed based on rumors rather than on preannouncements. Moreover, the preannouncements for an incremental innovation were less ambiguous than that for radical innovations. Companies intentionally remain ambiguous about radical innovations, while being clear on incremental innovations. This strategy is supported in study 2, which shows that people are more interested in radical innovations when the rumor is more ambiguous, while they are more interested in an incremental innovation when the rumor is unambiguous. It suggest that companies should be clear about their incremental innovations, while remain ambiguous about their radical innovations in order to make their product interesting in the eyes of the consumers.

## References

Allport, Gordon W. and Leo Postman (1947), *The Psychology of Rumor,* New York: Holt, Rinehart & Winston.

Berlyne, David E. (1954), "A Theory of Human Curiosity," *British Journal of Psychology*, Vol. 45, pp.180–191.

Berlyne, David E. (1960), *Conflict, Arousal, and Curiosity*, New York: McGraw -Hill

Dorge, Cornelia., Michael A. Stanko, and Wesley A. Pollitte (2010), "Lead Users and Early Adopters on the Web: The Role of New Technology Product Blogs," *The Journal of Product Innovation Management*, Vol. 27: pp. 66-82

Eliashberg, Jehoshua and Thomas S. Robertson (1988). "New Product Preannouncing Behavior: A Market Signaling Study," *Journal of Marketing Research*, 25. 282-292.

Garcia, Rosanna and Roger Calantone (2002), "A Critical Look at Technological Innovation Typology and Innovativeness Terminology: A Literature Review", *The Journal of Product Innovation Management*, Vol.19, pp.110—132

Herr, Paul M., Frank R. Kardes, and John Kim (1991), "Effects of Word-of-mouth and Product Attribute Information on Persuasion: An Accessibility-diagnosticity Perspective," *Journal of Consumer Research*, Vol. 17 (March), pp. 454-462.

Kamins, Michael. A., Valerie S. Folkes, and Lars Perner (1997), "Consumer Responses to Rumors: Good News, Bad News," *Journal of Consumer Psychology*, Vol. 6, No. 2, pp. 165-187

Kohli, Chiranjeev (1999), "Signaling New Product Announcements: A Framework Explaining the Timing of Announcements," *Journal of Business Research*, Vol. 46, pp.45-56.

Lilly, Bryan and Rockney Walters (1997), "Toward a Model of New Product Preannouncement Timing," *Journal of Product Innovation Management*, Vol.14, pp.4-20

Nagard-Assayag, Emmanuelle Le and Delphine Manceau (2001), "Modeling the Impact of Product Preannouncements in the Context of Indirect Network Externalities," *International Journal of Research in Marketing*, Vol.18, pp. 203–219.

Rogers, Everett M. (1962), *Diffusion of innovations*, New York: Free Press.

Schatzel, Kim and Roger Calantone (2006), "Creating Market Anticipation: An Exploratory Examination of the Effect of Preannouncement Behavior on a New Product's Launch," *Journal of the Academy of Marketing Science*, Vol. 34, No. 3, pp. 357-366

# Frisbee for Friends, Furniture for Family:
# The Influence of Products on Network Activation and WOM Intentions

Lalin Anik, Harvard Business School, USA
Michael Norton, Harvard Business School, USA

People use different products to signal desired identities to different social networks–iPods to impress their friends, briefcases to impress their employers. We suggest that this behavior causes those products to become linked to specific social networks, such that mere exposure to products can prime different social networks, making some relationships more salient than others. We furthermore explore how people perceive the closeness of these salient networks as a possible mechanism to examine subsequent WOM intentions.

Previous research has demonstrated that situational and environmental cues or primes can activate associated representations, making them more accessible (Berger and Fitzsimons 2008; Higgins, Rholes, and Jones 1977). As priming a given construct leads to the activation of related constructs in memory, it can also have impact on the perceptually-related objects, and furthermore on the product choice and evaluations (Lee and Labroo 2004; Whittlesea 1994). In this project, we use products belonging to different categories as our primes, and explore whether exposure to these primes makes certain social networks more accessible.

The literature on goal instrumentality previously showed that active goals lead to the activation of different relationship partners, specifically of those who are goal congruent (e.g., Fitzsimons and Shah 2008). We, however, look at the salience of relationship partners in relation to product categories rather than personal goals or motivations. Moreover, we argue that the products as primes influence social perceptions and as a result offer people's changing perceptions of network closeness as a mechanism for following WOM behavior. To examine this linkage of products to networks to WOM, we ran three studies.

In Study 1, we investigated whether exposure to products belonging to various categories make related networks more salient than others in the minds of people. One hundred and thirty-five participants were randomly assigned to one of four conditions: *family, friends, co-worker priming* and *control* conditions where they were presented with products belonging to family, friends, co-worker categories respectively, and asked to indicate their preference in a set of four. Those in the *control condition* didn't see any products. Subjects went through a total of twenty trials, viewing eighty different options. Afterwards, participants were asked to write down the initials of the first five people that came up to their mind and subsequently, instructed to indicate their relationship to each of the five people they listed.

The dependent variable was the number of family members, friends and co-workers listed in each of the four conditions. Our results showed that participants in the *family priming* condition listed significantly more family members than those in the *friends priming, co-worker priming,* and *control* conditions. These results were parallel for the *friends* and *co-worker priming* conditions, such that when primed with *friends* related products, people thought of their friends more so than when they saw *family* or *work* related products. Finally, those people in the *co-worker priming* condition reported significantly more number of colleagues than the participants in the other conditions.

Having shown the increase in the salience of networks as a result of being exposed to related products, next we wanted to examine whether exposure to products from different categories impacts people's perception of network closeness, and as a result who they think of passing on information to. In Study 2, one hundred and eight participants were again randomly assigned to one of the four (*family, friends, co-worker priming or control*) groups and exposed to the same product priming tasks as in Study 1. After the priming tasks, participants were randomly presented with five print ads and asked "Who would you forward this ad to?" With this question, we aimed to capture word of mouth intentions. Participants were furthermore instructed to specify the relationship of the person.

We predicted that the priming categories would impact who participants listed as possible recipients of print advertisements. In line with our previous findings, participants who were in the *friends priming* condition listed more friends who they would forward the ads to than those in the *family priming, co-worker priming,* and *control* conditions. Our results again held in the *family* and *co-worker priming* conditions as participants in those groups listed many more family members and co-workers, respectively, than those in the other conditions.

So far, we showed that exposure to different product categories increases salience of category-related network members, who are then considered more accessible in word of mouth considerations. Next, we tested whether product categories influenced the salience of network members in WOM considerations via changing the perception of network closeness. In Study 3, one hundred and twenty seven participants were randomly assigned to *family, friends* or *no priming* conditions where the products task was the same as in the previous two studies. Following the priming task, they were shown three products they had not seen before. Participants were presented with announcements about a new model of each of the three products (printer, MP3 player, coffee maker) and were asked to indicate three people to whom they thought of passing this info. In order to understand whether the WOM intentions were mediated by network closeness, we asked subjects how close they perceived their family and friends networks.

Replicating our previous findings, participants in the *family priming* condition listed significantly more friends and those in the *friends priming* condition significantly more friends when asked about their WOM intentions than the listings in the other conditions. Additionally, our results showed that people in corresponding priming conditions feel their networks to be both closer to themselves and also closer to each other. Further analysis showed that the relationship between *family priming* and preference for sharing information with family members was mediated by the perception of family network closeness. Perception of network closeness was also a significant mediator for the *friends priming* condition.

These initial experiments provide insights about how products can influence people's perception of and interaction with various networks they are a part of. Our investigation demonstrates how the self can be linked to specific networks, which can subsequently alter WOM intentions. We are currently running a field study where we manipulate social interactions of people via product primes and look forward to engaging in deeper discussions about our findings with ACR members.

**Selected References:**

Berger, Jonah and Gráinne M. Fitzsimons (2008), "Dogs on the Street, Pumas on Your Feet: How Cues in the Environment Influence Product Evaluation and Choice," *Journal of Marketing Research*, 45(1), 1-14.

Fitzsimons, Grainné M. and James Y. Shah (2008), "How Goal Instrumentality Shapes Relationship Evaluations," *Journal of Personality and Social Psychology*, 95, 319-337.

Higgins, Tory E., William S. Rholes, and Carl R. Jones (1977), "Category Accessibility and Impression Formation," *Journal of Social Psychology*, 13, 141-154.

Lee, Angela Y. and Aparna Labroo (2004), "Effects of Conceptual and Perceptual Fluency on Affective Judgment," *Journal of Marketing Research*, 41(2), 151-165.

Whittlesea, Bruce W.A. (1993), "Illusions of Familiarity," *Journal of Experimental Psychology: Learning, Memory, and Cognition*, 19 (6), 1235-53.

# Hopelessly Devoted? Word-of-Mouth and Diagnosticity in a Stable Preference Context

Martin Pyle, Queen's University, Canada
Peter Dacin, Queen's University, Canada
Ethan Pancer, Queen's University, Canada

Consumption-related word-of-mouth (WOM) is considered one of the more persuasive forms of information exchange among consumers (Dichter 1966), receiving considerable attention in the marketing literature (e.g., Bearden and Etzel 1982; Herr, Kardes and Kim 1991; Stephen, Lehmann and Toubia 2010). Much of the research on the persuasiveness of WOM occurs in contexts where the audience does not have an initial preference for a product (e.g., innovations), or in which the audience demonstrates no initial commitment to the product (e.g., Herr et al 1991). Many consumers, however, have strong, stable preferences for a given product, leading to questions of whether and how WOM can affect these preferences? We address these questions by examining conditions under which WOM might convince consumers with stable brand preferences to, at least, consider switching brands.

We hypothesize two conditions under which stable preferences may be swayed by WOM. These are the motivation of the consumer receiving the WOM and his or her perceptions regarding the diagnosticity of the WOM message. With respect to motivation, based on the concept of naïve realism, we suggest that although consumers may perceive that others use biased reasoning, consumers view their own evaluative judgments as objective and unbiased (Robinson, Keltner, Ward and Ross 1995). Consequently, consumers will tend to process information with an accuracy motivation, and likely view arguments that positively highlight a clear alternative choice, as opposed to suggesting something negative about their preferred brand, as more persuasive.

Although accuracy motivations tend to lead consumers to process information with an open mind and give greater diagnostic weight to negative information (Ahluwalia 2002), we argue that when consumers have stable preferences, the diagnosticity of WOM lies not in its valence, but rather in the degree to which it makes it easier for the consumer to provide reasons to discriminate between choices and highlight decisions (Darke and Chaiken 2005, Herr et al 1991). In short, diagnostic messages can provide the reasons to support a new choice (Shafir, Simonson and Tversky 1993). We also argue that the diagnosticity of WOM messages is related to the type of WOM message—be they WOM against the current preference (WOM-ACP) or WOM in favor of an alternate brand (WOM-IFA)—such that WOM-IFA will be seen as more diagnostic by clearly demonstrating reasons for a better choice. In addition, the speaker's expertise and evident biases will also affect the diagnosticity and persuasiveness of the WOM in that perceptions of WOM messages from a biased source should be neither diagnostic nor persuasive, while WOM messages from experts should be both diagnostic and persuasive. When both bias and expertise are low, however, we expect WOM-IFA rather than WOM-ACP to be more diagnostic and persuasive.

In the first of two studies, subjects listed a product that was important to them in a category (personal grooming products) in which pretests revealed consumers develop strong preferences. Participants then read a scenario describing a hypothetical exchange about the product with a colleague. In the scenario, we manipulated three factors, i) speaker's expertise (high vs. low), ii) speaker's bias (strong vs. weak), as well as iii) WOM type (WOM-IFA vs. WOM-ACP). We randomly assigned each of 145 participants to one of the eight cells and measured diagnosticity and persuasion (the latter via consideration of switching brands).

As expected, there was a significant main effect on persuasion for both bias (weak-bias was more persuasive) and expertise (higher expertise was more persuasive). WOM-IFA was significantly more persuasive than WOM-ACP. That is, when the bias manipulation offered a clear reason to dismiss the message (i.e., high bias) or the expertise manipulation gave a clear reason to accept the message (i.e., high expertise), we found no significant impact of WOM type on persuasion. However, when these reasons were absent, our participants revealed a noticeable difference in both diagnosticity and persuasion and WOM-IFA was more persuasive than WOM-ACP. This supports our expectation for greater persuasion when WOM offers a clear choice.

To ensure that accuracy goals formed the basis of the motivation for processing WOM, we conducted a second study in which we manipulated two factors: i) diagnosticity (higher vs. lower) and ii) WOM type (WOM-IFA vs. WOM-ACP). This second study also allowed us to demonstrate that the message valence (i.e., a positivity effect) was not driving the outcomes from Study 1. The procedure mirrored Study 1, as we again asked participants to think about a brand in a given product category (juice) for which they held strong preferences. In the higher diagnosticity condition, WOM either mentioned the alternative brand as the only one using fresh fruit (WOM-IFA) or the current preference as using frozen fruit (WOM-ACP). In the lower diagnosticity condition, WOM mentioned either the alternative brand or current preference as being *one of many* companies that used a certain process. We also included self-monitoring as a covariate to examine whether effects were driven by social impression goals.

With persuasion as the dependent variable the analysis revealed no effect for self-monitoring; no main effect for WOM type; a significant main effect for diagnosticity; and a significant interaction effect between WOM type and diagnosticity. In the lower diagnosticity condition, WOM-ACP was less persuasive than WOM-IFA, while in the higher diagnostic condition there was no difference in effect on persuasion between WOM types. This is consistent with our expectation of participants using an accuracy motivation to maintain their sense of naïve realism. Results also revealed no relationship between message valence and perceived diagnosticity.

We posed the questions of whether and how WOM can persuade consumers with stable preferences to consider switching brands. The results demonstrate that many consumers hold strong preferences only so long as they believe they can reasonably support their choice. When presented with unbiased, credible and diagnostic WOM highlighting a better choice, consumers' accuracy goals are activated, and they are willing to consider another option. Furthermore, reasons for preferring or switching brands do not appear to be rooted in the valence of the message but rather in their ability to clearly specify a better choice.

**Selected References**

Ahluwalia, Rohini (2002), "How Prevalent Is the Negativity Effect in Consumer Environments?," *Journal of Consumer Research*, 29 (September), 270-279.

Bearden, William O. and Michael J. Etzel (1982), "Reference Group Influence on Product and Brand Purchase Decisions," *Journal of Consumer Research*, 9 (September), 183-194.

Darke, Peter R. and Shelly Chaiken (2005) "The Pursuit of Self-Interest: Self-Interest Bias in Attitude Judgment and Persuasion," *Journal of Personality and Social Psychology*, 89 (6), 864-883.

Dichter, Ernest (1966) "How Word-of-Mouth Advertising Works," *Harvard Business Review*, 44 (November-December), 147-166.

Herr, Paul M., Frank R. Kardes and John Kim (1991), "Effects of Word-of-Mouth and Product-Attribute Information on Persuasion: An Accessibility-Diagnosticity Perspective," *Journal of Consumer Research,* 17 (March), 454-462.

Robinson, Robert J., Dacher Keltner, Andrew Ward and Lee Ross (1995), "Actual Versus Assumed Differences in Construal: 'Naïve Realism' in Intergroup Perception and Conflict," *Journal of Personality and Social Psychology,* 68 (3), 404-417.

Shafir, Eldar, Simonson, Itamar & Tversky, Amos. (1993), "Reason-based Choice," *Cognition*, 49, 11–36.

Stephen, Andrew, Donald Lehmann and Olivier Toubia (2010), "Why Do Consumers Talk, Does Anyone Listen, and What Happens?," in *Advances in Consumer* Research Volume 37, eds. Margaret C. Campbell and Jeff Inman and Rik Pieters, Duluth, MN : Association for Consumer Research.

# Information But at What Cost?
# The Positive and Negative Impact of Informational Social Influence

Kashef Majid, George Washington University, USA
Vanessa Perry, George Washington University, USA
Johny K. Johansson, Georgetown University, USA

Under conditions of uncertainty the presence of an informational social influence has long been thought to impact consumer judgments (Asch 1955). Originally conceptualized as the influence to accept information from another as evidence of reality (Deutsch and Gerrard 1955, pg. 629), prior work has found that informational social influence can positively impact consumer judgments, encourages product usage, and creates positive perceptions towards products (Cohen and Golden 1972). However, the creation of informational social influence is not without its harmful consequences. A nightclub owner may keep patrons waiting in long lines outside of the establishment in order to signal the popularity of the venue; by doing so potential patrons may be scared away at having to wait for a long period of time or the possibility of not being afforded enough personal space once inside. When assessing the validity of informational social influence consumers must ascertain whether the informational social influence signals a positive or negative outcome. The purpose of the present paper is to explore the conditions under which the deployment of informational social influence causes impacts negative judgments and when informational social influence impacts positive judgments.

The context for the present study was a virtual environment. Over 30 years has passed since the pioneering work on informational social influence and product judgments conducted by (Cohen and Golden 1972) as well as (Pincus and Waters 1977). However, the impact of the construct in judgments towards products is as relevant if not more so than ever. The growth of virtual environments and e-commerce in particular, has fueled an environment rich in informational social influence. Much of this influence is deliberately created by consumers as a means to share their experiences and communicate their recommendations, such as the writing of user reviews or the rating of certain products (Chevalier and Mayzlin 2006). However, in a virtual environment, informational social influence is also created inadvertently by consumers. For example, each time a consumer downloads a piece of music or software online that download is accumulated and then displayed to other potential users as a sign that others have made the same decision that the consumer is considering. Thus, when forming a product judgment regarding a product viewed in a virtual environment, consumers must interpret the informational social influence that they are faced with and use it to assess the product either positively or negatively.

One of the greatest concerns consumers have when purchasing products in a virtual environment is that the product will appear to be one thing online and then actually be something else once it arrives (Trocchia and Janda 2003). At best the product in question has slight deviations from what was expected; at worse, the product is a fake or a forgery. Through exposure and experience, consumers have gained a level of knowledge that helps them to ascertain the quality of the product before purchase (Pavlou and Gefen 2004). For example, consumers which purchase certain luxury brand name apparel may be apprehensive of purchasing the product online if it is selling for a third of the price that it does at the local retailer regardless of the number of the consumers that have purchased the product before. We argue that when knowledge of the product category is high consumers may be less susceptible to informational social influence and would be more likely to view the negative aspects of the informational social influence. Conversely, when consumers are uncertain as to the quality of the product then we believe that informational influence will play an enhanced role in reducing that uncertainty and will positively impact judgment towards the product.

The predictions above were tested using a 2 (familiarity: high vs. low) x 2 (informational social presence: present vs. absent) study design. A total of 133 undergraduate students from a large private university in the South Eastern United States participated in the study in exchange for course credit. Familiarity was manipulated by product category. A total of 22 participants drawn from the same sample as the study population participated in the pretest and were asked to rate their familiarity and purchase frequency of several different product categories. We ultimately chose DVDs and a universal remote control as our products for this study based on the differing levels of familiarity that the sample had of these two products ($M\_DVD=5.87$ vs. $M\_Remote=3.35$, $F(1, 43)=4.46$, $p<0.05$) and the high rate of counterfeiting in each of these two product categories. Two popular DVDs were chosen so as to eliminate unique effects of using one DVD that the participants may be familiar with.

The research team then searched for versions of these products for sale on the popular online marketplace "eBay.com". Once found, the web pages displaying these items for sale was then saved and edited by a graphics design team in order to remove any previous feedback the seller of the products had previously received and to standardize the information given by each seller for each of the products. Informational social influence was manipulated by either adding bidders for the item or removing any bidders from the item. In the informational social influence condition several bidders were competing for the item while in the non informational social influence condition there were no other bidders. All of the DVDs were priced at $9.50 while all of the Universal Remote Controls were priced at $79.95. Participants used their personal computers to log into the school's intranet where they were then able to access the study. Once the study was activated the participants would then see the edited eBay seller page and were asked to state the probability that they thought the product was counterfeit and to state the maximum amount of money that they would pay for the item.

Our findings revealed a significant interaction between product familiarity and informational social presence in terms of the product being viewed as counterfeit ($F(1, 110=3.95$, $p<0.05$). Participants rated the DVDs as more likely to be counterfeit if others had bid on it (Mdvd_social presence=43.86 vs. Mdvd_social presence absent=35.43); conversely, the universal remote control was viewed as less likely to be counterfeit if others were bidding on it than if there were no other bidders (MRemote_social presence=51.67 vs. MRemote_social presence absent=35.43). Main effects for familiarity or social presence were not significant.

For the DVDs the presence of other bidders adds cost increases to the price of the DVDs but provides little value in terms of signaling the authenticity of the product. The presence of others may actually have signaled to consumers that the price was previously lower and thus more likely to be counterfeit. With the unfamiliar good, the universal remote control, the presence of other bidders seems to have provided a signal to consumers that the product is authentic. Furthermore, we tested between group differences on the maximum amount that participants were willing to pay for the both products. A between groups analysis revealed that participants were willing to pay significantly more for the DVDs when there were no other bidders versus the condition where there were multiple bidders (F(1, 59)=7.93, $p<0.01$, M$DVD_social presence=10.114 vs. M$DVD_social presence absent=7.749). There were no observed differences between the two groups in the willingness to pay for the universal remote control.

In conclusion, our findings demonstrate that under conditions of uncertainty, informational social influence can enhance the perceived quality of products. However, when consumers are familiar with the products in question, informational social influence can create negative byproducts through its employment which we have demonstrated can decrease the value of the product as well as its perceived quality.

**Selected References:**

Asch, Solomon. E. (1955), Opinions and social pressure. *Scientific American,* 193(5), 31-35.

Chevalier, Judith A. and Dina Mayzlin (2006), The Effect of Word of Mouth on Sales, *Journal of Marketing Research*, 43 (3), 345-354.

Cohen, Joel B. and Golden, Ellen (1972), Informational Social Influence and Product Evaluation. *Journal of Applied Psychology,* 56 (1), 54-59.

Deutsch, Morton and Harold B. Gerard (1955), A study of normative and informational social influences upon individual judgment. *The Journal of Abnormal and Social Psychology,* 51, 629-636.

Pavlou, Paul A. and David Gefen (2004), Building Effective Online Marketplaces with Institution-Based Trust. *Information Systems Research*, 15 (1), 37-59.

Pincus, Steven and L.K. Waters (1977), Informational Social Influence and Product Quality Judgments. *Journal of Applied Psychology, 62 (5),* 615-619.

Trocchia, Philip J. and Swinder Janda (2003), How do consumers evaluate Internet retail service quality? *Journal of Services Marketing*, 17 (3), 243-253.

# Investigation of Differences in Diffusion Between Positive and Negative Word-of-Mouth

Andreas M. Kaplan, ESCP Europe, France
Michael Haenlein, ESCP Europe, France

## Extended Abstract

Word-of-Mouth (WoM) is a topic that has received regular interest among Marketing researchers over the last 50 years in both traditional (e.g. Day 1971; Katz and Lazarsfeld 1955; Thorelli 1971; Udell 1966) and electronic settings (e.g. Dellarocas 2003; Dwyer 2007; Godes and Mayzlin 2004; Hennig-Thurau et al. 2004; Kozinets 2002). Within this stream of research, we investigate how WoM valence (i.e. positive vs. negative WoM) influences WoM diffusion characteristics based on data from a French virtual world, similar to the US-based "Second Life" application.

## Study 1

Study 1 investigates the impact of valence on WoM diffusion frequency (i.e. the number of contacts WoM is spread to) and speed (i.e. the time elapsed between receiving and retransmitting the information). With respect to WoM diffusion frequency, it is commonly believed that negative WoM is spread to more contacts than positive WoM (e.g. Silverman 1997), triggered by several research studies showing that negative WoM from dissatisfied customers exceeds the amount of positive WoM by satisfied clients (e.g. Bearden and Teel 1983; Richins 1983a, b; Westbrook 1987). However, East, Hammond, and Wright (2007) show that differences in aggregated WoM volume are caused by differences in WoM penetration (i.e. the share of the population spreading WoM) instead of differences in individual-level diffusion frequencies. Given that people take account of the needs of others when engaging in information transmission, the same customers are likely to spread both positive and negative WoM (with equal frequency), depending on the information needs of the receiver (East et al. 2007; Mangold, Miller, and Brockway 1999). We therefore assume that WoM diffusion frequency is independent from WoM valence. Regarding diffusion speed, we expect negative WoM to spread faster than positive WoM as unpleasant or potentially dangerous situations lead to a strong negative reaction, the negativity bias (e.g. Ito et al. 1998). This is supported by studies in the Finance discipline showing that stock prices tend to reflect bad news faster than good news (Lobo 2000) and that good news have more pronounced lagged effects than bad news (Marshall and Walker 2002). This leads to the following two hypotheses:

H₁: There is no impact of WoM valence on individual-level WoM diffusion frequency.

H₂: WoM diffusion speed is higher for negative WoM than for positive WoM.

## Study 2

Study 1 provides insight into the impact of WoM valence on basic WoM diffusion characteristics (i.e. how often and when). Study 2 analyzes the influence of social network-related variables on WoM transmission (i.e. to whom). We expect that strong ties are activated more frequently than weak ties in WoM diffusion as strong tie relationships tend to be more influential as information sources (Brown and Reingen 1987; Reingen and Kernan 1986) and their presence leads to higher levels of WoM (Fitzgerald Bone 1992; Wirtz and Chew 2002). Concerning WoM valence, we assume a moderating influence in the sense that this strong-tie preference will be even more pronounced for negative than for positive WoM. One the on hand, we expect people to be reluctant to transmit negative WoM to weak tie relationships as it tends to be associated with unpleasant messages and a notion of complaining, potentially resulting in a negative impression that the transmitter may want to avoid (Sperduto, Calhoun, and Ciminero 1978; Tice et al. 1995). On the other hand, WoM to strong ties is likely to be caused by altruistic motives and the desire to help the receiver making better decisions. Given that the sender is likely to have a good level of understanding of the needs and likes of strong ties (Kiecker and Hartman 1994), s/he may be sufficiently confident sharing even negative information (Frenzen and Nakamoto 1993; Wirtz and Chew 2002). This leads to the following two hypotheses:

H3: Strong ties are activated more often than weak ties in the WoM diffusion process.

H4: The preference for strong ties gets stronger with increasing WoM negativity.

**Study 3**

Studies 1 and 2 analyze WoM diffusion by focusing on messages received by some source and passed on to social contacts of varying degree of closeness. Study 3 addresses the question whether WoM that reflects hearsay shows different diffusion patterns than WoM originating from a personal and direct experience made by the WoM sender. Generally, we expect that personal experiences lead to higher degree of WoM than hearsay as they result in unique and less ambiguous information that people feel more confident to transmit (Fazio and Zanna 1981; Kardes, Allen, and Pontes 1993). With respect to WoM valence, we expect a moderating impact in the sense that information based on hearsay is more likely to be transmitted when it is of negative compared to positive valence. This is based on Kamins, Folkes, and Perner (1997) who showed that consumers are more inclined to spread negative than positive rumors and (Donavan, Mowen, and Chakraborty (1999) who indicate that urban legends with negative information are associated with higher levels of communication intent. This leads to the following two hypotheses:

H5: WoM based on personal experience will be transferred more often than WoM based on hearsay.

H6: For WoM based on hearsay, negative WoM is more likely to be transmitted than positive WoM.

**Research Methodology**

We plan to investigate the aforementioned hypotheses based on data we collected from a French virtual world, which is targeted toward children and teenagers. We chose this setting over traditional laboratory-style experiments as we expect it to provide a higher degree of external validity. Within this virtual world we launched 16 different messages (4 message per cell within a 2 levels of message strength x 2 levels of message valence design) and recorded the resulting WoM activities generated by the virtual world users (diffusion frequency, diffusion speed, type of social tie activation). Currently, we are in the process of coding the data obtained form the virtual world platform (weblogs) in order to prepare our data analysis.

**References**
Bearden, William O. and Jesse E. Teel (1983), "Selected Determinants of Consumer Satisfaction and Complaint Reports," *Journal of marketing research*, 20 (1), 21-28.
Brown, Jacqueline Johnson and Peter H. Reingen (1987), "Social Ties and Word-of-Mouth Referral Behavior," *Journal of consumer research*, 14 (3), 350-62.
Day, George S. (1971), "Attitude Change, Media and Word of Mouth," *Journal of advertising research*, 11 (6), 31-40.
Dellarocas, Chrysanthos (2003), "The Digitization of Word of Mouth: Promise and Challenges of Online Feedback Mechanisms," *Management science*, 49 (10), 1407-24.
Donavan, D. Todd, John C. Mowen, and Goutam Chakraborty (1999), "Urban Legends: The Word-of-Mouth Communication of Morality through Negative Story Content," *Marketing letters*, 10 (1), 23-34.
Dwyer, Paul (2007), "Measuring the Value of Electronic Word-of-Mouth and Its Impact in Consumer Communities," *Journal of interactive marketing*, 21 (2), 63-79.
East, Robert, Kathy Hammond, and Malcolm Wright (2007), "The Relative Incidence of Positive and Negative Word of Mouth: A Multi-Category Study," *International journal of research in marketing*, 24 (2), 175-84.
Fazio, Russell H. and Mark P. Zanna (1981), "Direct Experience and Attitude-Behavior Consistency," *Advances in experimental social psychology*, 14, 161-202.
Fitzgerald Bone, Paula (1992), "Determinants of Word-of-Mouth Communications During Product Consumption," *Advances in consumer research*, 19 (1), 579-83.
Frenzen, Jonathan and Kent Nakamoto (1993), "Structure, Cooperation and the Flow of Market Information," *Journal of consumer research*, 20 (3), 360-75.
Godes, David and Dina Mayzlin (2004), "Using Online Conversations to Study Word-of-Mouth Communication," *Marketing science*, 23 (4), 545-60.
Hennig-Thurau, Thorsten, Kevin P. Gwinner, Gianfranco Walsh, and Dwayne D. Gremler (2004), "Electronic Word-of-Mouth Via Consumer-Opinion Platforms: What Motivates Consumers to Articulate Themselves on the Internet?," *Journal of interactive marketing*, 18 (1), 38-52.
Ito, Tiffany A., Jeff T. Larsen, N. Kyle Smith, and John T. Cacioppo (1998), "Negative Information Weights More Heavily on the Brain: The Negativity Bias in Evaluating Categorizations," *Journal of personality and social psychology*, 75 (4), 887-900.
Kamins, Michael A., Valerie S. Folkes, and Lars Perner (1997), "Consumer Responses to Rumors: Good News, Bad News," *Journal of consumer psychology*, 6 (2), 165-87.

Kardes, Frank R., Chris T. Allen, and Manuel J. Pontes (1993), "Effects of Multiple Measurement Operations on Consumer Judgment: Measurement Reliability or Reactivity?," *Advances in consumer research*, 20 (1), 280-83.

Katz, Elihu and Paul F. Lazarsfeld (1955), *Personal Influence: The Part Played by People in the Flow of Mass Communications*, Glencoe, Illinois: The Free Press.

Kiecker, Pamela and Cathy L. Hartman (1994), "Predicting Buyers' Selection of Interpersonal Sources: The Role of Strong Ties and Weak Ties," *Advances in consumer research*, 21 (1), 464-69.

Kozinets, Robert V. (2002), "The Field Behind the Screen: Using Netnography for Marketing Research in Online Communities," *Journal of marketing research*, 39 (1), 61-72.

Lobo, Bento J. (2000), "Asymmetric Effects of Interest Rate Changes on Stock Prices," *The financial review*, 35 (3), 125-44.

Mangold, W. Glynn, Fred Miller, and Gary R. Brockway (1999), "Word-of-Mouth Communication in the Service Marketplace," *Journal of services marketing*, 13 (1), 73-89.

Marshall, Pablo and Eduardo Walker (2002), "Asymmetric Reaction to Information and Serial Dependence of Short-Run Returns," *Journal of applied economics*, 5 (2), 273-92.

Reingen, Peter H. and Jerome B. Kernan (1986), "Analysis of Referral Networks in Marketing: Methods and Illustration," *Journal of marketing research*, 23 (4), 370-78.

Richins, Marsha L. (1983a), "An Analysis of Consumer Interaction Styles in the Marketplace," *Journal of consumer research*, 10 (1), 73-82.

_____ (1983b), "Negative Word-of-Mouth by Dissatisfied Customers: A Pilot Study," *Journal of marketing*, 47 (1), 68-78.

Silverman, George (1997), "How to Harness the Awesome Power of Word of Mouth," *Direct marketing*, 60 (7), 32-37.

Sperduto, Gary R., Karen S. Calhoun, and Anthony R. Ciminero (1978), "The Effects of Reciprocal Reactivity on Positively and Negatively Valenced Self-Rated Behaviors," *Behavior research and therapy*, 16 (6), 429-34.

Thorelli, Hans B. (1971), "Concentration of Information Power among Consumers," *Journal of marketing research*, 8 (4), 427-32.

Tice, Dianne M., Jennifer L. Butler, Mark B. Muraven, and Arlene M. Stillwell (1995), "When Modesty Prevails: Differential Favorability of Self-Presentation to Friends and Strangers," *Journal of personality and social psychology*, 69 (6), 1120-38.

Udell, Jon G. (1966), "Prepurchase Behavior of Buyers of Small Electrical Appliances," *Journal of marketing*, 30 (4), 50-52.

Westbrook, Robert A. (1987), "Product/ Consumption-Based Affective Responses and Postpurchase Processes," *Journal of marketing research*, 24 (3), 258-70.

Wirtz, Jochen and Patricia Chew (2002), "The Effects of Incentives, Deal Proneness, Satisfaction and Tie Strength on Word-of-Mouth Behavior," *International journal of service industry management*, 13 (2), 141

# Are Bad Reviews Stronger than Good?
## Asymmetric Negativity Biases in the Formation of Online Consumer Trust

Dezhi Yin, Georgia Tech, USA
Samuel Bond, Georgia Tech, USA
Han Zhang, Georgia Tech, USA

This research examines biases in the formation of trusting beliefs and intentions in an online environment. Interactions with unfamiliar sellers contain an element of uncertainty and risk (Reichheld and Schefter 2000), but modern consumers have access to various forms of information to help resolve this uncertainty, including online consumer reviews. Empirical studies have demonstrated a negativity bias whereby even a limited number of "bad" reviews from prior consumers have stronger impact than good reviews on sales and price premiums (Ba and Pavlou 2002; Chevalier and Mayzlin 2006). However, measurements of trust and corresponding beliefs are generally unavailable in secondary data. On the other hand, survey-based studies in the trust literature have tended to measure relevant constructs without regard to potential biases. To address this gap, we take an experimental approach and ask the following: Do consumers exposed to online reviews of a seller exhibit bias in the formation of trusting beliefs and intentions? If so, is the bias always negative? Drawing upon prospect theory and models of person perception, we propose that although consumers may exhibit a general negativity bias, the magnitude of this bias will depend on the dimension of seller behavior involved.

That tendency to weigh negative information more heavily than positive information has been established as a general principle of human judgment (Baumeister et al. 2001; Rozin and Royzman 2001). This tendency follows directly from Kahneman and Tversky's (1979) prospect theory, which posits that people derive value from gains and losses according to a nonlinear "value function" that is concave for gains and convex for losses; losses loom larger than gains. Applied to the risky environment of e-commerce, consumers will be more concerned with potential losses than with potential gains. In particular, when considering positive and negative information related to the trustworthiness of a seller, they will overweight the negative information, and this bias will subsequently lead to more negative trusting beliefs and eventual intentions

However, evidence from the arena of person perception suggests that when judging others' behavior, "bad is not always stronger than good". For example, Skowronski and Carlston's (1987) category diagnosticity model separates person-relevant information into 'competence' and 'morality' domains. The model suggests that most individuals possess schemas in which moral people exhibit moral behaviors all the time; therefore, a single immoral behavior is a reliable indicator of immorality. The same is not true for competence, where even competent individuals occasionally fail; a single success is a more reliable indicator of competence, while a single failure is generally discounted. Online trust literature also breaks trusting beliefs into "competence" and "integrity" dimensions among others

(McKnight, Cummings, and Chervany 1998). Applying this domain-specific approach to the current setting, we predict that consumers' trusting beliefs pertaining to a seller's integrity will be more negatively biased than their trusting beliefs pertaining to a seller's competence.

We conducted two studies to test our hypothesis in a typical e-commerce setting involving word-of-mouth. Study 1 presented 36 undergraduate participants with aggregated profile 'ratings' regarding different characteristics of online sellers. The study utilized a 2 (profile dimension: competence, integrity) × 2 (store rating manipulation: treatment, control) within-subject design. Participants were told that they were shopping for a camera and asked to read profiles summarizing consumer reviews of four different online stores. Each store's profile was composed of two sections, one related to competence and the other related to integrity; each section listed three relevant items along with an average rating for each item. All ratings were presented using a 5-point "smiley face" scale ranging from "very negative" to "very positive". The ratings for treatment stores' first profile section were (0, -2, 2) or (0, 2, -2), while those for control stores were all neutral; ratings in the second profile section were identical between treatment and control stores. Participants were asked their competence and integrity beliefs after the first profile section, and their overall trust and purchasing intention after the whole profile of a store. As predicted, results indicated that negativity bias implied by a lower evaluation of the treatment stores was not universal, but rather depended on the category of seller behavior involved. Participants in the *integrity* condition were negatively biased in their trusting beliefs, overall trust and purchasing intention; however, none of these biases were significant for participants in the *competence* condition.

Study 2 extended our investigation from simple, numeric seller ratings to the more elaborate domain of written reviews. The study involved a mixed design in which participants were asked to read five consumer reviews about a particular online store before deciding whether to buy a camera from that store. The first three 'baseline reviews' were the same for all participants and had been pretested to be neutral in their implications regarding the sellers' competence and integrity. Next, participants read two additional 'treatment' reviews pertaining to either competence or integrity, depending on condition. The two treatment reviews were pretested to be opposite in valence and similar in extremity. In order to capture belief changes, participants were asked to report their trusting beliefs and overall trust before and after reading the two treatment reviews. Analysis of belief changes revealed that as predicted, both groups exhibited significant negativity bias, but the extent of bias was dramatically greater for the integrity condition. Furthermore, analysis of overall trust revealed a negativity bias for participants in the integrity condition, but no significant bias for the competence condition.

This research contributes to literature on trust formation and e-commerce in several ways. Theoretically, we break new ground by identifying the existence of negativity biases in the formation of trusting beliefs and intentions and by exploring whether "bad is always stronger" in B2C commerce. Our studies indicate that although negativity bias does impact trust formation in this setting, it is much more prevalent for information regarding sellers' integrity than for information regarding their competence. Our results also have practical implications for retailers seeking to establish trust among potential customers: e.g., negative word-of-mouth regarding integrity is particularly difficult to overcome, and should be handled proactively.

## Selected References

Ba, S. L. and P. A. Pavlou (2002), "Evidence of the Effect of Trust Building Technology in Electronic Markets: Price Premiums and Buyer Behavior," *Mis Quarterly*, 26 (3), 243-68.

Baumeister, Roy F., Ellen Bratslavsky, Catrin Finkenauer, and Kathleen D. Vohs (2001), "Bad Is Stronger Than Good," *Review of General Psychology*, 5 (4), 323-70.

Chevalier, J. A. and D. Mayzlin (2006), "The Effect of Word of Mouth on Sales: Online Book Reviews," *Journal of Marketing Research*, 43 (3), 345-54.

Kahneman, D. and A. Tversky (1979), "Prospect Theory-Analysis of Decision under Risk," *Econometrica*, 47 (2), 263-91.

McKnight, D. H., L. L. Cummings, and N. L. Chervany (1998), "Initial Trust Formation in New Organizational Relationships," *Academy of Management Review*, 23 (3), 473-90.

Reichheld, F. F. and P. Schefter (2000), "E-Loyalty-Your Secret Weapon on the Web," *Harvard Business Review*, 78 (4), 105-13.

Rozin, P. and E. B. Royzman (2001), "Negativity Bias, Negativity Dominance, and Contagion," *Personality and Social Psychology Review*, 5 (4), 296-320.

Skowronski, J. J. and D. E. Carlston (1987), "Social Judgment and Social Memory-the Role of Cue Diagnosticity in Negativity, Positivity, and Extremity Biases," *Journal of Personality and Social Psychology*, 52 (4), 689-99.

# The Impact of Negative Online Reviews: When Does Reviewer Similarity Make a Difference?

Ali Faraji-Rad, BI Norwegian School of Management, Norway
Radu-Mihai Dimitriu, BI Norwegian School of Management, Norway

## Extended Abstract

The advent of the internet has brought major changes to the way consumers search for information and express their opinions about products or services. Message boards, blogs, user review websites, etc. have become increasingly important for today's online consumers to exchange opinions and experiences related to both companies and their offerings. Although online reviews have been mainly perceived to be anonymous, recent improvements in the design of websites have enabled individuals to have different degrees of profile disclosure (picture, name, age, gender, short biography) which, contrary to the general assumption in the word of mouth literature, introduces cues on which consumers can rely and base their judgments on. We conduct a study to investigate whether the perceived homophily between the reader and the reviewer has any impact on the influence of the word of mouth message. Homophily is defined as "the degree to which pairs of individuals who interact are similar with respect to attributes, such as beliefs, values, education, socials status, age, gender, lifestyle, etc"(Rogers & Bhowmik, 1970). We also seek to qualify this effect by focusing on the different nature of hedonic and utilitarian consumption (Adaval, 2001; Batra & Ahtola, 1991). Because utility maximization is considered to be more tangible and objective, consumers should be just as willing to rely on other consumers' evaluations whether that consumer is similar to them or not. In contrast, the evaluation of hedonic products is linked to expectations which could be subject to individual lifestyle. Therefore, we hypothesize that *higher (vs. lower) homophily influences the effect of negative product reviews on product evaluation for hedonic products, but not for utilitarian ones.*

The hotel industry was chosen as the context of the study. One hundred and eleven bachelor students participated in a 2 (Hedonic vs. Utilitarian) X 2 (Homophilous vs. Non-homophilous) between-subjects experiment in class. The dependent variable was participants' evaluation of the hotel.

After an introductory first page, participants read a scenario which was designed to manipulate the hedonic or utilitarian consumption situations. In the utilitarian case, participants were asked to imagine themselves trying to book a hotel for a stay in Frankfurt with a colleague. In the hedonic scenario, they were asked to imagine themselves going to Paris with their partner and choosing a hotel which would ensure their enjoyment. Participants were then presented with two online reviews about the hotel. Each review included a profile, a comment (one-two lines explaining how the reviewer saw the hotel), and a rating (a star ranking of the hotel given by the reviewer on a seven star system). The first review and its corresponding profile were kept constant for all the groups and was a neutral review (rating of 5 out of 7) coming from a journalist. Negative word of mouth and homophily were manipulated through the second review and its corresponding profile. The negative comment (rating of 2 out of 7) was kept constant for all the groups. For the homophilous group, the reviewer was a business student and in the non-homophilous group the reviewer was a researcher for "a major chemical company". Next, eleven items measured the product evaluation, manipulation checks and two covariates. Two questions were asked to measure the participants' product evaluation (good choice; favorable attitude). Homophily manipulations were checked using a three item scale. Two items measured the extent to which participants perceived the hotel to be hedonic (fun; enjoyable and exciting) and two items the extent to which they perceived it to be functional (cover functional needs; practical considerations). The two covariates were the perceived degree of expertise of the reviewer and importance of the decision of choosing the hotel. Manipulation checks and covariate question were presented last in order.

An analysis of the data revealed that the manipulations worked as intended. For testing the hypothesis we first ran an ANOVA test with hotel evaluation as a dependent variable and "homophily" and "product type" as independent factors, and using the two covariates mentioned earlier. The expertise covariate had a significant effect on the dependent variable $(F(1,105)=3.93)$, $p=.05)$, whereas the choice importance did not $(p>.7)$. The ANCOVA model suggested that the main effect of "homophily" failed to reach significance $(3.86$ vs. $4.19$, $F(1,105)=2.74$, $p>.1)$. Meanwhile, the main effect of "product type" was significant, with the evaluation of the hedonic product being significantly lower than the one for of utilitarian one $(3.81$ vs. $4.23$, $F(1,105)=4.26$, $p<.05)$. Supporting the hypothesis, the interaction was significant $(F(1,105)=4.49$, $p<.04)$. Planned contrasts analyses revealed that the effect of "homophily" was not significant when the hotel was perceived to be utilitarian $(4.28$ vs. $4.19$, $F(1,105)=.13$, $p>.7)$. However, when the hotel was perceived to be hedonic, the hotel evaluation was significantly lower when the reviewer was "homophilous" rather than not $(3.44$ vs. $4.19$, $F(1,105)=7.26$, $p<.01)$. Also, a similar analysis revealed the same results, not including the covariates.

Therefore, consistent with the hypothesis, homophily increases the influence of negative product reviews only in case of hedonic products.

From a theoretical perspective, this study sheds light on how the cues consumers use in the face-to-face environments map into online environments. To our knowledge, this is also the first research that qualifies the influence of homophily in the word of mouth literature.

From a managerial perspective, the study provides insights into how reviews on websites can influence consumers' product evaluations. It shows that negative word of mouth is riskier for experiential (hedonic) products and that this risk is higher when it comes from similar consumers providing reviews. In terms of segmentation, mangers should be encouraged to pay more attention to consumer complaints about experiential products, especially when they are coming from company's target or core customers. Such customers are more likely to form a unitary and similar group. This will prevent target customers from engaging in word of mouth that is most harmful for the company.

**Selected References**

Adaval, R., 2001. Sometimes It Just Feels Right: The Differential Weighting of Affect-Consistent and Affect- Inconsistent Product Information. *Journal of Consumer Research*, 28(1), 1-17.

Batra, R. & Ahtola, O., 1991. Measuring the hedonic and utilitarian sources of consumer attitudes. *Marketing letters*, 2(2), 159170.

Rogers, E. & Bhowmik, D., 1970. Homophily-heterophily: Relational concepts for communication research. *The Public opinion quarterly*, 34(4), 523538.

# Best-Seller or Your-Style Recommendation Sign?:
## Effect of Self-Construal on Inclination Towards Inter- vs. Intrapersonal Norm

Jae-Eun Namkoong, University of Texas at Austin, USA
Susan Broniarczyk, University of Texas at Austin, USA

## Extended Abstract

Modern consumers are often loaded with options. Despite the initial pleasure one might feel when provided with many goods to choose from, it is very likely that s/he will feel frustrated by how difficult a choice is to make (Iyengar & Lepper, 2000; Schwartz, 2005). Product recommendations are intended to aid consumers with their decision making process and to promote sales by highlighting a particular product. The present research focuses on two broad types of norm-based product recommendations and demonstrates how the level of self-construal determines the way consumers react to these recommendations.

Recommendations can be based on in*tra*personal norm or in*ter*personal norm. An in*tra*personal norm is realized through a repeated behavioral pattern within a single individual (Kahneman & Miller, 1986). People have the need to act in a coherent manner (Swann Jr, 1983), and technology has allowed retailers to generate recommendations designating a product alternative as "Your-Style" based on consumers' purchase histories, browsing patterns, and preferences. On the other hand, an *inter*personal norm is formed through observing other people's behavior. Simply observing what other people are doing could influence one's own decision, even when there is no apparent pressure (Aarts, Gollwitzer, & Hassin, 2004). The most common example of an interpersonal norm in a consumption setting would be the indication of "Best-Seller" that captures consensus between individuals.

Which norm-based recommendation is more effective, however, will depend on one's level of self-construal. An independent construal of the self "requires construing oneself as an individual whose behavior is organized and made meaningful by reference to one's own internal repertoire of thoughts, feelings, and actions," whereas the in*ter*dependent self-construal entails understanding oneself "as part of an encompassing social relationship and recognizing that one's behavior is determined, contingent on, and, to a large extent organized by what the actor perceives to be the thoughts, feelings, and actions of others in the relationship" (Markus & Kitayama, 1991, pp. 226–227). Because of the differential sensitivity towards internal vs. external repertoires among independent vs. interdependent individuals, we predict that interpersonal (vs. intrapersonal) norm-based recommendations have a stronger effect on recommendation evaluation, choice of the recommendation, and post-choice evaluation among highly interdependent (vs. low interdependent or independent) people. Specifically, we compare inter- and intrapersonal norm recommendations operationalized as Best-Seller and Your-Style recommendation signs, respectively. Three studies examine the moderating effect of self construal via priming (pilot study), measured as a chronic trait (study 1), or operationalized by culture (study 2).

A pilot study confirms that evaluation of the two norm-based recommendations differed as a function of self-construal. Participants read a scenario describing either a Best Seller or Your Style recommendation. Self construal was primed using the established scenario of Trafimow, Triandis, and Goto (1991). Supporting our prediction, a Norm Recommendation Type x Self-Construal interaction showed that interdependence-primed (vs. independence-primed) participants reported the Best-Seller (vs. Your-Style) recommendation as more attractive ($F_{(1,90)}$=3.569, p=.062) and had stronger intentions to follow ($F_{(1,90)}$=3.698, *p*=.058).

Study 1 examines how the presence of either a Best-Seller or a Your-Style sign affects participants' choice of office chairs as a function of self-construal. Although the product recommendations were in fact placed on the same product across all conditions, participants were lead to believe that the Best-Seller sign was generated based on the retailer's customer database and the Your-Style sign based on their own previously revealed preferences. In order to make it a strong test, the recommendation was always placed on the second most attractive product. Self construal was measured using the classic self-construal scale of Singelis (1994). Consistent with our prediction, the Norm Recommendation Type x Self Construal interaction revealed the likelihood of participants choosing a recommended product over the most attractive product was higher when the product recommendation was based on a norm that was highly relevant to their given self-construal (*b*=1.432, *t*=1.737, *p*=.082). Specifically, highly interdependent (vs. independent) participants were more likely to choose the recommended product when presented with a Best-Seller (vs. Your-Style) sign recommendation.

Study 2 then explores whether the interaction between norm recommendation type and self-construal extends to post-choice satisfaction. Moreover, instead of examining compliance behavior, study 2 looks at the effect of *deviating* from recommendations. Norm based recommendation was manipulated similar to Study 1 and self construal was operationalized as individualistic vs. collectivist cultures (Markus & Kitayama, 1991). The product stimuli was sofa chairs. In all conditions, the recommendation was placed on an objectively unattractive option so subjects would choose a non-recommended option (93%). This allowed us to gauge the effect of deviating from a recommendation on participants' choice satisfaction after choosing a non-recommended option. Supporting our conceptualization that the presence of a self-relevant recommendation would impact people's post-choice evaluations, there was a significant Norm Recommendation Type x Self Construal interaction on post-choice satisfaction ($F_{(1,90)}$=5.425, *p*=.022). Specifically, when participants from a highly interdependent (vs. independent) cultural background were presented with a Best-Seller (vs. Your-Style) recommendation and rejected it, they felt lower choice satisfaction. This result suggests that even when a person strongly disagrees with a recommendation and decides not to follow it, the fact that s/he has been presented with and had to forgo a self-relevant recommendation can undermine his consumption experience.

The present research introduces self-construal as a meaningful predictor in determining which type of norm-based recommendation has a more powerful influence on people's evaluation of the recommendation, compliance to recommendation, and post-choice satisfaction after deviating from recommendation. Presenting consumers with a self-relevant norm could be an efficient way to aid consumers' decision as it increases the appeal of the recommendation and the probability of choosing the recommended item. However, when a relevant norm is misplaced it could also be a source of consumer dissatisfaction and regret. Practical implications and future research extensions are discussed.

## References

Aarts, H., Gollwitzer, P., & Hassin, R. (2004). Goal contagion: Perceiving is for pursuing. *Journal of Personality and Social Psychology, 87*, 23-37.

Iyengar, S., & Lepper, M. (2000). When choice is demotivating: Can one desire too much of a good thing? *Journal of Personality and Social Psychology, 79*(6), 995-1006.

Kahneman, D., & Miller, D. (1986). Norm theory: Comparing reality to its alternatives. *Psychological review, 93*(2), 136-153.

Markus, H., & Kitayama, S. (1991). Culture and the self: Implications for cognition, emotion, and motivation. *Psychological review, 98*(2), 224-253.

Schwartz, B. (2005). *The paradox of choice: Why more is less*: Harper Perennial.

Singelis, T. (1994). The measurement of independent and interdependent self-construals. *Personality and Social Psychology Bulletin,* *20*(5), 580.

Swann Jr, W. (1983). Self-verification: Bringing social reality into harmony with the self. *Psychological perspectives on the self, 2,* 33-66.

Trafimow, D., Triandis, H., & Goto, S. (1991). Some tests of the distinction between the private self and the collective self. *Journal of Personality and Social Psychology, 60*(5), 649-655.

# Prospective Motivated Reasoning in Charitable Giving: Making Sense of Our Future Behavior and Protecting Our Future Self

Jae-Eun Namkoong, University of Texas at Austin, USA
Julie Erwin, University of Texas at Austin, USA

## Extended Abstract

The present research also falls under the large umbrella of motivated or biased reasoning (Bem 1972, Greenwald & Ronis 1978, Wicklund & Brehm 1976). It is similar to previous work showing that people alter their attitude to reduce the gap between what they believe and how they have behaved, in order to restore a favorable self-view. However, our design differs from previous research in two ways. First, our research looks at people's tendency to make sense of their *prospective* (rather than retrospective) behavior, and second, our findings do not depend on the respondents actually behaving in the way they fear they might behave. While a decision has not yet been made, people may reason in a forward looking manner, preparing a basis or a safety net for their potentially undesirable future behavior. We look into this effect of prospective biased reasoning in the context of donation or charitable giving. Even without the conventional form of "products" involved, the topic of altruistic consumer behavior is highly relevant to marketing because the structure or relationship between providers and suppliers remains largely similar. Moreover, understanding people's altruistic behavior gives insight into the consumption of ethically enhanced products.

Acting against one's own self-interest to satisfy a moral imperative (such as helping others) is likely to involve struggle or conflict between one's actual and ideal self. The present research examines how this struggle or conflict plays a role in people's prospective reasoning–specifically, how people prepare a safe pathway to escape from the perceived obligation to help others, without hurting their positive and moral self-view.

In our experiment, participants were told that the study was a collaborative project with a non-profit organization. Before starting, they were given information about this organization to read and learn about its identity, goal, and activity. One group of participants were informed at the beginning of the survey that they will be asked to donate a part of their compensation to the organization at the end of the experiment, while the other group was not told that they would be asked to make donations to this organization. Whether the donation was made by real or hypothetical money was also manipulated as a proxy for motivational strength to talk oneself out of making a donation. Thus, there was a 2 (donation request revealed at beginning vs. not revealed) X 2 (real vs. hypothetical donation) design. We were particularly interested in the change in participants' beliefs regarding the seriousness of the social issues being addressed by the organization (AIDS and poverty). We found a number of two-way interactions, including for rated seriousness of the AIDS problem ($b$=.199, $t$=.230, $p$=.022) and rated seriousness of poverty ($b$=.146, $t$=1.772, $p$=.078). Participants in the real money condition who were informed (vs. not informed) about the donation opportunity prior to the evaluation of social issues were more likely to believe that the social issues were less serious. ($b$=-.437, $t$=-3.005, $p$=.003 for AIDS and $b$=-.281, $t$=-2.039, $p$=.043 for poverty).

We were also interested in the effect on behavior. Those who saw (vs. did not see) the donation information prior to the evaluation questions donated significantly less hypothetical money ($b$=-.411, $t$=-2.744, $p$=.007). However, this behavioral effect was non-significant in the real money condition, probably because most people in this condition did not donate (i.e., a floor effect). Interestingly, however, when participants were asked to donate their real money, those who were informed about the donation opportunity ahead of time perceived higher level of financial constraint, compared to those who were informed about the donation opportunity later ($b$=.477, $t$=1.805, $p$=.076). We also found a mediating pattern where a set of negative moods (e.g. afraid, scared, and hostile) explained why knowing ahead about the donation opportunity led to lowered perception of issue seriousness ($z$=-1.69, $p$=.08).

Overall, our findings suggest that informing people that they may be asked to donate in the future causes a particular type of "potential dissonance" reduction process in a prospective direction, even when respondents do not donate anyway. That is, knowing about a donation opportunity earlier makes people feel uncomfortable because there is a potential threat on one's positive self-view in case one decides not behave in an altruistic manner in the future. While people have not yet made any decision, they may still prepare for this potential threat by creating a safety pathway to escape if necessary, while keeping their positive self-view intact. Consequent (proposed) studies aim to discover whether people have already made their decision to donate at an implicit (or may even at an explicit) level once they are informed about the donation opportunity. This will clarify the question about how similar or different the effect is from classic dissonance theories. Another research direction is to examine whether one's level of self-esteem serves as a moderator, as the motivation seems to come from the restoration or defense of positive self-view. In addition, whether or not the changes in attitudes persist after the experiment also a matter of interest; it would be good to know whether the denigration of the issue and the organization persists after the threat is gone.

## References

Bem, D. J. (1972). Self-perception theory. In L. Berkowitz (Ed.), *Advances in experimental social psychology* (Vol. 6, pp. 1-62). New York: Academic Press.

Greenwald, A., & Ronis, D. (1978). Twenty years of cognitive dissonance: Case study of the evolution of a theory. *Psychological Review, 85*(1), 53-57.

Wicklund, R. A., & Brehm, J. W. (1976). *Perspectives on cognitive dissonance*: Oxford, England: Lawrence Erlbaum.

# Promoting Products versus Outcomes to impact the Decision Making Process: the Power of Recommending One Product

Mirjam van Ginkel, Erasmus University Rotterdam, The Netherlands
Benedict Dellaert, Erasmus University Rotterdam, The Netherlands

## Extended Abstract

When going online to buy a product, consumers are often exposed to several product variants instantly on the introductory page of the website. This can be a presentation of the web shops' bestsellers, or a presentation of the available assortment within the specific product category. An immediate confrontation with concrete products may stimulate consumers to buy, but it may suppress consumers' goal oriented thinking. In other words, consumers may choose a product to buy, but may neglect to formulate personal goals or benefits previously. Although it might have a positive effect on sales, this can be unfavorable in situations in which you want consumers to think about their decision behavior in a structured way. For example, in the current health debate we want to make people more conscious about their food decisions.

We distinguish two types of messages in purchase settings. Specific product exposures, on the one hand, recommend specific products because of a certain benefit. Generic messages, on the other hand, recommend a product category because of a certain benefit–for example "Yoghurt is healthy-and are not specific on product level.

Within the decision making process of daily goods, we distinguish two decision stages. In the first stage consumers investigate their need for the product being considered and weigh the pros and contras of buying a product. This leads to a goal-oriented mental representation with more attention and better recall of goal related information. The second stage incorporates the decision which of the alternatives consumers prefer. This type of decision making leads to a comparative mental representation (Xu, Wyer, 2008).

A message functions as a stimulus, which leads to a mental representation. Exposing consumers to a generic recommendation, moves consumers in a goal-oriented mental representation. Exposing consumers to a specific multiple product recommendation moves consumers in a comparative mental representation (Xu, Wyer 2008). These mental representations in turn impact the processes of benefit activation and choice. A good understanding of the impact of different types of messages on the mental representations in the defined decision stages is still lacking. In this paper a theoretical framework is developed to understand the impact of different types of messages on the decision making process.

Our contribution is to give insight in how generic and specific product recommendations can be combined best to steer consumers' mental representations of daily decisions and therefore to promote the product choices anticipated by the recommender. The first contribution of this paper is that we show that generic recommendations are more effective in activating benefits than specific multiple product recommendations. We give evidence why specific multiple product recommendations are not very effective in benefit activation. Recommendations are more effective in benefit activation when generating a goal-oriented mindset. Specific multiple product recommendations seem to bring people in a comparative mindset. The second contribution is that specific multiple product recommendations are more effective in activating choices, which are anticipated by the recommender, than generic recommendations. The third and main contribution of this paper is that it shows that a specific single product recommendation has best of both worlds; it is able to activate benefits-as well as a generic recommendation-and to translate these activated benefits into choice activation–as well as a multiple product recommendation. In the end we show that the above relationship between recommendation type and task performance is moderated by the focus of the respondent. For example, for respondents with a health focus, health benefit activation is attenuated for the reason that health benefits already are activated.

In five experiments under students in between-subject designs, we examined the impact of the different types of health recommendations on health benefit activation and healthy product choice.

## Selected references:

Dhar, Huber, Kahn (2007) The Shopping Momentum Effect, *Journal of Marketing Research*, Vol 44, p. 370-378

Escalas, Luce (2004) Understanding the Effects of Process-Focused versus Outcome-Focused Thought in Response to Advertising, Journal of Consumer Research, Vol 31, p. 274-285

Gollwitzer, Heckhausen, Steller (1990) Deliberative and Implemental Mind-sets: Cognitive tuning toward congruous thoughts and information, *Journal of Personality and Social Psychology*, Vol. 59(6), p 1119-1127

Gollwitzer, P.M. (1990) Action phases and mind-sets. In E.T. Higgins & R.M. Sorrentino (Eds.), *Handbook of motivation and cognition* (Vol. 2, pp. 53-92). New York: Guilford Press.

Kahneman and Tversky (1979) "Prospect theory: An analysis of decision under risk" *Econometrica*, Vol 47, p. 263-291

Xu, Wyer (2007) The Effect of mind-Sets on Consumer Decision Strategies, *Journal of Consumer Research*, Vol. 34, p. 556-566

Xu, Wyer (2008) The Comparative Mind-set; From Animal Comparison to Increased Purchase Intentions, *Psychological Science*, Vol 19 (9), p. 859-864

# The Use of Rankings in Uncertainty Reduction Efforts: A Basis Paradigm

Simon Quaschning, Ghent University, Belgium
Iris Vermeir, Ghent University, Belgium
Mario Pandelaere, Ghent University, Belgium

During the last years there has been a huge increase in available choice options for customers (Schwartz et al. 2002), a phenomenon called hyperchoice (Mick, Broniarczyk, and Haidt 2004). But confrontation with an overload of alternatives makes decision making more difficult (Schwartz 2004), partly because customers feel more responsible for their choices (Iyengar, and Lepper 2000). The result is a decrease in choice confidence (Chernev 2003), leading to greater uncertainty (Anderson 2003). In addition, consumers often face decisions involving unfamiliar goods (Chocarro, Cortiñas, and Elorz 2009). According to Berger and Calabrese (1975) there is a human drive to reduce uncertainty. Consumer will engage in uncertainty reduction efforts by searching information, where especially the opinions of others are often consulted (Weiss, Lurie, and MacInnis 2008). One possible source of information is rankings. Ranking are applied in an increasing number of situations, yet no relevant research has been conducted so far. In this study we will explore the effect of rankings on consumer decisions.

Making a choice in the modern purchasing environment, that is characterized by an ever growing consumption, increasing assortment sizes, and a growing number of brands and products (Mick 2008), requires the access to information. It has repeatedly demonstrated that information search increases systematically with experienced uncertainty (Lanzetta, and Driscoll 1968; Urbany, Dickson, and Wilkie 1989). It enables the decision maker to evaluate alternatives on relevant traits and to make a thoughtful choice, reducing the risk and probability of a non-optimal outcome (Mitchell 1992). Additionally, in situations where the consumer possesses little knowledge about the products, no prior experience is present and it is assumed that consumers depend on information available in the choice itself (Bettman, and Park 1980). One kind of information often consulted for this is the opinion of others. Available in numerous forms, other's opinion have been shown to influence consumers' evaluations, when relevant product attribute information was not accessible (Bearden, and Etzel 1982). Information sources in the form of online forums, book recommendations and newspaper columns are therefore of great value for the customer.

While former research focused on some of this information sources, we will investigate the effect of rankings. From the New York Times Best Seller list, the Nielsen Ratings and Billboard charts, to the top 10 lists in our local video and music stores, rankings are a part of our everyday life. They structure our ways of thinking about comparisons, contrasts and order and may be another way for consumers to reduce their uncertainty (Hakanen 1998). The purpose of this study is to investigate what role rankings play in the preference formation task. We hypothesize that in a situation of uncertainty, consumers will use rankings in order to form their preferences.

In order to test our hypothesis, we administered a questionnaire to eighty-eight respondents, asking them to express their preferences for 10 rather unknown brands of champagne. We randomly divided the respondents into 4 conditions each facing a different ranking. Condition 1 provided a simple top 10 list, while condition 2 additionally included expert scores. Condition 3 also was a simple ranking, but the 2 top brands of condition 1 were ranked as the two "worst" brands, and vice versa. Condition 4 simply was a list, without any ranking implied. Respondents had to indicate their willingness to pay (WTP) for each of the brands. We also included measures concerning the familiarity with the product category and the different brands (showing no familiarity with the brands included), and a scale measuring respondents' preference for numerical information. In order to test our hypothesis we estimated a multilevel regression model.

Our results indicate that rankings may indeed strongly affect consumer preferences. In particular, we found that our respondents' evaluation of a given brand (expressed by the WTP) depended on the rank of the brand in the list. Respondents are willing to pay more for brands that are ranked higher (versus lower). In addition, for the 10 brands involved, respondents indicate a higher WTP than for those same brands when the order of presentation reflected no ranking (condition 4). We assume that the ranking itself could offer respondents some indication about the value of the brand. Interestingly, the effect of rank was moderated by preference for numerical information (PNI). A high PNI indicates that respondents have an eye for numerical information and use it in their decision making, especially in settings that require only a minimum level of mathematical ability (Viswanathan 1993). Our results show that individuals with a high PNI are more likely to use rankings, compared to individuals with a low PNI. The effect of rank was also moderated by familiarity with the product category. For respondents not familiar with champagne, rankings show less effect. That is, the slope relating rank position and WTP was less steep for them. Finally, we also observed a main effect of product category familiarity: respondents unfamiliar with champagne indicated a lower WTP for champagne brands.

To conclude, our results show that rankings have an influence on the preference formulation in uncertain situations. Further research must indicate the robustness and generalizability of the current findings. Investigating the potential moderation by other customer characteristics, such as the difference between maximizers and satisficers or the need for closure on the use of specific rankings would also add to the literature.

## References

Anderson, Christopher J. (2003), "The Psychology of Doing Nothing: Forms of Decision Avoidance Result from Reason and Emotion," *Psychological Bulletin,* 129(1), 139-66.

Bearden, William O. and Michael J. Etzel (1982), "Reference Group Influence on Product and Brand Purchase Decisions," *Journal of Consumer Research,* 9(2), 183-94.

Berger, Charles. R. and Richard J. Calabrese (1975), "Some Exploration in Initial Interaction and Beyond: Toward a Development Theory of Interpersonal Communication," *Human Communication Research,* 1, 99-112.

Bettman, James R. and C. Whan Park (1980), "Effects of Prior Knowledge and Experience and Phase of the Choice Process on Consumer Decision Processes: A Protocol Analysis," *Journal of Consumer Research,* 7(3), 234-48.

Chernev, Alexander (2003), "When More is Less and Less is More: The Role of Ideal Point Availability and Assortment in Consumer Choice," *Journal of Consumer Research,* 30, 170-83.

Chocarro, Raquel, Monica Cortiñas and Margarita Elorz (2009), "The Impact of Product Category Knowledge on Consumer Use of Extrinsic Cues: A Study Involving Agrifood Products," *Food Quality and Preference,* 20(3), 176-86.

Hakanen, Ernest. A. (1998), "Counting Down to Number One: The Evolution of the Meaning of Popular Music Charts," *Popular Music,* 17(1), 95-111.

Iyengar, Sheena. S. and Mark R. Lepper (2000), "When Choice is Demotivating: Can One Desire Too Much of a Good Thing?," *Journal of Personality and Social Psychology,* 79(6), 995-1006.

Lanzetta, John T. and James M. Driscoll (1968), "Effects of Uncertainty and Importance on Information Search in Decision Making," *Journal of Personality and Social Psychology,* 10(4), 479-86.

Mick, David G., Susan M. Broniarczyk and Jonathan Haidt (2004), "Choose, Choose, Choose, Choose, Choose, Choose, Choose: Emerging and Prospective Research on the Deleterious Effects of Living in Consumer Hyperchoice," *Journal of Business Ethics, 52(2),* 207-11.

Mick, David G. (2008), "Degrees of Freedom of Will: An Essential Endless Question in Consumer Behavior," *Journal of Consumer Psychology,* 18(1), 17-21.

Mitchell, Vincent W. (1992), "Understanding Consumers' Behavior: Can Perceived Risk Theory Help?," *Management Decision,* 30(3), 26-31.

Schwartz, Barry, Andrew Ward, John Monterosso, Sonja Lyubomirsky, Katherine White and Darrin R. Lehman (2002), "Maximizing Versus Satisficing: Happiness Is a Matter of Choice," *Journal of Personality and Social Psychology,* 83(5), 1178-197.

Schwartz, Barry (2004), *The Paradox of Choice: Why Less is More,* New York, NY: HarperCollins.

Urbany, Joel E., Peter R. Dickson and William L. Wilkie (1989), "Buyer Uncertainty and Information Search," *Journal of Consumer Research,* 16, 208-15.

Viswanathan, Madhubalan (1993), "Measurement of Individual Differences in Preference for Numerical Information," *Journal of Applied Psychology,* 78(5), 741-52.

Weiss, Allen M., Nicholas H. Lurie and Deborah J. MacInnis (2008), "Listening to Strangers: Whose Responses Are Valuable, How Valuable Are They, and Why?," *Journal of Marketing Research,* 45(4), 425-36.

# Citations and Herding: Why One Article Makes It and Another Doesn't

Simon Quaschning, Ghent University, Belgium

Mario Pandelaere, Ghent University, Belgium

Iris Vermeir, Ghent University, Belgium

The information era has brought with it the well-known problem of 'information explosion' (Hanani, and Frank 2000): researchers face an ever-increasing amount of information and with the arrival of the internet and search engines they have more options in seeking and obtaining information than ever before (Junni 2007). At the same time, the number of marketing-related journals has increased rapidly in recent years (Baumgartner, and Pieters 2003) and journals expand into broader fields of research. This proliferation of information comes with greater uncertainty (Anderson 2003) and increases the difficulty to select an option (Schwartz et al. 2002). According to the uncertainty reduction theory (Berger, and Calabrese 1975), people will engage in uncertainty reduction efforts to alleviate and eliminate the risk caused by uncertainty and to maximize outcome value. One kind of information often used in these efforts is the number of citations. While the number of citations may not be a perfect indicator of quality (Walter et al. 2003) it does play an important role in the evaluation of academics and papers (Stremersch, Verniers, and Verhoef 2007). In this study we will explore the role of herding in citing behavior.

In order to select sources for their research, one has to make a choice out of a seemingly endless amount of articles. In such a context of uncertainty, Parker and Prechter (2005) have seen a default to a herding impulse: people may imitate each other out of a desire to be safe. They may believe that persons before them had better information on the quality of articles than they themselves do, and therefore may include the articles in their own research (Bonabeau 2004). We assume that the number of citations serves as a quality cue for a given paper. As individuals follow the previous citing behavior of others without taking their own information into account, they will concentrate on a limited amount of articles with an established citation record. When this imitation occurs in large numbers, informational cascades can be formed (Banerjee 1992; Bikhchandani Hirshleifer, and Welch 1992). The limited number of papers that is already cited tends to accumulate citations increasingly rapidly while a larger set of initially uncited papers tends to be (virtually) ignored.

While former research (Stremersch et al. 2007) focused on static determinants of citations (e.g. quality and domain of the article, visibility and personal promotion), we focus on herding behavior of researchers, a dynamic determinant. In order to investigate our hypothesis, our study will be divided into two parts, the demand and the supply side: On the one hand, we will examine the herding effect of citations by the means of citation counts. On the other hand, we will look at the possible increase in the supply of journals and its articles.

For the first part of our study we collected citation data via Web of Science. We sampled six major marketing journals: *JCR, JRM, JM, MKS, JCP* and *IJRM.* We inventoried all articles published in these journals in 1985, 1990, 1995, 2000 and 2005. For each article we tallied the number of citations made in each of the 5 years following its year of publication. The herding effect will be examined by means of a mixed model approach, where the number an article got cited each year is the dependent variable and the year of publication, the year after publication, the journal and the number of citations in the first year serve as independent variables. In the absence of herding, the cites that a paper receives in the first five years after publication should be distributed uniformly over those five years. In case of herding, on the other hand, a steady increase of the number of cites that a paper attracts should be observed. Moreover, this increase should be more pronounced for papers that are already heavily cited in the first year after publication.

The results confirm our expectations. We can see a significant increase in the number of citations each year, therefore indicating a more than linear rise in the cumulative number of citations. This herding effect is moderated by the year of publication, the specific journal as well as by the number of citations in the first year. The herding effect is more pronounced in 2005 than in 2000 ($p$=.07). In addition, stronger herding is observed in 2000 than in 1985, 1990 and 1995; the latter three do not significantly differ. The stronger herding in 2000 and 2005 can partly be explained by the growing use of electronically retrieved information, causing a larger amount of information. The difference between 2005 and 2000 can be explained by the introduction of Web of Science, making citation-oriented search even more convenient and common. The herding behavior observed for *JM* also differs significantly from that of *JCR, JMR, MKS, JCP* and *IJRM*. It exhibits strong herding. We also found stronger herding for articles that are heavily cited in the first year.

The second part of the study investigates whether the information supply for researcher has increased over the past decade (years 1998 to 2008). To do so, we developed a list of the different journals that were cited in the 6 target journals. We also tallied how often a specific journal was cited. If the supply of relevant information has increased, we would expect that the number of cited journals has also steadily increased.

Our findings confirm this expectation. Interestingly, the number of cites that come from the Top 5–cited journals have increased. This implies that the distribution of citations has become more lopsided: an increasing amount of journals are hardly cited while another, small proportion is heavily cited. This again testifies to the herding phenomenon in citing behavior.

To conclude, our results show that citing behavior is characterized by significant herding. In addition, herding has become more pronounced over the past decade. Finally, increased herding may be attributed to the increased supply of relevant information. The latter is exhibited by an increase of the number of used journals.

## References

Anderson, Christopher J. (2003), "The Psychology of Doing Nothing: Forms of Decision Avoidance Result From Reason and Emotion," *Psychological Bulletin,* 129(1), 139-66.

Banerjee, Abhijit V. (1992), "A Simple Model of Herd Behavior," *The Quarterly Journal of Economics,* 107(3), 797-817.

Baumgartner, Hans and Rik Pieters (2003), "The Structural Influence of Marketing Journals: A Citation Analysis of the Discipline and Its Subareas Over Time," *Journal of Marketing,* 67(2), 123-39.

Berger, Charles R. and Rik J. Calabrese (1975), "Some Exploration in Initial Interaction and Beyond: Toward a Development Theory of Interpersonal Communication," *Human Communication Research,* 1, 99-112.

Bikhchandani, Sushil, David Hirshleifer and Ivo Welch (1992), "A Theory of Fads, Fashion, Custom, and Cultural Change as Informational Cascades," *Journal of Political Economy,* 100 (5), 992-1026.

Bonabeau, Eric (2004), "The Perils of the Imitation Age," *Harvard Business Review,* 82(6), 45-54

Hanani, Uri and Ariel J. Frank (2000), "The Parallel Evolution of Search Engines and Digital Libraries: Their Convergence to the Mega-Portal. Paper presented at the Kyoto International Conference on Digital Libraries: Research and Practice, 13-16 November 2000. Retrieved from the Bar Ilan University Web Site: http://u.cs.biu.ac.il/~ariel/download/ird665/kyoto.pdf

Junni, Paulina (2007). Students Seeking Information for their Master's Tthesis: The Effect of the Internet. *Information Research,* 12(2), 1-19.

Parker, Wayne D. and Robert R. Prechter (2005), "Herding: An Interdisciplinary Integrative Review From a Socionomic Perspective," In Kokinov & Boicho (Eds.), Advances in cognitive economics: Proceedings of the international conference on cognitive economics (271-280). Sofia, Bulgaria: New Bulgarian University Press.

Schwartz, Barry, Andrew Ward, John Monterosso, Sonja Lyubomirsky, Katherine White and Darrin R. Lehman (2002), "Maximizing Versus Satisficing: Happiness Is a Matter of Choice," *Journal of Personality and Social Psychology,* 83(5), 1178-197.

Stremersch, Stefan, Isabel Verniers and Peter C. Verhoef (2007), "The Quest for Citations: Drivers of Article Impact," *Journal of Marketing,* 71(3), 171-93.

Walter, Garry, Sidney Bloch, Glenn Hunt and Karen Fisher (2003), "Counting on Citations: A Flawed Way to Measure Quality. *Medical Journal of Australia,* 178(6), 253-54.

# Living a Second Life: The Role of Goals and Mental Imagery on Satisfaction Online

Diogo Hildebrand, Baruch College, USA

Sankar Sen, Baruch College, USA

Online Virtual Environments (OVE), a new technology launched during the late 1980s, are revolutionizing the way products are consumed. OVEs are environments in which synthetic sensory information leads users to perceive the virtual environment as if it was not synthetic (Blascovitch et al. 2002). Because of this unique characteristic, OVEs allow users not only to buy or sell products, but also to consume products online. For instance, in Second Life, a virtual world available on the web, consumers may purchase and drive a virtual Mercedes-Benz, wear virtual Giorgio Armani shirts or visit the Smithsonian's Virtual Latino Museum.

Because of its ability to enable online consumption, OVEs are gradually gaining attention from both managers and consumers. Recently, the CIO of the Smithsonian Institute affirmed that the institution's investment in the virtual world is supported by the prediction that 80% of active Internet users in 2008 will be consumers in virtual worlds by the year 2011 (Smithsonian Institute 2008). Furthermore, consumers in the virtual world spent, in 2009 alone, around $400 million in products and services from thousands of companies such as Mercedes-Benz, Nike, and Dell. However, although the importance of the OVE as a marketing channel and branding tool is increasing (Barnes and Mattsson 2008), the main determinants of individual satisfaction with online consumption are still unknown (Hoffman and Novak 2009).

In the present research, we rely on literature from the general web-browsing context to build a model of online consumption. As a starting point, state of flow is a central antecedent of user satisfaction on the web (Hoffman and Novak 1996; Novak, Hoffman and Yung 2000). Furthermore, researchers have presented significant evidence of the importance of website content in inducing state of flow and user satisfaction with online experience (Novak, Hoffman and Duhachek 2003). Building on this basic idea, because use of OVEs is strongly associated with the satisfaction of experiential and symbolic needs (Vicdam and Ulusoy 2008; Yee 2006), we propose that the extent to which the OVE allows users to satisfy experiential and symbolic needs will be an alternative content feature that influences both state of flow and user evaluation of online consumption experience.

Moreover, the dynamics of online experiences are structurally different than those of real world experiences. Specifically, unlike in the real world, the consumption in OVEs is reportedly an indirect experience (Hamilton and Thompson 2007). Importantly, in indirect experiences, sensory information is not presented directly, but depends on individual capability to emulate the sensations elicited by the OVE. As a result, the extent to which sensory information is presented in working memory (i.e., level of mental imagery processing (MacInnis and Price 1987)) will be a key moderator of the extent to which an OVE can satisfy aroused individual goals. Particularly, for high mental imagery processing, consumers will process the sensory information elicited by the OVE intensively. In this case, since consumers will have a significant amount of sensory information to support assessments of progress toward their aroused goals, the extent to which the OVE can satisfy these goals will have a positive effect on flow and, consequently, on individual evaluation of the online consumption experience. On the contrary, because under low imagery processing, consumers will process a lesser amount of sensory information, they will have a limited basis to judge the extent to which goals are being satisfied. As a result, even though consumers might still present moderate levels of flow (Novak et al. 2003), consumers under low imagery processing will not be sensitive to the extent to which experiential goals can be satisfied online. We test these hypotheses in one study.

We manipulated level of mental imagery and the extent to which goals can be satisfied online and measured individual state of flow and satisfaction with the online experience. Seventy-seven undergraduate students participated in the research. The virtual environment of the National Museum of Natural History of the Smithsonian Institute was chosen as the OVE. Participants were first asked to write an essay to arouse goals that either could (i.e., learn new things) or could not (i.e., share experience with others) be satisfied online. Next, following previous manipulations of mental imagery (Petrova and Cialdini 2005), participants read the instructions to browse in the museum's virtual environment, being either encouraged or discouraged to use their imagination.

The results of an ANOVA supported the hypotheses. Particularly, the extent to which a goal can be satisfied online had a positive effect on both flow ($p<0.05$) and evaluation of the online experience ($p<0.01$). Additionally, we found a significant interaction between the extent to which goals can be satisfied in the OVE and level of mental imagery on both flow ($p<0.05$) and satisfaction with the online experience ($p<0.01$). Specifically, individuals in high mental imagery processing felt higher state of flow and evaluated better the online consumption experience when they were able to satisfy aroused goals online. On the other hand, individuals in low imagery processing presented no difference in both state of flow and experience evaluation, regardless of the extent to which their goals could be satisfied in the OVE. Finally, using the bootstrap technique (Preacher, Rucker and Hayes 2007), we verified that flow is a significant mediator of the interaction on the "evaluation of online experience" for individuals in high mental imagery processing but not for those low in imagery processing.

The present research is, to the best of our knowledge, the first attempt to unveil the process underlying consumers' consumption in this novel environment. Past research in psychology and marketing has linked individual state of flow with the pleasantness of the activity. In the present research we show that the extent to which goals can be satisfied in the OVE and level of mental imagery processing will be important variables in the process of online consumption experience.

## References

Barnes, S. J., & Mattsson, J. (2008). "Measuring Brand Value in Real and Virtual Worlds: An Axiological Approach using PLS". *American Marketing Association Educators' Proceedings*, 19, 374-81.

Blascovich, J., Loomis, J., Beall, A. C., Swinth, K. R., Hoyt, C. L., & Bailenson, J. N. (2002). "Immersive virtual environment technology as a methodological tool for social psychology". *Psychological Inquiry, 13*(2), 103-124.

Hamilton, R. W., & Thompson, D. V. (2007). "Is there a substitute for direct experience? comparing consumers' preferences after direct and indirect product experiences". *Journal of Consumer Research, 34*(4), 546-555.

Hoffman, D. L., & Novak, T. P. (2009). "Flow online: Lessons learned and future prospects". *Journal of Interactive Marketing, 23*(1), 23-34.

Hoffman, D. L., & Novak, T. P. (1996). Marketing in hypermedia computer-mediated environments: Conceptual foundations. *Journal of Marketing, 60*(3), 50-68.

MacInnis, D. J., & Price, L. L. (1987). "The role of imagery in information processing: Review and extensions". *Journal of Consumer Research, 13*(4), 473-491.

Novak, T. P., Hoffman, D. L., & Duhachek, A. (2003). "The influence of goal-directed and experiential activities on online flow experiences". *Journal of Consumer Psychology, 13*(1), 3.

Novak, T. P., Hoffman, D. L., & Yung, Y. (2000). "Measuring the customer experience in online environments: A structural modeling approach". *Marketing Science, 19*(1), 22.

Petrova, P. K., & Cialdini, R. B. (2005). "Fluency of consumption imagery and the backfire effects of imagery appeals". *Journal of Consumer Research, 32*(3), 442-452.

Preacher, K. J., Rucker, D. D., & Hayes, A. F. (2007). "Addressing moderated mediation hypotheses: Theory, methods, and prescriptions". *Multivariate Behavioral Research, 42*(1), 185-227.

Smithsonian Institute. (2008). Minutes of the Meeting of the Board of Regents of the Smithsonian Institute, May 5, http://www.si.edu/about/regents/documents/5-5-08%20Minutes%20for%20Web.pdf.

Vicdam, H., & Ulusoy, E. (2008). "Symbolic and Experiential Consumption of Body in Virtual Worlds: from (Dis)Embodiment to Symembodiment". *Virtual Worlds Research: Consumer Behavior in Virtual Worlds*, 1(2), 1-22.

Yee, N. (2006). "The Demographics, Motivations, and Derived Experiences of Users of Massively Multi-User Online Graphical Environments". *Presence: Teleoperators and Virtual Environments*, 15, 309-329.

# Putting the Roots Back in Grassroots: Consumer Activism through Social Media

Pia A. Albinsson, Appalachian State University, USA

B. Yasanthi Perera, New Mexico State University, USA

"The existence of united groups of online consumers implies that power is shifting away from marketers and flowing to consumers" (Kozinets 1999:258).

Social movements are activists' collective efforts to transform the social order (Buechler 2000) often with respect to consumption and marketing (Kozinets and Handleman 2004) in terms of anti-brands (Hollenbeck and Zinkhan 2006) and other forms of resistance to consumption (Penaloza and Price 1993). Such movements organized to resist various industrial or marketing practices, comprises of the goal, the activists, and their adversary (Melucci 1989; Touraine 1981). While activism traditionally entailed activists meeting and engaging in protests, the Internet has given rise to web-based activism. Vegh (2003) classifies web-based, or web-enhanced, activism into three categories: awareness/advocacy, organization/mobilization, and action/reaction. Awareness/Advocacy entail providing contrary information to raise awareness on a given issue, organizing the movement, and engaging in lobbying efforts; Organization/Mobilization may comprise of calling for offline action, and calling for offline action that maybe more effectively conducted through the internet; finally, Action/Reaction involves online attacks on various sites of interest by hackers or "hacktivists" (Vegh 2003).

Social media has facilitated the rise of a new form of activist known as the 'slactivist.' While this term is somewhat derisive, it aptly describes consumers who care for social causes but only up to a certain point of engagement and effort. These consumers will sign on-line petitions and join Facebook activist pages but do not have the desire, and/or resources to engage in traditional activism such as protests (Caplan 2009). We contend that Internet activists who influence slactivists to the point that they engage in real-life action ways create win-win situations. The consumers win in terms of garnering psychological well-being thorough their contributions towards societal welfare; the corporations win through being rewarded for their efforts to adopt socially responsible practices; the society at large benefits through these practices; and the activists win through achieving their goals of encouraging corporations to adopt socially responsible practices, thereby planting seeds for industry-wide changes. This win-win situation mirrors the latest AMA definition of marketing perfectly and illustrates the power of consumers in today's world. In this paper we focus on examining the way consumer activists, interested in forming cooperative relationships with firms, engage with other consumers using social media to influence their typical purchasing behaviors in order to create a win-win situation for all involved parties. Therefore, we explore Carrotmob, an online consumer activists' movement, which exemplifies cooperative consumer activism and word-of-mouth (WOM) activities facilitated by Internet and social media.

## Carrotmob

Carrotmob, focusing upon fostering cooperation between consumers and corporations, are organized in cities across the US and the world. The organization hosts events that entail businesses competing to do the most social good (e.g., increasing energy efficiency, reducing carbon footprints or start recycling). Carrotmob is essentially a viral phenomenon that is spread through consumer word-of-mouth (WOM) through YouTube, Facebook, Twitter and the Carrotmob blog. Consumers register on Carrotmob's website, (www.carrotmob.org) and organizers send alerts (through email, blog, Twitter and Facebook) when a local store or firm adopts socially responsible practices. Carrotmobbers then mob the business or perform a "buycott" (Friedman 1996) and purchase products that they normally would en masse. In addition to their primary Facebook site with nearly 6,000 members, organizers create a new page for each town in which a mob is organized (e.g., carrotmob NYC, carrotmob Berlin, carrotmob Portland). As the company's website notes Carrotmob's master plan and "model is not threatening, not expensive, not time-consuming, not uncomfortable, not "radical," not confusing, and not negative." (www.carrotmob.org). Through engaging in friendly competition, the Carrotmob movements for specific locales generate new ideas, urge new cities to participate, and challenge existing movements to continue their efforts.

## Method

The authors engage in netnography (Kozinets 2002), otherwise known as online ethnographic research (Maclaran and Catterall 2002) of the Carrotmob website, its blog and affiliated social media pages on Twitter and Facebook and other media coverage of their events. Both authors accessed the above social media cites and made individual field notes of their experiences, thoughts and ideas as they emerged from the member's interactions and commentaries before any comparisons were made in the analysis stage.

## Discussion and Conclusion

Our data analysis illustrates how consumers use social media to transform consumer behavior to reward companies that choose engage in practices that benefit the society at large, for example green efforts focusing on benefiting the environment. We present a model of how contemporary social media drive consumer action through the power of viral marketing where consumer activists target other consumers.

Due to the widespread use of computers and the Internet, online consumer activists have the means to reach a wide range of fellow consumers through listservs, online communities, and even spam e-mails similar to Kozinets et al.'s (2010) *The Network Coproduction*

*Model.* However, the present research involves consumer activists, not outside marketers, marketing their own events to other consumers in the network. Consumers in the social media network become one-time participants in the events that generate excitement and, we contend, are of some psychological benefit to the participants. In response, companies who wins a bid for a mob event may promote their business as being "more green" to other consumers at a later stage.

We contend that the ever-rising popularity and access to the internet has given rise to this class of 'casual' activists. Thus, the key to effective consumer activism that targets the casual consumer is to propose action, on the consumers' part, that does not require much effort. In addition, we posit that Carrotmobs essentially entail value co-creation. While consumers may not co-create an actual product, or a service, they contribute to co-creating the firm's overall value chain proposition through the firm adopting greener practices that, for this consumer segment, adds value to products or services. In the bargain, these consumers change the industry as corporations compete to gain the carrotmobbers' business realize that consumers are essentially rewarding them for adopting greener practices. This insight may encourage more firms to become green, thus contributing to changing industry practices, as they realize that socially responsible behavior can be profitable.

## References

Buechler, Steven M. (2000), *Social Movements in Advancec Capitalism*, New York: Oxford University Press.
Caplan, Jeremy (2009), "Shoppers, Unite! Carrotmobs Are Coller than Boycotts," Time Magazine, online article, May 15, 2009 available at http://www.time.com/time/business/article/0,8599,1898728,00.html). Accessed December 15, 2009.
Friedman, Monroe (1996), "A Positive Approach to Organized Consumer Action: They "Buycott" as an Alternative to the Boycott," *Journal of Consumer Policy*, 19, 439-451.
Hollenbeck, Candice R. and George M. Zinkhan (2006), "Consumer Activism on the Internet: The Role of Anti-brand communities," *Advances in Consumer Research*, 33, 479-485.
Kozinets, Robert V., Kristine de Valck, Andrea C. Wojnicki, and Sarah J.S. Wilner (2010), "Networked Narratives: Understanding Word-of-Mouth Marketing in Online Communities," *Journal of Marketing,* 74 (March), 71-89.
Kozinets, Robert V., (2002), "The Field Behind the Screen. Using Netnography for Market Research in Online Communities, *Journal of Marketing Research,* (39) February, 61-72.
Kozinets, Robert.V. (1999), "E-Tribalized Marketing? The Strategic Implications of Virtual Communities of Consumption," *European Management Journal*, 17 (June), 252-264.
Kozinets, Robert V. and Jay M. Handelman (1998), "Adversaries of Consumption: Consumer Movements, Activism and Ideology," *Journal of Consumer Research,* 31 (December), 691-704.
Maclaran Pauline and Miriam Catterall (2002), "Researching the social Web: Marketing information from virtual communities," *Marketing Intelligence & Planning,* 20 (6), 319-326.
Melucci, Alberto (1989), *Nomads of the Present*, London: Macmillan.
Penaloza, Lisa and Linda L. Price (1993), "Consumer Resistance: A Conceptual Overview," *Advances in Consumer Research,* 20, 123-128.
Touraine, Alain (1981), *The Voice and the Eye,* Cambridge: Cambridge University Press.
Vegh, Sandor (2003), "Classifying Forms of Online Activism: The Case of Cyber Protests Against the World Bank," in *Cyber Activism: Online Activism in Theory and Practice (*Martha McCaughey and Michael D. Ayers (Eds)), New York, NY: Routledge.

# Source 2.0: Reading Source Cues in Online Communities
Catherine Coleman, Texas Christian University, USA
Marie-Agnès Parmentier, HEC Montreal, Canada

"Granted when he is actually playing basketball there maybe scowls on Lebron's face but darn this is Vogue not Sports Illustrated! He should have been in a great suit.

You also have to keep in mind that Vogue has only had a handful of Black People on their covers in their 100 plus history so when they do it stands out. This is the reason why diversity is needed in the editorial rooms of these magazines that we enjoy so much. If I saw the proofs of those pictures I would have vetoed it right away. And maybe just maybe it wouldn't kill Vogue and other fashion magazines to try models/actresses of different hues on their covers.

This is about perspective and the acknowledgement that loyal readers of this magazine have different perspective and that should be taken into account.

Vogue you are not alone in this. There's plenty of blame out there." (Style.com; March 27, 2008; online participant DcetStyle30)

The quotation above is from an online discussion of a controversial *Vogue* magazine cover that some critics deemed racist and derogatory. African American NBA player Lebron James and supermodel Gisele Bündchen are featured together to promote the magazine's annual "shape" issue celebrating the human body. The controversy arose when an image was circulated online and in the media that juxtaposed the cover with a WWI propoganda poster for the U.S. Army featuring King Kong and its demsel in distress (see appendix). Claims that the two celebrities had re-enacted the essence of the poster and that the black athlete had been portrayed as a dangerous predator of the white woman brought up heated discussions amongst Internet forums posters. In this paper, we develop theoretical insight on how consumers interpret and negotiate source cues both in relation to historical, experiential, and cultural knowledge they bring to the interpretation and in relation to their engament with community and the development of shared meaning.

In basic communication models, the source is a person or organization with information to share. In advertising, a source can be the sponsor (i.e., a company or organization), the agency that authors the advertisement, or the persona within the text, often in the form of a spokesperson or model (Arens et al. 2009). The latter source, the spokesperson or model, has been a topic of great interest in scholarly works. To date, the advertising and marketing literatures have focused on experimental research perspectives derived from psychology (e.g., Micu et al. 2009; Bower and Landreth 2001; Kamins 1990; Petty et al. 1983). This stream of research emphasizes individual responses and attends to source characteristics such as credibility (expertise and trustworthiness) and attractiveness (similarity, familiarity and likeability).

While we acknowledge the valuable contributions these models have made, we heed the call of McCracken (1989), whose meaning model incorporates cues that include cultural codes such as gender, race and class and how they interact and inform people's interpretation of the advertisement. For example, if we take the instance described above and adopt the point of view of the source literature to date, we most likely would attend to elements of credibility and trustworthiness of the two celebrities. We would not, however, account for the complex and dynamic ways that audiences may attribute meaning to the celebrity based on their own cultural knowledge, such as historical and contemporary understanding of race, gender, sports, fashion, specific media vehicles, knowledge about celebrity personal and professional lives, and the ways in which these various factors may interact. A more encompassing view of advertising sources is needed because the source literature to date has yet to treat consumers as readers of ads (Scott 1994; Scott and Vargas 2007).

McCracken's model also implies that certain audiences share cultural codes and, because culture is not static, neither are shared meanings. Interpretation and negotiation of sources frequently happens at the collective level via the information, knowledge and opinions that people share. Consumer culture researchers have investigated the influence of interpretive communities in creating meaning in the consumer world (Arnould and Thompson 2005). However, there is still little theoretically and empirically informed insight into the collective reading of source cues. When McCracken developed his meaning model, the web 2.0 had not yet developed. We have found it timely to re-envision the source literature to accommodate more complex aspects of consumer engagement with meaning; with social media we now have the opportunity to observe these effects in sites such as online forums that extend beyond traditional boundaries of space and time. Our inductive, qualitative study thus draws on over 500 pages of netnographic data (Kozinets 2002) collected from two online communities, Foxsports.com and Style.com, following the controversy surrounding the infamous *Vogue* cover. This context is an ideal site to develop theory about how collectives read source cues. In brief, it is characterized by multiple layers of meaning, emerging from both the ad itself and from the dynamics between online posters who bring in their own knowledge and subjectivity.

The intended contribution of this paper is to extend the prior literature by examining interpretive practices of readers of ads in consumer collectives as they negotiate the dynamic interaction of various source cues. It posits that as readers engage in discussions with one another, interpretations of source cues do not remain static but evolve over short periods of time and shape further readings. Data analysis is ongoing but has already begun to illuminate the complex, socially constructed ways in which people engage with and create meaning through source cues. We find that various source cues move from the periphery to the center of the discussion, and back to the periphery again and so on, as readers negotiate interpretations of the cover and its sources' representations and intentions. For example, race, gender, celebrity meaning, intentionality of image encoding and media context move and develop in relation to the controversy and to audience articulation of subjectivity. We anticipate that our findings will further articulate contemporary reading of source cues and offer nuances of readings in consumer collectives.

## REFERENCES

Arens, William F, Michael F. Weigold, and Christian Arens (2009), *Contemporary Advertising*, Boston: McGraw Hill.

Arnould, Eric J. and Craig J. Thompson (2005), "Consumer Culture Theory (CCT): Twenty Years of Research," Journal of Consumer Research, 31(4), 868-882.

Bower, A.B. and S. Landreth (2001), "Is Beauty Best? Highly Versus Normally Attractive Models in Advertising," *Journal of Advertising*, 30 (1), 1-12.

Kamins, M.A. (1990), "An Investigation into the "Match-Up" Hypothesis in Celebrity Advertising: When Beauty May Only be Skin Deep," *Journal of Advertising*, 19 (1), 4-13.

Kozinets, Robert V. (2002), "The Field Behind the Screen: Using Netnography for Marketing Research in Online Communities," *Journal of Marketing Research* 39 (1), 61-72.

McCracken, Grant (1989), "Who is the Celebrity Endorser? Cultural Foundations of the Endorsement Process," *Journal of Consumer Research*, 16 (December), 310-321.

Micu, Camelia C., Robin A. Coulter and Lindal L. Price (2009), "How Product Trial Alters the Effects of Model Attractiveness," *Journal of Advertising*, 38 (2), 69-81.

Petty, R. E., J.T. Cacioppo and D. Shuman (1983), "Central and Peripheral Routes to Advertising Effectiveness: The Moderating Role of Involvement," *Journal of Consumer Research*, 10 (September), 135-146.

Scott, L.M. (1994), "The Bridge from Text to Mind: Adapting Reader-Response Theory to Consumer Research," *Journal of Consumer Research*, 21 (December), 461-480.

Scott, Linda M. and Patrick Vargas (2007), "Writing with Pictures: Toward a Unifying Theory of Consumer Response to Images," *Journal of Consumer Research*, 34 (October), 341-356.

**Appendix**

# Virtual Worlds: New Marketing Channels or Emperor's New Clothes? (Consumer Perceptions of Innovation in Product-oriented vs. Service-oriented Companies)

Sonja Propopec, ESSEC Business School, France
Lakshmi Goel, University of South Florida, USA

## Abstract

We examine the impact of brand presence in virtual worlds on consumers' perceptions of brand innovativeness for product-oriented and service-oriented companies. Results from a pilot study show that the consumer's perception of innovativeness significantly decreases with brand presence in virtual world for product-oriented companies, but significantly increases for service-oriented companies.

## Outline

Virtual worlds are increasingly gaining attention in popular media as well as academia (Nelson, 2007), and growth in the virtual worlds is now building at a more reasonable and sustainable level. For example, consumers are spending more time online, there is has been an increase in the revenues generated as well as in the number of interactions (McCormick, 2009). Second Life continues to be an active playground for brands and there are more than 1000 virtual worlds in production around the globe (McCormick, 2009).

Research on what constitutes a successful strategy for entering and operating in virtual worlds is still limited (Goel and Mousavidin, 2007). Previous research shows that virtual worlds differ from traditional websites along several dimensions in terms of their interface and user experience (Goel et al., 2009), warranting further investigation. To better understand the success of an entry strategy one could look at the change in consumer perceptions after visiting the virtual world store for the first time. More specifically, we examine how the brand presence in virtual worlds impacts consumer perceptions of brand innovativeness, a factor that has been shown as important (Christensen, 1997; Christensen and Raynor, 2003; Keller, 2003). Additionally, our research aims to examine whether consumers in virtual worlds perceive product-oriented and service-oriented companies differently.

Majority of the research in virtual words has until now focused on marketing of products (e.g. Goel and Prokopec, 2009; Hemp, 2006). However, with more and more service-oriented companies opening their stores in virtual worlds such as Second Life, it is important to examine whether the consumer perceptions change and if so, in which aspect does the change occur. Services are different from products because they are intangible, unique (heterogeneous) and co-produced with the customer (inseparable) (Anderson, Fornell, and

Rust, 1997). The production and consumption of service occurs simultaneously, whereas the production and consumption of products occurs sequentially. Furthermore, customers are often co-producers of the services they consume (e.g. social networking sites)(Prahalad and Ramaswamy, 2004). Inseparability means that consumers ultimately buy the organization's capabilities and expertise, not merely their immediate offers.

Intuitively, it might seem that presence in a new channel like virtual worlds would be perceived as being innovative. In our research, we propose to explore this line of thought. We argue that perceptions of innovativeness may depend on whether the company is product oriented, or service oriented. In product-oriented companies, a new channel may not yield benefits in terms of consumer perception since innovativeness may be tied to the actual product offering (e.g. a car), and not necessarily the channel (e.g. a dealership/ website). On the other hand, for service-oriented companies, due to the intangibility of the offering and the inseparability between the production and the consumption part of the offering, a consumer visiting the virtual world store (i.e. an university) is more likely to perceive the brand to be more innovative.

Thus we hypothesize:

H1: Virtual world brand presence will not impact the perceived level of innovativeness of product-oriented companies.

H2: Virtual world brand presence will positively impact the perceived level of innovativeness of service-oriented companies.

In order to measure the impact of virtual world brand presence, we plan to conduct an experiment that measures consumers' perceptions of innovativeness before and after they have visited the virtual world. Since there are several factors that need to be considered to ensure internal and external validity of such a study, we conducted a preliminary pilot to help guide our future data collection and analysis. We present details of our pilot next.

**Pilot Study Methodology**

Thirty-five subjects participated in the pilot study. The virtual world selected was Second Life (SL). None of the subjects had a SL avatar prior to the study, although they were very familiar with using computers, the Internet, and social networking sites.

A survey was administered to the subjects that asked questions pertaining to their perceptions of brand innovativeness. Of the four companies selected, Toyota[1] and Sony/BMG were considered representative of product-oriented companies, and Princeton and University of Southern California (USC) of service-oriented. The subjects were asked the question "Rate the brand on the level of innovativeness" for each of the four companies. Next, the subjects were asked to create SL avatars, and spend two weeks exploring the virtual world. After the subjects had completed their assignment, a second survey was administered with the same question for each of the four companies.

**Preliminary Results**

Given that n=35, we present our results with the caveat that this is intended to be a pilot study. Paired sample t-tests were conducted to measure differences between brand perceptions before and after the virtual world exposure. We find support for H2, i.e. perceptions of innovativeness increased for service-oriented companies (Princeton: $M_{PRE}$: 3.26, $M_{POST}$: 4.11, $p<.001$ and USC: $M_{PRE}$: 3.14, $M_{POST}$, $p<.001$). However, for H1, we find that perceptions significantly decreased due to brand presence in virtual worlds for product-oriented companies (Sony/BMG: $M_{PRE}$: 4.26, $M_{POST}$: 3.09, $p<.001$ and Toyota: $M_{PRE}$: 4.2, $M_{POST}$: 3.20, $p<.001$). These results, though simple, have significant implications for companies that wish to leverage the new channel of virtual worlds. A significant negative change in perception of innovativeness may result in harming the brand image, rather than helping, and it might be better for such companies to steer clear of the virtual world channel. Though this study is focused on innovativeness, consumer focus, and brand quality were also measured as part of the pre-and post- tests. These factors also significantly dropped for product-oriented companies. However, service-oriented companies, such as universities, would benefit significantly from a presence in the virtual world channel.

**Next Steps**

The study presented is intended to spur a broad research agenda in virtual worlds that includes several brand perception dimensions. We are interested in how consumers react to the virtual world channel, thus providing practitioners with guidelines for entry strategies in virtual worlds. A wider range of product and service-oriented companies need to be sampled to represent different types of products and services (e.g. hedonic, utilitarian etc).

**References**

Anderson , E . W . , Fornell , C . and Rust , R . T . ( 1997 ) ' Customer satisfaction, productivity, and profitability: Differences between goods and services ' , *Marketing Science* , Vol. 16 , No. 2 , pp. 129–145 .

Christensen, C.M. (1997) "The Innovator's Dilemma," Boston: Harvard Business School Press.

Christensen, C.M. and Raynor, M.E. (2003), "The Innovator's Solution," Boston: Harvard Business School Press.

Goel, L., Junglas, I., and Ives, B. (2009) "Virtual Worlds as Platforms for Communities of Practice," Knowledge Management and Organizational Learning, Volume 4, pp. 180-196.

Goel, L., & Mousavidin, E. (2007). vCRM: Virtual customer relationship management. *Database*, 38(4), 56–60.

Hemp, P. (2006) "Avatar-based marketing," Harvard Business Review, pp. 48-57.

Keller, K.L. (2003), "Strategic Brand Management: Building, Measuring, and Managing Brand Equity," (2d ed.). Sydney: Prentice Hall.

McCormack, A. (2009), " New Virtual Worlds to cater for brands," Revolution, http://www.revolutionmagazine.com. Accessed 20 january, 2010.

Nelson, M. (2007). Virtual world marketing gets reality check in 2007. The ClickZ Network online. http://www.clickz.com/
showPage.html?page=3627979. Accessed 23 February, 2010.

Prahalad , C . K . and Ramaswamy , V . ( 2004 ) ' Co-creation experiences: The next practice in value creation', *Journal of Interactive Marketing* , Vol. 18 ,No. 3 , p. 5 .

Footnote
[1]The pilot was conducted before the press releases regarding quality issues surrounding Toyota.

# Social Production Of Medicine in a Virtual Health Community Organization
## Handan Vicdan, Eastern Kentucky University, USA

## Extended Abstract

This research explores new systems of marketing developing as a result of transformations in technology (Web 2.0), consumer/ marketer value systems, forms of discourse and institutional roles. I aim to provide insights into developments in healthcare provision as systems that utilize social networking and engage in reconstitution of roles and relations in healthcare develop. I revisit previous theories of market relations to understand why/how new perspectives need to be incorporated into our frameworks. Scholars have articulated the structure of relationships between consumers and organizations in the market largely exhibiting dialectical processes: (1) Marketer/ Consumer constitution in dominant/dominated dialectic (Peñaloza and Price 1993; Slater and Tonkiss 2001; Zwick et al. 2008), and (2) unidirectional provisioning and hierarchical relations that give control and primacy to the marketer (Firat and Dholakia 2006). These views rest mainly on modern conceptions of power including domination, confrontation (Venn 2007) and unilateral govern-mentality, and emphasize maximizing/normalizing discourses by marketers. Such discourses in healthcare include fear of loss of life, normalization of body and maximization of lifespan (Rose 2007), and make human body an object of one-way surveillance by a superior medical gaze (Foucault 1975).

I aim to discover new forms of organizing roles and relationships in healthcare through a non-participatory netnographic inquiry (Kozinets 2002) of a web-based Medicine 2.0 community organization, *patientslikeme.com* (PLM). PLM is a co-mediated market platform for real-time partnership among patients, physicians, pharmaceutical companies, healthcare researchers, and administrators of the website. PLM cultivates collaboration through proactive and complementary relations, intensifies connectedness among market actors, and contributes to social production of medicine. These relations seem to be qualitatively different from conventional market relations that treat organizations and consumers as distinct entities (Firat and Dholakia 2006; Peñaloza and Venkatesh 2006). Patients actively engage in real-time clinical research and generation of new medical knowledge, and determine their and others' care along with other market actors. I attract attention to the meso level institution(alization)s or legitimation processes that develop and maintain these new forms of interaction, make people become a part of these systems and enable their continued participation in sharing their private health data and experiences as a result of synergistic discourses among actors with an increasing appreciation for difference, and decreasing desire to contest, confront and establish supremacy. Findings are organized in two core themes: (1) provisioning diluted in healthcare through reorganization of business by PLM, and new roles patients and physicians/researchers adopt in this community, and (2) meso level dynamics of how actors relate to each other and maintain their participation in the market order constructed in PLM, and how these relations influence relations among market actors outside of the community. In doing so, sharing/privacy distinction will be articulated, forms of sharing in PLM–which encourage disclosure of private health information–will be exemplified, and the why and how of sharing/not sharing in this community will be explicated.

I reconsider Foucauldian notions of govern-mentality (1982) and biopower (1990) to articulate the theoretical/conceptual explanations of how and why such a system may be attracting patients and other healthcare actors and (re)organizing their relationships, and how their interest and participation in the system are maintained. I attract attention to the shift from government intervention to the multitude of diverse healthcare market actors in organizing sharing of private health information, and negotiating meanings of privacy/disclosure. PLM enables organized decentralization of private health data sharing, and mobilizes market actors as a non-state institution through non-dominating discursive regimes (Rose 2007) (e.g., hope based versus fear based culture, sharing/openness versus privacy, quality of life and personalization). Consumers are governed by and govern through different institutionalizations that produce discourses through which roles and relations are legitimized and institutionalized (Thompson 2004). Through institution(alization)s grown out of these new business models, community participants make decisions to share private health information and stay in the community, which emerge from mutual, non-linear, and multi-way negotiations. Govern-mentality increasingly takes multiple forms that may not be categorized as either top down (domination) or bottom-up (domination over consumers through constituting them as free subjects) (Zwick et al. 2008) perspectives. As we observe the abandonment of unidirectional provisioning and overly deterministic actions of marketers –prominent in dominant marketing approaches –, and the realization that consumers and marketers are both a part of a social system and a market system, reflecting the multifaceted and multilayered nature of organizing roles and governing relations among market actors in the world of social networking necessitate the theorization of govern-mentality in productive and meridian (Cova 2005, p.210) terms. PLM as a meso level institution also becomes the locus of legitimation in sharing and organizing private health information and generating medical knowledge, and contributes to (re)institutionalizing surveillance in healthcare through clinical research with and intensified multilevel connectedness among healthcare actors.

**References**

Cova, Bernard (2005), "Thinking of Marketing in Meridian Terms," *Marketing Theory,* 5 (2), 205-214.

Firat, A. Fuat, and Nikhilesh Dholakia (2006), "Theoretical and Philosophical Implications of Postmodern Debates: Some Challenges to Postmodern Marketing," *Marketing Theory,* 6 (2), 123-162.

Foucault, Michel (1975), *The Birth of the Clinic: An Archeology of Medical Perception.* New York: Vintage Books.

_____ (1982), "The Subject and Power," in H. L. Dreyfus and P. Rabinow (ed.), *Michel Foucault. Beyond Structuralism and Hermeneutics.* Harvester Press, 208-226.

_____ (1990), *The History of Sexuality.* New York: Vintage Books.

Kozinets, Robert V. (2002) "The Field Behind the Screen: Using Netnography for Marketing Research in Online Communities," *Journal of Marketing Research,* 39 (1), 61-72. _

Peñaloza, Lisa, and Linda L. Price (1993), "Consumer Resistance: A Conceptual Overview," *Advances in Consumer Research,* 20, 123-128.

_____ , and Alladi Venkatesh (2006), "Further Evolving the New Dominant Logic of Marketing: From Services to the Social Construction of Markets," *Marketing Theory,* 6 (3), 299-316.

Rose, Nikolas (2007), *The Politics of Life Itself: Biomedicine, Power, and Subjectivity in the Twenty-First Century.* Princeton University Press: NJ.

Slater, Don, and Fran Tonkiss (2001), *Market Society: Markets and Modern Social Theory,* Polity Press, London.

Thompson, Craig J. (2004), "Marketplace Mythology and Discourses of Power," *Journal of Consumer Research,* 31 (1), 162-180.

Venn, Couze (2007), "Cultural Theory, Biopolitics, and the Question of Power," *Theory, Culture & Society,* 24 (3), 111-124.

Zwick, Detlev, Samuel K. Bonsu, and Aron Darmody (2008), "Putting Consumers to Work: 'Co-Creation' and New Marketing Govern-mentality," *Journal of Consumer Culture,* 8 (2), 163-196.

## APPENDIX

**Theoretical Articulation Based on Initial Findings:**

A.  How PLM has developed and is functioning in the healthcare market?: Cultivating Biopower-Biopolitical Production-Biosociality Triangle in Healthcare through PLM:

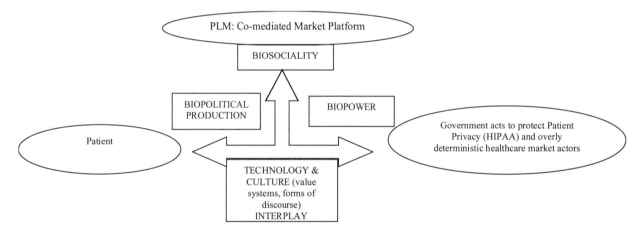

B.  Based on the themes discovered, this graph shows different levels of governing relations among healthcare actors as a result of connectedness intensified by/through PLM:

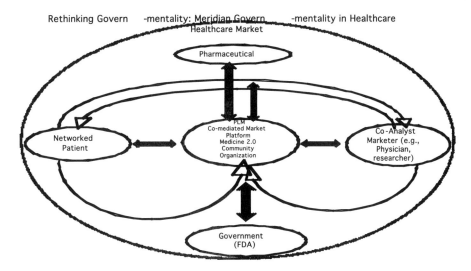

Rethinking Govern    -mentality: Meridian Govern    -mentality in Healthcare
Healthcare Market

# The Consequence of Screening Strategies on Decision Accuracy:  The Roles of Perceived Uncertainty and Consideration Set Size

Rajani Genesh Pillai, North Dakota State University, USA
Xin He, University of Central Florida, USA
Raj Echambadi, University of Illinois at Urbana-Champaign, USA

## Extended Abstract

Consumers screen from all available alternatives (Beach 1993) and consider a smaller subset of alternatives for further evaluation, called the consideration set (Bettman 1979; Nedungadi 1990). Two types of screening strategies are commonly utilized by consumers to form consideration sets: an *exclusion (rejection) strategy* wherein alternatives not worthy of further consideration are eliminated and an *inclusion (choice) strategy* wherein worthy alternatives are included into the consideration set (Shafir 1993; Yaniv and Schul 1997; 2000). Despite the understanding that an important motivation for consumers to engage in screening is to search and choose the best option (Beach 1993; Beach and Mitchell 1990), there is limited understanding of the consequences of the screening strategy on decision quality. This paper attempts to fill the void by investigating how screening strategies impact decision quality as well as the factors that moderate this relationship.

Two outcomes of using the screening strategy that have been investigated are the number of alternatives considered (consideration set size) and the accuracy of the decision (Heller, Levin, and Gorannson 2002; Levin et al. 2001; Yaniv and Schul 1997, 2000). Evidence for the impact of the screening strategy on the size of consideration set is robust, such that sets created by exclusion screening strategy are significantly larger than those created by inclusion (Heller et al. 2002; Levin et al. 2001; Yaniv and Schul 1997, 2000). However, there is little consensus about the impact of the screening strategy on decision quality. Past studies demonstrated that consideration sets created by exclusion strategy are more accurate, but only when the consideration set size is not taken into account. Accuracy in these studies was defined by the outcome of the screening strategy itself (i.e. the percentage of sets that contain the correct answer) which is different from the accuracy of the final choice. In addition, existing research does not consider a wide range of contingent factors that might influence the screening strategy—decision accuracy relationship. In this paper, we focus on the accuracy of the final choice because it is the ultimate performance criterion of the screen strategy employed. We contend that, the accuracy of the decision should be analyzed in terms of the ability of the screening strategy to improve the likelihood of making a good decision, depending on both perceived uncertainty and consideration set size.

Consumers frequently experience varying levels of uncertainty while making choices (Hansen 1976; Kahn and Sarin 1988). We argue that highly uncertain consumers who use inclusion screening strategy make more accurate decisions and consumers with low perceived uncertainty are better off using exclusion screening strategy. We draw upon the literature on decision making to suggest that screening by inclusion involves greater search for information (Levin, Huneke, and Jasper 2000). Greater search intensity of the inclusion strategy would facilitate highly uncertain consumers to improve decision accuracy by helping to clarify their preferences. Conversely, it would distract consumers with low perceived uncertainty from making accurate decision because more information encountered during search will dilute their true preferences. Because search intensity of a screening strategy depends on consideration set size, we further argue for an interesting reversal of this interactive effect when consideration set sizes are varied. Since exclusion screening strategy involves greater search than inclusion strategy when forming larger consideration sets, we predict that highly uncertain consumers are better off using exclusion screening strategy in such context while consumers with low perceived uncertainty make better decisions using inclusion screening strategy.

**Empirical Study**

We conducted an experimental study (n=130) using an actual choice task that followed a 2 (perceived uncertainty: high or low) x 2 (screening strategy: inclusion or exclusion) x 2 (consideration set size: high or low) design. In this study, perceived uncertainty was measured whereas screening strategy and consideration set size were manipulated. Following Creyer, Bettman, and Payne (1990), the measure of decision accuracy is derived by comparing the weighted additive value of the chosen alternative to that of the best and worst alternatives in the set. Consistent with our predictions, there was a significant three-way interaction among screening strategies, perceived uncertainty, and consideration set size on decision accuracy ($F(1,122)=8.34$, $p<.01$). Initial results were directionally supportive for our predictions under smaller consideration sets (such that participants with low perceived uncertainty made slightly more accurate decisions with exclusion strategy while participants with high perceived uncertainty made slightly more accurate decisions using inclusion strategy) although the effects failed to reach statistical significance. More importantly, the pattern of results was reversed when participants formed larger consideration sets. Those with low perceived uncertainty made higher quality decisions with inclusion as compared to exclusion screening strategy when forming larger consideration sets. On the other hand, participants with high perceived uncertainty made more accurate decision with exclusion as compared to inclusion screening strategy and both mean comparisons were significant. Thus, results were generally supportive of our predictions as indicated by a significant three-way interaction, although the effects under large consideration sets seem to be stronger than those under small consideration sets.

**Discussion**

This paper seeks to address the issue of decision accuracy of screening strategies, given the perceived uncertainty consumers experience during the choice process. Further, it also highlights the important moderating role played by consideration set size on the interactive relationship between perceived uncertainty and screening strategy on decision accuracy. Drawing upon literature in consumer decision making, we show that, the process benefits of information search and learning that are obtained by choosing and applying the right screening strategy can greatly enhance the quality of decisions. This paper contributes to our understanding regarding the consequence of using the screening strategies. Decision accuracy is an important outcome of the decision making process and has huge public policy and consumer welfare implications. For instance, this research highlights that consumers could make suboptimal choices through the use of a wrong screening strategy. Such suboptimal choices can have seriously negative and long lasting consequences in various situations like medical decision making, financial and investment decision making, and partner selection that are rife with uncertainty.

**References**

Beach, Lee R (1993), "Broadening the Definition of Decision Making: The Role of Prechoice Screening of Options," *Psychological Science*, 4 (July), 215-20.
Beach, Lee R and Terence. R Mitchell (1990), "Image Theory: A Behavioral Theory of Decisions in Organizations," in *Research in Organizational Behavior,* Vol. 12, ed. B.M. Staw and L.L. Cummins, 12, Greenwich, CT: JAI Press, 1-4.
Bettman, James R. (1979), *An Information Processing Theory of Consumer Choice*, MA: Addison- Wesley.
Creyer, Elizabeth H., James R. Bettman and John W. Payne (1990), "The Impact of Accuracy and Effort Feedback and Goals on Adaptive Decision Behavior," Journal of Behavioral Decision Making, 3, 1-16.
Hansen, Flemming (1976), "Psychological Theories of Consumer Choice," Journal of Consumer Research, 3 (December), 117-42.
Heller, Daniel., Levin P. Irwin, and Martin Goransson (2002), "Selection of Strategies for Narrowing Choice Options: Antecedents and Consequences," *Organizational Behavior and Human Decision Processes*, 89 (November), 1194-213.
Kahn, Barbara E. and Rakesh K. Sarin (1988), "Modeling Ambiguity in Decisions Under Uncertainty," Journal of Consumer Research, 15 (September), 265-72.
Levin, Irwin .P., Caryn M. Prosansky, Daniel Heller, and Brad M. Brunick (2001), "Prescreening of Choice Options in Positive and Negative Decision Making Tasks," Journal of Behavioral Decision Making, 14 (October), 279-93.
Levin, Irwin .P. , J. D. Jasper, and Wendy S. Forbes (1998), "Choosing Versus Rejecting at Different Stages of Decision Making," *Journal of Behavioral Decision Making*, 11 (September), 193-210.
Levin, Irwin .P., Mary E. Huneke, and J.D. Jasper (2000), "Information Processing at Successive Stages of Decision Making: Need for Cognition and Inclusion-Exclusion Effects," *Organizational Behavior and Human Decision Processes*, 82 (July), 171-93.
Nedungadi, Prakash (1990), "Recall and Consideration Sets Influencing Choice without Altering Brand Evaluations," *Journal of Consumer Research*, 17 (December), 263-76.
Shafir, Eldar (1993), "Choosing Versus Rejecting: Why Some Options are Both Better and Worse Than Others," *Memory and Cognition*, 21 (July), 546-56.
Yaniv, Ilan and Yaacov Schul (1997), "Elimination and Inclusion Procedures in Judgment," *Journal of Behavioral Decision Making*, 10 (September), 211-20.
Yaniv, Ilan and Yaacov Schul (2000), "Acceptance and Elimination Procedures in Choice: Non Complementarity and the Role of Implied Status Quo," *Organizational Behavior and Human Decision Processes*, 82 (July), 293-313.

# The Influence of Assortment Size on Preference-Consistent Choice

Maarten Elen, Ghent University, Belgium
Ineke Uyttersprot, University College Ghent, Belgium
Maggie Geuens, Ghent University and Vlerick Leuven Gent Management School, Belgium
Iris Vermeir, Ghent University, Belgium

## Extended Abstract

Decades of research on the effects of variety and assortment size have focused on the affective and motivational consequences of having personal choice (Iyengar, & Lepper, 2000). Providing consumers with choice has been linked to increases in perceived control, task performance and life satisfaction (Iyengar, & Lepper, 2000). When choosing from a large number of options, the likelihood that decision makers will be successful in finding an option that matches their preferences, increases (Chernev, 2003; Iyengar, & Lepper, 2000). Large assortments also help people satisfy their needs for variety, whether the reason for seeking variety simply reflects some desire for change or having multiple needs to satisfy (Hermann, & Heitmann, 2006).

While much of the earlier work on variety provided support for the notion that more variety is better, a growing body of research suggests that more variety does not always lead to better choices. Research on the choice overload hypothesis suggests that having much choice can initially seem desirable, but prove to be demotivating in the end (Iyengar, & Lepper, 2000). Choosing from larger assortments demands a greater amount of cognitive effort from the decision maker and increases choice difficulty (Chernev, & Hamilton, 2009). An increased number of options to choose from has also been associated with greater anticipation of post-decisional regret (Hermann, & Heitmann, 2006; Sela, Berger, & Liu, 2009). These cognitive and emotional costs of decision-making out of large assortments have been shown to lead consumers to defer decision, choose the default option or to simply not choose at all (Iyengar, & Lepper, 2000; Sela et al., 2009; Scheibehenne, Greifeneder, & Todd, 2009).

Both positive and negative consequences of assortment size on choice difficulty, choice likelihood and satisfaction are thus well-documented. Studies assessing the impact of assortment size on the option people actually choose are limited.

In this study we will examine how assortment size influences the choice of the preferred option and preference-consistent behavior. We argue that assortment size can have an important influence on preference-consistent choice. More specifically, we suggest that in small assortments; where making a choice is less difficult and results from a deliberative decision-making process (Hermann, Heitmann, Morgan, Henneberg, & Landwehr, 2009), people might not always choose their preferred option, even if this option is available. To support this claim, we integrate two research streams; assortment size and deliberation.

Studies on the influence of assortment size on decision-making processes have shown that as the complexity of making choices rises, people tend to simplify their decision-making process by relying on simple heuristics (Iyengar, & Lepper, 2000; Hermann et al., 2009). Therefore, we suggest that when choosing from larger assortments consumers will rely on readily available "cues", whereas in small assortments they will evaluate the alternatives and compare and contrast different attributes before making a choice. Recent research has demonstrated that this kind of conscious thought and deliberation can have an influence on people's judgments and preferences, often reducing the consistency of preferences over time (Dijksterhuis en Nordgren, 2006; Nordgren & Dijksterhuis, 2009).

As heuristics are often used in decision-making in large assortments, we hypothesize that when the most preferred option is available in a choice set, this option will be chosen in case of a large assortment. Consumers will use their initial positive evaluation of this option as a cue to select it. When choosing from a small assortment, the deliberative decision-making process might lead consumers to focus on attributes of the attitude object that seem like plausible causes of the evaluation but were not weighted heavily before (Nordgren, & Dijksterhuis, 2009), resulting in less preference-consistent choices.

The experiment examining this prediction comprised two stages. In the first stage, participants' preferences for twenty different ice cream flavors were measured. They were asked to rank their top six from a menu of twenty flavors (e.g. vanilla, pistachio, strawberry, …), and rate every flavor on a 7-item scale ranging from "totally unfavorable" to "totally favorable". After this preference-measure task, respondents participated in an unrelated study of about 45 minutes to divert attention from the current study. In the second stage, participants were informed that they could win a bucket of ice cream and were asked which flavor they wanted if they would win. The assortment they could choose from consisted of either six (i.e. small assortment) or twenty (i.e. large assortment) different ice cream flavors. The latter assortment consisted of all twenty initial flavors, while the former assortment consisted only of the top six ice cream flavors they ranked earlier. Thus, participants' top six flavors were presented in both the large and the small assortment. This was done to enhance comparability between choices from both assortments.

In order to test our hypothesis regarding the effect of assortment size on preference-choice consistency, we first calculated whether there was a match between the participants' preferences in the first stage and their choice in the last stage. Thus, for each subject, we calculated whether their choice was consistent with the option they had ranked at the top in the first stage. This comprised the dependent measure of the study.

Next, we looked at the influence of assortment size on the preference-choice consistency. Chi-square analysis revealed a significant effect. Significantly more subjects were consistent in the large assortment condition (67.1%) than in the small assortment condition (52.4% %) ($\chi^2(1)=3.853$, p<.05). Thus, this result supports our hypothesis.

Our results seem to indicate that as the variety of options to choose from decreases, the likelihood of choosing the most preferred option decreases as well–supposedly confirming the idea that, in terms of preference-choice consistency, more is indeed better. However, we propose that in other situations, preference-inconsistent choices will be more likely in large than small assortments. Specifically, we hypothesize that when readily available cues favor a less-preferred option, the likelihood of this option being chosen over the most-preferred option increases. Several experiments are being set up to investigate this prediction.

## Selected References

Chernev, A. (2003). When More Is Less and Less Is More: The Role of Ideal Point Availability and Assortment in Consumer Choice. Journal of Consumer Research, 30, 170-183.

Chernev, A., & Hamilton, R. (2009). Assortment Size and Option Attractiveness in Consumer Choice Among Retailers. Journal of Marketing Research, 46, 410-420.

Dijksterhuis, A.P., & Nordrgen, L.F. (2006). A Theory of Unconscious Thought. Perspectives on Psychological Science, 1(2), 95-109.

Hermann, A., & Heitmann, M. (2006). Providing more or providing less? Accounting for cultural differences in consumers' preference for variety. International Marketing Review, 23(1), 7-24.

Herrmann, A., Heitmann, M., Morgan, R., Henneberg, S.C., & Landwehr, J. (2009). Consumer Decision Making and Variety of Offerings: The Effect of Attribute Alignability. Psychology & Marketing, 26(4), 333-358.

Iyengar, S.S., & Lepper, M.R. (2000). When Choice is Demotivating: Can One Desire Too Much of a Good Thing? Journal of Personality and Social Psychology, 79(6), 995-1006.

Nordgren, L.F., & Dijksterhuis, A.P. (2009). The Devil Is in the Deliberation: Thinking Too Much Reduces Preference Consistency. Journal of Consumer Research, 36, 39-46.

Scheibehenne, B., Greifeneder, R., & Todd, P.M. (2009). What Moderates the Too-Much-Choice Effect? Psychology & Marketing, 26(3), 229-253.

Sela, A., Berger, J., & Liu, W. (2009). Variety, Vice, and Virtue: How Assortment Size Influences Option Choice. Journal of Consumer Research, 35, 941-951.

# Investigating the Strength of Affectively and Cognitively Based Attitudes

Ineke Uyttersprot, Ghent University, Belgium
Iris Vermeir, Ghent University, Belgium
Maggie Geuens, Ghent University and Vlerick Leuven Gent Management, Belgium

## Extended abstract

Attitude strength is often defined in terms of four characterizing features which strong attitudes are thought to possess. That is, strong attitudes are said to be persistent over time, more resistant to attack, more influential of information processing and more predictive of judgments and behavior (Krosnick & Petty, 1995). Affective attitudes are supposed to be stronger than cognitively based ones (Giner-Sorolla, 2001) because empirical evidence shows that attitudes based on emotions tend to resist cognitive persuasion appeals, whereas attitudes based on cognitive beliefs do not resist affective appeals, and affective attitudes appear to be more stable over time.

Several studies exploring the accessibility of affect-based attitudes compared to cognition-based ones tend to support this supposition. Accessibility has been indicated as one of the strength-related dimensions of attitudes, with highly accessible attitudes being stronger than less accessible ones (Fazio, 1995). Responses to affective evaluations have been shown to be formed more quickly than responses to cognitive evaluations (Huskinson & Haddock, 2006; Verplanken, Hofstee & Janssen, 1998), possibly indicating that evaluations based on emotions and feelings are more accessible in memory than evaluations based on cognitive beliefs. Giner-Sorolla (2001) also found an accessibility advantage of affective over cognitive base, but only when attitudes were more extreme; when attitudes were less extreme, affective attitudes tended to be expressed more slowly, whereas cognitive attitudes were expressed faster (Giner-Sorolla, 2001). In some situations then, cognitively based attitudes seemingly are stronger than affectively based attitudes.

Accessibility, however, is not the only attitudinal variable proposed as a measure of attitude strength; several other dimensions have been identified as well, such as certainty, knowledge, importance, extremity, … (Krosnick, Boninger, Chuang, Berent & Carnot, 1993; Visser, Bizer & Krosnick, 2006). Yet, besides accessibility, none of these strength-related dimensions has been examined in relation to the structural base of attitudes.

In this study we take a look at two other strength-related dimensions, certainty and knowledge, and explore whether affectively versus cognitively based attitudes differ on these dimensions. We hypothesize that cognitively based attitudes are held with more certainty and more subjective knowledge, since some of the main antecedents of attitude certainty are made up of cognitive factors such as the amount, clarity and consistency of the information available (Gross, Holtz & Miller, 1995). Further, the amount of cognitive elaboration of attitude-relevant information has been proposed as a determinant of attitude certainty, mediated by subjective perceptions of knowledge (Smith, Fabrigar, Macdougall, & Wiesenthal, 2008). Since cognitions about an attitude object are believed to be formed based on deliberative and controlled information processing, whereas affective reactions are formed in a relatively automatic manner without much deliberate elaboration (Shiv, & Fedorikhin, 1999), a certainty and knowledge advantage for attitudes based on cognitive beliefs over attitudes based on affective reactions is proposed.

To investigate the level of certainty and amount of subjective knowledge associated with affectively versus cognitively based attitudes, an experiment was conducted. We manipulated the structural base of participants' attitude toward a fictional animal by exposing them to either an affective or cognitive passage about the animal (see Fabrigar & Petty, 1999). The affective passage described a person's encounter with the animal and was designed to evoke positive emotions about the animal. The passage designed to induce a cognitive attitude contained positive information about the same fictitious animal and was presented as an excerpt from an encyclopedia of marine life. Following the attitude base manipulation, participants were asked to complete the measures of attitude, affect and cognition validated by Crites et al. (1994). Next, attitude certainty and subjective knowledge were assessed.

In order to investigate whether the attitude formation manipulation resulted in affective and cognitive attitudes, we tested whether attitude-affect and attitude-cognition consistency differed across both formation conditions. This was done by computing two discrepancy scores, obtained by calculating the absolute value of the difference between the attitude score on the one hand and the affect and cognition score on the other hand. High consistency between the attitudinal base and the overall attitude is indicated by small numbers on these discrepancy scores.

A 2 (attitude-affect discrepancy vs. attitude-cognition discrepancy) x 2 (affective attitude formation condition vs. cognitive attitude formation condition) mixed-design ANOVA indicated that we were successful in creating affectively or cognitively based attitudes, since the predicted crossover interaction between type of discrepancy score and attitude formation condition was obtained, $F(1,118)=9.134$, $p<.01$. In the affective formation condition the affective discrepancy scores ($M=.53$) were significantly smaller than the cognitive discrepancy scores ($M=.76$), $t(59)=3.605$, $p<.01$; whereas in the cognitive formation condition a nonsignificant tendency for cognitive discrepancy scores ($M=.41$) to be smaller than affective discrepancy scores ($M=.51$) was obtained, $t(59)$, $p=.374$.

To assess the difference between affective and cognitive attitudes concerning attitude certainty and subjective knowledge, an Independent Samples T-test was conducted with attitude basis as the independent variable. Both for certainty, $t(109)=-2.599$, $p<.05$, and subjective knowledge, $t(109)=-3.845$, $p<.001$, a significant effect of attitude basis was found. Cognitive attitudes were both held with greater certainty ($M=5.13$) as well as associated with greater subjective knowledge ($M=2.95$) than affective attitudes (respectively $M=4.57$ and $M=2.00$), thus supporting our hypothesis.

Based on these results we can conclude that, contrary to previous research where affectively based attitudes seemingly are stronger than cognitively based attitudes when accessibility was used as a strength measure, cognitively based attitudes appear to be stronger than affectively based ones in terms of certainty and knowledge. These results provide useful insights in light of future studies. Possible research entails to explore which type of persuasive appeal, cognitive or affective, is most suitable to create strong attitudes.

## Selected References

Crites, S.L., Fabrigar, L.R., & Petty, R.E. (1994). Measuring the affective and cognitive properties of attitudes: Conceptual and methodological issues. Personality and Social Psychology Bulletin, 20, 619-634.

Fabrigar, L.R., & Petty, R.E. (1999). The Role of Affective and Cognitive Bases of Attitudes in Susceptibility to Affectively and Cognitively Based Persuasion. Personality and Social Psychology Bulletin, 25, 363-381.

Fazio, R.H., (1995). Attitudes as object-evaluations associations: Determinants, consequences, and correlates of attitude accessibility. In R.E. Petty & J.A. Krosnick (Eds.), Attitude strength: Antecedents and consequences (pp. 247-282). Mahwah, NJ: Lawrence Erlbaum.

Giner-Sorolla, R. (2001). Affective Attitudes Are not Always Faster: The Moderating Role of Extremity. Personality and Social Psychology Bulletin, 27, 666-677.

Gross, S.R., Holtz, R., & Miller, N. (1995). Attitude Certainty. In R.E. Petty & J.A. Krosnick (Eds.), Attitude strength: Antecedents and consequences (pp. 215-245). Mahwah, NJ: Lawrence Erlbaum.

Huskinson, T.L.H, & Haddock, G. (2006). Individual differences in attitude structure and the accessibility of the affective and cognitive components of attitude. Social Cognition, 24 (4), 453-468.

Krosnick, J.A., & Petty, R.E. (1995). Attitude strength: An overview. In R.E. Petty & J.A. Krosnick (Eds.), Attitude strength: Antecedents and consequences (pp. 1-24). Mahwah, NJ: Lawrence Erlbaum.

Krosnick, J.A., Boninger, D.S., Chuang, Y.C., Berent, M.K., & Carnot, C.G. (1993). Attitude Strength: One Construct or Many Related Constructs? Journal of Personality and Social Psychology, 65 (6), 1132-1151.

Shiv, B., & Fedorikhin, A. (1999). Heart and Mind in Conflict: The Interplay of Affect and Cognition in Consumer Decision Making. Journal of Consumer Research, 26, 278-292.

Smith, S.M., Fabrigar, L.R., Macdougall, B.L., & Wiesenthal, N.L. (2008). The role of amount, cognitive elaboration, and structural consistency of attitude-relevant knowledge in the formation of attitude certainty. European Journal of Social Psychology, 38 (2), 280-295.

Verplanken, B., Hofstee, G., & Janssen, H.J.W. (1998). Accessibility of affective versus cognitive components of attitudes. European Journal of Social Psychology, 28, 23-35.

Visser, P.S., Bizer, G.Y., & Krosnick, J.A. (2006). Exploring the Latent Structure of Strength-Related Attitude Attributes. Advances in Experimental Social Psychology, 38, 1-67.

# When More is Merrier Indeed: The Impact of Product Involvement on Choice

Maria Aladjem, VU University Amsterdam, The Netherlands

Ulf Böckenholt, McGill University, Canada and Northwestern University, USA

## Extended Abstract

Although generally extensive assortments are believed to benefit consumers, more recent research has highlighted the negative consequences of large assortments. Notably, research on the "More-is-Less" effect (Iyengar and Lepper 2000, Chernev 2003) established that extensive assortments can hinder choice and lower choice satisfaction. These adverse consequences are often explained with the decision difficulty consumers experience when choosing from extensive (as opposed to limited) choice sets. However, a recent meta-analysis (Scheibehenne, Greifender and Todd, forthcoming) invites a discussion on the generality of the "More-is-Less" effect since multiple studies failed to replicate the adverse effects of large assortments on choice satisfaction (Scheibehenne, Greifender and Todd 2009). Clearly, there is a need for a deeper understanding of the possible effects of extensive assortments on consumer choice and a thorough investigation of possible moderator variables and boundary conditions of the More-is-Less effect.

This work argues that choice from extensive assortments can trigger multiple sources of experiential information that affect choice satisfaction. Thus, going beyond experienced difficulty, we show that intrinsic pleasure from exploring the choice options can increase choice satisfaction and lead participants to be more satisfied when choosing from a larger assortment size. We refer to this finding as the "More-is-Merrier" effect. The involvement level of a consumer is an important moderator variable for this effect: Larger assortments can lead to greater choice-process difficulty and thus reduce the choice satisfaction of consumers with low levels of product involvement. In contrast, consumers with high levels of involvement experience choosing from the same large assortments as more enjoyable and report greater choice satisfaction. Perhaps similar to baseball fans enjoying recalling arcane statistics or splitting hairs over particular teams, high-involved consumers enjoy exploring and comparing options and are–if at all-to a much smaller degree affected by the difficulty of a choice task than low-involved consumers.

Experiment 1 examined whether choice-set size would differentially affect the choice satisfaction of consumers with different levels of product involvement. Based on a large-scale online pretest, we selected participants with high and low levels of involvement with night clubs based on the Personal Involvement Inventory (Zaichkowsky 1994). Several weeks later, the same participants were randomly assigned to one of two conditions with either a limited (6) or an extensive (16) choice set of night clubs and were instructed to choose a night club for a company party paid for by the firm. Care was taken to ensure that not the composition of the choice sets, but their size would be the underlying reason for the ease or the difficulty of the choice task. As predicted, we found that high-involved consumers liked better their choice after choosing from the extensive choice set and that this effect was mediated by involvement-induced task enjoyment measured by a three-item scale. Conversely, low-involved consumers liked better their choice when choosing from the limited choice set and this effect was mediated by experienced difficulty, in agreement with previous findings on the More-is-Less effect (Iyengar and Lepper 2000, Chernev 2003). Importantly, perceived variety in the choice sets and experienced difficulty were both found to increase significantly with choice set size and not to vary across involvement conditions.

The objectives of Experiment 2 were two-fold: First, the experiment was designed to test the sensitivity of high- and low-involved consumers to choice task difficulty in their judgment of choice satisfaction. For this purpose, we introduced a default option in the choice task that was expected to lower choice task difficulty and hence to increase the choice satisfaction of low-involved consumers. For high-involved consumers we expected no effect of the default option on choice satisfaction. Second, we selected a customization task to demonstrate that choice-option exploration can trigger task difficulty for low-involved consumers and enjoyment for high-involved consumers.

Participants were asked to customize a weekend trip, consisting of multiple choices among hotels, restaurants and activities. For each choice, we provided a default option in the low-difficulty condition. As in Study 1, we conducted a large-scale pretest to identify respondents' involvement levels with planning and going on trips. Several weeks later, high- and low-involvement participants were invited to the lab and asked to customize a hypothetical complementary weekend escape for two in a popular winter resort. As predicted, we found that although the presence of a default option in a self-customization task reduced significantly the perceived difficulty of the task, it increased satisfaction with the customized offer only among respondents with low levels of involvement. Further, the exploration of the choice option mediated the effect of task enjoyment on choice satisfaction for high-involved respondents.

Study 3 considered temporal distance as a moderator variable of task-induced enjoyment. High-involvement participants were asked to plan their weekend trip–as in Study 2–but with the additional instruction that the trip would take place a year later. We predicted and found that this temporal distance manipulation both reduced significantly the exploration of choice alternatives and lowered experienced enjoyment: Compared to participants of Study 2 who did not have to wait for the trip to take place, participants of Study 3 reported significantly lower choice satisfaction with their customized weekend trip.

In sum, the contributions of this research are three-fold. First, the findings point to the importance of affective consequences of involvement, in addition to the motivational and cognitive ones considered in the Elaboration Likelihood Model (Petty et al. 2005, Petty and Cacioppo 1990). Critically, it demonstrates that unlike task-unrelated affect (Bless et al. 1990), task-related affect increases the depth with which people explore and compare choice options. Experienced difficulty has no adverse affects on choice satisfaction. Second, this work adds to the literature on the More-is-Less effect by showing that involvement is an important moderator of this effect. Finally, this work is also of clear importance to practitioners since it demonstrates the need for differentiation of marketing strategies for consumers with high and low levels of involvement with a product category.

### References

Bless H., G. Bohner, N. Schwarz, and A. Strack (1990), "Mood and Persuasion–a Cognitive Response Analysis," *Personality and Social Psychology Bulletin* ,106, 331-345

Chernev, A. (2003), "When More is Less and Less is More: The Role of Ideal Point Availability and Assortment in Consumer Choice," *Journal of Consumer Research*, 30 (2), 170-83.

Iyengar, S. S. and M. R. Lepper (2000), "When Choice is Demotivating: Can One Desire Too Much of a Good Thing?," *Journal of Personality and Social Psychology*, 79 (6), 995-1006.

Petty, R. E. and J.T. Cacioppo (1990), "Involvement and Persuasion: Tradition versus Integration," *Psychological Bulletin*, 107, 367-374.

Petty, R. E., J.T. Cacioppo, A. Strathman, and J.R.Priester (2005), "To Think or not to Think? Exploring Two Routes to Persuasion," in T. C. Brock & M. C. Green (Eds.), *Persuasion: Psychological insights and perspectives* (2nd ed., 81-116). Thousand Oaks, CA: Sage Publications

Scheibehenne, B., R. Greifeneder, and P.M. Todd (2010). Can There Ever be Too Many Options? A Meta-Analytic Review of Choice Overload. *Journal of Consumer Research.* In Press.

Scheibehenne, B., R. Greifeneder, and P.M. Todd (2009), "What Moderates the Too-much-choice Effect?," *Psychology & Marketing*, 26, 229-253

Zaichkowsky, J. L. (1994), "The Personal Involvement Inventory: Reduction, Revision, and Application to Advertising," *Journal of Advertising*, 23 (4), 59–70.

# Should Variety Seeking Be Measured at the SKU, Brand, or Category Level? Does It Matter

Marina Girju, University of Texas at Dallas, USA
B. P. S. Murthi, University of Texas at Dallas, USA

In a two-week period, the average US consumer snacks 32 times on 17 different brands coming from 4.5 different snack categories, e.g. salty, sweet, salsa/dips, fuel, grain and non-macro (fruits, vegetables). She switches among the brands 29 times and among the categories 22 times. Virtually no brand is eaten twice in a row and only 1.5 brands are from the same category. Thus, the US consumer seeks high variety in her snack consumption. Past research has focused on only one form of variety-seeking, usually at the brand level. In this research, we offer a comprehensive view of individual variety-seeking behavior in the snacks market, in which we associate consumer variety-seeking behavior at the SKU, brand, and category levels. We seek to understand the correlations between the different types of variety-seeking and study the effect of demographic, psychographic, environment (location), and consumption factors (needs, time of day/week, activity) on different types of variety-seeking.

Extensive consumer behavior and empirical marketing literature provides a benchmark of variety-seeking models and findings (Khan 1995, McAlister & Pessemier 1982). More recent research shows that variety-seeking is more likely to occur on taste than on brand (Inman 2001) or when consumers derive greater hedonic characteristics from the product category (Van Trijp, Hoyer and Inman 1996). However, past research had several restrictions. It looked at variety-seeking as a trade-off between flavor and brand (Inman 2001, 2008). It analyzed single product categories, e.g. potato chips (Maier et al. 2007) and considered variety-seeking at the brand level. Variety-seeking research that is based on scanner data explains variety-seeking at the household level, not the individual level. Last, it did not explain how variety-seeking changes over time, around holidays or seasons. Our proposed research circumvents these restrictions. We focus on consumption patterns at the individual level, thus, avoid the aggregation bias in studies of household demand. We measure variety-seeking across the entire US snack market, and get a better view on consumers' overall snacking behavior and their consumption trade-offs when switching among brands/categories. The length of our study (2004-2009) allows us to show how variety-seeking evolved and how consumers seek more variety in some categories at the expense of others. Using over 80 variables of consumption, we can explain how variety-seeking changes with time of day (Roehm and Roehm 2004) or week, location, activity, needs, social occasion (Ratner and Kahn 2002).

To analyze variety-seeking in snacking for the whole US population, we rely on an extensive dataset monitoring the entire snacking behavior of 30,000 consumers located across the US. The respondents, chosen randomly, are weighted on six demographic variables that ensure a nationally representative sample. They self-report their snack consumption over 2-week periods and provide demographics and other personal information, such as weight/height, physical activity levels, household size, age, gender, race, marital status, income, etc. At each snack occasion, the panelist also records the consumption details: time of day/week, location, consumed on its own or with food or drinks, in public/private, needs (e.g. good to eat with others, to relax) and the activity the consumer was doing during the consumption (shopping, watching TV, socializing) etc. Each consumer reports the exact brand-flavor consumed by choosing from a list of 900 snacks ranging from leading brands (Pringles, Hersheys, etc) to regional and private label. Using the industry's market structure, these brands are further categorized into 60 subcategories (potato chips, gum, salsa) and 6 snack categories (salty, sweet, accompaniments, fuel, grain, non-macro). Thus, this comprehensive dataset allows us to create a detailed map of the whole US snack market and to understand the overall snack consumption not only at the individual consumer level but also aggregated for the whole US population.

We use several measures of variety-seeking at the brand, subcategory, and category level and employ a model with a linear system of equations to understand and paint a comprehensive picture of overall variety-seeking in US snack consumption. First, we draw on the previous research literature and quantify variety-seeking as 1.) number of unique brands consumed, and 2.) number of switches among the brands consumed. Second, accounting for the brands' dissimilarity, we perform the analysis not only at the brand level, but also at the subcategory and category level, e.g. when a consumer snacks on Lays, Orbit, and Hersheys, we record 3 different brands, 3 subcategories (potato chips, gum, candy) and 2 different snack categories (salty, sweet). Third, due to high correlation among the variety-seeking measures either within or across categories, and endogeneity, we use system of equations analysis to understand what factors explain variety-seeking. We model the different measures of variety-seeking at the brand and category levels, within and across categories as dependent variables, regressed on 80-140 independent variables: demographics, psychographics, situational factors, seasonality, trend in consumption. With high R-squares (60%-80%), the models fit the data well and give a comprehensive understanding of the factors that explain variety-seeking.

Some of the research questions we asked and the partial results we obtained are:

1. The correlation between brand and category level variety-seeking is high but not for all individuals.
2. What consumption factors impact VS?–An interesting finding is that doing sports and shopping/running errands decreases variety-seeking.
3. How do demographics influence VS?–Heavier and older people switch less on brands; Men snack on fewer brands/categories and switch less; Hispanics seek more variety. Less educated consumers are high variety-seekers.
4. Is variety-seeking seasonal?–Overall, variety-seeking does not change throughout the year, but consumers seek more salty variety in the Fall and more non-macro variety in the Summer and Fall. Some holidays also impact variety-seeking positively, e.g. Valentine, Halloween for sweets.

The research seeks to understand the big picture idea "Should variety-seeking be studied at the category, brand or SKU level?" How do different measures of variety-seeking change if the analysis is done at different levels of variety-seeking? What is the magnitude of correlation between the different types of variety-seeking? This is the first research study that offers a comprehensive map of brand and within-across category variety-seeking for snacks for the whole US population.

**References**

J. Jeffrey Inman, Joonwook Park, and Ashish Sinha (2008), "A Dynamic Choice Map Approach to Modeling Attribute-Level Varied Behavior Among Stockkeeping Units," Journal of Marketing Research, 45 (February), 94-103.

Cassie Mogilner, Tamar Rudnick, and Sheena S. Iyengar. (2008) The Mere Categorization Effect: How the Presence of Categories Increases Choosers' Perceptions of Assortment Variety and Outcome Satisfaction. *Journal of Consumer Research* 35:2, 202-215

Andrea Maier, Zata Vickers, and J. Jeffrey Inman (2007), "Sensory-Specific Satiety. Its Crossovers, and Subsequent Choice of Potato Chip Flavors," Appetite, 49 (2), 419-428.

Roehm Jr., H. A., & Roehm, M. L. (2004). Variety-Seeking and Time of Day: Why Leader Brands Hope Young Adults Shop in the Afternoon, but Follower Brands Hope for Morning. *Marketing Letters*, 15 (4), 213-221.

Ratner, R.K., & Kahn, B.K. (2002). "The Impact of Private versus Public consumption on Variety-Seeking Behavior." *Journal of Consumer Research, 29*, pp. 246-257.

J. Jeffrey Inman (2001), "The Role of Sensory-Specific Satiety in Attribute-Level Variety-seeking," Journal of Consumer Research, 28 (June), 105-120.

Hans C. M. Van Trijp, Wayne D. Hoyer and J. Jeffrey Inman (1996). "Why Switch? Product Category: Level Explanations for True Variety-Seeking Behavior ." *Journal of Marketing Research*, Vol. 33, No. 3 (Aug., 1996), pp. 281-292

Minakshi Trivedi, Frank M. Bass and Ram C. Rao (1994). "A Model of Stochastic Variety-Seeking." *Marketing Science*, Vol. 13, No. 3 (Summer, 1994), pp. 274-297

Barbara E. Kahn (1995). "Consumer variety-seeking among goods and services : An integrative review." Journal of Retailing and Consumer Services, Volume 2, Issue 3, pp. 139-148

McAlister and Pessemier (1982). "Variety-seeking behavior: an interdisciplinary review." *Journal of Consumer Research* 9 (1982), pp. 311–322 (December)

# Leaky Preferences: Fluency Effects in Perception and Choice

Mark Schneider, University of Connecticut, USA

Keys and Schwartz (2007) have argued that "psychological processes that affect decisions may be said also to "leak" into one's experience." Perhaps analogously, the ease of certain computational tasks may leak into one's perception of the content that is being processed. That is, certain stimuli or environmental features may be preferred *because* they are easier to process. We will refer to this hypothesis as the "leaky preferences" assumption.

The leaky preferences assumption can be applied to both abstract and concrete stimuli, with different implications. When applied to abstract stimuli, the assumption predicts consumers to systematically share a set of aesthetic preferences for features such as symmetry, consistency, straightness, similarity, simplicity, familiarity, and certainty. Each of these environmental features serves to reduce the processing load and aids in the efficient compression of information.

It should be noted that the "leaky preferences" assumption is an instance of a more general fluency effect. Research which varies the ease or difficulty of reading certain fonts, or of searching for information from memory, for instance, can lead people to make attribution errors, generally favoring stimuli which can be processed with a greater degree of fluency. Oppenheimer (2008) notes, that "Fluency–the subjective experience of ease or difficulty associated with completing a mental task- has been shown to be an influential cue in a wide array of judgments…. Fluency impacts whether information is represented in working memory and what aspects of that information are attended to." In applying the "leaky preferences" assumption we are proposing that certain environmental features are routinely processed with high degrees of fluency, and thus these stimuli are generally preferred.

The leaky preferences assumption may also operate on a more concrete level. Specifically, we propose that when no available option in a choice assortment is clearly superior to the others (and hence, preference uncertainty is high) people will base their decision on effort-reduction factors rather than on the content of the choice. That is, when appeal to preference is uninformative, people choose the option which simplifies the decision process. We will call this tendency, the *choice-simplicity heuristic.*

In the standard dual-process framework (e.g. Kahneman and Frederick, 2002), consumers are postulated to have two families of cognitive processes- one that is relatively automatic, affective, and intuitive (System 1) and the other that is more effortful, deliberative, and logical (System 2). In our view, the choice-simplicity heuristic applies to both cognitive systems. When System 2 is dominant (and preference uncertainty is high), the choice simplicity heuristic selects the option which simplifies the decision process *by calculation.* Likewise, when System 1 is dominant, the choice simplicity heuristic selects the option which simplifies the decision process *by affect.* In both cases, the decision process can be simplified by attending to certain cues in the choice environment.

Seemingly irrelevant contextual cues (i.e. features of the choice environment which do not relate to the content of the choices being considered), can nevertheless simplify the decision process. For instance, we can simplify the decision process for System 2 by selecting the option which involves the least tradeoffs. Selecting the option which minimizes tradeoffs *between products* leads to variety seeking behavior (Simonson, 1990). Similarly, selecting the option which minimizes tradeoffs *between attributes* leads to the compromise effect (Simonson, 1989; Simonson and Tversky, 1992). This approach significantly simplifies the calculations and deliberations in the choice process.

The choice-simplicity heuristic suggests that people often look for simplifying cues in the choice environment to aid them in the decision process. In particular, consumers may consider objective cues (such as the presence of a default option), perceptual cues (such as the recognition that one option dominates another), affective cues (such as a positive affective response toward a stimulus) or cognitive cues (such as minimizing the need to make tradeoffs). This perspective suggests that extremeness seeking, endowment effects, and asymmetric dominance effects are under the purview of system 1 since the (objective, perceptual, and affective) cues which generate these effects are relatively automatic. Similarly, we would suspect that variety seeking and compromise effects result from System 2 processing since making tradeoffs is a more deliberative activity. This hypothesis gains some support in recent work (e.g. Bettman et al. (2008), Pocheptsova et al. (2009)).

Overall, the leaky preferences assumption may serve to integrate aspects of computational efficiency (ease of processing), aesthetic preferences (easily processed abstract stimuli), and difficult choices (easily processed concrete stimuli), into a basic model of perception, preference, and choice. At the abstract level, this assumption provides a simple framework for identifying potentially universal aesthetic preferences, and determining how these preferences are related. At a more concrete level, the leaky preferences assumption suggests that in the face of preference uncertainty, consumers may select an option simply because the structure of the choice environment makes that option easier to process. This leads to the choice simplicity heuristic which, in turn, can account for some notable behavioral anomalies.

### Selected References

Bettman, J.R., Luce, M. F. and J.W. Payne. (2008). Consumer Decision Making: A Choice Goals Approach. Pp. 589-610 in *Handbook of Consumer Psychology.* Haugtvedt, C.P., Herr, P., and Frank R. Kardes [eds].

Kahneman, D, and Frederick, S. (2002). Representativeness revisited: Attribute substitution in intuitive Judgment. Pp. 49-81 in T. Gilovich, D. Griffin, and D. Kahneman [eds]. *Heuristics & Biases: The Psychology of Intuitive Judgment.* New York. Cambridge University Press.

Keys, D., and B. Schwartz (2007): "Leaky" Rationality: How Research on Behavioral Decision Making Challenges Normative Standards of Rationality," *Perspectives on Psychological Science.* Vol. 2, No. 2, pp. 162-180.

Oppenheimer, D. (2008): "The Secret Life of Fluency". Trends in Cognitive Sciences. Vol. 12, No. 6. pp. 237-241.

Pocheptsova, A., Amir, O., Dhar, R., and R.F. Baumeister. (2009). Deciding Without Resources:Psychological Depletion and Choice in Context. Unpublished working paper.

Simonson, I. (1989). Choice Based on Reasons: The Case of Attraction and Compromise Effects. *The Journal of Consumer Research.* 16(2): 158-174.

Simonson, I. (1990). The Effect of Purchase Quantity and Timing on Variety-Seeking Behavior. *Journal of Marketing Research.* 27(2): 150-162.

Simonson, I, and A. Tversky (1992). Choice in Context: Tradeoff Contrast and Extremeness Aversion. *Journal of Marketing Research.* 29(3): 281-295.

# Choice Under Pressure: Perverse Outcomes of Enhanced Familiarity Preference

Ab Litt, Stanford University, USA
Taly Reich, Stanford University, USA
Senia Maymin, Stanford University, USA
Baba Shiv, Stanford University, USA

### Extended Abstract

Consumers often have to evaluate options and make decisions under time pressure, which can affect these behaviors in diverse and important ways (Chowdhury et al., 2009; Nowlis, 1995). Extensively documented in both animal research (Griebel et al. 1993; Heinrichs & Koob, 1992; Shephard & Estall, 1984) and cases such as preferences for "comfort foods" (Kandiah et al., 2006) is that pressure of various forms increases preferences for familiar stimuli and options. Familiarity signals safety, which gains heightened importance and appeal under stress. Similarly, in a converse case, happy moods can eliminate preferences for familiar stimuli by independently signaling safety (de Vries et al., 2010).

Sometimes, however, a familiar option is also the most *disaligned* with the very source of one's felt pressure. Imagine that you drive the same route to work every day, along a frequently congested highway. You know of a likely quicker route involving various side-streets, but have only taken it a few times. When you're running late and have a big meeting to make, the pressure to arrive on-time, by magnifying the attractiveness of taking the familiar but longer route, may make it *more* likely that you'll be late. Similarly, time pressure may increase a consumer's willingness to wait for their "usual" option (such as a regularly called cab driver, but who is ten minutes away) and foregoing other, more immediately available alternatives.

Of course, it is not that these familiar options are guaranteed to have worse outcomes: an unfamiliar driving-route might take longer if you get lost; an unfamiliar cab driver may drive slowly, get lost, or choose a bad route. But even with no objective evidence for these possibilities, pressure may increase worry over their prospect and conversely enhance the "warm glow" of safety associated with a familiar option, even if evidence suggests it is a worse choice.

*Study Method.* We tested such counterposing of familiarity and communicated option-characteristics in the case of selection between task options for completion under time pressure. In part 1 of the experiment, participants (*n*=145, from a national pool) encountered ancillary biographical information about a pictured person (name, birthday, number of siblings, hometown, etc.). In the second part, they were told that, if they solved a word-puzzle task correctly, they would be entered into a prize-drawing. In the *No-Pressure* condition, participants were told they could take as long as they wished to complete the task. In the *Time-Pressure* condition, they were told they would have at most four minutes to complete the task.

Participants were offered a choice between two puzzle-task options: one listed as having two passages of text to work through, and the other listed as having three. The only other information provided about these options was the name of the person who created each of them. In the *Both-Unfamiliar* condition, neither of these individuals had been encountered in the experiment. In the *Longer-Familiar* condition, the person associated with the three-passage option was the same one for whom participants encountered irrelevant biographical information in part 1 of the experiment. Crossing the pressure and familiarity manipulations, we explored how time pressure affected preferences for seemingly longer but incidentally familiar options.

*Results.* Cross-tabulations yielded significant differences in task-choice between the four cells (Chi-sq(3)=12.25, p<.01). As hypothesized, time pressure increased choice of the three-passage (i.e., objectively longer-seeming) option when it was associated with a familiar person, in comparison to when both options were associated with unfamiliar people (p<.01), and also compared to both No-Pressure cases, regardless of whether a familiar option was given (p<.05). Thus, time pressure enhanced familiarity bias, even when objective information indicated the familiar choice would actually take longer, and when the shorter option was preferred in the absence of any familiarity difference between options.

We also queried several process measures after the primary experimental sections that support our results. In both No-Pressure conditions and the Time-Pressure/Both-Unfamiliar condition, concern prior to the puzzle task about finishing in time was significantly correlated with choosing the *two*-passage task (r's>.43), whereas in the Time-Pressure/Longer-Familiar case, this concern significantly correlated with choice of the *three*-passage task (r=.34). In contrast, perceived stress and pressure *during* the task was greater amongst those who chose the three-passage task, regardless of associated familiarity. Thus, despite their preference for the familiar option, individuals under time pressure choosing the longer task did not experience less stress or find the task less difficult.

As evidence for the bases of familiar-option preferences, under time pressure, choosing the longer task was correlated with higher risk aversion, as measured by lower minimum sure-gains preferred to a 95% chance to win $100 (r=-.29). In both Longer-Familiar conditions, choice of this longer option correlated with beliefs (for which no objective evidence existed) that this task would be easier (r's>.35) and give a greater chance of success (r's>.30), and also with beliefs that this choice was less risky (r's>.34) and fit better with one's "gut feeling" about the best choice to make (r's>.50).

*Ongoing Work and Extensions.* In follow-up investigations we are exploring familiarity established through *negative* experiences, such as unpleasant interpersonal encounters. Whereas such familiarity commonly leads to biases *against* associated stimuli (Lewicki, 1986), our results suggest perceived pressure may reverse this preference. As well, we are exploring non-time forms of stress, such as performance pressure, and cases where objective evidence indicates familiar options are again more likely to aggravate such pressure.

*Conclusions.* Results indicate that not only does pressure magnify the attractiveness of familiar choice options, it can do so even when such options are contrary to the very source of the pressure one feels. These results are driven by heightened perceptions of safety and comfort with familiar options, even when objective evidence disfavors them. Consumers may thus make perversely distorted choices when available alternatives differ in their perceived familiarity, and objectively superior choices when choice-sets are limited to unfamiliar options.

### References

Chowdhury, T. G., Ratneshwar, S., & Mohanty, P. (2009). The time-harried shopper: Exploring the differences between maximizers and satisficers. *Marketing Letters, 20*(2), 155-167.

de Vries, M., Holland, R. W., Chenier, T., Starr, M. J., & Winkielman, P. (2010). Happiness cools the warm glow of familiarity: Psychophysiological evidence that mood modulates the familiarity-affect link. Forthcoming, *Psychological Science*.

Griebel, G., Belzung, C., Misslin, R., & Vogel, E. (1993). The free-exploratory paradigm: An effective method for measuring neophobic behaviour in mice and testing potential neophobia-reducing drugs. *Behavioural Pharmacology, 4*, 637-644.

Heinrichs, S. C., & Koob, G. F. (1992). Corticotropin-releasing factor modulates dietary preference in nutritionally and physically stressed rats. *Psychopharmacology, 109*(1), 177-184.

Kandiah, J., Yake, M., Jones, J., & Meyer, M. (2006). Stress influences appetite and comfort food preferences in college women. *Nutrition Research, 26*(3), 118-123.

Lewicki, P. (1986). *Nonconscious social information processing*. New York: Academic Press.

Nowlis, S. M. (1995). The effect of time pressure on the choice between brands that differ in quality, price, and product features. *Marketing Letters, 6*(4), 287-295.

Shephard, R. A., & Estall, L. B. (1984). Anxiolytic actions of chlordiazepoxide determine its effects on hyponeophagia in rats. *Psychopharmacology, 82*(4), 343-347.

# When Ambivalence Increases Attitude-Behavior Correspondence

Lifeng Yang, Ohio State University, USA
H. Rao Unnava, Ohio State University, USA

Much of the past research has focused on the consequences of attitudinal ambivalence in terms of reduced attitude-behavior consistency, and the antecedents of ambivalence (Priester et al, 1996; Conner et al, 2002; Cavazza et al, 2008). There has not been much attention devoted to studying *conditions under which attitudes may be predictive of behavior even when they are held with high ambivalence.* The objective of this research therefore is to study ambivalent individuals' attitude-behavior correspondence under conditions where one's positive (negative) reactions are made more (less) diagnostic at the time of choice. We use different levels of mood to manipulate individual's perceived diagnosticity of their initial reactions toward the attitudinal object. We argue that when individuals are put in a happy mood, they would perceive mood congruent (thus positive) aspects the product as of being more diagnostic; however when individuals are put in a sad mood, they would perceive mood congruent (thus negative) aspects of the product to be more diagnostic. The perception of reaction diagnosticity is believed to act as the key role determining whether an individual is more or less likely to behavior according to their attitude.

**Theoretical Conceptualization**

Attitudinal ambivalence is characterized by a person experiencing both positive and negative reactions to an object. Dominant reactions are those that are greater in number, whether positive or negative; Conflicting reactions, on the other hand, are those that are fewer in number, and are opposite in valence with the dominant reactions (Priester et al., 1996; Priester & Petty, 2001; Priester, Petty & Park, 2007). The idea that ambivalence is linked separately in memory to positive and negative components is important because it suggests that a different attitudinal reaction emerges depending on which of the components is activated in memory (e.g., Petty & Briñol, 2009). In normal conditions, if people hold a positive attitude without ambivalence, it is expected that primarily the positive reactions would come to their mind whenever they think about the attitudinal object. However, if individuals have ambivalence in their attitude, even though their overall evaluation of the attitudinal object is one-directional, the encountering of the object may invoke both positive and negative reactions within these individuals. Whether ambivalent individuals' choice consistent with their overall attitude would depend on which reactions are perceived to be more diagnostic at the moment.

Thus, while ambivalent attitudes are characterized by positive and negative components of the attitude being retrieved simultaneously, they may experience a hard time making up their mind for decisions. At this time, the mood one is in may serve as the trigger for spreading activations of the positive aspects of the attitudinal object. Ambivalent individuals may have an easier time retrieving the positive (negative) associations about the attitudinal object when they are in a happy (sad) mood. The easier retrieval of the positive (negative) associations may increase the perceived diagnosticity of the retrieved associations thus affects the later behavior.

Explicitly, we predict that:

$H_1$: For highly ambivalent attitudes, being in a happy (sad) mood will affect choice to be more (less) consistent with the positive component of the attitude while being in a neutral mood will make the choice to be less consistent with the positive component of the attitude.

$H_2$: For attitudes held with low ambivalence, being in a happy (sad) mood will affect choice no differently from being in a neutral mood, in terms of consistency between the positive (negative) component of an attitude and choice.

**Methods & Results**

We conducted a 2 (low vs. high ambivalence) X 3 (happy vs. neutral vs. sad mood) study to test our hypotheses above. We randomly assigned subjects to different mood induction conditions then had them responded to a choice question of either a free order of French fries or a free order of parfait as reward for the participation of the study. The attitudinal object of the study was Wendy's French fries. Subjects for the study all hold an overall positive attitude toward French fries (attitude scores >6 in a 9-point scale where 1=extremely negative and 9=extremely positive). Among all, sixty of these individuals hold a positive but low ambivalent attitude toward French fries ($M_{attitude}$= 6.85, SD=1.04; $M_{ambivalence}$=3.73, SD=.69); and the other seventy four participants hold a positive but high ambivalent attitude toward French fries ($M_{attitude}$=6.63, SD= .88; $M_{ambivalence}$=6.81, SD=.99). Subjects from the low vs. high ambivalent groups were significantly different in ambivalence ($F_{(1, 132)}$ =418.057, p<.000) but they did not differ much in their attitude or attitude extremity toward French fries ($F_{(1, 132)}$ =1.723, p>.192 NS).

Our hypotheses call for an interaction between mood and ambivalence such that choice probabilities of French fries are unaffected by mood in the low ambivalence conditions, but affected positively in the happy mood condition and negatively in the sad mood condition. In other words, while choice probabilities are about equal in four experimental conditions (low ambivalence neutral, happy and sad mood conditions; and high ambivalence neutral mood condition), there would be an increase (decrease) in the choice probability of French fries in the happy (sad) mood, high ambivalence condition(s).

For the whole sample, 66.4 % of the participants (89 out of 134) chose French fries with the rest of the sample choosing Parfait. Overall, individuals' attitude toward French fries was positively correlated with their choice (r=.22, p<.01). The fact that more than 50% of the participants choosing French fries was not surprising but was predicted because all participants chosen for this study had indicated that they had an overall positive attitude toward French fries (M=6.73 in a 9-point scale where "1"= very negative "9"=very positive). Choice probabilities for French fries do not vary much for the low ambivalent groups ($\beta$=.158, p>.68) (

$Probability_{Low+neutral} = 68.6\%$  $Probability_{Low+sad} = 71.9\%$  $Probability_{Low+happy} = 66.1\%$

*p for each pair-comparison all >.60*). However, attitude consists with behavior the most likely for those the high ambivalent

individuals in happy mood condition ($Probability_{High+happy} = 93.7\%$, $Probability_{High+neutral} = 68.8\%$,

$Probability_{High+sad} = 83.7\%$).

Consistent with past literature pertaining that ambivalent attitudes are less predictive of behavior than less ambivalent attitudes, we find in this research that individuals who hold a positive but less ambivalent attitude toward French fries to show a more stable attitude-behavior correspondence than those who hold a positive but high ambivalent attitude. Further, individuals with less ambivalent attitude should tend to choose toward French fries regardless of what mood condition they are in. In contrast, high ambivalent individuals would have a more fluctuated behavior pattern in choosing for French fries because of the existence of conflicting reactions, and that the conflicting reactions can be perceived as deterministically diagnostic if they are made salient to them.

**Selective References**

Adaval, R. (2001). Sometimes It Just Feels Right: The Differential Weighting of Affect-Consistent And Affect Inconsistent Product Information. *Journal of Consumer Research,* 28(3), 1-17.

Bell, David W., & Esses, V. M. (2002). Ambivalence and Response Amplification: A Motivational Perspective. *Personality and Social Psychology Bulletin*, 28(8), 1143-1152.

Cavazza, N., & Butera, F. (2008). Bending without Breaking: Examining the Role of Attitudinal Ambivalence in Resisting Persuasive Communication. *European Journal of Social Psychology*, 38(1), 1-15.

Conner, M., Sparks, P., Povey, R., James, R., Shepherd, R., & Armitage, C. J. (2002). Moderator Effects of Attitudinal Ambivalence on Attitude-behaviour Relationships. *European Journal of Social Psychology*, 32(5), 705-718.

Kaplan, K. J. (1972). On the Ambivalence-difference Problem in Attitude Theory and Measurement: A Suggested Modification of the Semantic Differential Technique. *Psychological Bulletin*, 77(5), 361-372.

Petty, R. E., & Briñol, P. (2009). Implicit Ambivalence: A Meta-cognitive Approach. In R. E. Petty, R. H. Fazio, and P. Briñol (Eds.), *Attitudes: Insights from the New Implicit Measure*, (pp.119-161), New York, NY: Psychology Press.

Petty, R. E., & Krosnick, J. A. (1995). Attitude Strength: An Overview. In R. E. Petty, and J. A. Krosnick (Eds.), *Attitude Strength: Antecedents and Consequences*, (pp. 1-24), Mahwah, NJ: Lawrence Erlbaum Associates.

Priester, J. R., & Petty, R. E. (1996). The Gradual Threshold Model of Ambivalence: Relating the Positive and Negative Bases of Attitudes to Subjective Ambivalence. *Journal of Personality and Social Psychology*, 71(3), 431-449.

# It's More Likely...But Can It Be Worth It?
# Perceived Similarity, Probability and Outcome Value

Hui-Yun Chen, Virginia Tech, USA

Elise Chandon Ince, Virginia Tech, USA

## Extended Abstract

Individuals are prone to developing naïve theories about the likelihood of event occurrences because what is reckoned to happen determines their subsequent judgments and actions. Prior research suggests that intuitive probability judgments are susceptible to extraneous cues such as descriptions of the event (Tversky and Koehler 1994), the representativeness or availability of exemplars (Kahneman, Slovic, and Tversky 1982), moods (Wright and Bower 1992), and cognitive orientation (Wakslak and Trope 2009). In this research, we propose that individuals employ an extraneous cue, perceived similarity, to infer the probability of an event, and in turn, use the probability judgment to evaluate the impact level of the event.

In order to understand, evaluate, and predict the outside world, individuals are motivated to develop naïve theories from cumulated life experiences (Strevens 2000) or knowledge (Springer 1995). For most daily life cases, the proximity to the target person and the likelihood of event occurrence are highly correlated. For example, sharing a living space with someone with a cold makes us more likely to get sick. Another common example is that individuals who have a family history of heart disease are high in risk as well because of genetic factors. Recently, research on probability judgment has also shown that lottery participants estimate their chance of winning as higher when the winner of previous round is similar to them than when the former winner is dissimilar (Laporte and Laurent 2009). Thus we posit that individuals build from the observations and experiences of such events the naïve theory that they are more prone to experience events that strike their close others than events that strike unknown individuals. Moreover, even though this naïve theory facilitates and leads to correct judgments in general, it does lead to inflated likelihood when people infer higher probabilities from proximities that are irrelevant.

Intuitive probability judgments in turn affect individuals' judgments of the target event. For example, increasing individuals' perceptions of their own risk leads to more favorable attitudes and intentions toward practicing HIV precautionary behaviors (Raghubir 1998). However, we argue that probability judgments would undercut the perceived impact level of events in situations where the outcome of an event is ambiguous or unknown. That is, when the information about event outcome is absent, event probability serves as indirect information and signals the impact level of events. Previous research has shown that limited, scarce resources are deemed more desirable (Inman, Peter, and Raghubir 1997; Lynn 1992). Drawing on this logic, we further hypothesize that the inflated probability judgment based on perceived proximity would downplay perceived impact level of the event. In other words, an event that is related to a similar individual will appear more likely to occur, which in turn, will render the event less impactful.

Two studies tested the present predictions. Study 1 investigated the influence of probability information on perceived impact level. Participants read scenarios about winning a store gift card in a store lottery and getting a flight upgrade on a trip and then judged the outcome values. We manipulated the probability of each event (70%, 30%, and 5%). The dependent variable was the outcome value (i.e., value of the store gift card and value of the flight upgrade). The results confirmed our hypothesis. When the event is of lowest likelihood (5%), the highest outcome value estimation was achieved. Furthermore, the estimated outcome value decreased as the event probability increased.

Study 2 directly tested whether embedding a similar social cue (vs. dissimilar) in the description of events (winning a store gift card in a lottery and getting a flight upgrade on a trip) would construe the events to be more likely to occur, and the inflated probability would subsequently decrease the perceived impact level of the events. Participants were asked to read scenarios that contained different social cues (e.g., a friend or a stranger) and then rated the likelihood that the events would occur to them and how long the effect of events would last. As expected, we found that the presence of a similar social cue leads to a higher probability judgment. Furthermore, probability judgments negatively predicted the number of days participants believed the positive effect would last.

Probabilities are often difficult to assess objectively, and research has indicated various cues employed to infer probabilities. The present studies suggest that perceived proximity acts as such a cue. Specifically, our initial findings demonstrate that probability judgments may be biased by the presence of social cues because individuals make probability inferences from perceived proximity to the target person. In addition, the probability judgment itself serves as a cue when the information about the event outcome is ambiguous, and thus affects the perceived impact level of an event. When an event is judged as more likely to occur due to perceived proximity, it is also judged as less impactful.

References

Inman, J. Jeffrey, Anil C. Peter, and Priya Raghubir (1997), "Framing the Deal: The Role of Restrictions in Accentuating Deal Value," *The Journal of Consumer Research*, 24 (1), 68-79.
Kahneman, D, P Slovic, and A Tversky (1982), *Judgment under Uncertainty: Heuristics and Biases*: Cambridge Univ Pr.
Laporte, Sandra and Gilles Laurent (2009), "The Interpersonal Hot Hand Fallacy: How Similarity with Previous Winners Increases Subjective Probability of Winning," in *2009 ACR North American Conference*, Pittsburgh.
Lynn, Michael (1992), "Scarcity's Enhancement of Desirability: The Role of Naive Economic Theories," *Basic and Applied Social Psychology*, 13 (1), 67-78.
Raghubir, Priya (1998), "Coupon Value: A Signal for Price?," *Journal of Marketing Research*, 35 (3), 316-24.
Springer, Ken (1995), "Acquiring a Naive Theory of Kinship through Inference," *Child Development*, 66 (2), 547-58.
Strevens, Michael (2000), "The Essentialist Aspect of Naive Theories," *Cognition*, 74 (2), 149-75.
Tversky, Amos and Derek J. Koehler (1994), "Support Theory: A Nonextensional Representation of Subjective Probability," *Psychological Review*, 101 (4), 547-67.
Wakslak, Cheryl and Yaacov Trope (2009), "The Effect of Construal Level on Subjective Probability Estimates," *Psychological Science*, 20 (1), 52-58.
Wright, William F. and Gordon H. Bower (1992), "Mood Effects on Subjective Probability Assessment," *Organizational Behavior and Human Decision Processes*, 52 (2), 276-91.

# Consumers Do Compare Apples with Oranges:
## Investigating Cross Category Referencing in Consumer Decision-making
Vanessa Patrick, University of Houston, USA
Weixing Ma, University of Houston, USA

Apples have a golden skin or red without and white within. An orange has a tangy rind and a color that is distinct. Unless you have an axe to grind or some other devious design then I would say that the differences are like night and day. - Anonymous

Prior research has demonstrated that consumers use references to facilitate decision-making. The literature examined consumer's reliance on reference points with comparable attributes within a product category (Rajendran and Tellis 1994; Rosch 1975). The current research aims to reveal that consumers often rely on a previous purchase from a different, often unrelated product category in order to justify a current purchase decision.

## Literature
Consumers usually need various strategies to make/justify a purchase decision. In classical economics, a consumer's decision is derived from her preferences for competing alternatives, as revealed by the indifference curve given a budget constraint. Little attention has been devoted to the formation of such indifference curve due to the subjective nature of preferences (Georgescu-Roegen 1936; Hauer and Urban 1986). Marketing scholars, especially consumer behavior researchers, have been dedicated to explore such subjectivity of consumers' preferences.

Prior research focused on *how* consumers discover their own preferences through various decision-making strategies or tactics, for instance, framing (Kahneman and Tversky 1984), anchoring (Strack and Mussweiler 1997; Tversky and Kahneman 1974), and relying on a reference (Rosch 1975; Rajendran and Tellis 1994; Huber et al. 2008). Notably this research stream focuses on the comparison between products or attributes that are closely related or comparable, for example, different brands or different prices, respectively, within a given product category.

Recent research also acknowledged the possible influence of unrelated or cross-category products on consumer decision-making: for instance, the shopping momentum phenomenon (Dhar et al. 2007), the devaluation effect (Brendl et al. 2003), and the role of incidentally activated shopping goals (Chartrand et al. 2008). In these studies, unrelated or cross category purchases or products emerge as situational/ environmental influences or consumer mindsets, rather than as references consumers actively use to evaluate a focal purchase decision.

The current research aims to broaden the view of reference by investigating situations in which consumers refer to an unrelated (cross-category) product as a reference to make a current purchase decision. We present a theory of "motivated anchoring" to understand (1) when consumers rely on cross-category referencing, (2) its impact on consumer decision-making, and 3) its underlying mechanism.

## Cross Category Reference in Consumer Decision-making
The literature on motivated reasoning has studied how people's motivational states can influence their perceptions and judgments (Kunda 1990). We present a theory of "motivated anchoring" to understand how a consumer may use seemingly incomparable references to help her justify a highly (less) desired target product as being more (less) worthy of purchase.

We argue that when a consumer desires to own a product, this form of biased evaluation will justify the purchase. In other words, a consumer driven by her desire for the target product is motivated to retrieve a cross category reference that helps justify her purchase decision and ease the pain of paying the price. Consider the following: a consumer is debating whether she should buy another pair of designer shoes. She then thinks about the tax she "gives away" to the government every year. Suddenly, the price of the shoes is no longer hefty and in fact, is very reasonable for such gorgeous shoes. Similarly, "motivated anchoring" can also justify *not* making a purchase.

## Empirical Investigation

We already conducted an exploratory critical incident analysis and one experiment. Additional studies are underway.

Eighty-eight undergraduate students participated in the critical incident survey. We collected open-ended data of participants' experience of using cross category references in their decision-making. The survey provided ample evidence for the phenomenon. Coding of the open-ended data revealed the following key findings: 1) consumers were more likely to use cross-category references to help make/justify purchase decisions of discretionary and hedonic products, 2) most references were at a similar price range as the target product, and 3) individuals were more likely to rely on a less expensive unrelated (cross-category) reference to justify a spontaneous purchase.

Next, we conducted an experiment to demonstrate how different references can have different impact on consumers' decisions. We propose that a negative reference which emphasizes negative utility upon consumption such as medical expense and tax payment will make consumers increase their subjective evaluation of the utility of the target product and downplay its cost, and hence, they are more likely to purchase the target product. On the other hand, a positive reference which focuses on the pleasure of consumption such as a wonderful dinner at one's favorite restaurant will make the current target product appear to be more costly and less enjoyable, and therefore a less attractive purchase option.

We recruited 150 real world consumers to participate in a between-subjects experiment in which the nature of a reference product (negative vs. positive) was manipulated. We measured its impact on consumers willingness to select from a set of vacation options that varied from being very expensive (hedonic), moderately expensive, cheap to forgoing the vacation. The results reveal that participants who were exposed to a negative reference (paying tax) were more likely to choose the most expensive vacation plan compared to participants exposed to the positive reference (purchase of an electronic product; 36.4% vs. 20%, p<.05). The positive reference was more likely to induce the choice of the compromise option compared to the negative reference (49.1% vs. 34.5%, p<.05).

We aim to contribute to the literature in the following ways: 1) establish the impact of an unrelated purchase on consumer decision-making, 2) present and test a theory of motivated anchoring to illustrate how consumers use unrelated products from different product categories to view a target product as more or less desirable and worthy of purchase, and, 3) to identify managerial and public policy implications that stem from these findings.

## Selected References

Brendl, C. Miguel, Arthur B. Markman, and Claude Messner (2003), "The Devaluation Effect: Activating a Need Devalues Unrelated Objects," *Journal of Consumer Research*, 29 (4), 463-473.
Chartrand, Tanya A., Joel Huber, Baba Shiv and Robin J. Tanner (2008), "Nonconscious Goals and Consumer Choice," *Journal of Consumer Research*, 35 (2), 189-201.
Dhar, Ravi, Joel Huber and Uzma Khan (2007), "The Shopping Momentum Effect," *Journal of Marketing Research*, 44(3), 370-378.
Georgescu-Roegen, Nicholas (1936), "The Pure Theory of Consumer Behavior," *Quarterly Journal of Economics*, 50 (4), 545-593.
Hauser, John R. and Glen L. Urban (1986), "The Value Priority Hypotheses for Consumer Budget Plans," *Journal of Consumer Research*, 12 (4), 446-462.
Huber, Joel, W. Kip Viscusi and Jason Bell (2008), "Reference Dependence in Iterative Choices," *Organizational Behavior and Human Decision Process*, 106 (2), 143-152.
Kahneman, Daniel and Amos Tversky (1984), "Choices, Values and Frames," *American Psychologist*, 39 (4), 341-350.
Kunda, Ziva (1990), "The Case for Motivated Reasoning," *Psychological Bulletin*, 108 (3), 480-498.
Rajendran, K. N and Gerard J. Tellis (1994), "Contextual and Temporal Components of Reference Price," *Journal of Marketing*, 58 (1), 22-34.
Rosch, Eleanor (1975), "Cognitive Reference Points," *Cognitive Psychology*, 7 (4), 532-547.
Strack, Fritz and Thomas Mussweiler (1997), "Explaining the Enigmatic Anchoring Effect: Mechanisms of Selective Accessibility," *Journal of Personality and Social Psychology*, 73 (3), 437-446.
Tversky, Amos and Daniel Kahneman (1974), "Judgment under Uncertainty: Heuristics and Biases," *Science*, 185 (4157), 1124-1131.

# Should You Kill Two Birds with One Stone?
# The Diluting Influence of Having Multiple Goals on Goal Pursuit

Weixing Ma, University of Houston, USA
Vanessa Patrick, University of Houston, USA

One man; two loves. No good ever comes of that. --------Euripides, Greece

People are often engaged in a single activity which serves multiple goals simultaneously. Intuitively, we applaud the efficiency of "killing two birds with one stone". But is "more" necessarily better? This research aims to demonstrate the dilution effect of multiple goals on the effort level exerted through a single activity. Moreover, we investigate this, keeping in mind the between-goal relationships, by asking: Are all goals created "equal"? Does the commitment to one goal strengthen or undermine the attention to other goals? This research seeks answers to these questions, and discovers the structure of these multiple goals and their relationship with the single means.

## Literature

Goals constitute the focal points around which human behavior is organized (Fishbach and Ferguson 1996). Prior literature on goals has examined the cognitive, affective, interactive and dynamic perspectives of goal related phenomena and mechanisms. The recently developed goal system theory explored the cognitive perspective of goals and their related means (Bargh et al. 2001; Kruglanski et al. 2002; Shah and Kruglanski 2003; Fishbach et al. 2003; Fishbach et al. 2004). Successful goal attainment typically results in positive affect (Dweck and Leggett 1988; Carver and Scheier 1990). Conversely, such affect may be transferred to its cognitively associated means (Fishbach et al. 2004). The research which focused on the interactive and dynamic aspects of goals has explored three configurations of multiple goals: multiple goals of similar centrality (Shah and Kruglanski 2002), different centrality and the effect of multiple goals on a sequence of actions that unfold over time (Fishbach and Ferguson 1996).

The same dilution effect of multiple goals served by a single means was previously examined by Zhang, Fishbach and Kruglanski (2007), but from a different vantage point than the current research. In their study (Zhang et al. 2007), the dilution effect was observed only through the perceived instrumentality of a shared goal-means path, where goal distinctiveness and perceived means-goal associative strength were considered as mediating factors.

The current research aims to tap into the interplay and dynamics between affect and cognition in the multiple goals-single means relationship. Specifically, we not only replicate the dilution effect of multiple goals (Zhang et al. 2007) on the shared single means, but aim to uncover a unique mechanism that leads to the dilution effect.

## Theory and Hypotheses

We first propose a general construct of 'goal-means linkage", which is the general indicator for the relationship between a goal and a single means that serves the goal. Then we explore the major facets of this general construct, namely, cognitive, affective, dynamic, and interactive, which compose the second level refined constructs for the general "goal-means linkage": goal momentum (dynamic and interactive), goal valence (affective), and goal instrumentality (cognitive).

We then investigate how such cognitive, affective, interactive and dynamic aspects of the multiple goals have impact on the efforts exerted through their shared single means. Furthermore, we examine what happens to the effort level when the number of the goals served by a means increases. We propose the following key hypotheses: (1) when multiple goals are served by a single means, as the number of the goals increases, the effort level exerted through the means decreases. This is the dilution effect in the multiple goals-single means setting. (2) A goal of higher momentum is likely to result in the exertion of greater effort (3) A goal of positive valence is likely to exert more effort than the goals of negative valence, and, (4) A goal with higher perceived instrumentality is likely to exert more effort through the single means.

## Studies

We have conducted two preliminary studies. The first was a survey in order to develop the scales for the constructs and examine the multiple goals-single means relationship. Next, we conducted a study using donation-to-a-charity as the decision-making context to test the basic proposition: Does increasing number of identified goals lead to increased dilution (lower donation)?

In the survey, we first gave the participants some examples of people engaging in a single activity in order to achieve more than just one goal. Participants were then asked to recall similar multiple goals-single means situations which they have experienced in the past. After they wrote down the single means and all the goals served by this means, they were instructed to rate each goal-means pair on a seven-point semantic differential scale on the following: effectiveness, measurability, pleasantness, importance, urgency, uniqueness, and attentiveness. Each variable was followed by a brief description and a detailed example. The descriptions and examples were pretested to ensure clarity of instruction. Seventy-eight undergraduate students participated in the survey. Three constructs were refined through exploratory factor analysis of the survey data: (1) *goal momentum* as measured by importance, urgency, uniqueness, and attentiveness, (2) *goal instrumentality* as measured by effectiveness and measurability, and (3) *goal valence* as measured by pleasantness. Confirmatory factor analysis was conducted to assess the convergent and discriminate validity of these constructs. The survey data also supported the four hypotheses on goal structure and the dilution effect.

Next an experiment was conducted using a charity donation decision-making context, in which participants identified the goal(s) they would like to achieve via their charitable donation, and then determined the amount they would like to donate. The data indicated that as the number of goals increased, individuals tended to donate significantly less money ($\beta$=-21.1, $p$=.015).

The preliminary results are promising and a set of experiments are planned to further develop this research. We expect to have completed a comprehensive set of studies by ACR.

## Summary

This research aims to contribute to the literature on the multiple goals-single means setting in the following ways: (1) we demonstrate that goals are not created equal in terms of their momentum, instrumentality and valence; (2) more goals are not necessarily better in terms of the effort level they exert through the shared single means.

## Selected References

Bargh, John A, Peter M. Gollwitzer, Annette Lee-Chai, Kimberly Barndollar and Roman Trötschel (2001), "The Automated Will: Nonconscious Activation and Pursuit of Behavioral Goals," *Journal of Personality and Social Psychology*, 81(6), 1014-1027.

Carver, Charles S. and Michael F. Scheier (1990), "Principles of Self-regulation: Action and Emotion," in *Handbook of Motivation and Cognition: Foundations of Social Behavior*, Vol. 2, eds. Higgins, E.Tory & Sorrentino, R.M., Guilford Press, New York, 3-52.

Dweck, Carol S. and Ellen L. Leggett (1988), "A Social-cognitive Approach to Motivation and Personality," *Psychological Review*, 95(2), 256-273.

Fishbach, Ayelet and Melissa J. Ferguson (1996), "The Goal Construct in Social Psychology," in *Social Psychology: Handbook of Basic Principles*, Vol. 2, eds. Kruglanski A.W. & Higgins E. Tory, Guilford Press, New York, 490-515.

Fishbach, Ayelet, Ronald S. Friedman and Arie W. Kruglanski (2003), "Leading Us Not Into Temptation: Momentary Allurements Elicit Overriding Goal Activation," *Journal of Personality and Social Psychology*, 84 (2), 296-309.

Fishbach, Ayelet, James Y. Shah and Arie. W. Kruglanski (2004), "Emotional Transfer in Goal Systems," *Journal of Experimental Social Psychology*, 40 (6), 723-738.

Kruglanski, Arie, James Y. Shah, Ayelet Fishbach, Ronald Friedman, Woo Y. Chun and David Sleeth-Keppler (2002), "A Theory of Goal Systems," in *Advances in Experimental Social Psychology*, Vol. 34, ed. M. P. Zanna, Academic Press, San Diego, 331-378.

Shah, James Y. and Arie W. Kruglanski (2002), "Priming Against Your Will: How Goal Pursuit Is Affected by Accessible Alternatives," *Journal of Experimental Social Psychology*, 38 (4), 368-383.

Shah, James Y. and Arie W. Kruglanski (2003), "When Opportunity Knocks: Bottom-up Priming of Goals by Means and Its Effects on Self-regulation," *Journal of Personality and Social Psychology*, 84 (6), 1109-1122.

Zhang, Ying, Ayelet Fishbach and Arie W. Kruglanski (2007), "The Dilution Model: How Additional Goals Undermine the Perceived Instrumentality of a Shared Path," *Journal of Personality and Social Psychology*, 92(3), 389-401.

# How Goals Affect the Impact of Product Attributes on Product Evaluation: The Role of Attribute Ability, Goal Activation and Goal-Product Fit

Na Xiao, Queen's University, Canada
Laurence Ashworth, Queen's University, Canada

## Extended Abstract

Understanding how consumers evaluate products is a central topic in marketing research. Most approaches focus on the way in which consumers use information about specific features of the product to reach an overall judgment. Some research focuses on the way consumers *compare* attributes across products (e.g. Bettman, Luce and Payne, 2008), while other research examines how consumers *combine* attribute information (e.g. Cohen, Fishbein and Ahtola, 1972). Still other research focuses on the way consumers *process* arguments (e.g. information about attributes; e.g. Chen and Chaiken, 1999). While each approach is clearly important, very little work examines what makes particular attributes important to consumers in the first place.

The current work adopts the broad perspective that product attributes are important to the extent that they can fulfill consumers' activated goals. Product evaluation involves judging the "goodness" or "usefulness" of a product, which implicitly involves references to consumers' underlying goals. This is consistent with the perspective that objects, more generally, are evaluated as good or bad depending on their ability to help meet or hinder individuals' goals (Markman and Brendl 2000).

This leads to a number of specific predictions about the way in which goals and attributes are likely to jointly impact product evaluation. First, attributes related to goals should be more likely to impact product evaluation. Specifically, the better able the attribute is perceived to fulfill the activated goal, the more positive the product evaluation. There is some evidence consistent with this in the satisfaction literature. Garbarino and Johnson (2001) found that consumers were more satisfied with a theatre performance when it fulfilled the particular goals they held (e.g. cultural enrichment versus relaxation). Moreover, this effect should be moderated by the activation of the goal (i.e., whether it occupies consumers' thoughts)–this means that the ability of an attribute to fulfill a goal should have a greater impact on overall product evaluation when the goal is activated than not. We test this idea in our first study.

Second, while activated goals might render relevant attributes more important to the overall evaluation of the product, not all goals are likely to be relevant to all products. In fact, some products are likely to be viewed as unlikely candidates for fulfilling certain goals. For example, consumers rarely seem to consider the environmental impact of the wine they purchase, or whether or not the tea they drink comes from fair trade sources. Yet many consumers fret about the environmental impact of the bottles their water comes in and frequently consider whether their coffee is fairly traded. In short, certain products are likely to "fit" well with certain goals, and poorly with others. If the product and goal do not fit, then attributes relevant to that goal should be unlikely to exert an important influence on the overall evaluation, even when the goal is important. We test this idea in our second study. Specifically, we attempt to manipulate the extent to which consumers perceive a "fit" between a particular product and goal, as well as the ability of the product to fulfill that goal.

## Study 1

One hundred and thirty-nine students participated in a 2 (Attribute Ability: Low vs. High) x 2 (Goal Activation: Yes vs. No) between-subjects factorial design. Students were presented with information for a brand of coffee that, among other attributes, was said to contain either 5% (low ability) or 75% (high ability) fair trade beans. Goal activation was manipulated in an article ostensibly from an online coffee guide that participants read prior to product evaluation. Both articles were identical except for a short addition in the Goal Activation condition that mentioned fair trade could bring many benefits to coffee farmers. Participants then completed thought listings (i.e. to measure goal activation) and measures of their evaluation of the coffee. Examination of the thoughts listings showed that participants generated more thoughts related to the fair trade in the Goal Activation conditions ($X^2(136)=4.53$, $p<.05$). Consistent with our predictions, a significant Attribute Ability x Goal Activation interaction ($F(1, 135)=5.59$, $p<.05$) indicated that the effect of attribute ability on product evaluation was more pronounced when the goal was activated (goal activated: $Ms=3.69$ vs. 5.06; $F(1, 135)=21.72$, $p<.05$; goal not activated: $Ms=4.20$ vs. 4.58; $F(1, 135)=1.72$, $p>.1$).

**Study 2**

One hundred and twenty-one students participated in a 2 (Attribute Ability: Low vs. High) x 2 (Goal-Product Fit: Low vs. High) between-subjects factorial design. Participants saw information about a pair of binoculars that, among other attributes, contained information about the lens material. Half of the participants were told that the lenses were made from optical eco-glass (a lead and arsenic free product) (high ability to fulfill environmental goals). The remaining participants were told simply that the lenses were constructed out of optical glass (low ability to fulfill environmental goals). Goal-product fit was manipulated in an article, ostensibly from an online binocular guide, that participants read prior to product evaluation. The article was identical in each condition except for a short addition in the High Goal-Product Fit conditions that mentioned binoculars, as with all products, are associated with certain environmental impact. A significant Attribute Ability x Goal-Product Fit interaction ($F(1, 117)=5.13$, $p<.05$) indicated that High Ability led to more favorable product attitudes when Goal-Product Fit was high ($M$s=5.23 vs. 4.30; $F(1, 117)=6.22$, $p<.05$), but not when it was low ($M$s=5.13 vs. 5.41; $F<1$).

To summarize, existing work shows that individual product attributes contribute to its overall evaluation, but little work addresses the question of what makes particular attributes important to consumers. The current work demonstrates that the importance of individual attributes depends, in part, on the extent to which they can fulfill activated consumer goals. Our research further contributes to this literature by making specific predictions about the way in which goals influence the role of attributes in product evaluation. First, goals that are activated were more likely to strengthen the impact of goal-relevant attributes on product evaluation. When a goal not activated, the ability of the attribute to fulfill the goal had little effect on product evaluation. Second, for goals to influence the impact of attributes on product evaluation there needs to be a perceived fit with the product. That is, products should be seen as appropriate means to fulfill particular goals if relevant attributes are to impact the overall evaluation of the product. Consistent with this, good performance on an attribute was more likely to result in more favorable product attitudes when goal-product fit was high.

**References**

Bettman, James R., Mary Frances Luce, and John W Payne (2008), "Consumer Decision Making: A Choice Goals Approach", in *Handbook of Consumer Psychology*, Ed. Curtis P. Haugtvedt, Paul M. Herr, Frank R. Kardes, Psychology Press, 589-610

Chen, Serena, Chaiken, Shelly. (1999), "The Heuristic-systematic Model in Its Broader Context", *Dual-process Theories in Social Psychology*, edited by Shelly Chaiken and Yaacov Trope. 1999, 73–96

Cohen, Joel B., Martin Fishbein, Olli T Ahtola (1972), "the Nature and Uses of Expectancy-value Models in Consumer Attitude Research. *Journal of Marketing Research*, 9 (Nov), 456-460

Garbarino, Ellen, Mark S Johnson (2001), "Effects of Consumer Goals on Attribute Weighting, Overall Satisfaction, and Product Usage", *Psychology and Marketing*, 18, 9, 929-949

Markman, Arthur B., C Miguel Brendl (2000), "The Influence of Goals on Value and Choice", *The Psychology of Learning and Motivation*, 39, 97-128

# The Rebound of the Forgone Alternative
Zachary Arens, University of Maryland, USA
Rebecca Hamilton, University of Maryland, USA

Consumers often face choices requiring a trade-off between valued alternatives. Consider a consumer who wants to purchase a relaxing massage as well as a new pair of sneakers for exercising. Looking in her wallet, she finds that she only has enough money for one of these purchases. After difficult consideration, she decides to purchase the massage and forgo the sneakers. In this research, we examine what happens to her desire for the forgone alternative, the sneakers, after she has chosen and consumed the massage.

There are two bodies of literature that offer conflicting predictions as to the fate of the forgone alternative. The free choice paradigm suggests that consumers derogate the value of forgone alternative relative to the value of the chosen alternative. This spreading-of-alternatives effect is based on cognitive dissonance theory, which argues that dissonance is created by focusing on the positive attributes of the forgone alternative and negative attributes of the chosen one (Brehm 1956; Festinger 1957). Thus, consumers alter their attitudes towards these alternatives postchoice to support their choice behavior. In the first demonstration of this effect, Brehm (1956) asked participants to rank the desirability of a variety of small gift items (e.g., a toaster, coffee-maker, art book) and then choose between two products to take home as a thank-you gift. After participants made their choices, Brehm re-measured the desirability of each item and found that when the choice produced dissonance (i.e., the choice set alternatives were both highly valued) the desirability of the selected alternative increased but the forgone alternative decreased.

However, research on motivation suggests a different outcome. It proposes that the forgone alternative will remain desirable regardless of the choice. In other words, choosing one alternative does not deactivate the goal associated with the forgone alternatives and thus, goal instrumental objects should remain desirable (Markman and Brendl 2000).

This research seeks to reconcile these two views by demonstrating that both are correct depending on the stage in the consumption process. Once a choice has been made, potential distractions, such as the forgone alternative, are automatically devalued to help ensure effective action toward achieving the chosen alternative (Brendl, Markman, and Messner 2003; Harmon-Jones and Harmon-Jones 2002). After the action is complete (i.e., the chosen alternative is consumed), though, the desirability of the forgone alternative will rebound. Specifically, we predict that *after choice but prior to consumption* consumers will derogate the desirability of the forgone alternative relative to the desirability of the chosen alternative, in accordance with the cognitive dissonance paradigm. However, *after consumption*, consumers will enhance the desirability of the forgone alternative but derogate the desirability of the chosen alternative. In short, the value of the forgone alternative will rebound.

Our first study sought to replicate the free choice paradigm and show that after consuming the chosen alternative, the desirability of the forgone alternative rebounds. Participants read short descriptions of the eight questionnaire topics (fashion, restaurants, movies, vacations, music, cell phones, beverages and books) and rated how much they would like to complete each questionnaire. Based on these ratings, participants were asked to choose between two of these alternatives. Those in the high dissonance condition chose between two highly desirable alternatives, while those in the low dissonance condition chose between a highly desirable and a less desirable alternative. Half of the participants then re-rated all eight alternatives before completing the questionnaire (postchoice-preconsumption stage), while the other half re-rated them after completing it (postconsumption stage). The results replicated the free choice paradigm, showing that in the high dissonance condition, the desirability of the forgone alternative declined from the prechoice stage to the postchoice-preconsumption stage in comparison to the chosen alternative. Supporting our predictions, however, the desirability of the forgone alternative rebounded after participants completed the chosen questionnaire.

The second study used a similar procedure which involved rating nine different activities, making a choice between two and then re-rating the activities. However, this study sought to demonstrate that the rebound effect was moderated by whether the forgone and chosen alternatives were substitutes. The substitutability of the choice set was manipulated by varying the similarity of the other activities in the rated set. While the alternatives in the choice set always involved viewing photographs of wild animals (e.g., gorillas, penguins), the other activities were either similar (e.g., viewing photographs of kangaroos, bison) or dissimilar (e.g., reading a news article about Asia, playing a math puzzle game). Thus, by comparison, the forgone appeared to be a non-substitute or a substitute for the chosen alternative, respectively. As expected, when the forgone did not appear to substitute for the chosen alternative, the desirability of the forgone alternative decreased in the postchoice-preconsumption stage, but not in the postconsumption stage, replicating the findings of the first study. However, when the forgone alternative was viewed as a substitute for the chosen alternative, the desirability of the forgone and chosen alternatives exhibited the same pattern: they decreased in desirability in the postconsumption stage but not in the postchoice-preconsumption stage.

Our second study also ruled out regret and option attachment (Carmon, Wertenbroch, and Zeelenberg 2003) as alternative explanations. Regret did not differ by condition, nor did it correlate with desirability of the forgone alternative, suggesting that it does not explain the results. Option attachment, which was manipulated by having participants list three reasons why they would enjoy viewing the photographs in the choice set, did not affect the change in the desirability of the forgone alternative across consumption stages, suggesting that it is not an alternative explanation.

These studies reconcile earlier work on cognitive dissonance with later work on goals by demonstrating that consumers' attitudes towards a forgone alternative vary with the stage in the consumption process. Our results suggest that consumers will be unlikely to purchase a forgone alternative until their chosen alternative has been consumed, at which time their motivation to obtain the forgone alternative rebounds. As the familiar adage suggests, timing is everything.

## References

Brehm, Jack W. (1956), "Postdecision Changes in the Desirability of Alternatives," *The Journal of Abnormal and Social Psychology*, 52 (3), 384-89.

Brendl, C. Miguel, Arthur B. Markman, and Claude Messner (2003), "The Devaluation Effect: Activating a Need Devalues Unrelated Objects," *Journal of Consumer Research*, 29 (4), 463-73.

Carmon, Ziv, Klaus Wertenbroch, and Marcel Zeelenberg (2003), "Option Attachment: When Deliberating Makes Choosing Feel Like Losing," *Journal of Consumer Research*, 30 (1), 15-29.

Festinger, Leon A. (1957), *A Theory of Cognitive Dissonance*, Stanford, CA: Stanford University Press.

Harmon-Jones, Eddie and Cindy Harmon-Jones (2002), "Testing the Action-Based Model of Cognitive Dissonance: The Effect of Action Orientation on Postdecision Attitudes," *Personality & Social Psychology Bulletin*, 28 (6), 711-23.

Markman, Arthur B. and C. Miguel Brendl (2000), "The Influence of Goals on Value and Choice," in *The Psychology of Learning and Motivation: Advances in Research and Theory*, Vol. 39, ed. Douglas L. Medin, New York: Academic Press, 97-128.

# The Impact of Negative Information on Perceptions of Own Country Products: A New Perspective on Country of Origin and its Influence on Consumer Behavior

Rania Semaan, Baruch College, USA
Chen-Ho, Baruch College, USA
Andreas Grein, Baruch College, USA

## Extended Abstract

Country of origin (COO) research has examined how consumers evaluate products and make purchasing decisions based on their perceptions of country image. Country of origin refers to "information pertaining to where a product is made" (Zhang, 1996: 51). Negative country images cause consumers to evaluate products from that country poorly (Han & Terpstra, 1988). Although useful, the existing evidence of country of origin and country image effects on product evaluations is somehow limited. Researchers have mainly studied *foreign* consumers' product evaluations and purchase intentions relative to negative country image. To the best of our knowledge, the literature has overlooked *domestic* consumers' perception of their own products relative to their own country's negative image.

An interesting example occurred in summer 2007, when Mattel announced massive recalls of toys manufactured in China, due to lead contamination (in the paint) and small parts which could be accidentally swallowed by children resulting in creating a negative image to China (Anonymous, 2007). Not only was this an international trade conflict event, but also, it occurred at the same time as

Chinese consumers' preferences were shifting towards Chinese products over foreign-made products (Dyer, 2007). And so contrary to the evidence provided by previous literature and to conventional wisdom, in China's case a negative country image resulted in a positive evaluation of products.

In this research, we aim at investigating how consumers' preferences change when confronted with negative information about their *own country's* products.

Social Identity Theory argues that groups become part of the self affecting thoughts, feelings, and behavior (Tjafel & Turner, 1986). Moreover, strong emotions can develop as a result of group memberships (Smith, Seger, and Mackie 2007), for example anger when a source of information from outside the group presents negative information about the group. Intergroup Emotions Theory (Mackie, Devos & Smith, 2000; Mackie & Smith 1998) states that when an individual acquires in-group social and emotional significance, events that intrude on the in-group are appraised for their emotional relevance, just like events that occur in an individual's personal life (Smith & Henry 1996). Further, Anger has been shown to be elicited when social identity is threatened (Yzerbyt et al. 2003). Building on Social Identity Theory and Intergroup Emotions Theory, we propose that exposure to own country negative information increases the level of anger and the willingness to buy domestic products.

## Study 1

The objective of study one is to investigate the main effect of negative information on domestic consumers' willingness to buy products of their own country. Chinese subjects living in China were recruited for this study based on Hofstede's (1980) intercultural dimensions such as collectivism and individualism. For example, a person is seen as a separate entity in individualist societies, whereas the person's identity is defined as part of a larger group in collectivist societies.

*Method*: Undergraduate Chinese students participated in this study. Nagashima (1970) has shown that highly ethnocentric consumers may prefer products from their own country. Specifically, Chinese consumers' ethnocentrism was positively correlated to favorable attitudes towards domestic products (Wang and Zou 2003). Moreover, country of origin effects may be exacerbated if other countries may engage or have engaged in military, political or economic acts which a consumer finds difficult to tolerate and hence may cause animosity towards the offending country's products (Klein *et al.*, 1998). Therefore, First participants filled out the ethnocentricity scale developed by Shimp and Sharma (1987) followed by the animosity scale (Klein *et al.*, 1998), followed by a filler task.

Participants then moved to the second portion of the study, which involves reading an article and evaluating it. This serves as our information manipulation. Participants in the negative news read a fictitious article about an American Firm recalling children's sleepwear from China. Participants in the neutral news read a real article adapted from the Wall Street Journal, "Seeing through Buyers' Eyes" Jan 29, 2007, WSJ, B4.

Next, participants were given a scenario where they are in need of a laptop. They were also told that the store they visited only had two brands, Chinese (Made in China) and American (Made in USA). Finally, participants were asked to evaluate the article using a seven-point four item scale anchored at, dislike–like, favorable–unfavorable, negative–positive, and bad-good. This serves as a manipulation check.

*Results:* The manipulation check indicated that the negative news elicited more negative evaluations (M=4.86) than did the neutral news (M=6.77, F (1, 238)=62.21, p=0.00).

As mentioned above, ethnocentricity and animosity need to be accounted for; therefore they were used as covariates. A one way analysis of variance indicated that there was a main effect of the news manipulation on choice. Those in the bad news condition chose the Chinese product (M=0.704) more than those in the neutral news condition (M=0.467, F(1, 224, p=0.00). Both the covariates were not significant (p>0.05).

## Discussion

Several studies have shown that negative country image leads to lower willingness to buy products made in that country. Study 1 showed that this is not always the case. Negative country image of consumers' own country actually increases their preference for their own products. However, there are many other issues to consider and in ongoing research, Study 2 aims to explore two gaps in Study 1. First, the study does not assess the mediating role of intergroup emotions on domestic product preferences. Second, it does not assess whether consumers' choices differ if the domestic product were not only pitted against a hostile outgroup product but also against a neutral one.

## References

Anonymous (2007), "Mattel Issues New Massive China Toy Recall," *The Associated Press*

Dyer, Geoff (2007), "Chinese Consumers Prefer Own Products," *Financial Times,* 29, October, 2007

Han, Min and Vern Terpstra (1988), "Country-of-Origin Effects for Uni-national and Bi-national Products," *Journal of International Business Studies,* 19 (2) 235-255

Hofstede, Geert (1980) *Culture's Consequences.* Sage: Beverly Hills, CA.

Klein, Jill J., Richard Ettenson, and Marlene D. Morris (1998), "The Animosity Model of Foreign Product Purchase: An Empirical Test in the People's Republic of China," *Journal of Marketing,* 11 (4), 5-24

Mackie, Diane M. and Eliot R. Smith (1998), "Intergroup Relations: Insights from a Theoretically Integrative Approach," *Psychological Review,* 105(3), 499-529

Mackie, Diane M., Thierry Devos, and Eliot R. Smith (2000) "Intergroup Emotions: Explaining Offensive Action Tendencies in an Intergroup Context," *Journal of Personality and Social Psychology,* 79(4), 602-616

Nagashima, Akira (1970), "A Comparison of Japanese and U.S. Attitudes Toward Foreign Products," *Journal of Marketing,* 34 (January), 68-74

Shimp, Terence A. and Subhash Sharma (1987), "Consumer Ethnocentrism: Construction and Validation of the CETSCALE," *Journal of Marketing Research,* 24 (August), 280-289

Smith, Eliot R., Charles R. Seger, and Diane M. Mackie (2007), "Can Emotions be Truly Group Level? Evidence Regarding Four Conceptual Criteria," *Journal of Personality and Social Psychology*, 93(3), 431-446

Tajfel, Henri and John Turner (1986) "The Social Identity Theory of Intergroup Behavior," *The Psychology of Intergroup Relations*: 7.24. Chicago: Nelson-Hall.

Wang Hongzu, and Pengcheng Zhao (2003), "Brand-of Origin Effect and Marketing Strategy: A Survey of Country Images of Europe, USA, Japan and China," *Chinese Industrial Economy*, 1, 78-86

Yzerbyt, Vincent, Muriel Dumont, Daniel Wigboldus, and Ernestine Gordijin (2003), "I Feel for Us: The Impact of Categorization and Identification on Emotions and Action Tendencies," *British Journal of Social Psychology*, 42, 533-549

Zhang, Young (1996), "Chinese Consumers' Evaluation of Foreign Products: The Influence of Culture, Product Type, and Product Presentation Format," *European Journal of Marketing*, 30 (12), 50

# The Compromise Effect in Choosing for Others

Shih-Chieh Chuang, National Chung Cheng University, Taiwan
Yih-Hui Cheng, National TaiChung University, Taiwan
Sun Ya-Chung, Vanung University, Taiwan
Sui-Min Wang, National Chung Cheng University, Taiwan

## Extended Abstract

In daily life, people need, or are forced to, make choices for others, such as buying souvenirs for relatives, helping others, at their invitation, to buy something, or buying a birthday gift for a friend. Such decision making is a common but little-discussed phenomenon. People are often faced with situations in which they have to predict whether others, not themselves, will be satisfied with the choices they have made. Do people make the same choices for others as they do for themselves? When choosing for others rather than oneself, uncertainty arises and makes one more concerned about the judgment of others.

Early social, psychological, and decision-making research found that people have a variety of motives for justifying their decisions to themselves and others. The need to justify decisions to oneself and others reflects a desire to enhance one's self-esteem (Hall and Lindzey, 1978), cognitive dissonance (Festinger 1957), the anticipation of the possibility of regret (Bell 1983), and people's perception of themselves as rational beings with reasons for preferring one option over another (Abelson 1964). Therefore, people expecting to be judged by others may make the safest option (averaged) to be favorably evaluated by others, decrease criticism, and minimize potential errors (Simonson 1989).

The compromise effect is a crucial determinant in the decision-making process that is based on the context effect. This effect is based on the notion that "an alternative would tend to gain market share when it becomes a compromise or middle option in the choice set" (Simonson, 1989). Consumer preference is dynamic with new alternatives in choice sets (Bettman, Luce, and Payne, 1998), and is based on the principle of value maximization. Therefore, the difference between choosing for oneself and for others should be analyzed in relation to the compromise effect.

One is more familiar with the needs and conditions of people with whom one is friends or with whom one frequently communicates. When people make choices for those with whom they are intimate, they are confident that their decisions will take into account the preferences of the latter. Hence, making choices for people to whom one is not close and with whom one communicates infrequently will result in greater uncertainty, and decision makers may easily overestimate unknown negative outcomes and tend to choose the middle option as the safe one.

Making choices for others is deeply influenced by interpersonal relationships. Bearden and Etzel (1982) stated that susceptibility to interpersonal influence can be defined as an individual's willingness to accept information from other people about purchase decisions. Then, that the compromise effect will greater among those who are highly susceptible to interpersonal influence.

Accountability leads people to be more concerned about decision accuracy and helps strengthen the beliefs of decision makers. It increases decision accuracy because the need to justify past decisions leads decision makers to engage in more unbiased evaluation of alternatives (Tetlock 1983) and to focus more on cues (Johnson and Kaplan 1991). In addition, accountability leads people to consider additional relevant evidence and improve their estimates (Kruglanski and Freund 1983).

Anticipation of regret is used to examine the prediction. It refers to the regret that consumers anticipate that they will feel if their decision results in negative outcomes. Cox and Rich (1967) proposed that risk is composed of negative consequence and uncertainty. However, choosing for others induces anticipation of regret, compared to no anticipation of regret, will correspond to an increase in the fear of making a wrong choice (negative outcome) and result in the greater likelihood of choosing the compromise option as the safe option.

Because of the influence of interpersonal relations, it is useful to investigate whether people will be more inclined to choose a compromise option to reduce the effect of the loss or tend to choose what they favor when choosing for others. Building on the findings of Simonson (1989), this paper aims to uncover the underlying mechanisms of the self-other difference in the compromise effect.

## Study 1

The goal of Study 1 was to test the hypothesis that the compromise effect is greater when choosing for others than for oneself. Two factors were manipulated in a 2 X 2 (self or others vs. either two or three options in the choice set) between-participants design. A total of 160 undergraduate and graduate students participated in Study 1. In the experiment, participants were randomly assigned to two conditions (self or others), and in these two conditions randomly assigned to a binary (A, B–two alternatives) or trinary (A, B, C–three alternatives) scenario to choose for themselves or others.

The results confirmed our hypotheses. It is show that choosing for others leads to a greater compromise effect compared to choosing for oneself.

## Study 2

To broaden the knowledge of others, Study 2 tests whether the level of intimacy of a relationship influences the compromise effect, and whether this influence depends on the level of susceptibility to interpersonal influence of the decision maker. Participants were randomly assigned to one of eight cells in a 2 (two or three options in the choice set) X 4 (target person: self, family member, friend, or classmate) between-participants design. A total of 120 undergraduate students participated in this experiment.

The results support the prediction that the compromise effect varies with the level of intimacy of the relationship with others of the decision maker, and is not as different among those with a low level of susceptibility compared to those with a high level of susceptibility.

## Study 3

Study 3 examined the effect of accountability on the choice of the middle option. Participants were randomly assigned to one of eight cells in a 2 (two or three options in the choice set) X 2 (self or others) X 2 (accountability or no accountability) between-participants design. A total of 320 students participated in this experiment.

The results support the hypotheses. The findings of study show that the compromise effect when choosing for others is weaker under the accountability condition than under the no accountability one.

## Study 4

The goal of this experiment was to test the impact of the anticipation of regret (negative outcome) on the compromise effect. Participants were randomly assigned to one of eight cells in a 2 (two or three options in the choice set) X 2 (self or others) X 2 (anticipation of regret or no anticipation of regret) between-participants design. A total of 320 students participated in this experiment.

The results are as expected, the compromise effect in choosing for others is significantly greater in the anticipation of regret than in the no anticipation of regret condition.

## General Discussion

The purpose of this paper is to explore the relationship between self-other difference and the compromise effect. This research can explaining why one has chosen one product over another for someone else makes one more concerned about decision accuracy. It also helps strengthen the beliefs of decision makers such that they will be less likely to choose the compromise option. In addition, this paper has general implications for the marketing of new and existing products. The positioning of new products, especially those often bought for others (e.g., gifts, souvenirs, domestic products) could focus on developing the average attributes to avoid the product becoming the extreme option. For existing products, sales staff could be trained to ask consumers for whom they are buying and then give appropriate advice.

## References

Abelson, Robert (1964), The Choice of Choice Theory in Decision and Choice, New York: McGraw-Hill.
Bearden, William O. and Michael J. Etzel, (1982), "Reference group Influence on Product and Brand Purchase Decisions," Journal of Consumer Research, 9, 183-194.
Bell, David E. (1983), "Risk Premiums for Decision Regret," Management Science, 29, 1156-1166.
Bettman, James R., Mary Frances Luce, and John W. Payne (1998), "Constructive Consumer Choice Processes," Journal of Consumer Research, 25, 187-217.
Cox, Donald F. (1967), Risk Taking and Information Handling in Consumer Behavior, Boston: Harvard University Press, 1-22, 604-639.
Festinger, Leon (1957), Theory of Cognitive Dissonance, Standford University Press.
Hall, C. S. and Lindzey, G (1978), Theories of Personality, New York: John Wiley.
Johnson,Van E. and Steven E. Kaplan (1991), "Experimental Evidence on the Effects of Accountability on Auditor Judgments," Journal of Accounting Research, 35, 227-237.
Kruglanski, Arie W. and Tallie Freund (1983), "The Freezing and Unfreezing of Lay-inferences: Effects on Impressional Primacy, Ethnic Stereotyping and Numerical Anchoring," Experimental Social Psychology, 19, 448-468.
Simonson, Itamar (1989), "Choice Based on Reasons: The Case of Attraction and Compromise Effects," Journal of Consumer Research, 16, 158-74.
Tetlock, Philip E. (1983), "Accountability and Complexity of Thought," Journal of Personality & Social Psychology, 45, 74-83.

# Skill- versus Effort-Based Difficulty: The Role of Emotion in Motivating Difficult Actions
Kirsten Passyn, Salisbury University, USA
Mita Sujan, Tulane University, USA

## Extended Abstract
Health protection campaigns have traditionally relied on fear appeals to promote behaviors. These campaigns have also demonstrated the necessity of self-efficacy and the particular problems of motivating difficult behaviors (Sturges & Rogers, 1996; Keller & Block, 1996). For difficult behaviors, for which individuals generally have low self-efficacy, fear appeals have been found to be particularly ineffective.

More recent research has looked at the motivating influence of other emotions over fear including anger, (Lerner & Keltner, 2000, 2001), pride (Higgins et al, 2001) and regret (Zeelenberg & Pieters, 2007). Specifically, in the health domain Passyn & Sujan (2006) found the motivated action response of regret which is to prevent or correct wrongs, to be more effective at motivating simple health-preventative behaviors, such as using sunscreen and choosing high fiber foods, than fear with its action response to avoid or deny. Higgins et al. found that pride was positively related to diet maintenance. However, the conditions of the study were an imagined diet and an imagined piece of pizza likely limiting perceptions of task difficulty.

This research makes several important contributions to understanding task difficulty. First, we delineate the independence of the constructs of self-efficacy and task difficulty. These constructs have often been confounded in research as procedures used to enhance perceptions of self-efficacy typically make the task less difficult resulting in the constructs being treated as synonymous (Hu, Huhman, & Hyman, 2007). However, we show that perceptions of task difficulty and perceptions of self-efficacy are indeed independent. Second, we distinguish among different types of task difficulty. Based on the aptitude versus effort distinction for outcomes, we forward the argument that a task can be perceived as difficult for two main reasons: a task can be perceived as difficult because it requires skill–skill-based difficulty–or because it requires exerting effort–effort-based difficulty.

The main purpose of this research is to understand what type of emotions best spur different types of difficult health behaviors. Specifically, we examine if anticipated regret for the mistake and the heightened potential for failure–and hence regret–when task effort-difficulty is made salient will erase self-efficacy doubts, and motivate effortful action. In addition, we examine if anticipated pride for task accomplishment and the heightened potential for pride when the behavior is considered challenging will erase self-efficacy doubts, and motivate challenging action. In pretests and two studies, we examine the effectiveness of these emotions in comparison to each other and fear. The first study compares the effectiveness of fear versus regret at motivating simple versus effortful behaviors in the context of condom usage. The second study compares regret and pride at motivating simple, effortful, versus challenging behaviors in the context of CPR training.

Surveys (Essien, Ross, Eugiena, & Williams 2006) suggest that condom usage on campus is so low because young adults find it too effortful to interrupt the mood and say, "We need to use a condom." Study one a 2(emotion: fear versus regret) X 2 (task difficulty: easy versus effortful) demonstrates how consumers can be motivated to act when taking action is effortful. A pretest confirmed that undergraduate students report that condoms are effective protection against STDs. Furthermore, we document the reality of "in-the-moment" feelings during a sexual encounter at heightening task effort difficulty, reducing perceptions of self-efficacy, and intentions to use condoms. The results of study 1 confirm our predictions that regret will motivate effortful behaviors with a task difficulty x emotion interaction ($F(1, 67)=5.87, p<.02$). Specifically, we replicate the general finding of Protection Motivation Theory that under conditions of fear, increasing the salience of the difficulty of the task significantly decreases perceptions of self-efficacy ($M_{fear-control}=3.68$ vs. $M_{fear-difficult}=2.76; t(67)=3.24, p<.01$) and behavioral intentions (($t(67)=1.92, p<.05; M_{fear-control}=5.45$ vs. $M_{fear-difficult}=4.14$). However, under conditions of regret, we find a reversal effect; increasing the salience of the difficulty of the task, significantly enhances perceptions of self-efficacy($M_{regret-control}=3.77$ vs. $M_{regret-difficult}=4.30; t(67)=2.56, p<.01$) and behavioral intentions ($t(67)=1.95, p<.05; M_{regret-control}=6.97$ vs. $M_{regret-difficult}=8.12$). Thus not only is regret robust in its ability to promote both easy and effortful behaviors, but the motivational impact of regret is improved under conditions that make the task effort-difficulty salient.

Study 2 is a 2(emotion: pride versus guilt) X 3 (task difficulty: easy versus skill-based versus effort-based) between-subjects design. Half the participants were primed by words that cue pride (mastery type words) and the other half by words that cue regret (repentance type words). In an "unrelated" study that follows, participants were asked to sign up for a CPR class. Administering CPR was described as potentially life saving in all conditions to produce the necessary level of arousal for emotion and action. In addition CPR was described as easy (for 1/3 of the participants), described as a difficult skill that not everyone can perform correctly (for 1/3 of the participants), or described as needing significant time commitment (for 1/3 of the participants). Pretests confirmed that the priming tasks produced felt pride and regret and that the three descriptions of CPR resulted in easy, skillful, and effortful assessments of task difficulty. Although, data collection and analysis is still in progress preliminary results confirm that as in study one regret results in a reversal effect under conditions of effort-based task difficulty, with significantly enhanced perceptions of self-efficacy, increased behavioral intentions and increased behavior (as measured by on-line signing up for CPR courses). In addition, pride also results in a reversal effect for skill-based task difficulty, with significantly enhanced perceptions of self-efficacy, increased behavioral intentions, and increased behaviors. However, regret was not effective at motivating skill-based task difficulty and pride was not effective at motivating effort-based task difficulty.

In summary, the big impact of this research is finding how to best motivate big health behaviors, those that require a big effort are best motivated by regret, those that require big time skills are best motivated by pride.

## Selected References

Passyn, K., & Sujan, M. (2006). Self-Accountability emotions and fear appeals: Motivating behavior. Journal of Consumer Research 32, 583-589.

Sturges, J. W. & Rogers R.W. (1996). Preventive health psychology from a developmental perspective: An extenuation of protection motivation theory. Health Psychology, 15, 158-166.

Higgins, T.H., Friedman, F.S., Harlow, R.E., Idson, L.S., Ayduk, O.A., & Taylor A. (2001). Achievement orientations and subjective histories of success: promotion pride versus prevention pride. European Journal of Social Psychology, 31, 3-23.

Hu, J. Humann, B.A., & Hyman M. R. (2007). The relationship between task complexity and information search: The role of self-efficacy. Psychology & Marketing. 24, 253-270.

Keller, P.A. & Block, L.G. (1996). Increasing the persuasiveness of fear appeals: The effect of arousal and elaboration. Journal of Consumer Research, 22, 448-459.

Lerner, J.S., & Keltner, D. (2001). Fear, anger, and risk. Journal of Personality and Social Psychology, 81, 146-159.

Zeelenberg, M. & Pieters R. (2007). A theory of regret regulation 1.0. Journal of Consumer Psychology, 17, 3-18.

# Emotion in Isolation: Crossing Valence with Certainty Leads to Unexpected Results

Julian Saint Clair, University of Washington, USA

## Extended Abstract

Emotions have multiple dimensions (Smith & Ellsworth, 1985; see Han et al., 2007 for a review). One such dimension receiving more recent attention is that of certainty. A positive relationship between emotional certainty and risk taking has been demonstrated (e.g. Raghunathan & Pham, 1999; Lerner & Keltner, 2001). Specifically, the experience of emotional certainty reverses the pervasive risk-aversion tendency for gains while uncertainty reverses the risk-seeking tendency for losses.

Two theories have been proffered to explain these results: one states that certainty influences motivation via mood regulation goals (Raghunathan & Pham, 1999), the other states that certainty influences risk perceptions (i.e. optimism; Lerner & Keltner, 2001). The present study tests these two theories by isolating and manipulating the dimensions of interest rather than priming specific emotions. Results show that neither theory is sufficient. Instead, certainty is interacting with valence in an unpredicted fashion.

Specifically, it appears that while certainty is indeed impacting perceptions of risk, valence is determining which outcome is receiving the subjects' certain/uncertain attention. This theoretical explanation put forward to explain this interaction is that negative (positive) valence leads to increased (decreased) depth of processing, causing subjects to focus attention on less (more) salient aspects of the decision task – the more salient possibilities of gains and losses vs. the less salient possibilities of non-gains and non-losses.

In the remainder of this document, I describe the above statements in more detail. I summarize the two previous theories and the results they are based on, I describe the present study and outline the theoretical predictions, and I report the unexpected results and describe the new explanatory theory.

### Certainty and Mood Regulation Goals

*Raghunathan & Pham, 1999.* Across three studies, Negative/Uncertainty (Anxiety) primed subjects selected risk-averse choices for gains (i.e. prefer a 6/10 chance to win $5 vs. 3/10 chance to win $10). The choice was theorized to be motivated by the underlying mood regulation goal of Uncertainty Reduction.

Comparatively, the authors also demonstrated that Negative/Certainty (Sadness) primed subjects selected risk-seeking choices for gains (i.e. the 3/10 chance to win $10). It is contended that sadness, associated with loss or absence of reward (Lazarus, 1991), results in reward seeking behavior motivated by the mood regulation goal of Mood Repair.

### Certainty and Risk Perception

*Lerner & Keltner, 2001.* Using the classic Asian Disease Problem, subjects primed with Negative/Uncertainty (Fear; Negative/Certainty: Anger) were risk-averse (risk-seeking) across choices framed as gains as well as choices framed as losses, preferring the sure (risky) gain and the sure (risky) loss. The explanation was that the sense of uncertainty (certainty) associated with fear (anger) leads to perceptions of high (low) risk (i.e. pessimism/optimism). This in turn causes subjects to focus on worst (best) case scenarios and prefer the riskless (risky) options. To support their theory, the authors showed in a separate study that increased certainty led to increased optimism

### The Present Study and Predictions

Is the certainty dimension impacting perceptions of risk or is it impacting mood regulation goals?

In our study, we simply crossed valence by certainty in a 2 (positive/negative) by 2 (certain/uncertain) between subjects design. Rather than cloud the results by using specific emotions with varying underlying dimensional properties, we isolated the dimensions of interest by directly manipulated emotional certainty and valence themselves. For example, we asked subjects to describe in detail an emotional event in which they felt extremely negative and uncertain. We then administered the 'Financial Decision Making' task as an onstensible filler task before a manipulation check, suspicion probe, and demographics questions completed the study. The decision task was similar to Raghunathan and Pham (1999), e.g. 60% chance to win (lose) $5 vs. 30% chance to win (lose) $10.

Both the 'mood regulation goals' theory and the 'risk perceptions' theory would predict that negative/certainty (vs. negative/uncertainty) leads to increased risk taking for losses and gains. However, they have differing predictions for *positive* emotions. Specifically, due to 'mood maintenance' goals, mood regulation theory would predict that positive/certainty (vs. positive/uncertainty) would lead to decreased risk-taking for gains and increased risk-taking for losses. Risk perception theory would predict no difference between gains and losses – that positive/certainty leads to increased risk-taking for both.

### Results and Discussion

*Gains.* Subjects in the positive/certain (vs. positive/uncertain) were more risk-seeking, choosing the 30% $10 gain more often than the 60% $5 gain. Subjects in the negative condition were the exact opposite. Negative/certain (vs. negative/uncertain) were *less* risk seeking.

*Losses.* Subjects in the negative/certain (vs. negative/uncertain) were more risk-seeking, choosing the 30% $10 loss over the 60% $5 loss. The positive-valence subjects were the opposite: positive/certain (vs. positive/uncertain) subjects were *less* risk seeking.

These actual results supported neither the Mood Regulation Theory nor the Risk Perceptions Theory as conceptualized by previous research. However, the results are consistent with a new theoretical framework wherein depth of processing interacts with risk perceptions. This interaction is further described below.

I manipulated 2 dimensions that have been shown to impact both content of processing and depth of processing. The content of processing argument is what I sought to test: do these dimensions affect content via Mood Regulation Theory or Risk Perceptions Theory? However, it is possible that I actually influenced *depth* of processing as well as content, and results show that the two interact.

Results suggest that certainty simply influenced cognition in a manner consistent with risk perceptions theory: subjects who felt more certain perceived 'unlikely' events as more likely. However, the events on which subjects directed this certain/uncertain attention seemed to be moderated by the depth of processing caused by valence (see Schwarz, Bless, and Bohner, 1991 for a review on valence and processing). Results suggest that subjects in the positive valence conditions attended more to surface cues (i.e. heuristic processing) while those in negative valence conditions attended to information implied but not overtly highlighted (i.e. systematic processing).

Specifically, subjects in positive valence conditions focused their attention on the highlighted possibilities of gains and losses while subjects in the negative valence conditions attended to the implied possibilities of non-gains and non-losses.

# Retail Therapy or Rose-Tinted Glasses? The Effect of Mood on Impulse Buying
Debra Trampe, University of Groningen, The Netherlands

## Extended Abstract

Opportunities to give in to the sudden impulse to buy have never been more abundant. Marketing developments like 24-hour retailing, outlet stores, credit cards, and online shopping make it easier than ever for consumers to purchase products or services when they experience the impulse to do so. Paralleling consumers' often heard claim that they were "overwhelmed by an irresistible impulse to buy" (Rook 1987) are estimations that impulsive consumption annually accounts for over $4 billion of sales in the US alone (Mogelonsky, 1998). At the same time, household debts are at an unprecedented high and show no sign of diminishing (Vohs & Faber 2007). Considering its potentially self-destructive nature, increasing our insight into impulse buying is essential.

Though a number of factors that may contribute to impulse buying have been investigated, one important but relatively understudied factor is mood. Ironically, in recent reviews of the relevant literature, impulse buying has been related to positive as well as negative mood states. Consumers are more likely to act on their buying impulses when they are in a positive mood … and when they are in a negative mood (Rook and Gardner 1993; Silvera, Lavack, and Kropp 2008). How is that possible? We argue that people may engage in impulse buying to repair negative moods, whereas in positive moods impulse buying may occur because happy consumers are more likely to act relatively capriciously and carefree. And indeed, shoppers report making impulsive purchases to alter an unpleasant mood (Baumeister 2002; Silvera, Lavack, and Kropp 2008), reflecting the idea of "retail therapy". Also, research on self-gifting (Mick and DeMoss 1990) has observed that consumers tend to indulge after stress or depression by acquiring self-gifts. Conversely, impulse buying in positive mood states seems common as well. For example, when a group of consumers were asked to select the one mood that would be most likely to encourage them to make an impulse purchase, "pleasure" was most frequently named, followed by "carefree" and "excitement" (Rook and Gardner 1993). On a more general level, research has shown that objects are typically evaluated more positively when individuals are in a positive rather than a negative mood (Cohen, Pham, and Andrade 2008; Gardner 1995). Thus, a positive affective state may make mood congruent associations more accessible, and the offerings consumers encounter to be evaluated more positively, which in turn leads consumers to engage in impulsive purchasing. Stated otherwise, consumers can at times engage in mood-congruent behavior, by looking at the (consumption) world through so-called "rose-tinted glasses."

In three experiments we aim to clarify the role of mood in impulse buying and uncover the mechanisms at work in positive and negative moods in promoting impulse buying. As experimental research is still lacking, our first goal is to offer a straightforward demonstration that both positive and negative moods compared to a control condition would increase impulse buying tendencies. Our second goal is to shed more light on the mechanisms underlying the positive and negative antecedents of impulse buying. We hypothesize that increased impulse buying results from a motivation to improve one's mood, whereas increased impulse buying in a positive mood is driven by mood-congruent behavior. This hypothesis should manifest itself in at least two ways: first, the type of products that are bought on impulse in positive and negative moods should differ. As hedonic products provide more fun and pleasure and more so than utilitarian products trigger an urge for immediate consumption (Dhar and Wertenbroch 2000), consumers in a negative mood (vs. a positive mood) should be more likely to impulse buy hedonic products. Utilitarian products are primarily functional and instrumental and hence the likelihood that they are bought on impulse should not differ between positive and negative moods. Second, the motivational component in impulse buying in response to negative moods should make it more goal-directed in nature than impulse buying in response to positive moods. Goal-directed behavior is known to be different from non-goal-directed behavior: it is persistent through obstacles, it increases following a delay, and decreases when the goal is fulfilled (Förster, Liberman, and Freedman 2007). Thus, if impulse buying in negative moods is a motivational process, impulse buying tendencies should be larger after a delay than immediately after the mood induction.

In the first two experiments, following Vohs and Faber (2007), impulse buying was conceptualized as willingness to pay (WTP). In Study 1, both positive and negative moods, relative to a control condition, were found to increase WTP for a number of diverse products. In Study 2, we differentiated between hedonic and utilitarian products. Results showed that the pattern for utilitarian products replicated Study 1: both positive and negative moods enhanced WTP, compared with a control condition. For hedonic products, however, the pattern was different. For hedonic products, a negative mood produced higher WTP compared to both a positive and a control mood. The latter two conditions did not differ in WTP for hedonic products. In Study 3, the impulse buying measurement was modeled after Rook and Fisher (1995). Participants were presented with a scenario that described a shopping situation with an opportunity to make an impulse purchase. They then indicated their level of impulsive urge and buying behavior. In addition, Study 3 also explored the moderating role of trait impulsiveness. Using a 3 (mood: positive vs. negative vs. control) x 2 (delay: yes vs. no) between-subjects design, participants in a negative mood experienced stronger urges to buy after a delay and indicated that they were more likely to make an impulse purchase than participants in the no-delay condition. For participants in a positive and neutral mood, there was no such difference.

As impulse buying has been suggested to account for up to 80% of all purchases in certain categories (Kacen and Lee 2002), insight into this widespread phenomenon is imperative. This research focused on the role of mood in impulse buying and illustrates that (1) both positive and negative mood states enhance impulse buying relative to neutral moods, and (2) the mechanisms underlying both mood states differ profoundly.

References

Baumeister, Roy F. (2002), "Yielding to Temptation: Self-Control Failure, Impulsive Purchasing, and Consumer Behavior," *Journal of Consumer Research, 28, 670-76.*

Cohen, Joel B., Michel Tuan Pham, and Eduardo B. Andrade (2008), The Nature and Role of Affect in Consumer Behavior," In *Handbook of Consumer Psychology*, ed. Curtis P. Haugtvedt, Paul Herr, and Frank Kardes, Mahwah, NJ: Erlbaum, 297-348.

Dhar, Ravi and Klaus Wertenbroch (2000), "Consumer Choice Between Hedonic and Utilitarian Goods," *Journal of Marketing Research,* 37, 60-71.

Förster, Jens, Nira Liberman, and Ronald S. Freedman (1999), "Seven Principles of Goal Activation: A Systematic Approach to Distinguishing Goal Priming from Priming of Non-goal Constructs," *Personality and Social Psychology Review*, 11 (3), 211-35.

Gardner, Meryl Paula (1995), "Mood States and Consumer Behavior: A Critical Review," *Journal of Consumer Research,* 12, 281-300.

Kacen, Jacqueline J. and Julie Anne Lee (2002), "The Influence of Culture on Consumer Impulsive Buying Behavior," *Journal of Consumer Psychology,* 12 (2), 163-76.

Mick, David Glen and Michelle DeMoss (1990), "Self-Gifts: Phenomenological Insights from Four Contexts," *Journal of Consumer Research,* 17, 322-32.

Mogelonsky, Marcia (1998), "Keep Candy in the Aisles," *American Demographics,* 20, 32.

Rook, Dennis W. (1987), "The Buying Impulse", *Journal of Consumer Research* 14, 189-99.

_____ and Robert J. Fisher (1995), "Normative Influences on Impulsive Behavior," *Journal of Consumer Research,* 22, 305-13.

_____ and Meryl Paula Gardner (1993), "In the Mood: Impulse Buying's Affective Consequences," *Research in Consumer Behavior,* 6, 1-28.

Silvera, David H., Anne M. Lavack, and Frederic Kropp (2008), "Impulse Buying: The Role of Affect, Social Influence, and Subjective Well-Being," *Journal of Consumer Marketing,* 25 (1), 23-33.

Vohs, Kathleen D. and Ronald J. Faber (2007), "Spent Resources: Self-Regulatory Resource Availability Affects Impulse Spending," *Journal of Consumer Research,* 33, 537-47.

# When Is It Better To Be Bad? Schema-Congruency Effects in Moral Evaluations of Products

Jennifer S. Danilowitz, Yale University, USA

George E. Newman, Yale University, USA

## Extended Abstract

All things being equal, people prefer good things over bad. People seek pleasure, and avoid pain (Bentham 1779, James 1890, Higgins 1997). Within psychology, the approach-avoidance hierarchy has dominated the motivation literature (Elliot 2006). Perception researchers have shown that stimuli are classified into positive and negative with only 30 milliseconds of subliminal presentation (Stapel, Koomen & Ruys, 2002, Osgood 1955). Across multiple disciplines, people are believed to quickly classify targets into high level categories of "good/approach" and "bad/avoid".

Managers have embraced this perspective in their marketing communication tactics. Brands spend hundreds of millions of dollars each year on celebrity endorsements, with the logic of associating their product with a persona that consumers already like to gain some halo affect. Recent events have shown that if a spokesperson's image shifts to bad or immoral, mangers are quick to disassociate themselves from the disgraced endorser. Yet is it always the case that any association with an immoral figure is bad for a product? The present research proposes that in certain cases a product may benefit from association with an immoral persona.

Previous research has demonstrated that individuals' appraisals of a new product may be dependent on the degree to which the product's features and the activated category schema are congruent (Aggarawal and McGill 2007; Meyers-Levy and Tybout 1989). In general, objects that are schema congruent are evaluated more favorably than objects that are schema incongruent because people tend to like objects that conform to their expectations. People may transfer positive affect about the fit between the product's features and their beliefs about the category (e.g., satisfaction for schema congruent products) to the object itself (Fiske 1982).

Consistent with the findings of previous schema congruency research, we hypothesized that consumers would be more likely to prefer vice products invented by immoral creators as compared to vice products invented by moral creators or virtue products invented by immoral creators. Specifically, if a product is framed for use in a vice behavior context, we predict that consumers will be more interested in purchasing it when it was created by an immoral person.

The present studies directly tested the effects of a product's moral history on consumer preferences. Across four studies we manipulated the moral history of the product and the product's framing. In study 1 participants read a story describing the inventor of an energy drink as moral or immoral, then were told that the energy drink was intended to "provide the extra energy needed for studying for exams and working hard (partying with friends and having fun) throughout the long hours of the night". The results of Study 1 support our predictions. Specifically, when a product (e.g., an energy drink) is positioned for use in a virtuous context, people prefer the moral inventor, $F (1,190)=6.92, p=.009, M_{study/moral}=3.82, M_{study/immoral}=2.82$). However, when the same product was framed in a vice behavior context (i.e., partying), participants instead preferred the product to have been invented by the immoral person compared to a moral person ($M_{party/moral}=2.25, M_{party/immoral}=2.78$).

We believe that Study 1 provides initial evidence for a congruency effect between the moral valence of the product's creator and the moral valence of a product's intended use, such that people prefer the immoral inventor when the drink is intended for a vice-like use. However, these results might be due to a general semantic priming of a vice-like frame of mind, which could result in increased purchase intent for any party aid. Another possibility is that people believe that an immoral inventor would make a better party-aid than a moral inventor–perhaps due to expertise on the part of the inventor in the behavioral domains. We conducted Study 2 in order to rule out these alternate explanations, and to investigate the role of similarity between inventor and framing as a possible mediator of the effect. In Study 2 participants read the same history and framing background story, but we added additional conditions so that some subjects were told that the manufacturer had been unable to secure the rights to that formula invented by the immoral(moral inventor), and instead was using a different recipe to produce the energy drink. The results indicate that participants prefer the energy drink as a party aid only when it was made from the EXACT FORMULA of the immoral inventor $F(1, 637)=5.36$, $p=.021$. Next, when probed for beliefs about the effectiveness of the drink at keeping them awake, subjects in the vice (virtuous) framing did not believe that the drink would be less effective for a virtuous (vice) activity, $(M_{party}=2.25, M_{study}=2.32, F(1,641)=2.38$, ns.). Study 2 replicated our initial findings, ruled out two major alternative explanations, and provides initial evidence of schema congruency as a mediator.

Study 3 replicated the effect in another domain: that of art and artists. Subjects were presented shown an ambiguous piece of art ("Tunnel") and the moral history of the artist and his intended framing of the art were manipulated. The predicted interaction emerged for history (moral, immoral, very immoral) X framing (positive or dark), $F(2,165)=3.02$, $p=.051$, providing further evidence that when products are framed in dark or vice ways, people tend to prefer immoral creators.

This congruency effect persists across multiple product domains and in spite of the fact that participants explicitly rate the immoral target as morally corrupt and unlikable. Therefore, in addition to providing a test of the effects of moral judgments on product evaluations, these studies provide some of the first experimental evidence that in certain contexts, people may prefer products associated with immoral individuals. These patterns are interpreted within the broader framework of essentialism and schema congruency, and the implications for marketing, social policy and academic theory are discussed.

## Selected References

Aggarwal, P., & McGill, A. L. (2007). Is that car smiling at me? Schema congruity as a basis for evaluating anthropomorphized products. *Journal of Consumer Research, 34*(4), 468-479.

Bentham, J. (1779/1879). *Introduction to the principles of morals and legislation*. Oxford: Clarendon Press.

Fiske, S. T. (1982). Schema-triggered affect: Applications to social perception. In M. S. Clark & S. T. Fiske (Eds.), Affect and cognition: The 17th Annual Carnegie Symposium on Cognition (pp. 55-78). Hillsdale, NJ: Erlbaum.

Gelman, Susan ( 2005). "Essentialism in Everyday Thought," *Psychological Science Agenda* Volume 19: No. 5.

Gray, H., Gray, K., Wegner D. (2007) "Dimensions of Mind Perception" *Science* Vol 315 2 February 2007.

Haidt, J. (2001). The emotional dog and its rational tail: A social intuitionist approach to moral judgment. *Psychological Review. 108*, 814-834.

Higgins, E. T. (1997). "Beyond pleasure and pain," *American Psychologist*, 52, 1280–1300.

James, W. (1890). *The Principles of Psychology* (vol. 2). NY: Henry Holt & Co.

Joyce, R. (2006) "Is human morality innate?" in P. Carruthers, S. Laurence, & S. Stich (eds.), *The Innate Mind: Culture and Cognition*, Oxford University Press, 257-279.

Meyers-Levy, J., & Tybout, A. M. (1989). Schema congruity as a basis for product evaluation. *The Journal of Consumer Research, 16*(1), 39-54.

Osgood, Charles E.; Suci, George J., (1955) "Factor analysis of meaning," *Journal of Experimental Psychology*. Vol 50(5), 325-338.

Ruedy & Schweitzer (2009). Cheaters Never Win? Affective Consequences of Unethical Behavior. Poster at Association for Consumer Research Conference, Pittsburg, PA.

Stapel, D. A., Koomen, W., & Ruys, K. I. (2002). "The effects of diffuse and distinct affect," *Journal of Personality and Social Psychology, 83*, 60–74.

# Anchoring Unveiled

Jennifer S. Danilowitz, Yale University, USA
Shane Frederick, Yale University, USA
Daniel Mochon, Yale University, USA

## Extended Abstract

Nearly all studies of anchoring ask participants to first make a comparative judgment, and then render an estimate. Within this paradigm, the dominant psychological account of anchoring is that people actively compare their estimate to the anchor, thereby increasing the accessibility of anchor consistent information (Strack and Mussweiler 1997). A second account suggests a more deliberate process in which people start with the anchor value, and then adjust it until the proximate boundary of plausible ranges is reached (Jacowitz and Kahneman 1995). A third account implicates the conversational norm that provided information is relevant (Grice 1975, Schwarz 1999).

Though anchoring effects have been found even in contexts that should help control for some of these possibilities (like the use of manifestly random anchors, Tversky and Kahneman 1974), little work has attempted to assess the comparative influence of these different forces either between or within studies.

The present research is intended to test the comparative importance of these mechanisms in the traditional paradigm. We manipulated the source of the anchor and quantified the magnitude of the anchoring effect. In condition A, anchors were manifestly unrelated to the comparative question: they were generated by the participants (e.g. by taking a bill out of their wallet and entering the first two digits of the serial number as the anchor). This design was intended to minimize inferences about the informational value of the anchor. The other three conditions were "yoked" to the numbers these respondents self generated, resulting in 90 perfectly yoked "quartets". Within each quartet, for each value entered by a participant in condition A there was one and only one condition B, C and D participant who saw that value as their respective anchors. In condition B, the yoked anchors were provided and the instructions indicated (falsely) that the anchor was randomly generated by the computer. In condition C, there was no mention of anchor origin included in the instructions, but the anchors were presented in red and participants had to re-type the value. In the final condition D, the anchor appeared as a comparative question, as in the traditional paradigm.

Each respondent made 6 judgments. Because each value generated in Condition A was a two digit number, the judgments were chosen such that the range of possible answers was naturally bounded between 0 and 100. Three of the questions asked for a percent estimate, and three of the questions asked for estimates where the only possible answers would be between 0 and 100. Specifically, the six items were:

1.  Is the percentage of American adults who have a passport higher or lower than that number?

2.  Is the number of U.S. senators who have law degrees higher or lower than that number?

3.  Is the percentage of adults in the world who are Christian higher or lower than that number?

4.  Last year, was the average interception return in the National Football League higher or lower than that number of yards?

5.  Among all Major League Baseball players currently playing, is the percentage who are married higher or lower than that number?

6.  During the last century in the U.S., is the number of years in which Michael was the most common name for baby boys higher or lower than that number?

To compare the strength of an anchor's influence on the estimates across conditions, we regressed numeric judgments against anchor values and measured the size of the coefficient. For the transparently random anchor condition A, there was a small but significant positive relationship between anchor and estimate; $b_A$=.08, $SE$=.03, $p$<.01. For conditions B and C the anchor interaction term also predicted the estimates in a positive direction, and the relationship is slightly steeper than in condition A, 1; $b_B$=.11, $SE$=.05, $p$<.01, and $b_C$=.13, $SE$=.05, $p$<.01. Finally, condition D, which closely mirrors the traditional comparative anchoring paradigm, showed the strongest effect of anchor on the estimate, $b_D$= .25, $SE$=.05, $p$<.01. In a secondary analysis, we also observed an interaction between question type and anchoring effect. There was markedly less anchoring for items involving a percentage response than items involving a count, even though for both types all responses ranged from 0 to 99.

In sum the values ranged from a small (but significant) value of 0.08 in the "dollar bill" condition to 0.25 in the "standard" paradigm. Conditions B and C yielded similar results and the results were intermediate. These findings suggest that in the standard paradigm, inference plays a very substantial role in generating the anchoring effect, and increases the size of the effect threefold.

**Key Results**
    Condition A–*Anchor is generated by participants and transparently irrelevant.* Effect: *b=.08*
    Condition B–*Instructions explain that anchors are "randomly generated".* Effect: *b=.11*
    Condition C-*Anchor is presented in odd font/color and had to be retyped.* Effect: *b=.13*
    Condition D-*Anchor included in the comparative question.* Effect: *b=.25*
    *All p's <.01*

**Selected References**

Grice, H. P. (1975). Logic and conversation. In P. Cole & J. Morgan (Eds.), *Syntax and semantics 3: Speech acts* (pp. 41–58). New York: Academic Press.

Jacowitz, K. E., & Kahneman, D. (1995). Measures of anchoring in estimation tasks. *Personality Social Psychology Bulletin*, 21, 1161–1166.

Schwarz, N. (1999). Self-reports: How the questions shape the answers. *American Psychologist, 54*, 93-105.

Strack, F., & Mussweiler, T. (1997). Explaining the enigmatic anchoring effect: Mechanisms of selective accessibility. *Journal of Personality and Social Psychology*, 73, 437-446.

Tversky, A., & Kahneman, D. (1974). Judgment under uncertainty: heuristics and biases. *Science*, 185, 1124-1131.

# Aligning Consumers Around Low-carbon Competitiveness:
# Evidence from an Online Experiment
Julia Joo-A Lee, Harvard Kennedy School, USA

Behavioral change in consumer demand is not only critical in determining the size of an individual's carbon footprint, but also motivates business leaders to respond to increased climate-awareness among consumers by supplying lower carbon products. Thus, many public and non-profit organizations are concerned with creating credible and reliable messages that will help motivate consumers to change their consumption decision-making and to reduce their carbon footprint. This study addresses an important question of how behavioral economics could encourage more environmentally sustainable consumer behavior. The goal of this study is to improve the ways in which government and non-profit organizations communicate consumption and climate-related information to consumers.

What are the factors that influence change in consumer behavior? First of all, a consumer's need for more information in part confirms what the standard economic theory of the rational choice model predicts: consumers should have access to sufficient information to make optimal, informed decisions about available options (Bord et al. 2000; Viscusi & Zeckhauser, 2006; Fischer, 2008). However, providing more information to the public does not necessarily change the consumer's environmentally significant behavior. Among the many reasons for the difficulty in behavioral change, including cognitive and motivated biases that distort how people process information, recent research found that emotions could powerfully influence individual processing of information and decision-making related to climate change (Leiserowitz, 2007).

Drawing on the recent theoretical and empirical developments in the study of emotions, this research project is designed to test whether incidental emotions such as guilt and shame can elicit different degrees of pro-environmental consumption behavior. Due to the difficulty in observing consumer behavioral change directly, it is important to identify dependent variables that are strong predictors of behavioral change in environmental decision-making; i) consumer's willingness-to-pay (WTP) for more pro-environmental products, ii) consumer's perceived self-efficacy, measured by their willingness to address the climate change problems, and to act on their intentions. Given the two dependent variables, it was hypothesized that consumers who know their own carbon footprint to be higher than the national average are more likely to show higher measures of pro-environmental consumption behavioral predictors. It was also hypothesized that eliciting guilt prior to calculating carbon footprint is more effective in changing consumer behavior than eliciting shame.

One hundred participants were recruited using the subject pool at the Harvard Decision Science Lab, which ensured a reasonably representative subject population. A general introduction informed the subjects about the experimental procedure. Participants were notified that they would be asked to answer two different surveys that are unrelated. The format of the two surveys differed in order to enhance the "unrelatedness" of the two surveys.

In the first survey, all participants were randomly assigned to one of three different emotion conditions of the survey (guilt, shame, and control). The first two groups of participants were asked to complete the emotion induction exercise, which consists of a directed-writing task designed to manipulate their emotions. This study replicated the guilt and shame elicitation method developed and administered by Shaver et al. (1987) and Tangney (1996: p. 1259). This exercise asked participants to "describe in detail the one situation that has made you feel the most [guilty/ashamed]." In order to help participants bring up memories of the emotional experience more vividly, additional prompts were given. Questions included "Why did it happen? Describe as much detail as you can what you were feeling and thinking. How did you respond? What did you say, if anything, and how did you say it? What are the physical signs of guilt you showed, if any?" Participants in the control group received a set of neutral questions asking them to describe their emotions that they feel at the moment. These incidental emotions were unrelated to the subsequent questions asked in the second part of the survey.

The second part of the survey included measurement of one's own carbon footprint, using a link to a publicly available carbon footprint calculator. After reporting one's own carbon footprint, participants were also asked to compare their carbon footprint with the U.S. average of national carbon emissions, and then to report whether their footprint was above, or below, average. After completing this task, participants were asked to report their WTP for environmentally friendly products in percentage terms, as well as their PSE. Calculating one's own carbon footprint was designed to improve the external validity of this study by realistically measuring one's culpability.

Results from this study demonstrate that the mean dependent variables (WTP and PSE) differed for consumers who had done three different writing tasks (guilt, shame, and control). That is, consumers who received guilt induction had statistically significantly higher ratings of both WTP and PSE measures, compared to those who received shame induction. Also, the differences in WTP and PSE between guilt and shame conditions were more pronounced in the low-carbon group than in the high-carbon group. It is also important to note that the level of carbon footprint could be a boundary condition for the influence of emotional states on environmental decisions; unlike what was hypothesized, high-carbon consumers were not particularly different in their decisions from low-carbon consumers.

## References

Bord, R., O'Connor, R., & Fisher, A. 2000. "In what sense does the public need to understand global climate change?" *Public Understanding of Science,* 9(3): pp. 205-218.

Leiserowitz, A. 2007. "Communicating the risks of global warming: American risk perceptions, affective images and interpretive communities," in Moser, S. C., and Dilling, L. (eds.) *Creating a Climate for Change: Communicating Climate Change and Facilitating Social Change,* New York: Cambridge University Press.

Lerner, J. S., & Keltner, D. 2000. "Beyond valence: Toward a model of emotion-specific influences on judgment and choice," *Cognition & Emotion,* 14(4), 473–493.

Loewenstein, G. and Lerner J. S., 2003. "The role of affect on decision-making," in Richard D., Klaus, Scherer, and Goldsmith, H. H. eds., *The Handbook of Affective Science,* New York: Oxford University Press, pp. 619-642.

Meinhold, J. L. & Malkus, A. J. 2005. "Adolescent environmental behaviors: Can knowledge, attitudes, and self-efficacy make a difference?," *Environment and Behavior,* 37: pp. 511-532.

Niedenthal, P. M., Tangney, J. P., & Gavanski, I. 1994. "'If only I weren't' versus 'If only I hadn't': Distinguishing shame and guilt in counterfactual thinking," *Journal of Personality and Social Psychology,* 67: pp. 585-595.

Norgaard, K. M. 2009. "Cognitive and behavioral challenges in responding to climate change," *Background Paper to the 2010 World Development Report,* The World Bank, Policy Research Working Paper 4940, pp. 1-74.

Tangney, J. P. 1991. "Moral affect: The good, the bad, and the ugly," *Journal of Personality and Social Psychology,* 61(4): pp. 598-607.

Tangney, J. 2003. "Self-relevant emotions," in M. Leary & J. Tangney (eds.), *Handbook of Self and Identity.* New York: Guilford, pp. 384-400.

Tangney, J. P., Miller, R. S., Flicker, L, & Barlow, D. B. 1996. "Are shame, guilt, and embarrassment distinct emotions?," *Journal of Personality and Social Psychology*, 70: pp. 1256-1269.

# Hiding Guilt

Christina I. Anthony, University of Sydney, Australia
Elizabeth Cowley, University of Sydney, Australia
Mario Pandelaere, Ghent University, Belgium

Consider Jane who is shopping for a present for a friend's birthday party that evening. She gets distracted and ends up shopping for a new pair of jeans for herself. She hears an announcement, that the store will close in 5 minutes, and that customers need to make their way to the check out. She buys her new jeans, but did buy a present. Jane feels guilty about this transgression. Will this affect Jane's liking of her new jeans? This paper investigates whether feeling guilty affects the liking of the product that reminds people of a transgression. We propose that guilty people, compared to non-guilty people, will evaluate the jeans less favorably, but only if the jeans are visible after the transgression. Why? Because people believe that seeing the jeans will interfere with effective affect regulation efforts, therefore reducing their evaluation of the reminder. Our results provide the first insight into why people adopt covert coping behaviors, such as hiding the tainted product in the closet (Dahl, Honea, and Manchanda 2003).

Consumers engage in affect regulation to alleviate feelings of guilt, such as suppressing unwanted thoughts and feelings about the event (Tice and Bratslavsky 2000). Different strategies exist for this process (Gross 1998). The strategy chosen depends not only on the effectiveness of the tactic, but also on people's metacognitive intuitions regarding the perceived effectiveness of the strategy (Loewenstein 2007). Therefore, having the object involved in the transgression subsequently in sight, may be perceived as interfering with this process, and result in a devaluation of the object.

## Method

One hundred participants were randomly assigned to dyads. In the no-guilt condition, one member of each dyad was presented with a black pen and two green pens and asked to choose one and give another pen to the other dyad member. In the guilt-condition, the dyad member that was allowed to choose a pen was informed that participants with a green pen would have to stay 20 minutes longer than participants with a black pen. We expected participants to choose the black pen and to feel guilty. This is exactly what happened. Participants in the not guilty condition were not given a choice, nor were they aware of any differences in the timing of their condition.

Participants were assigned to one of the four conditions of a 2 (guilt: guilt, no guilt) X 2 (pen visibility: visible, not visible) design. There were two different color pens: green and black. Participants were informed that if they chose the green pen, they would not have to do an extra task, but that the person next to them would have to stay for an extra 20 minutes. However, if they chose the black pen, they would have to stay instead. A manipulation check confirmed that participants in the guilty condition felt more guilty than those in the not guilty condition.

Following the guilt manipulation, participants were required to complete a second consumer choice task During this task the pen was either removed, and participants completed the choices on a computer (not visible) or the pen was placed in a clear plastic pen holder beside the computer. Finally, participants evaluated the perceived cognitive difficulty of the consumer choice task, and evaluated the pen (0=very bad, 100=very good) as part of a general survey of the lab experience.

## Results

*Guilt Compliance Rate.* Overall, 87% of participants in the guilt condition chose the 'leave early' pen. Therefore, the analysis comprised of 87 participants.

*Pen Evaluation.* A 2 (guilt: guilt, no guilt) X 2 (pen visibility: visible, not visible) ANOVA conducted on participants pen evaluation revealed a significant interaction ($F(1, 83)=5.70, p<.02$). Guilty participants rated the pen less favorably when the pen was in sight ($M=66.96$) compared to out of sight ($M=81.74$). In contrast, in the non-guilty participants, participants rated the pen more favorably when visible after the pen choice task ($M=82.25$), compared to when the pen was removed from sight ($M=67.38$).

*Perceived Difficulty.* A 2 (guilt: guilt, no guilt) X 2 (pen visibility: visible, not visible) ANOVA conducted on participants perceived difficultly revealed a significant interaction ($F(1, 83)=3.70, p<.05$). Guilty participants rated found the binary choice task more difficult when the pen was visible, compared to the not visible condition. The perceived difficulty suggests that guilty participants with a visible reminder were engaged in more effortful affect regulation, which is cognitively taxing (Richards and Gross 2000).

## Discussion

We show that guilt may result in a less favorable evaluation of a reminder object when in sight. We propose that this occurs because guilty participants believe that a visible reminder interferes with attempts at affect regulation. Our current work examines whether the effect is driven by the pen in sight (interfering with affect regulation 'haunting effect') or the pen removed from sight (allowing for successful regulation). We did not include a subsequent measure of guilt in the present study. Alternatively, the reminder may merely support intuitive beliefs that thought suppression is an effective strategy for regulating guilt, regardless of whether there is an actual reduction in experienced guilt. If this is the case, we might expect a misattribution of anger to the reminder object due to perceptions of goal inhibition. Hence, we are also investigating how people monitor their progress when affectively regulating. To sum, our results suggest that hiding a guilt ridden reminder–a seemingly unusual reaction–may in fact be an adaptive strategy for guilt regulation.

**References**

Dahl., Darren W., Heather Honea, and Rajesh V. Manchanda (2003), "The Nature of Self-Reported Guilt in Consumption Contexts," *Marketing Letters*, 14 (October), 159-71.

Gross, James J. (1998), "Antecedent and Response-Focused Emotion Regulation: Divergent Consequences for Experience, Expression, and Physiology," *Journal of Personality and Social Psychology*, 74 (1), 224-37.

Loewenstein, George, ed. (2007), *Handbook of Emotion Regulation: Chapter Name: Affect Regulation and Affective Forecasting.*

Richards, Jane M. and James J. Gross (2000), "Emotion Regulation and Memory: The Cognitive Costs of Keeping One's Cool," *Journal of Personality and Social Psychology*, 79 (3), 410-24.

Tice, Dianne M. and Ellen Bratslavsky (2000), "Giving in to Feel: The Place of Emotion Regulation in the Context of General Self-Control," *Psychological Inquiry*, 11 (3), 149-59.

# The Big Cost of Small Problems: Ironic Effects of Malfunction Severity on Enjoyment

Neil Brigden, University of Alberta, Canada
Gerald Häubl, University of Alberta, Canada

Consumers frequently face product malfunctions that vary in severity. One might reasonably assume that the negative impact of a malfunction on consumer enjoyment is proportional to the severity of the malfunction. In other words, larger malfunctions should lower enjoyment more than smaller malfunctions. In this paper, we propose that this is not always true and that more minor malfunctions can reduce enjoyment more than objectively larger malfunctions. This paradoxical result is possible because of the persistence of smaller malfunctions. Consumers tend to address larger malfunctions immediately while allowing smaller malfunctions to persist.

We hypothesize that smaller malfunctions are allowed to persist because of an affective forecasting error in which the long-term impact of the malfunction is underestimated. We also hypothesize that following an initial decision to not repair a product problem, inaction inertia takes over reducing the likelihood that the decision will be revisited.

The underestimation of a smaller malfunction's long-term negative impact on enjoyment is an affective forecasting error where the individual inaccurately predicts how a future state will make them feel. The idea that small problems could be more harmful than larger ones has been suggested previously in the affective forecasting literature (e.g. Wilson & Gilbert 2003). Wilson, Gilbert and colleagues have also demonstrated that this effect can occur in the domain of emotional experience because psychological processes that ameliorate distress are only triggered when a certain threshold of distress is reached (Gilbert et al. 2004).

The affective forecasting error that we explore in the domain of product repairs is atypical in its direction. In general, research has found evidence of a consistent impact bias, whereby individuals *overestimate* the continued impact a specific event will have on their future emotional experience (Wilson & Gilbert 2003). Here we believe underestimation is more likely because the malfunction is a persistent state rather than a discrete event and because consumers may fail to account for the malfunction at all in there forecasts due to a perception that the malfunction is too minor to impact enjoyment.

Once a consumer has decided not to repair a malfunction, inaction inertia prolongs the malfunction. Inaction inertia refers to the decreased likelihood of taking an attractive course of action when a similar and superior course of action has been previously foregone (Tykocinski & Pittman 1998; Tykocinski, Pittman & Tuttle 1995). Therefore, even if consumers recognize that a persistent malfunction should be repaired, they will be unlikely to repair it because they have missed a superior opportunity to repair in a previous time period.

Two experiments tested these hypotheses. In both experiments, participants experienced a malfunction with a hedonic product, had the option of repairing it and then continued to use the product in its repaired or unrepaired state. The key dependent measure in both studies was participants' self reports of enjoyment with the product.

Experiment 1 used a video viewing experience in which participants watched stand-up comedy on a computer screen. The malfunctions in this study were 2-4 second bursts of audio static. In the larger malfunction condition they occurred 8 times per minute, while in the smaller malfunction condition they occurred 2 times per minute. Malfunction severity was manipulated between subject. In both conditions, participants saw a 30 second preview clip and then watched a 10 minute clip. Participants could fix the malfunction at any time during the 10 minute clip by pressing a button. The cost of fixing the problem was one minute of mute (no audio at all). As predicted, participants in the larger malfunction condition were more likely to fix the problem, fixed the problem earlier in the clip and reported enjoying the video more than participants in the smaller malfunction condition.

Experiment 2 used a computer game experience in which a repair to the malfunction could only be made prior to the start of the experience. Participants played a game called Snake, in which they used the arrow keys to control a snake on screen and attempted to eat apples without crashing into the sides of the game area or the snake's body. The malfunctions in this study were random moves that turned the snake without the participant's control. These occurred 20 times per minute in the larger malfunction condition and 5 times per minute in the smaller malfunction condition. In line with our predictions, participants in the larger malfunction condition were more likely to repair the malfunction and reported enjoying the game more than participants in the smaller malfunction condition.

The decision of whether or not to fix a minor malfunction has important consequences for both the consumer and the marketer. The decision will directly affect the consumer's short and long-term enjoyment of the product. The marketer will be indirectly affected by the consumer's retrospective evaluation of the product experience which in turn will influence behaviors such as repeat purchase and word-of-mouth communications with other consumers.

It is not the case that all malfunctions should be fixed, but we find evidence suggesting that there is a class of minor malfunctions that consumers typically do not fix that significantly impair enjoyment. Our results suggest that consumers may not always make normative repair decisions and that marketers might improve consumer experience by offering decision assistance to the consumer.

**References:**

Gilbert, D. T., Lieberman, M. D., Morewedge, C. K., & Wilson, T. D. (2004), "The peculiar longevity of things not so bad," *Psychological Science, 15*, 14-19.

Tykocinski, Orit E. & Thane S. Pittman (1998), "The Consequences of Doing Nothing: Inaction Inertia as Avoidance of Anticipated Counterfactual Regret," *Journal of Personality and Social Psychology, 75*, 607-615.

Tykocinski, Orit E., Thane S. Pittman, & Erin E. Tuttle (1995), "Inaction Inertia: Foregoing Future Benefits as a Result of an Initial Failure to Act," *Journal of Personality and Social Psychology, 68*, 793-803.

Wilson, Tim. D. & Daniel. T. Gilbert (2003). Affective forecasting. In M. Zanna (Ed.), *Advances in experimental social psychology*, Vol. 35 (pp. 345-411). New York: Elsevier.

# The Abandonment of Unprofitable Customer Relationships:
## An Analysis of Emotional Reactions

Michael Haenlein, ESCP Europe, France

Andreas M. Kaplan, ESCP Europe, France

The proactive termination of customer relationships that lack profitability ("unprofitable customer abandonment") has previously been discussed in academic literature and shown to be associated with substantial value (Haenlein et al. 2006). Nevertheless, there is only insufficient insight into its impact on existing customers the abandoning firm would like to retain. Our study therefore investigates (a) the emotional reactions of the abandoning firm's current customers in response to unprofitable customer abandonment, (b) how the tie strength towards the abandoned customer influences these reactions, and (c) the relationship between emotional reactions and behavioral intentions in response to unprofitable customer abandonment.

Following the work of Clore et al. (1987) we use the term emotion to describe internal mental affective conditions. We classify emotions along the two dimensions valence (positive/ negative) and focus (ego-focused/other-focused) (Kitayama et al. 2000; Kitayama et al. 2006). Consistent with attribution theory (Mizerski et al. 1979), we assume that unprofitable customer abandonment will result in causal attributions that lead to emotional reactions (Weiner 1985). We furthermore assume that strong tie relationships are more consistent with an interdependent (vs. independent) construal of the self and therefore with other-focused (vs. ego-focused) emotions (Clark 1984; Clark et al. 1986; Frenzen and Nakamoto 1993):

$H_1$: The tie strength toward the abandoned customer will have (a) a negative impact on the occurrence of ego-focused emotional reactions and (b) a positive impact on the occurrence of other-focused emotional reactions.

Prior research indicates that different emotions are related to different action tendencies (Roseman et al. 1994; Shaver et al. 1987). We assume that the valence of emotional reactions will have a relationship to the choice between positive (i.e. loyalty, positive WoM) and negative behavioral intentions (i.e. exit, negative WoM, boycott). In addition, we postulate that the focus of emotional reactions will be associated with the choice between individualistic (i.e. exit, voice, loyalty) and collective (i.e. boycott) reactions (Klein et al. 2004; McGraw and Tetlock 2005; Sen et al. 2001):

$H_2$: Positive emotional reactions will have a stronger association with positive and a weaker association with negative behavioral intentions than negative emotional reactions.

$H_3$: Other-focused emotional reactions will have a stronger association with collective and a weaker association with individualistic behavioral intentions than ego-focused emotional reactions.

Data collection was carried using an online experiment. We collaborated with a US market research firm who distributed our questionnaire via e-Mail to an online consumer panel. This resulted in a usable sample size of 428 respondents. Respondents were first asked to provide the name or initials of "a casual acquaintance" (weak tie condition) or of "one of their closest friends" (strong tie condition, Frenzen and Nakamoto 1993). They were then exposed to a scenario text describing an unprofitable customer abandonment decision implemented by a mobile phone provider. Respondents are approximately equally split by gender, on average 43 years old with an annual income of approximately $40,000.

Emotional reactions were measured following the work of Kitayama and Markus (2000; 2006). Behavioral intentions were measured building on Hibbard et al. (2001) for threatened withdrawal, constructive discussion, passive acceptance, and venting; Ping (1993) for exit, voice, and loyalty intentions; Bougie et al. (2003) for negative WoM; Sen et al. (2001) for boycott; and East et al. (2007) for positive WoM. To test for demand artifacts we asked respondents whether they could imagine an actual mobile phone provider behaving in the way described in the situation (M=3.11, SD=1.07) and whether they believed that the described situation could happen in real life (M=3.49, SD=1.01) on a scale from 1 to 5. The effectiveness of our tie strength manipulation was verified based on four items used by Frenzen and Nakamoto (1993).

Our analysis shows that hearing about unprofitable customer abandonment leads to emotional reactions among the abandoning firm's current customers. Surprisingly, we observe a relative high occurrence of positive ego-focused emotions: 20% of respondents report to (very) likely feel good about themselves while 15% feel self-esteem and 11% pride. With respect to the impact of tie strength, other-focused emotions are significantly more likely for the abandonment of strong tie than of weak tie relationships. $H_1$ is therefore supported.

Regarding behavioral intentions in response to unprofitable customer abandonment, negative emotional reactions are more strongly correlated with negative action tendencies (i.e. exit, threatened withdrawal, venting, negative WoM, boycott) while positive emotional reactions show higher correlation with positive action tendencies (i.e. collaborative voice, loyalty). Combined, this provides overall support for $H_2$. Yet, although other-focused emotions are experienced more frequently than ego-focused ones, virtually all action tendencies (with the exception of collaborative voice) show a stronger correlation with ego-focused than with other-focused emotions, leading to rejection of $H_3$.

These findings result in three theoretical contributions: First, we show that unprofitable customer abandonment can lead to positive ego-focused emotions and that these emotions are associated with positive behavioral intentions (i.e. loyalty). Second, we show that by terminating some client relationships and maintaining others, the company signals to its remaining customers that they are of higher importance to the firm. This apparently leads to the same positive ego-focused emotions as formally upgrading them to a higher loyalty program tier (Dreze and Nunes 2009). Finally, our work enhances the concept of ego- and other-focused emotions by extending it from a cross-cultural to an interpersonal context.

From a managerial perspective, our work provides two important insights: First, we show that unprofitable customer abandonment does not necessarily only lead to negative emotions within the current customer base. Second, our results indicate that the type of relationship toward the abandoned customer matters and influences the emotional reactions experienced in response to unprofitable customer abandonment. Although it is mainly ego-focused emotions that drive subsequent behavioral intentions, customers who are related to the abandoned customer through strong ties should be of specific concern to the abandoning firm.

## References

Bougie, Roger, Rik Pieters, and Marcel Zeelenberg (2003), "Angry customers don't come back, they get back: The experience and behavioral implications of anger and dissatisfaction in services," *Journal of the academy of marketing science*, 31 (4), 377-93.

Clark, Margaret S. (1984), "Record keeping in two types of relationships," *Journal of personality and social psychology*, 47 (3), 549-57.

Clark, Margaret S., Judson Mills, and Martha C. Powell (1986), "Keeping track of needs in communal and exchange relationships," *Journal of personality and social psychology*, 51 (2), 333-38.

Clore, Gerald L., Andrew Ortony, and Mark A. Foss (1987), "The psychological foundations of the affective lexicon," *Journal of personality and social psychology*, 53 (4), 751-66.

Dreze, Xavier and Joseph C. Nunes (2009), "Feeling superior: The impact of loyalty program structure on consumers' perceptions of status," *Journal of consumer research*, 35 (6), 890-905.

East, Robert, Kathy Hammond, and Malcolm Wright (2007), "The relative incidence of positive and negative word of mouth: A multi-category study," *International journal of research in marketing*, 24 (2), 175-84.

Frenzen, Jonathan and Kent Nakamoto (1993), "Structure, cooperation and the flow of market information," *Journal of consumer research*, 20 (3), 360-75.

Haenlein, Michael, Andreas M. Kaplan, and Detlef Schoder (2006), "Valuing the real option of abandoning unprofitable customers when calculating customer lifetime value," *Journal of Marketing*, 70 (3), 5-20.

Hibbard, Jonathan D., Nirmalya Kumar, and Louis W. Stern (2001), "Examining the impact of destructive acts in Marketing channel relationships," *Journal of marketing research*, 38 (1), 45-61.

Kitayama, Shinobu, Hazel Rose Markus, and Masaru Kurokawa (2000), "Culture, emotion, and well-being: Good feelings in Japan and the United States," *Cognition and emotion*, 14 (1), 93-124.

Kitayama, Shinobu, Batja Mesquita, and Mayumi Karasawa (2006), "Cultural affordances and emotional experience: Socially engaging and disengaging emotions in Japan and the United States," *Journal of personality and social psychology*, 91 (5), 890-903.

Klein, Jill Gabrielle, N. Craig Smith, and Andrew John (2004), "Why we boycott: Consumer motivations for boycott participation," *Journal of marketing*, 68 (3), 92-109.

McGraw, A. Peter and Philip E. Tetlock (2005), "Taboo trade-offs, relational framing, and the acceptability of exchanges," *Journal of consumer psychology*, 15 (1), 2-15.

Mizerski, Richard W., Linda L. Golden, and Jerome B. Kernan (1979), "The attribution process in consumer decision making," *Journal of consumer research*, 6 (2), 123-40.

Ping, Robert A. Jr. (1993), "The effects of satisfaction and structural constraints on retailer exiting, voice, loyalty, opportunism, and neglect," *Journal of retailing*, 69 (3), 320-52.

Roseman, Ira J., Cynthia Wiest, and Tamara S. Swartz (1994), "Phenomenology, behaviors, and goals differentiate discrete emotions," *Journal of personality and social psychology*, 67 (2), 206-21.

Sen, Sankar, Zeynep Gürhan-Canli, and Vicki Morwitz (2001), "Withholding consumption: A social dilemma perspective on consumer boycotts," *Journal of consumer research*, 28 (3), 399-417.

Shaver, Phillip, Judith Schwartz, Donald Kirson, and Cary O'Connor (1987), "Emotion knowledge: Further explanation of a prototype approach," *Journal of personality and social psychology*, 52 (6), 1061-86.

Weiner, Bernard (1985), "An attributional theory of achievement motivation and emotion," *Psychological review*, 92 (4), 548-73.

# Understanding Conformity in Consumption Contexts: Individual Differences in Need for Approval and the Propensity to Conform

Victor Barger, University of Wisconsin-Madison, USA
Joann Peck, University of Wisconsin-Madison, USA

## Extended Abstract

The propensity of consumers to conform to social pressure is of great consequence to the marketing community. This is due in part to the wide-ranging implications of social conformity, from its influence on rates of adoption to the attractiveness of market segments. To date the marketing literature has focused mainly on personality traits that predispose individuals to conform to or resist social pressure. Research on traits that lead to acquiescence has revolved around constructs such as consumer susceptibility to interpersonal influence (Bearden, Netemeyer, & Teel, 1989) and attention to social comparison information (Bearden & Rose, 1990). Studies of factors that encourage resistance to social pressure are less common, but constructs such as consumers' need for uniqueness (Tian, Bearden, & Hunter, 2001) have been identified.

This paper hypothesizes that a hitherto overlooked individual trait, consumers' need for approval, underlies social conformity in consumption contexts. A review of prior attempts to measure need for approval sheds light on the construct, but reveals significant flaws in the extant measures. Currently, the primary measures of need for approval are the Demand for Approval dimension of the General Attitude and Belief Scale, the Approval by Others dimension of the Dysfunctional Attitude Scale, and the Crowne & Marlowe Social Desirability Scale. All three have roots in research conducted in the 1960's, the first two drawing on work in clinical psychology by Ellis (1962) and Beck (1967), respectively, and the third resulting from Crowne & Marlowe's (1960) research on accurate measurement of personality traits.

Based on our review of the literature, we define need for approval as *the extent to which an individual behaves in ways that he thinks others will approve of in order to get them to like him.* This conceptual definition proposes three features common to individuals who are high on need for approval: (1) they believe that they can get others to like them by behaving in ways that others approve of, (2) they are motivated to act on this belief, even if it requires subjugating their own desires and preferences, and (3) although they try to behave in ways that others approve of, they may or may not be successful at anticipating the behaviors that will garner the approval of others.

Consistent with the domain sampling model of measurement (Churchill, 1979), a pool of items was generated to capture the construct of need for approval. This was accomplished in three stages: (1) items were developed based on personal experience and understanding of the construct; (2) items from extant personality inventories were screened for appropriateness given the construct definition; and (3) undergraduate students were provided with the construct definition and asked to generate lists of items. Overlapping items from the pool were deleted and the remaining items were edited for clarity. The pool of items was then evaluated for content validity, and those that met the criteria were retained for further evaluation. In total, 64 items were obtained.

The pool of items was administered to a sample of undergraduate students at a large Midwestern university. Specifically, students enrolled in an introductory course in marketing were invited to participate in the study for extra credit. The questionnaire was administered in a computer lab, and responses were coded on 5-point Likert scales. Of the 425 students enrolled, 397 completed the questionnaire, for a response rate of 93%. After purification of the items using item-total correlations, Cronbach's alpha, and factor analysis, six items remained.

The purified measure was administered to a second sample of undergraduate students to assess construct validity. In addition to the need for approval items, items from related measures, such as need to belong (Leary, Kelly, Cottrell, & Schreindorfer, 2007), need for uniqueness (Snyder & Fromkin, 1977, 1980), and self-esteem (Rosenberg, 1965), were included. The 181-item questionnaire was administered in a computer lab, and responses were coded on 5-point Likert scales. Of the 264 students enrolled, 226 completed the questionnaire, for a response rate of 86%. Analysis of the responses support the convergent validity, discriminant validity, and nomological validity of the six-item measure of consumers' need for approval. In addition, support was found for the hypothesis that consumers' need for approval predicts consumer susceptibility to interpersonal influence when moderated by attention to social comparison information.

Similar to Bearden & Rose (1990), a conformity study in the guise of a soda pop taste test was conducted to ascertain the predictive validity of the measure. Undergraduate students who had previously completed the need for approval questionnaire were invited to participate. A 2 (social pressure vs. no social pressure) × 2 (need for approval: high vs. low [determined by a median split]) design was employed, with the first factor manipulated between subjects and the second factor measured between subjects. In the no social pressure condition, subjects were asked to taste two sodas, Soda A and Soda B, and privately indicate their preferences on ballots. In the social pressure condition, subjects participated in the taste test one at a time with three student confederates; after tasting the two sodas, each student was asked to state their preference. The confederates were instructed to say that they preferred Soda B, and the subject was always asked last. A pre-test had revealed a strong preference for Soda A among students in general. A total of 238 subjects participated in the study, with 107 in the social pressure condition and 131 in the no social pressure condition. As hypothesized, subjects high in need for approval were more likely to choose Soda B than subjects low in need for approval when social pressure was exerted.

Social conformity lies at the heart of a wide range of marketing phenomena. As a driver of social conformity, need for approval offers promise for enhancing our understanding of social conformity. This paper proposes a measure of consumers' need for approval and demonstrates its utility in ascertaining the propensity of individuals to conform to social pressure in consumption contexts.

## References

Bearden, William O., Netemeyer, Richard G., & Teel, Jesse E. (1989). Measurement of consumer susceptibility to interpersonal influence. *Journal of Consumer Research, 15*(4), 473-481.

Bearden, William O., & Rose, Randall L. (1990). Attention to social comparison information: An individual difference factor affecting consumer conformity. *Journal of Consumer Research, 16*(4), 461-471.

Beck, Aaron T. (1967). *Depression: Clinical, experimental, and theoretical aspects*. New York: Harper and Row.

Churchill, Jr., Gilbert A. (1979). A paradigm for developing better measures of marketing constructs. *Journal of Marketing Research, 16*(1), 64-73.

Crowne, Douglas P., & Marlowe, David (1960). A new scale of social desirability independent of psychopathology. *Journal of Consulting Psychology, 24*(4), 349-354.

Ellis, Albert (1962). *Reason and emotion in psychotherapy*. New York: Citadel Press.

Leary, Mark R., Kelly, Kristine M., Cottrell, Catherine A., & Schreindorfer, Lisa S. (2007). Individual differences in the need to belong: Mapping the nomological network. Duke University.

Rosenberg, Morris (1965). *Society and the adolescent self-image*. Princeton, New Jersey: Princeton University Press.

Snyder, C. R., & Fromkin, Howard L. (1977). Abnormality as a positive characteristic: The development and validation of a scale measuring need for uniqueness. *Journal of Abnormal Psychology, 86*(5), 518-527.

Snyder, C. R., & Fromkin, Howard L. (1980). *Uniqueness: The human pursuit of difference*. New York: Plenum Press.

Tian, Kelly Tepper, Bearden, William O., & Hunter, Gary L. (2001). Consumers' need for uniqueness: Scale development and validation. *Journal of Consumer Research, 28*(1), 50-66.

# Trust or Not: The Role of Self-construal in Interacting with Salespeople

Wenxia Guo, University of Manitoba, Canada
Kelley Main, University of Manitoba, Canada

## Extended Abstract

Today's marketplace is one that is internationally diverse. Individuals from different cultures have distinct self-construals (Resnick 1991), which suggest that marketing messages need to be tailored to their individual backgrounds. Individualist (Western) cultures tend to hold independence in high regard which makes the independent self chronically accessible, while collectivist (Eastern) cultures focus on interdependence which makes the interdependent self chronically accessible (Cousins, 1994). Cultural research on persuasion reveals that North American consumers have more favourable attitudes toward persuasion appeals that focus on the independent self, whereas persuasion appeals that focus on interdependent self have more positive effects on Asian consumers (Han & Shavitt, 1994). However, these persuasion appeals that are effective in advertisements may not operate the same way in retailing contexts in which salespeople interact directly with consumers. The current paper attempts to investigate the potential ways for salespeople to communicate with consumers from different cultures in which people may form distinct self-construals (independence vs. interdependence).

In a dynamic interaction between salespeople and consumers, trust is crucial to facilitate the purchase experience. As a result, it is important to understand how culture and trust interact and how to develop trust based on cultural differences in an interpersonal marketplace. Over time, consumers develop knowledge about the behaviours of salespeople they encounter and persuasion attempts used by advertisements. Persuasion knowledge (Friestad & Wright, 1994) is a resource that influences how, when, and why consumers respond to marketer's persuasion attempts. The situation in which persuasion messages match with consumers' self-construals has been applied in advertisements, so the same situation that occurs in retailing contexts may make consumers easily activate persuasion knowledge and lead to low trustworthiness. However, the situation in which persuasion messages from salespeople mismatch their self-construals is less used in advertisements, so the situation used by salespeople may be less likely to activate persuasion knowledge and result in higher trustworthiness. But, this effect may be moderated by situational salient self-construal.

Self-construal is a way in which people think about themselves. An independent self-construal emphasizes uniqueness or distinctiveness from others, while an interdependent self tends to focus on harmony and connectedness with others (e.g., Markus & Kitayama, 1991). Further research has provided evidence that the two selves can coexist within an individual (e.g., Zhang & Shrum, 2009). Accordingly, people's perceptions and cognition styles are influenced by a salient self-construal activated at a given time (Trafimow, et. al., 1991). The coexistence of two types of self-construals makes it possible for markers to link their marketing communications with consumers' activated self-construals by making it salient through the use of external cues (Reed II, 2004). An independent self-construal is oriented toward people instead of social contexts (Morris & Peng 1994) and is likely to apply a context-independent cognitive style (Nisbett et al. 2001), so a consumer with a salient independent self-view may form impressions toward a salesperson based on dispositional attributions, leading to higher persuasion knowledge and lower trustworthiness toward salespeople who are perceived as making a sale regardless of whether persuasion messages from salespeople do or do not match the salient independent identity. In contrast, an interdependent self tends to apply a context-dependent cognitive style (Nisbett et al. 2001) and is oriented toward social contexts rather than people (Miller 1984), so a consumer with a salient interdependent identity may rely more on situational attributions as opposed to dispositional ones.

> H1: When an independent self is salient, persuasion attempts either matching or mismatching with salient independent self will make no difference in terms of consumers' perceptions of trustworthiness toward salespeople. However, when interdependent self is primed, persuasion attempts mismatching with a salient interdependent self will lead to higher trustworthiness than matching persuasion attempts.

## Study 1

This was a 2 (Persuasion attempt: focus on independent self-construal vs. focus on interdependent self-construal) X 2 (self-construal priming: independence vs. interdependence) between-subjects design (N=60). Half of the participants were presented with 18 scrambled sentences to activate an independent self and the other half were given sentences to activate an interdependent self (Skrull, 1978). Next, all participants were asked to image an interaction with a salesclerk where they were going to buy a camera. Half of participants were told

"That's a great camera. Whenever you are together with family and friends, you can take pictures with them…." (focus on interdependent self-construal). The remaining was told: "That's a great camera. Whenever you go for a trip, you can take those impressive and unique pictures…." (focus on independent self-construal). The primary dependent measure was trustworthiness ($\alpha$=0.74).

Results showed a significant interaction between persuasion attempt and self-construal priming (F (1,55)=4.52, p<0.05) and a main effect of priming (F=5.52, p<0.05). As expected, when participants were primed with an independent self-construal, a persuasion attempt that either matched or mismatched their salient independent self-identity made no difference in terms of trustworthiness toward the salesperson, whereas when participants were primed with an interdependent self-construal, a persuasion attempt mismatching the salient interdependent self resulted in higher trustworthiness than one matching with salient interdependent self. This result supported H1.

## Discussion

Overall, this study contributes to the literature by demonstrating the different effect of persuasion attempts which match or mismatch with consumers' temporarily activated self-construals (interdependence versus independence) in retailing contexts as compared to its effect in advertisement. Prior research finds that when persuasion attempts match with either an independent or interdependent self, there is a positive evaluation toward ads (e.g., Aaker & Maheswaran 1997). However, the current study indicates that in interpersonal settings, messages from salespeople have little influence for consumers whose independent self-view is accessible. In contrast, messages mismatching with consumers' interdependent self led to higher trustworthiness than matching messages. This finding suggests that a salient self may play a role when trying persuasion attempts. In future, we would like to identify marketing related self-construal priming and also test the robustness of the result by using participants from different cultures, as research shows that people in Western cultures tend to hold independent self, while people from Eastern cultures focus on interdependent self (Cousins, 1994).

## References

Aaker, J. & Maheswaran, D. (1997). The effect of cultural orientation on persuasion. *Journal of Consumer Research*, 24 (December), 315-328.

Babin, B.J., Boles, J.S., & Darden, W.R. (1995). Salesperson stereotypes, consumer emotions, and their impact on information processing. *Journal of the Academy of Marketing Science*, 32(2), 94-105.

Cousins, S. & Maheswaran, D. (1994). Heuristic processing can bias systematic processing: Effects of source credibility, argument ambiguity and task importance on evaluation judgments. *Journal of Personality and Social Psychology*, 56, 124-131.

Friestad, M.R., & Wright, P. (1994). The persuasion knowledge model: How people cope with persuasion attempts. *Journal of Consumer Research*, 21, 1-31.

Han, S-P. & Sharon, S. (1994). Persuasion and culture: Advertising appeals in individualistic and collectivistic societies. *Journal of Experimental Social Psychology*, 30(4), 326-35.

Main, K.J., Dahl, D.W., & Darke, P.R. (2007). Deliberative and automatic bases of suspicion: empirical evidence of the sinister attribution error. *Journal of Consumer Psychology*, 17(1), 59-69.

Markus, H.R. & Kitayama, S. (1991). Culture and the self: Implications for cognition, emotion, and motivation. *Psychological Review*, 20, 569-579.

Miller, J.G. (1984). Culture and the development of everyday social explanation. *Journal of Personality and Social Psychology*, 46, 961-978.

Morris, M.W. & Peng, K. (1994). Culture and cause: American and Chinese attributions for social and physical events. *Journal of Personality and Social Psychology*, 67, 949-971.

Nisbett, R.E., Peng, K., Choi, I., & Norenzayan, A. (2001). Cultureand systems of thought: Holistic versus analytic cognition. *Psychological Review*, 108, 291-310.

Reed II, A. (2004). Activating the self-importance of consumer selves: Exploring identity salience effects on judgments. *Journal of Consumer Research*, 31(September), 286-295.

Resnick, L.B. (1991). Shared cognition: Thinking as social practice, in *Perspectives on Socially Shared Cognition*, Lauren B. Resnick, John M.Levine, and Stephanie D. Teasley, Washington, DC: American Psychological Association, 1-20.

Trafimow, D., Triandis, H.C., & Goto, S.G. (1991). Some tests of the distinction between the private self and the collective self. *Journal of Personality and Social Psychology*, 60, 649-655.

Zhang, Y. & Shrum, L.J. (2009). The influence of self-construal on impulsive consumption. *Journal of Consumer Research*, 35(February), 838-850.

# The Fundamental Attribution Error in Salespeople and Its Correction by Stealing Thunder: Evidence from Agents and Consumers

Wenxia Guo, University of Manitoba, Canada
Kelley Main, University of Manitoba, Cananda

## Extended Abstract

When you go shopping and encounter a salesperson, what is your first impression? Do you spontaneously think "untrustworthy" or "helpful"? When you automatically think untrustworthy, a stereotype toward salespeople is activated. Research has demonstrated that people are suspicious of salespeople's behavior (Main, Dahl, & Darke, 2007) and have a negative stereotype toward salespeople (Babin, Boles, & Darden, 1995). This negative stereotype may influence consumers' perceptions. Specifically, when dealing with salespeople, consumers may fall prey to the fundamental attribution error (Ross, 1977), which holds that when forming impressions, people tend to misattribute others' behavior to dispositional factors (e.g., untrustworthy) while underestimating the impact of situational factors.

We argue that consumers who have no work experience as salespeople may easily apply FAE when processing feedback from salespeople, as their early negative impressions may bias the interpretation of later information. In turn, the application of FAE may lead to high persuasion knowledge (Friestad & Wright 1994). In contrast, consumers who have worked as salespeople may hold relatively accurate perceptions of salespeople, so they are less likely to apply the FAE.

H1: Consumers with experience as salespeople will have higher perceptions of trust toward salespeople who provide them with positive feedback than consumers without experience as salespeople.

A second question is how to counteract the negatively biased judgments of salespeople's trustworthiness (i.e. the sinister attribution error) evidenced in retail settings (Main et al. 2007). One possibility is the use of stealing thunder which is a dissuasion tactic in which people self-disclose potential weaknesses to reduce its negative impact on others' evaluations (Dolink et al, 2003). That is, salespeople may use the stealing thunder tactic by self-disclosing a plausible ulterior motive to increase their perceived trustworthiness. However, this effect may be moderated by work experience as salespeople. Consumers who have worked as salespeople may recognize stealing thunder as a tactic, so they are less likely to trust the message. Therefore:

H2: Flattery with stealing thunder will lead to higher perceptions of trust toward salespeople than flattery alone for consumers without salesclerk experience. However, this stealing thunder will have negative effects on consumers who have worked as salespeople.

## Study 1

*Method.* This was a 2 (flattery: alone vs. combined with stealing thunder) × 2 (consumer types: salesperson experience vs. no experience) quasi experimental between-subjects design (N=74). Participants self identified whether they worked as salespeople previously. They imaged an interaction with a salesclerk where they were going to buy a pair of sunglasses. Participants were either told that: "That's a great pair of sunglasses. ... (flattery)" or "You may think that I am just trying to make a sale, but that's a great pair of sunglasses. ... (stealing thunder)" The dependent measure was trust (Main et al., 2007; $\alpha$=0.81).

Results showed a significant interaction (F (1,70)=6.41, p<0.05). Planned contrasts showed that for flattery alone, participants with sales experience had higher trust in the salesclerk than those without experience (F(1,70)=8,48, p<0.01), as per H1. Planned contrasts also supported H2. Participants without experience perceived salespeople as more trustworthy when flattery was combined with stealing thunder than when provided alone (F(1,70)=3.43, p=0.068). In contrast, participants with sales experience rated lower trust for flattery used with stealing thunder than flattery alone (F(1,70)=3.0, p=0.088).

## Study 2

It is well established that motivations have an influence on information processing (Chen & Chaiken, 1999). A motivation for accuracy may drive people to "use all attribution-relevant information" (Vonk, 1999, p.383) instead of dispositional bias like the FAE. Consequently, under accuracy motivation, flattery combined with or without other tactics (e.g., stealing thunder) will have little influence on consumer's information processing. On the contrary, defense motivation is a desire to hold attitudes that are congruent with one's prior beliefs (Chaiken, Giner-Sorolla, & Chen, 1996). In retailing contexts, when defense motivated, flattery may lead to lower perceptions of trust for consumers without sales experience than consumers who have, as the former may be more likely to attribute causation to salespeople's dispositions than the latter. However, flattery combined with stealing thunder will result in the opposite effect under defense motivation.

H3: Stealing thunder will be only effective for consumers without sales experience under defense motivation, while it will make no difference under accuracy motivation.

*Method.* It was a 2 (flattery: alone vs. combined with stealing thunder) X 2 (consumer types: salesperson experience vs. none) X 2 (motivation: accuracy vs. defense) between-subjects design (N=141). The manipulation of flattery was the same as Study 1. Participants were asked to image an interaction with a salesclerk. Half of them were told to buy a pair of sunglasses. Given that buying sunglasses is the primary shopping goal, this should lead them to want to avoid being tricked by the salesclerk (defense motivation). The remaining participants were asked to go shopping for a jacket and try on sunglasses beforehand (accuracy motivation).

*Trustworthiness.* A 2 X 2 X 2 ANOVA on trust yielded significant two-way interaction between flattery type and consumer types in support of H2 ($F(1, 133) = 5.14$, $p < 0.05$) and three-way interaction ($F(1, 133) = 4.87$, $p < 0.05$). Planned contrasts supported H3. Under defense-motivation, participants without experience rated higher trust with the use of stealing thunder than the use of flattery alone ($F = 8.48$, $p < 0.01$), while under accuracy-motivation, there were no significant effects ($F = 0.28$, $p = 0.60$ (flattery) and $F = 0.24$, $p = 0.63$ (stealing thunder)). Further, under defense-motivation, higher trust was evidenced with the use of stealing thunder for participants without experience than those with experience ($F = 7.74$, $p < 0.01$), while for flattery alone, participants with experience had higher trust than participants without experience ($F = 4.04$, $p < 0.05$).

## General Discussion

This research demonstrates that after flattery, consumers with sales experience rated trust higher than consumers with no experience. Salesclerks can provide positive feedback to consumers without experience when used in combination with stealing thunder. Defense-motivation influences the interpretation of these tactics, while accuracy-motivation does not. The present study contributes to the literature by: (1) identifying when salesclerks can provide positive feedback and be trusted, (2) demonstrating evidence of the application of FAE by salespeople, and (3) demonstrating the impact of motivations.

## Reference

Babin, B.J., Boles, J.S., & Darden, W.R. (1995). Salesperson stereotypes, consumer emotions, and their impact on information processing. *Journal of the Academy of Marketing Science*, 32(2), 94-105.

Chen S. & Chaiken, S. (1999). The heuristic-systematic model in its broader context. *In Dual-Process Theories in Social Psychology* (pp. 73-96). S. Chaiken & Y. Tropecde, New York: Guilford Press.

Chaiken, S., Giner-Sorolla, R., & Chen, S. (1996). Beyond accuracy: Defense and impression motives in heuristic and systematic information processing. In P.M.Gollwitzer & J.A. Bargh (Ed.), *The psychology of action: Linking cognition and motivation to behavior* (pp. 553-578). New York: Guilford Press.

Cowley, E. (2005). Views from consumers next in line: The fundamental attribution error in a service setting. *Journal of the Academy of Marketing Science*, 33(2), 139-152.

Dolnik, L., Case, T.I., & Williams, K.D. (2003). Stealing thunder as a courtroom tactic revisited: Processes and boundaries. *Law and Human Behavior*, 27(3), 267-287.

Easley, R.W., Bearden, W.O., & Teel, J.E. (1995). Testing predictions derived from inoculation theory and the effectiveness of self-disclosure communications strategies. *Journal of Business Research*, 34, 93-105.

Friestad, M.R., & Wright, P. (1994). The persuasion knowledge model: How people cope with persuasion attempts. *Journal of Consumer Research*, 21, 1-31.

Lopez, T.B., Hopkins, C.D., & Raymond, M.A. (2006). Reward preferences of salespeople: How do commission rate? *Journal of Personal Selling and Sales Management*, 26(4), 381-390.

Main, K.J., Dahl, D.W., & Darke, P.R. (2007). Deliberative and automatic bases of suspicion: empirical evidence of the sinister attribution error. *Journal of Consumer Psychology*, 17(1), 59-69.

Ondrus, S.A., & Williams, K.D. (1996). Effects of stealing thunder by a political candidate: Admit or deny? Paper presented at Midwest Psychological Association annual conference, Chicago.

Ross, L. (1977). The intuitive psychologist and his shortcomings: Distortions in the attribution process. In L. Berkowtiz (Ed.), *Advances in experimental social psychology* (Vol.10, pp.174-221). New York: Academic Press.

Sabini, J., Garvery, B., & Hall, A.L. (2001). Shame and embarrassment revisited. *Personality and Social Psychology Bulletin*, 27(1),104-117.

Vonk, R. (1999). Effects of outcome dependency on correspondence bias. *Personality and Social Psychology Bulletin*, 25(3), 382-389.

Wood, W., & Eagly, A.H. (1981). Stages in analysis of persuasive messages: The role of causal attributions and message comprehension. *Journal of Personality and Social Psychology*, 40, 246-259.

Williams, K.D., Bourgeois, M.J., & Croyle, R.T. (1993). The effects of stealing thunder in criminal and civil trials. *Law and Human Behavior*, 17, 597-609.

# To Punish or to Forgive: Examining the Effects of Consumer Penalties on Perceptions and Behavioral Intentions towards the Service Provider

Lan Xia, Bentley University, USA
Monika Kukar-Kinney, University of Richmond, USA

Price penalties are imposed on consumers in various industries especially services. For example, retailers charge a restocking fee when consumers return unwanted products; airlines charge a cancellation or re-ticketing fee when travelers change their plans; and banks charge a late payment fee when consumers fail to pay their credit card bills on time. While service providers claim that penalties are imposed to enhance compliance and compensate for the loss when customers fail to comply, consumers may not agree. Research showed that the presence of a penalty only slightly enhances compliance (Fram and McCarthy 2000). In contrast, there is a prevalent feeling among consumers that service providers abuse their power and perceive the penalties as revenue enhancement rather than covering costs (Fram and Callahan 2001). As a result, many penalties are perceived as unfair and consumers develop negative emotions and vengeful feelings. These undesirable perceptions and emotions subsequently lead to behavioral consequences including switching service provider and negative word-of-mouth (Fram and McCarthy 2000, Kim and Smith 2005).

Research on consumer penalties is sparse. The existing research is exploratory in nature and has mostly focused on consumer negative perceptions and behavioral intentions. However, research showed that about 50% people challenge the penalties (Fram and Callahan 2001). Consequently, not all penalties will result in negative consequences for the consumer, as the provider may decide to lift the penalty after the consumer contacts them. The way in which service providers handle the interactions with customers who challenge the penalties should significantly influence subsequent consumer behaviors. Service provider's flexible handling of penalties may have a positive influence on customers' responses (Kim and Smith 2005). Penalties also create opportunities for service providers to interact with their customers. Therefore, the long-term effect of the penalty may well depend on these interactions.

In this research, we focus on potential positive effects of a penalty arising from customer-service provider interaction (see Figure 1). We propose that consumers perceive flexibility of service provider in handling requests regarding penalties based on various factors arising during the interaction (e.g., outcome, whether consumers' specific situation is considered, the emotional exchanges, etc.). Perception of provider's flexibility will induce feeling of gratitude as well as reduce unfairness perceptions associated with the penalty procedure or outcome. Recent research shows that emotions, such as gratitude, play an important role in strong relationship building (Palmatier et al. 2009). Thus, it is expected that customers who positively resolve the penalty will appreciate provider's flexibility and will consequently develop a stronger relationship with the provider. Therefore, grateful customers will not only stay loyal, but will also serve as an advocate for the service provider via generating positive word-of-mouth, and will be more likely to comply with the providers' requirements in the future. In addition, perceived provider's flexibility will also enhance consumers' fairness perceptions and hence loyalty intentions. We also propose that the effects of customer-service provider interactions are moderated by additional consumer characteristics. Finkel (2001) suggested that when misfortune happens (e.g., being penalized), fairness judgment is influenced by assessment of whether the person is flawed (e.g., a bad person deserves to get a bad outcome) or at fault (e.g., the person is responsible for the bad outcome). In the context of penalties, consumers' consideration of factors such as whether the penalty is due to their fault and whether they have a good record with the provider may influence their feeling of entitlement and expectation of the penalty resolution, and hence the feeling of gratitude and fairness judgment.

To test the above propositions, we conducted an online experiment in the context of late fee for credit card payment (n=290). We manipulated customer relationship with the bank (loyal vs. new customer), whether the customer is at fault (controllable vs. non-controllable situation), and resolution outcome upon contact (penalty imposed vs. lifted). Participants were provided a scenario describing the late fee penalty, reasons for being late, customer relationship with the service provider, and interactions with the provider upon contact. Then they responded to a set questions including their emotions, feeling of entitlement, perceived flexibility of the bank, perceived fairness of the late fee procedure and outcome, and their future behavioral intentions with respect to the provider (loyalty, intention to advocate, and future compliance).

Results show that participants who get the penalty due to their own fault feel less entitled to have the penalty lifted than those who are late due to uncontrollable factors. Loyal customers feel more entitled to have the penalty lifted than new customers. Feeling of entitlement reduces fairness perceptions of the penalty procedure. Consumers who perceive the penalty practice and outcome as more fair are more likely to stay loyal to the provider. However, entitlement does not reduce feeling of gratitude. On the other hand, we find that the perceived provider's flexibility in handling the penalty (induced by whether the service provider lifted the penalty upon request) has an important positive effect on perceived fairness. In addition, outcome resolution influences perceived flexibility which contributes to feeling of gratitude. When consumers feel grateful, they not only stay loyal to the provider, but also express greater intention to advocate for the provider. Finally, neither fairness nor gratitude has a direct effect on tendency to comply in the future. Loyalty intentions are the only driver of increased future compliance.

In addition to the above study, we are planning new studies to examine both consumer and consumer-provider relationship factors in other contexts as well as additional factors influencing perceived flexibility of the service provider in handling penalties such as whether they adapt to consumers' specific background or situation.

Given the potential tensions, conflicts, and opportunities created by consumer penalties between service providers and their customers, it is important to fully understand the effects of these punishments on customers' evaluations in order to properly administer and manage these penalties. We believe our research will provide important theoretical and empirical implications.

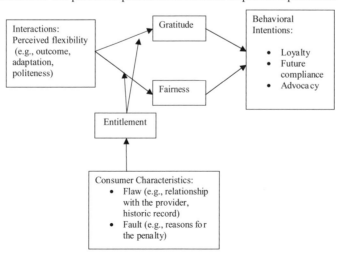

**References**

Finkel, Norman (2001), Not Fair! The Typology of Commonsense Unfairness, American Psychological Association, Washington, DC.

Fram, Eugene H. and Andrew Callahan (2001), Do You Know What The Customer You Penalized Yesterday is Doing Today? A Pilot Analysis. *The Journal of Services Marketing*, 16, 6/7, 496-509.

Fram, Eugene H. and Michael S. McCarthy (2000), An Exploratory Investigation Of Customer Penalties: Assessment of Efficacy, Consequences, And Fairness Perceptions, *Journal of Services Marketing*, 14 (6), 479-501.

Palmatier, Robert W., Cheryl Burke Jarvis, Jennifer R. Bechkoff, and Frank R. Kardes (2009), The Role of Customer Gratitude in Relationship Marketing, *Journal of Marketing*, 73 (September), 1-18.

Young "Sally" K. Kim and Amy K. Smith (2005), Crime and Punishment: Examining Customers' Responses To Service Organizations' Penalties, *Journal of Service Research*, 8(2), 162-180.

# Make a Funny: Humor Production and the Benign Violation Theory

Bridget Leonard, University of Colorado, USA

Caleb Warren, University of Colorado, USA

A. Peter McGraw, University of Colorado, USA

Popular sentiment maintains that if you can make someone laugh, you can make someone buy. Humor attempts are common in marketing communications (e.g., commercial interludes, print ads) and entertainment products (e.g., television, web-content). Humorous products, such as hit films like *The Hangover*, can generate hundreds of millions of dollars in revenue (www.the-numbers.com 2010), and an estimated 10% to 30% of advertisements attempt to elicit humor (Lee and Lim 2008; Krishnan and Chakravarti 2003; Weinberger and Spotts 1989). Consequently, understanding how to create humor is important for both marketers and consumers.

Since Plato, scholars have offered many explanations of what makes things humorous (Morreal 1987; Provine 2000). Some of these explanations account for particular types of humor, such as verbal humor (Raskin 1985) or irony (Giora 1995). As discussed below, others attempt to account for all types of humor. Although many empirical tests address how well different humor theories explain humor (see Martin 2007 for a review), we are unaware of research that examines how understanding a theory of humor improves humor production. Knowing how to create humor, however, is far more useful for marketers than simply knowing how to explain it.

We investigate if learning about a humor theory will facilitate the creation of humor. The three most prevalent general theories of humor are superiority theory, incongruity theory, and relief theory (Martin 2007; Raskin 1985; Speck 1991). Incongruity theories suggest that humor occurs when one perceives something that does not match their expectations or is inconsistent with their beliefs (Elpers, Mukherjee and Hoyer 2004; Suls 1972). Superiority theory suggests that humor requires feeling better than someone else and typically requires some form of aggression or disparagement. Relief theory suggests that humor occurs when arousal from repressed drives is released (Freud 1928; Spencer 1860). Relief theory, however, has largely fallen out of favor because (1) it proposes mechanisms most researchers consider implausible, and (2) its predictions are not supported by empirical evidence (Martin 2007).

Recently, McGraw and Warren (2010) proposed a general humor theory called the benign violation theory (BVT). The BVT suggests that humor occurs when people perceive a violation, or something that threatens their beliefs about how the world ought to be, but simultaneously see the violation as benign. We suspect the BVT may facilitate the production of humor relative to other humor theories because it suggests a wide array of potentially humorous stimuli. For example, unlike incongruity theory and superiority theory, the BVT predicts that the mock aggression in play fighting and tickling will arouse humor in the recipient (Gervais and Wilson 2005; Koestler 1964; Matsusaka 2004). Additionally, we suspect that incongruity theory and superiority theory may encourage the production of stimuli that are incongruous and disparaging but are distressing because the attempt "goes too far."

Our study tests which general humor theory best facilitates the production of humor for a print advertisement. We asked 57 marketing undergraduates to create a humorous headline for an advertisement for an online thrift store (thriftonline.com) that contained a photo of a male and female couple wearing mismatched clothing. Participants were randomly assigned to one of four conditions. In three experimental conditions participants were instructed to create a funny headline using a (randomly assigned) description of a humor theory: superiority theory, incongruity theory, or the benign violation theory. In the control condition participants were simply instructed to create a funny headline. Participants were told that they had ten minutes in which to make their headline as funny as possible for an audience of their peers. Afterwards, participants answered manipulation check questions to determine the degree to which they had used the theory for the task.

In a second phase of the study, 26 undergraduate students rated the funniness of each headline on a scale from 1 to 5 with higher numbers indicating higher levels of perceived humor. Perceptions of humor were reliably correlated ($\alpha$=.76) so we averaged the ratings of the 26 judges for each headline. Participants who used the BVT created the funniest headlines ($M$=2.38), followed by participants in the control condition ($M$=2.30), participants who used incongruity theory ($M$=2.17), and finally, participants who used superiority theory ($M$=2.13). Contrast analysis revealed that participants who used the BVT produced funnier headlines than participants who used either superiority theory or incongruity theory ($F$=3.26, p<.08). The analysis reached standard levels of significance when we controlled for the participant's gender ($F$=4.3, p<.05).

We examined the degree to which participants used the humor theory that they were assigned. Participants reported using the BVT to the same degree, on average, as the other theories ($M_{BVT}$=4.50, $M_{Others}$=4.46). Participants, however, were more likely to report using superiority theory than incongruity theory ($M_{superiority}$=5.50, $M_{Incongruity}$=3.46, $t$=-3.2, p<.01.). Importantly, the judged use of the humor theory helped participants who used the BVT but not participants who used either incongruity theory or superiority theory. For participants in the BVT condition, use of the theory had a strong positive correlation with the average funniness rating ($r$=.70, p<0.01). For participants in the other humor theory conditions, however, use of the theory was uncorrelated with average funniness rating ($r$=-.14, p>.6 and $r$=-.07, p>.8, respectively). That is, participants who reported using the BVT created funnier headlines than participants who learned about the BVT but did not use it. Conversely, using the theory did not appear to help participants exposed to either incongruity theory or superiority theory.

## References

Elpers, J.L.C., Mukherjee, A., and Hoyer, W.D. (2004). Humor in television advertising: A moment-to-moment analysis. *Journal of Consumer Research, 31*(1), 592-598.

Freud, S. (1928). Humor. *International Journal of Psychoanalysis, 9*, 1-6.

Gervais, M., & Wilson, D. S. (2005). The evolution and functions of laughter and humor: A synthetic approach. *Quarterly Review of Biology, 80*(4), 395-430.

Giora, R. (1995). On irony and negation. *Discourse Processes, 19*(2), 239-264.

Koestler, A. (1964). *The act of creation.* New York: Macmillan.

Krishnan, H.S., and Chakraverti, D. (2003). A process analysis of the effects of humorous advertising executions on brand claims memory. *Journal of Consumer Psychology, 13*, 230-245.

Lee, Y.H., and Lim, E.A.C. (2008). What's funny and what's not: The moderating role of cultural orientation in ad humor. *Journal of Advertising, 37*(2), 71-84.

Martin, R.A. (2007) *The psychology of humor: An integrative approach.* Elsevier Academic Press: Burlington, MA.

Matsusaka, T. (2004). When does play panting occur during social play in wild chimpanzees? *Primates 45*(4), 221-229.

McGraw, A.P. & Warren, C., Benign violations: Making immoral behavior funny. (Forthcoming). Psychological Science.

Morreal, J. (1987). *The Philosophy of Laughter and Humor.* Albany: State University of New York Press.

Provine, R.R. (2000). *Laughter: A scientific investigation.* New York: Viking.

Raskin, V. (1985). Jokes. *Psychology Today, 19*(10), 34-&

Speck, P.S. (1991). The Humorous Message Taxonomy: A Framework for the Study of Humorous Ads. In J.Leigh and C.R. Martin (Eds.) *Current Issues and Research in Advertising*, Vol. 13. Ann Arbor: Michigan Business School.

Spencer, H. (1860). On the physiology of laughter. *Macmillian's Magazine, 1*, 395-402.

Suls, J. (1972). A two-stage model for the appreciation of jokes and cartoons: An information-processing analysis. In J. H. Goldstein & P. E. McGhee (Eds.), *The Psychology of Humor: Theoretical Perspectives and Empirical Issues* (pp. 81-100). New York: Academic Press.

Weinberger, G.M., and Spotts, H.E. (1989). Humor in U.S. vs. U.K. TV commercials: A comparison. *Journal of Advertising, 18*(2), 39-44.

# "Is That a Real Song or Did You Just Make It Up?"
# Styles of Authenticity in the Cultural (Re)production of Music

Jon Littlefield, Berry College, USA
Robert Siudzinski, Washington College, USA

## Extended Abstract

Music as an art form has many linkages to consumption. While music itself is consumed in the form of songs, videos, and concerts, its consumption is also integral in the consumption of other art forms such as films (Holbrook 2008; Suisman 2009) and commercial forms such as advertising (Scott 1990) and retail atmospherics (Kellaris and Kent 1993; Kotler 1973/1974; Milliman 1986). Similarly, music often serves as the background in consumers' lives—commercial radio accompanies us on our daily errands or newer subscription-based services free us from the commercial (usually including musical) intrusion into our otherwise quiet lives while we dine, shop, or ride elevators (Bradshaw and Holbrook 2008).

Music is also consumed in its live form (Deighton 1992). Bands perform publicly and privately in venues as diverse as symphony halls and local blues clubs, and from marching band performances during athletic events to weddings and other gatherings. While we see performances as consumption, we might also see the production of music as a consumption activity (Bradshaw, Sherlock, and McDonagh 2003; Kerrigan, O'Reilly, and Lehn 2009). Musicians use instruments, amplification equipment, and pursue education; and put a great deal of effort into both individual practice and group rehearsal. Distinctions between musicians and non-musicians are difficult because musical groups may perform frequently, occasionally, or not at all. Similarly, the lines between professional and amateur musicians (Stebbins 1979; Thompson and Tambyah 1999) and between performer and audience member (Drew 1997; Minor et al. 2004) may at times be vague or nonexistent. Simply getting together with other musicians and "jamming" represents a community activity with its own set of norms and values that include respect for others' abilities, turn-taking, and providing support; and songwriters gain particular respect in this community for their originality[1] and authenticity.

### FOOTNOTE
[1]The title of this paper is derived from a CD of original music produced by a local songwriter's group.

In consumer research, authenticity is desired when cultural resources are used in the production of the self-identity (Beverland and Farrelly 2009; Hesmondhalgh 2008; Holt 2002). Authenticity is seen in opposition to the commercial (Belk, Wallendorf, and Sherry 1989;

Kozinets 2002) and may be seen as "staged" if a commercial connection becomes apparent to consumers (Murray 2002). In contrast, authenticity may be seen as a desirable consequence of a commercial transaction (Arnould and Price 1993) and may serve the role as a marker of status (Schouten and McAlexander 1995; Belk and Costa 2001). This paper reports the preliminary results of a study of local musicians' expressions of authenticity. We were interested in assessing the varied nature of authenticities found in the culture of musicians (Bennett 1991), and in learning the degree to which the equipment required to produce music would be associated with these expressions.

The study uses qualitative methodology, including participant observation and depth interviews. The first author became immersed in the local music community by playing in a band, attending musical performances, participating in guitar circles, and attending meetings and monthly performances of a local songwriter's group. We have, to date, conducted in-depth interviews with 8 musicians. Interview participants were recruited through the first author's contacts within the community, and were questioned about their early influences, performance experiences, and equipment. As the topic of authenticity emerged early in the study, the interview guide was altered in order to more thoroughly capture what is authentic to these musicians. Data are analyzed using a hermeneutic approach (Thompson, Pollio, and Locander 1994; Thompson 1997). First, each interview was read to develop a perspective of each informant's lived experience as a musician. This involved constructing a summary of that musician's data and writing a narrative summary for each musician. Second, the interviews were thematically coded, the coded texts were sorted, and each code was analyzed across interview participants.

Preliminary findings suggest that, while authenticity is a moving target (Beverland and Farrelly 2009; Holt 2002; Rose and Wood 2005), musicians seek to capture and signal authenticity in a number of ways, some of them related to their equipment. Moreover, musicians' legitimacy as performers is potentially contested terrain, and they seek to signal this legitimacy through use of appropriate equipment. For instance, some brands represented a higher degree of authenticity and use of equipment from previous eras in music was one path to legitimacy and authenticity (Grayson and Martinec 2004; Grayson and Shulman 2000; Holbrook 1993).

During the early phases of the study, we suspected that an authentic music experience was related to a nostalgic connection with the past (Holbrook 1993) or with particular music groups, and this expectation was consistent with our first finding. Perhaps ironically, other participants suggested that authenticity is attained through transcendence of the awareness of equipment and brands in favor of a focus of being in the moment with the music. For them, equipment and its use are necessary in creating music, but focus on equipment takes the artist away from that creational process (Heidegger 1962). This group was likely to suggest that authenticity is located in creativity and is represented in originality of music. For these musicians, often singer-songwriters, authenticity derived from a movement away from the ordinary into new musical terrain. Routes to this authenticity included writing music that was lyrically complex, melodic, and new.

## Selected References

Arnould, Eric J., and Linda L. Price (1993), "River Majic: Extraordinary Experience and the Extended Service Encounter," *Journal of Consumer Research*, 20(June), 24-45.

Belk, Russell W., and Janeen Arnold Costa (1998), "The Mountain Man Myth: A Contemporary Consuming Fantasy," *Journal of Consumer Research*, 25(December), 218-240.

Belk, Russell W., Melanie Wallendorf, and John F. Sherry, Jr. (1989), "The Sacred and the Profane in Consumer Behavior: Theodicy on the Odyssey," *Journal of Consumer Research*, 16(June), 1-38.

Bennett, Andy (2001), *Cultures of Popular Music*, Buckingham: Open University Press.

Beverland, Michael B., and Francis J. Farrelly (2010), "The Quest for Authenticity in Consumption: Consumers' Purposive Choice of Authentic Cues to Shape Experienced Outcomes," *Journal of Consumer Research*, 36 (February), 838-856.

Bradshaw, Alan, and Morris B. Holbrook (2008), "Must We Have Muzak Wherever We Go? A Critical Consideration of the Consumer Culture," *Consumption Markets & Culture*, 11(March), 25-43.

Bradshaw, Alan, Roger Sherlock, and Pierre McDonagh (2003), "On the Methods of Researching Music in Everyday Life: Assessing the Musician as Producer of Commercialized Music," in *European Advances in Consumer Research*, 6 (ed. Darach Turley and Stephen Brown), Provo, UT: Association for Consumer Research, 193-198.

Deighton, John (1992), "The Consumption of Performance," *Journal of Consumer Research*, 19(December), 362-372.

Drew, Robert S. (1997), "Embracing the Role of Amateur: How Karaoke Bar Patrons Become Regular Performers," *Journal of Contemporary Ethnography*, 25(January), 449-468.

Grayson, Kent, and Radan Martinec (2004), "Consumer Perceptions of Iconicity and Indexicality and Their Influence on Assessments of Authentic Market Offerings," *Journal of Consumer Research*, 31(September), 296-312.

Grayson, Kent, and David Shulman (2000), "Indexicality and the Verification Function of Irreplaceable Possessions: A Semiotic Analysis," *Journal of Consumer Research*, 27(June), 17-30.

Heidegger, Martin (1962). *Being and Time.* (J. MacQuarrie & E. Robinson, Trans.). London: SCM Press. (Original work published in 1927).

Hesmondhalgh, David (2008), "Towards a Critical Understanding of Music, Emotion and Self-identity," *Consumption Markets & Culture*, 11(December), 329-343.

Holbrook, Morris B. (1993), "Nostalgia and Consumption Preferences: Some Emerging Patterns of Consumer Tastes, *Journal of Consumer Research*, 20(September), 245-256.

Holbrook, Morris B. (2008), "Music Meanings in Movies: The Case of the Crime-plus-jazz Genre," *Consumption Markets & Culture*, 11(December), 307-327.

Holt, Douglas B. (2002), "Why Do Brands Cause Trouble? A Dialectical Theory of Consumer Culture and Branding," *Journal of Consumer Research*, 29(June), 70-90.

Kates, Steven M. (2002), "The Protean Quality of Subcultural Consumption: An Ethnographic Account of Gay Consumers," *Journal of Consumer Research* 29(December), 383-399.

Kellaris, James J., and Robert J. Kent (1993), "An Exploratory Investigation of Responses Elicited by Music Varying in Tempo, Tonality, and Texture," *Journal of Consumer Psychology*, 2(4), 381-401.

Kerrigan, Finola, Daragh O'Reilly, and Dirk vom Lehn (2009), "Producing and Consuming Arts: A Marketing Perspective," *Consumption Markets & Culture*, 12(3), 203-207.

Kotler, Phillip (1973/1974), "Atmospherics as a Marketing Tool," *Journal of Retailing* 49(Winter), 40-64.

Kozinets, Robert V. (2002), "Can Consumers Escape the Market? Emancipatory Illuminations from Burning Man," *Journal of Consumer Research* 29(June), 20-38.

Milliman, Ronald E. (1986), "The Influence of Background Music on the Behavior of Restaurant Patrons," *Journal of Consumer Research*, 13(September), 286-289.

Minor, Michael S., Tillmann Wagner, F.J. Brewerton, and Angela Hausman (2004), "Rock On! An Elementary Model of Customer Satisfaction with Musical Performances," *Journal of Services Marketing*, 18(1), 7-18.

Murray, Jeff B. (2002), "The Politics of Consumption: A Re-Inquiry on Thompson and Haytko's (1997) 'Speaking of Fashion,'" *Journal of Consumer Research*, 29(December), 427-440.

Rose, Randall L., and Stacy L. Wood (2005), "Paradox and the Consumption of Authenticity through Reality Television," *Journal of Consumer Research* 32(September), 284-296.

Schouten, John W. and James H. McAlexander (1995), "Subcultures of Consumption: An Ethnography of the New Bikers," *Journal of Consumer Research*, 22 (June), 43-61.

Scott, Linda M. (1990), "Understanding Jingles and Needledrop: A Rhetorical Approach to Music in Advertising," *Journal of Consumer Research*, 17(September), 223-236.

Stebbins, Robert A. (1979), *Amateurs: On the Margin between Work and Leisure*, Beverly Hills, CA: Sage.

Suisman, David (2009), *Selling Sounds: The Commercial Revolution in American Music*, Cambridge: Harvard University Press.

Thompson, Craig J. (1997), "Interpreting Consumers: A Hermeneutical Framework for Deriving Marketing Insights from the Texts of Consumers' Consumption Stories," *Journal of Marketing Research*, 34(November), 438-455.

Thompson, Craig J., Howard R. Pollio, and William B. Locander (1994), "The Spoken and the Unspoken: A Hermeneutic Approach to Understanding the Cultural Viewpoints That Underlie Consumers' Expressed Meanings," *Journal of Consumer Research*, 21(December), 432-452.

Thompson, Craig J., and Siok Kuan Tambyah (1999), "Trying to Be Cosmopolitan," *Journal of Consumer Research*, 26(December), 214-241.

# In Search of an Authentic Conceptualization for Authenticity in Marketing Offerings

Kisson Lin, University of Hong Kong, China
Felix Tang, Hang Seng School of Commerce, China
Michelle So, University of Hong Kong, China

## Extended Abstract

This research reviews and synthesizes the existing conceptualizations of authenticity. Authenticity is becoming a popular topic in contemporary literature and business practices. It has been applied to tourism experience (e.g., Wang 1999), music (e.g., Peterson 2005), leadership behavior (e.g., Bass and Steidlmeier 1999), culture (e.g., Linnekin 1991), education (e.g., Breen 1985), social study (e.g., Erickson 1995) and in marketing domains such as service delivery (e.g., Chalmers 2008), consumer rituals (e.g., Wallendorf and Amould 1991), consumer possessions (e.g., Grayson and Shulman 2000) and advertising (e.g., Stern 1994). However, the different conceptualizations of authenticity create great confusion for both academic researchers and marketing practitioners.

Confusion still exists when the scope of investigation in narrowed down to the domain of describing authenticity in marketing offering. In some articles, while authenticity has been named differently, their meanings are very similar if not identical. For instance, an offering which has the characteristic of unbroken commitments to tradition and place of origin, Beverland et al. (2008) calls it *pure authenticity*, while Grayson and Martinec (2004) refer to it as *indexical authenticity*. More commonly, authenticity (or its component) are named the same but referring to totally different aspects of it. For example, it means being genuine and natural when describing a commodity or person (e.g., Trilling 1972); trustworthiness when describing messages like advertisements (e.g., Chalmers 2008); being historically grounded and/or rooted in traditional modes of production (e.g., Peterson 2005); or similarity between two objects when describing products or individuals (e.g., Grayson and Martinec 2004). Therefore, it is vital to clear up this confusion to allow progress to be made in this stream of research.

This research provides a qualitative review on the existing literature on authenticity in marketing and identifies fourteen existing concepts, namely, indexical, iconic (Grayson and Radan Martinec 2004), natural, original, exceptional, referential, influential (Gilmore and Pine II 2007), existential, absolute, symbolic (Leigh, Peters and Shelton 2006), synthetic (Cloud, John, Time 2008), pure, approximate and moral (Beverland, Lindgreen, and Vink 2008).

The qualitative review includes two stages. In the first stage, the authors compare and contrast the fourteen conceptualizations of authenticity through logical induction. For each dimension, we review the definitions and examples from the article. Then, a panel of expert judges in linguistic and in communication reviews each of the conceptualizations and categorize them into four groups based on each of their definition and explanation. Afterward, the authors review and pick a conceptualization that best represents the group. We avoid creating new names that would lead to more confusion.

The four groups are: 1) indexical authenticity, which contains originality (which further includes true self or true origin, not a copy or imitation), and absolute connection with some time, venue, or person. It incorporates pure authenticity and absolute authenticity. The definition of exceptional authenticity is also partially incorporated; 2) iconic authenticity, on the other hand, requires no connection, but instead emphasizes on being similar to the object one resembles. It incorporates referential, approximate, symbolic, moral, and synthetic authenticity; 3) existential authenticity, which describes one's sensation in the whole purchasing experience vis-à-vis the offering alone, incorporates the concept of influential authenticity; 4) natural authenticity, which focuses on the natural state of an object, represents a unique dimension of authenticity.

In the second stage, we run four focus groups in a large university in Hong Kong. The four groups comprise a good mix of student and non-student informants. The purpose is to examine the conceptualization's similarities and differences from a consumer's perspective and to explore how the four dimensions may link to different consumption behaviors. Informants shares their past consumptions and views on various market offerings. Attentions were drawn to their perception of various conceptualization of authenticity describing marketing offerings, along with other marketing concepts, such as ethicality, loyalty, satisfaction, and quality.

Some interesting insights are found. Consumers may use indexical authenticity in judging the quality of a marketing offering and the ethically of a purchase (e.g., counterfeits), but their satisfaction evaluation may be associated more with the iconic and existential dimensions. Natural authenticity is highlighted when the marketing offering is edible (e.g., ice-cream) or when it can be applied to the skin (e.g., skin care product). Furthermore, consumers focus on different dimensions of authenticity when describing different types of products and services. In general, the informants find that it is simple and easy to use the four proposed dimensions to describe the authenticity of their past consumptions.

This research contributes to the existing literature by reviewing fourteen existing conceptualizations of authenticity and synthesizing them into a simple and systemized four-dimensional framework. For academicians, our theoretically based framework eliminates overlapping categories in the existing conceptualizations and avoids confusion when one looks up the concept of authenticity. Perception of authenticity seems to be product category-specific. The framework should facilitate discussion from different stream of research on authenticity. Specifically, future research should explore which dimensions of authenticity are more important in different product categories. For practitioners, our framework gives them a simplified big picture as to the major dimension of authenticity that customers care about when they evaluate the authenticity of a marketing offering. From a strategic perspective, the four dimensions should be studied when offerings are positioned to be authentic.

## References

Bass, Bernard M. and Paul Steidlmeier (1999), "Ethics, Character, and Authentic Transformational Leadership Behavior," *The Leadership Quarterly*, 10 (2), 181-217.
Beverland, Michael B., Adam Lindgreen, and Michiel W Vink (2008), "Projecting Authenticity through Advertising: Consumer Judgments of Advertisers' Claims," *Journal of Advertising*, 37 (1), 5-14.
Beverland, Michael B., Adam Lindgreen, and Michiel W Vink (2008), "Projecting Authenticity through Advertising: Consumer Judgments of Advertisers' Claims," *Journal of Advertising*, 37 (1), 5-14.
Breen, Michael P. (1985), "Authenticity in the Language Classroom," *Applied Linguistics*, 6 (1), 60-70.
Chalmers, Tandy D. (2008), "Advertising Authenticity: Resonating Replications of Real Life," *European Advances in Consumer Research*, 8, 442.
Cloud, John, John, Time (2008), "Synthetic Authenticity," *Time Inc*, 171 (12), 1-2.
Erickson, Rebecca J. (1995), "The Importance of Authenticity for Self and Society," *Symbolic Interaction*, 18 (2), 121-44.
Gilmore, James H. and B. Joseph Pine II (2007), *Authenticity: What Consumers Really Want?* Boston, Mass: Harvard Business School Press.
Grayson, Kent and Radan Martinec (2004), "Consumer Perceptions of Iconicity and Indexicality and Their Influence on Assessments of Authentic market Offerings," *Journal of Consumer Research*, 31 (September), 296-97.
Leigh, Thomas W., Cara Peters, and Jeremy Shelton (2006), "The Consumer Quest for Authenticity: The Multiplicity of Meanings Within the MG Subculture of consumption," *Academy of Marketing Science Journal*, 34 (4), 481-83.
Linnekin, Jocelyn (1991), "Cultural Invention and the Dilemma of Authenticity," *American Anthropologist*, 93 (2), 446-49.
Peterson, Richard A. (2005), "In Search of Authenticity," *Journal of Management Studies*, 42 (July), 1083-98.
Stern, Barbara (1994), "Authenticity and the Textural Persona: Postmodern Paradoxes in Advertising Narrative," *International Journal of Research in Marketing*, 11, 387-400.
Trilling, Lionel (1972), *Sincerity and Authenticity*, Cambridge, MA: Harvard University Press.
Wallendorf, Melanie and Eric J. Amould (1991), ""We Gather Together": Consumption Rituals of Thanksgiving Day," *Journal of Consumer Research*, 18 (June), 13-31.
Wang, Ning (1999), "Rethinking Authenticity in Tourism Experience," *Annuals of Tourism Research,* 26 (2), 349-70.

# Experiential Consumption: A Look at the Performing Arts
Gail Leizerovici, Richard Ivey School of Business, University of Western Ontario, Canada

Today's marketplace can be described as one which provides and sells experiences. Our economy has seen a natural progression from one which started with a focus on commodities during the early part of the 20th century, moving to a goods and services focus, with a final orientation on experiences (Pine and Gilmore, 1998). The question of what comprises positive experiences is difficult for consumers to articulate (Arnould and Price, 1993). Experiences are vague, and consumers do not necessarily know what to expect nor how to evaluate them. In the performing arts context, a more complicated question of how such experiences are received and assessed arises. Specifically, this context does not provide a tangible good for a consumer to take home at the end of a performance (except for the show program, for example). Arguably, the only "take-away" for the money rendered is the individual's memory of that experience.

This research is, to the best of my knowledge, the first attempt to unravel the underlying mechanisms that influence why individuals choose to consume performing arts experiences and, what makes these experiences successful for those involved. A four stage process is proposed in order to demonstrate the underlying mechanisms. These four proposed stages are: 1) Engagement, 2) Absorption, 3) Attachment of Meanings, and 4) Moment(s) of Utopia. While literature in philosophy and psychology have touched upon these various concepts using a variety of language, the ultimate contribution of this research is to develop a parsimonious, comprehensive framework of the relationships among these concepts. At this point in the research, it is hoped that this framework will provide a better understanding of the uniqueness of performing arts experiences, while also providing some insight into how these experiences typically unfold.

In support of this framework, the first proposed stage is *engagement* and is defined as the individual's willingness to attend the performance and therefore be involved in the impending experience. According to Arnould and Price (1993), individuals undergo a "rite of integration" when engaging in an experience-related event. Rites of integration can be defined as "planned social interactions that consolidate various forms of cultural artifacts...with the objective of achieving 'a temporary sense of closeness'..." (Siehl, Bowen, and Pearson, 1993). This *engagement* can be further described as one where the individual allows a "letting be of the process" (Arnould and Price, 1993) and where a converging of moods can occur (Totterdell, 2000). This emotion or mood component is further supported in Joy and Sherry's (2003) description of multi-sensory engagement. That is, the individual is not only aware of the surrounding environment and context in which they have become engaged in, but they have also submitted themselves to the impending power and emotion of the performance experience.

The next step proposed in this framework is *absorption*. This stage can be characterized by a complete focus and high level of involvement where the individual becomes disengaged from external distractions and constraints (Charters, 2006). According to Arnould and Price (1993), in a group consumption context individuals can experience an intensely positive experience due to the merging of actions, sharpness of focus, personal integration and awareness of enjoyment. Such intensity of experience and level of involvement reflects a high level of attention, interest and excitement, which can be a direct result of the individual's physical and sensual engagement. This can be observed via emotional responses among audience members, as well as the underlying cognitive processes which characterize such events (Holbrook and Hirschman 1982).

Following the engagement and absorption stages, the next proposed level in this framework is described as *attachment of meanings*. Research has shown that people imbue goods with symbolic meaning to supplement concrete attributes (Hirschman and Holbrook 1982). This is done in order to facilitate in imagining alternate realities, subsequently allowing a certain degree of disengagement from "real world" boundaries or constraints. Such psychological processes are said to occur because individuals like to pretend that something else is happening during consumption. An example relevant to the performing arts context is when individuals choose to attend a theatrical production because they identify with a particular character and imagine that they are the actor (Hirschman and Holbrook 1982). Performances are said to only acquire meaning because consumers attach meanings to them (Deighton, 1992). This imposition and attachment of meanings is what gives the consumer a greater level pleasure, allowing this process to facilitate their disengagement from external, worldly distractions.

The last stage in this framework is *moment(s) of utopia*. Utopia can be defined in this context as an ideal state. Literature in the areas of psychology and philosophy has also provided similar concepts to describe such a state, namely peak experience and flow (Csikszentmihalyi and LeFevre, 1989; Wild et al, 1995). This moment of utopia is a direct result of the build-up and integrative process proposed thus far (engagement, absorption, and attachment of meanings). Specifically, when the attachment of meanings is undertaken, and the individual perceives that their skill in interpreting and attaching these personal meanings matches the complexity of material from the multi-sensory input, then a state of utopia, flow or peak experience is achieved. When a moment of utopia, flow or peak experience is achieved, the temporal frame can be described as "standing still". Time no longer has a salient influence on the individual at this particular moment; instead, one is completely immersed with the experience (Thompson et al., 1990).

Ultimately, this paper presents a conceptual framework suggesting a number of interesting avenues for future empirical work. The initial phase of the data collection is on-going, and involves the use of semi-structured depth interviews with both performers and audience members at local musical performances. Future work could explore additional performing arts contexts as well as a broader range of geographic locations.

## Selected References

Arnould, E. J., & Price, L. L. (1993). River Magic: Extraordinary Experience and the Extended Service Encounter. *Journal of Consumer Research*, *20* (1), 24-45.

Charters, S. (2006). Aesthetic Products and Aesthetic Consumption: A Review. *Consumption, Markets and Culture*, *9* (3), 235-255.

Csikszentmihalyi, M., & LeFevre, J. (1989). Optimal Experience in Work and Leisure. *Journal of Personality and Social Psychology*, *56* (5), 815-822.

Deighton, J. (1992). The Consumption of Performance. *Journal of Consumer Research*, *19* (3), 362-372.

Hirschman, E. C., & Holbrook, M. B. (1982). Hedonic Consumption: Emerging Concepts, Methods and Propositions. *Journal of Marketing*, *46* (3), 92-101.

Holbrook, M. B., & Hirschman, E. C. (1982). The Experiential Aspects of Consumption: Consumer Fantasies, Feelings, and Fun. *Journal of Consumer Research*, *9* (2), 132-140.

Joy, A., & Shery, J. F. (2003). Speaking of Art as Embodied Imagination: A Multisensory Approach to Understanding Aesthetic Experience. *Journal of Consumer Research*, *30* (2), 259-282.

Pine, J. I., & Gilmore, J. H. (1998). Welcome to the Experience Economy. *Harvard Business Review*, *July-August*, 97-105.

Siehl, C., Bowen, D. E., & Pearson, C. M. (1993). Service Encounters as Rites of Integration: An Information Processing Model. *Organization Science*, *3* (November), 537-555.

Thompson, C. J., Locander, W. B., & Pollio, H. R. (1990). The Lived Meaning of Free Choice: An Existential-Phenomenological Description of Everyday Consumer Experiences of Contemporary Married Women. *Journal of Consumer Research , 17* (3), 346-361.

Totterdell, P. (2000). Catching Moods and Hitting Runs: Mood Linkage and Subjective Performance in Professional Sport Teams. *Journal of Applied Psychology , 85* (6), 848-859.

Wild, T. C., Kuiken, D., & Schopflocher, D. (1995). The Role of Absorption in Experiential Involvement. *Journal of Personality and Social Psychology , 69* (3), 569-579.

# Adolescent Motivations to Watch Reality Television

Anthony Patino, Loyola Marymount University, USA
Velitchka Kalcheva, Loyola Marymount University, USA
Michael Smith, Loyola Marymount University, USA

Amongst the most watched programs on television today are reality programs (Nielsen 2008). For example, four of the ten most popular 2005-2006 television programs among viewers under 17 were reality programs, such as *American Idol* (Nielsen 2006). Because reality programs influence the buying behavior and consumption habits of adolescents (Strasburger, Wilson, and Jordan 2009), it becomes vital to investigate the popularity of reality television with adolescent viewers. We therefore conducted an exploratory study with the objective to examine adolescents' motivations to watch reality programming. In the next section, we review earlier research investigating people's motivations to watch television programming.

## Prior Research on Television Viewer Motivations

Television motivation research is based on the Uses and Gratifications Theory developed by Blumler and Katz (1974). The central tenet of the Uses and Gratifications Theory is that viewers differ in their motivations for media use (Blumler 1979). People make decisions as to what program to watch—and whether to watch television at all—based on the needs and wants they seek to satisfy.

Adopting the tenets of the Uses and Gratifications Theory, earlier research identified motivations of adult viewers across multiple television genres (McQuail 1987; Rubin 1984) and for reality television specifically (Barton 2009). Prior research however did not investigate adolescents' motivations for watching reality programming. Studying adolescent viewers separately from adults is important for two reasons. First, there are significant age-related differences in social and cognitive development between adolescents and adults (for a review, see Roedder-John 1999), which are likely to result in dissimilar viewer motivations. Second, as previously discussed, research shows that adolescents are increasingly knowledgeable and influenced by reality television (Strasburger, Wilson, and Jordan 2009). We therefore conducted an exploratory study that begins to address this gap in the literature. Because our study is designed to generate preliminary insights into adolescent viewer motivations for reality programming, we do not offer formal hypotheses. Next, we describe the sample and measures, and then discuss the results.

## Method

A national random sample of 800 adolescents, ranging from 13 through 18 years of age, completed online surveys. The sample was obtained from the Harris Poll Online (HPOL) opt-in panel. Respondents were first asked "What is the name of your favorite reality television show? If you do not have a favorite reality television show, please type 'none.'" Those who wrote the name of a program were then asked: "Why is [the listed program] your favorite reality television program?" Participants responded in their own words.

## Results

Of the 800 respondents, 339 (46.13%) did not list a favorite reality program, and 30 (3.75%) listed a favorite program that was not a reality program. These 369 respondents were not included in the analyses. Of the 431 respondents who were included in the analyses, each listed on average 1.55 motivations. We divided the sample into two age groups: younger teens (12 to 15 year olds) and older teens (16 to 18 year olds), and analyzed adolescents' viewer motivations separately for males and females within each of the two age groups.

Two coders who were unfamiliar with the objectives of the study were asked to independently code participants' viewer motivations. Because of the exploratory objective of this research, we refrained from imposing an a priori structure on the data by suggesting content categories (viewer motivations) to the coders. We adopted the procedure described by Kaltcheva and Weitz (2006). First, each coder independently coded the responses to determine a set of relevant content categories. Next, through discussion, the two coders established a common set of content categories, and the definitions of those categories. Then, each coder used the established common categorization scheme and independently coded all responses. The intercoder reliability, evaluated with Perreault and Leigh's (1989) reliability index, was 86%, which is considered to be an acceptable level of inter-coder reliability (Saldana 2009). The coders resolved disagreements through discussion.

Because both the independent (four age x gender groups) and the dependent (viewer motivation categories) variables in our study are nominal variables, the data was analyzed using correspondence analysis, which is known as "factor analysis for categorical data" (Myers and Mullet 2003, p. 305). Correspondence analysis creates a two-dimensional space. The categories of the independent and dependent variables are located in that space in such a way that categories with similar (dissimilar) distributions are close to each other (far apart) (Clausen 1998).

In our study, the two dimensions accounted for 88% of the variance. One viewer motivation—entertainment/excitement—was located in the center of the two-dimensional space, and it was approximately equidistant from all age x gender groups, suggesting that watching reality programs for entertainment is an equally important motivation for all adolescents. Other viewer motivations were differentially important across the four age x gender groups. Both male and female adolescents in the 16 to 18 age range (older teens) seek reality programs that incorporate dramatic situations and relationships among the program participants. Gender differences were found for the younger adolescents (the 13 to 15 age range). Whereas younger males prefer reality programs that involve humorous and/ or inspirational elements, females of the same age watch a reality program because of one or more of the participants/characters featured in the program and the program's realism (real people placed in real-life situations).

Our results are consistent with extant developmental theories which show that the appreciation of dramatic content and human relationships typically requires a higher level of cognitive and emotional sophistication, which is gradually developed throughout adolescence (Vorderer and Knobloch 2000; Zillman 2000). Our research offers insights that would be helpful to television programmers, advertisers, and public policy makers. For example, television programmers and advertisers can utilize motivation-based segmentation when developing more targeted programming schedules and media buys with quality rationale. By understanding adolescent motivations to watch reality programming, public policy experts can appeal to the same motivations and encourage adolescents to engage in non-television activities, such as reading and exercise.

## References

Blumler, J.G. (1979). The role of theory in Uses and Gratifications research. *Communication Research*, 6, 9-36.

Blumler, J.G. and Katz, E (Eds.). (1974). The uses of mass communications: Current perspectives on gratifications research. Beverly Hills: Sage.

Clausen, Sten-Erik (1998). *Applied Correspondence Analysis: An Introduction*, Thousand Oaks, CA: Sage Publications.

Kaltcheva, V.D. and Weitz B.A. (2006). When Should a Retailer Create an Exciting Store Environment? *Journal of Marketing*, 70 (January), 107-118.

McQuail, D (1987). Mass communication theory: An introduction, Second edition. London: Sage.

Myers, James H. and Gary M. Mullet (2003). *Managerial Applications of Multivariate Analysis in Marketing*, Chicago, Illinois: American Marketing Association.

*Nielsen 2007 Report on Television.* (2007). Nielsen Media Research, New York.

*Nielsen 2008 Report on Television.* (2008). Nielsen Media Research, New York.

*Nielsen 2009 Report on Television.* (2009). Nielsen Media Research, New York.

Perrault, W.D. and Leigh L.E. (1989). Reliability of Nominal Data Based on Qualitative Judgments. *Journal of Marketing Research*, 26 (May), 135-148.

Roedder-John, D. (1999). Consumer Socialization of Children: A retrospective at twenty-five years of research. *Journal of Consumer Research*, 26 (3), 183-212.

Rubin, A.M. (1984). Ritualized and instrumental television viewing. Journal of Communication, 34(3), 67-77.

Saldana, Johnny (2009). The Coding Manual for Qualitative Researchers. London: Sage Publishing, Ltd.

Shrum, L.J. (1999). Television and Persuasion: Effects of the programs between the ads. *Psychology and Marketing*, 16 (2): 119-140.

Strasburger, V.C., Wilson, B.J., and Jordan, A.B. (2009). Children, Adolescents and the Media. Thousand Oaks, CA.: Sage Publishing.

Van Evra, J.P. (1995). Advertising's Impact on Children as a Function of Viewing Purpose. *Psychology and Marketing*, 12 (5), 423-432.

Vorderer, P and Knobloch, S. (2000). Conflict and Suspense in Drama. In D. Zillman and P Vorderer (Eds.), *Media Entertainment: The psychology of its appeal* (pp. 59-72). Mahwah, NJ: Lawrence Erlbaum Associates.

Zillman, D. (2000). Humor and Comedy. In D. Zillman and P Vorderer (Eds.). *Media Entertainment: The psychology of its appeal* (pp. 37-58). Mahwah, NJ: Lawrence Erlbaum Associates.

## Consuming Stardust: The Consumption of Celebrities Beyond Product Endorsements

Diego Rinallo, Bocconi University, Italy
Eduardo Savi, Independent Scholar

We live in a world obsessed with celebrity. Michael Jackson. Madonna. Sofia Loren. Paris Hilton. Tiger Woods. These names are familiar to many people around the world and bring with them memories and emotions, positive and negative, both in those who actively follow their careers and life vicissitudes and in those passively exposed to the media hype surrounding the famous. Consumer researchers have long investigated celebrities for their role as product endorsers. Research in this domain, initially conducted from a social psychological perspective, views celebrities as particularly source of advertising messages (for a review see Erdogan 1999). In the consumer culture theory tradition (Arnould and Thompson 2005), celebrities are understood as receptacles of cultural meanings that are transferred to consumption goods through the act of endorsement (McCracken 1986, 1989). Both psychological and cultural perspectives have thus investigated celebrities from a narrow point of view. Following this year's call for big picture research at the North American ACR conference, in this paper we draw attention to the complex and multifaceted manners through which consumers consume celebrities–beyond the consumption of endorsed products.

Our study draws on data obtained from 18 informants (half men, half women; aged 13 to 50; mostly Italian) with varying levels of interest in celebrities (i.e., worship/fandom; active search for information; passive exposure to news). We conducted phenomenological interviews (McCracken 1988; Thompson 1997) lasting on overage 90 to 120 minutes. Informants were asked about their views on celebrities, what they like/dislike about them, and several narratives of consumption stories and rituals centered upon the famous were elicited. We also resorted to photo-elicitation and autodriving (Heisley and Levy 1991) by showing informants pictures of appropriately selected celebrities and by asking them to bring pictures, videos and other relevant material (e.g., autographs). Interviews were transcribed verbatim from digital records. Informants were given access to their transcribed interviews for correction and/or amplification. The interviews totaled more than 30 hours of conversation, resulting in approximately 360 pages of single-spaced discursive material and 47 auto-driven artifacts.

We found that celebrities can be consumed in highly complex manners. Specifically, in this paper we introduce the idea of three different layers of celebrity: the performer, the character, and the private self. These layers represent specific aspects of the flow of goods, news, performances and media images based on the celebrity. The *performer* refers to the celebrity's recognized performances–for instance, the Oscar-winning actor or the professional athlete whose skills earn her a gold medal at the Olympics. The *character* consists of the attitudes, looks, narratives, lifestyle and those other aspects that constitute the celebrity's public image beyond performances. Celebrities are sometimes known more for these aspects than for their professional achievements and a theme that reverberated throughout our interviews is the opposition between the "real" celebrities and the new brand of people "who are famous because they are famous" through the exposure gained with Big Brother, American Idol and countless other television shows. The third layer, the *private self*, is not easy to see through the looking glass of celebrities' manufactured public image. This aspect can only be imagined or glimpsed at by most consumers.

Each of these layers is consumed in its own specific manners. The performer is consumed through the output of his/her profession. The *consumption of professional excellence* entails a variety of consumption practices. For example, in the case of an actor, such practices include going to a movie theatre in the opening weekend of the star's new film; watching DVDs of those movies alone, with the partner or with friends; downloading legally or illegally those movies and collecting them. A second way to consume the performer is the *integration of their skills*. Dancers who imitate Michael Jackson's moonwalk, young kids' emulating famous skaters' moves, drummers who play according to Jimmy Hendrix's style are just a few examples of how this consumption practice can be expressed. This is particularly frequent in sports, where amateurism is widespread and champion role models are sought after.

Also the character is consumed in multifaceted ways. The *consumption of products* endorsed, designed or somehow linked to the celebrity is the most visible way of consuming the character. Consumers are willing to buy books, make-up, perfumes, fashion and other products because they are a way to feel close to their idols. However, the character may be consumed in other manners, without the mediation of consumer goods, by *reading/watching the news stories* regarding the celebrity, by *imitating their looks and attitudes* and, in some cases, by *integrating their ideas and values* into one's own life.

The person behind the media image is both the most difficult layer of celebrity and the most satisfactory object of consumption for a fan. The primary consumption practice involving the private self of a celebrity is the highly craved *personal contact* during or, even better, outside of professional contexts. Meeting a celebrity is often a fulfilling moment leading to cherished memories– although consumers may also be disappointed by the real person behind the celebrity's character. A less intense experience is the *indirect contact* with the celebrity through acquaintances' storytelling of personal encounters that give a voyeuristic look at the idol's private self. Another related set of consumption activities involves *artifacts*, pictures of or with the celebrity and autographs being the most recurring ones.

Our emerging research findings extend understanding of celebrities' role in today's consumer culture by highlighting the multifaceted consumption practices centered upon the famous, which as we show go much beyond the consumption of endorsed products. We show that shared believes, social practices, consumption rituals and cultural meanings circulate also among non-fans, including those who are even annoyed by the media hype centered and consider them as anti-heroes, negative role models and scapegoats for society's ills. Our findings also have implications for celebrities themselves, who may be viewed as iconic brands (Rein et al. 1987). Specifically, the three layers of celebrity we identify lend themselves to different paths of celebrity legitimization through authentication acts that may converge or conflict among themselves.

**Selected References**

Arnould, E. J., & Thompson, C. J. (2005). Consumer Culture Theory (CCT): Twenty Years of Research. *Journal of Consumer Research, 31* (4), 868-882.
Erdogan, B. Z. (1999). Celebrity Endorsement: A Literature Review. *Journal of Marketing Management, 15* (4), 291-314.
Heisley, D. D., Levy, S. J. (1991). Autodriving: A Photoelicitation Technique. *Journal of Consumer Research 18* (12), 257-272.
McCracken, G. (1986). Culture and Consumption: A Theoretical Account of the Structure and Movement of the Cultural Meaning of Consumer Goods. *Journal of Consumer Research, 13* (1), 71-84.
McCracken, G. (1988). *The Long Interview.* Newbury Park, CA: SAGE Publications.
McCracken, G. (1989). Who is the Celebrity Endorser? Cultural Foundations of the Endorsement Process. *Journal of Consumer Research, 16* (3), 310-321.
Rein, I., Kotler, P., & Stoller, M. (1987). *High Visibility.* New York, NY: Dodd Mead & Company.
Thompson, C. J. (1997). Interpreting Consumers: a hermeneutical framework for deriving marketing insights from the texts of consumers' consumption stories. *Journal of Marketing Research, 34* (11), 438-455.

# Logo Image Effects on Consumer Perceptions of Packages
Adriana Madzharov, Baruch College, USA
Lauren G. Block, Baruch College, USA

Extant research has established that package size plays an important role in consumers' choice, preference and purchase quantity decisions (Raghubir and Greenleaf 2006; Wansink and Van Ittersum 2003). In addition, it has been found that consumers rarely search for and utilize volume information on package labels (Cole and Balasunbramanian 1993). Instead, in order to conserve mental effort, consumers make visual judgments of size easily and automatically using external and sometimes unrelated cues (Krishna 2007).

Consumers tend to utilize the most salient to them cue which leads to biased judgments of package size (e.g.: container shape, Folkes and Matta 2004; elongation of package, Raghubir and Krishna 1999).

So far research on perceptual biases has only looked at the structural elements of packaging (e.g., size, shape). In the present research, we argue that package size estimations are also biased by the graphics (images) displayed on the package. In particular, we examine how the size of the image on the package interacts with individual differences in visual processing and leads to differences in perceptions of package size, purchase intentions and opinion of the brand. We examine this effect in the context of package shelf facings that display a logo and a background frame that surrounds the logo.

We base our argument on visual perception theories which posit that appearance and perception of a visual entity depend on the attributes of the images presented on it (Arnheim 1954); and that the magnitude and accuracy of size judgments of a target depend upon its visual attributes (Baird 1970). Thus, we propose that the sizes of the images displayed on the package influence size estimations for the whole package. In addition, there are consistent individual differences in the relevant salience of cues (Kahneman 1973) where depending on their level of visual processing people articulate on different parts of the visual entity and find some cues more salient than others. In particular, people with high level of visual processing apply more global, top-down processing (Kirby, Moore and Schofield 1988). They are field dependent and are more influenced by the frame in a visual entity (Witkin 1950). Therefore, we propose that people with high visual processing will articulate more on the background area and will use its size as a cue for size of the whole package. On the contrary, people with low level of visual processing are more internally directed and apply detailed, bottom-up processing (Kirby et al., 1988). They are field-independent and are more influenced by the smaller figures in the visual entity (Witkin 1950). Therefore, we propose that people with a low level of visual processing will articulate more on the logo and will use its size to estimate size of the whole package. We hypothesize that people at low level of visual processing will perceive the package as bigger in size when the logo is larger; and that people at high level of visual processing will perceive the package as bigger when the background area around the logo is larger. Furthermore, previous studies have demonstrated greater preference for larger packages (Raghubir and Krishna 1999), thus we hypothesize that subjects will have higher purchase intent for packages they perceive as bigger.

We conducted one study with 108 participants that were randomly assigned to two conditions (size of images displayed on the package: small logo and large background; large logo and small background). Level of visual processing was measured using the Style of Processing Scale (Childers, Houston and Heckler 1985). Participants saw packages of detergents on a computer screen. Three regression analyses revealed significant interactions between condition and mean-centered visual processing on package size, purchase intent and opinion of the brand. Consistent with our hypotheses when the logo was big, subjects at low level of visual processing perceived the package as having more loads, and had higher purchase intentions and opinion of the brand. When the background area was large (the logo was small) subjects at high level of visual processing perceived the package as having more loads, and had higher purchase intentions and opinion of the brand.

The present research contributes to perceptional biases theory in the context of packaging by incorporating package images and individual differences in visual perception. Package size influences consumers in their preferences, willingness to pay and consumption, thus extending research on perception biases in packaging has not only theoretical significance but also important managerial implications.

**References**

Arnheim, Rudolf (1954), in *Art and Visual Perception*, Berkeley: University of California Press.

Baird, John C. (1970), in *Psychophysical Analysis of Visual Space*, New York: Pergamon Press.

Childers, Terry L., Michael J. Houston, and Susan E. Heckler (1985), "Measurement of Individual Differences in Visual versus Verbal Information Processing", *Journal of Consumer Research,* 12 (9), 125-134.

Cole, Catherine A. and Siva K. Balasubramanian (1993), "Age Differences in Consumers' Search for Information: Public Policy Implications," *Journal of Consumer Research,* 20 (June), 157-69.

Folkes, Valerie and Shashi Matta (2004), "The Effect of Package Shape on Consumers' Judgments of Product Volume: Attention as a Mental Contaminant," *Journal of Consumer Research,* 31 (2), 390-401.

Kahneman, Daniel (1973), in *Attention and Effort*, Englewood Cliffs, New Jersey: Prentice Hall.

Kirby, John R., Philip J. Moore, and Neville J. Schofield (1988), "Verbal and Visual Learning Styles," *Contemporary Educational Psychology,* 13, 169–84.

Krishna, Aradhna (2007) "Spatial Perception Research: An Integrative Review of Length, Area, Volume, and Number Perception," in *Visual Marketing: From Attention to Action*, Michel Wedel and Rik Pieters, eds. Mahwah, New Jersey, Lawrence Erlbaum Associates, 167-92.

Raghubir, Priya and Eric A. Greenleaf (2006), "Ratios in Proportion: What Should the Shape of the Package Should Be?" *Journal of Marketing,* 70 (2), 95-107.

Raghubir, Priya and Aradhna Krishna (1999), "Vital Dimensions in Volume Perception: Can the Eye Fool the Stomach," *Journal of Marketing Research*, 36 (August), 313–26.

Wansink, Brian and Koert Van Ittersum (2003), "Bottoms Up! The Influence of Elongation on Pouring and Consumption Volume," *Journal of Consumer Research,* 30 (December), 455-463.

Witkin, H. A. (1950), "Individual Differences in the Ease of Perception of Embedded Figures," *Journal of Personality,* 19, 1-15.

# The Psychology of Color in Promotion Design: A Regulatory Fit Perspective

He Jia, Nanjing University, China

## Extended Abstract

Sales promotion is an important component of the marketing mix, which provides a direct and effective stimulus for purchasing behavior. Several studies have investigated the differentiated effects of free offer and monetary discount from a behavioral perspective. On the one hand, researchers have analyzed the advantage of the free offer over the monetary discount. For example, a free offer is processed more independently of price than a monetary discount (Chandran and Morwitz 2006; Nunes and Park 2003). Based on this assumption, Nunes and Park (2003) argue that compared with an equivalent cash discount, a free offer is less likely to suffer from diminishing marginal returns, and Chandran and Morwitz (2006) find that free offers appear more salient to consumers and therefore can isolate target products from the influences of negative product quality information.

On the other hand, there is a stream of research focusing on the different perceptions related to the two basic types of promotion. A monetary discount may be perceived as a nonloss by consumers since consumers can save some money by enjoying the discount, compared with the original price of the product. In contrast, a free offer may be perceived as a gain by consumers since consumers obtain additional utility beyond what the base product originally provides when they get free offers (Palazon and Delgado-Ballester 2009; Ramanathan and Dhar 2010). This conceptualization opens up an avenue for us to investigate how to enhance the effectiveness of promotional offers from a perspective of regulatory fit theory (Higgins 2000).

Drawing on regulatory fit theory and prior findings of promotion research and color research, this research aims to examine (1) which color to use in the poster of a specific type of promotional offer in order to enhance consumers' evaluation, (2) the mechanism underlying this effect, and (3) the boundary condition for the effects of color and promotion type on consumers' evaluation of the promotional offer.

Recent research in color implies that red can activate a prevention focus, whereas blue can stimulate a promotion focus (Mehta and Zhu 2009). As regulatory focus theory suggests, promotion-focused people are more sensitive to gains and nongains, whereas prevention-focused people are more sensitive to losses and nonlosses (Higgins 1997). When people with a prevention focus (versus a promotion focus) process a piece of information framed with losses/nonlosses (versus gains/nongains), they will experience regulatory fit which is driven by processing fluency (Lee and Aaker 2004). Regulatory fit can enhance consumers' evaluation of the focal object (Higgins 2000; Lee and Aaker 2004). Since consumers may perceive a free offer (versus a monetary discount) as a gain (versus a nonloss), and the blue color (versus the red color) can stimulate a promotion focus (versus a prevention focus), I hypothesize:

H1:  A free offer is evaluated more favorably when its poster is colored with blue than red, whereas a monetary discount is evaluated more favorably when its poster is colored with red than blue.

H2:  Processing fluency mediates the interaction effect between promotion type and color on consumers' evaluation of the promotion.

Since the effect of color and promotion type on consumers' evaluation of the promotional offer is driven by processing fluency, this effect is expected to occur when consumers in low involvement rely on heuristic processing (Wang and Lee 2006). Therefore, the price level of the focal product may moderate the effects of color and promotion type on consumers' evaluation of the promotional offer through altering consumers' involvement. When the price of the focal product is low, consumers are less motivated to process the relevant promotion and therefore more susceptible to the effect of processing fluency. On the contrary, when the price level of the focal product is high, consumers tend to elaborate on the relevant promotion information. In this condition, the effect of processing fluency will disappear. Hence, I propose the high price level as a boundary condition for the effects of color and promotion type on promotion evaluation:

H3: The interaction effect between promotion type and color on consumers' evaluation of the promotional offer is evident when the price level of the focal product is low.

Three experiments are scheduled to provide convergent support to the relevant hypothesis. In Experiment 1, I plan to adopt a 2 (Promotion-type: free offer versus monetary discount) ×2 (Color of the poster: blue versus red) between-subjects design and measure participations' evaluation of the promotional offer. Using this design, I can investigate how promotion type and color of the poster interactively influence consumers' promotion evaluation (H1).

The purpose of Experiment 2 is to generalize the findings of Experiment 1 and obtain evidence for the process underlying the effects of promotion type and color of the poster on consumers' evaluation of the promotional offer (H2). Experiment 2 will be different from Experiment 1 in two ways: (1) Experiment 2 will adopt a different stimulus and (2) a process measure of processing fluency will be adopted.

Experiment 3 will be designed to clarify the mechanism in which color and promotion type influence consumers' evaluation of the promotional offer by investigating the boundary condition for the proposed effect (H3). This experiment will modify the design adopted by Experiment 2 by adding one more between-subjects factor (Price level: high versus low).

From a theoretical perspective, the current research investigates the relationship between the two ostensibly unrelated variables, color and promotion type, and therefore adds new knowledge to the promotion literature. Given that color is a common visual element to shoppers, this research is of special significance to practice in designing the poster of promotional offer. The findings of this research can provide practitioners with managerial implications which are highly actionable, since color of the poster is very easy to manipulate. The suggestion is that when presenting consumers with a free offer, the marketers had better use the blue color in the poster rather than the red color. On the contrary, it is more advantageous for marketers to color the poster of a monetary discount with red rather than blue.

**References**

Chandran, Sucharita and Vicki G. Morwitz (2006), "The Price of "Free"-dom: Consumer Sensitivity to Promotions with Negative Contextual Influences," *Journal of Consumer Research*, 33 (December), 384-392.

Higgins, E. Tory (1997), "Beyond Pleasure and Pain," *American Psychologist*, 52 (12), 1280-1300.

Higgins, E. Tory (2000), "Making a Good Decision: Value From Fit," *American Psychologist*, 55 (11), 1217-1230.

Lee, Angela Y. and Jennifer L. Aaker (2004), "Bringing the Frame into Focus: The Influence of Regulatory Fit on Processing Fluency and Persuasion," *Journal of Personality and Social Psychology*, 86 (2), 205-218.

Mehta, Ravi and Rui (Juliet) Zhu (2009), "Blue or Red? Exploring the Effect of Color on Cognitive Task Performance," *Science*, 323, 1226-1229.

Nunes, Joseph C. and C. Whan Park (2003), "Incommensurate Resources: Not Just More of the Same," *Journal of Marketing Research*, 40 (February), 26-38.

Palazon, Mariola and Elena Delgado-Ballester (2009), "Effectiveness of Price Discounts and Premium Promotions," *Psychology and Marketing*, 26 (12), 1108-1129.

Ramanathan, Suresh and Sanjay K. Dhar (2010), "The Effect of Sales Promotions on Size and Composition of the Shopping Basket: Regulatory Compatibility from Framing and Temporal Restrictions," *Journal of Marketing Research*, forthcoming.

Wang, Jing and Angela Y. Lee (2006), "The Role of Regulatory Focus in Preference Construction," *Journal of Marketing Research*, 43 (February), 28-38.

# Unanticipated Marketing Effects of Color: Empirical Tests in Two Contexts

Jungsil Choi, University of Kansas, USA
Surendra Singh, University of Kansas, USA

## Extended Abstract

Marketers use colors extensively for a variety of reasons, from attempting to induce positive product attitudes and beliefs(Middlestadt 1990) to making customers linger longer in malls and have a more positive shopping experience (Bellizzi and Hite 1992).

Interestingly, humans perceive colors as cold (e.g., blue) and warm (e.g., red, orange) regardless of actual temperature (Stone 1998). [Note: A color consists of hue determined by its wavelength, chroma, and value, only hue is commonly used to describe a color]. And, cold colors tend to have shorter wavelengths compared to warm colors (Yildirim et al. 2007). Research shows that people feel more comfortable if they stay in cold-colored environments when feeling hot and warm-colored environments when feeling cold (Kearney 1966). Blue-colored workplaces tend to feel colder than warm-colored ones (Stone 1998). It is surmised that different temperature perceptions of color occur due to associative learning by associating the colors red and orange with objects such as fire and the sun, and associating the color blue with objects such as a deep sea and ice.

Furthermore, colors also influence emotional responses to the stimuli. For instance, warm colors are perceived as arousing and exciting, while cold colors as relaxing and calming (Bellizzi et al. 1983, 1992; Crowley 1993; Gorn et al. 2004; Valdez and Mehrabian 1994; Dijkstra et al. 2008).

Surprisingly, to date no one has investigated the effect of these inherent qualities of color (warm/cold; arousing/calming) on marketing communications and on consumer choice behavior. In two studies, we demonstrate that the type of color used affects the effectiveness of persuasive messages as well as the degree of risk-taking behavior. More specifically, we show how the type of color used in designing a message interacts with the type of message appeal to determine its effectiveness and how the type of color used for a stimuli background affects risk-taking behavior in terms of a positive and a negative event.

## Color and Message Effectiveness of a Charitable Appeal

Charitable appeals can be broadly classified as either heartwarming, depicting hope, or heartbreaking, depicting desperation and misery (Bendapudi, Singh, Bendapudi (1996). We design two types of flyers soliciting help. A pretest showed that the heartwarming flyer aroused emotionally warm feelings of pleasantness and happiness, whereas the heartbreaking flyer aroused emotionally cold feelings of guilt, depression and sadness. Reasoning that it is a natural human tendency to find a warm place when feeling cold and a cool place when feeling warm, we propose that a heartbreaking (heartwarming) message will be more effective when presented in warm (cold) colors.

Using a 2 (message type: heartwarming vs. heartbreaking) x 2 (background color of the flyer: blue vs. orange) between subjects design, we randomly assigned 129 student participants to the various conditions. We measured informativeness, persuasiveness, and intention to donate. The results show an interaction effect of the type of color and the type of message on informativeness ($p<0.01$). The post hoc analysis shows that the heartbreaking (heartwarming) flyer is more informative with orange (blue) background (respectively, $p<0.05$). [Note: In designing stimuli, we control chroma and value but vary the hue]. We also find an interaction effect on persuasiveness ($p<0.05$), such that the heartbreaking flyer with the color orange is more persuasive than that with blue ($p<0.1$), but the heartwarming flyer with blue is not more persuasive than that with orange ($p>0.1$).

The results also show an interaction effect on the intention to donate ($p<0.01$). The post-hoc analysis shows that the heartwarming (heartbreaking) flyer with blue (orange) is more effective in enhancing the intention to donate ($p<0.1$). It appears that the informativeness of the message mediates the interaction between the type of color and the type of message on the intention to donate. A color compatible with the message enhances the informativeness of the message. Although we did not measure it, it appears that the effect is due to greater attention derived to the message processing. The increased informativeness in turn affects the effectiveness of the message. Previous studies have shown that perceived sensory quality enhanced by a suitable atmosphere affects buyer's information and affective state

(Menon and Kahn 2002; Kotler 1973) and enhances consumers' attention, purchase intentions and shopping time (Baker, Grewal, & Levy 1992; Kotler 1973) in an online shopping mall as well as in a traditional store.

## Effect of Color on Risk-Taking

We hypothesize that warm colors boost the felt excitement associated with risk-taking behavior in a positive event. Likewise cold colors dampen tension associated with a negative event. We use Hsee and Weber's (1999) stimuli to manipulate risk-taking behavior. In a 2 (background color: blue and orange) x 2 (event type: a lottery prize vs. a traffic fine) design, 86 students were randomly assigned to various conditions. We find the interaction effect between the type of color and the type of event on risk-taking behavior ($p<0.05$). The post-hoc analysis shows that orange, compared to blue, induced more risk-taking in choices ($p<0.05$) in a positive event but that blue, compared to orange, does not significantly increase risk-taking in choices ($p=0.144$) in a negative event. In a follow-up study, we raise the stakes (by increasing the amount of prize and fine) and find that the effect of color on risk-taking behavior vanishes. These results demonstrate that color is likely a peripheral cue, and that its effects are attenuated under high involvement conditions.

These findings have clear implications for managers. Colors, be they in the background of a message or in a store could have profound effects on consumers and we need to take this fact into account in all facets of marketing decisions.

## References

Ayn E. Crowley (1993), "The Two-Dimensional Impact of Color on Shopping," Marketing Letters, 4(1), 56-69

Baker, Julie, Michael Levy, and Dhruv Grewal (1992), "An Experimental Approach to Making Retail Store Environmental Decisions," Journal of Retailing, 68(4), 445-460

Bellizzi, Joseph A., Ayn E. Crowley, and Ronald W. Hasty (1983), "The Effects of Color in Store Design," Journal or Retailing, 59(1), 21-45

Bellizzi, Joseph A. and Robert E. Hite (1992), "Environmental Color, Consumer Feelings, and Purchase Likelihood," Psychology and Marketing, 9(5), 347-363

Bendapudi, Neeli, Surendra N. Singh, and Venkat Bendapudi (1996) "Enhancing Helping Behavior: An Integrative Framework for Promotion Planning," Journal of Marketing, 60, 33-49

Dijkstra, K, M.E. Pieterse, A.Th.H. Pruyn (2008), "Individual Differences in Reactions towards Color in Simulated Healthcare Environments: The Role of Stimulus Screening Ability," journal of Environmental Psychology, 28(3), 268-277

Gorn, Gerald J., Amitava Chattopadhyay, Jaideep Sengupta, and Shashank Tripathi (2004), "Waiting for the Web: How Screen Color Affects Time Perception," Journal of Marketing Research, 41(2), 215-225

Hsee, Christopher K. and Elke U. Weber (1999), "Cross-National Differences in Risk Preference and Lay Predictions," Journal of Behavioral Decision Making, 12, 165-179

Kearney, G.E. (1966), "Hue Preferences as a Function of Ambient Temperatures," Australian Journal of Psychology, 18(3), 271-275

Kotler, Philip (1973), "Atmospherics as a Marketing Tool," Journal of Retailing, 49(4), 48-64

Menon, Satya and Barbara Kahn (2002), "Cross-Category Effects of Induced Arousal and Pleasure on the Internet Shopping Experience," Journal of Retailing, 78(1), 31-40

Middlestadt, Susan E (1990), "The Effect of Background and Ambient Color on Product Attitudes and Beliefs," ACR, 17(1), 244-249

Ross, R.T. (1938), "Studies in the Psychology of the Theater," Psychological Record, 2, 127-190

Stone, Nancy J. (1998), "Task Type, Posters, and Workspace Color on Mood, Satisfaction, and Performance," Journal of Environmental Psychology, 18, 175-185

Valdez, Patricia and Albert Mehrabian (1994), "Effects of Color on Emotions" Journal of Experimental Psychology, 123(4), 394-409

Yildirim, K., A. Akalin-Baskaya, and M.L. Hidayetoglu (2007), "Effects of Indoor Color on Mood and Cognitive Performance," Building and Environment, 42(9), 3233-3240

# Empathy Drivers in the Uncanny Valley

Kristen Smirnov, University of Alberta, Canada
John Pracejus, University of Alberta, Canada

## Extended Abstract

For several decades the idea has existed that there exists a state of "almost real" for humanoid figures that causes a strong negative reaction in the viewer (Mori, 1970). First suggested by a Japanese roboticist who had noticed the phenomenon in his daily work, Mori's concept of the "Uncanny Valley" went relatively unstudied for decades after its proposal. The past decade has seen a sudden surge of interest in the behaviors it describes. Robotics researchers have looked at this idea of poor reactions to something that cannot quite pass as real, but the idea has yet to be seriously studied outside their field; furthermore, their focus has been largely on elements of applied practicality to physical designs.

While this lack of research is understandable in decades prior, marketers are now studying consumers who are exposed to unreal figures in their daily lives. These figures range from entirely virtual to actual humans with a veneer of artificiality over them. Films that are entirely created with computer animation software earn hundreds of millions of dollars in the global box office. Photographs of models and celebrities are modified to remove imperfections and improve their proportions to a rigid standard of beauty (Reaves et al., 2004). Web sites use computer-generated avatars to guide users through the site's activities (Holzwarth, Janiszewski, & Neumann, 2006; McGoldrick, Keeling, & Beatty, 2008; Bauer & Neumann, 2005). Some companies choose to pursue the most realistic creations they can manage in this arena, with such film examples as *The Polar Express* and *Beowolf*; others like Nintendo state that "[their] goal has never exclusively been to make things as likelike as possible" (MacMillan, 2007).

Research into portrayal of unrealistic figures has been relatively uncommon in the marketing field despite its presence in consumers' daily lives. It tends, unsurprisingly, to focus on elements related to commercial applications (e.g. Holzwarth, Janiszewski, & Neumann, 2006). There has been no apparent attempt within marketing to investigate the concept of the Uncanny Valley from a more fundamental approach: how do people react in general to a figure that is not quite real, and why? We sought to investigate these behaviors through a series of studies.

Multiple hypotheses were in place as the studies began. Firstly, under Mori's proposition, there should be a greater identification of inhuman features for an uncanny figure relative to a cartoonish one, even though the cartoon is by definition less human. Secondly, we expected to find that people's own typical empathetic behaviors have an impact on how they react to uncanny figures. This, if true, would be an entirely new addition to the literature.

*Poser* software was used to model a woman's face. (This particular software was chosen due to its previous use in psychological research on virtual facial imagery and its accessibility to business operations as a source of virtual figures (Karpouzis et al. 2003; Riva 1997; Spencer-Smith et al. 2001).) A rendering at maximum detail was made, including such specific levels of detail as individual hairs, freckles and pores. After this woman, dubbed "Aiko", was rendered, a simplified cartoon version was made that traced her facial proportions but reduced the three-dimensional presentation of her face into a two-dimensional cartoon. This served as Condition 1 and the full rendering as Condition 5; Conditions 2, 3, and 4 blended these two images together at 75/25%, 50/50%, and 25/75% strengths, respectively. This mimics previous stimuli presentations for Uncanny work (MacDorman 2006).

A large single study has been the primary work so far on this research. Subjects (N=264) were randomly assigned to one of these five facial presentation conditions. They looked at Aiko's picture for ten seconds after being told a cover story, at which point they were told to proceed to the next page and begin answering questions. Four empathy measures previously used toward Uncanny figures (Lee 2006) were taken on seven-point center-anchored scales: (1) "Do you hope this person succeeds?", (2) "Would you let this person comfort you if you were upset?", (3) "Do you think you know what this person feels?", and (4) "Would you go to this person if they were crying?" Following this page was an adapted version of the PANAS (Watson, Clark, & Tellegen 1988) to measure the affective response to Aiko, where participants responded (also on a seven-point center-anchored scale) how strongly the picture had made them feel "bad," "fearful," "joyful," etc. Participants then completed the 28-question Interpersonal Reactivity Index (Davis 1980, 1983) for measures of their own empathetic behaviors.

Results related to the figure itself were significant at a $p < .001$ level across the extremes (i.e. between the fully uncanny and fully cartoon image) in the expected direction, but were only significant at better than a $p < .05$ level between conditions 3 and 4. This suggests two things: one, that we have found the point at which behaviors begin to dramatically change, but also that we may have not used the best possible stimulus in this first attempt at a study. New figures will also be used in future work to avoid reactions specific to one model. However, we believe that a key finding here is that one element of individual empathy was significantly ($p < .05$) related to reactions to uncanny figures: the "fantasy" factor in Davis' scale. Those people, possessing strong imaginations, both liked the cartoon version more and were more unsettled by the uncanny version. Considering these are the types of consumers who would likely be most interested in presentations of fictional characters and spokespeople, this seems a highly relevant finding to investigate further, to see if modern design choices will only serve to alienate this consumer group. We believe pursuing this type of subject with a greater variety of figure types, as well as showing moving figures rather than simply static ones, will help us further understand this topic which would be an entirely new entry into the consumer behavior field.

**References:**

Bauer, Hans H., and Marcus M. Neumann (2005), "Investigating The Effects Of Avatars As Virtual Representatives In Electronic Commerce," in *ANZMAC 2005 Conference: Electronic Marketing*, Perth, Australia.

Holzwarth, Martin, Chris Janiszewski, and Marcus M. Neumann (2006), "The Influence of Avatars on Online Consumer Shopping Behavior." *Journal of Marketing, 70*(4), 19-36.

Karpouzis, K., A. Raouzaiou, P. Tzouveli, S. Iaonnou, and S. Kollias (2003), "MPEG-4: One Multimedia Standard to Unite All," in *2003 International Conference on Multimedia and Expo*.

Lee, Billy (2006), "Empathy, Androids and 'Authentic Experience'," *Connection Science*, 18 (4), 419-28.

MacDorman, Karl F. (2006), "Subjective Ratings of Robot Video Clips for Human Likeness, Familiarity, and Eeriness: An Exploration of the Uncanny Valley," in *ICCS/CogSci-2006 Long Symposium: Toward Social Mechanisms of Android Science*, Vancouver, Canada.

MacMillan, Douglas (2007), "Navigating the Uncanny Valley." *BusinessWeek*. Accessed January 7, 2009 from http://www.businessweek.com/innovate/content/aug2007/id20070817_955317.htm?chan=innovation_special+report+--+the+power+of+gaming_the+power+of+gaming.

McGoldrick, Peter J., Kathleen, A. Keeling, and Susan F Beatty, (2008). "A Typology of Roles for Avatars in Online Retailing." *Journal of Marketing Management, 24*(3-4), 433-461.

Mori, Masuhiro (1970), "The Uncanny Valley," *Energy*, 7 (4), 33-35.

Reaves, Shiela, Jacqueline Bush Hitchon, Sung-Yeon Park, and Gi Woong Yun (2004). If Looks Could Kill: Digital Manipulation of Fashion Models. *Journal of Mass Media Ethics, 19* (1), 56-71.

Riva, Giuseppe (1997), "Virtual Reality as Assessment Tool in Psychology," in *Virtual Reality in Neuro-Psycho-Physiology*, ed. Giuseppe Riva, Amsterdam, Netherlands: Ios Press, 71-79.

Spencer-Smith, Jesse, Heather Wild, Åse H. Innes-Ker, James Townsend, Christy Duffy, Chad Edwards, Kristina Ervin, Nicole Merritt, and Jae Won Pak (2001), "Making Faces: Creating Three-Dimensional Parameterized Models of Facial Expression," *Behavior Research Methods, Instruments, & Computers*, 33 (2), 115-23.

Watson, D., LA Clark, and A. Tellegen (1988), "Development and Validation of Brief Measures of Positive and Negative Affect: the PANAS Scales." *Journal of Personality and Social Psychology, 54*(6), 1063-1070.

Davis, Mark H. (1980), "A Multidimensional Approach to Individual Differences in Empathy," *JSAS Catalog of Selected Documents in Psychology*, 10, 85.

_____ (1983), "Measuring Individual Differences in Empathy: Evidence for a Multidimensional Approach," *Journal of Personality and Social Psychology*, 44, 113-26.

# Come Closer: Anthropomorphized Products as Intimate Companions

Ana Valenzuela, Baruch College, CUNY, USA
Rhonda Hadi, Baruch College, CUNY, USA

## Extended Abstract

Many of us have heard a friend say: "I just want to go home and curl up with a good book." Likewise, it is not rare to see a person eating at a restaurant alone, with only a book as his or her dining companion. These observations motivate the question: to what extent do books function as "friends"? The idea that books potentially assume roles of human companions is linked to the more general study of anthropomorphism. Anthropomorphism can be described as the inclination to attribute humanlike properties, characteristics or mental states to nonhuman agents and objects (Guthrie 1993; Epley et al. 2007).

In a consumer behavior context, anthropomorphism is most often examined with regards to brand personality, which refers to the set of human-like traits associated with a brand (Aaker 1997). Research has suggested that brands with strong positive brand personalities are perceived to be more familiar and less risky to consumers (Freling 2005). While anthropomorphism of *brands* has been explored, research regarding the anthropomorphism of *objects* is rare in consumer behavior journals. One notable exception is research by Agaarwal and Mcgill (2007), which investigated the role of schema congruity on product anthropomorphism. Their research, using cars and beverage bottles as stimuli, indicated that the ease with which a product is anthropomorphized depends on the congruity between the proposed human schema and the product features.

Since researchers have examined constructs such as product attachment and product involvement (Schultz et al. 1989; Kleine et al. 1995; Zaichkowsky 1985), it is not far-fetched to propose that consumers may develop relationships with products as well. In fact, Shimp & Madden (1988) applied Sternberg's (1986) triangular theory of love to the study of consumer-object relations. One component of consumer-object relations highlighted by Shimp & Madden (in reference to Sternberg's theory) was intimacy, which they described as the feelings of closeness and connectedness with consumption objects (Shimp & Madden 1988, pg. 163). The study of product intimacy and the conditions under which it develops defines the focus of our research.

Researchers have attempted to pinpoint potential explanations for why people anthropomorphize. One explanation is sociality, which refers to our innate need to establish social connections with other people (Maslow 1943; Epley et al. 2007). One recent set of studies found that people who are either chronically lonely or induced to feel lonely are more likely to anthropomorphize objects and religious agents (Epley et al. 2008). In fact, research by Luczak and colleagues (2003) suggests that individuals may compensate for their social interaction deficiencies by relating to technical products. That indicates that a lack of traditional socialization may lead to increased anthropomorphization. We expect that people with a high preference for solitude would be more likely to anthropomorphize products in general. Further, we hypothesize that these participants will anthropomorphize products with human traits (e.g., a book with a human face on the front cover) more than products without those traits, and that product anthropomorphism will lead to an enhanced role of the book as an intimate companion.

Study 1 examined the hypotheses above. Specifically, it examined whether people with a high preference for solitude differed from people with a low preference for solitude, in that the former would more likely anthropomorphize and bond with a product (a book) with human traits (a book with a human face on the cover as opposed to a book with a geometrical pattern on the cover). We employed a 2 (preference for solitude (measured): high vs. low) × 2 (book cover prime: human vs. non-human) between-subject design. Participants completed the preference for solitude scale items (Burger 1995) before evaluating one of the two book covers. The dependent variables measured companionship tendencies, as the participant's indication of whether he/she would take the product along to undertake certain activities (e.g., sit in a cafe, travel, eat in a restaurant). Further, respondents answered the question "Can a book become a best friend?" on a 7-point Likert scale.

A significant book cover by preference for solitude interaction was found for all activities to be undertaken with the book (F (1, 45)=3.242, *p*<.08) and their agreement with the statement that a book could be a best friend (F (1, 45)=5.184, *p*<.03). The results show that participants with a high preference for solitude reported to be more likely to undertake these activities with the book that had a human face on the cover (as compared to the book with a geometrical pattern), while responses of participants with a low preference for solitude did not show such pattern. Similarly, participants with a high preference for solitude were more likely to agree with the idea that a book could be a best friend when primed with the human face cover (as compared to the non-face cover), while participants with a low preference for solitude did not. These results may seem counterintuitive at first. However, the previously mentioned literature regarding compensatory anthropomorphic tendencies (Epley et al. 2007; Luczak et al. 2003) indicate that to make up for their lack of socialization, those with a high preference for solitude may gravitate towards products with more outwardly human-like traits. This same lack of socialization may be the cause of what makes them more prone to taking a book with a human face in the cover as a companion.

This research builds upon previous findings by further examining to what extent an object can actually take on the functions of a human friend. Further, it highlights that while anthropomorphism may lead to increased companionship for some people (those with a high preference for solitude), other people may not display the same pattern, and may even prefer objects that are *non* human-like.

These results may also have implications for research regarding the endowment effect (Thaler 1980, Kahneman et al. 1990). Recent research has documented that emotions play a role in the endowment effect, and that merely touching an object results in increased perceived ownership of that object (Lin et al. 2006; Peck & Shu 2009). It is possible that anthropomorphism of an object partially explains the tendency to over-value objects once they have come into one's possession. Further, research by Ruble (2008) suggests a "proximity effect" based on the idea that affective stimuli reactions are polarized when proximal. In the context of anthropomorphism, this finding suggests that the extent to which human-like traits lead consumers to treat products as an intimate companion may be moderated by the physical and perceived closeness of the product's humanity. In our next study we will consider these moderators, and broaden its scope by including stimuli from product categories other than books. Further, we will attempt to measure consumer-object intimacy by relying on additional constructs in the literature (Sternberg 1986; Shimp & Madden 1988).

## References

Aggarwal, P., & Mcgill, A. (2007). Is That Car Smiling at Me? Schema Congruity as a Basis for Evaluating Anthropomorphized Products. *Journal of Consumer Research, 34*, 468–479.

Aaker, J. (1997) Dimensions of Brand Personality. *Journal of Marketing Research, 34*, 347-356.

Burger, J. M. (1995). Individual Differences in Preference for Solitude. *Journal of Research in Personality, 29*, 85–108.

Epley, N., Akalis, S., Waytz, A. & Cacioppo, J. (2008). Creating Social Connection Through Inferential Reproduction: Loneliness and Perceived Agency in Gadgets, Gods, and Greyhounds. *Psychological Science, 19 (2)*, 114–120.

Epley, N., Waytz, A., & Cacioppo, J. T. (2007). On seeing human: A three factor theory of anthropomorphism. *Psychological Review*, 114, 864–886.

Freling, T., & Forbes, P. (2005). An examination of brand personality through methodological triangulation. *Journal of Brand Management*, 13 (2), 148–162.

Guthrie, S. E. (1993). *Faces in the clouds: A new theory of religion.* New York: Oxford University Press.

Kahneman, D., Knetsch, J. L., & Thaler, R. (1990). Experimental tests of the endowment effect and the coase theorem. *Journal of Political Economy*, 99, 1325–1348.

Kleine, S. S., Kleine, R. E., & Allen, C. T. (1995). How Is a Possession ''Me'' or ''Not Me''? Characterizing Types and an Antecedent of Material Possession Attachment. *Journal of Consumer Research*, 22, 327–343.

Lin, C., Chuang, S., Kao, T. K., & Kung C. (2006). The role of emotions in the endowment effect. *Journal of Economic Psychology*, 27, 589–597.

Luczak, H., Roetting, M. & Schmidt, L. (2003). Let's talk: Anthropomorphization as Means to Cope with Stress of Interacting with Technical Devices. *Ergonomics*, 46 (13/14), 1361–1374.

Maslow, A. (1943). A Theory of Human Motivation. *Psychological Review*, 50(4), 370-96.

Peck, J., & Shu, S. B. (2009). The effect of mere touch on perceived ownership. *Journal of Consumer Research,* 36, 434–447.

Ruble, R. M. (2008). How distance influences evaluations and choice. *Dissertation Abstracts International Section A: Humanities and Social Sciences*, 68 (7A), 3043.

Schultz, S. E., Kleine, R. E., & Kernan, J. B. (1989). "These Are A Few of My Favorite Things" Toward an Explication of Attachment as a Consumer Behavior Construct. *Advances in Consumer Research*, 16, 359–366.

Shimp, T. A., & Madden, T. J. (1988). Consumer-Object Relations: A Conceptual Framework Based Analogously on Sternberg's Triangular Theory of Love. *Advances in Consumer Research*, 15, 163–168.

Sternberg, R J. (1986). A Triangular Theory of Love. *Psychological Review,* 93 (2), 119-135.

Thaler, R. (1980). "Toward a Positive Theory of Consumer Choice." *Journal of Economic Behavior and Organization*, 1, 36–90.

Zaichkowsky, J. L. (1985). Measuring the Involvement Construct. *Journal of Consumer Research*, 12, 341–352.

# The Interplay between Form, Function, and Expertise in Consumer Choice

Jianping Liang, SunYat-sen University, Taiwan
Kyle B. Murray, University of Alberta, Canada

## Extended Abstract

We know that consumers make purchase decisions based both on what products do (i.e., functionality) and how they appear (i.e., form) (e.g., Bloch 1995; Chitturi, Raghunathan and Mahajan 2007; Veryzer and Hutchinson 1998). For example, when the compact fluorescent (CFL) light bulb was first introduced, many consumers were hesitant to switch from their traditional bulbs, in part, because the CFL's "swirl" shape was so unusual (Fishman 2006). The early adopters of CFLs were consumers who put more emphasis on the functional improvement in energy efficiency than on the bulb's unconventional appearance. Yet, although marketing research has extensively examined how differences in functionality affect the choices that consumers make between new and existing products, very little research has addressed how product form affects such decisions (Bloch 1995; Rogers 2003).

Nevertheless, form is becoming an increasingly important part of new product development. Electronics companies are relying more and more on form to differentiate products whose core functionally[1] varies little between competitors (e.g., TVs, computers, cameras, coffee makers, toasters, etc.). Even when the core functionality of these products does differ in important ways, those differences are not always clear or meaningful to the average consumer. For example, what will the impact be on my television viewing experience of a 120Hz versus 240Hz refresh rate or a screen resolution of 1080p versus 1080i? Similarly, will I notice a difference in picture quality between a 2 versus 8 megapixels camera or one with an ISO rating of 400 versus 1600? For consumers that do have the required expertise, these differences in functional attributes may very well play a key role in the products that they choose. However, in this paper we predict that for the many consumers that do not have the requisite knowledge, the form of a new product will be a critical determinant of the choices that they make. Specifically, we predict that consumers lacking product expertise (i.e., novices) will be risk averse and tend to select products that have a conventional appearance over those that have an unconventional form.[2]

### FOOTNOTES

[1]In this paper we define *core functionality* as the ability of a product to fulfill its fundamental utility (such as transportation for a vehicle, writing for a pencil, picture taking for a digital camera, and information processing for a computer).

[2]We define *form* as a combination of attributes related to the appearance of the product (e.g., size, shape and color), which does not affect the product's core functionality.

We hypothesize that expertise plays a critical role in determining the weight that consumers place on these two general types of products attributes. In addition, we propose two key boundary conditions on the basic effect: 1) experts discount product form only when they have enough time to systematically process functional information; and, 2) novices discount product form when they expect to have experience with the product that compensates for their lack of functional knowledge (e.g., they are able to try using a new camera before committing to buy it). Finally, we predict that differences in the decision weight given to form versus function by novices and experts can be explained by the level of risk that they perceive in different product forms–that is, the perceived risk of adopting a new product mediates the impact of form on preference. We test, and find strong support for, these hypotheses in a series of three laboratory experiments.

In Study 1, we manipulated the form and the core functionality of a new product and measured the participants' expertise to conduct a 2 (form: same-as-status-quo vs. unconventional) by 2 (core functionality: same-as-status-quo vs. improved) by 2 (consumer expertise: experts vs. novices) experiment. We found that that expertise plays a critical role in determining the weight between form and function.

Study 2 was designed to test the assumption that experts give less weight to form in new product adoption decisions because they are better able to process functional information. Study 2 employed a 2 (expertise: experts vs. novices) by 2 (time pressure: low vs. high) between subjects design and found supportive evidence for the above assumption.

Study 3 was designed to explore the role that risk plays in consumers' willingness to adopt a new product in an unconventional form. Study 3 employed a 2 (form: conventional vs. unconventional) by 2 (expertise: experts vs. novices) by 2 (type of decision: try vs. switch) between subjects experimental design. Moderated mediation test found supportive evidence that the perceived risk of adopting a new product mediates the impact of form on preference.

In these studies, we ruled out alternative explanations such as Need for Variety (NFV), Need for Uniqueness (NFU), and innovativeness. Variables such as demographic variables (i.e., age, gender, and native language), product involvement, task involvement, and aesthetic evaluation were controlled.

We aim to make four key contributions to the extant literature. First, this paper demonstrates that form can play a critical role in the choices that consumers make between new and existing (i.e., status quo) products. Second, we show that the effect of form on consumer choice is especially strong among novice consumers, but can also affect expert decision making under specific conditions (e.g., time pressure). Third, we show that the potentially negative impact on choice of an unconventional form can be overcome if consumers are given the option to try the product out without committing to purchasing it. Fourth, our results provide insight into the psychological mechanism that underlies the effect of form on consumer choice–specifically, novice consumers tend to avoid products with unconventional forms because they perceive greater risk in the adoption of such products.

### References

Bloch, P. H. (1995), "Seeking the Ideal Form: Product Design and Consumer Response," *Journal of Marketing*, Vol. 59, July, 16-29.

Chitturi, Ravindra, Rajagopal Raghunathan, and Vijay Mahajan (2007), "Form Versus Function: How the Intensities of Specific Emotions Evoked in Functional Versus Hedonic Trade-Offs Mediate Product Preferences," *Journal of Marketing Research*, Vol. XLIV, November, 702-714.

Fishman, Charles (2006), "How Many Lightbulbs Does it Take to Change the World?" *Fast Company*, 108 (September).

Rogers, E. M. (2003). *Diffusion of Innovations* (5th ed.), New York: The Free Press.

Veryzer, Robert W. Jr. and J. W. Hutchinson (1998), "The Influence of Unity and Prototypicality on Aesthetic Responses to New Product Design," *Journal of Consumer Research*, Vol. 24, No. 4, 374-394.

# Gender Differences in Responses to Form and Function

Jianping Liang, Sun Yat-sen University, Taiwan

Kyle B. Murray, University of Alberta, Canada

### Extended Abstract

It has been argued for decades that stereotypically, women are associated with concepts of feeling, imagination, intuition, and subjectivity, while men are associated with concepts of mind, rationality, and objectivity (Korsmeyer 2004). However, it is still not clear whether such a stereotypical perception exists and how it may influence consumers' decision making. Consumers make purchase decisions based both on what products do (i.e., functionality) and how they appear (i.e., form) (e.g., Bloch 1995; Chitturi, Raghunathan and Mahajan 2007; Veryzer and Hutchinson 1998). Recent research demonstrated that information processing on form may be more superficial and heuristic whereas processing of functional information may be deeper and more rational (Liang and Murray 2009; Townsend and Sood 2010). If males and females have access to the gendered stereotypical perceptions in minds when making purchase decisions, they are very likely to exhibit different behavioural patterns, compared with the situation where they do not have access to such perceptions. In other words, males (females) consumers are more likely to make purchase decisions on functionality (form) when they take the stereotypical perceptions between genders into consideration. However, little research in the marketing and consumer research has investigated similar issues. Therefore, this paper attempts to explore whether such stereotypical perceptions of gendered preference on form and function exist in consumers' mind and under what conditions such perceptions may or may not influence consumers' decision making.

Methodology. To the best of our knowledge, this is the first study to explore the perceived gender differences in responses to form and function of products in the consumer literature. We conducted in-depth interviews with twenty-seven college students at a large North American university. The informants' responses were coded by two research assistants blind to the study hypotheses. Generally accepted criteria (including credibility, transferability, dependability, and confirmability; Hirschman 1986) were used to assess the quality of the data, which were subsequently analyzed.

Major Findings. From the in-depth interviews, participants were found to perceive that gender difference may exist in consumers' response to form and functionality of products, depending on the product types, the product's usage situations, and the consumer's background and characteristics.

In particular, we found that the perceived gender differences may be smaller for highly utilitarian products (e.g., food and medicine) and highly hedonic products (e.g., paintings) than for products that are somewhat in the middle (e.g., highlighters, shoes, bags, wallets, digital cameras, laptops, watches and cars).

We also found that the perceived gender difference may exist when the product is consumed in public. One (female) said: "*Men will choose the most comfortable shoes to go out even if they are not the most stylish or brand names. Women will spend a night with blisters just to be more stylish and wear the Steve Madden heels.*" Even though some products are consumed in private, they may be shown in public, which could also lead to the gender difference, as one (male) said: "*While she (my sister) went for the one (shower) that looked like a waterfall, I choose the one that had a giant face and more pressure. Now anyone who visits her washroom complements her shower and no one has anything to say about my mine. While she was really happy with her shower for that reason, she would often use mine when she wanted to take a quick shower because hers was too slow!*"

However, it does not mean that the perceived gender difference won't exist when the product is consumed in private. One (female) said: "*A huge gender difference of aesthetics versus functionality would be decorating a room/house. Men want comfort and practical furniture such as a table by their TV chair, where they can put their drink. Women want to put things where they look pretty, even if it is not practical.*"

In addition, the perceived gender difference may be larger for products that one gender happens to be more interested in, more knowledgeable about, and use more frequently than the other gender, as one (male) said: "*If a person is more familiar with a product they will care about its functions. If they aren't too familiar with a product they will choose one that looks better*".

But this is not always the case. In the cosmetic category, one (female) said: "*women's perfume is usually in fun-shaped, colourful, pretty-looking bottles, and men's cologne is usually in a more simply-designed bottle*". Another (male) said: "*Women tend to have more facial products even though most of them serve the same function. They overbuy them because of the new scent, or some added ingredients. Men usually wouldn't mind too much about that as they believe all facial cleansers serve the same function.*"

Furthermore, the perceived gender difference may indicate potential conflicts in relationships between females and males in situations where they have to deal with each other's purchases (e.g., shopping for both genders or gift giving for the other gender): "*As we were looking at the cameras, I focused more on the models that come with a variety of colours to choose from. My brother, on the other hand, compared all the different functions among the models. At last, we couldn't compromise*" (female). "*Our family decided to buy my sister a camera as her birthday present. We bought a petite and easy handle camera which we all thought it will be suitable for her, but turn out that she rather wants a SLR camera, which is heavier to carry and more complicated to use. We are all surprised*" (male).

However, in certain situation, males and females may agree with each other on the importance of form over function, as one (male) said: "*When a guy takes a girl out for the first date, the guy would also think of aesthetics as important. He wouldn't bring her to a fast food chain restaurant for the first date as fast food just serves as an eating function. Instead, he would bring her to a more upscale restaurant for dinner, which serves the eating function as well but with the addition of atmosphere*".

## REFERENCES

Bloch, P. H. (1995), "Seeking the Ideal Form: Product Design and Consumer Response," *Journal of Marketing*, Vol. 59, July, 16-29.

Chitturi, Ravindra, Rajagopal Raghunathan, and Vijay Mahajan (2007), "Form Versus Function: How the Intensities of Specific Emotions Evoked in Functional Versus Hedonic Trade-Offs Mediate Product Preferences," *Journal of Marketing Research*, Vol. XLIV, November, 702-714.

Hirschman, Elizabeth C. (1986), "Humanistic Inquiry in Marketing Research: Philosophy, Method, and Criteria," *Journal of Marketing Research*, 23, 237-249.

Korsmeyer, Carol (2004), *Gender and Aesthetics: An Introduction (Understanding Feminist Philosophy)*, Routledge, 1st edition.

Liang, Jianping and Kyle B. Murray (2009), "The Interplay between Form, Function and Consumer Expertise in New Product Adoptions," *Proceedings of the 2009 Society of Consumer Psychology Conference*, eds. Alexander Chernev, Michal Herzenstein, and Shailendra Pratap Jain, San Diego: Society of Consumer Psychology.

Townsend, Claudia and Sanjay Sood (2010), "On the Impact of Product Aesthetics on Choice: A Dual-Processing Perspective," *Proceedings of the 2010 Society of Consumer Psychology Conference*, eds. Adam Duhachek and Meg Meloy, St. Pete Beach, FL: Society of Consumer Psychology.

Veryzer, Robert W. Jr. and J. W. Hutchinson (1998), "The Influence of Unity and Prototypicality on Aesthetic Responses to New Product Design," *Journal of Consumer Research*, Vol. 24, No. 4, 374-394.

# Is there a Universal Positivity Effect? A Cross-Cultural Perspective

Jianping Liang, Sun Yat-sen University, Taiwan
Zengxiang Chen, School of Business, Sun Yat-sen University, Taiwan
Haizhong Wang, Sun Yat-sen University, Taiwan
Kyle B. Murray, University of Alberta, Canada

## Extended Abstract

Literature in the judgment and decision making and consumer behaviour found prevalently that consumers tend to evaluate the negative information to a larger extent than the positive information ("loss aversion", Kahneman and Tversky 1979; or "negative bias", Herr, Kardes and Kim 1991). Some researchers argued that such results are found in the product domain because negative information is considered as more diagnostic (Skowronski and Carlson 1989) or permits categorization of a product more easily (Herr et al. 1991). However, when it comes to service perceptions, it is totally different. As indicated in Folkes and Patrick (2003), services are not as homogenous as products are. Instead, consumers have heterogeneous service experience. They also have positive expectation for service provider's behaviour. Hence, for a novice consumer, negative information about an individual service provider is not diagnostic of the firm and s/he may consider negative individual as an outlier (Herr et al. 1991). Folkes and Patrick (2003) found that American consumers who have little experience with a service tend to have a "positivity effect", i.e., from positive information about one employee, American consumers infer the firm's other service providers to be similarly positive to a greater extent than, from negative information, they infer the firm's other service providers to be similarly negative.

More research is called for to examine the boundaries and the underlying cognitive processes of this positivity effect (Folkes and Patrick 2003). To the best of our knowledge, the literature is still silent on two important assumptions: although it is true that services tend to be more heterogeneous than products in reality, consumers may *NOT* necessarily perceived (1) that services are heterogeneous and (2) that negative information in such a situation is not diagnostic, even when the other conditions are met (e.g., novice consumer and positive expectation). Therefore, this paper attempts to investigate these issues from a cross-cultural perspective: whether and how a different inference mechanism in a collectivist culture, Chinese culture in particular (i.e., a stronger tendency to infer and generalize from one individual sample to others, including both service experience and members in the same group) (Spencer-Rodgers et al. 2007) may influence the positivity effect.

### Study 1: Positivity Effect for Chinese Consumers: Correction of Cultural-Based Judgments?

Spencer-Rodgers et al. (2007) found that Chinese may view diverse groups as more entitative, to attribute more internally consistent dispositions to groups and their members, and to stereotype more readily than do Americans. Thus, in the context of service experience, it is possible that Chinese may be more likely than Americans to not only consider service experience to be more homogeneous (generalization from one service experience), but also infer and generalize behaviours from one individual employee to the other members in the same firm. Consequently, negativity effect, instead of positivity effect, may be the default effect for Chinese consumers. In other words, Chinese consumers are more likely to infer the firm's other service providers to behave negatively from information that one individual service provider behaved negatively than they are to infer the firm's other service providers to behave positively from information that one individual service provider behaved positively.

However, the generalization from one individual to the whole group is not a logical and persuasive reasoning, especially when consumers have positive expectation and can make thoughtful deliberation (e.g., negative information about an individual is not diagnostic of the firm and they should consider him/her as an outlier), regardless of their cultural background. Briley and Aaker (2006) found that culture-based judgments can be corrected by personal knowledge (e.g., logical and persuasive internal reasoning), in particular, when processing is thoughtful and more deliberative. Therefore, negativity (positivity) effect may occur when Chinese consumers make initial and automatic (deliberate) reactions to the individual sample.

Study One was a 2 (behaviour valence: positive vs. negative) X 2 (deliberate vs. intuitive thinking) between-subject experiment, in which 101 Chinese consumers participated. We found that Chinese consumers exhibited positivity effects when they were asked to think deliberately. When they were asked to think intuitively, they exhibited a strong negativity effect.

### Study 2: Why does culture matter?

Spencer-Rodgers et al. (2007) argued that private interests are expected to be suppressed and personal attributes are to be adjusted for members of collectivist cultures to fit in with the group (Markus & Kitayama 1991; Triandis, 1995). Hence, the cultural difference between Chinese and Americans on the inference from one individual sample to a whole group may be due to different modes of thinking: interdependent (Chinese) vs. independent (Americans) thinking (Kühnen, Hannover and Schubert 2001). Thus, we predict that when Chinese consumers are in a mode of interdependent thinking (about their relationship with others), they may be more likely to consider the individual to be part of the group and thus s/he represents the group's attributes, which should be the same for other members in the group. However, when Chinese consumers are in a mode of independent thinking, they may be more likely to think that each individual is independent from others and does not represent the group. It has been found that both culture and situational priming may lead to the accessibility of different mode of thinking (Kühnen et al. 2001). Briley and Wyer (2001) found that after a contextual prime (e.g., exposing Chinese people to pictures of American cultural icons) prompting a challenge to the cultural guidance, Chinese people feel no more emotionally connected to important others than American people do. Therefore, we propose that by priming an independent mode of thinking, Chinese consumers may show a positivity effect as Americans, while by priming an interdependent mode of thinking, Chinese consumers may show negativity effect.

Study Two was a 2 (behaviour valence: positive vs. negative) X 2 (mode of thinking: independent vs. interdependent thinking) between-subject experiment, in which 120 Chinese consumers participated. We found that Chinese consumers showed negativity effects when they were primed to think interdependently, while they showed positivity effects when they were primed to think independently.

**References**

Briley, Donnel and Robert S. Wyer (2001), "Transitory Determinants of Values and Decisions: The Utility (or Nonutility) of Individualism and Collectivism in Understanding Cultural Differences," *Social Cognition*, 19 (June), 197-227.

Briley, Donnel A. and Aaker Jennifer L. (2006), "When Does Culture Matter? Effects of Personal Knowledge on the Correction of Culture-Based Judgments," *Journal of Marketing Research*, Vol. XLIII (August), 395-408.

Folkes, Valerie S. and Vanessa M. Patrick (2003), "The Positivity Effect in Perceptions of Services: Seen One, Seen Them All?" *Journal of Consumer Research*, Vol. 30, June, 125-137.

Herr, Paul M., Frank Kardes, and John Kim (1991), "Effects of Word-of-Mouth and Product-Attribute Information on Persuasion: An Accessibility-Diagnosticity Perspective," *Journal of Consumer Research*, 17 (March), 454-462.

Kahneman, Daniel and Amos Tversky (1979), "Prospect Theory: An Analysis of Decision Under Risk," *Econometrica*, March, 47 (2), 263-292.

Kühnen, Ulrich, Bettina Hannover, and Benjamin Schubert (2001), "The Semantic-Procedural Interface Model of the Self: The Role of Self-Knowledge for Context-Dependent Versus Context-Independent Modes of Thinking," *Journal of Personality and Social Psychology*, Vol. 80, No. 3, 397-409.

Markus, H. R., & Kitayama, S. (1991), "Culture and the self: Implications for cognition, emotion, and motivation," *Psychological Review*, 98, 224–253.

Skowronski, John J. and Donal E. Carlston (1989), "Negativity and Extremity Biases in Impression Formation: A Review of Explanations," *Psychological Bulletin*, 105 (January), 131-142.

Spencer-Rodgers, Julie, Melissa J. Williams, David L. Hamilton, Kaiping Peng, and Lei Wang (2007), "Culture and Group Perception: Dispositional and Stereotypic Inferences About Novel and National Groups," *Journal of Personality and Social Psychology*, Vol. 93, No. 4, 525-543.

Triandis, H. C. (1995), *Individualism and collectivism*, Boulder, CO: Westview Press.

# The Link between Usability, Preference Reversal, and Decision Making

Na Wen, Georgia Institute of Technology, USA
Nicholas Lurie, Georgia Institute of Technology, USA

Whether it's browsing thousands of digital cameras on eBay or making sense of a myriad number of coffee makers on Amazon.com, it is clear that today's consumers face large amounts of information. Online retailers have tried many approaches to help consumers deal with increasing amounts of information; including electronic agents that recommend particular products based on consumer preferences or the similarity of their shopping histories to other consumers (Diehl 2005; Häubl and Murray 2003); presenting information in matrix format that allows alternatives and attributes to easily be compared (Häubl and Trifts 2000); and providing tools for sorting, selecting, and filtering alternatives (Todd and Benbasat 1991; 1992; 1999).

Prior research suggests that the navigability of a retail website is a key determinant of the likelihood that browsers turn into buyers, the extent to which they learn to efficiently use the website, and the likelihood they return to the website for future purchases (Johnson, Bellman, and Lohse 2003; Nielsen 1993; Palmer 2002). One widely used approach to improve navigability is to use visual design elements such as visual separators between rows or between columns of data in a product matrix. For example, both Travelocity and Intel display alternatives in columns and attributes in rows on their websites but Travelocity uses vertical lines to separate alternatives while Intel uses horizontal lines to separate attributes. Although each approach may increase consumer understanding of the environment by making navigation easier (Huizingh 2000; Nielsen 1993), it is unclear which is better from a decision-making perspective.

Most assessments of website design involve usability testing, with a focus on user understanding, the extent to which users get lost, and the speed of information retrieval (Huizingh 2000; Nielsen 1993; Palmer 2002). In contrast, research on decision making tends to examine how task aspects of a decision problem, such as the amount of information in a choice set; or context aspects, such as the correlation among product attributes, affect decision processes and outcomes (Bettman, Johnson, Luce, and Payne 1993; Payne, Bettman, and Johnson 1993; Lurie 2004). In general there has been little examination of how design elements, that make no changes to task or context variables, affect consumer preferences and decision making.

In this article, we propose that design elements, such as visual separators, can act as cognitive constraints that systematically affect the acquisition and processing of information with implications for preferences as well as decision processes and choices. To the extent that consumers adapt their decision processes to the task and context variables in the decision environment (Bettman et al. 1993; Payne, Bettman, and Johnson 1988; Payne et al. 1993), visual separators may discourage these adaptive responses. However, by encouraging the uniform use of particular information acquisition strategies, visual separators should also serve to enhance decision efficiency. To the extent that decision processes have a larger impact on choice quality in environments where consumers need to make tradeoffs among attributes (Bettman et al. 1993; Payne et al. 1988), we expect that visual separators will have the greatest effect on choice quality in such environments.

In a series of studies we examine how design elements such as visual separators affect decision processes and outcomes in different choice contexts. Although a pretest suggests that there is no clear agreement, even among computer science students, on whether it is better to visually separate alternatives or attributes, experimental results show these design elements affect choice quality. These effects, however, depend on the characteristics of the decision context; in particular, the intercorrelation among product attributes.

Study 1 shows that visual separators shift the preference reversal effect between joint and separate evaluations of alternatives found in Hsee (1996) such that visual separators between alternatives increase the difference of willingness to pay for two alternatives while visual separators between attributes reduce such a difference. A second process-tracing study shows that visual separators reduce the extent to which consumers adapt their choice processes to the choice context but enhance decision efficiency (i.e., lead to faster decisions). A third study process-tracing study manipulates time pressure. Results show that, under time pressure, visual separators between attributes as well as between alternatives improve decision quality when product attributes are negatively correlated. Process tracing measures show that under time pressure, visual separators lead to more systematic information acquisition, faster processing of information, and consideration of more information. Under time pressure, this more systematic and comprehensive processing of information appears to compensate for reductions in decision quality due to by-attribute versus by-alternative information acquisition.

By examining how visual aspects of electronic environments affect preferences as well as decision processes and outcomes, this article provides a link between research on design and usability of information environments (Huizingh 2000; Nielsen 1993) and research on decision making (Bettman et al. 1993; Payne et al. 1988; Payne et al. 1993). More generally, this research adds to understanding about the links between perception and cognition (Fiske 1993; Johnson et al. 2003), with implications for decision making. From a managerial perspective, this research provides insights into how seemingly innocuous design changes may affect consumer decision making and those conditions in which visual separators are likely to be helpful or harmful to consumers.

**Selected References:**

Bettman, James R., Eric J. Johnson, Mary Frances Luce, and John W. Payne (1993), "Correlation, Conflict and Choice," *Journal of Experimental Psychology: Learning, Memory, and Cognition*, 19 (4), 931-51.

Diehl, Kristin (2005), "When Two Rights Make a Wrong: Searching Too Much in Ordered Environments," *Journal of Marketing Research*, 42 (3), 313-22.

Fiske, Susan T. (1993), "Controlling Other People: The Impact of Power on Stereotyping," *American Psychologist*, 48 (6), 621-28.

Häubl, Gerald and Kyle B. Murray (2003), "Preference Construction and Persistence in Digital Marketplaces: The Role of Electronic Recommendation Agents," *Journal of Consumer Psychology*, 13 (1&2), 75-91.

Häubl, Gerald and Valerie Trifts (2000), "Consumer Decision Making in Online Shopping Environments: The Effects of Interactive Decision Aids," *Marketing Science*, 19 (1), 4-21.

Hsee, Christopher K. (1996), "The Evaluability Hypothesis: An Explanation for Preference Reversals between Joint and Separate Evaluations of Alternatives," *Organizational* Behavior *and Human Decision Processes*, 67 (3), 247-57.

Huizingh, Eelko K.R.E. (2000), "The Content and Design of Web Sites: An Empirical Study," *Information & Management*, 37 (2000), 127-34.

Johnson, Eric J., Steven Bellman, and Gerald L. Lohse (2003), "Cognitive Lock-In and the Power Law of Practice," *Journal of Marketing*, 67 (2), 62-75.

Lurie, Nicholas H. (2004), "Decision Making in Information-Rich Environments: The Role of Information Structure," *Journal of Consumer Research*, 30 (4), 473-86.

Nielsen, Jakob (1993), *Usability Engineering*. San Francisco, CA.

Palmer W. Jonathan (2002), "Web Usability, Design, and Performance Metrics," *Information Systems Research*, 13 (2), 151-67.

Payne, John W, James R. Bettman, and Eric J. Johnson (1988), "Adaptive Strategy Selection in Decision Making," *Journal of Experimental* Psychology*: Learning, Memory & Cognition*, 14 (3), 534-52.

Payne, John W, James R. Bettman, and Eric J. Johnson (1993), *The Adaptive Decision Maker*. New York, NY: Cambridge.

Todd, Peter and Izak Benbasat (1991), "An Experimental Investigation of the Impact of Computer Based Decision Aids on Decision Making Strategies," *Information Systems Research*, 2 (2), 87-115.

Todd, Peter and Izak Benbasat (1992), "The Use of Information in Decision Making: An Experimental Investigation of the Impact of Computer-Based Decision Aids," *Management Information Systems Quarterly*, 16 (1), 373-93.

Todd, Peter and Izak Benbasat (1999), "Evaluating the Impact of DSS, Cognitive Effort, and Incentives on Strategy Selection," *Information Systems Research*, 10 (4), 356-74.

## Retail, Beauty Services and Masculinity: When Brands Face Retailers' Resistance to Changing Masculine Market

Nacima Ourahmoune, ESSEC Business School, France

Gender is an important issue in consumer research. Yet few studies have addressed the relationship between retail strategies and masculine consumption and values. Some scholars developed a framework to understand male consumption (Holt and Thompson, 2004, Schroder and Zwick, 2004, Elliott and Elliott, 2005, Rinallo 2007, Ourahmoune and Nyeck 2008). While sociocultural changes are taking place, traditional masculine and feminine values are evolving, leading to changing gender roles and having impact on the market place (Kimmel and Tissier-Desbordes, 1999).

Men are becoming concerned with appearance and beauty, in the traditional feminine way, and sales of male cosmetics and fashion are increasing. Trendy words are used to describe this "new man" sensitive to appearance, body conscious: metrosexual, übersexual... (Tuncay 2006, Rinallo, 2007).

### Context

This paper intends to understand and describe how the new postmodern masculine values and codes shape retailing strategies and services. Despite the fact that hair beauty brands developed recently a range of professional products dedicated to men (Tigi, Wella,

Goldwell, Redken, L'Oreal Professionnel…), they face haircut salons managers' reluctance to engage in transformations of their salons' aesthetic codes and practices. The vast majority of them believe men are less profitable customers than women and neglect adaptation to changing beauty market for men. Moreover, hairdressers are the unique retail channel for professional hair products in France. They are the key contact with male consumers and brands rely on them. Then, it seems relevant to explore their rep about this new masculine segment.

Then, This research deciphers existing and emerging masculine codes in merchant beauty spaces. It also identifies lagging factors to the emergence of new beauty services for men expressed by salons managers.

**Methodology**

A multi-method study is performed to get a "thick description" (Geertz 1982) of the phenomenon under study. We use structural semiotics (Floch 2005) to discover the meaning of very diverse hair salons narratives: 20 in Paris, 10 in London, 8 in Barcelona, 5 in Spanish Pays Basque, 7 in Athens. Salons are unique retail spaces for professional hair beauty brands (Redken, L'Oreal professional…). Also, 19 semi-structured interviews with hair salon managers were performed in Paris to understand their representations of male consumers as well as lagging factors to a renewed offer for men. In addition, 2 managers from a worldwide beauty company were interviewed to better understand challenges they face on the Male Market. Finally, 200 men in Paris answered our questionnaire about their practices and expectations as regard hair salons. Men were from 15 up to 68 years old, with very diverse occupations and backgrounds.

**Results**

Hair salons are Gendered spaces: 18% go to *only for men* hair salons, 37% Unisex salons, 40% both in Unisex and only for men salons 5% never go to hair salons (home). Male who prefer *Only for men* salons emphasize male hairdressers expertise- *A masculine "in between us" know how. Instrumental/ utilitarian values prevail* in terms male consumers expectations: Hygiene (86%), next-door salon (82%) nice haircut (84%). However, nice atmosphere and beautiful design were important criteria for consumers under 39 years old (42%) as well as nice scalp massages (64%). These results express *the rise of hedonic/ aesthetic values*. Also, a vast majority of men would like more of insights and tips from their hairdresser. If most of them never buy male professional hair products and are not able to quote professional brands, 76% state they were never offered to buy them in a salon AND 81% say they would buy them if it were the case! Then, there is a gap between male consumers expectations and retailers' rep and practices as observed in salons and through retailers' discourse analysis.

We refer in our semio-analysis to the 5 masculine archetypes (i.e "Traditional Man", "Tough guy", "Melancholic Man", "Postmodern Man" and "Effeminate Man") that were identified by previous research on brand communication and masculinity (Ourahmoune and Nyeck 2008). We use the same semiotic square (Floch 2005) to compare and analyze our international salons gender narratives. We then were abe to map salons rep of gender identity in terms multiple masculinities (Schroder and Zwick 2004). We discovered that most of the salons address "traditional men" and « tough guys » in their communications on POS (visuals, space organization, staff behavior, practices and offer). Very few emphasize other masculine values: new territories are then left empty. *In Unisex salons, feminine values prevail* and lead to social conformity: men do not often dare cross the barrier by asking "unexpected/illegitimate masculine services". Some men in touch with new masculine beauty trends might find an offer that suits them better in traditional *only for men* salons (scalp massage, manicure…). However, those salons are not appealing to Melancholic and Postmodern customers who do not identify with the very traditional mise-en-scène.

Yet, hair product brands are captive of their retailing channel. Professional hair products do sell only in a selective channel (salons).« *We just launched our professional hair product dedicated to men, we believe it should really perform very well…but we do face a serious obstacle when it comes to our retailers… » (Hair professional manager, Leader international cosmetic brand, Paris).* Then, the brand engaged in an expensive change process through events, learning sessions and communication with their retailers …

**Implications**

Existing literature on changing masculinity and consumer research is mainly consumer or brand discourse oriented; this paper proposes to address a lack by exploring services, retailing/ retailers' point of view.

This research identifies that retailers' resistance consists in internalized traditional gender schemes connecting with "social fears" identified in the literature on male consumers (Kimmel and Tissier-Desbordes 2000, Rinallo 2007, Ourahmoune 2009). This resistance impacts the way beauty services providers address new male consumers beside an evidence of renewed expectations from a significant number of consumers in our sample.

In addition, our research suggests that business resistance to changing socio-cultural values is an insufficiently researched area.

**References**

Badinter, E. (1992), *XY, de l'identité masculine*, Paris, Odile Jacob.

Baudrillard, J. *(1988), De la séduction*, Galilée, Paris, 1979, Gallimard, Folio Essais 81.

Barthes R., (1957), *Mythologies*, Paris, Seuil

Belk, R. W. & Costa, J. A. (1998), The mountain man myth: A contemporary consuming fantasy. *Journal of Consumer Research, 25*, 218-240.

Bourdieu, P. (1998), *La domination masculine*, Paris, Seuil.

Caru, A., Cova B., & Tissier Desbordes E. (2004), Consumerscapes as enclaves of masculinity, *ACR Conference on Gender, Marketing and Consumer Behaviour*, Madison, Wisconsin, June 24-27.

Elliott R. & Elliott C. (2005), Idealized images of the male body in advertising: a reader-response exploration, *Journal of Marketing Communications*, 11, 1, 3-19.

Floch, J-M. (2005), *Semiotics, marketing and communication: Beneath the signs, the strategies*, translated by R. Orr Bodkin from the 1995 french version, New York: Palgrave Macmillan.

Holt D. B. & Thompson C. J. (2004), Man-of-action heroes: The pursuit of heroic masculinity in everyday consumption. *Journal of Consumer Research*, 31, 2, 425.

Kimmel, A. J. & Tissier-Desbordes E. (2000), Males, masculinity, and consumption: An exploratory investigation, *European Advances in Consumer Research*, 4, 243-251.

Mick, D.G., Burroughs, J.E., Hetzel, P. & Brannen, M.Y. (2004), Pursuing the meaning of meaning in the commercial world: An international review of marketing and consumer research founded on semiotics, *Semiotica*, 152, 1/4, 1-74.

Otnes, C. C. & McGrath, M. A. (2001), Perceptions and realities of male shopping behaviour, *Journal of Retailing, 77,* 111-137.

Ourahmoune, N. & Nyeck, S. (2008), Gender values and brand communication: The transfer of masculine representations to brand narratives, *in European Advances in Consumer Research*, 8, 181-188.

Ourahmoune, N. (2009), Intimacy-related male consumption and masculine identity construction: a consumer point of view, in *Asia-Pacific Advances in Consumer Research,* 8.

Patterson, M. & R. Elliott (2002), Negotiating masculinities: Advertising and the inversion of the male gaze. *Consumption Markets and Culture*, 5, 231-246.

Rinallo, D. (2007), Metro/Fashion/Tribes of men: Negotiating the boundaries of men's legitimate consumption, in *Consumer Tribes*, chapter 6 , B. Cova, R. Kozinets & A. Shankar (Edts), Routlege.

Schroeder, J, & Zwick D. (2004), Mirrors of masculinity: Representation and identity in advertising images. *Consumption, Markets and Culture*, March, 7, 1, 21-52.

Spiggle S. (1994), Analysis and interpretation of qualitative data in consumer research, *Journal of Consumer Research*, December, 491-503.

Tuncay, L. & Otnes C.(2007), Exploring the link between masculinity and consumption, in T. M. Lowrey (edts.), *Brick & Mortar Shopping in the 21st Century*, (Erlbaum).

# Investment of Self through Process Involvement

Sukriye Atakan, University of Michigan, USA
Richard P. Bagozzi, University of Michigan, USA
Carolyn Yoon, University of Michigan, USA

## Extended Abstract

Imagine that you are working on your car, building a patio, or making a bookshelf. The process may require your physical involvement (changing a particular part of the engine, placing stones for the patio, cutting and staining the wood for the shelves) and/or intellectual involvement (determining the problem with the car, designing the patio or choosing the color of the shelves). How would these types of involvement affect your evaluation of the final product? Which factor will be the most important for you? Do you think intellectual involvement in the production process will have different results than physical involvement?

These questions are important if companies want to influence and optimize value derived from consumers' involvement in the production process. Little is known about participation of consumers in the production process (i.e. what Toffler referred to as "prosumption"). Our goal is to investigate the factors that affect the value derived from prosumption behavior and the specific consequences of being involved in the production process.

We draw on findings from person-object literature (Belk 1988; Richins 1994; Pierce, Kostova and Dirks 2003) to investigate prosumption. This stream of research indicates that investing the self into the target (creating, shaping or producing an object) results in the most powerful association between the self and the object since one invests labor, time and one's self in this process. During the production or modification process, investment of self into the product can be through intellectual and/or physical involvement. Intellectual involvement entails intellectual stimulation, creativity and/or choice in the process. If one uses his/her intellectual labor during production of the product, then the product may represent the ideas the person has generated and become part of the extended self. Therefore, intellectual stimulation in the process may transfer part of the self to the focal product, and affect personal relevance and evaluation of the product.

Labor creates a sense of ownership. Marx (1867) indicated that a person is the owner of his labor and has rights over production that involves his labor. You may feel that a sweater you have knitted, or a car you have worked on, is special since it absorbed your labor and time. In some cases, people may value self-made products even more than expert-made ones (Norton and Ariely, 2007). Therefore, physical labor may contribute to the value derived from prosumption.

The first study examined the relationship between products and consumers in detail by looking at how intellectual investment during production shapes how consumers relate to products. We hypothesized that higher levels of intellectual investment will enhance product evaluation. Also, we proposed that identification with (hypothesized to be the cognitive dimension of person-object relationship) and attachment to the product (hypothesized to be the affective dimension) mediate the impact of intellectual investment on product evaluation. The study was a three-group between-subjects design where intellectual investment in the process was manipulated at three levels; high, low, none (control condition). In all conditions, participants were given a travel mug with a customizable blank insert. One could remove the insert, draw/write on it and place it back. In the low condition, participants were provided with 12 stickers from which they could choose one to stick onto the blank mug insert. In the high condition, participants were provided with colored pencils and an example sheet which included the same 12 figures from the low intellectual investment condition. They could use this to get ideas, or they could use other figures/shapes they wanted. In the control condition, participants were encouraged to examine the mug but couldn't modify/change it. To equate the time spent with the product, in the control and the low intellectual investment conditions, participants worked on a filler task while the mug was in front of them. Then, all the participants answered identification, attachment, and product evaluation questions. As predicted, the product was valued more highly when the production process allowed higher levels of intellectual investment. Moreover, results showed that identification and attachment mediated the impact of intellectual investment on product evaluation.

Next, we investigated how physical investment in the production process affects person-object relationship. Participants were randomly assigned to one of the three physical investment conditions: high, low and none (control condition). In the high condition, participants were provided with all the supplies to make a picture frame from cardboard. In the low condition, the participants were given pre-made pieces that would be used to make the same frame. In both conditions, detailed step-by-step instructions allowed no creativity or choice. In the control condition, participants were given a pre-made cardboard frame and asked to examine it. To equate the time spent with the product, in the control and the low physical investment conditions, the participants worked on a filler task before evaluating the frame. Then, they answered the same dependent variables from the previous study. Results indicated that even low levels of physical investment enhanced product evaluation. Attachment to the product increased as the level of physical investment in the production process increased. However, identification didn't differ among the three conditions. Physical labor alone doesn't result in identification. Analysis indicated that attachment fully mediated the effect of physical investment on product evaluation. When consumers can invest their physical labor into the product through the production process, they become more attached to but not necessarily identify with the product.

We make several contributions to the literature. First, we operationalize identification with and attachment to a product in measurable terms. This enables us to measure personal relevance of products when consumers are involved in the production process. Next, we demonstrate that intellectual investment enhances product evaluation by enhancing both attachment to and identification with the product. On the other hand, we show that physical investment affects only attachment to but not identification with the product. Physical involvement alone doesn't give the consumer the opportunity to reflect his/her taste, preferences, that's his/her identity, through the product. Therefore, physical involvement affects product evaluation only through attachment. Furthermore, we show that attachment and identification are two different dimensions of person-object relationship.

## Selected References
Belk, Russell W. (1988) "Possessions and the Extended Self," *Journal of Consumer Research*, 15, Sept, 139-168
Norton, Michael and Dan Ariely (2007), "The IKEA Effect: How Labor Leads to Love" ACR Presentation
Pierce, Jon L., Tatiana Kostova and Kurt T. Dirks (2003) "The State of Psychological Ownership: Integrating and Extending a Century of Research," Review of General Psychology, 7(1), 84-107.
Richins, Marsha L. (1994) "Special Possessions and the Expression of Material Values," *Journal of Consumer Research*, 21 (3), 522-533.

# Consumer-based Perceived Product Innovativeness: the Big Seven
Jean Boisvert, American University of Sharjaj, United Arab Emirates

Growing market competition in consumer goods has led to increased concerns regarding the competitive advantage conferred to firms offering innovative products. While insights from consumers are often used as starting point in the design process, what is thought to be innovative by a team of engineers and designers may not be perceived in the same way by target market consumers. Marketers would benefit by knowing more about the specific dimensions underlying consumer perceptions of innovative products.

Personal innovativeness as a personality trait has been addressed in the literature (Cotte and Wood, 2004; Manning et al., 1995; Midgley, 1977; Midgley and Dowling, 1978). The goal of this paper, however, is to clarify the construct of consumer-based perceived product innovativeness. Perceived product innovativeness from the firm's and customer's perspective has been addressed in previous research (Garcia and Calantone, 2002; Danneels and Kleinschmidt, 2001) but definitive construct dimensions have not been identified and systematically tested (cf. Calantone et al., 2006). In reviews of the literature, Danneels and Kleinschmidt (2001) as well as Garcia and Calantone (2002) identified many dimensions that may underlie perceived innovativeness. They noted that specific dimensions have not been employed consistently across studies. Our ultimate goal is to develop a standardized measure that can be employed across future studies so results of studies can be more comparable.

In their meta-analysis on antecedents of product performance, Henard and Szymanski (2001) specified product characteristics as a predictor of product innovativeness. According to the authors, product innovativeness can be defined as perceived newness, originality, uniqueness and radicalness of the product. Sethi et al. (2001) used two factors to define product innovativeness: a) novelty broken down into novel and original, and b) appropriateness broken down into useful and appropriate. Product innovativeness has also been confounded with product uniqueness as defined by customers (Daneels and Kleinschmidt, 2001; Troy et al., 2000; Ali et al., 1995). Uniqueness has also been viewed as a distinct measure of innovativeness in defining product advantage (Henard and Szymanski, 2001; Langerak et al., 2004). Conversely, product newness and uniqueness have also been used as sub-measures of product innovativeness (Salavou, 2005).

Positive product attitudes have been associated with new products perceived to be innovative (i.e., novel and useful to consumers; Troy and Davidow, 1998). It also appears that when the innovativeness measure includes a "meaningfulness" dimension it yields a stronger relationship with product success (Szymanski et al., 2007). In addition to novelty dimension, Fang (2008) found dimensions like "challenging existing ideas," "creative and interesting," underlying perceived product innovativeness. In one of the original studies identifying factors underlying perceptions of new product launches, Cooper (1979) identified product uniqueness superiority further broken down into newness, uniqueness, and superiority to meet customer's needs, cost reduction and higher quality.

In sum, inconsistencies exist in the literature in terms of how to define the construct and dimensions underlying product innovativeness as perceived by consumers. The ultimate is our research to provide a tool that will allow more consistency across studies. In addition to using concepts identified in the reviews of the literature, in-depth interviews were conducted in order to gather the widest possible range of adjectives related to perceived product innovativeness from the consumer point of view. Inspired by a methodology used by Li et al. (2008), 34 student interviewers were asked to conduct several in-depth interviews each. They were required to recruit campus across ages, genders and education among students and non-students of over twenty years of age. Based on a methodology used by Krishnan (1996) for generating brand associations, 340 participants were asked to provide top-of-mind thoughts using open-ended questioning. The initial set of statements / items was screened by faculty judges, independent of the study, to group the ones with similar meanings but also to eliminate redundant and non relevant attributes in order to reduce the pool of adjectives to a manageable size (Bearden et al., 2001). As a result, a final list of 68 attributes was compiled.

A questionnaire was developed based on a 7 point bipolar Likert scale where the resulting set of 68 items was submitted to principal component analysis. The decision to use principal component analysis was driven by the fact that the theory behind consumer-based perceived product innovativeness has not been clearly conceptualized and sufficiently detailed regarding the relations between indicators and the construct (Gerbing and Anderson, 1988). A survey was conducted and the questionnaires administrated to a sample of 218 adults around a campus community of an American university. Participants were selected based on a wide range of ages, gender and education. After a series of iterations, an optimal 7-factor solution accounting for a significant 61.4% of the variance explained appeared to be meaningful and interpretable. The uncovered factors are in order: 1) Usability, 2) Novelty, 3) Desirability, 4) Newness, 5) Sophistication, 6) Uniqueness and, 7) Worthiness.

In conclusion, this study confirmed underlying dimensions of consumer-based perceived product innovativeness found in past research and, importantly, also uncovered distinct dimensions that have not been addressed in previous research. Results of our research confirm that consumer-based perceived product innovativeness is a multi-dimensional construct. The conclusion of our study proposes that a new scale be developed and tested across different types of product categories. This scale would then be used in future research on perceptions of innovative products.

## Selected References

Ali, A., Krapfel R Jr., and D. LaBahn (1995), "Product Innovativeness and Entry Strategy: Impact on Cycle Time and Break-even Time." *Journal of Product Innovation Management,* 12(1), 54–69.

Bearden, W. O., Hardesty, D.M., & R.L. Rose (2001), "Consumer Self-confidence: Refinements in Conceptualization and Measurement," *Journal of Consumer Research,* 28 (1), 121–134.

Calantone, R. J., Kwong, C. and A.S. Cui (2006), "Decomposing Product Innovativeness and Its Effects on New Product Success," *Journal of Product Innovation Management,* 23 (4), 420-421.

Cooper, R. G. (1979), "The Dimensions of Industrial New Product Success and Failure," *Journal of Marketing,* 43 (3), 93-103.

Cotte, J. and S.L. Wood (2004), "Families and Innovative Consumer Behavior: a Triadic Analysis of Sibling and Parental Influence," *Journal of Consumer Research,* 31 (1), 78-86.

Daneels E. and E.J. Kleinschmidt (2001), "Product Innovativeness from the Firm's Perspective: Its Dimensions and Their Relation with Project Selection and Performance," *Journal of Product Innovation Management,* 18 (4), 357-373.

Fang, E. (2008), Customer participation and the trade-off between new product innovativeness and speed to market, *Journal of Marketing, 72 (4),* 98-104.

Garcia, R. and R.J. Calantone (2002), "A Critical Look at Technological Innovation Typology and Innovativeness Terminology: a Literature Review, *Journal of Product Innovation Management,* 19 (3), 110-132.

Gerbing, D. W., & Anderson, J. C. (1988), "An Updated Paradigm for Scale Development Incorporating Unidimensionality and its Assessment," *Journal of Marketing Research,* 25 (2), 186–192.

Henard, D. H. and D.M. Szymanski (2001), "Why Some New Products Are More Successful Than Others, *Journal of Marketing Research,* 38 (3), 362-375.

Krishnan, H. S. (1996), "Characteristics of Memory Associations: A Consumer-based Brand Equity Perspective," *International Journal of Research in Marketing,* 13 (4), 389-405.

Langerak, F., Hultink, E. J. and H. Robben. (2004), "The Impact of Market Orientation, Product Advantage, and Launch Proficiency on New Product Performance and Organizational Performance," *Journal of Product Innovation Management,*21(2), 79–94.

Li, F., Zhou, N., Kashyap, R. and Z. Yang (2008), "Brand Trust as a Second-order Factor: An Alternative Measurement Model, *International Journal of Market Research,* 50 (6), 817-839.

Manning, K. C., Bearden, W. O. and T.J. Madden (1995), "Consumer Innovativeness and The Adoption Process, *Journal of Consumer Psychology,* 4 (4), 329-346.

Midgley, D. F. (1977), "Innovation and New Product Marketing," New York: Halsted Press; John Wiley & Sons.

Midgley, D. F. and G.R. Dowling (1978), "Innovativeness: The Concept and Its Measurement," *Journal of Consumer Research,* 4 (4), 229-242.

Salavou, H. (2005), "Do Customer and Technology Orientations Influence Product Innovativeness in SMEs? Some New Evidence," *Journal of Marketing Management,* 21 (3-4), 307-338.

Sethi, R., Smith, D. C. and C.W. Park (2001), "Cross-functional Product Development Teams, Creativity, and Innovativeness of New Consumer Products," *Journal of Marketing Research,* 38 (1), 73-85.

Szymanski, D. M., Kroff M. W. and L.C. Troy (2007), "Innovativeness and New Product Success: Insights from the Cumulative Evidence," *Journal of the Academy of Marketing Science,* 35 (1), 35-52.

Troy, L. C., White J. C. and R.N. Gerlich (2000), "The Influence of Product Uniqueness on
Retailer's Acceptance of New Products: A Contigency Investigation," AMA Conference Proceedings, American Marketing Association Winter Conference, p. 54.

Troy, L. C. and M. Davidow (1998), "The Relationship Between Customer-perceived Product Innovativeness and New Products Potential for Success," AMA Conference Proceedings, American Marketing Association Winter Conference, p. 127.

# Negative Dimensions of Brand Personality

Jenny Jiao, Virginia Tech, USA
Jane Machin, Virginia Tech, USA

## Extended Abstract

Brand personality is the set of human characteristics or traits that consumers attribute to a brand (Aaker, 1997). Brand personality is of great importance to both consumers and marketers. Among other outcomes, research demonstrates that the brand personality construct helps consumers to: evaluate brands and build relationships (Fournier, 1998); develop emotional attachments to brands (Landon, 1974); differentiate brands (Crask & Laskey, 1990) and increase brand preference and usage (Sirgy, 1982).

This research seeks to extend our understanding of the brand personality construct by focusing specifically on the *negative* dimensions of a brand's personality. We define negative brand personality as the set of *negative* human characteristics or traits that consumers attribute to a brand. For example, some consumers might associate Paris Hilton perfume with the human personality traits of "fickle" and "naïve." We believe prior work has overlooked the negative dimensions of brand personality.

The study design in Aaker's (1997) seminal paper on brand personality promoted the generation of predominantly positive personality dimensions. First, the process likely led to the complete omission of some negative traits. Participants were asked to assess the descriptiveness of an initial pool of traits by imagining how descriptive the trait was when thinking about *positive, liked* brands such as Wrangler jeans. It is likely that many initial negative traits were not considered descriptive of such positive brands and thus omitted from the subsequent generation of dimensions.

Second, participants were presented with the positively valenced end-point of any particular trait pair (e.g. "exciting" not "boring"). This was purposeful, because "the ultimate use of the scale is to determine the extent to which brand personality affects the probability that consumers approach (versus avoid) products (Aaker, 1997, p 350)." However research in many different domains such as attitudes (Thompson & Zanna, 1995), emotions (Watson, Clark, & Tellegen, 1988), decision making (Park, Jun, & Macinnis, 2000; Shafir, 1993; Tversky & Kahneman, 1986) and motivation (Higgins, 1997)suggests that approach and avoid processes are independent and not mirror images of one another. In a similar manner, consumers may associate brands with both negative and positive personality traits simultaneously. Examining the negatively valenced end-point therefore may lead to a richer conceptualization of the brand personality construct.

Indeed, while many brands are positively viewed, by no means are all of them (Winchester, Romaniuk, & Bogomolova, 2008). Oftentimes we believe that brands are avoided because consumers dislike aspects of the brand's personality, not because of defective functional performance. For example, previous research suggests that consumers boycott brands they view as "egregious," "unintelligent" or "foolish" (Kleine & Hubbert, 1993; Kozinets & Handelman, 2004). In some extreme cases, we believe this can even lead consumers to avoid brands whose performance they enjoy but whose personality they do not. For example, the lead author likes the smell of Paris Hilton perfume but will never use it because she dislikes the negative personality traits associated with it.

Finally, noteworthy that while Aaker's dimensions map closely to three of the original "Big Five" human personality factors (Briggs, 1992), there is no equivalent for the most negative of the human dimensions–neuroticism. The equivalent brand traits that this dimension captures–"disturbing," "irritating," "fickle"–are thus missing from current brand personality construct.

In these studies we seek to understand the number and nature of negative brand personality. Planned research that examines the interaction between negative and positive personality dimensions on decision making is also outlined.

## Personality Trait Generation

We began by collecting negative personality traits from academic literature and original qualitative studies.

First, 281 non-redundant personality traits were collected from literature, including Big Five, International Personality Item Pool, Traits of Human Consciousness, 16 Personality Factors (Cattell 1946, 1947). Second, we took the antonyms of the positive traits in Aaker's (1997) study to add a further 202 traits. We also collected 219 unique negative traits from five focus group studies. In total, 530 non-redundant negative personality traits were generated.

Next, we reduced these 530 traits to a more manageable number by asking 93 participants to rate how descriptive of brands they considered the traits. Similar to Aaker (1997) we wanted participants at this stage to think about lots of different brands, not one in particular. Unlike Aaker however, the brand examples we gave, as well as the personality traits, were more negative (e.g. State Farm–boring, old-fashioned, and slow). Participants rated how descriptive the 530 traits were of brands in general on a 7-point scale (1=Not at all descriptive to 7=Extremely descriptive.) The ratings ranged from 2.25 to 5.35. We set the cut off at one standard deviation (0.55) above the mean (3.37) for each trait leaving 158 personality traits for the next stage.

## Stimuli Selection

Drawing from extant research (Aaker, 1997; Batra and Ahtola, 1991; Subodh & Srinivas, 1998) sixty representative brands were selected from twenty product categories. Each product category included hedonic (e.g., Cardiac Car), utilitarian (e.g., Ford Car) and both hedonic &utilitarian (e.g., Toyota) brands, as determined by a pre-test.

## Negative Brand Personality Dimensions

We are currently in the process of asking participants to rate the extent to which the 158 negative personality traits describe each of the sixty specific brands. (To eliminate, participants only rate a subset of the brands, with one brand being rated by all to ensure inter-rater agreement. Procedures mimic Aaker (1997) and are omitted for brevity's sake). These ratings will be subjected to factor analysis to identify the underlying negative brand personality dimensions. Finally, facet analysis will be conducted to identify the three traits that best represent each dimension. *The results from these two stages will be available by the conference.*

Future research will investigate how the positive and negative dimensions of a brand's personality interact. For example, if consumers are *uncertain* about the options in a choice set, we hypothesize they will focus more on negative personality traits. We also believe that negative personality traits may help to find stronger support for brand-self congruity effects. This study fills up the gap between brand personality and brand avoidance, by demonstrating that a brand not only has positive personality traits but also negative brand personality traits. This study contributes to the anti-consumption and consumer-avoidance research by exploring the phenomenon of negative brand personality and brand avoidance, this study also contributes to the measurement research by building the first measurement for negative brand personality.

### References
Aaker, J. L. (1997). Dimensions of Brand Personality. *Journal of Marketing Research, 34*(3), 347-356.
Batra, Rajeev, and Olli T. Ahtola. (1991). Measuring the Hedonic and Utilitarian Sources of Con- sumer Attitudes," *Marketing Letters*, 2 (April), 159-170.
Bhat, Subodh, and Srinivas K. Reddy (1998). Symbolic and Functional Positioning of Brands. *Journal of Consumer. Marketing,* Vol. 15 (1), 32-43.
Briggs, S. R. (1992). Assessing the 5-Factor Model of Personality Description. *Journal of Personality, 60*(2), 253-293.
Cattell, R. B. (1946). The Description and Measurement of Personality. New York: Harcourt, Brace, & World.
Cattell, R. B. (1957). Personality and Motivation Structure and Measurement. New York: World Book.
Crask, M. R., & Laskey, H. A. (1990). A Positioning-Based Decision-Model for Selecting Advertising Messages. *Journal of Advertising Research, 30*(4), 32-38.
Fournier, S. (1998). Consumers and their brands: Developing relationship theory in consumer research. *Journal of Consumer Research, 24*(4), 343-373.
Higgins, E. T. (1997). Beyond pleasure and pain. *American Psychologist, 52*(12), 1280-1300.
Kleine, S. S., & Hubbert, A. R. (1993). How Do Consumers Acquire a New Food-Consumption System When It Is Vegetarian. *Advances in Consumer Research, Vol 20, 20*, 196-201.
Kozinets, R. V., & Handelman, J. M. (2004). Adversaries of consumption: Consumer movements, activism, and ideology. *Journal of Consumer Research, 31*(3), 691-704.
Landon, E. L. (1974). Self-Concept, Ideal Self-Concept, and Consumer Purchase Intentions. *Journal of Consumer Research, 1*(2), 44-51.
Park, C. W., Jun, S. Y., & Macinnis, D. J. (2000). Choosing what I want versus rejecting what I do not want: An application of decision framing to product option choice decisions. *Journal of Marketing Research, 37*(2), 187-202.
Shafir, E. (1993). Choosing Versus Rejecting-Why Some Options Are Both Better and Worse Than Others. *Memory & Cognition, 21*(4), 546-556.
Sirgy, M. J. (1982). Self-Concept in Consumer-Behavior-a Critical-Review. *Journal of Consumer Research, 9*(3), 287-300.
Thompson, M. M., & Zanna, M. P. (1995). The Conflicted Individual-Personality-Based and Domain-Specific Antecedents of Ambivalent Social-Attitudes. *Journal of Personality, 63*(2), 259-288.
Tversky, A., & Kahneman, D. (1986). Rational Choice and the Framing of Decisions. *Journal of Business, 59*(4), S251-S278.
Watson, D., Clark, L. A., & Tellegen, A. (1988). Development and Validation of Brief Measures of Positive and Negative Affect-the Panas Scales. *Journal of Personality and Social Psychology, 54*(6), 1063-1070.
Winchester, M., Romaniuk, J., & Bogomolova, S. (2008). Positive and negative brand beliefs and brand defection/uptake. *European Journal of Marketing, 42*(5-6), 553-570.

# Is Abercrombie Making Me Arrogant?
## The Impact of Brand Personality Traits on Post-Consumption Behavior

Lauren Trabold, Baruch College, USA
Pragya Mathur, Baruch College, USA

Research has documented that consumers are influenced by brands that they encounter (Ferraro et al. 2009). In general, brand influence on behavior has been explained through a motivational account in which the brand's traits activate an underlying goal, which subsequently elicits goal-directed consumer behavior (Fitzsimons et al. 2008). This is possible when the brand is associated with a goal that represents a desirable end-state (Sela & Shiv 2009). Although extant literature documents robust findings across positive traits, the influence of negative brand traits has yet to be explored. Furthermore, the potential effect on downstream behavioral intentions has not been addressed. We explore these two important areas of interest in our research.

Brands may have positive trait associations (e.g. upper-class: Calvin Klein) or negative trait associations (e.g. arrogance: Abercrombie). Although consumers may be influenced by brands through goal-activation, this account is limited to desirable outcomes and does not explain the influence of brands with negative trait associations. A possible explanation is semantic priming, in which exposure to a brand subsequently elicits congruent behavior which is not restricted to desirable outcomes (Sela & Shiv 2009).

Beyond the immediate effect of brand exposure, the downstream effect on behavioral intentions is not well understood (Chartrand et al. 2008). In the current research, we propose that brands may influence consumers even when the end-state is not desirable. Importantly, we suggest that brand exposure may influence consumer perceptions of their own traits. In three studies using real brands, we suggest that brands may influence consumers through trait priming, and show that this influence may impact downstream behavior.

Study 1 was designed to test if brands associated with specific traits can influence both self-trait perceptions and downstream behaviors, even when the respondent does not possess chronicity for the given trait. Respondents participated in a 3(brand: Calvin Klein, Gap, Timberland) x 2(time: pre and post brand exposure) mixed design study. Brands were pre-tested for associated traits: Calvin Klein: up-to-date, successful, and upper class; Gap: down to earth, honest, and reliable; Timberland: outdoorsy, tough, and rugged. Respondents first filled out a self-reported personality trait index adapted from Aaker's brand personality scale (1997); then they began an ostensibly unrelated study, guised with the intent to "Get to know the undergraduate student." Respondents imagined that they were planning to get dressed for the day and were shown a picture of a closet from which they would take their clothes; their clothes for the day were a t-shirt and jeans branded with Calvin Klein, Gap, or Timberland depending upon the experimental condition. Subjects then indicated their plans to engage in various activities including pro-social behaviors and, finally, completed the self-reported personality trait scale again.

Analysis revealed that, as expected, brand consumption significantly impacted downstream behavioral intentions. Respondents were asked to indicate the activities that they were likely to engage in from a diverse list which included pro-social behaviors (volunteering, community service), prestigious behaviors (shopping in prominent neighborhoods, vacationing in exclusive places), daring behaviors (bungee jumping), and everyday behaviors (spending time with family, cleaning). Importantly, significant results were concentrated in the area of pro-social activities.

After imagining the consumption of Calvin Klein and Timberland (versus Gap), respondents rated themselves significantly more likely to engage in behaviors such as volunteering (Calvin Klein: $p<.05$; Timberland: $p<.01$) and performing community service (Calvin Klein: $p<.05$). Respondents' increased likelihood of engaging in pro-social behaviors suggests that trait adoption has ramifications beyond the consumption domain and reveals an alternative way of influencing consumers to adopt pro-social behaviors. While neither Calvin Klein nor Timberland actively promote community service or volunteering, respondents were significantly more likely to do so after consuming these brands versus Gap, a brand that does engage in social marketing.

Study 2 was designed to illuminate the process by which downstream behavioral intentions are influenced (as shown in Study 1) and to establish that consumers can be influenced by negative traits. We offer evidence that impact on downstream behaviors is due to trait priming and not goal-activation due to the undesirable outcomes elicited by negative trait influence. Respondents participated in a 4(brand: Calvin Klein, Timberland, Everlast, Abercrombie) x 2(time: pre and post brand exposure) mixed design study. The two negative brands introduced in this study were pretested for trait associations. Everlast: lethargic, old-fashioned; Abercrombie: arrogant, deceptive. The procedure was identical to that of Study 1.

Analysis illustrated that consumers can be influenced by negative traits and that they may elicit undesirable downstream behaviors. After imagining consumption of Abercrombie, Everlast, or Timberland, subjects were significantly more likely than those who consumed Calvin Klein to joke about someone's appearance (Abercrombie: $p<.01$, Everlast: $p<.05$, Timberland: $p<.01$), to make fun of others (Abercrombie: $p<.05$), to skip school (Abercrombie: $p<.05$, Everlast: $p<.05$), and to lay on the couch all day (Abercrombie: $p<.05$). Of further interest, the measure of several self-reported negative personality traits (deceptive, lazy, selfish) varied between pre and post brand exposure such that respondent's rated themselves significantly lower post exposure. We expect that this is due to social desirability effects. We plan to run Study 3 to address this issue.

A proposed Study 3 will be nearly identical to Study 2, with the addition of a cognitive load task after the pre-exposure personality trait inventory. We expect that in the cognitive load condition, respondents' ability to adjust their self-reported negative traits post -brand exposure will be diminished, resulting in post-traits that may be consistent with behavioral intentions, thereby supporting our process.

In three studies, we expect to demonstrate that consumers may be influenced by brands that have both positive and negative trait associations and that these associations may result in important downstream behaviors. Our work aims to add to the growing understanding on how incidental brand influences alter human behavior.

### References

Aaker, Jennifer L. (1997), "Dimensions of Brand Personality," *Journal of Marketing Research*, 34(August), 347-356.

Chartrand, Tanya L., Joel Huber, Baba Shiv, and Robin J. Tanner (2008), "Nonconscious Goals and Consumer Choice," *Journal of Consumer Research*, 35(August), 189-201.

Ferraro, Rosellina, James R. Bettman, and Tanya L. Chartrand (2009), "The Power of Strangers: The Effect of Incidental Consumer Brand Encounters on Brand Choice," *Journal of Consumer Research*, 35(February), 729-741.

Fitzsimons, Grainne M., Tanya L. Chartrand, and Gavan J. Fitzsimons (2008), "Automatic Effects of Brand Exposure on Motivated Behavior: How Apple Makes You "Think Different," *Journal of Consumer Research*, 35(June), 21-35.

Sela, Aner and Baba Shiv (2009), "Unraveling Priming: When Does the Same Prime Activate a Goal versus a Trait?," *Journal of Consumer Research*, 36(October), 418-433.

# Sharing the Reward or Blaming the Failure:
## The Moderating Role of Self-Brand Connection on Attitude towards the Brand

Marina Carnevale, Baruch College, USA

### Extended Abstract

Imagine that Susan and Jenny would like to purchase a Gucci handbag. Susan has just received a job promotion and decides to reward herself shopping. Jenny, instead, has just learned that the promotion she was hoping to have didn't go through; to cheer herself up, she decides to do some shopping. Will these differences in the psychological contexts that prompt the purchase decision be reflected in Susan and Jenny's attitude towards Gucci? Will it vary depending on the extent to which they feel connected to the brand? The purpose of this research is to address these questions by exploring how the psychological context in which attitude towards a brand is solicited may affect the way consumers evaluate such brand.

Self-Brand Connection (SBC) represents the extent to which individuals have incorporated brands into their self-concept (Escalas and Bettman 2003). Research suggests that increasing one's feeling that a brand is "me" will lead to more favorable attitude towards that brand (Mogliner and Aaker, 2009). The assumption is that individuals are motivated to view themselves favorably (Allport 1961; Taylor and Brown 1988). Consequently, people hold positive automatic associations with almost anything that is associated with themselves (Greenwald and Banajj 1995; Hetts, Sakuma, and Pelham, 1999). This might explain why when individuals feel that they had achieved some extraordinary work, a need to gratify the self prompts towards the consumption of products that would reward such feeling (Kivetz and Zheng 2006), likely those that consumers feel connected to. Hence, it is expected that the positive associations that consumers hold about themselves should transfer to such "reward" brands by means of self-connection. Simply put, when self-brand connection is high, consumers seeking to gratify the self are likely to exhibit positive post-purchase evaluations, such as attitude towards the brand.

The abovementioned effects would suggest that when individuals instead view themselves unfavorably, negative associations to the self tend to transfer to anything individuals feel connected to, and thus decrease the attitude towards a brand they feel connected to. Interestingly, however, research has shown that the act of purchasing a product might on the contrary be prompt by the need to compensate for some bad feeling about the self (Tice, Bratslavsky, and Baumeister 2001). For example, the inability to make the self perform or monitor specific actions may motivate individuals towards some immediate pleasure (i.e., purchase) that could compensate for such bad feeling (Baumeister 2002). I expect that purchases made as self-compensation will reflect such negative feelings about the self in less favorable post-purchase attitudes. These effects, however, should only happen when consumers feel connected to the brand. The case of "prestige possessions", such as designer jeans or handbags, appears to be particularly interesting since they are a category of goods where spending a large amount of money on the products reflects one's identity (Bearden and Etzel 1982).

Study 1 examines whether purchases made as self-gratification (self-compensation) will evoke more (less) favorable post-purchase attitudes as opposed to a control condition. Further, I expect that such effects arise only in the case of high self-brand connection.

## Study 1

*Method.* Eighty-two undergraduate students participated in the study. Subjects were randomly assigned to one of three conditions (Motivation to purchase: self-gratification vs. self-compensation vs. control). Then, participants were asked to list the brand that they had considered in the purchase scenario. Next, participants' feelings of self-brand connection were measured by adapting Escalas and Bettman's (2003) scale. Next, subjects reported their attitudes towards the brand using a two item 7-point scale (Like/Good), anchored at "not at all" and "very much so". Manipulation checks followed. Also, measures of self-esteem and of involvement with the product category were taken to avoid potential confounds (Escalas and Bettman 2003).

Participants in the self-gratification [self compensation] condition read the following scenario: "It is the end of the semester. You just got your grades and learned that you received an A [C] in your marketing course. This was really exciting [devastating] because you worked really hard all semester. To reward yourself [compensate] for this good [bad] grade you decide to go out and buy yourself a pair of designer jeans. Even though you don't need them, you decide to buy them anyway to reward yourself [make up] for the A [C] grade". In the control condition there was no mention of the class grade.

*Results.* Findings showed that the manipulation worked successfully. The key dependent variable was attitude towards the brand. Motivation to purchase, mean-centered SBC, and the interaction between motivation to purchase and SBC were included as independent variables. As expected, results showed a significant interaction of motivation to purchase and SBC. To explore the nature of the interaction, I compared whether there were significant differences across motivation to purchase conditions at both low and high levels of SBC. As SBC is a continuous measure, I performed a spotlight analysis at plus and minus one standard deviation from the mean of SBC (Aiken and West 1991; Fitzsimons 2008). The planned contrasts revealed that for low SBC, individuals' attitudes towards the brand do not significantly vary across motivation to purchase conditions ($p > .1$). However, as hypothesized, for those individuals who hold high levels of SBC, attitude towards the brand significantly differs across motivation to purchase conditions ($p < 0.05$). No other measures (i.e., self-esteem and product category involvement) varied significantly across conditions ($p > .1$).

## Discussion

By illustrating how individuals' feelings about the self may affect post purchase evaluations for brands they feel connected to, this research develops a greater understanding of how brands are related to the self concept. In study 2 I want to explore whether the different psychological contexts that solicit attitude may also directly influence consumers' brand choice. Consumers might be very strategic in their choices when there is some asset they feel should be protected (Zauberman, Ratner, and Kim 2009). This suggests that individuals might decide to preserve their favorite brand from the negative feelings associated with the choice they are about to do. On the contrary, consumers might be "strategically" motivated to choose their favorite brand when such brand is going to be associated with the positive feelings about the self and the reward achieved.

## References

Aiken, Leona and Stephen G. West (1991), *Multiple Regression: Testing and Interpreting Interactions*, Newbury Park, CA: Sage.

Allport, Gordon W. (1961), *Pattern and Growth in Personality*, New York: Holt, Rinehart & Winston.

Baumeister, Roy F. (2002), "Yielding to Temptation: Self-Control Failure, Impulsive Purchasing, and Consumer Behavior," *Journal of Consumer Research*, 28 (March), 670-676.

Bearden, William and Michael J. Etzel (1982), "Reference Group Influence on Product and Brand Purchase Decisions," *Journal of Consumer Research*, 9 (September), 183–94.

Escalas, Jennifer E. and James R. Bettman (2003), "You Are What They Eat: The Influence of Reference Groups on Consumer Connections to Brands," *Journal of Consumer Psychology*, 13 (3), 339-48.

Fitzsimons, Gavan J. (2008), "Death to Dichotomizing," *Journal of Consumer Research*, 35 (1), 5–8.

Greenwald, Anthony G. and Mahzarin R. Banaji (1995), "Implicit Social Cognition: Attitudes, Self-Esteem, and Stereotypes," *Psychological Review*, 102 (January), 4–27.

Hetts, John J., Michiko Sakuma, and BrettW. Pelham (1999), "Two Roads to Positive Regard: Implicit and Explicit Self-Evaluation and Culture," *Journal of Experimental Social Psychology*, 35 (November), 512–59.

Kivetz, Ran and Yuhuang Zheng (2006), "Determinants of Justification and Self-Control", *Journal of Experimental Psychology*, 135 (4), 572-587.

Mogilner, Cassie and Jennifer Aaker (2009), "The Time vs. Money Effect": Shifting Product Attitudes and Decisions through Personal Connection," *Journal of Consumer Research*, 36 (2), 277-91.

Taylor, Shelley and Jonathon Brown (1988), "Illusion and Well-Being: A Social Psychological Perspective on Mental Health," *Psychological Bulletin*, 103 (March), 193–210.

Tice, Dianne M., Ellen Bratslavsky, and Roy F. Baumeister (2001), "Emotional Distress Regulation Takes Precedence Over Impulse Control: If You Feel Bad, Do It!," *Journal of Personality and Social Psychology*, 80 (1), 53-67.

Zauberman, Gal, Rebecca K. Ratner, and B. Kyu Kim (2009), "Memories as Assets: Strategic Memory Protection in Choice over Time," *Journal of Consumer Research*, 35 (5), 715-28.

# Determinants of Consumer-Brand Reunion After a Break-up

Svetlana Bogomolova, University of South Australia, Australia

## Extended Abstract

This research uses a framework of consumer-brand relationships (Fournier 1998) and extends the work into consumer-brand 'break-ups' (Fajer and Schouten 1995; Mai and Canti 2008) by examining which factors influence consumers to restore relationships with previously abandoned brands.

Breaking up with a brand could be a significant event in consumers' lives (Fajer and Schouten 1995; Mai and Canti 2008). Terminating brand relationships can take a lot of consumers' time, resources and emotions (Keaveney 1995). Therefore, the break-up experience might have a strong impact on consumers' future decisions, in particular, whether to deal with the same brand again (Stauss and Friege 1999). Consequently, it is important to understand the effects circumstances prior, during and following a consumer-brand break-up have on consumers' future propensities to revive those relationships.

Only a few academic studies have directly examined the notion of lost customers' reunion with their former brands (Homburg, Hoyer, and Stock 2007; Stauss and Friege 1999; Thomas, Blattberg, and Fox 2004; Tokman, Davis, and Lemon 2007). Stauss and Friedge (1999) presented a conceptual base for profitable regain management and segmentation of lost customers. Thomas et al. (2004) proposed an optimal pricing strategy for winback offers. Homburg et al (2007) focused on factors during a revival process that increase the winback propensity. Finally, Tokman et al. (2007) proposed a model of the perceived value of winback offer. Principally, these studies examined the issue from the brand's perspective, assessing what managers can do to lure lost customers back. However, there is a need for a study that looks into the focal issue from the consumers' perspective, taking into account the dynamic nature of the consumer-brand break-up process.

Firstly, it is important to understand the relationship consumers held with a brand before the break-up (Fajer and Schouten 1995). Focusing on more objective determinants (such as facts of prior behaviour) avoids potential bias in consumers' post-termination responses (as per Cognitive Dissonance Theory (Festinger 1957)). The first determinant of prior relationship is its length before termination (Thomas et al. 2004). Another determinant is consumer loyalty or disloyalty to the brand, in a form of variety-seeking behaviour (Givon 1984) that results in sole or multiple brand usage (Bird, Channon, and Ehrenberg 1970).

The next set of items describes the process of relationship termination. Attribution Theory (Weiner 2000) suggests that depending on whom consumers hold responsible for the break-up (the brand itself, attraction of competition or themselves-in case of changes in personal circumstances), it will affect how consumers evaluate the experience. Indeed, the reasons for defection were found to have a strong impact on the likelihood of winning back lost customers (Stauss and Friege 1999; Tokman et al. 2007). In a multi-product financial relationship, complete or partial termination could also describe the nature of a break-up.

Finally, factors occurring after the break-up include consumers' post-defection opinions of the former brand, in the form of positive or negative associations and overall evaluations (Bogomolova and Romaniuk 2009). The time lapsed since the event has also been described as an important moderator of consumers' opinions (for example, due to the Cognitive Dissonance Adjustment (Festinger 1957)). Additionally, consumers' demographic characteristics are also believed to have an impact on consumer decisions (Homburg et al. 2007; Tokman et al. 2007).

This research used the context of financial service relationships, which is typically characterised with high involvement (both financial and emotional), long-term (due to its subscription nature) and multi-product relationships, with personal interaction components (Berry 2000). Customers who have terminated relationships with a financial service provider were identified using the provider's records. They were approached by phone for a 15-minute interview, achieving a 30% response rate. The demographic profile of the final sample (141 respondents) was similar to the profile of all provider's lost customers. A hierarchical regression model estimated the relative impact of each factor on the propensity of consumers who have previously terminated relationships to return to their former provider (measured by an 11-point Juster probability scale (Juster 1966)). The factors were inputted in four consecutive models, starting with demographic characteristics, followed by groups of factors occurring before, during and after the termination.

The results showed that the following five (out of eleven) factors significantly contributed to the propensity of lost customers' reunion with the former brand. First, the higher was the number of positive attributes associated with the former brand ($\beta=0.26$, $p<.01$) and the higher was the overall evaluation (ß=0.47, *p*<.01), the higher was the propensity for consumers to return. This suggests that consumers who feel positive about their former provider (even after defection) are more likely to consider returning. Furthermore, the number of different brands respondents had used, had a significant negative impact on the propensity to return (ß=-0.18, *p*<.01), suggesting that consumers who have other providers or are experienced in switching providers are less likely to return. Next, the longer the time lapse since defection (but still within a year), the higher was the propensity of winback (ß=0.15, *p*<.05). This suggests that consumers are more likely to return after they had some time to reflect on the decision ('to cool their heads off'), but not so long that they could forget about those relationships. Finally, an increase in household income had a negative relationship with the propensity of return (ß=-0.11, *p*<.01). This suggests that consumers who have more money (who are perhaps, more savvy at managing finances) are less likely to return to their former brand.

In summary, this study offers a contribution to consumer research in the area of consumer-brand reunion after break-up, by identifying factors that moderate the likelihood of future reunion.

## References

Barry, Leonard L (2000), "Cultivating Service Brand Equity," *Journal of the Academy of Marketing Science*, 28 (1), 128-37.

Bird, Michael, Charles Channon, and A.S.C. Ehrenberg (1970), "Brand Image and Brand Usage," *Journal of Marketing Research*, 7 (3), 307-14.

Bogomolova, Svetlana and Jenni Romaniuk (2009), "Brand Defection in a Business-to-Business Financial Service," *Journal of Business Research*, 62 (3), 291-96.

Fajer, Mary T and John W Schouten (1995), "Breakdown and Dissolution of Person-Brand Relationships," *Advances in consumer research*, 22 (1), 663-67.

Festinger, L (1957), *A Theory of Cognitive Dissonance*, Stanford: Stanford University Press.

Fournier, Susan (1998), "Consumers and Their Brands: Developing Relationship Theory in Consumer Research," *Journal of Consumer Research*, 24 (4), 343-53.

Givon, Moshe (1984), "Variety Seeking through Brand Switching," *Marketing Science*, 3 (1, Winter), 1-22.

Homburg, Christian, Wayne D Hoyer, and Ruth Maria Stock (2007), "How to Get Lost Customers Back? A Study of Antecedents of Relationship Revival," *Journal of the Academy of Marketing Science*, 35 (4), 461-74.

Juster, F. Thomas (1966), *Consumer Buying Intentions and Purchase Probability: An Experiment in Survey Design*, New York: National Bureau of Economic Research, Columbia University Press.

Keaveney, Susan M (1995), "Customer Switching Behavior in Service Industries: An Exploratory Study," *Journal of Marketing*, 59 (April), 71-82.

Mai, L W and P G Canti (2008), "Dissolution of a Person-Brand Relationship: An Understanding of Brand-Detachment," *European Advances in Consumer Research*, 8, 424-30.

Stauss, Bernd and Christian Friege (1999), "Regaining Service Customers: Costs and Benefits of Regain Management," *Journal of Service Research*, 1 (4), 347-61.

Thomas, Jacquelyn S, Robert C Blattberg, and Edward J Fox (2004), "Recapturing Lost Customers," *Journal of Marketing Research*, 41 (1), 31-45.

Tokman, Mert, Lenita M Davis, and Katherine N Lemon (2007), "The Wow Factor: Creating Value through Win-Back Offers to Reacquire Lost Customers," *Journal of Retailing*, 83 (1), 47-64.

Weiner, Bernard (2000), "Attributional Thoughts About Consumer Behaviour," *Journal of Consumer Research*, 27 (December), 382-87.

# Consumers' Investments in Brand Relationships:
# An Explorative Investigation of Specific Investments in Consumer-Brand Relationships

Tarje Gaustad, Norwegian School of Management, Norway

## Extended Abstract

The literature on consumer-brand relationships is heavily influenced by research on inter-personal relationships from social psychology (Fournier 2009). One factor known to influence persistence in an inter-personal relationship is the size of relational specific investments (Rusbult, Martz & Agnew 1998). Such investments are defined as resources that are invested in the relationship and that lose a significant part of their value if the relationship is ended (Rusbult 1980). Invested resources enhance commitment to the relationship because the act of investment serves as a powerful psychological inducement to persist and it increases the costs of termination (Cox, Wexler, Rusbult & Gaines 1997).

In a similar vein, the concept of asset specificity and specific investments is common in the literature on inter-organizational relationships (Heide & Stump 1995). In the transaction cost perspective, specific assets create dependence on the transaction partner and, if not balanced, create a potential threat of opportunism (Wathne & Heide 2000).

Despite the focus on specific investments in both inter-personal and inter-organizational relationships, there have been a few attempts to understand the nature of such investments in consumer-brand relationships. The lack of learning from the inter-organizational literature is addressed as a shortcoming in the research on brand relationships (Fournier 2009).

30 semi structured in-dept interviews on consumers' investments in brand relationships related to three different contexts (Apple Inc., a national soccer team, and the mobile phone brands the participants had at the time, with 10 interviews in each context) were conducted.

Based on this, and existing research on specific investments in related disciplines, a typology of consumers' specific investments in brand relationships is proposed.

The in-dept interviews indicate that consumers, both directly and indirectly, invest in their relationships with brands. The investments are found to be both of an economic nature, as well as time, effort, and other psychological investments. These are investments that are uniquely related to a specific brand relationship and consequently lose their value outside the relationship. Therefore, consumers' specific investments increase commitment to the brand relationship and build brand loyalty, safeguarding the brand in situations of dissatisfaction and/or presence of attractive alternatives. The proposed typology distinguishes between investments that are direct and indirect to the relationship, as well as extrinsic (directed towards external objects) and intrinsic (driven by internal dynamics) motivations for the investments.

*Explicit investments* are resources that are directly invested in the relationship and that create commitment as a consequence of external objects and conditions. Examples identified are direct financial investment in physical products and start-up costs, direct financial investments in complementary products, contractual commitment, and other direct switching costs.

*Exertion investments* in the brand relationship are direct in nature and create commitment as a consequence of the consumer's intrinsic involvement and efforts. The examples found in the present explorative research are efforts the participants have made in terms of learning and personalization, existing knowledge about the brand, as well as past engagement in word-of-mouth, and brand related feelings and memories.

*Social investments* are indirectly related to the relationship and create commitment based on extrinsic motivations. This type of investments can be related to Holt's (1995) typology of consumption as play, meaning that the consumption act is a part of socialization and a basis for relations and networks among consumers. Such relations among consumers are likely to also create an indirect commitment towards the brand, as it forms the hub of the consumer networks. The types of social investment identified in this research are group identification, sense of belonging to a larger group, friends, user networks, and special objects and events.

*Integrated investments* are indirect and create commitment as a consequence of intrinsic motivation. This form of relationship investment can be related to Holt's (1995) classification of consumption as integration and classification. One could argue that classification also could be understood as a form of social investment. However, it is probably driven by an inner motivation related to the definition of the users self, and thereby best understood as an intrinsic indirect investment. Examples are assimilation of values and associations of the brand and its reference groups, as well as dissimilation of associations and values of other brands and out groups.

The types of specific investments presented in this work are based on different motivations and have diverging implications for brand relationship management. *Explicit* and *Exertion* investments are assumed to create constraint-based commitment (Johnson 1982) and exchange norms (Aggarwal 2004), as they are instrumental, create dependence and are based on a negative motivation not to loose resources that are invested in the relationship. On the other hand, *Social* and *Integrated* investments are assumed to create dedication-based commitment (Johnson 1982) and communal norms (Aggarwal 2004), because of the value of social networks, affiliation and consumers' self-construal through identification with the brand.

Knowledge about the motivations for the relationship, and the types of investments that function as antecedents of commitment is vital for strategies employed in brand relationship management. For example, the use of tactics based on an instrumental logic and exchange norms might be successful in the case of relationships mainly based on explicit investments, but detrimental for relationships that are heavily based on integrated investments.

Further research should investigate to what extent type of investment influence relationship commitment at different stages of the relationship life cycle, and eventually relationship outcome (behavioral loyalty, interest in alternatives, functional conflict, word-of-mouth, and more), in order to enable companies to craft more tailored and effective strategies for brand relationship management.

## Selected References

Aggarwal, Pankaj. 2004. The Effects of Brand Relationship Norms on Consumer Attitudes and Behaviour. *Journal of Consumer Research*, 31, 87-101.

Cox, C. L., Wexler, M. O, Rusbult, C. E., & Gaines Jr. S. O. (1997). Prescriptive Support and Commitment Processes in Close Relationships. *Social Psychology Quarterly*, 60(1), 79-90.

Fournier, S. (2009). Lessons Learned About Consumers' Relationships With Their Brands. In D. J. McInnis, C. W. Park & J. R. Priester (eds.), The Handbook of Brand Relationships (pp. 5-). New York : M. E. Sharpe.

Heide, J. B., & Stump, R. L. (1995). Performance Implications of Buyer-Supplier Relationships in Industrial markets. *Journal of Business Research*, 32, 57-66.

Johnson, M. P. (1982). The Social and Cognitive Features of the Dissolution of Commitment to Relationships. In S. Duck (ed.), Personal Relationships: Dissolving Personal Relationships (pp. 51-73). New York: Academic Press.

Rusbult, C. E. (1980). Satisfaction and Commitment in Friendships. *Representative Research in Social Psychology*, 11, 96-105.

Rusbult, C. E., Martz, J. M., & Agnew, C. R. (1998). The Investment Model Scale: Measuring Commitment, Satisfaction Level, Quality of Alternatives, and Investment Size. *Personal Relationships*, 5, 357-391.

Wathne, K,, & Heide J. B. (2000). Opportunism in Interfirm Relationships: Forms, Outcomes, and Solutions. *Journal of Marketing*, 64(4), 36-51.

# Does Consumers' Product Involvement with Sponsors' Products Matter in Sponsorship?

Cindy Lee, West Virginia University, USA

Boyun Woo, Endicott College, USA

The growth of corporate sponsorship has been phenomenal throughout the world for the past two decades. For example, in the U.S., corporate investment in sponsorship has increased from $850 million to $12.1 billion between 1985 and 2005 (IEG, 2005). In addition, the areas of sponsorship have been diversified including art, social cause, sports, and entertainment tour. Yet, among the different areas of sponsorship, sports has been one of the most popular venues because of its abilities to attract public interest and reach almost all classes in a more subtle way. Therefore, marketers increasingly view sports sponsorship as an alternative to traditional marketing communications making corporate sponsorship as one of the fastest growing types of marketing communications (Roy & Cornwell, 2003).

As the amount of money spent on sponsorship increases and as the needs to justify the money spent on sponsorship increases, there is more interest in measuring sponsorship effects and its influencing factors. Although many influencing factors on sponsorship effects have been studied (e.g., congruency between sponsors and sponsored events/products, fan identification toward sponsored entities, terms of sponsorship contract, and brand dominance in market), consumers' product involvement with sponsors' products has not been studied much. This is surprising considering the fact that product involvement is a critical factor in explaining various consumer behaviors (e.g., attitude change, decision making). Therefore, this study attempts to see whether consumers' involvement with sponsors' products influences sponsorship effects. In addition, fan identification was included as a variable because much literature (Branscomb & Wann, 1993; Trail, Anderson, & Fink, 2000) attests that fan identification is an essential component which makes sponsorship effects possible.

Product involvement refers to the degree to which an individual is involved with a given product on a regular basis (Zaichkowsky, 1985). Products can be classified as high- or low-involvement depending on factors such as price, importance to self, the level of risk involved in the product's purchase, frequency of purchase, and durability (Dholakia, 1997). There are many companies with different ranges of products that sponsor sport teams, and consumers have various levels of involvement with sponsoring companies' products. For example, sponsorship companies includes Buick(automobile), Coke(soft drink), Geico(insurance) and Campbell(soup). In fact, changing attitudes or behaviors toward high involvement products is harder than low involvement products, because consumers are involved very much in information gathering, decision making, and information processing for high involvement products. This notion is supported by Meenaghan (2001) who assumed that influence of sponsorship for high-involvement products would not be great. Elaboration Likelihood Model (Petty, Cacioppo, & Schumann 1983) and the Consumer Decision Process model (Blackwell, Miniard, & Engel, 2001) provide theoretical background of this phenomenon.

Fan identification makes it possible for sports sponsors to achieve their marketing objectives. The influence of fan identification on sponsorship can be explained by three mechanisms: mere exposure effects, extension of goodwill, and/or social identity/group norms. In essence, fans' responses to sponsors are influenced by their identification level and sponsorship effects tend to be more evident among highly identified fans compared to casual fans.

The objectives of corporate sponsorship varies from increasing sales, generating and raising awareness, reaching new target markets, to enhancing corporate image, and sponsorship effects have been measured in terms of increased awareness (i.e., recall and recognition), attitude change, and increases in sales. In this study, consumers' attitudes and purchase intention toward product were measured. An experiment study format was adopted to control any external factors such as promotion, advertising, or any other marketing communication activities.

Six potential product categories were selected as sponsor products. Using Zaichkowsky's Product Involvement Inventory (PII), the level of involvement toward each product category was measured. Top two (i.e., auto insurance and athletic shoes) and bottom two (soft drink and soup) product categories were selected, and t- test was conducted and confirmed that there is a significant difference between high ($M = 26.71$, $t(39) = 38.29$) and low ($M = 14.28$, $t(39) = 14.05$) product categories at the $p < .001$ level. Next, a brief advertisement/ description was developed for each product and a pilot test was conducted with 40 students. Participants' attitude and intention to purchase were measured after they read the description of each product. Then, participants' level of team identification with a professional football team in the region was measured. Lastly, participants were told that the brands were actually the sponsors of this team and asked to rerate their attitude and purchase intention to see whether there are any changes due to this newly revealed association between the brands and the sponsored team.

A series of MANOVA was conducted for each high and low involvement product with independent variable of fan identification and dependent variables of changed attitudes and changed purchase intention. The results showed that there was a significant difference between highly identified and lowly identified groups. Highly identified fans evaluated sponsoring brands more favorably and showed more willingness to purchase the products than those people with low level of fan identification after they were told that the brands were sponsors (Auto insurance, $F(2,37) = 4.29$, $p < .05$; Athletic shoes, $F(2,37) = 7.47$, $p < .05$; Soft drink, $F(2,37) = 5.76$, $p < .05$; Soup $F(2,37) = 6.38$, $p < .05$). However, there were no significant differences found between high and low involvement products.

As seen in the previous studies, this study confirmed that fan identification is an important factor in sponsorship effects. However, the current study failed to show the role of product involvement in sponsorship. This may be due to the fact that fictitious brands were used in the study. It seems that fictitious brands made it hard for the participants to actually evaluate each brand in purchase situation. Therefore, further study with actual sponsors will be needed with combination of qualitative methods. However, controlling other external factors in the market could be challenging with real brands.

## Selected References

Blackwell, R. D., Miniard, P. W., & Engel, J. F. (2001). *Consumer behavior* (9th ed.). Orlando, FL: Harcourt Inc.

Branscomb, N. R., & Wann, D. L. (1993). The positive social and self-concept consequences of sports team identification. *Journal of Sport and Social Issues, 15*, 115-127.

Dholakia, U. M. (1997). An investigation of the relationship between perceived risk and product involvement. *Advances in Consumer Research, 24*(1), 159-157.

IEG Sponsorship Report. (2005). Annual estimates of sponsorship expenditure. Chicago, IL: IEG LLC.

Meenaghan, T. (2001). Understanding sponsorship effects. *Psychology and Marketing, 18*(2), 95-122.

Petty, R. E., Cacioppo, J. T., & Schumann, D. (1983). Central and peripheral routes to advertising effectiveness: The moderating role of involvement. *Journal of Consumer Research, 10*(2), 135-146.

Roy, D. P., & Cornwell, T. B. (2003). Brand equity's influence on response to event sponsorships. *Journal of Product & Brand Management, 12*(6), 377-393.

Trail, G. T., Anderson, D., & Fink, J. S. (2000). A theoretical model of sport consumer behavior. *International Journal of Sport Management, 1,* 154-180.

Zaichkowsky, J. L. (1985). Measuring the involvement construct. *Journal of Consumer Research, 12,* 341-352.

# Consumer Chronic Affect and Persuasiveness of Nostalgia Advertising Appeals

Guangzhi Zhao, University of Kansas, USA
Darrel Muehling, Washington State University, USA
Surendra Singh, University of Kansas, USA
Junwu Chai, University of Electronic Science and Technology of China, China

**Extended Abstract**

As the nostalgia boom in the popular culture continues to expand in its depth and scope, nostalgic themes are frequently seen in advertising campaigns as well (Crain 2003; Goulding 2001; Muehling and Sprott 2004; Naughton and Vlasic 1998; Stern 1992). A growing number of marketers (e.g., Ford, Mars, PepsiCo, and GE) often connect or pair their brands with words, pictures, scenes, or music in their promotions by portraying a by-gone era to evoke nostalgia among viewers (Bussey 2008; Naughton and Vlasic 1998; Vranica 2009).

Even though the use of nostalgia as a promotional tool is on the rise, research on the topic–especially nostalgia in an advertising context–remains scarce, and the effectiveness of such marketing practice is not well understood (Bussey 2008; Crain 2003; Muehling and Sprott 2004; Stern 1992). Some research has found that nostalgic cues are capable of triggering positive thoughts in consumers and may result in positive attitude toward the advertised brand (Muehling and Sprott 2004). Nevertheless, others have viewed the use of nostalgia ads as a minefield (Bussey 2008; Crain 2003), noting that although nostalgia may be a useful approach for advertising, it has the likelihood of potentially alienating consumers and may even cause boomerang effects if nostalgic appeals are not accurately matched with target consumers.

Though previous research has demonstrated that nostalgia advertising can evoke positive thoughts and emotions in viewers and can subsequently enhance persuasion, few studies have examined the role of viewers' characteristics on the effectiveness of nostalgia advertising. In the literature, researchers have long hinted that consumers' characteristics play an important role in understanding individuals' nostalgic experience. For example, Baker and Kennedy (1994) proposed that individuals' responses to nostalgia would vary by gender and personal life experience. Holbrook (1993) proposed and empirically demonstrated that consumers could be segmented by their nostalgia proneness (i.e., individuals' susceptibility and tendency to feel nostalgic). Extending this line of research to nostalgia advertising, it seems reasonable to expect there are important individual differences in how consumers will respond to nostalgia advertising, i.e., other individual characteristics may moderate the persuasiveness of nostalgia advertising.

One individual characteristic that bears consideration is consumers' affective state. A considerable body of research has shown the impact of consumers' affective state on the advertising persuasion process (see Cohen, Pham, and Andrade (2008) for a review). In addition, consumers' affective state can usefully be differentiated by time frame, e.g., feelings at the present moment, chronic feelings during the past few days, and chronic feelings during the past few weeks and beyond (Watson, Clark, and Tellegen 1988). In our opinion, consumers' chronic affect is especially important for nostalgia advertising since it is expected to influence viewers by evoking memories of the past, thereby, activating positive emotional resonance. In general, the more positive the emotional resonance, the more effective is the nostalgia advertising in influencing ad and brand attitudes. It is our contention, however, that the efficacy of nostalgia advertising at evoking positive emotional resonance depends on both the ad itself and on the viewer's affective state (i.e., is the viewer's general state of mind one that would be considered positive?). Holding the nostalgia advertising constant, we expect that the higher the viewers' chronic positive affective state, the more positive emotional resonance will be evoked and subsequently the more persuasive the nostalgia advertising will be.

Thus, we expect the persuasiveness of nostalgia advertising to be moderated by viewers' affective state, specifically, viewers' chronic positive affect. For viewers who are high on chronic positive affect, nostalgia ads will work together with affective state (i.e., an additive effect) and subsequently arouse more positive emotional resonance in viewers, which in turn should boost nostalgia advertising persuasiveness. For viewers who are low on chronic positive affect, nostalgia ads are expected to mismatch with viewers' affective state and, as a result, are expected to be less effective at arousing positive emotional resonance and be persuasive.

In the preliminary research reported here, one hundred thirty-seven undergraduate students (54.7% male, ranging in age from 18 to 25) participated in a two-factor between subject factorial experiment for course credits: 2 (Ad appeal: nostalgia ad vs. control) x 2 (viewers' chronic positive affect: high vs. low). Participants' chronic positive affect was measured using the positive affect sub-scale of the PANAS Scale, which measures the extent to which participants perceived they had experienced positive affect during the past few weeks (Watson, Clark, and Tellegen 1988). Consumer researchers have widely adopted and relied heavily on the scale in consumer studies as well (Cohen, Pham, and Andrade 2008). Participants were placed into high and low chronic positive affect groups via a median-split procedure.

Two fictitious ads for Kodak digital cameras were adapted from the literature: one nostalgia ad and one non-nostalgia ad (i.e., control) (cf. Muehling and Sprott 2004). The ads featured a picture of a group of boys posing after a backyard basketball game on a summer afternoon. The two ads were comparable in visual format, color, illustration, length of ad copy, description of product features, and placement of brand logo, but differed in several important ways. Nostalgic cues replaced comparable, though non-nostalgic, cues in the headline ("Re-live the Moment" for the nostalgia ad versus "Capture the Moment" for the control ad), in the date inserted below the dominant picture ("Last day of Summer, August 28, 1998" versus "Last day of Summer, August 28, 2009"), in several statements placed in the ad copy (e.g., "It was a time like no other. . . . Remember?" versus "A moment just like this. . . . A stop in the action"), and in the tag line ("And, Kodak was there" versus "And, Kodak is there"). It is important to note that the highlighted product features (e.g., 10.2 MP. 3X optical zoom lens, etc.) were held constant across the two ads.

A set of two-way ANOVA analyses were conducted on the dependent measures including *purchase intention, brand attitude, ad attitude, and ad-aroused positive emotion*. Standard scale items were borrowed from the literature. Our hypotheses were all supported. A two-way ANOVA on intention to purchase revealed a significant interaction effect between ad appeal and viewers' chronic positive affective state (F (1, 133)=6.47, p<.05). Subsequent pair-wise comparisons showed that, when participants were in a high chronic positive affect, those who viewed the nostalgia ad had a higher intention to purchase the advertised product (M=4.28) than those who viewed the non-nostalgia ad (M=3.75) (t (133)=2.00, p<.05). On the other hand, when participants were in a low chronic positive affect, those who viewed the nostalgia ad reported an intention to purchase the advertised product (M=3.52) comparable to those who viewed the non-nostalgia ad (M=3.92) (t (133)=1.59, p=.11). Similar results were found on other dependent measures.

## REFERENCES

Baker, Stacy M. and Patricia F. Kennedy (1994), "Death by Nostalgia: A Diagnosis of Context-Specific Cases," in Allen, C. T. and John, D. R. (eds) *Advances in Consumer Research*, Vol. 21, Association for Consumer Research, Provo, UT, 169–174.

Bussey, Noel (2008), "Does nostalgic advertising work?" *Campaign*, (March 07), 11.

Casey, Nicolas (2009), "Toy Makers Reach Into Product Attic," the *Wall Street Journal*, March (09), B1.

Cohen, Joel B., Michel Tuan Pham, and Eduardo B. Andrade (2008), "The Nature and Role of Affect in Consumer Behavior," in *Handbook of Consumer Psychology*, Ed. C. P. Haugtvedt, P. M. Herr, and F. R. Kardes, Psychology Press, New York, 297-348.

Crain, Rance (2003), "If Consumers Crave Familiar, Bring Back the Golden Oldies," *Advertising Age*, 74 (16), 20.

Goulding, Christina (2001), "Romancing the Past: Heritage Visiting and the Nostalgic Consumer," *Psychology and Marketing*, 18(6), 565–580.

Holbrook, Morris. B. (1993), "Nostalgia and Consumption Preferences: Some Emerging Patterns of Consumer Tastes," *Journal of Consumer Research*, 20 (September), 245–256.

Muehling, Darrel D and David E Sprott (2004), "The Power of Reflection: An Empirical Examination of Nostalgia Advertising Effects," *Journal of Advertising*. 33 (3), 25-35.

Naughton, Keith and Bill Vlasic (1998), "The Nostalgia Boom," *Business Week*, (March 23), 58-64.

Stern, Barbara (1992), "Historical and Personal Nostalgia in Advertising Text: The Fin de Siècle Effect," *Journal of Advertising*, 21 (4), 11-22.

Vranica, Suzanne (2009), "Super Bowl Ads Try Hard-Sell," the *Wall Street Journal*, Jan (30), B1.

Watson, D., Clark, L. A., & Tellegen, A. (1988). Development and validation of brief measures of positive and negative affect: The PANAS scales. *Journal of Personality and Social Psychology, 54,* 1063–1070.

# Temporal Construal, Categorization Processes, and Brand Extension Evaluation

Pronabesh Banerjee, University of Kansas, USA
Sanjay Mishra, University of Kansas, USA
Guangzhi Zhao, University of Kansas, USA
Junwu Chai, University of Electronic Science and Technology of China, China

**Extended Abstract**

Categorization involves treating two or more distinct entities as equivalent (Medin 1989). Research in categorization has shown that perceptual similarity and conceptual coherence often serve as the two most common bases for judging the equivalence and subsequent categorization of objects into a particular group. For example, a robin and a nightingale can be classified into the same category of bird since they are perceptually similar such that both have feathers, wings and beak. In contrast, children, money, photo album and pets cannot be grouped together based on their physical appearance (i.e., perceptual similarity), but they may form a group based on their conceptual coherence (e.g., "things to take out of one's house in case of fire") (Barsalou 1983).

The basic difference in the above two types of categorization (which we term as perceptual and conceptual categorization, respectively hereafter) is that perceptual categorization involves mainly feature-matching among the category members, while conceptual categorization requires the identification of causal relationships or conceptual relatedness among the category members.

Various factors (e.g., cultural background and expertise) are found to moderate use of perceptual similarity or conceptual coherence in forming groups (Murphy and Medin 1985). We propose that the way an individual construes an event in time (near vs. distant future)–temporal construal of an individual, as another factor moderating the use of the two bases of categorization. Temporal construal theory proposes that events which are closer to the present (e.g., taking a trip tomorrow) are likely to be construe as containing more concrete, peripheral and situation specific details of the event. Conversely, construing the same event six months from now leads to the consideration of more abstract, central and goal related features of the event (Trope and Liberman 2003). Thus, we propose that more concrete (abstract) features or perceptual similarity (conceptual relatedness) will be used for forming a group when one thinks in near (distant) future terms.

In the first study participants' temporal construal was manipulated by asking them to enlist the thoughts while thinking of taking an exam either tomorrow (near future prime) or six months from now (distant future prime). Then they were presented with a focal brand (Nike) and asked to pick three brands from a set of ten brands (Asics, Hush puppies, Timberland, Prince, Wilson, Casio, Polo Ralph Lauren, Dr Scholl's, Caterpillar and Esprit) that forms a "coherent" group with the focal brand. The meaning of the word "coherent" was neither defined nor explained to the participants. Supporting our propositions, we found participants in the near (distant) future prime used perceptual (conceptual) similarity for forming a "coherent" group with Nike–as is evident in the analysis of the following dependent measures, (i) reasons for forming the group (ii) listing of common characteristics between Nike and the chosen brands (iii) the thoughts which went through the participants' mind as they were making the choices and (iv) names given to the chosen group.

Recent research has demonstrated that the way in which products are categorized influences subsequent decision making in an unrelated context (Ulkumen. Chakravarti and Morwitz forthcoming in JMR). For example, the purchase of a new type of candy at the checkout counter is influenced by a prior categorization task–categorizing a DVD into a narrow (e.g. comedy movie) vs. a broad category (e.g., movie). Arguing on a similar vein, we posit that categorizing objects on perceptual similarities or narrower categories (e.g., Nike running shoes) vs. conceptual coherence or broader categories (e.g., Nike for sports) will influence a subsequent decision making task later in the study–evaluation of an ad. In a second study, supporting our hypothesis we find that participants in the near (distant) future prime evaluated the ad promoting brands' perceptual similarity (e.g., NIKE RUNNING SHOES) more favorably than the one promoting brands' conceptual coherence (e.g., NIKE EMPOWER YOURSELF) ($F (1,105)=14.41$, $p<0.00$).

In a third study, we seek to extend our findings in the context of brand extensions, as extensions are often evaluated on the basis of similarity to the category that the brand stands for (Boush and Loken 1991). However, extensions like Jeep strollers and Godiva ice-cream are notable exceptions to the above logic. Bridges, Keller and Sood (2000) argues that as long as the target customers are able to find an explanatory link between the extension and the parent brand, perceptual similarity is not deemed necessary for evaluating an extension's similarity with the parent brand. We propose that consumers' ability in finding such exploratory links will be enhanced when they are primed with distant vs. near temporal orientation.

The hypotheses was tested in a 2 (temporal orientation–near vs. far) $\times$ 2 (type of brand extension–perceptual similarity vs. conceptual coherence) between subjects design. Johnson & Johnson skin care lotion (perceptually similar to the line of J & J lotion) and stuffed toys (conceptually related to the brand–a brand known for babies) were used as experimental stimuli. As expected, J&J stuffed toys was more similar to the parent brand in the distant (vs. near) future prime (M=6.44(1.20) vs. M=4.07(1.88), p<0.00) and the participants listed more exploratory links between stuffed toys and the J&J brand when they were in the distant (vs. near) future prime. However, due to the obvious similarity of the skin care lotion to the J&J brand no differences either in similarity judgment or listing of exploratory links was found was observed across conditions.

Findings of our research contribute to the categorization literature by identifying temporal construal as another factor influencing such a process. Categorization is found to be the basic cognitive mechanism underlying several key decision making processes like consideration set formation (Desai and Hoyer 2000), brand extension evaluation (Boush and Loken 1991) and assimilation and contrast (Levy 1993). Thus, future research may explore temporal construal as a key factor moderating the above cognitive factors and its attendant marketing implications.

## References

Barsalou, Lawrence W. (1983), "Ad hoc categories," *Memory and Cognition*, 11(3), 211-27.

Boush, David M. and Barbara Loken (1991), "A Process -Tracing Study of Brand Extension Evaluation," *Journal of Marketing Research*, 28(1), 16-28.

Bridges, Sheri, Kevin Lane Keller, and Sanjay Sood (2000), "Communication Strategies for Brand Extensions: Enhancing Perceived Fit by Establishing Explanatory Links," *Journal of Advertising*, 29(4), 1-11.

Desai, Kalpesh K. and Wayne D. Hoyer (2000), "The Descriptive Characteristics of Memory-Based Consideration Sets: Influence of Usage Occasion Frequency and Usage Location Familiarity," *Journal of Consumer Research*, 27(3), 309-23.

Medin, Douglas L. (1989), "Concepts and Conceptual Structure," *The American Psychologist*, 44(12), 1469-81.

Meyers-Levy, Joan and Brian Sternthal (1993), "A Two-Factor Explanation of Assimilation and Contrast," *Journal of Marketing Research*, 30(3), 359-68.

Murphy, Gregory L. and Douglas L. Medin (1985), "The Role of Theories in Conceptual Coherence," *Psychological Review*, 92(3), 289-315.

Trope, Yaacov and Nira Liberman (2003), "Temporal Construal," *Psychological Review*, 110(3), 403-421.

Ülkümen, Gülden, Amitav Chakravarti, Vicki G. Morwitz, "Categories Create Mindsets: The Effect of Exposure to Broad versus Narrow Categorizations on Subsequent, unrelated Decisions," *Journal of Marketing Research*, forthcoming.

# How Does Power Affect Evaluation of Brand Extensions?
Youngseon Kim, University of Texas at San Antonio, USA

## Extended Abstract

Brand extension is an important topic in consumer behavior research. Extant research highlights fit between a parent brand and its extension product as a major determinant of brand extension success, and focuses on identifying brand related factors or individual factors that affect the perceived fit and the evaluation (Ahluwalia 2008; Keller 2002; Park, Milberg, and Lawson 1991). However, a very important aspect of social factor such as power has been largely ignored in the literature. Power has recently gained attention from the consumer scholars, who found that power has a systematic effect on consumer decisions such as spending propensities (e.g., Rucker and Galinsky 2008).

Power has been defined as an individual's relative capacity to control resources and outcomes, both one's own and others' (Keltner, Gruenfeld, and Anderson 2003; Thibaut and Kelley 1959). It has been well documented that people with high power tend to engage in more abstract thinking than those with low power. For example, Smith and Trope (2006) found that high power primed participants in the task of categorization were more inclusive in their categorization than low power primed participants, and rated the weak exemplars as less atypical. High power primed participants chose a greater number of a higher level of alternatives than low power primed participants in a Behavior Identification Form (BIF) task, a measure of different levels of abstractness of behaviors (Vallacher and Wegner 1989). The research findings on the relationship between power and abstract thinking suggest that power might have a role in brand extension evaluations.

Perceiving fit is a global judgment of the relations that exist between a brand extension and its parent brand, based on factors such as being in similar product categories, sharing important attributes (Aaker and Keller 1990; Kim and John 2008). People who process information at an abstract level may perceive more fit between the brand extension and the parent brand (Aggarwal and Law 2005; Monga and John 2007). Thus, I propose that high power people will process brand extension evaluations at a higher level of abstraction, perceive a moderate brand extension as being more similar to the parent brand category, and evaluate the extension more favorably than low power people. Previous research has shown that consumers tend to be likely influenced by situational factors in their brand extension evaluations when the brand extension was moderate than extreme (Barone, Miniard, and Romeo 2000). However, no differences between high power people and low power people are predicted in the evaluation of a near brand extension since it would already be rated as a member of the parent brand category, regardless of the different status of power. Thus, the formal hypotheses are as follows:

H1: High power people will evaluate a moderate brand extension more favorably than low power people.

H2: High power people and low power people will not show a difference in the evaluation of a near brand extension.

## EXPERIMENT

### Method

*Design and Participants.* Seventy eight undergraduate students from a large southwestern university participated in a 2 (power priming: high vs. low) x 2 (extension fit: near vs. moderate) between-participants study. They were randomly assigned to one of the four conditions.

*Stimuli.* BMW was used as the parent brand. Two hypothetical extensions for BMW were chosen after a pretest (N=25): BMW motorboat as a near extension, and BMW golf clubs as a moderate extension ($t=4.32$, $p<.001$).

*Measures.* Participants' evaluation of a proposed brand extension (1=poor to 7=excellent scale), brand extension fit judgment (1=inconsistent/not fit to 7=consistent/fit scales), and their familiarity (1= not familiar to 7=familiar scale) and attitude toward BMW (1=poor to 7=excellent scale). The two items for brand extension fit judgment was averaged ($r=.74$).

### Results and Discussion

Brand familiarity and brand attitude were used as covariates in the analyses. A 2 x 2 ANOVA was run on the brand extension evaluation. The interaction between power and extension fit on the evaluation emerged ($F$ (1, 76)=4.52, $p<.05$). Specifically, simple contrasts showed that high power-primed participants evaluated the moderate extension more favorably than low power-primed participants ($M_{\text{high power}}=4.52$, $M_{\text{low power}}=3.28$, $F$ (1, 76)=5.64, $p<.05$), whereas such a difference was not observed in the evaluation of the near extension ($M_{\text{high power}}=5.1$, $M_{\text{low power}}=5.0$, $F$ (1, 76)=.11, $p=.74$). Therefore, H1 and H2 were supported.

Mediation analyses (Baron and Kenny 1986) confirmed mediation by perceived fit on the extension evaluation. Power emerged as a predictor of the evaluation ($\beta=.22$, t=1.92, $p<.06$) as well as brand extension fit judgment ($\beta=.23$, t=2.03, $p<.05$). When both power and the fit judgment were included in the same regression equation, the effect of power became insignificant ($\beta=.09$, t=.96, $p=.34$), whereas brand extension fit judgment was significant ($\beta=.53$, t=5.44, $p<.001$). The analyses suggest complete mediation of the effect of power on the evaluation by perceived fit (Sobel test-statistic=1.91, $p<.05$).

This research makes important contributions with implications for further research. Foremost, it discovers the new role of power as moderator in brand extension evaluations while most current research has focused on the effect of power on consumers' spending propensities such as status consumption. Second, it is the first study that investigated the role of social power in brand extension research, whereas most research in the literature has examined individual factors or brand related factors to affect the evaluation of brand extension. Third, it demonstrates that different social power groups tend to view the same brand extension differently. The finding signals that brand extensions may be more segment specific phenomena rather than universal ones.

Finally, the next step for this research is to generalize the findings in different settings, and to further test whether the moderating role of power in the brand extension evaluation would be tempered by a parent brand factor, e.g., whether the parent brand is status-associated.

## References

Aaker, David A. and Kevin L. Keller (1990), "Consumer Evaluations of Brand Extensions," *Journal of Marketing*, 54 (January), 27-41.

Aggawal, Pankaj and Sharmistha Law (2005), "Role of Relationship Norms in Processing Brand Information," *Journal of Consumer Research*, 32 (December), 453-64.

Ahluwalia, Rohini (2008), "How Far Can a Brand Stretch? Understanding the Role of Self-Construal," *Journal of Marketing Research*, 45 (June), 337-50.

Baron, Reuben M. and David A. Kenny (1986), "The Moderator-Mediator Variable Distinction in Social Psychological Research: Conceptual, Strategic, and Statistical Considerations," *Journal of Personality and Social Psychology*, 51 (6), 1173-82.

Barone, Michael J., Paul W. Miniard, and Jean B. Romeo (2000), "The Influence of Positive Mood on Brand Extension Evaluations," *Journal of Consumer Research*, 26 (March), 386-400.

Keller, Kevin Lane (2002), *Branding and Brand Equity*, Cambridge, MA: Marketing Science Institute.

Keltner, Dacher, Deborah H. Gruenfeld, and Cameron Anderson (2003), "Power, Approach, and Inhibition," *Psychological Review*, 110 (2), 265-84.

Kim, Hakkyun and Deborah R. John (2008), "Consumer Response to Brand Extensions: Construal Level as a Moderator of the Importance of Perceived Fit," *Journal of Consumer Psychology*, 18 (2), 116-26.

Monga, Alokparna B. and Deborah R. John (2007), "Cultural Differences in Brand Extension Evaluation: The Influence of Analytic versus Holistic Thinking," *Journal of consumer research*, 33 (March), 529-36.

Park, C. Whan, Sandra Milberg, and Robert Lawson (1991), "Evaluation of Brand Extensions: The role of Product Feature Similarity and Brand Concept Consistency," *Journal of Consumer Research*, 18 (September), 185-93.

Rucker, Derek and Adam D. Galinsky (2008), "Desire to Acquire: Powerlessness and Compensatory Consumption," *Journal of Consumer Research*, 35 (August), 257-67.

Smith, Pamela K. and Yaacov Trope (2006), "You Focus on the Forest When You're in Charge of the Trees: Power Priming and Abstract Information Processing," *Journal of Personality and Social Psychology*, 90 (April), 578-96.

Thibaut, John W. and Harold H. Kelley (1959), *The Social Psychology of Groups*, New York: Wiley.

Vallacher, Robin R. and Daniel M. Wegner (1989), "Levels of Personal Agency: Individual Variation in Action Identification," *Journal of Personality and Social Psychology*, 57 (4), 660-71.

# Brand Synergy in Multi-Product Experiences

Ryan Rahinel, University of Minnesota, USA
Joseph Redden, University of Minnesota, USA

Products are often used together to form a single experience (e.g, toothpaste and toothbrushes jointly form a teeth cleaning experiences). A natural question stemming from this phenomenon is: "How does the set of brands used across the multiple products affect the consumption experience?" Surprisingly, there has been little research on the experience of using two products in tandem. In this research, we demonstrate that experiences involving products of the same brand are evaluated more positively than experiences involving products of different brands. Our data suggests that a sizable part of this effect can be attributed to consumers' desire to have a single "coordinator" for experiences.

Previous research has shown that evaluations of a consumption experience are formed through a combination of intrinsic and extrinsic cues. For example, the primary intrinsic cue in the experience of eating a potato chip is the gustatory perception. In contrast, extrinsic cues are cues that arise from the context of consumption or the external environment (Shiv et al., 2005; Allison and Uhl, 1996; Bellizzi & Martin, 1982; LeClerc, Schmitt, & Dube, 1994). As shown by Allison and Uhl's (1964) classic beer study, brands can serve as an extrinsic cue for the consumption experience, particularly through the brand's function as a signal of quality.

In this research we investigate a new function of brands, namely as agents of coordination. In single product experiences, brands can be seen as coordinating the component parts of the product, essentially ensuring that all the parts work together effectively. Research in the area of co-branding lends some preliminary support to this idea. A common phenomenon examined in this literature is the effect of header and modifier brands (e.g., in the co-branded product Oral-B Rembrandt whitening strips, Oral-B is the header brand and Rembrandt is the modifier brand; Kumar, 2005; Park, Jun, and Shocker, 1996). That these co-branded products tend to have header and modifier brands points to the possibility that consumers wish to think of these products as having been coordinated primarily by the one brand (the header) with only specific component expertise provided by the modifier brand. In this work we extend this thought into where the evaluation target is the joint experience of two products. If consumers really do prefer to have one coordinator of experiences, then one should observe that (1) consumers tend to prefer multi-product experiences involving one (vs. two) brands (which we term the brand synergy effect), (2) the effect should be for brands only (not for other benign matching properties), and (3) the effect should be larger for experiences with more risk or complexity. We tested these predictions in five studies.

The first study tested whether people's liking ratings in a range of product categories would display the brand synergy effect. This study employed a 2 (Product 1 Brand: Brand A vs. Brand B) x 2 (Product 2 Brand: Brand A vs. Brand B) X 4 (Product Category Pair: laundry detergent + fabric softener, toothbrush + toothpaste, chips + dip, MP3 player + headphones) within-subjects design using real brands (brand names available upon request). On each of the 16 trials, subjects were asked to consider using two brands of products together. As the dependent variable, the subject was asked to "Imagine using these products together. How do you think they would be for [insert experiential goal here]?" The subject then provided their rating on a 101-point visual analog scale anchored by very bad/very good. Results across all four categories showed the brand synergy effect. That is, subjects' ratings for experiences involving one brand were significantly higher than those for two different brands.

The second study and third studies tested the effect actual experiences. Study 2 employed a 2 (Product 1 Brand: Brand A vs. Brand B) x 2 (Product 2 Brand: Brand A vs. Brand B) x (2 Product Category Pair: jellybean flavors vs. chips and salsa) mixed design using real brands. Product category pair was a within subjects factor, with the other two factors varying between subjects. Although subjects were told that the foods were from particular brands, the foods themselves were actually from the same brand for all subjects. Subjects were asked to indicate how the foods tasted together on a 131mm line scale. Contrasts from a repeated measures ANOVA showed that across the two product category pairs, subjects perceived that the foods tasted better together when they were of the same (vs. different) brands. We replicated this finding in a third study using the same basic setup (i.e., crossing real brands in a factorial design) for a more utilitarian category pair–printer and ink. Subjects were asked to evaluate the quality of a picture on a printout. Results showed that subjects felt the picture was sharper when the printout was generated using a printer and ink from the same (vs. different) brands.

In the fourth and fifth studies, we sought to gain some process evidence for the synergy effect. Study 4 tested whether the effect was local to brands or any other matching attribute. We asked subjects to consume and rate the taste of chips and dip that were either described using generic labels ("festivity" or "party time") or as brands ("Festivity® brand" or "Party Time® brand"). As expected, we observed the brand synergy effect emerge when we described the chips and dip as registered brands, but not when they were merely described using generic labels. Study 5 again used the printer and ink paradigm. If brands are truly seen as coordinators, then the effect should be enlarged when there is risk in the quality of experiences. Thus, we used reports from *Consumer Reports* to frame the risk of the experiential category as either being high or low prior to the printout evaluation task described in the third study. Results showed that those in the high risk category showed the brand synergy effect much more-so than those in the low risk category.

## References

Allison Ralph. I., and Kenneth. P. Uhl (1964), "Influence of beer brand identification on taste perception," *Journal of Marketing Research*, 1, 36-39.

Bellizzi, Joseph A., and Warren S. Martin (1982), "The influence of national versus generic branding on taste perceptions," *Journal of Business Research*, 10(3), 385-396.

Kumar, Piyush (2005), "The impact of cobranding on customer evaluation of brand counterextensions," *Journal of Marketing*, 69 (July), 1-18.

LeClerc, France, Bernd Schmitt, and Laurette Dube (1994), "Foreign branding and its effect on product perceptions and attitudes," *Journal of Marketing Research*, 31(2), 263-270.

Nowlis Stephen M., and Baba Shiv (2005), "The influence of consumer distractions on the effectiveness of food-sampling programs," *Journal of Marketing Research*, 42, 157-168.

Park, C.Whan, S. Youl Jun and Allan D. Shocker (1996), "Composite branding alliances: an investigation of extension and feedback effects." *Journal of Marketing Research*, 33 (November), 453-466.

Shiv, Baba, Ziv Carmon, and Dan Ariely (2005), "Placebo effects of marketing actions: Consumers may get what they pay for," *Journal of Marketing Research*, November, 383-393.

# Can Moral Identity Enhance Out-Group Brand Evaluations?:
## The Moderating Role of Thinking Style

Woo Jin Choi, Texas A&M University, USA
Karen Page Winterich, Pennsylvania State University, USA

**Extended Abstract**

The pervasive impact of moral identity (hereafter, MI) has largely been limited to altruistic or prosocial behaviors (e.g., Reed and Aquino 2003; Shang et al. 2008; Winterich et al. 2009). Can MI influence other consumer behaviors, such as brand evaluations? If so, how and under what conditions? We examine the influence of MI on evaluations of brands associated with an out-group (hereafter, out-group brand evaluations), demonstrating that consumers' thinking styles moderate the effect of MI on out-group brands and brand extension evaluations.

Due to the general tendency of people toward in-group favoritism and out-group hostility (Reed and Aquino 2003; White and Dhal 2007), brands associated with in-groups receive more favorable brand evaluations and have stronger self-brand connections whereas brands associated with out-groups are evaluated less favorably (Escalas and Bettman 2005). Therefore, it is plausible that the evaluation of an out-group brand will depend on the amount of "social distance" (Sagiv and Schwartz 1995) that an individual perceives as existing between himself/herself and the outgroup. We predict that MI will play an important role in determining consumers' out-group brand evaluations.

MI refers to "a commitment to one's sense of self to lines of action that promote or protect the welfare of others" (Hart et al. 1998). Building on this work, Reed and Aquino (2003) suggest that MI can influence out-group hostility by altering the psychological boundaries that define in-group membership such that a highly self-important MI is associated with an expansive circle of moral regard toward out-group members. We draw upon this prior research on MI and out-group evaluations to theorize that consumers with a highly self-important MI will evaluate out-group brands more favorably. We reason that this effect occurs because consumers with high MI importance tend to expand the boundaries of ingroups to include more individuals, including individuals otherwise perceived as out-group members. In doing so, these consumers perceive themselves as being closer to members of outgroups, responding less negatively toward out-group brands, even if the brands are perceived as out-group brands.

Furthermore, we predict that consumers' thinking styles will moderate the effect of MI on out-group brand evaluations. Thinking style refers to individuals' preferred ways of processing information (Zhang and Higgins 2008). Prior research on thinking styles acknowledges that individuals' thinking styles can vary between cultures (Nisbett et al. 2001; Nisbett and Miyamoto 2005) as well within cultures (Choi et al. 2007). Considering that social identity is just one piece of information used in brand evaluations and that consumers hold multiple identities that may differ in salience at any specific point in time (Reed 2004), consumers' cognitive mechanisms may systematically affect the way in which they select which self-identities form the basis of their brand evaluations.

Although holistic thinkers take into consideration the salient identity (herein, MI) as well as their other identities (herein, their customary beliefs and attitudes towards the out-group), the latter will have a stronger effect on holistic than analytic thinkers because comprehensive thinking styles of holistic thinkers better enable them to recall their habitual attitudes toward out-groups. In contrast, individuals with analytic thinking styles are more likely to limit their attention to the currently salient MI, thereby resulting in their evaluations being less affected by their habitual attitudes toward the out-group.

We conducted two studies to test these hypotheses. The first study was a 2 (brand: in-group vs. out-group) X 2 (moral identity: low vs. high (measured continuously)) X 2 (thinking styles: analytic vs. holistic (measured continuously)) mixed design with brand as a within-subjects factor. Participants listed a brand associated with an ingroup and an outgroup. Then participants completed the 24-item thinking style scale (Choi et al. 2007) and the 10-item MI scale (Reed and Aquino 2003). We expected that participants' MI would be heightened, or made salient, while responding to the MI scale. Then, participants evaluated both the in-group and the out-group brand as well as several other filler brands, randomly ordered.

Results indicated that consumers evaluated their in-group brands more favorably than out-group brands, which is consistent with results reported in previous studies (White and Dhal 2007). Furthermore, as we theorized, MI was positively associated with out-group brand evaluations but did not affect in-group brand evaluations. Most importantly, the results demonstrated that the three-way interaction of thinking style, MI, and reference group influenced brand evaluations. Exploring the pattern of this interaction, we found that the effect of MI on out-group brand evaluations was significant for analytic thinkers but not for holistic thinkers. Among analytic thinkers, those with higher MI evaluated the out-group brands more favorably than those with lower MI, demonstrating that they reflect their MI in an unbiased manner. However, the evaluations of holistic thinkers did not differ according to their MI, suggesting that they evaluate out-group brands mainly based on their customary attitudes, rather than their MI.

Study 2 extends the results of Study 1 to consumers' evaluation of brand extensions. The design was the same as that of Study 1 with three important distinctions: 1) MI was manipulating using the procedure from Aquino et al. (2007), 2) all participants saw the same in-group (Nike, Polo) and out-group (Toms, American Apparel) brands, based on a pretest, and 3) evaluation of each brand's extension into the jewelry category was the dependent variable.

The results replicated those of Study 1 for brand extension evaluations. For out-group brand extensions, analytic thinkers reported more favorable evaluations when they were in the high MI salience condition. In contrast, holistic thinkers evaluated the out-group brand extensions less favorably, irrespective of their MI condition. Thinking style and moral identity did not influence in-group brand extension evaluations.

This research makes two important contributions to the literature. First, we demonstrate that MI, which has been neglected in the previous research on consumer-brand relationships except for CSR, is a means through which marketers can enhance consumers' brand evaluations, particularly for out-group brands. Second, we provide insights into the effect of social identity on brand evaluations, demonstrating that the identity salience effects (herein, MI) can vary according to consumers' thinking styles.

### References

Aquino, Karl and Americus Reed II (2002), "The Self-Importance of Moral Identity," *Journal of Personality and Social Psychology*, 83 (December), 1423-40.

Aquino, Karl, Americus Reed II, Stefan Thau, and Dan Freeman (2007), "A Grotesque and Dark Beauty: How moral Identity and Mechanisms of Moral Disengagement Influence Cognitive and Emotional Reactions to War," *Journal of Experimental Social Psychology*, 43 (May), 385-92.

Choi, Incheol, Minkyung Koo and Jong An Choi (2007), "Individual Differences in Analytic Versus Holistic Thinking," *Personality and Social Psychology Bulletin*, 33 (5), 691-705.

Escalas, Jennifer E. and James R. Bettman (2005), "Self-Construal, Reference Groups, and Brand Meaning," *Journal of Consumer Research*, 32 (December), 378-89.

Hart, Daniel, Robert Atkins, and Debra Ford (1998), "Urban America as a Context for the Development of Moral Identity in Adolescence," *Journal of Social Issues*, 54, 513-30.

Nisbett, Richard E., Kaiping Peng, Incheol Choi, and Ara Norenzayan (2001), "Culture and Systems of Thought: Holistic versus Analytic Cognition," *Psychological Review*, 108 (April), 291-310.

_____ and Yuri Miyamoto (2005), "The Influence of Culture: Holistic versus Analytic Perception," *Trends in Cognitive Sciences*, 9 (10), 467-73.

Sagiv, Lilach and Shalom H. Schwartz (1995), "Value priorities and readiness for out-group social contact," *Journal of Personality and Social Psychology*, 69 (September), 437-48.

Shang, Jen, Americus Reed II, and Rachel Croson (2008), "Identity Congruency Effects on Donations," *Journal of Marketing Research*, 45 (June), 351-61.

Reed, Americus, II and Karl Aquino (2003), "Moral Identity and the Expanding Circle of Moral Regard toward Out-Groups," *Journal of Personality and Social Psychology*, 84 (June), 1270-86.

Reed, Americus II (2004), "Activating the Self-Importance of Consumer Selves: Exploring Identity Salience Effects on Judgments," *Journal of Consumer Research*, 31 (September), 286-95.

White, Kate and Darren Dahl (2007), "Are All Out–Groups Created Equal? Consumer Identity and Dissociative Influence," *Journal of Consumer Research*, 34 (December), 525-36.

Winterich, Karen P., Vikas Mittal, and William T. Ross Jr. (2009), "Donation Behavior toward In-Groups and Out-Groups: The Role of Gender and Moral Identity," *Journal of Consumer Research*, 36 (August), 199-214.

Zhang, Li-fang and Paul Higgins (2008), "The Predictive Power of Socialization Variables for Thinking Styles among Adults in the Workplace," *Learning and Individual Differences*, 18 (1), 11-8.

# Consumer Memory for Easy-to-Pronounce Non-Word Brand Names: The Effect of Attitudes

Paula Chesley, University of Minnesota, USA
Dawn Lerman, Fordham University, USA

## Extended abstract

Among the many criteria that marketers should consider when creating new brands names is ease of pronunciation (Kohli and LaBahn, 1997). An easy-to-pronounce name may be critical when the consumer must ask for the brand (Lerman, 2003) and as Bao, Shao and Rivers (2008) argue may also aid processing and retrieval. This is important as brand name memorability is considered important for marketplace success (Keller, 1993).

Generally, word names best fit the ease-of-pronunciation criterion as they have been learned previously by the consumer and are already represented in the consumer's lexicon. However, the task of finding new easy-to-pronounce and thus memorable brand names is complicated by the fact that the vast majority of English words have already been trademarked. This challenges marketers to create non-word brand names that are easily pronounceable. Two types of non-word brands names fitting this criterion are acronyms (e.g., UPS) and morphemic non-words. A morphemic non-word may be a derivation (base + affix as in *Wheatables*=Wheat + -able + -s) or a blend (combination of two words, e.g., *flackers*=flax + crackers or *dunch*=dinner + lunch).

Conventional wisdom (see, for example, Robertson, 1989) suggests that the use of acronyms and/or morphemes in brand naming aids memorability. However, the results of empirical research are mixed, particularly for morphemic non-word names. For example, Lerman (2003) found that the use of morphemes aids memory whereas Lowrey, Shrum and Dubitsky (2003) found that at least one type of morphemic device–blends–impedes memory, particularly for less familiar brands. In the case of acronyms, consumer researchers cite a single study conducted by Bower in 1972 suggesting that acronyms aid memory.

Our study seeks to address this gap in the literature by examining consumer memory for easy to pronounce non-word brand names. We propose that memory for easy-to-pronounce brand names is a function not only of name type (i.e., acronym, blend, morphemic derivation) but also of consumer attitudes toward the name. We expect, for example, that the perceived utility or humor that a consumer associates with a name will influence memory. The results of an empirical study suggest that name type and consumer attitudes toward the name do indeed influence memory retention of new words.

We ran a combined lexical decision and eye-tracking experiment with new acronyms, blends, and derivations that have appeared on websites and in a variety of media including television. A pre-test determined that our 45 participants were unlikely to have seen these words beforehand. Each word appeared with its definition one at a time on a computer screen. With the word and definition still visible, participants responded to a series of attitudinal questions about the word's perceived utility (Corbin, 1987), emotional content (Kensinger & Corkin, 2003), humor (Metcalf, 2004), and degree of formality. Immediately following completion of the attitudinal measures for the last word, half of the participants were tested on recall. We tested the other half after one night's sleep; this allowed us to examine the consolidation of new words into long-term memory.

We fit mixed-effects models for reaction time (RT), lexical decision accuracy, number of fixations, number of regressions, and free recall. Control variables included participant sex, age, and education level, word length, and frequencies of initial component words. Although shorter in length overall, acronyms took significantly longer than blends or derivations to read, and decision accuracy for acronyms was significantly lower than for blends and derivations. This effect holds for acronyms that can be pronounced as letters (*FSBO*, "For Sale By Owner") as well as words (*BITGOD*, "Back In The Good Old Days"). Both groups of participants (i.e., immediate and delayed recall groups) fared worse on acronyms, as an intervening night's sleep significantly shortened RTs and improved accuracy for only blends and derivations. This improvement after one night's sleep is in line with recent research suggesting sleep is helpful in memory consolidation of new vocabulary items (Dumay and Gaskell, 2007). Unlike Lowrey et al. (2003), we find no inhibitory effect for blends: no significant difference between blends and derivations appeared in any dependent variable. Furthermore, the only significant attitudinal question that was consistently significant was, "Would you use this word at a party with your friends?" The more participants said they would use a new word at a party, the shorter their RT and the better their accuracy and free recall. Hypothetical use in other social contexts like "at work or school" was only a significant predictor for free recall and was negatively correlated with memory retention.

These findings indicate that both word formation type and attitudes about the social utility of a new word are important factors in whether consumers remember words that are new to them. There are several implications of this work for marketing. First, by any measurement of memory retention, acronyms appear especially difficult to remember. Moreover, participants often volunteered their distaste for acronyms with comments like "I hate acronyms. . . they sound like jargon." These findings suggest that at least new brand names that are acronyms will be more difficult to remember than blends and derivations. Blends, for their part, were less problematic than expected–perhaps this is due to their ever-increasing presence in advertising and the lexicon in general.

The findings concerning consumer attitudes highlight the importance of social context in remembering new lexical items. In addition to examining responses to individual questions such as "Would you use this word at a party with your friends?", we also took the first and second factors in a principal component analysis as predictor variables. Responses to the party question were more robust than the first principal component, which implies a specific judgment concerning utility and social context as opposed to an overall impression about the word. The "party effect" could be an exciting link between individual cognitive entrenchment and in-group vocabulary choice. This suggests that marketing for new brand names which focuses on in-group usage of the word, if applicable, could be an effective strategy for consumer memory retention.

## References

Bao, Yeqing, Alan T. Shao and Drew Rivers (2008), "Creating New Brand Names: Effects of Relevance, Connotation, and Pronunciation," *Journal of Advertising Research*, 48 (March), 148-162.

Bower, Gordon H. (1972), "Perceptual Groups as Coding Units in Immediate Memory," *Psychonomic Science*, 27 (4), 217-219.

Corbin, D. 1987. *Morphologie dérivationelle et structuration du lexique* . Tübingen: Niemeyer.

Dumay, N., & M. G. Gaskell. 2007. Sleep-associated changes in the mental representation of spoken words. *Psychological Science* 18.35–39.

Keller, Kevin Lane (1993), "Conceptualizing, Measuring, and Managing Customer-Based Brand Equity," *Journal of Marketing*, 57 (January), 1-22.

Kensinger, E., & S. Corkin. 2003. Memory enhancement for emotional words: Are emotional words more vividly remembered than neutral words? *Memory and Cognition* 31.1169–1180.

Kohli, Chiranjeev and Douglas LaBahn (1997), "Creating Effective Brand Names: A Study of the Naming Process," *Journal of Advertising Research*, 37 (1), 67-75.

Lerman, Dawn (2003), "The Effect of Morphemic Familiarity and Exposure Mode on Recall and Recognition of Brand Names," in *Advances in Consumer Research, Volume 30*, eds. Punam Anaud Keller and Dennis W. Rook, Valdosta, GA: Association for Consumer Research, 80-81.

Lowrey, T., L.J. Shrum, & T.M. Dubitsky. 2003. The relation between brand-name linguistic characteristics and brand-name memory. *Journal of Adv*ertising 32.7–17.

Markson, L., & P. Bloom. 2001. Evidence against a dedicated system for word learning in children. In *Language development: the essential readings* , ed. by E. Bates & M. Tomasello, 151–163. Oxford: Blackwell Publishers.

Metcalf, A. 2004. Predicting New Words: The Secrets of Their Success . Boston: Houghton Mifflin Harcourt.

Robertson, Kim R. (1989), "Strategically Desirable Brand Name Characteristics," *Journal of Consumer Marketing*, 6 (4), 61-71.

# Two Small Steps, One Giant Leap: Effect of Movement Signals on Consumers' Walking Speed

Gaby Schellekens, Erasmus University Rotterdam, The Netherlands
Bram Van den Bergh, Erasmus University Rotterdam, The Netherlands

This research examined the effects of movement signals, such as path of footprints or squares on consumers walking path and walking speed. Three studies demonstrated that exposure to a path of movement signals causes following behavior even if the route is less attractive, and that the distance between of movement signals has an effect on walking speed.

In-store shopping movement paths of consumers have received increasing attention lately (Hui and colleagues, 2009; 2010). Arrows or a depicted path of footprints on the floor of the store are attempts to guide consumers movements paths. It avoids inconvenient store traffic flow, and can pull customers deeper into a store. Rather surprisingly, the actual effect of these movement signals on the travel patterns has remained unstudied. This research examined the implicit effects of depicting a path of movement signals on consumers walking behavior.

From past experiences, people know that a path of footprints, stripes or arrows indicate a route to follow. For instance, arrows in a subway station or a row of light dots in an airplane direct the route to the nearest exit. Frequent exposure to these environmental cues can lead to an automatic association between exposure to a depicted path and the behavior of following this path, which leads to automatic following behavior (H1). When consumers are exposed to footprints in a path, they may attempt to mimic the indicated steps by placing their feet on the footprints. Mimicry of other people's behavior is an inborn tendency, based on the notion that we simply *do* what we *see* (Dijksterhuis & Bargh, 2001). Evidence for the mimicry of other people's body posture, facial expression and speech related variables is abundant (Chartrand & Bargh, 1999; Chartrand, Maddux & Lakin, 2005). While, previous research mainly focused on the mimicry of observable human behavior, we argue that even in the absence of a human model, human-like cues, like a depicted path of footsteps suggestive of a human walking path could also automatically trigger mimicry. Correspondingly, it is hypothesized that when the distance between the depicted movement signals is larger (vs. smaller) than an average human footstep, consumers will walk faster (H2). We argue that consumers do not have to be aware of the influence of (the distance of) the footprints on their motion path, nor of their walking speed for these effects to occur.

In study 1 we used footprints that look like the print of a shoe placed on a human walking rhythm. For a *smaller distance* between the footprints the average foot size is used, which is about 30 cm (Agnihotri, Shukla, & Purwar, 2007). For a *larger distance* between the footprints, an average foot size was added to the average footstep (which is 74 cm: Judge, Davis, & Ounpuu, 1996), summing up to about 100 cm. The movement signals were printed on white sticker paper, and were pasted on a grey linoleum floor.

In study 1 the participants (N=60) were randomly assigned to one of three movement signal conditions (small distance vs. large distance vs. no footsteps). First, this study tested if peoples' walking paths can be affected by a path of footprints; footprints were placed on a non dominant path ('alternative route') of an Y-junction on the participants walking route after finishing a filler study. The participant's walking time and chosen route unobtrusively recorded by research assistant. As expected, without a depiction of footprints,

70% of the participants choose the dominant route, while this dropped to 40% when footprints (both smaller and larger distances) were depicted on the alternative route ($\chi^2(1)$=4.13, p<.05). Second, this study revealed (contrast analyses of an ANOVA) that participants walked faster with a larger distance between the depicted footprints (M=18.77, SD=5.60), compared to a smaller distance between the footprints (M=24.15, SD=2.84; $F(1, 56)$=12.79, p<.001)(one outlier was removed according to Interquartile Range; Tukey, 1977).

The goal of study 2 was to replicate these findings with non human shapes (squares) on a human walking rhythm. This study (N=50) had a between subject design (small vs. large distance between footsteps), and the participants' walking behavior was taped by the surveillance camera of the research lab. Afterwards an independent judges coded the walking time of the participants. As expected, a t-test revealed with a smaller distance between the depicted squares the participants walked slower (M =11.639, SD=1.1858), than with a larger distance between the squares (M=11, SD=0.922), ($t(48)$=2.03, p<.05)(one outlier was removed).

The goal of study 3 (N=78) was to examine if people follow an indicated rhythm of movement signals *independent* of both human shape and human walking placement by placing squares in a row. We used a between subject design (small distance vs. large distance vs. no footsteps), and the procedure was equal to study 2. As expected, we found (contrast analyses of ANOVA) that participants walked slower when there was a smaller (M=8.57, SD=1.45) compared to a larger distance between the squares (M=7.87, SD=0.73; $F(1, 65)$=3.24, p=.077). Planned contrasts also revealed that participants in both the smaller ($F(1, 65)$=46.57, p<.001), and larger distance conditions ($F(1, 65)$=59.53, p<.001) walked significantly faster than participants in the control condition (M=11.16, SD=1.49)(four outliers were removed).

The influence of a shopping environment on consumer behaviour is an important aspect of marketing research. We showed that walking route and speed are significantly influenced by movement signals: the bigger the distances between the depicted signals, the faster people walk. Our findings have important marketing implications. For instance, to achieve high profits, a store manager can try to 'lead' the consumer to high margin products, and 'sway' customers to walk slowly in the vicinity of these products. We argued that movement signals automatically trigger mimicry of these signals, but based on the current studies we cannot exclude possible alternative processes, such as visual information.

### References

Agnihotri, A.K., Shukla, S., & Purwar, B. (2007). Determination Of Sex From The Foot Measurements, *The Internet Journal of Forensic Science, 2(1)*

Chartrand, T. L., & Bargh, J. A. (1999). The chameleon effect: The perception-behavior link and social interaction. *Journal of Personality and Social Psychology, 76*, 893–910.

Chartrand, T. L., Maddux, W. W., & Lakin, J. L. (2005). Beyond the perception-behavior link: The ubiquitous utility and motivational moderators of nonconscious mimicry. In R. Hassin, J. S. Uleman, & J. A. Bargh (Eds.), *The new unconscious* (pp. 334–361). New York: Oxford University Press.

Dijksterhuis, A., & Bargh, J.A. (2001). The Perception-Behavior Expressway: The Automatic Effects of Social Perception on Social Behavior. *Advances in Experimental Social Psychology, 33*, 1–40.

Hui, S. K., Bradlow, E. T., & Fader, P. S. (in press). Testing Behavioral Hypotheses Using an Integrated Model of Grocery Store Shopping Path and Purchase Behavior, *Journal of Consumer Research*, 36.

Hui, S. K., Fader, P. S., & Bradlow, E. T. (2009). Path Data in Marketing: An Integrative Framework and Prospectus for Model Building. *Marketing Science, 28(2)*, 320-335.

Judge, R. J. O., Davis, B., & Ounpuu, S. (1996). Step Length Reductions in Advanced Age: The Role of Ankle and Hip Kinetics. *The Journals of Gerontology Series A: Biological Sciences and Medical Sciences, 51(6)*, 303-312.

Tukey, J. W. (1977). *Exploratory Data Analysis*. Reading, MA: Addison-Wesley.

# Consumer Willingness to Purchase Counterfeit Brands: Frequent Change in Fashion as a Determinant

Kaleel Rahman, American University in Dubai, United Arab Emirates

## Extended Abstract

The objective of this research is to examine the determinants of consumers' willingness to buy counterfeit brands within the context of UAE market. According to the International Anticounterfeiting Coalition (IACC, 2008), almost five percent of all products are counterfeits. Hence, from different perspectives, many consumer researchers have attempted to identity the non-price related factors as to why consumers buy counterfeits (e. g., Bamossy, and Scammon, 1985; Ferreira and Pereira, 2010; Kim et. al., 2010). Although actions to limit counterfeit can arise from both supply side and demand side, supply side has dominated most of the research work to date, where issues of controlling the source and flow of counterfeit products are examined to make recommendations to policy makers (Albers-Miller, 1999). This practice is very clear in UAE. For example, a cursory scan of over four hundred newspaper clippings in regards to counterfeiting in UAE demonstrates this trend where most of them relate to some form of seizures but nothing about understanding why consumers like or are willing to buy counterfeits.

Until recently, the UAE government may have been turning a blind eye on the counterfeit industry as it has been a large aspect of tourism. However, since becoming a member of WTO in 1996, the government has been combating counterfeit trade. A massive amount of counterfeit trade currently present in the country is inconsistent with its attempt to portray a positive image in terms of luxury, tourism, business and real estate developments. The following points provide an overview of the scale of counterfeit trade in UAE and its impacts: About 35 per cent of software sold in the UAE is counterfeit (Gulfnews, November 15, 2008); value of fake products in the

UAE reached $696 million in 2006 (Gulf News, January 18, 2008); compared to the year 2006, 2007 shows a greater loss for concerned industries seeing a 52% increase in counterfeits (Gulf News, August 8, 2007). Despite counterfeit dilemma often being attributed to UAE (IACC, 2008), no study on counterfeit has been conducted in UAE from a consumer research perspective. Hence, in this research we examine the reasons why consumers prefer counterfeit brands, in the UAE market in particular.

We developed our measures using a projective technique in that fifty seven respondents (as part of their class exercises) were asked to write as many non-price related reasons as possible as to "why people buy counterfeit brands". These responses were then categorized into eight meaningful themes (i.e., reasons as constructs). Several of these constructs overlapped determinants identified in prior studies (e. g., Gentry et. al., 2006). We then developed scales to measure these constructs using the procedures suggested by authorities in construct development in marketing (e.g., Churchill, 1979; Nunnally, 1978). We adapted scales from prior studies to measure attitudes toward counterfeit (Huang et. al., 2004) and intention to buy counterfeits (Ang et. al., 2001). Constructs are listed below with respective coefficient alpha, number of items, and a sample item in parenthesis:

*Fashion changes quickly* ($\alpha$=.78, 3 items, "Fashion changes so quickly so it is ok to buy counterfeits")
*Superior quality of counterfeits* ($\alpha$=.61, 3 items, "The quality of counterfeits measure up to the quality of the original brands")
*Trialability of new brands* ($\alpha$=.64, 3 items, "Some consumers use counterfeits to test it, then buy the original if they like it")
*Novelty/ curiosity of brand names* ($\alpha$=.68, 4 items, "I like counterfeit for the novelty of having that brand name")
*Aspect of tourism* ($\alpha$=.74, 3 items, "It is quite acceptable for tourists to buy counterfeits")
*Friendly/ approachable sellers* ($\alpha$=.66, 6 items, "Sellers of counterfeit products are friendlier than sellers of original brands")
*Availability/ accessibility* ($\alpha$=.76, 2 items, "Sometimes counterfeits are available before the originals are released")
*Household usability* ($\alpha$=.55, 2 items, "For rough and in-house wear, I got no problem with counterfeits")
*Attitudes toward counterfeit* ($\alpha$=.86, 4 items, "Buying counterfeit goods generally benefits the consumer")
*Intention to buy counterfeit* ($\alpha$=.88, 4 items, "What is the chance that you think about a counterfeit product as a choice when buying something?")

We collected data using a 7-point Likert scale from a total of 348 consumers, both students and non-students who live in UAE. The questionnaire also included several other items beyond the scope of this paper. We averaged the items under each construct to create a single item measure. In analyzing the data, we used stepwise regression analysis in SPSS in order to gain some preliminary insight. Using standardized beta coefficients, we summarize the results below:

*Attitudes toward counterfeits* (R Squared=0.63, F=135, p=0.000)
= $\beta$1 fashion changes + $\beta$2 trialability + $\beta$3 superior quality + $\beta$4 household use
= [.51 fashion changes] + [.17 trialability] + [.14 superior quality] + [.13 household use]
*Intention to buy counterfeits* (R Squared=0.40, F=152, p=0.000)
= $\beta$1 fashion changes + $\beta$2 superior quality + $\beta$3 household use
= [.33 fashion changes] + [.25 superior quality] + [.17 household use]

This can be interpreted that 63% of total variance in *attitudes toward counterfeit* was explained by fashion changes, trialability, superior quality and household usability of counterfeits. Other variables mentioned by respondents in the projective technique did not make a statistically significant contribution. When it comes to *intention to buy counterfeit* brands, the result was somewhat different where trialability of counterfeit was not a predictor of intention. These results are quite insightful as frequent changes in fashion emerged as the strongest determinant of consumers' preference for counterfeit brands, a determinant ignored in prior research. Interestingly, several factors strongly expressed by projective technique respondents were not supported by our large-sample regression model. For example, "counterfeit sellers are very friendly", "they come to your door", "they are available even before the originals" were reasons frequently mentioned by respondents. Currently, we have planned to do further modeling using Amos and analysis on differences between groups such as Arabs versus non-Arabs, and the users versus non-users of counterfeits.

## Selected References

Albers-Miller, Nancy D, (1999), "Consumer Misbehavior: Why People Buy Illicit Goods", *Journal of Consumer Marketing*, 76(3), 273-287,

Ang, Swee Hoon, Peng Sim Cheng, Elison A,C, Lim, and Siok Kuan Tambyah, (2001). "Spot the Difference: Consumer Responses Towards Counterfeits", *Journal of Consumer Marketing, 18(3), 219-235*.

Bamossy , G . and Scammon , D . ( 1985 ) ' Produce counterfeiting: Consumers and manufacturers beware ' , *Advances in Consumer Research* , Vol. 12 , pp. 334–340 .

Churchill, Jr., G. A. (1979) A paradigm for developing better measures of marketing constructs, *Journal of Marketing Research*, vol. 16, no. 1, pp. 64-73

Ferreira, Marcia Christina and Bill Pereira (2010), "IT'S FAKE!? CONSUMERS' SELF CREATION IN A MARKET WITH EASY ACCESS TO COUNTERFEIT GOODS", in Advances in Consumer Research Volume 37

Gentry, J. W., Putrevu, S. and Schultz, C. (2006) "The effects of counterfeiting on consumer search, Journal of Consumer Behaviour, Vol 5, May-June, pp 245-256

International Anticounterfeiting Coalition (2008), "Facts on fakes", available at: www.iacc.org/Facts.html (accessed September 27, 2008).

Kim, Jungkeun, Jae-Eun Kim, Jongwon Park (2010), "EFFECTS OF RESOURCE AVAILABILITY ON CONSUMER DECISIONS ON COUNTERFEIT PRODUCTS: ROLE OF JUSTIFICATION", in Advances in Consumer Research Volume 37

Nunnally, J.C. (1978), Psychometric Theory, 2nd ed., McGraw-Hill, New York, NY.

Wang, F., Zang, H. and Ouyang, M. (2005) Purchasing pirated software: an initial examination of Chinese consumers, Journal of Consumer Marketing, Vol 22, No. 6, pp. 340-351

# New Business, New Babies: Proposing a Sociological Analysis of Consuming Early Childhood Development Service in China

### Gehui Zhang, University of Illinois at Urbana-Champaign, USA

China's Early Childhood Development (ECD) industry is at its very outset; however, by all means uprising. It was estimated that the current China ECD market scale is approximately worth four billion US dollars per year and will maintain a fast growth compared with other industries[1]. It was reported in 2006 that over 50% urban Chinese parents are willing to purchase professional ECD services for their young children[2]. This research aims to examine the cultural contexts in which the development of this relatively new market and the consumption of ECD service have embedded in China.

FOOTNOTE 1 and 2

[1]"An Analysis of Early Childhood Education Industry," retrieved from http://www.ci123.com/article.php/22877

[2]Yang, Gu (2007), "Early childhood education on fast track in China," retrieved from http://en.ce.cn/Insight/200707/26/t20070726_12321002.shtml

Consumption on young kids' early development education is an economic action, a consumer behavior, a familial practice, and with a more general view, a reflection of the interaction between social institutions and individual agents. Gary Becker (1991) uses rational choice theory to explain a series of familial relations and activities, such as marriage, fertility, education investment, and domestic division of labor. In his theoretical model, individual are not only social beings but foremost economic agents. Social and culture forces such as traditions and values may shape individuals' decision making process however say little about how people act. Instead, one can only understand individual's action as a consequence of a careful calculation on efficiency and utility maximization, regardless conforming or challenge social norms. Zelizer (2005), however, argues that the context-free analysis of market and the rational choice orthodox advocated in neoclassical approach of economic activities are inadequate to understand economic exchange. Adopting Weberian tradition, Zelizer (2005) proposed an "alternative approach" to analyze the interaction between social and cultural characters and market as well as economic activities, in which a market is neither treated in dominance nor in subordination, but recognized as one of the social categories (Zelizer 1988).

In current capitalist markets, child is one of the most central subjects which have been commercialized in most of the social aspects. However, parents' consumption on early childhood development (ECD) services has been portrayed as either an investment or altruism based on parents' sacred love, which may contribute to its understudies in existing literatures. Scholars, such as D. Cook (2000), argue about the reconciliation between "scared" childhood and the "profane" market was achieved through redefining certain commodities or services beneficial or useful to child's development—the process of f the early life course moving through predictable, specifiable, and sequential stages (Seiter 1993). However, the "naturally" perceived child development periods and their commoditification are nothing given but culturally and historically constructed. The dominant moral standard of economically useless but emotionally priceless child was a consequence of an ideological victory of the sacred view of childhood over the productive one (Zelizer 1985).

Gymborre, recognized as "the global leader" in early childhood development program, was founded in 1976 in the United States and became an international brand in offering classes, trainings, and programs in early childhood development for under 5-year old children and their parents globally. The key philosophy as it publicizes is to "focus on the whole child in order to help children acquire the key ingredients--motor skills, social skills and self-esteem--they need to grow up to be confident, happy and successful adults.[3]" Gymboree Play & Music Program entered Mainland China's market in 2003 and the franchise business has grown rapidly through licensing over 50 Gymboree centers within four years. Market operators expect to have over 200 centers by 2010, which will make China the biggest market for Gymborre's ECD business. This working paper, using Gymborre, one of the best renowned global brands in early childhood development industry as a case study, aims to provide an alternative theoretical framework to understand the recent development of ECD market in China through a preliminary analysis of Gymborre's rapid franchise expansion in China. By reviewing the literatures on parents' consumption on children's education, I propose the cultural embeddedness approach as a valuable tool to study the markets which are ingrained in the "presumable" or "unquestionable" moralities, such as consumption in ECD services. I argue that the booming ECD market and its swift popularity in China is culturally embedded phenomenon which deserves a more careful examination on the impact of social values and relations out of the money nexus on the formation of consumer culture and culture of consumption. The creation of consumption discourse in ECD market, I suggest, parallels with the on-going transformation of parenting and childhood ideologies in Chinese society, which needs to be understood with the formation of modern child and personhood in neo-liberalism social condition.

FOOTNOTE

[3]rettrieved from http://www.gymboree.com.cn/app/web_en/aboutus_6.jsp

## Selected References

Becker, Gary (1991). *A Treatise on the Family (enlarged edition)*, Harvard University Press.

Cook, Daniel (2000). "The Rise of 'the Toddler' as Subject and as Merchandising

Category in the 1930s," Pp111-29 in *New Forms of Consumption: Consumers, Culture, and Commodification*, edited by Mark Gottdiener. Rowman & Littlefield.

Seiter, Ellen (1993). *Sold Separately: Children and Parents in Consumer Culture,* Rutgers University Press

Zelizer, Viviana (1985). *Pricing and Priceless Child: The Changing Social Value of Children,* Harper Collins Press.

_____ (1988). "Beyond the Polemics on the Market: Establishing a Theoretical and Empirical Agenda," *Sociological Forum,* 3(4), 614-34.

_____ (2005). "Enter Culture," Pp 101-29 in *The New Economic Sociology: Developments in an Emerging Field,* edited by Mauro Guillen, R. Collins, P. England, and M. Meyer. Russell Sage Foundation Press.

# It Leaves a Bad Taste In Your Mouth: The Impact of Negative Company Information on Consumption Experience

John Peloza, Simon Fraser University, Canada

Jingzhi Shang, Simon Fraser University, Canada

## Extended Abstract

Consumers' attitudes toward brands are impacted by corporate social responsibility (CSR) information, and firm-level CSR can translate into improved attitudes toward products of the firm (e.g., Brown and Dacin 1997). But attitudes stemming from CSR information aren't always good predictors of actual consumer behaviors. For example, products that have social attributes are sometimes perceived as inferior in quality to those that do not (Obermiller et al. 2009), and consumers will not sacrifice quality for social features (Auger and Devinney 2008). This gap between CSR attitudes and behaviors (see Cotte and Trudel (2009) for a review) suggests additional research is necessary to understand how CSR information can impact consumers beyond attitudes. Further, the impact of CSR information on subjective, post-purchase consumption experiences remains unstudied. This represents a theoretical and managerial gap since many consumers acquire CSR information *after* they have already purchased a product or developed a relationship with a brand.

On the other hand, research examining how information can alter subjective consumption experience is plentiful. One of the consumption experiences most fertile for researchers is taste (Lee, Frederick and Ariely 2006). This is because consumers generally lack taste discrimination and are unaware of their ineptitude (Lau, Post, and Kagan 1995), making it highly susceptible to the forces of information. Indeed, taste is a commonly used dependent variable (e.g., Allison and Uhl 1964; Braun 1999; Hoegg and Alba 2007; Lee et al. 2006; Levin and Gaeth 1988; Obermiller et al. 2009; Wansink, Payne and North 2007). Further, a wide variety of information has been used to manipulate taste evaluations including product labels (Allison and Uhl 1964; Nevid 1981), advertising copy (Braun 1999; Elder and Krishna 2010), product color (Hoegg and Alba 2007), and nutritional content (Wardle and Solomons 1994). However, the information used in these studies is closely linked to product attributes with high salience to product performance (i.e., taste). For example, Elder and Krishna (2010) prime multiple senses through advertising copy since taste is enhanced when multiple senses are engaged. Despite broad consensus that information can influence consumption experiences, the impacts of firm-level information such as CSR (as opposed to attributes more salient to product performance) are relatively unknown.

Our research aims to address the gaps in these two disparate research streams, contributing to each in the process. Across two studies we examine how CSR information impacts consumer evaluations of product taste.

Our research is based on the idea that CSR information can activate emotions in consumers, and those emotions in turn will impact their taste evaluations of products. The prevailing social norm is that consumers who support firms that perform CSR are engaging in positive behavior, and those who support firms engaged in corporate social irresponsibility (CSIR) are engaging in negative behavior. This effect is particularly strong for CSIR; consumers are much more willing to punish firms who engage in CSIR then they are to reward firms who perform CSR (Sen and Bhattacharya 2001). With CSIR, the perceived violation of a social norm stimulates guilt which in turn diminishes enjoyment.

Study 1 tests this hypothesis through a chocolate taste test. Participants were told that a company was market testing a new line of chocolate. Company information was presented in one of three conditions. The first condition was neutral, and merely presented some generic company information (years in business, etc.). The positive condition stated that the firm had been a leader in employee policies, and the negative condition described several violations in the area of employee policies. The issue of employment was chosen because a pretest rated it as most important from a range of other social and environmental issues.

The results from study 1 support the hypothesis that CSIR information can diminish taste perceptions. However, CSR information does not enhance taste perceptions. The neutral and CSR conditions were not significantly different ($M_{NEUTRAL}$=7.10 and $M_{CSR}$=7.01 on a taste scale of 1 to 10) but the CSIR ratings were significantly lower ($M_{CSIR}$=6.15; $F_{(2, 107)}$=4.865, p<.01). Bonferroni tests confirm that the CSR and neutral conditions are not statistically distinct, but that the CSIR condition was statistically different from both the CSR and neutral conditions.

Study 2 seeks to examine the underlying process behind this effect. Enjoyment of food is not only determined by the quality of the food itself (bottom-up processes) but by knowledge of how the food was prepared and other information about the manufacturer (top-down processes). Information received prior to evaluation should lead to greater coding of the information (Hoch and Ha 1986; Lee et al. 2006). Therefore, the cognitive top-down process related to CSIR should have a greater effect on taste perceptions when consumers receive the information prior to tasting rather than after. This is because the consumer is in a negative mindset prior to experiencing the relatively enjoyable taste of chocolate. When they taste the chocolate first, the enjoyment is more likely to overshadow the negative valence from CSIR. Study 2 used the same procedure as study 1, except only the CSIR condition was used, and participants were instructed to taste the chocolate either before or after the information was provided.

The results from study 2 are significant, but in the opposite direction than predicted. Participants who received the CSIR information before they tasted the chocolate rated the taste significantly *higher* than those who received it after ($M_{BEFORE}$=7.04, $M_{AFTER}$=6.26, $F_{(1, 82)}$=4.288, p=.042).

Study 2 suggests that when consumers learn about CSIR from a brand they currently consume it is more damaging than if they are not current consumers, and provides fruitful direction for future studies. One possible explanation is that the relatively pleasant taste of chocolate did not conform to the negative expectations intended by the CSIR information. On the other hand, the presentation of CSIR information after the taste has the effect of "tainting" the memory of the taste. Future studies will further examine the role of guilt as well as memory and recency.

## References

Allison, Ralph I. and Kenneth P. Uhl (1964), "Influence of Beer Brand Identification on Taste Perception," *Journal of Marketing Research*, 1, 36-39.

Auger, Pat, Timothy Devinney, Jordan Louviere, and Paul Burke (2008), "Do Social Product Features Have Value to Consumers?" *International Journal of Research in Marketing*, 25 (3), 183-91.

Braun, Kathryn A. (1999), "Postexperience Advertising Effects on Consumer Memory," *Journal of Consumer Research*, 25 (March), 319-334.

Brown, T. J., & Dacin, P. A. (1997). The Company and the Product: Corporate Associations and Consumer Product Responses. *Journal of Marketing, 61* (January), 68-84.

Cotte, June and Remi Trudel (2009), *Socially Conscious Consumerism: A Systematic Review of the Body of Knowledge*, Network for Business Sustainability: London.

Elder, Ryan S. and Aradhna Krishna (2010), "The Effects of Advertising Copy on Sensory Thoughts and Perceived Taste," *Journal of Consumer Research*, 36 (February), 748-756.

Hoch, Stephen J. and Young-Won Ha (1986), "Consumer Learning: Advertising and the Ambiguity of Product Experience," *Journal of Consumer Research*, 13 (September), 221-233.

Hoegg, Joandrea and Joseph W. Alba (2007), "Taste Perception: More than Meets the Tongue," *Journal of Consumer Research*, 33 (March), 490-498.

Lau, Kin-Nam, Gerald Post, and Albert Kagan (1995), "Using Economic Incentives to Distinguish Perception Bias from Discrimination Ability in Taste Tests," *Journal of Marketing Research*, 32 (May), 140-151.

Lee, Leonard, Shane Frederick, and Dan Ariely (2006), "Try It, You'll Like It: The Influence of Expectation, Consumption, and Revelation on Preferences for Beer," *Psychological Science*, 17 (12), 1054-1058.

Levin, Irwin P. and Gary J. Gaeth (1988), "How Consumers Are Affected by the Framing of Attribute Information Before and After Consuming the Product," *Journal of Consumer Research*, 15 (December), 374-378.

Nevid, Jeffrey S. (1981), "Effects of Brand Labeling on Ratings of Product Quality," *Perceptual and Motor Skills, 53*, 407–10.

Obermiller, Carl, Chauncey Burke, Erin Talbott and Gareth P. Green (2009), "'Taste Great or More Fulfilling': The Effect of Brand Reputation on Consumer Social Responsibility Advertising for Fair Trade Coffee," *Corporate Reputation Review*, 12 (2), 159-176.

Sen, Sanka and C.B. Bhattacharya (2001), "Does Doing Good Always Lead to Doing Better? Consumer Reactions to Corporate Social Responsibility," *Journal of Marketing Research*, 38 (May), 225-243.

Wansink, Brian, Collin R. Payne, and Jill North (2007), "Fine as North Dakota Wine: Sensory Expectations and the Intake of Companion Foods," *Physiology & Behavior*, 90, 712-716.

Wardle, Jane and Wendy Solomons (1994), "Naughty But Nice: A Laboratory Study of Health Information and Food Preferences in a Community Sample," *Health Psychology*, 13 (2), 180-183.

# The Effect of Systems of Thought on Brand Scandal Spillover: Holistic versus Analytic Cognition Moderating Scandal Spillover and Denial Effects

Yun Lee, University of Iowa, USA
Nara Youn, Hongik University, Korea

## Extended Abstract

Recent high-profile product recalls (Tang 2008) and more stringent product-safety legislation (Birch 1994; Patterson 1993) have led to increased consumers' exposure to negative brand publicity. Product-harm crises or brand scandals lead to significantly decreased preferences and purchases for the scandalized brands and their family (Sullivan 1990) as well as their competing brands (Roehm and Tybout 2006). Recent research has demonstrated that consumers engaged in different systems of thought are more or less susceptible to negative brand publicity (Monga and John 2008).

Extending prior work, our research examines how different contents of negative publicity and systems of thought jointly affect consumer reactions to brand scandals and the spillover correction effects of denials. We argue that whether the contents of negative brand publicity are intrinsic or extrinsic to the product itself determines the degree to which individuals process the negative information as a focal point versus a context and that this relative difference subsequently affects the type of judgment bias they make. Holistic thinkers tend to focus more on relationships among objects and events and analytic thinkers tend to focus more on a discrete focal point from its context (Nisbett et al. 2001).

These distinct differences between holistic versus analytic cognitive styles lead us to predict that when negative publicity is directly associated with issues intrinsic to the product itself, for example, poor product quality or risks of injury threatening consumer safety, the focal components of negative publicity become more salient, and thus analytic thinkers might make more biased judgments for the scandalized brand than holistic thinkers might. Monga and John (2008) depicted this case and showed that when participants were presented with negative publicity about a new car with manufacturing problems, analytic thinkers were prone to more biases than holistic thinkers. We argue that the converse should show the opposite results. When negative publicity is not directly associated with the product itself, but related with issues extrinsic to the product, for example, manufacturing process causing a water pollution or recent Tiger Woods' multiple mistress scandal linked with brands using him in their ads (e.g., Nike or Gatorade), consumers would attend more to the contexts of the brand scandals than the focal points of the scandalized brand itself, thus it leads to more biased judgments of holistic thinkers.

Furthermore, we argue that the effects of brand scandal denials will also depend on which cognitive thinking mode is active. Since scandal denials are perceived to be informative, when consumers consider the brand scandal as diagnostic, but to be redundant when they do not we argue that when the contents of the negative brand publicity are intrinsic to the product itself (Roehm and Tybout 2006), denials will attenuate the harmful effects of the brand scandal for analytic thinkers, but not for holistic thinkers. In contrast, when negative brand publicity information is extrinsic to the product itself, scandal denials will be more effective for holistic thinkers than for analytic thinkers.

We begin our hypothesis testing by demonstrating the effects of holistic versus analytic cognitive styles on brand scandal spillover in a fictitious situation where a brand scandal is extrinsic to the brand itself (Experiment 1). Next, we investigate the moderating role of thinking modes on the effects of scandal denials involved with the negative publicity extrinsic (Experiment 2), and intrinsic (Experiment 3) to the brand.

In Experiment 1, participants were asked to read a fictitiously created water pollution scandal regarding Nike athletic shoe factories and then indicate brand attitudes for Nike in general and the likelihood of its competing brand, Reebok, polluting nearby waters. Then they responded to ten items on a holistic scale (Choi et al. 2003). Regressing thinking styles (holistic versus analytic) on brand scandal spillover supported our prediction. In the context of negative publicity involved in the issues extrinsic to the product itself, holistic thinkers evaluated its parent brand more negatively and indicated the higher likelihood of Reebok's water pollution than analytic thinkers did ($\beta$Nike= -.490, $t$= -2.694, $p$=.013; $\beta$Reebok= .51, $t$= -2.65, $p$=.015).

To investigate the role of cognitive modes moderating the effects of brand scandal denials, in Experiment 2, participants were primed with holistic versus analytic thinking styles by completing sentences in a short story about a trip to a city by filling in proper pronouns (i.e., I, my, me, mine versus we, our, us, ours; Kühnen et al. 2001). Then they were presented with a brand scandal about Nike's water pollution and then an article introducing its competing brands, Adidas or Converse's launching new athletic shoes with or without the denial of water pollution. Participants indicated the likelihood of Adidas or Converse' polluting nearby waters. A 2(thinking styles: holistic versus analytic) $\times$ 2 (brand similarity: high, Adidas versus low, Converse) $\times$ 2(denial: yes versus no) between-subjects ANOVA revealed a significant three-way interaction ($F(1,103)$=9.277, $p$=.003). Subsequent analyses showed that there was a two-way significant interaction between thinking styles and denial in the high brand similarity condition ($F$adidas$(1,53)$=9.245, $p$=.004). We also found a marginally significant main effect for thinking style, indicating that holistic thinkers are more susceptible to the brand scandal spillover ($F(1,53)$=3.258, $p$=.077) than analytic thinkers are. Contrasts revealed a marginally significant brand scandal spillover correction effect of a denial for holistic thinkers, but its boomerang effects for analytic thinkers. When denial was provided in the article, holistic thinkers indicated decreased likelihood of Adidas' water pollution compared to when denial was not included in the article ($M$no= 4.69, $M$yes=4.408; $F(1,25)$=3.021, $p$=.09). In contrast, analytic thinkers indicated significantly increased likelihood of Adidas' water pollution when denial was included in the article ($M$no= 3.292, $M$yes=4.405; $F(1,28)$=6.547, $p$=.016).

In Experiment 3, we tested our prediction in the context of negative publicity intrinsic to the product itself. Thinking style manipulation was the same as used in Experiment 2. Participants were presented with a fictitiously created McDonald's food hygiene law violation scandal about using expired hamburger meat and breads. After reading the scandal story, they indicated the likelihood of Burger King and Outback's food hygiene law violations and also of other filler brands. They then read an article introducing KFC or Outback's new programs employing organic produce from environmentally friendly farming methods. The new program article was also varied with or without denial of food hygiene law violation. Participants then indicated the likelihood of KFC or Outback's food hygiene law violation. A 2(thinking styles: holistic versus analytic) X 2 (brand similarity: high, Burger King versus low, Outback) repeated-measures ANOVA with thinking styles as a between-subjects factor and brand similarity as a within-subjects factor revealed a marginally significant main effect for thinking styles ($F(1,220)$=3.048, $p$=.08) and a significant main effect for brand similarity ($F(1,220)$=73.33, $p$<.001).

Replicating the results of Monga and John (2008), the data showed that holistic thinkers were less susceptible to the negative brand publicity than analytic thinkers were ($M$holistic= 5.095, $M$yes=5.603). This effect was greater for the participants in the conditions of Burger King than Outback ($M$buerger king= 5.919, $M$outback=4.779). As expected, a 2(thinking styles: holistic versus analytic) $\times$ 2 (brand similarity: high, KFC versus low, Outback) $\times$ 2(denial: yes versus no) between-subjects ANOVA revealed a significant three-way interaction ($F(1,211)$=8.207, $p$=.005). This interaction effect qualified the main effects for thinking styles ($F(1,220)$=4.459, $p$=.036), indicating that the brand scandal spillover effects occurred to analytic thinkers than holistic thinkers ($M$holistic= 5.104, $M$analytic=5.760). Subsequent analyses revealed a marginally significant two-way interaction between thinking styles and denial in the condition of KFC ($F(1,138)$=3.119, $p$=.08). As expected, contrasts indicated that the brand scandal spillover correction effects occurred to analytic thinkers, when the article was with the brand scandal denial compared to when it was not ($M$no= 6.72, $M$yes=5.5; $F(1,69)$=6.752, $p$=.01), whereas denial or no denial was equally effective to holistic thinkers.

By employing a 2(thinking styles: holistic versus analytic) X 2 (brand similarity: high versus low) X 2(denial: yes versus no) $\times$ 2(scandal content: intrinsic versus extrinsic) between-subjects design in Experiment 4, we intend to increase the robustness of previous results and directly test the effect of the scandal content. The results of Experiment 4 will be presented at ACR 2010 with a complete working paper.

**References**

Birch, John (1994), "New Factors in Crisis Planning and Response," *Public Relations Quarterly,* 39 (Spring), 31-4.

Choi, Incheol, Reeshad Dalal, Chu Kim-Prieto, and Hyekyung Park (2003), "Culture and Judgment of Causal Relevance," *Journal of Personality and Social Psychology,* 84 (January), 46–59.

Klein, Jill and Niraj Dawar (2004), "Corporate social responsibility and consumer's attributions and brand evaluations in a product harm crisis," *International Journal of Research in Marketing,* 21, 203-17.

Kühnen, Ulrich, Bettina Hannover, and Benjamin Schubert (2001), "The Semantic-Procedural Interface Model of the Self: The Role of Self-Knowledge for Context-Dependent versus Context- Independent Modes of Thinking," *Journal of Personality and Social Psychology,* 80 (March), 397–409.

Monga, Alokparna Basu and Deborah Roedder John (2008), "When Does Negative Brand Publicity Hurt? The Moderating Influence of Analytic versus Holistic Thinking," *Journal of Consumer Psychology,* 18, 320-32.

Nisbett, Richard E., Kaiping Peng, Incheol Choi, and Ara Norenzayan (2001), "Culture and Systems of Thought: Holistic versus Analytic Cognition," *Psychological Review,* 108 (April), 291-310.

Patterson, Bill (1993), "Crises Impact on Reputation Management," *Public Relations Journal,* 49 (November), 47-8.

Roehm, Michelle, L. and Alice M. Tybout (2006), "When Will a Brand Scandal Spill Over, and How Should Competitors Respond?," *Journal of Marketing Research,* 43 (August), 366- 73.

Sullivan, M. (1990), "Measuring image spillovers in umbrella-branded products," *The Journal of Business,* 63, 309-21.

Tang, Christoper S. (2008), "Making Products Safe: Process and Challenges," *International Consumer Review,* 8 (Autumn), 48-55.

Tybout, Alice M., Bobby J. Calder and Brian Sternthal (1981), "Using Information Processing Theory to Design Marketing Strategies," *Journal of Marketing Research,* 18 (February), 73-9.

# Is Negative Brand Publicity Always Damaging? The Moderating Role of Power

David A. Norton, University of South Carolina, USA
Alokparna (Sonia) Monga, University of South Carolina, USA
William O. Bearden, University of South Carolina, USA

As consumers have increasing access to multiple sources for product information (e.g., blogs, television, news outlets, etc.), the ability to manage negative publicity becomes increasingly difficult. Prior research has demonstrated that consumers place more weight on negative than positive information in forming judgments (Eagly and Chaiken, 1993) showing that negative publicity can cause substantial harm. For example, the recent events surrounding Toyota's faulty accelerator and brake pedals have led to detrimental effects on the brand.

Surprisingly, little research has focused on characteristics of the message recipients and how they might influence responses to negative publicity. In this vein, we examine the effect of consumers' power on responses to negative publicity. Power is an important characteristic to study, as it is ubiquitous and highly malleable. In many instances throughout our daily life, we may be shifting between a powerful (e.g., meeting with a subordinate) and a powerless (e.g., meeting with a boss) mindset. Further, ambient marketing activity (e.g., advertising, point-of-sale displays, etc.) can influence a consumer's sense of power. Aside from these situational variations, power may also be conceptualized as an individual difference variable which varies across consumers (Anderson et al. 2005).

We know that negative publicity can be damaging for brands (Ahluwalia, Unnava and Burnkrant 2000; Monga and John 2008). In this research, we suggest that powerful individuals are less likely to be affected by negative publicity than powerless individuals. Galinsky et al. (2008) find that powerful people possess more freedom from influence of external forces compared to powerless people. Powerful people are less influenced and constrained by salient information in the environment, because power increases sensitivity to internal states and increases confidence in one's own thoughts (Brinol et al. 2007). This sensitivity to internal states suggests that powerful individuals may rely more on their own thoughts about the brand and are less likely to be influenced by negative publicity information, compared to powerless individuals. Thus, upon exposure to negative publicity, brand evaluations of powerful individuals would be more favorable than those of powerless individuals.

In study 1, we test our hypothesis using a power manipulation (Galinksy et al. 2008). In the powerful condition, participants wrote about a situation in which he/she controlled the ability of another person or persons to get something they wanted. In the powerless condition, participants wrote about a situation in which another person controlled the ability of the participant to get something he/she wanted. Next, participants were exposed to a press release stating that Mercedes Benz was experiencing manufacturing problems on their new line of cars. Subsequently, participants rated the new line of cars and the Mercedes Benz brand. As expected, participants in the powerful condition rated the brand more favorably than participants in the powerless condition.

In study 2, we examine the role of source credibility (Brinol et al. 2004). We anticipate that for a less credible source, we would expect that powerful individuals would be less susceptible to the negative publicity than powerless individuals (as in our prior study). However, for a more credible source, we expect that powerful individuals would be more likely to attend to the negative publicity and their brand evaluations would decrease. As a result, differences in brand evaluations between powerful and powerless individuals would dissipate.

In study 2, participants were exposed to the same power manipulation as in study 1. The source of the press release was indicated as either a highly credible source (*The Wall Street Journal*) or a significantly less credible source (*The National Enquirer*). We also included a control condition to assess baseline evaluations for the brand. Participants in this condition were not exposed to the negative publicity. Thus, we used a 2 (Power: High, Low) x 3 (Source Credibility: High, Low, Control) between subjects design. Our results show a significant interaction between power and credibility on brand evaluations, such that in the low credibility condition powerful individuals evaluate the brand higher than powerless individuals. However, this difference is not significant in the high credibility condition or in the control condition.

The findings in our paper contribute to the negative publicity literature and to the largely understudied area of consumer power. Prior research shows that negative publicity can adversely affect the brand. We show that this effect is more likely to happen for powerless than powerful consumers.

## References

Ahluwalia, R., Burnkrant, R. E., & Unnava. H. R. (2000). Consumer response to negative publicity: The moderating role of commitment, *Journal of Marketing Research, 37,* 203-214.

Briñol, P., Petty, R. E., Valle, C., Rucker, D. D., & Becerra, A. (2007). The effects of message recipients' power before and after persuasion: A self-validation analysis. Journal of Personality and Social Psychology, 93, 1040-1053.

Eagly, A., & Chaiken, S. (1993). *The psychology of attitudes,* Fort Worth, TX: Harcourt Brace Jovanovich.

Galinsky, A. D., Magee, J. C., Gruenfeld, D. H, Whitson, J., & Liljenquist, K. A. (2008). Social power reduces the strength of the situation: Implications for creativity, conformity, and dissonance. *Journal of Personality and Social Psychology,* 95, 1450-1466.

Monga, A. B. and D. R. John (2008), "When Does Negative Brand Publicity Hurt? The Moderating Influence of Analytic Versus Holistic Thinking," *Journal of Consumer Psychology*, 18 (4), 320-332.

# Disaster Zone! Maximizing the Impact of Corporate Contributions to Disasters or a Different Way of Thinking of Fit

Yoshiko DeMotta, Baruch College, USA
Diogo Heldebrand, Baruch College, USA
Ana Valenzuela, Baruch College, USA
Sankar Sen, Baruch College, USA

Corporations are often willing to help when a major disaster, such as the recent earthquake in Haiti or the 9/11 terrorist attacks, happens. For example, American companies already donated $146.8 million to the relief of the earthquake victims in Haiti (U.S. Chamber of Commerce 2010). Regardless on the motives behind these humanitarian contributions (e.g., altruistic or strategic nature), it is of chief importance to maximize corporate return in terms of consumers' attitudes and corporate image (Porter and Kramer 2006). Along this line, the concept of fit, or perceived link between a brand and a CSR cause, has been pointed as having central importance in consumers' attitudes (Pracejus and Olsen 2004). For example, support for breast cancer research by Yoplait yogurt is considered to have a good fit since both brand and cause serve a similar customer base (Nan and Hao 2007). Although this conceptualization of fit is useful in order to understand the effect of firms' ongoing CSR programs, we propose that consumers may use different dimensions of fit to evaluate CSR programs directed toward non-recurring causes such as disaster relief efforts. In this paper, we research the idea that type of contribution (monetary vs. non-monetary) may be pertinent to this judgment of fit, having an important effect on consumers attitudes toward the company after the disaster relief.

There are two main approaches used by companies to contribute to the relief of victims in disasters–monetary contributions and non-monetary contributions (i.e., products, services and employee volunteerism). Because the later are considered more effortful than the former, it is generally accepted that non-monetary contributions will have a more positive impact on consumers' attitudes toward the company (Ellen, Webb and Mohr 2000). However, we propose that sometimes monetary contributions may be considered more adequate. Specifically, we suggest that the fit between characteristics of the cause (i.e., nature-made or man-made) and the contribution type (monetary or non-monetary) will influence consumers' attributions and attitudes toward the company that helped in the disaster relief.

A disaster is the tragedy of a natural-made or human-made hazard that negatively affects society. Consumers may perceive nature-made disasters as phenomena beyond human control, but from predictable sources (Quarantelli 1993). In this case, non-monetary contributions, for being considered less flexible but more hands-on and specialized, will be considered more adequate. On the contrary, since human-made disasters are originated on much more varied and unpredictable number of sources (Quarantelli 1993), more flexible and versatile monetary contributions might be considered more adequate. We formalize our hypotheses as follows:

H1: Fit between contribution type and cause of disaster will increase consumer evaluations of corporate contributions for disaster relief.

Consumers will evaluate a firm's non-monetary contribution to nature-made disasters more positively than a firm's monetary contribution to such disasters.

Consumers will evaluate a firm's monetary contribution to man-made disasters more positively than a firm's non-monetary contribution to such disasters.

We examined this hypothesis using a 2 (contribution type) x 2 (cause of disaster) between-subjects design. One hundred and sixty undergraduate students participated in this study. Participants read fictitious news about a large scale fire in California and a disaster relief effort of a logistics company. In the news, the company's contribution was either one million dollars (monetary) or logistic services that worth one million dollars (non-monetary). Disaster was caused either by arson (man-made disaster) or lightening (human-made disaster). After reading the story, participants assessed their evaluations of the company in a three items ($\alpha=0.87$) 7-point semantic differential scale (favorable, effective, helpful).

Results of an ANOVA analysis supported our hypotheses. Personal relevance of the disaster was included as a covariate. Contribution type and cause of disaster presented significant main effects on consumer evaluations. More importantly, the interaction term was significant (p<0.02). In the nature-made disaster condition, the evaluation was more positive when the company made non-monetary contributions, whereas in the man-made disaster condition, the evaluation was more positive when the company made monetary contributions.

Moreover, Ellen, Webb and Mohr (2006) observed that if there is a perceived lack of fit on CSR initiatives, consumers will attribute corporate efforts to be of a negative self-centered nature. Hence, if it is perception of fit the mechanism underlying consumers' evaluation, negative self-centered attributions shall mediate the effect of the interaction between contribution type and disaster characteristics on company evaluation. We measured consumer negative self-centered attributions using 4 items (α=0.84) (Ellen et al. 2006). Meditational analysis (Baron and Kenny 1986) corroborates our process explanation. Particularly, the interaction between contribution type and cause of disaster significantly affected negative self-centered attributions (p<0.01). Furthermore, egoistic attributions, contribution type, cause of disaster and the interaction term significantly affected individual evaluation of the company (p<0.05). Nevertheless, when regressing company evaluation on egoistic attributions, contribution type, cause of disaster and the interaction term, the interaction term had its significance reduced (from p=0.013 to p=0.038).

The partial mediation effect of negative self-centered is a clear indicative that consumers evaluations of the company is centered on consumers perception of fit, explanation that demands closer attention in future studies. Furthermore, future studies should also verify the robustness of the effect here presented under different operationalizations of corporate contributions and disaster characteristics.

Corporate contributions to the community are considered a strategic tool for company survival and success (Porter and Kramer 2006). The present paper contributes to the literature of consumer response to CSR by showing the effect of a new dimension of fit between contribution type and non-recurring causes on consumers' evaluations of the company.

## References

Ellen, Pam Scholder, Deborah J. Webb, and Lois A. Mohr (2006), "Building Corporate Associations: Consumer Attributions for Corporate Socially Responsible Programs," *Journal of Academy of Marketing Science,* 34 (2), 147-157.

Ellen, Pam Scholder, Lois A. Mohr, and Deborah J. Webb (2000), "Charitable programs and the retailer: Do they mix?" *Journal of Retailing*, 76 (3), 393-406.

Nan, Xiaoli and Kwangjun Heo (2007), "Consumer Responses to Corporate Social Responsibility (CSR) Initiatives," *Journal of Advertising*, 36 (2), 63-74.

Porter, Michael E. and Mark R. Kramer (2006), Strategy & Society: The Link between Competitive Advantage and Corporate Social Responsibility, *Harvard Business Review*, 84 (12), 78-92.

Pracejus, John W. and G. Douglas Olsen (2004), "The Role of Brand/Cause Fit in the Effectiveness of Cause-Related Marketing Campaigns," *Journal of Business Research*, 57 (6), 635-640.

Quarantelli E.L. (1993), "Community Crises: An Exploratory Comparison of the Characteristics and Consequences of Disasters and Riots," *Journal of Contingencies and Crisis Management*, 1 (2), 67-78.

U.S. Chamber of Commerce (2010), Corporate Donations in Response to Earthquake in Haiti, http://www.uschamber.com.

# Impact of Primary-Secondary Control on Donation Behavior

Yoshiko DeMotta, Baruch College, USA

Lauren G. Block, Baruch College, USA

Stephen Gould, Baruch College, USA

Control, one of fundamental human motives (Baumeister 2005; Fiske 2002), is so valued that individuals rarely abandon their quest for it, even in uncontrollable circumstances (Rothbaum, Weisz, and Snyder 1982). Donation requests often imply external, uncontrollable factors that cause beneficiary's needs (e.g., poverty, disease). In such seemingly uncontrollable circumstances, a quest for control may serve as a motive to help, but effects of control are unexamined in existing frameworks in the donation literature. Drawing on primary-secondary control theory (Rothbaum et al. 1982), we develop and test a new theory of persuasion that induces people to help social causes.

Primary-secondary control theory posits two paths to a feeling of control (primary vs. secondary control) (Rothbaum et al. 1982); primary control occurs when individuals attempt to alter the environment (e.g., circumstances, symptoms, other people) so that the environment fits the self's needs, whereas secondary control occurs when individuals attempt to align themselves with the environment by accepting the environment and adjusting the self (e.g., expectations, perceptions, attitudes). Although seemingly passive, secondary control differs from helplessness; in this process, an individual believes that the situation, or a part of it, can be improved through acceptance (Thompson, Nanni, and Levine 1994). An individual tends to emphasize one type of control, either primary or secondary, as a central role in everyday life, but often shifts from one type of striving for control to another (Rothbaum et al. 1982). We conceptualize donation behaviors as both primary control and secondary control. It is an act of primary control when a person donates in order to change the environment to his desired wishes. It is an act of secondary control when a person donates in order to adjust himself to the environment.

In a persuasion context, we suggest that compliance to a donation request is a behavior that falls into the category of secondary control because implicit within any prosocial act is the individual's acknowledgement of an unchangeable environment, resulting in the adjustment of the individual's behavior to fit within that environment. For example, when a donation request for cancer research is presented, an individual who uses secondary control may accept that cancer affects people's life (i.e., an unchangeable environment) and may adjust his action to this environment by donating—even though this individual may perceive that his single action is insignificant to the magnitude of the environment as a whole. On the other hand, an individual who relies on primary control is unlikely to comply with this request because the request itself may not provoke the self's needs.

Within the secondary control process, we further propose that the effectiveness of donation requests may be enhanced through the use of positive frames. Past research found that when individuals are highly motivated to process information, they tend to perceive that negatively framed information is more persuasive (Block and Keller 1995; Maheswaran and Meyers-Levy 1990). From a perspective of secondary control, however, even in a high motivation setting, positively framed messages may be more effective because positive frames are more likely to appeal to people's goal of accepting the positive environment that is described in a request and adjusting the self to that environment. Negative frames are not directly tied with desired outcomes and thus will not motivate people to exert compliance to a request.

H1: Individuals with high primary control are less likely to donate than those with low primary control.

H2: Individuals with high secondary control are more likely to donate than those with low secondary control when positively framed messages are presented. This effect will diminish when negatively framed messages are presented.

One experimental study examined our hypotheses. One hundred and sixty three undergraduate students participated in this study. Participants were presented with a one page donation request ostensibly written by a non-profit organization (animal shelter) and are asked to answer series of questions. The participants are randomly assigned to two conditions, which manipulated the type of message framing. In the positive (negative) frame condition, the message read: "With (Without) your help, the life of homeless animals will improve (deteriorate)." After presented with the description, participants are asked to choose one of donation options. After making a donation choice, degrees of primary-secondary control were measured using a scale developed by Heeps (2000).

Binary logistic regression was used to examine the impact of framing and primary-secondary control on donation behavior. IVs are framing (positive vs. negative), primary control, secondary control. DV is donation choice (1 if donated and 0 if did not donate). Consistent with H1, there was a main effect of primary control on donation; as primary control increased, the probability of donation decreased ($p=.010$). There was also a main effect of secondary control; as secondary control increased, the probability of donation increased ($p=.005$). Supporting H2, the interaction between message framing and secondary control was significant ($p=.003$). In a positive frame condition, participants high (vs. low) in secondary control were likely to donate more frequently. In a negative frame condition, degrees of secondary control did not make a difference on donation likelihood. There was no interaction effect between framing and primary control.

In conclusion, these results demonstrate that the effectiveness of donation requests can be enhanced through the use of a specific type of message framing moderated by control strategies. Our next study will further investigate the underlying psychological processes of the effects found in study 1.

## References

Baumeister, Roy F. (2005), *The cultural animal: Human nature, meaning, and social life,* Oxford, England: Oxford University Press.

Block, Lauren G. and Punam Anand Keller (1995), "When to accentuate the negative: The effects of perceived efficacy and message framing on intentions to perform a health-related behavior," *Journal of Marketing Research*, 32 (2), 192-203.

Fiske, Susan T. (2002), Five core social motives, plus or minus five. In S. J. Spencer, S. Fein, M. P. Zanna, & J. Olson (Eds.), *Motivated social perception: The Ontario Symposium* (Vol. 9, pp. 233–46), Mahwah, NJ: Erlbaum.

Heeps, Luke J. (2000), "The Role of Primary/Secondary Control in Positive Psychological Adjustment," unpublished dissertation, Deakin University.

Maheswaran, Durairaj and Joan Meyers-Levy (1990), "The influence of message framing and issue involvement," *Journal of Marketing Research*, 27 (3), 361-67.

Rothbaum, Fred M., John R. Weisz, and Samuel S. Snyder (1982), "Changing the world and changing the self: A two-process model of perceived control," Journal of Personality and Social Psychology, *42*, 5-37.

Thompson, Suzanne C., Christopher Nanni, and Alexandra Levine (1994), "Primary versus secondary and central versus consequence-related control in HIV-positive men," Journal of Personality and Social Psychology, *67*, 540–47.

# Expanding Time: Altering Consumers' Experience of Time through Temporal Perspective

Melanie Rudd, Sanford University, USA
Jennifer Aaker, Stanford University, USA

The consumer of today lives in a fast paced society. Over the years, technological breakthroughs allowed them to trade in their bicycles for cars and their handwritten letters for emails. Although these advancements enabled consumers to save time by performing tasks more quickly, they also altered consumers' perceptions of time. As a result, consumers often struggle to keep up with the pace of technology and meet the expectations of a society that highly values time efficiency. Indeed, the percentage of adult Americans who feel "always rushed" increased from 22 percent in 1971 to 35 percent in 1992 (Robinson and Godbey 1997).

This tendency for consumers to live rushed lives often leads to negative consequences. For instance, feeling pressed for time can result in high stress levels. If poorly managed, stress leads to a wide range of health issues, such as fatigue, heart disease, and obesity (American Psychological Association 2007). Feeling rushed also encourages dangerous behaviors, such as multitasking at inappropriate times (e.g., while driving; Nationwide Mutual Insurance Company 2007).

Our research addresses the question of how consumers can avoid some of the consequences of living fast-paced lives. Specifically, how can consumers feel less rushed and hurried? We propose if the perceived passage of time is slowed down, consumers' feelings of being rushed and hurried will be reduced. This research focuses on how one specific factor, attention to a particular temporal domain (the present vs. the future), is capable of altering the subjective passage of time, and thus able to reduce these negative feelings.

To date, the subjective experience of time has been predominantly assessed by retrospective duration estimates (Danckert and Allman 2005). Though duration judgments are important for assessing time estimate accuracy, this research focuses on a relatively overlooked measure, the perceived passage of time (the subjective impression of how slowly or quickly time is passing), as it is better equipped to measure how time is experienced "in the moment." Additionally, prior research has yet to investigate the influence temporal perspective (Liberman and Trope 1998) has on the subjective passage of time. This research concentrates on temporal domain attention (Mogilner, Kamvar, and Aaker 2010), one specific aspect of temporal perspective, because this factor can be manipulated, and illuminate conditions under which the perceived passage of time can be deliberately altered. This is important, as most extant research focuses on how the experience of time is influenced by relatively unalterable factors, such as age (McCormack et al. 1999), gender (Block, Hancock, and Zakay 2000), and culture (Hill, Block, and Buggie 2000).

We hypothesize focusing on the present (vs. the future) slows down the subjective passage of time. Support for this idea comes from research on self-regulation and time perception. Specifically, prior research found the perception of time lengthens during self-regulation. This occurs because self-regulation increases awareness of current behaviors and emotions, which is thought to better attune one to the passage of time (Vohs and Schmeichel 2003). We propose focusing on the present results in an attention to the time that is lacking when focusing on the future. When thinking about the present (vs. the future), current emotions and behaviors should increase in salience. This heightened awareness of the "present self" could promote greater attention to time passage, just as it does during self-regulation. And, as attention to time elongates one's perception of time (Block and Zakay 1997), this could decrease the perceived passage of time. We also hypothesize slowing the perceived passage of time in turn reduces feelings of being hurried and rushed, because when time is perceived to be passing at a slower rate, individuals may feel they have more time to complete or experience the task at hand.

Study 1 was a qualitative exploration of the predicted relationship between temporal domain attention and feelings of being rushed. All participants (28 students) responded to two open-ended questions that asked them to describe how they feel when they think about the present and how they feel when they think about the future. The feelings participants provided as answers to these questions were analyzed by two independent judges who were blind to the hypotheses. Each distinct feeling was classified as either (a) highly related to being rushed, (b) highly related to being unrushed, or (c) neither. Repeated measures t-tests revealed the mean number of rushed-related thoughts reported per subject was greater and the mean number of unrushed-related thoughts reported per subject was fewer when participants described how they feel when they think about the future as opposed to the present.

Study 2 directly manipulated temporal domain attention and measured the resulting effect on the subjective experience of time and feelings of being rushed and hurried. Participants were told we were interested in how people communicate information about themselves on social networking sites. Participants first responded to questions "sometimes used by social networking sites to elicit status updates from their members." To manipulate temporal domain attention, participants in the present [future] condition were asked to use up to 140 characters to answer the following: "What are you doing right now? [What are you going to do later?]," and "Where are you right now? [Where are you going to go later?]" Participants then reported how slowly or quickly time was currently passing, and how rushed and how hurried they were feeling. One-way ANOVAs showed those in the future (vs. the present) condition felt time was currently passing by more quickly, and felt more rushed and hurried. Importantly, mediation analyses confirmed the perceived passage of time mediated the relationship between temporal domain attention and feeling hurried or rushed.

In conclusion, this research both indentifies a novel way in which the perceived passage of time can be altered and assists consumers who wish to reduce the feelings of being rushed that are often brought about by a fast-paced lifestyle. Future studies will be aimed at better understanding the precise mechanisms through which temporal domain attention exerts its influence on the subjective experience of time.

## Selected References

American Psychological Association (2007, October), "Stress in America," Retrieved December 7, 2009, from http://www.apa.org/pubs/info/reports/2007-stress.doc.

Block, Richard A., Peter A. Hancock, and Dan Zakay (2000), "Sex differences in duration judgments: A meta-analytic review," *Memory and Cognition,* 28 (8), 1333–1346.

Block, Richard A. and Dan Zakay (1997), "Prospective and retrospective duration judgments: A meta-analytic review," *Psychonomic Bulletin & Review,* 4 (2), 184–197.

Danckert, James A. and Ava-Ann A. Allman (2005), "Time flies when you`re having fun: temporal estimation and the experience of boredom," *Brain and Cognition*, 59 (3), 236- 245.

Hill, Oliver W., Richard A. Block, Stephen E. Buggie (2000), "Culture and beliefs about time: Comparisons among Black Americans, Black African and White Americans," *Journal of Psychology,* 134 (4), 443-461.

Liberman, Nira and Yaacov Trope (1998), "The role of feasibility and desirability considerations in near and distant future decisions: A test of temporal construal theory," *Journal of Personality and Social Psychology*, 75(1), 5-18.

McCormack, Teresa, Gordon D. A. Brown, Elizabeth A. Maylor, Richard J. Darby, and Dina Green (1999), "Developmental changes in time estimation: Comparing childhood and old age," *Developmental Psychology*, 35 (4), 1143–1155.

Mogilner, Cassie, Sep Kamvar and Jennifer Aaker (2010), "The Shifting Meaning of Happiness," working paper.

Nationwide Mutual Insurance Company (2007), "Driving While Distracted Public Relations Research," Retrieved December 7, 2009 from http://www.nationwide.com/pdf/dwd- 2007-survey-results.pdf

Robinson, John P. and Geoffrey Godbey (1997), *Time for Life: The Surprising Ways Americans Use Their Time*, University Park: Pennsylvania State University Press.

Vohs, Kathleen D., and Brandon J. Schmeichel (2003), "Self-regulation and the extended now: Controlling the self alters the subjective experience of time," *Journal of Personality and Social Psychology,* 85 (2), 217–230.

# I'd Rather Wait 30 Days Than One Month: The Unit Effect in Time Perception

Charles Y. Z. Zhang, University of Michigan, USA
Norbert Schwarz, University of Michigan, USA

## Extended Abstract

Suppose you inquire how long it would take for your order to arrive if you placed it today. Would it make a difference if the merchant told you that it takes "one month" vs. "four weeks" vs. "30 days"? Although those terms are often used interchangeably ways, they may convey different information about the speaker's knowledge about the likely arrival of your order. Three experiments show that this is the case: time estimates expressed in more fine-grained units are perceived as more precise and consumers infer a more uncertain waiting period from "one month" than from "30 days".

As the philosopher Paul Grice (1975) noted, conversations follow the tacit assumptions of a cooperative principle. Speakers should provide as much information as the listener needs (maxim of quantity), but not more information than the speaker actually has (maxim of quality). One implication is that estimates should be neither unnecessarily vague, nor more precise than the speaker's knowledge warrants. One familiar way in which speakers hedge their bets is the use of vague quantifiers, such as "some" or "many", which recipients interpret by drawing on contextual information (Pepper 1981). In many cases, the purposeful vagueness of the expression serves to convey the speaker's uncertainty about the quantity (Powell 1985).

Going beyond the use of vague quantifiers as indicators of uncertainty, we propose that different levels of certainty can also be conveyed by the speaker's choice of a coarse (e.g., "one month") rather than fine-grained (e.g., "29 days") unit. Indeed, the maxim of quantity would urge a speaker who is aware that an order will take 29 days to convey this knowledge, which is insufficiently captured by "one month". If recipients are sensitive to this implication of the maxim of quantity, they should have more confidence in estimates that are expressed in fine-grained rather than coarse units, even if the quantity conveyed is largely identical. Three experiments test this rationale, which has important implications for the format in which information should be conveyed to customers.

In *Study 1*, 90 business undergraduate students were told that a construction team just started a project that would take "1 year" vs. "12 months" vs. "52 weeks" to complete; however, the project might be finished earlier or later. Participants then received a calendar for the next year and circled the *earliest* and *latest* date on which they thought the project might be finished.

The difference these two dates serves as the measure of participants' perception of how precisely the construction team's estimate captures the actual completion time. As expected, the difference between the estimated earliest and latest completion date was 140 days in the "one year", 105 days in the "12 months", and 84 days in the "52 weeks" condition, indicating a significant unit effect ($\beta$=0.33, $p$=.001).

*Study 2* replicated this finding in a different context. University of Michigan students (N=267) were approached on campus and asked to imagine that their cars needed repair. The dealership estimated that it would take 1 month vs. 30 or 31 days to receive the relevant parts and repair the car. Participants were asked for their best and worst case estimates–that is, the minimum and maximum number of days they might have to wait. As expected, the difference between their best and worst case estimates was larger in the one month (M=24.8 days) than in the "30" (M=20.6 days) and "31 days" (M=20.3 days) conditions; $t$(266)=1.97, $p$<.05, for the contrast between 1-month vs. 30/31-days conditions.

In *Study 3*, 188 participants from an online sample were asked to imagine that they needed to buy a camera for an upcoming vacation trip. They were presented with two options, a currently available model and an upgraded new model, said to become available in "3 months" vs. "13 weeks", which is about 10 days before the start date of their vacation trip. The new model dominated the available model on all attributes, except current availability. Participants estimated the latest possible date on which the new model may actually be available in the store and indicated their purchase preference on a 7-point scale (1= definitely buy old model; 7=definitely buy new model). Replicating the earlier findings, participants in the one-month condition assumed that it might take up to 47 extra days for the new camera to be in the store; for participants in the 13-weeks condition the same estimate was 41.6 extra days. More important, participants were more willing to wait for the new model when the unit "week" (M=3.6) rather than "month" (M=4.3) was used to describe the wait period, $t$(186)=2.00, $p$<.05). Lastly, this difference in preference was fully mediated by the difference in perceived wait length.

The present studies consistently show that consumers are sensitive to the unit in which firms express time estimates: The finer the unit used, the more precise consumers assume the estimate to be. This has important implications for marketing and public relations communication. On the one hand, coarse unit are likely to make consumers wonder whether the estimate is reliable; on the other hand, fine units are likely to elicit increased anger when delivery is delayed beyond the apparently precise estimate. Ongoing studies address these implications.

### References

Grice, H.P. (1975). Logic and conversation. In Cole, P. and Morgan, J. (eds.) *Syntax and semantics, vol 3*. New York: Academic Press.

Pepper, S.C. (1981). Problems in the quantification of frequency expressions. In D.W. Fiske (Ed.), *Problems with language imprecision* (New Directions for Methodology of Social and Behavioral Science, Vol. 9). San Francisco: Jossey-Bass.

Powell, M.J., (1985). Purposive vagueness: an evaluative dimension of vague quantifying expressions. Journal of Linguistics, 21, pp 31-50.

# "I Like Goods and I Want Them As Soon As Possible":
# The Impact of Materialism on the Time-Money Trade-Off in Consumer Decisions

Christophe Lembregts, Ghent University, Belgium
Mario Pandelaere, Ghent University, Belgium

### Extended Abstract

Time is an important factor influencing consumer's decisions. For instance, during an online purchase, consumers can often choose between a normal delivery and a faster, but more expensive express delivery. This requires making a time-money trade-off. It has been repeatedly shown that people perceive an amount of money to be received in the future as worth somewhat less compared to the equivalent amount received in the present (Frederick, Loewenstein & O'Donoghue, 2002; Thaler, 1981). Several factors have been shown to be influencing this time-money trade-off. For instance, future outcomes that are equivalent in magnitude, but different in valence (i.e. a gain vs. a loss) are valued differently. People need a larger amount of money to defer gains, but are only willing to pay a small amount to defer losses (Thaler, 1981).

In this study, one of potentially most important psychological determinants of temporal discounting, namely materialism, is examined. Materialism refers to a value system in which material goods and their acquisition are central determinant of a successful and happy life (Richins & Dawson, 1992). In the temporal discounting literature, there are few studies about the psychological factors such as materialism underlying this temporal bias. This paper proposes that materialism is an important determinant of temporal impatience. Given the importance materialists attribute to the possession material goods, it could be that materialists are growing more impatient when confronted with a delay in a consumer good delivery, compared to non-materialists. If the acquisition of goods is central in one's life, one could argue that the sooner one receives a consumer good, the better. Dittmar and Bond (2010, in press) provided some support for this claim when they found that materialists are more impulsive buyers of identity expressive goods compared to non-materialists. These propositions will be tested in two studies.

Study 1 assessed if materialists are more willing to pay a surcharge for an earlier delivery of a commodity. 221 participants were exposed to 18 product offers which consisted of 2 choice options: a sooner but more expensive offer and a later but cheaper option. In particular, participants had to make a choice for all combinations of 3 products, which differed in price. We used 3 prices differences (5%, 10%, 15% surcharge for sooner delivery) and 2 temporal distances (delivery in 2 vs. 3 months or delivery in 11 vs. 12 months). Materialism was measured using the Material Values Scale by Richins and Dawson (2004). Results confirm that participants who value the possession of material goods as central in their lives and as an important source of success were more prepared to pay an amount of money to avoid a delay of one month.

Study 2 had two objectives. First, we wanted to replicate the findings of study 1. Second, instead of including only a delay for material goods, we included two other delays: for experiental purchases and money. It has been shown that money and experiental purchases elicit different discounting. For instance, consumers are more patient for money compared to consumable goods (Estle, Green, Myerson & Holt, 2007; Odum, Baumann & Rimington, 2006; Rosati, Stevens, Hare & Hauser, 2007). Furthermore, experiental purchases tend to make people happier than material purchases (Van Boven & Gilovich, 2003). From this, it can be argued that respondents will be more impatient for experiences. 154 participants were asked to repeatedly choose between 2 different offers. The delay difference (1 month) and surcharges for an early delivery were identical to study 1. Type of outcome (money, experiences, goods) was manipulated between subjects. In the experiental and material goods conditions, participants were repeatedly exposed a buying offer containing two choice options, similar to study 1. Participants in the money condition were told to imagine they possessed two identical goods, and decided to sell one of them. Due to time constraints, they were only able to sell it after two months for a certain selling price; if they waited one month longer (after three months), resulted this in a better selling price. So participants had to make a choice between either receiving a smaller amount of money earlier or receiving a larger amount later. Four amounts were chosen for the money condition. Identical amounts were used in the goods and activities conditions. Overall, results indicated that participants were more impatient when exposed to experiences compared to money and goods. For materialists, an interesting pattern emerged. In the goods condition, participants who indicated that the possession of material goods is central in their life preferred the expensive offer more compared to non-materialists. This replicated in part the findings of study 1. When experiental purchases were stalled, participants who regard the possession of material goods as a necessary condition for a happy life opted *less* for the more expensive offer compared to participants who scored low on the happiness subscale of materialism. In the selling condition, materialists (success subscale) opted more for the sooner offer compared to non-materialists.

Results indicated that materialists and non-materialists differ in trading off time and money. Materialists are more impatient (compared to non-materialists) for consumer goods and money. In the money condition, a substantial number of materialists was prepared to sell a consumer good (which is seen as an important sign of success) earlier even when they received less money for it. This is quite striking given the importance materialists attribute to material goods. A potential explanation for this could be our use of a manipulation where two identical products were involved. Materialists possibly want to buy another good with the received money as soon as possible, even when this results in a lower selling price. Non-materialists spend more money on having pleasant experiences sooner. This could be attributed to a possible preference of materialists for consumer goods, which are central in their lives, and money, which can be used to buy consumer goods, over experiences.

## References

Dittmar, H., &, Bond, R. (2010, in press). "I want it and I want it now". Using a temporal discounting paradigm to examine predictors of consumer impulsivity. *British Journal of Psychology.*

Estle, S.J., Green ,L. ,Myerson, J. , &, Holt, D.D.(2007).Discounting of monetary and directly consumable rewards. *Psychological Science, 18*, 58–63.

Frederick, S., Loewenstein, G., & O'Donoghue, T. (2002). Time Discounting and Time Preference: A Critical Review. *Journal of Economic Literature, 40*(2), 351-401.

Odum,A.L., Baumann, A.A.L., & Rimington, D.D.(2006). Discounting of delayed hypothetical money and food: Effects of amount. *Behavioural Processes, 73*, 278–284.

Richins, M. (2004). The Material Values Scale: Measurement Properties and Development of a Short Form. *Journal of Consumer Research, 31*(1), 209-219.

Richins, M., & Dawson, S. (1992). A Consumer Values Orientation for Materialism and Its Measurement: Scale Development and Validation. *Journal of Consumer Research, 19*(3), 303-316.

Rosati, A.G., Stevens, J.R., Hare, B., &, Hauser, M.D. (2007). The evolutionary origins of human patience: Temporal preferences in chimpanzees, bonobos, and human adults. *Current Biology, 17*(19), 1663-1668.

Thaler, Richard H. (1981). "Some Empirical Evidence on Dynamic Inconsistency," *Economic Letters, 8*, pp. 201–07.

Van Boven, L. & Gilovich, T. (2003). To do or to have? That is the question. *Journal of Personality and Social Psychology, 85*(6), 1193-1202.

# Comparability as the Determinant of Reward Evaluation in Frequency Program

Lei Su, The Chinese University of Hong Kong, China
Leilei Gao, The Chinese University of Hong Kong, China
Jianmin Jia, The Chinese University of Hong Kong, China

## Extended Abstract

Frequency programs have two main components: required effort and earned rewards. A question that naturally arises is how the two interact to affect consumer behavior. We propose the effort consumers need to make to earn rewards can influence perceptions of those rewards in two opposite directions. The comparability of effort and reward determines which direction dominates. Specifically, when effort and reward are comparable, relative processing is employed to evaluate the reward. Effort made decrease the perceived value of a reward by shifting the reference point of the reward's value function. In contrast, when effort and reward are non-comparable, the reward is evaluated holistically by referring to both the effort made and the additional value derived from actually making that effort. Consequently, the value function of the reward is steepened by the effort requirement.

## Research Hypothesis

The expenditure of effort can shift the preference point in the value function of a reward. According to traditional economic theory, consumers always calculate what they get by subtracting costs from gains, which means that the perceived value of the reward is always considered relative to the effort made to obtain it. Kivetz (2003) argues that the effort made can serve as the reference point when gauging the reward's utility by providing a higher level of expectation. Based on prospect theory (Kaheman and Tversky 1979), an increased reference point will lead to a decreased perceived value of the reward. Relative processing of effort and reward is conducted in this situation.

Effort can also add value to a reward, which results in a steeper value function for that reward. Recent behavioral decision theory has suggested that a reward acquired from protracted effort is different from that acquired normally. Prior research has indicated that making effort can enhance the personal connection or attachment with the final result (Morales 2005). According to Moglinear and Aaker (2009), personal connections can boost consumer attitudes about products. Ariely and Simonson (2003) find that products with increased attachment are more attractive. Effort can also be an indicator of the value of a reward when consumers cannot judge it clearly (Hoch and Deighton 1989). Taken together, these findings suggest that the perceived value of a reward increases with the effort required to obtain it.

Product comparability is the degree to which consumers consider products using the same attributes (Johnson 1984). The comparability between effort and reward can thus be defined as the comparability between the product involved in the accumulated consumption (effort) and the free product (reward). While relative processing is pervasive among comparable alternatives, holistic processing dominates for non-comparative alternatives when consumers need to incorporate all related information (Johnson 1984). Taken together with our argument about the two different effects of effort in frequency programs, we hypothesize that the perceived value of reward decreases with an increase in the effort requirement when effort and reward are comparable, and the opposite is the case when effort and reward are non-comparable. According to construal level theory (Liberman, Trope, and Wakslak 2007), high level construal results in holistic information processing, and even the most non-comparable alternatives can be compared according to overall worth or utility using this type of processing. Thus, we further propose that the aforementioned effect is attenuated at a high (vs. low) construal level.

**Method and Results**

In experiment 1, a total of 114 participants were first presented with one of four frequency programs, in which a certain reward was given after accumulated cups of coffee were consumed. The magnitude of effort needed to receive the reward was manipulated by changing the number of the cups of coffee to be consumed. The comparability of effort and reward was manipulated by changing the product category of the reward (another cup of coffee vs. an umbrella). The results were consistent with the predicted direction, and there was a significant interaction effect between the magnitude of effort and comparability ($p<.01$). The results of the thought listing and choice task provided further evidence that relative evaluation was employed when effort and reward were comparable and holistic evaluation was employed when they were not.

In experiment 2, a total of 120 participants were required to make real efforts of different magnitudes (solving easy vs. difficult mathematic questions) to gain a real reward (postcards) after being primed with construal levels (high or low). After completing a construal-level manipulation developed by Freitas, Gollwitzer, and Trope (2004), the participants were then required to solve several mathematic questions with the ostensible purpose of evaluating teaching materials for a middle school. Several online postcards were distributed as a reward, and the participants' evaluations of the postcards were measured at the end of the experiment. The results revealed a significant interaction effect between effort magnitude and construal level ($p<.01$). In addition, participants' evaluation of the reward decreased with the level of effort needed to obtain it at the low level of construal, with the opposite direction prevailing at the high level.

**References**

Ariely, Dan and Itamar Simonson (2003), "Buying, Bidding, Playing, or Competing? Value Assessment and Decision Dynamics in Online Auctions", *Journal of Consumer Psychology*, 13 (1/2), 113-23.

Freitas, Antonio, Peter Gollwitzer, and Yaacov Trope (2004), "The Influence of Abstract and Concrete Mindsets on Anticipating and Guiding Others' Self-regulatory Efforts", *Journal of Experimental Social Psychology*, 40 (6), 739-52.

Hoch, Stephen J. and John Deighton (1989), "Managing What Consumers Learn from Experience," *Journal of Marketing*, 53 (2), 1-20.

Johnson, Michael D. (1984), "Consumer Choice Strategies for Comparing Noncomparable Alternatives," *Journal of Consumer Research*, 11 (December), 741-53.

Kivetz, Ran (2003), "The Effects of Effort and Intrinsic Motivation on Risky Choice", *Marketing Science*, 22 (4), 477-502.

Liberman, Nira, Trope Yaacov, and Cheryl Wakslak (2007), "Construal Level Theory and Consumer Behavior", *Journal of Consumer Psychology*, 17 (2), 113-7.

Mogilner, Cassie and Jennifer Aaker (2009), " 'The Time vs. Money Effect': Shifting Product Attitudes through Personal Connection," *Journal of Consumer Research*, 36 (August), 277-91.

Morales, Andrea C. (2005), "Giving Firms an 'E' for Effort: Consumer Responses to High-Effort Firms," *Journal of Consumer Research*, 31 (March), 806-12.

# Small Change: Subjective Valuation Of Coins And Paper Money

Eric Dolansky, Brock University, Canada

**Extended Abstract**

According to the official website of the U.S. Mint, the U.S. treasury would save $500 million per year if individuals used one-dollar coins rather than bills. As a result, on several occasions in the past, the U.S. mint has issued dollar coins, most recently in 2007. None have proven to be very popular (Unser, 2009). So what is preventing Americans from adopting dollar coins?

Individuals tend to exhibit biases when valuing money, despite the explicit denomination of the coin or bill. Mishra, Mishra and Nayakankuppam (2006) found that individuals valued large-denomination bills more highly than an equivalent amount of money presented in smaller bills. Work by Alter and Oppenheimer (2008) indicates that familiarity of the money has an impact on how highly it is valued. A more recent finding ties denomination of money to self-control in spending (Raghubir and Srivistava 2009).

This research aims to extend previous findings by determining if individuals have a bias towards higher valuation of bills as opposed to coins. This topic has been mentioned in the relevant literature (Alter and Oppenheimer 2008; Mishra et al 2006; Raghubir 2006) as worthy of further exploration, however the idea has not been empirically tested. Raghubir and Srivistava (2009) incorporated coins vs. bills as a condition in one of their studies, but it was inconclusive.

In nearly every currency in the world bills are of a higher denomination than coins. This difference in objective valuation could have an impact on subjective valuation, as a representativeness bias (Kahneman and Tversky 1973). As such, coins would tend to be valued less than bills, even when the denominations are the same. It has also been found that people will take an instance and average it to its own category. Thus a coin would be valued to the average value in its category, which would be lower than the average for the bills category (Huttenlocher, Hedges and Bradburn 1990). This leads to the key hypothesis of this paper:

H₁: An amount of money presented in paper form (i.e. bill) will be valued higher than an equivalent amount of money presented in coin form.

To test this prediction, study 1 was conducted. Participants (*n*=52) were given either one Trinidad and Tobago dollar bill or one Trinidad and Tobago dollar coin and were asked how much of each of nine inexpensive items (e.g. pencils, paper clips) they could buy with that money. Participants were also asked to estimate how many Canadian dollars they could purchase with the money.

Unfamiliar currency was used to eliminate the possibility that familiarity with the money was a cause for any differences found, as in previous research (Alter and Oppenheimer 2008). Participants were told that the exchange rate was approximately 1:1 (the real exchange rate is $5 TT to $1 CDN and would result in too little purchasing power for useful estimates) and were instructed that the purchase amounts they estimated should reflect costs in Canada. Participants were also asked how familiar they were with the currency prior to the experiment. Four participants were removed from the analysis because they were previously familiar with the currency.

While some of the results are mixed, overall H$_1$ is supported. When all of the estimates are standardized, there is a marginally significant difference between the objects purchasable with bills (1.34 standard deviations above the mean) than with coins (1.39 standard deviations below the mean, *p*=0.096). Some individual items exhibited significant or marginally significant effects as well, such as paper clips (*p*=0.046), napkins (*p*=0.05), and thumbtacks (*p*=0.073). The lack of strong results in the individual item estimates is likely due to the high variance in the estimates from one participant to another.

The exchange valuation prediction is more conclusive: participants given coins estimated they could exchange their $1 TT for $0.798 CDN and those given bills estimated $1.192 (*p*=0.02), despite being told that both the coins and bills were worth approximately $1 CDN.

Study 2 is planned to refine and extend this effect. It is believed that the effects found here would be moderated by the relative value of coins or bills in an individual's home country. For example, in Canada, coins are used up to the two-dollar denomination and bills are used for denominations of five dollars and larger. This is in contrast to the U.S., where denominations of one dollar or larger are represented by bills, and denominations less than one dollar use coins. A study that includes both Canadians and Americans could find such a difference. Study 2 will be conducted at Niagara Falls, Ontario, and will use nationality as a found condition.

Study 3 is an investigation into the physical properties of coins and bills themselves. At the most basic level, coins are metal tokens and bills paper certificates. Would individuals value non-money tokens and certificates the same way? It is expected that they would not; in fact, the opposite valuation is predicted. This is because of the relative weight and permanence of a metal token as opposed to a paper certificate. Furthermore, even real money, when abstracted from its role as money, may have reduced subjective value. As in study 1, it is expected that money coins will be valued less than money bills (demonstrated as the difference between the number of ounces participants drink). The opposite effect is expected for the non-monetary rewards: it is believed that participants receiving non-monetary tokens will drink more than those receiving non-monetary paper certificates.

This work provides insight into how individuals value money and implications for research, management, and policy. Policy implications are the most salient here, as it is possible that a shift from bills to coins for a particular denomination (e.g., one dollar in the U.S.) could have an impact on valuation of money overall, as individuals ascribe less purchasing power to the coin than to the bill.

### References

Alter, Adam L. and Daniel M. Oppenheimer (2008), "Easy on the Mind, Easy on the Wallet: The Roles of Familiarity and Processing Fluency in Valuation Judgments," *Psychonomic Bulletin and Review*, 15 (5), 985-990.

Huttenlocher, Janellen, Larry V. Hedges and Norman M. Bradburn (1990), "Reports of Elapsed Time: Bounding and Rounding Processes in Estimation," *Journal of Experimental Psychology: Learning, Memory and Cognition*, 16 (March), 196-213.

Kahneman, Daniel, and Amos Tversky (1973), "On the psychology of prediction," *Psychological Review*, 80, 237-251.

Mishra, Himanshu, Arul Mishra and Dhananjay Nayakankuppam (2006), "Money: A Bias for the Whole," *Journal of Consumer Research*, 32 (March), 541-549.

Raghubir, Priya (2006), "An Information Processing Review of the Subjective Value of Money and Prices," *Journal of Business Research*, 59, 1053-1062.

Raghubir, Priya and Joydeep Srivistava (2009), "The Denomination Effect," *Journal of Consumer Research*, 36 (December), 701-713.

Unser, Darrin Lee (2009), "US Dollar Coins Glut, Supply Far Exceeds Demand," http://www.coinnews.net.

# Can Money and Religion Substitute for Each Other?

Ezgi Akpinar, Erasmus University Rotterdam, The Netherlands
Kathleen Vohs, University of Minnesota, USA

Money and religion both act as coping aids that people can call upon to make themselves feel strong. A growing stream of research on money has shown that activating the concept of money evokes a state of self-efficacy that implies that each person can and will take care of him/herself (Vohs, Mead, and Goode 2006; Zhou, Vohs, and Baumeister 2009). In parallel, religion too is associated with a feeling of strength or efficacy. When people face threatening, stressful events, religious coping can offset some of the negative consequences of such events (Pargament, Koenig, and Perez 2000). In this research, we investigated to what extent these two sources of strength can substitute each other. Specifically, we tested whether being reminded of money would lessen a need for religious coping, and whether reminders of religion would produce a weakened desire for money.

There is a growing research on the psychological effects of money. Money is a distinct entity, which implies that it is attached to a meaning apart from its incentive and functional abilities (Lea and Webley 2006). Empirically, participants reminded of money evince higher personal goal pursuit and reduced dependency on others compared to participants not reminded of money (Vohs et al. 2008). Additionally, money stimulates a general sense of confidence and strength, which therefore helps people to cope with difficulties such as physical pain or social exclusion. Money provides a feeling of confidence that problems can be solved and needs can be met (Zhou et al. 2009).

Like money, religion is another source of support within the social system. When people are confronted with threatening events, religion offers a sense of mastery and control. Religion can provide internal and external sources for coping stressful life events such as terrorism or the death of an infant child (Kay, Gaucher, McGregor, and Nash 2010; McIntosh, Silver, and Wortman 1993).

The commonality between the psychological effects of money and religion suggests that money and religion might be interchangeable, in their ability to help people cope with negative life events. Because money stimulates self-sufficient state, being reminded of it was predicted to reduce participants' need to cope via religious resources. Because religion also seems to draw out a sense of efficacy, we predicted that mentally activating it would lessen a desire for money.

In Study 1, we manipulated the salience of money by having some of the participants count coins and Euro bills and then list their monetary expenditures for the past 30 days. Participants in the neutral condition counted glass beads and listed the weather conditions over the past 30 days. Then, all participants remembered a negative event that had occurred in their life and wrote down the event and their reactions towards it. Thinking on the negative event they had described, participants completed RCOPE scale (Pargament et al. 2000). RCOPE is a scale developed to assess the degree to which various types of religious coping are involved in dealing with negative events. In line with the substitution hypothesis, there was a main effect of money priming on religious coping. Participants who were reminded of money reported being less likely to rely on religious coping compared to participants under neutral conditions.

In Study 2, half of the participants were primed with religious concepts using the scrambled-sentence paradigm (Shariff and Norenzayan 2007). The other half completed the scramble task using neutral words. Next, participants were given a list of eleven pleasant things (watching TV, sunshine, spring, chocolate, beach, mobile phone, sport, dancing, Internet, snow, holiday) and asked how willing they would be to forgo those items permanently in exchange for 1 million Euros (Zhou et al. 2009). As predicted, there was a significant effect of religious priming on desire for money. Participants primed with religious concepts were less willing to exchange pleasant things for money. This finding suggests too that money and religion can compensation for each other.

Study 3 sought to replicate the effects and to test whether self efficacy mediated the effect of religion on desire for money. Religion-primed participants completed a word-search puzzle that consisted of religious words (Pichon, Boccato, and Saroglou 2007). In control condition, participants completed a word-search puzzle with neutral words. Next, perceived self-efficacy was measured by the General Self-Efficacy Scale (Schwarzer and Jerusalem 1995). Last, desire for money was measured again using the likelihood of exchanging pleasant items in life for 1 million Euros (see study 2). Our results confirmed that religious priming reduces the desire for money, and that this was partially mediated by self efficacy.

This research takes a broad look at the interconnectedness of money and religion, two powerful forces in human life. Although there is growing literature on the consequences of reminding people of money, an understanding of religion vis-à-vis other key constructs such as money remains poor. The present studies demonstrate that money and religion can compensate for one another, such that being reminded of money lessens a desire to have the other. What links these two disparate constructs is that they both stimulate a feeling of efficacy, which is elicited by small, subtle reminders. In addition to theoretical value, our results imply exercising caution when using religion to promote products for marketers.

## References

Lea, Stephen E. G., and Paul Webley (2006), "Money as tool, money as drug: The biological psychology of a strong incentive," *Behavioral and Brain Sciences,* 29 (02), 161-209.

Kay, Aaron C., Danielle Gaucher, Ian McGregor, and Kyle Nash (2010), "Religious belief as compensatory control," *Personality and Social Psychology Review,* 14 (1), 37-48.

McIntosh, Daniel N., Roxane C. Silver, and Camille B. Wortman (1993), "Religion's role in adjustment to a negative life event: Coping with the loss of a child," *Journal of Personality,* 65 (4), 812-21.

Pargament, Kenneth I., Harold G. Koenig, and Lisa M. Perez (2000), "The many methods of religious coping: Development and initial validation of the RCOPE," *Journal of Clinical Psychology,* 56 (4), 519-43.

Pichon, Isabelle, Giulio Boccato, and Vassilis Saroglou (2007), "Nonconscious influences of religion on prosociality: A priming study," *European Journal of Social Psychology,* 37 (5), 1032-45.

Schwarzer, Ralf, and Jerusalem, Matthias (1995). *Generalized Self-Efficacy scale. In Measures in health psychology: A user's portfolio. Causal and control beliefs,* ed. J. Weinman, S. Wright, and M. Johnston,Windsor, UK: NFER-NELSON, 35-37.

Shariff, Azim F., and Ara Norenzayan (2007), "God is watching you: Priming god concepts increases prosocial behavior in an anonymous economic game," *Psychological Science,* 18 (9), 803-9.

Vohs, Kathleen D., Nicole L. Mead, and Miranda R. Goode (2006), "The psychological consequences of money," *Science,* 314, 1154-6.

_____ (2008), "Merely activating the concept of money changes personal and interpersonal behavior," *Current Directions in Psychological Science,* 17 (3), 208-12.

Zhou, Xinyue, Kathleen D. Vohs, and Roy F. Baumeister (2009), "The symbolic power of money: Reminders of money alter social distress and physical pain," *Psychological Science,* 20 (6), 700-6

# The Effect of Evaluation Mode on Nine-Ending Price Perception:
## Separate, Joint, and Sequential Evaluation

Shih-Chieh Chuang, National Chung Cheng University, Taiwan
Yih-Hui Cheng, National TaiChung University, Taiwan
Chih-Cheng Huang, National Formosa University, Taiwan
Hsiu-Chu Li, National Chung Cheng University, Taiwan

## Extended Abstract

The evaluation of nine-ending prices usually is used in the actual purchasing behavior. Those digits are converted into an analog quantity for each price, which is allocated a magnitude based on an internal analog magnitude scale. It is this conversion from numerical symbol to magnitude that affects number encoding precision (Dehaene 1997). The evidence of the effectiveness of nine-ending pricing from prior studies has significant experimental value; however, the models used are inconsistent with real-life consumer evaluation settings. Nine-ending and zero-ending prices are mostly evaluated separately in experimental designs, whereas they are generally evaluated side by side by consumers during actual in-store purchasing. This difference in the form of evaluation creates a gap between theoretical results and reality. Hence, the development of new evaluation models that examine the nine-ending pricing effect from a practical purchasing perspective is important.

This research offers further evidence of the effect of nine-ending pricing on the magnitude perception of price. The conceptual framework of the present study is developed based on the left-digit effect (Bizer and Schindler 2005), drop-off mechanism (Thomas and Morwitz 2005), and separate and joint evaluation conditions (Hsee 1996) to examine the varying effect of nine-ending pricing on consumer magnitude perception under different conditions. Bizer and Schindler (2005) developed a new experimental approach to demonstrate numerical drop-off and avoid two major causes of failures in research into the nine-ending pricing effect: high variation among open-ended responses in free-recall tasks (e.g., short-term price recall in the study of Schindler and Kibarian 1993) and unrealistic conditions (e.g., respondents were given several minutes to examine an advertisement showing only one price in the study of Schindler and Kibarian 1993). Another commonly proposed explanation of the nine-ending pricing effect is the left-digit effect (Thomas and Morwitz 2005), which suggests that it is the change in the leftmost digit, rather than the ending digit(s) to its right, that influences the magnitude perception of numerical symbols. This research adopts the left-digit effect as the fundamental explanation of the nine-ending pricing effect, with the drop-off mechanism supporting certain aspects of the study. Based on Hsee's (1996) evaluability hypothesis, separate and joint evaluations are utilized herein for further analysis of this effect. In addition, extending Hsee's (1996) evaluability hypothesis of the separate evaluation (SE) and joint evaluation (JE) conditions, this study is interested in investigating a third condition together with the existing two. Thus, a new evaluation condition is proposed, termed the "sequential evaluation" ("SQE") condition, which serves as a bridge between the two abovementioned evaluation conditions. It is constructed as the midpoint between the SE and JE conditions with the stimulus options evaluated back-to-back in a sequence.

Although various experimental conditions have been constructed to investigate the nine-ending pricing effect, they often do not correspond to real purchasing settings. In the latter, consumers do not evaluate nine-ending and zero-ending prices separately; rather, they evaluate both simultaneously. Therefore, to determine whether nine-ending pricing influences actual purchasing decisions when nine-ending and zero-ending prices are presented side by side (e.g., product prices printed on DM and in-store shelves), this study investigates different evaluation conditions.

## Study 1

The aim of Study 1 was to examine whether the difference in magnitude perception between nine-ending and zero-ending prices is greater in the separate evaluation (SE) condition, in which the nine-ending pricing effect manifests, than in the joint evaluation (JE) condition, in which the nine-ending pricing effect diminishes. This study utilized a one-factor three-level (separate nine ending, separate zero ending, and joint nine ending and zero ending) design. The stimuli for this study were nail clippers, batteries, and baseball caps. A total of 146 undergraduate students were recruited from a large southern university. The participants were randomly divided into three subgroups, each of which was randomly assigned to one of three conditions.

The results support our hypotheses, which postulated that the nine-ending pricing effect increased the difference in perceived magnitude of price between nine-ending and zero-ending prices in the SE but not the JE condition.

## Study 2

Study 2 was conducted to further examine the difference in the nine-ending pricing effect in the separate and joint evaluation conditions. Its aim was to examine whether the difference in quantitative estimations between nine-ending and zero-ending prices is greater in the separate evaluation (SE) than in the joint evaluation (JE) condition. This study utilized a one-factor three-level (separate nine ending, separate zero ending, and joint nine ending and zero ending) design. A total of 130 undergraduate students were recruited from a large southern university. The participants were randomly divided into three subgroups, each of which was randomly assigned to one of three conditions.

The results support the hypotheses, which postulated that the nine-ending pricing effect increased the difference in perceived quantitative estimations between nine-ending and zero-ending prices in the SE condition, but less so in the JE condition.

## Study 3

Study 3 was conducted to further examine the differences in the nine-ending pricing effect among the separate, sequential, and joint evaluation conditions. Its aim was to examine whether the difference in quantitative estimation between nine-ending and zero-ending prices is greatest in the separate evaluation (SE) condition, followed by the sequential evaluation (SQE) and the joint evaluation (JE) condition. This study utilized a one-factor, four-level (separate nine ending, separate zero ending, joint nine ending and zero ending, and sequential nine ending and zero ending) design. A total of 158 undergraduate students, seventy-eight males and eighty females, were recruited from a large southern university. The participants were randomly divided into four subgroups, each of which was randomly assigned to one of four conditions.

The results also support the hypotheses. These findings demonstrate that the nine-ending pricing effect manifests in the SQE condition more strongly than in the JE condition but less strongly than in the SE condition.

## General Discussion

The results of the present research offer practical implications for predicting actual purchasing behavior, as people constantly encounter buying circumstances involving either separate or joint evaluations in daily life (Hsee 1996). The diversity in evaluation conditions provides an advantage in marketing campaigns depending on the managerial approach. Alternatively, a zero-ending priced item could be advertised jointly with the comparable nine-ending priced items of competitors if a retailer wishes to generate the perception of equivalent prices.

## Reference

Bizer, George Y. and Robert M. Schindler (2005), "Direct Evidence of Ending-digit Drop-off in Price Information Processing," *Psychology & Marketing, 22*, 771-783.

Dehaene, Stanislas (1997), *The Number Sense*. New York: Oxford.

Hsee, Christopher K. (1996), "The Evaluability Hypothesis: An Explanation for Preference Reversals Between Joint and Separate Evaluations of Alternatives," *Organizational Behavior and human Decision Processes, 67*, 247-257.

Schindler, Robert M. and Thomas Kibarian (1993), "Testing for Perceptual Underestimation of 9-ending Prices," *Advances in Consumer Research*, 20, 580-585.

Thomas Manoj and Vicki Morwitz (2005), "Penny Wise and Pound Foolish: The Left-digit Effect in Price Cognition," *Journal of Consumer Research, 32*, 54-64.

# Maneuvering or Cheating? Perspective-taking and Numerical Anchoring in Price Negotiation

Guang-Xin Xie, University of Massachusetts–Boston, USA

Hua Chang, Drexel University, USA

## Extended Abstract

Extant research has examined the extent to which externally presented numerical anchors on buyers' perceptions of sellers in price negotiation (e.g. Bolton Warlop, and Alba 2003; Ofir 2004; Rajendran and Tellis 1994). However, the existing literature remains relatively silent on the effect of buyers' self-generated anchors and the related boundary conditions. Based on the recent studies on perspective-taking (e.g. Galinsky, Maddux, Gilin, and White 2008) and numerical anchoring (e.g. Wegener, Petty, Blankenship, and Detweiler-Bedell 2010), we propose that buyers have a "comfort zone" about the degree to which sellers can deviate from the fact (i.e. some tactics are acceptable). Further, buyers' capacity to consider the market norms from a seller's perspective can shape the range of the comfort zone and affect the perceived deceptiveness of the seller (i.e. tactics may be considered cheating anyway).

In general, when sellers provide a false numeric anchor that deviates from the fact, buyers are more likely to think they are deceptive and not acceptable. In this study, we intend to find out whether perspective-taking could change the extrinsic numeric anchor when buyers (e.g. consumers) evaluate the deceptiveness of sellers (e.g. a salesperson working for a car dealer). Perspective-taking is a cognitive capacity to consider the world from other viewpoints and allows an individual to anticipate the behavior and reactions of others (Galinsky and Mussweiler 2001). As Mazar, Amir and Ariely (2008) suggested, even honest people sometimes cheat, as long as the deviation is small enough to maintain a positive self-concept. Therefore, if buyers think from a seller's perspective, they may be more forgiving because they will probably cheat as well in that position. The perspective-taking heuristic, however, may or may not be factored in when buyers bargain with a seller. We speculate that without this mindset, buyers are more likely to focus on the factual aspect of a seller's negotiation tactic and therefore remain defensive. In comparison, buyers can be more tolerant about the fact-claim discrepancies if they will also cheat as a seller given a chance. In three experiments, we tested this hypothesis and the related boundary condition.

In study 1, seventy-one undergraduate students were randomly assigned to two experimental conditions. First, participants in both conditions were told to imagine they work at a car dealership as a salesperson who is selling a car with a markup of 7%. Next, they were asked what they would tell their customer if the customer asked what the markup is. After a filler task, participants were presented the same scenario from the customers' standpoint. They were told that a salesperson said the markup rate is 7.5% in one condition and 15% in another condition, while the true rate is 7%. Then they were asked to rate the salesperson in terms of being deceptive, misleading, trustworthy, and appropriate.

We first distinguished the participants by how much they would like to cheat as a salesperson. The absolute values of deviation from the true rate (7%) were calculated, followed by a median split to categorize participants as high or low deviation from the true markup. We ran a 2 (salesperson's deviation: low 7.5% vs. high 15%) x 2 (participants' deviation from the true markup: high vs. low) ANOVA. As expected, the main effect of the salesperson's deviation was significant: participants across conditions rated the salesperson as more deceptive when he said the true rate was 15% compared to 7.5%, $F (1, 67)=7.60$, $p=.008$. The main effect of participant's willingness to deviate was not significant. Interestingly, the interaction was significant, $F (1, 67)=3.97$, $p=.04$. Those who didn't cheat or cheated just a little as a seller considered the 7.5% rate much less deceptive than the 15% rate. In comparison, those who cheat a lot as a seller considered the salesperson equally non-deceptive despite the deviation. The role of perspective-taking was evident.

One possible explanation for the observed effect is that the perspective-taking task prior to the deviation manipulation adds an anchor about how much deviation is appropriate. Participants used this self-generated anchor rather than the actual anchor 7% to evaluate the salesperson. To test this hypothesis, we flipped the task order in Study 2.

Two-hundred and seventy-four undergraduate students participated in Study 2. They were first presented with the seller evaluation task, comparing the deceptiveness of 7.5% and 15% markup rates. After a filler task, they indicated the markup rate to tell their customer if they assumed the role as a salesperson. The results indicate a significant main effect of seller deviation: 15% rate was considered more deceptive than the 7.5% rate. As expected, the interaction was not significant anymore. Participants who deviated a lot from 7% as a seller considered 15% rate was more deceptive than 7.5% as well. More interestingly, we found that participants were less likely to cheat when the evaluation task was presented first. Much more participants in terms of percentage (53%) were willing to tell the customer the true rate 7% than those in Study 1 (18%), $\chi^2$ (1, 355)=21.57, $p<.001$. Participants in Study 2 appeared to be much more honest because they engaged in the seller evaluation task first. In Study 3, we further pushed the boundary of deviation to test whether the findings hold.

One hundred and forty-five undergraduate students participated in Study 3. The design was the same as Study 2, except that the salesperson told the customer the true rate 7% or a much higher rate 21%. The rate 21% was chosen to exceed the upper bound of participants' self-reported deviation in Study 2, while maintains some level of realism. The results replicated the patterns found in Study 2.

Combined, the results in three studies supported that at least three heuristics could influence the perceived deceptiveness of a seller: 1). how much the deviation from the fact is; 2). how much buyers would like to cheat as sellers, and 3). the extent to which the perspective-taking mindset is activated. This study contributes to the literature by offering one of the first empirical evidence about the effect of self-generated anchor on judgments: the internal anchor is a moving target bounded by the situational salience and market norms.

## References

Bolton, Lisa E., Luk, Warlop, and Joseph W. Alba (2003), "Consumer Perceptions of Price (Un)Fairness," *Journal of Consumer Research*, 29 (4), 474-91.

Galinsky, Adam D., William W. Maddux, Debra Gilin, and Judith B. White (2008), "Why It Pays to Get Inside the Head of Your Opponent: The Differential Effects of Perspective Taking and Empathy in Negotiations," *Psychological Science*, 19(4), 378-84.

Galinsky, Adam D. and Thomas Mussweiler (2001), "First Offers as Anchors: The Role of Perspective-Taking and Negotiator Focus," *Journal of Personality & Social Psychology*, 81(4), 657-69.

Mazar, Nina, On Amir, and Dan Ariely (2008), "The Dishonesty of Honest People: A Theory of Self-Concept Maintenance. *Journal of Marketing Research*, 45(6), 633-44.

Ofir, Chezy (2004), "Reexamining Latitude of Price Acceptability and Price Thresholds: Predicting Basic Consumer Reaction to Price," *Journal of Consumer Research*, 30 (4), 612-21.

Rajendran, K. N. and Gerard J. Tellis (1994), "Contextual and Temporal Components of Reference Price," *Journal of Marketing*, 58(1), 22-34.

Wegener, Duane T., Richard E. Petty, Kevin L. Blankenship, and Brian Detweiler-Bedell (2010), "Elaboration and numerical anchoring: Implications of attitude theories for consumer judgment and decision making," *Journal of Consumer Psychology*," 20(1), 5-16.

# SAS (Un)fairness

Sungchui Choe, University of Northern British Columbia, Canada
Mike Stanyer, University of Northern British Columbia, Canada

**Extended Abstract**

The "Scratch and Save (SAS)" promotion is emerging in North America as a store-level promotional strategy. SAS promotions offer potential discounts on all regular-price items in the store for a very short time period. Unlike the more established Tensile Price Claim (TPC), for which consumers are given the exact discount on a *specific* product, the SAS offers a variable discount on all products: the exact discount is determined from the deal's parameters (e.g. "up to 40% off" or "5%-30% off") by a scratch-off card at the point of purchase. Therefore, the SAS discount is characterized by uncertainty of savings until purchase. The variable outcome introduces a gambling component (note that a similar mechanism is used in "scratch-off" lottery cards) and customers buying the exact same item will inevitably receive different discounts from each other. The variable and unequal outcomes introduced by SAS promotions raise concerns about fairness. Two studies presented here explore how consumers approach (un)fairness in SAS promotions, and how their (un)fairness judgments influence emotion, satisfaction, and post-purchase behavior. In study 1, we employed a one-factor (actual discount), three-level (10%, 15%, and 20%), between-subjects design using a 15% reference discount. Study 2 manipulated levels of reference discount and inequality with a 2 (reference discount level: low (15%) vs. high (25%)) x 2 (inequality: advantageous vs. disadvangeous) x 2 (inequality level: low (±5%) vs. high (±10%))

We propose that consumers consider disadvantageous inequality to be more unfair than advantageous inequality. Furthermore, consumers will consider a deal to be unfair, even though they receive a discount, if the discount is lower than the average discount received by other customers. Therefore, we distinguish between dissatisfaction, as discussed in the "disconfirmation" (e.g., Oliver, 1980; Oliver and Swan, 1989) and "counterfactual-thinking" (e.g., Walchli and Landman, 2003) literature, and unfairness as prompted by a comparison to deals that other customers receive.

SAS promotions provide a maximum ceiling for their discounts (i.e., "up to 30%"), a minimum guaranteed discount (i.e., "10% or more"), or a range with explicit minimum and maximum bounds (i.e., "10% to 30%"). Regardless of the discount parameters, consumers will arguable consider the possibility of receiving the lowest possible discount, as they must commit to the purchase in order to discover the exact discount. The price, after applying the minimum discount, is then assumed to be satisfactory. This judgment is informed by consumers' internal and external reference prices: their expectations of what the price should be. Assuming that prices have not been increased to compensate for discounts, a consumer's reference price may very well be similar to the regular price, or base price (without any discount applied) in the SAS deal. It is intuitive, then, that the price can be satisfactory with little or no discount. But consumers will also have internal and external reference discounts, and it is important to distinguish between reference *discounts* and reference *prices*. For the sake of brevity, this study does not discuss the multitude of influences that can affect a consumer's internal and external reference price. Instead, the reference *discount* is under examination: particularly the external reference discount. While the resulting price from the SAS deal may be satisfactory, consumers may be unsatisfied if they regard the discount as unfair.

The fairness literature makes frequent reference to distributive fairness (the equal balance of inputs and outputs in a transaction) and the dual entitlement principle (stating that sellers are entitled to a fair profit). A deep discount, then, may be considered unfair because consumers are giving too little and receiving too much. Recent fairness studies, however, show that consumers do not perceive fairness objectively: they tend to report fairness in an egotistical manner (e.g., Maxwell, Nye and Maxwell, 1999). A result that is not in their favor is regarded as unfair, while an outcome to their advantage is regarded as "fair," regardless of the seller's outputs. Meanwhile, a consumer's inputs, even in a retail transaction, are not necessarily monetary; consumers may invest trust in the offer. Despite receiving a guaranteed discount, they could feel that the discount (particularly one below the reference discount) is too low, weighed against their expectation of a higher discount (meeting or exceeding the reference discount). For this reason, perhaps, consumers may consider their own outcome as unfair, despite getting a deal and clearly receiving a benefit compared to the seller.

The studies herein establish consumers' subjective, egocentric approach to fairness, and also find that unfairness and fairness perceptions operate according to the Prospect Theory: the loss function is steeper than the gain function (Thaler, 1985; Kahneman & Tversky, 1979), or perceptions of unfairness are more severe than those of fairness. Participants report the negative outcome of low discounts (inequality in the seller's favor) as severely unfair, but report the positive outcome of high discounts (inequality in their own favor) as only minimally fair. Even when the deviation from the average savings is equal (i.e., plus or minus 5%), consumers' evaluation of unfairness is unequal, being more sensitive to their losses than their gains.

These studies also collect participants' affective, satisfaction and post purchase responses to positive and negative outcomes. As expected, the level of perceived unfairness increases the magnitude of emotional responses such as anger, happiness, surprise and perceptions of exploitation and obligation. These responses are measured in addition to satisfaction because SAS discounts offer a unique situation in which discount inequality exists for the same item being purchased by different customers. Resulting affective reactions based on perceptions of unfairness, therefore, may sully an otherwise satisfactory price. Furthermore, the level of perceived unfairness influences post-purchase behavior, particularly the possibility of returning an item and repurchasing it. Dissatisfaction with the outcome of a purchase may encourage consumers to make a gamble by repurchasing an item in hopes of scratching a greater discount.

This paper continues research concerning fairness, affect and satisfaction. It extends research on (un)fairness to the new "Scratch and Save" form of discount, in which (un)fairness is a prominent concern in due to the discount's variable outcomes between customers.

**References**
Kahneman, D., & Tversky, A. (1979). Prospect Theory: an analysis of decision under risk. *Econometrica*, 47, 263-291.
Maxwell, S., Nye, P. & Maxwell, N. (1999). Less pain, same gain: the effects of priming fairness on price negotiations. *Psychology an Marketing*, 16(7), 545-562.
Oliver, R. L. (1980). A cognitive model of the antecedents and consequences of satisfaction decisions. *Journal of Marketing Research*, 17, 460–469.
Oliver, R.L. & Swan., J. (1989). Equity and disconfirmation perceptions as influences on merchant and product satisfaction. *Journal of Consumer Research*, 16(3), 372-383.
Thaler, R. (1985). Mental accounting and consumer choice. *Marketing Science*, 4, 199-214.
Walchi, S.B. & Landman, J. (2003). Effects of counterfactual thought on postpurchase consumer affect. *Psychology and Marketing*, 20(1), 23–46.

# Do "Locally Made" Products Affect Price Perceptions? Not Always
Rajneesh Suri, Drexel University, USA
Mrugank Thakor, Concordia University, Canada
Umit Koc, LeBrow College of Business, Drexel University, USA

Consumers often use an array of extrinsic and intrinsic attributes to infer product quality and to assess intentions to pay. Though an intrinsic attribute normally dominates extrinsic cues when formulating evaluations because it is deemed more useful, such intrinsic information is often scarce, not useful or consumers might have little opportunity to process it (Miyazaki, Grewal and Goodstein 2005). Hence it is not surprising that extrinsic cues are more often used to make product decisions. Though research suggests positive relationships between a positive country-of-origin and perceptions of product quality, the literature reveals little about how and if consumers would use cues like country-of-origin (e.g., made in USA) differently than a region-of-origin cue like "locally made" when evaluating a product. Furthermore, since consumers when making purchases integrate inferences about product quality derived from an extrinsic cue with assessments of monetary sacrifice derived from another extrinsic cue, price, an intriguing question remains as to how consumers will integrate information from two cues, price and region-of-origin, to form product assessments. Though Miyazaki, Grewal and Goodstein (2005) concluded that consumers form stronger price-quality associations in the presence of consistent pairing between the price and other cues to product quality research is elusive as to how a dual cue like price which provides inferences about not only quality but also monetary sacrifice will be integrated with inferences from region-of-origin when determining product quality and also willingness to pay for such products.

Following Krishnan, Biswas and Netemeyer (2006) it is argued that compared to a national origin, a local region-of-origin will be perceived as a more relevant and a concrete extrinsic cue making such cues less ambiguous and more effective in reducing additional search for quality information. We also use insights from cue-consistency theory (Maheswaran and Chaiken 1991) and information integration approaches to suggest that region-of-origin will be integrated with price cues to form perceptions of quality when both are positive. Furthermore since integration of information requires cognitive resources it is predicted that an enhanced impact of region-of-origin cue on product evaluations would be observed when consumers are otherwise motivated to process information. Consequently when motivated to process information, consumers would be willing to pay a higher price for a locally made product while there would be no difference between the region-of-origin and country-of-origin cues on consumers' willingness to pay when motivation to process information is otherwise low.

In two studies we collect initial information on whether a region-of-origin cue affects consumers' willingness to pay for products differently than a country-of-origin cue. Study 1 assessed the proposition directly by measuring consumers' price acceptability limits and price they expected to pay for locally made office furniture. Participants (105 undergraduate students) randomly assigned to a 2(motivation: low vs. high) x 2 (product origin: local vs. national) between subjects design read a scenario manipulating their purchasing goals (or lack thereof) for the target product before indicating their price acceptability limits. Results revealed that motivated participants had significantly higher willingness when the target was associated with region-of-origin information than "made in USA." In low motivation conditions, there was however no difference between these two cues on participant's willingness to pay for the target product.

Study 2 further assessed the evaluation of a relatively high price target. To assess participant's integration of information from multiple extrinsic cues to quality, past consumers' product quality reviews for this product were included. Study design and execution was similar to study 1 but with an additional variable of quality reviews (superior vs. inferior) for the target product. Perceptions of product quality and monetary sacrifice for the target product along with individual difference measures of regional attachment and price sensitivity were collected. Results were interesting and revealed that motivated participants perceived this high price target that was "locally made" to be less expensive than the one with "made in USA" provided that the target accompanied superior product quality reviews. Interestingly in low motivation conditions, participants perceived the target with the national origin and superior product reviews as less expensive than that with regional credentials. The cognitive response further revealed an enhanced depth of processing was associated with the region-of-origin cue in high motivation conditions but with heuristic processing of quality reviews and the country-of- origin cue in low motivation conditions.

Though research suggests that for agricultural commodities state-level appeals enhance consumer willingness to pay (Govindasamy et al. 2000), little marketing research has examined the effects of such "buy local" campaigns on price perceptions for other manufactured non-agrarian products (e.g., Noble et al 2006). The initial evidence from this research suggests interesting effects of locally made products on consumers' price perceptions. While it may be assumed that a cue like region-of-origin is likely to affect product evaluations in a manner similar to the country-of-origin, we argue that the concreteness and relevance of a regional cue will have a more positive effect on consumers' price perceptions for consumers motivated to process information. These results also add to our understanding of how integration of multiple cues will be impacted by consumers' processing goals extending our current understanding of the impact of multiple cues on price perceptions.

### Selected References

Govindasamy, R., Italia J., & Thatch D. (2000). Direct market retailer perceptions of state-sponsored marketing programs. *Review of Agricultural Economics*, 22 (1), 77-88.

Noble, S. M., Griffith D. A., & Adjei M. T. (2006). Drivers of local merchant loyalty: understanding the influence of gender and shopping motives. *Journal of Retailing, 82 (3)*, 177-188.

Krishnan, Balaji C., Abhijit Biswas and Richard G. Netemeyer (2006), "Semantic cues in reference price advertisements: The moderating role of cue concreteness." *Journal of Retailing*, 82, 2, 95-104.

Maheswaran Durairaj and Shelly Chaiken (1991), "Promoting Systematic Processing in Low Motivation settings: Effects of Incongruent Information on Processing and Judgments," *Journal of Personality and Social Psychology*, 61, July, 13-25.

Miyazaki, Anthony D., Dhruv Grewal and Ronald C. Goodstein (2005), "The Effect of Multiple Extrinsic Cues on Quality Perceptions: A Matter of Consistency," *Journal of Consumer Research*, 32, June, 146- 153.

# Effects of Sorting Competitive Prices on Product Evaluations

Rajneesh Suri, Drexel University, USA
Prabakar Kothandaraman, Drexel University, USA
Shan Feng, Drexel University, USA
Umit Koc, LeBow College of Business, Drexel University, USA

Online shopping has not only increased the availability of information to consumers but also resulted in an increased reliance on electronic decision aids that assist shoppers in organizing information. Decision aids that arrange products on utility have been shown to influence overall evaluations of the sorted set of alternatives (Diehl and Zauberman 2005) and also consumers' choice quality (Haubl and Trifts 2000). Though this research used customers' expected utility to create sorted sets of alternatives, several online retailers are likely to provide decision aids that simply arrange alternatives on attributes like price. Furthermore, brick and mortar retailers might not have access to consumers' utility and arrange their merchandise displays simply on basis of an attribute like price. Such marketplace reality of using price instead of consumers' utility suggests a research gap and our understanding of the effects of price sorts. Available results from past research on decision aids that focused on utility may not shed light on the impact of alternatives arranged on price. This is because the relationship between price and consumers utility is not straightforward and depends upon whether consumers use price more in its role to assess monetary sacrifice or product quality (Monroe 2003).

Past research on numerical cognition suggests that infants often grow up learning natural numbers that are arranged in ascending order from one upwards (Ripps, Bloomfield and Asmuth 2008). Hence adults have an innate tendency to similarly order numeric information (prices) in memory and are distracted by tasks that uses a descending numeric order (Nairne 1983). More importantly descending numeric orders constrain cognitive resources to process task relevant information. Integrating these conclusions with research on cost benefit effects of information presentation and information flow (Ariely 2000), we predict that compared to alternatives sorted on ascending prices, a descending price sort will constrain cognitive resources to process target information especially when participants are motivated to process such information. Specifically, in high motivation conditions, a low price target would be perceived lower in monetary sacrifice when alternatives are sorted on ascending than on descending prices. In low motivation conditions, however, there will be no difference in the effects of the two sorts on the evaluation of a target product.

In four studies, we gather initial evidence for the effects of price sort on the evaluation of a target product. Study 1 used a 2 (motivation: low, high) x 2 (price sort: ascending, descending) between subjects design to assess perceptions of sacrifice for a relatively low price target DVD player accompanied by a sorted list of 20 other players. The results revealed that in high motivation conditions the target was perceived low on monetary sacrifice when the accompanying alternatives were arranged on ascending than on descending prices. In low motivation conditions there was no significant difference between the two sorts on evaluation of the target product.

Study 2 replicated the effects of sorting using an online website with the server inconspicuously capturing participants' mouse clicks and assessed depth of information processing for both the target product and the accompanying alternatives. The effects of price sort on evaluation of the target's monetary sacrifice were similar to those observed in study 1. More informative was the result that in high motivation conditions, compared to an ascending price sort, those exposed to descending prices viewed far fewer alternatives and spent significantly less time on the target.

Using a dual task approach, study 3 assessed cognitive constraints imposed by price sort by including an additional variable, memory load (low, high) to the research design used in the previous studies. In high motivation conditions, the higher memory load disrupted processing of target information more when the alternatives were sorted on ascending prices but not when they were sorted on descending prices. Thus descending prices were cognitively onerous and consequently the target's evaluation was not impacted by the memory load on participants.

Study 4 used another manipulation of motivation conditions and replicated the debilitating effects of memory load on ascending price sort observed in study 3 by using different range of prices for the accompanying alternatives. In high motivation conditions, despite the alternatives being sorted on ascending prices, the perceptions of sacrifice for a low price target increased when wider range of prices was used for the accompanying alternatives.

Overall, the results appear to indicate that compared to an ascending price sort, a descending price sort made it harder for consumers to assess monetary sacrifice. Interestingly, results also indicate that though ascending prices are more amenable to a thorough assessment of monetary sacrifice, such evaluations can be impeded by contextual influences like cognitive loads on memory or the uncertainty created by price range of the accompanying alternatives. Additional research is however needed to understand processing differences due to such sorting of alternatives and to examine whether location of a target's price in a sorted list of alternatives will influence consumers' assessment of its monetary sacrifice.

## Selected References

Ariely, Dan. (2000), "Controlling the Information Flow: Effects on Consumers' Decision Making and Preferences." *Journal of Consumer Research* 27 (September): 233-248.

Diehl, Kristin and Gal Zauberman (2005), "Searching Ordered Sets: Evaluations from Sequences under Search." *Journal of Consumer Research* 31 (4): 824-832.

Haubl, Gerald and Valerie Trifts (2000), "Consumer Decision Making in Online Shopping Environments: The Effects of Interactive Decision Aids." *Marketing Science* 19 (1): 4-21.

Monroe, Kent B. (2003), *Pricing: Making Profitable Decisions.* Burr Ridge, IL: McGraw-Hill/Irwin.

Nairne, J. S. (1983), "Associate Processing during Rote Rehearsal," *Journal of Experimental Psychology: Learning, Memory and Cognition*, 9, 3-20.

Ripps, Lance. J., Amber Bloomfield, and Jennifer Asmuth (2008), "From Numerical Concepts to Concepts of Number," *Behavioral and Brain Sciences*, 31, 623-687.

# Not Everyone Loves Buffets: Pricing Preference of Frugal Consumers

Olivia (Wan-Ting) Lin, Texas A&M University, USA

Kelly Haws, Texas A&M University, USA

## Extended Abstract

*"Being frugal is back in fashion again... People who spent every dime of their disposable income two years ago are now saving... They're scrimping with more vigor and tenacity than economists have seen in decades,"* reported the Los Angeles Times. The recent recession has significantly changed Americans' spending habits and consumption attitudes (Time magazine, 2009). For example, many

mobile phone users, who used to opt for a fixed-fee, unlimited postpaid plan, are pursuing frugality and switching to a usage-based prepaid plan. *"Prepaid is growing at an unprecedented rate with consumers keenly focused on value,"* said Sprint's Chief Executive Officer Dan Hesse (CNET 2009). The return to frugal living seems to offer counter-evidence for the flat-rate bias–a term dubbed by Train (1991) to describe the phenomenon that many users prefer a flat rate even though their billing amount would be lower with a pay-per-use tariff.

Lambrecht and Skiera (2006) attribute consumers' bias toward flat rates to three causes: 1) insurance against sudden large bills due to fluctuating demands, 2) reduction of the taxi meter effect (The ticking of the taxi meter reduces the pleasure of a taxi ride.), and 3) overestimation of product demand. Several studies have demonstrated the prevalence of flat-rate bias in product categories such as internet access (Lambrecht and Skiera 2006), health club membership (DellaVigna and Malmendier 2006), online grocery shopping services (Nunes 2000), cruises (Prelec and Loewenstein 1998), and telephone service (e.g., Kridel, Lehman, and Weisman 1993; Train, McFadden, and Ben-Akiva 1987). However, consumers' preference for pay-per-use rates receives scarce attention in extant literature. An exception is Miravete (2002), who claims that underestimation of product demand could also lead to a pay-per-use bias. In response to Lambrecht and Skiera's (2006) call for further research into pay-per-use preference, the present paper seeks to address this literature gap.

Lastovicka et al. (1999) define frugality as *"the degree to which consumers are both restrained in acquiring and in resourcefully using economic goods and services to achieve longer-term goals"* (p.88). DeYoung (1986) investigates the psychological aspects of reduced consumption behaviors and finds that careful use of resources and avoidance of waste can contribute to individuals' satisfaction. Frugal consumers enjoy (or are accustomed to) minimizing the quantity purchased or the money spent, and maximizing the utility of each product acquired. Thus, while their non-frugal counterparts resent the taxi meter effect, frugal consumers may enjoy (or cannot help but) carrying their own mental meters and keeping track of how carefully they have managed anything valuable. Accordingly, frugality can potentially lead to preference for pay-per-use rates, which facilitate achieving the goals of restrained acquisition and resourceful usage.

Just and Wansink (2008) as well as Litvak and Morewedge (2009) find that owing to consumers' loss aversion and sunk-cost psychology, they usually adopt a breakeven strategy after paying flat rates. Choosing between flat rates and pay-per-use rates is relatively easy when the breakeven quantity falls far above or below the expected demand quantity. However, the decision gets complicated when no clear gap exists between the breakeven and the expected demand quantities. The present research thus investigates how frugal consumers' pricing preference changes under varying demand uncertainty levels. We present two pricing options (one-day pass and pay-per-ride) in an amusement park scenario (and in an all-you-can-eat buffet restaurant scenario in another study). We manipulate the variances of our subjects' anticipated consumption quantities and then ask them to choose their favorite pricing method. After seeing some filler pictures for distraction purposes, our college student participants answer questions designed to measure their frugality levels. We adopt Lastovicka et al.'s (1999) eight-item scale for the measurement of frugality.

The preliminary results of our experimental studies indicate that frugal consumers show stronger preference for pay-per-use pricing under low demand variance and equal liking for flat rates under high demand uncertainty compared with their non-frugal counterparts. Under low demand uncertainty, frugal consumers deem it more likely or more favorable for them to consume under the breakeven quantity. Accordingly, they choose the usage-based pricing to accomplish their goals of restrained spending and resourceful utilization. However, under high demand uncertainty, their confidence in consuming under the breakeven quantity decreases. Since losses loom larger than gains, frugal consumers increase their preference for a flat rate plan that provides insurance against potential large bills.

An interesting extension of the current research is to study frugal consumers' consumption quantity and satisfaction under a flat-rate pricing policy. Do frugal consumers, compared to their non-frugal counterparts, suffer greater pain of paying, feel more vulnerable to the sunk cost psychology, and accordingly have a greater increase in their consumption quantity? As flat rates relieve their restraint on spending, frugal consumers may increase their consumption of the goods that incur no marginal cost to them. However, since frugal consumers resent wasting resources, they could end up consuming well beyond their satiety level and below their optimal satisfaction level.

Findings of our research should help retailers understand the pricing preference of frugal consumers and design pricing structures that meet their needs and increase their consumption satisfaction. Moreover, our findings have policy-making implications. Since overconsumption and resource wastage are contributing to environmental depletion and degradation (Cohen et al. 2005), the answer to a sustainable future seems to point to the re-establishment of frugality (Bove, Nagpal, and Dorsett 2009). Government should consider promoting pricing methods that encourage frugal behaviors to alleviate problems such as increasing economic debt, diminishing natural resources, global warming and disposal of waste. For instance, the U.S. Environmental Protection Agency developed a Pay-As-You-Throw (PAYT) system, where households pay directly for collection services based on the amount of waste thrown away. Some communities that have implemented the PAYT system have seen their overall waste disposal decline 25~45 percent (EPA 2009).

## References

Bove, Liliana L., Anish Nagpal, and Adlai David S. Dorsett (2009), "Exploring the Determinants of the Frugal Shopper," *Journal of Retailing and Consumer Services*, 16, 291–297.

Cohen, Maurie J., Aaron Comrov, and Brian Hoffner (2005), "The New Politics of Consumption: Promoting Sustainability in the American Marketplace," *Sustainability: Science, Practice, & Policy*, 1 (1), 58–76.

DellaVigna, Stefano and Ulrike Malmendier (2006), "Paying Not to Go to the Gym," *American Economic Review*, 96, 694-719.

DeYoung, Raymond (1986), "Encouraging Environmentally Appropriate Behavior: The Role of Intrinsic Motivation," *Journal of Environmental Systems,* 15 (4), 281–291.

CNET (2009), "Sprint Nextel bets big on prepaid wireless," http://news.cnet.com/8301-1035_3-10297395-94.html, July 28, 2009.

EPA (2009), "Pay-As-You-Throw," U.S. Environmental Protection Agency, http://www.epa.gov/region7/waste/solidwaste/reduce_waste.htm, November 23, 2009.

Just, David R. and Brian Wansink (2008), "The Fixed Price Paradox: Conflicting Effects of 'all-You-Can-Eat' Pricing," *Review of Economics and Statistics*, Forthcoming.

Kridel, Donald J., Dale E. Lehman, and Dennis L. Weisman (1993), "Option Value, Telecommunication Demand, and Policy," *Information Economics and Policy*, 5 (2), 125–144.

Lambrecht, Anja and Bernd Skiera (2006), "Paying Too Much and Being Happy About It: Existence, Causes, and Consequences of Tariff-choice Biases," *Journal of Marketing Research*, 43(2), 212-223.

Lastovicka, John L., Lance A. Bettencourt, Renée Shaw Hugher, and Ronald J. Kuntze (1999), "Lifestyle of the Tight and Frugal: Theory and Measurement," *Journal of Consumer Research,* 26 (1), 85-98.

Litvak, Paul M. and Carey K. Morewedge (2009), "Breakeven Strategy in the Consumption of Flat-Rate Goods," *working paper.*

Los Angeles Times (2009), "Being Frugal Is Back In Fashion," http://articles.latimes.com/2009/dec/12/business/la-fi-cover-frugal13-2009dec13, December 12, 2009.

Miravete, Eugenio J. (2002), "Choosing the Wrong Calling Plan? Ignorance and Learning," *American Economic Review*, 93 (1), 297–310.

Nunes, Joseph C. (2000), "A Cognitive Model of People's Usage Estimations," *Journal of Marketing Research*, 37 (November), 397–409.

Prelec, Drazen and George Loewenstein (1998), "The Red and the Black: Mental Accounting of Savings and Debt," *Marketing Science*, 17 (1), 4-28.

Time magazine (2010), "How Americans Spend Now," http://www.time.com/time/specials/packages/article/0,28804,1891475_1891477,00.html.

Train, Kenneth E., Daniel L. McFadden, and Moshe Ben-Akiva (1987), "The Demand for Local Telephone Service: A Fully Discrete Model of Residential Calling Patterns and Service Choices," *Rand Journal of Economics*, 18 (1), 109–123.

# Can Consumers Cope with Visual Rhetorical Figures in Advertising?

Steven Andrews, University of Oregon, USA

Guang-Xin Xie, University of Massachusetts–Boston, USA

Over the past several decades print advertisements relied less on verbal language in either the headline or the body of the ad and more on complex, stylized visual messages delivered with rhetorical devices such as metaphor (Phillips and McQuarrie, 2002). McQuarrie and Mick (1996) defined rhetorical devices used in advertisements as "artful deviations" from the typical, expected communication structure. These deviations are generally pleasant to process and they encourage reinterpretation and/or reading additional meanings; therefore, rhetorical devices inherently yield weak persuasive arguments (McQuarrie and Phillips, 2005). Previous research suggests that ads with rhetorical devices generate greater ad liking, greater ad elaboration, and greater ad recall compared to ads without rhetorical devices. Specifically, visual rhetoric in ads are complex information devices (Scott, 1994a, 1994b) that enjoy universal processing advantages over ads with verbal rhetoric devices (McQuarrie and Mick, 2003b). Visual rhetoric elicits strong, immediate persuasive impact (McQuarrie and Phillips, 2005) which persists during incidental exposure (McQuarrie and Mick, 2003a) when verbal ads of any kind have virtually no persuasive impact. Given the pervasiveness of metaphor (Hirschman, 2007) in the marketplace and given the important differences in how the visual and the verbal systems process information (Franks, 2003) the present study examined more deeply the persuasive impact of visual metaphor ads in contrast to verbal ads. Specifically, we looked more closely at how effectively consumers cope with visual metaphor as a persuasive tactic.

The Persuasion Knowledge Model (PKM: Friestad and Wright, 1994) described how consumers cope with persuasive attempts in the marketplace. The PKM considers consumer beliefs, attitudes, and choices about persuaders and their tactics, and consumer perceptions of the effectiveness and appropriateness of persuasion attempts. Previous research examined the persuasive impact of rhetorical devices in ads within a persuasion knowledge context. Aluwhalia and Burnkrandt (2004) showed that the persuasion knowledge (PK) dimension of consumer self-confidence (Bearden, Hardesty, and Rose, 2001) determined how people processed rhetorical questions— a non-sensory rhetorical device—in the headlines and/or the body of verbal ads. People high in PK (based on median splits of the 6-item scale) rated the ads based more on source perceptions of a well-known brand. Conversely, people low in PK rated the ads based more on the strength of the persuasive claim. Persuasion was enhanced (weakened) by stronger (weaker) persuasive claims.

Based on previous research using visual rhetoric in print advertisements we hypothesized that in contrast to verbal metaphors, visual metaphors would not conform to the Aluwhalia et al (2004) model. Specifically, even though visual metaphors yield weak persuasive arguments print ads using these devices would show strong persuasive impact irrespective of PK scale scores. With 646 student subjects we used a 3 (ad style: verbal literal, verbal metaphor, visual metaphor) x 2 (PK scale score: high, low) between groups design. Ad stimuli were taken from previous research (McQuarrie & Phillips, 2005) on the persuasive impact of visual rhetorical ads. Factorial ANOVAs confirmed our expectations that consumers perceived visual metaphor as a persuasive tactic to a much greater extent than the other ads. Despite that visual metaphors showed much higher ad and brand attitude regardless of PK level. In contrast, verbal metaphor had much lower attitude scores for the low PK vs. high PK consumers as shown previously for weak arguments. Consistent with previous research (McQuarrie & Mick, 2003a), consumers in study one rated the ads with visual metaphors more interesting, more artistic, and more likely to possess multiple meanings than the verbal ads. Consumer PK scale scores did not impact elaboration ratings.

Based on the higher involvement ratings for visual metaphors in study one, study two explored the possibility that visual rhetorical ads penetrated PKM persuasion filters more thoroughly because the visuals worked through affective, meta-cognitive processes such as visual fluency (Winkielman, Schwarz, Reber, and Fazendeiro, 2003). Specifically, visual fluency theory suggests that the pleasant experience consumers have when processing more fluent stimuli gets interpreted as relevant information regarding the stimulus being processed. Stimuli that are more perceptually fluent and more conceptually fluent are liked better and they are perceived to be more truthful (Reber, Schwarz, and Winkielman, 2004). Perceptual fluency studies have shown that when a visual stimulus is limited in the duration of exposure, putting stress on the viewer's mind, the stimuli are liked less and perceived as less truthful (Reber, Winkielman, and Schwarz, 1998).

Study two explored whether perceptual fluency effects influenced the positive ratings of visual metaphors despite the greater perception that the ads were using a persuasive tactic. Using the same ads, we manipulated exposure duration: 110 student subjects either had unlimited time to view the ads or were restricted to one standard deviation below the pre-tested mean for adequate minimum processing time for all the ads (3-seconds). A two (exposure duration) x 3 (ad styles) mixed design based on McQuarrie and Phillips (2005) showed that the limited duration exposure resulted in decreased ad attitude ratings and decreased perception of honesty ratings for both verbal ads. The limited exposure duration had no effect on attitude or honesty ratings for visual metaphors, which remained higher than both the verbal ads across both exposure conditions.

In summary, study one demonstrated that persuasion knowledge: a rational, cognitive measure of persuasion coping (Campbell and Kirmani, 2008) had virtually no effect on consumer coping with print ads using visual metaphors. This finding has strong implications regarding the persuasive power of rhetorical figures used in visual advertising, particularly given how popular the tactic is in practice. Results from both studies suggested that the visual metaphors elicited strong affective reactions. But apparently the exposure duration manipulation in study two was not strong enough to affect the instant impact of visual rhetorical figures on consumer response. Future research should also consider the possibility that the rhetorical "artful deviations" elicit perceptual feelings of familiarity (Whittlesea, 1993). Another possibility worthy of future consideration is that visual processing fluency may moderate more traditional levels of processing effects on visual ads: attention, elaboration, and the formation of new knowledge structures from existing knowledge structures (Petty and Krosnick, 1995).

## Selected References

Ahluwalia, and Burnkrant, 2004. Answering Questions about Questions: A Persuasion Knowledge Perspective for Understanding the Effects of Rhetorical Questions. [Article]. *Journal of Consumer Research*. 31:26-42.

Bearden, Hardesty, and Rose, 2001. Consumer Self-Confidence: Refinements in Conceptualization and Measurement. *Journal of Consumer Research*. 28(1):121-134.

Campbell, and Kirmani. (2008). I Know What You're Doing and Why You're Doing it: The Use of the Persuasion Knowledge Model in Consumer Research. In C. P. Haugtvedt, P. M. Herr andF. R. Kardes (Eds.), *Handbook of Consumer Psychology* (pp. 549-574). New York: Psychology Press.

Franks. (2003). The Neuroscience of Emotions. In J. S. J. Turner (Ed.), *Handbook of the Sociology of Emotions* (pp. 38-65). New York: Springer Science + Business Media, LLC.

Friestad, and Wright, 1994. The Persuasion Knowledge Model: How People Cope with Persuasion Attempts. *Journal of Consumer Research*. 21(June):1-31.

Hirschman, 2007. Metaphor in the marketplace. *Marketing Theory*. 7(3):227-248.

McQuarrie, and Mick, 1996. Figures of rhetoric in advertising language. [Article]. *Journal of Consumer Research*. 22(4):424-438.

McQuarrie, and Mick, 2003a. Visual and Verbal Rhetorical Figures under Directed Processing versus Incidental Exposure to Advertising. [Article]. *Journal of Consumer Research*. 29(4):579-587.

McQuarrie, and Mick. (2003b). The Contribution of Semiotic and Rhetorical Perspectives to the Explanation of Visual Persuasion in Advertising. In L. S. R. Batra (Ed.), *Persuasive Imagery: A Consumer Response Perspective* (pp. 191-222). Mahwah, NJ: Lawrence Earlbaum Associates, Inc.

McQuarrie, and Phillips, 2005. Indirect Persuasion in Advertising. [Article]. *Journal of Advertising*. 34(2):7-20.

Petty, and Krosnick. 1995. *Attitude Strength: Antecedents and Consequences*. Mahwah, NJ: Lawrence Erlbaum Associates, Inc.

Phillips, and McQuarrie, 2002. The Development, Change, and Transformation of Rhetorical Style in Magazine Advertisements 1954-1999. [Article]. *Journal of Advertising*. 31(4):1-13.

Reber, Schwarz, and Winkielman, 2004. Processing Fluency and Aesthetic Pleasure: Is Beauty in the Perceiver's Processing Experience? *Personality and Social Psychology Review*. 8(4):364-382.

Reber, Winkielman, and Schwarz, 1998. Effects of Perceptual Fluency on Affective Judgments. *Psychological Science*. 9(1):45-48.

Scott, 1994a. The Bridge from Text to Mind: Adapting Reader-Response Theory to Consumer Research. *Journal of Consumer Research*. 21:461-480.

Scott, 1994b. Images in advertising: The need for a theory of visual rhetoric. [Article]. *Journal of Consumer Research*. 21(2):252.

Whittlesea, 1993. Illusions of familiarity. *Journal of Experimental Psychology: Learning, Memory, and Cognition*. 19(6):1235-1253.

Winkielman, Schwarz, Reber, and Fazendeiro. (2003). Cognitive and affective consequences of visual fluency: When seeing is easy on the mind. In *Persuasive imagery: A consumer response perspective*. (pp. 75-89): Mahwah, NJ, US: Lawrence Erlbaum Associates Publishers.

# Using Visual Interference to Establish New Brand-Attribute Linkages

Christina Saenger, Kent State University, USA
Robert Jewell, Kent State University, USA
Jennifer Wiggins Johnson, Kent State University, USA

Memory interference occurs when a memory cue is associated with more than one brand through similar advertisements (Burke and Srull 1988). At retrieval, the cue triggers associations with both brands, yielding response competition and confusion between the brands. Research has found that confusion can interfere with an individual's ability to correctly recall brand-attribute associations, potentially harming the brand (Unnava and Sirdeshmukh 1994). However, research has also suggested that interference can be used for repositioning when a brand uses an advertisement that communicates similar brand attributes as a competitor's ad (Jewell and Unnava 2003) as recall for new attribute information is enhanced by the common association between the brands.

Most research has focused on text-based interference. However, trends in print advertising show that marketers rely more on images, and use fewer verbal claims (McQuarrie and Phillips 2008), suggesting a new interference problem. An informal content analysis of three fashion magazines revealed ten sets of advertisements for different brands using similar pictures. Research has shown that ads with similar pictures can foster competing associations to the common picture cue at retrieval, leading to the same harmful interference effects (Kumar 2000; Kumar and Krishnan 2004). If similar pictures can lead to interference, then picture similarity may also yield the positive effects observed with text cues when used to reposition a brand. This paper explores whether the repositioning effect of text-based interference also occurs with visual interference.

For a brand to experience the repositioning effect of visual interference, the pictures used need to be similar enough to prompt a common association between two brands and a single picture cue. When consumers view advertising pictures, they extract inferences about the attributes possessed by the brand (Scott and Vargas 2007). This finding is in line with referential processing, where verbal representations of visual stimuli are encoded in memory (Paivio 1971, 1990). Recall for pictoral information relies on this verbal recoding (Walker et al. 1997). Therefore, we propose that when a picture becomes associated with both a target brand and a brand that possesses a new, desirable attribute, response competition during interference may facilitate recall of the desirable attribute for the target brand, effectively repositioning the target brand.

In addition to visual similarity, the use of a picture that communicates the meaning of the repositioning attribute is a second necessary condition in visual interference-based repositioning. If verbal recoding of pictoral information occurs in memory, visual interference-based repositioning is more likely to occur when the picture is communicative of the attribute's meaning. If the picture is similar but not communicative of the intended meaning, it may be verbally-recoded and cause interference, but the desired repositioning is unlikely. If the picture is communicative but not similar to another brand's advertising, interference will not occur and the brand is less likely to reposition due to the lack of competing associations. Therefore, we expect the effectiveness of visual interference in repositioning to depend on the similarity of the picture cue and the meaning extracted from the picture.

We tested this prediction in the context of repositioning a hotel brand. Pretests revealed that our participants were familiar with this product category and the brands Holiday Inn and Hilton. Holiday Inn was perceived to be related to the attribute, "appropriate for vacation," and Hilton was perceived to be related to the attribute, "appropriate for business," with each brand unrelated to the other attribute. The goal of this study was to reposition Holiday Inn as "appropriate for business" using visual interference. Several pictures were pretested, and a briefcase was determined to mean "appropriate for business" while a beach bag meant "appropriate for vacation." We created advertisements for Holiday Inn and Hilton featuring these focal images embedded into images of hotel rooms. The images were accompanied by headlines and text copy that did not make any reference to the focal attributes. Pretesting determined the headlines, text copy, and full ads for each brand were equally persuasive and informative.

We employed a 2 (meaning of target image: conveyed /did not convey the business attribute) x 2 (image similarity: similar/different) design. The meaning and similarity of the ads was manipulated using the focal images in the ads, creating four conditions for the Holiday Inn/Hilton ads: briefcase/briefcase, briefcase/beach bag, beach bag/briefcase, and beach bag/beach bag. 108 business undergraduates viewed a 10-advertisement sequence that included the Holiday Inn and Hilton ads, counterbalanced for order effects, including other competing ads to mask the manipulated ads. The dependent variable, measured via 7-point Likert scale, indicated participants' agreement with the statements, "Holiday Inn is appropriate for business travel" and "Holiday Inn is appropriate for a business conference," which we combined into a single index ($r = .65$).

We found a significant interaction effect between similarity and meaning ($F (1,104)=4.37$, $p<.05$). Ratings of Holiday Inn's appropriateness for business were higher when both ads featured the briefcase ($M=5.65$) than when the Holiday Inn ad featured the briefcase and the Hilton ad featured the beach bag ($M=4.71$, $p<.01$), when the Holiday Inn ad featured the beach bag and the Hilton ad featured the briefcase ($M=4.65$, $p<.01$), or when both ads featured the beach bag ($M=4.67$, $p<.01$). There were no significant differences between the other three conditions.

This suggests that picture meaning or similarity alone are no more effective at repositioning the brand than an advertisement that does not communicate the repositioning attribute at all. We conclude that similarity and meaning are necessary but not sufficient conditions to link a brand to a new attribute using visual interference. Additional studies will investigate how similar the pictures must be when the appropriate meaning is conveyed, how effectively the pictures must communicate the meaning when they are similar, and cross-category effects.

This research contributes to advertising research by demonstrating that visual interference can be an effective repositioning tool. Since visual advertising is dominant and often employs similar imagery, this research demonstrates how advertising's competitive environment can be used to a brand's advantage.

## Selected References

Burke, Raymond R. and Thomas K. Srull (1988), "Competitive Interference and Consumer Memory for Advertising," *Journal of Consumer Research*, 15 (June), 55-68.

Jewell, Robert D. and H. Rao Unnava (2003), "When Competitive Interference Can Be Beneficial," *Journal of Consumer Research*, 30 (September), 283-91.

Kumar, Anand (2000), "Interference Effects of Contextual Cues in Advertisements on Memory for Ad Context," *Journal of Consumer Psychology*, 3 (9), 155-66.

Kumar, Anand and Shanker Krishnan (2004), "Memory Interference in Advertising: A Replication and Extension," *Journal of Consumer Research*, 30 (March), 602-11.

McQuarrie, Edward F. and Barbara J. Phillips (2008), "It's Not Your Father's Magazine Ad," *Journal of Advertising*, 37 (3), 95-106.

Paivio, Allan (1971/1986), *Mental Representations: A Dual Coding Approach*, New York: Oxford.

Scott, Linda M. and Patrick Vargas (2007), "Writing with Pictures: Toward a Unifying Theory of Consumer Response to Images," *Journal of Consumer Research*, 34 (October), 341-56.

Unnava, H. Rao and Deepak Sirdeshmukh (1994), "Reducing Competitive Ad Interference," *Journal of Marketing Research*, 31 (August), 403-11.

Walker, Peter, Graham J. Hitch, Stephen A. Dewhurst, Helen E. Whiteley, and Maria A. Brandimonte (1997), "The Representation of Nonstructural Information in Visual Memory: Evidence from Image Combination," *Memory & Cognition*, 25 (July), 484-91.

# The Bleeding Effect:
# How Interference in Advertising Messaging Influences Perceptions and Impacts Behavior

Bryan Greenberg, Elizabethtown College, USA
David Ruggeri, St. Louis University, USA

The question of how advertising effectiveness is influenced by competitive messages, both for similar products as well as for those falling into a different product class, has been an important area of inquiry for researchers. Two areas that researchers have focused on are the impact of messages pertaining to similar types of products and the impact of messages containing similar creative elements. The former, generally referred to as competitive interference, refers to the way that competitive brands, i.e. those brands that represent similar or substitutable products, can interfere with recall measures. Various studies (Burke and Srull, 1988; Keller, 1991) have found that brand recall is significantly lower when an ad for a similar product is present. The second area of research, known as contextual interference, is focused more on the creative decisions that go into the development of an advertisement, such as the use of similar pictures or imagery. Results have shown that contextual interference can diminish recall when multiple products, regardless of their product class, rely on similar executions (Kumar and Krishnan, 2004; Kumar, 2000).

While general brand name and messaging recall has been shown to decrease or become muddled in the face of interference, research into how this may influence consumer perception or interpretation is scarcer. Is interference just problematic for processing and retrieval tasks, or does it alter how consumers view and interpret a product? Some of the research into interference begins to address these questions, including that into contextual interference, which has shown that similarity in executional elements can confuse consumers, leading them to mistake one brand for another when cued with the advertising executional elements both brands shared (Kumar and Krishnan, 2004). Jewell and Unnava (2003) also offered some insight into this issue when they studied the potential positive impact of competitive interference. They found that such interference could be beneficial to established brands attempting to promote a new product attribute.

The primary goal of this research is to further examine how interference influences how and what consumers interpret when faced with such interference effects. This study includes an examination of what specific information consumers recall, and whether that information matches the brand's messaging, the competitive messaging, or is unrelated to both. It also measures consumer intent to purchase, seeking to connect interpretation of messaging to purchasing behavior. In addition, qualitative analysis is also utilized to better understand the link between messaging, processing, interpretation, and behavior.

A secondary goal of this research is to apply what has traditionally been a lab-based approach to studying interference effects to a more natural setting. This project therefore included a field experiment followed by replication in a laboratory setting to compare effects.

To accomplish the above goals, a field experiment was first conducted over the course of one week (Friday through Thursday) at a large multiplex movie theater. Theater management agreed to allow the manipulation of pre-show elements for two prints, both of the same film playing on two of the theater's screens. The messaging tested consisted of movie trailers, what we define as extended commercials. To control for outside variables, each print consisted of only two movie trailers and the film. No additional advertising, theater promotional messaging, or other entertainment content was present. There were three conditions–interference-ad-present, interference-ad-absent, control–with each rotated across screens and dayparts to account for potential bias. The trailer for *Flightplan* served as the target advertisement. The trailer for *Red Eye* version A served as the interference-inducing advertisement (*Red Eye* A contained similar imagery, with both it and *Flightplan* featuring scenes taking place on a plane). *Red Eye* version B was used in the interference-ad-absent condition (this version did not feature any scenes on a plane). A trailer for a romantic comedy, unrelated thematically and executionally to *Flightplan*, was used in the control group.

To test the results from study 1 in a controlled environment, a second study was designed to replicate the first in a laboratory setting. Students, staff, and local residents were invited to attend a free film screening. There were three showings of the film, each representing one of the three conditions found in the first study.

Subjects in both groups were told that a study on the moviegoing experience was being conducted and were asked to complete two surveys. The first was completed prior to entering the theater/screening room, while the second was completed at the completion of the film. Upon completion of survey one, respondents were provided a raffle ticket for free movie tickets and told it would be collected upon completion of survey two. The code on this ticket was used to match both surveys.

The primary measures to understand interference and consumer interpretation in the face of interference were a variety of unaided and aided recall measures. These included three specially-designed thematic recall scores: Correct recall, confused recall, and incorrect recall. For these respondents were asked to list as many themes/elements they could recall from each trailer. These responses were categorized as correct (matched one of a pre-determined set of elements for that trailer), confused (matched a pre-determined set of elements for the alternative trailer the subject viewed), or incorrect (matched neither set of elements). Likelihood to purchase scores, as well as open-ended questions designed to elicit additional details as to why that was the case, were utilized to offer additional insight into the behavioral impact of interference effects.

Results showed a statistically significant difference across all thematic recall measures for those subjects exposed to the trailers featuring similar executions. Those in the interference-ad-absent and control conditions were not significantly different. In addition, those in the interference-ad-present condition were much more likely to interpret the *Flightplan* trailer in a way that did not match its execution or its actual theme. For example, many subjects thought the film included a plane crash when, in fact, it did not (nor did either of the two trailers they saw). Thus consumers were creating alternative interpretations that matched neither the target advertisement nor the test advertisement. Other results include lower unaided recall (of the trailers viewed) and decreased intention to purchase (to see the film advertised).

## Selected References

Burke, Raymond R. and Thomas K. Srull (1988). "Competitive Interference and Consumer Memory for Advertising," *Journal of Consumer Research*, 15 (June), 55-68.

Keller, Kevin L. (1991). "Memory and Evaluation Effects in Competitive Advertising Environments," *Journal of Consumer Research*, 17 (March), 463-476.

Kumar, Anand (2000), "Interference Effects of Contextual Cues in Advertisements on Memory for Ad Content," *Journal of Consumer Psychology*, 9 (3), 155-166

Kumar, Anand and Shanker Krishnan (2004), "Memory Interference in Advertising: A Replication and Extension," *Journal of Consumer Research*, 30 (March), 602-611.

Jewel, Robert D. and H. Rao Unnava (2003), "When Competitive Interference Can be Beneficial," *Journal of Consumer Research*, 30 (September), 283-291.

# Is a Diamond Really Forever?
# Effects of Lay Theories of Love on Responses to Romance Appeals in Advertising

Li Huang, HKUST, Hong Kong

Anirban Mukhopadhyay, Hong Kong University of Science and Technology, China

## Extended Abstract

The theme of romantic love is commonly used in advertising as marketing practitioners strive to generate favorable attitudes towards advertised products (Galician and Merskin 2007; Huang 2004). It is therefore interesting to observe that consumer researchers have paid scarce attention to this theme (choosing instead to focus their efforts on the study of a possibly related area, namely, sex in advertising, cf. Dahl, Sengupta, and Vohs 2009). The aim of this research is to address this gap in the literature, by exploring consumers' responses to romance appeals in advertising and how these may depend on their lay theories.

Lay theories, the basic and often naïve assumptions that people hold about their world, guide many aspects of social behavior (Dweck 1999; Wyer 2004). Consumer researchers have recently begun to uncover some of these diverse effects of lay theories on various aspects of consumer judgment and decision making (e.g., Mukhopadhyay and Yeung 2010; Mukhopadhyay and Johar 2005; Raghunathan, Naylor, and Hoyer 2006; Wang, Keh, and Bolton 2010). Particularly relevant to this research, Hung and Wyer (2008) demonstrated that consumer's responses to advertising may be influenced by their lay theories. Along similar lines, we seek to understand how lay theories that are specific to love might influence consumers' responses to romantic appeals in advertising.

Various literatures have proposed different beliefs regarding love (Lindholm 1998). Some ideally believe that love is forever and eternal; in contrast, some strongly believe that love is transitory and destined to change (Peck 1978). This distinction corresponds to Labroo and Mukhopadhyay's (2009) study of lay theories of emotions, according to which people's beliefs about the transience of emotions range along a continuum from "lasting" to "fleeting". Correspondingly, we too suggest that lay theories of love may vary–from *lasting* to *fleeting*.

What effect might these lay theories have on the appraisals of romantic messages in advertising? Wheeler, Petty and Bizer (2005) demonstrate that self-schemata matching, or presenting individuals with a message that appeals or conforms to some aspect of their self-conception, enhances favorable reactions to that message. Romantic love often entails feelings of attachment and wishes of long-lasting relationships (Hazan and Shaver 1987), which is more consistent with the belief of lasting-theorists. Therefore, our first prediction is that lasting-theorists will have more favorable attitudes towards romance appeals than will fleeting-theorists.

What if the relationship is threatened? Optimism may lead to a false sense of security (Weinstein 1980), and hence lasting-theorists who optimistically believe love is eternal may perceive their relationships to be more secure than they really are. This would make them less inclined to take actions to maintain their relationships. Knee (1998) found that people who held a "destiny" theory of relationship (potential partners are meant for each other) were more likely to engage in avoidance coping in response to a stressful relationship event as compared to "growth" theorists (relationship is cultivated and developed over time). In our context, this would imply that lasting-theorists would have an avoidant reaction to relationship threats, and therefore the presence of a relationship threat would make them less likely to buy products advertised using romantic appeals. In contrast, since fleeting-theorists do not hold such over-optimistic beliefs about perennial love, the presence of threat should not affect their responses to romantic appeals.

Till date, we have tested our hypotheses in two completed experiments. In Study 1a (*N*=144), participants viewed a target ad for chocolates, featuring a romantic appeal, and a filler ad for mobile phones, and reported their attitudes towards both ads ($\alpha$=.95). They then responded to some demographic measures, following which we assessed lay theories of love based on six items including statements such as "Love is forever" and "love is transitory"($\alpha$=.87). Lower (higher) scores on this scale represent a greater fleeting (lasting) orientation. Regression analyses showed that lay theories of love significantly predicted attitudes towards the romance appeal ad, such that lasting-theorists had more positive attitudes than fleeting-theorists ($\beta$=.40, $t(143)$=5.18, $p<.001$). An analysis using median splits for ease of explication indicates the difference between the two groups ($M_{lasting}$=5.84, $M_{fleeting}$=4.94, $t(143)$=4.84, $p<.001$). There were no significant differences in attitudes for the filler ad. Study 1b ($N$=65) replicated these results on a different sample, with the stimuli consisting only of the target ad and no filler ($\beta$=.47, $M_{lasting}$=6.24, $M_{fleeting}$=5.04, $t(64)$=4.29, $p<.001$).

Study 2 assessed whether threat moderates the effect of lay theories of love on the purchase intention for the advertised product. Participants ($N$=48) in a 2 (threat vs. no threat) × 2 (lasting vs. fleeting) between-subjects design read a scenario in which their romantic relationship was in conflict vs. not. They then saw an ad featuring a romantic appeal for chocolates, and indicated their intention of buying the advertised product as a gift to resolve the conflict ($\alpha$=.88). Participants in the no-threat condition merely indicated how likely they were to buy the chocolates as gifts for their lovers. The analysis reveals a significant interaction between threat and lay theories of love ($F(1, 44)$=55.16, $p<.01$).In the absence of threat, the previous results obtain, such that lasting-theorists had higher purchase intentions than fleeting-theorists ($M_{lasting}$=4.58, $M_{fleeting}$=3.98; $F(1, 44)$=5.25, $p<.01$). In contrast, under threat, there was no difference in purchase intentions ($M_{lasting}$=3.94, $M_{fleeting}$=3.79, $F(1, 48)$=1.78, $ns$). As expected, relationship threat does not affect fleeting-theorists' responses to romance appeals, but strongly affect lasting-theorists' behavior.

To summarize, this research investigates romantic appeals in advertising, and our results till date demonstrate that responses to such appeals vary based on consumers' lay theories of love as well as the presence of relationship threat. These results are among the first in consumer research to investigate the effects of romantic appeals, a perennial theme in advertising. Subsequent studies will explore the mechanisms underlying the observed effects.

## References

Dahl, Darren W., Jaideep Sengupta and Kathleen D. Vohs (2009), "Sex in Advertising: Gender Differences and the Role of Relationship Commitment," *Journal of Consumer Research,* 36(2), 215-231.

Dweck, Carol S. (1999), *Self Theories: Their Role in Motivation, Personality and Development*, Philadelphia: Taylor and Francis.

Galician, Mary-Lou and Debra L. Mersk (2007), *Critical Thinking about Sex, Love, and Romance in the Mass Media: Media Literacy Application*, London: Routledge.

Hazan, Cindy and Philip Shaver (1987), "Romantic Love Conceptualized as an Attachment Process," *Journal of Personality and Social Psychology*, 52(3), 511-524.

Huang, Ming-Hui (2004), "Romantic Love and Sex: Their Relationship and Impacts on Ad Attitudes," *Psychology and Marketing,* 21(1), 53-73.

Hung, Iris and Robert S. Wyer (2008), "The Impact of Implicit Theories on Responses to Problem-Solving Print Advertisements," *Journal of Consumer Psychology*, 18(3), 223-235.

Knee, Raymond C. (1998), "Implicit Theories of Relationships: Assessment and Prediction of Romantic Relationship Initiation, Coping, and Longevity," *Journal of Personality and Social Psychology*, 74(2), 360-370.

Labroo, Aparna A. and Anirban Mukhopadhyay (2009), "Lay Theories of Emotion Transience and the Search for Happiness: A Fresh Perspective on Affect Regulation," *Journal of Consumer Research*, 36(2), 242-254.

Lindholm, Charles (1998), "The Future of Love" in *Romantic Love and Sexual Behavior: Perspectives from Social Sciences*, Vol. 1, ed. De Munck,Victor C., Westport CT: Praeger, 17-32.

Mukhopadhyay, Anirban and Gita V. Johar (2005), "Where There Is a Will, Is There a Way? Effects of Lay Theories of Self-Control on Setting and Keeping Resolutions," *Journal of Consumer Research*, 31(March), 779-786.

Mukhopadhyay, Anirban and Catherine W. M. Yeung (2010), "Building Character: Effects of Lay Theories of Self-Control on the Selection of Products for Children," *Journal of Marketing Research*, forthcoming.

Peck, Scott M. (1978), *The Road Less Traveled: A New Psychology of Love, Traditional Values, and Spiritual Growth*, New York: Simon and Schuster.

Raghunathan, Rajagopal, Rebecca W. Naylor, and Wayne D. Hoyer (2006), "The Unhealthy=Tasty Intuition and Its Effects on Taste Inferences, Enjoyment, and Choice of Food Products," *Journal of Marketing*, 70(4), 170-184.

Wang, Wenbo, Hean Tat Keh, and Lisa E. Bolton (2010), "Lay Theories of Medicine and a Healthy Lifestyle," *Journal of Consumer Research*, forthcoming.

Weinstein Neal D. (1980), "Unrealistic Optimism about Future Life Events," *Journal of Personality and Social Psychology*, 39(5), 806-820.

Wheeler, Christian S., Richard E. Petty, and George Y. Bizer (2005), "Self-Schema Matching and Attitude change: Situational and Dispositional Determinants of Message Elaboration," *Journal of Consumer Research*, 31(4), 787-797.

Wyer, Robert S. (2004), *Social comprehension and judgment: The role of situation models, narratives, and implicit theories*, Mahwah, NJ, US: Lawrence Erlbaum Associates Publishers.

# The Effect of Cultural Orientation on Responses to Comparative Advertising

Ozge Yucel-Aybat, Baruch College, CUNY, USA
Thomas Kramer, Baruch College, CUNY, USA

Nowadays, brands often try to differentiate themselves from competitors, and comparative advertisements are used as traditional tactics to persuade consumers of their superiority over other brands. To that effect, advertisers state that their product is better than the competitor's product or even better than any other product. Many of us are familiar with Subway's advertisement targeting McDonald's and these practices are increasingly used by industry giants such as Pizza Hut, Diet Pepsi and Apple (McArthur and Cuneo, 2007). Extant research has examined the effects of comparative message claims. For example, Grewal et al (1997) found that comparative ads are more effective than noncomparative ads in terms of brand awareness, attitudes and purchase intentions. Research has also examined the effectiveness of comparative ads by concentrating on valence of framing (Jain et al., 2007), on information processing (Thompson and Hamilton, 2006) and on brand positioning (Pechmann and Ratneshwar, 1991). In this research, we propose that comparative ads may not be universally effective and that individual differences associated with distinct cultural values may affect consumers' perceptions.

We focus on the extent to which consumers accept "inequality" as a legitimate result of their cultural values, which is defined as "power distance" in Hofstede's (1980) cross-cultural studies. It is assumed that cultures are distinguished by the way they are accustomed to deal with inequalities, in other words by how individuals handle inequality in society and hierarchy of powers (Hofstede, 1991). For some cultures (low power distance), inequality and inconsistencies among various areas are often problematic. On contrary, for others (high power distance), unequal power distribution is generally accepted: people do not and should not question the power of others; they should accept the hierarchy as it is. Thus, the more their culture encourages rigid social hierarchy in different positions of power, the more they are expected to be comfortable in accepting this inequality. We argue that this acceptance of inequality may in turn affect how consumers cope with companies' claims of being superior to their competitors in comparative ads. Therefore, the aim of this research is to extend the comparative advertisement literature by investigating potential differences in consumer responses due to the cultural orientation construct of power distance.

One of the first cross-country investigations about comparative advertisement is conducted by Donthu (1998). This research suggests that although consumers recall these ads better, their attitudes toward comparative ads are not very positive in countries where these practices are rarely used. However, Jeon and Beatty (2002) show that in countries where consumers are unfamiliar with direct comparative ad (explicitly naming the well-known competitor), this type of advertisement is more effective than indirect comparative ad (e.g., "our brand is better than any other brand"). Choi and Miracle (2004) on the other hand examine the mediating effect of self-construal on the relationship between national culture and effectiveness of comparative advertisement. Polyorat and Alden (2005) also investigate the effectiveness of indirect comparative ads by using two different samples (US and Thai) and test the effects of self-construal and need for cognition. In this research, we extend Polyorat and Alden's work (2005) by investigating the effects of direct comparison, indirect comparison and noncomparison advertisements by considering cultural differences. Researchers examining comparative advertisement through cross-country investigation conducted studies with participants born in different countries. However, even individuals of the same country may differ in terms of how they are affected by the same culture. Therefore, instead of differentiating based on the country, we try to differentiate among consumers based on their personality traits as Hofstede (1991) suggests.

## Study

We manipulated presence of comparison in the ads by using direct, indirect and noncomparative arguments in the ads. Three ad versions of a fictitious brand were used as in Pechmann and Ratneshwar's studies (1991) to control for subjects' familiarity with the ad. 137 undergraduate students enrolled in marketing courses at an East Cost University participated in the study in exchange for course credit. Participants were first presented with brief information about the target fictitious brand (Star) and some of them saw direct comparative version (comparing Star with Ajax), some indirect comparative version (claiming that Star is the best) and some noncomparative version (only stating Star's positive attributes) of the ad. We then measured participants' power distance scores as a second factor. Manipulation checks were conducted to make sure that participants can easily distinguish between the comparative and noncomparative ads.

Data supported our hypothesis that comparative ads may not be universally effective and participants' willingness to accept inequality (power distance) may affect this process. An ANOVA on ad effectiveness revealed a significant interaction ($p<.05$) between the ad type and power distance measures. Direct comparison ads were more effective for participants with lower power distance scores (less willing to accept inequality); whereas indirect comparison ads were more effective for participants with higher power distance scores than those with lower power distance scores.

## Discussion

Using power distance as a construct to differentiate between individuals' perceptions of inequality, this research tries to contribute to literature by showing that individual differences caused by cultural differences can moderate the way consumers perceive comparative advertisements. This research also has practical implications for managers, suggesting under which conditions comparative ads are likely to be most effective.

The current stimuli use a fictitious brand name and compare it with a well-known competitor. To increase the external validity and to comply with real-life settings, in the next study we will use familiar brand names. We will also manipulate the credibility of comparative claims (direct and indirect). In direct comparison condition, for the incredible version, the ad will compare an inferior brand with a high quality brand and claim its superiority; whereas for the credible version an equally powerful brand will claim that is superior to its competitor. We will use pretests to make sure we use the appropriate brand names for inferior, equally powerful and best-known competitor brands. In addition, in a follow-up study, we will investigate how cognitive load impacts the effect of power distance on effectiveness of comparative ads.

## References

Choi, Y. K., & Miracle, G. E. (2004). The Effectiveness of Comparative Advertising in Korea and the United States, *Journal of Advertising,* 33 (4), 75- 87.

Donthu, N. (1998). A Cross-Country Investigation of Recall and Attitude Toward Comparative Advertising, *Journal of Advertising,* 27 (2), 111-122.

Grewal, D., Kavanoor, S., Fern, E. F., Costley, C., & Barnes, J. (1997). Comparative versus Noncomparative Advertising: A Meta-Analysis, *Journal of Marketing,* 61 (4), 1-15.

Hofstede, G. (1980). Culture's Consequences: International Differences in Work-Related Values, Beverly Hills, CA: Sage.

Hofstede, G. (1991). Cultures and Organizations: Software of the Mind, McGraw-Hill, London.

Jain, S. P., Lindsey, C., Agrawal, N., & Maheswaran, D. (2007). For Better or For Worse? Valenced Comparative Frames and Regulatory Focus, *Journal of Consumer Research*, 34, 57-65.

Jeon, J. O., & Beatty, S. E. (2002). Comparative Advertising Effectiveness in Different National Cultures, *Journal of Business Research,* 55, 907-913,

McArthur, K., & Cuneo, A. (2007). Why Big Brands Are Getting Into the Ring, *Advertising Age,* 78 (21), 6-6.

Pechmann, C., & Ratneshwar, S. (1991). The Use of Comparative Advertising For Brand Positioning: Association versus Differentiation, *Journal of Consumer Research*, 18 (2), 145-160.

Polyorat, K., & Alden, D. L. (2005). Self-Construal and Need for Cognition Effects on Brand Attitudes and Purchase Intentions in Response to Comparative Advertising in Thailand and the United States, *Journal of Advertising,* 34 (1), 37-48.

Singelis, T. M., & Brown, W. J. (1995). Culture, Self, and Collectivist Communication: Linking Culture to Individual Behavior, *Human Communication Research,* 21, 354-389.

Thompson, D. V., & Hamilton, R. W. (2006). The Effects of Information Processing Mode on Consumers' Responses to Comparative Advertising, *Journal of Consumer Research*, 32, 530-540.

# Effects of Metaphor on Goal-Oriented Appeals in Advertising

Hongmin Ahn, The University of Texas at Austin, USA
Yongjun Sung, The University of Texas at Austin, USA
Jason Crandall, The University of Texas at Austin, USA

Advertising messages influence one's motivations, views, and perceptions in achieving goals. One of the key techniques to encourage consumers to reinforce or alter their goals is the use of rhetorical figures, such as metaphorical expression (McQuarrie and Mick 1996). While metaphorical claim is the most widely used rhetoric in current advertising practice, little is known about the circumstances under which metaphorical claims are most persuasive. Previous studies tend to focus on the advantages of metaphoric claims as compared with literal claims (e.g., McQuarrie and Phillips 2005), and the persuasive nature of metaphorical claims themselves is not fully investigated. In this article, we adopt regulatory focus theory to investigate the effectiveness of metaphor on enhancing one's goal achievement.

Regulatory focus theory (Higgins 1997) suggests two basic motivational orientations that individuals adopt to achieve their goals: prevention-focus and promotion-focus. Prevention-focus oriented individuals seek to avoid negative outcomes; thus, their concerns are about safety, responsibilities, and obligations (Higgins 1997, 2000). Conversely, promotion-focus oriented individuals, seek to achieve positive goals and are concerned with growth, accomplishment, and aspirations. When people adopt the goal pursuit strategies and engage in activities that are consistent with their regulatory orientation, they experience "feels-it-right" sensation and their motivations become heightened (Aaker and Lee 2006).

Researchers of regulatory orientation have also suggested that not only a match between a manner in which a person pursue a goal and his or her goal orientation, but also the types of message framing (i.e., promotion vs. prevention) in a given context determine the persuasiveness of information. That is, prevention-focused messages are most persuasive at a concrete, detail-oriented level because they allow consumers to maximize the accuracy of their decision outcomes (Mogilner, Aaker, and Pennington 2008). Promotion-focused messages, however, are most persuasive when framed at an abstract level because people who are presented with promotion-focused messages would focus more on the ultimate meaning of an event, as opposed to its concrete details. Mogilner et al. (2008) empirically tested this notion by suggesting that prevention-framed products were more favorable when consumers' purchase decisions are imminent while promotion-framed products were preferred when the purchases did not need to be made immediately.

Given the different characteristics of prevention/promotion goal orientations, it is expected that prevention-focused messages would be more effective when the ad employs literal rhetorical techniques to persuade consumers because these messages provide explicit, concrete means to avoid the negative outcomes. On the other hand, it is expected that promotion-focused messages will be more persuasive when the ad uses metaphorical rhetorical technique because promotion-oriented individuals will focus more on the ultimate meaning of an event. The promotion-focused messages should motivate people to achieve positive outcomes rather than emphasizing a concrete focus (Mogilner et al. 2008). Furthermore, metaphorical claims have been shown to be more advantageous in providing positive outcomes as compared to literal claims because they render consumers more receptive to diverse and positive influences about advertised brands while still conveying the main message of the ad (McQuarrie and Phillips 2005). We conducted an experiment to test these expectations.

## Method

*Stimulus Development.* To develop a set of rigorous metaphoric advertising stimuli, stimulus development procedure followed a multiple-step process. First, professional advertising artists initially created 10 sets of ads carrying various themes of metaphorical verbal expressions that emphasize the benefits of eating cereals. The prevention-focused ads conveyed messages such as, "This cereal helps prevent heart disease" whereas the promotion-focused ads had messages such as, "This cereal helps enhance your heart health." Since the quality of metaphorical expression critically influences participants' evaluations of ads, we conducted several pre-tests to screen out dead or inapt metaphors among these ads. Undergraduate students at a large southern American university evaluated whether ads were creative/imaginative or plain/matter-of-fact (McQuarrie and Mick 1996). Participants also rated the levels of implications of these ads on a seven-point scale anchored by "Almost everyone/no reasonable person would draw this conclusion from the ad." (McQuarrie and Phillips 2005). Through these procedures, we selected a final set of metaphorical ads for the preliminary study.

*Preliminary Analysis.* In order to investigate these hypotheses, we used a 2 (rhetorical styles: metaphorical vs. literal) ´ 2 (goal orientation: prevention vs. promotion) between-subjects factorial design. The dependent variable was attitude toward the advertised brand (a cereal brand). The results of ANOVA indicated that there was a marginally significant interaction effect of rhetorical styles and goal orientations ($F= 3.78, p=. 058$). Direction of the effect was consistent with our expectations. That is, the prevention-focused ad was more favorable ($M= 4.92$) than the promotion focused ad ($M= 4.05$) when participants were shown a set of ads containing literal claims. The promotion-focused ads, however, became more appealing ($M= 4.60$) than prevention-focused ads ($M= 4. 25$) when participants were presented with metaphorical claims.

### Implications and Limitations

McQuarrie and Phillips (2005) argued that, in general, the use of metaphorical claims (vs. literal claims) in ads is more effective to evoke positive attitudes among consumers given its ability to provide diverse references about advertised brands. Our initial phase of the study, however, shows that the goal orientation of the message-framing influences the persuasiveness of metaphors in ads, thus demonstrating a potential limitation on the suitability of metaphorical claims. The results provide useful guidelines for advertising practitioners in effectively utilizing metaphoric techniques in ads. At this stage, we only tested the effectiveness of metaphor in terms of verbal expression (i.e., ad copies) for a routinely purchased commodity. To a better understanding of the nature of persuasiveness in metaphor, future study should incorporate visual metaphors. It may also be worthwhile to investigate if this interaction occurs in other types of purchases.

### Selected References

Aaker, Jennifer L., and Angela Y. Lee (2006), "Understanding Regulatory Fit," *Journal of Marketing Research,* 43(1), 15-19.

Higgins, E. Tory (1987), "Self-Discrepancy: A Theory Relating Self and Affect," *Psychological Review*, 94 (July), 319-40.

_____ (1997), "Beyond Pleasure and Pain," *American Psychologist*, 52 (December), 1280-1300.

McQuarrie, Edward F., and David G. Mick (1996), "Figures of Rhetoric in Advertising Language," *Journal of Consumer Research*, 22 (March), 424-438

_____ , and Barbara J. Phillips (2005), "Indirect Persuasion in Advertising: How Consumers Process Metaphors Presented in Pictures and Words," *Journal of Advertising*, 34(2), 7-20.

Mogilner, Cassie, Jennifer L. Aaker, Ginger L. Pennington (2008), "Time Will Tell: The Distant Appeal of Promotion and Imminent Appeal of Prevention," *Journal of Consumer Research*, 34, 670-681.

# Do I Really Have to Prove Who I Am? The Impact of Identity Denial and Targeted Ads

Bruno Kocher, HEC Paris, France
Luna David, Baruch College, USA

### Extended Abstract

American citizens of foreign origins, who might be born and raised in the United States, frequently have to answer questions such as "do you speak English" or "where are you really from? (Cheryan and Monin 2005). Since they do not match the prototype of the in-group, their belonging to that group is questioned. This phenomenon has been labeled as "identity denial" (Cheryan and Monin 2005). The purpose of this research is to assess consumers' reaction to such an acceptance threat (Branscombe, Ellemers, Spears, and Doosje 1999).

Past consumer research has assessed the impact of in-groups, out-groups and dissociative groups from different perspectives (e.g. Bearden and Etzel 1982; White and Dahl 2007). Consumption (or abandon) of brands/products was advocated to help individuals build their self-concept (e.g. Escalas and Bettman 2005) or to differentiate them from out-group members adopting these tastes (Berger and Heath 2007, 2008).

However, to the best of our knowledge, no research has assessed the impact of identity denial on consumers' attitudes. Cheryan and Monin (2005) demonstrate that identity denial leads to an increase in respondents' effort to show cultural knowledge and claims to participate in in-group practices. Nevertheless, we currently do not know to which extent this phenomenon affects consumers' consumption decisions, brand/product attitudes and perception of advertisement executions.

### Theoretical Background

*Ethnic identities.* Advertisers frequently use ethnic cues in order to target members of ethnic groups. Past research has shown that, in general, consumers targeted by this tactic respond in a positive manner (Whittler 1989, 1991). According to Deshpandé and Stayman (1994), ethnic minorities (vs. ethnic majorities) evaluate spokespersons from the same ethnic background as more trustworthy. Subsequently, this increased trustworthiness leads to higher brand attitudes. Most of past research has assessed ethnic cues from an in-group versus out-group perspective. Respondents were primed by (or exposed to) ads containing (vs. not containing) a cue specific to their ethnicity. As Deshpandé and Stayman (1994), we are interested in trustworthiness or honesty of advertisers. However, the present study takes a different look at the implementation of ethnic primes. More precisely, we are interested by the impact of a prime which denies membership to a group, even though the person objectively belongs to that group. In other words, the purpose is to assess how consumers react to ethnically targeted ads when they are denied one of their identities and, concomitantly remembered of another one.

*Identity denial.* As stated by Cheryan and Monin (2005, p. 718) "whereas stereotypes threat (Steele 1997) is the fear of being seen in a negative light because of one's group membership, identity denial is the fear of not being seen as part of the in-group at all". Rejection from an important group may frustrate the basic need of belonging (Baumeister and Leary 1995; Eisenberger, Liberman and Williams 2003). As demonstrated by Schmitt and Branscombe (2001), when people are targeted by a social identity threat, they alter their subsequent behavior. The reaction to an identity denial is to assert one's identity in order to prove to others than one really belongs to that in-group (Cheryan and Monin 2005).

**Study**

*Procedure.* Forty-three American citizens from Chinese origins were recruited through flyers on the campus of a major East Coast university. After entering the lab, subjects were asked (or not) about their knowledge of English (do you speak English?). This question represents the identity denial manipulation. As shown by previous researchers (Cheryan and Monin 2005), this interrogation makes respondents think about their membership of the group. After this question, they received a fake magazine directed toward Chinese American or American respondents. The magazine contained the ad for a fictitious brand (Expert Financial Services) as well as some filler ads and articles. In the magazine directed toward Americans, the ad was in English. The magazine directed toward Chinese Americans was exactly the same, except that the brand name in the ads was written in English and in Chinese characters. After having scanned the magazine, respondents were asked to respond to a short survey.

*Results.* A 2 X 2 ANOVA was conducted with perceived honesty (2 items: dishonest-honest, insincere-sincere) of the magazine and the ad as dependent variables and identity denial (identity denial vs. no identity denial) and type of ad (ad targeted toward Americans vs. ad targeted toward Chinese) as independent variables. The two-way interaction between identity denial and type of ad was significant for the perceived honesty toward the magazine ($F(1, 42)=4.17$, $p<.05$). Planned contrasts revealed that when the respondents' identity was denied, they rated the magazine directed toward Americans ($M_{american}=5.75$, SD=.84) as more honest than the magazine directed toward Chinese Americans ($M_{chinese-american}=4.94$, SD=0.85; $F(1, 39)=4.03$, p=.052). However, this was not the case when their identity was not denied ($M_{american}=5.00$, SD=.97, $M_{chinese-american}=5.38$, SD=1.06; $F(1, 39)=.81$, p=.375).

The two-way interaction between identity denial and type of ad was marginally significant for the perceived honesty toward the brand ($F(1, 43)=3.63$, p=.06). Planned contrasts revealed that when the respondents' identity was denied, they rated the brand directed toward Americans ($M_{american}=5.33$, SD=1.02) as more honest than the brand directed toward Chinese Americans ($M_{chinese-american}=4.40$, SD=1.79; $F(1, 40)=3.17$, p=.083). However, this was not the case when their identity was not denied ($M_{american}=4.55$, SD=.86, $M_{chinese-american}=5.04$, SD=1.12; $F(1, 40)=.85$, p=.363). These results support our proposition that identity denial affects consumers' perception toward the magazines as well as toward brands targeting certain type of consumers.

As a next step, a series of experiments, which are currently executed, are testing the effect of other moderators on this relationship. These moderators include the impact of acculturation and strength of identity. Moreover, we also varied the identity denial manipulation in order to increase its external validity. We hope this research will be a first step in the understanding of the relationship between denial and consumption.

**References**

Baumeister, Roy .F., and Mark R. Leary (1995), "The need to belong: Desire for interpersonal attachments as a fundamental human motivation", *Psychological Bulletin*, 117, 497-529.

Bearden, William O. and Michael Etzel (1982), "Reference group influence on product and brand purchase decisions", *Journal of Consumer Research*, 9 (September), 183-194.

Berger, Jonah and Chip Heath (2007), "Where consumers diverge from others: Identity signaling and product domains", *Journal of Consumer Research*, 34 (August), 121-134.

_____ (2008), "Who drives divergence? Identity signaling, outgroup dissimilarity and the abandonment of cultural tastes", *Journal of Personality and Social Psychology*, 95 (3), 593-607.

Branscombe, Nyla R., Noami Ellemers, Russell Spears, and Bertjan Doosje (1999), "The context and content of social identity threat", In N. Ellemers, R. Spears, & B. Doosje (Eds.), *Social identity: Context, commitment, content* (pp. 35-58). Oxford, UK: Blackwell.

Cheryan, Sapna and Benoît Monin (2005), ""Where are you really from?" Asian American and identity denial", *Journal of Personality and Social Psychology*, 89 (5), 717-730.

Deshpandé, Rohit and Douglas M. Stayman (1994), "A tale of two cities: Distinctiveness theory and advertising effectiveness", *Journal of Marketing Research*, 31 (February), 57-64.

Eisenberger, Naomi I., Matthew D. Lieberman, and Kipling D. Williams (2003), "Does rejection hurt? An fMRI study of social exclusion", *Science*, 302, 290-292.

Escalas, Jennifer and James Bettman (2005), "Self-construal, reference groups, and brand meaning", *Journal of Consumer Research*, 32 (December), 378-389.

Schmitt, Michael T. and Nyla R. Branscombe (2001), "The good, the bad, and the manly: Threats to one's prototypicality and evaluations of fellow in-group members", *Journal of Experimental Social Psychology*, 37, 510–17.

White, Katherine and Darren W. Dahl (2007), "Are all out-groups created equal? Consumer identity and dissociative influence", *Journal of Consumer Research*, 34 (December), 525-536.

Whittler, Tommy E. (1989), "Viewers' Pro-cessing of Actor's Race and Message Claims in Advertising Stimuli", *Psychology and Marketing*, 6 (2), 287-309.

_____ (1991), "The effects of actors' race in commercial advertising: Review and extension", *Journal of Advertising*, 20 (1), 54-60.

# Do Males Endorse Thin Ideal for Women When the Price is High?

Maxim Polonsky, University of Connecticut, USA

Ioannis Kareklas, University of Connecticut, USA

## Extended Abstract

Marketers claim that thin models are very efficient in selling products (Gillian, 2000). Research findings show that consumers generally associate thin with happiness, desirability, and status (Tiggermann, 2003). On the other hand, marketers and advertisers have been criticized for using thin models which adversely affect young women's self-esteem and body satisfaction (Martin and Gentry 1997). Hence, marketer's dilemma is evident: images that are most effective in selling products may also harm consumers the most. For example, Dittmar and Howard (2004) have shown that while the exposure to thin ideals in ads may harm an individual's body esteem, there is no difference between thin and average-size models in terms of advertising effectiveness (i.e. product and ad evaluation, and purchase intention).

Further, research indicates that omnipresence of idealized thin models has a cross-gender effect (Lavine, Sweeney, and Wagner 1999). Proliferation of thin-ideal images in male consumed media may lead to males' endorsement of thinness for women. Because men often influence, advice and participate in women's shopping decisions, we focus our investigation on males and ask whether body size of advertising models influences males' perception of product quality, price, and willingness to recommend and/or buy the advertised product for women.

Our experiment employs a between-subject 3 x 2 factorial design, investigating the effect of exposure condition (ads featuring thin models, plus-size models, and average models) and price (low and high) on the following outcomes: 1) advertising effectiveness (ad attitude, perceived product quality, model attitude, and purchase intention and 2) body-esteem and intentions to diet and lose weight. We introduce price variable as an important and potentially powerful moderator of body size effects on aforementioned dependent variables. Furthermore, because thin is associated with status, the absence of research on body size and price interaction is puzzling. We manipulate price in order to investigate whether price interacts with model body size and to determine under which conditions body and price create the perception of quality and elicit generally more favorable attitudes toward advertisements.

One hundred and sixty males participated in the online experiment. Upon login onto the website, participants were randomized into one of the six conditions and told that that they are participating in a marketing research study that explores different communication and appeal strategies (print vs. video, reading detailed information versus watching a short ad, etc.) for two product categories–computers and women shoes. After completing pre-test, participants in each condition were referred to CNET.com page "Best 5 desktops" (http://reviews.cnet.com/best-desktops/?tag=leftColumnArea1.0) or similar updated page, and asked to read short one-paragraph review for each of the five computers. Next, participants answered filler questions about their liking, preference, and purchase intention for any of the reviewed computers. Upon the completion, study participants saw the experimental ad and filled a post-test questionnaire that consisted of a) questions about advertising effectiveness (e.g. ad evaluation, purchase intention), and b) questions about attitudes toward and behavioral intentions to diet and lose weight. Participants were deceived that the later part of the post-test was an unrelated small scale study that would be used to design local health marketing campaign. Six ads used in the study were separately pre-tested on one hundred and twenty undergraduate students. Our manipulation was successful.

To examine the effects of price and model body size on our dependent variables, we conducted a 2 (price: high and low) x 3 (model body size: thin, average, plus size) MANOVA Our results showed significant main effects of price [Wilks' $\lambda$=.71, $F(6, 120)$=8.13, $p$<.001], of model body size [Wilks' $\lambda$=.81, $F(12, 240)$=2.83, $p$=.013], and a significant two-way interaction (Wilks' $\lambda$=.80, $F(12, 240)$=2.24, $p$=.011). For two independent variables, there were four significant main effects: the effects of body size on perception of price (F (2, 147)=3.31, p=.04), and model attitude (F (2, 147)=4.82, p=.01), and the effect of price on model attitude (F (1, 148)=4.27, p=.04) and perceived product quality (F (1, 146)=4.43, p=.037). The interaction of price with model body size was significant for all dependent variables, save body esteem, price perception, and product quality.

We describe main effects that are not complicated by the presence of significant interaction first. We find that price was evaluated least favorably in a plus-size model condition, and there were no statistically significant difference in price evaluations between the ads featuring thin and average models (p=.18). Main effect of price on product quality revealed that higher price signaled higher quality (p=.037). Follow-up univariate post-hoc comparisons between groups revealed that consumers' attitude toward the ad was the least favorable in a high price average body condition; in a low price condition, however, average model elicited more positive ad attitudes relative to thin and plus-size models. Further, our findings indicate that thin model was evaluated more positively relative to plus size and average models only in a high price condition. In a low price condition average model was preferred. We expected higher values of purchase intention when thin model was paired with high price. Although mean value for purchase intention for this particular condition was the highest, it was not significantly different from plus size model in the same condition. Again, we find that average model had a positive effect on purchase intention in a low price condition and negative effect in a high price condition. In a low price condition, the purchase intention was the lowest for thin model.

Last but not least, although price and body size manipulation did not affect males' body-esteem, there was an interaction effect of two independent variables on intention to diet. Specifically, males exposed to a thin model paired with high price, were more likely to indicate their intention to diet and lose weight. We focus our discussion on these controversial findings while more data is being collected.

## References

Dittmar, Helga and Sarah Howard (2004), "Thin-ideal Internalization and Social Comparison Tendency as Moderators of Media Models' Impact on Women's Body-focused Anxiety," *Journal of Social and Clinical Psychology,* 23, 747-770.

Gillian, A. (2000, may 31). Skinny models 'send unhealthy message'. The Guardian, p. 7.

Lavine, Howard, Donna Sweeney, and Stephen H. Wagner (1999), "Depicting Women as Sex Objects in Television Adverting: Effects on Body Dissatisfaction," *Personality and Social Psychology Bulletin,* 25 (August), 1049-1058.

Martin, Mary C. and James W. Gentry (1997), "Stuck in the Model Trap: The Effects of Beautiful Models in Ads on Female Pre-Adolescents and Adolescents," *Journal of Advertising,* 26 (Summer), 19–33.

Tiggemann, M. (2003). Media exposure, body dissatisfaction and disordered eating: Television and magazines are not the same! *European Eating Disorders Review, 11,* 418-430.

# Who Said Multitasking is Bad? The Benefits of Doing Two Things at The Same Time

Sydney Chinchanachokchai, University of Illinois, USA
Brittany Duff, University of Illinois, USA
Robert S. Wyer, University of Illinois, USA

Consumers are often multitaskers, turning on a TV while flipping through a magazine or talking on a cell phone while browsing through grocery aisles. In everyday life, people often engage in multiple tasks at the same time. Multitasking behavior in consumers is an area underexplored yet important for marketers to understand in its impact on advertising effectiveness.

Although multitasking has been explored in psychology and consumer research, most studies show that when people perform two tasks simultaneously, their performance on one or both tasks decreases (Hembrooke & Gay 2003). In some cases, however, performing a secondary task can actually increase one's attention to a primary task by preventing one's mind from wandering and, therefore, may increase performance on the primary task and memory for the material that is relevant to it (Andrade 2009). This paper presents a preliminary look at why this difference may occur, particularly in an advertising context, and how multitasking affects memory under different levels of involvement.

In the situation where the two tasks are not equally cognitive demanding, the performance of one task may benefit the others. Performance decrements through competition for task-specific resources are moderated when the secondary task reduces the mind-wandering that can be a hidden feature of single task control conditions (Smallwood et al 2007). fMRI studies have also shown that as central executive demands of tasks decrease, stimulus-independent thought (mind-wandering) increases (Mason et al 2007). These stimulus-irrelevant thoughts have been shown to lower performance on memory tasks (Seibert& Ellis 1991), showing that there might not always be straightforward effects of multitasking on consumer memory.

One exception to the lack of research on multitasking and advertising is Shapiro and Krishnan (2001). In this study, attention was divided by playing an audio program at the same time ads were shown on slides. However, this study compared dual-task groups and did not look at possible detrimental effects of a single-task, particularly when the single-task is not involving.

The concept of involvement is an important moderator of the amount and type of information processing elicited by a persuasive communication (Petty & Cacioppo 1981). High-involvement messages have greater personal relevance and consequences or elicit more personal connections than low-involvement messages (Krugman 1965). According to the elaboration likelihood model, as product increases in personal relevance or consequences, people are more motivated to devote cognitive effort required to evaluate it when involvement is high rather than low (Petty et al 1983). High involvement also leads to greater attention and comprehension (Celsi& Olson 1988). When the level of involvement is high, consumers are more motivated to process salient product information in advertisements. They also exert greater cognitive effort during comprehension of the ads, increasingly focusing their attention on the product-related information (Celsi & Olson 1988). Therefore, people who are performing a low cognitive-demand task (such as doodling) while low-involvement ads are presented should recognize product and ad points more than those who are not performing the task. A high-involvement ad may be able to draw attention from the audience by itself, therefore, the low demand task should not help ad memory in this case.

A study was conducted to examine the effect of a low cognitive demand secondary task on memory. In this experiment, we used doodling as a secondary task. Participants (n= 77; 2x2 (Task x Involvement)) were told to listen to a series of monotonous radio commercials as if they were listening to the radio at home and form an impression toward the ads. Participants were randomly assigned into one of the two conditions (dual-task vs. single-task). In the dual-task condition, they performed a "doodling task" while listening to the commercials. Participants were provided paper with shapes on the left hand side and asked to copy the target shapes into the blank spaces. The single-task group only listened to the ads. There were two versions of the target commercial: high and low involvement. Each group heard five radio ads with four ads that were the same for all groups. The target commercial (high or low involvement) was placed at the end in order to generate a boredom effect. After the commercials finished playing, participants wrote down their impression and answered filler questions about the other ads that played and then performed a recognition task on 15 product and ad points (correct and foil).

A separate group (n= 23) rated only the high or low involvement ad (no other ads or tasks) confirmed the high-involvement ad was easier to pay attention to, was less boring, and had a more interesting product than the low-involvement ad

The results supported the hypotheses. There was a significant interaction effect between doodle task and the level of involvement on the ad recognition [$F(1,73)=7.89, p< 0.01$]. Participants in the dual-task group scored lower than the single-task group in the recognition task when the target ad was high-involvement. Importantly, the opposite was true for the low-involvement condition. Dual-task participants actually scored higher in the ad recognition task than the single-task participants.

There is a significant main effect of involvement on the target ad [$F(1,73)=8.65, p< 0.01$]. Participants in both groups rated the target ad in the high-involvement condition as more interesting than in the low-involvement condition. As expected, the effect was not significant for other ads (p's>.1, n.s.), Indicating the manipulation worked as intended. There was also a significant interaction in self-reported boredom between two groups $F(1,73)=6.7, p< 0.05$. Specifically, for those that listened to the low-involvement ad, the dual-task condition was less bored than the single-task condition. However, in the high-involvement condition, the difference in boredom was not significant. This indicates that the secondary task keeps participants from being bored especially when they are not interested in the primary task (ads).

Multitasking is not always inefficient and sometimes can actually help memory, particularly in low-involvement conditions. Future studies will examine in more depth the role of mind-wandering and stimulus independent thought as well as the limits of the effect in terms of task load, the role of goals in multitasking. as well as individual differences such as attentional control.

## Selected References

Andrade, Jackie (2009), "What Does Doodling Do?", *Applied Cognitive Psychology*, Published online by Wiley InterScience.

Celsi, Richard. L. and Jerry C. Olson (1988), "The Role of Involvement in Attention and Comprehension Processes," *Journal of Consumer Research*, 15, 210-224.

Hembrooke, Helene and Geri Gay (2003), "The Laptop and the Lecture: The Effects of Multitasking in Learning Environments," *Journal of Computing in Higher Education*, 15(1).

Kahneman, Daniel (1973), "Attention and Effort," Englewood Cliffs, NJ: Prentice-Hall.

Krugman, Herbert E. (1965), "The Impact of Television Advertising: Learning Without Involvement," *Public Opinion Quarterly*, 29(Fall), 349-356.

Maison, Malia, et al (2007), "Wandering Minds: The Default Network and Stimulus-Independent Thought," *Science*, 315, 393-395.

Petty, Richard E. and John T. Cacioppo (1981), "Attitudes and Persuasion: Classic and Contemporary Approaches," Dubuque, IA: William C.Brown.

Petty, Richard E. and John T. Cacioppo, and David Schumann (1983) "Central and Peripheral Routes to Advertising Effectiveness: The Moderating Rold of Involvement," *Journal of Consumer Research*, 10, 135-146.

Seibert, Pennie and Henry Ellis (1991), "Irrelevant Thoughts, emotional mood states and cognitive task performance," *Memory & Cognition*, 19(5), 507-513

Shapiro, Stewart and H. Shanker Krishnan (2001), "Memory-Based Measures for Assessing Advertising Effects: A comparison of Explicit and Implicit Memory Effects," *Journal of Advertising*, 30(3), 1-13.

Smallwood, Jonathan, Rory C. O'Connor, Megan Sudbery, and Marc Obonsawin (2007), "Mind-wandering and Dysphoria," *Cognition and Emotion*, 21, 816–842.

# Increasing Persuasion While Decreasing Recognition: Exploring the Interactive Effects of Product Placements on Consumers in a State of Ego-Depletion

Brian Gillespie, Washington State University, USA

Jeff Joireman, Washington State University, USA

The majority of people who watch television, watch during evening "primetime" hours. While they watch, they are frequently exposed to product placements stemming from a $3.36 billion dollar industry (PQ Media 2007). Importantly, before people sit down to watch primetime television, most spend their day regulating their behavior (e.g. being at work when they would rather be golfing, or working to put their kids to bed when it would be easier to just let them stay up). Past research suggests that engaging in such tasks is likely to lead to a state of "ego-depletion" (Baumeister 2002). This is important because past research shows that ego-depletion interferes with cognitive functioning on challenging intellectual tasks (Schmeichel, Vohs and Baumeister 2003). Furthermore, past research has shown when cognitive resources are limited and individuals have no motivation to process a message, the message is processed peripherally and persuasiveness (positive impact on attitudes) increases (Petty, Cacioppo and Schumann 1983).

This suggests two hypotheses. First, when viewers are in a state of ego-depletion, they may be more positively influenced by lower plot connection (LPC) product placements—products that are subtle and not connected to the plot in a meaningful manner—because LPC placements offering no motivation for the viewer to process the placement. Motivation to process higher plot connection (HPC) product placements—products that are blatant and connected to the plot in a meaningful manner—does exist, so no differences between conditions are expected. Second, the lack of cognitive resources available will interfere with ego-depleted viewers' ability to recognize LPC placements. HPC placements, however, are so blatant that all individuals will recognize them. This reasoning led to the following two hypotheses:

H1: For LPC product placements, individuals in an ego-depleted condition will experience a significant increase in brand attitudes. There will be no difference for HPC product placements.

H2: For LPC product placements, individuals in an ego-depleted condition will experience a significant decrease in brand recognition. There will be no difference for HPC product placements.

## Method

Participants were 50 undergraduate students participating for course credit. Two participants' results were dropped due to their inability to follow instructions. Participants arrived and participated in the study individually. The experimenter was blind to participants' condition.

Upon arrival, half the participants were given instructions designed to result in ego-depletion. We used a standard attention regulation based ego-depletion manipulation (Schmeichel et al. 2003). Following the ego-depletion manipulation, participants watched an episode of a popular 30 minute primetime comedy television show from a major television network. The episode used in this study was chosen because pilot testing—on a different group of participants—indicated that participants liked the show, recognized the brands involved in the product placements, and had neutral brand attitudes toward those products. After participants watched the show, they reported their attitudes toward brands that were and were not placed in the show using a 7-point likert scale (1=strongly dislike to 7=strongly like). After participants evaluated the brands, they completed a recognition task in which they indicated the brands they recognized seeing in the show.

## Major Findings

*Manipulation Checks.* After the ego-depletion manipulation, participants rated the difficultly of the video-viewing task. As expected, participants in the ego-depletion condition reported that the task was significantly more difficult than participants in the control condition ( $p$=.001). To rule out mood as an alternative explanation, participants also completed a mood scale. Results showed no significant difference between the conditions in negative or positive mood ($p$>.58). These results suggest a successful ego-depletion manipulation that is not confounded with mood.

*Hypothesis Tests.* To begin the analysis, we first standardized the participant's reported brand attitudes and recognition using z-scores. We did this for two reasons. First, in standardizing scores, we were able to control for previous participant attitudes toward products. Second, in standardizing the data, we were able to compare brand recognition and brand attitudes on the same scale.

A 2 x 2 x 3 (Control vs. Ego-depletion, Attitudes vs. Recognition, LPC vs. HPC vs. Not placed) mixed model ANOVA, revealed a significant three way interaction, $F(2,45)$=6.14, $p$<.01. We followed this up by examining the simple 2 x 2 (Control vs. Ego-depletion, Attitudes vs. Recognition) interaction within each level of "plot connection" (low, high, not placed).

The 2 x 2 interaction was not significant within either the not placed or the high plot connection conditions. However, in the LPC condition, there was a significant interaction between conditions, $F(1,46)$=7.42, $p$<.01. We further explored the simple effect of ego depletion on attitudes and recognition. Consistent with hypothesis 1, brand attitudes were higher among those in the ego depletion condition (M=.24) than those in the control condition (M=-.24), $F(1,46)$=2.77, $p$=.05 (one-tailed). Also, consistent with hypothesis 2, recognition was higher among those in the control condition (M=.29) than those in the ego depletion condition (M=-.29), $F(1,46)$=4.18, $p$<.05 (one-tailed).

## Conclusion

To date, most product placement research has focused on either the nature of the placement, such as its connection to the plot (Russell 2002), or pre-existing differences between viewers such as viewers' connection to the show (Cowley and Barron 2008) or its actors (Russell and Stern 2006). The current paper expands product placement research by exploring whether the effectiveness of product placements depends on temporary variations in viewers' self-regulatory strength. Assuming that there is little motivation for individuals to process LPC product placements, we hypothesized (and found) that ego-depletion increased brand attitudes toward LPC product placements while at the same time decreasing recognition of those same brands. These effects suggest that while ego-depleted individuals are less aware of LPC placements than non ego-depleted individuals, they are more positively persuaded by those placements. The present results underscore the importance of ego-depletion for research on product placement.

## References

Baumeister, Roy F. (2002), "Yielding to Temptation: Self-Control Failure, Impulsive Purchasing, and Consumer Behavior," *Journal of Consumer Research*, 28 (March), 670-676.

Cowley, Elizabeth and Chris Barron (2008), "When Product Placement Goes Wrong: The Effects of Program Liking and Placement Prominence," *Journal of Advertising*, 37 (1), 89-98.

Petty, Richard E., John T. Cacioppo and David Schumann (1983), "Central and Peripheral Routes to Advertising Effectiveness: The Moderating Role of Involvement," *Journal of Consumer Research*, 10 (Sept), 135-146.

PQ Media (2007), "Global Product Placement Forecast 2006-2010," available at http://www.pqmedia.com/global-product-placement-2006.html.

Russell, Cristel (2002), "Investigating the Effectiveness of Product Placements in Television Shows: The Role of Modality and Plot Connection Congruence on Brand Memory and Attitude," *Journal of Consumer Research*, 29 (Dec), 306-318.

_____ and Barbara B. Stern (2006), "Consumers, Characters, and Products: A Balance Model of Sitcom Product Placement Effects," *Journal of Advertising*, 35 (1), 7-21.

Schmeichel, Brandon, Kathleen D. Vohs and Roy F. Baumeister (2003), "Intellectual Performance and Ego Depletion: Role of the Self in Logical Reasoning and Other Information Processing," *Journal of Personality and Social Psychology*, 85 (1), 33-46.

# True Lies in Online Research: How to Determine Accuracy in Web Surveys

Boris Toma, University of Mannheim, Germany
Daniel Heinrich, University of Mannheim, Germany
Hans H. Bauer, University of Mannheim, Germany

## Extended Abstract

The growth and diffusion of the Internet have led to a rapid devlopment of surveys on the World Wide Web (WWW) by opening new opportunities for collecting and disseminating research information. Existing research on web surveys has mainly focused on comparing internet-based and traditional mail surveys or on combining existing evidence into a meta-analysis (Cook, Heath, and Thompson 2000; Ilieva, Baron, and Healey 2002; Sheehan 2001; Shermis and Lombard 1999). Main focus has thereby been placed on response rates. While methodological research around response quality in online surveys is still limited (O'Neil and Penrod 2001; Deutskens et al.

2004), past research has mainly determined data quality by strictly quantitative measures such as the number of omitted items (item-nonresponse) or dropouts (Goeritz 2004; O'Neil and Penrod 2001; Tuten, Galesic, and Bosnjak 2004; Frick, Baechtiger, and Reips 2001). Little or no attention has been paid to the motivation and attitude of respondents, and the question whether respondents give accurate answers to survey questions.

In two experimental studies, we propose mechanisms, which are appropriate to identify inaccurate response behavior. In our first survey, we provide an intencive and examine three groups, which have been recruited by (1) email, (2) online panel and (3) virtual communities. By determining the data quality of the three experimental groups, we are able to draw conclusions on effective indicators for accurate response behavior in online surveys. In order to explore whether results will vary when no incentives are given, we conduct a second study replicating our first one.

In the context of surveys, data quality is merely a function of the amount of error in the data. The more accurate the data (or: the less erroneous the data), the higher is the quality of the data (Biemer and Lyberg 2003). An approach that focuses on accuracy and that is often used for analyzing the several different sources of error in surveys is the total survey error (Groves et al. 2009). Following Assael and Keon (1982, 115), total survey error is "a function of the difference between the overall population's mean true value and the mean observed value obtained from the respondents of a particular sample" and can be measured by the mean squared error. But even though Weisberg (2005) elaborates the importance of response behavior within the concept of total survey error, existing literature mostly examines data quality on the basis of indicators such as item-nonresponse or dropouts and gives recommendations on how to design questionnaires in order to minimize error (MacElroy 2000; Deutskens et al. 2004). However, even a perfect questionnaire does not necessarily prevent respondents from giving inaccurate answers.

Thus, it is imperative to broaden the scope on the response process when determining data quality. An accurate response requires going through all of the four stages of the response process (Tourangeau 1984), but not all of the respondents do so. In fact, this depends on the respondent's motivation and other factors (Tourangeau, Rips, and Rasinski 2000). Incentives are a widely spread means of motivating people (Manfreda and Vehovar 2008). Past research shows that incentives do raise response rates and motivate respondents to finish surveys (Tuten, Bosnjak and Bandilla 2000). Nevertheless, the impact of the incentive depends on the whole context of the web survey, especially on the way of recruiting and the population targeted (Manfreda and Vehovar 2008).

Hence, in study 1 we conducted an experimental web survey by using a 1x3 design, with the form of recruiting (email, online panel, and virtual community) as the independant variable and the data quality as the dependant variable. Respondents in the first group were invited by an email that was sent from their e-mail hosting service. The second group was made up of online panelists, who regularly participate in online surveys. Respondents from group three were acquired by web banners in virtual communities such as facebook. The three groups (n=532) were exposed to the same questionnaire, which consisted of several questions and items. These mechanisms allow us to check the respondent's motivation and manipulation attempts and thus the response accuracy. For instance, we asked the same question on different scales (semantic differential versus Likert scaling). We also checked the length of answers in an open question as well as the misspelling. Alltogether we developed more than 15 of these mechanisms. The three groups in our first study were promised an incentive for completing the questionnaire. As the panelists were paid in bonus points, we set a voucher for an online music store as incentive for the email and virtual community group. To ensure comparability, the voucher amounted to the cash equivalent of the bonus points (€ 1). In order to determine data quality we used the total survey error approach. The empirical values for each group were externally validated so that the mean squared error could be computed. By this means, the mean squared error compared empirical and true values and alluded to accuracy of data within the three groups. By using this measure, we were able to determine data quality.

In study 2 the experrriment was replicated with the same parameters but without an incentive for the respondents. We ought to examine whether intrinsic motivation, such as altruistic or issue-oriented factors, results in higher data quality than extrinsic motivation, and if yes whether different mechanisms of response behavior account for that.

Our research shows that the respondents who were acquired in virtual communities give the most accurate answers. This is in accordance with prior research, as people in virtual communities tend to be more faithful and talkative (Williams 2001). In opposition to the academic literature, the virtual community group that received an incentive features higher data quality than the non-incentive group, but still the quality of the group without incentive is high. Moreover, first results show that we identified several mechanisms (questions and items) with focus on the respondent's motivation that effectively determine data quality. We therefore propose to implement these mechanisms into future studies and surveys in order to revise our findings.

## References

Assael, Henry and John Keon (1982), "Nonsampling vs. sampling errors in survey research," *Journal of Marketing*, 46(2), 114-23.

Biemer, Paul P. and Lars E. Lyberg (2003), *Introduction to Survey Quality*, Hoboken, NJ: Wiley.

Cook, Colleen, Fred Heath, and Russell Thompson (2000), "A Meta-Analysis of Response Rates in Web- or Internet-Based Surveys," *Educational & Psychological Measurement*, 60(6), 821-36.

Deutskens, Elisabeth, Ko de Ruyter, Martin Wetzels, and Paul Oosterveld (2004), "Response Rate and Response Quality of Internet-Based Surveys: An Experimental Study," *Marketing Letters*, 15(1), 21-36.

Frick, Andrea, Marie T. Baechtiger, and Ulf D. Reips (2001), "Financial Incentives, Personal Information and Drop Out in Online Studies," in *Dimensions of Internet Science*, ed. Ulf D. Reips, Michael Bosnjak, Lengerich: Pabst Science Publishers, 209-20.

Goeritz, Anja S. (2004), "The Impact of Material Incentives on Response Quantity, Response Quality, Sample Composition, Survey Outcome, and Cost in Online Access Panels," *International Journal of Market Research*, 46(3), 327-45.

Groves, Robert M., Floyd J Fowler Jr., Mick P. Couper, James M. Lepkowski, Eleanor Singer, and Roger Tourangeau (2009), *Survey Methodology*, Hoboken, NJ: Wiley.

Ilieva, Janet, Steve Baron, and Nigel M. Healey (2002), "Online Surveys in Marketing Research: Pros and Cons," *International Journal of Market Research*, 44(3), 361-82.

MacElroy, Bill (2000), "Variables influencing dropout rates in Web-based surveys", *Quirk's Marketing Research Review*, 2000 (June).

Manfreda, Katja L. and Vasja Vehovar (2008), "Internet Surveys," in *The International Handbook of Survey Methodology*, ed. Edit D. De Leeuw, Joop J. Hox, Don A. Dillman, New York, NY: Erlbaum, 264-84.

O'Neil, Kevin M. and Steven D. Penrod (2001), "Webbased Research: Methodological Variables' Effects on Dropout and Sample Characteristics," *Behavior Research Methods, Instruments, & Computers*, 33(2), 226-33.

Sheehan, Kim B. (2001), "E-mail Survey Response Rates: A Review," *Journal of Computer-Mediated Communication*, 6(2), 1-20.

Shermis, Mark D. and Danielle Lombard (1999), "A Comparison of Survey Data Collected by Regular Mail and Electronic Mail Questionnaires," *Journal of Business & Psychology*, 14(2), 341-54.

Tourangeau, Roger (1984), "Cognitive Sciences and Survey Methods," in *Cognitive Aspects of Survey Methodology: Building a Bridge Between Disciplines*, ed. Thomas B. Jabine, Miron L. Straf, Judith M. Tanur, and Roger Tourangeau, Washington D.C.: National Academy Press, 73-100.

Tourangeau, Roger, Lance J. Rips, and Kenneth Rasinski (2000), *The Psychology of Survey Response*, New York, NY: Cambridge University Press.

Tuten, Tracy L., Michael Bosnjak, and Wolfgang Bandilla (2000), "Banner-advertised Web surveys," *Marketing Research*, 11(4), 17-21.

Tuten, Tracy L., Mirta Galesic, and Michael Bosnjak (2004), "Effects of Immediate Versus Delayed Notification of Prize Draw Results on Response Behavior in Web Surveys: An Experiment," *Social Science Computer Review*, 22 (3), 377-84.

Weisberg, Herbert F. (2005), *The Total Survey Error Approach*, Chicago: University of Chicago Press.

Williams, Michele (2001), "In whom we trust: Group membership as an affective context for trust development," *Academy of Management Review*, 26(3), 377-96.

# Attitudes and Behaviors Assessment: The Impact of the Hypothetical Bias

Caroline Roux, McGill University, Canada

Ulf Böckenholt, McGill University, Canada and Northwestern University, USA

## Extended Abstract

Surveys consistently show that people are voicing strong support for environmental protection, but they seem to be paying lip service when an investigator asks whether they are taking actions to save the planet from climate change (Dolliver 2008). But why do environmentally conscious consumers tend to express recurrent equivocal or "aspirational" commitment to the environment (Dolliver 2008)? According to Cotte and Trudel (2009), we should not be surprised that consumers state to hold very positive attitudes toward the environment when surveyed about their environmental opinions, since survey researchers seem to rarely try to find subtle ways of eliciting more "true" responding. This suggests that the way consumers are surveyed about their pro-environmental attitudes and behavioral intentions can hinder their "true" reporting, and the goal of this paper is to better understand how survey formats can influence attitudinal and behavioral assessments.

## Background

The hypothetical bias is an overestimation of willingness to pay in hypothetical or contingent markets, when compared to actual payments in otherwise identical real cash markets (Ajzen, Brown, and Carvajal 2004). This bias also applies to contingent valuation in the context of a referendum, where individuals that are confronted with a real referendum about contributing money to a worthy goal express less favorable reactions with respect to voting yes than individuals who are confronted with a hypothetical referendum (Ajzen, Brown, and Carvajal 2004). This suggests that hypothetical and real contexts are construed in very different ways, that they are qualitatively different, and that questions posed in such contexts can elicit very different responses (Ajzen, Brown, and Carvajal 2004). Moreover, according to Ajzen, Brown and Carvajal (2004), statements of willingness to pay in a hypothetical situation can be equated to behavioral intentions and the hypothetical bias to a discrepancy between intentions and behavior. We thus hypothesize that people should express different levels of attitudes in different contexts:

H1: People express stronger attitudes and behavioral intentions in a hypothetical context than in a real one.

Different ways to adjust for the bias have been demonstrated, but they mainly apply to contingent valuation studies (e.g., asking participants to respond as if they were really spending their money; Ajzen, Brown, and Carvajal 2004). However, it seems that for contingent valuation survey to elicit useful information about willingness-to-pay, respondents must understand exactly what they are being asked to value (Johnston 2006). Hence, familiarity may lead to closer correspondence between intentions and behavior, and thus reduce or even eliminate the hypothetical bias (Johnston 2006). We thus hypothesize that familiarity could moderate the effect:

H2: People express similar attitudes and behavioral intentions in both concrete and hypothetical conditions when surveyed about familiar behaviors.

Furthermore, when people are asked to report an attitude, they often infer this attitude from the implications of a past behavior that happens to be salient to them at the time of the reporting (Albarracin and Wyer 2000). In fact, subjective judgments of attitude certainty, intensity, and importance are affected by the subjective ease of retrieval of experiences that accompany the recollection of attitude-relevant information (Haddock et al. 1999). In addition, construal level theory states that people represent hypothetical tasks in a more abstract, high-level terms, and real tasks in a more concrete, low-level terms (Armor and Sackett 2006; Trope, Liberman, and Wakslak 2007). Consequently, we hypothesize that reporting behavioral intentions could have the same effect as making salient past behavior on people's attitude assessment, and that the hypothetical bias should moderate the informational value of behavioral intentions:

H3: Behavioral intentions are used as more abstract information in a hypothetical context and as more concrete information in a real context in further assessments.

## Study

These propositions were tested within the realm of environmental protection. Respondents (114 undergraduate students) pledged to perform behaviors from statements (Roberts 1996) that were formulated either in a hypothetical or a concrete way. Results from the study provided support for our hypotheses.

When asked to pledge to perform hypothetical behaviors (e.g., I pledge that I would buy), participants expressed greater behavioral intentions than when asked to pledge to perform actual behaviors (e.g., I pledge to buy; 4.26 vs. 3.31, p<0.001), which supports H1. Moreover, familiarity seems to moderate this effect, since there is no significant difference between the hypothetical and the concrete conditions (4.15 vs. 3.98, p>0.1) for what appears to be more familiar behaviors (i.e., behaviors that are performed inside the home–e.g., recycle, save energy and water), while there is a significant effect (4.03 vs. 3.54, p<0.05) on less familiar, and maybe less concrete behaviors (i.e., behaviors that are performed outside the home or related to social activities in support of the cause–e.g., buying fair-trade or organic products, convincing friends to be more eco-friendly), thus supporting H2.

Furthermore, when in a hypothetical condition, participants expressed stronger attitudinal self-relevance with the environment than in the concrete condition (3.97 vs. 3.76). On the other hand, when in a concrete condition, participants stated that they perform more actual behaviors that in the hypothetical condition (3.48 vs. 3.81). The interaction effect is significant (p=0.05). People thus seem to be inferring their attitudes from the actions that they are willing to do and their level of hypotheticality, since there is a match between "would-behavior" and self-relevance and between "do-behavior" and reported behaviors, providing support for H3.

## Discussion

Our study shows that there is a hypothetical bias in the pro-environmental domain, that this bias affects how people assess their attitudes and behaviors, and that it is moderated by familiarity. Moreover, making people think more abstractly or more concretely about their behaviors affects their self-relevance perception or their retrieval memory of past behaviors, respectively.

The next step is to try to better understand the process underlying the hypothetical bias, and to establish a link with actual behavior, in order to determine whether the hypothetical bias results in more or less actual behavioral consistency.

## References

Ajzen, Icek, Thomas C. Brown and Franklin Carvajal (2004). Explaining the Discrepancy between Intentions and Actions: The Case of Hypothetical Bias in Contingent Valuation, *Personality and Social Psychology Bulletin*, 30, 1108-20.
Albarracin, Dolores and Robert S. Wyer, Jr. (2000). "The Cognitive Impact of Past Behavior: Influences on Beliefs, Attitudes, and Future Behavioral Decisions." *Journal of Personality and Social Psychology*, 79 (1), 5-22.
Armor, David A. and Aaron M. Sackett (2006). "Accuracy, Error, and Bias in Predictions for Real Versus Hypothetical Events," *Journal of Personality and Social Psychology*, 91 (4), 583–600.
Cotte, June and Remi Trudel (2009). *Socially Conscious Consumerism, A Systematic Review of the Body of Knowledge*, Report from the Network for Business Sustainability Knowledge Project Series.
Dolliver, Mark (2008), "Deflating a Myth, Consumers aren't as devoted to the planet as you wish they were," Adweek, (accessed November 2, 2009), [available at http://www.adweek.com /aw/ content_display/news/strategy/e3i5e732e045deaaba3ef1cd271cfd0d102].
Haddock, Geoffrey, Alexander J. Rothman, Rolf Reber, and Norbert Schwarz (1999). "Forming Judgments of Attitude Certainty, Intensity, and Importance: The Role of Subjective Experiences," *Personality and Social Psychology Bulletin*, 25 (7), 771-782.
Johnston, Robert J. (2006). "Is hypothetical bias universal? Validating contingent valuation responses using a binding public referendum," *Journal of Environmental Economics and Management*, 52 (1), 469-81.
Roberts, James A. (1996). "Green Consumers in the 1990s: Profile and Implications for Advertising," *Journal of Business Research*, 36, 217-31.
Trope, Yaacov, Nira Liberman, and Cheryl Wakslak (2007). "Construal Levels and Psychological Distance: Effects on Representation, Prediction, Evaluation, and Behavior," *Journal of Consumer Psychology*, 17 (2), 83-95.

# The Abstractness of Luxury
Jochim Hansen, New York University, USA
Michaela Wänke, University of Basel, Switzerland

Almost everyday, consumers buy and use commodities such as food, clothing, or other necessities. Sometimes, however, they may indulge in luxurious goods (Kivetz and Simonson, 2002). Yet, luxury purchases are exceptions to the rule as they occur rather seldom and often are merely hypothetical.

Moreover, luxury cannot be purchased everywhere; it is usually limited and for most people difficult to attain (Miyazaki, Grewal, and Goodstein, 2005; Nuemo and Quelch, 1998; Silverstein and Fiske, 2003). As such, luxury is something that only a few people can afford; and luxurious goods are usually consumed especially by the higher upper-class society, which implies a connection between luxury and exclusiveness. Since luxurious goods are relatively exclusive and their acquisition is limited and often only hypothetical, they generally are perceived as more psychologically distant than ordinary objects.

Construal Level Theory (Trope and Liberman, 2000, 2003) assumes that psychologically distant objects are construed abstractly, whereas proximal objects are construed concretely. An abstract representation of an object consists of its high-level features which capture the central and stable aspects of an object. A concrete representation, on the other hand, includes more low-level aspects such as incidental details that are peripheral to the object's core representation.

Because luxury appears to be psychologically distant, and because psychologically distant objects are mentally represented more abstractly than psychologically proximal objects, we propose that luxury is mentally construed abstractly instead of concretely. In three studies, we investigated the bi-directional relationship between luxury and abstractness of mental representations. Study 1 tested whether consumers describe situations that involve luxury objects in a more abstract language than situations that involve comparably mundane objects. Study 2 tested the converse relationship and showed that products that are described in abstract language are perceived as more luxurious than products that are described in concrete language. Finally, study 3 showed that actual product descriptions of luxury goods are more abstract than descriptions of ordinary goods.

In study 1 which was framed as a creativity study, we asked participants to write a short story by using 12 specific words that should appear in their text at least once. For half of the participants, the list included 6 words that are associated with luxury (i.e., mansion, gourmet restaurant, limousine, 5-stars hotel, candelabra, and gemstone). For the other half of the participants, the target words were exchanged with their ordinary counterpart (i.e., house, canteen, car, hostel, lamp, and stone). The stories were analyzed with the Linguistic Category Model (Semin and Fiedler, 1988, 1991). This model distinguishes between several classes of word (descriptive action verbs, interpretive action verbs, state verbs, and adjectives) that can be located on the concreteness–abstractness continuum. The relative proportions of words of the different classes were determined by two coders who were unaware of the hypothesis, in order to measure the abstractness of the texts. As hypothesized, the findings indicated that stories that included luxurious objects were linguistically more abstract than stories that included ordinary objects.

In study 2, we tested the converse relationship and hypothesized that abstract descriptions of products cause consumers to perceive them as more luxurious than concrete descriptions. Participants were presented with short descriptions of six product types (i.e., yacht trips, dog food, cars, TV sets, vacuum cleaners, and watches). For each product type, we presented two descriptions—one abstract and one concrete. For the vacuum cleaners, for instance, one feature of the abstract description reads "…this unit has a very good vacuum pump, a low sound level, and a clever filtration." The more concrete counterpart reads "…this unit vacuums very well, does not make much sound, and filtrates dust cleverly." The content of the descriptions was counterbalanced in such way that specific features appeared either only in an abstract language or only in a concrete language. Participants were asked to judge for each product type on an 8-point scale which of two descriptions (concrete vs. abstract) they perceived as more luxurious, more expensive, and more exclusive. As expected, the findings indicated that the abstract descriptions were judged as more luxurious for these items.

Finally, in study 3, we were interested in the link between luxury and abstractness in real-world product descriptions. Forty-six descriptions of diverse products (23 luxury, 23 mundane products) were located on the Internet and analyzed regarding their linguistic abstractness. In line with the results of studies 1 and 2, we found that luxurious goods were described with more abstract language than mundane objects. This effect emerged (1) when comparing luxurious products with mundane products (e.g., fragrances vs. detergents), (2) when comparing two instances of the same product type (e.g., luxury cars vs. cheap cars), and (3) when comparing products within specific brands (e.g., the most expensive razor vs. the cheapest razor of the same brand). These findings give a first indication that advertisers may intuitively use the abstractness-luxury link in promoting their products.

In summary, the findings of the present research document that luxury is associated with an abstract representation: Luxury caused a more abstract language (both in study participants and in advertisers), and abstract language caused perceptions of luxury. The findings have important implication for advertising: An abstract presentation may lead consumers to perceive products as more exclusive, more luxurious, but also as more expensive.

## References

Kivetz, Ran and Itamar Simonson (2002), "Self-Control for the Righteous: Toward a Theory of Precommitment to Indulge," *Journal of Consumer Research*, 29 (September), 199-217.

Miyazaki, Anthony D., Dhruv Grewal, and Ronald C. Goodstein (2005), "The Effect of Multiple Extrinsic Cues on Quality Perceptions: A Matter of Consistency," *Journal of Consumer Research*, 32 (June), 146-53.

Nuemo, Jose Luis and John A. Quelch (1998), "The Mass Marketing of Luxury," *Business Horizons*, 41 (November-December), 61-68.

Semin, Gün R. and Klaus Fiedler (1988), "The Cognitive Functions of Linguistic Categories in Describing Persons: Social Cognition and Language," *Journal of Personality and Social Psychology*, 54 (4, April), 558-68.

_____ (1991), "The Linguistic Category Model, Its Bases, Applications and Range," in *European Review of Social Psychology*, Vol. 2, ed. Wolfgang Stroebe & Miles Hewstone, Chichester, UK: Wiley, 1-30.

Silverstein, Michael J. and Neil Fiske (2003), *Trading Up: The New American Luxury*, New York: Penguin.

Trope, Yaacov and Nira Liberman (2000), "Temporal Construal and Time-Dependent Changes in Preference," *Journal of Personality and Social Psychology*, 79 (6, December), 876-89.

_____ (2003), "Temporal Construal," *Psychological Review*, 110 (3, July), 403-21.

# When Closer is Better:
# The Influence of Physical Distance on Consumer Judgment of Product Effectiveness

Xiuping Li, National University of Singapore, Singapore
Boyoun (Grace) Chae, University of British Columbia, Canada
Rui (Juliet) Zhu, University of British Columbia, Canada

## Extended Abstract

This study was motivated by new drug-failure cases in real life. The most prominent case is Pfizer's $2.8 billion withdraw of its needle-free insulin inhaler when it failed to convince the patients about the effectiveness of the new format of the medicine (Johnson, 2007). This case makes us wonder what influences people's judgment of the efficacy of a drug, or in a broader sense, the effectiveness of a product on addressing a particular problem. This research will investigate the effect of spatial distance on perception of product effectiveness.

It has been found that spatial distance (i.e.,"near-far") influences individuals' judgment. For example, people who were primed with spatial closeness (versus distance) showed an increase in emotional intensity toward stimuli (Williams & Bargh, 2008). People also use spatial distance to avoid influence from unfamiliar (Patterson & Sechrest, 1970) and undesirable objects (Kim, Ellen, & Margaret, 1992). Based on these observations about the relationship between spatial distance and intensity, we predict that people will judge a product to be more effective when it is physically close to the focal problem. Moreover, we also posit that the effect of spatial distance on effectiveness judgment is moderated by how long it takes the product to become effective. Last, we argue that people's lay theories about distance and effectiveness will moderate the demonstrated impact of spatial distance. These predictions are tested and supported by 4 studies we have conducted in our labs.

In Study 1, participants were asked to judge how effective a new over the counter (OTC) drug was at treating allergies with nasal symptoms. The perceived spatial distance was manipulated by different drug types: nasal spray versus tablet that people take orally. Since spray works closer to the affected area (nose) than the tablet, we predicted that people would judge the product in the spray format to be more effective than that in the tablet format. Participants read similar product information and the only differences were drug formats and corresponding images of the new drug. As anticipated, we found that people evaluated the drug to be more effective when the product was in closer contact to the symptomatic problem areas (i.e., nasal spray vs. table). The aim of study 2 was to replicate experiment 1 results and to further test how people's belief of the relationship between the spatial distance and efficacy of the product in general might moderate the observed effect. The procedure of Study 2 was similar to that of Study 1 except that participants indicated the extent to which they believed that closer (vs. farther) distance between a solution (e.g., product) and a problem would imply greater effectiveness. As anticipated, regression analysis revealed that the belief strength moderated the main effect of spatial distance. Specifically, people who strongly believed there was a relationship between closeness and efficacy judged the nasal spray format as more effective than the tablet format. However, such a pattern was absent among participants who did not hold such strong beliefs.

Study 3 aimed to demonstrate another boundary condition for the effect of spatial distance on efficacy judgment. We predicted that the closeness is more related to immediate effectiveness. When a drug was intended to solve a problem gradually, over the long term, the closeness would not impact the efficacy judgment to the same extent. A 2 (nasal spray vs. tablet) X 2 (immediate solution vs. gradual solution) factorial design was applied. Consistent with our prediction, the results revealed a significant interaction. In particular, when the drug claimed to have immediate relief, consumers judged the drug in nasal spray format to be more effective than in a tablet format. However, no effect was found when the drug was introduced as a gradual relief to the problem.

Study 4 further investigated our theorizing by manipulating spatial distance in a different manner. Here, we manipulated the perceived spatial distance by varying the distance between a drug image and an agent image (e.g., a picture of patient) in the advertisement. In the spatially close condition, the product was placed next to problem agent; whereas in the remote condition, the two images were put relatively far away from each other on the same page. Participants were assigned in a 2 (spatial distance close vs. far) X 2 (immediate relief vs. long term relief) between-subjects design study. In order to test the role of lay theory (i.e., general belief about the relationship between distance and effectiveness), we also measured the strength of each participant's belief in this relationship. Regression analyses revealed a significant three-way interaction. Only those people who had relatively strong belief in the relationship between distance and effectiveness judged the drug to be more effective when the images of the drug and the agent were proximal rather than distant to each other.

In sum, across four studies and using different methods to manipulate spatial distance, we showed the role of spatial-distance on judgment of product effectiveness. We also demonstrated that the lay beliefs about the distance-effectiveness relationship moderated the effect.

## References

Johnson, A. (2007, October 19). Insulin flop costs Pfizer $2.8 billion. *The Wall Street Journal.*

Kim, M. M., Ellen, S. C., & Margaret, B. S. (1992). Physical distance and AIDS: too close for comfort? *Journal of Applied Social Psychology*, 22(18), 1442-1452.

Mukhopadhyay, A., & Johar, G. (2005). Where there is a will, is there a way? Effects of lay theories of self-control on setting and keeping resolutions. *Journal of Consumer Research*, 31(4), 779-786.

Novemsky, N., & Ratner, R. (2003). The time course and impact of consumers' erroneous beliefs about hedonic contrast effects. *Journal of Consumer Research*, 29(4), 507-516.

Patterson, M. L., & Sechrest, L. B. (1970). Interpersonal distance and impression formation. *Journal of Personality*, 38, 161-166.

Pocheptsova, A., & Novemsky, N. (Forthcoming) When do incidental mood effects last? Lay beliefs versus actual effects. *Journal of Consumer Research.*

Williams, L. E., & Bargh, J. A. (2008). Keeping one's distance: the influence of spatial distance cues on affect and evaluation. *Psychological Science*, 19(3), 302-308.

# Does Bodily Feedback Signal Differential Psychological Distance? The Effect of Approach and Avoidance Motor Action Signals on the Level of Construal for Mental Representation

Fang-Chi Lu, University of Iowa, USA
Dhananjay Nayakankuppam, University of Iowa, USA

## Extended Abstract

A body of literature has suggested that the chronic-built association between isometric arm flexion/extension contraction and approach/ avoidance motivational orientations influences people's judgment and attitude formation (Cacioppo, Priester, & Berntson, 1993; Peiester, Cacioppo, & Petty, 1996). Arm flexion (by pressing upward on a table) produces bodily feedback which is associated with approaching positive stimuli; while arm extension (by pressing downward on a table) provides the association with avoiding negative stimuli (Forster, 1998; Forster, & Strack, 1997). This motor action effect is bidirectional. Performing arm flexion vs. extension makes people evaluate a neutral object more positively or negatively; presenting people with positive vs. negative valenced stimuli also automatically activates an approach vs. avoidance motor tendency (Bargh, 1997).

Construal level theory was recently suggested by Liberman and Trope (1998) as a framework linking psychological distance and abstraction. According to their theory, the chronic association between psychological distance (temporal, social, spatial or hypothetical) and abstraction in cognition leads to the tendency to mentally represent a distant object with higher-level (abstract) construals, while represent a near object with lower-level (concrete) construals.

We propose that the approach vs. avoidance motor actions, bringing things toward or away from oneself, might signal differential psychological distance. That is, the arm flexion contraction is associated with near psychological distance and arm extension is associated with far psychological distance. Therefore, performing arm flexion might lead to the tendency of construing objects with more concrete, subordinate terms; while performing arm extension leads to a more high-level construal mental representation of objects. Two studies were conducted to test this proposition.

In Study 1, participants were presented with a series of pictures of objects from four different categories (vehicle, clothing, furniture, and fruit) on the computers. The choice of exemplars for each category is following Rosch's (1975) norms, with exemplars having differential typicality to their corresponding categories. The presentation order of the objects was randomized. After seeing each picture, participants were asked to assign the item to a superordinate or a subordinate category (i.e. a picture of apple followed by two categorization choices: apple and fruit). Response time on categorization decision was also measured. While performing the categorization task, participants were asked to either place their palm on the bottom (flexion) or on the top (extension) of the table. We predict that when an objects is presented under arm flexion, less psychological distance of the object is perceived, thus people are more likely to represent it at more concrete construals, which in turn leads to a more subordinate categorization. On the other hand, arm extension will lead to a more superordinate categorization. Repeated measure ANOVA was performed with isometric exercise (flexion vs. extension) as between-subjects variable, and we looked at the isometric exercise effect on both binary categorization choice and response time. Results from the vehicle category support our hypothesis. A significant categorization by motor action interaction effect was shown on the response time (P=.01). When performing arm flexion, people were faster at assigning items to a subordinate category (i.e. car) ($RT_{superordinate}$=2087; $RT_{subordinate}$ =1449 mini sec.); while performing arm extension, people were faster at assigning items to a superordinate category (vehicle) ($RT_{superordinate}$ =1393 ; $RT_{subordinate}$ =1567 mini sec.).

In Study 2, Vallacher and Wegner's Behavioral Identification Form (BIF) (1989) was used as the test stimuli to measure the construal level of people's action identification under different motor action conditions. Specifically, while performing isometric exercise, participants were asked to choose between a high-level and a low-level identity on the 25 action items from the BIF scale (i.e. Reading: a. following lines of print; b. gaining knowledge). The presentation order of the two alternatives was counterbalanced. We predict that people under arm flexion are more likely to choose low-level identity of the actions; while people in the arm extension are more likely to choose high-level identity of the actions. Results of analyses support our prediction (p=.06)

Taken these two studies together, we found the effects of bodily feedback on the level of construals being used to represent objects or events. When people are performing arm extension contraction, they tend to form a mental representation in higher-level, more abstract terms, and categorize things at a superordinate category; while performing arm flexion contraction leads to a lower-level, more concrete mental representation and a more subordinate categorization.

Previous research has suggested that effect between construal and psychological distance is bidirectional. Manipulations of construal would affect distance perceptions in the same way as the distance of an event influences its construal. Therefore, one of the future research directions will be to test the direct effect of approach/avoidance motor actions on the perception of various dimensions of psychological distance. For example, in the temporal distance dimension, while performing arm flexion vs. extension contraction, participants will be presented with descriptions of a series of events (i.e. imagine that you're considering "opening a bank account", "enrolling in a fitness program"), and then be asked to answer how much time from now the activity would be performed (Liberman et al., 2007). It will be interesting to know if people's perception of psychological distance shifts with the motor actions being performed.

## References

Bargh, J. A. (1997), The automaticity of everyday life. In R. S. Wyer Jr. (Ed.), *Advances in social cognition* (Vol. 10, pp1-61). Mahwah, NJ: Erlbaum.

Cacioppo, J. T., Priester, J. R., & Berntson, G. G. (1993), Rudimentary determinants of attitudes: II. Arm flexion and extension have differential effects on attitudes. *Journal of Personality and Social Psychology, 65*, 5-17.

Forster, J., & Strack, F. (1997). Motor actions in retrieval of valenced information: A motor congruence effect. *Perceptual and Motor Skills, 85*, 1419-1427.

Forster, J., & Strack, F. (1998). Motor actions in retrieval of valenced information: II Boundary conditions for motor congruence effects. *Perceptual and Motor Skills, 86*, 1423-1426.

Liberman, N., Macrae, S., Sherman, S. & Trope, Y. (2007). The effect of level of construal on temporal distance. *Journal of Experimental Social Psychology*, 43, 143–149.

Liberman, N., & Trope, Y. (1998). The role of feasibility and desirability considerations in near and distant future decisions: A test of temporal construal theory. *Journal of Personality and Social Psychology, 75*, 5–18.

Priester, J. R., Cacioppo, J. T., & Petty, R. E. (1996). The influence of motor processes on attitude toward novel versus familiar semantic stimuli. *Personality and Social Psychology Bulletin, 22*, 442-447.

Rosch, E., (1975). Cognitive representation of semantic categories, *Journal of Experimental Psychology: General*, 104, 192-233.

Vallacher, R. R., & Wegner, D. M., (1989), Levels of Personal Agency: Individual Variation in Action Identification. *Journal of Personality and Social Psychology, 57*, 660-671.

# A Regulatory Focus–Reactance Perspective of Consumer Reward Preferences in Loyalty Programs

Meltem Tugut, Saint Louis University, USA

Mark J. Arnold, Saint Louis University, USA

## Extended Abstract

Regulatory focus theory (Higgins 1997) suggests that individuals differ in how they approach pleasure and avoid pain. These differences are manifested in two distinct regulatory systems which govern how people pursue goals: promotion focus and prevention focus (Higgins 1997). When it comes to consumption, different product attributes help individuals fulfill different regulatory focus goals. It has been shown that hedonic products allow consumers to reach their promotion-focus goals whereas utilitarian products permit them to realize their prevention-focus goals (Chernev 2004; Dhar and Wertenbroch 2000). In this research, we explore whether the "fit" between hedonic products and promotion-focus and that between utilitarian products and prevention-focus holds true in the context of loyalty rewards programs. Specifically, we propose that psychological reactance aroused by loyalty programs may result in reward preferences that do not necessarily match individuals' regulatory goals.

Regulatory focus can be a chronic individual trait or situationally induced (Aaker and Lee 2001; Higgins et al. 2001). Promotion-focused individuals are concerned with the presence and absence of positive outcomes (gains and non-gains) to pursue maximal goals of advancement, growth, and accomplishment (Camacho, Higgins, and Lugar 2003; Higgins 2000). On the other hand, prevention-focused individuals are interested in the presence and absence of negative outcomes (losses and non-losses) to attain minimal goals of protection, safety, and responsibility (Brendl and Higgins 1996; Idson, Liberman, and Higgins 2000).

Hedonic goods provide individuals with an affect-based consumption experience that delivers benefits of sensual fun, pleasure, and excitement (Hirschman and Holbrook 1982). Since individuals with promotion goals are inclined to maximize their potential gains, they place more emphasis on products that provide hedonic benefits in order to realize their "maximal" goals (Chernev 2004; Chitturi, Raghunathan, and Mahajan 2007). On the other hand, consumption of utilitarian goods is often cognition-based and driven by a need to acquire functional, practical, and instrumental benefits (Strahilevitz and Myers 1998). As individuals with prevention goals are concerned with minimizing their losses, they show a tendency toward products that present utilitarian benefits in order to fulfill their "minimal" goals (Kivetz and Simonson 2002).

However, this regulatory focus–product fit may not hold for consumers who choose between loyalty programs offering a hedonic vs. a utilitarian reward of equal monetary value. Loyalty programs are known to activate reactance among consumers (Kivetz 2005). Since loyalty programs demand commitment over a period of time in order to prevent switching behavior, consumers may perceive these programs as a restriction to their future freedom of choice and express reactance toward them (Kivetz 2005). The situational reactance experienced by individuals is partly driven by their level of chronic reactance (Hong and Faedda 1996).

We expect promotion-focused individuals to experience higher levels of chronic reactance than prevention-focused individuals. While promotion-focused individuals often adopt a more risky bias and consider various alternatives in consumption choice contexts, prevention-focused consumers usually follow a more risk-averse strategy and limit themselves to fewer alternatives. "Variety-seeking" people tend to express intense reactance toward threats to their freedom of choice.

When an extrinsic reward becomes salient as a potential reason for a particular behavior, people attribute their behavior to this outside influence (Kivetz 2005). Utilitarian rewards do not provide a strong extrinsic reason for consumers to exhibit specific consumption behaviors. Therefore, consumers believe that their behavior is not influenced by utilitarian rewards and do not perceive them as a threat. In contrast, hedonic rewards present a salient extrinsic explanation for particular consumption behaviors. Hence, consumers usually attribute their behavior to these incentives and see them as a threat to their freedom.

Since promotion-focused consumers are expected to have higher levels of chronic reactance, they are more likely to prefer loyalty programs that offer utilitarian rewards in order to alleviate their reactance toward such programs. On the other hand, as prevention-focused consumers are expected to have lower levels of chronic reactance and do not face the need to alleviate their reactance, they are expected to be indifferent toward loyalty programs that offer hedonic or utilitarian rewards.

We tested the present predictions in two studies. In Study 1, we used a regulatory focus (promotion vs. prevention) x loyalty reward (hedonic vs. utilitarian) two-factor design where the reward was manipulated as a between-subject factor through loyalty program scenarios and the regulatory focus was measured as an individual difference factor (N=236). Wine and a gasoline coupon (equal monetary value) were used as hedonic and utilitarian rewards respectively. The dependent variables were preference toward the loyalty program and the likelihood of joining the program. A MANOVA revealed that promotion-focused consumers are more likely to prefer and join loyalty programs offering utilitarian rewards compared to those offering hedonic rewards. Prevention-consumers were indifferent toward either type of loyalty program. Participants' chronic reactance was also measured and an ANOVA indicated that promotion-focused consumers were indeed higher in chronic reactance compared to prevention-focused consumers.

Study 2 utilized a regulatory focus (promotion vs. prevention) x loyalty reward (hedonic vs. utilitarian) two-factor design where both the reward and the regulatory focus were manipulated as between-subject factors through loyalty program scenarios (N=143). A restaurant certificate and a grocery coupon (equal monetary value) were used as hedonic and utilitarian rewards respectively. The dependent variables were the same as in Study 1. The MANOVA replicated Study 1 results. When individuals' promotion goals were made accessible, they showed a tendency to prefer and join loyalty programs offering utilitarian rewards vs. hedonic rewards. When prevention goals were induced, individuals were indifferent toward either type of loyalty program. An ANOVA indicated that promotion-primed consumers exhibited higher reactance compared to prevention-primed consumers.

The present research showed that consumers' preferences toward hedonic and utilitarian rewards in the context of loyalty programs may not necessarily fit their regulatory goals. The differences in the level of reactance experienced seem to influence consumers' reward preferences. Promotion-focused consumers, for whom reactance becomes a salient factor, tend to prefer utilitarian loyalty rewards to alleviate the resulting unpleasant state. Prevention-focused consumers, who are less concerned with reactance, are indifferent toward either loyalty reward.

## References

Aaker, Jennifer L. and Angela Y. Lee (2001), "'I' Seek Pleasures And 'We' Avoid Pains: The Role Of Self-Regulatory Goals In Information Processing And Persuasion," *Journal of Consumer Research*, 28 (1), 33-49.

Chernev, Alexander (2004), "Goal-Attribute Compatibility in Consumer Choice," *Journal of Consumer Psychology*, 14 (1-2), 141-50.

Chitturi, Ravindra, Rajagopal Raghunathan, and Vijay Mahajan (2007), "Form Versus Function: How the Intensities of Specific Emotions Evoked in Functional Versus Hedonic Trade-Offs Mediate Product Preferences," *Journal of Marketing Research*, 44 (November), 702-14.

Dhar, Ravi and Klaus Wertenbroch (2000), "Consumer Choice Between Hedonic and Utilitarian Goods," *Journal of Marketing Research*, 37 (February), 60-71.

Higgins, E. Tory (1997), "Beyond Pleasure and Pain," *American Psychologist*, 52 (December), 1280-300.

Kivetz, Ran (2005), "Promotion Reactance: The Role of Effort-Reward Congruity," *Journal of Consumer Research*, 31 (March), 725-36.

_____ and Itamar Simonson (2002), "Earning the Right to Indulge: Effort as a Determinant of Customer Preferences Toward Frequency Program Rewards," *Journal of Marketing Research*, 39 (May), 155-70.

# The Impact of Counterfactual Mindset on Consumer Information Processing

Guangzhi Zhao, Univerity of Kansas, USA

Kai-Yu Wang, Brock University, Canada

## Extended Abstract

Counterfactual thinking is the process of looking back at events and thinking how things could have turned out differently. Whenever individuals consider how the past might have turned out differently, they are engaging in counterfactual thinking. For example, in consumption context, imagine that one consumer finds her HDTV needs repair just after the warranty expires. This consumer may think to herself: "If only I had purchased a TV with an extended warranty, I would not have to incur so much cost on this repair."

A large body of research has documented a wide variety of psychological (e.g., emotional and judgmental) consequences of engaging in counterfactual thinking. Two basic routes through which counterfactual thinking influences individuals have been differentiated in the literature: the content-specific route and the content-neutral route (Epstude and Roese 2008). Through the content-specific route, counterfactual thinking influences the same behavior specified by the counterfactual. In contrast, through the content-neutral route, counterfactual thinking influences individuals' behavior in domains that are independent of the counterfactual context. That is, independent of the meaning contained in a counterfactual thought, the process of counterfactual thinking can ignite attentional, cognitive, or motivational processes that will linger after counterfactual thinking and alter individuals' subsequent behavior in another domain. For example, counterfactual thinking in one domain (e.g., missing a flight) can influence behavior in a different domain (e.g., buying a book, ordering meal in the airport).

Recently, an emerging stream of research starts to study the content-neutral route, especially, the influence of counterfactual mind-set (or cognition orientations) that results from constructing counterfactual thoughts (Galinsky and Moskowitz 2000). A counterfactual mind-set may involve a range of cognitive operations, including attention shifts to specific classes of information and the use of specific inferential strategies (Galinsky and Kray 2004; Krishnamurthy and Sivaraman 2002). In this research we explored how counterfactual thinking might activate another cognition orientation and influence consumers' preferences. Specifically, we propose that counterfactual thinking can activate a process/procedure-focused (i.e., "how to") cognition orientation, which leads consumers to construe activities more often as "how to," overweight product feasibility attributes in choice, and be persuaded more by ad messages promoting ease-of-use product features.

Counterfactual thinking often takes the form of a conditional proposition, in which individuals identify alternative routes or processes to mutate factual events. For example, Krishnamurthy and Sivaraman (2002) view counterfactual thinking as a problem-solving process which involves generating alternatives, steps, and solutions to solve problems. That is, counterfactual thinking involves mentally mutating a past event by re-running the sequence of the event and also simulating the necessary alternative steps or procedures needed to alter what has happened. In this way, counterfactual thinking may activate a process-focused information processing mentality and sensitize individuals to procedural information. This is especially true for counterfactual thinking involving a sequence of actions (e.g., one missed an important meeting because of first alarm clock failure, then being caught in traffic jams, and also getting lost the building) instead of single event (e.g., one missed the chance to win a trip to Hawaii because of seat switching) (Roese 1997).

In consumption context, the mindset of focusing on processes or procedural relationships created through counterfactual thinking will increase consumers' ability to perceive, understand, and valuate product ease-of-use or product feasibility in judgment and choice. Product feasibility, in addition to desirability, is a prominent consideration of consumer choices. Many times consumer decision making involves a trade-off between these two product attributes (Zhao, Hoeffler, Zauberman 2007). Several moderating conditions for consumers' preference for product feasibility and desirability have been identified in the literature, e.g., product trial experience, decision time distance, decision stage, etc. (Hamilton and Thompson 2007; Rothman 2000; Trope and Liberman 2000).

We propose that consumers' preference for product feasibility and desirability will be moderated by counterfactual thinking (vs. control). Specifically, consumers' preference for product feasibility will be boosted after going through counterfactual thinking in an unrelated domain. We conducted three experiments to test our hypotheses.

In Study 1, we examined how counterfactual thinking (vs. control) impacts the way in which individuals construe activities. 124 participants were randomly assigned to either a control condition or a counterfactual thinking group. Participants in the counterfactual thinking group were instructed to engage in counterfactual thinking with a standard procedure borrowed from the literature. Then, all the participants completed the Behavior Identification Form (BIF). The BIF, a 25-item, dichotomous-response questionnaire, assesses individual differences in level of action identification. For each item, participants read about an action (e.g., "voting") and circled which of two identifications more appropriately described it. The choices corresponded to "how to" (i.e., procedural) identifications (e.g., "marking a ballot") and ends identifications (e.g., "influencing the election"). A one-way ANOVA on the total number of "how to" identifications revealed a significant main effect for counterfactual thinking such that individuals gone through counterfactual thinking had a higher total number of "how to" identifications (M=5.75) than the control group (M=4.70, F (1, 122)=6.52, p<.05).

In Study 2, we employed a 2 (counterfactual thinking vs. control) x 2 (high-desirability and low-feasibility product vs. low-desirability and high-feasibility product) between subject factorial design to study how counterfactual thinking will impact consumer choices of product that are presented either in terms of product feasibility or desirability. A total 171 students participated in the study. The counterfactual scenario was modeled after the literature (Roese 1997). The scenario asked the participants to imagine that they experienced a broken camera on a beach during a vacation and later found out that the camera was broken because the camera was left on the beach too long and the battery was damaged. After reading the scenario, participants were asked to complete a series of "If only _____" counterfactual thinking sentences. The control group read the same scenario without going through counterfactual thinking and only wrote down their thoughts that went through their minds as they read the story. Then, participants read a product review from the CNET about MP3 voice recorder. The high-desirability and low-feasibility product was rated high on desirability attributes (e.g., recording quality, overall rating); whereas the high-feasibility and low-desirability product was rated high on feasibility (e.g., ease of use, quick to set up). Two-way ANOVAs revealed a significant two-way interaction between the two factors (F (1, 167)=5.30, p<.05). Further analyses showed that individuals gone through counterfactual thinking indicated higher intentions to choose the high-feasibility and low-desirability option (M=4.79) than the high-desirability and low-feasibility option (M=4.09, t=2.43, p<.05). There was no difference in the control condition. Similar results were found on other dependent measures including likelihood to buy and product attitude.

In Study 3, we seek to replicate the finings in Study 2 in persuasion context to further explore the role of counterfactual thinking on consumer information processing. It was a two-factor between subject factorial: 2 (counterfactual thinking vs. control) x 2 (ad promoting feasibility attributes vs. ad promoting desirability attributes). A total of 136 students participated in the study. A similar procedure was used to manipulated counterfactual thinking, but with a scenario about missing an important interview. Then participants were shown two digital camera ads promoting a pseudo brand. One ad had a headline of "An Easy Way to Capture Important Moments!" and highlighted the feasibility attributes of the camera (e.g., easy to frame and shoot pictures and videos, automatic face detection, etc.); the other ad had a headline of "An Perfect Camera for Important Moments!" and highlighted the desirability attributes of the camera (e.g., large LCD, true HD quality, etc). Two-way ANOVAs revealed a significant two-way interaction between the two factors on intention to use (F (1, 132)=5.60, p<.05). Further analyses showed that, for individuals gone through counterfactual thinking, they indicated higher intentions to use the camera after reading the ad promoting feasibility attributes (M=5.02) than the ad promoting desirability attributes (M=3.84, t=2.68, p<.01). The two ads were equally persuasive in the control condition (t=.67, p=.51). Similar results were found on other dependent measures including likelihood to buy and product attitude.

Taken together, these three experiments support our proposed theorizing that consumers' preference for product feasibility will be boosted after going through counterfactual thinking in an unrelated domain.

## References

Bagozzi, Richard P. and Utpal M. Dholakia (1999), "Goal setting and goal striving in consumer behavior," *Journal of Marketing*, 63, 19-32.

Beck, S. R., Robinson, E. J., Carroll, D.J., & Apperly, I. A. (2006), "Children's thinking about counterfactuals and future hypotheticals as possibilities," *Child Development*, 77, 413-426.

Epstude, Kai and Neal J. Roese (2008), "The Functional Theory of Counterfactual Thinking," *Personality and Social Psychology Bulletin*, 12 (2), 168-192

Galinsky, A. D., & Kray, L. J. (2004), "From thinking about what might have been to sharing what we know: The effects of counterfactual mind-sets on information sharing in groups," *Journal of Experimental Social Psychology*, 40, 606–618.

Galinsky, A. D., & Moskowitz, G. B. (2000), "Counterfactuals as behavioral primes: Priming the simulation heuristic and consideration of alternatives," *Journal of Experimental Social Psychology*, 36, 257–383.

Gilovich, T., Wang, R. F., Regan, D., & Nishina, S. (2003), "Regrets of action and inaction across cultures," *Journal of Cross-Cultural Psychology*, 34, 61-71.

Hamilton, Rebecca W. and Debora V. Thompson (2007), "Is there a Substitute for Direct Experience? Comparing Consumers' Preferences After Direct and Indirect Product Experiences," *Journal of Consumer Research*, 34 (December), 546-555.

Krishnamurthy, Parthasarathy and Anuradha Sivaraman (2002), "The Impact of Counterfactual Thinking on Processing of Subsequently Encountered Stimuli", *Journal of Consumer Research*, 28 (March), 650-658.

Liberman, N., & Trope, Y. (1998), "The role of feasibility and desirability considerations in near and distant future decisions: A test of temporal construal theory," *Journal of Personality and Social Psychology*, 75, 5-18.

Markman, K. D., & McMullen, M. N. (2003), "A reflection and evaluation model of comparative thinking," *Personality and Social Psychology Review*, 7, 244–267.

Rothman, Alexander J. (2000), "Toward a theory-based analysis of behavioral maintenance," *Health Psychology*, 19, 64-69.

Roese, Neal J. (1997), "Counterfactual thinking," *Psychological Bulletin*, 121, 133-148.

Trope, Y., & Liberman N. (2000), "Temporal construal and time-dependent changes in preference," *Journal of Personality and Social Psychology*, 79, 876-889.

Vallacher, R. R., & Wegner, D. M. (1989), "Levels of personal agency: Individual variation in action identification," *Journal of Personality and Social Psychology*, 57, 660-671.

Zhao, Min, Steve Hoeffler, and Gal Zauberman (2007), "Mental Simulation and Preference Consistency over Time: The Role of Process- Versus Outcome-Focused Thoughts," *Journal of Marketing Research*, 44 (2), 379-388.

# Counterfactual Priming Effects on Advertising Persuasion

Kai-Yu Wang, Brock University, Canada

Xiaojing Yang, University of Wisconsin-Milwaukee, USA

## Extended Abstract

Counterfactual thinking (CFT) refers to the process of reflecting on past events and simulating alternative possible outcomes. CFT impacts consumers in many ways, including their emotions, judgments, and decision making. Consumers engage in CFT, either upward or downward, after experiencing purchase events. For example, imagine that your new plasma TV needs to be repaired immediately after the warranty expires. As you consider this repair, you might engage in upward counterfactual thinking, generating alternatives that are better than actuality, when you think, if only I had purchased a TV with an extended warranty, I would not have to spend so much money on this repair. Conversely, if you engage in downward counterfactual thinking as you contemplate the repair, you would generate alternatives that are worse than actuality. You might think, at least I did not purchase the model with the longer warranty and smaller screen, because I enjoy my large screen TV. CFT occurs in a variety of consumer contexts, regardless of the valence, positive or negative, of purchase outcomes.

In consumer contexts, it is important to understand how CFT affects consumers' future decision making. Such understanding will help marketers develop effective marketing strategies. Little consumer research has investigated related issues on this topic. Given that CFT may influence information processing (Krishnamurthy and Sivaraman 2002), it is important to determine how and when such effects occur. This research investigates how cognitive activities (i.e., CFT) initiated by previously encountered events (e.g., a negative purchase experience) impact consumers' subsequent processing of ad messages. Such motivational priming processes are only beginning to be understood in social psychology (Roese, Hur, and Pennington 1999, Galinsky and Moskowitz 2000), and have not received much attention in the consumer behavior literature.

After experiencing a purchase event, particularly following a negative outcome, consumers engage in either upward or downward CFT (Walchli and Landman 2003). Recent research has indicated that upward CFT impacts consumers' processing of subsequently encountered ad messages (Krishnamurthy and Sivaraman 2002). Consumers who engage in upward CFT scrutinize ad claims, and thus they are more persuaded by strong arguments than by weak arguments. Roese (1994) indicates that upward counterfactuals serve a preparative function and help to improve performance in the future. Following this logic, after a negative purchase outcome, consumers who engage in upward CFT should seek improvements over their previous experience. Thus, these consumers should process subsequent information via a central route, while those who do not engage in upward CFT via peripheral route, according to the elaboration-likelihood model, ELM (Petty, Cacioppo, and Schumann 1983). We argue that this mentality primed should affect consumers' preference for comparative appeals vs. noncomparative appeals.

Specifically, we conducted two experiments demonstrating the impact of CFT in response to previous consumption experience on the effectiveness of comparative advertising appeals that consumers subsequently get exposed to. In experiment 1, we show the effect of CFT on consumers' processing of subsequently encountered ad messages (comparative vs. noncomparative) that is relevant to prior consumption experience. In experiment 2, the effects observed in experiment 1 are replicated when subsequently encountered ad information is unrelated to the previous consumption experience, providing an extension of experiment 1 and establishing the robustness of the documented findings.

In experiment 1, counterfactual thinking (CFT and control) and ad format (comparative and noncomparative) were manipulated. We hypothesized that when presented with a comparative ad, respondents who receive instructions (vs. those who do not receive instructions) to think counterfactually generate higher ad evaluations, brand evaluations, and purchase intentions than in a subsequent related context. In contrast, when presented with a noncomparative ad, respondents who do not receive instructions (vs. those who receive instructions) to think counterfactually generate higher ad evaluations, brand evaluations, and purchase intentions in a subsequent related context. The results were consistent with our predictions. Examination of thought measures provided additional support for the hypotheses.

Experiment 2 replicated findings in experiment 1 in a subsequent unrelated context. All of our predictions were supported. Examination of thought measures also provided additional support for the predictions.

Taken together, these two studies support most of our proposed theorizing regarding the effect of CFT on consumers' processing of subsequently encountered ad messages (comparative vs. noncomparative) that is relevant/irrelevant to prior consumption experience. The studies reveal that respondents who engage in upward CFT process ad information via a central route whereas those who do not engage in upward CFT process ad information via a peripheral route and consequently, they prefer different ad formats. This is the first attempt to apply CFT to comparative advertising contexts and advances our current knowledge by identifying the importance of understanding the impact of CFT on comparative advertising persuasion. This research also extends CFT priming effects to subsequent information processing in unrelated consumption contexts.

## References

Krishnamurthy, Parthasarathy and Anuradha Sivaraman (2002), "Counterfactual thinking and advertising responses," *Journal of Consumer Research,* 28 (March), 650-658.

Galinsky, Adam D. and Gordon B. Moskowitz (2000), "Counterfactuals as Behavioral Primes: Priming the Simulation Heuristic and Consideration of Alternatives," Journal of Experimental Social Psychology, 36, 384-409.

Petty, Richard E., John T. Cacioppo, and David Schumann (1983), "Central and peripheral routes to advertising effectiveness: The moderating role of involvement." *Journal of Consumer Research*, 10 (September): 135-46.

Roese, Neal (1994), "The functional basis of counterfactual thinking," *Journal of Personality and Social Psychology*, 66 (May), 805-818.

Roese, Neal, Taekyun Hur, and Ginger L. Pennington (1999), "Counterfactual thinking and regulatory focus: Implications for action versus inaction and sufficiency versus necessity." *Journal of Personality and Social Psychology,* 77 (6), 1109-20.

Walchli, Suzanne B. and Janet Landman (2003), "Effects of counterfactual thought on postpurchase consumer affect," *Psychology & Marketing*, 20 (January), 23-46.

# Avoiding Poor Health or Approaching Good Health: Does it Matter? Conceptualization, Measurement and Consequences of Health Regulatory Focus

Pierrick Gomez, Reims Management School and Université Paris Dauphine, France

Adilson Borges, Reims Management School, France

## Extended Abstract

The motivational underpinnings of health behavior have been largely ignored in the marketing literature (Briley and Aaker, 2006). The regulatory focus theory (Higgins, 1997) offers a relevant theoretical framework to understand how basic motivations influence health behaviors. In this regard, some researchers have proposed that hoped selves or feared selves could act as motivational incentives (Hooker et Kaus, 1994). However, although regulatory focus theory has already been applied to health message persuasion and health behavior (e.g.: Keller, 2006; Fuglestad, Rothman and Jeffery, 2008), no effort has been made until now to adapt it to the health domain. The present research proposes that individuals could vary in their spontaneous tendency to represent their health in terms of desired state or undesired state and that this individual difference influence their health beliefs and behaviors. Because other variables has been successfully adapted to the health domain (e.g.: Wallston *et alii*, 1978 ; Schwarzer and Renner, 2000) and because past researches using general measure of regulatory focus has lead to mitigated results (e.g.: Vartanian, Herman, and Polivy 2006), conceptualize health regulatory focus and build a specific tool of measurement seem to be an important step to engage.

### Development and Validation of the Health Regulatory Focus Scale

To generate items our initial set of 50 items for the HRFS, we first closely examined instruments used to measure general regulatory focus and second conducted in-depth discussions with 8 consumers. 31 items were finally selected by four expert judges and administered to a sample of 187 consumers. The factorial analysis with oblimin rotation was used to check the factorial structure of the measure. A two factors solution is obtained and explained 58% of the variance. Moreover, the correlation between the two dimensions is low ($r$=.16, $p$<.001). The final version of the HRFS includes 8 items (five items for promotion dimension and three for prevention dimension). To assess the relationship between, general regulatory focus and health regulatory focus, the RFQ (Higgins, 2001) has also been administered to the sample: no significant correlation exists between these two constructs.

To validate the HRFS, the items were administered to a sample of 1600 consumers. After checking for the items multinormality, we adopted the maximum likelihood and the bootstrap procedures to conduct the analysis. All the indicators have confirmed that the model fits the data well ($\chi2$=151.67; GFI=.98 AGFI=.95, CFI=.97, TLI=.97, RMSEA<.08). The model shows that the correlation between the latent constructs and its items are always over .5, and that the error terms variance is bellow the acceptable threshold of 2.58 (Hu and Bentler 1998). However, the correlation between the two latent constructs is much higher than in study 2 ($r$=.79, p<.001). This result threatens our two dimensions solution. To avoid any doubt about this issue, we conducted a model comparison using the chi-square difference tests recommended by Anderson and Gerbing (1988). The results argue that a two constructs model solution fits the data better. The increase in chi square is 283.37, which is significant at $p<0.01$. These results support the discriminant validity of the HRFS. Each of the resulting scales exhibits good internal reliability: Cronbach alpha and Joreskog's Rhô were superior to recommended thresholds.

**Nomological Studies: Consequences of Health Regulatory Focus on Health Beliefs, Health Behaviors and Subjective Health State**

Using the data described earlier (n=1600), the goal of the study 2 is to test the ability of the HRFS to predict health beliefs, health behavior and subjective health state. To test our hypothesis, we create an HRF index by subtracting participants' promotion scores from their prevention scores. We then perform a tertiary split on this index, creating a predominant promotion group and a predominant prevention group (Camacho, Luger and Higgins, 2003). Concerning health beliefs, based on prior existing research, we expect a relationship between health regulatory focus and health locus of control (Pham and Higgins, 2005) and health risk (Leikas *et alii*, 2006). Confirming our expectations, the results showed that people with higher prevention score have a stronger external locus of control (doctors and chance). However, no significant relationship is found between internal locus of control and promotion orientation contrary to what we expected. To test the influence of health regulatory focus on health risk assessment, two scenarios manipulating health risk due to a *decrease* in *immune system* function were presented to respondents. There was a significant relationship between health risk perception and health regulatory focus. In comparison to promotion oriented respondents, prevention oriented respondents have higher scores of perceived severity and susceptibility. Promotion oriented consumers were also more likely to adopt approach health behaviors (e.g. sport practice, eat 5 fruits and veggies). We have also found that promotion oriented consumers initiate a larger number of health behavior. This result is consisting with the fact that promotion-oriented consumers exhibit a greater need for variety in their self-regulation strategies (Pham and Higgins, 2005). It appears also clearly that promotion-oriented consumer demonstrate greater ability to maintain these health behaviors. It could be explained by the fact that promotion orientation influences positively the motivation to persist on a complex task (Crowe and Higgins, 1997). Finally, consumers who are promotion-oriented have higher score of subjective health state. This result supports the idea that under prevention, consumers are more likely to perceive their current health state as a source of potential problem. Additionally, a significant relationship between promotion orientation and optimism and between prevention orientation and neuroticism provide further evidence of the good validity of the HRFS.

To conclude, health regulatory focus seems to be an important concept to understand consumers' health motivation and especially how this motivation influence health outcomes. More research is needed to assess the additional contribution of the HRFS versus more domain-general alternative and explore its impact on consumers' health status and health information processing.

**References**

Briley D.A. and Aaker J.L. (2006), Bridging the culture chasm: Ensuring that consumers are healthy, wealthy and wise, *Journal of Public Policy & Marketing*, 25,1, 53-66.

Camacho C.J., Higgins E.T. and Luger L. (2003), Moral value transfer from regulatory fit: What feels right is right and what feels wrong is wrong. *Journal of Personality and Social Psychology*, 84, 3, 498-510.

Fuglestad P.T., Rothman A.J. and Jeffery R.W. (2008). Getting there and hanging on: The effect of regulatory focus on performance in smoking, *Health Psychology*, 27 (3), 260-270.

Higgins, E. T. (1997), Beyond pleasure and pain, *American Psychologist*, 52, 12, 1280-1300.

Hooker K. and Kaus C.R. (1994), Health-related possible selves in young and middle adulthood, *Psychology and Aging*, 9, 126-133.

Keller P.A. (2006), Regulatory focus and efficacy of health messages, *Journal of Consumer Research*, 33, 1, 109-114.

Leikas, S., Lindeman, M., Roininen, K. and Latheenmaki, N. (2006), Regulatory focus and food risk perception, *Appetite*, 47, 257-279.

Pham, M. T. and Higgins, E. T. (2005), Promotion and prevention in consumer decision making: The state of the art and theoretical propositions, *Inside consumption: Consumer motives, goals, and desires*, S. Ratneshwar & D. G. Mick (eds.), Londres, Routledge, 8-43.

Vartanian, L. R., C. P, Herman and Polivy, J. (2006), The role of regulatory focus on dietary restraint, *Eating Behaviour*, 7, 333-341.

Wallston K.A., Wallston B.S. and DeVellis R. (1978), Development of the multidimensional health locus of control (MHLC) scales, *Health Education Monographs*, 6, 160-170.

# The Effect of Self-Construal and Regulatory Focus on Persuasion: The Moderating Role of Perceived Risk

Ying-Ching Lin, National Dong Hwa University, Taiwan
Chiu-Chi Angela Chang, Shippensburg University, USA
Yu-Fang Lin, National Dong Hwa University, Taiwan

**Extended Abstract**

Consider an example regarding marketing nutritional supplements. Advertising for supplements may evoke the importance of good health for oneself or for loved ones. The advertisements may focus on either attaining a positive outcome (e.g., boosting energy) for your health, or preventing a negative outcome (e.g., preventing fatigue). The risk perception of a consumer is often influenced by information presented in the ads (e.g., a significant number of people died from heart diseases every year). Different combinations of self-construal (independent versus interdependent), regulatory focus (promotion-focused versus prevention-focused), and risk perceptions are likely in any given communication. It begs the question: what kind of combination would be the most persuasive? It is the motivation for the present research to investigate the persuasion effect of the interplay of self-construal, regulatory focus, and perceived risk.

Considerable research has been done on self construal and regulatory focus. The independent self is defined by unique attributes and independence from others. This is a dominant self-view in cultures where independence and achievement are emphasized. In contrast, the interdependent self is defined by others and appreciates fitting in and being harmoniously interdependent with each other. This self-view is predominant in cultures where obligations and responsibilities are emphasized (e.g., Fiske et al. 1998). In addition, according to regulatory focus theory (Higgins 2002), individuals with a promotion focus regulate their attitudes and behaviors to attain advancement, growth, and accomplishment. These individuals are inclined against committing errors of omission and are associated with eagerness strategies and openness to change. In contrast, individuals with a prevention focus regulate their attitudes and behaviors to attain safety and security. They are inclined against making errors of commission and prefer vigilance strategies and stability.

Self-construal and regulatory focus have been found to interact to influence consumer behavior. Lee, Aaker, and Gardner (2000) found that individuals with an accessible independent self perceive promotion-focused information as being more important than prevention-focused information, and that the converse is true for individuals with an accessible interdependent self. Aaker and Lee (2001) further showed that a promotion-focused message is considered more persuasive than a prevention-focused message for individuals with an independent self-view, and that the converse is true for individuals with an interdependent self-view. The present research extends the above mentioned literature by proposing a situational factor, perceived risk, to moderate the aforementioned persuasion effects.

As noted earlier, risk perceptions may be manipulated in a communication in order to attract consumers' attention. It is conceivable that consumers may react differently in a high versus low risk context to promotions (e.g., Bolton et al. 2008). The present research hypothesizes that when perceived risk is high, a prevention- (versus promotion-) focused message is more persuasive, no matter the individual's self-view. The reason for this is that a risk that is perceived to be high will sensitize consumers to focus on the possible negative outcomes and on vigilance (Lee and Aaker 2004), which is consistent with a prevention focus. Conversely, when perceived risk is low, the findings by Aaker and Lee (2001) should be replicated.

Three studies tested the proposition that perceived risk moderates the interaction effect of self-construal and regulatory focus on persuasion. Study 1 replicated the original findings in Aaker and Lee (2001) and Studies 2 and 3 manipulated the perceived risk in different ways and obtained results that were in agreement with our premise. Specifically, Study 1 asked participants to think about either themselves or their family (i.e., an independent versus interdependent self-construal; self-construal was manipulated this way across the three studies). The advertisement for the target product, cranberry juice, focused on the belief that it enhanced youthfulness and energy or that it could prevent heart disease (i.e., a promotion versus prevention focus). In Study 2 where a yogurt drink was the target product, the promotion-focused message mentioned that the product could benefit and strengthen the immune system as well as the digestive system, while the prevention-focused message mentioned the drink's ability to prevent digestive system diseases and reduce cholesterol and cancer-causing toxins. To manipulate perceived risk, half of the participants in Study 2 were told that "six people died of colon cancer *every day* in this country," while the other half learned that "two thousand people died of colon cancer *every year* in this country." This manipulation was based on Chandran and Menon (2004), whose findings showed that risk estimates are higher on a per day versus a per year basis. Finally, Study 3 used another target product, Essence of Golden Clam, which was advertised to either enhance the health of one's liver and boost energy, or prevent liver disease (promotion versus prevention focus). Perceived risk was manipulated based on the frequency of engaging in risk behavior (Menon, Block, & Ramanathan, 2002). Participants were told by the advertisement that hepatitis B could be contracted either by not bandaging a cut (a frequent risk behavior; high perceived risk) or by getting a tattoo (an infrequent behavior; low perceived risk). Consistent with our proposition, both Studies 2 and 3 found that in a high (versus low) perceived risk situation, a prevention-focused message led to more favorable brand attitudes and purchase intentions for both independent- and interdependent-self construal groups.

In summary, the present research proposes that perceived risk moderates the effect of self-construal and regulatory focus on persuasion. In particular, when perceived risk is high, a prevention-focused message should be considered more persuasive, no matter the type of self-construal. Empirical findings from three studies support our proposition, where perceived risk was manipulated by using a day versus year frame, and by highlighting a frequent versus infrequent risk behavior. The theoretical contribution of this research is that it clarifies the moderating role of perceived risk in the findings of Aaker and Lee (2001). From a practical perspective, advertising strategies targeting consumers who are likely to perceive the message in the advertisement as a high risk issue should utilize a prevention-focused appeal to enhance persuasion, irrespective of the consumers' self-views.

## References

Aaker, Jennifer L. and Angela Y. Lee (2001), "'I' Seek Pleasures and 'We' Avoid Pains: The Role of Self-Regulatory Goals in Information Processing and Persuasion, *Journal of Consumer Research*, 28 (June), 33-49.

Bolton, Lisa E., Americus Reed II, Kevin G. Volpp, and Katrina Armstrong, (2008), "How Does Drug and Supplement Marketing Affect a Healthy Lifestyle?" *Journal of Consumer Research* 34 (February), 713-726.

Chandran, Sucharita and Geeta Menon (2004), "When a Day Means More than a Year: Effects of Temporal Framing on Judgments of Health Risk," *Journal of Consumer Research*, 31 (September), 375-389.

Fiske, Alan, Shinobu Kitayama, Hazel R. Markus, and Richard Nisbett (1998), "The Cultural Matrix of Social Psychology," in *The Handbook of Social Psychology*, Vol. 2, ed. Daniel T. Gilbert and Susan T. Fiske, Boston: McGraw-Hill, 915–981.

Higgins, E. Tory, (2002), "How Self-Regulation Creates Distinct Values: The Case of Promotion and Prevention Decision Making," *Journal of Consumer Psychology,* 12 (3), 177-191.

Lee, Angela Y., and Jennifer L. Aaker, (2004), "Bringing the Frame into Focus: The Influence of Regulatory Fit on Processing fluency and Persuasion," *Journal of Personality & Social Psychology* 86 (2), 205-218.

Lee, Angela Y., Jennifer L. Aaker, and Wendi L. Gardner (2000), "The Pleasures and Pains of Distinct Self-Construals: The Role of Interdependence in Regulatory Focus," *Journal of Personality and Social Psychology*, 78 (June), 1122–1134.

Menon, Geeta, Lauren G. Block, and Suresh Ramanathan (2002), "We're at as Much Risk as We Are Led to Believe: Effects of Message Cues on Judgments of Health Risk," *Journal of Consumer Research*, 28 (March), 533-549.

# Self-control and the Differential Weighting of the Components of Risk

Shi Jia, Stanford University, USA
Ab Litt, Stanford University, USA
Uzma Khan, Stanford University, USA
Tatiana Andreyeva, Yale University, USA

## Extended Abstract

Harmful consumption decisions like smoking, overeating, and drinking are commonly blamed on self-control problems. Rather than assume that people with low self-control simply fail to rein in their impulses, this work explores whether such people view the fundamental nature of risks differently.

Risk perception is often divided into two distinct components: probability and consequences of negative outcomes. In this work we show systematic differences in the weighting of these basic risk components by individuals varying in self-control. In particular, we find that low-self-control leads to heightened focus on probability, but relative neglect of consequences. This divergent construction of perceived risk may be influenced by motivating factors and defensive mechanisms. When faced with threatening information, people often engage in defensive or motivated reasoning, even if such processes make a person objectively worse off (Kunda 1987, 1990, Sherman, Nelson, and Steele 2000).

By disentangling the individual components of risk from an overall conception of risk, our approach yields deeper insight into self-control and systematic patterns of risk underestimation and relative focus on distinct components during threat assessment.

In consumer behavior research, perceived risk been modeled as a function of uncertainty and consequences dimensions (Bauer 1960, Cunningham, 1967, Cox 1967):

$$R = v\,(x)^a\, p(x)^b \qquad (1)$$

where $R$ is the overall perceived risk of $x$, $v(x)$ represents the negative consequences of $x$, $p(x)$ is the probability of $x$ occurring, and $a$ and $b$ are the relative weights of probability and consequences. We apply a log-linear transformation for regression analyses to obtain

$$\ln(R) = \mathrm{h}\,c + a\,\mathrm{h}\,v(x) + b\,\mathrm{h}\,p(x) \qquad (2)$$

By measuring overall threat, $R$, the probability of $x$ occurring, $p(x)$, and the value of the negative consequence of $x$, $v(x)$, we will be able to derive the relative weighting of consequence and probability ($a$ and $b$, respectively). One may think of the weighting coefficient as telling us how much one's overall sense of risk increases with a one unit increase in consequence or probability

We may add two interaction terms, the interaction between self-control ($S$) and consequence and the interaction between self-control and probability, to see how people with different levels of self-control differentially weight the components of risk;

$$\ln(R) = \mathrm{h}\,c + a\,\mathrm{h}\,v(x) + b\,\mathrm{h}\,p(x) + c\ln[v(x)*S] + d\,\mathrm{h}[p(x)*S] \qquad (3)$$

## Study 1: Dietary Disinhibition and Overeating-related Risk Perception

After completing a measure for self-control in eating habits (Karlsson et al., 2000), participants (n=76) completed a three-stage rating of perceived risk for heart attack and diabetes due to overeating. Participants rated their perceptions of the consequences, probability, and overall threat for each risk.

In within group analysis using our estimated log-linear model (3), both interaction terms are significant in different directions. For both heart attack and diabetes from overeating, the interaction between consequence and self-control was positive and significant (p<0.05), while the interaction between probability and self-control was negative and significant (p<0.05). The results show that the negative *consequences* of diet-related health problems appeared to be a more important component of perceived risk among high-self-control eaters than high-self-control eaters. In contrast, the perceived *probability* proved relatively more important for low-self-control eaters.

## Study 2: General Perceived Risks and Self-Control

Study 2 explores whether study 1's results can be generalized into other domains or risky behavior outside of overeating-related diseases. Subjects (n=124) complete the same risk elicitation procedures and perceived risk model as in study 1. However, we now use a general self-control scale that measures Cognitive Restraint (Karlsson et al 2000).

Results indicated a pattern analogous with the results of Study 1—low-self-control leading to relative probability-focus, high-self-control to relative consequences-focus—was observed in non-overeating-related domains characterized by a *high self-agency for control*. We find this pattern for overeating related diseases (p<0.05), speeding-related car crashes (p<0.), smoking-related lung cancer (p<0.01), food hygiene issues (p<0.05), and MSG poisoning (p<0.01 for *c* and *d*).

In contrast, risks with *low potential-for-control* (e.g., genetic-related cancer, avian flu, hard drive crash) did not show similar results. None of the low self-agency risks had any statistically significant interaction terms between self-control and probability or consequence. The necessity of self-agency for differential weighting to occur hints at some motivational process: when adverse consequences are not attributable to self-control failings, low-self-control individuals need not underweight consequences when formulating overall risk.

## Study 3: Manipulating Felt Self-Control

Study 3 shows that manipulating one's sense of self-control can cause the differential weighting of the components of risk. In this study, we induce different levels of felt self-control through an ease of retrieval paradigm (Schwarz et al 1991). Participants (n=133) are asked to recall two or ten instances in which they were able to 'exercise self-control, discipline, or willpower in the face of temptation' (2 instances=easy, 10 instances=difficult). The difficulty of the task is supposed to cause participants to infer that they are not very good at that particular action or behavior. After the recall task, subjects' risk attitudes are elicited in the same manner as studies 1 and 2. There is also a control condition against which we compare the recall conditions.

Our results once again show that people with lower felt-self-control focus more on probabilities and less on consequences. In the 'hard recall' condition, where subjects feel lower self-control, our regression analyses finds significant interaction terms between self-control level (now a dummy variable) and risk components. We find that compared to the control condition, subjects who are induced to feel lower self-control weight consequence less and weight probability more (predictors sig. p<0.05 for heart attack and hypertension from overeating, speeding, drinking, smoking, and job loss from shirking).

None of these interactions are significant for people induced to feel 'high control', suggesting that 'high self-control' people do not engage in differential weighting of the risk components.

## Conclusions

Differential weighting of the components of perceived risk, probability and consequences, may differentially contribute to the estimation of risk for people with low versus high self-control. This is especially prevalent when defensive and motivated reasoning strategies are both possible and desirable. Such motivated processing may lead to the persistence of both risky and non-risky behavioral patterns, and also to irrational and counter-intuitive underestimations of overall threat by those individuals most at risk of being affected by specific negative outcomes.

## Selected References

Bauer, Raymond A. "Consumer Behavior as Risk Taking," in Donald F. Cox, ed., *Risk Taking and Information Handling in Consumer Behavior*. Boston: Graduate School of Business Administration, Harvard University, 1967, 23-33.

Cox, Donald F., ed., *Risk Taking and Information Handling in Consumer Behavior*. Boston: Graduate School of Business Administration, Harvard University, 1967.

Karlsson, Jan, Lars-Olof Persson, Lars Sjöström, and Marriane Sullivan (2000), "Psychometric properties and factor structure of the Three-Factor Eating Questionnaire (TFEQ) in obese men and women. Results from the Swedish Obese Subjects (SOS) study," *International Journal of Obesity*, 24 (December), 1715-1725.

Kunda, Ziv (1987), "The Case for Motivated Reasoning," *Psychological Bulletin*, 108 (3), 480-498.

Kunda, Ziv (1990), "Motivation and inference: Self-serving generation and evaluation of evidence," *Journal of Personality and Social Psychology*, 53, 636-647.

Sherman, David A.K., Leif D. Nelson, and Claude M. Steele (2000), "Do Messages about Health Risks Threaten the Self? Increasing the Acceptance of Threatening Health Messages Via Self-Affirmation," *Personality and Social Psychology Bulletin*, 26 (9), 1046-1058.

# Risk Acculturation Through Marketplace and Technology

Gulnur Tumbat, San Francisco State University, USA
Markus Giesler, York University, Canada

## Extended Abstract

The theory of risk acculturation explains the process of normalization of risk through socialization and experience. According to Celsi, Rose, and Leigh's (1993) great account of skydiving, risk perceptions become normalized with socialization to a subculture and through gaining experience and the participant achieves an insider status and thus accepted by the skydiving community. For an outsider, the risky activity is deviant and it requires learning and adaptation process to see it as normal. The risk becomes normalized through the process of socialization and thus gradually assuming/adapting the ideology of the subculture. The high-risk subculture is considered as a tight community that places properties of high-risk behavior within the realm of normal. With full acculturation to this community, high-risk performers *learn* to be risk managers and the differences among insiders and outsiders are limited to the stages of their socialization into the high-risk subculture and to the stages of their risk perception evolution trajectories. Furthermore, participants acculturated to risk also become able to attend higher-level transcendent motives such as flow, communitas, and phatic communion (Celsi, Rose, and Leigh's 1993).

Yet risk acculturation theory as it currently stands falls short of explaining the implications of the easier access to and participation into high-risk performances by an increasing number of people with various levels of experience in today's marketplace. The availability of the high-risk performance stages, service providers, and technological developments in the marketplace help novices to become high-risk performers. In order to illustrate, personal GPS tracker devices provide location-based communication and notifies friends, families, or professional services such as rescue coordination services "all with the push of a button." These devices are designed for backpackers, boaters, campers, cyclists, climbers, hikers, kayakers/canoeists, off-road enthusiasts, sailors, snowmobilers, and many others. This is an example of a case that enables people to rely on a technological tool to manage the risk of getting lost or being hurt. In other words, in this case, one can argue that risk is normalized through the help of a tool available in the marketplace. Furthermore, relying on such tools while lacking the necessary understanding and experience may create tensions within the (sub)culture. When people, with a variety of experience and skill levels and physical conditions, end up in situations that would require outside help, discussions arise as to who should pay for their rescue costs. Taxpayers raise their concerns over those rescues of inexperienced people who get lost in the wilderness due to their inexperience. After exploring the relevant consumer behavior literature including the more general acculturation studies (we don't list the extensive review here due to space limitations), we came to realize that risk acculturation theory ascribes little or no potential for the increasingly commercial nature of such performances and its effects on the interactions among (insider or outsider) participants and non-participants. The aim of this study is thus to address this theoretical gap.

The context of our study is commercially guided climbing expeditions on big mountains as part of the growing adventure industry. It provides a suitable area to explore marketplace dynamics of risk acculturation process. People with different backgrounds and various levels of experience hire professional mountain guides and use high-tech gear and tools to improve their chances to climb mountains and claim a mountaineer identity. We collected data through extensive participant observation and in-depth interviews within various mountaineering communities. Active participant observation for over five years took place at several high-altitude mountains in the world, including Elbrus in Russia, Everest in Nepal, McKinley in the US, and Aconcagua in Argentina. Our data set includes 17 on-site interviews with climbers who pay for guide services on the mountains and their guides. These on-site in-depth interviews were followed by 20 more off-site in-depth interviews with some of the same participants along with the new ones after their climbs. We focused on the commercial nature of the activity as a general topic in our conversations. Standard IRB procedures were followed to gather consent from the participants. The interviews lasted on average 50 minutes and were transcribed verbatim. We analyzed the field notes and in-depth interviews that are close to 1,000 single spaced pages as a whole with the help of the Atlas data analysis software and through a hermeneutic and iterative process. We also incorporated extensive secondary data from sources including but not limited to mountaineering books, adventure magazines, and web blogs.

We found that participants in this high-risk leisure activity do not necessarily follow the path identified by Celsi *et al.* (1993) on their way to claim a high-risk identity. For many, marketplace provides a stage and an opportunity to experience such an identity with the help of high-tech tools, gear, and guide services. Thus, although they lack experience and never truly socialize into a mountaineering subculture, they normalize risk through the marketplace–the missing path in the prior risk acculturation conceptualization. Socialization and gaining experience are not very convenient since they both take time and effort. They instead take an alternate path which allows them to normalize risk and claim a mountaineer identity. Thus, we contend that risk acculturation occurs not only through experience and socialization but also through commercialization of services and tools (Figure 1). This is seen as an illegitimate short cut for some aficionados and results in conflicts and tensions rather than communitas. Furthermore, these participants never fully experience flow since they lack the necessary skills and delegate dealing with challenges to guides as commercial service providers.

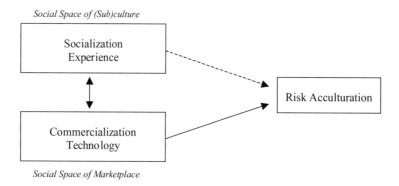

**Figure 1.** Marketplace and Risk Acculturation

The theoretical contribution of this study is therefore twofold. First, it unpacks the underappreciated commercial dimension in high-risk performances. Second, it explicates how marketplace dynamics in terms of commercialization and technology significantly shapes the risk acculturation process which is theorized as related only with experience and socialization to a high-risk consumption community. We further argue that this updated risk acculturation process does not necessarily result in higher end states such as flow, communitas, or phatic communion (Celsi, Rose, and Leigh 1993). Expanding the theory by accounting the commercialization and marketplace availability has significant implications to a variety of different areas not only for leisure activities (hiring a guide service to climb a mountain, using a GPS tracking device in wilderness, signing up for a rescue service before stepping to the outdoors) but also bigger picture items as encouraged by this ACR's organizers, such as various financial investments through hiring a financial advisor or signing on a loan from a financial institution that is believed to manage the risk in an uncertain economic environment. Thus, we believe the extended conceptualization of risk acculturation within marketplace will generate great interest and discussion within the ACR audience which help us improve this study significantly.

### References

Celsi, Richard L., Randall L. Rose, and Thomas W. Leigh, (1993), "An Exploration of High-Risk Leisure Consumption through Skydiving," *Journal of Consumer Research*, 20 (June), 1-23.

# An Identity Approach to Prosumption- A Case of Bacalhau Prosumption in Brazil

Lúcia Fátima Martins Guilhoto, Fandação Instituto de Administração, Brazil
Chunyan Xie, Stord/Haugesund University College, Norway
Kjell Gronhaug, Norwegian School of Economics and Business Administration, Norway
Jens Ostli, Nofima marked, Norway

## Extended Abstract

The phenomenon of "prosumption" has attracted substantial interest both among researchers and practitioners since this term was first coined by Toffler (1980). In existent research literature, the phenomenon has been addressed from different perspectives. Here we explore the phenomenon of prosumption from the perspectives of role-based identity (Burke 1991) and social identity (Turner et al. 1987), which is a rather novel approach to gain insight into the phenomenon.

Prosumption can be defined as "value creation activities undertaken by the consumer that result in the production of products they eventually consume and that become their consumption experiences" (Xie, Bagozzi and Troye 2008). Furthermore, prosumption can be conceived as a process consisting of two phases: production and consumption. All the activities before the beginning point of consumption are included in the production process, and those after the point are included in the consumption process. Both phases consist of a flow of behaviors, appraisal of those behaviors and emotional experiences. The inputs to the prosumption process are time, effort and monetary resources. The outputs are experiences and values created through the prosumption process.

The prosumption process is embedded in a social world that is constituted not only by formal rules, but also by the wide variety of conventions, habits and styles from different people. That is why our theoretical perspectives of role-based identity and social identity are so relevant to a deeper understanding of the whole process. Key aspects of these theories are people' self-views emerging from the reflexive activity of self-categorization or identification in terms of roles (role-based identity) or membership in particular groups (social identity).

For instance, from the perspective of role-based identity, a prosumer categorizes herself as an occupant of a role (i.e. a hostess), and incorporates into herself of the meanings and expectations associated with that role and its performance. A prosumption process can be, then, conceived as an identity control system that consists of a feedback loop (Burke 1991). The loop has four components: a standard (the set of self-meaning, a prosumer's standard, e.g., to be a good hostess); an input from the social situation (including one's reflected appraisal); a process that compares the input with the standard (a comparator); and an output to the environment (meaningful behavior) that is a results of the comparison. The system works by modifying output to the social situation in attempts to change the input (reflected appraisals) to match the internal standard. Prosumers increase their self-esteem and self-efficacy by performing a role well, because they go through a self-verification process by comparing the what a person perceives in the situation (reflected appraisal) and the self-meaning held by the individual (standard) (Burke and Stets 1999).

A social identity is a person's knowledge that he or she belongs to a social category or group. Such a group-based knowledge may account for the closeness of the social relations among persons who are involved in the prosumption process. Our empirical context is bacalhau prosumption in Brazil. Bacalhau is a Portuguese word for a particular preparation of cod fish and is synonymous with salted and dried cod. It is the tradition that bacalhau meal is served as a centerpiece of family celebrations and social solidarity during important holidays such as Easter and Christmas. Great part of such kind of social gathering relies on symbolic interactive activities that show mutual appreciation, respect, and esteem among the members, helping shaping social identities. To sum up, one way to understand such a prosumption process can be to conceive it as a process where prosumers carry out various production and consumption activities in order to create, maintain and regulate their identities.

We approached this empirical context in an explorative, discovery-oriented basis. Our paper draws upon 13 qualitative focus groups interviews that were developed with 104 consumers from different social classes, genders and geographic locations in Brazil. The guiding heuristic principle is that the informal discussion of all the phases of the prosumption process (namely, planning, shopping, desalting, cooking and serving) can bring to surface several aspects of role-based identity and social identity such as environments, perceived self-meaning, reflected appraisals from others and shared experiences and provide insights on how people interact in order to reinforce social identity in their groups assuming specific roles supported by rituals, behaviors and social connections.

We found empirical evidence on role identity for every phase of the bacalhau prosumption. We verified that for each phase several quality standards are established by a person when she assumes the role of host of the dinner. These standards are controlled once different tasks are performed; if consistency is found between what was established and what was observed the role identity loop is closed and the person experiences feelings of self-accomplishment, pride and satisfaction. For instance, we have found out that for the shopping phase of the bacalhau prosumption the most common standards established are size of the piece of bacalhau, color, kind of package and expiration date. These pre-established standards are checked during the purchase of bacalhau and if this purchase meets all the standards established the host feels that the loop is closed, reinforces her self-accomplishment feeling and passes to the following phase. We also found empirical evidence that the prosumption of bacalhau involves meanings and interactive processes that are deeply based on the reinforcement of the social identity. For instance, we found that although much of the prosumption of bacalhau is done by one person that assumes the role of the host of the dinner everything is done having in mind the rules and expectations of the group; if these rules and expectations are not met ingredients and attitudes are rearranged in order to conform to the groups' social identity.

In sum, we develop and apply a model that integrates the prosumption process and the theoretical perspectives on role-based identity and social identity to better understand prosumption. It provides novel understanding of the prosumption process-especially related to food-related prosumption. Both theoretical and managerial implications are highlighted, and avenues for future research indicated.

### References

Burke, Peter J. (1991) "Identity processes and social stress", *American Sociological Review*, Vol. 56, No. 6, 836-849.

Burke Peter J. and Stets Jan E. (1999), "Trust and Commitment through Self-Verification", *Social Psychology Quarterly*, Vol. 62, No.4, 347-366.

Toffler, A. (1980). The third wave. New York: William Collins Sons & Co. Ltd.

Turner, J.C., Hogg, M.A., Oakes, P.J., Reicher, S.D., Wetherell, M.S. (1987), *Rediscovering the social group: A self-categorization theory*, Basil Blackwell Oxford Toffler (1980).

Chunyan Xie, Richard Bagozzi and Sigurd Troye (2008), "Trying to prosume: Toward a theory of consumers as co-creators of value", Journal of Academy of Marketing Science.

# I Show You Only Who I Am If Needed: Identity Signaling as a Result of the Interaction Between Personal Motives and Situational Factors

Hendrik Slabbinck, Ghent University, Belgium
Patrick Van Kenhove, Ghent University, Belgium

Consumers often make choices that diverge from those of others to ensure that they effectively communicate desired identities. Teens, for instance, regularly want to distinguish themselves from their parents and therefore choose for music styles, clothes, … their parents dislike. Previous studies demonstrate this drive to differentiate from others through product choices to vary across individuals (Snyder and Fromkin 1977) and situations (Byrne and Griffitt 1969). Further, research shows that for product categories symbolizing one's identity, individuals abandon product options which the majority prefers (Berger and Heath 2007).

In addition, identity signaling is partially driven by price and explicitness of brand logos. Consumers, for instance, who strive for broader public recognition like to show others they can afford expensive products. Therefore, they choose expensive products that are well know by a broad range of consumers. They further prefer loud or large brand logos because it helps them broadcasting their desired identity. Very expensive top-class products that are only recognizable by connoisseurs are for these consumers less suitable for identity signaling.(Berger and Ward 2009).

The data of our three studies, however, display a more nuanced pattern. In Study 1, we asked 56 undergraduate students to enumerate brands that are typically bought or avoided by students who strive for broader recognition by showing their possessions to others. When analyzing the product categories, product categories that are seen as symbolic of identity were, as expected, most frequently listed (i.e. clothes (n= 36) and cars (n=30)). When analyzing brands, results were also straightforward. In general, the rather expensive well known brands that are still affordable by a rather broad range of consumers were top listed as typical signaling brands. These were BMW (n=16) and Mercedes Benz (n=15) for cars and Tommy Hilfiger (n=11) and Armani (n=6) for clothing. Further and in line with our expectations, lower priced well known brands were enumerated as brands these people rather avoid. For cars, these were Volkswagen (n=5) and Opel (n=5), and for clothing, Esprit (n=9) and H&M (n=5). So far, all results were in line with the existing literature.

In study 2 (n=137), we measured the degree to which undergraduate students strive for broader recognition by showing his/her personal wealth to others. The focal product category was clothing because it was top listed as identity signaling product category in Study1. Surprisingly, we could not find any relation between the degree for striving for broader public recognition and the percentage of the clothes of signaling brands that the participant had in his wardrobe (r=.07; p>.05). Based on previous studies as well as the results of our first study, we expected people high (low) in need for public recognition to own relatively more (less) clothes of signaling brands.

These unexpected results indicated that the activation of signaling related behavior is more complex than just the straightforward relationship between need for public recognition and an individual's number of signaling brands. According to McClelland et al. (1989), behavior is the result of the interaction between motives and the environment. In brief, a person with a certain motive or need will only engage in motive relevant behavior under the presence of appropriate environmental stimuli. Without the presence of these environmental stimuli, motive relevant behavior is less likely to occur. In terms of identity signaling, this means that a consumer high in need for public recognition should be more likely to buy an expensive shirt with a large and loud imprint of a brand logo in a multi-brand store than in a mono-brand store. This because the presence of unwanted, cheap brands in the multi-brand store could act as an environmental stimulus that activates the consumer's need for public recognition. Once this need is activated, the consumer's purchase behavior should be channeled towards signaling brands with large brand logos. If this explanation is true, then the relationship between need for public recognition and intended purchase behavior of signaling brands must be higher in the presence of unwanted brands, certainly if the brands have explicit brand logos. To test this hypothesis, we set up a third study (n=131) in which we measured need for public recognition and intended purchase behaviour of two brands (within subjects): a signaling brand (Tommy Hilfiger) and an unwanted brand (Esprit). Signal explicitness was manipulated between subjects. We created two conditions for each brand. In the first condition, all t-shirts had large brand logos. In the second condition, we showed exactly the same t-shirts, but with brand logos erased. Each picture was tagged with a short description and brand name. To assess intended purchase behavior, each participant (all females) got virtually 100 Euros which they needed to spend in our online t-shirt shop. Difference tests on Fisher r-to-z transformations fully supported our hypothesis. The correlation, for instance, between need for public recognition and intended purchase behavior for the signaling brand was .41 (p<.05) when both the signaling and unwanted brand had explicit brand logos. This correlation was significantly higher than when both brands had no brand logos (r=.08, p>.1; $z_{diff}$=1.98, p<.05).

The results of these three studies add important insights to identity signaling theory. We clearly showed that individual differences and situational factors must be studied jointly instead of separately. As shown in our third study, the effect of individual differences on identity signaling is only activated in a specific situation. In future research, we will incorporate additional situational factors and individual difference variables (e.g. self-esteem). Another interesting avenue for further research concerns the question how identity signaling works for symbolic products that are less visible for the general public (e.g. pajamas, bathroom accessories, …).

## Selected References

Berger, J. and C. Heath (2007), "Where Consumers Diverge from Others: Identity Signaling and Product Domains," *Journal of Consumer Research*, 34 (2), 121-34.

Berger, Jonah and Morgan Ward (2009), "The Subtle Signals of Inconspicuous Consumption," in *Advances in Consumer Research*, Vol. 36, ed. Ann L. McGill and Sharon Shavitt, Duluth, MN Association for Consumer Research, 90-92.

Byrne, D. and W. Griffitt (1969), "Similarity and Awareness of Similarity of Personality Characteristics as Determinants of Attraction," *Journal of Experimental Research in Personality*, 3 (3), 179-86.

McClelland, D. C., R. Koestner, and J. Weinberger (1989), "How Do Self-Attributed and Implicit Motives Differ," *Psychological Review*, 96 (4), 690-702.

Snyder, C. R. and H. L. Fromkin (1977), "Abnormality as a Positive Characteristic-Development and Validation of a Scales Measuring Need for Uniqueness," *Journal of Abnormal Psychology*, 86 (5), 518-27.

# Who Determines the Ideal Self?: A Comparative Analysis of Non-Verbal Communication

Junko Kimura, Hosei University, Japan
Mototaka Sakashita, Keio Business School, Japan

## Extended Abstract

Self-concept must be treated as having two components; the actual self-concept and the ideal self-concept. Ideal self-concept is defined as the image of oneself as one would like to be. The ideal self-concept has been referred to as the "ideal self," "idealized image," and "desired self" (Sirgy 1982). Consumers hold their own ideal self images, and often try to alter their appearance by changing their outfits, in order to get closer to those images. Ideal self is the self-concept where an individual puts the highest value (Rogers 1959). Consumers use purchasing in order to approach their ideal self (Belk 1988; McCracken 1988). A desirable self-concept can be created through consumption, and it can also be extended into products. (Belk 1988; Schouten 1991). Most scholars seem to agree that the term "self-concept" denotes the "totality of the individual's thoughts and feelings having reference to him as an object" (Rosenberg 1979). Actual self refers to how a person perceives herself. Ideal self refers to how a person would like to perceive herself. Social self refers to how a person presents herself to others.

Since the concept of ideal self is highly important to the consumers, they independently search for their ideal self-image, and often decide on it. When they decide on their ideal self, their significant others approve it. Significant others are specific others who influence the self-formation of consumers. Parents and teachers can be significant others; also, friends, classmates, and mass media can become such influential people (Mead 1934). They have long proposed that parents are the most influential socializing agents for their children (Cooley 1902; Sullivan 1947; Turner 1962).

Mothers might be significant socializers for their daughters and control them by using social power. Social power consists of reward power, coercive power, legitimate power, referent power, and expert power (French and Raven 1959). Significant others may not only approve of the ideal self that the consumers decided on, but also occasionally decide on the consumers' ideal self itself. It seems reasonable to look at mothers as primary socializing agents for the formation of their daughters' attitudes (Bohannon and Blanton 1999). The ideal self determination process under mother-daughter situation can be described as "coercive," since the mother has already formed a clear idea of her daughter's ideal self image prior to the shopping experience. Here, the mother tries to force her daughter to accept whatever ideal self image she has. According to Nobuta and Ueno (2008), in contemporary Japan, identification with mothers does not simply mean identifying with the actual existing mothers. Mothers try to get their daughters to identify with their ideal self.

Female friendship is affective. Women expect their female friends to feel and react in the same manner as they do (Wheeler & Nezlek 1977). Female friends mutually request sympathy from the other party. Sympathy can be created by self-monitoring. Self-monitoring is to observe whether one's expression, action or self-presentation of one's self is socially appropriate. In female friendship context, one's behavior is modified according to the other's reaction (Snyder 1974). The ideal self determination process under friend-daughter situation can be described as "collaborative," since the daughter and her female friend are both engage in the daughter's ideal self determination process.

We set our proposition: a different nature of relationship results in a different ideal self determination process. Specifically, in a mother-daughter relationship, the mother has already decided on the daughter's ideal self before the actual process starts. The mother then forces her daughter to accept her own idea. This is called a "coercive process", and the entire process is often omitted. In the friend-daughter relationship, the friend and the daughter act as if they mutually sympathize to the other, and cooperatively decide on the daughter's ideal self. This is called a "collaborative process", where they even enjoy spending time together until they reach to the daughter's desirable ideal self.

We use interpretive approach and directly observe actions at catalogue shopping of mother-daughter pair and friend-daughter pair. We conducted a unique comparative analysis of the collected quantity data; using three types of Non Verbal Communication (NVC), we compared frequencies of those NVC in each pair and interpret them with supplemental verbal data. The study consists of [STUDY 1] and [STUDY 2], and there were twelve sets of pair altogether. Six daughters participated in both studies. The daughters brought her mothers for [STUDY 1] to form M-D relationship condition. Under this context, they performed the daughter's ideal self decision process. Not only verbal data but also nonverbal data were collected because the Japanese people tend to use many subtle body language cues in daily conversation.

Results of the comparative analysis were consistent with the proposition. Important future research directions were addressed.

### References

Belk, Russell W. (1988), "Possessions and the Extended Self," *Journal of Consumer Research*, 15, 139-168.

Bohannon, Judy Rollins. and Blanton, Priscilla White. (1999), "Gender Role Attitudes of American Mothers and Daughters Over Time," *Journal of Social Psychology*, 139(2), 173-179.

Cooley, C.H. (1902), Human Nature and the Social Order. New York: Scribner.

French, J.R., Jr. and Raven, B. (1959), "The Bases of Social Power," Cartwright, D. (ed.) *Studies in Social Power*. Ann Arbor, MI: Institute for Social Research, University of Michigan.

Rosenberg, Morris. (1979) *Conceiving the Self*. New York: Basic Books.

Sirgy, Joseph M. (1982), "Self-Concept in Consumer Behavior: A Critical Review," *Journal of Consumer Research*, 9 (December), 287-300.

Sullivan, H.S. (1947), *Conceptions of Modern Psychology*. Washington, DC: William A. White Psychiatric Foundation.

Turner, R.H. (1962), "Role-Taking Process versus Conformity," Rose, A. (ed.) *Human Behavior and Social Processes: An Interactionist Approach*. Boston: Houghton Mifflin.

# Narcissists as Consumers: Using Scarce Products to Validate Excessively Positive Self-View

Seung Yun Lee, McGill University, Canada
Sung Hoon Park, Yonsei University, Korea

### Extended Abstract

Narcissists can be defined as people who can be characterized as self–centered, self–aggrandizing, dominant, and manipulative[1,2]. Recently, narcissism as an individual difference dimension has been operationalized as a higher scorer on the Narcissistic Personality Inventory (NPI) [3,4]. Several researchers have shown interest in the characteristic and behavior patterns of narcissists as consumers [5,6]. They proposed that narcissists as consumers are likely to purchase prestigious and exclusive products to sustain and elevate their self-positivity. That is to say, narcissism can drive people to purchase highly exclusive and luxurious products because the consumptions of such products potentially serve as a means of validating excessively positive self–views. As a result, narcissists may, in order to validate their excessively positive self–views, try to purchase prestigious and exclusive products which are believed to have higher symbolic values than other products. In so doing, they try to regulate their own self–esteem by increasing their apparent status, hence obtaining others' admiration and envy[5,6]. Past research suggests that when narcissistic consumers make a choice, they may have much higher tendency to sacrifice utilitarian aspects for attaining symbolic ones, compared to non-narcissistic consumers[6]. That is, for narcissists as consumers, it may not be important whether a product will serve their own practical needs or not. The utilitarian value of a product is likely to be of lesser importance to them, whereas a product's symbolic value is of greater importance.

Scarcity can be defined as insufficiency of product supply or time of availability[7]. Past research suggests that consumers can use scarcity as a cue (i.e. "What is rare is good") for good value, whereby they infer that a highly scarce product must be more valuable than a less scarce product[8,9]. The underlying mechanism for this inference of scarcity as value is based on the assumption that people tend to desire uniqueness[10]. In this case, people evaluate scarce products as being more valuable because they believe that possessing something scarce can produce positive feelings of personal uniqueness. In the present research, we show that narcissistic individuals are more likely to strive to purchase a scarce product in order to obtain others' admiration and envy, albeit at the cost of utilitarian aspects, compared to non-narcissistic counterparts, because they believe that the possession of a scarce product can show their own exclusive uniqueness, hence validating their excessively self-positive view through such consumption.

In study 1, we propose that for consumers with high narcissism (HN), scarcity will have strong positive effect on product evaluation, while consumers with low narcissism (LN) are less unaffected by scarcity (H1). One hundred participants were randomly assigned to a 2 (Scarcity: High versus Low) between-subject design. Participants were asked to complete the forty–item ($\alpha$=.92) questionnaire from Narcissistic Personality Inventory (NPI), with the purpose of assessing the participants' propensity for self–narcissism. Consistent with other studies in this area[11], participants scoring in the top third of the NPI were considered as having high narcissism and those who scored in the bottom third of the NPI were considered as having low narcissism. After then, participants were presented with a hypothetical retail scenario, which included an ad for a wristwatch. The ad manipulated scarcity, in terms of limited quantities. The dependent variable of product evaluation was measured by an item assessing willingness to pay (WTP). We predicted and found that participants with HN reported higher WTP toward the product promoted with scarcity claim than that without scarcity claim ($M$=\$163.73 vs. \$80.91, $t$(35)=2.63, $p$=.012). However, this effect did not happen for LN participants ($M$=\$90.26 vs. \$83.12, $t$(33)=.355, $p$=.725). This result indicates that HN consumers have a stronger desire for a scarce product, compared to LN counterparts.

The literatures on scarcity have shown that an increase in arousal due to scarcity tends to motivates consumers to pay more attention to task relevant cues, resulting in a systematic processing of relevant information[12,13]. In study 2, we argue that narcissistic consumers are likely to have a stronger propensity to purchase the scarce product without scrutinizing information because they want to validate their excessively positive self-views by purchasing a scarce product and can sacrifice utilitarian needs for attaining symbolic ones. Therefore, we predict that for consumers with high narcissism (HN), increasing scarcity will reduce depth of processing (H2a). On the other hand, for consumers with low narcissism (LN), consistent with past scarcity research, increasing scarcity will increase depth of processing (H2b). These different effects of scarcity on depth of processing outlined in H2a and H2b, in turn, have consequences for product evaluation, depending on argument quality. We hypothesize that for consumers with HN, the effect of scarcity on product evaluation will not be affected by argument quality (H3a). In contrast, for consumers with LN, scarcity will have a stronger positive effect on product evaluation when argument quality is strong than when argument quality is weak (H3b). The study 2 was designed as a 2 (High Scarcity versus Low Scarcity) x 2 (Strong product argument versus Weak product argument) between-subjects ANOVA, with one hundred fifty participants recruited. The high and low narcissistic Participants were chosen by the same procedure as in study 1. Two-level Narcissism (Low or High) was the third between-subjects factor in the analysis. As study 1, participants were presented with a hypothetical retail scenario, which included an ad for a wristwatch. The ad manipulated scarcity and argument quality using methods validated in past research[14,15]. Finally, participants responded to the dependent variables, and listed their thoughts while reading the ad. The dependent variable of product evaluation was measured by a single item, nine point scale for purchase intent and a three item, nine-point scale for product attitude. Participants' thoughts were coded into message-related thoughts and irrelevant thoughts by two judges blind to experimental conditions. The number of message-related thoughts served as one measure of depth of processing. A second measure of depth of processing was a two-item scale for cognitive effort anchored by effortful/thought validated in past research[16]. We predicted and found that HN participants in the high scarcity condition reported less message-related thoughts than did HN participants in the low scarcity condition (M=2.96 vs. 4.11, $t(44)$ =-2.02, $p$=.049). However, as predicted by H2b, this effect was reversed for LN participant (M=5.04 vs. 3.76, $t(52)$=1.158, $p$=.02). The cognitive effort scale showed the same pattern of results. Consistent with H3a, the effect of scarcity on purchase intent for HN participants was not affected by argument quality (M=4.15 vs. M=3.47, $t(26)$=1.051, $p$=.30). In contrast, as predicted by H3b, for LN participants, scarcity increased purchase intent when argument quality was strong, but not when argument quality was weak (M=3.57 vs. 2.18, $t(23)$=2.152, $p$=.04). The effect of scarcity on attitude toward the target product showed the same pattern of results.

This research makes a theoretical contribution by identifying how narcissistic consumers are motivated to validate their excessively positive self-view by obtaining a scarce product which can give a unique value.

**Reference**

1. Emmons, R. A. (1987). "Narcissism: Theory and measurement," *Journal of Personality and Social Psychology,* 11-17.
2. Sedikides, C., Campbell, W. K., Reeder, G., Elliot, A. J., and Gregg, A. (2002). "The self in relationships: Whether, how, and when close others put the self in its place," European review of social psychology, 12, 237-265.
3. Raskin, R., & Hall, C. S. (1979). "A narcissistic personality inventory," *Psychological Reports*, 45, 590.
4. Raskin, R., & Terry, H. (1988). "A principle components analysis of the Narcissistic Personality Inventory and further evidence of its construct validity," *Journal of Personality and Social Psychology*, 54, 890–902.
5. Dunning, D. (2007). "Self–Image motives and consumer behavior: How sacrosanct self–beliefs sway preferences in the marketplace," *Journal of Consumer Psychology*, 17, 237-249.
6. Sedikides, C., Gregg, A., Cisek, S & Hart, C. (2007). "The I that Buys: Narcissists as Consumers," *Journal of Consumer Psychology*, 17(4), 254-257.
7. Brock, T. C. (1968). Implications of Commodity Theory for Value Change. In: A.G. Greenwald, T. C. Brock and T. M. Ostrom (eds.), *Psychological foundations of attitudes*. New York: Academic Press. pp. 243-275.
8. Cialdini, R. B. (2001). *Influence Science and Practice*. Allyn and Bacon *(4th eds)*.
9. Cialdini, R. B. and Trost, M. R. (1998). Social Influence: Social Norms, Conformity and Compliance. In D. T. Gilbert, S. T. Fiske, and G. Lindzey (Eds.), *The Handbook of Social Psychology* (4th ed., Vol. 2, 151–192). Boston: McGraw-Hill.
10. Snyder, C. R., and Fromkin, H. L. (1980). *Uniqueness: The human pursuit of difference*. New York: Plenum.
11. Morf, C. C., Weir, C. R., and Davidov, M. (2000). "Narcissism and intrinsic motivation: The role of goal congruence," *Journal of Experimental Social Psychology*, 36, 424–438.
12. Inman, J. J., Peter, A. C. and Raghubir, R. P. (1997). Framing the deal: The role of restrictions in accentuating deal value. *Journal of Consumer Research*, 24 (June), 68-79.
13. Ditto, P. H. and Jemmott III, J. B (1989), "From Rarity to Evaluative Extremity: Effects of Prevalence Information on Evaluations of Positive and Negative Characteristics," *Journal of Personality and Social Psychology*, 57 (1), 16-26.
14. Lynn, M. (1989). Scarcity effects on value: Mediated by assumed expensiveness? *Journal of Economic Psychology*, 10, 257-274.
15. Li, W. and Wyer, J, R, S. (1994). The Role of Country of Origin in Product Evaluations: Informational and Standard–of– Comparison Effects. *Journal of Consumer Psychology*, 3 (2), 187- 212.
16. Menon, Geeta. (1997). "Are the Parts Better than the Whole? The Effects of Decompositional Questions on Judgments of Frequent Behaviors," *Journal of Marketing Research*, 32 (August), 335–346.

# Because I'm Worth It (And You're Not):
# Separating The Effects Of Narcissism And Self-Esteem On Prestige Purchases

Mary Ann Cunningham-Kim, York University, Canada
Peter Darke, York University, Canada

## Extended Abstract

Consumer researchers typically assume that higher self-regard indicates greater benefits to the individual than lower self-regard. High self-regard is associated with ability to resist high calorie treats following mortality salience (Mandel and Smeesters 2008), lower materialism in adolescents (Chaplin and John 2007), and lower proclivity toward compulsive buying (O'Guinn and Faber 1989). However, evidence in the psychology literature suggests that high self-regard is not simply a de facto "good thing;" for example, it has been implicated as a predictor of violence and aggression (Baumeister et al. 1996); perceived invulnerability to health threats, resulting in lower levels of compliance (Lin et al. 2003), and self-protection at the cost of interpersonal relationships (Heatherton and Vohs 2000). Overall, there seem to be two somewhat contradictory patterns of behavior: one suggesting high regard leads to better decision making or more functional behavior, and another pattern suggesting it leads to negative or less functional behavior.

These somewhat contradictory findings may relate to whether self-regard reflects a stable, "true" sense of self, or an attempt to create an overly positive identity by inflating feelings of self-worth. In order to better understand the relationship between self-regard and consumption choices, the current research compares the effects of self-regard in terms of both self-esteem and narcissism under varying conditions of ego-threat. While these measures are typically correlated, the construct of self-esteem is concerned with an individual's feelings about the self in terms of worthiness, likeableness and acceptance (Kernis 2003), whereas narcissism is concerned more with a chronic tendency to inflate or exaggerate self-regard (Raskin, Novacek, and Hogan 1991).

Galinsky and Rucker (2008) suggest consumption of luxury items serves as a method of regaining equilibrium following ego-threat. Since narcissism involves the goal of protecting fragile self-image from threat, it is proposed that narcissists will tend to use consumption of prestige products to reinforce high self-regard more than non-narcissists. The chronic nature of their self-esteem goals should lead narcissists to prefer prestige items even in the absence of any obvious external ego-threats.

In contrast, self-esteem is thought to function in part to help consumers make better decisions (Baumeister 2002), which might be expected to lead to a preference for value based options rather than items that provide prestige without corresponding performance. Also, since low self-esteem indicates a tendency to experience global changes in feelings of self-worth in response to changing circumstances (Deci and Ryan 1985; Kernis 2003), it is predicted that low esteem individuals will be more reactive to external sources of threat, leading to a greater need to choose prestige products. In contrast, high self-esteem individuals should show greater ego-strength in the face of threat (Steele 1988), and should therefore be in a position to stay focused on making better, value-based decisions (Baumeister et al. 2000). The theoretical contribution of this research is that it helps broaden our understanding of the different ways in which self-regard can relate to consumer choice, as well as identifying a new subset of consumers who are particularly vulnerable to self-esteem or prestige based marketing.

Study 1 tested the relationship between narcissism, self-esteem, and the choice of prestige products. Participants completed the Narcissistic Personality Inventory (NPI) and the Rosenberg Self-Esteem Scale (RSE). They were randomly assigned to either an ego-threat condition, where they were provided with unsolvable puzzles and informed that most college students could complete them within 5 minutes and that the results would be displayed publicly; or a non-threat condition with solvable puzzles and no display threat. Under the guise of a separate study, participants were asked for feedback on a new consumer guide that rated products according to whether they provided fair performance at a lower price, superior performance at a reasonable price, or provided prestige to owners. The reviews for the prestige products contained information suggesting that performance was similar to the lower cost items. For the dependent measure, participants were asked which item they would select for purchase in each of 4 product categories. As expected, narcissism predicted a greater number of prestige items chosen ($\beta$=.436, p<.001), and this effect was not moderated by ego-threat. A spotlight analysis on the interaction between threat and self-esteem indicated that low self-esteem participants in the threat condition increased their preference for prestige items ($\beta$=.645, p=.05) while high self-esteem participants were unlikely to choose the prestige products regardless of threat.

For study 2, advertisement based ego-threats were used to examine the more subtle forms of ego-threat that occur in marketing settings. After completing the NPI and RSE, participants received 4 advertisements, which provided either threats to self-image associated with the product (e.g. an ad for The Economist stated "I never read The Economist: 42-year old management trainee") or non-threatening messages (e.g. "The Economist: Turning Average Joe into Mr. Joe.") Dependent measures were attitudes to the ads and the products, as well as purchase intentions toward the products. As predicted, narcissism was marginally associated with higher purchase intentions regardless of the condition ($\beta$=.176, p=.07). Spotlight analysis showed an interaction between threat and self-esteem, with low self-esteem participants more likely to express interest in purchasing the products in the threat condition ($\beta$=.411, p=.07). The effects here show that the basic pattern of ego threat replicated when this took the form of threatening advertising messages, although the significance levels of these results were more marginal in strength. We attribute the latter to more subtle forms of threat in marketing versus the achievement related contexts used in study 1.

Both studies showed narcissists were vulnerable to marketing tactics/options that suggested a means for creating a positive self-image. Consumers with low self-esteem were similarly vulnerable following a threat. In contrast, high self-esteem consumers made better choices in the sense that they tended to disregard the highly expensive prestige items, regardless of threat. These findings suggest that some of the mixed conclusions concerning the relation of self-regard to purchase decisions may be explainable in terms of the manner in which this construct is operationalized.

## References

Baumeister, RF, M Muraven, and DM Tice (2000), "Ego Depletion: A Resource Model of Volition, Self-Regulation, and Controlled Processing," *Social Cognition*, 18 (2), 130-50.

Baumeister, RF, L Smart, and JM Boden (1996), "Relation of Threatened Egotism to Violence and Aggression: The Dark Side of High Self-Esteem," *Psychological review*, 103 (1), 5-33.

Baumeister, Roy F. (2002), "Yielding to Temptation: Self-Control Failure, Impulsive Purchasing, and Consumer Behavior," *Journal of Consumer Research*, 28 (4), 670-76.

Chaplin, Lan Nguyen and Deborah Roedder John (2007), "Growing up in a Material World: Age Differences in Materialism in Children and Adolescents," *Journal of Consumer Research*, 34 (4), 480-93.

Deci, EL and RM Ryan (1985), *Intrinsic Motivation and Self-Determination in Human Behavior*: Springer.

Heatherton, TF and KD Vohs (2000), "Interpersonal Evaluations Following Threats to Self: Role of Self-Esteem," *Journal of Personality and Social Psychology*, 78 (4), 725-36.

Kernis, MH (2003), "Toward a Conceptualization of Optimal Self-Esteem," *Psychological Inquiry*, 14 (1), 1-26.

Lin, YC, CH Lin, and P Raghubir (2003), "Avoiding Anxiety, Being in Denial, or Simply Stroking Self-Esteem: Why Self-Positivity?," *Journal of Consumer Psychology*, 13 (4), 464-77.

Mandel, Naomi and Dirk Smeesters (2008), "The Sweet Escape: Effects of Mortality Salience on Consumption Quantities for High- and Low- Self-Esteem Consumers," *Journal of Consumer Research*, 35 (2), 309-23.

O'Guinn, Thomas C. and Ronald J. Faber (1989), "Compulsive Buying: A Phenomenological Exploration," *Journal of Consumer Research*, 16 (2), 147-57.

Raskin, R, J Novacek, and R Hogan (1991), "Narcissistic Self-Esteem Management," *Journal of Personality and Social Psychology*, 60 (6), 911-18.

Rucker, DD and AD Galinsky (2008), "Desire to Acquire: Powerlessness and Compensatory Consumption," *Journal of Consumer Research*, 35 (2), 257-67.

# Self-Construal And Socially Responsible Consumer Behavior

Irina Cojuharenco, Universidade Católica Portuguesa, Portugal
Gert Cornelissen, Pompeu Fabra University, Spain
Natalia Karelaia, INSEAD, France

Current ecological and economical upheaval demonstrates the need for individuals to rethink their consumption pattern and its impact on their social, ideological and ecological environment. Public and private initiatives undertaken with this goal have been proven to be of limited success. Therefore, further research on the factors associated with socially responsible behavior is warranted. In the current paper, we investigate the potential role of the individual's self-construal (e.g., Sedikides & Brewer, 2001) on the shaping of ethical consumer behavior (e.g., choosing fair trade and locally produced products, or boycotting firms with poor ethical standards). From a public policy perspective, an interesting aspect of self-construal is that individualism and collectivism represent separate dimensions within the individual (Triandis & Gelfand, 1998). In other words, a person possesses both individualistic and collectivistic tendencies to a smaller or larger extent (Sinha & Tripathi, 1994). This implies that if, as hypothesized, collective selfconstrual is associated with socially responsible behavior, such behavior can be promoted by emphasizing or activating the collective self.

Self-construal refers to different ways of defining one's identity. Sedikides and Brewer (2001) distinguish between three types of self-construal: the individual self, the relational self, and the collective self. Defining the self by emphasizing unique traits and independence from others is characteristic for the independent self. The relational and collective self are typically defined in terms of relationships with other individuals and group membership, respectively. At the individual level, multiple tendencies can exist within the same person (Trafimow, Triandis, & Goto, 1991). Recent research has demonstrated that socially conscious consumer behavior, like its ecological counterpart, appears to be an expression of prosocial values, like universalism and benevolence (Pepper, Jackson, & Uzzell, 2009). These are the values that are typically associated with collectivism, as opposed to individualism (Triandis, 1995). For example, people with an interdependent self construal (i.e., relational or collective) emphasize group goals over personal goals (e.g., Utz, 2004). Therefore we expect selfconstrual to be related to socially responsible consumer behavior. Rather than to merely ascertain this relationship, we are interested in uncovering the process which connects both constructs. Additionally, we intend to test whether it is possible to temporarily alter one's dominant selfconstrual through a priming procedure and thus influence the likelihood of engaging in socially responsible consumption.

Using data from a large scale survey we verified the relation between selfconstrual and the tendency to engage in socially responsible consumer behavior. A representative sample of 754 US citizens completed a number of measures related to selfconstrual (Selenta & Lord, 2005), socially responsible consumer behavior (Vitell & Muncy, 2005; Webb, Mohr, & Harris, 2008), and Perceived Consumer Effectiveness (PCE; Roberts, 1996), among others.

As expected, we found a strong relationship between relational and collective selfconstrual on the one hand and ethical consumption on the other. The more the individual describes him/herself in interdependent terms, the more s/he is inclined to make ethical consumer decisions. Relations between ethical consumption and the independent self were smaller or non-significant. More interestingly, we found that PCE mediated the relationship between selfconstrual and ethical consumption using a bootstrapping procedure (Preacher & Hayes, 2008). We used this method because it offers a number of advantages compared to other procedures based on multiple regressions (e.g., Baron and Kenny's procedure). Bootstrapping allows for examining all hypotheses in one statistical model, it does not rely on the assumption of normal distribution, and it provides a direct evaluation of the size and significance of the indirect effect. The analysis suggested that the relational self (*Z*=8.43, *p*<0.01) and the collective self (*Z*=8.65, *p*<0.01) have an indirect effect on ethical consumption, mediated by PCE. The independent self does not have such an indirect effect (*Z*=-0.58, *p*=0.56)[1], because there is no relationship between independent selfconstrual and PCE (*r*=-0.02, *p*=0.56).

Footnote 1
[1]The results of only one DV are reported on here, due to space restrictions. Results were consistent over all DV's.

In follow-up research, which is ongoing and will be completed by the date of the conference, we are further testing the role of PCE and other constructs as mediators of the relationship between selfconstrual and ethical consumption experimentally. PCE refers to the fact that people believe, to a larger or smaller extent, that their actions can make a difference on the large scale. Previous research has demonstrated that PCE is the single largest predictor of socially responsible consumer behaviour (Roberts, 1996). We propose that selfconstrual is linked to PCE through projected expectations. Collectivists (as opposed to individualists), who think in terms of collective rationality, expect others to do so as well (Iedema & Poppe, 1995). As a result, collectivists assume that a larger proportion of the population pursues societal interests and therefore it is more likely that the individual (as part of an aggregate) can make a difference. We are testing this hypothesis against a number of alternatives (differences in levels of trust in others, care for others, and a different judgment of the relevance of socially responsible behavior). Additionally, we are testing whether a priming procedure can temporarily override trait selfconstrual and can successfully activate or emphasize one's relational or collective self. Using behavioral measures, we subsequently test whether such manipulation is successful at influencing an individual's level of socially responsible consumption. If this is the case, and if a subtle priming procedure is successful at manipulating PCE, this idea could be developed into an interesting social marketing tool.

## References

Iedema, J., & Poppe, M. (1995). Perceived consensus of one's social value orientation in different populations in public and private circumstances. *European Journal of Social Psychology, 25*(5), 497-507.

Pepper, M., Jackson, T., & Uzzell, D. (2009). An examination of the values that motivate socially conscious and frugal consumer behaviours. *International Journal of Consumer Studies, 33*(2), 126-136.

Preacher, K. J., & Hayes, A. F. (2008). Asymptotic and resampling strategies for assessing and comparing indirect effects in multiple mediator models. *Behavior Research Methods, 40*(3), 879-891.

Roberts, J. A. (1996). Green consumers in the 1990s: Profile and implications for advertising. *Journal of Business Research, 36*(3), 217-231.

Sedikides, C., & Brewer, M. B. (2001). *Individual self, relational self, collective self.* New York, NY US: Psychology Press.

Selenta, C., & Lord, R. G. (2005). Development of the levels of selfconcept scale: Measuring the individual, relational, and collective levels. Unpublished manuscript.

Sinha, D., & Tripathi, R. C. (1994). Individualism in a collectivist culture: A case of coexistence of opposites. In U. Kim, H. C. Triandis, Ç. Kağitçibaşi, S.-C. Choi & G. Yoon (Eds.), *Individualism and collectivism: Theory, method, and applications.* (pp. 123-136). Thousand Oaks, CA US: Sage Publications, Inc.

Trafimow, D., Triandis, H. C., & Goto, S. G. (1991). Some tests of the distinction between the private self and the collective self. *Journal of Personality and Social Psychology, 60*(5), 649-655.

Triandis, H. C. (1995). *Individualism & collectivism.* Boulder, CO US: Westview Press.

Triandis, H. C., & Gelfand, M. J. (1998). Converging measurement of horizontal and vertical individualism and collectivism. *Journal of Personality and Social Psychology, 74*(1), 118-128.

Utz, S. (2004). Self-Construal and Cooperation: Is the Interdependent Self More Cooperative Than the Independent Self? *Self and Identity, 3*, 177-190.

Vitell, S., & Muncy, J. (2005). The Muncy–Vitell Consumer Ethics Scale: A Modification and Application. *Journal of Business Ethics, 62*(3), 267-275.

Webb, D. J., Mohr, L. A., & Harris, K. E. (2008). A re-examination of socially responsible consumption and its measurement. *Journal of Business Research, 61*(2), 91-98.

# How Self-View Influences Consumers' Propensity to Adopt New Products: Role of Product Newness and Risk-Relieving Information

Zhenfeng Ma, University of Ontario Institute of Technology, Canada
Zhiyong Yang, University of Texas at Arlington, USA

Prior research has shown that certain national cultural traits influence consumers' propensity to adopt new products. The examination of the relationships between collectivism/individualism and innovation adoption across different nations consistently shows that collectivism is negatively associated with innovation adoption, whereas individualism is positively associated with it (Steenkamp, Hofstede, and Wedel 1999; Tellis, Stremersch, and Yin 2003). However, how situationally activated cultural orientations may affect individuals' innovation adoption *within a nation* has not been examined by previous studies.

According to Markus and Kitayama (1991), within a cultural environment, multiple cultural values coexist in an individual's memory. A person in any cultural environment has both an individualist orientation (i.e., an independent self-view), perceiving the self as unique and different from others, and a collectivist orientation (i.e., an interdependent self-view), perceiving the self as part of a group and connected with others. In addition, a self-view can be made more salient by situational cues: consumers in a predominantly individualistic cultural environment can be temporarily primed with a collectivist orientation, or vice versa (Aaker and Lee 2001; Gardner, Gabriel, and Lee 1999).

Following this dynamic view of culture, we posit that situationally activated self-views would influence an individual's new product adoption decision. This proposition is grounded in the differences in regulatory focus between individuals with a situationally activated independent self-view (the 'independents') and those with a situationally activated interdependent self-view (the 'interdependents'). The independents are promotion-oriented, focusing on seeking benefits and gains. In contrast, the interdependents are prevention-oriented, focusing on avoiding mistakes and losses. Prior research on innovation classified products along a spectrum of innovation newness, ranging from really new products (RNP), incrementally new product (INP), to existing products (EP) (Herzenstein, Posavac, and Brakus 2007; Hoeffler 2003). The different regulatory foci between the independents and the interdependents could result in differential responses toward RNP. As a one-of-its-kind product, RNP offers unique benefits, but is associated with high risk and uncertainty (Hoeffler 2003). Because of their promotion focus, the independents would attend more to the unique benefits than the potential risks of RNP. Conversely, given their prevention focus, the interdependents would attend more to the potential risks than the benefits of RNP. Thus, the independents would be more likely to adopt RNP than the interdependents. However, the independents and the interdependents would not differ in their adoption propensity toward INP or EP, because the low to moderate benefits and risks associated with those products are not sufficient to induce differential responses between the two groups.

H1:  The independents exhibit higher adoption propensity than the interdependents toward RNP, whereas these two groups do not differ in the adoption propensity toward INP or EP. This is because:

H2:  The independents perceive higher benefits and lower risks than the interdependents when the product is a RNP, whereas they do not differ in perceived benefits/risks when the product is an INP/EP.

It is further expected that the independents and the interdependents would react differently to risk-reduction information (e.g., product warranty) about RNP versus INP/EP. Because the interdependents are more inclined to avoid risks and uncertainty than the independents when the product is a RNP, risk-relieving information would be more effective in enhancing the adoption propensity of the interdependents than the independents when the product is a RNP. However, the two groups would not differ in response to risk-relieving information about INP/EP, given the relatively low risk associated with those products.

H3:  The interdependents react more favourably toward the risk-relieving information than the independents when the product is a RNP, whereas the two groups do not differ in their reactions toward the risk-relieving information about an INP/EP.

We tested hypotheses H1 through H3 using two experimental studies. In Experiment 1, we examined how situationally activated self-views influence adoption propensity toward products that vary in innovation newness (H1) and the psychological processes underlying such effects (H2). Ninety-eight undergraduate students were primed with either an independent or an interdependent self-view, using a sports-related scenario (Aaker and Lee 2001). Afterwards, each participant read the descriptions of three different cars (the order of presentation was counterbalanced), whose innovation newness was pretested to be high (RNP), moderate (INP), or low (EP). We measured participants' perceived benefits, perceived risks, and adoption propensity toward each car. Consistent with H1, a repeated-measure ANOVA indicated that the independents reported higher adoption propensity than the interdependents toward RNP. In contrast, the two groups did not differ in adoption propensity toward INP or EP. Further, repeated-measure ANOVAs of perceived benefits and risks indicated that when the product was a RNP, the independents reported higher perceived benefits but lower perceived risks than the interdependents. When the product was an INP or EP, however, perceived benefits/risks did not differ between the two groups. Thus, H2 was also supported. Moreover, a follow-up mediation analysis shows that the observed effect of self-view and innovation newness on adoption propensity was mediated by perceived benefits and risks.

In Experiment 2, we examined how risk-relieving information (i.e., product warranty) influences the adoption propensity of the independents versus the interdependents toward RNP and INP/EP (H3). Eighty undergraduate students were primed with either an independent or an interdependent self-view through a life-event recounting task (Trafimow et al. 1991; Zhu and Myers-Lev 2009). Participants were then presented with a description of a TV, which was pretested to be either an EP or RNP. After reporting their baseline adoption propensity, the participants were informed that the manufacturer of the TV offers a 90-day money-back guarantee, compared with a 30-day limited guarantee commonly offered by TV manufacturers. After reading the product warranty, participants then indicated their adoption propensity again. The increment in adoption propensity, measured by the change score of adoption propensity from its baseline, was used as the dependent variable. A two-way ANOVA indicated that when the product was a RNP, the interdependents exhibited larger increment in adoption propensity than the independents. In contrast, when the product was an INP, the two groups did not differ in their increment of adoption propensity. These results supported H3.

Overall, our findings suggest that situationally activated self-views influence consumers' new product adoption decisions, and that such influences were contingent on the newness of the products. The effects of self-view and innovation newness on adoption decisions was mediated by perceived benefits and risks. Moreover, situationally activated self-views also influence consumers' reactions toward risk-relieving information, and such reactions were again contingent on the newness of the products.

## References

Aaker, Jennifer L. Angela Y. Lee (2001), "'I' Seek pleasures and 'We' Avoid Pains: The Role of Self-Regulatory Goals in Information Processing and Persuasion," *Journal of Consumer Research,* 28 (June), 33-49.

Gardner, Wendi L., Shira Gabriel, and Angela Y. Lee (1999), "'I' Value Freedom But 'We' Value Relationship: Self-Construal Priming Mirrors Cultural Differences In Judgment," *Psychological Science,* 10 (4), 321–326.

Herzenstein, Michal, Stevens S. Posavac, and J. Josko Brakus (2007), "Adoption of New and Really New Products: The Effects of Self-Regulation Systems and Risk Salience," *Journal of Marketing Research,* 44 (May), 251-260.

Hoeffler, Steve (2003), "Measuring Preferences for Really New Products," *Journal of Marketing Research,* 40(4), 406-420.

Markus, Hazel and Shinobu Kitayama (1991), "Culture and the Self: Implications for Cognition, Emotion, and Motivation," *Psychological Review,* 98 (April), 224-53.

Steenkamp, Jan-Benedict E.M., Frenkel ter Hofstede, and Michael Wedel (1999), "A Cross-National Investigation into the Individual and National Cultural Antecedents of Consumer Innovativeness," *Journal of Marketing,* 63 (April), 55-69.

Tellis, Gerad J., Stefan Stremersch, and Eden Yin (2003), "The International Takeoff of New Products: The Role of Economics, Culture, and Country Innovativeness," Marketing Science, 22 (2), 188-208.

Trafimow, David, Harry C. Triandis, and Sharon G. Goto (1991), "Some Tests of the Distinction Between the Private Self and the Collective Self," *Journal of Personality and Social Psychology,* 60 (5), 649-655.

Zhu, Rui and Joan Meyers-Levy (2009), "The Influence of Self-View on Context Effects: How Display Fixtures Can Affect Product Evaluations," *Journal of Marketing Research,* 46 (February), 37-45.

# Defensive Reactions to Self Threat in Consumption: The Moderating Role of Affirmation

Pingping Qiu, Monash University, Australia
Fang Wan, University of Manitoba, Canada
Darren W. Dahl, University of British Columbia, Canada

## Extended Abstract

Consumers often receive information posing threats to self in advertising and consumption contexts. For example, the exposure to idealized images in advertising media poses a threat to one's own physical attractiveness (Richins 1991). In these cases, we could expect two competing outcomes of self threat. On the one hand, consumers who are made insecure about their positive self views could engage in a defensive reaction toward the threat (Baumeister, Dale, and Sommer 1998) and dismiss products and brands that claim to boost their self images in the threatened domain. We label it as a *defensive consumption strategy*. On the other hand, consumers could perceive the same products and brands to be an important means of self improvement (Eisenstadt, Leippe, and Rivers 2002), therefore, would be more likely to welcome and adopt these products and brands. We label it as a *compliant consumption strategy*.

Surprisingly, scanty consumer research has been done to address the conditions in which a defensive (vs. compliant) consumption mode can be activated and how defensive or compliant reactions toward self threat would affect subsequent consumption behaviors. Recent consumer research on this topic demonstrated a compliant consumption mode resulting from self threat. That is, consumers who experience self threat would resort to products that can directly repair and bolster the threatened self domain (Gao, Wheeler, and Shiv 2009). What is missing from this stream of research is the lack of identification of those factors in consumer contexts activating a defensive consumption mode.

Our research addresses this issue by first uncover consumer contexts where self threat can activate a defensive consumption mode. We then investigate that consumers who experience self threat would be more likely to reject products that offer low affirmation value or signal self deficiency (i.e., self improvement products) (Study 1). Furthermore, we address the relationship between the two competing coping mechanisms of self threat: compliance and defense. We argue that there are two key factors in modulating whether a defensive or a compliant strategy takes place: 1) opportunities for self affirmation (including general affirmation opportunities and affirmation value offered by products or brands) and 2) the mode of threat (blatant vs. subtle). Specifically, when there are external opportunities for self affirmation, consumers who experience self threat are less likely to engage in defensive consumption (Study 2). This effect is exacerbated when self threat is activated in blatant manner than in a subtle manner (Study 3). We test these propositions in three experiments.

*Study 1* explored a consumer context where a defensive reaction to self threat leads to the dismissal of self improvement products. Specifically, we examined consumers' evaluations of a body enhancement product after a prior exposure to idealized images in a preceding and seemingly unrelated advertisement evaluation task. We expected to find that subjects whose self views on physical appearance are threatened by the exposure to idealized images are more likely to show less favorable attitude toward the product. In addition, we considered the self domain importance as a moderator of the proposed relationship. That is, defensive consumption is only evident when the threatening source is in an important self domain. We used gender as a proxy of domain importance, since physical appearance has been identified to be important for females but not males. ANOVA results of a 2 (self threat: idealized image vs. no image) × 2 (gender) between-subjects experiment yielded a significant interaction ($F(1,104)=4.89, p<.05$). Planned contrast revealed that females who viewed idealized images (vs. no images) devaluated the product ($M=2.99$ vs. $4.04$; $F=8.26, p<.01$), whereas no such effect emerged among males ($F<1$).

*Study 2* addresses opportunities for self affirmation as the underlying mechanism of a defensive consumption mode. We argue that the reason for consumers to dismiss self improvement products when their self images were threatened is that these products focus on the domain where self image is threatened, therefore providing no opportunities for self affirmation. We test this proposition by adopting affirmation tasks from Sherman and Cohen (2006). We employed the same research context as in Study 1. We expected that for threatened consumers, when self can be affirmed immediately after the threat (i.e., receiving bogus positive feedback in intelligence domain), the overall self-worth will be maintained and the subsequent defensive reactions toward self improvement products will be mitigated. We also argue that self esteem can moderate the relationship between self affirmation and defensive consumption strategy. High self-esteem individuals are more likely to utilize external opportunities to replenish self worth when threatened than low self-esteem individuals (Vohs and Heatherton 2004). Results of a 2 (self affirmation: affirming vs. control) by 2 (measured trait self-esteem, high vs. low) between-subjects experiment confirmed our hypothesis, showing that the affirmation task (vs. no affirmation) reduced defensive consumption among high self-esteem individuals ($A_{product}$ $M$=3.59 vs. 2.97; $F$=2.87, $p$<.10) but not low self-esteem individuals ($F$<1).

*Study 3* intends to reconcile the discrepancy between the present research and prior research on compliant consumption. We propose that a defensive (vs. compliant) consumption mode is activated by available (vs. absent) opportunities to affirm and blatant (vs. subtle) self threat. In this study, participants' self views were threatened either blatantly (receiving bogus negative feedback) or subtly (performing a difficult task) in intelligence domain. Subsequently, they evaluated products with high affirmation value (products signaling high intelligence of the user) or products with low affirmation value (intelligence improving products signaling low intelligence of the user). Results revealed that defensive consumption mode emerged only in the blatant threat and low-affirmation-value product condition. That is, when participants were threatened blatantly, they held significantly less favorable attitude toward products with low (vs. high) affirmation value ($M$=3.38 vs. 4.21; $F(1,54)$=5.22, $p$<.05). Moreover, even if the product offers low affirmation value, participants receiving subtle (vs. blatant) threat held more positive attitude toward the products, signaling a compliant consumption strategy ($M$=4.13 vs. 3.38; $F(1,54)$=4.09, $p$<.05).

Taken together, our research echoes with the recent calls from consumer researchers (Dunning 2007) that we need to understand more about the relationship between consumers' self views and their consumption behaviors. Whereas previous research has painted a rosy picture of how products and brands are empowering consumers by providing important symbolic values, this research deviates and presents a darker side of the story. That is, when there is a mismatch between products symbolic value and consumers' fluid self views, consumers would reject these choices as a way to defend their self views. In addition, by delineating how consumers switch between compliant and defensive consumption on the basis of contextual factors (such as the way self is threatened, or affirmation value of products), this research enriches our understanding of the nature of adaptive consumer behaviors.

**Selected References**

Bargh, John A. (2002), "Losing Consciousness: Automatic Influences on Consumer Judgment, Behavior and Motivation," *Journal of Consumer Research*, 29(September), 280-85.

Baumeister, Roy F., Karen Dale, and Kristin L. Sommer (1998), "Freudian Defense Mechanisms and Empirical Findings in Modern Social Psychology: Reaction Formation, Projection, Displacement, Undoing, Isolation, Sublimation, and Denial," *Journal of Personality*, 66(December), 1081-1124.

Dunning, David (2007), "Self-Image Motives and Consumer Behavior: How Sacrosanct Self-Beliefs Sway Preferences in the Marketplace," *Journal of Consumer Psychology*, 17 (4), 237-49.

Elliott, Richard (1994), "Exploring the Symbolic Meaning of Brands," *British Journal of Management*, 5 (June), S13-S19.

Eisenstadt, Donna, Michael R. Leippe, and Jennifer A. Rivers (2002), "Asymmetry and Defense in Self-Comparison: Differential Reactions to Feedback about the Rejected and Ideal Selves," *Self and Identity*, 1 (4), 289-311.

Gao, Leilei, S. Christian Wheeler, and Baba Shiv (2009), "The 'Shaken Self': Product Choices as a Means of Restoring Self-View Confidence," *Journal of Consumer Research*, 36 (June), 29-38.

Richins, Marsha L. (1991), "Social Comparison and the Idealized Images of Advertising," *Journal of Consumer Research*, 19 (June), 71-83.

Sherman, David K. and Geoffrey L. Cohen (2006), "The Psychology of Self-Defense: Self-Affirmation Theory," in *Advances in Experimental Social Psychology,* 38, ed. M. P. Zanna, San Diego, CA: Academic Press, 183-242.

Tesser, Abraham (2000), "On the Confluence of Self-Esteem Maintenance Mechanisms," *Personality and Social Psychology Review*, 4 (4), 290-99.

Willer, Robb (2006), "Overdoing Gender: A Test of the Masculine Overcompensation Thesis," working paper, University of California.

Vohs, Kathleen D. and Todd F. Heatherton (2004), "Ego Threat Elicits Different Social Comparison Processes Among High and Low Self-esteem People: Implications for Interpersonal Perceptions," *Social Cognition,* 22 (February), 168–191.

# Co-Branding with an Emotional Brand:
# Identity Threat and Coping Strategies among Loyal Consumers

Na Xiao, Queen's University, Canada
Fang Wan, University of Manitoba, Canada

**Extended Abstract**

Emotional branding is heralded as a key strategy to build stronger consumer-brand relationships compared to functional brand strategies (e.g., Thompson, Rindfleisch, and Arsel, 2006). For example, the success of Apple speaks largely to this type of brand strategy. That is, emotional branding strategy involves crafting brands' visions and values in lieu of consumers' deep-seated emotional needs, dreams, and goals, which allows such brands become spokesperson or substitute of consumers' identity (e.g., Gobe, 2001). In spite its success, in a competitive brand world, a well-crafted emotional brand alone can hardly maintain its success without working together with brands with complementary strength to reach broader consumer segments (co-branding, Leuthesser et al. 2003). For example,

Apple aligned co-branded with HP to release its Ipod products to reach out to HP's Window users of PCs and notebooks. As a result, HP Window users will have a pre-installed Apple's iTunes jukebox software and an easy-reference desktop icon to access the iTunes Music Store (Mahr 2004). However, will this type of brand alliance be successful?

Whereas previous research on co-branding tend to focus on issues such as the perceived fit of brand partners (Taylor and Bearden 2002), we take the perspectives of loyal consumers of an emotional brand and investigate whether or not they perceive co-branding to be an identity threat and how they defend for their identity and reconcile with the incongruence between brand partners. We propose that a co-branding strategy can pose an identity threat to loyal consumers of an emotional brand when the co-brand is perceived to provide an incongruent value. Specifically, loyal consumers would view the co-brand to be a transgressor of their brand's culture, value, promises and a threat to their own identity. We employ qualitative depth interviews to uncover the whether loyal consumers of an emotional brand perceive co-branding as an identity threat and how they cope with such threat (Pretest), and test how two coping strategies affect their evaluation of the brand alliance (Study 1) and how co-branding with different partners can affect consumers attitude and loyalty toward the original brand (Study 2).

*Pretest*. The goal of Study 1 is to understand whether loyal consumers of an emotional brand perceive its alliance with an incongruent brand to be an identity threat and how they cope with such threat. To do this, we conducted depth interviews with six loyal Apple Mac users. We asked the informants about their views on the release of new Mac computers (i.e., emotional brand, Belk and Tumbat 2002) which uses Intel hardware (a functional brand, Ritson 2006).

Results revealed that informants felt humiliated by the brand alliance between Apple and Intel and were concerned that Apple users' identity was impaired by Intel, strongly associated with PCs. In addition, we discovered two coping strategies informants employed to buttress their support of Apple brand vis-à-vis the incongruent co-branding efforts: 1)"decoupling", the efforts of some informants to single out Intel and dismissing its impact on Apple brand (e.g., "Intel is just an ingredient and will not affect the myth, easiness, and openness that Apple represents" (Informant G)) and 2) "biased assimilation," intending to boost the evaluation of Intel so that it can be assimilated into positive associations of Apple brand. For example, "Apple and Intel are both to make money and to create passion" (Informant F).

*Study 1*. The goal of Study 1 is to uncover in an experiment setting which coping strategy is more effective in what context. We propose that the perceived fit between brand partners is low, *decoupling* is more effective than *biased assimilation* because the latter requires relatively positive associations with the co-brand to be activated. When the perceived fit is high, this perceived congruence between brand partners itself can trigger positive evaluations of the brand alliance, which makes coping strategies unnecessary and ineffective. We test this argument in Study 2.

A 2 (coping strategy: decoupling vs. biased assimilation) by 2 (fit: low vs. high, measured factor) between-subject design was adopted. Eighty six Apple users (based on screening questions) participated in the study. Coping strategies were manipulated by exposing subjects to difference versions of consumers reviews (elaborating on either decoupling or biased assimilation) preceding brand evaluations. Perceived fit between Apple and Intel (Taylor and Bearden 2002) was measured, split based on its median value and used as a between-subject factor.

ANOVA yielded a significant interaction between coping strategies and fit on attitude towards the brand alliance ($F(1, 82)=8.94$, $p<.05$). Specifically, when the perceived fit was low, attitude towards brand alliance was more positive when a decoupling strategy (vs. biased assimilation) is activated (M=5.08 v.s. 4.22; $F(1, 81)=3.64$, p=.05). However, when the perceived fit was high, coping strategy has no impact ($M_{decoupling}=5.19$ vs. $M_{biased}=5.47$, F<1, p>.05). The results supported our hypothesis.

*Study 2*. Study 2 addresses two issues. First, it addresses the fit between brand partners by manipulating the types of co-branding partners (emotional and emotional vs. emotional and functional). Two, it investigates consumers with varying degrees of identification with the original brand can respond to co-brand differently. For loyal consumers with high identification with an emotional brand, they are motivated to buttress their support for their brand, and the brand alliance regardless of the types of brand alliance (e.g., Einwiller et al., 2006). However, for consumers with low identification with an emotional brand, they would evaluate emotional brand-functional brand alliance more positively because the functional benefits (vs. cultural meanings) of resulting co-brand are more intuitive to them.

A 2 (co-branding type: emotional-emotional versus emotional-functional) X 2 (identification with emotional brand, measured: high versus low) between-subject design was adopted. Eighty four current Apple users participated in the study. Co-branding types were manipulated as co-branding between either Apple with Intel or Apple with Nintendo based on pretest results (Nintendo was chosen as pretest subjects perceived it to be cool, active and trendy). Identification with Apple was measured on 5 items (Bhattacharya et al., 1995) first and was entered as between-subject factor based on a median split. Participants read one of the two co-branding scenarios (Apple with Intel, or Nintendo co-launched a new product, Intel's chip or Nintendo's game software in Apple's computers). They lastly responded to questions with regard to the fit between brands (manipulation check questions) and their attitudes toward the brand alliance.

ANOVA analyses revealed that manipulations were successful. Results indicated that there were significant interactions between co-branding types and identification on attitude toward the brand alliance ($F(1, 80)=6.31, p<.05$). Specifically, when consumers' identification with Apple is low, they rated emotional-functional brand alliance (Apple+Intel) to be more positive than emotional-emotional brand alliance (Apple+Nintendo) (M=5.93 vs 4.72, $F(1, 80)=6.86$ p<.05). However, when brand identification is high, consumers prefer emotional and emotional brand alliance over emotional and functional one (M=5.56 vs. 5.50; $F<1$).

Put together, our findings help us understand that for brand alliance such as Apple and HP (incongruent co-branding), it will be perceived positively among HP users who may not have a strong identification with Apple users. At the same time, Apple users with high identification with the brand are not sensitive to brand alliances that Apple is striking as they already have a very strong emotional and identity buy-in with the brand.

## References

Ashforth, B. E., & Mael, F. A. (1989), "Social Identity Theory and the Organization" *Academy of Management Review*, 14, 20-39.

Bhattacharya, C B, Rao, Hayagreeva, Glynn, Mary Ann (1995), "Understanding the Bond of Identification: An Investigation of Its Correlates among Art Museum Members", *Journal of Marketing*, 59 (4), 46-58

Belk, Russell W. and Tumbat G. (2002), *The Cult of Mac. Odyssey Films*, Salt Lake City, Utah

Borden, Mark (2001), "Let the Games Begin", Fortune, New York: Nov 26, 144 (11), 237-9

Einwiller, S. A., Fedorikhin, A., Johnson, A. R., & Kamins, M. A. (2006). Enough Is Enough! When Identification No Longer Prevents Negative Corporate Associations. *Academy of Marketing Science*, 34(2), 185.

Gobe, Marc (2001), *Emotional Branding: The New Paradigm for Connecting Brands to People*. New York: Allworth Press

Leuthesser, Lance, Chiranjeev Kohli, Rajneesh Suri (2003), "2 + 2=5? A Framework for Using Co-branding to Leverage a Brand" *Journal of Brand Management*, 11(Sep), 35-47

Mahr, Jackson (2004), "HP & iPod out of Sync," www.brandchannel.com/features_profile.asp?pr_id=205, November 8, 2004 issue.

Ritson, Mark (2006), "Intel Attitude Does Not Compute", *Marketing*, 25.

Taylor, V.A. and Bearden, W.O. (2002), "The effects of price on brand extension evaluations: the moderating role of extension similarity", *Journal of the Academy of Marketing Science*, Vol. 30 No. 2, pp. 131-40.

Thompson, Craig J, Aric Rindfleisch, Zeynep Arsel(2006), "Emotional Branding and the Strategic Value of the Doppelganger Brand Image", *Journal of Marketing*, 70(Jan), 50-64

You, Xueming and Naveen Donthu (2001), "Developing and Validating a Multidimensional Consumer-Based Brand Equity Scale," *Journal of Business Research*, 52 (April), 1–14.

# Do I Remember More When I Feel More Knowledgeable?

Charles Lebar, HEC Paris, France
Sandor Czellar, University of Lausanne, Switzerland

## Extended Abstract

"Familiar with sustainable developmental issues, are you? But did you actually notice the picture was upside down?" To their surprise, most of the readers of this humanitarian ad probably did not. We can indeed wonder what reactions will result from situations in which consumers are induced to feel more or less ignorant than initially believed. Will they become more attentive to subsequent information or, on the contrary, give up to process any related incoming information? Answers to this question may have important implications not only for brand marketers willing to enhance consumer brand knowledge but also for consumers who wish to optimize the way they select information from the marketplace.

Subjective knowledge (SK) is consumers' degree of confidence in their knowledge, as opposed to objective knowledge (OK) that refers to what an individual actually knows in a specific domain (Carlson et al. 2009). Whereas the impact of OK on information search (Bettman and Park 1980; Brucks 1985; Radecki and Jaccard 1995; Swasy and Rethans 1986) and processing strategies (Maheswaran, and Sternthal 1990; Sujan 1985) has been extensively studied, extant research on the impact of SK remains scarce and leads to inconclusive results (Moorman et al. 2004; Park, Gardner, and Thurkal 1988; Park and Lessig 1981; Raju, Lonia, and Mangold 1995; See 2009).

The present research focuses on a potential effect of SK manipulation that has not yet been investigated: the mechanisms through which SK manipulations may impact actual memory for information. Are consumers who are given the illusion that they know more (less) than they actually do will be able to retain more (v. less) information when exposed to a message?

We assess the extent of SK change as a result of experimental manipulation using two measurements: SK before the manipulation and after the manipulation. Extant research has so far typically used self-reported assessments of SK after false feedback on a task, showing that participants in high (vs. low) SK conditions indeed provide higher SK scores (Moorman et al. 2004). Such procedures, however, do not allow to evaluate the directionality and extent of SK change compared to an initial baseline. This can only be done if SK perceptions are assessed both before and after the critical knowledge manipulations.

We also argue that moderating personality traits as well as mediating variables need to be to be taken into account to explain contradictory evidence found in the literature. Building upon the ego protection and self-esteem literatures (Baumeister 1993; Brockner and Chen 1996; Rosenberg 1965; Wiener 1973), we propose that a manipulation of SK may have a different impact on information processing depending on the initial level of consumer self-esteem. Chronic low self-esteem individuals tend to be doubtful about their capacities. Following self-consistency theory, a decrease in their SK may increase the negative perception they have of their capacities and discourage them to process any additional information. Opposed to this, positive feedback may increase their confidence in their capacity and motivate them to further process domain-related information. On the other hand, high self-esteem individuals are generally confident in their capacities. Increasing confidence in their capacity may drive them to become over-confident, rest on their laurel and possibly retain less information. However, decreasing their perceptions of knowledge may actually boost their motivation to search for additional information.

We conducted a pilot study to gain initial insights about the feasibility of this research. After reporting their SK on different domains including our focal topic (computer knowledge), 34 undergraduate marketing students took part in a moderately difficult quiz about computers. Subjective knowledge was manipulated via false feedback on the quiz using two conditions (low vs. high score compared to a school average), following which SK was re-assessed. Finally, participants were asked to complete a domain-related information processing task. The manipulation of perceived knowledge occurred as predicted, as individuals in the low (vs. high) SK condition reported lower levels of perceived domain-related knowledge. However, no main effect of SK manipulation on memory for information was found, thus supporting the need to investigate possible moderating variables.

One-hundred and twenty undergraduate students participated in our first experiment, which differed from the pilot in the following way. We included a measure of trait self-esteem (Rosenberg 1965) in an unrelated survey and used four memorization measures: recall (answer to open ended-questions); recognition (choosing the correct answer in multiple-choice items); discrimination task (ability to recognize whether a piece of information was present or not in the message); and the number of items left unanswered. In line with our pilot study, we found no main effect of SK on any of our memory measures. However, the analysis of the interaction between self-esteem and SK manipulation revealed insightful results. Converging patterns were found for each of our four measures of memory for low SE consumers: an increase (decrease) of SK was associated with higher (lower) scores on recall, recognition, and discrimination tasks and with higher number of unanswered items. The opposite pattern of results was found for high SE consumers.

The next steps of this research involve experiments identifying possible extensions of our findings. The first area we investigate is the possible mediating effect of state (vs. trait) self-esteem on the relation between subjective knowledge change and information processing. A key challenge is to overcome a potential demand effect induced by a repeated explicit measure of self-esteem. To do so, a study-in-progress measures self-esteem using the IAT procedure (Greenwald 1995; Greenwald and Farnham 2000) right after the SK manipulation. In addition, we measure General Self-Efficacy to test whether other personality traits might moderate the relationship between SK change and memory for information. We also test whether our SK manipulation, in addition to memory for information, also impacts attitude change and normative quality of decision-making.

The present research promises important insights for our understanding of the underlying mechanisms of the relationship between SK manipulation and information processing strategies. Our research may also have important applied implications as the findings will likely prove useful in improving information retention in public policy and health-related communications.

## References

Alba, Joseph W. and J. Wesley Hutchinson (1987), "Dimensions of Consumer Expertise," *Journal of Consumer Research*, 13 (4), 411-454.

Baker, William, Wesley Hutchinson, Danny Moore and Prakash Nedungadi (1986), "Brand Familiarity and Advertising: Effects on the Evoked Set and Brand Preference," *Advances in Consumer Research*, *13*, 637-642

Bettman, James R. and C. Whan Park (1980), "Effects of Prior Knowledge and Experience and Phase of the Choice Process on Consumer Decision Processes: A Protocol Analysis," *Journal of Consumer Research*, 7 (3), 234-248.

Brockner, Joel, David De Cremer, Kees van den Bos, and Ya-Ru Chen (2005), "The Influence of Interdependent Self-Construal on Procedural Fairness Effects," *Organizational behavior and human decision processes*, 96 (2), 155.

Brucks, Merrie (1985), "The Effects of Product Class Knowledge on Information Search Behavior," *Journal of Consumer Research*, 12 (1), 1-16.

Carlson, Jay P., William O. Bearden, and David M. Hardesty (2007), "Influences on What Consumers Know and What They Think They Know Regarding Marketer Pricing Tactics," *Psychology & Marketing*, 24 (2), 117.

Carlson, Jay P., Leslie H. Vincent, David M. Hardesty, and William O. Bearden (2009), "Objective and Subjective Knowledge Relationships: A Quantitative Analysis of Consumer Research Findings," Journal of Consumer Research, 35 (February), 864-876.

Greenwald, Anthony G. and Shelly D. Farnham (2000), "Using the Implicit Association Test to Measure Self-Esteem and Self-Concept," *Journal of Personality and Social Psychology*, 79 (6), 1022-38.

Greenwald, Anthony G. and Mahzarin R. Banaji (1995), "Implicit Social Cognition: Attitudes, Self-Esteem, and Stereotypes," *Psychological Review*, 102 (1), 4-27.

Maheswaran, Durairaj and Brian Sternthal (1990), "The Effects of Knowledge, Motivation, and Type of Message on Ad Processing and Product Judgments," *Journal of Consumer Research*, 17 (1), 66-73.

Moorman, Christine, Kristin Diehl, David Brinberg, and Blair Kidwell (2004), "Subjective Knowledge, Search Locations, and Consumer Choice," *Journal of Consumer Research*, 31 (3), 673-680.

Park, C. Whan, Meryl P. Gardner, and Vinod K. Thukral (1988), "Self-Perceived Knowledge: Some Effects on Information Processing for a Choice Task," *The American Journal of Psychology*, 101 (3), 401-424.

Park, C. Whan and V. Parker Lessig (1981), "Familiarity and Its Impact on Consumer Decision Biases and Heuristics," *Journal of Consumer Research*, 8 (2), 223-230.

Radecki, Carmen M. and James Jaccard (1995), "Perceptions of Knowledge, Actual Knowledge, and Information Search Behavior," *Journal of Experimental Social Psychology*, 31 (2), 107-138.

Raju, P. S., Subhash C. Lonial, and W. Glynn Mangold (1995), "Differential Effects of Subjective Knowledge, Objective Knowledge, and Usage Experience on Decision Making: An Exploratory Investigation," *Journal of Consumer Psychology*, 4 (2), 153.

See, Kelly E. (2009), "Reactions to Decisions with Uncertain Consequences: Reliance on Perceived Fairness Versus Predicted Outcomes Depends on Knowledge," *Journal of personality and social psychology*, 96 (1), 104-118.

Sujan, Mita (1985), "Consumer Knowledge: Effects on Evaluation Strategies Mediating Consumer Judgments," *Journal of Consumer Research*, 12 (1), 31-46.

Wiener, Yoash (1973), "Task Ego-Involvement and Self-Esteem as Moderators of Situationally Devalued Self-Esteem," *Journal of Applied Psychology*, 58 (2), 225-232.

# When Does National Identity Matter?
## Two Contrasting Symbolic Meaning of Brands in Emerging Countries

Man Ching Kwan, Hong Kong Baptist University, Hong Kong

## Extended Abstract

Under increasing globalization, cultural convergence occurs and people are exposed to multiple cultures simultaneously. Living in such a multiplex atmosphere, people risk an identity crisis in every aspect of their lives, even during consumption. One of the most salient incongruence lies between identities and brand perceptions. This has merited much attention in marketing literature. For example, a research stream on nationalism and patriotism highlighted some potential hazardous outcomes, like anti-consumption movement (Varman & Belk, 2009) and repulsion to foreign brands (Wang and Wang, 2007), are resulted from the infringement of nationhood or ethnic identity. However, some research suggested "foreignness" is not essentially bad. For many occasions, global appeal is more valued by consumers due to its connotation of cosmopolitanism, modernity and high quality (Zhou & Belk, 2004; Steenkamp, Batra & Alden, 2001). Dong & Tian (2009) even suggested consumers might use foreign brands to assert a desired national identity.

Apparently, there exists the ambiguity in consumer choice between the protection of embraced ideology and the pursuit of social development. In light of this, this research investigated how this would impact on brand perceptions, especially in the emerging countries like China. More specifically, it was suggested that the congruity of brand personality with people's believes held for their nation (i.e. national identity), either actual or ideal, impacts on brand favorability.

Based on self-concept theories (Levy, 1959; Rogers, 1951; Sirgy, 1986), consumers purchase and use goods that have a user image consistent with their own self-image in order to express and communicate their "self". This process is known as self-congruity (or "self-image congruence"), which is driven by the two twin motives, the self-esteem motive (the tendency to seek experiences that enhances self-concepts) and the self-consistency motive (the tendency for an individual to behave consistently with her view of herself) (Malhotra, 1981, 1988; Sirgy, 1982a, 1982b, 1982c). This research tried to tease out their effects on different dimensions of a "self", i.e. actual (referring to how a person perceive herself) and ideal (refers to how a person would like to perceive herself) (Rogers, 1951). It is suggested the relatively more salient the actual self (vs. ideal self) strives the decision making process, the stronger impact the self-esteem motive (vs. self-enhancement motive) exerts.

To operationalize the self-congruity conditions, an important pair of ideology related to national identity (i.e. traditionalism and modernism) was identified. In the research, "Traditional" referred to the values of respecting the past, customs and conventions, and venerating the quality of being historical, time-honored and legendary; whereas "Modern" represented a notion of being new, contemporary, up-to-date, and ahead of times (Pollay, 1983; Zhang & Shavitt, 2003). While many traditional values might have been deeply rooted in consumers' mind over decades, the influence of modern values has been intensifying and challenging the status quo of the existing ideology in commercial world. The trade-off among them perfectly illustrates the conflicts between the actual self (i.e. what the Chinese believe they are) and the ideal self (i.e. what they desire to become).

On the other hand, recognized as an important symbolic brand attribute through which consumers are enabled to express different dimensions of the self, such as the personal-self (Belk, 1988), the ideal self (Malhotra, 1988) and etc., brand personality is another important variable considered in the research. Two personalities, sincerity and excitement, are selected from the Big-five brand personality model (Aaker, 1997), in regarded to their robustness across cultures (Aaker, 2004) and prominence in variance explanation (Aaker, 1997). Embedding a pursuit of harmony, true sentiment and collective goals, sincere traits are found consistently across the East countries (e.g. Sung and Tinkham, 2005; Aaker, Benet-Martinez & Garolera, 2001; Huang and Lu, 2003). Alternatively, excitement connotes imaginativeness, innovativeness, independence and youthfulness (Aaker, 1997), which are not prevalent and accepted in these traditional societies. Consequently, congruence occurs when sincerity (vs. excitement) matches with traditionalism (vs. modernism) whereas incongruence occurs when reversing the match. In this sense, self-congruity was operationalized in a 2 (brand personality: sincerity vs. excitement) x2 (national identity: traditional vs. modern) between-subject design and four conditions (i.e. actual/ideal vs. congruent/incongruent) were resulted.

To examine the hypotheses, several experiments would be conducted. Experiment 1 investigated the dynamics of congruity effect. Participants were given one version of the four manipulated advertisements and asked to rate "how much they like about the brand captured in the ads", and "how much they identify with traditional (vs. modern) national images". Results revealed that there exists a crossover interaction effect between brand personality and national identity, consistent with our predictions. It was found that consumers who possess stronger traditional (vs. modern) values prefer brands with coherent brand personalities, i.e. sincerity (vs. excitement). Surprisingly, for sincere brands, brand favorability does not differ significantly among the two country image perceptions; whereas there is significant difference among the two incongruent conditions (i.e. sincere/modern vs. exciting/traditional). This implied a prominent persistence of long-lasting cultural values regardless of social transforms and changes, offering insights unique to the transitioning national state. Meanwhile, the result obtained was encouraging. However, stronger evidence and support were sought to confirm the effect of the two motives and rule out other confining factors. Therefore, additional experiments were designing and would be conducted in parallel to Experiment 1.

In sum, this research enriched the understandings about the dynamics of consumer preferences in transforming economy and brought about both valuable theoretical and managerial implications. Particularly, this research applied self congruity theory to a "collective" self-belief about a nation (i.e. national identity). It also extended some interpretative researches on western brand meaning (e.g. Dong & Tian, 2009; Zhou & Belk, 2004; Zhang & Shavitt, 2003). Through conducting experiments, it was illustrated empirically in what circumstances consumers prefer brands reflecting their desired national identity rather than the one reflecting a consistent identity. Moreover, it supplemented the existing self-concept theory (Levy, 1959; Roger, 1951; Grubb & Grathwohl, 1967; Sirgy, 1982) and offered additional insights to the conflicting congruity/incongruity situations. Most importantly, some valuable insights of understanding a transitioning economy are provided, consolidating the foundation for future research.

### References

Aaker, Jennifer, Benet-Martinez Veronica and Garolera, Jordi (2001), "Consumption symbols as carriers of culture: A study of Japanese and Spanish brand personality constructs", *Journal of Personality and social Psychology*, 81 (3), 492-508.
Aaker, Jennifer, Fournier, Susan and Brasel, S. Adam (2004), "When good brands do bad", *Jounral of Consumer Research*, 31(6), 1-16
Aaker, Jennifer (1997), "Dimensions of brand personality", *Journal of Marketing Research*, 34(3), 347-56.
Belk, R.W. (1988). Possessions and the Extended Self. Journal of consumer Research, 15 (2), 139-168.

Dong, Lily and Tian, Kelly (2009), "The Use of Western Brands in Asserting Chinese National Identity", *Journal of Consumer Research*, 36(3), 504-523.

Huang, Shengbing and Lu, Taihong (2003), "Localized Study of Brand Dimensions", *Nankai business review*, 6(1), 4-9

Levy, Sidney J. (1959), "Symbols for Sales", *Harvard Business Review*, 27(4), 117-124.

Malhotra, Naresh K. (1981), "A Scale to Measure Self-Concepts, Person Concepts, and Product Concepts", *Journal of Marketing Research*, 18, 456-464.

Malhotra, Naresh K. (1988), "Self-Concept and Product Choice: an Integrated Perspective", *Journal of Economic Psychology*, 9(March), 1-28

Pollay, Richard W. (1983), "Measuring the cultural values manifest in advertising", in *Current Issues and Research in Advertising*, ed. James H. Leigh and Claude R. Martin, Jr., Ann Arbor: University of Michigan Graduate School of Business Division Research, 71-91

Rogers, Carl (1951), *Client-Centred Therapy: Its Current Practices, Implications, and Theory*, Boston: Hougton Mifflin.

Sirgy, M. Joseph (1982a), "Self-concept in consumer behavior: a critical review", *Journal of Consumer Research*, 9(3), 287-300

Sirgy, M. Joseph (1982b), "Self-Image/Product Image Congruity and Purchase Motivation: A Role Playing Experiment", *Proceedings of the American Psychological Association–Consumer Psychology Division*, 90.

Sirgy, M. Joseph (1986), *Self-congruity: toward a theory of personality and cybernetics*, New York, NY: Praeger.

Steenkamp, Jan-Benedict EM., Batra, Rajeev and Alden, Dana L. (2001), "How Perceived Brand Globalness Creates Brand Value", *Journal of International Business Studies*, 34, 53-65.

Sung, Yongjun and Tinkham, Spencer F. (2005), "Brand Personality Structures in the United States and Korea: Common and Culture-Specific Factors", *Journal of Consumer Psychology*, 15(4), 334-350.

Varman Rohit, and Belk, Russell W. (2009), "Nationalism and Ideology in an Anti-consumption Movement", *Journal of Consumer Research*, 36(4), 686-700.

Wang, Jian and Wang, Zhiying (2007), "Consumer Goods as Dialogue about Development: Colonial time and Television Time in Belize", In *Consumption and Identity*, ed. Jonathan Friedman, New York: Routledege, 97-118

Zhang, Jing and Shavitt, Sharon (2003), "Cultural Values in Advertisements to the Chinese X-Generation–Promoting Modernity and Individualism", *Journal of Advertising*, 32(1), 23-33.

Zhou, Nan and Belk, Russell W. (2004), "Chinese Consumer Readings of Global and Local Advertising Appeals", *Journal of Advertising*, 33(3), 63-76.

# Mortality Salience and Foreign Product Evaluation: An Important Moderator

Mark Mulder, Washington State University, Australia
Fang Wan, University of Manitoba, Canada
Darren W. Dahl, University of British Columbia, Canada

## EXTENDED ABSTRACT

### Motivation and Conceptualization

Terror Management Theory (TMT) (Greenberg et al., 1997) assumes that thoughts of death create anxiety, and that people have developed worldviews as a buffer against this anxiety. In 2004, Arndt et al. suggested that much can be learned regarding the relationship between terror management and consumer behavior. Indeed, at least two studies have shown consumers' tendency to prefer domestic products (over foreign products) is magnified under conditions of MS. In one study, for example, Jonas et al. (2005) found Germans in an MS condition showed more support for the German Mark and less support for the Euro. In another related study, Friese and Hofmann (2008) found Swiss consumers in an MS condition showed a stronger preference for Swiss Chocolate over other foreign options. While these studies support the basic propositions of TMT, previous research leaves at least two interesting questions unanswered. First, past research has focused on a somewhat narrow band of products (foreign currency and chocolates). Accordingly, it is relevant to ask whether similar findings will emerge based on more common products such as cameras or MP3 players. Second, past research has not, to our knowledge, examined whether the impact of MS on foreign product evaluation depends on theoretically-meaningful individual differences.

According to TMT, MS enhances the impact of people's worldviews on judgments of in-groups (e.g., domestic products) and out-groups (e.g., foreign products). One relevant individual difference in this regard is consumer ethnocentrism (CE), which Shimp and Sharma (1987) define as "the belief among consumers that it is inappropriate, or even immoral, to purchase foreign products because to do so is damaging to the domestic economy, costs domestic jobs and is unpatriotic" (p. 281). In theory, the impact of MS on foreign product evaluation should be stronger among consumers high in CE. The present study tests that hypothesis by asking consumers to evaluate products produced in the U.S. and Iran. Prior to evaluating the products, consumers complete the CE scale and write down their thoughts about death or dental pain (a commonly used control condition in TMT research).

Overall, we expected that consumers would prefer products made in the U.S. to products made in Iran (i.e., a main effect of country of production; *Hypothesis 1*). We also expected this tendency to be stronger among those high in CE (i.e., a two-way interaction between country of production and CE; *Hypothesis 2*). Finally, we anticipated that the tendency to prefer U.S. products would be the strongest among consumers high in CE who were assigned to the MS condition (i.e., a three-way interaction between CE, country of production and MS condition; *Hypothesis 3*). We chose to compare products made in the U.S. to products made in Iran because prior research has suggested that it is important to look at the impact of MS on foreign product evaluation using a country which is considered antagonistic

(Maheswaran & Agrawal, 2004), and recent research on consumer animosity suggests that consumers hold a high degree of animosity toward Iran (Funk, Arthurs, Trevino, and Joireman, 2010).

## Method

American university students completed the survey in exchange for course credit (38 females, 48 males; median age=21). Participants first completed a shortened ethnocentrism scale (6 items; alpha=.90). Next, participants were randomly assigned to a mortality salience (MS) or dental pain (DP) control condition (cf. Jonas, Schimel, Greenberg, and Pyszczynski, 2002). In the *MS condition*, participants were asked to briefly describe the emotions that the thought of their own death aroused in them, and to jot down, as specifically as they could, what they thought would happen to them (personally) as they die and once they are physically dead. In the *DP condition*, participants responded to similar questions about dental pain. After writing down their thoughts about death or dental pain, participants completed a 60-item mood scale (PANAS–X; Watson, Clark, and Tellegen, 1988) as a delay task (cf., Greenberg, Pyszczynski, Solomon, Simon, & Breus, 1994). Following the mood scale, participants received ads of a camera and an MP3 player and evaluated each product, each of which had a suggested retail of $99.00. One product was said to be made in the U.S. and one product was said to be made in Iran. To avoid confounding product with country, assignment of product to country was counterbalanced. Brand names were based on a pretest (N=16) which indicated that the brand names chosen were viewed as both likable and believable. Participants evaluated each product using a four-item (7-point Likert type) scale (alphas>.93; bad/good; unfavorable/favorable; worthless/valuable; dislike/like).

## Major Findings

To test our hypotheses, we conducted a 2 (MS Condition: MS vs. DP) x 2 (CE: low vs. high) x 2 (Country of Production: U.S. vs. Iran) mixed-model ANOVA, treating the first two variables as between-subject variables and the latter variable as a within-subject variable. Supporting H1, participants evaluated the U.S. product more favorably than the Iranian product ($p<.001$). Consistent with H2, results also revealed a marginally significant two-way interaction between Country of Production and CE (p=.07). This interaction revealed that the tendency to prefer U.S. products was stronger among those high in CE. Finally, in line with H3, results revealed a marginally-significant three-way interaction between Country of Production, CE and MS condition (p=.11). The tendency to evaluate U.S. products more favorably was strongest among participants high in CE who had also been assigned to the MS condition.

## Conclusion

The present findings suggest that the impact of MS on foreign product evaluations depends on consumer ethnocentrism. By integrating CE into this line of work, we have helped to extend past research which has shown that MS leads to a stronger preference for domestic products. The current study's sample size was relatively small, and some of the findings did not reach conventional levels of statistical significance. Nevertheless, the overall patterns were consistent with hypotheses and suggest future research in this area is warranted.

## References

Arndt, J., Solomon, S., Kasser, T. & Sheldon, K. (2004). The Urge to Splurge Revisited: Further Reflections on Applying Terror Management Theory to Materialism and Consumer Behavior. *Journal of Consumer Psychology*, 14, 225-229.

Friese, M. & Hofmann, W. (2008). What Would You Have as a Last Supper? Thoughts About Death Influence Evaluation and Consumption of Food Products. *Journal of Experimental Social Psychology*, 44, 1388-1394.

Funk, C.A., Arthurs, J.D., Trevino, L.J. & Joireman, J. (2010). Consumer Animosity in the Global Value Chain: The Effect of International Production Shifts on Willingness to Purchase Hybrid Products. *Journal of International Business Studies* (forthcoming).

Greenberg, J., Solomon, S., & Pyszczynski, T. (1997). *Terror Management Theory of Self-esteem and Cultural Worldviews: Empirical Assessments and Conceptual Refinements*. In M. Zanna (Ed.), Advances in experimental social psychology (Vol. 29, pp. 61–139). Orlando, FL: Academic Press.

Jonas, E., Schimel, J., Greenberg, J., & Pyszczynski, T. (2002). The Scrooge Effect: Evidence that Mortality Salience increases Prosocial Attitudes and Behavior. *Personality and Social Psychology Bulletin*, 28, 1342–1353.

Jonas, E., Fritsche, I., & Greenberg, J. (2005). Currencies as Cultural Symbols–An Existential Psychological Perspective on Reactions of Germans Towards the Euro. *Journal of Economic Psychology*, 26, 129-146.

Maheswaran, D. & Agrawal, N. (2004). Motivational and Cultural Variations in Mortality Salience Effects: Contemplations on Terror Management Theory and Consumer Behavior. *Journal of Consumer Psychology*, 14, 213-218.

Shimp, T. A., & Sharma, S. (1987). Consumer Ethnocentrism: Construction and Validation of the CETSCALE. *Journal of Marketing Research*, 24, 280-289.

Watson, D., Clark, L. A., & Tellegen, A. (1988). Development and validation of brief measures of positive and negative affect: The PANAS scales. *Journal of Personality and Social Psychology,* 54, 1063-1070.

# Family Obligations and Time Management

Therese A. Louie, San Jose State University, USA
Judy Hanh Vo, San Jose State University, USA

## Extended Abstract

The core of successful marketing is providing consumers with products and services that help them spend time in the way they find most meaningful. Addressing their needs is becoming more challenging as the population diversifies ethnically (Kennedy, Lawton, and Walker, 2001). For example, there are disparate cultural norms regarding how much time is spent on family responsibilities such as care-giving, household chores, and financial support. This research explores how ethnic customs influence consumers' time management.

Much research on family responsibilities has focused upon the Latino subculture. Fuligni and Pedersen (2002) found that Latin American and Filipino students had a strong sense of familial duty, and were more likely than their counterparts to help their families financially. Traditional Latinos' partake in high levels of care-giving (Kuperminc, Jurkovic, and Casey, 2009). In addition, historically the Asian subculture--for which there is a norm of relative interdependence (Aaker and Lee, 2001)--has emphasized family-related activities. Tseng (2004) found that Asian respondents provided large levels of assistance at home (e.g., running errands that the family needs done).

Hence, research has established that Latinos and Asians are inclined to be dedicated to family. This paper extends past work by investigating how they manage those responsibilities. In a given month, how much of their schedule is spent focusing on familial obligations versus on other chores characteristic of their age group? Although individuals from all ethnic backgrounds may have such family duties, it is anticipated that Latinos and Asians from traditional backgrounds will have many such tasks on their to-do lists. In addition, when completing the tasks, it is expected that Latinos and Asians will spend more energy on items family members request that they do.

A total of 57 undergraduates (45% male) taking Marketing classes were asked to participate. First, participants were asked to list all the tasks unrelated to school that they planned to complete within a four-week period; the researcher collected these materials. Then, four weeks later the lists were returned. Participants put a plus sign (+) next to each task they had completed. In addition, they noted throughout their initial lists which tasks family members had asked them to do.

Measures were taken to ascertain participant ethnicity. It was important to identify those who were from families that continued to emphasize customs prevalent in the nations from which they emigrated. Therefore, participants were asked if they spoke a language other than English growing up in their household. A total of 23 participants (40% of the sample) learned Spanish or an Asian language at home. The survey responses from these participants were compared to their classmates during the data analysis.

As anticipated, the type of tasks enumerated on participants' to-do lists reveals an ethnic "familial responsibilities" norm. It was predicted that those with Spanish or Asian language skills would list more tasks that were requests from family members. Indeed, they provided a statistically significant higher percentage of family-related tasks on their to-do lists than did the non-Spanish/Asian language group ($t(55)=2.22$, $p<.05$). In addition, Spanish and Asian language participants focused proportionately more of their task completion on family duties. Of the tasks that were finished, they had a higher percentage of family-related items ($t(55)=2.42$, $p<.05$).

Marketers targeting ethnic subcultures might do well to recognize scheduling constraints they may face. Latinos' and Asians' purchase decisions may include strong "family" components that are relevant even to young adults who do not yet have children of their own. For example, familial considerations may influence the neighborhoods in which they want to live, the number of seats in their cars, and the type of employment they seek (e.g., in terms of time flexibility). Furthermore, research can outline practices and products that might help Latinos and Asians organize their days. Those whose lives are disrupted by multiple family activities might learn to develop tactics that help them refocus upon returning to professional and student responsibilities. (For example, before errand-running one scheduling expert takes a moment to list three to-do items that help to ease the transition back to the office.) Note that although norms within the Latino and Asian cultures might prompt higher levels of family duties, many participants from both research groups in this study provided such responsibilities on their to-do lists. Therefore, efforts to help consumers successfully schedule their time might be especially relevant to Latinos and Asians, and are more generally applicable to individuals from all backgrounds.

Extensions of this work include a fuller investigation of demographic factors that influence time management. Although Latinos and Asians may have heightened family obligations, there is a risk in generalizing in-depth similarities across, and even within, the subcultures. It is worthwhile to explore cross-nationality differences in how consumers cope with family responsibilities. In addition, with larger cell sizes it will be possible to explore the effect of gender, as this factor may have a heavier influence on time management in some cultures (Sy and Romero, 2008). In the meantime, it is hoped that this research stimulates more investigations into ethnic differences that influence how consumers spend their time.

## References

Aaker, Jennifer L. and Angela Y. Lee (2001), "'I' Seek Pleasures and 'We' Avoid Pains: The Role of Self-Regulatory Goals in Information Processing and Persuasion," *Journal of Consumer Research,* 28(1), 33-49.

Fuligni Andrew .J, and Sara Pedersen (2002), "Family Obligation and the Transition to Young Adulthood," *Developmental Psychology*, 38(5), 856-868.

Kennedy Ellen J., Leigh Lawton, and Erika Walker, "The Case for Using Live Cases: Shifting the Paradigm in Marketing Education," Journal of Marketing Education, 23( 2), 145-151.

Kuperminc Gabriel P., Gregory J. Jurkovic, and Sean Casey (2009), "Relation of Filial Responsibility to the Personal and Social Adjustment of Latino Adolescents from Immigrant Families, *Journal of Family Psychology*, 23(1), 14-22.

Sy, Susan R., and Jessica Romero (2008), "Family Responsibilities Among Latina College Students from Immigrant Families," *Journal of Hispanic Higher Education*, 7(3), 212-227.

Tseng, Vivian (2004), "Family Interdependence and Academic Adjustment in College: Youth from Immigrant and U.S.-Born Families," *Child Development*, 75(3), 966-983.

# Male Interpretation of Idealized Model Images in Advertising–A Cross Cultural Study

Hazel H. Huang, Durham Business School
Richard Elliott, Bath School of Management, UK

## Extended Abstract

Traditionally, females are seen to take the predominant consumer role and much research has been conducted in this area. Because of the change of social structure, the role of males as consumers has become more and more important. However, the attention to males as consumers is still inadequate. This paper aims to investigate this area by focusing on male interpretation of idealized model images (both females and males) in advertising.

This study explores how males from different cultural backgrounds, i.e. Western versus Far Eastern, define idealized model images. That gender is seen as a cultural construct is a consensus among sociologists (Massé and Rosenblum 1988) and marketers (Costa 1994). Thus, the perception of idealized model images (i.e. physical attractiveness) may differ across cultures. However, little is known regarding how males in different cultures evaluate physical attractiveness of males as well as females. To explore the differences between two distinct cultures, it attempts to understand how males respond to male and female portrayals in various forms. Current research on male portrayals is limited to content analysis (Kolbe and Albanese 1996; Patterson and England 2000; Rohlinger 2002). If content analysis is not used, the studies mainly examine male sexual representations (Elliott and Elliott 2005; Rohlinger 2002), social comparison theory (Gulas and McKeage 2000), or gender identity congruity (Martin and Gnoth 2009). These studies came to the conclusion that realistic masculinity is appealing, but is masculinity the only factor in evaluating male images? These studies overlooked how an idealized image is identified, and more importantly, identified by males with different cultural backgrounds. In addition to male interpretation of male images, focus is also directed towards male interpretation of female portrayals. Studies on female portrayals date back to the beginning of the liberation of women. Traditionally, the female role in adverts is decorative and usually features gender stereotyping. Early studies focusing on objectification of females utilized content analysis to demonstrate how society saw females (Goffman 1976). This view is a predominantly a male view of females (Stern 1999). Later, research started to center around females as audience through social comparison theory (Richins 1991) with an emphasis on female well-being (Martin and Gentry 1997). However, three decades have passed since Goffman's (1976) benchmarking study and the balance of social power between men and women has changed greatly. A renewed male view of female images is in need for an update.

These objectives prompt the research questions: how do males from different cultural backgrounds respond to the male and female representations in advertising? And what are considered to be idealized images? To explore these questions, the study adopts Scott's (1994) reader-response theory, which signifies the negotiation between the meaning of the images and the reader, because *beauty is in the eyes of the beholder*. Twenty interviews were carried out among heterosexual males; ten were Taiwanese (representing a Far-Eastern culture) and ten were British Caucasian (representing a Western culture). Twelve print adverts, each featuring only one sex, were selected from women's and men's lifestyle magazines in Western and Far Eastern countries.

One similarity between Taiwanese and British males has been identified: their views on the idealized levels of femininity/masculinity for females and males. Both British and Taiwanese view a moderately masculine male image and a moderately feminine female image more favorably than the extreme masculine or feminine forms. This finding is consistent with the ideas of new men (Cramer, Cupp, and Kuhn 1993) and new women (Peck and Loken 2004). In spite of this similarity, the cultural differences in male interpretation of idealized model images are overwhelming and can be classified into three categories: (1) judgment of appearances, (2) evaluation of realistically idealized images, and (3) the relationship between the perception of good adverts and good-looking images.

The first difference lies in how British and Taiwanese see an idealized model image. British informants focus on bodies and facial appearances when describing idealized appearances of males and females. On the other hand, Taiwanese males ignore physical appearances. They focus on 'inner beauty', such as charisma for males and 'qi-zhi' (an inner grace put forward by a mixture of behavior and presence) for females. They tend to read facial expression, rather than facial appearances, in discussing the model images. Another variation in their views of realistically idealized images is observed. While images considered as naturally beautiful or handsome are appealing to Taiwanese males, images close to an unachievable perfection interest them even more. Taiwanese believe that an idealized image should be perfect and that a sense of unattainability increases their curiosity (or fantasy) and wish to worship the person. This is not the case from the responses of their British counterparts, who strongly suggest that realistically beautiful/handsome images are idealized. A final deviation on the relationship between model images and adverts is identified. British informants are able to detach their evaluation of the model images from that of the adverts. Similarly, they are able to isolate how good-looking the model images are from how much they like the models presented in the adverts. By contrast, their Taiwanese counterparts do not display such detachment. In other words, if the Taiwanese interviewees like the model images, they see them as good-looking and develop positive attitudes towards the adverts.

The study supports a sociocultural view of physical attractiveness. The findings are in line with Callow and Schiffman's (2003) argument that a high-context culture (i.e. Taiwanese) is inclined to over-read into the meaning of the model images and connect the dots (e.g. the images) to develop a story (e.g. a positive relationship between the images and adverts). Moreover, the worship of idealized model images observed in Taiwan and the appreciation of realistically idealized model images in Britain may be a transformation from Hofstede's power distance: hierarchy does not only exist in social status; it exists in physical attractiveness. These differences in interpreting idealized model images encourage advertising companies to re-evaluate the effectiveness of using idealized model images in different countries.

## References

Callow, Michael and Leon G. Schiffman (2003), "Sociocultural Meanings in Visually Standardized Print Ads," *European Journal of Marketing*, 38 (9/10), 1113-1128.

Costa, Janeen Arnold (1994), "Gender Issues: Gender as a Cultural Construct," in *Advances in Consumer Research*, Vol. 21, ed. Chris T. Allen and Deborah Roedder John, Provo, UT: Association for Consumer Research, 372-373.

Cramer, Robert Ervin, Robert G. Cupp, and Jill A. Kuhn (1993), "Male Attractiveness: Masculinity with a Feminine Touch," *Current Psychology*, 12 (2), 142-150.

Elliott, Richard and Christine Elliott (2005), "Idealized Images of the Male Body in Advertising: A Reader-Response Exploration," *Journal of Marketing Communications*, 11 (March), 3-19.

Goffman, Erving (1976), *Gender Advertisements*, Cambridge, MA: Harvard University Press.

Gulas, Charles S. and Kim McKeage (2000), "Extending Social Comparison: An Examination of the Unintended Consequences of Idealized Advertising Imagery," *Journal of Advertising*, 29 (2), 17-28.

Hofstede, Geert H. (1980), *Culture's Consequences: International Differences in Work-Related Values*, London: Sage.

Kolbe, Richard H. and Paul J. Albanese (1996), "Man to Man: A Content Analysis of Sole-Male Images in Male-Audience Magazines," *Journal of Advertising*, 25 (4), 1-20.

Martin, Brett A. S. and Juergen Gnoth (2009), "Is The Marlboro Man the Only Alternative? The Role of Gender Identity and Self-Construal Salience in Evaluations of Male Models," *Marketing Letters*, 20 (4), 353-367.

Martin, Mary C. and James W. Gentry (1997), "Stuck in the Model Trap: The Effects of Beautiful Models in Ads on Female Pre-Adolescents and Adolescents," *Journal of Advertising*, 26 (2), 19-33.

Massé, Michelle A. and Karen Rosenblum (1988), "Male and Female Created They Them: The Depiction of Gender in the Advertising of Traditional Women's and Men's Magazines," *Women's Studies International Forum*, 11 (2), 127-144.

Patterson, Maurice and G. England (2000), "Body Work: Depicting the Male Body in Men's Lifestyle Magazines," in *Proceedings of the Academy of Marketing Annual Conference*: University of Derby.

Peck, Joann and Barbara Loken (2004), "When Will Larger-Sized Female Models in Advertisements Be Viewed Positively? The Moderating Effects of Instructional Frame, Gender, and Need for Cognition," *Psychology & Marketing*, 21 (6), 425-442.

Richins, Marsha L. (1991), "Social Comparison and the Idealized Images of Advertising," *Journal of Consumer Research*, 18 (June), 71-83.

Rohlinger, Deana A. (2002), "Eroticizing Men: Cultural Influences on Advertising and Male Objectification," *Sex Roles*, 46 (3/4), 61-74.

Scott, Linda M. (1994), "The Bridge from Text to Mind: Adapting Reader-Response Theory to Consumer Research," *Journal of Consumer Research*, 21 (December), 461-480.

Stern, Barbara B. (1999), "Gender and Multicultural Issues in Advertising: Stages on the Research Highway," *Journal of Advertising*, 1999 (1), 1-9.

# Sunglasses, Hierarchy, and Negotiations: Gender Differences in Eye Gaze During Interpersonal Communication

Todd Pezzuti, University of California-Irvine, USA
Connie Pechmann, University of California-Irvine, USA
Adilson Borges, Reims Management School, France
Dante Pirouz, University of Western Ontario, Canada

**Extended Abstract**

Sales negotiations are an important facet of marketing and consumer behavior because many products and services are sold face to face and the terms are negotiated, e.g., on car lots and golf courses. The impact of visual contact during sales negotiations may differ for males and females. This effect was demonstrated in a recent study that found direct eye contact benefited females negotiating with females, but not males negotiating with males (Swaab and Swaab 2009). That direct eye contact impairs negotiation performance for males is surprising in the light of media richness theory which suggests that performance on complex tasks such as negotiations should be enhanced by visual contact since visual contact provides information about ambiguous or equivocal messages and allows people to communicate more quickly (Daft and Lengel 1986).

Swaab and Swaab (2009) draw on several different areas of research to explain the contrasting effects of eye contact for males and females. The authors explain that females are more comfortable with eye contact and use eye contact to understand others (Connelan et al. 2000; Troemel-Ploetz 1991). Moreover, females communicate in order to discuss and understand the perspectives of others (Tannen 2002). Males, on the other hand, are less comfortable with eye contact (Connelan et al. 2000) and focus on winning discussions (Tannen 2002). Consequently, the competitive intentions communicated by the eyes may distract males from the task at hand, and in turn, interfere with communication.

The present study adds a new layer to the understanding of how eye contact influences complex interactions for males and females by studying the behavior of a buyer and seller as they negotiate the terms of a hypothetical automobile purchase while wearing sunglasses. We illustrate that eye contact does not always benefit negotiations between females, nor does eye contact always impair negotiations between males.

An important methodological difference between the present study and previous work leads to very different assumptions and results. Swaab and Swaab (2009) developed a device that allowed participants to see their partners on a computer monitor. The angle of the cameras was manipulated so that the eyes of ones partner were looking straight ahead (direct eye contact) or appeared to be looking down (no direct eye contact). As Swaab and Swaab (2009) explain, the communication of competitive intentions signaled through direct eye contact was attenuated in the no eye contact condition since participants could not look directly into the eyes of their partner. Moreover, because of the placement of the cameras, all of the participants in the no direct eye contact condition appeared to be looking down towards the ground, which is a nonverbal cue of submission. Therefore, although the participants in the no eye contact condition did not signal competitive intentions with their eyes, participants may have viewed their partners as submissive since participants looked straight ahead at the computer screen, but were perceived by their partners to be looking down.

The present study differs from Swaab and Swaab (2009) in that participants cannot determine the direction of their partner's gaze since the eyes are completely blocked by sunglasses. Gaze, importantly, facilitates the establishment of hierarchies in social interactions (Hall, Coats, and LeBeau 2005). For instance, looking down as someone gazes in one's direction signals submission. Therefore, completely blocking the eyes impedes establishing a hierarchy. This is particularly significant since research indicates that status hierarchies actually enhance interactions and that individuals like and are more comfortable with people who complement their dominant and submissive nonverbal behaviors (Tiedens and Fragale 2003). Additionally, evidence indicates that individuals have an unconscious drive for hierarchy (Tiedens, Unzueta, and Young 2007). Importantly, however, females are generally viewed as less concerned with hierarchy and are less hierarchically organized than males during initial interactions (Mast 2002). With these considerations in mind, a lack of hierarchy-related cues should lead to less satisfying negotiations for males, but not females. This reasoning leads to the following hypotheses:

H1: When the eyes of a negotiation partner are blocked with sunglasses, males, but not females, evaluate their partners less favorably and like their partners less than do participants who can see the eyes of their partner.

H2: For males, but not females, it takes more effort to reach agreements when the eyes of a negotiation partner are blocked by sunglasses than when the eyes are not blocked, which will impair subsequent performance on a cognitive task for males in the sunglass condition.

Participants (92 students) were assigned the role of buyer or seller and paired together to negotiate the terms of a hypothetical automobile sale (for more details see, Thompson 1991). Buyers and sellers were matched on gender. Groups were randomly assigned to negotiate without sunglasses or to negotiate while wearing sunglasses designed to fit over regular eye glasses. Participants were given 25 minutes to agree on the terms of the sales transaction. After the negotiation, participants descrambled as many groups of letters into words (anagram task) as possible to measure cognitive resource depletion. After the anagram task, participants completed a survey.

The results confirm the hypotheses. Males, but not females, in the sunglass condition liked their partners less and reported less interpersonal attraction when compared to the control condition. Males in the sunglass condition also perceived their partners as less intelligent, less competent, less sincere, less trustworthy, and more manipulative. Furthermore, performance on the anagram task was impaired for males in the sunglass condition, indicating that extra effort was needed in order to reach agreements.

The present study demonstrates that eye contact does not always impair negotiations for males and that eye contact does not always benefit females. In line with the literature on social hierarchy, the presence of subtle cues related to status benefit males in face-to-face interactions. Females, on the other hand, are less concerned with hierarchy and are impacted less when their partner's eyes are covered with sunglasses.

**Selected References**

Connelan, Jennifer, Simon Baron-Cohen, Sally Wheelwright, Anna Batki, and Jag Ahluwalia (2000), "Sex Differences in Human Neonatal Social Perception," *Infant Behavior and Development*, 32 (January), 113-18.

Daft, Richard L. and Robert H. Lengel (1986), "Organizational Information Requirements, Media Richness, and Structural Designs," *Management Science*, 32 (May), 554-71.

Hall, Judith A., Erik J. Coats, and Lavonia S. LeBeau (2005), "Nonverbal Behavior and the Vertical Dimension of Social Relationships: A Meta-Analysis," *Psychological Bulletin*, 131 (November), 898-924.

Mast, Marianne S. (2008), "Female Dominance Hierarchies: Are They Any Different from Males?," *Personality and Social Psychology Bulletin*, 28 (January), 29-39.

Swaab, Roderick I. and Dick F. Swaab (2009), "Sex Differences in the Effects of Visual Contact and Eye Contact in Negotiations," *Journal of Experimental Social Psychology*, 45 (January), 129-36.

Tannen, Deborah (2001), *You Just Don't Understand: Men and Women in Conversation*, New York, NY: Quill.

Thompson, Leigh L. (1991), "Information Exchange in Negotiation," *Journal of Experimental Social Psychology*, 27 (March), 161-79.

Tiedens, Larissa Z. and Alison R. Fragale (2003), "Power Moves: Complementarity in Dominant and Submissive Nonverbal Behavior," *Journal of Personality and Social Psychology*, 84 (March), 558-68.

Tiedens, Larissa Z., Miguel M. Unzueta, and Maia J. Young (2007), "An Unconscious Desire for Hierarchy? The Motivated Perception of Dominance Complementarity in Task Partners," *Journal of Personality and Social Psychology*, 93 (September), 402-14.

Tromel-Ploetz, Senta (1991), "Review Essay: Selling the Apolitical," *Discourse and Society*, 2, 489-502.

# The Role of Culture in the Assimilation of Materialistic Values:
## The Case of South African Society

James M. Hunt, Temple University, USA
Carol Kaufman Scarborough, Rutgers University-Camden, USA
Scott Hoenig, Witwatersrand University, South Africa
Nicola Klein, University of Pretoria, South Africa
Kerry Chip, Witwatersrand University, South Africa

**Extended Abstract**

The concept of materialism continues to play an enduring role in the consumer literature because it is widely viewed as a driving force in western society as well as a salient expression of an individual's self-concept (see Richins 1999). Anecdotally, materialism appears to be a central concern for social commentators and scholars alike. As Richins (2004) notes, the topic has spawned more than 100 empirical studies in addition to numerous articles in the popular press focusing on materialism's role in contemporary society. However, much of our formal understanding of materialism comes from research conducted to define and measure the concept or studies that attempt to isolate its individual factors and affirm its basis in possessions. Not only has this research produced viable scales with which to measure materialism (Belk 1984; Richins and Dawson 1992), but it also has demonstrated the relationship between consumption decisions and the values the construct rests on (Belk 1985; Burroughs and Rindfleish 2002; Dittmar and Pepper 1992; Richins 1994).

Surprisingly, little attention has been paid to the process by which materialism is inculcated from a cultural perspective. Although some studies have shed light on factors effecting materialistic values (Belk 1987; Churchill and Moschis 1979; Flouri 1999 Rindfleisch, Burroughs, and Denton 1997 research on the acculturation of materialistic values remains dormant. This is particularly surprising given that materialism is widely viewed as a value orientation (Burroughs and Rindfleish 2002). In a series of depth interviews in South Africa, we investigate what happens to the personal values associated with materialism when individuals move from one cultural setting to another, particularly when the new environment is considerably more materialistic than that of the original one.

In the case of South Africa, society has been, and continues to be dominated by western culture (Klein 2007; Thomas and Bendixen 2000), although it is far from uniform in its makeup. In fact, South African society has a fairly extensive tribal heritage, which derives from various subgroups such as Xhosa, Vendi, Zulu, Tsonga, and Sotho. Most of these share a patrilineal clan based system of kinship, resulting in strong individual values.

As South Africa, with its western dominance, has become more economically advanced, it might be expected that it also become more materialistic in nature. On the other hand, given the strong set of individual values formed through a socialization process largely tribal in nature, it is possible that many South Africans may resist the self-centered nature of materialism (Cf., Burroghs and Rindfleish 2002). To investigate this question, we conducted depth interviews with individuals who had migrated, for one reason or another, from the tribal areas to the major city of Johannesburg. We anticipated that these individuals would experience cross pressures from the conflict between materialism and individual values learned in the tribal socialization process. As a result, they would exhibit less receptivity to a materialistic value system.

Our data set regarding this question originates from six long, interviews employing the theme of value confrontation. Informants were individuals who had come from various tribal areas of southern Africa to Johannesburg. Interviews were conducted on the campus of Witwatersrand University and lasted approximately one hour each. They sought to locate individuals' encounter with modern western culture in the context of personal values.

Interviews were conducted in English and taped; transcription followed. Axial coding across transcripts was used to uncover common themes and patterns underlying the interviews. Themes were identified and bracketed, and coded with examples. Further verification, discussion, and file development remain to be completed at this point in time. However, we present our initial findings here from repeated readings to date.

Emergent themes and key differences across informants are best exhibited in the responses of two of our informants–Thandi, from Limpopo, once called Northern Province, or the Transvaal, and Bobby from Botswanan Xhosa society. The first theme attendant to moving from tribal areas to Johannesburg was that of <u>marginalization</u>. All of our informants felt out of place in moving to a large modern western city. For instance, Thandi indicated that the move was "quite a challenge for me, having grown up in a slow paced life where you see a car once a day [and where] it is more bushy like, more homeland like, more opened. Here, you have got more buildings…" This is noteworthy because both Richins (1999) and Belk (1984) suggest that marginalization associated with moving encourages the use of possessions to regain a sense of self. A second theme was that of the <u>use of possessions to define self</u>. While both recognized this tendency in their new society at large, each responded differently. Bobby admitted that, having become more aware of possessions, he conscientiously attempted to change his appearance to that which was "stylish" in western terms–"the guys I wanted to relate to were more into All-Stars, flat shoes, etc, a more Italian style, so I cut my hair short…" On the other hand, Thandi moderated her adoption of western style products, eschewing western makeup and those who used it while at the same time adopting western clothing. We suggest that this difference is due to Thandi's closer ties to family and tribal past, which can be seen in her response to questions about current associations. While she listed friends from the past and the "rurals" as close entities, Bobby was more focused on finding new friends who were class and brand conscious. Our final theme is <u>valued possessions</u>. While Thandi placed primary emphasis on house and yard, which, with its gardens, reminded her of her tribal setting, Bobby fixated on clothing, shoes, and designer glasses.

In sum, our data (of which an abbreviated portion is shown here) suggest that acculturation of materialistic values in advancing societies such as that of South Africa occurs in variable yet systematic fashion. Individuals who have strong anchorage in personal values, learned through earlier socialization are able to resist the full impact of materialism and the cross pressure it brings. Those lacking in such moorings are more apt to absorb the full force of materialism. Although our work here is preliminary, we see little controversy or limitation to this proposition.

**References**

Belk, Russell W. (1984), "Three Scales to Measure Constructs Related to Materialism: Reliability, Validity, and Relationships to Measures of Happiness," in *Advances in Consumer Research*, Vol. 11, ed. T. Kinnear, Provo, UT: Associate for Consumer Research, 291-97.

Belk, Russell W. (1985), "Materialism: Trait Aspects of Living in the Material World," *Journal of Consumer Research*, 12(December), 265-280.

Belk, Russell W. (1987), "Material Values in the Comics: A Content Analysis of Comic Books Featuring Themes of Wealth," *Journal of Consumer Research*, 14(June), 26-42.

Churchill Jr., Gilbert A., and George P. Moschis (1979), "Television and Interpersonal Influences on Adolescent Consumer Learning," *Journal of Consumer Research*, 6(June), 23-35.

Dittmar, Helga, and Lucy Pepper (1992), "Materialistic Values, Relative Wealth and Person Perception: Social Psychological Belief System of Adolescents from Different Socio-Economic Backgrounds," in *Meaning, Measure and Morality of Materialism*, ed. F. Rudmin and M. Richins, Provo, UT: Associate for Consumer Research, 40-45.

Faber, Ronald J., Thomas C. O'Guinn, and John A. McCarty (1987), "Ethnicity, Acculturation, and the Importance of Product Attributes," *Psychology & Marketing*, 4(Summer), 121-134.

Flouri, Eirini (1999), "An Integrated Model of Consumer Materialism: Can Economic Socialization and Maternal Values Predict Materialistic Attitudes in Adolescents?" *Journal of Socio-Economics*, 28(6), 707-24.

Lipset, Seymour Martin (1963), *The Value Patterns of Democracy: a Case Study in Comparative Analysis*, University of California, Berkeley.

Klein, Naomi (2007) *The Shock Doctrine,* Henry Holt and Company, New York.

Mehta, Raj, and Russell W. Belk (1991), "Artifacts, Identity, and Transition: Favorite Possessions of Indians and Indian Immigrants to the United States," *Journal of Consumer Research*, 17(March), 398-411.

Parsons, Talcott (1964), *The Social System*, The Free Press, New York.

Richins, Marsha L. (1994), "Special Possessions and the Expression of Material Values," *Journal of Consumer Research*, 21(December), 522-531.

Richins, Marsha L. (1999), "Possessions, Materialism, and Other-directedness in the Expression of Self," in *Consumer Value: A Framework for Analysis and Research*, ed. Morris B. Holbrook, London: Routledge, 85-104.

Richins, Marsha L. (2004), "The Material Values Scale: Measurement Properties and Development of a Short Form," *Journal of Consumer Research*, 31(June), 209-19.

Richins, Marsha L., and Scott Dawson (1992), "Materialism as a Consumer Value: Measure Development and Validation," *Journal of Consumer Research*, 19(December), 303-317.

Rindfleisch, Aric, James E. Burroughs and Frank Denton (1997), "Family Structure, Materialism, and Compulsive Consumption," *Journal of Consumer Research*, 23(March), 312-25.

Shrum, L.J., Burroughs, J.E., and Rindfleisch, A. (2005), "Television's Cultivation of Material Values," *Journal of Consumer Research*, 32(December), 473-479.

# Exploring the Relationship between Types of TV Programs, Advertising, and Materialism: A Cultivation Theory Perspective

Eda Gurel-Atay, University of Oregon, USA
Lynn Kahle, University of Oregon, USA
Karen Ring, Universal McCann, USA

**Extended Abstract**

Because materialism has important negative consequences, it is important to understand what causes materialism. Television viewership is one of the most examined antecedents of materialism. Cultivation theory (Gerbner et al. 1977) suggests that television programs present a distorted reality and heavy exposure to that distorted reality makes people believe that the real world is similar to what they see on television. For instance, television programs tend to portray a more affluent (O'Guinn and Shrum 1997) and violent (Gerbner et al. 1980b) world full of with doctors and lawyers (Lichter, Lichter, and Rothman 1994).

Many television programs also portray a luxurious lifestyle, making heavy viewers have higher estimates of ownership of luxury products by average people (O'Guinn and Shrum 1997). Moreover, those programs show how people in those programs are happy with their expensive clothes, large homes, luxury cars, and other expensive possessions. Because materialism is a belief that acquiring possessions brings happiness and signals status and success (Belk 1984; Richins 2004) and because TV programs portray people with many possessions as being happy and successful, heavy viewers of TV tend to be more materialistic.

According to the cultivation theory, TV viewing leads to distorted perceptions of reality regardless of the TV program types (Shrum, Burroughs, and Rindfleisch 2004). However, it is also suggested that the cultivation effect might be program-specific (Gunter 1994). For instance, crime-related reality programs might affect people's perceptions of crime rates while family dramas might affect people's perceptions of family relationships. Therefore, in order to examine the cultivation effect of TV viewing, it is important to consider the differences between TV program types (Weimann, Broisus, and Wober 1992).

This research proposes that different kinds of TV programs have different effects on materialism. As suggested by Holt (1995, pg. 13), "materialism can be conceptualized as the consumption style that results when consumers perceive that value inheres in consumption objects rather than in experiences or in other people." Accordingly, it can be argued that TV programs that emphasize acquiring objects over sharing experiences and portray a luxurious, materialistic lifestyle will be more associated to materialism: (*H1a*) People who generally watch TV programs that portray a luxurious, materialistic lifestyle will be more materialistic than people who do not generally watch those TV programs; (*H1b*) People who generally watch TV programs that do not portray a luxurious, materialistic lifestyle will not differ from people who do not watch those TV programs in terms of materialism.

It can also be argued that different specials of a certain TV program type are more related to materialism than others. For instance, some sports specials, such as golf or tennis tournaments, might be associated with materialism because those sports are more related to affluent people, thereby implying a luxurious, materialistic lifestyle. However, we believe that a broader definition of a TV program type will be a better determinant of materialism because specials still reflect the nature of certain TV program types: (*H2a*) People who watch TV specials related to genres that portray a luxurious, materialistic lifestyle will be more materialistic than people who do not watch those TV specials; (*H2b*) People who watch TV specials related to genres that do not portray a luxurious, materialistic lifestyle will not differ from people who do not watch those TV specials in terms of materialism.

It is also possible that people who watch certain types of programs might report higher levels of materialism because of the commercials that air in those programs. TV commercials might make people believe that possession of products promoted in advertisements is important to obtain desired qualities, such as happiness, beauty, uniqueness, and success (Pollay 1986). Impact of advertising on materialism is also expected to be stronger when people pay more attention to commercials. Accordingly, paying more attention to commercials aired in favorite TV programs might mediate the relationship between TV viewing and materialism. However, this mediation effect will hold only for the TV programs that portray a luxurious, materialistic lifestyle (*H3a*). Because one of the conditions of mediation (i.e., a significant relationship between the independent variable and dependent variable; Baron and Kenny 1986) is not satisfied for TV programs that do not portray a luxurious, materialistic lifestyle, there will be no relationship to be mediated by paying attention to commercials (*H3b*).

To test the proposed hypotheses, data from a national survey conducted by Universal McCann-Ericson in 2005 were used. The survey was completed by 5,508 adults aged 18 and over in 2005.

The results of independent samples t-tests showed that people who generally watch TV programs that portray a luxurious, materialistic lifestyle (i.e., awards shows, celebrity interviews, films/movies, financial/stock market analysis, and reality programs) are more materialistic compared to people who do not generally watch those TV programs. In contrast, there is no significant difference between the materialism level of people who generally watch TV programs that do not portray a luxurious, materialistic lifestyle (i.e., biographies, documentary/nature, do-it-yourself shows, history, news, and sports) and the materialism level of people who do not generally watch those TV programs. Both H1a and H1b were confirmed.

Two different TV specials were used to test for H2a and H2b: one portraying a luxurious lifestyle (i.e., awards specials), and one not portraying a luxurious lifestyle (i.e., sports specials). The results demonstrated that people who watched awards specials on TV are more likely to be materialistic than people who did not watch awards specials, regardless of the type of the awards special, supporting H2a. In contrast to what was proposed in H2b, however, significant differences were found for two sports specials. People who watched March Madness basketball and people who watched the US Open Tennis Tournament on TV are more materialistic compared to people who did not watch those specials. Therefore, H2b was partially supported.

To test the mediating effect of paying attention to commercials ("attention"), blocked multiple regression analyses were conducted for each of the independent variables: Watching TV programs that portray a luxurious, materialistic lifestyle (i.e., materialistic TV viewing), and watching TV programs that do not portray a luxurious, materialistic lifestyle (i.e., nonmaterialistic TV viewing). In each of the analyses, TV viewing was entered in the first step and attention was entered in the second step. The results showed that paying attention to commercials in favorite TV programs partially mediates the relationship between materialistic TV viewing and materialism. H3a and H3b were confirmed.

This study, to our knowledge, is the first attempt to reveal the TV program types that are more related to materialism. However, our findings do not contradict with the cultivation theory. Instead, they emphasize that not all TV programs present the same message and heavy viewing of different TV programs or TV specials might lead to different distorted realities. In fact, focusing on program types (as opposed to total amount of time spent in TV viewing) might increase the effectiveness and validity of the cultivation theory by providing more concrete results.

## References

Baron, Reuben M. and David A. Kenny (1986), "The Moderator-Mediator Variable Distinction in Social Psychological Research: Conceptual, Strategic, and Statistical Considerations," *Journal of Personality and Social Psychology*, 51 (6), 1173–1182.

Belk, Russell W. (1984), "Three Scales to Measure Constructs Related to Materialism: Reliability, Validity, and Relationships to Measures of Happiness," in *Advances in Consumer Research*, Vol. 11, T. Kinnear, ed., Provo, UT: Association for Consumer Research, 291-97.

Gerbner, George, Larry Gross, Michael F. Eleey, Marilyn Jackson-Beeck, Suzanne Jeffries-Fox, and Nancy Sigronielli (1977), "TV Violence Profile No. 8: The Highlights," *Journal of Communication*, 27 (June), 171-180.

Gerbner, George, Larry Gross, Michael Morgan, and Nancy Sigronielli (1980b), "The Main Streaming of America: Violence Profile No. 11," *Journal of Communication*, 30 (Summer), 10-29.

Gunter, B. (1994), "The Question of Media Violence," in *Media Effects: Advances in Theory and Research,* eds. J. Bryant and D. Zilhnann, Hillsdale, NJ: Erlbaum, 163-211.

Holt, Douglas B. (1995), "How Consumers Consume: A Typology of Consumption Practices," *Journal of Consumer Research*, 22 (June), 1-16.

Lichter, S. R., L. S. Lichter, and S. Rothman (1994), *Prime Time: How TV Portrays American Culture*, Washington DC: Regnery Publishing.

O'Guinn, Thomas C. and L. J. Shrum (1997), "The Role of Television in the Construct of Social Reality," *Journal of Consumer Research*, 23 (4), 278-94.

Pollay, R.W. (1986), "The Distorted Mirror: Reflections on the Unintended Consequences of Advertising," *Journal of Marketing*, 50 (2), 18-36.

Richins, Martha L. (2004), "The Material Values Scale: Measurement Properties and Development of a Short Form," *Journal of Consumer Research*, 31 (1), 209-19.

Shrum, L. J., James E. Burroughs, and Aric Rindfleisch (2004), "A Process Model of Consumer Cultivation: The Role of Television Is a Function of the Type of Judgment," in *The Psychology of Entertainment Media: Blurring the Lines Between Entertainment and Persuasion*, ed. L. J. Shrum, Mahwah, NJ: Lawrence Erlbaum Associates, Inc, 177-192.

Weimann, Gabriel, H. B. Buisus, and M. Wobel (1992), "TV Diets: Toward a Typology of TV Viewership," *European Journal of Communication,* 7, 491-515.

# Exploring the Antecedents and Consequences of Physical Appearance Concern

Eda Gurel-Atay, University of Oregon, USA
Leslie Koppenhafer, University of Oregon, USA
Jae-Gu Yu, University of Oregon, USA
Lynn Kahle, University of Oregon, USA
Karen Ring, Universal McCann, USA

**Extended Abstract**

In today's Westernized and competitive environment, both women and men experience increasing pressures of physical appearance. For most people, the discrepancy between ideal body image and actual body image enlarges as the media continually endorses "thinner" and "sexier" bodies. For instance, previous studies demonstrated that heavy TV viewers are more likely to perceive unrealistic thin female bodies as a standard (Hendriks 2002) and have biased perceptions of body images (Eisend and Moller 2006).

The idealized images conveyed by media vehicles also create a sense of displeasure in consumers with their current personal appearance (Hirschman and Thompson 1997), which in turn affects their consumption behaviors. For instance, as people become more concerned with their physical appearances, they become more interested in clothes and apparels (Burton, Netemeyer, and Lichtenstein 1994), their likelihood of purchasing apparels online decreases (Rosa, Garbarino, and Malter 2006), their attitudes toward cosmetic surgery becomes more positive (Burton, Netemeyer, and Lichtenstein 1994), their usage of cosmetics increases (Netemeyer, Burton, and Lichtenstein 1995), and their usage of tanning salons increases (Burton, Netemeyer, and Lichtenstein 1994).

Physical appearance concern can also affect health-related behaviors. For instance, excessive physical appearance concern might lead to excessive exercise (Tiggemann and Lynch 2001) or unhealthy eating behaviors (Armstrong and Mallory 1992). However, it can also be argued that some types of healthful behaviors are practiced because people are concerned with their appearance as much as their health (Hayes and Ross 1987). Moreover, people who are highly concerned with their concern might want to be look healthy.

In this study, we explore the relationship between media consumption, physical appearance concern, cloths/apparel consumption, and health-related behaviors. It is hypothesized that people who read certain magazines (e.g. InStyle, People, and Vogue) and watch particular types of TV programs (e.g., awards shows, celebrity interviews, and news magazine shows) will be more likely to be concerned with their physical appearance (*H1*). High physical appearance concern, on the other hand, will be associated with both negative outcomes (related to cloths/apparel consumption–*H2*: amount of money spent on clothes, apparel, and luxury items; and frequency of cloth/apparel shopping) and positive outcomes (health-related behaviors–*H3*: healthy food consumption; consumption of foods that help weight-management; and frequency of exercising).

To test the proposed hypotheses, data from a national survey conducted by Universal McCann-Ericson in 2005 were used. The survey, called *Media in Mind*, is conducted each year and focuses on lifestyles, media consumption, and other consumption related attitudes and opinions. Of 4,990 adults who completed the survey, 40% were male, 50% were older than 50-years-old, 83.5% were White, and 65% were married. Measures related to media consumption (TV programs that portray thin and sexy body images, and favorite magazines that are related to fashion and celebrities), physical appearance concern, amount of money spent on clothes/apparels and luxury items, frequency of cloth/apparel shopping, and consumption of healthy food, consumption of food that help weight-management, and frequency of exercising were used to test proposed hypotheses. Also, because there is a significant difference between men (Mean=3.36) and women (Mean=3.65; *t*=-12.830, *p*<.001) in terms of physical appearance concern, gender was treated as a control variable in all analyses.

To test for the impact of media consumption on physical appearance concern, a blocked multiple regression analysis was conducted by entering gender in the first step and entering media consumption variables in the second step. The inclusion of media consumption variables in the regression model resulted in a significant F change ($F_{\text{increment}}$=190.503; *df*=2, 4983; *p*<.001; $\Delta R^2$=.07). The predictors explained 10% of the variance in physical appearance concern in the second step ($F$=186.044; *df*=3,4983; $MS_{\text{res}}$=.561; *p*<.001; $R^2$=.101; adjusted $R^2$=.100). Both media consumption variables have positive and significant effects on physical appearance concern, meaning that as people watched more TV programs that portray thin and sexy bodies ($\beta$=.184, *t*=12.593, *p*<.001) and as people read more fashion-related magazines ($\beta$=.138, *t*=9.480, *p*<.001), they become more concerned with their physical appearances. Therefore, H1 was confirmed.

A series of blocked multiple regression analyses were also conducted to examine the impact of physical appearance concern on proposed dependent variables. In all of these analyses, gender was entered in the first step and physical appearance concern was entered in the second step. The inclusion of physical appearance in the second step resulted in significant F changes in all analyses.

The results showed that as physical appearance concern increases, people spend more money on clothes and apparel ($\beta$=.193, $t$=12.773, $p$<.001) and luxury items ($\beta$=.208, $t$=14.679, $p$<.001). Also, they go shopping for clothes and apparel more frequently ($\beta$=.222, $t$=16.145, $p$<.001). These results provided support for H2.

Our results also showed that people who are highly concerned with their physical appearance are more likely to consume healthy foods ($\beta$=.196, $t$=13.934, $p$<.001) and more likely to consume foods that help them manage their weight ($\beta$=.192, $t$=13.571, $p$<.001). However, no significant relationship between physical appearance concern and frequency of exercising was found ($\beta$=.-0.009, $t$=-.443, $p$=.658). Therefore, H3 was partially supported.

Overall, our study shows that, as the cultivation theory suggested (Gerbner et al. 1977), media consumption affects the level of physical appearance concern. People who consume certain types of TV programs and magazines are more likely to be concerned with their physical appearances. Similar to previous studies, our study shows that physical appearance concern has negative impacts on clothes/apparel-related consumption behaviors. As opposed to previous studies, on the other hand, our study provides some evidence that physical appearance concern might lead to healthy behaviors, such as healthy food consumption. Future studies should examine these issues through experiments and longitudinal studies in order to establish direct cause-effect relationships between media, physical appearance concern, consumption behaviors, and health-related behaviors.

## References

Armstrong, L. and Maria Mallory (1992), "The Diet Business Starts Sweating," *Business Week*, (June 22), 22-23.

Burton, S., Netemeyer, R., and Lichtenstein, D. (1994), "Gender Differences for Appearance-Related Attitudes and Behaviors: Implications for Consumer Welfare," *Journal of Public Policy and Marketing*, 13 (2), 60-75.

Eisend, Martin, and Jana Möller, (2007), "The Influence of TV Viewing on Consumers' Body Images and Related Consumption Behavior," *Marketing Letters*, 18 (1/2), 101-116.

Gerbner, George, Larry Gross, Michael F. Eleey, Marilyn Jackson-Beeck, Suzanne Jeffries-Fox, and Nancy Sigronielli (1977), "TV Violence Profile No. 8: The Highlights," *Journal of Communication*, 27 (June), 171-180.

Hendriks, A. (2002), "Examining the Effects of Hegemonic Depictions of Female Bodies on Television: A Call for Theory and Programmatic Research," *Critical Studies in Media Communication*, 19, 106–123.

Hayes, Diane and Catherine E. Ross (1987), "Concern with Appearance, Health Beliefs and Eating Habits," *Journal of Health and Social Behavior*, 28 (June), 120-130.

Hirschman, Elizabeth C. and Craig Thompson (1997), "Why Media Matter: Toward a Richer Understanding of Consumers' Relationships with Advertising and Mass Media," *Journal of Advertising*, 26 (Spring), 43-60.

Netemeyer, Richard G., Scot Burton, and Donald Lichtenstein (1995), "Trait Aspects of Vanity: Measurement and Relevance to Consumer Behavior," *Journal of Consumer Research*, 21 (March), 46-60.

Rosa, J. A., Garbarino, E. C., and Malter, A. J. (2006), "Keeping the Body in Mind: The Influence of Body Esteem and Body Boundary Aberration on Consumer Beliefs and Purchase Intentions," *Journal of Consumer Psychology*, 16 (1), 79-91.

Tiggemann, M. & Lynch, J. E. (2001), "Body Image Across the Life Span in Adult Women: The Role of Self-Objectification," *Developmental Psychology*, 37, 243–253.

# Don't Go to the Grocery Store Hungry?

Christine Ringler, Arizona State University, USA
Andrea Morales, Arizona State University, USA
Steve Nowlis, Arizona State University, USA

The focus of the current research, is to identify whether consumers show preference for hedonic and utilitarian food and non-food items when hungry, explain why such differences exist, and demonstrate the relationship between hunger and self-control (manipulated through cognitive load) on our consumption of hedonic and utilitarian items. Research on palatability and preference ratings (Rolls et al. 1981), the role of external cues (Cornier et al. 2004), and variety seeking behavior (Menon and Kahn 1995) have explored how hunger affects our preferences and choices. This literature shows that consumers are not very good at understanding their body, instead they respond to external cues like time of day or the smell of pizza (Schachter 1968). Additionally, they tend to seek items that will satiate their hunger (Goukens et al. 2007), which results in increased attractiveness of the items when hungry. Only after they have eaten a large amount of one item does the attractiveness of that item decrease (Rolls et al. 1981). However, research does not offer predictions regarding cases of consumption where the most attractive item is not the most consumed. We hypothesize that while self-control does not affect the attractiveness of an item, self-control is in effect when the individual is ready for consumption, thus extending previous work on the effects of hunger in consumption settings and self-control in general. We extend this research by gaining a better understanding of the effects of self-control as a moderator between hunger and consumption. Specifically, we consider the case where consumers report their individual levels of hunger, then participate in consumption of utilitarian and hedonic foods. This leads us to propose a theory of hunger that demonstrates that when hungry, consumers have a tendency to eat more than they should, therefore, they tend to employ self-control tactics, which stop them from eating excessive quantities of the hedonic foods, but allows them to eat the utilitarian foods. Research on self-regulation has investigated cases where consumer impose measures of self-control (restrained eaters), but has not examined cases where consumers are "normal" eaters and impose measures of self-control when presented with hedonic food items in a hunger situation.

Although prior research on hunger has identified reasons why consumers ignore internal signals of hunger (i.e. impulsiveness) and in particular when external cues are present; we extend the research to explain why hungry consumers eat more of the utilitarian product even though the hedonic is more attractive. Research on hedonic versus utilitarian consumption has shown that consumers rate a hedonic alternative higher than a utilitarian alternative when each is presented by itself, but the utilitarian alternative tends to be chosen over the hedonic alternative when the two are presented together (Okada 2005). To the degree that presenting the utilitarian and hedonic products separately but within the same survey constitutes them being looked at singularly, we would expect the preference for hedonic products to be higher than utilitarian products, this effect being magnified when consumers are hungry and the hedonic products are food. The goal of study 1 is to examine whether hedonic items, (food and non-food), are shown more preference when hungry then when not hungry. We are interested in testing whether self-control moderates the relationship between hunger and preference for hedonic food items, specifically we will examine utilitarian food and non-food item preference when hungry and not hungry. As such, in study 1 we assess whether consumers find hedonic items more attractive than utilitarian items by asking them to rate them individually under situations of low and high cognitive load and under feelings of hungry and not hungry. The results of study 1 indicate that consumers view hedonic food items as being more attractive than hedonic non-food items and utilitarian items when hungry compared to not hungry. Participants rated food items as being preferred only when they were hedonic in nature. Additionally, participants did not consider non-food items more attractive when hungry. This demonstrates that hunger impacts consumer choices when evaluating food products, however this is only applicable to hedonic food products and does not appear to extend beyond this category. Previous research indicates that high cognitive load causes us to make choices based on impulse (choosing hedonic items), which might not occur if consumer's choices were free of cognitive load. These findings suggest that cognitive load moderates the relationship between hunger and product preferences in that only under high load and hunger do consumers prefer hedonic food items. Lastly, we identified no differentiation in product preference when participants were under low load. Study 2 attempts to test our second hypothesis by measuring actual consumption, as it relates to hunger using hedonic and utilitarian food items, under conditions of high and low cognitive load. We test consumption by using hedonic and utilitarian food items (M&M's versus Carrots) under conditions of hungry and not hungry. While attempting to replicate the results of study 1 under low load, study 2 shows that when we present the food item to the participant, hunger has no impact on the preference for hedonic food item (M&M's), which is consistent with the results of study 1. Additionally, results indicate that participants are able to employ self-control tactics when hungry that allowed them to avoid eating more of the hedonic food item but allowed them to eat more of the utilitarian food item. To better understand this, study 3 seeks to replicate the results of study 2 and turn off the over consumption of hedonic food items when hungry and under high load by providing participants with calorie or no calorie information. Study 3 finds that under high load with no calorie information present, participants ate significantly more when hungry than when not hungry. Under high load with calorie information present, the difference between hungry and not hungry failed to reach significance. Additionally, when no calorie information is present and participants were not hungry, the difference between low load and high load failed to reach significance. Study 4 seeks to understand the underlying processes associated with these results.

### References

Cornier, Marc-Andre, Gary K. Grunwald, Susan L. Johnson, and Daniel H. Bessesen (2004), "Effects of Short-Term Overfeeding on Hunger, Satiety, and Energy Intake in Thin and Reduced-Obese Individuals," *Appetite*, 43(3), 253-59.

Goukens, Caroline, Siegfried Dewitte, Mario Pandelaere, and Luk Warlop (2007), "Wanting a Bit(e) of Everything: Extending the Valuation Effect to Variety Seeking," *Journal of Consumer Research*, 34(3), 386-94.

Menon, Satya and Barbara E. Kahn (1995), "The Impact of Context on Variety Seeking in Product Choices," *Journal of Consumer Research*, 22(3), 285-95.

Okada, Erica Mina (2005), "Justification Effects on Consumer Choice of Hedonic and Utilitarian Goods," *Journal of Marketing Research*, 42(1), 43-53.

Rolls, Barbara J., Edmund T. Rolls, Edward A. Rowe, and Kevin Sweeney (1981), "Sensory Specific Satiety in Man," *Physiology & Behavior*, 27(1), 137-42.

Schachter, Stanley (1968), "Obesity and Eating," *Science*, 161(3843), 751-56.

# Environmental Cues and Food Consumption

Beth Vallen, Loyola University, USA
Lauren G. Block, Baruch College, USA
Chrissy Mitakakis, Baruch College, USA

### Extended Abstract

Individuals often face self-control dilemmas, whereby temptations interfere with the pursuit of long term goals (Fishbach and Shah 2006). Choosing between vices, which provide immediate pleasure, and virtues, which are in line with long-term goals, is likely to generate guilt and intrapersonal conflict. Along these lines, individuals often seek justification for indulging in vices to reduce feelings of guilt (Giner-Sorolla 2001). Recent research provides support for the contention that specific occasions or special events (i.e., holidays, birthdays, etc.) engender a sense of entitlement for individuals in terms of their consumption behavior; this justification cue results in a greater likelihood of relaxing self-control and selecting vices (e.g., chocolate cake) over virtues (e.g., fruit salad; Kivetz and Zheng 2006). On the contrary, such cues can also result in a heightened defensive state for people who are particularly guarding against indulgence, such as dieters.

In this research, we explore how individual differences in dieting behavior interact with the presence of an environmental cue, such as a special occasion or holiday, to either justify indulgence or bolster self-control, leading to a choice of more versus less indulgent food items, respectively. We posit that dieters will exert more self-control when such environmental cues are present (vs. absent). We argue that for these individuals, cues involving a holiday or special event are interpreted as situations that are characteristic of indulging and, therefore, can automatically signal higher efforts at self-control. Instead of acting as justification for indulgence, these cues will act as triggers for guarding against dieters' long-term eating goals (Myrseth, Fishbach, and Trope 2009; Trope and Fishbach 2005). Additionally, we hypothesize that the absence of such cues will lead dieters to be unprepared to bolster their self-control efforts, thus resulting in a self-control failure and indulgence. On the other hand, since non-dieters do not exert the constant attempts at self-control and monitoring that dieters do, we expect that non-dieters will utilize holiday cues as justifications to indulge.

For our first study, we examined the effect of a specific environmental cue (i.e., a birthday) on people's consumption behavior. Participants were given a questionnaire in which they read about a hypothetical scenario where they were going to dinner with some friends. Half of the participants were told that the dinner was hold in honor of their own birthday, while the other half were told that it was for a friend's birthday. All participants were then asked to choose the specific dessert they would order at the dinner. Dessert choices ranged from extremely unindulgent (i.e., a healthy fruit salad), to extremely indulgent (chocolate cake à la mode). A series of self-report measures followed, including measures of self-control and dieting behavior. Results support our hypotheses; dieting participants who were told that they were out to dinner in celebration of a friends' birthday chose the most indulgent dessert significantly more than dieting participants who were told that they were out to dinner celebrating their own birthday. By contrast, non-dieting participants chose the most indulgent dessert more when they were told that they were celebrating their own birthday. Additionally, we found that choice for the most indulgent option was significantly higher for dieting participants than non-dieting participants overall.

In our second study, we explored the impact of dieters' defense bolstering in the presence of a holiday justification cue on actual food consumption. We varied the saliency of the holiday cue by administering half our study on Halloween, and the other half on another day the week following the holiday. All participants were given a bag with 50 M&M candies and a questionnaire to complete. Participants were told that they could enjoy the candy as they filled out the questionnaire. Included on the questionnaire were questions assessing participants' self-control and dieting behavior. At the end of the study, participants were asked to count the number of candies remaining in their bag, which we used to calculate the amount consumed. Our results again support the hypothesis that dieters experience a bolstering of self-control when the holiday cue (i.e., Halloween) is available and consequently eat less than dieters who do not have such cues available (i.e., an ordinary day). Moreover, the opposite effects occurs for non-dieting participants, who consumed less of the candy on an ordinary day compared to Halloween.

A third study (currently underway) seeks to examine the proposed psychological mechanisms underlying the effects found in our prior studies, with a particular emphasis on the processes involved in the heightened efforts of self-control for dieters when holiday cues are present. As in study 2, in this study we assess participants' actual consumption behavior, this time in the presence or absence of holiday-related food cues (i.e., highlighting the food-related characteristics of Thanksgiving versus the non-food characteristics). In addition to measures of self-control and dieting behavior, we implicitly assess the specific efforts involved in self-control that act to guard against indulgent consumption. It is hypothesized that, in line with our prior results, dieters will exhibit heightened self-control with the presence of a holiday cue, but will relax efforts at self-control when the holiday cue is framed as a non-eating holiday. We predict that these varying levels of self-control will impact actual food consumption.

In sum, our research demonstrates that certain cues in the environment that have been traditionally considered justifications for indulgence can also have the opposite effects for certain individuals, namely dieters. On one hand, this bodes well for dieters, who may be better equipped to handle holiday-related consumption cues (e.g., a big bowl of mashed potatoes and gravy). On the other hand, it also demonstrates that these individuals might be less well equipped to deal with everyday indulgences (e.g., the candy jar on a co-worker's desk). These findings carry implications for dieters as well as those individuals striving for weight maintenance. Future research might explore other factors that contribute to the bolstering versus licensing effects so that individuals might be better equipped to handle environmental cues linked to overconsumption.

**References**

Fishbach, Ayelet, Ronald S. Friedman, and Arie W. Kruglanski (2003), "Leading Us Not Unto Temptation: Momentary Allurements Elicit Overriding Goal Activation," *Journal of Personality and Social Psychology*, 84(2), 296-309.

Fishbach, Ayelet and James Y. Shah (2006), "Self-Control in Action: Implicit Dispositions Toward Goals and Away from Temptations, *Journal of Personality and Social Psychology*, 90(5), 820-832.

Giner-Sorolla, Roger (2001), "Guilty Pleasures and Grim Necessities: Affective Attitudes in Dilemmas of Self-Control," *Journal of Personality and Social Psychology*, 80 (2), 206–21.

Kivetz, Ran and Yuhuang Zheng (2006), "Determinants of Justification and Self-Control," *Journal of Experimental Psychology: General*, 135(4), 572-587.

Myrseth, Kristian Ove R., Yaacov Trope, and Ayelet Fishbach (2009), "Counteractive Self-Control: When Making Temptation Available Makes Temptation Less Tempting," *Psychological Bulletin*, 20(2), 159–163.

Trope, Yaacov and Ayelet Fishbach (2005), "Going Beyond the Motivation Given: Self-Control and Situational Control over Behavior," Pp.537-565 in *The New Unconscious,* Ran. R. Hassin, James S. Uleman, and John A. Bargh (eds.). New York: Oxford University Press.

# Quality and Quantity of Food Consumption: Role of Emotion and Social Capital

Alice Labban, McGill University, Canada
Spencer Moore, Queen's University, Canada
Laurette Dubé, Canada

## EXTENDED ABSTRACT

### Research Background

In times in which obesity represents a problematic issue in different countries, it is becoming more and more important to understand individuals' food consumption habits[1-2]. The present work provides a clearer picture of what drives or inhibits healthy/unhealthy eating building on regulatory focus theory and temporal construal theory to explain how emotions and social capital predict quantity and quality of individuals' food consumption. Previous research has suggested that both emotions[3-4] and social capital[5-6-7], here measured by social participation[6-8] are assumed to play an important role in food consumption, but we need a clearer understanding of the underlying mechanisms that justify the nature of the relationships and its specific outcomes.

Regulatory focus theory posits that individuals approach desired states and avoid undesired states through promotion and prevention respectively[9]. All behaviors could be categorized as either approach or avoidance behaviors[10]. Approach behaviors are the all positive behaviors directed towards a certain environment and avoidance behaviors are the opposite[11]. We use quantity and quality of food consumed compared to individual's perceived eating norm as indicators of approach and avoidance behaviors. Choosing to conform to the eating norm is considered as an avoidance behavior and choosing to consume healthier/unhealthier to the eating norm is considered to be an approach behavior.

Temporal construal theory posits that the value individuals' give to outcomes is time dependant and individuals sometimes put more weight on short-term rewards while other times focus more on the long-term rewards[12-13]. When it comes to quantity/quality of food consumed, individuals have a short-termed desired state of fulfillment and pleasure when eating more quantities/unhealthy that could lead to long-term undesirable state of gaining weight. However, consuming fewer quantities/healthy have a short-term undesirable state of un-satisfaction and perceived bad taste but a long-term desirable state of maintaining or losing weight[14]. Therefore, both healthier and unhealthier food consumption could prompt individuals either to approach or avoid them.

We argue that individuals focusing on short-term rewards are more likely to approach unhealthy items and avoid healthy items. However, those focusing on the long-term rewards are more likely to approach healthy items and avoid unhealthy items. Previous literature found that individuals in a positive state are preoccupied, in the short-term, to maintain that positive state while individuals in a negative state are preoccupied in the short-term to alleviate immediately that negative state[15]. Therefore, we hypothesize that when it comes to emotions (calm and depression) individuals focus on the short-term rewards. Positive emotions like calmness lead individuals to approach objects around them[11-17] and in this case approach unhealthy behaviors. Negative emotions such as depression lead individuals to avoid objects around them[11-17] and in this case avoid healthy behaviors. As for participation, it was found to provide affective support and increase self-esteem[18] and contributes to individuals' health by promoting positive affect[19], by decreasing negative affects[20] and by buffering stress[21]. Participation provides individuals with a general sense of contentment and fulfills individuals need to belong and therefore we hypothesize that participation makes individuals less preoccupied by short-term rewards and more focused on the long-term rewards making them more prompt to conform with others and thus avoid unhealthier behaviors. Moreover, as participation could act as buffer to negative emotions[20] we hypothesize that participation will help depressed individuals succumb their negative emotions and thus making them avoid unhealthy behaviors.

## METHOD

### Design and Procedures

Questionnaires administered through a computer assisted telephone interviewing system were used to test our hypotheses. In total 787 participants completed the questionnaire. These participants were randomly selected from census data from the Montreal Metropolitan Area.

### Measures

Participants were asked to rate the quantity and quality of food consumed in comparison to their perceived eating norm (what they perceive others like them usually eat). We operationalize approach behaviors in terms of participants choosing either to consume healthier or unhealthier quantity and quality of food compared to the eating norm. As for avoidance behaviors, we operationalize them in terms of consuming the same quantity and quality of food as the perceived eating norm. Choosing to conform to the eating norm is considered to be an avoidance behavior since it fulfills the prevention goals that individuals think should be met. Consuming healthier or unhealthier than the eating norm is considered to be an approach behavior since it meets individuals' promotion goals that are those goals that individuals aspire to meet[22]. A 5-point Likert scale measured three types of emotion: Calm, Energy and Depression. A dichotomous measure of Participation showed whether individuals participated or not in any of four form of social participation[23].

### Results

A multinomial analysis showed that both emotions and social participation play an important role in the quality and quantity consumed. Actually, we found that the calmer participants are the more likely they were to say that they consumed more quantities than the perceived eating norm. Those that have high levels of depression were less likely to say that they consumed fewer quantities than the perceived eating norm. Those who participate in social activities are less likely to eat less healthy food compared to the perceived eating norm.

Furthermore, social participation played a moderating role on the relationship between depression and the quantity and quality of food consumed. Participation seems to buffer the effect of depression on the quality of the food consumed making depressed individuals less likely to consume less healthy quality than the perceived eating norm. Moreover, it seems that depressed individuals that participate in social activities are better off than non depressed individuals that do not participate in social activities.

**Conclusion and Discussion**

In conclusion, this research shows that emotion and social capital captured through social participation have a great effect on food consumption and on whether individuals decide to either approach or avoid healthy or unhealthy items. This research also shows that participation could be a good mood restoration management tool aiding depressed people in their health habits. Finally, this research differs from other research on food consumption in that it shows that different predictors could play differential roles in terms of either prompting or preventing individuals from conducting healthy or unhealthy behaviors.

**References**

Seiders K. and Petty R.D. (2004). Obesity and the Role of Food Marketing: A Policy Analysis of Issues and Remedies. *Journal of Public Policy and Marketing, 23(2)*, 153-169.

Centers for Disease Control and Prevention (2005). The burden of obesity in the United States: A problem of massive proportions. *Chronic Disease Notes and Reports, 17*, 4-9.

Macht M. and Simons G. (2000). Emotions and Eating in Everyday Life. *Appetite, 35*, 65-71.

Christensen L. and Redig C. (1993). Effect of Meal Composition on Mood. *Behav Neuroscience, 107*, 346-353.

Kawachi, I., Kennedy, B., Lochner, K., Prothrow-Stith, D., 1997. Social capital, income inequality and mortality. *American Journal of Public Health 87*, 1491-1498.

Moore S., Daniel M., Paquet C., Dube L. and Gauvin L. (2009). Association of Individual Network Social Capital with Abdominal adiposity, Overweight and obesity. *Journal of Public Health*, 1-9.

Veenstra, G., Lomas, J. (1999). Home is where the governing is: Social capital and regional health governance. *Health and Place, 5*, 1-12.

Putnam, R.D., Leonardi, R., Nanetti, R.Y., 1993. *Making Democracy Work: Civic Traditions in Modern Italy.* Princeton University Press, New Jersey.

Higgins E.T. (2002). How Self-Regulation Creates Distinct Values: The Case of Promotion and Prevention Decision Making. *Journal of Consumer Psychology, 12(3)*, 177-191.

Mehrabian A. and Russell J.A. (1974). *An Approach to Environmental Psychology.* Cambridge, MA: Massachusetts Institute of Technology.

Bitner M.J. (1992). Servicescapes: The Impact of Physical Surroundings on Customers and Employees. *The Journal of Marketing, 56(2)*, 57-71.

Ainslie G. and Haslam N. (1992). Hyperbolic Discounting. In G. Loewenstein and Elster J. (Eds). *Choice over Time* (pp. 57-92). New York: Russell Sage Foundation.

Elster J. and Loewenstein G. (1992). Utility from Memory and Anticipation. In G. Loewenstein and Elster J. (Eds). *Choice over Time* (pp. 57-92). New York: Russell Sage Foundation.

Raghunathan R., Naylor R.W., and Hoyer W.D. (2006). The Unhealthy=Tasty Intuition and Its Effects on Taste Inferences, Enjoyment, and Choice of Food Products. *Journal of Marketing, 70 (4)*, 170–84.

LeBel J.L., Lu J. and Dube L. (2008). Weakened Biological Signals: Highly-Developed Eating Schemas amongst Women are Associated with Maladaptive Patterns of Comfort Food Consumption. *Physiology and Behavior, 94*, 384-392.

Ridgway N.M., Dawson S.A. and Bloch P.H. (1989). Pleasure and Arousal in the Marketplace: Interpersonal Differences in Approach-Avoidance Responses.

Wilkinson, R.G., 1996. *Unhealthy Societies: The Afflictions of Inequality.* Routledge, London.

Hull R.B. (1990). Mood as a Product of Leisure: Causes and Consequences. *Journal of Leisure Research, 22*, 99-111.

Caldwell L.L. and Smith E.A. (1998). Leisure: An Overlooked Component of Health Promotion. *Canadian Journal of Public Health, 79 (April/May)*, S44-S48.

Coleman D. and Iso-Ahola S.E. (1993). Leisure and Health: The Role of Social Support and Self-Determination. *Journal of Leisure Research, 25*, 111-128

Chitturi R., Raghunathan R. and Mahajan V. (2008). Delight by Design: The Role of Hedonic Versus Utilitarian Benefits. *Journal of Marketing*, 72(May), 48-63.

Swaroop, S., & Morenoff, J. (2006). Building community: The neighborhood context of social organization. *Social Forces, 84(3)*, 1665-1695.

# Everything in Moderation? When Moderation Leads to Indulgence

Ashley Rae Arsena, The University of Texas at San Antonio, USA
David H. Silvera, The University of Texas at San Antonio, USA

## Extended Abstract

"Everything in moderation" is often recommended as a way to achieve balance and limit consumption. From chocolate to wine to eating out, acting in moderation is expected to combat many problems that deal with consumption excess (e.g., obesity, binge drinking, impulsive buying, alcoholism). For example, a recent public service announcement aiming to reduce alcohol consumption features a picture of vodka with the slogan "It's not what you drink. It's how much you drink that counts. Moderation in all things." Similarly, another advertisement advocating the practice of moderation illustrates a body builder with unnaturally large grotesque muscles accompanied by the slogan "Too much of a good thing is still too much. Moderation."

However, although the practice of moderation has been prescribed by many, there is no empirical research investigating whether moderation actually succeeds in promoting healthy behavior. The objective of this research is to provide a much needed understanding of the role moderation plays in consumption behavior.

Past research has shown that individuals license themselves to indulge when they have previously acted in line with a long-term goal (Fishback and Dhar 2005; Khan and Dhar 2006). That is, when individuals feel they have made progress toward a long term goal, they have less motivation to engage in self-control directed at achieving this goal. This phenomenon, called the licensing effect, indicates that when progress toward a long term goal is perceived, individuals often disengage from that goal and act in opposition to it.

The licensing effect has been observed in many domains. For example, dieters' who felt they made sufficient progress in losing weight were more likely to choose unhealthy options (Fishback and Dhar 2005). Similarly, individuals who were induced to feel moral showed less inclination to engage in moral action (i.e., by donating blood) compared to people who were not induced to feel moral (Sachdeva, Iliev, and Medin 2009).

The present research applies this logic to the concept of moderation. Thus, we hypothesize that activation of the moderation concept leads to a temporary satisfaction of health goals, which in turn makes the individual feel that they are licensed to indulge. Consequently, the activation of moderation should result in greater preference for more indulgent items in a choice set.

Furthermore, individual differences in self-control should moderate this effect. Specifically, individuals who are high in self-control can more easily access past behaviors or project future behaviors where they will engage in healthy eating (Wilcox et al. 2009), and the resulting increase in activation of past and/or future health behaviors consequently makes these individuals feel more licensed to indulge. Thus, the concept of moderation is likely to lead to greater preference for indulgent items in a choice set for individuals who are high in self-control.

To test this hypothesis, participants were assigned to one of two conditions. Participants in the moderation prime condition were asked to elaborate on the concept "everything in moderation." In contrast, participants in the neutral prime condition were asked to provide a summary of their favorite movie. Participants were then shown pictures of 5 dessert choices. Based on a pre-test, these choices varied in their degree of perceived healthiness (from least to most healthy: chocolate brownie with 6 scoops of ice cream, chocolate cake, carrot cake, strawberries with whipped cream, and a bowl of fruit). Participants were asked to indicate their dessert preference. After participants completed the prime and the decision task, trait self-control was measured using the 36-item Self-Control Scale (Tangney et al. 2004). A regression analysis showed a significant interaction between trait self-control and the priming manipulation in predicting the healthiness of food choices. Specifically, among low self-control individuals, the moderation prime was associated with healthier choices than the neutral prime, whereas among high self-control individuals the moderation prime was associated with more indulgent choices than the neutral prime. These results suggest that moderation has the desired effect on low self-control individuals, but that moderation can backfire for high self-control individuals and lead them to prefer indulgent options.

This study demonstrates a relatively novel effect: the impact of activation of the moderation concept on consumption. Thus, the present research makes an important contribution by providing empirical evidence addressing the question of how moderation influences consumption decisions. Moreover, these results support the counterintuitive proposition that moderation actually leads to indulgent preferences for high self-control individuals, which has serious implications for the use of moderation in efforts to promote healthy behavior.

Future studies will examine the underlying mechanism for this effect. That is, how does moderation satisfy health goals? Presumably, moderation puts one in a healthy mindset by invoking past instances where one has satisfied a health goal (e.g., I ate healthy last week) or future behavior where one will satisfy a health goal (e.g., I'll eat healthy tomorrow). This mindset would potentially connect the present findings with research on the effect of future choices on self-control, which indicates that when a decision is presented in the context of sequential future choices, people optimistically believe they will be virtuous in the future and are thus more likely to indulge in the present (Khan and Dhar 2007). In other words, individuals might feel licensed to engage in short-term transgressions because they believe they can make up for them in the future. This suggests that the effect of moderation on indulgence might be attenuated if participants are asked to think about a choice in isolation rather than a choice that is part of a sequence of choices. If this is the case, then (a) high self-control individuals should prefer indulgent items when the choice is made as part of a sequence but not when the choice is made in isolation, and (b) it is possible that priming moderation spontaneously invokes thoughts of sequential choices (i.e., the realization that moderation can be achieved by balancing past, future, and present choices), and that these thoughts mediate the relation between moderation and feeling licensed to indulge.

## References

Fishbach, Ayelet and Ravi Dhar (2005), "Goals as Excuses or Guides: The Liberating Effect of Perceived Goal Progress on Choice," *Journal of Consumer Research*, 32 (3), 370–77.

Khan, Uzma and Ravi Dhar (2007), "Where There Is a Way, Is There a Will? The Effect of Future Choices on Self-Control," *Journal of Experimental Psychology: General*, 136 (2), 277-288.

Khan, Uzma and Ravi Dhar (2007). "Licensing effect in consumer choice." *Journal of Marketing Research*, 43 (1), 259–266. 136 (2), 277-88

Sachdeva, Sonya, Rumen Iliev, and Douglas L. Medin (2009), "Sinning Saints and Saintly Sinners: The Paradox of Moral Self-Regulation," *Psychological Science*, 29 (4), 523-528.

Tangney, June P., Roy F. Baumeister, and Angie L. Boone (2004), "High Self-Control Predicts Good Adjustment, Less pathology, Better Grades, and Interpersonal Success," *Journal of Personality*, 72 (2), 271-322.

Wilcox, K., Beth Vallen, Lauren Block, and Gavan J. Fitzsimons (2009), "Vicarious Goal Fulfillment: When the Mere Presence of a Healthy Option Leads to an Ironically Indulgent Decision," *Journal of Consumer Resarch*, 36 (2), 380–393.

# Overweight and Self-Control Failure: Is There a Way Out?

Thomas Rudolph, University of St. Gallen, Switzerland
Alexandra Glas, University of St. Gallen, Switzerland
Peter Kenning, Zeppelin University, Switzerland

**Extended Abstract**

Persuading people to eat healthier is a major challenge in modern societies. To prevent diet-related diseases, there are to the best of our knowledge two research approaches being discussed. One approach applies powerful economic mechanisms, e.g. higher taxes for unhealthy food products. Studies showed that the demand for sugar-sweetened beverages can be reduced significantly by increasing prices (Epstein et al. 2010; Brownell and Frieden 2009). The other approach under discussion uses instruments that are grounded in psychology (Garg, Wansink, and Inman 2007; Chandon and Wansink 2007). However, both ways are often discussed unrelated to each other. This is astonishing assuming that a combination of both ways might positively affect the power of prevention. This holds particularly true considering that taxes might have serious consequences for markets and competition and are insofar second best. Against this background the aim of our study is to shed light on the interaction between economic and psychological approaches.

Literature both in psychology and economics ties habits and self-control. A pivotal tenet of economics is that incentives promote effort and performance (Gibbons 1997; Lazear 2000). In other words, rewards serve as positive reinforcers for the desired behavior (Bénabou and Tirole 2004). For psychologists, in contrast, the effect of rewards is more controversial (Deci, Koester, and Ryan 1999). They rather argue that self-regulatory strategies promote the initiation of goal-directed behaviors (Gollwitzer 1999; Baumeister and Heatherton 1996).

In this research we test whether implementation intention as a self-regulation mechanism and monetary incentives can be used in combination to overcome the self-control dilemma and to foster healthy eating behavior. Furthermore we aim to examine which of these approaches have a stronger influence and whether interactions might accrue. Thus comparing the two interventions provides insight into the interplay between psychological and economic processes underlying the healthy eating behavior.

To achieve this aim we conducted a controlled field experiment using a 2 *(Implementation Intention: Formed/Not Formed)* x 2 *(Monetary Incentive: Available/Not Available)* between-subjects design.

The study was conducted in three sequences with 176 Swiss consumers. Firstly, participants completed a baseline questionnaire which was combined with the implementation intention manipulation. The second sequence contained the incentive manipulation followed by the redemption of the voucher which measured actual eating behavior. Participants could choose between high-calorie, unhealthy snacks (croissants) and low-calorie, healthy snacks (mandarins/grapes). We counted the number of snacks chosen and converted the amount into calories (kcal). One week later, all participants completed a follow-up questionnaire being asked for the amount of unhealthy snacks they had consumed during the manipulation week.

Following this setup we are able to observe eating behavior before, during, and for one week after the intervention. Our main predictions are strongly confirmed. Firstly, the short-term interventions "implementation intention" and "monetary incentives" foster to choose the healthy snack. Secondly, participants are dynamically inconsistent: they chose more unhealthy snacks for immediate than for advance choice.

Analyses were conducted with SPSS. In a first step, we checked randomization and intercorrelations between all antecedents, as postulated by the theory of planned behavior as well as whether these antecedents predicted behavioral intention. Therefore, a multivariate analysis (MANOVA) was conducted between participants in the experimental and control groups with respect to the antecedent variables. The Levene's test for each variable was not significant ($p>.05$), suggesting that the randomization had been successful.

Secondly, healthy eating behavior correlated significantly ($p<.01$) with all antecedent variables, except subjective norm. As expected, habits correlated negatively (-.238, $p<.01$) with healthy behavior. To test whether the antecedents predicted behavioral intention, we regressed behavioral intention on all antecedents. In the regression analysis ($R^2=.45$) both the beta weights of attitude and perceived behavioral control were highly significant, $\beta=.56, p<.01$, and $\beta=.19, p<.01$, respectively, demonstrating that both variables contributed uniquely to the prediction of intention.

In a second step, we analyzed the interventions. Overall, 131 of 176 participants redeemed their voucher. As expected, the percentage of participants redeeming their voucher for a healthy snack in the control group was low-only 50%. In the experimental group "implementation intention" this percentage rises to 78.1%. In the experimental group "monetary incentive" 85.3% choose a healthy snack and in the combined experimental group this percentage is 82.9%. A chi-square-test shows high significance among the observed frequencies ($p<.05$).

The relative power of the three experimental manipulations was tested with an ANOVA. The overall F-test of this ANOVA is significant, $F(3,131)=4.101, p<.05$. The multiple mean comparisons (Student-Newman-Keuls-test) show a significant difference between the behavioral reaction of the control group and that of all three experimental groups. For the behavioral differences between the three experimental groups the multiple mean comparisons show no statistically significant differences.

To test whether the two interventions reduced the self-reported snack behavior during the follow-up week, we conducted an ANOVA. The main effect of the interventions was not significant $F(3,160)=1.72$. Following a Wilcoxon-test there was a highly significant ($p<.05$) effect of "Time" for the combined experimental group. Thus, those subjects who received both interventions reduced their snack consumption significantly during the follow-up compared to the baseline week ($M_{baseline}=7.81$; $M_{follow-up}=6.45$).

To conclude, our study provides first insights about the effect of the combination of economic and psychological interventions on consumers' food choices. Our data reveal that incentives *and* self-regulation mechanisms encourage consumers to engage in healthy snack behavior. Incentives seem to have the strongest power. Moreover, the result provides evidence that the combined effect is more overlapping than additive. This finding initiates the discussion of how independent psychological and economic processes are. It could be argued that in daily life strong incentives encourage consumers to engage in self-regulation activities. From the food industry's point of view, such a combined approach may be more attractive–in contrast to taxation-because it gives leeway for communication activities rather than just following policies. Further research should determine details about the long-term effects of combined interventions.

## Selected References

Baumeister, Roy and Todd Heatherton (1996), "Self-Regulation Failure: An Overview," *Psychological Inquiry*, 7 (1), 1-15.

Bénabou, Roland and Jean Tirole (2003), "Intrinsic and Extrinsic Motivation," *Review of Economic Studies*, 70 (244), 489-520.

Brownell, Kelly D., and Thomas R. Frieden (2009), "Ounces of Prevention-The Public Policy Case for Taxes on Sugared Beverages," *The New England Journal of Medicine*, 306 (18), 1805-08.

Chandon, Pierre and Brian Wansink (2007), "The Biasing Health Halos of Fast-Food Restaurant health Claims: Lower Calorie Estimates and Higher Side-Dish Consumption Intentions," *Journal of Consumer Research*, 34 (3), 301-14.

Deci, Edward, Richard Koester, and Richard M. Ryan (1999), "A Meta-Analytic Review of Experiments Examining the Effects of Extrinsic Rewards on Intrinsic Motivation," *Psychological Bulletin*, 125 (6), 627-68.

Epstein, Leonard H., Kelly K. Dearing, Lora G. Roba, and Eric Finkelstein (2010), "The Influence of Taxes and Subsidies on Energy Purchased in an Experimental Purchasing Study," Psychological Science, 21 (2), 1-9.

Garg, Nitika, Brian Wansink, and J. Jeffrey Inman, (2007), "The Influence of Incidental Affect on Consumers' Food Intake," *Journal of Marketing*, 71 (1), 194-206.

Gibbons, Robert (1997), "Incentives and Careers in Organizations," in D. Kreps and K. Wallis (eds.) *Advances in Economic Theory and Econometrics*, Vol. II (Cambridge, U.K.: Cambridge University Press).

Gollwitzer, Peter M. (1999), "Implementation Intentions: Strong Effects of Simple plans," *American Psychologist*, 54, 493-503.

Lazear, Edward P. (2000), "Performance Pay and Productivity," *American Economic Review*, 90 (5), 1346-61.

# The Boomerang Effect of Mandatory Sanitary Messages to Prevent Obesity

Caroline Cuny, Grenoble Ecole de Management, France

Carolina Werle, Grenoble Ecole de Management, France

The prevalence of overweight and obesity increases in a tremendous way in France, especially since the beginning of the 1990s. To counter this problem, French authorities establish new guidelines and, since 2007, companies are obliged to include health sanitary messages on their advertisements for foods and beverages. Four health message ("For your health, eat at least five fruit and vegetables a day"; "For your health, avoid foods that are too fatty, too salty or too sweet"; "For your health, avoid snacking between meals"; and "For your health, practice a regular physical activity"). These health messages must "be presented in a way they are easily readable and clearly differentiated from the advertising message" and must occupy at least 7 % of the advertising space.

The inclusion of sanitary messages on advertisements is based on the assumption that food advertisements favour obesity among children. Previous studies emphasized the influence of advertisements on the gain of weight among children (Pécheux, Derbaix and Charry, 2006). The objective of the inclusion of sanitary messages in the food advertisements was to prevent obesity and to easily disseminate health messages to the population.

However, the presence of sanitary messages can have a different effect on consumers' perception of a hedonic product. Indeed, the consumption of hedonic products is associated with a need for justification and feelings of guilt (Kivetz and Simonson, 2002). Although hedonic products' consumption generates positive emotions (Chitturi, Raghunathan and Mahajan, 2007), this choice is difficult to justify (Okada, 2005) and may have negative consequences in the long run, increasing guilt (Hoch and Loewenstein, 1991). The policy makers' objective including sanitary messages in advertisements for foods is to increase the guilt associated with the product, reducing its consumption. Nevertheless, the presence of the health message can be a justification for the hedonic choice. Previous research indicates that presenting a justification for the choice of a hedonic product increases its consumption (Kivetz and Simonson, 2002; Lee, Shavitt, 2009). Making a hedonic decision and claiming to do something good for your health just after it reduces the feeling of guilt and finally encourages the hedonic choice (Strahilevitz and Myers, 1998). Here, presenting a hedonic food simultaneously with the solution to face the consequences of its consumption (sanitary message) may have an unexpected opposite effect.

The objective of this article is to verify the effects of the sanitary messages on the explicit and implicit attitudes towards hedonic foods. Following the conceptualisation above, we propose that attitudes towards the product will be more positive when the sanitary message is present in the advertisement than when it is absent, because the message provide a justification for the hedonic consumption.

One-hundred thirty-one students (average age 20 years old) participated in the study. A single health message was tested in the present study: "For your health, eat at least five fruit and vegetables per day". This message was chosen because it is the best recalled message among the four mandatory messages imposed by the French government (INPES study, 2007). The hedonic food advertisement used was a real advertisement for McDonald's showing the picture of a BigMac. To measure the implicit attitude towards the product, we developed a visuo-semantic priming protocol. In a task unrelated to the test, participants were instructed to determine as quickly as possible if character strings were real French words or not (lexical decision task). The test comprised a total of 96 sequences including 12 test sequences and 84 distractive sequences designed to prevent participants from understanding the real objective of the study. The 12 test sequences were constituted by the presentation of the Big Mac advertisement followed by the presentation of a real French word. The words used as semantic concepts targets were the following: health, nutrition, wellness, pleasure, taste, credibility, obesity, constraint, casual, guilt, weakness, confusion; they represented 6 positive concepts and 6 negative concepts. The Big Mac advertisement was presented alone in half of the trials and including the sanitary message in the other half.

Participants were then asked to fill in a questionnaire. Before answering they were presented the Big Mac picture with or without the sanitary message for 5 seconds. Participants answered questions about their attitudes towards the product (adapted from Voss, Spangenberg & Grohmann, 2003; Homer, 1990) and general questions, such as gender, age, weight and height, and when was their last meal. After finishing the questionnaire participants received a McDonald's coupon as a thank-you gift for their participation in the study. They had the choice between two coupons for a McDonald dessert: a sundae (unhealthy option) or a bag of fruits (healthy option).

Results indicated no effects of the sanitary messages on the explicit attitudes towards the product, neither on the behavioural measure (choice of dessert). However, results of the lexical decision task demonstrated greater reaction times to process the negative concepts when the Big Mac advertisement was presented with a health message that when it was not. Thus, implicit measures showed that participants associated more easily negative concepts to the product when the advertisement was presented without the sanitary message than when it was presented with a health sanitary message. This result is consistent with our conceptualization.

The presence of the health message can automatically activate representations associated to a justification for the product consumption, leading to a less negative perception of the product. Thanks to implicit and explicit data collection protocols, our research shows that the presence of a health sanitary message on an advertisement for a hedonic product made it less negative. These results highlight an unconscious automatic process which could lead to the association of health messages to a justification for an indulgent behaviour, leading therefore to opposite effects than those expected. Further research should replicate these findings using other products and other health messages in order to design new ways to communicate obesity prevention messages.

### References

Chitturi R., Raghunathan R. et Mahajan V. (2007), Form Versus Function: How the Intensities of Specific Emotions Evoked in Functional Versus Hedonic Trade-Offs Mediate Product Preferences, *Journal of Marketing Research*, 44, 4, 702-714.

Hoch S. J. et Loewenstein G.F. (1991), Time-inconsistent Preferences and Consumer Self-Control, *Journal of Consumer Research*, 17, 4, 492-507.

Homer P. M. (1990), The Mediating Role of Attitude Toward the Ad: Some Additional Evidence, *Journal of Marketing Research*, 27, 1, 78-86.

INPES (2007). Post-Test des messages sanitaires apposés sur les publicités alimentaires auprès des 8 ans et plus, Ministère de la santé, de la jeunesse et des sports et l'Institut National de Prévention et d'Education pour la Santé.

Kivetz R. et Simonson I. (2002a), Earning the Right to Indulge: Effort as a Determinant of Customer Preferences Toward Frequency Program Rewards, *Journal of Marketing Research*, 39, 2, 155-70.

Kivetz R. et Simonson I. (2002b), Self-Control for the Righteous: Toward a Theory of Precommitment to Indulgence, *Journal of Consumer Research*, 29, 2, 199-217.

Lee K. et Shavitt S. (2009), Can McDonald's Food Ever Be Considered Healthful? Metacognitive Experiences Affect the Perceived Understanding of a Brand, *Journal of Marketing Research*, 46, 222-233.

Okada E. M. (2005), Justification Effects on Consumer Choice of Hedonic and Utilitarian Goods, *Journal of Marketing Research*, 42, 1, 43-53.

Pécheux C., Derbaix C. et Charry K. (2006), Enfants, Alimentation et obésité : quels rôles pour la publicité ?, *Actes du XXIIème Congrès de l'Association Française du Marketing*, Nantes.

Strahilevitz M. et Myers J.G. (1998), Donations to Charity as Purchase Incentives: How Well They Work May Depend on What You Are Trying to Sell, *Journal of Consumer Research*, 24, 434-446.

Voss K. E., Spangenberg E.R. et Grohmann B. (2003), Measuring the Hedonic and Utilitarian Dimensions of Consumer Attitude, *Journal of Marketing Research*, 40, 3, 310-320.

# The Dove Effect:
# How the Normalization of Obesity Can Influence Food Consumption

Lily Lin, University of British Columbia, Canada
Brent McFerran, University of British Columbia, Canada

### Extended Abstract

Several years ago, Dove introduced the "Real Beauty" campaign, which featured "real women with real curves" as the models in its advertisements. While one of the goals of this campaign was to counter the stigma often faced by overweight individuals, the campaign also set out to enhance women's self-esteem by encouraging them to embrace their physical appearance. Although there is no question that finding ways to reduce the stigma many obese individuals face and promoting a healthy body-esteem are laudable and important goals (e.g., Smeesters et al. 2010), it may be equally important to examine whether such campaigns and advertisements can influence people's food consumption choices. For instance, if one is told that women who are overweight are "normal" or "real", perhaps this *reduces* consumers' motivation to eat healthy and lose weight. Given the problem of obesity, and how it is largely driven by food intake (Young and Nesle 2002), this is a relevant concern.

We examined this research question in two studies. In both studies, we manipulated perceptions about what a plus size and what an average size person looks like. We then investigated how viewing a single advertisement could influence people's decisions during a food selection task, their attitudes toward healthy eating and weight loss, and their actual consumption behavior. While previous research had shown that exposures to certain figures in the media can impact consumers' perceptions about their own appearances (Smeesters and Mandel 2006; Trampe et al. 2007), our research examined if "normalizing" larger body sizes would change consumers' food choices. Furthermore, we examined whether the normalization of obesity would influence people's selections of menu items and their motivation to pursue a healthier lifestyle.

The purpose of Study 1 was to examine how the normalization of obesity would influence people's actual food consumption tendencies. The study was a one factor between-subjects design, where 49 participants were either assigned to a "plus size" or "normal" condition. Following past research (McFerran et al. 2010, Smeesters and Mandel 2006, and Trampe et al. 2007), only females were included in the study. In both conditions, participants were asked to view an advertisement for a new clothing store that had a photo of an obese female model posing in the center of the ad. While the model and ad copy were the same between conditions, the tag line that was shown with the model was different between the two groups. In the "plus size" condition, the tag line that appeared with the model was "For Plus-Size Women". In the "normal" condition, the tag line that appeared with the model was "For Real Women". Participants then completed a number of dummy measures related to the ad copy and brand, as well as studies unrelated to the present experiment that served to disguise the true purposes of the research. To measure how the exposure of the advertisement affected people's consumption choices, ten chocolates were placed on the table where the participants were seated. Participants were told that the chocolates were left over from a previous study, and that they should feel free to eat as many of them as they wished. The number of chocolates consumed during the course of the study served as the behavioral measure. We found that participants in the "normal" condition consumed more chocolates by the end of the session than those in the "plus size" condition.

Study 2 was designed to replicate the effect from study 1 using a different measure containing several food choices as well as caloric information. The second purpose of the study was to increase the generalizability of the previous study by including both genders in our sample. The third purpose was to extend the previous results by measuring one's motivation to engage in a healthier lifestyle, which would provide some process evidence for the effect. The participants were 95 Amazon.com users, and the study employed the identical design and manipulation for the "plus size" and "normal" conditions as the first study. After the participants viewed the advertisement for a few minutes, they were asked to create their ideal meal from a list of 15 food items. Pictures of the food and caloric counts of the items were shown, and participants could select as many or as few items as they wished. Participants also rated their current motivation to exercise more, lose weight, and eat a more healthy diet on 7-point Likert Scales. Results showed that the meals created by those in the "normal" condition contained significantly more calories in total than those in the "plus size" condition. Additionally, those in "normal" condition provided *lower* ratings on questions related to motivation to be in better shape, to get down to one's desired weight, and to eat a more healthy diet. Importantly, in both studies, the participants' own BMI did not have any mediating or moderating effects.

Two studies showed that while presenting obesity as "normal" or more socially acceptable may be intended to increase consumers' feelings towards their own body image, in doing so consumers may have a reduced desire to make healthy lifestyle decisions. Our research dovetails with that of Christakis and Fowler (2007), who showed that obesity can spread through social networks, but provided little evidence for the mechanism. Perhaps if one's social network is made up of a greater percentage of people who are obese, obesity would become increasingly "normal" to a given individual, and the stigma would be attenuated. While reducing the stigma of obesity is important, normalizing it may also have adverse public health effects.

**References**

Christakis, Nicholas A. and James H. Fowler (2007), "The Spread of Obesity in a Large Social Network Over 32 Years," *The New England Journal of Medicine*, 357 (4), 370-79.

McFerran, Brent, Darren W. Dahl, Gavan J. Fitzsimons, and Andrea C. Morales (2010), "I'll Have What She's Having: Effects of Social Influence and Body Type on the Food Choices of Others", *Journal of Consumer Research*, 36 (6) forthcoming.

Smeesters, Dirk and Naomi Mandel (2006), "Positive and Negative Media Image Effects on the Self," *Journal of Consumer Research*, 32 (4), 576-82.

Smeesters, Dirk, Thomas Mussweiler, and Naomi Mandel (2010), "The Effects of Thin and Heavy Media Images on Overweight and Underweight Consumers: Social Comparison Processes and Behavioral Implications," *Journal of Consumer Research*, 36 (6), forthcoming.

Trampe Debra, Diederik A. Stapel, and Frans W. Siero (2007), "On Models and Vases: Body Dissatisfaction and Proneness to Social Comparison Effects," *Journal of Personality and Social Psychology*, 92 (1), 106-18.

Young, Lisa R. and Marion Nestle (2002), "The Contribution of Expanding Portion Sizes to the US Obesity Epidemic," *American Journal of Public Health*, 92 (2), 246–49.

# Social Risk Efficacy in Preventing Youth Obesity

Carolina Werle, Grenoble Ecole de Management, France
Sabine Boesen-Mariani, Université Pierre Mendes France, Grenoble, France
Marie-Laure Gavard-Perret, Université Pierre Mendes France, CERAG, France
Stéphanie Berthaud, Université Pierre Mendes France, CERAG, France

## Extended Abstract

Obesity prevention campaigns highlighting health risks are omnipresent in France nowadays. A content analysis of official prevention messages in use since 2001 revealed the pervasive use of arguments based on health risks or benefits linked to prevention behaviors (eat healthy, exercise, etc). However, these campaigns neglect social risks and adolescents are especially sensitive to social norms and the positive or negative consideration of their peers (Steinberg and Scott 2003).

Previous research on anti-smoking advertisements shows that the use of social arguments can be more efficient in the short term because they address concerns that are important to adolescents (Ho 1998; Pechmann and Knight 2002; Pechmann and Ratneshwar 1994). In an exploratory study, we found that adolescents are especially susceptible to social risks associated with obesity, such as disapproval or rejection from the group. We therefore suggest that arguments focusing on social issues are likely to be more efficient in the short term because they address concerns of importance to adolescents. Therefore, the first objective of this study is to verify the efficacy of using social risks in obesity prevention campaigns targeting youths.

A second objective is to verify if the message regulatory orientation (Higgins 1997; Zhao and Pechmann 2007) can moderate the impact of the type of obesity prevention argument being used (social vs. health). Other prevention campaigns unrelated to obesity, such as anti-smoking or anti-alcohol campaigns, frequently use prevention-oriented messages. They highlight the negative consequences of an undesired behavior, while obesity prevention campaigns in France use the opposite approach. They put forth the benefits of healthy eating and rarely bring up the negative consequences of obesity. We propose that obesity prevention messages using a prevention orientation will be more efficient in changing behaviors and intentions than messages using a promotion approach.

We conducted an experiment with 797 adolescents (mean age=14 years old) from low- income middle schools and high schools in Grenoble, France. The low income population is, in fact, the most affected by obesity. Parental and student consent were obtained prior to the study. Of the subjects, 57% are male and 88% have a normal body-mass-index.

The design was a between-subjects factorial with two factors: obesity prevention argument (health vs. social) and message orientation (prevention vs. promotion), and control. A professional advertisement agency created five advertisements; four obesity prevention advertisements and a control advertisement about ecology. All advertisements had the same design (colors and typo) and they used characters to avoid stigmatization of obese kids. The health prevention oriented message slogan was "Too many forms, not in shape!" and the image showed characters representing fast-foods (hamburger, fries) in the top of a scale that was breaking down. The social promotion oriented message slogan message was "Balanced meals, lots of friends!") and the image showed characters representing fruits and vegetables (carrots, orange, tomato) playing together.

Target advertisements were placed into a brochure with four filler advertisements about unrelated topics (local public transportation system, a videogame, clothes, and recycling), to reproduce a realistic exposition context. The target ad was shown twice to ensure a strong exposure. Participants received the brochure and were asked to look at each advertisement for a given time (15 seconds, controlled by a research assistant) and then turn the page. After seeing all the pages of the brochure, research assistants collected the brochures and distributed questionnaires. In the first part of the questionnaire, participants were asked to indicate their choice for a thank-you snack to be received at the end of the study; there were two options: a cereal bar (healthy) or a chocolate bar (less healthy). Then participants indicated their intentions to watch what they eat in the future on 5-point Likert scale, but also responded to filler questions about their intentions related to the filler ads (i.e., intention to buy clothes, to use the public transportation system). The order of the questions about intentions and choice was counterbalanced among participants. Finally, participants answered a set of manipulation checks, questions about their eating habits, family model (parenting feeding styles and family food environment), and personal questions (age, gender, height, and weight).

Our behavioral results show that 65% of the participants exposed to the messages using a social argument chose the healthy snack option (cereal bar), while only 55% of those exposed to the health argument made the same choice (Chi-square=6.16; $p=.01$). There was no effect of the regulatory orientation of the message on the snack choice. These results indicate that the social message leads participants' to healthier food choices than the health argument.

Concerning their intentions to watch what they eat, we found an interaction between the message argument (social vs. health) and the regulatory orientation (promotion vs. prevention) of the message ($p=.060$). The prevention orientation works better for messages using the health argument, while the promotion orientation generates higher intentions in conjunction with the social argument. Pair-wise comparisons show that intentions of participants exposed to the message using a health argument and a promotion orientation is not different than intentions of the control group. The other three messages elicited intentions higher than control. Thus, a health message using a prevention orientation and both social messages (prevention and promotion oriented) are efficient to prevent obesity among adolescents.

Our results confirm that an argument based on social consequences of obesity is more efficient because it is closer to the current concerns of young people. Public policymakers should consider including social risks and prevention oriented messages when designing obesity prevention campaigns.

## References

Higgins, E. Tory (1997), "Beyond Pleasure and Pain," *American Psychologist*, 52 (12), 1280-300.
Ho, Robert (1998), "The Intention to Give up Smoking: Disease Versus Social Dimensions," *Journal of Social Psychology*, 138 (3), 368-80.

Pechmann, Cornelia and Susan J. Knight (2002), "An Experimental Investigation of the Joint Effects of Advertising and Peers on Adolescents' Beliefs and Intentions About Cigarette Consumption," *Journal of Consumer Research*, 29 (1), 5-19.

Pechmann, Cornelia and S. Ratneshwar (1994), "The Effects of Antismoking and Cigarette Advertising on Young Adolescents' Perceptions of Peers," *Journal of Consumer Research*, 21 (2), 236.

Steinberg, Laurence and Elizabeth S. Scott (2003), "Less Guilty by Reason of Adolescence: Developmental Immaturity, Diminished Responsibility, and the Juvenile Death Penalty," *American Psychologist*, 58 (12), 1009-18.

Zhao, Guangzhi and Cornelia Pechmann (2007), "The Impact of Regulatory Focus on Adolescents' Response to Antismoking Advertising Campaigns," *Journal of Marketing Research*, 44 (4), 671-87.

# Partnership in Healthcare: The Impact of Co-Production on Healthcare Outcomes

Stephanie J. Lawson, Florida State University, USA

Healthcare in the United States is facing a crisis. The United States spends $6,401 per capita on healthcare which is far greater than other developed economies (in comparison, Switzerland comes in second and spends $4,177 per person). This crisis stems the fact that although healthcare spending is high, the United States ranks last among 19 industrialized countries in preventing death from treatable conditions (Ginsburg, Doherty, Ralston, and Senkeeto, 2008). The majority of deaths related to treatable conditions are the result of modifiable behavior choices (e.g. diet, smoking, physical activity). Consumer lifestyle choices contribute to 40% of the deaths in America (McGinnis, Williams-Russo, and Knickman, 2002). Consumers hold responsibility for their lifestyle choices; however, making behavioral changes requires not only self discipline but access to information and resources through healthcare and social systems. How can consumers and healthcare providers work together to improve the quality of life in the United States? The purpose of this research is to explore how consumers and healthcare practitioners, through co-production impact healthcare outcomes. The importance of this research lies is the fact that due to the rising cost of care our current healthcare system is not sustainable (Berry 2008). Berry and Bendapudi (2007) call for more research in healthcare as its problems are, "perennial (mortality and suffering) but also mutable (technology, advances in science, and social mores continually affect the delivery of health care)."

The commitment-trust theory of relationship marketing provides a framework from which to investigate this issue (Morgan and Hunt 1994). Past research suggests shared values positively impact the level of relationship commitment and trust leading to outcomes of improved compliance and cooperation while reducing uncertainty. Social exchange theory suggests shared values with the firm make customers more likely to voluntarily participate in the firm's initiatives (Bettencourt 1997). Healthcare practitioners represent the firm to consumers, thus, it is reasonable to conclude that shared values (i.e. treatment or therapy goals) between practitioner and patient would yield similar outcomes. Successful health outcomes often require patient participation both during (i.e. answering questions) and after (i.e. taking medication) the service encounter (Berry and Bendapudi 2007). Co-production is a growing trend and past research suggests examining the role customers play in the service production process (Lengnick-Hall 1996). However, the impact of co-production on the relationship between shared values and relationship commitment and trust has yet to be illuminated.

Customer participation is defined as, "the degree to which the customer is involved in producing and delivering the service" (Dabholkar 1990). Co-production represents a shift towards active creation of service encounter• (Wind and Rangaswamy 2000). Past research suggests consumer cooperation during the service encounter contributes to their own and others' satisfaction and service quality perceptions (Bendapudi and Leone 2003; Bettencourt 1997). Patients are often suffering from an illness and feel a great amount of stress during health encounters (Berry and Bendapudi 2007). By involving consumers in the creation of their health encounter the moderating effect of co-production on the relationships between shared values (i.e. health goals) and relationship commitment and trust should be positively affected.

Shared values are defined as, "the extent to which partners have beliefs in common about what behaviors, goals, and policies are important or unimportant, appropriate or inappropriate, and right or wrong" (Morgan and Hunt 1994). Past research suggests shared values lead to the development of relationship commitment and trust (Dwyer, Schurr, and Oh 1987). Patients and practitioners share a common goal of positive health outcomes. However, many patients suffer from anxiety and engage in avoidance coping strategies due to the fear associated with making behavioral changes or undergoing a medical procedure (Berry and Bendapudi 2007). The introduction of co-production opportunities for consumers creates an opportunity for control which has been found to increase satisfaction (Bendapudi and Leone 2003).

Berry and Parasuraman (1991, p. 139) suggest, "relationships are built on the foundation of mutual commitment." Relationship commitment is defined as, "the exchange partner believing the ongoing relationship with another is worth maintaining" (Morgan and Hunt 1994). Trust exists when one party has confidence in the exchange partner's reliability and integrity (Morgan and Hunt 1994). Healthcare is a service that is unique from many other services in that consumers need it but often do not want it. Health encounters (between practitioners and patients) are of an interpersonal nature owing to the fact that healthcare is one of the most personal and important services consumers purchase. The relationships between healthcare providers and consumers are inherently personal and, aside from acute care, usually persist over an extended period of time and require trust in technical abilities (Berry and Bendapudi 2007). Social exchange theory supports the idea that customers exhibiting cooperative attitudes toward the firm feel the firm values their contributions and cares about their well-being (Eisenberger, Huntington, Hutchison, and Sowa 1986). If patients feel health providers care about their well-being then it is reasonable to conclude that relationship commitment and trust will have an impact on outcomes related to care compliance, cooperation in care, and uncertainty reduction.

An empirical study using scenario-based surveys is planned to investigate the impact of co-creation on healthcare outcomes. Survey respondents will be adults from a large southeastern city with experience in healthcare encounters. The relationships between the constructs will be analyzed using structural equation modeling. Coproduced healthcare experiences are hypothesized to positively impact relationship commitment and trust. Relationship commitment and trust are hypothesized to positively impact consumer compliance and consumer cooperation while negatively impacting or reducing consumer uncertainty.

In conclusion, the relationships between shared values and relationship commitment and trust have been established in the literature acting as mediating variables between shared values and outcomes (Morgan and Hunt 1994). However, within the healthcare context, the impact to co-production has not been examined. Recent research calls healthcare a "fertile field for services research" (Berry and Bendapudi 2007). This research contributes to understanding the impact of consumer participation on outcomes and offers healthcare practitioners the opportunity to create innovative care programs aimed at reducing the percentage of preventable deaths in the United States.

## References

Bendapudi, N., & Leone, R. P (2003), "Psychological implications of customer participation in co-production," *Journal of Marketing*, 67, 14–28, (January).

Bettencourt, Lance A. (1997), "Customer Voluntary Performance: Customers as Partners in Service Delivery," *Journal of Retailing*, 73(3), 383-406.

Berry, Leonard L. (2008), "Confronting America's Healthcare Crisis," Business Horizons, 51, 273–280.

Berry, Leonard L *and Neeli Bendapudi (2007), "Health Care: A Fertile Field for Services Research," Journal of Service Research* 2007; 10; 111

Berry, Leonard L. and A. Parasuraman (1991), *Marketing Services*. New York: The Free Press.

Dabholkar, Pratibha (1990), "How to Improve Perceived Service Quality by Improving Customer Participation," in *Developments in Marketing Science*, B.J. Dunlap, ed. Cullowhee, NC: Academy of Marketing Science, 483–87.

Dwyer, F. Robert, Paul H. Schurr, and Sejo Oh (1987), "Developing Buyer-Seller Relationships," *Journal of Marketing*, 51, 11-27 (April).

Eisenberger, Robert, Robin Huntington, Steven Hutchison, and Debora Sowa (1986), "Perceived Organizational Support," *Journal of Applied Psychology*, 71 (August), 500-507.

Ginsburg, J. A., Doherty, R. B., Ralston, J. F., Jr., & Senkeeto, N. (2008). "Achieving a high-performance health care system with universal access: What the United States can learn from other countries," *Annals of Internal Medicine*, 148(1), 55—75.

Lengnick-Hall, Cynthia A. (1996), "Customer Contributions to Quality: A Different View of the Customer-Oriented Firm," *The Academy of Management Review*, 21 (3), 791–824.

McGinnis, M. J., Williams-Russo, P., & Knickman, J. R. (2002), "The case for more active policy attention to health promotion," *Health Affairs*, 21(2), 78—93.

Morgan, Robert M. and Shelby D. Hunt (1994), "The Commitment-Trust Theory of Relationship Marketing," *Journal of Marketing*, 58, 20-28, (July).

Wind, Jerry and Arvind Rangaswamy (2000), "Customerization: The Next Revolution in Mass Customization," *Marketing Science Institute Working Paper No. 00-108*. Cambridge, MA: Marketing Science Institute.

# Can You Say "No" to Being a Sustainable Consumer?

Sangdo Oh, University of Illinois, USA
Sukki Yoon, Bryant University, USA
Patrick Vargas, University of Illinois, USA

Promoting sustainable consumption is a key goal of numerous academic researchers, corporations, government agencies, and non-government organizations. Across the world, various campaigns are being carried out to promote sustainable consumption among various publics (Nisbet, 2009). However, 'sustainability' remains a concept that is yet to be clearly understood (Oepen and Hamacher, 2000), indicating a fundamental problem relating to a lack of appropriate communication strategy. A lack of understanding of the meaning of 'sustainable consumption' may hinder their interests towards the necessity for change in current consumption behavior, thus it must be explained in carefully framed information-based campaigns to increase public awareness (Kolandai-Matchett, 2009).

A sizeable literature has accumulated testing message framing effect on persuasion, extensively in how self-regulatory goal framing influence the effectiveness of advertising messages. Higgins (2002) used the terminology *regulatory fit* to describe two distinctive processing styles by which goals are perused: promotion and prevention, and its strategic means during goal pursuits. A promotion focus is geared to motivate to attain advancement and achievement by approaching matches to end-state. A prevention focus, in contrast, is geared to motivate people to achieve protection and security by avoiding mismatches to desired end-state. When the persuasive message serves self-regulatory goal and compatible strategic, message recipients *feel right* during message reception, thus, attitude becomes more favorable (Avnet and Higgins, 2006).

When measuring the effectiveness of environment-related message, the most controversial issue is how to capture the construct of 'Environmental Attitude', a crucial construct in environmental psychology. Studies measuring environmental attitudes have generally used direct self-report. However, research has shown a weak link between explicit environmental attitudes and behavior (e.g., Bamberg 2003). As noted by Beckmann (2005), "Who actually would dare to admit disinterest or even anti-environment attitudes?" (p. 281), there is a strong social desirability element with the self-report measures that may systematically increase the mean ratings or decrease the variability of evaluations (e.g., Bruni & Schultz, 2010). Although several researchers developed scales while acknowledging participants' impression management occurs in survey responses (e.g., Connectedness to Nature Scale, Mayer & Frantz, 2004), these alternative measures may not entirely rule out social desirability effect.

The study outlined in this presentation drew upon the literature on regulatory fit and how to effectively measure attitudes about the environments. Specifically, we tested whether message recipients are affected by goal framing, targeted recipient and pre-existing implicit attitude. Implicit attitude toward sustainable consumption was measured using modified version of the implicit association test (Greenwald, 1998). This modified version of IAT assessed a person's implicit associations between "sustainable product" and "positive affect" by rapid categorization tasks. Participants received regulatory focus priming about positive (or negative) end-state of the self (or the earth), evaluated sustainable product using 7-point affect scales (Crites, et al., 1994). We hypothesized that promotion-primed participants would evaluate a sustainable product more favorably when the usage of product benefits the planet (compatible) than when it benefits the self (incompatible), and the reverse would be true for prevention-primed participants. However, this goal compatibility effect would be observed only among low-IAT participants.

We analyzed the data by means of an analysis of variance as a 2 (IAT: high or low) x 2 (recipient: the planet or self) 2 (regulatory focus prime: promotion or prevention) between-subjects factorial design. The results showed that high-IAT participants evaluated the sustainable product more favorable than low-IAT participants (5.33 versus 4.88; $F(1, 394)=11.65$, $p<.00$). Furthermore, regulatory focus prime × recipient interaction was marginally significant ($p=.05$); prevention-primed participants evaluated the sustainable product more favorably when the usage benefits the planet than the individual, whereas promotion-primed does not differ by proposed recipients. More central to our hypothesis, we observed the predicted three-way interaction among regulatory focus, recipient, and implicit attitude ($p<.001$). Subsequent analyses conducted separately for the two implicit attitude groups showed a regulatory focus × recipient interaction in the low-implicit attitude group ($F(1, 199)=9.68$, $p<.01$), conceptually replicating Aaker and Lee's (2001) findings. The results of planned contrasts showed that prevention-primed participants evaluated a sustainable product benefitting the planet more favorably than did promotion-primed participants ($M=5.74$ versus $5.28$; $F(1, 103)=5.34$, $p<.05$). The reverse was true for a self as a recipient ($M=4.58$ versus $5.18$; $p<.05$). For the high implicit attitude group, participants evaluated a sustainable product more favorably when promotion-primed than prevention-primed ($M=5.51$ versus $M=5.17$; $F(1, 195)=4.00$, $p<.05$), regardless of a recipient.

After three weeks, 250 participants returned to the lab for the post measures. We asked participants to indicate use of household goods in the past three weeks. These items were selected from the General Ecological Behavior (GEB) scale (Kaiser, & Wilson, 2000); 4 items were measuring sustainable product consumption behavior, and the other half was about instant use products. The results of 2 (compatibility: compatible versus incompatible) x 2 (implicit attitude: high versus low) ANOVA on the recent ecological behavior index yielded a main effect of compatibility. As predicted, frame-recipient compatibility had a significant effect on recent behavioral change; participants who received compatible priming ($M=3.67$) to the recipient of the product use showed higher score in ecological behavior index than the participants who received incompatible priming ($M=3.39$) to the recipient of the action ($F(1, 249)=6.19$, $p<.05$). In addition, a main effect for implicit attitude emerged revealing that high-IAT participants ($M=3.68$) scored higher in ECCB index than low-IAT participants ($M=3.40$). However, the interaction was marginally significant ($p=.08$).

Consistent with our predictions, we observed the goal compatibility effect, in immediate evaluations and post-exposure behavior, only when participants' implicit attitude toward sustainable product is relatively low; the effect disappeared when participants' implicit attitude toward sustainable product is high. This implies that environmental message should be carefully framed upon the context, and social desirability concerns should be factor in further development in environmental attitude measures.

**References**

Aaker, Jennifer L. and Angela Y. Lee (2001), 'I' Seek Pleasures and 'We' Avoid Pains: The Role of Self Regulatory Goals in Information Processing and Persuasion, *Journal of Consumer Research*, 28 (June), 33–49.

Avnet, T., & Higgins, E. T. (2006). How regulatory fit affects value in consumer choices and opinions. *Journal of Marketing Research*, 43, 1–10.

Bamberg S (2003) How does environmental concern influence specific environmentally related behaviours? A new answer to an old question. *Journal of Environmental Psychology*, 23, 21–32

Beckmann SC (2005) In the eye of the beholder: Danish consumer- citizens and sustainability. In: Grunert KG, Thøgersen J (eds) Consumers, policy and the environment: a tribute to Folke Olander. Springer, Berlin, pp 265–299

Bruni, C. & Schultz, W. (2010) Implicit beliefs about self and nature: Evidence from a IAT game. *Journal of Environmental Psychology*, 30, 95-102

Crites, S. L., Jr., Fabrigar, L. R., & Petty, R. E. (1994). Measuring the affective and cognitive properties of attitudes: Conceptual and methodological issues. *Personality and Social Psychology Bulletin*, 20, 619-634.

Greenwald, A. G., McGhee, D. E., & Schwartz, J. L. K. (1998). Measuring individual differences in implicit cognition: The Implicit Association Test. *Journal of Personality and Social Psychology, 74,* 1464–1480.

Higgins, E. Tory (2002), How Self-Regulation Creates Distinct Values: The Case of Promotion and Prevention Decision Making, *Journal of Consumer Psychology*, 12 (3), 177–191.

Kolandai-Matchett, K. (2009) Mediated communication of 'sustainable consumption' in the alternative media: a case study exploring a message framing strategy. *International Journal of Consumer Studies*, 33(2), 113-125

Nisbet, M. (2009). Communicating Climate Change: Why Frames Matter for Public Engagement. *Environment*, 51(2), 514-518.

Oepen, M. & Hamacher, W. (eds) (2000) Communicating the Environment: Environmental Communication for Sustainable Development. Peter Lang GmbH, Frankfurt.

# Examining the Relationship of Locus of Control, Pro-environmental Attitude and Pro-environmental Behavior

Emine Sarigollu, McGill University, Canada
Rong Huang, Shanghai University of Economics and Finance, China

This research examines the role of locus of control in the context of pro-environmental behavior. As a personality characteristic, locus of control is defined as an individual's generalized expectancies regarding the forces that determine reward and punishments (Rotter, 1966). In the realm of responsible environmental behavior studies, plenty of studies explore the relationship of locus of control, attitude and pro-environment behavior/behavior intentions. However, the extant literature provides inconsistent findings regarding the relationship between locus of control, attitude and pro-environmental behavior/behavior intention. In general, three different associations between locus control and the other two constructs are identified in the existing studies, namely, locus of control as direct predictor to pro-environmental behavior/behavior intention (e.g., Allen & Ferrand, 1999; Bamberg & Moser, 2007; Cleveland, Kalamas, & Laroche, 2005; Hamid & Cheng, 1995; e.g., Hines, Hungerford, & Tomera, 1986/87; Kim, 2005) , effect of locus of control on pro-environmental behavior being mediated by attitude (e.g., Balderjahn, 1988; McCarty & Shrum, 2001), and locus of control moderating the impact of attitude on pro-environmental behavior/behavior intention (e.g., Berger & Corbin, 1992).

The present research contributes a better understanding of the role of locus of control on ecological behavior. This work studies both the direct impact of locus of control on behavior and the moderating effects of it on attitude-behavior relationship. Moreover, the current study includes a rather comprehensive assessment of ecological attitude and behavior in Turkey. Currently, most researches in environmental domain are taken in developed countries. As locus of control is a stable, general status being influence greatly by culture, Turkey would be a good context for such studies with it mosaic of eastern and western cultures.

Data were gathered from 1000 randomly selected residences of Istanbul via at-home personal interviews using standard surveys. Attitudinal, behavioral, socioeconomic and demographic variables that were frequently employed in previous studies were used in this research. Appropriateness of the attitude and behavior items for the Turkish context was verified by first testing them on a sample of consumers. Attitudes toward the environment were assessed using a number of items adapted from a Roper study (1990). Behavior was measured by asking respondents for self-reports of nine different behaviors, given the opportunity, on a scale from 1 (never) to 5 (always). Similarly a scale of 1 (strongly disagree) to 5 (strongly agree) was used for measuring attitudinal characteristics. Appropriateness of adopting scales (1-5) typically used in the North American context to Turkey was verified with a local market research industry representative who asserted that these scales are commonly used in Turkey as they nicely correspond with the grading system (1-5) of Turkish schools and hence were easily comprehended by anyone who had at least some level of elementary education. Locus of control was assessed via three items selected from Rotter's (1966) I-E scale. Four items from the general control dimension were selected and those of political control ignored since they were not relevant to the current study.

Data were analyzed in three stages. In the first stage, the various dimensions underlying the behavior and attitude toward environment are uncovered by a factor analysis using the principal component method with varimax rotation (Hair et al. 1998). In the second stage, confirmatory factor analysis (CFA) was applied to purify the measurement of attitude and behavior dimensions. In the third stage, structural equation modeling (SEM) is used to explore the relationship between locus of control, attitude dimensions and behavior dimensions. For moderating effects, the most widely used technique to test for moderating effects in structural equation modeling is the multisample approach (Ridgon et al. 1998). Two groups are created with the dataset; the internal and external locus of control groups in our case. The interaction effect is assessed by comparing parameters from the two groups.

The study finds two dimensions underlying pro-environmental attitude. One dimension named as "general attitude" summarizes the respondents' overall concern regarding environmental protection. The other dimension named as "activity attitude" represents the respondents' attitude about taking activities to protect environment. In addition, two dimensions are also found for pro-environmental behaviour. One dimension named as "EXPRESS" indicates the respondents' behavior to express their concern of attitude and advocate the environmentally behavior. Named as "PROTECT", the second factor summarizes the some specific actions of respondents to protect the environment.

Analyses of the relationship between locus of control, attitude and behavior are conducted for all the four combinations of attitude and behavior dimensions respectively. The current research finds that the locus of control does not moderate the impact of pro-environmental attitude on pro-environmental behavior. In addition, locus of control neither has direct impact on pro-environmental behavior. Rather, locus of control is directly related to pro-environmental attitude. That is, respondents with internal locus of control are more concerned of environment. Hence, they are more likely to conduct activities to protect the environment. On the contrary, respondents who believe fate or luck more are less likely to do something for the environment.

## References

Allen, J. B., & Ferrand, J. L. (1999). Environmental Locus of Control, Sympathy, and proenvironmental Behavior: A Test of Geller's Actively Caring Hypothesis. *Environment and Behavior, 31*(3), 338-353.

Balderjahn, I. (1988). Personality Variables and Environmental Attitudes as Predictors of Ecologically Responsible Consumption Patterns. *Journal of Business Research*(17), 51-56.

Bamberg, S., & Moser, G. (2007). Twenty Years after Hines, Hungerford, and Tomera: A New Meta-analysis of Psycho-social Determinants of Pro-environmental Behavior. *Journal of Environmental Psychology*(27), 14-25.

Berger, I. E., & Corbin, R. M. (1992). Perceived Consumer Effectiveness and Faith in Others as Moderators of Environmentally Responsible Behaviors. *Journal of Public Policy and Marketing, 11*(2), 79-100.

Cleveland, M., Kalamas, M., & Laroche, M. (2005). Shade of Green: Linking Environmental Locus of Control and Pro-environmental Behaviors. *Journal of Consumer Marketing, 22*(4), 198-212.

Hamid, P. N., & Cheng, S.-T. (1995). Predicting Antipollution Behavior: The Role of Molar Behavioral Intentions, Past Behavior, and Locus of Control. *Environment and Behavior, 27*(5), 679-697.

Hines, J. M., Hungerford, H. R., & Tomera, A. N. (1986/87). Analysis and Synthesis of Research on Responsible Environmental Behavior: a Meta-Analysis. *Journal of Environmental Education, 18*, 1-8.

Kim, Y. (2005). Antecedents of Green Purchase Behavior: An Examination of Collectivism, Environmental Concern, and PCE. *Advances in Consumer Research, 32*(592-599).

McCarty, J. A., & Shrum, L. J. (2001). The Influence of Individualism, Collectivism, and Locus of Control on Environmental Belief's and Behavior. *Journal of Public Policy and Marketing, 20*(1), 93-104.

Roper, O. (1990). *The Environment: Public Attitudes and Individual Behavior*: Commissioned by S.C. Johnson and Son, Inc.

Rotter, J. B. (1966). Generalized Expectancies for Internal versus External Control of Reinforcement. *Psychological Monographs, 80*(1), 609

# Breaking the Status Quo:
# Using Ideology and Conviction to Increase Adoption of Green Behaviors

Blair Kidwell, University of Kentucky, USA
Adam Farmer, University of Kentucky, USA
David Hardesty, University of Kentucky, USA

## Extended Abstract

Central issues confronting transformative researchers are how to get consumers to adopt consumption (e.g., healthy food choices) and disposition behaviors (e.g., recycling). A better understanding is needed for why adoption of these behaviors has been slow to catch on, and why these behaviors tend to fall along ideological lines. In this research, we explore the psychological mechanisms underlying conviction, the impact of conviction on consumer decision making, and ways to appeal to different ideologies in promoting the adoption of green behaviors and healthy consumption.

In study 1, we develop a conceptual model for how conviction can be altered via mortality salience manipulation to influence consumer decision making, leading to status quo choices and suboptimal decisions. Study 2 examines the theoretical framework underlying these effects and demonstrates how consumers who have lowered conviction can become more open-minded and consider new information. Finally, in study 3, we extend our understanding of conviction and ideology by examining a green behavior (recycling) from 10,000 households relative to our theoretical model. In addition, we develop tailored messages that may appeal to both conservatives and liberals in promoting this green behavior.

## Review of the Literature

The subject of ideology has been pervasive in the behavioral literature in recent years. Ideology has been examined across multiple disciplines in many different ways. This area has recently been extended to understanding differences between conservatives and liberals. For example, McAdams et al. (2008) used life-narrative interviews of self-labeled psychological conservatives and liberals. Liberals were found to recall stories of lessons learned regarding openness and empathy while finding the values of harm and fairness as being the most relevant to them. In contrast, conservatives were more likely to recall lessons learned in regards to authority, strict rules, and self discipline while finding the values of purity, authority, and in-group as being the most relevant. Furthermore, Morrison and Miller (2008) describe conservatives as descriptive deviants in that they tend to move toward and conform to the desirable group attitude, while liberals can be referred to as prescriptive deviants who tend to move away from the desirable group attitude. In line with this theorizing, Janoff-Bulman, Sheikh, and Hepp (2009) recently described differences between liberals and conservatives in terms of prescriptive and proscriptive morality. Prescriptive morality involves activating positive behavior, whereas proscriptive morality is defined as inhibiting negative behavior. Conservatives were found to be more proscriptive in that they restrain undesired behaviors to better the overall social order, whereas liberals are more prescriptive in that they focus on desired behaviors to improve the overall social justice (Janoff-Bulman et al., 2009).

## Proposed Conceptual Framework

While the characteristics and moral orientations underlying ideology are apparent, it is important to note that one's views can be significantly polarized by incoming information that often leads to significant strengthening of one's ideology. Such polarization is referred to as eliciting closed-mindedness or conviction (Ledgerwood and Chaiken, 2007). While little is actually known about conviction, how it manifests, or how it might influence behavior, research has begun to indicate that self-affirming information may increase openness to information even if the new information conflicts with a salient identity (Cohen et al., 2007).

*Conservatives.* Recent research suggests that conservatives are likely to exhibit a motivated tendency to construe the status quo as the most desirable and reasonable state of affairs (Kay et al., 2009). This tendency is increased when personal control is threatened (Kay, et al. 2008). Thus, strategies for behavior change that invoke negative emotion that threatens personal control toward a behavior often does not lead to the intended behavior, rather, it potentially leads to the opposite—adhering to the status quo. However, Kay et al. (2008) also found that some reduction in status quo tendencies was exhibited when the system was perceived as being benevolent. Thus, it may be possible to break the status quo tendency with positively primed messages based on self-affirmation of in-group norms to increase openness to information (Cohen et al., 2007).

*Liberals*. Liberals are likely to engage in green behaviors because they are desirable behaviors for the social good. Moreover, liberals are prescriptive deviants who tend to move away from the desirable group attitude, and thus, may hold positive views of green behaviors because they deem them as the right thing to do regardless of whether others are engaging in these behaviors. While many liberals may currently adhere to green behaviors, it may be possible to elicit further adoption by evoking positive consequences (as opposed to thoughts about their death) by priming that green behaviors are the right thing to do and help society as a whole.

## Plan of Studies and Methodology

*Study 1*. Study 1 was an experimental study with college students at a large eastern university who were administered a survey about their PFC (preference for consistency), followed by either a mortality salience manipulation or a positive consequence (control) condition where they wrote about watching TV, and follow up conviction items. Participants low in PFC (liberals) who received the mortality salience prime vs. a control condition, exhibited increased conviction (M=4.9), while those conservatives high in PFC who received the positive consequences prime, exhibited lowered conviction (M=3.7), and thus be more likely to adopt green behaviors (t264=4.26, p<.05).

*Study 2*. Study 2 will involve an experimental design to develop tailored messages for both liberals and conservatives. For conservatives, the message will elicit vulnerability but be self-affirming relative to their in-group's participation in green behaviors. For liberals, the tailored message will be positive in tone, illustrating the favorable consequences of engaging in green behaviors and that it is the right thing to do. Several green behaviors will be examined relative to their adoption of these behaviors.

*Study 3*. Study 3 will examine the implementation of our theoretical framework to better understand adoption of green behaviors in a field setting. Specifically, we will examine the effects of psychological ideology and conviction relative to message priming in on actual recycling behavior across 10,000 households in support of our conceptual framework.

## References

Cohen, G. L., Sherman, D. K., Bastardi, A., Hsu, L., McGoey, M., & Ross, L. (2007). Bridging the Partisan Divide: Self-Affirmation Reduces Ideological Closed-Mindedness and Inflexibility in Negotiation. *Journal of Personality & Social Psychology, 93*(3), 415-430.

Graham, J., Haidt, J., & Nosek, B. A. (2009). Liberals and Conservatives Rely on Different Sets of Moral Foundations. *Journal of Personality & Social Psychology, 96*(5), 1029-1046.

Janoff-Bulman, R., Sheikh, S., & Hepp, S. (2009). Proscriptive Versus Prescriptive Morality: Two Faces of Moral Regulation. *Journal of Personality & Social Psychology, 96*(3), 521-537.

Jost, J. T., Glaser, J., Kruglanski, A. W., & Sulloway, F. J. (2003). Exceptions That Prove the Rule--Using a Theory of Motivated Social Cognition to Account for Ideological Incongruities and Political Anomalies: Reply to Greenberg and Jonas (2003). *Psychological Bulletin, 129*(3), 383.

Kay, A. C., Gaucher, D., Napier, J. L., Callan, M. J., & Laurin, K. (2008). God and the Government: Testing a Compensatory Control Mechanism for the Support of External Systems. *Journal of Personality & Social Psychology, 95*(1), 18-35.

Kay, A. C., Gaucher, D., Peach, J. M., Laurin, K., Friesen, J., Zanna, M. P., et al. (2009). Inequality, Discrimination, and the Power of the Status Quo: Direct Evidence for a Motivation to See the Way Things Are as the Way They Should Be. *Journal of Personality & Social Psychology, 97*(3), 421-434.

Kosloff, S., Greenberg, J., Weise, D., & Solomon, S. (2010). The Effects of Mortality Salience on Politcal Preferences: The Roles of Charisma and Political Orientation. *Journal of Experimental Social Psychology, 46*(1), 139-147.

Ledgerwood, A., & Chaiken, S. (2007). Priming Us and Them: Automatic Assimilation and Contrast in Group Attitudes. *Journal of Personality & Social Psychology, 93*(6), 940-956.

McAdams, D. P., Albaugh, M., Farber, E., Daniels, J., Logan, R. L., & Olson, B. (2008). Family Metaphors and Moral Intuitions: How Conservatives and Liberals Narrate Their Lives. *Journal of Personality & Social Psychology, 95*(4), 978-990.

Morrison, K. R., & Miller, D. T. (2008). Distinguishing Between Silent and Vocal Minorities: Not All Deviants Feel Marginal. *Journal of Personality & Social Psychology, 94*(5), 871-882.

Nail, P. R., McGregor, I., Drinkwater, A. E., Steele, G. M., & Thompson, A. W. (2009). Threat Causes Liberals to Think Like Conservatives. *Journal of Experimental Social Psychology, 45*, 901-907

# Process Versus Outcome Focus: How to Encourage Consumer to Increase Repayment Amount

Lili Wang, Shanghai Jiao Tong University, China
Wei Lv, Shanghai Jiao Tong University, China

Most decision research on credit cards has focused on understanding why consumers over-spend with credit. In order to solve debt problem, it is necessary to encourage individual to repay more each month to reduce the debt amount. Taylor and Schneider (1989) suggested that mental simulation served problem-solving functions and emotional regulation functions for turning imagined experience into action. So in present paper, we tried to manipulate mental simulation to encourage consumer to increase repayment amount. Meanwhile, we

There are two kinds of mental simulation—process simulation and outcome simulation (Pham and Taylor 1999; Escalas and Luce 2003, 2004). Process simulation help individual to rehearse the process to reach an envisioned end state, so individual can identify and organize the steps involved in the activities needed to get there, which, in turn, yields a plan. At the same time as one is mentally walking through these activities, the emotions that will be involved may be evoked, at least in a modest state, such that one can anticipate what these emotional states will be and develop some degree of control over them. Outcome simulation espouses an "I can do it" effect on goal pursuit. It helps individual to envision the outcome that one wants to achieve may facilitate efforts to achieve the goal or enhance perception of self-efficacy. Although, previous literature has already shown that process to some extent are more efficient to increase goal achievement because it provide a detail plan (Pham and Taylor 1999). In contrast, outcome simulations may make people feel good in the present without providing a basis for achievement in the future, so it is much easier for individual to fall into planning fallacy (Oettingen 1995). With the reference of credit debt, researchers generally accepted that unrealistic optimism is the main reason to account for credit debt (Yang, Markoczy and Qi 2007). So in present research we propose that process simulation is more efficient to increase repayment amount than outcome simulation. Moreover, we further propose that process simulation decrease individual's optimistic.

Five studies tested the present prediction. Study 1 and 2 tested that process simulation would increase repayment amount. In study 1, we directly manipulated the information related with the repayment using process or outcome simulation. We randomly assigned participants into process, outcome or control groups. Consistent with prior research (Escalas and Luce 2003,2004), process simulation instructions focused on the activities, procedures associated with paying off the debt, whereas outcome simulation instructions focused on the benefits associated with paying off the debt. The dependent variable was the amount of payment. We found that participants under process simulation would have a significantly higher repayment amount than participants in control group. Meanwhile, there are no significant different amount of payment between participants in outcome simulation situation and control group.

In order to generalize the result of study 1, before we provided the repayment information, we first randomly assigned participants to process or outcome simulation situation. For participants under process simulation, we asked them to image that how to plan a trip, meanwhile asked them to write down the basic procedure to plan a trip. For participants under outcome simulation, we asked them to image that the benefits of a trip, meanwhile asked them to write down the happiness and benefits of the trip. We also found that participants under process simulation would have a higher repayment amount than participants under outcome simulation. From study 1 and study 2, we found that process simulation would increase repayment amount regardless of manipulated information related with repayment or not.

Study 3 tested that consumer under process simulation would have a higher repayment amount depended on the amount of the debt. In study 3, we employed a 2 (mental simulation: process simulation vs. outcome simulation) ×2 (amount of debt: ¥500 vs. ¥5000) between-subject design. Manipulations of process and outcome simulation are similar to study 1. The dependent variable was repayment amount. We found that participants under process simulation would have a higher repayment amount only when they owned more debt rather than less debt.

Study 4 tested that optimistic bias played as a mediator. Latest research indicated that the main reason for consumer falling into debt was unrealistic optimism (Yang, Markoczy and Qi 2007), which means that individual normal have optimistic bias. Taylor et al (1998) also found that a mental simulation of the process of goal pursuit attenuates optimistic bias. So we hypothesized that process simulation induced optimistic bias thus increased repayment amount. We used the same method of study 1 to manipulated process simulation and outcome simulation. After participants read the process simulated information, we used 7-likert scales to measure optimistic bias. In order to rule out that planning played as a mediator. We also measured planning (Pham and Taylor 1999). After analysis, we found that process simulation significantly decreased individual's optimistic bias. Meanwhile, optimistic bias was positively related with repayment amount. But when we control optimistic bias, the relationship between process simulation and repayment amount would not exist. Although planning was negatively related with repayment amount, when we control planning, the relationship between process simulation and repayment amount also existed. So we made the conclusion that optimistic bias played as mediator rather than planning.

In study 5, we tried to find the boundary of our previous results. We found that all of results we received previously were valid for individuals who were high self-efficacy. For consumer with low self-efficacy, process simulation and outcome simulation didn't function significantly different.

In order to help individual escape from credit debt, we try to use mental simulation to encourage repaying more each month. In present research, we documented that due to optimistic bias, individual normally underestimated the ponderance of financial situation. If we asked individual to imagine the process of repayment rather than the outcome of repayment, it would help them to repay more each month. Thus, process simulation would be more efficient to help individual out of debt.

## References

Escalas, Jennifer E and Mary F. Luce (2003), "Process versus outcome thought focus and advertising," *Journal of Consumer Psychology,* 13(3), 246-254

Escalas, Jennifer E and Mary F. Luce (2003), "Understanding the Effect of Process-Focused versus Outcome-Focused Thought in Response to Advertising," *Journal of Consumer Psychology,* 31(2), 274-285

Jain, Shailendra P, Pragya Mathur, and Durairaj Maheswaran (2009), "The Influence of consumers' Lay Theories on Approach/ Avoidance Motivation," *Journal of Marketing Research,* 46(1), 56-65

Lee, Yin H and Cheng Qiu (2009), "When Uncertainty Brings Pleasure: The Role of Prospect Imageability and Mental Imagery," *Journal of Consumer Research,* 36(4), 624-633

Mishra, Himanshu, Baba Shiv and Dhananjay Nayakankuppam (2008), "The Blissful Ignorance Effect: Pre-versus Post-action Effect on Outcome Expectancies Arising from Premise and Vague Information," *Journal of Consumer Research,* 35(4), 573-585

Petrova, Petia K and Robert B. Claldini (2005), "Fluency of Consumption Imagery and the Backfire Effect of Imagery Appeals," *Journal of Consumer Research,* 32(3), 442-452

Pham, Lien B and Shelley E. Taylor (1999), "From Thought to Action: Effect of Process-versus Outcome-Based Mental Simulations on Performance," *Personality and Social Psychology Bulletin,* 25 (2), 250-260

Pham, Lien B and Shelley E. Taylor (1999), "The Effect of Mental Simulation on Goal-Directed performance," *Imagination, Cognition and Performance,* 18 (4), 253-263

Taylor, S.E and Schneider, S. K (1989), "Coping and the Simulation of events," *Social Cognition,* 7, 174-194

Taylor, Shelley E, Lien B. Pham and Inna D. Rivkin, and David A. Armor (1998), "Harnessing the Imagination-mental Simulation, Self-regulation, and Coping," *American Psychologist,* 53 (4), 429-439

Thompson, Debora V, Rebecca W. and Petia K. Petrova (2009), "When Mental Simulation Hinders Behavior: The effect of Process-Oriented Thinking on Decision Difficulty and Performance," *Journal of Consumer Research,* 36(4), 562-574

Ulkumen, Gulden, Manoj Thomas and Vicki G. Morwitz (2008), "Will I Spend More in 12 Months or a Year? The effect of Ease of Estimation and Confidence on budget Estimates," *Journal of Consumer Research,* 35(2), 245-256

Yang, S., L. Markoczy, et al. (2007), "Unrealistic Optimism in Consumer Credit Card Adoption," *Journal of Economic Psychology,* 28(2), 170-185

Zhang, Ying, Ayelet Fishbach and Ravi Dhar (2007), "When Thinking Beats Doing: The Role of Optimistic Expectations in Goal-Based Choice," *Journal of Consumer Research,* 34(4), 567-578

Zhang, Yinlong and Vikas Mittal (2005), "Decision Difficulty: Effects of Procedural and Outcome Accountability," *Journal of Consumer Research,* 32(3), 465-472

Zhao, Ming, Steve Hoeffler, and Gal Zauberman (2007), "Mental Simulation and Preference Consistency over Time: The Role of Process-Versus Outcome-Focused Thought," *Journal of Marketing,* 44(3), 379-388

# Understanding the Impact of Parents-Provided Financial Education on the Satisfaction with Life: The Moderating and Mediating Role of Consumer Characteristics

Vladimir Pashkevich, Marymount Manhattan College, USA

## Extended Abstract

Deregulated and very innovative financial system demands of its users a high level of financial sophistication. Consumers have to choose from among bewildering array of financial products, such as credit cards and mortgages, which grow more complex. In fact, there is a virtual requirement that consumers bear increasing responsibility for their financial and retirement security. Some argue that it's most important to improve government regulation to make financial products more transparent and fair. Others argue that financial-literacy programs aimed at students and other consumers are effective: we cannot expect consumers to make optimal choices if they are not equipped with the personal resources for doing so. Consumers need to be taught how to do so. The fundamental questions I am asking: what is the best way to structure financial education efforts? There is growing evidence that many consumers lack the basic financial literacy necessary to make decisions in their own best interest. Nevertheless, many researchers debate the value of financial-education programs and some researchers admit that we know very little about whether financial literacy programs actually work. Moreover, there is growing evidence that while higher levels of education and cognitive ability cause increased participation in financial markets, that financial-literacy education does not affect individual savings decision. High-school seniors who take personal-finance courses tend to score no better on the personal finance tests than those who don't. What's more, whites have tended to do better than blacks and Hispanics, and students from wealthy families have tended to score better than those from low-income backgrounds. It seems that one factor that differentiates those who do well on the personal finance tests and go on to make optimal financial choices in the future and those who don't when their "formal" financial literacy training is basically the same, is a better understanding of economic and personal finance issues gained in the families. It seems that personal financial skills are well internalized when they are taught starting at an early age and the learning is hands-on, real-time and involves something that belongs to the child' family. High school or college personal finance courses are unlikely to replace family education where children can start getting the training early enough and this training can be repeated often enough in the context of the decision points that are faced on a daily basis. The financial education received at home is more likely to address social and emotional influences, is more likely to change long-term financial behavior and enhance financial well-being than one-semester course in financial literacy.

However, many adults are ill-equipped to teach their children about budgeting and saving, and are not prepared to guide their teenagers on investing. Therefore, social marketers should target parents with future-oriented educational interventions that have real-world applications and motivate parents to reach their children at their most 'teachable' moments. As a result, parents should become less of a financial 'safety-net' and more of strong normative influence with respect to financial planning and taking responsibility for future financial choices.

In this paper, I deal with empirical issues about whether involving parents into teaching financial literacy has a positive effect on their children's future well being and financial literacy. I also focus on the mechanisms that seem promising for explaining the impact of parental normative influence on their children's future financial well being. I also consider the impact of various moderators on the parental financial education- financial well-being relationship.

Based on a survey study using adult consumers, I explore how different levels of acquiring financial decision-making skills at home during a childhood and adolescence affect the satisfaction with life. Based on the data from 200 respondents, I find support for the expectation that the parental financial education leads to higher satisfaction with life. It is shown that the effect of the parental financial education on the satisfaction with life is fully mediated by its effect of financial literacy and economic locus of control. Finally, the hypothesized moderating effect of materialism and social-economic status is also confirmed.

Finally, I will formulate some suggestions for public policy. Given that many consumers lack the basic financial literacy necessary to make decisions in their own best interest and the "formal" financial literacy training is basically not as effective as expected, this research has clear implications for consumer welfare and public policy administrators.

## References

Nasser, R., Abouchedid K. (2006). Locus of control and the attribution for poverty: comparing Lebanese and south African university students. *Social Behavior and Personality*, 34(7), 777-796

Diener E., Emmons R., Larsen R., and Griffin S. (1985). The satisfaction with life scale. *Journal of Personality Assessment*, 49(1), 71-75.

Furnham A. (1986). Economic Locus of Control. *Human Relations*, 39(1), 29-43.

Gallo L., Smith T., and Cox C. (2006). Socioeconomic status, psychosocial processes, and perceived health: an interpersonal perspective. *Annals of Behavioral Medicine*, 31(2), 109-119.

Plunkett H., Buehner M. (2007). The relation of general and specific locus of control to intertemporal monetary choice. *Personality and Individual Differences*, 42, 1233-1242.

Kirby K., Herrnstein R. (1995). *Preference reversals to myopic discounting of delayed reward.* 6(2), 83-89.

Andreasen A. (2002). Marketing social marketing in the social change marketplace. *Journal of Public Policy & Marketing*, 21(1), 3-13.

Kirby K., Petry N., and Bickel W. (1999). Heroin addicts have higher discount rates for delayed rewards than non-drug-using controls. *Journal of Experimental Psychology: General*, 128(1), 78-87.

MacLeod A. and Conway C. (2005). Well-being and the anticipation of future positive experiences" the role of income, social networks, and planning ability, *Cognition and Emotion*, 19(3), 357-374

Hilgert M. and Hogarth J. (2003). Household Financial Management: the connection between knowledge and behavior. *Federal Reserve Bulletin*, July, 309-322.

Braunstein S. and Welch C. (2002). Financial literacy: an overview of practice, research, and policy. *Federal Reserve Bulletin*, November, 446-457.

Smith D., Langa K., Kabeto M., and Ubel P. (2005). Health, wealth, and happiness: financial resources buffer subjective well-being after the onset of a disability. *Psychological Science*, 16(9), 663-666.

Reifner U. ad Herwig I. (2003). Consumer education and information rights in financial services. *Information& Communication Technology Law*, 12(2), 125-142.

Hira T. and Loibil G. (2005). Understanding the impact of employer-provided financial education on workplace satisfaction. *The Journal of Consumer Affairs*, 39(1), 173-194.

# Embiggeners and Ensmalleners:
## A Scale Measure of Perceived Risk and Benefits in Sharing Resources

Sommer Kapitan, University of Texas at San Antonio, USA
Rajesh Bhargave, University of Texas at San Antonio, USA

**Extended Abstract**

Sharing has emerged as a "theoretical terra incognita" in consumer behavior research (Belk 2010, 716), an unexplored arena of social life that guides consumer spending at home as well as among those who extend resources beyond the family circle (Widlock 2004). Motivations vary in the sparse literature that documents sharing behavior, from socially desirable attempts to appear nice to maintaining a balance in reciprocity (Staub and Sherk 1970). From Belk's (2010) call for future research to the paucity of information in the literature, it is clear that further investigations in sharing would benefit from empirically established constructs that pinpoint individual differences within this arena. We propose an 18-item measure of individual differences in perceived risk and benefits in sharing resources.

According to Belk (2010), consumers share resources when they desire connection, with co-management of resources cementing social bonds both within and outside the family unit. However, Marcoux (2009) notes that consumers may sometimes prefer social divestment and autonomy due to risks involved in common property, such as obligation and indebtedness. We argue that these different perspectives may characterize consumer types. Embiggeners view mutual resources as a means of establishing social bonds. They enjoy a sense of belonging and caring for others through extending their resources. Ensmalleners emphasize the risk inherent in lending or co-managing ownership of resources. They prefer to maintain a balance in interactions with others to avoid indebtedness. Whereas embiggeners seek to extend themselves through possessions borrowed and shared, ensmalleners seek differentiation and prefer responsibility and control of their domains. We hypothesize that embiggeners will be more agreeable to sharing resources than ensmalleners. Yet, the Embiggener/Ensmallener distinction goes beyond just willingness to share: We expect that ensmalleners will be as likely to share if the context diminishes sharing-related risks.

A pilot test (n=113 undergraduate students) examined the validity of an Embiggener/Ensmallener scale, tested hypothesized predictions from the scale, and compared predictions from other relevant scales to establish convergent and discriminant validity. We first piloted an initial pool of 29 items expected to tap into the construct. The first 12 items were true/false (0/1) values statements; these were summed, with higher scores associated with embiggeners. The remaining 17 items were subjected to exploratory factor analysis. Eigenvalues indicated five possible factor loadings, though only one factor loading was reliable, at $\alpha=.68$. Our proposed overall Embiggener/Ensmallener scale is the sum of the mean of the 12 true/false items and the mean of the six items in the one reliable factor. As a result, the reliable factor gets a heavier weighting in the overall scale. Representative true/false scale items include responses to "Sharing things with someone brings you closer together" and "I always repay someone for a favor, right away" (reverse coded). The six-item factor identified also includes items such as "I always offer a bite of my dessert to friends I'm eating with," and "I never leave my things out where others can use them" (reverse coded).

We also exposed participants to scenarios with two conditions, varying sharing context. Support for the predictive power of Embiggener/Ensmallener was found in two main effects and two interactions. As a main effect, we found that willingness to loan luggage to a friend was positively related to Embiggener score ($F(1,111)=9.47, p<.01$). A median split of the scale finds that participants classified as embiggeners were more willing to share than participants classified as ensmalleners ($M_{embiggener}$=3.47 vs. $M_{ensmallener}$=2.78). Results were significant in another scenario that involved sharing gum with a classmate.

Willingness to share also depended on the context, which interacted with Embiggener score. One interaction showed ensmalleners were more likely to view sharing as fair when reciprocity was in effect ($F(1,104)$= 4.09, $p$<.05). After being handed a tissue by a fellow student, ensmalleners were more likely to see it as fair to offer use of their pen ($M$=4.39) than if the tissue had not been offered ($M$=3.79), whereas embiggeners' perceived fairness did not depend on the scenario ($M_{no-reciprocity}$=4.37 vs $M_{reciprocity}$=4.19). In another scenario in which participants were asked to share a textbook, we varied the situation as either splitting usage of the textbook over a semester or lending the textbook after a course was complete. There was an Embiggener score X context interaction ($F$ (1, 104)=2.68, $p$<.05) when controlling for demographics. Ensmalleners—but not embiggeners—were more likely to view sharing as fair when asked to lend, as opposed to splitting usage time and co-managing the textbook ($M_{co-manage}$=3.82 vs. $M_{lend}$=4.26). Together, these results indicate that ensmalleners are more willing to share if the context encourages autonomy and diminishes indebtedness.

A final goal of the pilot study was to establish convergent and discriminant validity of the scale. During the study, responses were gathered for other extant scales. For space, only significant correlations are reported below. Embiggener/Ensmallener scale was positively and significantly correlated with John, Naumann and Soto's (2008) Big Five Extraversion ($r$(113)=.28,$p$<.01) and Big Five Agreeableness ($r$(113)=.38, $p$<.001); Rushton, Chrisjohn and Fekken's (1981) altruism self-report scale ($r$(113)=.28, $p$<.001); and Mills and Clark's (1994) scale for communal orientation ($r$(113)=.36, $p$<.001). Some overlap with related constructs shows convergent validity with well-established theoretical ground. However, discriminant validity in predicting responses is necessary to establish that the construct differentially explains variance in consumer sharing practices. A chief concern was the overlap with communal orientation. People high in communal orientation view exchange as grounded in the social market and prefer equality and cooperation. Yet, communal orientation failed to predict responses to the tested scenarios.

Through future research, we expect to pare down the present 18-item scale, validate it across different groups of participants to increase generalizability, and compare it with additional scales to further establish validity. We also plan to examine other factors that influence whether ensmalleners are willing to share. For instance, we will examine the effect of relationship length, predicting that ensmalleners are more likely to share if engaging in a short-term relationship. Likewise, we expect that ensmalleners are more likely to share when property is clearly engraved or marked (i.e., when there is no chance of confusing ownership).

## References

Belk, Russell P. (2010), "Sharing," *Journal of Consumer Research*, 36 (February), 715-734.

John, Oliver P., L.P. Naumann, and C.J. Soto (2008), "Paradigm Shift to the Integrative Big Five Trait Taxonomy: History, Measurement, and Conceptual Issues," in *Handbook of Personality: Theory and Research*, eds. Oliver P. John, Richard W. Robins, and L. A. Pervin, New York: Guilford, 114-158.

Marcoux, Jean-Sébastian (2009), "Escaping the Gift Economy," *Journal of Consumer Research*, 36 (December), 671-685.

Mills, Judson and Margaret S. Clark (1994), "Communal and Exchange Relationships: Controversies and Research," in *Theoretical Frameworks for Personal Relationships*, eds. Ralph Erber and Robin Gilmour, Hillsdale, NJ: Erlbaum, 29-42.

Rushton, J. Phillipe, Roland D. Chrisjohn, and G. Cynthia Fekken (1981), "The Altruistic Perosnality and the Self-Report Altruism Scale," *Personality and Individual Differences*, 2 (4), 293-302.

Staub, Ervin and Linda Sherk (1970), "Need for Approval, Children's Sharing Behavior, and Reciprocity in Sharing," *Child Development*, 41 (March), 243-252.

Wildock, Thomas (2004), "Sharing by Default: Outline of an Anthropology of Virtue," *Anthropological Theory*, 4 (1), 53-70.

# The Influence of the Entertainment Industry on the Perception of Ethics

Arne Baruca, UTPA, USA
Greg Selber, UTPA, USA

Historically, different philosophies presented the perception of what is moral or immoral differently. Utilitarians, represented by Mill, argue that the morality right action is the one that provides the most happiness for all those affected of actions. Kant on the other hand, argues that action have moral worth only when we act from duty (Shaw, 2008). Nowadays, even though some people developed genuine moral principles, they act differently in different occasions. Thus, it is not unusual to encounter an individual that finds it immoral to copy a hard copy of a book, but yet, uses the internet to download a pirate electronic version of the same books. The question is why double moral standards? Why people behave differently when faced with similar phenomena, but yet different occasions? In accordance with the cultivation theory we argue that the entertainment industry helps to shape the moral standards of today's society. The main goal of the present research is to shed the light on the effects that the entertainment industry has on the perception of what is moral or immoral for the consumers of that industry.

People are bombarded with messages daily and as Snyder (2008) noted the advertising industry spends 200 billions annually. That is the industry that practically largely funds our entertainment, and programming and informs consumers about products and services (Snyder, 2008). Therefore through constant mass communication certain truths are seen differently. To be more precise, we believe that in accordance with cultivation theory (Morgan and Shanahan ,1996) the constant exposure to communication of certain fabricated realities, like TV commercials, TV shows, and so forth, people somehow change their moral standards. A possible example of such phenomena is a comparison study of Zimmerman and Dahlberg (2008) where their result suggested that females do agree that female bodies were portrayed as sex objects in advertisement, but females nowadays are less offended about these portrayals than females in 1991.

As explained before, people have double moral standards when it comes to the same ethical dilemmas. Sometimes they see a certain thing as immoral, but on the other time they see it as moral. One of the reasons why this happens can be found in the philosophical literature. Currently, we live in moment where humanity is moving from the modern era into the so called postmodern era.

The modern era is categorized as an ordinate era. An era, where we as humans have better plans for the future. Humans work today, for benefits they would have in the future. Everything must have a plan and everything is under control. On the other hand, the postmodern society wants to have a meaning right away. Nothing is seen as the "best" thing, the difference is appreciated, and pretty much everything goes. Live now, and do not wait for tomorrow. Post-modernity is chaotic, and so are the people who live in it (Firat and Dholakia, 1998). Fragmentation and consequently multiple (fragmented) personalities are one of the most representative descriptions of post-modernity (Firat and Dholakia, 1998). Each person has a different role at different points in time. The fragmentation can also be a reasonable explanation, why certain actions are explained differently in different occasions. The morality of the situation depends from the role people play at a specific moment.

Howver, the process of the ethics change can be analyzed through the *change equation model*. The Change Equation model borrows from Hegel and McLuhan (1989) along with the Social Change Model of Leadership Development created in 1996 by the Higher Education Research Institute of UCLA in an effort to enhance student learning and facilitate positive social change. Hegel's notion of the dialectic argues that each action will eventually receive a reaction, creating a new reality. In terms of the Change Equation, public opinion can be seen to be affected by the reception and perception of media messages, whereby the original idea becomes an opinion which is altered by media exposure into a new opinion, often publically mediated and perceived. Institutions such as mass media or government act as mediating devices for the change, and the key here is for everyday citizens to grab ahold of the mechanism themselves through various means such as involvement in public affairs, publication of ideas, or feedback using interactivity offered on the Internet, i.e. message boards.

Change is achieved as a matter of course due to the dialectical process; whoever controls the power of discourse can guide the perceptions that become new public opinion. McLuhan stated that each new communication technology alters the previous ones, but he was less optimistic that citizens would able to harness the power of electronic technology, mainly due to the constant distraction such innovation visits on its users.

The Change Equation therefore describes the mechanics of how ideas turn into action, through a mediating device. It combines the structure of Hegel's dialectic with the electronic dimension McLuhan wrote about and adapts the UCLA model to show how normal citizens not connected with media or government can raise awareness, be active manipulators of message reception and perception, and implement social change agendas by getting out in front of the process and becoming active users with a goal in mind. Therefore, the model consists of six parts; *the thought, the idea, the discourse, power, institution and finally the change*. Each part of the model is analyzed for the case of the entertainment industry, and sheds the light on how ethics of its consumers change.

To conclude, people do not generalize their moral standards, but they rather adjust them according to the situation in which they find themselves in. The main point here is that the context matters, not the deontological behavior that teaches us that we can only be right or wrong, no matter where we are. The same thing can be right in one context, but totally wrong in the other one. The dilemma is not the problem, but the context is. And if something is seen on TV, it is even easier to accept it.

**References**
Firat, A.F., & Dholakia N. (1998). Consuming People: From Political Economy to Theaters of Consumption. London, Uk: Routledge.
Higher Education Research Institute. (1996). A social change model of leadershio development: Guidebook version III. Los Angelese: The Regents of the University of California.
Johnson, S. (2005). Everything bad is good for you. Riverhead Book, New York, NY.
McLuhan, M. & Powers, B.R. (1989). The Global Village. NY:Oxford University Press.
McTaggart J.& McTaggart E. (2005) Studies in the Hegelian Dialectic. Boston: Adamant Media Corporation
Morgan, M. & Shanahan, J. (1996). Two decades of cultivation research: An appraisal and meta-analysis. In B.R. Burleson (Ed), Communication yearbook 20 (p 1 -45). Newburry Park, CA: Sage.
Shaw, W.M. (2008). Business Ethics 6th edition. Thomson Wadforth: Belmont, CA.
Snyder, W.S. (2008). The Ethical Consequences of Your Advertisement Matter. Journal of Advertising. March, 8-9.
Zimmerman, A. & Dahlber J. (2008). The Sexual Objectification of Women Advertising: A Contemporary Perspective. Journal of Advertising, March, 71-79.

# Counter-stigma and Achievement of Happiness through the Freegan Ideology

Hieu Nguyen, California State University, Long Beach, USA
Steven Chen, California State, Fullerton, USA
Sayantani Mukherjee, California State University, Long Beach, USA

## Introduction and Research Questions
The purpose of this study is to investigate how stigmatized practices that are rooted in anti-consumption ideology are different from other forms of social stigma, such as disease (Goffman 1963), obesity (Hebl and Mannix 2003), and low literacy (Adkins and Ozanne 2005), and to introduce a theory of "counter-stigma," where anti-consumption ideology is leveraged to invert the stigma into a heroic morality play, while simultaneously redirecting stigma onto mainstream culture. We also look at how voluntary participation in a stigmatized practice brings about happiness.

To investigate these issues, we focused on Freeganism, a form of activism that involves employing strategies for living based on limited participation in the conventional economy and minimized consumption. A signature practice of Freeganism is dumpster diving—reclaiming food, clothes and other basic needs from dumpsters. For mainstream culture, consuming used, disposed goods and food past the date of expiration is associated with dirtiness, health risks and lower class status (Sen and Block 2008)—a stigma. But for freegans, dumpster diving is central to their freeganism beliefs emphasizing the message that much of what mainstream consumers consider "waste" is still usable, edible goods.

**Relevant Literature**

Stigma, often examined under the guise of a birth defect or medical condition, is a deeply discrediting attribute that makes the stigmatized individual de-valued by others (Goffman 1963). However, stigma could also result from ingrained cultural beliefs about practices and attributes that are unacceptable by mainstream culture (Sandickci and Ger 2010) such as low literacy (Adkins and Ozanne 2005), living in a mobile home (Kusenbach 2009), obesity (Hebl and Mannix 2003) and sexual orientation (Neuberg et al. 1994). Thus, to mitigate or avoid problematic encounters with mainstream culture, stigmatized individuals often adopt stigma management strategies such as avoidance of contact, defensive cowering, hostile bravado, masking, and identity ambivalence (Adkins and Ozanne 2005; Goffman 1963; Kusenbach 2009; Rochlen et al. 2008).

While these studies offer insights into social stigma and stigma management strategies, there is little research that 1) investigates an instance of social stigma where the stigmatized practice is voluntary and ideologically motivated; 2) examines instances where the stigma is redirected to the mainstream culture, thereby cleansing itself of the taint; and 3) studies social stigma that results in subjective positive outcomes.

**Methodology**

To address these areas of inquiry, we conducted an ethnographic study on the Freegan community. We conducted long interviews with eight freegans in Los Angeles, Chicago, New York City and London. We also engaged in participant observation of freegan dumpster dives, community meetups, and online discussion forums over a one year period. All interview transcripts, photography and ethnographers' notes were converted to text and subjected to the three iterative stages of grounded theory—open, axial, and selective coding.

**Findings**

Findings revealed that Freeganism practices represent a unique form of social stigma that is voluntary and politically and morally motivated. Specifically, freeganism is founded on three ideological principles: anti-capitalism, spirituality of nature, and the ethic of sharing. These ideological principles inform the unique practices of freegans, which include dumpster diving, dispossession, squatting/rent-free housing, and voluntary joblessness.

Second, we found evidence of "counter stigma," when freegans leverage their ideology to invert the stigma of waste onto mainstream consumers. While mainstream consumers see *consuming waste* as a tainted practice, Freegans view *being wasteful* as the stigmatized practice. Findings revealed that the stigma of "eating trash" was inverted into a heroic morality play through three important processes germane to the Freegan practice: de-branding marketplace resources, reclaiming and reusing disposed marketplace resources, and sharing reclaimed resources within communities and anyone else who need them.

Finally, by enacting their heroic morality play centered on waste reduction, living on less, and sharing, Freeganism provided its devotees with a vehicle to achieve happiness. In their quest to save Mother Nature from an overconsumption society, freegans become moral saviors who have shredded themselves of the mundane needs often encouraged by marketers. They achieve a heightened sense of self-actualization and self-liberation which leads to a unique sense of happiness, one not based on possession and consumption but moral purity.

**Discussion**

In this research, we examine social stigma that is voluntarily adopted by consumers within the context of "freeganism". By doing so, we add to existing research, which has primarily focused on different forms of stigma of which individuals have little locus of control or choice. These are often attached to biological or cultural situations such as disease (Goffman 1963), sexual orientation (Hebl and Mannix 2003), or courtesy stigma (Argo and Main 2008),

Second, we introduce a theory of counter-stigma that is distinct from theories of stigma management and theories of de-stigmatization. Stigma management assumes that the stigmatized individual acknowledges his or her discredited status (Adkins and Ozanne 2005; Henry and Caldwell 2006), and takes actions to reduce problematic encounters with mainstream culture. De-stigmatization occurs when the taint of a stigmatized practice gets naturalized or erased through routine exposure over time (Sandickci and Ger 2010). However, our examination of the freegans revealed that they did not merely "cope" with the stigma, nor did the stigma get naturalized. Indeed, freegans not only acknowledged the stigma associated with practices such as dumpster-diving, but also reframed the stigma into a heroic practice linked to conservation, sharing and saving the world-that is they transformed the stigma into a "heroic morality play" (Luedicke, Thompson and Giesler 2010). Importantly freegans engaged in a form of "counter-stigma", whereby they redirected the stigma of waste(fullness) onto the mainstream consumer culture.

Third, our findings provide evidence where a stigmatized practice serves as a vehicle to help individuals achieve self-actualization and happiness. This finding is novel, because past research has stressed the negative outcomes of social stigma, which include alienation, shame, self-hate and self-derogation (Goffman 1963). Social stigma also has been shown to negatively impact self-esteem (Brenda 2006; Crocker 1999; Crocker and Quinn 2003; Twenge and Crocker 2002), academic achievement (McCown and Weinstein 2003), and health (American Heart Association 2003).

Finally, our findings provide an ideological perspective as to why people consume past expired goods. Strong sentiments of anti-capitalism, moral responsibility to save the earth from an overconsumption society, and self-liberation underlie Dumpster diving. This understanding contributes to existing research that posit economic theories (e.g. sunk cost, search cost) and psychological theories (endowment effect) to explain why consumers will consume goods past the date of expiration (Sen and Block 2008).

## References

Adkins, Natalie R. and Julie L. Ozanne (2005), "The Low Literate Consumer," *Journal of Consumer Research*, 32 (June), 93-106.

American Heart Association (2003). *Stroke risk factors*. Http://www.americanheart.org/presenter.jhtml?identifier=237.

Argo, Jennifer J. and Kelley J. Main (2008), "Stigma by Association in coupon Redemption: Looking Cheap Because of Others," *Journal of Consumer Research*, 35 (December), 559-572.

Ashforth, Blake E., Glen E. Kreiner, Mark A. Clark, and Mel Fugate (forthcoming), "Normalizing Dirty Work: Managerial Tactics for Countering Occupational Taint," *Academy of Management Journal*.

Crocker, Jennifer (1999), "Social Stigma and Self-esteem: Situational Construction of Self-worth," *Journal of Experimental Social Psychology*, 35(1), 89-107.

Crocker, Jennifer and Dianne M. Quinn (2003), "Social Stigmas and The Self: Meanings, Situations, and Self-esteem," in *The Social Psychology of Stigma*, ed. Todd F. Heatherton, Robert E. Kleck, Michelle R. Helb, and Jay G. Hull, New York: Guilford, 153-83.

Goffman, Erving (1963), *Stigma: Notes on The Management of Spoiled Identity*, New York: Simon & Schuster.

Hebl, Michelle and Laura M. Mannix (2003), "The Weight of Obesity in Evaluating Others: A Mere Proximity Effect," *Personality and Social Psychology Bulletin*, 29(1), 28-38.

Henry, Paul C. and Mary L. Caldwell (2006), "Self-Empowerment and Consumption: Consumer Remedies for Prolonged Stigmatization," *European Journal of Marketing*, 40 (9-10), 1031-48.

Kusenbach, Margarethe (2009), "Salvaging Decency: Mobile Home Residents' Strategies of Managing the Stigma of 'Trailer' Living," *Qualitative Sociology*, 32, 399-428.

Luedicke, Marius K., Craig J. Thompson and Markus Giesler (2010), "Consumer Identity Work as Moral Protagonism: How Myth and Ideology Animate a Brand-Mediated Moral Conflict," *Journal of Consumer Research*, 36 (April), forthcoming.

Major, Brenda (2006), "New Perspectives on Stigma and Psychological Well-being," in S. Levin & C. van Laar (Ed.), Stigma and Group Inequality: Social Psychological Perspectives, (193-210), Mahwah, NJ: Erlbaum.

McKown Clark, and Rhona S. Weinstein (2003), "The Development Consequences of Stereotyped Consciousness in Middle Childhood," *Child development*, 74, 498-515.

Neuberg, Steven L., Dylan M. Smith, Honna C. Hoffman and Frank J. Russell (1994), "When We Observe Stigmatized and 'Normal' Individuals Interacting: Stigma by Association," *Personality and Social Psychology Bulletin*, 20 (2), 196-209.

Rochlen, Aaron B., Marie-Anne Suizzo, Ryan A. McKelley and Vanessa Scaringi (2008), "I'm Just Providing for My Family": A Qualitiative Study of Stay-at-home Fathers," *Psychology of Men and Masculinity*, 9 (4), 193-206.

Sandikci, Ozlem and Guliz Ger (2010), "Veiling in Style: How Does a Stigmatized Practice Become Fashionable?," *Journal of Consumer Research*, 37 (June), forthcoming.

Sen, Sankar and Lauren G. Block (2008), " 'Why My Mother Never Threw Anything Out': The Effect of Product Freshness on Consumption," *Journal of Consumer Research*, 36 (June), 47-55.

Twenge, Jean and Jennifer Crocker (2002, "Race and self-esteem: Meta-analyses Comparing Whites, Blacks, Hispanics, Asians and American Indians and a commentary on Gray-Little and Hafdahl (2000)", *Psychological Bulletin*, 128, 371-408.

# Anticipate, Go Big, Enjoy, Repeat:
## Towards an Optimal Consumption Strategy and Well-Being

Michael Lowe, Texas A&M University, USA
Kelly Haws, Texas A&M University, USA

## Extended Abstract

*"Happiness is the meaning and the purpose of life, the whole aim and end of human existence"–Aristotle*

The ultimate "big picture" of understanding consumer behavior is understanding what maximizes well-being of both individual consumers and society. If we accept happiness as the aim of human existence, it is an enduring obligation to examine the role of marketers in either contributing to or detracting from this goal. It should be troublesome to any in the field of marketing that accusations continue to be raised regarding marketing's detraction from happiness through the promoting of a hedonistic and materialistic society. Marketers, in turn, defend their trade by pointing to the other end of the spectrum where sub-optimal happiness prevails because human needs or desires are left unaddressed (Diener 2000; Haws and Poynor 2008). Similarly, while researchers have contributed much to the understanding of how exercising self-control can lead to more positive long-term outcomes, there is also evidence to suggest that becoming overly focused on future outcomes results in lower overall enjoyment of life (Haws and Poynor 2008; Keinan and Kivetz 2006; Rick et al. 2008).

Research has shown that high levels of consumption do not promote happiness, and the two may actually be negatively correlated (Csikszentmihalyi and Schneider 2000; Diener 2000; Myers 2000). However, research has also illustrated the detrimental effects of the inability (or failure) to consume at sufficient levels to ensure happiness (Diener 2000; Haws and Poynor 2008). There are inherent costs and benefits to consumption, and this relationship is apparently quadratic in nature. This realization, supported by further research, led Csikszentmihalyi (2000) to pose the following; "Up to a certain point, material resources add greatly to the quality of life. *But where is the point of inflection after which the relationship may no longer exist, or actually become negative?"* (Italics added) This is a question we seek to answer in this research.

As such, we build on past research that shows engaging in experiences rather than buying material goods enhances happiness (Van Boven and Gilovich 2003; Mogilner and Aaker 2009), while spending money on others seems to have a more positive boost on happiness than does spending money on ourselves (Dunn et al. 2008, Harbaugh et al. 2007; McGowan 2006).

While our objectives of learning more about what might generally represent optimal patterns of consumption are admittedly lofty, we begin our research by trying to understand what consumers believe will make them the happiest. This investigations into the intuitions of consumers is consistent with recent perspectives in consumer research examining lay theories (Mukhopadhyay and Johar 2005; Labroo and Mukhopadhyay 2009). For our initial investigation, we have focused specifically on understanding the role of frequency and magnitude of indulgent types of consumption. We will briefly report the results of two studies. Further studies are in progress.

In study 1, we examine beliefs about happiness relating to consumption frequency (i.e., often vs. rarely), and magnitude of consumption experience (relatively smaller vs. larger). We also separately examined beliefs about consuming goods and experiences. Respondents who were undergraduate students (n=109) were presented two hypothetical situations (counterbalanced), each of which utilized a projective technique to try to capture beliefs about the relationship between consumption decisions and happiness. The first situation featured two individuals deciding how to spend vacation days (experience) under constrained resources (time). Respondents strongly agreed that the individual who took one larger vacation rather than an equivalent amount of smaller vacations would be happier with the vacation usage itself (p<.051), but that the individual using his vacation time in smaller, more frequent increments would be happier with his life overall (p<.001). As such, we see evidence for the general predictions of prospect theory (Tversky and Kahneman 1979) when segregating positive experiences increases overall happiness, but the larger vacation may have a more lasting impact in terms of long-term happiness. The second situation examined the use of another constrained resource, money, and the consumption of indulgent material goods. Two hypothetical individuals facing the same constraint decided between saving up for an infrequent, larger indulgence or spreading out indulgences in smaller, more frequent intervals. Results showed that restraint followed by a large, planned indulgence was expected to lead to greater happiness with the expenditure (p<.001), lower guilt over the indulgence (p<.001) and overall greater life happiness (p=.01) than would spending on a series of smaller indulgences. These results highlight the psychological benefits associated with the anticipation of positive consumption experiences (Caplin and Leahy 2001; Loewenstein 1987), as waiting for one larger good enhanced estimates of happiness.

In study 2, we used a critical incidence technique by asking participants (n=122) to recall a recent indulgence of their own by providing instructions between subjects for one of four conditions representing a 2 (size of indulgence: small or large) X 2 (type of indulgence: good or experience). After describing the indulgence, participants were asked about how long their happiness related to the indulgence lasted. Also, we asked participants to indicate the level of planning that had gone into their consumption decision. A 2 X 2 ANOVA indicate an interaction between product type and magnitude of consumption. Mean value suggested that happiness had latest longest when consumers were asked to consider large purchases of material goods. Further, the level of planning that went into such purchases appeared to be driving these effects, suggesting the benefits associated with anticipating such a purchase may have cause the resulting happiness to last longer. These results provide support consistent with the second part of study 1.

Overall, understanding the factors that enhance consumer happiness and well-being is an important part of understanding the big picture of what we as consumer researchers are seeking to understanding. What and who we spend our time and money on, how often and in what amounts, and the amount of planning we put into our decisions can all impact are ultimate enjoyment of consumption, and we present a small step in enhancing this understanding.

# Materialism and Affective Forecasting Error: Implications for Subjective Well-Being

Miguel Hernandez, The University of Texas at San Antonio, USA
Ashley Rae Arsena, The University of Texas at San Antonio, USA
Jaehoon Lee, The University of Texas at San Antonio, USA
L. J. Shrum, The University of Texas at San Antonio, USA

## Extended Abstract

Materialism as a construct is an area of interest in consumer research for the simple reason that materialism by definition is consumption, but with a twist. Consumption through the eyes of the materialist differs from the "norm" in that the pursuit of material possessions is more of a value to the consumer than just merely the act of acquisition to satisfy a need. The materialist views their possessions beyond their actual physical properties and designated purposes and attaches meaning to these objects beyond the scope of the non-materialist. Richins and Dawson (1992) provided a comprehensive measurement scale of materialism with three defining factors for the way material objects affect the way materialists perceive their world. In essence, materialists acquire possessions to pursue happiness, define their success and establish self-meaning in their lives.

The materialist appears to have a rigid and streamlined path to the attainment of life satisfaction, but research investigating the relation between materialism and subjective well-being has indicated that the two constructs appear to move in opposite directions (Burroughs and Rindfleisch 2002; Richins and Dawson 1992). Several hypotheses have been purported in the explanation of this inverse relation. Burroughs and Rindfleisch (2002) investigated this negative relation in the context of conflicting values, indicating that the individualistic path of the materialist conflicts with the collectivist-oriented values of family and religion, thus providing a sense of psychological tension that culminates in a reduction in subjective well-being. Richins and Dawson (1992) also indicated that this negative relation might be due in part to a lack of importance placed on interpersonal interaction with more emphasis put toward the attainment of financial success. Finally, Kasser (2002) materialists may constantly strive for more material goods with the expectation that these goods will bring happiness. However, when these expectations are unfulfilled, happiness and life satisfaction may be reduced.

The research presented here addresses the latter proposition. Specifically, we were interested in determining whether high materialists may be more likely to overestimate the happiness the acquisition of products will bring them. Such an overestimation is known as affective forecasting error (Wilson and Gilbert 2002). More specifically, when an individual makes a purchase of an item they feel will make them happy, they may overestimate how happy this item will continue to make them feel in the future. If high materialists are more prone to affective forecasting error than are low materialists, it may explain why high materialists tend to be less happy with their lives than do low materialists.

Although the affective forecasting error has the potential to explain the negative relation between materialism and life satisfaction, there is also reason to think that high materialists may be more accurate than low materialists. Because products likely play a more central role in the lives of high materialists than low materialists, high materialists may be more involved with their purchases and the benefits that products may bring them. If so, then high materialists should actually be better calibrated than low materialists, and thus exhibit less affective forecasting error.

The current studies test these competing hypotheses. In study 1, participants were given the opportunity to be both predictors and experiencers for a list of several hedonic products and utilitarian products. The difference between the ratings of the predictors and experiencers served as the dependent variable and level of materialism (centrality dimension; Richins and Dawson 1992) was a measured independent variable. Individuals scoring in the top and bottom third of the distribution were used to maximize differentiation on materialism. The results indicate that high materialists showed no significant affective forecasting error, whereas low materialists did, suggesting that high materialists were more accurate in their forecasts. In study 2 (in progress), we further test these results in a within subjects, longitudinal design.

## References

Burroughs, James E. and Rindfleisch, Aric (2002), "Materialism and Well–Being: A Conflicting Values Perspective," *Journal of Consumer Research*, 29 (December), 348-70.

Gilbert, Daniel T., Gill, Michael J. and Wilson, Timothy D. (2002), "The Future is Now: Temporal Correction in Affective Forecasting," *Organizational Behavior and Human Decision Processes*, 88 (May), 430-44.

Kasser, Tim (2002), *The High Price of Materialism*, Cambridge, MA: MIT Press.

Richins, Marsha L. and Dawson, Scott (1992), "A Consumer Values Orientation for Materialism and Its Measurement: Scale Development and Validation," *Journal of Consumer Research*, 19 (December), 303-16.

Wilson, Timothy D. and Daniel T. Gilbert (2005), "Affective Forecasting: Knowing What to Want," *Current Directions in Psychological Science*, 14 (3), 131-34.

# Exposure to Extreme Luxury: Effects of Well-Being

Katrien Meert, Ghent University, Belgium
Mario Pandelaere, Ghent University, Belgium

## Extended Abstract

The current paper deals with the (unintended) effect of exposure to extreme luxury on consumer well-being. We use various dependent variables that are in one way or another related to consumer well-being.

Study 1 focuses on goal pursuit, entitlement and individualism. With regard to goal pursuit, we distinguish between *extrinsic* goals (e.g. wealth, fame, image) to *intrinsic* goals (e.g. growth, relationships, community) (Ryan & Deci, 2000). Individualism also comes in two varieties (Sivadas, Bruvold & Nelson, 2008). *Horizontal individualists* do not want to stand out from a group by aiming at status or achievement. By contrast, *vertical individualists* want to be "the best" and always strive for achievement. *Entitlement* is a stable and pervasive sense that one deserves more and is entitled to more than others and is linked to a pattern of selfish and self-serving beliefs and behaviors (Campbell, Bonacci, Shelton, et al., 2004).

Common sense suggests that marketing, like exposure to luxury, can make people somewhat more extrinsically motivated, entitled or vertical individualistic. However, we believe that this common sense does not apply for exposure to *unattainable* luxury. We suggest that, in the face of unattainable luxury, consumers may engage in self-protection and downplay the importance of luxury. This may affect their goal pursuit. In particular, exposure to extreme luxury may lead consumers to attach more importance to intrinsic goals than to extrinsic ones. In addition, we propose that exposure to extreme luxury leads consumers to derogate status differences between people. Hence, we expect that exposure to extreme luxury will not affect *vertical* individualism but rather *horizontal* individualism. Finally, images of extreme luxury may lead to the realization that life does not give you what you want all the time. This may, in turn, lead to a decreased sense of entitlement.

Study 1 was set up as an online survey to provide test of the hypotheses. 194 participants were asked to indicate on a 9-point Likert scale how much they wanted the object depicted. In the 'extreme luxury' condition, participants rated thirty extreme luxury pictures (e.g. master bedroom with spectacular view, private jet, private sauna); in the 'functional' condition, they rated thirty photos depicting functional products (e.g. rolling pin, hammer, ballpoint, calculator). Participants were randomly assigned to one of the two conditions. The order of the pictures (who were all pretested) was counterbalanced across participants. After this manipulation, our dependent measures were administered, namely *motivation* (Vansteenkiste & Lens, 2006), *entitlement* (Campbell et al., 2004) and *individualism* (Sivadas et al., 2008).

First, our manipulation proved to be successful. Respondents' mean scores of how much they wanted the object depicted differed significantly between the two conditions.

Second, results confirmed our predictions and showed that participants who were exposed to extreme luxury received a lower entitlement score and were more intrinsically motivated than participants in the functional condition. Moreover, a significant interaction effect between condition (extreme luxury/functionality) and individualism (vertical/horizontal) showed no difference for horizontal individualism, but a significant lower score for vertical individualism after exposure to extreme luxury.

In study 2, we focus on goal pursuit, materialism, and willingness-to-pay for luxury items. 136 students participated in a lab study. To manipulate 'extreme luxury' versus 'functionality', respondents had to decorate respectively a residence versus a small house. Therefore, they received a paper floor plan and three paper photos with possible interiors per room to choose from (either luxury interiors or not). Participants had to place their choice of interior on the right room of the floor plan to really make them involved in the task. During the experiment, a manipulation boost was used: participants had to choose additional products from a list to use in their newly decorated house (e.g. surround system, 150" plasma TV versus watering can, garbage can). We measured goal pursuit as in Study 1, materialism using Belk's (1985) scale, and willingness-to-pay for a room in a luxury hotel.

Again, our manipulation proved successful. As in study 1, exposure to luxury caused the importance of intrinsic values to increase. Exposure to luxury also affected materialism, albeit in a rather complex fashion. On the one hand, envy increased in the luxury condition compared to the functional condition. This is consistent with the finding that the possession of anything desirable by another person can cause one to feel envy (Schoeck, 1966). After all, the extreme luxury images signals the wealth others may have but is out of reach for the ordinary consumer. On the other hand, exposure to extreme luxury decreased the importance one attached to one's possessions. Possibly, individuals devaluate the importance of their own possessions after repeated exposure to extreme luxury. Although possessiveness and envy are typically positively related, the opposing effect of exposure to luxury causes the relation to become nonsignificant. Still, both increased envy and decreased possessiveness may signal a diminished satisfaction with life. Finally, after exposure to extreme luxury, people were willing to pay more for a given luxury room in a hotel. This implies that when people visit a website to book a room in a luxury hotel, they would pay more after seeing luxury pages on the internet.

In two studies we found evidence that exposure to luxury may threaten consumers' well-being. They feel more envy and think their possessions are worth less. The decreased entitlement seems to suggest that they become more accepting of huge differences in wealth and income. To cope, consumers may increase the value they attach to intrinsic goals. Additional research is needed to further investigate the effect of exposure to luxury on well-being. For instance, what will happen when regarding attainable luxury instead of unattainable luxury? Moreover, this research project will be expanded as we intend to include regulatory focus as a potential moderator because luxury aspects receive more attention when in a promotion focus than in a prevention focus (Werth & Foerster, 2007).

## References

Belk, R.W. (1985). Materialism: Trait Aspects of Living in the Material World. Journal of Consumer Research, 12 (3), 265-280.

Campbell, W.K., Bonacci, A.M., Shelton, J. et al. (2004). Psychological Entitlement: Interpersonal Consequences and Validation of a Self-Report Measure. Journal of Personality Assessment, 83 (1), 29-45.

Nelson, M.R. & Shavitt S. (2002). Horizontal and Vertical Individualism and Achievement Values. Journal of Cross-Cultural Psychology, 33 (5), 439-458.

Ryan, R.M. & Deci, E.L. (2000). Self-Determination Theory and the Facilitation of Intrinsic Motivation, Social Development, and Well-Being. American Psychologist, 55 (1), 68-78.

Schoeck, H. (1966). Envy: A Theory of Social Behavior, trans. Michael Glennyard and Betty Ross, New York: Harcourt, Brace and World.

Sivadas, E., Bruvold, N.T. & Nelson, M.R. (2008). A Reduced Version of the Horizontal and Vertical Individualism and Collectivism Scale: A Four-Country Assessment. Journal of Business Research, 61 (3), 201-210.

Vansteenkiste, M. & Lens, W. (2006). Intrinsic versus Extrinsic Goal Contents in Self-Determination Theory: Another Look at the Quality of Academic Motivation. Educational Psychologist, 41 (1), 19-31.

Werth, L. & Foerster, J. (2007). How Regulatory Focus influences Consumer Behavior. European Journal of Social Psychology, 37 (1), 33-51.

# The Effects of Desire: Desire as Motivator

Mario Pandelaere, Ghent University, Belgium
Maarten Elen, Ghent University, Belgium
Christophe Lembregts, Ghent University, Belgium
Katrien Meert, Ghent University, Belgium
Tina Tessitore, Ghent University, Belgium

## Extended Abstract

The current paper deals with the effect of desire on a person's self-esteem, subjective happiness and satisfaction with life.

Desire is an important determinant of contemporary consumption. Consumer culture constantly exposes people to a stream of advertisements for goods. Consequently, people participating in consumer culture are continuously encouraged to desire goods. Due to this constant promotion of desire in consumer culture, it is useful to examine the consequences. Belk, Ger and Askegaard (2003) found that desire was seen by consumers as a powerful positive affective state that is both uncomfortable and pleasant. Additionally, perceived discrepancies between a current and a desired state lead to a decrease in satisfaction with life (Michalos, 1985; Solberg, Diener, Wirtz, Lucas & Oishi, 2002). For instance, Brown, Kasser, Ryan, Linley and Orzech (2009) found that a financial desire discrepancy was inversely related to satisfaction with life. In this study we further examine the consequences of desiring goods. First, when confronted with a desire, we predict that self-esteem will rise. This increase is needed for the achievement of a desire. Here, self-esteem works as a functional resource from which one can draw. Hence, we expect a positive effect of desire on self-esteem (Hypothesis 1). Next to an increase in self-esteem, a positive effect of desire on subjective happiness (Lyubomirsky & Lepper, 1999) is expected (Hypothesis 2). When one desires something, this generally generates positive affective feelings. Possibly these positive feelings are transferred to an overall feeling of subjective happiness. Contrary to satisfaction with life, which gauges more to the cognitive component of happiness, subjective happiness assesses the more affective part of happiness. Simultaneously, we expect a decrease in satisfaction with life (Hypothesis 3). Desiring something also means that something is missing in life, so when people realize this, a decrease in satisfaction with life can be foreseen. It has already been shown that the discrepancy between what people actually have and what they want leads to a decrease in satisfaction with life (Larsen & McKibban, 2008; Solberg et al, 2002).

To test these hypotheses, a first online study was set up. A total of 81 respondents participated in an online experiment. First, the participants' feelings of desire were manipulated. One group of subjects (i.e. 'desire condition') were exposed to thirty desirable pictures (e.g. palm tree, cruise ship, etc...), whereas another group of subjects (i.e. 'no desire condition') were shown undesirable pictures (e.g. pen, calculator, etc...). As a manipulation check, respondents reported on a scale from 0 to 100 how much they desired what was shown in each picture. After this manipulation, our dependent measures were administered, namely self-esteem (Rosenberg, 1965), satisfaction with life (Diener, Emmons, Larsen & Griffin, 1985) and subjective happiness (Lyubomirsky & Lepper, 1999).

First, our manipulation proved to be successful. Respondents' mean desire scores differed significantly between the two conditions $(F(1,79)=80.482, p<.001)$. Second, results revealed a significant main effect of condition on self-esteem $(F(1,79)=5.711, p=.019)$. Subjects who were exposed to desirable pictures scored significantly higher on self-esteem than subjects who were shown undesirable pictures, hence supporting hypothesis 1. Third, also subjective happiness differed significantly across groups $(F(1,79)=3.966, p<.05)$. Respondents from the 'desire condition' reported to be significantly happier than respondents from the 'no desire condition'. Thus, the second hypothesis was supported by the data. Fourth, concerning satisfaction with life, no significances were found. Hence, we found no support for the third hypothesis.

Therefore, in study 2, we focused only on satisfaction with life. 75 subjects participated in a lab study. To manipulate desire, one group of participants was asked to imagine themselves organizing a world trip. Each participant had to situate twelve pictures of desirable destinations in order of preference on a world map. The second group of participants was given a similar task, with the exception that it concerned a regional trip. Moreover, the twelve destinations were less desirable (all material was pretested).

Again, our manipulation proved to be successful. Respondents' mean desire scores differed significantly between the two conditions $(F(1,72)=14.403, p<.001)$. Furthermore, results revealed a marginal significant effect of desire on satisfaction with life, hence marginally supporting the third hypothesis. People who organized the regional trip were more satisfied with their lives than people who organized the world trip $(F(1,72)=1.178, p=.084)$. Probably, organizing (and actually undertaking) a world trip might seem unattainable, which produces a discrepancy between an actual and a desired state, entailing an effect on people's satisfaction with life.

In two studies we found evidence that desire has implications on one's self-esteem, subjective happiness and satisfaction with life. When consumers are confronted with a feeling of desire, they get a higher self-esteem, feel happier, but are less satisfied with their lives.

Additional research is needed to further investigate the effect of desire on previous discussed dependent variables, especially satisfaction with life, because of its marginally significance. Besides, other dependent variables might be considered as well. For instance, what will be the effect of desire on risk-taking behavior? Probably, consumers who are confronted with a higher self-esteem, due to desire, might be more risk-taking than consumers without an induced feeling of desire.

**References**

Belk, R.W., Ger, G., Askegaard, S. (2003). The fire of desire: A multisited inquiry into consumer passion. *Journal of Consumer Research, 30*(3), 326-351.

Brown, K.W., Kasser, T., Ryan, R.M., Linley, P.A., & Orzech, K. (2009). When what one has enough: Mindfulness, financial desire discrepancy and subjective well-being. *Journal of Research in Personality, 43*(5), 727-736.

Diener, E., Emmons, R.A., Larsen, R.J., & Griffin, S. (1985). The satisfaction with life scale. *Journal of Personality Assessment*, 49, 71-75.

Larsen, J..T., & McKibban, A.R. (2008) Is happiness having what you want, wanting what you have or both? *Psychological Science, 19*(4), 371-377.

Lyubomirsky, S. & Lepper, H.S. (1999). A measure of subjective happiness: Preliminary reliability and construct validation. *Social Indicators Research, 46*(2), 137-155.

Michalos, A. C. (1985). Multiple discrepancies theory (MDT). *Social Indicators Research*, 16, 347–413.

Rosenberg, M. (1965). Society and the adolescent self-image. Princeton, NJ: Princeton University Press.

Solberg, E. C., Diener, E., Wirtz, D., Lucas, R. E., & Oishi, S. (2002). Wanting, having, and satisfaction: Examining the role of desire discrepancies in satisfaction with income. *Journal of Personality and Social Psychology*, 83, 725–734.

Watson, D., Clark, L. A., & Tellegen, A. (1988). Development and validation of brief measures of positive and negative affect: The PANAS scale. *Journal of Personality and Social Psychology*, 54, 1063-1070.

# Ovulatory Cycle Effects on Women's Attention to High-Status Products

Inge Lens, K. U. Leuven, Belgium
Karolien Driesmans, K. U. Leuven, Belgium
Luk Warlop, Catholic University Leuven, Belgium
Mario Pandelaere, Ghent University, Belgium

## Extended Abstract

An important life-goal of many species, including humans, is to find an appropriate sexual partner. A number of studies have shown that a woman benefits from selecting a mate with strong genes, who is also willing and able to invest in her and her children (Bjorklund and Shackelford 1999; Brase 2006). Consequently, women are attracted to men with social status and sufficient financial resources (e.g., Li et al. 2002). In response to this, men in a mating-mindset show an increased intention to spend money on luxury products (Griskevicius et al. 2007). Various studies found that women's mating motivations change or increase during the most fertile period of their monthly cycle. For instance, near ovulation women are attracted to more masculine, taller and more socially dominant men (Gangestad, Thornhill, and Garver-Apgar 2005) and they are willing to pay more for products that increase their attractiveness (Hill and Durante 2009). These findings suggest that around ovulation women are more receptive to stimuli that highlight the qualities of a potential mate (mate selection) and are more willing to attract a suitable sexual partner (mate attraction). With respect to the mate selection goal, most research focused on menstrual cycle effects on women's interest in physical signs of genetic quality. Only few studies investigated cycle effects on the appreciation of mate values related to investment capacity (e.g., Gangestad et al. 2007). We aim to fill this gap, yet we focus on attention to material signs of status (i.e., high-status products), rather than on the appreciation of males carrying these products. In particular, we test whether ovulating women pay more attention to status products, even in the absence of an explicit mating context (i.e., without potential partner present). In addition, we test whether attention to high-status products is predicted by levels of estrogen (positively) and progesterone (negatively), consistent with previous findings that hormones underlie menstrual cycle effects on mate preferences (e.g., Lukaszewski and Roney 2009; Roney and Simmons 2008). For women using hormonal contraceptives, such as the Pill, no effect of cycle phase is expected as Pill usage suppresses the regular flow of female hormones. Therefore, Pill use is expected to moderate the effect of cycle phase on attention to high-status products.

In a (quasi)experiment, 124 Pill users and 38 normally cycling women ($M_{age}$=22.34) were exposed to ten computerized, visual displays consisting of six products (cf. Roskos-Ewoldsen and Fazio 1992). One product in each display was a high-status product (expensive car, exclusive watch,…), the remaining five products were low-status products (bucket, umbrella,…). A pretest confirmed that high-status products were perceived to be more prestigious than low-status products, $t(57)$=-17.2, $p<.001$. Exposure to each display lasted one second after which participants had 20 seconds to write down the objects they had noticed. The dependent variable used in further analyses is the absolute number, as well as the proportion of listed high-status products (taking into account the total number of products listed). We also calculated a score indicating the position of each high-status product in the list of recalled items for each display. Higher scores indicate quicker recall/more attention.

Next, participants indicated whether they take a contraceptive Pill or other hormone based medicine. Subsequently, they reported the start of their last menstruation (cycle day 1). We divided participants in three groups: Participants in days 1-5 are in the menstrual phase (9 normally cycling women, 23 Pill users), participants in days 9-15 are in the fertile phase (11 normally cycling women, 25 Pill users) and participants in days 18-28 are in the luteal phase (12 normally cycling women, 47 Pill users). We dropped participants who were in the ambiguous zones between two phases (cf. Miller, Tybur, and Jordan 2007) or who reported an unusual cycle length. Finally, based on the cycle day we estimated levels of estrogen and progesterone in normally cycling participants (cf. Martin and Behbehani 2006).

Empirical evidence confirms our predictions. For normally cycling women cycle phase has a significant effect on the absolute number, $F(2, 29)$=7.14, $p$=.003, and proportion of listed high-status products, $F(2, 29)$=8.32, $p$=.001. Women around ovulation notice more high-status products than women in other phases do, consistent with the notion that the activation of a goal (e.g., mate selection goal) directs attention to goal-consistent stimuli (Moskowitz 2002). In addition, high-status products are recalled quicker during ovulation than during other phases, $F(2, 29)$=7.63, $p$=.002. As expected, Pill use moderates the effect of cycle phase on the absolute number, $F(2, 121)$=5.07, $p$=.008, and proportion of listed high-status products, $F(2, 121)$=5.51, $p$=.005, as well as on the position of the listed high-status products, $F(2, 121)$=3.79, $p$=.03. In all cases, attention to high-status products does not differ across the cycle for Pill users. In addition, estrogen and progesterone levels significantly influence attention to high-status products. Higher levels of estrogen lead to higher absolute, $\beta$=.85, $t(29)$=2.03, $p$=.05, and relative numbers of noticed high-status products, $\beta$=.03, $t(29)$=2.31, $p$=.03, and to quicker recall, $\beta$=.06, $t(29)$=2.07, $p$=.047. Progesterone levels are associated with smaller absolute numbers, $\beta$=-.23, $t(29)$=-2.05, $p$=.049, and proportions of listed high-status products, $\beta$=-.008, $t(29)$=-2.22, $p$=.03, and with slower recall, $\beta$=-.02, $t(29)$=-2.57, $p$=.02.

In sum, our research relates women's attention to status products to the evolutionary principles of mate selection by showing that attention to high-status products increases during days of high fertility. This finding may have interesting implications, as more diverse consumer preferences or behaviours may differ depending on hormonal fluctuations. Future research might, for instance, address whether heightened attention to luxury products during ovulation leads to increased spending intentions or willingness to pay for status products or to greater acceptance of advertising messages for luxuries.

## References

Bjorklund, David F. and Todd K. Shackelford (1999), "Differences in Parental Investment Contribute to Important Differences Between Men and Women," *Current directions in Psychological Science,* 8 (June), 86-9.

Brase, Gary L. (2006), "Cues of Parental Investment as a Factor in Attractiveness," *Evolution and Human Behavior,* 27, 145-57.

Gangestad, Steven W., Christine E. Garver-Apgar, Jeffry A. Simpson, and Alita J. Cousins, (2007), "Changes In Women's Mate Preferences Across The Cycle. *Journal of Personality and Social Psychology,* 92, 151–63.

Gangestad, Steven W., Randy Thornhill, and Christine E.Garver-Apgar, (2005), "Adaptations to Ovulation," In *Handbook of evolutionary psychology.* Ed. David M. Buss, New York: Wiley, 344–71.

Griskevicius, Vladas, Joshua M. Tybur, Jill M. Sundie, Robert B. Cialdini, Geoffrey F. Miller, and Douglas T. Kenrick (2007), "Blatant Benevolence and Conspicuous Consumption: When Romantic Motives Elicit Strategic Costly Signals," *Journal of Personality and Social Psychology,* 93 (1), 85–102.

Hill, Sarah .E. and Kristina M. Durante (2009), "Do Women Feel Worse to Look Their Best? Testing the Relationship Between Self-Esteem and Fertility Status Across the Menstrual Cycle," *Personality and Social Psychology Bulletin,* 35 (12), 1592-601.

Li, Norman P., J. Michael Bailey, Douglas T. Kenrick, and Joan A.W. Linsenmeier (2002), "The Necessities and Luxuries of Mate Preferences: Testing the Tradeoffs," *Journal of Personality and Social Psychology,* 82 (6), 947-55.

Lukaszewski, Aaron W. and James R. Roney (2009), "Estimated Hormones Predict Women's Mate Preferences for Dominant Personality Traits," *Personality and Individual Differences,* 47, 191–6.

Martin, Vincent T. and Michael Behbehani, (2006). "Ovarian Hormones and Migraine Headache: Understanding Mechanisms and Pathogenesis-Part 2," Headache, 46 (3), 365–86.

Miller, Geoffrey F., Joshua M. Tybur , and Brent D. Jordan (2007), "Ovulatory Cycle Effects on Tip Earnings by Lap Dancers: Economic Evidence for Human Estrus?" *Evolution and Human Behavior,* 28 (6), 375-81.

Moskowitz, Gordon B. (2002), "Preconscious Effects of Temporary Goals on Attention," *Journal of Experimental Social Psychology,* 38, 397-404.

Roney, James R. and Zachary L. Simmons (2008), "Women's Estradiol Predicts Preference for Facial Cues of Men's Testosterone," *Hormones and Behavior,* 53 (1), 14–9.

Roskos-Ewoldsen, David R. and Russell H. Fazio (1992), "On the Orienting Value of Attitudes: Attitude Accessibility as a Determinant of an Object's Attraction of Visual Attention," *Journal of Personality and Social Psychology,* 63 (2), 198-211.

# Testosterone and Context-Specific Risk:
# Digit Ratios as Predictors of Recreational, Financial, and Social Risk-taking

Eric Stanstrom, Concordia Univesity, Canada
Gad Saad, Concordia Univesity, Canada
Marcelo V. Nepomuceno, Concordia Univesity, Canada
Zack Mendenhall, Concordia Univesity, Canada

Consumers frequently make choices between options that entail varying degrees of risk. Whether it is within financial, recreational, or health contexts, consumers differ a great deal in their appetite for risk. While prior research has identified numerous antecedents of risk-taking proclivities (e.g., Baker and Maner 2009; Loewenstein et al. 2001; Levenson 1990), the physiological correlates of risk-taking remain relatively unexplored. We investigate the impact of testosterone on risk preferences across a variety of contexts. Specifically, we examine the association between digit length ratio (a proxy of prenatal testosterone exposure) and risk-taking behavior across financial, recreational, social, health and ethical domains.

Prenatal androgens have significant effects on brain organization and future behavior (Archer 2006; Auyeung et al. 2009; Udry 2000). This exposure also stunts the growth of the second digit relative to the other fingers. As a result, the second (index) to fourth (ring) digit length ratio (2D:4D) has been used as a proxy of exposure to prenatal testosterone (Lutchmaya et al. 2004; Manning et al. 1998). This association has spurred considerable interest in 2D:4D, which has been associated to an array of masculine traits including aggression (Bailey and Hurd 2005), athletic ability (Manning and Hill 2009), and perceived dominance (Neave et al. 2003). Even among females, a lower 2D:4D tends to predict masculine behavioral traits (Csathó et al. 2003; Paul et al. 2006).

Recent research has linked 2D:4D to financial risk-taking (Coates, Gurnell, and Rustichini 2009; Coates and Page 2009; Dreber and Hoffman 2007). However, there is a paucity of research exploring the link between digit ratio and other forms of risk-taking. Risk-taking preferences are typically assessed via a financially-related measure subsequent to which the findings are generalized to all domains of risk (i.e., one index of risk is associated equally to all risk-related contexts). While this operationalization of risk preferences is consistent with the expected utility framework and prospect theory (Kahneman and Tversky 1979), more recent research suggests that risk-taking proclivity is a domain-specific phenomenon in which an individual's risk proclivities are different across domains (Weber et al. 2002; Blais and Weber 2006; Kruger, Wang, and Wilke 2009). In other words, an individual may display a strong appetite for financial risk and a strong aversion to risk in other domains such as recreational activities or social situations. Accordingly, the current paper examines if digit ratio is predictive of risk-taking propensity across recreational, financial, social, ethical, and health domains. We propose that lower, more masculine digit ratios are predictive of riskier behaviors across all five domains among men and women.

A sample of four hundred and thirteen students completed a survey and had the lengths of all right-hand digits measured by a trained experimenter. The 2D:4D and *rel*2 (the length of the second finger relative to the sum of the lengths of all four fingers) ratios were computed for each participant. The *rel*2 ratio was included because it has recently been shown to be more accurate than 2D:4D in discriminating between males and females (Loehlin, Medland, and Martin 2008). Risk was assessed via a domain-specific risk-taking behavior scale as described in Weber, Blais and Betz (2002). Each of the five domains contained 10 five-point Likert-type items (1 to 5) assessing one's likelihood of engaging in a given risky activity (all alphas above .67). Items include "periodically engaging in a dangerous sports (e.g., mountain climbing or sky diving)" (recreational), "investing 10% of your annual income in a very speculative stock" (financial), "speaking your mind about an unpopular issue at a social occasion" (social), "shoplifting a small item (e.g., a lipstick or pen)" (ethical), and "eating 'expired' food products that still 'look okay' " (health).

To control for the potentially confounding effects of sex and ethnic heterogeneity (Manning et al. 2007), Pearson correlations between digit ratios and risk measures were performed on the following four subsamples: male Caucasians (n=130), female Caucasians (n=109), all males (n=219), and all females (n=194). In the subsample of male Caucasians, lower *rel2* was predictive of greater financial, social, and recreational risk-taking. Lower 2D:4D was predictive of greater risk-taking in two domains (social and recreational) in this group. In the full male sample (ethnically heterogeneous), the only significant correlation was a negative association between 2D:4D and financial risk. In other words, all significant correlations were in the predicted direction. Surprisingly, no significant correlations were found in the female subsamples. Finally, men were more risk-seeking than women across all five contexts.

In sum, our results indicate that prenatal testosterone exposure has organizational effects on a man's recreational, financial, and social risk-taking propensity. Furthermore, our findings suggest that future digit ratio research should account for ethnic heterogeneity and that *rel2* should be considered as a potential alternative proxy of prenatal testosterone exposure. Moreover, our study highlights the potential of using physiological markers to predict individual differences in consumer behavior. Ultimately, the digit ratio might serve as a test case for the applicability of morphological segmentation as a viable marketing strategy. Morphological segmentation might be used by marketers perhaps not to identify singular individuals but rather to create segments of similar consumers (e.g., high testosterone men), all of whom can then be targeted with tailored advertising messages and promotional campaigns.

## Selected References

Auyeung, Bonnie, Simon Baron-Cohen, Emma Ashwin, Rebecca Knickmeyer, Kevin Taylor, Gerald Hackett, and Melissa Hines (2009), "Fetal Testosterone Predicts Sexually Differentiated Childhood Behavior in Girls and in Boys," *Psychological Science*, 20 (2), 144-48.

Coates, John M., Mark Gurnell, and Aldo Rustichini (2009), "Second-to-Fourth Digit Ratio Predicts Success among High-Frequency Financial Traders," *Proceedings of the National Academy of Sciences of the United States of America*, 106 (2), 623-28.

Kahneman, Daniel and Amos Tversky (1979), "Prospect Theory: An Analysis of Decision under Risk," *Econometrica*, 47 (2), 263-91.

Levenson, Michael R. (1990), "Risk-Taking and Personality," *Journal of Personality and Social Psychology*, 58 (6), 1073-80.

Loewenstein, George F., Elke U. Weber, Christopher K. Hsee, and Ned Welch (2001), "Risk as Feelings," *Psychological Bulletin*, 127 (2), 267-86.

Manning, John T., Diane Scutt, James Wilson, and D. Iwan Lewis-Jones (1998), "The Ratio of 2nd to 4th Digit Length: A Predictor of Sperm Numbers and Concentrations of Testosterone, Luteinizing Hormone and Oestrogen," *Human Reproduction*, 13 (11), 3000-04.

Udry, J. Richard (2000), "Biological Limits of Gender Construction," *American Sociological Review*, 65 (3), 443-57.

Weber, Elke U., Ann-Renée Blais, and Nancy E. Betz (2002), "A Domain-Specific Risk-Attitude Scale: Measuring Risk Perceptions and Risk Behaviors," *Journal of Behavioral Decision Making*, 15 (4), 263-90.

# The Effects of the Menstrual Cycle on Food Appearance-related Consumption

Gad Saad, Concordia University, Canada
Eric Stenstrom, Concordia University, Canada

Consumer behavior is influenced by a wide variety of situational variables (e.g., Argo, Dahl, and Manchanda 2005). We focus on a physiologically-based situational factor unique to women, namely the menstrual cycle. Despite the mounting evidence demonstrating the profound effect that the menstrual cycle has on women's desires, preferences, and behaviors (e.g., Gangestad et al. 2007), its role in the consumption arena remains relatively unexplored. In the current work, we show that a woman's appearance- and food-related desires, product usage, and purchasing behavior are influenced by her menstrual cycle.

The menstrual cycle begins with the menstrual phase (usually days one to four of a 28-day cycle), followed by the follicular phase (days five to 14), and ending with the luteal phase (days 15 to 28). Women can only conceive during a short fertile window of roughly six days during the late follicular phase, typically occurring between days eight and 15 of a 28-day cycle. Given the evidence suggesting a late follicular peak in mating-related drives (Gangestad, Thornhill, and Garver-Apgar 2005) and associated styling behaviors (Haselton et al. 2007; Durante, Li, and Haselton 2008; Roder, Brewer, and Fink 2009), we expect that women will increase their appearance-related consumption on fertile days in order to maximise their attractiveness to potential mates at this time. Specifically, we predict that women's appearance-related desires, purchases, and product usage, will be greater during the fertile phase compared to during the luteal phase. Further, given the evidence indicating a peak in caloric intake during the luteal phase (Buffenstein et al. 1995; Fessler 2003), we expect that women's food-related desires, purchases, and consumption choices will be greater on luteal days compared to fertile days.

Fifty-nine normally cycling women who were not taking any hormonal contraceptives were asked to track their expenditures in a shopping diary and to answer online survey questions every evening for a period of 35 days. Participants were asked to complete a short survey consisting of a number of survey items every evening (denoted as survey 1) and to complete a much longer survey containing many additional items on three specific evenings (denoted as survey 2). The reported food and clothing-related Likert-type items were included in both surveys. Participants were asked to track the exact amounts of money that they had spent on food and clothing in a paper shopping diary and to indicate their totals every evening in survey 1. To assess food and appearance-related desires and product usage, participants provided ratings in surveys 1 and 2. Specifically, on a nine-point Likert-type scale anchored by -4 ("far less than usual"), 0 ("about average"), and +4 ("far more than usual"), they were requested to indicate "Over the last 24 hours, compared to most days in the last 12 months, I ..." In survey 1, desire for food was measured by "felt hungry today" and "craved highly caloric foods," whereas actual food consumption was assessed by the items "consumed calories," and "ate highly caloric foods." In survey 2, appearance-related desires were measured by the item "felt a desire to look sexy," while a variety of items assessed appearance-related product usage including "wore sexy clothes," "wore clothes that showed lots of skin," "wore a skirt," and "went sun tanning." Of the 59 women who began the 35-day study, 48 women completed survey 1 at least once each during the luteal and fertile phases, while 20 did so for survey 2. After excluding the data from 12 women who did not have regular cycles between 27 and 39 days in length and one who reported taking a hormonal contraceptive during the study, the final sample sizes were 35 participants for survey 1 (the food-related Likert-type items and the expenditures in both categories) and 17 for survey 2 (the appearance-related Likert-type items). Each participant's follicular and luteal phases were estimated based on menstruation information collected via survey 1 (i.e., "did you menstruate today?") and on subsequent post-study email correspondences.

As hypothesized, women reported feeling greater appearance-related desires and engaging in greater appearance-related product usage on fertile days than on luteal days. Despite the large mean difference in the predicted direction, there were no significant differences between the daily amount of money spent on clothing on fertile days and the amount spent on luteal days. However, a more granular split of the data revealed that women spent significantly more money during the fertile phase than during the early follicular phase. Recall that we predict the opposite menstrual cycle effect for food, such that consumption will be greater during the luteal phase than during the fertile phase. As expected, women reported feeling hungrier and stronger cravings for highly caloric foods on luteal days than on fertile days. Similarly, women in their luteal phase reported consuming more calories and more highly caloric foods compared to when they were in their fertile phase. The amounts of money that women spent on food were also significantly influenced by menstrual cycle phase, such that women reported spending significantly more money on food on luteal days than on fertile days. Mediation analyses revealed that the menstrual cycle effect on appearance-related product usage was significantly mediated by appearance-related desires. Further, food-related desires significantly mediated the menstrual cycle effects on food consumption and on food expenditures.

The obtained findings relating to actual purchases constitute the first direct economic evidence of a menstrual cycle effect on women's consumer behavior. Our research is of relevance to consumer welfare in that we are highlighting when women are most vulnerable to succumbing to cyclical temptations for high-calorie foods and appearance-enhancing products. From a managerial perspective, practitioners having access to detailed purchasing data can deduce a particular consumer's menstrual cycle phase from her food and/or clothing buying patterns and employ direct marketing strategies accordingly (e.g., send food-related promotions to consumers who are likely to be in their luteal phase). Overall, our findings add to the growing body of work at the nexus of physiology and consumer behavior (Miller, Tybur, and Jordan 2007; Plassmann, O'Doherty, Shiv, and Rangel 2008; Saad and Vongas 2009).

**Selected References**
Argo, Jennifer J., Darren W. Dahl, and Rajesh V. Manchanda (2005), "The Influence of a Mere Social Presence in a Retail Context," *Journal of Consumer Research*, 32 (2), 207-12.
Buffenstein, Rochelle, Sally. D. Poppitt, Regina M. McDevitt, & Andrew M. Prentice (1995), "Food Intake and the Menstrual Cycle: A Retrospective Analysis, with Implications for Appetite Research," *Physiology and Behavior*, 58 (6), 1067-77.
Durante, Kristina M., Norman P. Li, and Martie G. Haselton (2008), "Changes in Women's Choice of Dress across the Ovulatory Cycle: Naturalistic and Laboratory Task-Based Evidence," *Personality and Social Psychology Bulletin*, 34 (11), 1451-60.
Gangestad, Steven W., Christine E. Garver-Apgar, Jeffry A. Simpson, and Alita J. Cousins (2007), "Changes in Women's Mate Preferences across the Ovulatory Cycle," *Journal of Personality and Social Psychology*, 92 (1), 151-63.
Haselton, Martie G., Mina Mortezaie, Elizabeth G. Pillsworth, April Bleske-Rechek, and David A. Frederick (2007), "Ovulatory Shifts in Human Female Ornamentation: Near Ovulation, Women Dress to Impress," *Hormones and Behavior*, 51 (1), 40-45.
Miller, Geoffrey, Joshua M. Tybur, and Brent D. Jordan (2007), "Ovulatory Cycle Effects on Tip Earnings by Lap Dancers: Economic Evidence for Human Estrus?," *Evolution and Human Behavior*, 28 (6), 375-81.
Plassmann, Hilke, John O'Doherty, Baba Shiv, and Antonio Rangel (2008), "Marketing Actions can Modulate Neural Representations of Experienced Pleasantness," *Proceedings of the National Academy of Sciences*, 105 (3), 1050-54.
Saad, Gad and John G. Vongas (2009), "The Effect of Conspicuous Consumption on Men's Testosterone Levels," *Organizational Behavior and Human Decision Processes*, 110 (2), 80-92.

# Compulsive Buying–Also a Male Problem?

Mirja Hubert, Zeppelin University, Germany
Marco Hubert, Zeppelin University, Germany
Oliver B. Büttner, Zeppelin University, Germany
Arnd Florack, Zeppelin University, Germany
Peter Kenning, Zeppelin University, Germany

**Extended Abstract**
Compulsive Buying (CB) is a problem with increasing relevance for individuals and society. Earlier studies show that the fraction of people who exhibit a strong tendency toward CB is between 5% and 8% of the population in Western societies (Faber and O'Guinn 1992; Koran et al. 2006; Reisch, Neuner, and Raab 2004; Ridgway, Kukar-Kinney, and Monroe 2008). However, previous investigations provide evidence that between 80-95% of compulsive buyers are female (Black 2007; Faber and O'Guinn 1992; Müller and de Zwaan 2004). Remarkably, research indicates that men rarely evidence CB tendencies.

In general, compulsive buyers are prone to run into indebtedness because they are characterized by a tendency for repetitive buying with a loss of impulse control over buying (Ridgway et al. 2008). Evidence that overspending and debts are problems that often affect men more seriously than they do women (www.creditreform.de) suggests that CB is a more severe problem among men than is reflected in the current literature (Dittmar and Drury 2000, Koran et al. 2006). There are two possible reasons why CB is often not reported for men: First, excessive shopping might be more socially accepted among women. Second, the scales for measuring CB seem to be more representative for female types of shopping behavior (e.g., Ridgway et al. 2008). Thus, CB among men might be underreported and, consequently, underestimated (Koran et al. 2006; Müller et al. 2005).

Against this background, we ran two studies with male participants in order to provide new insights about CB in men. In Study 1 we applied the Implicit-Association-Test (IAT; Greenwald, McGhee, and Schwartz 1998) to examine correlations between indicators of overspending and automatically activated evaluative associations of brands of the high-price segment. In Study 2 we used fMRI (functional magnetic resonance imaging) to measure activity changes in brain areas related to reward experiences or anticipation in men with, and without, CB tendencies.

In Study 1, automatically activated evaluative associations of brands were assessed using a single target IAT (Bluemke and Friese 2008). The IAT is a response-time-based measure that can be used to assess the strength of associations between concepts (Lane et al. 2007). Our study included 28 male participants ($M_{age}$=29 years). The target category was "brands," which was represented by thirteen brand-logos assumed to be relevant for a male sample. The attribute categories were "positive" and "negative" valences, represented by a mix of pictures. The sequence of the different IAT blocks followed the standard procedure for a single target IAT (Karpinksi and Steinmann 2006). After answering a number of questions unrelated to our study, participants were asked about financial problems using two five-point rating items for the two problems of overdrawing a bank account and of settling debts. Both items showed significant correlation ($r$=.30, $p$=.06). Based on the response times of the IAT, we calculated the $D$ measure (Greenwald, Nosek, and Banaji 2003), with higher values representing more positive associations of the selected brands. As predicted, the more positive the brand associations were, the more problems with overdrawing one's account ($r$=.43, $p$<.05), and with settling one's debts ($r$=.32, $p$<.05) were reported. This result shows that adverse financial consequences of CB are correlated with positive brand associations that are activated on an automatic level.

In Study 2 we applied fMRI in order to observe these automatic processes during the perception of brands on a neural level. Taking into account that the underlying neural mechanisms of CB are still not known, we wanted to investigate whether men with CB tendencies exhibit different neural activation patterns compared to men without CB tendencies. Ten men participated in the study (age: $M$=31.2) that was executed on a 3T fMRI-scanner. Data processing and statistical analyses were conducted with SPM5 by using the General Linear Model (Huettel, Song, and McCarthy 2008). The stimulus material consisted of the same brands as in Study 1. The participants' task was to judge the brand as attractive or unattractive. After the scanning session, participants were asked to fill out a questionnaire that included a demographic information section and a 16-item scale to measure CB tendencies (Scherhorn, Reisch, and Raab, 1990). Using this scale, we classified participants as either having a tendency toward CB (TCB group, $N$=3; $M_{CBscale}$=35.67) or having no tendency toward CB (NTCB group, $N$=6; $M_{CBscale}$=27.00) (Scherhorn et al., 1990). An ANOVA confirmed significant differences between the two groups ($F$(1, 8)=32.19, $p$<.001). Based on this classification, the fMRI analysis revealed different neural activation patterns for the TCB and NTCB groups. We observed neural activity changes in, for example, the caudate, the putamen, or the amygdala. These structures are often associated with reward and emotions (Delgado et al. 2003; Haruno and Kawato 2006; O'Doherty 2004). These results suggest that the "reward system" (Dalgleish 2004; Dalgleish, Dunn, and Mobbs 2009; Elliot, Friston, and Dolan 2000; O'Doherty 2004; Phillips and Stanton 2004; Weber and Johnson 2009) might be crucial for the development of CB. The exhibited activations can be explained by increased emotional arousal and reward expectations regarding attractive brands. This is consistent with the satisfaction experience that compulsive buyers report within the buying situation (Boundy 2004, Faber 2004). Furthermore, our study reveals that male consumers who are prone to CB show activity changes within brain regions that are often seen in studies of psychological diseases, that is, impulsive compulsive disorders, addiction, and obsessive compulsive disorders (e.g., Lubman, Yücel, and Pantelis 2004; Maltby et al. 2005; Saxena et al. 1998).

Our studies show that there is a correlation between the adverse financial consequences of CB and the positive brand associations on an automatic level, and that attractive brands lead to activity changes in reward-related brain areas in men with CB tendencies. Thus, if attractive brands act as strong reward stimuli in the brain and evoke positive associations on an automatic level, men are more likely to show CB characteristics. This indication that CB is also a male phenomenon suggests a need for further attention by consumer researchers.

## References

Black, D.W. (2007), "A review of compulsive buying disorder," *World Psychiatry,* 6, 14-18.

Bluemke, M. and Friese, M. (2008), "Reliability and validity of the Single-Target IAT (ST-IAT): Assessing automatic affect towards multiple attitude objects," *European Journal of Social Psychology,* 38, 977-997.

Boundy, D. (2004), "When Money is the Drug," In A. L. Benson (Ed.), *I Shop Therefore I Am Compulsive Buying and the Search for Self.* Maryland: Rowman & Littlefield Publisher.

Dalgleish, Tim. (2004), "The emotional brain," *Nature Reviews/Neuroscience,* 5, 582-589.

Dalgleish, Tim, Dunn, B. D., and Mobbs, D. (2009), „Affective Neuroscience: Past, Present, and Future," Emotion Review, 1 (4), 355-68.

Delgado, M.R., Locke, H.M, Stenger, V.A., and Fiez, J.A (2003), "Dorsal striatum responses to reward and punishment: Effects of valence and magnitude manipulations," *Cognitive, Affective, and Behavioral Neuroscience,* 3, 27-38.

Dittmar, H., & Drury, J. (2000), "Self-image–is it in the bag? A qualitative comparison between "ordinary" and "excessive" consumers," *Journal of Economic Psychology,* 21, 109-142.

Elliot, R., Friston, K.J., and Dolan, R.J. (2000), "Dissociable Neural Responses in Human Reward Systems," *The Journal of Neuroscience,* 20, 6159-6165.

Faber, R.J. (2004), "A Systematic Investigation into Compulsive Buying," In A. L. Benson (Ed.), *I Shop Therefore I Am Compulsive Buying and the Search for Self.* Maryland: Rowman & Littlefield Publisher

Faber, R.J., and O'Guinn, T. (1992), "A Clinical Screener for Compulsive Buying," *Journal of Consumer Research,* 19, 459-469.

Greenwald, A. G., McGhee, D. E., and Schwartz, J. L. L. (1998), „Measuring individual differences in implicit cognition: The Implicit Association Test," *Journal of Personality and Social Psychology,* 74, 1464-1480.

Greenwald, A. G., Nosek, B. A., & Banaji, M. R. (2003), "Understanding and using the Implicit Association Test: I. An improved scoring algorithm," *Journal of Personality and Social Psychology,* 85, 197-216.

Haruno, M. and Kawato, M. (2006), "Different Neural Correlates of Reward Expectation and Reward Expectation Error in the Putamen and Caudate Nucleus During Stimulus-Action-Reward Association Learning," *Journal of Neurophysiology*, 95, 948-59.

Huettel, Scott A., Allen W. Song, and Gregory McCarthy (2008), "Functional Magnetic Resonance Imaging," (2nd ed.), MA: Sinauer.

Karpinski, A. and Steinman, R. B. (2006), „The Single Category Implicit Association Test as a measure of implicit social cognition," *Journal of Personality and Social Psychology,* 91, 16-32.

Koran, M. L., Faber, R.J., Aboujaoude, E., Large, M.D., and Serpe, R.T. (2006), « Estimated Prevalence of Compulsive Buying Behavior in the United States," *American Journal of Psychiatry,* 163, 1806-1812.

Lane, K. A., Banaji, M. R., Nosek, B. A., and Greenwald, A. G. (2007), "Understanding and using the Implicit Association Test: What we know (so far) about the method," In B. Wittenbrink & N. Schwarz (Eds.), *Implicit Measures of Attitudes*, New York: Guilford (59-102).

Lubman, D. I., Yücel, M. and Pantelis, C. (2004), "Addiction, a condition of compulsive behaviour? Neuroimaging and neurpsychological evidence of inhibitory dysregulation," *Addiction*, 99, 1491-502.

Maltby, N., Tolin, D. F., Worhunsky, P., O'Keefe, T. M., and Kiehl, K. A. (2005), "Dysfunctional action monitoring hyperactivates frontal-striatal circuits in obsessive-compulsive disorder: an event-related fMRI study," *NeuroImage*, 24, 495-503.

Müller, A., Reinecker, H., Jacobi, C., Reisch, L., and de Zwaan, M. (2005), „Pathologisches Kaufen–Eine Literaturübersicht/ Pathological Buying–A Literature Review," *Psychat Prax,* 32, 3-12.

Müller, A., and de Zwaan, M. (2004), „Aktueller Stand der Therapieforschung bei pathologischem Kaufen [Actual state of therapy research in compulsive buying]. *Verhaltenstherapie*," 14, 112-119 (in German).

O'Doherty, J.P. (2004), "Reward representations and reward-related learning in the human brain: insights from neuroimaging," *Current opinion in Neurobiology*, 14, 769-776.

Phillips, D. M., and Stanton, J. L. (2004), "Age-related differences in advertising: Recall and persuasion," *Journal of Targeting, Measurement & Analysis for Marketing*, 13, 7-20.

Reisch, L. A., Neuner, M., & Raab, G. (2004), "Ein Jahrzehnt verhaltenswissenschaftlicher Kaufsuchtforschung in Deutschland [A decade of compulsive buying research in germany]," *Verhaltenstherapie*, 14, 120-125 (in German).

Ridgway, N.M., Kukar-Kinney, M., & Monroe, K.B. (2008), „An Expanded Conceptualization and a New Measure of Compulsive Buying," *Journal of Consumer Research*, 35, 622-639.

Saxena, S. Brody, A.L., Schwartz, J.M., and Baxter, L.R. (1998), "Neuroimaging and frontal subcortical circuitry in obsessive-compulsive disorder," *British Journal of Psychiatry Supplement*, 35, 26-37.

Scherhorn, G., Reisch, L.A., & Raab, G. (1990), "Addictive Buying in West Germany: An Empirical Study," *Journal of Consumer Policy*, 13, 355-387.

Weber, E.U., and Johnson, E.J. (2009), "Mindful Judgement and Decision Making," *Annu. Rev. Psychol.*, 60, 53–85.

http://www.creditreform.de/Deutsch/Creditreform/Aktuelles/Creditreform_Analysen/SchuldnerAtlas/7_Geschlecht.jsp (27.11.09).

# Do Retail Brands Bias Consumer Decision-Making?
# –An fMRI Study on Retail Brand Frames and the Evaluation of Product Packaging

Mirja Hubert, Zeppelin University, Germany
Marco Hubert, Zeppelin University, Germany
Peter Kenning, Zeppelin University, Germany

**Extended Abstract**

Research in the field of retail marketing is important for manufacturers, in order to select the best marketing strategy, the most appropriate distribution channels, the optimal price policy, and the best retailers (Choi 1991; Lee and Staelin 1997; Pasternack 1985). However, very little is known about optimal strategies of product positioning, or about how different retail brands influence ("frame") customers' product perception and evaluation (Martenson 2007).

In contrast, in economic and psychological theory the "framing effect" is a very well-known and important concept for the identification of judgment biases within subjects' choices (Gonzalez et al. 2005; Tversky and Kahneman 1981). Recent studies provide evidence that the "framing effect" occurs due to the integration of conscious and unconscious implicit and explicit background knowledge in the decision-making process. In addition, recent evidence indicates that specific neural processes play a central role for susceptibility to the manner in which a choice-problem is presented (Deppe et al. 2005a, Deppe et al. 2007).

Against this background, we applied fMRI in order to understand how the product evaluation of consumers is influenced by retail-brand-frames. In this regard, the application of fMRI could offer a new theoretical perspective and may help to reach a higher level of explained variance regarding the susceptibility of consumers to retail brands.

In our study, we investigated the behavioral decision-making and the correlating neural activity pattern of 21 subjects (11 female, $M_{age}$=25.91, SD=.44; 10 male, $M_{age}$=28.6, SD=5.502), by comparing individual attractiveness evaluations of 30 packages within an unframed task and a framed task. The unframed task consisted of the attractiveness evaluation of product packages alone, whereas in the framed task we presented product packages together with selected retail brands. Both tasks were pseudo-randomized, and repeated four times. Because of this structure, the 30 product package images had to be evaluated four times in the unframed task and, respectively, four times--in combination with the retail brand--in the framed task.

The stimulus material for the fMRI-experiment was selected in a pretest. In this pilot study, 51 randomly selected subjects (23 female, 28 male) evaluated, according to their attractiveness, 130 original paper-based packages of current supermarket products. The packages had to be rated on a score ranging from 1="very unattractive" to 10="very attractive." We then selected only the 10 most attractive packages ("P+"), the 10 least attractive packages ("P-"). and 10 neutral packages ("P0") for the neuroimaging experiment (Deppe et al. 2005a; 2007; Stoll, Baecke and Kenning 2008).

The study was executed on a 3T scanner (Magnetom Trio, SIEMENS, Erlangen, Germany). The protocol included a 3D isotropic T1-weighted data set of the entire head, with a measured voxelsize of 1.0 mm edge length for anatomical identification and coregistration into the Talairachspace. The data set consisted of 36 transversal slices of 3.6 mm thickness without a gap, FOV 230 mm x 230 mm, acquired matrix 64 x 64, that is, isotropic voxels with 3.6 mm edge length. Contrast parameters were TR=3000 ms, TE=50 ms, flip angle=90°. The stimuli were projected onto a transparent screen with an LCD beamer, and viewed from the other side via a 45° mirror mounted on an element phase array coil.

First, we compared the behavioral data (the attractiveness rating) of the framed task with the behavioral data of the unframed task. For this we used the evaluations of each participant within the scanner. We calculated an individual attractiveness ratio (AR) for the framed (AR [framing]) and the unframed task (AR [packaging]), by subtracting the number of negative evaluations (not attractive) from the number of positive evaluations (attractive) in the scanner, divided by the total number of all evaluations for each participant (Deppe et al. 2007). The Response Bias (RB), a measure of susceptibility toward framing information, was assessed by subtracting the absolute values of the AR (packaging) from the absolute value of the AR (framing). The expected value of the RB for an individual participant should be zero if the framing information has no influence on the participant's decision-making. We identified 15 of 21 participants who were influenced by the framing information with an RB unequal 0 on a range from RB=0.03 to RB=0.45. A paired t-test for AR (packaging) and AR (framing) confirmed these differences to be significant (t= 2.155, p< 0.05).

Second, results from the fMRI data analysis indicated that people who are susceptible to framing information (RB unequal 0) also show different neural activity changes compared to people who show an RB=0. We found activity changes in the dorsolateral prefrontal cortex (DLPFC) and the ventral anterior cingulate cortex (vACC). The DLPFC is suggested to play a prominent role for cognitive control, working memory, and decision-making (McClure et al. 2004a; Sanfey et al. 2003). The vACC is linked to emotions and to reward-based learning, and seems to play an important role in visual attention, the integration of incoming information with background knowledge, the retrieval of episodic memory, and self-reflection (Bush et al. 2002; Deppe et al. 2005a, 2005b, 2007; Devinsky, Morrell and Vogt 1995; Lamm et al. 2007). Moreover, activity changes in the vACC are also associated with the general susceptibility of a person (Deppe et al. 2007). Our results are in accordance with the study conducted by Deppe et al. (2007) and their findings that the anterior cingulate cortex is associated with the general susceptibility of a person and plays a decisive role in behavioral adjustments and the integration of framing information in the decision-making process.

Our findings suggest that the application of fMRI can offer a new perspective in order to better understand unconscious processes that influence consumer decision-making. We found neural correlates of judgment biases within the DLPFC and the vACC. This confirmed recent findings in other studies regarding the influence of the "framing effect" on marketing-relevant decisions (e.g., Deppe et al. 2007). Because of the strong influence of the psychological "framing-effect," it should be important for manufacturers to implement consumer susceptibility, product positioning, and the biasing effects of retail brands in their product and price strategy portfolios.

**References**

Bush, George, Brent A. Vogt, Jennifer Holmes, Anders M. Dale, Douglas Greve, Michael A. Jenike, and Bruce R. Rosen (2002), „Dorsal anterior cingulate cortex: A role in reward-based decision-making," *PNAS*, 8 (January), 523-28.

Choi, S. Chan (1991), "Price Competition in a Channel Structure with a Common Retailer", *Marketing Science*, 10(4), 271-96.

Deppe, Michael, Wolfram Schwindt, Julia Krämer, Harald Kugel, Hilke Plassmann, Peter Kenning, and E. Bernd Ringelstein (2005a), "Evidence for a neural correlate of a framing effect: Bias–specific activity in the ventromedial prefrontal cortex during credibility judgments", *Brain Research Bulletin*, 67, 413-421.

Deppe, Michael, Wolfram Schwindt, Harald Kugel, Hilke Plassmann, and Peter Kenning (2005b)"Nonlinear Responses Within the Medial Prefrontal Cortex Reveal When Specific Implicit Information Influences Economic Decision Making", *Journal of Neuroimaging*, 15, 171-182.

Deppe, Michael, Wolfram Schwindt, Anna Pieper, Harald Kugel, Hilke Plassmann, Peter Kenning, Katja Deppe, and E. Bernd Ringelstein (2007), „Anterior cingulate reflects susceptibility to framing during attractiveness evaluation", *NeuroReport*, 18 (11), 1119-1123.

Devinsky Orrin, Martha J.Morrell and Brent A.Vogt (1995), "Contributions of anterior cingulated cortex to behaviour," *Brain*, 118 (1), 279-306.

Gonzalez, Cleotilde, Jason Dana, Hideya Koshino, and Marcel Just (2005), "The framing effect and risky decisions: Examining cognitive functions with fMRI", *Journal of Economic Psychology*, 26, 1-20.

Lamm, Claus, Howard C. Nussbaum, Andrew N. Meltzoff, and Jean Decety (2007),"What are you feeling? Using functional magnetic resonance imaging to assess the modulation of sensory and affective responses during empathy for pain," *PLoS ONE*, 2 (12).

Lee, Eunkyu and Richard Staelin (1997), "Vertical Strategy Interaction: Implications for Channel Pricing Strategy", *Marketing Science*, 16(3), 185-207.

Martenson, Rita (2007), "Corporate brand image, satisfaction and store loyalty: A study of the store as a brand, store brands and manufacturer brands", *International Journal of Retail and Distribution Management*, 35(7), 544-555.

McClure, Samuel M., Jian Li, Damon Tomlin, Kim S. Cypert, Latané M. Montague, and P. Read Montague (2004), "Neural Correlates of Behavioral Preference for Culturally Familiar Drinks", *Neuron*, 44 (14), 379-387.

Pasternack, Barry Alan (1985), "Optimal Pricing and Return Policies for Perishable Commodities" *Marketing Science*, 4(2), 166-176.

Sanfey, Alan G., James K. Rilling, Jessica A. Aronson, Leigh E. Nystrom, and Jonathan D. Cohen (2003), "The Neural Basis of Economic Decision-Making in the Ultimatum Game", *Science*, 300 (June), 1755-1758.

Stoll, Marco, Sebastian Baecke, and Peter Kenning (2008), "What they see is what they get? An fMRI-study on neural correlates of attractive packaging," *Journal of Consumer Behaviour*, 7 (4-5), 342-59.

Tversky, Amos and Daniel Kahneman (1981), "The Framing of Decisions and the Psychology of Choice", *Science*, 211 (4481), 453-458.

# Author Index